ofFossils&Foxes

The official definitive history of Leicester City Football Club

Dave Smith & Paul Taylor

POLAR PUBLISHING

DEDICATION

PT: *To the London Branch, and all travelling Foxiles.*

DS: *To Helen, for her unfailing love and support, and to Tom, Jenny, Paul and Sally.*

First published 1989 by Polar Publishing (Leicester) Limited,
This revised and updated edition published 2001 by Polar Publishing, part of the Polar Group Ltd
9-17 Tuxford Road, Hamilton, Leicester LE4 9TZ

Text copyright © 2001 Dave Smith & Paul Taylor

Design copyright © 2001 Polar Group Ltd

ISBN 1 899538 21 6

British Library Cataloguing in Publication Data. A catalogue record for this book is available from the
British Library.

General Editor   Julian Baskcomb
Design   Trevor Hartley
Printed by   Polar Print Group Ltd
                  9-17 Tuxford Road, Hamilton,
                  Leicester LE4 9TZ
                  Tel: 0116 274 4700

Photographs and illustrations are courtesy of:
Leicester City FC, Neville Chadwick Photography, Associated Sports Photography, Empics Ltd, Action Images, Colorsport,
Leicester Mercury, David Munden Photography, Raymonds Press Agency, Leicester Records Office, Linda Carruthers-Watt and
The National Film & Television Archive.
Many of the photographs are from original material in the files of Leicester City FC, who also retain the rights to official
photocall pictures from the present era taken by the appointed Club Photographer. Most remaining photographs are from the
private collections of the authors or from albums owned by various Leicester City supporters or former players. We have been
unable to trace the sources of all these pictures, but any photographer involved is cordially invited to contact the publishers in
writing providing proof of copyright.

Cover photographs:
Front: (clockwise) Sep Smith; Gordon Banks and Peter Shilton; 27th February 2000, Wembley, Martin O'Neill and Matt
Elliott; 27th May 1996, Wembley, post match celebrations.
Back: (from top) Fosse in action at Filbert Street in the 1890s; 12th September 1925, Arthur Chandler challenges Willis
Edwards of Leeds; the 1968/9 squad, the last season in which City reached the FA Cup Final; Adam Black; 16th April 1997,
Hillsborough, Steve Walsh and Steve Claridge.
Title page: 16th April 1997, Hillsborough, Steve Claridge's winning goal.
Contents page: The forward line that shot City to promotion in 1924/5; Hughie Adcock, John Duncan, Arthur Chandler,
George Carr, Harold Wadsworth.

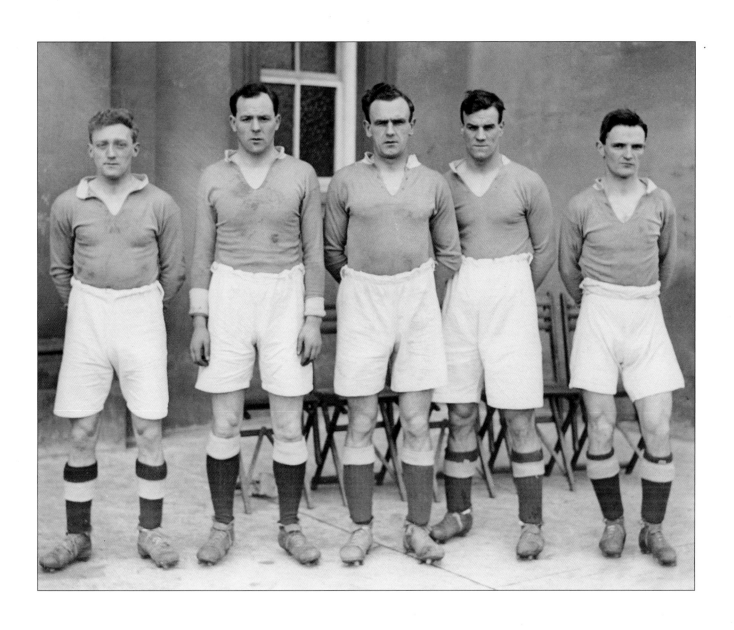

Contents of Fossils & Foxes

ACKNOWLEDGEMENTS

> The acknowledgements pages of the first edition of this volume, together with that from it's companion publication, *The Foxes Alphabet*, both bear testimony to the debt of gratitude owed by the authors to an increasing list of individuals and institutions that are involved in the research, compilation and collation of any addition to world of football history.

Supporters, former players, football historians and fellow members of the Association of Football Statisticians have all contributed crucially towards making this updated version of our original tome even more comprehensive than our initial attempt of a decade ago. Hopefully, this volume will again be regarded as the definitive club history and will prove invaluable in settling a host of arguments of the sort that arise in public bars across the county and further afield, as well as providing our friends in the media with the factual basis for a score of future articles or informed comment.

Of the institutions that have provided assistance we would express our sincere thanks to the staff of the Football League, Leicester City Football Club, the Leicester Records Office, the Leicester Mercury Library and the British Library's Newspaper Library at Colindale.

Of the individuals who are worthy of special thanks for their contribution to the genesis of this work, pride of place, as always, must go to Mike Davage for sharing the results of his unstinting football research with us. Without Mike, this publication, along with countless other football volumes over the years, would certainly be the poorer.

Other individuals that have contributed from the birth of the project over a decade ago up to the present day, are listed here alphabetically. Sadly, not all of the following are still with us, but their contributions are gratefully remembered and acknowledged by the authors: Charlie Adam, John Aldridge, Bill Anderson, Liz Ashforth, Bill Barradell, Dr John Batterbee, Reg Beaumont, John Belton, Alan Bennett, Jenny Blackhurst, John G Blackmore, Graham Blackwood, Jill Bocock, John Borthwick, Steve Botting, Colin Boulter, Phil Brown, Beryl Burridge, John Byrne, Stephen Byrne, Joe Calvert, Colin Cameron, Irene Cave, Gary Chalk, Denis Clarebrough, Michael Clarke, Tom Coates, Alan Craft, Ian Crosland, Jack Curtis, Gareth M Davies, Steven Day, Derek Deadman, David Dennison, Bill Donnachie, Garth Dykes, John Eastwood, Steve England, Stuart Farmer, Michael Featherstone, Alan Futter, Michael Gardner, Ian Garland, John Garner, John Gaustad, Stan Goddard, Alan Harding, Roger Harris, Carl Harrison, Jimmy Harrison, John Hayes, Stewart Henry, Charles Hine, Sam Holmes, Chris Horner, Bill Hume, Gerald Hutchinson, Mimi Inoue, Roy Jones, Trefor Jones, Colin Jose, Doug Kemp, Ray Kirby, David Kirkby, Douglas Lamming, Rob Lee, Syd Lee, John Litster, Eugene MacBride, Gordon McKenzie, Garrow McLaren, Clive Major, Colin Martin, Wade Martin, John Marvin, Brian Mellowship, J.M. Melrose, Gerald Mortimer, Barry Muir, Balbi Murrell, John Northcutt, Martin O'Connor, Mark Osborne, G.H. Park, Geraint Parry, Jim Pennington, Steven Phillips, Paul Plowman, Ed Pointon, Jenny Schofield, Maurice Scott, Tony Sealy, Gary Silke, Rosemary Simpson, David Smith (no relation), Ray Spiller, Barbara Taylor, Paul Taylor (no relation), Tise Vahimagi, Len Walker, Ian Weller, Richard Wells, Lars-Olaf Wendler, Chris Wigginton, Mike Wilbur, Ernest Wiles, Alex Wilson, Ian Wilson, Bob Wood and to anyone else that we have inadvertently overlooked.

Also, to all those who have subscribed to or purchased this or earlier volumes, for without your faith and support there would be no books.

Finally, and most crucially of all, we would wish to express our deep and sincere gratitude to our publishers, Polar, and in particular to Julian Baskcomb, Julia Byrne, Sarah Hefford, Gerald Toon and Trevor Hartley, for your continued support and belief in us and for maintaining the highest of production values, as always.

Foreword

by Gary Lineker

It is a genuine honour and a real pleasure for me to write a few words to kick-off this completely revised and re-designed version of the official history of Leicester City Football Club "Of Fossils & Foxes".

When this book first appeared in 1989, I like every other true-blue Foxes fan, found it a fascinating read as nothing before had ever covered the history of our football club, its results and its players in such great detail.

Yet so many marvellous things have happened to our club in the 12 years since then, with no less than seven visits to Wembley, two promotions into the Premiership and a pair of League Cup triumphs, that the time is surely right for this huge new volume charting the club's progress.

Leicester City is the club I have supported all my life and, of course, it was a particularly proud day for me when I made my debut on a freezing cold New Year's Day back in 1979 against Oldham at Filbert Street. We won 2-0 that afternoon and turning out and scoring goals for City over the next seven years were some of the happiest days of my playing career.

They were good times, but there have been many other memorable moments across the years of Leicester City's history and whenever a football competition has been created, City has more than made its mark.

Below: Gary meets up with City manager Peter Taylor in July 2001.

We have produced some fantastic players as well. A new generation of supporters will be able to discover more about the deeds of great names from the past such as Arthur Chandler, Sep Smith and Arthur Rowley, as well as the wonderful City team of the early 1960's and Jimmy Bloomfield's stylish squad of the 1970's.

Two of the finest goalkeepers in the history of the game, Gordon Banks and Peter Shilton, just happened to follow each other into the Leicester team around 30 years ago, while David Nish was the youngest-ever FA Cup Final captain when he led us out at Wembley in 1969. Frank Worthington, Alan Smith and Gary McAllister are just three others who have all enjoyed excellent careers and entertained us while at Filbert Street.

The last decade proved a great time to be a follower of Leicester City with three play-off Wembley finals under Brian Little ending in that unforgettable Steve Walsh-inspired 1994 triumph against Derby County.

Further memorable seasons followed as Martin O'Neill then steered the club to a dramatic last-minute promotion at Wembley in 1996 and two triumphs in three League Cup Finals as well as a taste of European football during the established Premiership years that followed.

Football is big business now, but Leicester City have much to look forward to with a superb new stadium being developed close by and I am sure they will continue to add to the pages of their playing history by striving for even greater heights and achievements in the future.

Gary Lineker
July 2001

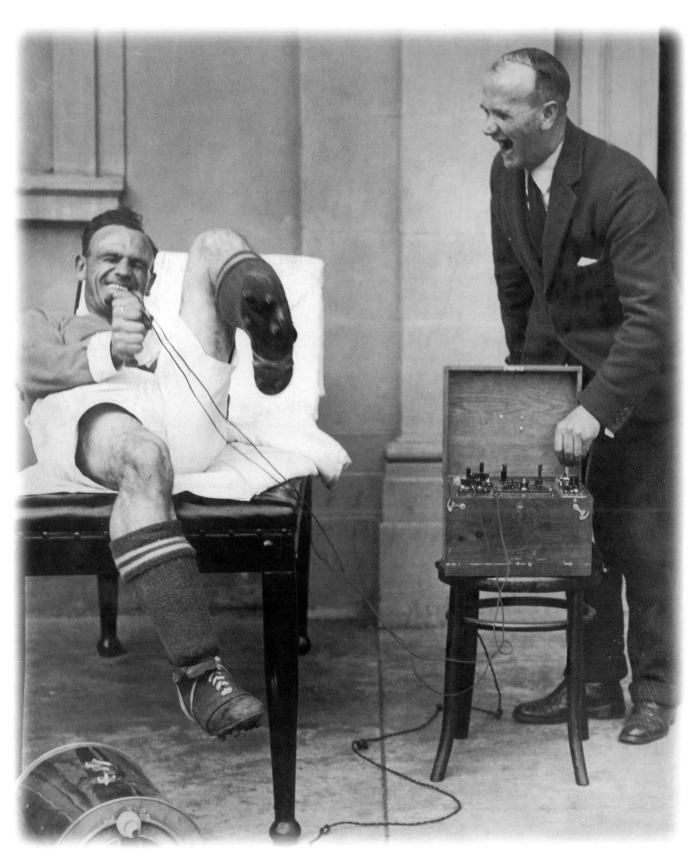

Leicester City clearly provided the very latest in physiotherapy technology to spark Arthur Chandler's electric goalscoring performances during the 1920s!

# of Fossils & Foxes

> Following the basic format employed in the 1989 edition of 'Of Fossils & Foxes', this book is essentially divided into three parts: an expanded narrative history of the club; a statistical and records section; and a biographical index to players, managers, coaches and administrators. Hence, aspects of the same story are related from three different perspectives – making the authors acutely aware of the need to avoid undue repetition.

The bulk of the narrative is carried forward in season-by-season fashion. There is clearly no need for a match-by-match commentary, as the bare facts of every senior competitive game the club has ever played are tabulated in the statistical section. Likewise, there has been no temptation to mention every single player's arrival or departure in this part of the book, for fuller details on careers and contributions follow in the third section, as do retrospective summaries of each manager's period of control. Instead there is a concentration on context, development, salient incident and, hopefully, flavoursome anecdote.

It is still beyond the remit and the competence of the authors to flesh out the purely sociological context of the story in any but the most sketchy of terms; and we acknowledge that as great a leap of imagination on the part of the reader will be required to picture, say, the everyday Victorian life of Leicester and its people (including those associated with the Fosse), as will be needed to envisage the game of football itself of that era: played to still-changing rules, and in differing tactical formations, on seemingly oddly-marked pitches, before spectators whose world-view and expectations we can barely guess at.

Accordingly, speculations about the vital varying relationships between The People and The People's Game have not really been attempted. We have again had to limit ourselves to a book for Leicester's supporters, rather than about them; though the present authors would dearly love to see someone, someday, attempt that intriguing project.

The match-by-match statistical section – incorporating team line-ups and scorers for every first-class match played by Fosse and City – is substantially grounded in the painstaking research

The 1989 edition of 'Of Fossils & Foxes' and 'The Foxes Alphabet', published in 1995, both by the same authors.

carried out by Dave Smith and presented in copy form to the club on the occasion of its Centenary in 1984. It has subsequently been marginally amended and massively expanded (now additionally incorporating attendances, opposition goalscorers and fluctuations in League position), with both authors confident of its value for comprehensively settling the sort of arguments that eternally arise whenever supporters or old players begin to match rather misted memories. We have also endeavoured to make the records section relating to the club and its players as authoritative as possible.

The ongoing attempt to construct a full career biography and assessment for every player to have represented Fosse and City in senior competition here appears in its third and most developed incarnation. It currently represents a twenty-two year research task (principally on the part of Paul Taylor): doomed, probably, never to be definitively completed; yet, for the authors, representing perhaps the most exacting and exciting detective work involved in this book's genesis.

All records and data are correct up to the end of the 2000/1 season.

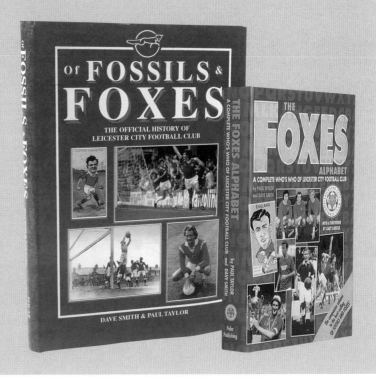

> It is such a commonplace these days to find the game of football and the law of the land in convoluted conflict – over matters as diverse as the transfer market, ground development and crowd control – that it is difficult to suppress an ironic smile in citing one of the earliest known records of The People's Game in Leicester and environs.

For over 400 years ago, in April 1592, the pastime and the principles of order were first reported locally as being at odds. The county magistrates were exercised by the case of one Matthewe Puchin, who, with eleven others, had been summoned for playing football on a Sunday at Oadby. Sensibly, they dismissed the charge.

The sport Puchin and his fellow pioneer miscreants were indulging in was doubtless barely recognisable as the game of today. Every locality at that time had its own variant on the basic notion of opposing teams (or mobs) projecting some vaguely spherical object towards some sort of 'goal': such rural folk-forms of football still exist today as quaint feast-day traditions in many parts of the country, and are still associated with notions of disorderly conduct.

The development of the 'modern' game – and its rise to a long-guarded respectability – really got underway in the second half of the nineteenth century. The impetus came from the universities and the public schools, where the knack of the youthful leisured classes lay in codifying rules for their competitive sport; and sanction came from the church, via then-popular notions of 'muscular Christianity' – 'a healthy mind in a healthy body', and all that. The social and moral benefits of well-ordered team sport were thus propounded with due missionary zeal by way of the grammar schools, the Sunday Schools, the temperance societies and suchlike avenues of influence, and quickly took root throughout the social fabric, especially – in the case of association football – among the men of the urban working class, many of whom were now being granted Saturday half-holidays for the first time.

The context for this development in Leicester was little different from that pertaining elsewhere in England. For years the term 'sport', especially as used in the press, referred exclusively to horse racing, although there was occasional acknowledgement of cricket as the pastime of the gentlemen of the county during the summer months. By the mid-nineteenth century, however, cricket matches had become frequent on parks and village greens, and the growing interest in competitive rivalry had led the local press regularly to print scorecards of the more important games.

The Leicestershire County Cricket Club was organised into its present-day form in February 1879, and by 1884 had regular fixtures with the MCC as well as meetings with the touring Australian teams. Within a further year they would become officially part of the County Championship. They were also fortunate enough to have a private ground to play on, at Grace Road. (Where they would remain until 1900, and where they would return in 1946, having played in the interim at Aylestone Road).

When the cricket season ended each autumn, and only then, the parks were given over to winter games. Rugby was the premier pastime for the men of Leicester at this time. The first clubs appeared in the county in the 1860s, but the Leicester Football Club, the now famous Tigers, did not come into existence until 1880. In their initial season they played their home fixtures on the Belgrave Road Sports Ground, a venue long since demolished, but subsequently moved to Victoria Park. By 1884, they had established a sizeable following there, with fixtures against the likes of Moseley, Coventry, Northampton and Bedford – all leading Midland clubs who exploited the new ease of transport to broaden their sporting horizons.

In contrast, the round-ball game was struggling to gain a foothold within the town. The local press only gave room to match reports when the handling code did not fill all available space (and even then hardly in graphic detail), and it was clear that players, then drawn primarily from the well-educated middle classes, outnumbered spectators on most occasions. These diehards maintained a limited local fixture list, however – even the town's premier rugby club ran a subsidiary soccer team for three years – and took their cue from the national scene to await optimistically for reinforcements.

For the London-based Football Association had been formed in 1863; had instituted their English Cup in 1871/2; and had finally agreed a uniform set of Laws of the Game in 1877. Professionalism amongst some players was a covert fact from the mid 1870s, and would be legalised in 1885. And, by the 1880s, club rivalries were spilling across city, county, and even international boundaries as 'football fever' spread at a remarkable rate. Leicester, a thriving town at the heart of an expanding rail nexus, could not remain a soccer backwater for long.

Friendly Fossils

> The formation of the Leicester Fosse Football Club took place in the spring of 1884. The event was regarded as possessing little significance at the time, and was certainly not recorded in the local press. While it is certain that a number of Old Wyggestonians were amongst the founders, and that several of these were additionally members of the Bible class run by the Rev Llewellyn H Parsons at the old Emmanuel Church in New Parks Street (thus giving the club a wholly typical background for the period in emerging from the rugged philosophies of private education and 'muscular Christianity'), we have only the much later testimony of co-founder Frank Gardner to trust for the enduring suggestion that the decision to form the club was reached at a meeting in a garden shed just off the old Fosse Road, behind a house adjacent to the King Richards Road Chapel.

The youthfully enterprising Gardner was elected as the first secretary and treasurer, and it is to him that the naming of the club is attributable. It is open to question whether he actually ever did utter the oft-quoted, prophetic statement – "As the Fosse is known throughout the land, so the new club shall be known to the future" – but, nevertheless, the football club was to be sustained through many a trial and tribulation by just such optimistic enthusiasm.

Messrs Ashby, Bromwich and West additionally formed the first club committee – they were, of course, also players – and the captaincy was voted into the hands of William Johnson. All members donated ninepence each towards a ball, and a further ninepence each as subscriptions. A local carpenter was engaged to make a set of goalposts, which he is reputed to have painted amber and black, and preparations were made for an inaugural fixture.

The first game to be played by Leicester Fosse actually took place on 1st November, 1884, the venue being a private field off the Fosse Road, and the opposition being Syston Fosse (the new club's name, as can be seen, hardly being unique). Leicester wore black jerseys with a diagonal blue sash and long white

"As the Fosse is known throughout the land, so the new club shall be known to the future"

Co-founder Frank Gardner

Emmanuel Church

9

trousers, and goals from West (2), Dingley and Hilton Johnson (2) steered the club to an initial triumph by 5-0. The way in which the team lined up for that historic fixture, as detailed in the local press, shows the tenacious influence of rugby on tactical thinking at that time:

HOW FOSSE LOOKED IN FIRST GAME

E Smith
(goal)

F Burdett
(three-quarter back)

E Johnson　　**W Johnson**　　**F Gardner**
(half-backs)

H Johnson　**B Lewitt**　　**A West**　**F Bromwich**　　**A Ashby**　**S Dingley**
(right wing)　　　　　(centres)　　　　　　(left wing)

One of the earliest 'old chestnuts' associated with the club's history is the assertion that this initial game was a 12-a-side affair. This claim first appeared in a pamphlet about the club produced in 1894, and has been oft-repeated since. In fact, the fourth fixture that the club played was the 12-a-side game; the confusion arising from the fact that this time the opponents were Syston St Peters.

For the rest of that initial 1884/5 season, Leicester Fosse played their fixtures on Victoria Park – still then often referred to as The Racecourse, which indeed it had been until as recently as 1883 – but at no time did they record such a spectacular scoreline again as in that opening match.

During that debut season, Fosse also played the odd game under the Union code. Local sources claim that two fixtures were probably played, but only one appears to have been reported – in February, when Holy Trinity Band of Hope provided the opposition, scoring one try to the four minor points achieved by the Fosse. All soccer opposition consisted of local clubs, with Mill Hill House, Melbourne Hall and St Mary's swelling the remainder of the fixture list. By the end of that first campaign, the new club had actually made a profit of one shilling and tenpence.

For 1885/6, Victoria Park remained the club's established venue, although most spectators continued to turn their backs on the Fosse's efforts and watch Rugby Union on the adjoining pitches. The weekly tactical and selection meetings initially took place in the West Bridge Coffee House, but later switched to the Eastgates Coffee House, overlooking the Clock Tower in the centre of town. William Johnson was again captain, but subscriptions had been raised to three shillings, together with a joining fee of a further

The club colours changed to chocolate and blue for the 1886/7 season.

OUTNUMBERED

> One incident, in March 1885, demonstrates the lack of organisation in the game in those days, for, when facing Wyggeston Boys School, Fosse were having particular problems coping with the opposition until a half-time tally-up established that the School team had actually fielded 13 men throughout the first period!

shilling. Even these early examples of inflation couldn't balance the Fosse's books, though, and the season ended with the club two shillings and a ha'penny in the red.

The campaign itself was very poorly reported in the local press, as indeed, curiously, was that of the Rugby Union club. Sport was definitely not deemed fashionable reading during the winter of 1885/6. Of the games which did get noted, a record 6-0 victory was recorded when Trinity Band of Hope were entertained at Victoria Park; revenge therefore being well and truly exacted for the previous season's defeat at the oval ball game. At the end of January, when playing Mill Hill House, the Fosse suffered their first recorded instance of completing a fixture with only ten men.

The fixture list was again predominantly local, but a game was secured with a team from Market Harborough. Another fixture, in March, was due to be played in Loughborough, with Old Loughburians scheduled to provide the opposition. However, Fosse could not find their hosts' ground, and are popularly believed to have spent the afternoon at the races instead.

By the start of the 1886/7 campaign, the club membership had increased to 40, and a reserve team, Leicester Fosse Rovers, was founded. The club colours had changed to chocolate and blue halved shirts, and the first 'outsider' joined the club. He was Sam Sudbury, from Lincoln, who had recently moved to the Leicester area when he was spotted by Frank Gardner kicking a ball about on Spinney Hill Park. By the following weekend he was playing for the Fosse's first eleven!

The fixture list was gradually encompassing opposition from further afield. Barwell, Coalville, Loughborough and even Nottingham were all visited during the campaign, though not always with success. In November, the Coalville team walked off the pitch before the end of the game in disagreement with a decision made by the umpire. The same month, at Belgrave, Fosse turned up with only ten men, but persuaded a spectator to make up their numbers. Twice during the season Fosse met opposition made up of only ten men – first St Marks and then Belgrave in the return fixture. Once again a record victory was established, Wyggeston School Past & Present being thrashed 9-0 at Victoria Park in March. Off the field, the AGM was presented with a balance sheet showing a credit of £1 12s 9d. Things were beginning to look up.

So much so that for the 1887/8 season membership had risen to 65 and the club was able to field three teams. Another pointer to the steady rise in the status of the club was the decision to move to a private ground. The Belgrave Road Sports Ground (built in 1880 by local entrepreneur Colonel Burnaby, and featuring athletics and cycle tracks around a central area large enough for cricket) was hired, although strangely it did not possess changing facilities. The teams got ready and later washed down, in fact, at the White Hart Hotel, almost a mile away from the enclosure. The arrangement of matches against the likes of Kettering, Burton Swifts and Notts County Reserves also indexed the club's growing status; and it was the November fixture with Burton Swifts that saw another landmark notched in the club's history, with gate money being taken from home spectators for the first time. Encouragement from the local press, especially from the journalist revelling in the soubriquet 'Referee', now extended to the characterisation of the club as 'that go-ahead, fear nothing, tackle anything Society'. Some things did not change, however, and on 10th December, when Castle Donington failed to put in a scheduled appearance, Fosse were reduced to playing a full-scale practice match against their own reserves, which ended in a 1-1 draw.

By the end of the season Fosse's membership had crept up to 72, total gate receipts for the season amounted to £8 4s 0d, and the club was in credit with a balance of £2 13s 4d showing on the books. Reporting of football in the local press had also improved considerably, and one regular correspondent was responsible for dubbing the club with their first pair of popular nicknames – 'The Fossils', of obvious derivation, or 'The Ancients', which contrived to imply a club of rather longer traditions than a mere three or four years. In fact, 'Old Fossil' was to become the pen-name of the reporter himself as he continued to log the club's deeds over many years in the old *Daily Post*.

17th April 1888, was a date of major significance in football history. On that day the second meeting called by Aston Villa committee man William McGregor ended in the formation of the Football League, initially to comprise twelve of the strongest clubs from the North and Midlands. In Leicestershire, however, there were other summer events to claim the sporting headlines. Firstly, the County Cricket Club became the toast of the land when their first ever victory over the touring Australians was hailed as the sensation of the season. Then, unfortunately for Fosse, they were outbid for the use of the Belgrave Road Grounds by the Rugby Union Club, who had become somewhat jealous of their upstart soccer rivals' rise in prestige. The Tigers were, in fact, to remain at this ground until September 1892, when they would move

COUNTY CUP

> The 1887/8 season saw the formation of the Leicestershire Football Association, reported in the local press in September, and the institution of the Leicestershire Association Challenge Cup. Again, Frank Gardner had been a leading light in agitation to form the LFA, partly to regularise fixture organisation in the county, and he was soon to be honoured with the Association's Presidency. Fosse of course entered the new cup competition, but soon hit trouble. Their first round tie with St Saviours, at Belgrave Road, finished in a 4-2 victory, but the result was declared void after a protest from the visitors over the poor light in which the game was completed. When the tie was replayed, Fosse were clearly in the mood to stifle further argument, and ran out winners by five clear goals. Rivalry between the Leicester town clubs and those based in the Loughborough area was particularly keen, and when Fosse were paired with Shepshed in Round Two anticipation ran high. In the event, it took three attempts to settle the issue in favour of the North Leicestershire club (formed back in 1879), who subsequently went on to become the first holders of the trophy, defeating Mill Hill House 8-0 at Kegworth, after a 1-1 draw at Coalville.

to the Welford Road site that they still occupy today; but the turn of events left a crestfallen Fosse with no alternative but to return to Victoria Park for the 1888/9 season. (Belgrave Road Sports Ground itself was to last only until 1901, when it was built over by shops, houses and part of the British United Co factory).

To call this retrogressive move a body blow for the ambitious soccer club would be an understatement, and the first effect was the immediate defection to rivals Loughborough, who possessed a private ground, of skipper Tommy Ashmole and goalkeeper Tom DeVille. In the reshuffle, G A Knight was made captain and William Johnson assumed the role of assistant secretary to Frank Gardner. They did their best to ensure that performances on the field did not suffer and, to show that the club was still progressive in spite of setbacks, Fosse engaged the first professional to don their colours. His name was Harry Webb, and he was lured from Stafford Rangers with the promise of 2s 6d per week plus travelling expenses.

Webb's debut came against Coalville Town on 13th October, but his biggest impact was made a month later in the first round of the Leicestershire Association Challenge Cup. Syston Wreake Valley provided the opposition and Webb scored six times as Fosse ran up a club record victory by 12-1. This was, however, to prove a false dawn in the Cup as, after receiving a bye in Round Two, Fosse were despatched 0-2 at Loughborough at the next hurdle. Despite the drawbacks of the parks pitch, the fixture list continued to expand and gain in quality, and games were played during the season against Long Eaton Midland, Bulwell United, Sawley Rangers and Nottingham Forest Reserves.

If the Fosse were to continue to pursue their intention of becoming the premier town club, it was imperative that a private ground be found for 1889/90. This was duly secured with the rental of an enclosed canal-side pitch on Mill Lane, owned by the Town Council. The season itself did not kick off in an auspicious fashion as, for the opening fixture at Bulwell, two Fosse players missed the train and the team had to complete the match with only nine men. This occurrence was actually repeated in December, when Grantham was the venue. Unsurprisingly, both games ended in 0-3 reverses. Still, nine men was better than none at all, which was what Long Eaton Midland contrived to deliver to Mill Lane just after Christmas. This resulted in the first occasion on which Fosse had to refund all gate money to the disgruntled would-be spectators. (How much is not recorded, but the local press were adamant that gates had grown appreciably from the start of the season, when all of 3s 10d had been the 'take' from the opening Mill Lane fixture).

Not all was doom, gloom and cock-ups, though, for meetings with the reserve teams of both Notts County and Nottingham Forest were retained on the fixture list, and the likes of Grantham Rovers, Stafford Rangers and Sheffield Montrose added. Jimmy Johnson had taken over as club captain, and it was to him that the honour would fall of lifting the club's first ever trophy.

The Leicestershire FA had decided to run two Cup competitions for their Senior and Junior members, reflecting the massive growth of the game throughout the county as it had taken hold of the working population's imagination, and Fosse were at last to make their mark in the Senior Cup. Rivalry with Loughborough was becoming more intense, and when the two clubs were paired in the semi-final, fireworks were expected. In the event, all the playing pyrotechnics came from Fosse, who won 4-0, though there was an acrimonious sequel when the Luffs put in a protest over the eligibility of J Eggleton in Fosse's team. The accusation was that Fosse had illegally approached the amateur player after he'd appeared for Hinckley against Fosse Rovers, had paid him excessive travelling expenses, and had provided him with tea; but no substantive evidence was placed before the adjudicating Cup committee, and Eggleton himself had left the area to work in the south by the time of the hearing. Fosse were censured for obtaining no receipt for his expenses, but allowed to face Coalville Town in the final – ironically to be played at Loughborough. A 1-1 draw in the first clash (which Fosse finished with nine men after injuries to Cliff Bentley and Dick Perry) was followed by a 4-0 replay victory for Fosse, and silverware was in the hands of the youthful Ancients at last.

Fosse's home pasture at Mill Lane was chosen as the venue for the first Junior Cup final, between Gresley Rovers and Loughborough Athletic, the Luffs' reserve team, as well as for an inter-Association match between Birmingham and Leicester. These extra fixtures did not swell the coffers appreciably, though, so despite their success the club still made a loss of £6 7s 10d. on the season. The AGM, undaunted, resolved that the club should consolidate its status by applying for membership of the Football Association. Fosse were duly accepted by the national body on 21st July 1890, and immediately lodged their initial entry for the English Cup.

The Mill Lane ground was retained for 1890/1, and Fosse changed their colours again, to white shirts and dark blue trousers. They started the season with their first-ever 'guarantee' game, away to Boston

Harry Webb became the club's first professional player.

Jimmy Johnson - the first Fosse captain to lift a trophy.

Town, who had offered a minimum of £5 plus refreshments to secure the fixture. The first English Cup tie came at Mill Lane on 4th October. Hopes were high and gate receipts totalled £15 as Fosse took the field against Burton Wanderers, but the visitors, steeled by regular competitive football in their second season in the new Midland League, ran out rather easy victors by 4-0. (Even so, the winners were to be themselves embarrassed in the next round: thrashed 1-8 by Midland Alliance members Loughborough).

Fosse's own friendly fare now encompassed meetings with the original Northampton Town club, the reserves of both Aston Villa and Derby County and, at Christmas, with London Casuals. Yet most interest was still aroused by the local derbies with Loughborough, for by now Fosse could rightly claim to be the premier club in the town, while the Luffs were top of the heap in the county surrounds.

Because a December meeting was spoiled by the weather (see panel story), the two clubs agreed to play a charity match over the Christmas period. This was staged at the Belgrave Road Grounds and £27 13s 3d was raised as the teams again drew 1-1. For the third meeting of the local rivals on 7th February at Loughborough, some 1500 fans travelled to cheer on the Fosse on the first-ever 'football special' train to run from Leicester. It was all to no avail, though, as the Luffs recorded a comfortable 3-1 victory.

To round off the campaign, the Fosse committee invited the beaten English Cup finalists from Notts County to Mill Lane. A record crowd paid nearly £30 to watch Fosse's first opponents from the Football League being held to a 2-2 draw. Turnover for the season had risen to £334 and the club showed a profit of £15, while the Leicestershire Senior Cup had been retained with a 2-0 victory over Gresley Rovers at Loughborough. The club had additionally supplied ten of the eleven players for the inter-county match between Leicestershire and Huntingdonshire.

Clearly, if the club was to continue to improve its standing, steps had to be taken towards an eventual application to join the Football League. With this ambitious goal in mind, Fosse took intelligent stock of the immediately achievable, applied to be granted a place in the Midland League and, on 23rd May 1891, were duly accepted (as, indeed, were Loughborough). In just seven short years of the club's existence so much progress had been achieved already, and future prospects looked nothing but golden.

The Midland League Years

> The Midland League was one of the most prestigious of several senior competitions established in the wake of the acknowledged success of the Football League, and had already completed two seasons (in which Lincoln City and Gainsborough Trinity had finished as champions) by the time it accepted Fosse into its ranks.

Twelve teams were to compete in season 1891/2, though Staveley would resign early in the campaign, so Fosse's first experience of 'a fixity of fixtures' eventually gave them a 20-game league programme, under the captaincy of 'Snooks' Nuttall. This initial adventure was not exactly to be a roaring success but, in mitigation, there were several severe handicaps to be overcome along the way.

The most serious cloud over the start of the campaign was the recurrent problem of a home ground. The Mill Lane enclosure was required by the Leicester Corporation for building purposes, and Fosse were stymied until graciously offered temporary rental of the Aylestone Road cricket ground as an interim headquarters. It was here, despite much correspondence of complaint from the cricketing fraternity to the local press, that Fosse started their still substantial supplementary programme of friendlies with a home defeat by Derby County; here that the first Midland League game against Derby Junction (with a 4.50pm kick-off, and refereed by future Fosse manager William Clark) was won by a single goal from star winger Jimmy Atter; and here that Fosse received their first-hurdle FA Cup mauling at the hands of Small Heath, by 2-6. (The latter match rather went with the strong wind: the visitors were five goals to the good at half-time with its assistance). The eighth and final game at Aylestone Road was a 6-1 friendly win over Notts Olympic, for the hectic search for a permanent playing base had at last come to an end.

Open land nearby – between Aylestone Road and Walnut Street – had been earmarked (at the suggestion of, legend has it, a Miss Westland, niece of senior Fosse committee-man Joseph Johnson), and three and three-quarter acres secured on lease from the Corporation to serve as Fosse's new home. Mr Johnson (a boot and shoe manufacturer, who had seen four sons turn out for Fosse at various times) himself guaranteed the rent, and work proceeded apace to lay out a pitch and a rudimentary enclosure, bounded at one end by Filbert Street. It was initially deemed that few potential patrons would know the whereabouts of this relatively minor thoroughfare, so

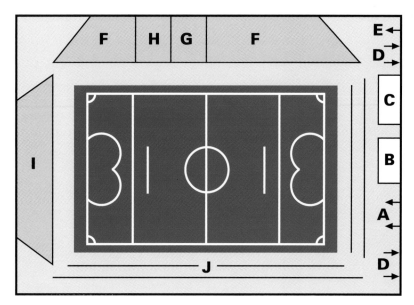

advertisements drew the crowds to what was called the Walnut Street Ground for the inaugural senior game, a friendly drawn 1-1 on 7th November against Nottingham Forest's reserve side; in which Jimmy Atter equalised Kearsley's opener. (In fact, Fosse's own reserves had had prior use of the new pitch, on 17th October, when beating Melton Swifts 3-2. The visitors' Paddy Slawson drew first blood on that day, with Billy Davis the first Fossil on the scoresheet).

Loughborough were the initial Midland League guests on the new ground, but it was not until 9th January that Fosse fans could cheer a League victory at Walnut Street, when champions-to-be Rotherham Town succumbed by 4-1. Indeed, it had long been apparent even by this juncture that Fosse were ill-equipped in playing terms for the regular competitive challenge. They had done little to strengthen their squad from the previous campaign, and a succession of reverses and dents to morale was topped in the return game at Rotherham, when a ten-man Fosse shipped eleven goals without reply. Outside-left Amos Atkins was the man who failed to turn up for this fixture, on only the second occasion he'd been selected.

The season ended with Fosse sharing the wooden spoon with Derby Junction. They had failed to win any of their final eight fixtures, and would have been stranded on rock-bottom had goal-average or goal-difference then entered the calculations. Gate receipts had amounted to only £599, but both the financial and playing state of the club had come under intense discussion on March 18th, when a public meeting at the Co-Operative Hall chaired by J T Hincks had been called to "consider the question of raising the standard of Association football in Leicester, and the best means of helping the Fosse Football Club to attain this end". A fund-raising committee was elected, and an immediate infusion of £200 added to club coffers.

Public support for the novelty of regular competitive soccer was not yet massive – and competing demands for patronage included such

Above: A plan of the ground in the mid 1890s. Filbert Street ran along the right hand side.

KEY

A Ground Entrance
B Refreshments Room
C Secretary's Office
D Exits
E Members Entrance
F Members Stand
G Subscribers Reserved Seats
H Press & Committee
I Open Stand
J Unreserved

'Kiddy' Lowe acted as both goalkeeper and goalscorer against Mansfield.

events as a week of performances on the Belgrave Road Grounds by Buffalo Bill's Wild West Show, coinciding with the start of Fosse's season – but at least it was wholehearted. There was to be no turning back to less rigorous local fare for Fosse.

Neither was there to be the prospect of an under-strength team representing the club for 1892/3. Close-season dealings by newly-elected honorary secretary Ernest Marson had brought several new faces to Leicester, including former Notts County goalkeeper Jimmy Thraves and dashing winger Billy Dorrell, who helped demolish his former Singers (Coventry) team-mates by 10-1 in Fosse's initial friendly. The club had now switched its official headquarters from the Victoria Hotel to the Freeman's Arms Hotel, and had also invested in considerable improvements to the Walnut Street ground, so that a record crowd of 13,000 (paying £254) could be accommodated when Fosse met Loughborough late in the Midland League campaign.

Two heavy defeats heralded the start of competitive fare (with forward Kiddy Lowe conceding three Mansfield goals while awaiting the late arrival of keeper Thraves, then claiming Fosse's consolation), but Fosse soon perked up with a record 7-1 win over Newark and more than held their own, finishing the 24-game league season in a commendable fourth place. Rotherham Town were again champions and, as an encouraging sign to increasingly ambitious Fosse, were immediately elected to the Second Division of the Football League.

Fosse also registered their first FA Cup success this term. In the Qualifying competition, they removed each of Rushden and Notts Olympic by the score of 7-0 (the latter in a replay) before bowing the knee rather disappointingly to Buxton. Indeed, the growing respect for the club beyond the confines of City and County was indexed by the selection of Thraves, Dorrell and Nuttall to represent the Midland League in inter-league competition; by the selection of Leicester to host the AGM of the Midland League executive; and by the use of Walnut Street for the then-annual Champions v Rest of the League fixture.

Another pointer to the season's satisfactions was the increased turnover of £1,640. Admission charges had been amended in October: they were 4d for Midland League games, and 3d for friendlies. There was still some hedging over the relative 'pull' of Fosse in their home town, though: the scheduled home and away fixtures with Gainsborough Trinity were switched to avoid the Walnut Street encounter clashing with the Tigers v Guys Hospital rugby match in January.

It was not so much a lack of self-confidence,

however, as a desire to honour contracts and commitments, that led Fosse's committee to pass up an unexpected chance to leap straight into the Football League. For it was not until 22nd August, when the 1893/4 fixtures had long been settled and nineteen professionals contracted for a Midland League campaign starting less than a fortnight later, that Fosse received an invitation to replace Bootle upon their belated resignation from the Second Division. Fosse, via president Frank Ashwell, deemed themselves 'bound by honour to the Midland League', graciously declined the elevation, and Second Division expansion was limited to fifteen members rather than the envisaged sixteen.

A concerted attempt on the Midland League championship, then, would become Fosse's seasonal ambition after all. An opening-day defeat by Burton Wanderers was soon shrugged off, but would, in the long run, prove crucial. For Fosse, Burton and Loughborough soon turned the title chase into a three-horse race. An attractive, free-scoring Fosse won 15 of their 20 fixtures, and lost only 3, but Burton remained unbeaten all term to take the title despite having two points docked for fielding an ineligible player in one game. Fosse did, however, pip their county rivals for runners-up spot.

Dorrell and Thraves were still starring weekly (the latter donning an overcoat for the duration of an eventually-abandoned, snow-shrouded game against Doncaster Rovers in November), and the gradual addition of ex-League expertise was helping consolidate Fosse's progressive reputation. Defender Arthur Henrys had arrived from Newton Heath before the end of the previous season, while influential Scotsman Jimmy Brown was recruited from Aston Villa in October to display his playmaking and goalscoring versatility, and centre-forward Willie McArthur signed on from Bolton Wanderers in April. Fosse had opened the campaign with a new Members' Stand, holding 1,400 patrons at 1s 4d per head (and raising £9 2s 6d in season-ticket sales), adding a prestigious air to their home enclosure – to which entry otherwise remained a mere 4d or 7d. Indeed, it was probably the seeking of prestige on all fronts which cost Fosse the coveted championship.

Their supplementary programme of friendlies now took in sapping encounters with League teams of the calibre of West Brom, Sheffield United, Newcastle

Billy Dorrell (above) and Jimmy Thraves (below) were starring weekly for Fosse in the 1893/4 season.

Above: A Fosse season ticket from the last pre-League season - for 'Member and Lady'.

and Wolves, and both the famous amateur Corinthians and mighty Glasgow Rangers were also added to the home fixture list for the first time (with Rangers' skipper Davie Mitchell becoming one of the first players dismissed at Walnut Street). In addition, the FA Cup campaign this season garnered wholly unaccustomed national kudos to the club, while nonetheless stretching resources.

Three Qualifying rounds had to be played through, and Mansfield Town, Mansfield Greenhalgh's and local rivals Loughborough were each dispatched without a goal conceded — though the latter tie was a fraught affair, involving a 34-minute delay while Luffs defender Jack Kent had his broken leg set by a doctor while still lying on the pitch, and drawing from the Leicester press the accusation of 'downright ruffianism' against the Luffs. These successes saw Fosse in the First Round Proper for the first time, and a home tie with South Shore (later to amalgamate with their neighbours Blackpool) produced a 2-1 win.

In the Second Round, the might of Derby County (3rd in the First Division that season) had to be faced at Walnut Street, and 12,000 squashed in to witness Fosse come close to a shock result. They could not quite breach the Rams' rearguard, however, and the goalless draw was followed by an honourable exit by 0-3 in the replay. (It was also followed by a hospital trip for Steve Bloomer, who broke his collarbone, and a day in court for Derby skipper Archie Goodall, fined £5 for assaulting a spectator). Later, a little consolation silverware was captured in the shape of the Kettering Charity Cup, after Wolverton L&NWR had been vanquished at Kettering.

By far the most exciting and rewarding of Fosse's three seasons at Midland League level, this term ended with two serious decisions to be made by the club committee. The first, though saddening, was comparatively minor: Fosse at last succumbing to the lure of a hefty transfer offer of around £250 from Aston Villa for Billy Dorrell. The second concerned Fosse's assessment of their own potential for continued progress. Would they continue to seek success in the Midland League or, with the invitation of the previous August as distinct encouragement, submit an application to enter the truly national arena represented by the Football League? The verdict was as unanimous then as it now sounds inevitable: Fosse would stand for election to the Second Division.

Some early action photos showing Filbert Street in the 1890s.

Election to Re-election

Into the League...

The Fosse committee, having definitively set their sights on Football League status for the club, spent a hectic first month of the 1894 close season lobbying their counterparts among existing League members, and their representatives travelled to the AGM on 21st May in confident mood. Division Two, now two seasons old, was to be extended to a membership of sixteen regardless, and Northwich Victoria had resigned from the competition; while the fact that Ardwick (newly reconstructed as Manchester City) and Rotherham Town were seeking re-election meant that four places were being contested by eight applicants.

Joy among the Leicester contingent was unrestrained when the election figures were announced: both Fosse and Manchester City had garnered a maximum 20 votes, and were to be joined in Division Two by Bury and Burton Wanderers (17 votes each). Rotherham Town (15), Blackpool (8), Accrington (7) and Rossendale (nil) were the disappointed candidates, but in fact Rotherham regained their place only a week later when Middlesbrough Ironopolis folded.

Team-building for the new challenge (at a time when no player signed anything longer than a season's contract, and wholesale personnel changes in the close season were the norm) became a priority for new secretary Mr Lee and his committee-men, though a lot of faith was riding on the Midland League stalwarts. The fixture calendar was negotiated directly with the new opposition, and the first day of September impatiently awaited by the likes of trainer Bob Roberts and skipper Jimmy Brown....

> In a season highlighted, naturally enough, by a series of 'firsts', Fosse kicked off their initial Football League encounter at Grimsby Town's Abbey Park ground. Newcomer David Skea claimed Fosse's opening goal, but a close tussle ended in a 3-4 defeat. A Harry Bailey own goal proved crucial in a match that earned the debutants generally favourable press comment. One paper quoted Grimsby keeper Whitehouse's admission that a Priestman shot had also crossed the line behind him, unseen by the referee; while also reporting that McArthur's legitimate goal had been scored 'while Whitehouse was pulling up his socks!'

A friendly victory over First Division Derby County on the following Monday boosted confidence, and the club's first points came from their first home fixture, with McArthur getting on the Walnut Street scoresheet after only 7 minutes, and Skea netting a hat-trick in a 4-2 eclipse of Rotherham Town. Duly jubilant home supporters were now paying 6d or 9d for their view from the newly 'banked-up' Aylestone Road side or Gasworks End, or 1s 6d to enjoy the relative comforts of the stand.

Alarm bells sounded when a subsequent run of four League defeats followed, but a remarkable 13-0 cakewalk against minnows Notts Olympic in the First Qualifying Round of the FA Cup (still the club's record score in the competition) heralded a turnaround in fortunes. A week later, Fosse were 0-4 down against Newcastle United but fought back to draw, and would have claimed both points had centre-forward 'Tout' Miller not missed the first penalty awarded the club at League level.

Fosse didn't lose again until Christmas Day, when they conceded their first hat-trick to Bury's Henderson, and in the interim both the first successful penalty (by Skea against Notts County) and the first own goal (by Burton Swifts' Hackett) had been recorded to Leicester's credit. A gate of around 10,000 had seen the first of three ties with Loughborough as Fosse continued their progress through the Cup's Qualifying rounds, but this run, too, came to an end at Bury in the First Round proper.

A League win by 9-1 over Walsall Town Swifts (who were only 0-2 down at the interval) established one seasonal record, while a 2-8 defeat at Darwen set its opposite, though this game was something of a farce. The original fixture on 30th December had been abandoned after only two minutes when the goalposts were blown down by a gale, and a 50-minute friendly substituted (which a bedraggled Fosse lost 0-6); while the rematch was deemed playable only by the referee, who allowed one set of posts to be moved back onto the adjacent cricket pitch, the playing field to be hastily re-marked, and the Darwen players to strap their boots in swathes of felt to help them traverse the mud, puddles and sand! The scoreline seems almost respectable considering a half-time deficit of seven goals.

Cricket grounds played quite a part in Fosse's season: they met Notts County at their then home, Trent Bridge; played Woolwich Arsenal on the Essex CCC ground at Leyton while their hosts' own Plumstead enclosure was under closure by FA order; and later faced Sheffield United at Bramall Lane in a United Counties League fixture. This latter competition was a supplementary first-XI league which had initially been set up for senior clubs who had made early FA Cup exits: Fosse's only season in contention was in fact the league's last.

The Football League, though, was soon appearing a less daunting arena for Fosse. Unbeaten in their final thirteen games, they came within a whisker of qualifying for the Test Matches which then decided promotion and relegation between the First Division's bottom three and Division Two's top trio. Finishing fourth with 38 points, despite losing the injured Henrys and suspended Archie Hughes for the run-in, only goal difference separated them from Newton Heath. Indeed, they were but a single point behind second-placed Notts County, and had only their poor start to the season to blame. David Skea took top

Above: A season ticket from Fosse's first ever season in the Football League, 1894/5. The opened out first pages (below) show a list of club officials. Club offices were at 5½ St. Martins!

scorer's honours with 23 League strikes and 8 in the Cup as an ever-present inside-left, while goalkeeper Jimmy Thraves was the other Fossil not to miss a game.

Perhaps ironically, Fosse hosted the crucial Test Match between Derby and Notts, in which a 2-1 win for the Rams kept them in Division One. Earlier, the Walnut Street ground had been the venue for the semi-final of the Birmingham Cup, when Loughborough crashed 2-6 to Aston Villa; while Villa themselves had been one of Fosse's most notable scalps of the season when Leicester had triumphed 2-1 in the Bass Charity Vase semi-final. Fosse unfortunately fell in extra time of the final of this prestigious competition to Burton Wanderers, who were also their conquerors in the final of the Kettering Charity Cup.

It was left to the reserve team to claim the season's silverware, adding the Wellingborough Cup to their championship trophy from the Leics & Northants League.

Overall, though, Fosse's first season as a League club had been the cause of quiet satisfaction. On the field, they were clearly not out of their depth, though there was a worrying note intruding from the accounts book, which showed a £200 loss on a season which had seen gate receipts of £2,587, and an expenditure on wages of £1,434. The minimum admission price had, however, been reduced to 4d in March, coincident with a lock-out in the local shoe trade. There had been only one brush with authority, when the FA had censured the club in November over an illegal approach to Wrexham's Welsh international forward Harry Trainer. 1894/5 was barely over, however, before Trainer was legitimately signed for the next assault on the promotion goal.

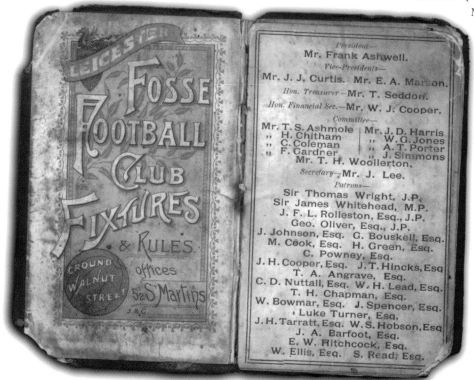

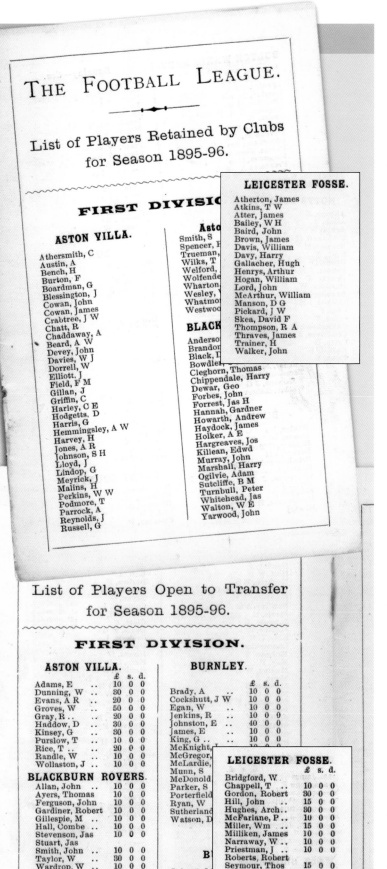

THE FOOTBALL LEAGUE.

List of Players Retained by Clubs for Season 1895-96.

FIRST DIVISION

ASTON VILLA.

Athersmith, C
Austin, A
Bench, H
Burton, F
Boardman, G
Blessington, J
Cowan, John
Cowan, James
Crabtree, J W
Chatt, R
Chaddaway, A
Beard, A W
Devey, John
Davies, W J
Dorrell, W
Elliott, J
Field, F M
Gillan, J
Griffin, C
Harley, C E
Hodgetts, D
Harris, G
Hemmingsley, A W
Harvey, H
Jones, A R
Johnson, S H
Lloyd, J
Lindop, G
Meyrick, J
Malins, H
Perkins, W W
Podmore, T
Parrock, A
Reynolds, J
Russell, G

ASTON [VILLA]

Smith, S
Spencer, F
Trueman,
Wilks, T
Welford,
Wolfende
Wharton,
Wesley,
Whatmo
Westwoo

BLACK[BURN]

Anderso
Brandon
Black, D
Bowdler
Cleghorn, Thomas
Chippendale, Harry
Dewar, Geo
Forbes, John
Forrest, Jas H
Hannah, Gardner
Howarth, Andrew
Haydock, James
Holker, A E
Hargreaves, Jos
Killean, Edwd
Murray, John
Marshall, Harry
Ogilvie, Adam
Sutcliffe, B M
Turnbull, Peter
Whitehead, Jas
Walton, W E
Yarwood, John

LEICESTER FOSSE.

Atherton, James
Atkins, T W
Atter, James
Bailey, W H
Baird, John
Brown, James
Davis, William
Davy, Harry
Gallacher, Hugh
Henrys, Arthur
Hogan, William
Lord, John
McArthur, William
Manson, D G
Pickard, J W
Skea, David F
Thompson, R A
Thraves, James
Trainer, H
Walker, John

List of Players Open to Transfer for Season 1895-96.

FIRST DIVISION.

ASTON VILLA.	£	s.	d.
Adams, E ..	10	0	0
Dunning, W ..	30	0	0
Evans, A R ..	20	0	0
Groves, W ..	50	0	0
Gray, R	20	0	0
Haddow, D ..	30	0	0
Kinsey, G ..	30	0	0
Purslow, T ..	10	0	0
Rice, T	20	0	0
Randle, W ..	10	0	0
Wollaston, J ..	10	0	0

BLACKBURN ROVERS.			
Allan, John ..	10	0	0
Ayers, Thomas	10	0	0
Ferguson, John	10	0	0
Gardiner, Robert	10	0	0
Gillespie, M ..	10	0	0
Hall, Combe ..	10	0	0
Stevenson, Jas	10	0	0
Stuart, Jas			
Smith, John ..	10	0	0
Taylor, W ..	30	0	0
Wardrop, W ..	10	0	0
Walton, N ..	10	0	0

BOLTON WANDERERS.			
Bracelin, J ..	10	0	0
Burns, W ..	30	0	0
Bentley, H ..	50	0	0
Docherty, J ..	30	0	0
Gardiner, H ..	50	0	0
McGinn, J ..	30	0	0
Mates, J ..	10	0	0
Spence, A ..	10	0	0
Stevenson, J ..	20	0	0
Weir, D	20	0	0
Wilson, J ..	20	0	0

BURNLEY.	£	s.	d.
Brady, A ..	10	0	0
Cockshutt, J W	10	0	0
Egan, W ..	10	0	0
Jenkins, R ..	10	0	0
Johnston, E ..	40	0	0
James, E ..	10	0	0
King, G ..	10	0	0
McKnight,			
McGregor,			
McLardie,			
Munn, S			
McDonald			
Parker, S			
Porterfield			
Ryan, W			
Sutherland			
Watson, D			

LEICESTER FOSSE.	£	s.	d.
Bridgford, W			
Chappell, T ..	10	0	0
Gordon, Robert	30	0	0
Hill, John ..	15	0	0
Hughes, Arch..	30	0	0
McFarlane, P ..	10	0	0
Miller, Wm ..	15	0	0
Milliken, James	10	0	0
Narraway, W ..	10	0	0
Priestman, J ..	10	0	0
Roberts, Robert			
Seymour, Thos	15	0	0
Stirling, James	10	0	0
Smith, George	20	0	0
Whitelaw, A ..	10	0	0

B[...]			
Calvert, J			
Crowther,			
Edwards, J			
Gillespie,			
Heath, R			
Hislop, A ..	20	0	0
Kirkland, J ..	10	0	0
Morris, A G ..	20	0	0
Murdoch, M ..	20	0	0
Ostler, J ..	5	0	0
Park, W ..	5	0	0
Perry, J W			
Templeton, R			
White, J ..	10	0	0

> The omens looked good for Fosse after their inaugural near-miss, but events were soon to sour. Near-neighbours and old rivals Loughborough had joined Fosse in Division Two, guaranteeing a couple of derby fixtures, and there were five new players in the opening line-up, prepared for the fray by a new trainer, Joe Newton. In fact, Fosse had celebrated a double over the Luffs by the middle of November (5-0 at home and 4-1 away), but there had been few other victories to cheer, and in that month secretary Lee resigned. He was presented with a gold medal by the players, with whom he had been extremely popular, and replaced by former West Bromwich Albion administrator Henry 'Swin' Jackson.

Quite what was going on in the background was unclear, though regular half-back Arthur Henrys was twice suspended by the committee for indiscipline, but it was evident that Fosse had lost their on-field consistency. A win over champions-to-be Liverpool and a draw at Woolwich Arsenal were followed seven days later by a humbling home FA Cup exit at the hands of Midland Leaguers Kettering.

Fosse were removed from three lesser cup competitions in January, and only climbed to mid-table League respectability with a revival in March which coincided with the return of old hero Billy Dorrell. Dorrell in fact missed his train to the home fixture with Rotherham Town, in which a reshuffled Fosse scored eight without reply (Harry Trainer belatedly coming good with a nap hand), but he was unfortunate enough to be present at Grimsby for the season's final game, when leading scorer Willie McArthur was experimented with at centre-half, and the Mariners' hot-shot Tommy McCairns helped himself to a six-goal haul from a 1-7 debacle.

The reserves again took the championship of the Leics & Northants League, but their triumph was a little hollow, as only nine teams competed, and the league itself was disbanded in May. Fosse's home ground was chosen to host the FA Amateur Cup final on 28th March, when Bishop Auckland scraped a 1-0 win over Royal Artillery (Portsmouth). Finally, it was noted that the finances were getting little better: gate receipts had dropped by over £200, and the players' wage bill had risen by almost the same amount. 25th May saw Fosse promote an athletic Sports Day, the first of many such fund-raising events over the next few years.

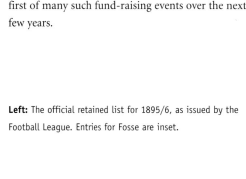

Left: The official retained list for 1895/6, as issued by the Football League. Entries for Fosse are inset.

Above: Early action from Filbert Street.

> New faces abounded as Fosse faced their third season of League combat. Club President Frank Ashwell stepped down from office (six months before his death in December 1896) and was replaced by JFL Rolleston, while club trainer Joe Newton departed for Dundee (and had his role assumed by former Wolves, Liverpool and Loughborough mentor John Jackson). Six new players graced the Fosse line-up for the opening game against Darwen, and three of them got on the scoresheet in a 4-1 win, on the first occasion that neutral linesmen became mandatory.

Poor away form soon scuttled hopes of a promotion challenge, though, and a mid-table placing was on the cards from early in the season. All-too-typical inconsistency saw League victories over higher placed Newton Heath and Newcastle (5-0) bracketing a second successive Cup surrender to Kettering, for whom Fossil-to-be Alf Ball claimed a crucial goal.

Wages for the team who took Fosse to their lowest-yet placing of 9th were now up to £1,834, while gate receipts had fallen again to £2,344, with 10% of that total accounted for by the Christmas Day derby with Loughborough (who were again despatched home and away). A week-long Bazaar had been organised by the club at the Floral Hall in October to boost depleted funds, but the only substantial boosts to depleted spirits were the capture of both the Burford and Rushden Cups.

In the former, more highly regarded competition, Fosse humbled Nottingham Forest 3-0 in the semi-

final and beat Second Division champions Notts County with two Billy Dorrell goals in the final; while the latter pot was secured with a 4-0 final win over Rushden themselves. Fosse's reserves, meanwhile, had claimed runners-up spot in the Leicestershire Senior League, won by Hinckley Town.

Back at League level, goalkeeper Jimmy Thraves bowed out in February after not having missed a senior game since 1892; and outside-right Willie Freebairn disgraced himself by becoming the first Fossil sent off in the League when he harangued a linesman at Lincoln. Both disgraced and disgruntled was Burton Wanderers full-back Cunningham, who parted from his teammates after the January fixture in Leicester, toured a few pubs challenging all and sundry to take him on, and eventually found enough takers to hospitalise him!

There was more chatter of a positive nature to come in the early weeks of the close season, though. There had been several of the classic pre-meetings in smoke-filled rooms in the run-up to the club's AGM on 26th May 1897, at the Temperance Hall, and a substantial motion was on the agenda as a result. Mr Rolleston chaired the meeting, and from the floor Mr George Boyling held forth on the failure of the current committee – 'hamstrung by cliques', as he put it – and proposed the setting up of a Limited Company. His motion was seconded by existing committee member Samuel Hudson, and eventually passed, amidst some acrimonious argument.

Below: Note the linesman's attire and 'flag' in this early Filbert Street picture!

> The behind-the-scenes shuffles of the summer meant Fosse now had their first board of directors (inheriting a debt of £1,086 from the old committee), with Samuel Hudson in the chair, and a new secretary/manager in William D Clark, formerly with Burton Wanderers and Derby County. The latter's first innovation was to promote an exhibition game of baseball at Filbert Street, when Crystal Palace met Derby on 21st August, and a series of 100-yard handicap races for footballers, eventually won by Billy Dorrell. When he turned to soccer, it was to put out a reshaped Fosse side as Luton Town's first-ever opponents in the League, but the home draw achieved brought Fosse one of only two points garnered from the first five matches.

Fosse's season thereafter was a matter of fits and starts, with a seven-game unbeaten run putting them back on course for another mid-table finale, though this time in the improved position of 7th. Clark's eye for a novelty led him to precede the Darwen home game with a 440-yard challenge race between Dorrell and visiting American half-miler C H Kilpatrick, which won the Fosse flyer £10, but which presumably tired him out for the game in hand, which was lost 0-1.

Only a week or so later, the board's response to indiscipline and insubordination (almost certainly alcohol-related) on the part of some players led to six of them being suspended indefinitely, and indeed several were never again heard of in a Football League context. (The fact that Fosse retained their registrations for that competition suitably indexed the then-pertaining state of 'soccer slavery' professionals found themselves in).

By this time Fosse were out of the FA Cup as well as the hunt for League honours. Though trainer Jackson's special regime for the Cup-tie at Southampton rather charmingly included 'paperchasing', the strong Southern League outfit proved too strong on the day of Fosse's first automatic entry to the First Round proper. The Burford Cup was also surrendered during the season (to Nottingham Forest in the final, in the last game they ever played on their old Town Ground, prior to moving to the current City Ground site), as was the Rushden trophy (again in the final, but this time to Midland League outfit Wellingborough).

The closing stages of the season were brightened in one regard for Fosse, however, when left-half Dick Jones and reserve forward Alfred Watkins together won Welsh caps against Scotland, the first international honours to be earned by players while on Fosse's books.

Above: Johnny McMillan was an early hero of the local fans.

Below: More early action from Filbert Street, where the cameras of the period struggled to keep pace with the play.

> Transfer activity around the Fosse was, if anything, noticeably less hectic than the close season norm during the summer months of 1898 – the departure of trainer Jackson to Brighton United and his replacement by Bob Dunmore initially occasioning more comment than the movement of players. It was therefore quite a surprise just how much dust and dirt was kicked up in the early weeks of September as William Clark's dealings came under official scrutiny.

First, rivals Loughborough charged Fosse with poaching goalkeeper Godfrey Beardsley, but withdrew the accusation when accepting £25 and the promise of a friendly game. This climbdown pleased neither the FA, who instigated an enquiry, nor the outvoted chairman and secretary-manager of the Luffs, who both resigned. Fosse director Ernest Marson also resigned, and secretary Clark was suspended pending the FA's findings. But a second bombshell was to fall almost immediately, for Clark had signed former England 'keeper (and more recently Stoke secretary) Billy Rowley for the opening League game at Lincoln, and had paid this veteran amateur an illegal signing-on fee.

It was October before the FA delivered their judgement: for the Rowley affair, Fosse were fined £10, and both Rowley and Clark suspended for 12 months from all involvement with football; while for their parts in the Beardsley matter, Fosse were fined £50, and Clark suspended sine die. In November, the club were still applying for more time to pay!

Fall-out from these upheavals was still being felt some time later, with Fosse chairman Samuel Hudson resigning in January 1899, and director Arthur Staines being suspended for eight months from April, when Clark's first appeal against his sentence was unsuccessful. (It would eventually be lifted in October, after which Clark took up a post with Burton United).

While all this was going on, replacement secretary George Johnson was marshalling his inherited forces into credible promotion challengers. A run of twelve wins in fifteen games ended in late January with Fosse

atop the Second Division chart for the first time ever. A home win over Barnsley put them there, though a remarkable 6-1 win at Luton the week before had set them up, in a game marred by crowd disturbances and attempts by the home fans to assault referee Kingswell – Luton's ground was closed for a fortnight as a result.

Another instance of disciplinary ground closure was brought to light a fortnight later, for while Fosse were being toppled from their lofty perch with a 0-4 defeat at Gainsborough, Filbert Street was hosting another Division Two game, between Loughborough and Blackpool. The long-suffering Luffs' fans had also been demonstrating their agitation rather too strongly for the local FA, and not for the last time were being forced to travel to Leicester to watch another 'home' defeat, by 1-3.

Fosse took their best receipts of the season (£344) from a 14,000 crowd at the February home game with Manchester City, but the result heralded a series of draws which cost Fosse dear; and it was another draw, at Newton Heath with two games to go, which finally stymied their promotion hopes. The penultimate game brought an impressive win over New Brighton Tower which killed off that team's hopes, but Fosse finished a point adrift of second-placed Glossop in the

Above: The top picture looks across the pitch towards Grasmere Street. The original Main Stand is featured in the lower picture, in a view that looks northwards towards the Filbert Street end.

first season that automatic promotion and relegation had taken the place of Test Matches. Few were more disappointed than Alfred Watkins, now a regular first-teamer, who turned down a further Welsh cap against Ireland to aid Fosse's cause.

Right-half Alf Ball (ever-present for the second season), Dick Jones and left-back and skipper George Swift were the defensive stalwarts of Fosse's vain struggle, while forwards Tommy Galbraith, Watkins and Rab King all reached double figures on the scoresheet as Fosse negotiated their first 34-game season with an unbeaten home record. The FA Cup, in which Fosse were forced to plough through the Qualifying rounds once more, brought almost predictable disappointment in the shape of a replay defeat by bogey team Kettering.

A season which had seen Fosse shrug off its backstage embarrassments so well (despite a £189 loss), and come so close to elevation, could surely have no other sequel but a successful promotion bid next time round ... could it? Fosse were almost at the stage of consulting the timetables to First Division venues at the new Great Central Station (opened in March 1899), but, as someone surely must once have said, football's a funny game...

> Fosse were certainly laughing for the opening weeks of the new season. With only centre-half Herbert Dainty and centre-forward Tommy Brown added to the previous term's squad, the team went for the first eleven games without defeat, at which point they were sitting level at the top of the table with Sheffield Wednesday; and drawing from the *Athletic News* the tribute that, 'For a team of genuine triers, that which does duty for Leicester Fosse would be hard to beat'. In fact, the eleventh fixture saw Wednesday as the Filbert Street visitors in front of a record crowd of 12,000 paying customers and several thousand more who poured in when the gates gave way.

A goalless draw in this game meant that Godfrey Beardsley had only conceded four in eleven games, but it was Wednesday who maintained their momentum throughout the campaign to finish as champions, while Fosse inexplicably fell away somewhat after the New Year, to fifth place. They would have finished higher, though in no less a frustrated state, had it not been for two disastrous final games.

The penultimate match, at home to New Brighton Tower, ended in 1-2 defeat – Fosse's first home reverse in two full seasons; while the final game once more took the team to Grimsby for a thrashing. McCairns may have gone, but both Hemingfield and Ratcliffe notched hat-tricks on behalf of the 6-1 victors.

Some Fosse supporters may have been tempted to blame the club's change of colours for the reverse in fortunes – this was the first season that the white shirts and black breeches had given way to an ensemble of Cambridge blue shirts and dark blue shorts – but a lack of punch up front was in the long run costly, and could not be compensated for by a defence which maintained admirable tightness until its regular collapse at Grimsby. Fosse could even risk playing non-specialist goalkeepers in two fixtures which Beardsley missed through injury: former

"For a team of genuine triers, that which does duty for Leicester Fosse would be hard to beat"

Athletic News

stalwart full-back Harry Bailey was an emergency stand-in for the 2-1 win at Walsall, while inside-forward Herbert Lyon was chosen in advance for the crucial home fixture with Bolton Wanderers, and kept a clean sheet behind a consistent, experienced set of full- and half-backs.

Right back on the opening day of the season, Filbert Street – now officially known as such on the club's display advertisements in the local press – had again hosted a Division Two game for the temporarily 'locked out' Loughborough, in which the Luffs had been beaten 2-3 by Bolton Wanderers; and this term unfortunately marked the last-ever round of inter-county rivalry at League level. Fosse were far from the only team to claim a double off the Luffs this season, for their neighbours garnered only one win and eight points from the entire campaign. Finishing rock bottom for the second time in three seasons, Loughborough predictably failed to gain re-election in May, and in fact folded a month or so later, with massive debts. In five seasons of derby encounters, Fosse had taken 19 of the 20 available League points.

Another pair of notable fixtures at Filbert Street this season were provided first by the friendly encounter with a touring South African side, The Kaffirs (reportedly comprising 'two Hottentots and nine Basutos', and presumably somewhat pleased to be out of range of the Boer War concurrently raging in their homeland), which Fosse won 7-3; and secondly by the FA's choice once more of the Fosse ground for the Amateur Cup final in March, which Bishop Auckland again won, this time by a convincing 5-1 margin against Lowestoft Town.

Fosse's own Cup hopes had again been dashed at the First Round proper stage, when Sheffield United's Bennett had claimed the lone goal of the tie, and the massive, 20-stone-plus goalkeeper Willie Foulke barred the way to an equaliser against the First Division leaders.

To date the authors have been unable to precisely identify the fixtures featured in this series of early action views and would welcome any input from readers.

> Ground improvements were on the Filbert Street agenda during the summer of 1900, with the pitch being slightly enlarged and the wooden terracing replaced by earthwork banking at what would soon become known, in reference to the hill battle of the Boer War, as the Spion Kop end. But improvements to the playing blend were harder to achieve.

Four new Fosse forwards faced League newcomers Stockport County in the opening fixture of the term (when an embarrassed referee had to borrow a coin from a spectator to toss for ends), yet the team's goalmouth failings were amplified and accentuated this year. Despite Johnny McMillan and Archie Brash each claiming four goals in a game at different stages, and Tommy Brown notching a hat-trick later, Fosse amassed their lowest goal-haul to date as they slipped to a moribund 11th place. In fact goals were at a premium all round for dedicated Fosse-watchers: the 34 League games produced 39 for and 37 against, and featured 12 matches in which Fosse failed to score at all (including six goalless draws).

Not only chances were getting away. Wragg, McMillan and Henderson were all transferred to Small Heath during the season, and helped the Brummies to promotion, while former Fosse favourite Rab King was quick to rub his ex-comrades' noses in the mud with a strike in Glossop's 3-1 win.

In a campaign that took an unexpected mid-season break in late January and early February – as the entire fixture list was cancelled for two weeks following the death of Queen Victoria – the only thing Fosse were first to do was complete their calendar.

George Swift marked another ever-present record by scoring from the half-way line in the season's-best 5-0 win over Walsall, and Brown completed his triple in this match by dribbling round an over-adventurous goalkeeper at the same spot and proceeding unmolested to the goal-line.

Only one goal came from close season signing Harry Hammond, but in fairness he was sidelined with typhoid fever for nearly six months after his transfer, and did not make his debut until the FA Cup tie at Nottingham Forest, which the Reds won easily by 5-1, with the help of a Calvey hat-trick.

One honour came the way of a Fossil this season, but right-back Mick Cochrane was perhaps not in any mood to celebrate it. The former Distillery player was chosen at left-half to win his eighth cap for Ireland, but Scotland rather spoilt his day by winning 11-0 in Glasgow!

NO ALE

> September 1900 had seen the failure of Fosse's first-ever attempt to gain an alcohol license for the ground, with the local council deeming the club's support excitable enough without extra stimulation. Such support was leaking away worryingly, however, and a seasonal loss of £615 ensued.

> Change, perhaps inevitably, was in the air after Fosse's recent disappointments. Nationally, the maximum wage for professional footballers at League level had come into force: allowing only for a £10 signing-on fee, a wage of no more than £4 per week, and for no match bonuses whatsoever. Against this background, Fosse's directorate, through secretary George Johnson, announced they were following a policy of assembling a 'cheaper' team than had been the case with the previous term's collection of 'stars'. (Leicester businessmen knew all about relativity before Einstein theorised it).

Additionally, the Fosse team would appear in a new strip: a rather attractive two-tone combination of dark blue shirts with light blue collars and sleeves, and white knickers.

The campaign began with a routine series of home wins and away defeats, but form in general was uninspiring, home gates fell fairly alarmingly (a late December fixture with West Brom attracting an all-too-characteristic 2,034 patrons), and Fosse were soon languishing nearer the bottom of the table than the top. Indeed, they were to finish in fourteenth place, not far enough above the re-election places for total comfort.

December saw a first-hurdle FA Cup exit (in the Intermediate Round) at the hands of Glossop, for whom veteran player-manager John Goodall scored the only goal, after having played the first ten minutes between the sticks before delayed goalkeeper Birchenough arrived. The same month brought the indefinite suspension of Tommy Brown, for a serious breach of Fosse's training rules.

Fosse's lack of firepower was again illuminated in March in the home game with Blackpool: the visitors' goalkeeper this time missed his train altogether, their secretary T A Barcroft stood in as last line, and only a long-range fluke by George Swift beat him all afternoon. The first-team forwards even failed when Fosse and Barnsley agreed to play the nominal Midland League reserve games between them at full strength: a goalless draw and a 0-6 defeat resulted, though ironically the Tykes did provide Fosse with their only double at normal Second Division level.

Desperation was becoming evident in several spheres. Not only were several local youngsters and amateurs inappropriately boosted into the League fray, but the club also felt the need for a little gimmickry in presentation, as on 26th April when an

CLYDE CYCLES are Best.

OFFICIAL PROGRAMME. Price 2d.

Leicester Fosse Football Club
(Affiliated to the M.C.A.A. and N.C.U.)

The Tenth Annual Amateur Athletic
SPORTS,

WILL BE HELD ON THE

New County Cricket Ground
AYLESTONE ROAD.

On SATURDAY, JUNE 15, 1901,
COMMENCING AT THREE O'CLOCK PROMPT.

The GAS DEPARTMENT BAND

Will be in attendance during the Sports, and play for
in the Evening

LADY ROLLESTON

Has kindly consented to Distribute the Prizes to the
Competitors at the conclusion of the Sports.

Admission 2s., 1s. & 6d ; After 6 o'clock

RIDE CLYDE CYCLES. LONDON

(side text) CLYDE BEARINGS are guaranteed 3 years.
(side text) CLYDE CYCLES for Quality and

> After a summer of recruitment on the cheap, Fosse's management clearly felt duty bound to offer a concomitant discount to their faithful support: cutting the price of a season ticket from 12s 6d to 10s 6d! It was initially announced that the former Blackburn and England winger Joe Lofthouse, recently returned from a Hungarian coaching stint, was to be the new trainer. But terms could not be agreed, and it was under the guidance of Alick Stewart, who had scored for Burnley against Fosse the previous season, that a Leicester side featuring seven new faces – including an entire debut-making forward line – fell to a wholly inauspicious home defeat to Small Heath on the campaign's opening day. After five games had brought only one win – and that, against Burnley, aided by another flukey up-and-under from the half-way line by full-back Andy Mills – it was clear that Fosse's decline had yet to bottom out.

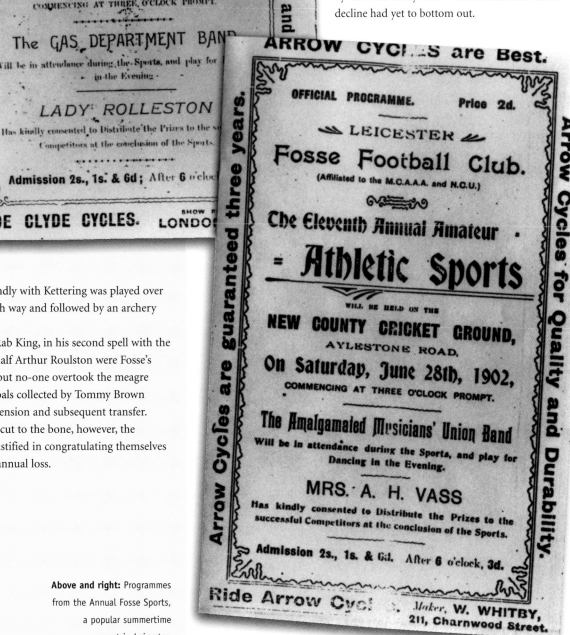

ARROW CYCLES are Best.

OFFICIAL PROGRAMME. Price 2d.

LEICESTER
Fosse Football Club.
(Affiliated to the M.C.A.A.A. and N.C.U.)

The Eleventh Annual Amateur
Athletic Sports

WILL BE HELD ON THE

NEW COUNTY CRICKET GROUND,
AYLESTONE ROAD,

On Saturday, June 28th, 1902,
COMMENCING AT THREE O'CLOCK PROMPT.

The Amalgamated Musicians' Union Band
Will be in attendance during the Sports, and play for
Dancing in the Evening.

MRS. A. H. VASS

Has kindly consented to Distribute the Prizes to the
successful Competitors at the conclusion of the Sports.

Admission 2s., 1s. & 6d. After 6 o'clock, 3d.

Ride Arrow Cycles. Maker, W. WHITBY,
211, Charnwood Street.

(side text) Arrow Cycles are guaranteed three years.
(side text) Arrow Cycles for Quality and Durability.

exhibition friendly with Kettering was played over 30 minutes each way and followed by an archery tournament!

Forward Rab King, in his second spell with the club, and left-half Arthur Roulston were Fosse's ever-presents, but no-one overtook the meagre total of nine goals collected by Tommy Brown before his suspension and subsequent transfer. With expenses cut to the bone, however, the directors felt justified in congratulating themselves on only a £20 annual loss.

Above and right: Programmes from the Annual Fosse Sports, a popular summertime event in Leicester.

There were spasmodic signs of recovery, especially when the errant Tommy Brown returned to become top scorer, but consistency could not be achieved at any price, and Fosse ended the term grateful that their away form had improved marginally – in finishing in the dangerously low position of fifteenth, their record included five wins both at Filbert Street and on their travels.

A 2-1 win at Glossop was prompted by an opening goal and inspirational performance from trainer Stewart, coaxed out of retirement for the occasion. This, incidentally, was the only one of the final seven fixtures in which Fosse managed to score at all. Luckily, three goalless draws closed the campaign, and the point so gained in the penultimate match, at home to Lincoln, finally ensured Fosse's avoidance of a re-election slot.

The Cup brought no relief from Fosse's misery. It was back to the Qualifying rounds route this time out, and while Fosse squeezed through on a roped-off, standless field at Irthlingborough, they then departed the slightly less modest surroundings of Wellingborough with jeers ringing in their ears after a ludicrous 1-4 defeat, marked by Andy Mills' second penalty miss in two weeks, and two first-half goals from that scourge of Fosse defences, Tom McCairns.

Injuries took their toll of Fosse's already fairly ragged forces: Mills was sidelined after being carried off during a Welsh international trial in February; while promising trialist Sandy Simpson broke his collarbone in a reserve game against Whitwick White Cross, and attendant Fosse director Tom Collins reacted with such 'improper conduct' during the near-riot which followed that he was subsequently suspended for a month by the FA.

Remarkably, though, the directorate announced a seasonal profit of £115. At the end of the term a home friendly with Reading was organised from which the receipts were specifically earmarked for the summer transfer fund; an unexpected windfall accrued when Notts County returned Herbert Dainty to the League sphere from Northampton; and winger Tom Simpson earned the club a £175 transfer fee from Everton. Disappointed not to secure Sheffield United's Winterhalder as a replacement, Fosse nonetheless went about their annual reconstruction of the team in fairly cheery mood; confident that League fortunes couldn't possibly get worse. Or could they?

RESERVES FAIL TO LIFT THE GLOOM

> In their fourth season in the Midland League, Fosse's reserves ended rock bottom for the second time, and subsequently withdrew for the less strenuous competition of the Leicestershire Senior League. In failing to agree a second replay date for the County Cup final with Whitwick White Cross, they also forfeited even that consolation trophy.

> Fosse tried another change of kit as 1903-04 got under way – turning out for the first time in the royal blue shirts/white shorts ensemble we now think of as traditional – but the only change in fortune was adverse. Despite the presence of a new on-field 'general' in veteran Scottish international Jimmy Blessington, League form dipped from bad to worse.

It was November, and the tenth fixture, before a win was recorded, and that, surprisingly, away from home at Blackpool. Already, a stinging 0-8 reverse had been experienced at Woolwich Arsenal, where a future Fossil in Tommy Shanks had helped himself to a hat-trick, and it was not long before a former Fossil, Johnny McMillan, repeated the feat for Bradford City.

Fosse's mixture of ageing veterans and callow youngsters could hardly be called a blend, and Second Division sides ruthlessly exploited the side's lack of defensive combination. Glossop's Goodall, Preston's Percy Smith and Lincoln's Dennis O'Donnell were others to plunder hat-tricks against Fosse as they slumped to the bottom of the table; there to become rooted until the season's end.

The board voted to extend its composition from 7 to 10 members in February as they flailed about for an infusion of ideas and capital; but they got an early lesson in how a football team is kicked when it's down, as respected amateur full-back Ernest Vickerstaffe was drafted in for the away match at Burslem Port Vale, and promptly suffered a serious

Right: Former Scottish international Jimmy Blessington.

Arthur Collins and Ike Evenson were two of the Fosse stalwarts through the club's tribulations during the early years of the twentieth century.

> Fosse sighed with relief at their reprieve, and George Johnson set about the annual task of rebuilding the senior squad on an almost wholesale basis. Goalkeeper Walter Smith had been a promising discovery of the previous term, but in front of him on the opening day at Blackpool were no less than seven newcomers, including former England centre-half Billy Bannister, recruited at a total cost of £395. Two days later, a friendly at Northampton spelt the beginning and end of the senior Fosse career of young local outside-left A Sullivan, who broke his collarbone in this sole appearance for the first team.

Overall, though, there was a slight upswing in Fosse's fortunes. The fans were slow to rally round as Fosse battled to a mid-table slot, and there was a falling-away in results once survival appeared secure, but a final placing of fourteenth at least showed the corner had been turned. Fighting spirit manifested itself in several ways; though not all were positive, as Walter Robinson (at Barnsley) and both Bob Pollock and Ike Evenson (at Bolton) were sent off in the course of the campaign. The severely-depleted Fosse (Hubbard was stretchered off in the same game!) yet managed a highly unlikely, but highly valuable win at Burnden, though.

The defence could still be charitable on occasions: Liverpool's Robinson scored all four at Anfield, and Manchester United's Peddie and Preston's O'Donnell (for the second season running) took hat-tricks off the Fosse; who had only Evenson as a three-goal man in the League this season.

There were, however, goals galore in the FA Cup, from which Fosse at last earned a bit of giant-killing

leg-break on his debut. In December, Fosse had fought for a 2-1 lead at Manchester United (helped by debutant scorer George Warren), only for the game to be abandoned 12 minutes from time because of fog. By the time the rematch was eventually contested in April (after an interim postponement), Fosse had already known for three weeks that they would have to seek re-election.

They had no FA Cup run to point to in mitigation: while Market Harborough had been slammed to the tune of double figures, and revenge extracted from Wellingborough, a three-game marathon with Burton United, abandoned during extra-time in the Leicester replay, was finally settled in the Brewers' favour on Derby County's ground, after full-back George Mountain had become the first Fossil to be sent off in this competition. A cumulative share of the gates from these five ties gained Fosse only a derisory £136.

Yet Fosse (worriedly posting a £564 loss on the season) clearly had the goodwill of most of the football community. Only a single vote went against them in the League's re-election poll, which they topped with 33 votes. Glossop were also re-elected with 27 votes, but Stockport County, who had finished two League places above Leicester, garnered only 11 responses to Doncaster Rovers' 21, and lost their status to the Yorkshiremen. Crewe Alexandra, with 10 votes, were the other unsuccessful candidates.

Right: Former England centre-half Billy Bannister joined from Woolwich Arsenal in May 1904.

glory. The Qualifying run started with another ten-goal hammering of minnows (Linby Church on this occasion), and eventually led Fosse into an Intermediate Round encounter at West Bromwich Albion. The form book suggested an easy passage for the Baggies, but Fosse overturned it with a superb 5-2 away victory. Three of their goals came in a whirlwind four minutes, and 'Pecker' Mounteney completed a hat-trick in 16 minutes. The subsequent draw for the First Round proper was hardly kind to Fosse, though, and they bowed out at that stage by 1-5 to a still-aristocratic Aston Villa in front of 26,091 at Villa Park.

Fosse's own gates were still too low to make economic sense of League competition, though. Director W H Squires wrote an open letter to the *Leicester Daily Mercury* in January inviting stay-away grumblers to put their money where their mouths were; yet was almost ironically mocked only days later when the FA added to Fosse's financial woes by fining the club one guinea. This nominal penalty was also levied on Bolton Wanderers: some over-zealous official had noted that when the two teams met at Filbert Street in December, the players' knickers had been too short – an arcane rule of the time demanded that they cover the knees!

As ever, a concerned group of fans were keen to assist the club through its monetary travails. In May 1905, George Johnson addressed the subscribers of the Fosse Supporters Fund, and explained the vicious circle in which the poverty-stricken club was apparently trapped. Basically, even after cutting the seasonal loss to £169 this time around, Fosse had to borrow to pay summer wages (when there was no gate income) and, therefore always being deeply in debt at the start of the season, were unable to invest in players afterwards to fill up any weak spots that might become noticeable. Looking to ancillary summer income, the supporters organised a race for professional walkers, and the club rang the changes on its hitherto-annual athletics day by promoting a Military Tournament (accompanying the local Yeomanry's exertions with pony races and a tug-of-war). Yet only playing success could tip the balance sheet into the black. Maybe next year...?

Above: Right back Harry Ashby was in consistent form during the 1905/6 season.

Above: 'Ranji' Hubbard top scored for Fosse in 1905/6 with 12 League goals.

> Team-building this year was a matter of self-congratulatory penny-pinching. Three departures (Robinson, Evenson and Webb) raised a combined £125; while five newcomers required a total outlay of only £195. The only directorial change saw the refusal to stand for re-election of G Woodford, who memorably left citing his tiredness 'of being collared and blackguarded every Saturday'.

Division Two was extended to a twenty-club competition for the new season, and one of the newly elected, Clapton Orient, travelled to Leicester for their inaugural League game, only to be sent away on the wrong end of an inhospitable 2-1 scoreline. Fosse remarkably found the weather against them the next week, as they splashed through 75 minutes at Burnley before the referee called a halt. A few nervy performances followed – including the gifting of their first League win to the other neophytes, Leeds City – before Fosse got into an unaccustomed points-gathering stride.

In fact, a seven-match unbeaten run on either side of Christmas raised hopes of a genuine promotion challenge materialising, and a further eight-game spell without defeat from late January to mid-March kept Fosse on the fringes of the race. However, hopes were pitched too high, and a subsequent miserable haul of only two points from the final seven games saw the club finish in a creditable but disappointing seventh place.

The rot set in when Bradford City visited Leicester, bringing with them 3,000 supporters on their 'annual club trip', and escaped with a 4-2 win, courtesy of a hat-trick from Wallace Smith, himself later to join Fosse. A further hat-trick the following week by Manchester United's Peddie (for the second successive season) merely emphasised Fosse's frailties at a time when they should have been gearing up for a final challenge.

By far their best performance of the season had come with a win at Ashton Gate in February. Bristol City were runaway divisional champions, and this defeat by a ten-man team (Oakes being badly injured) was the only one they suffered all term after the opening fixture.

Close-season signing Harry Ashby, at right-back, was a significant success in a consistent Fosse defence which featured centre-half Bannister and goalkeeper Smith as ever-presents, while up front it was left to local youngster 'Ranji' Hubbard to claim the lion's share of the goalscoring burden.

Fosse's Cup exploits of the previous season had won them immunity from the Qualifying competition this time round, but the draw was again unkind, pitting them against Liverpool at Anfield. A ding-dong battle ensued, which Fosse lost 1-2, but not before Walter Smith had distinguished himself by saving two penalties, and Bannister had blotted his copybook by missing one for Fosse.

The spectre of impecunity was inevitably another ever-present, however. The Fosse Supporters' Fund had been running for over a year with only a modicum of cash-raising success, and was superceded in March 1906 by the institution of the Million Farthing Fund, which again proved unequal to calming the worries of the bank over the size of Fosse's overdraft; as summer events would demonstrate.

Above: Uncompromising full back Joe Blackett came to Fosse from Southern League side Luton Town.

COUNTY CRICKETERS.

A. E. LEWIS.
SOMERSETSHIRE.

LEWIS

Three different views of Tal Lewis, the Somerset cricketer and Fosse goalkeeper of the period.

> Before the new season got under way, Walter Smith had departed to Manchester City, at the insistence of the club's bankers, for an incoming record fee of £600, and Tal Lewis, better known as a Somerset cricketer, took up his place between the Fosse sticks. Another £165 came in from Bury for winger Albert Hodgkinson, while also on the incoming turn of the transfer roundabout arrived left-back Joe Blackett, wing-half Billy Leech, and forwards Harry Wilcox and Frank Middleton, with Irish schemer Tommy Shanks being added to the squad in October.

A nine-point haul from the opening five games registered notice of intent and optimistic resurgence on Fosse's part, and established them amongst the early divisional leaders, while the crowds flocked back at this hint of success. And for once Fosse maintained much of their momentum. They were beaten only once at home all season, and then only in their final Filbert Street fixture, when Nottingham Forest lowered their colours by the odd goal of three to secure their own status as champions. But eventually Leicester had to be satisfied with third place, nine points behind runners-up Chelsea.

The lack of a consistent marksman was the main factor in keeping Fosse down. Wilcox was the only forward to reach a double-figure tally, with 14. The defence was generally sound, with 'keeper Lewis an ever-present in his only Fosse campaign. Harry Ashby was the unluckiest Fossil of the season; a broken leg sustained in a challenge on amateur international E G D Wright at Hull in March bringing his career to a tragically premature conclusion.

Fosse had to travel again to meet top-flight opposition in the Cup – they had yet to be drawn at home in the competition proper since becoming a League club, despite qualifying on seven occasions – and this time returned from Sunderland well beaten.

The reserve side were once again the club's only trophy-winners. They had now spent four seasons in the Leicestershire Senior League, and this year completed a hat-trick of successive championship titles, after an initial term in the runners-up spot behind Loughborough Corinthians. Henceforth, they would compete again in the stronger Midland League.

The upsurge of interest in Fosse's League challenge was reflected in the accounts book at the end of the term, when a club record profit of £1,167 was announced. Leicester fans now looked forward to seeing it wisely invested in additional players who could take their club at least one placing higher in the League table next year, and on to the heights of the First Division. They had at least one underdog success story to inspire them: in 1906 Ramsay MacDonald had become Leicester's first-ever socialist MP.

> There was a staunch conviction in the air that this would be Leicester Fosse's year. Season-ticket sales were running at an all-time record (£1,167); substantial ground improvements had seen the stand extended and the Kop enlarged to bring capacity to a notional 22,000; quality new players in the shape of left-back Harry Thorpe and forwards Jimmy Donnelly and Percy Humphreys had been signed up; and commerce was climbing aboard the anticipated bandwagon. Clothiers W H Thompson of Granby Street were offering a free mackintosh to the best Fosse player of each month – a change of tack, as their previous offer of a coat for each first-team hat-trick had remained unclaimed for two seasons!

The Great Central Railway were now offering regular rail excursions to away matches (a day return fare of 2s.9d to Grimsby being typical), and local publishers, Messrs Hill Brothers of Gallowtree Gate, were even attempting to launch a weekly sports paper, called *Half Time*, onto a market already saturated by the local dailies. *Half Time* itself only lasted until Christmas, and hardly endeared itself to Fosse fans in the interim with editorial suggestions that the club follow a policy of signing local players only, and withdraw entirely from the transfer market!

Fosse certainly kicked off full of self-belief. Only one defeat was registered in their first eleven fixtures, but form then wavered a little. An exchange deal brought popular centre-forward Fred Shinton from West Brom to stiffen the challenge, and even though the free-scoring Humphreys was allowed to move to Chelsea in February for £350 (the amount of a short-lived ceiling on fees imposed by the League), and

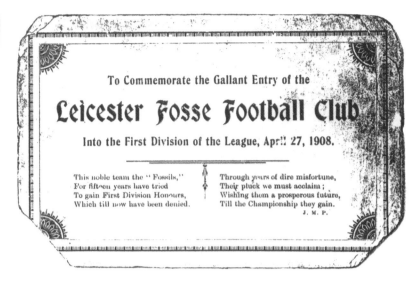

Above: A card commemorating Fosse's 'Gallant Entry' into the First Division.

Below and opposite: A pair of souvenir postcards issued to mark Fosse's promotion to Division One for the first time in 1908. Both give a good impression of the Filbert Street ground of that era.

illness removed Thorpe from the fray, Fosse were by then into unstoppable stride.

Even though, ironically, the local correspondence columns continued to feature an unceasing range of grumbles about transfer policy, team-selection and reserve strength, Fosse lost only one of their final eighteen games as they battled towards the promotion target. Nevertheless, a top-two placing was always tantalisingly out of their grasp, and Fosse were still in third position after the final scheduled Saturday of the season, behind Bradford City and Oldham Athletic, but with a game in hand.

Bradford, whom Fosse had already thrashed 5-1 away (a feat which earned them a brass band reception back in Leicester), were sure of the championship with 54 points. Oldham, whom Fosse had held to a crucial draw on the previous Tuesday at Boundary Park, were on 50 points with a goal average of 1.809. Fosse also had 50 points, but a lesser goal average of 1.511. They also had to face Stoke, away from home on Monday 27th April – needing at least a point to reach their long-fought-for goal.

As it turned out, they claimed both points from the nailbiter at Stoke, thanks to a solitary goal from Tommy Shanks (a close-range effort after Shinton's shot had been parried) and a characteristically solid performance from newly capped England 'keeper Horace Bailey. By the time the Fosse party arrived back at the Midland Station in Leicester at 10.25 that evening, the surrounding streets were overflowing with a celebrating throng, and

the players were cheered, sung at and played to for hours as they attempted to negotiate London Road and Granby Street.

The promotion effort was a triumph for professionalism – the players had been taken away to sample the restful delights of such places as Matlock, Quorn, Skegness and Hornsea before important matches – yet the season had not been without its reminders that the pre-Great War game belonged to a different world. Fosse had started the fixture at Barnsley in December with only ten men – Fred Shinton arriving on a delayed train in time only to feature in the final 60 minutes. They had also played several matches without star goalkeeper Bailey – never thinking of denying him the chance of an amateur cap, and thereby innocently contributing to his rapid elevation to the full England team. And amidst all the relatively high financial dealing of the season (leading to an eventual pleasing profit of £521), the board saw fit to award the takings of the home League game with Grimsby to stalwart defender Bob Pollock as his benefit payment. They had also, though, refused the use of Filbert Street for the Northern Union v New Zealand fixture, setting themselves firmly against any potential encroachment into their constituency by the increasingly popular Rugby League game.

The Cup might well have proved a costly diversion this season, so there were few tears shed when Fosse made a dignified exit in the Second Round, and were left to concentrate on their League challenge. They had proved a point to themselves by toppling First Division Blackburn Rovers, and took consolation that the Portsmouth goal that defeated them at Fratton Park was scored very much against the run of play.

Ultimately, there would seem to be no more appropriate way to close comment on this happy season than to quote the wonderful self-conscious hyperbole of 'Old Fossil' from the May 2nd edition of the *Leicester Daily Post*:

"In port! Tempest-tossed and weather-beaten, the stout old barque of the Fosse FC has at long last negotiated the shoals and rocks of the Second League, and reached a land of smiling promise - Division One".

Above: The Grimsby home game in February 1908 proved truly beneficial for Bob Pollock.

> Famed football-ground architect Archibald Leach advised the Fosse directorate on ground improvements during the 1908 close season, but a commitment to roof over the Spion Kop terrace was the only first-phase upshot. Season ticket receipts were now up to £1,223.

About 15,000 spectators gathered at Filbert Street on 1st September for their initial glimpse of Fosse in First Division action, and saw a goal from Jimmy Donnelly earn a point from a 1-1 draw with Sheffield Wednesday. Fosse's first win in the top drawer came almost three weeks later, at Preston, but already by then a cloud had shadowed the sunny prospect of the season. For full-back Harry Thorpe had failed to recover from the illness he contracted during the promotion push, had died on 15th September at his Chesterfield home, and had been buried by many of his former team-mates.

Lesser omens of gloom were also accumulating. Former Liverpool half-back Jim Gorman was injured on his debut at Manchester City and sidelined for many months, while former England goalgetter Billy Garraty failed to settle at all with Fosse, and soon moved on. Amateur forward Sidney Owen was often kept out of the reckoning by business commitments, and it was soon clear that the oft-changed team would not be setting the Division alight.

On a brighter note, keeper Horace Bailey took time out in October to help the United Kingdom to gold-medal victory in the Olympic Games football tournament.

What really darkened the horizon, though, was the appalling run of results from late November, when

Fosse picked up only three draws from a run of
fourteen matches without a win. Not unnaturally, this
sequence sent Fosse to the bottom of the table, and a
brief revival in March wasn't sustained enough to lift
them from the wooden spoon position. New centre-
half and captain Andy Aitken inspired this flurry, and
was rewarded at the end of the season with the post of
player-manager, but he had arrived rather too late to
substantially alter matters.

The fate of instant relegation was settled long
before the fixtures were finished; but it wouldn't have
been characteristic of a Leicester team to merely
accept their destiny quietly. On 17th April, they beat
Cup finalists Manchester United 3-2, a week before
United beat Bristol City to take the trophy. Then, only
four days later, Fosse contested (if that's the right
word) the game which put them into the record books
for all the wrong reasons.

Nottingham Forest put twelve goals past a
beleaguered Bailey, and might have had more but for a
spectacular display by the custodian; there was
certainly little in the display of the ten men in front of
him to pose a credible barrier to the Trentsiders' far-
from-subtle plundering, which featured hat-tricks
from each of Spouncer, Hooper and West. Questions
were bound to be asked after such a lacklustre display,
meaningless though the result may have been in
League placing terms; and it was the Football League
that asked them, when hastily convening a
commission at Leicester's Grand Hotel, chaired by
J J Bentley.

The answers presented by Fosse's representatives
(secretary George Johnson, director Orson Wright,
and players Horace Bailey and George Hedley)

ODDITIES...

*In October 1908,
Fosse met Blackburn
Rovers at Peel Croft,
Burton in a floodlit
game. This
experimental friendly,
which Rovers won 3-1,
was Fosse's first and
only experience of
night-time football,
played by the light of
"electric arc lamps
suspended around and
over the ground".*

*Fosse reserves
experienced a unique
case of a referee's
ignorance actually
being officially
acknowledged. Their
away Midland League
fixture with Sheffield
Wednesday had to be
replayed in its entirety
after the official had
awarded Fosse a last-
minute penalty and
then blown for time
before it could be
taken.*

centred on the fact that the Fosse team had rather
overdone the celebrating on the day before the game,
after former team-mate 'Leggy' Turner, recently
transferred to Everton, had got married in Leicester.
Accordingly, the League accepted that their dozy
performance by the Trent could be put down to a
collective hangover. (The 0-12 defeat equalled the
1891/2 scoreline of West Brom v Darwen, and still
stands as a joint top-echelon record; it was not
exceeded at any League level until January 1934, when
Stockport triumphed 13-0 against Halifax).

Fosse's pot-hunting aspirations drew mixed
success this year. They got past Watford after a replay
in the FA Cup, then drew 22,000 to Filbert Street for
the Second Round tie with Derby County, who spoilt
the party with a 2-0 win. A relaxed Fosse
did, however, pick up the Bass Charity
Vase in April, with a 2-0 final victory over
Southern League Coventry City.

Little, though, could compensate for
the loss of top-flight status for which the
club had waited so long. 'Old Fossil', still
waxing lyrical, but now in mournful vein,
should once more have the last word on
Fosse's predicament: "Brief and transient
has been their period of exaltation, and
woeful their experience...".

IN LOVING MEMORY

OF

LEICESTER FOSSE.

After the game had started,
After the whistle did blow,
Long had the County been
pressing,
Just then Barnes shot through.

Many a heart was aching,
If you could read them all,
When Bentley knocked Starbuck
through the goal
After the ball.

R.I.P. (rest in pieces.)

No flowers by request.

Left: Mocked-up funeral cards were a common
feature of pre-WW1 football. This example,
produced by a Derby County supporter after
they'd knocked Fosse out of the F.A. Cup in
1908/9, has the merits neither of poetry nor
accuracy - Derby's goals came from a Bentley
penalty and from Trueman.

> The close season of 1909 was marked by a new spirit of activism amongst members of the Players' Union, and when negotiations over a limited form of freedom of contract met a stonewall from League representatives, a strike was threatened. As the due date for the campaign's opening drew near, each club's players were asked to declare their loyalty to their employers and the FA, and Fosse's less-than-radical professional muster duly complied; though the mooted strike itself never happened.

Such matters hardly impinged, then, on Fosse's preparations for a renewed attempt to struggle out of the Second Division. But finance certainly did. Outstanding liabilities of £3,894 had been carried over from the relegation campaign; and season ticket sales had dropped precipitously to only £880. By December an 'acute financial position' was being declared to shareholders, and a scheme proposed to issue an extra 2,500 shares at £1, to be paid for at one shilling per week. Season ticket holders were asked to pay at the gate for the two home games over Christmas, and terrace prices for these fixtures raised by 3d to 9d and 1s. Crisis was narrowly averted, but boardroom gloom was a disturbing backdrop to the on-field fightback.

Full-backs Billy Henry and Dick Pudan and forwards Fred Threlfall and Johnny Lang had joined the senior squad under the supervision of new player-manager Andy Aitken and trainer Harley Thompson, but there was never quite enough conviction to Fosse's challenge for the top spots.

They notched up some impressive results, and Fred Shinton alone claimed four hat-tricks during the season, but there was yet again a serious falling-off in form over the latter stages, with not a single win coming from the last nine games, and Fosse eventually trailed in 5th place, some nine points behind the three teams separated by goal average immediately above.

An early home victory over Clapton Orient was unedifyingly enlivened by the half-time spectacle of an Orient player fighting a spectator, while a Filbert Street goal-feast around Christmas time brought eighteen goals for Fosse in three games, half of them in a 9-1 mauling of Gainsborough Trinity, who lost their goalkeeper when the score was a mere 5-1. Dave Walker bagged four goals in this game, which also contributed one of top-scorer Shinton's threesomes. Old Fosse goalkeeper Teddy Daw came out of retirement for the game at Stockport, but rustily conceded six.

The FA Cup provided the highlights of the season, though, with Fosse reaching the giddy heights of the quarter-finals (Round Four) after never previously having attained the Third Round. A fine 4-1 win at Birmingham started the run, then Fosse

Billy Henry was one of a number of new signings made by Andy Aitken.

Below: Sid Owen was a regular for the England amateur international team, as well as for Fosse during the season.

garnered receipts of £565 and a 3-2 win from the home tie with First Division Bury. A trip to Southern League Leyton, for whom ex-Fossil Jamie Durrant was now starring, attracted a ground-record 21,005 crowd, and produced a 1-0 win thanks to Fred Threlfall's 7th-minute goal. But Fosse finally exited in front of 52,544 at St James' Park, where Newcastle gradually wore down a Leicester side reduced to ten men after Shirley Hubbard broke his collarbone, and added insult to injury with two late goals for a 3-0 victory. The Magpies went on to win the Cup.

Otherwise, interest briefly shifted to the international arena, where Andy Aitken was reviving his Scotland career at centre-half in their 2-0 beating of the Auld Enemy, and where Sidney Owen was claiming several amateur caps for England as a goalscorer. One of Owen's former Burslem Port Vale teammates almost joined him at Filbert Street, but the amateur spirit was still a stark contrast to the prevailing professional ethos: Fosse announced that centre-forward Albert Cook would definitely make his debut in March 1910, only to find that on the day he was alternatively drawn to his accountancy duties.

> Tragedy clouded Fosse's preparations for the new campaign. They were determined not to overreach themselves in the transfer market, but had pulled off a promising-looking bit of business in persuading the 33-year-old former Wolves and West Brom centre-half Ted Pheasant to sign in July. However, within two weeks of his transfer, Pheasant died of peritonitis in Leicester Infirmary.

With the due period of mourning over, though, minds had to be concentrated once more on the game. At first, with Andy Aitken leaving himself out of the team and giving Teddy King a run of games in the pivotal position, Fosse looked as if they might put together a renewed promotion challenge. They claimed six victories from the opening nine games, but soon slumped alarmingly. Neither of the new forwards, Jack Hall nor George Travers, showed much firepower, and Fosse (who had now formally adopted Leicester Imperial as a nursery club), were soon forced into blooding a set of local youngsters of decidedly variable quality.

Results accordingly see-sawed, even when crowd favourite Fred Shinton returned from a brief spell with Bolton Wanderers, until a by-now-traditional end of season slump saw only one win garnered from the final eight games. A placing of 15th saw Fosse only five points above the re-election zone. With such a lack of charisma about the side, it was something of a surprise when Andy Aitken was awarded his final two Scottish caps during the campaign, and was indeed entrusted with his national side's captaincy against England, shortly before announcing his impending homeward return.

There was little cheer from the Cup this year, either. Southampton were despatched at Filbert Street in front of a 13,500 crowd, but First Division Middlesbrough disappointed 14,000 Leicester fans with a replay win in extra time after Fosse had returned from Ayresome with a goalless draw. Faithful goalkeeper Jonty Starbuck stood down after this game, to be replaced by well-travelled Fred Mearns, whom Fosse secured in an exchange deal with Barnsley which saw Travers depart.

Pretty much at a loss to explain Leicester failings this year was chairman W H Squires, though he had his own lengthy weekly column in the local *Mail*, headlined 'Doings of the Fosse', in which to try. At least the accumulated deficit was now down to a more manageable £1,189.

IN-AND-OUT

> Fosse reserves were seemingly intent on mirroring their seniors' in-and-out form: on the final day of October they walloped Worksop by 8-0, with Tommy Benfield netting six; while three days later they succumbed to Barnsley reserves by 2-9. They performed a home-and-away double over Chesterfield, then languishing in the Midland League after failing re-election in 1909, yet finished only two places off the bottom of the table. Indeed, they tried to resign from the Midland League in the summer of 1911, having been involved in the mooted establishment of a rival Midland Football Alliance; but this did not gain FA sanction.

> Mr Squires, with his column now redubbed 'Fosse Fancies', never quite resorted to mangling the old football cliche into a comment on this being a season of two halves, but he would have been justified in doing so. None of the four experienced imports who saw Fosse to a deceptive opening burst of two wins were in the side by the end of the season, for a dangerous nosedive in results up to the turn of the year prompted the directors, now back in charge of team selection, to declare a policy of pinning their faith on youth, and it was a predominantly locally-recruited squad who saw Fosse to the safety of 10th place.

By early February, Fosse had just completed a run of eleven League games without a win, and were out of the Cup. As if this weren't enough, the directors were prompted to their public policy statement by a couple of other events in January. On the 5th, long-serving secretary George Johnson announced his resignation to concentrate on his printing business, leaving director S Scattergood to take up the reins on a pro tem basis, and only a day later Fosse were involved in a bizarre spectacle at Grimsby.

In appalling conditions of rain, sleet and gale-force wind, referee Adams of Nottingham refused to do the expected and either postpone or abandon the game, which started and continued as a waterlogged farce. With 15 minutes left and Grimsby holding a single-goal lead from the first minute, King and Thompson left the field exhausted, to be followed five minutes later by Harper, Clay and Rollinson. In the final minute Allman joined them in the shelter of the dressing room, leaving only five Fossils on the pitch. Unsurprisingly, the game ended in a 4-0 win for Grimsby, and there was an equally inevitable sequel when the League ordered an enquiry. Each of the six players was fined £5 but, more controversially, trainer Harley Thompson was suspended for two months for allegedly enticing them off. This apparent injustice followed hard on the FA suspension of Fosse's young Cockney forward Billy Mills for having dared to play football on a Sunday.

The Cup ties of January were also to have a longer-term effect on Fosse. They found themselves two down away to Southern League side Croydon Common before fighting back to draw, and though they took the replay honours by 6-1, they had been mightily impressed by the opposition. They soon signed centre-forward Harry Sparrow (who'd actually missed the Cup ties), arranged a further friendly meeting, and then on March 20th appointed 34-year-old Croydon boss Jack Bartlett as their new secretary-manager; the youngest in the League. An advertisement for the post in the *Athletic News* had brought forth 102 applications, but Mr Laing of Darlington was the only other candidate interviewed at the Fosse offices; then still in Stanley Chambers, Gallowtree Gate, rather than at the ground.

Fosse had in the interim experienced their Cup exit at Barnsley, where full-back Sam Currie had a penalty saved, but were reviving admirably in the League thanks to the efforts of such local youngsters as right-back Tommy Clay, inside-forward Fred Osborn, and wingers Tommy Benfield and George Harrison.

There were also a couple of minor talking points thrown up this season. Back in September, there had been much muttering over crowd behaviour: seven Chelsea supporters had been arrested on breach of the peace charges after the match at Filbert Street. Officials were also in the eye: the Croydon Common Cup replay had been refereed by Mr J Talks, who at 4ft 9ins was the smallest in the League, while the whistler for the home game with Hull failed to put in an appearance until half-time. His role was assumed by a linesman, and that gentleman's flag taken over by Wallace Smith, the former Fosse forward now on Hull's injury list. Finally, the season was extended into May for the first time when a series of friendlies for the Titanic Disaster Fund were sanctioned by the FA. Fosse drew 3-3 with a Leicestershire XI in helping to boost the charitable coffers.

Their own coffers could have done with a boost, too; as a seasonal loss of £1,498 was reported. About a third of this figure had been accounted for by the unsuccessful re-recruitment of old favourite Percy Humphreys; who was, in fact, to become the last-ever of Fosse's even half-way expensive imports.

Seven Chelsea supporters arrested on breach of the peace charges after match at Filbert Street

> New boss Bartlett had begun recruiting players to his squad before the 1911/12 season was over, and it was perhaps to be expected that a combination of Fosse's budgetary stringency and his own background should lead him to concentrate on men from both professional and amateur non-League circles in the South. His reshaping of the Second Division team paid few dividends, however, and this was very much a campaign of struggle for Fosse.

Right-half Douglas McWhirter (an Olympic gold-medallist from his summer jaunt in Stockholm) and, later, winger George Douglas and centre-half Jim Harrold (both also being current England amateur internationals) were among the few Bartlett signings convincingly to make the step up to the demands of League football, and once more it was predominantly a case of the locally-produced stars keeping Fosse's heads above the water-line of the re-election zone. Fred Osborn was top scorer with 14 goals, and George Harrison the only ever-present, but both were snapped up at season's end by First Division clubs, with the former going to Preston and the latter to Everton, on his way to England recognition.

Fosse had few alternatives but to sell their most valuable players. Attendances had fallen again, to the point where an appeal was made to season-ticket holders to voluntarily pay at the gate for the final two home games, to help alleviate the financial straits. The professional players, as Teddy King later testified, did not know whether, or how much, they'd be paid weekly as they queued following Saturday's games outside Bartlett's office. The loss on the season was

Right: Two current and one future Fosse player featured in the England Amateur international line-up to face Germany in Berlin in March 1913. They are Douglas McWhirter (second from left), Ron Brebner (fourth) and George Douglas (eighth). Douglas scored twice as England won 3-0.

—AND "CROWDS" AT LEICESTER.

DECEMBER 14, 1912.

—for our "Dollar" or "Double Dollar" Prize.

The Victorious Preston Team.

Taylor the Preston Goalie.

Sparrow, the Fosse Centre, gets in some clever head work.

Mearns, the Fosse goalie.

More "RINGS."

There was a record number of copies of "Lotinga's," in the crowd, and wherever our camera pointed they were held aloft for the "Double Dollar." Unfortunately, some of the enthusiasts, in the excitement of the moment, held the paper *in front* of their faces, making identification impossible.

—(with photo and autograph) in NEXT week's issue.

EXCLUSIVE PICTURES OF THE PLAY—

DECEMBER 14, 1912.

See if you and your friend are ringed.

The Fosse Team.

EXCLUSIVE PICTURES BY OUR OWN PHOTOGRAPHERS

Another attack on the Fosse goal. Mearns (the goalie) clears with difficulty.

Dollar & Double Dollar Winners.

Above is the result of our photographer's visit to Leicester on Saturday, on the occasion of the "Fosse's" match with Preston North End. The "home" supporters were provided with a capital game, the only drawback being the result—3-0 in favour of Preston North End.

"Celebrities" in EVERY sport give their experiences—

First tour for Fosse

> Fosse's fortunes, in both monetary and metaphorical terms, may have been at a low ebb in the summer of 1913, but spirits were briefly raised by an invitation for the club to undertake its first ever foreign tour. Whether because of their residual reputation, or simply because they had just given a half-season's worth of competitive (reserve and friendly) football to international wing-half Karl Gustafsson, Fosse were offered an all-expenses-paid trip to Sweden by that country's FA, and set off on June 16th for a 46-hour sea-and-rail journey to Gothenburg and a whirlwind five-match tour.

What looked suspiciously like over-confidence at the outset actually paid off, for while Fosse took only eleven players (plus three directors) on the exhausting jaunt, and played their first game only two hours after arrival, they managed to avoid injuries and completed their schedule with five straight wins in ten days, culminating in a second 4-2 victory over the full Swedish international side at Rasunda, where Prince Eugene was amongst the crowd. New forward Fred Mortimer scored in every game, notching ten in total; all the matches were refereed by Danish international Nils Middleboe (just about to commence a nine-year playing career at Chelsea); each player received a commemorative silver cup; and arrangements were made for another young Swedish international, Helge Ekroth, to follow Gustafsson's path to Filbert Street during the following season.

Fosse clearly enjoyed their spell as ambassadors of English football, and the diversion was adjudged a diplomatic triumph, even if the FA at home – suspiciously aware of Fosse's otherwise impecunious circumstances –took some of the icing off the cake by demanding to see a full set of expense accounts when the party returned!

£634, contributing to an alarming accumulated deficit of around £7,700; and the fact that the club had taken over the publication of its own matchday programme, *The Fosse Chronicle*, formerly independently produced, made little impact on the income side.

There had certainly been few Filbert Street highlights to attract the fans. Osborn shot four past Stockport, but the season was on its last legs by then. And Cup hopes had been extinguished at the first glimmer. Southern League Norwich City had already given Fosse a scare when the first attempt to play the Filbert Street tie was aborted after 65 minutes in the midst of a snowstorm, with the game goalless. But Fosse failed to take the hint in the rematch, as they slid on a treacherous surface to a humiliating 1-4 defeat. Sparrow was lost to injury before half-time, but ex-Fossil Willie Bauchop had already laid on the Canaries' opening pair by then.

One rather cruel commentator claimed that the best football seen all season at Leicester had been that played in the benefit match held on behalf of former secretary George Johnson on March 6th, when First Division Bradford City had beaten Steve Bloomer's XI of all-stars by 2-0.

Above: A benefit game for George Johnson was staged at Filbert Street in March 1913.

> At least Fosse could make a bit of publicity capital out of their dire financial situation. As the season got under way, they were known nationally as 'The £105 Team', for only three members of their early selections had cost a fee: Sparrow £90, Mills £5, and newcomer Tom Waterall £10. Ironically, their initial away game was the first match ever to be played at Highbury, into which Arsenal's backers were sinking thousands of pounds in a gamble on North London support being more substantial than that found at their former Plumstead base.

Fine amateur international keeper Ronald Brebner was now between the sticks, but sadly his career came to an abrupt end with a Boxing Day injury at Lincoln, and a few fellow recruits from the unpaid ranks found the Second Division going generally too tough. Indeed, Fosse as a whole were almost out of their depth this season. A few choice results in the early weeks provided much-needed insurance cover, for a sequence of only three wins from 21 mid-season games had disaster beckoning, and eventually Fosse escaped having to apply for re-election by the narrowest margin possible – goal average.

With three games to go, a 2-0 home win over Lincoln City proved crucial, though it was a point gained with a Whitfield goal at Bury on the following

Above: On Christmas Day 1913 Tom Waterall played for the reserves in the morning and then the first team in the afternoon!

Saturday, while Lincoln were losing at home to promotion-chasing Bradford, that actually allowed Fosse to finish above the Sincil Bank club. Both sides had a meagre 26 points, Fosse finishing with a goal average of 0.737 to Lincoln's 0.545. It was little cause for complacency when both Lincoln and bottom club Nottingham Forest later duly secured re-election.

The rot had initially set in with the first home reverse. Four Filbert Street wins had preceded the fixture against Stockport County; and Fosse were 2-0 up after 38 minutes. Two dodgy penalties brought the scores level before a collapse to 2-5 defeat; and scenes at the final whistle featured Stockport keeper Tommy Evans receiving a kicking from fans unable to get at the police-escorted referee.

Not unnaturally, Fosse's on-field travails were accompanied by much backstage activity. The board, under chairman W Smith, had made itself unpopular with the Leicester public in January when prices for the Cup tie with Spurs were raised appreciably, and had also scored something of an own goal, as the smaller-than-expected crowd paid only £543, not much above the minimum guarantee Spurs were offering to host the tie at White Hart Lane.

Then the club fell foul of an FA commission, being fined £10 for making an illegal approach to an Ilford amateur, F J C Blake, via an agent. Clubs at this

Action from February 1914 at Filbert Street as Fosse 'keeper Herbert Bown thwarts a rare Leeds City attack in a game Fosse won 5-1.

time often used third parties to negotiate transfer deals, but the practice was frowned on by the authorities, and they were always on the look out for breaches of rule. In this instance the agent, former Walthamstow Grange secretary Bert Fish, was banned for life from entry to any FA-affiliated ground.

Only a week later, on 1st March, Jack Bartlett – who, unremarked, had already landed four ex-Walthamstow players at Filbert Street – resigned. Director J M Hawkes was temporarily installed in his place, but less than a month elapsed before the appointment to the secretary-manager's role of Louis Ford, a veteran administrator with both West Bromwich and Walsall who had been involved in drawing up the Football League's rules way back at its inception.

Almost his first act was to sell Tommy Benfield to Derby to raise cash, for Fosse's finances were still in a critical state, with a further seasonal loss of £365 being reported despite the sale earlier in the campaign of the likes of Clay and Sparrow. Both these promising players went to Spurs immediately after the Cup ties, in which the Londoners gained a 2-0 replay triumph following a remarkable 5-5 draw at Filbert Street which Fosse had come very close to shading – a Claude Stoodley hat-trick helping them to a 5-3 lead before they lost Teddy King to injury.

Though Fosse's seniors closed their campaign with a sigh of relief, it must have been one less exhausted than that uttered by their second string. The reserves had been switching Leagues quite regularly, most recently from the Midland League in 1911/12 to the Central Alliance the following term. For some reason, though, they had supplemented their 30 Central Alliance fixtures this term with an additional 40-game calendar in the South Eastern League. Remarkably, they finished 5th of 16 in the former competition, and 19th of 21 in the latter, with a composite goals record of 130 for, 129 against; and still found the energy for the four knockout games required to win the Leicestershire Senior Cup, beating Holwell Works 2-1 in the final at Coalville! Perhaps they took their cue from Tom Waterall who, on Christmas Day, represented the reserves in the morning and the seniors against Blackpool in the afternoon.

Outraged commentators either saw the continuance of professional sport at home as an insult to those fighting abroad, or believed that men able-bodied enough to play football should automatically demonstrate blind patriotism by enlisting for the front.

> In Leicester as much as around the rest of the country, it was a matter of much heated debate whether or not this League season should take place. Britain was already embroiled in the Great War, and the first casualty lists were being published when the League and FA jointly decided on business as usual. Outraged commentators either saw the continuance of professional sport at home as an insult to those fighting abroad, or believed that men able-bodied enough to play football should automatically demonstrate blind patriotism by enlisting for the front. Those in favour of the kick-off adduced that the game would provide a sorely-needed diversion at a time of crisis. No-one, of course, knew at this time just how long the conflict would continue, or the likely dimensions of its carnage.

The War evidently put Fosse's problems into stark perspective, but it could not hide the club's own crisis entirely. Summer team-building had, as was now customary, been done on the cheap, but at least Louis Ford and his directors had spread their net a little more widely for professionals from Glasgow, the North-East and the South-West.

The new-look Fosse only briefly flattered to deceive, though. After gaining three points from the opening two games, they were beaten in six successive games, and soon were shipping goals alarmingly. Wolves and Leeds City both claimed seven (a Herbert Bown penalty save keeping the score down against the former), Arsenal and Derby County six apiece (with Bown off the field injured during the latter game). Fosse were removed from the Cup by former boss Jack Bartlett's lowly Southern League Second Division side Swansea Town (in Leicester's last-ever appearance at the Qualifying stage, and last defeat by non-League opposition until the Harlow debacle of 1980), and spirits dropped terribly. In fact the Football League Management Committee were asked to advise on Fosse's internal problems when they met at Leicester on 19th January, and interviewed players Teddy King, Billy Mills and Sam Currie, plus Messrs Squires, Scattergood and Ford.

Their communique was published locally on 2nd February, containing the claim that they had been able to "adjust difficulties" in the relationship between the club and its players, but noting ominously that here was a "club shrouded in an atmosphere of pessimism ...(which) lacks vitality and confidence". The implied criticism was of the directors, but it was Louis Ford who resigned in the hiatus between the League meeting and the issuing of its statement. Director Harry Linney took over the secretarial duties; while the players pulled together in accepting half-wages.

No change in playing fortunes ensued, however. Fosse had only Glossop below them in the Second Division table, and were trailing the rest by some margin for the remainder of the campaign, which they finished five points behind 18th-placed Nottingham Forest.

What turned out to be Fosse's final League game under that title was a 0-2 defeat away to Clapton Orient (marked, like their very first, by an own goal conceded, this time by the unfortunate Charles Barron), but at least they had said farewell to Filbert Street in this context with a 5-1 win over Leeds City a week earlier. The Orient game was also the occasion of a concerted army recruitment drive; the last of the term's reminders of the context of conflict. Filbert Street had been used as a drilling ground for Territorial units all season; first-day visitors Lincoln City had de-trained at Leicester amidst throngs of people awaiting homeward-bound casualties; and the Nottingham Forest home gate was appreciably augmented by the presence of Belgian refugees.

Above: Fosse's final League game prior to the suspension of the Football League due to World War One. Skipper Horace Burton greets his Clapton Orient counterpart at Millfields Road in April 1915.

Reconstruction, though an obvious remedy to Fosse's perpetual problems (a further seasonal loss of £711, and a £2,250 write-off of the players' transfer values, only partly offset by receipt of £934 from the League relief fund, now contributed to an accumulated deficit of £7,307), would have to wait until the war was over. In the short term, thoughts strayed anxiously to the League AGM at which re-election had to be sought.

That AGM actually decided that League football would henceforth be suspended for the duration of the War, but not until after the voting had taken place to settle the membership. Fosse came top of the poll with 33 votes, Glossop bottom with only one. Stoke (21) were elected, and the other unsuccessful applicants were South Shields (11), Chesterfield (8) and Darlington (4). The immediate future for Fosse was one of uncertainty; but at least they had a future.

Fosse at War

> The decision to suspend the Football League and FA Cup programmes was in many ways overdue. The public could not really raise much enthusiasm for sporting events whilst so many of the country's young men were giving up their lives in the carnage just across the Channel.

Leicester Tigers had ceased their Rugby activities immediately upon the outbreak of hostilities in August 1914 and the Welford Road ground was actually acting as headquarters for two artillery units and a pioneer corps. Rugby was not resumed until Boxing Day 1918. The outbreak of war had also caused the cancellation of Leicestershire's final cricket fixture of the summer of 1914, and there would be no more first class cricket at Aylestone Road until 1919. This ground, too, was pressed into war-related service, being used as HQ for the 53rd ASC and for the Leicestershire Volunteer Regiment.

In contrast, Filbert Street was to remain open throughout the war years, as the Fosse continued to compete in the Regional Leagues that were created to replace national fare. However, in deference to the seriousness of the war effort, there were no cups to be played for, no medals to be awarded, and even league points were officially eliminated. This latter ruling was largely lost, however, on the popular press, who continued to publish league tables every weekend. No wages were paid to footballers during this period, though, and the only recompense to which they were entitled was for genuine out-of-pocket expenses.

The first obvious change for Fosse during 1915/16 was in their playing strip. Nominally because blue dye was hard to obtain, the now traditional blue shirts were abandoned in favour of blue and white stripes, an arrangement which continued sporadically until the end of the 1920/1 season. Fosse competed in the Midland Section of the League that first winter, achieving a moderate degree of success in eventually finishing fifth of the fourteen teams taking part – not that there were any official tables, of course. In a subsidiary tournament running through March and April, third place out of six was the end result.

As might be expected at such a time of disruption, the campaign did not pass without incident. Matches were compulsorily reduced to 80 minutes duration during December, but, due to inclement weather, the home clash with Bradford City on 4th December only lasted 73 minutes, and without any half-time break at that. Such matters were entirely at the discretion of the referee.

The introduction of compulsory military

service in 1916 brought about the official introduction of the guest player system in football. However, guests were being used regularly some time before that as clubs struggled to field full-strength teams. Some players returned to the seat of their families during the hostilities, whilst those in the forces could be stationed anywhere in the country. Consequently, guests who appeared in wartime football constituted a wide mixture of ages and allegiances, as well as a range of abilities from that of local enthusiast to international star.

Two old Fossils who had last represented the club over a decade earlier, but who found themselves treading the Filbert Street turf again, were Sep Atterbury of Plymouth Argyle and Arthur Collins of Norwich City. Another to return in the early weeks of 1915/16 was George Harrison, who actually missed the train for what would have been his final appearance, at Bradford Park Avenue on 16th October. Accordingly, a friend of regular guest Richard Gibson, named Cope, who had gone along as a spectator, was press-ganged into donning a Fosse jersey for the afternoon. This sort of occurrence was oft repeated throughout the wartime seasons.

The necessity to field an eleven-man team was no respecter of reputations or positions. So, when Fosse arrived two men short for the 22nd January fixture with Leeds City, the home club provided one guest, Fox, from their reserves, while Fosse had to persuade Billy Green, the former Burnley goalkeeper, to step from the crowd and chase up and down their right wing. Among other notable guests who represented Fosse in that 1915/16 season were Alec Donaldson of Bolton Wanderers, Jimmy Leach of Aston Villa, Neddy Freeman of Northampton Town, and the Birmingham pair of Gibson and Billy Walker.

Walker had the honour of recording Fosse's first wartime hat-tricks – at home to Leeds City on 23rd October and Hull City on 29th January, when both games yielded 4-0 victories. He eventually finished the term as the club's leading marksman, finding the net on 13 occasions in 26 matches. There were no ever-presents for the 36 fixtures, but leading the appearance chart were Sep Atterbury and Teddy King on 32, with Arthur Collins just one behind.

As the 1916/17 season got under way, teams were beginning to come to terms with the specific demands of wartime football. As more and more of Britain's young men were called up for military service the guest player system flourished, and Fosse would eventually call upon 72 players to see them through their 36 fixtures. Even this figure looked frugal compared to Blackburn Rovers, who used no less than 95 different players throughout the campaign! The

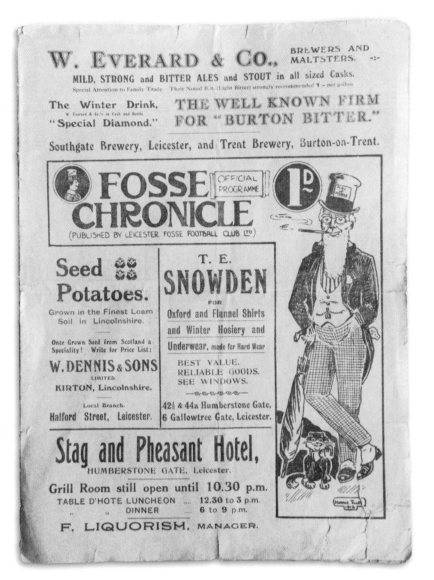

Above: The *Fosse Chronicle* also managed to soldier on during the hostilities.

Fosse turned out in an all magenta borrowed kit at Grimsby!

Football League altered regulations for the winter months, and the 80 minute match duration was now in force from mid-November to mid-January.

None of these circumstances seemed to help Fosse in any way as, after remaining unbeaten over their first six matches (five of which were drawn), their form fell away badly and they eventually finished in the penultimate position of the 16 teams in the Midland Section. Throughout November and December, the club actually recorded a sequence of ten successive defeats; one of which, at home to Hull, saw Fosse unable to score past visiting half-back Joe Edelston, who played in goal throughout. Incredibly, the circumstances surrounding the trip to Grimsby on 6th January, the day on which the sequence was broken, were perhaps the most unfavourable of the season. The team were not only three players short on arrival at Blundell Park, but were also minus their kit, which had been lost somewhere on the journey. Eventually Fosse managed to secure the services of three guests – Pykett of Notts County, George Padley of Worksop Town and Colin Stainsby from a local Grimsby team – as well as to borrow a set of strip from a local club. The borrowed kit may well have dazzled the opposition, for it was described as 'all magenta', and certainly the guests played their part, as goals from Padley and Stainsby, together with an own goal, clinched an unlikely 3-1 win for Fosse.

In fact, the earlier home fixture with Grimsby Town that season provided another headache, with Fosse playing one man short for the opening quarter of an hour, until former Fossil 'Nigger' Trueman was spotted in the stand and persuaded to make up the full complement. One presumed guest from 1916/17 who has so far eluded all detective work was the bearer of the name 'A Newman' who played at outside-right for Fosse in the home game with Lincoln City on 28th October. This time-honoured pseudonym was increasingly being adopted by players attempting to keep their identities secret, especially from either the police or military authorities, who may have had other ideas as to how the individual should be spending his time.

The six fixtures played in the subsidiary tournament at the end of the season brought about an upturn in the team's fortunes. A finish with a flourish, resulting in four successive victories, enabled Fosse to finish in fourth place out of the sixteen entrants. Of those who represented Fosse throughout the campaign, goalkeeper Herbert Bown was not only the sole ever-present, but also managed to get himself onto the scoresheet. At Hull on March 3rd he scored from the penalty spot in a 1-2 defeat. Full-back Sam Currie only missed two games, whilst Teddy King and Jimmy Leach were the others who regularly supplied the backbone of the team. A Coalville youngster named Cliff Price was brought into the side in January and went on to become leading goalscorer with a mere 7 strikes. Fosse director W H Squires made the first of two unsuccessful attempts to gain election to the Football League Management Committee.

By the time the 1917/18 season began, much of the original public hostility towards wartime football had disappeared. Travel arrangements, however, continued to cause major headaches, and on 22nd December, when Fosse visited Bradford Park Avenue, the train carrying the team arrived so late that the match only lasted 52 minutes before darkness set in. The referee was so impatient to make a start that he ordered the kick-off to take place as soon as Fosse had their statutory eight players changed and ready to begin; unsurprisingly, Bradford notched the game's only goal against this complement after two minutes.

Overall, the season's record showed an improvement on the previous winter. A final placing of seventh out of fifteen was achieved thanks mainly to a haul of eleven wins at Filbert Street. A slump followed in the end-of-season subsidiary tournament, though, and the club eventually ranked twelfth out of sixteen.

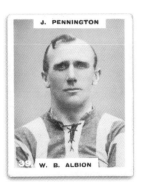

Above: David Donald, Harold Edgley, Jimmy Leach and Jesse Pennington all guested for Fosse during the Wartime seasons.

Guests were less numerous than in the previous season, but one who reappeared to figure in an unusual incident was Alec Donaldson. When Sheffield United visited on 9th February, he netted direct from a corner kick. Unfortunately, the rules of the game as then applied did not allow this, so only a goal-kick resulted.

Once again, Herbert Bown was the only ever-present, and his season did not pass without incident either. Against Sheffield Wednesday at Filbert Street on 6th October he missed from the penalty spot, and such a panic ensued that he was not entrusted with the duty again. Two weeks later, when visiting Bradford City, he was involved in more bizarrerie. A dog happened to run from the crowd behind him just as he prepared to take a goal-kick, and Bown unwittingly landed his hefty punt on the canine intruder instead of the ball. Luckily, no permanent damage was done to either man or beast. A number of other players turned out in 30 or more games, with Sam Currie, David Donald (QPR), the ill-starred George Draycott, Jimmy Leach (Villa), Cliff Price and Charlie Storer contributing to the more settled aspect of the side. Price was again top scorer, this time notching 14 goals.

The season of 1918/19 was destined to be the last of regional fare, as hostilities drew to a close and the Armistice was signed in November. With so many players in transit around the end of the war, the guest system again flourished, and 57 players were used to see Fosse through their fixture list. Unsurprisingly, Fosse again failed to make any substantial impact in the Midland Section, finishing tenth out of sixteen. Results in the subsidiary tournament evened out rather more, and a ranking of second in a group of four was achieved with 3 wins and 3 defeats.

The season did prove to be just as haphazardly eventful as previous ones during wartime and, once again, the trip to Grimsby was to prove jinxed. This time no less than four players missed the train and local substitutes had to be drafted in. In fact, Fosse played for the first 40 minutes with only ten men, so the 1-4 defeat was no real shock. There was also another instance of the club literally losing their shirts, as the kit went astray en route to Hull, and a spare set had to be borrowed from the home side.

The popularity of the game, once peace was declared, was further increased, and this was particularly demonstrated at Filbert Street on Boxing Day when the gates were stormed and hundreds of fans managed to gain a free viewing of the game against Birmingham. Fosse gave them value for their non-contribution by losing 0-4.

For the third consecutive season, Herbert Bown

topped the appearance chart, taking part in 35 of the 36 fixtures. His remarkable wartime sequence of 94 consecutive appearances, stretching from the opening day of the 1916/17 season to February 8th, 1919, was finally interrupted when he had to withdraw from the trip to Sheffield United because he was needed to help out at home during his wife's illness. Sam Currie and Teddy King were, again, the most regular of the outfield players, whilst Cliff Price made it a hat-trick of seasons as leading marksman. The movement of Allied troops throughout the season brought about the appearance of one interesting guest. Honoré Vlaminck of the Belgian Army played in four matches in November, and his three goals included a brace in the 7-3 victory over Sheffield Wednesday. He won four post-war caps for Belgium on returning to Daring FC.

Throughout the four seasons of regional football, Fosse had played 142 matches in total, winning 55 but losing 64. Four individual players managed to reach three figures in terms of appearances: Sam Currie topped the chart with 123, followed by Teddy King 121, Herbert Bown 112 and Jimmy Leach (still officially a Villa player) with 102. Cliff Price was the club's top marksman during the period with 33 in 75 matches; though the Fosse striker of this era

Above: Tommy Benfield was one of a number of ex-Fossils who perished during the Great War, shot by a sniper less than two months before the Armistice.

subsequently to build the biggest footballing reputation was Tommy Roberts, who moved from Leicester via Southport Vulcan to Preston North End, and on to England international honours.

Several men associated with the Fosse playing staff over the years failed to return from the continental battlefields: Arthur Beadsworth, Tommy Benfield, George Draycott, William Sharpley, Jack Sheffield, Bernard Vann VC and Bert Waterfield were amongst those on the posthumous roll of honour. More suffered severe wounds, and both Tommy Codd and Billy Mills had their careers terminated by the loss, respectively, of an eye and a foot.

Losses of a financial nature, however, were exercising the Fosse directorate as soon as peace returned. The club's balance sheet was making no better reading now than in the pre-war days of pauperdom; and as early as March 1919 came first mention of a 'Fosse Reconstruction Scheme'. Off-field events in the summer of 1919 would revolve around something more serious than a mere casual preparation for the return of Second Division combat. Rather more substantial processes of transition were being negotiated.

Reconstruction 1919

The front pages and editorial leaders of the local press were full of satisfied comment on the implications of the first change; the sports pages taking longer (and much less column space) to interpret the upheaval which is more the concern of this narrative.

A concerted campaign to whip up parochial pride was mounted for the impending visit of King George V and Queen Mary on 10th June, as speculation was rife that this event would portend the town of Leicester's restoration to the status of a City, after an interval of some 700 years. In fact it was four days after the flag-waving royal reception that the Home Secretary wrote to the Mayor confirming the restoration. There would soon be capitalisation on this event by the Football Club, but not until a more radical reconstruction had been carried out at Filbert Street.

By the end of the 1918/19 season, Fosse owed the United Counties Bank the sum of £3,150 3s 3d, and there seemed little chance of raising cash infusions for an essentially moribund business set-up. Accordingly, a winding-up and take-over by a new company was mooted at an extraordinary general meeting of the shareholders on May 16th, at the offices of Messrs Herbert, Simpson and Bennett, solicitors. The resolution (proposed by chairman W H Squires) was carried unanimously, and a liquidator appointed. A creditors' meeting at the end of May was told that, after realising the club's assets, there was still a deficiency to meet the claims of unsecured creditors of £940 18s 10d, and the resolution passed by the shareholders was confirmed. The take-over plans (already sanctioned in outline by the Football League back in late April) were set in motion.

The new company was ready for business by mid-July, by which time the change in status of Leicester itself had taken place. On 5th July, the new directors gained the assent of the Football League Management Committee for the club to change its name to Leicester City.

The following text, extracted from the share prospectus issued by the new concern, explains the terms of the take-over:

"...The Fosse club enjoyed a considerable measure of popularity, and became well known in Football circles throughout England, but for some time past it has been suffering from financial difficulties by reason of the adverse conditions under which it has had to be carried on, and it is felt that the time has arrived when in the interest of true sport, and for the credit of the City of Leicester (with the name of which the Fosse has always been associated), some effort should be made to free the Club from its embarrassments and reorganise the same on a better basis. It was therefore decided to wind up the affairs of the old Company and to reorganise the Club under the auspices of a new Company which has been registered under the name of The Leicester City Football Club Company, Limited.

"In order to accomplish this object and to make the Club worthy of the City of Leicester, it is considered that a sum of £10,000 will be required, and the Directors whose names appear at the head of this prospectus ask for sympathetic consideration and support, and trust that the people of Leicester will respond to the appeal to provide that sum.

"...The Directors have arranged for the purchase of the old Company's assets (including the value of the players' transfers) from Mr John Fowler Beale ... the liquidator of the Leicester Fosse Football Club Company, Limited, at the price of £4,500, payable in cash out of this issue. Nothing is being paid for goodwill..."

The new board consisted of five former Fosse directors (William Herbert Squires, Louis Henry Burridge, Harry Collins, Carter Crossland and Harry Linney), plus four new men – William Archibald Jennings, Arthur Needham, William Tompkins and former player Albert Ernest Pudan – though for some time the FA were to block the last-named from acting in his new capacity. The directors stated they would strengthen the team, embark on a series of ground improvements, and renegotiate the lease of Filbert Street with the City Corporation; while the new Articles of Association they signed seemed to cover almost any eventuality in terms of having amongst the club's 25 stated objects a paragraph enabling it to "promote the practice and play of Football, Cricket, Lacrosse, Lawn Tennis, Hockey, Bowls, Bicycle and Tricycle riding, running, jumping, the physical training and development of the human frame, and other athletic sports, games and pastimes and exercises...".

The new club offices were set up at 17 Market Place – where they remained until a move to the ground in June 1920 – and Harry Linney retained his role of honorary secretary until a professional appointment could be made. A sidelight on the times is provided by the fact that one of the numerous legal documents Leicester City had to file before they could commence business was a declaration under The Trading With The Enemy Amendment Act! Paperwork done, though, a return to sporting combat for the new-look club was less than a month away.

Certificate No. 157760.

THE COMPANIES ACTS, 1908 to 1917.

COMPANY LIMITED BY SHARES.

Memorandum

AND

Articles of Association

OF

The Leicester City Football Club Company, Limited.

Incorporated the 7th day of August, 1919.

SOLICITORS :
HERBERT SIMPSON & BENNETT,
LEICESTER,

City's halcyon days

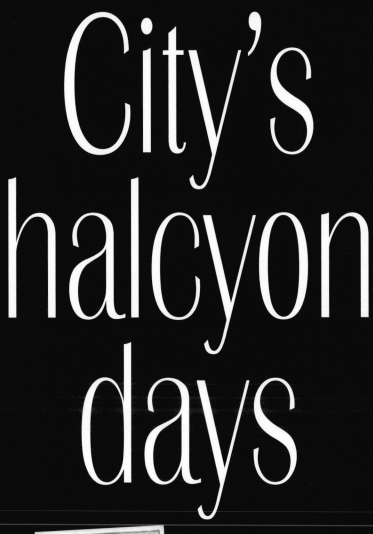

> August 1919 found a strange commingling of moods around Leicester. The euphoria that accompanied the restoration of peace was dying down, and intimations of social strife were growing (especially among returning servicemen and the unemployed, who were all too often one and the same). The elevation of the borough to City status satisfied the civic pride of the great and good, but offered no tangible benefit to anyone else. While the reconstruction of the Football Club – focus of interest for the bulk of Leicester's sporting public – encouraged a rather warily quizzical response; especially when it was revealed that the subscription appeal for £10,000 had initially raised only just over a quarter of that amount.

Would the new set-up be able to break the cycle of economic and playing poverty which had bedevilled the Fosse? Would the re-election trauma of the last pre-war League season be experienced again? Would the new board cleave like its predecessors to a style of amateurish administration of its professional playing staff?

It was a couple of weeks into the new season before the third question was answered first. Initially, local football administrator Jack Linthwaite was sounded out for the key post of secretary-manager. But he realised what the directors should have done: that outside experience was required as a signal of progress. Happily, this resulted in the recruitment of Peter Hodge.

The former Raith Rovers and Stoke boss was to be given full responsibility for team matters, and was to prove an astutely inspired choice to lead the new club towards unparalleled success. His initial tasks, however, were more modest – assessing and altering the balance of playing strengths (between veterans of the Fosse's final struggles and a posse of largely untried youngsters), and aiming at Second Division consolidation.

The squad he inherited was, characteristically for the time, an odd blend of experience and callowness. Remaining from pre-war campaigns were Herbert Bown, Sam Currie, George Douglas, Teddy King, Norman Whitfield and skipper Jim Harrold; while former Fossils Billy Thomson and Shirley Hubbard had also been persuaded to re-sign after spells away. More recent discoveries, untested beyond the bounds of wartime competition, included Sid Harrold, Ike Smith, Billy Barrett and Cliff Price; while 'name' players fixed up by the directorate before Hodge's arrival included Irish international Jim Macauley and former Newcastle and Arsenal stalwart George Jobey. It was around this nucleus that Hodge would begin his long-term team-building exercise, though neither

he nor trainer Dave Gardner were to be tardy in recognising the need for short-term shoring-up.

City's first season opened with a home defeat by Wolves in front of an expectant crowd estimated at 10,000, now paying a 1s minimum admission (or having invested in season tickets ranging from 17s 6d to 2 guineas). George Douglas became the first scorer for the new club, but goals from Bate and Harrison negated his effort. The first victory did not arrive until the fifth fixture, when Fulham were beaten 3-2 at Filbert Street. Teddy King claimed the decisive goal, but was less happy in the return fixture a week later – a 0-5 defeat which featured a Donald Cock hat-trick – when sent off along with Fulham's McIntyre for fighting. Goalscoring was an early problem for City, and the centre-forward position was proving hard to fill effectively. Hodge made a double signing from Arsenal in October of Harry King and Billy Spittle, but both forwards soon suffered from injuries, and it was December before a genuinely consistent striker was bought. Jock Paterson arrived from Dundee for a reportedly 'hefty' fee, and soon proceeded to justify it.

He it was who claimed City's first hat-trick (in a 4-0 home win over Lincoln City), just a couple of weeks before becoming the new club's first full international, when playing at inside-left for Scotland against England on the Wednesday's ground at Sheffield. Jock would finish the season as the side's

Above: King George V is introduced to the Leicester City team by chairman W.A. Jennings before the FA Cup tie at Stamford Bridge in February 1920. City players (left to right) are Billy Thomson, Jimmy Harrold, Tom Smith, Sam Currie, Billy Barrett, Herbert Bown and skipper George Jobey.

undisputed top marksman, with 11 League goals from his 20 appearances, and one more in the Cup. Only one signing this term was, eventually, to outshine that of Paterson, and that followed in January, when Hodge secured a young full-back from Bathgate, named Adam Black.

Despite all Hodge's experimentation with personnel (no less than 30 players made senior appearances during the season) and the concomitant inconsistency of results, City comfortably secured a mid-table position. Leicester crowds apparently appreciated the City's efforts, with 18,214 turning up on Christmas Day to see the 1-0 win over Birmingham and producing the club's first ever match receipts total of over £1,000.

Crowd and receipts records were both to be quickly updated, though, in the course of a Cup run which took City into the last 16. The board made efforts to get Southern League strugglers Newport County to switch their first round tie with City to Filbert Street, but were rebuffed despite offering a £600 guarantee. The team, however, ensured the Leicester public would get to see them through by drawing 0-0 on Welsh soil. The replay drew 20,212 (£1202) for a 2-0 win, and then 23,109 turned up to watch First Division Manchester City despatched 3-0, paying £1945 for the privilege. What they didn't see was the heroism of Jim Harrold, concussed in the first half, and playing on throughout despite fainting at half time. City made their exit at Stamford Bridge, where no less an honoured spectator than King George V watched a bad-tempered game in which City succumbed to three second-half goals.

One trophy made its way to Filbert Street, though, with the Reserves taking the Leicestershire Senior Cup via a record 11-2 final win over Moira United in April. Earlier, the 'stiffs' had remained unbeaten in the Central Alliance until November 22nd, but had then fallen away in a competition they were to dominate for the next three seasons.

However, the biggest smiles around Filbert Street in the close season of 1920 were those of the new board. The return on their investment and optimism had resulted in a profit of £463, and earned the club the rare accolade of an editorial comment of congratulation from the *Daily Post*. A year of looking back fearfully at the former travails of the Fosse was over; the firm foundations of the City had been laid; Peter Hodge could start to dream of promotion and perhaps even primacy for his new club.

OGDEN'S CIGARETTES

LEICESTER CITY

> The consolidation process continued this season, with progress to a final position of 12th in the Second Division representing a leap of two places over the previous term. Peter Hodge's influence – and especially its Scottish tinge – was becoming ever more apparent, though. Young Adam Black quickly established himself as a regular first-choice full-back in the early stages of creating the club record for League appearances; the amateur Roxburgh brothers were given sporadic chances in the forward line; and in mid-season a schemer from the classic Caledonian mould arrived in the shape of Harry Graham from Hearts. Jock Paterson was still the main scoring threat (claiming 16 League goals and one in the Cup); while the Reserves – who took the Central Alliance championship – instituted the distinctly Scottish practice of pseudonymously naming trialists as 'Newman'.

The Reserves, in fact, hogged many of the local headlines over the course of the season, due to the outstanding scoring prowess of newcomer Albert Pynegar, an inside-forward who celebrated the

Below: A crowd scene from the 'Popular Side' of the (then) Grasmere Street side of the ground in the early 1920s. Note that the early press boxes were exactly that!

season's opening day with a six-goal haul against Derby County, and finished with 49 goals from 25 second-team appearances. The Senior Cup was also retained by City's shadow-squad, with Loughborough Corinthians vanquished 3-0 in the final at Filbert Street. An end-of-term attempt to switch the Seconds into the Central League was, however, unsuccessful.

Back in Division Two, the first team's efforts were significantly stymied by a poor away record, with only two victories being registered on their travels, at West Ham and Nottingham Forest. The Upton Park game saw not only City's first points haul from London, but featured the club's first League or Cup goal in the capital since March 1914, after nine scoreless visits. At Filbert Street, the record League attendance was increased twice before Christmas, with 19,681 seeing Fulham take a point and 21,228 cheering a win over Cardiff City. It was again left to the FA Cup to generate the major interest in the season, though. Only one tie was played, but what a game! The visitors to Filbert Street were League leaders Burnley, who were in the middle of their record-breaking run of 30 League games without defeat, and well on their way to the championship. They drew a record crowd of 29,149 to Leicester, paying a record £2,323, to witness a scintillating display in which they ran out victors by 7-3.

Off the pitch, the most significant development at Filbert Street was the start made in March on erecting the new main stand, built behind the existing structure to plans drawn up by Leicester architect W E Moore, at an eventual cost of £26,482. The pitch itself would be moved ten yards towards the new edifice before the official opening ceremony in the following November.

Two effective changes to the City board occurred towards the end of the season. In March, the FA finally sanctioned the appointment of former player Dick Pudan as a director, while in April came news of the untimely death of chairman W A Jennings, at the age of 49. A self-made boot and shoe manufacturer and prominent Liberal, Jennings was borne to his grave by six City players.

Earlier, other harsh realities had impinged more tangentially on the club. A friendly fixture at Merthyr Town in November had to be cancelled when the home club were almost crippled by the effects of a coal strike, while in the same month Filbert Street hosted a women's football match between the famous Dick, Kerr's Ladies and St Helens Ladies (won 4-0 by the former) which raised £700 for the Leicester Unemployment Fund. On the monetary theme, City themselves raised their seasonal profit to £1,499.

ODD NUMBER

> In a season which saw Filbert Street's biggest crowd to date a 'record' was set at the other end of the attendance scale at the final League game of 1920-21, away to relegation-doomed Stockport County on May 7th. County's own Edgeley Park ground had been closed by disciplinary order of the FA, so the fixture was belatedly arranged to be played at Old Trafford with a 6.30 kick-off, effectively as part of a 'double-header', following the First Division game between Manchester United and Derby County. The official attendance at the City match was a League record low of 13. However, this figure merely represented those who paid for entry between the two games, and masks an overall attendance estimated between 1,000 and 2,000. Such is the stuff that some carelessly-quoted 'records' are made of!

> If Peter Hodge had been subject to a school report his assessment might well have read 'steady progress maintained' by the end of this season. The club was now established in the top half of Division Two and remained on the fringe of the promotion battle throughout the season, without ever really mounting a serious challenge; finally finishing the campaign in ninth place. The defence was much tighter than in previous seasons but the attack was still far from prolific. No-one reached a double-figure goal tally, with Jock Paterson and Sandy Trotter claiming eight apiece, and deficiencies in marksmanship were primarily responsible for the high number of away draws which drained City's upward aspirations of conviction. Indeed the campaign featured a record of nine goalless games in total.

It is probable that Paterson would have led the charts on his own for a third season, but his City days were cut short in March, when Sunderland stepped in to effect his transfer, and he went on to net another five goals for the Rokerites in a dozen appearances this season. In fact, the most noteworthy scoring feat of this curiously lacklustre campaign occurred at the wrong end of the field: with the three-goal defeat at Leeds being the single-handed work of United centre-forward Bill Poyntz, celebrating his marriage earlier that very day!

A fortnight after Paterson's departure, City themselves parted with a substantial fee. The target was inveterate wanderer Mick O'Brien, latterly the QPR centre-half, and a fine player who immediately added to his tally of Irish caps with appearances against Scotland and Wales. The club's other significant outgoings were charitable: in January they endowed a bed at the Royal Infirmary to the tune of £1,000 from the proceeds of 1921's practice matches and friendlies, and mentioned at the time that they had passed on a further £1,000 to other local charities. They also distributed 1,500 free passes to the local unemployed to boost the home gate against Bristol City to some 16,000.

City's Cup campaign consisted of a trio of meetings with clubs from the capital. Clapton Orient and Fulham were both despatched at Filbert Street (with the *Daily Express* noting that City 'produced surprising virility in attack' against the Cottagers), but Arsenal at Highbury were too sharp for Leicester.

On the international scene, Filbert Street was chosen as the venue for an amateur international between England and Ireland on November 12th. Unfortunately, the game had to be postponed because of thick fog, but it was played two days later, England winning 4-1.

Two weeks later, on November 26th, the new

> The close season of 1922 saw the next and, so far, most significant piece added to Peter Hodge's jigsaw. In July, John Duncan was tempted to leave Hodge's old club, Raith Rovers, to try his luck south of the border. A goal-scoring inside-forward, he was to be the pivotal figure around whom City's first major promotion campaign revolved. He scored twice on his debut, a spectacular 5-4 win away to Stockport County and, at last, the goals which had dried up in previous seasons began to flow. Centre-forward George Waite (another former Raith player, as were Harry Graham and John Duncan's brother, Tom) also began to find the net regularly, and even Albert Pynegar enjoyed a brief resurgence, culminating in a four-goal haul in March as Wolves were humbled 7-0 at Filbert Street.

By the end of the season, City were the leading goalscorers in Division Two, but ironically were to be denied promotion by virtue of an inferior goal average to that of West Ham United. City's record of 65 goals for and 44 against resulted in an average of 1.477 while the Hammers recorded 63-38 for an average of 1.657.

Indeed, the eventual position of third was a huge disappointment to Leicester supporters, for promotion had looked likely for much of the season. A 2-0 home win over Bradford City on 14th October (in the midst of a then-record nine-game run with an unchanged side) had taken the club to the top of the table, and they rarely dropped out of the top three from then onwards. On 28th April, after 41 matches, City again stood in top spot, but a 0-2 reverse at Bury

main stand was officially opened by John McKenna, President of the Football League, before City's 1-1 draw with Coventry City. Season tickets for the new structure had been available from the start of the campaign at three guineas (ladies two guineas) for the reserved section, and two guineas (ladies one guinea) for the unreserved seats; and the increased gate income contributed to a seasonal profit of £1,960.

While the first team consolidated their position, the Reserves again dominated the Central Alliance, retaining their title with a haul of 58 points from their 34 fixtures, and peaking with a 15-0 win over Sutton Junction, as well as no less than four 9-0 scorelines.

Above: A rare aerial view of Filbert Street in the 1920s before the double-decker stand was constructed.

Below: Herbert Bown is beaten as City go out of the Cup at Arsenal. It was to be London's revenge for both Clapton Orient and Fulham having fallen at Filbert Street in previous rounds.

on the final day (with John Duncan, Mick O'Brien, Billy Thomson and Albert Pynegar all out injured, and future City boss Norman Bullock on the Shakers' scoresheet) was to deny them glory. Beaten Wembley Cup-finalists West Ham had won a game in hand on Monday 30th April to lead the table on goal average from City and Notts County; then, on that final day, the Hammers lost at home to the Magpies, who themselves clinched the title, leaving City to ponder on might-have-beens. Head of the hindsight list of nightmares must have been the February home game against the Hammers, lost by a clear six goals.

However, Hodge's pattern was beginning to take shape. Reg Osborne and Norman Watson were introduced to the first team during the latter weeks of the season, whilst, during March, a youngster named Hugh Adcock joined the club from Loughborough Corinthians. He would not make his debut until the following season, but his role would be significant in City's future. By the end of the campaign Adam Black and goalkeeper George Hebden had become the club's first 'ever-presents' since the reconstruction.

City were beginning to be recognised as a decent footballing force well beyond the confines of Leicester, but this factor wasn't universal: back in September a London charabanc driver had delivered the team to the Crystal Palace, believing them to be competitors in a band festival, before bemusedly re-routing to Selhurst Park just in time for kick-off.

Away from League business, the Filbert Street record attendance was again broken as 35,728 people paid £2805 to witness the second round Cup exit at the hands of Cardiff City; and, for the third consecutive season, the Reserve team clinched the championship of the Central Alliance. At the business end of the business, a heartening profit of £4,152 was recorded.

Goalkeeper George Hebden was an ever-present in season 1922/3.

1923-24

> The disappointments of the near-miss campaign were, of course, tempered by optimistic expectations among City supporters that elevation to the top flight would almost certainly ensue this season, and such hopes were bolstered in the summer with news of Peter Hodge's acquisition of a new centre-forward. Arthur Chandler had not been a particularly prolific goalscorer with Queens Park Rangers, but Hodge had spotted clear potential in his robust style – though it is doubtful that even the manager could have imagined in June 1923 just what an impact on City's history his new signing eventually would have.

Chandler and Hughie Adcock both made their debuts in the opening game, a 1-1 draw at Hull, and both registered their first goals two days later, as Stoke were thrashed 5-0 at Filbert Street. Optimism seemed indeed well founded as the goals continued to flow from City over the early weeks of the season, and the club fringed the promotion race for a spell. But a bad crop of injuries, and a series of inconsistent performances away from home, saw the team's challenge fade badly. Eventually, a position of 12th had to be settled for, with Hodge utilising the second half of the season to further his team-strengthening exercise in earnest. Only 'Channy' finished the term as an ever-present, hitting the first two of his seventeen City hat-tricks on the way to a chart-topping goals total of 24. (In fact, he took in-person congratulations from Winston Churchill for the first threesome, when the politician was gladhanding at Filbert Street on the occasion of the South Shields fixture). Introduced around the City spearhead at various stages of the campaign were Pat Carrigan, John Bamber, George Carr, Billy Newton and Albert Godderidge, as the formidable team of the mid-20s began to take discernible shape.

There would henceforth be no place for Mick O'Brien, who had succeeded Jim Harrold as club captain and who had been capped twice more this year for Ireland; or for Teddy King, who had been on the club's books since the summer of 1906, and was about to take up the new position of club coach after a couple of seasons lending his vast experience to the Reserves. That team had just completed its first season in the Southern League, Eastern Section, to which competition it had switched in search of sterner opposition, and in which it had to settle for runners-up spot, behind Peterborough and Fletton United. The second team also regained the Leicestershire Senior Cup by defeating Barwell United 5-1 in a replayed Final, after having run up their all-time record score of 22-0 in an earlier round against the hapless Ibstock Colliery.

FRUSTRATED RAMS!

> Strangely enough, in view of the generally deflationary aspect of the 1923/4 campaign (which additionally saw a financial loss of £1,699, and the death in March of director Harry Linney), the final day of the League season had, for the second season running, involved City's seniors in high drama. They were at the Baseball Ground, where Derby knew they required a 5-0 win to pip Bury for the second promotion place on goal average. City, in no mood for over-neighbourly gestures after their own high hopes had died, somehow contrived to keep the bitterly frustrated Rams down to four unanswered goals, despite being three adrift at half-time!

PLAYER'S CIGARETTES.

HUGH ADCOCK

Hugh Adcock had become established as a key member of the promotion winning team.

Below: Hanging around during training are Jack Bamber, Harold Wadsworth, George Carr and Arthur Chandler.

> The final game of this season would produce far from hollow glory, though, for at the end of it City would be in possession of the Second Division championship shield, and contemplating life among the elite.

During the close season of 1924 the final pieces of Peter Hodge's jigsaw were nudged into place. Two key signings were made, full-back Harry Hooper from Southampton and outside-left Harold Wadsworth from Liverpool; while, in recognition of his motivational role, John Duncan was appointed club captain in succession to O'Brien.

The season did not get off to a particularly auspicious start; although as City went down to a penalty at Manchester United on the opening day, no less than 10,000 turned up at Filbert Street to watch the Reserves lock Southern League horns with Peterborough & Fletton. The second fixture saw Arthur Chandler thwarted from the penalty spot by Chelsea's Ben Howard Baker; and the third game had Channy denied a winner by the referee, who failed to see his free-kick rebound from Middlesbrough's stanchion. The fourth game, at Stamford Bridge, turned on a first-half injury to keeper Albert Godderidge. In fact, only three points were taken from the opening five League fixtures, but once Black and Newton regained their places, forfeited through pre-

season injuries, events took a distinct upturn, and goals began to flow with consummate ease, particularly from the boots of Duncan and Chandler.

The former claimed 30 League and four Cup goals, while the latter notched 32 in the Second Division and a further six in the knockout competition. Duncan set a club record with six goals in succession (past Measham-born keeper Tom Fern) in the 7-0 Christmas Day thrashing of Port Vale, whilst Chandler failed by only one goal to equal the feat as Barnsley were crushed 6-0 on February 28th. Chandler's consistency as a marksman was most amply demonstrated in mid-season when he scored in eight successive games at one stage, and actually found the net in 14 out of 15 consecutive matches. The odd game out, a 0-2 League defeat by Blackpool, immediately preceded a record unbeaten run which proved the crux of the championship effort.

From 6th December to 30th March there stretched a magnificent run of 18 League games without defeat, 14 of which were won, during which City took pole position following a victory at Oldham. After this, only an aberrant sequence of goalless draws postponed City's celebrations. A George Carr goal in the penultimate game, at home to Bradford City on Cup Final day, finally sealed promotion (after a Reg Osborne penalty miss – City's fifth out of nine

awarded this term – looked like delaying it), and a 4-0 cakewalk in the last home game against Stockport (marred only by an elbow injury to Duncan after he'd scored twice) guaranteed the top spot. Other club records amassed along the way included those for number of League wins, number of goals scored, and number of points attained. A *Mercury* editorial deemed that the readership should feel 'healthily pleased'.

Success, however, was not confined solely to League matters. In the FA Cup, the club equalled its best ever performance by reaching the quarter-finals, and dreams of a first Wembley trip were still very much alive when Cardiff City grabbed a last-minute winner at Ninian Park with a goal scored by Willie Davies direct from a corner kick. As this was, in fact, the first time the feat had been achieved since a rule change had allowed for the possibility, much confusion followed. As no time had remained in which to restart the tie, several City players actually left the field in the genuine belief that they had earned a replay against the Wembley-bound Welshmen.

City ever-presents were Chandler and Wadsworth, and six other players missed three games or less, so the consistency was in marked contrast to the tribulations of the previous season. There was also a surprise at the lower end of the scorers' list: Adam Black having briefly assumed the mantle of penalty taker and successfully converted three spot-kicks. This apparently unremarkable feat is put into its proper perspective when one realises that in a career spanning 557 games for Leicester, Adam only managed four goals in total! Ironically he lost this role after missing from the spot against Southampton, during his own benefit match.

With the club having now reached Division One for only the second time in its history, and having profited to the tune of £3,685, the question was whether this time the elevated status could be maintained for longer than a single season? City would not only contend with classier company, but they would be playing from August to the new offside law, which required only two defenders (rather than three) to be between an attacker and the goal for him to be onside. With rare foresight, Arthur Chandler suggested that the end-of-season hospital-benefit friendly at Port Vale be played to the new rules: on all-round agreement, he rendered thanks with a hat-trick in a 5-3 win!

Ernie Hine scored twice on his City debut against Burnley in January 1926.

Below: A souvenir postcard issued to mark the local 'derby' between Notts County and Leicester City in the FA Cup Third Round in January 1926.

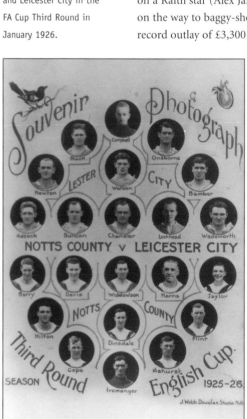

> The acquisition of First Division status was physically marked by the summer extension of the new main stand, with an additional bay of seating at each end now seeing it stretch the full length of the pitch. In the boardroom, it heralded a confident resistance to the predatory attentions of several bigger clubs. Everton had enquiries for Duncan, Chandler and Carr rejected, and Preston North End received short shrift when chasing Adam Black. If City were indeed to consolidate amongst the elite, they would require every bit of the class, character and consistency represented by this quartet, and would almost certainly need to augment it.

An opening-day home win over Liverpool sent hopes soaring, and City showed excellent spirit in fighting back for a point from their first away game, at Highbury, after going two down to Arsenal. But a hat-trick for Burnley by former wartime Fossil Tom Roberts initiated a sequence of five consecutive defeats, plunging City towards the depths, and their resources were severely stretched when George Carr broke a leg in the home defeat by Leeds, causing several spectators to faint at the sight, and ruling himself out for the rest of the season. Nevertheless, City crowds remained loyal, and a new record gate of 37,483 was registered at Filbert Street for the October game with Aston Villa.

October also saw Peter Hodge's first significant foray into the transfer market: he missed out for once on a Raith star (Alex James being whisked to Preston, on the way to baggy-shorted fame at Arsenal), but a record outlay of £3,300 enticed Manchester United to part with inside-forward Arthur Lochhead. The intelligent Scot, who had already scored against City at Old Trafford this season, netted twice on his debut against West Brom in compensation. However, despite Lochhead's impact, the introduction of Scottish international 'keeper Kenny Campbell and Chandler's continued goalscoring consistency, City remained locked in the relegation struggle throughout the first half of the season. Their occasional frailty was perhaps best evinced, ironically enough, by a 5-3 home win over Spurs: apparently a fine result, but

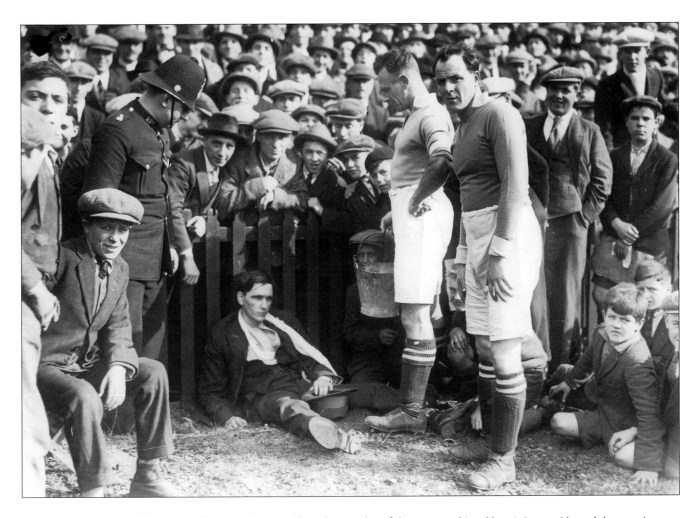

achieved against a nervy debutant goalkeeper and, from the third minute, only 9-man opposition, with Grimsdell a broken ankle victim and former Fossil Tommy Clay having suffered a head wound.

Again, Hodge was allowed to chase and secure a major signing; expending another £3,000 on Barnsley marksman Ernie Hine. And, again, a two-goal debut was the immediate reward – though Hine blotted the margin of his copybook by missing a penalty late in the same game against Burnley. With results picking up, a mid-table finish seemed likely, but a couple of late slips left the club in 17th place at the season's conclusion. Still, it was the highest League ranking

Above: Some members of the crowd fainted with shock at the sight of George Carr's broken leg against Leeds. Here Arthur Chandler and John Duncan come to the aid of one unfortunate fan.

Below: Arthur Chandler nets in the home fixture with Liverpool in August 1925.

ever achieved by a Leicester side, and the promise was of better to come.

Amidst all the activity of October 1925, John Duncan had won his sole Scottish cap, scoring once in a 3-0 demolition of Wales; and Arthur Chandler had become the first Leicester player to notch 100 consecutive appearances. Injury interrupted Chandler's run after 118 games, though he was again City's top scorer with 26 League goals; but mystery surrounds the failure of the Scottish selectors to further recognise Duncan's genius. The near-cliché view of Leicester as 'unfashionable' is something that the likes of Chandler, Sep Smith and Arthur Rowley would also later have to contend with in mulling over the disparity between their evident weekly achievement and the dearth of international honours accruing to them.

There were matters of greater weight and immediacy on the minds of all concerned with Leicester at the close of this term, however, and they were not just anxieties over the impending General Strike or the complete relaying of the Filbert Street pitch and drainage system. Peter Hodge had done perhaps more than anyone to strengthen both the club's self-esteem and their status, and had guided City from the embers of wartime to hitherto undreamed-of heights. Consequently it came as a great shock to the club when, in May 1926, he resigned to take over as manager of relegated Manchester City.

> Shocked and distressed though the City board may have been, they wasted no time in finding a replacement for Hodge. Their choice in July was Willie Orr, a former Scottish international left-half who had become a successful manager with Airdrieonians; and by mid-September they must have been toasting themselves on their perspicacity. The previous season's signings had reduced the club's profit to £714, and Orr's only initial outlay was on reserve full-back Davie Moyes, but he certainly saw early value from his inheritance.

With the less restrictive offside rule in its second season of operation, the campaign opened with an avalanche of goals all round, and City were quick to claim their share. On the evening of 18th September, Orr and everyone at the City experienced a wholly new and heady sensation. City, three goals down at half-time at Goodison Park, had stormed back to lead 4-3, survived a last-minute Everton penalty, and attained top place in Division One:

Kenny Campbell was an early example of "personality" goalkeepers to stand between the sticks at Filbert Street.

	P	W	D	L	F	A	Pts
Leicester City	7	3	4	0	23	17	10
Birmingham	6	4	1	1	11	7	9
Sheffield United	6	4	1	1	12	9	9
Arsenal	7	3	3	1	12	12	9
Burnley	6	3	2	1	18	13	8
Huddersfield Town	7	2	4	1	12	10	8

On the following Monday, Birmingham beat Everton 1-0 to take over the top spot. Then, on the next Saturday, City crushed Blackburn Rovers 4-0 to regain the pinnacle, but one week later a 3-5 reverse at Huddersfield dropped the team to third place. The goal rush at both ends of the park continued, but City could not quite maintain the impetus of their title bid, and eventually a disappointing final month to the

Right: A newspaper cutting covers the first time ever that Leicester City had found themselves on top of Division One.

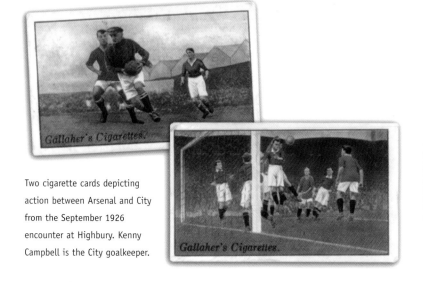

Two cigarette cards depicting action between Arsenal and City from the September 1926 encounter at Highbury. Kenny Campbell is the City goalkeeper.

EVENTFUL DAY
FOR
LEADING CLUBS
TRIUMPHANT LEICESTER CITY.

(By Our Own Correspondent.)

All the leaders in the League had a day of pain and perspiration yesterday, for not one of the exalted was wholly successful. Indeed, it is necessary to travel all the way to Lanarkshire, in fact to Motherwell, to find a match in which the team in the premier position of its competition secured the full points. There Dundee, by free scoring in the second half, retained their place at the head of the Scottish League.

There is quite another story concerning the matches in England, for Burnley, Manchester City, and Swindon, who were at the head of affairs in their several tournaments, each suffered their first reverse of the season, and Stoke City surrendered a point at Chesterfield. It is true that all these unbeaten teams were appearing as visitors, but they were all presumed to have reasonable hope of victory. Such changes as these supply spice to sport, and in some instances bring new leaders in the different groups.

The most startling development arising from these events is to see Leicester City occupying the place of honour in the First Division. This is a novelty, but it will not astonish any of the clubs which have played Leicester. Those who have drawn with the Midlanders have been inclined to consider themselves fortunate, and those who have been vanquished have had no just cause for complaint. Indeed the keenest judges among the team-managers have made no secret of their opinion that Leicester City are at the moment the best balanced and the most thrustful set of players in the country. But the way that Leicester climbed to the top of the pedestal at Everton is indeed interesting.

In consequence of their failures, Everton have been shuffling their players as if they were a pack of cards. The re-arrangements must have seemed very satisfactory at Goodwin Park yesterday, when they were leading by three clear goals at the interval. This adverse score did not daunt Leicester, who scored four goals in the second half and gained an exhilarating victory. In Hine, Lockhead, and Chandler they have clever inside forwards, and they are plied with good passes and choice centres. Considering the steady progress of Leicester City during the past four years the club deserves to be heartily congratulated on their achievement, which is the reward of merit and not of fortune—although no doubt they have been suited by the fast grounds caused by the Indian summer. Whether they will play quite so fast and so finished football on the heavy turf to come remains to be seen. How some of the players must be sighing for grey skies and soft grass.

season meant the club having to settle for 7th position, ten points behind champions Newcastle.

There could be no complaints about entertainment value this season, though, and memorable individual performances dotted the campaign. Chandler notched a hat-trick on the opening day at West Ham, and completed his first century of City goals in the first minute of his 140th game, at home to Sunderland. Watched by two England selectors in this match, he scored again five minutes later, but then went off with a knee injury that kept him out for seven weeks; only to bounce back to twice achieve five-goal hauls, against Aston Villa and West Brom. During his absence the returning George Carr banished unhappy memories of the previous season's injury against Leeds by claiming a hat-trick off them this time. At the other end of the pitch, Kenny Campbell saved two penalties at St James's Park as City drew 1-1; but conceded two strikes from George Camsell in the Cup as City bowed out 3-5 and the Middlesbrough forward barged on towards a seasonal record of 64 goals.

Billy Lane scored for Spurs against City at Filbert Street and then arrived as cover for the injured Chandler, netting on his debut against Derby. The latter match also marked the initial City appearance of Sid Bishop, the classy former West Ham skipper who became Willie Orr's first major purchase, and who won England caps before the season's end.

Also gaining a representative honour at last was Arthur Chandler, who led the line for the Football League against the Scottish League in March in Filbert Street's second Auld Enemy tussle of the season: the first-ever amateur international between England and Scotland having also been hosted by Leicester on December 18th, when former Fossil Robert Noble and ex-City man Jack Roxburgh helped the Scots to a 4-1 win.

The final League game of the season saw City eclipse champions Newcastle United with an Arthur Lochhead double; and when this campaign's balance sheet was eventually totted up, it showed a healthy profit of £5,503.

In an attempt to further improve the quality of young players coming through the ranks, the Reserves – who the previous season had completed a hat-trick of Senior Cup wins – were entered into the extended London Combination as well as the Southern League. Undaunted by their strenuous programme, they eventually finished as runners-up in the former competition (with Billy Findlay and George Carr chosen for its representative eleven), and would continue in that League only from then onwards.

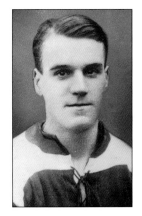

Back to full fitness, George Carr took his revenge on Leeds with a hat-trick.

Below: England international Reg Osborne and Scotland international John Duncan take a break on the golf course.

> The summer landscape at Filbert Street was one of a hive of industry. The roof from the Spion Kop end terrace was dismantled and re-erected at the Filbert Street end; while work commenced on the new Double Decker stand. That this £31,000 structure bore quite a strong resemblance to the main stand at Upton Park was no coincidence: the designers and contractors for both were those employed by West Ham director W J Cearns of Stratford.

There was no doubt by this time that Leicester City had become a First Division force to be reckoned with, well respected throughout the land, and despite manager Willie Orr's failure to land an eve-of-season transfer coup when Motherwell rejected his enquiry for Bob Ferrier, another good start to the season was exactly what the supporters demanded. They were not to be disappointed, for, after four games, City once more sat atop the early League table, holding off Arsenal on goal average:

	P	W	D	L	F	A	Pts
Leicester City	4	2	2	0	10	5	6
Arsenal	4	3	0	1	13	8	6
Manchester United	3	2	1	0	5	0	5
Newcastle United	3	2	1	0	8	3	5

Their reign, however, was to be short lived (of two days duration, to be exact!), and a subsequent run

Left: John Duncan, Norman Watson, George Ritchie and George Carr.

of four successive defeats rather comprehensively took the gloss off the early success. To compound the problems skipper Johnny Duncan suffered a dislocated elbow and broken arm at Portsmouth and would be missing until the New Year.

Orr was quick to respond to the setbacks. The captaincy passed to Reg Osborne and a new-look half-back line was introduced. Billy Findlay, Norman Watson and George Carr took over from the injured Duncan and the out-of-form Carrigan and Bishop. The forward-line, too, was strengthened, with the acquisition of outside-left Len Barry from Notts County for a £3,450 fee. The effect was the desired one, with City showing new steel to climb back into the top half of the table and eventually to the fringe of the championship battle. Such was the extra competitiveness shown that Adam Black was actually severely censured by the FA for an 'improper expression' made to Arsenal's Charles Buchan during the October fixture!

By the end of the season City had elevated themselves to third place, five points adrift of champions Everton. They had established a new record goal tally of 96, of which Chandler contributed 34, including two hat-tricks and one four-goal haul at Newcastle. (In the debit column, incidentally, was included a hat-trick from Dixie Dean: one-twentieth of his record seasonal goal-haul). International recognition was also forthcoming for City players, with Reg Osborne playing for England against Wales and Len Barry donning the white shirt in the games against France and Belgium. In fact, City's willingness to allow their stars to appear in representative games cost them dearly, for they lost a couple of important League matches while Bishop (Football League), Duncan and Lochhead (both in the Scottish trial) were so absent.

Osborne was one of three players granted a benefit that season; Duncan and Watson being the others. By a strange quirk of fate, all three were injured and unable to play in their respective benefit matches.

Filbert Street by this time was becoming a fitting setting for top-flight football. The Double-Decker Stand was officially opened on 26th November, when Newcastle United were the visitors. Coincidentally, this was six years to the day since the official opening of the main stand, which might have disappeared in December had not a fire in the trainers' room been spotted early enough. Fortunately, the only damage was to kit, for which the insurance company paid up £130. The Newcastle fixture was additionally the instance of another Filbert Street innovation: with BBC radio broadcasting live from the ground for the

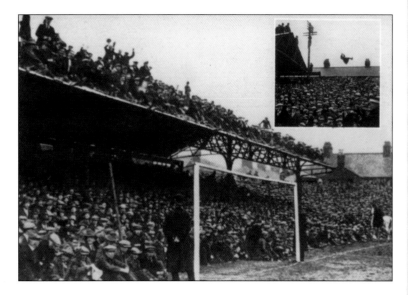

first time, utilising the commentary skills of local *Mercury* editor H W Bourne.

The addition of the Double Decker increased the notional capacity of the ground to around 45,000, but even that was insufficient to accommodate all those who wanted to see the Fifth Round FA Cup tie with Tottenham Hotspur in February. By the time the gates were closed on the heaving throng, a ground record crowd of 47,298 had paid £4702 10s 6d to witness City's exit by 0-3. Not included in this total, however, were the hundreds who stormed the directors' entrance, and the adventurous souls who scaled the Filbert Street end roof.

Such was the enhanced status of Filbert Street that it was chosen to stage the FA Cup Semi-Final between Arsenal and Blackburn Rovers on 24th March. A disappointing turn-out of 25,633 saw Rovers win 1-0, on their way to a surprise Final victory over Huddersfield Town. Blackburn actually brought the Cup with them for the final League game of the season at Leicester, and went home with a 6-0 thrashing from an unimpressed City. A further, interim prestige game on the ground had seen a Raich Carter-inspired England Schoolboys beat their Scottish counterparts by 5-0 on April 21st. (City themselves had beaten a Scottish League XI, chosen by Celtic boss Willie Maley, in an earlier April friendly for Leicestershire CCC funds, by conjuring a six-goal avalanche in the final thirty minutes to register a 7-2 scoreline).

Questions for end-of-season debate by the board (depleted by the April death of Shipstone Arms licensee Carter Crossland; but celebrating a profit of £2,508) included an application for the summer use of Filbert Street for greyhound racing (summarily rejected), and the more usual ones around prospective transfer moves. Hearts were given short shrift when cheekily chasing Arthur Chandler, but lengthy negotiations with Chelsea ended in the sale of Sid Bishop for £3,800, after the apparently homesick Londoner had attempted to get permission to live and train in the capital and commute to City's games.

Above: Fans in the record crowd for the FA Cup tie with Tottenham Hotspur even braved sitting on the roof of the stand at Filbert Street. **Inset:** A daring spectator climbs in via a telegraph wire!

> Both Willie Orr and his directors (whose boardroom was oak-panelled over the summer) were now further determined to hold on to the spine of the City squad for a renewed title challenge. Enquiries from Manchester City for Watson and from Everton for Duncan were firmly rebuffed, and while protracted negotiations continued with Falkirk to set up a deal which would see classy left-half George Ritchie replace Bishop, overtures from the Scottish club to take either Carrigan or Watson in part-exchange were also refused. Eventually, Ritchie arrived in late September, with City reserves Andy Russell and George Wyness going north as makeweights in the complex transaction.

Oddly enough, in what was to turn out to be City's finest and most convincing challenge for the title, the club never actually reached the top of the table at any time during the season. After suffering mixed fortunes in the early weeks of the campaign and finding themselves down in 14th position after ten games, City effectively launched their

Club archivist Jack Curtis shows off items from the City collection: the ball that Arthur Chandler scored six goals with against Portsmouth in 1928 and the FA representative cap Chandler won on the 1929 tour to South Africa.

with two fixtures outstanding, had 48 points and a goal average only minutely inferior to Wednesday's. Two victories may well have brought the title to Filbert Street at last.

Alas, City's one-goal lead at Huddersfield that afternoon was cut back by an 81st-minute equaliser from George Brown, following a rare mistake by keeper McLaren; Wednesday's Jack Allen equalised against Burnley at Hillsborough in the 85th minute; and the pair of 1-1 draws meant the dream was shattered. Even a 6-1 spree in the final fixture against Bolton Wanderers (FA Cup winners after earlier edging City out in the Fifth Round) proved little consolation as the club finished in the runners-up spot, just one point adrift of the Owls, who relaxedly lost their final game on the same day.

As ever, saddened backward glances were cast at points lost. City didn't have far to look: despite their record score against Portsmouth at home, they'd surrendered 0-1 to the same opposition at Fratton Park in April.

City couldn't even mark their achievement with any proper reward for the players: a request from the directors to the Football League in May that they be allowed to show their appreciation to the twelve regulars, by way of a gift to the approximate value of £10, was refused out of hand! And even though the club were in demand abroad, the directors themselves felt unable to accept offers to tour either Denmark or Sweden on the grounds of finance. Rather inexplicable grounds, it should be said, when set against a new record seasonal profit of £11,505!

At least Hughie Adcock and Len Barry managed to tour Europe with England at the end of a season in which Ernie Hine also won his first cap, but there was still no full international call for Arthur Chandler, despite his impressive performance in the trial match: he and Reg Osborne would be off to South Africa with an FA touring party instead. Chandler and Hine had both topped the 30-goal mark as City equalled their 96 goals of the previous season, and Adcock completed a new record run of 119 consecutive appearances in February. In remaining unbeaten at home throughout the campaign, City had equalled the feat of the Fosse in the shorter 1898/9 season, and set a record the club has still to parallel to this day.

There existed, of course, an optimistic strain of thought that City would automatically continue their recent progression through the top three positions of the First Division, and at last capture the Championship trophy in 1930. Such hopes, though, were soon to be dashed. And hindsight would prove that City's heyday as consistent contenders for the highest football honour was unfortunately at an end.

championship bid on 20th October, when Portsmouth were the visitors to Filbert Street.

Despite losing both Osborne and Duncan on the morning of the match, and being skippered for the first time by George Carr, City ran in five goals in the first half, with Chandler collecting a hat-trick in the space of 14 minutes. After 70 minutes, as Channy collected his fifth and City's seventh, five swans flew over the ground as if to mark the occasion. A few minutes later, after Hine added number eight, a sixth swan straggled overhead. The crowd were quick to call for another Chandler special, and the popular centre-forward duly obliged to equal John Duncan's club record of six goals in a game. Eventually Ernie Hine, celebrating his first England call-up, completed a hat-trick of his own and City had registered their record League victory, by 10-0. They had even managed to burst the ball as well! City scribe 'Touch' in the local *Mail* could barely contain his enthusiasm over such 'artistry at times almost amounting to wizardry'.

With this boost to their morale, and despite never winning more than four games in succession throughout the campaign, City rapidly climbed the table and continued to chase hard for the title. By the morning of Cup Final day, 27th April, they stood in second place in the table. Sheffield Wednesday, with two games to play, led with 51 points; whilst City, also

CONFUSING

A sidelight on the numbers game was provided by the home reserve game against Arsenal. The authorities were still resistant to growing agitation for the universal numbering of players' shirts (and would senselessly ban them for a further decade at League level). Official programmes nonetheless gave line-ups in notional 1-22 formation. The pitfall here was that Arsenal's stiffs wore 1-11, while spectators tried to match them up with a team-sheet marking them 22 (goalkeeper) to 12 (outside left)!

> By most yardsticks, a season which resulted in a final position of eighth in the top echelon would be one to look back on with some degree of satisfaction. In view of what had happened in the previous two years, however, the campaign was largely one of disappointment for City's followers. Filbert Street was this summer graced with the finishing touch to the main stand – a classical stone portico over the players' entrance – but that's where extravagance stopped.

Defeat at Huddersfield in the opening fixture, where a Jack Brown own-goal proved the decisive one of five, and where the 17-year-old Sep Smith made an unexpected debut, heralded a shaky start in which

Above: Roger Heywood, injured soon after joining.

Below: Arthur Chandler and Ernie Hine.

only one victory was gained from the first six outings. A commendable recovery ensued, to quickly banish any relegation fears, and the top half of the table was soon reached. But fifth place in March was the summit of City's achievement, and they never looked likely to sustain a realistic challenge for honours.

Goals again flowed freely, with Chandler once more topping the 30 mark (and claiming four hat-tricks to set alongside the one scored by his deputy, Lovatt), but it was the goals conceded column which gave the most cause for concern. The total of 90 goals against was the highest since the relegation season of 1908/9, and was a foretaste of things to come. In

January City visited Sheffield United and received a 1-7 hiding, with Irishman Jimmy Dunne notching four to set alongside his earlier Filbert Street hat-trick. A week later they returned to Bramall Lane on FA Cup duty. The 1-2 defeat they suffered that day (with Dunne restricted to a single goal) seemed almost a good result in the circumstances, but it only served to emphasise the now-unaccustomed lack of interest the later stages of the season would generate.

The highlights of the campaign unsurprisingly revolved around high-scoring games. A double was achieved over Everton, with both games incredibly ending 5-4, whilst Cup-finalists Arsenal came to Filbert Street in April to share in a League record 6-6 draw (only ever equalled by Charlton and Middlesbrough in 1960/1). David Halliday, destined to become a City manager, scored four goals for the Gunners that day, including a hat-trick in the space of 5 minutes, yet was left out of their Wembley side the following Saturday. (In February, he'd notched five against City Reserves).

Newcomers to the City scene included centre-half Albert Harrison, bought for a substantial fee from Nottingham Forest in December, and wing-

> George Ritchie took over as club captain for 1930-31, but John Duncan's departure (see panel story) definitively signalled that City's brief golden era was over. There was never really a whiff of disaster about the term, with City bobbing around in mid-table most of the time before settling into 16th place, but vital sparks were clearly missing. Ernie Hine passed the 30-goal target, broke the net at the Filbert Street end with his Boxing Day scorcher against Sunderland, and also took a well-earned benefit during the season (as did Findlay and Lochhead), but he generally lacked support. Chandler was not as prolific as in recent seasons, whilst the goals conceded total continued to rise, to 95.

Both regular goalkeepers suffered their share of criticism – Jim McLaren conceding eight goals at Grimsby and Jack Beby being beaten seven times by Arsenal at Filbert Street, shortly before putting in a transfer request on 'health' grounds, claiming the 'climate of Leicester did not agree with him or his wife'. Grimsby's Coleman, with four goals, and Arsenal's Lambert, Villa's Beresford, Blackpool's Hampson, Manchester United's Bullock and Sheffield Wednesday's Ball, each with hat-tricks, were amongst First Division forwards who enjoyed field-days against City's oft-changed reaguard, in which only Adam Black was a fixture.

The most evident sign of slipping standards at Leicester, though, came with the embarrassment of a Third Round Cup exit at home to Brighton & Hove Albion, from the Third Division (South), in front of a 25,722 crowd. Many of Brighton's train-borne support failed to arrive in time to witness Lochhead's fifth-minute opener, but they certainly cheered 'Potter' Smith's second-half double on a rock-hard, grassless pitch. A more tragically sobering incident came in March, when 19-year-old reserve right-winger Paul Moss collapsed in midweek training, and died of meningitis on the following Sunday. Three days later, City's visit to Old Trafford, for a goalless game with relegation-bound Manchester United, drew the lowest First Division crowd of the season: 3,679.

At the end of the campaign, the board once more rejected the opportunity of a summer tour, this time to Holland, on cash grounds (there was a nett loss of £179 on the year); yet also rejected two requests to lease Filbert Street for boxing tournaments during the close season. City might now have been deemed to be struggling, but not as much as their local footballing competition: this had been the first season of four in which the Leicestershire Senior League would fail to operate.

half Roger Heywood, who was immediately ruled out by injury after signing from Chorley; while, indexing defensive indecision, no less than four goalkeepers took turns between the City sticks, including giant South African trialist Aubrey Mandy. Forward stalwarts Adcock and Hine each added two more England caps to their tally; and the directorate were happy enough to publicise a seasonal profit of £5,343; but, behind the scenes, rumblings of discontent were beginning to be heard.

CITY ROCKED BY BUSINESS DISPUTES

> In January 1930, George Carr approached the board to ask for permission to open a greengrocer's shop and off-licence in the city. As any business interests concerning the sale of alcohol were specifically banned by the directors, permission was refused. Carr's immediate transfer request attracted only a derisory £1,000 bid from Grimsby, which was rejected, but it was April before Carr patched up his differences with the club. The case, however, proved to be the forerunner of a major dispute that would rock the club during the summer.

At a board meeting on 12th August, it was reported that club captain John Duncan had taken over the licence of a public house in Leicester. As this was specifically against club policy, it was agreed that the player was deemed to have automatically terminated his agreement with Leicester City, without prejudicing the club's rights to retain his registration or any transfer fee which might accrue. Strangely, Northampton Town were the only League club to show any solid interest in Duncan. In September their offer of £800 fell far short of City's valuation of £2,500, but, the following month, a bid of £1,000 was accepted. However, the player could not agree personal terms, wishing to choose his matches on a loan basis, and decided instead to retire to concentrate on his new business. City, of course, continued to maintain the name of one of their greatest-ever players on their official open-to-transfer list for another year.

> If the campaign of 1930/1 had seemed near-disastrous to some eyes, it was nothing compared to what was to follow. A summer disappointment for Willie Orr was the eleventh-hour decision of young Yoker Athletic centre-forward Sam English to reject City for Rangers (where within weeks he would be involved in the haunting episode of Celtic keeper John Thomson's death). But the events of the opening day might well have been heeded as more pertinent portents. The train taking the City team to their away fixture at Villa Park arrived late at Birmingham station, and then the charabanc driver transporting the party from the station to the ground took the wrong route. The game eventually kicked off eleven minutes late, an ill-prepared City lost 2-3, and a detailed explanation had to be supplied to the Football League to avert a hefty fine.

Three weeks later, City's railway carriage crashed while being shunted at Woodhouse Junction on the way to Grimsby; but fortunately even cut-knee casualty Reg Osborne was able to turn out with his badly-shaken teammates (including 17-year-old debutant Jack Calder) in a 0-3 defeat. Such early results were far from encouraging and team spirit inevitably suffered throughout the club. This was amply demonstrated before a reserve match at Brentford in November when two of the fringe members of the first-team squad, Jack Beby and Billy Jackson, were involved in a petty dispute over changing room pegs, which escalated to blows being struck. Jackson was ruled the aggressor and fined £5 by the board, whilst Beby was severely censured. £3 of the fine was subsequently remitted when Jackson proffered a letter of apology, but the incident was symptomatic of the new atmosphere within the club.

Team-mates Jack Beby (above) and Billy Jackson (below) came to blows in the dressing room.

RUGBY AND BOXING GRAB PUBLIC ATTENTION

> As if the nationwide trade depression were not a discouraging enough backdrop (with attendant mutterings of possible enforced wage-cuts for footballers), there even seemed to be a localised conspiracy in Leicester to divert sporting attention away from Filbert Street. On 14th November, at Welford Road, Leics & East Midlands inflicted the sole defeat on the touring Springbok XIV, by 30-21; and only two days later, local Great Bowden fighter Reggie Meen took the British heavyweight title by outpointing Charlie Smith at the Granby Halls, after a well-ballyhooed training build-up at the Narborough Hotel.

City certainly reclaimed the back-page headlines on 14th January, though, when Willie Orr resigned as secretary-manager, on the heels of six successive League defeats. Dave Gardner, the club's long-serving trainer, had died the previous November, having suffered a heart-attack whilst playing golf at Longcliffe, so the team had, within a short space of time, lost both of its main guiding influences. (Vice-

chairman William Tompkins would also pass away during the course of the campaign).

A string of atrocious results, including a 2-9 defeat at Goodison in which Dixie Dean claimed four goals and a 3-8 home defeat by Aston Villa in which George Brown went nap, had borne eloquent testimony to the lack of leadership. (Incidentally, those present for the latter game probably unwittingly watched history in the making: never before or since has any other Football League game finished with a 3-8 scoreline in favour of the away team).

In their hour of need, the board initially advertised ('Manager required at once. Must be competent, reliable and a good judge of players. No secretarial duties'), then, after crowd demonstrations ('Leicester City directors were entertained to a mild form of public disapproval on Saturday'), turned to their former mentor, Peter Hodge. The announcement of his return was made on February 15th, but it would not take effect until a chagrined Manchester City released him at the end of March, immediately after their FA Cup semi-final defeat; though his interim advice would prove useful to the immediate task of ensuring survival in the top flight. At the end of the season, under his direct control, a return of three wins and a draw from the final four fixtures enabled City to finish in 19th position, five points clear of relegation.

Hodge then set about a rebuilding programme and sizeable fees were paid for Jim Paterson (£1,025), Joe Calvert (£1,200) and Danny Liddle and Ted Lowery (together £1,320), to add to the mid-season expenditure of £1,700 on young Ernie Keeley. Considering the club's financial state (worsened by a seasonal loss of £2,702), this money had to be recouped from somewhere, and the most marketable possession was new skipper Ernie Hine, who had again been capped by England during the campaign. The £6,000 price tag set by City attracted enquiries from both Bradford Park Avenue and Huddersfield Town, though when the latter duly signed Hine in May, the accepted fee was only £4,000.

Hine had ended his final City season as the club's leading goalscorer once more and, in January, had joined Duncan, Chandler and Fossil Harry Trainer in the very select band of men who had scored five goals in a game for City – a feat achieved with the opening quintet of the 7-0 thrashing of non-League Crook Town in the FA Cup Third Round. (City would be KO'd in the Fifth by Wembley winners-to-be Newcastle United).

Perhaps the saddest departure, though, was that of Teddy King, whose position as club coach was deemed now redundant – an unfortunate way to end a 26-year association with the club.

> Try as he might, Peter Hodge could not reverse the downward trajectory of City's fortunes this season. Reg Osborne took over again as club captain, but was soon replaced by Adam Black, now nearing the veteran stage himself. Adcock was still a regular but had lost some of the sparkle of his youth, and Chandler could no longer command a regular place. Lochhead, too, was coming towards the end of a distinguished playing career. So often great teams that have grown up together also grow old together, and this was what was happening to Leicester. They did possess, however, at least one rising star in Sep Smith, whose cultured displays at half-back or inside-forward prompted a rapidly-dismissed enquiry from Bradford City.

City were early marked as relegation candidates, and had gained only one win by Christmas, by which stage they were understandably at rock-bottom in the chart. They did not win on a Saturday until 13th February; then chose Anfield a week later as the site of their first away victory. Yet somehow they managed to maintain slim hopes of avoiding the drop, and a remarkable run of three successive high-scoring victories in the final three fixtures once again ensured last-match safety, this time with just two points to spare. The season's final day saw City, Wolves, Bolton and Blackpool all threatened with demotion: wins for all four saw the Lancashire duo down. In fact, City would have stayed up with a draw at home to West Brom: they mudlarked instead to a 6-2 victory in a thunderstorm, which reduced the pitch to a quagmire before giving way to a celebratory rainbow. Two mid-match crowd invasions were neither hostile nor celebratory: they featured soaking Popular Side patrons dashing towards covered accommodation!

Hodge had in fact made two further significant signings. Inside-forward Arthur 'Digger' Maw had arrived from Notts County back in July, while Scottish international 'keeper Sandy McLaren was bought for £2,500 from St Johnstone in February. Both were introduced into the team in the later stages of the campaign, and both played their part in the final escape; as did full-back Sandy Wood, newly repatriated from the United States, whom he had represented at World Cup level.

Maw collected seven goals in those final three fixtures as City uncharacteristically crushed Sunderland (4-2; including a fluke Adam Black free-kick from his own half), Birmingham (4-0 away) and West Brom, and actually ended the season as the club's leading marksman, albeit with a tally of just 14 goals. This was the first time since 1921/2 that no City player had reached the 20-goal mark for the season.

Throughout January, when a heavily injury-hit

Above: Joe Calvert, Adam Black and Roger Heywood are powerless to prevent this Arsenal goal at Highbury in October 1932. City lost 8-2 to sink to the foot of the table.

City propped up the table and had just received their Cup quietus from Everton, there was much agitation amongst the non-directorial shareholders (partly stirred by the local *Evening Mail* columnist, and a *Mercury* 'open letter' editorial) for extra representation at board level. But even a deputation led by Cllr Charles Keene to confront chairman W H Squires met a stonewall. As, later, did an invitation to the board for City to tour South America during June. Squires himself would assume the club presidency that month, following the death of Montague Rice, and at a meeting announcing a £410 profit on the year.

City could probably have done with the broadening experience of foreign football: in January they'd welcomed the touring Rapid Vienna side to Filbert Street as the ground's first-ever continental visitors, and had lost 1-3. Internationals Binder, Wesilik and Bican scored past trialist goalkeeper Arthur Gourlay (from Dunipace Juniors), Jim Paterson replied, Johnny Campbell missed a penalty, only around 5,000 turned up to watch, and the Austrian coach subsequently condemned City's over-rigorous tactical adherence to the W-formation, saying it left them too short-handed in the penalty area. Hodge actually listened to this unsolicited advice, for the relegation escape was achieved with an old-fashioned 'flat' front five.

At least the Reserves (who finished their second successive Combination term with over a hundred goals in each of the 'for' and 'against' columns) were beginning to enjoy more localised success again as they retained the Leicestershire Senior Cup by defeating Loughborough Corinthians 3-0 in the final at Filbert Street. The previous season they had brought the trophy back to the club by overcoming the challenge of Market Harborough in a replayed final at Springfield Road. The Thirties was to be a decade in which City Reserves would dominate this particular competition.

CLOSED RANKS

> One other bit of local news brightened the season for ironists: the City Police's football club announced in November that their Melton Road home matches would henceforth be open only to members of the force and their relatives: they had been suffering persistent barracking and other rowdyism from a gang of 'City roughs'!

> Though, in the wake of 1949 and 1969, City have gained something of a reputation for overturning the form-book when it comes to their FA Cup exploits, there was no precedent for their Jekyll and Hyde act this season. During the club's heyday in the Twenties they had never met with much success in the Cup, reaching the Quarter-Finals only once. Yet now the team was struggling each season against relegation, and was going through a desperate transitional period, City found themselves qualifying for their first ever Semi-Final, and only 90 minutes from Wembley. More of that in a moment.

With Chandler no longer being the force he was in the previous decade, Hodge's main priority was to find a replacement centre-forward. As City again battled to keep out of the relegation zone throughout the season, much of the behind-the-scenes activity surrounded this subject, together with the eventual fate of Channy himself.

As early as September, City made enquiries for Jack Bowers of Derby and Middlesbrough's George Camsell, but both were rejected. City then baulked at the £3,000 asking fee for Arsenal's Jack Lambert. The following month, Gurney of Sunderland was the

Above: Archie Gardiner scored four of City's five goals against Portsmouth on his debut.

Below: Arthur Chandler demonstrates that a footballer's life is not without its relaxing moments.

target, but the price tag of £5,000 was beyond City. By November, with pressure mounting in the local press, the board went back to Sunderland with an offer of £3,500, but this was rejected by the Rokerites.

By February, Hodge had turned his attention north of the border. George Mutch of Arbroath (and later Preston) was watched, but eventually Archie Gardiner of Hearts was signed for a £1,000 fee. He exploded onto the Football League scene with four goals on his debut, a 5-3 win at Portsmouth, and recorded another hat-trick two weeks later as champions-to-be Arsenal were toppled 4-1 at Filbert Street; and his goals did indeed help keep City up.

In the meantime, Chandler had often looked set to end his association with the club. Millwall made an enquiry for his services in September but were dissuaded by the £1,000 fee asked by City. The following month, Norwich City sniffed, City asked £750, and the Canaries promptly lost interest. The following week it was Bournemouth who were after Channy. This time City asked £600, but the Dean Court club wouldn't stump up. By the end of November, City received a letter from Norwich City offering to take Chandler off their hands for free. The assistant secretary, George Smith, was asked to draft a reply acknowledging their impertinence! Eventually, in May 1934, Queens Park Rangers came up with an offer of £500 to buy back their former centre-forward. The two clubs agreed terms, but Chandler himself rejected the move, stating that he would prefer to end his career with Leicester, for whom he had developed so much affection over the years.

Before leaving the topic of transfers, there was one further incident, back in October, which is worthy of note. One of the directors had been sent to Stoke to watch their young outside-right, Matthews by name. He reported back that the youngster seemed to be of above average ability, but no further action was recommended – and the rest, as they say, is history!

Back on the field, City once more managed to cling on to their First Division status – by a safety margin of four places and five points. They couldn't have asked for a better start: Arthur Maw netted after four minutes of the Villa Park opener, won 3-2 (while reserve forward Jack Gurry was off the mark within 30 seconds at Filbert Street on his way to a hat-trick in a 5-1 beating of Charlton Athletic's seconds); and Danny Liddle's four-goal haul saw off Sheffield United in fixture number two. Indeed, City eventually earned the luxury of being able to lose their final four games and still feel safe (on the way reprieving Birmingham, who stayed up courtesy of a 7-3 win at Filbert Street). But it was definitely a case of the 'cup that cheered' in 1934.

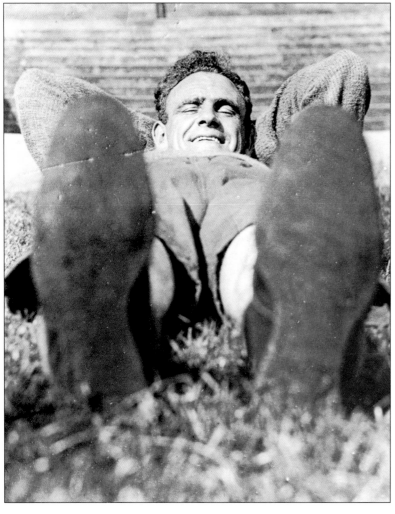

The Third and Fourth Round ties saw City emerge victorious at home to Lincoln City and away to Millwall, the two clubs who would eventually be relegated from Division Two. Scorelines of 3-0 and 6-3 resulted, with the recalled Chandler netting a brace at The Den. Next up was a trip to Birmingham, one of the few First Division clubs to finish below City this season, and Chandler again scored twice to clinch a 2-1 victory. City's reward was another away tie. This time the opposition was high-flying Preston, later destined to fill one of the promotion places from Division Two. Once more it was Channy, with the only goal of the game, who saw City through.

Thus the big day came on 17th March. St Andrews, Birmingham was the venue (welcoming its then-record crowd of 66,544) and Portsmouth the opposition. Three of the footballing Smith brothers were on the pitch (Sep for City; Jack and Willie for Pompey), but on the day it was the Pompey centre-forward Weddle, one of the survivors of their 0-10 defeat in 1928, who emerged as the hero. Scoring early as City were distracted by the fencing behind their goal giving way and fans spilling onto the touchline, he went on to collect a hat-trick as City's Wembley dream was dashed 1-4, despite them having more of the play. Arthur Lochhead's first-half strike couldn't compensate for defensive raggedness that was partly caused by a freak injury to Sandy Wood, semi-dazed after breaking his nose in collision with a touchline photographer. It would be another fifteen years before City extracted their sweet revenge.

As for the rest of the season's happenings, Roger Heywood had taken over from Black as captain and assumed the honour of leading City out on their most famous occasion to date; Sandy Wood took months to disentangle himself from Home Office work-permit red-tape; new full back Dai Jones was capped twice for Wales; Maw was named as travelling reserve for both the Football League and the full England team in October; winger Liddle topped the scoring list; and George Dewis joined the club from Nuneaton Town. This last event drew little attention at the time, but Dewis would eventually prove a key figure in the development of the club over many years, both in his centre-forward role and in his backroom capacity as prime motivator of young City talent.

Behind the scenes, City announced a £2,230 seasonal profit and successfully renegotiated their Filbert Street lease with the Council: extending it by 14 years, but having to swallow a rise in annual rental from £88 10s to £200!

MEN IN BLACK

> Two incidents put officials in the news in 1933/4. In September, Burnley-based referee H E Hull, due to take City v Chelsea, reached the Welford Road dressing room and pitch before realising he was at the Tigers' ground; and in April, during an unsavoury encounter with Wolves that saw Arthur Lochhead following opposition defender Crook to an early bath, a linesman was knocked unconscious by a 'stray' ball as the half-time whistle blew.

Below: 1934/5 saw the club celebrating its Golden Jubilee.

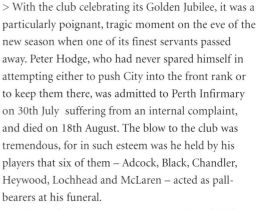

> With the club celebrating its Golden Jubilee, it was a particularly poignant, tragic moment on the eve of the new season when one of its finest servants passed away. Peter Hodge, who had never spared himself in attempting either to push City into the front rank or to keep them there, was admitted to Perth Infirmary on 30th July suffering from an internal complaint, and died on 18th August. The blow to the club was tremendous, for in such esteem was he held by his players that six of them – Adcock, Black, Chandler, Heywood, Lochhead and McLaren – acted as pall-bearers at his funeral.

His replacement was not appointed until 17th October, when the board persuaded Arthur Lochhead to retire from the playing staff and take over the role of manager. Whoever took charge of team affairs, though, was on the proverbial hiding to nothing. The Cup run of the previous season had been the last gasp of City's ageing, ailing heroes, and had barely masked the side's deficiency as a top flight unit; while the loss of Hodge had torn the heart from the club. Relegation was written on the wall for City from early in the campaign and, bravely as he tried, Lochhead could not smudge it out.

Amazingly, as veteran forces were shuffled and new faces tried (including close-season buy Tommy Mills, capped twice for Wales during the campaign, and young full-back Willie Frame, who soon recovered from the trauma of scoring an 89th minute own-goal on his debut at White Hart Lane), City maintained slim hopes of avoiding the drop for a considerable time. Indeed, cash was made available to Lochhead in February to recruit two forwards to the survival battle. But Tony Carroll (£2,200 from Clyde) and Gene O'Callaghan (£2,250 from Spurs) eventually proved unable to stem the tide. Their purchases also stretched the club's finances to the limit. There was no way City could afford the £4,000 asked by Sheffield Wednesday in March for Harry Burgess (who moved to Chelsea

instead); and even the plan to build another double-decker stand on the Popular Side had to be abandoned, with the directors (facing an overall £4,208 loss on the year) settling instead for a cheaper scheme to roof the terracing.

In the end, City failed to win any of their last six games (taking just four points from the twelve available) and were relegated by a single point, with Middlesbrough escaping the drop, one place above. There was, almost inevitably with City, last-day drama involved: but only if City won at Portsmouth and Middlesbrough lost at Chelsea would their positions be reversed. A Dai Jones own goal after six minutes hardly aided City's cause; and both games in fact ended in draws. The crucial encounter over which regrets and recriminations would be held, though, had come a fortnight earlier at Hillsborough: Sandy Wood broke his collarbone, but 10-man City were denied victory, and that vital extra point, when the referee failed to register a Carroll cross-shot going over the line before being scooped out.

Earlier, in December, referee F W Wort almost failed to register at all; not arriving at Filbert Street until half-time of the game against Portsmouth. One of his linesman was also delayed until the third minute, and the only 'official' official at kick-off, A W Smith, found himself in the midst of a goal-rush. The scoreline read 2-2 after only seven minutes, and City went on to temporarily brighten their Christmas preparations with a 6-3 victory. Despite this sort of rare incident, the FA were giving serious consideration at this time to the proposition of utilising two referees per match; and City's friendly at Coventry in May was experimentally so officiated before the idea was once more shelved.

Above: The City team, with manager Arthur Lochhead, pictured at Leicester Station en route to Middlesbrough in October 1934.

Below: Action from the FA Cup tie against Blackpool in 1935.

Eventually, even relegation gloom had to be put into some sort of perspective. Loughborough Corinthians had been forced out of business before the season started, and Rugby Town disbanded in December 1934 (to be followed a year later by Market Harborough Town). In March, long-serving blind masseur Bill Fox had committed suicide after a spell in hospital. In April, the streets of Leicester had erupted in oppositional response to a Granby Halls rant by fascist leader Sir Oswald Mosley to his assembled, and heavily police-protected, blackshirts. And when the football club's retain and transfer list was issued in May, stalwarts Black and Chandler were to be given frees, whilst Adcock was listed for just £250. This time it really was the end of an era.

> During the summer of 1935, Arthur Chandler joined Notts County and Hugh Adcock moved on to Bristol Rovers for an eventual fee of £150. They would face each other in a scoreless opening-day game at Eastville. Adam Black, meanwhile, had chosen to retire from the first-class game.

Considering the fact that no money was available to spend on new players, Lochhead did well to guide his team to a final place of 6th in Division Two. The financial state of the club was causing great concern and, in October, the club's bankers, Barclays, refused to grant an overdraft of more than £1,000. The directors felt this limit to be unreasonable and hastily arranged with Martins Bank to take over the club's account, with an agreed overdraft limit of £5,000. This move at least allowed Lochhead to secure one newcomer during the season, the peripatetic Owen McNally from Distillery for £1,000.

Despite their troubles, the directors staunchly refused to sell off their few assets. Sep Smith was the subject of enquiries by Liverpool and Tottenham; Spurs were also interested in Fred Sharman; whilst Middlesbrough wanted to sign Sandy McLaren and Danny Liddle. The board knew as well as any the need to signal their ambitions for a return to the top flight, and were willing to augment their own number if an injection of new capital resulted. Such was the club's parlous state, however, that all invitations to potential new directors met with rejection — though the infighting that would emerge at the summer AGM may have had as much to do with this.

Very little more need be detailed about this particular – and peculiar – campaign. Lochhead directed his team to top spot in each of September, October, November and December before they fell away; and to the Fifth Round of the Cup, where narrow defeat at Middlesbrough ensued. (The home Fourth Round eclipse of Watford, won 6-3, had featured a hat-trick from visiting forward Frank MacPherson, ten years after he'd notched a threesome at Filbert Street for Manchester United; and nine after another double on his only other appearance at the ground).

Gene O'Callaghan was given the task of leading the team and did a reasonably effective job (turning down a Welsh cap in October to aid the club cause); Fred Sharman showed his versatility by regularly switching between the centre-half and centre-forward positions, and scoring only one goal less than joint top-scorers Tony Carroll and Digger Maw; Sep Smith won long overdue international recognition for England against Ireland; Dai Jones again won two Welsh caps during the season, so emulating his achievement of the previous two campaigns; and

POOLS PLAN

> The peculiarity of the season was one in which City shared with all their fellow League clubs. For February saw the Football League escalate their long-smouldering conflict with the Pools companies into absurdity. The copyright of the fixture list was the issue, so the League, in mid-season, ripped it up; and delayed announcements of each following Saturday's fixtures until the day before. Thus on 29th February, City travelled to Hull at 24 hours notice: they had been expecting a day off as scheduled opponents Spurs were still in the Cup. The next Thursday, the *Evening Mail* reported: 'Leicester City last night selected their team for their probable home match at Filbert Street on Saturday with opponents yet to be announced'. As it happened, they entertained Fulham, and won 5-2. The League soon retreated from this farce, in the face of mass protest by their member clubs and the transport authorities.

former favourite Ernie Hine induced a bout of nostalgia (or envy) amongst City's small band of travelling fans by hitting a hat-trick for Barnsley in the drawn December fixture (including an 88th-minute equaliser direct from a corner).

The Reserves were once again successful in the Leicestershire Senior Cup. This was their fourth victory in the past five seasons, and it saw them put five without reply past a Leicestershire Nomads goalkeeper called Shilton – Peter's uncle Fred.

The summer of 1936, however, was distinctly soured by a stormy club AGM. Amidst vitriolic accusations of backstabbing, former president W H Squires failed to win a vote back on to the board he had left in February; and after deeming this an 'action that will stink in the nostrils of every sportsman', got involved in a slanging match with chairman Emmanuel Gregson and director Louis Burridge that bore eloquent testimony to the sort of political divisions that were as much cause as outcome of City's recent decline. The AGM (at which a seasonal profit of £356 was announced) also voted to abolish the post of club president; though somehow wounds were sufficiently healed later in the year for Squires actually to rejoin his boardroom antagonists.

Right: Goalkeeper Sandy McLaren was a stalwart of the 1930s.

> The season of 1936/7 provided something of an oasis in the wilderness of the Thirties; one which initially took shape as the haziest of mirages, yet eventually proved to be sweetly refreshing. The trek began with a setback, as Arthur Lochhead abruptly resigned as manager on September 2nd, after only two games. He had himself come under barely-veiled criticism at the stormy summer AGM, and it was clear that certain directors deemed him to possess too much autonomy.

The board were accordingly careful in appointing a replacement. Frank Womack, a stalwart international full-back at Birmingham, and more recently manager of Worcester City, Torquay United and First Division Grimsby Town, was the man chosen to prompt City's revival; while other interviewees for the vacancy had included Jackie Carr (George's brother, then boss at Tranmere), Andy Cunningham (Newcastle), Jimmy McMullan (ex-Aston Villa) and Billy McCracken (ex-Millwall). When Womack took over in October, City had collected a meagre six points from their first ten fixtures and, one place off rock-bottom, were contemplating the real

Above: Jack Bowers became the club's record signing when he moved from Derby in November 1936.

Below: The Board of Directors with the Second Division Championship Shield in June 1937. Back (l to r): G Smith (Secretary), WSG Needham, LH Burridge, WA Tompkins, FS Smith, F Womack (Manager). Front: A Rice, WH Squires, E Gregson (Chairman), AE Pudan.

possibility of dropping into Division Three for the first time in their history.

Of necessity, then, the new boss was quick to act. In November, on the heels of the morale-boosting return of Arthur Chandler to the coaching and scouting staff, he persuaded the board to increase their financial commitment and part with a club record fee of £7,500 to bring Jack Bowers to Filbert Street from Derby. Bowers' impact was truly amazing. In just 27 League outings he rattled in 33 goals, and if ever one man can be said to have won a team promotion, then Jack was that man. Not that he performed miracles quite without support, of course. New skipper Sep Smith provided inspired generalship, whilst big Eric Stubbs, signed from Nottingham Forest a week before Bowers arrived, was the winger who gave Jack the service he required to act as the scourge of Second Division defences.

So far behind the promotion race were City when Womack took over that it took until February for the club to climb into the top two. The impetus provided by Bowers might be judged by the fact that he scored in each of his first six appearances, all victories,

registering 12 goals in total during that spell, and actually found the net in eleven of his first dozen League games for City to spearhead the ascent.

City remained in second place from February onwards, and might well have finished there, which would have been creditable enough. But on 24th April, as City secured promotion with a home win over Nottingham Forest, fellow promotion club Blackpool threw away their guarantee of the title with a 1-1 home draw against bottom club Doncaster Rovers in their final match, and City knew that a home win over Tottenham on May 1st would secure them their second championship shield. A fine 4-1 victory ensued, with Bowers claiming a characteristic brace, then narrowly escaping the massive crowd which thronged the pitch at the end and briefly engulfed most of his team-mates.

The crowd on this joyful occasion strangely only numbered 22,761 (the simultaneous radio broadcast of the Cup Final perhaps proving a strong counter-attraction; rather than any sense of collective mourning for the victims of Guernica, bombed into oblivion only days earlier); but the Filbert Street record for a League game had been broken a few weeks previously, when 39,127 watched Bowers score the only goal separating City and Aston Villa. A couple of weeks before that, the Filbert Street faithful had also seen one of only two games that ended with a blank sheet for City after Bowers' arrival. The goalless draw with Swansea might not have been worthy of note, but for the fact that the visitors had to field their veteran full-back Wilf Milne in goal throughout!

Despite the promotion triumph, one substantial embarrassment attached to Womack's side. In the FA Cup, City brushed aside the Eastville challenge of a Bristol Rovers side bossed by Burbage-born Percy Smith, but then exited to Division Three (South) re-election candidates Exeter City. The 1-3 away defeat saw City, down to ten men after ten minutes following injury to Sep Smith, unable to cope with a pitch of deep mud and slush.

Although the rewards were great, the huge financial outlay needed to build the promotion team (inclusive of a further £2,000 expended on Sunderland's Bert Davis, who failed to fit in) was bound to leave its mark – a red one, to the seasonal

Leicester City Football Club

PROMOTION CELEBRATION
DINNER
and
PRESENTATION OF MEDALS

Chairman – Mr. E. GREGSON

The Grand Hotel, Leicester
Monday, 16th August, 1937
at 7 p.m.

Below: A picture taken on City's tour of Eastern Europe in 1937. On the train are coach Arthur Chandler, Dai Jones, Gene O'Callaghan and manager Frank Womack.

tune of £7,776. City's directors were more than aware of events this winter at nearby Aylestone Road, where Leicestershire CCC had come within weeks of closing down entirely as a result of financial crisis, ameliorated only by a subscription drive in the local press. And they'd seen non-league neighbours Nuneaton Town give up the ghost this term, following the 1934 collapse of both Loughborough Corinthians and Rugby Town, and that in 1935 of Market Harborough Town.

Even so, the board still refused to submit to what they saw as gimmicky fund-raising requests. Consequently a suggestion that a special challenge tennis match between Fred Perry and Ellsworth Vines be staged at the ground during the summer was turned down flat.

There was nonetheless one spirit of adventure acceded to, when City agreed at short notice to assume an East European touring itinerary initially drawn up for Wolves, who were prevented from undertaking it by the FA because of their disciplinary record. The culture-shock proved enormous: from the first sight of the cinder pitch of Bucharest, through eccentric refereeing customs and the novelty of floodlights in Belgrade, to an injury list featuring gravel-rash, mosquito bites and sunburn. Five defeats (to Venus and Ripensia in Bucharest, to Hungaria Budapest, BSK Belgrade and Bratislava) bore eloquent testimony to the drawbacks of English tactical isolationism.

> City's return 'home' to the top flight was greeted with great enthusiasm by their supporters, and in early September another 39,000-plus gate was accommodated at Filbert Street to witness a 1-1 draw with Arsenal (in which Joe Calvert saved a Cliff Bastin penalty). Indeed, City's keepers were virtually unbeatable from the spot in the opening weeks: McLaren also saving Filbert Street efforts from both Derby and Huddersfield. But it was soon evident to all but the most myopic that such brinkmanship was hardly a healthy trait, and that City were finding it hard going to cope with their new elevated status.

Jack Bowers again led the line, but with much less success than he had during the promotion campaign. It was clear that he needed support up front. In October, City made an offer of £1,000 to Arsenal for Joe Hulme, but the figure did not match up to the Gunners' valuation. Nor did a higher bid for Belfast Celtic's Norman Kernaghan prove successful. By November, however, Matt Moralee had been signed from Aston Villa. He had attracted City's attention the previous season while playing for Grimsby Town, but the Villains had acted more quickly on that occasion.

Above: Percy Grosvenor — the only ever-present for City in 1937/8.

Right: No tabloid titillation here – former favourite Ernie Hine's low key retrospective on his career was hardly the stuff of controversy, and rattled no Filbert Street skeletons.

TOPICAL TIMES WEEK ENDING JULY 24, 1937.

Striking New Articles **Confessions of the Perfect Valet** No. 1 in This Issue

TOPICAL TIMES

NO. 923. REGISTERED AS A NEWSPAPER AT G.P.O. WEEK ENDING JULY 24, 1937. PRICE 2D.

Grand New Football Revelations

SECRETS OF MY 15 YEARS in FOOTBALL by Ernie Hine

BEGINS INSIDE

George Dewis, Billy Coutts and Peter Hodge's final signing, Willie Muncie, were also tried in the forward line as City desperately sought to find the right balance.

In the end, an unbeaten run of eight games in February and March, only two of which were won, proved sufficient to lift City clear of relegation. They were brought down to earth by Good Friday, though, when trounced 1-10 at Molineux, with Westcott and Dorsett each notching four goals against an eccentrically experimental City line-up, and even City's lone reply was gifted by Wolves' centre-half Stan Cullis! Ironically, three days later, the same two teams drew 1-1 at Filbert Street. A City defence which now regularly included Maurice Reeday also shipped hat-tricks from Birmingham's Jones, Manchester City's Doherty and Portsmouth's Beattie during the campaign; while future City signings Frank Soo (for Stoke) and Dave McCulloch (for Brentford) also exposed current frailties. Only left-half Percy Grosvenor ended the season as an ever-present, seeing City to a final placing of 16th after a tight home win against Charlton (achieved thanks to another Calvert penalty save) had finally banished anxieties. A final-day collapse at home to Birmingham also kept the Brummies up.

Once again, despite financial difficulties which at one stage resulted in a very public row between Womack and chairman Emmanuel Gregson (over available transfer funds), the directors refused to part with their more valuable players. Young Dewis' potential had been noted by both Stockport County and Newcastle United, but all enquiries were rebuffed. West Bromwich Albion were keen enough to capture Bowers to offer Richardson in exchange, but the board would not entertain the suggestion. Nor, however, would they sanction the proposed takeover of Hinckley United as a nursery club.

By season's end, despite a profit of £1,466, more finance simply had to be generated, virtually to keep the club standing still. A bank loan of £15,000 was eventually agreed, with the directors personally guaranteeing £10,000 of this figure. Unfortunately, much of the money was required to pay for the covering of the old Popular Side terrace, the plans for which had been drawn up as long ago as 1934. The work was eventually completed between November and February of the subsequent season; finally blocking out the Burnmoor Street bedroom-window vista which had earned many a local resident a little supplementary income over the previous forty-odd years.

Above: Matt Moralee was re-united with his former Grimsby boss, Frank Womack, at Filbert Street after a brief spell with Aston Villa.

Below: Even Sep Smith's sterling efforts could not stop City's relegation back into the Second Division.

> There are problems of common good taste, as well as of perspective, automatically raised if one attempts to cast City's struggles of this unfortunate season in too apocalyptic a light. That the club's hopes and mid-term prospects lay in ruins by the end of the campaign, and that its very future once more looked bleak, are undeniable facts. But description of a relegation campaign could hardly command all the usual adjectival notations – tragic, disastrous, shattering – when football's tensions were at the time so overwhelmingly minimised by those afflicting the country and the culture as a whole.

The entire term was to be played out against the gathering threat of war, and under the looming shadow of pan-European fascism. At the end of September the Munich Agreement was signed by Chamberlain, Daladier, Hitler and Mussolini, and anxieties eased temporarily, but there was still little confidence that conflict could be averted.

Football was a valuable diversion for those who had little say in the power politics of the time, but who knew they would be in the front line if war indeed came. It was not, however, a particularly joyful diversion for those watching their football in Leicester.

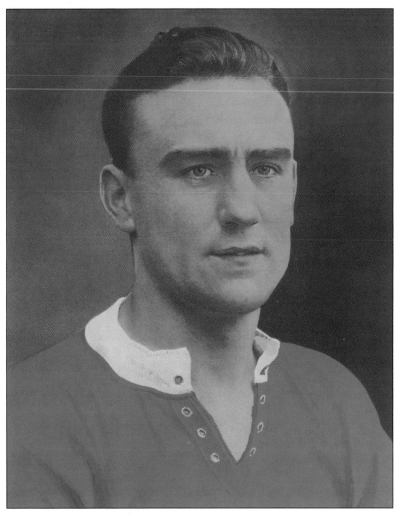

City had been in no position to substantially alter their floundering team of the previous term; and lowly early gates pointed to public disapproval of their pauperish policies. Tony Carroll had left for Luton, and in September young Mal Griffiths arrived from Arsenal to assume his place on the right wing, after the only summer newcomer, Arthur Smith, proved inadequate to the task. But despite Griffiths' evident promise, and the sterling efforts of Sep Smith, City could not hit on a successful blend. George Dewis shouldered too much of the front-line responsibility, and Fred Sharman too often stood exposed at the heart of the defence. City tenuously held on to a mid-table placing in the early months (demolishing champions-to-be Everton in the term's undisputed classic), but confidence wilted, the goal supply dried up, and the slide into the relegation zone was rapid.

Sandy McLaren was lost for a spell after being injured in a 2-8 mauling at Leeds in which Gordon Hodgson claimed his five goals against two stand-in goalkeepers (Sharman and Frame taking over in turn); while his specialist deputy, Joe Calvert, conceded four from Grimsby's Howe in a 1-6 defeat at Blundell Park. Calvert did, however, frustrate Cliff Bastin for the second season running with a penalty save from the Arsenal ace; this time at Highbury. Fred Sharman finished the campaign with two penalties to his credit, but haplessly by then had already got on the scoresheet for each of Birmingham, Blackpool and Charlton with own goals.

The prospect for City and their followers seemed almost as arid as it had for Fosse just prior to the First World War

This time there would be no upturn in fortunes, no dramatic finale. From early February onwards, only two victories were achieved, and City finally finished rock bottom of the table. Their sole League double came against Cup-winners-to-be Portsmouth; while they exited the Cup to beaten finalists Wolves in the Fourth Round. The sense of depression was compounded before the final game of the season when the announcement was made of the resignation of manager Frank Womack – much criticised for not securing a single pre-deadline signing, despite bids for Lincoln youngster James Wilson and Hearts forward Andy Black, and the refusal to move of Newcastle's Harry Clifton. Meanwhile chairman Arch Tompkins, having been involved in a motoring accident in Hertfordshire in which two motor-cyclists died, had to wait and worry until June to be cleared of manslaughter charges.

Even the minor consolation of the Reserves' accomplishment in taking the Senior Cup for the fifth successive season was itself tempered by the thought that quite a few members of that side would effectively lose the promise of their footballing careers to the demands of the national crisis.

With the German army having already been mobilised, conscription having begun in Great Britain, and the club doomed to what looked likely to be a lengthy spell in Division Two, the prospect for City and their followers seemed almost as arid as it had for Fosse just prior to the First World War.

Left: Action from a reserve encounter with Southampton in the late 1930s — Joe Calvert is the City goalkeeper in the picture. Of particular note is the size of the crowd for a second team game in those days.

City at War

> The summer of 1939 was no time for optimism. Chamberlain's 'peace in our time' message was increasingly looking open to ridicule, and the likelihood of war fearfully accepted. At Filbert Street little was happening to relieve the gloom. Following Frank Womack's resignation, a number of the other backroom staff also departed. June saw trainers Laurie Edwards and Walter McLean, and coach Arthur Chandler, each dispensed with; while director Arthur Needham resigned owing to failing health. Once more, former Fossil and veteran director Dick Pudan was, despite ongoing health problems, regarded as a valid managerial candidate.

Conscious of the club's ever-worsening financial state (the previous term's loss having amounted to £4,097), the directors finally bowed to pressure and made Sep Smith available for transfer at an asking price of £8,000. But, before any firm offer was ever received, outside events would intervene to shelve all such dealings.

On 14th July, Tom Bromilow – a former Liverpool player and Burnley and Crystal Palace manager – took over Womack's office. Two weeks later, Jim Metcalf from Preston North End and Fred Rose from Oldham Athletic were appointed as senior and second-team trainers respectively. The new management team prepared their squad for the coming season with as much spirit as could be mustered under the circumstances, but everyone's thoughts were now more firmly focussed on events on the other side of the Channel.

The first few days of the 1939/40 season coincided with some of the most momentous in history as world events rapidly overwhelmed the Football League programme. The Second Division campaign had opened with a victory over Manchester City and a defeat at Birmingham. In the boardroom, arrangements were being made to bid for Jimmy Cunliffe of Everton, and a benefit game for Billy Coutts was under discussion. Elsewhere, Poland had been invaded by the Germans; Great Britain and France had mobilised their forces, and evacuation schemes had been put into motion in England and Wales. On 2nd September, military service for men between the ages of 18 and 41 was made compulsory, City won at Upton Park, and their return journey from London was made in the blackout. The following day, war was declared.

The Football League, accused by many of being a year late in responding to the outbreak of the First World War, this time acted immediately to abandon their fixtures. In fact, all forms of sport came to a halt as there came into force a universal ban on the assembly of crowds. This ban only lasted a few days, and in the meantime the Football Association held talks with the Home Office to authorise the continuation of football on a regional basis, as had been done from 1915-19. The difference this time was that football was to help boost public morale and cup competitions would be actively encouraged.

Elsewhere in Leicester, the Aylestone Road Cricket Ground was again loaned for war purposes. It was eventually used by the US Army Pioneer Corps and the National Fire Service, and was so badly damaged that a new home for Leicestershire County Cricket Club was required for the resumption of first-class cricket in 1946, resulting in the return to Grace Road.

After a makeshift opening game to the season, Leicester Tigers played no more Rugby Union until 1945/6, although a Leicester Harlequins team was formed to play games for charity. Over £10,700 would eventually be raised by this team.

Left: Tommy Lawton netted five goals in three games as a City guest, but never tasted victory.

However, Leicester City decided to soldier on. The wages of both players and ground staff were initially suspended, but despite that the lack of income was becoming a serious problem. On 13th September, City played an Army XI in a friendly at Filbert Street, winning 7-2. This was one of the first fixtures to be played anywhere after the abandonment of the League programme. From then until late October, when Regional fare began, a series of further friendlies were undertaken.

When the new League began, Leicester found themselves in the Midland Division along with seven other clubs. It was not to prove a successful season, with the team finishing in the penultimate position. That first winter of the war was actually the coldest since 1894, and football suffered its share of problems. Postponements were frequent, with no football on four successive Saturdays during January and February due to snow and ice. However, the censor decreed that no weather information should appear in the press lest it should help the enemy, so no advance warning of these postponements was published. Unsurprisingly, attendances plummeted as the season advanced, and things got worse following the introduction of rationing in January. Only 850 paid to watch the season's Filbert Street closer against Northampton.

The guest player system, so necessary during WW1, was reintroduced (with Northampton winger Bobby King the first outsider to don City's colours, and many others arriving from Aston Villa, who suspended operations). The most notable effect seen in Leicester in 1939/40 was the appearance of the legendary Tommy Lawton in three games during November and December, scoring five goals, yet never tasting victory. Of the regulars, Sep Smith, Dai Jones, Sandy McLaren and Jack Bowers were the main stalwarts, with Bowers heading the scorers' list, just ahead of Billy Coutts.

City's trips to the West Midlands threw up a couple of the season's characteristic curiosities. For the November fixture against West Brom, City arrived to find access to the Hawthorns possible only from the Staffordshire side of the border-straddling ground: Warwickshire police had still to raise a ban on football at this stage, and closed all turnstiles in their jurisdiction. And for the away fixture with Birmingham in January, played by arrangement at Leamington Spa, City turned out in borrowed blue-and-yellow quartered shirts.

The first ever League War Cup began in April and City bowed out in the second round at the hands of the eventual winners, West Ham United. The final took place at Wembley during the week of the retreat from Dunkirk, and some survivors were admitted free of charge. Thus that first wartime season drew to a close just as England faced her darkest hour, with an invasion appearing imminent.

Leicester City, too, was facing its own darkest hour. Off the field, the financial situation had become critical during the season. Three new directors, Alf Pallett, Leslie Green and Len Shipman, had joined the board in November, to provide an influx of capital, but a major reconstruction of the club's finances was proposed in January. The members of the board were each asked to either increase their own liability or to resign. Three of the long-serving directors, Pudan, Squires and Emmanuel Gregson, were all asked to step down in due course; whilst even more seriously, George Smith was suspended from his duties as club secretary, pending the deliberations of a Football Association commission which began investigating the club's books in April. Leslie Green was not cut out for such proceedings and he also resigned his directorship, hinting at scandal, only a few months after taking up the post.

On 20th and 21st May, the FA held an inquiry into the affairs of the club. They were primarily concerned with the payment of excessive bonuses and signing-on fees and the provision of irregular payments to amateur players over a lengthy period of time. The club was found guilty and fined £500 plus costs, and the former manager, Frank Womack, was suspended from football for twelve months. Five current or former directors – Tompkins, Squires, Gregson, Pudan and Frank Smith – were all suspended sine die, whilst other suspensions were handed out to Arthur Needham and Louis Burridge, three years each, Arthur Rice, two years, and Sid Needham, one year. The newcomers, Pallett and Shipman, were of course absolved from blame and were the only directors present at the subsequent board meeting on May 28th. George Smith was also cleared and invited to resume his duties, which he did until later in the year when resigning to run a pub at Groby. Eventually, after investigations finally concluded in September, a total of twelve current and former players (including Sep Smith and Jack Bowers) would also be suspended for one year. Such was the impact on the individual directors that several suffered serious illness shortly thereafter, and Arthur Rice died in January 1941.

At one stage during the summer of 1940 the talk was of liquidation, but a new board of directors was formed under Alf Pallett's chairmanship, and the club set itself to begin the 1940/1 season under the shadow of the Battle of Britain, which had been raging since July. Two local signs of optimism were the initiation of

Above: Now a veteran, Fred Sharman continued to turn out for City during the war years.

Below: The guest system again flourished and Stoke's Freddie Steele was recruited to bolster the forward line.

a Colts scheme for 15 to 17-year-olds, mixing Filbert Street coaching with civilian work of national importance, and the August launch of a City Supporters Club (with Johnny Duncan on the initial committee).

The season overall was probably the most arduous of the whole war, with play being automatically suspended whenever the air-raid signals sounded. A sign of the times, which raised many a much-needed laugh around the terraces, was that the Football League, desperate to keep competitions running, allowed referees who wore spectacles to officiate at Regional matches.

Oddly enough, just as things seemed to be at their lowest ebb for the club, performances on the field picked up considerably. City competed in the South Regional League this time, eventually attaining 14th place of the 34 member clubs. For the one and only time, final positions were determined by goal average rather than points. One of the prime reasons for City's improvement could be directly attributed to the decision by Wolverhampton Wanderers not to compete that season. Consequently, all their players were loaned out to other clubs, and two of their most promising young forwards, Jimmy Mullen and Billy Wright (only later to revert to centre-half), played for City for much of the campaign.

Coincidentally, it was another Wright, Dennis of that ilk, who made the headlines in November when City visited Mansfield. He was the Stags' reserve goalkeeper, but played at outside-right for City, who had arrived with only ten men, and scored both goals in a 2-4 defeat. Generally, the City forward-line proved to be prolific marksmen throughout the season, though the defence suffered the occasional disaster. This was amply illustrated on Christmas Day when two fixtures with Northampton Town were undertaken. A 10.45am kick-off at the County Ground saw City crash 2-5, but at 3.00pm at Filbert Street (with debutant Jack Lee for Jimmy Harrison the only team change), instant revenge was extracted by 7-2.

The improvement in fortunes was not confined to League games, for the club also completed a most successful season in cup competitions. The Midland Cup was secured with a 2-0 win over Walsall at Filbert Street on 3rd May, with Mullen and Wright getting the goals; whilst, a week earlier, the club had been on the verge of a first ever appearance at Wembley, only to be foiled by Arsenal in a two-legged semi-final of the League War Cup.

Having returned from White Hart Lane – where Arsenal were wartime tenants – with only a single goal reverse in front of a 9,242 crowd, hopes were high for a second-leg comeback. But Arsenal negotiated the release of three players from the same day's England v Wales international, and City also lost this game, by 1-2, with a Leslie Compton penalty decisive, to be denied their walk down Wembley Way. The crowd of 26,500 for the Filbert Street leg was somewhat unrepresentative of the season's norm (and indeed transpired to be the biggest of the entire wartime period): the previous highest gate had been for QPR's visit in the quarter-final, when 8,267 had turned out.

When the season ended, Billy Frame was the only ever-present, although several players managed over 30 appearances, whilst George Dewis proved to be the prince of strikers, collecting 24 goals from 30 outings, and at one stage netting in ten consecutive games. The Colts finished as runners-up to Loughborough Brush in the Leicestershire Senior League; and one of their number who failed to break through for City, forward Des Arnold from Syston, took a modicum of compensation by guesting for each of Tottenham and Nottingham Forest's seniors against City during the campaign (and would do so again for Bristol City the next term).

Off the field, times were almost as eventful. On 14th November, the night of the major blitz on Coventry, Filbert Street was hit by a German bomb. Damage was done primarily to the Main Stand, towards the Double Decker end, but affected the roof, seats, kitchen, toilets, gymnasium and boardroom, and a vain request to the FA for a loan left City facing an estimated repair bill for £15,000 alone. City were more successful in gaining the Football League's assistance, albeit only in resolving a contract dispute with Wolves over Arthur Smith, who was found to be registered for both clubs!

In order to raise funds, the directors sanctioned a boxing tournament (featuring Freddie Mills on the bill) taking place at Filbert Street on 4th August – a decision which reminded everyone how precarious was the state of the club's finances, given the stance previously taken against such ventures.

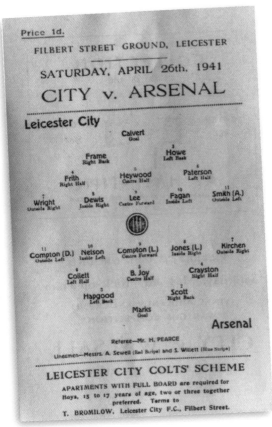

City came within 90 minutes of a first ever trip to Wembley in the 1940/1 League War Cup. They did, however, collect some silverware in the shape of the Midland Cup that season.

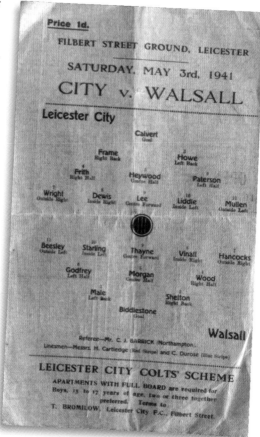

However, the outlook for the club and for Britain in general had improved considerably over the previous twelve months, and the 1941/2 season was greeted with cautious optimism. Owing to the breakaway of the London clubs, who wished to form their own Regional section, there was a late restructuring of fixtures this season, with the championship being split into two separate halves; the first running up to Christmas Day, and the second, incorporating the War Cup, occupying the remainder of the season.

Against a background of commodity shortages (new kit coming under coupon legislation, petrol not being given priority for sporting purposes, and even a drop in the number of footballs being manufactured!), City exploited the absence of the metropolitan clubs from the South Regional League, and clinched the 14-club championship on Christmas Day with a 2-0 home win over Nottingham Forest. This climaxed a sequence of six successive victories and was enough to bring the title to Leicester by a margin of 0.17 of a point from West Bromwich Albion, who did not have a match on that final day. The criteria for deciding positions was one of average points, based on an assumed norm of 18 games per club, and City accrued 26.47 against West Brom's 26.30. The Filbert Street crowd for the festive decider was 7,687; a substantial increase from the 2,790 who'd attended the campaign's opener against Norwich City.

Thus, barely two weeks after the Japanese attack on Pearl Harbour, City had affirmed their comeback from the depths and, moreover, made their name without the illustrious guests of the previous season. Mullen and Wright had returned to Wolves, who themselves had resumed business with a new youth policy. Their team which visited Filbert Street on 27th September had an average age of 17, with the veteran of the side being 19-year-old Derek Ashton! The policy was to prove the foundation of considerable postwar success for the Wolves, but was not to pay immediate dividends.

The second half of the campaign saw City as a target for other clubs to shoot down, and not a terribly durable one at that – they slid to 17th place of the 22 clubs who actually completed enough fixtures to qualify for the final table.

On an individual basis, Billy Frame was again an ever-present, a distinction he shared with Bert Howe, whilst youngster Gordon Jayes, Sep Smith and guest Harry Barratt all played in 30 or more of the 35 fixtures. Dennis Cheney and Jayes were the chief marksmen, finishing with 15 and 14 goals respectively. The most notable guest to don the blue and white of the City during the season was Ted Drake of Arsenal, who appeared in the 1-2 defeat at Walsall on 8th November.

The Colts took the Senior League title by a huge margin (on the way beating Holwell Works 17-0, with Vernon Chapman netting ten, Dennis Cheney five and Ray Iggleden two), but were beaten in the County Cup final 1-3 by Loughborough Brush, when their consolation goal was scored by a deaf-mute winger named Felstead. City additionally fielded a Junior team this term in the City & Mutual League, utilising the YMCA ground at Belvoir Drive. The club also 'adopted' the crew of the Grimsby trawler 'Leicester City', now on war work, as recipients of some of their charitable efforts.

Things were much quieter behind the scenes by now, but another setback occurred on 29th June 1942 when a fire in the Main Stand caused extensive damage. Starting at the Double Decker end, it quickly spread to destroy the dressing rooms, trainer's room, kit, referee's room and gymnasium as well as much of the upper seating. In addition, the boardroom and offices suffered water damage in the fire-fighting operation.

By the time the Football League's AGM came round, also in June, the changing face of the war was considered, and a committee established to discuss postwar arrangements. During the season a Victory Cup was purchased, though this seemed a somewhat premature move as the Allies' fortunes continued to fluctuate. At a League meeting in January 1943, the decision was made that a transitional season would be implemented once hostilities ended, prior to the normal peacetime formula being resumed.

Above: Wartime tribulations for the Filbert Street ground, which was bombed in 1941 and later caught fire in June 1942.

Above: Billy Wright was a more than useful guest for City before returning to Wolves to become part of that club's inspired youth policy.

The 1942/3 season itself, covering roughly the period from the battle for El Alamein to the flight of the famous Dambusters, was a fairly indifferent one for City, who this time were placed in the Northern Section of the Regional League, and had to fulfil their first quartet of fixtures in borrowed maroon shirts. The unavailability of many of the club stalwarts on a regular basis led to major problems of team selection: the average age of the senior XI was often under-21, and a total of 58 players were used to complete the 38 fixtures, including the high number of 26 listed guests. Once again the campaign consisted of two separate championships. Final placings of 33rd out of 48 and 22nd out of 54 accurately indexed City's mediocrity over the season.

In October, Danny Liddle, Fred Sharman, Jack Bowers and Dai Jones all featured for Notts County against City and aided the Magpies to a 3-1 Filbert Street win. In November, the 2-1 home win against Forest was played at Coalville Town's Ashby Road ground, but the attendance of 2,300 was a huge disappointment to both the club and the Leicestershire Mine Owners Association, who had laid on the game on a rare pitmen's rest day. In March, it was Forest who put City out of the War Cup (North), amid much Filbert Street controversy. Forest led 1-0 at 90 minutes, levelling the tie on aggregate, and there was no further scoring in 20 minutes of extra-time. A sudden-death period was now embarked on, and the referee allowed Hindley's 119th-minute winner to stand despite the linesman's offside flag. Lieutenant F J A Bear's rank stood for nothing as a mass pitch invasion saw him smuggled to safety by the police. The Leicester crowd had been seen in disorderly mode on Christmas Day too, with a thousand or so breaking down a gate to join the 8,534 who'd paid to watch visitors Aston Villa

Two wartime records were established, however, during 1942/3. On 12th December, as Wolves were humbled 5-0 at Filbert Street, Freddie Steele, a guest from Stoke City, became the first player to score four goals in a game; whilst, on January 2nd, City ran up a record victory of 9-0 over West Brom.

Sep Smith, Bert Howe and goalkeeper Alick Grant were the only players to top the 30 appearance mark and Freddie Steele, with 13, was the only marksman to reach double figures. The Colts took the Senior League title again, but this time only with a last-match win over rivals Central Ordnance Depot (Old Dalby). Conscious of the need to raise outside income, despite a seasonal profit of £1,032, the directors actually hired out the ground for a gymkhana on two occasions, as well as contacting American forces stationed in the area with a view to staging baseball at Filbert Street for the first time since 1897! Nothing came of this 'new' initiative until the following Christmas, though.

1943/4 was a season played out against a background of considerable optimism throughout the country as the tide of war began to turn significantly in the Allies' favour. Shortages at home were beginning to bite harder, and German air-raids actually intensified (the FA offices being hit by an incendiary bomb), but football attendances rose appreciably in tune with spirits (City's leaping from 3,579 to 4,674 to 6,328 over their first trio of home games).

City's season was again moderate. 28th position out of 50 was achieved in the first championship, whilst a respectable 14th slot of the 56 participants in the second brought the season to a satisfactory close. The highlights on the field were reserved for two of

Above: Frank Soo moved from Stoke to Leicester, but never really settled in the East Midlands.

Left: George Dewis scored more wartime goals for City than any other player.

the clashes with Notts County. On 30th October, George Dewis and Arthur Smith hit four goals apiece as City triumphed 9-1 at Meadow Lane. (On the very same day, the Colts beat Pegsons 9-1 and the Juniors ran up a 9-2 scoreline against Petronians!) Then on New Year's Day, it was the turn of Sep Smith and guest Norman Bowden to record hat-tricks in a 7-2 frolic against the Magpies at Filbert Street.

Once again, Billy Frame, Alick Grant and Sep Smith (this term one of nine Smiths on the club's books) were the mainstays of the team. No-one emerged as a regular goalscorer, though, with Arsenal reserve Bowden leading the way with 11 goals from his 9 appearances. On Boxing Day, a 3,000 crowd watched two American service teams in baseball action at Filbert Street: a fair turnout considering Aston Villa had only tempted 4,737 to the ground a week earlier.

As the season drew to a close, the Second Front invasion of Europe was imminent, and finally took place on 6th June. In the City boardroom D-Day was marked by the decision to adopt Middlesbrough Swifts as an official nursery club. This followed a recommendation by ex-City stalwart George Carr, and hopes were high that some of the talent emerging from that footballing hotbed of the North-East could be diverted to Filbert Street. Indeed, Don Revie soon arrived from that very source, but the promising theory was destined never to be tested during peacetime.

City also re-arranged their reserve set-up for this term: the Reserves were to play in the newly-formed, nine-club, Midland Senior League (under Fred Sharman), and the Colts in the Leics Senior League; while the Juniors were to be disbanded.

The success of the D-Day landings had raised expectations throughout the country of an early end to hostilities, and talk at the postponed AGMs of both the FA and League was of plans for the transitional season. In the meantime, though, the despatch of military personnel into Europe in the wake of the Second Front had led to the guest system again being overworked during the 1944/5 season. Leicester suffered as much as anyone and a total of 62 players, the highest of any season during World War Two, was used to complete the campaign. The disruption was particularly bad during the early part of the season, when City even started their home game against West Brom with only nine men, and a dismal final placing of 52nd in the first championship, with only two clubs faring worse, was no surprise. As things settled down after Christmas, a steady improvement was made and the club rose to 34th position of the 60 clubs in the second competition.

Much of the credit for this amelioration was due to the inclusion of Motherwell's Billy Leitch as a regular guest after Christmas. The Scottish centre-forward scored a dozen times at the rate of a goal per game, and also seemed to bring the best out of Sep Smith, who reached double figures in post-Xmas goals, having found the net only twice previously. Leitch's hat-trick was the highlight of the 8-3 thumping of Mansfield Town in January, and it was only after his departure that four of the final five fixtures were lost. Gates were on the rise, too, with five-figure returns becoming less unusual, and a season's best of 19,074 paying to see Derby at Filbert Street in March.

Throughout the season, Sep Smith and Billy Frame were yet again the stalwarts, with Frank Sheard also establishing himself as a regular defensive pivot. No-one else came near to matching the dozen goals of Leitch and Smith, but that fact paled into insignificance as the season closed with reports of Hitler's suicide and the final surrender of Germany.

Closer to home, the season's end was marked by the resignation of Tom Bromilow as manager. He had steered the club through an immensely difficult period, but his relationship with the board had deteriorated, and he felt it was no longer possible to continue. His successor was Tom Mather, a former boss at Stoke and Newcastle, and a man with a

Above: Some of the City squad, with mascot, at the station ready to depart for their FA Cup tie at Chelsea in January 1946.
Left to right: Dai Jones, John Grogan, John Osborne, mascot, Joe Calvert, Bill Towers, Frank Sheard, Charlie Adam, Sep Smith, Danny Liddle, Billy Frame, Don Revie.

reputation as a talent-spotter. He had, in fact, signed Stanley Matthews for the Potteries club, and the Leicester board were hopeful that he might unearth similar class in the East Midlands.

As he made his plans for the transitional season of 1945/6, the world was rocked by the use of the atomic bombs on Hiroshima and Nagasaki. Within days Japan had surrendered, and the Second World War came to an official end just two weeks into the footballing campaign.

Putting City on the front pages of the local press at this time was a major row over the future of Filbert Street itself. The City Council would not agree an extension of the club's lease on the ground beyond the end of 1948, owing to the possible expansion of the neighbouring electricity generating station. City lobbied for political support, claiming the loss of the ground would kill the club; but it was not until nine months later, in March 1946, that a single-vote majority decision was made by the Council to give the club a 14-year lease at £200 per annum, subject to two-year notice after September 1953, with compensation then payable up to an amount of £20,000.

The arrangements for the transitional season were slightly different to those during the previous few years. The old First and Second Division clubs were combined, then split into North and South

Above: Danny Liddle made over 100 wartime appearances for City.

Divisions, whilst the Third Divisions were split into four smaller sections. The popular League War Cup competitions were scrapped, but the FA Cup was reinstated, though ties were to be played on a two-leg basis at the request of the clubs to generate extra revenue.

Leicester City were placed in the League South and met with little success, ultimately being placed 20th of the 22 competitors. They also made an early Cup exit, losing on aggregate to Chelsea at the first hurdle. In October the club's official nursery, Middlesbrough Swifts, was reported as folding up due to lack of funds, and a potential source of fresh talent was lost.

The previous month, Mather had persuaded one of his discoveries from Stoke to make the move to Filbert Street. Wartime international Frank Soo was a highly-prized signing, and a skilful playmaker much admired by the crowd, but he was destined for only a short stay with City. On Christmas Eve he turned out for Port Vale without previously having obtained the board's permission and, following a heated dispute, was placed on the transfer list. The rift was never healed and, during the summer, Soo moved on to Luton Town.

Tom Mather himself never really settled at Leicester, and in mid-March handed in his resignation. He had occupied the managerial chair for a mere ten months. Before his departure, however, he had recognised City's need for an experienced general to marshal his young team. To this end he tried to persuade Wolves to part with Stan Cullis, but the Molineux club rejected his proposals.

Two days after Mather resigned, John Duncan, the man who had captained City in their halcyon days of the late 1920s, was appointed to take over the managerial reins. It was too late for him to change the club's fortunes for that season but his day would come.

Sep Smith and Billy Frame once more led the appearance charts as wartime football drew to a close, whilst Stan Mercer was the leading marksman with 10 goals. Crowds had returned to reasonable levels despite the 'artificial' nature of the competitive fare on offer, but the remarkable Filbert Street attendance of 32,904 attracted in May by a schoolboy match – albeit the first leg of the final of the English Schools FA Trophy – indexed the potential peacetime drawing power of the game. (Incidentally, Leicester Boys – under the captaincy of future County Cricket skipper Maurice Hallam, and under the management of Jack Curtis, later City's youth liaison officer – overcame their Stockton counterparts with a 4-1 home win and a further 3-0 victory at Ayresome Park to bring this particular pot home for the first time).

Over the seven seasons covered by World War Two, City had played 273 competitive matches, including the three League games of 1939/40 and the two FA Cup ties of 1945/6, winning 96 and losing 122. Three players topped the 200 appearance mark – Billy Frame with 220, Sep Smith 213 and Bert Howe 209 – yet such were the outside demands on players' time during this period that only one other, Danny Liddle with 115, reached three figures. Of the goalscorers, George Dewis earned pride of place with 62 goals in 81 games. Sep Smith managed to accumulate 48 goals over the period; his total being boosted by 12 successful spot kicks. Two of City's managers had come and gone without selecting a side for an official League game. So far as we are aware, all of the 63 club staff who had signed up for military or civil service during the period emerged relatively unscathed.

Wartime fare was hardly going to be mourned by City. The period of makeshift competition and major internal upheaval had, however, seen City emerge on a sounder footing than that on which they entered it. And the prospect of a fresh start in Division Two, free of the stigma of the pre-war relegation debacle, was one to be relished.

Peace & Progress

WILLS'S CIGARETTES

D. McCULLOCH

WILLS'S CIGARETTES

S. SMITH (LEICESTER CITY)

> The prospect of Leicester City's return to peacetime soccer and genuine Football League fare remarkably resembled that which had faced the club at the end of the Great War. The team were once again in Division Two, were under new management, and the club had undergone a major financial and structural overhaul during the break occasioned by the hostilities.

Once again, the backbone of the City squad would be formed from two groups of players – the handful of mainly youthful discoveries who had staked their claim during the years of Regional football, and several hardy survivors from the pre-war era. Each of the players in the latter category had, of course, had some seven seasons of their professional careers claimed by the war, and some, like skipper Sep Smith, were now very much at the veteran stage.

Behind the scenes, as Johnny Duncan plotted his first campaign with the assistance of trainers George Ritchie and Bill McLean, there was one other significant change, with the appointment of Charles Maley as Club Secretary. Wing-half Tommy Eggleston and the veteran Dave McCulloch, together from Derby, were the only major signings, though Rangers' soon-to-be Scottish international centre-half Willie Woodburn turned Duncan down after his club had accepted terms.

The fixture list for 1946/7 duplicated that originally drawn up for the abandoned season of 1939/40, but this time City did not get off to such a good start. Initially being thwarted by a Frank Swift 'blinder' for Manchester City, and then returning goalless and pointless from St Andrews, they did manage to get off the mark by exactly replicating their pre-war result at Upton Park with a 2-0 win, courtesy of a lofted Dai Jones free-kick and Bobby Anderson's 40-yard dribble and cross-shot. (Jones, Mal Griffiths and George Dewis were the only City men to have played in both fixtures against West Ham, seven years apart).

For the first midweek home game, City had to wait until a half-hour before the 6.00 kick off for the arrival of each of Anderson, Don Revie and Jimmy Dawson from a full day's work – without lunch-break – at their respective industrial apprenticeships. Football was not to be exempted from the prevailing social mood of austerity, and for a while the fare City were serving up looked more austere than most. In fact only five points were gleaned from the first eight fixtures, and Duncan was quick to ring the team changes, discarding among others his new centre-forward McCulloch, who could not rediscover his pre-war scoring consistency.

But the team's form picked up in October to such

an extent that only one defeat was suffered in the next ten outings, and a useful attacking partnership between Jack Lee and George Dewis began to emerge, materially assisted by the stylish promptings of Don Revie. A spot of hooliganism attended the goalless draw at Burnley during this sequence, with keeper Joe Calvert hit by a stone and a pitch invader wrestled away. Calvert played on here, but was three times stretchered from the fray to be replaced by outfield players before the season was out. Indeed, his final departure, at Plymouth, was part of a dark farce: he injured his back trying to keep out a Sep Smith own goal, was replaced in turn by Dewis and Eggleston, and watched Dai Jones contribute another own goal to a 0-4 defeat.

Eventually, a crop of such niggling injuries disrupted the balance of the side, but the final League placing of ninth gave modest grounds for optimism. The twin effect of those injuries and of Duncan's search for an effective blend can best be seen from the fact that no player managed to turn out in more than 36 of the 42 League fixtures. Mal Griffiths was the man to top the appearance charts, and also the first City player capped after the war, when chosen on the Welsh right wing against Ireland in April. Jack Lee led the scoring list with 18 League goals from only 24 games, though George Dewis supplemented his League tally of 16 with three Cup strikes.

Overall, the season was not quite the boom year that nostalgic myth would have it; even if it produced a welcome £4,336 profit. The fixture list was severely disrupted by what was the worst winter on record to that date, and the combination of this with a temporary Government ban on midweek sport led to the season being extended into June. Supporters' enthusiasm was understandably somewhat dimmed, and City's final home game with Fulham drew a gate of only 8,006 – which remained a postwar record low for a League match at Filbert Street for over 35 years.

City did, though, manage to stir their fans' interest with their FA Cup exploits. A fine away win over West Ham in Round Three was followed by a long-drawn-out affair with First Division Brentford, dogged by ice and snow, and it took a third-game victory at neutral Villa Park (where the terraces were almost deserted, and an army of helpers constantly brushed the lines as play continued in a blizzard) to bring the reward of a Fifth Round tie with Newcastle United. 50,309 witnessed City emerge from St James's Park with a brave draw, but the Geordies triumphed in another icy spectacular at Leicester to end City's Wembley hopes.

Above: Jack Haines came and went in the same season.

> Although some degree of stability had been achieved during Johnny Duncan's first season in charge, it was clear that the team needed to be strengthened if a promotion bid was to be made. To this end, the club paid out a fee of £4,600 to Swansea Town in July to secure the services of the versatile Jack Haines.

The future England international did not settle in particularly well, though, and by March was transferred to West Bromwich Albion in part exchange for Scottish playmaker Peter McKennan. City also expended £6,000 in cash to complete this deal so, although a value was never formally put on the transfer, it may legitimately be regarded as the equivalent of a club record.

The other transaction of significance during the season occurred in January, when no less than five City players moved to Watford on the same day – a deal thought to be unique in football history. Joe Calvert, Tommy Eggleston, Johnny Osborne and Tom Hartley all made a permanent switch to Vicarage Road, whilst Dennis Cheney was loaned until the end of the season. Hartley, incidentally, was a reserve inside-forward who had only been on City's books for a month. Watford, who were managerless at the time, had initially made a board-level enquiry to cost the entire City reserve team; and had then attempted to take a sextet including George Dewis!

The club did make further attempts to reinforce the senior squad, including enquiries for Joe Arnison of Rangers and Reg Lewis of Arsenal, but no actual bids were tabled. Another young player watched during the season was Danny Blanchflower of Glentoran, but again no action was taken, and City's loss would much later be Spurs' decided gain.

The season itself pretty closely mirrored the previous one; excepting the fact that the opening day fixture nearly fell to postponement when City's Leeds-

Below: A record transfer deal in January 1948 as five City players are transferred to Watford on the same day. John Duncan bids farewell to Dennis Cheney, Tom Eggleston, Tom Hartley, Joe Calvert and John Osborne.

bound coach broke down near Doncaster. Frantic use of the thumb saw the majority of the party delivered part-way to Elland Road in a furniture van! (A tragic sequel to the day saw the returning replacement coach fatally knock down a Leicester woman in Belgrave Road that evening).

City again finished ninth in Division Two, generally betraying elegant approach work with penalty-area profligacy, and again reached the Fifth Round of the FA Cup, this time tasting defeat at White Hart Lane after removing Bury and Sheffield Wednesday from the competition. A massive 69,049 gate saw three Spurs goals in three minutes kill off City's plucky challenge after the score had stood at 2-2 with 64 minutes gone.

Injuries again took their toll, with Revie and Lee both being sidelined for long periods, and once more no player came close to being ever-present. Lee, with 13 League goals and two more in the Cup, was the only scorer in double figures, but young Derek Hines burst onto the scene towards the end of the campaign, notching six in nine games and linking productively with old hand McKennan, after some remarkable scoring feats in the Reserves, the County Youth team, and for England Youth.

Indeed, it was from the less experienced members of Duncan's quietly reshaped squad that City drew most encouragement in this generally mediocre

season, with the Reserves demonstrating their promise by capturing the Combination Cup after beating Bournemouth & Boscombe Athletic 2-1 in the Filbert Street final, with Sandy Scott's penalty and Arthur Smith's header wiping out the half-time lead Holland had given the visitors. A gate of 13,073 resisted the counter-attractions of the same day's FA Cup Final and the City seniors' fixture at Bury.

The site of Filbert Street itself was the subject of some boardroom discussion. Even though the lease had been renewed and extended in 1946, the directors took the opportunity to consider other sites for a ground the club might itself own. Possible moves to Enderby, Abbey Lane or Saffron Lane were all eventually rejected, though, and continuing tenancy of the club's traditional home confirmed. The state of the pitch, however, required urgent attention. A 'glutinous mess' for most of the campaign, it was ripped up and relaid over a new drainage system as soon as the campaign closed, thus eating severely into the seasonal profit of £4,103.

This term also saw the initial serialisation (in the *Evening Mail*), and eventual pocket-sized publication, of journalist Noel Tarbotton's club history 'From Fosse To City', by far the most comprehensive approach to logging the Leicester soccer saga to that date. Within a year, even its most stirring tales would be rivalled and eclipsed for drama.

> During the summer of 1948, the board decided that a club crest would henceforth be worn on the players' jerseys. The design chosen, representing the hunting traditions of the county, was that of a fox's head, surrounded by the letters 'LCFC'. Little could the directors have imagined that, within a year, City's unlikely trophy-hunting ambitions would lead to the new badge being proudly worn at Wembley.

Indeed, it was worn initially in distinctly less hallowed surroundings, for City were forced to borrow the Dunlop Sports Ground, St Mary's Mills, for training purposes; while their 'A' team's home Birmingham League fixtures would be played at Barwell. City also took on the sponsorship of a local nursery team, Leicester Junior Imperial, which would produce two England Youth internationals (full-back Ken Hincks and centre-forward Reg Warner) this term.

Johnny Duncan was meanwhile sifting his senior squad for another attempt at producing a promotion-worthy blend. Record incoming fees for Arthur Smith and Jimmy Hernon (£14,750 to Bolton) eased any temptation to yield to enquiries for both Don Revie (from Notts County and Arsenal) and Jack Lee (from Nottingham Forest and Coventry City). But as the

Above: A fox appeared on City shirts for the first time in the 1948/9 season.

Below: A young boy hands out the kit as the players prepare for one of the season's Cup games.

season got underway in earnest, with the opening-day promise of a 6-2 slaughter of Leeds soon giving way to a worrying slide, Duncan played the market again, with decidedly mixed fortune. Out went Peter McKennan (to Brentford for £7,000) to be briefly replaced by Scottish junior Tom Paterson, and then by Third Lanark's Jimmy Ayton, a £7,750 signing who was soon sidelined by jaundice. Crewe pair Jack Meaney and Tony Waddington were targets out of Duncan's reach; then, when he failed to tempt Arsenal's Alec Forbes to Filbert Street, he swooped for three players in three days: with goalkeepers Johnny Anderson and Ian McGraw bracketing winger Tommy Edwards in the arrivals queue. Finally, as the slither into the relegation zone became precipitate, came Leeds inside-left and former wartime guest Ken Chisholm, for a record £11,000 outlay, in time for a New Year's Day debut.

Second Division failings were becoming a severe embarrassment by the time the diversion of the FA Cup came around. Charlie Wayman had helped himself to five of Southampton's six against City: but a shot-shy forward line was earning as much criticism as the occasionally rickety defence. The side was anything but settled: Sep Smith was coming to the end

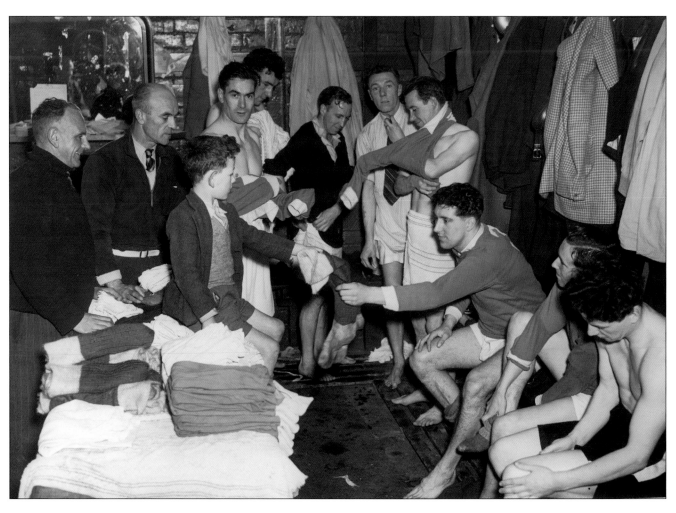

of an illustrious career, and he saw Norman Plummer take over both his centre-half position and the club captaincy; yet even the latter was uncertain of automatic selection.

As 400-1 shots City lined up for their Third Round tie away to Birmingham City, the League table showed them in 19th place in Division Two, with only Grimsby Town, Nottingham Forest and Lincoln City below them. It took some time – three games and 330 minutes, in fact – for City to register a heartening giant-killing over their top-flight rivals, but the tonic effect was welcome.

A 5-3 thumping of fellow strugglers Lincoln City (during which Plummer gave away two penalties and registered an own goal!) had lifted City to 17th place in the table when Preston North End came to Filbert Street in Round Four. The Lancastrians would eventually be relegated from Division One, and City had little trouble in building on an opening-minute penalty lead to complete another giant-killing act and reach Round Five for the third consecutive season.

This time fellow Second Division club Luton Town were to provide the opposition. The game, at Kenilworth Road, was one of the most exciting cup-ties ever staged. After 6 minutes City scored the opener, 4 minutes later Luton led 2-1, by half-time City had nosed in front by 3-2, and at the end of 90 minutes the score stood at 3-3. An extra half-hour was to be played, and City quickly restored their lead, but by the mid-point of the extra period, Luton again held the advantage, by 5-4. As the game drifted into injury time, it looked as though this would be the final result, but Mal Griffiths sent over a last-ditch corner

and Jack Lee rose to head home the equaliser. It was Lee's fourth goal of the game.

The replay, the following week, was no anti-climax. Luton netted in the first minute, but City stormed back to lead 4-1 shortly after half-time. The Hatters then staged a rally to reduce the arrears to 4-3 and keep the 38,822 crowd on tenterhooks before a late Griffiths goal ensured City's passage to the quarter-finals.

City were back down in 18th place when they travelled to meet Brentford in Round Six, in front of an all-time Griffin Park record crowd of 38,678. The Londoners, however, were only three places higher (even if a week before Peter McKennan had netted five for them against Bury), and Leicester, boosted by a classic diving header from Lee, won comfortably by 2-0 to reach the semi-final for only the second time in their history.

Highbury was the venue for City's clash with Portsmouth, leaders and eventual champions of Division One. City had slipped again, down to 20th position in Division Two, and were given next to no chance of extracting revenge for their defeat at this stage in 1934. What followed, though, is still regarded by many as among City's finest hours.

The Leicester performance that day was magnificent, with Don Revie the orchestrator as well as the scorer of two goals. This was no hit-and-run display: City simply outplayed their more illustrious opponents on the day, silenced the Pompey chimes, brought a frown to the face of Lord Montgomery of Alamein, and ran out 3-1 winners to clinch their first-ever appearance in the FA Cup Final.

Fate, however, stepped in to deal the club two cruel blows in the nine League games that had to be squeezed in before the trip to Wembley. Only a week after the Highbury success, as Wolves and Manchester United battled in a replay for the right to meet the giantkillers, City found themselves involved in a real rough-house of a battle against Grimsby at home. They scraped a point from the encounter, but suffered several injuries, including one to 'keeper McGraw's hand which would rule him out of the Final, and eventually lead to him losing a finger. Three weeks later, Revie, the architect of the Cup run, suffered a serious nose injury and a near-fatal loss of blood, and was barred even from making the trip to Wembley, let alone playing.

City were still very much on the brink of relegation to the Third Division, with only three League games still to play, when they faced Wolves at Wembley with something of a makeshift line-up, involving the experiment of playing full-back Jimmy Harrison at centre-forward, and shifting Jack Lee to an inside-forward role. The First Division outfit

The equivalent of just £1.05 for a Cup Final seat at Wembley and another 5p for the programme - those were the days!

Below: City followers get in the mood!

Top: Managers Stan Cullis and John Duncan lead the teams out at Wembley. **Left:** Skippers Norman Plummer and Billy Wright wish each other the best of luck. **Above:** Wright can only turn and watch as Mal Griffiths (out of picture) scores City's goal. **Below:** City 'keeper Gordon Bradley collects a cross.

SPORTS MAIL

L. C. F.C.

11971 : SATURDAY, APRIL 30th, 1949.   (GREEN 'UN)   TWOPENCE

TWO HELPINGS OF PYE WERE TOO MUCH
FOR THE CITY AT WEMBLEY

CITY

WOLVES

Goal By Live-Wire Griffiths Raised Leicester's Hopes, But They Missed The Revie Touch

FATE, in the shape of cruel injuries to Revie and McGraw, played a big part in the defeat of Leicester City in their first Cup Final this afternoon at Wembley, but full marks must go to the Wolves, who were deserved winners on the day. Pye (centre-forward) and Smyth (inside-right) netted the winners' goals, and Griffiths replied for the gallant losers, who fought every inch of the way against big odds.

LEICESTER CITY 1 WOLVERHAMPTON WANDERERS 3
By BILLY KING

PLUMMER

Bradley   Jelly

Scott   Harrison (W.)

King   Griffiths

Lee   Harrison (J.)

Chisholm   Adam

THIS is the story of the greatest afternoon in the long and honoured history of Leicester City. As the players came near to Wembley on their journey from Stevenage and saw the tens of thousands swarming towards the arena, an unmistakable thrill gripped these young players for whom the occasion was the most exciting adventure of their lives. Leicester supporters clustered round the coach as it moved slowly behind a police escort to the entrance. One of the City side said to me, "This is a schoolboy's dream come true."

The hundred thousand audience had settled down about half-an-hour before the start. The Wembley turf looked more beautiful than ever, and at 2.50 the teams appeared from the east end of the ground to be greeted by a massive roar.

The managers were at the head of their teams, and I could see Johnny Duncan as he walked beside Norman Plummer, talking eagerly and making his familiar gestures.

The players lined up and the green sward was painted with the red of the Guards, the black and gold of the Wolves and the brilliant royal blue of the City. The Duke of Gloucester and the Duke of Edinburgh, escorted by FA officials, came out to meet the teams.

Billy Wright introduced his men to the Royal visitors, and

SCOREBOARD

12 mins.—PYE (Wolves).
42 mins.—PYE (Wolves).
47 mins.—GRIFFITHS (City).
65 mins.—SMYTH (Wolves).

then it was Norman Plummer's turn.

I saw the Duke of Edinburgh in animated conversation with several of the City side, as he moved slowly behind the Duke of Gloucester.

This ceremony was soon over, and the teams gladly broke up, Leicester running to the west goal.

Then the toss. Plummer spun the coin and Wright made the wrong call.

SUN FADES

The City skipper at once called his men to the east end and the teams took their positions, only to be kept waiting more than a minute until three o'clock.

This was irksome for the actors in this great sporting drama and they danced about, fidgeting, until at last the game started.

Conditions were ideal, there

VOLUNTEERED—THEN BROKE A LEG

LOUIS CHURCHILL, the Taunton Rugby Union full-back, missed his club's last game of the season today because he broke a leg yesterday while he was playing soccer. Churchill works at Langport, and when the local team were a man short, he volunteered to fill the gap. The accident happened five minutes from the end.

LEICESTER CITY
Right   Left

Bradley

Jelly   Scott

Harrison (W.)   Plummer   King

Griffiths   Lee   Harrison (J.)   Chisholm   Adam

O

Mullen   Dunn   Pye   Smyth   Hancocks

Wright   Shorthouse   Crook (W.)

Springthorpe   Pritchard

Williams

Left   **WOLVERHAMPTON**   Right

Referee: R. A. Mortimer (Huddersfield). Linesmen: V. Rae (London) and R. L. Aldridge (Birmingham).

being practically no wind, and the sun's brilliance had faded.

Bradley had to gather a long ball through the middle in the first few seconds.

NIPPY BRADLEY

And then the Wolves made a sharp thrust on the left, where Dunn, their inside-left, drove the ball out of play.

A free-kick came to the Wolves out on the right just beyond the penalty area, and Bradley nipped across to hold the ball from Hancocks beautifully. No sign of wrist trouble in that save.

SWIFT PROGRESS

Griffiths figured in the first Leicester attack, being sent along the wing, to cut inside while Jim Harrison darted out to the flank.

The move was neatly cut off by the Wolves' defence, and then we saw a choice piece of work from the Wanderers' half-backs and left-wing pair.

They dovetailed smoothly, making swift progress with carpet-passes that confused the City.

Mullen bore in, and from 18 yards tried a shot that sailed well wide of the left-hand post.

SETTLING DOWN

Norman Plummer was hanging on to Pye like a leech, and chased him out to the touchline for a valuable clearance.

The City had shaken off that cup-tie tension in the first five minutes, and began settling down to some promising raiding.

A ball from Walter Harrison brought concern in the Wolves' ranks, and Lee cut out an opening of great possibilities

R. A. MORTIMER, of Huddersfield, the Cup Final referee.

which Chisholm could not find quite enough speed to take.

WOLVES STRIKE

Jim Harrison fed Griffiths very nicely, and the winger turned on his speed as he curved in.

We thought he would take the ball much closer than he did, and his long shot, that sailed high over the goal, was a disappointment.

There was a great thrill when Adam closed in, racing with Williams for possession, and the goalkeeper just pounced on it.

In the 12th minute Wolves struck the first crucial blow. It was rather tough luck on Scott, who had been holding

the fort steadily, that the goal should come from the right winger's cross.

PYE SCORES

It was slung over almost to the penalty spot by Hancocks, and PYE had no serious challenge as he jumped for a smashing header almost into the centre of goal.

The Wolves hammered away, and again it was Mullen, a strong hitter of the ball, who placed a cross drive so well that Bradley had to hurl himself out and turn it away.

The City half-backs were gradually asserting themselves, and the ball was reaching Chisholm quite often, one of his typical vigorous runs being spoiled when the ball was crossed to the right, and Griffiths could not reach it.

We could see how these Wolves depended on Wright for their inspiration.

He was finding the gaps in the Leicester half of the field and setting the pace for his clever forward line.

TOO MUCH ROPE

The Wolves were being allowed a dangerous length of rope when they got near the City penalty area, and it was as well for Leicester that the opposing forwards elected to shoot from unduly long range.

First Pye sent Dunn through for the inside-left to hammer a long one over the bar, and then Pye himself, with a pass from Wright, repeated the act.

We entered on a spell of midfield tussles with Johnny King playing a dominant part.

He made the running for Adam to trick Pritchard with a very clever run, and push the ball into the Wolves' penalty area to Lee.

Jack hesitated with the crowd shouting madly for him to shoot, but he was hemmed in, and very coolly slipped a back pass to King for the little half-back to take a hefty wallop at it.

TIGHT DEFENCE

It struck a Wolves' player and was cleared.

The City's share of the play, since the goal, had been considerable, but they could not find that final punch to beat a very tight defence.

In this Wright was going great guns.

Jim Harrison got his head to two or three balls from Walter Harrison and Griffiths, but only to send the ball into the air harmlessly.

We had been given powerful evidence of the Wolves' strength on the wing, where the delicate ball control of Hancocks was now giving Scott a bad headache.

Twice Hancocks got round the full-back, and each time

(Continued in Page Five)

Williams   Pritchard

Springthorpe   Crook (W.)

Shorthouse   Hancocks

Smyth   Pye

Dunn   Mullen

ROOKE TO MANAGE CRYSTAL PALACE

ARRANGEMENTS have been completed between Arsenal and Crystal Palace for Ronnie Rooke (centre-forward) to join the Selhurst club as player-manager, succeeding Jack Butler, the former Leicester City coach, who resigned from the Crystal Palace managership recently. Rooke was formerly with Fulham before going to Arsenal.

LEICESTER CITY'S YEAR

Leicester Mercury

2/6
Souvenir

Wembley 1949!

WEMBLEY STORY

Leicester Mercury

1/-
Final Souvenir

L.C.F.C.

Above: The *Leicester Mercury* produced excellent souvenir brochures before and after the Final.

unsurprisingly dominated the first half and two goals from Jesse Pye looked to have the game sewn up before the interval. Johnny Duncan reorganised his forward-line during the break, though, and, two minutes into the second half, City struck back. Mal Griffiths was the man who scored, latching on to Bert Williams' parry of Chisholm's power-drive, and Wolves suddenly began to totter.

A newly-confident City continued to press for the equaliser, but in the 64th minute came the incident that effectively settled the game. Taking a long cross from Jimmy Harrison, hooked on by Griffiths, Chisholm netted from an acute angle for City, only to be ruled marginally offside. With the players still deflated by referee Mortimer's decision, Wolves broke away and, within 60 seconds, Sammy Smyth had scored a stunning solo to make it 1-3. So the Cup was lost and City, with kudos for gallantry ringing in their ears, had to return to their desperate relegation battle.

Four days after the Final, City gained an invaluable win at Bury, but within 24 hours this advantage had been nullified by a crushing home defeat at the hands of West Bromwich Albion, who thereby sealed their own promotion. By this time, Lincoln already knew they would be relegated: it was a toss-up as to whether City or Nottingham Forest would accompany them into the Third.

Thus City came to their final match, against Cardiff City at Ninian Park, needing a point to ensure safety, assuming Forest would beat Bury in their final fixture. When news filtered through of Forest's duly accomplished victory, in a game with an earlier kick-

Right: Ken Chisholm nets from a tight angle, but City's 'equaliser' is negated by a linesman's flag.

Left: Beaten but not dispirited - City players can still smile, even with runners-up medals in their hands. Pictured are Lee, Griffiths, Jimmy Harrison, Jelly, Plummer, Adam and Chisholm.

Below: A celebration dinner for Leicester's first Wembley finalists was held at The Bell Hotel in the city on Monday 9th May, 1949.

LEICESTER CITY FOOTBALL CLUB
The Football Association Challenge Cup Finalists

CELEBRATION DINNER

MENU

Clear Madrilene

———

Roast Aylesbury Duckling, Sage Stuffing
Apple Sauce
New Boiled Potatoes, Roasted Potatoes
Fresh Garden Peas, Buttered New Carrots

———

Fresh Strawberry Flan Meringue
Vanilla Cream Ices

———

Coffee

———

Toast THE KING

Entertainers:
JACK TRAIN
PETER WARING
JIMMY HEARTH
CLIVE ALLEN *at Piano*

NORMAN PLUMMER
(Captain)

CHARLIE ADAM

JOHNNY KING

SANDY SCOTT

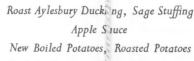

KEN CHISHOLM

GORDON BRADLEY

JIMMY HARRISON

WALLY HARRISON

GEORGE RITCHIE

JACK LEE

MAL GRIFFITHS

TED JELLY

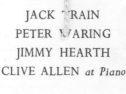

off time, City were clearly in deep trouble. They trailed to a 65th minute goal by Baker, yet were being urged on even by the Cardiff fans. Eventually though, with only 13 minutes of the season remaining, Jack Lee's head came to the rescue, and his rather soft equaliser banished the spectre of the big drop.

More recently, this match has been the subject of a suggestion (by Ken Chisholm) that the result was induced by collusion. (See Simon Inglis's 'Soccer In The Dock', Willow Books, 1985). However, such accusations are not that uncommon where vital games are concerned, and no evidence has been produced to adequately support the claim, which naturally has been refuted by all others concerned with either club. The final game was also notable in marking the last appearance of Sep Smith in a City shirt, almost 20 years after his debut. Later in May he took up a new position as club coach.

End-of-term honours devolved to Mal Griffiths, called up again for Wales in Portugal and Belgium, and Walter Harrison, who won England B caps in Finland and Holland. The still-recuperating Don Revie had been forced to withdraw from the latter tour.

A postscript to this dizzying season would note that the board, elated at the twin achievements of Cup glory and Second Division survival, and smiling over an £8,521 profit, definitively turned down the opportunity to purchase the Blackbird Road speedway and greyhound stadium, and once more committed the club to its Filbert Street base (where, incidentally, Bournemouth had taken revenge over City's Reserves two days before the Cup Final, with a Combination Cup semi-final replay victory). A sidelight, barely noted as even a glimmer in Leicester at the time, showed that at the other end of the League table a young forward named Arthur Rowley had contributed 19 priceless goals to Fulham's successful promotion push.

Below and right: These line drawings of the Secretary, Manager and Board of Directors in May 1949 are taken from the Cup Final Celebration Dinner menu (see left).

L. T. SHIPMAN

W. A. WILEMAN

T. S. BLOOR

W. S. G. NEEDHAM

A. E. PALLETT

CHARLES MALEY
(Secretary)

JOHNNY DUNCAN
(Manager)

D. E. SHARP

1949-50

> City fans could well have been forgiven for looking back from the summer of 1949 and reckoning they'd recently seen enough dramatic action to last them a couple of years. The phrase, if indeed it was ever uttered, would have been premonitory. The season of 1949/50 almost defined on-field mediocrity: pretty much all the drama involved the swinging to and fro of the main doors at Filbert Street, as backroom and playing personnel came and went with near-bewildering rapidity and regularity.

Jimmy Harrison, in a £12,000 deal with Aston Villa in July, was the first of the Cup Final eleven to depart, and when the League term started with a lacklustre performance at Hillsborough, Wembley skipper Norman Plummer also found himself out of favour, replaced by strongman Tom McArthur. Joint trainer Bill McLean was another to make a close season exit, with Jim Metcalfe assuming the role of head trainer. The rumour machine was cranking into action from Day One of the season, with allegations of dressing room dissension rife.

As if to give substance to the whispers, new captain Don Revie had a transfer request granted in September. A veritable flood of enquiries ensued, but Johnny Duncan held out for a part-exchange deal. By 11th October, with little sign of this materialising, with little improvement in results, and with little evidence of the side being otherwise substantially strengthened, the manager was asked to resign.

The City board, only briefly deflected by an inconclusive Football Association investigation into reports that the club had been party to Cup Final ticket profiteering (the appropriate evidential file of ticket applications having recently been destroyed!), set itself the dual task of progressing Revie's transfer and finding the club a new manager.

First a player-exchange deal with Arsenal foundered, then Revie himself turned down Manchester City after a £25,000 bid had been accepted. Eventually, Hull City stepped in to secure the services of the future England international for £20,000. At the same time, though, the board rejected outright Everton's overtures for Jack Lee.

Former Bury boss Norman Bullock was the man chosen to reinvigorate a struggling side, and he eased into the manager's chair at the beginning of December, by which time only four Second Division victories had accrued. Eire international goalkeeper Tommy Godwin arrived at Filbert Street only days before Duncan's departure, but there were to be six more senior purchases by new-broom Bullock before the end of the campaign.

One-time Pompey foe Bert Barlow joined the forward line, and Wrexham schoolteacher Ron

9 3

Jackson inherited Sandy Scott's No.3 shirt. Blackburn wing-half Jimmy Baldwin buttressed the side midway through its face-saving improvement in March, and no less than three newcomers arrived on transfer deadline day: wingers Peter Small and Ian Wilson, and inside forward Jack Marsh; the latter in a part-exchange deal that also saw Ken Chisholm move on to Coventry. Chisholm had been agitating for a move since February, and had previously rebuffed both Sheffield Wednesday and Plymouth Argyle.

It was a much shuffled side which ended the season in a lowly 15th place. A 2-0 White Hart Lane victory over runaway divisional champions Spurs, in front of no less than 60,595 (the biggest gate to watch City in League action until 2001), was the highlight that heralded a sufficiently decent spell in February and March to keep City out of the relegation zone, yet even that momentum hadn't been maintained to the end of the term. The defence had leaked badly, the forwards (apart from reliable Jack Lee) had rarely appeared incisive, and even the captaincy had passed from hand to hand, as Revie, Walter Harrison, the reinstated Plummer and new man Barlow each took

Above: 1949/50 saw Jack Lee and Don Revie in tandem for City for the last time.

Left: Skipper Don Revie was one of several departures from Filbert Street in 1949/50.

Above: Peter Small - 'The Horsham Flier' had faced City in the previous season's Cup epics with Luton.

spells leading out the team. Almost inevitably, this year's FA Cup effort had ended in meek surrender at the initial hurdle, at Bramall Lane, where Sheffield United could afford to coast on three first-half goals.

If few of this term's City debutants remain particularly noteworthy at this remove, one 21-year-old who made his League bow against City in September would continue in and around the game for a seeming eternity: a forward named Jimmy Hill. The day after City had beaten Hill's Brentford side in London, they made their own bit of club history by flying for the first time to a game: boarding at Northolt for the hop over to Belfast for a friendly against Linfield, won 5-1.

Norman Bullock, having achieved the immediate, consolidatory stage of what he maintained would be a five-year struggle for promotion, was still far from happy with the resources at his disposal (though these now included a seasonal profit of £6,352). May saw George Ritchie and Sep Smith having their long associations with the City severed as they followed head trainer Metcalfe out of Filbert Street; veterans Billy Frame and George Dewis given free transfers; and six more players with senior experience put on the list. June saw David Jones installed as new trainer.

But it was the transfer activity of July which would prove most important to the City story, diverting attention from the unfolding Korean War story on the front pages, and from England's World Cup embarrassment on the back. Controversy was the immediate upshot when two deals were announced on the same day – popular centre-forward Jack Lee being sold to Derby for £16,000, and £14,000 being invested in his little-heralded replacement from Fulham. It would not, however, take long for the new forward to stifle the initially heartfelt criticisms of this most shrewd bit of Bullock business: the City faithful would soon have a new hero indeed in Arthur Rowley.

> Making his City debut in a No 9 shirt, Arthur Rowley nabbed a late winner at Bury on the new season's opening day. But initial optimism that this was to be City's big year soon dissipated. After all five forwards had got themselves on the scoresheet in the opening home game against QPR, the team went seven games without a win, and it was soon apparent that a mid-table slot would again perforce represent the height of the season's Second Division ambitions.

Norman Bullock once more played the transfer market. He'd ousted nine first-teamers during the summer, but then failed to bring in his prime targets of Wolves' Roy Pritchard or Stoke's ex-England skipper Neil Franklin. The latter was the subject of what would have been a club record-breaking £20,000 offer, at a time when he was under six months suspension for having joined the brief but massively controversial exodus of British talent to Colombia, but he chose to move to Hull instead. Soon, however, full-back 'Buller' Lever arrived at Filbert Street from Cardiff City for a £15,000 fee, and was immediately installed as club captain. Wing-half Reg Halton rejoined his former Gigg Lane manager, and winger Tom Dryburgh buttressed the squad strength.

A more crucial managerial intervention, however, turned out to be the recall of young centre-forward Derek Hines, and the shifting of Rowley to the inside-left position; a berth from which he would henceforth terrorise defences for well over a decade. 'The Gunner' scored the clinching goal at Hull past Don Revie, on emergency duty between the sticks after an injury to the Tigers' goalie; took up the mantle of responsibility for City's penalties; notched his first Filbert Street hat-trick against Bury; and was soon on his way to a seasonal tally of 28 goals – the best post-war League return from a City marksman, and a total which placed him second in the Division Two scoring chart, behind Cecil McCormack of Barnsley.

That Rowley was such a crowd-pleaser was just as well, for his predecessor Jack Lee was finally called up to lead the England line against Ireland in October, when mutterings of discontent about the former favourite's release were still barely muted. City's own international, Mal Griffiths, added four Welsh caps to his collection during this term, and at least thereby showed that 'unfashionable' City weren't entirely out of the selectors' orbit.

City pulled themselves out of the early-season mire with a sequence of results between December and mid-March which saw only one defeat in ten fixtures, and eventually achieved a comfortable position of 14th. In the midst of the face-saving effort, champions-to-be Preston North End handed out a Third Round Cup drubbing at Filbert Street to quash

Right: Mal Griffiths, City's first Wembley goalscorer, was a popular winger at Filbert Street for many years.

TV TRIALS

> Gates had been a speculative concern during the season: the revived Leicester speedway team, in their second season at Blackbird Road, were pulling in a regular 20,000 attendees on Friday nights during a boom time for that sport; and there were worries about the effect of television on live football after a few trial broadcasts. One, and the first-ever from Filbert Street, was of the England v Wales amateur international in January, which nonetheless drew 13,398 to watch a 4-1 home win. (To be set against predictions that the new medium would harm the game at this particular time was the BBC's own count, at the time of City's Wembley appearance less than two years earlier, that there were only 35 sets licensed in the entire Leicester area)!

hopes of knock-out glory, and the same side followed up with an Easter League double over City; yet managing, however, to attract 37,233 spectators to the game at Leicester when the outcome was almost academic to the homesters.

Bullock strengthened the ex-Bury contingent at Filbert Street with the acquisition of inside-right Fred Worthington late in March, but otherwise seemed quite happy with his senior playing resources as the basis for a renewed promotion push in the autumn. Boardroom smiles centred on a £9,674 seasonal profit.

At reserve level, City had been withdrawn by the County FA from the Senior Cup, and joined by a trio of local semi-pro clubs in the new County Challenge Cup, duly lifted at the first attempt after a 6-2 victory over Brush Sports in May. The same month, Leicestershire fought out their first-ever County Youth Cup final over two legs at Filbert Street and Wealdstone, but went down on a 1-3 aggregate to a Middlesex side containing such future League stars as Johnny Haynes, Tosh Chamberlain, Ernie Walley and John Hollowbread.

Belatedly, the Filbert Street curtain came down for the summer with City's contribution to the nationwide Festival of Britain, a home friendly with FK Austria, whose 2-1 win drew raves from the local *Mail's* Billy King about the 'scientific certainty of their remarkable football'. Four members of this side would aid their national eleven to a 4-0 win over Scotland a fortnight later, and a 2-2 draw with England at Wembley in November.

> 1951/2, the season which commenced with a rise in the maximum wage for players from £12 to £14 per week, saw City on the fringe of the promotion race throughout the winter, though always tantalisingly outside the top two. The forward combination of Hines and Rowley continued to torment opposing defences and, by the end of the season, Rowley was again ranked second in the Division Two goalscorers' list, this time behind Sheffield Wednesday's Derek Dooley, but this time with a club record of 38 goals. One sequence saw Rowley strike in seven consecutive games, collecting eleven credits; while the 'scorer's apprentice', Hines, himself amassed a 17-goal tally as City battled to maintain their promotion hopes.

In the end that target was missed by a mere four points, and City had to settle for 5th place in the table (behind the elevated Sheffield Wednesday and Cardiff, and similarly frustrated local rivals Birmingham City and Nottingham Forest) despite manager Bullock's tinkerings with his squad. Tom Dryburgh had now assumed Charlie Adam's left-flank position, and full-back Bill Webb, goalkeeper Adam Dickson and inside-forward Arthur Dixon were all given try-outs, but it was January before City made any significant splash in the transfer market, when persuading centre-half Matt Gillies to leave Bolton Wanderers to try his luck in the East Midlands. Upon his signing, Gillies also took over the captaincy from Lever. By mid-March, with promotion still a possibility, the club parted with a sizeable fee to secure the signature of England B full-back Stan Milburn from Chesterfield. Unfortunately, the final push did not ensure success, as three victories over the Easter weekend could not compensate for three desperately depressing defeats immediately prior to the holiday. In the first of these, City shipped five goals to the Sheffield United attack for the second time in the season; the Filbert Street meeting in

Above: Stan Milburn joined City from Chesterfield for a five figure fee in February 1952.

November having produced the third 5-5 draw in the club's history, after City had led 4-3 at the interval.

The home and away fixtures with Blackburn Rovers were also eventful this term. Former Ewood star Jimmy Baldwin returned with City to net an own goal and suffer a broken cheekbone in November, while the Filbert Street game in April was the occasion on which Rowley bettered Arthur Chandler's long-standing 34-goal club record, with a match-settling penalty.

The Third Round of the FA Cup proved to be an insurmountable hurdle for City for the third consecutive season – quite a let-down for a club that had just beforehand tasted the atmosphere of a Wembley final. This time it was Coventry City who did the damage. Like Preston the previous year, they were eventually destined to leave the Second Division at the end of the season, but unlike the Lancastrians, their exit would signal the beginning of a period of obscurity in the lower Divisions. Against Leicester, however, they fielded a team including Jimmy Harrison and Ken Chisholm, and achieved a draw at Filbert Street before handing City a 4-1 hiding in the replay, with Chisholm on the victors' scoresheet.

Seasonal sidelights were varied. The architectural extravagance of the old Main Stand players' entrance was compromised by the extension of the enclosure terracing on either side, leaving only a conventional tunnel's width. A City motion to the Football League, to restore the BBC's right to carry radio commentary on the second-half of a selected Saturday game per week, was carried by 28 votes to 21. A new Northern scout was added to the payroll, with former Bury player (and Manchester United and Accrington Stanley manager) Jimmy Porter supplementing the efforts of Tom Bromilow and Walter McLean. Goalkeeper Johnny Anderson, still on National Service, represented the Army in nine major games, and faced Billy Webb in the FA XI at Highbury in November. Derek Hines found himself called up as travelling reserve for England B's fixture in Holland in March. And a City side played its first-ever game under floodlights, when a largely reserve eleven fulfilled a friendly fixture at Cheltenham Town in March, winning 3-1.

The improvement in City's stature as credible promotion challengers was at least recognised at the season's end by the club's own directors, who (despite logging a loss of £9,868) arranged a four-game tour of Holland against regional representative sides. Three wins and a draw resulted, and the experience deemed extremely useful – while the fans back home sincerely hoped such 'away' form would be carried over to the next term's crack at securing a top-flight return.

Below: Arthur Chandler (left) congratulates Arthur Rowley on his breaking his club goalscoring record.

> To continue to fuel City's promotion hopes, Bullock again was ready to plunge into the transfer market. An early enquiry for Denis Wilshaw was rejected by Wolves, but in October the club again paid out a record fee. This time the target was Derby's unsettled Johnny Morris, and the sum involved was £21,500. The international inside-forward's signing was to prove the start of a stormy relationship; though niggling muscle injuries would in fact keep him out of the spotlight for much of this term.

By that time, City had already established themselves amongst the Division's front-runners. Four of the first five games were won, including two 6-goal romps against Fulham, and Rowley and Hines were once again the scourge of the penalty area, with 'The Gunner' claiming four and three goals from his previous club in the home and away fixtures. (In mitigation to Fulham, it should be said that they had to move goalkeeper Ian Black to centre-forward midway through the first game – yet it was he who claimed their consolation goal, with a fine header)!

However, in late November, it was City who were handed a salutary lesson in football skills, when Sheffield United ran out winners at Bramall Lane by 7-2. Unsurprisingly, the Blades would go on to become Second Division champions; while City, despite scoring more goals and winning more points than in the previous season, again had to settle for 5th place, this time fully ten points adrift of promotion.

Rowley finally managed to finish the season as the Division's leading scorer, setting a new club record of 39 League goals and, indeed, topping the entire Football League list. Hines (despite frequent Army representative calls) continued to provide support, this time with 14 goals, and so well noted had the pairing become that Portsmouth actually made an enquiry during December as to whether they might be able to purchase both. Needless to say, Bullock firmly rejected the approach.

For the fourth successive year, the FA Cup challenge ended in disaster. This time the Third Round visitors were a Notts County team well below City in the table and destined to finish 19th, but once more the story was a familiar one as the Magpies triumphed by 4-2. Thus City had still not tasted success in a cup-tie since their famous semi-final against Portsmouth in 1949. Arthur Rowley also collected

Below: Arthur Rowley nets against Rotherham at Filbert Street in April 1953 to complete a century of goals for the club in just 122 games.

both City's goals in this game, giving him an overall total of 41 for the season – again a new club record.

Nonetheless, the City public were proving themselves something of a perverse bunch of perfectionists. A fine turn-out of 39,908 cheered the November victory over Huddersfield (a first versus third clash, with the visitors previously unbeaten away), but a hard-core amongst the smaller post-Christmas gates were intent on barracking anyone they felt responsible for the slide from the promotion zone, and even Rowley became a target. Misplaced verbals were also behind an FA fine of £5 for manager Bullock, after he had queried the referee at West Ham over a disallowed goal.

City's reserves, playing for the first time in the Second Division of the recently reorganised Football Combination, at least achieved the promotion target their seniors had missed, finishing as runners-up. The A-team were not quite so successful, and in September the club found itself unable to fulfil a fixture at this level as no less than 14 of their youth players were on National Service duties. Later, it was junior football which rang down the seasonal curtain at Filbert Street, with Bobby Charlton one of the starlets on view in May's goalless England v Scotland schoolboy international.

When Norman Bullock had taken over from John Duncan in 1949, he had informed the board that he could take the club back to Division One within five years provided he was given a free hand and enough money to buy the players he required. The directors (who oversaw a modest £881 loss on the season's workings) had lived up to their part of the bargain admirably. Now Bullock had just one more season to go to justify his prophecy.

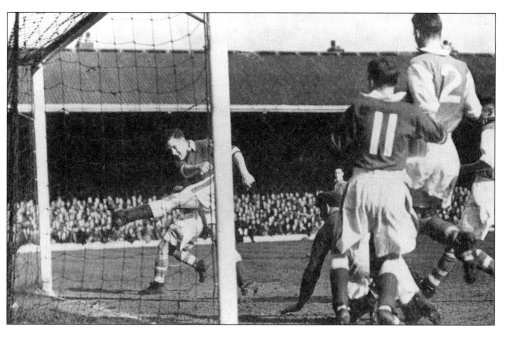

Above: Johnny Anderson won his sole Scottish cap against Finland.

Below: The menu for the champions' "Celebration Dinner' on July 20th 1954.

> For the first time since the days of the Fosse, the Football League season kicked off on a Wednesday, as all the nominal 1st May fixtures were brought forward to avoid clashing with the live television transmission of the Cup Final. However, draws at home to Derby County and Fulham (both achieved after being 0-2 down), and an intervening 1-4 reverse in London at the hands of West Ham, hardly represented the opening to the season that City's players or supporters were looking for. If promotion was to be a realistic aim, the team could not afford to drop too far behind the leaders in the early weeks of the campaign.

Bullock quickly roused his men, however, convincing them that their forward-line was the most feared in the Division. As if on cue, in September, his assessment was backed up by Arsenal, who enquired vainly whether City might part with Morris, Hines and Rowley – quite a compliment to a Second Division outfit.

The goals indeed began to flow regularly again from the forwards as City embarked on an unbeaten run covering 14 matches to establish themselves firmly in the promotion race, culminating in a 2-1 victory over Everton at Goodison Park, achieved despite the late loss of goalkeeper Johnny Anderson, that was eventually to prove absolutely crucial. In late November, Lincoln City were crushed 9-2 at Filbert Street with Derek Hines netting no less than five times after getting off the mark in 10 seconds, and the fans were beginning to believe in Bullock's powers of prophecy. (They also took to his one touch of gimmickry – this game was the first in which he had oxygen administered to the team at half-time, prompting a seven-goal second-half return).

LEICESTER CITY FOOTBALL CLUB

CHAMPIONS OF THE FOOTBALL LEAGUE 2ND DIVISION 1953-4
CELEBRATION DINNER

Toasts

The Queen

The Football Association and The Football League
Proposed by LESLIE L. GREEN, Esq., M.B.E., J.P., C.C.
Response: SIR STANLEY ROUS, C.B.E., J.P.
Secretary, The Football Association
A. H. OAKLEY, Esq., J.P.
Vice-President, The Football League

Leicester City Football Club
Proposed by J. RICHARDS, Esq., J.P.
Chairman, Barnsley Football Club,
Member of the Management Committee, The Football League
Response: L. T. SHIPMAN, Esq.
Chairman, Leicester City Football Club

Our Guests
Proposed by W. A. WILEMAN, Esq., C.C.
Vice-Chairman, Leicester City Football Club
Response: S. BOLTON, Esq.
Chairman, Leeds United Football Club

Entertainers:
CLIVE ALLEN   BOBBIE JOY
WAL RAYNER

Menu

STRAWS   OLIVES   ALMONDS

CREAM OF CHICKEN SOUP

SCOTCH SALMON
Shrimp Sauce

FILLET OF ENGLISH BEEF
Mushroom and Red Wine Sauce
Noisette-Potatoes
Fresh Garden Peas

STRAWBERRY MELBA

SWEETMEATS

CHEESE   BISCUITS
COFFEE

Music during Dinner:
THE AMBASSADORS SALON
QUINTET

Standing:
N. Bullock, *Manager*
J. Baldwin
S. Milburn
A. Rowley
J. Anderson
E. Russell
D. Hines
D. Jones, *Trainer*

Seated:
M. Griffiths
J. Morris
M. Gillies, *Capt.*
R. Jackson
P. Small

With the Manager and Trainer are members of the City Team who played in the last vital match

England's humiliation at the hands of Hungary during the following midweek portended a hiccup in City's table-topping progress, but there was soon another slaughter for Filbert Street regulars to enjoy: a 6-0 romp against Brentford.

Then, at the turn of the year, came an alarming turnabout in fortunes. The three League fixtures played during January were all lost, and a 1-7 thumping at Elland Road (featuring a hat-trick by City reject Ray Iggleden) threatened a severe denting of confidence. That this essential was restored quickly was in no small way due to a Third Round FA Cup replay victory over First Division Middlesbrough – City's first Cup win since 1949.

The team were able to pull themselves together with five successive League wins, whilst enjoying an eight-game Cup run which only came to an end in a quarter-final second replay, when Tom Finney inspired eventual finalists Preston North End to a Hillsborough triumph.

As Easter approached, the promotion battle had settled into a three-horse race between City, Everton and Blackburn Rovers. Just as the supporters were getting ready to celebrate, City very nearly managed to throw everything away. A three-goal defeat at Blackburn on Good Friday and a draw with Notts County at Filbert Street the following day put the club's position in jeopardy, but the response was all that could be asked. On Easter Monday, City slammed Blackburn 4-0 in the return fixture (in front of a new record League crowd of 40,047) and, on the following Saturday, won 3-1 at Brentford in the final game to guarantee promotion. With Everton still to play a game in hand, and likely to draw level on points with City, there was still a wait to establish the top team. But when the Merseysiders' final fixture at Oldham produced a 4-0 scoreline, rather than the 6-0 outcome they needed, the upshot was the Second Division Championship shield returning to Filbert Street for the third time.

Above: Captain Matt Gillies receives the Second Division Championship shield from Football League Vice-President AH Oakley.

Below: Peter Small scores with a header at home to Everton in March.

City had triumphed on goal average from Everton with a final calculation of 1.62 as opposed to the Toffees' 1.59. Blackburn had finished just one point behind with a far superior goal average, so anything less than victory in those last two matches would have meant that City would have missed promotion altogether.

Manager Bullock, in seeing his 'five-year plan' come to fruition, had largely shown faith in the forces he had assembled over the previous four years. There had been no close-season signings, and the only additions to the first-team squad during the campaign had been those of left-half Eddie Russell from Middlesbrough in October, and of Portsmouth's versatile former England international, Jack Froggatt, in March. (In February, a bid to unite the Rowley brothers had failed when Manchester United declined to sell Jack to Leicester). A £14,709 profit proved one sort of icing on the championship cake; while the presentation of the shield itself was a bit of a low-key affair: taking place after the reserves had overcome Brush Sports for the fourth year running in the invitational County Challenge Cup.

The first team's final total of 97 League goals was a new club record, with all five regular forwards reaching double figures. Arthur Rowley, inevitably, led the way, though his total of 30 League goals was almost an anti-climax in the light of the previous two seasons' hauls; whilst Derek Hines again provided the main supporting role with 19.

Mal Griffiths, with his final cap for Wales in Vienna, and Johnny Anderson, with his sole selection for Scotland in Helsinki, both won end-of-term international recognition, but there was still no sign of a call-up for Rowley. Perhaps the chance to display his talents in Division One would change things?

> Norman Bullock was shrewd enough to know that his squad needed strengthening further if the club's new status was to be consolidated, but close-season interest in Brentford's Jimmy Bloomfield was thwarted when the player signed for Arsenal, and it was only the reserve roster that was augmented in the short term. Worryingly, Johnny Morris, who had never managed to form a good relationship with Bullock, was briefly listed during the summer (citing a desire to be allowed to train with former club Derby), but a dearth of bids meant that the promotion team was in fact the one which started the new campaign. A substantial rise in revenue from season-ticket sales (at the new prices of £7 17s 6d for the Centre Stand, £5 10s for the Wing Stands, and £4 4s for the Double Decker) at least indicated supporter confidence.

A home draw with Chelsea and a 3-2 win at The Valley gave brief justification for such optimism, but four straight defeats followed, and the writing was well and truly on the wall by the end of October, when City had only two wins out of fifteen fixtures to their credit. Bullock's attempts to introduce new faces – making enquiries for Bolton's Eric Bell, Villa's Danny Blanchflower (both out of City's price range), and the Newcastle pair of George Hannah and Bob Stokoe – all foundered, and a series of injury problems, with a dozen seniors out at one stage, led to the early blooding of several reserves. The initial defeat at Cardiff was symptomatic of early-season problems piling up – City were down to nine men, with Stan Milburn deputising in goal for 65 minutes, when they conceded a late, decisive goal.

Willie Cunningham was signed from St Mirren for £4,750 in November to bolster an ailing defence but, at the same time, a £15,000 bid for Burnley wing-half Les Shannon was firmly rebuffed. Eventually, in December, with Derek Hines sidelined through injury, City paid out a club record fee of £27,600 for Lincoln's free-scoring centre-forward Andy Graver. The new man scored on his debut at Stamford Bridge, but it was one of the goals at the other end, contributing to a 1-3 defeat, which summed up City's plight: with Stan Milburn (attempting to concede a corner) and Jack Froggatt (aiming for touch) contriving to kick the ball simultaneously past Johnny Anderson and find themselves credited with a unique 'shared' own-goal!

The club's confidence in Bullock was eroding quickly and, at the end of the year, the directors asked him to resign once the season was over. As it happened, though, an incident at a Whitley Bay hotel in February, following a defeat away to Newcastle, brought matters to a head somewhat prematurely. An emergency board meeting the following day resulted in a statement being issued that "it is impossible for

Above: City in action at Chelsea in December 1954, with Johnny Anderson leaping to deny Roy Bentley. This was the fixture in which Stan Milburn and Jack Froggatt recorded their unique 'joint own goal'!

the manager to conduct the affairs of the club or be able to control the playing staff". As a consequence, Norman Bullock was given the opportunity of resigning immediately, and this he did. Johnny Morris, Bullock's main adversary, was himself suspended for 14 days for his part in the incidents at Whitley Bay.

The managerless City briefly rallied, but could find no consistency before season's end. Their attempt to avoid relegation failed, but eventually they had the right to consider themselves a shade unlucky, as their total of 35 points was the highest for a relegated club since 1937/8. Additionally, an extremely tight First Division table had seen second-placed Wolves only eight points clear of 17th-placed West Brom, so a more settled City side, or one pulled together by a replacement manager, might well have saved itself.

Lack of support from the terraces and stands could certainly not be blamed for the fall from grace, though. Not only had a new (and definitive) Filbert Street record gate for a League game been established – 42,486 being attracted by the October visit of Arsenal, when there were two pre-match fatalities recorded, along with a 3-3 draw secured via Johnny Anderson's late penalty save from Roper – but the average home attendance for the season represented the highest-ever at 31,067. Even the latest new diversion for a sport-crazy Leicester public – stock-car racing at Blackbird Road, which drew 17,000 to its opening meeting in September – failed to dent the Filbert Street figures. Away from home, the Shah of Persia was among the VIPs who watched the February draw at Highbury.

The unhappy Andy Graver, who had failed to settle and had given way to a fit-again Hines, was the target for a deadline bid from Stoke City, who sniffed again in the close season, along with Sheffield Wednesday and Preston, but he eventually rejoined Lincoln City for a record outgoing fee of £26,000. This recoupment more than covered the seasonal loss of £3,797.

Above: Derek Hogg, a regular in the number 11 shirt.

The board (who, under chairman Len Shipman, had assumed team selection duties since February, and had left 60 unsolicited applications on the table in the interim) got around to considering candidates for the vacant manager's post early in the close season. They enquired after Barnsley's Tim Ward, but then interviewed two more strong candidates: David Halliday and Joe Mercer. After some debate, the directors decided to entrust the former with the task of resurrecting City's fortunes and prompting them to an early return to the top Division.

> The previous season, Halliday had guided Aberdeen to the Scottish League Championship, and his faith in Caledonian quality was manifestly strong as, during his first year at Filbert Street, he signed no less than eleven players from north of the border. Of this initial influx, the most significant recruit turned out to be Willie Gardiner, a centre-forward from Rangers, who actually achieved the barely credible feat of toppling Arthur Rowley from the head of the club's scoring list.

In fact, the gangling Gardiner finished the season as the leading goalscorer in Division Two, with 34 goals; and in one fertile patch notched a foursome and two hat-tricks in three successive home fixtures. Rowley was five behind his new partner in the League but, when FA Cup goals were accounted for, the pair of them finished up with 35 apiece. At last, too, Rowley gained a modicum of recognition for his prolific efforts: an England B cap against Switzerland in March, when he contributed a headed goal from a Bryan Douglas cross to a 4-1 win.

Mainly on the strength of this duo's spectacular efforts, City were able to remain on the fringe of the promotion race throughout the season. Jack Froggatt retained the captaincy he had taken over from Matt Gillies the previous term, Derek Hogg was now a left-flank regular (and an Arsenal target in September), and ex-Hibernian defenders John Ogilvie and Pat Ward were other Halliday acquisitions to shine. Seventeen-year-old Howard Riley was the revelation of the local discoveries.

Consistency was hardly the side's keynote, though. City reaped nine goals from their opening two wins, but within a fortnight, with a distinctly youthful line-up, had conceded thirteen in two successive away defeats! They went on to thrash then-leaders Swansea by 6-1 (when BBC cameras captured the action for highlights to be shown on the Saturday evening *Sportsview*), and promotion-winners Leeds by 5-2, yet soon surrendered at home to relegation-bound Hull. They also conceded the first League goal ever registered by Middlesbrough youngster Brian Clough during a seven-goal thriller at Ayresome.

Ultimately it was a home defeat at the hands of champions-elect Sheffield Wednesday on Easter Monday that dashed hopes of an immediate return to Division One, and City had to be content with 5th position, four points adrift of their target. Cup consolation was absent, too, as Andy Graver poached the decisive Stoke goal in a Fourth Round replay from his former teammates. (The previous round had been negotiated thanks to a Rowley hat-trick on a Kenilworth Road mudheap, in a midweek game that had originally suffered postponement only 15 minutes before scheduled kick-off in a fogbound Luton).

Above: Arthur Rowley pressurises the Newcastle defence at St James' Park in February.

Left: Johnny Morris' turbulent Filbert Street career peaked with two Second Division Championship medals, won in 1954 and 1957.

> The close season of 1956 was marked primarily by a series of negotiations between the Football League and the television companies over conflicting bids to broadcast live the second-half of selected games over the coming season. ATV proposed to put 35 such matches on the small screen on Saturday evenings, while the BBC responded with an offer to cover the final 45 minutes of twelve games on Tuesday evenings. No agreement was reached, however – the fact that still relatively few clubs possessed floodlights having some bearing – and it was very much 'business as usual' when the new campaign kicked off in August. In the wider world, the Suez crisis was boiling up, and Britain was coming to terms with the Teddy Boy phenomenon.

For Leicester City, however, the season turned out to be something rather special. The Championship of Division Two was brought to Filbert Street for the fourth time and with it came no less than six new club records. Fresh benchmarks were set for most wins (25), most away wins (11), fewest defeats (6), most points (61), most goals (109), and for highest individual scoring: Arthur Rowley claiming 44 and, unsurprisingly, again topping the marksmanship list for the entire Football League. Runner-up to him in the Division Two chart was Brian Clough of Middlesbrough, with 38.

Yet clearly Halliday had succeeded in reshaping his team in readiness for a major assault during the following campaign; and would continue his Scots-accented shake-up throughout the summer.

Other matters of reconstruction on the agenda involved the shape of the League itself: a major conference of the clubs in March prompted City's board to advocate the effective restructuring of the competition into five divisions. No change was the predictable outcome, though general worries over declining gates were not necessarily shared by City anyway, as they were soon contemplating a record £19,585 profit on the seasonal balance sheet.

Above: Arthur Rowley scored 44 goals as the Second Division Championship shield returned to Filbert Street in 1956/7.

The campaign started with another minor, but telling, record, with City's first eleven (in their new V-necked kit) going unchanged for eight games. Indeed, with few newcomers to the senior squad (the right wing-berth being taken successively by Tommy McDonald and Billy Wright, and goalkeeper Dave MacLaren arriving from Dundee in January to replace the injured Anderson), the team spirit in the City camp was superb throughout the campaign. Testament to this could be found in the fact that not only did the team never lose successive games, but also managed seven victories in matches when they had trailed at the interval. Their positive attitude (which had seen them go top as early as mid-September, with a 5-4 win at Bury) shone through perhaps most brightly on 30th March, when City, as League leaders, travelled to second-placed Nottingham Forest to face one of their most demanding tests. Ian McNeill found the net within 10 seconds, City produced a masterly display to win 2-1, and their Trentside rivals effectively conceded the Championship.

The return passage to Division One was nominally clinched the following Saturday as West Ham were beaten 5-3, largely thanks to Rowley's fourth hat-trick of the campaign, and in the course of this game City reached their seasonal century of League goals for the first time. The Championship was formally sealed with a 5-1 win at Leyton Orient on Easter Monday and, despite an irrelevant hiccup in the return game, City closed their account with a seven-point margin over Forest.

City had strangely conceded more goals at home (36) than they had away (31), and one of the Filbert Street debits was down to an 89th-minute header from former keeper Gordon Bradley, injured and then playing outfield during City's 6-3 win against Notts County. His net-minding stand-in, future City winger Gordon Wills, was also on the Magpies' scoresheet in this game. One player who would give City keepers much back-bending work over future seasons made his senior debut against City in a Stamford Bridge testimonial game in May: Jimmy Greaves was the youngster concerned.

The FA Cup was no distraction for City this year: a 0-2 defeat at Tottenham would have been worse but for Anderson's penalty save from Tommy Harmer; though the goalkeeper was adamant that Spurs' credited opener never crossed the line. The reserves took the County Challenge Cup for the seventh season since its inception, with a 9-0 win over Anstey Nomads; but City's first entry into the FA Youth Cup

Above: Willie Cunningham won six Irish caps during the season, despite making only one first team appearance.

Below: The new champions of Division Two are cheered off the field despite the hiccup of a home defeat by Leyton Orient in the final match of the season.

ended in a 1-8 embarrassment at West Brom in the Second Round. The youngsters nonetheless took the championship of the Leicestershire Senior League for the second time in three seasons.

For the second successive season Willie Cunningham had earned Irish caps while turning out regularly in City's reserves, but the nearest that Arthur Rowley came to international honours was an appearance for the Football League against the Irish League at Newcastle, as a replacement for Denis Viollet. Rowley was also a two-goal scorer for the Football Combination XI in Amsterdam in October, though his qualification was questionable – he'd never once appeared for City's reserves since joining the club!

There was no international travel for City's victorious squad, though: a mooted end-of-season tour of Israel and Turkey was cancelled, and a three-day holiday in Blackpool substituted! Finance was probably not the reason: there may have been a £6,913 loss on the season's workings, but the Government had just cheered the City board immensely with the lifting of Entertainment Tax.

As the promotion celebrations died down, work began on the installation of a floodlighting system at Filbert Street, and City began sending out invitations to several famous European clubs in the hope of bringing the fans a series of notable floodlit friendlies in the future. Though none of Real Madrid, Juventus or AC Milan would actually grace the Filbert Street turf during the following season, the directors' outlook was certainly a positive one as City stood on the threshold of a new era back in Division One.

> Work may have been proceeding apace on the new Filbert Street pylons, but David Halliday and his board were slower off the mark in applying reconstruction plans to City's playing resources. A degree of confidence in the Second Division record-breakers of the previous term was understandable, but the harsh lessons of the club's 1954/5 top flight misadventure might profitably have been heeded earlier.

City's combativeness for the challenge was in little doubt: Johnny Morris even contrived to get himself sent off in the pre-season Blues v Reds public practice match, albeit for querying the referee's eyesight. But the cliche that Division One was a whole new ball game was rammed home emphatically in the campaign's early weeks. Six of the first seven fixtures ended in defeat (a second-half Billy Whelan hat-trick separating City and reigning champs Manchester United on opening day; a last-minute penalty spelling defeat at Leeds), and only five victories accrued before Christmas. City were marked early as relegation favourites, and rocked by a series of seven formal transfer requests in October and November.

Halliday shuffled his playing pack ceaselessly, and then entered the market for reinforcements. Busby Babe John Doherty arrived for £6,500, but was soon found to be carrying a long-term injury problem. Then, as veteran skipper Jack Froggatt moved on to Kettering for £6,000, in came Birmingham centre-half John Newman at twice the price, only to make his debut at the heart of a City defence which shipped seven Burnley goals. Doherty scored after 30 seconds at Turf Moor, but the subsequent capitulation was sparked by a hat-trick from future City forward Albert Cheesebrough.

Carefree, slapdash defending of this sort was no longer being wholly compensated for by a once brilliant attack. Rowley, Gardiner and Hines were all in partial or relative decline (even if each were the target of several new transfer bids), and only the consistent peak form of Derek Hogg kept City in the picture until their fortunes were boosted after the New Year by the emergence of Jimmy Walsh and the availability of Howard Riley. Riley, then a private in the Royal Leicestershire Regiment, became City's first Under-23 cap, while Willie Cunningham, who took over the captaincy after Froggatt's departure, added two further Irish international appearances to his record during this term, and went on to perform wonderfully during the summer World Cup in Sweden.

Despite a distinct imbalance between such individual encouragements and severe collective embarrassments, however, Leicester kept in close

Above: The City squad train at Filbert Street during the summer of 1957 as the new floodlight pylons are under construction.

enough contact with their similarly inconsistent partners in First Division distress, and were not about to give up their new status without a supreme struggle.

Or without entertaining a public which could afford to be almost blasé about goals. In fact City claimed 91 successes over the season to set against the new record tally of 112 conceded. In seven matches City scored four or more goals, while they let in at least four on eleven occasions; and they achieved both feats simultaneously when meeting Manchester City at Filbert Street on 22nd February – running out 8-4 winners, with Walsh claiming four himself. The very same day, the out-of-favour Arthur Rowley played his first-ever reserve game for City in a 1-7 thrashing at White Hart Lane, and a Frank McLintock-skippered junior team collapsed to an 0-9 FA Youth Cup humiliation at Molineux.

A 4-1 away win at Tottenham in December was another seasonal highlight of the League struggle, though Spurs later removed City from the FA Cup at the initial hurdle for the second successive season, and then threatened to hasten City's downward doom when winning at Filbert Street in the campaign's penultimate match.

Only one escape route presented itself: a point from a draw at St Andrews on the final day would keep City up. Halliday gambled on five team changes, introduced young Len Chalmers for a nerve-wracking debut, and saw Ian McNeill (replacing Rowley) poach the 50th-minute goal which beat Birmingham, lifted City to eighteenth place and condemned Sunderland to a first-ever relegation. This was only City's second clean sheet of the season, and the first registered away from home.

Relief was followed immediately by the realisation that genuine consolidation required reinvestment in the team. At various stages of the season, Halliday had made enquiries for Manchester United's Ronnie Cope and Freddie Goodwin, Cardiff's Danny Malloy, Derby's Jack Parry and Tottenham's Jim Iley, and had been frustrated each time. He had also despatched scouts to monitor the progress of a young Preston wing-half, but Gordon Milne's role in City's history would not be assumed until much later. Now, though, Halliday's dealings bore fruit.

In April, promising Northampton forward Ken Leek guested against Brazilians Canto do Rio in the third of the season's international floodlit friendlies (the lights had been christened back in October, when 18,398 watched City beat German champions Borussia Dortmund with a Gardiner goal), and signed days later for £5,750. Then, using most of the £20,000 received from the surprise sale of Derek Hogg to West Brom, Halliday captured wing-half Ken Keyworth from Rotherham, full-back Ian MacFarlane from Chelsea and winger Gordon Wills from Notts County. These new faces were as surprised as the City management when they arrived in Germany in May unaware that a return friendly with Borussia Dortmund had been cancelled; but it was the May publication of the manager's retained list which forewarned of one rather larger close-season shock.

Above: Willie Gardiner netted the first goal scored under floodlights at Filbert Street.

Below: Ken Leek took over the number 10 shirt after the bombshell of Arthur Rowley's departure.

> Arthur Rowley had rattled up a total of 265 goals in 321 appearances for City, and looked suitably poised to overtake Arthur Chandler as the club's all-time record marksman, when David Halliday stunned Leicester supporters with the news that 'The Gunner' was to be allowed to move on. As a close-season controversy, there had been nothing to match this particular bombshell since 1950, when Jack Lee had departed and Rowley himself arrived.

Initially approached by Rugby Town, and an applicant himself for a player/manager role at Doncaster Rovers, Rowley was soon fixed up with joint responsibilities at lowly Shrewsbury Town, for a fee of £4,250. In fact, by the end of the summer, no less than four of the previous season's cast-list were ensconced in player/manager roles: Froggatt at Kettering, Morris at Corby, Rowley at Gay Meadow and young John Doherty at Rugby Town. Perhaps this was one way of circumventing the new Football League maximum wage: raised during the summer only as far as £20 per week.

Ken Leek donned Rowley's No 10 shirt in the season's curtain-raiser, and netted in a 2-0 home win over Everton that would actually prove to be the club's

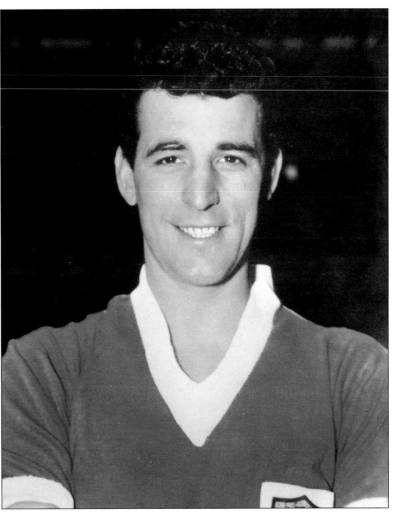

last opening-day victory for twelve seasons. It would also prove to be a false dawn for 1958, for City conceded ten goals in their next two fixtures to paint a more accurate picture of their immediate First Division prospects.

These soon swung from bad to worse, and four successive dismal defeats (marked by the opposition's easy rumbling of the deep-lying centre-forward game City had utilised to stay up) led to the resignation of David Halliday on 6th November, two days after receiving a vote of confidence from new chairman Tom Bloor. Two days later, coach Matt Gillies took over as acting manager, and eventually the former centre-half was confirmed in post on 28th January.

Gillies had his own ideas of the kind of player needed to transform City into a solid First Division outfit, and he had a 1957/8 profit of £16,330 on which to fall back, so behind-the-scenes activity intensified during the following months. Little of this resulted in actual deals, though the ambition of the man could be judged by the calibre of players for whom unsuccessful enquiries were made: Gordon Harris and John Connelly (Burnley), Geoff Strong (Arsenal), Peter McParland (Aston Villa), Tony Kay (Sheffield Wednesday) and Bobby Robson (West Brom). Later, definite and substantial bids for both Swansea's Mel Charles and Burnley's Albert Cheesebrough proved equally futile; and another Turf Moor forward, Roy Stephenson, arrived as the sole pre-deadline purchase.

By and large, then, City had to soldier on with their established squad. The first home game with Gillies in charge produced a 6-3 win over Aston Villa in which Derek Hines notched four goals after the visitors had taken a three-goal lead; and a good spell around Christmas relieved some of the gloom from Filbert Street. Twelve games without a win, however, (bracketing an all-time record of five successive home defeats), left City squarely in the relegation zone, and Good Friday arrived with the club in 21st place and seemingly doomed.

A Houdini act was once more called for, and duly delivered. Of the nine fixtures remaining, four were won and three drawn. A 4-1 win on Trentside helped set up a grandstand finale, but a predictable setback saw Wolves clinch the First Division championship by easily eclipsing City at Molineux. Three days later, 38,466 watched a tense 2-1 home victory over League runners-up Manchester United in the penultimate game confirm the team's status for another year. Defeat in the last match at Maine Road therefore hardly worried nineteenth-placed Leicester, but it still had a crucial bearing on the relegation issue, with Manchester City thereby saving themselves at Aston Villa's expense.

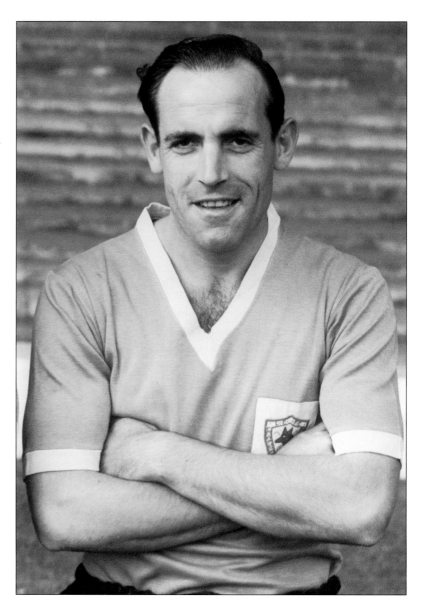

Above: Derek Hines netted four goals in City's comeback win over Villa in November.

The nick-of-time escapology aside, though, the campaign had been illuminated less by highlights than sidelights; one of which saw both FA Cup finalists having progressed to Wembley via Filbert Street. Luton Town had drawn there before despatching City in a Fourth Round replay, while Nottingham Forest had eliminated a troublesome Birmingham City at the third attempt on the neutral Leicester ground, when a Monday afternoon crowd of 34,458 brought unforeseen chaos to the city's roads. Birmingham had also been the visitors in March when Filbert Street hosted its first-ever scheduled all-floodlit evening League game.

Perhaps ironically in view of the seniors' struggles, City's reserves captured the Football Combination title for the first (and only) time, pipping reigning champions Chelsea by a point with a final-game 2-1 win at Tottenham, thanks to a brace from top-scorer Jack Lornie. Clearly, the club's complement of up-and-coming talent – bolstered by Matt Gillies' end-of-season capture of promising young goalkeeper Gordon Banks and long-term target Albert Cheesebrough – offered a substantial cause for renewed optimism.

The Cups that (almost) cheered!

> The arrivals of Banks and Cheesebrough (for £19,775) represented the only dents in the club's newly-announced record profit of £36,797 during the summer, and Matt Gillies otherwise contented himself with taking on former wartime colleague Bert Johnson, latterly manager of Cambridge United, initially as chief scout. (Former manager Tom Bromilow, who'd most recently held this role, had died in March; while Northern scout Louis Page would pass on in October).

But another poor start to the season soon had the manager chasing quality new blood for City, only to find on-field disappointments being matched by rebuffs off it. Offers were made for John White of Falkirk (£15,000 plus Walsh, or £10,000 plus Cunningham), who signed days later for Spurs, and for Joe Baker of Hibernian (whose club resisted City's proffered £30,000). Enquiries for Brian Clough (Middlesbrough) and Billy Bingham (Luton) met with no encouragement. And scouting missions to watch Huddersfield's young Denis Law found him actually turning in unimpressive displays on two separate occasions!

Early in September, Dave MacLaren was carried off after 30 minutes at the Hawthorns and a 0-5 scoreline resulted. This accident opened the way for Gordon Banks to make his debut in the following match and, by not much more than a month later, he had established himself as first choice 'keeper. Also promoted from the reserves during September was a young, slim wing-half: Frank McLintock.

Above: Tommy McDonald, still a threat on the right wing.

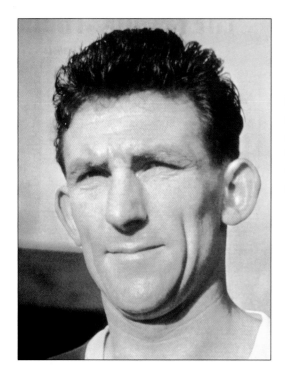

> Whatever the expectations of the City faithful – and even the committed optimists were not looking far beyond their favourites managing to avoid the annual relegation scare – none could have been quite prepared for the events of the new campaign. Change was in the air, but only some of it universally welcomed. The new apprenticeship scheme for young players was introduced at the League's summer meeting, as was the Football League Cup. Clubs would now be allowed postponements if two or more of their regular team were on international duty, while admission charges would rise to a minimum of 2s 6d. Leicester courted criticism by raising theirs (for the Popular Side) from two to three shillings. Moreover, there would be rumblings throughout the winter of possible strike action, as the League and Jimmy Hill's PFA repeatedly went head-to-head over contract restrictions and the maximum wage; with the players eventually claiming victory in January.

Tottenham Hotspur grabbed all the early-season headlines with an opening sequence of eleven successive victories (the ninth being achieved at Filbert Street), and continued to show every sign of carrying all before them. City, meanwhile, with much the same line-up as in the previous campaign, recovered from an initial wobbly patch to settle comfortably into the middle of the table by the season's midway point. A Banks penalty save helped City to a first-ever win at Stamford Bridge (at the 18th attempt), and later in the term would come a similar

To talk of immediate impact from the new stars-to-be, however, would be to ignore the uncomfortable facts of First Division life. By December, City were once more in 21st place in the table (and Cheesebrough had already missed two penalties). One result, though, seemed to turn their season around. Wolves were reigning champions, and the only top-flight club to have maintained an unbeaten home record, when City went to Molineux and triumphed 3-0. A fine, steady revival from Leicester thereafter lifted them well up the table to an eventual twelfth place, with the significant factor being that more away points (17) had been secured by the club than ever before in a Division One campaign.

In the FA Cup, too, City finally put together a noteworthy run. Negotiating a difficult away tie at Wrexham and eclipsing Fulham at Filbert Street, City met West Brom (with a certain Jock Wallace in goal) in the Fifth Round, and got through for the third time by a 2-1 scoreline, in a match clouded by the tragedy of the half-time death of referee Jack Husband. In the quarter-final game with Wolves, however, the share-out of the three goals went in the visitors' favour, with young skipper Len Chalmers heartbroken over his own-goal contribution. Wolves went on to win the Cup, but City at least completed the League double over them, ironically only a week after the Cup exit.

On the representative front, Willie Cunningham won three more Irish caps to bring his tally to 23 gained whilst with City, making him then the club's most-capped player. Tony Knapp played for the Football League, acted as reserve to the Under-23s, and was also a member of the full England party for their European tour during May, though, frustratingly, he was fated never to win a full cap.

TICKET RUSH

> The Wolves Cup-tie gave rise to one of the ironies of the 1959/60 season. With tickets for the game being much coveted items (this was Filbert Street's second-ever all-ticket game, after the WBA tie of the previous round), the decision to sell them at the turnstiles on 27th February led to a crowd of 22,800 attending the reserves' Combination fixture with Bournemouth – on the same day that only 18,691 watched City's seniors take on Luton at Kenilworth Road!

hoodoo-breaking effort at Highbury (with an away win over Arsenal 62 years distant from Fosse's only such triumph at Plumstead). As a result of a linesman being pelted with missiles from the Popular Side during the opening game against Blackpool, the FA ordered City to display warning notices at Filbert Street throughout October.

Matt Gillies, whose only summer acquisitions had been Leeds winger George Meek and Rochdale keeper George Heyes, was again frustrated in early efforts to strengthen his team, having a £30,000 bid for Arsenal's David Herd rejected, and receiving no joy from enquiries for Terry Medwin (Spurs), Alan Gilzean (Dundee) or Pat Crerand (Celtic). Jimmy Walsh had taken over the captaincy from Len Chalmers, and made his mark on the new Football League Cup competition, introduced in low-key fashion amid much hostility from the leading clubs (six of whom declined to enter). Walsh claimed the competition's inaugural hat-trick in City's First Round victory over Mansfield Town (after Albert Cheesebrough had recorded the club's opening goal), but the ignominy of a home defeat at the next hurdle by Rotherham United (eventual finalists) was City's backhanded reward.

Certainly, there was little evidence here (or in a second-half collapse at Fulham, when a Graham Leggat hat-trick sparked the Cottagers' four-goal reply to City's 2-0 lead) to suggest the imminent upturn in Leicester's fortunes. But a Boxing Day win over Bolton sparked an unbeaten thirteen-game run into March, by which time City were well established in the upper reaches of the League table, and were confirmed as Cup semi-finalists. While League form peaked with fine home wins over Everton and Newcastle (with Magpies debutant George Dalton contributing an own goal to the 5-3 scoreline), a magnificent 6-0 demolition of Manchester United, and a record-breaking 3-2 win at White Hart Lane (where Super Spurs were hitherto unbeaten), City's most significant FA Cup run for twelve years was getting into stride.

Non-Leaguers Oxford United were City's Round Three victims at Filbert Street, but the Cup run hiccupped to a temporary halt three weeks later when a quagmire of a pitch forced the half-time abandonment of the home tie with Bristol City. A Richie Norman own goal was the first meaningful action when the tie was re-staged, but the Robins were then swept aside by a 20-minute whirlwind of five City goals.

It took a home replay to dispose of a physical

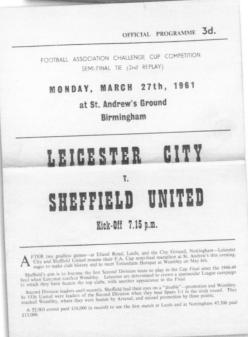

Above: The programmes from the semi-final trilogy with Second Division Sheffield United.

Birmingham City side in Round Five, and extra-time in an Oakwell replay to overcome the plucky challenge of Third Division Barnsley, who had kept City scoreless for the first time since Christmas when drawing at Leicester. Ken Leek's late winner meant he had scored in each round to date.

A 0-1 League defeat at the Hawthorns (with Heyes deputising for Banks) ended City's unbeaten run, but they entered the Cup semi-final at Elland Road as clear favourites to beat Second Division Sheffield United and reach Wembley for the second time. In the event, the game was a goalless anti-climax, with the most significant occurrence being an injury to winger Gordon Wills that brought his season to a sadly premature close.

The replay, staged by Nottingham Forest, was a dour carbon copy, with both sides seemingly inhibited by fear of failure; but the third meeting, at St Andrews, possessed more than its fair share of drama. After just 11 minutes, Ian King saw his penalty saved when he stubbed his toe into the ground at the moment of impact. Then, after 24 minutes, Jimmy Walsh headed City into the lead (signalling the end of an overall sequence of 451 minutes' play without a goal by City since the Barnsley matchwinner). Ken Leek added a second just after half-time, but the Blades were given an opportunity to revive their hopes with a penalty after 65 minutes. Graham Shaw stepped up, pulled his shot wide, and City were effectively through to meet Double-chasing Spurs.

The team continued to impress in League performance after the semi-final marathon, and eventually finished sixth, their highest placing for 32 years. Banks and Riley were both honoured with England Under-23 appearances, Tony Knapp (sidelined at City) maintained his frustrating England squad place, Ken Leek was capped by Wales, and Colin Appleton chosen for the FA XI's summer tour of the Far East and New

Cup Final Day was television's big sporting showpiece.

Matt Gillies and Bill Nicholson lead the
teams out for the Wembley final.

Left: Injured Len Chalmers with trainer Dave Jones. There were no substitutes in those days and Chalmers returned in a 'nuisance' role!

Below: Bobby Smith breaks Leicester's resistance.

Zealand. Two youngsters were drafted in towards the end of the campaign, and both made scoring debuts. Local discovery Graham Cross would go on to play a major role in the City story over the next fifteen years; but Scottish junior Hugh McIlmoyle could hardly guess at the mark he would make almost immediately in City annals.

City's preparations for the Wembley showcase were outwardly unremarkable. Wills had been ruled out for weeks, and a cheek injury to Keyworth hardly impinged on Gillies' plans to tackle Tottenham. Spurs already had the League title in the bag, but nagging away at their confidence, as they sought to become the first side this century to take the Double, was the memory of how City had mastered them at White Hart Lane, and especially of how Ken Leek had always given Maurice Norman a torrid time.

Then, only two days before the match, came

City's bombshell. Leading scorer Leek was dropped, and young McIlmoyle handed his place. Matt Gillies claimed it was a matter of current form: since the semi-final, Leek had played four League games, scoring in three, while McIlmoyle's seven appearances (the extent of his senior experience) had netted him four goals. The public could not believe it. Every sort of rumour flew around Leicester, but the club stuck by Gillies' explanation, and has done ever since. (Only those directly concerned could possibly contradict: the pages of the boardroom minute book which cover the pre-Cup Final meeting have been removed!)

When City strode out at a blustery, rainy Wembley, though, there were no discernible ill-effects on their spirit from this rumpus. They settled to their game faster than Spurs, and it should be emphasised that McIlmoyle's deeper-lying style posed a considerable threat to a Tottenham defence that was probably better prepared to face the more conventional spearhead of a Leek.

It was the old Wembley hoodoo which had most bearing on the outcome, though. Len Chalmers came out of a first-half challenge by Les Allen with a crippling leg injury, and for 70 minutes City were effectively reduced to ten men, despite the full-back gallantly remaining on the field for pure nuisance value at outside-left. McLintock was pulled back into defence and Keyworth into the middle line, City's

attacks were almost invariably confined to the right wing, and Spurs cannily exploited their advantage by virtually running City's depleted forces off their feet.

A tiring but ever-game City conceded two late goals to Bobby Smith and Terry Dyson (the latter finishing a break emanating from a Chalmers mishit), but were far from disgraced as the North Londoners celebrated their historic achievement.

The team's reward for their efforts was a relaxed five-game tour of Rhodesia and South Africa, and the board's a record profit of £44,088.

LEICESTER CITY FOOTBALL CLUB

BANQUET

to celebrate the occasion of the appearance of the Club in the Final of the Football Association Cup

SATURDAY, 6th MAY, 1961

THE DORCHESTER
Park Lane, London

Left: The menu card from City's Cup Final banquet at the Dorchester Hotel in Park Lane.

Leicester Evening Mail
SPORTS MAIL

GREEN UN

15,038 SATURDAY, MAY 6, 1961

Price 2½d

TOTTENHAM'S CUP

CITY

JIMMY WALSH

Gordon Banks   Len Chalmers

Richie Norman | Frank McLintock | Ian King | Colin Appleton

Howard Riley | Hugh McIlmoyle | Ken Keyworth | Albert Cheesebrough

Cliff Jones | Dave Mackay | Maurice Norman | Ron Henry

Terry Dyson | Les Allen | Bobby Smith | John White

SPURS

DANNY BLANCHFLOWER

Peter Baker   Bill Brown

NOT SO SPECIAL

A special train for South Leicestershire cup fans which started at Hinckley and called at all stations to Kettering this morning began its journey with only 26 passengers aboard.

Fine fight by City 10

TOTTENHAM HOTSPUR 2   LEICESTER CITY 0

WITH full-back Chalmers injured and a passenger from the 18th minute, Leicester City's ten fit men put up a glorious fight against Tottenham Hotspur in the F.A. Cup Final this afternoon at Wembley. The handicap, however, was too great, and Spurs eventually pierced a gallant defence in the 69th minute through Smith, and 76th minute through Dyson.

The Wembley hoodoo had struck again, and hard though the City fought, they could not fight both the rampant Spurs and fate.

Thus Spurs completed the double for the first time since 1897.

Blanchflower won the toss and Leicester played into the breeze.

In the first 10 seconds a free-kick was taken by Chalmers and gathered by Cliff Jones, who had

WHY LEEK WAS DROPPED
—Gillies

WHY was Ken Leek dropped from Leicester City's Cup Final team? Leicester has seethed with rumours of "other reasons" which have not been divulged.

I put the matter to manager Matt Gillies, writes BILLY KING, shortly before the team left for Wembley today.

He said: "There appears to be some kind of mystery in the minds of many people. It is quite absurd to suggest that I made the change for any reason but the interest of the side. I made the change purely and simply because I consider McIlmoyle to be the player in form, and that is all."

Hoodoo strikes

THE agony of Chalmers — Dramatic picture in the Cup Final Picture Souvenir, Page Seven.

fallen back to help his defence. The winger was coolly checked by Norman, but the Spurs came back and this time Dyson failed to gather a ball which ran out of play on the right wing.

Play stayed in the City's half and Mackay tried one of his long throws before the ball came back for him to cross it.

It reached Allen, who had taken position on the right, and he slipped a quick pass inside. When the ball reached the feet of White at about 12 yards range, I thought it was all up for the City, but White hoisted his shot over the bar.

Leicester pulled out, trying to organise on the right. A move from the right to left saw McIlmoyle serving Cheesebrough, but the winger could not get the ball into the middle

Like an arrow

The Spurs sprang out of defence very dangerously, and Cliff Jones was off like an arrow, out Norman had come to meet him and his tackle stopped the Welshman in great style.

City organised two useful

SCOREBOARD

69 mins.—SMITH (Tottenham).
76 mins.—DYSON (Tottenham).

By BILLY KING

The flag kick was taken coolly by the Spurs' defence.

Spurs tried doggedly to build their game, and a series of short passes finished weakly, with Jones sending the ball out of play.

A free-kick when Riley was bowled over, landed in the goalmouth, and McIlmoyle glanced it across goal, but no colleague was on his right to take it.

Mackay fouled Riley on the edge of the penalty area, and again the Spurs' goal was under

raids. Keyworth sauntered to the wing, and from the left put in a ball which was headed away coolly by Blanchflower.

Then came the long-striding McIlmoyle on the right, heading for goal and trying a low shot which skipped off a Spurs foot, for Brown to dive in a vain attempt to avert a corner.

Crowd gasped

City's half-backs were swinging into top power and Appleton was bold enough to move deep and try a shot at 25 yards. The crowd gasped and Brown was grateful for the let-off.

City had developed their

(Continued in Back Page)

threat from Riley's free-kick.

King made a superb interception to cut off the ball from White, who was trying hard to make up for his first minute blunder. The game swung Spurs way once more, and we saw all their forwards weaving closely when King again broke up the move by checking Smith.

His pass to Cheesebrough something good was coming, but Cheesebrough was held.

In the 12th minute Riley had moved inside to share in sweeping the ball to the other wing, and his long kick found McIlmoyle lurking at left-wing. He darted outside the back, the target was open for him at a difficult angle, and he hooked over the bar

Leicester City / Tottenham line-up

RIGHT	LEICESTER CITY		LEFT
	Banks		
	Chalmers		Norman
McLintock		King	Appleton
	Walsh		Keyworth
Riley		McIlmoyle	Cheesebrough
		O	
Dyson	Allen	Smith	White	Jones
Mackay		Norman		Blanchflower
	Henry		Baker
	Brown		
LEFT	TOTTENHAM		RIGHT

Referee: J. Kelly (Chorley). Linesmen: H. New (Hants) and W. Downey (Durham).

> Unsurprisingly, in view of the events of May, Ken Leek was a summer departure from Filbert Street, joining Newcastle United for £24,700. Also leaving City was another class performer, Tony Knapp, who had lost out to Ian King in a close contest for the No 5 shirt. Liverpool and Wolves were interested, and City proposed an exchange deal with the latter that would have involved Peter Broadbent, but Knapp eventually moved to Southampton for an initial fee of £25,000, which would rise by 10 per cent after he'd made 25 senior appearances. Otherwise, Matt Gillies' satisfaction with his squad seemed complete: the only incoming transfer during the summer heralded a frustrating City sojourn for Dunfermline's Scottish Cup-winning hero David Thomson, while trialist winger John Mitten was the only first-team newcomer over the first half of the season.

A new experience awaited City this term – one which would take them 36 years to partake of again. A spin-off of Spurs' Double achievement was that beaten Cup Finalists City would compete as English representatives in the European Cup Winners Cup, while Spurs carried the banner in the premier continental competition. Comfortable victories over Irish Cup-holders Glenavon at both Windsor Park (a four-goal riposte to Sid Weatherup's opener) and Filbert Street (a trio of headed goals) earned City a glamorous clash with Spanish stylists Atletico Madrid in Round Two. A classic first leg at Filbert Street ended at 1-1 when Mendoza managed a last-minute reply to Ken Keyworth's opener; but City frustrations were doubled over the matter of Keyworth having had an additional 19th minute strike rubbed off, and a City free-kick awarded instead. Gordon Banks, incidentally, had arrived only 40 minutes before kick-off, having spent the afternoon on the Wembley bench for the England v Portugal international.

The second leg drew over 50,000 to watch a stubborn City exit 0-2 to the eventual trophy winners: but not before Graham Cross had distinguished himself with a fine centre-half performance on his eighteenth birthday, and Gordon Banks had kept out the first of two Atletico penalties. Matt Gillies would not be the last Leicester manager to air his grievances over the performance of a French referee.

This night was one of the few proud memories that City could retain from a generally anti-climactic season. The League challenge never got off the ground, and City were anchored around the middle of the table throughout the campaign, eventually finishing fourteenth. Two September defeats by Burnley were among the term's most noteworthy

Above: Frank McLintock.
Below: Mike Stringfellow.

Ian King, while the 2-6 reverse at home had the Filbert Street fans granting a heartfelt standing ovation to the visitors for a breathtaking display. Burnley in fact returned to Leicester later in the season, to earn their trip to Wembley by overcoming Fulham in an FA Cup semi-final replay.

City's own domestic pot-hunting efforts both proved disastrous. In the League Cup, Fourth Division York City delivered a humiliating knockout; and the board later debated the wisdom of continuing to enter this competition, before concluding that they would do so until it was discontinued. In the FA Cup, Leicester were ousted in a Third Round replay by Stoke City, losing 2-5 and having two 'goals' disallowed for offside. Essentially, though, the tie hinged on a wondrous performance by the almost 47-year-old Stanley Matthews, who gave poor Richie Norman the runaround of his career.

This latter Cup exit prompted Gillies into the transfer market to try to salvage something from the season. He had met a rebuff when enquiring about Airdrie's centre-forward Jim Storrie, but was then successful with two bids of £25,000 each – to be repaid in kind many times over – for Mansfield's rangy left-winger Mike Stringfellow and Hibernian's superbly skilful schemer David Gibson. Gibson was still on National Service, and his appearances for the rest of the term therefore restricted, while Stringfellow initially struggled to find his shooting boots, but soon there were glimpses of just what an exciting left-flank partnership this pair would forge.

There was also a glimpse of the effectiveness of another City hero-to-be this year. Derek Dougan claimed one of Aston Villa's goals in their 2-0 win at Filbert Street, and two more in their 8-3 crushing of City at Villa Park in April; the last occasion Leicester conceded so many goals. Gordon Banks was rarely so embarrassed, and his justifiably growing reputation was acknowledged by selection for the Football League. A Scottish Under-23 honour for Frank McLintock, and England Youth recognition for Graham Cross, completed City's representative haul this term.

City applied for entry to the 1962/3 Inter-Cities Fairs Cup, only to find that League-position qualification would henceforth be necessary to enter this previously invitational tournament; and they were surprisingly barred by the FA from providing opposition in planned matches at Santander and Bilbao to the Spanish national team preparing for the Chile World Cup. Then, at the end of the season, long-serving club secretary Charles Maley retired. He was

> One-time Birmingham goalkeeping hopeful Eddie Plumley was appointed club secretary in July, and was immediately involved in the formation of the Leicester City Development Association. A weekly pool and daily tote was to be run to fund ground improvements now that the club had sole responsibility for such matters. Money was still available to Matt Gillies for team-strengthening, but he chose not to expend any during the summer, and was rewarded for his faith in his side by seeing City make their best start to a First Division campaign since 1925/6, taking 18 points from the first 13 fixtures to lie in 5th place.

For once, in fact, Gillies was now in the enviable position of having to fend off enquiries for his players: from Wolves (McLintock), Arsenal and Newcastle (Banks), Preston and Bury (Cheesebrough) and Blackpool and Northampton (Riley). Indeed, during December, Arsenal manager Billy Wright was actually reported to the League for an illegal approach to Banks.

City's inventive tactical approach to their campaign (often involving an elegant interchange of roles between McLintock and Cross; essentially predicated on a counter-attacking style; and very much the product of coach Bert Johnson's promptings) was already being remarked upon by the national press as Christmas neared with City still up among the challengers. The League Cup had again provided a hiccup of embarrassment, as City squandered a clear four-goal lead over Charlton at

City were about to earn their tabloid tag of 'Ice-Age Champs'

Below: When second-placed City entertained League leaders Tottenham in March, the crowd was supplemented by several onlookers on the roof of the Popular Side. Here Mike Stringfellow nets Leicester's first goal in the 2-2 draw.

Filbert Street (when Gordon Banks contributed an own goal, and the loudest cheers greeted the announcement that elsewhere Arthur Rowley had just broken the British scoring record). They then lost the replay at The Valley (where Len Chalmers was sent off, and both Howard Riley and Charlton's Matthews missed penalties before a young Len Glover prodded the winner); but League form was distinctly and contrastingly pleasing.

Boxing Day, 1962, proved to be a particularly significant date. It heralded the beginning of the most severe winter of the century, which would eventually throw fixture lists into chaos, though City's astute use of chemically-treated topsoil would generate enough warmth to break the icy Filbert Street surface and allow most home fixtures to be completed. It was also the date on which Colin Appleton took over from Jimmy Walsh as captain, a stylish new round-necked kit was unveiled, Leyton Orient were trounced 5-1 at Filbert Street, and a record-breaking run of 16 games undefeated, including 10 successive victories, got underway. City were about to earn their tabloid tag of 'Ice-Age Champs'.

No League games were played during January, but Grimsby and Ipswich were each dismissed in potentially tricky FA Cup ties, and City divided their training routines between the Granby Halls and bracing Brighton. Four straight League victories followed in February, then, on 2nd March, City completed a League double over Liverpool with a 2-0

triumph at Anfield — the first time the Merseysiders had failed to score in 55 successive home games. It was City's eighth consecutive victory. A Fifth Round Cup win at Leyton Orient and a League success against Blackburn took the sequence into double figures to set the scene for the visit of League leaders Tottenham.

Spurs themselves were unbeaten in League matches since 8th December, and stood just one place above City. A crowd of 41,622 witnessed high drama on the stroke of half-time as Jimmy Greaves netted (apparently putting Spurs 3-1 up), only to find that the referee's whistle had blown a split second too early for Spurs. The final scoreline was 2-2 and City continued their unbeaten run, including a Sixth Round Cup victory in front of Norwich City's all-time record crowd, to Monday 8th April. On that night, following a 1-1 draw at Blackpool, the First Division tables showed City in top position for the first time since September 1927.

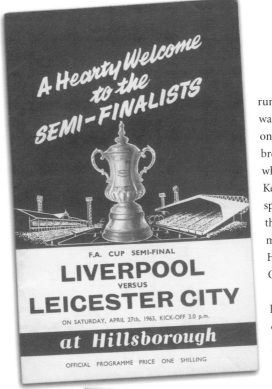

	P	W	D	L	F	A	Pts
Leicester City	34	19	10	5	68	35	48
Tottenham Hotspur	33	20	7	6	92	45	47
Everton	33	18	9	6	66	36	45
Burnley	31	16	8	7	60	42	40
Wolverhampton W.	32	15	8	9	74	51	38
Liverpool	31	14	8	9	57	40	36

The following Saturday, at Easter, the run ended at Upton Park and top place was lost. However, a draw at Old Trafford on Easter Monday was followed by a breathtaking return fixture the next day when the pinnacle was regained. Ken Keyworth notched a hat-trick in the space of six minutes, Denis Law claimed three for United (including a miraculous bicycle kick), and a Terry Heath goal split the two sides, 4-3 in City's favour.

City's fourth game in eight days, a home draw against Wolves, saw them once more toppled from premier position. A brief respite followed, before City travelled to Hillsborough to take on Liverpool in the FA Cup semi-final. Mike Stringfellow headed the decisive goal after 18 minutes in one of City's few attacks, and a magnificent rearguard action, with Banks outstanding, saw City safely through to Wembley for the third time. Surely no-one could possibly envisage that this was to be City's last victory of the season.

Above: Matt Gillies and Colin Appleton lead out City at Wembley, resplendent in all white to avoid a 'colour clash' for monochrome TV viewers.

Matt Gillies had made pre-deadline attempts to bolster his squad for the anticipated run-in towards the elusive League and Cup Double. An enquiry for Bradford's Kevin Hector was rebuffed, as were two bids for Motherwell's Bobby Roberts. This failure to reinforce would prove costly, as City's League challenge petered out with four successive away defeats, including a last-day St Andrews cliffhanger which guaranteed Birmingham City's safety. A final First Division placing of fourth was a crushing disappointment, despite being the club's best performance since 1928/9!

City's hopes were nonetheless high that Cup glory was at hand. Their opponents Manchester United had been involved in the relegation battle all season, and the credit balance from the

THE FOOTBALL ASSOCIATION CHALLENGE CUP COMPETITION

THE FOOTBALL ASSOCIATION · 1863-1963 · CENTENARY YEAR

FINAL TIE
LEICESTER CITY
V
MANCHESTER UNITED

OFFICIAL PROGRAMME   ONE SHILLING

WEMBLEY
EMPIRE STADIUM

SATURDAY, MAY 25th   Kick-off 3 p.m.

WEST STANDING ENCLOSURE   ENTER AT H TURNSTILES
(See plan and conditions on back)
ENTRANCE 55

EMPIRE STADIUM WEMBLEY
The Football Association
Cup Competition
FINAL TIE
SATURDAY, MAY 4th, 1963
KICK-OFF 3 P.M.
WEMBLEY
Price 7/6

THIS PORTION TO BE RETAINED
This Ticket is issued on the condition that it is not re-sold for more than its face value

117

Easter clashes was definitely in City's favour. Three new full internationals would be in City colours – Banks, McLintock and Gibson – whilst Appleton had represented the Football League and Cross had gained his first Under-23 cap. Surely it would be a case of third time lucky for City?

Alas, on the big day, City's stars froze into something approaching dazed ineptitude, whilst United's talented individuals blossomed, cohering around Pat Crerand's mastery of the midfield. Denis Law turned on a sixpence to shoot United ahead, Banks mishandled to allow David Herd to slot home a second, Ken Keyworth lifted City hopes with a superb diving header with just nine minutes remaining, but Banks erred again for Herd to seal United's victory by 3-1. City simply had not done themselves justice.

The bigger the stakes, the harder it had become to swallow the disappointments. Certainly, Gillies had established the club amongst the elite. But would anything tangible, trophy-wise, ever result?

Above left: Opposing captains Noel Cantwell and Colin Appleton shake hands before the 1963 Final.

Left: Close, but not close enough, as a City chance runs just wide.

Above: Ken Keyworth's goal makes it 1-2 with nine minutes remaining.

Below: The goal that finally ended City's hopes, crashed in by David Herd three minutes from time.

IT WASN'T CITY'S DAY

Denis Was One Law Too Many For City

An early Leicester raid. Gaskell punches clear as Stringfellow comes in.

THIRD TIME DIDN'T PROVE LUCKY FOR LEICESTER CITY AT WEMBLEY TODAY. BRILLIANTLY INSPIRED BY DENNIS LAW AND FIRED BY MAN-OF-THE-MATCH PAT CRERAND, MANCHESTER UNITED ALWAYS CARRIED TOO MUCH PACE AND IDEA FOR A CITY SIDE WHO LOOKED JADED IN ATTACK AND OVERWORKED IN DEFENCE.

Keyworth boosted City hopes with an 80th-minute goal to start a rare rally that came too late.

Leicester City 1   Man. Utd. 3

KEYWORTH .... 81 minutes	LAW .... 29 minutes
Attendance 100,000 Receipts £89,000.	HERD .... 57 minutes
	HERD .... 85 minutes

"Better put this lot in pawn until next year."

The roof nearly came off the Stadium when the teams took the field parading behind their managers.' Sartorially they were splendid, with United's brilliant red track suit tops really standing out.

City did not wear anything on top of their match uniform, but looked more relaxed—waving to the crowd and as they waited for the presentation to His Royal Highness the Duke of Edinburgh—David Gibson even tried a spot of ball juggling. The National Anthem put an end to that.

ONCE THE DUKE HAD PASSED HALF WAY DOWN THE LEICESTER LINE

THE LINE-UP

LEICESTER CITY

Banks

Norman .... Sjoberg
Appleton   King   McIntock
Gibson   Cross
Stringfellow Keyworth   Riley

O

Giles   Herd   Charlton
  Quixall   Law
  Crerand Foulkes Setters
  Dunne   Cantwell

Gaskell

MANCHESTER UNITED

Referee: K. Aston, Ilford.
Linesmen: C. H. Pegg, Spalding; W. G. Handley, Cannock.

when they moved smartly down the right Gaskell hastened out to pick up. Both attacks were doing a lot to help their defenders when the necessity arose, and Giles popped up at the wrong end to dispossess Stringfellow.

But the Nottinghamshire lad quickly got it away again to send a low shot just wide of the far post.

It was deflected for a corner from which the same player headed over the bar, and had it not been for that first touch Keyworth moving through well might have had the first goal.

Leicester were drawing applause for their quick confident redistribution, looking really cool as they played their way out of defence.

But defenders helped attackers too, and Setters gave away a free kick for a hard tackle on Riley after Sjoberg had joined in an offensive.

Then came a real scramble around the United goal in which Gaskell twice looked unhappy punching under pressure.

Stringfellow was the man jumping with the young 'keeper twice as United hearts fell into their boots, but strength of numbers got them out of trouble and an offside ruling as Appleton chipped the ball forward raised the siege. United went away with a corner which Cross headed away splendidly.

Crerand was getting through a lot of work, and as he tried to go through himself Appleton was booed for a tackle which the referee thought rated as an obstruction. Anyway, Banks pulled Quixall's lob down with the ease of a boy scrumping apples.

The Crerand-Giles combination was the best for United so

★ Continued on Back Page

THE LINE-UP

WHITE SHIRTED CITY BEGAN TO PRACTISE THEIR BALL SKILLS FORTUNATELY NO ONE MISKICKED.

As the teams kicked in the Leicester chant was more predominant. Colin Appleton won the toss and Banks defended the goal at the tunnel end of the Stadium. Then Riley, nearly level with the edge of his own penalty area, fell back to stop Charlton.

Through Ball Misplaced

Quixall planted a ball through the Leicester defence, but it was too far advanced for Giles to make anything of it. Gibson too, came back to stop Law and soon Leicester were moving forward once more, Quixall checking Keyworth unfairly. But Appleton wasted the free kick and it was Crerand's turn to show up well, putting Herd away but the leader pulled the ball back badly.

United moved down the right, but King came quickly into action to check them and Appleton drove a pass forward parallel to the side line for Stringfellow but Foulkes moved over to give away a throw in from which Gibson and Cross moved forward without getting anywhere.

Even in the early moments Leicester were stroking the ball about confidently and

Just Eluded Gibson

Cross was mainly a midfield worker, and he slipped one ball down the middle after ten minutes which only just eluded Gibson to run through to Gaskell.

UNITED WERE HAVING PROBLEMS ALREADY WITH THE CITY DEFENCE, AND THE BEST HERD COULD MANAGE AFTER A FIVE PASS MOVEMENT WAS A HARMLESS, AIMLESS 25 YARDER THAT WAS WIDE.

BY

Laurie Simpkin

Left-back Cantwell sees the ball go across his goal as Stringfellow corners in.

Crerand And Setters Established Grip

ALTHOUGH Leicester did most of the early pressing, United's beginning was brisk enough and Herd should have made better use of a perfect through pass from Quixall with the City defence out of position.

Quixall had taken on the responsibility of midfield schemer but Leicester's tight marking and close covering prevented Law from taking a quick return pass down the inside right.

United's defence was lying a little too square for my liking at this point.

Twice Riley almost swept past Cantwell on the inside and

Manchester supporters sighed with relief when Keyworth just failed to get to Stringfellow's inviting cross.

Crerand's flair for the accurate long ball was soon evident, but Charlton, challenged in turn by Riley and Keyworth was again in his indifferent Wembley form. Patchy distribution by Herd ended two bright moves but Busby's men were now finding their feet and quick and precise midfield moves showed some promise.

Thankfully, United had put their dismal League form behind them.

GILES AND CHARLTON WERE TRYING TO FIND A WAY ROUND THE FLANKS OF LEICESTER'S COMPACT DEFENCE AND CHARLTON, BRIGHTENING UP ALMOST DID THE TRICK WITH A SPARKLING RUN AND CENTRE

of City's attack was disappointing, to say the least.

On the run of play Leicester were fortunate not to be further behind at the break.

even the close attentions of two, and sometimes three, City defenders failed to contain Law.

The volatile inside left should have had a second goal after a glorious "one-two" link with Herd but give McLintock credit for getting back to make a goal line clearance after his first tackle on the Scot had failed.

Leicester's first real shot came in the 37th minute from Cross, and Banks was undoubtedly the busier goalkeeper.

Crerand and Setters had established a firm midfield grip and the first half performances

Leicester needed a quick second half goal but United's defence, even with Gaskell a jittery and uncertain goalkeeper, was in no mood to fall for the hopeful and haphazard City attacks which were tinged with desperation.

Where was Leicester's famed quick strike from defence? Where was the build up.

★★ Continued on Back Page

Law scores. The Manchester inside left fires across Appleton and Norman into the net.

> With a profit of £19,567 to invest, the Double Decker was re-roofed, and the Enclosure re-terraced during the summer. Papering over cracks in squad morale fell to Matt Gillies, who spent much of this time pacifying Frank McLintock and Gordon Banks over their opposition to the club policy of pay parity for the whole first-team pool. The manager's bid to sign Bury centre-forward George Jones having failed, it was the familiar Cup Final eleven who lined up for the start of the new season – only the second time in the club's history, and the first since 1937, that exactly the same team selection had been made for both the final game of one season and the first of the next. (1976 would mark the third and most recent example of this phenomenon).

Again, City flattered to deceive. A draw at the Hawthorns, a 3-0 home victory over Birmingham City and a spectacular 7-2 Filbert Street win against Arsenal (handicapped by the early loss of goalkeeper Jack McClelland) saw City head the first published tables of the season. But inconsistency dogged the side thereafter, nullifying the effect of five straight League wins around Christmas; and despite a double over champions-to-be Liverpool (received with a hail of both abuse and missiles at Anfield), the mere respectability of eleventh place was the final return from the League campaign. For the first time since 1906, City lost more games at home (8) than they did away (7).

Bargain signings Jimmy Goodfellow and Billy Hodgson flitted in and out of the team, and even the eventual capture of Bobby Roberts from Motherwell (at a club record fee of £41,000) did not pay immediate dividends. Additional City interest in Swindon's Don Rogers and Manchester City's Neil Young was quashed at the enquiry stage.

The FA Cup proved to be a huge disappointment, with a surprise 2-3 home defeat coming at the hands of Leyton Orient in Round Three. Malcolm Musgrove, later to become City's coach, netted twice for the Second Division visitors on the day. But substantial consolation accrued, however, from the less vaunted Football League Cup.

A series of competent performances in the early rounds accounted for Aldershot, Tranmere, Gillingham and

Above: The menu from City's post-Cup Final banquet at The Dorchester.

Left: The *Mercury's* Cup Final special carried the first reports on Saturday night.

Right: Gordon Banks celebrates his position as England's first choice custodian with a cover apprearance on *Football Monthly*.

Norwich, and allowed for first-team bloodings for youngsters Bob Newton, Max Dougan and Tom Sweenie. An extra-time winner from Howard Riley in the home replay against the Canaries set City up for a semi-final clash with West Ham, and a 4-3 thriller in the first leg at Filbert Street left the tie finely balanced. The second leg was a football connoisseur's delight, with City pulling out their best performance of the season to triumph 2-0.

The similarly two-legged Final got underway with a slightly fortunate 1-1 draw at Stoke City's Victoria Ground, with Bebbington poaching from a Banks parry of Asprey's skidder, and David Gibson netting the equaliser for Leicester after a Skeels clearance bounced off Terry Heath into his path. The denouement at Filbert Street, however, finally and deservedly brought the club its first-ever major trophy. Mike Stringfellow's goal – a sixth-minute drive after he'd latched on to Sjoberg's long-ball – separated the teams at half-time. Stoke were level two minutes later via Viollet, but then capitulated to Gibson's rare near-post header and Howard Riley's left-footer before finding injury-time consolation from Kinnell. A thoroughly intriguing contest finished 3-2 to City on the night, and 4-3 on aggregate, with League secretary Alan Hardaker (very much the 'godfather' of this competition) enthusing that "This is the cure for most of soccer's ills ... more games such as this. We should want bigger grounds". Skipper Colin Appleton was able to display the silverware the following week at his well-earned testimonial game.

During the season, Richie Norman took his club record for consecutive appearances to 194 games before a pulled muscle ended the run; 16-year-old goalkeeper David Timson became City's youngest peacetime debutant to date; and both Banks and Gibson added to their tally of full international caps.

Right: Mike Stringfellow puts City ahead against Stoke in the League Cup Final second leg.
Below: David Gibson's header makes it 2-1.
Bottom: The third goal from Howard Riley clinches the Cup for City.
Bottom right: Colin Appleton collects the club's first major trophy.

Above: David Gibson was one of six senior players in dispute with the club at the start of the 1964/5 season.

> Hopes for another season of success were rocked as early as the summer months of 1964. Several players were involved in contractual disputes and, by the opening day of the campaign, six senior players – Appleton, Banks, Cross, Gibson, McLintock and Roberts – had all still failed to reach agreement. Most of the negotiations were over improved terms, though Gibson had requested permission to run a licensed bar at Filbert Street on matchdays, and had the idea rejected summarily by the directors. In addition, Banks had been transfer-listed during June following an unauthorised outburst in the press. Eventually, most problems were settled, though not before Frank McLintock moved to Arsenal for a record incoming fee of £80,000 in early October, after City had rejected enquiries for him from both Wolves and Coventry.

Against this backdrop of turmoil, it was somewhat surprising that City did not taste defeat until their seventh game, but it was not long before they flagged badly. In contrast to their winter form of recent seasons, City actually embarked on a run of 13 League games without a win from November to February, and they were grateful for their earlier points haul when defeat in each of the last three fixtures saw them drop to eighteenth spot. Gillies was wholly unable to spend any of the McLintock cash, having no luck with enquiries for Colin Bell (Bury),

Martin Chivers (Southampton) or Peter Knowles (Wolves).

There was, however, distinct relief from the League travails in two substantial Cup runs. The FA Cup produced an exciting, hard-fought slog to the last eight before eventual winners Liverpool triumphed by the only goal in an Anfield replay, while City also conjured a valiant attempt to retain the League Cup, which for the first time would carry with it the incentive of a place in the Inter-Cities Fairs Cup for the winners.

Leicester in fact made heavy weather of a couple of their early League Cup clashes as they disposed of Peterborough, Grimsby and Crystal Palace, but they really startled their fans with an uncharacteristic local derby display against Second Division Coventry City in the Highfield Road quarter-final. Sky Blues skipper George Curtis netted an own goal and then departed with an injury; City keeper Banks also went off injured, although only temporarily; full-back Richie Norman scored twice; and City eventually romped home by 8-1 (still the competition's record away win). Norman, who also scored in Round Three at Grimsby, thus notched three goals during this Cup run – significant because he only scored two others in his entire City career, spanning some 365 matches in total!

Plymouth Argyle were toppled in the semi-final, by 4-2 on aggregate (City had also removed the Pilgrims from the FA Cup, skating to a 5-0 win on an icy Filbert Street), but Chelsea posed a sterner threat in the Final. Goals from Colin Appleton and Jimmy Goodfellow could not prevent a 2-3 reverse in the first leg at Stamford Bridge (where they still talk in awe of Eddie McCreadie's individualist goal that night), and

Above: Plenty of City pressure but no breakthrough as Chelsea hang on to a goalless draw to win the Cup 3-2 on aggregate.

Left: An early City attack is thwarted by Chelsea in the second leg of the League Cup Final.

constant one-way pressure could not unlock the well-drilled Chelsea defence at Filbert Street, where a 0-0 scoreline saw the trophy wrenched from City's grasp.

(Incidentally, a draw resulted in Filbert Street's other national Cup final of this year: with Leicester Boys and Swansea Boys sharing the English Schools FA Trophy after a hearteningly skilful second-leg display had failed to separate the teams. Many City fans got their first glimpse of Peter Shilton and Jeff Blockley in this game).

In total, City packed 58 senior competitive games into their season, from the August day they faced newly-promoted Sunderland's 15-year-old keeper Derek Forster at Roker, via their BBC2 'Match of the Day' debut in the October home win over Forest, to their dull-as-ditchwater April home defeat by Stoke: more than ever before. But the passed-up opportunity to add two friendlies to this roster reflected badly on the City board (who were otherwise celebrating turning a 1963/4 loss of £61,624 into a 1964/5 profit of £43,284).

In September, they rejected terms offered by the FA for a match against top Brazilian club Santos, featuring the incomparable Pele; whilst in January they turned down a request by Arthur Rowley to stage a Testimonial game at Filbert Street. At the end of the season, Shrewsbury player-manager Rowley finally hung up his shooting boots, having registered a Football League record of 434 goals, 251 of them for City. The fans were left wondering if a forward of such character would ever don a City jersey again.

> Character, in fact, was one of the words most often used to describe City's major summer signing. Derek Dougan cost £21,000 from Third Division Peterborough, and quickly grasped City's lifeline to put his colourful career back on the rails. The charismatic centre-forward soon became the fans' favourite, especially in harness with fellow-newcomer Jackie Sinclair, a bargain £25,000 capture from Dunfermline. Not all the auguries for the campaign ahead were good, though. An ill-fated pre-season friendly with Northampton saw Gordon Banks break a wrist, so George Heyes, an unheralded understudy for so long, began the season with a guaranteed place for several weeks.

An innovation in League football this term was the permitted use of a substitute to replace an injured player. Jimmy Goodfellow was City's first nominated No 12, and was called on to replace Graham Cross in the 80th minute of the opening fixture. This game, a 1-3 home reverse to Liverpool, signalled a shaky start to the campaign, which did not really pick up until Banks returned in late September, and Dougan and Sinclair developed an effective understanding with their new team-mates.

In fact, Matt Gillies made a club record bid of £50,000 to Chelsea in an attempt to add Barry Bridges to his forward line at this time, but the deal fell through. City's record fee was eventually increased at the end of the year, though, when full-back Peter Rodrigues was signed from Cardiff for £42,500.

Above: Graham Cross, the first City player to be substituted, when replaced by Jimmy Goodfellow against Liverpool.

Below: A rare view from the Double Decker, taken during City's clash with West Ham in May 1966.

On the field, matters were rarely dull this term, and November pretty well encapsulated City's roller-coaster fortunes. They began the month with a 2-1 win at Goodison that would have been better had not the referee's half-time whistle cancelled out a Sinclair scorcher. The following week Manchester United triumphed at Filbert Street, but the bare 0-5 scoreline hid the story of a superb game to which City had contributed marvellously. The Reds may have given City a lesson in the economy of finishing, but Leicester were still cheered off by their own fans after gaining 36 corner kicks without reward! And they simply took out their frustrations on Newcastle a week later, waltzing to a 5-1 win at St James' Park.

By Easter, City's fortunes had picked up considerably. Two goals by Mike Stringfellow at Old Trafford exacted revenge for the November mauling and ended United's run of 41 home games without defeat. Days later, Tom Sweenie became City's first scoring substitute after replacing Stringfellow against Blackburn. Such efforts also helped lift City to sixth place, and briefly encouraged hopes of Fairs Cup qualification at season's end.

Stutters over the final fixtures, however, left them seventh in the final chart. John Sjoberg contributed two own goals to West Brom's cause in a 1-5 defeat at the Hawthorns, while a week later Graham Cross netted all three goals in a 2-1 Filbert Street win over Nottingham Forest (gifting them the lead after 20 minutes, equalising after 21, and notching the winner

12 minutes later). The next game, at home to Cup winners-elect Everton, saw 16-year-old Peter Shilton keep a characteristic clean sheet on his debut, as the club's youngest senior player at that date; while the next and penultimate fixture saw Banks return from international duty to find himself once more under fire from his own defence, with Rodrigues this time netting the decider in Arsenal's favour.

Youth was very much on the agenda this term: in March, David Nish had thrice warmed the City substitute's bench while still a pupil at Ashby Grammar School. And former City stalwart Charlie Adam guided his Leicestershire & Rutland charges (Nish and Rodney Fern included) to victory in the FA County Youth Cup; a 3-1 second-leg win at Loughborough securing a 6-5 aggregate over London. The season also saw the institution of the Plumley Cup, a tournament for under-15 sides played at Filbert Street in the hour prior to home-game kick-off time. Named after the City secretary, this initiative grew out of a series of exhibition games played the previous term by Blaby Boys Club, and added immeasurably to the notion of pre-match entertainment.

For once, there was little to report on City's own knockout front. Manchester City closed their interest in the League Cup at the first hurdle, and also shocked Filbert Street by shading a Fifth Round FA Cup replay after it appeared that City's fine away form was going to carry them through their third awkward draw – they'd already had to visit Birmingham twice to oust Villa and Blues. Neil Young, a real Cup bogey-man for City this decade, scored twice at Maine Road and got a mishit bobbler past Banks in the replay.

Representative honours accumulated interestingly this term. All three newcomers – Dougan (Northern Ireland), Sinclair (Scotland) and Rodrigues (Wales) – won full caps, as did Banks for England; giving City the rare distinction of current internationals for all four home countries. There was also celebration in the boardroom, especially for the Shipman family. Len was elected President of the Football League, whilst son Terry became a fellow City director. A seasonal loss of £4,331 was pretty much shrugged off.

> The summer of 1966 was dominated by the World Cup finals. England's eventual victory at Wembley over West Germany was a source of much national pride, and a particular parochial slice of that pride attached to Leicester City, who had provided the faultless Gordon Banks for the winning team, and had seen him hailed as successor to Lev Yashin as the world's premier goalkeeper. Football in general was to receive a terrific boost to its image and status from the events of July, but the question remained as to how much effect would be felt at Filbert Street.

There were no new faces in the City side as the season got underway with an unfortunate defeat at Anfield, and only a change in the team's strip (to all blue) impinged on the still fairly pleasurable sense of déja vu which stretched – almost – to the end of the campaign. Indeed, at one stage City's very line-up remained unchanged for nine League games and two League Cup ties. Sinclair hit a hat-trick in the first home fixture, a characteristically entertaining 5-4 win over West Ham; while Dougan subjected his former Villa comrades to a similar torment a few weeks later as City notched five without reply. Another hat-trick game was at Southampton, where Ron Davies's triple gave the Saints a 3-1 half-time lead, which City pulled back to 4-4 despite a Sinclair penalty miss. Both regular goalscorers passed the 20-goal mark in League and Cup matches for the second season running, and it was scant surprise that other aspects of the campaign seemed to mirror fairly accurately the events of the term before.

An eighth place finish resulted from the League challenge, and Manchester City again removed City

Right: English football's finest moment and the Leicester City goalkeeper was a key part of it.

FILBERT STREET WELCOMES ALCOHOL

> A significant off-field development was the opening of licensed bars at the ground for the first time, and such was the financial success of this move that in April the directors decided to plan for the summer construction of the Fosse Bar at the Double Decker end of the Main Stand. The irony of all this was that, in March, former club stalwart John Duncan had passed away: the first man to challenge openly the club's original principled objections that drink and football did not mix.

Above: Derek Dougan scores his third in the 5-0 win against Aston Villa in September 1966. By the following March the popular Dougan had been transferred.

Below: England goalkeepers present and future, as Gordon Banks hands over the reins to Peter Shilton before departing to Stoke in April 1967.

from the FA Cup, this time at Maine Road in Round Three. This year City also set out on an alternative route to Wembley, where the League Cup final was for the first time to be staged. But, after 5-0 victories over both Reading and Lincoln, they came a cropper at Loftus Road and went down 2-4 to an inspired Queens Park Rangers, who would eventually capture the trophy itself, as the first Third Division club to appear in a Wembley Final.

Sidelights to the seasonal flow came in September, when Denis Howell, the Government Minister with special responsibility for sport, officially opened the new Fosse Bar, and when manager Matt Gillies was appointed to the local magistrates' bench. Transfer activity was minimal around this time. Nothing arose from enquiries about Luton's Bruce Rioch or Sheffield United's Alan Birchenall, and when Sunderland's Nick Sharkey did arrive at Filbert Street in October for a small fee, he lost his place after one game to goalscoring debutant David Nish.

It was transfer activity, though, that was to prompt a pair of major controversies that overshadowed all else (even including a shameful outbreak of violent hooliganism at a Filbert Street friendly against Rangers) in the final months of the season. Swiftly and unexpectedly, City were to part with two of their genuine stars. In March, Derek Dougan was sold to Wolves for £50,000 to help seal their promotion effort; and then in April another £50,000 fee was accepted from Stoke City for Gordon Banks. 'The Doog' was a prolific scorer and an immensely popular hero with the Filbert Street fans, while Banks had won a record 37 caps during his time with City, and was thought by many still to be approaching his peak.

There was little forgiveness for Gillies or his directors over the Dougan sale; even if there was a general realisation that a difficult decision had to be made over the goalkeeping dilemma, especially once the prodigiously talented Peter Shilton had made his ambitions plain. The sheer speed of the Banks move, however, caught out even Liverpool's legendary boss Bill Shankly, who rang to table a bid literally seconds after the keeper had signed for Stoke.

Neither the knowledge that the club now had money in the bank, nor that it possessed a fine crop of youngsters, did much to placate the comprehensively disgruntled supporters. The reserves did, however, manage to draw 8,804 of them to Filbert Street for the second leg of the Football Combination Cup Final, and pulled back a deficit to draw 2-2 on aggregate with Spurs and share the trophy. Here, apparently, was long-term promise; but could either City or their fans find the patience to wait for its fulfilment?

Above: John Sjoberg led the attack at Old Trafford in 1967/8.

Below: An aerial view of Filbert Street, showing that the ground had not substantially altered since the roofing of the Popular Side before World War Two.

> To the outsider's eye, it looked all too apparent that City were letting the grass grow under their feet. Literally, in the sense that Filbert Street was wholly returfed this close season with a surface cut from the Belvoir Drive training ground; and metaphorically, in that nothing tangible by way of signings resulted from Matt Gillies' attempts at team-building. Enquiries were made for Jim McCalliog (Sheffield Wednesday), Ron Davies (Southampton), Mike Doyle (Manchester City), Fred Pickering (Everton), Alf Arrowsmith (Liverpool), Allan Clarke (Fulham) and Maurice Setters (Stoke), but not a single deal developed.

The goalkeeping situation was somewhat absurd. There was literally no cover for Peter Shilton on the books. Scottish trialist Jim Eadie suffered torn ligaments on his first day's training; Fulham, themselves injury-hit, recalled Jack McClelland on the day his loan spell was due to start; and local teenage amateurs were pressed into City's reserve and A-team service.

The League season opened with two defeats and, in what looked to be the ultimate in panic measures, centre-half John Sjoberg was switched to lead the attack in the third fixture, at Old Trafford. City did salvage their first point in that match, but not before suffering a real scare. Shilton was carried off injured, and Bobby Roberts had to don the keeper's jersey for the final eight minutes. The sale of Banks had rebounded on City in unexpected fashion and, after failing to come to terms with United's David Gaskell, Gillies had to persuade Forest reserve Brian

Williamson to join the club on loan to cover Shilton's absence.

The manager suffered more disappointments when bids of £70,000 for Hull striker Chris Chilton and of £110,000 for Burnley's Andy Lochhead were each rejected, and was successful only in shoring up the defence with Willie Bell from Leeds. The team was also experiencing mixed emotions. A fit-again Shilton actually scored a last-minute goal with a punt from his own area in a 5-1 victory over Southampton at The Dell (the club's first-ever there, and their last for over thirty years!); but Graham Cross suffered a broken leg in a friendly in Strasbourg.

Significant signings finally came in November. Much-travelled Frank Large arrived from Northampton in time to take part in a 0-6 hammering at Maine Road, but was joined a week later by Charlton winger Len Glover, who cost a record £80,000. Glover's impact with City was initially muted by injuries, but the enthusiastic Large was an almost instant hit. City were by now in a lowly League position, but gradually lifted themselves towards the relative comfort of a thirteenth place finish, mainly thanks to the overspill impetus from another memorable Cup run.

Manchester City again ended City's interest in the League Cup, and when the two teams were paired in the FA Cup for the third successive season, there was little optimism in the City camp. Leicester held out, however, at Maine Road, and brought their rivals back home for a scintillating classic of a Fourth Round replay. Two goals down inside the opening half-hour, City appeared to be heading for their customary exit. But a Large-inspired fightback on either side of half-time heralded a four-goal salvo, and City eventually won 4-3 with the Filbert Street crowd in raptures.

The regular 60s ritual of all-night queueing for tickets at Filbert Street (indulged in by both authors, amongst several hundreds of the faithful!) preceded the Fifth Round trip to Rotherham, and a home replay win over the Millers further kindled Cup fever. The adventure ended, though, at the quarter-final stage, with Everton pouncing on home defensive errors to produce a 1-3 scoreline.

Matt Gillies missed most of the New Year excitements, having been ordered in January to take a three-month rest from the game on medical grounds. His chief coach Bert Johnson stood in temporarily, and it was he who was responsible for first blooding another hero of the Manchester City tie, Rodney Fern. Brian Potts, Don Hutchins and Malcolm Manley also earned later promotions from the Combination ranks. Gillies would return in the summer to continue his search for a more consistently successful City blend.

Above: Frank Large proved to be an inspirational signing.

Below: British record signing Allan Clarke (centre) lines up the wall with Brian Potts (left) and Rodney Fern (right) in the October 1968 fixture with Tottenham.

> This year it was intended that there should be no slurs that City had underbid for a coveted player, or had settled for second-best. Gillies got his board's backing to go out and break the British transfer record, and the target he returned with was Fulham's young forward star, Allan Clarke, in a deal valued at £150,000. City paid £110,000 in cash, but also had to let proven inspiration Frank Large move to Craven Cottage to make up the full fee; so even before hindsight could be applied, there were those who questioned the wisdom of such a deal. Ironically, the other main summer arrival at Filbert Street was Ray Shaw, a former manager of Clarke's at Walsall, and now City's chief scout. One man close to departure was Graham Cross. City accepted an £80,000 offer from Derby, but the player himself rejected the move.

Indeed, Cross lined up alongside Clarke for City's opener at Loftus Road, and the new man's debut goal gave City a share of the points. A glorious hat-trick from Clarke a few weeks later against Manchester City was another early highlight, but on the whole City's start to the campaign was disappointingly unimpressive, and generally goals were proving hard

to come by. Thoughts perforce turned from expectancy of a title challenge to the reality of a relegation struggle. In October, Gillies tried to buy back Large for £20,000, but Fulham turned him down, and it was to another long-time target, Burnley's Andy Lochhead, that he turned; expending £80,000 on the centre-forward's experience.

By November, Derby returned with further enquiries for Cross, David Nish and Malcolm Manley, but City rebuffed their approach. It was clear, however, that something was amiss at the club, with dressing-room morale and harmony at a low ebb. At a special meeting on 28th November involving the directors, three senior players and the manager, the following three points were resolved:

i) The board expressed their confidence in the manager.
ii) The assistant manager (Bert Johnson) and the assistant coach (George Dewis) were to be relieved of their duties.
iii) Dewis was to be offered the post of A-team trainer.

On 29th November, Gillies, who was not in agreement with these resolutions, tendered his resignation, with the announcement to be made officially at 4pm the following day. Ironically, earlier the same month, Gillies had celebrated becoming the first City manager to survive 10 years in the post. On that following day, City crashed 1-7 at Goodison to complete the miserable picture.

During December, Torquay's Frank O'Farrell was appointed manager. (The other shortlisted candidate, Allan Brown, met a double disappointment: being sacked by Luton as soon as news of his application was publicised.) By January, Malcolm Musgrove had been employed as coach; taking over from caretaker Willie Bell. Thus, within a short space of time, all the key members of the club's

backroom staff had changed, for secretary Eddie Plumley had left in October for Coventry, and had been replaced by John Smith, recently returned from Stateside football administration.

Bad weather during February (and a disgraceful playing surface) led to a clutch of postponements and an unhealthy backlog of fixtures as City continued to battle against relegation. This fixture pile-up was exacerbated by another inexplicably good run in the FA Cup. Barnsley and Millwall had been conquered during January, but a much-postponed Fifth Round tie with Liverpool could not take place until March.

A goalless draw at Filbert Street took the teams to Anfield two days later, with struggling City expected to be lambs to the slaughter. However, a bullet header from Andy Lochhead, combined with a superb Peter Shilton penalty save from Tommy Smith, inspired City to another memorable Cup-tie victory. Five days later, Rodney Fern's far-post header saw off Mansfield at an overflowing Field Mill, and suddenly City were unlikely semi-finalists once more.

Hillsborough was again the venue, Cup-holders West Brom the opposition. Allan Clarke, ever appearing to take less interest in mundane League affairs, proved to be the man for the big occasion, snatching the only goal of the day with barely three minutes remaining. So City were in their fifth Cup Final of the decade, and this time their opponents would be none other than Manchester City, for the fourth successive year in the FA Cup.

131

There was hardly time for euphoria. Not with eleven League fixtures still to play, and a crucial encounter with fellow-strugglers Coventry City away on the Tuesday. Crucial, indeed, this tension-soaked game turned out to be. City were holding their own comfortably when, with seven minutes to go, substitute Brian Greenhalgh was scythed down in the Coventry box and City awarded a penalty. The ball was on the spot before the referee consulted his linesman, and mayhem ensued as he changed his decision and gave the Sky Blues a free kick. A totally

Above: Graham Cross, Andy Lochhead and David Nish celebrate at Hillsborough.

Below and top right: The Cup Final teams are led out by Frank O'Farrell and Joe Mercer.

Below right: David Nish became the youngest captain of a Wembley Cup Final side.

deflated Leicester team were helpless as Coventry raced away to score immediately through Neil Martin at the other end.

Only two more points accrued from the next five games before, on 26th April, David Nish became the youngest captain to lead his Cup team out at Wembley. Despite City's spirited and sometimes elegant contribution to a decent footballing Final, however, Nish was destined to suffer the same fate as all Leicester skippers before him. John Sjoberg was missing at the back; Len Glover's fitness was suspect;

SPORTS MERCURY SPECIAL CUP FINAL EDITION

1946   Saturday, April 26, 1969   5d.

FOUR TIME LOSERS

City Pipped Again At Wembley

THE LAW OF AVERAGES DIDN'T WORK OUT AT WEMBLEY AFTER ALL THIS AFTERNOON. LEICESTER CAME TO WEMBLEY FOR THE FOURTH TIME AND THEY'RE STILL WAITING TO BRING THAT ELUSIVE F.A. CUP HOME.

Manchester City were clearly the more polished assured side and deserved their 1-0 victory. Yet for all their skill they found the Leicester defence extremely hard to break and it is a fact that on chances this game might well have been a 3-3 draw.

Leicester City	**0**
Manchester City . .	**1**

YOUNG (Manchester City) ...... 23 minutes
OFFICIAL ATTENDANCE 100,000
RECEIPTS £128,000

DOGGED DEFENCE IN THE BOX

by JIMMY MARTIN

The goal that rocked Leicester in today's Cup Final at Wembley. The scorer, Neil Young, Manchester City, is not in the picture, but his shot completely beat the leaping Peter Shilton. Alan Woollett and Peter Rodrigues are also helpless.

After very heavy rain in the morning, the weather cleared considerably, there was some sunshine but still sufficient cloud around to give the impression of showers.

The famous Wembley pitch is now only a travesty of its former self with ugly scars on the turf. There is certainly nothing lush about this surface.

The teams came on and were presented to Princess Anne who was making her first appearance at a football occasion.

The teams came on headed by their respective managers Frank O'Farrell and Joe Mercer.

Leicester were wearing white track suit jackets and Manchester in blue. But the colours for the afternoon were Leicester in their usual blue jerseys and white shorts and their stockngs are blue with white rings on the top. Manchester were wearing their Italian-style red and black stripes with black shorts.

Leicester made a nervous start and indifferent passing twice had them in minor spots of trouble.

LEICESTER	MANCHESTER
1 Shilton	1 Dowd
2 Rodrigues	2 Book
3 Nish	3 Pardoe
4 Roberts	4 Doyle
5 Woollett	5 Booth
6 Cross	6 Oakes
7 Fern	7 Summerbee
8 Gibson	8 Bell
9 Lochhead	9 Lee
10 Clarke	10 Young
11 Glover	11 Coleman
12 Manley	12 Connor

Referee: G. McCabe (Sheffield), linesmen K. H. Burns (Birmingham), H. C. Lane (Horsham).

One quick passing raid by Manchester could have been serious but Doyle ruined the move in the box.

Leicester's first throat was engineered mainly by Clarke and it produced the initial corner of the game. Taken by Fern, it was a low ball which Gibson headed on into the box but Manchester cleared.

An excellent run by Summerbee, who beat Nish, raised Manchester's hopes but Cross got there in time to give away a corner.

A good cross by Young was cleverly headed away by Clarke and certainly in the first seven minutes or so Manchester had been the quicker of the teams to settle although Shilton had not yet made a save and the only real effort of a shot came from Coleman that raged across the goalmouth and past.

Another Manchester shot came from Young, but he blasted over the bar.

IT WAS A NOT UNFAMILIAR STORY OF LEICESTER'S PROGRESS IN THE CUP. THEY WERE BEING BEATEN IN MIDFIELD BUT THEIR DEFENCE WAS DETERMINEDLY PROTECTING THE BOX.

A solo run by Clarke soon petered out and then suddenly came the first real chance of the game.

Lee raced away down the wing and Summerbee intelligently streaked into the open space, collected the

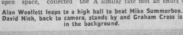
Alan Woollett leaps to a high ball to beat Mike Summerbee. David Nish, back to camera, stands by and Graham Cross is in the background.

ball and whipped it across the goalmouth. It went to Coleman who was left with a clear chance. But he tried to sidefoot it into the net and sliced the ball past. This was all rather depressing for Leicester then suddenly they started to hit out.

A run by Lochhead started the move and after gaining considerable ground the centre forward slipped the ball back to Clarke.

He cut across and let go a tremendous right-footer — the first shot on target in the game, which Dowd brilliantly tipped over for a corner.

From the flag kick, Leicester nearly scored, Fern's shot racing across and away for a goal kick.

A similar fate met an effort by

Summerbee was having a rare game for Manchester and most of the danger emanated from him.

David Gibson, one of the doubtful players this week, appeared to be standing up to things well and his use of the ball was excellent.

Occasionally Leicester would play with the fluency of the opposition but it was not a sustained effort.

The game quietened a bit and there was a lot of midfield play that led to little.

On the whole it had been a fairly good final so far with plenty of good football — mostly from Manchester, although it was a fact that Shilton and Dowd had been given very little to do.

Booth occasionally looked a little bit shaky and he was

Glover who took a shot on the run after a great pass by Gibson.

Shilton saved a nasty situation by going down bravely at the feet of Young then shortly afterwards Leicester ought to have taken the lead.

Roberts dribbled his way into the box and suddenly transferred the ball to Gibson out on the left.

HIS SHORT CROSS ELUDED THE MANCHESTER DEFENCE BUT TWO LEICESTER MEN, ALMOST ON THE LINE, COULDN'T QUITE GET AT THE BALL. RODRIGUES DID, HOWEVER AND FROM ONLY FIVE YARDS SHOT PAST.

Leicester had suddenly come back with a vengeance and were playing good attacking football and the Manchester defence was looking anything but assured.

So it was all the more disappointing for the Blues when they lost a goal in the 23rd minute.

Summerbee eluded a tackle, cut the ball back from the goal line to YOUNG who was left with a clear sight of the target about 12 yards out. He took it without hesitation and blasted the ball home to give Manchester the lead.

It was rather ironic that Leicester should withstand the early sustained pressure and then go behind just as they seemed to be getting a grip of the game.

certainly finding Lochhead far from easy to keep quiet.

Young was injured but recovered after attention without leaving the field.

Bell, after surviving two desperate tackles, began to bear down on the Leicester goal but he was brought down from behind by Nish, and eventually cleared from the free kick.

Manchester often played exhibition stuff with their famous forward line moving at great speed. But Cross and his fellow defenders refused to be drawn and were keeping Shilton well protected.

A fast move by Lochhead and Fern put Gibson away on the left but he made a mess of his cross.

Lee forced a good corner with a solo effort and got himself injured in the process. He recovered but Coleman put the flag kick past.

Manchester, with players like Bell buzzing around in midfield, were always that little bit sharper than Leicester.

Just on half time, Shilton had to go down to an angled shot from Coleman.

Half time: Leicester City nil, Manchester City 1.

Young nearly got Manchester into bother in the very first minute of the resumption when Fern robbed him around the box. But nothing came of it.

Only a minute later, however, Dowd brought off a great save from an angled shot by

Continued on Back Page

Above: Allan Clarke's performance earned him the Man of the Match award.

Left: Peter Rodrigues slides in to deny Neil Young.

Below: Andy Lochhead appears to be fouled as Tommy Booth heads clear.

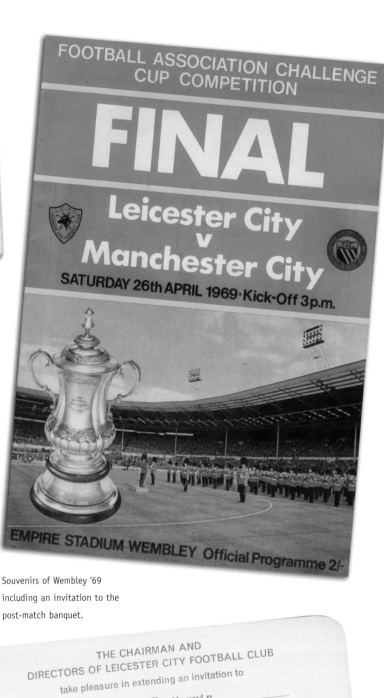

both Rodrigues and Lochhead spurned pottable chances; Neil Young drove home the only goal of the game for the Mancunians; and City were vanquished at the last once again.

Following the Final, such was the imbalance in fixtures that Coventry, City's main relegation rivals, had completed their League programme, whilst Leicester still had five games to play in three weeks. At least City knew their target for survival – a further seven points.

A Clarke goal brought victory over Tottenham, but the same could not prevent defeat at Ipswich. Young debutant Ally Brown's two goals edged out Sunderland, and Graham Cross netted to salvage a draw against Everton in a bad-tempered home encounter. So City came to their final fixture requiring a victory to avoid relegation. Manchester United were the opposition, Old Trafford the venue, and the Reds were motivated by the fact that this was Sir Matt Busby's final game as team manager. Skipper Nish gave City the lead in the opening minute, but by the fourth minute they were in arrears to an unfortunate own goal and a typical piece of George Best magic. Eventually City went down 2-3, and so ended the club's longest-ever spell in the top flight.

The attempt to climb back under O'Farrell's guidance would be witnessed by virtually a generation of fans who had never known City to be anything other than a First Division outfit – quite a contrast to earlier days! One aspect of tradition, though, had been restored during this campaign, with the reversion to a playing strip once more featuring white shorts.

Souvenirs of Wembley '69 including an invitation to the post-match banquet.

Touches of Class

> The major transfer activity of the summer once more involved a British record fee for Allan Clarke, who had taken the Man of the Match award from the Cup Final, but whose temperament was unlikely to be of much value to City in the Second Division. This time Leeds were the purchasers, at £165,000. Veteran full-back Billy Houghton was the only newcomer to Filbert Street, at the merest fraction of the Clarke fee.

The season itself started in early August, with its close scheduled for mid-April: a move designed to give the England team time to acclimatise to conditions in Mexico, where they would attempt to retain the World Cup in 1970. City seemed to like the early start; uncharacteristically opening with a victory over Birmingham that featured a Shilton penalty save and a spectacular overhead kick from Rodney Fern that notched the club's first Second Division goal in over 12 years. The side continued to prosper during the first half of the season, keeping well up with the front-runners, and actually finding the net in each of their opening 21 League fixtures – the best sequence in the entire competition.

Andy Lochhead initially hit a rich vein of goals, but was later jettisoned to Aston Villa for £30,000. Wolves winger John Farrington arrived for the same fee, but higher bids from O'Farrell for Watford's Stewart Scullion (£55,000) and Birmingham's Bob Latchford (£35,000) were unsuccessful. Reserve forwards Murray Brodie and David Tearse made contrasting breakthroughs: the former scoring in his first two games, the latter being pressed into service as an emergency right-back at Blackburn. Kenny Sandercock, a youthful buy from Torquay, was a first-minute injury victim on his full debut. And Rodney Fern hit a hat-trick at Bolton that represented the first by a City player on opposition soil since the days of Arthur Rowley.

Tangential off-field controversies adhered to the club as the promotion drive seemed to be going well; rather more serious rows would follow later in the term. In September the Football League objected to the design of goalkeeping jersey being worn and marketed by Peter Shilton, deeming the collar fastening to be potentially dangerous. A few months on, disagreements were of a distinctly local nature, with the *Leicester Mercury* complaining of Frank O'Farrell's policy of naming a 14-man squad on the Friday before a match, rather than the actual team line-up. A diminution of press coverage was at one stage threatened, but common sense eventually prevailed.

Back on the field, by Easter, Huddersfield looked clear favourites for promotion, with City sitting just behind Blackpool and vying strongly for the runners-up spot. The Seasiders' visit to Filbert Street on Easter Tuesday would prove vital. On the night the weather was diabolical, with torrential rain rendering the pitch a mudbath. A postponement looked likely, but referee Jim Finney decided to make a start. Abandonment then looked certain, especially when Fern's goalbound shot actually stuck in the cloying mud just inches short of the line, but incredibly proceedings were allowed to continue. The inevitable 0-0 scoreline was sufficient to cost City promotion.

There was one further controversy in store, however. The following Saturday, relegation-threatened Aston Villa visited Filbert Street. City won 1-0, but not before Pat McMahon's shot had clearly entered the City net, hit the rear stanchion and rebounded into play. The referee waved the game on and an incensed Villa were doomed to Division Three. After the incident, the City directors resolved to alter the type of stanchion used for the following season.

City's distractions from the near-miss promotion bid included fair runs in both Cup competitions. Seven games were played in the League Cup, from which West Brom removed City at the quarter-final replay stage, having attracted a new record Filbert Street crowd for the competition to the first game. And a further five matches, all against First Division opposition, saw City to a Fifth Round home replay against Liverpool in the FA Cup. Two goals from Alun Evans spelled the end of City's Wembley hopes for the season; and Evans would prove, some eight years later, in rather more embarrassing circumstances, to hold a cup hoodoo over City.

Another competition was exercising the thoughts of O'Farrell by season's end. Conscious of the ever-pressing need for Leicester to develop their own youngsters, he applied for the club's reserves to transfer to the Central League for 1970/1, but found that no vacancies then existed.

Below: Football goes decimal and City set the prices for Filbert Street.

> Having just failed to point his men to promotion at the first attempt, O'Farrell looked once more to the transfer market as a means of stiffening City's renewed challenge. During the summer he had bids of £55,000 for Celtic's Tommy Gemmell and £40,000 for Sheffield United's John Tudor turned down, but prior to the opening day he expended £48,500 on Bristol City's tenacious midfielder Bobby Kellard, and continued to wheel and deal for the next few months as City recovered from the shock of an initial home defeat to get up amongst the divisional leaders.

Investments in youthful promise brought Joe Jopling and Malcolm Partridge to Filbert Street, but it was the bargain £35,000 purchase in October of Derby's wily and experienced Willie Carlin that proved the manager's masterstroke. David Gibson and Peter Rodrigues moved on with City's thanks for sterling service (the latter deposed by local discovery Steve Whitworth), and a now settled squad knuckled down to meet O'Farrell's aims. In fact, the soft-spoken Irishman's methods were at this time the subject of an eight-week television documentary series on goal-oriented business management techniques ('Can You Manage?'), and the City boss would, eventually, thoroughly justify such exemplary status.

Despite having lost Partridge with a broken elbow during a goalless draw at St Andrews, City ended November nicely tucked into the leading pack. But December and January brought only three points from six League games, and the last of these – a 1-4 home defeat by Birmingham sustained while Colin Mackleworth was standing in for the injured (and temporarily transfer-seeking) Shilton – seemed to imply that City were going backwards.

On the contrary, however, City thereafter conceded only five more goals all season as they put together a magnificent closing run

PRESENTED BY LEICESTER CITY FOOTBALL CLUB

THE MAN INSIDE SAYS
"BEFORE YE ENTER THESE GATES"

EXACT MONEY READY PLEASE

'THINK DECIMAL'

GROUND 30p · CHILDREN 15p

ENCLOSURE 35p · CHILDREN 20p

DOUBLE DECKER 50p

WING STAND 70p

MAIN STAND 80p

ADMISSION CHARGES REMAIN THE SAME

CONVERSION GUIDE . . . .

NEW	£1	50p	10p	5p	2½p	2p	1p	½p
OLD	£1	10/-	2/-	1/-	6d	ABOUT 5d	OVER 2d	OVER 1d

Printed by E. Hannibal & Co. Ltd., Pinfold Road, Thurmaston, Leicester

LEICESTER CITY finished the season as Second Division champions with yet another away win. This extended their unbeaten run to 17 games – a fine record.

Pompey's incentive of £500 a man if they drew or won encouraged them to fight to the end and in fact they did score in the last minute of the game. But it came too late and they lacked the class to beat the poise and assurance of Leicester who looked worthy champions. Hundreds of Leicester fans streamed onto the pitch at the finish to acclaim their heroes.

SCOREBOARD

Portsmouth	1
CITY	- - 2

FARRINGTON (City) 6 mins.
BROWN (City) 35 mins.
NIXON (Pompey) 89 mins.

Above: David Nish with the Second Division Championship trophy. The old shield won by City in 1937, 1954 and 1957 had been destroyed in a fire at Coventry in 1968.

of 17 unbeaten League games. The 1-0 victory at Swindon on 13th March, which took City to the top of the table, was a characteristic display of ultra-cool defending and breakaway incisiveness; while the crucial Easter Monday clash at Luton was a model illustration of City's belief in their own class, with an inspired Rodney Fern orchestrating the comeback after an own-goal reverse to secure a 3-1 win.

Another 1-0 away win, by courtesy of top-scorer Ally Brown's strike at Bristol City on the night of 27th April, clinched both promotion and the championship (though only after a scare involving the Robins hitting City's post, two players being carried off after they clashed for the rebound and burst the ball, and a resultant, dodgily defended bounce-up eight yards out). Accordingly, David Nish was handed the trophy at Fratton Park four days later, in front of a mass of pitch-swarming City fans, following yet another victory on opposition soil. Particularly elated amongst the City squad was veteran defender John Sjoberg, for the silverware would be on show at Filbert Street a few weeks later when City met Derby in his testimonial game.

Supplemented by the ever-competitive midfield guile of Carlin and Kellard, City's defence was the cornerstone of the championship success, setting new records for niggardliness with only 30 League goals conceded throughout the campaign (14 at home, 16 away). Peter Shilton managed to keep no less than 23 clean sheets – his elevation to the full England international side during the season being fully vindicated.

Shilton had, though, been beaten once more during the course of the League season. Despite the introduction of differently designed goal stanchions at Filbert Street following the previous season's incident in the Villa game, the self-same thing occurred when

THE CITY TENT

> February 1971 was a busy month for the club, with the introduction of decimalisation and the decision to order a giant inflatable 'balloon', or polysphere, to protect the pitch from severe weather *(see pictures above)*. **The initial investment of £5,000 in this structure, soon popularly dubbed 'the tent', would reap substantial rewards in future seasons.**

Portsmouth were the visitors, and Jim Storrie's header rebounded back into play with the referee unaware that it had entered the net.

In a season of high excitement, City even managed to generate some more in the Cup competitions. Bristol City removed them from the League Cup after extra-time in a Fourth Round replay at Ashton Gate, while FA Cup progress was stymied only in controversial fashion. Notts County and Torquay were dismissed in the early rounds, then a brave fight by Oxford was overcome in extra-time in a Manor Ground replay. Both clubs had requested a change of referee for this game, so poorly had he performed in the original tie, but the FA refused the plea.

The quarter-final brought Double-chasing Arsenal to Filbert Street and an excruciatingly tense goalless draw resulted. But in the Highbury replay, Fern had a perfect headed goal inexcusably disallowed by Jim Finney, nominally for pushing, and the Gunners scraped a single-goal win on their way to joint Cup and League success.

Behind the Filbert Street scenes, there had been plenty of activity, too. Back in the summer, secretary John Smith had raised the subject of ground development, mentioning factors such as members' clubs, the presentation of other sports, more seating, and general modernisation. The board decided to consider the appointment of a Public Relations Officer to examine such possibilities. Mike Turner was approached, but felt he could not accept because of his moral committment to Leicestershire CCC, and the idea faded for a while.

Above: Steve Whitworth's goal won the FA Charity Shield for the Foxes.

> Preparations for First Division football took a radical change as early as June. Manager O'Farrell accepted an offer to take over the reins at Manchester United, and coach Malcolm Musgrove followed him. The City board wasted no time in finding a successor, appointing Orient boss Jimmy Bloomfield to usher in a new era at the club.

Bloomfield was to have no truck with sentiment, barely giving the promotion side a chance to prove itself at the higher level before setting about a comprehensive rebuilding job. Arsenal midfielder Jon Sammels was the first import, at £100,000; arriving in time to help City to a morale-boosting FA Charity Shield win over Liverpool at Filbert Street (achieved via that genuine collector's item, a Steve Whitworth goal).

Ally Brown netted the first goal of the entire Football League season, after just 45 seconds, as City brought home a point from Huddersfield, but only two wins had accrued by October, prompting Bloomfield to lash out again. This time his captures were forwards Keith Weller (Chelsea, £100,000) and Alan Birchenall (Crystal Palace, £45,450 plus Bobby Kellard), and City were soon on course for consolidation.

Bloomfield also had to battle to hold on to his inherited talents, though. Peter Shilton attracted an enquiry from Everton, a £175,000 bid from Derby, and an Arsenal offer of an exchange deal. City asked for £150,000 plus Bob Wilson, but no moves materialised. David Nish was the other prime target, with Manchester United expressing interest, and Derby suggesting John Robson, John McGovern, Alan Durban or Frank Wignall as bait for a possible part-exchange.

Adapting to Bloomfield's attacking gospel took Leicester some time, but they were rarely in danger of the drop. Sheffield United, promoted behind City, were the early pacemakers, and retained top spot in September when Alan Woodward netted a last-minute goal direct from a corner to sink City 0-1 at Filbert Street. A fruitful January brought another home win over Liverpool, though there was a mini-slump a month later as City got over the embarrassment of FA Cup defeat at home by Bloomfield's former charges, Orient. City were forced to blood young keeper Carl Jayes in this Fourth Round tie, and he was badly at fault with the visitors' clincher.

City would eventually play the market again to secure Mark Wallington from Walsall as cover for Shilton, and to let top-scorer Ally Brown move on to West Brom for £55,000. By the end of the term, a wholly respectable First Division position of twelfth was attained; partly on the back of the rare statistic that saw City having scored five more goals away than at Filbert Street. One such came from Jon Sammels via the penalty spot in the final fixture at Spurs: the first City had been awarded in 76 games since David Nish had seen Norwich's Kevin Keelan save his twelve-yard effort back in November 1970.

A fair bit of publicity was also garnered during the campaign by the club's efforts in two other tourneys. In a football-themed television quiz show, 'Quizball', City's representatives (plus Nicholas Parsons) reached the final before bowing to a team from Dunfermline Athletic; while in the *Daily Express* 5-a-Side tournament at Wembley, City disposed of Everton, Celtic and West Brom before confronting Southampton in the final. They eventually lost on penalties, but Keith Weller ended the evening as the event's top scorer.

The board, too, despite facing a seasonal loss of £156,355 on the back of the transfer roundabout, were evincing a more progressive attitude than in the past. But though they agreed in principle to a major rock concert (to have headlined local band Family) being staged at Filbert Street, and to the building of squash courts at the stadium, neither development actually took place. The directors also commissioned, for £100, a club history from Billy King, doyen of local sports journalists. Though this never materialised as a comprehensive publication, it was several times utilised in serialised, skeletal form in club programmes over the next decade.

Below: Jimmy Bloomfield's early signings from London clubs, Jon Sammels (Arsenal), Keith Weller (Chelsea) and Alan Birchenall (Crystal Palace).

> The summer of 1972 was nothing if not eventful. At Filbert Street, new floodlighting, with double the power of the old system, was installed at a cost of £10,000, and a penning arrangement introduced onto the Spion Kop terraces, to facilitate crowd control and segregation. The Football League and FA joined forces in an unavailing attempt to fight off the imposition of VAT on sporting admission prices, and the League introduced its own 'penalty' system of points awarded for bookable offences leading to automatic suspensions for on-field sinners. The most evidently dramatic change for City, however, was Bloomfield's decision to alter the team's strip to an all-white outfit – partly in imitation of the successful Leeds side of the era, and partly on the dubious grounds that the players looked bigger when so attired!

Midsummer and early season transfer traffic was again heavy. Fern moved to Luton for £45,000, and Frank Worthington belatedly signed from Huddersfield for six figures in August, after it had looked like Liverpool's intervention might deny City a long-coveted acquisition. A week later David Nish moved to champions Derby for a British record fee of £250,000, and to fill his No 3 shirt Bloomfield expended approximately half that amount on Orient's Dennis Rofe.

Five games had been played without a victory when Liverpool visited Filbert Street, and went two goals up through John Toshack. But a remarkable Keith Weller hat-trick turned the tables, and even if only the woodwork denied Toshack an equaliser on the night, City's 3-2 win had them up and running. (Weller's achievement could best be put in context by pointing out that no other player would net a triple against Liverpool until Coventry's Terry Gibson managed the feat in December 1983).

Results generally, though, were poor, and when a flu epidemic led

Above: When manager Jimmy Bloomfield signed Frank Worthington in August 1972 the mould was set for one of the most entertaining teams in the club's history to take shape.

to the postponement of the fixture with Newcastle at the end of November, City actually sank to the bottom of the table. Talented as the team appeared on paper, goals were increasingly hard to come by. However the defence, ably marshalled by Manley and Cross, proved equally miserly, and eventually survival was assured with a final placement of sixteenth looking deceptively comfortable.

Worthington (against West Brom) was City's second hat-trick scorer of the term; a Birchenall double brought down high-flying Leeds; and in the final game of the season, City's obdurate defence denied champions Liverpool an Anfield celebration victory. There was little to shout about in first-hurdle Cup defeats, unless it was once more to berate the referee for a ludicrous decision against Leicester at Highbury. John Farrington seemed to have added to City's opener with a fine 20-yard drive, but the point was disallowed for an offside decision against Birchenall, standing way out on the wing in no position to interfere with play. For all City's classy entertainment value that day, a late George Amstrong equaliser meant a 2-2 scoreline, and Arsenal nicked the replay by the odd goal in three.

Two boardroom decisions this season would take effect from the next. In January a promise was made to revert to a blue and white playing kit (the change having been neither successful nor popular), and in February plans were put in hand to build a number of Executive Boxes at the Filbert Street end of the ground. These would replace the roof at that end and offer a close-up, elevated view of proceedings for City's wealthier business clientele. What was desperately needed, though, was some on-field success to generate more income through the regular turnstiles.

Left: The all-white strip introduced in 1972, worn here by Keith Weller, was supposed to make the players look more imposing, but it was not popular with the fans.

> Despite the disappointing outcome to the previous season, Bloomfield kept a low profile during the summer of 1973, preferring to work on instilling confidence in the players already at his disposal rather than searching for replacements.

A few changes were in the air, though. The League introduced a three-up, three-down system of promotion and relegation between the top divisions, hoping to diminish the number of effectively meaningless games towards the end of the term. City, in an attempt to encourage more youngsters to attend games, opened a Family Enclosure in front of the Main Stand, where safety from any hooligan element amongst the crowd could be assured. Also, to help generate more income, the idea of individual match sponsorship was introduced. The Audnel Group were the first company to be associated with this scheme, backing the initial home game, against Liverpool.

This game brought City's third successive draw, and though they remained unbeaten in their first eight fixtures, five returns of only a single point prevented them challenging for top spot. That was the place held by the formidable Leeds outfit who visited Filbert Street on 13th October. City actually led by two goals after 20 minutes, but had to settle for a 2-2 draw by the end. Leeds went on to compile a League record run of 29 unbeaten games from the start of the season, and never came quite so close to defeat again during the sequence.

The following week, City were onlookers at a major demonstration staged by Derby County fans in

Above: Mike Stringfellow had scored the semi-final winner against Liverpool in 1963, but could not repeat the feat 11 years later.

Below: The City team thank the fans for their support during their thrilling FA Cup run, at the home fixture with Birmingham in April, just three days after losing the semi-final.

protest at the departure of Brian Clough. Whether such signs of discord prompted complacency or not, City went down 1-2 when the match got underway.

December saw the debut of Bloomfield's only significant signing of the season, Steve Earle. The former Fulham striker effectively replaced the veteran, injury-blighted Mike Stringfellow in the regular line-up, which now boasted a centre-back pairing of Graham Cross, in his testimonial year, and young Malcolm Munro. The same month, the first effects of the strike-hit 'winter of discontent', with its attendant three-day working week, were felt in football, when the use of floodlights was banned. By January, permission was given for the first time for games to be staged on Sundays, though City themselves took no advantage.

With some often entrancing entertainment being served up by City, but still too many games resulting in a share of the points, they finished the season in a creditable ninth place. Worthington was again a hat-trick scorer in City's best win (5-0 over Ipswich), but triples were conceded in each game against Birmingham, to Bob Latchford at St Andrews and to Kenny Burns at Filbert Street.

However, it was City's exploits in the FA Cup which this year once more captured the public's imagination. Steve Earle netted a late goal to defeat Tottenham in Round Three; Len Glover replied to Alan Mullery's 'Goal of the Season' volley at Fulham, and then helped clinch success in the replay; and the whole team turned on a breathtaking performance to

trounce Luton 4-0 away in Round Five. This masterpiece of a match was climaxed by a superb individual goal by Keith Weller, and drew from no less than *The Sunday Times* a heartfelt comparison between City's football and that of Brazil!

So City came to the quarter-finals, drawn away to QPR and facing an injury crisis. Alan Birchenall had been ruled out two weeks earlier and regular deputy Alan Woollett was also sidelined. Bloomfield decided to gamble on debutant midfielder Joe Waters, and the game turned into a fairy tale come true – Waters notched both the goals which took City through to their sixth semi-final.

The ensuing encounter with favourites Liverpool was a different matter. City only just survived the first goalless game at Old Trafford, when a late Kevin Keegan header struck a post and rebounded into Shilton's arms. They fell behind in the Villa Park replay, but equalised immediately through Glover, and for 15 minutes looked on the brink of another Wembley final. But a dazzling snap shot by Keegan turned the game, City wilted, and ultimately succumbed 1-3.

Still, Bloomfield's faith in City's quicksilver flair was being partially rewarded, and recognition of the high individual skill factor within the side came from England's caretaker manager, Joe Mercer, who called up both Weller and Worthington for their first caps during his short term in post.

Below: Summer 1974 marked the start of a long period of transformation at Filbert Street, as the first four executive boxes were to be built behind the goal at the Filbert Street end of the ground.

> The relative success of the previous season soon seemed a distant memory as the new campaign got underway. Bloomfield had refrained from summer dealing, but soon found himself deep in a series of frustrating negotiations as City got off to a shaky start. Peter Shilton was refusing to sign a new contract, and Mark Wallington started the season in goal. A ding-dong affair that ended in a 4-3 win for City at St Andrews, thanks to Dennis Rofe's last-minute solo run, gave deceptive hope that City would be in for another carefree jaunt into the First Division's upper reaches.

But such was not to be. Points were being given away far too freely. Bloomfield moved in September for Ipswich iron-man Allan Hunter, but the player could not agree terms. He tempted Manchester United forward Brian Kidd, but when publicity broke about the projected deal, Arsenal nipped in with a better offer. Then, in November, Bloomfield sincerely believed he had got his man. A £160,000 deal was agreed with Liverpool for John Toshack, and the Welsh striker actually trained with City before the results of a club medical quashed the deal. The only transfer actually concluded that month involved Shilton once more emulating his mentor Gordon Banks by signing for Stoke, at a record fee for a goalkeeper of £325,000.

From early November to late February, City could not register a solitary League victory, and dressing-room discontent was all too apparent. Shortly before Christmas, Keith Weller had a transfer request turned down and, days later, refused to take the field for the second half of the home game against Ipswich. The Suffolk club won the game 1-0 to move to the top of

Division One, whereas Weller was subsequently fined two weeks' wages and placed on the transfer list. Norwich manager John Bond made a strong attack on the player through the media, and wrote to all First and Second Division club managers asking them to blacklist Weller. However, the player eventually settled his differences with the club, and no repeat of such an incident ever occurred again.

Shortly before this bombshell, City had got into a real mess with their goalkeeping resources. Wallington replaced the departed Shilton, but broke a bone in his hand for the second time in the season. Stoke's John Farmer arrived on loan, but was also injured; and Carl Jayes had to hold the position until Wallington returned in January to commence his record-breaking run of consecutive appearances.

City hit rock bottom on 11th January, when they were one of three clubs – Carlisle and Luton were the others – who found themselves five points adrift of Chelsea in 19th place. But Cup progress gave League form a little boost, and then two successful Bloomfield captures proved absolutely inspirational in helping City climb from the mire. Centre-back Jeff Blockley stiffened the rearguard, and striker Chris Garland galvanised a forward line that also now featured local lad Bob Lee as a regular. Garland's eight goals in ten games were the icing on the cake of a fine City recovery that lifted them eventually to sixteenth place.

Remarkably, City could laugh off a spectacular Weller own goal at Luton, and could honourably sit back and allow Derby to take away from Filbert Street the point they needed for the championship in the penultimate game.

The Cup competitions this year provided further lashings of incident. Arsenal and Leicester just could not bear to be apart. City triumphed over the Gunners in a League Cup replay, but the roles were reversed after three nailbiting Fifth Round games in the FA Cup. Arsenal, incidentally, also took three points from the League meetings between the clubs.

The League Cup adventure ended mundanely at Middlesbrough (where earlier the first attempt at a First Division meeting had been cut short after 24 minutes by a complete floodlight failure), but the Cup tie of the season for most people was in the Fourth Round of the premier competition. Drawn away to Isthmian League Leatherhead, City negotiated a switch of the venue to Filbert Street, and TV cameras were present to record their acute embarrassment at going 0-2 down to the minnows. Only a goal-line clearance kept the deficit within reason and reach until City fortunately regained form and stormed back with a three-goal reply.

On the year's individual front, Steve Whitworth was added to City's list of current internationals – providing further evidence that the team possessed the talent if only Bloomfield could mould them into a consistently effective unit – and long-serving Mike Stringfellow took a well deserved testimonial game against Wolves.

1975-76

> The summer of 1975 was a famous one for Leicestershire. The County Cricket Club generated immense excitement and pride as they captured the Championship for the first time; though not quite everyone was as delighted as they might have been. City's directors decided to suspend Graham Cross for continuing to play cricket during July rather than report back for pre-season football training, and his subsequent dropping from the Anglo-Scottish Cup pipe-openers spelled the beginning of the end of a magnificent City career. At Filbert Street, seating had been introduced on the old Popular Side terraces, substantially reducing the ground capacity, while Bloomfield had supplemented his squad with the purchase of Steve Kember from Chelsea and Brian Alderson from Coventry.

The opening fixture, a topsy-turvy 3-3 draw at home to Birmingham, saw City finish – and indeed twice equalise – with only nine men; Garland being sent off and Blockley carried off with a knee injury after the substitute had already been used. Such fortune was to prove a portent of things to come as City put together an unwanted run of fifteen games without a League victory: though as ten of these were draws (including a Maine Road match which went on and on until a Birchenall own goal gave the homesters a 98th-minute point), there was neither undue panic nor total surprise when Burnley were edged out by 3-2 at Filbert Street in November.

Matters picked up healthily after this, though a further nine draws were interleaved in the seasonal record, which finally saw City finish in a good seventh place in a tightly contested Division.

The Cups this year provided only marginally less distraction than usual. In the League Cup, it took extra-time in a Filbert Street replay to separate City and Portsmouth, and Graham Taylor's Lincoln stretched the home team, too, before Burnley administered a Turf Moor knockout. A Chris Garland hat-trick saw off Sheffield United in the Third Round of the FA Cup, and Bob Lee's strike eliminated lowly Bury, but Manchester United shaded a 2-1 win in front of a Filbert Street full house. Gerry Daly claimed United's opener, but City were left smarting over two disallowed 'goals' at crucial stages of the tie.

Frustration, however, was becoming something of a permanent state of mind at Leicester City: there was still no real sign of Bloomfield's side realising their much-vaunted potential.

OGs AND GKs

> Much of the incidental drama of season 1975/6 seemed to have been saved for the month of March. On the 13th, a Stuart Boam own goal gave City a 1-0 win at Ayresome Park. A week later, Aston Villa's Chris Nicholl scored all four goals in a 2-2 draw at Filbert Street. Then, a week after that, Mark Wallington suffered a bad ankle injury in trying to prevent the goal that gave Wolves a 2-1 lead, and while Keith Weller and Brian Alderson in turn assumed the green jersey, Frank Worthington claimed an unlikely but deserved equaliser to bring a useful point back from Molineux. Also during March, Graham Cross notched up his 600th senior game while on loan to Chesterfield.

Below: Radical rebuilding now forcibly rose to the top of the agenda, but at least it would take place at Filbert Street. In March 1977, development plans for the Beaumont Leys area of Leicester had been published, and included speculative proposals for a 35,000-capacity, all-seater stadium, complete with synthetic pitch. The City board, however, soon firmly resolved not to consider a move.

1976-77

> The only summer additions to the City roster this year were new directors Bill Page and Colin McLeod, while their colleague Len Shipman was awarded the CBE in the Queen's birthday honours list. Jimmy Bloomfield seemed content to persevere with his existing squad and look, eventually, to some of the youthful talent at the club for new blood. A squad of City youngsters (including future first-teamers Tommy Williams, Winston White and Dean Smith) in fact represented the club at Wembley in August, playing in the final of the Pontins Six-A-Side tournament before the Charity Shield game, but losing out to Arsenal.

Their seniors made a sluggish start when the season proper began a week later, with six successive draws. In the last of these, at home to QPR, Dennis Rofe claimed his side's fourth goal of the campaign by floating a free-kick from his own half over an embarrassed Phil Parkes. In September, Frank Worthington publicly criticised the team's style of play, and was fined a week's wages. Discontent was again rife, and a voluble 'Bloomfield Out' campaign flourished among some sections of the crowd, gaining in intensity when strikers Lee and Garland were both allowed to move, despite the team's low scoring rate.

An air of unreality held sway for a while. After 13 games, City were fifth in the table, yet had only scored 13 goals. From this nominal high-point, a slide was ensured by characteristic inconsistency. Even a hitherto solid defence occasionally crumbled, as when Birmingham exploited their speed over a frozen Filbert Street pitch to register a 2-6 defeat on City (replete with another Kenny Burns hat-trick), and when Brian Kidd, once so nearly a City player, plundered four of Manchester City's five goals without reply at Maine Road.

Yet even with only one victory accruing from the final ten games, City still somehow managed to finish the term in eleventh place. In itself, this would be a pointer to a reasonable season, but sights had definitely been set higher, on European qualification at least; and the abiding spectre of City being comprehensively taken apart by West Brom at home was one that haunted the under-pressure manager as he looked back over a year that had also featured two first-hurdle Cup exits. Barely a week after the action stopped, Bloomfield resigned.

Yo-Yo Years

> The board took a gamble on the Old Boy network in appointing Bloomfield's successor. Frank McLintock, the former City favourite who had just completed his splendid playing career, was deemed the man to lift the club's fortunes; and the new boss's first additions to the staff (former QPR team-mate Eddie Kelly bolstering the midfield complement, and the experienced Ian MacFarlane returning to Filbert Street as coach) gave rise to renewed optimism.

High hopes soon, however, lay in ruins. Three unbeaten League games had been negotiated when City tamely surrendered to Portsmouth in the League Cup, and then confidence and coherence utterly collapsed as McLintock set about a haphazard new-broom approach to restructuring his team. Thrust into the side in successive weeks were new signings Lammie Robertson, Alan Waddle, George Armstrong, David Webb and Geoff Salmons (plus youngster Tommy Williams), but none could effect a turnaround in City's rock-bottom form, which saw them lodged firmly in the relegation slot from October onwards. None did much for the fans' morale, either, which was hit as much by the departure of folk hero Frank Worthington as by a series of disastrous results. There were few smiles even when McLintock idly threatened to re-register himself as a player to bolster his spiritless squad.

December saw another transfer flurry as McLintock became desperate. While City could not match the wage demands of Liverpool's David Johnson, the board backed McLintock in gambling the club's record outlay of £250,000 on former Derby star Roger Davies, returning to English football from Bruges. Within weeks Davies would have a new

Right: The Frank McLintock era was eagerly anticipated in the summer of 1977 but soon proved to be a disaster for the club, culminating in relegation the following year.

partner in Billy Hughes, bought directly from the Baseball Ground. Almost all the new faces at Filbert Street were forwards or attacking midfielders, but City goals were by now like gold dust: precisely 11 having been registered in 23 games by the turn of the year.

The FA Cup brought no relief from the pervading misery. A win at Hull only set up City for further humiliation at Third Division Walsall, where the veteran Alun Evans once more delivered the KO punch. Soon, relegation was a certainty in all but mathematical terms, and when that particular statistical guarantee was fulfilled, all that was left for City fans to do was bet on precisely how many of the club's all-time 'worst' records would fall by season's end.

They would have found few willing to take odds on McLintock's contract being renewed. By 5th April, the board's inevitable decision was made known to the manager, who had incurred their displeasure throughout his tenure for his refusal to move his home base from London (where he had business interests) to Leicester, and McLintock made his exit early, with MacFarlane assuming caretaker duties for the campaign's finale.

A last-game home victory over relegation companions Newcastle, by 3-0, saw City to a total of 26 in the 'goals for' column – a record low for a 42-game First Division season that would stand until Stoke City's even more shot-shy strugglers contrived a 24-goal haul during 1984/5. The same game also saw Davies and Salmons climb to the top of the City scoring charts – with four apiece! Club records to fall in this dire term included those for least wins (5), most defeats (25), most home defeats (10) and lowest points tally (22). Even Steve Whitworth's (then) record run of consecutive appearances came to end on number 198 during the season.

And as if First Division rivalry hadn't already proved overwhelming to City, there was now even a renewed home-town challenge to the club's hold on its support: for the Tigers' exploits with the oval ball had this year taken them to their first Twickenham Cup Final.

> City were now potentially a club in severe crisis. Rudderless, there was every chance they would find the Second Division seas as rocky as those of the First. Confidence in (or even amongst) their playing resources was in short supply. There was little spare cash available (and a fair amount had to be expended this summer on the stadium, to meet the new requirements of the Safety of Sports Grounds Act). The club's future literally hung on the board's ability to act decisively to stop the rot.

The decisive act in fact shocked the football world; for City somehow prised away from Ibrox one of the most successful managers of the decade: Jock Wallace. This formidable, charismatic figure – a disciplinarian and fitness fanatic – immediately stamped his inspirational mark on Filbert Street, instituting new training regimes, clearing out both the

Below: Ex Rangers boss Jock Wallace rebuilt the team, with a vigorous fitness campaign and a policy of giving youth its head.

backroom and playing staffs, embarking on an ambitious youth policy and, crucially, forging a warm, rousing rapport with the supporters.

Wallace's first season was always going to be one of struggle; but at least it was one that could now be faced with spirit under his motivational management. Bold team selections marked the campaign's early weeks: young John O'Neill made an opening day debut at centre-back as City (in borrowed yellow shorts) battled to a draw at Turf Moor. More juniors stepped up as the makeshift side contrived to keep its feet out of the relegation mire, supplemented by low-cost buys Martin Henderson, John Ridley and Bobby Smith.

The latter arrived from Hibernian over Christmas, and lined up on New Year's Day against Oldham alongside two other debutants: David

Above: Gary Lineker celebrated the New Year in 1979 with a Leicester debut against Oldham.

Buchanan and Gary Lineker. While Smith and 16-year-old Buchanan claimed the winning goals and took the plaudits, the rather overawed Lineker retreated to the reserves: his impact would be made (and sustained) in years to come.

Wallace's winning penchant for the unpredictable was now ready to be exposed to a wider audience. On a day when only three Third Round FA Cup ties went ahead, City's hot-air pitch cover allowed them to face First Division Norwich in front of the TV cameras, and the 3-0 success was marked equally by an individualist goal from Keith Weller (resplendent in white tights) and an incredibly mature midfield display from yet another teenage apprentice, Andy Peake.

Such was the whirl of movement and incident at Leicester, however, that by the time the much-postponed Fourth Round tie at Oldham was played (and lost, to an Alan Young hat-trick), Weller was playing in America, Peake was on England Youth duty, and the Latics' programme contained pen pictures for no less than twelve departed City players. Even the hitherto reliable polysphere had collapsed under heavy overnight snow, causing the postponement of an interim home fixture with Fulham.

The odd whiff of danger still attended some of City's remaining League fixtures as the inconsistencies of inexperience occasionally told, but this really was a season in which a final placing of 17th in Division Two could legitimately be regarded as a triumph. Further individual baptisms had brought mixed results (Neil Grewcock became another 16-year-old debut goalscorer; Lineker hit his first strike to win important points at Notts County; poor Everton Carr was sent off, and Alan Lee attacked on the pitch, during a farcical final game at Bramall Lane that also saw relegated Sheffield United awarded two ludicrous penalties). But there was no denying that City had been genuinely rejuvenated.

Though long service to the club, too, still brought reward. Back at the start of the campaign, director Sid Needham (awarded an OBE the year previously) joined his colleague Len Shipman as one of only six Life Members of the FA in the country; while in mid-term another senior boardroom figure, Tom Bloor, retired to become the first-ever Life Member of the club itself. Steve Whitworth moved on in March, part-way through his well-earned testimonial year, but he would nevertheless be allowed to stage a game (against Coventry) the following autumn. Finally, another ten-year club servant, secretary John Smith, took up an executive appointment at Luton, and was replaced by Alan Bennett.

> The all-change ambience at Filbert Street remained as City prepared to face their second campaign in the lower Division. Top scorer Trevor Christie was allowed to move on as City made their first signing under the new Freedom of Contract arrangement for players: capturing last February's Cup scourge Alan Young for a record-equalling, tribunal-set fee of £250,000 after he had declined to re-sign for Oldham.

Other newcomers were defender Gregor Stevens and midfielders Ian Wilson and Pat Byrne; and all four made their bow as City commenced their season early, in First Round League Cup combat with Rotherham. Defeat home and away against Third Division opposition hardly augured well for the League campaign to follow, but it didn't take long for the side to hit its stride. They were Divisional leaders when the initial League tables were published, after playing superbly to win 4-1 at Loftus Road, and thereafter never slipped below sixth position in a tight promotion race.

Young hit a useful early scoring seam, the hapless Stevens was quickly jettisoned, and valuable goals began coming from unexpected quarters (Dennis Rofe claiming two scorchers at Swansea; the returning Lineker shattering Sunderland with sheer pace; and young Derek Strickland starting Wrexham's downfall in his first full game). Indeed, City scored in every game up until their 0-2 defeat at The Valley in mid-December (only their second setback away from home).

Below: Skipper Mark Wallington leads the City team on a lap of honour to display the Second Division Championship trophy.

Handily placed as the New Year dawned, however, City were about to receive a blow that could have shattered their young side's confidence had Wallace ever allowed heads to drop. For a hiding-to-nothing FA Cup draw against Isthmian League outsiders Harlow Town turned utterly nightmarish, with a late Filbert Street equaliser earning the 'minnows' another shot at giant-killing glory, and accountant John Mackenzie enjoying his fifteen minutes of fame with the only goal of the replay at the tiny Hammarskjold Road Sportcentre. It was the first time since 1914/15 that Leicester had fallen to non-League opposition in the Cup.

It therefore spoke volumes about City's character and resilience that, three games later, a 1-0 home win over Newcastle put them back on top of Division Two. Jitters did set in subsequently, as Chelsea, Sunderland and Birmingham joined the promotion fight in earnest; and captain Dennis Rofe actually moved to Chelsea, citing his belief that they were better bets to go up. Geoff Scott, from Stoke, assumed the No 3 shirt, and young winger Paul Edmunds made crucial contributions as City got back on course.

City held Sunderland at Roker, hiccupped badly at home to Preston, but then won each of the crunch home games against Chelsea and Birmingham. A foul on Edmunds at Wrexham left him with a broken wrist and ended his season, but from the free kick Eddie Kelly blasted the invaluable winner. Two games later, after a tense 2-1 home win over Charlton, City were

all but assured of promotion, with Chelsea needing to make up a goal difference of eight to pip them. The mathematics proved irrelevant, however, when Larry May's goal secured a final-day win at Brisbane Road: with Sunderland dropping a point on the same day, City were Champions once more.

John O'Neill, the supporters' Player of the Season, was capped for the first time by Northern Ireland during the campaign; but experienced Eddie Kelly, who had assumed the captaincy on Rofe's departure and had done much to steady the side, was rewarded only with a free transfer at the end of the term. Sadness had tinged the final month of the promotion push, with City mourning the death of chief scout Ray Shaw; while boardroom changes earlier had seen the recruitment of new directors Bill Shooter and Tom Smeaton, and the shift to Life Member status of long-serving former club chairmen Len Shipman, Sid Needham and Alf Pallett.

Work had been put in hand to build a new, stylish function room at Filbert Street, to be known as the Belvoir Suite, for City's more well-heeled clientele; but the vast majority of the supporters were wondering if Jock Wallace's young side, promoted earlier than anticipated, could survive their elevation in any style at all.

Left: Within two seasons, Jock Wallace's young team had won the Second Division title. Central defender Larry May almost qualified as a veteran in the line up.

> Characteristically, Jock Wallace stated his ambition for the new season to be the capture of the First Division title. Characteristically, his only close-season capture was a player of youthful promise rather than profound experience; though it did take another record-equalling £250,000 to bring Partick Thistle striker Jim Melrose to Leicester. And, characteristically, Wallace threw into the deep end of the opening fixture yet another untried junior, left-back Billy Gibson.

City disappointed in their opening defeats by Ipswich and Everton, but showed just what they were capable of with a fine 2-0 win over Liverpool, cued by a spectacular long-range strike from Andy Peake. An Elland Road victory followed, but soon the 'goals against' column was bulging, with successive 0-5 reverses at Manchester United and Nottingham Forest pointing to a campaign of scrabbling at the wrong end of the table.

Introducing more youngsters like Stewart Hamill, Kevin MacDonald and Paul Friar, and confident that the conveyor belt of cost-free talent would continue to roll in the charge of recent appointee Dave Richardson, Wallace could take sporadic encouragement from City's performances against the 'bigger' clubs, but time was running out before his side could cohere around one style or system. Melrose finally hit the mark for the first time in a win at St Andrews in December; the cocky MacDonald stepped up calmly to slot home the winning spot-kick against Middlesbrough in his first full game at Filbert Street. Four early Southampton goals put paid to City at The Dell, but the fact City had 'drawn' the second half led Wallace half-seriously to propose an alteration to the points system!

Another Cup embarrassment, at Exeter, where Tony Kellow's hat-trick did the damage in a Fourth Round replay, could once more have been the prelude to collapse: in typically paradoxical fashion, it actually inspired City to complete the double over Liverpool with a 2-1 win at Anfield on the following Saturday – the Reds' first home defeat in 85 games. Manchester United, Spurs (further double victims) and Arsenal all fell to a semi-revived City – bolstered by February purchase Steve Lynex on the right wing – but the club's hopes of saving themselves disappeared in a tempestuous match at Brighton on Easter Monday. Kevin MacDonald's header gave City the lead, but both he and Alan Young were sent off before Brighton turned the tables.

Two wins after this were of no real value to City, though Melrose's carefree hat-trick at Norwich helped send the Canaries down as well. Paul Ramsey and Norman Leet were both given a place in the starting line-up for this game, but the biggest headlines of the second half of City's season had revolved around one player with a rather larger reputation than either of these could realistically aspire to.

In February, Wallace had decided to gamble for high stakes, opening negotiations to try to secure the services of Johan Cruyff, then 33 but formerly the world's top-rated individual player. By 24th February, Wallace had agreed terms for Cruyff to be paid on a match-by-match basis until the end of the season, giving the Dutchman between £4,000 and £5,000 per game, which Wallace was certain could be recouped from the bumper crowds he would attract. Then came a telephone call from Cruyff's agent with the news that Spanish club Levanthe had decided to 'exercise their option' on the player. It was claimed that the Spaniards were offering a deal involving Cruyff pocketing 50% of the gate receipts for each match. By 26th February, the deal with Leicester had emphatically fallen through. Some cynics claimed the whole affair had been a publicity gimmick in the first place, but Wallace had indeed been sincere in attempting to lure the best talent available to aid his youngsters in their relegation battle.

City certainly needed to maintain their crowd-pulling traditions somehow, for the ups and downs of the Wallace management period – and especially the lack of knock-out success – were set in contrast to the remarkable run being enjoyed by the club's Welford Road near-neighbours. This year the Tigers returned from Twickenham for the fourth successive season, with a hat-trick of John Player Cup wins behind them, and it was not hard to envisage a subtle shift in the interests of the Leicester sporting public if City continued to fail to come up with the goods.

Above: Mark Wallington, who registered more ever-present seasons than any other City player.

Below: The popular Jim Melrose in action against West Brom in January 1981.

> This summer there were no major signings. Wallace had decided that the year's top-flight experience gained by most of his charges would stand them in good stead for an immediate return, and he also stuck by his choice of goalkeeper Mark Wallington as captain. His opening line-up was, however, notable for the inclusion of Gary Lineker in place of the injured Alan Young. Hitherto very much a fringe player in Wallace's squads, Lineker would emerge this term as both a regular senior performer and leading goalscorer – a process he initiated with City's opening goal in the draw at Grimsby.

The capriciousness of football fate was never better illustrated, though, than by that befalling Stewart Hamill, who claimed the winning goal in each of City's next two games, and never returned to first-team action again with Leicester. Each of these single-goal home wins was now worth three points; the Football League having introduced this amendment to encourage attacking play and to maintain interest in the season for more teams for a greater length of time.

In City's case, promotion-oriented interest was indeed maintained until very late in the campaign. Early season form was unspectacular, and neither the arrival of comparative veteran Keith Robson nor that on loan of Southampton's Trevor Hebberd did much to imbue the side with consistency. The return of Eddie Kelly was a more significant spark to improvement, but City had left themselves a lot to do if they were seriously to challenge the sides above them by the end of the year.

They had already ceded points to many of their rivals (notably experiencing an initial pointless return from QPR's new artificial pitch at Loftus Road), but revived strongly in February, March and April; by which time they had games in hand and a decent rhythm. Indeed, despite the odd setback, City were still in with a shout as, with three games to play, they faced two apparent home bankers against Grimsby and Shrewsbury. Nervily scrambling only a single point off this pair meant that City had frittered away a genuine opportunity, though an eventual placing of eighth rather diguises just how frustratingly close they had come to an immediate return 'upstairs'.

Frustration was in fact the entire season's keynote, for the Cups brought their share, too. In the League Cup, City actually got past the first hurdle for the first time since 1975, only to go down away to Aston Villa in a Third Round replay. In the FA Cup, however, City put together a fine, exciting run; starting with a 3-1 demolition of First Division Southampton, and gathering pace with competent victories over Hereford and Watford, to set up a Filbert Street quarter-final clash with Shrewsbury.

CUP DRAMA

> When Larry May headed City into an early lead (right) in the FA Cup Sixth Round tie against Shrewsbury, there was little sign of the drama that was about to unfold...

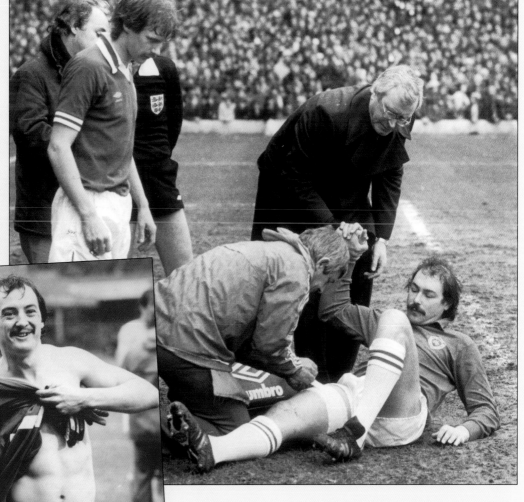

... Mark Wallington's injury (above) not only brought to an end his record run of 331 consecutive appearances but led to City eventually using three goalkeepers during the game, with Alan Young (above left) and Steve Lynex (left) taking their turn between the sticks before City won dramatically by 5-2. Young took over from the injured Wallington before himself being replaced by the diminutive Lynex, and then later returned for a second spell between the posts.

Unexpectedly, this all-Second Division encounter turned out to be a story-book affair, complete with tortuous plot, heroes and villains. Larry May gave City an early lead, then Mark Wallington was badly injured in a clash with Town's Chic Bates. The severely hampered goalkeeper was powerless to prevent the visitors equalising then taking the lead and, as he inevitably limped out of the game, fate seemed to have struck City a cruel blow. But fate produced another twist on the stroke of half-time, this time in the shape of a bizarre Shrewsbury own goal to level things up. By the time the second period started, the crowd were frantic and the City team inspired. It mattered little that three goalkeepers were eventually used: stand-in Alan Young was himself injured in another clash with Bates, and Steve Lynex took over the green jersey for a spell before Young's head had cleared sufficiently for him to return. City simply swept the Shrews aside on a rush of adrenalin and passion, with substitute Jim Melrose netting twice and Gary Lineker once to clinch a 5-2 victory, and a place in another Villa Park semi-final, this time against Cup-holders Tottenham Hotspur.

This time, though, there was no fairy-tale ending for City. Ossie Ardiles helped prompt Spurs forward on his last appearance for the club for some time, only the day after the Falklands/Malvinas conflict had erupted, and Garth Crooks' opening strike in the second half was followed by a double dose of tragedy for City, with Tommy Williams breaking his leg and Ian Wilson conceding an own goal. The better team on the day had won the Wembley passage, but there was much post-match criticism of Jock Wallace's decision to play Alan Young from the start of the game and leave the in-form Melrose on the bench.

Wallington had recovered in time for the semi-final disappointment, but the injury he'd received in the previous round at last broke his club record sequence of consecutive appearances on the 331 mark, allowing young Nicky Walker a six-game run in his stead.

As the season ended, the City board first celebrated director Bill Page's new status as Lord Mayor of Leicester, but then were soon pitched into acrimony. For manager Wallace abruptly resigned to take up a similar post with Motherwell. From the outside it looked a simple case of City's 'so near, so far away' season disheartening their boss. But initially the directors refused to accept Wallace's resignation, accusing the Scottish club of poaching. Eventually, they had little option but to allow him to leave, but vigorously pursued their claims for compensation from Motherwell for enticing him to break his contract, while themselves searching for a successor.

> The search ended in August with the appointment of Gordon Milne from Coventry, a man who appeared the temperamental antithesis of Wallace, but who had developed a shrewd business sense at Highfield Road while keeping his charges in the top flight against the odds.

On surveying the Filbert Street scene, Milne immediately prioritised a drastic pruning of the playing staff at all levels. One player he would not dispose of, though, was newcomer Alan Smith. The tall Brummie had been signed from Alvechurch by acting manager Ian MacFarlane during the summer, and would soon forge a powerful striking partnership with Lineker.

Milne also had his own ideas about the playing style he wanted his team to adopt, and soon released MacFarlane, replacing him with Gerry Summers as coach. City responded, in the early weeks of the season, with characteristic inconsistency, and Milne's acceptance by a wary Leicester public was not aided by his decision to exchange the popular Jim Melrose for his former Coventry striker Tom English. The manager was confident of pulling off another deal in September, but the prevarication of Ipswich's Mick

Below: City celebrate with the fans after the vital win at Craven Cottage in April 1983 that was the catalyst for Fulham being overhauled in the promotion race.

Mills led to City withdrawing their offer, and the player went to Southampton instead.

Certainly, there were few early omens that this might be another promotion-chasing campaign. Three of the opening four home fixtures were lost (though the exception saw both Lynex and Lineker claim hat-tricks against Carlisle), while a fine burst of winning League form in October (with Lineker bagging another treble at Derby) was bracketed by defeat in both legs of the League Cup (Milk Cup) tie against little Lincoln.

By the time the FA Cup came round, City were comfortably placed in the top half of the table, but the leading trio of QPR, Wolves and Fulham were beginning to pull well away from the pack. Third Round home defeat by Notts County, who took an authoritative three-goal lead before City pulled two

Above: Robbie Jones runs to celebrate his debut goal with Kevin MacDonald in the win at Oldham in May that kept City in third place.

back in injury time as flattering consolation, seemed to signal the end of City's glory-hunting for at least another year.

But an unlikely turning point was reached in February, initially marked by the arrival of cultured midfielder Gerry Daly, on loan from Coventry for the remainder of the season. It is a classic case of the benefit of hindsight to point to a routine home win over Shrewsbury as the moment City's climb took off in earnest: the match itself attracted only 6,155 spectators; the lowest home League gate since the war. But a 5-0 walloping of high-flying Wolves followed, and with confidence growing, City were embarked on a lengthy unbeaten run.

As City continued to make ground on the top three, so Fulham began to falter. The points gap closed inexorably until the vital head-to-head encounter came at Craven Cottage on 23rd April. Ian Wilson's goal clinched the points in a tension-filled atmosphere, and the balance looked to have been tipped in City's favour.

Still, however, it was neck and neck between the two clubs for the third promotion spot and, when it came to the final game of the season, City entertained an already

SPORTS FINAL EDITION

Leicester Mercury

SATURDAY, MAY 14, 1983   Twelve Pence

Today's results check

CONGRATULATIONS

No goals—but City clinch promotion

by Bill Anderson

No goals but glory for Leicester City at Filbert Street this afternoon. The 0-0 draw against Burnley was enough to bring the return of First Division football.

The tension in the closing minutes was eased by the news from Derby and as soon as the final whistle went, the City fans in the 29,000 crowd were celebrating.

It was by no means classic action — not surprising under the circumstances — and there were some anxious moments for City in the first half. But they over-

CITY 0, BURNLEY 0

O'Neill put them in trouble. Ramsey cleared the danger. There was another anxious moment when Donovan got his head to a Young on Phelan as the visitors looked every bit as promising as the home side.

Half-time: City 0, Burn-ley 0.

155

relegation-doomed Burnley knowing a win would secure promotion, whilst Fulham travelled to Derby hoping to take advantage of any City slip.

On the day City could only manage a goalless draw. It was their 15th unbeaten game since February, but the supporters would have an anxious wait to find out whether it was to be enough. For there was drama indeed at the Baseball Ground where, late in the game, the crowd had literally spilled over the running track and encroached over the touchlines. Conditions were clearly difficult and an incident involving a spectator and a Fulham player eventually led to the game being abandoned some 75 seconds before the 90 minute mark, with Fulham trailing 0-1.

The Football League held an enquiry, and City had a few worrying days before learning their fate. The League finally decided that the Derby-Fulham result should stand, and it was Malcolm Macdonald, the Fulham manager, who was the first to telephone Filbert Street to congratulate City on their promotion – a fine gesture in the midst of his own disappointment.

Several individual landmarks peppered a campaign that was latterly notable for a remarkable degree of systematic teamwork. Mark Wallington, back to ever-present status, took a testimonial game against Nottingham Forest in October; Gary Lineker broke the twenty-goal barrier for the first time to close with 26 League counters; Kevin MacDonald illustrated his confident versatility by filling in superbly at centre-back while Larry May was sidelined for much of the run-in; and young Robbie Jones came through his baptism of fire in the penultimate game at Oldham with the vital opening goal to his credit. One record set this term, however, was far from a source of pride: no less than five City players were sent off in its course.

Other significant developments during the season included the first-time sponsorship of the youth team, whose shirts now bore the brand-name legend of 'Fresha' on behalf of local bakery Squires & Kintons; and the February appointment of the club's first-ever Vice President, Trevor Bennett; a local businessman who had, over the years, been a benefactor of both the Football Club and the County Cricket Club, where he would shortly take up a similar post.

There was, however, a further spectre at the promotion feast. The manner of City's challenge, coming from behind on the last lap, had led to significantly less spectator interest than usual being generated, and the club actually showed a loss of over £300,000 on the season. All of Milne's business acumen, as well as his footballing brain, would be required to keep City in Division One this time.

Above: The new green and gold away kit, worn here by Gary Lineker, was popular with neither players nor fans.

Above: Peter Eastoe arrived on loan in October 1983, and would return in the same capacity a year later.

> The summer of 1983 proved to be quite hectic in terms of Filbert Street comings and goings. George Dewis finally retired from his backroom duties at the age of 70; former player Alan Birchenall returned as Public Relations Officer; two more Vice Presidents arrived in Martin George and John Elsom; and Gordon Milne's transfer dealings landed West Brom keeper Mark Grew and Barnsley midfielder Ian Banks. Surprisingly, however, there was no contract deal for Gerry Daly, and Larry May was another to depart.

Sponsorship also made its mark during the summer. The Football League became the Canon League, and City adopted a new strip incorporating the name of brewers Ind Coope. The new look was further enhanced by the change of the club badge, with a copyrighted running fox logo replacing the former fox head and crossed riding crops design.

By kick-off day, Mark Wallington was still in contractual dispute, so Grew was given an early opportunity. He was also given plenty of practice, as the team patently failed to come to terms with the demands of top-level football. Old-boy Trevor Christie snatched a hat-trick against City in the opener (after Notts County debutant Martin O'Neill had put his side ahead with a 30-yard free-kick), and six successive defeats represented the club's worst-ever start to a season, labelling them early as relegation favourites.

Against this backdrop, the club was a hive of activity. An attempt to take Liverpool's Phil Thompson on loan failed, as did lengthy negotiations for another former England defender, Dave Watson, newly returned from Vancouver Whitecaps. The National Westminster Bank submitted a demand that the club reduce its £800,000 overdraft, further thwarting Milne's team-strengthening ambitions, and leading to Martin George becoming a club director. Additionally, crowd trouble at the game with Tottenham confirmed the need to fence the main stand enclosure, again diverting slender financial resources.

City's first point came from a 2-2 home draw with Stoke on 24th September (a painful experience for Alan Smith, who had to retrieve three teeth from the pitch after they'd been kicked out), but their first League win was delayed until 29th October, when Everton were the visitors. In the interim, Bob Hazell had been signed to bolster the central defence, Peter Eastoe had come on loan to find his debut game against Southampton abandoned during a torrential downpour, and City had departed the League Cup following a penalty shoot-out at Chelsea. Two goals down from the home leg of this tie, City really regained their pride and their shape in the 2-0

fightback at Stamford Bridge (the only game they would 'win' all season in their apparently jinxed new change colours of green and gold).

Form definitely picked up after this, though luck was still against City. When Manchester United visited in November, Lynex was the player to lose a tooth, but more seriously Eastoe broke his jaw, and would be out of action for months (with City committed to paying his wages until he was fit enough to conclude his loan period). City had their first taste of Sunday football during December, at Nottingham Forest and Sunderland; and during the same month saw Smith collect his first hat-trick (against Wolves), and a last-minute Wallington penalty-save secure a point from Anfield.

There was now genuine substance to City's survival battle, and eventually relegation was formally avoided when Forest were beaten 2-1 at Filbert Street in May, with two games to spare. Home defeat by Sunderland in the final fixture kept the Wearsiders up too, and saw City finish in 15th place. A cumulative 50-goal haul from the striking trio of Lineker, Smith and Lynex was effectively City's salvation; the consistently prolific Lineker earned his first England call-up for a substitute appearance against Scotland, while young midfielder Paul Ramsey finished the season with three Irish caps to his name.

Above: Atrocious conditions during the last game to be abandoned at Filbert Street, against Southampton in October 1983.

> The prelude to the club's Centenary season, in which Milne would hope to consolidate City's top-flight acclimatisation, was unfortunately the arrival of bad news: one of Leicester's finest servants, Arthur Chandler, passed away in hospital during the summer.

In June, the boardroom complement was strengthened by the elevation of John Elsom to director level, and backstage changes would continue throughout the campaign, with Trevor Bennett becoming the club's first post-war President in October, and Ken Brigstock being appointed Vice President in March.

The regular pre-season friendly fare, in which former Port Vale striker Mark Bright got to know his new colleagues, and Ian Wilson received his marching orders during a 2-2 draw at Ibrox, this year culminated in City's Centenary match. Aberdeen provided the tough Filbert Street opposition, drawing 1-1, but as much interest was generated by the pre-match entertainment, featuring a game between ex-City players of earlier eras, and the return to Leicester of numerous old favourites.

Competitive action brought the now customary stuttering start. Consistency was as elusive a quality as ever, as successive League games in October demonstrated: City crashed 0-5 at Hillsborough, then at home blasted Aston Villa 5-0. The month before, a single game, against Brentford in the League Cup, had also illustrated City's 'Jekyll & Hyde' act: two goals down with only nine minutes remaining, they contrived a blistering four-goal revival. A Third Round exit at Luton awaited, however.

This maddening mixture of the superb and the

Right: Leicester City Football Club celebrated its Centenary in 1984, with a pre-season challenge match against Aberdeen. Skipper Kevin MacDonald exchanges pennants with Willie Miller prior to kick-off.

Above: Ian Banks scores the second of City's four goals in the final nine minutes to overcome Brentford 4-2 in the League Cup tie at Filbert Street.

diabolical continued throughout the League calendar. City plundered four-goal returns from both North-Eastern citadels, Roker and St James', and hit Coventry for five on the occasion of the first Sunday game at Filbert Street (when David Rennie notched the club's 5,000th League goal). They managed another shock win at Anfield, but many of their other matches were best quietly forgotten, as they ended up in 15th place once more.

The FA Cup this year prompted sensational headlines of the wrong sort. In the Third Round, City were drawn away to Burton Albion, of the Northern Premier League, and the tie was switched to Derby's Baseball Ground. City skated home by 6-1, but an incident occurred when the scores were level which eventually nullified the victory. With hundreds of Derby 'supporters' in the crowd already having clashed with their equally troublesome Leicester counterparts, a missile had been thrown from behind the Burton goal and had struck keeper Paul Evans on the head, temporarily stunning him. An FA enquiry into the incident ruled that the game should be replayed behind closed doors.

Originally scheduled again for Derby, the re-match was in fact switched to Coventry because of pitch conditions, and City duly won through by a single Ramsey goal, greeted with eerie silence from the virtually empty stands and terraces. Carlisle were ousted from the competition in the next round, but on a freezing winter night at The Den when City's finishing went badly awry, Third Division Millwall ended any thoughts of a Wembley march.

Above: David Rennie, scorer of City's 5,000th League goal.

The season had also seen skipper Kevin MacDonald's transfer to Liverpool in November bring in a club record fee of £400,000; the emergence of Ian Andrews as goalkeeping successor to Mark Wallington (who would move to Derby in July); and the introduction of a partial Membership scheme for home supporters at Filbert Street, with the Main Stand being redesignated the Members' Stand in January.

Lineker, Smith and Lynex had combined to produce 59 goals this time; and Lineker's first full England game, against the Republic of Ireland in March, brought him his first international goal. New striker Bright had made little impact at senior level, but with the reserves he claimed 28 goals in only 27 appearances, as they romped away with the Second Division championship of the Central League in their first season in the competition, having switched from the Football Combination at Milne's insistence.

However, events elsewhere as the season closed left a cloud hanging over the whole of English football. The Valley Parade fire and the Heysel Stadium disaster, with their attendant heavy death tolls, scarred the game's image badly, and caused City's Centenary campaign to end on the most sombre of notes.

> A busy summer in the transfer market was dominated by one deal. Gary Lineker's contract was at an end, and in June he signed for Champions Everton. The fee was set by an independent tribunal at a club record of £800,000, plus a share of any future profits should the player be resold within two years. City had made Lineker a generous offer, but he felt the need to join a 'glamour' club if he was significantly to further his career. He had become only the sixth City player to complete a century of goals, and would clearly be a hard man to replace.

Mark Wallington and Andy Peake also departed during the close season, whilst new signings came in the shape of Ipswich defender Russell Osman and Motherwell midfielders Ali Mauchlen and Gary McAllister. Milne's dealings had brought an income in excess of £1.3 million in recent months, compared to an expenditure in the region of £0.5 million. The books were being balanced and the overdraft cut, but would the team be up to the task in hand, especially without its talismanic striker?

The fates conspired to send Everton to Filbert Street on the opening day of the season. Mark Bright assumed Lineker's position, then assured himself of the headlines as he netted twice in a 3-1 win over the Champions. This result soon, however, proved a false augury, for only one of the next 13 games ended in victory. A 0-5 hiding from divisional newcomers Oxford United was the low point of this sequence; a double dismissal of Ian Wilson and Chelsea's David Speedie at Filbert Street a marginal distraction; and there developed a groundswell of public disquiet over Milne's management. In October, only 7,237 turned up to see City struggle to salvage a 2-2 draw with West Brom. It was bottom club Albion's first away point of the season, and City's lowest post-war First Division gate.

Tony Sealy was by now augmenting the forward line, and young Simon Morgan had grasped the left-back slot, while Milne cast his net abroad for reinforcements. Danish forward Tommy Christensen arrived briefly on loan, then former England winger Laurie Cunningham settled in for a lengthier and rather more effective loan stint, albeit one bedevilled by injuries.

Above: Bobby Smith

Below: Ian Andrews

Below: Laurie Cunningham makes his City debut against another of his former loan clubs, Manchester United.

The League Cup brought no respite from League struggles. Derby, now languishing in Division Three, ousted City with some comfort at the first hurdle. The Filbert Street evening leg was followed by a night of rioting in the Highfields area of the city; its start being widely (but dubiously) ascribed to clashes between opposing football hooligans. City had decided that they would give a further knockout opportunity a miss – standing aloof from the inaugural term of the Full Members Cup, in which there were, in fact, only 21 entrants.

The League campaign continued to be an uphill struggle, punctuated by some excellent displays, such as a 3-0 home win over Manchester United in November and a 2-1 success at Everton, to complete a double, in December. There were, however, a rather greater number of shoddy performances, with results to match. City's FA Cup exit – humiliated by Third Division Bristol Rovers at Eastville – definitely fell into this category.

Right up until the season's final day, City looked good bets for relegation. And even the ultimate 2-0 home win over Newcastle proved to be a lifeline only because Ipswich lost at Sheffield Wednesday the same afternoon, leaving City safe in 19th place.

John O'Neill had by now taken his tally of Irish caps to 39, a record total for a City player; Alan Smith had continued to find the net regularly; and Osman, McAllister and Mauchlen had all settled reasonably well. Yet a frankly poor campaign gave few grounds for optimism.

During May the directors held discussions with Swindon manager Lou Macari over the manager's position at Filbert Street, but he rejected any overtures. Milne's position was, at best, uncertain.

> That uncertainty was compounded for a while in June when Bryan Hamilton, the former Wigan boss, joined the Filbert Street payroll to share duties with Milne. The latter was redesignated as General Manager, whilst Hamilton assumed the title of Team Manager.

Other changes were in prospect for 1986/7. Canon had withdrawn from their sponsorship of the Football League, eventually to be replaced by the Today newspaper; Ind Coope chose to display the 'John Bull' logo on City's shirts, to promote a particular brand of bitter; and the League introduced a play-off system for some promotion and relegation places, with the First Division due to be reduced to 21 clubs in 1987/8 and to 20 by 1988/9; the Second Division increasing in size accordingly.

Long-serving Tommy Williams moved on to Birmingham during the summer, but still was allowed to stage a hugely successful testimonial game in the autumn, featuring City's current side against a team of former Filbert Street favourites which included both Frank Worthington and Gary Lineker. Lineker was by now a Barcelona player: he had flourished in the media glare at Goodison, his recent World Cup exploits had made him a national hero, and City had received an unexpected windfall of £250,000 in July as their share of the deal between Everton and the Spaniards. This brought the local lad's club record fee up to £1,050,000; but had only deepened the genuine sense of loss in Leicester: how City missed his talents now.

In fact, in a make-do spirit, City got off to their best start to a First Division season for some time, finding themselves briefly in the top half of that table for the first time since 1977. Central defender Steve Walsh had joined his former boss in the summer, and Hamilton soon made a club record outlay of £300,000 on Southampton's Steve Moran in an attempt to provide support for Alan Smith. Liverpool had once more been vanquished at Filbert Street, and away wins at both QPR and Manchester City were on the board when City's season started to fall apart.

A game at Charlton was thrown away following the dismissal of Walsh, and proved to be merely the first of 17

Above: On-loan Mich D'Avray threatens the Norwich defence at Filbert Street in February 1987.

Below: Record signing Steve Moran cost £300,000 from Southampton.

successive away defeats – a dismal record which proved too great a burden for sporadic home form to offset. The Cups brought equal misery: an Anfield exit from the newly-dubbed Littlewoods Challenge Cup (League Cup), and a 2-5 thrashing on QPR's plastic in the premier competition.

By December, leading scorer Alan Smith, in the final year of his contract, had been reluctantly transfer-listed at £1 million. Chelsea were prepared to meet City's asking price, but Smith himself rejected the move. In March, though, Smith finally signed for Arsenal for £800,000, but was immediately loaned back to City until the end of the season. The same month, a below-form Steve Lynex was offloaded to West Brom; so City's once formidable striking trio were now definitively scattered.

Youngsters and loan-spell trialists came and went as City fought on, but by the time they broke their horrendous away run with a goalless draw at Oxford on the season's final day, their fate – 20th place and automatic relegation – was sealed.

Early confidence, such as had seen Andrews and Morgan called up for England Under-21 duty, had dissipated entirely, and when next the consoling representative spotlight fell on Leicester, the result was a real mixed blessing. Both McAllister and Wilson starred for Scotland in a rare 'B' international, but the injury the former received kept him out of City's final three games, when they still had a nominal chance of surviving the drop. At least Wilson went on to win full caps at season's end.

There was no way in which City's experiment with dual management could be regarded as a success; but neither was there much taste for assigning can-carrying duties to either boss on the immediate heels of the club's downfall. Gordon Milne, however, was missing day-to-day involvement with the players, and he parted company with the club in May, leaving Hamilton in sole charge of their immediate Second Division future.

> Bryan Hamilton's forays into the summer transfer market brought three experienced heads to Leicester – goalkeeper Paul Cooper from Ipswich, midfielder Gary Ford from York, and the versatile Robbie James from QPR – plus one promising young striker in Nick Cusack from Alvechurch. He had, however, apparently been able to do little to repair morale over the break, and City suffered five deeply disheartening defeats in their initial six Second Division fixtures.

Worse still, on-field discipline was at a similarly low ebb. Steve Walsh was sent off on the opening day for breaking the jaw of Shrewsbury's goalscorer, David Geddis, and would eventually be forced to miss eleven matches through suspension.

As metaphorical alarm bells sounded, Hamilton adopted a gambler's response. He snapped up Finnish international forward Jari Rantanen from IFK Gothenburg despite never having seen him in senior action, then broke the club transfer record to expend £350,000 on another central striker, Luton's Mike Newell. Prospects immediately looked brighter with three successive victories, but left-side impetus was then lost with Ian Wilson's move to Everton, and form dipped drastically again. Even the use of two substitutes, allowed for the first time in League matches, could not help Hamilton effectively juggle his resources. New club sponsors Walkers Crisps (who'd prompted predictable headlines of the 'crunch season' variety) must have wondered what they had let themselves in for as City slid down the Second Division chart.

Steve Moran moved on to Reading for £200,000 in November, ironically at the start of a record seven-game spell of scoreless performances from City. The loan system brought full-back David Langan and midfielder Kjetil Osvold briefly into the rather bleak

Above: Job advert in the *Daily Mail* in December 1987.

Right: New record signing Mike Newell joined from Luton.

Below: Gary McAllister, seen in action here at Villa Park in February, continued to display his creative skills throughout a difficult season.

picture, and then saw a sadly less than match-fit Kevin MacDonald fleetingly return.

The latter deal was sealed by coach and acting manager Peter Morris, for in early December the City board had decided to relieve Hamilton of his responsibilities. It was not long before they announced his permanent replacement, but David Pleat, the former Tottenham boss, left team matters in the hands of Morris over the Christmas period before assuming complete control.

Pleat's priority had to be a turnaround in League fortunes, for Oxford had supplied the killing blow in both major Cup competitions, and City were by now well mired amongst those scrabbling to avoid the drop to Division Three. The new manager's method was time-honoured, in the sense that it involved a rapid turnover of playing personnel, but it also hinged on a wonderfully effective tactical transformation of the side.

Out went Ford, James, Mark Venus and Kevin Jobling. In came Aberdeen winger Peter Weir, Walsall striker Nicky Cross, Grimsby utility man Phil Turner and, later, Burton Albion midfielder Paul Groves. And upwards and onwards went a City side that now also featured young left-footed striker Paul Reid on the right wing, Ali Mauchlen's battling qualities at right-back, and Paul Cooper as settled first-choice keeper. Alongside Weir, McAllister felt able to express creative skills which soon renewed covetous attention from the likes of Celtic and Spurs; while at the heart of the defence Steve Walsh was now demonstrating genuine disciplined maturity.

Pleat's new-look team performed as well as any in the Division during the second half of the season and,

1988-89

scoring in each of their final 16 games, climbed to a comfortable 13th place. Their spirit was restored, and their accurate passing game was too much for most rivals, as was seen to superb advantage when they stylishly and relaxedly eclipsed Middlesbrough in the final fixture, which the Ayresome side had needed to win to secure automatic promotion.

Sidelights on the season tended towards the ironic, and were probably only appreciated by supporters grateful to have had their faith rekindled. One involved City's eventual fate in their initial foray into the fledgling Full Members Cup (a competition they had shunned for two years, but which now carried attractive sponsorship from shoe firm Simod). For, having brushed past Huddersfield and Charlton, City were ousted by Stoke on penalties. The grim jest here was that acknowledged spot-kick stopper Paul Cooper had already pulled off one such save during the game itself, but proved unable to get in the way of any in the ensuing shootout! A further irony was that neither of the two men who had been added this term to City's roster of full internationals – James and Rantanen – figured remotely in Pleat's plans; while the one capped player who apparently did – QPR's versatile Israeli, David Pizanti – was denied a loan spell with City by the restrictive terms of his work permit.

The plans themselves, of course, centred on mounting a realistic promotion bid next time out. Up the street at Welford Road, Tigers were celebrating their installation as inaugural winners of Rugby Union's Courage Championship, while Filbert Street regulars were busy convincing themselves that City had, under Pleat, cracked a championship code of their own. Optimism was back in fashion at Leicester.

Above: The 'mighty Finn', Jari Rantanen, seen here in action against Bradford City in November 1987, did not figure in Pleat's plans.

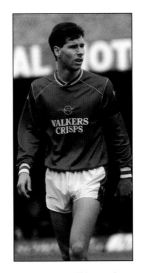

Above: Steve Wilkinson also failed to win a regular place in Pleat's line-up.

> Those justifiably eternal optimists, the bookies, shared the view that City were not to be long for the Second Division; quoting the club as second favourites for promotion (behind Chelsea) before a ball was kicked in anger. There seemed little evidence – beyond the fact that this term would see the longest-ever Second Division fixture list, involving 24 clubs – to contradict the opinion that 1988/9 would mark the end of City's fifth successive two-year spell at the lower level, following the down-up pattern of 1955-57, 1969-71, 1978-80 and 1981-83.

Certainly, the ins and outs of summer transfer dealing hardly suggested anything other than that City's resources were, overall, being augmented. The loss of the cultured and experienced Russell Osman was a blow, but appeared to be compensated for by the purchase of defenders Alan Paris, Tony Spearing and Steve Thompson. Jimmy Quinn, the previous season's overall divisional top scorer, arrived to challenge for a striker's role; while the outgoing Ian Andrews was replaced by Martin Hodge.

However the script – which involved City either finishing among the automatically-promoted top two, or at least qualifying for the Play-Offs by virtue of a placing between third and sixth — proved surprisingly difficult to follow; and City's powers of improvisation rather failed them, too. There were a few unforeseen casting blows: Thompson missing most of the pre-season build-up (and in fact soon moving on after being stuck with an understudy's role), Hodge aggravating a serious stomach injury only minutes into his debut, Quinn finding difficulty in interrupting the Cross/Newell partnership, and Peter Weir falling prey to homesickness. But it was too often an apparently collective belief on the part of City's players that they were giving charity performances which brought them some deservedly stinging reviews.

At League level they developed an unfortunate knack of taking and then surrendering a hard-won lead (no less than thirteen times!); failed utterly to put two consecutive wins together all season (a record matched only in the 1977/8 relegation term); and could not even carry over fine Littlewoods Cup form (which saw them past the respective leaders of the top two divisions, Watford and Norwich, and to honourable replay defeat against eventual winners Nottingham Forest) into League fare. In too many games, it was left to a few isolated individuals to furnish the only real competitive spirit on show; and frustrations mounted on the back of those few sporadic occasions when City's skills and Pleat's system genuinely gelled to produce a classy spectacle.

Watford took extra-time Simod Cup revenge for

their Littlewoods pasting, and a disputed penalty removed City from the FA Cup at Maine Road, so there were few distractions from the League table, which showed City always out of reach of a top-six placing after the season's mid-point. In fact, 9th position in December proved the seasonal high-water mark, after a climb from 18th, the lowest point, in October. The final placing of 15th meant that City had fetched up in the lower half of Division Two for a second successive season: a fate they hadn't known since 1951.

The only positive seasonal doubles came with the only two away wins, against relegated Birmingham and Walsall; while virtual repeats of the previous campaign's displays occurred in the home games with Swindon (a point-saving comeback from a 0-3 deficit) and Bournemouth (an utterly frustrating single-goal Boxing Day defeat). The latter club were amongst four to put the home-and-away hoodoo on City (along with Ipswich, Barnsley and Oldham), and surrender at Dean Court was accompanied by a depressing illustration of just how unfitted Pleat's current squad were to the five-man-midfield formation he'd favoured successfully at Tottenham.

Jimmy Quinn contrived to score both the winner for City against Bradford City at home, and for the Valley Paraders in the return fixture, following his transfer; while Gary McAllister persevered as penalty-taker until the last match, despite a less than 50% success rate. That said, twice as many spot-kicks were conceded throughout the term as were awarded to City.

A 4-0 trouncing of high-flying Blackburn represented the statistical high-point, while a battling 2-0 triumph over champions-to-be Chelsea was the most satisfying result, delaying their promotion celebrations and bringing to an end a 27-match unbeaten run just short of the Divisional record. As befitted a term where inconsistency was virtually institutionalised, the latter win proved to be the only three-pointer of the final eight fixtures. The date of its achievement, however, proved one that will forever be edged in black in the game's calendar: for the Hillsborough disaster that day cast a pall of gloom over the nation, and once again football's more regular dramas were put into decidedly diminished perspective.

City's travelling support paid their respects before the Watford game a week later; many of them had been similarly hushed a month earlier at Maine Road, when Manchester City youngster Paul Lake collapsed on the pitch following an accidental collision of heads, and had to receive emergency life-saving treatment after swallowing his tongue.

Above: Alan Paris became established in defence during the season.

Below: Nicky Cross fires narrowly wide during the home defeat by Ipswich in September 1988.

Throughout the season, Pleat always seemed to be on the verge of a major, morale-boosting signing, but his prey usually slipped away (as in the publicised cases of Bournemouth full-back Mark Newson and Spurs' £350,000-rated centre-back Chris Fairclough), or he was frustrated by fate (as when giant Romanian defender Gino Iorgolescu had his February trial period curtailed by early injury); and even the manager's burst of deadline dealing was cut back by the refusal of out-of-favour Paul Ramsey to agree to an exchange with Walsall's Craig Shakespeare.

Though most of the term's newcomers settled to a senior niche of sorts, only Alan Paris (in a central defensive role) made major progressive strides, while City's best bit of business in regard to new blood turned out to be the belated introduction on loan of Forest youngster Gary Charles, who showed up many of his elders in both aptitude and attitude. Non-contract trialists to flit across the Filbert Street scene were, incidentally, a cosmopolitan bunch. In addition to the aforementioned Iorgolescu, three other internationals were briefly subjects of City scrutiny: the Nigerian Emeka Nwaijobi, the Moroccan Al Fadir, and the Northern Irishman Ian Stewart.

Senior friendly fare saw City beat Trinidad and Tobago's World Cup team (replete with a substitute named Philbert Jones); while the Reserves had to mount a late run to avoid relegation from the Central League's top flight, but won the County Challenge Cup. The youth team similarly won a knock-out pot, the Midland Purity Youth League Cup, while just missing out on their League title. Prospects Ian Baraclough and Paul Kitson each represented the League's Under-18 XI in Moscow, and the latter scored in a 2-1 win against their Soviet counterparts.

> Condemned to their longest sojourn in Division Two since the immediate post-war era, City prepared for the new campaign by indulging in another of those player-exchange transfers that would have the fans up in arms. The popular Mike Newell was allowed to leave for Everton, with a cash adjustment of £600,000 plus Wayne Clarke, younger brother of one-time record signing Allan, heading down the motorway to Filbert Street. In fact, the summer was a particularly busy one in the transfer market, as David Pleat built a new team with the capture of Kevin Russell from Wrexham, Tommy Wright from Oldham, Allan Evans from Aston Villa, Rob Johnson from Luton and Tony James from Lincoln. He also secured the signature of supposed free-agent Pat Gavin, though a registration dispute with Gillingham eventually led to the young striker being loaned back to the Gills for the entire season.

Nonetheless, it was not the turnover in playing staff that dominated interest over the summer months, but the potential effects of the interim publication of the Taylor Report, commissioned after the dreadful events at Hillsborough earlier in the year. In fact, the initial impact was fairly minor at Filbert Street, with gates to be left open in the perimeter fences to provide extra safety exits, and the capacity being reduced by over 3,000 to speed up evacuation times.

The campaign opened promisingly, with Clarke registering the opening strike in a draw on Humberside, but quickly fell apart in the early months as injuries ravaged the squad. A total of 22 different players were utilised during the first seven fixtures, and results suffered as a consequence. In early September, City actually occupied bottom position in the Division, an experience that had not been endured

Above: Tony James was destined for a key role in the club's history.

Below: City and Leeds players all in a row in the November 1989 fixture at Filbert Street. Note that City 'keeper Martin Hodge is on the far left, whilst the goal is actually out of picture on the right, behind Allan Evans.

since the Fosse days of February 1915; and only one win came from the first dozen League fixtures. A single goal from on-loan Lee Glover, against Brighton, won those three points, and it was to the loan system that Pleat turned again to effect a major upturn in City's fortunes. The temporary signings of Tottenham's Paul Moran and Arsenal's raw reserve striker Kevin Campbell paid utterly unexpected inspirational dividends, and a run of six wins in seven outings at the end of the year propelled the Foxes into mid-table. A remarkable 4-3 home win over Leeds, featuring a super-sub contribution from Paul Ramsey, marked Campbell's debut; while the first game in City colours of David Oldfield, newly signed from Manchester City in part-exchange for the disappointing Clarke, was another high-scoring affair. City were poised to move within five points of a Play-Off place when they led 4-2 at St James' Park with 13 minutes remaining, but collapsed to a 4-5 defeat, with Mark McGhee scoring twice for Newcastle. Soon both loanees were back with their own clubs, excitement subsided, and City settled for mid-table security, from which vantage they had to host a Sheffield United promotion party on the season's final day.

By this time, City had used 32 players on first-team duty, a record for a peacetime campaign, whilst the goals-against column showed a total of 79 conceded, the worst for 25 years and the second-highest total in the entire League: only lowly Hartlepool United in Division Four fared worse defensively. The record would have been even more damning but for five penalty saves by Martin Hodge across the campaign, including two in the drawn March fixture at Swindon. City's last major signing of the season, David Kelly, notched his first City goal in that game, and in fact claimed seven strikes in his first

seven outings. Another plus-point was that back in November, victory at Stoke finally brought to an end a record sequence of 23 away games without a win.

In each of the Cup competitions, City suffered the ignominy of first-hurdle exits. Crystal Palace edged an aggregate victory on away goals in the League Cup after City had returned with a first leg lead from Selhurst Park; while even the luxury of the first home draw since 1983 in Round Three of the FA Cup failed to inspire anything but tame surrender to a rather ordinary Barnsley outfit. Another Selhurst visit had seen City knocked out of the Full Members (Zenith Data Systems) Cup in a fog-shrouded encounter with ground-sharing Charlton Athletic.

There were few individual highlights to record, beyond the impact made by Moran and Campbell, but Gary Mills did manage to pick up the awards for both Player of the Season, despite only totalling 28 out of a possible 50 appearances, and Goal of the Season, for a superb solo effort against Watford. International recognition came for Kelly and for Gary McAllister, who began an ultimately long and distinguished Scotland career against East Germany at Hampden in April; having previously turned down a possible £1.15 million move from City to Nottingham Forest. Paul Ramsey was rewarded for a decade of loyal service with a testimonial, and City fans were treated to the sight of former favourites Frank Worthington and Gary Lineker in tandem as the Foxes entertained Tottenham Hotspur.

The Filbert Street ground had gained a new addition early in the season, with the construction of an electronic scoreboard, sited on the roof of the East Stand; and perimeter fencing was removed from in front of the seated areas after Christmas, following final publication of the Taylor Report. The effects of this document would be much more wide-ranging in the near future, however. For while it endorsed the football authorities' stance in rejecting governmental plans for an identity-card scheme for supporters, its major conclusion was that all First and Second Division grounds must become all-seater by 1994.

This prospect was not the only matter of import exercising the City boardroom. Club President Trevor Bennett – a significant benefactor to both the Foxes and the County Cricket Club – resigned in December after the board threw out his reasoned blueprint for the restructuring of the business and its ambitions. Though he later renewed football interest with an associate director's role at Newcastle, City would henceforth miss his financial support and acumen. Another chapter in boardroom history closed in March, with the death at the age of 87 of Len Shipman.

ACTION GROUP

> There was anger on the terraces and in the stands in the autumn of 1990, though a gallows humour sometimes prevailed – even the *Sports Mercury* caught the tone of dark irony with a mock-triumphant headline of 'Two in a Row' after City had taken six points from Bristol City and Notts County in an uncharacteristic four-day burst in October. A supporters' action group – Ambitious Leicester Fans – was formed in October to apply additional pressure to the board and management.

Leicester Mercury cutting, just prior to the departure of David Pleat.

> With the club still anchored unprofitably in Division Two, the board reluctantly agreed to release Gary McAllister during the summer, and his move to Leeds United eventually brought in a tribunal-set fee of £1 million. So at least David Pleat had some cash to spend in the transfer market, even if it was as yet unclear how much would have to be set aside to help the club meet the demands of the Taylor Report.

In his build-up to the new campaign, Pleat was quick to point out that the decision to restore Division One to 22 clubs meant that there were four promotion places to chase this term; a real incentive to the club. What he did not emphasise, though, was that consequently there would be only two relegation spots to avoid this time. Ultimately, it was the latter arrangement that was to prove far more significant to the club's future by the season's end, even if Pleat himself was destined not to be around to direct the dramatic denouement.

He initially invested only some £300,000 of the 'McAllister Million' in the playing staff, and neither of the two new midfielders, Billy Davies and Ricky Hill, would settle in their new surroundings. A first-fixture win proved a false dawn. David Kelly scored after only two minutes of the home encounter with Bristol Rovers, City had two 'goals' rubbed off for offside, and the eventual 3-2 victory featured Hill's arrival from the bench as the 750th first-team player to serve Fosse and City. To follow immediately, though, was the equalling of a club-record sequence of seven successive League defeats, culminating in a 0-6 thrashing at Ayresome Park after Steve Walsh's dismissal. The only surprising statistic at this stage was that City were still one place off the bottom of the table, as hapless Watford had managed only two draws over the same period.

More loan players arrived in the shape of goalkeeper Mike Hooper and defender Terry Fenwick, and one more signing to bolster the ailing defence in left-back Colin Gibson; though an attempt to lure the latter's one-time Old Trafford partner Viv Anderson to Leicester was not successful. Yet City continued to leak goals like a colander and could not break away from the relegation battle.

No comfort could be gained from the Cups, with another hat-trick of first-hurdle tumbles representing the seasonal record. The Full Members competition brought both Wolves and the BSB Sports Channel's cameras to Filbert Street for the first live transmission of a home City game; while the FA Cup exit at The Den – City's sixth successive Third Round defeat – was a deeply dispiriting affair, with Paul Ramsey and Steve Walsh both being sent off and Millwall turning the game with goals in the 86th and 89th minutes.

A fortnight later, Pleat's final throw of the dice was another ill-judged foray into the loan market, to engage veteran Sheffield Wednesday defender Lawrie Madden, but after a 1-3 home defeat by Blackburn at the end of January, the inevitable happened and Pleat was sacked. Chairman Terry Shipman also chose to stand down at the same time, leaving Martin George to take over in the boardroom, assistant manager Gordon Lee to assume control of team matters for the remainder of the season, and skipper Ali Mauchlen to add coaching duties to his portfolio. Another backroom change, which would have far-reaching effects in years to come, was the appointment of the club's first full-time Director of Marketing. Barrie Pierpoint, who arrived in April confessing to knowing nothing about football but everything about commerce – prophetic words indeed!

The hoped-for revival on the pitch proved a stop-go affair, with a team still low on confidence cancelling out the odd heartening win with rather more defeats and plummeting to 22nd place in March; though Kevin Russell inspired a fine comeback at home to Middlesbrough, and substantially raised spirits with his energetic front-running and goalscoring success. A trip to The Hawthorns in mid-April had all the makings of a crucial six-pointer, and a fired-up City took an early lead through 'Rooster'. But former City winger Winston White levelled the scores before West Brom grabbed a vital winner. It was now mathematically possible for City to win all five of their remaining games and still go down, and a defeat at Ipswich in the penultimate fixture left the club

Above: Tony James' goal against Oxford in May 1991 proves enough to save City from relegation to Division Three, sending West Brom down instead.

The job advert in *The Guardian* that led to the arrival of Barrie Pierpoint at Filbert Street.

firmly in the relegation frame, trailing the Baggies on goal difference, with their fate now out of their own hands. A first-ever drop to Division Three loomed dauntingly large as the final fixture, at home to Oxford United, kicked off amid excruciating tension. To their credit, City took the approach that only a win would suffice and it was no use worrying about what West Brom were doing at Twerton Park until after the final whistle – though the number of transistors in the crowd meant this wasn't an approach shared by worried fans. A concerted attacking effort took 24 minutes to bear fruit. Then Player of the Season Tony James turned the ball home from close range to give City a slim lifeline. After that, in truth, Oxford rarely threatened, and the Foxes gleefully accepted all three points. Minutes later came confirmation that Albion had only drawn against a ten-man Bristol Rovers, and City were safe. The Baggies had actually remained unbeaten in their final nine fixtures, but seven draws in that sequence denied them sufficient points to beat the drop, so it was they who would taste Third Division fare for the first time instead. The scenes of relieved, abandoned celebration at Filbert Street mirrored those last seen in 1983, when promotion had been the spur.

Although Gordon Lee had proved popular with players and supporters, the board believed that the only way forward from The Great Escape was to effect a complete managerial clean sweep, and Martin George swiftly narrowed his sights on two men from whom he'd make his choice of the manager he believed would reverse recent Filbert Street fortunes.

Play-Offs, Premier Days & Pot-hunting

> First in the frame for the managerial vacancy was John Beck. A success with Cambridge United, he was unfortunately identified with the worst excesses of route-one football; and to have appointed him would have run counter to the club's footballing traditions. So it was to general approval that Martin George turned to the second of his candidates. Brian Little had created his managerial reputation with unfashionable Darlington, capturing the Conference and Fourth Division championships in successive seasons, and the former Villa forward soon accepted the chance to move up a further flight, quickly appointing a bevy of former Villains – Allan Evans, John Gregory and Steve Hunt – to his backroom staff. He was fast off the mark, too, in starting his team rebuilding, though without any lavish spending and without, initially, returning to his former employers. Five new faces were in the squad by the time the new campaign got underway, costing a grand total of only £160,000 between them.

In stark contrast to the previous year, Little's City started with a draw and then registered six consecutive victories in the Second Division and the League Cup. Suddenly in contention at the right end of the table, City's players and supporters alike began to exude an unaccustomed self-belief. This was boosted immensely in late September, when League Champions Arsenal came visiting in the League Cup. A never-say-die performance from the Foxes culminated in Steve Walsh ramming home a bullet header to equalise in the final minute. It hardly mattered that City fell at Highbury a fortnight later, for a new spirit was abroad.

Right: The arrival of Brian Little as manager signalled a change of direction for the club, and the beginning of a decade unparalleled in City's history.

More new faces arrived, with Luton's Steve Thompson adding some culture to midfield and, finally, three former Quakers in Coatsworth, Willis and Trotter relocated to the East Midlands. City continued to harry the divisional leaders, but it was the sudden-death fixtures that did even more to define the season for City. In the much-maligned Full Members Cup, top-flight Everton were comprehensively outplayed at Filbert Street, then Notts County were overcome in extra time on a foul night at Meadow Lane, when the City supporters packing the open terrace cared not a jot about their soaking. Those victories put City one round away from an unlikely Wembley appearance, but neighbours Forest proved too strong over two legs and the chance slipped by. Even the FA Cup finally brought a cheer to Filbert Street, and what a cheer as local lad Richard Smith netted the decider against Crystal Palace in the dying seconds of the Third Round encounter. A frosty slither to home defeat by Bristol City was the ensuing anti-climax here.

With promotion still a possibility, Little again moved boldly into the transfer market as deadline day approached. Paul Kitson, whose early-season form and goalscoring record had been inspirational, but who handled his sudden fame less well, was jettisoned to Derby in a record part-exchange deal which brought Ian Ormondroyd and Phil Gee to Leicester, and financed the capture soon afterwards of Simon Grayson and Mike Whitlow from Leeds. Additionally, Irish international defender Colin Hill arrived on loan

Above: Jimmy Willis was one of three new faces eventually signed from Little's former club.

Below: City's 5-0 destruction of Cambridge United in the 1992 Play-Off semi-final second leg took the club back to Wembley for the first time in 23 years. Here Tommy Wright opens the scoring at Filbert Street.

from Sheffield United. The upshot was a run of seven wins in eight games to move the Foxes into second place in the table. Suddenly, the prospect of automatic promotion beckoned. But it was dulled just as quickly in the penultimate fixture, when City offered a lacklustre performance to their travelling hordes, losing 0-2 to Charlton in a game more notable for setting the attendance record for the Addicks' temporary tenure at Upton Park. Drama still attended the final game, at home to Newcastle, with both clubs now seemingly in need of a victory to achieve their respective targets of automatic promotion and the avoidance of relegation. Steve Walsh contrived to score at both ends as Kevin Keegan's Magpies won 2-1 on a day marked by serious crowd trouble, but results elsewhere actually rendered this fixture meaningless. City had to settle for fourth place in the final table and a new experience, a battle for promotion through the Play-Offs.

City were paired with Cambridge United in the semi-finals. John Beck's team were still plying their long-ball game, and had suckered City by 5-1 earlier in the season with a team including Dion Dublin, Steve Claridge and Lee Philpott, so the journey to the Abbey Stadium was made with some trepidation. But by then Kevin Russell had re-emerged as a City goalscoring hero, and his strike enabled City to escape from the first leg with a 1-1 draw, and set up a night of high drama for the Filbert Street return. It was as if all City's Christmases had arrived at once as Tommy Wright, another who had achieved cult status with the

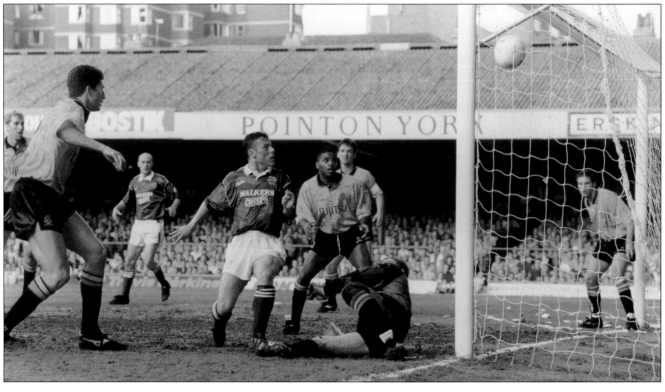

Steve Walsh leads the team out for the 1992
Play-Off Final against Blackburn Rovers.

fans, netted twice, Russell headed another, and the Foxes stormed to a 5-0 win that led to long celebrations of the club's first trip to Wembley for 23 years.

The Final, traditionally played on Bank Holiday Monday at the end of May, saw City facing a Blackburn Rovers team that had been radically reconstructed during the season. Local millionaire Jack Walker had tempted Kenny Dalglish out of retirement to sit in the manager's chair, and had bankrolled a substantial transfer investment. Even so, Kevin Russell's slightly fortuitous goal had downed them at Ewood on Easter Saturday, so there were grounds for City optimism. The prize at stake was not, however, promotion to Division One. Instead the winners would take their place in the newly-formed Premier League, the mutant elitist offspring of heavy

Above: City pressure fails to break a stout Blackburn defence.

Below: Carl Muggleton joins a select band of goalkeepers who have saved a penalty at Wembley, but Mike Newell's earlier spotkick proved decisive.

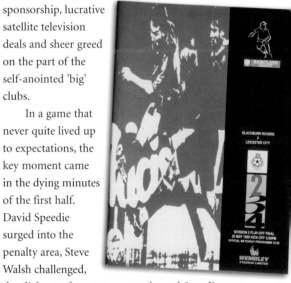

sponsorship, lucrative satellite television deals and sheer greed on the part of the self-anointed 'big' clubs.

In a game that never quite lived up to expectations, the key moment came in the dying minutes of the first half. David Speedie surged into the penalty area, Steve Walsh challenged, the slightest of contact was made, and Speedie went easily to ground. A spot-kick was awarded, City and their fans were incensed, but former Fox Mike Newell confidently converted from twelve yards. City's pressure in the second period forced a couple of goalline clearances, but it was a Blackburn breakaway that came closest to altering the scoreline. Carl Muggleton floored Mark Atkins for a second penalty – clear-cut this time – but made amends by diving left to Newell's effort and joining an elite band of Wembley penalty savers. Thereafter Rovers held out fairly comfortably to earn their elevation. Many of City's fans were satisfied that real progress had been

Home of the Foxes

> After the upsurge in fortunes in 1991/2, there was no doubt that the goal for the new campaign could be nothing less than an emphatic promotion challenge. Yet, strangely, there was little activity on the summer transfer front. Colin Hill's loan move was made permanent, Bobby Davison arrived from Leeds and David Lowe was snapped up from Ipswich Town. The most noticeable change was City's adoption of an all-blue playing strip (Jimmy Bloomfield's old pop-psychological preference for a single-colour kit getting a 20-years-on airing from Brian Little). But there was also a new name for the competition City were playing in: the old Second Division having mutated into the Football League Division One as a consequence of the formation of the FA's Premier League.

Left: A Royal visit, to mark the club's contribution to Leicester's environmental drive, occurred in November 1991, with The Prince of Wales being shown around by chairman Martin George.

made following the lean years under David Pleat, and the trip to the Twin Towers had been a real bonus. Not so Little and his team, who had set their ambitions considerably higher.

On the individual front, it was ironically one of Pleat's signings, Gary Mills, who captured the Player of the Season award for the second time in three years. Ever-present throughout City's most hectic season ever, he played in no less than 61 games in the No 2 shirt. City's only full international cap of the season was won by David Kelly, who failed to settle under the new regime at Filbert Street, and who was transferred to Newcastle shortly after his outing for the Republic of Ireland. But the Leicester focus on the international arena predominantly fell on an 'old boy': Gary Lineker's magnificent England career coming to a sad end this summer, and his fluffed spot-kick against Brazil leaving him agonisingly one goal short of matching Bobby Charlton's representative tally.

Throughout the year, the club had been celebrating 100 years at Filbert Street. Prince Charles visited in November to check out the ground's new 'green' credentials, and a Grand Ball later that month formally marked the enclosure's centenary – even if the headlines that night were stolen by the arrest for fighting of celebrity guest Alex Higgins. Plans for a radical revamp of the ground were disappointingly stymied, however. The idea was to turn the pitch through 90 degrees, build a new Main Stand along Filbert Street itself and a new West Stand over the existing car park area, but the council vetoed the scheme on the grounds of its impact on Filbert Street residents.

David Lowe was a pre-season casualty, fracturing his cheekbone in a home friendly against Borussia Mönchengladbach, but City got off to a winning start – just – in their re-dubbed league, with an injury-time Mike Whitlow goal sealing a 2-1 scoreline against Luton. A few weeks later, Carl Muggleton became a pre-match casualty, injuring his back in the warm-up prior to the home game with Wolves. A game that already bore the landmark status of being the first league fixture to be televised live from Filbert Street thus saw the drama of young reserve keeper Russell Hoult being summoned from the stand – and from a hot-dog lunch – to make his debut. The youngster kept a clean sheet and took most of the plaudits, while Neil Lewis also made his bow as substitute in this match.

The hoped-for challenge for automatic promotion, however, never really materialised, and inconsistency became the keyword for the season. The team mixed the very good with the very bad in quite liberal proportions; such that, by late February, even a Play-Off place seemed seriously under threat. Davison had not really proved the answer to the lack of firepower up front so, just before Christmas, Little made the tactical decision that would ultimately have far-reaching effects. Central defensive linchpin Steve Walsh was switched to a striking role, and was to act as a foil for the emerging, exciting talent of 18-year-old Julian Joachim.

Joachim had sprung to prominence with three early-season hat-tricks for the youth team, and had gleefully seized the opportunities of early first-eleven elevation. As the season unfolded, his blistering speed and eye for the spectacular goal would shape many a headline. Walsh was also to demonstrate a subtlety of touch that was rarely required from him at the back, and an instinct for goal that would lift him to the head of the seasonal scoring charts.

Above: Bobby Davison was the third player to arrive from Leeds in the space of six months.

Nevertheless, City's season stuttered along for several months, with the humiliation of a 1-7 thrashing at Hillsborough in the League Cup, and the heartache of an FA Cup exit in a penalty shoot-out at Oakwell, to contend with on top of the league travails. That game at Barnsley had shot young Joachim to national prominence, however, as a stunning strike clinched the BBC 'Goal of the Month' award for January.

Suddenly, however, in early March, the Foxes' season was fired into top gear; with the impetus emanating from an unlikely source. Rugged defender Gary Coatsworth slammed two goals in a 3-2 away win against Barnsley, one of his former clubs, to extract some measure of revenge for the Cup disappointment, and to prompt City to the second of seven successive wins. Six featured three-goal performances, and six featured counters from Steve Walsh. By the time that fellow Play-Off contenders Millwall were toppled at Easter, also courtesy of a three-goal return, City harboured genuine promotion hopes once more.

With a Play-Off berth secure, the Foxes took the field for the final home fixture against Bristol City to play for the last time in front of the old Main Stand. The mainly wooden structure, built in 1921, would no longer stand up to rigorous new safety regulations, and plans were in place for a £5.35 million replacement, an imposing edifice that would also house an infrastructure capable of generating income for the club on a seven-day-a-week basis. The goalless draw that followed was hardly a fitting end for such a monument, but it was infinitely better than what followed in the final league fixture. Live television cameras were on hand to capture all the Geordie euphoria as Newcastle were to celebrate the capture of the Football League championship as well as promotion to the elite. The Tynesiders went up in style, handing City their second 1-7 reverse of the season after scoring six times unanswered in the first half, with former Fox David Kelly collecting a hat-trick to counter the one he'd scored for City against Newcastle two seasons earlier.

The question now was to what extent such a drubbing might affect confidence for the Play-Offs. This time the opposition was to be a Portsmouth team that had finished fully twelve points clear of City and had only missed automatic promotion on the final afternoon. This fact garnered Pompey all the public sympathy, even though City had to stage the home leg of the tie at Nottingham Forest's City Ground, as demolition work was proceeding at Filbert Street. A

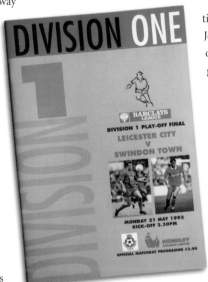

Top right: Julian Joachim scores to make it 1-3.

Centre right: Steve Walsh's header reduces the arrears further.

Bottom right: Steve Thompson's equaliser rounds off the club's most sensational 12 minutes ever.

tight first leg was settled by another piece of Joachim magic. A pacy dribble through the heart of the defence set up a magnificent individualist goal to give City a priceless lead. Equally important was the fact that no away goal had been conceded, and an eventual 2-2 draw at Fratton Park, which sparked a riotous response from shattered home fans, was enough to clinch a return to Wembley.

Glen Hoddle's Swindon Town were to provide the opposition, and a neatly balanced game suddenly fell apart for City either side of half-time, as defensive hesitancy contributed to a 0-3 deficit. What followed, for a time at least, was real 'Roy of the Rovers' stuff. No team had ever recovered from such a scoreline in Wembley's long history, yet the Foxes managed it in a glorious twelve-minute spell that saw Joachim, Walsh and Steve Thompson cut Swindon to ribbons. Alas, the fairy tale was to end there as, in the closing minutes, another controversial penalty award went against the team. The 3-4 reverse left the fans with some magnificent memories but, once again, the grail had been snatched from Little's grasp, and City had left the Twin Towers luckless and winless for a sixth time.

Above: Swindon's Steve White is floored by Kevin Poole and City's promotion dream dies.

173

Above: 1991 had marked the centenary of the Filbert Street stadium. Plans were then already afoot to knock down the Main Stand (bottom left of picture), which had stood since 1921, and build a new modern construction in its place.

Below: May 1993 and a last look at the old Main Stand. Its demolition meant that the first leg of the Play-Off semi-final had to be staged at Nottingham Forest, the first time a Leicester home game had been played outside of the city in peacetime.

> The summer of 1993 was dominated, as would be the Filbert Street skyline, by the new stand's construction. To the same design as previously rejected, its positioning now on the west side of the site gave no grounds for council concern, even though it soon became clear that it would dwarf even the old Double Decker. At least part of the ground would now enter the modern era, and allow for a significant expansion of commercial activity. A minor part of that activity would be the auction of assorted fixtures and fittings from the demolished edifice, and the *Mercury's* football correspondent Bill Anderson was to the fore among bidders for the door to the visiting team's dressing room!

Meanwhile, in the manager's portakabin, perhaps the most unlikely face of all was to be found signing for the club. David Speedie had been the fans' bête noir ever since the 1992 Play-Off Final, and had proved an on-field irritant since, but now he was deemed by Brian Little the ideal man to play alongside Steve Walsh, and allow Julian Joachim's talent to develop in a less pressured wide position. But if the deal seemed a dicey move, it took only a matter of weeks before even the hardiest of doubters were won over, and Speedie installed as the latest cult hero on the terraces.

The season actually commenced amid the strangest of atmospheres, with Filbert Street temporarily a three-sided ground, and no away supporters present at either of the first two home league games. A midweek Anglo-Italian Cup qualifier against West Brom even had to kick off at 6.00 as only two floodlight pylons remained. City were nonetheless quickly into stride, but a customary reverse at Ayresome Park in late September, just as a top three challenge was taking shape, left Little's plans in disarray, with Walsh being carried off with a cruciate ligament injury that threatened to end his season.

City continued to keep in touch with the top, even hitting the summit on a couple of brief occasions, but the injury list continued to grow, and even the goals of new striker Iwan Roberts, a November purchase, were insufficient to keep the club in the hunt for automatic promotion. By the time April came around, ten players who would have been considered as first choices were simultaneously sidelined with injuries, although City had made one interim addition to their squad in midfielder Mark Blake, whose fee upped the club record by £10,000 to £360,000. Yet, in what appeared their darkest hour, Little's makeshift selection simply rolled up their sleeves and contrived an unbeaten nine-match run to the end of the term. Seven of these games were drawn; with the most spectacular being a 3-3 encounter

May 1993: A strange view of Filbert Street, with a pile of rubble where the Main Stand used to be.

September 1993: The new Carling Stand begins to take shape.

October 1993, City v Rochdale (League Cup): The view from the rear of the new Carling Stand adds a new dimension to watching football at Filbert Street.

against Derby, in which all six goals arrived in a 29-minute spell – three of them from Roberts, two from old-boy Paul Kitson, and one own goal from Jimmy Willis. The football was not always pretty to watch, but the spirit carrying City to their third successive tilt at the Play-Off route to the big time was unquenchable.

The Foxes faced Tranmere in the semi-final and started by grinding out a goalless draw at Prenton Park, aided by some excellent saves from goalkeeper Gavin Ward and a slightly suspect goalline clearance from skipper Simon Grayson. For the return leg, Little took a huge gamble, recalling Walsh, who had made a spectacular recovery from his injury, but was clearly not match-fit. City grabbed a vital goal on the break, after Walsh's quick thinking at a throw-in set up the opportunity, but the Merseysiders levelled early in the second period, taking the advantage by virtue of the away strike. City, though, were in no mood to succumb, and David Speedie claimed the faintest of touches to a cross that also deflected netwards off the keeper and a defender to send the club once more to Wembley. Even then the drama was not complete, as a flare-up in the few seconds that remained saw Speedie red-carded (along with Eric Nixon) and so banned from the Final. No-one realised it at the time, but that was to be the player's last act in a Leicester shirt.

Iwan Roberts returned from injury to replace Speedie on the big day, forming a less than fully fit front pairing with Walsh. Local rivals Derby provided the opposition and looked worthy favourites when Tommy Johnson outpaced the City defence to fire them ahead. But, for once, luck was to smile on Leicester at Wembley. Another couple of good chances for the Rams went begging, before a hopefully-punted long centre from Gary Coatsworth was headed goalwards by Walsh. Amidst appeals for a foul on the goalkeeper by Roberts, and a piece of woeful covering on the line by a Derby defender, the ball somehow found the net, and the teams turned round all square.

City continued to hang on, with Jimmy Willis marshalling the defence superbly to earn the Man of the Match trophy, and Derby missed another gilt-edged chance late in the game. Then, with four minutes remaining, the Foxes produced the one class move of the match. Joachim fed Grayson on the right; the skipper's centre was headed powerfully goalwards by Ian Ormondroyd; the keeper parried and there was Steve Walsh on hand to turn the rebound home. It had only taken City 626 minutes of playing time, spread over 45 years, to finally take the lead at the home of football, and they were not about to relinquish it easily. Derby, in fact,

Above: Simon Grayson leads out City for their third successive Play-Off Final at Wembley.

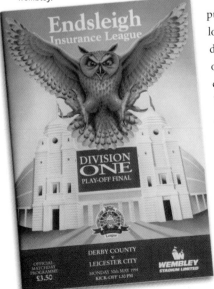

were broken, and Grayson became the first-ever Leicester captain to climb those famous 39 steps to the Royal Box to hold silverware aloft.

The style of victory was hardly a purist's delight, and Little's squad actually looked less well-equipped to face the demands of the Premier League than that of twelve months previously, but nothing could detract from the glory of that first Wembley win – seventh heaven indeed. All the way back to Leicester, service stations and bridges along the M1 motorway were festooned in blue and white, and the fans celebrated long and loud. Those who did not make the trip, but listened to the commentary on Radio Leicester instead, were also treated to an unforgettable moment in broadcasting annals as match summariser, the injured Gary Mills,

Right: An early setback as Tommy Johnson fires Derby ahead.

Above: Steve Walsh, assisted by Iwan Roberts, heads the equaliser just before the break.

Right: Steve Walsh's winning goal with six minutes remaining takes City to the Premier League.

Above: Simon Grayson becomes the first City captain to lift a trophy beneath the Twin Towers.

Left: Jimmy Willis celebrates with his 'Man of the Match' award for a brilliant defensive display against Derby.

let out a massive involuntary roar to greet Walsh's winner.

Back at Filbert Street, the new stand was now fully ready to welcome the nation's premier clubs. City's flirtations this term with clubs from the elite, however, had come in the shape of heavy defeats in both main Cup competitions at the hands of each of the Manchester clubs, and would prove a grim warning for City of what to expect after seven seasons away from the top flight. The advent of the Premier League, with its own sponsorship deals and financial structure, was definitely already beginning to create an ever-widening gulf between the haves and have-nots of the game, and promoted clubs were already finding they'd have to produce something special just to survive.

One area in which the club was more than holding its own with the Premier outfits, however, was in commercial innovation. Reserve-team matches were re-designated as Family Night Football in January, with extra entertainment for youngsters and a drive to bring families back to the game with attractive pricing packages. The plan was a roaring success, with the average Central League gate rising from 400 to 4,000 (and Manchester United's second-team attracting around 16,000 in February) as City became the envy of many of the so-called 'bigger' clubs.

> Clearly, City's first-team squad required strengthening if the Foxes were to stand any chance of survival in the upper echelon, but that proved to be surprisingly difficult to achieve for Brian Little. By the time the opening Premier League fixture came round, only two new men were found wearing obligatory squad numbers. Nicky Mohan had been captured from Middlesbrough to bolster the defence, whilst a substantially upped new club record of £1.25 million was paid to Notts County for midfielder Mark Draper. On the debit side, Tony James, City's saviour of just over three years earlier, was released to join Hereford United; David Speedie was sidelined by a career-ending injury; and the club also bade farewell to secretary Alan Bennett after 15 years of service.

That opening game, a 1-3 reverse to Newcastle at Filbert Street – kicking off at 4.00 on a Sunday for the benefit of Sky Sports – was an early taste of just how tough life at the top was set to become. Draper, showing plenty of confidence, stepped forward to take a spot-kick when City were just a goal in arrears, missed, and the first lesson in having to take chances as they arose was harshly learned. More would follow, although easier to get used to were two further innovations: the 15-minute half-time break, and the potential for using three substitutes, including a goalkeeper.

As City began living down to their pre-season status as relegation favourites, another series of injuries exacerbated their problems. Steve Walsh required a cartilage operation and would play only five times all season, while Julian Joachim was also sidelined for the bulk of the campaign, though not before he had represented England's Under-21 side at Filbert Street, against Portugal. The story otherwise was fairly consistent in the early months, with decent performances earning no reward as the team were punished for virtually every odd error at the back. Even Wembley hero Jimmy Willis suffered the misfortune of recording own goals in successive games at one stage, as City failed to keep a clean sheet until mid-December. By that time, though, events off the field had comprehensively taken over the headlines.

A series of managerial changes in early November soon led to rife speculation linking Little with the vacancy at Aston Villa. Little claimed to be content at Leicester, but a live televised Sunday afternoon game against Manchester City had all the pundits talking in terms of 'when' rather than 'if' the boss would return to the club he'd spent his playing career serving. A day later, after an Everton win in the Merseyside derby, City plunged to the bottom of the table; and a day after that came the news that Little had resigned as manager for personal reasons. Wednesday morning

Above: Ian Ormondroyd lost his sole Premiership strike to the Dubious Goals Panel.

Above: David Oldfield was the culprit for City's fourth successive missed spotkick during the season.

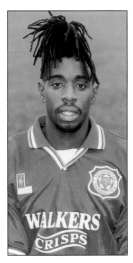

Above: Jamie Lawrence, signed from Doncaster for £125,000, was distinguishable by his 'pineapple' cut.

saw coach John Gregory relinquish his duties, leaving Allan Evans to prepare the team for the visit of Arsenal that evening. Incredibly, the team produced one of their best performances of the season to win 2-1 and climb to 20th position. Ian Ormondroyd later suffered the indignity of having what would have been his only Premier League strike for City ruled out by the newly installed Premiership Panel, who were convened to adjudicate on deflected goals, and whose verdicts meant that there were to be official goalscorers for the first time in over a century of league football.

Events continued apace with Evans resigning on the Friday and Little being appointed as the new Villa boss the same day. Youth-team coaches Tony McAndrew and Kevin MacDonald were thus temporarily handed the duty of selecting the senior side. Meanwhile the City board failed in the High Court to obtain an injunction preventing Little taking up his new post, and also failed to convince the promising young Wycombe manager, Martin O'Neill, to abandon the Chairboys. So it was an ironic twist of fate that the next Filbert Street fixture was to bring Villa to town. The crowd reaction was severely hostile, with banners reading 'Judas' and 'Liar' leaving the former manager in no doubt as to how the supporters felt about his desertion. Perhaps it was just as well that honours were even on the field on this occasion.

Early speculation had Sheffield United's Dave Bassett as a target for the City post, but it was Mark McGhee of Reading who soon emerged as the popular favourite. McGhee's appointment was confirmed in mid-December, though only after he'd had an overnight change of mind to accept City's offer. His first game in charge was against league leaders Blackburn, and a more organised defensive performance was rewarded with that first clean sheet at last.

But there was to be no magic wand, alas, and the team continued to look just out of its depth. (It also continued to spurn penalty opportunities, with David Oldfield's miss in the Cup-tie against non-league Enfield being the fourth successive failure from twelve yards). Walsh, it was announced, would require a second operation, though new faces arrived in the shape of Jamie Lawrence from Doncaster and, for £1m, Mark Robins from Norwich. Robins had to watch fellow strugglers Crystal Palace break an 838-minute goal-drought of their own in toppling the Foxes at Selhurst Park, then had his potential debut at home to Leeds postponed due to a midday downpour. So it was the following Wednesday night, on a Maine Road pitch that looked far worse than Filbert Street had done days previously, that Robins finally wore a

City shirt. Atrocious weather meant that some supporters' coaches only arrived twenty minutes before the final whistle, whilst several did not make it to Manchester at all. By then, Robins had headed the only goal of the game from a Lawrence cross, much to the joy of the drenched souls occupying an unroofed, under-development Kippax side. These latter witnesses to City's only Premiership away win of the term were later rewarded for their endurance when the club issued a limited-edition T-shirt, offered free to all those who'd eventually dried out their ticket stubs from the fixture.

In truth, there was little else to get excited about as the remainder of the season unfolded and relegation became a reality. Loan signing Mike Galloway added some steel to midfield and became a real favourite with the fans, while protracted negotiations with Villa over compensation for Little and his coaches were finally concluded in a complex deal that saw Franz Carr move to the West Midlands and Garry Parker join the Foxes. One brief moment of relief then came in the return fixture with Little's new charges, as City pulled back a 1-4 deficit with 13 minutes remaining to snatch a point. However, as early as mid-April, City were mathematically doomed, and a closing run of three games unbeaten proved irrelevant. By then, an unknown striker from the youth team had been pressed into service in a much-depleted side at Loftus Road. He'd not uprooted any trees, but Emile Heskey looked like he might soon be able to, as the signs were that he'd become a big lad once he grew up!

League Cup embarrassment added to the overall gloom, with Second Division Brighton winning both legs in Round Two; though progress to the last sixteen of the FA Cup, for the first time since 1985, raised a few whispers that the club might emulate its 1969 double of relegation and Wembley. Former City striker David Kelly put paid to that sort of speculation with the winner at Molineux: on the day Parker made his City bow, and when the Foxes first utilised a substitute goalie.

Above: Julian Joachim in action against Forest in August 1994, on a day when Stan Collymore's goal sent City to the foot of the initial table.

Below: The completed Carling Stand gives a new look to the Filbert Street Stadium by August 1995.

> With disappointment turning to anticipatory resolve that the club would return to the top flight immediately, McGhee set about reshaping his squad. Most of the financial wherewithal came from the sale of Mark Draper to Little's Villa, though £500,000 of the record £3.25m fee had to be passed on as a windfall to Notts County. Three players (Ward, Mohan and Ormondroyd) moved jointly to Bradford City in a deal that had old timers recalling the Watford transfer saga of 1948, but the market was now becoming rather more cosmopolitan. McGhee returned to his old club, Reading, for midfielder Scott Taylor, his only English buy, but otherwise cast his net wide. Landed were two Australians in Steve Corica and giant goalkeeper Zeljko Kalac (who promptly underwent a lengthy work-permit dispute); while thrown back were pre-season and early-season trialists from Slovakia (Vladimir Kinder), Poland (Dariusz Adamczuk) and Germany (Markus Kranz).

City started stylishly, racing to the head of the table with a passing game that was far more elaborate than anything seen in the Little era, although it was a frenzied fixture at Derby, on the occasion of City's final visit to the old Baseball Ground, that saw them to the summit. The single-goal win that day was achieved against a backdrop of Kevin Poole saving a penalty, Iwan Roberts being sent off, and Colin Hill being stretchered off. Two more foreign signings swelled the squad, with Frenchman Franck Rolling joining from Ayr United after trials, and Sweden's Pontus Kåmark arriving after helping IFK to their domestic title, and both lined up in front of the debutant Kalac at The Hawthorns on Guy Fawkes Day. A dazzlingly confident first-half display had City three goals ahead and oozing class but, after the break, cracks began to appear. Two errors by Kalac left City hanging on and the fans wondering just what the

Aussie international's reputation was based on. Three days later, in a League Cup tie against Bolton, Kalac again came up with a hapless performance that cost City the match, Kåmark was carried off with serious knee ligament trouble, and the side's early confidence soon disappeared.

Within weeks, so too had McGhee. Just one year after Little had left, his successor was also tempted away to the West Midlands. This time, though, there was no pull of a club with long personal associations; instead it was the supposed ambition of a 'bigger' club that tempted McGhee to 'sleeping giants' Wolves. Once again, City tried to block the move and, once again, all the senior coaching staff followed, leaving the club back at square one, twelve months on. In fact, the club had initially refused to accept the resignations of McGhee, Colin Lee and Mike Hickman, after which the trio simply failed to report for work. David Nish, Chris Turner, Garry Parker and Steve Walsh took charge of training and Nish assumed caretaker manager duties in the interim, while City bowed to the inevitable and agreed a record compensation deal with Wolves.

It looked as though former Norwich and Everton boss Mike Walker was favourite to take the Filbert Street reins but, on the morning of 17th December, came the news that would preface a reshaping of the club's future. Martin O'Neill, a target for the managerial post a year previously, resigned his position at Norwich on the very day the two clubs were due to meet at Filbert Street. The Leicester vacancy remained open for a few days longer, Martin George obtained permission from Norwich to approach their former boss, and O'Neill was duly appointed in time for the following fixture.

The new manager's preferred style of play was somewhat different from that of his predecessor, and it took a while for the players to adjust. Indeed, by the time the Foxes visited Molineux to face McGhee's new outfit in late February, they had not won in nine games under their new boss. They had exited the FA Cup, 0-5 at Maine Road, by their widest losing margin ever in this competition, and the promotion challenge was beginning to fade. O'Neill's first win as a Leicester manager turned out to be one to savour: the rapidly emerging Emile Heskey scored twice and City overcame their hosts 3-2. After that, the first new faces

Above: Steve Walsh leads the Foxes out for their fourth Play-Off Final in five years.

began to arrive, as the Irishman set about building his own team.

No string of household names arrived, nor any particularly expensive signings, but Neil Lennon, Steve Claridge, Julian Watts and loanee Muzzy Izzet signified the move into a new era. Not that results improved after the Wolves win. In fact, the Play-Offs looked the remotest of possibilities on the afternoon that Watts and Izzet made their debuts: a truly dire home defeat by Sheffield United that was the absolute nadir of O'Neill's entire tenure, and that was marked by vocal unrest from some sections of the crowd.

Suddenly, though, with everything seemingly lost, the team found a new strength from their inner depths. Successive away wins in London against fellow promotion-chasers Charlton and Crystal Palace got the train back on the tracks, and an eventual four victories from the four final fixtures was enough to clinch another crack at the Play-Offs. Before City could contemplate the possibility of a return to what was rapidly becoming their second home in North London, O'Neill had to pay Chelsea a £75,000 fee to extend the loan of Izzet, whose goal at Watford had sealed qualification. The investment would prove justified.

This time it was Stoke City who stood in the way of another May Bank Holiday outing, and a tight first leg at Filbert Street ended goalless, thanks in the main to a magnificent early save from Kevin Poole. City then turned on the style in the second leg, controlling the tempo of the game and suckering the Potters with a Garry Parker goal that caught them cold at the start of the second half. This decisive strike marked the welcome rehabilitation of the former skipper, who had earlier been stripped of both his status and his senior place after a well-publicised argument with O'Neill.

It nonetheless fell to Steve Walsh to lead out the team at Wembley, where Crystal Palace provided the opposition, just as he had in 1992. The Eagles took a first-half lead through Andy Roberts, but City looked the better team, playing their most controlled and attractive game yet beneath the Twin Towers. Even so, it was not until the 76th minute that the scores were finally levelled. Izzet was felled in the area by Edworthy, and Parker coolly planted the spot-kick beyond Nigel Martyn for the equaliser. The game passed into extra time and the spectre of a penalty shoot-out to decide promotion was looming large. Then O'Neill made a change that was to stun all 73,573 present and, indirectly, was to decide the game. With only seconds remaining, and Parker about to take a City free-kick, O'Neill withdrew goalkeeper

Above: Garry Parker's late penalty takes the 1996 Play-Off Final into extra time. **Below:** Steve Claridge's last gasp goal clinches victory, though he can hardly believe it.

Kevin Poole and sent on the giant substitute Kalac. The Australian had not played since the Bolton nightmare, and in the interim had been the subject of a transfer agreement Wolves had pulled out of, so the gamble was huge, but the manager believed that Kalac's sheer presence would prove intimidatory in the expected sudden-death lottery. It was likely to be an experience to make or break a career but, incredibly, it didn't happen. Parker took the free-kick, Watts headed the ball down along the edge of the area and, with half the players seemingly distracted or stunned, Steve Claridge stepped forward to mishit the perfect shot into the top corner past a static Martyn. There was a palpable delay in the crowd reaction as the moment sunk in; then sheer delirium at the Leicester end. Just four seconds were played after the restart, Kalac never got near the ball, (indeed, he never kicked a ball in anger again for Leicester), and City were back in the top flight once more.

Above: Steve Walsh collects the trophy that meant promotion had been secured.   **Below:** City's two goalscorers, Garry Parker and Steve Claridge, enjoy their moment.

183

> In the space of two months, Martin O'Neill had risen from scorn to virtual sainthood in the eyes of some supporters, and the fickleness of footballing fortune had never been better illustrated. But his short-term achievements soon began to pale in significance as his pre-season relegation favourites set about the new Premiership campaign with renewed vigour, revelling on a home pitch that had been completely relaid during the summer. The chairman who'd brought O'Neill to Leicester, Martin George, had stepped down, with successor Tom Smeaton promising a sizeable cash infusion for the club, but the manager initially had difficulties strengthening his squad. Muzzy Izzet's loan was turned into a permanent deal, but IFK Göteborg winger Jesper Blomqvist spurned City's advances, and it was not until virtually the very eve of the new season that Kasey Keller and Spencer Prior joined to bolster playing resources.

But there would be a gradual accretion of talent over the course of the season, with O'Neill's shrewdness in the home market, and in spotting underdeveloped lower-division potential, particularly evident. Ian Marshall, Matt Elliott, Rob Ullathorne and Steve Guppy arrived at different junctures of the year, while trialists such as former Under-21 midfielder Stuart Slater, German winger Sascha Lenhart and Dutch international Pieter Huistra briefly flitted across the Filbert Street scene. The reshaped squad showed plenty of appetite for the top-flight fray, and soon had the bookies recalculating their odds. Team spirit and a never-say-die attitude were the qualities underpinning some fine football from

Top: Mark Robins strikes to oust Ipswich in the quarter final of the League Cup in 1996/7.

Above: Rob Ullathorne suffers a broken leg after just 11 minutes of his debut against Wimbledon in the semi-final first leg.

Below: Simon Grayson heads City's vital away goal in the second leg of the semi-final at Selhurst Park.

City, though a myopic press tended to harp only on the former attributes as explanation for the side's refusal to settle for their supposed fall-guy destiny. As several well-beaten sets of 'big boys' repeated the mantra that they'd 'had an off-day' against City, O'Neill happily capitalised on the sense of embattled defiance shared by players and fans.

City never dropped below sixteenth place in the table, and eventually finished as high as ninth, though just how tight the Premiership battle had become was illustrated by the fact that it took Matt Elliott's goal in the penultimate fixture, at home to Sheffield Wednesday, to formally fend off the possibility of relegation. Survival, though, was far from the only issue this term, for a mark was finally to be made in the Cup competitions.

The FA Cup brought another run to the last 16, and a fine recovery from a two-goal deficit against Chelsea, by an injury-hit team, earned a replay at Stamford Bridge. Deep into extra-time, with penalties looming, just one such spot-kick was to cause almost unprecedented controversy. The award to Chelsea made by referee Mike Reed, when no contact whatsoever had been made on the diving Erland Johnsen, proved decisive in the game, ushered Chelsea onwards to to raise the Cup itself, and prompted a fall-out that included the sacking of a radio personality and a Prime Ministerial comment. For once, it also drew a widespread public sympathy to City that their against-the-odds league performances had strangely failed to elicit.

The Coca-Cola Cup Final 1997 Leicester City v Middlesbrough

Nonetheless, this excitement was well and truly eclipsed by that raised by City's exploits in the League Cup. From humble beginnings at Scarborough and York, via victories over a predominantly second-string Manchester United outfit and an awkwardly resilient Ipswich, the Foxes found themselves facing Wimbledon in the two-legged semi-final. Ullathorne made his debut in the Filbert Street game and lasted only eleven minutes before suffering a broken leg, stumbling without an opposition player anywhere nearby. A goalless draw resulted from a tight encounter, and there was equivalent toughness and tension to the Selhurst Park return. The Dons took a first-half lead after an uncharacteristic error by Julian Watts, but Simon Grayson rose to head a famous equaliser. Garry Parker made two goalline clearances deep into extra time, and City won through on the away goals ruling after a real war of attrition.

Again, the Final, against Middlesbrough, proved a close-fought, nerve-wracking affair. Weeks earlier, Boro had torn City to shreds at Filbert Street with the diminutive Brazilian, Juninho, outstanding. O'Neill duly took note, and handed Pontus Kåmark the job of marking the midfielder out of the game; a task the Swede performed to perfection. Even so, it was Boro's Italian striker Fabrizio Ravanelli who broke the Wembley deadlock in extra time; and it took a scrambled goal,

Above: Emile Heskey's late equaliser in extra time at Wembley earns City another chance.

Left: The key to Cup glory was the duel between Pontus Kåmark and Juninho.

Below: The *Mercury* ilustrates City's relief.

forced home by Emile Heskey with just three minutes remaining, to earn the Foxes another tilt at the trophy. The replay was staged at Hillsborough and ran to predictable form as yet another tightly tactical spectacle. Extra time was again required, but this time, with 100 minutes on the clock, a Garry Parker free-kick was headed back across goal by Steve Walsh, and there was Steve Claridge to volley home from an awkward height. Within a minute, Kasey Keller made a top-class save at the other end and, after that, Walsh marshalled his defence magnificently to deny Boro any further chances back into the game. Amid a mayhem of delirious joy from the City support, Walsh then collected both the Cup and the Man of the Match award. Major silverware was thus returned to the Filbert Street trophy cabinet for the first time since 1964 and, better still, this time the additional reward was to be a place in the UEFA Cup; with City returning to European competition for the first time in 36 years.

Individually, Keller (a regular transatlantic flyer), Kåmark, Hill and Lennon (redefining perpetual motion in midfield) added to their various full international honours, whilst Heskey was elevated to the England Under-21 team and also voted runner-up in the PFA Young Player of the Year awards. Walsh could not have asked for a better testimonial year; while there were numerous unsung or under-rated heroes in the squad. The power of Heskey and Marshall (a 21-minute hat-trick scorer against Derby),

plus the ragamuffin opportunism of Claridge, had accounted for the bulk of the goal tally, while Elliott had proved a new defensive colossus, and Simon Grayson was a revelation at right back, taking the club's Player of the Year award. Overall, this Leicester team had suddenly become the benchmark for other clubs aspiring to make the transition from Football League to Premier League. What was required now was to disabuse of their prejudice those who grudgingly claimed it all as a flash in the pan.

Below: The replay at Hillsborough and Steve Claridge strikes in extra time to win the Cup for City.

Right: The front page of the next day's *Mercury* summed up every City fans feelings.

Above: Martin O'Neill, John Robertson and the rest of the City bench jump for joy as the final whistle goes at Hillsborough.

Below: Skipper and 'Man of the Match' Steve Walsh celebrates with goalscorer Steve Claridge at Hillsborough.

> It was another busy summer for O'Neill – rewarded with a new three-year contract after rumours of an approach by Everton – as he attempted to build on the achievements of the previous campaign. He missed out on Norwich's midfielder Andy Johnson, and lost Scott Taylor to long-term injury, but in came a Welshman, Robbie Savage, a Frenchman, Pegguy Arphexad, and two Englishmen, Graham Fenton and Tony Cottee; the latter rescued from the obscurity of Malaysian football and the supposed twilight of a lengthy striking career. The Nigerian Mobi Oparaku, the Italian Felice Centofanti, the Scotsman Iain Nicolson and the German Dietmar Beiersdorfer were also given brief chances to impress as City looked to cast their net ever wider, but options on this quartet were not taken up.

By the middle of the season, Greek international captain Theo Zagorakis had, though, joined the increasingly cosmopolitan City throng and, by the end, the general opinion was that this had been a term of solid progress. This was despite the fact that the club finished one place lower in the table than in 1997 (even if they exceeded their points total), and exited each of the three knockout competitions in the early stages.

The key to the banishment of league anxieties was a good start made from a particularly tough-looking early fixture list, earning O'Neill the first Manager of the Month award as City sat 3rd in the

Above: Tony Cottee netted the winner at Old Trafford to relaunch his career with a bang!

Below: On City's return to Europe after 36 years, Ian Marshall strikes to open the scoring in the first leg away to Atletico Madrid.

Premiership at the end of September. Victories over Aston Villa and at Anfield were followed by creditable home draws with both Manchester United and Arsenal; the latter game ending in an incredible 3-3 scoreline after City had been 0-2 down in 83 minutes, and three goals were scored in seven long minutes of added time. Later in the campaign, City followed up by completing the double over Liverpool and inflicting a rare home defeat on United. This was achieved by way of Tony Cottee's first league goal for the Foxes: a moment that effectively relaunched the former England forward's career in a way few could have anticipated. The crowning glory of the league season then came in a televised game at Pride Park in April, when four headed goals in the first 15 minutes simply blew the Rams away; though earlier City had also indicated the new balance of Midlands football by winning at Coventry for the first time in 22 years.

Despite all this, there was no doubting that the centrepiece of the season was the return to European competition for the first time since 1961. By a strange quirk of fate, the UEFA Cup draw paired the Foxes with the same club they had faced back then, Atletico Madrid. The club made arrangements for supporters to follow the team to Spain, either by air or overland by coach, and it was the latter move which brought them embarrassing headlines, as a nightmare journey left many travellers sadly disillusioned – while others, who'd risked setting their own itinerary, had the time

of their lives in the Spanish capital. There were no
complaints, however, about the performance on the
pitch, as Ian Marshall fired City into an early lead.
The defence then held firm until the closing stages
before Juninho, now plying his artistry in the Iberian
sunshine, carved out an equaliser that deflected off
Steve Walsh's outstretched leg, and a controversial
penalty gave Atletico a slight advantage. A thrilling
return leg at Leicester saw more controversy, as City
were twice denied clear spot-kicks and Garry Parker
was red-carded, effectively for taking a free-kick too
quickly. Two late goals on the break, as City continued
to press forward, finally ended the dream, but the
experience had been fun while it had lasted. A
postscript of the most minor consolation was that
UEFA removed French referee Remi Harrel from their
list less than a month later.

No consolation at all came from the domestic

Above: The special
atmosphere of floodlit
football is captured vividly on
the night of the return leg
with Atletico.

cups, with a Kevin Jobling equaliser setting City on
the slide to a 1-3 League Cup defeat at Grimsby, and a
nightmare game for Matt Elliott contributing to the
Bruce Dyer hat-trick by which Crystal Palace ousted
City from the FA Cup. The otherwise impeccable
Elliott earned himself recognition by Scotland this
term, and each of Keller, Kåmark, Savage, Lennon
and Zagorakis added to their full international
records, while Heskey and Stuart Campbell were
Under-21 regulars for England and Scotland
respectively.

Off the field, activity was intense. The board had
been in discussions with a stock market-listed
company called Soccer Investments since July, with a
view to a reverse takeover that would see Leicester
City floated as a plc on the Alternative Investment
Market. This status was achieved on 24th October,
with a sale of shares priced initially at 110p, and the

club nominally valued at around £36m; although trading fluctuations would soon see the share value fall to a more realistic level. There were soon plans on the table to spend some of the concomitant cash infusion: and they centred on a search for a new home for the club. It was recognised that a larger capacity was necessary to generate extra matchday revenue, and even more resources than the Carling Stand could provide would be needed to further increase ancillary commercial income, if City were to compete on anything like level terms with some of their Premier League rivals. Mere redevelopment of the Filbert Street site was deemed unfeasible. Much speculation attended the proposed siting of the planned 40,000-capacity stadium, until an announcement was eventually made that a brownfield site on Bede Island South, just across the canal from the existing ground, was the favoured option. An ambitious timescale would have City relocated by the millennium, but fears that progress on this matter would be far from problem-free gained ground as early as May, when Tom Smeaton resigned the chairmanship of the Football Club.

The chairman of the plc, Sir Rodney Walker, had earlier earned himself mild opprobrium by suggesting, in his parallel guise of chairman of the Rugby Football League, that he'd like to see his particular oval-ball game tried out at Filbert Street to gauge local interest in the sport. Instead, Leicester's status as a sporting city was confirmed by the hosting, in summer 1998, of the first-ever World Cup tournament for players with learning difficulties, at the Filbert Street climax of which Poland beat Brazil 4-0.

Above: Gerry Taggart was a bargain capture under the Bosman ruling.

Below: City's dramatic comeback against Leeds in the League Cup fourth round is crowned by Garry Parker's last minute penalty.

> By virtue of his exploits in firmly establishing City in the top half of the Premier League, Martin O'Neill was rapidly gaining a reputation as one of the most sought-after young managers in the game. His name would constantly be linked with any vacancy that may arise at any so-called 'bigger' or 'more fashionable' club. And so it was, in the summer of 1998, that Everton approached Leicester for permission to sound out O'Neill regarding the open post at Goodison Park, where Howard Kendall had returned unsuccessfully since the Merseysiders last expressed interest in the City boss. O'Neill was deemed to be vulnerable to a new approach, as he'd been irked by the cursory consultation he'd been allowed into the summer's boardroom reconstruction, and had delayed pledging his future to City until after his stint of World Cup TV punditry in France; but the new City board, under John Elsom, stood firm in refusing Everton permission to speak formally to the manager.

O'Neill expressed a little discontent but was soon re-committed to City's immediate on-field development; though the saga of outside tugs on his loyalty was far from over. He picked up the signature of defender Gerry Taggart on a free transfer under the Bosman ruling, and spent £2m on Frank Sinclair on the season's eve, after rejecting Belgian trialist full-back Olivier Suray. (Argentinian forward prospect Walter Otta would similarly soon be jettisoned; while Spencer Prior would raise £700,000 from Derby). An opening-day draw at Old Trafford could now be regarded as a disappointment (as, in this instance, it followed City taking a two-goal lead), and City were soon re-emphasising that they were nobody's mugs at the Premiership game.

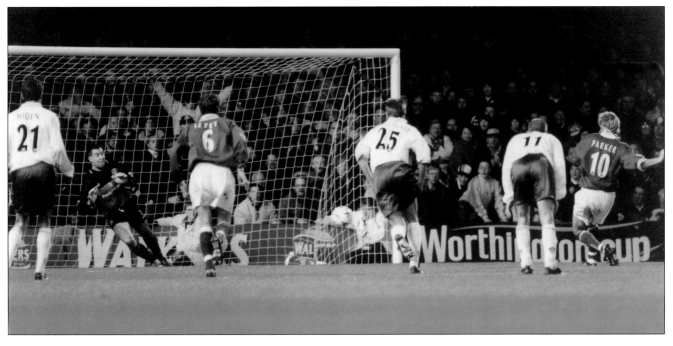

They were soon embroiled once more, though, in agonies over their totemic mentor. At the very end of September, George Graham resigned his post at Leeds to return to London with Tottenham Hotspur. His assistant, David O'Leary, took temporary charge, but it soon became clear that O'Neill was the number one target for the Elland Road club. Ironically, the clubs faced each other in West Yorkshire just as the speculation broke, with City grabbing an important win to further enhance the Ulsterman's standing. City chairman John Elsom stubbornly refused permission for Leeds to approach O'Neill, even though the manager believed that this attitude was a breach of a gentleman's agreement reached after the Everton affair. The whole business, featuring announcements via the Stock Exchange, seemed to drag out for an eternity as Elsom was forced by a quirk of the fixture list to wait a further 16 days before his trump card was played for him. The next game at Filbert Street saw Graham's Spurs arrive for a televised Monday night fixture, and the crowd finally seized their chance to make their feelings known. A mammoth show of impassioned support for O'Neill was displayed, and an emotionally draining evening was climaxed by a breathtaking Muzzy Izzet volley for City's winner. Days later, O'Neill announced he would be staying at Filbert Street, and Leicestershire heaved a collective sigh of relief. Ironically, but worthily, O'Neill then picked up the Manager of the Month award for October!

Amazingly enough, as the two clubs' fates seemed to become inextricably linked, Leeds had to visit Filbert Street on League Cup business in early November, and City turned near-certain defeat into

Top: Tony Cottee's first goal in the semi-final victory at Sunderland set the Foxes on the Wembley path once more.

Above: Kasey Keller's late save from Niall Quinn in the second leg kept City's slender lead intact.

victory with two very late goals, including another piece of spectacularly skilful opportunism from Izzet. Ten days later, Leeds then secured the services of City secretary Ian Silvester. In the background, ongoing negotiations were proving necessary to the attempt to secure planning permission for the new stadium at Bede Island South.

A return to the transfer market confirmed the renewal of focus on football itself. Seven-figure fees added each of Andrew Impey and Arnar Gunnlaugsson to the City squad, as league form went through a bit of a rollercoaster period; and both Manchester United at Filbert Street and Arsenal at Highbury delivered heavy defeats to ward off complacency. But the main story taking shape on the pitch was the re-emergence of Tony Cottee as a top

flight striker at the age of 33. Not only was he heading the club's goalscoring chart in the league, but he was also grabbing the glory in another fine League Cup run for City. His two goals had seen off Charlton's challenge in Round Three, and now he would prove the decisive influence at the semi-final stage. Two opportunist strikes at the daunting Stadium of Light gave City a precious first-leg lead over Division One leaders Sunderland, then another to equalise at Filbert Street sealed the Foxes' sixth trip to Wembley in the space of just eight years. On the very same night it was announced that the City Council had passed the plans for the new stadium development, so suddenly everything seemed to be cast in a rosy hue.

There was still, however, drama in store, and much of it revolved around the linkage of City and George Graham's Spurs, echoing the earlier intertwining with his previous club. Tottenham were to be City's Wembley opponents, and an intriguing stalemate developed, with the game leaning marginally in City's favour at the point Justin Edinburgh was sent off for striking Robbie Savage. There were no doubts that the offence was worthy of the red card, but Savage's late reaction to the incident won him few friends and stirred Spurs to repeated attempts at retribution. City held their concentration until the dying seconds of the game, when a break down the right led to Kasey Keller parrying a cross-shot directly into the path of Allan Nielsen, whose header proved a heartbreaking finale for the Foxes. National pressmen on duty were hastily instructed to change their selection of Man of the Match from Rob Ullathorne, who had accomplished a fine marking job on danger-man David Ginola, to the goalscorer; and many of the same metrocentric journalists were subsequently to go way over the top in their criticisms of Savage in particular, and City's defensive orientation in general. To make matters worse on the day, there had been an outbreak of crowd trouble caused by the presence of Spurs fans in the Leicester end, and an enquiry showed that the

Typical Wembley scenes created by the City fans as the teams emerge for the 1999 League Cup Final.

193

tickets acquired by the London supporters had emanated from sources within the City club – a major embarrassment that quickly led to the tightening of restrictions on allocations for future events.

The League Cup kerfuffle had no chance to die down, however, with City due at White Hart Lane on league business a week later. Savage was greeted with much hostility, but it was Cottee who stole the show for a highly motivated City, scoring the 200th league goal of his career to clinch maximum points from opponents against whom he'd netted both his first and 100th strikes. This game was the third in a sequence of eight unbeaten Premiership outings, and by the end of the term City had managed their third successive top-ten finish. Another double over Liverpool had accrued courtesy of Ian Marshall's last-minute strike, a fond Filbert Street farewell had been made to Pontus Kåmark, and young Stefan Oakes had won his introduction to the senior side. City topped the English Fair Play League for the least bookings and dismissals received during the season, but failed to have their name drawn in a June ballot for a possible entry to the UEFA Cup via this achievement. Steve Guppy finished the campaign as the only Premiership player to have completed 90 minutes of every single fixture, and Emile Heskey finally made his full England bow as a late substitute against Hungary, adding to City's roster this term of active internationals for the USA, Sweden, Jamaica, Greece, Iceland, Northern Ireland, Wales and Scotland.

City had mourned the death of one of their finest former managers, Matt Gillies, back in December; but were cheered in June when their current magician of a boss finally put pen to paper on his new contract, to expire in 2002. However, there was still a nagging feeling that storm clouds were gathering on the club's horizon, especially as the plans for the new ground were called in by the Government for further appraisal, amid worries that the essential accompanying retail developments breached planning guidelines.

Above: In a Final of few chances, Tony Cottee is denied by Tottenham's Ian Walker.
Below: Justin Edinburgh is dismissed after a clash with Robbie Savage.
Bottom: Steffen Iversen's cross that led to Spurs' late winner.

> When those clouds arrived, the result was not so much a storm as a full-blown hurricane. For some time there had been an unease between the footballing and commercial sides of the administration, exacerbated by an easily apparent hostility between Martin O'Neill and the club's CEO, Barrie Pierpoint. Indeed, football affairs were now run exclusively from the Belvoir Drive training ground, whilst the commercial team operated out of Filbert Street. This division had already led to trouble in the aftermath of the FA enquiry into the Wembley ticketing fiasco, when a breakdown in communication had resulted in several players being charged with failure to co-operate by missing a deadline for returning questionnaires about which they hadn't been informed. The board was clearly divided on the matter of assigning responsibility for this, and the matter came swiftly and dramatically to a head at a Friday evening board meeting in September.

Sir Rodney Walker, chairman of the plc, and John Elsom, chairman of the Football Club, departed early from the acrimonious meeting, and an announcement to the Stock Exchange soon followed that the pair had resigned. Their swift action to deny this was accompanied by the resignation of the club's stockbrokers, though the majority of their fellow directors continued to insist that this was the case. Both parties soon became entrenched in their antagonism, with claims and counter-claims being aired through the local media, and it became clear that the only way to resolve the impasse would be through an EGM. Walker and Elsom crucially appeared to have the support not only of Martin O'Neill, but also of former City favourite Gary Lineker, by now a presenter on BBC's 'Match of the Day'. O'Neill's backing ensured that the majority of small shareholders, the fans, would vote for Elsom, while Walker's reputation in the business world also seemed to carry sufficient weight to see off the challenge of the 'Gang of Four'. The meeting at Donington Park, when it came, was something of an anti-climax. Three of the four directors – Roy Parker, Gilbert Kinch and Philip Smith – resigned prior to the EGM, whilst Barrie Pierpoint was the only rebel to see himself voted off the board on the day itself. Elsom's new board was to welcome back former chairman Martin George and ex-director Bill Shooter, and encouraged City fans to believe they could now turn back to a concentration on events on the field.

Well, not quite, as the new stadium plans had also run into more trouble. The public enquiry, planned to start in December, had to be postponed after a late and extraordinary argument between the club and their proposed co-developers of the site, Goldwing

Above: Pressure from supporters preceded the removal of Chief Executive Barrie Pierpoint.

Below: Muzzy Izzet fires home the decisive penalty in the shoot-out against Leeds in the fourth round of the League Cup.

Bottom: Steve Walsh crowns a late comeback against Fulham in round five.

Properties. Rearranged for January, the enquiry was eventually called off when the new board announced it was pulling out of the scheme. In the face of falling gates, as football became ever more expensive for the traditional supporter, City announced that the plan for a 40,000-capacity stadium was to be shelved. Instead, options for a ground capable of seating 32,000 were to be investigated, with potential new sites coming under consideration as well as the possibility of looking once more at redeveloping the present ground. What became crystal clear, however, was that any new stadium would not be ready until 2001 at the earliest, and probably not until some time beyond that.

Now it was virtually inconceivable that such turmoil behind the scenes would fail to have a detrimental effect on the playing side of the club. Yet O'Neill's team seemed to derive strength from defying convention. They started the term with Lennon and Heskey on new contracts, with Tim Flowers having

City's attacking armoury, that would also come in handy elsewhere.

The parallel League Cup trail, once more a-winding towards Wembley in that stadium's final season as a venue for club competitions, was even more incident-packed and exciting. A comfortable two-leg win over Crystal Palace featured a cameo in goal from Theo Zagorakis, after both Pegguy Arphexad and Tim Flowers had been lost to injuries at Selhurst. A Flowers penalty save eased City's task against Grimsby, but he was not able actually to stop any of Leeds' spot-kicks, a couple of which were wayward, when City triumphed in the shoot-out following a goalless Filbert Street draw. In the next round, where City found themselves trailing 0-2 to First Division big spenders Fulham after 84 minutes, and fought back via inspirational veterans Ian Marshall and Steve Walsh to a 3-3 scoreline after extra time, it was Arphexad who was required to perform shoot-out heroics.

City utterly frustrated Aston Villa in the first leg of the semi-final, leading the ungracious John Gregory to join a chorus of wrong-headed criticism of City as a 'boring', spoiling side. Bad-loser Arsène Wenger and Chelsea's 'boardroom buffoon' Ken Bates had started this particular bandwagon rolling, paying no regard to how far the Foxes' squad was stretched, or to such tactically adventurous moves as sending defensive kingpin Elliott up front; but it was City's fans who would stop it in its tracks with their gleefully ironic rendering of "Boring, Boring Leicester" as a satisfyingly positive display in the second leg against Villa – and a decisive Elliott goal – clinched a date at Wembley for the seventh time in just nine seasons.

succeeded Kasey Keller in goal, and soon buttressed the squad with the acquisition of defender Phil Gilchrist. A point was dropped at Highbury, and two at home to Chelsea, when Frank Sinclair conceded injury-time own goals on each of the first two Saturdays, but he, just like the rest of a fairly settled selection, soon bounced back. Muzzy Izzet hit a fine goalscoring seam, becoming at the end of September the first City player to take a Carling Player of the Month award; Steve Guppy was capped for England against Belgium; and a position in the top half of the table was again soon achieved. O'Neill missed out on signing Sheffield Wednesday striker Andy Booth, but later added long-time target Darren Eadie to his playing strength at a club record £3m. Which was just as well, for suddenly a crippling list of injuries stripped the senior squad to the bare bones, and sometimes beyond.

Above: Matt Elliott heads City's 'Wembley goal' against Aston Villa in the League Cup semi-final.

In the face of this adversity, the season started to reshape itself around a string of epic cup battles, in which extra time and penalty shoot-outs became almost a new norm. In the FA Cup, Conference side Hereford United lasted 210 minutes against City, and took the lead, before succumbing in the Filbert Street replay. City and Arsenal couldn't be separated, and couldn't score, in an equivalent time-span, but sudden-death penalties did the trick for the Foxes. Defeat in Round Five at Chelsea was both predictable and predictably controversial, as a makeshift line-up fought hard to overcome their disbelief that the home side's second goal had been allowed to stand despite a clear foul on Gilchrist in its lead-up. Matt Elliott's last-minute consolation instanced in its sure-footed deadliness a new aspect of

This time the opposition was First Division Tranmere Rovers, a team blessed with a defender with a freakishly long throw, and captained by former Fox David Kelly. An open, lively Final, with plenty of goalmouth incident, provided a complete contrast to the events of twelve months earlier; though there was another red card for an opponent – with the substitute referee having no choice but to dismiss Clint Hill when he floored Emile Heskey from behind

Above: Manager Martin O'Neill and captain Matt Elliott lead out City at Wembley for the League Cup Final with Tranmere Rovers in 2000.

Right: Matt Elliott's header puts City into a first half lead.

Below right: Elliott's Cup winning header.

after the striker had turned him on the edge of the box. City's hero was again skipper Elliott, who headed home a brace of Steve Guppy corners, one in each half; with the second coming just three minutes after Kelly had snatched a late equaliser for the Birkenhead team. These goals, plus a near-faultless defensive display, earned Elliott the Man of the Match award, whilst all the time he'd been keeping one eye on his wife – due to give birth to their fourth child that very day – in the crowd. Though Tranmere took due plaudits for a spirited contribution to the game, City had in truth looked fairly comfortable throughout, and had squandered a few chances to stretch their lead. After all that had gone before during this campaign, this was a sweet victory indeed; and of course made City the first Premiership side to qualify for European competition in 2000.

Yet another set of adverse headlines had preceded the Final, when the club's pre-Wembley preparations at La Manga in Spain were abruptly terminated. Martin O'Neill had taken what many saw as a gamble in signing striker Stan Collymore – a deeply troubled individual in recent years – from Aston Villa. The terms of the transfer presented minimal risk to the club, and the newcomer had already indicated his willingness to work in a debut outing at Watford, so there was disappointment when his prank with a fire extinguisher on a boisterous first evening away led to the whole party being asked to leave. A suitably contrite Collymore accepted his substantial club fine,

Above: Matt Elliott, Neil Lennon and Robbie Savage celebrate City's third League Cup triumph.

Below: A proud moment for Martin O'Neill and 'Man of the Match' Elliott.

and then made an indelible mark on his home debut – scoring a fine hat-trick against Sunderland in a 5-2 victory. City fans could hardly wait for the partnership of Collymore and Heskey to develop from these stunningly effective beginnings, but were sadly to be denied the mouthwatering prospect. Only days later, both Leicester's and Liverpool's transfer records were updated by the £11m move of 'Bruno' to Anfield, and it was but a matter of weeks before Collymore would

Leicester Mercury

OUR HERO!

How City won the Worthington Cup
- 12-page picture special inside | Martin O'Neill's leap
year - Back Page

fall in agony at Derby, his leg broken in a freak accident during a game City dominated but lost 0-3.

Liverpool would also take a fancy to Pegguy Arphexad after the popular reserve 'keeper helped City to a third successive win at Anfield, yet even with such results adding to their legend, the Foxes couldn't quite bear to rest on their considerable campaign laurels until the very end of 1999/2000. A first win at The Dell since the late 60s cheered travelling supporters, while a 3-0 home win against Bradford City guaranteed the club its record Premiership points total. Even an abysmal final-day defeat at Hillsborough ended with City in their highest-ever Premiership placing of 8th.

Theo Zagorakis took his final Filbert Street bow in PRO Alan Birchenall's May testimonial game, and Ian Marshall was listed on a free transfer; while Muzzy Izzet would make his international bow during Euro 2000 after committing himself to the land of his father, Turkey. But the summer news was to be dominated by another chapter in the Martin O'Neill saga. The major job of restoring Celtic to their former glory had become vacant, and the attraction of that post to a Catholic Irishman could not be denied. In June, after chairman John Elsom had mounted a considerable effort to hold on to City's talismanic manager, Martin O'Neill left Leicester to pursue a dream in Glasgow. There wasn't a Foxes fan who wanted to lose him, but there were few who begrudged him the well-earned right to gamble on his ability to turn around an under-achieving club as comprehensively as he had done Leicester City.

Below: The peripatetic Stan Collymore, seen here in action against Ipswich in September 2000, would soon be off on his travels once more.

> Conversely, there were many commentators, both dispassionate and committed, ready to deem City's four successive top-ten Premiership finishes, and their recent pair of League Cup triumphs, as some sort of over-achievement. When the managerial role at Filbert Street was offered to Gillingham's Peter Taylor, however, he was clearly not among them. Like O'Neill, he was a former international player who had learned the managerial ropes in the straitened circumstances of non-league football, and had then tasted lower-division success on his return to the senior sphere. He had also made a name for himself during a spell as the Glenn Hoddle-appointed coach of the England Under-21 side, and arrived with quite a reputation for coaxing the best from younger players under his tutelage.

The initial fear around Filbert Street was that O'Neill's departure might spark a mass exodus to Glasgow. This was borne out in terms of key coaching staff following him northwards (with coach Steve Walford's loss a severe one), but was otherwise allayed when skipper Matt Elliott and, eventually, the hugely influential Neil Lennon signed new contracts, while other squad members seemed content to give life under the new regime a try.

Taylor's first objective was to add greater strength in depth to his inherited squad and, with the Heskey transfer fund at his disposal, he embarked earnestly on a recruitment campaign that quickly landed a quintet of newcomers; both equalling and then breaking the club transfer record in the process. Defenders Gary Rowett and Callum Davidson, goalkeeper Simon Royce and promising young striker

Above: City's record signing
Ade Akinbiyi puts the
Sunderland defence under
pressure at the Stadium of
Light in October 2000. The
goalless draw earned that
afternoon was enough to take
the Foxes to the top of the
Premiership.

Trevor Benjamin were the first through the door; and though Taylor suffered a knock-back when targeting his former Under-21 protegé Carl Cort, losing out to Newcastle for the forward, he soon turned instead to Wolves' Nigerian international Ade Akinbiyi, on whom the outlay was a record fee of £5m. Taylor would also initiate a fairly comprehensive new broom approach to other elements of the club's staffing, bringing in the experienced Colin Murphy (last at Filbert Street under David Pleat) as Football Co-Ordinator, former Gillingham player Steve Butler as head coach, and ex-Forest and Leeds starfinder Alan Hill to reorganise the entire Academy set-up.

As the team lined up for their opening Premiership fixture, with Rowett, Davidson and Akinbiyi set to make their debuts, most supporters were anticipating a transitional term and would gladly have settled for a mid-table position, an absence of relegation fears, and perhaps the bonus of a cup run. If, ultimately, that was exactly what they would get, none of them could have foreseen the rather crazy rollercoaster ride that would take them there. Indeed, any season that could see the club both sit on top of the league and also register a record sequence of consecutive defeats has to go down in the annals as unique. (As, probably, does a term in which a City fan would be ejected from the ground, and his season-ticket temporarily withdrawn, for falling asleep during a match!)

Perhaps it was the string of results in the early weeks that really defied logic. A run of particularly solid away performances was the key, including long overdue victories at both Upton Park and Stamford Bridge. Tim Flowers was in outstanding form in goal,

being beaten only once in open play in the first eight League fixtures and winning the Carling Player of the Month award for September. This was coupled with Manager of the Month kudos accruing to Taylor as the Foxes confounded the pundits to scale the heights.

An opportunity arose to move to the top of the table on 24th September, when City entertained Everton in front of the live TV cameras. A confident first-half display suggested everything was on course, but a stuttering second period led to a draw, and the chance was missed. At that moment, there were few who could have read the long-term portents of that second 45 minutes. Particularly as, a week later, on Sunday 1st October, a purposeful performance at the Stadium of Light earned another draw, and this time it would prove highly significant. An hour later, Arsenal's Thierry Henry spun on the edge of the box to deliver a spectacular winner against Manchester United, and the Foxes found themselves at the head of the league for the first time since August 1963.

	P	W	D	L	F	A	Pts
Leicester City	8	4	4	0	7	2	16
Manchester United	8	4	3	1	20	8	15
Arsenal	8	4	3	1	14	9	15
Newcastle United	8	4	1	3	8	7	13
Aston Villa	7	3	3	1	11	7	12
Charlton Athletic	8	3	3	2	14	13	12

By a quirk of the fixture list, with no games scheduled for the following week due to World Cup qualifiers, the Foxes were able to enjoy their longest-ever spell at the pinnacle, of 13 days.

Yet, even in the midst of the euphoria that

Below: Arnar Gunnlaugsson was a great favourite with the 'Blue Army'.

surrounded this achievement, the seeds of future problems were being sown. Two of City's most experienced players, Steve Walsh and Tony Cottee, who had made a joint application for the vacant managerial post in the summer, had been allowed to leave on the premise that their first-team opportunities would be limited as part of the rebuilt squad. Oddly, both moved to Norwich in September, in separate deals. Walsh had become 'Mr Leicester' over the past 14 years, and his departure was deeply lamented by the support. Cottee had also proved an astute investment for the club and, in a personally unsettled season, he would eventually play in all four divisions during the campaign; have his first taste of club management with a Barnet outfit destined to lose their League status; and end the term celebrating the Second Division championship with Mark McGhee's Millwall.

Stan Collymore was also proving something of a problem for Taylor. His match fitness was in question, yet the striker himself was unhappy at being a regular on the bench, and was seeking a pay rise. Before October was out, he too would have departed, with Bradford City the first stop on a rapid journey, via Spain, to the self-willed oblivion of retirement. In Collymore's case the parting was hastened by a serious and well-publicised half-time dispute with Trevor Benjamin during a reserve fixture against Charlton.

Almost imperceptibly, amidst the on-field success, the squad was becoming depleted of experience, and the first to really suffer was record buy Akinbiyi, who was now denied the opportunity to develop alongside a regular partner, and was expected to carry the main weight of leading the line himself. It was not part of Taylor's blueprint for Akinbiyi's progress, and it would prove a heavy burden as the season unfolded.

City's sojourn at the top of the table was brought to an abrupt halt by Manchester United, who cruised to a 3-0 victory at Filbert Street as City froze; taking over the leadership, and soon stretching it to win the title at a canter.

By that time, the European adventure had also come off the rails. Although seeded as an English entrant, City were given possibly the most difficult draw of all, having to face Yugoslav Double-winners (and former European Cup winners) Red Star Belgrade. A flurry of flares from the visitors' section of the East Stand gave Filbert Street a particularly European flavour as the first leg kicked off, and the smoke had yet to clear by the time the Yugoslavs had taken a grip on the tie, scoring a stunning 25-yarder in the opening minute. City did manage to equalise through Gerry Taggart, and missed the odd late

Above: The arrival of Roberto Mancini at Filbert Street in February 2001 brought a touch of genuine world class to the team. He is seen here in action against Chelsea's Dennis Wise.

Above: Kevin Ellison was a surprise debutant at Old Trafford in March 2001.

chance to take the lead, but looked to be severely up against it for the return leg. By order of UEFA, this was switched at the last minute to Vienna as a consequence of the turbulent political situation in Serbia, and while there were none of the travel problems for the fans that Madrid had prompted three years earlier, the matchday 'welcome' was hostile in the extreme. The team gave a good account of themselves in the first half, equalising Red Star's opener with a close-range Izzet goal, and suffering a series of near-misses from Darren Eadie, but the 'home' team stepped up a gear after the break, and ran out clear winners.

Back on the domestic scene, City continued to hold a place in the top six, having taken 14 points from the opening seven away games; giving rise to expectations of a further European qualification via their Premiership position. Ironically, the only defeat on their travels, and only away goal conceded during this spell, was attributable to Emile Heskey at Anfield. In light of this, it seemed all the more inexplicable when the wheels came off away from Filbert Street. An utterly undeserved hammering at White Hart Lane, featuring a Les Ferdinand hat-trick, was the signal for a lengthy run of defeats on their travels that would last until the end of the season and significantly undermine those European hopes. Even worse, a team accustomed to applying a degree of attacking flair on their travels now seemed directed to withdraw into a negative defensive shell for eminently winnable away games, and confidence drained after they came away pointless from several matches where a draw sadly looked to be the height of their ambition.

Increasingly, City had to rely on their home form

to maintain their challenge and, generally, this held firm until March, culminating in a fine display in the return fixture with Liverpool that saw the Foxes end the afternoon still in fourth place in the Premiership. By that time another experienced player, Neil Lennon, had finally elected to rejoin his mentor at Celtic Park (there to share in eventual Treble-winning glory), though his Filbert Street swansong had been one of the more memorable displays of the campaign, a 3-1 home victory over a Leeds side parading British record signing Rio Ferdinand for a debut at the heart of a defence City soon reduced to disarray. Also, Tim Flowers had picked up a hip injury that had kept him sidelined since New Year's Day. His deputy Simon Royce had put well behind him a traumatic debut of his own (though he was actually blameless for the home League Cup humiliation at the hands of First Division strugglers Crystal Palace), and was performing creditably between the sticks without ever quite replicating the imposing presence of the ex-England man.

Promising progress was nonetheless being made in the FA Cup. Fairly routine home victories over York and Bristol City bracketed a Villa Park humdinger eventually settled by supersub Arnar Gunnlaugsson's ferocious shot over David James; later adjudged City's Goal of the Season. And City were already counting on a semi-final slot when they prepared to follow up that Liverpool victory with, a week later, a home encounter with lowly Second Division visitors Wycombe Wanderers. Such were the latter's problems with injuries and suspensions that they had even advertised on the internet for an eligible striker, and actually recruited Roy Essandoh on a trialist's contract as a result of that initiative. Though the game should have been a formality, instead City froze into ineptitude once more; and it was substitute Essandoh who completed the nightmare / fairy-tale by heading the winning goal deep into stoppage time. Leicester were devastated and, even worse, had suffered serious injuries to key midfielders Izzet and Savage during the game. Their loss, and the absences of Elliott and Taggart which followed, led to the fielding of some distinctly inexperienced line-ups over the next few weeks, with interim buys like Matthew Jones, Junior Lewis, Lee Marshall and the highly promising Damien Delaney having to shoulder immense responsibilities. Results unsurprisingly suffered, with even home points being gifted in succession to relegation strugglers Coventry, Manchester City and Middlesbrough, and the upshot was the establishment of a new overall club record of nine consecutive defeats. A tumble into the bottom half of the table was inevitable, and prayers of thanks given that City had

Above: Peter Taylor turned to his former club, Gillingham, in April 2001 to sign midfield anchorman Junior Lewis, seen here in action against Paul Ince of Middlesbrough.

accumulated sufficient points early in the campaign to avert any danger of being dragged into the relegation mire themselves.

Inevitably, some factions of the public questioned Taylor's managerial and coaching abilities during this abysmal sequence. Yet the City boss was so highly thought of elsewhere that he had been invited by the FA to take temporary charge of the England team back in October, after Kevin Keegan's resignation, and had continued to work alongside the new manager, Sven-Goran Eriksson, thereafter. Taylor's initial elevation completed a unique treble for the City of Leicester, as both James Whitaker and John Wells already held managerial and coaching roles respectively in the England cricket and rugby union set-ups.

Taylor's first England squad, for a friendly against Italy in Turin, contained no players over the age of 30; a clear signal that the Leicester boss still preferred to work with the younger element. This came as a particular disappointment for the in-form Flowers, who was being widely touted for an England recall at the time. More successful in adding to their tallies of caps during the term were Elliott, Davidson, Savage, Izzet, Lennon, Jones and Taggart; while Benjamin made a belated breakthrough to the Under-21 side, and Young Player of the Year Jordan Stewart was capped at Under-18 level.

One fascinating spin-off from Taylor's links with ex-Lazio boss Eriksson was the arrival on a short-term deal in January of football legend Roberto Mancini, who had nominally retired to the Roman club's coaching staff, but was deemed fit enough to add experience to City's Premiership side. It was unfortunate, given the flashes of artistry he had produced while getting to know both his teammates and the idiosyncracies of English football, that he would cut short his stay after only a month, when the Fiorentina coaching job became available. City's other January recruit was Derby striker Dean Sturridge, who at least offered a seasoned foil to Akinbiyi for much of the rest of the term.

Off the field, a whole new set of plans were drawn up for the future stadium, this time with a 32,000 capacity, to be sited on Freeman's Wharf, a decent goal-kick away from the present home and just across the river from the now abandoned Bede Island footprint. Initial plans were approved by the Council and the land acquired from its owners, Powergen. The date for the move could turn out to be as early as 2002 if the outstanding planning issues are dealt with promptly, the financial bond is raised without hindrance, and building work proceeds without

Above: Andrew Impey began to blossom at Filbert Street under the tutelage of Peter Taylor.

Below: A computer generated impression of the new stadium, for which construction began in the summer of 2001.

undue disruption from the weather; though it should be no later than 2003 at worst. Even so, Filbert Street itself, made available for future sale in June, was still chosen to host an Under-21 international in May, when England entertained Mexico on the night before the senior side met the same opponents at Derby's Pride Park.

Another change, which will be in evidence much earlier, is the ending of the shirt sponsorship deal with Walkers Crisps which has run since 1987. The logo of LG Electronics will henceforth adorn the royal blue; with the income of some £2.5m thereby derived being added to the massively increased pot of gold that is City's share of the Premiership's renegotiated TV deals.

Just how wisely Peter Taylor may spend the proportion of these riches the Board allow him will be for future chroniclers of Leicester City Football Club to gauge with the wisdom of hindsight. Just how far he may extend his preferred investment in younger talent (bolstered by the club's imaginative youth development tie-up with Cork City), or whether in the short term he will send out teams characterised by either fear or flamboyance, are questions soon to be answered. There is one certainty, though. That there will have been another whole hatful of highs and lows enjoyed or endured by the Filbert Street faithful by the time the next update of this volume comes about. Though, of course, they'll not actually be referred to as the Filbert Street faithful any more!

> In a slightly portentous Afterword to our narrative back in 1989, we waxed rather philosophical about the game, and its relation to its supporters – looking for signs of optimism in those dark days for football as a whole and pretty grey ones for Leicester City in particular. We could still make glibly downbeat observations on some of the excesses and injustices the current football world is prey to (especially about the way that the financial and sports pages of the press now seem all-too-naturally interchangeable); though we'd definitely be justified in putting a more upbeat complexion on Fox-specific matters. I think we've realised, though, that there is no postscript possible in regard to a sport which inhabits an eternal present. The professionals really do take each game as it comes (and, the cynical might add, each pay-cheque, and each transfer...); and it is only really the committed punter for whom the game's and the club's tradition – or history – holds value. We sincerely hope this version of that history contributes in some way to the rich experience of being – proudly –a supporter.

Below: The old and new will go side by side, barely a hefty goal-kick apart, when the club make the move from Filbert Street to Freeman's Wharf in the near future.

Statistics&Records

Only a few notes of explanation should be required to buttress the largely self-explanatory tabulation of records on a season-by-season, match-by-match basis which follows in this section.

FOOTBALL LEAGUE

In the case of two fixtures, the scoreline we record is at variance with that entered in the Football League records. Meticulous rechecking of contemporary reports in both local and national newspapers assures us of our own accuracy in noting the home fixture against Walsall on 28.11.1896 as having ended 4-2 (rather than 4-1) and the away game against Hull City on 26.04.1913 as having ended 0-2 (rather than 1-2).

FA CUP

The structure of the FA Cup as we now know it, with clubs from the top two divisions exempt until the Third Round Proper, was only settled on in 1925. Here we chart the equivalent rounds for competitions in which Fosse and City took part before season 1925/6:

1925-date	(Qual Rds)			Rd1	Rd2	Rd3	Rd4	Rd5	Rd6	S/F	F
1914-1925					Q6	Rd1	Rd2	Rd3	Rd4	S/F	F
1906-1914					(Q5)	Rd1	Rd2	Rd3	Rd4	S/F	F
1905/6					(Q4)	Rd1	Rd2	Rd3	Rd4	S/F	F
1904/5	Q3	Q4	Q5	Q6	Int	Rd1	Rd2	Rd3		S/F	F
1900-1904		Q3	Q4	Q5	Int	Rd1	Rd2	Rd3		S/F	F
1896-1900			Q3	Q4	Q5	Rd1	Rd2	Rd3		S/F	F
1890-1896		Q1	Q2	Q3	Q4	Rd1	Rd2	Rd3		S/F	F

(eg: Fosse's achievement in reaching Rd2 in 1893/4 was the equivalent of reaching the modern Rd5; while their exit at Qual Rd6 in 1914/15 equated to a failure to attain the modern Rd3)

Fosse's exemption status varied from season to season: the round of their entry into the competition for any given season is marked appropriately in the following pages. City automatically entered the competition at the Rd1 stage between 1919-25, and have continued to do so ever since at the equivalent Rd3 stage.

FOOTBALL LEAGUE CUP

The number and format of rounds in this competition has also varied over the years since its inception in 1960, as has City's exemption status; as this chart, compiled on the same basis as above, indicates:

1979-2001	Rd1/1	Rd1/2	Rd2/1	Rd2/2	Rd3	Rd4	Rd5	SF/1	SF/2		F
1975-1979	Rd1/1	Rd1/2		Rd2	Rd3	Rd4	Rd5	SF/1	SF/2		F
1966-1975		Rd1		Rd2	Rd3	Rd4	Rd5	SF/1	SF/2		F
1961-1966		Rd1		Rd2	Rd3	Rd4	Rd5	SF/1	SF/2	F/1	F/2
1960/1				Rd1	Rd2	Rd3	Rd4	SF/1	SF/2	F/1	F/2

City's entry into the competition was in Rd1 in 1961/2, but has been at the Rd2 stage ever since, apart from 1979/80 and 1991/2, when the previous seasons' lowly Second Division positions were taken into account and necessitated Rd1 entry, and 1997/8 and 2000/1, when byes to Rd3 were granted in acknowledgement of UEFA Cup qualification.

NUMBERING

Though players did not wear numbered shirts until 1939, we have taken notice of the widespread tactical adherence to specialist positional play before this date, and have followed the traditional practice of assigning numbers in the line-up grids as follows:

1 - Goalkeeper; 2 - Right-back; 3 - Left-back; 4 - Right-half; 5 - Centre-half; 6 - Left-half; 7 - Outside-right; 8 - Inside-right; 9 - Centre-forward; 10 - Inside-left; 11 - Outside-left.

Perhaps more contentiously, we have also consistently maintained a 1 - 11 numbering system for recent seasons when players have actually worn squad numbers (which are nonetheless indicated). Positional relevance here is admittedly tenuous, but at least this practice allows easy differentiation of the starting line up from the substitutes who are numbered from 12 to 14.

We record substitutes only if they actually played for any part of the game in question. For the period from 1965 to 1986, we mark the player withdrawn with *. For the period from 1986 to 1994, we note the number (12 or 14) the substitute actually wore, and mark the player withdrawn with * when replaced by 12 and † when replaced by 14.

For 1994/5 when two substitutes were allowed but squad numbers utilised, the first player withdrawn is marked with * and replaced by 12, the second player withdrawn is marked with † and replaced by 13.

For 1995/6, actual shirt numbers are used but three substitutes were allowed. Player number 12 replaces *; player number 13 replaces †; player number 14 replaces ‡.

For 1996 to date, three substitutes had been allowed but players wore squad numbers. Player number 12 replaces *, the first to be withdrawn; player 13 replaces †, the second to be withdrawn; player 14 replaces ‡, the third to be withdrawn.

Match No	Date	Opponents	Result	Scorers	Att	Charlie Walker	Sammy Rowson	Billy Davis	Ernest Nuttall	Dick Perry	Jimmy Johnson	Jimmy Flint	Jimmy Murdoch	Harry Webb	Teddy Johnson	Jimmy Atter									Match No
FA CUP																									
1	Oct 4 H	Burton Wanderers (Q1)	L 0-4	- / Brown 2, Dicken 2		1	2	3	4	5	6	7	8	9	10	11									1

Note: Oct 4, played at Mill Lane.

1886-87
Back: Hurndall, Hassell, W Johnson, Taylor (umpire), H Johnson, De Ville, Knight.
Middle: Smith, Ashmole, Gardner, West;
Front: J Johnson, Bankart, E Johnson.

1888-89
No caption available

Champions: Rotherham Town

MIDLAND LEAGUE

Match No	Date		Opponents	Result	Points	Scorers	Att
1	Sep 12	H	Derby Junction	W 1-0	2	J Atter	
2	Oct 10	H	Grantham Rovers	W 3-1	4	Lord, Webb, J Atter / Southwell	
3	17	A	Burton Wanderers	L 0-6	4	- / S Holmes 3, Miller 2, Lowe	
4	Nov 14	A	Loughborough Town	L 2-6	4	Mouel, J Atter / Carnelly 3, Freestone, Shelton, Lowe	4000
5	28	H	Loughborough Town	L 1-2	4	Mouel / W Kelham, Freestone	2000
6	Dec 5	A	Wednesbury Old Athletic	W 4-3	6	Hufton, Mouel, J Atter, Webb / Longmore, Danks, Harvey	2000
7	19	A	Grantham Rovers	L 0-2	6	- / Pulling, Mulvey	
8	26	A	Doncaster Rovers	L 0-1	6	- / Edwards	1800
9	Jan 2	H	Burton Wanderers	L 1-6	6	Bennett / Orton 3, S Holmes, F Holmes 2	1000
10	9	H	Rotherham Town	W 4-1	8	J Atter 2, Mouel 2 / Oxley	800
11	23	A	Long Eaton Rangers	L 1-5	8	Bennett / Plackett, Saxton 3, Osborne	
12	30	H	Wednesbury Old Athletic	W 1-0	10	Johnson	
13	Feb 13	H	Gainsborough Trinity	L 0-3	10	- / Cook 2, Cookson	
14	Mar 12	A	Derby Junction	D 0-0	11		
15	19	A	Gainsborough Trinity	L 0-1	11	- / DeVille (og)	
16	Apr 9	H	Long Eaton Rangers	D 0-0	12		
17	16	A	Rotherham Town	L 0-11	12	- / Leather 5, McCormick 2, Longden 2, Cutts, Rogers	
18	19	H	Burslem Port Vale	L 1-3	12	Herbert Bailey / McGinnis 2, Dean	4000
19	28	A	Burslem Port Vale	L 0-4	12	- / McGinnis 2, unknown 2	150
20	30	H	Doncaster Rovers	D 0-0	13		3000

Final League Position: 11

League Appearances: 7 6 17 20 3 18 7 15 5 18 16 4 15 2 13 2 5 1 1 10 3 2 3 1 1 4 1 1 1

League Goals: 1 — 2 2 1 6 1 — 5 — — — — — — — — — — — 1 —

FA CUP

Match No	Date		Opponents	Result		Scorers	Att
1	Oct 3	H	Small Heath (Q1)	L 2-6		Nuttall, Herrod / Hands, Millard 2, Hallam, Wheldon 2	1000

Player columns: George Old, Sammy Rowson, Harry Bailey, Jack Lord, Billy Davis, Ernest Nuttall, Bob Herrod, Harry Webb, A Bennett, Teddy Johnson, Jimmy Atter, Sammy Hufton, Albert Vickers, Ernest Mouel, Benny Wood, James Owen, Charlie Walker, Dick Perry, Frank Gardner, Charles Atter, W Harris, Tom DeVille, Harry Taylor, J King, R Lewis, C Lisle, Amos Atkins, Herbert Bailey, R Winter, J Mabbott, E Wilkins

Note: Sep 12, Oct 3, Oct 10, played at Aylestone Road; Apr 16, Fosse played with 10 men, Atkins failed to turn up;
Staveley withdrew from the Midland League after the competition began and their record was expunged; Fosse had not played them at that time.

1889-90
Back: Gardner (Secretary), Rowson, Walker, Davis, Cooper (umpire).
Middle: Squire, J Johnson, Murdoch, Perry, Vickers.
Front: Bentley, Thompson, West, E Johnson, Atter.

1890-91
Back: Stubbs, Cooper (Treasurer), Rowson, Walker, Gardner (Secretary), Hillman.
Middle: Flint, Murdoch, J Johnson, Davis, Nuttall.
Front: E Johnson, Perry, Atter.

Champions: Rotherham Town

MIDLAND LEAGUE

Match No	Date		Opponents	Result	Points	Scorers	Att	Jimmy Thraves	Harry Bailey	Harry Taylor	Ernest Nuttall	Edward Silvester	Jack Lord	William Lowe	Alf Slack	Alf Carter	Levi Freeman	Billy Dorrell	James Owen	Harry Webb	J Mabbott	George Smith	Walter Hardy	Jack Frettingham	Jimmy Atter	J Stott	James Priestman	Arthur Henrys	Arthur Worrall	Match No
1	Sep 17	A	Mansfield Town	L 1-4		Lowe / Emmerson, Leivers, Fazey, Elliman		1	2	3	4	5	6	7	8	9	10	11												1
2	26	A	Rotherham Town	L 1-6		Freeman / unknown 6		1		3	4		5	6	7		9	10	11	2	8									2
3	Oct 1	H	Newark	W 7-1	2	Slack 3, Freeman 2, Silvester, Dorrell / Parlby	3000	1		3	4		5	6	7		9	10	11	2	8									3
4	8	A	Kettering	W 4-0	4	Webb 3, Mabelstone (og)	1500	1		3	4		5	6	7		9	10	11	2	8									4
5	22	H	Derby Junction	W 4-0	6	Lowe, Dorrell, Freeman, Webb		1		3	4		5	6	7		9	10	11	2	8									5
6	Nov 12	A	Loughborough Town	L 1-2	6	Slack / Carnelly, J Start	5000	1		3	4		5	6	7		9	10	11	2	8									6
7	26	H	Grantham Rovers	W 2-0	8	Mabbott, Slack	2000	1		3	4		5	6	7		9	10	11		2	8								7
8	Dec 17	H	Doncaster Rovers	W 1-0	10	Freeman	1000	1		3	4	6	5		8	9		10	11		7	2								8
9	24	A	Wednesbury Old Athletic	L 2-3	10	Hardy, Slack / Cooper 2, Longmore		1		3	4	6	5			9			11		8	2	7	10						9
10	Jan 7	H	Doncaster Rovers	L 0-1	10	- / W Smith	4000	1		3	4	6	5		8	9			11		10	2	7							10
11	14	H	Burton Wanderers	L 1-2	10	Hardy / A Capes, Harley		1		3	4	6	5		8	9			11		10	2	7							11
12	21	A	Gainsborough Trinity	W 2-1	12	Carter, Slack / Gordon		1		3	4	6			8	9	10		11			2	7							12
13	28	A	Grantham Rovers	W 2-1	14	Dorrell, Lowe / Watson		1		3	4	6	5		8	9	10		11			2	7							13
14	Feb 4	H	Wednesbury Old Athletic	W 3-1	16	Lowe 2, Slack / Longmore		1		3	4	6	5		8	9	10		11			2	7							14
15	18	H	Gainsborough Trinity	W 2-1	18	Taylor, Lowe / Prentice		1		3	4	6	5			9	10		7			2	8	11						15
16	25	A	Burton Wanderers	L 0-3	18	- / Hearne 2, A Capes		1		3	4	6			5	10			7			2	8	11	9					16
17	Mar 4	H	Rotherham Town	D 1-1	19	Lowe / Leatherbarrow		1		3	4	6		5	9	10			7			2	8	11						17
18	11	A	Long Eaton Rangers	L 1-2	19	Nuttall / Saxton, Plackett		1		3	4	6		5	9	10			7			2	8		11					18
19	18	H	Loughborough Town	D 1-1	20	Dorrell / J Start	13000	1		3	4	6		5	9	10			7			2	8	11						19
20	Apr 1	A	Newark	D 3-3	21	Dorrell, Nuttall, Lowe / Oswald, Frettingham, Walton		1		3	4	6		5	9	10			7			2		11			8			20
21	3	H	Long Eaton Rangers	L 0-1	21	- / Sheppard		1		3	4	6		5		9		10	7			2		11			8			21
22	8	H	Kettering	W 3-1	23	Dorrell 2, Slack / Garfield		1		3	5	4			9		10	7	8			2		11			6			22
23	22	H	Mansfield Town	W 5-1	25	Worrall, Lowe, Priestman 2, Slack / Gill (p)		1		3	5	4			7	8		10				2		11			6	9		23
24	27	A	Derby Junction	W 3-1	27	Webb 2, Dorrell / Wood		1		3	4		5		9			7				2		11	10	6				24

| Final League Position: | | | **4** | | | League Appearances | | 24 | 24 | 24 | 17 | 11 | 17 | 20 | 24 | 4 | 10 | 24 | 5 | 11 | 1 | 18 | 11 | 1 | 8 | 1 | 3 | 5 | 1 | |
| | | | | | | League Goals | | | 1 | 2 | 1 | | | 9 | 10 | 1 | 5 | 8 | | 6 | 1 | | 2 | | | | 2 | 1 | | |

FA CUP

Match No	Date		Opponents	Result	Scorers	Att	Thr	Tay	Nut	Lord	Lowe	Slack	Freeman	Dorrell	Owen	Webb	Mabbott		Match No
1	Oct 15	H	Rushden (Q1)	W 7-0	Lowe, Webb 3, Dorrell 3 (1p)	3000	1	3	4	5	6	7	9	10	11	2	8		1
2	29	A	Notts Olympic (Q2)	D 3-3 aet	Lowe, Freeman, Thompson (og) / Geary, Mann, Buck		1	3	4	5	6	7	9	10	11	2	8		2
3	Nov 5	H	Notts Olympic (Q2 rep)	W 7-0	Dorrell 4, Webb 2, Slack	4000	1	3	4	5	6	7	9	10	11	2	8		3
4	19	H	Buxton (Q3)	L 1-2	Freeman / F Kitchen, C Finney	5000	1	3		4	5	6	7	9	10	11	2	8	4

Stand-in Goalkeepers: Sep 17, Lowe for Thraves (temporary), Mansfield Town (a), for first 35 minutes until Thraves turned up.
Note: Oct 29, abandoned during extra time, result at 90 minutes stood; Mar 18, record attendance at Filbert Street.
Nov 26, George Smith made his debut under the pseudonym of Bob Thompson

1892-93
Back: Marson (Secretary), Carter, Lord, Bailey, Silvester, Smith (Trainer). **Middle:** Thraves, Lowe, Nuttall, Slack, Webb. **Front:** Dorrell, Taylor.

Season **1893-94**

Champions: Burton Wanderers

MIDLAND LEAGUE

Match No	Date		Opponents	Result	Points	Scorers	Att	Jimmy Thraves	George Smith	Harry Bailey	Tom Seymour	Arthur Henrys	Jack Lord	Jacky Hill	William Miller	Arthur Worrall	H Shaw	Billy Dorrell	Jack Rickus	Alf Slack	Harry Taylor	Harry Edwards	Jimmy Brown	Billy Davis	James Priestman	Herbert Bailey	Willie McArthur	Match No
1	Sep 9	H	Burton Wanderers	L 1-2		Worrall / A Capes, AJ Capes	5000	1	2	3	4	5	6	7	8	9	10	11										1
2	23	H	Long Eaton Rangers	W 3-0	2	Hill, Worrall, Henrys	4000	1	2	3	4	5	6	7	8	9		11	10									2
3	30	A	Gainsborough Trinity	D 0-0	3		2000	1	2	3	4	5	6	7	8	9		11	8	10								3
4	Oct 7	A	Loughborough Town	L 0-1	3	- / W Storer	6000	1	2	3	10	5	6	7	8	9		11			4							4
5	21	H	Mansfield Town	W 4-0	5	Miller, Dorrell, Seymour, Edwards	3000	1	2	3	4	5	6	7	9			11	10			8						5
6	Nov 18	H	Doncaster Rovers	W 2-1	7	Brown, Dorrell / Cartwright	2000	1	2	3	4	5	6	7	10			11				8	9					6
7	Dec 2	H	Newark	W 3-0	9	Hill 2, Miller	3000	1	2	3	4		6	7	10			11				8	9	5				7
8	9	H	Mansfield Greenhalghs	W 4-2	11	Dorrell, Brown 3 / Roper, May	2000	1		3	4		6	7	10			11		2		8	9	5				8
9	23	H	Grantham Rovers	W 4-0	13	Miller 2, Brown 2	4000	1	2	3	4	5	6	7	10			11				8	9					9
10	Jan 6	H	Loughborough Town	W 4-0	15	Dorrell, Hill, Brown, Lord	6000	1	2	3	4	5	6	7	10			11				8	9					10
11	13	H	Gainsborough Trinity	W 3-1	17	Brown, Edwards, Hill / Haynes	3000	1	2	3	4	5	6	7	10			11				8	9					11
12	20	A	Doncaster Rovers	W 2-1	19	Slack, Guild (og) / Lees	1500	1	2	3	4	5	6	7	10			11		9		8						12
13	Feb 3	A	Long Eaton Rangers	W 2-0	21	Miller, Fairbrother (og)	1000	1		3	4	5	6	7	10			11			2	8	9					13
14	24	H	Kettering	W 4-0	23	Brown, Hill, Miller, McDermott (og)	4000	1	2	3	4	5	6	7	10			11				8	9					14
15	Mar 3	A	Mansfield Greenhalghs	W 3-0	25	Hill, Brown 2		1	2	3	4	5	6	7	10			11				8	9		11			15
16	10	A	Burton Wanderers	L 1-2	25	Dorrell / A Capes, Garfield	3500	1	2	3	4	5	6	7	10			11				8	9					16
17	17	A	Newark	W 2-0	27	Dorrell 2		1	2	3	4	5	6	7	10			11					9		8			17
18	24	A	Kettering	D 1-1	28	Brown / Dixon	2000	1	2	3	4	5	6	7	10			11					9		8			18
19	Apr 4	A	Mansfield Town	W 3-0	30	Lord, Priestman, Brown		1	2	3	4	5	6	8	10			11					9		7			19
20	28	A	Grantham Rovers	W 3-2	32	Miller, Brown, Dorrell / Mulvey, Senior		1	2	3	4		6	7	10			11				8	9		5	8	9	20

Final League Position:				2		**League Appearances**		20	18	20	20	18	19	20	20	3	1	19	3	2	3	12	14	2	4	1	1	
						League Goals					1	1	2	7	7	2		8		1		2	14		1			

FA CUP

Match No	Date		Opponents	Result	Scorers	Att	Jimmy Thraves	George Smith	Harry Bailey	Tom Seymour	Arthur Henrys	Jack Lord	Jacky Hill	William Miller	Billy Dorrell	Harry Taylor	Harry Edwards	Jimmy Brown	James Priestman	Match No
1	Nov 4	H	Mansfield Town (Q2)	W 1-0	Dorrell	4000	1	2	3	10	5	6	7	9	11	4	8			1
2	25	A	Mansfield Greenhalghs (Q3)	W 5-0	Brown, Hill, Lord, Miller, Haslam (og)	5000	1	2	3	4	5	6	7	10	11		8	9		2
3	Dec 16	A	Loughborough Town (Q4)	W 1-0	Dorrell	8000	1		2	6	5	4	7	10	11	3	8	9		3
4	Jan 27	H	South Shore (1)	W 2-1	Hill, Brown / S Parkinson	4000	1	2	3	4	5	6	7	10	11		8	9		4
5	Feb 10	H	Derby County (2)	D 0-0		12000	1	2	3	4	5	6	7	10	11		8	9		5
6	17	A	Derby County (2 rep)	L 0-3	- / Allan, McMillan, Francis	4000	1	2	3	4	5	6	7	10	11		8	9		6

Note: Nov 18, abandoned after 50 minutes when Doncaster Rovers walked off, Midland League directed that result should stand; Nov 25, drawn away, but tie switched to Filbert Street;

Football League re-election voting: Ardwick 20 (re-elected), Leicester Fosse 20, Burton Wanderers 17, Bury 17 (all elected), Rotherham Town 15, Blackpool 8, Loughborough Town 8, Accrington 7, Rossendale 0. Rotherham Town subsequently re-elected after Middlesbrough Ironopolis went into liquidation.

1893-94 (with various committee members)
Back: unknown, Hartopp, Lee, Curtis.
Second Row: Jones, Cooper, W Brown, Smith, Thraves, Bailey, unknown, Ashwell, Porter, Seddon.
Third Row: Kilby, Marson (Secretary), Hughes, J Brown, McArthur, Henrys, Lord, Gardner.
Front: Hill, Priestman, Miller, Dorrell.

Season 1894-95

Promoted: Bury
Re-election: Lincoln City (elected), Walsall Town Swifts (not elected), Burslem Port Vale, Crewe Alexandra (both elected)

FOOTBALL LEAGUE DIVISION TWO

Match No	Date		Opponents	Result	Pts	Pos	Scorers	Att	Thraves	Smith	Bailey	Seymour	Brown	Henrys	Hill	Hughes	McArthur	Skea	Priestman	Whitelaw	Gallacher	Lord	Miller	Stirling	Gordon	McFarlane	Thompson	Match No
1	Sep 1	A	Grimsby Town	L 3-4		-	Skea 2, McArthur / McCairns, Fletcher 2, Bailey (og)	5000	1	2	3	4	5	6	7	8	9	10	11									1
2	8	H	Rotherham Town	W 4-2	2	5	Skea 3, Gallacher / Bryant, McCormick	4000	1		2	4	5	6	7	8	9	10			3	11						2
3	15	H	Burton Wanderers	L 1-2	2	9	Skea / Moore, R Brown	8000	1		2	4		6	7	8	9	10			3	11	5					3
4	22	H	Newton Heath	L 2-3	2	12	Skea, McArthur / Dow 2, Smith	6000	1		2	4	5	6	7	8	9	10			3		11					4
5	29	A	Newcastle United	L 0-2	2	14	- / Thompson 2	5000	1		2	4	5	6	7		8	9			3	11	10					5
6	Oct 6	A	Notts County	L 0-3	2	15	- / Allsopp 2, Daft	10000	1	2		4	5	6	7	8		10			3	11			9			6
7	20	H	Newcastle United	D 4-4	3	15	McArthur, Henrys, Miller 2 / Dickson, Thompson, Willis, Smith (p)	8000	1	2		4	5	6	7		8	10			3	11			9			7
8	27	A	Newton Heath	D 2-2	4	15	Skea 2 / McNaught, Smith	3000	1	2		4	5	6	7		8	10			3	11			9			8
9	Nov 10	H	Darwen	W 2-1	6	12	Hill, McArthur / Hartley	5000	1	2		4		6	11	5	8	10			3		7		9			9
10	17	H	Burton Swifts	D 2-2	7	14	Skea, Hackett (og) / West, Ekins	6000	1	2		4	5	6	7		8	10			3	11			9			10
11	Dec 1	H	Notts County	W 5-1	9	10	Skea 3 (1p), Gordon, McArthur / Fletcher	5000	1	2		4		6	7	5	8	10			3	11			9			11
12	8	A	Walsall Town Swifts	W 3-1	11	9	McArthur 2, Skea / O'Brien	2000	1	2		4		6	7	5	8	10			3	11			9			12
13	25	A	Bury	L 1-4	11	11	McArthur / Plant, Henderson 3	5041	1	2		4	5	6	7		8	10			3	11			9			13
14	Jan 5	H	Walsall Town Swifts	W 9-1	13	11	McArthur, Gordon 2, Brown, Skea 2, Gallacher, Seymour, Forsyth (og) / Devey	2000	1	2	3	4		6	7	5	8	10		11					9			14
15	7	H	Woolwich Arsenal	W 3-1	15	10	McArthur, Gordon, Hill / Mortimer	3000	1	2		4	5	6	7		8	10			3	11			9			15
16	12	A	Crewe Alexandra	D 2-2	16	9	Gallacher 2 / Riley, T Jones	600	1	2		4	5	6			8	10		11	3		7		9			16
17	15	A	Darwen	L 2-8	16	9	Skea, Gordon / Maxwell 2, A King 3, Townsend 3	500	1	2		4	5	6			8	10		11	3		7		9			17
18	26	A	Rotherham Town	W 1-0	18	10	McArthur	2000	1	2	3	4	5	6	7		8	10		11					9			18
19	Feb 9	A	Burton Wanderers	D 1-1	19	11	Brown / Garfield	2000	1	2	3	4		6	7	5		10		11			8		9			19
20	18	H	Crewe Alexandra	W 4-0	21	8	McArthur, Priestman, Stirling, Gordon	1000	1		3	4		6		5	8	10	11	2				7	9			20
21	23	A	Burslem Port Vale	D 1-1	22	9	Priestman / Evans		1	2	3		5	6	7		8	10	11					4	9			21
22	Mar 2	A	Burton Swifts	W 5-0	24	7	Hughes, Skea 2, Gordon, McArthur		1	2	3	4		6		5	8	10		11			7		9			22
23	4	H	Lincoln City	W 2-1	26	6	Skea, Gallacher / Burke		1	2	3	4		6		5	8	10		11			7		9			23
24	9	A	Woolwich Arsenal	D 3-3	27	6	McArthur, Gordon, Skea / O'Brien, Sharpe, Mortimer	4000	1	2	3	4		6		5	8	10		11			7		9			24
25	16	H	Manchester City	W 3-1	29	6	Gordon, Hughes, McArthur / Sharples	4000	1	2	3	4		6		5	8	10		11			7		9			25
26	23	H	Burslem Port Vale	W 2-1	31	6	Gordon, Skea / Evans	3000	1		3	4		6		5	8	10	11				7		9	2		26
27	30	A	Manchester City	D 1-1	32	6	Gordon / McReddie	4000	1	2	3	4		6	7	5	8	10		11					9			27
28	Apr 6	A	Lincoln City	W 2-1	34	6	Gallacher, McArthur / Blades		1	2	3	4		6	7		8	10		11		5			9			28
29	15	H	Grimsby Town	W 1-0	36	4	Skea	3000	1	2	3		5		7		8	10		11		4	9		6			29
30	20	H	Bury	W 1-0	38	4	Gordon	3000	1	2	3		5		7		8	10		11		4	9		6			30

| | | | | | | | | League Appearances | 30 | 24 | 19 | 19 | 27 | 26 | 20 | 18 | 28 | 30 | 8 | 16 | 25 | 3 | 10 | 4 | 21 | 1 | 1 | |
| | | | | | | | | League Goals | | 1 | | 1 | 2 | 1 | 2 | 2 | 16 | 23 | 2 | | 6 | | 2 | 1 | 12 | | | |

Final League Position: 4
Average Home League Attendance: 6000

FA CUP

	Date		Opponents	Result	Scorers	Att	Thraves	Smith	Bailey	Seymour	Brown	Henrys	Hill	Hughes	McArthur	Skea	Priestman	Whitelaw	Gallacher	Miller	Gordon	
1	Oct 13	A	Notts Olympic (Q1)	W 13-0	Skea 3, Miller 4, McArthur 4, Hill 2	2000	1	2	3	4	5	6	7		8	10		11			9	1
2	Nov 3	H	Kimberley (Q2)	W 7-2	Gordon 2, Gallacher, Skea 2, McArthur, Hill / Norman 2	1000	1	2		4	5	6	7		8	10		11	3		9	2
3	24	A	Rushden (Q3)	W 3-2	Seymour, Gallacher, Skea (p) / Lichfield, Church	1000	1	2		4	5	6	7		8	10		11	3		9	3
4	Dec 15	H	Loughborough Town (Q4)	D 1-1	Hill / Edge	10000	1	2		4	5	6	7		8	10		11	3		9	4
5	19	A	Loughborough T (Q4 rep)	D 2-2	Skea, Gallacher / Edge 2	3000	1	2		4	5		7		8	10		11	3	6	9	5
6	22	H	Loughborough T (Q4 rep 2)	W 3-0	Gallacher, Hill, Skea (p)		1	2		4	5	6	7		8	10		11	3		9	6
7	Feb 2	A	Bury (1)	L 1-4	McArthur / Henderson 2, Lee, Plant	3200	1	2	3	4		6	7	5	8	10		11			9	7

Note: Oct 13, drawn away, but tie switched to Filbert Street;
Jan 5, Brown generally credited with a goal from an indirect free kick which deflected off an unnamed defender;
Mar 9, played at the Lyttleton Ground, Leyton;
Notts County and Newton Heath both failed to win promotion via the Test Matches.

1894-95
Back: Lee (Secretary), Smith, Chappell, Priestman, Bailey, Whitelaw, Miller, Brown (Trainer).
Front: Hill, Hughes, McArthur, Brown, Thraves, Skea, Gallacher.
On Ground: Seymour, Henrys.

Promoted: Liverpool
Re-election: Burslem Port Vale (not elected), Rotherham Town (did not apply), Crewe Alexandra (not elected)

FOOTBALL LEAGUE DIVISION TWO

Player columns (left to right): Jimmy Thraves, John Baird, Harry Davy, Jimmy Brown, Jack Walker, Arthur Henrys, David Manson, Willie McArthur, Harry Trainer, David Skea, Hugh Gallacher, Richard Davies, Harry Bailey, James Atherton, John Pickard, Peter McWhirter, Matt Bishop, James Lynes, Jack Lord, Billy Dorrell, Bob Thompson, John Hibberd

Match No	Date		Opponents	Result	Points	Position	Scorers	Att	Thr	Bai	Dav	Bro	Wal	Hen	Man	McA	Tra	Ske	Gal	RDa	Bai	Ath	Pic	McW	Bis	Lyn	Lor	Dor	Tho	Hib
1	Sep 7	H	Burton Swifts	W 2-1	2	-	Gallacher, Skea / Drysdale	5000	1	2	3	4	5	6	7	8	9	10	11											
2	14	A	Manchester City	L 0-2	2	10	- / Finnerhan, Rowan	9000	1	3	2	4	5	6	7	8	9	10	11											
3	21	A	Darwen	L 1-4	2	12	Skea / Burton 2, McAvoy, Tyrer	1000	1	2	3	4	5	6	7	8			11	9										
4	28	H	Burton Wanderers	L 1-3	2	13	McArthur / Garfield 2, R Brown	6000	1	2			4	5		7	9	8	10	11		3	6							
5	Oct 5	H	Loughborough Town	W 5-0	4	10	Brown, Skea, McArthur, Gallacher 2	7000	1	2			4	5	6		8	9	10	11		3		7						
6	19	A	Burton Wanderers	D 0-0	5	11		2000	1	2	4		7	5	6		8	9	10	11		3								
7	26	H	Darwen	L 2-3	5	12	Davies, Trainer / Shaw, F Hunt, Maxwell	5000	1	2			6	5	4		8	9				10	3			7	11			
8	Nov 9	A	Liverpool	L 1-3	5	12	Bishop / Geary 2, Wilkie	7000	1		2	4	5	6		8	9	10					3			11	7			
9	16	A	Loughborough Town	W 4-1	7	11	Bishop, Davies 2, Lynes / Davy (og)	7000	1		2	4	5	6		8						10	3			7	11	9		
10	30	H	Liverpool	W 2-0	9	10	Davies, McArthur	8000	1		2	4	5	6		8						10	3			7	11	9		
11	Dec 7	A	Woolwich Arsenal	D 1-1	10	11	Lynes / Boyd	5000	1		2	4	5	6		8						10	3			7	11	9		
12	21	H	Crewe Alexandra	W 4-1	12	10	Skea 2, McArthur, Stafford (og) / Peake	3000	1		2	4	5			9				10		8	3			7	11	6		
13	Jan 1	A	Newcastle United	L 0-1	12	11	- / Aitken	7000	1		2	4	5			8	9			10	11		3			7		6		
14	4	H	Newton Heath	W 3-0	14	11	McArthur 2, Manson	7000	1		2	4	5			8	9			10	11		3			7		6		
15	11	H	Notts County	W 2-1	16	10	Manson, Skea (p) / Bull	10000	1		2	4	5			8	9						3			7		6		
16	18	A	Rotherham Town	L 0-2	16	10	- / Wheatcroft (p), McCabe	1000	1		2	4	5	6	8		9			11	10	3			7					
17	25	H	Woolwich Arsenal	W 1-0	18	10	Lynes	6000	1		2	4	5		8	10				11			3			7		9	6	
18	Feb 3	A	Newton Heath	L 0-2	18	10	- / Kennedy, Smith	1000	1		2	4	5		8	10							3			7	11	9	6	
19	8	A	Notts County	W 2-1	20	9	McArthur, Manson / Bull	11000	1		2	4	5		8	9				10	11		3			7		6		
20	15	A	Lincoln City	W 3-2	22	8	McWhirter, Manson, Boullemier (og) / M Gillespie, Shearman	2000	1		2	4	5		8	9				10	11		3			7		6		
21	22	A	Crewe Alexandra	D 1-1	23	8	McArthur / Riley	3000	1		2	4	5		8	9				10	11		3			7		6		
22	29	H	Lincoln City	L 1-3	23	8	Trainer / M Gillespie, Shearman, Davy (og)	3000	1		2	4	5		8	9	10				11		3			7		6		
23	Mar 7	A	Burslem Port Vale	D 1-1	24	8	Moss / Beckett	1500	1		2	4	5		8			10			11		3			7	9	6		
24	21	H	Burslem Port Vale	W 5-0	26	8	Lord 2, Gallacher, Trainer, Dorrell	5000	1	3	2	4	5		8			10	9	7							6	11		
25	28	A	Burton Swifts	W 2-0	28	7	McArthur, Gallacher	3000	1	2	3	4	5		8	9	10			7							6	11		
26	Apr 3	H	Rotherham Town	W 8-0	30	6	Trainer 5, McArthur, Manson, Hobson (og)			1	3		7	5	8	9	10			11		2					6		4	
27	4	H	Manchester City	L 1-2	30	7	McArthur / Meredith, Robson	4000	1	2		4	5		8	9	10			7		3					6	11		
28	6	H	Grimsby Town	L 1-2	30	8	Dorrell / McCairns, Gray	4000	1	2		4	5		8	9	10			7		3					6	11		
29	7	H	Newcastle United	W 2-0	32	7	Trainer 2	5000	1			3			8	4	10	9				2	5	7			6	11		
30	11	A	Grimsby Town	L 1-7	32	8	Manson / McCairns 6, Higgins	3000	1	2		9	5		8	4	10			7		3					6	11		

Final League Position:	8	
Average Home League Attendance:	6100	

League Appearances: 30 13 22 29 30 11 23 27 17 15 22 7 25 2 1 17 7 7 18 6 1

League Goals: 1   6 11 10 6 5 4   1 2 3 2 2

FA CUP

Match No	Date		Opponents	Result	Scorers	Att																							
1	Oct 12	H	Hinckley Town (Q1)	W 4-0	Trainer 2, Bishop, McArthur	2500	1	2			4	5	6		8	9				10	3		7		11			
2	Nov 2	H	Hucknall St Johns (Q2)	W 3-1	Manson, Hibberd, Trainer / Murphy		1		2	4	5		10		9						3			11	7	6		8
3	23	A	Kimberley (Q3)	W 3-1	McArthur 2, Rowley (og) / Lilley		1		2	4	5	6		8						10	3			7	11	9		
4	Dec 14	H	Kettering (Q4)	L 1-2	Trainer / Ashworth, Whitehouse	7000	1		2	4	5	6		8	9					10	3			11	7			

Note: Oct 26, Trainer credited with second goal after a scramble also involving Davies; Nov 2, Nov 9, Lynes made his first two appearances under the pseudonym of "James"; Manchester City failed to win promotion via the Test Matches.

1895-96
Back: Lee (Secretary), Baird, Atherton, Thompson, Strachan, Lord, Walker, Bailey, Newton (Trainer).
Middle: Hogan, Manson, Thraves, Davies, Pickard, Gallacher, Henrys.
Front: McArthur, Trainer, Skea, Brown.

Season 1896-97

Promoted: Notts County
Re-election: Burton Swifts (elected), Burton Wanderers (not elected), Lincoln City (elected)

FOOTBALL LEAGUE DIVISION TWO

No	Date	Opponents	Result	Pts	Pos	Scorers	Att	Thraves	Davy	Swift	Lord	Walker	Leighton	Dorrell	Freebairn	Lonie	Carnelly	McMillan	Brown	Manson	Bailey	Trainer	McDonald	Proudfoot	Bishop	Howes	Wood	No
1	Sep 5 H	Darwen	W 4-1	2	-	McMillan, Lonie, Walker, Freebairn / Lees	4000	1	2	3	4	5	6	7	8	9	10	11										1
2	12 H	Notts County	L 2-3	2	6	Manson 2 / Murphy, Bull, Smith	6000	1	2	3		5	6		7	9	10	11	4	8								2
3	19 A	Burton Swifts	L 1-2	2	12	Dorrell / Leigh, Yardley	4000	1	2	3		5	6	7	8	9	10	11	4									3
4	26 A	Loughborough Town	W 2-0	4	10	McMillan 2	5000	1	2	3		5	6	11	7	9	8	10	4									4
5	Oct 3 H	Blackpool	W 2-1	6	7	Dorrell, Carnelly / Donnelly	6000	1	2	3		5	6	11	7	9	8	10	4									5
6	17 A	Notts County	L 0-6	6	12	- / Murphy 2, Allan 2, Bull, Calderhead	5000	1		3		5	6	10	9	8	11	4			2	7						6
7	24 A	Darwen	L 1-4	6	13	Lonie / Hunt 2 (1p), Tyrer, McKee	2000	1	2	3	6	5		7	10	9	8	11	4									7
8	Nov 7 H	Lincoln City	W 4-1	8	12	McMillan 2, Carnelly, Freebairn / M Gillespie	2000	1	2	3	6	4		11	7	10	9	5					8					8
9	14 A	Newcastle United	L 1-3	8	12	McMillan / Wardrope 2, Smellie	6000	1	2	3	6	4		11	7	10	9	5					8					9
10	28 H	Walsall	W 4-2	10	12	Freebairn, Carnelly 2, McDonald / Griffin, J Aston	4000	1	2	3	6	4		11	7	10	9	5					8					10
11	Dec 5 H	Grimsby Town	W 4-2	12	11	McMillan 2, Dorrell, McDonald / Gray, Fletcher	8000	1	2	3	6			11	7		10	9	4				8	5				11
12	19 A	Burton Wanderers	L 1-2	12	11	McDonald / Lowe, Daniels	3000	1	2	3	6			11	7		10	9	4				8	5				12
13	25 H	Loughborough Town	W 4-2	14	9	McDonald, Dorrell, Freebairn 2 / Brailsford, Jones	11000	1	2	3			6	11	7		10	9	4				8	5				13
14	28 H	Newton Heath	W 1-0	16	9	Dorrell	8000	1	2	3	6			11	7		10		4			5	9	8				14
15	Jan 9 H	Newcastle United	W 5-0	18	8	Trainer, McDonald 2, Carnelly, Dorrell	3000	1		3	6			11	7		10		4		2	9	8	5				15
16	16 A	Burton Wanderers	W 2-1	20	7	Brown, Trainer / W Devey	8000	1	2	3	6				7		10		4			5	9	8	11			16
17	23 A	Grimsby Town	L 1-4	20	7	Dorrell / McCairns, Gray 2, Fletcher	3000	1	2	3	6			8	7		10		4				9	5	11			17
18	Feb 6 A	Gainsborough Trinity	W 2-0	22	5	McMillan 2	2000	1	2	3	6			11	7		10	8	4				9	5				18
19	13 H	Woolwich Arsenal	W 6-3	24	5	Dorrell 2, Carnelly 2, Freebairn, Sinclair (og) / O'Brien 2, Haywood	6000	1	2	3	6			11	7		10	8	4				9	5				19
20	20 A	Newton Heath	L 1-2	24	5	Carnelly / Boyd, Donaldson	8000	1	2	3	6			11	7		10	9	4				8	5				20
21	27 A	Blackpool	L 0-3	24	7	- / Bradshaw, J Parkinson, Clarke	1000		2	3	6			11	7		10	9	4				8	5		1		21
22	Mar 6 H	Burton Swifts	W 3-0	26	5	Carnelly, Dorrell, Freebairn	7000		2	3	6			11	7				4				8	5		1		22
23	13 A	Manchester City	L 0-4	26	6	- / Holmes, Meredith, Gillespie, Williams	6000		2	3	6			7			10	11	4				9	8	5	1		23
24	20 A	Walsall	D 1-1	27	6	Wood / Wilkes	2500		2	3	6			7			10						9	5	11	1	8	24
25	27 H	Small Heath	L 0-1	27	8	- / Hodgetts	5500		2	3	6			11	7		10	9					5			1	8	25
26	Apr 10 A	Lincoln City	L 1-2	27	9	Freebairn / Hartley, Lynes			2	3	6			11	7		10	9	4				8	5		1		26
27	12 H	Manchester City	D 3-3	28	9	McMillan, Carnelly, Ray (og) / Meredith 2, Howes (og)	1000		2	3	6			11	7		10	9	4				8	5		1		27
28	16 A	Small Heath	D 2-2	29	8	McDonald, Freebairn / Hare, Inglis	2000		2	3	6			11	7		10		4				9	8	5	1		28
29	17 A	Woolwich Arsenal	L 1-2	29	8	Dorrell / Caie, Brock	5000		2	3	6			11	7		10		4				9	8	5	1		29
30	19 H	Gainsborough Trinity	D 0-0	30	9		2000		2	3	6			11	7		10	9	4					8	5	1		30

| | | | | | | | League Appearances | 20 | 28 | 30 | 8 | 24 | 14 | 26 | 30 | 7 | 28 | 22 | 26 | 1 | 2 | 14 | 16 | 19 | 3 | 10 | 2 | |
| | | | | | | | League Goals | | | | | 1 | | 11 | 9 | 2 | 10 | 11 | 1 | 2 | | 2 | 7 | | | | 1 | |

Final League Position: 9

Average Home League Attendance: 5900

FA CUP

No	Date	Opponents	Result	Scorers	Att	Thraves	Davy	Swift	Lord	Walker	Leighton	Dorrell	Freebairn	Lonie	Carnelly	McMillan	Brown	Manson	Bailey	Trainer	McDonald	Proudfoot	Bishop	Howes	Wood	No
1	Nov 21 H	Bulwell United (Q3)	W 3-1	Freebairn 2, Lord / Lowe	1000	1	2	3	6	4		11	7		10	9	5				8					1
2	Dec 12 A	Wellingborough Town (Q4)	W 3-2	McMillan, Dorrell, Freebairn / Murray, Walker	1500	1	2	3	6	4		11	7		10	9	5				8					2
3	Jan 2 A	Kettering (Q5)	L 1-2	Dorrell / Ball, Dixon	5000	1	2	3	6	4		11	8		10		7				9	5				3

Dismissals: Apr 10, Freebairn, Lincoln City (a).
Note: Newton Heath failed to win promotion via the Test Matches.

1896-97
Back: J Jackson (Trainer), Lord, Davy, Bailey, Swift, Dorrell, H Jackson (Secretary).
Middle: Brown, Lonie, Carnelly, Thraves, Leighton, Walker.
Front: Freebairn, McMillan, Manson.

Season 1897-98

Promoted: Burnley
Re-election: Lincoln City (elected), Darwen (not elected), Loughborough Town (elected)

FOOTBALL LEAGUE DIVISION TWO

Match No	Date		Opponents	Result	Points	Position	Scorers	Att	Arthur Howes	Jack Walker	George Swift	Dick Jones	David Proudfoot	Alf Ball	Willie Freebairn	Roddie McLeod	Harry Smith	Johnny McMillan	Billy Dorrell	Rab King	Charlie Saer	Alec Gillies	Tom Rowell	Jimmy Brown	William Flanagan	Alf Watkins	Sam Eaton	Harry Coulson	William Keech	Match No
1	Sep 4	H	Luton Town	D 1-1	1	-	Freebairn / Ekins	6000	1	2	3	4	5	6	7	8	9	10	11											1
2	11	A	Small Heath	L 1-2	1	10	Smith / Abbott, Gadsby	3000	1	2	3	4	5	6	7	8	9		10	11										2
3	18	A	Grimsby Town	D 0-0	2	9		3000		2	3	4	5	6	7	8	9		11		1		10							3
4	Oct 2	A	Newton Heath	L 0-2	2	13	- / Boyd 2	6000		2	3	6	5	4	7	8	9		11		1		10							4
5	9	H	Burnley	L 0-1	2	15	- / Bowes	6000		2	3	6	5	4		8	9		11	7	1		10							5
6	16	H	Walsall	W 3-1	4	13	Smith 2, King / Loynes	2500		2	3	6	5	4	7	8	9	10	11		1									6
7	23	A	Woolwich Arsenal	W 3-0	6	10	McMillan, McLeod, King	7000		2	3	6		4	7	8	9	10	11		1			5						7
8	Nov 6	H	Blackpool	W 4-1	8	8	Freebairn, McLeod 2, McMillan / Martin	6000		2	3	6		4	7	8	9	10	11		1			5						8
9	13	A	Loughborough Town	D 1-1	9	9	McLeod / Walker	5000		2	3	6		4		8	9	10	11	7	1			5						9
10	20	H	Newton Heath	D 1-1	10	8	McLeod / Wedge	6000		2	3	6		4		8	9	10	11	7	1			5						10
11	27	A	Burton Swifts	W 3-2	12	8	Dorrell, Freebairn, McMillan / Goodchild, Gray (p)	1000		2	3	6		4	7		9	10	11		1			5	8					11
12	Dec 4	H	Woolwich Arsenal	W 2-1	14	7	McLeod, Dorrell / Duff	4000		2	3	6		4			9	10	7		1	11		5	8					12
13	11	A	Manchester City	L 1-2	14	7	McMillan / Gillespie, Meredith	9000		2	3	6		4	7		9	10	11		1			5	8					13
14	18	A	Darwen	W 2-1	16	5	McLeod, McMillan / Crook (p)	600		2	3	6		4	7		9	10	11	8	1			5						14
15	25	H	Loughborough Town	W 4-0	18	5	McMillan, Smith, McLeod, Freebairn	9000		2	3	6		4	7		9	10	11		1			5						15
16	Jan 8	H	Blackpool	L 1-2	18	7	Freebairn / Parkinson, Martin	3000		2	3	6	5	4	7	8	9	10	11		1									16
17	15	A	Burnley	L 0-4	18	7	- / Ross 3 (1p), Walker (og)	3000		2	3	6		4	7	8	9	10	11		1			5						17
18	22	A	Newcastle United	L 2-4	18	8	McLeod, King / Aitken, Peddie 3	10000		2	3	6		4	7		9	10	11	8	1			5						18
19	Feb 5	A	Darwen	L 0-1	18	9	- / Earnshaw	5000		2	3	6		4	7	8	9		11		1		10	5						19
20	12	H	Lincoln City	W 3-1	20	8	Coulson, McLeod, Dorrell / Ross	3000		2	3	6		4		8		10	11		1			5			7		9	20
21	26	A	Walsall	L 1-2	20	8	McLeod / Johnson, Griffin	2000		2	3	6		4		8		10	11		1			5			7		9	21
22	Mar 5	A	Lincoln City	W 4-1	22	8	McLeod, McMillan, Dorrell, Keech / Fletcher	2000		2	3	6		4		8		10	11	7	1			5					9	22
23	12	H	Burton Swifts	W 1-0	23	9	McMillan / Hutton	5000		2	3	6		4		8		10	11	7	1			5					9	23
24	19	A	Gainsborough Trinity	L 0-1	23	10	- / McRoberts	2000		2	3	6		4		8	9	10	11	7	1			5						24
25	26	H	Small Heath	W 2-0	25	9	McLeod, Keech	2000		2	3	6		4		8		10	11	7	1			5					9	25
26	Apr 2	H	Manchester City	D 0-0	26	9		6000		2	3	6		4		8		10	11	7	1			5					9	26
27	8	A	Luton Town	W 1-0	28	8	Dorrell	4000		2	3	6		4				10	11	7	1			5				3	9	27
28	9	H	Newcastle United	D 1-1	29	6	Dorrell (p) / Peddie	6000		2	3	6		4		8		10	11	7	1			5					9	28
29	11	H	Grimsby Town	W 1-0	31	6	McMillan	4000		2	3	6		4				10	11	7	1			5		8			9	29
30	16	H	Gainsborough Trinity	W 3-1	33	7	Dorrell, Watkins, Keech / Wigmore	5000		2	3	6		4		8		10	7		1			5		11			9	30

| **Final League Position:** | 7 | | | | | | | **League Appearances** | 2 | 29 | 30 | 28 | 6 | 30 | 14 | 28 | 15 | 26 | 26 | 18 | 28 | 4 | 5 | 22 | 4 | 2 | 3 | 1 | 9 | |
| **Average Home League Attendance:** | 6000 | | | | | | | **League Goals** | | | | | | | 5 | 13 | 4 | 9 | 7 | 3 | | | | | | 1 | | 1 | 3 | |

FA CUP

	Date		Opponents	Result			Scorers	Att		Jack Walker	George Swift	Dick Jones		Alf Ball	Willie Freebairn	Roddie McLeod	Harry Smith	Johnny McMillan	Billy Dorrell		Charlie Saer			Jimmy Brown						
1	Jan 29	A	Southampton (1)	L 1-2			McLeod / Meston, Buchanan	10000		2	3	6		4	7	8	9	10	11		1			5						1

Note: Newcastle United failed to gain promotion via the Test Matches, subsequently elected to extended Division One;
Darwen subsequently elected to extended Division Two.

1897-98
Back: Clark (Secretary), Gillies, Bailey, Walker, Ball, Leese, Rowell, Howes, Jackson (Trainer). **Middle:** McLeod, Proudfoot, Lord, Swift, Jones, Dorrell, Smith.
Front: King, Flanagan, McMillan, Freebairn

Season 1898-99

Promoted: Manchester City, Glossop
Re-election: Blackpool (not elected), Loughborough Town (elected), Darwen (did not apply)

FOOTBALL LEAGUE DIVISION TWO

Match No	Date		Opponents	Result	Points	Position	Scorers	Att	Billy Rowley	Jack Walker	George Swift	Alf Ball	Jimmy Brown	Dick Jones	Tommy Galbraith	Billy Dorrell	Johnny McMillan	Rab King	Alf Watkins	Godfrey Beardsley	Maurice Parry	William Keech	Arthur Howes	Sam Eaton	Bennie Fulwood	Frank Ballard	Bob Thompson	Walter Robinson	Peter Goudie	Bertie Lyon	Billy Wragg	Tom Bradshaw	Matt Bishop	Match No
1	Sep 3	H	Lincoln City	W 3-2	2	-	Watkins 2, King / Robertson 2 (1p)	8000	1	2	3	4	5	6	7	8	9	10	11															1
2	10	A	Woolwich Arsenal	L 0-4	2	10	- / White 2, Hunt 2	6000		2	3	4	5		7		10	8	11	1	6	9												2
3	17	H	Luton Town	D 1-1	3	10	King / Kempley	3000		2	3	4	5	6	7		10	8	11	1		9												3
4	24	A	Barnsley St Peters	W 4-3	5	7	Galbraith 2, Keech 2 / Hepworth, Lees, Davis	3000		2	3	4	5	6	7		10	8	11	1		9												4
5	26	A	Walsall	D 1-1	6	7	Galbraith / Griffin	2500		2	3	4	5	6	7		10	8	11			9	1											5
6	Oct 1	A	Darwen	L 0-3	6	9	- / Bleasdale, Dewhurst 2	1500		2	3	4	5	6	7		10	8	11	1		9												6
7	8	H	Gainsborough Trinity	W 1-0	8	6	Galbraith	4000		2	3	4	5	6	7		10					9	1	8	11									7
8	15	A	Manchester City	L 1-3	8	9	Eaton / Meredith, S Smith, Gillespie	8000	5		3	4		6	7		10	9	11	1				8		2								8
9	22	H	Glossop North End	W 4-2	10	7	King, Eaton, Watkins, Fulwood / Gallacher 2	3000		2	3	4	5	6	7		9		11	1				8	10									9
10	Nov 5	H	Burton Swifts	W 1-0	12	7	Watkins	4000		2	3	4	5	6	7		9	10	1					8	11									10
11	12	A	Burslem Port Vale	W 2-0	14	5	King, Galbraith	2000		2	3	4	5	6	7		11	9	10	1				8										11
12	26	A	Loughborough Town	W 3-0	16	5	Eaton, Fulwood, King	3000		2	3	4	5	6	7		10	9		1				8	11									12
13	Dec 3	H	Blackpool	W 4-0	18	3	Galbraith 2, King, Watkins	4000		2	3	4	5	6	7		9	10	1					8	11									13
14	17	H	Newton Heath	W 1-0	20	3	Fulwood	8000			3	4		6	7		9	10	1					8	11	2	5							14
15	24	A	New Brighton Tower	L 0-1	20	5	- / Hammond	2000		2	3	4		6	7		10		9	1				8	11		5							15
16	26	H	Darwen	W 4-0	22	4	Eaton, Galbraith, McMillan, Watkins	5000		2	3	4		6	7		10		9	1				8	11		5							16
17	27	H	Loughborough Town	W 1-0	24	3	Ball	2000		2				6	7		10		9	1				8	11	3	5							17
18	31	A	Lincoln City	L 1-3	24	5	Robinson / Robertson 2 (1p), Pugh	1500		2	3	4		6	7		10	9						8	11		5							18
19	Jan 7	H	Woolwich Arsenal	W 2-1	26	4	King / Haywood	4000		2	3	4		6	7		10	9	11	1				8			5							19
20	14	A	Luton Town	W 6-1	28	3	King, Watkins, Galbraith 2, McMillan, Lyon / W Ford	2000		2	3	4		6	7		10	9	11								5	1	8					20
21	21	H	Barnsley St Peters	W 3-1	30	1	Galbraith 2, King / Lees	3000		2	3	4		6	7		10	9					1		11		5		8					21
22	Feb 4	A	Gainsborough Trinity	L 0-4	30	3	- / Wigmore, Fenton, Spence 2	1000		2	3	4		6	7		10	9	11	1							5		8					22
23	11	H	Manchester City	D 1-1	31	3	McMillan / F Williams	10000		2	3	4		6	7		10	9	11	1							5		8					23
24	18	A	Glossop North End	W 3-1	33	2	King, Galbraith, Watkins / Lumsden	1000		2	3	4		6	7		10	9	11	1							5		8					24
25	25	H	Walsall	D 2-2	34	2	Watkins, Lyon / J Aston 2	1700		2	3	4		6	7		10	9	11	1							5		8					25
26	Mar 4	A	Burton Swifts	D 1-1	35	3	McMillan / Swift (og)	4000		2	3	4		6	7		10	9	11	1							5		8					26
27	11	H	Burslem Port Vale	D 1-1	36	3	McMillan / Harvey	12000		2	3	4		6	7		10	9	11	1							5		8					27
28	18	A	Small Heath	W 3-0	38	3	Galbraith, Eaton, King	10000		2	3	4		6	7		10	9	11	1				8			5							28
29	31	A	Grimsby Town	L 0-1	38	4	- / Jenkinson	5000		2	3	4		6	7		10	9	11	1				8			5							29
30	Apr 1	A	Blackpool	D 2-2	39	5	Galbraith, McMillan / Scott, Morris	2500		2		4		6	7		10	9	11	1				8			5				3			30
31	3	H	Grimsby Town	W 2-0	41	4	Watkins, Eaton	6000		2		4		6			10	11	9	1				8			5				3	7		31
32	15	H	Newton Heath	D 2-2	42	5	Bradshaw, McMillan / Cassidy, Gillespie	6000			2	4		6			10	9	11	1				8			5				3	7		32
33	22	H	New Brighton Tower	W 4-1	44	3	Galbraith, Bradshaw, Ball, King / Hammond	10000			3	4		6	7		10	9	11	1							2				5	8		33
34	29	H	Small Heath	D 0-0	45	3		4000			3	4		6	7			9		1				8			2	5				11	10	34

Final League Position:	3	
Average Home League Attendance:	8000	

League Appearances: 1 30 31 34 12 33 32 1 29 30 29 1 6 3 19 11 2 2 21 1 8 4 4 1

League Goals: 2 16 7 12 11 2 6 3 1 2 2

FA CUP

Match No	Date		Opponents	Result	Scorers	Att	Players
1	Oct 29	H	Kimberley (Q3)	W 9-0	King 4, Watkins 2, Fulwood, Swift (p), Brown (p)	2000	2 3 4 5 6 7 9 10 1 8 11
2	Nov 19	H	Rushden (Q4)	W 2-1	Galbraith, McMillan / Hingerty	6000	2 3 4 5 6 7 11 9 10 1 8
3	Dec 10	A	Kettering (Q5)	D 1-1	Fulwood / Panter	5000	2 3 4 5 6 7 9 10 1 8 11
4	15	H	Kettering (Q5 rep)	L 1-2	Eaton / Beaver, Winterhalder	5000	2 3 4 5 6 7 11 9 10 1 8

Note: Apr 3, Most reports credit Watkins with first goal, some credit Eaton.

1898-99
Back: Ball, Galbraith, Watkins, Beardsley, Dorrell, Dunmore (Trainer).
Middle: Johnson (Secretary), Brown, Eaton, Swift, Walker, McMillan.
Front: Jones, King.

Season 1899-1900

Promoted: Sheffield Wednesday, Bolton Wanderers
Re-election: Barnsley (elected), Luton Town, Loughborough Town (not elected)

FOOTBALL LEAGUE DIVISION TWO

Match No	Date		Opponents	Result	Points	Position	Scorers	Att	Godfrey Beardsley	Billy Wragg	George Swift	Alf Ball	Walter Robinson	Dick Jones	Tommy Galbraith	Tom Bradshaw	Tommy Brown	Johnny McMillan	Rab King	Sam Eaton	Herbert Dainty	Matt Bishop	Harry Bailey	Harry Allen	Bertie Lyon	Roger Carter	Johnny Mercer	Cecil Wood	Match No
1	Sep 2	A	Woolwich Arsenal	W 2-0	2	-	King, Brown	10000	1	2	3	4	5	6	7	8	9	10	11										1
2	9	H	Barnsley	W 1-0	4	1	Wragg	6000	1	2	3	4	5	6	7	8	9	10	11										2
3	16	H	Burton Swifts	W 1-0	6	1	Ball	5000	1	2	3	4	5	6	7	9		10	11	8									3
4	23	A	Luton Town	D 0-0	7	2		4000	1	2	3	4		6	7			10	9	8	5	11							4
5	25	A	Walsall	W 2-1	9	1	Bradshaw, Brown / Dean	2500		2	3	4		6	8	7	9	10	11		5		1						5
6	30	H	Burslem Port Vale	W 2-0	11	1	Bradshaw, McMillan	5000	1	2	3		4	6	8	7	9	10	11		5								6
7	Oct 14	H	Middlesbrough	W 4-1	13	2	Brown, King 2, McMillan / Lamb	8000	1	2	3	4		6	8	7	9	10	11		5								7
8	21	A	Chesterfield	D 0-0	14	3		7000	1	2	3	4		6	8	7	9	10	11		5								8
9	Nov 4	A	Bolton Wanderers	D 2-2	15	3	McMillan, Dainty / Bell, Morgan	5000	1	2	3		4	6	8	7	9	10	11		5								9
10	11	A	Loughborough Town	W 2-0	17	3	Wragg, Brown	6000	1	2	3		4	6	8	7	9	10	11		5								10
11	25	H	Sheffield Wednesday	D 0-0	18	2		12000	1	2	3		4	6	8	7	9	10	11		5								11
12	Dec 2	A	Lincoln City	L 0-2	18	3	- / Hartley 2 (1p)	4000	1	2	3		4	6	8	7	9	10	11		5								12
13	16	A	New Brighton Tower	D 2-2	19	3	McMillan, Bradshaw / Hargreaves, Goodall	2000	1	2	3	4		6	8	7		10	9		5				11				13
14	23	H	Grimsby Town	W 3-0	21	3	McMillan 2, Mountain (og)	5000	1	2	3		4	6	8	7		10	9		5				11				14
15	25	H	Loughborough Town	W 5-0	23	2	Bradshaw, King 2, Galbraith, Allen	7000	1	2	3		4	6	8	7		10	9		5				11				15
16	27	H	Walsall	W 2-1	25	2	McMillan, King / Dailly	2500	1	2	3		4	6	8	7		10	9		5				11				16
17	30	H	Woolwich Arsenal	D 0-0	26	1		8500	1	2	3		4	6	8	7		10	9		5				11				17
18	Jan 6	A	Barnsley	W 2-1	28	3	King, Dainty / Campbell	1000	1	2	3		4	6	8	7		10	9		5				11				18
19	13	A	Burton Swifts	L 0-2	28	3	- / Wildes, Mainman (p)	2000	1	2	3		4	6		7		10	9			5	11			8			19
20	20	H	Luton Town	D 2-2	29	3	Allen, McMillan / Draper 2	6000	1	2	3	4	5	6			7	8	10	9					11				20
21	Feb 3	A	Burslem Port Vale	W 2-0	31	3	Eaton 2	600		2	3		4	6	7			10	9	8	5				11	1			21
22	17	A	Middlesbrough	W 1-0	33	2	Brown	8000	1	2	3		4	6	7		9	10			8	5			11				22
23	24	H	Chesterfield	D 2-2	34	2	McMillan, King / Geary, Arnold	5000	1	2	3		4	6				10	9	8	5				11		7		23
24	Mar 3	A	Gainsborough Trinity	L 0-3	34	4	- / Vail 2, Ball (og)	2000	1	2	3	4		6				10	9	8	5				11		7		24
25	10	H	Bolton Wanderers	D 0-0	35	4		10000		2	3	4		6				9	10	8		5			11	1	7		25
26	24	H	Newton Heath	W 2-0	37	4	King, Brown	8000	1	2	3				6	7	8	9	10	11	5							4	26
27	31	A	Sheffield Wednesday	L 0-2	37	4	- / Wright, Beech	12000	1	2	3		4	6	8	7	9		10		5			11					27
28	Apr 7	H	Lincoln City	W 2-0	39	4	Mercer, King	4000	1	2	3		4	6	8		9	10	11		5						7		28
29	13	A	Newton Heath	L 2-3	39	5	Mercer, Wragg / Gillespie, Griffiths, Leigh	10000	1	2	3		4		6		9				11	8	5			10	7		29
30	14	A	Small Heath	L 1-4	39	5	Lyon / McRoberts, Wharton, Main, Wragg (og)	6000	1	2	3		4		6		9				11	8	5			10	7		30
31	16	H	Gainsborough Trinity	W 5-0	41	4	Wragg 2, Lyon, Dainty, King	1500	1	5	3		2		4	8	9				11	6				10	7		31
32	17	H	Small Heath	W 2-0	43	4	Bradshaw, Lyon	6000	1	5	3		2		4	8	9				11	7	6			10			32
33	21	H	New Brighton Tower	L 1-2	43	4	King / Hargreaves 2	3000	1	5	3		2		4	8	9	10	11		6						7		33
34	28	A	Grimsby Town	L 1-6	43	5	King / Hemingfield 2, Ratcliffe 2, Lakey, Jenkinson	3000	1	5	3		2		4	8			10	11	6					9	7		34

Final League Position:	5	**League Appearances**	31 34 34 11 26 28 30 24 21 29 33 9 30 2 1 13 7 1 9 1	
Average Home League Attendance:	7125	**League Goals**	5 1 1 5 6 9 13 2 3 2 3 2	

FA CUP

	Date		Opponents	Result	Scorers	Att																				
1	Oct 28	H	Wellingborough (Q3)	W 3-1	McMillan, Bishop, Brown / Hulme	4000	1	2	3			4	6	8	7	9	10		5	11						1
2	Nov 27	A	Burton Swifts (Q4)	W 3-1	Brown 2, Swift (p) / Sellars	2000	1	2	3			4	6	8	7	9	10	11	5							2
3	Dec 9	A	Hucknall Portland (Q5)	W 6-1	King, Bradshaw, McMillan 2, Lyon 2 / Jayes	2000	1	2	3	4		6		7		8	11		5	10			9			3
4	Jan 27	A	Sheffield United (1)	L 0-1	- / Bennett	12000	1	2	3			4	6		7	8	10	9	5			11				4

Note: Sep 25, Bailey (goalkeeper) is the same player who played full back 1894-97;
Nov 25, Fans stormed gates, estimated 25000 inside ground to watch fixture;
Nov 27, drawn away, but tie played at Filbert Street;
Dec 9, drawn away, but tie played at Filbert Street;
Dec 23, Most reports credit McMillan with second goal, some credit King;
Mar 10, Lyon (goalkeeper) is the same player who played as a forward during the season;
Apr 16, Most reports credit Wragg with second goal, some credit Lyon.

Herbert Dainty

Cecil Wood in more familiar guise, playing cricket for Leicestershire.

Promoted: Grimsby Town, Small Heath
Re-election: Walsall (not elected), Stockport County, Burton Swifts (both elected)

FOOTBALL LEAGUE DIVISION TWO

Match No	Date		Opponents	Result	Points	Position	Scorers	Att
1	Sep 1	H	Stockport County	D 2-2	1	-	McMillan, Connachan / Betteley, Smith	7000
2	8	A	Small Heath	D 0-0	2	10		7000
3	15	H	Grimsby Town	W 4-0	4	4	McMillan 4 (1p)	6000
4	22	A	Lincoln City	L 0-1	4	9	- / Swift (og)	3000
5	29	H	Newton Heath	W 1-0	6	4	McMillan (p)	6000
6	Oct 1	A	Burton Swifts	W 1-0	8	3	McMillan	3000
7	6	A	Glossop	L 1-3	8	5	Connachan / Goddard 2, King	1000
8	13	H	Middlesbrough	W 1-0	10	4	Connachan	5000
9	20	A	Burnley	D 0-0	11	4		3000
10	27	H	Burslem Port Vale	D 0-0	12	4		5000
11	Nov 3	A	Woolwich Arsenal	L 1-2	12	5	Jones / Blackwood, Gaudie	7000
12	10	A	New Brighton Tower	D 0-0	13	5		3000
13	17	H	Burnley	D 1-1	14	6	Connachan / Savage	7000
14	24	A	Walsall	L 0-2	14	7	- / McLean, Martin	3000
15	Dec 1	H	Burton Swifts	W 5-2	16	6	Brash 4, Robertson / Burton, Bunting	5000
16	15	H	Woolwich Arsenal	W 1-0	18	5	Kyle	9000
17	22	A	Blackpool	L 0-1	18	5	- / Birkett	2000
18	25	H	Barnsley	W 2-0	20	5	Brash, Connachan	6000
19	29	A	Stockport County	L 1-3	20	6	Swift (p) / Ashworth, McLachlan, Jack Foster	3000
20	Jan 1	A	Barnsley	L 0-1	20	6	- / Mawson	2000
21	5	H	Small Heath	D 1-1	21	6	Brown / Aston	6000
22	12	A	Grimsby Town	L 1-4	21	7	Brown / Mellor 2, Lakey, Hall	5000
23	19	H	Lincoln City	L 0-2	21	7	- / McCairns, Smith	2000
24	Feb 16	A	Middlesbrough	L 1-2	21	10	Hammond / Wardrope 2	8000
25	21	H	Glossop	L 1-2	21	10	Kyle / Kennedy, Crump	1000
26	Mar 2	A	Burslem Port Vale	D 0-0	22	12		2000
27	9	H	Chesterfield	L 1-3	22	12	Allsopp / Munday, Gooing 2	3000
28	16	A	New Brighton Tower	D 1-1	23	13	Brown / Cunliffe	2000
29	20	A	Newton Heath	W 3-2	25	12	Swift, Connachan, Brown / Fisher, Jackson	2000
30	23	A	Gainsborough Trinity	D 0-0	26	12		3000
31	30	H	Walsall	W 5-0	28	10	Brown 3, Langham, Swift	2500
32	Apr 5	A	Chesterfield	L 0-1	28	12	- / Gooing	4000
33	8	H	Gainsborough Trinity	W 1-0	30	11	Kyle	4000
34	9	H	Blackpool	W 3-1	32	8	Brown 2, Langham / Parkinson	3000

Final League Position:	11	
Average Home League Attendance:	5500	

Player appearances grid (shirt number worn; blank = did not appear)

Match	Godfrey Beardsley	Andy Mills	George Swift	Billy Wragg	James Foster	Dick Jones	Archie Brash	Peter Kyle	Jamie Connachan	Johnny McMillan	Albert Dunkley	Mick Cochrane	John Woolridge	Jack Hamilton	Tommy Brown	Arthur Beadsworth	Teddy Daw	Walter Robinson	Hugh Robertson	Billy Langham	John Henderson	Harry Hammond	Tommy Allsopp	Arthur Berry
1	1	2	3	4	5	6	7	8	9	10	11													
2	1	4	3		5	6	7	8	9	10		2	11											
3	1	4	3			6	7	8	9	10	11	2		5										
4	1	4	3			6	7	8	9	10	11	2		5										
5	1	4	3	6				10	8	7		2		5	9	11								
6		4	3	6				10	8	7		2	11	5	9	1								
7	1	4	3				7	9	8	10		2	11	5										
8	1		3	4		6	7	9	8	10	11	2		5										
9	1		3	4	5		8	7		10	11	2		6	9									
10	1		3	4	5		8	7		10	11	2		6	9									
11		9	3	4		6	7	8		10	11	2		5			1							
12			3	4		6		7	8	9	11	2		5			1	10						
13			3	4		6		7	8	9	11	2		5			1	10						
14			3	4		6		7	8	9	11	2		5			1	10						
15			3			6	7	8			11	2		5			1		4	9				
16			3					8	10			2		5			1			9	7	11		
17			3	4		6		8	10			2		5			1			9	7	11		
18			3	4		6	7	8	10			2		5			1			9		11		
19			3			6	7	8	10			2		5			1		4	9		11		
20		6	3				7	8	10			2		5	9							11		
21		6	3	4					10		11	2		5	9		1				7	8		
22		6	3	4					10		11	2			9		1	5			7	8		
23			3	4		6		8	10		11	2		5	9		1				7			
24			3	4					10			2		5			1	6			7	8	9	11
25			3	4				10				2		5			1	6			7	8	9	11
26			3	4		6			10			2		5			1				7	8	9	11
27			3	4					10			2		5			1	6			7	8	9	11
28									10	7		2		5	9		1	6				8	11	4
29		2	3						10	7				5	9		1	6				8	11	4
30		2	3						10	8				5	9		1	6		7			11	4
31		2	3						10	8				5	9		1	6		7			11	4
32		2	3						10	8					9		1	5		7			11	4
33		2	3			6			10	8					9		1	5		7			11	4
34		2	3			6			10	8					9		1	5		7			11	4
League Appearances	9	16	34	11	20	15	14	31	29	16	10	27	3	28	15	4	25	13	5	14	13	4	11	7
League Goals			3			1	5	3	6	7					9				1	2		1	1	

FA CUP

Match No	Date		Opponents	Result			Scorers	Att
1	Feb 9	A	Nottingham Forest (1)	L 1-5			Kyle / Calvey 3, Morris, FR Forman	9000

FA Cup appearances: Swift 3, Wragg 4, Jones 6, Connachan 10, Dunkley 11, Cochrane 2, Hamilton 5, Robinson 8, Daw 1, Henderson 7, Hammond 9

Note: New Brighton Tower subsequently resigned from the Football League, with the club going into liquidation; Burton Swifts amalgamated with Burton Wanderers during the close season to form Burton United.

Godfrey Beardsley

Peter Kyle

Season 1901-02

Promoted: West Bromwich Albion, Middlesbrough
Re-election: Chesterfield, Stockport County, Gainsborough Trinity (all elected)

FOOTBALL LEAGUE DIVISION TWO

Match No	Date		Opponents	Result	Points	Position	Scorers	Att
1	Sep 7	A	Woolwich Arsenal	L 0-2	–	–	– / J Anderson, Briercliffe	10000
2	14	H	Barnsley	W 2-0	2	9	Brown, King	4000
3	21	H	Burton United	W 4-0	4	6	Webb 2, Brown 2	3000
4	28	A	Preston North End	L 0-5	4	11	– / Wilcox 2 (2p), Green 2, Rogers	5000
5	Oct 5	H	Burnley	W 2-1	6	8	Richards, Brown / Stewart	3000
6	12	A	Burslem Port Vale	L 0-3	6	12	– / Rushton, Capes, Jones	3000
7	19	H	Chesterfield	W 3-0	8	8	Brown 3	3000
8	26	A	Gainsborough Trinity	D 3-3	9	8	Richards, Brown, Allsopp / Gettins 2, Fenton	1000
9	Nov 2	H	Middlesbrough	L 0-2	9	8	– / Brearley, Tennant	6000
10	9	A	Bristol City	L 1-2	9	9	Brown / Davies (p), O'Brien	5000
11	23	A	Stockport County	D 1-1	10	10	Burgess / Davies	4000
12	30	H	Newton Heath	W 3-2	12	8	Richards, Webb, Marshall / Cartwright, Preston	4000
13	Dec 7	A	Glossop	D 1-1	13	10	Marshall / Goodall	1000
14	21	A	Lincoln City	L 0-2	13	10	– / Smith, Hartley	2000
15	26	H	Doncaster Rovers	W 1-0	15	10	King	2000
16	28	H	West Bromwich Albion	L 0-3	15	10	– / Simmons 2, McLean	2034
17	Jan 4	H	Woolwich Arsenal	W 2-1	17	8	King, Marshall / Gooing	7000
18	6	A	West Bromwich Albion	L 0-1	17	8	– / Nurse	6483
19	11	A	Barnsley	W 3-2	19	8	Marshall 2, King / Travers 2	2000
20	18	A	Burton United	L 0-2	19	8	– / Arkesden 2	3000
21	25	H	Burslem Port Vale	L 0-1	19	8	– / Boullemeir	2000
22	Feb 1	A	Burnley	L 0-1	19	9	– / Taylor	2000
23	15	A	Chesterfield	D 3-3	20	11	King, Richards 2 / McCowie 2, England	2000
24	22	H	Gainsborough Trinity	W 2-0	22	9	King, Stevenson	2500
25	Mar 1	A	Middlesbrough	L 0-5	22	9	– / DW Smith (p), Cassidy 2, Leslie, Crawford	10000
26	8	H	Bristol City	L 0-1	22	10	– / S Jones	4000
27	15	H	Blackpool	W 1-0	24	10	Swift	1500
28	22	A	Stockport County	L 0-2	24	11	– / Marshall, Davies	2000
29	28	A	Blackpool	L 0-4	24	13	– / Anderson, Foster 2, Parkinson	3000
30	29	A	Newton Heath	L 0-2	24	14	– / Griffiths, Hayes	2000
31	31	H	Preston North End	W 1-0	26	13	Eaton	3000
32	Apr 1	A	Glossop	D 1-1	27	11	Eaton / Crump	2500
33	12	A	Doncaster Rovers	L 1-2	27	12	Fletcher / Price, Drake	2000
34	19	H	Lincoln City	W 3-1	29	12	Spriggs 2, Eaton / Hartley	2000

Final League Position: 14
Average Home League Attendance: 4100

Player appearances grid (shirt numbers)

Players (left to right): Teddy Daw, Andy Mills, George Swift, Walter Robinson, Herbert Dainty, Arthur Roulston, Charles Webb, Charles Richards, Tommy Brown, Arthur Marshall, Rab King, W T Wilson, Ernest Gill, Tommy Allsopp, Arthur Berry, Tommy Burgess, A Hackett, James Stevenson, Ewart Benskin, Sam Eaton, Arthur Collins, R Atherley, C Rosevear, Herbert Betts, Tommy Fletcher, Sam Peers, Frank Spriggs

M	Daw	Mills	Swift	Robinson	Dainty	Roulston	Webb	Richards	Brown	Marshall	King	Wilson	Gill	Allsopp	Berry	Burgess	Hackett	Stevenson	Benskin	Eaton	Collins	Atherley	Rosevear	Betts	Fletcher	Peers	Spriggs
1	1	2	3	4	5	6	7	8	9	10	11																
2		2	3	4	5	6	7	8	9	10	11	1															
3	1	2	3	4	5	6	7	8	9	10	11																
4	1	2	3	4	5	6	7	8	9	10	11																
5		2	3	4	5	6	7	8	9	10	11	1															
6		2	3	4	5	6	7	8	9	10	11	1															
7	1	2	3	4	5	6	7	8	9	10	11																
8	1	2			4	5	6	7	8	9	10			3	11												
9	1	2	3	4	5	6	7	8	9		10			11													
10	1	2	3	4	5	6	7	8	9		10			11													
11	1	2	3		5	6	7		9	10	11					4	8										
12	1	2	3	4	5	6	7	8	9	10	11																
13	1	2	3	4	5	6	7	8	9	10	11																
14	1	2	3	4	5	6	7	8		10	9			11													
15	1	2	3		5	6	7	8		10	9			11	4												
16	1	2	3		5	6	7	8		10	9			11	4												
17	1	2	3	4	5	6	7	8		10	9			11													
18	1	2	3	4	5	6	7	8			9			11				10									
19	1	2	3	4	5	6	7	8		10	9			11	4	7											
20	1	2	3	4	5	6		8			9			11	7			10									
21	1	2	3	4		6	7	8			9			11				10	5								
22	1	2	3	4	5	6	7	8			9			11				10									
23	1		3		2	5	6	7		9	8			11	4			10									
24	1	2	3	4	5	6	7	8			9			11				10									
25	1		3		2	5	6	7		9	8			11	4			10									
26	1	2			5	6	3	7		8	9			10	4			11									
27	1	2	3		6	5	10	7			9			11	4					8							
28	1	2	3	5		6	7				9			11	4			10		8							
29	1	2	3			6	7				10			11	4					8	5		9				
30	1	2	3			6	7				10			11	4					8	5		9				
31	1	2	3	4		6	7				10			11						8	5		9				
32	1	2	3	4		6	7				10			11						8	5				9	6	
33	1	2	3	4		6	7				9			11						8	5				10		
34		2	3	4		6	7				11	1						8						10		5	9

	Daw	Mills	Swift	Robinson	Dainty	Roulston	Webb	Richards	Brown	Marshall	King	Wilson	Gill	Allsopp	Berry	Burgess	Hackett	Stevenson	Benskin	Eaton	Collins	Atherley	Rosevear	Betts	Fletcher	Peers	Spriggs
League Appearances	30	33	27	33	23	34	32	25	13	15	34	4	1	23	11	3	2	7	1	8	5	1	3	2	2	1	1
League Goals			1				3	5	9	5	6			1		1		1		3					1		2

FA CUP

	Date		Opponents	Result	Scorers	Att	Daw	Mills	Swift	Robinson	Dainty	Roulston	Webb	Richards	Brown	Marshall	King
1	Dec 14	H	Glossop (Int)	L 0-1	– / Goodall	3000	1	2	3	4	5	6	7	8	9	10	11

Note: Jan 4, Most reports credit Marshall with second goal, some credit Swift;
Apr 19, Most reports credit Spriggs with third goal, some credit Fletcher.

1901-02
Back: Brown (Trainer), Roulston, Dainty, Webb, Richards, Smith (Director).
Middle: Marshall, Mills, Swift, Daw, Gill, Johnson (Secretary).
Front: Robinson, Brown, King.

Season 1902-03

Promoted: Manchester City, Small Heath
Re-election: Doncaster Rovers (not elected), Stockport County, Burnley (both elected)

Player columns (left to right): Archie Ling, Harry Whitehead, Andy Mills, Walter Robinson, Sam Peers, Arthur Roulston, Arthur Hadley, Tom Belton, George Lewis, John Binney, John Staples, Donald Coles, Arthur Berry, Sam Eaton, A Hales, Bob Pollock, Arthur Collins, Tom Simpson, Tommy Brown, W T Wilson, Sep Atterbury, W A Sharp, Sam Benskin, E Manship, Tommy Fletcher, Archie Wilde, Ewart Benskin, Alick Stewart, Frank Spriggs.

FOOTBALL LEAGUE DIVISION TWO

Match No	Date		Opponents	Result	Points	Position	Scorers	Att
1	Sep 6	H	Small Heath	L 1-3	-		Lewis / Field 2, McRoberts	5000
2	13	A	Chesterfield	L 0-5		17	- / Unwin, Newton 2, Munday 2	3000
3	20	A	Manchester City	L 1-3		17	Belton / Meredith, Gillespie, Mills (og)	12000
4	27	H	Burnley	W 2-1	2	15	Mills, Belton / Hogan	3000
5	Oct 4	A	Preston North End	L 0-2	2	16	- / Pearson, Wilcox	3000
6	11	H	Burslem Port Vale	W 2-0	4	15	Lewis, Mills (p)	3000
7	18	A	Barnsley	W 2-1	6	10	Belton / Bennett	2000
8	Nov 8	H	Bristol City	D 2-2	7	13	Belton, Mills (p) / Boucher, Gara	5000
9	22	H	Manchester United	D 1-1	8	14	Brown (p) / Downie	5000
10	29	A	Stockport County	D 2-2	9	13	Simpson, Roulston / Evenson, McKiernan	2000
11	Dec 6	H	Blackpool	W 2-1	11	10	Brown 2 / Cookson	2000
12	20	H	Doncaster Rovers	L 0-1	11	12	- / Pyle	2500
13	25	H	Gainsborough Trinity	W 4-1	13	11	Brown 2, Belton, Simpson / Dixon	7000
14	26	A	Burton United	W 3-2	15	9	Brown 2, Simpson / Arkesden 2	5000
15	27	A	Lincoln City	W 2-1	17	8	Simpson, Eaton / Proudfoot	4000
16	Jan 3	A	Small Heath	L 3-4	17	9	Lewis, Simpson, Brown / Leonard 2, Field, McRoberts	6000
17	10	H	Chesterfield	L 0-2	17	10	- / Steel, Taylor	5000
18	17	H	Manchester City	D 1-1	18	10	Pollock (p) / Threlfall	7000
19	24	A	Burnley	W 3-1	20	9	Brown 2, FS Benskin / Bell	1000
20	31	H	Preston North End	D 1-1	21	8	Robinson / Bond	8000
21	Feb 7	A	Burslem Port Vale	L 0-2	21	10	- / Eardley, Capes	1000
22	14	H	Barnsley	L 2-1	21	11	Brown / Lees, Albert Hellewell	3000
23	21	A	Gainsborough Trinity	L 1-5	21	11	Brown / Jacklin, Saul, Jenkinson, Greensell 2	2000
24	28	H	Burton United	L 0-1	21	13	- / Joyce	3000
25	Mar 7	A	Bristol City	L 1-6	21	14	Brown / Gara 2, Leigh 2, Banks, Barnes	5000
26	14	H	Glossop	W 3-2	23	12	Brown, Hadley, Belton / Ridgway, Thornley	1500
27	21	A	Manchester United	L 1-5	23	14	Fletcher / Fitchett, Griffiths, Morrison, Pegg, Smith	8000
28	26	H	Stockport County	L 0-2	23	14	- / Freeborough, Raby	2000
29	Apr 4	A	Blackpool	L 0-2	23	14	- / Duckworth 2	4000
30	10	A	Glossop	W 2-1	25	15	Stewart, Belton / Coates	4000
31	11	H	Woolwich Arsenal	L 0-2	25	15	- / Coleman, Gooing	10000
32	13	A	Woolwich Arsenal	D 0-0	26	15		12000
33	14	H	Lincoln City	D 0-0	27	14		4000
34	18	A	Doncaster Rovers	D 0-0	28	15		2500

Final League Position: 15
Average Home League Attendance: 5500

League Appearances: 33 3 15 34 10 34 29 29 30 2 5 1 4 13 1 28 22 27 23 1 21 1 1 2 1 2 1
League Goals: 3 1 1 1 8 3 1 1 5 14 1 1 1

FA CUP

	Date		Opponents	Result	Scorers	Att	
1	Nov 1	A	Irthlingborough (Q3)	W 1-0	Belton		
2	15	A	Wellingborough (Q4)	L 1-4	Hadley / McCairns 2, Darnell, Brett	4000	

Note: Nov 22, Most reports credit penalty to Brown, one report credits Pollock.

1902-03
Back: Collins, Spriggs, Stark, Smith, Wilson, Staples, Atterbury, E Benskin, Stewart (Trainer); **Middle:** Johnson (Secretary), Whitehead, Belton, Mills, Lewis, Ling, Berry. **Front:** Betts, Hadley, Eaton, Robinson, Peers, Roulston, Hales, FS Benskin.

Season 1903-04

Promoted: Preston North End, Woolwich Arsenal
Re-election: Stockport County (not elected), Glossop, Leicester Fosse (both elected)

FOOTBALL LEAGUE DIVISION TWO

Match No	Date		Opponents	Result		Points	Position	Scorers	Att	Archie Ling	George Mountain	Walter Robinson	Bob Pollock	Jack Bell	Arthur Collins	Arthur Hadley	Jimmy Blessington	Ike Evenson	John Barlow	Sam Peers	Arthur Berry	Billy Harper	Tom Belton	George Lewis	Tom Dilks	Ernest Gwynne	George Warren	Ewart Benskin	Tommy Fletcher	J Cheater	Ernest Coulson	Arthur Mounteney	Walter Smith	Alf West	Ernest Vickerstaffe	Frank Simpson	H Hougham	Match No
1	Sep 5	A	Barnsley	D	1-1	1	-	Peers / Sherman	5000	1	2	3	4	5	6	7	8	9	10	11																		1
2	12	H	Lincoln City	D	2-2	2	9	Blessington, Pollock (p) / CF Simpson, Pallister	4000	1	2	3	4	5	6	7	8	9	10	11																		2
3	19	A	Stockport County	L	0-2	2	12	- / Williams, Broomfield	3000	1	2	3	4	5			7	8	9	10	11	6																3
4	26	H	Chesterfield	D	0-0	3	13		3000	1	2	3	4	5	6	7	8	9	10			11																4
5	Oct 3	A	Bolton Wanderers	L	1-3	3	15	Barlow / Wright 2, Marsh	8000	1	2	3	4	5	6	7	8		10			11	9															5
6	10	H	Burnley	D	0-0	4	15		4000	1	2			5	6	7	8		10			11	9	3														6
7	17	A	Preston North End	L	3-4	4	15	Pollock (p), Blessington, Belton / Bell 2, Wilcox 2	10000	1	2	9	4	5	6		8		10			11	7	3														7
8	24	H	Grimsby Town	D	1-1	5	16	Hadley / Roberts	5000	1	2	6	4	5		7	8		10			9	3	11														8
9	26	A	Woolwich Arsenal	L	0-8	5	16	- / Shanks 3, Pratt 2, Gooing, Briercliffe, Busby	5000	1	2		4	5	6	7	8		10				3	11	9													9
10	Nov 7	A	Blackpool	W	2-1	7	14	Barlow, Robinson / Carthy	2500	1	2	5	4		6	7	8	9	11			10	3															10
11	21	A	Burton United	D	0-0	8	14		2000	1	2	5	4		6	7	8	9	11			10	3															11
12	Dec 12	H	Glossop	W	4-2	10	13	Belton 2, Blessington 2 / Green, Murphy	2000	1	2	5	4		6	7	8		11			10	3			9												12
13	19	A	Bradford City	L	0-4	10	14	- / McMillan 3, Robinson (og)	3000	1	2	5	4		6	7	8		11			10	3			9												13
14	25	H	Burslem Port Vale	D	1-1	11	13	Pollock / Capes	10000	1	2	6	4			5	7	8	11			10	3			9												14
15	26	A	Woolwich Arsenal	D	0-0	12	12		14000	1	2	3	4			5	7	8	11			10				9	6											15
16	Jan 2	H	Barnsley	W	2-0	14	13	Warren, Hadley	4000	1	2	3	4			5	7	8				10				9	6	11										16
17	9	A	Lincoln City	L	1-6	14	13	Blessington / D O'Donnell 3, CF Simpson, Brown 2	3000	1		3	4	5	2	7	8		11		6	10				9												17
18	16	H	Stockport County	W	3-0	16	13	Collins, Warren, Belton	3000	1		3	4		5	7	8		11			10				9	6		2									18
19	23	A	Chesterfield	L	0-2	16	14	- / Munday, Newton	2000	1		3	4			5	8	10				11				9	6		2	7								19
20	30	A	Bolton Wanderers	D	2-2	17	13	Blessington, Pollock (p) / Boyd, Marsh	2000	1		3	4			5	7	8				11				9	6		2		10							20
21	Feb 6	A	Burnley	L	1-2	17	14	Warren / Dixon (p), Williams	3000	1	2	3	4			5	7	8				10	11			9	6											21
22	13	H	Preston North End	L	1-4	17	14	Blessington / P Smith 3, Bell	6000	1	2	3	4			5	7	8		10			11			9	6											22
23	20	A	Grimsby Town	L	3-4	17	14	Warren 2, Evenson / Lappin, Nelmes, Elkins, Roberts	4000	1		3	6		4	5	7	8	10				11			9			2									23
24	25	H	Bristol City	W	1-0	19	13	Evenson	3000			3	6	4	5	7	8	10					11			9								1	2			24
25	27	A	Burslem Port Vale	L	2-6	19	13	Evenson, Mullineux (og) / Capes 2, Simpson, Price, Croxton, Eardley	1000			3		4	5	7	8	10				6	11			9								1	2			25
26	Mar 5	H	Blackpool	W	5-1	21	13	Evenson 2, Collins, Hadley, Birkett (og) / Bennett	5000		2	3	6	4	5	7	8	10	11				9											1				26
27	12	A	Gainsborough Trinity	L	0-4	21	15	- / Langham 2, Dixon, F Foxall	2000	1	2	3	6	4	5	7	8	10	11				9															27
28	19	H	Burton United	L	1-3	21	16	Evenson / Lewis 2, Gilchrist	3000		2	3	4		5		8	10	11				7		9	6						1						28
29	26	A	Bristol City	L	0-4	21	17	- / Corbett 2, Dean, Hosie	5000			3	4	6	5		8	10	11				9					2			1		7				29
30	Apr 2	H	Manchester United	L	0-1	21	18	- / McCartney	4000		2		4	6	5	7	8	10				11	9								1	3					30
31	4	H	Gainsborough Trinity	D	2-2	22	17	Evenson 2 / Dixon, Richardson	5000		2		4	6	5	7	8	10				9									1	3		11			31
32	9	A	Glossop	L	0-5	22	18	- / Green, Goodall 3, Boden	3000		2	3	4	6	5	7	8	10				11	9								1						32
33	16	H	Bradford City	L	1-2	22	18	Mounteney / Graham, McMillan	4000		2		4	6	5	7	8	10										3		9	1			11		33
34	30	A	Manchester United	L	2-5	22	18	Warren 2 / A Schofield 2, Bonthron, Griffiths, A Robertson	7000		2		4	6	5	7	8	10						3		9					1			11		34

Final League Position:	18	League Appearances	24	26	28	33	21	32	30	34	19	22	3	2	4	20	10	8	1	21	8	1	6	1	2	10	3	1	2	2
Average Home League Attendance:	5400	League Goals		1	4		2	3	7	8	2	1			4			7				1								

FA CUP

	Date		Opponents	Result		Scorers	Att	Archie Ling	George Mountain	Walter Robinson	Bob Pollock	Jack Bell	Arthur Collins	Arthur Hadley	Jimmy Blessington	Ike Evenson	John Barlow	Tom Belton	George Lewis	Tom Dilks	Ewart Benskin	Frank Simpson		
1	Oct 31	A	Market Harborough (Q3)	W	10-0	Hadley 2, Evenson 3, Barlow, Belton 3, Blessington	2000	1		2	4	5	6	7	8	9	11	10	3					1
2	Nov 14	A	Wellingborough (Q4)	W	2-1	Pollock (p), Belton / Lamberton	4000	1	2	5	4		6	7	8	9	11	10	3					2
3	28	A	Burton United (Q5)	D	1-1	Evenson / Lewis	5000	1	2	5	4		6	7	8	9	10	11	3					3
4	Dec 3	H	Burton United (Q5 rep)	D	2-2 aet	Pollock 2 (1p) / Lewis, Hargreaves	1000	1	2	5	4		6	7	8	9	10		3	11				4
5	7		Burton United (Q5 rep 2)	L	0-2	- / Reynolds, Gould	600	1	2	5	4		6	7	8	9	10		3			11		5

Dismissals: Dec 7, Mountain, Burton United (Derby) FAC.

Note: Oct 31, drawn away, but tie played at Filbert Street; Dec 3, abandoned during extra time, result at 90 minutes stood; Dec 7, played at Baseball Ground (Derby County);

Re-election voting: Leicester Fosse 33, Glossop 27, Doncaster Rovers 21(all elected), Stockport County 11, Crewe Alexandra 10.

1903-04
Back: Johnson (Secretary), Berry, Evenson, Jayes, Swift, Turner, Pollock, Ling, Stewart (Trainer).
Middle: Collins, Hadley, Belton, Bell, Barlow, Gwynne, Blessington, Robinson.
Front: Mountain.

Season 1904-05

Promoted: Liverpool, Bolton Wanderers
Re-election: Burslem Port Vale (elected), Burton United, Doncaster Rovers (both not elected)

FOOTBALL LEAGUE DIVISION TWO

Match No	Date		Opponents	Result	Points	Position	Scorers	Att	Walter Smith	Jack Bennett	Billy Oakes	Billy Morgan	Billy Bannister	Bob Pollock	Jamie Durrant	Alf Watkins	Matt Brunton	Ike Evenson	Tommy Allsopp	Walter Robinson	Jimmy Blessington	Arthur Mounteney	Jack Sheffield	George Perkins	Arthur Collins	Archie Hubbard	Joe Moran	Archie Ling	Ernest Harper	James Hyett	Albert Lee	Arthur Hadley	Match No
1	Sep 3	A	Blackpool	D 0-0	1	-		4300	1	2	3	4	5	6	7	8	9	10	11														1
2	10	H	Doncaster Rovers	W 3-2	3	7	Evenson 2, Morgan (p) / Law, Davies	5000	1	2	3	4	5	6	7	8	9	10	11														2
3	17	A	Gainsborough Trinity	L 0-2	3	10	- / Langham, Twigg	3000	1	2		4	5	6	7	8	9	10	11	3													3
4	24	H	Burton United	W 2-0	5	5	Mounteney, Bennett (p)	5000	1	2		6	5	4	7			10	11	3	8	9											4
5	Oct 1	A	Liverpool	L 0-4	5	11	- / Robinson 4	12000	1	2		4	5	6				10	11	3	8	9	7										5
6	8	H	Burslem Port Vale	W 3-0	7	7	Morgan, Evenson, Mounteney	3000	1	2		4	5	6	7			10	11	3	8	9											6
7	15	A	Bristol City	L 0-3	7	9	- / Gilligan 2, Robinson (og)	9000	1	2		4	5	6	7			10	11	3	8	9											7
8	22	H	Manchester United	L 0-3	7	12	- / Arkesden, Peddie, Schofield	7000	1	2		4	5	6				10	11	3	8	9	7										8
9	Nov 5	H	Chesterfield Town	D 1-1	8	12	Mounteney / Newton	3000	1	2		4	5	6	7	8		9	11	3		10											9
10	19	A	Lincoln City	L 0-1	8	13	- / M O'Donnell	4000		2		9	5	4	7					3		10		1	6	8	11						10
11	Dec 3	A	Barnsley	L 1-2	8	15	Allsopp / Edwards (p), Silto	4000		2		9	5	4	7			10	11	3	8				6			1					11
12	15	H	West Bromwich Albion	W 3-1	10	13	Collins, Mounteney, Morgan / Aston	7890	1	2		9	5	4	7			10		3	8	11			6								12
13	17	A	Burnley	L 0-2	10	15	- / Marshall, McFarlane	4000	1	2		4	5	6	7		9	10	11	3	8												13
14	24	H	Grimsby Town	W 5-1	12	13	Allsopp, Mounteney 2, Morgan 2 / Higgins	4000	1	2		9	5	4	7				11	3	8	10			6								14
15	26	H	Glossop	L 0-2	12	15	- / Goodall 2	8000	1	2		9	5	4	7				11	3	8	10			6								15
16	27	H	Bolton Wanderers	L 2-4	12	15	Durrant, Morgan / Stokes, White 2, Marsh	8000	1	2		9	5	4	7				11	3	8	10			6								16
17	31	H	Blackpool	W 3-1	14	13	Blessington 2, Mounteney / Scott (p)	4000	1	2		9	5		7	4			11	3	8	10			6								17
18	Jan 7	A	Doncaster Rovers	L 0-3	14	14	- / Moralee, Hyde, Magee	2000	1	2	3	9	5		7	4			11		8	10			6								18
19	21	A	Burton United	W 3-0	16	12	Evenson 3	2000	1	2		4		6	7			9	11		8	10			5				3				19
20	28	H	Liverpool	L 0-3	16	13	- / Robinson, West, Goddard	12000	1	2	3	4		6	7			8	10			11			5					9			20
21	Feb 11	H	Bristol City	W 2-1	18	13	Durrant, Mounteney (p) / Gilson	6000	1	2			5	4	7			9	11	3	8	10			6								21
22	18	A	Manchester United	L 1-4	18	14	Durrant / Peddie 3, Allan	7000	1	2			5	4	7			9	11	3	8	10			6								22
23	23	H	Gainsborough Trinity	D 1-1	19	12	Durrant / Thompson	1500	1	2			5	4	7			9	11	3	8	10			6								23
24	Mar 4	A	Chesterfield Town	D 0-0	20	13		2000	1	2		4	5	3	7			9	11		8	10			6								24
25	11	H	Bradford City	L 1-2	20	15	Allsopp / Graham, McGeachan	3000	1	2		4	5	3	7			9	11		8	10			6								25
26	18	A	Lincoln City	L 1-5	20	16	Allsopp / Martin, D O'Donnell 3 (1p), CF Simpson	3000		2		4	5	3	7				11		8				6	9		1			10		26
27	25	A	Bolton Wanderers	W 1-0	22	15	Collins	10000	1	2		4		3				8	11	5	7	10			6	9							27
28	Apr 1	H	Barnsley	W 2-0	24	14	Hubbard, Collins	6000	1	2		4		3					11	5	8	10			6	9						7	28
29	3	A	Burslem Port Vale	W 3-1	26	9	Hubbard 2, Mounteney / Allman	2000	1	2		4		3				6	11	5	8	10				9						7	29
30	8	A	West Bromwich Albion	L 0-2	26	12	- / Pheasant 2	3104	1	2		4		3					11	5	8	10			6	9						7	30
31	15	H	Burnley	D 2-2	27	12	Mounteney, Hubbard / Hogan, R Smith	5000	1			2	4	5	3				11		8	10			6	9						7	31
32	21	A	Glossop	D 0-0	28	12		3000	1			2	4	5	3	7					8	10			6	9						11	32
33	22	A	Grimsby Town	L 0-2	28	14	- / Padley 2	2500	1			2	4	5	3	7			11		8	10			6	9							33
34	24	A	Bradford City	D 0-0	29	13		11000	1			2	4	5	3	7			11		8	10			6	9							34

| | | | | | | | League Appearances | | 31 | 27 | 11 | 31 | 28 | 32 | 27 | 4 | 5 | 23 | 30 | 22 | 28 | 28 | 2 | 1 | 23 | 10 | 1 | 2 | 1 | 1 | 1 | 5 | |
| | | | | | | | League Goals | | | 1 | | 6 | | 4 | | | | 6 | 4 | | 2 | 10 | | | 3 | 4 | | | | | | | |

Final League Position: 14
Average Home League Attendance: 5900

FA CUP

Match No	Date		Opponents	Result	Scorers	Att	Walter Smith	Jack Bennett	Billy Oakes	Billy Morgan	Billy Bannister	Bob Pollock	Jamie Durrant	Alf Watkins	Matt Brunton	Ike Evenson	Tommy Allsopp	Walter Robinson	Jimmy Blessington	Arthur Mounteney	Jack Sheffield	George Perkins	Arthur Collins	Archie Hubbard	Match No
1	Oct 29	H	Linby Church (Q3)	W 10-1	Mounteney 4, Bannister 2, Watkins 2, Durrant 2 / Clarke (p)	800	1	2		4	5		7	8	9		11	3		10			6		1
2	Nov 12	H	Gresley Rovers (Q4)	W 5-0	Morgan, Mounteney 2, Hubbard 2	2000	1	2		9	5	4	7					3	8	10			6	11	2
3	26	A	Northampton (Q5)	D 2-2	Pollock (p), Blessington / Benbow 2	5000	1	2		9	5	4	7			10	11	3	8				6		3
4	Dec 1	A	Northampton (Q5 rep)	W 2-0	Morgan 2	3500	1	2		9	5	4	7			10	11	3	8				6		4
5	10	A	Southall (Q6)	W 4-0	Evenson 2, Durrant, Snarry (og)	500	1	2		9	5	4	7			10	11	3	8				6		5
6	Jan 5	A	West Bromwich A. (Int)	W 5-2	Mounteney 3, Allsopp, Blessington / Aston, Pheasant	5230	1	2			4	5	3	7		9	11		8	10			6		6
7	Feb 4	A	Aston Villa (1)	L 1-5	Mounteney (p) / Bache 2, Hampton, Leake, Hall	26091	1	2			5	4	7			9	11	3	8	10			6		7

Dismissals: Dec 3, Robinson, Barnsley (a); Mar 25, Pollock and Evenson, Bolton Wanderers (a).
Note: Subsequently, the Football League was extended by four clubs, with Burton United elected to one of the extra places. An election was held to select the two clubs to join the extended Division One; both relegated clubs were elected.

1904-05
Back: Hubbard, Sheffield, Mounteney, Pollock, Oakes, Perkins, Harper, Stubbings, Lee, Johnson (Secretary), Berry.
Middle: Durrant, Blessington, Morgan, Bennett, Bannister, Evenson, Collins, Allsopp.
Front: Brunton, Watkins, Smith, Robinson.

Season 1905-06

Promoted: Bristol City, Manchester United
Re-election: Chesterfield Town, Burton United, Clapton Orient (all elected)

FOOTBALL LEAGUE DIVISION TWO

Match No	Date		Opponents	Result	Points	Position	Scorers	Att	Walter Smith	Harry Ashby	Billy Oakes	Billy Morgan	Billy Bannister	Albert Trueman	Jamie Durrant	Jimmy Blessington	William Cox	Harry Moody	Albert Hodgkinson	Bob Pollock	Willie Gould	Archie Hubbard	Tom Bradshaw	Fred Bracey	George Keogh	Billy Turner	Bernard Hughes	Match No
1	Sep 2	H	Clapton Orient	W 2-1	2	-	Moody, Morgan / Kingaby	6000	1	2	3	4	5	6	7	8	9	10	11									1
2	16	H	Leeds City	L 0-1	2	16	- / Singleton	5000	1	2	3	4	5		7		9		11	6	10							2
3	23	A	Burton United	D 0-0	3	14		2000	1	2	3	4	5		7	8	9	10	11	6								3
4	30	H	Chelsea	L 0-1	3	17	- / J Robertson	7000	1	2	3	4	5		7	8		10	11	6	9							4
5	Oct 2	A	Burnley	W 2-0	5	12	Hubbard, Durrant	2000	1	2	3	4	5		7	8		10	11	6	9							5
6	7	A	Gainsborough Trinity	W 1-0	7	5	Blessington	3000	1	2	3	4	5		7	8		10	11	6		9						6
7	14	H	Bristol City	L 1-2	7	11	Hubbard / Bennett 2 (1p)	7000	1		2	4	5	6	7	8		10	11	3		9						7
8	21	A	Manchester United	L 2-3	7	15	Hubbard, Pollock (p) / Peddie 2, Sagar	12000	1	2	3	4	5		7			10	11	6		9	8					8
9	28	H	Glossop	W 2-1	9	11	Hubbard, Hodgkinson / Ross	5000	1	2	3	4	5		7			10	11	6		9	8					9
10	Nov 4	A	Stockport County	D 1-1	10	10	Blessington / Waters (p)	4000	1	2	3	4	5			8		10	11	6		9	7					10
11	11	H	Blackpool	W 2-0	12	8	Hubbard 2	4000	1	2	3	4	5		7			10	11	6		9	8					11
12	18	A	Bradford City	D 3-3	13	7	Bradshaw 2, Durrant / Smith 2, Robinson	9000	1	2	3	4	5		7			10	11	6		9	8					12
13	25	H	West Bromwich Albion	D 0-0	14	8		6500	1	2	3	4	5		7			10	11	6		9	8					13
14	Dec 2	A	Grimsby Town	D 1-1	15	7	Moody / Padley	3000	1	2	3	4	5		7			10	11	6		9	8					14
15	7	H	Hull City	L 1-2	15	7	Bannister (p) / Raisbeck, Manning	3000	1	2	3	4	5					10	11	6		9	8	7				15
16	9	H	Chesterfield Town	D 1-1	16	6	Bannister (p) / Munday	4000	1	2		4	5	6				10	11	3		9	8	7				16
17	16	H	Lincoln City	W 3-1	18	5	Durrant, Moody, Hodgkinson / Martin	5000	1	2		4	5	6	7	8		9	11	3		10						17
18	23	A	Chesterfield Town	D 3-3	19	6	Durrant, Blessington 2 / Munday 2, Banner	4000	1	2	3	4	5		7	8		9	11	6		10						18
19	25	H	Barnsley	W 1-0	21	6	Hodgkinson	8000	1	2	3	4	5		7	8		9	11	6		10						19
20	26	H	Burslem Port Vale	W 2-1	23	6	Moody 2 / Mountford	10000	1	2	3	4	5		7	8		9	11	6		10						20
21	30	A	Clapton Orient	W 2-0	25	5	Gould, Bannister (p)	2000	1	2	3	4	5		7	8		9	11	6	10							21
22	Jan 6	H	Burnley	W 2-0	27	5	Hubbard, Morgan	3000	1	2	3	4	5		7	8		9	11	6		10						22
23	20	A	Leeds City	L 1-4	27	6	Morgan / Murray (p), Drain, Watson, Hargraves	8000	1	2		4	5	6	7	8		9	11			10			3			23
24	27	A	Burton United	D 1-1	28	6	Durrant / Trueman (og)	5000	1	2	3	4	5	6	7	8		9	11			10						24
25	Feb 5	A	Chelsea	D 3-3	29	5	Hodgkinson, Blessington, Hubbard / Pearson, Windridge, J Robertson	6000	1	2	3	4	5		7	8		9	11	6		10						25
26	10	H	Gainsborough Trinity	W 4-0	31	5	Hodgkinson, Hubbard, Durrant, Moody	3000	1	2	3	4	5		7	8		9	11	6		10						26
27	17	H	Bristol City	W 2-1	33	5	Bannister, Blessington / Gilligan	8000	1	2	3	4	5		7	8		9	11	6		10						27
28	24	H	Grimsby Town	W 2-0	35	5	Bannister, Hubbard	7000	1	2		4	5	6	7	8		9	11	3		10						28
29	Mar 3	A	Glossop	D 0-0	36	5		2000	1	2		4	5	6		8		9	11	3		10		7				29
30	10	H	Stockport County	W 2-0	38	5	Durrant, Hubbard	6000	1	2		4	5	6	7	8		9	11	3		10						30
31	17	H	Blackpool	W 1-0	40	5	Hubbard	1500	1	2		4	5	6	7	8		9	11	3		10						31
32	24	H	Bradford City	L 2-4	40	5	Durrant, Pollock / Smith 3, Clarke	10000	1	2		4	5	6	7	8			11	3		9				10		32
33	29	H	Manchester United	L 2-5	40	5	Trueman 2 / Peddie 3, Picken, Sagar	5000	1	2		4	5	6	7	8		9	11	3		10						33
34	31	A	West Bromwich Albion	L 0-3	40	5	- / Shinton, Haycock 2	10067	1	2		4	5	6	7	8		9		3		10	11					34
35	Apr 13	A	Burslem Port Vale	L 0-2	40	5	- / Carter, Mountford	5000	1	2		4	5	6	7	8		9				10	11					35
36	14	H	Hull City	D 0-0	41	5		10000	1	2	3		5	6	7	8		9				10	11				4	36
37	16	A	Barnsley	D 0-0	42	6		5000	1	2	3		5	6	7	8		9			4	10	11					37
38	21	A	Lincoln City	L 1-3	42	6	Blessington / Machin, Martin (p), Hood	3000	1	2	3		5	6	7	8		9			4	10	11					38

Final League Position:	7	**League Appearances**	38 37 28 35 38 17 34 29 3 33 33 33 6 28 15 8 1 1 1
Average Home League Attendance:	6175	**League Goals**	3 5 2 8 7 6 5 2 12 2

FA CUP

	Date		Opponents	Result			Scorers	Att	Players		
1	Jan 13	A	Liverpool (1)	L 1-2			Moody / Raybould, Goddard	12000	1 2 3 4 5 / 7 8 / 9 11 6 / 10		1

1905-06
Back: Morgan, Gould, Blessington, Smith, Moody, Trueman, Pollock, Thompson (Trainer).
Middle: Johnson (Secretary), Bradshaw, Hubbard, Bannister, Oakes, Ashby, Hodgkinson.
Front: Durrant.

Season 1906-07

Promoted: Nottingham Forest, Chelsea
Re-election: Chesterfield Town, Lincoln City (both elected), Burton United (not elected)

FOOTBALL LEAGUE DIVISION TWO

Match No	Date		Opponents	Result	Points	Position	Scorers	Att	Tal Lewis	Harry Ashby	Joe Blackett	Billy Leech	Billy Bannister	Bob Pollock	Jamie Durrant	Harry Moody	Harry Wilcox	Archie Hubbard	Frank Middleton	Bob Turner	Billy Oakes	Tommy Shanks	Albert Trueman	Alf Norman	Jimmy Blessington	George Wesley	Shirley Hubbard	Teddy King	Fred Milnes	Match No
1	Sep 1	A	Burslem Port Vale	W 2-1	2	-	Middleton, Wilcox / Dodds	6000	1	2	3	4	5	6	7	8	9	10	11											1
2	3	H	Grimsby Town	W 2-0	4	-	Middleton, Wilcox	6000	1	2	3	4	5	6	7	8	9	10	11											2
3	8	H	Burnley	W 2-0	6	1	Middleton, Moody	10000	1	2	3	4	5	6	7	8	9	10	11											3
4	15	A	Leeds City	D 1-1	7	1	Middleton / Jefferson	11000	1	2	3	4	5	6	7	8	9	10	11											4
5	22	H	Barnsley	W 2-1	9	1	Wilcox, Moody / Griffiths	8000	1	2	3	4	5	6	7	8	9	10					11							5
6	29	A	Chelsea	L 0-1	9	2	- / Hilsdon	20000	1	2	3	4	5	6	7	8	9	10					11							6
7	Oct 6	H	Wolverhampton W.	W 2-0	11	1	Durrant, Wilcox	6000	1	2	3	4	5	6	7	8	9	10	11											7
8	13	A	Clapton Orient	L 0-1	11	4	- / Thacker	4000	1	2		4	5	6	7	8	9		11		3	10								8
9	20	H	Gainsborough Trinity	W 3-1	13	2	Moody, Leech, Wilcox / F Foxall	11000	1	2	3	4	5	6	7	8	9		11			10								9
10	27	A	Stockport County	L 0-1	13	3	- / Crump	5000	1	2	3	4	5	6	7	8	9		11			10								10
11	Nov 3	H	Hull City	W 3-0	15	2	Durrant, Shanks 2 (2p)	14000	1	2	3	4	5	6	7	9	8		11			10								11
12	10	A	Glossop	D 2-2	16	3	Pollock, Durrant / Napier 2	3000	1	2	3	4	5	6	7	9	8	10	11											12
13	17	H	Blackpool	W 5-1	18	3	Wilcox 2, Bannister, Shanks, A Hubbard / Grundy	7000	1	2	3	4	5		7	9	8	11				10	6							13
14	24	A	Bradford City	L 1-3	18	4	Shanks / Robinson, Handley, Clarke	17000	1	2	3	4	5			9	8	11				10	6	7						14
15	Dec 1	H	West Bromwich Albion	W 3-0	20	4	Wilcox 2, Blessington	19820	1	2	3	4	5	6	7		9		11			10			8					15
16	8	A	Chesterfield Town	W 2-0	22	3	Shanks (p), Wilcox	10000	1	2	3	4	5	6	7		9		11			10			8					16
17	15	A	Nottingham Forest	L 1-2	22	4	Middleton / Morris, West	20000	1	2	3	4	5	6	7		9		11			10			8					17
18	22	H	Lincoln City	W 3-0	24	4	Wilcox, Shanks, Norman	10000	1	2		4	5	3		9	8	11				10	6	7						18
19	25	H	Stockport County	W 1-0	26	4	Durrant	14000	1	2		4	5	3	7	8	9		11			10	6							19
20	26	H	Burton United	W 3-0	28	2	Moody, Middleton, Blessington	8000	1	2		4	5	3	7	9			11			10	6		8					20
21	29	H	Burslem Port Vale	W 4-1	30	2	Bannister 2, Moody, Durrant / Beats	8000	1	2		4	5	3	7	9			11			10	6		8					21
22	Jan 5	A	Burnley	L 0-5	30	3	- / Whittaker 2, R Smith 2, Ogden	6000	1	2	3	4	5	6	7	9			11			10			8					22
23	19	H	Leeds City	D 2-2	31	3	A Hubbard, Wilcox / McLeod, Kirk	8000	1	2	3	5	4		7		9	10	11				6		8					23
24	26	A	Barnsley	D 2-2	32	3	Durrant, Bannister (p) / Hellewell, Reeves	4000	1	2	3	5	4		7	8		10	11				6			9				24
25	Feb 2	A	Chelsea	D 1-1	33	2	Bannister (p) / Birnie	17000	1	2	3	4	5	6	7	9	8	10	11											25
26	9	A	Wolverhampton W.	L 0-1	33	3	- / Roberts	4000	1	2	3	4	5		7	9		10	11				6		8					26
27	16	H	Clapton Orient	W 2-1	35	3	Wilcox, Shanks / Oliver	8000	1	2	3	4	5	6	7	8	9		11			10								27
28	23	A	Gainsborough Trinity	W 2-1	37	3	A Hubbard, Durrant / Holmes	2000	1	2	3	4	5	6	7	8		9	11			10								28
29	Mar 9	A	Hull City	D 1-1	38	3	Shanks / Hedley	7000	1	2	3	4	5	6	7	8	9		11			10								29
30	16	H	Glossop	D 2-2	39	3	Leech, A Hubbard / Kelly, JT Robertson	7000	1		2	4	5	3	7	8		9	11			10	6							30
31	23	A	Blackpool	L 0-1	39	4	- / Grundy	6000	1		2	4	5	3	7	8		9	11			10	6							31
32	29	A	Burton United	W 1-0	41	3	Wilcox	8000	1		2	4	5	3	7		8		11			10	6				9			32
33	30	H	Bradford City	W 1-0	43	3	Durrant	10000	1		2	4	5	3	7		8		11			10	6				9			33
34	Apr 1	A	Grimsby Town	W 1-0	45	3	Bannister (p)	10000	1		2	4	5	3	7	9	8		11			10	6							34
35	6	A	West Bromwich Albion	W 1-0	47	3	S Hubbard	5034	1		2	4		3	7	8			11			10	6				9	5		35
36	13	A	Chesterfield Town	L 1-2	47	3	Bannister / Wheatley, Baker	5000	1		2	4	5	3	7	8			11			10	6				9			36
37	20	H	Nottingham Forest	L 1-2	47	3	Middleton / Morris, West	12000	1		2	4	5	3	7	8			11			10	6				9			37
38	27	A	Lincoln City	D 2-2	48	3	S Hubbard, A Hubbard / Langham 2	5000	1		3	4	5		7	8		11				10	6				9		2	38

									Tal Lewis	Harry Ashby	Joe Blackett	Billy Leech	Billy Bannister	Bob Pollock	Jamie Durrant	Harry Moody	Harry Wilcox	Archie Hubbard	Frank Middleton	Bob Turner	Billy Oakes	Tommy Shanks	Albert Trueman	Alf Norman	Jimmy Blessington	George Wesley	Shirley Hubbard	Teddy King	Fred Milnes	
Final League Position:	3						**League Appearances**		38	29	33	36	37	34	35	21	35	20	27	9	1	27	18	2	7	1	6	1	1	
Average Home League Attendance:	10200						**League Goals**					2	7	1	8	5	14	5	7			8		1	2		2			

FA CUP

Match No	Date		Opponents	Result			Scorers	Att	Tal Lewis	Harry Ashby	Joe Blackett	Billy Leech	Billy Bannister	Bob Pollock	Jamie Durrant	Harry Moody	Harry Wilcox	Archie Hubbard	Frank Middleton	Bob Turner	Billy Oakes	Tommy Shanks	Albert Trueman	Alf Norman	Jimmy Blessington	George Wesley	Shirley Hubbard	Teddy King	Fred Milnes	Match No
1	Jan 12	A	Sunderland (1)	L 1-4			Bannister / McIntosh 2, Raine, Bridgett	20000	1	2	3	5	4		7		9	10	11				6		8					1

Note: Burslem Port Vale subsequently resigned from the Football League, with the club going into liquidation.

1906-07
Back: Thompson (Trainer), Blessington, Oakes, Lewis, Pollock, Trueman, Leech.
Middle: Johnson (Secretary), Durrant, Moody, Bannister, Wilcox, Middleton, Blackett.
Front: Hubbard, Ashby.

Season 1907-08

Promoted: Bradford City, Leicester Fosse
Re-election: Grimsby Town, Chesterfield Town (both elected), Lincoln City (not elected)

FOOTBALL LEAGUE DIVISION TWO

Match No	Date		Opponents	Result	Pts	Pos	Scorers	Att	Jonty Starbuck	Joe Blackett	Harry Thorpe	Billy Leech	Billy Bannister	Bob Pollock	Jamie Durrant	Jimmy Donnelly	Percy Humphreys	Tommy Shanks	Frank Middleton	Horace Bailey	Shirley Hubbard	Harry Wilcox	Albert Trueman	Bob Mackie	Fred Shinton	Jimmy Blessington	Fred Bracey	Bob Turner	George Hedley	Billy Turner	Match No
1	Sep 7	H	Leeds City	D 2-2	1	-	Pollock (p), Middleton / Watson, McLeod	10000	1	2	3	4	5	6	7	8	9	10	11												1
2	9	H	Wolverhampton W.	W 1-0	3	-	Humphreys	8000		2	3	4	5	6	7	8	9		11	1		10									2
3	14	A	Wolverhampton W.	D 0-0	4	9		6000		2	3	4	5	6	7		9	10	11	1		8									3
4	21	H	Gainsborough Trinity	W 3-0	6	4	Humphreys 2, Wilcox	13000		2	3	4	5	6	7		9	10	11	1		8									4
5	28	A	Stockport County	L 1-2	6	8	Humphreys / Crump, Green	8000		2	3	4	5		7		9	10	11	1		8		6							5
6	Oct 5	H	Glossop	W 3-1	8	6	Humphreys 2, Leech / Mackenzie	9000		2	3	4	5	6	7		9	10	11	1		8									6
7	12	A	Grimsby Town	D 1-1	9	5	Bannister / Jewel	4500		2	3	4	5	6	7		9	10	11	1		8									7
8	19	A	Blackpool	D 2-2	10	6	Humphreys, Pollock (p) / Whittingham, Grundy	8000		2	3	4	5	6	7		9	10	11	1		8									8
9	26	H	Stoke	W 1-0	12	6	Pollock	18000		2	3	4	5	6	7	8			11	1	9	10									9
10	Nov 2	A	West Bromwich Albion	D 1-1	13	6	Wilcox / Bradley	17000		2	3	4	5	6	7		9	10	11	1		8									10
11	9	H	Bradford City	W 2-1	15	6	Humphreys, Donnelly / Handley	15000		2	3	4	5	6	7	8	9	10	11	1											11
12	16	A	Hull City	L 2-3	15	6	Humphreys, Donnelly / Temple 3	6000		2	3	4	5		7	8	9	10	11	1				6							12
13	23	H	Derby County	L 1-3	15	10	Donnelly / Bevan, Long, G Davis	18000			3	4	5	6	7	8	9		11	1	10			2							13
14	30	A	Lincoln City	W 3-0	17	8	Shinton, Humphreys 2	6000			3	4	5	6	7	8	9		11	1				2	10						14
15	Dec 7	H	Fulham	L 2-3	17	9	Durrant, Donnelly / Harrison 2, Threlfall	12000		2	3	4	5	6	7	8	9		11	1	10										15
16	14	A	Barnsley	W 3-1	19	8	Middleton 2, Hubbard / Tomlinson	10000		2	3	4	5		7	8			11	1	10			6	9						16
17	21	H	Chesterfield Town	W 3-1	21	7	Humphreys 3 / Wheatley	15000		2	3	4	5		7	8	9		11	1	10			6							17
18	25	H	Oldham Athletic	W 4-1	23	6	Hubbard, Humphreys 2, Shinton / Shadbolt	20000		2	3	4	5	6	7		9		11	1	10				8						18
19	26	H	Clapton Orient	L 0-2	23	7	- / Goffin, Parker	12000		2	3	4	5	6			9		11	1	10				8				7		19
20	28	A	Burnley	L 1-4	23	8	Humphreys / Parker, Donaghey 2, A Smith	11000	1	2	3	4	5	6			9				10				8			11	7		20
21	Jan 4	A	Leeds City	D 0-0	24	9		10000		2	3	4	5	6	7		9		11	1	10				8						21
22	18	A	Gainsborough Trinity	D 1-1	25	9	Pollock (p) / Murphy	4000			3	4	5	6	7		9			1	10			2	8			11			22
23	25	H	Stockport County	W 2-1	27	9	Hubbard, Pollock (p) / Bannister (og)	6000			3	4	5	6	7		9		11	1	10			2	8						23
24	Feb 8	H	Grimsby Town	D 1-1	28	8	Donnelly / Hakin	8000		2	3	4	5	6	7	8	9		11	1	10										24
25	15	H	Blackpool	W 2-1	30	8	Humphreys 2 / Gow	10000			3	4	5	6	7		9			1	10			2	8			11			25
26	22	A	Derby County	W 2-1	32	8	Shinton 2 / Bentley	6000	1	2		4	5	6	7		9				10			3	8			11			26
27	29	H	West Bromwich Albion	W 3-0	34	8	Donnelly, Shinton 2	6337		2		4	5	6	7	8				1	10			3	9			11			27
28	Mar 7	A	Bradford City	W 5-1	36	7	Shanks 2, Donnelly, Shinton, RF Turner / McDonald	17000		2		4	5	6	7	8		10		1				3	9			11			28
29	14	H	Hull City	W 3-2	38	4	Donnelly, Hubbard, RF Turner / Jack Smith, Shaw	12000		2		4	5	6	7	8				1	10			3	9			11			29
30	24	A	Glossop	W 3-2	40	3	Donnelly 3 / Galvin, JT Robertson	2500			3	4	5	6	7	8				1	10			2	9			11			30
31	28	H	Lincoln City	W 1-0	42	3	Shinton	8000			3	4	5	6	7	8				1	10			2	9			11			31
32	Apr 4	H	Fulham	L 1-5	42	7	Durrant / Harrison, Dalrymple, Carter, Brown 2	30000		2		4	5	6	7	8				1	10			3	9			11			32
33	11	H	Barnsley	W 4-0	44	4	Shinton, Hubbard, Bannister, Shanks	8000		2		4	5	6	7			8		1	10			3	9			11			33
34	18	A	Chesterfield Town	D 2-2	45	6	Shinton, Donnelly / Lee, Allen	6000		2		4	5	6	7	8				1	10			3	9			11			34
35	20	H	Clapton Orient	W 1-0	47	4	Hubbard	5000	1	2		4	5	6	7	8					10			3	9			11			35
36	21	A	Oldham Athletic	D 1-1	48	3	Shanks / Hancock	27000	1	2		4	5	6	7	8		10						3	9			11			36
37	25	H	Burnley	W 3-1	50	3	RF Turner 2, Hubbard / R Smith	16000		2		4	5	6	7	8				1	10			3	9			11			37
38	27	A	Stoke	W 1-0	52	2	Shanks	1500		2		4	5	6	7	8		10		1				3	9			11			38

									Sta	Bla	Tho	Lee	Ban	Pol	Dur	Don	Hum	Sha	Mid	Bai	Hub	Wil	Tru	Mac	Shi	Ble	Bra	BTu	Hed	BiT	
Final League Position:		2					**League Appearances**		5	27	26	38	33	35	21	25	26	20	22	33	25	9	8	18	24	1	2	16	3	1	
Average Home League Attendance:		12775					**League Goals**					1	2	5	2	12	19	5	3		7	2			10			4			

FA CUP

	Date		Opponents	Result			Scorers	Att	Sta	Bla	Tho	Lee	Ban	Pol	Dur	Don	Hum	Sha	Mid	Bai	Hub	Wil	Tru	Mac	Shi	Ble	Bra	BTu	Hed	BiT	
1	Jan 11	H	Blackburn Rovers (1)	W 2-0			Humphreys, Pollock (p)	13749		2	3	4	5	6	7		9		11	1	10				8						1
2	Feb 1	A	Portsmouth (2)	L 0-1			- / McDonald	20000		2	3	4	5	6	7	8	9		11	1	10										2

Note: Stoke subsequently resigned from Football League, with the club going into liquidation.

1907-08
Back: Blessington (Player/Manager), Ashby, Lavery, Davies, Starbuck, Mackie, Cummings, Bracey, Blackett, Thompson (Trainer).
Middle: Johnson (Secretary), RF Turner, Donnelly, Trueman, Humphreys, Bannister, Pollock, Thorpe, Bailey, Middleton.
Front: Shanks, Leech, Durrant, Hubbard, Shinton.

Champions: Newcastle United
Relegated: Manchester City, Leicester Fosse

FOOTBALL LEAGUE DIVISION ONE

Match No	Date		Opponents	Result	Points	Position	Scorers	Att	Bailey	Hedley	Blackett	Randle	Bannister	Goldie	Donnelly	Walker	Hubbard	Shanks	Turner	Garraty	Gorman	Durrant	Mackie	Shinton	Starbuck	Pollock	King	Owen	Leech	Blessington	Vincett	Webster	Smith	Aitken	Holding	West	B.Turner	Match No
1	Sep 1	H	Sheffield Wednesday	D 1-1	1	-	Donnelly / Wilson	16000	1	2	3	4	5	6	7	8	9	10	11																			1
2	5	A	Newcastle United	L 0-2	1	-	- / Howie, Veitch	32000	1	2	3	4	5	6	7	8	9	10	11																			2
3	12	H	Bristol City	D 1-1	2	17	Shanks / Burton	17000	1	2	3	4	5	6	7	8		10	11	9																		3
4	19	A	Preston North End	W 1-0	4	12	Hubbard		1	2	3	4	5	6	7		9	10	11	8																		4
5	26	H	Middlesbrough	D 1-1	5	12	Shanks (p) / Wilcox	20000	1	2	3	4	5	6	7		9	10	11	8																		5
6	Oct 3	A	Manchester City	L 2-5	5	16	Walker, Hubbard / Grieve 2, Ross 2, Dorsett	15000	1	2	3	4		6		10	9		11	8	5	7																6
7	10	H	Liverpool	W 3-2	7	11	Walker 2, RF Turner / Orr 2	12000	1	2		4	5	6		10	9		11	8	7	3																7
8	17	H	Bury	D 2-2	8	14	Shinton, Bannister / Hibbert, Duffy	7399	1	2	3	4	5	6		10	9		11		7		8															8
9	24	H	Sheffield United	D 1-1	9	12	Durrant / Evans	10000		2	3	4	5	6		10	9		11	8	7			1														9
10	31	A	Aston Villa	D 1-1	10	13	Hubbard / Bache	25000		2		4		6		10	9		11		7	8	1	3	5													10
11	Nov 7	A	Nottingham Forest	L 0-3	10	14	- / Marrison, Hooper 2	20000		2		4		6			10		11		7	8		3	5	9												11
12	14	A	Sunderland	L 1-3	10	15	RF Turner / Mordue, Holley, Bridgett	8000	1	2		5		6	8		9		11		7			3		10	4											12
13	21	H	Chelsea	W 5-2	12	13	Hubbard 2, Owen, RF Turner, Donnelly / Warren, Hilsdon	15000	1	2		5		6	8		9		11		7			3		10	4											13
14	28	A	Blackburn Rovers	L 0-3	12	15	- / Kyle 2, Davies		1	2		5		6	8		9		11		7			3		10	4											14
15	Dec 5	H	Bradford City	L 1-4	12	17	Donnelly / Lintott, Whittaker, O'Rourke 2	10000	1		2	4	5	6	8	10	9		11					3				7										15
16	12	A	Manchester United	L 2-4	12	19	Hubbard, Donnelly / Wall 3, Picken	10000	1	2		4			8		9	10	11		7			6						3	5							16
17	19	H	Everton	L 0-2	12	20	- / Sharp, Young	15000		2			6	8		9		11			7	3		1	4			10				5						17
18	25	H	Woolwich Arsenal	D 1-1	13	19	Owen / Satterthwaite	16000		2			6	8		9		11			7	3		1	4			10				5						18
19	26	A	Woolwich Arsenal	L 1-2	13	19	Pollock (p) / Fitchie 2	20000		2		4	5		8	10	9		11		7	3		1	6													19
20	Jan 1	A	Sheffield Wednesday	L 1-3	13	20	Owen / Wilson 2, Bradshaw			2		5		8		9		11			7	3		1	6			10	4									20
21	2	H	Newcastle United	L 0-4	13	20	- / Higgins 2, Shepherd, Stewart	15000		2		4	5		8			10	11		7	3	9	1	6													21
22	9	A	Bristol City	D 1-1	14	20	Shinton / Gilligan	12000	1	2		4						9	11		7	3	8	6								5	10					22
23	23	H	Preston North End	D 0-0	15	19		10000		2				6		10			11		7	3	8	1				4				5	9					23
24	30	A	Middlesbrough	L 2-6	15	19	Walker, Hubbard / Hall 3, Thackeray, Cail, Hedley (og)	10000		2				6	7	10	9	8	11			3	1					4				5						24
25	Feb 13	A	Liverpool	L 1-4	15	20	Walker / Bradley, Goddard 2, Bowyer	10000	1		2	4			7	9		10	11			3										6	8	5				25
26	20	H	Bury	L 2-5	15	20	Shanks, Walker / Tufnell, Kay, Hibbert, Duffy, Hughes	8000	1	2		4		6	7	9		10	11			3											8	5				26
27	27	A	Sheffield United	L 1-2	15	20	Walker / Hardinge, Gallimore	5000	1	2	3	4		6		9			11					10								8	5	7				27
28	Mar 11	A	Manchester City	W 3-1	17	19	Shinton, Walker, Donnelly / Thornley	8000		2	3			6	7	9			11			8	1					10	4				5					28
29	20	H	Sunderland	W 4-3	19	20	Walker, Shinton 2, Donnelly / Jarvie, Clark, Bridgett	12000		2	3	4		6	7	9	10		11			8	1										5					29
30	27	A	Aston Villa	W 4-2	21	20	Hedley (p), Owen 2, Shinton / Walters 2	8000		2	3	4		6	7	9			11			8	1					10					5					30
31	Apr 3	H	Blackburn Rovers	L 2-4	21	20	Donnelly, Shinton / Garbutt, Latherton 2, Kyle	8000		2		4		6	7	9			11			3	8	1				10					5					31
32	9	A	Notts County	W 3-2	23	20	Owen, Donnelly, Durrant / Cantrell, Flint	16000		2		4		6	8					7	3	9	1					10					5			11		32
33	10	A	Bradford City	L 1-4	23	20	Owen / O'Rourke, Whittingham 2, Hardman	18000		2		4		6	8					7	3	9	1					10					5			11		33
34	17	A	Notts County	L 0-2	23	20	- / Dodd, Cantrell	8000		2		4		6	7	9				11	3	8	1										5				10	34
35	17	H	Manchester United	W 3-2	25	20	RW Turner, West, Shinton / J Turnbull, Wall	8000	1	2		4		6	9			5	7	8												3				11	10	35
36	21	A	Nottingham Forest	L 0-12	25	20	- / Morris 2, Spouncer 3, Hooper 3, West 3, Hughes	7000	1	2		4		6	9				5		8		3											7		11	10	36
37	24	A	Everton	L 2-4	25	20	Donnelly 2 / Coleman 2, Freeman 2			2		4			9					7	3	8	1		6								5			11	10	37
38	29	A	Chelsea	L 0-1	25	20	- / Bridgeman	10000		2		4			8	9				7	3		1		6								5			11	10	38

Final League Position:	20	League Appearances	20	32	18	32	12	30	29	22	21	10	31	6	3	23	15	16	18	16	4	13	7	1	1	7	5	13	2	6	5
Average Home League Attendance:	12790	League Goals		1		1			10	9	7	3	3			2		8		1		7								1	1

FA CUP

	Date		Opponents	Result			Scorers	Att	Bailey	Hedley	Blackett	Randle	Bannister	Goldie	Donnelly	Walker	Hubbard	Shanks	Turner	Garraty	Gorman	Durrant	Mackie	Shinton	Starbuck	Pollock	King	Owen	Leech	Blessington	Vincett	Webster	Smith	Aitken	Holding	West	B.Turner	
1	Jan 16	A	Watford (1)	D 1-1			Shinton / Cleaver	4913		2		4					9		11		7	3	8	1	6			10				5					1
2	20	H	Watford (1 rep)	W 3-1			Donnelly, Walker, RF Turner / Maclaine	7000		2		4		6	7	9		10	11			3	8	1								5					2
3	Feb 6	H	Derby County (2)	L 0-2			- / Bentley (p), Trueman	22000		2					10	9			11		7	3		1	6				4			5	8				3

Note: Feb 6, record attendance to date at Filbert Street.

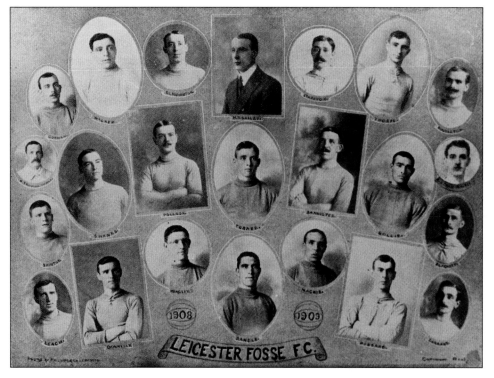

1908-09
Back: Thompson (Trainer), Gorman, Walker, Blessington, Bailey, Starbuck, Thorpe, Middleton, Owen.
Middle: Shinton, Shanks, Pollock, RF Turner, Bannister, Goldie, Blackett.
Front: Leech, Donnelly, Hedley, Randle, Mackie, Hubbard, Durrant.

Season 1909-10

Promoted: Manchester City, Oldham Athletic
Re-election: Grimsby Town (not elected), Birmingham (elected)

FOOTBALL LEAGUE DIVISION TWO

Match No	Date		Opponents	Result	Points	Position	Scorers	Att	Horace Bailey	Billy Henry	Dick Pudan	Arthur Randle	Andy Aitken	Billy Goldie	Jimmy Donnelly	Fred Shinton	Shirley Hubbard	Dave Walker	Fred Threlfall	William Holding	Jonty Starbuck	Billy Turner	Jack West	John Lang	Frank Spriggs	Syd Owen	Billy Leech	Teddy King	Billy Bannister	Sam Currie	Harry Simpson	Teddy Daw	Ernest Darby	Percy Hanger	Match No
1	Sep 1	H	Wolverhampton W.	W 2-1	2	-	Shinton, Threlfall / Hedley	5000	1	2	3	4	5	6	7	8	9	10	11																1
2	4	H	Manchester City	L 1-3	2	-	Shinton / Stewart, Ross, Conlin	9000	1	2	3	4	5	6		8	9	10	11	7															2
3	11	A	Bradford Park Avenue	W 3-1	4	7	Shinton, Pudan (p), Walker / McClarance			2	3	4	5	6		8		9	7		1	10	11												3
4	18	A	Lincoln City	L 1-3	4	9	Pudan (p) / Barrell, Scanlow, Wadsley			2	3	4	5	6		8		9	11		1	10		7											4
5	25	H	Clapton Orient	W 4-0	6	6	Walker 2, Threlfall, Hind (og)	10000		2	3	4	5	6		8	10	9	11		1			7											5
6	Oct 2	A	Blackpool	W 1-0	8	6	Shinton			2	3	4	5	6		8	10		11		1			7	9										6
7	9	H	Hull City	W 3-1	10	6	Donnelly, Hubbard 2 / Temple	12000		2	3	4	5	6	8	9	10		11		1			7											7
8	16	A	Derby County	W 1-0	12	5	Shinton	12000		2	3	4	5	6	8	9	10				1			7		11									8
9	23	H	Stockport County	W 1-0	14	3	Donnelly	8000		2	3	4	5	6	8	9	10				1			7		11									9
10	30	A	Glossop	L 0-1	14	6	- / Craigie		1	2	3	4	5	6	7	8	10	9	11																10
11	Nov 6	H	Birmingham	W 3-1	16	4	Shinton 2, King / Freeman	10000	1	2	3		5		7	8	10	9	11								4	6							11
12	13	A	West Bromwich Albion	W 2-1	18	2	Hubbard, Shinton / Hewitt	9040	1	2	3	4	5		7	8	10	9	11									6							12
13	20	H	Oldham Athletic	W 3-0	20	2	Shinton 3	18000	1	2	3	4	5		7	8	10	9	11									6							13
14	27	A	Barnsley	L 1-3	20	2	Hubbard / Gadsby, Tufnell, Lillycrop		1	2	3	4	5	6		8	10	9	11					7											14
15	Dec 4	H	Fulham	L 2-3	20	5	Walker, Shinton / Dalrymple, Mavin, Henry (og)	4000	1	2	3	4	5	6		8	9	10						7		11									15
16	11	A	Burnley	L 2-5	20	6	Hubbard, Shinton / Green 2, Chadburn, Abbott, Morley		1	2	3		5	6	7	9	8	10	11								4								16
17	18	H	Leeds City	W 6-2	22	6	Pudan (p), Hubbard, Shinton 3, Walker / McLeod, Halligan	12000	1	2	3	4	5	6	7	9	8	10	11																17
18	25	H	Grimsby Town	W 3-1	24	6	Randle, Owen, Walker / Bell	18000		2	3	4	5	6		9	8	10	7		1					11									18
19	27	H	Gainsborough Trinity	W 9-1	26	4	Shinton 3, Walker 4, Owen, Floyd (og) / Mettam	10000		2	3	4	5	6		9	8	10	7		1					11									19
20	28	A	Wolverhampton W.	L 1-4	26	4	Hubbard / Blunt 4	7000		2	3	4		6	7	9	8	10	11		1							5							20
21	Jan 8	A	Manchester City	L 0-2	26	6	- / Jones, Holford	25000		2	3			6		9	8	10	7		1					11		4	5						21
22	22	H	Bradford Park Avenue	W 3-0	28	6	Pudan (p), Shinton 2	15000		2	3		5	6		9	8	10	7		1					11		4							22
23	29	H	Lincoln City	W 4-1	30	4	Lang 2, Shinton, Goldie / Hunter	6000		2	3		5	6		9	8	10	11		1			7				4							23
24	Feb 12	H	Blackpool	W 3-2	32	3	Shinton 2, Pudan (p) / Beare 2	10000		2	3	4	5	6		9	8	10	7		1					11									24
25	26	H	Derby County	W 6-0	34	3	Hubbard 2, Shinton 3, Pudan (p)	18000		2	3	4	5	6		9	8	10	7		1					11									25
26	Mar 12	H	Glossop	W 3-1	36	3	Shinton, Donnelly, Threlfall / H Stapley	11000		2		4	3	6	8	9		10	7		1					11		5							26
27	19	A	Birmingham	L 1-2	36	5	Turner / Burton, Buckley	10000		2		4	5	6	8	9			7		1	10				11				3					27
28	25	A	Gainsborough Trinity	W 1-0	38	3	Turner			2	3	4	5	6	8	9			11		1	10		7											28
29	26	H	West Bromwich Albion	W 2-1	40	3	Walker, Shinton / Bowser	7000	1	2	3	4	5	6	8	9		10	11					7											29
30	28	A	Grimsby Town	D 0-0	41	3		10000	1	2	3	4	5	6	8	9		10	11					7											30
31	Apr 2	A	Oldham Athletic	L 1-2	41	5	Pudan / Donnachie, Fay	14000	1	2	3	4		6		9		10						7		11		5			8				31
32	6	A	Stockport County	L 2-6	41	5	Simpson, Shinton / Makin 2, Abram 2 (1p), Nixon, Greechan			2		4	5	6		9		10						7		11				3	8	1			32
33	9	H	Barnsley	D 1-1	42	5	West / Lillycrop	6000	1	2		4	5	6		9		10					11	7						3	8				33
34	14	A	Hull City	L 1-2	42	5	Shinton / Jack Smith, W Smith	8000		2		4		6	7	9		10					11					5		3	8		1		34
35	16	A	Fulham	L 0-2	42	5	- / Brown, Smith	14000		2		4	5	6		9		10					11	7						3	8		1		35
36	23	H	Burnley	D 1-1	43	5	Donnelly / Lomas	5000	1	2		4		6	7	9	10					11								3	8			5	36
37	25	A	Clapton Orient	L 0-3	43	5	- / Louch, Bevan 2			2		4		6	7	9	10					11								3	8		1	5	37
38	30	A	Leeds City	D 1-1	44	5	Shinton / McLeod	2000		2				6	8	9	10					11		7				4		3			1	5	38
Final League Position:				5				**League Appearances**	15	38	29	32	31	35	20	38	26	29	27	1	18	7	4	17	1	13	2	11	1	8	7	1	4	3	
Average Home League Attendance:				9825				**League Goals**			7	1		1	4	32	9	11	3			2	1	2		2		1			1				

FA CUP

Match No	Date		Opponents	Result	Scorers	Att	Horace Bailey	Billy Henry	Dick Pudan	Arthur Randle	Andy Aitken	Billy Goldie	Jimmy Donnelly	Fred Shinton	Shirley Hubbard	Dave Walker	Fred Threlfall	William Holding	Jonty Starbuck	Billy Turner	Jack West	John Lang	Frank Spriggs	Syd Owen	Billy Leech	Teddy King	Billy Bannister	Sam Currie	Harry Simpson	Teddy Daw	Ernest Darby	Percy Hanger	Match No
1	Jan 15	A	Birmingham (1)	W 4-1	Hubbard 2, Shinton 2 / Lappin	15119		2	3		5	6		9	8	10	7		1					11		4							1
2	Feb 5	H	Bury (2)	W 3-2	Threlfall 2, Owen / Hibbert, Currie	16468		2	3		5	6		9	8	10	7		1					11		4							2
3	19	A	Leyton (3)	W 1-0	Threlfall	21005		2	3	4	5	6		9	8	10	7		1					11									3
4	Mar 5	A	Newcastle United (4)	L 0-3	- / Wilson, Shepherd, Howie	52544		2	3	4	5	6		9	8	10	7		1					11									4

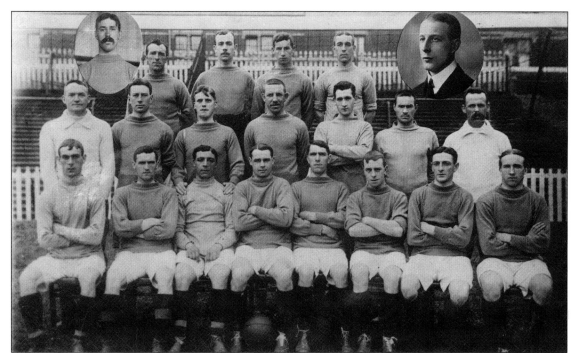

1909-10
Inset: Starbuck, Bailey;
Back: Leech, Gorman, West, King.
Middle: Hurley (Asst Trainer), Pudan, Shinton, Bannister, Currie, Goldie, Thompson (Trainer).
Front: Hubbard, Donnelly, Walker, Aitken, Randle, W Turner, Threlfall, Henry.

Promoted: West Bromwich Albion, Bolton Wanderers
Re-election: Barnsley (elected), Lincoln City (not elected)

FOOTBALL LEAGUE DIVISION TWO

Player columns (left to right): Jonty Starbuck, Billy Henry, Sam Currie, Arthur Randle, Teddy King, Billy Goldie, Fred Threlfall, George Travers, Jack Hall, Shirley Hubbard, Syd Owen, Dave Walker, Andy Aitken, Robert Messer, Billy Leech, Fred Osborn, Tommy Benfield, George King, Bill Williamson, Dick Butler, Bob Grieve, Fred Shinton, Frank Watkin, Fred Mearns, Percy Hanger, Paul Haig, Arthur Starkey, Horace Burton, George Harrison

Match No	Date		Opponents	Result	Points	Position	Scorers	Att
1	Sep 3	H	Bolton Wanderers	W 5-0	2	-	Threlfall, Travers 2, Hall 2	10000
2	10	A	Wolverhampton W.	L 0-1	2	10	- / J Needham	6000
3	17	H	Chelsea	W 1-0	4	8	Hall	16000
4	24	A	Clapton Orient	L 1-3	4	11	Aitken / Scott 2, Goffin	
5	Oct 1	H	Blackpool	W 2-0	6	10	Hubbard, Owen	10000
6	8	A	Glossop	L 0-1	6	14	- / Porter	
7	15	H	Lincoln City	W 2-0	8	9	Walker, Owen	12000
8	22	A	Huddersfield Town	W 2-1	10	7	Owen, Hall / Hamilton	6800
9	29	H	Birmingham	W 2-0	12	4	Osborn, Threlfall	10000
10	Nov 5	A	West Bromwich Albion	L 1-5	12	8	Osborn / Bowser, Lloyd 2, Wollaston, Buck (p)	15200
11	12	H	Hull City	L 0-2	12	9	- / Joe Smith, G Browell	8000
12	19	A	Fulham	L 1-3	12	10	Osborn / Smith, White, Mavin	15000
13	26	H	Bradford Park Avenue	W 2-0	14	10	Hall, Walker	8000
14	Dec 3	A	Burnley	L 1-2	14	12	Walker / Watson (p), Green	
15	10	H	Gainsborough Trinity	W 1-0	16	10	E King	8000
16	17	A	Leeds City	W 3-2	18	9	Walker, Travers, Creichton (og) / Enright, Morris	5000
17	24	H	Stockport County	W 5-1	20	9	Walker, Travers 2, E King, Hubbard / Prout	8000
18	26	A	Derby County	L 0-3	20	10	- / Bloomer 2, Hall	20000
19	27	H	Barnsley	D 1-1	21	10	Threlfall (p) / Forman	10000
20	31	A	Bolton Wanderers	L 2-6	21	10	Osborn, Hubbard / Hughes 3, Smith 2, Greenhalgh	
21	Jan 7	H	Wolverhampton W.	L 2-3	21	11	Grieve 2 / Harrison, Hedley, J Needham	6000
22	21	A	Chelsea	L 0-2	21	12	- / Whittingham, Hilsdon	18000
23	28	H	Clapton Orient	W 2-1	23	12	Shinton, Walker / Dalrymple	6000
24	Feb 11	H	Glossop	D 1-1	24	11	Watkin / Wilson	4000
25	18	A	Lincoln City	L 0-2	24	13	- / Robson, Gardner	
26	25	H	Huddersfield Town	W 2-1	26	13	Benfield 2 / Richardson	4000
27	Mar 4	A	Birmingham	L 0-1	26	14	- / Buckley	8000
28	11	H	West Bromwich Albion	L 2-3	26	14	Randle, Walker / Bowser 2, Wright	10547
29	18	A	Hull City	D 2-2	27	13	Currie (p), Benfield / Joe Smith 2	7000
30	25	H	Fulham	W 3-2	29	12	Shinton, Haig, Mavin (og) / Mavin, Brown	6000
31	29	A	Blackpool	L 0-2	29	13	- / Morley, Mearns (og)	3000
32	Apr 1	A	Bradford Park Avenue	L 1-3	29	14	Shinton / Little 2, Turnbull	
33	8	H	Burnley	D 1-1	30	14	Haig / Newton	5000
34	14	A	Barnsley	D 1-1	31	14	Shinton / Tufnell	
35	15	A	Gainsborough Trinity	L 0-2	31	14	- / J Foxall 2	
36	17	H	Derby County	L 1-2	31	14	Shinton / Bloomer 2	12000
37	22	H	Leeds City	W 2-1	33	14	Currie (p), Hubbard / Croot	5000
38	29	A	Stockport County	L 0-1	33	15	- / Prout	

Final League Position:	15
Average Home League Attendance:	8515

League Appearances: 24 37 32 35 30 17 23 12 15 26 17 22 20 2 1 12 16 1 2 7 4 14 4 14 12 8 2 1

League Goals: 2 1 2 — 3 5 5 4 3 7 1 — 4 3 — 2 5 1 2

FA CUP

	Date		Opponents	Result	Scorers	Att
1	Jan 14	H	Southampton (1)	W 3-1	Walker, Osborn, Threlfall / H Brown	13500
2	Feb 4	A	Middlesbrough (2)	D 0-0		17220
3	9	H	Middlesbrough (2 rep)	L 1-2 aet	Currie (p) / Cail, Dixon	14000

Dismissals: Jan 28, Walker, Clapton Orient (h).

1910-11
Back: Benfield, Hanger, Osborn, Messer, G King.
Middle: Henry, Threlfall, Starbuck, Walker, Cameron, Hall, Currie.
Front: Randle, E King, Goldie, Aitken, Travers, Hubbard, Owen.

Season 1911-12

Promoted: Derby County, Chelsea
Re-election: Leeds City (elected), Gainsborough Trinity (not elected)

FOOTBALL LEAGUE DIVISION TWO

No	Date		Opponents	Result	Pts	Pos	Scorers	Att	FM	BH	SC	DB	BnH	TK	WC	SH	FO	FR	WB	TB	BT	WK	AR	PH	HB	JT	PcH	DA	GH	TC	BM	JS	HS	DM	TL	JSh	WS	JM
1	Sep 2	A	Gainsborough Trinity	W 1-0	2	-	Osborn		1	2	3	4	5	6	7	8	9	10	11																			
2	4	H	Gainsborough Trinity	W 2-0	4	-	Hubbard, Rollinson	10000	1	2	3	4	5	6	7	8	9	10	11																			
3	9	H	Grimsby Town	L 0-2	4	4	- / Rampton, Hubbard (p)	10000	1	2	3	4	5	6	7	8	9	10	11																			
4	11	A	Burnley	L 0-3	4	6	- / Mountford (p), Freeman, Lindley		1	2	3	4	5	6	7		9	10	11	8																		
5	16	A	Nottingham Forest	L 1-4	4	13	Hubbard / Derrick, Hooper, Morris, Saunders		1	2		4	5	6		8		10	11	7	3	9																
6	23	H	Chelsea	W 2-0	6	9	W King, Bauchop	15000	1	2			6	5		8		10	11	7	3	9	4															
7	30	A	Clapton Orient	L 1-4	6	12	W King / Scott 3, Willis		1	2	3		6	5		8		10	11	7		9	4															
8	Oct 7	H	Bristol City	W 2-0	8	11	Benfield, Humphreys	12000	1	2	3		6	5		8		10	11	7			4	9														
9	14	A	Birmingham	L 0-4	8	12	- / Hall 2, Graham 2	15000	1	2			6	5		8		10	11	7	3		9	4														
10	21	H	Huddersfield Town	L 0-2	8	14	- / Hall, Cowley	5000	1	2	3		6		5		8	10		11	7			9		4												
11	28	A	Blackpool	D 1-1	9	13	W King / Quinn		1	2	3		6	5				10	11	7		8	4	9														
12	Nov 4	H	Glossop	W 1-0	11	12	Rollinson	6000	1	2	3		6	5				10	11	7		8	4	9														
13	11	A	Hull City	L 1-4	11	12	Clark / T Browell 4	10000	1	2	3		6	5			7	10	11	8			4	9														
14	18	H	Barnsley	D 0-0	12	13		8000	1	2	3	4		6				10		7				9					5	8	11							
15	25	A	Bradford Park Avenue	D 1-1	13	13	Humphreys / Turnbull		1			4		6			8			7	3			9					5	10	11	2						
16	Dec 2	H	Fulham	L 2-5	13	14	Benfield (p), Allman / Pearce 2, Coleman, Collins, Walker	8000	1			4		6			8			7	3			9					5	10	11	2						
17	9	A	Derby County	L 0-5	13	15	- / Bloomer 2, Leonard 2, Wright	12000	1		3	4	5	6			8			10			7						9		11	2						
18	16	H	Stockport County	D 1-1	14	15	Mills / Norton	7000	1		3		5	6		10				7			4	9						11	2	8*						
19	23	A	Leeds City	L 1-2	14	15	Allman / Enright 2	6000	1		3			6				10	11	7							4	5	9		2	8						
20	25	H	Wolverhampton W.	D 1-1	15	15	Allman / Harrison	10000	1		3			6				10	11	7			4					5	9		2	8						
21	26	A	Wolverhampton W.	L 0-1	15	15	- / Hedley	18000						7	10				11		3		4		6			5	9		2	8	1					
22	Jan 6	A	Grimsby Town	L 0-4	15	16	- / Gordon, Staniforth, Mounteney, Martin	3000	1		3			6		4		10	11	7	3							5	9		2	8						
23	27	H	Chelsea	L 1-2	15	18	Osborn / Ormiston, Whittingham	27000	1		3			6		10	8		11	7			4	9				5			2							
24	Feb 10	A	Bristol City	W 1-0	17	18	Sparrow	6000			3			6		10	8			7			4					5		11	2		1	9				
25	17	H	Birmingham	W 5-2	19	18	Hubbard, Osborn 2 (1p), Sparrow 2 / Conlin, Jones (p)	10000			3			6		10	8			7			4					5		11	2		1	9				
26	24	A	Huddersfield Town	W 2-1	21	18	Harrison, Sparrow / Macaulay	5000			3			6		10	8			7			4					5		11	2		1	9				
27	29	H	Nottingham Forest	D 1-1	22	16	Benfield / Ford	3000			3			6		10	8			7			4					5		11	2		1	9				
28	Mar 2	H	Blackpool	W 4-0	24	14	Osborn 3 (1p), E King	5000			3			6			8			7			4	10				5		11	2		1	9				
29	9	A	Glossop	L 0-6	24	15	- / Hoare, Littlewort, Moore 2, H Stapley 2				3	6					8			7			4	10				5		11	2		1	9				
30	16	H	Hull City	W 3-0	26	14	Benfield, Sparrow, Osborn	6000			3			6		10	8			7			4					5		11	2		1	9				
31	23	A	Barnsley	D 0-0	27	14					3			6		10	8			7			4					5		11	2		1	9				
32	30	H	Bradford Park Avenue	W 3-0	29	12	Sparrow 3 (1p)	8000			3			6		10	8			7								5		11	2		1	9	4			
33	Apr 6	A	Fulham	L 1-4	29	16	Osborn / Pearce 3, Coleman	9000			3			6		10	8			7								5		11	2		1	9	4			
34	8	H	Burnley	W 3-2	31	14	Sparrow 2, Benfield / Hodgson, Freeman	10000			3			6		10	8			7			4					5		11	2		1	9				
35	9	H	Clapton Orient	W 2-0	33	10	Harrison, W King	5000	1			6							7	3	9	4						5		11	2	10			5			
36	13	H	Derby County	L 0-1	33	11	- / Bloomer	15000	1		3			6		10	8			7			9	4				5		11	2							
37	20	A	Stockport County	W 3-2	35	10	Benfield, Mills, Osborn / Charlton (p), Rodgers		1		3			6			9			7								5		11	2	8			4		10	
38	27	H	Leeds City	W 2-1	37	10	Sparrow, Harrison / Enright	10000	1							10				7								5		11	2	8		9	4		3	6

Final League Position:	10	**League Appearances**	26 14 29 19 14 27 6 26 21 17 18 34 8 7 21 14 2 2 22 7 20 24 8 12 12 4 1 1 1 1
Average Home League Attendance:	9265	**League Goals**	1 1 3 10 2 1 6 4 2 3 3 2 11

FA CUP

No	Date		Opponents	Result	Scorers	Att																						
1	Jan 13	A	Croydon Common (1)	D 2-2	Mills, Humphreys / Yenson, Wood	7500				6		10			11	7	3		4	9		5		2	8	1	
2	22	H	Croydon Common (1 rep)	W 6-1	Hubbard, Osborn, Humphreys 2, Hanger, Lee (og) / Yenson	2500		3		6		10	8		11	7			4	9		5		2		1	
3	Feb 3	A	Barnsley (2)	L 0-1	- / Lillycrop	15113	1	3		6		10	8		11	7		9	4			5		2			

Note: Jan 22, own goal originally uncredited in local press due to scorer not being visible in fog.

Shirley Hubbard and **Jonty Starbuck** (far right)

Season 1912-13

Promoted: Preston North End, Burnley
Re-election: Stockport County, Blackpool (both elected)

Player columns (left to right): Fred Mearns, Tommy Clay, Sam Currie, Douglas McWhirter, Percy Hanger, Teddy King, Tommy Benfield, Bob Noble, Harry Sparrow, Fred Osborn, George Harrison, Arthur Randle, Bob Thompson, Shirley Hubbard, Harold Furr, Horace Burton, Willie Furr, Billy Mills, Alex Crews, James Straughton, James Proctor, Dick Pudan, Tom Lightbody, George Douglas, Walter Reynolds, Bill Pepper, Jimmy Harrold, Charles Barnett

FOOTBALL LEAGUE DIVISION TWO

Match No	Date		Opponents	Result	Points	Position	Scorers	Att
1	Sep 7	H	Nottingham Forest	W 3-1	2	-	Sparrow 2, Osborn (p) / Currie (og)	13000
2	9	A	Lincoln City	L 0-3	2	-	- / Miller, Barrell 2	
3	14	A	Bristol City	L 0-1	2	15	- / Owers	13000
4	21	H	Birmingham	L 1-2	2	17	Hubbard / Jones, Robertson	14000
5	28	A	Huddersfield Town	L 0-3	2	19	- / Howie, Macaulay 2	6500
6	Oct 5	H	Leeds City	D 1-1	3	19	Harrison / Robertson	10000
7	12	A	Grimsby Town	L 0-2	3	19	- / T Rippon, Staniforth	
8	19	H	Bury	W 3-0	5	18	Sparrow 2, Osborn	8000
9	26	A	Fulham	D 1-1	6	17	Osborn / Pearce	6000
10	Nov 2	H	Barnsley	W 1-0	8	15	Sparrow	
11	4	A	Stockport County	W 2-1	10	12	Osborn, Sparrow / Charlton (p)	1500
12	9	A	Bradford Park Avenue	D 2-2	11	14	King, Mills / McCandless 2	
13	16	H	Wolverhampton W.	L 0-1	11	14	- / Brooks	7500
14	23	A	Blackpool	L 1-2	11	15	Benfield / Gillow, Wilson	2000
15	30	H	Fulham	W 1-0	13	11	Osborn	9000
16	Dec 7	H	Preston North End	L 0-3	13	15	- / Green, Halliwell 2	7000
17	14	A	Burnley	L 1-5	13	16	Osborn (p) / Freeman 4, Hodgson	
18	21	H	Hull City	W 3-2	15	14	Hubbard, Harrison, Straughton / Fazackerley 2	5000
19	25	A	Clapton Orient	D 1-1	16	14	Straughton / Dryden	13000
20	26	H	Glossop	L 1-4	16	16	Harrison / Moore 4	
21	28	A	Nottingham Forest	L 2-4	16	16	Sparrow 2 / Derrick 3, Morris	
22	Jan 4	A	Bristol City	W 3-1	18	16	Osborn, Benfield, Sparrow / Brough	3000
23	18	A	Birmingham	L 1-5	18	16	Proctor / AR Smith, Hall 2, Jones, King (og)	12000
24	25	H	Huddersfield Town	D 0-0	19	17		10000
25	Feb 8	A	Leeds City	L 1-5	19	18	Harrison (p) / Price 2, Speirs, Fenwick, McLeod	10000
26	15	H	Grimsby Town	W 1-0	21	18	McWhirter	
27	22	A	Bury	D 2-2	22	18	Mills, Hubbard / Smith, Perry (p)	4166
28	Mar 8	A	Barnsley	L 0-1	22	18	- / Utley	
29	15	H	Bradford Park Avenue	W 3-0	24	18	McWhirter, Osborn, Harrison (p)	
30	21	A	Glossop	L 0-3	24	18	- / Moore 3 (1p)	
31	22	H	Wolverhampton W.	D 1-1	25	18	Sparrow / Harrison	4000
32	24	H	Clapton Orient	W 1-0	27	18	Mills	
33	25	H	Lincoln City	W 1-0	29	16	Benfield	
34	29	H	Blackpool	W 5-1	31	15	Osborn 4, Sparrow / Bainbridge	
35	Apr 5	A	Stockport County	W 4-1	33	11	Harrison (p), Mills, Douglas, Osborn / Rodgers	
36	12	A	Preston North End	L 0-1	33	12	- / Holdsworth	
37	19	H	Burnley	L 2-3	33	14	Osborn, Sparrow / Hodgson 2, Freeman	
38	26	A	Hull City	L 0-2	33	15	- / Fenwick 2	5000

Final League Position:	15	
Average Home League Attendance:	7940	

League Appearances: 28 19 29 31 21 31 20 4 27 34 38 3 19 7 8 15 1 28 1 10 7 8 2 13 1 1 11 1

League Goals: 2 1 3 12 14 6 3 4 2 1 1

FA CUP

	Date		Opponents	Result	Scorers	Att
1	Jan 16	H	Norwich City (1)	L 1-4	Proctor / Wolstenholme, Woodlands, Hughes, Osborne	8610

Stand-in Goalkeepers: Nov 9, Currie for Mearns (temporary), Bradford Park Avenue (a).

1912-13 (v Preston North End, 7 December 1912)
McWhirter, Hanger, Mills, Osborn, Clay, Currie, Sparrow, King, Harrison, Proctor, Mearns.

228

OF FOSSILS & FOXES

Promoted: Notts County, Bradford Park Avenue
Re-election: Lincoln City, Nottingham Forest (both elected)

FOOTBALL LEAGUE DIVISION TWO

Match No	Date		Opponents	Result	Points	Position	Scorers	Att	Ron Brebner	Tommy Clay	Sam Currie	Douglas McWhirter	Jimmy Harrold	Horace Burton	George Douglas	Billy Mills	Harry Sparrow	Tommy Benfield	Tom Waterall	Teddy King	Claude Stoodley	Fred Mortimer	Fred Ridley	Herbert Bown	William Russell	Vic Walters	James Straughton	Dick Pudan	Saville Pilkington	Albert Berrington	Angus Seed	Maurice Woodward	Norman Whitfield	Match No
1	Sep 3	A	Nottingham Forest	W 3-1	2	-	Benfield, Waterall, Sparrow / Firth		1	2	3	4	5	6	7	8	9	10	11															1
2	6	A	Woolwich Arsenal	L 1-2	2	-	Benfield / Jobey, Devine (p)	20000	1	2	3	4	5	6	7	8	9	10	11															2
3	11	H	Nottingham Forest	W 5-1	4	4	Mills 2, Sparrow, Benfield 2 / Gibson		1	2	3	4	5		7	8	9	10	11	6														3
4	13	H	Grimsby Town	W 2-0	6	1	Benfield, Waterall	17000	1	2	3	4	5		7	8	9	10	11	6														4
5	20	A	Birmingham	L 0-1	6	2	- / Ballantyne	20000	1	2	3	4	5					10	7	6	8	9	11											5
6	27	H	Bristol City	W 3-0	8	1	Mortimer 3	16000	1	2	3	4	5		7			10	11	6	8	9												6
7	Oct 4	A	Leeds City	L 1-2	8	4	Mortimer / Bainbridge, Price	18000	1	2	3	4	5		7			10	11	6	8	9												7
8	11	H	Clapton Orient	W 1-0	10	4	King		1	2	3	4	5		7			10	11	6	8	9												8
9	18	A	Glossop	W 2-0	12	2	Waterall 2		1	2	3	4	5		7			10	11	6	8	9												9
10	25	H	Stockport County	L 2-5	12	5	Benfield, Mortimer / Waterall 2 (2p), Garrett, Gault, Wood		1	2	3	4	5		7	8		10	11	6		9												10
11	Nov 1	A	Bradford Park Avenue	L 2-3	12	7	Mills, Waterall / Smith 2 (1p), Clay (og)		1	2	3	4	5		7	8		10	11	6		9												11
12	8	H	Notts County	L 0-2	12	9	- / Peart, Richards	12000		2	3	4	5		7	8		10	11	6		9		1										12
13	15	H	Fulham	W 3-0	14	7	Harrold, Sparrow 2	10000		2	3	4	5	6	7	8	9	10	11					1										13
14	22	A	Wolverhampton W.	L 1-2	14	9	Sparrow / Lockett, Francis	10000	1	2	3	4	5	6	7	8	9		11			10												14
15	29	H	Hull City	L 0-4	14	11	- / Halligan 2, Stevens, J Lyon	10000	1	2	3	4	5	6		8	9		11		7	10												15
16	Dec 6	A	Barnsley	L 0-3	14	13	- / Bratley, Moore, Travers		1	2	3	4	5	6	7	8	9	10	11															16
17	13	H	Bury	D 0-0	15	13		8000	1	2	3	4		6		8		7	11	5	10	9												17
18	20	A	Huddersfield Town	W 2-1	17	12	Sparrow, King / James	5500	1	2	3	4		6			9	8		5		10			7	11								18
19	25	H	Blackpool	L 0-1	17	11	- / Charlton	10000	1	2	3	4	5	6				8	9			10			7	11								19
20	26	A	Lincoln City	L 0-3	17	13	- / Miller, Brindley, Barrell		1	2	3	4	5	6				10	11			8				7	9							20
21	27	H	Woolwich Arsenal	L 1-2	17	16	Mortimer / Bell 2	10000		2	4	3		6				9		5	8	10		1	7	11								21
22	Jan 3	A	Grimsby Town	L 0-3	17	16	- / W Rippon 2, Gregson				3		5	4	7			9		6	8	10		1		11		2						22
23	17	H	Birmingham	D 0-0	18	16		6000			3	4		6	7			10		5	8	9		1	2	11								23
24	24	A	Bristol City	L 0-1	18	16	- / Broad	7000			5	3					11	4	10	6	8	9		1	7			2						24
25	Feb 7	H	Leeds City	W 5-1	20	16	Walters 2, Waterall, Benfield 2 / Speirs	4000			2		5	6	7			10	9	4	8			1		11					3			25
26	14	A	Clapton Orient	L 0-1	20	16	- / Jonas				2		5	6	7			10	9	4	8			1		11					3			26
27	21	H	Glossop	L 1-3	20	17	Stoodley / Carney (p), Doncaster 2				3		5	6	7			10	9	4	8			1		11				2				27
28	28	A	Stockport County	L 0-3	20	17	- / Rodgers, Ashmole, Proctor				3		5	6	7			10	9					1		11				2	4	8		28
29	Mar 7	H	Bradford Park Avenue	L 2-3	20	17	Mortimer, King / Bauchop, Little, Smith				3		5	6	7			10	11	4	8	9		1				2						29
30	14	A	Notts County	L 1-4	20	18	Stoodley / Peart 2, Richards, Flint	14000			3		5	6	7			10	11	4	8	9		1				2						30
31	21	A	Fulham	W 2-1	22	17	Benfield, Mortimer (p) / Coleman	6000			3		5	6	7			10	11	4	8	9		1				2						31
32	28	H	Wolverhampton W.	L 2-3	22	17	Stoodley, King / Harrison, Hughes 2	6000		2	4	5	3		7			10	11	6	8	9		1										32
33	Apr 4	A	Hull City	D 0-0	23	17		6000			3		5	6	7			10	11	4	8			1			9	2						33
34	10	A	Blackpool	L 0-1	23	19	- / Connor	4000			3		5	6	7			10	11	4	8			1			9	2						34
35	11	H	Barnsley	L 0-2	23	19	- / Tufnell, Moore				3		5	6	7			10	11	4	8			1			9	2						35
36	13	H	Lincoln City	W 2-0	25	19	Benfield 2				3		5	6	7			10		4	8			1		11		2					9	36
37	18	A	Bury	D 1-1	26	18	Whitfield / Peake	3683			3		5	6	7			10		4	8			1		11		2					9	37
38	25	H	Huddersfield Town	L 0-1	26	18	- / Islip	6000			3		5	2	7			10		4	8			1		11						6	9	38

| | | | | | | | League Appearances | | 18 | 20 | 37 | 23 | 35 | 28 | 30 | 12 | 9 | 36 | 31 | 29 | 25 | 22 | 1 | 20 | 5 | 11 | 5 | 9 | 1 | 2 | 3 | 2 | 4 | |
| | | | | | | | League Goals | | | | 1 | | | | 3 | 6 | 11 | 6 | 4 | 3 | 8 | | | | | 2 | | | | | | | 1 | |

Final League Position: 18
Average Home League Attendance: 9365

FA CUP

	Date		Opponents	Result	Scorers	Att	Tommy Clay	Sam Currie	Douglas McWhirter	Jimmy Harrold	Horace Burton	George Douglas	Harry Sparrow	Tom Waterall	Teddy King	Claude Stoodley	Fred Mortimer	Herbert Bown	
1	Jan 10	H	Tottenham Hotspur (1)	D 5-5	Mortimer, Currie, Stoodley 3 / Walden, Minter, Cantrell, Bliss 2	9454	2	3		5	6	7	9	11	4	8	10	1	1
2	15	A	Tottenham H. (1 rep)	L 0-2	- / Walden, Bliss	20252	2	3	4	5	6	7	9	11		8	10	1	2

Stand-in Goalkeepers: Dec 26, Currie for Brebner, Lincoln City (a).

1913-14
Back: Barnett, Scoon, Woodward, Berrington, Straughton, Pudan.
Middle: Leech (Trainer), Brebner, Russell, Webber, Burton, Harrold, Mortimer, Clay, Waterall, Bown, Thompson (Asst Trainer).
Front: Tillson, Ridley, Sparrow, Stoodley, Douglas, Mills, King, Benfield, Currie.

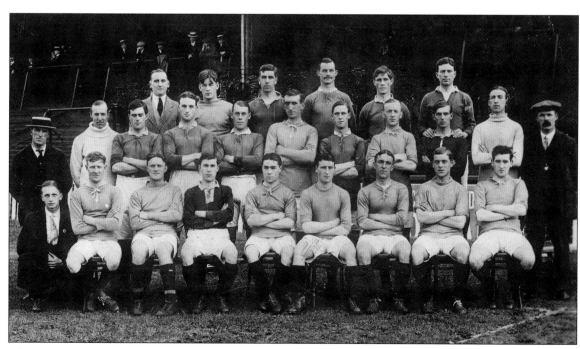

Promoted: Derby County, Preston North End
Re-election: Leicester Fosse (elected), Glossop (not elected)

FOOTBALL LEAGUE DIVISION TWO

Match No	Date		Opponents	Result	Points	Position	Scorers	Att	Herbert Bown	Billy Troughear	Sam Currie	Teddy King	Jimmy Harrold	Horace Burton	George Douglas	Stephen Sims	Sam Simms	George Hastie	Andy Anderson	Billy Mills	Bill Thomson	Norman Whitfield	Dick Taylor	Harold Wise	Charles Barnett	Tommy Codd	Charles Barron	Charlie Hogg	A Legge	Alf Barrett	Match No
1	Sep 2	H	Lincoln City	D 2-2	1	-	Simms 2 / Gardner (p), Egerton		1	2	3	4	5	6	7	8	9	10	11												1
2	5	H	Birmingham	W 1-0	3	-	Harrold (p)	4000	1	2	3	4	5	6	7			9	10	11	8										2
3	12	A	Grimsby Town	L 0-1	3	12	- / Rampton		1	2	3		5	6	7	9			10	11			4	8							3
4	19	H	Huddersfield Town	L 1-2	3	13	Harrold / Slade, Jee		1		2	4	5		7	9				11	8	6	10	3							4
5	21	A	Huddersfield Town	L 1-3	3	15	Whitfield / Shields 2, Slade	6000	1		2	4	5	3	7		9			11		6	10		8						5
6	26	A	Bristol City	L 0-1	3	16	- / Morton	10000	1		2	4	5		7	9				11		6	10	3	8						6
7	Oct 3	H	Bury	L 1-3	3	18	King / Connor, McKnight, Mercer	7000	1		2	9	5	6	7				10	11		4	8	3							7
8	10	A	Preston North End	L 0-1	3	19	- / Osborn		1		2	4	5	3	7	9			10	11	8	6									8
9	17	H	Nottingham Forest	W 3-1	5	17	Harrold, King, Anderson / Coleman		1	2	3	4	5		7	9				11	8	6	10								9
10	24	A	Blackpool	W 2-1	7	17	Sims, Thomson / Sibbald		1	2	3	7	5	4		9				11	8	6	10								10
11	31	A	Barnsley	L 0-1	7	18	- / Halliwell		1	2	3		5		7	9			4	11	8	6	10								11
12	Nov 7	H	Glossop	W 3-2	9	17	Sims, Whitfield 2 / Thompson, Cuffe (p)		1	2	3	4	5		7	9				11	8	6	10								12
13	14	A	Wolverhampton W.	L 0-7	9	18	- / Curtis 4, Needham 3	5500	1	2	3	7	5	4		9				11	8	6	10								13
14	21	H	Fulham	L 0-2	9	19	- / Lee 2	4000		2	3	5		4	7	9	10			11	8	6				1					14
15	28	A	Stockport County	L 0-3	9	19	- / Gault 2, Waterall			2	3	5		4	7				10	11	8	6	9			1					15
16	Dec 5	H	Hull City	D 1-1	10	19	King / Halligan	4000		2	3	4	5		7			9	10	11	8	6				1					16
17	12	A	Leeds City	L 2-7	10	19	Mills, Douglas / Bainbridge 2, McLeod 2, Price 3	5000		2	3	9	5	4	7					11	8	6	10			1					17
18	25	H	Arsenal	L 1-4	10	19	Mills / Grant, King, Benson, Blyth	13000	1	2	3	6		4	7			9	10	11	8	5									18
19	26	A	Arsenal	L 0-6	10	19	- / Lewis 3, McKinnon, King, Flanagan	6000	1	2			5	4	7		3	10	9	8	6										19
20	28	H	Derby County	L 0-6	10	19	- / Leonard 2, Moore 2, Benfield 2	5000	1	2		9	5	4	10					8	6		3	7			11				20
21	Jan 2	A	Birmingham	L 0-2	10	20	- / Gibson, Windridge	15000			5	4	7				10	11	8	6		3	9	1		2					21
22	16	H	Grimsby Town	W 2-0	12	19	Mills 2				9	5	4	7					10	6		3	8	1	11	2					22
23	30	H	Clapton Orient	D 1-1	13	19	Mills / Scott				9	5	4	7					10	6		3	8	1	11	2					23
24	Feb 6	A	Bury	L 1-3	13	20	King / Lythgoe 2, Goldie	2950	1		9	5	4	7					10	6		3	8		11	2					24
25	13	H	Preston North End	L 2-3	13	20	King, Burton / Macauley, Osborn, Toward				9	5	4	7					10	6		3	8	1	11	2					25
26	20	A	Nottingham Forest	W 3-1	15	19	King, Harrold (p), Douglas / Mercer				9	5	4	7			8		10	6		3		1	11	2					26
27	27	H	Blackpool	D 2-2	16	19	Mills, Hogg / Lane 2				9	5	4	7					11	10	6		3	1		2	8				27
28	Mar 6	A	Barnsley	L 0-1	16	19	- / Moore				9		4	7			5			10	6		3	8	1	11	2				28
29	13	A	Glossop	W 3-2	18	19	Mills 2, Wise / Thompson 2			3		5	4	7					11	10	6			8	1		2		9		29
30	20	H	Wolverhampton W.	L 0-3	18	19	- / Harrison, S Brooks 2	3000		3		5	4	7					11	10	6			8	1		2		9		30
31	25	H	Bristol City	L 1-3	18	19	Mills / Brown 2, Batey		1		2	6	5	4	7		9			8			3		11		10				31
32	27	A	Fulham	L 0-1	18	19	- / Maughan	4000		3	8	5	4	7			9		11	10	6				1		2				32
33	Apr 2	A	Lincoln City	W 3-2	20	19	King, Hastie, Simms / Ball, Egerton			3	8	5	4	7			9	10		6			1		2			11		33
34	3	H	Stockport County	W 5-4	22	19	Simms 2, King, Hogg, Harrold (p) / Waterall 2, Gault, Rodgers			2	8	5	4	7			9			6		3		1	11		10				34
35	5	A	Derby County	L 0-1	22	19	- / Baker	10000		3	8	5		7			9	4		6				1	11	2	10				35
36	10	A	Hull City	L 1-2	22	19	Douglas / Stevens, Halligan	5500	1		3	8		4	7		9	5		6					11	2	10				36
37	17	H	Leeds City	W 5-1	24	19	Mills 2, Douglas, King 2 / Jackson	3000			8		3	7			5	4		9	6				1	11	2				37
38	24	A	Clapton Orient	L 0-2	24	19	- / Layton, Barron (og)					5	3	7			8	4	11	9	6				1		2	10			38

Final League Position:	19	League Appearances	19	15	26	31	32	31	36	11	16	17	25	29	35	12	14	11	19	13	16	7	2	1
Average Home League Attendance:	3600	League Goals			10	5	1	4	2	5	1	1	11	1	3		1				2			

FA CUP

	Date		Opponents	Result			Scorers	Att	Herbert Bown	Billy Troughear	Sam Currie	Teddy King	Jimmy Harrold	Horace Burton	George Douglas	Stephen Sims	Sam Simms	George Hastie	Andy Anderson	Billy Mills	Bill Thomson		
1	Dec 19	A	Swansea Town (Q6)	L 0-1			- / Lloyd	5000	1	2	3	4		6	7		9	10	11	8	5		1

Dismissals: Mar 20, Currie, Wolverhampton Wanderers (h).
Stand-in Goalkeepers: Dec 28, Taylor for Bown (temporary), Derby County (h).
Note: Arsenal subsequently elected to extended Division One after World War One;
Re-election voting: Leicester Fosse 33, Stoke 21 (both elected), South Shields 11, Chesterfield 8, Darlington 4, Glossop 1; Division Two subsequently extended with further election.

1914-15 (v Wolverhampton Wanderers, 14 November 1914, players only named)
Back: Troughear, Burton, Harrold, Bown, Currie, Anderson.
Front: Mills, Sims, King, Whitfield, Thomson.

Champions: Main Tournament: Nottingham Forest; Subsidiary Tournament: Nottingham Forest.

FOOTBALL LEAGUE MIDLAND SECTION

No	Date	Ven	Opponents	Result	Scorers	Att	1	2	3	4	5	6	7	8	9	10	11
1	Sep 4	A	Bradford City	L 0-2	- / Hillam 2	4500	Barnett	Bettridge	Currie	Collins	King	Calderhead	Gibson	Hogg	Freeman E	Freeman C	Harrison
2	11	H	Huddersfield Town	W 3-0	Harrison, E Freeman, Hogg	3000	Smith	Bettridge	Currie	Collins	King	Calderhead	Gibson	Hogg	Freeman E	Freeman C	Harrison
3	18	A	Grimsby Town	D 0-0		3000	Smith	Bettridge	Currie	Collins	Hall	Calderhead	Gibson	Hogg	King	Freeman C	Harrison
4	Oct 2	A	Derby County	D 1-1	Gibson / Leigh	8000	Smith	Bettridge	Atterbury	Collins	King	Calderhead	Donaldson	Gibson	Hogg	Freeman C	Harrison
5	9	H	Sheffield Wednesday	W 3-1	E Freeman 2, Harrison (p) / Burkinshaw	5000	Smith	Bettridge	Atterbury	Collins	King	Bailey	Donaldson	Mills	Freeman E	Freeman C	Harrison
6	16	A	Bradford Park Avenue	W 2-1	Gibson, Walker / Waite	5000	Smith	Bettridge	Atterbury	Collins	King	Calderhead	Douglas	Gibson	Walker	Hogg	Cope
7	23	H	Leeds City	W 4-0	Walker 3, Gibson	5000	Smith	Bettridge	Atterbury	Collins	King	Bailey	Donaldson	Gibson	Walker	Benfield	Freeman E
8	30	H	Hull City	D 2-2	Walker, Hogg / Stevens, McQuillan	4000	Smith	Bettridge	Atterbury	Collins	King	Calderhead	Donaldson	Hogg	Walker	Benfield	Bailey
9	Nov 6	H	Nottingham Forest	L 1-3	Gibson / Bell, Birch, Tinsley	5000	Smith	Bettridge	Atterbury	Collins	King	Bailey	Donaldson	Gibson	Walker	Benfield	Freeman E
10	13	A	Barnsley	L 2-3	King 2 / Moore, Bratley, Birtles		Smith	Collins	Atterbury	Calderhead	King	Dunne	Donaldson	Gibson	Walker	Benfield	Freeman E
11	20	A	Lincoln City	L 0-1	- / Chesser	4000	Smith	Pullen	Atterbury	Collins	Calderhead	Bailey	Lambert	Gibson	Walker	Hogg	Bailey
12	27	H	Sheffield United	L 2-5	Hogg, Gibson / Gillespie 2, Kitchen 2, Shearman	1000	Smith	Barron	Atterbury	Benfield	King	Bailey	Donaldson	Gibson	Walker	Hogg	Freeman E
13	Dec 4	H	Bradford City	W 2-1	King, E Freeman / McIlvenny	500	Smith	Barron	Atterbury	Lane	King	Bailey	Gibson	Benfield	Freeman E	Hogg	Edgley
14	11	A	Huddersfield Town	L 1-2	Benfield / Elliott 2	3000	Smith	Barron	Atterbury	Bailey	King	Leach	Gibson	Benfield	Freeman E	Hogg	Edgley
15	18	H	Grimsby Town	W 2-0	E Freeman, Edgley	4000	Smith	Currie	Currie	Barron	Harrold	Leach	Gibson	Walker	Freeman E	Hogg	Edgley
16	25	A	Notts County	W 2-1	King, Benfield / Henshall	3000	Smith	Currie	Atterbury	Collins	King	Lane	Benfield	King	Walker	Hogg	Bailey
17	27	H	Notts County	W 2-1	Walker, Benfield / Henshall (p)	10000	Smith	Currie	Atterbury	Collins	King	Leach	Benfield	Lane	Walker	Freeman E	Freeman E
18	Jan 1	H	Derby County	W 2-0	Lane, E Freeman	5000	Smith	Currie	Atterbury	Collins	King	Leach	Douglas	Lane	Freeman E	Benfield	Edgley
19	8	A	Sheffield Wednesday	L 1-3	E Freeman / Wilson, Burkinshaw, Cawley	5000	Smith	Currie	Atterbury	Collins	King	Leach	Benfield	Gibson	Freeman E	Freeman E	Edgley
20	15	H	Bradford Park Avenue	W 2-1	Hogg, Walker / Crozier	4000	Smith	Currie	Atterbury	Collins	King	Leach	Green	Hogg	Walker	Freeman E	Edgley
21	22	A	Leeds City	L 0-1	- / Bainbridge	3000	Smith	Currie	Atterbury	Collins	King	Leach	Benfield	Fox	Bailey	Freeman E	Edgley
22	29	H	Hull City	W 4-0	Walker 3, Leach	6000	Smith	Currie	Atterbury	Bailey	Collins	Leach	Gibson	Whitfield	Walker	Freeman E	Edgley
23	Feb 5	A	Nottingham Forest	L 0-1	- / Bell		Barnett	Currie	Atterbury	Collins	King	Leach	Benfield	Benfield	Walker	Freeman E	Edgley
24	12	H	Barnsley	D 2-2	King, Walker / Burkinshaw, Bratley		Bown	Currie	Atterbury	Collins	King	Leach	Benfield	Morrell	Walker	Freeman E	Edgley
25	19	H	Lincoln City	D 1-1	E Freeman (p) / Parrish		Bown	Currie	Atterbury	Collins	King	Leach	Gibson	Whitfield	Walker	Freeman E	Edgley
26	Apr 25	A	Sheffield United	D 1-1	Gibson / Masterman	7500	Bown	Currie	Atterbury	Collins	King	Hibbert	Gibson	Benfield	Parker	Walker	Sharpe

FOOTBALL LEAGUE MIDLAND SECTION (SUBSIDIARY TOURNAMENT - SOUTHERN SECTION)

No	Date	Ven	Opponents	Result	Scorers	Att	1	2	3	4	5	6	7	8	9	10	11
1	Mar 4	H	Notts County	D 0-0		3000	Bown	Currie	Atterbury	Collins	King	Leach	Benfield	Bailey	Walker	Freeman E	Edgley
2	11	A	Derby County	W 5-2	Montgomery, Walker 2, Atterbury (p), Haynes (og) / Burton, Leigh	7500	Barnett	Currie	Atterbury	Collins	Bailey	Leach	Benfield	Montgomery	Walker	Freeman E	Edgley
3	18	H	Stoke	W 2-1	King, Benfield / Whittingham		Smith	Currie	Atterbury	Bailey	Collins	Leach	Benfield	King	Freeman E	Montgomery	Montgomery
4	25	A	Nottingham Forest	L 0-4	- / Tinsley 2, Bell 2	4000	Smith	Currie	Atterbury	Collins	King	Leach	Benfield	Montgomery	Walker	Freeman E	Edgley
5	Apr 1	A	Chesterfield	L 1-3	Bailey / Revell, Cook, Sankey		Smith	Currie	Atterbury	Collins	King	Leach	Benfield	Bailey	Parker	Walker	Edgley
6	8	A	Notts County	D 1-1	Atterbury (p) / Bird	3000	Bown	Currie	Atterbury	Collins	King	Leach	Gibson	Benfield	Freeman E	Walker	Edgley
7	15	H	Derby County	W 3-2	Parker 2, King / Whitehouse 2		Bown	Currie	Atterbury	Collins	King	Leach	Benfield	Freeman E	Parker	Walker	Edgley
8	22	A	Stoke	L 0-1	- / Bailey (og)	6000	Bown	Waterfield	Atterbury	Bailey	Harrold	Webber	Goddard	Benfield	Parker	Currie	Freeman E
9	24	H	Chesterfield	D 2-2	Atterbury (p), Benfield / Sharp, Smith	3000	Bown	Currie	Atterbury	Waterfield	King	Bailey	Collins	Benfield	Parker	Walker	Freeman E
10	29	H	Nottingham Forest	L 1-3	King / Tinsley, Bell, Sharp	3000	Barnett	Currie	Atterbury	Collins	King	Leach	Douglas	Benfield	Freeman E	Walker	Edgley

Final League Position: Main Tournament: 5 of 14; Subsidiary Tournament: 3 of 6.

Note: Apr 25, postponed from Feb 26.

Champions: Main Tournament: Leeds City; Subsidiary Tournament: Bradford Park Avenue.

FOOTBALL LEAGUE MIDLAND SECTION

Match No	Date		Opponents	Result	Scorers	Att	1	2	3	4	5	6	7	8	9	10	11
1	Sep 2	A	Leeds City	D 2-2	Parsonage, Sturdy / Price 2	3000	Bown	Currie	Atterbury	Collins	King	Leach	Hawden	Sturdy	Boyne	Parsonage	Edgley
2	9	H	Sheffield United	D 2-2	Edgley, Parsonage / Uttley, Buddery	4000	Bown	Currie	Atterbury	Collins	King	Leach	Benfield	Leigh	Boyne	Parsonage	Edgley
3	16	A	Bradford City	D 1-1	Benfield / McIlvenny	3000	Bown	Currie	Atterbury	Collins	King	Leach	Benfield	Leigh	Boyne	Parsonage	Edgley
4	23	H	Chesterfield	W 2-0	King, Leigh		Bown	Currie	Atterbury	Collins	King	Leach	Freeman	Leigh	Boyne	Parsonage	Edgley
5	30	H	Grimsby Town	D 0-0			Bown	Currie	Atterbury	Trueman	King	Leach	Collins	Leigh	Boyne	Parsonage	Freeman
6	Oct 7	A	Notts County	L 1-5	Leigh / Cantrell 3, Housley 2	3000	Bown	Currie	Cullin	Collins	Collins	Leach	Freeman	Leigh	Boyne	Parsonage	Edgley
7	14	H	Rotherham County	W 3-1	Parsonage 2, Freeman / Hopkinson		Bown	Currie	Atterbury	Bailey	Collins	Leach	Broadley	Boyne	Freeman	Parsonage	Edgley
8	21	A	Huddersfield Town	L 1-4	Freeman / Mann, Connor 2, Moore	4000	Bown	Currie	Atterbury	Bailey	Collins	Leach	Boyne	Joyce	Freeman	Parsonage	Edgley
9	28	H	Lincoln City	D 1-1	Boyne / Barrell		Bown	Currie	Atterbury	Bailey	Collins	Leach	Newman	Boyne	Freeman	Parsonage	Edgley
10	Nov 4	A	Sheffield Wednesday	L 0-3	- / T Brelsford, Glennon, Cawley		Bown	Currie	Atterbury	Bailey	King	Leach	Collins	Boyne	Parsonage	Thurman	Edgley
11	11	H	Bradford Park Avenue	L 0-2	- / Kemp 2		Bown	Currie	Atterbury	Crutchley	King	Leach	Goddard S	Boyne	Freeman	Parsonage	Edgley
12	18	A	Birmingham	L 1-2	Parsonage / S Brooks, Gardner	13000	Bown	Currie	Atterbury	Crutchley	Collins	Leach	Day T	King	Day T	Parsonage	Edgley
13	25	H	Hull City	L 0-2	- / Grimshaw, Leigh	2000	Bown	Currie	Atterbury	Collins	King	Leach	Southwell	Freeman	Day T	Parsonage	Edgley
14	Dec 2	A	Nottingham Forest	L 0-2	- / Godfrey 2	3000	Bown	Currie	Atterbury	Collins	King	Leach	Boyne	Parsonage	Storer C	Edgley	Timmins
15	9	H	Leeds City	L 1-4	King / Price 3, Thorpe	3000	Bown	Currie	Atterbury	Collins	King	Bailey	Barratt	Bennett	Storer C	Hubbard	Marriott
16	16	A	Sheffield United	L 0-1	- / Brown	4000	Bown	Currie	Atterbury	Bailey	Benfield	Roulson	Smith S	Boyne	Storer C	Hubbard	Marriott
17	25	H	Barnsley	L 1-2	King / Birtles 2		Bown	Currie	Atterbury	Collins	Hall	Leach	Barratt	Parsonage	Hubbard	King	Webber
18	26	A	Barnsley	L 0-5	- / Keenlyside, Brattley, Burkinshaw 3		Bown	Stern	Atterbury	Bee	Hall	Leach	Barratt	Botterill	Hubbard	Longlands	Currie
19	30	H	Chesterfield	L 0-2	- / Revill, Goodwin		Bown	Draycott	Currie	Smith F	Collins	Leach	Barratt	Sharpe	Storer C	Parsonage	Marriott
20	Jan 6	A	Grimsby Town	W 3-1	Padley, Stainsby, Webster (og) / T Rippon		Bown	Draycott	Currie	Storer S	Storer C	Atterbury	Goddard J	Stainsby	Pykett	Padley	Marriott
21	13	H	Notts County	L 0-1	- / Walker (p)	1600	Bown	Draycott	Currie	Smith F	Storer C	Leach	Goddard S	Goddard J	King	Parsonage	Price
22	20	A	Rotherham County	L 0-1	- / Reed		Bown	Draycott	Currie	Smith F	Storer C	Leach	Boyne	Brown	King	Whitworth	Price
23	27	H	Huddersfield Town	W 2-0	Boyne, Price		Bown	Draycott	Currie	Storer S	Storer C	Webber	Smith S	King	Boyne	Price	Sharpe
24	Feb 3	A	Lincoln City	L 1-3	Sharp / Addinall, Egerton, Jackson		Bown	Currie	Leach	Leyland	Storer C	Dunne	Willmott	Nash	Boyne	Price	Sharpe
25	10	H	Sheffield Wednesday	W 3-0	C Storer, Benfield 2		Bown	Draycott	Currie	Smith S	Storer C	Leach	Benfield	Nash	Boyne	Price	Sharpe
26	17	A	Bradford Park Avenue	W 1-0	S Smith		Bown	Draycott	Currie	King	Storer C	Leach	Smith S	Fearnley	Boyne	Price	Clarke
27	24	H	Birmingham	D 1-1	Price / Turner	10000	Bown	Draycott	Currie	King	Storer C	Leach	Smith S	Nash	Boyne	Price	Sharpe
28	Mar 3	A	Hull City	L 1-2	Bown (p) / Mercer 2	2000	Bown	Day	Currie	King	Storer C	Leach	Barrow	Willoughby	Pace	Price	Sharpe
29	10	H	Nottingham Forest	D 1-1	Price / Godfrey	1500	Bown	Draycott	Currie	Storer S	Storer C	King	Starkey	Bird	Boyne	Price	Sharpe
30	Apr 10	A	Bradford City	L 0-2	- / Walker, Mann		Bown	Hampton	Walker	Storer S	King	Hall	Swain	Bird	Cantrell	Price	Brownlow

FOOTBALL LEAGUE MIDLAND SECTION (SUBSIDIARY TOURNAMENT)

Match No	Date		Opponents	Result	Scorers	Att	1	2	3	4	5	6	7	8	9	10	11
1	Mar 24	A	Birmingham	L 1-5	Swain / Whitehouse, Moore, Bell, Bowser, McClure	5000	Bown	Draycott	Hampton	King	Storer C	Leach	Swain	Nash	Boyne	Price	Sharpe
2	31	H	Nottingham Forest	L 0-1	- / Tinsley	3000	Bown	Draycott	Currie	King	Storer C	Leach	Burton	Bird	Boyne	Price	Mullins
3	Apr 7	A	Notts County	W 2-1	Price, Roberts / Cantrell		Bown	Draycott	Currie	Storer S	King	Hall	Swain	Bird	Roberts	Price	Edwards
4	9	A	Notts County	W 3-2	Roberts 2, Bird / Cantrell, Richards	3000	Bown	Hampton	Currie	Storer S	King	Hall	Swain	Bird	Roberts	Price	Brownlow
5	14	H	Birmingham	W 4-2	Price 2, Roberts, Swain / Bell, Whitehouse	2000	Bown	Draycott	Currie	Hall	King	Leach	Swain	Bird	Roberts	Price	Mortimer
6	21	H	Nottingham Forest	W 2-1	Price, Bird / Wightman	2000	Bown	Draycott	Currie	Hall	King	Leach	Swain	Bird	Roberts	Price	Webber

Final League Position: Main Tournament: 15 of 16; **Subsidiary Tournament:** 4 of 16.

Dismissals: Dec 26, Atterbury, Barnsley (a).

Note: Oct 28, A. Newman is probably a pseudonym. Football League records credit T. Benfield with an appearance; Apr 10, postponed from Dec 23.

Season 1917-18

Champions: Main Tournament: Leeds City; Subsidiary Tournament: Grimsby Town.

FOOTBALL LEAGUE MIDLAND SECTION

Match No	Date		Opponents	Result	Scorers	Att	1	2	3	4	5	6	7	8	9	10	11
1	Sep 1	A	Notts County	L 1-2	Roberts / Richards, Tremelling		Bown	Draycott	Currie	Hall	Storer C	Leach	Moore	King	Roberts	Price	Donald
2	8	H	Notts County	W 1-0	Roberts		Bown	Draycott	Currie	King	Storer C	Leach	Swain	Bird	Roberts	Price	Donald
3	15	A	Huddersfield Town	W 2-1	Bird, Price / Mann		Bown	Draycott	Currie	King	Storer C	Leach	Swain	Bird	Roberts	Price	Donald
4	22	H	Huddersfield Town	W 4-1	Bird 2, Benfield, Price / Baker (p)	5500	Bown	Draycott	Currie	King	Storer C	Leach	Benfield	Bird	Roberts	Price	Donald
5	29	A	Sheffield Wednesday	W 3-1	Roberts 2, King / Glennon		Bown	Draycott	Currie	King	Storer C	Leach	Swain	Bird	Roberts	Price	Donald
6	Oct 6	H	Sheffield Wednesday	L 1-2	Donaldson / Wilson, Burkinshaw		Bown	Draycott	Currie	King	Storer C	Leach	Donaldson	Bird	Roberts	Price	Donald
7	13	H	Bradford City	W 2-0	Donald, Currie (p)	3000	Bown	Draycott	Currie	King	Storer C	Leach	Donaldson	Bird	Roberts	Price	Donald
8	20	A	Bradford City	L 1-4	Bird / McIlvenney (p), G Wild, Thompson 2		Bown	Draycott	Currie	King	Storer C	Leach	Donaldson	Bird	Roberts	Price	Donald
9	27	H	Rotherham County	W 2-0	Roberts, Price		Bown	Draycott	Currie	King	Storer C	Leach	Donaldson	Bird	Roberts	Price	Donald
10	Nov 3	A	Rotherham County	L 2-4	Price, Roberts / Taylor, Hibbert, Lloyd, Spratt		Bown	Draycott	Currie	King	Hall	Leach	Smelt	Benfield	Roberts	Price	Donald
11	10	H	Lincoln City	W 4-0	Roberts 2, Currie, Jackson (og)		Bown	Draycott	Currie	King	Storer C	Leach	Donaldson	Benfield	Roberts	Price	Donald
12	17	A	Lincoln City	D 1-1	Roberts / Egerton		Bown	Draycott	Currie	Storer S	Storer C	Leach	King	Bird	Roberts	Price	Donald
13	24	H	Grimsby Town	W 6-1	Bird, Roberts 2, Price, King, Donaldson / Knighton		Bown	Draycott	Currie	King	Storer C	Leach	Donaldson	Bird	Roberts	Price	Donald
14	Dec 1	A	Grimsby Town	D 1-1	Bird / Fenny		Bown	Draycott	Currie	Burton	Wale	Leach	Foreman	Bird	Storer C	Price	Buckley
15	8	A	Hull City	L 1-3	Price / Mercer 2, Hughes	2500	Bown	Currie	Storer C	King	Bird	Leach	Datton	Donaldson	Roberts	Price	Donald
16	15	H	Hull City	W 3-1	Price 2, King / Mercer	2000	Bown	Hall	Currie	King	Storer C	Leach	Donaldson	Bird	Roberts	Price	Donald
17	22	A	Bradford Park Avenue	L 0-1	- / Elliott		Bown	Draycott	Hall	King	Storer C	Leach	Pollard	Fearnley	Roberts	Price	Murray
18	25	A	Birmingham	D 0-0		20000	Bown	Draycott	Currie	Hall	Storer C	Leach	Donaldson	Millington	Roberts	Turner	Donald
19	26	H	Birmingham	W 3-0	Donaldson, Price, Donald	5000	Bown	Draycott	Currie	King	Storer C	Leach	Donaldson	King	Roberts	Price	Donald
20	29	H	Bradford Park Avenue	W 2-0	Roberts 2		Bown	Hall	Currie	King	Storer C	Leach	Donaldson	Osborn	Roberts	Price	Donald
21	Jan 5	H	Nottingham Forest	W 2-0	King, Price	2000	Bown	Draycott	Currie	King	Storer C	Leach	Donaldson	Osborn	Roberts	Price	Donald
22	12	A	Nottingham Forest	L 0-2	- / Tinsley, Godfrey	4000	Bown	Draycott	Hall	Benfield	Storer C	Leach	Donaldson	Osborn	Roberts	Price	Donald
23	19	H	Leeds City	L 2-4	King, Donaldson / Sherwin, C Stephenson, Cawley 2	3000	Bown	Draycott	Hall	Storer S	Storer C	Leach	Donaldson	King	Longlands	Price	Donald
24	26	A	Leeds City	L 0-4	- / Price, Peart, Goodwin, C Stephenson	5000	Bown	Draycott	Gittins	Hall	Storer C	Leach	Bowden	King	Chapman	Price	Currie
25	Feb 2	A	Sheffield United	L 2-6	Price, Mills / Kitchen 3, Tummon, Johnson, Shearman	8000	Bown	Draycott	Currie	King	Brown	Hall	Barrett	Mills	Storer C	Price	Donald
26	9	H	Sheffield United	L 1-2	Currie (p) / Johnson, Shearman	2500	Bown	Draycott	Currie	Hall	Storer C	Leach	Donaldson	Sarson	Goddard	Price	Donald
27	16	H	Barnsley	L 0-1	- / Bratley		Bown	Hall	Currie	Whiteman	Storer C	Leach	Sarson	Tyler	Mortimer	Price	Donald
28	23	H	Barnsley	W 5-1	Sarson, C Storer, Price 3 / Donkin		Bown	Draycott	Currie	Hall	Storer C	Leach	Donaldson	Sarson	Mortimer	Price	Donald

FOOTBALL LEAGUE MIDLAND SECTION (SUBSIDIARY TOURNAMENT)

Match No	Date		Opponents	Result	Scorers	Att	1	2	3	4	5	6	7	8	9	10	11
1	Mar 16	A	Notts County	L 1-5	Mortimer / Short 2, Cantrell, Charlesworth (p), Richards		Bown	Draycott	Currie	King	Storer C	Leach	Donaldson	Mortimer	Benfield	Price	Donald
2	23	H	Notts County	W 3-1	Mortimer 2, Currie (p) / Cantrell		Bown	Draycott	Currie	Hall	King	Leach	Donaldson	Bird	Mortimer	Price	Donald
3	30	H	Nottingham Forest	W 1-0	Mortimer		Bown	Draycott	Currie	Hall	Storer C	Leach	Ellis	Sarson	Mortimer	Price	King
4	Apr 6	A	Nottingham Forest	L 0-2	- / Poole 2	1000	Bown	Draycott	Currie	Hall	Storer C	Leach	Donaldson	King	Mortimer	Price	Donald
5	13	H	Birmingham	D 1-1	Mortimer / Butler	4000	Bown	Draycott	Currie	Hall	Storer C	Leach	Donaldson	King	Mortimer	Price	Donald
6	20	A	Birmingham	L 0-1	- / J Godfrey	5000	Bown	Draycott	Currie	Hall	King	Leach	Burton E	King	Mortimer	Crowe	Donald

Final League Position: Main Tournament: 7 of 15; Subsidiary Tournament: 12 of 16.

Season 1918-19

Champions: Main Tournament: Nottingham Forest; Subsidiary Tournament: Birmingham.

FOOTBALL LEAGUE MIDLAND SECTION

Match No	Date	Opponents	Result	Scorers	Att	1	2	3	4	5	6	7	8	9	10	11
1	Sep 7 H	Rotherham County	W 4-1	Roberts 2, Price 2 / Taylor		Bown	Underwood	Currie	Parker	King	Leach	Donaldson	Mortimer	Roberts	Price	Donald
2	14 A	Rotherham County	W 3-0	Roberts 3		Bown	Underwood	Currie	Bailey	King	Leach	Donaldson	Mortimer	Roberts	Price	Donald
3	21 H	Lincoln City	W 2-0	Currie (p). Price		Bown	Underwood	Currie	Bailey	King	Leach	Donaldson	Mortimer	Roberts	Price	Donald
4	28 A	Lincoln City	L 0-4	- / Egerton 2, Parrish, Cavanagh		Bown	Underwood	Currie	Bailey	King	Leach	Donaldson	Mortimer	Roberts	Price	Donald
5	Oct 5 H	Grimsby Town	W 5-3	Roberts 2, G Davis, Price, King / Wilkinson, Knighton, Sankey		Bown	Underwood	Currie	Bailey	King	Leach	Donaldson	Davis G	Roberts	Price	Donald
6	12 A	Grimsby Town	L 1-4	Hubbard / Kitchen, Sankey 2, Stainsby		Bown	Currie	Lowe	Bailey	King	Leach	Smith S	Hubbard	Roach	Barber	Faulconer
7	19 A	Bradford City	L 0-2	- / Grimshaw, Bauchop	5000	Bown	Underwood	Currie	Bailey	Storer	Leach	King	Davis G	Hubbard	Price	Jordan
8	26 H	Bradford City	W 3-2	King 2, Hubbard / Duckett 2	3000	Bown	Underwood	Currie	Bailey	Storer	King	Donaldson	King	Hubbard	Price	Donald
9	Nov 2 A	Sheffield Wednesday	W 2-0	Donaldson, Hubbard		Bown	Underwood	Currie	Bailey	Storer	King	Donaldson	Hubbard	Vlaminck	Price	Donald
10	9 H	Sheffield Wednesday	W 7-3	Hubbard, Donald, Vlaminck 2, King, Price, Stapleton (og) / J Burkinshaw 2, R Burkinshaw		Bown	Underwood	Currie	Bailey	King	Hall	Donaldson	Hubbard	Vlaminck	Price	Donald
11	16 A	Huddersfield Town	L 0-2	- / Crowther, Foster	2500	Bown	Underwood	Currie	Bailey	King	Hall	Donaldson	Hubbard	Vlaminck	Price	Donald
12	23 H	Huddersfield Town	W 3-1	Price 2, Vlaminck / J Baker	3000	Bown	Underwood	Currie	Bailey	Storer	Hall	Donaldson	Hubbard	Vlaminck	Price	Dennis
13	30 A	Notts County	L 0-1	- / Short		Bown	Underwood	Currie	Davis G	Storer	Hall	Donaldson	Green	Mortimer	Price	Dennis
14	Dec 7 H	Notts County	W 3-0	Price 2, King		Bown	Underwood	Currie	Storer	Harrold J	Leach	Donaldson	King	Hubbard	Price	Donald
15	14 H	Barnsley	W 2-1	Currie (p), A Davis / Moore		Bown	Underwood	Currie	King	Storer	Leach	Donaldson	Davis A	Hubbard	Price	Donald
16	21 A	Barnsley	L 2-3	A Davis, Dennis / Moore, Barson, Newton		Bown	Underwood	Currie	May	Storer	Leach	Donaldson	Davis A	Roberts	King	Dennis
17	25 A	Birmingham	W 2-0	Donaldson, Hubbard	10000	Bown	Underwood	Pennington	King	Storer	Leach	Donaldson	Davis A	Roberts	Hubbard	Dennis
18	26 H	Birmingham	L 0-4	- / Whitehouse 2, J Godfrey 2	15000	Bown	Underwood	Pennington	King	Storer	Leach	Donaldson	Price	Roberts	Hubbard	Dennis
19	28 H	Bradford Park Avenue	L 1-2	A Davis / Taylor, Bauchop		Bown	Underwood	Currie	King	Storer	Leach	Minney	Davis A	Hubbard	Price	Dennis
20	Jan 11 A	Nottingham Forest	D 1-1	A Davis / Holford	8000	Bown	Underwood	Currie	King	Storer	Leach	Donaldson	Davis A	Hopkins	Price	Harold S
21	18 H	Nottingham Forest	L 0-1	- / Burton	10000	Bown	Underwood	Currie	King	Storer	Leach	Donaldson	Davis A	Leonard	Price	Harold S
22	25 A	Leeds City	L 2-4	Kirrage, Gibson / C Stephenson, Price 2, Peart	3000	Bown	Smith T	Currie	King	Storer	Leach	Donaldson	Gibson	Kirrage	Price	Harold S
23	Feb 1 H	Leeds City	D 0-0		4000	Bown	Peel	Currie	King	Storer	Leach	Donaldson	Gibson	Kirrage	Price	Stanton
24	8 H	Sheffield United	W 2-1	Stanton, Price / Kitchen	6000	Bown	Underwood	Currie	King	Storer	Leach	Donaldson	Price	Smart	Machin	Stanton
25	15 A	Sheffield United	L 0-1	- / Masterman	10000	Blackwell	Smith G	Currie	Storer	Harrold J	Leach	Donaldson	King	Stanton	Price	Harold S
26	22 H	Hull City	W 3-2	King, Nock 2 / Potter, Mercer	7000	Bown	Mugglestone	Smith G	Storer	Harrold J	Leach	Donaldson	King	Nock	Price	Harold S
27	Mar 1 A	Hull City	L 2-5	S Harrold, Price / Stevens, Hughes, Mercer, Lyon, Deacey	8000	Bown	Smith G	Currie	King	Storer	Leach	Read	Brittain	Nock	Price	Harold S
28	8 H	Coventry City	D 2-2	King 2 / Johnstone, Craig	10000	Bown	Smith G	Currie	Storer	Harrold J	King	Donaldson	Brittain	Nock	Price	Harold S
29	15 A	Coventry City	L 0-1	- / Lowes	12000	Bown	Smith G	Currie	George	Storer	King	Norton	Phipps	Nock	Dobson	Harold S
30	Apr 21 A	Bradford Park Avenue	L 1-2	Richmond / Crowther, Little		Bown	Barron	Currie	King	Harrold J	Smith I	Armstrong	Richmond	Nock	Whitfield	Harold S

FOOTBALL LEAGUE MIDLAND SECTION (SUBSIDIARY TOURNAMENT)

Match No	Date	Opponents	Result	Scorers	Att	1	2	3	4	5	6	7	8	9	10	11
1	Mar 22 H	Notts County	W 5-1	Richmond 2, Price, Nock, S Harrold / Cook		Bown	Smith G	Currie	Storer	Harrold J	Smith I	Norton	Richmond	Nock	Price	Harold S
2	29 A	Notts County	L 0-5	- / Richards 2, Cantrell, Dale, Henshall		Bown	Smith G	Currie	Storer	Harrold J	King	Norton	Richmond	Nock	Price	Harold S
3	Apr 5 A	Nottingham Forest	W 2-0	Osborne, Nock	10000	Bown	Smith G	Currie	King	Harrold J	Smith I	Norton	Osborne	Nock	Whitfield	Harold S
4	12 H	Nottingham Forest	W 1-0	Nock	6000	Bown	Smith G	Currie	King	Harrold J	Smith I	Norton	Osborne	Nock	Whitfield	Harold S
5	19 A	Birmingham	L 0-3	- / Short, Walker, Morgan	5000	Bown	Barron	Currie	King	Harrold J	Smith I	Norton	Richmond	Nock	Whitfield	Harold S
6	26 H	Birmingham	L 2-4	Richmond, Currie (p) / Crowe, J Godfrey 3	6000	Bown	Watson	Currie	King	Harrold J	Smith I	Norton	Richmond	Nock	Whitfield	Harold S

Final League Position: Main Tournament: 10 of 16; Subsidiary Tournament: 2 of 4.

Note: Apr 21, postponed from Jan 4.

Season 1915-16

NAME	CLUB	Apps FLM	Apps FLMS	Goals FLM	Goals FLMS
Sep Atterbury	Plymouth Argyle	22	10		3
Tom Bailey	Gresley Rovers	13	6		1
Charlie Barnett		3	2		
Charles Barron		4			
Tommy Benfield	Derby County	18	10	3	2
Walter Bettridge	Chelsea	9		3	
Herbert Bown		2	5		
David Calderhead	Motherwell	8			
Arthur Collins	Jnr club (Birmingham area)	22	9		
T Cope					
Sam Currie		15	10		
Alec Donaldson	Bolton Wanderers	7			
George Douglas		2	1		1
John Dunne	Lincoln City		1		
Harold Edgley	Aston Villa	11	8	1	
N Fox	Leeds City	1			
Charlie Freeman	Chelsea	5			
Edwin Freeman	Northampton Town	18	9	8	
Richard Gibson	Birmingham	16	1	6	
Sid Goddard	Leicester Imperial	1			
Billy Green	Bradford P.A. (retired)				
Ben Hall		1			
George Harrison	Everton	5		2	
Jimmy Harrold		1	1		
Harry Hibbert	Chesterfield Town	13		4	
Charlie Hogg					
Teddy King		24	8	5	3
J W Lambert	Belvoir S S				
Harry Lane	Sutton Town	4	1	1	
Jimmy Leach	Aston Villa	11	8	1	1
Billy Mills		1			
W Montgomery	Bellis & Morcom		3	1	
T Morrell	Redditch	1			
P Parker	Army	1	4		2
Harry Pullen	Queens Park Rangers	1			
George Sharpe	Chesterfield Town				
Walter Smith	Manchester City	21	3		
Billy Walker	Birmingham	18	8	11	2
Bert Waterfield	Leicester Imperial	2			
George Webber		1			
Norman Whitfield		2			

Season 1916-17

NAME	CLUB	Apps FLM	Apps FLMS	Goals FLM	Goals FLMS
Sep Atterbury	Plymouth Argyle	18			
Tom Bailey	Gresley Rovers	6			
Joe Barratt	Nuneaton Town	4			
C H Barrow	Army	1			
T Bee	Balmoral United	1			
Tommy Benfield	Derby County	4			3
F Bennett	Queens Park Rangers	1			
Walter Bird	Coalville Swifts	2	5		2
C Botterill	Jnr club (Leicester area)				
Herbert Bown	Aston Villa	30	6	1	
Reg Boyne	Leicester Tigers RUFC	21	2	2	
F R Broadley	Gresley Rovers	1			
A Brown	Coalville Swifts	1			
Tommy Brownlow		1			
E Burton	Jnr club (Birmingham area)	1			
Jimmy Cantrell	Notts County	1			
W Clarke		1			
Arthur Collins	Norwich City	16			
J Crutchley	Jnr club (Birmingham area)	2			
Percy Cullin	Chesterfield Town	1			
Sam Currie		29	5		
T Day	Jnr club (Birmingham area)	2			
- Day	Leicestershire Regiment	1			
George Draycott	Bradford City	9	5		
John Dunne	Lincoln City	1			
Harold Edgley	Aston Villa	13		1	
N Edwards	Jnr club (Birmingham area)	1			
E Fearnley	Bradford City	1			
Edwin Freeman	Northampton Town	8		2	
J W Goddard	Jnr club (Mansfield area)	2			
Sid Goddard	Leicester Imperial	2			
Ben Hall		3	4		
G Hampton	Derby County	1			
H Hawden	Junior club (Leeds area)	1			
Shirley Hubbard		4			
J H Joyce	Aston Villa	1			
Teddy King		21	6	3	
Jimmy Leach	Aston Villa	24	4		
Syd Leigh	Derby County	5		2	
A Leyland	Lincoln City	1			
Jimmy Longlands	Balmoral United	1			
E Marriott	Pinxton	4			
Fred Mortimer		1			
E Mullins	Shirebrook	1			
Harry Nash	Aston Villa	3	1		
A Newman	(pseudonym?)	1			
Arthur Pace	Hull City	1			
George Padley	Worksop Town	1		1	
Harry Parsonage	Shrewsbury Town	17		5	
Cliff Price	Coalville Swifts	10	6	3	4
B Pykett	Notts County	1			
Tommy Roberts		1			
Joe Roulson	Birmingham	1			
George Sharpe	Chesterfield Town	7	1	1	
F Smith	Whitwick Imperial	3			
S Smith	Newhall Swifts	5	1	1	
J Southwell	Jnr club (Birmingham area)	1			
Colin Stainsby	Grimsby Town	1			
A E Starkey					

Season 1916-17 continued

NAME	CLUB	Apps FLM	Apps FLMS	Goals FLM	Goals FLMS
J Stern	Mexborough	1			
Charley Storer	Bradford City	14	2	1	
Sid Storer	Coalville Swifts	4	2		
E F Sturdy	Leeds City	1		1	
Aaron Swain	Coalville Swifts	1	5		2
Bert Thurman	Loughborough Corinthians	1			
W Timmins	Nottingham Forest	1			
Albert Trueman		1			
Harry Walker	Derby County	1			
George Webber	Balmoral United	2	1		
G W Whitworth	Rotherham County	1			
A Willmott	Army	1			
G Willoughby	Jnr club (Sheffield area)	1			

Season 1917-18

NAME	CLUB	Apps FLM	Apps FLMS	Goals FLM	Goals FLMS
G Barrett	Bradford Park Avenue	1			
Tommy Benfield		3	1	1	
Walter Bird	Coalville Swifts	14	1	6	
V H Bowden	Balmoral United	1			
Herbert Bown		28	6		
Tommy Brown	Bradford Park Avenue	1			
J E C Buckley	Army	1			
E Burton	Jnr club (Birmingham area)	1			
- Burton		1			
G Chapman	Barnsley	1			
Frank Crowe	Birmingham	1			
Sam Currie		25	6	3	1
- Dalton	Army	1			
David Donald	Queens Park Rangers	25	5	2	
Alec Donaldson	Bolton Wanderers	16	4	4	
George Draycott	Bradford City	24	6		
A Ellis	Jnr club (Leicester area)	1			
E Fearnley	Bradford City	1			
G A Foreman	Navy	1			
Jack Gittins	Barnsley	1			
Sid Goddard	Leicester Imperial	1			
Ben Hall		13	5		
Teddy King	Bradford City	23	6	5	
Jimmy Leach	Aston Villa	27	6		
J Longlands	Balmoral United	1			
Charley Millington	Stourbridge	1			
Billy Mills		1			
Andy Moore	Whitwick Imperial	1		1	
Fred Mortimer		2	6		5
T Murray	Jnr club (Bradford area)	1			
George Osborn	Hinckley United	3			
S Pollard	Jnr club (Bradford area)	1			
Cliff Price	Coalville Swifts	27	5	14	
Tommy Roberts	Coalville Swifts	21		13	
H Sarson	Leicestershire Regiment	3	1		
Jack Smelt	Rotherham County	1			
Charley Storer	Bradford City	27	5	1	
Sid Storer	Coalville Swifts	2			
Aaron Swain	Coalville Swifts	3			
A Turner	Notts County	1			
Joe Tyler		1			
L Wale	Jnr club (Birmingham area)	1			
A Whiteman	Barnsley	1			

Season 1918-19

NAME	CLUB	Apps FLM	Apps FLMS	Goals FLM	Goals FLMS
A Armstrong	Loughborough Corinthians	1			
Tom Bailey	Gresley Rovers	11			
J Barber	Jnr club (Grimsby area)	1	1		
C W Barron		1	1		
Ernest Blackwell	Sheffield United	1			
Herbert Bown	Chelsea	29	6		
Harry Brittain	Chelsea	2			
Sam Currie		27	6	2	1
Arthur Davis	Evesham	6		4	
George Davis	Asfordby	3		1	
George Dennis	Newhall Swifts	5		1	
Harry Dobson	Coventry City	1			
David Donald	Queens Park Rangers	12		1	
Alec Donaldson	Bolton Wanderers	24		2	
A Faulconer	Jnr club (Grimsby area)	1			
Billy George	Austin Motor Works	1			
Richard Gibson	Birmingham	2		1	
- Green		1			
Ben Hall		4			
Jimmy Harrold		5	6	1	1
Sid Harrold	Cardiff City	10	6	1	1
Len Hopkins		6			
Shirley Hubbard		13		5	
George Jordan	Overseal	1			
Teddy King	Nottingham Forest	28	5	8	
Frank Kirrage	Nottingham Forest	1		1	
Jimmy Leach	Aston Villa	22			
Harry Leonard	Derby County	1			
W R Lowe	Jnr club (Grimsby area)	1			
J Machin	Jnr club (Birmingham area)	1			
R May	Huddersfield Town	1			
H Minney	Standard Engineering	1			
Fred Mortimer		5			
Emanuel Mugglestone	Coalville Swifts	1			
Jimmy Nock	Millwall	5	6	2	3
Joe Norton	Barnsley	1	6		
Fred Osborne	Lincoln City	1	2		
George Parker		1			
A Peel	Junior club (North)	1			
Jesse Pennington	West Bromwich Albion	2			
Harry Phipps		1			
Cliff Price	Coalville Swifts	25	2	11	1
William Read	Swansea Town	1			
Hugh Richmond	Kilmarnock	5	4	1	3
- Roach		1			
Tommy Roberts		7	7		
Herbert Smart	Aston Villa	1			
George Smith	Wednesbury	5	4		
Ike Smith	Stanton	1	5		
S Smith	Army	1			
T Smith	Army	1			
Mick Stanton	Hinckley United	2		1	
Charley Storer	Bradford City	21	2		
J "Gent" Underwood	Coalville Swifts	21			
Honore Vlaminck	Belgian Army	4		3	
J Watson	Jnr club (Nottingham area)	1	4		
Norman Whitfield		1	4		

Wartime guests **Edwin Freeman** (left) and **Alec Donaldson** (right).

Promoted: Tottenham Hotspur, Huddersfield Town
Relegated: Lincoln City (not re-elected), Grimsby Town

FOOTBALL LEAGUE DIVISION TWO

Player columns (left to right): Herbert Bown, Billy Barrett, Sam Currie, Teddy King, Jimmy Harrold, Ike Smith, George Douglas, William Thornton, Hugh Richmond, Jim Macauley, Sid Harrold, Bill Thomson, Joe Norton, Brendel Anstey, George Jobey, Cliff Price, Walter Essom, Ernest Bacon, Jack Parker, Shirley Hubbard, Billy Spittle, Harry King, Ernie Walker, Norman Whitfield, Billy Dorrell, Tom Smith, Jock Paterson, Adam Black, Walter Currie, Chris Duffy

Match No	Date		Opponents	Result	Points	Position	Scorers	Att	Match No
1	Aug 30	H	Wolverhampton W.	L 1-2	-		Douglas / Harrison, Bate	10000	1
2	Sep 1	A	Tottenham Hotspur	L 0-4	-		- / Clay (p), Cantrell 2, Bliss	21060	2
3	6	A	Wolverhampton W.	D 1-1	1	19	Richmond / Bate	12000	3
4	11	H	Tottenham Hotspur	L 2-4	1	19	Price 2 / Clay (p), Minter, Cantrell, Bliss	20000	4
5	13	H	Fulham	W 3-2	3	18	Price, Thomson, E King / Cock 2	12000	5
6	20	A	Fulham	L 0-5	3	19	- / Cock 3, McIntyre 2	16000	6
7	27	H	Coventry City	W 1-0	5	18	Douglas	10000	7
8	Oct 4	A	Coventry City	W 2-1	7	15	Hubbard, S Harrold / Lowes	17500	8
9	11	H	Huddersfield Town	L 0-4	7	17	- / Taylor 2, Mann, Shields	12000	9
10	18	A	Huddersfield Town	D 0-0	8	17		4000	10
11	25	H	Blackpool	L 2-3	8	17	Spittle, H King / Lane 2, Booth	12000	11
12	Nov 1	A	Blackpool	L 0-3	8	17	- / Charles, Booth, Lane	6000	12
13	8	H	West Ham United	D 0-0	9	18		14181	13
14	15	A	West Ham United	L 0-1	9	19	- / Burton	23000	14
15	22	H	South Shields	D 0-0	10	18		11000	15
16	29	A	South Shields	L 0-2	10	19	- / G Smith, J Smith	10000	16
17	Dec 6	H	Rotherham County	D 1-1	11	19	S Currie (p) / Glennon	8000	17
18	13	A	Rotherham County	L 0-1	11	19	- / Millership (p)	7000	18
19	20	H	Stoke	W 3-1	13	19	S Harrold, Walker, Paterson / Brown	19641	19
20	25	H	Birmingham	W 1-0	15	17	Paterson	18214	20
21	26	A	Birmingham	W 1-0	17	16	Whitfield	20000	21
22	27	A	Stoke	L 0-3	17	17	- / Brown 2, Whittingham	15000	22
23	Jan 3	A	Grimsby Town	W 2-1	19	15	Macauley, Paterson / Broom (p)	5000	23
24	17	H	Grimsby Town	W 2-0	21	15	Paterson, Macauley	14315	24
25	24	H	Hull City	W 3-2	23	15	Paterson (p), Walker, Douglas / Stevens, D Mercer	15000	25
26	Feb 7	H	Stockport County	L 0-2	23	16	- / Rodgers, Metcalf	16000	26
27	12	A	Hull City	L 1-5	23	16	Thornton / Morrall 3, Stevens, Deacey	6000	27
28	14	A	Stockport County	W 2-0	25	16	Paterson, Walker	9000	28
29	28	A	Barnsley	W 1-0	27	15	Paterson	7000	29
30	Mar 4	H	Barnsley	D 0-0	28	15		10000	30
31	6	A	Nottingham Forest	D 0-0	29	14		10000	31
32	13	H	Nottingham Forest	D 0-0	30	15		15706	32
33	20	A	Lincoln City	W 3-0	32	15	S Currie (p), Thornton, Whitfield	9000	33
34	27	H	Lincoln City	W 4-0	34	13	Paterson 3, Douglas	11324	34
35	Apr 3	A	Bury	L 0-1	34	15	- / F Heap	13370	35
36	5	A	Bristol City	D 0-0	35	15		20000	36
37	6	H	Bristol City	W 2-1	37	11	Duffy, Paterson / Wilcox	21162	37
38	10	H	Bury	L 0-5	37	14	- / Peake, Hird 2, Lomas, Ritchie	13000	38
39	17	A	Port Vale	W 2-1	39	11	Douglas, Parker / Blood (p)	13000	39
40	24	H	Port Vale	L 0-1	39	13	- / Aitken	14000	40
41	26	A	Clapton Orient	L 0-3	39	14	- / S Tonner, J Tonner, Dixon	8000	41
42	May 1	H	Clapton Orient	D 1-1	40	14	W Currie / Dixon	12000	42

Final League Position:	14	
Average Home League Attendance:	13355	

League Appearances: 35 38 38 18 30 2 34 11 7 19 18 34 11 7 30 9 2 4 5 3 8 8 27 8 1 15 20 6 10 4

League Goals: 2 1 / 5 2 1 2 2 1 / 3 / 1 1 1 1 3 2 / 11 1 1

FA CUP

	Date		Opponents	Result		Scorers	Att	
1	Jan 10	A	Newport County (1)	D 0-0			7523	1
2	15	H	Newport County (1 rep)	W 2-0		Walker, Paterson	20212	2
3	31	H	Manchester City (2)	W 3-0		Douglas, Walker, T Smith	23109	3
4	Feb 21	A	Chelsea (3)	L 0-3		- / Ford, Cock, Browning	42756	4

Dismissals: Sep 20, Teddy King, Fulham (a).
Note: Jan 31, record attendance to date at Filbert Street;
Port Vale took over the Leeds City fixtures after Oct 14 when the latter were disbanded by order of the F.A. following alleged illegal practices.

1919-20
(v Birmingham, 26 December 1919, players only named)
Back: Barrett, Jobey, Bown, Harrold, S Currie, Paterson (in cap & tie), Thomson.
Front: Norton, T Smith, Whitfield, Macauley, Walker.

Season 1920-21

Promoted: Birmingham, Cardiff City
Relegated: Stockport County

FOOTBALL LEAGUE DIVISION TWO

Match No	Date		Opponents	Result	Points	Position	Scorers	Att	Herbert Bown	Bernard Clarke	Sam Currie	Bob Villiers	Jimmy Harrold	Bill Thomson	George Douglas	Billy Spittle	Jock Paterson	Andy Roxburgh	Ernie Walker	Adam Black	Teddy King	Sandy Trotter	Albert Pynegar	Percy Tompkin	Billy Barrett	Hugh Richmond	Walter Currie	Tom Smith	John Roxburgh	Cliff Price	Harry Graham	George Hebden	Match No
1	Aug 28	A	Clapton Orient	L 0-2	-	-	- / Williams, Smith	18000	1	2	3	4	5	6	7	8	9	10	11														1
2	Sep 2	H	Bury	W 4-0	2	-	Tompkin, Pynegar 2, Trotter	15000	1	2			5	6	7	8				3	4	9	10	11									2
3	4	H	Clapton Orient	W 2-1	4	6	Pynegar, Spittle / Smith	17632	1	2			5	6	7	8				3	4	9	10	11									3
4	8	A	Bury	L 0-4	4	13	- / Peake, Ritchie, Trotter 2	10144	1			4		6	7	8				3		9	10	11	2	5							4
5	11	H	Leeds United	D 1-1	5	10	Pynegar / Ellson	16000	1				5	6	7		9			3		10	8	11	2		4						5
6	18	A	Leeds United	L 1-3	5	15	Spittle / Ellson, Goldthorpe 2 (1p)	11000	1		3		5	6	7	10				4	9	8	11	2									6
7	25	H	Birmingham	W 3-0	7	14	Smith, Pynegar, Paterson	17805	1		3		5	6	7		9			4		10	11	2			8						7
8	Oct 2	A	Birmingham	L 0-5	7	16	- / Lane 2, Hampton 3	18000	1		3		5	6	7		9			2	4	10	11				8						8
9	9	H	West Ham United	W 1-0	9	14	Tompkin	17000	1		3		5	6		8	9			2	4		11							7	10		9
10	16	A	West Ham United	W 1-0	11	11	Price	25000	1		3		5	6		8				2	4		11				9			7	10		10
11	23	H	Fulham	D 1-1	12	11	Smith / Torrance	19681	1		3		5	6		8				2	4		11				9			7	10		11
12	30	A	Fulham	D 1-1	13	9	Price / Banks	20000	1		3		5	6		8				2	4		11				9			7	10		12
13	Nov 6	H	Cardiff City	W 2-0	15	8	Harrold, Paterson	21228	1		3		5	6			8	9		2	4		11							7	10		13
14	13	A	Cardiff City	L 0-2	15	12	- / Cashmore, Gill	23000	1		3		5			7	8	9		2	4		11			6					10		14
15	20	A	Notts County	D 1-1	16	11	Paterson / Richards	18000	1		3		5				8	9		2	4		11			6				7	10		15
16	27	A	Notts County	L 0-3	16	11	- / Richards, Henshall, Hill	21914	1		3		5	6			8	9		2	4		11				7				10		16
17	Dec 4	A	Blackpool	L 0-2	16	15	- / Reid, Barrass	8000	1		3		5				8	9		2	4	10	11			6				7			17
18	11	H	Blackpool	L 0-1	16	16	- / Barrass	13000	1		3		5			9	8			2	4	10	11			6				7			18
19	18	A	Sheffield Wednesday	D 0-0	17	17		15000	1		3		5	6			9			2	4		11				8			7	10		19
20	25	H	Stoke	W 3-1	19	14	Paterson 3 / Watkin	20000	1		3		5	6			9			11	2	4					8			7	10		20
21	27	H	Stoke	D 1-1	20	13	Smith / Tempest	15000	1		3			6			9			2			11		5	4	8	7			10		21
22	Jan 1	H	Sheffield Wednesday	W 2-1	22	12	Paterson 2 / McIntyre	14000	1		3		5	6			9			2	4						8	7			10		22
23	15	A	Barnsley	L 1-2	22	15	Paterson / Wainscoat 2	8000	1				5		7		9			3	4		11	2			6	8			10		23
24	22	H	Barnsley	W 2-0	24	12	King 2	13000	1				5		7		9			3	4		11	2			6	8			10		24
25	29	A	Bristol City	L 0-1	24	12	- / Bown	15000	1				5		7		9			3	4		11	2			6	8			10		25
26	Feb 5	H	Bristol City	D 0-0	25	13		20000	1				5		7					3	4		9	11	2			6	10		8		26
27	12	A	Nottingham Forest	W 2-1	27	11	Paterson 2 / Elliott	16000	1						7		9			3	4	11			2	5	6	10			8		27
28	19	H	Nottingham Forest	W 2-0	29	9	Paterson, Pynegar	17300	1								9			3	4	11	8		2	5	6			7	10		28
29	26	A	Rotherham County	D 1-1	30	8	Richmond / Glennon	12000	1		3		5				9					11	8		2	4	6			7	10		29
30	Mar 5	H	Rotherham County	D 1-1	31	8	Paterson / Glennon	17000	1		3		5				9					11	8		2	4	6			7	10		30
31	12	A	Port Vale	D 0-0	32	8		12000	1		3		5			8	9					11			2	4	6			7	10		31
32	19	H	Port Vale	D 0-0	33	8		15000	1		3			4		8	9					11			2	5	6			7	10		32
33	26	H	South Shields	W 2-0	35	8	J Roxburgh, Paterson	18000	1		3	6		4		8	9					11			2	5				7	10		33
34	28	H	Coventry City	L 0-1	35	10	- / Millard	20000	1		3	6	5	4		8	9					11			2					7	10		34
35	29	A	Coventry City	L 0-1	35	10	- / Mercer	20000	1			6	5	4			9	10		3		11			2			8	7				35
36	Apr 2	A	South Shields	L 3-4	35	10	Paterson 2, A Roxburgh / Lillycrop, Oxberry, Keenlyside, Richardson	10000	1								9	8		3		11			2	5	6	7			10		36
37	9	H	Hull City	D 0-0	36	11		12000									9	8		3		11			2	5	6	7			10	1	37
38	16	A	Hull City	D 1-1	37	11	Trotter / Mills	9000									9			3		11			2	5	6	7		10	8	1	38
39	28	H	Wolverhampton W.	D 0-0	38	11		16000					5							3		11	9		2	4	6		7	10	8	1	39
40	30	A	Wolverhampton W.	L 0-3	38	13	- / Riley, Edmonds, Brooks	17203					5							3		9	11	2	4	6	7			10	8	1	40
41	May 2	H	Stockport County	D 0-0	39	12		8000	1				5	6			9	10		3		11			2	4		7			8		41
42	7	A	Stockport County	D 0-0	40	12		13	1				5	6			9	10		3		11			2	4		7			8		42

| | | | | | | | **League Appearances** | | 38 | 3 | 24 | 5 | 33 | 27 | 14 | 18 | 32 | 7 | 2 | 33 | 24 | 22 | 13 | 25 | 24 | 16 | 21 | 21 | 22 | 12 | 22 | 4 | |
| | | | | | | | **League Goals** | | | | | | 1 | | | 2 | 16 | 1 | | | | 2 | 2 | 6 | 2 | | 1 | 3 | 1 | 2 | | | |

Final League Position:	12
Average Home League Attendance:	17175

FA CUP

Match No	Date		Opponents	Result	Points	Position	Scorers	Att	Herbert Bown	Jimmy Harrold	Bill Thomson	Jock Paterson	Adam Black	Teddy King	Albert Pynegar	Billy Barrett	Hugh Richmond	Tom Smith	John Roxburgh	Harry Graham	Match No
1	Jan 8	H	Burnley (1)	L 3-7			Smith, J Roxburgh, Paterson / Anderson 4, Kelly, Cross, King (og)	29149	1	5	6	9	3	4	11	2		8	7	10	1

Note: Jan 8, record attendance to date at Filbert Street;
May 7, played at Old Trafford (Manchester United) due to suspension of Edgeley Park for disciplinary reasons, official record low attendance denotes spectactors who only arrived for second game of double header.

1920-21 (v Birmingham, 2 October 1920)
Back: Thomson, King, Bown, Harrold, S Currie.
Front: Douglas, Smith, Paterson, Pynegar, Tompkin, Black.

Season 1921-22

Promoted: Nottingham Forest, Stoke
Relegated: Bradford Park Avenue, Bristol City

FOOTBALL LEAGUE DIVISION TWO

No	Date		Opponents	Result	Pts	Pos	Scorers	Att	Herbert Bown	Billy Barrett	Adam Black	Teddy King	Jimmy Harrold	Bill Thomson	John Roxburgh	George Greatorex	Jock Paterson	Harry Graham	Sandy Trotter	Cliff Price	Sam Currie	Dennis Jones	Ernie Walker	Andy Roxburgh	Hugh Richmond	Tom Smith	Albert Pynegar	Percy Tompkin	Walter Currie	Ernie Brooks	Jack King	George Hebden	Mick O'Brien	George Waite	No
1	Aug 27	A	Bradford Park Avenue	W 1-0	2	-	Paterson	13000	1	2	3	4	5	6	7	8	9	10	11																1
2	29	H	Fulham	L 1-2	2	-	Greatorex / Shea, Cock	17774	1	2	3	4	5	6	7	8	9	10	11																2
3	Sep 3	H	Bradford Park Avenue	W 2-1	4	7	Greatorex, Trotter / Bauchop	18000	1	2	3	4	5	6	7	8	9	10	11																3
4	5	A	Fulham	D 0-0	5	7		16000	1	2	3	4	5	6	7	8	9	10	11																4
5	10	H	South Shields	W 1-0	7	5	E King	16000	1	2	3	4	5	6	7	8	9	10	11																5
6	17	A	South Shields	L 0-1	7	9	- / Richardson	11000	1	2	3	4	5	6	7	8	9	10	11																6
7	24	H	Bristol City	W 4-1	9	5	Paterson 2, E King, J Roxburgh / Pocock	16000	1	2	3	4	5	6	7		9	8	11	10															7
8	Oct 1	A	Bristol City	D 1-1	10	4	Trotter / Wilcox	14000	1	2	3	4	5	6	7		9	8	11	10															8
9	8	H	Nottingham Forest	D 2-2	11	5	Price 2 / Burton, Spaven	25000	1	2	3	4	5	6	7		9	8	11	10															9
10	15	A	Nottingham Forest	D 0-0	12	5		24000	1	2		4	5	6	7		9	8	11	10	3														10
11	22	A	Wolverhampton W.	L 0-1	12	9	- / Brooks	9000	1	2		4	5	6	7		9	8	11	10	3														11
12	29	A	Wolverhampton W.	D 1-1	13	7	Price / Edmonds	7760	1	2		4	5	6	7	8	9		11	10	3														12
13	Nov 5	H	Barnsley	W 1-0	15	7	Paterson	17000	1	2		4		6	7	8	9		11		3	5	10												13
14	12	A	Barnsley	D 0-0	16	7		10000	1	2		4	5	6	7	8	9		11		3		10												14
15	19	A	Coventry City	D 0-0	17	9		18000	1	2		4	5	6	7		9	8	11		3		10												15
16	26	H	Coventry City	D 1-1	18	9	Smith / Morgan	17900	1	2		4	5	6	7				11		3			10	8	9									16
17	Dec 3	A	Derby County	W 1-0	20	7	Smith	10000	1	2		4	5	6				8		10	3					9	7	11							17
18	10	H	Derby County	D 1-1	21	8	Pynegar / Moore	19698	1	2		4	5	6				8		10	3					9	7	11							18
19	17	A	Bury	W 1-0	23	6	Paterson	9292	1	2			5	6	7		9	10	11		3	4				8									19
20	24	H	Bury	D 0-0	24	6		15000	1	2	3		5	6	7		9	10	11			4				8									20
21	26	A	Blackpool	L 0-2	24	6	- / Bedford 2	13000	1	2		4	5	6	7		9		11		3					8	10								21
22	27	H	Blackpool	W 1-0	26	5	Trotter	22750	1	2			5	6	7		9		11		4	3				10	8								22
23	31	A	West Ham United	L 0-1	26	8	- / Tresadern	20000	1	2			5	6	7		9		11		4	3				10	8								23
24	Jan 14	H	West Ham United	W 2-1	28	7	Paterson, Smith / Watson	16000	1	2			5	6			9	8	11		4	3				10	7								24
25	21	A	Clapton Orient	D 0-0	29	7		7000	1	2			5	6			9	8	11		4	3				10	7								25
26	Feb 4	A	Stoke	D 1-1	30	7	Pynegar (p) / Groves	9000	1	2			5	6			9	8	11		4	3				10	7								26
27	9	H	Clapton Orient	W 1-0	32	6	Paterson	11300	1	2			5				9		11		4	3				8				6	7		10		27
28	11	H	Stoke	L 3-4	32	6	E King 2, J King / Groves 2, J Broad, Tempest	21000	1		2	5		6			9	8	11		4	3									7		10		28
29	20	A	Leeds United	L 0-3	32	6	- / Poyntz 3	5000		2		6	5				9				4	3		10		8	7	11				1			29
30	25	H	Leeds United	D 0-0	33	7		14000		2			5	6		8		10			3	4		9			7	11				1			30
31	Mar 4	A	Hull City	L 2-5	33	8	Pynegar (p), A Roxburgh / McKinney 3, Flood 2	8000		2			5	6				10			3	4		9		8	7	11				1			31
32	11	H	Hull City	L 0-1	33	9	- / Stansfield	12000		2	3		5	6		8			11		4			10		9	7					1			32
33	18	H	Notts County	W 3-0	35	8	Graham 2, Trotter	14500		2	3			6				8	9		4					7		11			10	1	5		33
34	Apr 1	H	Crystal Palace	W 2-0	37	8	J King 2	12000		2	3		5	6				8	9		4					7		11			10	1			34
35	8	A	Crystal Palace	L 0-1	37	8	- / McCracken	10000		2	3			6				8	9		4			10		7		11				1	5		35
36	14	A	Port Vale	D 1-1	38	9	Trotter / Fitchford	10000		2	3			6				8	9		4			10		7		11				1	5		36
37	15	H	Rotherham County	W 1-0	40	9	Graham	11000		2	3			6				8	9		4			10		7		11				1	5		37
38	17	H	Port Vale	W 3-0	42	9	Trotter, Thomson, Graham	15000		2	3		5	6				8	9		4			10		7		11				1			38
39	22	A	Rotherham County	D 0-0	43	8		5000		2	3		5	6				8	9		4			10		7		11				1			39
40	26	A	Notts County	D 0-0	44	7		12000	1	2	3		5	6				8	9		4			10		7		11							40
41	29	H	Sheffield Wednesday	D 1-1	45	7	Trotter / Lofthouse	13000	1	2	3	4		6				8	9	10						7		11					5		41
42	May 6	A	Sheffield Wednesday	L 0-1	45	9	- / Petrie	10000	1	2	3			6				8		10	4					7		11					5	9	42

| Final League Position: | 9 | | | | | | | League Appearances | 31 | 40 | 23 | 21 | 36 | 39 | 20 | 11 | 29 | 31 | 38 | 7 | 13 | 23 | 9 | 12 | 1 | 20 | 15 | 16 | 1 | 4 | 4 | 11 | 6 | 1 | |
| Average Home League Attendance: | 15885 | | | | | | | League Goals | | | | 4 | | 1 | 1 | 2 | 7 | 4 | 7 | 3 | | | | 1 | | 3 | 3 | | | | 3 | | | | |

FA CUP

No	Date		Opponents	Result			Scorers	Att	Herbert Bown	Billy Barrett	Adam Black	Teddy King	Jimmy Harrold	Bill Thomson	John Roxburgh	George Greatorex	Jock Paterson	Harry Graham	Sandy Trotter	Cliff Price	Sam Currie	Dennis Jones	Ernie Walker	Andy Roxburgh	Hugh Richmond	Tom Smith	Albert Pynegar	Percy Tompkin							No
1	Jan 7	H	Clapton Orient (1)	W 2-0			Pynegar (p), Trotter	20757	1	2			5	6	7		9		11		4	3				10	8								1
2	28	H	Fulham (2)	W 2-0			Graham, Paterson	30022	1	2			5	6			9	8	11		4	3				10	7								2
3	Feb 18	A	Arsenal (3)	L 0-3			- / Rutherford, White 2	39421	1	2			5	6			9	8	11		4	3				10	7								3

Note: Jan 28, record attendance to date at Filbert Street.

1921-22
(Although this photograph is listed in the club's 1928-29 handbook as representing 1921-22, the players correspond exactly to the line-ups for the public practice match in August 1920. However, no other team photograph for 1921-22 has yet been found.)
Back: Gardner (Trainer), Linney (Director), Walker, Paterson, Fox (Masseur), Black, Richmond, Bown, Harrold, Hebden, Price, Nixon (Asst Trainer), Needham (Director), Hodge (Manager).
Middle: King, Spittle, Douglas, Thomson, Barrett, S Currie, W Currie, Clarke.
Front: Villiers, Trotter, Smith, A Roxburgh, J Roxburgh, Tompkin, Pynegar.

Season **1922-23**

Promoted: Notts County, West Ham United
Relegated: Rotherham County, Wolverhampton Wanderers

FOOTBALL LEAGUE DIVISION TWO

No	Date		Opponents	Result	Pts	Pos	Scorers	Att	Hebden	Barrett	Black	Thomson	Harrold	O'Brien	Roxburgh	J.Duncan	Waite	Graham	Trotter	T.Duncan	Walker	Jones	Tompkin	Smith	Pynegar	Price	Osborne	Watson	Middleton	No
1	Aug 26	A	Stockport County	W 5-4	2	-	J Duncan 2, Graham, Waite, Waterall (og) / Crossthwaite, Green 2, Woodcock	14000	1	2	3	4	5	6	7	8	9	10	11											1
2	28	H	Rotherham County	W 3-0	4		Trotter, J Duncan, Waite	16000	1	2	3	4	5	6	7	8	9	10	11											2
3	Sep 2	H	Stockport County	W 2-0	6	3	Graham 2	20000	1	2	3	4	5	6	7	8	9	10	11											3
4	4	A	Rotherham County	D 0-0	7	1		9000	1	2	3	4	5	6		8	9	10	11	7										4
5	9	A	Clapton Orient	L 0-2	7	8	- / J Tonner, Galbraith	12000	1	2	3	4	5	6	7	8	9	10	11											5
6	16	A	Clapton Orient	W 2-0	9	4	J Duncan, Waite (p)	17000	1		2		6	5	7	8	9	10	11		3	4								6
7	23	A	Crystal Palace	W 1-0	11	2	Jones	10000	1		2		6	5	7	8	9	10	11		3	4								7
8	30	H	Crystal Palace	W 3-0	13	2	Waite, J Duncan 2	16000	1		2		6	5		8	9	10		7	3	4	11							8
9	Oct 7	A	Bradford City	D 2-2	14	2	J Duncan, Waite / Cheetham (p), Logan	12000	1		2		6	5		8	9	10		7	3	4	11							9
10	14	H	Bradford City	W 2-0	16	1	J Duncan, T Duncan	20503	1		2		6	5		8	9	10		7	3	4	11							10
11	21	A	Leeds United	D 0-0	17	1		12000	1		2		6	5		8	9	10		7	3	4	11							11
12	28	H	Leeds United	W 2-1	19	1	Graham, J Duncan / Harris	20000	1		2		6	5		8	9	10		7	3	4	11							12
13	Nov 4	H	Hull City	L 0-1	19	2	- / Martin	16987	1		2		6	5		8	9	10		7	3	4	11							13
14	11	A	Hull City	W 3-1	21	1	J Duncan, Waite, T Duncan / Martin	10000	1		2		6	5		8	9	10		7	3	4	11							14
15	18	H	Southampton	W 2-1	23	1	T Duncan 2 / Dominy	19000	1		2		6	5		8	9	10		7	3	4	11							15
16	25	A	Southampton	D 0-0	24	1		17000	1		2		6	5		8	9	10		7	3	4	11							16
17	Dec 2	H	Sheffield Wednesday	W 3-1	26	1	J Duncan, Graham, T Duncan / Taylor	19000	1		2		6	5	3	8	9	10		7		4	11							17
18	9	A	Sheffield Wednesday	L 1-2	26	1	Waite (p) / Williams, Smailes	18000	1	2	3		6	5		8	9	10		7		4	11							18
19	16	A	Derby County	L 0-2	26	3	- / Galloway 2	14000	1	2	3		6	5		8	9	10		7		4	11							19
20	23	H	Derby County	L 0-1	26	3	- / Murphy	20000	1	2	3		6	5		8	10	9		7		4	11							20
21	25	H	Blackpool	L 1-2	26	5	J Duncan / Bedford 2	16000	1	2	3		6	5	4	8	9	10		7			11							21
22	26	A	Blackpool	W 2-1	28	3	Tompkin, J Duncan / McIvenney	15000	1	2	3		6	5		8	9	10				4	11	7						22
23	30	H	Barnsley	W 1-0	30	3	Waite	10000	1		2		6	5		8	9	10			3	4	11	7						23
24	Jan 6	H	Barnsley	D 2-2	31	5	Waite 2 (2p) / Halliwell, Beaumont	15000	1		2		6	5		8	9	10			3	4	11	7						24
25	20	H	Notts County	W 2-1	33	2	Waite 2 (1p) / Daly	23604	1		2		6	5	4	8	9	10			3		11	7						25
26	27	A	Notts County	L 0-1	33	4	- / Dinsdale	29337	1		2		6	5		8	9	10			3	4	11	7						26
27	Feb 10	H	West Ham United	D 2-2	34	3	J Duncan 2 / Richards, Brown	16000	1		2		6	5	4	8		10		7	3		11		9					27
28	15	A	West Ham United	L 0-6	34	4	- / Moore 3, Richards, Ruffell, Tresadern	6000	1		2		6	5	4	8		7		10	3		11		9					28
29	17	A	South Shields	L 1-2	34	7	Pynegar / Oxberry, J Smith	8000	1		2		6		5	8		10		7	3	4	11		9					29
30	26	H	South Shields	W 3-0	36	3	Pynegar 2, J Duncan	8000	1		2		6		5	8		10		7	3	4			9	11				30
31	Mar 3	A	Wolverhampton W.	W 2-1	38	2	Pynegar, J Duncan / Fazackerley	10999	1		2		6		5	8		10		7	3	4			9	11				31
32	10	H	Wolverhampton W.	W 7-0	40	2	Pynegar 4 (1p), J Duncan, Graham, O'Brien	11460	1		2		6		5	8		10	11	7	3	4			9					32
33	17	H	Coventry City	W 2-1	42	1	Pynegar, Smith / Herbert	19750	1		2		6		5	8			11	7	3	4		10	9					33
34	24	A	Coventry City	D 1-1	43	1	Smith / Dougall	17000	1		2		6		5	8			11	7	3	4		10	9					34
35	30	A	Fulham	L 0-2	43	2	- / Shea, McKay	25000	1		2		6		5	8		10		7	3	4	11		9					35
36	31	H	Port Vale	W 3-0	45	2	Pynegar 2, O'Brien	20000	1		2		6		5	8		10		7	3	4	11		9					36
37	Apr 2	H	Fulham	D 1-1	46	1	J Duncan / McKay	24527	1		2		6		5	8		10		7		4	11		9		3			37
38	7	A	Port Vale	D 0-0	47	1		12000	1		2		6		5	8		10		7		4	11		9		3			38
39	14	H	Manchester United	L 0-1	47	4	- / Bain	25000	1		2		5			8		10		7		4	11		9		3	6	8	39
40	21	A	Manchester United	W 2-0	49	3	J Duncan, Smith	31000	1		2		5			6		10	11	7		4		8	9		3			40
41	28	H	Bury	W 2-0	51	1	Smith 2	21323	1		2		5			6		10	11	7		4		9			3		8	41
42	May 5	A	Bury	L 0-2	51	3	- / Bullock, Robbie	9467	1		2		5					10	11	7		4		9			3	6	8	42
			League Appearances						42	10	42	38	29	24	6	41	27	39	15	29	25	32	27	10	14	2	6	2	2	
			League Goals									2		20	12	6	1	5			1	1	5	11					

Final League Position:	3
Average Home League Attendance:	19040

FA CUP

No	Date		Opponents	Result	Scorers	Att	Hebden	Black	Harrold	O'Brien	Roxburgh	J.Duncan	Waite	Graham	Walker	Tompkin	Smith	Pynegar	No
1	Jan 13	H	Fulham (1)	W 4-0	J Duncan 2, Smith, Graham	25870	1	2	6	5	4	8	9	10	3	11	7		1
2	Feb 3	H	Cardiff City (2)	L 0-1	- / L Davies	35728	1	2	6	5	4	8	9	10	3	11		7	2

Stand-in Goalkeepers: Oct 7, Harrold for Hebden (temporary), Bradford City (a).
Note: Feb 3, record attendance to date at Filbert Street.

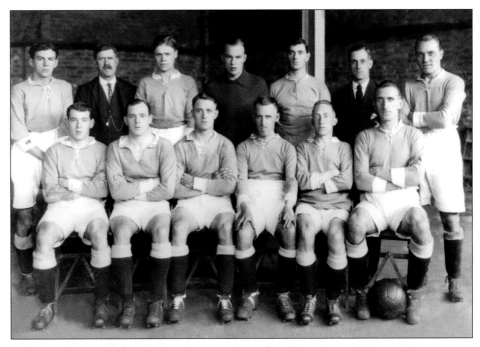

1922-23
Back: Jones, Gardner (Trainer), Black, Hebden, Walker, Trotter, Thomson.
Front: T Duncan, J Duncan, Waite, Graham, Tompkin, Harrold.

Season 1923-24

Promoted: Leeds United, Bury
Relegated: Nelson, Bristol City

FOOTBALL LEAGUE DIVISION TWO

Player columns (left→right): George Hebden, Adam Black, Reg Osborne, Dennis Jones, Mick O'Brien, Bill Thomson, Hughie Adcock, John Duncan, Arthur Chandler, Harry Graham, Percy Tompkin, Tom Smith, Sandy Trotter, Billy Newton, Jack King, Norman Watson, Billy Barrett, Tom Duncan, Albert Pynegar, Ben Davies, Ernie Walker, Pat Carrigan, Jack Middleton, Jack Bamber, Fred Price, George Carr, Albert Godderidge

No	Date	V	Opponents	Result	Pts	Pos	Scorers	Att	Heb	Bla	Osb	Jon	OBr	Tho	Adc	JDu	Cha	Gra	Tmp	Smi	Tro	New	Kin	Wat	Bar	TDu	Pyn	Dav	Wal	Crg	Mid	Bam	Pri	Carr	God
1	Aug 25	A	Hull City	D 1-1	1	-	Graham / Thom	12500	1	2	3	4	5	6	7	8	9	10	11																
2	27	H	Stoke	W 5-0	3	-	Chandler 2, Smith, O'Brien, Adcock	18300	1	2	3	4	5	6	7	8	9			10	11														
3	Sep 1	H	Hull City	D 1-1	4	6	Chandler / Smith	22036	1	2	3	4	5	6	7	8	9			10	11														
4	3	A	Stoke	L 0-1	4	8	- / Davies	11000	1	2	3	4	5	6	7	8	9			10	11														
5	8	H	Leeds United	W 2-0	6	5	Chandler, Jones	17500	1	2	3	4	5	6	7	8	9	10	11																
6	15	A	Leeds United	W 2-1	8	3	Chandler, J Duncan / Swan	15000	1	2	3	4	5	6	7	8	9	10	11																
7	22	H	Port Vale	W 2-0	10	3	Chandler, J Duncan	18000	1	2	3	4	5	6	7	8	9	10	11																
8	29	A	Port Vale	L 1-2	10	4	Graham / Page, Connelly	12000	1	2	3	4	5	6	7	8	9	10	11																
9	Oct 6	H	Bradford City	L 0-1	10	10	- / Chalmers	20000	1	2	3	4	5	6	7	8	9	10	11																
10	13	A	Bradford City	D 2-2	11	9	O'Brien, Chandler / Rhodes, Chalmers	21500	1	2	3		5	6	7	8	9				11	4	10												
11	20	H	Barnsley	W 2-0	13	5	J Duncan, King	17000	1	2	3		5		7	8	9				11	4	10	6											
12	27	A	Barnsley	L 1-3	13	8	J Duncan / Halliwell 3	10000	1	2	3		5		7	8	9				11	4	10	6											
13	Nov 3	H	Manchester United	D 2-2	14	9	O'Brien, J Duncan / Lochhead 2	17000	1		3		5	6		8		10			11	4			2	7	9								
14	10	A	Manchester United	L 0-3	14	13	- / Lochhead, Mann, Spence	20000	1		3		5	6		8	9	10			11	4			2	7									
15	17	H	Bury	W 3-0	16	7	Chandler 2, F Heap (og)	15000	1		3		5	6		8	9	10			11	4			2	7									
16	Dec 1	H	South Shields	W 4-1	18	6	Graham, Chandler 3 / Simms	18000	1		3		5	6		8	9	10			11	4			2	7									
17	8	A	South Shields	W 2-1	20	6	J Duncan, Chandler / Simms	9000			3		5	6		8	9	10			11	4			2	7		1							
18	15	H	Oldham Athletic	D 1-1	21	5	J Duncan / Staniforth	17000			3		5	6		8	9	10			11	4			2	7		1							
19	22	A	Oldham Athletic	D 0-0	22	6		7089	1		3		5	6		8	9	10			11	4			2	7									
20	25	A	Clapton Orient	L 0-1	22	6	- / Townrow	15000	1		3		5	6		8	9			10	11	4			2	7									
21	26	H	Clapton Orient	L 1-2	22	7	J Duncan / Bliss 2	23500	1		3		5	6		8	9			10	11	4			2	7									
22	29	H	Stockport County	D 1-1	23	9	T Duncan / Critchley	16000			3		5	6		8	9			10	11	4			2	7		1							
23	Jan 2	A	Bury	L 0-2	23	11	- / Matthews, Ball	8274	1					6			9	10			11	4			2	7					3	5		8	
24	5	A	Stockport County	L 1-3	23	14	Middleton / Swan, Simms 2	12000	1		3		5	6				10			11	4			2	7	9							8	
25	19	A	Crystal Palace	L 3-4	23	15	Chandler, Middleton, Cracknell (og) / Whitworth 2, Hoddinott, Morgan	10000	1		3			6	7		9	10	11			4			2								5	8	
26	26	H	Crystal Palace	W 1-0	25	13	Chandler	14000	1		3		5	6	7		9	10	11			4			2									8	
27	Feb 9	A	Sheffield Wednesday	W 2-1	27	12	Chandler, J Duncan / Binks	15000	1		3		5		7	8	9	10	11			4			2									6	
28	11	A	Sheffield Wednesday	L 1-2	27	13	Graham / Binks 2	10000	1		3		5		7	8	9	10	11			4			2									6	
29	16	A	Coventry City	W 4-2	29	12	Chandler 3, J Duncan / Shea, Wood	12000	1		3		5		7	8	9	10				4			2								6	11	
30	23	H	Coventry City	W 2-0	31	11	Chandler, Carr	22500	1		3		5		7	8	9					4			2								6	11	10
31	Mar 1	A	Bristol City	W 1-0	33	8	Carr	11000	1		3				7	8	9		11			4			2					5				6	10
32	8	A	Bristol City	W 5-1	35	7	Chandler, Carr, J Duncan 3 / Smailes	22000	1		3		5		7	8	9		11			4			2								6	10	
33	15	H	Southampton	L 0-1	35	8	- / Dominy	20000	1		3				7	8	9		11			4			2					5			6	10	
34	22	A	Southampton	L 0-1	35	10	- / Parker	9000	1		3		5		7	8	9		11			4			2								6	10	
35	29	H	Fulham	W 2-1	37	8	Adcock 2 / Chaplin	14000			3		5		7	8	9		11			4			2							6		10	1
36	Apr 5	A	Fulham	L 0-1	37	10	- / Edmonds	17000			3		5		7		9		11			4			2						8	6		10	1
37	12	H	Blackpool	L 1-2	37	10	Chandler / Butler, Bedford	15000		2	3		5		7		9		11			4			2						8	6		10	1
38	19	A	Blackpool	L 1-3	37	14	O'Brien / White 2, Watson	15000	1	2	3		5		7		9		11			4									8	6		10	
39	21	A	Nelson	D 1-1	38	14	Tompkin / Eddleston	11000	1		3		5		7		9		11			4			2						8	6		10	
40	22	H	Nelson	W 3-1	40	12	Chandler 2, Adcock / McCulloch	18000			3		5		7		9		11			4			2						8	6		10	1
41	26	H	Derby County	W 3-0	42	11	Carr 2, Middleton	16000			3				7		9		11			4			2						8	6	5	10	1
42	May 3	A	Derby County	L 0-4	42	12	- / Moore 2, Storer, Galloway	20000			3				7		9		11			4			2						8	6	5	10	1
	Final League Position: 12						**League Appearances**		33	22	33	9	35	24	30	34	42	18	19	6	21	30	3	7	28	12	2	3	1	4	9	16	2	13	6
	Average Home League Attendance: 17335						**League Goals**				1	4			4	13	24	4	1	1		1			1							3		5	

FA CUP

No	Date	V	Opponents	Result	Scorers	Att	Heb	Osb	OBr	Tho	Adc	Cha	Gra	Tmp	New	Bar	TDu	Bam
1	Jan 12	A	Sheffield Wednesday (1)	L 1-4	Barrett (p) / Taylor 2, Binks (p), Petrie	39127	1	3	5			9	10	11	4	2	7	8

Stand-in Goalkeepers: Dec 26, Trotter for Hebden, Clapton Orient (h).

1923-24
Back: Jones, J King, Black, Hebden, Osborne, Gardner (Trainer), Thomson.
Front: Adcock, J Duncan, O'Brien, Chandler, Graham, Tompkin.

Season 1924-25

Promoted: Leicester City, Manchester United
Relegated: Crystal Palace, Coventry City

FOOTBALL LEAGUE DIVISION TWO

Match No	Date		Opponents	Result		Points	Position	Scorers	Att	Albert Godderidge	Harry Hooper	Reg Osborne	Jack Bamber	Pat Carrigan	John Duncan	Hughie Adcock	Norman Proctor	Arthur Chandler	George Carr	Harold Wadsworth	Jack Middleton	Billy Barrett	Adam Black	Norman Watson	George Hebden	Billy Newton	Buchanan Sharp	Match No
1	Aug 30	A	Manchester United	L	0-1	-	-	- / Goldthorpe	21250	1	2	3	4	5	6	7	8	9	10	11								1
2	Sep 1	H	Chelsea	W	4-0	2	-	Adcock, Chandler, Carr 2	22687	1	2	3	4	5	6	7	8	9	10	11								2
3	6	H	Middlesbrough	D	0-0	3	9		24000	1	2	3	4	5	6	7	10	9			11	8						3
4	8	A	Chelsea	L	0-4	3	14	- / Whitton 4	32000	1			4	5	10	7	8	9		11			2	3	6			4
5	13	H	Stoke	L	0-1	3	17	- / Armitage	15000				4	5	6	7	8	9	10	11			2	3	1			5
6	15	A	Stockport County	W	2-0	5	11	Duncan, Barrett (p)	18000				6	5	8	7		9	10	11			2	3	1	4		6
7	20	A	Coventry City	L	2-4	5	17	Carr, Chandler / Shea 2, Morris, Herbert	18000			3	6	5	8	7		9	10	11			2		1	4		7
8	27	H	Oldham Athletic	W	3-0	7	13	Carrigan, Chandler, Duncan	18000			3	6	5	8	7		9	10	11			2		1	4		8
9	Oct 4	A	Sheffield Wednesday	W	4-1	9	10	Chandler, Wadsworth, Duncan 2 / Trotter	15000			3	6	5	8	7		9	10	11			2		1	4		9
10	11	H	Clapton Orient	W	4-2	11	7	Carr 2, Duncan 2 / Rennox, Bliss	15000			3	6	5	8	7		9	10	11			2		1	4		10
11	18	A	Crystal Palace	W	2-0	13	5	Duncan, Chandler	20000			3	6	5	8	7		9	10	11			2		1	4		11
12	25	A	Barnsley	D	1-1	14	5	Chandler / Beaumont	8000	1		3	6	5	8	7		9	10	11			2			4		12
13	Nov 1	H	Wolverhampton W.	W	2-0	16	4	Chandler, Duncan	10000			3	6	5	8	7		9	10	11			2		1	4		13
14	8	A	Fulham	D	2-2	17	5	Chandler, Bamber / Prouse 2	18000			3	6	5	8	7		9	10	11			2		1	4		14
15	15	H	Portsmouth	W	4-0	19	3	Chandler, Carr, Duncan, Newton	22300			3	6	5	8	7		9	10	11			2		1	4		15
16	22	A	Hull City	L	1-2	19	4	Chandler / Mills 2	11000			3	6	5	8	7		9	10	11			2		1	4		16
17	29	H	Blackpool	L	0-2	19	6	- / Bedford, Meredith	20000	1	3		6	5	8	7		9	10	11			2			4		17
18	Dec 6	A	Derby County	W	3-0	21	4	Duncan, Carrigan, Chandler	25381	1	3		6	5	8	7		9	10	11			2			4		18
19	13	H	South Shields	D	1-1	22	4	Chandler / J Smith	14000	1	3		6	5	8	7		9	10	11			2			4		19
20	20	A	Bradford City	D	1-1	23	4	Chandler / Butler	12500	1	3		6	5	8	7		9	10	11			2			4		20
21	25	H	Port Vale	W	7-0	25	4	Chandler, Duncan 6	22000	1	3		6	5	8	7		9	10	11			2			4		21
22	26	A	Port Vale	W	2-1	27	4	Chandler, Carr / Kirkham	17000	1	3		6	5	8	7		9	10	11			2			4		22
23	27	H	Manchester United	W	3-0	29	4	Chandler 2, Duncan	18250	1	3		6	5	8	7		9	10	11			2			4		23
24	Jan 3	A	Middlesbrough	W	5-1	31	4	Duncan 2, Chandler, Carr, Adcock / Hick (p)	12000	1	3		6	5	8	7		9	10	11			2			4		24
25	17	A	Stoke	D	1-1	32	4	Adcock / Watkin	11705	1	3		6	5	8	7		9	10	11			2			4		25
26	24	H	Coventry City	W	5-1	34	3	Sharp, Carr, Chandler 3 / Richmond	17000	1	3		6	5		7		9	10	11			2			4	8	26
27	Feb 7	H	Sheffield Wednesday	W	6-1	36	3	Duncan 2, Black 2 (2p), Chandler 2 / Trotter		1	3		6		8	7		9	10	11			2	5		4		27
28	14	A	Clapton Orient	W	1-0	38	2	Duncan	20000	1	3		6	5	8	7		9	10	11			2			4		28
29	28	H	Barnsley	W	6-0	40	3	Chandler 5, Duncan	18000	1	3		6	5	8			9	10	11			2	7		4		29
30	Mar 12	H	Crystal Palace	W	3-1	42	2	Carrigan, Black (p), Duncan / Groves		1	3			5	8	7		9	10	11			2	6		4		30
31	14	H	Fulham	W	4-0	44	2	Duncan 3, Adcock	22000	1	3			5	8	7		9	10	11			2	6		4		31
32	17	A	Oldham Athletic	W	1-0	46	1	Chandler	11278	1	3			5		7		9	10	11			2	6		4	8	32
33	21	A	Portsmouth	D	1-1	47	2	Chandler / Beedie	16000	1	3		6	5	8	7		9	10	11			2			4		33
34	28	H	Hull City	W	1-0	49	1	Carr	23000	1	3		6	5	8	7		9	10	11			2			4		34
35	30	A	Wolverhampton W.	W	1-0	51	1	Chandler	15530	1	3		6	5	8	7		9	10	11			2			4		35
36	Apr 4	A	Blackpool	L	1-2	51	1	Duncan / Bedford (p), Meredith	9000	1	3		6	5	8			9	10	11			2	7		4		36
37	11	H	Derby County	D	0-0	52	1		33269	1	3		6	5	8	7		9	10	11			2			4		37
38	13	A	Southampton	D	0-0	53	1		6000	1	3		6	5	8	7		9	10	11			2			4		38
39	14	H	Southampton	D	0-0	54	1		25000	1	3		6	5	8	7		9	10	11			2			4		39
40	18	H	South Shields	D	1-1	55	1	Bamber / Oxberry	5000	1	3		6		8	7		9	5	11			2			4	10	40
41	25	H	Bradford City	W	1-0	57	1	Carr	25000	1	3		6		8	7		9	10	11			2			4		41
42	May 2	H	Stockport County	W	4-0	59	1	Duncan 2, Chandler, Carr	22000	1	3		6	5	8	7		9	10	11						4		42

Final League Position:	1	**League Appearances**	31 26 16 39 40 40 40 5 42 40 42 1 3 39 10 11 34 3
Average Home League Attendance:	20455	**League Goals**	2 3 30 4 32 12 1 3 1 1

FA CUP

	Date		Opponents	Result		Scorers	Att	Gd	Ho	Os	Ba	Ca	Du	Ad	Pr	Ch	Cr	Wa	Mi	Br	Bl	Wt	He	Ne	Sh	
1	Jan 10	H	Stoke (1)	W	3-0	Duncan 2, Chandler	28713	1	3		6	5	8	7		9	10	11			2			4		1
2	31	A	Newcastle United (2)	D	2-2	Chandler 2 / McDonald (p), Cowan	58713	1	3		6	5	8	7		9	10	11			2			4		2
3	Feb 5	H	Newcastle United (2 rep)	W	1-0	Carr	37434	1	3		6	5	8	7		9	10	11			2			4		3
4	21	A	Hull City (3)	D	1-1	Duncan / O'Brien	27000	1	3		6	5	8	7		9	10	11			2			4		4
5	26	H	Hull City (3 rep)	W	3-1	Chandler 3 / Hamilton	19864	1	3		6	5	8			9	10	11			2	7		4		5
6	Mar 7	A	Cardiff City (4)	L	1-2	Duncan / Beadles, W Davies	50272	1	3		6	5	8	7		9	10	11			2			4		6

Stand-in Goalkeepers: Sep 8, Watson for Godderidge, Chelsea (a); Sep 20, Osborne for Hebden (temporary), Coventry City (a).
Note: Feb 5, record attendance to date at Filbert Street.

1924-25
Carr, Godderidge, Chandler, Duncan, Adcock, Wadsworth, Newton, Hooper, Black, Carrigan, Bamber.

Season 1925-26

Champions: Huddersfield Town
Relegated: Manchester City, Notts County

FOOTBALL LEAGUE DIVISION ONE

Match No	Date		Opponents	Result	Points	Position	Scorers	Att
1	Aug 29	H	Liverpool	W 3-1	2	-	Chandler 2, Adcock / McKinlay	32000
2	31	A	Arsenal	D 2-2	3	-	Duncan 2 (1p) / Neil, Brain	23823
3	Sep 5	A	Burnley	L 0-4	3	12	- / Roberts 3, Beel	18372
4	7	H	Arsenal	L 0-1	3	13	- / Brain	25401
5	12	H	Leeds United	L 1-3	3	20	Chandler / Jennings, Turnbull 2	23592
6	16	A	Manchester United	L 2-3	3	20	Chandler, Duncan (p) / Rennox 2, Lochhead	21275
7	19	A	Newcastle United	L 2-3	3	21	Bamber 2 / Loughlin 3	31000
8	26	H	Bolton Wanderers	W 5-2	5	19	Chandler 2, Duncan 2, Wadsworth / JR Smith, D Jack	23820
9	Oct 3	A	Notts County	D 2-2	6	21	Chandler 2 / Davis, Newton (og)	34508
10	10	A	Aston Villa	L 1-2	6	21	Duncan (p) / Capewell, Walker	37483
11	17	H	West Bromwich Albion	W 3-0	8	18	Chandler, Lochhead 2	24500
12	24	A	Birmingham	D 1-1	9	18	Chandler / Islip	30000
13	31	H	Tottenham Hotspur	W 5-3	11	16	Chandler 2, Sharp, Lochhead, Wadsworth / Osborne 3	28076
14	Nov 7	A	Cardiff City	L 2-5	11	18	Chandler, Lochhead / Cassidy 3, W Davies, Ferguson	30000
15	14	H	Sunderland	W 4-1	13	16	Duncan 2, Chandler, Lochhead / Halliday	24000
16	21	A	Huddersfield Town	L 0-3	13	18	- / Brown 2, Williams	14386
17	28	H	Everton	D 1-1	14	18	Lochhead / Dean	20044
18	Dec 5	A	Manchester City	L 1-5	14	19	Chandler / Roberts 2, Johnson 2, Dennison	20000
19	12	H	Bury	L 0-2	14	21	- / Stage, Ball	18000
20	19	A	Blackburn Rovers	D 0-0	15	21		13679
21	25	A	Sheffield United	W 4-2	17	19	Lochhead 2, Adcock, Duncan / Waugh, Tunstall	28789
22	26	H	Sheffield United	D 2-2	18	19	Lochhead, Duncan / Johnson, Boyle	31958
23	28	H	Manchester United	L 1-3	18	19	Chandler / McPherson 3	28367
24	Jan 2	A	Liverpool	W 3-0	20	16	Lochhead, Adcock, Chandler	35000
25	16	H	Burnley	W 3-2	22	15	Chandler, Hine 2 / Roberts, Page	16423
26	23	A	Leeds United	L 0-1	22	16	- / Chadwick	19569
27	30	A	Everton	L 0-1	22	17	- / Watson (og)	31515
28	Feb 6	A	Bolton Wanderers	D 2-2	23	17	Chandler, Bamber / J Smith 2 (2p)	17939
29	13	H	Notts County	W 1-0	25	16	Chandler	30938
30	20	H	Blackburn Rovers	W 2-1	27	15	Chandler, Duncan / Mitchell	23612
31	22	H	Newcastle United	W 3-2	29	14	Chandler, Lochhead, Duncan / Gallacher 2	17000
32	27	A	West Bromwich Albion	L 1-3	29	15	Hine / Glidden (p), James, Byers	19532
33	Mar 6	H	Birmingham	W 1-0	31	13	Lochhead (p)	20000
34	10	A	Aston Villa	D 2-2	32	10	Hine, Lochhead / York 2	10000
35	13	A	Tottenham Hotspur	W 3-1	34	8	Lochhead, Hine, Chandler / Osborne	23911
36	20	H	Cardiff City	L 1-2	34	11	Chandler / W Davies 2	23000
37	27	A	Sunderland	L 0-3	34	12	- / Prior, Kelly, Halliday	12000
38	Apr 2	A	West Ham United	D 1-1	35	12	Lochhead / Watson	30000
39	3	H	Huddersfield Town	W 2-0	37	10	Bell, Hine	29903
40	5	H	West Ham United	D 1-1	38	10	Chandler / Campbell	20000
41	17	H	Manchester City	L 2-3	38	14	Hine, Chandler / Roberts 2, Browell	20000
42	24	A	Bury	L 0-4	38	17	- / Ball, Bullock, Amos 2	11878

Player appearances by match (shirt numbers)

Match No	Albert Godderidge	Adam Black	Harry Hooper	Billy Newton	Norman Watson	Jack Bamber	Hughie Adcock	John Duncan	Arthur Chandler	George Carr	Harold Wadsworth	Pat Carrigan	Reg Osborne	John Jarvie	Buchanan Sharp	Billy Findlay	Jack Brown	Arthur Lochhead	Kenny Campbell	Ernie Hine	Willie Webb	Billy Bell	Jimmy Baxter
1	1	2	3	4	5	6	7	8	9	10	11												
2	1	2	3	4	5	6	7	8	9	10	11												
3	1	2	3	4		6	7	8	9	10	11	5											
4	1	2	3	4		6	7	8	9	10	11	5											
5	1	2		4		6	7	8	9	10	11	5	3										
6		2		4	5	6	7	8	9		11		3			1		10					
7		2			5	6	7	8	9		11		3			1	4	10					
8		2		4	5	6	7	8	9		11		3			1		10					
9		2		4	5	6	7	8	9		11		3			1		10					
10		2		4	5	6	7	8	9		11			1				10					
11	1	2		4	5	6	7	8	9		11		3					10					
12	1	2		4	5	6	7	8	9		11		3					10					
13	1	2		4	5	6	7		9		11		3		8			10					
14	1	2		4	5	6	7	8	9		11		3					10					
15		2		4	5	6	7	8	9		11		3					10	1				
16		2		4	5	6	7	8	9		11		3					10	1				
17		2		4		6	7	8	9		11	5	3					10	1				
18		2		4		6	7		9		11	5	3		8			10	1				
19		2	3	4		6	7		9		11	5			8			10	1				
20		2		4	5	6	7	8	9		11		3					10	1				
21		2		4		6	7	8	9		11		3		5			10	1				
22		2		4		6	7	8	9		11		3		5			10	1				
23		2		4		6	7	8	9		11		3		5			10	1				
24		2		4	5	6	7	8	9		11		3					10	1				
25		2		4	5	6	7		9		11		3					10	1	8			
26		2		4	5	6	7		9		11		3					10	1	8			
27		2		4	5	6	7				11		10					9	1	8			
28		2			5	6	7		9				3	4				10	1	8	11		
29		2			5	6	7		9		11		3	4				10	1	8			
30		2			5	6	7	10	9				3	4				11	1	8			
31	1	2			5	6	7		9		11		3	4				10		8			
32		2			5	6	7		9				3	4				10	1	8			11
33		2			5	6	7		9				3	4				10	1	8		11	
34		2	3		5	6	7		9		11			4				10	1	8			
35		2			5	6	7		9		11		3	4				10	1	8			
36		2			5	6	7		9		11		3	4				10	1	8			
37		2	3		5	6			9				7	4				10	1	8			11
38		2			5	6			9				7	4		3		10	1	8			11
39		2			5	6			4				7			3		10	1	9		8	
40	1	2			5	6			9				7	4		3		10		8		11	
41		2			5	6			9				7	4		3		10	1	8		11	
42		2			5	6							7	4	8	3		10	1			9	11

Final League Position: 17	**League Appearances**	11	42	7	23	36	42	35	34	38	5	38	6	31	5	9	10	4	32	26	18	1	8	1
Average Home League Attendance: 24692	**League Goals**						3	3	12	26		2				1			15		7		1	

FA CUP

Match No	Date		Opponents	Result	Scorers	Att
1	Jan 9	A	Notts County (3)	L 0-2	- / Widdowson, Taylor	33495

FA Cup line-up (shirt numbers): Black 2, Newton 4, Watson 5, Bamber 6, Adcock 7, Duncan 8, Chandler 9, Wadsworth 11, Osborne 3, Lochhead 10, Campbell 1.

Note: Oct 10, record attendance to date at Filbert Street.

1925-26
(v Birmingham, 24 October 1925)
Back: Newton, Black, Godderidge, Bamber, Wadsworth, Gardner (Trainer).
Front: Watson, Adcock, Duncan, Chandler, Lochhead, Brown.

Season 1926-27

Champions: Newcastle United
Relegated: Leeds United, West Bromwich Albion

FOOTBALL LEAGUE DIVISION ONE

Match No	Date		Opponents	Result	Points	Position	Scorers	Att	Campbell	Black	Osborne	Duncan	Watson	Bamber	Adcock	Hine	Chandler	Carr	Bell	Lochhead	Carrigan	Brown	Moyes	Bishop	Lane	Godderidge	Wadsworth	Heathcock	Findlay	McLaren	Match No
1	Aug 28	A	West Ham United	D 3-3	1	-	Chandler 3 / Earle, Ruffell, Watson	20000	1	2	3	4	5	6	7	8	9	10	11												1
2	30	H	Birmingham	W 5-2	3	-	Bell, Lochhead, Chandler, Hine, Duncan / Bradford, Harris	25000	1	2	3	4	5	6	7	8	9		11	10											2
3	Sep 4	H	Sheffield Wednesday	W 5-3	5	3	Hine 3, Chandler, Bell / Trotter, Hill, Froggatt	24275	1	2	3	4	5	6	7	8	9		11	10											3
4	6	A	Tottenham Hotspur	D 2-2	6	2	Hine, Lochhead (p) / Dimmock 2	19461	1	2	3	4	5	6	7	8	9		11	10											4
5	11	A	Arsenal	D 2-2	7	3	Chandler, Lochhead (p) / Brain, Hulme	30800	1	2	3	4	5	6	7	8	9		11	10											5
6	13	H	Tottenham Hotspur	D 2-2	8	2	Chandler, Bell / Lane, Dimmock	24928	1	2	3	4	5	6	7	8	9		11	10											6
7	18	A	Everton	W 4-3	10	1	Chandler 2, Hine, Duncan / Irvine 2, Bain	29049	1	2	3	4			6	7	8	9	11	10					5						7
8	25	H	Blackburn Rovers	W 4-0	12	1	Lochhead, Hine, Duncan, Chandler	26087	1	2	3	4	5	6	7	8	9		11	10											8
9	Oct 2	A	Huddersfield Town	L 3-5	12	3	Bamber 2, Chandler / Brown 3, Slicer 2	25288	1	2	3	4	5	6	7	8	9		11	10											9
10	9	H	Sunderland	W 2-1	14	2	Chandler 2 / Coglin	30000	1	2	3	4	5	6	7	9	8		11	10											10
11	16	H	Leeds United	W 3-2	16	2	Carr 3 / Jennings 2 (1p)	27753	1		3	4	5	6	7	8		10	11	9	2										11
12	23	A	Liverpool	L 0-1	16	3	- / Chambers	35000	1			4	5	6	7	8		10	11	9	2	3									12
13	30	H	Sheffield United	D 2-2	17	3	Lochhead 2 (1p) / Green, Johnson	24748	1			4	5	6	7	9		10	11	8	2	3									13
14	Nov 6	A	Derby County	L 1-4	17	7	Lane / Bedford 2, Gill 2	22234	1					8	5	6	7	10		11	2	3	4		9						14
15	13	H	Manchester United	L 2-3	17	8	Lane, Hine / McPherson 2, Rennox	18521	1		3	4	5	6	7	8		10	11		2				9						15
16	20	A	Bolton Wanderers	L 0-2	17	10	- / Butler, D Jack	15255	1	2	3	4	5	6	7	8		10	11						9						16
17	27	H	Aston Villa	W 5-1	19	8	Chandler 5 / Walker	30000	1	2	3	4	5		7	8	9		11	10				6							17
18	Dec 4	A	Cardiff City	W 1-0	21	7	Lochhead	15000	1	2	3	4	5		7	8	9		11	10				6							18
19	11	H	Burnley	L 0-3	21	8	- / Beel, Page, Bruton	26591	1	2	3	4	5		7	9	8		11	10				6							19
20	18	A	Newcastle United	D 1-1	22	7	Chandler / Seymour	25000	1	2	3	4			7	9	8		11	10		5		6							20
21	25	H	West Bromwich Albion	W 5-0	24	6	Chandler 5	25017	1	2	3	4			7	8	9		11	10		5		6							21
22	27	A	West Bromwich Albion	W 1-0	26	5	Lochhead	31286	1	2	3	4			7	8	9		11	10		5		6							22
23	Jan 1	A	Birmingham	L 1-2	26	6	Cringan (og) / Bradford 2	34500		2	3	4			7	8	9			10		5		6		1	11				23
24	15	H	West Ham United	W 3-0	28	6	Adcock, Bishop, Hebden (og)	20000	1		3	4			7	8	9			10	2	5		6			11				24
25	22	A	Sheffield Wednesday	D 2-2	29	6	Chandler, Hine / Hill, Powell	19796	1		3	4	2		7	8	9			10		5		6			11				25
26	29	A	Sunderland	L 0-3	29	6	- / Halliday 2, Gurney	20000	1		3	4	2		7	8	9			10		5		6			11				26
27	Feb 5	H	Everton	W 6-2	31	5	Chandler, Wadsworth 2, Hine 2, Lochhead / Dean 2	21369	1	2	3	4			7	8	9			10		5		6			11				27
28	10	H	Arsenal	W 2-1	33	5	Adcock, Bishop / Brain	16736	1	2	3	4	5		7	8	9			10				6			11				28
29	12	A	Blackburn Rovers	L 1-2	33	5	Lochhead (p) / Harper 2	17802	1	2	3	4	5		7	8	9			10				6			11				29
30	19	H	Huddersfield Town	L 2-4	33	5	Wadsworth, Duncan / W Smith, Devlin, Brown, Osborne (og)	34142		2	3	4			7	8	9			10		5		6		1	11				30
31	Mar 5	A	Leeds United	D 1-1	34	7	Bishop / Jennings	21420	1		3	4	5		7	8	9	10			2			6			11				31
32	12	H	Liverpool	W 3-2	36	6	Wadsworth, Hine, Chandler / Reid 2	25000	1		3	4	5		7	8	9	10			2			6			11				32
33	19	A	Sheffield United	W 3-0	38	6	Hine, Heathcock 2	20504	1		3	4	5		7	8		10			2			6			11	9			33
34	26	H	Derby County	D 1-1	39	6	Duncan / Whitehouse	25391	1		3	4	5		7	8	9	10			2			6			11				34
35	Apr 2	A	Manchester United	L 0-1	39	6	- / Spence	17119	1		3	4	5		7	8	9	10			2						11		6		35
36	7	H	Cardiff City	W 3-1	41	5	Hine 2, Chandler / Ferguson	12000	1		3	4		6	7	8	9	10			2			5			11				36
37	9	H	Bolton Wanderers	L 0-1	41	5	- / Blackmore	20768	1		3	4		6	7	8	9	10			2			5			11				37
38	15	A	Bury	D 0-0	42	5		19755	1		3	4	5		7	8	9	10			2			6			11				38
39	16	A	Aston Villa	L 0-2	42		- / Cook, Johnstone	34000	1		3	4	5		7	8	9	10			2			6			11				39
40	18	H	Bury	D 1-1	43	7	Hine / Ball	22000	1		3	4	5		7	8	9	10			2			6			11				40
41	30	A	Burnley	D 1-1	44	7	Lochhead / Page	11072	1		3	4	5		7	8			11	10	2			6			9				41
42	May 7	H	Newcastle United	W 2-1	46	7	Lochhead 2 (1p) / Low	26621			3	4	5		7	8	9		11	10	2			6						1	42

									Campbell	Black	Osborne	Duncan	Watson	Bamber	Adcock	Hine	Chandler	Carr	Bell	Lochhead	Carrigan	Brown	Moyes	Bishop	Lane	Godderidge	Wadsworth	Heathcock	Findlay	McLaren	
Final League Position:			7				**League Appearances**		39	23	38	42	34	16	42	39	34	19	23	29	10	18	3	26	4	2	18	1	1	1	
Average Home League Attendance:			23718				**League Goals**			5		2	2		16	28	3	3	13			3	2			4	2				

FA CUP

Match No	Date		Opponents	Result			Scorers	Att	Campbell	Black	Osborne	Duncan	Watson	Bamber	Adcock	Hine	Chandler	Carr	Bell	Lochhead	Carrigan	Brown	Moyes	Bishop	Lane	Godderidge	Wadsworth	Heathcock	Findlay	McLaren	Match No
1	Jan 8	A	Middlesbrough (3)	L 3-5			Duncan, Hine, Chandler / O Williams, Pease, Birrell 2, Camsell	30000	1		3	4	2		7	8	9			10		5		6			11				1

1926-27
Back: McLachlan, Bamber, Brown, Godderidge, Campbell, Findlay, Gibbs, Webb.
Middle: Fox (Masseur), Smith (Asst Secretary), Carrigan, Watson, Carr, Viner, Lochhead, Osborne, Garner, Gouch, King (Coach).
Front: Nixon (Asst Trainer), Moyes, Adcock, Hine, Chandler, Duncan, Bell, Bishop, Heathcock, Hackett, Gardner (Trainer).

Champions: Everton
Relegated: Tottenham Hotspur, Middlesbrough

FOOTBALL LEAGUE DIVISION ONE

Match No	Date		Opponents	Result	Points	Position	Scorers	Att	McLaren	Brown	Osborne	Duncan	Carrigan	Bishop	Adcock	Hine	Chandler	Lochhead	Bell	Black	Findlay	Watson	Carr	Barry	Baxter	Lane	Gibson	Campbell	Callachan	Russell	Match No
1	Aug 27	A	Aston Villa	W 3-0	2	-	Adcock, Bishop, Bell	45000	1	2	3	4	5	6	7	8	9	10	11												1
2	29	H	Sheffield United	W 3-1	4	-	Duncan, Hine, Adcock / Johnson	27117	1		3	4	5	6	7	8	9	10	11	2											2
3	Sep 3	H	Sunderland	D 3-3	5	2	Lochhead 2, Chandler / Halliday 2, Ellis	30000	1		3	4	5	6	7	8	9	10	11	2											3
4	5	A	Sheffield United	D 1-1	6	1	Chandler / Johnson	13096	1		3	4	5	6	7	8	9	10	11	2											4
5	10	A	Derby County	L 1-2	6	4	Chandler / Gill, Whitehouse	26008	1		3	4	5		7	8	9	10	11	2			6								5
6	17	H	West Ham United	L 2-3	6	10	Chandler, Adcock / Yews, Ruffell, Earle	30000	1		3	4		6	7	8	9	10	11	2			5								6
7	22	H	Tottenham Hotspur	L 1-2	6	12	Hine / Osborne, Blair	9436	1		3				7	8	9	10	11	2	4		5								7
8	24	A	Portsmouth	L 0-2	6	14	- / Forward, Watson	25000	1		3	4		6	7	8	9	10		2			5	11							8
9	Oct 1	H	Manchester United	W 1-0	8	11	Adcock	22385	1		3				7	8	9	10		2	4	6	5	11							9
10	8	H	Liverpool	D 1-1	9	10	Hine / Hodgson	30000	1		3				7	8	9	10		2	4	6	5	11							10
11	15	A	Arsenal	D 2-2	10	10	Adcock, Hine / Brain, Hoar	36640	1		3				7	8	9	10		2	4	6	5	11							11
12	22	A	Blackburn Rovers	D 0-0	11	9		11115	1		3				7	8	9	10		2	4	6	5	11							12
13	29	H	Cardiff City	W 4-1	13	8	Lochhead, Hine 2, Chandler / Smith	26000	1		3				7	8	9	10		2	4	6	5	11							13
14	Nov 5	A	Everton	L 1-7	13	11	Chandler / Dean 3, Weldon 2, Critchley, Troup	30392	1		3		5		7	8	9	10		2	4	6		11							14
15	12	A	Bolton Wanderers	W 4-2	15	8	Lochhead 2, Hine, Chandler / Wright, Blackmore	21249	1		3			6	7	8	9	10		2	4		5	11							15
16	19	H	Sheffield Wednesday	W 2-1	17	5	Chandler, Hine / Trotter	15969	1		3				7	8	9	10		2	4	6	5	11							16
17	26	H	Newcastle United	W 3-0	19	3	Chandler 2, Lochhead	33375	1		3				7	8	9	10		2	4	6	5	11							17
18	Dec 3	A	Birmingham	W 2-0	21	3	Lochhead, Hine	15000	1		3				7	8	9	10		2	4		5	11	6						18
19	10	H	Middlesbrough	D 3-3	22	4	Chandler 2, Lochhead / Pease, Camsell 2	26815	1		3				7	8	9	10		2	4		5	11	6						19
20	17	A	Huddersfield Town	L 1-3	22	5	Chandler / Brown 2, R Kelly	13717	1		3				7	8	9	10		2	4		5	11	6						20
21	24	H	Tottenham Hotspur	W 6-1	24	2	Bishop, Chandler 3, Lochhead, Adcock / Handley	19987	1		3			6	7	8	9	10		2	4		5	11							21
22	26	H	Burnley	W 5-0	26	2	Adcock, Bishop, Lochhead 2, Hine	20063	1		3			6	7	8	9	10		2	4		5	11							22
23	27	A	Burnley	L 1-5	26	3	McCluggage (og) / Beel 2, Page 2, P Dougall	24824	1		3			6	7	8	9	10		2	4		5	11							23
24	31	A	Aston Villa	W 3-0	28	3	Hine 2, Chandler	25000	1		3			6	7	8	9	10		2	4		5	11							24
25	Jan 2	A	Bury	L 1-2	28	3	Chandler / Chambers, Ball	15902	1		3			6	7	8	9	10		2	4		5	11							25
26	7	A	Sunderland	D 2-2	29	3	Lochhead, Barry / Ramsay, Halliday	20000	1		3			6	7	8	9	10		2	4		5	11							26
27	21	H	Derby County	W 4-0	31	3	Chandler 2, Lochhead, Adcock	36094	1		3	4		6	7	8	9	10		2			5	11							27
28	Feb 4	A	Portsmouth	W 6-2	33	3	Lochhead 2, Hine, Chandler 2, Barry / Watson 2	25000	1		3	4		6	7	8	9	10		2			5	11							28
29	11	A	Manchester United	L 2-5	33	3	Chandler, Duncan / Nicol 2, Spence 2, Hanson	16640	1		3	4			7	8	9	10		2		6	5	11							29
30	25	H	Arsenal	W 3-2	35	3	Bishop, Adcock, Duncan / Hoar, Buchan	25835	1		3	4		6	7	8	9	10		2			5	11							30
31	Mar 10	A	Cardiff City	L 0-3	35	5	- / Ferguson 2, McLachlan	15000	1		3			6	7	8		10		2	4		5	11			9				31
32	12	A	West Ham United	L 0-4	35	5	- / Watson 3, Yews	6211	1		3				7	8	9			2	4		5	11		10					32
33	17	H	Everton	W 1-0	37	4	Adcock	26625	1		3	4		6	7	8		10		2			5	11							33
34	24	A	Bolton Wanderers	D 3-3	38	3	Hine 2, Chandler / McClelland 2, Butler	18142	1		3	4		6	7	8	9	10		2			5	11							34
35	31	H	Sheffield Wednesday	D 2-2	39	3	Hine, Chandler / Prince, Trotter	18634	1		3			6	7	8	9	10		2	4		5	11							35
36	Apr 7	A	Newcastle United	W 5-1	41	3	Chandler 4, Hine / Chalmers	32492						6	7	8	9	10		2	4		5	11				1	3		36
37	9	H	Bury	D 2-2	42	3	Hine, Lochhead / T Bradshaw, Robbie	25000						6	7	8	9	10		2	4		5	11				1	3		37
38	14	H	Birmingham	W 3-0	44	3	Barry, Chandler, Hine	15000						6	7	8	9	10		2			5	11				1	3	4	38
39	21	A	Middlesbrough	D 1-1	45	3	Carr / Pease	18854			3			6	7	8	9	10		2	4		5	11				1			39
40	25	A	Liverpool	D 1-1	46	3	Chandler / Reid	30000			3	4		6	7	8	9	10		2			5	11			8	1			40
41	28	A	Huddersfield Town	L 1-2	46	3	Carr / Raw, Barkas (p)	29191			3	4		6	7	8	9	10		2			5	11				1			41
42	30	H	Blackburn Rovers	W 6-0	48	3	Hine, Chandler 3, Barry, Lochhead	14914	1		3			6	7	8	9	10		2	4		5	11							42
			League Appearances						36	8	32	21	6	23	42	41	41	41	7	41	28	10	35	34	3	1	2	6	3	1	
			League Goals									3		4	10	20	34	17	1				2	4							

Final League Position: 3

Average Home League Attendance: 24758

FA CUP

	Date		Opponents	Result			Scorers	Att	McLaren	Brown	Osborne	Duncan	Carrigan	Bishop	Adcock	Hine	Chandler	Lochhead	Bell	Black	Findlay	Watson	Carr	Barry							
1	Jan 14	A	Hull City (3)	W 1-0			Barry	23141	1		3	4		6	7	8	9	10		2			5	11							1
2	28	A	Reading (4)	W 1-0			Adcock	27243	1		3	4		6	7	8	9	10		2			5	11							2
3	Feb 18	H	Tottenham Hotspur (5)	L 0-3			- / O'Callaghan 2, Dimmock	47298	1		3	4		6	7	8	9	10		2			5	11							3

Note: Feb 18, all time record attendance at Filbert Street.

1927-28

Back: Lane, Callachan, Osborne, McLaren, Campbell, Brown, Carrigan, Bishop. **Middle:** Smith (Secretary), Gibbs, Smith, Findlay, Black, Watson, Orr (Manager), Chandler, Barry, Baxter, Garner, King (Coach). **Front:** Nixon (Asst Trainer), Bell, Carr, Adcock, Hine, Gibson, Lochhead, Heathcock, Hackett, Gouch, Gardner (Trainer).

Champions: Sheffield Wednesday
Relegated: Bury, Cardiff City

FOOTBALL LEAGUE DIVISION ONE

Match No	Date	H/A	Opponents	Result	Pts	Pos	Scorers	Att	Kenny Campbell	Adam Black	Jack Brown	Billy Findlay	George Carr	John Duncan	Hughie Adcock	Ernie Hine	Arthur Chandler	Arthur Lochhead	Len Barry	Reg Osborne	Jimmy Baxter	Tom Gibson	Jim McLaren	Norman Watson	George Ritchie	Pat Carrigan	Billy Bell	Walter Langford	Harry Lovatt	Match No
1	Aug 25	A	Manchester United	D 1-1	1	-	Hine / Rawlings	20129	1	2	3	4	5	6	7	8	9	10	11											1
2	27	H	Birmingham	W 5-3	3	-	Hine, Chandler 2, Lochhead 2 / Briggs, Crosbie, Ellis	20000	1	2	3	4	5	6	7	8	9	10	11											2
3	Sep 1	H	Leeds United	D 4-4	4	6	Barry, Hine, Chandler 2 / Keetley 2, Turnbull, Armand	27507	1	2	3	4	5	6	7	8	9	10	11											3
4	8	A	Liverpool	L 3-6	4	12	Baxter, Chandler, Gibson / Edmed, Done, McDougall, Reid, Hodgson 2	25000	1	2			5	4	7	8	9		11		3	6	10							4
5	10	A	Birmingham	L 0-1	4	14	- / Briggs	20000	1	2			5	4	7	8	9		11		3	6	10							5
6	15	H	West Ham United	W 5-0	6	11	Barry, Chandler 2, Lochhead, Hine	25000		2			5	4	7	8	9	10	11		3	6		1						6
7	22	A	Newcastle United	L 0-1	6	14	- / Hudspeth	30816		2				4	7	8	9	10	11		3	6	5	1						7
8	29	H	Burnley	D 1-1	7	14	Chandler / Beel	26506		2			5	4	7	8	9	10	11		3	6		1						8
9	Oct 6	A	Cardiff City	W 2-1	9	12	Carr, Hine / Harris	15000		2		4	10		7	8	9		11		3	6	5	1						9
10	13	H	Sheffield United	W 3-1	11	9	Chandler 2, Hine / Phillipson	25438		2		4	10		7	8	9		11		3	6	5	1						10
11	20	H	Portsmouth	W 10-0	13	5	Hine 3, Barry, Chandler 6	25000		2	3	4	5		7	8	9	10	11			6		1						11
12	27	A	Manchester City	W 3-2	15	5	Lochhead, Adcock, Hine / Roberts 2	30000		2	3	4	5		7	8	9	10	11			6		1						12
13	Nov 3	H	Sheffield Wednesday	D 1-1	16	5	Hine / Allen	29522		2	3	4	5		7	8	9	10	11			6		1						13
14	10	A	Derby County	L 2-5	16	5	Hine, Lochhead / Whitehouse 2, McIntyre, Stephenson, JC Robson	24673		2	3	4	5		7	8	9	10	11			6		1						14
15	17	H	Sunderland	W 1-0	18	4	Chandler	25000		2	3	4	5	8	7		9	10	11			6		1						15
16	24	A	Blackburn Rovers	D 1-1	19	5	Chandler / Puddefoot	10831		2	3	4	5		7	8	9	10				6		1				11		16
17	Dec 1	H	Arsenal	D 1-1	20	4	Hine / Brain	26851	1	2	3	4	5		7	8	9	10				6						11		17
18	8	A	Everton	L 1-3	20	7	Chandler / Dean, Martin, Troup	25226		2	3	4	5		7	8	9	10	11			6		1						18
19	15	H	Huddersfield Town	W 4-1	22	5	Hine 2, Chandler 2 / Jackson	19528		2	3	4	5		7	8	9	10	11			6		1						19
20	22	A	Bolton Wanderers	L 0-5	22	6	- / Butler, McClelland, Gibson, Blackmore 2	16030		2	3	4	5		7	8	9	10	11			6		1						20
21	25	A	Bury	L 1-3	22	8	Chandler / Ball, Gayle, Amos	19805		2	3		5	4	7	8	9	10	11			6		1						21
22	26	H	Bury	W 5-2	24	6	Hine 3, Adcock, Lochhead / Gale, Amos	30000		2	3		5	4	7	8	9	10	11			6		1						22
23	29	H	Manchester United	W 2-1	26	5	Hine 2 / Hanson	21535		2	3		5		7	8	9	10	11			6	4	1						23
24	Jan 5	A	Leeds United	L 3-4	26	10	Chandler, Lochhead, Hine / Keetley 3, Turnbull	18870		2	3		5		7	8	9	10	11			6	4	1						24
25	19	H	Liverpool	W 2-0	28	7	Hine 2 (1p)	28000		2	3		5		7	8	9	10	11			6	4	1						25
26	Feb 2	H	Newcastle United	D 1-1	29	8	Adcock / Gallacher	20796		2	3		5		7	8	9		11			6	4	1			10			26
27	9	A	Burnley	W 1-0	31	6	Chandler	14879		2	3		5	4	7	8	9		11			6		1			10			27
28	21	H	Cardiff City	W 2-0	33	5	Lovatt, Hine (p)	21000		2	3			4	7	8		10	11			6	5	1					9	28
29	23	A	Sheffield United	W 4-1	35	5	Lochhead, Chandler 2, Hine / S Gibson	19045		2	3			4		8	9	10	11			6		1	5				7	29
30	Mar 4	A	West Ham United	L 1-2	35	6	Lovatt / Ruffell, Earle	10000		2	3			4		8	9	10	11			6		1	5				7	30
31	9	H	Manchester City	W 3-2	37	3	Hine 2, Lochhead / Johnson, Tilson	15000		2	3		5	4	7	8	9	10	11			6		1						31
32	16	A	Sheffield Wednesday	L 0-1	37	5	- / Allen	30176		2	3		5	4	7	8	9	10	11			6		1						32
33	23	H	Derby County	W 1-0	39	3	Hine	23622		2	3		5	4	7	8	9	10	11			6		1						33
34	30	A	Sunderland	W 2-1	41	3	Lochhead, Chandler / McLean	18000		2	3	4	5	8	7		9	10	11			6		1						34
35	Apr 1	H	Aston Villa	W 4-1	43	2	Adcock (p), Lochhead, Duncan, Chandler / Capewell	21000		2	3		5	8	7		9	10	11			6	4	1						35
36	2	A	Aston Villa	L 2-4	43	3	Chandler 2 / Walker 2, Chester, Waring	26000		2	3		5	8	7		9	10	11			6	4	1						36
37	6	H	Blackburn Rovers	W 2-1	45	2	Chandler 2 / Rigby	19328	1	2	3	4	5	8	7		9	10	11			6								37
38	10	A	Portsmouth	L 0-1	45	2	- / Weddle	21000		2	3	4	5	8	7		9	10	11			6		1						38
39	13	A	Arsenal	D 1-1	46	2	Chandler / Parker (p)	19139		2	3	4	5	8	7		9	10	11			6		1						39
40	20	H	Everton	W 4-1	48	2	Chandler, Hine 2, Lochhead / White	19006		2	3		5	4	7	8	9	10	11			6		1						40
41	27	A	Huddersfield Town	D 1-1	49	2	Duncan / Brown	8778		2	3		5	4	7	8	9	10	11			6		1						41
42	May 4	H	Bolton Wanderers	W 6-1	51	2	Lochhead, Lovatt 3, Hine 2 / Blackmore	19912		2	3		5	4	7	8		10	11			6		1					9	42

Final League Position:	2	**League Appearances**	8 40 31 19 39 27 40 35 40 36 12 2 2 34 16 28 5 2 2 4
Average Home League Attendance:	23773	**League Goals**	1 2 4 32 34 13 3 1 1 5

FA CUP

Match No	Date	H/A	Opponents	Result	Scorers	Att	Black	Brown	Carr	Duncan	Adcock	Hine	Chandler	Lochhead	Barry	Gibson	McLaren	Watson	Match No
1	Jan 12	A	Lincoln City (3)	W 1-0	Lochhead	16849	2	3	5		7	8	9	10	11	6	4	1	1
2	26	H	Swansea Town (4)	W 1-0	Lochhead	39188	2	3	5		7	8	9	10	11	6	4	1	2
3	Feb 16	H	Bolton Wanderers (5)	L 1-2	Lochhead / Seddon, Blackmore	30591	2	3	5	4	7	8	9	10	11	6		1	3

1928-29 (v Birmingham, 10 September 1928)
Back: Carr, Black, Campbell, Osborne, Watson, Gibson.
Front: Adcock, Baxter, Hine, Chandler, Duncan, Barry.

1928-29
Back: High, J Smith, Brown, A Smith, Campbell, G Smith (Asst Secretary), McLaren, Callachan, Wiggins, Carrigan.
Middle: Fox (Masseur), Chandler, Langford, Black, Osborne, Watson, Orr (Manager), Garner, Carr, Raynor, Cairns, Bushell, Gardner (Trainer).
Front: Nixon (Asst Trainer), Lochhead, Findlay, Hine, Duncan, Adcock, Lovatt, Barry, Bell, King (Coach). **On Ground:** Wyness, Baxter.

1929-30
Back: Callachan, Lovatt, Nixon (Asst Trainer), Wiggins, McLaren, Carrigan, Wright, Brown, Raynor.
Middle: King (Coach), Fox (Masseur), J Smith, Black, Orr (Manager), Watson, Osborne, Smith (Asst Secretary), Gardiner (Trainer).
Front: Ritchie, Adcock, Hine, Duncan, Chandler, Carr, Findlay, Barry.
On Ground: Bell, Garner, Bushell, Langford, S Smith, Woolliscroft.

Season 1929-30

Champions: Sheffield Wednesday
Relegated: Burnley, Everton

FOOTBALL LEAGUE DIVISION ONE

Match No	Date		Opponents	Result	Points	Position	Scorers	Att	Jim McLaren	Adam Black	Jack Brown	John Duncan	George Carr	George Ritchie	Hughie Adcock	Ernie Hine	Arthur Chandler	Sep Smith	Len Barry	Joe Wright	Pat Carrigan	Walter Langford	Norman Watson	Harry Lovatt	Arthur Lochhead	Billy Findlay	Willie Bushell	Arthur Woolliscroft	Albert Harrison	Aubrey Mandy	Billy Bell	Reg Osborne	John Beby	Roger Heywood	Match No
1	Aug 31	A	Huddersfield Town	L 2-3		-	Chandler 2 / Dent, Smith, Jackson	16646	1	2	3	4	5	6	7	8	9	10	11																1
2	Sep 2	H	Manchester United	W 4-1	2	-	Hine 2, Carr, Chandler / Rowley	20490		2	3	4	10	6	7	8	9		11	1	5														2
3	7	H	Sheffield United	D 3-3	3	10	Chandler 3 / Dunne 3	26141	1	2	3	4	10	6	7	8	9		11		5														3
4	11	A	Manchester United	L 1-2	3	12	Barry / Ball, Spence	16445		2	3	4	5	6	7	8	9		11	1		10													4
5	14	A	Newcastle United	L 1-2	3	15	Hine / Gallacher 2 (1p)	29791		2	3	4	10	6	7	8	9		11	1				5											5
6	21	H	Blackburn Rovers	D 1-1	4	18	Chandler / Groves	22793	1	2	3	4	5	6	7	8	10		11				9												6
7	28	A	Middlesbrough	W 2-0	6	17	Adcock, Chandler	26851		2	3	4	5	6	7	8	9		11	1					10										7
8	Oct 5	H	Liverpool	W 2-1	8	13	Lochhead, Hine / Smith	20000		2	3	4	5	6	7	8	9		11	1					10										8
9	12	A	West Ham United	W 2-1	10	9	Hine, Barry / Watson	30000		2	3	4	5	6	7	8	9		11	1					10										9
10	17	H	Birmingham	W 2-1	12	5	Chandler, Bushell / Curtis	20000		2	3	8	5	6			9		11	1					10	4	7								10
11	19	A	Aston Villa	L 0-3	12	7	- / Brown 2, Tate	40000		2	3	8	5	6			9		11	1					10	4	7								11
12	26	H	Leeds United	D 2-2	13	6	Hine, Lochhead / Mitchell, Mangnall	27242		2	3	4			7	8	9		11	1	5		6		10										12
13	Nov 2	A	Sheffield Wednesday	L 0-4	13	9	- / Allen 3, Burgess	19159		2	3	4					9		11	1	5		6		10			7	8						13
14	9	H	Portsmouth	L 0-5	13	15	- / Forward 2, J Smith, Weddle, Cook	20000		2	3		5		7	8	9		11	1					10	4									14
15	16	A	Sunderland	L 1-2	13	18	Hine / Clunas, Gunson	18000	1	2	3	4	5	6	7	8			11					9	10										15
16	23	H	Bolton Wanderers	W 5-2	15	12	Lovatt 3, Adcock, Duncan / Butler, Blackmore	15330	1	2	3	4		6	7	8			11					10	5	9									16
17	30	A	Everton	W 5-4	17	10	Langford 2, Lovatt, Barry, Adcock / Rigby 2, Martin, White	18836	1	2	3	4		6	7				11					10	5	9	8								17
18	Dec 7	H	Derby County	D 0-0	18	9		25363	1	2	3	4		6	7	8			11					9	10				5						18
19	14	A	Manchester City	L 2-3	18	12	Chandler 2 / Johnson 2, Brook	10000	1	2	3	4		6	7	8	9		11						10				5						19
20	21	H	Burnley	W 4-3	20	10	Hine 2, Chandler, Duncan / McCluggage, Devine, Heslop	16188	1	2	3	4		6	7	8	9		11						10				5						20
21	25	A	Grimsby Town	W 4-1	22	7	Hine 2, Chandler, Lochhead / Barley	16173	1	2	3	4	5	6	7	8	9		11						10										21
22	26	H	Grimsby Town	W 1-0	24	6	Chandler	35644		2	3	4	5	6	7	8	9		11						10					1					22
23	28	H	Huddersfield Town	L 1-2	24	8	Adcock / Raw 2	23463		2	3	4	5	6	7	8	9		11						10						1	11			23
24	Jan 4	A	Sheffield United	L 1-7	24	13	Lochhead / Dunne 4, Pickering, Phillipson, S Gibson	22637		2	3	4		6	7	8	9		11						10				5	1					24
25	18	H	Newcastle United	W 6-1	26	10	Chandler 3, Hine 2, Langford / Hutchinson	15000	1	2		4		6	7	8	9		11			10							5			3			25
26	27	A	Blackburn Rovers	L 1-3	26	11	Adcock / McLean, Cunliffe 2	10444	1	2		4		6	7	8	9		11			10							5			3			26
27	Feb 1	H	Middlesbrough	W 4-1	28	9	Chandler 2, Hine 2 / Camsell	19057	1	2		4			7	8	9		11				6		10				5			3			27
28	8	A	Liverpool	D 1-1	29	9	Lochhead / Hodgson	30000	1	2		4			7	8	9		11				6		10				5			3			28
29	15	A	Burnley	D 1-1	30	7	Chandler / Page	10717	1	2		4			7	8	9		11				6		10				5			3			29
30	20	A	West Ham United	L 1-2	30	8	Lochhead / Watson, Wood	10000	1	2		4			7	8	9		11				6		10				5			3			30
31	22	H	Aston Villa	W 4-3	32	7	Chandler 3, Lochhead / Houghton, York 2	17000	1	2	3	4			7	8	9		11				6		10				5						31
32	Mar 1	A	Leeds United	W 2-1	34	5	Hine 2 / Jennings	18486	1	2	3	4			7	8	9		11				6		10				5						32
33	8	H	Sheffield Wednesday	W 2-1	36	5	Hine, Chandler / Marsden	29664	1	2	3	4			7	8	9		11				6		10				5						33
34	15	A	Portsmouth	L 0-3	36	6	- / Nichol, Weddle, Easson	20000		2	3	4			7	8	9		11	1			6		10				5						34
35	22	H	Sunderland	L 1-2	36	7	Chandler / Eden, McLean	18000		2	3	4			7	8	9		11	1			6		10				5						35
36	29	A	Bolton Wanderers	L 0-1	36	8	- / Wright	13644	1	2	3	4			7	8	9		11				6		10				5						36
37	Apr 5	H	Everton	W 5-4	38	8	Lochhead, Chandler 3, Barry / Martin 2, Critchley, Johnson	13897	1	2	3	4			7	8	9		11				6		10				5						37
38	12	A	Derby County	D 2-2	39	9	Chandler 2 / Bedford, Davison	19044	1	2	3	4			7	8	9		11				6		10				5						38
39	18	A	Arsenal	D 1-1	40	8	Chandler / James	46663	1	2	3			4	7	8	9		11				6		10				5						39
40	19	H	Manchester City	W 3-1	42	5	Duncan, Hine, Chandler / Tait	10000		2	3	4			7	8	9		11	1			6		10				5						40
41	21	H	Arsenal	D 6-6	43	5	Adcock 2, Lochhead 2, Hine, Barry / Halliday 4, Bastin 2	27241		2	3	4			7	8	9		11	1			6		10				5						41
42	May 3	A	Birmingham	L 0-3	43	8	- / Bradford 3	9340		2	3	4			7	8	9		11				6		10								1	5	42

									Jim McLaren	Adam Black	Jack Brown	John Duncan	George Carr	George Ritchie	Hughie Adcock	Ernie Hine	Arthur Chandler	Sep Smith	Len Barry	Joe Wright	Pat Carrigan	Walter Langford	Norman Watson	Harry Lovatt	Arthur Lochhead	Billy Findlay	Willie Bushell	Arthur Woolliscroft	Albert Harrison	Aubrey Mandy	Billy Bell	Reg Osborne	John Beby	Roger Heywood	
Final League Position:		8					**League Appearances**		23	42	36	40	16	24	39	38	38	1	41	15	4	5	22	5	33	3	3	1	21	3	1	6	1	1	
Average Home League Attendance:		21344					**League Goals**						3	1	7	20	32		5			3		4	10				1						

FA CUP

Match No	Date		Opponents	Result		Scorers	Att	Jim McLaren	Adam Black	Jack Brown	John Duncan	George Carr	George Ritchie	Hughie Adcock	Ernie Hine	Arthur Chandler	Sep Smith	Len Barry						Arthur Lochhead				Albert Harrison						Match No
1	Jan 11	A	Sheffield United (3)	L 1-2		Hine / S Gibson, Dunne	31476	1	2	3	4		6	7	8	9		11						10				5						1

1929-30
(v Arsenal, 18 April 1930)
Back: Watson, Carr, Lochhead, Brown, McLaren, Harrison, Black, Gardner (Trainer).
Front: Adcock, Hine, Chandler, Ritchie, Barry.

Season 1930-31

Champions: Arsenal
Relegated: Leeds United, Manchester United

FOOTBALL LEAGUE DIVISION ONE

Match No	Date		Opponents	Result	Points	Position	Scorers	Att	Jim McLaren	Adam Black	Jack Brown	George Ritchie	Albert Harrison	Norman Watson	Hughie Adcock	Ernie Hine	Arthur Chandler	Arthur Lochhead	Len Barry	John Beby	Reg Osborne	George Carr	Sep Smith	Roger Heywood	Jim Bulling	Harry Lovatt	Billy Findlay	Percy Richards	George Dumbrell	Joe Wiggins	Match No
1	Aug 30	H	Derby County	D 1-1	1	-	Ritchie / Stephenson	20824	1	2	3	4	5	6	7	8	9	10	11												1
2	Sep 1	H	Birmingham	W 2-1	3	-	Chandler, Hine / Briggs	15000		2	3	4	5	6	7	8	9	10	11	1											2
3	6	A	Manchester City	W 2-0	5	3	Chandler, Cowan (og)	25000		2	3	4	5	6	7	8	9	10	11	1											3
4	8	H	Sheffield United	D 2-2	6	3	Adcock, Hine / Dunne, Gillespie	15352		2	3	4	5	6	7	8	9	10	11	1											4
5	13	H	Portsmouth	W 3-1	8	3	Chandler, Lochhead 2 / Easson	15000		2	3	6	5	4	7	8	9	10	11	1											5
6	20	A	Arsenal	L 1-4	8	7	Hine / Hulme, Lambert 2, Bastin	37851		2	3	6	5	4	7	8	9	10	11	1											6
7	24	A	Sheffield United	W 2-0	10	5	Chandler, Lochhead	13293	1	2	3	6	5	4	7	8	9	10	11												7
8	27	H	Blackburn Rovers	W 3-1	12	5	Chandler, Adcock 2 / Imrie (p)	18820	1	2	3	6	5	4	7	8	9	10	11												8
9	Oct 4	A	Blackpool	L 4-5	12	6	Lochhead, Hine 2, Harrison / Hampson 3, Oxberry, Upton	24105	1	2	3	6	5	4	7	8	9	10	11												9
10	11	H	Leeds United	W 4-0	14	4	Hine 3 (1p), Chandler	19405	1	2		6		4	7	8	9		11		3	5	10								10
11	18	A	Huddersfield Town	L 1-4	14	6	Adcock / Smith, Davies 2, Crownshaw	15125	1	2		6		4	7	8	9		11		3	5	10								11
12	25	H	Aston Villa	W 4-1	16	5	Smith, Hine 3 / Waring	37483	1	2		6	5	4	7	8	9		11		3		10								12
13	Nov 1	A	Grimsby Town	L 2-8	16	7	Chandler, Watson / Coleman 4, Prior 2, Priestley, Fielding	9868	1	2		6	5	4	7	8	9	10	11		3										13
14	8	H	Manchester United	W 5-4	18	6	Lochhead 2, Hine 2, Chandler / Bullock 3, McLachlan	17466		2		6		4	7	8	9	10	11	1	3			5							14
15	15	A	Liverpool	L 1-3	18	8	Lochhead / Smith 2, Black (og)	20000		2				4	7	8	9	10	11	1	3		5	6							15
16	22	H	Sheffield Wednesday	L 2-5	18	8	Chandler 2 / Ball 3, Burgess 2	18794		2				4	7	8	9	10	11	1	3		5	6							16
17	29	A	West Ham United	L 0-2	18	9	- / Ruffell 2	25000		2				4	7	8		10	11	1	3		5	6			9				17
18	Dec 6	A	Middlesbrough	L 0-3	18	11	- / Warren, Cameron, Camsell	14467		2	3			4	7	8	9		11	1			10	5			6				18
19	13	A	Newcastle United	L 2-5	18	12	Ritchie, Lochhead / Bedford, Boyd, Hutchinson 2, Black (og)	25000		2	3	6			7	8	9	10	11	1		5					4				19
20	20	H	Bolton Wanderers	W 2-1	20	11	Chandler 2 / Blackmore	12660		2	3	6			7	8	9	10	11	1		5					4				20
21	25	A	Sunderland	W 5-2	22	7	Hine 3, Barry 2 / Eden, Leonard	25000		2	3	6			7	8	9	10	11	1		5					4				21
22	26	H	Sunderland	D 1-1	23	7	Hine / Gallacher	25000		2	3	6			7	8	9	10	11	1		5					4				22
23	27	A	Derby County	L 0-1	23	12	- / Ramage	19706		2	3	6			7	8	9	10	11	1		5					4				23
24	Jan 3	H	Manchester City	W 3-2	25	9	Chandler, Hine 2 (1p) / Halliday 2	15000		2	3	6			7	8	9	10	11	1		5					4				24
25	17	A	Portsmouth	L 1-2	25	13	Adcock / Forward 2	18000		2		6		4	7	8	9			1	3		10	11			5				25
26	Feb 5	H	Arsenal	L 2-7	25	15	Hine 2 (1p) / Lambert 3, Bastin 2, Jack, Hulme	17416		2		6			7	8	9	10		1	3	5					4	11			26
27	7	H	Blackpool	W 6-0	27	13	Adcock, Chandler, Hine 4	14581	1	2		6			7	8	9	10			3	5					4	11			27
28	18	A	Leeds United	W 3-1	29	12	Hine 2, Adcock / Duggan	5572	1	2		6			7	8	9	10			3	5					4	11			28
29	21	H	Huddersfield Town	L 1-2	29	13	Hine / Mangnall 2	18242	1	2		6			7	8	9	10			3			5			4	11			29
30	28	A	Aston Villa	L 2-4	29	14	Smith, Richards / Waring, Beresford 3	24000	1	2		6		4	7		9	10			3		8	5				11			30
31	Mar 2	A	Blackburn Rovers	L 0-3	29	14	- / McLean, Cunliffe, L Bruton	6699	1			6		4	7		9	10			3		8	5				11	2		31
32	7	H	Grimsby Town	L 0-1	29	15	- / Coleman	12163		2		6			7	8	9		11	1			10	5			4		3		32
33	21	H	Liverpool	W 3-2	31	15	Hine 2 (1p), Adcock / Barton 2	15000		2		6			7	8		10	11	1	3			5			4			9	33
34	25	A	Manchester United	D 0-0	32	14		3679		2		6			7	8		10	11	1				5			4		3	9	34
35	28	A	Sheffield Wednesday	L 0-4	32	16	- / Rimmer 2, Ball 2	10525		2		6			7	8	9		11	1			10	5			4		3		35
36	Apr 4	H	West Ham United	D 1-1	33	17	Chandler / Gamble	18000	1	2	3	6			7	8	9	10	11					5			4				36
37	6	A	Chelsea	L 0-1	33	18	- / Pearson	26157	1	2		6			7		9	10	11		3		8	5			4				37
38	7	H	Chelsea	W 2-1	35	15	Chandler. Lochhead / Rankin	19848	1	2		6			7	8	9	10	11		3			5			4				38
39	11	A	Middlesbrough	D 2-2	36	14	Barry, Lochhead / McPhail, Cameron	10934	1	2		6			7		9	10	11		3		8	5			4				39
40	18	H	Newcastle United	W 3-1	38	12	Chandler, Adcock, Lochhead / Bedford	12148	1	2		6			7	8	9	10	11		3			5			4				40
41	25	A	Bolton Wanderers	L 1-4	38	15	Chandler / Butler, Blackmore, Gibson 2	8962	1	2				6	7	8	9	10	11		3			5			4				41
42	May 2	A	Birmingham	L 1-2	38	16	Hine / Curtis, Bradford	10365	1	2				6	7	8	9	10	11		3			5			4				42

Final League Position:			16				**League Appearances**		20	41	17	36	11	23	42	40	37	35	35	22	22	11	11	21	4	1	21	6	4	2	
Average Home League Attendance:			17075				**League Goals**			2	1	1			9	31	18	11	3				2				1				

FA CUP

Match No	Date		Opponents	Result	Points	Position	Scorers	Att	Jim McLaren	Adam Black	Jack Brown	George Ritchie	Albert Harrison	Norman Watson	Hughie Adcock	Ernie Hine	Arthur Chandler	Arthur Lochhead	Len Barry	John Beby	Reg Osborne	George Carr	Sep Smith	Roger Heywood	Jim Bulling	Harry Lovatt	Billy Findlay	Percy Richards	George Dumbrell	Joe Wiggins	Match No
1	Jan 10	H	Brighton & Hove A. (3)	L 1-2			Lochhead / Smith 2	25722		2	3	6			7	8	9	10	11	1			5				4				1

Stand-in Goalkeepers: Sep 20, Chandler for Beby, Arsenal (a); Mar 2, Watson for McLaren, Blackburn Rovers (a).

1930-31
Back: Osborne, Findlay, Brown, McLaren, Gardner (Trainer), Black, Langford, Watson.
Front: Harrison, Adcock, Hine, Chandler, Lochhead, Barry.
On Ground: Ritchie, Lovatt.

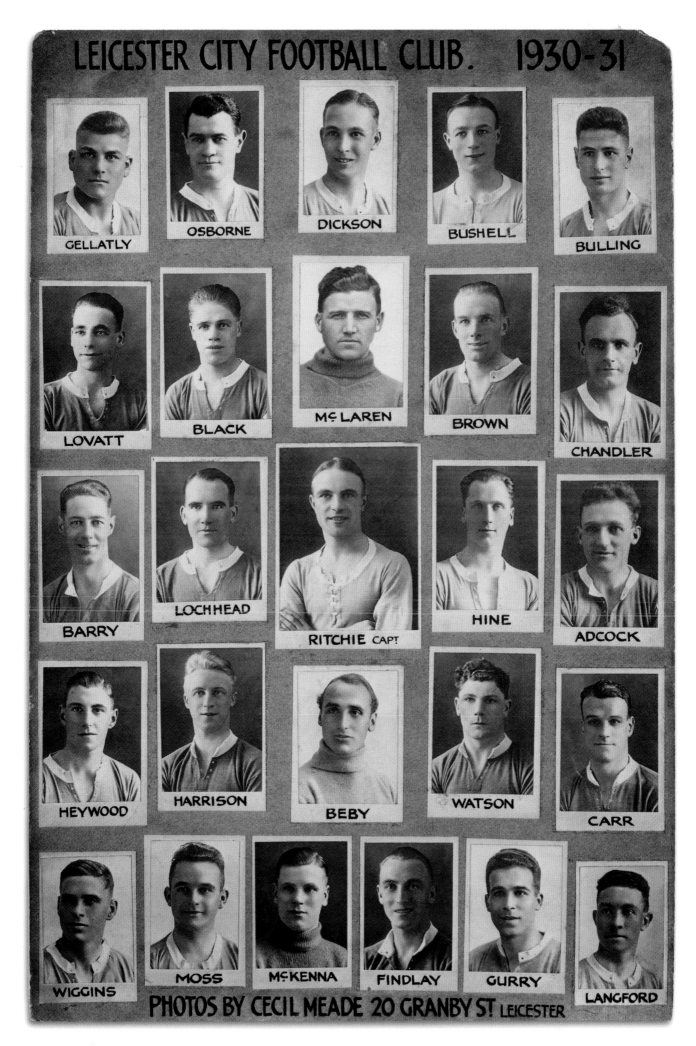

LEICESTER CITY FOOTBALL CLUB. 1930-31

GELLATLY   OSBORNE   DICKSON   BUSHELL   BULLING

LOVATT   BLACK   McLAREN   BROWN   CHANDLER

BARRY   LOCHHEAD   RITCHIE CAPT.   HINE   ADCOCK

HEYWOOD   HARRISON   BEBY   WATSON   CARR

WIGGINS   MOSS   McKENNA   FINDLAY   GURRY   LANGFORD

PHOTOS BY CECIL MEADE 20 GRANBY ST LEICESTER

249

Season 1931-32

Champions: Everton
Relegated: Grimsby Town, West Ham United

FOOTBALL LEAGUE DIVISION ONE

Match No	Date		Opponents	Result	Points	Position	Scorers	Att
1	Aug 29	A	Aston Villa	L 2-3	-	-	Smith 2 / Houghton, Waring 2	21000
2	31	H	Middlesbrough	D 2-2	1	-	Smith, Barry / Pease, Warren	15339
3	Sep 5	H	Manchester City	W 4-0	3	9	Hine, Smith 2, Ritchie	12000
4	7	A	Huddersfield Town	L 1-2	3	11	Hine (p) / Mangnall, R Kelly	9875
5	12	H	Liverpool	W 2-1	5	9	Smith, Hine / Gunson	15000
6	19	A	Grimsby Town	L 0-3	5	16	- / Glover 2, Marshall	13156
7	26	H	Chelsea	W 1-0	7	12	Odell (og)	19189
8	Oct 3	A	West Ham United	W 4-1	9	10	Hine 2, Chandler 2 / Gibbins	25000
9	10	H	Sheffield Wednesday	W 3-2	11	7	Hine 2, Barry / Ball, Strange	30100
10	15	H	Huddersfield Town	L 2-4	11	8	Chandler, Smith / McLean, Fogg, R Kelly, Black (og)	11420
11	17	A	Derby County	D 1-1	12	11	Langford / Lewis	14707
12	24	H	Arsenal	L 1-2	12	12	Barry / Jack, Osborne (og)	26233
13	31	A	Blackpool	W 3-2	14	9	Lochhead, Chandler 2 / Hampson 2	9542
14	Nov 7	H	Sheffield United	W 4-3	16	10	Lochhead 2, Chandler 2 / Oswald, Dunne, Pickering	15216
15	14	A	Birmingham	L 0-2	16	10	- / Grosvenor, Bradford	16000
16	21	H	Sunderland	W 5-0	18	9	Hine 2, Barry, Chandler, Osborne (p)	10000
17	28	A	Everton	L 2-9	18	12	Hine, Barry / Dean 4, Johnson 2, White 2, Clark	33513
18	Dec 5	H	West Bromwich Albion	L 2-3	18	12	Hine 2 / Richardson, Glidden, Wood	30000
19	12	A	Blackburn Rovers	L 0-6	18	12	- / J Bruton, Thompson 2, Cunliffe, T McLean, Osborne (og)	7885
20	25	A	Bolton Wanderers	L 0-1	18	15	- / Blackmore	32544
21	26	H	Bolton Wanderers	L 1-3	18	18	Hine / Milsom, Taylor 2	24675
22	Jan 2	H	Aston Villa	L 3-8	18	19	Smith, Hine (p), Langford / Brown 5, Walker 2, Beresford	25000
23	16	A	Manchester City	L 1-5	18	19	Hine / Marshall 2, Halliday, Tilson, Brook	20000
24	27	A	Liverpool	D 3-3	19	19	Hine 2 (1p), Adcock / Hodgson, McRorie, Gunson	30000
25	30	H	Grimsby Town	L 1-2	19	19	Richards / Marshall, Coleman	13907
26	Feb 4	H	Portsmouth	W 2-1	21	19	Smith 2 / W Smith	6000
27	6	A	Chelsea	L 0-1	21	19	- / Miller	34077
28	18	H	West Ham United	W 2-1	23	19	Chandler, Barry / Ruffell	12000
29	20	A	Sheffield Wednesday	L 1-3	23	19	Chandler / Ball 2, Rimmer	11391
30	27	H	Derby County	D 1-1	24	19	Smith / JC Robson	17990
31	Mar 5	A	Arsenal	L 1-2	24	19	Barry / Bastin (p), Hulme	53920
32	12	H	Blackpool	D 2-2	25	20	Barry, Hine (p) / A Watson 2 (1p)	14558
33	19	A	Sheffield United	D 2-2	26	20	Chandler, Lochhead / Barclay, Black (og)	14275
34	25	A	Newcastle United	L 2-3	26	20	Lochhead, Chandler / Starling, Allen, Boyd	34697
35	26	H	Birmingham	W 3-1	28	20	Adcock, Lochhead 2 / Smith	20000
36	29	H	Newcastle United	W 4-2	30	19	Ritchie, Hine 3 / Allen, Weaver (p)	25000
37	Apr 2	A	Sunderland	L 1-4	30	20	Osborne (p) / Shaw, Temple, Gurney, Devine	15000
38	9	H	Everton	L 0-1	30	20	- / Dean	23229
39	16	A	West Bromwich Albion	W 2-1	32	19	Lochhead, Hine / Sandford	15014
40	23	H	Blackburn Rovers	W 1-0	34	19	Ritchie	15645
41	30	A	Portsmouth	W 1-0	36	19	Lochhead	15000
42	May 7	A	Middlesbrough	D 1-1	37	19	Barry / Cameron	5410

Player shirt numbers by match

Match	McLaren	Black	Osborne	Bulling	Heywood	Ritchie	Adcock	Hine	Smith	Lochhead	Barry	Wiggins	Findlay	Jackson	Watson	Calder	Chandler	Langford	Beby	Carr	Edwards	Dumbrell	Richards	Keeley	McKenna
1	1	2	3	4	5	6	7	8	9	10	11														
2	1	2	3	4	5	6	7	8	9	10	11														
3	1	2	3	4	5	6	7	8	9	10					11										
4	1	2	3	6	5		7	8	9	10					11			4							
5	1	2	3	6	5		7	8	9	10					11			4							
6	1	2	3	6	5		7	8	9	10					11			4							
7	1	2	3		5	6	7	8		10	11		4				9								
8	1	2	3		5	6	7	8		10	11		4				9								
9	1	2	3		5	6	7	8		10	11		4				9								
10	1	2	3		5	6	7	8		10	11		4				9								
11	1	2	3		5	6	7	8		10	11		4				9								
12	1	2	3		5	6	7	8		10	11		4				9								
13	1	2	3		5	6	7	8		10	11		4				9								
14	1	2	3	4	5	6	7			10	11	8					9								
15	1	2	3		5	6	7	8		10	11		4				9								
16	1	2	3		5	6	7	8		10	11		4				9								
17	1	2	3		5	6	7	8		10	11		4				9								
18		2	3			6	7	8		10	11		4				9		1		5				
19	1	2	3		5	6	7	8		10	11						9	4							
20	1	2			5		7	8		10			4	6			9					3	11		
21	1	2			5		7	8		10			4	6			9					3	11		
22	1	2			5		7	8		10	11		4	6			9					3			
23	1	2	3		5	6	7	8		10	11		4				9								
24		2	3		5	6	7	8		10	11					1	9	4							
25		2		4	5	6	7	8		10							9		1			3	11		
26		2			5	6	7	8	9	10			4						1			3	11		
27	1	2			5	6	7	8		10	11		4				9					3			
28	1	2			5	6	7	8		10	11						9					3		4	
29	1	2			5	6	7	8		10	11						9					3		4	
30	1	2			5	6	7	8		10	11		4				9					3			
31	1	2			5	6	7	8		10	11		4				9					3			
32	1	2			5	6	7	8		10	11		4				9					3			
33	1	2			5	6	7	8		10	11		4				9					3			
34	1	2			5	6	7	8		10	11		4				9					3			
35		2			5	6	7	8		10	11		4				9					3			1
36		2	3		5	6	7	8		10	11		4				9		1						
37		2	3		5	6	7	8		10	11		4				9		1						
38	1	2	3		5	6	7			10	11	8	4				9								
39	1	2	3		5	6	7	8		10	11		4				9								
40	1	2	3		5	6	7	8		10	11		4				9								
41	1	2	3		5	6	7	8		10	11		4				9								
42	1	2	3		5	6	7	8		10	11		4				9								
League Appearances	35	42	28	8	41	33	37	36	22	31	38	3	18	4	13	1	33	4	6	1	3	18	4	2	1
League Goals			2			3	2	22	11	9	9						12	2					1		

Final League Position: 19
Average Home League Attendance: 16241

FA CUP

Match	Date		Opponents	Result	Scorers	Att
1	Jan 9	A	Crook Town (3)	W 7-0	Hine 5, Langford, Chandler	21875
2	23	A	Port Vale (4)	W 2-1	Hine, Chandler / Nolan	20637
3	Feb 13	A	Newcastle United (5)	L 1-3	Lochhead / Allen, Lang, Weaver	43354

Match	McLaren	Black	Osborne	Heywood	Ritchie	Adcock	Hine	Smith	Lochhead	Barry	Findlay	Chandler	Langford	Dumbrell
1	1	2		5	6	7	8		10	11	4	9		3
2	1	2	3	5	6	7	8		10	11	4	9		
3	1	2		5	6	7	8		10	11	4	9		3

Note: Jan 9, drawn away, but tie played at Filbert Street.

1931-32
Back: Smith, Dumbrell, Black, Beby, Gardner (Trainer), McLaren, Heywood, Watson, Osborne.
Front: Barry, Findlay, Chandler, Hine, Adcock, Lochhead, Carr, Jackson.
On Ground: Wiggins, Langford.

Season 1932-33

Champions: Arsenal
Relegated: Bolton Wanderers, Blackpool

FOOTBALL LEAGUE DIVISION ONE

Match No	Date		Opponents	Result	Points	Position	Scorers	Att	Joe Calvert	Adam Black	Reg Osborne	Sep Smith	Roger Heywood	George Ritchie	Hughie Adcock	Ted Lowery	Jim Paterson	Arthur Lochhead	Danny Liddle	Arthur Chandler	Jim McLaren	Len Barry	Ernest Keeley	George Dumbrell	Idris Miles	Archie Young	Jack Gurry	John Campbell	Arthur Maw	Walter Langford	Joe Wiggins	Sandy McLaren	Sandy Wood	Match No
1	Aug 27	H	Sheffield United	D 1-1	1	-	Paterson / Pickering	20204	1	2	3	4	5	6	7	8	9	10	11															1
2	29	A	Huddersfield Town	L 1-4	1	-	Chandler / McLean 2, Hine, Calvert (og)	10596	1	2	3	4	5	6	7	8		10	11	9														2
3	Sep 3	A	Wolverhampton W.	D 1-1	2	18	Lowery / Deacon	32889		2	3	4	5	6	7	8		10		9	1	11												3
4	5	H	Huddersfield Town	W 3-1	4	10	Ritchie, Lochhead 2 / W Smith	15594		2	3	4	5	6	7	8		10		9	1	11												4
5	10	H	Newcastle United	L 0-3	4	18	- / Boyd 2, Lang	22103		2	3	4	5	6	7	8	9	10			1	11												5
6	17	A	Aston Villa	L 2-4	4	19	Paterson, Heywood / Brown 2, Walker, Houghton	25000		2	3	4	5	6	7	8	9	10			1	11												6
7	24	H	Middlesbrough	D 1-1	5	19	Lochhead / Rigby	16628		2	3	4	5	6	7	8	9	10			1	11												7
8	Oct 1	A	Bolton Wanderers	L 0-5	5	21	- / Westwood 2, Gibson, Cook, Milsom	12342	1	2	3	4	5	6	7	8		10	11	9														8
9	8	H	Liverpool	L 1-2	5	21	Liddle / Roberts, Hodgson	15000	1	2	3	10	5	6	7	8			11	9			4											9
10	15	A	Blackpool	L 1-2	5	21	Paterson / Hampson, Crawford	16898	1	2		4	5	6	7	8	9	10	11						3									10
11	22	H	Everton	D 2-2	6	21	Liddle, Miles / McGourty, Stein	17770	1	2		4	5	6				10	11	9				8	3	7								11
12	29	A	Arsenal	L 2-8	6	22	Chandler, Ritchie / Hulme 3, Bastin 2, Coleman 2, Jack	36714	1	2		4	5	6				8	11	9					3	7	10							12
13	Nov 5	H	Sheffield Wednesday	D 0-0	7	21		16044		2		4	5	6				8	11	9	1				3	7	10							13
14	12	A	Leeds United	D 1-1	8	21	Chandler / Hydes	12426		2			5	6		8		10	11	9	1				3	7	4							14
15	19	H	Blackburn Rovers	D 1-1	9	21	Lochhead / Thompson	12680		2			5	6		8		10	11	9	1				3	7	4							15
16	26	A	Derby County	L 2-3	9	21	Lochhead, Smith / Bowers 3	16605		2	3	8	5	6				10		9	1	11				7	4							16
17	Dec 3	H	Manchester City	L 1-2	9	22	Chandler / Tilson, Brook	15000		2		8	5	6				10		9	1	11			3	7	4							17
18	10	A	Sunderland	L 1-2	9	22	Smith / Carter 2	9000		2		8	5	6	7	10				9	1	11			3		4							18
19	17	H	Birmingham	D 2-2	10	22	Smith (p), Campbell / Cringan, Gregg	10000		2		8	5	6	7			10	11		1				3		4	9						19
20	24	A	West Bromwich Albion	L 3-4	10	22	Lochhead, Campbell, Smith / Richardson 3, Sandford	15905		2		8	5	6	7			10	11		1				3		4	9						20
21	26	A	Portsmouth	L 1-2	10	22	Lochhead / Weddle, Worrall	20000		2		8	5	6	7			10	11		1				3		4	9						21
22	27	H	Portsmouth	W 2-1	12	21	Campbell, Smith (p) / Weddle	25000		2		8	5	6	7			10	11		1				3		4	9						22
23	31	A	Sheffield United	L 2-5	12	21	Liddle, Adcock / Williams 2, Pickering 2, Dunne	15732		2		8	5	6	7	10			11		1				3		4	9						23
24	Jan 7	A	Wolverhampton W.	D 2-2	13	21	Campbell, Liddle / Crook, Hetherington	15000		2			5	6	7				11		1				3		4	9		8	10			24
25	21	A	Newcastle United	L 1-2	13	22	Campbell / Boyd, JR Richardson	12659	1	2		10	5	6	7				11								4	9		8			3	25
26	Feb 4	A	Middlesbrough	D 1-1	14	22	Barry / JJ Williams	11255		2	3	4	5	6	7			10			1	11						9	8					26
27	9	H	Aston Villa	W 3-0	16	22	Maw 3	16000		2	3	4	5	6	7			10			1	11						9	8					27
28	11	H	Bolton Wanderers	W 2-0	18	22	Maw, Campbell	14178		2	3	4	5		7			10			1	11						9	8		6			28
29	18	A	Liverpool	W 2-1	20	21	Campbell, Heywood / Roberts	15000		2	3	4	5	6	7			10			1	11						9	8					29
30	Mar 8	A	Everton	L 3-6	20	22	Maw, Campbell, Cresswell (og) / Dean 3, Dunn 2, White	12745		2	3	4	5	6	7			10				11						9	8			1		30
31	11	H	Arsenal	D 1-1	21	22	Lochhead / James	32228		2		4	5	6	7			10				11						9	8		3	1		31
32	18	A	Sheffield Wednesday	L 1-4	21	22	Lochhead / Ball 3, Burgess	13964		2		4	5	6	7			10				11						9	8		3	1		32
33	25	A	Leeds United	W 3-1	23	22	Paterson 2, Lochhead / Furness	13669		2		4	5	6	7		9	10	11										8		3	1		33
34	30	H	Blackpool	W 3-0	25	22	Paterson, Lochhead, Maw	7904		2		4	5	6	7		9	10	11										8			1	3	34
35	Apr 1	A	Blackburn Rovers	D 1-1	26	22	Liddle / Thompson	7562		2		4	5	6	7		9	10	11										8			1	3	35
36	8	H	Derby County	W 4-0	28	21	Adcock, Paterson 2, Maw	18233		2			5	6	7		9	10	11							4			8			1	3	36
37	14	A	Chelsea	L 1-4	28	21	Paterson / Oakton, Gallacher, Horton 2	45608		2		4	5	6	7		9	10	11										8			1	3	37
38	15	A	Manchester City	L 1-4	28	22	Cann (og) / Herd 2, Toseland, Marshall	22000		2		4	5	6	7		9	10	11										8			1	3	38
39	18	H	Chelsea	D 1-1	29	22	Liddle / Gallacher	22647		2		5		6	7			10	11							4	8	9				1	3	39
40	22	H	Sunderland	W 4-2	31	21	Maw 2, Lochhead, Black / Gurney, Gallacher	10000		2		4	5	6	7		9	10	11										8			1	3	40
41	29	A	Birmingham	W 4-0	33	19	Ritchie, Paterson, Maw 2	9894		2		4	5	6	7		9	10	11										8			1	3	41
42	May 6	H	West Bromwich Albion	W 6-2	35	19	Liddle 2, Maw 3, Paterson / Carter, Sandford	19000		2		4	5	6	7		9	10	11										8			1	3	42

									Joe Calvert	Adam Black	Reg Osborne	Sep Smith	Roger Heywood	George Ritchie	Hughie Adcock	Ted Lowery	Jim Paterson	Arthur Lochhead	Danny Liddle	Arthur Chandler	Jim McLaren	Len Barry	Ernest Keeley	George Dumbrell	Idris Miles	Archie Young	Jack Gurry	John Campbell	Arthur Maw	Walter Langford	Joe Wiggins	Sandy McLaren	Sandy Wood	
League Appearances									8	41	16	37	41	40	35	10	19	37	27	13	21	15	2	14	7	5	14	14	18	2	4	13	9	
League Goals										1		5	2	3	2	1	11	12	8	4		1			1			8	14					

Final League Position: 19
Average Home League Attendance: 16822

FA CUP

Match No	Date		Opponents	Result	Scorers	Att	Joe Calvert	Adam Black	Reg Osborne	Sep Smith	Roger Heywood	George Ritchie	Hughie Adcock	Ted Lowery	Jim Paterson	Arthur Lochhead	Danny Liddle	Arthur Chandler	Jim McLaren	Len Barry	Ernest Keeley	George Dumbrell	Idris Miles	Archie Young	Jack Gurry	John Campbell	Arthur Maw	Walter Langford	Joe Wiggins	Sandy McLaren	Sandy Wood	Match No
1	Jan 14	H	Everton (3)	L 2-3	Campbell 2 / Dean, Dunn, Stein	21845	1	2	3	10	5	6	7				11								4	9	8					1

1932-33
Back: Young, Heywood, Black, Dumbrell, Calvert, Smith;
Front: Adcock, Lowery, Paterson, Hodge (Manager), Chandler, Lochhead, Barry.
On Ground: Ritchie, Liddle, Osborne.

Season 1933-34

Champions: Arsenal
Relegated: Newcastle United, Sheffield United

FOOTBALL LEAGUE DIVISION ONE

Match No	Date		Opponents	Result	Points	Position	Scorers	Att	McLaren	Black	Jones	Smith	Heywood	Ritchie	Adcock	Maw	Paterson	Lochhead	Liddle	Gurry	Chandler	Lowery	Dumbrell	Philp	Young	Campbell	Wood	Dewis	Grosvenor	Sharman	Gardiner	Match No
1	Aug 26	A	Aston Villa	W 3-2	2	-	Maw 2, Lochhead / Astley, Waring	42555	1	2	3	4	5	6	7	8	9	10	11													1
2	28	H	Sheffield United	W 4-0	4	-	Liddle 4	20878	1	2	3	4	5	6	7			10	11	8	9											2
3	Sep 2	H	Manchester City	D 0-0	5	1		24682	1	2	3	4	5	6	7	8	9		11			10										3
4	4	A	Sheffield United	L 1-2	5	3	Paterson / Barclay 2	9521	1	2	3	4	5		7	8	9		11			10	6									4
5	9	H	Tottenham Hotspur	L 1-3	5	11	Paterson / McCormick 3	26112	1	2	3		5	6	7	8	9		11			10		4								5
6	16	A	Liverpool	W 3-1	7	5	Adcock, Lochhead, Maw / Hanson	29723	1	2	3		5		7	8	9	10	11	4					6							6
7	23	H	Chelsea	D 1-1	8	3	Liddle / Gibson	21164	1	2	3		5	6	7	8		10	11	4						9						7
8	30	A	Sunderland	L 1-2	8	9	Campbell / Davis, Yorston	21083	1	2	3		5	6	7	8		10	11	4						9						8
9	Oct 7	A	Portsmouth	W 2-1	10	4	Liddle, Campbell / Rutherford	19352	1	2	3	4	5	6	7	8		10	11							9						9
10	14	A	Huddersfield Town	L 1-5	10	12	Liddle / McLean, Luke 2, Bott, W Smith	10251	1	2	3	4	5	6	7			10	11	8						9						10
11	21	A	Arsenal	L 0-2	10	16	- / Dunne 2	44014	1	2	3	4	5	6	7			10	11						6	9						11
12	28	H	Everton	W 3-1	12	11	Maw, Adcock, Campbell / White	15538	1	2	3	4	5		7	8		10	11						6	9						12
13	Nov 4	A	Derby County	L 1-2	12	14	Campbell / Bowers, Crooks	22102	1	2		4	5		7	8		10	11						6	9	3					13
14	11	H	Blackburn Rovers	L 1-2	12	15	Chandler / Harper, Bruton	17364	1	2	3	4	5	6	7	10	8		11		9											14
15	18	A	Newcastle United	D 1-1	13	16	Liddle / McMenemy	8098	1	2	3	4	5	6	7	8		10	11		9											15
16	25	H	Leeds United	D 2-2	14	16	Paterson 2 / Duggan, Hydes	14022	1	2	3	4	5	6	7	8		10	11		9											16
17	Dec 2	H	Sheffield Wednesday	D 1-1	15	17	Chandler / Strange	10313	1	2	3	4	5	6	7	8		10	11		9											17
18	9	H	West Bromwich Albion	L 0-1	15	17	- / Carter	20614	1	2	3	4	5	6	7	8		10	11									9				18
19	23	H	Middlesbrough	L 1-2	15	19	Dewis / Camsell, JJ Williams	9980	1	2	3	4	5	6	7	8		10	11									9				19
20	25	A	Stoke City	L 1-2	15	20	Paterson / Bamber, Sale	21588	1	2	3	4	5	6	7	8		10	11									9				20
21	26	H	Stoke City	W 3-1	17	19	Liddle, Adcock, Chandler / Matthews	21517	1	2			5	6	7		8	10	11	4	9						3					21
22	30	H	Aston Villa	D 1-1	18	19	Liddle / Astley	15140	1	2	3	4	5		7		9	10	11	8										6		22
23	Jan 6	A	Manchester City	D 1-1	19	19	Maw / Herd	21496	1	2	3	4	5		7	8	9	10	11											6		23
24	20	A	Tottenham Hotspur	W 1-0	21	18	Lochhead	31393	1	2		4	5		7	8		10	11		9						3			6		24
25	Feb 1	H	Liverpool	W 1-0	23	16	Liddle	11855	1	2		4			7	8		10	11		9						3		5	6		25
26	10	H	Sunderland	D 0-0	24	17		18919	1	2		4			7	8		10	11		9						3		5	6		26
27	21	A	Portsmouth	W 5-3	26	16	Gardiner 4, Liddle / J Smith 2, Weddle	10678	1	2		4	5		7	8			11		10						3		6		9	27
28	24	H	Huddersfield Town	W 1-0	28	13	Maw	29533	1	2		4	5		7	8		10	11								3		6		9	28
29	Mar 8	H	Arsenal	W 4-1	30	12	Gardiner 3, Chandler / Bowden	23976	1	2		4	5		7			10	11		9						3		6		8	29
30	10	A	Everton	D 1-1	31	13	Gardiner / Stein	21959	1	2		4	5		7			10	11		9						3		6		8	30
31	24	A	Blackburn Rovers	L 0-3	31	14	- / Harper 3	6670	1	2		4	5	6	7	8		10	11								3				9	31
32	28	A	Birmingham	L 0-3	31	14	- / Moffatt, Mangnall, Sharman (og)	7846	1	2		4		6	7	10	8		11								3		5		9	32
33	31	H	Newcastle United	W 3-2	33	14	Maw, Lochhead, Paterson / Allen, Pearson	17920	1		2	4		6	7	8		10	11								3		5		9	33
34	Apr 2	A	Wolverhampton W.	D 1-1	34	14	Maw / Phillips	29088	1		2	4		6	7	8		10	11								3		5		9	34
35	3	H	Wolverhampton W.	D 1-1	35	13	Maw / Goddard	23335	1		2	4		6	7	8		10	11								3		5		9	35
36	7	A	Leeds United	L 0-8	35	14	- / Duggan 2, Mahon 2, Furness 2, Firth 2	11871	1		2	4		6	7	8		10	11								3		5		9	36
37	14	H	Sheffield Wednesday	W 2-0	37	14	Gardiner, Adcock	11731	1	2	3	4	5	6	7	10	8		11												9	37
38	19	H	Derby County	W 2-0	39	11	Liddle, Gardiner	8864	1	2	3	4	5	6	7	10	8		11												9	38
39	21	A	West Bromwich Albion	L 0-2	39	13	- / Richardson, Boyes	11309	1	2	3	4	5	6	7	10	8		11												9	39
40	23	A	Chelsea	L 0-2	39	13	- / Mills 2	16304	1	2	3	4	5	6	7	10		8	11												9	40
41	28	H	Birmingham	L 3-7	39	15	Chandler 2, Maw / Moffatt, Guest 3, Mangnall, Roberts, Jones (og)	6981	1	2	3	4	5	6	7	8		10	11		9											41
42	May 5	A	Middlesbrough	L 1-4	39	17	Maw / Yorston 2, Stuart, Warren	4758	1	2	3	4	5	6	7	8		10	11												9	42

									McLaren	Black	Jones	Smith	Heywood	Ritchie	Adcock	Maw	Paterson	Lochhead	Liddle	Gurry	Chandler	Lowery	Dumbrell	Philp	Young	Campbell	Wood	Dewis	Grosvenor	Sharman	Gardiner	
Final League Position:				**17**			**League Appearances**		42	37	32	39	35	26	38	36	24	25	42	8	12	4	1	1	4	7	15	3	9	7	15	
Average Home League Attendance:				**18349**			**League Goals**								4	11	6	4	13		6					4		1			10	

FA CUP

	Date		Opponents	Result			Scorers	Att	McLaren	Black	Jones	Smith	Heywood	Ritchie	Adcock	Maw	Paterson	Lochhead	Liddle	Gurry	Chandler	Lowery	Dumbrell	Philp	Young	Campbell	Wood	Dewis	Grosvenor	Sharman	Gardiner	
1	Jan 13	H	Lincoln City (3)	W 3-0			Maw, Lochhead, Paterson	25987	1	2	3	4	5		7	8	9	10	11							6						1
2	27	A	Millwall (4)	W 6-3			Smith, Chandler 2, Maw, Liddle, Lochhead / Phillips, Yardley 2	31449	1	2		4	5		7	8		10	11		9					6	3					2
3	Feb 17	A	Birmingham (5)	W 2-1			Chandler 2 / Haywood	48563	1	2		4	5		7	8		10	11		9					6	3					3
4	Mar 3	A	Preston North End (6)	W 1-0			Chandler	38605	1	2		4	5		7	8		10	11		9					6	3					4
5	17		Portsmouth (sf)	L 1-4			Lochhead / Weddle 3, Rutherford	66544	1	2		4	5		7			10	11		9					6	3				8	5

Dismissals: Apr 3, Lochhead, Wolverhampton Wanderers (h).
Note: Mar 17, at St Andrews (Birmingham).

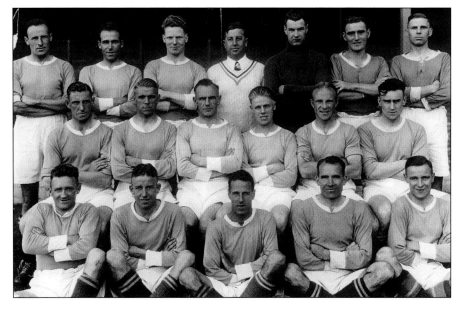

1933-34
Back: Young, Gurry, Dumbrell, Edwards (Trainer), McLaren, Jones, Wiggins.
Middle: Heywood, Lowery, Chandler, Black, Ritchie, Smith.
Front: Adcock, Maw, Paterson, Lochhead, Liddle.

Season 1934-35

Champions: Arsenal
Relegated: Leicester City, Tottenham Hotspur

FOOTBALL LEAGUE DIVISION ONE

Match No	Date		Opponents	Result	Points	Position	Scorers	Att	Sandy McLaren	Adam Black	Dai Jones	Sep Smith	Roger Heywood	George Ritchie	Hughie Adcock	Arthur Maw	Archie Gardiner	Billy Coutts	Danny Liddle	Jim Paterson	John Summers	Tommy Mills	Arthur Chandler	Arthur Lochhead	Fred Sharman	Sandy Wood	Jack Gurry	Billy Frame	Willie Muncie	George Dewis	George Gibson	Jack Liggins	Percy Grosvenor	Archie Young	Pat Clarke	Tony Carroll	Gene O'Callaghan	Match No
1	Aug 25	H	Wolverhampton W.	D 1-1	1	-	Coutts / Hartill	21891	1	2	3	4	5	6	7	8	9	10	11																			1
2	29	A	Everton	L 1-2	1	-	Gardiner / Dean, Leyfield	20475	1	2	3	4	5	6		8	9	10	11	7																		2
3	Sep 1	A	Chelsea	L 1-3	1	20	Summers / Mills 2, Cheyne	20084	1	2	3	4	5	6		8	9	10	11		7																	3
4	3	H	Everton	W 5-2	3	14	Lochhead 2, Liddle, Chandler, Mills / Dean, Leyfield	15975	1	2	3	4	5	6					11			7	8	9	10													4
5	8	H	Aston Villa	W 5-0	5	9	Chandler 3, Liddle, Mills	28548	1	2	3	4		6					11			7	8	9	10	5												5
6	15	A	Derby County	D 1-1	6	9	Summers / Bowers	25211	1	2	3	4		6					11			7	8	9	10	5												6
7	22	H	Manchester City	L 1-3	6	14	Mills / Herd 2, Busby	21359	1	2	3	4		6					11			7	8	9	10	5												7
8	29	H	Sunderland	L 0-2	6	16	- / Davis, Gurney	16002	1	2			8			6			11	10	7		9			5	3	4										8
9	Oct 6	A	Tottenham Hotspur	D 2-2	7	15	Liddle, Maw / Hedley, Frame (og)	37409	1		3	4		6	7	8			11				10	9		5			2									9
10	13	H	Preston North End	D 0-0	8	17		19652	1		3	4		6	7	8			11				10	9		5			2									10
11	20	A	Middlesbrough	L 0-1	8	18	- / Baxter	12363	1		3	4	5	6		8			11				10	9					2	7								11
12	27	H	Blackburn Rovers	L 0-1	8	19	- / Thompson	13041	1		3	4	5	6	7	8						10		9					2	11								12
13	Nov 3	A	Birmingham	W 3-2	10	17	Liddle, Smith (p), Booton (og) / Jones 2	16799	1		3	4	5	6	7	10		8	11										2		9							13
14	10	H	Stoke City	L 0-3	10	18	- / Sale 2, Matthews	15981	1		3	4	5	6		10		8	11	7									2			9						14
15	17	A	Liverpool	L 1-5	10	19	Liddle / Hodgson 3, Wright, Taylor	18790	1		3	4	5	6		10			11			7	8										9					15
16	24	H	Leeds United	W 1-0	12	20	Liggins	12785	1	2	3	4		6		10			11			7	8			5						9						16
17	Dec 1	A	West Bromwich Albion	L 1-4	12	21	Maw / Boyes 2, Glidden 2	17174	1	2	3	4		6		10			11			7	8			5						9						17
18	8	H	Sheffield Wednesday	L 0-1	12	22	- / Burgess	13288	1		3	4		6		10			11	8	7					5	2					9						18
19	15	A	Arsenal	L 0-8	12	22	- / Drake 3, Hulme 3, Bastin 2	23689	1		3	4						10	11	8				7		5	2				9			6				19
20	22	H	Portsmouth	W 6-3	14	22	Mills, Maw, Chandler 2, Liddle, Salmond (og) / Nichol, Bagley, Weddle	9010	1	2		4			7	8			11			10	9			5	3							6				20
21	25	H	Huddersfield Town	L 0-3	14	22	- / Malam 2, Morris	24064	1			4			7	8			11			10	9			5	3		2					6				21
22	26	A	Huddersfield Town	W 3-2	16	22	Muncie, Chandler 2 / Morris, Young	25718	1			8			6	7							9			5	3			2	11			4	10			22
23	29	A	Wolverhampton W.	L 1-3	16	22	Chandler / Phillips, Hartill, Crook	24288	1			8			6	7			11				9			5	3			2				4	10			23
24	Jan 5	H	Chelsea	W 1-0	18	22	Liddle	14593	1		3	4			6	7	8		11				9			5	2								10			24
25	19	A	Aston Villa	L 0-5	18	22	- / Astley 3, Cunliffe, Beresford	27608	1		3	4			6	7	8		11				9			5	2								10			25
26	31	H	Derby County	L 0-1	18	22	- / Gallacher	14011	1	2	3	4			6	7	8		11			10	9			5												26
27	Feb 2	A	Manchester City	L 3-6	18	22	Muncie, Liddle, Smith (p) / Brook 2, Bray, Toseland, Herd, Tilson	24224	1		2	8	5	6									9						7					4	10	3		27
28	9	A	Sunderland	L 0-2	18	22	- / Gurney, Carter	18048	1	2		4	5			8			11			10	9			3			7					6				28
29	23	A	Preston North End	L 0-2	18	22	- / Maxwell, Friar	18276	1			4	5			8			11			10	9			2	3							6		7		29
30	Mar 2	H	Middlesbrough	W 3-1	20	22	Dewis 2, Maw / Chadwick	16120	1				5	6		10			11							2	3					9		4		7	8	30
31	9	A	Blackburn Rovers	D 0-0	21	22		9299	1			4	5	6		10			11							2	3					9				7	8	31
32	16	H	Birmingham	W 2-1	23	22	Dewis 2 / Stoker	18540	1	2				6		10			11							5	3					9		4		7	8	32
33	23	A	Stoke City	L 0-3	23	22	- / Matthews 2, Turner	8471	1	2				6		10			11							5	3					9		4		7	8	33
34	28	H	Tottenham Hotspur	W 6-0	25	21	Liggins 2, Carroll, Liddle 2, Channell (og)	13061	1	2				6		10			11							5	3					9	4			7	8	34
35	30	H	Liverpool	W 3-1	27	21	Liddle, Maw, O'Callaghan / Johnson	16302	1	2		4		6		10			11					9		5	3									7	8	35
36	Apr 6	A	Leeds United	W 2-0	29	21	Liggins, Liddle	12086	1	2		4	5	6		10			11							3						9				7	8	36
37	13	H	West Bromwich Albion	D 0-0	30	21		21508	1	2		4	5	6	7	10			11							3						9					8	37
38	19	A	Grimsby Town	L 1-3	30	21	Maw / Craven 2, Dyson	19531	1	2		4	5	6	7	10			11							3					9					7	8	38
39	20	A	Sheffield Wednesday	D 1-1	31	21	O'Callaghan / Sharp	15654	1			4	5			10			11				9			2	3							6		7	8	39
40	22	H	Grimsby Town	D 2-2	32	20	Liddle 2 / Craven 2	25195	1		3	4	5			10			11				9			2								6		7	8	40
41	27	H	Arsenal	L 3-5	32	21	Maw, Dewis, Ritchie / Beasley 2, Crayston 2, Davidson	26958	1		3	4	5	6		10			11							2						9				7	8	41
42	May 4	A	Portsmouth	D 1-1	33	21	O'Callaghan / Jones (og)	12605	1		3	4	5	6		10			11							2						9				7	8	42

Final League Position:	21	
Average Home League Attendance:	17994	

League Appearances: 42 14 32 38 21 35 14 33 3 6 40 5 11 15 23 4 28 21 1 9 5 8 2 7 14 5 1 12 13

League Goals: 2 1 7 1 1 14 2 4 9 2 2 5 4 1 3

FA CUP

	Date		Opponents	Result			Scorers	Att	Sandy McLaren	Adam Black	Dai Jones	Sep Smith	Roger Heywood	George Ritchie	Hughie Adcock	Arthur Maw	Archie Gardiner	Billy Coutts	Danny Liddle	Jim Paterson	John Summers	Tommy Mills	Arthur Chandler	Arthur Lochhead	Fred Sharman	Sandy Wood	Jack Gurry	Billy Frame	Willie Muncie	George Dewis	George Gibson	Jack Liggins	Percy Grosvenor	Archie Young	Pat Clarke	Tony Carroll	Gene O'Callaghan	Match No
1	Jan 12	H	Blackpool (3)	W 2-1			Maw, Ritchie / Hall	25000	1		3	4		6	7	8			11				9			5	2							10				1
2	26	H	Arsenal (4)	L 0-1			- / Hulme	39494	1	2	3	4		6	7	8			11			10	9			5												2

1934-35
Back: Edwards (Trainer), Jones, McLaren, Heywood, Calvert, Smith, Lochhead.
Middle: Black, Maw, Grosvenor, Chandler, Wood, Liddle.
Front: Adcock, Ritchie, Gardiner, Paterson, Gurry.

Season 1935-36

Promoted: Manchester United, Charlton Athletic
Relegated: Port Vale, Hull City

FOOTBALL LEAGUE DIVISION TWO

Match No	Date		Opponents	Result	Points	Position	Scorers	Att	Sandy McLaren	Dai Jones	Sandy Wood	Sep Smith	Fred Sharman	George Ritchie	Tony Carroll	Gene O'Callaghan	George Dewis	Arthur Maw	Danny Liddle	Percy Grosvenor	Roger Heywood	Joe Calvert	Billy Frame	Tommy Mills	Billy Coutts	John Grogan	Jack Liggins	George Bedford	Willie Muncie	Owen McNally	David Bruce	Match No
1	Aug 31	A	Sheffield United	W 2-1	2	-	O'Callaghan 2 / Dodds	16049	1	2	3	4	5	6	7	8	9	10	11													1
2	Sep 2	A	Swansea Town	L 0-2	2	-	- / Bussey, Martin	12530	1	2	3	4	5	6	7	8	9	10	11													2
3	7	H	Southampton	D 1-1	3	11	Carroll / Neal	15793	1	2	3	4	5		7	8	9	10	11	6												3
4	9	H	Swansea Town	W 4-1	5	4	Carroll 3, Maw / Olsen	8498	1	2	3	4	9		7	8		10	11	6	5											4
5	14	A	Norwich City	W 2-1	7	3	Sharman, Maw / Goffey	20571	1	2	3	4	9		7	8		10	11	6	5											5
6	16	H	Bradford City	W 2-1	9	2	Sharman, Mills / Hallows	9954		3		4	9		7	8			11	6	5	1	2	10								6
7	21	H	Nottingham Forest	W 2-1	11	1	O'Callaghan, Liddle / Dent	19426		3		4	9		7	8		10	11	6	5	1	2									7
8	28	A	Blackpool	W 5-3	13	1	Maw 2, O'Callaghan, Carroll, Liddle / Middleton 2, Watmough	24409	1	3		4	9		7	8		10	11	6	5		2									8
9	Oct 5	H	Doncaster Rovers	W 6-0	15	1	O'Callaghan 2, Sharman 3, Liddle	16672	1	3		4	9		7	8		10	11	6	5		2									9
10	12	A	Bury	L 0-3	15	1	- / Buttery, Matthews, Graham	12164	1	3		4			7	8	9		11	6	5		2	10								10
11	19	A	Newcastle United	L 1-3	15	4	Liggins / Cairns, Harris, Ware	14017	1	3					7	8		10	11	6	5		2			4	9					11
12	26	H	Tottenham Hotspur	W 4-1	17	1	Carroll 2, Maw, Sharman / Morrison	24721	1	3		4	9		7	8		10	11	6	5		2									12
13	Nov 2	A	Manchester United	W 1-0	19	1	Sharman	39074	1	3		4	9		7	8		10	11	6	5		2									13
14	9	H	Port Vale	W 2-0	21	1	Maw, Carroll	16349	1	3		4	9		7	8		10	11	6	5		2									14
15	16	A	Fulham	L 0-2	21	2	- / Hammond, Perry	13948	1	3		4	9		7	8		10	11	6	5		2									15
16	23	H	Plymouth Argyle	W 2-0	23	1	Carroll, O'Callaghan	16251	1	3		4	9		7	8		10	11	6	5		2									16
17	30	A	Charlton Athletic	L 0-1	23	2	- / Robinson	25555	1	3		4	9		7	8		10	11	6	5		2									17
18	Dec 7	H	Hull City	D 2-2	24	1	O'Callaghan, Carroll / Cameron, Cassidy	8561	1	3		4	9		7	8		10	11	6	5		2									18
19	14	A	Barnsley	D 3-3	25	1	Maw, Sharman 2 / Hine 3	9783	1	3		4	9		7	8		10	11	6			2					5				19
20	21	H	Burnley	W 2-0	27	1	Maw 2	9042	1	3		4	9		7	8		10	11	6	5		2									20
21	25	H	Bradford Park Avenue	W 5-0	29	1	Carroll, O'Callaghan, Sharman, Maw, Liddle	18097	1	3		4	9		7	8		10	11	6	5		2									21
22	28	H	Sheffield United	L 1-3	29	1	Maw / Dodds 2, Barclay	19382	1	3		4	9		7	8		10	11	6	5		2									22
23	Jan 1	A	Bradford Park Avenue	L 1-3	29	1	O'Callaghan / Meek 2, Lewis	9218	1	3		4	5	6		8	9		11				2	10					7			23
24	4	A	Southampton	L 0-1	29	4	- / Neal	11848	1	3		4	9			8		10	11	6			2					5	7			24
25	18	H	Norwich City	D 1-1	30	4	Jones / Vinall	13236	1	3		4	5			8	9	10	11	6			2						7			25
26	30	A	Nottingham Forest	W 1-0	32	2	Maw	12878	1	3		4	5		7	8		10	11	6			2							9		26
27	Feb 1	H	Blackpool	W 4-1	34	2	Liddle, McNally 2, Muncie / T Jones	18095	1	3		4	5			8		10	11	6			2						7	9		27
28	8	A	Doncaster Rovers	L 0-1	34	5	- / A Turner	15479	1	3		4	5			8		10	11	6			2						7	9		28
29	20	H	Bury	L 1-2	34	5	Ritchie / Matthews, Chalmers	10162	1	3		4	5	6		8		10	11				2						7	9		29
30	29	A	Hull City	D 3-3	35	6	O'Callaghan, McNally 2 / Nicol, Acquroff, Cameron	2284	1	3		4	5	6		8		10	11				2						7	9		30
31	Mar 7	H	Fulham	W 5-2	37	6	Maw, Smith (p), Carroll, Muncie, McNally / Smith 2	12755	1	3		4	5	6	7	8		10					2						11	9		31
32	14	A	Port Vale	D 1-1	38	6	Carroll / Roberts	8331	1	3		4	5	6	7	8		10					2						11	9		32
33	19	H	Newcastle United	W 1-0	40	5	Sharman	13499	1	3			9	6		8		10	11		5		2		4				7			33
34	21	H	Manchester United	D 1-1	41	6	Maw / Bryant	18200	1	3			9	6	7	8		10	11		5		2		4							34
35	28	H	Plymouth Argyle	L 1-2	41	6	Sharman / Eggleston, Hunter	17208	1	3			9	6	7	8		10	11		5		2		4							35
36	Apr 4	H	Charlton Athletic	W 4-1	43	6	Sharman, Carroll, Jones, Coutts / Hobbis	12992	1	3			9	6	7	8		10	11		5		2		4							36
37	10	A	West Ham United	L 2-3	43	6	Carroll, O'Callaghan / Fenton, Goulden, Simpson	38332	1	3		4	9	6	7	8		10	11		5		2									37
38	11	A	Tottenham Hotspur	D 1-1	44	6	Sharman / G Hunt	35286	1	3		4	9		7	8		10	11	6	5		2									38
39	13	H	West Ham United	D 1-1	45	6	Dewis / Simpson	24892	1	3		4			7	8	9		11	6	5		2							10		39
40	18	H	Barnsley	W 2-0	47	6	Muncie, Maw	11109	1	3	2			6	7	8		9			5				4				11	10		40
41	25	A	Burnley	D 2-2	48	6	Dewis, Ritchie / Brocklebank, T Lawton	5543	1	3				6		8	9				5		2		4				11	10	7	41
42	May 2	A	Bradford City	L 0-2	48	6	- / Travis, Murphy	6006	1	3				6		8	9		11		5		2		4				7	10		42

									Sandy McLaren	Dai Jones	Sandy Wood	Sep Smith	Fred Sharman	George Ritchie	Tony Carroll	Gene O'Callaghan	George Dewis	Arthur Maw	Danny Liddle	Percy Grosvenor	Roger Heywood	Joe Calvert	Billy Frame	Tommy Mills	Billy Coutts	John Grogan	Jack Liggins	George Bedford	Willie Muncie	Owen McNally	David Bruce	
Final League Position:			6				**League Appearances**		40	41	7	36	37	15	31	36	8	37	38	33	28	2	36	2	6	2	1	2	13	10	1	
Average Home League Attendance:			15126				**League Goals**			2		1	14	2	15	12	2	15	5					1	1		1		3	5		

FA CUP

	Date		Opponents	Result			Scorers	Att	McLaren	Jones	Wood	Smith	Sharman	Ritchie	Carroll	O'Callaghan	Dewis	Maw	Liddle	Grosvenor	Heywood	Calvert	Frame	Mills	Coutts	Grogan	Liggins	Bedford	Muncie	McNally	Bruce	
1	Jan 11	H	Brentford (3)	W 1-0			Maw	29750	1	3		4	5			8	9	10	11	6			2						7			1
2	25	H	Watford (4)	W 6-3			Maw 2, Dewis, Liddle 3 / McPherson 3 (1p)	32650	1	3		4	5		7	8	9	10	11	6			2									2
3	Feb 15	A	Middlesbrough (5)	L 1-2			McNally / Camsell, Forrest	42214	1	3		4	5	6	7	8		10	11				2							9		3

Stand-in Goalkeepers: Sep 21, Frame for Calvert, Nottingham Forest (h).

1935-36
Back: Sharman, Coutts, Heywood, Edwards (Trainer), McLaren, Jones, Frame, Grosvenor.
Middle: Dewis, Ritchie, O'Callaghan, Lochhead (Manager), Liggins, Maw, Wood.
Front: Mills, Carroll, Muncie, Liddle, Clarke.

Season 1936-37

Promoted: Leicester City, Blackpool
Relegated: Bradford City, Doncaster Rovers

FOOTBALL LEAGUE DIVISION TWO

Match No	Date		Opponents	Result	Points	Position	Scorers	Att	McLaren	Frame	Jones	Smith	Heywood	Ritchie	Muncie	O'Callaghan	Dewis	Maw	Liddle	Calvert	Sharman	McNally	Coutts	Grosvenor	Grogan	Carroll	Bedford	Stubbs	Bowers	Davis	Match No
1	Aug 29	H	Blackpool	L 1-2		-	O'Callaghan / Finan 2	14417	1	2	3	4	5	6	7	8	9	10	11												1
2	31	H	Bradford Park Avenue	W 5-0	2	-	Muncie 2, Ritchie, O'Callaghan, McNally	8036			3	4	5	6	7	8			11	1		2	9	10							2
3	Sep 5	A	Blackburn Rovers	D 0-0	3	8		14757			3	4	5	6	7				11	1		2	9	10	8						3
4	9	A	Bradford Park Avenue	W 2-1	5	4	O'Callaghan, McNally / Danskin	9223			3	4	5	6	7	8			11	1		2	9	10							4
5	12	H	Bury	L 0-3	5	8	- / Graham 2, Matthews	10251			3	4	5	6	7	8			11	1		2	9	10							5
6	14	A	Tottenham Hotspur	L 2-4	5	13	O'Callaghan 2 (1p) / Morrison 2, Bell, W Evans	17913		2	3				7	8			11	1	5		9	10		6	4				6
7	19	A	Plymouth Argyle	L 1-2	5	17	Gorman (og) / Eggleston 2	20542	1	2	3				7	8	9	10	11		5					6	4				7
8	26	A	West Ham United	L 1-4	5	20	O'Callaghan / Marshall 2, Goulden, Martin	24286	1	2	3				7	8	9		11		5		10			6	4				8
9	Oct 3	H	Norwich City	D 2-2	6	20	O'Callaghan 2 / Warnes 2	9736	1	2	3	4			7	8			11		5		9	10		6					9
10	10	A	Newcastle United	L 0-1	6	21	- / Cairns	34877	1	2	3	4			11		8	9	10		5			6		7					10
11	17	H	Coventry City	W 1-0	8	19	Dewis	25554	1	2	3	4			11		8	9	10		5			6		7					11
12	24	A	Doncaster Rovers	D 0-0	9	19		14434	1	2	3	4			11		8	9	10		5			6		7					12
13	31	H	Fulham	W 2-0	11	15	Dewis, O'Callaghan	12704	1	2	3	4					8	9	11		5		10	6		7					13
14	Nov 7	A	Burnley	D 0-0	12	16		10208	1	2	3	4					8	9	11		5			6		7	10				14
15	14	H	Southampton	D 2-2	13	17	Liddle, Sharman / Dunne 2	15291	1	2	3	4				8			10		5			6		7	9	11			15
16	21	A	Swansea Town	W 3-1	15	11	Muncie, Bowers, Liddle / Brain	13269	1	2	3	4			7	8			10		5			6				11	9		16
17	28	H	Bradford City	W 4-1	17	10	Bowers 2, Stubbs 2 / Travis	18818	1	2	3	4			7	8			10		5			6				11	9		17
18	Dec 5	A	Aston Villa	W 3-1	19	9	Bowers 2, O'Callaghan / Massie	29981	1	2	3	4				8		7	10		5			6				11	9		18
19	12	A	Chesterfield	W 3-1	21	7	Bowers 2, Wass (og) / Read	19857	1	2	3	4							10		5			6	8			11	9	7	19
20	19	A	Nottingham Forest	W 3-0	23	6	Bowers 2 (1p), O'Callaghan	24015	1	2	3	4				8			10		5			6		7		11	9		20
21	25	H	Barnsley	W 5-1	25	5	Bowers 3, Stubbs, Liddle / Hallows	35610	1	2	3	4				8			10		5			6		7		11	9		21
22	26	A	Blackpool	L 2-6	25	6	O'Callaghan, Stubbs / Finan 2, Hill, Farrow (p), Watmough, T Jones	30759	1	2	3	4				8			10		5			6		7		11	9		22
23	28	A	Barnsley	W 2-1	27	5	Grosvenor, Bowers / Hine	10639	1	2	3	4				8			10		5			6				11	9	7	23
24	Jan 1	A	Sheffield United	L 1-3	27	7	Bowers (p) / Barton, Jones (og), Grosvenor (og)	21985	1	2	3	4				8					5		10	6				11	9	7	24
25	2	H	Blackburn Rovers	W 1-0	29	6	Bowers	15823	1	2	3					8					5		10	6		4		11	9	7	25
26	9	A	Bury	W 1-0	31	4	Bowers	13887	1	2	3	4		6		8			10		5					7		11	9		26
27	23	H	Plymouth Argyle	W 3-2	33	3	Bowers, Stubbs, O'Callaghan / Connor 2	19910	1	2	3	4		6		8			10		5					7		11	9		27
28	Feb 4	H	West Ham United	D 2-2	34	3	O'Callaghan, Liddle / Goulden, Foxall	12541	1	2	3			6		8			10		5					4		11	9	7	28
29	6	A	Norwich City	W 2-1	36	3	Sharman (p), Liddle / Goffey	13507	1	2	3			6		8			10		5					4		11	9	7	29
30	13	H	Newcastle United	W 3-2	38	2	Liddle, Carroll, Stubbs / Cairns, Smith	24252	1	2	3			6		8			10		5					7	4	11	9		30
31	25	H	Coventry City	W 2-0	40	2	Bowers 2	14109	1	2	3					8			10		5			6		7	4	11	9		31
32	27	H	Doncaster Rovers	W 7-1	42	2	Bowers 3, Carroll 2, O'Callaghan, Jacobson (og) / Burton	18170	1	2	3					8			10		5			6		7	4	11	9		32
33	Mar 6	A	Fulham	L 0-2	42	2	- / Woodward, Smith	19534	1	2	3					8			10		5			6		7	4	11	9		33
34	13	H	Burnley	W 7-3	44	2	Liddle, Carroll 2, Bowers 4 / Gastall, Brocklebank, Fletcher	19747	1	2	3					8			10		5			6		7	4	11	9		34
35	20	A	Southampton	D 1-1	45	2	Bowers / Dunne	13601	1	2	3	4				8			10		5			6		7		11	9		35
36	27	H	Swansea Town	D 0-0	46	2		24244	1	2	3	4				8			10		5			6		7		11	9		36
37	29	H	Sheffield United	L 1-2	46	2	Liddle / Thompson, Graham	36293	1	2	3	4				8			10		5			6		7		11	9		37
38	Apr 3	A	Bradford City	W 2-1	48	2	Liddle, Bowers / Buttery	13010	1	2	3	4						8	10		5			6				11	9	7	38
39	10	H	Aston Villa	W 1-0	50	2	Bowers	39127	1	2	3	4						8	10		5			6				11	9	7	39
40	17	A	Chesterfield	W 5-2	52	2	Stubbs 2, Bowers, Maw, Smith / Bonass, Ponting	13200	1	2	3	4						8	10		5			6		7		11	9		40
41	24	A	Nottingham Forest	W 2-1	54	2	Bowers, Maw / Pugh	24267	1	2	3	4						8	10		5			6		7		11	9		41
42	May 1	H	Tottenham Hotspur	W 4-1	56	1	Bowers 2, Maw, Carroll / Morrison	22761	1	2	3	4						8	10		5			6		7		11	9		42

| | | | | | | | League Appearances | | 37 | 38 | 42 | 31 | 5 | 10 | 14 | 34 | 8 | 9 | 40 | 5 | 41 | 6 | 11 | 34 | 10 | 22 | 2 | 28 | 27 | 8 | |
| | | | | | | | League Goals | | | 1 | | | | 1 | 3 | 15 | 2 | 3 | 9 | | 2 | 2 | | 1 | | 6 | | 8 | 33 | | |

Final League Position: 1

Average Home League Attendance: 20257

FA CUP

Match No	Date		Opponents	Result			Scorers	Att	McLaren	Frame	Jones	Smith	Heywood	Ritchie	Muncie	O'Callaghan	Dewis	Maw	Liddle	Calvert	Sharman	McNally	Coutts	Grosvenor	Grogan	Carroll	Bedford	Stubbs	Bowers	Davis	Match No
1	Jan 16	A	Bristol Rovers (3)	W 5-2			Bowers 2, Carroll, O'Callaghan, Stubbs / Butterworth, McArthur	25156	1	2	3	4		6		8			10		5					7		11	9		1
2	30	A	Exeter City (4)	L 1-3			Liddle / Bussey, Williams 2	11984	1	2	3	4		6		8			10		5							11	9	7	2

Dismissals: Mar 6, Jones, Fulham (a).
Note: Feb 27, most reports credit Jacobson (og), some credit Carroll.

1936-37
Back: Ritchie, Smith, Calvert, Heywood, McLaren, Jones, Dewis.
Middle: Coutts, Frame, Edwards (Trainer), Maw, Lochhead (Manager), Sharman, Grosvenor.
Front: Carroll, Muncie, O'Callaghan, McNally, Liddle.

Season 1937-38

Champions: Arsenal
Relegated: Manchester City, West Bromwich Albion

FOOTBALL LEAGUE DIVISION ONE

Player columns (left→right): Sandy McLaren, Billy Frame, Dai Jones, Sep Smith, Fred Sharman, Percy Grosvenor, Tony Carroll, Arthur Maw, Jack Bowers, Danny Liddle, Eric Stubbs, John Grogan, Joe Calvert, Maurice Reeday, Gene O'Callaghan, Matt Moralee, George Dewis, Roger Heywood, Albert Woodvine, Billy Coutts, Willie Muncie, Maurice Tompkin.

No	Date		Opponents	Result	Pts	Pos	Scorers	Att	McL	Fra	Jon	Smi	Sha	Gro	Car	Maw	Bow	Lid	Stu	Grn	Cal	Ree	OCa	Mor	Dew	Hey	Woo	Cou	Mun	Tom	No
1	Aug 28	H	Derby County	D 0-0	1	-		37874	1	2	3	4	5	6	7	8	9	10	11												1
2	30	H	Sunderland	W 4-0	3	-	Stubbs, Liddle 2, Bowers	23906	1	2	3		5	6	7	8	9	10	11	4											2
3	Sep 4	A	Manchester City	L 0-3	3	11	- / Bray, Herd, Brook	37687	1	2	3		5	6	7	8	9	10	11	4											3
4	8	A	Sunderland	L 0-1	3	15	- / Duns	23635	1	2	3		5	6	7	8	9	10	11	4											4
5	11	H	Arsenal	D 1-1	4	14	Bowers / Drake	39106		3			5	6	7	8	9	10	11	4	1	2									5
6	15	A	Birmingham	L 1-4	4	19	Maw / Jones 3, White	14441		3			5	6	7	8	9	10	11	4	1	2									6
7	18	A	Blackpool	W 4-2	6	17	Bowers, Stubbs, Maw 2 / Hampson, J Blair	31443		3		4	5	6	7	8	9	10	11		1	2									7
8	25	H	Brentford	L 0-1	6	19	- / McCulloch	23416		3		4	5	6	7	8	9	10	11		1	2									8
9	Oct 2	A	Bolton Wanderers	L 1-6	6	20	Tennant (og) / Carruthers, Westwood 2, Milsom, Goslin 2	26498	1		3	4	5	6	7	8	9		11			2		10							9
10	9	H	Huddersfield Town	W 2-1	8	17	Carroll, Bowers / Richardson	18442	1		3	4	5	6	7	8	9	10	11			2									10
11	16	H	West Bromwich Albion	W 4-1	10	14	Bowers 3, Liddle / Robbins	18772	1		3	4	5	6	7	8	9	10	11			2									11
12	23	A	Liverpool	D 1-1	11	16	Stubbs / Hanson	18841	1		3		5	6	7	8	9	10	11	4		2									12
13	30	H	Leeds United	L 2-4	11	16	Stubbs, Liddle / Hodgson 2, Milburn (p), Buckley	18833	1		3	4	5	6	7	8	9	10	11			2									13
14	Nov 6	A	Portsmouth	D 1-1	12	18	Bowers / Groves	17307	1		3	8	5	6		10	9	11	7	4		2									14
15	13	H	Preston North End	W 1-0	14	15	A Beattie (og)	19968	1		3	4	5	6	7	8	9		11			2		10							15
16	20	A	Middlesbrough	L 2-4	14	16	Carroll, Little / Fenton 3, Reeday (og)	18426	1		3	4	5	6	7	8	9		11			2		10							16
17	27	H	Chelsea	W 1-0	16	16	Liddle	18883	1		3	4	5	6	7		9	10	11			2			8						17
18	Dec 4	A	Grimsby Town	L 1-2	16	17	Smith (p) / Tomlinson, Lewis	8246	1		3	4	5	6	7		9	10	11			2			8						18
19	11	H	Stoke City	W 2-0	18	17	Liddle, Smith (p)	17787	1		3	4	5	6	7		9	10	11			2			8						19
20	18	A	Charlton Athletic	L 0-2	18	17	- / Robinson, Boulter	17533	1		3	4	5	6	7		9	10	11			2			8						20
21	25	H	Everton	W 3-1	20	12	Bowers, Moralee, Britton (og) / Trentham	17268	1		3	4	5	6	7	8	9		11			2		10							21
22	27	A	Everton	L 0-3	20	15	- / Lawton 2, Trentham	38693	1		3	4	5	6	7	8	9		11			2		10							22
23	Jan 1	H	Derby County	W 1-0	22	13	Dewis	24357	1	2		4	5	6	7	8			11			3		10	9						23
24	15	H	Manchester City	L 1-4	22	14	Moralee / Doherty 3, Heale	17332	1		3		5	6	7	8			11	4		2		10	9						24
25	29	H	Blackpool	L 0-1	22	18	- / Finan	13873	1		3		5	6	7	8	9		11	4		2		10							25
26	Feb 2	H	Arsenal	L 1-3	22	18	Smith (p) / Drake, Bastin, L Jones	23839	1		3	8	5	6	7		9		11	4		2		10							26
27	5	A	Brentford	D 1-1	23	18	Muncie / McCulloch	21309	1	2		4		6			9				3		5		8	7			10	11	27
28	12	H	Bolton Wanderers	D 1-1	24	17	Bowers / Howe	15069	1	2		4		6			9		11		3				8	5		7	10		28
29	19	A	Huddersfield Town	D 0-0	25	17		14999	1	2		4		6		8	9		11		3				10	5		7			29
30	26	A	West Bromwich Albion	W 3-1	27	13	Moralee, Liddle, Smith (p) / Johnson	21563	1	2		4		6			9	10	11		1	3		8		5		7			30
31	Mar 5	H	Liverpool	D 2-2	28	12	Muncie 2 / Hanson 2	18116	1	2		4		6			9	10	11		1	3			8	5		7			31
32	9	A	Preston North End	D 0-0	29	12		9150	1	2		4	5	6	7				11			3			8	9		10			32
33	12	A	Leeds United	W 2-0	31	10	Dewis, Stubbs	19839	1	2	3	4	5	6	7				8						9			10			33
34	19	H	Portsmouth	D 3-3	32	11	Dewis 2, Coutts / Beattie 3	16682	1	2	3	4	5	6	7				8						9			10			34
35	Apr 2	A	Middlesbrough	L 0-1	32	15	- / Cochrane	17759	1	2	3	4	5	6	7	8			11						9			10			35
36	9	A	Chelsea	L 1-4	32	16	Maw / Weaver, Spence, Chitty, Sharman (og)	20211	1	2	3		5	6	7	8	9		11								4	10			36
37	15	A	Wolverhampton W.	L 1-10	32	19	Cullis (og) / Maguire, Westcott 4, Jones, Dorsett 4	25540	1		3	4			7		9	10	11			2			8	5		6			37
38	16	H	Grimsby Town	W 1-0	34	17	Smith (p)	16733	1	2		4	5	6	7		9					3			8			10	11		38
39	18	H	Wolverhampton W.	D 1-1	35	15	Coutts / Jones	30572	1	2	3	4	5	6	7									10	9			8	11		39
40	23	A	Stoke City	W 2-1	37	14	Dewis, Carroll / Soo	16355		2			5	6	7					4	1	3		10	9			8	11		40
41	30	H	Charlton Athletic	W 1-0	39	14	Liddle	12916		2			5	6	7			10		4	1	3			9			8	11		41
42	May 7	H	Birmingham	L 1-4	39	16	Liddle / Dearson, Clarke, White 2	13255	1	2			5	6				10		4		3			9			8	11	7	42

									McL	Fra	Jon	Smi	Sha	Gro	Car	Maw	Bow	Lid	Stu	Grn	Cal	Ree	OCa	Mor	Dew	Hey	Woo	Cou	Mun	Tom	
Final League Position:	16						**League Appearances**		34	20	30	30	36	42	29	25	34	39	25	13	8	34	1	14	16	7	1	13	10	1	
Average Home League Attendance:	20402						**League Goals**					5			3	4	10	10	5					3	5			2	3		

FA CUP

No	Date		Opponents	Result			Scorers	Att	McL	Fra	Jon	Smi	Sha	Gro	Car	Maw	Bow	Lid	Stu	Grn	Cal	Ree	OCa	Mor	Dew	Hey	Woo	Cou	Mun	Tom	No
1	Jan 8	A	Mansfield Town (3)	W 2-1			Liddle, Bowers / Johnston	15890	1	2		4	5	6	7	8	9	10	11			3		10							1
2	22	A	Preston North End (4)	L 0-2			- / Mutch, H O'Donnell	32000	1		3		5	6	7	8	9	10	11	4		2		10							2

Note: Nov 13, most reports credit A Beattie (og), some credit Bowers.

1937-38
Back: Coutts, Frame, Calvert, Grogan, Stubbs.
Middle: Edwards (Trainer), Bedford, Sharman, McLaren, Grosvenor, Jones, Heywood.
Front: Smith (Secretary), Bowers, Carroll, Maw, Smith, Dewis, Liddle, Womack (Manager).
On Ground: Muncie, O'Callaghan.

Season 1938-39

Champions: Everton
Relegated: Birmingham, Leicester City

FOOTBALL LEAGUE DIVISION ONE

Match No	Date		Opponents	Result	Pts	Pos	Scorers	Att	Sandy McLaren	Billy Frame	Maurice Reeday	Sep Smith	Fred Sharman	Percy Grosvenor	Arthur H Smith	Arthur Maw	George Dewis	Matt Moralee	Danny Liddle	Stan Baines	Jack Bowers	Mal Griffiths	Billy Coutts	Joe Calvert	Roger Heywood	Eric Stubbs	Dai Jones	John Grogan	Bert Howe	Match No
1	Aug 27	H	Stoke City	D 2-2	1	-	Dewis 2 / Steele 2	15582	1	2	3	4	5	6	7	8	9	10	11											1
2	29	A	Wolverhampton W.	D 0-0	2	-		25882	1	2	3	4	5	6	7	8	9	10	11											2
3	Sep 3	A	Chelsea	L 0-3	2	17	- / Mills 2, Hanson	37323	1	2	3	4	5	6	7	8	9	10	11											3
4	7	A	Birmingham	L 1-2	2	21	Moralee / Kelly, Jones	14092	1	2	3	4	5	6	7	8	9	10	11											4
5	10	H	Preston North End	W 2-1	4	17	Dewis, S Smith (p) / Mutch	17507	1	2	3	4	5	6	7	8	9	10					11							5
6	12	H	Birmingham	W 2-1	6	8	Bowers, Dewis / Farrage	10778	1	2	3	4	5	6	7			8	10	11	9									6
7	17	A	Charlton Athletic	L 0-1	6	15	- / Brown	26939	1	2	3	4	5	6	7			10	8	11	9									7
8	24	H	Bolton Wanderers	D 0-0	7	13		18263	1	2	3	4	5	6		8		10		11	9	7								8
9	Oct 1	A	Leeds United	L 2-8	7	18	Baines, Bowers / Hodgson 5, Cochrane, Milburn (p), Hargreaves	15001	1	2	3	4	5	6				10		11	9	7	8							9
10	8	H	Liverpool	D 2-2	8	17	Griffiths, Dewis / Nieuwenhuys, Van Den Berg	13559		2	3	4	5	6			9	10		11		7	8	1						10
11	15	H	Sunderland	L 0-2	8	18	- / Spuhler, Smeaton	17208		2	3	4	5	6			9		10	11		7	8	1						11
12	22	A	Aston Villa	W 2-1	10	16	Dewis, Reeday (p) / Haycock	46233		2	3		5	6		8	9	10				7		1	4	11				12
13	29	H	Everton	W 3-0	12	12	Maw, Dewis, Griffiths	23964		2	3		5	6		8	9	10				7		1	4	11				13
14	Nov 5	A	Huddersfield Town	L 0-2	12	13	- / Beasley, Barlow	16102		2	3		5	6		8	9	10				7		1	4	11				14
15	12	H	Portsmouth	W 5-0	14	10	Stubbs, Griffiths, Maw 3	14885		2	3		5	6		8	9	10				7		1	4	11				15
16	19	A	Arsenal	D 0-0	15	11		36407		2	3		5	6		8	9	10				7		1	4	11				16
17	26	H	Brentford	D 1-1	16	10	Moralee / Scott	16634		2	3		5	6		8	9	10				7		1	4	11				17
18	Dec 3	A	Blackpool	D 1-1	17	11	Griffiths / Jones	14255		2			5	6		8	9		10			7		1	4	11	3			18
19	10	H	Derby County	L 2-3	17	13	Liddle 2 / McCulloch 2, Dix	29723		2			5	6		8	9		10			7		1	4	11	3			19
20	17	A	Grimsby Town	L 1-6	17	16	Reeday (p) / Boyd, Howe 4, Beattie	9389		2	3		5	6		8	9	10				7		1	4	11				20
21	24	A	Stoke City	L 0-1	17	19	- / Steele	15201	1	2	3		5	6		8			10				9	7	4	11				21
22	26	A	Manchester United	L 0-3	17	20	- / Wrigglesworth 2, Carey	26332	1	2	3		5	6		8			10	11			9	7	4					22
23	27	H	Manchester United	D 1-1	18	20	Griffiths / Hanlon	21434	1	2	3		5	6		8	9		10	11		7			4					23
24	31	H	Chelsea	W 3-2	20	16	S Smith 2, Liddle / Argue 2	13180	1	2	3	8	5	6			9		10	11		7			4					24
25	Jan 14	A	Preston North End	L 1-2	20	19	Bowers / R Beattie, Mutch	15724	1	2	3	8		6					10	11			9	7	4	5				25
26	28	A	Bolton Wanderers	L 0-4	20	20	- / Sinclair, Howe 2, Hunt	18621	1	2	3	8	5		7		9		10					6	4	11				26
27	Feb 4	A	Leeds United	W 2-0	22	17	Liddle, Dewis	12618	1	2	3	8	5				9		10				7	10	4					27
28	9	H	Charlton Athletic	L 1-5	22	17	S Smith / Tadman 2, Brown, Welsh, Sharman (og)	9467	1	2	3	4	5				9	8					7	10	6	11				28
29	18	A	Sunderland	L 0-2	22	19	- / Carter, Smeaton	15631	1		3		5	6		8		10	11		9	7			4		2			29
30	25	H	Aston Villa	D 1-1	23	19	Bowers / O'Donnell	22266	1		3	8	5	6				10	11		9	7			4		2			30
31	Mar 4	A	Liverpool	D 1-1	24	18	S Smith / Taylor	25451	1		3	8	5	6					11		9	7	10		4		2			31
32	8	A	Everton	L 0-4	24	19	- / Boyes, Greenhalgh, Lawton, Stevenson	8199	1		3	8	5	6					11		9	7	10		4		2			32
33	11	H	Huddersfield Town	L 0-1	24	21	- / Isaac	13898	1		3	8	5	6					11		9	7	10		4		2			33
34	18	A	Portsmouth	W 1-0	26	21	Dewis	23410	1		3	8	5	6			9		10			7			4	11	2			34
35	25	H	Arsenal	L 0-2	26	21	- / Kirchen, Drake	22565	1		3	8	5	6			9		10			7			4	11	2			35
36	Apr 1	A	Brentford	L 0-2	26	21	- / Smith, Hopkins	17238	1		3	8	5	6			9		10			7			4	11	2			36
37	8	H	Blackpool	L 3-4	26	21	Bowers 2, Moralee / Dodds 2, Eastham, Sharman (og)	14679	1		3		5	6	7			10	8		9				4	11	2			37
38	10	A	Middlesbrough	L 2-3	26	21	Bowers 2 / Camsell, Mannion, McKenzie	19764	1		3	8		6		10					9	7		5		11	2	4		38
39	11	H	Middlesbrough	W 5-3	28	21	Sharman 2 (2p), Dewis, Bowers, Jones / Fenton 2, Mannion	12143	1		3		5	6				8			10	9	7		4	11	2			39
40	15	A	Derby County	D 1-1	29	20	Liddle / Stamps	11922	1		3		5				8		10		9	7	6			11	2	4		40
41	22	H	Grimsby Town	L 0-2	29	22	- / Crack 2	17326	1		3		5				8		10		9	7	6			11	2	4		41
42	May 4	H	Wolverhampton W.	L 0-2	29	22	- / Westcott 2	9055	1		3		5				8		10		9	7				11	2	4	6	42

Final League Position:			22				**League Appearances**		31	28	40	24	41	36	8	21	29	24	29	7	18	33	12	11	28	21	16	4	1	
Average Home League Attendance:			16225				**League Goals**				2	5	2			4	10	3	5	1	9	5				1	1			

FA CUP

Match No	Date		Opponents	Result	Scorers	Att	Sandy McLaren	Billy Frame	Maurice Reeday	Sep Smith	Fred Sharman	Percy Grosvenor	Arthur H Smith	Arthur Maw	George Dewis	Matt Moralee	Danny Liddle	Stan Baines	Jack Bowers	Mal Griffiths	Billy Coutts	Joe Calvert	Roger Heywood	Eric Stubbs	Dai Jones	John Grogan	Bert Howe	Match No
1	Jan 7	H	Stoke City (3)	D 1-1	Dewis / Soo	21167	1	2	3	8		6			9		10	11		7			4	5				1
2	11	A	Stoke City (3 rep)	W 2-1	Dewis, Liddle / Steele	18488	1	2	3	8		6			9		10	11		7			4	5				2
3	21	A	Wolverhampton W (4)	L 1-5	Bowers / Westcott 2, Dorsett, Maguire 2	43205	1	2	3	8	5	6			9		10	11		7			4					3

Stand-in Goalkeepers: Oct 1, Sharman and Frame for McLaren, Leeds United (a).

1938-39
Back: Sharman, Holdham, Howe, Bedford, Dewis, Frame, Grogan, Moralee.
Middle: Edwards (Trainer), Norton, Hubbard, Gummer, McLaren, Stubbs, Calvert, Heywood, Jones, McLean (Asst Trainer).
Front: Thompson, Woodvine, Osborne, Jayes, Womack (Manager), Baines, Coutts, Liddle, Smith (Secretary).
On Ground: AH Smith, Reeday, S Smith, Bowers, Maw, Grosvenor.

FOOTBALL LEAGUE DIVISION TWO

Match No	Date		Opponents	Result	Points	Position	Scorers	Att	Sandy McLaren	Dai Jones	Maurice Reeday	John Osborne	Fred Sharman	Billy Coutts	Arthur H Smith	Sep Smith	Jack Bowers	Danny Liddle	Eric Stubbs	Roger Heywood	Percy Grosvenor	Mal Griffiths	George Dewis	Match No
1	Aug 26	H	Manchester City	W 4-3	2	-	A Smith 2, Sharman (p), Stubbs / Dunkley, Doherty, Brook	12000	1	2	3	4	5	6	7	8	9	10	11					1
2	30	A	Birmingham	L 0-2	2	-	- / Farrage, Sharman (og)	15000	1	2	3		5		7	8	9	10	11	4	6			2
3	Sep 2	A	West Ham United	W 2-0	4	5	Dewis, Griffiths	13400	1	2	3		5	6		4	8	10	11			7	9	3
			League Position at Abandonment	5			**League Appearances**		3	3	3	1	3	2	2	3	3	3	3	1	1	1	1	
			Average Home League Attendance:	12000			**League Goals**						1		2				1			1	1	

Note: Season abandoned due to outbreak of Second World War; These three matches were subsequently excluded from players' first class records.
In promotion positions: Luton Town, Birmingham
In relegation positions: Fulham, Burnley

1939-40
Back: AH Smith, Heywood, Sharman, Rose (Asst Trainer), Bedford, Howe, Bowers.
Middle: Frame, Reeday, Calvert, S Smith, Jones, McLaren, Grosvenor, Stubbs.
Front: Metcalfe (Trainer), Griffiths, Grogan, Woodvine, Bromilow (Manager), Osborne, Adam, Forrest, Smith (Secretary).
On Ground: Coutts, Dewis, Thompson, Liddle.

1941-42
(v West Bromwich Albion, 13 September 1941)
Back: Sheard, Frith, Frame, Parker, Calvert, Howe, Mansfield, Butler (Trainer).
Front: Barratt, S Smith, Jayes, AE Smith, Adam, Paterson.

Champions: Wolverhampton Wanderers

REGIONAL LEAGUE MIDLAND DIVISION

Match No	Date		Opponents	Result	Scorers	Att	1	2	3	4	5	6	7	8	9	10	11
1	Oct 21	H	Walsall	W 6-1	King, Bowers 3, Barron, Williams (og) / Alsop	2500	McLaren	Frame	Jones	Smith S	Bedford	Coutts	King	Dewis	Bowers	Liddle	Barron
2	28	A	Luton Town	L 2-4	Liddle, Dewis / Billington 3, Finlayson	3000	McLaren	Frame	Jones	Smith S	Bedford	Coutts	King	Dewis	Bowers	Liddle	Barron
3	Nov 4	H	Coventry City	W 4-2	S Smith, Bowers, Dewis 2 / Green, Lowrie	3000	McLaren	Frame	Jones	Smith S	Bedford	Coutts	Thompson	Dewis	Bowers	Liddle	Barron
4	11	A	West Bromwich Albion	L 0-1	- / H Jones	4265	McLaren	Frame	Jones	Smith S	Bedford	Coutts	Dewis	Jayes	Bowers	Howe	Pritchard
5	18	A	Northampton Town	D 2-2	Bowers 2 / Lyman, Henson	3000	McLaren	Frame	Jones	Smith S	Bedford	Coutts	Thompson	Dewis	Bowers	Shell	Pritchard
6	25	H	Birmingham	L 1-3	Lawton / Jones, Bye, Edwards	4104	McLaren	Jones	Howe	Smith S	Bedford	Coutts	Thompson	Liddle	Lawton	Bowers	Barron
7	Dec 2	A	Wolverhampton Wanderers	L 0-5	- / Westcott 3, King, Dorsett	5147	McLaren	Sharman	Jones	Smith S	Bedford	Coutts	Thompson	Jayes	Lawton	Eastham	Pritchard
8	9	A	Walsall	L 3-4	Lawton 3 / Alsop 2, Wood, Bulger	1645	McLaren	Frame	Jones	Sharman	Bedford	Grosvenor	Thompson	Eastham	Lawton	Bowers	Pritchard
9	16	H	Luton Town	D 3-3	Lawton, Bowers 2 / Vinall, Billington 2	3000	McLaren	Jones	Beattie	Sharman	Bedford	Grosvenor	Thompson	Eastham	Lawton	Bowers	Barron
10	23	A	Coventry City	W 1-0	Bowers (p)	1200	McLaren	Jones	Beattie	Grogan	Sharman	Grosvenor	Thompson	Eastham	Dewis	Bowers	Kingham
11	30	H	West Bromwich Albion	L 2-5	Kingham, Jayes / Connelly, Johnson, H Jones (p), Newsome, Witcomb	1939	McLaren	Frame	Jones	Smith S	Sharman	Coutts	Pritchard	Jayes	Dewis	Eastham	Kingham
12	Jan 6	H	Northampton Town	D 1-1	S Smith / Billingham	1500	Calvert	Frame	Beattie	Smith S	Sharman	Grosvenor	Thompson	Grogan	Jones	Bowers	Pritchard
13	13	A	Birmingham	D 3-3	Smith, Bowers, Turner (og) / Guest 2, Duckhouse	2000	Calvert	Frame	Beattie	Grogan	Sharman	Howe	Thompson	Smith S	Bowers	Eastham	Barron
14	20	H	Wolverhampton Wanderers	L 1-2	Jayes / Dorsett, McIntosh	1800	Calvert	Frame	Jones	Grogan	Sharman	Grosvenor	Thompson	Smith S	Bowers	Haycock	Pritchard
15	Feb 24	A	Northampton Town	L 2-4	Jones, Thompson / Liddle, Shell, Billingham 2	3500	McLaren	Frame	Jones	Grogan	Sharman	Howe	Thompson	Smith S	Bowers	Haycock	Ansell
16	Mar 2	H	Birmingham	W 2-1	Dewis 2 / Jones	2140	McLaren	Frame	Jones	Grogan	Sharman	Howe	Thompson	Smith S	Dewis	Haycock	Pritchard
17	9	A	Wolverhampton Wanderers	L 1-5	S Smith / Mullen, McIntosh, McMahon 3	2446	McLaren	Frame	Jones	Grogan	Sharman	Howe	Pritchard	Smith S	Dewis	Iverson	Houghton
18	16	A	Walsall	L 2-3	S Smith, Pritchard / Alsop 2, Edwards	2509	McLaren	Frame	Jones	Grogan	Sharman	Howe	Pritchard	Smith S	Dewis	Haycock	Houghton
19	23	H	Luton Town	L 1-2	Haycock / Duggan, Vinall	3000	McLaren	Frame	Howe	Grogan	Sharman	Iverson	Thompson	Smith S	Dewis	Haycock	Houghton
20	26	A	West Bromwich Albion	L 1-5	S Smith / H Jones 2, Newsome 2 (1p), Connelly	6088	McLaren	Frame	Howe	Smith S	Sharman	Iverson	Thompson	Jayes	Bowers	Haycock	Houghton
21	30	A	Coventry City	L 1-4	Dewis / Barratt, Davidson, Green, Crawley	4036	McLaren	Jones	Howe	Grogan	Sharman	Iverson	Thompson	Smith S	Dewis	Haycock	Houghton
22	Apr 6	H	West Bromwich Albion	W 5-2	Dewis 3, Houghton, S Smith / H Jones, Heaselgrave	5006	McLaren	Jones	Howe	Grogan	Sharman	Iverson	Sansome	Smith S	Dewis	Haycock	Houghton
23	May 18	A	Luton Town	L 1-5	Bowers / Billington 5		McLaren	Frame	Jones	Grogan	Heywood	Iverson	Bowers	Smith S	Bowers	Iverson	Houghton
24	20	A	Birmingham	D 0-0		1500	Queenborough	Frame	Jones	Smith S	Bedford	Howe	Haycock	Smith J	Bowers	Iverson	Houghton
25	25	H	Wolverhampton Wanderers	W 3-1	J Smith 2, Bowers / Somerfield	3340	Queenborough	Frame	Jones	Smith S	Bedford	Howe	Rochester	Smith J	Bowers	Jayes	Houghton
26	30	H	Coventry City	L 1-3	Bowers / Lauderdale, Crawley, Murray	2000	McLaren	Frame	Jones	Smith S	Bedford	Dewis	Sansome	Smith J	Bowers	Jayes	Houghton
27	Jun 1	H	Walsall	D 0-0		4000	McLaren	Frame	Howe	Smith S	Bedford	Dewis	Sansome	Smith J	Bowers	Jayes	Houghton
28	8	H	Northampton Town	W 2-0	Logan, Houghton	850	McLaren	Frame	Jones	Smith S	Sharman	Howe	Sansome	Smith J	Bowers	Logan	Houghton

LEAGUE WAR CUP

Match No	Date		Opponents	Result	Scorers	Att	1	2	3	4	5	6	7	8	9	10	11
1	Apr 20	H	Clapton Orient (1 leg 1)	W 5-2	Bowers, Haycock 2, S Smith, Dewis / Smith 2	3500	McLaren	Frame	Jones	Grogan	Sharman	Iverson	Dewis	Smith S	Bowers	Haycock	Houghton
2	27	A	Clapton Orient (1 leg 2)	L 0-2	- / Smith, Shankly	4800	McLaren	Frame	Jones	Grogan	Sharman	Iverson	Dewis	Smith S	Bowers	Haycock	Barron
3	May 4	H	West Ham United (2 leg 1)	D 1-1	S Smith / Macaulay	6320	McLaren	Frame	Jones	Heywood	Sharman	Iverson	Dewis	Smith S	Bowers	Haycock	Houghton
4	11	A	West Ham United (2 leg 2)	L 0-3	- / Foreman 2, Foxall	15500	McLaren	Frame	Jones	Grogan	Heywood	Iverson	Bowers	Smith S	Sharman	Jayes	Houghton

Final League Position: 7 of 8

Note: Jan 13, at Leamington.

Season 1940-41

Champions: Crystal Palace

SOUTH REGIONAL LEAGUE

No	Date		Opponents	Supp. Comp.	Result	Att	Scorers	1	2	3	4	5	6	7	8	9	10	11
1	Aug 31	A	Coventry City		D 1-1	2165	Bowers / Lowrie	Calvert	Frame	Howe	Smith S	Heywood	Thornhill	Wright W	Smith J	Bowers	Smith L	Mullen
2	Sep 7	H	Coventry City		L 0-2	2106	- / Lowrie, Crawley	Calvert	Frame	Howe	Towers	Heywood	Thornhill	Wright W	Smith J	Dewis	Smith L	Mullen
3	14	A	Nottingham Forest		L 3-6	200	W Wright, Dewis 2 / Peacock 2, Smith 3, Barks	Calvert	Frame	Howe	Towers	Heywood	Grogan	Wright W	Smith J	Dewis	Smith L	Mullen
4	21	H	Nottingham Forest		D 2-2	3000	Heywood (p), J Smith / Hunter, Antonio	Calvert	Frame	Jones	Sharman	Heywood	Thornhill	Wright W	Smith J	Steele	Liddle	Mullen
5	28	H	Stoke City		W 1-0	2814	Liddle	Calvert	Frame	Howe	Sharman	Heywood	Howe	Wright W	Smith J	Dewis	Liddle	Mullen
6	Oct 5	A	Stoke City		D 3-3	800	Dewis, Liddle, Heywood (p) / Sale, F Mountford 2	Calvert	Frame	Howe	Sharman	Heywood	Johnston	Wright W	Smith J	Dewis	Liddle	Liddle
7	12	A	Luton Town		L 0-2	2500	- / Duggan, Smith	Calvert	Frame	Howe	Towers	Heywood	Wilson	Cunningham	Smith J	Steele	Johnston	Liddle
8	19	H	Luton Town		W 4-0	3000	Steele, Mullen 2, Liddle	Calvert	Frame	Howe	Sharman	Heywood	Johnston	Cunningham	Smith J	Steele	Liddle	Mullen
9	26	H	Birmingham		W 2-1	500	Liddle, Steele / Gardner	Calvert	Frame	Howe	Rochester	Heywood	Johnston	Wright W	Jayes	Steele	Liddle	Mullen
10	Nov 2	A	Birmingham		W 2-1	1500	Mullen, W Wright / Trigg	Calvert	Frame	Howe	Rochester	Heywood	Dewis	Wright W	Smith J	Steele	Liddle	Mullen
11	9	H	Mansfield Town		W 3-2	2000	W Wright, Steele 2 / Robertson, Barke	Calvert	Frame	Howe	Rochester	Heywood	Liddle	Wright W	Smith J	Steele	Cheney	Mullen
12	16	A	Mansfield Town		L 2-4	1472	D Wright 2 / Rickards, Egan, Robertson 2	Calvert	Frame	Howe	Rochester	Heywood	Liddle	Wright D	Smith J	Wright W	Cheney	Mullen
13	23	A	Walsall		L 0-5	600	- / Hancocks 2, Brown, Rowley 2	Calvert	Frame	Dewis	Rochester	Heywood	Liddle	Wright W	Smith J	Steele	Cheney	Mullen
14	30	H	Walsall		D 1-1	1500	Steele / Brown	Calvert	Frame	Howe	Rochester	Heywood	Liddle	Wright W	Jayes	Steele	Smith A	Mullen
15	Dec 7	H	Notts County		W 6-0	939	Mullen 3, Dewis 2, W Wright	Calvert	Harrison	Howe	Frame	Heywood	Liddle	Wright W	Rochester	Dewis	Smith A	Mullen
16	14	H	West Bromwich Albion		W 4-3	765	A Smith, Dewis 2, Mullen / Heaselgrave 2, Richardson	Calvert	Harrison	Howe	Frame	Heywood	Liddle	Wright W	Rochester	Dewis	Smith A	Mullen
17	21	A	West Bromwich Albion		W 5-4	2500	Dewis 2, Mullen 3 (1p) / Richardson 3, Elliott	Calvert	Harrison	Springthorpe	Frame	Heywood	Liddle	Wright W	Rochester	Dewis	Smith A	Mullen
18	25	A	Northampton Town		L 2-5	2500	Dewis 2 / Alsop 2, Billingham 2, Dunkley	Calvert	Harrison	Howe	Frame	Heywood	Liddle	Wright W	Rochester	Dewis	Smith A	Mullen
19	25	H	Northampton Town		W 7-2	2000	Mullen 2 (1p), A Smith 2, Dewis, W Wright, Lee / Billingham 2	Calvert	Harrison	Howe	Rochester	Heywood	Liddle	Wright W	Dewis	Lee	Smith A	Mullen
20	28	A	Notts County		L 2-4	3000	W Wright, Dewis / Broome 2, Duncan 2	Calvert	Harrison	Howe	Frame	Heywood	Liddle	Wright W	Rochester	Dewis	Smith A	Mullen
21	Jan 4	H	Stoke City	MC 1 leg 1	W 6-2	2000	Mullen, A Smith 2, W Wright 2, Dewis / F Mountford, Sale	Calvert	Frame	Howe	Rochester	Frith	Liddle	Wright W	Dewis	Lee	Smith A	Mullen
22	11	A	Stoke City	MC 1 leg 2	W 5-3	2868	Dewis, Mullen, Lee, A Smith, Challinor (og) / F Mountford 2, Sale	Calvert	Frame	Howe	Frith	Heywood	Liddle	Wright W	Lee	Dewis	Smith A	Mullen
23	Feb 1	H	Nottingham Forest	MC 2	W 6-2	4000	Dewis, Howe 2 (2p), W Wright, Lee 2 / Lowrie, Crisp	Calvert	Frame	Howe	Frith	Heywood	Liddle	Wright W	Lee	Lee	Smith A	Mullen
24	8	H	Lincoln City	MC sf leg 1	W 4-1		A Smith, Dewis 2, Sanderson / Dunderdale	Calvert	Frame	Howe	Rochester	Heywood	Liddle	Wright W	Dewis	Sanderson	Smith A	Mullen
25	Apr 12	A	Lincoln City	MC sf leg 2	L 4-5		Lee 2, Jayes, W Wright / Meek, Clare, Towler 3	Calvert	Frame	Wyles	Grogan	Sheard	Paterson	Frost	Jayes	Lee	Liddle	Wright W
26	14	H	Lincoln City		D 1-1		Chapman / Towler	Calvert	Frame	Howe	Rochester	Heywood	Paterson	Wright W	Dewis	Lee	Burditt	Chapman
27	May 3	H	Walsall	MC f	W 2-0	6562	W Wright, Mullen	Calvert	Frame	Howe	Frith	Heywood	Liddle	Wright W	Dewis	Lee	Liddle	Mullen
28	10	A	Walsall		L 1-3	1250	Lee / Brown, Thayne, Hancocks	Calvert	Frame	Howe	Frith	Heywood	Liddle	Frost	Dewis	Lee	Rochester	Mullen
29	17	H	Tottenham Hotspur		L 1-2	3000	Jayes / Burgess 2	Ward	Frame	Howe	Frith	Heywood	Liddle	Frost	Jayes	Lee	Freer	Freer
30	24	A	Tottenham Hotspur		L 0-3	3400	- / Broadis, Gibbons, Ludford	Calvert	Frame	Howe	Frith	Heywood	Paterson	Sanderson	Burditt	Jayes	Witcomb	Adam
31	31	H	Northampton Town		W 3-2	1800	Liddle 2, Dewis / King 2	Calvert	Frame	Howe	Frith	Heywood	Paterson	Sanderson	Dewis	Jayes	Liddle	Adam
32	Jun 2	H	Nottingham Forest		W 2-0	1000	A Smith, Dewis	Calvert	Frame	Howe	Sheard	Heywood	Paterson	Sanderson	Smith A	Dewis	Burditt	Roome
33	7	H	Stoke City		W 2-1	1500	Dewis, A Smith / Brigham (p)	Calvert	Frame	Howe	Frith	Sheard	Paterson	Sanderson	Smith A	Dewis	Liddle	Adam

LEAGUE WAR CUP

No	Date		Opponents	Result	Att	Scorers	1	2	3	4	5	6	7	8	9	10	11
1	Feb 15	H	Birmingham (1 leg 1)	D 3-3	3917	Lee, Jayes, Foster / Dearson, Shaw, Gardner	Chesters	Frame	Howe	Frith	Heywood	Liddle	Jayes	Dewis	Lee	Cheney	Foster
2	22	H	Birmingham (1 leg 2)	W 3-2	4500	Liddle, Dewis, A Smith / Gardner, Dearson	Calvert	Frame	Howe	Frith	Heywood	Liddle	Rochester	Dewis	Lee	Smith A	Lyman
3	Mar 1	A	Nottingham Forest (2 leg 1)	W 2-0	2000	Lee, A Smith	Chesters	Frame	Howe	Towers	Heywood	Liddle	Rochester	Dewis	Lee	Smith A	Lyman
4	8	H	Nottingham Forest (2 leg 2)	D 1-1	6000	Lee / Barks	Chesters	Frame	Howe	Towers	Heywood	Liddle	Wright W	Smith L	Lee	Smith A	Lyman
5	15	H	Mansfield Town (3 leg 1)	D 2-2	6000	W Wright, Lee / Beaumont, Robertson	Chesters	Jones	Howe	Frame	Heywood	Liddle	Wright W	Dewis	Lee	Smith A	Liddle
6	22	A	Mansfield Town (3 leg 2)	W 2-1	5000	Liddle, Dewis / Hubbard	Calvert	Frame	Howe	Frith	Sheard	Rochester	Wright W	Dewis	Lee	Smith A	Liddle
7	29	A	Queens Park R (4 leg 1)	L 1-2	5700	Dewis / Mangnall 2	Calvert	Frame	Howe	Frith	Heywood	Rochester	Wright W	Dewis	Lee	Smith A	Liddle
8	Apr 5	H	Queens Park R (4 leg 2)	W 6-1	8267	Lee, A Smith 3, Jayes 2 / Mallett	Calvert	Frame	Howe	Frith	Heywood	Paterson	Wright W	Jayes	Lee	Burditt	Smith A
9	19	A	Arsenal (sf leg 1)	L 0-1	9242	- / Crayston	Calvert	Frame	Howe	Frith	Heywood	Paterson	Wright W	Smith A	Dewis	Liddle	Chapman
10	26	H	Arsenal (sf leg 2)	L 1-2	26500	Lee / L Compton, Crayston	Calvert	Frame	Howe	Frith	Heywood	Paterson	Wright W	Dewis	Dewis	Fagan	Smith A

Final League Position: 14 of 34

Note: Dec 25, two fixtures played on same day, kick-offs 10.45 am and 3.00 pm;
Feb 15, Feb 22, both legs played at Filbert Street;
The six Midland Cup ties also counted towards the League table.

Champions: Southern Section: Leicester City; Championship: Manchester United

Season 1941-42

FOOTBALL LEAGUE SOUTHERN SECTION

Match No	Date	Opponents	Result	Supp. Comp.	Scorers	Att	1	2	3	4	5	6	7	8	9	10	11
1	Aug 30 H	Norwich City	D 1-1		Jayes / Plunkett	2790	Calvert	Frame	Howe	Frith	Sheard	Mansfield	Barratt	Jayes	Lee	Smith A	Adam
2	Sep 6 A	Norwich City	D 0-0			3972	Calvert	Frame	Howe	Rochester	Sheard	Mansfield	Barratt	Jayes	Lee	Smith A	Adam
3	13 A	West Bromwich Albion	L 1-4		S Smith / C Evans 2, Richardson, Johnson	3786	Parker	Frame	Howe	Frith	Paterson	Mansfield	Barratt	Smith S	Jayes	Smith A	Adam
4	20 H	West Bromwich Albion	W 3-2		Cheney 2, S Smith / Elliott, Sankey	3526	Parker	Frame	Howe	Smith S	Frith	Paterson	Barratt	Jayes	Chapman	Smith A	Cheney
5	27 H	Wolverhampton Wanderers	W 2-0		Chapman 2	3850	Morgan	Frame	Howe	Smith S	Frith	Paterson	Barratt	Jayes	Chapman	Smith A	Cheney
6	Oct 4 A	Wolverhampton Wanderers	D 0-0			4121	Morgan	Frame	Howe	Smith S	Frith	Jones L	Barratt	Smith A	Jayes	Iggleden	Cheney
7	11 A	Luton Town	L 2-3		Cheney, Barratt / Goodyear 2, T Joyer	2000	Morgan	Frame	Howe	Frith	Smith S	Liddle	Barratt	Jayes	Lee	Iggleden	Cheney
8	18 H	Luton Town	W 7-2		Cheney 3, A Smith 2, Jayes, L Smith / Sanderson, Duggan	3000	Morgan	Frame	Howe	Smith S	Smith S	Paterson	Barratt	Smith A	Jayes	Smith L	Cheney
9	25 H	Northampton Town	W 1-0		Jayes	4000	Morgan	Frame	Howe	Smith S	Frith	Paterson	Barratt	Iggleden	Jayes	Smith L	Cheney
10	Nov 1 A	Northampton Town	W 1-0		Barratt	2000	Morgan	Frame	Howe	Smith S	Frith	Paterson	Barratt	Mulraney	Jayes	Smith A	Cheney
11	8 A	Walsall	L 1-2		Jayes / Wood, Hancocks	3000	Morgan	Frame	Howe	Smith S	Sheard	Frith	Barratt	Drake	Jayes	Smith A	Cheney
12	15 H	Walsall	W 6-0		Cheney, Barratt 2, Jayes, S Smith, Shelton (og)	4000	Grant	Frame	Howe	Smith S	Frith	Paterson	Barratt	Jayes	Sanderson	Smith A	Cheney
13	22 H	Nottingham Forest	W 3-0		A Smith, Cheney, Sanderson	6000	Morgan	Frame	Howe	Smith S	Frith	Mansfield	Barratt	Rochester	Sanderson	Smith A	Cheney
14	29 A	Nottingham Forest	W 1-0		Sanderson	1700	Grant	Frame	Howe	Smith S	Frith	Paterson	Barratt	Rochester	Sanderson	Smith A	Cheney
15	Dec 6 H	Norwich City	W 6-1		Sanderson, Paterson, Cheney 2, S Smith, Jayes / Maskell	3000	Morgan	Frame	Howe	Smith S	Frith	Paterson	Barratt	Jayes	Sanderson	Smith A	Cheney
16	20 H	Nottingham Forest	W 3-2		Sanderson, Jayes, Cheney / J Smith 2	1471	Morgan	Frame	Howe	Smith S	Frith	Paterson	Barratt	Jayes	Sanderson	Smith A	Cheney
17	25 H	Nottingham Forest	W 2-0		Howe (p), Jayes	7687	Grant	Frame	Howe	Smith S	Sheard	Liddle	Barratt	Jayes	Sanderson	Smith A	Cheney

FOOTBALL LEAGUE CHAMPIONSHIP

Match No	Date	Opponents	Result	Supp. Comp.	Scorers	Att	1	2	3	4	5	6	7	8	9	10	11
1	Dec 27 A	Chesterfield	D 3-3	WCQ	Dewis 3 / Miller, Sinclair, Jones	5000	Calvert	Frame	Howe	Smith S	Frith	Liddle	Barratt	Jayes	Dewis	Smith A	Cheney
2	Jan 3 H	Chesterfield	W 4-1	WCQ	Cheney, Jayes, A Smith, Dewis / Miller	5000	Grant	Frame	Howe	Smith S	Frith	Liddle	Frost	Jayes	Dewis	Smith A	Cheney
3	10 H	Luton Town	W 3-0	WCQ	Liddle, Chapman, A Smith	5000	Calvert	Frame	Howe	Smith S	Frith	Paterson	Frost	Jayes	Chapman	Smith A	Liddle
4	17 A	Luton Town	D 2-2	WCQ	Cheney, A Smith / Duggan, Billington	2300	Grant	Frame	Howe	Smith S	Frith	Paterson	Frost	Barratt	Jayes	Smith A	Cheney
5	Feb 14 A	West Bromwich Albion	L 2-3	WCQ	Barratt, Jayes / Richardson 2, Elliott	4378	Calvert	Frame	Howe	Frith	Sheard	Paterson	Barratt	Smith S	Jayes	Smith A	Liddle
6	21 H	Norwich City	D 1-1	WCQ	Liddle / Howe	2000	Calvert	Frame	Howe	Smith S	Sheard	Paterson	Paterson	Jayes	Jayes	Smith A	Liddle
7	28 A	Norwich City	L 3-6	WCQ	Jayes, A Smith, Paterson / Maskell 3, Thornton, Howe, Furness (p)	5653	Grant	Frame	Howe	Smith S	Frith	Liddle	Barratt	Jayes	Paterson	Smith A	Cheney
8	Mar 14 H	Sheffield Wednesday	W 5-1	WCQ	Dewis 3, Barratt, S Smith / Rogers	6500	Grant	Frame	Howe	Smith S	Crawley	Paterson	Barratt	Jayes	Dewis	Buchan	Taylor
9	21 H	West Bromwich Albion	W 4-2	WCQ	S Smith, Buchan 2, Jayes / Sankey, Gripton	5685	Grant	Frame	Howe	Smith S	Crawley	Smith A	Barratt	Jayes	Bowers	Buchan	Cheney
10	28 A	Northampton Town	D 1-1		Taylor / Fagan	2500	Morgan	Frame	Howe	Smith S	Liddle	Liddle	Barratt	Jayes	Paterson	Smith A	Taylor
11	Apr 4 H	Norwich City	W 2-0	WC 1 leg 1	Jayes, Howe (p)	8500	Morgan	Frame	Howe	Smith S	Frith	Frith	Rochester	Jayes	Crawley	Smith A	Adam
12	6 A	Norwich City	L 0-3	WC 1 leg 2	- / Thornton 2, Roberts	8769	Morgan	Frame	Wyles	Smith S	Crawley	Paterson	Barratt	Jayes	Sanderson	Smith A	Cheney
13	11 A	Sheffield Wednesday	L 1-4		Cheney / Melling 2, Nelson, Howsam	2500	Morgan	Frame	Howe	Wyles	Frith	Paterson	Barratt	Lee	Howe	Smith A	Cheney
14	18 H	Sheffield Wednesday	L 0-1		- / Cockroft (p)	3000	Morgan	Frame	Howe	Harrison	Grogan	Paterson	Sanderson	Jayes	Lee	Buchan	Bulger
15	May 16 A	Northampton Town	L 1-3		Jayes / Johnston, Pritchard, Alsop	3000	Morgan	Frame	Howe	Smith S	Frith	Wyles	Barratt	Jayes	Jones D	Liddle	Hemon
16	23 H	Bristol City	W 5-1		Liddle 2, Barratt 2, Cheney / Bentley	2000	Morgan	Frame	Howe	Smith S	Wyles	Barnes	Barratt	Jayes	Cheney	Liddle	Hemon
17	25 H	Northampton Town	L 1-4		Sanderson / unknown 4		Graham	Frame	Howe	Smith S	Wyles	Paterson	Cheney	Jayes	Sanderson	Liddle	Hemon
18	30 A	Bristol City	L 1-3		Jayes / Bowers, Garrett, Tadman	1800	Morgan	Frame	Howe	Smith S	Wyles	Barnes	Barratt	Jayes	Sanderson	Buchan	Hemon

Final League Position: Southern Section: 1 of 13; Championship: 17 of 22.

Dismissals: May 16, Frame, Northampton Town (a).

Note: The eleven War Cup ties also counted towards the League Championship, though goals scored in extra time did not; Apr 6, after extra time, score at 90 minutes 0-2.

Season 1942-43

Champions: First Competition: Blackpool; Second Competition: Liverpool

FOOTBALL LEAGUE NORTH

Match No	Date		Opponents	Result	Supp. Comp.	Scorers	Att	1	2	3	4	5	6	7	8	9	10	11
1	Aug 29	H	Birmingham	L 0-1		- / McCormick	4000	Grant	Frame	Howe	Smith S	Wyles	Liddle	Dunkley	Kirkaldie	Jayes	Buchan	Hernon
2	Sep 5	A	Birmingham	L 1-2		Sanderson / Brown, Shaw	7000	Grant	Frame	Howe	Smith S	Sheard	Liddle	Kirkaldie	Walton R	Sanderson	Hernon	Cheney
3	12	A	West Bromwich Albion	L 2-3		Jayes, Hernon / Millard 3	4000	Grant	Frame	Howe	Smith S	Wyles	Liddle	Hilliard	Jayes	Sanderson	Hernon	Cheney
4	19	H	West Bromwich Albion	D 0-0			4029	Grant	Frame	Howe	Smith S	Wyles	Kendall	Walton H	Gallagher	Walton R	Hernon	Cheney
5	26	H	Coventry City	D 0-0			6025	Grant	Frame	Howe	Smith S	Sheard	Wyles	Cheney	Jayes	Walton R	Gallagher	Hernon
6	Oct 3	A	Coventry City	L 1-5		Plummer / Lowrie 3, Ashall, Simpson	9575	Grant	Frame	Howe	Smith S	Sheard	Wyles	Kirkaldie	Smith J	Cheney	Hernon	Plummer
7	10	H	Notts County	L 1-3		F Steele / Liddle 2, Booth	4000	Grant	Harrison	Howe	Smith S	Sheard	Wyles	Barratt	Jayes	Steele F	Hernon	Plummer
8	17	A	Notts County	D 1-1		Carver / Bowers	4000	Grant	Wyles	Howe	Smith S	Plummer	Paterson	Barratt	Smith J	Steele F	Carver	Hernon
9	24	A	Mansfield Town	W 2-1		Gardiner, Plummer / Rickards	1500	Grant	Snape	Howe	Smith S	Wyles	Robertson	McAskill	Gardiner	Plummer	Smith A	Hernon
10	31	H	Mansfield Town	W 5-2		F Steele 2, A Smith, Cheney 2 / Rickards, Bicknell	3000	Grant	Plummer	Howe	Smith S	Wyles	Hilliard	Cheney	Hughes	Steele F	Smith A	Hernon
11	Nov 7	H	Derby County	L 2-3		S Smith 2 (1p) / Weaver, Powell, Duncan	8500	Grant	Snape	Howe	Smith S	Sheard	Hilliard	Hughes	Jayes	Plummer	Steele F	Hernon
12	14	A	Derby County	L 3-5		Dunkley, Hughes, A Smith / Duncan 3, Lyman 2	9000	Bradley	Snape	Howe	Smith S	Bedford	Hilliard	Dunkley	Hughes	Plummer	Smith A	Steele E
13	21	H	Nottingham Forest	W 2-1		E Steele, F Steele / Egan	2300	Grant	Frame	Howe	Smith S	Snape	Plummer	Dunkley	Barratt	Steele F	Smith A	Steele E
14	28	A	Nottingham Forest	D 1-1		Hernon / Egan	3191	Grant	Walton R	Howe	Smith S	Gemmell	Snape	McAskill	Steele F	Chapman	Hernon	Flint
15	Dec 5	A	Wolverhampton Wanderers	W 2-0		F Steele 2	1954	Grant	Walton R	Howe	Smith S	Gemmell	Snape	Chapman	Barratt	Steele F	Smith A	Plummer
16	12	H	Wolverhampton Wanderers	W 5-0		Barratt, F Steele 4	5139	Grant	Walton R	Howe	Smith S	Gemmell	Plummer	Thompson	Barratt	Steele F	Hernon	Flint
17	19	A	Aston Villa	L 2-4		S Smith, F Steele / Broome, Houghton 3	4700	Bradley	Walton R	Howe	Smith S	Gemmell	Plummer	Thompson	Betteridge	Steele F	Hernon	Steele E
18	25	H	Aston Villa	L 2-5		Barratt, Chapman / Kerr 2, Broome 2, Edwards	8534	Grant	Walton R	Howe	Smith S	Gemmell	Plummer	Barratt	Gardiner	Chapman	Smith A	Hernon

FOOTBALL LEAGUE NORTH (Second Competition)

Match No	Date		Opponents	Result	Supp. Comp.	Scorers	Att	1	2	3	4	5	6	7	8	9	10	11
1	Dec 26	A	West Bromwich Albion	L 1-5	LNCQ	Chapman / Elliott 3 (1p), Hodgetts, Dudley	8119	Grant	Walton R	Howe	Smith S	Plummer	Hernon	Gemmell	Barratt	Chapman	Smith A	Flint
2	Jan 2	H	West Bromwich Albion	W 9-0	LNCQ	Dewis, F Steele 2, Barratt 2, Howe (p), Cheney 3	3578	Grant	Walton R	Howe	Smith S	Gemmell	Plummer	Barratt	Dewis	Steele F	Cheney	Steele E
3	9	A	Birmingham	L 0-5	LNCQ	- / McCormick, Jones 2, Craven, Howe (og)	1000	Grant	Walton R	Howe	Smith S	Gemmell	Plummer	Hernon	Dewis	Steele F	Sanderson	Liddle
4	16	H	Birmingham	W 2-1	LNCQ	Barratt, Frost / Acquaroff	5000	Grant	Walton R	Howe	Smith S	Gemmell	Wyles	Frost	Barratt	Sanderson	Smith A	Steele E
5	23	H	Nottingham Forest	W 5-0	LNCQ	Plummer 3, S Smith, Dunkley	5500	Grant	Walton R	Howe	Smith S	Gemmell	Wyles	Dunkley	Barratt	Plummer	Liddle	Frost
6	30	A	Nottingham Forest	L 0-2	LNCQ	- / Hindley 2, Beaumont, Egan	4267	Grant	Walton R	Howe	Smith S	Gemmell	Wyles	Barratt	Smith A	Plummer	Jayes	Cheney
7	Feb 6	A	Coventry City	L 0-2	LNCQ	- / Lowrie, Setchell	8187	Bradley	Walton R	Gemmell	Smith S	Sharman	Howe	Rochester	Barratt	Plummer	Smith A	Flint
8	13	A	Coventry City	W 3-1	LNCQ	S Smith, Dewis, Barratt / Lowrie	9544	Grant	Walton R	Gemmell	Smith S	Sharman	Hamilton	Barratt	Dewis	Plummer	Johnston	Liddle
9	20	A	Northampton Town	W 3-2	LNCQ	Plummer, Johnston, S Smith (p) / Macaulay, own goal	3000	Grant	Walton R	Gemmell	Smith S	Sharman	Hamilton	Hughes	Barratt	Plummer	Johnston	Liddle
10	27	A	Northampton Town	W 4-2	LNCQ	Barratt 2, S Smith (p), Johnston / Harris, Alsop	7000	Grant	Walton R	Gemmell	Smith S	Sharman	Hamilton	Hughes	Barratt	Dewis	Johnston	Cheney
11	Mar 6	A	Nottingham Forest	W 1-0	LNC 1 leg 1	Dewis	9064	King	Walton R	Howe	Smith S	Sharman	Hamilton	Pritchard	Jayes	Plummer	Johnston	Liddle
12	13	H	Nottingham Forest	L 0-2	LNC 1 leg 2	- / Clare, Hindley	9000	King	Walton R	Gemmell	Smith S	Sharman	Howe	Dunkley	Jayes	Harrison	Johnston	Liddle
13	20	H	Derby County	L 2-3		Liddle, Harrison / Attwood 2, Duncan	5000	King	Walton R	Howe	Smith S	Sharman	Jones	McCormick	Hughes	Harrison	Lewis	Liddle
14	27	H	Derby County	W 3-1		Howe, S Smith, Harrison / Attwood	4000	King	Walton R	Gemmell	Smith S	Sharman	Jones	Hughes	Phillips	Harrison	McCormick	Howe
15	Apr 3	H	Northampton Town	W 3-0		Phillips, Harrison, Dewis	3000	Grant	Walton R	Gemmell	Smith S	Sharman	Kendall	Hughes	Dewis	Harrison	Phillips	Howe
16	10	A	Northampton Town	D 2-2		Johnston, Rutherford / Harris, own goal	3000	Grant	Walton R	Howe	Smith S	Sharman	Kendall	Dunkley	Phillips	Harrison	Johnston	Rutherford
17	17	H	Coventry City	L 1-3		S Smith (p) / Lowrie 2, Simmons	3556	Grant	Walton R	Howe	Smith S	Gemmell	Kendall	McCormick	Phillips	Walton R	Johnston	Rutherford
18	24	A	Coventry City	D 0-0			4188	Grant	Sharman	Howe	Smith S	Gemmell	Kendall	Hughes	Phillips	Walton R	Johnston	Hernon
19	26	H	Stoke City	L 1-2		Liddle / F Mountford 2	2424	Grant	Walton R	Wyles	Johnston	Gemmell	Howe	Hughes	Phillips	Sharman	Browne	Liddle
20	May 1	A	Stoke City	L 0-3		- / Bowyer, G Mountford, Vallance	1500	Grant	Walton R	Gemmell	Smith S	Burditt	Johnston	Birks	Staples	Harrison	Dunkley	Longland

Final League Position: First Competition: 33 of 48; Second Competition: 22 of 54

Note: The twelve League North ties also counted towards the League North table, but goals scored in extra time did not; Nov 21, played at Coalville; Mar 13, after extra time, score at 90 minutes 0-1.

Season 1943-44

Champions: First Competition: Blackpool; Second Competition: Bath City

FOOTBALL LEAGUE NORTH

Match No	Date	V	Opponents	Result	Supp. Comp.	Att	1	2	3	4	5	6	7	8	9	10	11	Scorers
1	Aug 28	H	Mansfield Town	W 4-1		3579	Grant A	Frame	Howe	Smith S	Sharman	Liddle	McNeil	Phillips	Dewis	Dickie	Bulger	Phillips 3, Dewis / Chessell
2	Sep 4	H	Mansfield Town	D 0-0		2500	Grant A	Frame	Howe	Smith S	Sharman	Liddle	Staples	Phillips	Steward	Dickie	Bulger	
3	11	A	Birmingham	L 0-3		6000	Grant A	Frame	Howe	Smith S	Sharman	Liddle	Frost	Phillips	Chapman	North	Bulger	- / Hinsley 2 (1p), Acquaroff
4	18	H	Birmingham	D 2-2		4674	Grant A	Frame	Howe	Smith S	Gemmell	Liddle	Cronin	Phillips	Chapman	Dickie	Bulger	S Smith, Bulger / Hinsley, Bright
5	25	A	Coventry City	W 1-0		5962	Grant A	Frame	Howe	Smith S	Gemmell	Liddle	Cronin	Dickie	Bulger	Lycett	Roberts	Dickie
6	Oct 2	H	Coventry City	W 1-0		6328	Grant A	Frame	Howe	Smith S	Gemmell	Liddle	Cronin	Dewis	Bulger	Lycett	Jones LO	Cronin
7	9	H	West Bromwich Albion	L 0-3		6971	Grant A	Frame	Howe	Smith S	Gemmell	Liddle	Campbell	Dickie	Phillips	Lycett	Campbell	- / Richardson 2, Hodgetts
8	16	A	West Bromwich Albion	D 2-2		7090	Grant A	Frame	Becci	Sheard	Gemmell	Liddle	Campbell	Smith S	Bowden	Lycett	Hillard	Lycett, Campbell / Richardson 2
9	23	H	Notts County	W 5-0		3000	Grant A	Frame	Becci	Smith S	Gemmell	Liddle	Cronin	Dickie	Bowden	Lycett	Campbell	Campbell, Bowden 2, Lycett, Marshall (og)
10	30	A	Notts County	W 9-1		5000	Grant A	Frame	Becci	Smith S	Gemmell	Liddle	Cronin	Dickie	Dewis	Smith A	Campbell	Dewis 4, Campbell, A Smith 4 / Antonio
11	Nov 6	H	Derby County	L 0-1		9000	Grant A	Frame	Becci	Smith S	Gemmell	Liddle	Cronin	Smith A	Phillips	Dickie	Campbell	- / T Jones
12	13	A	Derby County	L 2-3		7000	Grant A	Frame	Howe	Smith S	Gemmell	Dickie	Little	Phillips	Sutton	Lycett	Alsop	Alsop, Vose (og) / Carter, Rodgers, Nicholas
13	20	A	Nottingham Forest	L 0-1		4759	Grant A	Frame	Howe	Smith S	Gemmell	Little	Little	Dickie	Cheney	Cheney	Bulger	- / Dulson
14	27	H	Nottingham Forest	D 3-3		3000	Grant A	Frame	Gemmell	Dickie	Smith S	Liddle	Campbell	Staples	Bowden	Cheney	Alsop	Bowden 2, Staples / Dulson, Johnston, Flewitt
15	Dec 4	H	Wolverhampton Wanderers	W 1-0		5223	Grant A	Frame	Becci	Smith S	Gemmell	Dickie	Hillard	Staples	Bowden	Lycett	Campbell	Bowden
16	11	A	Wolverhampton Wanderers	L 1-4		3869	Grant A	Frame	Harrison	Smith S	Gemmell	Liddle	Cronin	Staples	Alsop	Dickie	Campbell	Alsop / Stephens 2, McLean, Dunn
17	18	H	Aston Villa	L 1-3		4737	Major	Frame	Becci	Sheard	Gemmell	Dickie	Campbell	Lycett	Bowden	Dimond	Alsop	Campbell / Parkes 2, Houghton
18	25	A	Aston Villa	L 1-3		10000	Major	Frame	Becci	Smith S	Sheard	Plummer	Campbell	Lycett	Grant R	Dimond	Alsop	Lycett / Houghton 2 (1p), Broome

FOOTBALL LEAGUE NORTH (Second Competition)

Match No	Date	V	Opponents	Result	Supp. Comp.	Att	1	2	3	4	5	6	7	8	9	10	11	Scorers
1	Dec 26	A	Notts County	W 2-1	LNCQ	10000	Grant A	Frame	Becci	Sheard	Gemmell	Liddle	Goffin	Smith S	Bowden	Lycett	Campbell	Bowden 2 / Edwards
2	Jan 1	H	Notts County	W 7-2	LNCQ	6000	Grant A	Frame	Sharman	Sheard	Gemmell	Liddle	Goffin	Smith S	Bowden	Lycett	Campbell	S Smith 3 (1p), Bowden 3, Campbell / Knott, Towler
3	8	A	Derby County	W 1-0	LNCQ	10000	Grant A	Frame	Sharman	Sheard	Gemmell	Dickie	Alsop	Smith S	Bowden	Campbell	Goffin	Bowden
4	15	H	Derby County	W 1-0	LNCQ	10000	Grant A	Frame	Sharman	Sheard	Gemmell	Dickie	Goffin	Smith S	Bowden	Lycett	Campbell	Campbell
5	22	H	Mansfield Town	W 5-2	LNCQ	6000	Major	Frame	Sharman	Sheard	Gemmell	Liddle	Cronin	Smith S	Alsop	Dickie	Campbell	Campbell, S Smith 2, Cronin, Alsop / Rickards, own goal
6	29	A	Mansfield Town	D 1-1	LNCQ	5000	Grant A	Frame	Howe	Sheard	Gemmell	Liddle	Cronin	Smith S	Knott	Dickie	Campbell	Knott / Marlow
7	Feb 5	H	Sheffield Wednesday	D 1-1	LNCQ	8000	Grant A	Frame	Howe	Sheard	Sharman	Liddle	Morton	Smith S	Knott	Campbell	Alsop	Russell (og) / Froggatt
8	12	A	Sheffield Wednesday	W 3-0	LNCQ	15000	Grant A	Frame	Howe	Sheard	Gemmell	Dickie	Knott	Smith S	Dewis	Jayes	Campbell	Knott 2, Dewis
9	19	A	Nottingham Forest	L 0-1	LNCQ	5829	Grant A	Frame	Davidson	Sheard	Gemmell	Howe	Cronin	Smith S	Knott	Liddle	Little	- / Johnston
10	26	H	Nottingham Forest	D 1-1	LNC 1 leg 1	10000	Grant A	Frame	Howe	King	Gemmell	Sheard	Little	Smith S	Knott	Jones LJ	Campbell	LJ Jones / Wheatley
11	Mar 4	A	Birmingham	L 1-3	LNC 1 leg 2	12000	Grant A	Frame	Howe	Sheard	Gemmell	Jones LJ	Little	Smith S	Rickards	Knott	Campbell	LJ Jones / Mulraney, Trigg 2
12	11	H	Birmingham	W 2-1	LNC 1 leg 2	15000	Grant A	Frame	Howe	Sheard	Gemmell	Dickie	Little	Smith A	Knott	Jones LJ	Muncie	Muncie, Howe (p) / Bright
13	18	A	Stoke City	W 5-2	MC 1 leg 1	3279	Bradley	Frame	Howe	Smith S	Gemmell	Dickie	Little	Smith A	Knott	Jones LJ	Crossland	Knott 3, A Smith, Little / F Mountford, Sellars
14	25	H	Stoke City	D 2-2	MC 1 leg 2	7000	Bradley	Frame	Howe	Sparrow	Gemmell	Sheard	King	Smith S	Dewis	Dickie	Hillard	Dewis 2 / Bowyer, Ormston
15	Apr 1	H	Northampton Town	L 0-2	MC 2 leg 1	7000	Grant A	Frame	Howe	Smith S	Gemmell	Little	King	Dewis	Knott	Dickie	Campbell	- / Perry, Brooks
16	8	A	Northampton Town	L 1-3	MC 2 leg 2	7000	Grant A	Frame	Reeday	Smith S	Sheard	Howe	Frost	Little	Walton	Liddle	Wattie	Wattie / Barron, Fenton 2
17	10	A	Wolverhampton Wanderers	L 1-4		9941	Grant A	Sparrow	Wyles	King	Sharman	Howe	Little	Phillips	Sheard	Liddle	Wattie	Sheard (p) / McLean 2, Mullen 2
18	15	H	Coventry City	D 1-1		4037	Grant A	Frame	Walton	King	Gemmell	Sheard	Little	Phillips	Sharman	Kilshaw	Wattie	Phillips / Edwards
19	22	A	Coventry City	L 2-6		3420	Grant A	Frame	Walton	King	Sharman	Lycett	Hillard	Phillips	Sanderson	Middleton	Campbell	Sanderson 2 / Crawley 3, McKeown, Edwards, Barratt
20	29	A	Derby County	W 2-0		3000	Grant A	Frame	Sharman	King	Gemmell	Dickie	Campbell	Smith S	Sheard	Windle	Bulger	Sheard, Windle
21	May 6	H	Derby County	W 1-0		3000	Grant A	Frame	Howe	King	Gemmell	Kendall	Campbell	Smith S	Sheard	Dickie	Bulger	Leuty (og)

Final League Position: First Competition: 28 of 50; Second Competition: 14 of 56.

Note: The twelve League North Cup ties and four Midland Cup ties also counted towards the League North table, but goals scored in extra time did not; Mar 11, after extra time, score at 90 minutes 2-0.

Champions: First Competition: Huddersfield Town; Second Competition: Derby County

FOOTBALL LEAGUE NORTH

Match No	Date		Opponents	Result	Supp. Comp.	Att	Scorers	1	2	3	4	5	6	7	8	9	10	11
1	Aug 26	H	Wolverhampton Wanderers	D 2-2		10175	Dewis 2 / Haycock, Dorsett	Grant	Frame	Howe	King	Gemmell	Dickie	Revie	Smith S	Dewis	Jones LJ	Campbell
2	Sep 2	A	Wolverhampton Wanderers	L 0-4		7948	- / Acquaroff 2, Aldecoa, Finch	Grant	Frame	Harrison	King	Gemmell	Sheard	Revie	Smith S	Dewis	Dickie	Campbell
3	9	H	Walsall	L 2-3		7000	Phillips 2 / Beech, Kernick, White	Grant	Frame	Cobley	Smith S	Sheard	Dickie	Jones T	King	Phillips	Jones LJ	Smart
4	16	A	Walsall	W 1-0		5000	Mercer	Grant	Frame	Cobley	Smith S	Sheard	Paterson	Jones T	King	Mercer	Woodvine	Campbell
5	23	H	Birmingham	L 0-1		7000	- / Shaw	Grant	Frame	Howe	Smith S	Sheard	Dickie	Jones T	Smith A	Rickards	Jones LJ	Woodvine
6	30	A	Birmingham	D 3-3		10000	Rickards, Mercer 2 / Mulraney 2, Trigg	Grant	Frame	Howe	King	Sheard	Jones LJ	Jones T	Rickards	Mercer	Smith S	Campbell
7	Oct 7	A	West Bromwich Albion	D 1-1		9970	S Smith / Heaselgrave	Major	Frame	Howe	King	Sheard	Jones LJ	Jones T	Dewis	Mercer	Smith S	Campbell
8	14	H	West Bromwich Albion	L 0-2		7201	- / Evans, Clarke	Major	Frame	Howe	King	Sheard	Jones LJ	Campbell	Brown	Rickards	Smith S	Woodvine
9	21	H	Port Vale	W 4-1		5770	Campbell, Rickards 3 (1p) / E Prince	Major	Frame	Cobley	King	Sheard	Jones LJ	Campbell	Rickards	Bowden	Smith S	Douglas
10	28	A	Port Vale	L 1-2		4070	Rickards / Bellis, McDowell	Major	Frame	Howe	King	Sheard	Jones LJ	Campbell	Rickards	Bowden	Smith S	Douglas
11	Nov 4	H	Coventry City	W 2-1		5989	Campbell, S Smith / Paul	Major	Frame	Howe	King	Sheard	Jones LJ	Campbell	Rickards	Chapman	Smith S	Muncie
12	11	A	Coventry City	L 1-3		4829	Kelly / Paul 2, Frith	Major	Frame	Howe	King	Sheard	Jones LJ	Campbell	Rickards	Kelly	Smith S	Dickie
13	18	A	Northampton Town	L 1-3		3000	Dunkley / Morrall 2, Hughes	Major	Frame	Howe	Grogan	Sheard	Jones LJ	Dunkley	Rickards	Kelly	Smith S	Long
14	25	H	Northampton Town	D 2-2		5000	Bowden, Rickards / Morrall, Hughes	Major	Frame	Hubble	King	Sheard	Jones LJ	Kelly	Rickards	Bowden	Smith S	Dunkley
15	Dec 2	H	Aston Villa	L 0-3		10648	- / Edwards, Houghton 2	Major	Frame	Howe	Smith S	Sheard	King	Dunkley	Rickards	Mercer	Jones LJ	Hubble
16	9	A	Aston Villa	L 0-5		12000	- / Goffin, Houghton 3, Haycock	Major	Frame	Hubble	Smith S	Sheard	King	Smith A	Stephan	Kelly	Iddon	Chapman
17	16	H	Stoke City	L 2-5		5000	Iddon, Cheney / Matthews 2, Sale 2, Frame (og)	Major	Frame	Howe	Towers	Morby	Sheard	Dunkley	Smith S	Sanderson	Iddon	Cheney
18	23	H	Stoke City	L 1-5		8000	Rickards / Sale 2, Matthews, Bowyer, G Mountford	Bradley	Frame	Howe	Towers	Smith S	Sheard	Dunkley	Rickards	Sanderson	Iddon	Buckby

FOOTBALL LEAGUE NORTH (Second Competition)

Match No	Date		Opponents	Result	Supp. Comp.	Att	Scorers	1	2	3	4	5	6	7	8	9	10	11
1	Dec 30	A	Nottingham Forest	D 0-0	LNCQ	6800		Major	Frame	Howe	Smith S	Sheard	King	Dunkley	Rickards	Wyles	Riley	Campbell
2	Jan 6	A	Mansfield Town	D 2-2	LNCQ	5000	Kilshaw, S Smith (p) / Curry, Marlow	Grant	Frame	Howe	Kilshaw	Wyles	Lindley	Dunkley	Smith S	Dewis	Riley	Liddle
3	13	H	Mansfield Town	W 8-3	LNCQ	5000	Leitch 3, S Smith 2, Liddle 2, Dunkley / Rickards, Hewitt, Akers	Major	Frame	Howe	King	Sheard	Towers	Dunkley	Smith S	Leitch	Iddon	Liddle
4	20	A	Chesterfield	L 0-1	LNCQ	3000	- / Milburn	Major	Frame	Howe	Towers	Sheard	Lindley	Campbell	Smith S	Wyles	Iddon	Liddle
5	27	H	Chesterfield	D 2-2	LNCQ	4000	Leitch, S Smith (p) / Milburn 2	Major	Frame	Howe	Towers	Sheard	Wyles	Kilshaw	Smith S	Leitch	Iddon	Liddle
6	Feb 3	A	Notts County	W 4-1	LNCQ	5000	S Smith, Stephan, Leitch 2 / Southwell	Major	Frame	Howe	Jones R	Sheard	Towers	Buckby	Smith S	Leitch	Stephan	Liddle
7	10	H	Notts County	W 4-1	LNCQ	7500	Leitch, Liddle, Bowden, S Smith / Wright	Major	Frame	Howe	Towers	Sheard	Jones R	Bowden	Smith S	Leitch	Stephan	Liddle
8	17	H	Derby County	D 2-2	LNCQ	17546	Leitch 2 / Crooks, Duncan	Major	Frame	Howe	Kilshaw	Sheard	Towers	Dunkley	Bowden	Leitch	Stephan	Liddle
9	24	A	Derby County	L 0-3	LNCQ	18621	- / Doherty 2, Howe (og)	Major	Frame	Howe	Smith S	Sheard	Towers	Smith C	Mercer	Leitch	Bowden	Liddle
10	Mar 3	H	Nottingham Forest	D 1-1	LNCQ	10000	Leitch / Johnston	Major	Frame	Howe	Smith S	Sheard	Towers	Dunkley	Tapping	Leitch	Iddon	Liddle
11	10	A	Wolverhampton Wanderers	L 2-3		7856	Cronin, Ashton (og) / Fenton 2, Williams	Major	Hanford	Howe	Tapping	Leitch	Riley	Cronin	Smith S	Bowden	Iddon	Liddle
12	17	H	Coventry City	D 2-2		5133	Bowden, Douglas / Elliott, Edwards	Major	Frame	Hanford	Sheard	Plummer	Riley	Cronin	Smith S	Bowden	Thompson	Douglas
13	24	H	Derby County	W 2-1	LNC 1 leg 1	19074	Iddon, S Smith / Lyman	Major	McCall	Howe	Elliott	Sheard	Baxter	Bowden	Smith S	Leitch	Iddon	Clare
14	31	A	Derby County	L 0-2	LNC 1 leg 2	24900	- / Carter, Leuty	Major	McCall	Howe	Baxter	Sheard	Elliott	Cronin	Smith S	Leitch	Bowden	Cheney
15	Apr 2	H	Sheffield Wednesday	W 2-1		7500	Cheney, Tapping / Bates	Graham	Frame	Howe	Kilshaw	Sheard	Wyles	Cronin	Tapping	Bowden	Cheney	Liddle
16	7	H	Aston Villa	W 2-0		7000	Tapping, Leitch	Graham	Frame	Howe	Tapping	Sheard	Towers	Frost	Smith S	Leitch	Bowden	Morrison
17	14	A	Aston Villa	L 2-7		7500	Leitch, S Smith (p) / Edwards 2, Goffin, Houghton 3, Parkes	Major	Frame	Howe	Tapping	Sheard	Towers	Cronin	Smith S	Leitch	Thompson	Morrison
18	21	A	West Bromwich Albion	L 0-1	MC 1 leg 1	5002	- / Clarke	Graham	Frame	Howe	King	Sheard	Towers	Cronin	Smith S	Mercer	Thompson	Liddle
19	28	H	West Bromwich Albion	W 3-0	MC 1 leg 2	6166	S Smith 2, Dewis	Graham	Frame	Howe	Tapping	Sheard	Towers	Dunkley	Smith S	Dewis	Iddon	Liddle
20	May 5	A	Derby County	L 1-3	MC 2 leg 1	7270	Dewis / Doherty 2, Lyman	Graham	Frame	Howe	Tapping	Sheard	Towers	Dunkley	Smith S	Dewis	Iddon	Johnston
21	12	H	Derby County	L 1-2	MC 2 leg 2	9000	Dewis / Crooks, Doherty	Graham	Frame	Howe	Kilshaw	Sheard	Elliott	Dunkley	Smith S	Dewis	Bowden	Johnston

Final League Position: First Competition: 52 of 54; Second Competition: 34 of 60

Note: The twelve League North Cup ties and four Midland Cup ties also counted towards the League North title.

Champions: Birmingham

FOOTBALL LEAGUE SOUTH

Match No	Date	H/A	Opponents	Result	Supp. Comp.	Scorers	Att	1	2	3	4	5	6	7	8	9	10	11
1	Aug 25	H	Charlton Athletic	L 2-3		Mercer, Cronin / Welsh, Turner, Hobbis	14000	Graham R	Frame	Jones	Smith S	Sheard	Howe	Cronin	Revie	Mercer	Riley	Liddle
2	Sep 1	A	Charlton Athletic	L 1-2		Mercer / Welsh, Turner	18000	Graham R	Frame	Jones	Graham J	Grogan	Towers	Attwood	Revie	Mercer	Hernon	Liddle
3	6	A	Brentford	W 2-1		Liddle, Mercer / Sloan	11620	Graham R	Frame	Jones	Smith S	Grogan	Russell	Sinclair	Revie	Mercer	Liddle	Anderson
4	8	A	Fulham	D 1-1		Mercer / Rooke	18000	Graham R	Frame	Jones	Smith S	Grogan	Robinson	Revie	McInally	Mercer	Liddle	Anderson
5	12	A	Tottenham Hotspur	L 2-6		S Smith (p), Jones / Burgess 2, McCormick, AE Hall, Ludford 2	13294	Graham R	Frame	Jones	Smith S	Grogan	Robinson	Revie	McInally	Bowden	Liddle	Anderson
6	15	H	Fulham	L 0-1		- / Taylor	14000	Graham R	Frame	Jones	Smith S	Grogan	Towers	Anderson	Revie	Small	Liddle	Aldecoa
7	22	A	Plymouth Argyle	W 3-2		Aldecoa, Mercer, Campbell / Tinkler, R Brown	15000	Graham R	Frame	Jones	Smith S	Howe	Towers	Campbell	Revie	Mercer	Aldecoa	Stubbs
8	29	H	Plymouth Argyle	D 2-2		Revie, A Smith / Tinkler, D Thomas	24000	Graham R	Frame	Jones	Smith S	Howe	Soo	Revie	Smith A	Mercer	Liddle	Aldecoa
9	Oct 6	A	Portsmouth	L 0-2		- / Froggatt, Evans	21930	Graham R	Jones	Howe	Smith S	Davies	Soo	Campbell	Revie	Mercer	Smith A	Liddle
10	13	H	Portsmouth	W 3-2		A Smith, Soo, S Smith (p) / Evans, Barlow	18646	Calvert	Frame	Howe	Smith S	Davies	Soo	Campbell	Revie	Mercer	Smith A	Aldecoa
11	20	H	Nottingham Forest	D 0-0			14861	Calvert	Frame	Howe	Smith S	Sheard	Towers	Campbell	Revie	Dewis	Middleton	Poulton
12	27	A	Nottingham Forest	L 0-2		Soo / Barks	19807	Calvert	Frame	Howe	Smith S	Sheard	Soo	Anderson	Revie	Mercer	Towers	Liddle
13	Nov 3	A	Newport County	L 0-2		- / Derrick 2	10000	Graham R	Frame	Howe	Smith S	Smith E	Pearce	Campbell	King	Mercer	Towers	Liddle
14	10	H	Newport County	W 2-0		Liddle 2	10000	Grant	Frame	Howe	Smith S	Smith E	Soo	Campbell	Towers	Mercer	Lycett	Liddle
15	17	H	Wolverhampton Wanderers	L 1-2		Lycett / Chatham, Dunn	17486	Grant	Frame	Howe	Smith S	Smith E	Soo	Campbell	Revie	Jones	Lycett	Liddle
16	24	A	Wolverhampton Wanderers	L 0-3		- / Chatham 2, Mullen	22099	Grant	Frame	Howe	Smith S	Smith E	Soo	Dewis	Grogan	Mercer	Lycett	Johnson
17	Dec 1	A	West Ham United	D 2-2		Mercer, Revie / Macaulay, Small	20000	Grant	Frame	Howe	Grogan	Smith E	Towers	Revie	Smith S	Mercer	Lycett	Liddle
18	8	H	West Ham United	W 4-1		King, Mercer, Towers 2 / Woodgate	12345	Grant	Frame	Howe	Smith S	Smith E	Soo	Revie	King	Mercer	Towers	Liddle
19	15	H	West Bromwich Albion	L 1-3		Mercer / Elliott, Newsome, Millard	14227	Grant	Frame	Howe	Osborne	Smith E	Soo	Revie	King	Mercer	Towers	Liddle
20	22	A	West Bromwich Albion	L 2-3		Pimbley, Soo / Elliott 2, Newsome	15107	Grant	Frame	Watts	Smith S	Sheard	Soo	Campbell	Dewis	Mercer	Pimbley	Weatherston
21	25	A	Birmingham	L 2-6		Dewis 2 / Jones 2, Dougall, Bodle, Edwards, Mulraney	30000	Calvert	Frame	Howe	Smith S	Grogan	Soo	Revie	Hernon	Dewis	Pimbley	Liddle
22	26	H	Birmingham	L 0-1		- / Mulraney	24460	Calvert	Frame	Jones	Smith S	Grogan	Towers	Revie	Hernon	Dewis	Osborne	Weatherston
23	29	H	Tottenham Hotspur	W 4-0		Revie, Mercer, S Smith 2	15330	Calvert	Frame	Jones	Osborne	Sheard	Towers	Revie	Smith A	Mercer	Soo	Adam
24	Jan 12	A	Chelsea	L 1-7		Foster / Williams 3, Payne 2, Foss, Dolding	15894	Calvert	Watts	Howe	Smith S	Sheard	Grogan	Mercer	Smith A	Sutton	Chisholm	Foster
25	19	A	Chelsea	L 0-4		- / Williams 3, Payne	14349	Grant	Frame	Howe	Osborne	Sheard	Towers	King	Smith S	Mercer	Smith A	Foster
26	26	H	Arsenal	L 4-5		Foster 2, Mercer, Chisholm / Barnard 2, LJ Jones 2, Bremner	14723	Grant	Frame	Jones	Smith S	Sheard	Towers	Revie	Chisholm	Mercer	Smith A	Foster
27	Feb 9	H	Millwall	L 2-6		Osborne, Harrison / Hurrell 3, Osman, Johnson 2	10834	Calvert	Frame	Howe	Osborne	Sheard	Towers	Revie	Harrison	Lee	Osborne	Weatherston
28	16	A	Southampton	L 1-2		S Smith (p) / Evans, Veck	13826	Calvert	Frame	Jones	Osborne	Smith E	Towers	Revie	Smith S	Dewis	Chisholm	Letters
29	23	H	Southampton	L 1-3		Pimbley / Bradley, McGibbon, G Smith	10000	Calvert	Frame	Howe	Smith S	Smith E	King	Revie	Iggleden	Dewis	Pimbley	Foster
30	Mar 2	A	Derby County	D 1-1		Pimbley / Powell	21640	Calvert	Frame	Howe	Smith S	Smith E	Soo	Revie	Iggleden	Mercer	Pimbley	Foster
31	9	A	Swansea Town	L 3-4		Pimbley, Revie, Campbell / Ford 2, Roberts 2	24000	Calvert	Frame	Howe	Smith S	Smith E	King	Campbell	Revie	Cutting	Pimbley	Foster
32	16	H	Swansea Town	L 0-2		- / Ford, own goal	12534	Calvert	Frame	Howe	Smith S	Smith E	King	Campbell	Revie	Pimbley	Iggleden	Foster
33	23	A	Coventry City	L 1-3		Foster / Barratt 2, Crawley	13864	Calvert	Ashton	Howe	Smith S	Smith E	King	Griffiths	Osborne	Dewis	Harrison	Foster
34	30	H	Coventry City	W 1-0		Griffiths	14240	Calvert	Jones	Howe	Osborne	Grogan	King	Griffiths	Smith S	Dewis	Towers	Foster
35	Apr 6	A	Luton Town	L 1-2		Dewis / Billington, Lee	14000	Grant	Jones	Howe	Osborne	Grogan	King	Griffiths	Smith S	Dewis	Towers	Cutting
36	10	H	Derby County	L 1-4		King / Duncan 2, Doherty (p), Carter	15541	Grant	Jones	Howe	Osborne	Grogan	Soo	Griffiths	Revie	Lee	King	Lycett
37	13	H	Luton Town	L 0-2		- / Billington 2	9195	Grant	Frame	Howe	Smith S	Grogan	Towers	Griffiths	Smith A	Osborne	King	Lycett
38	15	A	Millwall	D 2-2		S Smith (p), A Smith / Jinks, Ford	11500	Grant	Frame	Howe	Smith S	Grogan	Towers	Revie	King	Griffiths	Smith A	Cutting
39	20	A	Arsenal	W 2-1		A Smith, Griffiths / Roffi	20000	Calvert	Frame	Howe	Smith S	Grogan	Towers	Revie	King	Griffiths	Smith A	Liddle
40	22	A	Aston Villa	L 0-3		- / Dixon, Goffin 2	30000	Grant	Frame	Jones	Smith S	Grogan	Towers	Griffiths	Revie	Pimbley	Smith A	Woodvine
41	23	H	Aston Villa	L 0-1		- / Martin	20000	Grant	Frame	Jones	Smith S	Grogan	Towers	Revie	Smith S	Griffiths	King	Pimbley
42	May 4	H	Brentford	L 1-3		Heathcote / Durrant, McAloon 2	10000	Calvert	Jones	Howe	Smith S	Grogan	Towers	Griffiths	Edwards	Heathcote	King	Goffin

Final League Position: 20 of 22

Season 1939-40

NAME	CLUB	Apps RLM	LWC	Goals RLM	LWC
Tom Ansell	Petronians	1			
Bill Barron	Northampton Town	6	1		1
Andy Beattie	Preston North End	4			
George Bedford		13			
Jack Bowers		22	4	13	1
Joe Calvert		3			
Billy Coutts		8			
George Dewis		14	3	9	1
Harry Eastham	Liverpool	6			
Billy Frame		22	4		
John Grogan		12	3		
Percy Grosvenor		5			
Fred Haycock	Aston Villa	10	3	1	2
Roger Heywood		1	2		
Eric Houghton	Aston Villa	12	3	2	
Bert Howe		16			
Bob Iverson	Aston Villa	7	4		
Gordon Jayes		7	1	2	
Dai Jones		24	4	1	
Bobby King	Northampton Town	2		1	
Bill Kinghorn	Liverpool	3		5	
Tommy Lawton	Everton	3		1	
Danny Liddle		4		1	
Stanley Logan	Highfields United	1			
Sandy McLaren		23	4		
Jack Pritchard	Manchester City	10		1	
Arthur Queenborough	Wigston COB	2			
Alan Rochester	Hexham United	1			
Fred Sansome	Oadby Imperial	4			
Fred Sharman		17	4		
Frank Shell	Aston Villa	1			
Jack Smith	Fairfax United	5	4	2	
Sep Smith		25	4	7	2
Tommy Thompson		15		1	

Season 1940-41

NAME	CLUB	Apps SRL	LWC	Goals SRL	LWC
Charlie Adam		3			
Jack Bowers		1		1	
Ken Burditt	Colchester United	3	1		
Joe Calvert		32	6		
Vernon Chapman		1	1	1	
Denis Cheney		3	1		
Arthur Chesters	Crystal Palace				
Edwin Cunningham	Bristol City	1		4	
George Dewis		22	8	20	
Willie Fagan	Liverpool	1			
Walter Foster	Western Athletic	1		1	
Billy Frame		33	10		
Billy Freer	Syston Imperial	1			
Billy Frith	Coventry City	9	7		
Stan Frost		3			
John Grogan		2			
Jimmy Harrison		5		2	
Roger Heywood		28	9	2	
Bert Howe		30	10	2	
Gordon Jayes		8	2	3	2
Harry Johnston	Blackpool	4	1		
Dai Jones		1	1		
Jack Lee		9	10	7	6
Danny Liddle		27	8	6	2
Colin Lyman	Tottenham Hotspur	4			
Jimmy Mullen	Wolverhampton W.	25		15	
George Paterson	Celtic	7	3		
Alan Rochester		17	4		
George Roome	Gresley Rovers	1			
Don Sanderson	Coalville Town	5		1	
Fred Sharman		4			
Frank Sheard		5	1		
Arthur E Smith	Wolverhampton W.	13	8	9	5
Jack Smith		11	1	1	
Les G Smith	Junior club (Leicester area)	3	1		
Sep Smith		1			
Terry Springthorpe	Wolverhampton W.	1			
Fred Steele	Stoke City	7	5	5	
Dennis Thornhill	Wolverhampton W.	3	1		
Bill Towers		3	2		
Eric Ward	Gresley Rovers	1			
Fred Wilson	Bournemouth & B.A.	1			
Doug Witcomb	West Bromwich Albion	1			
Dennis Wright	Mansfield Town	1		2	
Billy Wright	Wolverhampton W.	26	7	11	1
Harold Wyles		1			

Season 1941-42

NAME	CLUB	Apps FLS	FLC	Goals FLS	FLC
Charlie Adam		3			
William Barnes	Hinckley ATC	1	2		
Harry Barratt	Coventry City	17	13	4	4
Jack Bowers		13			
Willie Buchan	Blackpool	4		2	
Charles Bulger	Walsall	1			
Joe Calvert		2	4		
Vernon Chapman		2	1	2	1
Denis Cheney	Coventry City	14	10	11	4
Tom Crawley		4			
George Dewis		3		7	
Ted Drake	Arsenal	1			
Billy Frame		17	18		
Billy Frith	Coventry City	15	11	4	
Stan Frost		1			
Dick Graham		1			
Alick Grant		4	5		
John Grogan		1		1	
Jimmy Harrison		1			
Jimmy Hemon		4		1	
Bert Howe		17	18	1	1
Ray Iggleden		3			
Gordon Jayes		15	17	8	6
Dai Jones		1			
Les J Jones	Arsenal	1			
Jack Lee		3	2		
Danny Liddle		2	10	4	
Reg Mansfield		4			
Bill Morgan	Coventry City	9	8		
Ambrose Mulraney	Ipswich Town	1			
Harry Parker	Holwell Works	2			
George Paterson	Celtic	10	10		
Alan Rochester		3	1		
Don Sanderson		6	4	4	
Frank Sheard		4	2		
Arthur E Smith		15	12	3	4
Les Smith	Brentford	1			
Sep Smith		15	17	4	2
George Taylor	Coventry City	2	1		
Harold Wyles		5		1	

John Grogan

Season 1942-43

NAME	CLUB	Apps FLN	FLN2	Goals FLN	FLN2
Harry Barratt	Coventry City	6	9	2	6
George Bedford	Northampton Town	1			
Mick Betteridge	Loughborough College	1			
William Birks	Port Vale	1			
Gordon Bradley		2	1		
JH Browne	Aston Villa	1			
Willie Buchan	Blackpool				
Ken Burditt	Colchester United	1			
Willie Carver		1		1	
Vernon Chapman		3	1	1	1
Denis Cheney		6	3	2	3
George Dewis		6		4	
Maurice Dunkley	Manchester City	3	4	1	1
Ken Flint	Bedford Town	2	2		
Billy Frame		7			
Stan Frost		2		1	
Patsy Gallagher	Stoke City	2			
Charlie Gardiner	Mansfield Town	2	1	1	
Jimmy Gemmell	Bury	5	16		
Alick Grant		16	15		
Willie Hamilton	Preston North End	4			
Jimmy Harrison		1	6		
Jimmy Hemon		15	3	2	
Jock Hillard		4			
Bert Howe		18	16	2	
Gwyn Hughes	BTH (Rugby)	3	7	1	
Gordon Jayes		5	3	1	
Tom Johnston	Northampton Town	10	3		
Les O Jones		2			
Jack Kendall		1	4		
Sid King	Birmingham	4			
Jack Kirkaldie	Doncaster Rovers	3			
Glyn Lewis	Crystal Palace	1			
Danny Liddle		3	8	2	
Eric Longland	Stoke City	2			
A McAskill	Third Lanark	2			
Jim McCormick	Tottenham Hotspur	3			
George Paterson	Celtic	6		1	
Russell Phillips					
Norman Plummer		12	10	2	4
Jack Pritchard	Manchester City	1			
Jimmy Robertson	Bradford City	1			
Alan Rochester		1			
Bill Rutherford	Army	2	1	1	
Don Sanderson		2	2	1	
Fred Sharman		13			
Frank Sheard		5			
Arthur E Smith		6	4	2	
Jack Smith		2			
Sep Smith		18	19	3	6
John Snape	Coventry City	6			
Len Staples					
Ernie Steele	Rochdale	3	2	1	
Fred Steele	Stoke City	9	2	11	2
Tommy Thompson		1			
Harry Walton		13			
Dick Walton		8	20		
Harold Wyles		9	3		

Joe Calvert

O F   F O S S I L S   &   F O X E S

Willie Muncie

Billy Frame

Season 1943-44

NAME	CLUB	Apps FLN	FLN2	Goals FLN	FLN2
Gilbert Alsop	Walsall	5	3	2	1
Attilio Becci	Arbroath	7	1		
Norman Bowden	Arsenal	5	4	5	6
Gordon Bradley		2	2		
Charles Bulger	Walsall	7	2	2	1
Jim Campbell		10	14	4	3
George Chapman		2			
Denis Cheney		2			
David Cronin	BTH Sports (Rugby)	8	3	1	1
Ben Crossland	Burnley		1		
David Davidson	Bradford Park Avenue		1		
George Dewis		4	3	5	3
Percy Dickie	Blackburn Rovers	14	12	1	
Stuart Dimond	Manchester United	2			
Billy Frame		18	20		
Stan Frost		1	1		
Jimmy Gemmell	Bury	14	16		
Billy Goffin	Aston Villa		4		
Alick Grant		16	18		
Ron Grant		1			
Jimmy Harrison		1			
Jock Hillard		2	2		
Bert Howe		9	13		
Gordon Jayes			4		
Les J Jones	Arsenal		1		2
Leslie O Jones		1			
Jack Kendall			1		
Fred Kilshaw	Everton		1		
Johnny King			7		
Herbert Knott	Hull City		8		6
Danny Liddle		13	7		
George Little	Doncaster Rovers	2	9	1	
Tim Lycett		9	4	3	
Bobby McNeil	Hamilton Academicals	1			
Les Major		2	1		
William Middleton	Pegsons Athletic		1		
Alex Morton	Morris Motors		1		
Willie Muncie		1			
Tom North	Brush Sports	1			
Russell Phillips		8	3	3	1
Norman Plummer		1			
Maurice Reeday	Mansfield Town		1		
Charlie Rickards	Wolverhampton W.	1			
Gordon Roberts			2		
Don Sanderson		3	10		
Fred Sharman		3	19	2	
Frank Sheard		2	2	4	1
Arthur E Smith		17	18	1	5
Sep Smith		2			
Terry Sparrow	Navy	4	1		
Len Staples	Junior club (Leicester area)	1			
A Sutton	Third Lanark	1			
Dick Walton			3		1
John Wattie	Dundee		3		
Eric Windle	Derby County		1		1
Harold Wyles			1		1

Season 1944-45

NAME	CLUB	Apps FLN	FLN2	Goals FLN	FLN2
Bill Baxter	Nottingham Forest	3	2		
Norman Bowden	Arsenal	3	10	1	2
Gordon Bradley		1			
Robert Brown	Charlton Athletic	1			
Maurice Buckby	Wigston	1	1		
Jim Campbell		10	2	2	
Vernon Chapman		2			
Denis Cheney		1	2	1	1
Joe Clare	Lincoln City		1		
William Cobley	Aston Villa	1			
David Cronin			6		
George Dewis	Blackburn Rovers	3	4	2	3
Percy Dickie	RAF	5			
David Douglas	Manchester City	2	1	1	
Maurice Dunkley	Nottingham Forest	5	8	1	1
Bryn Elliott			3		
Billy Frame		18	18		
Stan Frost			1		
Jimmy Gemmell	Bury	2			
Dick Graham			6		
Alick Grant		6	1		
John Grogan		1			
Norman Hanford		1	2		
Jimmy Harrison					
Bert Howe		12	20		
Len Hubble	Newcastle United	3			
Harry Iddon	Preston North End	3	8	1	1
Tom Johnston	Nottingham Forest	2			
Les J Jones	Arsenal	13			
Ralph Jones			2		
Tommy Jones	Derby County	5			
Don Kelly		4		1	
Fred Kilshaw		14	5		
Johnny King		3			
Bill Leitch	Motherwell	12	13	12	3
Danny Liddle		13			
Maurice Lindley	Everton	2			
Danny Long	Jnr club (Nottingham area)	1			
Bob McCall	Nottingham Forest	2			
Les Major		11	14		
Stan Mercer		4	2	3	
John Mordy	Aston Villa	1			
Angus Morrison	Derby County		2		
Willie Muncie		1			
George Paterson	Glasgow Celtic	1			
Russell Phillips		1		2	
Norman Plummer			1		
Don Revie		2			
Charlie Rickards	Mansfield Town	11	1	7	
Dick Riley			4		
Don Sanderson					
Frank Sheard		2			
Ian Smart	Dundee United	1			
Arthur E Smith		17	19		
Charlie Smith	Aberdeen	2	1		
Sep Smith		18	19	2	10
Harry Stephan	Blackburn Rovers	1	3		
Fred Tapping	Blackpool		7	2	
Ron Thompson	Sheffield Wednesday		3		
Bill Towers		2	13		
Albert Woodvine		3	1		
Harold Wyles			5		

Season 1945-46

NAME	CLUB	Apps FLS	Goals FLS
Charlie Adam		1	
Emilio Aldecoa	Wolverhampton Wanderers	4	1
Robert Anderson		5	
Derek Ashton	Wolverhampton Wanderers	1	
Arthur Attwood	ex Northfleet	1	
Norman Bowden	Arsenal	1	
Joe Calvert		15	
Jim Campbell		10	2
Ken Chisholm	Queens Park	3	1
David Cronin		1	1
Fred Cutting	Norwich City	3	
Bob Davies	Nottingham Forest	2	
George Dewis		10	3
George Edwards	Aston Villa	1	
Walter Foster		9	4
Billy Frame		35	
Billy Goffin	Aston Villa	1	
Jim Graham	ex York City	11	
Dick Graham		16	
Alick Grant		16	
Mal Griffiths		10	2
John Grogan		19	
Walter Harrison		2	1
Wilf Heathcote	Queens Park Rangers	1	1
Jimmy Hemon		3	
Bert Howe		30	
Ray Iggleden		3	
Joe Johnson	West Bromwich Albion	1	
Dai Jones		20	1
Johnny King		16	2
Jack Lee		2	
WJ Letters	Rangers	1	
Tim Lycett		17	3
Danny Liddle		6	1
John McInally	Motherwell	2	
Stan Mercer		21	10
William Middleton	Pegsons Athletic	1	
John Osborne		12	1
George Pearce	RAF	1	
Doug Pimbley	RAOC Chilwell	8	4
Wallace Poulton	Stoke City	1	
Don Revie		31	4
Dick Riley		1	
Peter Robinson	Manchester City	2	
Robert Russell	Chelsea	1	
Frank Sheard		9	
Tommy Sinclair	Bolton Wanderers	1	
Sam Small	West Ham United	1	
Arthur E Smith		10	4
Eric Smith		13	
Sep Smith		39	6
Frank Soo		14	3
Eric Stubbs		1	
Len Sutton	Quorn Methodists	1	
Bill Towers		24	2
Ray Watts		2	
Andy Weatherston		3	
Albert Woodvine		1	

Match No	Date		Opponents	Result	Points	Position	Scorers	Att	Joe Calvert	Dai Jones	Bert Howe	John Osborne	Frank Sheard	Bill Towers	Jim Campbell	Sep Smith	Stan Mercer	Frank Soo	Charlie Adam	Billy Frame	Danny Liddle	Match No
FA CUP																							
1	Jan 5	A	Chelsea (3 leg 1)	D 1-1			Adam / Lawton	39678	1	2	3	4	5	6	7	8	9	10	11			1
2	10	H	Chelsea (3 leg 2)	L 0-2			- / Goulden, Williams	25368	1		3	4	5	6		8	9	10	7	2	11	2

Note: The F.A. Cup recommenced one year ahead of the normal Football League on a two legged basis, but the two F.A. Cup ties did not count towards the War League South title.

1945-46 (v Aston Villa, 22 April 1946)
Back: S Smith, Frame, Grant, Butler (Trainer), Jones, Towers. **Front:** Griffiths, Revie, Pimbley, AE Smith, Woodvine, Grogan.

Season 1946-47

Promoted: Manchester City, Burnley
Relegated: Swansea Town, Newport County

FOOTBALL LEAGUE DIVISION TWO

Match No	Date		Opponents	Result	Points	Position	Scorers	Att
1	Aug 31	H	Manchester City	L 0-3	–		– / McDowall, Walsh, Jackson	33000
2	Sep 4	A	Birmingham City	L 0-4	–		– / Jones 2, Mulraney, Dougall	35000
3	7	A	West Ham United	W 2-0	2	19	Jones, Anderson	28000
4	12	H	Birmingham City	W 2-1	4	12	King, S Smith (p) / Mulraney	20885
5	14	H	Sheffield Wednesday	L 3-5	4	15	McCulloch 2, Adam / Robinson 2, Ward 2, Tomlinson	26181
6	19	H	Chesterfield	L 0-1	4	17	– / Swinscoe	16481
7	21	A	Fulham	L 2-4	4	19	Adam, J Harrison / Stevens, Shepherd, McCormick, Rooke	30000
8	28	H	Bury	D 0-0	5	19		20134
9	Oct 5	A	Luton Town	W 2-1	7	16	Lee 2 / Gager	18073
10	12	H	Plymouth Argyle	W 4-1	9	13	Lee, Dewis 2, Revie / Strauss	20177
11	19	H	Coventry City	W 1-0	11	12	Adam	28583
12	26	A	Nottingham Forest	L 0-2	11	14	– / Lyman, Mee	30010
13	Nov 2	A	Southampton	W 2-0	13	13	Dewis 2	20000
14	9	A	Newport County	W 3-2	15	12	Lee 2, Dewis / Rawcliffe 2	12350
15	16	H	Barnsley	W 6-0	17	10	Eggleston 2, Lee 2, Dewis, Pallister (og)	28524
16	23	A	Burnley	D 0-0	18	8		19062
17	30	A	Tottenham Hotspur	D 1-1	19	8	Dewis / Foreman	34543
18	Dec 7	A	Swansea Town	W 4-3	21	7	Lee 3, Dewis / Haines 2, McCrory	16697
19	14	H	Newcastle United	L 2-4	21	8	Lee 2 / Bentley, Pearson, Shackleton, Wayman	35262
20	21	A	West Bromwich Albion	L 2-4	21	8	Lee, Dewis / Duggan 2, Millard, Walsh	18820
21	25	A	Bradford Park Avenue	W 2-1	23	8	S Smith (p), Griffiths / Gibbons	14839
22	26	H	Bradford Park Avenue	W 2-1	25	8	Griffiths 2 / Horsman	36075
23	28	A	Manchester City	L 0-1	25	8	– / Constantine	43910
24	Jan 4	H	West Ham United	W 4-0	27	8	Lee 2, Dewis, Griffiths	29000
25	18	A	Sheffield Wednesday	W 3-1	29	6	Dewis 2, Revie (p) / Dailey	34858
26	Feb 1	A	Bury	W 3-2	31	5	Dewis, Griffiths, Revie / Mutch 2	12014
27	15	A	Plymouth Argyle	L 0-4	31	6	– / D Thomas, Tinkler, S Smith (og), Jones (og)	18298
28	Mar 1	H	Nottingham Forest	D 1-1	32	5	Revie (p) / Barks	26071
29	15	H	Newport County	W 3-0	34	5	King 2, Griffiths	20267
30	22	A	Barnsley	L 0-1	34	6	– / Kelly	13936
31	Apr 4	A	Millwall	L 0-1	34	7	– / Jinks (p)	25000
32	5	A	Tottenham Hotspur	L 1-2	34	8	A Smith / Rundle 2	37843
33	8	H	Millwall	W 5-0	36	7	Dewis 3, Griffiths 2	19572
34	12	H	Swansea Town	L 0-1	36	7	– / Burns	21515
35	19	A	Newcastle United	D 1-1	37	8	Corbett (og) / Wayman	36739
36	26	H	West Bromwich Albion	D 1-1	38	8	Revie / Clarke	30017
37	May 3	H	Luton Town	W 2-1	40	8	Adam, Revie / Driver	18578
38	10	A	Coventry City	L 1-2	40	9	Lee / Lowrie, Jones (og)	13522
39	17	A	Chesterfield	L 0-2	40	9	– / Swinscoe, Ottewell	12902
40	24	H	Burnley	L 1-4	40	9	Lee / Billingham 2, Hays 2	21626
41	26	A	Southampton	D 1-1	41	9	Lee / Bradley	9905
42	Jun 7	H	Fulham	W 2-0	43	9	Adam, Revie	8036

Final League Position:	9
Average Home League Attendance:	23783

League Appearances: Alick Grant 2, Billy Frame 15, Dai Jones 33, Sep Smith 35, Eric Smith 5, Tom Eggleston 30, Mal Griffiths 36, Don Revie 32, Dave McCulloch 4, Johnny King 21, Charlie Adam 34, Bill Towers 4, George Dewis 32, Joe Calvert 32, Bert Howe 27, Bob Anderson 13, Walter Harrison 28, Jim Dawson 1, John Grogan 17, Jimmy Harrison 10, Jack Lee 24, Ray Iggleden 3, Stan Mercer 1, Gordon Bradley 8, Arthur E Smith 5, Vernon Chapman 1, Tom McArthur 3, Jim Garvey 3, Ted Jelly 2, Jimmy Hernon 1

League Goals: Dai Jones 1, Sep Smith 2, Tom Eggleston 2, Mal Griffiths 8, Don Revie 7, Dave McCulloch 2, Johnny King 3, Charlie Adam 5, George Dewis 16, Bob Anderson 1, Jack Lee 18, + 1

FA CUP

	Date		Opponents	Result	Scorers	Att	
1	Jan 11	A	West Ham United (3)	W 2-1	Adam, Dewis / Woodgate	25858	1
2	25	A	Brentford (4)	D 0-0		32112	2
3	30	H	Brentford (4 rep)	D 0-0 aet		20339	3
4	Feb 3	H	Brentford (4 rep 2)	W 4-1	Griffiths, A Smith 2, Dewis / Scott	7500	4
5	8	A	Newcastle United (5)	D 1-1	Dewis / Shackleton	50309	5
6	20	H	Newcastle United (5 rep)	L 1-2	S Smith (p) / Bentley, Pearson	28424	6

Stand-in Goalkeepers:
Sep 12, Howe for Calvert (temporary), Birmingham City (h);
Dec 14, Howe for Calvert, Newcastle United (h);
Feb 15, Dewis and Eggleston for Calvert, Plymouth Argyle (a).
Note: The fixture list used for 1946-47 was identical to that designed for 1939-40; Feb 3, at Villa Park (Aston Villa).

1946-47 (v Birmingham City, 4 September 1946)
Back: Ritchie (Trainer), S Smith, Frame, Grant, Jones, McLean (Asst Trainer), Towers, Iggleden.
Front: Griffiths, Dewis, McCulloch, King, Adam, E Smith.

Promoted: Birmingham City, Newcastle United
Relegated: Doncaster Rovers, Millwall

FOOTBALL LEAGUE DIVISION TWO

Player columns (left to right): Joe Calvert, Billy Frame, Jimmy Harrison, Walter Harrison, Sep Smith, Jack Haines, Mal Griffiths, Don Revie, Jack Lee, Jimmy Hernon, Charlie Adam, Les Major, Tom Eggleston, Dennis Cheney, Tom McArthur, Johnny King, George Dewis, Arthur E Smith, Gordon Bradley, Ted Jelly, Ray Iggleden, Norman Plummer, Bob Anderson, Sandy Scott, Jim Garvey, Peter McKennan, Bill McGregor, Derek Hines, Alf Barratt

Match No	Date		Opponents	Result	Points	Position	Scorers	Att
1	Aug 23	A	Leeds United	L 1-3	-		Griffiths / Short, Ainsley 2	34937
2	25	H	Plymouth Argyle	W 2-1	2	-	Lee 2 / D Thomas	19845
3	30	H	Fulham	L 0-2	2	16	- / McGibbon 2	23000
4	Sep 3	A	Plymouth Argyle	D 0-0	3	16		17060
5	6	A	Coventry City	W 1-0	5	14	Griffiths	28628
6	8	H	Luton Town	W 3-2	7	7	Griffiths, Haines 2 / Duggan 2	22011
7	13	H	Newcastle United	D 2-2	8	10	Griffiths, Revie / Donaldson, Shackleton	35472
8	17	H	Luton Town	L 1-2	8	13	Dewis / Duggan 2	17597
9	20	A	Birmingham City	L 0-1	8	17	- / Dougall	30000
10	27	H	West Bromwich Albion	D 1-1	9	16	Revie (p) / Elliott	30266
11	Oct 4	A	Barnsley	L 0-2	9	17	- / Smith, Frame (og)	20765
12	11	H	Nottingham Forest	W 3-1	11	15	Dewis, Lee 2 / G Lee	27717
13	18	A	Bradford Park Avenue	W 2-0	13	11	Griffiths, Stephen (og)	16404
14	25	H	Cardiff City	W 2-1	15	9	Lee 2 / Frame (og)	36940
15	Nov 1	A	Sheffield Wednesday	D 1-1	16	10	A Smith / Froggatt	38992
16	8	H	Tottenham Hotspur	L 0-3	16	11	- / Cox, Stevens 2	34426
17	15	A	Millwall	W 4-0	18	9	Hernon, Lee 2, A Smith	22000
18	22	H	Chesterfield	L 1-2	18	10	Adam / Marron, Machant	26326
19	29	A	West Ham United	D 1-1	19	10	Adam / Woodgate	23000
20	Dec 6	H	Bury	W 2-1	21	9	Dewis, Adam / Constantine	21757
21	13	A	Southampton	L 1-3	21	10	Adam / Day, Wrigglesworth, Bates	18441
22	20	H	Leeds United	W 2-0	23	10	Griffiths, Lee	22252
23	25	A	Brentford	D 2-2	24	8	Hernon 2 / Dawson 2	21151
24	27	H	Brentford	L 1-2	24	12	W Harrison / Dawson, Girling	33040
25	Jan 3	A	Fulham	L 1-3	24	13	Lee / Stevens 2, Freeman	17000
26	17	H	Coventry City	D 2-2	25	13	Lee 2 / Warner, Dearson	27168
27	31	A	Newcastle United	L 0-2	25	15	- / McCall, Sibley	51675
28	Feb 14	A	West Bromwich Albion	W 3-1	27	14	Lee, Haines, Griffiths / McKennan	29322
29	28	A	Nottingham Forest	L 0-1	27	16	- / G Lee	32073
30	Mar 6	A	Bradford Park Avenue	W 2-0	29	13	Hernon, King	22293
31	13	A	Cardiff City	L 0-3	29	16	- / Hullett 2, Wardle	40000
32	20	H	Sheffield Wednesday	L 2-3	29	17	Dewis, Hernon (p) / Quigley 2, Jordan	26963
33	26	A	Doncaster Rovers	D 1-1	30	15	McKennan / Todd	24044
34	27	A	Tottenham Hotspur	D 0-0	31	16		33108
35	29	H	Doncaster Rovers	W 3-2	33	13	Hines 2, McKennan / Lowes, Bennett	30107
36	Apr 3	H	Millwall	W 3-0	35	14	Hines, Anderson, Hernon	27110
37	5	H	Barnsley	W 4-1	37	9	W Harrison, Iggleden 2, Hernon / Griffiths	21273
38	10	A	Chesterfield	W 3-2	39	9	Hines 2, McKennan / Capel 2	14362
39	17	H	West Ham United	L 1-3	39	11	McKennan (p) / Woodgate, Hall, Wade	24856
40	19	H	Birmingham City	D 0-0	40	9		32187
41	24	A	Bury	W 2-0	42	9	S Smith, Hines	7727
42	28	H	Southampton	D 0-0	43	9		17874

Final League Position:	9
Average Home League Attendance:	27110

League Appearances: 6 37 37 35 34 12 36 15 22 30 32 15 4 1 8 38 10 12 21 3 8 8 6 6 2 11 9 3
League Goals: 2 1 3 7 2 13 7 4 1 4 2 2 1 4 6

FA CUP

	Date		Opponents	Result	Scorers	Att	
1	Jan 10	H	Bury (3)	W 1-0	Lee	27499	1
2	24	H	Sheffield Wednesday (4)	W 2-1	W Harrison, Haines / Lowes	36517	2
3	Feb 7	A	Tottenham Hotspur (5)	L 2-5	W Harrison, Lee / Cox (p), Duquemin 3, S Smith (og)	69049	3

Stand-in Goalkeepers: Nov 22, W Harrison for Calvert, Chesterfield (h); Jan 24, W Harrison for Bradley, Sheffield Wednesday (h), FAC; Mar 20, W Harrison for Bradley, Sheffield Wednesday (h).

1947-48
Back: Ritchie (Trainer), McArthur, Eggleston, Grogan, Calvert, Dewis, W Harrison, Jones, McLean (Asst Trainer).
Middle: Griffiths, Frame, Adam, Duncan (Manager), Smith, Anderson, Lee.
Front: Jelly, King, J Harrison, Revie, Hernon, Haines.

Season 1948-49

Promoted: Fulham, West Bromwich Albion
Relegated: Nottingham Forest, Lincoln City

FOOTBALL LEAGUE DIVISION TWO

Match No	Date		Opponents	Result	Points	Position	Scorers	Att
1	Aug 21	H	Leeds United	W 6-2	2	-	Revie 2, Lee 2, McKennan 2 / Chisholm, Short	34937
2	26	A	Queens Park Rangers	L 1-4	2	-	Jefferson (og) / Addinall 3, Hartburn	24200
3	28	A	Coventry City	W 2-1	4	5	Revie, Griffiths / Roberts	32461
4	30	H	Queens Park Rangers	L 2-3	4	9	Lee 2 / Hatton 2, Mills	33961
5	Sep 4	H	Sheffield Wednesday	D 2-2	5	9	McKennan, Revie / Quigley, Jordan	32046
6	6	H	Brentford	D 0-0	6	8		24561
7	11	A	Lincoln City	L 0-2	6	15	- / Bean (p), Hutchinson	17103
8	15	A	Brentford	W 2-1	8	10	Revie (p), Paterson / Buchanan	18006
9	18	H	Chesterfield	D 2-2	9	11	Revie (p), Hines / Hudson, Capel	27257
10	25	A	West Bromwich Albion	L 1-2	9	16	Revie / Williams, Walsh	32517
11	Oct 2	H	Bury	W 3-2	11	11	Adam, Lee, Hart (og) / Kilshaw, Whitworth	27852
12	9	A	Luton Town	D 1-1	12	10	W Harrison / Duggan	16663
13	16	H	Bradford Park Avenue	D 2-2	13	12	Adam, Lee / Glover, Crowther	27150
14	23	A	Southampton	L 0-6	13	14	- / Wayman 5, Bates	23907
15	30	H	Barnsley	D 1-1	14	14	Lee / Troops	28178
16	Nov 6	A	Grimsby Town	L 0-1	14	18	- / Galley	14774
17	13	H	Nottingham Forest	W 4-2	16	14	Lee, Revie 3 (1p) / Ottewell, Linaker	26060
18	20	A	Fulham	L 0-1	16	17	- / R Thomas	20000
19	27	A	Plymouth Argyle	D 1-1	17	17	Ayton / Tadman	24350
20	Dec 4	A	Blackburn Rovers	L 0-2	17	18	- / Westcott 2	22476
21	11	H	Cardiff City	D 2-2	18	18	Revie (p), Lee / Rees, Gorin	24039
22	18	A	Leeds United	L 1-3	18	18	Edwards / Heaton 2, Chisholm	22600
23	25	H	Tottenham Hotspur	L 1-2	18	20	Paterson / Burgess, Bennett	30949
24	27	A	Tottenham Hotspur	D 1-1	19	19	Griffiths / Rundle	49411
25	Jan 1	H	Coventry City	W 3-1	21	19	Revie, Lee, Barrett (og) / Dearson	33230
26	22	H	Lincoln City	W 5-3	23	16	Revie, Lee 3, Chisholm / Bean 2 (2p), Plummer (og)	35340
27	Feb 5	A	Chesterfield	D 1-1	24	17	Lee / Halton (p)	16894
28	Mar 5	H	Luton Town	D 1-1	25	20	Hall (og) / Owen	26321
29	12	A	Bradford Park Avenue	D 3-3	26	20	Revie 2, Lee / Henry, Layton, Ainsley	14770
30	19	H	Southampton	L 1-3	26	20	Lee / Wayman 2, Bates	32700
31	Apr 2	H	Grimsby Town	D 1-1	27	20	Chisholm / Briggs	35847
32	6	A	Barnsley	L 1-3	27	20	Chisholm / Wright 2, Baxter	12010
33	9	A	Nottingham Forest	L 1-2	27	20	Gager (og) / Scott, Love	30724
34	11	A	Sheffield Wednesday	W 1-0	29	20	Lee	25081
35	15	A	West Ham United	L 1-4	29	20	Griffiths / Robinson 3, Woodgate	33000
36	16	H	Fulham	L 0-3	29	20	- / Jezzard, R Thomas, Rowley	35592
37	18	H	West Ham United	D 1-1	30	21	Lee / Robinson	29700
38	21	H	Blackburn Rovers	W 3-1	32	20	Lee, Griffiths, Revie / Eckersley (p)	30414
39	23	A	Plymouth Argyle	D 1-1	33	20	Chisholm / Strauss	25654
40	May 4	A	Bury	W 2-1	35	20	Lee, Griffiths, Massart	15222
41	5	H	West Bromwich Albion	L 0-3	35	20	- / Walsh, Kennedy, Barlow	34585
42	7	A	Cardiff City	D 1-1	36	19	Lee / Baker	35000

Final League Position:	19
Average Home League Attendance:	30384

League Appearances: 22 27 34 36 12 10 41 7 38 36 29 26 11 6 16 11 1 1 4 25 5 8 3 8 14 17 11 1 1 1

League Goals: 1 5 3 21 16 2 1 2 1 1 4

FA CUP

	Date		Opponents	Result	Scorers	Att
1	Jan 8	A	Birmingham City (3)	D 1-1 aet	Revie (p) / Roberts	41000
2	15	H	Birmingham City (3 rep)	D 1-1 aet	Griffiths / Bodle	35367
3	17	A	Birmingham City (3 rep 2)	W 2-1	J Harrison, Revie / Dorman	31609
4	29	H	Preston North End (4)	W 2-0	Lee (p), Griffiths	37775
5	Feb 12	A	Luton Town (5)	D 5-5 aet	Lee 4, Griffiths / Kiernan 2, Small, Brennan, Watkins	26280
6	19	H	Luton Town (5 rep)	W 5-3	Lee 2 (1p), Griffiths 2, Chisholm / Brennan 2, Arnison	38822
7	26	A	Brentford (6)	W 2-0	Lee, Griffiths	38678
8	Mar 26		Portsmouth (sf)	W 3-1	Revie 2, Chisholm / P Harris	62000
9	Apr 30		Wolverhampton W (f)	L 1-3	Griffiths / Pye 2, Smyth	98920

Stand-in Goalkeepers:
Sep 18, W Harrison for Major, Chesterfield (h);
Apr 2, Jelly for McGraw, Grimsby Town (h).
Note: Jan 17, tie staged at St Andrews after toss of coin;
Mar 26, at Highbury (Arsenal); Apr 30, at Wembley.

1948-49
Back: Siddon (Asst Secretary), Barratt, Iggleden, Revie, Paterson, Garvey, Johnston, Cheney, Chandler (Training Staff).
Middle: Ritchie (Trainer), Plummer, Scott, J Harrison, Major, Churchill, Bradley, Dewis, W Harrison, Jelly, McLean (Asst Trainer).
Front: Duncan (Manager), Griffiths, Frame, McArthur, Adam, Smith, Lee, McKennan.
On Ground: Staples, Moran, McGregor.

Promoted: Tottenham Hotspur, Sheffield Wednesday
Relegated: Plymouth Argyle, Bradford Park Avenue

FOOTBALL LEAGUE DIVISION TWO

Match No	Date		Opponents	Result	Points	Position	Scorers	Att	Gordon Bradley	Ted Jelly	Sandy Scott	Walter Harrison	Tom McArthur	Johnny King	Mal Griffiths	Don Revie	Jack Lee	Ken Chisholm	Charlie Adam	Norman Kirkman	Bill McGregor	Jimmy Ayton	Eddie Moran	Billy Frame	Willie Corbett	Jim Johnston	Derek Hines	Norman Plummer	Tom Paterson	Tom Godwin	George Dewis	Bert Barlow	Ron Jackson	Jimmy Baldwin	Peter Small	Jack Marsh	Ian Wilson	Johnny Anderson	Match No
1	Aug 20	A	Sheffield Wednesday	L 1-3	-		Adam / Quigley 2, Froggatt	35431	1	2	3	4	5	6	7	8	9	10	11																				1
2	24	A	Bradford Park Avenue	D 2-2	1	-	Griffiths, Chisholm / Glover, Smith	14642	1	2	3	4	5	6	7	8	9	10	11																				2
3	27	H	Hull City	L 1-2	1	18	Lee / Carter, Burbanks	37659	1	2			4	5	6	7	8	9	10	11	3																		3
4	29	A	Bradford Park Avenue	W 4-1	3	13	Lee 3, Chisholm / Deplidge	25232	1	2	3	4	5	6	7	8	9	10	11																				4
5	Sep 3	A	Brentford	W 1-0	5	11	Chisholm	20325	1	2	3	4	5	6	7	8	9	10	11																				5
6	10	H	Blackburn Rovers	D 3-3	6	12	Chisholm 2, Griffiths / Westcott 2, Bell	31735	1	2	3	4	5	6	7	8	9	10	11																				6
7	12	L	Chesterfield	L 0-1	6	13	- / McJarrow	13841				3	4	5	6	7	8	9	10	11		2																	7
8	17	A	Cardiff City	W 4-2	8	11	Chisholm 2, Lee, Griffiths / Best, Edwards	35000	1				5	6	7	4	9	10	11	3	2	8																	8
9	19	H	Chesterfield	L 0-1	8	11	- / Donaldson	29253	1				5	6	7	4	9	10	11	3	2		8																9
10	24	H	Tottenham Hotspur	L 1-2	8	13	Adam / Walters, Duquemin	36846	1			4	5	6	7	8	9	10	11	3			2																10
11	Oct 1	A	Bury	L 0-3	8	18	- / W Griffiths (p), Worthington, Bodle	17178	1				4	7	8	9	10	11	3					2	5	6													11
12	8	A	Luton Town	L 0-1	8	18	- / Walsh	20816	1	2	3			4	7	8		10	11						5	6	9												12
13	15	H	Barnsley	D 2-2	9	20	Scott, Chisholm / Wright, Griffiths	27966	1	2	3	7		6			8	9	10						5			4	11										13
14	22	A	West Ham United	D 2-2	10	18	Lee, Chisholm / Parsons, Bainbridge	23000	1	2	3	8		6	7		9	10	11						5			4											14
15	29	H	Sheffield United	D 1-1	11	18	Plummer / Brook	29387	1	2	3	8		6	7		9	10	11						5			4											15
16	Nov 5	A	Grimsby Town	L 1-2	11	18	Lee / Cairns, Briggs	14114	1	2	3	8		6	7		9	10	11						5			4											16
17	12	H	Queens Park Rangers	W 3-2	13	17	Lee 2, Chisholm / Addinall, Parkinson	26048	1	2	3	8			7		9	10	11						5	6		4											17
18	19	A	Preston North End	L 1-2	13	18	Lee / Horton, Knight	28722	1	2	3	4			7		9	10	11						5	6		8											18
19	26	H	Swansea Town	D 0-0	14	17		26500			3	4		8	7		9	10	11						2	5	6			1									19
20	Dec 3	A	Leeds United	D 1-1	15	18	Adam / P Harrison	26768		3		4		8	7		9	10	11						2	5	6			1									20
21	10	A	Southampton	D 2-2	16	18	Griffiths, Lee / Wayman, Bates	22167		3		4		8	7		9		11						2	5	6			1	10								21
22	17	H	Sheffield Wednesday	D 2-2	17	18	Lee 2 / Froggatt 2	27513			3	4		10	7		9		11						2	5	6			1		8							22
23	24	A	Hull City	L 0-4	17	20	- / Moore 2, Harrison 2	35207		2		4		10	7		9		11							5	6			1		8	3						23
24	26	H	Coventry City	W 1-0	19	18	Adam (p)	37903				4		10	7		9		11						2	5	6			1		8	3						24
25	27	A	Coventry City	W 2-1	21	17	Adam, Paterson / G Mason	36981					4	7			9		10						2	5	6		11	1		8	3						25
26	31	H	Brentford	D 1-1	22	16	Paterson / Dare	31000					4	7			9		10						2	5	6		11	1		8	3						26
27	Jan 14	A	Blackburn Rovers	L 0-3	22	18	- / Horton, Westcott, Graham	21826				5	4	7			10		11						2		6	9		1		8	3						27
28	21	A	Cardiff City	W 1-0	24	17	Chisholm	24500				4	5	6	7			10	11		2						9			1		8	3						28
29	Feb 4	A	Tottenham Hotspur	W 2-0	26	15	Adam (p), Barlow	60595		2		4		6	7		9		10									5	11	1		8	3						29
30	11	H	Plymouth Argyle	D 0-0	27	13		27912		2		4		6	7		9		10									5	11	1		8	3						30
31	18	H	Bury	L 0-2	27	16	- / Bodle, Hazlett	27514		2		4		6	7		9		11									10	5	1		8	3						31
32	25	A	Luton Town	W 3-2	29	15	Chisholm 2, Lee / Wyldes, Watkins	25071		2				6	7		9	10	11							5			1		8	3	4					32
33	Mar 4	A	Barnsley	D 2-2	30	12	Barlow 2 / Wright 2	16637		2				6	7		9	10	11							5			1		8	3	4					33
34	11	H	West Ham United	W 2-1	32	10	Lee 2 / Robinson	28040		2				6	7		9	10	11							5			1		8	3	4					34
35	18	A	Sheffield United	D 2-2	33	10	Jelly, Lee (p) / Collindridge, Hoyland	30870		2				6			9								4	5			1		8	3		7	10	11			35
36	25	H	Grimsby Town	W 1-0	35	8	Lee	31635		2					9					3					6	5			1		8		4	7	10	11			36
37	Apr 1	A	Swansea Town	D 0-0	36	8		25000		2					9					3					6	5			1		8		4	7	10	11			37
38	8	H	Leeds United	D 1-1	37	11	Lee / McMorran	33881		2					9					3					6	5			1		8		4	7	10	11			38
39	10	A	Plymouth Argyle	L 1-2	37	11	Lee / Strauss, Dews	14576		2					9				11	3					6	5			1		8		4	7	10				39
40	15	A	Queens Park Rangers	L 0-2	37	11	- / Addinall 2	15000		2					9				11	3					6	5			1		8		4	7	10				40
41	22	H	Preston North End	W 1-0	39	11	Barlow	22873		2				6	7		9		11	3						5			1		8		4		10		1		41
42	29	A	Southampton	L 3-5	39	13	Lee 2, Barlow / Wayman 2, Bates 2, Stevenson	21091		2				6	7		9		11	3						5			8			4			10		1		42

Final League Position:		15				**League Appearances**		18 31 14 24 12 35 35 13 39 25 37 12 4 1 1 10 16 19 4 19 6 22 1 21 13 10 6 8 4 2
Average Home League Attendance:		30266				**League Goals**		1 1 4 22 13 6 1 2 5

FA CUP

1	Jan 7	A	Sheffield United (3)	L 1-3			Adam / Thompson, Collindridge, Brook	41598	3 ... 4 7 9 10 11 ... 2 5 6 ... 1 8 ... 1

1949-50
Back: Kirkman, Metcalfe (Trainer), Corbett, Bradley, McArthur, Jelly, McGraw, Plummer.
Front: Duncan (Manager), Griffiths, Harrison, Revie, Ayton, Chisholm, Adam, Maley (Secretary).
On Ground: King, Lee, Scott.

Season 1950-51

Promoted: Preston North End, Manchester City
Relegated: Chesterfield, Grimsby Town

FOOTBALL LEAGUE DIVISION TWO

Match No	Date	Opponents	Result	Pts	Pos	Scorers	Att	Tom Godwin	Ted Jelly	Ron Jackson	Jimmy Baldwin	Norman Plummer	Johnny King	Mal Griffiths	Bert Barlow	Arthur Rowley	Jack Marsh	Ian Wilson	Walter Harrison	Ian McGraw	Tom McArthur	Peter Small	Tom Dryburgh	Arthur Lever	Jimmy Ayton	Derek Hines	Reg Halton	Charlie Adam	Eddie Moran	Johnny Anderson	Bill McGregor	Jimmy Crawford	Tommy Dunne	Fred Worthington	Match No
1	Aug 19 A	Bury	W 3-2	2	-	Marsh 2, Rowley / Bodle, Massart	17535	1	2	3	4	5	6	7	8	9	10	11																	1
2	23 A	Birmingham City	L 0-2	2	-	- / Trigg, Smith	28000	1	2	3	4	5	6	7	8	9	10	11																	2
3	26 H	Queens Park Rangers	W 6-2	4	7	Marsh 2, Griffiths, Rowley, Barlow, Wilson / Addinall, Shepherd	28600	1	2	3	4	5	6	7	8	9	10	11																	3
4	28 H	Birmingham City	L 1-3	4	10	Rowley / Trigg, Smith, Stewart	31100	1	2	3	4	5	6	7		9	10	11	8																4
5	Sep 2 A	Chesterfield	L 0-1	4	12	- / Bacci	14768		2	3	4		6	7	8	9	10	11		1	5														5
6	4 H	Notts County	D 1-1	5	12	Barlow / Johnston	36069		2	3	4		6		8	9	10			1	5	7	11												6
7	9 H	Sheffield United	D 2-2	6	11	Wilson, Barlow / Hutchinson, Brook	31162			3	4		6		8	9		11		1	5	7		2	10										7
8	16 H	Manchester City	L 1-2	6	18	Rowley / Turnbull, Smith	32856			3	4		6		8	9		11		1	5	7		2	10										8
9	23 A	Coventry City	L 1-2	6	18	Rowley (p) / Chisholm 2	33240	1		3	4		6		8	10		11			5	7		2		9									9
10	30 H	Cardiff City	D 1-1	7	18	Hines / Blair	23066	1		3	4			7	8	10					5		11	2		9	6								10
11	Oct 7 A	Hull City	W 3-1	9	16	Hines, Rowley 2 / Ackerman	33609	1		3	4			7	8	10					5		11	2		9	6								11
12	14 H	Doncaster Rovers	W 2-0	11	13	Rowley, Hines	33782	1		3	4			7	8	10					5		11	2		9	6								12
13	21 A	West Ham United	D 0-0	12	14		25000	1		3	4			7	8	10					5		11	2		9	6								13
14	28 H	Swansea Town	L 2-3	12	16	Griffiths, Dryburgh / C Beech, Thomas, Allchurch	26114	1		3	4			7	8	10					5		11	2		9	6								14
15	Nov 4 A	Luton Town	W 2-0	14	12	Adam, Hines	12967	1		3	4			7	8	10					5			2		9	6	11							15
16	11 H	Leeds United	L 1-5	14	15	Rowley / Burden, Dudley 3, Williams	26573	1		3				7	8	10			4		5			2		9	6	11							16
17	18 A	Brentford	D 0-0	15	15		16259	1		3	4			7		10					5			2		9	6	11	8						17
18	25 H	Blackburn Rovers	W 2-0	17	14	Rowley (p), Moran	22361	1		3	4			7		10					5			2		9	6	11	8						18
19	Dec 2 A	Southampton	D 2-2	18	14	Adam, Rowley / Brown, Bates	22375	1		3	4			7		10					5			2		9	6	11	8						19
20	9 H	Barnsley	L 1-2	18	14	Rowley (p) / McMorran, Taylor	20000	1		3	4			7		10					5			2		9	6	11	8						20
21	16 H	Bury	W 4-0	20	13	Rowley 3, Hines	16052	1		3	4			7		10					5			2		9	6	11	8						21
22	23 A	Queens Park Rangers	L 0-3	20	14	- / Addinall, Hatton, Shepherd	11017	1		3	4			7		10					5			2		9	6	11	8						22
23	25 H	Grimsby Town	W 2-0	22	13	Rowley, Hines	17565			3	4				8	10					5	7		2		9	6	11		1					23
24	26 H	Grimsby Town	D 0-0	23	14		28296			3	4					10					5	7	11			9	6			1	2		8		24
25	30 H	Chesterfield	W 1-0	25	13	Griffiths	19297			3	4			7	8	10					5					9	6	11		1	2				25
26	Jan 13 A	Sheffield United	L 1-2	25	15	Rowley / Hawksworth, Halton (og)	28380			3	4			7	8	10					5			2		9	6	11		1					26
27	20 A	Manchester City	D 1-1	26	15	Rowley / Hart	30198			3	4			7	8	9					5			2			6	11		1		10			27
28	Feb 3 A	Coventry City	W 3-0	28	12	Griffiths, Hines, Rowley	33485			3	4			7	8	10					5			2		9	6	11		1					28
29	17 A	Cardiff City	D 2-2	29	14	Rowley (p), Hines / Marchant, Baker	25000			3	4			7	8	10				1	5			2		9		11				6			29
30	24 H	Hull City	W 4-0	31	10	Rowley, Hines, Griffiths, Adam	35451			3	4			7	8	10					5			2		9	6	11		1					30
31	Mar 3 H	Doncaster Rovers	D 2-2	32	9	Adam, Rowley (p) / Harrison, Tindill	22403			3	4			7	8	10					5			2		9	6	11		1					31
32	10 H	West Ham United	W 1-0	34	7	Hines	22571			3	4			7	8	10					5			2		9	6	11		1					32
33	17 A	Swansea Town	L 1-2	34	10	Baldwin / Turnbull 2	12914			3	4			7	8	10					5			2		9	6	11		1					33
34	24 H	Luton Town	W 3-1	36	9	Hines, Rowley 2 / Stobbart	23360			3	4			7	8	10					5			2		9	6	11		1					34
35	26 A	Preston North End	L 2-3	36	11	Adam, Rowley (p) / Wayman 2, Finney	36474			3	4			7	8	10					5			2		9	6	11		1					35
36	27 H	Preston North End	L 2-3	36	11	Rowley 2 / Beattie, Horton, Morrison	37233			3	4			7	8	10					5			2		9	6	11		1					36
37	31 A	Leeds United	L 1-2	36	13	Hines / Burden 2	14397			3	4			7		10					5			2		9	6	11		1				8	37
38	Apr 7 A	Brentford	L 1-2	36	14	Halton (p) / Goodwin, Dare	20284			3	4			7		10					5			2		9	6	11		1				8	38
39	14 A	Blackburn Rovers	L 0-1	36	16	- / Leaver	10867	1		3	4					10					5			2		9	6	11	7					8	39
40	21 A	Southampton	W 3-1	38	15	Baldwin, Dryburgh 2 / Dudley	17000	1			4			7		10					5		11	2		9	6				3			8	40
41	28 A	Barnsley	D 0-0	39	15		9819	1		3	4					10					5	7	11	2		9	6							8	41
42	May 5 A	Notts County	W 3-2	41	14	Hines, Rowley, Barlow / Crookes, Lawton	24092	1		3	4			7	8	10					5			2		9	6	11							42

								Godwin	Jelly	Jackson	Baldwin	Plummer	King	Griffiths	Barlow	Rowley	Marsh	Wilson	Harrison	McGraw	McArthur	Small	Dryburgh	Lever	Ayton	Hines	Halton	Adam	Moran	Anderson	McGregor	Crawford	Dunne	Worthington	
Final League Position:		14				**League Appearances**		22	6	41	31	4	31	34	19	39	6	8	2	5	38	7	10	34	2	33	32	26	6	15	3	2	1	5	
Average Home League Attendance:		27293				**League Goals**					2			5	4	28	4	2			,		3			13	1	5	1						

FA CUP

Match No	Date	Opponents	Result	Scorers	Att	Jackson	Baldwin	Griffiths	Barlow	Rowley	McArthur	Lever	Hines	Halton	Adam	Anderson	McGregor	Match No
1	Jan 6 H	Preston North End (3)	L 0-3	- / Wayman 2, Horton	31078	3	4	7	8	10	5	2	9	6	11	1	2	1

1950-51
Back: King, Griffiths, Harrison, Plummer, Dewis (Trainer), Smyth, Marsh, Bruce, Murray.
Middle: Jones (Trainer), Armstrong, McArthur, Godwin, Jelly, McGraw, Dunne, Brews, Chandler (Training Staff).
Front: Bullock (Manager), Jackson, Barlow, Ayton, Dryburgh, Rowley, Wilson, Maley (Secretary).
On Ground: McGregor, Small, Baldwin, Moran.

Promoted: Sheffield Wednesday, Cardiff City
Relegated: Coventry City, Queens Park Rangers

FOOTBALL LEAGUE DIVISION TWO

Match No	Date		Opponents	Result	Points	Position	Scorers	Att	Johnny Anderson	Arthur Lever	Ron Jackson	Jimmy Baldwin	Tom McArthur	Reg Halton	Mal Griffiths	Bert Barlow	Derek Hines	Arthur Rowley	Tom Dryburgh	Fred Worthington	Bill Webb	Norman Plummer	Peter Small	Arthur Dixon	Tom Godwin	Adam Dickson	Johnny King	Tommy Dunne	Matt Gillies	Bill McGregor	Stan Milburn	Eric Littler	Match No
1	Aug 18	A	Cardiff City	L 0-4		-	- / Edwards, Grant 2, R Williams	35000	1	2	3	4	5	6	7	8	9	10	11														1
2	20	H	Sheffield Wednesday	W 3-1	2	-	Rowley 2, Hines / Sewell	23395	1	2	3	4	5	6	7	8	9	10	11														2
3	25	H	Birmingham City	W 4-0	4	5	Worthington, Rowley 3	25000	1	2	3	4	5	6	7		9	10	11	8													3
4	27	A	Sheffield Wednesday	L 0-1	4	7	- / Sewell	28517	1	2	3	4	5	6	7		9	10	11	8	3												4
5	Sep 1	H	Luton Town	D 3-3	5	9	Dryburgh, Hines 2 / Taylor 3	25735	1	2		4		6			9	10	11	8	3	5	7										5
6	3	H	Southampton	W 3-0	7	4	Dryburgh, Hines 2	21183	1	2		4	5	6			9	10	11	8	3		7										6
7	8	A	Nottingham Forest	D 2-2	8	6	Dryburgh, Small / Scott, Ardron	37483	1	2		4	5	6			9	10	11	8	3		7										7
8	15	H	Brentford	D 1-1	9	8	Halton / Monk	23656	1	2		4	5	6			9	10	11	8	3		7										8
9	22	A	Doncaster Rovers	D 2-2	10	8	Dryburgh, Rowley / Dubois, Harrison	19732	1	2		4	5	6			9	10	11	8	3		7										9
10	29	H	Everton	L 1-2	10	12	Rowley / Buckle, McNamara	28114	1	2		4	5	6			9	10	11	8	3		7										10
11	Oct 6	H	Bury	D 1-1	11	11	Hines / Bodle	24340	1	2		4	5	6	7		9	10	11		3			8									11
12	13	A	Swansea Town	L 0-1	11	16	- / O'Driscoll	21338	1	2		4		6	7		9	10	11		3	5		8		1							12
13	20	H	Coventry City	W 3-1	13	11	Griffiths, Hines, Rowley / Roberts	25097	1	2		4		6	7		9	10	11		3	5		8									13
14	27	A	West Ham United	W 3-2	15	10	Rowley, Hines 2 / Woodgate, Bing	21000		2		4		6	7		9	10	11		3	5		8		1							14
15	Nov 3	H	Sheffield United	D 5-5	16	10	Rowley 2, Hines, Dryburgh, Griffiths / Brook, FA Smith 2, Hagan 2	33775	1	2		4		6	7		9	10	11		3	5		8									15
16	10	A	Barnsley	D 3-3	17	12	Dryburgh, Rowley 2 / McCormack, Baxter, Webb (og)	11133	1	2		4		6	7		9	10	11		3	5		8									16
17	17	H	Hull City	W 1-0	19	9	Rowley	25041	1	2		4	5		7		9	10	11	8	3								6				17
18	24	A	Blackburn Rovers	L 1-2	19	11	Rowley / Quigley, Baldwin (og)	24931	1	2	3	4	5		7		9	10	11	8									6				18
19	Dec 1	H	Queens Park Rangers	W 4-0	21	10	Rowley 3, Dryburgh	23193	1	2	3		5	6	7		9	10	11	8							4						19
20	8	A	Notts County	W 3-2	23	8	Worthington, Hines, Halton (p) / Crookes 2	27065	1	2	3		5	6	7		9	10	11	8							4						20
21	15	H	Cardiff City	W 3-0	25	6	Rowley, Hines, Worthington	25000	1	2	3		5	6	7		9	10	11	8							4						21
22	22	A	Birmingham City	L 0-2	25	9	- / Briggs, Wardle	22500	1	2	3		5	6	7		9	10	11	8							4						22
23	25	H	Leeds United	L 1-2	25	9	Hines / Iggleden, Mills	24498	1	2	3		5	6	7		9	10	11	8							4						23
24	26	A	Leeds United	L 1-2	25	10	Hines / Fidler 2	29422	1	2	3		5	6	7		9	10	11	8							4						24
25	29	A	Luton Town	W 2-1	27	9	Dryburgh 2 / Watkins	17992	1	2	3	4	5				9	10	11	8									6				25
26	Jan 5	H	Nottingham Forest	W 3-1	29	7	Rowley, Griffiths 2 / Ardron	31294		2	3	4	5	6	7		9	10	11	8					1								26
27	19	A	Brentford	W 3-1	31	4	Rowley 3 / Dare	20000	1	2	3	4	5		7		9	10	11	8									6				27
28	26	H	Doncaster Rovers	W 2-1	33	3	Rowley 2 / Lawlor	30405	1	2	3	4			7		9	10	11	8									6		5		28
29	Feb 9	A	Everton	L 0-2	33	6	- / Hickson, McNamara	40535	1	2	3	4			7		9	10	11	8									6		5		29
30	16	A	Bury	W 4-1	35	2	Hines 2, Rowley 2 / Bodle	11232	1	2	3	4			7		9	10	11	8									6		5		30
31	23	A	Southampton	L 0-2	35	3	- / Judd, Day	19121	1	2	3	4			7		9	10	11	8									6				31
32	Mar 1	H	Swansea Town	D 1-1	36	3	Rowley / C Beech	31429	1	2	3	4			7		9	10	11	8									6		5		32
33	8	A	Coventry City	W 3-1	38	2	Rowley 2 (1p), Dryburgh / Lockhart	30244		2	3	4			7		9	10	11	8						1			6		5		33
34	15	H	West Ham United	W 3-1	40	3	Griffiths, Rowley 2 / Andrews	30038	1		3	4			7		9	10	11	8									6	2	5		34
35	22	A	Sheffield United	L 0-5	40	4	- / Browning 2, Ringstead, Hagan, Hawksworth	33477	1		3	4			7		9	10	11	8									6	2	5		35
36	29	H	Barnsley	L 1-2	40	5	Rowley / Lumley 2	17446	1		3	4		6	7		9	10	11						8					2	5		36
37	Apr 5	A	Hull City	L 1-3	40	7	Rowley / Carter, Harrison, Gerrie	24378	1		3	4			7		9	10	11	8									6	2	5		37
38	12	H	Blackburn Rovers	W 2-1	42	6	Rowley 2 (1p) / Quigley	24418	1		3	4			7		9	10	11	8									6	2	5		38
39	14	A	Rotherham United	W 2-0	44	6	Dryburgh, Rowley	16171	1		3	4		6	7			10	11	8		9								2	5		39
40	15	H	Rotherham United	W 2-0	46	6	Rowley 2	27875	1		3	4		6	7			10	11	8		9								2	5		40
41	19	A	Queens Park Rangers	L 0-1	46	6	- / Addinall	16731	1			4		6	7			10	11	8	3	9								2	5		41
42	26	H	Notts County	D 1-1	47	5	Littler / McPherson	21318	1			4		6	7			10	11	8	3			8						2	5	9	42

							League Appearances		38	33	26	36	18	32	36	2	39	42	41	32	16	9	6	8	1	3	15	5	14	1	8	1	
Final League Position:		5					League Goals							2	5		17	38	11	3				1								1	
Average Home League Attendance:		26080																																

FA CUP

	Date		Opponents	Result			Scorers	Att	Anderson	Lever	Jackson	Baldwin	McArthur	Halton	Griffiths		Hines	Rowley	Dryburgh	Worthington							King		Gillies				
1	Jan 12	H	Coventry City (3)	D 1-1			Griffiths / Allen	36116	1	2	3	4	5	6	7		9	10	11	8													1
2	14	A	Coventry City (3 rep)	L 1-4			Dryburgh / Roberts, Chisholm, Lockhart 2	24240	1	2	3		5		7		9	10	11	8							4		6				2

1951-52
Back: Chandler (Training Staff), Rowley, McArthur, Godwin, Halton, McGraw, Lever, Wilson, Jones (Trainer).
Front: Maley (Secretary), Baldwin, Griffiths, Dryburgh, Worthington, Barlow, Jackson, Bullock (Manager).
On Ground: Small, McGregor, King.

Season 1952-53

Promoted: Sheffield United, Huddersfield Town
Relegated: Southampton, Barnsley

FOOTBALL LEAGUE DIVISION TWO

Match No	Date		Opponents	Result	Points	Position	Scorers	Att	Johnny Anderson	Arthur Lever	Stan Milburn	Jimmy Baldwin	Matt Gillies	Johnny King	Mal Griffiths	Fred Worthington	Derek Hines	Arthur Rowley	Tom Dryburgh	Eric Littler	Peter Small	Ron Burbeck	Arthur Dixon	Johnny Morris	Bill Webb	Reg Warner	Tom McArthur	Adam Dickson	Jimmy Crawford	Derek Hogg	Ron Jackson	Tommy Dunne	Gordon Fincham	Match No
1	Aug 23	H	Notts County	W 3-0	2	-	Hines, Griffiths, Rowley	29508	1	2	3	4	5	6	7	8	9	10	11															1
2	25	H	Fulham	W 6-1	4	-	Rowley 4 (1p), Worthington, Griffiths / Black	24605	1	2	3	4	5	6	7	8	9	10	11															2
3	30	A	Southampton	L 2-5	4	5	Dryburgh, Elliott (og) / Day 2, Purves, Judd, McDonald	17089	1	2	3	4	5	6	7	8	9	10	11															3
4	Sep 3	A	Fulham	W 6-4	6	5	Rowley 3, King, Dryburgh 2 / Stevens, Jezzard 2, Mitten	22176	1	2	3	4	5	6	7	8	9	10	11															4
5	6	H	Bury	W 3-2	8	5	Griffiths, Worthington, Hines / Kelly 2	27308	1	2	3	4	5	6	7	8	9	10	11															5
6	8	H	West Ham United	D 0-0	9	3		23382	1	2	3	4	5	6	7	8		10	11	9														6
7	13	A	Birmingham City	L 1-3	9	4	Rowley / Briggs, Murphy, K Rowley	30000	1	2	3	4	5	6	7	8	9	10	11															7
8	15	A	West Ham United	L 1-4	9	5	Rowley (p) / Barrett 2, Woodgate, Kearns	14889	1	2	3	4	5	6		8	9	10			7	11												8
9	20	H	Luton Town	D 1-1	10	8	Rowley / Turner	24052	1	2	3	4					9	10	11		7			8										9
10	27	A	Leeds United	W 1-0	12	6	Hines	19724	1	2	3	4	5	6	7		9	10	11					8										10
11	Oct 4	H	Plymouth Argyle	W 2-0	14	3	Rowley, Hines	33036	1	2	3	4	5	6	7		9	10	11					8										11
12	11	A	Nottingham Forest	W 3-1	16	3	Dryburgh, Hines, Rowley / Capel	39132	1	2	3	4	5	6	7		9	10	11					8										12
13	18	A	Everton	W 4-2	18	2	Dryburgh, Morris 2, Rowley / Harris, Parker	36819	1	2		4	5	6	7		9	10	11					8	3									13
14	25	A	Brentford	L 2-4	18	5	Baldwin, Griffiths / Goodwin, Lawton 2, Dare	22000	1	2	3	4	5	6	7		9	10	11					8										14
15	Nov 1	H	Doncaster Rovers	W 4-2	20	4	Dryburgh, Hines 2, Rowley / Walker, Doherty (p)	29719	1	2	3	4	5	6	7		9	10	11					8										15
16	8	A	Swansea Town	D 1-1	21	5	Morris / Kiley	21179	1	2	3	4	5		7		9	10	11				6	8										16
17	15	H	Huddersfield Town	W 2-1	23	3	Rowley, Quested (og) / Glazzard	39908	1	2	3	4	5	6	7		9	10	11					8										17
18	22	A	Sheffield United	L 2-7	23	4	Rowley, Hines / Ringstead 2, Hagan 2, Furniss (p), Browning, Lever (og)	33489	1	2	3	4	5	6	7		9	10	11					8										18
19	29	H	Barnsley	D 2-2	24	5	Dryburgh, Rowley (p) / Taylor, McMorran	20497	1	2	3	8	5	6	7		9	10	11								4							19
20	Dec 6	A	Lincoln City	L 2-3	24	5	Hines, Rowley / Birch 2, Green (p)	17221	1	2	3	4	5	6	7		9	10	11					8										20
21	13	A	Hull City	W 5-0	26	4	Hines, Rowley 3, Dryburgh	16466	1	2	3	4		6	7		9	10	11					8				5						21
22	20	A	Notts County	D 2-2	27	3	Rowley 2 / Evans, McPherson	16168	1	2	3	4		6	7		9	10	11					8				5						22
23	25	A	Blackburn Rovers	L 0-2	27	4	- / Quigley 2	29410	1	2	3	4		6	7		9		11					8				5						23
24	27	H	Blackburn Rovers	W 2-1	29	3	Griffiths, Hines / Briggs	32015		2	3	4		6	7		9		11					8			1	5	10					24
25	Jan 3	H	Southampton	W 4-1	31	3	Dryburgh, Griffiths, Rowley (p), Crawford / Day	22889		2		4		6	7		9	10	11						3		1	5	8					25
26	17	A	Bury	W 4-1	33	3	Griffiths, Crawford, Rowley, Hines / Fletcher	15668	1	2		4	5		7		9	10	11				6		3				8					26
27	24	H	Birmingham City	L 3-4	33	4	Hines, Rowley (p), Griffiths / Murphy 3, Trigg	27478	1	2		4	5		7		9	10	11				6		3				8					27
28	Feb 7	A	Luton Town	L 0-2	33	5	- / Mitchell (p), Turner	22489		2		4		6	7		9	10	11					8	3	1	5							28
29	14	H	Leeds United	D 3-3	34	5	Morris, Rowley 2 / Meek, Charles 2	21754		2		4		6			9	10	11					8	3	1	5		7					29
30	21	A	Plymouth Argyle	L 1-2	34	5	Worthington / Dougall, Willis	19181		2		4		6		8	9	10	11						3	1	5		7					30
31	28	H	Nottingham Forest	D 1-1	35	5	Hogg / Moore	27009		2		4		6		8	9		11						3	1	5		7	10				31
32	Mar 7	A	Everton	D 2-2	36	5	Worthington, Dryburgh / Buckle, Hickson	41005	1	2		4	5	6	7	8	9	10	11						3									32
33	14	A	Brentford	L 2-3	36	7	Rowley 2 (1p) / Morrad, Latimer 2	21307	1	2		4	5	6	7	8	9	10	11						3									33
34	21	A	Doncaster Rovers	D 0-0	37	7		15141	1	2		4	5	6	7		9	10	11					8	3									34
35	28	H	Swansea Town	W 2-1	39	7	Dryburgh, Morris / Allchurch	15226	1	2		4	5		7		9	10	11					8							3	6		35
36	Apr 4	A	Huddersfield Town	L 0-1	39	7	- / Shiner	26822	1	2		4	5		7		9	10	11					8							3	6		36
37	6	A	Rotherham United	D 0-0	40	8		14330	1	2		4					9	10			8								7	11	3	6	5	37
38	7	H	Rotherham United	W 3-2	42	6	Hines, Rowley 2 / Shaw, Burke	24809	1	2		4	5				9	10	11		8								7		3	6		38
39	11	H	Sheffield United	D 0-0	43	7		32468	1	2		4	5				9	10			8								7		3	6		39
40	16	A	Hull City	D 1-1	44	6	Rowley / Gerrie	16692	1	4		2	5			8	9	10											7	11	3	6		40
41	18	A	Barnsley	W 3-0	46	5	Small, Rowley 2 (1p)	4697	1	4		2	5				9	10			8								7		3	6		41
42	25	H	Lincoln City	W 3-2	48	5	Rowley 3 (2p) / Birch, Whittle (p)	20923	1	2		4	5		9			10											7		3	6		42
			Final League Position:	5			**League Appearances**		36	29	39	38	34	31	32	13	38	41	35	1	9	1	3	20	11	4	9	6	7	8	8	8	1	
			Average Home League Attendance:	26250			**League Goals**					1		1	8	4	14	39	11		1			5					2	1				

FA CUP

Match No	Date		Opponents	Result			Scorers	Att	Johnny Anderson	Arthur Lever	Stan Milburn	Jimmy Baldwin	Matt Gillies	Johnny King	Mal Griffiths	Fred Worthington	Derek Hines	Arthur Rowley	Tom Dryburgh	Eric Littler	Peter Small	Ron Burbeck	Arthur Dixon	Johnny Morris	Bill Webb	Reg Warner	Tom McArthur	Adam Dickson	Jimmy Crawford	Derek Hogg	Ron Jackson	Tommy Dunne	Gordon Fincham	Match No
1	Jan 10	H	Notts County (3)	L 2-4			Rowley 2 (1p) / Crookes, McPherson 2, Broome (p)	30889		2	3	4	5	6	7		9	10	11								1		8					1

1952-53
Back: Dixon, Littler, Gillies, Anderson, Halton, Baldwin, McGregor.
Front: Bullock (Manager), Milburn, Worthington, Lever, Rowley, Small, Jones (Trainer).
On Ground: Griffiths, Dryburgh, King.

Promoted: Leicester City, Everton
Relegated: Brentford, Oldham Athletic

FOOTBALL LEAGUE DIVISION TWO

Match No	Date		Opponents	Result	Points	Position	Scorers	Att	Johnny Anderson	Arthur Lever	Ron Jackson	Jimmy Baldwin	Matt Gillies	Tommy Dunne	Mal Griffiths	Johnny Morris	Derek Hines	Arthur Rowley	Tom Dryburgh	Reg Warner	Peter Small	Bill Webb	Derek Hogg	Jimmy Crawford	Eddie Russell	Stan Milburn	Tom McArthur	Eric Littler	Gordon Fincham	Jack Froggatt	Fred Worthington	Match No
1	Aug 19	H	Derby County	D 2-2	1	-	Rowley, Hines / Dunn, Lee	35686	1	2	3	4	5	6	7	8	9	10	11													1
2	22	A	West Ham United	L 1-4	1	-	Rowley (p) / Kearns 3, Andrews	22300	1	2	3	4	5	6	7	8	9	10	11													2
3	24	H	Fulham	D 2-2	2	16	Morris 2 / Haynes, Jezzard	19950	1	2	3	4	5	6	7	8	9	10	11													3
4	29	H	Leeds United	W 5-0	4	10	Rowley 2, Hines 3	21984	1	2	3		5	6	7	8	9	10		4	11											4
5	Sep 2	A	Fulham	D 1-1	5	10	Hines / Mitten	16927	1	2	3		5	6	7	8	9	10		4	11											5
6	5	A	Birmingham City	W 2-1	7	7	Rowley, Hines / Stewart	30885	1	2	3		5	6	7	8	9	10		4		11										6
7	7	H	Stoke City	W 4-0	9	4	Griffiths 3, Rowley	20907	1	2	3	4	5	6	7	8	9	10			11											7
8	12	H	Nottingham Forest	W 1-0	11	3	Small	29839	1	2	3	4	5	6	7	8	9	10			11											8
9	14	A	Stoke City	D 2-2	12	4	Small 2 / Malkin 2	19367	1	2	3	4	5	6	7	8	9	10			11											9
10	19	A	Luton Town	D 2-2	13	4	Griffiths, Rowley (p) / Downie, Dunne (og)	19188	1	2	3	4	5	6	7	8	9	10			11											10
11	26	H	Plymouth Argyle	W 4-2	15	4	Griffiths, Small 2, Rowley / Davis 2	24495	1	2	3	4	5	6	7	8	9	10			11											11
12	Oct 3	A	Swansea Town	D 0-0	16	4		21721	1	2	3	4	5	6	7	8	9	10			11											12
13	10	H	Doncaster Rovers	W 2-0	18	2	Small, Rowley	31299	1	2	3	4	5	6	7	8	9	10			11											13
14	17	A	Bury	W 5-2	20	2	Rowley, Morris 2, Small, Hines / Plant, Fletcher	18163	1	2	3	4	5	6		8	9	10			11		7									14
15	24	H	Oldham Athletic	W 1-0	22	1	Rowley	28449	1	2	3	4	5	6		8	9	10			11			7								15
16	31	A	Everton	W 2-1	24	1	Morris, Hines / Eglington	51811	1	2	3	4	5	6	7	8	9	10			11											16
17	Nov 7	A	Hull City	L 1-3	24	1	Morris / Crosbie 2, Jensen	28726	1	2	3	4	5	6	7	8	9	10			11											17
18	14	A	Notts County	D 1-1	25	2	Small / McCormack	27806	1	2	3	4	5		7	8	9	10			11				6							18
19	21	H	Lincoln City	W 9-2	27	1	Hines 5, Morris, Griffiths, Rowley 2 (1p) / Whittle, Graver	30243	1	2	3	4	5		7	8	9	10			11				6							19
20	28	A	Bristol Rovers	L 0-3	27	1	- / McIlvenny, Hale, Meyer	26491	1	2	3	4	5		7	8	9	10			11				6							20
21	Dec 5	A	Brentford	W 6-0	29	1	Rowley 2, Morris, Dryburgh, Small, Baldwin	23896	1		3	4	5		7	8		10	11	9					6	2						21
22	12	A	Derby County	L 1-2	29	1	Rowley (p) / Parry 2	28205	1		3	4	5		7	8	9	10			11				6	2						22
23	19	H	West Ham United	W 2-1	31	1	Rowley, Russell / Dixon	22976	1	2	3	4	5		7	8	9	10			11				6							23
24	25	H	Rotherham United	W 4-1	33	1	Rowley 3, Hines / Guest	30902	1		3	4	5		7	8	9	10			11				6	2						24
25	26	A	Rotherham United	D 1-1	34	1	Griffiths / Wilson	16757	1		3	4	5		7	8	9	10	11						6	2						25
26	Jan 2	A	Leeds United	L 1-7	34	1	Griffiths / Iggleden 3, Williams, Charles, Nightingale, Tyrer	21532	1		3	4			7	8		10			11				6	2	5	9				26
27	16	H	Birmingham City	L 3-4	34	1	Hines 2, Rowley / Murphy, K Rowley, Govan 2	34604	1	2	3	6			7	8	9	10			11				4				5			27
28	23	A	Nottingham Forest	L 1-3	34	5	Rowley / Capel, McLaren 2	34273	1	2	3	4			7	8	9	10			11				6				5			28
29	Feb 6	H	Luton Town	W 2-1	36	1	Rowley (p), Small / Turner	31892	1		3	4	5		7	8	9	10			11				6	2						29
30	13	A	Plymouth Argyle	W 3-0	38	1	Hines, Small, Rowley	17020	1		3	4	5		7	8	9	10			11				6	2						30
31	23	A	Swansea Town	W 4-1	40	1	Rowley, Morris 2, Dryburgh / Medwin	15085	1		3	4	5	6	7	8	9	10	11							2						31
32	27	A	Doncaster Rovers	W 2-0	42	1	Littler, Dryburgh	18766	1		3	4	5		7	8		10	11						6	2	9					32
33	Mar 6	H	Bury	W 2-0	44	1	Rowley, Dryburgh	35725	1		3	4	5		7	8		10	11						6	2		9				33
34	20	H	Everton	D 2-2	45	2	Hines, Small / Hickson 2	39046	1		3		5	4		8	9	10		7					6	2				11		34
35	27	A	Lincoln City	L 1-3	45	3	Rowley / Graver, Garvey, Munro	16990	1		3	4	5		7			10			11				6	2				9	8	35
36	Apr 3	H	Bristol Rovers	W 1-0	47	2	Froggatt	27369	1		3	4	5			8	9	10		7					6	2				11		36
37	6	A	Oldham Athletic	W 2-0	49	1	Small, Hines	8468	1		3	4	5			8	9	10		7					6	2				11		37
38	10	A	Hull City	W 3-0	51	1	Rowley, Griffiths, Froggatt	19087	1		3	4	5		7		9	10		8					6	2				11		38
39	16	A	Blackburn Rovers	L 0-3	51	2	- / Quigley, Bell, Kelly	45521	1		3	4	5		7		9	10		8					6	2				11		39
40	17	H	Notts County	D 2-2	52	2	Small, Griffiths / Johnston 2	32042	1		3	4	5		7	8		10	11	9					6	2						40
41	19	H	Blackburn Rovers	W 4-0	54	1	Rowley 2, Morris 2	40047	1		3	4	5		7	8	9	10			11				6	2						41
42	24	A	Brentford	W 3-1	56	1	Griffiths, Morris, Horne (og) / Dudley	22800	1		3	4	5		7	8	9	10			11				6	2						42

Final League Position:				1			**League Appearances**		42	23	42	38	39	19	37	39	36	42	9	3	34	1	1	1	24	19	1	2	2	7	1	
Average Home League Attendance:			28982				**League Goals**			1					11	13	19	30	4		14				1				1	2		

FA CUP

Match No	Date		Opponents	Result	Scorers	Att	Johnny Anderson	Arthur Lever	Ron Jackson	Jimmy Baldwin	Matt Gillies	Tommy Dunne	Mal Griffiths	Johnny Morris	Derek Hines	Arthur Rowley	Tom Dryburgh	Reg Warner	Peter Small	Bill Webb	Derek Hogg	Jimmy Crawford	Eddie Russell	Stan Milburn	Tom McArthur	Eric Littler	Gordon Fincham	Jack Froggatt	Fred Worthington	Match No
1	Jan 9	A	Middlesbrough (3)	D 0-0		38701	1	2	3	6			7	8		10			11				4				9	5		1
2	14	H	Middlesbrough (3 rep)	W 3-2	Rowley 3 / Spuhler, Mannion	29736	1	2	3	6			7	8	9	10		5	11				4							2
3	30	A	Stoke City (4)	D 0-0		39066	1		3	4	5		7	8	9	10			11				6	2						3
4	Feb 2	H	Stoke City (4 rep)	W 3-1	Morris, Small 2 / Malkin	20646	1		3	4	5		7	8	9	10			11				6	2						4
5	20	A	Norwich City (5)	W 2-1	Rowley (p), Small / Brennan	39973	1		3	4	5		7	8	9	10			11				6	2						5
6	Mar 13	H	Preston N.E. (6)	D 1-1	Jackson / Morrison	40065	1		3	4	5		7	8	9	10			11				6	2						6
7	17	A	Preston N.E. (6 rep)	D 2-2 aet	Small, Rowley / Wayman, Morrison	38130	1		3	4	5		7	8	9	10			11				6	2						7
8	22		Preston N.E. (6 rep 2)	L 1-3	Rowley / Baxter, Foster, Finney	44356	1		3	4	5		7	8	9	10	11						6	2						8

Stand-in Goalkeepers: Oct 31, Rowley for Anderson, Everton (a).
Note: Mar 22, at Hillsborough (Sheffield Wednesday).

1953-54
Back: Baldwin, Warner, Lever, Gillies, Anderson, Griffiths, McArthur, Rowley.
Front: Jones (Trainer), Jackson, Dunne, Morris, Small, King, Dryburgh, Bullock (Manager).
On Ground: Milburn, Worthington.

Season 1954-55

Champions: Chelsea
Relegated: Leicester City, Sheffield Wednesday

FOOTBALL LEAGUE DIVISION ONE

No	Date	H/A	Opponents	Result	Pts	Pos	Scorers	Att	Anderson	Milburn	Jackson	Baldwin	Gillies	Russell	Griffiths	Morris	Hines	Rowley	Froggatt	Dickson	King	Small	Appleton	Jakeman	Hogg	Richardson	Webb	Worthington	Cunningham	Littler	Graver	Thomas	Fincham	Dunne	No
1	Aug 21	H	Chelsea	D 1-1	1	-	Griffiths / Bentley	38541	1	2	3	4	5	6	7	8	9	10	11																1
2	26	A	Charlton Athletic	W 3-2	3	-	Froggatt, Hines, Rowley / Hewie, Leary	23685	1	2	3	4	5	6	7	8	9	10	11																2
3	28	A	Cardiff City	L 1-2	3	11	Froggatt / Northcott, Ford	35000	1	2	3	4	5	6	7	8	9	10	11																3
4	30	H	Charlton Athletic	L 0-1	3	14	- / White	32050		2	3		5		7	8	9	10	4	1	6	11													4
5	Sep 4	H	Manchester City	L 0-2	3	18	- / McAdams, Hart	32825		2	3		5		7	8	9	10	4	1	11	6													5
6	6	A	Burnley	L 1-3	3	19	Rowley / Gray, Stephenson, Holden	20602		2	3		5			8	9	10	11	1	6	4	7												6
7	11	A	Everton	D 2-2	4	20	Rowley, Froggatt / Hickson, Lewis	49684		2	3		5		7	8	9	10	4	1	11	6													7
8	13	H	Burnley	D 2-2	5	19	Rowley, Hines / Pilkington, Stephenson	26413		2	3		5		7	8	9	10	4	1	6	11													8
9	18	H	Newcastle United	W 3-2	7	15	Morris, Froggatt, Griffiths / R Mitchell (p), White	38038		2	3		5		7	8	9	10	4	1	11	6													9
10	25	A	West Bromwich Albion	L 4-6	7	16	Hines, Rowley, Griffiths, Morris / Allen, Griffin, Nicholls 3, Lee	48422		2	3		5		7	8	9	10	4	1	11	6													10
11	Oct 2	H	Arsenal	D 3-3	8	17	Rowley 2 (1p), Hines / Lawton 2, Logie	42486	1	2	3		5	6	7	8	9	10	4						11										11
12	9	A	Bolton Wanderers	L 1-4	8	17	Rowley / Moir 2, Lofthouse, Hassall	35328	1	2			5	6	7	8	9	10	4						11				3						12
13	16	H	Huddersfield Town	L 1-3	8	20	Rowley / Burrell, Glazzard, Cavanagh	30491	1	2			5	6	7	8	9	10	4						11				3						13
14	23	A	Portsmouth	L 1-2	8	21	Dickinson (og) / P Harris 2	34727	1	2			5	6	7	8	9	10							11				3						14
15	30	H	Blackpool	D 2-2	9	22	Rowley, Hines / Mortensen 2	40655	1	2	3	4	5	6	7	8	9	10							11										15
16	Nov 6	A	Aston Villa	W 5-2	11	20	Worthington 2, Rowley, Griffiths, Hines / Walsh, Lockhart	26875	1	2	3		5	6	7		9	10	4						11			8							16
17	13	H	Sunderland	D 1-1	12	20	Rowley (p) / Purdon	39446	1	2	3		5	6	7		9	10	4						11			8							17
18	20	A	Tottenham Hotspur	L 1-5	12	21	Rowley / Gavin 2, Baily, Robb 2	27874	1	2	3		5	6	7		9	10	4						11			8							18
19	27	H	Sheffield Wednesday	W 4-3	14	19	Russell 2, Morris, Rowley / Hukin 2, Sewell	28474	1	2	3	4		6	7	8	9	10	5						11										19
20	Dec 4	A	Manchester United	L 1-3	14	20	Hines / Webster, Rowley, Viollet	19369	1	2	3	4		6	7	8	9	10	5						11										20
21	11	H	Wolverhampton W.	L 1-2	14	21	Rowley / Hancocks 2	35760	1	2		4		6	7	8	9	10	5						11				3						21
22	18	A	Chelsea	L 1-3	14	21	Graver / Parsons, McNichol, Froggatt-Milburn (jt og)	33215	1	2	3	4		6	7			10	5						11			8			9				22
23	25	A	Sheffield United	D 1-1	15	21	Graver / Hawksworth	32550	1	2	3	4		6	7			10	5						11						9	8			23
24	27	H	Sheffield United	L 0-1	15	21	- / Furniss (p)	39006	1	2	3	4		6	7			10	5						11						9	8			24
25	Jan 1	H	Cardiff City	W 2-1	17	21	Hogg, Morris / Nutt	25408	1	2	3	4		6	7	8		10	5						11						9				25
26	15	A	Manchester City	D 2-2	18	21	Morris, Griffiths / Hayes, Clarke	13648	1	2	3		5	6	7	8		10	4						11						9				26
27	Feb 5	A	Newcastle United	L 0-2	18	21	- / Hannah, J Milburn	36061	1	2	3		5	6	7	8		10	4						11						9				27
28	12	H	West Bromwich Albion	W 6-3	20	21	Rowley 3, Griffiths, Hogg, Graver / Carter 2, Lee	28786	1		3		5	6	7			10	4						11				2		9		8		28
29	19	A	Arsenal	D 1-1	21	21	Rowley / Roper	27384	1		3			6	7			10	4				5		11				2		9		8		29
30	Mar 5	A	Wolverhampton W.	L 0-5	21	21	- / Hancocks 2, Swinbourne, Wilshaw, Smith	41666	1		3			6	7	8	9	10	4						11				2				5		30
31	12	H	Portsmouth	W 4-0	23	21	Rowley 2, Hines, Hogg	28282	1		3			6	7	8	9	10	4						11				2				5		31
32	19	A	Blackpool	L 0-2	23	21	- / Mudie 2	24185	1		3			6	7	8	9	10	4						11				2				5		32
33	26	H	Aston Villa	W 4-2	25	21	Hines, Froggatt, Hogg, Rowley (p) / Southren, Dixon	18897	1		3	4		6		8	9	10	11						7				2				5		33
34	Apr 2	A	Sunderland	D 1-1	26	21	Hines / Chisholm	30457	1		3	4		6		8	9	10	11						7				2				5		34
35	8	A	Preston North End	W 4-2	28	21	Rowley, Morris 2, Walton (og) / Docherty, Evans	18949	1		3	4		6		8	9	10	11						7				2				5		35
36	9	H	Manchester United	W 1-0	30	21	Froggatt	34362	1	2		4		6		8	9		11						7				3		10		5		36
37	11	A	Preston North End	L 0-1	30	21	- / Waterhouse	28282	1	2		4		6		8	9		11						7				3		10		5		37
38	16	A	Sheffield Wednesday	L 0-1	30	21	- / R Froggatt	20539	1	2				6	7	8	9		4						11				3				5	10	38
39	20	H	Everton	D 2-2	31	21	Hogg, Froggatt / Eglington, Hickson	21122	1	2				6	7	8			4						11				3		9		5	10	39
40	23	H	Tottenham Hotspur	W 2-0	33	21	Hines, Hogg	23908	1	2				6	7	8	9	10	4						11				3				5		40
41	30	A	Huddersfield Town	L 1-3	33	21	Morris / Glazzard, Watson 2	16498	1	2				6	10	7	8	9	4						11				3				5		41
42	May 4	H	Bolton Wanderers	W 4-0	35	21	Thomas 3, Hogg	12223	1	2		4		6	7	8	9		11										3			10	5		42

			Anderson	Milburn	Jackson	Baldwin	Gillies	Russell	Griffiths	Morris	Hines	Rowley	Froggatt	Dickson	King	Small	Appleton	Jakeman	Hogg	Richardson	Webb	Worthington	Cunningham	Littler	Graver	Thomas	Fincham	Dunne
Final League Position:	21	**League Appearances**	35	34	31	24	16	30	36	37	32	36	41	7	1	3	4	1	36	2	3	4	16	1	11	5	14	2
Average Home League Attendance:	31067	**League Goals**						2	6	8	11	23	7						7			2			3	3		

FA CUP

No	Date	H/A	Opponents	Result	Pts	Pos	Scorers	Att	Anderson	Milburn	Jackson	Baldwin	Gillies	Russell	Griffiths	Morris	Hines	Rowley	Froggatt	Dickson	King	Small	Appleton	Jakeman	Hogg	Richardson	Webb	Worthington	Cunningham	Littler	Graver	Thomas	Fincham	Dunne	No
1	Jan 8	A	Rotherham United (3)	L 0-1			- / Pell	20331	1	2	3		5	6		8		10	4						7		11				9				1

Stand-in Goalkeepers: Aug 28, Milburn for Anderson, Cardiff City (a).

Note: Dec 18, Froggatt and Milburn kicked the ball simultaneously.

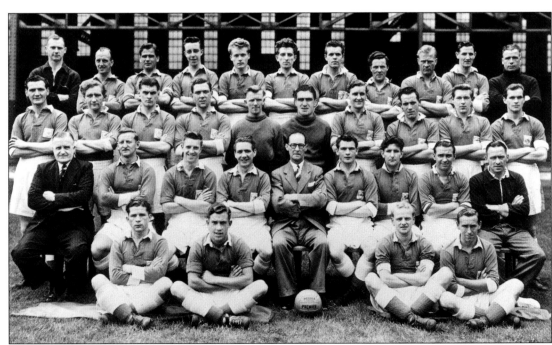

1954-55
Back: F King (Training Staff), Baldwin, Small, Reed, Dunne, Jayes, Heath, Morris, Froggatt, Hogg, Dewis (Trainer).
Middle: Gillies, Littler, Warner, Rowley, Dickson, Anderson, Russell, Hines, Knapp, Richardson.
Front: Maley (Secretary), Jackson, Milburn, Worthington, Bullock (Manager), Webb, Jakeman, Griffiths, Jones (Trainer).
On Ground: Wilson, Thomas, Jenkins, J King.

Season 1955-56

Promoted: Sheffield Wednesday, Leeds United
Relegated: Plymouth Argyle, Hull City

FOOTBALL LEAGUE DIVISION TWO

Match No	Date	V	Opponents	Result	Points	Position	Scorers	Att	Johnny Anderson	Stan Milburn	Willie Cunningham	Jimmy Baldwin	Jack Froggatt	Eddie Russell	Mal Griffiths	Johnny Morris	Derek Hines	Arthur Rowley	Derek Hogg	Howard Riley	Brian Jayes	Barrie Thomas	Jimmy Dunne	Oliver Beeby	Bill Webb	Gordon Fincham	Colin Appleton	Willie Gardiner	Billy Wright	Pat Ward	John Ogilvie	Tony Knapp	Ian McNeill	Ron Burbeck	Match No
1	Aug 20	A	Hull City	W 4-2	2	-	Morris, Rowley 2, Hines / Gerrie, Jensen	20431	1	2	3	4	5	6	7	8	9	10	11																1
2	22	H	Nottingham Forest	W 5-2	4	-	Morris, Hogg 2, Hines 2 / Higham, Imlach	29191	1	2	3	4	5	6	7	8	9	10	11																2
3	27	H	Blackburn Rovers	L 0-2	4	6	- / Briggs, Quigley	27380	1	2	3	4	5	6	7	8	9	10	11																3
4	31	A	Nottingham Forest	L 0-2	4	11	- / Imlach, Thomas	20661	1	2	3		5	6			9		11			8	4						7					10	4
5	Sep 3	A	Lincoln City	L 1-7	4	15	Hines / Finch 2, Munro 2, Graver, Northcott 2	11102	1	2	3		5	6			9		11			8	4						7					10	5
6	5	A	Doncaster Rovers	L 2-6	4	17	Rowley, Gardiner / Jeffrey 2, J Walker 2, Mooney, Herbert	11840	1	2	3		4	6	7	8		10	11							5		9							6
7	10	H	Barnsley	D 0-0	5	16		22856	1		2		4	6	7	8	9	10	11						3	5									7
8	12	A	Sheffield Wednesday	D 1-1	6	14	Rowley / Shiner	25819	1		2		4	6	7	8	9	10	11						3	5									8
9	17	H	Liverpool	W 3-1	8	12	Hogg, Gardiner 2 / Liddell	21356	1		2		4	6	7	8		10	11						3	5		9							9
10	24	A	Plymouth Argyle	W 1-0	10	11	Rowley	19454	1		2		4	6	7	8		10	11						3	5		9							10
11	Oct 1	H	Stoke City	W 3-1	12	10	Hogg, Gardiner, Rowley / Bowyer	28631	1		2		4	6	7	8		10	11						3	5		9							11
12	8	A	Middlesbrough	L 3-4	12	11	Rowley, Gardiner 2 / Clough, Fitzsimons, Delaphena (p), Harris	20642	1		2		4	6	7	8		10	11						3	5		9							12
13	15	H	Bristol City	D 2-2	13	12	Rowley 2 (1p) / Atyeo, Rogers	28254	1		2		4	6	7	8	9	10	11						3	5									13
14	22	A	Fulham	L 2-3	13	14	Rowley 2 / Robson 2, Jezzard	18000	1		2		4		7	8		10	11						3	5		9		6					14
15	29	H	Port Vale	W 4-1	15	10	Gardiner 4 / Stephenson	26486	1		2		4		7	8		10	11						3	5		9		6					15
16	Nov 5	A	Rotherham United	L 1-3	15	13	Rowley / Wilson, Keyworth, Farmer	11876	1		2		4		7	8		10	11						3	5		9		6					16
17	12	H	Swansea Town	W 6-1	17	11	Griffiths, Morris, Gardiner 3, Rowley / Thomas	31050	1		2		4		7	8		10	11							5		9		6	3				17
18	19	A	Notts County	D 1-1	18	11	Rowley / McGrath	25622	1		2		4		7	8		10	11							5		9		6	3				18
19	26	H	Leeds United	W 5-2	20	10	Rowley 2 (1p), Gardiner 3 / Charles 2 (2p)	30196	1		2		4		7	8		10	11							5		9		6	3				19
20	Dec 3	A	West Ham United	W 3-1	22	7	Rowley, Froggatt, Gardiner / Tucker	17500	1		2		4		7	8		10	11							5		9		6	3				20
21	10	H	Bury	W 5-0	24	5	Gardiner 2, Hogg, Rowley, Froggatt	27195	1		2		4		7	8		10	11							5		9		6	3				21
22	17	H	Hull City	L 1-2	24	9	Gardiner / Bradbury, Mortensen	27013	1		2		4		7	8		10	11							5		9		6	3				22
23	24	A	Blackburn Rovers	W 3-2	26	5	Morris, Rowley 2 1p / Briggs, Langton (p)	22771	1		2		4		7	8		10	11							5		9		6	3				23
24	26	A	Bristol Rovers	L 1-2	26	8	Morris / Biggs, Meyer	21652	1		2		4		7	8		10	11							5		9		6	3				24
25	27	H	Bristol Rovers	W 4-2	28	5	Froggatt, Gardiner 2, Rowley / Bradford, Meyer	35000	1		2		4			8		10	11							5		9		6	3				25
26	31	H	Lincoln City	W 4-0	30	2	Gardiner 2, Rowley 2 (1p)	34418	1		2		4			8		10	11							5		9		6	3				26
27	Jan 14	A	Barnsley	W 1-0	32	2	Gardiner	13188	1		2		4	6	7	8		10	11						3	5		9							27
28	21	A	Liverpool	L 1-3	32	4	Rowley / Liddell 2 (1p), Arnell	39917	1		2		4	6	7	8		10	11							5		9			3				28
29	Feb 4	H	Plymouth Argyle	W 5-1	34	3	Froggatt, Riley 2, Rowley 2 / Davis	23610	1		2		4			8		10	11	7						5		9		6	3				29
30	11	A	Stoke City	L 0-2	34	5	- / Coleman 2	21091	1		2		4			8		10	11	7						5		9		6	3				30
31	18	H	Notts County	W 4-0	36	2	Hogg, Gardiner 2, Rowley	25877	1		2		4			8		10	11	7						5		9		6	3				31
32	25	A	Bristol City	D 1-1	37	2	Riley / Burden	27419	1		2		4			8		10	11	7						5		9		6	3				32
33	Mar 3	H	Fulham	W 2-1	39	2	Froggatt 2 / Robson	35496	1		2		4			8		10	11	7					3	5		9		6					33
34	10	A	Bury	L 1-3	39	2	Rowley / Kelly 2, Pearson	16831	1		2		4			8	9	10	11	7						5				6	3				34
35	17	H	Rotherham United	W 3-1	41	2	Hogg, Rowley (p), Gardiner / Johnson	29031	1		2		4			8		10	11	7						5		9		6	3				35
36	24	A	Swansea Town	L 1-6	41	2	Froggatt / Griffiths 2, Medwin 3, L Allchurch	16920	1		2		4			8		10	11	7						5		9		6	3				36
37	31	H	Middlesbrough	D 1-1	42	3	Gardiner / Fitzsimons	28450	1	2			4		7	8		10	11							5		9		6	3				37
38	Apr 2	H	Sheffield Wednesday	L 1-2	42	6	Gardiner / R Froggatt 2	37624	1	2			10			8			11	7						5	4	9		6	3				38
39	7	A	Leeds United	L 0-4	42	9	- / Overfield, Brook, Charles 2 (1p)	26408	1	2			4			8		10	11							5		9		6	3				39
40	14	H	West Ham United	W 2-1	44	5	Griffiths, Gardiner / Blackburn	17432	1	2			4		7	8			11							5		9		6	3		10		40
41	21	A	Port Vale	W 3-2	46	5	Froggatt, Gardiner 2 / Done (p), Baily	14302	1	2			4			8			11	7						5		9		6	3		10		41
42	28	H	Doncaster Rovers	W 3-0	48	4	McNeill, Gardiner, Hogg	18267	1	2			4			8			11	7						5		9		6	3		10		42

									And	Mil	Cun	Bal	Fro	Rus	Gri	Mor	Hin	Row	Hog	Ril	Jay	Tho	Dun	Bee	Web	Fin	App	Gar	Wri	War	Ogi	Kna	McN	Bur	
Final League Position:			5				**League Appearances**		42	12	34	3	42	16	17	39	17	36	42	11	3	2	2	1	13	32	1	33	2	27	24	4	5	2	
Average Home League Attendance:			28134				**League Goals**						8		2	5	4	29	8	3								34					1		

FA CUP

	Date	V	Opponents	Result			Scorers	Att	And	Mil	Cun	Bal	Fro	Rus	Gri	Mor	Hin	Row	Hog	Ril	Jay	Tho	Dun	Bee	Web	Fin	App	Gar	Wri	War	Ogi	Kna	McN	Bur	
1	Jan 11	A	Luton Town (3)	W 4-0			Gardiner, Rowley 3	23221	1		2		4	6	7	8		10	11						3	5		9							1
2	28	H	Stoke City (4)	D 3-3			Rowley 2 (1p), Griffiths / Bowyer, Graver, King	35877	1		2		4	6	7	8		10	11							5		9			3				2
3	30	A	Stoke City (4 rep)	L 1-2			Rowley / Oscroft, Graver	34003	1		2		4		7	8	9	10	11							5				6	3				3

Dismissals: Mar 24, Ogilvie, Swansea Town (a).

1955-56
Back: Baldwin, Gillies, Fincham, Jones (Trainer), Anderson, Russell, Cunningham, Webb.
Front: Maley (Secretary), Griffiths, Morris, Thomas, Rowley, Hogg, Halliday (Manager).
On Ground: Milburn, Froggatt.

Promoted: Leicester City, Nottingham Forest
Relegated: Bury, Port Vale

FOOTBALL LEAGUE DIVISION TWO

Match No	Date		Opponents	Result	Points	Position	Scorers	Att	Johnny Anderson	Stan Milburn	John Ogilvie	Johnny Morris	Jack Froggatt	Pat Ward	Tommy McDonald	Ian McNeill	Willie Gardiner	Arthur Rowley	Derek Hogg	Bill Webb	Derek Hines	Colin Appleton	Billy Wright	Harvey Sinclair	Dave Maclaren	Jimmy Walsh	Jimmy Moran	Willie Cunningham	Match No
1	Aug 18	H	Doncaster Rovers	W 3-1	2	-	McDonald 2, Hogg / Jeffrey	26165	1	2	3	4	5	6	7	8	9	10	11										1
2	20	A	Huddersfield Town	W 2-1	4	-	McNeill, Rowley / Simpson	18978	1	2	3	4	5	6	7	8	9	10	11										2
3	25	A	Stoke City	L 1-3	4	8	Rowley / Oscroft, Coleman, Cairns (p)	23675	1	2	3	4	5	6	7	8	9	10	11										3
4	29	H	Huddersfield Town	D 2-2	5	7	Rowley, Gardiner / Hickson, McHale	28301	1	2	3	4	5	6	7	8	9	10	11										4
5	Sep 1	H	Middlesbrough	D 1-1	6	8	Gardiner / Clough	27227	1	2	3	4	5	6	7	8	9	10	11										5
6	8	A	Sheffield United	D 1-1	7	9	Rowley / Howitt	32141	1	2	3	4	5	6	7	8	9	10	11										6
7	12	H	Bury	W 3-0	9	4	Rowley 3	21104	1	2	3	4	5	6	7	8	9	10	11										7
8	15	A	Bristol Rovers	W 2-1	11	4	Rowley, McDonald / Meyer	28004	1	2	3	4	5	6	7	8	9	10	11										8
9	17	A	Bury	W 5-4	13	1	McNeill 2, Gardiner, Rowley, Milburn / Tilley 2, Pearson 2	11306	1	2		4	5	6	7	8	9	10	11	3									9
10	22	H	Notts County	W 6-3	15	1	Rowley 3, McDonald, Gardiner, McNeill / Wills, Jackson, Bradley	28806	1	2	3	4	5	6	7	8	9	10	11										10
11	29	A	Liverpool	L 0-2	15	2	- / Melia, Liddell	41126	1	2	3	4	5	6	7	8	9	10	11										11
12	Oct 6	H	Barnsley	W 5-2	17	1	McNeill 2, Rowley 2, Hines / Duggins, Kaye	27270	1	2	3	4	5	6	7	8		10	11		9								12
13	13	A	Port Vale	W 3-2	19	2	Hogg, Rowley 2 / Hayward 2	21687	1	2	3	4	5	6	7	8		10	11		9								13
14	20	H	Blackburn Rovers	W 6-0	21	1	Rowley 3 (1p), Hogg, McNeill, Hines	30710	1	2	3	4	5	6	7	8		10	11		9								14
15	27	A	Lincoln City	W 3-2	23	1	McNeill 2, Rowley / Hawkings, Withers	19450	1	2	3	4	5	6	7	8		10	11		9								15
16	Nov 3	H	Swansea Town	D 1-1	24	1	Rowley / Milburn (og)	32445	1	2	3	4	5	6	7	8		10	11		9								16
17	10	A	Fulham	D 2-2	25	1	Rowley, Hogg / Bentley 2	33700	1	2	3	4	5		7	8		10	11		9	6							17
18	17	H	Nottingham Forest	D 0-0	26	1		40830	1	2	3	4	5		7	8	9	10	11			6							18
19	24	A	West Ham United	L 1-2	26	2	Rowley / Lewis, Tucker	20000	1	2	3	4	5	6	7	8	9	10	11										19
20	Dec 1	H	Rotherham United	W 5-2	28	2	Hines 2, McNeill 2, Rowley / Jackson, Grainger	27841	1	2	3	4	5	6	7	8		10	11		9								20
21	8	A	Bristol City	W 2-0	30	1	McNeill 2	24518	1	2	3	4	5	6	7	8		10	11		9								21
22	15	A	Doncaster Rovers	W 2-0	32	1	Rowley, Graham (og)	13987	1	2	3	4	5	6	7	8		10	11		9								22
23	22	H	Stoke City	W 3-2	34	1	McNeill, Hines, Rowley / Kelly 2	27178	1	2	3	4	5		7	8		10	11		9	6							23
24	25	A	Grimsby Town	D 2-2	35	1	Rowley, Hines / Maddison 2 (1p)	16381	1	2	3	4	5		7	8		10			9	6	11						24
25	29	A	Middlesbrough	W 3-1	37	1	Wright, Appleton, Rowley / Fitzsimons	29704	1	2	3	4	5		7	8		10			9	6	11						25
26	Jan 12	A	Sheffield United	W 5-0	39	1	Hines, McNeill, Rowley 2	32752	1	2	3	4	5		7	8		10			9	6	11						26
27	19	H	Bristol Rovers	W 7-2	41	1	McDonald 2, Rowley 2 (1p), Wright 2, Hines / Hooper 2 (1p)	32288	1	2	3	4	5		7	8		10			9	6	11						27
28	26	H	Grimsby Town	W 4-3	43	1	Wright, Hines, Rowley, McNeill / Rafferty 2, Ogilvie (og)	34773		2	3	4	5		7	8		10			9	6	11	1					28
29	Feb 2	A	Notts County	D 0-0	44	1		43225		2	3	4	5		7	8		10			9	6	11		1				29
30	9	H	Liverpool	W 3-2	46	1	Hines, Rowley 2 (1p) / Liddell, Evans	39622		2	3	4	5			8		10	7		9	6	11		1				30
31	23	H	Port Vale	W 2-1	48	1	McDonald, Rowley / Spurdle	20765		2	3	4	5		7	8		10	11		9	6			1				31
32	27	A	Barnsley	L 0-2	48	1	- / Storey, Chappell	11109		2	3	4	5		7	8		10	11		9	6			1				32
33	Mar 2	A	Blackburn Rovers	D 1-1	49	1	Hines / Dobing	32380		2	3	4	5			8		10	11		9	6	7		1				33
34	9	H	Lincoln City	W 4-3	51	1	Rowley 2 (1p), Wright, Neal (og) / Smillie, Northcott, Bannan	33195		2	3	4	5			8		10	11		9	6	7		1				34
35	16	A	Swansea Town	W 3-2	53	1	Hines, McNeill, Rowley (p) / Palmer 2	14102		2	3	4	5	6		8		10	11		9		7		1				35
36	23	H	Fulham	L 1-3	53	1	Rowley / Bentley, Hill, Langley	36450		2	3	4	5					10	11		9	6	7		1	8			36
37	30	A	Nottingham Forest	W 2-1	55	1	McNeill, Hines / Barrett	38741		2	3	4	5	6		8		10	11		9		7		1				37
38	Apr 6	H	West Ham United	W 5-3	57	1	Rowley 3, Wright 2 / Musgrove 2, Allinson	33388		2	3	4	5	6		8		10	11		9		7		1				38
39	13	A	Rotherham United	D 1-1	58	1	Morris / Brown	10758		2	3	4	5	6		8		10	11		9		7		1				39
40	19	A	Leyton Orient	W 5-1	60	1	Wright, Moran, Rowley, Hogg, Facey (og) / Johnston	23695		2		4	5	6				10	11	3	9		7		1		8		40
41	20	H	Bristol City	D 1-1	61	1	Hines / Curtis	32653		2		4	5	6				10	11	3	9		7		1		8		41
42	22	H	Leyton Orient	L 1-4	61	1	Wright / White, McKnight, Andrews, Johnston	27582		2		4	5	6				10	11		9		7		1		8	3	42

									Johnny Anderson	Stan Milburn	John Ogilvie	Johnny Morris	Jack Froggatt	Pat Ward	Tommy McDonald	Ian McNeill	Willie Gardiner	Arthur Rowley	Derek Hogg	Bill Webb	Derek Hines	Colin Appleton	Billy Wright	Harvey Sinclair	Dave Maclaren	Jimmy Walsh	Jimmy Moran	Willie Cunningham	
Final League Position:	1						**League Appearances**		27	42	38	42	42	27	31	38	13	42	36	3	29	15	17	1	14	1	3	1	
Average Home League Attendance:	30624						**League Goals**			1		1			7	18	4	44	5		14	1	10				1		

FA CUP

| 1 | Jan 5 | A | Tottenham Hotspur (3) | L 0-2 | | | - / Blanchflower, Robb | 56492 | 1 | 2 | 3 | 4 | 5 | | 7 | 8 | | 10 | | | 9 | 6 | 11 | | | | | | 1 |

1956-57
Back: McDonald, Cunningham, Ogilvie, Anderson, Fincham, Froggatt, Milburn.
Front: Dowdells (Trainer), Russell, McNeill, Gardiner, Rowley, Hogg, Halliday (Manager).
On Ground: Webb, Morris, Ward, Hines.

Season 1957-58

Champions: Wolverhampton Wanderers
Relegated: Sunderland, Sheffield Wednesday

FOOTBALL LEAGUE DIVISION ONE

Match No	Date		Opponents	Result	Points	Position	Scorers	Att
1	Aug 24	H	Manchester United	L 0-3	-	-	- / Whelan 3	40214
2	28	H	Sunderland	W 4-1	2	-	McNeill 3, O'Neil / Grainger	34364
3	31	A	Leeds United	L 1-2	2	14	Rowley / Baird (p), Overfield	26660
4	Sep 4	A	Sunderland	L 2-3	2	18	McDonald, Hines / O'Neil 2, Goodchild	39629
5	7	H	Bolton Wanderers	L 2-3	2	22	Rowley (p), O'Neil / Holden, Stevens, Lofthouse	30033
6	11	A	Sheffield Wednesday	L 1-2	2	22	Rowley / J McAnearney, Ellis	18270
7	14	A	Arsenal	L 2-3	2	22	Froggatt / Groves 2, Herd	45321
8	18	H	Sheffield Wednesday	W 4-1	4	19	Gardiner 2, Rowley 2 / T McAnearney	22449
9	21	H	Wolverhampton W.	L 2-3	4	21	Russell, McNeill / Clamp, Murray 2	35388
10	28	A	Aston Villa	L 1-5	4	22	Morris / Sewell 2, Southren, Lynn (p), McParland	30851
11	Oct 5	H	Everton	D 2-2	5	22	Gardiner, Hogg / Fielding, Hickson	28992
12	12	A	Manchester City	L 3-4	5	22	Rowley 2 (1p), McDonald / Hayes 2, McAdams, Barlow	29884
13	19	H	Nottingham Forest	W 3-1	7	21	McDonald, Gardiner, Whare (og) / Wilson (p)	36836
14	26	A	Portsmouth	L 0-2	7	21	- / Mansell, Gordon	25947
15	Nov 2	H	Newcastle United	W 2-1	9	21	Gardiner, Russell / Batty	31884
16	9	A	Burnley	L 3-7	9	22	Doherty 2, Hogg / McIlroy 3, Cheesebrough 3, Pointer	20798
17	16	H	Preston North End	L 1-3	9	22	McDonald / Finney, Thompson, Taylor	27129
18	23	A	Chelsea	L 0-4	9	22	- / Tindall, Lewis 2, McNichol	27757
19	30	H	West Bromwich Albion	D 3-3	10	22	Rowley 2, Doherty / Robson 2, Allen	33855
20	Dec 7	A	Tottenham Hotspur	W 4-1	12	22	Doherty 2, McDonald, Rowley / Brooks	27855
21	14	H	Birmingham City	D 2-2	13	21	Rowley 2 / Kinsey, Astall	28610
22	21	H	Manchester United	L 0-4	13	22	- / Viollet 2, Charlton, Scanlon	41631
23	25	A	Blackpool	L 1-5	13	22	Gardiner / Mudie, Perry 2, Peterson 2	16696
24	26	H	Blackpool	W 2-1	15	22	Walsh, Gardiner / Durie	33052
25	28	H	Leeds United	W 3-0	17	21	Rowley 2 (1p), Walsh	31747
26	Jan 11	A	Bolton Wanderers	W 3-2	19	19	Walsh, Cunningham, Higgins (og) / Stevens, Parry	17884
27	18	H	Arsenal	L 0-1	19	21	- / Groves	31778
28	Feb 1	A	Wolverhampton W.	L 1-5	19	21	Walsh / Deeley, Broadbent, Murray 2, Mason	36400
29	8	H	Aston Villa	W 6-1	21	20	Walker, Hogg 2, Riley 2, Lynn (og) / Southren	27140
30	15	A	Everton	D 2-2	22	18	Walsh 2 / J Harris, Thomas	23460
31	22	H	Manchester City	W 8-4	24	15	Walsh 4, Riley 2 (1p), Hines, Hogg / Johnstone 2, McAdams, Barnes	31017
32	Mar 1	A	Nottingham Forest	L 1-3	24	17	Walsh / Gray, Baily, Imlach	38191
33	8	H	Portsmouth	D 2-2	25	17	Hines, Cunningham (p) / P Harris, Gordon	30951
34	15	A	Newcastle United	L 3-5	25	19	Walsh, Riley, McNeill / Bottom 2, White 3	33840
35	22	H	Chelsea	W 3-2	27	18	Hines 2, Cunningham (p) / P Sillett, Tindall	27849
36	29	A	Preston North End	L 1-4	27	19	Rowley / Thompson 2, Finney, Mayers	18389
37	Apr 5	H	Burnley	W 5-3	29	19	Rowley 2, Walsh, Riley 2 / McIlroy 2, Miller	26150
38	7	A	Luton Town	L 1-2	29	19	Hines / Gregory 2	14758
39	8	H	Luton Town	W 4-1	31	19	Rowley 2, Hines, Gardiner / Gregory	32480
40	12	A	West Bromwich Albion	L 2-6	31	19	Rowley, Gardiner / Robson 3, Whitehouse 2, Kevan	25389
41	19	H	Tottenham Hotspur	L 1-3	31	20	Gardiner / Medwin, Smith, Jones	37234
42	26	A	Birmingham City	W 1-0	33	18	McNeill	27614

Final League Position:	18	
Average Home League Attendance:	31359	

League Appearances: 24 19 15 29 11 5 22 17 23 25 38 23 20 8 28 23 19 18 3 1 2 12 28 1 16 10 21 1

League Goals: 1 1 2 5 6 7 20 5 10 2 3 13 5 1 7

FA CUP

	Date		Opponents	Result	Scorers	Att
1	Jan 4	A	Tottenham Hotspur (3)	L 0-4	- / Medwin, Smith 2, Stokes	42716

Dismissals: None, though Morris was sent off in the Public Practice Match for Blues v Whites at Filbert Street on Aug 17.

1957-58
Back: Currie, King, Hines, Gardiner, Froggatt, Ward, Fincham, Appleton, Chalmers, Ogilvie.
Middle: King (Asst Trainer), Walsh, Gammie, O'Neil, Maclaren, Anderson, Rowley, Knapp, Cunningham, Russell, Gillies (Coach).
Front: Dowdells (Trainer), McDonald, W Wright, Moran, McNeill, Hogg, Milburn, Calder, Halliday (Manager).
On Ground: Baillie, B Wright.

Season 1958-59

Champions: Wolverhampton Wanderers
Relegated: Aston Villa, Portsmouth

FOOTBALL LEAGUE DIVISION ONE

Match No	Date		Opponents	Result	Points	Position	Scorers	Att
1	Aug 23	H	Everton	W 2-0	2	-	Leek, Riley	34446
2	25	A	Blackburn Rovers	L 0-5	2	-	- / McGrath, Johnston, Dobing 2, Vernon	36451
3	30	A	Arsenal	L 1-5	2	18	Leek / Holton 2, Evans, Clapton, Nutt	35411
4	Sep 3	H	Blackburn Rovers	D 1-1	3	18	Walsh / Vernon	30669
5	6	H	Manchester City	W 3-1	5	15	McDonald, Kelly, Walsh / McAdams	29053
6	13	A	Leeds United	D 1-1	6	16	McDonald / Meek	23487
7	17	H	Preston North End	D 2-2	7	15	Kelly, Walsh / Thompson 2	34513
8	20	H	West Bromwich Albion	D 2-2	8	16	Walsh, Newman / Allen, Kevan	38751
9	22	A	Preston North End	L 1-3	8	16	Walsh / Finney, Thompson, Lambert	25436
10	27	A	Birmingham City	L 2-4	8	19	Kelly 2 / Gordon, Murphy, Hooper, Astall (p)	33291
11	Oct 4	H	Luton Town	W 3-1	10	14	McNeill, Walsh, Kelly / McLeod	32017
12	11	A	Newcastle United	L 1-3	10	18	Kelly (p) / Allchurch 2, White	46686
13	18	H	Tottenham Hotspur	L 3-4	10	18	Kelly, Walsh 2 / Harmer (p), Smith, Stokes 2	31509
14	25	A	Chelsea	L 2-5	10	21	Kelly, Walsh / P Sillett, Saunders, Brabrook, Tindall 2	40369
15	Nov 1	H	Blackpool	L 0-3	10	22	- / Durie, J Kelly, Garrett	31642
16	8	H	Portsmouth	L 1-4	10	22	Hines / H Harris 2, Saunders 2	20262
17	15	H	Aston Villa	W 6-3	12	21	Hines 4, Walsh, Kelly / Sewell, Hitchens 2	25079
18	22	A	West Ham United	W 3-0	14	21	Kelly, Keyworth, Hines	23500
19	29	A	Nottingham Forest	L 0-3	14	21	- / Dwight 3	26322
20	Dec 6	A	Manchester United	L 1-4	14	21	Kelly / Bradley, Charlton, Scanlon, Viollet	38482
21	13	H	Wolverhampton W.	W 1-0	16	21	Walsh	25964
22	20	A	Everton	W 1-0	18	19	Hines	27703
23	26	H	Burnley	D 1-1	19	18	Leek / Pointer	32182
24	27	A	Burnley	D 3-3	20	18	Riley 2, Leek / Pointer 2, Connelly	24468
25	Jan 3	H	Arsenal	L 2-3	20	18	Walsh, Kelly / Julians 2, Bloomfield	33979
26	31	H	Leeds United	L 0-1	20	19	- / Shackleton	23376
27	Feb 7	A	West Bromwich Albion	D 2-2	21	19	Lornie, Riley / Kevan, Allen	25375
28	21	A	Luton Town	L 3-4	21	20	Leek, Newman, Lornie / Morton, Brown, Cummins, Gregory	15786
29	28	H	Newcastle United	L 0-1	21	20	- / Eastham	24362
30	Mar 7	A	Tottenham Hotspur	L 0-6	21	21	- / Blanchflower, Medwin 4, Dunmore	30561
31	14	H	Chelsea	L 0-3	21	21	- / P Sillett, Brabrook, Greaves	20110
32	18	H	Birmingham City	L 2-4	21	21	Walsh 2 / Stubbs 3, Gordon	15413
33	21	A	Blackpool	L 1-2	21	22	Kelly / Perry 2	11479
34	27	A	Bolton Wanderers	D 3-3	22	21	Wills, Leek, Ogilvie (p) / Stevens, Lofthouse, Ogilvie (og)	21212
35	28	H	Portsmouth	W 3-1	24	21	Walsh, Ogilvie (p), Leek / Newman	17064
36	30	H	Bolton Wanderers	D 0-0	25	21		20329
37	Apr 4	A	Aston Villa	W 2-1	27	21	Walsh 2 / Dixon	40795
38	11	H	West Ham United	D 1-1	28	20	McDonald / Bond	23825
39	18	A	Nottingham Forest	W 4-1	30	19	Walsh, Keyworth, McDonald, Whare (og) / Dwight	24889
40	22	A	Wolverhampton W.	L 0-3	30	19	- / Lill, Murray, Deeley	41220
41	25	H	Manchester United	W 2-1	32	19	Walsh, Wills / Bradley	38466
42	29	A	Manchester City	L 1-3	32	19	Walsh / McAdams, Hayes, Sambrook	46936

Final League Position: 19
Average Home League Attendance: 27860

Player appearances (shirt numbers by match)

Player columns (left→right): Dave Maclaren, Willie Cunningham, Joe Baillie, John Newman, Ian King, Ken Keyworth, Howard Riley, Jimmy Walsh, Derek Hines, Ken Leek, Bill Calder, Tony Knapp, Tommy McDonald, Bernard Kelly, Gordon Wills, Ian McNeill, Ian MacFarlane, Johnny Anderson, Len Chalmers, Colin Appleton, Don Walker, Jack Lornie, John Ogilvie, Roy Stephenson

Match No	DMac	Cun	Bail	New	King	Key	Ril	Wal	Hin	Leek	Cal	Kna	McD	Kel	Wil	McN	MacF	And	Chal	App	Walk	Lor	Ogi	Step
League Appearances	37	28	37	42	22	32	13	38	16	31	3	23	29	24	22	12	1	5	11	12	4	5	5	10
League Goals		2		2		2	4	20	7	7			4	13	2	1						2	2	

FA CUP

Match No	Date		Opponents	Result	Scorers	Att
1	Jan 10	H	Lincoln City (3)	D 1-1	Kelly / McClelland	25623
2	14	A	Lincoln City (3 rep)	W 2-0	Kelly, Hines	7965
3	24	H	Luton Town (4)	D 1-1	McNeill / Bingham	36984
4	28	A	Luton Town (4 rep)	L 1-4	Leek / Brown 3, Gregory	27277

1958-59
Back: Newman, Chalmers, Gardiner, Maclaren, Anderson, King, Keyworth, Baillie.
Middle: Dowdells (Trainer), MacFarlane, Walker, Cunningham, Kelly, Wills, Halliday (Manager).
Front: Walsh, McDonald, McNeill, Hines, Leek.

Season 1959-60

Champions: Burnley
Relegated: Leeds United, Luton Town

FOOTBALL LEAGUE DIVISION ONE

Match No	Date		Opponents	Result	Points	Position	Scorers	Att	Dave Maclaren	Len Chalmers	Joe Baillie	John Newman	Tony Knapp	Colin Appleton	Howard Riley	Albert Cheesebrough	Derek Hines	Ken Leek	Gordon Wills	Willie Cunningham	Roy Stephenson	Tommy McDonald	Gordon Banks	Frank McLintock	Ken Keyworth	Ian White	Jimmy Walsh	Ian King	Jack Lormie	Richie Norman	Match No
1	Aug 22	A	West Ham United	L 0-3		-	- / Smith, Keeble, Grice	28000	1	2	3	4	5	6	7	8	9	10	11												1
2	26	H	Leeds United	W 3-2	2	-	Hines 2, Cheesebrough / Crowe, Cush	24790	1	2	3	4	5	6	7	8	9	10	11												2
3	29	H	Chelsea	W 3-1	4	8	Cheesebrough, Cunningham, Leek / Brabrook	29626	1	2		4	5	6	7	8	9	10	11		3										3
4	Sep 2	A	Leeds United	D 1-1	5	7	Leek / Crowe	18384	1	2	3	4	5	6		8	9	10	11		7										4
5	5	A	West Bromwich Albion	L 0-5	5	15	- / Dixon, Kevan, Jackson, Robson 2	27259	1	2	3	4	5	6		8	9	10	11							7					5
6	9	H	Blackpool	D 1-1	6	14	Leek / Mudie	28089		2	3	4	5	6		8	9	10	11				1			7					6
7	12	H	Newcastle United	L 0-2	6	16	- / Bell 2	24318		2	3	4	5	6		8	9	10	11				1			7					7
8	14	A	Blackpool	D 3-3	7	15	Wills 2, McDonald / J Kelly, Mudie, Armfield	20494	1	2	3		5	6			9	10	11			8		4		7					8
9	19	A	Birmingham City	W 4-3	9	11	Riley, Keyworth 2, Cheesebrough / Hooper 2 (1p), Smith	25003	1	2	3		5	6	7	8	9	10	11					4	8						9
10	26	H	Tottenham Hotspur	D 1-1	10	12	McDonald / Jones (p)	34445	1	2	3		5	6			9	10	11			8		4		7					10
11	Oct 3	A	Manchester United	L 1-4	10	14	Hines / Viollet 2, Charlton, Quixall	41637	1	2	3		5	6			9	10	11			8		4		7					11
12	10	H	Blackburn Rovers	L 2-3	10	19	Cheesebrough 2 / McGrath, Dobing, McEvoy	26107	1	2	3		5	6			9	10	11			8		4		7					12
13	17	A	Manchester City	L 2-3	10	20	McDonald 2 / McAdams 2, Hayes	33896		2	3		5	6			9	10	11			8	1	4		7					13
14	24	H	Arsenal	D 2-2	11	18	Wills, McDonald / Barnwell, Bloomfield	29152		2	3		5	6			9	10	11			8	1	4		7					14
15	31	A	Everton	L 1-6	11	20	McDonald / Thomas 2, Collins, B Harris, Parker, Shackleton	22587		2	3	4	5	6			9	10	11			8	1			7					15
16	Nov 7	H	Sheffield Wednesday	W 2-0	13	18	McDonald, Keyworth	21232		2	3		5	6				10	11			8	1	4	9	7					16
17	14	A	Nottingham Forest	L 0-1	13	20	- / Burkitt	20175		2	3		5	6	7			10	11			8	1	4	9						17
18	21	A	Fulham	L 0-1	13	21	- / Chamberlain	24165		2	3			6				10	11			8	1	4	9			5			18
19	28	A	Bolton Wanderers	L 1-3	13	21	Cheesebrough / Stevens, Hartle (p), Parry	19834		2	3			6		8		10	11				1	4	9	7		5			19
20	Dec 5	H	Luton Town	D 3-3	14	20	Appleton, Wills, McDonald / Bingham, Brown, Pacey	16700		2	3			6		8		10	11				1	4	9	7		5			20
21	12	A	Wolverhampton W.	W 3-0	16	19	McDonald, Leek, Cheesebrough	25370		2			5	6		8		10	11	3		9	1	4		7					21
22	19	H	West Ham United	W 2-1	18	18	White, Cheesebrough / Obeney	20000		2			5	6		8		10	11	3		9	1	4		7					22
23	26	H	Preston North End	D 2-2	19	18	Chalmers (p), Leek / Taylor, Thompson	32684		2			5	6		8		10	11	3		9	1	4		7					23
24	28	A	Preston North End	D 1-1	20	18	Cheesebrough / Knapp (og)	23545		2			5	6		8			11	3			1	4		7	10		9		24
25	Jan 2	A	Chelsea	D 2-2	21	17	Leek 2 / Livesey, Brooks	23719		2			5	6		8	9		11	3			1	4		7	10				25
26	16	A	West Bromwich Albion	L 0-1	21	19	- / Jackson	23802		2			5	6		8	9		11				1	4		7	10				26
27	23	A	Newcastle United	W 2-0	23	18	Walsh, McDonald	32353		2			5	6		8			11			9	1	4		7	10			3	27
28	Feb 6	H	Birmingham City	L 1-3	23	19	McDonald / Weston, Hume, Hooper	25946		2			5	6		8			11	3		9	1	4		7	10				28
29	13	A	Tottenham Hotspur	W 2-1	25	17	Walsh / R Smith	33504					5	6		8			11	2		9	1	4		7	10			3	29
30	24	A	Manchester United	W 3-1	27	16	McLintock, Cheesebrough, Wills / Scanlon	33191					5	6		8			11	3		9	1	4		7	10				30
31	27	A	Luton Town	L 0-2	27	18	- / Turner, McBride	18691		2				6		8			11	3		9	1	4		7	10	5			31
32	Mar 5	H	Manchester City	W 5-0	29	16	Wills 2, Cheesebrough, Leek 2	24009		2			5	6		8			11	3		9	1	4		7	10				32
33	15	A	Arsenal	D 1-1	30	15	Wills / Herd	27838		2			5	6		8			11	3		9	1	4		7	10				33
34	19	H	Wolverhampton W.	W 2-1	32	14	Walsh, Cheesebrough / Murray	25660		2			5	6		8			11	3		9	1	4		7	10				34
35	Apr 2	H	Nottingham Forest	L 0-1	32	15	- / Iley	25922		2			5					10	11	3			1	4	9	7	6	8			35
36	6	A	Sheffield Wednesday	D 2-2	33	15	Cheesebrough, Wills / Griffin, Ellis	26844		2			5	6		8			11			9	1	4		7	10			3	36
37	9	A	Fulham	D 1-1	34	16	Bentley (og) / Johnson	18664		2			5	6	7	8			11	3		9	1	4			10				37
38	15	A	Burnley	L 0-1	34	16	- / Connelly	23777		2			5	6		8			11	3		9	1	4		7	10				38
39	16	H	Everton	D 3-3	35	15	Chalmers (p), Cheesebrough, McLintock / Collins 2, Lill	22390		2			5	6		8			11	3		9	1	4		7	10				39
40	18	H	Burnley	W 2-1	37	13	Wills, Cheesebrough / Meredith	24429					5	6	7	8			11	2		9	1	4			10			3	40
41	23	A	Blackburn Rovers	W 1-0	39	12	Wills	18550					5	6	7	8			11	2		9	1	4			10			3	41
42	30	H	Bolton Wanderers	L 1-2	39	12	Riley / Deakin 2	19527		2			5	6	7	8			11			9	1	4			10			3	42

Final League Position:	12				**League Appearances**	10 39 17 9 39 42 9 41 12 32 39 20 2 31 32 17 20 18 22 4 1 6		
Average Home League Attendance:	25399				**League Goals**	2 1 2 15 3 9 11 1 11 2 3 1 4		

FA CUP

Match No	Date		Opponents	Result	Scorers	Att	Len Chalmers	Tony Knapp	Colin Appleton	Albert Cheesebrough	Tommy McDonald	Gordon Wills	Willie Cunningham	Ian White	Gordon Banks	Frank McLintock	Jimmy Walsh	Match No
1	Jan 9	A	Wrexham (3)	W 2-1	Cheesebrough, Leek / Weston	22561	2	5	6	8	9	11	3	7	1	4	10	1
2	30	H	Fulham (4)	W 2-1	McDonald, Wills / Cunningham (og)	34229	2	5	6	8	9	11	3	7	1	4	10	2
3	Feb 20	H	West Bromwich A. (5)	W 2-1	Walsh, Cheesebrough / Kennedy	37753	2	5	6	8	9	11	3	7	1	4	10	3
4	Mar 12	H	Wolverhampton W. (6)	L 1-2	McDonald / Broadbent, Chalmers (og)	39000	2	5	6	8	9	11	3	7	1	4	10	4

Stand-in Goalkeepers: Sep 5, Wills for Maclaren, West Bromwich Albion (a).
Note: Apr 9, goal credited to Bentley (og), some reports credit Cheesebrough.

1959-60
Back: Hines, Leek, Ogilvie, Maclaren, King, Chalmers, Appleton, Keyworth.
Front: Dowdells (Trainer), Baillie, Cheesebrough, Newman, Walsh, Stephenson, Wills, Gillies (Manager).
On Ground: McDonald, Cunningham.

Season 1960-61

Champions: Tottenham Hotspur
Relegated: Newcastle United, Preston North End

FOOTBALL LEAGUE DIVISION ONE

Player columns (left to right): Gordon Banks, Len Chalmers, Richie Norman, Ian White, Tony Knapp, Colin Appleton, George Meek, Albert Cheesebrough, Derek Hines, Jimmy Walsh, Gordon Wills, Frank McLintock, Howard Riley, Ken Leek, Ian King, Rodney Slack, Jack Lornie, John Sjoberg, Ken Keyworth, George Heyes, Hugh McIlmoyle, Graham Cross.

Match No	Date		Opponents	Result	Points	Position	Scorers	Att	Banks	Chalmers	Norman	White	Knapp	Appleton	Meek	Cheesebrough	Hines	Walsh	Wills	McLintock	Riley	Leek	King	Slack	Lornie	Sjoberg	Keyworth	Heyes	McIlmoyle	Cross
1	Aug 20	H	Blackpool	D 1-1	1	-	Appleton / Charnley	27062	1	2	3	4	5	6	7	8	9	10	11											
2	24	A	Chelsea	W 3-1	3	-	Wills 2, Walsh / Bradbury	24691	1	2	3	4	5	6	7	8	9	10	11											
3	27	A	Everton	L 1-3	3	13	Cheesebrough / Ring 2, Collins	45215	1	2	3	4	5	6	7	8	9	10	11											
4	31	H	Chelsea	L 1-3	3	17	Walsh / P Sillett, Greaves, Brooks	21087	1	2	3	4	5	6	7	8	9	10	11											
5	Sep 3	H	Blackburn Rovers	L 2-4	3	19	Walsh, Wills / Dobing 2 (1p), MacLeod, Douglas	17455	1	2	3		5	6		8		10	11	4	7	9								
6	7	A	Wolverhampton W.	L 2-3	3	18	Wills, Leek / Murray 2, Broadbent	33313	1	2	3		5	6		8		10	11	4	7	9								
7	10	A	Manchester United	D 1-1	4	18	Walsh / Giles	35493	1		3		5	6		8		10	11	4	7	9	2							
8	14	H	Wolverhampton W.	W 2-0	6	14	Walsh, King (p)	20044	1		3		5	6		8		10	11	4	7	9	2							
9	17	H	Tottenham Hotspur	L 1-2	6	16	Riley / R Smith 2	30129	1		3		5	6		8		10	11	4	7	9	2							
10	24	A	Newcastle United	W 3-1	8	13	Leek 2, Cheesebrough / McGuigan	21161	1		3		5	6		8		10	11	4	7	9	2							
11	Oct 1	A	Aston Villa	W 3-1	10	11	Walsh 2, Wills / McParland	29623	1		3		5	6		8		10	11	4	7	9	2							
12	8	H	Arsenal	W 2-1	12	10	Leek 2 / Henderson	22501	1		3		5	6		8		10	11	4	7	9	2							
13	15	A	Manchester City	L 1-3	12	12	Leek / Barlow, Hayes, Sambrook	30193	1		3		5	6		8		10	11	4	7	9	2							
14	22	H	West Bromwich Albion	D 2-2	13	11	Lornie, Cheesebrough / Burnside, Aitken	20770	1		3		5	6		8		10	11	4	7		2		9					
15	28	A	Cardiff City	L 1-2	13	11	Walsh / Donnelly, Hogg	15000	1		3			6		8		10	11	4	7	9	2			5				
16	Nov 4	H	Preston North End	W 5-2	15	10	Leek 2, Walsh, Cheesebrough, Riley / Sneddon, Norman (og)	16920	1	2	3		5	6		8		10	11	4	7	9								
17	12	A	Fulham	L 2-4	15	13	King (p), Cheesebrough / Leggat 3, Key	16617	1		3		5	6		8			11	4	7	9	2				10			
18	19	H	Sheffield Wednesday	W 2-1	17	13	Walsh, Wills / Griffin	25567	1	2	3			6		8		10	11	4	7	9	5							
19	26	A	Birmingham City	W 2-0	19	9	Leek, Wills	25583	1	2	3			6		8		10	11	4	7	9	5							
20	Dec 3	A	Nottingham Forest	D 1-1	20	10	Cheesebrough / Le Flem	20545	1	2	3			6		8		10	11	4	7	9	5							
21	10	A	Burnley	L 2-3	20	12	Wills, Leek / Connelly, Pointer, Robson	20640	1	2	3			6		8		10	11	4	7	9	5							
22	17	A	Blackpool	L 1-5	20	12	Walsh / Charnley 2, Mudie, J Kelly, Perry	8752	1	2	3			6		8		10	11	4	7	9	5							
23	24	A	Bolton Wanderers	L 0-2	20	13	- / Deakin, Stevens	11534	1	2	3			6		11	10	8		4	7	9	5							
24	26	H	Bolton Wanderers	W 2-0	22	11	Wills, Keyworth	23806	1	2	3			6		8		11		4	7	9	5				10			
25	31	H	Everton	W 4-1	24	9	Riley, Walsh, Leek 2 / B Harris	23495	1	2	3			6		8		11		4	7	9	5				10			
26	Jan 14	A	Blackburn Rovers	D 1-1	25	8	Leek / Dougan	14752	1	2	3			6		8		11		4	7	9	5				10			
27	21	H	Manchester United	W 6-0	27	8	Walsh 2, Keyworth 2, Wills, Riley (p)	31308	1	2	3			6		8		11		4	7	9	5				10			
28	Feb 4	A	Tottenham Hotspur	W 3-2	29	7	Leek, Walsh 2 / Blanchflower (p), Allen	53627	1	2	3			6		8		11		4	7	9	5				10			
29	11	H	Newcastle United	W 5-3	31	6	King 2 (2p), Cheesebrough, Leek, Dalton (og) / Allchurch, White 2	26449	1	2	3			6		11		8		4	7	9	5				10			
30	25	A	Arsenal	W 3-1	33	5	Keyworth 2, Appleton / Henderson	31721	1	2	3	4	5	6	11	8					7	9					10			
31	Mar 11	A	West Bromwich Albion	L 0-1	33	7	- / Clark	25168		2	3	6						10		8	11	4	7 9 5	1						
32	25	A	Preston North End	D 0-0	34	9		12567	1		3	4	5	6	11	8	9				7		2			10				
33	31	A	West Ham United	L 0-1	34	9	- / Dick	22010	1		3			6	11	8				4	7	9	5			2	10			
34	Apr 1	A	Burnley	D 2-2	35	9	Leek, Walsh / Connelly, McIlroy	27838	1		3			6	11	8				4	7	9	5			2	10			
35	3	H	West Ham United	W 5-1	37	8	Cheesebrough 3, Riley, McIlmoyle / Kirkup	23776	1		3	4	5		11	10		8		6	7					2			9	
36	8	A	Sheffield Wednesday	D 2-2	38	9	Walsh, McLintock / Wilkinson, Fantham	29904	1	2	3			6	11	10		8		4	7		5						9	
37	10	H	Cardiff City	W 3-0	40	7	Walsh 2, McIlmoyle	32042	1	2	3			6	11			8		4	7		5				10		9	
38	15	H	Fulham	L 1-2	40	10	Walsh / O'Connell, Leggat	30980	1	2	3			6	11			8		4	7		5				10		9	
39	19	H	Aston Villa	W 3-1	42	6	McIlmoyle 2, Keyworth / Hale	21219	1	2	3	4		6	7	11		8					5				10		9	
40	22	A	Nottingham Forest	D 2-2	43	7	Cheesebrough, Leek / Booth, Le Flem	25830	1	2	3	4		6		11		8			7	9	5				10			
41	26	H	Manchester City	L 1-2	43	7	Walsh / Baker 2	22248	1	2	3			6	11	8				4	7		5				10		9	
42	29	H	Birmingham City	W 3-2	45	6	Cross, Riley, Leek / Harris, Singer	19920		2	3			6	11					4	7	10	5	1					9	8

									Banks	Chalmers	Norman	White	Knapp	Appleton	Meek	Cheesebrough	Hines	Walsh	Wills	McLintock	Riley	Leek	King	Slack	Lornie	Sjoberg	Keyworth	Heyes	McIlmoyle	Cross
League Appearances									40	28	42	10	19	40	13	35	5	37	28	34	37	30	32	2	5	15	2	7	1	
League Goals														2		11		22	10	1	6	18	4		1		6		4	1

Final League Position: 6
Average Home League Attendance: 24056

FA CUP

	Date		Opponents	Result	Scorers	Att	Banks	Chalmers	Norman	White	Knapp	Appleton	Meek	Cheesebrough	Hines	Walsh	Wills	McLintock	Riley	Leek	King	Slack	Lornie	Sjoberg	Keyworth	Heyes	McIlmoyle	Cross
1	Jan 7	H	Oxford United (3)	W 3-1	Walsh, Leek, Riley / Jones	25601	1	2	3			6		8		11		4	7	9	5				10			
2	31	H	Bristol City (4)	W 5-1	Wills, Leek 2, Walsh 2 / Norman (og)	27701	1	2	3			6		8		11		4	7	9	5				10			
3	Feb 18	A	Birmingham City (5)	D 1-1	Riley / Harris (p)	53589	1	2	3			6		11		8		4	7	9	5				10			
4	22	H	Birmingham City (5 rep)	W 2-1	Leek 2 / Harris	41916	1	2	3			6		11		8		4	7	9	5				10			
5	Mar 4	H	Barnsley (6)	D 0-0		38744	1	2	3			6		8		11		4	7	9	5				10			
6	8	A	Barnsley (6 rep)	W 2-1 aet	Riley, Leek / Oliver	39250	1	2	3			6		8		11		4	7	9	5				10			
7	18		Sheffield Utd. (sf)	D 0-0		52095	1	2	3			6		8		11		4	7	9	5				10			
8	23		Sheffield Utd. (sf rep)	D 0-0 aet		43500	1	2	3			6		11		8		4	7	9	5				10			
9	27		Sheffield Utd. (sf rep 2)	W 2-0	Walsh, Leek	37190	1	2	3			6		11		8		4	7	9	5				10			
10	May 6		Tottenham Hotspur (f)	L 0-2	- / R Smith, Dyson	100000	1	2	3			6		11		8		4	7		5				10		9	

FOOTBALL LEAGUE CUP

	Date		Opponents	Result	Scorers	Att	Banks	Chalmers	Norman	White	Knapp	Appleton	Meek	Cheesebrough	Hines	Walsh	Wills	McLintock	Riley	Leek	King	Slack	Lornie	Sjoberg	Keyworth	Heyes	McIlmoyle	Cross
1	Oct 12	H	Mansfield Town (1)	W 4-0	Cheesebrough, Walsh 3	7070			3		5	6		8		10	11	4	7	9	2	1						
2	26	H	Rotherham United (2)	L 1-2	King (p) / Kettleborough, Darwin	6244	1		3		5	6		8		10	11	4	7		2		9					

Note: Mar 18, at Elland Road (Leeds United); Mar 23, at City Ground (Nottingham Forest); Mar 27, at St Andrews (Birmingham City); May 6, at Wembley.

6 May: Hugh McIlmoyle, the surprise replacement for Ken Leek, is thwarted by Spurs' goalkeeper, Bill Brown, during the early stages at Wembley.

1960-61

Back: Knapp, King, Heyes, Keyworth, Banks, Chalmers, Hines. **Front:** Dowdells (Trainer), Appleton, Riley, Cheesebrough, Leek, Walsh, Wills, Gillies (Manager).
On Ground: White, Norman.

1961-62

Back: McIlmoyle, McLintock, Hines, Banks, Dowdells (Trainer), King, Sjoberg, Knapp. **Front:** Appleton, Riley, Walsh, Gillies (Manager), Keyworth, Wills, Chalmers.
On Ground: White, Norman, Cheesebrough.

Season 1961-62

Champions: Ipswich Town
Relegated: Cardiff City, Chelsea

FOOTBALL LEAGUE DIVISION ONE

Match No	Date		Opponents	Result	Points	Position	Scorers	Att	Gordon Banks	Len Chalmers	Richie Norman	Ian White	Ian King	Colin Appleton	Howard Riley	Jimmy Walsh	Hugh McIlmoyle	Ken Keyworth	Gordon Wills	Albert Cheesebrough	Graham Cross	Frank McLintock	John Mitten	George Heyes	Mike Stringfellow	David Gibson	John Sjoberg	David Thomson
1	Aug 19	A	Manchester City	L 1-3	–	–	Wills / Kennedy, Barlow, Hayes	28899	1	2	3	4	5	6	7	8	9	10	11									
2	23	H	Arsenal	L 0-1	–	–	- / Eastham	29396	1	2	3	4	5	6	7	8	9	10	11									
3	26	H	West Bromwich Albion	W 1-0	2	17	Riley	20899	1	2	3	4	5	6	7	8		9	11	10								
4	29	A	Arsenal	D 4-4	3	15	Walsh, Cheesebrough 2, Keyworth / MacLeod, Eastham, Skirton, Charles	35055	1	2	3	4	5	6	7	8		9	11	10								
5	Sep 2	A	Birmingham City	W 5-1	5	10	Keyworth, Wills 2, Walsh 2 / Bloomfield	21950	1	2	3	4	5	6	7	8		9	11	10								
6	5	A	Burnley	L 0-2	5	11	- / Appleton (og), King (og)	22339	1	2	3	4	5	6	7	8	10	9	11									
7	9	H	Everton	W 2-0	7	9	Wills, Walsh	19889	1	2	3	4	5	6	7	8	10	9	11									
8	16	A	Fulham	L 1-2	7	12	Keyworth / Leggat, Chamberlain	19831	1	2	3	4	5	6	7	8		9	11	10								
9	20	H	Burnley	L 2-6	7	18	Walsh 2 / Connelly 2, Robson 2, Pointer, Harris	25567	1	2	3	4	5	6	7	8		9	11		10							
10	23	H	Sheffield Wednesday	W 1-0	9	13	Riley (p)	21338	1	2	3	4	5	6	7	8		9	11		10							
11	30	A	West Ham United	L 1-4	9	17	McLintock / Dick 2, Sealey, Woosnam	26746	1	2	3		5	6	7		9	8	10			4	11					
12	Oct 7	H	Sheffield United	W 4-1	11	13	Riley, Walsh, Wills, Chalmers / Allchurch	17952	1	2	3		5	6	7	8		9	10			4	11					
13	14	A	Chelsea	W 3-1	13	9	Wills, McLintock 2 / Block	21377	1	2	3	6	5	10	7	9	8		11			4						
14	21	H	Blackpool	L 0-2	13	14	- / Charnley 2 (1p)	17424	1	2	3	6	5	10	7	9	8		11			4						
15	28	A	Blackburn Rovers	L 1-2	13	17	Keyworth / McEvoy, Lawther	11113	1	2	3	6	5	10	7	8	9					4	11					
16	Nov 4	A	Wolverhampton W.	W 3-0	15	10	Riley (p), Wills, Appleton	18952	1	2	3	6	5	10	7	8	9					4	11					
17	11	A	Manchester United	D 2-2	16	10	McLintock, Appleton / Giles, Viollet	21567	1	2	3	6	5	10	7	8	9					4	11					
18	18	H	Cardiff City	W 3-0	18	7	Appleton, Keyworth, McIlmoyle	16992	1	2	3	4	5	10			9	8	7		6		11					
19	25	A	Tottenham Hotspur	W 2-1	20	7	Keyworth, Appleton / White	41745		2	3		5	10	7		9	6		8		4	11	1				
20	Dec 2	H	Aston Villa	L 0-2	20	9	- / Wylie, Dougan	21000	1	2	3		5	10	7		9	6		8		4	11					
21	9	A	Nottingham Forest	D 0-0	21	8		22524	1	2	3		5	10		8	9	6		7		4	11					
22	16	H	Manchester City	W 2-0	23	8	Cheesebrough, Walsh	15196	1	2	3		5	10		8	9	6		7		4	11					
23	23	A	West Bromwich Albion	L 0-2	23	9	- / Kevan, Smith	14286	1	2	3		5	10		8	9	6		7		4	11					
24	26	A	Ipswich Town	L 0-1	23	10	- / Crawford	18146	1	2	3		5	10	7	8		6	9			4	11					
25	Jan 13	H	Birmingham City	L 1-2	23	12	Cheesebrough / Harris, Auld	22681	1	2	3		5	6	7	8		9	11	10		4						
26	20	A	Everton	L 2-3	23	14	Walsh, Riley (p) / Collins, Green, Vernon	33934	1	2	3		5	6	7	8		9		10		4			11			
27	Feb 3	H	Fulham	W 4-1	25	12	Walsh 2, Keyworth, Riley (p) / Haynes	20272	1	2	3		5	6	7	8		9				4			11	10		
28	10	A	Sheffield Wednesday	W 2-1	27	11	Walsh, Johnson (og) / Finney	18179	1	2	3		5	6	7	8		9				4			11	10		
29	17	H	West Ham United	D 2-2	28	9	Keyworth 2 / Woosnam, Dick	21312	1	2	3	4	5	6	7	8		9							11	10		
30	24	A	Sheffield United	L 1-3	28	13	Keyworth / Allchurch 2, Kettleborough	24015	1	2	3		5	6	7	8		9				4			11	10		
31	Mar 10	A	Blackpool	L 1-2	28	16	Cheesebrough / Charnley, Hauser	10952	1	2	3		5	6	7	8		9		10		4			11			
32	17	H	Blackburn Rovers	W 2-0	30	15	Keyworth, Cheesebrough	16194	1	2	3		5	6	7	10		9		8		4			11			
33	24	A	Wolverhampton W.	D 1-1	31	15	Gibson / Hinton	22025	1	2	3		5	6	7	8		9				4			11	10		
34	28	H	Ipswich Town	L 0-2	31	16	- / Stephenson, Crawford	19068	1	2	3		5	6	7	9		10		8		4			11			
35	Apr 4	H	Manchester United	W 4-3	33	12	Cheesebrough 2, Keyworth / McMillan 2, Quixall	15318	1	2	3		5	6	7	9		8		10		4			11			
36	7	A	Cardiff City	W 4-0	35	10	Cheesebrough 2, Keyworth, King	11000	1	2	3		5	6	7	9		8		10		4			11			
37	11	H	Chelsea	W 2-0	37	9	Cheesebrough, Norman	15184	1	2	3		5	6	7	9		8		10		4			11			
38	21	A	Aston Villa	L 3-8	37	14	Walsh 2, Riley (p) / Thomson 3, Dougan 2, Burrows, Baker, Chalmers (og)	24184	1	2	3		5	6	7	9		8	11	10		4						
39	23	A	Bolton Wanderers	L 0-1	37	15	- / Davies	19264	1	2	3		5	6	7	9		8	11	10		4						
40	24	H	Bolton Wanderers	D 1-1	38	16	Walsh / McGarry	14093	1	2	3	4		6	7			10		11		9	8		5			
41	28	H	Nottingham Forest	W 2-1	40	14	McLintock 2 / Julians	14267	1	7	3	4	5	6				10		11		9	8				2	
42	30	H	Tottenham Hotspur	L 2-3	40	14	Cross, Thomson / Mackay, Medwin, Greaves	23929	1	2	3			6		8			11		7	9	4				5	10
League Appearances									41	42	42	19	40	42	36	33	13	39	22	23	6	30	12	1	12	5	3	1
League Goals										1	1		1	4	7	14	1	15	7	11	1	6			1			1

Final League Position:	14
Average Home League Attendance:	19459

FA CUP

Match No	Date		Opponents	Result		Scorers	Att	Banks	Chalmers	Norman	White	King	Appleton	Riley	Walsh	McIlmoyle	Keyworth	Wills	Cheesebrough	Cross	McLintock	Mitten
1	Jan 10	H	Stoke City (3)	D 1-1		Riley / Mudie	35663	1	2	3		5	10	7	8		6	9			4	11
2	15	A	Stoke City (3 rep)	L 2-5		Riley (p), Keyworth / Matthews, Allen, Bullock, Nibloe, Thompson	38315	1	2	3		5	6	7	8		9	11	10		4	

FOOTBALL LEAGUE CUP

Match No	Date		Opponents	Result		Scorers	Att	Banks	Chalmers	Norman	King	Appleton	Riley	Walsh	Keyworth	Wills	McLintock	Mitten
1	Oct 9	A	York City (2)	L 1-2		Mitten / Wragg, Stainsby	13275	1	2	3	5	6	7	8	9	10	4	11

EUROPEAN CUP WINNERS' CUP

Match No	Date		Opponents	Result		Scorers	Att	Banks	Chalmers	Norman	White	King	Appleton	Riley	Walsh	McIlmoyle	Keyworth	Wills	Cheesebrough	Cross	McLintock	Mitten
1	Sep 13	A	Glenavon (1 leg 1)	W 4-1		Walsh 2, Appleton, Keyworth / Weatherup	10000	1	2	3	4	5	6	7	8		9	11	10			
2	27	H	Glenavon (1 leg 2)	W 3-1		Wills, Keyworth, McIlmoyle / Wilson	10445	1	2	3	4	5	6	7		9	10	11	8			
3	Oct 25	H	Atletico Madrid (2 leg 1)	D 1-1		Keyworth / Mendoza	25527	1	2	3	6	5	10	7		8	9				4	11
4	Nov 15	A	Atletico Madrid (2 leg 2)	L 0-2		- / Collar (p), Jones	50000	1	4	3	6	2	10	7		8	9			5		11

Note: Sep 13, at Windsor Park, Belfast.

Gordon Banks added to his growing reputation as England's heir apparent with a series of stunning displays during the season, including a fine performance in Madrid during City's first European adventure.

Season 1962-63

Champions: Everton
Relegated: Manchester City, Leyton Orient

FOOTBALL LEAGUE DIVISION ONE

Match No	Date	V	Opponents	Result	Pts	Pos	Scorers	Att	Banks	Chalmers	Norman	McLintock	King	Appleton	Riley	Walsh	Keyworth	Gibson	Stringfellow	Cheesebrough	Cross	Sjoberg	Heath	Heyes	McDerment	Match No
1	Aug 18	A	Fulham	L 1-2	-		Stringfellow / Leggat 2	27064	1	2	3	4	5	6	7	8	9	10	11							1
2	22	H	Sheffield Wednesday	D 3-3	1	-	Walsh, Stringfellow, Riley / Layne 2, Dobson	21165	1	2	3	4	5	6	7	8	9	10	11							2
3	25	H	Nottingham Forest	W 2-1	3	10	Stringfellow 2 / Hockey	21573	1	2	3	4	5	6		8	9	10	11	7						3
4	29	A	Sheffield Wednesday	W 3-0	5	6	Stringfellow 2, Walsh	25307	1	2	3	4	5	6		8		10	11	7	9					4
5	Sep 1	H	Bolton Wanderers	W 4-1	7	4	Walsh 2, Cross, Gibson / Norman (og)	19113	1	2	3	4	5	6		8		10	11	7	9					5
6	4	A	Burnley	D 1-1	8	5	Gibson / Robson	23876	1	2	3	4	5	6		8		10	11	7	9					6
7	8	A	Everton	L 2-3	8	6	Walsh, Riley / Stevens, Vernon, Young	48738	1	2	3	4	5	6	7	8		10	11		9					7
8	15	H	West Bromwich Albion	W 1-0	10	6	Cross	21517	1	2	3	4	5	6				10	11		9					8
9	19	H	Burnley	D 3-3	11	5	Keyworth, McLintock, Riley / Pointer, Lochhead, McIlroy	26692	1	2	3	4	5	6	7	8	9	10	11							9
10	22	A	Arsenal	D 1-1	12	6	Keyworth / Baker	31291	1	2	3	4	5	6	7	8	9	10	11							10
11	29	A	Birmingham City	W 3-0	14	5	Keyworth, Cheesebrough, Foster (og)	22110	1	2	3	4	5	6	7	8	9	10	11							11
12	Oct 6	A	Ipswich Town	W 1-0	16	5	McLintock	18998	1	2	3	10	5	6	7	8	9		11		4					12
13	13	H	Liverpool	W 3-0	18	5	Gibson, Cheesebrough, Cross	24137	1	2	3	8	5	6	7		9	10	11		4					13
14	20	A	Blackburn Rovers	L 0-2	18	5	- / Douglas (p), Pickering	14197	1	2	3	8	5	6	7		9	10	11		4					14
15	27	H	Sheffield United	W 3-1	20	4	Keyworth 2, Cross / Pace	21315	1		3	10	5	6		8	9		11	7	4	2				15
16	Nov 3	A	Tottenham Hotspur	L 0-4	20	4	- / Blanchflower (p), Medwin, Greaves 2	52361	1	2	3	4	5	6		8	9	10	11							16
17	10	H	West Ham United	W 2-0	22	4	Stringfellow, McLintock	21064	1	2	3	4	5	6			9	10	11	7		8				17
18	17	A	Manchester City	D 1-1	23	4	Keyworth / Leivers	21053	1	2	3	4	5	6		8	9	10	11	7						18
19	24	H	Blackpool	D 0-0	24	4		21832	1	2	3	4	5	6		8	9	10	11	7						19
20	Dec 1	A	Wolverhampton W.	W 3-1	26	4	Gibson 2, Flowers (og) / Hinton	22305	1	2	3	4	5	6	7	8	9	10	11							20
21	8	H	Aston Villa	D 3-3	27	4	Gibson 2, Stringfellow / MacEwan, Burrows, Chalmers (og)	26773	1	2	3	4	5	6	7	8	9	10	11							21
22	15	A	Fulham	L 2-3	27	4	Walsh, Stringfellow / Leggat, Brown, Cook	18840	1	2	3	4	5	6	7	8	9	10	11							22
23	26	H	Leyton Orient	W 5-1	29	3	Keyworth 2, Cheesebrough, Appleton, Charlton (og) / Musgrove	17313	1		3	4	5	6		8	9	10		11	7	2				23
24	Feb 9	H	Arsenal	W 2-0	31	3	Keyworth 2	26320	1		3	4	5	6	7		9	10	11		8	2				24
25	12	H	Everton	W 3-1	33	3	Keyworth, Stringfellow, Cross / Vernon	35743	1		3	4	5	6	7		9	10	11		8	2				25
26	19	A	Nottingham Forest	W 2-0	35	2	Keyworth 2	27310	1		3	4	5	6	7		9	10	11		8	2				26
27	23	H	Ipswich Town	W 3-0	37	2	Gibson, Stringfellow, Riley	31258	1		3	4	5	6	7		9	10	11		8	2				27
28	Mar 2	A	Liverpool	W 2-0	39	2	Keyworth, Gibson	54842	1		3	4	5	6	7		9	10	11		8	2				28
29	9	H	Blackburn Rovers	W 2-0	41	2	Riley, Stringfellow	25624	1		3	4	5	6	7		9	10	11		8	2				29
30	23	H	Tottenham Hotspur	D 2-2	42	2	Stringfellow, Keyworth / R Smith, Greaves	41622	1		3	4	5	6	7		9	10	11		8	2				30
31	26	A	Sheffield United	D 0-0	43	2		26828	1		3	4	5	7		9	10	11	8	6	2					31
32	Apr 3	A	Leyton Orient	W 2-0	45	2	Stringfellow 2	14780	1	2	3	4	5	6	7		9		11		8		10			32
33	6	H	Manchester City	W 2-0	47	2	Stringfellow 2	27092	1		3	4	5	6	7		9	10	11		8	2		1		33
34	8	A	Blackpool	D 1-1	48	1	Keyworth / Charnley (p)	16765	1	2	3	4		6	7		9	10	11		8		5			34
35	13	A	West Ham United	L 0-2	48	2	- / Sealey 2	25689			3	4	5	6	7		9	10	11		8	2				35
36	15	A	Manchester United	D 2-2	49	2	Cross, Norman / Charlton, Herd	50005	1		3	4	5	6	7		9	10	11		8	2				36
37	16	H	Manchester United	W 4-3	51	1	Heath, Keyworth 3 / Law 3	37002	1		3	10	5	6	7		9		11		4	2	8			37
38	20	H	Wolverhampton W.	D 1-1	52	2	Keyworth / Hinton	32132	1		3	10	5	6	7		9		11		4	2	8			38
39	May 4	A	West Bromwich Albion	L 1-2	52	3	Cross / Fenton, Howe (p)	20564	1		3	4	5	6	7		9	10	11		8	2				39
40	11	A	Bolton Wanderers	L 0-2	52	3	- / Deakin, Russell	10374			3	4	5	6	7		9	10	11		8	2		1		40
41	15	A	Aston Villa	L 1-3	52	4	Keyworth / Lee, Fraser, Dougan	20720			3	4		6	7		10	9	11		8	2		1	5	41
42	18	A	Birmingham City	L 2-3	52	4	Heath, McLintock / Harris, Auld, Lynn (p)	23931			3	4		6	7		9	10	11			2	8	1	5	42

									Banks	Chalmers	Norman	McLintock	King	Appleton	Riley	Walsh	Keyworth	Gibson	Stringfellow	Cheesebrough	Cross	Sjoberg	Heath	Heyes	McDerment	
Final League Position:			4				**League Appearances**		38	23	42	42	39	40	32	26	32	36	29	23	29	20	5	4	2	
Average Home League Attendance:			25841				**League Goals**			1		4		1	5	6	21	9	17	3	7	2				

FA CUP

Match No	Date	V	Opponents	Result	Scorers	Att	Banks	Chalmers	Norman	McLintock	King	Appleton	Riley	Walsh	Keyworth	Gibson	Stringfellow	Cheesebrough	Cross	Sjoberg	Heath	Heyes	McDerment	Match No
1	Jan 8	A	Grimsby Town (3)	W 3-1	Gibson 2, Keyworth / Scott (p)	17103	1		3	4	5	6	7		9	10	11		8	2				1
2	30	H	Ipswich Town (4)	W 3-1	Cross, Keyworth 2 / Blackwood	26054	1		3	4	5	6	7		9	10	11		8	2				2
3	Mar 16	A	Leyton Orient (5)	W 1-0	Keyworth	25769	1		3	4	5	6	7		9	10	11		8	2				3
4	30	A	Norwich City (6)	W 2-0	Stringfellow, Gibson	43984	1		3	4	5	6	7		9	10	11		8	2				4
5	Apr 27		Liverpool (sf)	W 1-0	Stringfellow	65000	1		3	4	5	6	7		9	10	11		8	2				5
6	May 25		Manchester United (f)	L 1-3	Keyworth / Law, Herd 2	100000	1		3	4	5	6	7		9	10	11		8	2				6

FOOTBALL LEAGUE CUP

Match No	Date	V	Opponents	Result	Scorers	Att	Banks	Chalmers	Norman	McLintock	King	Appleton	Riley	Walsh	Keyworth	Gibson	Stringfellow	Cheesebrough	Cross	Sjoberg	Heath	Heyes	McDerment	Match No
1	Sep 26	H	Charlton Athletic (2)	D 4-4	Gibson, Walsh 2, Riley / Peacock 2, Lucas, Banks (og)	8049	1	2	3	4	5	6	7	8		10	11		9					1
2	Oct 2	A	Charlton Athletic (2 rep)	L 1-2	Keyworth / Matthews, Glover	10148	1	2	3	4	5	6	7		8	10	11		9					2

Dismissals: Oct 2, Chalmers, Charlton Athletic (a), FLC.
Note: Apr 27, at Hillsborough (Sheffield Wednesday); May 25, at Wembley.

25 May: It was a case of third time unlucky as City crashed to defeat at Wembley. Here Manchester United's Denis Law starts the slide with a typically instinctive strike that leaves Graham Cross, Richie Norman, Gordon Banks and Colin Appleton looking on dejected.

1962-63

Back: Svarc, Marshall, Smith, Walker, R Riley, Chandler (Training Staff), Sjoberg, Stringfellow, Chalmers, Norman, Hopewell, Knowles.
Middle: Dewis (Third Team Trainer), Gamble, McLintock, King, Heyes, Nesbit, Banks, McDerment, Thomson, McLean, Jones (Asst Trainer).
Front: Dowdells (Head Trainer), Appleton, Cheesebrough, H Riley, Walsh, Needham (Chairman), Keyworth, Heath, Tewley, Loughlan, Gillies (Manager).

1963-64

Back: Mitchellson, Nicholls, Tuckwood, Newton, McCaffrey, Balmer, Chandler (Training Staff), Muggleton, McLintock, McDerment, Gamble, Chalmers.
Middle: Appleton, Norman, King, Sjoberg, Heyes, Banks, Timson, Smith, Cross, M Dougan.
Front: Plumley (Secretary), Walsh, H Riley, Tewley, Gillies (Manager), Stringfellow, Heath, Keyworth, Dowdells (Trainer).
On Ground: Walker, Loughlan, R Riley, Gibson, Woollett, Goodfellow, Marshall.

Season 1963-64

Champions: Liverpool
Relegated: Bolton Wanderers, Ipswich Town

FOOTBALL LEAGUE DIVISION ONE

Match No	Date	Opponents	Result	Points	Position	Scorers	Att	Banks	Sjoberg	Norman	McLintock	King	Appleton	Riley	Cross	Keyworth	Gibson	Stringfellow	Goodfellow	Heyes	Hodgson	Roberts	McDerment	Newton	Chalmers	Dougan	Sweenie	Heath	Timson	Walker	Match No
1	Aug 24 A	West Bromwich Albion	D 1-1	1	-	Keyworth / Fenton	23078	1	2	3	4	5	6	7	8	9	10	11													1
2	28 H	Birmingham City	W 3-0	3	-	Riley, Keyworth, Stringfellow	27661	1	2	3	4	5	6	7	8	9	10	11													2
3	31 H	Arsenal	W 7-2	5	1	Riley, Keyworth 2, Gibson 2, Stringfellow, McLintock, Barnwell (p), MacLeod	29620	1	2	3	4	5	6	7	8	9	10	11													3
4	Sep 4 H	Birmingham City	L 0-2	5	5	- / Leek, Hellawell	23851	1	2	3	4	5	6	7	8	9	10	11													4
5	7 A	Stoke City	D 3-3	6	4	Appleton, Cross 2 / Viollet 2, Asprey	34453	1	2	3	4	5	6	7	8	9		11	10												5
6	11 H	Sheffield Wednesday	W 2-0	8	3	Keyworth, Stringfellow	27296	1	2	3	4	5	6	7	8	9	10	11													6
7	14 A	Bolton Wanderers	D 0-0	9	3		12753		2	3	4	5	6	7	8	9		11		1	10										7
8	21 H	Fulham	L 0-1	9	9	- / Marsh	26548	1	2	3	4	5		7	8	9	10	11				6									8
9	28 A	Manchester United	L 1-3	9	11	Gibson / Herd 2, Setters	41374	1	2	3	4	5		7	8	9	10				11	6									9
10	Oct 2 H	Sheffield Wednesday	W 2-1	11	9	Cross, Stringfellow / Quinn	21420	1		3	4	5	6		9		10	11			7	8			2						10
11	5 A	Burnley	D 0-0	12	11		26310	1		3	4	5	6	7	8	9	10	11							2						11
12	8 A	Nottingham Forest	L 0-2	12	11	- / Addison, Wignall	30982	1		3	4	5	6	7		9	10	11				8			2						12
13	14 H	Wolverhampton W.	L 0-1	12	11	- / Crawford	25067	1		3	4	5	6	7	8	9	10	11							2						13
14	19 A	Tottenham Hotspur	D 1-1	13	12	McLintock / Jones	50521	1		3	4	5	6	7	8	9	10	11							2						14
15	26 H	Blackburn Rovers	W 4-3	15	12	Gibson, McLintock 2, Keyworth / McEvoy 2, Douglas	24278	1		3	4	5	6	7	8	9	10	11							2						15
16	Nov 2 A	Liverpool	W 1-0	17	10	Keyworth	47438	1		3	4	5	6	7	8	9	10	11							2						16
17	9 H	Sheffield United	L 0-1	17	12	- / Kettleborough	28848	1		3	4	5	6	7	8	9	10	11							2						17
18	16 A	West Ham United	D 2-2	18	11	Stringfellow, Keyworth / Britt, Hurst	23073	1		3	4	5	6	7	8	9	10	11							2						18
19	23 H	Chelsea	L 2-4	18	13	Stringfellow, Cross / Venables 2 (1p), Tambling, Bridges	23315	1		3	4	5	6	7	8	9		11					10		2						19
20	30 A	Blackpool	D 3-3	19	14	Chalmers (p), Sweenie 2 / Ball, Charnley 2	10534	1		3	6	5		7					8		11	9	4		2		10				20
21	Dec 7 A	Aston Villa	D 0-0	20	13		21402	1		3	4	5	6		8				7		11	9			2		10				21
22	14 H	West Bromwich Albion	L 0-2	20	14	- / Fraser, Foggo	17740	1		3	4	5	6			9	10	11	7						2		8				22
23	21 A	Arsenal	W 1-0	22	12	McLintock	28019	1	2	3	4	5	6	7	8	9	10	11													23
24	26 H	Everton	W 2-0	24	12	Keyworth 2	30004	1		3	4	5	6	7	8	9	10	11							2						24
25	28 H	Everton	W 3-0	26	12	Stringfellow, Roberts 2	54808	1		3	4	5	6	7	8		10	11				9			2						25
26	Jan 11 H	Stoke City	W 2-1	28	11	Gibson, Stringfellow / Clamp	23333	1				5	6	7	4		10	11				8	9		2						26
27	18 H	Bolton Wanderers	W 1-0	30	9	Gibson	15902	1	2	3		5	6	7	4	9	10	11				8									27
28	Feb 1 H	Fulham	L 1-2	30	10	Cross / Metchick, Key	17583	1	2	3		5	6	7	4	9	10	11				8									28
29	8 H	Manchester United	W 3-2	32	9	Stringfellow, Hodgson 2 / Herd, Law	35538	1	2	3		5	6		4	9	10	11			7	8									29
30	22 A	Wolverhampton W.	W 2-1	34	9	Gibson, King / Broadbent	15286	1	2	3	4	5	6		8	9	10	11			7										30
31	29 H	Nottingham Forest	D 1-1	35	9	Hodgson / Whitefoot	23369	1	2	3	4	5	6		8	9	10	11			7										31
32	Mar 7 A	Blackburn Rovers	L 2-5	35	10	Hodgson, Stringfellow / McEvoy 4, Pickering	15118		2		4	5	3		6	9	10	11		1	7	8									32
33	10 A	Burnley	L 0-2	35	11	- / Morgan, Bellamy	12664		2		4	5	3		6	9	10	11		1	7	8									33
34	18 A	West Ham United	D 2-2	36	11	Gibson, Keyworth / Hugo, Burkett	11980		2		4	5	3		6	9	10	11		1	7							8			34
35	21 A	Sheffield United	W 1-0	38	9	McLintock	15571		2		4	5	3		6		10	11		1	7						9	8			35
36	28 H	Liverpool	L 0-2	38	11	- / Hunt, Arrowsmith	31209	1		3	4	5	2		6		10	11			7	9						8			36
37	30 A	Ipswich Town	D 1-1	39	10	Goodfellow / Colrain	16265	1	2	3	4		6		8		10		7		11	9				5					37
38	31 H	Ipswich Town	W 2-1	41	9	Stringfellow, Keyworth / Baker	15925	1	2	3	4		6	7		9	10	11				8				5					38
39	Apr 6 A	Chelsea	L 0-1	41	10	- / R Harris	25315	1	2			5	3	7		9	10	11							4	6	8				39
40	11 H	Blackpool	L 2-3	41	10	Stringfellow, Appleton (p) / Ball 2, Oates	15189		2		9	5	3	7	8		10	11							4	6				1	40
41	18 A	Aston Villa	W 3-1	43	9	Riley, Sweenie, Gibson / Deakin	17886	1	2			5		7	6		10	11				8			4		9		3		41
42	25 H	Tottenham Hotspur	L 0-1	43	11	- / White	26441	1	2	3		5	6	7	4	9	8	11									10				42

								Banks	Sjoberg	Norman	McLintock	King	Appleton	Riley	Cross	Keyworth	Gibson	Stringfellow	Goodfellow	Heyes	Hodgson	Roberts	McDerment	Newton	Chalmers	Dougan	Sweenie	Heath	Timson	Walker	
Final League Position:		11				**League Appearances**		36	25	35	35	40	38	30	39	30	37	38	5	5	16	17	3		16	5	7	3	1	1	
Average Home League Attendance:		24142				**League Goals**					6	1	2	3	5	12	9	12	1		4	2			1		3				

FA CUP

Match No	Date	Opponents	Result	Scorers	Att	Banks	Norman	McLintock	King	Appleton	Riley	Cross	Keyworth	Gibson	Stringfellow	Chalmers	Match No
1	Jan 4 A	Leyton Orient (3)	L 2-3	Cross, Keyworth / Musgrove 2, King (og)	21623	1	3	4	5	6	7	8	9	10	11	2	1

FOOTBALL LEAGUE CUP

Match No	Date	Opponents	Result	Scorers	Att	Banks	Sjoberg	Norman	McLintock	King	Appleton	Riley	Cross	Keyworth	Gibson	Stringfellow	Goodfellow	Heyes	Hodgson	Roberts	McDerment	Newton	Chalmers	Sweenie	Heath	Match No
1	Sep 25 H	Aldershot (2)	W 2-0	Newton, Keyworth	9843	1	2	3	4	5		7	8	9	10							6	11			1
2	Oct 16 A	Tranmere Rovers (3)	W 2-1	Hodgson, Roberts / Dyson	12985	1		3		5	6			9	10	11			7	8	4		2			2
3	Nov 27 H	Gillingham (4)	W 3-1	Keyworth, McLintock, Hodgson / Francis	10356	1		3	6	5			8				7		11		4		2	9	10	3
4	Dec 18 A	Norwich City (5)	D 1-1	Riley / Davies	19955			3	4	5	6	7	8	9	10	11		1					2			4
5	Jan 15 H	Norwich City (5 rep)	W 2-1 aet	Hodgson, Riley / Cross (og)	10645	1	2	3		5	6	7	4		10	11			8	9						5
6	Feb 5 H	West Ham Utd (sf leg 1)	W 4-3	Keyworth, Roberts, Stringfellow, McLintock / Hurst 2, Sealey	14087	1	2	3	4	5	6			9	10	11			7	8						6
7	Mar 23 A	West Ham Utd (sf leg 2)	W 2-0	McLintock, Roberts	27329	1	2	3	4	5	6		8		10	11			7	9						7
8	Apr 15 A	Stoke City (f leg 1)	D 1-1	Gibson / Bebbington	22309	1	2			5	3	7	4	9	10	11								6	8	8
9	22 H	Stoke City (f leg 2)	W 3-2	Stringfellow, Gibson, Riley / Viollet, Kinnell	25372	1	2	3		5	6	7	4	9	8	11								10		9

Dismissals: None, though McLintock was sent off in a friendly v Innsbruck (a), May 18.
Note: Jan 4, Goal credited to King (og), some reports initially credited Deeley.

22 April: Chairman Sid Needham pours after-match champagne to celebrate the club's first ever major trophy. Pictured are Bert Johnson, Richie Norman, Colin Appleton, Ian King, Matt Gillies, Tom Sweenie, Sid Needham and Eddie Plumley.

Season 1964-65

Champions: Manchester United
Relegated: Wolverhampton Wanderers, Birmingham City

FOOTBALL LEAGUE DIVISION ONE

Player columns: Gordon Banks, Graham Cross, Richie Norman, Frank McLintock, Ian King, Colin Appleton, Howard Riley, Tom Sweenie, Ken Keyworth, David Gibson, Mike Stringfellow, John Sjoberg, Len Chalmers, Bobby Roberts, Bobby Svarc, Billy Hodgson, Jimmy Goodfellow, George Heyes, Bill McDerment, Bob Newton, Clive Walker, Paul Matthews

Match No	Date		Opponents	Result	Pts	Pos	Scorers	Att	Ban	Cro	Nor	McL	Kin	App	Ril	Swe	Key	Gib	Str	Sjo	Cha	Rob	Sva	Hod	Goo	Hey	McD	New	Wal	Mat
1	Aug 22	A	Sunderland	D 3-3	1	-	Stringfellow, Sweenie, Keyworth / Herd, Mulhall 2	45465	1	2	3	4	5	6	7	8	9	10	11											
2	26	H	Wolverhampton W.	W 3-2	3	-	McLintock, Keyworth, Appleton (p) / Knowles, Wharton	25636	1		3	4	5	6	7	8	9	10	11	2										
3	29	H	Manchester United	D 2-2	4	8	Keyworth, Appleton / Law, Sadler	32373	1	3		4	5	6	7	8	9	10	11	2										
4	Sep 2	A	Wolverhampton W.	D 1-1	5	8	McLintock / Crawford	22907	1		3	4		6	7	8	9	10	11	2	5									
5	5	H	Chelsea	D 1-1	6	11	Appleton / Hollins	22176	1		3	4	5	6	7	8	9	10	11	2										
6	9	H	Liverpool	W 2-0	8	5	McLintock, Keyworth	27114	1		3	4	5	6	7	8	9	10	11	2										
7	12	A	Leeds United	L 2-3	8	10	Riley, Sweenie / Bremner 2 (1p), Johanneson	32300	1	8	3	4	5	6	7		9	10	11	2										
8	19	H	Arsenal	L 2-3	8	14	McLintock 2 / Baker, Court, Eastham	21364	1	8	3	4	5	6	7	11	9	10		2										
9	26	A	Blackburn Rovers	L 1-3	8	16	Gibson / McEvoy, Ferguson, Byrom	14964	1		3	4	5	6		8	9	10	11	2					7					
10	30	H	West Bromwich Albion	W 4-2	10	14	Appleton (p), Hodgson, McLintock, Svarc / Cram (p), Williams	17218	1		3	4	5	6				10	11	2		8	9	7						
11	Oct 5	H	Blackpool	W 3-2	12	10	Goodfellow, Stringfellow, Roberts / Oates, Charnley	18727	1	10	3		5	6					11	2		4	9	7	8					
12	10	A	Fulham	L 2-5	12	14	Roberts 2 / Marsh 2, Leggat 2, O'Connell	14300	1	10	3		5	6					11	2		4	9	7	8					
13	13	A	Liverpool	W 1-0	14	8	Stringfellow	42558	1		3		5	6			10		11	2		4	9	7	8					
14	17	H	Nottingham Forest	W 3-2	16	8	Hodgson, Appleton (p), Stringfellow / Crowe, Wignall	25859	1	8	3		5	6					11	2		4	9	7	10					
15	24	A	Stoke City	D 3-3	17	10	Goodfellow 2, Roberts / Palmer, Ritchie, Viollet	24551		8	3		5					10	11	2		6		7	9	1	4			
16	31	H	Tottenham Hotspur	W 4-2	19	6	Cross, Gibson, Stringfellow, Goodfellow / Greaves, Allen	29167	1	8	3		5	6				10	11	2		4		7	9					
17	Nov 7	A	Burnley	L 1-2	19	8	Roberts / Elder, Miller	13780	1	8	3		5					10	11	2		4		7	9		6			
18	14	H	Sheffield United	L 0-2	19	10	- / Hartle, Jones	18429	1	6	3		5				8	10	11	2		4		7	9					
19	21	A	Everton	D 2-2	20	10	Goodfellow, Sjoberg / Gabriel, Pickering	35015	1	6	3		5				8	10	11	2		4		7	9					
20	28	H	Birmingham City	D 4-4	21	10	Gibson, Goodfellow, Hodgson, Roberts / Thomson 2 (1p), Vowden, Thwaites	15848	1	6	3		5				8	10	11	2		4		7	9					
21	Dec 5	A	West Ham United	D 0-0	22	8		20515	1	8	3		5					10	11	2		4		7	9		6			
22	12	H	Sunderland	L 0-1	22	10	- / Sharkey	17946	1	8	3		5		10				11	2		4		7	9		6			
23	26	H	Sheffield Wednesday	D 2-2	23	12	Roberts 2 / Dobson, Fantham	25278	1	8	3		5		7			10	11	2		4			9		6			
24	28	A	Sheffield Wednesday	D 0-0	24	11		18045	1	8	3							10	11	2	5	4		7	9		6			
25	Jan 2	A	Chelsea	L 1-4	24	12	Stringfellow / McCreadie, Murray, Bridges, Graham	28344	1	8	3		5					10	11	2		4		7	9		6			
26	16	H	Leeds United	D 2-2	25	13	Cross, Stringfellow / Charlton, Johnson	23230	1	9	3			6				10	11	2	5	8			7		4			
27	23	A	Arsenal	L 3-4	25	13	Appleton (p), Stringfellow, McDerment / Baker 2, Eastham, Armstrong	31063	1	9	3			6				10	11	2	5	8			7		4			
28	Feb 6	H	Blackburn Rovers	L 2-3	25	14	Hodgson, Gibson / McEvoy, Anderson, Byrom	18001	1	8	3			6				10			5	4		7	9			11		
29	13	A	Blackpool	D 1-1	26	14	Goodfellow / Charnley	10367	1	8	3		5	6				10	11	2		4		7	9					
30	24	A	Fulham	W 5-1	28	14	Gibson, Goodfellow 3, Appleton (p) / Haynes	16760	1	8	3		5	6				10	11	2		4		7	9					
31	27	H	Nottingham Forest	L 1-2	28	14	Cross / Crowe, Storey-Moore	32985	1	8	3			6				10	11	2	5	4		7	9					
32	Mar 13	A	West Bromwich Albion	L 0-6	28	16	- / Astle 2, Howshall, Clark, Foggo, Williams	15162	1	8	3		5					10		2		4		7	9		6	11		
33	20	H	Burnley	L 0-2	28	18	- / Irvine, Coates	11929			3		5	6		8		10	11	2	4			7	9	1				
34	26	H	Sheffield United	W 2-0	30	16	Sweenie, Hodgson	15058	1	9	3			6		8		10	11		5			7			4		2	
35	Apr 3	A	Everton	W 2-1	32	16	Stringfellow, Appleton (p) / Temple	14377	1	9	3			6		8		10	11		5	4		7					2	
36	10	A	Birmingham City	L 0-2	32	17	- / Vowden, Jackson	12460		8	3							10	11		5	4		7	9	1	6		2	
37	12	A	Manchester United	L 0-1	32	17	- / Herd	34114	1	6	3					8		10	11		5	4		7	9				2	
38	17	H	West Ham United	W 1-0	34	16	Gibson	15880	1	4	3					8		10			5	9		7	11				2	
39	19	H	Aston Villa	D 1-1	35	16	Hodgson / Woosnam	14607	1	4	3		5	6										11	9	8	10		2	7
40	20	A	Aston Villa	L 0-1	35	16	- / Chatterley	22290	1	4	3		5	6		8		10	11						9				2	
41	24	A	Tottenham Hotspur	L 2-6	35	16	Stringfellow, Goodfellow / Greaves 2 (1p), Gilzean, Jones 3	32427	1	4	3		5	6		8		10	11					7	9				2	
42	26	H	Stoke City	L 0-1	35	17	- / Vernon	8717		4	3		5	6		8		10	11					9		1			2	7

Final League Position:	18							
Average Home League Attendance:	19963							

League Appearances	38	35	40	10	31	29	9	22	9	35	38	37	7	27	7	30	29	4	12	2	9	2
League Goals		3		6		8	1	3	4	6	10	1		8	1	6	11		1			

FA CUP

Match No	Date		Opponents	Result	Scorers	Att	Ban	Cro	Nor	McL	Kin	App	Ril	Swe	Key	Gib	Str	Sjo	Cha	Rob	Sva	Hod	Goo	Hey	McD	New	Wal	Mat
1	Jan 9	H	Blackburn Rovers (3)	D 2-2	Stringfellow, Roberts / Harrison, Douglas	23067	1		3			6				10	11	2	5	8		7	9		4			
2	14	A	Blackburn Rovers (3 rep)	W 2-1	Roberts, Cross / Byrom	25897	1	9	3			6				10	11	2	5	8		7			4			
3	30	H	Plymouth Argyle (4)	W 5-0	Stringfellow, Goodfellow 2, Gibson, Roberts	24618	1	8	3			6				10	11	2	5	4		7	9					
4	Feb 20	A	Middlesbrough (5)	W 3-0	Cross 2, Gibson	31099	1	8	3		5	6				10	11	2		4		7	9					
5	Mar 6	H	Liverpool (6)	D 0-0		39356	1	8	3		5	6				10	11	2		4		7	9					
6	10	A	Liverpool (6 rep)	L 0-1	- / Hunt	53524	1	8	3		5	6				10	11	2		4		7	9					

FOOTBALL LEAGUE CUP

Match No	Date		Opponents	Result	Scorers	Att	Ban	Cro	Nor	McL	Kin	App	Ril	Swe	Key	Gib	Str	Sjo	Cha	Rob	Sva	Hod	Goo	Hey	McD	New	Wal	Mat
1	Sep 23	H	Peterborough U. (2)	D 0-0		11503	1		3	4			7	11	9	10		2	5	6			8					
2	Oct 8	A	Peterborough U. (2 rep)	W 2-0	Appleton (p), Goodfellow	10562	1	10	3		5	6					11	2		4	9	7	8					
3	19	A	Grimsby Town (3)	W 5-0	Norman, Cross, Gibson, Stringfellow, Sjoberg	7270		8	3		5	6				10	11	2		4		7	9	1				
4	Nov 4	H	Crystal Palace (4)	W 1-1		11141	1	8	3		5	6				10	11	2		4		7	9					
5	11	A	Crystal Palace (4 rep)	W 2-1	Goodfellow 2 / Burridge	15808	1	6	3		5				8	10	11	2		4		7	9					
6	Dec 1	A	Coventry City (5)	W 8-1	Stringfellow 2, Hodgson 2, Gibson, Norman 2, Curtis (og) / Hudson	27433	1	8	3		5					10	11	2		4		7	9		6			
7	Jan 20	H	Plymouth A. (sf leg 1)	W 3-2	Roberts, Gibson, Williams (og) / Williams, Trebilcock	12470	1	9	3			6				10	11	2	5	8		7			4			
8	Feb 10	A	Plymouth A. (sf leg 2)	W 1-0	Sjoberg	20872	1	8	3		5	6				10	11	2		4		7	9					
9	Mar 15	A	Chelsea (f leg 1)	L 2-3	Appleton, Goodfellow / McCreadie, Tambling, Venables (p)	20690	1	8	3		5	6					11	2	10	4		7	9					
10	Apr 5	H	Chelsea (f leg 2)	D 0-0		26957	1	8	3			6				10	11	5		4		7	9				2	

Dismissals: Sep 12, Gibson, Leeds United (a).
Stand-in Goalkeepers: Dec 1, Cross for Banks (temporary), Coventry City (a), FLC.

289

1964-65
Back: King, Cross, Sjoberg, Heyes, Banks, Chalmers, Stringfellow, Appleton.
Front: Hodgson, Roberts, Goodfellow, Norman, Gibson; **On Ground:** McDerment, Sweenie.

1965-66
Back: Appleton, Chalmers, Goodfellow, Norman, Riley, Sweenie, Walker.
Middle: Sjoberg, Roberts, Stringfellow, Banks, King, Cross, D Dougan.
Front: Sinclair, Dewis (Asst Trainer), Johnson (Coach), Gillies (Manager), Sharp (Chairman), Plumley (Secretary), Jones (Trainer), Gibson.

Season **1965-66**

Champions: Liverpool
Relegated: Northampton Town, Blackburn Rovers

FOOTBALL LEAGUE DIVISION ONE

Player columns (left to right): George Heyes, Clive Walker, Richie Norman, Bobby Roberts, John Sjoberg, Graham Cross, Jackie Sinclair, David Gibson, Derek Dougan, Tom Sweenie, Mike Stringfellow, Jimmy Goodfellow, Len Chalmers, Ian King, Malcolm Clarke, Gordon Banks, Colin Appleton, Howard Riley, Bill McDermott, Paul Matthews, Max Dougan, Peter Rodrigues, Peter Shilton

Match No	Date		Opponents	Result	Points	Position	Scorers	Att	Line-up / Goalscorers by shirt number
1	Aug 21	H	Liverpool	L 1-3	-		Sinclair / Hunt 2, Strong	29696	1 2 3 4 5 6* 7 8 9 10 11 12
2	25	A	Tottenham Hotspur	L 2-4	-		Stringfellow, Sweenie / Knowles, Possee, Greaves, Robertson	39876	1 3 4 5 7 8 9 10 11 2 6
3	28	A	Aston Villa	D 2-2	1	18	Sjoberg, Sinclair / Hateley (p), Aitken	21052	1 3 4 5 6 7 8 9 10 11 2
4	Sep 1	H	Tottenham Hotspur	D 2-2	2	19	Gibson 2 / Possee, Greaves (p)	28463	1 2 3 4 5 6 7 8 9 11 10
5	4	H	Sunderland	W 4-1	4	14	Stringfellow, D Dougan, Gibson, Sinclair / O'Hare	24676	1 3 4 5 6 7 8 9 11 10 2
6	6	A	Blackpool	L 0-4	4	16	- / Robson, Moir, Ball, Armfield	15640	1 3 4 5 6 7 8 9 11 10 2
7	11	A	West Ham United	W 5-2	6	15	D Dougan 2, Sinclair 2, Goodfellow / Hurst 2	21400	1 2 3 4 5 6 7 8 9 11 10
8	14	H	Blackpool	L 0-3	6	16	- / Ball, Charnley, Robson	24153	1 2 3 4 5 6 7 8 10 11 9
9	18	H	Leeds United	D 3-3	7	16	D Dougan 2, Goodfellow / Peacock 2, Madeley	23276	1 3 4 2* 6 7 10 9 11 8 5 12
10	25	A	Sheffield United	D 2-2	8	15	Goodfellow, Sinclair / Reece, Jones	17504	3 4 2 8 11 10 9 5 1 6 7
11	Oct 2	H	Northampton Town	D 1-1	9	14	Goodfellow / Foley (p)	27484	3 4 2 7 10 11 9 5 1 6 8
12	9	A	Stoke City	L 0-1	9	16	- / Dobing	24025	3 4 2 8 7 10 9 11 5 1 6
13	16	H	Burnley	L 0-1	9	18	- / Morgan	17978	3 8 2 6 11 10 9 7 5 1 4
14	23	A	Chelsea	W 2-0	11	17	Sjoberg, D Dougan	30400	3 4 2 6 7 10 9 11 8 5 1
15	30	H	Arsenal	W 3-1	13	14	Cross, D Dougan, Goodfellow / Armstrong	22528	3 4 2 6 7 10 9 11 8 5 1
16	Nov 6	A	Everton	W 2-1	15	14	Goodfellow, Sinclair / Morrissey	30195	3 4 2 6 7 10 9 11 8 5 1
17	13	H	Manchester United	L 0-5	15	14	- / Herd 2, Best, Charlton, Connelly	34551	3 4 2 6 7 10 9 11 8 5 1
18	20	A	Newcastle United	W 5-1	17	12	Goodfellow, Sinclair 2, D Dougan, Stringfellow / Robson	27603	3 4 2 6 7 10 9 11 8 5 1
19	27	H	West Bromwich Albion	W 2-1	19	11	Goodfellow, D Dougan / Crawford	21124	3 4 2 6 7 10 9 11 8 5 1
20	Dec 4	A	Nottingham Forest	L 0-2	19	12	- / McArthur, Hinton	24435	3 4 2 6 7 10 9 11 8 5 1
21	11	H	Sheffield Wednesday	W 4-1	21	10	Stringfellow 2, D Dougan, Sinclair / Fantham	16438	3 4 5 2 7 10 9 11 8 1 6
22	18	A	Burnley	L 2-4	21	10	Gibson, Sinclair / Lochhead 2, Miller, Elder	13837	3 4 5 2 7 10 9 11 8 1 6
23	28	H	Fulham	W 5-0	23	11	Sinclair 2, Gibson, Roberts, Stringfellow	20164	3 4 5 2 7 10 9 11 8 1 6
24	Jan 1	H	Stoke City	W 1-0	25	10	D Dougan	26067	3 4 5 6 7 10 9 11 8 1 2
25	8	A	Sheffield Wednesday	W 2-1	27	9	Stringfellow, Goodfellow / Wilkinson	15165	3 4 5 6 7 10 9 11 8 1 2
26	29	A	Liverpool	L 0-1	27	10	- / Lawler	45409	3 4 5 6 7 10 9 11 8 1 12 2*
27	Feb 5	A	Aston Villa	W 2-1	29	9	Cross, Roberts / Hateley	21073	3 4 5 6 7 10 9 11 8 1 2
28	19	A	Sunderland	W 3-0	31	9	Sinclair 2, D Dougan	21722	3 5 4 7 10 9 11 8 1 6 2
29	Mar 12	A	Leeds United	L 2-3	31	11	Sinclair (p), Stringfellow / Charlton 2, Hunter	35597	3 4 5 6 7 10 9 11 8 1 2
30	19	H	Sheffield United	W 1-0	33	9	Stringfellow	16401	3 4 5 6 7 10 9 11 8 1 2
31	21	H	Chelsea	D 1-1	34	9	D Dougan / Bridges	25363	3 4 5 2 7 10 9 11 1 6 8
32	26	A	Northampton Town	D 2-2	35	9	Stringfellow, Sinclair / Hudson, Moore	21564	3 4 5 6 7 10 9 11 1 8 2
33	Apr 8	A	Blackburn Rovers	W 2-0	37	8	Matthews, D Dougan	13712	3 4 5 6 7 10 9 11 1 8 2
34	9	A	Manchester United	W 2-1	39	7	Stringfellow 2 / Connelly	42593	3 4 5 7 10 9 11 8 1 6 2
35	12	H	Blackburn Rovers	W 2-0	41	6	Sweenie, Sinclair	21224	3 4 5 7 10 12 11* 9 1 6 8 2
36	16	H	Newcastle United	L 1-2	41	7	Sweenie / Bennett, Robson (p)	18535	3 4 5 6 11 10 9 8 1 7 2
37	18	A	Fulham	W 4-0	43	5	D Dougan 2, Sinclair 2	18014	3 4 5 11 10 9 8 1 6 7 2
38	22	A	West Bromwich Albion	L 1-5	43	6	D Dougan / Kaye 2, Astle, Sjoberg 2 (2 og)	15229	3 4 5 6 11 10 9 8 1 7 2
39	30	H	Nottingham Forest	W 2-1	45	7	Cross 2 / Cross (og)	18485	3 4 5 6 11 10 9 8 1 7 2
40	May 4	H	Everton	W 3-0	47	6	Sinclair (p), D Dougan, Matthews	14504	3 4 5 11 10 9 8 6 7 2 1
41	7	A	Arsenal	L 0-1	47	7	- / Rodrigues (og)	16435	3 4 6 11 10 8* 9 1 12 7 5 2
42	9	H	West Ham United	W 2-1	49	7	Sinclair, D Dougan / Byrne	16066	2 3 4 5 7 10 9 11 8 1 6

Final League Position:	7	**League Appearances**	9 7 40 41 38 38 42 42 37 10 34 30 4 13 32 12 2 11 2 17 1
Average Home League Attendance:	22325	**Sub**	1 1 1 2
		League Goals	2 2 4 22 5 19 3 12 9 2

FA CUP

	Date		Opponents	Result	Scorers	Att	Line-up
1	Jan 22	A	Aston Villa (3)	W 2-1	D Dougan, Stringfellow / Woosnam	38015	3 4 5 7 10 9 11 8 1 6 2
2	Feb 12	A	Birmingham City (4)	W 2-1	Sinclair, Goodfellow / Thwaites	46623	3 4 5 6 7 10 9 11 8 1 2
3	Mar 5	A	Manchester City (5)	D 2-2	Sinclair, Stringfellow / Young 2	56787	3 8 5 4 7 10 9 11 1 6 2
4	9	H	Manchester City (5 rep)	L 0-1	- / Young	41892	3 4 5 6 7 10 9 11 8 1 2

FOOTBALL LEAGUE CUP

	Date		Opponents	Result	Scorers	Att	Line-up
1	Sep 22	A	Manchester City (2)	L 1-3	Roberts (p) / Murray, Pardoe, King (og)	13246	3 4 2 9 11 10 8 5 1 6 7

Note: Substitutes allowed in league fixtures for first time.

28 December: Derek Dougan quickly became revered as a folk hero on the Filbert Street terraces. Here the charismatic Irishman goes close with a header against Fulham.

Season 1966-67

Champions: Manchester United
Relegated: Aston Villa, Blackpool

FOOTBALL LEAGUE DIVISION ONE

Match No	Date		Opponents	Result	Points	Position	Scorers	Att	Gordon Banks	Peter Rodrigues	Richie Norman	Bobby Roberts	John Sjoberg	Graham Cross	Jackie Sinclair	Jimmy Goodfellow	Derek Dougan	David Gibson	Mike Stringfellow	Paul Matthews	Max Dougan	Tom Sweenie	Peter Shilton	Nick Sharkey	David Nish	Bill McDerment	Alan Woollett	David Timson	Alan Tewley	Match No
1	Aug 20	A	Liverpool	L 2-3		-	D Dougan 2 / Hunt, Strong, Stevenson (p)	49076	1	2	3	4	5	6	7	8	9	10	11											1
2	22	A	Blackpool	D 1-1	1	-	Goodfellow / Charnley	17031	1	2	3	4	5	6		8	9	10	11	7										2
3	27	H	West Ham United	W 5-4	3	11	D Dougan, Sinclair 3, Goodfellow / Brabrook 2, Hurst 2	26850	1	2	3	4	5	6	7	8	9	10	11											3
4	31	H	Blackpool	W 3-0	5	7	D Dougan 2, Roberts	22005	1	2	3	4	5	6	7	8	9	10	11											4
5	Sep 3	A	Sheffield Wednesday	D 1-1	6	7	D Dougan / Pugh	31252	1	2	3	4	5	6	7	8	9	10	11											5
6	7	A	Chelsea	D 2-2	7	8	D Dougan, Gibson / Osgood, Cooke	29760	1	2	3	4	5	6	10	8	9	7	11											6
7	10	H	Southampton	D 1-1	8	7	Sinclair (p) / Davies	23060	1	2	3	4	5	6	7	8	9	10	11											7
8	17	H	Sunderland	W 3-2	10	7	D Dougan, Roberts, Rodrigues / O'Hare, Martin	28586	1	2	3	4	5	6	7	8	9	10	11											8
9	24	H	Aston Villa	W 5-0	12	4	Goodfellow, D Dougan 3, Sinclair	22065	1	2	3	4	5	6	7	8	9	10	11											9
10	Oct 1	A	Arsenal	W 4-2	14	4	Sinclair, Stringfellow, Goodfellow, Simpson (og) / Addison, Graham	33945	1	2	3	4	5	6	7	8	9	10	11											10
11	8	H	Nottingham Forest	W 3-0	16	4	Gibson, Goodfellow, Stringfellow	39970	1	2	3	4	5	6	7	8	9	10	11											11
12	15	A	Burnley	L 2-5	16	5	Sinclair, D Dougan / Elder, Lochhead, Irvine, Harris, Coates	20642	1		3	6	5	2	7	8	9	10	11		4									12
13	29	A	Everton	L 0-2	16	7	- / Scott, Temple	47267	1	2	3	4	5	6	7	8	9		11			10								13
14	Nov 5	H	Burnley	W 5-1	18	5	Rodrigues, Sinclair 2, Gibson, Stringfellow / Elder	24394	1	2	3	4	5	6	7	8	9	10	11											14
15	12	A	Leeds United	L 1-3	18	7	D Dougan / Giles 2, Greenhoff	33803	1	2	3	4	5	6	7	8	9	10	11											15
16	19	H	West Bromwich Albion	W 2-1	20	6	Stringfellow, D Dougan / Foggo	25003		3	4	5	6	7	8	9	10	11		2		1								16
17	26	A	Sheffield United	W 1-0	22	5	Sinclair	19950	1	2	3	4	5	6	7	8	9	10	11											17
18	30	H	Manchester United	L 1-2	22	5	Gibson / Best, Law	39014	1	2	3	4	5	6	7		9	10	11					8						18
19	Dec 3	H	Stoke City	W 4-2	24	4	Rodrigues, D Dougan, Nish, Sinclair / Burrows (p), Vernon	26079	1	2	3	4	5	6	7		9	10	11	12					8*					19
20	10	A	Tottenham Hotspur	L 0-2	24	5	- / Greaves, Rodrigues (og)	41089	1	2	3	4	5	6	7		9	10	11					8						20
21	26	H	Fulham	L 0-2	24	8	- / Callaghan, Barrett	26936	1	2	3	4	5	6	7		9	10	11					8						21
22	27	H	Fulham	L 2-4	24	10	Sinclair, Gibson, Leggat 3, Haynes	25174	1	2	3	4	5	6	7		9	10	11	8										22
23	31	A	West Ham United	W 1-0	26	9	Sinclair	34168	1	2	3	4	5		7		9	10	11			8		6						23
24	Jan 7	H	Sheffield Wednesday	L 0-1	26	9	- / Ritchie	22241	1	2	3	4	5	6	7		9	10	11			8								24
25	14	A	Southampton	D 4-4	27	8	Sweenie 2, Gibson, Roberts / Davies 3, Chivers	25444	1	2	3	4	5	6	7		9	10	11			8								25
26	18	H	Liverpool	W 2-1	29	7	Stringfellow, Cross / Rodrigues (og)	32049	1	2	3	4	5	6	7		9	10	11			8								26
27	21	H	Sunderland	L 1-2	29	8	Sinclair (p) / O'Hare, Mulhall	25539	1	2	3	4	5	6	7		9	10	11			8								27
28	Feb 4	A	Aston Villa	W 1-0	31	8	Roberts	26571	1	2	3	4		5	7		9	10	11			8		6						28
29	11	H	Arsenal	W 2-1	33	8	Stringfellow, D Dougan / Graham	24587	1	2	3	4	5	6	7		9	10	11			8								29
30	25	A	Nottingham Forest	L 0-1	33	9	- / Storey-Moore	47188	1	2	3	4		5	7		9	10	11	12		8*								30
31	Mar 4	H	Everton	D 2-2	34	8	Roberts, Sinclair (p) / Hurst, Young	24757	1	2	3	4		5	7	8	9	10	11					6						31
32	18	A	Manchester United	L 2-5	34	9	Sinclair 2 / Aston, Charlton, Herd, Law, Sadler	50281	1	2	3	4		5	11	8		10	9	7				6						32
33	24	H	Manchester City	W 3-1	36	7	Sinclair 2 (2p), Stringfellow / Crossan (p)	35396	1	2	3	4		5	11	8		10	9	7				6						33
34	25	A	Tottenham Hotspur	L 0-1	36	8	- / Robertson	27711	1	2	3	4		5	11	8			9	7				6	10					34
35	28	H	Manchester City	W 2-1	38	7	Sinclair 2 / Jones	17361	1	2	3	4		5	7	8		10	9		11			6						35
36	Apr 1	A	Newcastle United	L 0-1	38	8	- / Hilley	35183	1	2	3	4		5	7	8		10	9		11			6						36
37	10	H	Leeds United	D 0-0	39	7		15437	1	2	3	4		5	11	8		10	9	7				6						37
38	15	A	West Bromwich Albion	L 0-1	39	7	- / Clark	22872		2	3	4		5	11	8		10	9	7			1	6*	12					38
39	22	H	Sheffield United	D 2-2	40	9	Stringfellow, Roberts / Hill, Woodward	17088		2	3	4		5	11	8		10	9	7*			1	6	12					39
40	29	A	Stoke City	L 1-3	40	11	Stringfellow / Dobing, Burrows, Mahoney	17870		2	3	4		5	11	7		10	9				1	8	6					40
41	May 6	H	Newcastle United	W 4-2	42	9	Stringfellow, Sharkey 2, McNamee (og) / Davies, Noble	13951		2	3	4		5	11*	7		10	9					8	6		1	12		41
42	9	H	Chelsea	W 3-2	44	8	Sharkey 2, Roberts / Houseman, Hamilton	17142		2	3	4		5	11	7		10	9					8	6		1			42

Final League Position:	8	**League Appearances**	36 40 42 42 28 41 41 29 31 40 42 8 2 11 4 3 18 1 1 2
Average Home League Attendance:	24463	**Sub**	2 1 1 1
		League Goals	3 7 1 21 5 16 6 10 2 4 1

FA CUP

	Date		Opponents	Result		Scorers	Att																						
1	Jan 28	A	Manchester City (3)	L 1-2		Sweenie / Doyle, Pardoe	38529	1	2	3	4	5	6	7		9	10	11			8								1

FOOTBALL LEAGUE CUP

	Date		Opponents	Result		Scorers	Att																						
1	Sep 14	H	Reading (2)	W 5-0		Stringfellow, Roberts, Goodfellow, D Dougan 2	11112	1	2	3	4	5	6	7	8	9	10	11											1
2	Oct 5	H	Lincoln City (3)	W 5-0		Goodfellow 2, D Dougan, Sinclair (p), Gibson	14491	1	2	3	4	5	6	7	8	9	10	11											2
3	25	A	Queens Park Rangers (4)	L 2-4		D Dougan 2 / Allen 2, R Morgan, Lazarus	20735	1	2	3	4	5	6	7	8	9	10*	11	12										3

Note: Substitutes allowed in cup competitions for first time.

1966-67
Back: Sjoberg, Stringfellow, Roberts, D Dougan, Cross, Shilton, McDerment, Woollett, Walker, Norman, Rodrigues, Goodfellow.
Front: Nish, Gibson, Sinclair, Dewis (Asst Trainer), Johnson (Coach), Gillies (Manager), Sharp (Chairman), Plumley (Secretary), Jones (Trainer), Sweenie, Tewley, Matthews.

Season 1967-68

Champions: Manchester City
Relegated: Sheffield United, Fulham

FOOTBALL LEAGUE DIVISION ONE

No	Date		Opponents	Result	Pts	Pos	Scorers	Att	Shilton	Rodrigues	Norman	Roberts	Sjoberg	Cross	Sinclair	Nish	Stringfellow	Gibson	Sharkey	Goodfellow	Woollett	Tewley	Williamson	Bell	Svarc	Large	Glover	Fern	Mackleworth	Potts	Hutchins	Manley	No
1	Aug 19	H	Tottenham Hotspur	L 2-3	-		Sharkey, Gibson / Kinnear, England, Saul	32552	1	2	3	4	5	6	7	8	9	10	11														1
2	23	A	Sheffield Wednesday	L 1-2	-		Sjoberg / Ritchie 2	30190	1	2	3	4	5	6	7	8	9	10	11*	12													2
3	26	A	Manchester United	D 1-1	1	18	Stringfellow / Foulkes	51256	1*	2	3	4	9	6	7	8	11	10			5	12											3
4	30	H	Sheffield Wednesday	W 3-0	3	12	Sinclair, Stringfellow, Sjoberg	20443		2	3	4	9	6	7	8	11	10			5		1										4
5	Sep 2	H	Sunderland	L 0-2	3	17	- / Suggett, Brand	23316		2	3	4		6	7	8	11	10	9		5		1										5
6	6	A	Stoke City	L 2-3	3	18	Sinclair, Sjoberg / Palmer, Burrows (p), Cross (og)	19032		2	3	4	9	6	7	8	11	10			5		1										6
7	9	A	Wolverhampton W.	W 3-1	5	15	Nish, Sinclair, Stringfellow / Knowles	31278		2	3	4	9	6	7	8	11	10			5		1										7
8	16	H	Fulham	L 1-2	5	19	Roberts / Clarke, Haynes	16441	1	2	3	4	9	6	7	8	11	10			5												8
9	23	A	Leeds United	L 2-3	5	22	Gibson, Nish / Lorimer 2 (1p), Greenhoff	37084		2	3	4	5		7	8	11	10	9	6			1										9
10	30	H	Everton	L 0-2	5	22	- / Ball 2	22768		2		4	5	6	7	8	11	10	9				1	3									10
11	Oct 7	H	Liverpool	W 2-1	7	20	Stringfellow 2 / St John	25609	1	2		4	5	6	7	8	11	10	9					3									11
12	14	A	Southampton	W 5-1	9	17	Stringfellow 2, Tewley, Sinclair, Shilton / Davies	21719	1	2	3	4	5		7	8	9	10*			12	11		6									12
13	25	H	Chelsea	D 2-2	10	17	Roberts 2 / Boyle, Bell (og)	24171	1	2	3	4	5		7	8	11	10						6	9								13
14	28	A	West Bromwich Albion	D 0-0	11	17		20961	1	2	3	4	5		7	8	11	10						6	9								14
15	Nov 4	H	Newcastle United	D 2-2	12	17	Sinclair, Stringfellow / Bennett, T Robson	18001	1	2	3	4	5		7	8	9	10			11			6									15
16	11	A	Manchester City	L 0-6	12	18	- / Young 2, Lee 2, Doyle, Oakes	29039	1	2	3	4			7	8	11	10			5			6	9								16
17	18	H	Arsenal	D 2-2	13	17	Large, Sinclair (p) / Radford, Johnston	28150	1	2		4*	5		7	6	9	10			12			3		8	11						17
18	25	A	Sheffield United	D 0-0	14	17		16132	1	2			5		7	6		10			4			3	9	8	11						18
19	Dec 2	H	Coventry City	D 0-0	15	18		30102	1	2		4	5		7	6	9	10						3		8	11						19
20	16	A	Tottenham Hotspur	W 1-0	17	15	Tewley	26036	1	2		4	5			6	9	10				7		3		8	11						20
21	23	H	Manchester United	D 2-2	18	15	Sjoberg, Tewley / Charlton, Law	40104	1	2		4	5			6	9	10				7		3		8	11						21
22	26	A	West Ham United	L 2-4	18	18	Large, Sinclair / Dear 3, Brooking	26520	1	2		4	5		11	6	9	10				7		3		8							22
23	30	H	West Ham United	L 2-4	18	18	Svarc, Large / Dear 2, Brooking, Sissons	24589	1	2		4	5			6		10*			12	7		3	9	8	11						23
24	Jan 6	A	Sunderland	W 2-0	20	16	Large 2	24703	1	2		4	5	10		6	9					7		3		8	11						24
25	13	H	Wolverhampton W.	W 3-1	22	14	Glover, Gibson, Large / Kenning	21463	1	2		4	5	10		6	9					7		3		8	11						25
26	20	A	Fulham	W 1-0	24	13	Stringfellow	16696	1	2		4	5	10		6	9				12	7		3		8	11*						26
27	Feb 3	H	Leeds United	D 2-2	25	14	Stringfellow, Large / Madeley, Giles	30081	1	2		4	5			6	10		11					3		8		9					27
28	24	A	Liverpool	L 1-3	25	14	Fern / Callaghan, Strong, Hateley	41451	1	2		4	5	6			9	10	11					3		8		7					28
29	Mar 2	H	Sheffield United	W 3-1	27	13	Large, Fern, Nish (p) / Reece	20239	1			4	5	6			10	9	11		2			3		8		7					29
30	16	A	Chelsea	L 1-4	27	14	Sjoberg / Tambling 2, Osgood (p), Baldwin	35990				4	5	6			10		11		2			3		8	7	9	1				30
31	19	A	Nottingham Forest	L 1-2	27	14	Tewley / Baker 2	30403	1			4	5	6			10		11		2	7		3		8		9					31
32	23	A	West Bromwich Albion	L 2-3	27	14	Nish, Tewley / Clark 2, Astle	23097	1			4	5	6			10		11		2	7		3		8		9					32
33	Apr 3	A	Newcastle United	D 0-0	28	15		33932	1	2*		4	5	6		8	11	10						3		9		7		12			33
34	6	H	Manchester City	W 1-0	30	14	Stringfellow	24925	1	2		4	5	6		8	11	10				7		3		9							34
35	9	A	Everton	L 1-2	30	14	Nish (p) / Morrissey, Royle	39156	1	2		4	5	6		8	11	10				7*		3		9		12					35
36	13	A	Arsenal	L 1-2	30	16	Nish / Gould, Graham	19108	1	2		4	5	6		8	11	10*			12	7		3		9							36
37	15	A	Burnley	D 1-1	31	15	Rodrigues (p) / Lochhead	12570	1	2		4	5	6		8	9				10			3		7					11		37
38	16	H	Burnley	L 0-2	31	16	- / Dobson, Casper	20032	1	2		4	5	6		8	11	10			12			3		9		7*					38
39	20	H	Southampton	W 4-1	33	16	Nish, Roberts, Gibson, Stringfellow / Davies	19518	1			8	5	2		4	11	10						3		9		7				6	39
40	27	H	Coventry City	W 1-0	35	16	Stringfellow	39888	1			8	5	2		4	11	10						3		9		7				6	40
41	May 4	H	Nottingham Forest	W 4-2	37	13	Fern 2, Roberts 2 / Storey-Moore, Chapman	26605	1			8	5	2		4	11	10						3		9		7				6	41
42	11	H	Stoke City	D 0-0	38	13		23852	1			8	5	2		4*	11	10						3		9	12	7				6	42
			League Appearances						35	34	14	41	40	29	20	42	37	41	3	3	14	12	6	33	4	26	9	13	1		1	4	
			Sub																	1	6	1						1	1		1			
			League Goals						1	1		6	5		7	7	13	4	1			5			1	8	1	4					

Final League Position: 13
Average Home League Attendance: 24528

FA CUP

No	Date		Opponents	Result	Scorers	Att	Shilton	Rodrigues	Norman	Roberts	Sjoberg	Cross	Sinclair	Nish	Stringfellow	Gibson	Sharkey	Goodfellow	Woollett	Tewley	Williamson	Bell	Svarc	Large	Glover	Fern	Mackleworth	No
1	Jan 27	A	Barrow (3)	W 2-1	Sjoberg, Arrowsmith (og) / Storf	16654	1	2		4	5	10		6	9					7		3	11	8				1
2	Feb 17	A	Manchester City (4)	D 0-0		51009	1	2		4	5	6		8	10							3		9	11	7		2
3	19	H	Manchester City (4 rep)	W 4-3	Fern, Large 2, Nish / Summerbee, Bell, Lee	39107	1	2		4	5	10		6	9		11					3		8		7		3
4	Mar 9	A	Rotherham Utd (5)	D 1-1	Nish (p) / Downs	23500		2		4	5	6			10	9	11					3		8		7	1	4
5	13	H	Rotherham Utd (5 rep)	W 2-0 aet	Large, Stringfellow	41856		2*		4	5	6			10	9	11					3		8	12	7	1	5
6	30	H	Everton (6)	L 1-3	Nish / Husband 2, Kendall	42000	1			4	5	6			10	9	11		2			3		8		7		6

FOOTBALL LEAGUE CUP

No	Date		Opponents	Result	Scorers	Att	Shilton	Rodrigues	Norman	Roberts	Sjoberg	Cross	Sinclair	Nish	Stringfellow	Gibson	Sharkey	Goodfellow	Woollett	Tewley	Williamson	No
1	Sep 13	A	Manchester City (2)	L 0-4	- / Bowles 2, Book, Young	25653		2	3	4	9	6	7	8	11	10			5		1	1

Dismissals: None, though Nish was sent off in a friendly v Kaiserslautern (a) on Aug 5.
Stand-in Goalkeepers: Aug 26, Roberts for Shilton, Manchester United (a).

1967-68
Back: Rodrigues, Cross, Shilton, Large, Woollett, Mackleworth, Bell, Gibson.
Front: Sjoberg, Stringfellow, Glover, Roberts, Fern, Tewley, Nish, Norman.

Season **1968-69**

Champions: Leeds United
Relegated: Leicester City, Queens Park Rangers

FOOTBALL LEAGUE DIVISION ONE

No	Date		Opponents	Result	Pts/Pos	Scorers	Att	Shilton	Woollett	Bell	Nish	Sjoberg	Manley	Gibson	Clarke	Stringfellow	Cross	Glover	Fern	Mackay	Roberts	Tewley	Svarc	Potts	Lochhead	Hutchins	Rodrigues	Matthews	Greenhalgh	Brown	No
1	Aug 10	A	Queens Park Rangers	D 1-1	1 -	Clarke / Allen	21494	1	2	3	4	5	6	7	8	9	10	11													1
2	13	A	Arsenal	L 0-3	1 -	- / Court, Gould 2	32164	1	2	3	4	5	6	7	8	9	10	11*	12												2
3	17	A	Ipswich Town	L 1-3	1 21	Nish (p) / Hegan, Crawford, O'Rourke	26014	1	2	3	4	5	6	7	8	9	10	11													3
4	21	H	Manchester City	W 3-0	3 17	Clarke 3	30076	1	2	3	10	5	6	11	8	9				7	4										4
5	24	A	Stoke City	L 0-1	3 20	- / Mahoney	18638	1	2	3	10	5	6	11	8	9*				7	4	12									5
6	28	A	Wolverhampton W.	L 0-1	3 20	- / Dougan	33474	1	2	3		5	6	10	8			11		4	9	7									6
7	31	H	Southampton	W 3-1	5 16	Clarke, Manley, Mackay / Kemp	21086	1	2	3*	9	5	6	10	8	11				4	12	7									7
8	Sep 7	A	Sunderland	L 0-2	5 20	- / Porterfield, Mulhall	26788	1	5	3				8	11	6		10	4	7	9	2									8
9	14	H	Leeds United	D 1-1	6 20	Gibson / Madeley	28564	1	2	3	9	5		10	8	11	6	7	12	4*											9
10	21	A	Liverpool	L 0-4	6 21	- / Yeats, Smith (p), Evans, Callaghan	48375	1	2	3	8	5		10		11	6	7	9	4											10
11	28	H	Coventry City	D 1-1	7 21	Fern / Hunt	32122	1	2	3	4	5		10	8*	11	6	7	9	12											11
12	Oct 5	A	Tottenham Hotspur	L 2-3	7 21	Clarke, Glover / Greaves 3	36622	1		3	4	5		10	8	11	6	7	9					2							12
13	9	H	Wolverhampton W.	W 2-0	9 19	Stringfellow, Fern	27048	1		3	4	5		10	8	11	6	7	9					2							13
14	12	H	West Bromwich Albion	L 0-2	9 19	- / Astle, Hartford	26348	1		3	4	5		10	8	11	6	7	9					2							14
15	19	A	Chelsea	L 0-3	9 20	- / Baldwin 3	33462	1		3	4	5		10	8		6	11		7		9	2								15
16	26	H	Burnley	L 0-2	9 22	- / Casper, Murray	21307	1	3		6	5		10	8	11	4	7	9					2							16
17	Nov 2	A	Newcastle United	D 0-0	10 21		20374	1	3		6	5		8	11	4	7	10						2	9						17
18	9	H	Nottingham Forest	D 2-2	11 21	Glover, Lochhead / Lyons, Storey-Moore	26828	1	3		6	5*		12	8		4	7	10					2	9	11					18
19	16	A	West Ham United	L 0-4	11 21	- / Dear 2, Peters, Woollett (og)	26328	1	3		6	12	5		8		4	7	10					2	9*	11					19
20	23	H	Sheffield Wednesday	D 1-1	12 20	Clarke / Fantham	21217	1			6	5	3	12	8	11*	4	7	10						9		2				20
21	30	A	Everton	L 1-7	12 20	Fern / Royle 3, Ball, Humphreys, Hurst, Husband	42492	1	3		6		5	11	8		4	7	9		10						2				21
22	Dec 7	H	Manchester United	W 2-1	14 20	Nish (p), Fern / Law	36303	1	3		6	5			11	8	7	10		4					9		2				22
23	14	A	West Bromwich Albion	D 1-1	15 19	Lochhead / Brown (p)	16483	1	3		6	5		10		11	4	7	8	2					9						23
24	21	H	Chelsea	L 1-4	15 20	Stringfellow / Tambling, Osgood 2, Birchenall	24037	1		3		6	5		12	11	8	7	10	4					9		2*				24
25	28	H	Burnley	L 1-2	15 20	Clarke / Collins, Kindon	15594	1	2	3	6	5			10	11	8	7		4					9						25
26	Jan 11	A	Newcastle United	W 2-1	17 19	Fern, Clarke, B Robson	21673	1		3	5	6	8	10		2	11	7		4					9						26
27	18	A	Nottingham Forest	D 0-0	18 19		27776	1		3	5		8	10		6	11	7		4					9		2				27
28	Feb 1	H	West Ham United	D 1-1	19 19	Clarke / Dear	31002	1	5	3			8	10		6	11	7		4					9		2				28
29	Mar 12	A	Queens Park Rangers	W 2-0	21 20	Lochhead 2	24554	1		3	5		8	10		6	11	7		4					9		2				29
30	15	H	Stoke City	D 0-0	22 20		24987	1		3	5		8	10		6	11	7		4					9		2				30
31	22	A	Southampton	L 0-1	22 21	- / Davies	18864	1	3		8	5		10		6	11	7		4					9						31
32	Apr 1	A	Coventry City	L 0-1	22 21	- / Martin	41486	1	3		2	5	4			11*	6	7		8					9			10	12		32
33	4	A	Manchester City	L 0-2	22 21	- / Summerbee 2	42022	1	3		10	5	4		11	6		12	8						9		2	7*			33
34	8	H	Arsenal	D 0-0	23 21		35573	1	3		8	5*	11		10		6	7		4					9		2	12			34
35	12	H	Liverpool	L 1-2	23 21	Rodrigues / Hughes, Callaghan	28671	1	3		8		5	7*	10		6	12		4					9	11	2				35
36	14	H	Sheffield Wednesday	W 3-1	25 21	Lochhead 2, Branfoot (og) / Woodall	18155	1	12		3		5	11*	10		6	7		4					9		2	8			36
37	19	A	Leeds United	L 0-2	25 21	- / Jones, Gray	38391	1	5		3				10		6	7		4	12				9*		2	8	11		37
38	29	H	Tottenham Hotspur	W 1-0	27 21	Clarke	35833	1	5		3		11	8*	10		6	12		4					9		2	7			38
39	May 3	A	Ipswich Town	L 1-2	27 21	Clarke / Viljoen, Lambert	22017	1	5		3		11	8	10	6*		12		4					9		2	7			39
40	5	H	Sunderland	W 2-1	29 21	Brown 2 / Kerr	32301	1	5		3		6	8	9			11		4*					12		2	7		10	40
41	14	H	Everton	D 1-1	30 21	Cross / Ball	41130	1	2		3		6	8*	10	5		12		4					9			7	11		41
42	17	A	Manchester United	L 2-3	30 21	Nish, Fern / Best, Law, Morgan	45860	1	3		4		5	8	10		6	11	7*						9		2	12			42

Final League Position:	21	League Appearances	42	32	16	40	23	28	29	36	22	37	27	29	6	25	3	2	9	24	3	18	7	2	2	
Average Home League Attendance:	28445	Sub		1			1			3				6	1	3	1		1			1	2			
		League Goals					3		1	1	12	2	1	2	6	1				6	1				2	

FA CUP

No	Date		Opponents	Result	Scorers	Att	Shilton	Woollett	Bell	Nish	Sjoberg	Manley	Gibson	Clarke	Stringfellow	Cross	Glover	Fern	Mackay	Roberts	Tewley	Svarc	Potts	Lochhead	Hutchins	Rodrigues	Matthews	Greenhalgh	Brown	No
1	Jan 4	A	Barnsley (3)	D 1-1	Glover / Evans	25099	1	2			6	5		7	10		8	11	12	3*	4			9						1
2	8	H	Barnsley (3 rep)	W 2-1	Fern, Glover / Loyden (p)	31814	1	3			6	5			10		8	11	7		4			9		2				2
3	25	A	Millwall (4)	W 1-0	Glover	31480	1			3	5			8	10		6	11	7		4			9		2				3
4	Mar 1	H	Liverpool (5)	D 0-0		42002	1			3	5			8	10		6	11	7		4			9		2				4
5	3	A	Liverpool (5 rep)	W 1-0	Lochhead	54666	1			3	5		12	8*	10		6	11	7		4			9		2				5
6	8	A	Mansfield Town (6)	W 1-0	Fern	23500	1			3	5			8	10		6	11	7		4			9		2				6
7	29		West Bromwich A. (sf)	W 1-0	Clarke	53207	1	3			4	5	12		10		6	11*	7		8			9		2				7
8	Apr 26		Manchester City (f)	L 0-1	- / Young	100000	1	5			3			12	8	10		6	11*	7				9		2				8

FOOTBALL LEAGUE CUP

No	Date		Opponents	Result	Scorers	Att	Shilton	Woollett	Bell	Nish	Sjoberg	Manley	Gibson	Clarke	Stringfellow	Cross	Glover	Fern	Mackay	Roberts	Tewley	Svarc	Potts	Lochhead	Hutchins	Rodrigues	Matthews	Greenhalgh	Brown	No
1	Sep 4	A	Darlington (2)	W 2-1	Clarke 2 / Felton	11653	1	2	3	6	5*			10	8	11			12	4	7	9								1
2	24	A	Carlisle United (3)	W 3-0	Clarke, Fern, Stringfellow	10894	1	2	3	4		5	10	8	11	6	7	9												2
3	Oct 16	A	Burnley (4)	L 0-4	- / Thomas, Murray 2, Casper	11605	1	3*		4	5	6	11		8	7	10		12		9	2								3

Dismissals: Oct 26, Clarke, Burnley (h).
Note: Mar 29, at Hillsborough (Sheffield Wednesday); Apr 26, at Wembley.

1 March: Andy Lochhead sends a header just over the bar in the first cup tie against Liverpool. His bullet header in the replay two days later would lead to a famous victory as City themselves headed for a Wembley and relegation double.

1968-69
Back: Fern, Cross, Roberts, Gibson. **Middle:** Sjoberg, Stringfellow, Shilton, Woollett, Mackleworth, Bell, Clarke. **Front:** Rodrigues, Nish, Tewley, Hutchins, Potts, Manley, Glover.

1969-70
Back: Nish, Woollett, Rodrigues, Shilton, Sjoberg, Cross, Roberts, Musgrove (Coach). **Front:** Farrington, Fern, Brown, Matthews, Glover.

Promoted: Huddersfield Town, Blackpool
Relegated: Aston Villa, Preston North End

Player columns (left to right): Peter Shilton, Peter Rodrigues, Billy Houghton, David Nish, John Sjoberg, Graham Cross, Len Glover, Rodney Fern, Andy Lochhead, David Gibson, Malcolm Manley, Bobby Roberts, Alan Woollett, Ally Brown, Derek Harrison, Bobby Mackay, Alan Tewley, Paul Matthews, Murray Brodie, David Tearse, John Farrington, Mike Stringfellow, Ken Sandercock, Colin Mackleworth, Graham Brown

FOOTBALL LEAGUE DIVISION TWO

Match No	Date		Opponents	Result	Points	Position	Scorers	Att
1	Aug 9	H	Birmingham City	W 3-1	2	-	Fern, Manley, Lochhead / Summerill	35168
2	16	A	Middlesbrough	L 1-2	2	11	Lochhead / Laidlaw, Hickton	22159
3	20	A	Bolton Wanderers	D 2-2	3	12	Cross, Lochhead / Wharton (p), Phillips	27673
4	23	H	Norwich City	W 3-0	5	10	Sjoberg, Lochhead, Forbes (og)	26716
5	27	A	Aston Villa	W 1-0	7	6	Glover	33838
6	30	A	Millwall	W 1-0	9	4	A Brown	14011
7	Sep 6	H	Portsmouth	W 2-1	11	2	Lochhead 2 / Atkins	25467
8	13	A	Cardiff City	D 1-1	12	3	Carver (og) / Toshack	26978
9	17	H	Carlisle United	L 1-2	12	3	Rodrigues / McIlmoyle, Woollett (og)	24434
10	20	H	Huddersfield Town	D 1-1	13	4	A Brown / McGill	24552
11	27	A	Swindon Town	D 1-1	14	5	Glover / Noble	22352
12	Oct 4	H	Watford	W 3-1	16	5	Glover, Nish (p), Brodie / Endean	25442
13	8	H	Middlesbrough	W 2-1	18	4	Brodie, Cross / Downing	26528
14	11	A	Preston North End	L 1-2	18	5	A Brown / Gemmill 2	14492
15	18	H	Bristol City	W 2-0	20	5	Fern, Glover	25954
16	25	A	Blackburn Rovers	L 1-3	20	5	Fern / Knighton, Hill, Darling	15362
17	Nov 1	H	Oxford United	W 2-1	22	5	Glover, Matthews / Shuker	25663
18	8	A	Blackpool	D 1-1	23	4	Matthews / Brown	13074
19	12	A	Bolton Wanderers	W 3-2	25	4	Fern 3 / Taylor, Wharton (p)	7219
20	15	H	Charlton Athletic	D 2-2	26	4	Fern, Nish (p) / Reddick, Treacy	23622
21	22	A	Queens Park Rangers	D 1-1	27	4	Stringfellow / Bridges	21067
22	Dec 6	A	Sheffield United	L 0-1	27	4	- / Reece	21326
23	13	H	Cardiff City	L 1-2	27	5	Fern / Clark, King	22590
24	17	H	Hull City	D 2-2	28	6	Nish, Fern / Chilton, Wagstaff	16059
25	20	A	Portsmouth	W 3-2	30	5	Farrington, Fern 2 / Trebilcock 2	12447
26	26	A	Norwich City	L 0-3	30	5	- / Conlon 2, Silvester	14905
27	27	H	Millwall	D 1-1	31	5	Tearse / Possee	24420
28	Jan 17	H	Swindon Town	L 0-2	31	9	- / Horsfield 2	24378
29	31	A	Watford	L 1-2	31	9	Glover / Eddy (p), Endean	19900
30	Feb 14	A	Birmingham City	W 1-0	33	10	Farrington	25990
31	25	H	Preston North End	W 3-0	35	9	Farrington, A Brown, Glover	21336
32	28	A	Bristol City	D 0-0	36	8		17044
33	Mar 10	H	Huddersfield Town	D 1-1	37	9	Fern / Worthington	20965
34	14	A	Hull City	L 1-4	37	9	Sjoberg / Chilton, Wagstaff, Simpkin, Nish (og)	11536
35	17	H	Blackburn Rovers	W 2-1	39	9	Farrington, Fern / Metcalfe	20225
36	21	H	Sheffield United	W 2-1	41	8	Glover, Fern / Reece	25770
37	27	A	Oxford United	W 1-0	43	7	Roberts	16741
38	28	A	Charlton Athletic	W 5-0	45	5	Matthews, Fern 2, Glover, A Brown	13514
39	31	H	Blackpool	D 0-0	46	5		32784
40	Apr 4	H	Aston Villa	W 1-0	48	3	A Brown	27481
41	14	A	Carlisle United	D 2-2	49	4	Fern, A Brown / Winstanley, Woollett (og)	6657
42	18	H	Queens Park Rangers	W 2-1	51	3	Nish, A Brown / Marsh (p)	20391

Final League Position:	3	League Appearances	39 29 6 42 39 42 37 39 16 9 9 31 27 26 24 3 5 24 7 5 3
Average Home League Attendance:	25104	Sub	1 1 1 3 3 2 2 5 1 1 5 1
		League Goals	1 4 2 2 9 17 6 1 1 8 3 2 1 4 1

FA CUP

	Date		Opponents	Result		Scorers	Att
1	Jan 3	H	Sunderland (3)	W 1-0		Roberts	24873
2	24	A	Southampton (4)	D 1-1		Farrington / Stokes	26660
3	28	H	Southampton (4 rep)	W 4-2		Lochhead 2, Farrington, Nish (p) / Paine, Channon	33399
4	Feb 7	A	Liverpool (5)	D 0-0			53788
5	11	H	Liverpool (5 rep)	L 0-2		- / Evans 2	42100

FOOTBALL LEAGUE CUP

	Date		Opponents	Result		Scorers	Att
1	Sep 2	A	Bristol City (2)	D 0-0			15883
2	10	A	Bristol City (2 rep)	D 0-0 aet			20797
3	15	H	Bristol City (2 rep 2)	W 3-1		Lochhead 3 / Galley	12600
4	24	A	Bournemouth & BA (3)	W 2-0		Manley, Fern	15857
5	Oct 15	H	Sheffield United (4)	W 2-0		A Brown, Lochhead	26627
6	29	H	West Bromwich A (5)	D 0-0			35121
7	Nov 5	A	West Bromwich A (5 rep)	L 1-2		Cross / Astle 2	25186

Note: Sep 15, tie staged at Filbert Street after toss of coin.

3 January: Eight months earlier, David Nish had become the youngest ever FA Cup Final captain. Here he tries to set City off on another cup run with this effort against Sunderland in Round Three.

Season 1970-71

Promoted: Leicester City, Sheffield United
Relegated: Blackburn Rovers, Bolton Wanderers

FOOTBALL LEAGUE DIVISION TWO

Match No	Date	H/A	Opponents	Result	Points	Position	Scorers	Att	Peter Shilton	Peter Rodrigues	Alan Woollett	David Nish	John Sjoberg	Graham Cross	John Farrington	Rodney Fern	Ally Brown	Bobby Kellard	Len Glover	Mike Stringfellow	Paul Matthews	Steve Whitworth	Malcolm Manley	Malcolm Partridge	Derek Harrison	Joe Jopling	Willie Carlin	David Tearse	Colin Mackleworth	Match No
1	Aug 15	H	Cardiff City	L 0-1		-	- / Clark	27578	1	2	3	4	5	6	7	8*	9	10	11	12										1
2	22	A	Queens Park Rangers	W 3-1	2	11	Kellard, Brown, Farrington / Venables (p)	17090	1	2	3		5	6	7	8	10*	4	11	9	12									2
3	29	H	Carlisle United	D 2-2	3	12	Nish, Glover / Barton, Hatton	20809	1	2	3		5	6	7	8	10	4	11	9										3
4	Sep 2	H	Bristol City	W 4-0	5	5	Farrington, Kellard, Brown, Nish (p)	20228	1		3		5	6	7	12	10	4	11	9*	8	2								4
5	5	A	Oxford United	L 0-1	5	9	- / Smithson (p)	12895	1		3		5	6	7		10*	4	11	9	8	2		12						5
6	12	H	Luton Town	W 1-0	7	6	Brown	24246	1		3		5	6	7	8	9	4	11			2	10							6
7	19	A	Charlton Athletic	W 1-0	9	5	Partridge	10940	1		3		5	6	7		9	10	11			2	4	8						7
8	26	H	Portsmouth	W 2-0	11	4	Glover, Farrington	25613	1		3		5	6	7		9	10	11			2	4	8						8
9	30	H	Middlesbrough	W 3-2	13	1	Brown 2, Kellard / Hickton 2	26260	1		3		5	6	7		9	10	11			2	4	8						9
10	Oct 3	A	Blackburn Rovers	D 2-2	14	1	Partridge, Nish (p) / Rogers, Manley (og)	9061	1		3		5	6	7		9	10	11			2	4	8						10
11	10	H	Sunderland	W 1-0	16	1	Glover	26580	1				5	6	7		9	10	11			2	4	8	3					11
12	17	A	Cardiff City	D 2-2	17	3	Farrington, Sjoberg / Gibson (p), Carver	26008	1		3*		5	6	7	12	9	10	11			2	4	8						12
13	20	A	Birmingham City	D 0-0	18	3		25381	1		3		5	6	7		9	4	11			2	12	8*		10				13
14	24	A	Sheffield Wednesday	W 3-0	20	3	Brown, Nish 2 (1p)	23160	1		3		5	6	7		9	4	11			2		8		10				14
15	31	H	Bolton Wanderers	W 1-0	22	1	Kellard	24623	1		3		5	6	7		9	4	11			2		8		10				15
16	Nov 7	A	Watford	W 1-0	24	1	Nish (p)	17107	1		3		5	6	7		9	10	11			2	4			8				16
17	14	H	Swindon Town	W 3-1	26	1	Brown, Jones (og), Harland (og) / Noble	26063	1		3		5	6	7		9	4	11			2	12			10	8*			17
18	21	A	Norwich City	D 2-2	27	1	Manley, Farrington / Silvester, Foggo	16342	1		3		5	6	7	12	9	10	11*			2	4			8				18
19	28	H	Orient	W 4-0	29	1	Manley, Brown 2, Kellard	23699	1		3		5	6	7		9	8	11			2	4			10				19
20	Dec 5	A	Hull City	L 0-3	29	1	- / Chilton, Houghton, Butler	21210	1		3		5	6	7	12	9	8	11*			2	4			10				20
21	12	H	Millwall	W 2-1	31	1	Kellard, Fern / Cripps	22062	1		3		5	6	7	8		4	11	9*		2	12			10				21
22	19	H	Queens Park Rangers	D 0-0	32	1		23866	1		3		5	6	7		8	4	11	9		2				10				22
23	26	A	Sheffield United	L 1-2	32	1	Farrington / Woodward, Nish (og)	31843	1		3		5	6	7		9	4	11			2		8		10				23
24	Jan 9	A	Middlesbrough	L 0-1	32	2	- / Hickton	30682			3		5	6	7		9	4	11	12		2		8		10*		1		24
25	16	H	Birmingham City	L 1-4	32	4	Sjoberg / B Latchford 2, Bowler, Summerill	25657			3		5	6	7	9				11		2	4	8		10		1		25
26	Feb 6	H	Hull City	D 0-0	33	4		31076	1		3		5	6	7	9		4	11			2		8		10				26
27	20	H	Norwich City	W 2-1	35	7	Fern, Partridge / Foggo	24866	1		3		5*	6	7	9	8	4				2	11	12		10				27
28	27	A	Bolton Wanderers	W 3-0	37	6	Brown, Sjoberg 2	8663	1		3		5	6	7	9	8	4	11			2		12		10*				28
29	Mar 1	A	Millwall	D 0-0	38	3		10738	1		3		5	6	7	9	8	4	11			2				10				29
30	10	H	Sheffield Wednesday	W 1-0	40	2	Brown	25843	1		3		5	6	7	9	8	4	11			2				10				30
31	13	A	Swindon Town	W 1-0	42	1	Kellard	17979	1	11	3		5	6	7	9	8	4				2				10				31
32	20	H	Watford	D 1-1	43	2	Nish / Walley	24817	1		5	3		6	7	9	8	4*	11			2	12			10				32
33	27	H	Oxford United	D 0-0	44	1		22233	1	12	3	5		6	7	9*			11			2	4			10	8			33
34	29	A	Orient	W 1-0	46	1	Glover	12736	1	3	7	5	6				9	8	4	11		2				10				34
35	Apr 3	A	Carlisle United	W 1-0	48	1	Brown	15325	1	3	7	5	6				9	8	4	11		2				10				35
36	10	H	Sheffield United	D 0-0	49	1		36752	1	3	7	5	6				9	8	4	11*		2	12			10				36
37	12	A	Luton Town	W 3-1	51	1	Manley, Farrington, Brown / Sjoberg (og)	24405	1		3	5	6	7	9	8				12		2	4*	11		10				37
38	13	H	Blackburn Rovers	D 1-1	52	1	Carlin / Pickering	32749	1		3	5	6	7	9	8	4					2	11			10				38
39	17	A	Sunderland	D 0-0	53	1		17353	1		3	5	6		9*	8	4			12		2	11	7		10				39
40	24	H	Charlton Athletic	W 1-0	55	1	Went (og)	29121	1		3	5	6		9	8	4			12		2	11	7*		10				40
41	27	A	Bristol City	W 1-0	57	1	Brown	16103	1		3	5*	6		9	8	4			12		2	11			10				41
42	May 1	A	Portsmouth	W 2-1	59	1	Farrington, Brown / Hiron	18795	1		3		6	7	9	8	4			11		2	5	12		10*				42

							League Appearances		40	1	9	40	40	42	37	23	38	39	33	7	4	39	20	15	1	30	2	2	
Final League Position:	1						Sub			1						4				5	2		4	5					
Average Home League Attendance:	25869						League Goals					7	4		8	2	15	7	4				3	3		1			

FA CUP

	Date	H/A	Opponents	Result			Scorers	Att																						
1	Jan 2	H	Notts County (3)	W 2-0			Brown, Partridge	33770			3		5	6	7		9	4	11			2		8		10	1			1
2	25	H	Torquay United (4)	W 3-0			Glover, Partridge, Cross	27265	1		3		5	6	7	9	12	4	11			2		8		10*				2
3	Feb 13	H	Oxford United (5)	D 1-1			Partridge / Lucas	34802	1		3		5	6	7	9	12	4	11*			2		8		10				3
4	17	A	Oxford United (5 rep)	W 3-1 aet			Brown, Fern 2 / R Atkinson	17948	1		3		5	6	7	9	8	4	11			2				10				4
5	Mar 6	H	Arsenal (6)	D 0-0				42000	1		3		5	6	7	9	8	4	11			2				10				5
6	15	A	Arsenal (6 rep)	L 0-1			- / George	57443	1		3		5	6	7	9	8*	4	11			2	12			10				6

FOOTBALL LEAGUE CUP

	Date	H/A	Opponents	Result			Scorers	Att																						
1	Sep 9	H	Southampton (2)	W 3-2			Farrington, Glover, Fern / Channon, Sjoberg (og)	20728	1	12	3*		5	6	7	8	9	10	11			2	4							1
2	Oct 7	A	Bolton Wanderers (3)	D 1-1			Farrington / Manning	8623	1	4	3*		6	7	8	9	10	11	12	2			5							2
3	12	H	Bolton Wanderers (3 rep)	W 1-0			Sjoberg	18068	1	3			5	6	7	8	9	10	11	2	4									3
4	28	H	Bristol City (4)	D 2-2			Farrington, Nish (p) / Garland, Sharpe	21577	1		3	5	6	7		8	10	11	9	2	4									4
5	Nov 3	A	Bristol City (4 rep)	L 1-2 aet			Nish (p) / Rodgers, Wimshurst	16575	1		3	5	6	7	8	12	10	11	9*	2	4									5

20 February: City pressurise the Canaries' defence at Filbert Street. Graham Cross and Rodney Fern are denied by Kevin Keelan, whilst Ally Brown looks on.

1970-71
Back: Woollett, Sjoberg, Brown, Cross, Shilton, Fern, Rodrigues. **Front:** Gibson, Glover, Roberts, Nish, Manley, Matthews, Farrington.

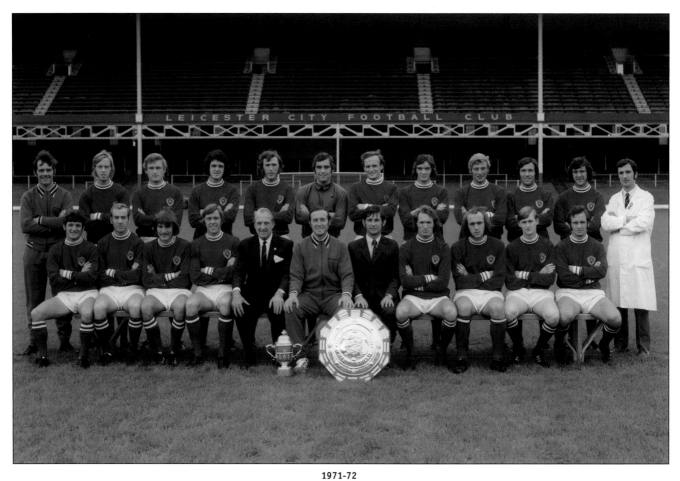

1971-72
Back: Coates (Trainer), Whitworth, Sjoberg, Jopling, Partridge, Shilton, Stringfellow, Brown, Cross, Sammels, Manley, Preston (Physio).
Front: Carlin, Woollett, Farrington, Nish, Shipman (Chairman), Bloomfield (Manager), Smith (Secretary), Glover, Fern, Matthews, Kellard.

Season **1971-72**

Champions: Derby County
Relegated: Nottingham Forest, Huddersfield Town

FOOTBALL LEAGUE DIVISION ONE

Match No	Date		Opponents	Result	Points	Position	Scorers	Att	Peter Shilton	Steve Whitworth	David Nish	Bobby Kellard	John Sjoberg	Graham Cross	John Farrington	Ally Brown	Rodney Fern	Jon Sammels	Len Glover	Willie Carlin	Malcolm Manley	Alan Woollett	Malcolm Partridge	Paul Matthews	Malcolm Munro	Keith Weller	Alan Birchenall	David Tomlin	Carl Jayes	Mark Wallington	Bob Lee	Match No
1	Aug 14	A	Huddersfield Town	D 2-2	1	-	Brown, Nish / Worthington, Cherry	16285	1	2	3	4	5	6	7	8	9	10	11													1
2	18	H	Nottingham Forest	W 2-1	3	-	Brown, O'Kane (og) / Cormack	32079	1	2	3	4	5	6	7	8	9	10	11													2
3	21	H	Derby County	L 0-2	3	12	- / Hector, Hinton (p)	35460	1	2	3	4	5	6	7	8	9	10	11													3
4	25	A	Stoke City	L 1-3	3	17	Brown / Ritchie, Bernard, Cross (og)	21678	1	2	3	4	5	6	7	8	9		11	10												4
5	28	A	Liverpool	L 2-3	3	17	Fern, Farrington / Heighway, Keegan, Toshack	50970	1	2	3	4	5	6	7	8	9	10	11													5
6	Sep 1	H	Southampton	L 0-1	3	20	- / Channon	22055	1	2	3	4	5*	6	7	8	9	10	11		12											6
7	4	H	Manchester City	D 0-0	4	20		25238	1	2	3	4		6	7	9		10	11		5	8										7
8	11	A	Ipswich Town	W 2-1	6	15	Sammels, Kellard / Clarke	18483	1	2	3*	4	5	6		8	9	10	11			12		7								8
9	18	H	Sheffield United	L 0-1	6	20	- / Woodward	30143	1	2	3	8	5	6		9	7	10	11		4											9
10	25	A	Arsenal	L 0-3	6	21	- / Radford 2, Rice	40201	1	2	3		5	6	7	9	8	10	11*		4		12									10
11	Oct 2	H	Crystal Palace	D 0-0	7	20		28493	1	2	3		5	4	7	9*	12	10			6					8	11					11
12	9	A	West Ham United	D 1-1	8	20	Cross / Hurst	31060	1	2	3		5	4		12	9	10	7		6*					8	11					12
13	16	H	Huddersfield Town	W 2-0	10	17	Sammels, Weller	22412	1	2	3		5	4		6	8	10								7	9	11				13
14	23	A	West Bromwich Albion	W 1-0	12	16	Weller	23088	1	2	3		5	4		6	8	10			11					7	9					14
15	30	H	Chelsea	D 1-1	13	16	Birchenall / Osgood	36574	1	2	3		5	4		6	8	10			12					7	9	11*				15
16	Nov 6	A	Leeds United	L 1-2	13	16	Brown / Bremner, Lorimer	39877	1	2	3		5	4		6	8	10	12		11*					7	9					16
17	13	H	Newcastle United	W 3-0	15	15	Brown, Sammels, Fern	28792	1	2	3		5	4		6	8	10	11							7	9					17
18	20	A	Manchester United	L 2-3	15	16	Birchenall, Glover / Law 2, Kidd	48757	1	2	3		5	4		6	8	10	11							7	9					18
19	27	H	Everton	D 0-0	16	16		29662	1	2	3		5	4		6	8	10	11							7	9					19
20	Dec 4	A	Coventry City	D 1-1	17	16	Brown / McGuire	26300	1	2	3		5	4		6	8	10	11							7	9					20
21	11	H	Tottenham Hotspur	L 0-1	17	16	- / Peters	30721	1	2	3		5	4		6	8	10	11							7	9					21
22	18	A	Manchester City	D 1-1	18	15	Weller / Lee	29524	1	2	3		5	4		6	10	8			11					7	9					22
23	27	A	Wolverhampton W.	L 1-2	18	15	Sammels / Munro, Dougan	37966	1	2	3		5	4		6	8	10	12		11*					7	9					23
24	Jan 1	A	Sheffield United	D 1-1	19	17	Sjoberg / Dearden	34406	1	2	3		5	4		6	8	10	11							7	9					24
25	8	H	Liverpool	W 1-0	21	15	Brown	26421	1	2	3			4	8	6		10	11		5					7	9					25
26	22	A	Nottingham Forest	W 2-1	23	14	Weller, Birchenall / Storey-Moore	27250	1	2	3		5	4	8	6*	12	10	11							7	9					26
27	29	H	Stoke City	W 2-1	25	12	Glover, Farrington / Greenhoff	26931	1	2	3		4	8	6	12	10	11		5						7	9*					27
28	Feb 12	A	West Bromwich Albion	L 0-1	25	13	- / Brown	24225	1	2	3		5	4*	8	12	6	10	11							7	9					28
29	19	A	Chelsea	L 1-2	25	15	Glover / Osgood 2	38783	1	2	3			4	12	8*		10	11		5	6				7	9					29
30	Mar 4	A	Newcastle United	L 0-2	25	16	- / Macdonald, Gibb	25256	1	2	3			4*	8	12	9	6	11		5					7	10					30
31	11	H	West Ham United	W 2-0	27	15	Nish 2	23345		2	3		5	4	7*		6	8	11							9	10		1			31
32	18	A	Derby County	L 0-3	27	16	- / O'Hare, Hector, Durban	34019		2	3			4		7*	8	11			5	6				9	10		1	12		32
33	22	H	Leeds United	D 0-0	28	16		32152	1	2	3			4			8	11			5	6				7	9	10				33
34	25	H	Ipswich Town	W 1-0	30	13	Tomlin	19769	1	2	3			4			8	11			5	6				7	9	10				34
35	Apr 1	H	Wolverhampton W.	W 1-0	32	13	Shaw (og)	23981	1	2	3			4			12	8	11			6	5			7	9*	10*				35
36	3	A	Crystal Palace	D 1-1	33	13	Fern / Craven	23736		2	3			4			9		11		5	6	8		12	7		10*	1			36
37	4	H	Arsenal	D 0-0	34	13		27431		2	3						6	8	11		5	4	10			7	9		1			37
38	8	H	Manchester United	W 2-0	36	11	Weller, Birchenall	35970	1	2	3						12	8	11		5	4	6			7	9	10*				38
39	11	A	Southampton	L 0-1	36	11	- / Davies	18752	1	2	3						12	8	11		5	4	6			7*	9	10				39
40	15	A	Everton	D 0-0	37	11		33342	1	2	3			4			9	8	11*		5	6	10			7		12				40
41	22	H	Coventry City	W 1-0	39	11	Glover	24254	1	2	3*			6			12	8	11		4	5	9			7		10				41
42	29	A	Tottenham Hotspur	L 3-4	39	11	Glover, Sammels (p), Partridge / Knowles 2 (1p), England, Pearce	19631		2	3			4				8	11		5	6	10			7	9			1		42

Final League Position:	12		**League Appearances**	37 42 42 9 26 39 15 27 29 40 35 1 23 13 8 1 32 29 9 5	
Average Home League Attendance:	28536		**Sub**	1 3 7 2 3 2 1 1 1	
			League Goals	3 1 1 1 2 7 3 5 5 1 5 4 1	

FA CUP

	Date		Opponents	Result	Scorers	Att	Shilton	Whitworth	Nish	Sjoberg	Cross	Brown	Fern	Sammels	Glover	Manley	Woollett	Weller	Birchenall	Jayes	
1	Jan 15	A	Wolverhampton W. (3)	D 1-1	Farrington / McCalliog	38121	1	2	3	5	4	8	6	10	11			7	9		1
2	19	H	Wolverhampton W. (3 rep)	W 2-0	Farrington, Glover	37060	1	2	3	5	4	8	6	10	11			7	9		2
3	Feb 5	H	Orient (4)	L 0-2	- / Bowyer, Allen	31402		2	3	5	4	8	6*	10	11	12		7	9	1	3

FOOTBALL LEAGUE CUP

	Date		Opponents	Result	Scorers	Att																
1	Sep 7	A	Charlton Athletic (2)	L 1-3	Partridge / Went, Peacock 2	11694	1	2	3	4	6	7	8	10	5	11*	9	12				1

Dismissals: None, though Weller was sent off in a friendly v Olympiakos (a) on May 9.

8 April: Keith Weller gets back to foil Bobby Charlton as Manchester United attempt to get back into the game at Filbert Street. City's massed defence includes David Nish, Steve Whitworth, Peter Shilton, Alan Woollett, Malcolm Partridge and Malcolm Manley.

Champions: Liverpool
Relegated: Crystal Palace, West Bromwich Albion

FOOTBALL LEAGUE DIVISION ONE

Match No	Date		Opponents	Result	Points	Position	Scorers	Att	Sh	Wh	Ni	Wo	Sj	Ma	Fa	Sa	We	Bi	Gl	Pa	Cr	St	Wr	Ro	Mu	Wa	To	Jo	Le	Match No
1	Aug 12	H	Arsenal	L 0-1	-	-	- / Ball (p)	28009	1	2	3	4*	5	6	7	8	9	10	11	12										1
2	16	H	Chelsea	D 1-1	1	-	Farrington / Garland	22873	1	2	3	4	5		7	8	9	10*	11	12	6									2
3	19	A	West Ham United	L 2-5	1	20	Stringfellow, Glover / Robson 2, Coker, Moore, Tyler	25490	1	2	3	4	5		7	8	9		11		6	10								3
4	23	A	Manchester United	D 1-1	2	19	Worthington / Best	40067	1	2	3		5		7	6	9	10			4		11	8						4
5	26	H	Coventry City	D 0-0	3	19		25894	1	2			5	6		8	7	10	11		4		9	3						5
6	30	H	Liverpool	W 3-2	5	15	Weller 3 / Toshack 2	28694	1	2			5	6	7	6	9	10	11		4		8	3						6
7	Sep 2	A	Manchester City	L 0-1	5	17	- / Marsh	27233	1	2			5		11	7	6	9			12	4	10	8	3*					7
8	9	H	Everton	L 1-2	5	19	Sammels / Connolly, Cross (og)	21080	1	2			5		7	6	9			11	12	4	10*	8	3					8
9	16	A	Leeds United	L 1-3	5	21	Glover / Clarke, Jones, Bates	33930	1	2		4			7	6	9	10	11		5		8	3						9
10	23	H	Wolverhampton W.	D 1-1	6	20	Farrington / Hegan	20817	1	2			5		7	4	9	8	11		6		10	3						10
11	30	A	Ipswich Town	W 2-0	8	17	Glover, Worthington	17811	1	2			5		7	4	9	8	11		6		10	3						11
12	Oct 7	H	Southampton	W 1-0	10	15	Sammels (p)	18092	1	2			5		7*	4	9	8	11		6	12	10	3						12
13	14	A	Derby County	L 1-2	10	16	Weller / Hinton (p), Hennessey	31841	1	2			5		7	4	9	8*	11		6	12	10	3						13
14	21	H	Norwich City	L 1-2	10	19	Weller / Cross, Paddon	19787	1	2		6	5		7	4	9	8	11				10	3						14
15	28	A	Stoke City	L 0-1	10	20	- / Hurst	24421	1	2	3			12	7	4		8	11	9*	5		10		6					15
16	Nov 4	H	Manchester United	D 2-2	11	20	Sammels, Farrington / Best, Davies	32575	1	2					7	4	9	8	11		6		10	3	5					16
17	11	A	Chelsea	D 1-1	12	19	Sammels / Garner	28456	1			2	5		7	4	9	8	11		6		10	3						17
18	18	H	Tottenham Hotspur	L 0-1	12	21	- / Chivers	22707		2		4	5*	12	7	8			10	11	6		9	3		1				18
19	Dec 2	H	West Bromwich Albion	W 3-1	14	21	Worthington 3 / Gould	15307	1	2		4			5	7	8*		10	11	6		9	3			12			19
20	9	A	Birmingham City	D 1-1	15	21	Cross / Calderwood	32481	1	2					5	7	8	4	10	11	6		9	3						20
21	16	A	Sheffield United	L 0-2	15	22	- / Woodward (p), Hockey	17111	1	2					5	7	4*	9	8	11	6		10	3			12			21
22	23	H	Crystal Palace	W 2-1	17	20	Worthington (p), Birchenall / Rogers	16962	1	2		4*			6	7		9	8	11	5		10	3			12			22
23	26	A	Wolverhampton W.	L 0-2	17	21	- / Richards, Dougan	22022	1	2		4*			5	7		9	8	11			10	3			12	6		23
24	30	H	West Ham United	W 2-1	19	17	Farrington, Worthington / Brooking	19341	1	2		4			5	7		9	8	11			10	3			6			24
25	Jan 1	A	Newcastle United	D 2-2	20	17	Birchenall, Worthington / Tudor, Smith	30868	1	2		4			5*	7		9	8	11	6	12	10	3						25
26	6	A	Coventry City	L 2-3	20	18	Worthington, Weller / Stein, Carr, Woollett (og)	25067	1	2		4			7		9	6	11		5	8*	10	3			12			26
27	20	H	Manchester City	D 1-1	21	17	Worthington / Bell	18761	1	2		4			5	7	9		11		6	8	10	3						27
28	27	A	Everton	W 1-0	23	16	Wright (og)	31531	1	2		4			5	7	9	8	11		6		10	3						28
29	Feb 10	H	Leeds United	W 2-0	25	15	Birchenall 2	35976	1	2		4			5	7	9	8	11		6		10	3						29
30	17	A	Arsenal	L 0-1	25	15	- / Manley (og)	42047	1	2		4*			5	7	12	9	8	11	6		10	3						30
31	24	H	Sheffield United	D 0-0	26	15		21821	1	2		4			5	7		8	9	11	6		10	3						31
32	Mar 3	A	Southampton	D 0-0	27	14		14134	1	2		4			5	7	9	8	11		6		10	3						32
33	10	H	Derby County	D 0-0	28	14		29690	1	2					5	7	4	9	8	11	6		10	3						33
34	17	A	Norwich City	D 1-1	29	14	Glover / Paddon	25299	1	2					5	7	4	9	8	11	6		10	3						34
35	24	H	Stoke City	W 2-0	31	13	Tomlin, Birchenall	18743	1	2					5	7	4	9	8	11*	6		10	3			12			35
36	31	A	Newcastle United	D 0-0	32	14		18712	1	2					5	7	4	9	8		6		10	3			11			36
37	Apr 7	A	West Bromwich Albion	L 0-1	32	18	- / Astle	15235	1	2		12			6	7	4	9	8		5		10	3			11*			37
38	14	H	Birmingham City	L 0-1	32	19	- / Campbell	27652	1	2		12			5	7*	4	9	8	11	6		10	3						38
39	20	A	Crystal Palace	W 1-0	34	18	Weller	36817	1	2		4			5	7		9	8	11	6		10	3						39
40	21	H	Tottenham Hotspur	D 1-1	35	17	Weller / Gilzean	23312	1	2		4			5		7	9	8	11*	6	12	10	3						40
41	24	H	Ipswich Town	D 1-1	36	17	Cross / Lambert	20373	1	2		4					9		11		6	12	10	3	5		7		8*	41
42	28	A	Liverpool	D 0-0	37	16		56202	1	2					5		7	9	8	11	6		4	10	3					42

						League Appearances			41	41	4	27	10	25	38	30	39	36	38	1	38	8	39	37	3	1	4	1	1	
Final League Position:	16						Sub							2		2				1		4			5		6			
Average Home League Attendance:	22706						League Goals								4	4	8	5	4		2	1	10				1			

FA CUP

Match No	Date		Opponents	Result	Scorers	Att	Sh	Wh	Ni	Wo	Sj	Ma	Fa	Sa	We	Bi	Gl	Pa	Cr	St	Wr	Ro	Mu	Wa	To	Jo	Le	Match No
1	Jan 13	A	Arsenal (3)	D 2-2	Worthington, Farrington / Kennedy, Armstrong	36433	1	2		4	5		7		9	8	11		6		10	3						1
2	17	H	Arsenal (3 rep)	L 1-2	Farrington / Radford, Kelly	32873	1	2		4			5	7		9	8*	11	6		10	3			12			2

FOOTBALL LEAGUE CUP

Match No	Date		Opponents	Result	Scorers	Att	Sh	Wh	Ni	Wo	Sj	Ma	Fa	Sa	We	Bi	Gl	Pa	Cr	St	Wr	Ro	Mu	Wa	To	Jo	Le	Match No
1	Sep 6	A	Norwich City (2)	L 1-2	Sammels / Bone 2	22498	1	2		4	3	5*	11	8	7				12	6	10	9						1

1972-73
Back: Woollett, Sjoberg, Yates, Stringfellow, Jopling, Munro, Manley, Matthews.
Middle: Coates (Trainer), Partridge, Birchenall, Jayes, Shilton, Wallington, Cross, Preston (Physio), Dewis (Coach), Smith (Secretary).
Front: Whitworth, Tomlin, Sammels, Shipman (Chairman), Weller, Bloomfield (Manager), Glover, Farrington, Nish.

Season 1973-74

Champions: Leeds United
Relegated: Southampton, Manchester United, Norwich City

FOOTBALL LEAGUE DIVISION ONE

No	Date	Opponents	Result	Pts	Pos	Scorers	Att	Shilton	Whitworth	Rofe	Stringfellow	Munro	Cross	Weller	Sammels	Worthington	Birchenall	Glover	Farrington	Partridge	Manley	Woollett	Jopling	Earle	Tomlin	Waters	Yates	Kruse	No
1	Aug 25 A	Ipswich Town	D 1-1	1	-	Sammels / Munro (og)	20116	1	2	3	4	5	6	7	8	9	10	11											1
2	28 A	Everton	D 1-1	2	-	Weller / Kenyon	33139	1	2	3	4	5	6	7	8	9	10	11											2
3	Sep 1 H	Liverpool	D 1-1	3	11	Birchenall / Toshack	29347	1	2	3	4	5	6	7	8	9	10	11											3
4	5 H	Manchester United	W 1-0	5	7	Worthington	29152	1	2	3	4	5	6	7	8	9	10	11											4
5	8 A	Arsenal	W 2-0	7	4	Glover, Stringfellow	28558	1	2	3	4	5	6	7	8	9	10	11											5
6	12 A	Manchester United	W 2-1	9	3	Weller, Stringfellow / Stepney (p)	40793	1	2	3	4	5	6	7	8	9	10	11											6
7	15 H	Manchester City	D 1-1	10	4	Weller / Bell	28466	1	2	3	4	5	6	7	8	9	10	11											7
8	22 A	West Ham United	D 1-1	11	5	Worthington / Robson	23567	1	2	3		5	6	7	8	9	10	11	4										8
9	29 H	Coventry City	L 0-2	11	6	- / Alderson, Cartwright	29319	1	2	3		5	6	7	8	9	10	11		4									9
10	Oct 6 H	Sheffield United	D 1-1	12	7	Weller / Woodward (p)	21589	1	2	3	4	5	6*	7	8	9	10	11	12										10
11	13 H	Leeds United	D 2-2	13	8	Worthington, Birchenall / Jones, Bremner	36978	1		3	4	5		7	8	9	10	11				6							11
12	20 A	Derby County	L 1-2	13	8	Worthington / McGovern, Hector	32203	1	2*	3	4	5		7	8	9	10	11	12			6							12
13	27 H	Southampton	L 0-1	13	11	- / Channon	18753	1		3	4	5	6	7	8	9	10	11				2							13
14	Nov 3 A	Norwich City	L 0-1	13	13	- / Rofe (og)	20565	1	2	3	4	5	6	7	8	9	10	11											14
15	10 H	Newcastle United	W 1-0	15	10	Weller	20726	1	2	3	4	5	6	7	8	9	10	11											15
16	17 H	Burnley	W 2-0	17	10	Glover, Stringfellow	21761	1	2	3	8	5	6	7	4	9	10	11											16
17	24 A	Birmingham City	L 0-3	17	10	- / B Latchford 3	27719	1	2	3	4*	5	6	7	8	9	10	11					12						17
18	Dec 1 A	Tottenham Hotspur	W 3-0	19	9	Glover 2, Earle	22088	1	2	3	12		6	7*	4	9	10	11				5		8					18
19	8 A	Chelsea	L 2-3	19	12	Worthington, Earle / Hollins 2 (2p), Osgood	20676	1	2	3	12	5	6	7	4	9	10	11						8*					19
20	15 H	Queens Park Rangers	W 2-0	21	10	Worthington, Glover	17614	1	2	3		5	6	7	8	9	10	11						4					20
21	22 H	Coventry City	W 2-1	23	5	Glover, Worthington / Cartwright	23324	1	2	3		5	6	7	8	9	10	11						4					21
22	26 H	Wolverhampton W.	D 2-2	24	8	Worthington 2 (1p) / Sunderland, Richards	30547	1	2	3		5	6	7	8	9	10	11						4					22
23	29 H	Arsenal	W 2-0	26	5	Worthington, Earle	25860	1	2	3		5	6	7	8	9	10*	11				12		4					23
24	Jan 1 A	Liverpool	D 1-1	27	4	Weller / Cormack	39110	1	2	3		5	6	7	8	9	10	11*				12		4					24
25	12 A	Manchester City	L 0-2	27	7	- / Marsh, Law	27488	1	2	3		5	6	7	8	9	10							4	11				25
26	19 H	Ipswich Town	W 5-0	29	4	Worthington 3 (2p), Munro, Beattie (og)	24280	1	2	3		5	6	7	8	9	10							4	11				26
27	Feb 2 A	Queens Park Rangers	D 0-0	30	5		22646	1	2	3		5	6	7	8	9	10	11						4					27
28	9 H	West Ham United	L 0-1	30	7	- / Best	27032	1	2	3		5	6	7	8	9	10	11						4					28
29	23 H	Sheffield United	D 1-1	31	7	Worthington / Salmons	24107	1	2	3	12	5	6	7	8	9	10*	11						4					29
30	26 A	Leeds United	D 1-1	32	6	Weller / Lorimer (p)	30489	1	2	3		5	6	7	8	9		11				10		4					30
31	Mar 2 H	Everton	W 2-1	34	6	Worthington, Earle / Latchford	22286	1	2	3	12	5	6	7	8	9		11				10*		4					31
32	16 H	Derby County	L 0-1	34	7	- / McFarland	30423	1	2	3	12	5	6	7	8	9								4	11*	10			32
33	18 A	Southampton	L 0-1	34	7	- / Stokes	26600	1	2	3	11	5	6	7	8	9								4		10			33
34	23 A	Newcastle United	D 1-1	35	8	Waters / McDermott (p)	32116	1	2	3*	11	5	6	7	8	9								4		10	12		34
35	Apr 6 H	Birmingham City	D 3-3	36	9	Cross, Glover 2 / Burns 3	28486	1	2	3		5	6	7	8	9		11						4		10			35
36	13 A	Burnley	D 0-0	37	9		18115	1	2	3		5	6	7	8	9		11						4		10			36
37	15 A	Stoke City	L 0-1	37	10	- / Hurst	21468	1	2	3		5	6	7*	8	9		11						4		10	12		37
38	16 H	Stoke City	D 1-1	38	9	Worthington / Hurst	21682	1	2	3		5	6	7	8	9		11						4		10			38
39	20 H	Chelsea	W 3-0	40	9	Worthington 2, Glover	22828	1	2	3		5	6	7		9	8	11						4		10			39
40	23 A	Wolverhampton W.	L 0-1	40	10	- / Sunderland	23574	1	2	3		5	6	7	8	9	10	11						4					40
41	27 A	Tottenham Hotspur	L 0-1	40	11	- / Chivers	20110	1	2	3			6	7	8	9	10	11						4				5	41
42	29 H	Norwich City	W 3-0	42	8	Worthington 2, Earle	16786	1	2	3	12		6	7	8	9	10							4	11*			5	42

								Shilton	Whitworth	Rofe	Stringfellow	Munro	Cross	Weller	Sammels	Worthington	Birchenall	Glover	Farrington	Partridge	Manley	Woollett	Jopling	Earle	Tomlin	Waters	Yates	Kruse	
Final League Position:		9				**League Appearances**		42	41	42	17	39	40	42	41	42	33	36	1	1		6		25	4	8		2	
Average Home League Attendance:		24825				**Sub**					6								2			2	1				2		
						League Goals					3	1	1	7	1	20	2	9						5		1			

FA CUP

No	Date	Opponents	Result		Scorers	Att	Shilton	Whitworth	Rofe	Stringfellow	Munro	Cross	Weller	Sammels	Worthington	Birchenall	Glover	Earle	Tomlin	Waters	No
1	Jan 5 H	Tottenham Hotspur (3)	W 1-0		Earle	28280	1	2	3	12	5	6	7	8	9	10		4	11*		1
2	26 A	Fulham (4)	D 1-1		Glover / Mullery	26105	1	2	3		5	6	7	8	9	10	11	4			2
3	30 H	Fulham (4 rep)	W 2-1 aet		Glover, Worthington / Barrett	37130	1	2	3		5	6	7	8	9	10	11	4			3
4	Feb 16 A	Luton Town (5)	W 4-0		Earle 2, Worthington, Weller	25712	1	2	3		5	6	7	8	9	10	11	4			4
5	Mar 9 A	Queens Park Rangers (6)	W 2-0		Waters 2	34078	1	2	3		5	6	7	8	9		11	4		10	5
6	30	Liverpool (sf)	D 0-0			60000	1	2	3		5	6	7	8	9		11	4		10	6
7	Apr 3	Liverpool (sf rep)	L 1-3		Glover / Hall, Keegan, Toshack	55619	1	2	3	10	5	6	7	8	9		11	4			7

FOOTBALL LEAGUE CUP

No	Date	Opponents	Result	Scorers	Att	Shilton	Whitworth	Rofe	Stringfellow	Munro	Cross	Weller	Sammels	Worthington	Birchenall	Glover	Farrington	Woollett	Jopling	No
1	Oct 8 H	Hull City (2)	D 3-3	Weller 2, Worthington / Wagstaff, Galvin, Whitworth (og)	9777	1	2*	3	4	5		7	8	9	10	11	12	6		1
2	31 A	Hull City (2 rep)	L 2-3	Stringfellow, Worthington / Pearson, Greenwood, de Vries	16003	1		3	4	5	6	7	8	9	10	11	12		2*	2

Note: Mar 30, at Old Trafford (Manchester United); Apr 3, at Villa Park (Aston Villa).

30 March: Joe Waters had made quite an impact in his debut, but he found Liverpool much stiffer opposition in the Semi-Final at Old Trafford. Here Ray Clemence and Phil Thompson combine to keep him out.

1973-74
Back: Rofe, Woollett, Kruse, Lee, Jopling, Yates, Tomlin, Farrington. **Middle:** Preston (Physio), Manley, Stringfellow, Jayes, Shilton, Wallington, Birchenall, Munro, Coates (Coach).
Front: Whitworth, Cross, Partridge, Bloomfield (Manager), Weller, Worthington, Sammels.

1974-75
Back: Rofe, Woollett, Kruse, Jayes, Yates, Tomlin, Earle, Waters. **Middle:** Coates (Coach), Stringfellow, Lee, Wallington, Shilton, Partridge, Munro, Preston (Physio).
Front: Glover, Cross, Whitworth, Smith (Secretary), Bloomfield (Manager), Weller, Worthington, Birchenall, Sammels.

OF FOSSILS & FOXES

Season 1974-75

Champions: Derby County
Relegated: Luton Town, Chelsea, Carlisle United

FOOTBALL LEAGUE DIVISION ONE

Match No	Date		Opponents	Result	Points	Position	Scorers	Att	Mark Wallington	Steve Whitworth	Dennis Rofe	Jon Sammels	Malcolm Munro	Graham Cross	Keith Weller	Steve Earle	Frank Worthington	Alan Birchenall	Len Glover	Joe Waters	Alan Woollett	Peter Shilton	Malcolm Partridge	Steve Yates	Mike Stringfellow	Carl Jayes	John Farmer	Bob Lee	David Tomlin	Jeff Blockley	Chris Garland	Match No
1	Aug 17	H	Arsenal	L 0-1	-	-	- / Kidd	26448	1	2	3	4	5	6	7	8	9	10	11													1
2	20	A	Birmingham City	W 4-3	2	-	Weller, Worthington 2, Rofe / Burns, Francis 2 (1p)	27961	1	2	3	4	5	6	7	8	9	10	11													2
3	24	A	Liverpool	L 1-2	2	14	Weller / Lindsay 2 (2p)	49398	1	2	3	4	5	6	7	8	9	10	11													3
4	27	H	Birmingham City	D 1-1	3	14	Worthington / Francis	24018	1	2	3	4	5	6	7	8	9	10	11													4
5	31	H	Carlisle United	D 1-1	4	15	Worthington (p) / McIlmoyle	20658	1	2	3	4	5	6	7	8*	9	10	11	12												5
6	Sep 7	A	Wolverhampton W.	D 1-1	5	14	Glover / Richards	20564	1	2	3	4	5		7	8	9	10	11		6											6
7	14	H	Queens Park Rangers	W 3-1	7	11	Worthington 2, Glover / Francis	19763	1	2	3	4	5		7	8	9	10	11		6											7
8	21	A	West Ham United	L 2-6	7	13	Worthington 2 (1p) / Gould 2, Jennings 2, Bonds, Robson	21377	1	2	3	4	5	12	7	8	9	10*	11		6											8
9	28	H	Coventry City	L 0-1	7	16	- / Holmes	21354		2	3	4	5	6	7	8	9		11		10	1										9
10	Oct 5	H	Luton Town	D 0-0	8	16		19024		2	3	4	5	12	7	8	9		11	10	6*	1										10
11	12	A	Derby County	L 0-1	8	19	- / Rioch	24753		2		4	5	6	7	8	9	10	11				1	3								11
12	19	H	Sheffield United	W 3-0	10	18	Worthington 2, Glover	18433		2		8	5	6	7	4	9	10	11				1	3								12
13	26	A	Newcastle United	W 1-0	12	16	Earle	34988		2	3*	8	5	6	7	4	9	10	11				1	12								13
14	Nov 2	H	Burnley	W 1-0	14	14	Sammels	19981	1	2		8	5	6	7	4	9	10	11					3								14
15	9	A	Chelsea	D 0-0	15	14		23915	1	2	3*	8	5	6	7	4	9	10	11					12								15
16	16	H	Tottenham Hotspur	L 1-2	15	14	Earle / Coates, Peters	23244	1	2		8	5	6	7	4	9	10	11					3*	12							16
17	23	A	Manchester City	L 1-4	15	18	Birchenall / Daniels 2, Bell, Tueart	31628	1	2		8	5	6*	7	4	9	10	11	12				3		1						17
18	30	A	Stoke City	L 0-1	15	19	- / Smith	29793		2		8	5	6	7	4	9	10	11					3	1							18
19	Dec 7	H	Everton	L 0-2	15	21	- / Hurst, Telfer	21451		2		8	5	6	7	4*	9	10	11					3	12	1						19
20	10	A	Middlesbrough	L 0-3	15	21	- / Foggon 2, Willey	22699		2		8	5	6	7	4	9	10	11					3		1						20
21	14	A	Arsenal	D 0-0	16	20		20849		2		8	5	6	7	4	9	10	11					3	1							21
22	20	H	Ipswich Town	L 0-1	16	20	- / Whymark	16636		2			5	6	7*	4	9	10	11	8				3	12	1						22
23	26	A	Queens Park Rangers	L 2-4	16	21	Lee 2 / Beck, Thomas, Givens, Westwood	17311		2		8	5	6		4	9	10	11		3					1	7					23
24	28	H	Leeds United	L 0-2	16	21	- / F Gray, McKenzie	29699		2		8	5	6			9	10	11	4	3					1	7					24
25	Jan 11	A	Everton	L 0-3	16	22	- / Jones, Lyons, Pearson	31985	1	2		8	5	6	7	4	9	10	11					3								25
26	18	H	Stoke City	D 1-1	17	21	Glover / Hurst	21736	1	2	3	8	5	6	7	4	9	10	11													26
27	Feb 1	H	Chelsea	D 1-1	18	21	Weller / Kember	23759	1	2	3	8		6	7	4	9	10	11											5		27
28	8	A	Burnley	L 0-2	18	22	- / Newton, Hankin	16352	1	2	3	8		6	7		9	10	11									4		5		28
29	22	A	Tottenham Hotspur	W 3-0	20	21	Stringfellow, Worthington, Sammels	20937	1	2	3	8		6	7		9	10							4			11		5		29
30	Mar 1	A	Carlisle United	W 1-0	22	20	Worthington	12676	1	2	3	8		6	7		9	10	11									4		5		30
31	8	H	Manchester City	W 1-0	24	20	Lee	23059	1	2	3	8		6	7	11*	9	10					12					4		5		31
32	15	A	Coventry City	D 2-2	25	19	Worthington, Lee / Green, Ferguson	23139	1	2	3	8		6	7		9	10										4		5	11	32
33	19	H	Liverpool	D 1-1	26	19	Worthington / Toshack	28012	1	2	3	8		6*	7		9	10					12					4		5	11	33
34	22	H	Wolverhampton W.	W 3-2	28	18	Garland 3 / Richards, Kindon	25070	1	2	3	8		6	7		9	10										4		5	11	34
35	29	A	Ipswich Town	L 1-2	28	20	Worthington / Viljoen, Woods	28745	1	2	3	8		6	7		9	10*	12									4		5	11	35
36	31	A	Leeds United	D 2-2	29	19	Lee, Garland / Clarke, Giles	29898	1	2	3	8		6	7		9	10	11*							12			5	4		36
37	Apr 1	H	West Ham United	W 3-0	31	18	Worthington (p), Garland 2	30408	1	2	3	8		6	7		9*	10	12									4		5	11	37
38	5	H	Newcastle United	W 4-0	33	17	Garland 2, Lee, Worthington	23638	1	2	3	8		6	7		9	10										4		5	11	38
39	9	H	Middlesbrough	W 1-0	35	15	Worthington	24531	1	2	3	8		6	7		9	10*		12								4		5	11	39
40	12	A	Luton Town	L 0-3	35	16	- / Alston, Husband, Weller (og)	18298	1	2	3	8		6*	7	12	9	10										4		5	11	40
41	19	H	Derby County	D 0-0	36	16		38143	1	2	3	8		6	7		9	10					12					4		5	11*	41
42	26	A	Sheffield United	L 0-4	36	18	- / Bradford, Flynn, Currie, Eddy (p)	28947	1	2	3	8		6	7	11*	9	10		12								4		5		42

Final League Position:	18	League Appearances	30	42	29	41	26	38	40	28	42	40	30	3	7	5	11	1	5	2	16		16	10
Average Home League Attendance:	23765	Sub						2		1				2	2	2		2	6		1			
		League Goals			1	2			3	2	18	1	4					1			6			8

FA CUP

1	Jan 4	H	Oxford United (3)	W 3-1			Worthington, Earle 2 / D Clarke	21643	1	2		8	5	6	7	4	9	10	11*				3					12				1
2	25	A	Leatherhead (4)	W 3-2			Sammels, Earle, Weller / McGillicuddy, Kelly	32090	1	2	3	8	5	6	7	4	9	10	11													2
3	Feb 15	A	Arsenal (5)	D 0-0				43841	1	2	3	8		6	7	4	9	10	11									5				3
4	19	H	Arsenal (5 rep)	D 1-1 aet			Birchenall / Radford	35009	1	2	3	8		6	7	4*	9	10	11				12					5				4
5	24	A	Arsenal (5 rep 2)	L 0-1 aet			- / Radford	39025	1	2	3	8		6	7	4*	9	10	11				12					5				5

FOOTBALL LEAGUE CUP

1	Sep 10	A	Arsenal (2)	D 1-1			Birchenall / Kidd	20788	1	2	3	4	5	6	7	8	9	10	11													1
2	18	H	Arsenal (2 rep)	W 2-1			Munro, Glover / Brady	17303	1	2	3	4	5		7	8	9	10	11		6											2
3	Oct 8	A	Middlesbrough (3)	L 0-1			- / Mills	23901		2	3*	4	5	6	7	8	9		11	10		1	12									3

Note: Jan 25, drawn away, but tie played at Filbert Street; Feb 24, tie staged at Filbert Street after toss of coin.

25 January: The cup tie against Leatherhead was a genuine classic. Steve Earle is seen here celebrating his equaliser, along with Graham Cross, as City came back from the brink against the Isthmian Leaguers.

Champions: Liverpool
Relegated: Wolverhampton Wanderers, Burnley, Sheffield United

FOOTBALL LEAGUE DIVISION ONE

Match No	Date		Opponents	Result	Points	Position	Scorers	Att	Mark Wallington	Steve Whitworth	Dennis Rofe	Jon Sammels	Jeff Blockley	Alan Birchenall	Steve Kember	Brian Alderson	Bob Lee	Chris Garland	David Tomlin	Steve Earle	Steve Sims	Graham Cross	Keith Weller	Frank Worthington	Alan Woollett	Steve Yates	Len Glover	Match No
1	Aug 16	H	Birmingham City	D 3-3	1	-	Sammels (p), Alderson, Roberts (og) / Hatton, Kendall 2 (1p)	25547	1	2	3	4	5	6	7	8	9	10	11*	12								1
2	20	A	Manchester City	D 1-1	2	-	Lee / Birchenall (og)	28557	1	2	3	10		6	4	7	9			11	8	5*	12					2
3	23	A	Newcastle United	L 0-3	2	16	- / Macdonald 2, Burns	36084	1	2	3	10		6	4	7	9	8*		5		12	11					3
4	27	H	Stoke City	D 1-1	3	18	Garland / Hudson	22878	1	2	3	10		6	4	8	11	5					7	9				4
5	30	H	Liverpool	D 1-1	4	18	Weller / Keegan	25008	1	2	3	10		6	4	12	8*	11		5			7	9				5
6	Sep 6	A	Arsenal	D 1-1	5	16	Sammels / Stapleton	22005	1	2	3	10		6	4	8	12	11		5*			7	9				6
7	13	H	West Ham United	D 3-3	6	17	Worthington, Sammels 2 / Bonds, Holland, Lampard	21413	1	2	3	10			4	8	11			5			7	9	6			7
8	20	A	Norwich City	L 0-2	6	18	- / MacDougall 2	22266	1	2	3	8			4	12	10*	11		5			7	9	6			8
9	23	A	Queens Park Rangers	L 0-1	6	19	- / Leach	19292	1	2	3	8			4		10	11		5			7	9	6			9
10	27	H	Coventry City	L 0-3	6	20	- / Craven, Cross 2	20411	1	2	3	8		6	4	11		10		5			7	9				10
11	Oct 4	A	Manchester United	D 0-0	7	20		47878	1	2	3	10			4	8		11		5			7	9	6			11
12	11	H	Middlesbrough	D 0-0	8	21		19095	1	2	3	10			4	8*	12	11		5			7	9	6			12
13	18	A	Ipswich Town	D 1-1	9	20	Lee / Whymark	23418	1	2	3	8	5		4	10	11						7	9	6			13
14	25	H	Tottenham Hotspur	L 2-3	9	20	Weller 2 / Coates, Perryman, Chivers	22088	1	2	3	10	5		4*	8	11	12					7	9	6			14
15	Nov 1	A	Everton	D 1-1	10	19	Lee / Smallman (p)	24930	1	2	3	8	5		4	10	11	9					7		6			15
16	8	H	Burnley	W 3-2	12	19	Weller, Kember, Garland / Noble (p), James	18344	1	2	3	8	5		4	10*	9	11					7	12	6			16
17	15	A	Sheffield United	W 2-1	14	17	Alderson, Rofe / Woodward	20165	1	2	3	8	5		4	10	12	9*					7	11	6			17
18	22	H	Ipswich Town	D 0-0	15	17		20115	1	2	3	8	5		4	10		9					7	11	6			18
19	29	A	Aston Villa	D 1-1	16	17	Worthington / Graydon	36388	1	2	3	10	5		4	8		11					7	9	6			19
20	Dec 6	A	Wolverhampton W.	W 2-0	18	17	Weller, Worthington	20012	1	2	3	8*	5		4	10	12	11					7	9	6			20
21	13	H	Newcastle United	W 1-0	20	14	Weller	18130	1	2	3		5	12	4	10	8	9*					7	11	6			21
22	20	A	Birmingham City	L 1-2	20	15	Lee / Withe, Francis (p)	21890	1	2	3		5		4	10	11					8	7	9	6			22
23	26	H	Derby County	W 2-1	22	14	Lee, Worthington / James	26870	1	2	3		5		4	10	8	9					7	11	6			23
24	27	A	Leeds United	L 0-4	22	15	- / Clarke, McKenzie 2, Lorimer	45139	1	2	3	4	5			8	10	9					7	11	6			24
25	Jan 10	A	West Ham United	D 1-1	23	16	Lee / A Taylor	24615	1	2	3	12	5		4	8	10	9*					7	11	6			25
26	17	A	Arsenal	W 2-1	25	15	Alderson, Lee / Ross	21331	1	2	3		5		4	10	8	9					7	11	6			26
27	31	H	Manchester City	W 1-0	27	13	Lee	21723	1	2	3		5		4	8	10	9					7	11	6			27
28	Feb 7	H	Stoke City	W 2-1	29	13	Worthington, Lee / Moores	21001	1	2	3	8	5		4	10	7	9						11	6			28
29	17	A	Burnley	L 0-1	29	13	- / Newton	13542	1	2	3	10	5		4		8	11					7	9	6			29
30	21	H	Sheffield United	D 1-1	30	11	Blockley / Woodward (p)	18698	1	2	3		5		4	10	8	11					7	9	6			30
31	25	H	Queens Park Rangers	L 0-1	30	12	- / Thomas	24340	1	2	3	12	5		4	10	8	11*					7	9	6			31
32	28	A	Tottenham Hotspur	D 1-1	31	11	Kember / Chivers	21427	1	2	3	11	5		4	10	8						7	9	6			32
33	Mar 6	H	Everton	W 1-0	33	11	Worthington	18490	1	2	3	8	5		4	10*	9						7	11	6		12	33
34	13	A	Middlesbrough	W 1-0	35	8	Boam (og)	17634	1	2	3	10	5		4	8	9						7	11	6			34
35	20	A	Aston Villa	W 2-1	36	10	Nicholl 2 (2 og) / Nicholl 2	24663	1	2	3	8	5		4	10	9						7	11	6			35
36	27	A	Wolverhampton W.	D 2-2	37	9	Sammels (p), Worthington / Hibbitt, Richards	18113	1*	2	3	8	5		4	10	9	12					7	11	6			36
37	Apr 3	A	Coventry City	W 2-0	39	8	Weller, Lee	18135	1	2	3	8	5		4	10	9						7	11	6			37
38	6	A	Liverpool	L 0-1	39	8	- / Keegan	36290	1	2	3	11	5		4	10	8						7	9	6			38
39	10	H	Norwich City	D 0-0	40	9		19856	1	2	3	11	5		4	10*	8						7	9	6		12	39
40	17	A	Derby County	D 2-2	41	9	Alderson, Garland / F Lee 2	30085	1	2	3		5		4	8	9	10					7	11	6			40
41	20	H	Leeds United	W 2-1	43	8	Worthington 2 / McKenzie	24240	1	2	3		5		4	10	8	11					7	9	6			41
42	24	H	Manchester United	W 2-1	45	7	Lee, Garland / Coyne	31053	1	2	3		5		4	10	8	11					7	9	6			42

									Mark Wallington	Steve Whitworth	Dennis Rofe	Jon Sammels	Jeff Blockley	Alan Birchenall	Steve Kember	Brian Alderson	Bob Lee	Chris Garland	David Tomlin	Steve Earle	Steve Sims	Graham Cross	Keith Weller	Frank Worthington	Alan Woollett	Steve Yates	Len Glover
Final League Position:	7						League Appearances		42	42	42	31	31	7	41	37	34	28	2	3	10	1	38	38	35		
Average Home League Attendance:	22049						Sub			2		1		2	4	2			1		1	1	1			2	
							League Goals					1	5		1	2	4	11			4		7	9			

FA CUP

	Date		Opponents	Result			Scorers	Att	MW	WHI	ROF		BLO		KEM	ALD	LEE	GAR					WEL	WOR	WOO			
1	Jan 3	H	Sheffield United (3)	W 3-0			Garland 3	24052	1	2	3		5		4	10	8	9					7	11	6			1
2	24	H	Bury (4)	W 1-0			Lee	27331	1	2	3		5		4	8	10	9					7	11	6			2
3	Feb 14	H	Manchester United (5)	L 1-2			Lee / Daly, Macari	34000	1	2	3	12	5		4	10*	8	9					7	11	6			3

FOOTBALL LEAGUE CUP

	Date		Opponents	Result			Scorers	Att	MW	WHI	ROF	SAM		BIR	KEM	ALD	LEE	GAR			SIM	CRO	WEL	WOR	WOO	YAT		
1	Sep 9	A	Portsmouth (2)	D 1-1			Garland / Eames	10629	1	2	3	10			4		8	11				5	7	9	6			1
2	17	H	Portsmouth (2 rep)	W 1-0 aet			Sammels	11055	1	2		10		6	4	12	8	11	9*			5	7			3		2
3	Oct 8	A	Lincoln City (3)	W 2-1			Weller, Sammels (p) / Smith	17060	1	2	3	10			4	8		11				5	7	9	6			3
4	Nov 11	A	Burnley (4)	L 0-2			- / Morgan (p), Hankin	15113	1	2	3*	8	5		4	10	11	9					7	12	6			4

Dismissals: Aug 16, Garland, Birmingham City (h).
Stand-in Goalkeepers: Mar 27, Weller and Alderson for Wallington, Wolverhampton Wanderers (a).

14 February: Despite a battling performance and two disallowed goals, City's Wembley hopes were dashed by Manchester United in Round Five. Here Bob Lee and Jon Sammels attempt to pierce the United rearguard, with Frank Worthington in close attendance.

1975-76
Back: Waters, Kember, Platt, Woollett, Trice, Tomlin, Earle, Rofe, Wilcox, Alderson.
Middle: Coates (Trainer), Carr, Sims, Lee, Plumley, Wallington, Jayes, Jackson, Shotton, Yates, Everitt (Trainer).
Front: Preston (Physio), Glover, Whitworth, Worthington, Smith (Secretary), Bloomfield (Manager), Sammels, Blockley, Birchenall, Weller, Garland, Shaw (Chief Scout).
On Ground: White, Bicknell, Bennett, Concannon, Williams, Green, May, Welsh, Langham, Steel, Gould, Smith, Warren.

1976-77
Back: Kember, Rofe, Gould, Coates (Coach), Williams, Hoult, Wilcox, Alderson. **Middle:** Everitt (Coach), Trice, Green, Wallington, Sims, Jayes, Yates, Tomlin, Preston (Physio).
Front: Garland, Woollett, Whitworth, Lee, Blockley, Bloomfield (Manager), Sammels, Birchenall, Weller, Earle.

Champions: Liverpool
Relegated: Sunderland, Stoke City, Tottenham Hotspur

FOOTBALL LEAGUE DIVISION ONE

Match No	Date	Opponents	Result	Points	Position	Scorers	Att	Mark Wallington	Steve Whitworth	Dennis Rofe	Steve Kember	Jeff Blockley	Alan Woollett	Keith Weller	Brian Alderson	Frank Worthington	Bob Lee	Chris Garland	Alan Birchenall	Steve Earle	Jon Sammels	Steve Sims	Steve Yates	Winston White	Larry May	Steve Bicknell	Peter Welsh	Match No
1	Aug 21 H	Manchester City	D 2-2	1	-	Alderson, Garland / Royle, Tueart	22612	1	2	3	4	5	6	7	8	9	10	11										1
2	24 A	Sunderland	D 0-0	2	-		36668	1	2	3	4	5	6	7	8	9	10	11										2
3	28 A	West Ham United	D 0-0	3	13		24960	1	2	3	4*	5	6	7	8	9	10	11	12									3
4	Sep 4 H	Everton	D 1-1	4	13	Worthington / Latchford	18083	1	2	3	4	5	6	7	8	9	10	11										4
5	11 A	Ipswich Town	D 0-0	5	11		19610	1	2	3	4	5	6	7	8*	9		11	12	10								5
6	18 H	Queens Park Rangers	D 2-2	6	13	Rofe, Garland / Givens, Hollins	18439	1	2	3	4	5	6	7		9		11	12	10*	8							6
7	25 A	Aston Villa	L 0-2	6	16	- / Graydon (p), Gray	36652	1	2	3	4	5	6	7		9		11		10	8							7
8	29 H	Stoke City	W 1-0	8	10	Worthington	15391	1	2	3	4	5	6	7		9		11	12	10	8*							8
9	Oct 2 H	Coventry City	D 1-1	9	9	Worthington / Ferguson	20957	1	2	3	4	5	6	7		9		11	12	10*	8							9
10	16 A	Bristol City	W 1-0	11	10	Worthington	20102	1	2	3	4		6	7	8	9		11		10		5						10
11	23 H	Arsenal	W 4-1	13	8	Weller 2, Earle, Worthington (p) / Stapleton	19351	1	2	3	4		6	7	10	9				11	8	5						11
12	27 A	Liverpool	L 0-1	13	8	- / Toshack	29384	1	2	3	4		6	7	10*	9			12	11	8	5						12
13	30 A	Middlesbrough	W 1-0	15	8	Worthington	24288	1	2	3	4		6	7	8	9			12	11*	10	5						13
14	Nov 6 H	Norwich City	D 1-1	16	6	Worthington / Boyer	17781	1	2	3	4		6	7	10	9				11	8	5						14
15	9 A	Liverpool	L 1-5	16	6	Worthington / Heighway, Toshack, Neal (p), Jones, Keegan (p)	39851	1	2	3	4		6	7	10	9				11	8	5						15
16	20 H	Manchester United	D 1-1	17	6	Garland / Daly	26421	1	2	3	4*		6	7	8	9			12	11	10	5						16
17	27 A	Leeds United	D 2-2	18	6	Worthington, Earle / Lorimer, McNiven	29713	1	2	3	4	5		7	8	9				11	10	6						17
18	Dec 4 H	Birmingham City	L 2-6	18	7	Kember, Worthington (p) / Emmanuel, Francis, Burns 3, Rofe (og)	20388	1	2	3	4	5		7	10	9			12	11*	8	6						18
19	11 A	West Bromwich Albion	D 2-2	19	8	Weller, Sims / Treacy, Cross	19049	1	2	3	4	5		7*	8	9			12	11	10	6						19
20	18 H	Tottenham Hotspur	W 2-1	21	7	Blockley, Earle / Coates	16397	1	2	3	4	5		7	10	9				11	8	6						20
21	27 A	Derby County	L 0-1	21	9	- / James	32892	1	2	3	4	5		7	10	9				11	8	6						21
22	Jan 1 A	Norwich City	L 2-3	21	9	Sammels, Earle / Busby 3	21531	1	2	3	4	5		7	10	9				11	8	6						22
23	15 H	Sunderland	W 2-0	23	8	Alderson, Earle	16051	1	2	3	4	5		7	10*	9			12	11	8	6						23
24	22 A	Manchester City	L 0-5	23	9	- / Kidd 4, Doyle	37609	1	2	3	4	5		7	10	9				11	8	6						24
25	Feb 5 H	West Ham United	W 2-0	25	9	Worthington, Weller	16201	1	2	3	4	5		7	10*	9			12	11	8	6						25
26	12 A	Everton	W 2-1	27	8	Earle, Alderson / Latchford	28024	1	2	3	4	5		7	10	9				11	8	6						26
27	19 H	Ipswich Town	W 1-0	29	7	Earle	21134	1	2	3	4	5		7	10	9				11	8	6						27
28	26 A	Queens Park Rangers	L 2-3	29	7	Earle, Sammels / Givens, Hollins, Francis (p)	20356	1	2	3	4	5		7	10	9				11	8	6						28
29	Mar 5 H	Aston Villa	D 1-1	30	9	Sammels (p) / Deehan	22038	1	2	3	4	5		7	10	9				11	8	6						29
30	12 H	Coventry City	W 3-1	32	7	Alderson, Earle, Worthington / Ferguson	16766	1	2	3	4		6	7	8	9				10	11	5						30
31	15 H	Middlesbrough	D 3-3	33	6	Worthington, Kember, Earle / Craggs, Mills, Wood	13483	1	2	3	4		6	7*	10	9			12	11	8	6						31
32	19 H	Stoke City	W 1-0	35	6	Worthington	14087	1	2	3	4*	5			10	9				11	8	6		7		12		32
33	26 H	Bristol City	D 0-0	36	6		16454	1	2	3*	4	5			10	9				11	8		6	7		12		33
34	Apr 2 A	Arsenal	L 0-3	36	7	- / Rix, O'Leary 2	23013	1	2	3	4	5			10	9				11	8	6		7				34
35	9 A	Newcastle United	D 0-0	37	8		32300	1	2	3	4		6		10	9					8	5		7		11		35
36	12 H	Derby County	D 1-1	38	7	Alderson / Powell	22393	1	2	3	4	5		7	10	9					8	6				11		36
37	16 A	Manchester United	D 1-1	39	8	Earle / J Greenhoff	49161	1	2	3	4		6	7	10	9					8	5				11		37
38	30 A	Birmingham City	D 1-1	40	9	Earle / Kendall	20836	1	2	3	4		6	7	10	9					8	5				11		38
39	May 4 H	Newcastle United	W 1-0	42	8	Earle	14289	1	2	3	4		6	7	10	9					8	5				11		39
40	7 H	West Bromwich Albion	L 0-5	42	9	- / Martin 2, Cross, Cunningham, T Brown	18139	1	2	3	4*		6	7	10	9					8	5			12	11		40
41	14 A	Tottenham Hotspur	L 0-2	42	9	- / Pratt, Holmes	26094	1	2	3			6	7	10	9		11			8	5				4		41
42	16 H	Leeds United	L 0-1	42	10	- / F Gray	13642	1	2	3			6	7	10	9		11*			8	5			4		12	42

								Mark Wallington	Steve Whitworth	Dennis Rofe	Steve Kember	Jeff Blockley	Alan Woollett	Keith Weller	Brian Alderson	Frank Worthington	Bob Lee	Chris Garland	Alan Birchenall	Steve Earle	Jon Sammels	Steve Sims	Steve Yates	Winston White	Larry May	Steve Bicknell	Peter Welsh	
Final League Position:	11					League Appearances		42	42	42	40	21	30	30	37	41	4	14	11	29	34	32	1	4	1	6	1	
Average Home League Attendance:	18806					Sub												2	1	6	4		3		1			
						League Goals				1	2	1		4	5	14		3		13	3	1						

FA CUP

Match No	Date	Opponents	Result	Points	Position	Scorers	Att	Mark Wallington	Steve Whitworth	Dennis Rofe	Steve Kember	Jeff Blockley	Alan Woollett	Keith Weller	Brian Alderson	Frank Worthington	Bob Lee	Chris Garland	Alan Birchenall	Steve Earle	Jon Sammels	Steve Sims						Match No
1	Jan 8 H	Aston Villa (3)	L 0-1			- / Gray	27112	1	2	3	4	5		7	10	9				11	8	6						1

FOOTBALL LEAGUE CUP

Match No	Date	Opponents	Result	Points	Position	Scorers	Att	Mark Wallington	Steve Whitworth	Dennis Rofe	Steve Kember	Jeff Blockley	Alan Woollett	Keith Weller	Brian Alderson	Frank Worthington	Bob Lee	Chris Garland										Match No
1	Sep 1 A	Wrexham (2)	L 0-1			- / Davies	9776	1	2	3	4	5	6	7	8	9	10	11										1

28 August: Frank Worthington puts West Ham's Billy Bonds under pressure at Upton Park during City's frustrating six-game drawn sequence that began the campaign. Alan Woollett looks on.

Season 1977-78

Champions: Nottingham Forest
Relegated: West Ham United, Newcastle United, Leicester City

FOOTBALL LEAGUE DIVISION ONE

Player columns (left to right): Mark Wallington, Steve Whitworth, Dennis Rofe, Eddie Kelly, Steve Sims, Alan Woollett, Brian Alderson, Steve Kember, Frank Worthington, Jon Sammels, Steve Earle, Jeff Blockley, Keith Weller, Larry May, Dean Smith, Lammie Robertson, Alan Waddle, George Armstrong, Dave Webb, Tommy Williams, Geoff Salmons, Winston White, Roger Davies, Mark Goodwin, Kevin Farmer, Billy Hughes, Nev Hamilton, Trevor Christie, Derek Dawkins.

Match No	Date		Opponents	Result		Points	Position	Scorers	Att
1	Aug 20	A	Manchester City	D 0-0		1	-		45963
2	24	H	West Ham United	W 1-0		3	-	Kember	18310
3	27	H	Bristol City	D 0-0		4	9		17011
4	Sep 3	A	Queens Park Rangers	L 0-3		4	13	- / Givens, Francis, Needham	14516
5	10	H	Everton	L 1-5		4	16	Sims / King 2, Latchford, McKenzie, Thomas	16425
6	17	A	Arsenal	L 1-2		4	19	Worthington / Stapleton, Macdonald	27371
7	24	A	Nottingham Forest	L 0-3		4	20	- / O'Neill, Woodcock, Robertson (p)	21447
8	Oct 1	A	Wolverhampton W.	L 0-3		4	21	- / Richards 3	20009
9	5	A	Chelsea	D 0-0		5	20		19575
10	8	H	Aston Villa	L 0-2		5	21	- / Cowans, Gray	20276
11	15	H	Coventry City	L 1-2		5	21	Sammels (p) / Coop 2 (2p)	20205
12	22	A	Norwich City	L 0-2		5	21	- / Ryan, Gibbins	17684
13	29	H	Leeds United	D 0-0		6	21		20128
14	Nov 5	A	West Bromwich Albion	L 0-2		6	22	- / T Brown, Cross	20082
15	12	H	Ipswich Town	W 2-1		8	21	Williams, Salmons / Talbot	13779
16	19	A	Birmingham City	D 1-1		9	21	Waddle / Francis	21208
17	26	H	Liverpool	L 0-4		9	21	- / Fairclough, Heighway, Dalglish, McDermott	26051
18	Dec 3	A	Newcastle United	L 0-2		9	21	- / Burns, Nattrass	20112
19	10	H	Derby County	D 1-1		10	22	Kelly / Hughes	21199
20	17	A	Ipswich Town	L 0-1		10	22	- / Whymark	16905
21	26	H	Middlesbrough	D 0-0		11	22		18476
22	27	A	Manchester United	L 1-3		11	22	Goodwin / Coppell, J Greenhoff, Hill	57396
23	31	A	West Ham United	L 2-3		11	22	Kember, Sims / Cross, Hales, McDowell	25455
24	Jan 2	H	Manchester City	L 0-1		11	22	- / Owen	24041
25	14	A	Bristol City	D 0-0		12	22		19704
26	21	H	Queens Park Rangers	D 0-0		13	22		16288
27	Feb 4	A	Everton	L 0-2		13	22	- / Latchford 2	33707
28	11	H	Arsenal	D 1-1		14	22	Williams / Brady (p)	15780
29	25	H	Wolverhampton W.	W 1-0		16	21	Goodwin	15763
30	Mar 4	A	Aston Villa	D 0-0		17	21		29971
31	11	A	Coventry City	L 0-1		17	21	- / Nardiello	24421
32	14	A	Nottingham Forest	L 0-1		17	21	- / Robertson (p)	32355
33	18	H	Norwich City	D 2-2		18	22	Williams, Davies / Ryan 2	13077
34	25	H	Manchester United	L 2-3		18	22	Smith, Salmons / J Greenhoff, Hill, Pearson	20299
35	27	A	Middlesbrough	W 1-0		20	21	Hughes	15534
36	28	A	Leeds United	L 1-5		20	21	Davies (p) / Hankin, F Gray, E Gray 3	21145
37	Apr 1	H	West Bromwich Albion	L 0-1		20	21	- / T Brown	14637
38	8	H	Liverpool	L 2-3		20	22	Hughes (p), White / Smith 2, Lee	42979
39	15	H	Birmingham City	L 1-4		20	22	Salmons / Hibbitt, Pendrey, Bertschin, Francis	15431
40	22	A	Derby County	L 1-4		20	22	Davies / George 2, Rioch, Buckley	18829
41	26	H	Chelsea	L 0-2		20	22	- / R Wilkins, Walker	12970
42	29	H	Newcastle United	W 3-0		22	22	Goodwin, Davies, Salmons	11530

Final League Position:	22	
Average Home League Attendance:	17768	

League Appearances: 42 34 33 24 28 12 13 26 7 19 6 7 23 3 8 6 11 11 29 31 25 5 14 14 1 18 4 5 3
Sub: 1 1 1 1 2 2 1 1 2 2 1 1 1 1 1 1 4
League Goals: 1 2 2 1 1 1 1 3 4 1 4 3 2

FA CUP

1	Jan 7	A	Hull City (3)	W 1-0	Armstrong		12374
2	28	A	Walsall (4)	L 0-1	- / Evans		17421

FOOTBALL LEAGUE CUP

1	Aug 30	A	Portsmouth (2)	L 0-2	- / Kemp, Green		13842

1977-78
Back: Alderson, Bicknell, Earle, Williams, Kelly, Kember, White.
Middle: MacFarlane (Asst Manager), Welsh, Wallington, Sims, May, Jayes, Yates, Peacock (Physio).
Front: Sammels, Worthington, Blockley, Smith (Secretary), McLintock (Manager), Rofe, Whitworth, Weller, Woollett.

Season 1978-79

Promoted: Crystal Palace, Brighton & Hove Albion, Stoke City
Relegated: Sheffield United, Millwall, Blackburn Rovers

FOOTBALL LEAGUE DIVISION TWO

Match No	Date		Opponents	Result	Points	Position	Scorers	Att	Wallington	Whitworth	Rofe	Kelly	O'Neill	Webb	Armstrong	Williams	Davies	Hughes	Christie	Goodwin	Kember	May	Sims	Weller	Duffy	White	Welsh	Henderson	Ridley	Reed	Lineker	Buchanan	Smith	Peake	Grewcock	Carr	Lee	Match No
1	Aug 19	A	Burnley	D 2-2	1	-	Hughes (p), Christie / Noble (p), Fletcher	12048	1	2	3	4	5	6	7	8	9	10	11*	12																		1
2	23	H	Sheffield United	L 0-1	1	-	- / Matthews	19381	1	2	3	4	5	6	11	8	10*	7	9	12																		2
3	26	H	Cambridge United	D 1-1	2	16	Christie / Biley	14148	1	2	3	4	5	6	7	8	9	10	11*	12																		3
4	Sep 2	A	Wrexham	D 0-0	3	16		12785	1						12	10*	9	11	8	7	4	5																4
5	9	H	Notts County	L 0-1	3	19	- / Vinter	14485	1	2	3	6		12		9		8	4	5	7	10	11*															5
6	16	A	Blackburn Rovers	D 1-1	4	19	Weller / Bradford	7908	1	2	3	10			9	11		8	6	5	7	4*		12														6
7	23	H	Brighton & Hove Albion	W 4-1	6	14	Christie, Hughes 2 (1p), Weller / Williams	14307	1	2	3	6*			11	9		8	4	5	7	10		12														7
8	30	A	Orient	W 1-0	8	11	Christie	5430	1	2	3	6			9	10		8	4	5	11			7														8
9	Oct 7	A	Newcastle United	L 0-1	8	13	- / Walker	25731	1	2	3	6		12	9	11		8	4	5	7			10*														9
10	14	H	Charlton Athletic	L 0-3	8	17	- / Flanagan 2, Brisley	14278	1	2	3	6		10	11	9		8	4	5	7*			12														10
11	21	A	Cardiff City	L 0-1	8	18	- / Stevens	8791	1	2	3	6			10	9	12	8*	4	5	7			11														11
12	28	H	Bristol Rovers	D 0-0	9	18		12498	1	2	3	6			11*	9			5		7	12		10	4													12
13	Nov 4	A	Luton Town	W 1-0	11	16	Christie	10608	1	2	3	6			4	11	9		5		7		12	10*	8													13
14	11	H	Burnley	W 2-1	13	15	Weller, Christie / Ingham	12842	1	2	3	6			4	11	9		5		7			10	8													14
15	18	A	Cambridge United	D 1-1	14	16	Henderson / Finney	8875	1	2	3	6	5		11	9			4		7			10	8													15
16	22	A	Wrexham	D 1-1	15	15	Christie / Thomas	14734	1	2	3	6	4		11	9*			7		5			10	8			12										16
17	25	H	West Ham United	L 1-2	15	17	Christie / Cross 2	16149	1	2	3	6	5		11	9	12		4		7			10*	8													17
18	Dec 2	H	Stoke City	D 0-0	16	14		15950	1	2	3	6	5		11	9			4		7			10	8													18
19	16	A	Crystal Palace	L 1-3	16	18	May / Cannon, Swindlehurst, Elwiss	17330	1	2	3		4	10		9	6		5		7			11	8													19
20	23	H	Preston North End	D 1-1	17	18	Davies / Bruce	10481	1	2	3		5	10		9	7		4		6			11	8													20
21	26	A	Sunderland	D 1-1	18	18	Henderson / Clarke	24544	1	2	3	6	4	10		9*	7		5		12			11	8													21
22	Jan 1	A	Oldham Athletic	W 2-0	20	16	Buchanan, Smith	12757	1	2	3	4				8	5							9	6			7	10			11						22
23	20	H	Blackburn Rovers	D 1-1	21	16	May / Garner	13234	1	2	3	6				12	5		7					10	4			11*	9			8						23
24	Feb 3	A	Brighton & Hove Albion	L 1-3	21	17	Davies / Maybank, Sayer, Ward	19973	1	2	3	4	6	10			5		9					8*				12	11			7						24
25	10	H	Orient	W 5-3	23	16	Smith, Buchanan, May, Williams, Goodwin / Chiedozie 2, Kitchen	12050	1	2	3	4	6			12	8		5					10*				11	9			7						25
26	17	H	Newcastle United	W 2-1	25	11	Peake, Buchanan / Nattrass	15106	1	2	3	5	6			12	8		4					10*				11	9			7						26
27	24	A	Charlton Athletic	L 0-1	25	14	- / Peacock (p)	7936	1	2	3	6	4				11		5					9				10	8			7						27
28	Mar 3	A	Cardiff City	L 1-2	25	16	Grewcock / Dwyer, Stevens	12820	1		3	6	4				2		5					9	12			11	10			7*	8					28
29	10	A	Bristol Rovers	D 1-1	26	16	Smith (p) / Williams	6381	1	2	3	5	4			11*	7		6					9	12			8	10									29
30	21	H	Fulham	W 1-0	28	14	Buchanan	10396	1	2*	3	8	4	6					7					9				10	11	12								30
31	28	H	Luton Town	W 3-0	30	12	May, Smith, Williams	10465	1		3	6	4	8					2					9	12			10*	11	7								31
32	31	H	West Ham United	D 1-1	31	12	Henderson / Robson	23992	1		3	6	4	8					2					9	12			10*	11	7								32
33	Apr 4	A	Millwall	L 0-2	31	12	- / Kitchener, Walker	4758	1		3	6	4	8					2					9	12			10	11	7*								33
34	7	H	Stoke City	D 1-1	32	13	Buchanan / Busby	17502	1		3	8	5	4					12	2	6			9				10*	11	7								34
35	14	H	Sunderland	L 1-2	32	13	Henderson / Docherty, Brown	20740	1		3	8	5	4		12			2	6				9				10*	11	7								35
36	16	A	Oldham Athletic	L 1-2	32	15	Smith / Hicks, Williams (og)	7179	1		3	6	4	8					2		5			9	12			10*	11	7								36
37	17	A	Preston North End	L 0-4	32	15	- / Robinson, Bruce 2, Coleman	10394	1		3	6*	5	10		8	9		2					12	4			7			11							37
38	20	H	Crystal Palace	D 1-1	33	14	Smith / Hinshelwood	16767	1		3			2			4		5					12				9	6		7	10	11*	8				38
39	24	A	Notts County	W 1-0	35	12	Lineker	8702	1		3*	4		2		8			5					12				9	6		7	10		11				39
40	28	A	Fulham	L 0-3	35	12	- / Strong, Davies 2	7002	1	2	3*	8				5			6					9	4			7				12		11				40
41	May 5	H	Millwall	D 0-0	36	15		12828	1			5				2								6*		4	9	12	8	10		7		3	11			41
42	8	A	Sheffield United	D 2-2	37	15	Peake, Duffy / Benjamin 2 (2p)	15178	1			4				6				2		5			10			9			7	12		8*		3	11	42

									Wallington	Whitworth	Rofe	Kelly	O'Neill	Webb	Armstrong	Williams	Davies	Hughes	Christie	Goodwin	Kember	May	Sims	Weller	Duffy	White	Welsh	Henderson	Ridley	Reed	Lineker	Buchanan	Smith	Peake	Grewcock	Carr	Lee	
Final League Position:	17						**League Appearances**		42	29	39	27	23	3	3	32	8	18	23	23	8	36	8	16	7	1	4	31	17		7	17	17	17	1	2	3	
Average Home League Attendance:	14187						**Sub**					3			1	3	5	1			4	1	2	2	7	1		2			1					1		
							League Goals					2	2	3	8	1		4			3	1		1	5	6	2	1										

FA CUP

	Date		Opponents	Result	Scorers	Att	Wallington	Whitworth	Rofe	Kelly	O'Neill	Webb	Armstrong	Williams	Davies	Hughes	Christie	Goodwin	Kember	May	Sims	Weller	Duffy	White	Welsh	Henderson	Ridley	Reed	Lineker	Buchanan	Smith	Peake	Grewcock	Carr	Lee	
1	Jan 6	H	Norwich City (3)	W 3-0	May, Weller, Henderson	19680	1	2			6			3			10		5	7		9	4			11			8							1
2	Feb 26	A	Oldham Athletic (4)	L 1-3	Henderson / Young 3	11972	1	2	3	12	4			8			7		5			9	6			11*	10									2

FOOTBALL LEAGUE CUP

	Date		Opponents	Result	Scorers	Att	Wallington	Whitworth	Rofe	Kelly	O'Neill	Webb	Armstrong	Williams	Davies	Hughes	Christie	Goodwin	Kember	May	Sims	Weller	Duffy	White	Welsh	Henderson	Ridley	Reed	Lineker	Buchanan	Smith	Peake	Grewcock	Carr	Lee	
1	Aug 30	H	Derby County (2)	L 0-1	- / Hill	18827	1	2	3	6			11	10	12	7	9*	8		4	5															1

Dismissals: Apr 16, May, Oldham Athletic (a); May 8, Carr, Sheffield United (a).

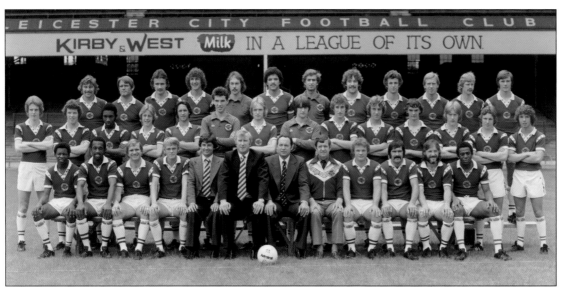

1978-79
Back: Salmons, Webb, Christie, Davies, Wallington, May, Rafter, Sims, Farmer, Whitworth, Williams, O'Neill.
Middle: Convey, Parsons, Carr, Buchanan, Lineker, Eason, Duffy, Hobby, Ratcliffe, Peake, Smith, Rowan, Grewcock, Reed.
Front: Hamilton, Dawkins, Kelly, Grewcock, Smith (Secretary), Wallace (Manager), MacFarlane (Asst Manager), McVey (Physio), Rofe, Hughes, Armstrong, White.

Champions: Leicester City, Sunderland, Birmingham City
Relegated: Fulham, Burnley, Charlton Athletic

FOOTBALL LEAGUE DIVISION TWO

Match No	Date		Opponents	Result		Points	Position	Scorers	Att	Mark Wallington	Tommy Williams	Everton Carr	Gregor Stevens	Larry May	Ian Wilson	Pat Byrne	Eddie Kelly	Alan Young	Martin Henderson	Bobby Smith	Dennis Rofe	Andy Peake	Mark Goodwin	Alan Lee	John O'Neill	Derek Strickland	Peter Welsh	Gary Lineker	Mick Duffy	Dave Buchanan	Geoff Scott	Paul Edmunds	Match No
1	Aug 18	H	Watford	W	2-0	2	-	Young 2	15772	1	2		4	5	6	7	8*	9	10	11	3	12											1
2	21	A	Cambridge United	D	1-1	3	-	Young / Finney	6042	1	2		4	5	6*	7		9	10		3	8	12	11									2
3	25	A	Queens Park Rangers	W	4-1	5	1	Peake 2, May, Goodwin / Allen (p)	13091	1	2		4	5		7	6	9	10		3	8	12	11*									3
4	Sep 1	H	Luton Town	L	1-3	5	3	May / Moss 2 (1p), Hill	16241	1	2		4	5		7	6	10	9		3	8	12	11*									4
5	8	H	Notts County	W	1-0	7	3	Young	16595	1	2		5			7	10	9	8	11	3*	4	12		6								5
6	15	A	Newcastle United	L	2-3	7	5	Smith 2 (1p) / Cartwright, Shoulder 2 (2p)	26443	1	2		5			7	10	9	8*	11	3	4	12		6								6
7	22	H	Fulham	D	3-3	8	5	Young 2, Smith / Davies 3	14875	1			5			7*	10	9	8	11	3	4	2		6	12							7
8	29	A	Swansea City	W	2-0	10	3	Rofe 2	15104	1	2		5			7	10	9	8*	11	3	4	12		6								8
9	Oct 6	A	Shrewsbury Town	D	2-2	11	4	Goodwin, Byrne / Chapman, King	9045	1	2		5	10	7		9			11	3	6	8		4								9
10	10	H	Cambridge United	W	2-1	13	5	Young, Wilson / Gibbins	15960	1	2		5	10	7		9	12	11		3	4	8*		6								10
11	13	A	West Ham United	L	1-2	13	6	Williams / Cross, Martin	22472	1	2		5	10	7*		9	8	11	3	4							6	12				11
12	20	A	Oldham Athletic	D	1-1	14	6	Young / Holt	10297	1	2		5	8*	7		9	11	10	3	6							4	12				12
13	27	H	Sunderland	W	2-1	16	6	Lineker 2 / Lee	19365	1	2		5				10	9	8	11	3	4						6	7				13
14	Nov 3	A	Watford	W	3-1	18	5	Smith 2 (1p), Peake / Pollard	14743	1	2		5				10	9*	8	11	3	4						6	7	12			14
15	10	H	Burnley	D	1-1	19	5	Young / James	17191	1	2		4				8*	9	11	10	3	6	12		5			7					15
16	17	A	Preston North End	D	1-1	20	5	Lineker / Bruce	10038	1	2		5	12			8*	9	11	10	3	6			4			7					16
17	24	H	Wrexham	W	2-0	22	5	Strickland, Henderson	15316	1	2		4	12	8		9*	11	10	3					5	6		7					17
18	Dec 1	A	Birmingham City	W	2-1	24	4	Smith, Henderson / Gallagher	25748	1	2		5		4		9	8	11	3					6	10*	12	7					18
19	8	H	Orient	D	2-2	25	3	Henderson, Goodwin / Mayo, Margerrison	16303	1	2		5		10*		9	8	11	3		12			6		4	7					19
20	15	A	Charlton Athletic	L	0-2	25	4	- / Hales, Berry	6717	1	2		5				10	9	8	11	3	4			6			7					20
21	21	H	Cardiff City	D	0-0	26	4		12877	1	2		5				10	9	8	11	3	4*	12		6			7					21
22	26	A	Chelsea	L	0-1	26	4	- / Fillery	25320	1	2		5	12	7*		10	9	8	11	3				4			6					22
23	29	H	Queens Park Rangers	W	2-0	28	3	Rofe, Henderson	20743	1	2		5	12	7		10	9	8	11*	3				4			6					23
24	Jan 1	H	Bristol Rovers	W	3-0	30	4	Smith 2, Goodwin	21579	1	2		5		7		10	9	8	11	3	4			6								24
25	12	A	Luton Town	D	0-0	31	4		14141	1	2		5	7			10*	9	8	11		4			6	12	3						25
26	19	A	Notts County	W	1-0	33	3	Strickland	14859	1			5	10		4	9			11		2			6	8*	3	7		12			26
27	Feb 2	H	Newcastle United	W	1-0	35	2	Smith (p)	22549	1	2		5	10		4	9	8*	11	3					6	12	7						27
28	9	A	Fulham	D	0-0	36	1		8691	1	2		5	10		4	9	8	11	3					6	12	7*						28
29	20	H	Swansea City	D	1-1	37	1	Henderson / Toshack	17597	1	2		5	10		4	9	8	11						6	7*			12	3			29
30	23	A	West Ham United	L	1-3	37	1	Young / Cross, Holland, Pike	27762	1	2		5			4	9	8	11		10	7			6					3			30
31	Mar 1	H	Oldham Athletic	L	0-1	37	4	- / Steel	16991	1	2		5	12			8	9	10	11		7	4*			6				3			31
32	8	A	Sunderland	D	0-0	38	3		29487	1	2		5				10	9*	11			4	12		6			8		3	7		32
33	15	H	Shrewsbury Town	W	2-0	40	3	Young, Edmunds	15391	1	2		5				10	9*	11			4	8		6			12		3	7		33
34	22	A	Burnley	W	2-1	42	2	Edmunds, Young / Scott	7173	1	2		5				8	9	10			4	7		6					3	11		34
35	29	H	Preston North End	L	1-2	42	3	Kelly / Elwiss 2	15293	1	2		5	12			10*	9	11			4	8		6					3	7		35
36	Apr 5	H	Chelsea	W	1-0	44	4	May	25826	1	2		5	11			10	9		3		4*	12		6			8			7		36
37	8	A	Cardiff City	W	1-0	46	4	Smith	10291	1	2		5	11			4	9		3		8	6					10			7		37
38	12	H	Birmingham City	W	2-1	48	2	Wilson, Young / Gemmill (p)	26075	1	2		5	10	7		4	9*	12	11		8			6					3			38
39	19	A	Wrexham	W	1-0	50	1	Kelly	10023	1	2		5	10	12		4	9		11		8			6					3	7*		39
40	23	A	Bristol Rovers	D	1-1	51	2	Smith / Bates	8205	1	2		5	10	7*		4	9	12	11		8			6					3			40
41	26	H	Charlton Athletic	W	2-1	53	1	Young, Smith / Gritt	23875	1	2		5	10	12		4	9		11		8			6			3	7*				41
42	May 3	A	Orient	W	1-0	55	1	May	13828	1	2		5	10	7		4	9	12	11		8*			6					3			42

Final League Position:	1		League Appearances	42	40		4	42	18	21	34	42	32	35	26	24	19	3	33	4	9	16			11	7	
Average Home League Attendance:	18636		Sub						6	2			4				1	11			3	2	3	1	2			
			League Goals	1			4	2	1	2	14	5	12	3	3	4			2		3			2			

FA CUP

1	Jan 5	H	Harlow Town (3)	D	1-1			Henderson / Prosser	21302	1	2		5			7	10	9	8	11	3				4			6					1
2	8	A	Harlow Town (3 rep)	L	0-1			- / Mackenzie	9723	1	2		5				10	9	8	11	3				4			6	7				2

FOOTBALL LEAGUE CUP

1	Aug 11	H	Rotherham Utd (1 leg 1)	L	1-2			Young / Finney, Gooding	11210	1	2	3	4	5	6	7	8	9	10	11														1
2	14	A	Rotherham Utd (1 leg 2)	L	0-3			- / Fern 2, Gooding	5179	1	2		4	5	6	7	8	9	10	11	3													2

Dismissals: Sep 15, Williams, Newcastle United (a); Feb 23, O'Neill, West Ham United (a).

1979-80
Back: Edmunds, Hughes, Lee, Stevens, O'Neill, Byrne, Grewcock, Buchanan.
Middle: MacFarlane (Asst Manager), Welsh, May, Ridley, Humphries, Wallington, Henderson, Young, Williams, Wallace (Manager).
Front: Lineker, Duffy, Smith, Kelly, Rofe, Peake, Goodwin, Wilson.

Season 1980-81

Champions: Aston Villa
Relegated: Norwich City, Leicester City, Crystal Palace

FOOTBALL LEAGUE DIVISION ONE

Match No	Date		Opponents	Result	Points	Position	Scorers	Att	Wallington	Williams	Gibson	Peake	May	O'Neill	Edmunds	Melrose	Young	Wilson	Smith	Henderson	Goodwin	Carr	Grewcock	Welsh	Scott	Buchanan	Lineker	Byrne	Hamill	MacDonald	Friar	Lynex	Ramsey	Leet	Match No
1	Aug 16	H	Ipswich Town	L 0-1	-		- / Wark	21640	1	2	3	4	5	6	7*	8	9	10	11	12															1
2	19	A	Everton	L 0-1	-		- / Eastoe	23337	1	2	3	4	5	6		8	9	10	11			7													2
3	23	H	Liverpool	W 2-0	2	16	Peake, Henderson	28455	1	2	3	4	5	6		8*	9	10	11	12		7													3
4	30	A	Leeds United	W 2-1	4	11	O'Neill, Henderson / Hart	18530	1	2	3	4	5	6		8*	9	10	11			7	12												4
5	Sep 6	H	Sunderland	L 0-1	4	14	- / Hawley	20638	1	2			5	6		12	9	10	8	11	4				7*										5
6	13	A	Manchester United	L 0-5	4	18	- / Jovanovic 2, Coppell, Grimes, Macari	43229	1	2	3		5	6		12	9	10	11	8	4				7*										6
7	20	A	Nottingham Forest	L 0-5	4	20	- / F Gray, Robertson (p), Birtles 2, Mills	27145	1	2	3		5	6*			9	10	11	8	4				7	12									7
8	27	H	Tottenham Hotspur	W 2-1	6	17	Smith, Buchanan / Villa	22616	1	4	3		5				9		10	8	7	2*			12	6	11								8
9	Oct 4	A	Arsenal	L 0-1	6	18	- / Stapleton	28490	1	4	3		5				9		10	8	7				2	6	11								9
10	8	H	Stoke City	D 1-1	7	19	Wilson / Chapman	14549	1	2	3		5			12	10	11	9	4					6	8*	7								10
11	11	H	Coventry City	L 1-3	7	19	Lineker / Dyson, Gooding, English	17104	1	2	3		5			12	10	11	9	4					6	8*	7								11
12	18	A	Crystal Palace	L 1-2	7	20	Young / Hilaire, Allen (p)	16387	1	2			5			12	9	10	11	8	7*	3			6		4								12
13	21	A	Middlesbrough	L 0-1	7	20	- / Armstrong	13114	1	4	3		5			7	9	10	11	8		2			6										13
14	25	H	Wolverhampton W.	W 2-0	9	19	Henderson, Young	18133	1	4	3		5			7	9	10	11	8*		2			6	12									14
15	Nov 1	A	Aston Villa	L 0-2	9	21	- / Shaw, Cowans	29953	1	4	3		5			7	9	10	11	8		2			6										15
16	8	H	Manchester City	D 1-1	10	20	Young / Tueart	19104	1	11		4	5	6		9	10		12						3	8	7*								16
17	12	H	Everton	L 0-1	10	21	- / Eastoe	15511	1	11		4	5	6		9	10			12	2				3	8	7*								17
18	15	A	Ipswich Town	L 1-3	10	22	Williams / Gates, D'Avray, Williams (og)	19892	1	11		4	5	6		9	10		12		2				3	8*	7								18
19	22	A	West Bromwich Albion	L 1-3	10	22	Lineker / Robson, Moses, Owen (p)	17752	1	11		4	5	6		9	10		12		2*				3	8	7								19
20	29	H	Norwich City	L 1-2	10	22	Young / Fashanu, Royle	13958	1	2	3	4		6		8	9	10	11				5					7*	12						20
21	Dec 6	A	Birmingham City	W 2-1	12	21	Melrose 2 / Scott (og)	18479	1	2	3	4				8	9*	10				12	5					7	11						21
22	13	H	Middlesbrough	W 1-0	14	21	MacDonald (p)	13998	1	2	3	4				8				12			5			9		7*	11						22
23	20	A	Stoke City	L 0-1	14	21	- / Chapman	13433	1	2	3	4				8	9	10				12	5					7*	11						23
24	26	H	Brighton & Hove Albion	L 1-1	14	21	- / Gregory	19570	1	2	3	4				8	9	10				7*			12	5			11						24
25	27	A	Southampton	L 0-4	14	21	- / Moran, Keegan, George, Baker	21886	1	2		4				8	9	10		7			3	5					11						25
26	Jan 10	H	West Bromwich Albion	L 0-2	14	22	- / Bennett, Deehan	17778	1	2	3	4*		6		9		10			12		5	8	7				11						26
27	17	H	Leeds United	L 0-1	14	22	- / Hart	16094	1	4	7*		6			12		10	11	9	2		5	8						3					27
28	31	A	Liverpool	W 2-1	16	21	Byrne, Melrose / Young (og)	35154	1	2		4	5	6		8	9	10		12							7*	11	3						28
29	Feb 7	H	Manchester United	W 1-0	18	21	Melrose	26085	1	2		4	5	6		8	9	10		12							7	11*	3						29
30	14	A	Sunderland	L 0-1	18	21	- / Cummins	22569	1	2		4*	5	6		8	9	10									7	12	3	11					30
31	21	A	Tottenham Hotspur	W 2-1	20	20	Lynex, Byrne / Archibald	27326	1	2		4	5	6		8*	9	10									12	11	3	7					31
32	28	H	Nottingham Forest	D 1-1	21	21	Lynex / Walsh	26608	1	2		4	5	6		8	9	10									12	11	3	7*					32
33	Mar 7	A	Arsenal	W 1-0	23	20	Williams	20198	1	2		4	5	6		8*	9	10									7	11	3		12				33
34	14	H	Coventry City	L 1-4	23	20	Young / English 3, Thompson	21430	1	2		4	5	6		8	9	10										11	3	7					34
35	21	H	Crystal Palace	D 1-1	24	21	O'Neill / Price	15176	1	2			5	6		8	9	10*	12						4			11	3	7					35
36	28	A	Wolverhampton W.	W 1-0	26	20	Melrose	21694	1	2			5	6*		8	9	10	12						4			11	3	7					36
37	31	H	Manchester City	D 3-3	27	20	Williams, Young, Melrose / Reeves 2, Henry	26144	1	2			5			8	9	10				11	6		4*			12	3	7					37
38	Apr 4	A	Aston Villa	L 2-4	27	21	Lynex 2 (1p) / Withe 2, Bremner, Morley	26032	1	2			5			8	9	10				11	6		4				3	7					38
39	18	H	Southampton	D 2-2	28	21	Young, Lynex (p) / Moran, Baker	21349	1	2			5	6		9	10	11	8*						4			12	3	7					39
40	20	A	Brighton & Hove Albion	L 1-2	28	21	MacDonald / Robinson, Gregory	21176	1	2			5	6		8	9	10				11*						12	4	3	7				40
41	25	H	Birmingham City	W 1-0	30	21	Williams	13666	1	2		4	5	6		8*		10		11					9				3	7	12				41
42	May 2	A	Norwich City	W 3-2	32	21	Melrose 3 / Fashanu, McGuire	24675	1	2			5	6		8		10							11			7	4	3*					42

							League Appearances		42	42	20	24	34	32	1	28	36	40	17	16	13	9	6	3	21	6	9	10	8	16	15	12	1	1	
Final League Position:	21						Sub									4			2		2	6	6		1	4		1	3	4		2		
Average Home League Attendance:	19476						League Goals			4		1		2		9	7	1	1	3					1	2	2			2		5			

FA CUP

	Date		Opponents	Result			Scorers	Att	Wallington	Williams	Gibson	Peake	May	O'Neill	Edmunds	Melrose	Young	Wilson	Smith	Henderson	Goodwin	Carr	Grewcock	Welsh	Scott	Buchanan	Lineker	Byrne	Hamill	MacDonald	Friar	Lynex	Ramsey	Leet	
1	Jan 3	H	Cardiff City (3)	W 3-0			Lineker, Buchanan, Melrose	17527	1	2	3	4		6		12	9	10					5		8*	7			11						1
2	24	H	Exeter City (4)	D 1-1			Henderson / Pullar	20996	1	2			5	6		7*	9	10	11	8			3	12	4										2
3	28	A	Exeter City (4 rep)	L 1-3			Melrose / Kellow 3 (1p)	15268	1	2		4*	5	6		8	9	10		12					7			11	3						3

FOOTBALL LEAGUE CUP

	Date		Opponents	Result			Scorers	Att	Wallington	Williams	Gibson	Peake	May	O'Neill	Edmunds	Melrose	Young	Wilson	Smith	Henderson	Goodwin	Carr	Grewcock	Welsh	Scott	Buchanan	Lineker	Byrne	Hamill	MacDonald	Friar	Lynex	Ramsey	Leet	
1	Aug 26	A	West Bromwich A (2/1)	L 0-1			- / Barnes	13810	1		3	4	5	6		8	9	10	11*	12	7	2													1
2	Sep 3	H	West Bromwich A (2/2)	L 0-1			- / Regis	17081	1	2	3	4*	5	6		8	9	10		11	7		12												2

Dismissals: Apr 20, Young and MacDonald, Brighton & Hove Albion (a); also Williams was sent off in a friendly v Karlsruhe (a) on Aug 5.

1980-81
Back: Grewcock, Buchanan, Goodwin, Welsh, MacDonald, Lee, Lineker, Edmunds.
Middle: MacFarlane (Asst Manager), Gibson, May, Young, Wallington, Humphries, Henderson, O'Neill, Scott, Wallace (Manager).
Front: Strickland, Byrne, Peake, Williams, Melrose, Carr, Smith, Wilson.

Season **1981-82**

Promoted: Luton Town, Watford, Norwich City
Relegated: Cardiff City, Wrexham, Orient

FOOTBALL LEAGUE DIVISION TWO

Match No	Date		Opponents	Result	Points	Position	Scorers	Att	Wallington	Williams	Gibson	Peake	May	O'Neill	Lynex	Melrose	Lineker	Wilson	MacDonald	Smith	Hamill	Young	Robson	Ramsey	Leet	Scott	Welsh	Hebberd	Kelly	Friar	Walker	Buchanan
1	Aug 29	A	Grimsby Town	D 2-2	1	-	Lineker, Melrose / Kilmore, Drinkell	11032	1	2	3	4*	5	6	7	8	9	10	11	12												
2	Sep 5	H	Wrexham	W 1-0	4	-	Hamill	12905	1	2	3	4	5	6	7	8*	9	10	12		11											
3	8	H	Barnsley	W 1-0	7	4	Hamill	15447	1	2	3	4	5	6	7	8	9	10				11										
4	12	A	Derby County	L 1-3	7	6	Melrose / Ramage, Hector, Buckley	16046	1	2	3	4	5	6	7	8	12	10				9*	11									
5	19	H	Luton Town	L 1-2	7	11	Lynex (p) / White 2	14159	1	2	3	4	5	6	7	8	9	10					11									
6	22	A	Rotherham United	D 1-1	8	11	May / Moore	7781	1	2	3	4	5	6	7	8		10				9	11									
7	26	A	Blackburn Rovers	W 2-0	11	7	May, Melrose	8925	1	2	3		5	6	7	8		10	11			9			4							
8	Oct 3	H	Crystal Palace	D 1-1	12	11	Lineker / Hilaire	12558	1	2	3		5	6	7	8	12	10*	11			9			4							
9	10	A	Bolton Wanderers	W 3-0	15	8	Melrose 2, Young	7361	1	2			6		12	8	7		11			9	10	4*	3	5						
10	16	H	Chelsea	D 1-1	16	6	Melrose / Fillery	18358	1	2			6			8	7		10			9	11	4	3	5						
11	24	A	Queens Park Rangers	L 0-2	16	11	- / Stainrod, Gregory	12419	1	2			6		12	8	7		10			9*	11	4	3	5						
12	31	H	Sheffield Wednesday	D 0-0	17	10		19125	1	2				6	7	8	9	10	4				11		3	5						
13	Nov 7	A	Charlton Athletic	W 4-1	20	9	Melrose, Lynex (p), Lineker 2 / Walsh	8212	1	2				6	7	8	9	10	4				11*		3	5	12					
14	14	H	Orient	L 0-1	20	9	- / McNeil	11733	1	2				6	7	8*	9	10	4			11			3	5	12					
15	21	A	Cardiff City	L 1-3	20	14	Welsh / Micallef, D Bennett, Stevens	6687	1	2		4		6	7		9	10	11	8						5	3					
16	28	H	Cambridge United	W 4-1	23	9	Lynex, Hebberd, Peake, Lineker / Christie	9524	1	2		4	5	6	7		9	10	11*	12						3	8					
17	Dec 5	A	Norwich City	D 0-0	24	9		12768	1	2		4	5	6	7		9	10								3	8	11				
18	12	H	Watford	D 1-1	25	9	Lineker / Jenkins	10340	1	2		4	5	6	7		9	10								3	8	11				
19	28	H	Oldham Athletic	D 1-1	26	9	Lynex / Wylde (p)	9174	1	2			5	6	7		8	10				9				3		11	4			
20	Jan 30	A	Luton Town	L 1-2	26	14	Lineker / White, Donaghy	11810	1	2		4	5	6	7	12	8	10				9		11*			3					
21	Feb 6	H	Derby County	W 2-1	29	12	Lynex (p), Lineker / Emson	14132	1	2		4	5	6	7	12	8	10				9						11*	3			
22	20	H	Blackburn Rovers	W 1-0	32	13	Peake	11667	1	2		4	5	6	7*	12	8	10				9							11	3		
23	27	H	Bolton Wanderers	W 1-0	35	13	Lynex (p)	10678	1	2		4	5	6	7	12	8	10				9*							11	3		
24	Mar 2	A	Newcastle United	W 3-0	38	12	Young, Lineker 2	12497	1	2		4	5	6	7	12	8	10				9							11*	3		
25	9	A	Chelsea	L 1-4	38	12	Lynex / Locke, Mayes 2, Hales	10586		2		4	5	6	7	12	8	10*				9							11	3	1	
26	13	H	Queens Park Rangers	W 3-2	41	12	Lynex (p), Young, Melrose / Currie, Stainrod	17821		2		4	5	6	7	12	8	10				9*							11	3	1	
27	17	H	Rotherham United	W 1-0	44	10	Melrose	21123		2		4	5	6	7*	9	8	10	11							12			3	1		
28	20	A	Sheffield Wednesday	L 0-2	44	11	- / Bannister, Pearson	18962		2		4	5	6	7*	12	8	10	11			9							3	1		
29	23	A	Crystal Palace	W 2-0	47	9	Lynex, Lineker	9506		2		4	5		7*	12	8	10	11			9		6					3	1		
30	27	H	Charlton Athletic	W 3-1	50	7	Young 2, MacDonald / Hales	13681		2		4	5	6*	7	12	8	10	11			9							3	1		
31	30	A	Shrewsbury Town	D 1-1	51	6	Lineker / Atkins (p)	5340	1	2		4	5	6	7	12	8	10				9*							11	3		
32	Apr 10	H	Newcastle United	D 0-0	52	10		25777	1			4	5	6	7	9*	8	10	11							3	12		2			
33	13	H	Oldham Athletic	W 2-1	55	6	Melrose, Lineker / Steel	14298	1			4	5	6	7	9*	8	10	11							3	12		2			
34	17	H	Cardiff City	W 3-1	58	5	Lineker 2, Lynex / Kitchen	13650	1				5	6	7		8	10*	11			9		4		3	12		2			
35	20	A	Wrexham	D 0-0	59	4		4913	1				5	6	9		8	10*	4					7		3	12	11	2			
36	24	A	Cambridge United	W 2-1	62	4	Lineker, Welsh / Fallon	7212	1				4	5	6	7	9	8								3	10	11	2			
37	May 1	H	Norwich City	L 1-4	62	8	May / Barham, Bertschin, Deehan, Leet (og)	19630	1				4	5	6	7	9	8								3	10	11	2			
38	4	A	Barnsley	W 2-0	65	4	Welsh, Lineker	15418	1				4	5	6	7	9	8	11					10			12	2*	3			
39	8	A	Watford	L 1-3	65	8	Melrose / Barnes 2, Blissett	20859	1				4	5	6	2	7	8*	11			9		10			12		3			
40	12	H	Grimsby Town	L 1-2	65	8	Welsh (p) / Whymark 2	13941	1				4	5	6	12	7	8	10*	11		9					2		3			
41	15	H	Shrewsbury Town	D 0-0	66	8		11368	1				4	5	6	12	7*	8	10	11		9					2		3			
42	18	A	Orient	L 0-3	66	8	- / Godfrey, Silkman, McNeil	2107	1				4		6	7	8		10*	11		9		5			2		3			12

							League Appearances		36	31	8	31	34	41	37	24	37	35	24	2	2	24	8	10	17	7	7	4	14	23	6	
							Sub						4		11	2			1	2						9				1		
							League Goals				2	3			10	11	17		1			2	5				4	1				

Final League Position: 8
Average Home League Attendance: 14183

FA CUP

	Date		Opponents	Result	Scorers	Att	Wallington	Williams	Peake	May	O'Neill	Lynex	Melrose	Lineker	Wilson	MacDonald	Young	Scott	Kelly	Friar
1	Jan 2	H	Southampton (3)	W 3-1	Young 2, Lineker / Keegan	20589	1	2	4	5	6	7	12	8	10		9*		11	3
2	23	A	Hereford United (4)	W 1-0	May	10602	1	2	4	5	6	7	12	8	10		9	11*		3
3	Feb 13	H	Watford (5)	W 2-0	O'Neill, Terry (og)	27991	1	2	4	5	6	7*	12	8	10		9		11	3
4	Mar 6	A	Shrewsbury Town (6)	W 5-2	May, Melrose 2, Lineker, Cross (og) / Bates, Keay	29117	1*	2	4	5	6	7	12	8	10		9		11	3
5	Apr 3		Tottenham Hotspur (sf)	L 0-2	- / Crooks, Wilson (og)	46606	1	2	4	5	6	7	12	8	10		9*		11	3

FOOTBALL LEAGUE CUP

	Date		Opponents	Result	Scorers	Att	Wallington	Williams	Gibson	Peake	May	O'Neill	Lynex	Melrose	Lineker	Wilson	MacDonald	Smith	Young	Scott	Kelly
1	Oct 6	A	Preston N.E. (2 leg 1)	L 0-1	- / Bruce	5382	1	2	3		5	6	7	8	11	10			9		4
2	28	H	Preston N.E. (2 leg 2)	W 4-0	Robson, Lynex, Melrose, O'Riordan (og)	7685	1	2		12	6	7	8	9	10*	4	11			3	5
3	Nov 11	A	Aston Villa (3)	D 0-0		19806	1	2			6	7	8	9	10	4	11			3	5
4	25	A	Aston Villa (3 rep)	L 0-2	- / Withe, Cowans (p)	23136	1	2		4	6	7	8	9	10	11	12			3*	5

Dismissals: Nov 21, Scott, Cardiff City (a); Mar 30, Kelly, Shrewsbury Town (a); Apr 10, MacDonald, Newcastle United (a).
Stand-in Goalkeepers: Mar 6, Young and Lynex for Wallington, Shrewsbury Town (h) FAC.
Note: Apr 3, played at Villa Park (Aston Villa).

6 February: Gary Lineker athletically manages to keep the ball in play against Derby County at Filbert Street. Steve Lynex awaits developments.

1981-82
Back: Lineker, Peake, Williams, O'Neill, MacDonald, Henderson, Gibson. **Middle:** Ramsey, Scott, Young, May, Walker, Wallington, Leet, Welsh, Hamill.
Front: MacFarlane (Asst Manager), Grewcock, Buchanan, Lynex, Melrose, Wilson, Smith, Friar, Wallace (Manager).

1982-83
Back: Robson, O'Neill, MacDonald, May, Walker, Wallington, Williams, Leet, A Smith, English.
Front: Peake, Lynex, Lineker, Kelly, B Smith, Ramsey, Friar, Wilson.

Season **1982-83**

Promoted: Queens Park Rangers, Wolverhampton Wanderers, Leicester City
Relegated: Rotherham United, Burnley, Bolton Wanderers

FOOTBALL LEAGUE DIVISION TWO

No	Date		Opponents	Result	Pts	Pos	Scorers	Att	Waltington	Ramsey	Friar	MacDonald	May	O'Neill	Lynex	Lineker	A Smith	Melrose	B Smith	Kelly	English	Wilson	Holmes	Buchanan	Leet	Williams	Brown	Robson	Daly	Peake	Jones	No
1	Aug 28	H	Charlton Athletic	L 1-2		-	B Smith / Walker 2	11038	1	2	3	4	5	6	7	8	9	10	11													1
2	31	A	Rotherham United	W 3-1	3	-	Melrose, A Smith, Lineker / Gow	9254	1	2	3	4	5	6	7*	12	9	10	11	8												2
3	Sep 4	A	Chelsea	D 1-1	4	8	Lineker / Droy	14127	1	2*	3	4	5	6	12	8	9	10	11	7												3
4	8	H	Leeds United	L 0-1	4	12	- / Butterworth	12963	1	2*	3	4	5	6	11	8	9	10		7												4
5	11	H	Carlisle United	W 6-0	7	9	Lynex 3 (2p), Lineker 3 (1p)	8440	1	2	3	4	5	6	11	8	9	10		7												5
6	18	A	Blackburn Rovers	L 1-3	7	11	A Smith / Garner, Bell, Barton	4963	1	2	3	4	5	6	7	8	9				10	11										6
7	25	H	Queens Park Rangers	L 0-1	7	13	- / O'Neill (og)	10647	1	2	3	4	5	6		8	9		11		10	7										7
8	Oct 2	A	Shrewsbury Town	W 2-0	10	11	MacDonald, O'Neill	5223	1	2	3	4	5	6	7	8		9			10	11										8
9	9	H	Grimsby Town	W 2-0	13	7	Lynex, Lineker	9640	1	2	3	4	5	6	7	8		9			10	11										9
10	16	A	Wolverhampton W.	W 3-0	16	6	Wilson, Lineker, English	15782	1	2	3	4	5	6	7	8			12		9*	10	11									10
11	23	A	Derby County	W 4-0	19	7	Lineker 3, A Smith	13191	1	2	3	4	5	6	7	8			12		9*	10	11									11
12	30	H	Sheffield Wednesday	L 0-2	19	7	- / Mirocevic, Shelton	17341	1	2	12	4	5	6	7	8	9				10*	11		3								12
13	Nov 6	A	Cambridge United	L 1-3	19	8	Lineker / Lockhart, Reilly, Finney	5011	1	2	12	4	5	6	7*	8	9				10	11		3								13
14	13	H	Newcastle United	D 2-2	20	8	English, Lineker / Keegan 2	15044	1	2	3	4	5	6	7	8		9			10	11										14
15	20	H	Crystal Palace	L 0-1	20	12	- / Mabbutt	8616	1	2	3	4	5	6	7	8			12		9*	10	11									15
16	27	A	Bolton Wanderers	L 1-3	20	15	Wilson / Foster, Doyle, C Thompson	5060	1	2	3	4	5	6	7	8			12		9	10*	11									16
17	Dec 4	H	Fulham	W 2-0	23	10	Buchanan, Lineker	9082	1	2	3*	4	5	6	7	8	10		9			11		12								17
18	11	A	Burnley	W 4-2	26	9	Lineker, Lynex (p), A Smith 2 / Steven, Taylor	6503	1	2		4	5	6	7	8	10		9			11		12		3*						18
19	18	H	Oldham Athletic	W 2-1	29	6	MacDonald (p), A Smith / Wylde	8125	1	2	3	4	5	6	12	8	10		9			11		7*								19
20	27	A	Middlesbrough	D 1-1	30	5	Lineker / S Bell (p)	12665	1		3	4	5	6	7	8	9				10	11			2							20
21	28	H	Barnsley	W 1-0	33	4	A Smith	14838	1		3	4	5	6		8	9		7	10		11			2							21
22	Jan 1	A	Crystal Palace	L 0-1	33	5	- / Langley	8801	1	2		4	5	6	12	8	10		7	9		11		3*								22
23	3	H	Chelsea	W 3-0	36	4	Lineker 2, A Smith	13745	1	2		4	5	6	12	8	9		7	10*		11		3								23
24	15	A	Charlton Athletic	L 1-2	36	5	Wilson / Simonsen 2	5971	1	2		4	5	6	7	8	9		3	10*		11					12					24
25	22	H	Blackburn Rovers	L 0-1	36	5	- / Lowey	8361	1	2		4	5	6	7*	8	9		3	10	12	11										25
26	Feb 5	A	Carlisle United	W 1-0	39	4	MacDonald	4402	1	2		4	5	6	7	8	9		3			11						10				26
27	19	A	Grimsby Town	L 0-2	39	6	- / Ford, Drinkell	6963	1	2*		4	5	6	7	8	9		3		12	11						10				27
28	22	H	Shrewsbury Town	W 3-2	42	4	Lineker 2, Wilson / Williams, Robinson	6155	1	2		4	5	6*	7	8	9		3		12	11						10				28
29	26	H	Wolverhampton W.	W 5-0	45	4	Lynex 2, A Smith, Lineker, Daly	13530	1	2		4	5		7	8	9		3		6	11						10*	12			29
30	Mar 5	H	Derby County	D 1-1	46	4	Lynex / Barton	15452	1	2		4		6	7	8	9		3		5	11						10				30
31	19	H	Cambridge United	W 4-0	49	4	A Smith 2, Lynex (p), Wilson	8305	1	2		4		6	7	8	9		3		5	11						10*	12			31
32	22	A	Sheffield Wednesday	D 2-2	50	4	MacDonald, A Smith / McCulloch, Megson	14036	1	2		4	12	6	7	8*	9		3		5	11						10				32
33	26	A	Newcastle United	D 2-2	51	4	Lineker 2 / McDermott, Keegan	22692	1	2		4		6	7	8	9		3		5	11						10				33
34	Apr 2	A	Barnsley	W 2-1	54	4	Wilson, English / McGuire	13278	1	2		4		6	7	8	9		3		5	11						10				34
35	5	H	Middlesbrough	W 1-0	57	4	O'Neill	12025	1	2		4		6	7	8	9		3		5	11						10				35
36	9	A	Queens Park Rangers	D 2-2	58	4	Lineker 2 / Gregory, Sealy	16301	1	2		4	12	6*	7	8	9		3		5	11						10				36
37	16	A	Rotherham United	W 3-1	61	4	Wilson, Lineker 2 / McBride	12978	1	2		4		6	7	8	9		3		5	11						10				37
38	23	A	Fulham	W 1-0	64	4	Wilson	24251	1	2		4		6	7	8	9		3		5	11						10				38
39	30	H	Bolton Wanderers	D 0-0	65	4		13959	1	2		4	12	6	7*	8	9		3		5	11						10				39
40	May 2	A	Leeds United	D 2-2	66	3	A Smith, May / F Gray, O'Neill (og)	14442	1	2		4	12	6		8*	9		3		5	11						10	7			40
41	7	A	Oldham Athletic	W 2-1	69	3	Jones, Ramsey / Palmer	9088	1	2		4		5	6		9		3		8			12				10	7*	11		41
42	14	H	Burnley	D 0-0	70	3		29453	1	2		4	12	6	7		9		3		8	11						10*		5		42

				League Appearances	42	40	18	42	30	41	34	39	35	5	26	20	25	36	2	1	1	4		17	2	2		
Final League Position:		3		Sub		2			5		4		1			4			3			3			1	2		
Average Home League Attendance:		12819		League Goals		1		4	1	2	9	26	13	1	1		3	8				1				1		1	

FA CUP

No	Date		Opponents	Result			Scorers	Att	Waltington	Ramsey	Friar	MacDonald	May	O'Neill	Lynex	Lineker	A Smith	Melrose	B Smith	Kelly	English	Wilson	Holmes	Buchanan	Leet	Williams	Brown	Robson	Daly	Peake	Jones	No
1	Jan 8	H	Notts County (3)	L 2-3			A Smith, Wilson / Fashanu 2, McCulloch	18384	1	2		4	5	6	7	8*	9					11		10			3	12				1

FOOTBALL LEAGUE CUP (Milk Cup)

No	Date		Opponents	Result			Scorers	Att	Waltington	Ramsey	Friar	MacDonald	May	O'Neill	Lynex	Lineker	A Smith	Melrose	B Smith	Kelly	English	Wilson	Holmes	Buchanan	Leet	Williams	Brown	Robson	Daly	Peake	Jones	No
1	Oct 6	A	Lincoln City (2 leg 1)	L 0-2			- / Bell, Shipley	6775	1	2	3	4	5	6	7	8		9	10	11												1
2	27	H	Lincoln City (2 leg 2)	L 0-1			- / Bell	10000	1	2	3	4	5	6	7	8	9		10	11												2

Dismissals: Aug 31, Kelly, Rotherham United (a); Sep 8, Lynex, Leeds United (h); Nov 27, Friar, Bolton Wanderers (a); Dec 11, Ramsey, Burnley (a); Feb 19, May, Grimsby Town (a).

16 April: Gary Lineker becomes the first City player since 1957 to net 25 league goals in a season with a brace against Rotherham United at Filbert Street. Kevin MacDonald joins in the celebrations.

Season 1983-84

Champions: Liverpool
Relegated: Birmingham City, Notts County, Wolverhampton Wanderers

FOOTBALL LEAGUE DIVISION ONE (Canon League)

Match No	Date	Opponents	Result	Points	Position	Scorers	Att	Mark Grew	Paul Ramsey	Bobby Smith	Kevin MacDonald	Ian Banks	John O'Neill	Steve Lynex	Gary Lineker	Alan Smith	Robert Jones	Ian Wilson	Andy Peake	David Rennie	Tom English	Mark Wallington	Tommy Williams	Bob Hazell	Peter Eastoe	Andy Feeley	Ian Andrews	Robert Kelly	Match No
1	Aug 27 H	Notts County	L 0-4	-		- / O'Neill, Christie 3	14838	1	2	3	4	5	6	7	8	9	10	11											1
2	31 H	Luton Town	L 0-3	-		- / Bunn, Moss, Hill	11929	1	2	3	4	5	6	7	8	9		11	10										2
3	Sep 3 H	West Bromwich Albion	L 0-1		22	- / Whitehead	12016	1	2	3	4	5*	6	7	8	9		11	10										3
4	6 A	West Ham United	L 1-3		22	Lineker / Cottee, Swindlehurst, Walford	22131	1	2	3	4			7	8	9	10*	11	6	5	12								4
5	10 H	Tottenham Hotspur	L 0-3		22	- / Stevens, Mabbutt, Crooks	15886	1	2	3	4			7*	8	9	10	11	6	5	12								5
6	17 A	Coventry City	L 1-2		22	Lineker / Platnauer, Gibson	12377		2	3	4		6		8	9	10*	11	7	5	12	1							6
7	24 H	Stoke City	D 2-2	1	22	Jones, Lineker / Painter, Maguire	10215		2	3	4		6	7	8	9*	10	11	12			1		5					7
8	Oct 1 A	Birmingham City	L 1-2	1	22	Lineker / Rees, Harford	15212		10	3	4		6	7	8	9*		11	12			1	2	5					8
9	19 A	Norwich City	L 1-3	1	22	Eastoe / Bertschin, Channon, Donowa	13780		10		4		6	7	8			11		3		1	2	5	9				9
10	22 A	Ipswich Town	D 0-0	2	22		14944		10		4		6	7	8*	12		11		3		1	2	5	9				10
11	29 H	Everton	W 2-0	5	21	A Smith, Ramsey	10953		10		4		6	7	8	9		11		3		1	2	5					11
12	Nov 5 A	Watford	D 3-3	6	21	Lynex 2 (1p), Banks / Callaghan, Richardson 2	15807		10		4	5*	6	7	8	12		11		3		1	2		9				12
13	12 H	Manchester United	D 1-1	7	21	Lynex / Robson	24409		10		4	12	6	7	8	9		11		3		1	2*	5					13
14	19 A	Aston Villa	L 1-3	7	21	Lynex (p) / Withe, Rideout, McMahon	19024		10		4		6	7	8	9		11		3	12	1	2	5*					14
15	26 H	Arsenal	W 3-0	10	21	Lineker, Lynex, A Smith	14777		10		4		6	7	8	9		11		3		1	2	5					15
16	30 A	Southampton	W 2-1	13	19	A Smith, Lineker / Worthington	14181		10		4		6	7	8*	9		11		3		1	2	5					16
17	Dec 4 H	Nottingham Forest	L 2-3	13	20	Jones, A Smith / Walsh, Bowyer, Thijssen	23248		10		4		6	7	8*	9	12	11		3		1	2	5					17
18	10 H	Wolverhampton W.	W 5-1	16	20	Lineker, A Smith 3, Lynex / Clarke	10969		10		4		6	7	8	9		11		3		1	2	5					18
19	18 A	Sunderland	D 1-1	17	19	Hazell / Rowell	16993		10		4		6	7	8	9		11		3		1	2	5					19
20	26 H	Queens Park Rangers	W 2-1	20	17	Lineker, Lynex / Fenwick (p)	17460		10		4		6	7*	8	9		11		3	12	1	2	5					20
21	27 A	Liverpool	D 2-2	21	17	A Smith, Banks / Lee, Rush	33664		10*		4	12	6	7	8	9		11		3		1	2	5					21
22	31 H	West Bromwich Albion	D 1-1	22	18	Lynex (p) / Thompson	15128		10*		4		6	7	8	9		11		3		1	2	5	12				22
23	Jan 2 A	Stoke City	W 1-0	25	18	A Smith	13728				4		6	7	8	9		11	10	3		1	2	5					23
24	14 A	Notts County	W 5-2	28	17	MacDonald, Lineker 3, Peake / Chiedozie, Harkouk	10607				4		6	7	8	9		11	10	3		1	2	5					24
25	21 H	Coventry City	D 1-1	29	18	Lineker / Daly	16262		10		4		6	7	8	9		11		3		1	2	5					25
26	Feb 4 H	Birmingham City	L 2-3	29	18	A Smith 2 / Gayle, Wright (p), Peake (og)	13770		10		4*		6	7	8	9		11		3	12	1	2	5					26
27	11 A	Tottenham Hotspur	L 2-3	29	19	Lineker 2 / Archibald, Falco, Galvin	28410		10*		4		6	7	8	9		11		3	12	1	2	5					27
28	25 H	Ipswich Town	W 2-0	32	18	A Smith, O'Neill	11399		10		4		6	7	8	9		11		3		1	2	5					28
29	Mar 3 H	Watford	W 4-1	35	16	Peake 2, Lineker, A Smith / Rostron	13295		10		4		6	7	8	9		11		3		1	2	5					29
30	10 A	Manchester United	L 0-2	35	17	- / Hughes, Moses	39473				4		6	7	8	9		11	12	3		1	2	5		10*			30
31	17 H	West Ham United	W 4-1	38	16	Hazell, Lynex 2 (2p), Lineker / Stewart	13533				4		6	7	8	9		11	10	3		1	2	5					31
32	20 H	Everton	D 1-1	39	16	Lineker / Richardson	15142				4		6	7	8	9		11	10	3		1	2*	5	12				32
33	24 A	Luton Town	D 0-0	40	15		10509				4		6	7	8	9		11	10	3		1	2	5					33
34	31 H	Norwich City	W 2-1	43	14	A Smith 2 / Deehan	11278		10		4		6	7	8	9		11		3		1	2	5					34
35	Apr 7 A	Southampton	D 2-2	44	14	Lineker 2 / Moran, Wallace	17455				4		6	7	8	9		11	10	3		1	2	5					35
36	14 A	Aston Villa	W 2-0	47	13	O'Neill, Banks	13366				4	12	6	7	8	9		11	10	3		1	2	5*					36
37	18 H	Liverpool	D 3-3	48	11	Peake, Lynex, Lineker / Whelan, Rush, Wark	26553				4	12	6*	7	8	9		11	10	3		1	2	5					37
38	21 A	Queens Park Rangers	L 0-2	48	13	- / Allen, Fereday	12360		10		4	12	6	7	8	9*		11		3		1	2	5					38
39	28 A	Arsenal	L 1-2	48	14	Lineker / Woodcock, Davis	24143		10		4		6	7	8	9		11		3		1	2	5					39
40	May 5 H	Nottingham Forest	W 2-1	51	12	Lynex, Lineker / Davenport	16600		10		4		6	7	8	9		11*	12	3		1	2	5					40
41	7 A	Wolverhampton W.	L 0-1	51	12	- / Smith	7405		10		4	12	6	7	8	9		11		3*		1	2	5					41
42	12 H	Sunderland	L 0-2	51	14	- / Robson, Chapman	12627		10				6	7	8*	9		11		3	12		2	5			1	4	42

								Grew	Ramsey	B.Smith	MacDonald	Banks	O'Neill	Lynex	Lineker	A.Smith	Jones	Wilson	Peake	Rennie	English	Wallington	Williams	Hazell	Eastoe	Feeley	Andrews	Kelly	
Final League Position:	15					**League Appearances**		5	33	35	38	22	31	40	38	39	6	41	22	15	4	35	21	27	5	2	2	1	
Average Home League Attendance:	14923					**Sub**			1			4			1	1	2		2		12				1	1			
						League Goals			1		1	3	2	12	22	15	2		4					2	1				

FA CUP

Match No	Date	Opponents	Result			Scorers	Att	Grew	Ramsey	B.Smith	MacDonald	Banks	O'Neill	Lynex	Lineker	A.Smith	Jones	Wilson	Peake	Rennie	English	Wallington	Williams	Hazell	Eastoe	Feeley	Andrews	Kelly	Match No
1	Jan 7 A	Crystal Palace (3)	L 0-1			- / Gilbert	11497				4		6	7	8	9		11	10*	3		1	2	5	12				1

FOOTBALL LEAGUE CUP (Milk Cup)

Match No	Date	Opponents	Result			Scorers	Att	Grew	Ramsey	B.Smith	MacDonald	Banks	O'Neill	Lynex	Lineker	A.Smith	Jones	Wilson	Peake	Rennie	English	Wallington	Williams	Hazell	Eastoe	Feeley	Andrews	Kelly	Match No
1	Oct 5 H	Chelsea (2 leg 1)	L 0-2			- / Dixon, Canoville	7798		10	3	4		6*	7	8	12	9	11				1	2	5					1
2	25 A	Chelsea (2 leg 2)	W 2-0 aet			A Smith, English	15666		10		4		6*	7	8			11		3	12	1	2	5	9				2

Dismissals: Jan 2, Peake, Stoke City (a); Apr 28, Peake, Arsenal (a).
Note: Oct 25, lost 3-4 on penalties (English, Hazell, Eastoe scored)

1983-84
Back: Williams, Ramsey, Forster, Grew, Andrews, Wallington, O'Neill, Robson, English. **Middle:** Richardson (Youth Team Coach), Hutchinson, Kelly, MacDonald, A Smith, May, Banks, Rennie, Cliff, McVey (Physio). **Front:** Lynex, Peake, Lineker, Milne (Manager), Summers (Coach), B Smith, Wilson, Jones.

Champions: Everton
Relegated: Norwich City, Sunderland, Stoke City

FOOTBALL LEAGUE DIVISION ONE (Canon League)

Match No	Date		Opponents	Result	Pts	Pos	Scorers	Att
1	Aug 25	H	Newcastle United	L 2-3		-	Lineker 2 / McCreery, Waddle, Carney	18636
2	27	A	Tottenham Hotspur	D 2-2	1	-	A Smith, Banks / Roberts 2 (1p)	30046
3	Sep 1	A	Coventry City	L 0-2	1	21	- / Bennett, Latchford	13510
4	5	H	Watford	D 1-1	2	21	Lineker / Taylor	12055
5	8	H	Ipswich Town	W 2-1	5	15	Lineker, Lynex / Gates	10737
6	15	A	Stoke City	D 2-2	6	16	Lineker, Lynex (p) / Bould, Hemming	11579
7	22	H	West Bromwich Albion	W 2-1	9	14	Lynex 2 (1p) / Cross	11960
8	29	A	Chelsea	L 0-3	9	16	- / Nevin, Dixon 2	18521
9	Oct 6	A	West Ham United	L 1-3	9	18	Lynex / Bonds, Cottee, Stewart	15306
10	13	H	Arsenal	L 1-4	9	20	Anderson (og) / Talbot 2 (1p), Anderson, Rix	19944
11	20	A	Sheffield Wednesday	L 0-5	9	20	- / Varadi 3, Blair, Ryan	23621
12	27	H	Aston Villa	W 5-0	12	18	Lineker 3, Lynex (p), Eastoe	11885
13	Nov 3	A	Everton	L 0-3	12	20	- / Heath, Sheedy, Steven	27784
14	10	H	Manchester United	L 2-3	12	21	Banks, Lineker / Brazil, Hughes, Strachan	23840
15	17	H	Norwich City	W 2-0	15	20	Banks, Lynex (p)	9693
16	25	A	Nottingham Forest	L 1-2	15	19	Banks / Davenport 2 (1p)	21463
17	Dec 1	H	Queens Park Rangers	W 4-0	18	17	Lineker, A Smith, Lynex, Banks	10218
18	8	A	Sunderland	W 4-0	21	17	A Smith 2, Lineker, Lynex	16441
19	15	H	Luton Town	D 2-2	22	15	Lynex, A Smith / Harford, B Stein	10476
20	23	H	Coventry City	W 5-1	25	14	Lynex (p), Rennie, Lineker 2, A Smith / Gynn	18016
21	26	A	Liverpool	W 2-1	28	12	A Smith, Lineker / Neal (p)	38419
22	29	A	Watford	L 1-4	28	14	O'Neill / Barnes, Reilly, Sterling, Terry	19491
23	Jan 1	H	Southampton	L 1-2	28	15	Banks / Armstrong, Wallace	15257
24	12	H	Stoke City	D 0-0	29	15		10111
25	Feb 2	H	Chelsea	D 1-1	30	15	Lineker / Speedie (p)	15657
26	23	H	Everton	L 1-2	30	16	Lynex / Gray 2	17345
27	Mar 2	H	Aston Villa	W 1-0	33	15	A Smith	16285
28	9	H	Sheffield Wednesday	W 3-1	36	13	Lineker, O'Neill, A Smith / Varadi	14037
29	16	A	Arsenal	L 0-2	36	15	- / Williams, Meade	20663
30	20	A	Newcastle United	W 4-1	39	11	Banks 2, Lineker, A Smith / Beardsley	21764
31	23	H	West Ham United	W 1-0	42	10	Lineker	11375
32	30	A	West Bromwich Albion	L 0-2	42	11	- / Hunt 2	9347
33	Apr 3	A	Manchester United	L 1-2	42	11	Lineker / Robson, Stapleton	35590
34	6	H	Liverpool	L 0-1	42	11	- / Whelan	22942
35	9	A	Southampton	L 1-3	42	13	Lynex (p) / Bond, Jordan, Lawrence	15638
36	13	H	Tottenham Hotspur	L 1-2	42	14	Peake / Falco, Hoddle	15609
37	20	A	Norwich City	W 3-1	45	12	A Smith 2, Banks / Donowa	12634
38	23	A	Ipswich Town	L 0-2	45	12	- / D'Avray, Sunderland	13666
39	27	H	Nottingham Forest	W 1-0	48	12	Lineker	13886
40	May 4	A	Queens Park Rangers	L 3-4	48	15	Lineker 2, Wilson / Fillery, Gregory, Bannister, Robinson	9071
41	6	H	Sunderland	W 2-0	51	11	Lineker 2	11455
42	11	A	Luton Town	L 0-4	51	15	- / Harford, Nwajiobi, Preece, B Stein	11802

Final League Position: 15
Average Home League Attendance: 14530

League appearances (shirt numbers)

Match	Wallington	Feeley	B.Smith	Banks	Rennie	O'Neill	Lynex	Lineker	A.Smith	Ramsey	Bright	MacDonald	Hazell	Peake	Wilson	Andrews	Williams	Eastoe	Jones
1	1	2	3	4	5	6	7	8	9	10	11								
2	1	2	3	12		6	7	8	9	10*	11			4	5				
3	1	2	3	12		6	7	8	9	10	11			4*	5				
4	1	2	3			6	7	8	9	10*	11	12		4	5				
5	1	2	3			6	7	8	9*	10	11	12		4	5				
6	1	2	3			6	7	8	9	10	11			4	5				
7	1	2	3*			6	7	8	9	10	11	12		4	5				
8	1	2	3			6	7	8	9	10*	11	12		4	5				
9	1	2	3			6	7	8	9	10	11*	12		4	5				
10	1	2	3			6	7	8	9	10	11	12		4*	5				
11	1	2	3			6	7*	8	9	10	11	12		4	5				
12		2	3	4		6	7	8	9	10*		12			5	1		11	
13		2	3	4		6	7	8	9	10					5	1		11	
14		2	3	4*		6	7	8	9	10		12			5	1		11	
15		2	3	4		6	7	8	9*	10		12			5	1		11	
16		2	3	4		6	7	8	9	10		12			5*	1		11	
17		2	3	4		6	7	8	9	10					5	1	11		
18		2	3	4		6	7	8	9	10					5	1	11		
19		2	3	4		6	7		9	10					5	1	11	8	
20		2	3	4		6	7	8	9	10					5	1	11		
21		2	3	4		6	7	8	9	10					5	1	11		
22		2	3	4		6	7	8	9	10					5	1	11		
23		2	3	4		6	7	8	9	10					5	1	11		
24		2	3	4		6	7	8	9	10					5	1	11		
25		2	3			6	7	8	9	10				4	5	1	11		
26		2	3			6	7	8	9*	10		12		4	5	1	11		
27		2	3			6	7	8	9	10				4	5	1	11		
28		2	3			6	7	8	9	10*		12		4	5	1	11		
29		2	3			6	7	8	9	10		12		4*	5	1	11		
30		2	3	4		6	7	8	9	10					5	1	11		
31		2*	3	4		6	7	8	9	10		12			5	1	11		
32		2*	3	4		6	7	8	9	10		12			5	1	11		
33		2	3	4		6	7	8	9	10					5	1	11		
34		2	3	4		6	7	8	9	10		12			5	1	11*		
35		2	3	4		6	7	8	9	10					5	1	11		
36		2	3	4		6	7	8	9*	10		12		11	5	1			
37		2	3	4		6	7	8	9	10					5	1	11		
38		2	3	4		6	7	8	9	10*		12			5	1	11		
39		2	3	4		6	7	8	9	10					5	1	11		
40			3	4		6	7	8	9	10					5	1	11		
41		2	3			6	7	8	9	10				4	5	1	11		
42		2*	3			6	7	8	9	10		12		4	5	1	11		

League Appearances: Wallington 11, Feeley 35, B.Smith 30, Banks 30, Rennie 3, O'Neill 42, Lynex 42, Lineker 41, A.Smith 36, Ramsey 38, Bright 2, MacDonald 13, Hazell 14, Peake 21, Wilson 38, Andrews 31, Williams 27, Eastoe 6, Jones 2

Sub: B.Smith 3, Bright 3, MacDonald 14, Peake 1, Eastoe 1

League Goals: Banks 9, Rennie 1, O'Neill 2, Lynex 13, Lineker 24, A.Smith 12, Ramsey 1, Wilson 1, Eastoe 1

FA CUP

No	Date		Opponents	Result	Scorers	Att
1	Jan 5	A	Burton Albion (3)	W 6-1	Lineker 3, A Smith 2, Lynex / Vaughan	22492
2	16		Burton Albion (3 rep)	W 1-0	Ramsey	
3	26	H	Carlisle United (4)	W 1-0	B Smith	14635
4	Feb 19	A	Millwall (5)	L 0-2	- / Fashanu, McLeary	16160

FA Cup teams (all four ties): Feeley 2, B.Smith 3, Banks 4, Wilson 5, O'Neill 6, Lynex 7, Lineker 8, A.Smith 9, Ramsey 10, Williams 11, Andrews 1.

FOOTBALL LEAGUE CUP (Milk Cup)

No	Date		Opponents	Result	Scorers	Att
1	Sep 26	H	Brentford (2 leg 1)	W 4-2	O'Neill, Banks, Lynex, Lineker / Alexander, Kamara	7638
2	Oct 9	A	Brentford (2 leg 2)	W 2-0	Ramsey, A Smith	6291
3	30	A	Luton Town (3)	L 1-3	Lineker / Moss, Donaghy, Williams (og)	11423

Milk Cup shirt numbers:
- Tie 1: Wallington 1, Feeley 2, B.Smith 3, Peake 4, Wilson 5, O'Neill 6, Lynex 7, Lineker 8, A.Smith 9, Ramsey 10, Bright 11
- Tie 2: Wallington 1, Feeley 2, B.Smith 3, Banks 4, Wilson 5, O'Neill 6, Lynex 7*, Lineker 8, A.Smith 9, Ramsey 10, Bright 11, MacDonald 12
- Tie 3: Feeley 2, B.Smith 3, Peake 4, Wilson 5, O'Neill 6, Lynex 7, Lineker 8, A.Smith 9, Ramsey 10, Eastoe 11*, Andrews 1, MacDonald 12

Dismissals: None, though Wilson was sent off in a friendly v Rangers (a) on Aug 8.

Note: Jan 5, drawn away but played at Baseball Ground (Derby County); tie subsequently ordered to be replayed behind closed doors by F.A. following crowd trouble;

Jan 16, originally scheduled for Baseball Ground (Derby County) but switched to Highfield Road (Coventry City) due to inclement weather and ground committments by order of the F.A.

13 October: Alongside Lineker and Lynex, Alan Smith was the third member of Gordon Milne's prolific triumverate of strikers that kept the Foxes in the top flight during this period. Here he is seen in action against the Arsenal side that he would later join with great success.

1984-85
Back: Kelly, Feeley, Peake, Hazell, A Smith, O'Neill, Bright, Williams.
Middle: Richardson (Youth Team Manager), Banks, Ramsey, MacDonald, Wallington, Andrews, Rennie, Lineker, Jones, McVey (Physio).
Front: Burnside, Lynex, Summers (Coach), Milne (Manager), B Smith, Wilson.

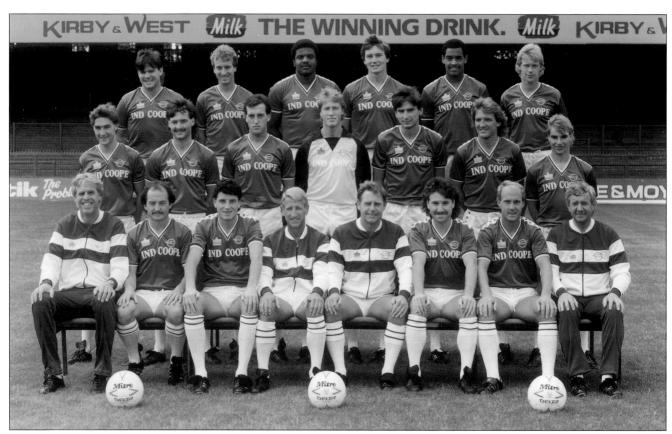

1985-86
Back: Feeley, Peake, Hazell, O'Neill, Bright, Williams.
Middle: Kelly, Banks, Rennie, Andrews, A Smith, Osman, Jones.
Front: Richardson (Youth Team Manager), Lynex, Ramsey, Summers (Coach), Milne (Manager), B Smith, Wilson, McVey (Physio).

Season 1985-86

Champions: Liverpool
Relegated: Ipswich Town, Birmingham City, West Bromwich Albion

FOOTBALL LEAGUE DIVISION ONE (Canon League)

Match No	Date		Opponents	Result	Pts	Pos	Scorers	Att	Ian Andrews	Paul Ramsey	Bobby Smith	Robert Kelly	Russell Osman	John O'Neill	Steve Lynex	Mark Bright	Alan Smith	Ian Wilson	Ian Banks	Ali Mauchlen	Tommy Williams	Robert Jones	Andy Feeley	Tony Sealy	David Rennie	Gary McAllister	Simon Morgan	Jerry Roberts	Tommy Christensen	Laurie Cunningham	Mark Venus
1	Aug 17	H	Everton	W 3-1	3	-	B Smith, Bright 2 / Mountfield	16932	1	2	3	4	5	6	7	8	9	10	11												
2	21	A	Manchester City	D 1-1	4	-	Wilson / Lillis	25528	1	2	3	4	5	6	7	8	9	10	11												
3	24	A	Oxford United	L 0-5	4	13	- / Hebberd, Hamilton 2, Charles, Trewick (p)	9626	1	2	3	4	5	6	7	8	9*	10	11	12											
4	28	H	Chelsea	D 0-0	5	13		11248	1	4	3		5	6	7	8	9	10	11		2										
5	31	A	Arsenal	L 0-1	5	15	- / Woodcock	18207	1	4		11	5	6	7	8	9*	10	12	3	2										
6	Sep 4	H	Watford	D 2-2	6	15	Ramsey, Bright / Rostron 2	9672	1	4			5	6	7	8	9*	3	12	10	2	11									
7	8	H	Nottingham Forest	L 0-3	6	19	- / Webb, Davenport, Rice	14247	1	4			5	6	7	8	12	3	11	10	2	9*									
8	14	A	West Ham United	L 0-3	6	21	- / Cottee, Devonshire, McAvennie	12125	1	4*	3	7	5	6		8	9		11	10	2	12									
9	21	A	Birmingham City	L 1-2	6	21	Sealy / Geddis 2	9834	1	4		11	5*	6		8	9		12	10	2		3	7							
10	28	H	Ipswich Town	W 1-0	9	19	A Smith	7290	1	2				6	7		9	12	11	10			5	8*		4	3				
11	Oct 2	H	Oxford United	D 4-4	10	18	A Smith, Wilson, McAllister, Lynex (p) / Thomas, Trewick (p), Aldridge 2	7711	1	2				6	7	8	9	11		10			5	12		4	3*				
12	6	A	Coventry City	L 0-3	10	19	- / Bowman, Gibson, Regis	10959	1	10				6	7	8	9		11				2	5		4	3				
13	12	H	West Bromwich Albion	D 2-2	11	19	A Smith, Lynex (p) / Crooks 2	7236					5	6	7	8	9		11				2	10		4	3	1			
14	19	H	Sheffield Wednesday	L 2-3	11	19	Lynex, A Smith / Marwood, Chapman, Jonsson	10259	1				5	6	7	8	9		11	12			2	10*		4	3				
15	26	A	Tottenham Hotspur	W 3-1	14	19	A Smith, Lynex (p), Bright / Falco	17944	1				5	6	7	8	9		11	10			2			4	3				
16	Nov 2	A	Liverpool	L 0-1	14	19	- / Rush	31718	1				5	6	7	8	9		11	10			2			4	3				
17	9	H	Southampton	D 2-2	15	19	A Smith, Lynex (p) / Puckett, Armstrong	8080	1				5	6	7	8*	9		11	10			2			4	3			12	
18	16	A	Queens Park Rangers	L 0-2	15	20	- / Wicks, Fereday	11085	1				5	6		8	9	11	12	10			2			4	3			7*	
19	23	H	Manchester United	W 3-0	18	19	McAllister, A Smith 2	22008	1				5	6			9	11	7	10			2			4	3			8	
20	30	A	Newcastle United	L 1-2	18	19	A Smith / Clarke, Beardsley	17311	1				5	6			9	11	7	10			2			4	3			8	
21	Dec 7	H	Manchester City	D 1-1	19	18	A Smith / Davies	10289	1				5	6			9	11	7	10			2			4	3			8	
22	14	A	Everton	W 2-1	22	17	McAllister (p), A Smith / Richardson	23347	1				5	6	12		9	11	7	10			2			4	3			8*	
23	26	H	Aston Villa	W 3-1	25	16	A Smith, Bright / Walters	13752	1				5	6	12		9	11	7	10			2			4	3			8*	
24	28	A	Watford	L 1-2	25	16	A Smith / West 2	14709	1				5	6		8	9	11	7	10			2			4	3				
25	Jan 1	A	Luton Town	L 1-3	25	16	Bright / Harford 3	10917	1	11			5	6	12	8	9		7	10			2			4*	3				
26	11	H	West Ham United	L 0-1	25	17	- / McAvennie	11359	1	12			5	6	7	8*	9		11	10			2			4	3				
27	18	H	Arsenal	D 2-2	26	16	Banks, Sealy / Robson, Nicholas	11246	1	8			5	6	7		9		11	10*			2	12		4	3				
28	Feb 1	A	Chelsea	D 2-2	27	17	Mauchlen, Lynex (p) / Jones, Shearer	12372	1				5	6	7		9	4	11	10			2	8			3				
29	Mar 8	A	Coventry City	W 2-1	30	17	McAllister, A Smith / Pickering	10744	1				5	6	7		9		11*	10			2	8		4	3			12	
30	12	H	Birmingham City	W 4-2	33	17	McAllister, Sealy, A Smith, Lynex (p) / Clarke, Kennedy	8458	1				5	6	7		9			10			2	8		4	3			11	
31	15	A	West Bromwich Albion	D 2-2	34	17	Sealy 2 / Varadi, Mackenzie	8337	1				5	6	7		9			10			2	8		4	3			11	
32	18	A	Sheffield Wednesday	L 0-1	34	17	- / Sterland	18874	1				5	6	7		9		11	10			2	8		4	3	1			
33	22	A	Nottingham Forest	L 3-4	34	17	A Smith 2, Sealy / Bowyer, Carr, Clough 2	14484	1				5	6	7*		9	12		10			2	8		4	3			11	
34	29	H	Luton Town	D 0-0	35	17		9912	1				5	6	7		9		12	10			2	8		4	3			11*	
35	31	A	Aston Villa	L 0-1	35	18	- / Stainrod	12200	1			12	5	6			9		7	10			2	8			3			11*	
36	Apr 5	H	Tottenham Hotspur	L 1-4	35	18	Lynex (p) / Bowen, Falco 3	9574	1				5	6	7		9		11	10			2	8		4	3				
37	8	A	Ipswich Town	W 2-0	38	16	McAllister, A Smith	11718	1	2			5	6	7		9		11	10				8		4	3				
38	12	A	Southampton	D 0-0	39	16		13403	1	2			5	6	7		9		11	10				8		4	3				
39	14	H	Queens Park Rangers	L 1-4	39	16	McAllister (p) / Allen, Bannister, Robinson, Byrne	7724			3		5	6	7		9		11	10				8		4	2*	1	12		
40	26	A	Manchester United	L 0-4	39	19	- / Blackmore, Davenport, Hughes, Stapleton	38840	1	7*	3		5	6		12			11	10				8		4	2			9	
41	30	H	Liverpool	L 0-2	39	20	- / Rush, Whelan	25799	1		3	11	5	6			9		12	10				8		4*	2			7	
42	May 3	H	Newcastle United	W 2-0	42	18	Mauchlen, Banks (p)	13171	1		3	4	5	6			9	11	12	10				8*			2			7	

							League Appearances		39	13	13	8	40	41	28	22	38	24	24	35	8	2	26	19	3	31	30	3	1	13	1
							Sub			1	1							2	2	2	1	7	2		1	2				1	2
							League Goals			1	1				8	6	19	2	2	2				6		7					

Final League Position: 19
Average Home League Attendance: 11792

FA CUP

Match No	Date		Opponents	Result	Scorers	Att	Ian Andrews	Paul Ramsey	Bobby Smith	Robert Kelly	Russell Osman	John O'Neill	Steve Lynex	Mark Bright	Alan Smith	Ian Wilson	Ian Banks	Ali Mauchlen	Tommy Williams	Robert Jones	Andy Feeley	Tony Sealy	David Rennie	Gary McAllister	Simon Morgan	Jerry Roberts	Tommy Christensen	Laurie Cunningham	Mark Venus
1	Jan 4	A	Bristol Rovers (3)	L 1-3	McAllister (p) / Stevenson, Morgan 2	9392	1	11			5	6		8	9		7	10			2			4	3				

FOOTBALL LEAGUE CUP (Milk Cup)

Match No	Date		Opponents	Result	Scorers	Att	Ian Andrews	Paul Ramsey	Bobby Smith	Robert Kelly	Russell Osman	John O'Neill	Steve Lynex	Mark Bright	Alan Smith	Ian Wilson	Ian Banks	Ali Mauchlen	Tommy Williams	Robert Jones	Andy Feeley	Tony Sealy	David Rennie	Gary McAllister	Simon Morgan	Jerry Roberts	Tommy Christensen	Laurie Cunningham	Mark Venus
1	Sep 25	A	Derby County (2 leg 1)	L 0-2	- / McLaren (p), Chandler	12504	1	4		12			7		9	3	11*	10		5	2	8	6						
2	Oct 9	H	Derby County (2 leg 2)	D 1-1	Wilson / Davison	10373	1	10*			5	6	7	8	9	11					2	12		4	3				

Dismissals: Aug 28, Wilson, Chelsea (h); Apr 14, Lynex, Queens Park Rangers (h).

Note: Leicester City did not enter the Full Members Cup.

26 December: Laurie Cunningham was a popular loan signing who helped to ensure City's top flight survival for one more season. He is pictured here in tandem with Ian Wilson battling for possession against Aston Villa on Boxing Day.

Champions: Everton
Relegated: Leicester City, Manchester City, Aston Villa

FOOTBALL LEAGUE DIVISION ONE (Today League)

Match No	Date		Opponents	Result	Pts	Pos	Scorers	Att
1	Aug 23	H	Luton Town	D 1-1	1	-	Smith / B Stein	9801
2	30	A	Wimbledon	L 0-1	1	20	- / Cork	5987
3	Sep 3	H	Liverpool	W 2-1	4	16	McAllister, Osman / Dalglish	16344
4	6	H	Manchester United	D 1-1	5	15	Kelly / Whiteside	16785
5	13	A	Sheffield Wednesday	D 2-2	6	14	McAllister, Moran / Chapman 2	21603
6	17	A	Norwich City	L 1-2	6	15	Smith / Barham, Biggins	14814
7	20	H	Tottenham Hotspur	L 1-2	6	17	Morgan / C Allen 2	13141
8	27	A	Queens Park Rangers	W 1-0	9	16	Smith	10021
9	Oct 4	A	Manchester City	W 2-1	12	13	Sealy, Smith / Hopkins	18033
10	11	H	Nottingham Forest	W 3-1	15	9	Smith, McAllister 2 (1p) / Birtles	18402
11	18	A	Charlton Athletic	L 0-2	15	10	- / Stuart 2	5770
12	25	H	Southampton	L 2-3	15	16	Osman, McAllister / Lawrence, Clarke, Wallace	9186
13	Nov 1	A	Aston Villa	L 0-2	15	18	- / Stainrod 2	14529
14	8	H	Newcastle United	D 1-1	16	17	Smith / McDonald (p)	9836
15	15	H	Everton	L 0-2	16	18	- / Heath, Sheedy	13450
16	22	A	Watford	L 1-5	16	19	Smith / Rostron, Barnes, Callaghan, Jackett (p), Falco	13605
17	29	H	Chelsea	D 2-2	17	18	McAllister (p), O'Neill / Bumstead, Speedie	10047
18	Dec 6	A	Coventry City	L 0-1	17	20	- / Regis	12320
19	14	H	Oxford United	W 2-0	20	17	Smith, Wilson	8480
20	20	A	Manchester United	L 0-2	20	18	- / C Gibson, Stapleton	34180
21	26	H	Arsenal	D 1-1	21	19	Moran / Hayes (p)	19205
22	28	A	Everton	L 1-5	21	22	Moran / Heath 2, Wilkinson, Sheedy, O'Neill (og)	39730
23	Jan 1	A	West Ham United	L 1-4	21	22	Moran / McAvennie, Dickens, Cottee 2	16625
24	3	H	Sheffield Wednesday	W 6-1	24	20	Ramsey, Smith 2, Moran 3 / Megson	10851
25	24	A	Luton Town	L 0-1	24	20	- / Newell	9102
26	Feb 7	H	Wimbledon	W 3-1	27	18	Smith, Ramsey 2 / Fairweather	8369
27	14	A	Liverpool	L 3-4	27	19	Smith 2, Johnston (og) / Walsh, Rush 3	34259
28	21	H	Norwich City	L 0-2	27	19	- / Crook, Putney	8742
29	25	A	Tottenham Hotspur	L 0-5	27	19	- / C Allen 2 (1p), P Allen, Claesen 2	16038
30	Mar 7	A	Southampton	L 0-4	27	20	- / Le Tissier 3, Hobson	11611
31	14	H	Charlton Athletic	W 1-0	30	18	Smith	8159
32	22	A	Nottingham Forest	L 1-2	30	19	Mauchlen / Carr, Clough	18679
33	25	H	Queens Park Rangers	W 4-1	33	18	McAllister 2 (1p), Ramsey, McDonald (og) / Rosenior	7384
34	28	H	Manchester City	W 4-0	36	18	Morgan, Smith, McAllister, Ramsey	10743
35	Apr 4	A	Newcastle United	L 0-2	36	18	- / Goddard, Wharton	23360
36	11	H	Aston Villa	D 1-1	37	19	Moran / Walters	11933
37	18	A	West Ham United	W 2-0	40	18	Smith, O'Neill	10434
38	20	A	Arsenal	L 1-4	40	19	Osman / Davis, Hayes 2 (1p), Nicholas	18767
39	25	H	Watford	L 1-2	40	19	Moran / Sterling, Bardsley	9448
40	May 2	A	Chelsea	L 1-3	40	19	Smith / Durie, Dixon 2	11975
41	4	H	Coventry City	D 1-1	41	20	Ramsey / Gynn	14903
42	9	A	Oxford United	D 0-0	42	20		10183

Player appearances (shirt numbers worn)

Columns: Ian Andrews, Paul Ramsey, Mark Venus, Russell Osman, Steve Walsh, Gary McAllister, Steve Lynex, Mark Bright, Alan Smith, Ian Wilson, Ian Banks, Tony Sealy, Robert Kelly, Simon Morgan, Steve Moran, Andy Feeley, Ali Mauchlen, Paul Bunce, John O'Neill, Robert Alleyne, Phil Horner, Mich D'Avray, Paul Reid, Steve Wilkinson, Kevin Jobling, John Buckley, Martin Russell

Match No	Andrews	Ramsey	Venus	Osman	Walsh	McAllister	Lynex	Bright	Smith	Wilson	Banks	Sealy	Kelly	Morgan	Moran	Feeley	Mauchlen	Bunce	O'Neill	Alleyne	Horner	D'Avray	Reid	Wilkinson	Jobling	Buckley	Russell
1	1	2	3	4	5	6*	7	8	9	10	11	12															
2	1	2	3	4	5	6	7	8	9	10	11*	12															
3	1	2	3	4	5	6	7*		9	10	11	12					8										
4	1	2	3	4	5	6	7		9	10	11	12					8*										
5	1	2	3	4	5	6	7*		9	10	11	12					8										
6	1	2	3	4	5	6	7*		9	10	11	12					8										
7	1	7	3	4	5	6			9	10	11	12		2*			8										
8	1		3	4	5	6			9	10	11	12		2	7		8*										
9	1		3	4	5	6			9	10	11	12		2	7		8*										
10	1		3	4	5	6			9	10	11	12		2	7		8*										
11	1		3	4	5	6			9	10	11*	12		2	7		8										
12	1		3	4	5	6			9	10	11	12		2	7		8*										
13	1		3	4					9	10	11*	12		2	7		8		5								
14	1		3	4*		6			9	10	11	12		2	7		8		5								
15	1		3	4		6			9	10	11	12		2	7		8*		5								
16	1		3	4		6			9	10	11	12		2	7*		8		5								
17	1		3	4		6			9	10	11			2	7		8		5								
18	1		3	4		6			9	10	11	12		2	7		8		5*								
19	1		3	4		6			9	10	11	12		2	7		8*		5								
20	1		3*	4		6			9	10	11	12		2	7		8		5								
21	1		3	4					9	10*	11	12		2	7		8		5								
22	1		3	4		6			9	10	11	12		2	7*		8		5								
23	1		3	4		6			9	10	11*	12		2	7		8		5								
24	1		3	4		6			9	10	11	12		2	7		8		5*								
25	1		3	4	5	6			9	10*	11	12		2	7		8										
26	1		3	4	5	6			9	10	11*	12		2	7		8										
27	1		3	4		6			9	10	11			2	7				5			8					
28	1		3*	4		6			9	10	11	12		2	7				5			8					
29	1		3	4		6			9		11	12		2	7				5*			8					
30	1		3	4	5				9	10	11	12		2	7							8*					
31	1	2	3	4	5	6			9	10		12			7	11	8*										
32	1	2	3	4	5	6			9	10		12			7	11	8*										
33	1	2	3	4		6			9	10					7	11	8		5								
34	1	2	3	4		6			9	10		12			7*	11	8		5								
35	1	2	3	4		6			9	10					7*	11	8		5				12				
36	1	2	3	4		6			9	10					7*	11	8		5				12				
37	1	2	3	4		6			9	10		12				11	8		5								7*
38	1	2	3	4	12	6			9	10						11	8		5								7*
39	1	2	3	4		6			9	10		12			7*	11			5								8
40	1	2	3	4		6			9	10		12				11	8		5								7*
41	1	2	3	4		6			9	10		12				11	8		5								7*
42	1	2	3	4		6			9	10		12				11	8		5								7*

Final League Position: 20																											
League Appearances	42	29	38	31	20	39	7	2	42	36	2	9	8	41	24	11	30	5	29	1	1	3	5		1	1	5
Sub		1		1		3					1	1		9	6		3	1		1		2	2		1	1	2	4
League Goals		6		3		9			17	1		1	1	2	9		1		2								

Average Home League Attendance: 11697

FA CUP

	Date		Opponents	Result	Scorers	Att
1	Jan 10	A	Queens Park Rangers (3)	L 2-5	Smith, McAllister (p) / Fenwick 2 (1p), Lee, James, Byrne	9684

Appearances: Andrews 1, Wilson 10, Venus 3, Walsh 5, McAllister 6, Moran 7†, Smith 9, Banks 11*, Mauchlen 8, Osman 4, Morgan 2, Sealy 12, (14).

FOOTBALL LEAGUE CUP (Littlewoods Cup)

	Date		Opponents	Result	Scorers	Att
1	Sep 23	A	Swansea City (2 leg 1)	W 2-0	McAllister, Smith	9590
2	Oct 8	H	Swansea City (2 leg 2)	W 4-2	Morgan, Smith, Moran 2 / Harrison, McCarthy	5884
3	29	A	Liverpool (3)	L 1-4	Moran / McMahon 3, Dalglish	20248

Dismissals: Oct 18, Walsh, Charlton Athletic (a); Dec 6, Venus, Coventry City (a).

Note: Leicester City did not enter the Full Members Cup.

1986-87
Back: Reid, Feeley, Banks, Andrews, Roberts, O'Neill, Kelly, Jobling.
Middle: Richardson (Youth Team Manager), Ramsey, Morgan, Venus, Horner, A Smith, Walsh, McAllister, Bright, Osman, McVey (Physio).
Front: Mauchlen, Lynex, Bunce, Milne (General Manager), Hamilton (Manager), Wilson, B Smith, Sealy.

Promoted: Millwall, Aston Villa, Middlesbrough
Relegated: Sheffield United, Reading, Huddersfield Town

Players (left to right): Ian Andrews, Simon Morgan, Robbie James, Russell Osman, Steve Walsh, Ian Wilson, Gary Ford, Gary McAllister, Nick Cusack, Paul Ramsey, Martin Russell, Mark Venus, Steve Moran, Steve Wilkinson, Phil Horner, Paul Reid, Paul Cooper, Ali Mauchlen, Jari Rantanen, Mike Newell, Tony Brien, Dave Langan, Kevin Jobling, Kjetil Osvold, Kevin MacDonald, Peter Weir, Steve Prindiville, Nicky Cross, Phil Turner, Grant Brown, Paul Groves

FOOTBALL LEAGUE DIVISION TWO (Barclays League)

Match No	Date		Opponents	Result	Points	Position	Scorers	Att
1	Aug 15	H	Shrewsbury Town	L 0-1	-	-	- / Geddis	8469
2	19	A	Leeds United	L 0-1	-	-	- / Sheridan (p)	21034
3	29	H	Millwall	W 1-0	3	17	Moran	7559
4	31	A	Stoke City	L 1-2	3	18	McAllister / Saunders, Heath	9948
5	Sep 5	H	Aston Villa	L 0-2	3	22	- / Walters, Lillis	10286
6	12	A	Crystal Palace	L 1-2	3	22	McAllister / Thomas, Wright	8925
7	16	H	Oldham Athletic	W 4-1	6	20	Newell, Rantanen, Ford, Wilson / Ritchie (p)	7358
8	19	H	Plymouth Argyle	W 4-0	9	17	Wilson, Ford, Newell, Rantanen	8872
9	26	A	Bournemouth	W 3-2	12	13	Newell, Osman, Mauchlen / Aylott, Newson (p)	7969
10	30	H	Ipswich Town	D 1-1	13	12	Moran / Woods	11533
11	Oct 3	A	Manchester City	L 2-4	13	15	Newell, Rantanen / Stewart 2, Varadi 2	16481
12	10	A	Barnsley	D 0-0	14	15		8665
13	17	A	Sheffield United	L 1-2	14	17	McAllister / Philliskirk 2	10593
14	21	H	West Bromwich Albion	W 3-0	17	14	Walsh, Moran 2	9262
15	24	A	Hull City	D 2-2	18	14	McAllister, Walsh / Roberts, Williams	8826
16	31	H	Blackburn Rovers	L 1-2	18	17	Moran / Garner, Hendry	8650
17	Nov 7	H	Swindon Town	W 3-2	21	15	Ramsey, Walsh, Venus / Barnes, Quinn	8346
18	14	A	Birmingham City	D 2-2	22	15	Walsh, Cusack / Whitton 2	8666
19	21	H	Bradford City	L 0-2	22	15	- / Futcher, Hendrie	11543
20	28	A	Huddersfield Town	L 0-1	22	16	- / Cooper	6704
21	Dec 5	H	Middlesbrough	D 0-0	23	16		9411
22	12	A	Oldham Athletic	L 0-2	23	16	- / Wright, Palmer	4785
23	26	H	Bournemouth	L 0-1	23	19	- / Cooke	11452
24	28	A	Plymouth Argyle	L 0-4	23	19	- / Smith, Tynan 2, Anderson	15581
25	Jan 1	A	Millwall	L 0-1	23	19	- / Briley	7220
26	2	H	Crystal Palace	D 4-4	24	21	Brien, McAllister (p), Reid, Wilkinson / Barber, Pennyfather, Wright 2	10104
27	16	A	Shrewsbury Town	D 0-0	25	21		5025
28	30	A	Reading	W 2-1	28	19	Osman, Walsh / Williams	6645
29	Feb 6	A	Aston Villa	L 1-2	28	20	Newell / Lillis, Evans	18867
30	13	H	Leeds United	W 3-2	31	19	McAllister 2 (1p), Cross / Williams, Sheridan (p)	11937
31	20	A	Ipswich Town	W 2-0	34	17	Reid, Newell	11084
32	27	H	Manchester City	W 1-0	37	17	Cross	13852
33	Mar 5	H	Sheffield United	W 1-0	40	16	Cross	12256
34	12	A	Barnsley	D 1-1	41	16	Walsh / Rees	7447
35	16	H	Stoke City	D 1-1	42	16	Mauchlen / Shaw	10502
36	19	A	Blackburn Rovers	D 3-3	43	16	Reid 2, Newell / Sellars, Hendry, Walsh (og)	12506
37	26	H	Hull City	W 2-1	46	16	Newell, Weir (p) / Edwards	10353
38	Apr 2	A	Swindon Town	L 2-3	46	16	Osman, McAllister / Quinn 2, Barnes	9450
39	5	H	Birmingham City	W 2-0	49	16	Osman 2	13541
40	9	A	West Bromwich Albion	D 1-1	50	16	Cross / Lynex	11013
41	23	H	Reading	W 1-0	53	16	Walsh	9603
42	30	A	Bradford City	L 1-4	53	16	Reid / Futcher (p), Ormondroyd, Mitchell, Hendrie	14393
43	May 2	H	Huddersfield Town	W 3-0	56	13	Cross 2, Groves	9803
44	7	A	Middlesbrough	W 2-1	59	13	Weir, McAllister / Slaven	27645

Final League Position:	13
Average Home League Attendance:	10157

FA CUP

	Date		Opponents	Result	Scorers	Att
1	Jan 9	A	Oxford United (3)	L 0-2	- / Foyle, Saunders	7557

FOOTBALL LEAGUE CUP (Littlewoods Cup)

	Date		Opponents	Result	Scorers	Att
1	Sep 23	H	Scunthorpe Utd (2 leg 1) W 2-1		McAllister, Newell / Flounders	7718
2	Oct 6	A	Scunthorpe Utd (2 leg 2) W 2-1		Reid, Rantanen / Johnson	4031
3	28	H	Oxford United (3)	D 0-0		6171
4	Nov 4	H	Oxford United (3 rep)	L 2-3	Newell 2 / Saunders, Shelton 2	10476

FULL MEMBERS CUP (Simod Cup)

	Date		Opponents	Result	Scorers	Att
1	Nov 10	H	Huddersfield Town (1)	W 1-0	Ford	3440
2	Dec 1	A	Charlton Athletic (2)	W 2-1 aet	Jobling 2 / Brien (og)	1327
3	Jan 19	H	Stoke City (3)	D 0-0 aet		5161

Dismissals: 15 Aug, Walsh, Shrewsbury Town (h); Dec 12, Newell, Oldham Athletic (a); Mar 19, Newell, Blackburn Rovers (a); Mar 26, McAllister, Hull City (h).
Note: Jan 19, lost 3-5 on penalties (McAllister, Weir, Venus scored)

1987-88
Back: Garwood, Williams, Russell, Andrews, Cooper, Muggleton, Alleyne, Prindiville, Reid.
Middle: Morgan, Horner, Ramsey, Walsh, McAllister, Cusack, Brien, Wilkinson.
Front: Davies (Kit Manager), Venus, Ford, Moran, James, Hamilton (Manager), Osman, Morris (Coach), Jobling, Mauchlen, Wilson, McVey (Physio).

Promoted: Chelsea, Manchester City, Crystal Palace
Relegated: Shrewsbury Town, Birmingham City, Walsall

FOOTBALL LEAGUE DIVISION TWO (Barclays League)

Match No	Date		Opponents	Result	Points	Position	Scorers	Att	Martin Hodge	Ali Mauchlen	Tony Spearing	Paul Ramsey	Steve Walsh	Grant Brown	Paul Reid	Nicky Cross	Mike Newell	Gary McAllister	Phil Turner	Jimmy Quinn	Paul Cooper	Alan Paris	Peter Weir	Simon Morgan	Martin Russell	Darren Williams	Paul Groves	Tony Brien	Carl Muggleton	Gary Mills	Mick Kennedy	Gary Charles	Marc North	Peter Eccles	Dave Puttnam	Steve Wilkinson	Match No
1	Aug 27	H	West Bromwich Albion	D 1-1	1	-	Mauchlen / Paskin	13082	1	2	3	4	5	6	7*	8	9	10	11	12																	1
2	29	A	Portsmouth	L 0-3	1	-	- / Quinn, Connor 2	10737		2	3	4†	5		14	8*	9	10	7	12	1	6	11														2
3	Sep 3	A	Birmingham City	W 3-2	4	12	Newell, Cross, Quinn / Robinson, Walsh (og)	7932		2	3	4	5	6	7	8*	9	10	11		1	12															3
4	10	H	Ipswich Town	L 0-1	4	13	- / Atkinson	10816		2*	3	4	5	6	7†	8	9	10	12	11	1	14															4
5	17	A	Oxford United	D 1-1	5	14	Cross / Shelton	6610		2	3	4	5	6	12	8*	9	10	11		1		7														5
6	21	H	Plymouth Argyle	W 1-0	8	11	Newell	9117		2†	3	4	5	6		8	9	10	11		1		7	14													6
7	24	H	Watford	D 2-2	9	11	Walsh, Reid / Porter, Wilkinson	10957		2		4	5	6	7	8	9	10			1		11	3													7
8	Oct 1	A	Chelsea	L 1-2	9	15	Quinn / Lee, Roberts (p)	7050		2		4	5	6	7	8	9	10	14		1		3	11†													8
9	4	A	Hull City	D 2-2	10	18	McAllister, Williams / Edwards, De Mange	5079		4		5			7	8	9	10	6		1	2	3			11											9
10	8	H	Brighton & Hove Albion	W 1-0	13	12	Quinn	9021		4		5	6	7	8	9	10	14	1	2†	3		11*	12													10
11	15	H	Stoke City	W 2-0	16	10	Newell 2	10312				5	6	7	8	9	10	1	2	11*	3		12	4													11
12	22	A	Leeds United	D 1-1	17	11	Quinn / Hilaire	17263			3		5	6	7	8	9	10	14	1	2	11*	12	4†													12
13	26	H	Swindon Town	D 3-3	18	10	McAllister 2 (1p), King (og) / King, White, Henry	9751			3		5	6*	7	8	9	10	4	1	2	11	12														13
14	29	A	Shrewsbury Town	L 0-3	18	14	- / Finley, Irvine 2	5178		4	3*		5		7	8	9	10	14	1	2	11†	6	12													14
15	Nov 5	H	Manchester City	D 0-0	19	16		14080		4	3		5		7	8	9	10	14	1	2		6	11†													15
16	12	A	Walsall	W 1-0	22	10	Newell	6895		4	3		5		7	8	9	10	14	1	2		6	11†													16
17	19	A	Crystal Palace	L 2-4	22	13	Newell, McAllister / Thomas, Barber 2, Bright	8843		4	3				7	8	9	10	11	1	2		6			5											17
18	26	H	Bradford City	W 1-0	25	10	Quinn	9533		4	3		5		7		9	10	11	1	2		6	8													18
19	Dec 3	A	Oldham Athletic	D 1-1	26	12	Quinn / Ritchie (p)	5789		4					7		9	10	3	11	1	2		6			8	5									19
20	10	H	Sunderland	W 3-1	29	9	Newell, Cross, Reid / Pascoe	11093		4†					7	12	9	10	3	11	1	2		6*	8	14	5										20
21	17	A	Barnsley	L 0-3	29	12	- / Currie (p), McGugan, Agnew	6477			3				7	8	9	10	4*	12	1	2		6	14	11	5†										21
22	26	H	Bournemouth	L 0-1	29	16	- / Clarke	13896			3	4*	5		7	14	9	10	12	11	1	2		6	8†												22
23	31	H	Blackburn Rovers	W 4-0	32	13	Turner, Cross, Newell, McAllister	10820	2†	3	4	5*		7	8	9	10	11	14	1		6		12													23
24	Jan 2	A	Ipswich Town	L 0-2	32	15	- / Linighan, Milton	14037	2	3	4†			7	8	9	10	11	1	5		6*		12													24
25	14	H	Portsmouth	W 2-1	35	14	Turner, Reid / Quinn	10567	2	3	4			7	8		10	11	9	1	5		6														25
26	21	A	West Bromwich Albion	D 1-1	36	14	Reid / Robson	15792	2	3	4*			7†	8	9	10	11	14		5		6		12		1										26
27	Feb 4	H	Hull City	L 0-2	36	15	- / Edwards 2	9996	2	3	4			7		9	10	11	8		5		6				1										27
28	11	A	Brighton & Hove Albion	D 1-1	37	17	McAllister / Nelson	9572	4	3		5		7	8	9	10	11	2		6		8†		1												28
29	18	H	Leeds United	L 1-2	37	17	Cross / Davison, Snodin	14151	1	2	3	4	5		7	8	9	10*	11†	14		6		12													29
30	25	A	Stoke City	D 2-2	38	16	Reid, Walsh / Beagrie, Bamber	9666	1	2	3	4*	5		7	8	9	10	11†	14		6		12													30
31	28	A	Swindon Town	L 1-2	38	16	Newell / Shearer, Jones (p)	7456	1	2	3		5		7	8	9	10	11	14		4†															31
32	Mar 4	H	Walsall	W 1-0	41	15	Cross	9375	1	2*	3	4	5		7	8	9	10			6			12					11								32
33	11	A	Manchester City	L 2-4	41	15	McAllister, Newell / Morley 3, Spearing (og)	22266	1	2	3†	4	5		7	8	9	10	14		6								11								33
34	15	H	Shrewsbury Town	D 1-1	42	15	McAllister / Williams	7750	1	2	3	4	5		7†	8	9	10	14		6								11								34
35	18	A	Plymouth Argyle	D 1-1	43	15	Cross / Stuart	6703	1	2	3		5		7	8	9	10			6								11	4							35
36	25	H	Birmingham City	W 2-0	46	15	Mauchlen 2	9564	1	2		5		7	8†	9	10	6*		3									11	4	12	14					36
37	27	A	Bournemouth	L 1-2	46	15	McAllister / Blissett, Newell (og)	8913	1	2		5		7	12	9	10	6		3*									11 4†	2	14						37
38	Apr 1	H	Oxford United	W 1-0	49	13	McAllister	8187	1	2		5		7	8†	9	10	6											11	4	3	14					38
39	8	A	Blackburn Rovers	D 0-0	50	16		8103	1		3	4*		7	8	9	10	6		14									11		2	12	5†				39
40	11	H	Barnsley	L 0-1	50	16	- / Lowndes	7266	1	4	3		7	8†	9	10	6	5											11		2*	14		12			40
41	15	H	Chelsea	W 2-0	53	13	Reid, Cross	19468	1	2	3		7	8	9	10	6	5											11	4							41
42	22	A	Watford	L 1-2	53	16	Newell / Wilkinson, Dean Holdsworth	11262	1	2	3		7	8†	9	10	6	5											11	4*	12	14					42
43	29	A	Bradford City	L 1-2	53	16	Paris / Jackson, Quinn	8703	1	2	3		7	8	9	10	6	5											11	4							43
44	May 1	H	Oldham Athletic	L 1-2	53	16	Newell / Wright, Kelly	7223	1	2	3		7	8†	9	10	6	5											11*	4	12	14					44
45	6	H	Crystal Palace	D 2-2	54	16	North, Cross, Madden 2 (2p)	9917	1		3	4†		7	12	9	10	6	5			14									2	8*	11				45
46	13	A	Sunderland	D 2-2	55	15	McAllister, Newell (p) / Bennett, Pascoe	15819	1		3	4		7	9	10	2	5								8								11†	14		46

Final League Position:	15	**League Appearances**	19 38 36 22 30 12 43 37 45 46 14 13 24 37 8 30 6 4 7 1 3 13 9 5 1 1 2
Average Home League Attendance:	10701	**Sub**	2 4 2 18 2 2 4 2 8 3 7 1 1
		League Goals	3 2 6 9 13 11 2 6 1 1 1

FA CUP

	Date		Opponents	Result		Scorers	Att		
1	Jan 7	A	Manchester City (3)	L 0-1		- / McNab (p)	23838	2 3 4* 7 8 9 10 11† 14 1 5 6 12	1

FOOTBALL LEAGUE CUP (Littlewoods Cup)

	Date		Opponents	Result		Scorers	Att		
1	Sep 28	H	Watford (2 leg 1)	W 4-1		Reid, Walsh, Cross, McAllister (p) / Wilkinson	9512	2 4* 5 6 7 8 9 10 14 1 12 11† 3	1
2	Oct 11	A	Watford (2 leg 2)	D 2-2		Mauchlen, Newell / Bamber, Rimmer	9087	4 5 6 7 8 9 10 1 2 3 11	2
3	Nov 2	H	Norwich City (3)	W 2-0		Newell, Reid	14586	4 3 5 7 8 9 10 1 2 6 11	3
4	30	H	Nottingham Forest (4)	D 0-0			26764	4 3 7* 12 9 10 14 11 1 2 6 8†	4
5	Dec 14	A	Nottingham Forest (4 rep)	L 1-2		Groves / Clough, Chapman	26676	4† 7 14 9 10 3 11 1 2 6 12 8 5*	5

FULL MEMBERS CUP (Simod Cup)

	Date		Opponents	Result		Scorers	Att		
1	Nov 8	A	Watford (1)	L 0-2 aet		- / Hodges, Porter (p)	3626	4 3 5* 7 8† 9 10 14 1 2 6 11 12	1

Dismissals: Oct 1, Mauchlen, Chelsea (h)

1988-89
Back: Turner, Brien, Weir, Paris, Morgan, Groves, Russell.
Middle: Lea (Coach), Roberts (Coach), Thompson, Rantanen, Muggleton, Walsh, Cooper, Quinn, Newell, Lee (Coach), McVey (Physio).
Front: Cross, McAllister, Ramsey, Pleat (Manager), Mauchlen, Spearing, Reid.

Season **1989-90**

Promoted: Leeds United, Sheffield United, Sunderland
Relegated: Bournemouth, Bradford City, Stoke City

Player columns (left to right): Martin Hodge, Rob Johnson, Tony Spearing, Ali Mauchlen, Alan Paris, Allan Evans, Kevin Russell, Wayne Clarke, Tommy Wright, Gary McAllister, Gary Mills, Paul Reid, Paul Ramsey, Dave Puttnam, Steve Walsh, Steve Wilkinson, Tony James, Simon Morgan, Paul Kitson, Lee Glover, Darren Williams, Marc North, Scott Oakes, Paul Moran, Kevin Campbell, Jason Peake, Ian Baraclough, David Oldfield, David Kelly, Richard Smith, Des Linton, Gary Fitzpatrick

FOOTBALL LEAGUE DIVISION TWO (Barclays League)

Match No	Date		Opponents	Result	Points	Position	Scorers	Att
1	Aug 19	A	Hull City	D 1-1	1	-	Clarke / Payton	8158
2	23	H	Blackburn Rovers	L 0-1	1	-	- / Sellars	11411
3	26	H	Newcastle United	D 2-2	2	16	McAllister, Spearing / Quinn, Gallacher	13693
4	Sep 2	A	Watford	L 1-3	2	21	McAllister / Wilkinson, Porter (p), Thompson	10252
5	9	H	West Bromwich Albion	L 1-3	2	24	Reid / West, Whyte, Goodman	10700
6	16	A	Bradford City	L 0-2	2	24	- / Leonard, Quinn	8732
7	23	H	Brighton & Hove Albion	W 1-0	5	24	Glover	8926
8	27	H	Sunderland	L 2-3	5	24	Williams, Paris / Armstrong, Hardyman (p), Owers	10843
9	30	A	Oldham Athletic	L 0-1	5	24	- / Ritchie	6407
10	Oct 7	H	Port Vale	L 1-2	5	24	Reid / Beckford, Cross	7268
11	14	H	Oxford United	D 0-0	6	24		8199
12	17	A	Plymouth Argyle	L 1-3	6	24	Reid / Hodges, Thomas 2	10037
13	21	H	Swindon Town	W 2-1	9	23	Reid 2 / McLoughlin	8547
14	28	A	Barnsley	D 2-2	10	23	North, Wright / Archdeacon, Currie (p)	6856
15	Nov 1	H	Wolverhampton W.	D 0-0	11	21		16580
16	4	A	Sheffield United	D 1-1	12	22	North / Evans (og)	15971
17	11	H	Leeds United	W 4-3	15	22	Ramsey 2, Moran, McAllister / Baird, Williams, Strachan (p)	18032
18	18	H	Ipswich Town	L 0-1	15	22	- / Stockwell	11661
19	25	A	Stoke City	W 1-0	18	22	Mills	12264
20	Dec 2	H	Hull City	W 2-1	21	19	Paris, McAllister (p) / Jacobs	8616
21	9	A	Blackburn Rovers	W 4-2	24	18	McAllister (p), Morgan, Campbell, Wright / Garner, Gayle	7538
22	16	A	Middlesbrough	L 1-4	24	19	McAllister (p) / Cooper 2, Slaven, Ripley	11428
23	26	H	Bournemouth	W 2-1	27	18	Campbell, Mills / Williams	14128
24	30	H	West Ham United	W 1-0	30	13	Mauchlen	16925
25	Jan 1	A	Portsmouth	W 3-2	33	13	Moran, Campbell 2 / Fillery, Wigley	9387
26	13	A	Newcastle United	L 4-5	33	15	Wright, Walsh, McAllister, Campbell / McGhee 2, Quinn 2, Gallacher	20785
27	20	H	Watford	D 1-1	34	15	Mills / Roeder	11466
28	Feb 10	H	Bradford City	D 1-1	35	14	Oldfield / Adcock	10281
29	17	A	Brighton & Hove Albion	L 0-1	35	16	- / Bremner	7498
30	21	A	West Bromwich Albion	W 1-0	38	14	Oldfield	10902
31	24	H	Stoke City	W 2-1	41	13	Oldfield, Reid / Biggins	12245
32	Mar 3	A	Ipswich Town	D 2-2	42	14	Walsh, Oldfield / Wark, Lowe	12237
33	10	A	Sunderland	D 2-2	43	15	Mills, James / Gabbiadini, Armstrong	13017
34	17	H	Port Vale	W 2-0	46	13	North, Walsh	10076
35	21	A	Oxford United	L 2-4	46	14	Reid, McAllister / Mustoe, Durnin, Stein, James (og)	5744
36	24	H	Plymouth Argyle	D 1-1	47	14	McAllister (p) / Marker	9395
37	31	A	Swindon Town	D 1-1	48	14	Kelly / Spearing (og)	8561
38	Apr 3	H	Oldham Athletic	W 3-0	51	12	North, Kelly 2	10368
39	7	H	Barnsley	D 2-2	52	12	Kelly 2 / Cooper, Agnew	8620
40	10	A	Wolverhampton W.	L 0-5	52	13	- / Bull 3, Dennison 2	18175
41	14	H	Portsmouth	D 1-1	53	13	James / Connor	8407
42	17	A	Bournemouth	W 3-2	56	12	North, Oldfield, Reid / Peacock, Aylott	6781
43	21	H	Middlesbrough	W 2-1	59	12	Kelly 2 / Slaven	9203
44	28	A	Leeds United	L 1-2	59	12	McAllister / Sterland, Strachan	32597
45	May 2	A	West Ham United	L 1-3	59	12	Ramsey / Rosenior, Keen, Morley	17939
46	5	H	Sheffield United	L 2-5	59	13	Mills, North / Wood, Deane, Agana 2, Rostron	21134

Final League Position: 13

Average Home League Attendance: 11715

League Appearances: 46 11 19 38 33 14 4 10 40 43 27 35 31 2 34 2 26 14 8 3 3 15 10 11 16 10 1

Sub: 2 1 5 6 1 1 2 5 4 2 5 3 5 2 1 9 2 4 4 1 1

League Goals: 1 1 2 1 3 10 5 8 3 3 2 1 1 1 6 2 5 5 7

FA CUP

	Date		Opponents	Result			Scorers	Att
1	Jan 6	H	Barnsley (3)	L 1-2			Paris / Currie, Lowndes	16278

FOOTBALL LEAGUE CUP (Littlewoods Cup)

	Date		Opponents	Result			Scorers	Att
1	Sep 19	A	Crystal Palace (2 leg 1)	W 2-1			Kitson, Reid / Wright	7382
2	Oct 4	H	Crystal Palace (2 leg 2)	L 2-3 aet			Clarke, Paris / Hopkins, Thomas, Bright	10283

FULL MEMBERS CUP (Zenith Data Systems Cup)

	Date		Opponents	Result			Scorers	Att
1	Nov 14	A	Charlton Athletic (2)	L 1-2			Campbell / Minto, Humphrey	1565

Dismissals: Sep 9, Wright, West Bromwich Albion (h); Mar 10, Spearing, Sunderland (a); Apr 17, Paris, Bournemouth (a).

Stand-in Goalkeepers:
May 5, North for Hodge, Sheffield United (h).

Note: Sep 2, McAllister generally credited with goal from indirect free kick which deflected off an unnamed defender; Oct 4, lost on away goals; Mar 10, goal credited to Mills, some reports credit Agboola (og).

1989-90

Back: Davies (Kit Manager), McAllister, Brown, Clarke, Paris, Rantanen, Walsh, Groves, Kitson, Roberts (Coach).
Middle: Geeson (Physio), Wilkinson, Ramsey, North, Muggleton, O'Connor, Hodge, Puttnam, Smith, Baraclough, Moore (Youth Coach).
Front: Pleat (Manager), Reid, Morgan, Mauchlen, Williams, Russell, Spearing, Mills, Kennedy, Lee (Coach).

Promoted: Oldham Athletic, West Ham United, Sheffield Wednesday, Notts County
Relegated: West Bromwich Albion, Hull City

FOOTBALL LEAGUE DIVISION TWO (Barclays League)

Match No	Date		Opponents	Result	Points	Position	Scorers	Att	Carl Muggleton	Gary Mills	Rob Johnson	Ali Mauchlen	Steve Walsh	Alan Paris	Tommy Wright	Marc North	David Oldfield	Billy Davies	David Kelly	Tony James	Ricky Hill	Paul Reid	Paul Kitson	Paul Ramsey	Martin Hodge	Tony Spearing	Mike Hooper	Des Linton	Pat Gavin	Terry Fenwick	Jason Peake	Colin Gibson	Lawrie Madden	Richard Smith	Kevin Russell	Match No
1	Aug 25	H	Bristol Rovers	W 3-2	3	-	Kelly, Wright, Alexander (og) / White, Jones	13648	1	2	3*	4	5	6	7	8	9	10†	11	12	14															1
2	28	A	Oldham Athletic	L 0-2	3	-	- / Marshall, Ritchie	13099	1	2	3	4	5	6†	7	8	9*	10	11	12	14															2
3	Sep 1	A	Port Vale	L 0-2	3	16	- / Earle, Beckford	8840	1	2	3	4	5	6*	7†	8	9	10	11		12	14														3
4	8	H	West Ham United	L 1-2	3	20	Mills / Morley, James (og)	14605	1	2	3	4†	5			8		10	11	6	7*	14	9	12												4
5	15	A	Plymouth Argyle	L 0-2	3	20	- / Hodges, Pickard	6336	2			5		7	14	8	10†	11	6	4	9*		12	1	3											5
6	18	A	Blackburn Rovers	L 1-4	3	20	Oldfield / Irvine, Atkins, Reid, Starbuck	5682	10	2		5	14	7		9	12	11	6	8*		4	1	3†												6
7	22	H	Sheffield Wednesday	L 2-4	3	22	Oldfield, Kelly / Hirst 2, Wilson, Williams	16156	10		2†	5	14	12	6	9		11		7*	8	4		3	1											7
8	29	A	Middlesbrough	L 0-6	3	23	- / Phillips, Kerr 2, Baird, Slaven, Hendrie	16178	10		2	5	3	7		9†		11*	6	14	8	4		1	12											8
9	Oct 3	H	Bristol City	W 3-0	6	20	James, Kelly 2	9815	10		2*	5	3	7	12	9		11	6		8	4		1												9
10	6	H	Notts County	W 2-1	9	19	Oldfield, Kelly / Johnson	13597	10		2	5	3	7	12	9*		11	6		8	4		1												10
11	13	A	Charlton Athletic	W 2-1	12	14	James, Balmer (og) / Dyer	6000	10		2		3	7	5†	9*		11	6		8	4		1		14	12									11
12	20	A	Portsmouth	L 1-3	12	17	Mills / Aspinall, Clarke, Black	9286	10		2		3	7	5	9		11	6	12	8	4*		1												12
13	24	H	Swindon Town	D 2-2	13	18	Mauchlen, North / Shearer, White	9592	10	12	2		3*	7	5	9		11	6	14	8	4†		1												13
14	27	H	Ipswich Town	L 1-2	13	20	Kelly (p) / Stockwell 2	11053	10		2	5		7	3*	9†		11		4	8	14	12	1					6							14
15	Nov 3	A	Oxford United	D 2-2	14	21	Wright, Kelly / Simpson, Foyle	5371	10		2	5*		7	3	12		11		4	8†	9		1					6	14						15
16	10	A	Barnsley	D 1-1	15	22	Wright / O'Connell	8581	10		2	5		7	3			11	6	4		9		1			3	1	5							16
17	17	H	Wolverhampton W.	W 1-0	18	21	Kelly	16574	10	9†	2			7*	8	12		11	6	4	14			1			3	1	5							17
18	23	A	Hull City	L 2-5	18	22	North, Reid / Payton 2, Swan 2, Palin	5855	10	9†	2			7	8	12		11	6	4	14			1		3*	1		5							18
19	Dec 1	H	Newcastle United	W 5-4	21	19	Fenwick, Kelly 3 (1p), Oldfield / Quinn 3, O'Brien	11045	10	4	2	5	14	12	3	8*		11			9			1			6	7†								19
20	15	A	Bristol Rovers	D 0-0	22	18		5791	10		2	5			14			11	12	8	7	4*		1		3	1	9†	6							20
21	23	H	Watford	D 0-0	23	19		16920	1	10		5			12	2	9*		11	8	7	4							6		3					21
22	26	A	Millwall	L 1-2	23	20	Oldfield / Sheringham 2 (1p)	6686	1			2	5	4	7	6	9		11		8	10†									14	3				22
23	Jan 1	H	West Bromwich Albion	W 2-1	26	20	Walsh, James / Ford	12210	1	10		2	5		7	4	9		11	6	8											3				23
24	12	H	Port Vale	D 1-1	27	19	Oldfield / Earle	9307	1	10		2	5		7*	4	9		11	6		8†							12		14	3				24
25	19	A	West Ham United	L 0-1	27	20	- / Parris	21652	1	10		2			12	4	9		11	6		8†								7*	3	5	14			25
26	26	H	Blackburn Rovers	L 1-3	27	21	Kelly / Livingstone, Gayle, Sulley (p)	8167	1	10		2			7	4	9		11			8									3	5	6			26
27	Feb 2	H	Plymouth Argyle	W 3-1	30	19	Wright, Kelly, James / Marker	8172	1	10†		4			7	2	9		11	6		8									14	3	5			27
28	20	A	Brighton & Hove Albion	L 0-3	30	20	- / Small, Wilkins, Wade	6455	1	10		4			7	2	9		11	6		8									3		5			28
29	23	H	Barnsley	W 2-1	33	17	James, Peake / Smith	9027	1	10		4	5		7	2	9†		11	6			14								8	3				29
30	Mar 2	A	Newcastle United	L 1-2	33	22	Wright / McGhee, Sloan	13575	1	10		4	5		7	2	9*		11	6		14	12								8†	3				30
31	5	A	Wolverhampton W.	L 1-2	33	22	Gibson / Bull, Mutch	15707	1	10		4	5		7	2	9*		11	6		12	14	8†								3				31
32	9	H	Hull City	L 0-1	33	22	- / Payton	8386	1	10		4	5		7	2	12		11	6			9*	8								3				32
33	12	A	Bristol City	L 0-1	33	22	- / Taylor	13297	1	10		4	5		7	2	9		11†	6		12	14	8								3*				33
34	16	H	Middlesbrough	W 4-3	36	20	Oldfield, Walsh, Russell, Phillips (og) / Putney, Phillips, McGee	8324	1	10		4	5		7	2	9			6			8	12								3*			11	34
35	20	H	Charlton Athletic	L 1-2	36	21	Mortimer (og) / Pitcher (p), Mortimer	8363	1	10		4	5		7	2	9			6		14	8	3†											11	35
36	23	A	Notts County	W 2-0	39	20	Mills, Russell (p)	11532	1	10*		4	5		7		9			14	6	12	8			2					3				11†	36
37	30	H	Millwall	L 1-2	39	21	Kelly / Sheringham 2	10783	1	10		4	5		7	2	9†			14	6		8			12					3*				11	37
38	Apr 1	A	Watford	L 0-1	39	21	- / Wilkinson	10078	1	10		4	5		7		9			14	6	12	8*	3		2									11†	38
39	6	H	Brighton & Hove Albion	W 3-0	42	21	Wright, Russell, Mills	8444		10	4*		7				12			9	6	8	2			1			5			3†		14	11	39
40	10	H	Oldham Athletic	D 0-0	43	21		11846		10	14		5†							8	6	4*	9			1	3		2						11	40
41	13	A	West Bromwich Albion	L 1-2	43	22	Russell / White, Goodman	13991		10			5		7†					8	6	4	9				1	3	2						11*	41
42	20	H	Portsmouth	W 2-1	46	20	Walsh, Russell / Wigley	10509		10	14	4	5		7†		2		12	8	6	9					1	3							11*	42
43	24	A	Sheffield Wednesday	D 0-0	47	21		31308		10			4	5		7	2	12			8	6	9					1	3							11*	43
44	27	A	Swindon Town	L 2-5	47	22	James, Wright / Foley 3, Hazard (p), James (og)	10404		10			4	5		7	2	12			8	6	9					1	3*						11	44
45	May 4	A	Ipswich Town	L 2-3	47	23	Reid, Mills (p) / Houghton, Gayle, Kiwomya	11347		10			5			7	2	9*			8	6	4					1	3					12	11	45
46	11	H	Oxford United	W 1-0	50	22	James	19011		10		4†	5		7	2					11	6			9			14	1	3					8	46

Final League Position:	22		League Appearances	22	45	8	40	35	10	40	35	32	5	41	35	19	24	2	20	10	16	14	5	1	8	4	17	3	2	13
Average Home League Attendance:	11546		Sub		4				3	4	4	10	1	3	3	7	9	5	4		1		3	2		4	1		2	
			League Goals	5		1	3		7	2	7		14	7		2								1	1	1				5

FA CUP

| 1 | Jan 5 | A | Millwall (3) | L 1-2 | | | James / Sheringham, Stephenson | 10766 | 1 | 10 | | 2 | 5 | | 7* | | 9 | | 11 | 6 | 8 | 12 | | 4 | | | | | | | 3 | | | | | 1 |

FOOTBALL LEAGUE CUP (Rumbelows League Cup)

| 1 | Sep 26 | H | Leeds United (2 leg 1) | W 1-0 | | | Kelly (p) | 13744 | 10 | | 2 | 5 | 3 | 7* | | 9 | | 11 | 6 | 14 | 8 | | 4† | 1 | | | | | 12 | | | | | | | 1 |
| 2 | Oct 10 | A | Leeds United (2 leg 2) | L 0-3 | | | - / Speed, Strachan, Walsh (og) | 19090 | 10 | | 2 | 5 | 3 | 7 | 12 | 9* | | 11 | 6 | 14 | 8 | | 4† | 1 | | | | | | | | | | | | 2 |

FULL MEMBERS CUP (Zenith Data Systems Cup)

| 1 | Nov 27 | H | Wolverhampton W (1) | L 0-1 | | | - / Bull | 4705 | 10 | | 2 | | 6 | 7 | 8 | 12 | | 11 | | 4 | 9* | | | | | 3† | 1 | | | 5 | 14 | | | | | 1 |

Dismissals: Sep 29, Walsh, Middlesbrough (a); Oct 27, Reid, Ipswich Town (h); Dec 23, Ramsey, Watford (h); Jan 5, Ramsey and Walsh, Millwall (a), FAC; Mar 20, Muggleton, Charlton Athletic (h); Mar 23, Walsh, Notts County (a).
Stand-in Goalkeepers: Mar 20, North for Muggleton (sent off), Charlton Athletic (h).
Note: Oct 27, both substitutes actually wore number 14, the error was not spotted by the officials; Mar 16, goal credited as Phillips (og), some reports credit James.

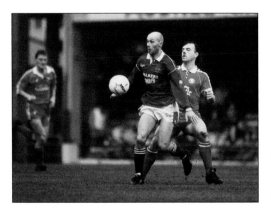

16 March: The return from injury of Kevin Russell was a key factor in City's successful battle against relegation. In his first outing of the season he inspired the Foxes to victory over Middlesbrough at Filbert Street.

1990-91

Back: Davies (Kit Manager), Geeson (Physio), Reid, Kitson, Linton, Holden, Walsh, Muggleton, Hoult, Hodge, James, Oldfield, Smith, Hyde, Hill, Roberts (Coach).
Front: Johnson, North, Spearing, Gibson, Wright, Kelly, Lee (Caretaker Manager), Mauchlen, Mills, Russell, Ramsey, Oakes.
On Ground: Jeffrey, G Fitzpatrick, Baraclough, Peake.

1991-92

Back: Linton, Gordon, Walsh, James, Muggleton, Poole, Hoult, P Fitzpatrick, Smith, Peake.
Middle: Mauchlen, Jeffrey, Gibson, Reid, Mills, Baraclough, Ramsey, Oldfield, Hill, Oakes.
Front: Platnauer, Russell, Wright, Kitson, Evans (Coach), Little (Manager), Gregory (Coach), Holden, Kelly, Ward, Johnson.

Season 1991-92

Promoted: Ipswich Town, Middlesbrough, Blackburn Rovers
Relegated: Plymouth Argyle, Brighton & Hove Albion, Port Vale

FOOTBALL LEAGUE DIVISION TWO (Barclays League)

Match No	Date		Opponents	Result	Points	Position	Scorers	Att	Kevin Poole	Gary Mills	Nicky Platnauer	Paul Fitzpatrick	Richard Smith	Tony James	Colin Gibson	Paul Reid	Ashley Ward	David Kelly	Paul Kitson	Tommy Wright	David Oldfield	Steve Walsh	Kevin Russell	Colin Gordon	Des Linton	Ali Mauchlen	Scott Oakes	Steve Thompson	Gary Coatsworth	Carl Muggleton	Jimmy Willis	Michael Trotter	Steve Holden	Ian Ormondroyd	Phil Gee	Simon Grayson	Colin Hill	Mike Whitlow	Match No
1	Aug 17	A	Swindon Town	D 0-0	1	-		12426	1	2	3	4	5	6	7	8	9†	10	11*	12	14																		1
2	24	H	Plymouth Argyle	W 2-0	4	6	Gibson, Kitson	11852	1	2	3	4		6	8		12	10*	11	9†	7	5	14																2
3	31	A	Southend United	W 2-1	7	5	Wright, Walsh / Martin	6944	1	2	3†	4*	14	6	8			10	11	9	7	5	12																3
4	Sep 4	H	Grimsby Town	W 2-0	10	3	Fitzpatrick, Gibson	16242	1	2	3	4		6	8			10	11	9	7	5																	4
5	7	H	Bristol City	W 2-1	13	2	Gibson, Fitzpatrick / Morgan	17815	1	2	3	4		6	8			10	11*	9†	7	5	12	14															5
6	14	A	Middlesbrough	L 0-3	13	3	- / Slaven, Wilkinson 2	16633	1	2	3†	4		6	8*			10	11	9	7	5	12		14														6
7	17	A	Barnsley	L 1-3	13	7	Kelly / Rammell, Taggart, Redfearn (p)	9318	1	2	3	4*		6		8	12	10	11	9	7	5																	7
8	21	H	Blackburn Rovers	W 3-0	16	3	Walsh, Kitson, Gordon	13278	1	2	3			6	8		12	10	11	9†	7	5		4*		14													8
9	29	A	Cambridge United	L 1-5	16	6	Gordon / Dublin 2, Claridge 2, Heathcote	12175	1	2	3	12		6	8†			10	11	9	7*	5		4		14													9
10	Oct 5	H	Charlton Athletic	L 0-2	16	9	- / Nelson, Dyer	11467	1	2	3	4*		6	8		12	10		9	7	5				11													10
11	12	A	Newcastle United	L 0-2	16	12	- / Hunt, Clark	16966	1	2			4	6	8		11*	10	12	9	7	5					3												11
12	19	H	Wolverhampton W.	W 3-0	19	7	Gordon 2, Wright	14428	1	2		14	4	6†	3		12		10	9	7	5		11*		8													12
13	26	A	Oxford United	W 2-1	22	7	Wright, Thompson / Simpson	5206	1	2		6	4		3				10	9	7	5		11		8†		14											13
14	30	A	Brighton & Hove Albion	W 2-1	25	7	Walsh, Kitson / Codner	6424	1	2		6	4		3				10	9†	7	5		11		14		8											14
15	Nov 2	H	Ipswich Town	D 2-2	26	6	Kitson, Oldfield / Wark, Johnson	11331	1	2		6	4		3				10	9	7	5		11				8											15
16	5	A	Portsmouth	L 0-1	26	6	- / Whittingham	7147	1	2		6†	4		3*				10	9	7	5		11		14		8	12										16
17	9	A	Watford	W 1-0	29	5	Kitson	9271	1	2		6	4		3				10	9	7	5		11		14		8†											17
18	20	H	Bristol Rovers	D 1-1	30	6	Wright / Mehew	10950	1	2		6	4		3†		12		10	9	7	5		11*		14		8											18
19	23	H	Port Vale	L 0-1	30	7	- / Jeffers	11450	1	2	3	6	4					9	10		7	5		11				8											19
20	30	A	Derby County	W 2-1	33	6	Fitzpatrick, Walsh / Ormondroyd	19306	1	2	3	6				12			10		7	5		9		11		8*	4										20
21	Dec 7	H	Millwall	D 1-1	34	7	Gordon / Kerr	12127	1	2	3	6	12						10†	14	7	5		9		11		8	4*										21
22	14	A	Sunderland	L 0-1	34	7	- / Goodman	15094	1	2	3†	6	4			14			10*	8	7	5		9		11		12											22
23	26	H	Brighton & Hove Albion	W 2-1	37	7	Mauchlen, Thompson / Gallacher	16767	1	2		12	4			3			10	11*	7	5		9		6		8											23
24	28	H	Southend United	W 2-0	40	6	Oldfield, Smith	15635	1	2		9	4			3			10	11	7	5				6		8											24
25	Jan 1	A	Bristol Rovers	D 1-1	41	6	Oldfield / Saunders	6673		2		12	4			3				11	7	5		9†		6		8		1	10*	14							25
26	11	A	Plymouth Argyle	D 2-2	42	7	Thompson, Turner (og) / Witter, Fiore	5486		2			4			3			11	9	7	5		6				8		1	10								26
27	18	H	Swindon Town	W 3-1	45	5	Fitzpatrick, Wright 2 / Bodin	14226		2		6	4			3			11	9	7	5						8		1	10*	12							27
28	Feb 1	A	Wolverhampton W.	L 0-1	45	6	- / Bull	18574	1	2		14	4			3	12		11	9	7*	5		10†				8			6								28
29	8	H	Oxford United	W 2-1	48	6	Kitson, Wright / Melville	12128	1	2	3		4						11	9	7	5	12			10		8*			6								29
30	15	A	Port Vale	W 2-1	51	4	Russell 2 / Foyle	8084	1	2	3		4						11	9	7†		8	6		10		14			5								30
31	22	H	Derby County	L 1-2	51	5	Mills (p) / Ormondroyd, Simpson	18148	1	2	14		4			3†			11	9			8	12		10		7			5		6*						31
32	29	A	Millwall	L 0-2	51	7	- / Cooper, Goodman	7562	1	2		6				3	14		11	9		5	8			10†		7			4								32
33	Mar 11	H	Portsmouth	D 2-2	52	8	Mills, Russell / Burns, Clarke	14207	1	2	3		4							9		5	8			6		7						10	11				33
34	14	A	Ipswich Town	D 0-0	53	9		16174	1	2	3		4							9		5	8					7						10	11	6			34
35	17	A	Grimsby Town	W 1-0	56	6	Wright	8377	1	2	3		4†							9		5	8					7			14			10	11	6			35
36	21	H	Watford	L 1-2	56	7	Walsh / Butler, Nogan	14519	1	2	3									9	12	5	8					7			4*			10	11	6			36
37	27	A	Tranmere Rovers	W 2-1	59	5	Ormondroyd, Gee / Muir	9061	1	2	3									9	8	5						7						10	11	6	4		37
38	Apr 1	H	Middlesbrough	W 2-1	62	4	Mills (p), Wright / Pollock	19352	1	2	14									9*	8	5	12					7						10	11	6	4	3†	38
39	4	A	Bristol City	L 1-2	62	6	Oldfield / Rosenior, Cole	13020	1	2										9	8	5	12					7*						10	11	6	4	3	39
40	8	H	Sunderland	W 3-2	65	5	Wright, Mills 2 (1p) / Bennett, Goodman	16533	1	2*										9	8	5	12					7						10	11	6	4	3	40
41	11	H	Barnsley	W 3-1	68	3	Walsh, Mills (p), Wright / Currie	14438	1	2	3									9	8	5						7						10	11	6	4		41
42	15	H	Tranmere Rovers	W 1-0	71	2	Russell	18555	1	2	3									9	8*	5	12	14				7						10†	11	6	4		42
43	18	A	Blackburn Rovers	W 1-0	74	2	Russell	18075	1	2	3									9	8	5	12					7						10	11*	6	4		43
44	21	H	Cambridge United	W 2-1	77	2	Wright, Gee / Claridge	21894	1	2	3†									9	8	5	12					7						10	11*	6	4	14	44
45	25	A	Charlton Athletic	L 0-2	77	2	- / Lee, Whyte	15537	1	2	14									9	8*	5	12					7						10	11†	6	4	3	45
46	May 2	H	Newcastle United	L 1-2	77	4	Walsh / Peacock, Walsh (og)	21844		2	3			14						9	8	5	12					7		1				10*	11†	6	4		46
Final League Position:				4				**League Appearances**	42	46	26	21	23	12	17	10	2	12	29	42	39	43	7	18		14	1	31	2	4	9		1	14	14	13	10	4	
Average Home League Attendance:				15184				**Sub**			3	5	2	1		2	8		1	2	2		13	3	1	6		3	1		1	2						1	
								League Goals		6		4	1		3			1	6	12	4	7	5	5		1		3						1	2				

PROMOTION PLAY-OFFS

Match No	Date		Opponents	Result	Points	Position	Scorers	Att	Kevin Poole	Gary Mills	Nicky Platnauer	Paul Fitzpatrick	Richard Smith	Tony James	Colin Gibson	Paul Reid	Ashley Ward	David Kelly	Paul Kitson	Tommy Wright	David Oldfield	Steve Walsh	Kevin Russell	Colin Gordon	Des Linton	Ali Mauchlen	Scott Oakes	Steve Thompson	Gary Coatsworth	Carl Muggleton	Jimmy Willis	Michael Trotter	Steve Holden	Ian Ormondroyd	Phil Gee	Simon Grayson	Colin Hill	Mike Whitlow	Match No
1	May 10	A	Cambridge Utd (sf leg 1)	D 1-1			Russell / O'Shea	9225		2				6						9		5	11					7		1				10		8	4	3	1
2	13	H	Cambridge Utd (sf leg 2)	W 5-0			Wright 2, Thompson, Russell, Ormondroyd	21024		2				6						9	12	5	11					7		1				10		8	4	3*	2
3	25		Blackburn Rovers (f)	L 0-1			- / Newell (p)	68147		2				6†						9		5	11					7		1				10	14	8	4	3	3

FA CUP

Match No	Date		Opponents	Result	Points	Position	Scorers	Att	Kevin Poole	Gary Mills	Nicky Platnauer	Paul Fitzpatrick	Richard Smith	Tony James	Colin Gibson	Paul Reid	Ashley Ward	David Kelly	Paul Kitson	Tommy Wright	David Oldfield	Steve Walsh	Kevin Russell	Colin Gordon	Des Linton	Ali Mauchlen	Scott Oakes	Steve Thompson	Gary Coatsworth	Carl Muggleton	Jimmy Willis	Michael Trotter	Steve Holden	Ian Ormondroyd	Phil Gee	Simon Grayson	Colin Hill	Mike Whitlow	Match No
1	Jan 4	H	Crystal Palace (3)	W 1-0			Smith	19613		2			4			3			12	11	7	5		9		6		8		1	10*								1
2	25	H	Bristol City (4)	L 1-2			Kitson / Bent, Dziekanowski	19313		2		6*	4			3	12		11	9	7	5						8		1	10								2

FOOTBALL LEAGUE CUP (Rumbelows League Cup)

Match No	Date		Opponents	Result	Points	Position	Scorers	Att	Kevin Poole	Gary Mills	Nicky Platnauer	Paul Fitzpatrick	Richard Smith	Tony James	Colin Gibson	Paul Reid	Ashley Ward	David Kelly	Paul Kitson	Tommy Wright	David Oldfield	Steve Walsh	Kevin Russell	Colin Gordon	Des Linton	Ali Mauchlen	Scott Oakes	Steve Thompson	Gary Coatsworth	Carl Muggleton	Jimmy Willis	Michael Trotter	Steve Holden	Ian Ormondroyd	Phil Gee	Simon Grayson	Colin Hill	Mike Whitlow	Match No
1	Aug 21	H	Maidstone Utd (1 leg 1)	W 3-0			Kitson, Kelly, Mills	9610	1	2	3	4		6	7	8†	9*	10	11	12	14	5																	1
2	28	A	Maidstone Utd (1 leg 2)	W 1-0			Kitson	1638	1	2	3	4		6	8†		12	10	11*	9	7	5	14																2
3	Sep 25	H	Arsenal (2 leg 1)	D 1-1			Walsh / Wright	20679	1	2	3			6	8			10	11	9	7	5		4†		14													3
4	Oct 8	A	Arsenal (2 leg 2)	L 0-2			- / Wright, Merson	28580	1	2	12		4	6	8		11	10		9	7	5				3*													4

FULL MEMBERS CUP (Zenith Data Systems Cup)

Match No	Date		Opponents	Result	Points	Position	Scorers	Att	Kevin Poole	Gary Mills	Nicky Platnauer	Paul Fitzpatrick	Richard Smith	Tony James	Colin Gibson	Paul Reid	Ashley Ward	David Kelly	Paul Kitson	Tommy Wright	David Oldfield	Steve Walsh	Kevin Russell	Colin Gordon	Des Linton	Ali Mauchlen	Scott Oakes	Steve Thompson	Gary Coatsworth	Carl Muggleton	Jimmy Willis	Michael Trotter	Steve Holden	Ian Ormondroyd	Phil Gee	Simon Grayson	Colin Hill	Mike Whitlow	Match No
1	Oct 2	H	Barnsley (1)	W 4-3	aet		Wright 2, Kelly, Walsh / Archdeacon, Currie, Saville	3995	1	2		4			8	12	14	10		9	7	5			6	11*	3†												1
2	23	H	Port Vale (2)	W 4-0			Wright 2, Kitson, Gordon	4858	1	2		6	4		3				10	9	7	5		11		8													2
3	Nov 27	H	Everton (3)	W 2-1			Oldfield, Thompson / Beardsley	13242	1	2	3	6	4*			14			10		7	5		9		11		8†	12										3
4	Jan 8	A	Notts County (Nsf)	W 2-1	aet		Wright, Fitzpatrick / Chris Short	11559		2		14	4			3			11	9	7†	5		12		6*		8		1	10								4
5	Feb 12	H	Nottingham F (Nf leg 1)	D 1-1			Gordon / Gemmill	19537	1	2	3		4						11	9	7	5	8	6†		10		14											5
6	26	A	Nottingham F (Nf leg 2)	L 0-2			- / Crosby, Wassall	21562	1	2		12	4†			3			11	9		5	8	6*		10		7			14								6

Dismissals: Sep 17, Kitson, Barnsley (a)
Note: May 25, at Wembley

Season 1992-93

Promoted: Newcastle United, West Ham United, Swindon Town
Relegated: Brentford, Cambridge United, Bristol Rovers

Match No	Date		Opponents	Result	Points	Position	Scorers	Att	Carl Muggleton	Gary Mills	Mike Whitlow	Richard Smith	Steve Walsh	Colin Hill	David Oldfield	Steve Thompson	Bobby Davison	Ian Ormondroyd	Phil Gee	Colin Gordon	Simon Grayson	Paul Fitzpatrick	Michael Trotter	Russell Hoult	Neil Lewis	David Lowe	Colin Gibson	Julian Joachim	Nicky Platnauer	Kevin Poole	Lee Philpott	Tony James	Steve Agnew	Gary Coatsworth	Match No
FOOTBALL LEAGUE DIVISION ONE (Barclays League)																																		
1	Aug 15	H	Luton Town	W 2-1	3	-	Walsh, Whitlow / Campbell	17428	1	2	3	4	5	6	7	8	9	10†	11	14															1
2	18	A	Wolverhampton W.	L 0-3	3	-	- / Bull, Mutch, Birch (p)	15821	1	2	3	4	5	6	7	8	9	10	11																2
3	22	A	Notts County	D 1-1	4	9	Gee / D Smith (p)	10501	1	2	3	4	5	6	7	8	9	10	11																3
4	26	H	Derby County	W 3-2	7	4	Gee 2, Thompson / Simpson 2	17739	1	2	3	4	5	6	7	8	9*	10	11		12														4
5	29	H	Portsmouth	W 1-0	10	3	Davison	14780	1	2	3	4*	5	6	7	8	9	10	11†		12	14													5
6	Sep 5	A	Southend United	L 1-3	10	6	Gee / Benjamin 2 (1 p), Ansah	5119	1	2	3	4		6	7	8	9	10	11		5														6
7	13	H	Wolverhampton W.	D 0-0	11	6		12965		2	3	4†		6	7	8	9	10	11		5			1	14										7
8	19	H	Brentford	D 0-0	12	7		12972		2	3	4	5	6	7*	8	9†	10	11					1	14	12									8
9	26	A	Watford	W 3-0	15	4	Davison, Lowe, Ormondroyd	8715		2	3	4	5	6		8	9	10		14			7*	1		11	12†								9
10	Oct 3	H	Barnsley	W 2-1	18	6	Grayson, Davison / Biggins	12290		2		4	5	6	7	8	9	10			3			1	14			11†							10
11	10	A	Birmingham City	W 2-0	21	4	Davison, Joachim	13443		2†	3	4	5	6	7	8	9	10	12		14			1				11*							11
12	18	H	Peterborough United	L 0-2	21	7	- / Philliskirk, Sterling	10952			3	4	5	6	7*	8	9†	10	12	14	2			1				11							12
13	24	A	Bristol City	L 1-2	21	7	Davison / Cole, Grayson (og)	10408			3*	4	5	6	7	8	9	10	12		2			1		14		11†							13
14	31	H	Newcastle United	W 2-1	24	3	Lowe, Davison / O'Brien	19687		2		4	5	6	7	8†	9*	14	11		12					10			3	1					14
15	Nov 4	A	Charlton Athletic	L 0-2	24	6	- / Nelson 2	4213		2		4	5	6	7		9	14	11†		8					10			3	1					15
16	7	H	Tranmere Rovers	L 0-1	24	9	- / Nevin	13538		2		4	5	6	7	8	9*	14	11†		12					10			3	1					16
17	15	A	Sunderland	W 2-1	27	6	Joachim 2 / Davenport	14945		2		4	5	6	7	8		9			11					14		10†	3	1					17
18	21	H	Cambridge United	D 2-2	28	7	Thompson 2 (1 p) / Claridge, Heathcote	12175		2		4		6	7*	8	12	9			5					14	11†	10	3	1					18
19	28	H	Bristol Rovers	L 0-1	28	9	- / Channing	12848		2		4		6	7	8	9	10*			5							12	3	1	11				19
20	Dec 5	A	Grimsby Town	W 3-1	31	7	Oldfield 2, Ormondroyd / Groves	7488		2†		4		5	6	8	9	12			3					10	14	7*		1	11				20
21	13	A	Oxford United	D 0-0	32	7		7949		2		4		5	6	8	9	12			3					10*		7		1	11				21
22	20	H	Swindon Town	W 4-2	35	5	Oldfield, Lowe 2, Joachim / Hazard, Walsh (og)	15088		2	3	4*	5	6	7	8		12								10		9		1	11				22
23	28	A	Millwall	L 0-2	35	6	- / Moralee, Goodman	12230		2		4	5	6	7	8		12			3					10*		9		1	11				23
24	Jan 9	A	Brentford	W 3-1	38	6	Walsh, Thompson 2 / Blissett	8517		2	3	4	5	6	7	8		10										9		1	11				24
25	16	H	Watford	W 5-2	41	5	Philpott 2, Walsh, Lowe, Joachim / Soloman, Nogan	12854		2	3	4	5	6	7	8										10		9		1	11				25
26	23	H	Notts County	D 1-1	42	6	Joachim / Draper	15716		2	3	4*	5	6	7	8			12					1		10	14	9†			11				26
27	30	H	West Ham United	L 1-2	42	6	Lowe / Robson, Gale	18838		2		4	5	6†	7	8			12					1		10	3	9*			11	14			27
28	Feb 6	A	Luton Town	L 0-2	42	8	- / Johnson, Gray	9140		2	3*	4	5	6	7	8		14						1		10	12	9†			11				28
29	20	A	Portsmouth	D 1-1	43	9	Philpott / Walsh	14160	1	2			5	6	7	8	9									10					3	4	11		29
30	24	A	Derby County	L 0-2	43	9	- / Forsyth, Gabbiadini	17507	1	2			5	6	7*	8	9	12	14							10†					3	4	11		30
31	28	H	Birmingham City	W 2-1	46	8	Walsh, Lowe / Matthewson	10284	1	7		4	5	6		8										10	3				11†	14	9	2	31
32	Mar 6	A	Barnsley	W 3-2	49	7	Coatsworth 2, Walsh / Rammell 2	9452	1			4	5	6	7	8	12									10*	3				11†	14	9	2	32
33	10	H	Sunderland	W 3-2	52	7	Walsh 2, Lowe / Goodman, Armstrong	15609	1	12		4	5	6	7	8	14									10	3*				11		9†	2	33
34	13	A	Tranmere Rovers	W 3-2	55	6	Walsh, Thompson, Lowe / Morrissey, Malkin	9680	1	3		4	5	6	7	8	14				9*					10					11†	12		2	34
35	20	H	Grimsby Town	W 3-0	58	6	Walsh, Oldfield, Groves (og)	15930	1	3		4	5	6	7	8					9*					10					11	12		2	35
36	23	A	Cambridge United	W 3-1	61	6	Joachim, Lowe 2 / Kimble (p)	6836	1	8		4	5	6	7						12				3	10		9*			11	14		2†	36
37	27	H	Charlton Athletic	W 3-1	64	5	Joachim, Walsh 2 / Dyer	17290	1	3		4	5	6	7	8										10		9*			11	12		2	37
38	Apr 3	A	Bristol Rovers	D 0-0	65	6		5270	1	3		4	5	6	7	8					14					10		9†			11	12		2*	38
39	7	H	Oxford United	W 2-1	68	5	Thompson (p), Walsh / Ford	16611	1*	3		4	5	6	7	8									14	10		9			11†	12		2	39
40	11	A	West Ham United	L 0-3	68	5	- / Speedie 2, Keen	13971		3	14	4	5	6	7	8										10		9		1	11*	12		2†	40
41	14	H	Millwall	W 3-0	71	5	Agnew, Thompson, Oldfield	19611		2	3	4	5	6	7	8										10				1	11		9		41
42	17	A	Swindon Town	D 1-1	72	5	Walsh / Taylor	15428		2	3	4	5	6	7	8					12							10		1	11†	14	9*		42
43	20	H	Southend United	W 4-1	75	5	Joachim 2, Walsh, Edwards (og) / Angell	18003		2	3	4†	5	6	7	8					12							10		1	11	14	9*		43
44	24	A	Peterborough United	L 0-3	75	5	- / Philliskirk, Adcock, Ebdon	15445		2	3	4	5	6	7	8										12		10		1	11†	14	9*		44
45	May 1	H	Bristol City	D 0-0	76	5		19294		2	3	4	5	6	7	8*									14	10		9†		1	11	12			45
46	9	A	Newcastle United	L 1-7	76	6	Walsh / Cole 3, Lee, Kelly 3	30129		2	3	4	5	6	7	8			14		12				11†	10		9*		1					46
Final League Position:				6				**League Appearances**	17	42	23	44	40	46	44	44	21	17	11		14		1	10	2	27	5	25	6	19	27	2	9	10	
Average Home League Attendance:				15326				**Sub**		1	1						4	9	7	3	10	1			5	5	4	1				14			
								League Goals			1		15		5	8	6	2	4		1					11		10			3		1	2	
PROMOTION PLAY-OFFS																																		
1	May 16	H	Portsmouth (sf leg 1)	W 1-0			Joachim	24538		2	3	4	5	6	7	8			9		14						10†	12		1	11*				1
2	19	A	Portsmouth (sf leg 2)	D 2-2			Ormondroyd, Thompson / McLoughlin, Kristensen	25438		2	3	4	5	6	7	8		10									12	9		1			11*		2
3	31		Swindon Town (f)	L 3-4			Joachim, Walsh, Thompson / Hoddle, Maskell, Taylor, Bodin (p)	73802		2	3	4	5	6	7	8												9		1	11		10		3
FA CUP																																		
1	Jan 13	H	Barnsley (3)	D 2-2			Thompson (p), Oldfield / Redfearn, Whitlow (og)	19137		2	3	4	5	6	7	8		10*								12		9		1	11				1
2	20	A	Barnsley (3 rep)	D 1-1 aet			Joachim / Archdeacon	15238		2	3†	4	5	6*	7	8		12								10	14	9		1	11				2
FOOTBALL LEAGUE CUP (Coca Cola Cup)																																		
1	Sep 23	H	Peterborough U (2 leg 1)	W 2-0			Lowe, Thompson	10366		2	3	4	5	6		8	9	10	11*				7	1		12									1
2	Oct 6	A	Peterborough U (2 leg 2)	L 1-2			Joachim / Halsall, Charlery	6936		2		4	5	6	7	8	9	10	12		3			1				11*							2
3	27	A	Sheffield Wednesday (3)	L 1-7			Davison / Hirst, Worthington, Bright 2, Watson 2, Bart-Williams	17326		2†		4	5	6	7	8	9	10*	11		14			1		12			3						3
ANGLO ITALIAN CUP																																		
1	Sep 2	H	Grimsby Town (p)	W 4-0			Davison 2, Gee 2	4112	1	2	3†	4		6	7*	8	9	10	11		5	14	12												1
2	30	A	Newcastle United (p)	L 0-4			- / Brock, Quinn 2 (1 p), Sheedy	14046		2	3	4	5	6		8	9†	10		14	7			1		11									2

Dismissals: Aug 18, Walsh, Wolverhampton Wanderers (a); Sep 5, Grayson, Southend United (a); Nov 4, Walsh, Charlton Athletic (a); Feb 6, Gibson, Luton Town (a); Apr 3, Lowe, Bristol Rovers (a); Apr 14, Agnew, Millwall (h); Apr 17, Joachim, Swindon Town (a).
Stand-In Goalkeepers: Apr 7, Smith for Muggleton, Oxford United (h).
Note: Divisions renumbered due to formation of F A Premier League;
Jan 20, lost 4-5 on penalties (Thompson, Oldfield, Gibson, Walsh scored);
May 16, at City Ground (Nottingham Forest) due to reconstruction work at Filbert Street; May 31, at Wembley.

1992-93
Back: Ward, Willis, Gordon, Walsh, Muggleton, Poole, Hoult, James, Trotter, Coatsworth, Smith.
Middle: Lewis, Gibson, Mogg, Mills, Fitzpatrick, Ormondroyd, Oldfield, Thompson, Platnauer, Hill.
Front: Lowe, Grayson, Haughton, Evans (Coach), Little (Manager), Gregory (Coach), Holden, Whitlow, Gee.

1993-94
Back: Willis, Eustace, Carey, Walsh, Poole, Hoult, Ward, Muggleton, Trotter, Coatsworth, I Thompson, Smith.
Middle: Lewis, Speedie, Gibson, Mills, James, Ormondroyd, Oldfield, S Thompson, Philpott, Hill, Crane.
Front: Bedder, Lowe, Grayson, Haughton, Evans (Asst Manager), Little (Manager), Gregory (Coach), Agnew, Whitlow, Gee, Davison.

Promoted: Crystal Palace, Nottingham Forest, Leicester City
Relegated: Birmingham City, Oxford United, Peterborough United

FOOTBALL LEAGUE DIVISION ONE (Endsleigh League)

No	Date		Opponents	Result	Pts	Pos	Scorers	Att	Players (shirt numbers)
1	Aug 14	H	Peterborough United	W 2-1	3	-	Thompson (p), James / Cooper (p)	13671	Ward 1, Hill 2, Whitlow 3†, Carey 4, Walsh 5, James 6, Mills 7, Thompson 8, Speedie 9, Agnew 10*, Philpott 11, Joachim 12, Smith 14
2	21	A	Tranmere Rovers	L 0-1	3	15	- / Malkin	8766	Hill 2, Whitlow 3, Carey 4, Walsh 5, James 6†, Mills 7, Thompson 8, Speedie 9, Agnew 10, Philpott 11, Smith 14, Poole 1
3	28	H	Millwall	W 4-0	6	8	Agnew, Walsh 2, Joachim	12219	Ward 1, Hill 6, Whitlow 3, Walsh 5, James 14, Mills 2, Thompson 8, Speedie 9, Agnew 10, Philpott 11, Grayson 4†, Lewis 11
4	Sep 12	H	Birmingham City	D 1-1	7	15	Walsh / Peschisolido	10366	Ward 1, Hill 6, Whitlow 3, Walsh 5, Mills 2, Thompson 8, Speedie 9, Agnew 10, Grayson 7, Lewis 4, Gee 11
5	14	A	Bristol City	W 3-1	10	6	Speedie 2, Walsh / Scott	7899	Ward 1, Hill 6, Whitlow 3, Carey 4, Walsh 5, Mills 2, Thompson 8, Speedie 9, Agnew 10, Lewis 11, Oldfield 7
6	18	A	Bolton Wanderers	W 2-1	13	5	Speedie 2 / McGinlay (p)	12049	Ward 1, Hill 6, Whitlow 3, Carey 4, Walsh 5, Thompson 2†, Speedie 8, Agnew 9*, Joachim 10, Ormondroyd 12, Grayson 11, Lewis 14, Oldfield 7
7	25	A	Barnsley	W 1-0	16	3	Oldfield	10392	Ward 1, Hill 6, Whitlow 3, Walsh 5, Thompson 8*, Speedie 9, Agnew 10, Ormondroyd 12, Grayson 4, Lewis 11, James 2, Oldfield 7
8	29	A	Middlesbrough	L 0-2	16	4	- / Wilkinson, Hendrie	11871	Ward 1, Hill 6, Whitlow 3, Walsh 5*, Thompson 14, Speedie 8, Agnew 9, Joachim 10, Ormondroyd 12, Grayson 4†, Lewis 11, James 2, Oldfield 7
9	Oct 2	H	Notts County	W 3-2	19	3	Speedie 2, Thompson (p) / Draper (p), McSwegan	16319	Ward 1, Hill 6, Whitlow 5, Speedie 8, Agnew 9, Joachim 10, Ormondroyd 14, Grayson 7, Lewis 11, James 2, Oldfield 3, Gee 4†
10	16	A	Charlton Athletic	L 1-2	19	4	Agnew / Chapple, Pitcher (p)	8316	Ward 1, Hill 6, Whitlow 3, Speedie 8, Agnew 9, Joachim 10, Ormondroyd 14, Grayson 7, Lewis 11*, James 2, Oldfield 5†, Gee 12, Roberts 4
11	24	H	Nottingham Forest	W 1-0	22	4	Speedie	17624	Ward 1, Hill 6, Whitlow 5, Speedie 12, Agnew 8, Joachim 9, Ormondroyd 10, Grayson 7, Lewis 11, James 2, Oldfield 3*
12	30	A	Luton Town	W 2-0	25	2	Thompson (p), Speedie	8813	Ward 1, Hill 6*, Whitlow 3, Walsh 5, Speedie 4, Agnew 8, Joachim 9, Ormondroyd 10, Grayson 7, Willis 12, James 2
13	Nov 2	A	Grimsby Town	D 0-0	26	5		6346	Ward 1, Hill 6, Whitlow 3, Walsh 5, Speedie 4, Agnew 8, Joachim 9, Ormondroyd 10, Grayson 7, James 2
14	6	H	Southend United	W 3-0	29	1	Joachim, Oldfield, Thompson (p)	15387	Ward 1, Hill 6, Whitlow 3, Walsh 5, Speedie 4, Agnew 8, Joachim 9, Ormondroyd 10†, Grayson 7, Oldfield 12, Gee 11*, James 2, Roberts 14
15	14	A	Stoke City	L 0-1	29	3	- / Gleghorn	15984	Ward 1, Hill 6, Whitlow 3, Walsh 5, Speedie 4*, Agnew 8, Joachim 9, Grayson 14, Lewis 7, Willis 12, James 2, Gee 11†, Oldfield 10
16	20	H	Oxford United	L 2-3	29	6	Thompson (p), Whitlow / Cusack, Rogan, Dyer	14070	Ward 1, Hill 6, Whitlow 3, Walsh 5, Speedie 4, Agnew 8, Joachim 9, Gibson 11†, Grayson 7, Lewis 14, James 2, Oldfield 10
17	27	H	Wolverhampton W.	D 2-2	30	5	Roberts 2 / Bull 2	18395	Ward 1, Hill 6†, Walsh 5*, Speedie 4, Agnew 8, Joachim 9, Gibson 11, Grayson 12, Lewis 7, James 14, Ormondroyd 2, Grayson 3, Roberts 10
18	Dec 5	A	Southend United	D 0-0	31	6		6114	Ward 1, Hill 6, Walsh 5, Speedie 4, Agnew 8, Joachim 9*, Gibson 7, Lewis 11, Ormondroyd 2, Grayson 3, Oldfield 12, Roberts 10
19	8	H	Crystal Palace	D 1-1	32	6	Roberts / Williams	16706	Ward 1, Hill 6†, Carey 12, Walsh 4*, Speedie 8, Agnew 9, Joachim 5, Gibson 11, Lewis 7, Ormondroyd 2, Grayson 3, Lowe 14, Roberts 10
20	11	A	Bristol City	W 3-0	35	5	Speedie 2, Joachim	13394	Ward 1, Hill 6, Speedie 8, Agnew 9, Joachim 5, Gibson 11, Lewis 7*, Ormondroyd 2, Grayson 3, Gee 12, Coatsworth 4†, Roberts 10, Blake 14
21	19	A	Peterborough United	D 1-1	36	5	Bradshaw (og) / Adcock	8595	Ward 1, Hill 6†, Carey 4, Speedie 8, Agnew 9, Joachim 5, Gibson 11, Lewis 7, Ormondroyd 2, Grayson 3*, Gee 12, Coatsworth 14, Roberts 10
22	27	H	Watford	D 4-4	37	6	Thompson (p), Oldfield 2, Ormondroyd / Dyer 2, Furlong 2	21744	Ward 1, Hill 6, Speedie 8, Agnew 9*, Joachim 5, Gibson 11†, Smith 3, Ormondroyd 14, Grayson 2, Lewis 12, Oldfield 7, Coatsworth 4, Roberts 10
23	28	A	Derby County	L 2-3	37	5	Joachim, Roberts / Pembridge, Gabbiadini, Johnson	17372	Ward 1, Hill 6, Speedie 8, Agnew 9, Joachim 5, Lewis 12, Grayson 11*, Ormondroyd 2, Smith 3, Oldfield 7, Coatsworth 4, Roberts 10
24	Jan 1	H	Sunderland	W 2-1	40	6	Speedie, Joachim / Gray (p)	19615	Hill 6, Speedie 8, Agnew 9†, Joachim 5, Gibson 12, Lewis 7*, Poole 1, Grayson 2, Smith 3, Neil 14, Oldfield 11, Coatsworth 4, Roberts 10
25	12	H	West Bromwich Albion	W 4-2	43	4	Roberts 2, Whitlow, Mardon (og) / Strodder, Mellon	15640	Hill 6, Whitlow 3, Speedie 4, Agnew 8, Joachim 9, Smith 5, Grayson 1, Lewis 11, Ormondroyd 2, Oldfield 7, Roberts 10
26	16	H	Charlton Athletic	W 2-1	46	4	Grayson, Roberts / Balmer	12577	Hill 6, Whitlow 3, Carey 14, Speedie 4, Agnew 8, Joachim 9†, Smith 5, Grayson 1, Gibson 11*, Ormondroyd 2, Lewis 12, Oldfield 7, Roberts 10
27	22	A	Crystal Palace	L 1-2	46	4	Thompson / Coleman, Armstrong	17045	Hill 6, Whitlow 3, Carey 12, Speedie 4, Agnew 8, Grayson 1, Gibson 11†, Ormondroyd 2, Willis 9*, Lowe 14, Oldfield 7, Roberts 5, Blake 10
28	Feb 6	A	Nottingham Forest	L 0-4	46	5	- / Gemmill 2, Glover, Woan	26616	Hill 6, Whitlow 3, Speedie 4, Agnew 8, Joachim 5, Gibson 9, Smith 1, Ormondroyd 2, Grayson 11†, Willis 14, Lowe 7, Roberts 10
29	12	H	Luton Town	W 2-1	49	4	Coatsworth, Roberts / James	16149	Ward 1, Hill 6, Carey 4, Thompson 7, Speedie 8, Agnew 9, Ormondroyd 11, Grayson 2, Smith 3, Coatsworth 5, Roberts 10
30	19	A	West Bromwich Albion	W 2-1	52	2	Roberts, Ormondroyd / Fenton	18153	Ward 1, Hill 12, Whitlow 6, Carey 4, Thompson 7, Speedie 8, Agnew 9*, Smith 14, Ormondroyd 11, Grayson 2, Neil 3†, Coatsworth 5, Roberts 10
31	23	H	Tranmere Rovers	D 1-1	53	2	McGreal (og) / McGreal	14028	Hill 6, Carey 4, Thompson 7*, Speedie 9, Smith 12, Ormondroyd 11, Grayson 2, Neil 3, Lowe 8, Coatsworth 5, Roberts 10
32	Mar 6	A	Millwall	D 0-0	54	3		8085	Ward 1, Whitlow 7, Carey 6, Carey 4, Speedie 9, Smith 5, Gibson 12, Grayson 14, Neil 11*, Willis 3†, Lowe 8, Roberts 2, Blake 10
33	12	H	Middlesbrough	W 2-0	57	2	Joachim, Speedie	16116	Ward 1, Hill 6, Whitlow 3, Carey 4, Joachim 9†, Speedie 5, Gibson 7*, Grayson 14, Neil 11, Lowe 8, Roberts 2, Blake 12, Kerr 10
34	15	A	Birmingham City	W 3-0	60	2	Joachim, Ormondroyd, Roberts	14681	Ward 1, Hill 6, Whitlow 3, Carey 4, Joachim 9, Speedie 5, Gibson 7, Neil 11, Lowe 8, Roberts 2, Blake 12, Kerr 10
35	19	A	Barnsley	L 0-1	60	3	- / Payton	15640	Ward 1, Hill 6†, Whitlow 3, Carey 4, Joachim 9, Speedie 5, Gibson 7, Grayson 14, Neil 11*, Lowe 8, Roberts 2, Blake 12, Kerr 10
36	26	A	Notts County	L 1-4	60	3	Ormondroyd / McSwegan, Matthews, Lund 2	11907	Ward 1, Carey 4, Mills 6, Joachim 9, Speedie 5, Gibson 7, Lewis 12, Grayson 11, Neil 2*, Coatsworth 3, Roberts 10, Blake 8
37	30	H	Portsmouth	L 0-3	60	3	- / Creaney, Hall, McLoughlin	15146	Ward 1, Hill 6, Carey 4, Walsh 14, Joachim 9†, Speedie 5, Gibson 7, Grayson 11*, Neil 2, Lowe 3, Roberts 10, Kerr 8, Blake 12
38	Apr 2	A	Watford	D 1-1	61	3	Agnew / Bailey	8645	Whitlow 5*, Walsh 11, Joachim 9†, Agnew 6, Gibson 12, Poole 1, Grayson 2, Neil 3, Lowe 4, Gee 14, Roberts 10, Kerr 8, Blake 7
39	5	A	Derby County	D 3-3	62	3	Roberts 3 / Kitson 2, Willis (og)	20050	Thompson 12, Agnew 6, Gibson 7, Poole 1, Grayson 11, Neil 2, Lowe 3, Gee 4, Oldfield 9*, Coatsworth 5†, Roberts 10, Kerr 8, Blake 14
40	9	A	Sunderland	W 3-2	65	3	Joachim 2, Kerr (p) / Goodman, Melville	17198	Thompson 12, Agnew 6, Gibson 7, Poole 1, Grayson 11, Neil 2, Lowe 3, Gee 4*, Oldfield 9†, Roberts 14, Roberts 10, Kerr 8, Blake 5
41	16	H	Grimsby Town	D 1-1	66	3	Joachim / Mendonca	15859	Agnew 6, Joachim 12, Gibson 7, Poole 1, Grayson 11, Neil 2, Lowe 3, Gee 4*, Oldfield 9, Roberts 5, Roberts 10, Kerr 8
42	23	A	Oxford United	D 2-2	67	6	Blake, Joachim / Elliott, Moody	8818	Walsh 5, Joachim 14, Gibson 7, Poole 1, Grayson 6, Neil 11, Lowe 2, Gee 3, Oldfield 9†, Eustace 10*, Blake 8
43	26	A	Portsmouth	W 1-0	70	4	Kerr	7869	Walsh 5, Gibson 7, Poole 1, Grayson 6, Neil 11, Lowe 2, Gee 3, Oldfield 4, Eustace 9, Kerr 8, Blake 10
44	30	H	Stoke City	D 1-1	71	4	Willis / Regis	19219	Walsh 5*, Gibson 12, Grayson 7, Neil 11, Lowe 2, Gee 3, Oldfield 4, Willis 10, Eustace 9, Kerr 8, Blake 14
45	May 3	A	Bolton Wanderers	D 1-1	72	4	Gee / McGinlay	18145	Joachim 9†, Agnew 6, Gibson 10, Poole 1, Grayson 11, Neil 2, Lowe 3, Gee 4, Willis 14, Eustace 7, Blake 5, Kerr 8
46	8	A	Wolverhampton W.	D 1-1	73	4	Coatsworth / Kelly	27229	Ward 1, Walsh 4, Joachim 12, Ormondroyd 10, Poole 6, Grayson 11, Neil 2, Lowe 3, Eustace 9*, Blake 7, Coatsworth 5, Roberts 14, Kerr 8†

Final League Position:	4	
Average Home League Attendance:	16005	

League Appearances: Ward 32, Hill 30, Whitlow 31, Carey 24, Walsh 9, James 4, Mills 21, Thompson 30, Speedie 37, Agnew 36, Philpott 10, Joachim 27, Smith 2, Poole 14, Gibson 11, Ormondroyd 30, Grayson 39, Lewis 24, Willis 9, Lowe 1, Gee 6, Oldfield 24, Coatsworth 15, Roberts 26, Blake 10, Kerr 4

Sub: Hill 1, Carey 3, Walsh 1, James 5, Mills 2, Philpott 9, Joachim 9, Smith 6, Ormondroyd 4, Grayson 1, Lewis 1, Gee 4, Oldfield 6, Davison 3, Roberts 4, Blake 1, Eustace 1, Kerr 3

League Goals: Hill 2, Walsh 4, James 1, Thompson 7, Speedie 12, Agnew 3, Joachim 11, Ormondroyd 4, Grayson 1, Lewis 1, Oldfield 1, Gee 4, Coatsworth 2, Roberts 13, Blake 1, Kerr 2

PROMOTION PLAY-OFFS

No	Date		Opponents	Result	Scorers	Att	Players
1	May 15	A	Tranmere Rov. (sf leg 1)	D 0-0		14962	Ward 1, Whitlow 3, Carey 6, Joachim 14, Speedie 7†, Poole 10, Grayson 11, Neil 2, Gee 4, Oldfield 9*, Roberts 12, Blake 5, Kerr 8
2	18	H	Tranmere Rov. (sf leg 2)	W 2-1	Ormondroyd, Speedie / Nevin	22593	Ward 1, Whitlow 3, Carey 6*, Walsh 9, Ormondroyd 14, Speedie 12, Grayson 7, Neil 10†, Gee 11, Oldfield 2, Blake 5, Kerr 8
3	30		Derby County (f)	W 2-1	Walsh 2 / Johnson	73671	Ward 1, Whitlow 3, Carey 6, Walsh 9, Ormondroyd 14, Grayson 12, Neil 7, Gee 11, Oldfield 2, Roberts 5†, Blake 10*, Kerr 8

FA CUP

No	Date		Opponents	Result	Scorers	Att	Players
1	Jan 8	A	Manchester City (3)	L 1-4	Oldfield / Ingebrigtsen 3, Kernaghan	22613	Hill 6, Carey 12, Thompson 10, Speedie 8, Agnew 9, Joachim 5, Smith 14, Grayson 7*, Ormondroyd 1, Lewis 2, Oldfield 3, Roberts 11, Blake 4†

FOOTBALL LEAGUE CUP (Coca Cola Cup)

No	Date		Opponents	Result	Scorers	Att	Players
1	Sep 21	A	Rochdale (2 leg 1)	W 6-1	Whitlow, Walsh, Thompson, Oldfield, Speedie, Ormondroyd / Graham	4491	Ward 1, Hill 6, Whitlow 3, Carey 4, Walsh 5*, Thompson 8, Speedie 9, Agnew 10, Joachim 12, Lewis 11, Oldfield 2, Gee 14, Roberts 7†
2	Oct 6	H	Rochdale (2 leg 2)	W 2-1	Ormondroyd, Joachim / Lancaster	7612	Ward 1, Hill 6, Speedie 8, Agnew 9*, Joachim 10†, Ormondroyd 14, Grayson 7, Lewis 11, James 2, Oldfield 3, Gee 5, Roberts 12, Blake 4
3	27	A	Manchester United (3)	L 1-5	Hill / Bruce 2, McClair, Sharpe, Hughes	41344	Ward 1, Hill 6, Whitlow 5, Speedie 12, Agnew 8, Joachim 9, Ormondroyd 10, Grayson 7, Lewis 11, James 2, Oldfield 3*

ANGLO ITALIAN CUP

No	Date		Opponents	Result	Scorers	Att	Players
1	Aug 31	A	Peterborough United (p)	L 3-4	Oldfield (p), Gee 2 / Iorfa, McGlashan, Cooper (p), Philliskirk	3830	Philpott 11, Joachim 4, Smith 1, Poole 6, Gibson 10, Ormondroyd 2, Grayson 3, Lewis 5, Willis 7, Gee 8, Oldfield 9
2	Sep 8	H	West Bromwich A. (p)	D 0-0		3588	Ward 1, Hill 6, Walsh 5, Joachim 10, Smith 2†, Ormondroyd 11, Grayson 9, Lewis 3, Gee 7, Willis 8*, Oldfield 4, Roberts 12, Blake 14

Dismissals: Dec 28, Coatsworth, Derby County (a); Feb 6, Hill, Nottingham Forest (a); Feb 19, Grayson, West Bromwich Albion (a); Mar 6, Oldfield, Millwall (a); Apr 23, Willis, Oxford United (a); May 18, Speedie, Tranmere Rovers (h), Play-Offs.
Note: May 18, goal credited to Speedie, some reports credit Garnett (og); May 30, at Wembley.

Champions: Blackburn Rovers
Relegated: Crystal Palace, Norwich City, Leicester City, Ipswich Town

Player columns (squad number / name):
(1) Gavin Ward, (2) Simon Grayson, (3) Mike Whitlow, (12) Richard Smith, (19) Colin Hill, (14) Nicky Mohan, (6) Steve Agnew, (8) Mark Blake, (10) Mark Draper, (5) Steve Walsh, (7) Julian Joachim, (17) Steve Thompson, (9) Iwan Roberts, (4) Jimmy Willis, (33) Kevin Poole, (21) Lee Philpott, (22) Gary Mills, (25) David Lowe, (26) Phil Gee, (24) Neil Lewis, (15) Brian Carey, (16) Franz Carr, (20) David Oldfield, (11) Ian Ormondroyd, (22) Jamie Lawrence, (6) Mark Robins, (34) Mike Galloway, (18) Garry Parker, (23) Emile Heskey, (29) Sam McMahon

FA PREMIER LEAGUE (Carling Premiership)

Match No	Date		Opponents	Result	Points	Position	Scorers	Att
1	Aug 21	H	Newcastle United	L 1-3	-		Joachim / Cole, Beardsley, Elliott	20048
2	23	A	Blackburn Rovers	L 0-3	-		- / Sutton, Berg, Shearer	21050
3	27	A	Nottingham Forest	L 0-1	22		- / Collymore	21601
4	31	H	Queens Park Rangers	D 1-1	1	20	Gee / Willis (og)	18695
5	Sep 10	A	Wimbledon	L 1-2	1	21	Lowe / Harford, Willis (og)	7683
6	17	H	Tottenham Hotspur	W 3-1	4	20	Joachim 2, Lowe / Klinsmann	21300
7	24	A	Everton	D 1-1	5	18	Draper / Ablett	28003
8	Oct 3	H	Coventry City	D 2-2	6	19	Roberts 2 / Wegerle, Dublin	19372
9	8	A	Chelsea	L 0-4	6	20	- / Spencer 2, Peacock, Shipperley	18397
10	15	H	Southampton	W 4-3	9	18	Blake 2, Roberts, Carr / Dowie 2, Le Tissier	20020
11	24	A	Leeds United	L 1-2	9	18	Blake / McAllister, Whelan	28547
12	29	H	Crystal Palace	L 0-1	9	19	- / Preece	20022
13	Nov 5	A	West Ham United	L 0-1	9	21	- / Dicks (p)	18780
14	20	H	Manchester City	L 0-1	9	21	- / Quinn	19006
15	23	A	Arsenal	W 2-1	12	20	Lowe, Seaman (og) / Wright (p)	20774
16	26	A	Norwich City	L 1-2	12	21	Draper / Newsome, Sutch	20657
17	Dec 3	H	Aston Villa	D 1-1	13	21	Gee / Whittingham	20896
18	10	A	Newcastle United	L 1-3	13	21	Oldfield / Albert 2, Howey	34400
19	17	H	Blackburn Rovers	D 0-0	14	21		20559
20	26	H	Liverpool	L 1-2	14	21	Roberts / Fowler (p), Rush	21393
21	28	A	Manchester United	D 1-1	15	21	Whitlow / Kanchelskis	43789
22	31	H	Sheffield Wednesday	L 0-1	15	21	- / Hyde	20624
23	Jan 2	A	Ipswich Town	L 1-4	15	22	Roberts / Kiwomya 2, Tanner, Yallop	15803
24	14	A	Crystal Palace	L 0-2	15	22	- / Newman, Ndah	12707
25	25	A	Manchester City	W 1-0	18	22	Robins	21007
26	Feb 4	H	West Ham United	L 1-2	18	22	Robins / Cottee, Dicks (p)	20375
27	11	A	Arsenal	D 1-1	19	22	Draper / Merson	31373
28	22	A	Aston Villa	D 4-4	20	21	Robins, Roberts, Lowe 2 / Saunders, Staunton, Yorke, Johnson	30825
29	25	A	Coventry City	L 2-4	20	22	Lowe, Roberts / Flynn 2, Marsh, Ndlovu	20633
30	Mar 4	H	Everton	D 2-2	21	22	Draper, Roberts / Limpar, Samways	20447
31	8	A	Queens Park Rangers	L 0-2	21	22	- / McDonald, Wilson	10189
32	11	H	Nottingham Forest	L 2-4	21	22	Lowe, Draper / Pearce (p), Collymore, Woan, Lee	20423
33	15	H	Leeds United	L 1-3	21	22	Roberts / Yeboah 2, Palmer	20068
34	18	A	Tottenham Hotspur	L 0-1	21	22	- / Klinsmann	30851
35	Apr 1	H	Wimbledon	L 3-4	21	22	Robins, Willis, Lawrence / Goodman 2, Leonhardsen 2	15489
36	5	H	Norwich City	W 1-0	24	21	Parker	15992
37	8	A	Sheffield Wednesday	L 0-1	24	21	- / Whittingham	22551
38	15	A	Manchester United	L 0-4	24	21	- / Sharpe, Cole 2, Ince	21281
39	17	H	Liverpool	L 0-2	24	21	- / Fowler, Rush	36012
40	29	H	Ipswich Town	W 2-0	27	21	Whitlow, Lowe	15248
41	May 6	H	Chelsea	D 1-1	28	21	Willis / Furlong	18140
42	14	A	Southampton	D 2-2	29	21	Parker, Robins / Monkou, Le Tissier	15101

Final League Position:	21	
Average Home League Attendance:	19532	

League Appearances: 6 34 28 10 24 23 7 26 39 5 11 16 32 29 36 19 1 19 3 13 11 12 8 6 9 16 4 14 1
Sub: 2 4 4 4 3 5 4 10 4 3 1 1 6 8 1 1 1
League Goals: 2 3 5 3 9 2 8 2 1 1 1 5 2

FA CUP (Littlewoods)

	Date		Opponents	Result	Scorers	Att	
1	Jan 7	H	Enfield (3)	W 2-0	Oldfield, Roberts	17351	1
2	28	A	Portsmouth (4)	W 1-0	Roberts	14928	2
3	Feb 18	A	Wolverhampton W (5)	L 0-1	- / Kelly	28544	3

FOOTBALL LEAGUE CUP (Coca Cola Cup)

	Date		Opponents	Result	Scorers	Att	
1	Sep 21	A	Brighton & H.A. (2 leg 1)	L 0-1	- / Nogan	11041	1
2	Oct 5	H	Brighton & H.A. (2 leg 2)	L 0-2	- / Munday, Nogan	14258	2

Dismissals: Aug 27, Mohan, Nottingham Forest (a); Sep 10, Lowe, Carey, Wimbledon (a); Oct 3, Willis, Coventry City (h); Nov 20, Smith, Manchester City (h); Dec 26, Grayson, Liverpool (h); Mar 11, Lewis, Nottingham Forest (h); Apr 17, Whitlow, Liverpool (a).

Note: Players actually wore squad numbers as denoted in column headings; some numbers were reallocated following mid-season transfers; Nov 23, Premiership panel credited Seaman (og), original reports credited Ormondroyd.

1994-95
Back: McMahon, Willis, Eustace, Carey, Walsh, Ormondroyd, Roberts, Coatsworth, I Thompson, Smith, Blyth.
Middle: Lewis, Speedie, Gibson, Mills, Mohan, Hoult, Poole, Ward, Oldfield, S Thompson, Philpott, Hill, Maisey.
Front: Draper, Lowe, Grayson, Joachim, Evans (Asst Manager), Little (Manager), Gregory (Coach), Agnew, Whitlow, Gee, Blake.

Promoted: Sunderland, Derby County, Leicester City
Relegated: Millwall, Watford, Luton Town

FOOTBALL LEAGUE DIVISION ONE (Endsleigh League)

Player columns (left to right): Kevin Poole, Simon Grayson, Mike Whitlow, Jimmy Willis, Steve Walsh, Garry Parker, Julian Joachim, Scott Taylor, Mark Robins, Steve Corica, Jamie Lawrence, Colin Hill, Iwan Roberts, Lee Philpott, Neil Lewis, David Lowe, Mark Blake, Phil Gee, Sam McMahon, Emile Heskey, Franck Rolling, Brian Carey, Zeljko Kalac, Pontus Kåmark, Richard Smith, Neil Lennon, Steve Claridge, Julian Watts, Muzzy Izzet

Match No	Date		Opponents	Result	Points	Position	Scorers	Att
1	Aug 12	A	Sunderland	W 2-1	3	-	Corica, Robins / Agnew	18593
2	19	H	Stoke City	L 2-3	3	-	Walsh, Parker (p) / Peschisolido 2, Gleghorn	17719
3	26	A	Luton Town	D 1-1	4	9	Parker / Hughes	7612
4	30	H	Portsmouth	W 4-2	7	3	Roberts 3, Parker / Creaney (p), Hall	15170
5	Sep 2	H	Wolverhampton W.	W 1-0	10	2	Whitlow	18441
6	10	A	Derby County	W 1-0	13	1	Joachim	11767
7	12	A	Port Vale	W 2-0	16	1	McMahon, Roberts	8814
8	16	H	Reading	D 1-1	17	1	Roberts / Bernal	19103
9	23	H	Southend United	L 1-3	17	1	Lowe / Hails 3	15276
10	30	A	Norwich City	W 1-0	20	1	Heskey	18435
11	Oct 7	A	Barnsley	D 2-2	21	1	Robins, Walsh / Payton, Bullock	13669
12	14	H	Charlton Athletic	D 1-1	22	1	Lowe / Leaburn	16771
13	21	A	Sheffield United	W 3-1	25	1	Roberts, Taylor, Lowe / Flo	13100
14	28	H	Crystal Palace	L 2-3	25	2	Robins, Taylor / Dyer 2, Hopkin	18376
15	Nov 5	A	West Bromwich Albion	W 3-2	28	2	Taylor 2, Roberts / Hamilton, Raven	16071
16	11	H	Watford	W 1-0	31	2	Roberts	16230
17	19	H	Tranmere Rovers	L 0-1	31	2	- / Moore	13125
18	21	A	Huddersfield Town	L 1-3	31	2	Robins / Bullock 2, Dalton	14300
19	26	A	Birmingham City	D 2-2	32	4	Roberts, Grayson / Hunt 2 (1p)	17350
20	Dec 2	H	Barnsley	D 2-2	33	2	Roberts, Grayson / Payton 2	15125
21	9	A	Southend United	L 1-2	33	8	Roberts / Dublin, Gridelet	5835
22	17	H	Norwich City	W 3-2	36	3	Whitlow, Roberts, Heskey / Eadie, Fleck	14251
23	23	A	Grimsby Town	D 2-2	37	3	Roberts, Walsh / Dobbin, Walsh (og)	7713
24	Jan 1	A	Millwall	D 1-1	38	3	Corica / Malkin	9953
25	13	A	Stoke City	L 0-1	38	5	- / Sturridge	13669
26	21	H	Sunderland	D 0-0	39	5		16130
27	Feb 3	H	Luton Town	D 1-1	40	7	Roberts / Thorpe	14821
28	10	A	Portsmouth	L 1-2	40	10	Roberts / Burton, Hall	9003
29	17	H	Port Vale	D 1-1	41	8	Taylor / McCarthy	13758
30	21	A	Wolverhampton W.	W 3-2	44	6	Roberts, Heskey 2 / Bull, Law	27381
31	24	A	Reading	D 1-1	45	6	Lewis / Lovell (p)	9817
32	28	H	Derby County	D 0-0	46	7		20911
33	Mar 3	A	Ipswich Town	L 2-4	46	8	Roberts 2 / Wark, Milton, Marshall 2	9817
34	9	H	Grimsby Town	W 2-1	49	7	Heskey 2 / Livingstone	13784
35	13	H	Ipswich Town	L 0-2	49	8	- / Marshall, Mathie	17783
36	16	A	Oldham Athletic	L 1-3	49	8	Whitlow / Barlow, Serrant, Richardson (p)	5582
37	23	H	Millwall	W 2-1	52	8	Carey, Taylor / Rae	12543
38	30	H	Sheffield United	L 0-2	52	9	- / Walker, Ward (p)	15230
39	Apr 2	A	Charlton Athletic	W 1-0	55	7	Claridge	11287
40	6	A	Crystal Palace	W 1-0	58	7	Roberts	17331
41	9	A	West Bromwich Albion	L 1-2	58	8	Robins / Sneekes, Raven	17889
42	13	A	Tranmere Rovers	D 1-1	59	8	Robins / Lennon (og)	8882
43	17	A	Oldham Athletic	W 2-0	62	7	Claridge 2	12790
44	20	H	Huddersfield Town	W 2-1	65	6	Walsh, Claridge / Bullock	17619
45	27	H	Birmingham City	W 3-0	68	6	Claridge, Heskey, Lennon	19702
46	May 5	A	Watford	W 1-0	71	5	Izzet	20089

Final League Position: 5
Average Home League Attendance: 16198

	Poole	Grayson	Whitlow	Willis	Walsh	Parker	Joachim	Taylor	Robins	Corica	Lawrence	Hill	Roberts	Philpott	Lewis	Lowe	Blake	Gee	McMahon	Heskey	Rolling	Carey	Kalac	Kåmark	Smith	Lennon	Claridge	Watts	Izzet
League Appearances	45	39	41	11	37	36	14	39	19	16	10	24	34	1	10	21	6	1	1	20	17	16	1	1	1	14	14	9	8
Sub		2	1	1		4	8		12		5	3	3	5	4	7	2	1	2	10		3			1		1		1
League Goals		2	3		4	3	1	6	6	2			19		1	3				7		1				1	5		1

PROMOTION PLAY-OFFS

	Date		Opponents	Result		Scorers	Att
1	May 12	H	Stoke City (sf leg 1)	D 0-0			20323
2	15	A	Stoke City (sf leg 2)	W 1-0		Parker	21037
3	27		Crystal Palace (f)	W 2-1	aet	Parker (p), Claridge / Roberts	73573

FA CUP (Littlewoods)

	Date		Opponents	Result	Scorers	Att
1	Jan 6	H	Manchester City (3)	D 0-0		20640
2	17	A	Manchester City (3 rep)	L 0-5	- / Rosler, Kinkladze, Quinn, Lomas, Creaney	19980

FOOTBALL LEAGUE CUP (Coca Cola Cup)

	Date		Opponents	Result	Scorers	Att
1	Sep 20	H	Burnley (2 leg 1)	W 2-0	Robins, Joachim	11142
2	Oct 3	H	Burnley (2 leg 2)	W 2-0	Robins 2	4553
3	24	A	Bolton Wanderers (3)	D 0-0		9166
4	Nov 8	H	Bolton Wanderers (3 rep)	L 2-3	Robins, Roberts / McGinlay, Sneekes, Curcic	14884

Dismissals: Sep 10, Roberts, Derby County (a);
Mar 16, Lennon, Oldham Athletic (a).
Note: May 27, at Wembley.

1995-96
Back: Lawrence, Philpott, Parker, Grayson, Hill, Blake, Gee, Hallam.
Middle: McGhee (Manager), Lee (Asst Manager), Smith, Willis, Roberts, Poole, Walsh, Carey, Whitlow, Hickman (Coach), Smith (Physio).
Front: Davies (Kit Manager), Joachim, McMahon, Lewis, Lowe, Taylor, Robins, Bedder, Yeoman (Physio).

Champions: Manchester United
Relegated: Sunderland, Middlesbrough, Nottingham Forest

FA PREMIER LEAGUE (Carling Premiership)

Match No	Date		Opponents	Result	Points	Position	Scorers	Att	(13) Kasey Keller	(2) Simon Grayson	(3) Mike Whitlow	(4) Julian Watts	(5) Steve Walsh	(17) Spencer Prior	(6) Muzzy Izzet	(7) Neil Lennon	(8) Scott Taylor	(12) Mark Robins	(11) Emile Heskey	(21) Jamie Lawrence	(9) Steve Claridge	(10) Garry Parker	(20) Ian Marshall	(22) Neil Lewis	(16) Franck Rolling	(26) Stuart Campbell	(1) Kevin Poole	(14) Colin Hill	(28) Sascha Lenhart	(15) Pontus Kåmark	(25) Stuart Wilson	(18) Matt Elliott	(19) Rob Ullathorne	(24) Steve Guppy	Match No
1	Aug 17	A	Sunderland	D 0-0	1	-		19262	1	2	3	4	5	6	7	8	9	10*	11	12															1
2	21	H	Southampton	W 2-1	4	7	Heskey 2 / Le Tissier (p)	17562	1	2	3	4	5	6	7*	8	9		11	12	10														2
3	24	H	Arsenal	L 0-2	4	12	- / Bergkamp, Wright	20429	1	2	3*	4	5	6	7	8			10	12															3
4	Sep 2	A	Sheffield Wednesday	L 1-2	4	13	Claridge / Humphreys, Booth	17657	1	2	3	4*	5	6	7	8	9†		11		10	13	12												4
5	7	A	Nottingham Forest	D 0-0	5	14		24105	1	2	3	4	5	6	7	8	9*		11		10†	12	13												5
6	15	H	Liverpool	L 0-3	5	16	- / Berger 2, Thomas	20987	1	2	3	4†	5	6*	7	8	9		11		10	12	13												6
7	22	A	Tottenham Hotspur	W 2-1	8	14	Claridge, Marshall / Wilson (p)	24159	1	2		4	5	6	7	8	9		11		10*	13	12	3†											7
8	28	H	Leeds United	W 1-0	11	10	Heskey	20359	1	2	3	4	5	6	7	8	9		11		12	10*													8
9	Oct 12	H	Chelsea	L 1-3	11	12	Watts / Vialli, Di Matteo, Hughes	20766	1	2	3	4	5	6	7	8			11		9	10													9
10	19	A	West Ham United	L 0-1	11	14	- / Moncur	22285	1	2	3	4	5	6	7	8	9†		11		12	13	10*												10
11	26	H	Newcastle United	W 2-0	14	11	Claridge, Heskey	21134	1	2	3	4	5	6	7†	8	9		11		10*	13	12	3†											11
12	Nov 2	A	Derby County	L 0-2	14	13	- / Ward, Whitlow (og)	18010		2	3	4		6*	7	8	9‡		11	12	10	14	13			1	5†								12
13	16	A	Aston Villa	W 3-1	17	10	Claridge, Parker (p), Izzet / Yorke	36193	1	2	3	4	5	6	7	8			11		10	9													13
14	23	H	Everton	L 1-2	17	12	Walsh / Hinchcliffe, Unsworth	20975		2	3	4*	5	6	7	8	13		11		10	9†	12		1										14
15	30	A	Manchester United	L 1-3	17	14	Lennon / Butt 2, Solskjaer	55196	1	2		4		6	7	8			11		9	5	12		3*										15
16	Dec 3	A	Middlesbrough	W 2-0	20	12	Claridge, Izzet	29709	1	2		4*		6	7	8	9‡		11†	14	10	3	5		13	12									16
17	7	H	Blackburn Rovers	D 1-1	21	12	Marshall / Sutton	19306	1	2		4		6	7	8	9		11		10	3*	5					12							17
18	21	H	Coventry City	L 0-2	21	13	- / Dublin 2	20038	1	2			6		7	8	9		11		10	12	5				4*		3						18
19	26	A	Liverpool	D 1-1	22	13	Claridge / Collymore	40786	1	2			6		7	8	13		11		10	5	12		9†		4		3*						19
20	28	H	Nottingham Forest	D 2-2	23	12	Heskey, Izzet / Clough, Cooper	20838	1	2			6	7		9			11	12	10	8	5	3*			4								20
21	Jan 11	A	Leeds United	L 0-3	23	16	- / Bowyer, Rush 2	29486	1	2			6	7†		9	14		11	12	10	8	5	3*		13	4†								21
22	18	H	Wimbledon	W 1-0	26	12	Heskey	18927	1	2			6	7	8				11		10	9	5				3		4						22
23	29	H	Sunderland	D 1-1	27	13	Parker (p) / Williams	17883	1	2		12		6	7	8	13		11		10	9	5†	3*					4						23
24	Feb 2	A	Newcastle United	L 3-4	27	14	Elliott, Claridge, Heskey / R Elliott, Shearer 3	36396	1	2		5		6	7	8	9*		11	12	10	3									4				24
25	22	H	Derby County	W 4-2	30	12	Marshall 3, Claridge / Sturridge 2	20323	1	2		4	5	6			9*				3	10	8	11		7			12						25
26	Mar 1	A	Wimbledon	W 3-1	33	10	Elliott 2, Robins / Holdsworth	11487		2			5	6	7	8	9*	10	11	12						1				4		3			26
27	5	H	Aston Villa	W 1-0	36	9	Claridge	20626	1	2		13	5	6†	7	8	14	10*11‡		12	9								4		3				27
28	8	A	Coventry City	D 0-0	37	10		19220	1	2		6	5		7	8	12	10*11*	13	9									4		3				28
29	15	H	Middlesbrough	L 1-3	37	11	Marshall / Blackmore, Juninho, Beck	20561	1	2		5		6	7	8		12		10*	9	11				1			4		3				29
30	19	H	Tottenham Hotspur	D 1-1	38	11	Claridge / Sheringham	20563	1	2			12		6	7	8		13	11*		10	9	5†		1			4		3				30
31	22	A	Southampton	D 2-2	39	11	Heskey, Dryden (og) / Ostenstad, van Gobbel	15044		2		12	5		7	8			11	13	10	9†				1			6*	4	3				31
32	Apr 9	A	Everton	D 1-1	40	11	Marshall / Branch	30368	1	2			5	6	7	8			11	9	10							2	4	3					32
33	12	A	Arsenal	L 0-2	40	13	- / Adams, Platt	38044	1		6	5			12	8	9†11†		7	13		10			14	2*		5	4	3					33
34	19	A	Chelsea	L 1-2	40	13	Sinclair (og) / Minto, Hughes	27723		2			6	7†	8		11	13	10*	9	12			1		5			4	3					34
35	23	H	West Ham United	L 0-1	40	14	- / Moncur	20327	1	2			5	6	7*	8			11		10	9	13		12				4		3†				35
36	May 3	H	Manchester United	D 2-2	41	16	Walsh, Marshall / Solskjaer 2	21068	1	2		14	5		7*	8			11		10†	9†	6			12			3	4		14			36
37	7	H	Sheffield Wednesday	W 1-0	44	12	Elliott	20793	1	2		12		5	14		8		11		10†	9*	6			13			7‡	4	3				37
38	11	A	Blackburn Rovers	W 4-2	47	9	Heskey 2, Claridge, Wilson / Flitcroft, Fenton	25881	1	2†	12			6*		8			11	13	10				5‡	9			7	14	4		3		38

Final League Position:			9					**League Appearances**	31	36	14	22	22	33	34	35	20	5	35	2	29	22	19	4	1	4	7	6	9	16	12			
Average Home League Attendance:			20182					**Sub**		3	4		1	1		5	3			13	3	9	9	2	6		1	1	2		1			
								League Goals		1	2		3	1		1	10		11	2	8					1	4								

FA CUP (Littlewoods)

1	Jan 15	H	Southend United (3)	W 2-0			Claridge, Marshall	13982	1	2		4		6	7*				11		10	9	5		8				3	12				
2	25	H	Norwich City (4)	W 2-1			Marshall, Parker (p) / Adams (p)	16703	1		12		6	7	8		13	11	2†	10	9	5					3*	4						
3	Feb 16	H	Chelsea (5)	D 2-2			Walsh, Newton (og) / Di Matteo, Hughes	19125	1	2		4	5	6		8	7*		13	10	9	11			3†			12						
4	26	A	Chelsea (5 rep)	L 0-1 aet			- / Leboeuf (p)	26053	1	2			5	6	7	8	12		11		10*	9	3					4						

FOOTBALL LEAGUE CUP (Coca Cola Cup)

1	Sep 17	A	Scarborough (2 leg 1)	W 2-0			Izzet, Lawrence	4168	1			4	5		7		9	11	12	2	10*	8		3	6†	13								1
2	25	H	Scarborough (2 leg 2)	W 2-1			Lawrence, Parker (p) / Ritchie	10793			5†		7	8		10	11	2*		9		3	6	13	1	4	12							2
3	Oct 22	A	York City (3)	W 2-0			Lennon, Grayson	8406	1	2	3	4	5	6		8	9*		11	12	10	7													3
4	Nov 27	H	Manchester United (4)	W 2-0			Claridge, Heskey	20428	1	2	3*	12	5	6	7	8	9†		11	13	10	4													4
5	Jan 21	A	Ipswich Town (5)	W 1-0			Robins	20793	1	2†		4		6	7	8	12	5	11		10	9						13	3						5
6	Feb 18	H	Wimbledon (sf leg 1)	D 0-0				16021	1	2		4	5	6	7		9		11	12	10	8							3*						6
7	Mar 11	A	Wimbledon (sf leg 2)	D 1-1 aet			Grayson / Gayle	17810	1	2		4	5	6	7	8		12	13	11	3*	10†	9												7
8	Apr 6		Middlesbrough (f)	D 1-1 aet			Heskey / Ravanelli	76757	1	2	3*		5	6	7†	8	13	12	11		10	9							4						8
9	16		Middlesbrough (f rep)	W 1-0 aet			Claridge	39500	1	2	3*		5	6	7	8		13	11	12	10†	9							4						9

Dismissals: Oct 19, Walsh, West Ham United (a); Jan 25, Lennon, Norwich City (h), FAC.
Note: Players actually wore squad numbers as denoted in column headings; Mar 11, won on away goals;
Mar 22, Premiership panel credited Dryden (og), original reports credited Claridge;
Apr 6, at Wembley; Apr 16, at Hillsborough (Sheffield Wednesday).

23 November: Once again, Steve Walsh was an inspired skipper, leading the Foxes to their first major trophy since 1964. Here he is pictured in typically robust fashion, brushing Emile Heskey aside to power in a header against Everton.

1996-97

Back: Hallam, Heskey, Grayson, Rolling, Walsh, Poole, Hyde, Watts, Willis, Whitlow, Hill.

Middle: Walford (Coach), Franklin (Coach), Robertson (Coach), Wenlock, Wilson, Skeldon, Quincey, Campbell, Dodds, Smith (Physio), Yeoman (Physio), McAndrew (Kit Manager).

Front: Lewis, McMahon, Kåmark, Claridge, Izzet, Smeaton (Chairman), O'Neill (Manager), Lennon, Taylor, Robins, Harrington, Lawrence.

1997-98

Back: Nish (Youth Coach), Hamilton (Youth Development), Heskey, Whitlow, Emerson, Parker, Steve Wilson, Keller, Prior, Watts, Elliott, Walsh, Claridge, McDonagh (Goalkeeping Coach), Smith (Physio).

Middle: Sims (Youth Development), Yeoman (Physio), McAndrew (Kit Manager), Savage, Neil, Fox, Arcos-Diaz, Robins, Branston, Oakes, Robertson (Asst Manager), Walford (Coach), Franklin (Coach).

Front: Jaffa, Wenlock, Stuart Wilson, McMahon, Campbell, Skeldon, Smeaton (Chairman), O'Neill (Manager), Lennon, Izzet, Taylor, Marshall, Guppy, Ullathorne.

Champions: Arsenal
Relegated: Bolton Wanderers, Barnsley, Crystal Palace

Player columns (squad number and name):
(1) Kasey Keller · (15) Pontus Kåmark · (24) Steve Guppy · (17) Spencer Prior · (18) Matt Elliott · (5) Steve Walsh · (6) Muzzy Izzet · (7) Neil Lennon · (16) Stuart Campbell · (20) Ian Marshall · (11) Emile Heskey · (14) Robbie Savage · (9) Steve Claridge · (21) Graham Fenton · (10) Garry Parker · (27) Tony Cottee · (4) Julian Watts · (25) Stuart Wilson · (23) Sam McMahon · (22) Pegguy Arphexad · (19) Rob Ullathorne · (37) Theo Zagorakis

FA PREMIER LEGUE (Carling Premiership)

Match No	Date		Opponents	Result	Points	Position	Scorers	Att	(1)	(15)	(24)	(17)	(18)	(5)	(6)	(7)	(16)	(20)	(11)	(14)	(9)	(21)	(10)	(27)	(4)	(25)	(23)	(22)	(19)	(37)	Match No
1	Aug 9	H	Aston Villa	W 1-0	3	-	Marshall	20304	1	2	3	4	5	6	7	8	9*	10†	11	12	13										1
2	13	A	Liverpool	W 2-1	6	4	Elliott, Fenton / Ince	35007	1	2	3	4	5	6	7*	8	9	10†	11	12			13								2
3	23	H	Manchester United	D 0-0	7	4		21221	1	2	3	4	5	6	7	8	9*	10†	11	12	13										3
4	27	H	Arsenal	D 3-3	8	4	Heskey, Elliott, Walsh / Bergkamp 3	21089	1	2	3	4	5	6	7†	8			11	10†	9*	12	13	14							4
5	30	A	Sheffield Wednesday	L 0-1	8	6	- / Carbone (p)	24851	1	2	3	4†	5	6	7	8			11	10*	9†	13	12	14							5
6	Sep 13	H	Tottenham Hotspur	W 3-0	11	5	Walsh, Guppy, Heskey	20683	1	2†	3†	4	5	6	7	8		9*	11		12	13	10	14							6
7	20	A	Leeds United	W 1-0	14	3	Walsh	29620	1	2	3	4	5	6*	7	8	13	9	11												7
8	24	H	Blackburn Rovers	D 1-1	15	4	Izzet / Sutton	19921	1	2	3	4	5		7	8	6	11	12		9†	10*	13								8
9	27	A	Barnsley	W 2-0	18	3	Marshall, Fenton	18660	1	2	3	4	5		7	8	6	11†	10	13	9*		12								9
10	Oct 6	H	Derby County	L 1-2	18	4	Elliott / Baiano 2	19585	1	2	3	4	5		7*	8	14	6†	11	12		13	10†	9							10
11	18	A	Chelsea	L 0-1	18	5	- / Leboeuf	33356	1	2	3	4	5		7	8	10*	11	6	9†	13		12				1				11
12	27	H	West Ham United	W 2-1	21	4	Heskey, Marshall / Berkovic	20201		2†	3	4	5		7	8	13	6	11	10*	9		12				1				12
13	Nov 1	A	Newcastle United	D 3-3	22	5	Marshall 2, Elliott / Barnes (p), Tomasson, Beresford	36754		2	3	4	5		7	8	6	11	12	9†	13		10*				1				13
14	10	H	Wimbledon	L 0-1	22	7	- / Gayle	18553		2	3	4	5	12	7	8	6	11	13	9*			10†				1				14
15	22	H	Bolton Wanderers	D 0-0	23	6		20464	1	2	3	4	5	6	7	8	11			9*	12		10†		13						15
16	29	A	Coventry City	W 2-0	26	6	Fenton, Elliott (p)	18309	1	2	3	4	5	6	7	8	11			10	9										16
17	Dec 6	H	Crystal Palace	D 1-1	27	6	Izzet / Padovano	19191	1	2	3*		4	5		7	8	10†		6	9†	11		13	12	14					17
18	13	A	Southampton	L 1-2	27	7	Savage / Le Tissier, Benali	15121	1	2	3	4†	5	6	7	8			11	10	13	9*			12						18
19	20	A	Everton	L 0-1	27	8	- / Speed (p)	20628	1	2†	3	4	5	6	7	8			11	10	12	9*			13						19
20	26	A	Arsenal	L 1-2	27	9	Lennon / Platt, Walsh (og)	38023	1		4	3		5	6	7	8	10*		11	2	9†		12	13						20
21	28	H	Sheffield Wednesday	D 1-1	28	9	Guppy / Booth	20800	1		4	3	12	5	6*	7	8		9†	11	2	13		10							21
22	Jan 10	A	Aston Villa	D 1-1	29	9	Parker (p) / Joachim	36429	1		4	3		5	6	7	8	9*	11	2			10	12							22
23	17	H	Liverpool	D 0-0	30	9		21633	1		4	3		5	6	7	8	9	11*	2			10	12							23
24	31	A	Manchester United	W 1-0	33	9	Cottee	55156	1		4	3	12	5	6*	7	8	13					10†	9‡	14		2				24
25	Feb 7	H	Leeds United	W 1-0	36	9	Parker (p)	21244	1		4	3	6	5		7	8		11	2*			10	9					12		25
26	14	A	Tottenham Hotspur	D 1-1	37	9	Cottee / Calderwood	28355			4	3	6	5		7	8		11	2			10*	9		1			12		26
27	21	H	Chelsea	W 2-0	40	7	Heskey 2	21335			4‡	3	6	5	12	7	8	14	11	2*		13	9†			1			10		27
28	28	A	Blackburn Rovers	L 3-5	40	7	Wilson, Izzet, Ullathorne / Dahlin, Sutton 3, Hendry	24854	1		3	4*	5		6	7	8		9†							13			12 10		28
29	Mar 14	A	Wimbledon	L 1-2	40	9	Savage / Roberts, Hughes	13229	1		3	4		6*		8		5†	11	2			9	12	13				7 10		29
30	28	A	Bolton Wanderers	L 0-2	40	12	- / Thompson 2	25000	1	6	3	4	5			8†			11	2		13	9		12				7 10*		30
31	Apr 4	H	Coventry City	D 1-1	41	12	Wilson / Whelan	21137	1	6	3	4†	5		7	8			11	2		12		9*	13				10		31
32	11	A	Crystal Palace	W 3-0	44	10	Heskey 2, Elliott	18771	1	6	3	4	5		7	8		14	11	2†	9‡	12		13					10*		32
33	14	H	Southampton	D 3-3	45	10	Lennon, Elliott, Parker (p) / Ostenstad 2, Hirst	20708	1	6	3	4‡	5	14	7	8	13	11	2		9†	12							10*		33
34	18	A	Everton	D 1-1	46	10	Marshall / Madar	33642	1	4	3		5	6	7		9	11	2		8	12							10*		34
35	26	A	Derby County	W 4-0	49	9	Heskey 2, Izzet, Marshall	29855	1	4	3†		5	6*	7	8	9	11	2	14		12						13	10‡		35
36	29	H	Newcastle United	D 0-0	50	9		21699	1	4	3		5	6	7	8	9†	11	2			13						12	10*		36
37	May 2	H	Barnsley	W 1-0	53	8	Zagorakis	21293	1		3		5	6	7	8	4	11	2		12	9*							10		37
38	10	A	West Ham United	L 3-4	53	10	Cottee 2, Heskey / Lampard, Abou 2, Sinclair	25781	1	4	3		5	6†	7	8	9‡	11	2			12	13	14					10*		38

Final League Position:	10								
Average Home League Attendance:	20615								

	(1)	(15)	(24)	(17)	(18)	(5)	(6)	(7)	(16)	(20)	(11)	(14)	(9)	(21)	(10)	(27)	(4)	(25)	(23)	(22)	(19)	(37)
League Appearances	32	35	37	28	37	23	36	37	6	22	35	28	10	9	15	7				6	3	12
Sub				2		3			5	2		7	7	14	7	12	3	11	1		3	2
League Goals			2		7	3	4	2		7	10	2		3	3	4	2				1	1

FA CUP (Littlewoods)

Match No	Date		Opponents	Result	Scorers	Att	(1)	(15)	(24)	(17)	(18)	(5)	(6)	(7)	(16)	(20)	(11)	(14)	(9)	(21)	(10)	(27)	(4)	(25)	(23)	(22)	(19)	(37)	Match No
1	Jan 3	H	Northampton Town (3)	W 4-0	Marshall, Parker (p), Savage, Cottee	20608	1	6	3‡	4	5		7†	8	9*	11	2			13	10	12	14						1
2	24	A	Crystal Palace (4)	L 0-3	- / Dyer 3	15489	1	4*	3		5	6	7	8	9†	11	2			10	12	13							2

FOOTBALL LEAGUE CUP (Coca Cola Cup)

Match No	Date		Opponents	Result	Scorers	Att	(1)	(15)	(24)	(17)	(18)	(5)	(6)	(7)	(16)	(20)	(11)	(14)	(9)	(21)	(10)	(27)	(4)	(25)	(23)	Match No
1	Oct 14	A	Grimsby Town (3)	L 1-3	Marshall / Jobling, Livingstone 2	7738	1		3		5	6†		8	7	9		2			10		11	4*	12 13	1

UEFA CUP

Match No	Date		Opponents	Result	Scorers	Att	(1)	(15)	(24)	(17)	(18)	(5)	(6)	(7)	(16)	(20)	(11)	(14)	(9)	(21)	(10)	(27)	(4)	(25)	(23)	Match No
1	Sep 16	A	Atletico Madrid (1 leg 1)	L 1-2	Marshall / Juninho, Vieri (p)	35000	1	2	3	4	5	6	7	8	14	9*	11		12‡	13	10†					1
2	30	H	Atletico Madrid (1 leg 2)	L 0-2	- / Juninho, Kiko	20776	1	2	3	4†	5		7	8		9‡	11	12		14	10	13	6*			2

Dismissals: Sep 30, Parker, Atletico Madrid (h), UEFA Cup; Nov 1, Heskey, Newcastle United (a); 28 Mar, Ullathorne, Bolton Wanderers (a).

Note: Players actually wore squad numbers as denoted in column headings; Sep 30, Tony Cottee wore number 8 (not 27) due to UEFA regulations.

31 January: City's victory at Old Trafford was one of the highlights of the season. Young Stuart Campbell, who came off the bench to play his part, is seen here powering past Manchester United's Paul Scholes.

Season 1998-99

Champions: Manchester United
Relegated: Charlton Athletic, Blackburn Rovers, Nottingham Forest

FA PREMIER LEAGUE (Carling Premiership)

Match No	Date		Opponents	Result	Points	Position	Scorers	Att	(1) Kasey Keller	(14) Robbie Savage	(11) Steve Guppy	(3) Frank Sinclair	(18) Matt Elliott	(5) Steve Walsh	(6) Muzzy Izzet	(7) Neil Lennon	(37) Theo Zagorakis	(27) Tony Cottee	(9) Emile Heskey	(22) Pegguy Arphexad	(25) Stuart Wilson	(4) Gerry Taggart	(16) Stuart Campbell	(10) Garry Parker	(15) Pontus Kåmark	(19) Rob Ullathorne	(21) Graham Fenton	(29) Stef Oakes	(24) Andy Impey	(20) Ian Marshall	(13) Arnar Gunnlaugsson	(17) Charlie Miller	Match No
1	Aug 15	A	Manchester United	D 2-2	1	-	Heskey, Cottee / Sheringham, Beckham	55052	1*	2	3	4	5‡	6	7	8	9	10†	11	12	13	14											1
2	22	H	Everton	W 2-0	4	2	Cottee, Izzet	21037	1	2	3	4	5	6	7	8	9	10	11														2
3	29	A	Blackburn Rovers	L 0-1	4	8	- / Gallacher	22544	1	2	3	4	5‡	6	7	8*	9†	10	11			14	12	13									3
4	Sep 9	H	Middlesbrough	L 0-1	4	13	- / Gascoigne	20635	1	2†	3	4	5		7	8	9†	10*	11			14	12	13		6							4
5	12	H	Arsenal	D 1-1	5	14	Heskey / Hughes	21628	1	2	3	4	5		7	8	9*	10	11				12			6							5
6	19	A	Derby County	L 0-2	5	17	- / Schnoor, Wanchope	26738	1	2†	3	4	5		7	8		10†	11			14	13	9*	12	6							6
7	27	H	Wimbledon	D 1-1	6	17	Elliott / Earle	17725	1	2	3	4	5		7	8		10†	11			13	6			12	9*						7
8	Oct 3	A	Leeds United	W 1-0	9	16	Cottee	32606	1	2	3		5		7	8	4*	10	11			6	12			9							8
9	19	H	Tottenham Hotspur	W 2-1	12	11	Heskey, Izzet / Ferdinand	20787	1	2	3	4	5		7	8		10	11			6*	12†	13		9							9
10	24	A	Aston Villa	D 1-1	13	11	Cottee / Ehiogu	39241	1	2	3	4	5		7	8	6*	10	11			12				9							10
11	31	H	Liverpool	W 1-0	16	7	Cottee	21837	1	2†	3	4	5	12	7	8	6*	10	11			13				9							11
12	Nov 7	A	Charlton Athletic	D 0-0	17	6		20021	1	2	3	4	5	6	7	8	10*		11			12				9							12
13	14	A	West Ham United	L 2-3	17	9	Izzet, Lampard (og) / Kitson, Lomas, Lampard	25642	1	2	3	4	5	6	7†	8		13				14		12	10*		9	11‡					13
14	21	H	Chelsea	L 2-4	17	12	Izzet, Guppy / Zola 2, Poyet, Flo	21401	1	2*	3	4	5	6	7	8	10						12			9	11†	13					14
15	28	A	Coventry City	D 1-1	18	13	Heskey / Huckerby	19984	1	2	3	4	5	6	7	8			11							9	10*		2				15
16	Dec 5	H	Southampton	W 2-0	21	12	Heskey, Walsh	18423	1	12	3	4	5	6†	7	8	10*		11			13				9			2				16
17	12	H	Nottingham Forest	W 3-1	24	8	Heskey, Elliott (p), Guppy / van Hooijdonk	20891	1	12	3		5	6†	7	8	10*		11†				14	4	9	13			2				17
18	19	A	Newcastle United	L 0-1	24	11	- / Glass	36718	1	12	3	4†	5		7*		10†	11			6			13	9	14			2				18
19	26	H	Sheffield Wednesday	W 1-0	27	10	Cottee	33513	1	12	3	4	5	6	7†	8		10	11			13				9			2*				19
20	28	H	Blackburn Rovers	D 1-1	28	10	Walsh / Gallacher	21083	1	2*	3	4	5	6	7	8	12†	10	11							9				13			20
21	Jan 9	A	Everton	D 0-0	29	10		32792	1		3	4	5	6	7	8		10	11							9			2				21
22	16	H	Manchester United	L 2-6	29	12	Zagorakis, Walsh / Yorke 3, Cole 2, Stam	22091	1		3			6	7	8	2	10†				11*	4	13	12	5†	9	14					22
23	30	A	Middlesbrough	D 0-0	30	12		34631	1		3		5	6†		8	10					4	12	11*	7	9	13		2				23
24	Feb 6	H	Sheffield Wednesday	L 0-2	30	13	- / Jonk, Carbone	20113	1		3	12	5	6†	7	8	14	10	11			4*			9			2†		13			24
25	20	A	Arsenal	L 0-5	30	14	- / Anelka 3, Parlour 2	38069	1	2	3	4	5	12	7	8	10†							6*	9	14		13		11‡			25
26	Mar 1	H	Leeds United	L 1-2	30	14	Cottee / Kewell, Smith	18101	1	2	3		5		7	8		10	11*					6	9			4†	12	13			26
27	6	A	Wimbledon	W 1-0	33	14	Guppy	11801	1*	2	3			6	7	8		10		12		4		9				11					27
28	13	H	Charlton Athletic	D 1-1	34	13	Lennon / Mendonca	20220	1	2	3		5	6	7	8		11*				4			9			10	12				28
29	Apr 3	A	Tottenham Hotspur	W 2-0	37	13	Elliott, Cottee	35415	1	2	3	4	5		7*	8		10	11						12	9		6					29
30	6	H	Aston Villa	D 2-2	38	14	Savage, Cottee / Hendrie, Joachim	20652	1	2	3	4	5			8		10	11						9			6		7*	12		30
31	10	H	West Ham United	D 0-0	39	13		20402	1	2	3	4	5			8		10	11						9			6*	13	7†	12		31
32	18	A	Chelsea	D 2-2	40	13	Guppy, Duberry (og) / Zola, Elliott (og)	34535	1	2	3	4	5			8		10	11						12	9*		6	13	7†			32
33	21	A	Liverpool	W 1-0	43	12	Marshall	36019	1	2	3	4	5			8		10						12	9			6	11	7*			33
34	24	H	Coventry City	W 1-0	46	11	Marshall	20224	1	2	3	4	5			8†		10*	11					12	9		13	6	7†	14			34
35	May 1	A	Southampton	L 1-2	46	11	Marshall / Marsden, Beattie	15228	1	2	3	4	5	13		8		10*	11					9†				6	7		12		35
36	5	H	Derby County	L 1-2	46	11	Sinclair / Sturridge, Beck	20535	1	2*	3	4	5	13	7	8		12	11					9				6	10†				36
37	8	H	Newcastle United	W 2-0	49	10	Izzet, Cottee	21125		2	3	4	5		7	8	12	10		1				9			6				11*		37
38	16	A	Nottingham Forest	L 0-1	49	10	- / Bart-Williams	25353		2	3	4†	5	13	7	8	11	10	12	1				9			6*						38

Final League Position:	10	League Appearances	36	29	38	30	37	17	31	37	16	29	29	2	1	9	1	2	15	25	3	2	17	6	5	1
Average Home League Attendance:	20469	Sub	5		1		5				3	2	1	2	8	6	11	5	4		6	1	1	4	4	3
		League Goals		1	4	1	3	3	5	1	1	10	6											3			

FA CUP (Axa)

	Date		Opponents	Result			Scorers	Att	(1)	(14)	(11)	(3)	(18)	(5)	(6)	(7)	(37)	(27)	(9)	(22)	(25)	(4)	(16)	(10)	(15)	(19)	(21)	(29)	(24)	(20)	(13)	(17)	
1	Jan 2	H	Birmingham City (3)	W 4-2			Sinclair, Ullathorne, Cottee, Guppy / Robinson, Adebola	19846	1		3	4	5		7†	8‡	14	10*	11			6	2	13		9			12				1
2	23	H	Coventry City (4)	L 0-3			- / Whelan, Telfer, Froggatt	21207	1		3	4	5	6	7	8	10*		11			13		12		9†		2					2

FOOTBALL LEAGUE CUP (Worthington Cup)

	Date		Opponents	Result			Scorers	Att	(1)	(14)	(11)	(3)	(18)	(5)	(6)	(7)	(37)	(27)	(9)	(22)	(25)	(4)	(16)	(10)	(15)	(19)	(21)	(29)	(24)	(20)	(13)	(17)	
1	Sep 16	H	Chesterfield (2 leg 1)	W 3-0			Heskey 2, Taggart	13480	1	2†	3	4	5			8‡	13	10*	11			12	6	9	7		14						1
2	22	A	Chesterfield (2 leg 2)	W 3-1			Heskey, Fenton, Wilson / Howard	4565		14	3		5			8*	2		11†	1	10	6	12	7	4	9‡	13						2
3	Oct 27	A	Charlton Athletic (3)	W 2-1			Cottee 2 / Mortimer	19671	1	2	3	4	5		7	8	6	10	11						9								3
4	Nov 11	H	Leeds United (4)	W 2-1			Izzet, Parker (p) / Kewell	20161	1	2	3	4	5	6	7	8	10*		11†			13		12	9								4
5	Dec 2	H	Blackburn Rovers (5)	W 1-0			Lennon	19442	1	2	3	4	5	6		8			11*			12	13	7	9	10†							5
6	Jan 26	A	Sunderland (sf leg 1)	W 2-1			Cottee 2 / McCann	38332	1		3	4†	5	6	7	8		10	11*			12	2		13	9							6
7	Feb 17	H	Sunderland (sf leg 2)	D 1-1			Cottee / Quinn	21231	1	12	3	4	5	6	7	8		10	11			2*			9								7
8	Mar 21		Tottenham Hotspur (f)	L 0-1			- / Nielsen	77892	1	2†	3		5	6	7	8	13	10	11*			4			9			12					8

Dismissals: Nov 28, Sinclair, Coventry City (a).
Note: Players actually wore squad numbers as denoted in column headings; Mar 21, at Wembley.

19 September: A plethora of Foxes, past and present, in action at Pride Park as City's Neil Lennon and Muzzy Izzet battle against Spencer Prior and Russell Hoult of the Rams.

1998-99

Back: Nish (Academy Manager), Sims (Youth Development Officer), Rudkin (Academy Asst Manager), Heskey, Parker, Taggart, Arphexad, Keller, Hodges, Prior, Elliott, Walsh, Neil, Smith (Physio), Yeoman (Physio), Andrews (Academy Physio).
Middle: McDonagh (Goalkeeping Coach), Hamilton (Academy Asst Manager), McAndrew (Kit Manager), Watts (Asst Kit Manager), Allen, Kåmark, Dudfield, Emerson, Goodwin, Taylor, Guppy, Fenton, Mitchell, Robertson (Asst Manager), Walford (First Team Coach), Franklin (Reserve Team Coach), Melrose (Scout).
Front: Cottee, McCann, Wenlock, McMahon, Wilson, Izzet, Savage, Elsom (Chairman), O'Neill (Manager), Campbell, Lennon, Zagorakis, Marshall, Fox, Oakes, Ullathorne.

1999-2000

Back: Watts (Asst Kit Manager), Yeoman (Physio), Smith (Physio), Dudfield, Heskey, Taggart, Elliott, Walsh, Oakes, Nish (Academy Director), Sims (Youth Development Officer), Hamilton (Academy Asst Director).
Second Row: Tucker (Academy Coach), McAndrew (Kit Manager), Gough, Branston, Arphexad, Flowers, Hodges, Goodwin, Savage, Rudkin (Academy Asst Director), Andrews (Physio).
Third Row: McDonagh (Goalkeeping Coach), Melrose (Chief Scout), McCann, Boateng, Izzet, Sinclair, Zagorakis, Fenton, Bacon, Guppy, Franklin (Reserve Team Coach), Parker (Coach).
Front: Robertson (Asst Manager), Brennan, Gunnlaugsson, Wilson, Cottee, O'Neill (Manager), Elsom (Chairman), Lennon, Campbell, Impey, Marshall, Walford (First Team Coach).

Season 1999-2000

Champions: Manchester United
Relegated: Wimbledon, Sheffield Wednesday, Watford

FA PREMIER LEAGUE (Carling Premiership)

Match No	Date		Opponents	Result	Points	Position	Scorers	Att	(1) Tim Flowers	(24) Andy Impey	(11) Steve Guppy	(3) Frank Sinclair	(18) Matt Elliott	(5) Steve Walsh	(6) Muzzy Izzet	(7) Neil Lennon	(14) Robbie Savage	(27) Tony Cottee	(9) Emile Heskey	(4) Gerry Taggart	(20) Ian Marshall	(16) Stuart Campbell	(15) Phil Gilchrist	(22) Pegguy Arphexad	(29) Stef Oakes	(37) Theo Zagorakis	(21) Graham Fenton	(25) Stuart Wilson	(13) Arnar Gunnlaugsson	(10) Darren Eadie	(34) Danny Thomas	(38) Tommy Goodwin	(46) Jordan Stewart	(8) Stan Collymore	(28) Lawrie Dudfield	Match No
1	Aug 7	A	Arsenal	L 1-2		-	Cottee / Bergkamp, Sinclair (og)	38026	1	2	3	4	5	6*	7	8	9	10	11†	12	13															1
2	11	H	Coventry City	W 1-0	3	12	Izzet (p)	19196	1	2	3	4	5		7	8	9	10		6†	11*	12	13													2
3	14	H	Chelsea	D 2-2	4	10	Heskey, Izzet (p) / Wise, Sinclair (og)	21068	1	2	3	4	5		7	8	9	10*	11	6†	11*	13														3
4	21	A	West Ham United	L 1-2	4	15	Heskey / Wanchope, Di Canio	23631	1	2	3	4	5		7	8	9*	10	11	6†	12	13														4
5	24	A	Middlesbrough	W 3-0	7	6	Heskey 2, Cottee	33126	1*	2	3	4	5		7	8	9	10†	11	6	13			12												5
6	30	H	Watford	W 1-0	10	5	Izzet	17920			3	4	5		7	8	9	10†	11	6	13			1	2*	12										6
7	Sep 11	A	Sunderland	L 0-2	10	10	- / Butler, McCann	40105	1	2	3	4	5		7	8	9†	10*	11	6	12	13														7
8	18	H	Liverpool	D 2-2	11	9	Cottee, Izzet / Owen 2 (1p)	21623		2*	3	4	5		7	8	9	10†	11	6		13	1	12												8
9	25	H	Aston Villa	W 3-1	14	7	Izzet, Cottee, Southgate (og) / Dublin	19917	1	2	3	4	5		7	8	9†	10*	11	6		12		6					13							9
10	Oct 3	A	Tottenham Hotspur	W 3-2	17	7	Izzet 2 (1p), Taggart / Iversen 2	35591	1	2	3		5		7	8	9	10	11	6	12	4*														10
11	16	H	Southampton	W 2-1	20	5	Guppy, Cottee / Pahars	19556	1	2	3	4	5		7	8	9†	10†	11	6*	13	12							14							11
12	23	A	Bradford City	L 1-3	20	6	Impey / Blake, Mills, Redfearn	17655	1	2	3	4	5	13	7	8	9*	10†	11	6		12		6												12
13	30	H	Sheffield Wednesday	W 3-0	23	5	Taggart 2, Cottee	19046	1	2	3	4	5		7	8	9†	10‡	11	6*		12							14	13						13
14	Nov 6	A	Manchester United	L 0-2	23	6	- / Cole 2	55191	1	2	3	4	5	12	7	8	9	10*	11	6																14
15	20	H	Wimbledon	W 2-1	26	7	Cottee 2 / Gayle	18255	1	2	3	4		5		8	9	10	11	6						7										15
16	27	H	Coventry City	W 1-0	29	5	Heskey	22021	1	2	3	4		5		8	9	10	11	6																16
17	Dec 4	A	Arsenal	L 0-3	29	5	- / Grimandi, Overmars, Guppy (og)	20495	1	2*	3	4	5		7	8	9†	10‡	11	6	12								13	14						17
18	18	H	Derby County	L 0-1	29	6	- / Powell	18591	1	2*			5	4	7		9	12	11	6						3	8			10						18
19	26	A	Leeds United	L 1-2	29	7	Cottee / Bridges, Bowyer	40105				4	5		7		9	10	11	6		2*	1	3	12				8							19
20	28	H	Newcastle United	L 1-2	29	7	Zagorakis / Ferguson, Shearer	21225	1			4	5		7*		9	10†	11	6		12	2			3				8	13					20
21	Jan 3	A	Everton	D 2-2	30	8	Elliott 2 / Hutchison, Unsworth (p)	30490	1*			4	5	2		8‡	9	10		6		13		12	3	7†				11	14					21
22	15	A	Chelsea	D 1-1	31	8	Taggart / Wise	35063		13	4	5					11	6	10*		2	1	3	7	12		9†	8								22
23	22	H	West Ham United	L 1-3	31	10	Heskey / Wanchope 2, Di Canio	19019			4	5					11				3	2	1		7†	10	9*	8	12	6	13					23
24	Feb 5	A	Middlesbrough	W 2-1	34	9	Impey, O'Neill (og) / Campbell	17550	1	2*		4	5	12	7	8	9		6		3	10								11						24
25	12	A	Watford	D 1-1	35	10	Elliott / Wooter	16814	1	2			5	6			10	11			4	8	7			3							9			25
26	Mar 5	H	Sunderland	W 5-2	38	10	Collymore 3, Heskey, Oakes / Phillips, Quinn	20432	1		3	4	5		7	8	9		11	6						12				2*				10		26
27	11	A	Wimbledon	L 1-2	38	11	Taggart / Ardley (p), Cort	14316	1	2	3	4	5		7	8	9*	10†		6	13	12												11		27
28	18	H	Manchester United	L 0-2	38	12	- / Beckham, Yorke	22170		3	4	5			7	8	9	12		6	13			2*						10†				11		28
29	26	H	Leeds United	W 2-1	41	11	Collymore, Guppy / Kewell	21059	1		3	4*	5		7	8	9	13		6		12	2							10†				11		29
30	Apr 2	A	Derby County	L 0-3	41	12	- / Burley, Delap, Sturridge	25763		14	3	4†	5		7	8	9			6	12	13	1	2						10‡				11*		30
31	8	H	Everton	D 1-1	42	13	Taggart / Hutchison	18705	1	2	3		5		7‡	8	9	10†		6	12		4			11*	14								13	31
32	15	A	Newcastle United	W 2-0	45	10	Cottee, Savage	36426	1	2	3	4	5			8	9†	10		6	12		7			11*	13									32
33	19	H	Tottenham Hotspur	L 0-1	45	11	- / Ginola	19764	1	2	3*	4	5			7		9	10†	6	13		8			11	12									33
34	22	A	Aston Villa	D 2-2	46	11	Elliott, Lennon / Thompson, Merson	31229	1	2			4	5		7†	8	9	10		6		3			11*	13							12		34
35	29	A	Southampton	W 2-1	49	11	Cottee, Izzet / Kachloul	15178	1	2	3	4	5	12	7	8	9	10†		6*		11														35
36	May 3	A	Liverpool	W 2-0	52	9	Cottee, Gilchrist	43456		2	3	4	5		7	8	9	10*			12		6	1	13				11†							36
37	6	H	Bradford City	W 3-0	55	8	Elliott 2, Cottee	21103	2*	3	4‡	5	13	7	8	9	10				6†	1	14	12					11							37
38	14	A	Sheffield Wednesday	L 0-4	55	8	- / Quinn, Booth, Alexandersson, de Bilde	21656	2†	3	4	5	12	7	8	9	10‡		14			6*	1	13					11							38

Final League Position:	8						League Appearances		29	28	29	34	37	5	32	31	35	30	23	30	2	1	17	9	15	6	1		2	15		1		6	
Average Home League Attendance:	19825						Sub			1	1			6					3		1	19	3	10	2	7	11	1			1	3		1		2
							League Goals			2	2		6		8	1	1	13	7	6					1		1	1						4	

FA CUP (Axa)

	Date		Opponents	Result			Scorers	Att																												
1	Dec 11	A	Hereford United (3)	D 0-0				7795	1	2	3	4*	5	12	7	8	9	10	11	6																1
2	22	H	Hereford United (3 rep)	W 2-1 aet			Elliott, Izzet / Fewings	12157		12		5	4*	7		9	10		6		13	2	1	3	8†	14	11†									2
3	Jan 9	A	Arsenal (4)	D 0-0				35710			4	5	2		8*	9		11	6	12	13	1	3	7†		10										3
4	19	H	Arsenal (4 rep)	D 0-0 aet				15235	1‡		3*	5			9			11	6		13	2	14	4	7	12	10	8†								4
5	30	A	Chelsea (5)	L 1-2			Elliott / Poyet, Weah	30141	2†		4	5	10		9			11‡	6		3	1		7*	12	14	8			13						5

FOOTBALL LEAGUE CUP (Worthington Cup)

	Date		Opponents	Result			Scorers	Att																												
1	Sep 14	A	Crystal Palace (2 leg 1)	D 3-3			Lennon, Taggart, Digby (og) / Morrison, Zhiyi, Mullins	5006	13		3	4	5*		7	8	9			11‡	12	10		6	1†				2	14						1
2	22	H	Crystal Palace (2 leg 2)	W 4-2			Oakes 2 (1p), Marshall, Fenton / Thomson, Bradbury	12762		2		4				8†	9			11*	6	10		5	1	3	7	12	13							2
3	Oct 13	H	Grimsby Town (3)	W 2-0			Izzet, Heskey	13701	1	2	3*	4			7	8			10†	11‡	6		5		9	14	13	12								3
4	Dec 15	H	Leeds United (4)	D 0-0 aet				16125	1	2			5	4	7	8*	9	10†	11	6			3	12			13									4
5	Jan 12	H	Fulham (5)	D 3-3 aet			Marshall 2, Walsh / Peschisolido, Horsfield, Coleman	13576		2*		4	5	7			9			11	6	10		13	1	3‡	8†	14		12						5
6	25	A	Aston Villa (sf leg 1)	D 0-0				28037	1	2†	3*	4	5	13	7†		9		11	6			14	8		10	12									6
7	Feb 2	H	Aston Villa (sf leg 2)	W 1-0			Elliott	21843	1	12	3*	4	5		7†	8‡	9		11	6			13	2		10	14									7
8	27		Tranmere Rovers (f)	W 2-1			Elliott 2 / Kelly	74313	1	12	3*	4	5		7	8	9	10†	11	6	13					2*										8

Dismissals: Sep 11, Taggart, Sunderland (a); Sep 18, Sinclair, Liverpool (h); Jan 9, Eadie, Arsenal (a), FAC; Jan 30, Walsh, Chelsea (a), FAC; Apr 2, Lennon, Derby County (a).
Stand-in Goalkeepers: Sep 14, Zagorakis for Flowers, Crystal Palace (a), FLC.
Note: Players actually wore squad numbers as denoted in column headings;
Dec 4, Premiership panel credited Guppy (og), original reports credited Dixon;
Dec 15, won 4-2 on penalties Gunnlaugsson, Elliott, Impey, Izzet scored);
Jan 12, won 3-0 on penalties (Gunnlaugsson, Savage, Fenton scored);
Jan 19, won 6-5 on penalties (Gunnlaugsson, Savage, Fenton, Elliott, Campbell, Heskey scored);
Feb 27, at Wembley.

22 January: City's deepening injury crisis led to several youngsters appearing against West Ham at Filbert Street; debutant Tommy Goodwin is pictured here outsmarting Paulo Wanchope. At the final whistle the crowd sang 'We are proud of you' despite a fourth successive home defeat.

Season 2000-01

Champions: Manchester United
Relegated: Manchester City, Coventry City, Bradford City

FA PREMIER LEAGUE (Carling Premiership)

Match No	Date		Opponents	Result	Points	Position	Scorers	Att
1	Aug 19	H	Aston Villa	D 0-0	1	-		21455
2	23	A	West Ham United	W 1-0	4	4	Eadie	25195
3	26	A	Bradford City	D 0-0	5	6		16766
4	Sep 6	H	Ipswich Town	W 2-1	8	3	Akinbiyi, Elliott / Magilton (p)	19598
5	9	H	Southampton	W 1-0	11	2	Taggart	18366
6	17	A	Chelsea	W 2-0	14	2	Izzet, Collymore	33697
7	24	H	Everton	D 1-1	15	2	Akinbiyi / Unsworth	18084
8	Oct 1	A	Sunderland	D 0-0	16	1		45338
9	14	H	Manchester United	L 0-3	16	3	- / Sheringham 2, Solskjaer	22132
10	21	A	Liverpool	L 0-1	16	5	- / Heskey	44395
11	28	H	Derby County	W 2-1	19	3	Izzet, Gunnlaugsson / Delap	20525
12	Nov 4	H	Manchester City	W 1-0	22	3	Savage	34279
13	11	H	Newcastle United	D 1-1	23	3	Gunnlaugsson / Speed	21406
14	18	A	Middlesbrough	W 3-0	26	3	Izzet (p), Benjamin, Eadie	27965
15	25	A	Tottenham Hotspur	L 0-3	26	4	- / Ferdinand 3	35636
16	Dec 2	H	Leeds United	W 3-1	29	3	Savage, Akinbiyi, Taggart / Viduka	21486
17	10	A	Coventry City	L 0-1	29	4	- / Bellamy	17283
18	16	H	Charlton Athletic	W 3-1	32	4	Akinbiyi, Elliott, Gunnlaugsson / Johansson	19371
19	23	H	West Ham United	W 2-1	35	3	Izzet, Savage / Kanoute	21524
20	26	A	Arsenal	L 1-6	35	4	Akinbiyi / Henry 3, Vieira, Ljungberg, Adams	38007
21	Jan 1	H	Bradford City	L 1-2	35	6	Izzet (p) / Jess, Jacobs	19278
22	14	A	Ipswich Town	L 0-2	35	6	- / Stewart, Scowcroft	22002
23	20	H	Arsenal	D 0-0	36	7		21872
24	31	A	Southampton	L 0-1	36	8	- / Petrescu	14909
25	Feb 3	H	Chelsea	W 2-1	39	6	Izzet, Rowett / Hasselbaink	21502
26	10	A	Everton	L 1-2	39	7	Sturridge / Jeffers, Campbell	30409
27	24	H	Sunderland	W 2-0	42	7	Sturridge, Akinbiyi	21086
28	Mar 3	H	Liverpool	W 2-0	45	4	Akinbiyi, Izzet	21924
29	17	A	Manchester United	L 0-2	45	7	- / Yorke, Silvestre	67516
30	Apr 1	H	Charlton Athletic	L 0-2	45	9	- / Todd, Bartlett	20043
31	4	A	Aston Villa	L 1-2	45	9	Davidson / Dublin, Hendrie	29043
32	7	H	Coventry City	L 1-3	45	10	Akinbiyi / Bellamy, Carsley, Hartson	19545
33	14	A	Manchester City	L 1-2	45	11	Akinbiyi / Goater, Wanchope	20224
34	16	A	Derby County	L 0-2	45	11	- / Boertien, Eranio	28387
35	21	H	Middlesbrough	L 0-3	45	12	- / Ricard, Boksic, Ince	18162
36	28	A	Newcastle United	L 0-1	45	13	- / Cort	50501
37	May 5	H	Tottenham Hotspur	W 4-2	48	10	Rowett, Sturridge, Guppy, Savage (p) / Davies, Carr	21056
38	19	A	Leeds United	L 1-3	48	13	Ferdinand (og) / Smith 2, Harte	39105

Final League Position: 13
Average Home League Attendance: 20452

Player columns: (1) Tim Flowers, (24) Andy Impey, (14) Callum Davidson, (2) Gary Rowett, (18) Matt Elliott, (4) Gerry Taggart, (6) Muzzy Izzet, (7) Neil Lennon, (8) Robbie Savage, (10) Stan Collymore, (22) Ade Akinbiyi, (9) Darren Eadie, (5) Steve Walsh, (11) Steve Guppy, (27) Tony Cottee, (15) Phil Gilchrist, (17) Stef Oakes, (23) Richard Cresswell, (13) Arnar Gunnlaugsson, (20) Trevor Benjamin, (3) Frank Sinclair, (12) Simon Royce, (21) Billy McKinlay, (7) Matthew Jones, (29) Damien Delaney, (10) Roberto Mancini, (21) Dean Sturridge, (25) Junior Lewis, (35) Kevin Ellison, (26) Lee Marshall

	Flowers	Impey	Davidson	Rowett	Elliott	Taggart	Izzet	Lennon	Savage	Collymore	Akinbiyi	Eadie	Walsh	Guppy	Cottee	Gilchrist	Oakes	Cresswell	Gunnlaugsson	Benjamin	Sinclair	Royce	McKinlay	Jones	Delaney	Mancini	Sturridge	Lewis	Ellison	Marshall
League Appearances	22	29	25	38	34	24	27	15	33	1	33	16	17	6	5	3	3	7	14	16	10	3	3	12	15	7				
Sub	4	3									4	4	8	1	11	2	6	8	5	14	14	3	3		1	2	1	1		1 2
League Goals		1	2	2	2	7		4	1	9	2	1		3	1							3								

FA CUP (Axa)

Match No	Date		Opponents	Result	Scorers	Att
1	Jan 6	H	York City (3)	W 3-0	Rowett, Izzet (p), Cresswell	16850
2	27	A	Aston Villa (4)	W 2-1	Akinbiyi, Gunnlaugsson / Joachim	26383
3	Feb 17	H	Bristol City (5)	W 3-0	Sturridge, Izzet (p), Hill (og)	20905
4	Mar 10	H	Wycombe Wanderers (6)	L 1-2	Izzet / McCarthy, Essandoh	21969

FOOTBALL LEAGUE CUP (Worthington Cup)

Match No	Date		Opponents	Result	Scorers	Att
1	Nov 1	H	Crystal Palace (3)	L 0-3	- / Morrison, Thomson, Rubins	12965

UEFA CUP

Match No	Date		Opponents	Result	Scorers	Att
1	Sep 14	H	Red Star Belgrade (1/1)	D 1-1	Taggart / Acimovic	21198
2	28	A	Red Star Belgrade (1/2)	L 1-3	Izzet / Drulic 2, Gvozdenovic	12700

Dismissals: Nov 25, Taggart, Tottenham Hotspur (a); Jan 20, Jones, Arsenal (h); Jan 27, Davidson, Aston Villa (a) FAC.
Note: Sep 14, Sep 28: opponents referred to as Crvena Zvezda in some publications; Sep 28, at Gerhard Hanappi Stadium, (Rapid) Vienna, by order of UEFA due to political situation in Yugoslavia.

1 April: Dean Sturridge arrived in January to add some much needed experience to the front line. Here he is seen in a tangle with Charlton's surprise England international, Chris Powell.

2000-01

Back: Yeoman (Physio), Benjamin, Oakes, Taggart, Elliott, Collymore, Walsh, Akinbiyi, Dudfield, Rennie (Physio).
Second Row: McAndrew (Kit Manager), M Savage, Stewart, Heath, Flowers, Price, Royce, Nurse, Goodwin, R Savage, Walls (Asst Kit Manager).
Third Row: McDonagh (Goalkeeping Coach), McCann, Boateng, Izzet, Sinclair, Rowett, Campbell, Gilchrist, Guppy, Reeves, Parker (Reserve Team Coach).
Front: Butler (First Team Coach), Davidson, Gunnlaugsson, Wilson, Cottee, Taylor (Manager), Elsom (Chairman), Lennon, Eadie, Impey, Thomas, Murphy (Football Co-ordinator).

The highly promising Damien Delaney was signed from Cork City as a forerunner of the arrangement made between the two clubs. By the end of the season he would have already won Under-21 honours.

Matthew Jones was a £3 million signing from Leeds United in December, having been initially viewed as a potential replacement for Neil Lennon, but who can adapt to a number of roles within the team.

337

Programme Gallery

In recent seasons the Leicester City matchday magazine has been a multiple award winner. The evolution of the publication, from the time of Leicester Fosse through to the present day is traced in detail over the next four pages.

OFFICIAL PROGRAMME - 3d.
LEICESTER CITY
FOOTBALL CLUB CO. LIMITED

LEICESTER CITY
versus
BURY

OFFICIAL PROGRAMME
1952   1953
LEICESTER
CITY
VERSUS
FULHAM
MONDAY
25 AUGUST, 1952
KICK-OFF 6-15 P.M.

OFFICIAL
PROGRAMME
LEICESTER
CITY
VERSUS
BRENTFORD
KICK-OFF
2-15 P.M.
SATURDAY, 5 DECEMBER, 1953

OFFICIAL PROGRAMME
LEICESTER CITY
VERSUS
HUDDERSFIELD TOWN
KICK-OFF 3 P.M.
SATURDAY, 16 OCT. 1954
Issued by the Leicester City Football Club

LEICESTER CITY
FOOTBALL CLUB
SEASON
1955-56
No. 8
FILBERT STREET GROUND

LEICESTER CITY
FOOTBALL CLUB
SEASON 1956-7
LEICESTER CITY v. PORT VALE

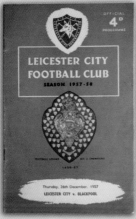

LEICESTER CITY
FOOTBALL CLUB
SEASON 1957-58
Thursday, 26th December, 1957
LEICESTER CITY v. BLACKPOOL

LEICESTER CITY
FOOTBALL CLUB
SEASON 1958-59
OFFICIAL 4d PROGRAMME
Saturday, 11th April, 1959
LEICESTER CITY v. WEST HAM UNITED

OFFICIAL PROGRAMME 4d.
LEICESTER CITY
FOOTBALL
CLUB
SEASON
1959-1960
Saturday, 29th August, 1959
LEICESTER CITY v. CHELSEA

OFFICIAL PROGRAMME 4d.
LEICESTER CITY
FOOTBALL
CLUB
SEASON
1960-1961
Saturday, 31st December 1960
LEICESTER CITY v. EVERTON

OFFICIAL PROGRAMME 4d.
LEICESTER CITY
FOOTBALL
CLUB
SEASON
1961-1962
Wednesday, 20th September 1961
LEICESTER CITY v. BURNLEY

OFFICIAL PROGRAMME 4d.
LEICESTER CITY
FOOTBALL CLUB
SEASON
1962
1963
LEICESTER CITY v
MANCHESTER CITY
Saturday 6th April 1963

OFFICIAL PROGRAMME 4d.
LEICESTER CITY
FOOTBALL CLUB
SEASON
1963
1964
LEICESTER CITY
v
STOKE CITY
SATURDAY 11th JANUARY 1964

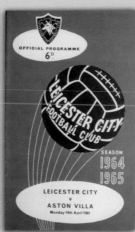

OFFICIAL PROGRAMME 6d.
LEICESTER CITY
FOOTBALL CLUB
SEASON
1964
1965
LEICESTER CITY
v
ASTON VILLA
Monday 19th April 1965

LEICESTER CITY
FOOTBALL CLUB
SEASON 1965-1966
NORTHAMPTON
SATURDAY OCTOBER 1 1965
OFFICIAL PROGRAMME 6d.

LEICESTER CITY
FOOTBALL CLUB
SEASON 1966-1967
SOUTHAMPTON
SATURDAY SEPTEMBER 10 1966
OFFICIAL PROGRAMME 6d.

Leicester
City
FOOTBALL CLUB
SEASON 1967-1968
MANCHESTER
CITY
SATURDAY 6 APRIL 1968
OFFICIAL PROGRAMME 6d.

Leicester City
FOOTBALL CLUB
Season 1968-69
FOOTBALL LEAGUE DIVISION 1
NOTTINGHAM
FOREST
SATURDAY NOVEMBER 9th
KICK-OFF 3 p.m.
OFFICIAL PROGRAMME 1/-

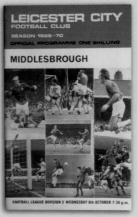

LEICESTER CITY
FOOTBALL CLUB
SEASON 1969-70
OFFICIAL PROGRAMME ONE SHILLING
MIDDLESBROUGH
FOOTBALL LEAGUE DIVISION 2 WEDNESDAY 8th OCTOBER 7-30 p.m.

SEASON 1970-71
LEICESTER
CITY F.C.
FOOTBALL LEAGUE
DIVISION 2
SATURDAY 3 p.m.
26th SEPTEMBER
PORTSMOUTH
OFFICIAL PROGRAMME
ONE SHILLING - FIVE NEW PENCE

339

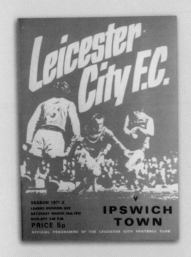

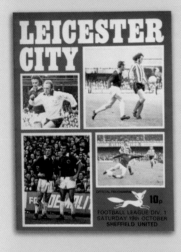

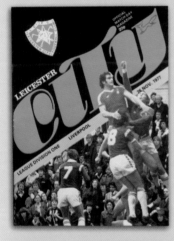

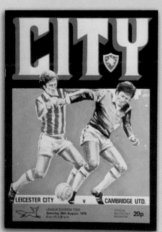

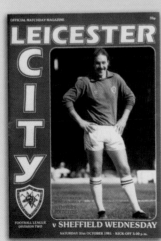

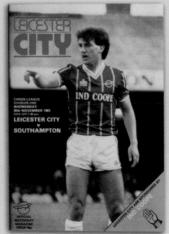

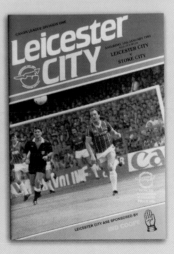

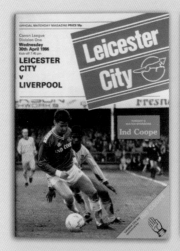

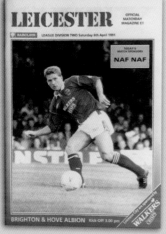

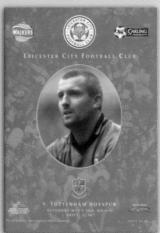

Facts&FiguresofFossils&Foxes

ABANDONED MATCHES

30.12.94	D2	Darwen (A)	2m	gale	0-0	-/-
28.12.95	D2	Newton Heath (A)	65m	waterlogged	0-2	-/Donaldson, Kennedy
16.11.01	D2	Blackpool (H)	67m	fog	1-0	Brown/-
05.12.03	D2	Manchester Utd (A)	78m	fog	2-1	Evenson, Warren/Duckworth
09.09.05	D2	Burnley (A)	79m	waterlogged	0-1	-/Wood
11.01.14	FAC1	Norwich City (H)	65m	snow	0-0	-/-
19.12.31	D1	Portsmouth (H)	63m	fog	1-0	Jackson/-
16.12.33	D1	Birmingham (A)	66m	fog	2-1	Liddle, Dewis/Horsman
03.02.34	D1	Chelsea (A)	78m	fog	1-1	Chandler/Priestley
22.02.36	D2	Newcastle Utd (H)	80m	snow/slush	2-1	O'Callaghan, Muncie/Weaver (p)
28.01.61	FAC4	Bristol City (H)	45m	waterlogged	0-0	-/-
09.12.67	D1	Nott'm Forest (A)	51m	ice/frost	1-0	Large/-
24.09.74	D1	Middlesbrough (A)	24m	f'light failure	0-1	-/Souness
15.10.83	D1	Southampton (H)	22m	waterlogged	0-0	-/-

Additionally, Fosse experienced two examples of drawn FA Cup games being abandoned during extra time because of bad light; though the unchanged 90-minute score was allowed to stand in both cases:

29.10.92	FAC QR2	Notts Olympic (H)	3-3
03.12.03	FAC QR5r	Burton United (H)	2-2

Only one Midland League fixture was abandoned, on 18.11.1893, when the Doncaster Rovers team left the field in protest at the conditions (a snowstorm) after 50 minutes, and conceded the points. The 2-1 scoreline to Fosse was entered into League records.

A friendly game at home to Derby Town on 3.12.1892 was abandoned after 83 minutes with the score at 1-1 when opposition player William Storer refused to leave the field when sent off by the referee for fighting.

A wartime League game at Nottingham Forest on 20.11.1943 was abandoned due to fog ten minutes from time with City 0-1 down. The result stood, while reporting restrictions then in force meant that no reason for the abandonment could be published at the time.

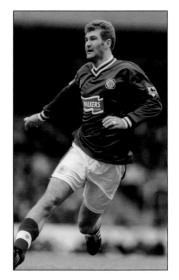

AGE

Right: The relatively youthful Ian Marshall is still City's oldest European marksman.

YOUNGEST PLAYERS

FL/D2	David Buchanan	16 years 192 days	01.01.1979	Oldham (H)
	Neil Grewcock	16 years 311 days	03.03.1979	Cardiff (H)
D1	Peter Shilton	16 years 228 days	04.05.1966	Everton (H)
	David Timson	16 years 231 days	11.04.1964	Blackpool (H)
Prem	Emile Heskey	17 years 56 days	08.03.1995	QPR (A)
	Jordan Stewart	17 years 264 days	22.01.2000	West Ham (H)
FAC	David Buchanan	16 years 197 days	06.01.1979	Norwich (H)
FLC	Bob Newton	17 years 249 days	25.09.1963	Aldershot (H)
	Emile Heskey	17 years 252 days	20.09.1995	Burnley (H)
Euro	Graham Cross	17 years 302 days	13.09.1961	Glenavon (A)
WW1	Cliff Price	16 years 214 days	13.01.1917	Notts County (H)
WW2	Gordon Jayes	16 years 46 days	11.11.1939	WBA (A)
	Dennis Cheney	16 years 132 days	09.11.1940	Mansfield (H)
	Ray Iggleden	16 years 201 days	04.11.1941	Wolves (A)
	Billy Wright	16 years 206 days	31.08.1940	Coventry (A)

YOUNGEST GOALSCORERS

FL/D2	David Buchanan	16 years 192 days	01.01.1979	Oldham (H)
D1	Graham Cross	17 years 169 days	29.04.1961	Birmingham (H)
Prem	Emile Heskey	18 years 222 days	21.08.1996	Southampton (H)
FAC	Julian Joachim	18 years 122 days	20.01.1993	Barnsley (A)
FLC	Bob Newton	17 years 249 days	25.09.1963	Aldershot (H)
Euro	Hugh McIlmoyle	21 years 241 days	27.09.1961	Glenavon (H)
WW1	Cliff Price	16 years 228 days	27.01.1917	Huddersfield (H)
WW2	Gordon Jayes	16 years 96 days	30.12.1939	WBA (H)

YOUNGEST HAT-TRICK SCORER

FL/D1	Barrie Thomas	17 years 350 days	04.05.1955	Bolton (H)

YOUNGEST CITY LINE-UP

Average Age 19 years 356 days   08.05.1979 v Sheffield United (A)
Wallington (26), Goodwin (19), Carr (18), O'Neill (21), May (20), Williams (21), Lineker (18), Peake (17) [sub Buchanan (16)], Henderson (23), Duffy (17), Lee (18).

OLDEST PLAYERS

FL/D2	Joe Calvert	40 years 313 days	13.12.1947	Southampton (A)
D1	Arthur Chandler	39 years 114 days	22.04.1935	Grimsby (H)
Prem	Roberto Mancini	36 years 75 days	10.02.2001	Everton (A)
FAC	Joe Calvert	40 years 5 days	08.02.1947	Newcastle (A)
FLC	Steve Walsh	35 years 83 days	25.01.2000	Aston Villa (A)
Euro	Tim Flowers	33 years 237 days	28.09.2000	Red Star Belgrade (A)
War	Arthur Attwood	43 years 275 days	01.09.1945	Charlton (A)

OLDEST DEBUTANTS

Prem	Roberto Mancini	36 years 54 days	20.01.2001	Arsenal (H)
D2	Ben Davies	35 years 182 days	08.12.1923	South Shields (A)
	Lawrie Madden	35 years 114 days	19.01.1991	West Ham (A)

OLDEST SCORERS

FL/D1	Arthur Chandler	39 years 32 days	29.12.1934	Wolves (A)
Prem	Tony Cottee	34 years 300 days	06.05.2000	Bradford C (H)
FAC	Arthur Chandler	38 years 96 days	03.03.1934	Preston (A)
FLC	Steve Walsh	35 years 70 days	12.01.2000	Fulham (H)
Euro	Ian Marshall	31 years 180 days	16.09.1997	Atletico Madrid (A)
War	Percy Dickie	35 years 288 days	25.09.1943	Coventry (A)

OLDEST HAT-TRICK SCORER

FL/D1	Arthur Chandler	38 years 285 days	08.09.1934	Aston Villa (H)

OLDEST CITY LINE-UP

Average Age 30 years 97 days
05.09.1932 v Huddersfield Town (H)
McLaren (35), Black (34), Osborne (34), Smith (20), Heywood (23), Ritchie (28), Adcock (29), Lowery (24), Chandler (36), Lochhead (34), Barry (30).

APPEARANCES

AGGREGATE
Graham Cross   29.04.61-23.08.75   599
(495+3 FL, 59 FAC, 40 FLC, 2 ECWC)

FOOTBALL LEAGUE
Adam Black   24.01.20-09.02.35   528

FA CUP
Graham Cross   08.01.63-24.02.75   59

FL CUP
Graham Cross   26.09.62-08.10.74   40
Steve Walsh   23.09.86- 25.01.00   40

CONSECUTIVE AGGREGATE
Mark Wallington   04.01.75-06.03.82   331
(294 FL, 22 FAC, 15 FLC)

CONSECUTIVE FOOTBALL LEAGUE
Mark Wallington   11.01.75-02.03.82   294

CONSECUTIVE FA CUP
Graham Cross   14.01.65-24.02.75   52

CONSECUTIVE FL CUP
John Sjoberg   15.01.64-04.09.68   21
Mark Wallington   09.09.75-09.10.84   21

SINGLE SEASON
Gary Mills   17.08.91-25.05.92   61
(46 FL, 3 PO, 2 FAC, 4 FLC, 6 FMC)

ALL COMPETITIVE GAMES
Graham Cross	599	[plus 10 others: ChSh 1; Ang-ItT 4; TexC 4; FAC3rd/4th 1.]
Sep Smith	586	[incl WW2]
Adam Black	557	
Hugh Adcock	460	
Mark Wallington	460	[plus 8 others: Ang-ItT 3; TexC 1; FAC 3rd/4th 1; Ang-ScT 3.]
Willie Frame	459	[incl WW2]
Steve Walsh	449	
Mal Griffiths	420	[incl WW2]
Arthur Chandler	419	
John Sjoberg	413	[plus 5 others: ChSh 1; Ang-ItT 2+2.]
Steve Whitworth	400	[plus 15 others: ChSh 1; Ang-ItT 3; TexC 8; Ang-ScT 3.]

FOOTBALL LEAGUE
Adam Black	528
Graham Cross	495+3
Hugh Adcock	434
Mark Wallington	412
Arthur Chandler	393
Mal Griffiths	373
Steve Walsh	352+17
Steve Whitworth	352+1
Sep Smith	350

FA CUP
Graham Cross	59
John Sjoberg	44
Mal Griffiths	36
Len Glover	35+1
Gordon Banks	34
Peter Shilton	33
Colin Appleton	32
Richie Norman	30
Bobby Roberts	30
Adam Black	29
David Gibson	29
Steve Whitworth	29

LEAGUE CUP
Graham Cross	40
Steve Walsh	39+1
John Sjoberg	34
David Gibson	30
Richie Norman	28
Mike Stringfellow	26+1
Emile Heskey	25+2
Gordon Banks	25
Mark Wallington	23
Neil Lennon	23
Ian King	22
Bobby Roberts	21+1

WW1
Sam Currie	123
Teddy King	121
Herbert Bown	112
Jimmy Leach	102

WW2
Willie Frame	220
Sep Smith	213
Bert Howe	209
Danny Liddle	115

LENGTHIEST FIRST-TEAM CAREERS
(In Unbroken Spell With Club)

Sep Smith	31.08.29-07.05.49	19 years 249 days
Mal Griffiths	24.09.38-14.04.56	17 years 202 days
George Dewis	09.12.33-10.12.49	16 years 1 day
Joe Calvert	27.08.32-13.12.47	15 years 108 days
Willie Frame	06.10.34-14.01.50	15 years 100 days
Adam Black	24.01.20-09.02.35	15 years 16 days
Teddy King	06.04.07-20.02.22	14 years 320 days
Graham Cross	29.04.61-23.08.75	14 years 116 days
Derek Hines	27.03.47-25.03.61	13 years 363 days
Steve Walsh	23.08.86-19.08.00	13 years 361 days
Dai Jones	26.08.33-17.05.47	13 years 264 days
Danny Liddle	27.08.32-20.04.46	13 years 236 days
Mike Stringfellow	20.01.62-19.04.75	13 years 89 days
Mark Wallington	11.03.72-20.10.84	12 years 223 days
John Sjoberg	28.10.60-02.12.72	12 years 35 days
Sam Currie	19.03.10-04.03.22	11 years 350 days
Colin Appleton	04.09.54-09.05.66	11 years 247 days
Arthur Chandler	25.08.23-22.04.35	11 years 240 days
Hughie Adcock	25.08.23-19.04.35	11 years 237 days
Johnny Grogan	19.10.35-05.04.47	11 years 168 days
Roger Heywood	03.05.30-02.06.41	11 years 30 days
Alan Woollett	22.04.67-15.04.78	10 years 358 days
Charlie Adam	24.05.40-05.05.51	10 years 346 days
Johnny King	26.02.44-30.08.54	10 years 185 days
Jimmy Harrold	15.02.13-05.05.23	10 years 79 days
Paul Ramsey	07.03.81-11.05.91	10 years 65 days

Above: Emile Heskey's crop of League Cup appearances include three Wembley trips with City.

Below: Graham Cross heads City's all-time appearances chart.

ATTENDANCES

HIGHEST : FILBERT STREET

OVERALL/FA CUP

18.02.1928	Tottenham Hotspur	FAC5	47,298

FOOTBALL LEAGUE

02.10.1954	Arsenal	Div1	42,486

DIVISION TWO

17.11.1956	Nottingham Forest	Div2	40,830

AS ALL-SEATER STADIUM/PREMIERSHIP

18.03.2000	Manchester United	Prem	22,170

FL CUP

29.10.1969	West Bromwich Albion	FLC5	35,121

FRIENDLY

18.02.1967	Rangers	Fr	24,408

FM CUP

12.02.1992	Nottingham Forest	NorthF/1	19,537

RESERVES

27.02.1960	Bournemouth & B Ath	FComb	22,800

NEUTRAL FIXTURE

13.03.1972	Arsenal v Derby C	FAC5r	36,534

> The highest estimate for a Filbert Street crowd in the Fosse era was that of 20,000-22,000 for the FA Cup Round Two tie v Derby County on 06.02.1909, but all such figures are unreliable. Between the wars, and until the ground record was set, the progressive rise in highest attendance figures was marked thus:

25.12.1919	Birmingham	Div2	18,214
	[First time receipts over £1,000]		
15.01.1920	Newport County	FAC1	20,212
31.01.1920	Manchester City	FAC2	23,109
08.01.1921	Burnley	FAC1	29,149
28.01.1922	Fulham	FAC2	30,022
03.02.1923	Cardiff City	FAC2	35,728
05.02.1925	Newcastle United	FAC2r	37,434
10.10.1925	Aston Villa	Div1	37,483
18.02.1928	Tottenham Hotspur	FAC5	47,298

For many years after WW2, the Filbert Street capacity was regarded as being 42,000. Between 1954 and 1971, this figure was reached – or severely tested by crowds of over 40,000 – on sixteen occasions (12 Saturdays; 4 midweek):

13.03.1954	Preston North End	FAC6	40,065
19.04.1954	Blackburn Rovers	Div2	40,047
02.10.1954	Arsenal	Div1	42,486
30.10.1954	Blackpool	Div1	40,655
17.11.1956	Nottingham Forest	Div2	40,930
24.08.1957	Manchester United	Div1	40,214
22.02.1961	Birmingham City	FAC5r	41,916
23.03.1963	Tottenham Hotspur	Div1	41,600
09.03.1966	Manchester City	FAC5	41,892
23.12.1967	Manchester United	Div1	40,104
13.03.1968	Rotherham United	FAC5r	41,856
30.03.1968	Everton	FAC6	42,000
01.03.1969	Liverpool	FAC5	42,002
14.05.1969	Everton	Div1	41,218
11.02.1970	Liverpool	FAC5r	42,100
06.03.1971	Arsenal	FAC6	42,000

> The capacity was lowered in 1975 to 34,000; a figure afterwards reached only once (14.02.1976 v Manchester United, FA Cup Round Five). Indeed, from then on, Filbert Street hosted only two further crowds of over 30,000.

Subsequently, the ground capacity was lowered again in stages commensurate with changes to the stadium layout and more stringent safety requirements; eventually leading to its adaptation to all-seater status in the early 1990s. Thereafter, the capacity was officially quoted at 22,517, but numerous 'sell-out' crowds have failed quite to register this figure.

HIGHEST : AWAY

OVERALL/FA CUP

07.02.1948	White Hart Lane/Tottenham H	FAC5	69,049

FOOTBALL LEAGUE

04.02.1950	White Hart Lane/Tottenham H	Div2	60,595

DIVISION ONE

27.12.1977	Old Trafford/Manchester U	Div1	57,396

PREMIERSHIP

17.03.2001	Old Trafford/Manchester U	Prem	67,516

FL CUP

27.10.1993	Old Trafford/Manchester U	FLC3	41,344

FM CUP

26.02.1992	City Ground/Nottm Forest	NorthF/2	21,562

Clearly, the above records discount the Wembley gates for City's FA Cup, League Cup and Play Off Finals, all ten of which fall into the range of 68,147 to 100,000.

LOWEST : FILBERT STREET

> The record for the smallest gate for a home senior game can never be reliably established due to the lack of official records for the Fosse period, when some abysmal gates were certainly experienced at both League and Cup games. The following figures therefore relate solely to the post-WW1 era of Leicester City:

DIVISION ONE

04.02.1932	Portsmouth		6,000 (est)
12.10.1985	West Bromwich Albion		7,237

DIVISION TWO

22.02.1983	Shrewsbury Town		6,155

PREMIERSHIP

29.04.1995	Ipswich Town		15,248

FA CUP

22.12.1999	Hereford United	Rd3 rep	12,157

FL CUP

08.10.1986	Swansea City	Rd2/2	5,884

FM CUP

10.11.1987	Huddersfield Town	Rd1	3,440

ANGLO-ITALIAN CUP

08.09.1993	West Bromwich Albion	Prelim Rd	3,058

NEUTRAL FIXTURE

20.09.1977	Brighton v Oldham	FLCRd2rep	1,840

LOWEST: AWAY

> Again it is far from certain what constitutes the lowest attendance Leicester have attracted for a competitive game away from home. (The oft-quoted record of only 13 paying customers at the Stockport County v City game in 1921 is explained and qualified in the narrative text; while the pre-WW1 annals are a morass of conflicting estimates). These figures once more relate, then, solely to Leicester City fixtures.

DIVISION TWO

07.05.1921	Old Trafford/Stockport C		1,000 (est)
18.05.1982	Brisbane Road/Orient		2,107

DIVISION ONE

05.05.1934	Ayresome Park/Middlesbrough		4,758

PREMIERSHIP

10.09.1994	Selhurst Park/Wimbledon		7,683

FA CUP

03.02.1947	Villa Park/Brentford	Rd4rep	7,500 (est)
10.01.1920	Somerton Park/Newport C	Rd1	7,523
16.01.1985	Highfield Road/Burton A	Rd3rep	nil/bcd

FL CUP

28.08.1991	Watling Street/Maidstone U	Rd1/2	1,638

FM CUP

01.12.1987	Selhurst Park/Charlton A	Rd2	1,327

Only two other League clubs still attribute their record attendances to games in which Leicester City were the visitors: Brentford's Griffin Park held 38,678 when City triumphed in the FA Cup Sixth Round tie of 20.02.1949; while Norwich City's Carrow Road had its record gate of 43,984 established by the FA Cup Sixth Round tie of 30.03.1963.

City's Cup visits to Sincil Bank (1929, Lincoln City, FAC3, 16,849), St Andrews, Birmingham (1934, Portsmouth, FACsf, 66,544), Field Mill (1938, Mansfield Town, FAC3, 15,890) and Loftus Road (1974, Queens Park Rangers, FAC6, 34,078) also set new ground records at the time, which have been subsequently bettered. The 1910 FA Cup game at the High Road ground of the now-defunct Leyton FC set an all-time record of 21,005 for that enclosure.

ARTIFICIAL PITCHES

> After Queens Park Rangers became the first League club (in 1981) to tear up their conventional grass playing area and replace it with an artificial Omniturf surface – to be followed later by Luton Town, Oldham Athletic and Preston North End – City played a total of 13 League and Cup games on such pitches, with fairly atrocious results. As the following record shows, City won once, drew twice, and lost ten of their games on 'plastic' pitches; scoring 10 and conceding 27 goals. Gary Lineker, with an aggregate four strikes against QPR, was City's leading marksman on such surfaces.

1981/2	QPR 0-2 (Div 2)
1982/3	QPR 2-2 (Div 2)
1983/4	QPR 0-2 (Div 1)
1984/5	QPR 3-4 (Div 1)
1985/6	Luton 1-3 (Div 1)
	QPR 0-2 (Div 1)
1986/7	Luton 0-1 (Div 1)
	QPR 1-0 (Div 1)
	QPR 2-5 (FA Cup)
1987/8	Oldham 0-2 (Div 2)
1988/9	Oldham 1-1 (Div 2)
1989/90	Oldham 0-1 (Div 2)
1990/1	Oldham 0-2 (Div 2)

BROADCASTING

First BBC radio commentary broadcast from Filbert St: 26.11.1927, City v Newcastle United.

First televised game involving City: 30.4.1949, City v Wolves, FA Cup Final, Wembley.
[Note, however, that there were only 35 sets in Leicester and district notionally capable of receiving the 'live' broadcast, and then only under 'freak' conditions. The Midland region did not get its own transmitter until Sutton Coldfield opened in the following December].

First BBC telecast from Filbert St: 20.1.1951, England v Wales, Amateur International.

First TV broadcast of City highlights from Filbert St: BBC 'Sportsview', 12.11.1955, City v Swansea Town.

First appearance on BBC 'Match of the Day': 17.10.1964, City v Nottm Forest.

First 'live' broadcast on satellite TV (BSkyB): 27.11.1990, City v Wolves, Full Members Cup.

First 'live' broadcast of Football League game (ITV): 13.9.1992, City v Wolves.

First fixture re-scheduled for 'live' satellite broadcast (Sky): 21.8.1994, City v Newcastle United.

First closed-circuit relay ('beamback') to Filbert St: 27.8.1994, Nottm Forest v City.

CHAMPIONS

> Fosse/City players who elsewhere accumulated appearances in First Division/Premier League championship campaigns. (Usually, a player would be awarded a championship medal only if he had turned out in at least a third of his club's fixtures).

			A	G
Andy Aitken	1905	Newcastle United	28	2
	1907	Newcastle United	3	-
Andy Anderson	1909	Newcastle United	19	3
George Armstrong	1971	Arsenal	42	7
John Baird	1894	Aston Villa	29	-
Jack Bamber	1922	Liverpool	8	-
	1923	Liverpool	4	-
Bert Barlow	1949	Portsmouth	29	8
	1950	Portsmouth	2	1
Kevin Campbell	1991	Arsenal	15+7	9
Allan Clarke	1974	Leeds United	34	13
Wayne Clarke	1987	Everton	10	5
Roger Davies	1975	Derby County	39+1	12
Bert Davis	1936	Sunderland	25	10
Jimmy Dawson	1950	Portsmouth	1	-
John Doherty	1956	Manchester United	16	4
	1957	Manchester United	3	-
Billy Dorrell	1896	Aston Villa	2	1
George Douglas	1921	Burnley	2	-
Chris Duffy	1907	Newcastle United	7	1
Allan Evans	1981	Aston Villa	39	7
Tim Flowers	1995	Blackburn Rovers	39	-
Jack Froggatt	1949	Portsmouth	41	15
	1950	Portsmouth	39	15
Billy Garraty	1899	Aston Villa	9	6
	1900	Aston Villa	33	27
Colin Gibson	1981	Aston Villa	19+2	-
Billy Goldie	1901	Liverpool	34	2
James Gorman	1906	Liverpool	1	-
Mal Griffiths	1938	Arsenal	9	5
George Harrison	1915	Everton	26	4
Mike Hooper	1988	Liverpool	2	-
George Jobey	1907	Newcastle United	1	-
	1909	Newcastle United	10	1
Eddie Kelly	1971	Arsenal	21+2	4
Gary McAllister	1992	Leeds United	41+1	5
Kevin MacDonald	1986	Liverpool	10+7	1
	1988	Liverpool	0+1	-
Frank McLintock	1971	Arsenal	42	5
Ian Marshall	1987	Everton	0+2	1
Fred Mearns	1902	Sunderland	2	-

			A	G
Mike Newell	1995	Blackburn Rovers	2+10	-
David Nish	1975	Derby County	38	2
Maurice Parry	1901	Liverpool	8	-
	1906	Liverpool	36	1
Dick Pudan	1909	Newcastle United	3	-
Jon Sammels	1971	Arsenal	13+2	1
Peter Shilton	1978	Nottingham Forest	37	-
Alan Smith	1989	Arsenal	36	23
	1991	Arsenal	35+2	23
Roy Stephenson	1962	Ipswich Town	41	7
Bob Thompson	1915	Everton	33	-
Billy Troughear	1913	Sunderland	6	-
Harold Wadsworth	1922	Liverpool	1	-
	1923	Liverpool	3	-
Alf Watkins	1900	Aston Villa	1	-
Mike Whitlow	1992	Leeds United	3+7	1

> Fosse/City players who elsewhere accumulated appearances in Scottish First/Premier Division championship campaigns:

			A	G
Joe Baillie	1954	Celtic	1	-
Jimmy Blessington	1893	Celtic	15	5
	1894	Celtic	18	4
	1896	Celtic	16	7
	1897	Celtic	5	1
Harry Callachan	1926	Celtic	6	-
Willie Gardiner	1953	Rangers	2	2
Alec Gillies	1897	Hearts	6	3
Martin Henderson	1976	Rangers	23+3	10
Neil Lennon	2001	Celtic	17	1
Jim Macauley	1911	Rangers	1	-
Kevin MacDonald	1989	Rangers	2+1	-
Tom McDonald	1952	Hibernian	?	?
Charlie Miller	1994	Rangers	2+1	-
	1995	Rangers	21	3
	1996	Rangers	17+6	3
	1997	Rangers	7+6	1
	1999	Rangers	2+15	3
John Ogilvie	1951	Hibernian	?	?
Joe O'Neil	1955	Aberdeen	12	4
Nicky Walker	1987	Rangers	2	-
Jimmy Walsh	1954	Celtic	19	5
Pat Ward	1951	Hibernian	?	?
	1952	Hibernian	?	?
Peter Weir	1984	Aberdeen	26+1	5
	1985	Aberdeen	15+1	3

The Newcastle United game in August 1994 was the first City game to be rescheduled at the behest of television.

CHAMPIONSHIPS & PROMOTION

> Though Leicester never won the old First Division championship, they share with Manchester City the record number of Second Division championship wins – six. In each having been promoted to the First Division or Premiership on ten occasions in total, City and Manchester City also level-peg in the record books.

CIVIL & MILITARY HONOURS

> Gordon Banks, Gary Lineker, Don Revie & Peter Shilton were each honoured with the OBE for services to football; former Fosse goalkeeper Charles Saer for public service in his post-football career. Frank McLintock's football achievements brought him the CBE; and Martin O'Neill earned the MBE for his.

> Former Fosse reserve Bernard Vann was posthumously awarded the Victoria Cross during WW1. From the same conflict emerged Adam Black with the Distinguished Conduct Medal and Angus Seed with the Military Medal; while William Sharpley also received the DCM before being killed in action.

Adam Black

COSMOPOLITANISM

> Ever since the rise of professionalism, English clubs have relied heavily on players from other corners of the British Isles, and to a lesser extent on imports from further afield. Neither Fosse nor City have bucked this general trend, though both have on rare occasions fielded a wholly English-born team. Fosse did so four times in total at Football League level [14.12.1907; 25.11.1911; 2.12.1911; 24.1.1914], and City debatably did twice in the inter-war years [26.4.1924 and 3.5.1924], when South African-born England international Reg Osborne was part of the eleven. Jimmy Bloomfield somewhat broke the mould by both

starting and finishing exactly 100 League and Cup games with an all-English line-up [between 1.4.1972 and 22.1.1977]; but no City boss since has followed suit. (Though several of Brian Little's selections for City came close; with Australian-born England Under-23 international David Oldfield and English-born Republic of Ireland cap David Kelly muddying the picture somewhat).

By far the greatest number of footballing imports have come from Scotland. Fosse's first-ever home League game [8.9.1894] saw no less than eight Scots in the line-up, and twice more during that inaugural season Fosse fielded a slightly different Caledonian octet. Only once has a City side had a similar constitution, on 27.12.1920, in Peter Hodge's selection for the game at Stoke. (Hodge later twice relied on seven Scots during 1932/3 and 1933/4, as once did the directors just after his death, in early 1934/5. David Halliday once chose seven during 1958/9; and Matt Gillies did so on seven occasions during 1963/4, 1964/5 and 1965/6).

The most cosmopolitan team ever fielded by Leicester City was at Highbury, for the 0-5 defeat by Arsenal on 20.2.1999, when representatives of nine different nations were included in the starting line-up: Keller (USA), Kåmark (Sweden), Sinclair (Jamaica), Elliott (Scotland), Savage (Wales), Zagorakis (Greece), Lennon (Northern Ireland) and Gunnlaugsson (Iceland) featuring alongside Englishmen Ullathorne, Guppy, and Izzet [before the latter represented Turkey]. Additionally, Arphexad (France) sat unused on the bench.

The most 'home-grown' players in a single City team – those who rose through the club's youth and reserve ranks – numbered ten of the twelve who faced Watford at home on 4.10.1969; while the highest number of Leicestershire-born players in a City team was eight of the twelve against Bolton Wanderers in the Football League Cup on 7.10.1970.

CRICKETERS

> There can be few Football League clubs who have included in their senior line-ups so many of the old breed of versatile footballer/cricketers as have Leicester over the years. Those who played at senior level both for Fosse or City and in first-class cricket are:

Tommy Allsopp, **Jimmy Atter**, **Harry**

Bailey, **Ewart Benskin**, **Graham Cross**, **Ernest Gill**, **Teddy King**, **Jack Lee**, **John Mitten**, **Arthur Mounteney**, **Fred Osborn**, **Maurice Tompkin**, **Bob Turner**, **Harry Whitehead** and **Cecil Wood** (all for Leicestershire); **Fred Bracey** and **Tom Fletcher** (Derbyshire); **Tal Lewis** (Somerset); **Jim Harrold** (Essex); **Tom Simpson** (Nottinghamshire) and **John Vincett** (Sussex & Surrey).

Additionally, **Gary Lineker** featured in MCC sides; **Archie Ling** played Minor Counties cricket for Cambridgeshire, **Jamie Durrant** for Bedfordshire, **Tom Smith** for Durham and **Reg Halton** for Staffordshire; **Steve Yates** was an England choice at schoolboy level; **Roger Heywood** played in the Lancashire League; while City trainer **David Jones** was a former Notts cricketer. Each of **Ron Burbeck**, **Reg Halton**, **Fred Price** and **Walter Smith** represented Leicestershire's Second XI; and both **Tommy Clay** and **Arthur Chandler** were County trialists. Of wartime guest players who turned out for Fosse or City, four were also first-class cricketers: **Bill Barron** (Lancashire & Northamptonshire), **Maurice Dunkley** and **Neddy Freeman** (both Northamptonshire) and **Eric Houghton** (Warwickshire).

Ewart Astill, **Les Berry**, **John Dickinson**, **Tom Jayes**, **Albert Matthews**, **Billy Odell**, **Harold Riley**, **George Shingler** and **Francis Stocks** are among Leicestershire players to have turned out for Fosse or City Reserves; and both **George Dawkes** and **Laurie Thursting** featured in City's Colts during WW2. **Maurice Hallam** and **Rodney Pratt** were City A-team players. In August 1937, **Arthur Chandler** appeared as fielding 12th man for both Leics and Notts at Aylestone Road.

Incidentally, Leicestershire CCC have also featured in first-class cricket several other all-rounders who have represented other football clubs at senior level, including **Chris Balderstone** (Huddersfield Town, Carlisle United, Doncaster Rovers, Queen of the South), **Les Berry** (Bristol Rovers, Swindon Town), **Walter Cornock** (Rochdale), **John Dickinson** (Distillery), **Ted Glennon** (Grimsby Town, Sheffield Wednesday, Rotherham County), **Harry Graham** (Linfield, Glentoran), **Aubrey Sharp** (Halifax Town), **Jeff Tolchard** (Torquay United, Exeter City), **George Watson** (Charlton Athletic, Crystal Palace, Clapton Orient, England Amateurs) and **Willie Watson** (Huddersfield Town, Sunderland, Halifax Town, England).

COUNTY CRICKETERS.

H. WHITEHEAD, LEICESTERSHIRE.

CUMULATIVE LEAGUE RECORD

(Football League & Premier League; to end 2000/1)

Grand Total [96 seasons]		Home/Away Breakdown	Home	Away
Played	3898	Played	1949	1949
Won	1446	Won	988	458
Drawn	986	Drawn	495	491
Lost	1466	Lost	466	1000
Goals For	5930	Goals For	3666	2264
Goals Against	6051	Goals Against	2377	3674

All Competitive Games

		P	W	D	L	F	A
Midland League	1891-94	64	32	8	24	118	105
FL/PL	1894-2001	3898	1446	986	1466	5930	6051
FL Play-Offs	1992-96	12	6	4	2	19	11
FA Cup	1890-2001	296	134	62	100	522	403
FL Cup	1960-2001	134	61	29	44	210	170
ECWC	1961/2	4	2	1	1	8	5
UEFA	1997-2001	4	-	1	3	3	8
FMC	1987-92	12	6	2	4	17	14
AIC	1992-94	4	1	1	2	7	8
Total		**4428**	**1688**	**1094**	**1646**	**6834**	**6775**

DISCIPLINE

> Almost hand in hand with City's reputation down the years as a 'footballing' side has gone an assessment of them as a 'fair' one: at no stage have they had to carry the 'cloggers' tag which still adheres to quite a few clubs whatever their turnover in personnel. Obviously though, cautions, bookings and dismissals have accrued against the club's players since League and Cup football commenced: what is perhaps most noteworthy about a full list of Fossils and City men sent off in the course of senior football is that a record of only 20 such instances from 1894 to 1975 has been augmented (and dwarfed) by no less than 75 more dismissals in the course of the twenty-two years since 1979. In fact, City went almost 15 years without a player sent off between 1919 and 1934, and a further near-14 year stretch between 1942 and 1956.

The first of a total of eight Fossils to receive their marching orders was Willie Freebairn, in the Second Division game at Lincoln on 10.04.1897. The first Leicester player to be sent off in an FA Cup tie was **George Mountain**, in the second replay of a Qualifying Round tie against Burton United on 07.12.1903. The first to take an early bath at Filbert Street was **David Walker**, on 28.01.1911, when Clapton Orient were the visitors.

Teddy King was the first villain for the reconstructed City, being dismissed at Fulham on 20.09.1919. **Johnny Morris**, sent off while playing for the Blues v Whites in the then-annual pre-season public practice match on 17.08.1957, was widely deemed to be the only player anywhere so disgraced in such a game. **Frank McLintock** (in Innsbruck in 1964), **David Nish** (at

Above: Ian Wilson – dismissed in a friendly in his native Scotland.

Kaiserslautern in 1967), **Keith Weller** (against Olympiakos in 1972), **Tommy Williams** (at Karlsruhe in 1980) and **Ian Wilson**, exiting the Ibrox pitch early during a 1984 clash with Rangers, are the only other City men to have been sent off in 'friendly' fixtures.

Len Chalmers remains the only City player dismissed in a League Cup tie (at Charlton on 02.10.1962); **David Speedie** the only one sent off in a Play Off game (at home to Tranmere on 18.05.1994); and **Garry Parker** the sole red-card victim in European competition (against Atletico Madrid on 30.09.1997). **Colin Gibson** (at Luton on 06.02.1993) and **David Speedie** (as above) are the only City substitutes to have both entered the game late and exited it early as a disciplinary measure.

There have been four instances of two Leicester players being sent off in the same game: **Bob Pollock** and **Ike Evenson** at Bolton on 25.03.1905; **Alan Young** and **Kevin MacDonald** at Brighton on 20.04.1981; **Paul Ramsey** and **Steve Walsh** at Millwall in the FA Cup on 05.01.1991; and **David Lowe** and **Brian Carey** away to Wimbledon on 10.09.1994.

Steve Walsh holds the unenviable club record of having been red-carded on a total of nine occasions while appearing for City. **Paul Ramsey**, **Simon Grayson** and **Neil Lennon**, with three dismissals apiece, are his distant runners-up.

City's initial Premiership campaign of 1994/5 saw the highest number of players sent off in one season: eight in total taking the early walk.

Though the Fosse directorate imposed fairly draconian suspensions on several players declared guilty of breaching internal disciplinary regulations, and several City players received one-year bans after the FA Commission on the club's financial dealings reported during WW2, the longest disciplinary suspension imposed on a Leicester player in modern times was served by **Steve Walsh** during 1987/8. Following his dismissal on the season's opening day, the cumulative upshot of an automatic 'sentence', and that imposed after a later hearing, was an eleven-game ban.

EVER-PRESENTS

> Fosse and City have had 76 players who have completed at least one season as an ever-present in League games since **Jack Lord** achieved the feat in the initial Midland League campaign of 1891/2. **Mark Wallington** did so on seven occasions (1975/6-1980/1 inclusive, plus 1982/3), while **Jimmy Thraves**, **George Swift**, **Adam Black**, **Richie Norman** and **Steve Whitworth** each did so four times, and **Hugh Adcock**, **Arthur Rowley**, **David Nish** and **Dennis Rofe** three times each.

There were five ever-presents in the second Midland League campaign (1892/3 - **Thraves**, **Bailey**, **Taylor**, **Dorrell** and **Slack**), and four in the Division One season of 1973/4 (**Shilton**, **Rofe**, **Weller** and **Worthington**). In 35 separate League seasons there have been no ever-present players at all. **Gary McAllister** became the club's first 46-game ever-present in 1988/9; **Steve Guppy** the first at Premiership level in 1998/9. The fact that only five players have achieved ever-present consistency since 1990 is probably testimony to the intensity of the modern game, with suspensions now accounting for almost as many absences as injury; even if City have yet to experience for themselves the luxury of adopting newly-fashionable 'squad rotation' principles.

FAMILIARITY

> Leicester's most familar opponents at competitive levels over the years have been those now known as Arsenal, Birmingham City, West Ham United and Manchester United.

Fosse and Woolwich Arsenal first met in Division Two in 1894/5: they have now encountered each other in 112 FL or PL games, 11 FA Cup and 4 League Cup ties [127 meetings in total]. Additionally the clubs clashed in WW2 football, and once in the Southern Professional Floodlit Cup.

Fosse and Small Heath contested an FA Cup tie in 1891/2: meetings between the clubs now total 114 FL games and 9 FA Cup ties [123 meetings in all]. Additionally, the clubs confronted each other in both WW1 and WW2 football, with a further encounter coming in the abandoned League season of 1939/40.

City and West Ham did not first meet competitively until 1919/20, yet they have since aggregated 115 meetings: 112 in FL and PL matches, one in the FA Cup and two in the League Cup. Additionally, the Hammers were another side met in the abandoned 1939/40 season, and later in WW2 football.

Fosse and Newton Heath were Second Division opponents in 1894/5: their 112 aggregate clashes are made up of 108 at FL and PL level, and two meetings in each of the FA Cup and League Cup.

In the FA Cup, Leicester & Manchester City have met 11 times after 8 pairings, and City & Arsenal 11 times after only 6 pairings; while Leicester & Spurs have also been paired on eight occasions. In the League Cup, City and Crystal Palace have had 7 games after 4 pairings.

In the course of one season, City and Arsenal met seven times. The two First Division fixtures of 1974/5 were supplemented by three FA Cup clashes and two in the League Cup.

In terms of meetings in most different competitions, the 'league table' of City opponents reads thus:

club	PL	D1*	D1	D2	FAC	FLC	FMC	PO
Derby County	●	●	●	●	●	●	●	●
Nottm Forest	●	●	●	●	●	●	●	
Crystal Palace	●	●	●	●	●	●		●
Watford		●	●	●	●	●	●	
Stoke City			●	●	●	●	●	●

Above: Steve Walsh in happier mood than when receiving an eleven match ban in 1987.

FILBERT STREET AS A NEUTRAL VENUE

> Some of the more important or prestigious games to have been held on the ground of Leicester Fosse/City:

International & Representative Matches:

14.11.1921	Amateur	England 4 Ireland 1	2,750
18.12.1926	Amateur	England 1 Scotland 4	14,000
19.03.1927	Inter-League	Football League 2 Scottish League 2	26,000
19.02.1938	Amateur	England 1 Ireland 1	4,800
20.01.1951	Amateur	England 4 Wales 1	13,398
14.10.1970	Under-23	England 3 West Germany 1	24,757
20.11.1979	Under-21	England 5 Bulgaria 0	5,758
06.09.1994	Under-21	England 0 Portugal 0	6,487
29.07.2000	Full	India 1 Bangladesh 0	2,588
24.05.2001	Under-21	England 3 Mexico 0	10,342

Football League:

27.04.1895	Test Match	Derby County 2 Notts County 1	8,000
04.02.1899	Division 2	Loughborough 1 Blackpool 3	4,000
02.09.1899	Division 2	Loughborough 2 Bolton Wanderers 3	5,000

FA Cup:

26.10.1903	2QR/2nd r	Burton United 5 Hinckley Town 1	-
18.01.1926	R3/2nd r	Derby County 2 Portsmouth 0	11,076
24.03.1928	Semi-final	Arsenal 0 Blackburn Rovers 1	25,633
23.02.1959	R5/2nd r	Birmingham City 0 Nott'm Forest 5	34,458
16.10.1961	3QR/2nd r	Hinckley Ath 3 Nuneaton Borough 1	3,000
09.04.1962	Semi-final r	Burnley 2 Fulham 1	31,477
13.03.1972	R5/2nd r	Arsenal 1 Derby County 0	36,534
29.01.1973	R3/2nd r	Nott'm Forest 1 West Brom 3	12,606
13.01.1975	R3/2nd r	Fulham 1 Hull City 0	4,929
25.03.1975	R5/2nd r	Ipswich Town 0 Leeds United 0	35,195
27.03.1975	R5/3rd r	Ipswich Town 3 Leeds United 2	19,510
16.01.1978	R3/2nd r	Grimsby Town 1 Southampton 4	11,356
15.01.1979	R3/2nd r	Arsenal 2 Sheffield Wednesday 2	25,011
17.01.1979	R3/3rd r	Arsenal 3 Sheffield Wednesday 3	17,008
22.01.1979	R3/4th r	Arsenal 2 Sheffield Wednesday 0	30,275
--.--.1986	1QR r	Leicester United 4 North Ferriby Utd 2	-

Football League Cup:

20.09.1977	R2/2nd r	Brighton & HA 1 Oldham Athletic 2	1,840
27.10.1987	R3	Luton Town 3 Coventry City 1	8,113

FA Amateur Cup:

28.03.1896	Final	Bishop Auckland 1 R.A. (Portsmouth) 0	-
31.03.1900	Final	Bishop Auckland 5 Lowestoft Town 1	-
05.03.1932	Semi-final	Marine 2 Yorkshire Amateurs 1	3,000

FA Trophy:

03.04.1971	Semi-final	Hereford United 0 Hillingdon Borough 2	-

Others:

20.04.1893	ML Ch/Rep	Rotherham Town 0 Rest of Midland Lge 3	-
09.03.1895	B'm Cup sf	Aston Villa 6 Loughborough 2	7,500

Schools Internationals:
1923 England 7 Wales 2; 1928 England 5 Scotland 0;
1953 England 0 Scotland 0; 1958 England 3 Wales 1;
1963 England 3 Rep.Ireland 2.; 1968 England 2 Wales 1.

FLOODLIGHTS

> The official illumination of the Filbert Street floodlights was celebrated with a midweek friendly on 23.10.1957 against Borussia Dortmund. The lights were used for the first time for a League game less than a month later, on 16.11.1957, when a First Division encounter with Preston North End was floodlit throughout to combat poor visibility, despite a 3.00 kick-off. The first competitive evening kick-off scheduled specifically to exploit City's possession of lights was a Division One game on 18.03.1959 against Birmingham City.

> Leicester Fosse played only one game under lights: a friendly against Blackburn Rovers at the Peel Croft ground, Burton-on-Trent, on 05.10.1908.

FOOTBALLER OF THE YEAR

> The Footballer of the Year award was instigated by the Football Writers' Association in 1947/8, and has been supplemented since 1974 by a Player of the Year award presented by the Professional Footballers' Association.

Don Revie

No player has won either award while on Leicester City's books; but several former stars have been so honoured after moving on: **Don Revie** (Manchester City, 1955), **Frank McLintock** (Arsenal, 1971), **Gordon Banks** (Stoke City, 1972), **Peter Shilton** (Nottingham Forest, 1978, PFA) and **Gary Lineker** (Everton, 1986, both awards, & Tottenham Hotspur, 1992, FWA).

Steve Moran (in 1982) and **Tony Cottee** (in 1986) both won the PFA's Young Player of the Year award prior to joining City; and **Charlie Miller** picked up the Scottish equivalent in 1995. **Pat Byrne** won the PFA of Ireland award in 1984, and the Sports Writers Association of Ireland Personality of the Year award in both 1985 and 1992. **Martin Russell** won the Irish PFA's Player of the Year award in 1992. **Kasey Keller** and **Theo Zagorakis** won equivalent American and Greek awards. **Emile Heskey** was runner-up in the voting for the PFA Young Player of the Year in 1997.

GOALKEEPERS

GOALS CONCEDED: AVERAGE PER GAME (Qualification: 100+ Lge & Cup games for Fosse/City):

	Total Apps/Gls	Ave per game
Peter Shilton	339/379	1.118
George Hebden	104/118	1.135
Kasey Keller	125/143	1.144
Mark Wallington	460/607	1.319
Herbert Bown	154/211	1.370
Kevin Poole	193/278	1.440
Jimmy Thraves	148/215	1.453
Gordon Banks	356/529	1.486
Ian Andrews	139/238	1.712
Sandy McLaren	256/448	1.750
Johnny Anderson	277/488	1.762
Jim McLaren	180/325	1.805

GOALSCORING GOALKEEPERS

For:

Herbert Bown (penalty)		
v Hull City	03.03.17	WW1
Peter Shilton (clearance)		
v Southampton	14.10.67	D1

Against:

Gray (penalty)		
for Burton Swifts	27.11.97	D2
Ian Black (playing outfield)		
for Fulham	25.08.52	D2
Gordon Bradley (playing outfield)		
for Notts County	22.09.56	D2
Alex Stepney (penalty)		
for Man United	12.09.73	D1

Above: Peter Shilton got his name on the scoresheet with a long clearance against Southampton in 1967.

Above: Frank Worthington, a regular marksman as well as a flamboyant character, and idolised on the terraces.

DOUBLE FIGURES CONCEDED

12	Horace Bailey		
	FOSSE v Nottm Forest	1908/9	
	D1		0-12
11	Tom DeVille		
	FOSSE v Rotherham T	1891/2	
	ML		0-11
11	Alick Grant		
	Newport Co v Notts Co	1948/9	
	D3S		1-11
11	Jack Beby		
	C Palace v Exeter C	1933/4	
	D3SC		6-11
10	Billy Rowley		
	Stoke v Preston NE	1889/0	
	FL		0-10
10	Joe Wright		
	Torquay Utd v Fulham	1931/2	
	D3S		2-10
10	Sandy McLaren		
	CITY v Wolves	1937/8	
	D1		1-10

GOALS AGAINST

CAREER GOAL RECORDS BY OPPONENTS IN LEAGUE & CUP MATCHES v FOSSE / CITY

Dixie Dean	18	(Everton 18)
Charlie Wayman	17	(Newcastle 2, Southampton 10, Preston 5)
George Brown	16	(Huddersfield 9, Aston Villa 7)
Jimmy Dunne	16	(Sheffield Utd 11, Arsenal 2, Southampton 3)
Gordon Hodgson	16	(Liverpool 9, Leeds United 7)
Jimmy Greaves	15	(Chelsea 2, Tottenham Hotspur 13)
Denis Law	14	(Man Utd 13, Man City 1)
Ray Charnley	13	(Blackpool 13)
Graham Leggat	13	(Fulham 13)
Jock Peddie	13	(Newcastle 4, Man Utd 9)
Dennis Westcott	13	(Wolves 8, Blackburn 5)

GOALSCORERS

Aggregate
(All competitive League, Cup & wartime football)

273	Arthur Chandler
265	Arthur Rowley
156	Ernie Hine
117	Derek Hines
114	Arthur Lochhead
113	George Dewis
103	Gary Lineker
97	Jack Lee
97	Mike Stringfellow
95	Johnny Duncan
92	Danny Liddle
92	Jimmy Walsh
85	Sep Smith
84	Alan Smith
79	Mal Griffiths
78	Frank Worthington
76	Ken Keyworth
71	Jack Bowers
64	Arthur Maw
62	Steve Walsh
60	Steve Lynex
58	Fred Shinton
53	Jackie Sinclair
53	David Gibson
52	Hughie Adcock
51	Gary McAllister
50	Teddy King

Gary McAllister

Football League

259	Arthur Chandler
251	Arthur Rowley
148	Ernie Hine
116	Derek Hines
106	Arthur Lochhead
95	Gary Lineker
88	Johnny Duncan
82	Mike Stringfellow
80	Jimmy Walsh
76	Alan Smith
74	Jack Lee

72	Frank Worthington			
66	Mal Griffiths			
64	Danny Liddle			
62	Ken Keyworth			
58	Arthur Maw			
57	Steve Lynex			
55	Fred Shinton			
53	Steve Walsh			
52	Jack Bowers			
51	Hughie Adcock			
50	Jackie Sinclair			

Danny Liddle

FA Cup

14	Arthur Chandler
14	Arthur Rowley
11	Billy Dorrell
10	Mal Griffiths
10	Jack Lee
10	Arthur Mounteney
9	Ken Leek
9	Willie McArthur
8	Len Glover
8	Ernie Hine
8	Arthur Lochhead
8	David Skea

FL Cup

8	Mike Stringfellow
7	David Gibson
7	Jimmy Goodfellow
6	Emile Heskey
6	Bobby Roberts
5	Tony Cottee
5	Derek Dougan
5	Billy Hodgson
5	Mike Newell
5	Mark Robins
5	Jimmy Walsh

WW1

33	Cliff Price
24	Teddy King

Mark Robins

WW2

62	George Dewis
48	Sep Smith

Most in One Game:

6	John Duncan
	25.12.1924 v Port Vale (H)
6	Arthur Chandler
	20.10.1928 v Portsmouth (H)

Most on Debut:

4	Archie Gardiner
	21.02.1934 v Portsmouth (A)

Scored in Successive Games:

8	Arthur Chandler
	[7 Lge + 1 FAC during 1924/5]
7	Arthur Rowley
	[7 Lge during 1951/2]
6	Dave Walker, Arthur Chandler (twice), Ernie Hine, Jack Bowers (twice; including first six games from debut), Arthur Rowley (four times), Ken Keyworth, Bob Lee, Alan Smith.

> Rowley also scored in 7 successive Lge games during 1956/7, but drew blank in an intervening FA Cup tie. George Dewis scored in 10 successive WW2 games during 1940/1.

> For scoring in successive games from the start of the season, the club record of 4 games is shared by David Skea (1894/5), Frank Middleton (1906/7), Tommy Benfield (1913/14), Mike Stringfellow (1962/3) and Andy Lochhead (1969/70).

Number of League & Cup Games Played to Reach 100 Goals for City:

122	Arthur Rowley
	07.04.53 v Rotherham U (H) Div 2
140	Arthur Chandler
	09.10.26 v Sunderland (H) Div 1
185	Ernie Hine
	20.09.30 v Arsenal (A) Div 1
214	Gary Lineker (207+7)
	04.05.85 v QPR (A) Div 1
259	Derek Hines
	04.09.57 v Sunderland (H) Div 1
267	Arthur Lochhead
	26.12.32 v Portsmouth (A) Div 1

Goals at Filbert Street:

Chandler: 168 Lge + 5 FAC : 173
Rowley: 156 Lge + 7 FAC : 163
(plus 1 Lge goal for Fulham v City)

Div One

203	Arthur Chandler
148	Ernie Hine
106	Arthur Lochhead
81	Mike Stringfellow
79	Jimmy Walsh
72	Frank Worthington
63	Ken Keyworth
63	Alan Smith
50	Danny Liddle
50	Jackie Sinclair

Div Two

208	Arthur Rowley
88	Derek Hines
74	Jack Lee
56	Arthur Chandler
50	Mal Griffiths

Premier League

33	Emile Heskey
27	Tony Cottee
27	Muzzy Izzet
22	Matt Elliott

Div One (post 1992)

32	Iwan Roberts
23	Steve Walsh
22	Julian Joachim

Muzzy Izzet

Progressive Record:

League Goals per season

1894/5	David Skea	23
1909/10	Fred Shinton	32
1924/5	Arthur Chandler	32
1927/8	Arthur Chandler	34
1928/9	Arthur Chandler	34
1951/2	Arthur Rowley	38
1952/3	Arthur Rowley	39
1956/7	Arthur Rowley	44

Quickest Goals

10 seconds	Tom Dryburgh v Swansea Town H D2 28.03.1953	
10 seconds	Derek Hines v Lincoln City H D2 21.11.1953	
10 seconds	Ian McNeill v Nottm Forest A D2 30.03.1957	
13 seconds	A Cheesebrough v Preston N E A D1 28.12.1959	

HAT-TRICKS

Occasions of Player Scoring Three or More:

For Leicester: 117 Lge; 20 FAC; 2 LC; 3 ML. (Total: 142)
Against Leicester: 142 Lge; 10 FAC; 1 LC; 4 ML. (Total: 157)

Leading Exponents (Fosse/City Hat-tricks or Better):

	6 gls	5 gls	4 gls	3 gls	
A Chandler	1	3	1	12	(17)
A Rowley		1		15	(16)
E Hine		1	1	7	(9)
G Lineker				5	(5)
J Bowers			1	3	(4)
J Lee			1	3	(4)
F Shinton				4	(4)

also scored 6 in game: J Duncan
also scored 5 in game: H Trainer, D Hines
also scored 4 in game: W Dorrell, W Miller, W McArthur, R King, J McMillan, A Brash, A Mounteney, D Walker, F Osborn, A Pynegar, D Liddle, A Gardiner, W Gardiner, J Walsh.

> The fastest hat-tricks for Leicester have come from Fred Shinton (in five minutes, 20.11.1909 v Oldham) and Ken Keyworth (in six minutes, 16.04.1963 v Manchester United).

> In first-class fixtures for Leicester, Tommy Brown (19.10.1901 v Chesterfield) and David Kelly (01.12.1990 v Newcastle) scored hat-tricks against clubs they would later serve. Arthur Rowley three times notched threesomes or better against clubs for whom he had previously played (25.08.1952 & 03.09.1952 v Fulham; 12.02.1955 v West Brom), and Derek Dougan (24.09.1966 v Aston Villa) once did likewise.

> In competitive games against Leicester, Tommy Shanks (Arsenal), Wallace Smith (Bradford City), Albert Cheesebrough (Burnley), Tommy English (Coventry), Jack Bowers (Derby), Albert Carnelly (Loughborough), Jack Hall (Middlesbrough) and Alan Young (Oldham) each notched hat-tricks before joining the club. Ernie Hine (Barnsley), Johnny McMillan (Bradford City), Ray Iggleden (Leeds), David Kelly (Newcastle) and Trevor Christie (Notts County) all claimed triples against Leicester after leaving the club.

> Arthur Rowley's 1952/3 feat of scoring home-and-away hat-tricks against Fulham is offset by Leicester twice being victims of such an occurrence: when Glossop's James Moore notched seven against Fosse in 1912/13, and when Sheffield United's Jimmy Dunne did likewise against City in 1929/30.

> Arthur Chandler is the only City man to have notched a 'hat-trick of hat-tricks' against the same opponents (Aston Villa); while Dixie Dean did the same for Everton against Leicester. Jock Peddie aggregated three triples against Fosse from his days with Newcastle United and Manchester United.

Players connected to Fosse/City who have scored 5 or more goals in a game:

8	Owen McNally	Arthurlie v Armadale	Scots Div 2	01.10.27
8	Jack Calder	Morton v Raith Rovers	Scots Div 2	18.04.36
6	John Duncan	CITY v Port Vale	Div 2	25.12.24
6	Arthur Chandler	CITY v Portsmouth	Div 1	20.10.28
6	Jack Calder	Morton v Cowdenbeath	Scots Div 2	14.12.35
6	Andy Graver	Lincoln v Crewe	Div 3N	29.09.51
5	Johnny McMillan	Derby v Wolves	F Lge	10.01.91
5	Harry Hammond	Sheff Utd v Bootle	Div 2	26.11.92
5	Harry Trainer	FOSSE v Rotherham Town	Div 2	03.04.96
5	Harry Hammond	New Brighton T v Darwen	Div 2	22.12.98
5	Harry Hammond	New Brighton T v Burton Sw	Div 2	24.03.00
5	Arthur Chandler	CITY v Barnsley	Div 2	28.02.25
5	Arthur Chandler	CITY v Aston Villa	Div 1	27.11.26
5	Arthur Chandler	CITY v WBA	Div 1	25.12.26
5	*Archie Waterston*	Southport v Nelson	Div 3N	01.01.31
5	Ernie Hine	CITY v Crook Town	FA Cup 3	09.01.32
5	Jack Calder	Morton v Kings Park	Scots Div 2	21.03.36
5	Jack Calder	Morton v Cowdenbeath	Scots Div 2	14.08.36
5	Johnny Campbell	Lincoln v Rochdale	Div 3N	21.11.36
5	Peter McKennan	Brentford v Bury	Div 2	19.02.49
5	Derek Hines	CITY v Lincoln City	Div 2	21.11.53
5	Nick Sharkey	Sunderland v Norwich	Div 2	20.03.63
5	Barrie Thomas	Scunthorpe v Luton	Div 3	24.04.65
5	Andy Lochhead	Burnley v Chelsea	Div 1	24.04.65
5	Andy Lochhead	Burnley v Bournemouth	FA Cup 3r	25.01.66
5	Steve Earle	Fulham v Halifax	Div 3	16.09.69
5	Roger Davies	Derby v Luton	Div 1	29.03.75
5	Steve Wilkinson	Mansfield v Birmingham	Div 3	03.04.90
5	Mark Robins	England U21 v France U21	U21 Intl	23.05.90

Running total of full caps won by players while on the books of Fosse / City

	59 players;	470 caps;	33 goals
Australia	1	2	-
England	15	116	12
Finland	1	10	1
Greece	1	18	-
Iceland	1	4	1
Ireland/NI	10	144	5
Jamaica	1	15	-
Rep Ireland	3	12	3
Scotland	11	39	6
Sweden	1	17	-
Turkey	1	4	-
USA	1	20	-
Wales	12	69	5

FULL INTERNATIONALS

AUSTRALIA

Zeljko Kalac [2 caps]

25.02.96	Sweden	Brisbane	0-2
28.02.96	Sweden	Sydney	0-0

[Also capped beforehand while with Sydney United, and subsequently while with Sydney United and Roda JC. Career total: 38 caps to date.]

ENGLAND

Hughie Adcock [5 caps; 1 goal]

09.05.29	France	Paris	4-1	
11.05.29	Belgium	Brussels	5-1	
15.05.29	Spain	Madrid	3-4	
19.10.29	N Ireland	Belfast	3-0	
20.11.29	Wales	Stamford Br	6-0	(1 gl)

Horace Bailey [5 caps]

16.03.08	Wales	Wrexham	7-1
06.06.08	Austria	Vienna	6-1
08.06.08	Austria	Vienna	11-1
10.06.08	Hungary	Budapest	7-0
13.06.08	Bohemia	Prague	4-0

Gordon Banks [37 caps]

06.04.63	Scotland	Wembley	1-2
08.05.63	Brazil	Wembley	1-1
20.05.63	Czechoslovakia	Bratislava	4-2
02.06.63	East Germany	Leipzig	2-1
12.10.63	Wales	Cardiff	4-0
23.10.63	Rest of the World	Wembley	2-1
20.11.63	N Ireland	Wembley	8-3
11.04.64	Scotland	Glasgow	0-1

Left: Sid Bishop won four England caps before becoming homesick for London.

06.05.64	Uruguay	Wembley	2-1
17.05.64	Portugal	Lisbon	4-3
27.05.64	USA	New York	10-0
04.06.64	Portugal	Sao Paolo	1-1
06.06.64	Argentina	Rio de Janeiro	0-1
03.10.64	N Ireland	Belfast	4-3
10.04.65	Scotland	Wembley	2-2
05.05.65	Hungary	Wembley	1-0
09.05.65	Yugoslavia	Belgrade	1-1
12.05.65	West Germany	Nuremberg	1-0
16.05.65	Sweden	Gothenburg	2-1
10.11.65	N Ireland	Wembley	2-1
08.12.65	Spain	Madrid	2-0
05.01.66	Poland	Goodison Pk	1-1
23.02.66	West Germany	Wembley	1-0
02.04.66	Scotland	Glasgow	4-3
04.05.66	Yugoslavia	Wembley	2-0
26.06.66	Finland	Helsinki	3-0
05.07.66	Poland	Chorzow	1-0
11.07.66	Uruguay [WCf]	Wembley	0-0
16.07.66	Mexico [WCf]	Wembley	2-0
20.07.66	France [WCf]	Wembley	2-0
23.07.66	Argentina [WCf]	Wembley	1-0
26.07.66	Portugal [WCf]	Wembley	2-1
30.07.66	W. Germany [WCf]	Wembley	4-2
22.10.66	N Ireland [ECq]	Belfast	2-0
02.11.66	Czechoslovakia	Wembley	0-0
16.11.66	Wales [ECq]	Wembley	5-1
15.04.67	Scotland [ECq]	Wembley	2-3

[Also capped subsequently while with Stoke City. Career total: 73 caps.]

Len Barry [5 caps]

17.05.28	France	Paris	5-1
19.05.28	Belgium	Antwerp	3-1
09.05.29	France	Paris	4-1
11.05.29	Belgium	Brussels	5-1
15.05.29	Spain	Madrid	3-4

Sid Bishop [4 caps; 1 goal]

02.04.27	Scotland	Glasgow	2-1	
11.05.27	Belgium	Brussels	9-1	
21.05.27	Luxembourg	Esch-sur-Alzette	5-2	(1 gl)
26.05.27	France	Paris	6-0	

Steve Guppy [1 cap]

10.10.99	Belgium	Sunderland	2-1

Emile Heskey [5 caps]

28.04.99	Hungary	Budapest	1-1	(sub)
09.06.99	Bulgaria [ECq]	Sofia	1-1	(sub)
10.10.99	Belgium	Sunderland	2-1	(sub)
17.11.99	Scotland [ECq]	Wembley	0-1	(sub)
23.02.00	Argentina	Wembley	0-0	

[Also capped subsequently while with Liverpool. Career total: 16 caps; 2 goals to date.]

Right: Steve Guppy's sole England cap was won away from Wembley.

Ernie Hine [6 caps; 4 goals]

22.10.28	N Ireland	Goodison Pk	2-1	
17.11.28	Wales	Swansea	3-2	(1 gl)
19.10.29	N Ireland	Belfast	3-0	(1 pen)
20.11.29	Wales	Stamford Br	6-0	
17.10.31	N Ireland	Belfast	6-2	(1 gl)
18.11.31	Wales	Anfield	3-1	(1 gl)

Gary Lineker [7 caps; 3 goals]

26.05.84	Scotland	Glasgow	1-1	(sub)
26.03.85	Rep Ireland	Wembley	2-1	(1 gl)
01.05.85	Romania [WCq]	Bucharest	0-0	(sub)
25.05.85	Scotland	Glasgow	0-1	(sub)
06.06.85	Italy	Mexico City	1-2	(sub)
12.06.85	West Germany	Mexico City	3-0	
16.06.85	USA	Los Angeles	5-0	(2 gls)

[Also capped subsequently while with Everton, Barcelona and Tottenham Hotspur. Career total: 80 caps; 48 goals.]

Reg Osborne [1 cap]

28.11.27	Wales	Turf Moor	1-2

Peter Shilton [20 caps]

25.11.70	East Germany	Wembley	3-1
19.05.71	Wales	Wembley	0-0
10.11.71	Switzerland [ECq]	Wembley	1-1
23.05.72	N Ireland	Wembley	0-1
11.10.72	Yugoslavia	Wembley	1-1
14.02.73	Scotland	Glasgow	5-0
12.05.73	N Ireland	Goodison Pk	2-1
15.05.73	Wales	Wembley	3-0
19.05.73	Scotland	Wembley	1-0
27.05.73	Czechoslovakia	Prague	1-1
06.06.73	Poland [WCq]	Chorzow	0-2
10.06.73	USSR	Moscow	2-1
14.06.73	Italy	Turin	0-2
26.09.73	Austria	Wembley	7-0
17.10.73	Poland [WCq]	Wembley	1-1
14.11.73	Italy	Wembley	0-1
11.05.74	Wales	Cardiff	2-0
15.05.74	N Ireland	Wembley	1-0
18.05.74	Scotland	Glasgow	0-2
22.05.74	Argentina	Wembley	2-2

[Also capped subsequently while with Stoke City, Nottingham Forest, Southampton and Derby County. Career total: 125 caps.]

Sep Smith [1 cap]

19.10.35	N Ireland	Belfast	3-1

Keith Weller [4 caps; 1 goal]

11.05.74	Wales	Cardiff	2-0	
15.05.74	N Ireland	Wembley	1-0	(1 gl)
18.05.74	Scotland	Glasgow	0-2	
22.05.74	Argentina	Wembley	2-2	

Steve Whitworth [7 caps]

12.03.75	West Germany	Wembley	2-0
11.05.75	Cyprus [ECq]	Limassol	1-0
17.05.75	N Ireland	Belfast	0-0
21.05.75	Wales	Wembley	2-2
24.05.75	Scotland	Wembley	5-1
03.09.75	Switzerland	Basle	2-1
19.11.75	Portugal [ECq]	Lisbon	1-1

Frank Worthington [8 caps; 2 goals]

15.05.74	N Ireland	Wembley	1-0	(sub)
18.05.74	Scotland	Glasgow	0-2	
22.05.74	Argentina	Wembley	2-2	(1 gl)
29.05.74	East Germany	Leipzig	1-1	
01.06.74	Bulgaria	Sofia	1-0	(1 gl)
05.06.74	Yugoslavia	Belgrade	2-2	
30.10.74	Czechoslovakia [ECq]	Wembley	3-0	
20.11.74	Portugal [ECq]	Wembley	0-0	(sub)

FINLAND

Jari Rantanen [10 caps; 1 goal]

09.09.87	Czechoslovakia [ECq]	Helsinki	3-0	
12.01.88	Czechoslovakia	Las Palmas	2-0	
15.01.88	Sweden	Las Palmas	0-1	(sent off)
19.05.88	Colombia	Helsinki	1-3	(1 gl)
04.08.88	Bulgaria	Vaasa	1-1	(sub)
17.08.88	USSR	Turku	0-0	
31.08.88	W. Germany [WCq]	Helsinki	0-4	
19.10.88	Wales [WCq]	Swansea	2-2	(sub)
11.01.89	Egypt	El Mahalla	1-2	(sub)
13.01.89	Egypt	Cairo	1-2	

[Also capped beforehand while with HJK Helsinki and IFK Göteborg. Career total: 28 caps; 4 goals. Also 7 apps; 4 goals in Olympic football.]

GREECE

Theo Zagorakis [18 caps]

18.02.98	Russia	Athens	1-1	(capt)
08.04.98	Romania	Bucharest	1-2	(capt)
06.09.98	Slovenia [ECq]	Athens	2-2	(capt)
14.10.98	Georgia [ECq]	Athens	3-0	(capt)
18.11.98	Albania [ECq]	Tirana	0-0	(capt)
10.03.99	Croatia	Athens	3-2	(capt)
27.03.99	Norway [ECq]	Athens	0-2	(capt)
31.03.99	Latvia [ECq]	Riga	0-0	(sub)
28.04.99	Switzerland	Athens	1-1	(sub)
05.06.99	Georgia [ECq]	Tbilisi	2-1	(capt)
09.06.99	Latvia [ECq]	Athens	1-2	(capt)
16.08.99	Mexico	Xanthi	3-2	(capt)
18.08.99	El Salvador	Kavala	3-1	(capt)
04.09.99	Norway [ECq]	Oslo	0-1	(capt)
06.10.99	Albania [ECq]	Athens	2-0	(capt)
09.10.99	Slovenia [ECq]	Maribor	3-0	(sub)
13.11.99	Nigeria	Kiklis	2-0	(capt)
17.11.99	Bulgaria	Kozani	1-0	(capt)

[Also capped beforehand while with PAOK, and subsequently while with AEK. Career total: 58 caps to date.]

ICELAND

Arnar Gunnlaugsson [4 caps; 1 goal to date]

10.03.99	Luxembourg	Luxembourg	2-1	(1 pen)
27.03.99	Andorra [ECq]	Andorra	2-0	
31.03.99	Ukraine [ECq]	Kiev	1-1	
28.04.99	Malta	Valletta	2-1	

[Also capped beforehand while with ÍA Akranes, Feyenoord, Nürnberg, Sochaux & Bolton Wanderers. Career total: 30 caps; 3 goals to date.]

IRELAND (to 1923) / NORTHERN IRELAND

Mick Cochrane [1 cap]

23.02.01	Scotland	Glasgow	0-11

[Also capped beforehand while with Distillery. Career total: 8 caps.]

Willie Cunningham [23 caps]

08.10.55	Scotland	Belfast	2-1
02.11.55	England	Wembley	0-3
11.04.56	Wales	Cardiff	1-1
06.10.56	England	Belfast	1-1
07.11.56	Scotland	Glasgow	0-1
16.01.57	Portugal [WCq]	Lisbon	1-1
10.04.57	Wales	Belfast	0-0
25.04.57	Italy [WCq]	Rome	0-1
01.05.57	Portugal [WCq]	Belfast	3-0
05.10.57	Scotland	Belfast	1-1
15.01.58	Italy [WCq]	Belfast	2-1
16.04.58	Wales	Cardiff	1-1
08.06.58	Czechoslovakia [WCf]	Halmstad	1-0
11.06.58	Argentina [WCf]	Halmstad	1-3
15.06.58	W.Germany [WCf]	Malmo	2-2
17.06.58	Czechoslovakia [WCf]	Malmo	2-1
19.06.58	France [WCf]	Norrkoping	0-4
04.10.58	England	Belfast	3-3
05.11.58	Scotland	Glasgow	2-2
22.04.59	Wales	Belfast	4-1
03.10.59	Scotland	Belfast	0-4
18.11.59	England	Wembley	1-2
06.04.60	Wales	Wrexham	2-3

[Also capped beforehand while with St Mirren, and subsequently while with Dunfermline Athletic. Career total: 30 caps.]

Derek Dougan [8 caps; 1 goal]

02.10.65	Scotland	Belfast	3-2	(1 gl)
10.11.65	England	Wembley	1-2	
24.11.65	Albania [WCq]	Tirana	1-1	
30.03.66	Wales	Cardiff	4-1	
07.05.66	West Germany	Belfast	0-2	
22.06.66	Mexico	Belfast	4-1	
22.10.66	England [ECq]	Belfast	0-2	
16.11.66	Scotland [ECq]	Glasgow	1-2	

[Also capped beforehand while with Portsmouth, Aston Villa and Blackburn Rovers, and subsequently while with Wolverhampton Wanderers. Career total: 43 caps; 8 goals.]

Colin Hill [16 caps]

29.03.95	Rep Ireland [ECq]	Dublin	1-1	
26.04.95	Latvia [ECq]	Riga	1-0	
03.09.95	Portugal [ECq]	Oporto	1-1	
11.10.95	Liechtenstein [ECq]	Eschen	4-0	
15.11.95	Austria [ECq]	Belfast	5-3	
27.03.96	Norway	Belfast	0-2	
24.04.96	Sweden	Belfast	1-2	
29.05.96	Germany	Belfast	1-1	
31.08.96	Ukraine [WCq]	Belfast	0-1	
05.10.96	Armenia [WCq]	Belfast	1-1	
09.11.96	Germany [WCq]	Nurnberg	1-1	
14.12.96	Albania [WCq]	Belfast	2-0	
29.03.97	Portugal [WCq]	Belfast	0-0	
02.04.97	Ukraine [WCq]	Kiev	1-2	
30.04.97	Armenia [WCq]	Yerevan	0-0	
21.05.97	Thailand	Bangkok	0-0	

[Also capped beforehand while with Sheffield United, and subsequently while with Trelleborgs and Northampton Town. Career total: 27 caps; 1 goal.]

Neil Lennon [30 caps; 2 goals]

27.03.96	Norway	Belfast	0-2	
31.08.96	Ukraine [WCq]	Belfast	0-1	
05.10.96	Armenia [WCq]	Belfast	1-1	(1 gl)
09.11.96	Germany [WCq]	Nurnberg	1-1	
14.12.96	Albania [WCq]	Belfast	2-0	

Above: *Neil Lennon*

11.02.97	Belgium	Belfast	3-0	
29.03.97	Portugal [WCq]	Belfast	0-0	
02.04.97	Ukraine [WCq]	Kiev	1-2	
30.04.97	Armenia [WCq]	Yerevan	0-0	
21.05.97	Thailand	Bangkok	0-0	
20.08.97	Germany [WCq]	Belfast	1-3	
10.09.97	Albania [WCq]	Zurich	0-1	
11.10.97	Portugal [WCq]	Lisbon	0-1	
25.03.98	Slovakia	Belfast	1-0	
22.04.98	Switzerland	Belfast	1-0	
03.06.98	Spain	Santander	1-4	
05.09.98	Turkey [ECq]	Istanbul	0-3	
10.10.98	Finland [ECq]	Belfast	1-0	
18.11.98	Moldova [ECq]	Belfast	2-2	(1 gl)
27.03.99	Germany [ECq]	Belfast	0-3	
31.03.99	Moldova [ECq]	Chisinau	0-0	
29.05.99	Rep Ireland	Dublin	1-0	
18.08.99	France	Belfast	0-1	
04.09.99	Turkey [ECq]	Belfast	0-3	
08.09.99	Germany [ECq]	Dortmund	0-4	
09.10.99	Finland [ECq]	Helsinki	1-4	(capt)
28.03.00	Malta	Valetta	3-0	
26.04.00	Hungary	Belfast	0-1	
07.10.00	Denmark [WCq]	Belfast	1-1	
11.10.00	Iceland [WCq]	Reykjavik	0-1	

[Also capped beforehand while with Crewe Alexandra, and subsequently while with Celtic. Career total: 39 caps; 2 goals to date]

Mick O'Brien [4 caps]

04.03.22	Scotland	Glasgow	1-2
01.04.22	Wales	Belfast	1-1
01.03.24	Scotland	Glasgow	0-2
15.03.24	Wales	Belfast	0-1

[Also capped beforehand while with Queens Park Rangers, and subsequently while with Hull City, Derby County, Walsall, Norwich City and Watford. Career total: (Ireland/N. Ireland) 10 caps; (Republic of Ireland) 4 caps.]

John O'Neill [39 caps; 1 goal]

26.03.80	Israel [WCq]	Tel Aviv	0-0	
16.05.80	Scotland	Belfast	1-0	
20.05.80	England	Wembley	1-1	
23.05.80	Wales	Cardiff	1-0	
11.06.80	Australia	Sydney	2-1	
15.06.80	Australia	Melbourne	1-1	
18.06.80	Australia	Adelaide	2-1	
19.11.80	Portugal [WCq]	Lisbon	0-1	
25.03.81	Scotland [WCq]	Glasgow	1-1	
29.04.81	Portugal [WCq]	Belfast	1-0	
19.05.81	Scotland	Glasgow	0-2	
03.06.81	Sweden [WCq]	Stockholm	0-1	
14.10.81	Scotland [WCq]	Belfast	0-0	
18.11.81	Israel [WCq]	Belfast	1-0	
23.01.82	England	Wembley	0-4	
24.03.82	France	Paris	0-4	
28.04.82	Scotland	Belfast	1-1	
04.06.82	France [WCf]	Madrid	1-4	(sub)
13.10.82	Austria [ECq]	Vienna	0-2	
17.11.82	W. Germany [ECq]	Belfast	1-0	
15.12.82	Albania [ECq]	Tirana	0-0	
30.03.83	Turkey [ECq]	Belfast	2-1	
27.04.83	Albania [ECq]	Belfast	1-0	
24.05.83	Scotland	Glasgow	0-0	
13.12.83	Scotland	Belfast	2-0	(sub)
16.10.84	Israel	Belfast	3-0	
14.11.84	Finland [WCq]	Belfast	2-1	(1 gl)
27.02.85	England [WCq]	Belfast	0-1	
27.03.85	Spain	Palma	0-0	
01.05.85	Turkey [WCq]	Belfast	2-0	
11.09.85	Turkey [WCq]	Izmir	0-0	
16.10.85	Rumania [WCq]	Bucharest	1-0	
13.11.85	England [WCq]	Wembley	0-0	
26.02.86	France	Paris	0-0	
26.03.86	Denmark	Belfast	1-1	
23.04.86	Morocco	Belfast	2-1	
03.06.86	Algeria [WCf]	Guadalajara	1-1	
07.06.86	Spain [WCf]	Guadalajara	1-2	
12.06.86	Brazil [WCf]	Guadalajara	0-3	

Jimmy Quinn [4 caps]
14.09.88	Rep Ireland [WCq]	Belfast	0-0	
19.10.88	Hungary [WCq]	Budapest	0-1	(sub)
21.12.88	Spain [WCq]	Seville	0-4	(sub)
08.02.89	Spain [WCq]	Belfast	0-2	

[Also capped beforehand while with Blackburn Rovers and Swindon Town, and subsequently while with Bradford City, West Ham United, Bournemouth and Reading. Career total: 46 caps; 12 goals.]

Paul Ramsey [14 caps]
21.09.83	Austria [ECq]	Belfast	3-1	
16.11.83	W. Germany [ECq]	Hamburg	1-0	
13.12.83	Scotland	Belfast	2-0	
16.10.84	Israel	Belfast	3-0	
27.02.85	England [WCq]	Belfast	0-1	
27.03.85	Spain	Palma	0-0	
01.05.85	Turkey [WCq]	Belfast	2-0	
11.09.85	Turkey [WCq]	Izmir	0-0	
23.04.86	Morocco	Belfast	2-1	
18.02.87	Israel	Tel Aviv	1-1	
01.04.87	England [ECq]	Belfast	0-2	
29.04.87	Yugoslavia [ECq]	Belfast	1-2	(sub)
14.10.87	Yugoslavia [ECq]	Sarajevo	0-3	
08.02.89	Spain [WCq]	Belfast	0-2	

Gerry Taggart [5 caps to date]
26.04.00	Hungary	Belfast	0-1	(capt)
02.09.00	Malta [WCq]	Belfast	1-0	
07.10.00	Denmark [WCq]	Belfast	1-1	
11.10.00	Iceland [WCq]	Reykjavik	0-1	
28.02.01	Norway	Belfast	0-4	(capt)

[Also capped beforehand while with Barnsley and Bolton Wanderers. Career total to date: 50 caps; 7 goals.]

Frank Sinclair [15 caps to date]
20.05.99	Norway	Oslo	0-6	
27.05.99	Sweden	Stockholm	1-2	
03.09.99	Canada	Toronto	0-1	
09.09.99	USA	Kingston	2-2	
10.02.00	Cayman Is	Kingston	1-0	
12.02.00	Colombia [Gold Cup]	Miami	0-1	
14.02.00	Honduras [Gold Cup]	Miami	0-2	
21.05.00	Romania	Ft Lauderdale	0-0	
27.05.00	Colombia	East Rutherford	0-3	
04.06.00	Morocco	Casablanca	0-1	(sub)
06.06.00	Japan	Casablanca	0-4	
10.06.01	Cuba	Kingston	4-1	
16.06.01	USA [WCq]	Kingston	0-0	
20.06.01	Costa Rica [WCq]	Alajuela	1-2	
30.06.01	Trinidad & Tob [WCq]	Port-of-Spain	2-1	

[Also capped beforehand while with Chelsea. Career total: 24 caps; 1 goal to date.]

Brian Carey [1 cap]
23.03.94	Russia	Dublin	0-0

[Also capped beforehand while with Manchester United. Career total: 3 caps.]

Tommy Godwin [4 caps]
09.10.49	Finland [WCq]	Helsinki	1-1
13.11.49	Sweden [WCq]	Dublin	1-3
10.05.50	Belgium	Brussels	1-5
26.11.50	Norway	Dublin	2-2

[Also capped beforehand while with Shamrock Rovers, and subsequently while with Bournemouth & Boscombe Athletic. Career total: 13 caps.]

David Kelly [7 caps; 3 goals]
25.04.90	USSR	Dublin	1-0	
02.06.90	Malta	Valetta	3-0	
12.09.90	Morocco	Dublin	1-0	(1 gl)

06.02.91	Wales	Wrexham	3-0	(sub)
22.05.91	Chile	Dublin	1-1	(1 gl)
01.06.91	USA	Boston, Mass.	1-1	
11.09.91	Hungary	Gyor	2-1	(1 gl)

[Also capped beforehand while with Walsall and West Ham United, and subsequently while with Newcastle United, Wolverhampton Wanderers, Sunderland and Tranmere Rovers. Career total: 26 caps; 9 goals.]

NB: **Gerry Daly** *was on loan to City from Coventry City when capped as a substitute in the 0-2 ECq defeat by Spain in Zaragoza on 27.04.83; a game which contributed to his career total of 48 caps; 13 goals.*

Andy Aitken [3 caps]
02.04.10	England	Hampden Pk	2-0	
18.03.11	Ireland	Parkhead	2-0	(capt)
01.04.11	England	Goodison Pk	1-1	(capt)

[Also capped beforehand while with Newcastle United and Middlesbrough. Career total: 14 caps.]

Johnny Anderson [1 cap]
25.05.54	Finland	Helsinki	2-1

Callum Davidson [2 caps to date]
02.09.00	Latvia [WCq]	Riga	1-0
25.04.01	Poland	Bydgoszcz	1-1

[Also capped beforehand while with Blackburn Rovers. Career total: 14 caps to date]

John Duncan [1 cap; 1 goal]
31.10.25	Wales	Cardiff	3-0	(1 gl)

Matt Elliott [15 caps; 1 goal to date]
12.11.97	France	Saint-Etienne	1-2	(sub)
25.03.98	Denmark	Ibrox	0-1	
22.04.98	Finland	Easter Road	1-1	
05.09.98	Lithuania [ECq]	Vilnius	0-0	

14.10.98	Faroe Is [ECq]	Pittodrie	2-1	
31.03.99	Czech Rep [ECq]	Celtic Park	1-2	(1 og)
05.06.99	Faroe Is [ECq]	Toftir	1-1	(sent off)
26.04.00	Holland	Arnhem	0-0	
30.05.00	Rep Ireland	Dublin	2-1	
02.09.00	Latvia [WCq]	Riga	1-0	
07.10.00	San Marino [WCq]	Serraville	2-0	(1 gl)
11.10.00	Croatia [WCq]	Zagreb	1-1	
15.11.00	Australia	Hampden Pk	0-2	(sub)
24.03.01	Belgium [WCq]	Hampden Pk	2-2	
28.03.01	San Marino [WCq]	Hampden Pk	4-0	

Davie Gibson [7 caps; 3 gls]
08.05.63	Austria	Hampden Pk	4-1	
		[aband.79m]		
04.06.63	Norway	Bergen	3-4	
09.06.63	Rep Ireland	Dublin	0-1	
13.06.63	Spain	Madrid	6-2	(1 gl)
12.10.63	N Ireland	Belfast	1-2	
03.10.64	Wales	Cardiff	2-3	(1 gl)
21.10.64	Finland [WCq]	Hampden Pk	3-1	(1 gl)

Gary McAllister [3 caps]
25.04.90	East Germany	Hampden Pk	0-1	
19.05.90	Poland	Hampden Pk	1-1	
28.05.90	Malta	Valetta	2-1	(sub)

[Also capped subsequently while with Leeds United and Coventry City. Career total: 57 caps; 5 goals.]

Frank McLintock [3 caps; 1 goal]
04.06.63	Norway	Bergen	3-4	(sub)
09.06.63	Rep Ireland	Dublin	0-1	
13.06.63	Spain	Madrid	6-2	(1 gl)

[Also capped subsequently while with Arsenal. Career total: 9 caps; 1 goal.]

Jock Paterson [1 cap]
10.04.20	England	Hillsborough	4-5

Jackie Sinclair [1 cap]
18.06.66	Portugal	Hampden Pk	0-1

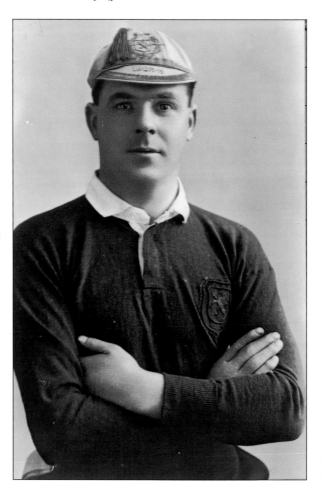

Left: John Duncan won just one Scottish cap in the 1920s.

Ian Wilson [2 caps]

23.05.87	England	Hampden Park	0-0
26.05.87	Brazil	Hampden Park	0-2

[Also capped subsequently while with Everton. Career total: 5 caps.]

SWEDEN

Pontus Kåmark [17 caps]

30.04.97	Scotland [WCq]	Gothenburg	2-1	
22.05.97	Poland	Stockholm	2-2	
06.08.97	Lithuania	Malmo	1-0	
20.08.97	Belarus [WCq]	Minsk	2-1	
06.09.97	Austria [WCq]	Vienna	0-1	
10.09.97	Latvia [WCq]	Stockholm	1-0	
22.04.98	France	Stockholm	0-0	
28.05.98	Denmark	Malmo	3-0	
02.06.98	Italy	Gothenburg	1-0	
19.08.98	Russia	Orebro	1-0	
05.09.98	England [ECq]	Stockholm	2-1	
10.02.99	Tunisia	Tunis	1-0	(sub)
27.03.99	Luxembourg [ECq]	Gothenburg	2-0	
31.03.99	Poland [ECq]	Chorzow	1-0	
28.04.99	Rep Ireland	Dublin	0-2	
27.05.99	Jamaica	Stockholm	2-1	
05.06.99	England [ECq]	Wembley	0-0	

[Also capped beforehand while with IFK Göteborg, and subsequently while with AIK. Career total: 49 caps.]

TURKEY

Muzzy Izzet [4 caps to date]

15.06.00	Sweden [ECf]	Eindhoven	0-0
07.10.00	Sweden [WCq]	Gothenburg	1-1
11.10.00	Azerbaijan [WCq]	Baku	1-0
15.11.00	France	Istanbul	0-4

U.S.A.

Kasey Keller [20 caps]

03.11.96	Guatemala [WCq]	Washington DC	2-0	
10.11.96	Trinidad & Tob. [WCq]	Richmond, Va	2-0	
24.11.96	Trinidad & Tob. [WCq]	Port-of-Spain	1-0	
02.03.97	Jamaica [WCq]	Kingston	0-0	
16.03.97	Canada [WCq]	San Francisco	3-0	
23.03.97	Costa Rica [WCq]	San Jose, Cal	2-3	
20.04.97	Mexico [WCq]	Foxboro, Mass	2-2	
07.09.97	Costa Rica [WCq]	Portland, Or	1-0	(capt)
03.10.97	Jamaica [WCq]	Washington DC	1-1	
10.02.98	Brazil [Concacaf GC]	Los Angeles	1-0	
15.02.98	Mexico [Concacaf GC]	Los Angeles	0-1	
21.02.98	Holland	Miami	0-2	
25.02.98	Belgium	Brussels	0-2	
22.04.98	Austria	Vienna	3-0	
16.05.98	Macedonia	San Jose, Cal	0-0	
23.05.98	Kuwait	Portland, Or	2-0	
30.05.98	Scotland	Washington DC	0-0	
15.06.98	Germany [WCf]	Paris	0-2	
21.06.98	Iran [WCf]	Lyon	1-2	
12.06.99	Argentina	Washington DC	1-0	

[Also capped beforehand while with University of Portland and Millwall, and subsequently while out of contract and with Rayo Vallecano. Career total: 49 caps to date. Plus 3 apps in Olympic football.]

WALES

Mal Griffiths [11 caps; 2 goals]

16.04.47	N Ireland	Belfast	1-2	
15.05.49	Portugal	Lisbon	2-3	
23.05.49	Belgium	Liege	1-3	
15.10.49	England [WCq]	Cardiff	1-4	(1 gl)
09.11.49	Scotland [WCq]	Glasgow	0-2	
23.11.49	Belgium	Cardiff	5-1	
15.11.50	England	Roker Park	2-4	

07.03.51	N Ireland	Belfast	2-1	
12.05.51	Portugal	Cardiff	2-1	(1 gl)
16.05.51	Switzerland	Wrexham	3-2	
09.05.54	Austria	Vienna	0-2	

Robbie James [2 caps]

09.09.87	Denmark [ECq]	Cardiff	1-0
14.10.87	Denmark [ECq]	Copenhagen	0-1

[Also capped beforehand while with Swansea City, Stoke City and Queens Park Rangers, and subsequently while with Swansea City. Career total: 47 caps; 8 goals.]

Dai Jones [7 caps]

04.11.33	N Ireland	Belfast	1-1
15.11.33	England	Newcastle	2-1
29.09.34	England	Cardiff	0-4
21.11.34	Scotland	Aberdeen	2-3
05.02.36	England	Molineux	2-1
11.03.36	N Ireland	Belfast	2-3
17.03.37	N Ireland	Wrexham	4-1

Dick Jones [1 cap]

19.03.1898	Scotland	Motherwell	2-5

Matthew Jones [3 caps to date]

24.03.01	Armenia [WCq]	Yerevan	2-2	(sub)
28.03.01	Ukraine [WCq]	Cardiff	1-1	
02.06.01	Poland [WCq]	Cardiff	1-2	(sub)

[Also capped beforehand while with Leeds United. Career total: 8 caps to date.]

Ken Leek [6 caps; 2 goals]

22.10.60	Scotland	Cardiff	2-0	
23.11.60	England	Wembley	1-5	(1 gl)
12.04.61	N Ireland	Belfast	5-1	(1 gl)
19.04.61	Spain [WCq]	Cardiff	1-2	
18.05.61	Spain [WCq]	Madrid	1-1	
28.05.61	Hungary	Budapest	2-3	

[Also capped subsequently while with Newcastle United, Birmingham City and Northampton Town. Career total: 13 caps; 5 goals.]

Arthur Lever [1 cap]

18.10.52	Scotland	Cardiff	1-2

Tommy Mills [2 caps]

29.09.34	England	Cardiff	0-4
21.11.34	Scotland	Aberdeen	2-3

[Also capped beforehand while with Clapton Orient. Career total: 4 caps; 1 goal.]

Iwan Roberts [3 caps]

20.04.94	Sweden	Wrexham	0-2	
07.09.94	Albania [ECq]	Cardiff	2-0	(sub)
12.10.94	Moldova [ECq]	Kishinev	2-3	

[Also capped beforehand while with Watford and Huddersfield Town, and subsequently while with Norwich City. Career total: 12 caps to date]

Peter Rodrigues [16 caps]

30.03.66	N Ireland	Cardiff	1-4
14.05.66	Brazil	Rio de Janeiro	1-3
18.05.66	Brazil	Belo Horizonte	0-1
22.05.66	Chile	Santiago	0-2
22.10.66	Scotland [ECq]	Cardiff	1-1
21.10.67	England [ECq]	Cardiff	0-3
22.11.67	Scotland [ECq]	Glasgow	2-3
28.02.68	N Ireland [ECq]	Wrexham	2-0
16.04.69	E. Germany [WCq]	Dresden	1-2
07.05.69	England	Wembley	1-2
10.05.69	N Ireland	Belfast	0-0
28.07.69	Rest of UK	Cardiff	0-1
22.10.69	E. Germany [WCq]	Cardiff	1-3
18.04.70	England	Cardiff	1-1
22.04.70	Scotland	Glasgow	0-0
25.04.70	N Ireland	Swansea	1-0

[Also capped beforehand while with Cardiff City, and subsequently while with Sheffield Wednesday. Career total: 40 caps.]

Robbie Savage [15 caps; 1 goal to date]

20.08.97	Turkey [WCq]	Istanbul	4-6	(1 gl)
11.10.97	Belgium [WCq]	Brussels	2-3	
25.03.98	Jamaica	Cardiff	0-0	
06.06.98	Tunisia	Tunis	0-4	
05.09.98	Italy [ECq]	Anfield	0-2	(sub)
10.10.98	Denmark [ECq]	Copenhagen	2-1	
14.10.98	Belarus [ECq]	Cardiff	3-2	
31.03.99	Switzerland [ECq]	Zurich	0-2	
09.10.99	Switzerland [ECq]	Wrexham	0-2	
29.03.00	Finland	Cardiff	1-2	
23.05.00	Brazil	Cardiff	0-3	
02.09.00	Belarus [WCq]	Minsk	1-2	
07.10.00	Norway [WCq]	Cardiff	1-1	
11.10.00	Poland [WCq]	Warsaw	0-0	
02.06.01	Poland [WCq]	Cardiff	1-2	

[Also capped beforehand while with Crewe Alexandra. Career total: 20 caps; 1 goal to date.]

Alf Watkins [2 caps]

19.03.1898	Scotland	Motherwell	2-5
28.03.1898	England	Wrexham	0-3

[Also capped subsequently while with Aston Villa and Millwall. Career total: 5 caps.]

Others to have won **FULL INTERNATIONAL CAPS** only before and/or after playing senior football for Leicester Fosse/City:
Australia: Steve Corica. **Denmark:** Tommy Christensen. **England:** Jack Bamber, Billy Bannister, Jeff Blockley, Jack Bowers, Gary Charles, Allan Clarke, Tommy Clay, Stan Collymore, Tony Cottee, Laurie Cunningham, Terry Fenwick, Tim Flowers, Jack Froggatt, Billy Garraty, Jack Haines, George Harrison, Ricky Hill, Percy Humphreys, Jack Lee, Johnny Morris, David Nish, Russell Osman, Don Revie, Charles Richards, Alan Smith. **Ireland:** Jim Macauley, Johnny Mercer, Tommy Shanks. **Italy:** Roberto Mancini. **Jamaica:** Jamie Lawrence. **Nigeria:** Ade Akinbiyi. **Norway:** Kjetil Osvold. **Republic of Ireland:** Pat Byrne, Peter Eccles, Jimmy Holmes, Mick Kennedy, David Langan, Joe Waters. **Scotland:** Willie Bell, Jimmy Blessington, Kenny Campbell, Allan Evans, Mike Galloway, Billy Hughes, Danny Liddle, Dave McCulloch, Billy McKinlay, Sandy McLaren, Charlie Miller, Jim Paterson, David Speedie, Nicky Walker, Peter Weir, Andrew Whitelaw. **South Africa:** Aubrey Mandy. **USA:** Sandy Wood. **Wales:** Albert Hodgkinson, Eugene O'Callaghan, Maurice Parry, Harry Trainer.

Others to have won **FULL INTERNATIONAL CAPS** only before and/or after playing non-senior football for Leicester Fosse/City (ie. wartime, reserve, trial or friendly matches):
Belgium: Honoré Vlaminck. **Canada:** Geoff Aunger. **Denmark:** Søren Frederiksen. **England:** Raich Carter, Ted Drake, Eric Houghton, Joe Johnson, Harry Johnston, Tommy Lawton, Jimmy Mullen, Jesse Pennington, Tommy Roberts, Les Smith, Freddie Steele, Billy Wright. **Germany:** Dietmar Beiersdorfer, Edwin Dutton. **Holland:** Pieter Huistra. **Iceland:** Petur Petursson, Arni Sveinsson. **Jamaica:** Dean Sewell. **Nigeria:** Mobi Oparaku. **Northern Ireland:** Alan Fettis, Ian Stewart. **Poland:** Dariusz Adamczuk. **Scotland:** Andy Beattie, Jimmy Blair, Alec Donaldson, Bobby Ferguson, Patsy Gallacher, George Paterson, Billy Steel. **Slovakia:** Vladimir Kinder. **Spain:** Emilio Aldecoa. **Sweden:** Helge Ekroth, Karl Gustafsson, Hakan Sandberg. **USA:** Terry Springthorpe. **Wales:** Les Jones, Doug Witcomb. **Yugoslavia:** Branko Miljus.

UNOFFICIAL INTERNATIONALS

Arthur Chandler

15.06.29	Test Match	FA XI v South Africa		
	Durban	3-2	(2 goals)	
13.07.29	Test Match	FA XI v South Africa		
	Jo'burg	2-1	(2 goals)	
17.07.29	Test Match	FA XI v South Africa		
	Cape Town	3-1	(2 goals)	

Allan Clarke

04.06.69	Unofficial	England v Mexico		
	Guadalajara	4-0	(2 goals)	

Peter Shilton

04.06.69	Unofficial	England v Mexico	
	Guadalajara	4-0	

Sep Smith

21.08.35	Jubilee Int'l	England v Scotland	
	Glasgow	2-4	(sub)

Frank Soo

20.10.45	Victory Int'l	England v Wales	
	Hawthorns	0-1	

[Also appeared beforehand in seven wartime internationals while with Stoke City.]

'B' INTERNATIONALS

ENGLAND

Steve Guppy

10.02.98	Chile	The Hawthorns	1-2	(sub)

Walter Harrison

15.05.49	Finland	Helsinki	4-0	
18.05.49	Holland	Amsterdam	4-0	

Emile Heskey

10.02.98	Chile	The Hawthorns	1-2	(1 gl)

Arthur Rowley

21.03.56	Switzerland	The Dell	4-1	(1 gl)

Steve Sims

30.05.78	Malaysia	Kuala Lumpur	1-1	

REPUBLIC OF IRELAND

David Kelly

27.03.90	England	Cork	4-1	(1 pen)

[Also appeared at this level subsequently, while with Newcastle United.]

SCOTLAND

Johnny Anderson

03.03.54	England	Roker Park	1-1	

Gary McAllister

29.04.87	France	Pittodrie	1-1	(1 gl)
27.03.90	Yugoslavia	Fir Park	0-0	

Ian Wilson

29.04.87	France	Pittodrie	1-1	

WALES

Iwan Roberts

02.02.94	Scotland	Wrexham	2-1	(1 gl)

Other **'B' INTERNATIONALS** who played senior football for Leicester City either before or after being capped at that level:
England: Kevin Campbell, Laurie Cunningham, Colin Gibson, Bob Hazell, Stan Milburn, Johnny Morris, Mike Newell, Russell Osman, Garry Parker, Don Revie, Alan Smith. **Northern Ireland:** Derek Dougan, Neil Lennon, Jimmy Quinn. **Republic of Ireland:** Martin Russell. **Scotland:** Joe Baillie, Willie Gardiner, Bernie Kelly, Tom McDonald, Billy McKinlay, Nicky Walker. **Wales:** Matthew Jones.

AMATEUR INTERNATIONALS

UNITED KINGDOM (Olympic Games)

Horace Bailey

20.10.08	Sweden	White City	12-1	
22.10.08	Holland	White City	4-0	
24.10.08	Denmark [Final]	White City	2-0	

Douglas McWhirter

04.07.12	Denmark [Final]	Stockholm	4-2	

ENGLAND

Horace Bailey

22.02.08	Wales	Edgeley Park	1-0	
23.03.08	France	Park Royal	12-0	
18.03.09	Germany	Oxford	9-0	

[Also appeared once subsequently while with Birmingham.]

Ronald Brebner

08.11.13	Ireland	Belfast	2-0	
15.11.13	Holland	Anlaby Rd, Hull	2-1	

[Also appeared 21 times beforehand while with Darlington, Northern Nomads, Huddersfield Town and Chelsea. Plus 3 Olympic Games apps.]

George Douglas

21.03.13	Germany	Berlin	3-0	(2 gls)
24.03.13	Holland	The Hague	1-2	

Jimmy Harrold

27.02.13	France	Paris	4-1	

[Also appeared once beforehand while with Custom House.]

Douglas McWhirter

03.10.12	Ireland	Belfast	2-3	
21.03.13	Germany	Berlin	3-0	
24.03.13	Holland	The Hague	1-2	

[Also appeared once beforehand while with Bromley.]

Sydney Owen

06.11.09	Sweden	Anlaby Rd, Hull	7-0	(3 gls)
20.11.09	Ireland	Leeds	4-4	(1 gl)
11.12.09	Holland	Stamford Bridge	9-1	(1 gl)
26.03.10	Belgium	Brussels	2-2	(1 gl)
19.11.10	Ireland	Belfast	2-3	

Other **AMATEUR INTERNATIONALS** who played senior football for Leicester Fosse/City before or after being capped at that level:
England: Len Barry, Fred Milnes, Reg Osborne.
Ireland: Jim Macauley. **Northern Ireland:** Derek Dougan. **Scotland:** Willie Bell, Max Dougan, Billy McDerment, Bob Noble, Jack Roxburgh.
[City reserve Jim Mitchell was also an England Amateur International].

FOOTBALL LEAGUE

Hughie Adcock

02.11.29	Scottish League	Ibrox	1-2	

Colin Appleton

31.10.62	Irish League	Carrow Road 3-1	

Gordon Banks

01.11.61	Irish League	Belfast	6-1	
31.10.62	Irish League	Carrow Road	3-1	
09.05.64	Italian League	Milan	0-1	(sub)
27.10.65	League of Ireland	Boothferry Pk	5-0	

[Also appeared twice subsequently while with Stoke City.]

Sid Bishop

10.03.28	Scottish League	Ibrox	6-2	

Arthur Chandler

19.03.27	Scottish League	Filbert St	2-2	

Ernie Hine

09.10.26	Irish League	Belfast	6-1	
07.11.28	Scottish League	Villa Park	2-1	(1 gl)
25.09.29	Irish League	Goodison Pk	7-2	(1 gl)
02.11.29	Scottish League	Ibrox	1-2	

[Also appeared once subsequently while with Huddersfield Town.]

Derek Hogg

26.10.55	Scottish League	Hillsborough	4-2	

Tony Knapp

23.03.60	Scottish League	Highbury	1-0	

David Nish

23.09.70	Irish League	Carrow Road	5-0	
22.09.71	League of Ireland	Dublin	2-1	
15.03.72	Scottish League	Ayresome Pk	3-2	

[Also appeared twice subsequently while with Derby County.]

Arthur Rowley

31.10.56	Irish League	St James's Pk	3-2	

Peter Shilton

23.09.70	Irish League	Carrow Road	5-0	
27.03.73	Scottish League	Hampden Pk	2-2	

[Also appeared twice subsequently while with Stoke City and Derby County].

Sep Smith

30.10.35	Scottish League	Ibrox	2-2	

Keith Weller

27.03.73	Scottish League	Hampden Pk	2-2	

Frank Worthington

27.03.73	Scottish League	Hampden Pk	2-2	

Other players to have appeared in representative **INTER-LEAGUE** games either before or after playing at senior level for Leicester Fosse/City:
Football League: Jack Bamber, Billy Bannister, Jeff Blockley, Jack Bowers, Allan Clarke, Tommy Clay, Billy Dorrell, Jack Froggatt, Percy Humphreys, Stan Milburn, Johnny Morris, Don Revie, Billy Rowley, Jon Sammels, Alan Smith, Walter Smith, George Swift.
Irish League: Mick Cochrane, James Macauley, Owen McNally, John Mercer, Martin Russell, Arthur Worrall.
League of Ireland: Pat Byrne, Tommy Godwin.
Scottish League: Joe Baillie, Jimmy Blessington, Kenny Campbell, Herbert Dainty, Harry Graham, Bernie Kelly, Dave McCulloch, Peter McKennan, Jimmy Melrose, Bobby Roberts, Gregor Stevens.
Southern League (pre-1920): Sep Atterbury, Harry Moody, Arthur Trueman, Harry Wilcox.

Additionally, Mick O'Brien represented the Football League v The Army, Jimmy Goodfellow played for the Scottish League v Scotland, Bob Gordon assisted the Southern League v London FA, and Peter McKennan twice appeared for the (wartime) Northern Ireland Regional League v the League of Ireland. Gary Lineker played for the Rest of the World against the Football League in the latter's 1987 Centenary match. Former Fosse and City reserves *Arthur Leonard Bamford, Billy Lavery, Gerry McCaffrey, Tommy Thompson* (all Irish League) and *Ted Leahy* (Welsh League), also appeared in senior Inter-League fare.

City players called up for the representative XIs of the London Combination and Football Combination (against other leagues, or in annual games versus League XIs from Holland and Belgium) included Johnny Anderson, Colin Appleton, Gordon Banks, George Carr, George Dewis, Billy Findlay, Johnny Grogan and Arthur Rowley.

UNDER-23 INTERNATIONALS

ENGLAND

Gordon Banks

08.02.61	Wales	Goodison Park	2-0
01.03.61	Scotland	Ayresome Park	0-1

Allan Clarke

16.04.69	Portugal	Highfield Rd	4-0 (2 gls)

[Also appeared five times beforehand while with Fulham.]

Graham Cross

21.03.63	Yugoslavia	Old Trafford	0-0
29.05.63	Yugoslavia	Belgrade	4-2 (1 pen)
02.06.63	Romania	Bucharest	0-1
13.11.63	Wales	Ashton Gate	1-1
27.11.63	West Germany	Anfield	4-1
05.02.64	Scotland	St James's Pk	3-2
08.04.64	France	Rouen	2-2
13.05.64	Hungary	Budapest	1-2
17.05.64	Israel	Tel Aviv	4-0
20.05.64	Turkey	Istanbul	0-3
20.04.66	Turkey	Ewood Park	2-0

David Nish

16.04.69	Portugal	Highfield Road	4-0 (sub)
25.05.69	Belgium	Ostend	1-0
28.05.69	Portugal	Funchal	1-1
01.10.69	Wales	Ashton Gate	2-0
22.10.69	USSR	Old Trafford	2-0
04.03.70	Scotland	Roker Park	3-1
		[aband 62m]	
08.04.70	Bulgaria	Home Park	4-1 (1 gl)
11.11.70	Sweden	Boothferry Pk	2-0
02.12.70	Wales	Wrexham	0-0
24.02.71	Scotland	Hampden Park	2-2

Howard Riley

23.04.58	Wales	Wrexham	1-2
08.02.61	Wales	Goodison Park	2-0

Dennis Rofe

01.06.73	Czechoslovakia	Bratislava	0-3 (sub)

Peter Shilton

02.10.68	Wales	Wrexham	3-1
13.11.68	Holland	St Andrews	2-2
16.04.69	Portugal	Highfield Road	4-0
22.05.69	Holland	Deventer	1-2
28.05.69	Portugal	Funchal	1-1
01.10.69	Wales	Ashton Gate	2-0
04.03.70	Scotland	Roker Park	3-1
		[aband 62m]	
08.04.70	Bulgaria	Home Park	4-1
14.10.70	West Germany	Filbert Street	3-1

24.11.71	Switzerland	Portman Road	1-1
01.06.72	East Germany	Leipzig	2-2
04.06.72	Poland	Warsaw	3-0
07.06.72	USSR	Kiev	0-0

Mark Wallington

10.03.76	Hungary	Budapest	0-3
23.03.76	Hungary	Old Trafford	3-1

Steve Whitworth

24.11.71	Switzerland	Portman Road	1-1
05.01.72	Wales	County Grd, Swindon	2-0
15.05.74	Yugoslavia	Zrenjanin	0-1
19.05.74	France	Valence	2-2
18.12.74	Scotland	Pittodrie	3-0 (1 gl)
21.01.75	Wales	Wrexham	2-0

NORTHERN IRELAND

Gerry McCaffrey

27.02.63	Wales	Vetch Field	1-5

SCOTLAND

Frank McLintock

28.02.62	England	Pittodrie	2-4

Other **UNDER-23 INTERNATIONALS** who played in senior football for Leicester City before or after being capped at that level:

England: George Armstrong, Alan Birchenall, Jeff Blockley, Albert Cheesebrough, Roger Davies, John Farmer, Chris Garland, Steve Kember, Jon Sammels, Frank Worthington. **Northern Ireland:** Neil Lennon, Gerry Taggart. **Republic of Ireland:** David Kelly, Martin Russell. **Scotland:** Brian Alderson, Eddie Kelly, Andy Lochhead, Bobby Roberts, Nick Sharkey, Jimmy Walsh. **Wales:** Ken Leek, Peter Rodrigues.

UNDER-21 INTERNATIONALS

ENGLAND

Ian Andrews

09.09.86	Sweden	Ostersund	1-1
		(over-age player)	

Trevor Benjamin

24.05.01	Mexico	Filbert Street	3-0 (sub)

Steve Guppy

24.03.98	Switzerland	Aarau	0-2
		(over-age player)	

Emile Heskey

08.10.96	Poland	Molineux	0-0
12.02.97	Italy	Ashton Gate	1-0
29.04.97	Georgia	The Valley	0-0
30.05.97	Poland	Katowice	1-1 (1 gl)
10.10.97	Italy	Rieti	1-0
13.11.97	Greece	Iraklion, Crete	0-2
17.12.97	Greece	Carrow Road	4-2 (2 gls)
24.03.98	Switzerland	Aarau	0-2
14.05.98	France	Nimes	1-1 (1 gl)
16.05.98	South Africa	Aubagne	3-1 (2 gls)
18.05.98	Argentina	Manosque	0-2
04.09.98	Sweden	Sundsvall	2-0
09.10.98	Bulgaria	Upton Park	1-0
13.10.98	Luxembourg	Grevenmacher	5-0
03.09.99	Luxembourg	Madejski, Reading	5-0

[Also appeared once subsequently while with Liverpool.]

Julian Joachim

08.03.94	Denmark	Griffin Park	1-0 (sub)
06.09.94	Portugal	Filbert Street	0-0
11.10.94	Austria	Kapfenberg	3-1

Above: Julian Joachim in action for England Under-21s against Portugal at Filbert Street in September 1994.

15.11.94	Rep Ireland	St James's Park	1-0
06.06.95	Brazil	Toulon	0-2
08.06.95	Malaysia	Toulon	2-0 (1 gl)
10.06.95	Angola	Toulon	1-0
12.06.95	France	Toulon	0-2
10.10.95	Norway	Stavanger	2-2

Paul Kitson

27.05.91	Senegal	Toulon	2-1 (sub)
29.05.91	Mexico	Toulon	6-0 (1 gl)
03.06.91	France	Toulon	1-0
12.11.91	Poland	Pila	1-2 (1 gl)

[Also appeared three times subsequently while with Derby County.]

Simon Morgan

09.09.86	Sweden	Ostersund	1-1
11.11.86	Yugoslavia	London Rd, P'boro	1-1

Carl Muggleton

23.05.90	France	Toulon	7-3

Andy Peake

07.04.82	Poland	Upton Park	2-2

Steve Sims

15.12.76	Wales	Molineux	0-0
27.04.77	Scotland	Bramall Lane	1-0
26.05.77	Finland	Helsinki	1-0
01.06.77	Norway	Bergen	2-1
06.09.77	Norway	Goldstone Grd	6-0
12.10.77	Finland	Boothferry Park	8-1 (1 gl)
08.03.78	Italy	Maine Road	2-1
05.04.78	Italy	Rome	0-0
19.04.78	Yugoslavia	Novi Sad	1-2 (1 og)
02.05.78	Yugoslavia	Maine Road	1-1

NORTHERN IRELAND

John O'Neill

08.03.78	Rep Ireland	Dublin	1-1

REPUBLIC OF IRELAND

Damien Delaney

05.06.01	Estonia	Tallinn	3-0

Martin Russell

28.04.87	Belgium	Dublin	1-1

[Also appeared once beforehand while with Manchester United.]

Stuart Campbell

24.03.98	Denmark	Stirling	1-2
21.04.98	Finland	Kirkcaldy	1-1 (sub)
18.05.98	Rep Ireland	Ballybofey	0-3
20.05.98	N Ireland	Sligo	1-1 (sub)
23.05.98	Italy	Castel di Sangro	0-4
04.09.98	Lithuania	Vilnius	0-0
09.10.98	Estonia	Airdrie	2-0
14.10.98	Belgium	Ghent	0-2
18.11.98	Belgium	Paisley	2-2
30.03.99	Czech Rep.	Fir Park	0-1
27.04.99	Germany	Meppen	1-2
31.05.99	Rep Ireland	Elgin	1-0
04.06.99	N Ireland	Inverness	1-1
08.06.99	Czech Rep.	Teplice	2-3 (sub)
04.09.99	Bosnia	Lukavac	5-2 (sub)

Gary McAllister

14.11.89	Norway	Perth	2-0
		(over-age player)	

Other **UNDER-21 INTERNATIONALS** who played in senior football for Leicester City before or after being capped at that level:
Australia: Steve Corica. **Denmark:** Tommy Christensen. **England:** Mark Blake, Kevin Campbell, Franz Carr, Gary Charles, Tony Cottee, Richard Cresswell, Laurie Cunningham, Mich D'Avray, Mark Draper, Darren Eadie, Graham Fenton, Terry Fenwick, Tim Flowers, Colin Gibson, Bob Hazell, Andrew Impey, David Lowe, Lee Marshall, Gary Mills, Steve Moran, Mike Newell, Scott Oakes, David Oldfield, Russell Osman, Garry Parker, Mark Robins.
Finland: Jari Rantanen. **France:** Pegguy Arphexad.
Italy: Roberto Mancini. **Greece:** Theo Zagorakis.
Northern Ireland: Neil Lennon. **Norway:** Kjetil Osvold. **Republic of Ireland:** Brian Carey, David Kelly. **Scotland:** Callum Davidson, Mike Galloway, Lee Glover, Billy McKinlay, Jimmy Melrose, Charlie Miller, David Speedie, Gregor Stevens, Tommy Wright.
Sweden: Pontus Kåmark. **USA:** Kasey Keller.
Wales: Robbie James, Matthew Jones, Robbie Savage.
[Additionally, unused City subs Stuart Slater (England) and Lars-Gunnar Carlstrand (Sweden) were Under-21 internationals].

Above: John O'Neill.

INTERNATIONAL TRIALS & MISCELLANEOUS SENIOR REPRESENTATIVE HONOURS

Hughie Adcock

12.03.30	England v The Rest	Anfield	1-6

Andy Aitken

21.03.10	Anglo Scots v Home Scots	Ibrox	4-0

Colin Appleton

04.10.61	FA XI v RAF	
	London Road, Peterborough	13-0

Horace Bailey

10.02.08	North v South (Amateur Int'l trial)	
	Stamford Bridge	1-1

Gordon Banks

21.09.60	England Under-23 v Vejle BK	
	Maine Road	5-1
19.10.60	FA XI v The Army Hillsborough	2-1
01.05.64	England v Young England	
	Stamford Bridge	3-0
30.04.65	England v Young England	
	Highbury	2-2

Len Barry

28.09.31	FA XI v Sheff Wed/Sheff Utd XI	
	Hillsborough	0-1

Sid Bishop

23.01.28	England v The Rest	
	The Hawthorns	5-1
08.02.28	England v The Rest	
	Ayresome Park	8-3

Adam Black

20.03.23	Anglo Scots v Home Scots	
	Cathkin Park	1-1

Ronald Brebner

06.10.13	Amateurs v Professionals (FA ChSh)	
	The Den	2-7

Ally Brown

10.01.72	Scotland U-23 v W Germany Olympic XI	
	Hampden Park	1-0

Arthur Chandler

19.01.25	The North v The South	
	Stamford Bridge	1-3 (1 gl)
07.02.27	The Rest v England	
	Burnden Park	3-2 (1 gl)
04.02.29	The Rest v England	
	Hillsborough	3-4 (1 gl)
07.10.29	Professionals v Amateurs (FAChSh)	
	The Den	3-0 (1 gl)

Graham Cross

01.05.64	Young England v England	
	Stamford Bridge	0-3
13.05.66	Young England v England	
	Stamford Bridge	1-1

Willie Cunningham

20.11.57	Irish FA v British Army	
	Elland Road	1-2

John Duncan

17.03.25	Scotland A XI v Scotland B XI	
	Shawfield	0-0
13.03.28	Anglo Scots v Home Scots	
	Firhill	1-1

Billy Henry

20.03.11	Anglo Scots v Home Scots	
	Cathkin Park	0-0

Ernie Hine

08.02.28	The Rest v England	
	Ayresome Park	3-8 (1 gl)
10.10.28	FA XI v Lancashire FA	
	Burnden Park	5-6 (1 gl)
04.02.29	England v The Rest	
	Hillsborough	4-3 (1 gl)
11.03.29	England v The Rest	
	White Hart Lane	1-2
12.03.30	England v The Rest	
	Anfield	1-6
28.09.31	FA XI v Sheff Wed/Sheff Utd XI	
	Hillsborough	0-1

Derek Hines

14.10.53	FA XI v RAF	
	White Hart Lane	4-0
30.04.54	Young England v England	
	Highbury	1-2 (1 gl)
06.05.55	Young England v England	
	Stamford Bridge	0-5

Derek Hogg

07.11.56	FA XI v The Army	
	Maine Road	7-3

Kasey Keller

09.06.98	USA v Gueugnon	
	Gueugnon (Fr)	4-0 (sub)

David Kelly

12.05.91	Rep Ireland XI v Celtic	
	Parkhead	2-3 (1 gl)

Johnny King

26.10.49	FA XI v RAF	
	Craven Cottage	2-1

Paul Kitson

04.03.92	F Lge Div 2 v Italian Serie B	
	Caserta	1-2 (1 gl)

Arthur Lochhead

13.02.28	Anglo Scots v Home Scots	
	Firhill	1-1

Frank McLintock

18.01.61	Scotland U-23 v 2nd Division XI	
	Brockville	10-2
13.02.61	Scotland U-23 v The Army	
	Fir Park	3-2
05.02.62	Scotland v Scottish League	
	Hampden Park	2-2
24.02.64	Scotland v Scottish League	
	Ibrox	3-1

Stan Milburn

--.11.52	FA XI v Cambridge University	
	Cambridge	8-0

Andy Mills

16.02.03	Whites v Stripes (Welsh trial)	
	Wrexham	4-4

John O'Neill

22.06.80	N Ireland v Western Australia	
	Perth	4-0 (1 gl)

Reg Osborne

23.01.28	England v The Rest	
	The Hawthorns	5-1
08.02.28	England v The Rest	
	Ayresome Park	8-3

Sydney Owen

01.02.09	North v South (Amateur Int'l trial)	
	Villa Park	2-5
31.01.10	Whites v Stripes	
	Anfield	1-1 (1 gl)

Jock Paterson
31.03.20 Anglo Scots v Home Scots
Cathkin Park   1-2   (1 gl)

Frank Sinclair
19.11.98 Jamaica v Botafogo
Kingston   1-1

Sep Smith
25.03.36 Possibles v Probables
Old Trafford   0-3

Frank Soo
06.04.46 FA XI v Army PT Corps
Wembley   4-5

Billy Webb
07.11.51 FA XI v The Army
Highbury   4-2

FA XI OVERSEAS TOURS

Colin Appleton
1961   Far East & New Zealand
        [apps n/k; 2 goals]

Len Barry
1931   Canada [14 apps; 7 goals]

Arthur Chandler
1929   South Africa [16 apps; 33 goals]

Ernie Hine
1931   Canada [12 apps; 20 goals]

Reg Osborne
1929   South Africa [2 apps; 0 goals]

Others to have toured abroad with FA Representative XI's before playing senior football for Leicester City: Jack Bamber, Albert Harrison, Stan Milburn, Eddie Russell, Keith Weller.

BRITISH ARMY REPRESENTATIVE HONOURS [PEACETIME]

Johnny Anderson
1950/1 (incl v) Essex, Queens Park Rangers, French Army.
1951/2 (incl v) Irish FA, Aston Villa, Everton, Aberdeen, FA XI, Belgian Army, Scottish FA, Royal Navy.

Colin Appleton
1957/8 (incl v) Portuguese Army, Aston Villa, FA XI, Irish FA.

Gordon Fincham
1953/4 (incl v) Plymouth Argyle.

Davie Gibson
1961/2 (incl v) Coventry City, French Army, Royal Navy, Belgian Army, Hong Kong XI.

Derek Hines
1952/3 (incl v) Irish FA, Everton, Aston Villa, FA XI, Brighton & Hove Albion, Scottish FA, RAF, Belgian Army, Sturm Graz.
1953/4 (incl v) Everton, FA XI, Exeter City.

Howard Riley
1957/8 (incl v) Watford.
1958/9 (incl v) French Army, Royal Navy, Irish FA, Belgian Army, RAF.

Billy Webb
1952/3 (incl v) Everton, Aston Villa, FA XI, Brighton & Hove Albion, Royal Navy, Belgian Army.

YOUTH INTERNATIONALS

[Italicised names are players who failed subsequently to graduate to senior football with Leicester City.]

ENGLAND

Ian Andrews, Oliver Beeby, David Buchanan, Ron Burbeck, *Martyn Capewell*, Graham Cross, *Keith Haines*, Emile Heskey, *Ken Hincks*, Derek Hines, Phil Horner, Julian Joachim, *Ralph Lockwood*, Malcolm Munro, David Nish, *Michael Oakes*, *John Pawley*, Andy Peake, Jason Peake, Howard Riley, *Jeremy Roberts*, Peter Shilton, Jordan Stewart, Barrie Thomas, Reg Warner, Steve Whitworth, *Richard Wilcox*, *Brian Wright*.

NORTHERN IRELAND

Steve Convey, Paul Emerson, Martin Linton, *Maurice Livingstone*, Tim McCann.

REPUBLIC OF IRELAND

Tony Brien, Gary Fitzpatrick, Robert Kelly, *Tom Kilkelly*, Joe Waters, *Alan Weldrick*.

SCOTLAND

Ally Brown, *Paul Crawford*, Paul Friar, Malcolm Manley, David Rennie, Nicky Walker.

WALES

Robbie Jones.

FOOTBALL LEAGUE U-18

Ian Baraclough, Paul Kitson.

UEFA INTERNATIONAL YOUTH TOURNAMENT FINALISTS

Peter Shilton	1967	England v USSR Istanbul	0-1
Andy Peake	1980	England v Poland Leipzig	2-1
David Rennie	1982	Scotland v Czechoslovakia Helsinki	3-1
Julian Joachim	1993	England v Turkey Nottingham	1-0

[Jon Sammels, Peter Eastoe and Tom English also represented England in the Final of this competition – in 1963, 1971 and 1980 respectively – before joining Leicester City].

SEMI PROFESSIONAL INTERNATIONALS

Before City: Steve Guppy, Alan Smith.
After City: David Buchanan, *Robert Codner*, Paul Culpin, Steve Holden, *Steve Humphries*, *Brendan Phillips*, Steve Prindiville.

The Nearly Men: Syd Owen, Arthur Maw and Tony Knapp came the closest to a full England cap without eventually being so honoured. Owen impressed in the international trial game of 1910 and was named reserve forward for the match against Wales in March 1910. Maw was sole travelling reserve for the fixture v Northern Ireland in October 1933 (as he had been weeks earlier for the Football League's fixture against the Irish League), while Knapp was four times a travelling reserve in 1960 for England's games with Yugoslavia, Spain, Hungary and Luxemburg. He'd previously twice held this frustrating role for the Under-23 clashes with Hungary and Scotland. Derek Hines was chosen as reserve to the England B team to face Holland in March 1952, and Russell Hoult was an unused substitute for England Under-21 in their games with Norway, Turkey and San Marino during 1992/3.

Two players capped for their countries prior to joining Leicester were selected for internationals while on the club's books, but failed to appear. Tommy Shanks was refused permission by Fosse to honour his Ireland call-up to face Wales in April 1908 (instead scoring in a key promotion battle against Barnsley); while Gene O'Callaghan – along with Dai Jones – preferred to assist City against Doncaster Rovers rather than Wales v Scotland in October 1935.

Captains: Fosse's Andy Aitken and City's Kasey Keller, Theo Zagorakis, Neil Lennon and Gerry Taggart each skippered their countries while on the club's books. Sid Bishop was the only Leicester player chosen to captain England, but had to withdraw through illness from the side to face Scotland in March 1928. After leaving Filbert Street, Gary Lineker led England on 18 occasions, and Peter Shilton on 15.

Managers: The following City managers represented their countries in full internationals during their playing careers – England: Tom Bromilow, Norman Bullock, Brian Little, Gordon Milne, Peter Taylor. Northern Ireland: Bryan Hamilton, Martin O'Neill. Republic of Ireland: Frank O'Farrell. Scotland: John Duncan, Mark McGhee, Frank McLintock, Willie Orr.

Most in one side: Three City men – Peter Shilton, Keith Weller and Frank Worthington – lined up together for England in the 1974 games against Northern Ireland, Scotland and Argentina. The recently-transferred David Nish also featured in the first two of these fixtures.

Most caps (with LCFC): John O'Neill 39
Most caps (career): Peter Shilton 125
Most int'l goals (with LCFC): Ernie Hine 4
Most int'l goals (career): Gary Lineker 48

LANDMARKS / MILESTONES

GOALS:

FL:	1000th:	James Proctor	v Birmingham (A)	18.01.1913	1-5	
	2000th:	Ernie Hine	v Everton (A)	28.11.1931	2-9	
	3000th:	Mal Griffiths	v Stoke City (H)	07.09.1953	4-0	
	4000th:	Jimmy Goodfellow	v Sheffield Wed. (A)	08.01.1966	2-1	
	5000th:	David Rennie	v Coventry City (H)	23.12.1984	5-1	
FAC:	500th:	Garry Parker (pen)	v Norwich C. (H)	25.01.1997	2-1	
FLC:	200th:	Ian Marshall	v Crystal Palace (H)	22.09.1999	4-2	

GAMES:

FL:	1000th:	v Aston Villa (H)	10.10.1925	1-2
	2000th:	v Huddersfield Town (A)	20.08.1956	2-1
	3000th:	v Cardiff City (A)	08.04.1980	1-0
FL Wins:	1000th:	v Queens Park Rangers (H)	18.04.1970	2-1
FL Defeats:	1000th:	v West Ham United (A)	19.08.1972	2-5

MEDALLISTS

> Fosse or City players who have accrued winners' or runners-up medals from major cup competitions at some point in their careers. Unused substitutes are excluded from this list.

EUROPEAN CHAMPIONS CUP
Winners: Allan Evans (Villa 1982), Gary Mills (Forest 1980), Peter Shilton (Forest 1979 & 1980).
Runners-Up: Laurie Cunningham (Real Madrid 1981), Allan Clarke (Leeds 1975), Roberto Mancini (Sampdoria 1992).

EUROPEAN CUP WINNERS CUP
Winners: Kevin Campbell (Arsenal 1994), Gary Lineker (Barcelona 1989), Roberto Mancini (Sampdoria 1990 & Lazio 1999), Alan Smith (Arsenal 1994), David Webb (Chelsea 1971), Peter Weir (Aberdeen 1983), Keith Weller (Chelsea 1971).
Runners-Up: Roberto Mancini (Sampdoria 1989), Keith Robson (West Ham 1976).

INTER-CITIES FAIRS CUP / UEFA CUP
Winners: George Armstrong (Arsenal 1970), Allan Clarke (Leeds 1971), Paul Cooper (Ipswich 1981), Emile Heskey (Liverpool 2001), Eddie Kelly (Arsenal 1970), Gary McAllister (Liverpool 2001), Frank McLintock (Arsenal 1970), Russell Osman (Ipswich 1981), Jon Sammels (Arsenal 1970), Jackie Sinclair (Newcastle 1969).
Runners-Up: Willie Bell (Leeds 1967), Derek Dougan (Wolves 1972), Roberto Mancini (Lazio 1998).

EUROPEAN SUPER CUP
Winners: Allan Evans (Villa 1982/3), Colin Gibson (Villa 1982/3), Roberto Mancini (Lazio 1999/2000), Peter Shilton (Forest 1979/80), Peter Weir (Aberdeen 1983/4).
Runners-Up: Kevin Campbell (Arsenal 1994/5), Kevin MacDonald (Liverpool 1984/5), Roberto Mancini (Sampdoria 1990/1), Peter Shilton (Forest 1980/1).

WORLD CLUB CHAMPIONSHIP
Runners-Up: Allan Evans (Villa 1982/3), Peter Shilton (Forest 1980/1).

FA CUP
Winners: George Armstrong (Arsenal 1971), Bert Barlow (Portsmouth 1939), Archie Brash (Sheff Wed 1896), Kevin Campbell (Arsenal 1993), Allan Clarke (Leeds 1972), Tommy Clay (Spurs 1921), Paul Cooper (Ipswich 1978), Laurie Cunningham (Wimbledon 1988), Billy Garraty (Villa 1905), Emile Heskey (Liverpool 2001), Billy Hughes (Sunderland 1973), Eddie Kelly (Arsenal 1971), Gary Lineker (Spurs 1991), Gary McAllister (Liverpool 2001), Kevin MacDonald (Liverpool 1986), Roddie McLeod (WBA 1892), Frank McLintock (Arsenal 1971), Johnny Morris (Man Utd 1948), Don Revie (Man City 1956), Charles Richards (Forest 1898), Mark Robins (Man Utd 1990, drawn game only), Peter Rodrigues (Southampton 1976), Frank Sinclair (Chelsea 1997), Alan Smith (Arsenal 1993), George Swift (Wolves 1893), George Travers (Barnsley 1912), David Webb (Chelsea 1970), William Wragg (Forest 1898).
Runners-Up: Charlie Adam (1949), Andy Aitken (Newcastle 1905 & 1906), Harry Allen (Derby 1899), Colin Appleton (1961 & 1963), George Armstrong (Arsenal 1972), John Baird (Villa 1892), Gordon Banks (1961 & 1963), Willie Bell (Leeds 1965), Sid Bishop (West Ham 1923), Gordon Bradley (1949), Mark Bright (C Palace 1990 & Sheff Wed 1993), Kenny Campbell (Liverpool 1914), Len Chalmers (1961), Gary Charles (Forest 1991), Albert Cheesebrough (1961), Ken Chisholm (1949), Allan Clarke (1969 & Leeds 1970 & 1973), Stan Collymore (Liverpool 1996), Tony Cottee (Everton 1989), Graham Cross (1963 & 1969), Gerry Daly (Man Utd 1976), Derek Dougan (Blackburn 1960), Terry Fenwick (QPR 1982), Rodney Fern (1969), David Gibson (1963 & 1969), Lee Glover (Forest 1991), Len Glover (1969), Mal Griffiths (1949), Jimmy Harrison (1949), Walter Harrison (1949), Bob Hazell (Bolton 1894), Ted Jelly (1949), Julian Joachim (Villa 2000), George Jobey (Newcastle 1911), Ken Keyworth (1961 & 1963), Ian King (1961 & 1963), Johnny King (1949), Jack Lee (1949), Gary Lineker (Everton 1986), Andy Lochhead (1969), Hugh McIlmoyle (1961), Roddie McLeod (WBA 1895), Frank McLintock (1961 & 1963 & Arsenal 1972), Malcolm Manley (1969), Fred Mearns (Barnsley 1910), *Jim Mitchell* (PNE 1922), John Newman (Birmingham 1956), David Nish (1969), Richie Norman (1961 & 1963), Garry Parker (Forest 1991), Norman Plummer (1949), Dick Pudan (Newcastle 1908), Don Revie (Man City 1955), Howard Riley (1961 & 1963), Bobby Roberts (1969), Tommy Roberts (Preston 1922), Peter Rodrigues (1969), Sandy Scott (1949), Frank Sinclair (Chelsea 1994), John Sjoberg (1963), Jimmy Stevenson (Derby 1898), Alick Stewart (Everton 1897), Mike Stringfellow (1963), Jimmy Thraves (Notts Co 1891), Jimmy Walsh (1961), Ian Wilson (Everton 1989), Maurice Woodward (Wolves 1921), Alan Woollett (1969).

FOOTBALL LEAGUE CUP
Winners: Colin Appleton (1964), Gordon Banks (1964 & Stoke 1972), Kevin Campbell (Arsenal 1993), Franz Carr (Forest 1990), Gary Charles (Villa 1996), Steve Claridge (1997), Tony Cottee (2000), Graham Cross (1964), Derek Dougan (Wolves 1974), Max Dougan (1964), Mark Draper (Villa 1996), Matt Elliott (2000), Graham Fenton (Villa 1994), Tim Flowers (2000), David Gibson (1964), Simon Grayson (1997), Steve Guppy (2000), Terry Heath (1964), Trevor Hebberd (Oxford 1986), Emile Heskey (1997, 2000 & Liverpool 2001), Ricky Hill (Luton 1988), Andrew Impey (2000), Muzzy Izzet (1997 & 2000), Rob Johnson (Luton 1988), Pontus Kåmark (1997), Kasey Keller (1997), Ken Keyworth (1964), Ian King (1964), David Langan (Oxford 1986), Jamie Lawrence (1997), Ken Leek (Birmingham 1963), Neil Lennon (1997 & 2000), Gary McAllister (Liverpool 2001), Lawrie Madden (Sheff Wed 1991), Ian Marshall (2000), Richie Norman (1964), Stefan Oakes (2000), Garry Parker (Forest 1989 & 1990; City 1997), Spencer Prior (1997), Howard Riley (1964), Mark Robins (1997), Robbie Savage (2000), Peter Shilton (Forest 1979), *Malcolm Shotton* (Oxford 1986), Frank Sinclair (Chelsea 1998; City 2000), John Sjoberg (1964), Mike Stringfellow (1964), Tom Sweenie (1964), Gerry Taggart (2000), Scott Taylor (1997, drawn game only), Steve Walsh (1997), Mike Whitlow (1997).
Runners-Up: Colin Appleton (1965), George Armstrong (Arsenal 1968 & 1969), Gordon Banks (1965), Mark Bright (Sheff Wed 1993), Len Chalmers (1965), Gary Charles (Forest 1992), Tony Cottee (Everton 1989), Graham Cross (1965), Matt Elliott (1999), Terry Fenwick (QPR 1986), Chris Garland (Chelsea 1972), David Gibson (1965), Jimmy Goodfellow (1965), Steve Guppy (1999), Emile Heskey (1999), Billy Hodgson (1965), Muzzy Izzet (1999), Robbie James (QPR 1986), Kasey Keller (1999), David Kelly (Tranmere 2000), Ian King (1965), Neil Lennon (1999), Andy Lochhead (Villa 1971), Gary McAllister (Leeds 1996), Frank McLintock (Arsenal 1968 & 1969), Ian Marshall (1999), Stan Milburn (Rochdale 1962), Richie Norman (1965), Bobby Roberts (1965), Jon Sammels (Arsenal 1968 & 1969), Robbie Savage (1999), Tony Sealy (Southampton 1979), Peter Shilton (Forest 1980), John Sjoberg (1965), Alan Smith (Arsenal 1988), Mike Stringfellow (1965), Tom Sweenie (1965), Gerry Taggart (1999), Rob Ullathorne (1999), Clive Walker (1965), Steve Walsh (1999), David Webb (Chelsea 1972), Theo Zagorakis (1999).

FULL MEMBERS CUPS (incl Simod, Zenith Data Systems, etc)
Winners: Mark Bright (C Palace 1991), Franz Carr (Forest 1989) Gary Charles (Forest 1992), Garry Parker (Forest 1989), David Speedie (Chelsea 1986).
Runners-Up: Tony Cottee (Everton 1989 & 1991), Tim Flowers (Southampton 1992), Rob Johnson (Luton 1988), *Owen McGee* (Middlesbrough 1990), Jim Melrose (Charlton 1987), Mike Newell (Everton 1991), Andy Peake (Charlton 1987), *Steve Thompson* (Charlton 1987).

TEXACO CUP
Winners: Roger Davies (Derby 1971/2), Derek Dougan (Wolves 1970/1).

ANGLO-SCOTTISH CUP
Winners: John Ridley (Chesterfield 1980/1), Geoff Salmons (Chesterfield 1980/1), Peter Weir (St Mirren 1979/80).
Runners-Up: Trevor Christie (Notts Co 1980/1), Laurie Cunningham (Orient 1976/7, first leg only), Mark Goodwin (Notts Co 1980/1), Eddie Kelly (Notts Co 1980/1, first leg only), Alan Young (Oldham 1978/9).

ANGLO-ITALIAN CUP
Winners: Gary Mills (Notts Co 1994/5), Phil Turner (Notts Co 1994/5).
Runners-Up: Mark Draper (Notts Co 1993/4), Lee Glover (Port Vale 1995/6), Steve Guppy (Port Vale 1995/6), Paul Kitson (Derby 1992/3), Phil Turner (Notts Co 1993/4).

WATNEY CUP
Winners: Willie Carlin (Derby 1970), John Farmer (Stoke 1973).
Runner-Up: Geoff Salmons (Sheff Utd 1972).

DIVISION THREE (NORTH) CUP
Winner: John Beby (Darlington 1934).

DIVISION THREE (SOUTH) CUP
Winner (shared): Jim McLaren (Watford 1937).
Runners-Up: Billy Lane (Watford 1935), Jim McLaren (Watford 1935).

ASSOCIATE MEMBERS CUP (incl.
League Group Cup, League Trophy, Freight/Rover, Sherpa Van, Leyland-DAF, Autoglass, Auto Windscreens, etc):
Winners: Steve Claridge (Birmingham 1995), Paul Groves (Grimsby 1998),

Arnar Gunnlaugsson (Stoke 2000), Kevin Jobling (Grimsby 1998), Paul Kerr (Port Vale 1993), David Lowe (Wigan 1985), Lawrie Madden (Millwall 1983), Nicky Mohan (Stoke 2000), Mike Newell (Wigan 1985), Steve Thompson (Bolton 1989), Steve Walsh (Wigan 1985), Gavin Ward (Stoke 2000), Joe Waters (Grimsby 1982).
Runners-Up: Matt Elliott (Torquay 1989), Paul Fitzpatrick (Bristol City 1987), Steve Thompson (Bolton 1986), *Tony Thorpe* (Bristol City 2000), Phil Turner (Lincoln 1983), *Paul Williams* (Stockport 1992).

SCREENSPORT SUPER CUP
Winners: Mike Hooper & Kevin MacDonald (Liverpool 1985/6, both first leg only).
Runner-Up: Ian Marshall (Everton 1985/6, first leg only).

FA AMATEUR CUP
Winners: Douglas McWhirter (Bromley 1911), Fred Milnes (Sheffield 1904), Bob Noble (Bromley 1911 & London Caledonians 1923).

FA TROPHY
Winners: Colin Appleton (Scarborough 1973), Steve Guppy (Wycombe 1991 & 1993), *Jon Pearson* (Kidderminster 1987, drawn game only), *Robin Taylor* (Woking 1997).
Runners-Up: *John Flannagan* (Kettering 1979), Paul Groves (Burton 1987), Phil Horner (Southport 1998), Bob Lee (Boston 1985), *Keith Mason* (Witton Albion 1992), *Stuart Slater* (Forest Green 2001), *Adam Sollitt* (Kettering 2000).

FA VASE
Winners: Andrew Impey (Yeading 1990), *Keith Mason* (Colne Dynamos 1988).
Runners-Up: *Paul O'Connor* (Bedlington Terriers 1999), *Alan Russell* (Stamford Town 1976).

FA YOUTH CUP
Winners: Kevin Campbell (Arsenal 1988), Terry Fenwick (C Palace 1977 & 1978), Mark Grew (WBA 1976), *Mark Hutchinson* (Villa 1980), Matthew Jones (Leeds 1997), Steve Lynex (WBA 1976, first leg only), Colin Mackleworth (West Ham 1963), Russell Osman (Ipswich 1975), Robbie Savage (Man Utd 1992), Tony Spearing (Norwich 1983).
Runners-Up: Gordon Banks (Chesterfield 1956), Colin Gibson (Villa 1978), Bob Hazell (Wolves 1976), Jimmy Holmes (Coventry 1970), Neil Lennon (Man City 1989), Robbie Savage (Man Utd 1993), Gerry Taggart (Man City 1989), Ashley Ward (Man City 1989).

SCOTTISH CUP
Winners: Joe Baillie (Celtic 1951), Kenny Campbell (Partick 1921), Willie Cunningham (Dunfermline 1961), Herbert Dainty (Dundee 1910), Martin Henderson (Rangers 1976), Neil Lennon (Celtic 2001), Gregor Stevens (Rangers 1981), David Thomson (Dunfermline 1961), Peter Weir

(Aberdeen 1983, 1984 & 1986).
Runners-Up: Andrew Anderson (St Mirren 1908), Willie Bauchop (Hearts 1907), Jimmy Blessington (Celtic 1893 & 1894), Billy Davies (Rangers 1983), Mike Galloway (Celtic 1990), Harry Graham (Raith 1913), Billy McKinlay (Dundee United 1988 & 1991), Jim Melrose (Celtic 1984), Jackie Sinclair (Dunfermline 1965), Gregor Stevens (Rangers 1980), Jimmy Walsh (Celtic 1955), Andrew Whitelaw (Vale of Leven 1890).

SCOTTISH LEAGUE CUP
Winners: Neil Lennon (Celtic 2000/1), Charlie Miller (Rangers 1996/7), Gregor Stevens (Rangers 1981/2), Nicky Walker (Rangers 1987/8), Jimmy Walsh (Celtic 1956/7, drawn game only).
Runners-Up: Billy Davies (Dunfermline 1991/2), Mike Galloway (Celtic 1994/5), *Andy Geddes* (Dundee 1980/1), Jim Melrose (Celtic 1983/4), John Ogilvie (Hibernian (1950/1), Bobby Smith (Hibernian 1974/5), Peter Weir (Aberdeen 1987/8).

SCOTTISH CHALLENGE CUP (incl Centenary Cup)
Runner-Up: Peter Weir (Ayr 1990/1).

SCOTTISH QUALIFYING CUP
Winners: Adam Black (Bathgate 1919/20), Willie Freebairn (East Stirlingshire 1898/9), George Hastie (Abercorn 1912/3), Harry Simpson (St Bernards 1907/8), *Bill Strachan* (Arbroath 1903/4).
Runner-Up: Tom Seymour (Arthurlie 1898/9).

SCOTTISH JUNIOR CUP
Winners: Jimmy Baxter (Parkhead 1924), *Maurice Buchanan* (Vale of Leven 1953), Sam Currie (Kilwinning Rangers 1909, drawn game only), Bill Findlay (Musselburgh Bruntonians 1923), Jack Lornie (Banks O'Dee 1957), *Archie Waterston* (Musselburgh Bruntonians 1923), Ian White (Petershill 1956).

DRYBURGH CUP
Winner: Bobby Smith (Hibernian 1973).
Runner-Up: Peter Weir (St Mirren 1980).

WELSH CUP
Winners: Dick Allman (Wrexham 1910), Malcolm Clarke (Cardiff 1968), Ben Davies (Cardiff 1922), John Farrington (Cardiff 1974, first leg only), Mike Ford (Cardiff 1988), George Heyes (Swansea 1966), Robbie James (Swansea 1981, 1982, 1983, 1989 & Cardiff 1993), Nicky Platnauer (Cardiff 1988), *Gary Plumley* (Newport 1980), Paul Ramsey (Cardiff 1992 & 1993), Peter Rodrigues (Cardiff 1964 & 1965, first leg only), Gavin Ward (Cardiff 1993).
Runners-Up: *Mick Betteridge* (Chester 1954), *Ken Brandon* (Chester 1955), Jack Brown (Wrexham 1932 & 1933), Jim Bulling (Wrexham 1933), George Heyes (Swansea 1969), Robbie Jones (Kidderminster 1989), *Dixie McNeil*

(Hereford 1976 & Wrexham 1979), *Jon Pearson* (Kidderminster 1989), *Brian Punter* (Hereford 1968), Kevin Russell (Wrexham 1988), Harry Trainer (Westminster Rovers 1894, Wrexham 1895), Winston White (Hereford 1981).

WELSH INVITATION CUP / WELSH PREMIER CUP
Winners: Brian Carey (Wrexham 1998).
Runners-Up: Brian Carey (Wrexham 1999), Kevin Russell (Wrexham 1999).

FAI CUP
Winners: Pat Byrne (Bohemians 1976 & Shamrock 1985, 1986, 1987), Jimmy Dunne (St Patrick's 1959), Tommy Dunne (Shamrock 1948), Peter Eccles (Shamrock 1986, 1987), Steve Lynex (Shamrock 1978).
Runners-Up: Pat Byrne (Shamrock 1984), Brian Carey (Cork 1989), Peter Eccles (Shamrock 1991), *Willie Hay* (Sligo 1939), *Ray McGuinness* (Derry 1988), *Neil Poutch* (Shamrock 1991).

IFA CUP
Winners: Derek Dougan (Distillery 1956), Jim Macauley (Cliftonville 1909), John Mercer (Linfield 1902 & Distillery 1903), *Tommy Thompson* (Linfield 1942, 1948, 1950 & 1953).
Runners-Up: Mick Cochrane (Distillery 1902), *Ian Hill* (Cliftonville 1997), Jim Macauley (Cliftonville 1910), *Gerry McCaffrey* (Distillery 1969).

BELGIAN CUP: Winner: Roger Davies (Club Brugge 1977). **FINNISH CUP:** Winner: Jari Rantanen (HJK 1996). **DUTCH CUP:** Winner: Zeljko Kalac (Roda JC 2000). **ITALIAN CUP:** Winner: Roberto Mancini (Sampdoria 1985, 1988, 1989, 1994 & Lazio 1998, 2000); Runner-Up: Roberto Mancini (Sampdoria 1986 & 1991). **NORWEGIAN CUP:** Winner: Kjetil Osvold (Lillestrom 1985). **SPANISH CUP:** Winners: Laurie Cunningham (Real Madrid 1980 & 1982), Gary Lineker (Barcelona 1988). **SWEDISH CUP:** Winner: Pontus Kåmark (IFK Göteborg 1991).

DURAND CUP (INDIA): Winner: Steve Prindiville (East Bengal 1991). **SOCCER BOWL(USA):** Runners-Up: Roger Davies & Gary Mills (both Seattle Sounders 1982).

Above: *Teddy King notched the first Leicester City own goal and the first in the FA Cup against the club.*

> Whilst often an area of dispute between statisticians, who occasionally wish to give the benefit of any doubt over a scorer's credit to an attacking player, the subject of own goals remains as much a source of fascination as one of embarrassment.

> Goalkeeper Tom DeVille was the first Fossil on the opposition's scoresheet at Midland League level with his decisive mistake at Gainsborough Trinity on 19.03.1892; while the very first Football League game the club played, at Grimsby Town on 01.09.1894, was the occasion Harry Bailey's own goal separated the teams at 3-4 [though some sources spared his blushes with an alternative credit to Mariners forward McCairns].

> Teddy King's own-goal contribution to Burnley's 7-3 FA Cup win at Filbert Street on 08.01.1921 was the first conceded both by the club in that competition and by the reconstructed Leicester City.

> The long-distance, up-and-under, own goal that Steve Walsh netted for Arsenal at Highbury on 26.12.1997 was his seventh against City; a somewhat undesired club record he had previously shared on six own goals with Dai Jones and Graham Cross.

> John Sjoberg remains the only Leicester player to have netted two own goals in one game: to the credit of West Bromwich Albion at the Hawthorns on 22.04.1966. On four occasions, however, two City players have netted against their own side in a single game: most recently when Colin Appleton and Ian King won the game for Burnley on 05.09.1961 at Turf Moor. In recent years, Jimmy Willis scored own goals in successive League matches, and Frank Sinclair in successive weeks.

> Willie Frame became the only City player to net an own goal on his League debut, when scoring in the final minute for Tottenham Hotspur in a 2-2 draw at White Hart Lane on 06.10.1934. Newcastle United's George Dalton gifted City an own goal on his debut on 11.02.1961, during a 5-3 home win for City.

> During City's defeat by Chelsea at Stamford Bridge on 18.12.1954, Leicester defenders Stan Milburn and Jack Froggatt simultaneously contrived to kick the ball into their own net while attempting a clearance, and were credited with a unique joint own goal.

> Graham Cross put Nottingham Forest ahead with an own goal at Filbert Street on 30.04.1966, but then completed a rare 'hat-trick' by scoring twice for City. Norman Plummer not

Above: *David Nish netted 14 spot kicks in succession.*

only registered an own goal on Lincoln City's behalf during City's 5-3 win on 22.01.1949, he also conceded the two penalties which completed their tally.

> Aston Villa defender Chris Nicholl netted all four goals in a 2-2 draw at Filbert Street on 20.03.1976. (City sources initially credited Brian Alderson with the first City goal, but were later amended). Nottingham Forest's Bill Whare was the only other opposition player to gift City two own goals; but these came in separate games on 19.10.1957 and 18.04.1959.

> Former City defender Pat Kruse, playing for Torquay United on 03.01.1977, registered the fastest own goal on record for the Football League, putting Cambridge United ahead after only six seconds. The quickest own goal conceded by City was by Len Chalmers after 15 seconds of the home game against Aston Villa on 08.12.1962, with the defender lobbing Gordon Banks while chasing a Derek Dougan through-ball.

> A remarkable coincidence attends the only occasions on which a player scored for Fosse before joining them, and for City after leaving them. George Mountain's own goal on 23.12.1899, and that scored by Paul Groves on 20.03.1993, both came in 3-0 home wins for Leicester over Grimsby Town. Frank Sinclair joined City after he'd already gifted them a goal against his own side, Chelsea, at Stamford Bridge on 19.04.1997, and uniquely returned the accidental favour at Filbert Street on 14.08.1999.

> Sinclair joined Tot Hedley (at Middlesbrough on 31.01.1909) and Jimmy Baldwin (at Blackburn Rovers on 24.11.1951) in having registered an own goal to the credit of a former club, while no less than four Leicester men have conceded own goals to clubs they would later serve: Billy Wragg to Small Heath (14.04.1900), Steve Whitworth to Mansfield Town (Anglo-Scottish Cup, 06.08.1975), Geoff Scott to Birmingham City (06.12.1980), and John O'Neill to Queens Park Rangers (25.09.1982).

PENALTIES

> City's leading penalty-kick scorers are Arthur Rowley 41 (38 Lge, 3 FAC); Sep Smith 26 (13 Lge, 1 FAC, 12 WW2); Steve Lynex 23 (all Lge); and Gary McAllister 15 (12 Lge, 2 FAC, 1 LC). David Nish's tally of 14 (10 Lge, 2 FAC, 2 LC) equals that of Fosse's spot-kick expert Bob Pollock (10 Lge, 4 FAC). Nish netted his fourteen in succession, until failing with a fifteenth and final effort. Pollock's fourteen were notched at a time when keepers could still advance from their goalline as the whistle sounded. Rowley, incidentally, failed eight times from the spot as a City player; while club top-scorer Arthur Chandler had both penalties he took for City saved.

> City registered their highest number of successful penalties in 1985/6: scoring ten in the League and one in the FA Cup. (There were also four spot-kicks missed or saved during this campaign). There have been eight full seasons in which City have netted no penalties at all (most recently in 1994/5, when four were wasted); and the club have twice gone 80 games without so scoring: from 20.03.1920 to 04.03.1922 (76 Lge & 4 FAC games), and from 27.12.1932 to 03.11.1934 (74 Lge & 6 FAC games). In the 75 League and Cup games from 28.11.1970 to 22.04.1972, City were not even awarded a spot-kick.

Steve Lynex

> Only once have City netted three penalties in one game: on 11.09.1982 at home to Carlisle United, when Steve Lynex claimed two and allowed Gary Lineker to take the third to complete the game's second hat-trick and the 6-0 scoreline. City have never conceded a trio of penalties in a single game.

> City Reserves were awarded no less than four penalties in their home Combination Cup game with Ipswich on 31.01.1948: Ray Iggleden scored one and missed one, Alex Scott scored one, and Derek Hines missed one. At first-team level, City and Coventry featured in a game of four penalties on 15.10.1977, when Mick Coop netted two for the Sky Blues, while Jon Sammels succeeded and Dennis Rofe failed in the home defeat.

> City conceded a penalty to Liverpool after only 19 seconds of the game at Anfield on 24.08.1974, and duly went behind to an Alec Lindsay spot-kick. This is often quoted as a League record for the fastest goal so scored. [City back-passed from the kick-off; a stray Malcolm Munro pass was intercepted by Steve Heighway, who was brought down by Mark Wallington; and Lindsay became only the second Liverpool player to have touched the

ball since the game's commencement. He netted a second penalty later in the same game].

> City first experienced the innovation of drawn knock-out ties being decided by a penalty shoot-out during their Texaco Cup games of 1972/3; so beating Dundee United away but so being eliminated in the next round at Norwich City. In first-class competitive games, City were beaten in such a manner in the League Cup by Chelsea at Stamford Bridge on 25.10.1983; in the Full Members Cup by Stoke City at Filbert Street on 19.01.1988; and in the FA Cup by Barnsley at Oakwell on 20.01.1993. They progressed in the League Cup by overcoming Leeds United (15.12.1999) and Fulham (12.01.2000), and in the FA Cup by eclipsing Arsenal (19.01.2000), in shoot-outs at home.

> Before he joined City, goalkeeper Paul Cooper established a League record by saving 8 of 10 penalties awarded against Ipswich Town in 1979/80.

> Harry Bailey scored Fosse's first-ever penalty, in a friendly against Notts County on 14.09.1891; and Billy Dorrell converted the first in competitive fare (in the FA Cup tie against Rushden on 15.10.1892). Fosse never scored a penalty during

their three seasons of Midland League football. 'Tout' Miller missed the first penalty awarded to Fosse at Football League level (v Newcastle United on 20.10.1894). Yet the same player had scored from the 12-yard mark for Burton Wanderers against Great Bridge Unity on the very day (01.09.1891) that the penalty-kick was first introduced. [See the note in the Who's Who section on Fosse goalkeeper Jimmy Thraves for details on his particular role in inspiring the penalty's introduction].

Above: *Harry Bailey successfully converted Fosse's first penalty kick.*

SCORELINES

CLUB RECORDS

Wins:

Premiership:	4-0	Derby County (A)	26.04.1998
League Div One:	10-0	Portsmouth (H)	20.10.1928
League Div Two:	9-1	Walsall Town Swifts (H)	05.01.1895
	9-1	Gainsborough Trinity (H)	27.12.1909
	9-2	Lincoln City (H)	21.11.1953
FAC Qualifying:	13-0	Notts Olympic (H)	13.10.1894
FAC Proper:	7-0	Crook Town (H)	09.01.1932
League Cup:	8-1	Coventry City (A)	01.12.1964
Midland League:	7-1	Newark (H)	01.10.1892

Defeats:

Premiership:	1-6	Arsenal (A)	26.12.2000
	0-5	Arsenal (A)	20.02.1999
	2-6	Manchester United (H)	16.01.1999
League Div One:	0-12	Nottingham Forest (A)	21.04.1909
	1-10	Wolverhampton W. (A)	15.04.1938
League Div Two:	0-8	Woolwich Arsenal (A)	26.10.1903
	2-8	Darwen (A)	15.01.1895
FAC Qualifying:	2-6	Small Heath (H)	03.10.1891
FAC Proper:	0-5	Manchester City (A)	17.01.1996
	3-7	Burnley (H)	08.01.1921
League Cup:	1-7	Sheffield Wednesday (A)	27.10.1992
Midland League:	0-11	Rotherham Town (A)	16.04.1892

Draws:

Premiership:	4-4	Aston Villa (A)	22.02.1995
League Div One:	6-6	Arsenal (H)	21.04.1930
League Div Two:	5-5	Sheffield United (H)	03.11.1951
FA Cup:	5-5	Tottenham Hotspur (H)	10.01.1914
	5-5	Luton Town (A)	12.02.1949
League Cup:	4-4	Charlton Athletic (H)	26.09.1962

Highest Seasonal H/A Aggregate:

19 goals:	City/West Bromwich Albion	1954/5	(H:6-3; A:4-6)
19 goals:	City/Manchester City	1957/8	(H:8-4; A:4-3)

SEASONAL RECORDS

BEST/WORST IN FOOTBALL LEAGUE/PREMIERSHIP

Most Wins:	25 of 42 (1956/7)
Most Home Wins:	16 of 21 (1928/9)
Most Away Wins:	11 of 21 (1956/7; 1970/1)
Most Defeats:	25 of 42 (1977/8; 1994/5)
Most Home Defeats:	10 of 21 (1977/8; 1994/5)
Most Away Defeats:	17 of 21 (1957/8; 1986/7)
Most Draws:	19 of 42 (1975/6)
Most Home Draws:	10 of 21 (1948/9)
	10 of 19 (1997/8)
Most Away Draws:	11 of 21 (1921/2)
Most Goalless Draws:	9 of 42 (1921/2)
Least Wins:	5 of 42 (1977/8)
Least Home Wins:	4 of 21 (1977/8)
Least Away Wins:	1 of 21 (1968/9; 1977/8; 1994/5)
Least Defeats:	6 of 42 (1956/7; 1970/1)
Least Home Defeats:	0 of 21 (1928/9)
	0 of 17 (1898/9)
Least Away Defeats:	4 of 21 (1956/7; 1970/1; 1979/80);
	4 of 19 (1907/8)
Least Draws:	5 of 42 (1957/8)
	4 of 38 (1909/10; 1913/14; 1914/15)
Least Home Draws:	2 of 21 (1922/3; 1961/2)
	0 of 15 (1895/6)
Least Away Draws:	1 of 21 (1957/8; 1980/1)
	0 of 19 (1914/15)
Most Goals:	109 in 42 (1956/7)
Most Home Goals:	68 in 21 (1956/7)
Most Away Goals:	41 in 21 (1956/7)
Most Goals Conceded:	112 in 42 (1957/8)
Most Home Goals Conceded:	41 in 21 (1957/8)
Most Away Goals Conceded:	71 in 21 (1957/8)
Least Goals:	26 in 42 (1977/8)
Least Home Goals:	16 in 21 (1977/8)
Least Away Goals:	9 in 21 (1921/2)
Least Goals Conceded:	30 in 42 (1970/1)
Least Home Goals Conceded:	9 in 21 (1924/5)
	8 in 17 (1899/1900)
Least Away Goals Conceded:	16 in 21 (1970/1)
Best Positive Goal Diff:	+58 from 42 (1924/5)
Worst Negative Goal Diff:	-44 from 42 (1977/8)
	-48 from 38 (1908/9)
Most Points (2 per win):	61 from poss 84 (1956/7)
Most Points (3 per win):	70 from poss 126 (1982/3)
	77 from poss 138 (1991/2)
Least Points (2 per win):	22 from poss 84 (1977/8)
	22 from poss 68 (1908/9)
Least Points (3 per win):	29 from poss 126 (1994/5)
Most Clean Sheets:	23 of 42 (1970/1)
Least Clean Sheets:	2 of 42 (1948/9; 1957/8)
Least Blank Scoresheets:	3 of 42 (1932/3; 1953/4)
	2 of 30 (1894/5)
Most Blank Scoresheets:	23 of 42 (1977/8)
Most Players Used:	31 (1987/8)
Least Players Used:	17 (1962/3)
Most Players on Scoresheet:	19 (1989/90)
Least Players on Scoresheet:	8 (1951/2)

SEQUENCES

These records relate to consecutive League games only

Consecutive Wins:	7	(from 15.02.1908;
		from 24.01.1925;
		from 26.12.1962;
		from 28.02.1993)
Consecutive Defeats:	8	(from 17.03.2001)
Consecutive Draws:	6	(from 21.04.1973;
		from 21.08.1976)
Consecutive Games Unbeaten:	19	(from 06.02.1971)
	18	(from 06.12.1924)
Consecutive Games without a Win:	18	(from 12.04.1975)
	17	(from 10.09.1932)
Consecutive Home Wins:	13	(from 03.09.1906)
Consecutive Home Defeats:	5	(from 03.01.1959)
Consecutive Home Draws:	5	(from 14.04.1903;
		from 19.04.1975)
Consecutive Away Wins:	4	(from 13.03.1971)
Consecutive Away Defeats:	15	(from 18.10.1986)
Consecutive Away Draws:	5	(from 01.10.1921)
Consecutive Home Games Unbeaten:	40	(from 12.02.1898)
Consecutive Home Games without a Win:	9	(from 03.12.1994)
Consecutive Away Games Unbeaten:	10	(from 27.02.1971)
Consecutive Away Games without a Win:	23	(from 19.11.1988)
Consecutive Clean Sheets:	7	(from 14.02.1920)
Consecutive Games without Scoring:	7	(from 21.11.1987)
Consecutive Goalless Draws:	3	(from 13.04.1903;
		from 04.03.1920;
		from 11.04.1925;
		from 24.02.1973)
Consecutive Games in which Scored:	31	(from 12.11.1932)
Consecutive Games in which Scored Against:	37	(from 09.02.1957)

City's overall record for consecutive wins was established in 1962/3, when the seven First Division wins noted above were supplemented by three victories in FA Cup ties. That for consecutive defeats stands at 9, with the above Premiership sequence being immediately preceded by the 2001 FA Cup exit.

FA Cup:

Consecutive Wins:	5	(1962/3)
Consecutive Unbeaten:	9	(1960/1)
Consecutive Defeats:	7	(1984/5-1990/1)
Consecutive Without a Win:	7	(1984/5-1990/1)

FL Cup:

Consecutive Wins:	6	(1998/9)
Consecutive Unbeaten:	17	(1963/4-1964/5)
Consecutive Defeats:	9	(1975/6-1981/2)
Consecutive Without a Win:	9	(1975/6-1981/2)

SPONSORSHIP

The commercial sponsorship of individual matches at Filbert Street started when the Audnel Group sponsored the match v Liverpool on 01.09.1973.

The first City side to wear sponsored shirts was the Youth squad of 1982/3, backed by the local bakery concern of Squires & Kintons and advertising their Fresha brand.

The initial club sponsorship deal with brewers Ind Coope was announced as a two-year link-up in May 1983 (later extended by a similar period), and City shirts bore this sponsor's name from 1983-86. For the 1986/7 season,

City's strip was adorned with the logo of John Bull, an Ind Coope brand-name.

The multiply-extended deal which identified Walkers Crisps as the club sponsor (until June 2001) was first struck to take effect from the beginning of season 1987/8; and is now to be succeeded by a link-up for at least two years with LG Electronics. The latter company had previously been associated with Leicester Tigers under their earlier brand name of Goldstar, and currently also sponsor the French and Australian international football squads.

SUBSTITUTES

QUOTA

1965/6 :	1	- Lge only	- injuries only
1966/7 :	1	- Lge/Cups	- injuries only
1967-86:	1	- Lge/Cups	
1986/7 :	1	- Lge	
	2	- Cups	
1987-93:	2	- Lge/Cups	
1993/4 :	2	- Lge/Cups	- from 3 named; incl gk.
1994/5 :	2+GK	- Lge/Cups	
1995/6 :	3	- Lge/Cups	
1996/7 :	3	- Lge/Cups	- from 5 named in PL, from 3 in Cups
1997/8 :	3	- Lge/Cups	- from 5 named in PL & FAC, from 3 in LC
1998-date	3	- Lge/Cups	- from 5 named in PL, FAC & FLC

FIRST CITY SUBS

Lge: Jimmy Goodfellow (for Graham Cross) 21.08.1965 v Liverpool (H)
LC : Paul Matthews (for David Gibson) 25.10.1966 v QPR (A)
FAC: Len Glover (for Peter Rodrigues) 13.03.1968 v Rotherham Utd (H)

First time 2 subs used: (Robert Kelly, Steve Lynex) 29.10.1986
v Liverpool (A) LC
First sub gk: Gavin Ward (for Kevin Poole) 18.02.1995 v Wolves (A) FAC
First time 3 subs used: (Lee Philpott, Iwan Roberts, Colin Hill) 12.08.1995
v Sunderland (A)
First sub to score: Tom Sweenie 12.04.1966 v Blackburn Rovers (H)
Scored on debut as sub: Paul Groves, Steve Thompson, Graham Fenton.
Most goals for City as sub: Mark Robins 5; Arnar Gunnlaugsson, David
Lowe, Jim Melrose 4.
Players having made only substitute apps for City: Graham Brown;
Malcolm Clarke; Lawrie Dudfield; Kevin Ellison [to date]; Scott Eustace; Gary
Fitzpatrick; Sascha Lenhart; Kevin Reed; Jordan Stewart [to date]; Danny
Thomas [to date].
Most sub apps before first start: Stuart Wilson 22 in Lge & Cups.
Subs named but never used:
Of 1: Alan Hoult, Derek Watts.
Of 2: Gary Hyde, Pat O'Toole.
Of 3: Richard Clay (gk).
Of 5: Lars-Gunnar Carlstrand, Alan Fettis (gk), Martin Fox, John Hodges
(gk), Paul Hyde (gk), Tim McCann, Michael Price (gk) [to date], Stuart
Slater.
Sub subbed for first time in competitive game: 26.09.1992 v Watford (A):
Colin Gibson replaced Michael Trotter after 45 mins, then injured and
replaced by Colin Gordon.
First sub sent off: Colin Gibson 06.02.1993 v Luton Town (A).
Running total of City goals scored by substitutes to end 2000/1: 92
(FL/PL 74; FAC 6; LC 9; FMC 1; PO 2)

TRANSFERS

Progressive Rises in Record Fees

Fees Paid

			(£)	
May 1904	W.Bannister	Woolwich Arsenal	300	
June 1907	P.Humphreys	Notts County	600	
Jan 1909	W.Smith	Bradford City	625	(a)
June 1923	A.C.H.Chandler	Queens Park Rangers	3,000	
Oct 1925	A.W.Lochhead	Manchester United	3,300	
Sept 1927	L.J.Barry	Notts County	3,450	
Nov 1936	J.W.A.Bowers	Derby County	7,500	
Mar 1948	P.S.McKennan	West Bromwich Albion	'record'	(b)
Oct 1948	J.Ayton	Third Lanark	7,750	
Jan 1949	K.M.Chisholm	Leeds United	'record'	(c)
July 1950	G.A.Rowley	Fulham	14,000	
Sept 1950	A.R.Lever	Cardiff City	15,000	
Oct 1952	J.Morris	Derby County	21,500	
Dec 1954	A.M.Graver	Lincoln City	27,600	(d)
Sept 1963	R.Roberts	Motherwell	41,000	
Dec 1965	P.J.Rodrigues	Cardiff City	42,500	
Nov 1967	L.Glover	Charlton Athletic	80,000	
June 1968	A.J.Clarke	Fulham	150,000	(e)
Dec 1977	R.Davies	Bruges	250,000	
July 1979	A.F.Young	Oldham Athletic	250,000	
July 1980	J.M.Melrose	Partick Thistle	250,000	
Sept 1986	S.J.Moran	Southampton	300,000	
Sept 1987	M.C.Newell	Luton Town	350,000	
Mar 1992	I.Ormondroyd	Derby County	350,000	(f)
Nov 1992	L.Philpott	Cambridge United	350,000	
Mar 1994	M.A.Blake	Portsmouth	360,000	
July 1994	M.A.Draper	Notts County	1,250,000	(g)
Jan 1997	M.S.Elliott	Oxford United	1,600,000	
Aug 1998	F.M.Sinclair	Chelsea	2,050,000	(h)
Dec 1999	D.M.Eadie	Norwich City	3,000,000	(i)
June 2000	G.Rowett	Birmingham City	3,000,000	(j)
July 2000	A.P.Akinbiyi	Wolverhampton W.	5,000,000	

Notes:

(a) Smith fee constituted a club record until at least 1919. Rise in fees 1919-23 unknown,
    though any of Macauley, Jobey or Paterson might have set a new figure.

(b) McKennan fee consisted of £6,000 + J.T.W.Haines – total value undisclosed.

(c) Chisholm fee consisted of £11,000 + H.Iggleden – total value undisclosed.

(d) Graver fee consisted of £27,000 + J.E.Littler.

(e) Clarke fee consisted of £110,000 + F.Large.

(f) Ormondoyd fee represented club valuation in part-exchange sale of P.Kitson.

(g) Draper fee eventually rose to £1.75m after passing on share of sell-on profit.

(h) Sinclair fee eventually rose to £2.55m after appearance-related instalments.

(i) Eadie fee has so far risen to £3.075m, and with further instalments may rise to £3.125m.

(j) Rowett fee has so far risen to £3.4m, and with further instalments may rise to £3.5m.

Fees Received

			(£)	
May 1894	W.Dorrell	Aston Villa	250	
May 1906	W.E.Smith	Manchester City	600	
Apr 1909	R.F.Turner	Everton	700	
Nov 1911	W.A.Henry	Manchester City	1,000	
Mar 1922	J.Paterson	Sunderland	3,790	
June 1928	S.M.Bishop	Chelsea	3,800	
May 1932	E.W.Hine	Huddersfield Town	4,000	
June 1948	A.E.Smith	West Bromwich Albion	5,000	
Sept 1948	J.Hernon	Bolton Wanderers	14,750	
Nov 1949	D.G.Revie	Hull City	20,000	
June 1955	A.M.Graver	Lincoln City	26,000	
Aug 1961	A.Knapp	Southampton	27,500	(a)
Oct 1964	F.McLintock	Arsenal	80,000	
June 1969	A.J.Clarke	Leeds United	165,000	
Sept 1972	D.J.Nish	Derby County	250,000	
Nov 1974	P.L.Shilton	Stoke City	325,000	
Nov 1984	K.D.MacDonald	Liverpool	400,000	
June 1985	G.W.Lineker	Everton	800,000	(b)
July 1990	G.McAllister	Leeds United	1,000,000	
Mar 1993	P.Kitson	Derby County	1,350,000	(c)
July 1995	M.A.Draper	Aston Villa	3,250,000	
Mar 2000	E.W.I.Heskey	Liverpool	11,000,000	(d)

Notes:

(a) Knapp fee consisted of £25,000 + £2,500 for first 25 apps.

(b) Lineker fee eventually rose to £1.05m after City took share of sell-on profit.

(c) Kitson fee consisted of £800,000 + I.Ormondroyd (£350,000) + P.J.Gee (£200,000).

(d) Heskey fee consisted of £10.5m + £0.5m for UEFA Cup qualification in 2000.

SUNDAY FOOTBALL

> City's first experience of League fixtures scheduled on Sundays came during 1983/4, with the First Division clashes at Nottingham Forest (04.12.1983) and Sunderland (18.12.1983). The first home game to take place on a Sunday was a season later, against Coventry City on 23.12.1984. First-team fixtures have now been undertaken on every day of the week.

VOID GAMES

> Fosse twice completed Midland League fixtures which were later declared void by the League authorities and ordered to be replayed.

On 02.04.1892, Fosse went down 0-2 away to Burslem Port Vale. They had played throughout with only ten men (Owen having missed his train), but a more crucial absentee had been the referee. A spectator had assumed whistling duties, and Fosse's later protests over his partiality were upheld. Ironically, a full-strength Fosse lost the rematch by 0-4.

On 25.03.1893, Fosse beat Derby Junction at Walnut Street by 6-0 (Slack 3, Lowe, Lord, Webb). However, Fosse had already met these opponents at home earlier in the campaign, and despite the Derby club's willingness to cede their scheduled home advantage on this occasion, the Midland League were not in agreement with this breach of their rules. The ordered rematch brought a 3-1 away win for Fosse.

The opening three games of 1939/40, played by City as Football League Division Two fixtures, were declared void upon the declaration of war, and the abandonment of the competition. [We have, however, included players' appearances and goals in these three fixtures amongst the wartime statistics appended to their biographical entries].

Allan Clarke cost the club a barrowload of cash when City broke the British transfer record to bring him to Filbert Street in 1968. A year later another British record saw him move to Leeds.

Complete League Record

SEASON	P	HOME					AWAY					OVERALL					Pts	Pos
		W	D	L	F	A	W	D	L	F	A	W	D	L	F	A		
MIDLAND LEAGUE																		
1891-92	20	4	2	4	12	16	1	1	8	7	39	5	3	12	19	55	13	11
1892-93	24	7	2	3	29	11	5	1	6	21	26	12	3	9	50	37	27	4
1893-94	20	9	0	1	32	6	6	2	2	17	7	15	2	3	49	13	32	2
FOOTBALL LEAGUE DIVISION TWO																		
1894-95	30	11	2	2	45	20	4	6	5	27	33	15	8	7	72	53	38	4
1895-96	30	10	0	5	40	16	4	4	7	17	28	14	4	12	57	44	32	8
1896-97	30	11	2	2	44	20	2	2	11	15	37	13	4	13	59	57	30	9
1897-98	30	8	5	2	26	11	5	2	8	20	24	13	7	10	46	35	33	7
1898-99	34	12	5	0	35	12	6	4	7	29	30	18	9	7	64	42	45	3
1899-1900	34	11	5	1	34	8	6	4	7	19	28	17	9	8	53	36	43	5
1900-01	34	9	5	3	30	15	2	5	10	9	22	11	10	13	39	37	32	11
1901-02	34	11	2	4	26	14	1	3	13	12	42	12	5	17	38	56	29	14
1902-03	34	5	5	7	20	23	5	3	9	21	42	10	8	16	41	65	28	15
1903-04	34	5	8	4	26	21	1	2	14	16	61	6	10	18	42	82	22	18
1904-05	34	8	3	6	30	25	3	4	10	10	30	11	7	16	40	55	29	14
1905-06	38	10	3	6	30	21	5	9	5	23	27	15	12	11	53	48	42	7
1906-07	38	15	3	1	44	12	5	5	9	18	27	20	8	10	62	39	48	3
1907-08	38	14	2	3	41	20	7	8	4	31	27	21	10	7	72	47	52	2
FOOTBALL LEAGUE DIVISION ONE																		
1908-09	38	6	6	7	32	41	2	3	14	22	61	8	9	21	54	102	25	20
FOOTBALL LEAGUE DIVISION TWO																		
1909-10	38	15	2	2	60	20	5	2	12	19	38	20	4	14	79	58	44	5
1910-11	38	12	3	4	37	19	2	2	15	15	43	14	5	19	52	62	33	15
1911-12	38	11	4	4	34	18	4	3	12	15	48	15	7	16	49	66	37	10
1912-13	38	12	2	5	34	20	1	5	13	15	45	13	7	18	49	65	33	15
1913-14	38	7	2	10	29	28	4	2	13	16	33	11	4	23	45	61	26	18
1914-15	38	6	4	9	31	41	4	0	15	16	47	10	4	24	47	88	24	19
1915-1919:	Competition suspended owing to First World War																	
1919-20	42	8	6	7	26	29	7	4	10	15	32	15	10	17	41	61	40	14
1920-21	42	10	8	3	26	11	2	8	11	13	35	12	16	14	39	46	40	12
1921-22	42	11	6	4	30	16	3	11	7	9	18	14	17	11	39	34	45	9
1922-23	42	14	2	5	42	19	7	7	7	23	25	21	9	12	65	44	51	3
1923-24	42	13	4	4	43	16	4	4	13	21	38	17	8	17	64	54	42	12
1924-25	42	15	4	2	58	9	9	7	5	32	23	24	11	7	90	32	59	1
FOOTBALL LEAGUE DIVISION ONE																		
1925-26	42	11	3	7	42	32	3	7	11	28	48	14	10	18	70	80	38	17
1926-27	42	13	4	4	58	33	4	8	9	27	37	17	12	13	85	70	46	7
1927-28	42	14	5	2	66	25	4	7	10	30	47	18	12	12	96	72	48	3
1928-29	42	16	5	0	67	22	5	4	12	29	45	21	9	12	96	67	51	2
1929-30	42	12	5	4	57	42	5	4	12	29	48	17	9	16	86	90	43	8
1930-31	42	12	4	5	50	38	4	2	15	30	57	16	6	20	80	95	38	16
1931-32	42	11	3	7	46	39	4	4	13	28	55	15	7	20	74	94	37	19
1932-33	42	9	9	3	43	25	2	4	15	32	64	11	13	18	75	89	35	19
1933-34	42	10	6	5	36	26	4	5	12	23	48	14	11	17	59	74	39	17
1934-35	42	9	4	8	39	30	3	5	13	22	56	12	9	21	61	86	33	21
FOOTBALL LEAGUE DIVISION TWO																		
1935-36	42	14	5	2	53	19	5	5	11	26	38	19	10	13	79	57	48	6
1936-37	42	14	4	3	56	26	10	4	7	33	31	24	8	10	89	57	56	1
FOOTBALL LEAGUE DIVISION ONE																		
1937-38	42	9	6	6	31	26	5	5	11	23	49	14	11	17	54	75	39	16
1938-39	42	7	6	8	35	35	2	5	14	13	47	9	11	22	48	82	29	22
1939-1946:	Competition suspended owing to Second World War																	
FOOTBALL LEAGUE DIVISION TWO																		
1946-47	42	11	4	6	42	25	7	3	11	27	39	18	7	17	69	64	43	9
1947-48	42	10	5	6	36	29	6	6	9	24	28	16	11	15	60	57	43	9
1948-49	42	6	10	5	41	38	4	6	11	21	41	10	16	16	62	79	36	19
1949-50	42	8	9	4	30	25	4	6	11	25	40	12	15	15	55	65	39	15
1950-51	42	10	4	7	42	28	5	7	9	26	30	15	11	16	68	58	41	14
1951-52	42	12	6	3	48	24	7	3	11	30	40	19	9	14	78	64	47	5
1952-53	42	13	6	2	55	29	5	6	10	34	45	18	12	12	89	74	48	5
1953-54	42	15	4	2	63	23	8	6	7	34	37	23	10	9	97	60	56	1

SEASON	P	HOME					AWAY					OVERALL					Pts	Pos
		W	D	L	F	A	W	D	L	F	A	W	D	L	F	A		
FOOTBALL LEAGUE DIVISION ONE																		
1954-55	42	9	6	6	43	32	3	5	13	31	54	12	11	19	74	86	35	21
FOOTBALL LEAGUE DIVISION TWO																		
1955-56	42	15	3	3	63	23	6	3	12	31	55	21	6	15	94	78	48	5
1956-57	42	14	5	2	68	36	11	6	4	41	31	25	11	6	109	67	61	1
FOOTBALL LEAGUE DIVISION ONE																		
1957-58	42	11	4	6	59	41	3	1	17	32	71	14	5	23	91	112	33	18
1958-59	42	7	6	8	34	36	4	4	13	33	62	11	10	21	67	98	32	19
1959-60	42	8	6	7	38	32	5	7	9	28	43	13	13	16	66	75	39	12
1960-61	42	12	4	5	54	31	6	5	10	33	39	18	9	15	87	70	45	6
1961-62	42	12	2	7	38	27	5	4	12	34	44	17	6	19	72	71	40	14
1962-63	42	14	6	1	53	23	6	6	9	26	30	20	12	10	79	53	52	4
1963-64	42	9	4	8	33	27	7	7	7	28	31	16	11	15	61	58	43	11
1964-65	42	9	6	6	43	36	2	7	12	26	49	11	13	18	69	85	35	18
1965-66	42	12	4	5	40	28	9	3	9	40	37	21	7	14	80	65	49	7
1966-67	42	12	4	5	47	28	6	4	11	31	43	18	8	16	78	71	44	8
1967-68	42	7	7	7	37	34	6	5	10	27	35	13	12	17	64	69	38	13
1968-69	42	8	8	5	27	24	1	4	16	12	44	9	12	21	39	68	30	21
FOOTBALL LEAGUE DIVISION TWO																		
1969-70	42	12	6	3	37	22	7	7	7	27	28	19	13	10	64	50	51	3
1970-71	42	12	7	2	30	14	11	6	4	27	16	23	13	6	57	30	59	1
FOOTBALL LEAGUE DIVISION ONE																		
1971-72	42	9	6	6	18	11	4	7	10	23	35	13	13	16	41	46	39	12
1972-73	42	7	9	5	23	18	3	8	10	17	28	10	17	15	40	46	37	16
1973-74	42	10	7	4	35	17	3	9	9	16	24	13	16	13	51	41	42	9
1974-75	42	8	7	6	25	17	4	5	12	21	43	12	12	18	46	60	36	18
1975-76	42	9	9	3	29	24	4	10	7	19	27	13	19	10	48	51	45	7
1976-77	42	8	9	4	30	28	4	9	8	17	32	12	18	12	47	60	42	11
1977-78	42	4	7	10	16	32	1	5	15	10	38	5	12	25	26	70	22	22
FOOTBALL LEAGUE DIVISION TWO																		
1978-79	42	7	8	6	28	23	3	9	9	15	29	10	17	15	43	52	37	17
1979-80	42	12	5	4	32	19	9	8	4	26	19	21	13	8	58	38	55	1
FOOTBALL LEAGUE DIVISION ONE																		
1980-81	42	7	5	9	20	23	6	1	14	20	44	13	6	23	40	67	32	21
FOOTBALL LEAGUE DIVISION TWO																		
1981-82	42	12	5	4	31	19	6	7	8	25	29	18	12	12	56	48	66	8
1982-83	42	11	4	6	36	15	9	6	6	36	29	20	10	12	72	44	70	3
FOOTBALL LEAGUE DIVISION ONE																		
1983-84	42	11	5	5	40	30	2	7	12	25	38	13	12	17	65	68	51	15
1984-85	42	10	4	7	39	25	5	2	14	26	48	15	6	21	65	73	51	15
1985-86	42	7	8	6	35	35	3	4	14	19	41	10	12	20	54	76	42	19
1986-87	42	9	7	5	39	24	2	2	17	15	52	11	9	22	54	76	42	20
FOOTBALL LEAGUE DIVISION TWO																		
1987-88	44	12	5	5	35	20	4	6	12	27	41	16	11	17	62	61	59	13
1988-89	46	11	6	6	31	20	2	10	11	25	43	13	16	17	56	63	55	15
1989-90	46	10	8	5	34	29	5	6	12	33	50	15	14	17	67	79	59	13
1990-91	46	12	4	7	41	33	2	4	17	19	50	14	8	24	60	83	50	22
1991-92	46	14	4	5	41	24	9	4	10	21	31	23	8	15	62	55	77	4
FOOTBALL LEAGUE DIVISION ONE * (renamed)																		
1992-93	46	14	5	4	43	24	8	5	10	28	40	22	10	14	71	64	76	6
1993-94	46	11	9	3	45	30	8	7	8	27	29	19	16	11	72	59	73	4
F A PREMIER LEAGUE																		
1994-95	42	5	6	10	28	37	1	5	15	17	43	6	11	25	45	80	29	21
FOOTBALL LEAGUE DIVISION ONE *																		
1995-96	46	9	7	7	32	29	10	7	6	34	31	19	14	13	66	60	71	5
F A PREMIER LEAGUE																		
1996-97	38	7	5	7	22	26	5	6	8	24	28	12	11	15	46	54	47	9
1997-98	38	6	10	3	21	15	7	4	8	30	26	13	14	11	51	41	53	10
1998-99	38	7	6	6	25	25	5	7	7	15	21	12	13	13	40	46	49	10
1999-2000	38	10	3	6	31	24	6	4	9	24	31	16	7	15	55	55	55	8
2000-01	38	10	4	5	28	23	4	2	13	11	28	14	6	18	39	51	48	13

TOTALS

	P																	
Midland League	64	20	4	8	73	33	12	4	16	45	72	32	8	24	118	105		
Premier League	232	45	34	37	155	150	28	28	60	121	177	73	62	97	276	327		
Division One	1592	368	216	212	1497	1097	151	194	451	945	1694	519	410	663	2442	2791		
Division One *	138	34	21	14	120	83	26	19	24	89	100	60	40	38	209	183		
Division Two	1936	541	224	203	1894	1047	253	250	465	1109	1703	794	474	668	3003	2750		
FL/PL Total	3898	988	495	466	3666	2377	458	491	1000	2264	3674	1446	986	1466	5930	6051		

Note: 1896-97: Official Football League table incorrect: 28 November 1896: Walsall (h) 4-2 not 4-1 as recorded in Football League records.

1912-13: Official Football League table incorrect: 26 April 1913: Hull City (a) 0-2 not 1-2 as recorded in Football League records.

Complete League Record

LEICESTER FOSSE/CITY AGAINST OTHER LEAGUE CLUBS FROM 1894

CLUB	First Played	P	HOME					AWAY					OVERALL					Divisions Met In			
			W	D	L	F	A	W	D	L	F	A	W	D	L	F	A	P	1	1*	2
Arsenal	1894-95	112	21	18	17	94	88	6	16	34	57	133	27	34	51	151	221	P	1		2
Aston Villa	1908-09	78	22	11	6	94	51	12	9	18	60	80	34	20	24	154	131	P	1		2
Barnsley	1898-99	88	25	12	7	79	33	15	15	14	57	61	40	27	21	136	94	P	1	1*	2
Birmingham City	1896-97	114	30	11	16	118	93	17	9	31	73	105	47	20	47	191	198		1	1*	2
Blackburn Rovers	1908-09	84	21	10	11	80	47	7	12	23	40	85	28	22	34	120	132	P	1		2
Blackpool	1896-97	84	22	7	13	87	52	8	11	23	51	89	30	18	36	138	141		1		2
Bolton Wanderers	1899-1900	56	13	10	5	55	29	6	5	17	33	69	19	15	22	88	98	P	1	1*	2
Bournemouth	1987-88	6	1	0	2	2	3	2	0	1	7	6	3	0	3	9	9				2
Bradford City	1903-04	32	8	1	7	23	21	2	6	8	20	34	10	7	15	43	55	P	1		2
Bradford Park Avenue	1909-10	24	10	1	1	35	8	5	4	3	22	20	15	5	4	57	28				2
Brentford	1937-38	20	1	5	4	13	11	5	3	2	17	13	6	8	6	30	24		1	1*	2
Brighton & Hove Albion	1978-79	12	5	0	1	11	3	1	1	4	5	11	6	1	5	16	14		1		
Bristol City	1901-02	48	13	8	3	44	18	7	6	11	18	29	20	14	14	62	47		1	1*	2
Bristol Rovers	1953-54	16	5	2	1	19	8	1	5	2	6	9	6	7	3	25	17			1*	2
Burnley	1897-98	80	18	13	9	75	60	5	11	24	42	91	23	24	33	117	151		1		2
Burton Swifts	1894-95	14	5	2	0	15	6	4	1	2	13	7	9	3	2	28	13				2
Burton United	1901-02	12	3	1	2	11	5	3	2	1	7	4	6	3	3	18	9				2
Burton Wanderers	1894-95	6	1	0	2	4	6	0	2	1	2	3	1	2	3	6	9				2
Bury	1894-95	52	13	6	7	48	33	10	4	12	40	52	23	10	19	88	85		1		2
Cambridge United	1978-79	12	4	2	0	15	6	2	2	2	9	12	6	4	2	24	18			1*	2
Cardiff City	1920-21	36	11	3	4	34	15	5	4	9	23	34	16	7	13	57	49		1		2
Carlisle United	1969-70	8	1	2	1	10	5	3	1	0	5	2	4	3	1	15	7		1		2
Charlton Athletic	1935-36	36	9	3	6	27	25	6	1	11	18	23	15	4	17	45	48	P	1	1*	2
Chelsea	1905-06	86	19	16	8	69	53	4	10	29	40	93	23	26	37	109	146	P	1		2
Chesterfield	1899-1900	30	5	5	5	20	17	2	6	7	18	27	7	11	12	38	44				2
Coventry City	1919-20	66	16	9	8	47	33	12	7	14	40	44	28	16	22	87	77	P	1		2
Crewe Alexandra	1894-95	4	2	0	0	8	1	0	2	0	3	3	2	2	0	11	4				2
Crystal Palace	1921-22	32	5	8	3	24	18	6	1	9	20	22	11	9	12	44	40	P	1	1*	2
Darwen	1894-95	10	3	0	2	12	6	1	0	4	6	20	4	0	6	18	26				2
Derby County	1907-08	78	11	15	13	52	46	9	5	25	40	73	20	20	38	92	119	P	1	1*	2
Doncaster Rovers	1901-02	24	11	0	1	36	10	2	6	4	12	17	13	6	5	48	27				2
Everton	1908-09	92	21	13	12	87	62	9	14	23	59	111	30	27	35	146	173	P	1		2
Fulham	1907-08	68	16	4	14	69	52	5	8	21	39	73	21	12	35	108	125		1		2
Gainsborough Trinity	1896-97	30	12	3	0	41	7	5	3	7	12	26	17	6	7	53	33				2
Glossop	1898-99	30	8	3	4	30	26	5	4	6	17	28	13	7	10	47	54				2
Grimsby Town	1894-95	68	22	6	6	59	25	6	8	20	37	80	28	14	26	96	105		1	1*	2
Huddersfield Town	1910-11	50	10	3	12	35	39	5	5	15	28	55	15	8	27	63	94		1	1*	2
Hull City	1905-06	56	12	6	10	43	35	4	11	13	40	62	16	17	23	83	97				2
Ipswich Town	1961-62	46	11	4	8	29	21	5	7	11	22	32	16	11	19	51	53	P	1	1*	2
Leeds City	1905-06	18	5	3	1	25	12	1	3	5	11	24	6	6	6	36	36				2
Leeds United	1920-21	96	21	15	12	90	68	9	11	28	55	108	30	26	40	145	176	P	1		2
Lincoln City	1894-95	50	19	3	3	67	28	8	1	16	35	61	27	4	19	102	89				2
Liverpool	1895-96	84	22	9	11	67	56	11	9	22	52	80	33	18	33	119	136	P	1		2
Loughborough Town	1895-96	10	5	0	0	19	2	4	1	0	12	2	9	1	0	31	4				2
Luton Town	1897-98	52	11	12	3	46	35	8	6	12	30	36	19	18	15	76	71		1	1*	2
Manchester City	1894-95	86	18	12	13	73	54	6	10	27	50	108	24	22	40	123	162	P	1		2
Manchester United	1894-95	108	25	13	16	94	89	6	13	35	56	125	31	26	51	150	214	P	1		2
Middlesbrough	1899-1900	66	15	11	7	51	42	11	6	16	43	60	26	17	23	94	102	P	1	1*	2
Millwall	1946-47	22	7	3	1	23	6	2	3	6	7	11	9	6	7	30	17			1*	2
Nelson	1923-24	2	1	0	0	3	1	0	1	0	1	1	1	1	0	4	2				2
New Brighton Tower	1898-99	6	1	1	1	6	4	0	2	1	2	3	1	3	2	8	7				2
Newcastle United	1894-95	102	30	11	10	107	68	7	11	33	62	100	37	22	43	169	168	P	1	1*	2
Newport County	1946-47	2	1	0	0	3	0	1	0	0	3	2	2	0	0	6	2				2
Northampton Town	1965-66	2	0	1	0	1	1	0	1	0	2	2	0	2	0	3	3		1		
Norwich City	1935-36	32	7	5	4	25	20	5	3	8	19	26	12	8	12	44	46	P	1	1*	2
Nottingham Forest	1906-07	84	24	11	7	79	54	10	7	25	45	79	34	18	32	124	133	P	1	1*	2
Notts County	1894-95	42	11	4	6	39	29	8	8	5	30	35	19	12	11	69	64		1	1*	2
Oldham Athletic	1907-08	28	10	2	2	28	8	3	5	6	12	17	13	7	8	40	25			1*	2
Orient	1905-06	42	14	3	4	43	23	8	2	11	17	27	22	5	15	60	50		1		2
Oxford United	1969-70	20	6	3	1	16	10	2	5	3	10	16	8	8	4	26	26		1	1*	2
Peterborough United	1992-93	4	1	0	1	2	3	0	1	1	1	4	1	1	2	3	7			1*	
Plymouth Argyle	1935-36	28	11	3	0	34	10	2	4	8	13	25	13	7	8	47	35				2
Portsmouth	1924-25	46	17	4	2	68	31	7	4	12	26	39	24	8	14	94	70		1	1*	2

CLUB	First Played	P	HOME					AWAY					OVERALL					Divisions Met In			
			W	D	L	F	A	W	D	L	F	A	W	D	L	F	A	P	1	1*	2
Port Vale	1894-95	48	15	6	3	49	12	10	7	7	31	32	25	13	10	80	44			1*	2
Preston North End	1901-02	38	6	6	7	26	28	2	4	13	17	39	8	10	20	43	67		1		2
Queens Park Rangers	1948-49	40	12	4	4	43	22	3	4	13	20	39	15	8	17	63	61	P	1		2
Reading	1987-88	4	1	1	0	2	1	1	1	0	3	2	2	2	0	5	3			1*	2
Rotherham County	1919-20	8	2	2	0	6	2	0	3	1	1	2	2	5	1	7	4				2
Rotherham Town	1894-95	4	2	0	0	12	2	1	0	1	1	2	3	0	1	13	4				2
Rotherham United	1951-52	14	7	0	0	21	7	2	4	1	9	7	9	4	1	30	14				2
Sheffield United	1908-09	72	12	15	9	63	50	10	12	14	50	67	22	27	23	113	117		1	1*	2
Sheffield Wednesday	1899-1900	92	22	13	11	92	64	11	13	22	50	73	33	26	33	142	137	P	1		2
Shrewsbury Town	1979-80	10	2	2	1	6	4	1	3	1	5	6	3	5	2	11	10				2
Southampton	1922-23	58	14	9	6	52	35	2	11	16	30	58	16	20	22	82	93	P	1		2
Southend United	1991-92	8	3	0	1	10	4	1	1	2	4	6	4	1	3	14	10			1*	2
South Shields	1919-20	12	4	2	0	11	2	1	1	4	7	11	5	3	4	18	13				2
Stockport County	1900-01	36	10	5	3	36	21	5	3	10	22	36	15	8	13	58	57				2
Stoke City	1907-08	68	17	12	5	59	34	6	9	19	30	51	23	21	24	89	85		1	1*	2
Sunderland	1908-09	72	20	6	10	70	44	9	12	15	45	54	29	18	25	115	98	P	1	1*	2
Swansea City	1935-36	22	4	5	2	21	11	4	3	4	15	18	8	8	6	36	29				2
Swindon Town	1969-70	16	5	2	1	20	14	1	4	3	9	13	6	6	4	29	27			1*	2
Tottenham Hotspur	1919-20	84	15	6	21	80	73	14	10	18	61	84	29	16	39	141	157	P	1		2
Tranmere Rovers	1991-92	8	1	1	2	2	3	2	1	1	6	5	3	2	3	8	8			1*	2
Walsall	1894-95	14	6	1	0	26	7	3	2	2	9	8	9	3	2	35	15				2
Watford	1969-70	32	6	8	2	30	20	5	3	8	21	28	11	11	10	51	48	P	1	1*	2
West Bromwich Albion	1901-02	88	19	10	15	80	65	10	9	25	49	93	29	19	40	129	158		1	1*	2
West Ham United	1919-20	112	29	13	14	98	69	10	13	33	68	119	39	26	47	166	188	P	1	1*	2
Wimbledon	1986-87	12	3	1	2	10	8	2	0	4	7	8	5	1	6	17	16	P	1		
Wolverhampton Wanderers	1906-07	88	21	12	11	74	43	10	12	22	41	84	31	24	33	115	127		1	1*	2
Wrexham	1978-79	6	2	1	0	4	1	1	2	0	1	0	3	3	0	5	1				2
Total		3898	988	495	466	3666	2377	458	491	1000	2264	3674	1446	986	1466	5930	6051				

Leicester Fosse/City have met 90 other clubs in Premier/Football League fixtures. Of the League's members in 2001/2, the following have never played Leicester in either League or Cup competitions:

Cheltenham Town, Colchester United, Halifax Town, Hartlepool United, Kidderminster Harriers, Macclesfield Town, Rushden & Diamonds, Wigan Athletic.

Of the former members of the League, the following fall into the same category:

Aberdare Athletic, Accrington, Accrington Stanley, Ashington, Barnet, Bootle, Chester City, Durham City, Merthyr Tydfil, Middlesbrough Ironopolis, New Brighton, Northwich Victoria, Stalybridge Celtic, Thames, Wigan Borough, Workington.

The following list represents League clubs, past and present, that have met Leicester in Cup ties but never in League fixtures:

Aldershot, Barrow, Darlington, Exeter City, Gillingham, Hereford United, Maidstone United, Mansfield Town, Rochdale, Scarborough, Scunthorpe United, Torquay United, Wycombe Wanderers, York City.
Note that Leicester Fosse met two early forerunners, Rushden and Irthlingborough, in cup ties, although the club has never met the amalgamated Rushden & Diamonds.

Apart from Leicester, the only other clubs never to have played League football outside of the top two divisions are:

Arsenal, Chelsea, Everton, Leeds United, Liverpool, Manchester United, Newcastle United, Tottenham Hotspur, West Ham United.

Note: Accrington and Accrington Stanley were separate clubs.
Arsenal incorporates games played against Woolwich Arsenal
Barnsley incorporates games played against Barnsley St Peters.
Birmingham City incorporates games played against Small Heath and Birmingham.
Leicester previously played an F A Cup tie against South Shore; that club amalgamated with Blackpool in 1899.
Bournemouth formerly met Leicester in the League Cup when known as Bournemouth & Boscombe Athletic.
Burton Swifts and Burton Wanderers amalgamated to form Burton United in 1901.
Chesterfield incorporates games played against Chesterfield Town.
Glossop incorporates games played against Glossop North End.
Leeds City and Leeds United were separate clubs.
Manchester United incorporates games played against Newton Heath.
New Brighton Tower and New Brighton were separate clubs.
Orient incorporates games played against Clapton Orient and Leyton Orient; the club have reverted to the name of Leyton Orient since the latest meeting.
Port Vale incorporates games played against Burslem Port Vale.
Rotherham County and Rotherham Town amalgamated to form Rotherham United in 1925.
Rushden Town and Irthlingborough Diamonds amalgamated to form Rushden & Diamonds in 1992.
South Shields later became known as Gateshead.
Stoke City incorporates games played against Stoke.
Swansea City incorporates games played against Swansea Town.
Walsall incorporates games played against Walsall Town Swifts.

Complete Wartime Record

Leicester Fosse, during World War One, and Leicester City during World War Two, took part in a variety of Official Football League competitions, with the season often split into separate competitions part-way through the campaign.

SEASON	COMPETITION	P	HOME						AWAY					OVERALL					Pts	Pos
			W	D	L	F	A	W	D	L	F	A	W	D	L	F	A		
FIRST WORLD WAR																			
1915-16	Midland (1)	26	9	2	2	30	15	2	4	7	12	19	11	6	9	42	34	28	5/14
	Midland (2)	10	2	2	1	8	8	1	1	3	7	11	3	3	4	15	19	9	3/6
1916-17	Midland (1)	30	4	5	6	17	19	2	2	11	12	34	6	7	17	29	53	19	15/16
	Midland (2)	6	3	0	0	8	4	1	0	2	4	8	4	0	2	12	12	8	4/16
1917-18	Midland (1)	28	11	0	3	38	12	2	3	9	14	31	13	3	12	52	43	29	7/15
	Midland (2)	6	2	1	0	5	2	0	0	3	1	8	2	1	3	6	10	5	12/16
1918-19	Midland (1)	30	10	2	3	37	23	3	1	11	16	30	13	3	14	53	53	29	10/16
	Midland (2)	6	2	0	1	8	5	1	0	2	2	8	3	0	3	10	13	6	2/4
WORLD WAR TWO																			
1939-40	Midland	28	6	3	5	32	26	1	3	10	19	45	7	6	15	51	71	20	7/8
1940-41	South	33	14	3	2	57	24	3	2	9	30	49	17	5	11	87	73	-	14/34
1941-42	South (1)	17	8	1	0	31	6	3	2	3	9	11	11	3	3	40	17	26.40	1/13
	National (2)	18	6	1	2	25	11	0	3	6	14	27	6	4	8	39	38	20.44	17/22
1942-43	North (1)	18	3	2	4	17	15	2	2	5	15	22	5	4	9	32	37	14	33/48
	North (2)	20	6	0	4	28	12	3	2	5	12	25	9	2	9	40	37	20	22/54
1943-44	North (1)	18	4	2	3	17	13	2	2	5	16	17	6	4	8	33	30	16	28/50
	North (2)	21	5	4	1	21	11	5	1	5	19	21	10	5	6	40	32	25	14/56
1944-45	North (1)	18	2	2	5	13	20	1	2	6	10	26	3	4	11	23	46	10	52/54
	North (2)	21	6	4	1	29	15	1	2	7	11	23	7	6	8	40	38	20	34/60
1945-46	South	42	4	3	14	30	47	4	4	13	27	54	8	7	27	57	101	23	20/22

Note: 1940-41: Competition decided on goal average (goals scored divided by goals conceeded) instead of points.

1941-42: In both competitions, points were calculated on the basis of all teams playing a standard number of matches.

Above: *The Vice President of The Football League, Arthur Oakley, presents the War League Southern Section Championship trophy to Leicester City captain Sep Smith after the first championship of 1941/2. Pictured (left to right) are: Arthur Oakley, Tom Bromilow, W. Taylor, Sep Smith, Alf Pallett, E. McLachlen and Frank Sheard.*

Non First Class Competitive Matches

	Date	Opponents	Result	1	2	3	4	5	6	7	8	9	10	11	

LEICESTERSHIRE F. A. SENIOR CUP 1887-88

	Date	Opponents	Result	1	2	3	4	5	6	7	8	9	10	11	
1	Oct 29 B	St Saviours (1)	W 4-2	West	De Ville	Ashmole	**Bankart 1**	Poyner	Gardner F	**James 1**	**Hassell 1**	**Knight 1**	Wright	Johnson E	1
2	Nov 26 B	St Saviours (1)	W 5-0	De Ville	Johnson W	Sudbury	Gardner F	Frost	Ashmole	**James 1**	**Bentley 2**	**Thompson 2**	Knight	Johnson E	2
3	Dec 24 A	Shepshed (2)	D 3-3	West	Johnson W	Sudbury	Poyner	Ashmole	Staines	James	**Thompson 2**	**Knight 1**	Johnson E	Gardner F	3
4	Jan 21 A	Shepshed (2 rep)	D 2-2	West	Johnson W	Staines	Ashmole	Poyner	Wright	James	Foster	Thompson	Knight	Johnson E	4
5	28	Shepshed (2 rep 2)	L 1-2	West	Johnson W	Ashmole	Sudbury	Poyner	Wright	James	Foster	Thompson	**Knight 1**	Johnson E	5

Note: B = Belgrave Road; Oct 29, declared void due to poor light; Jan 21, scorers not listed; Jan 28, at Loughborough.

LEICESTERSHIRE F. A. SENIOR CUP 1888-89

	Date	Opponents	Result	1	2	3	4	5	6	7	8	9	10	11	
1	Nov 10 V	Syston Wreake Valley (1)	W 12-1	De Ville	Gardner G	Sudbury	Johnson J	Johnson W	Poyner	**Glover 1**	Bentley	**Webb 6**	**Knight 4**	**Johnson E 1**	1
2	Feb 23 A	Loughborough Town (3)	L 0-2	Radford	Gardner G	Simpson	Johnson J	Timson	Sudbury	Rippon	Brady	Webb	Knight	Johnson E	2

Note: V = Victoria Park; Fosse received a bye in Round 2.

LEICESTERSHIRE F. A. SENIOR CUP 1889-90

	Date	Opponents	Result	1	2	3	4	5	6	7	8	9	10	11	
1	Dec 14 M	Leicester Teachers (2)	W 2-0	Walker	Simmonds	Davis	Johnson J	Perry	Vickers	Bentley	Murdoch	**Webb 1**	Parr	**Johnson E 1**	1
2	Mar 1	Loughborough Town (sf)	W 4-0	Walker	Rowson	Davis	Johnson J	Perry	Vickers	Bentley	**Murdoch 1**	**Webb 2**	**Johnson E 1**	Eggleton	2
3	29	Coalville Town (f)	D 1-1	Walker	Rowson	Davis	Johnson J	Perry	Vickers	Bentley	Murdoch	**Webb 1**	Squire	Johnson E	3
4	Apr 12	Coalville Town (f rep)	W 4-0	Walker	**Rowson 1**	Davis	Johnson J	**Murdoch 1**	Vickers	**Gardner F 1**	Bentley	**Thompson 1**	Johnson E	West	4

Note: M = Mill Lane; Fosse received a bye in Round 1; Mar 1, at Coalville; Mar 29, Apr 12, at Loughborough.

LEICESTERSHIRE F. A. SENIOR CUP 1890-91

	Date	Opponents	Result	1	2	3	4	5	6	7	8	9	10	11	
1	Jan 24 M	Melton Rovers (1)	W 10-0	Walker	Rowson	**Davis 1**	Johnson J	Perry	Nuttall	**Flint 1**	**Murdoch 2**	**Webb 2**	**Johnson E 2**	**Atter 2**	1
2	Feb 21	Leicester Teachers (sf)	W 3-1	Walker	Rowson	Davis	Johnson J	Perry	Gardner F	Flint	Murdoch	**Webb 1**	Johnson E	**Atter 2**	2
3	Mar 21	Gresley Rovers (f)	W 2-0	Walker	Rowson	Davis	Johnson J	Perry	Nuttall	Flint	Murdoch	**Webb 1**	**Johnson E 1**	Atter	3

Note: M = Mill Lane; Feb 21, at Coalville; Mar 21, at Loughborough.

UNITED COUNTIES LEAGUE 1894-95

	Date	Opponents	Result	1	2	3	4	5	6	7	8	9	10	11	
1	Feb 16 A	Derby County	D 2-2	Thraves	Whitelaw	Bailey	Seymour	Hughes	Henrys	Brown	**McArthur 1**	**Gordon 1**	Skea	Priestman	1
2	Mar 14 A	Notts County	W 2-0	Thraves	Bailey	Thompson	Lord	Hughes	Henrys	Stirling	Milliken	Miller	**Skea 2**	Hill	2
3	25 A	Sheffield United	L 2-3	Thraves	Bailey	Whitelaw	**Brown 1**	Hughes	Henrys	Hill	Miller	**Gordon 1**	Milliken	Stirling	3
4	Apr 1 H	Derby County	L 1-4	Thraves	Smith	Bailey	Lord	Hughes	Henrys	Hill	McArthur	Gordon	**Milliken 1**	Gallacher	4
5	4 A	Nottingham Forest	L 0-3	Chappell	Smith	Bailey	Lord	Brown	Henrys	Priestman	Milliken	Miller	Skea	Gallacher	5
6	13 H	Notts County	W 2-1	Chappell	Thompson	**McFarlane 1**	Miller	Seymour	Lord	Stirling	Pickard	Milliken	**Narraway 1**	Priestman	6
7	22 H	Nottingham Forest	D 1-1	Chappell	Thompson	McFarlane	Davis	McAlpin	Whitelaw	Tyler	**Stirling 1**	Milliken	Narraway	Priestman	7

SOUTHERN PROFESSIONAL FLOODLIT CUP 1959-60

	Date	Opponents	Result	1	2	3	4	5	6	7	8	9	10	11	
1	Oct 21 H	Charlton Athletic (1)	W 4-0	Slack	Chalmers	Baillie	**McLintock 1**	Knapp	**Appleton 1**	**Riley 1**	Keyworth	Leek	**Cheesebrough 1**	Wills	1
2	Nov 23 A	Arsenal (2)	L 2-4	Banks	Chalmers	Norman	White	Cunningham	Appleton	Riley	Stephenson	**Walsh 1**	Leek	**Wills 1**	2

F. A. CHARITY SHIELD 1971-72

	Date	Opponents	Result	1	2	3	4	5	6	7	8	9	10	11	
1	Aug 7 H	Liverpool	W 1-0	Shilton	**Whitworth 1**	Nish	Kellard	Sjoberg	Cross	Farrington	Brown	Fern	Sammels	Glover * (Manley)	1

ANGLO-ITALIAN TOURNAMENT 1971-72

	Date	Opponents	Result	1	2	3	4	5	6	7	8	9	10	11	
1	Jun 1 A	Cagliari	L 0-1	Wallington	Whitworth * (Farrington)	Nish	Cross	Sjoberg * (Fern)	Manley	Partridge	Sammels	Weller	Birchenall	Glover	1
2	4 A	Atalanta	L 3-5	Wallington	Whitworth	Nish	Cross	Sjoberg	Manley	Partridge	**Sammels 2**	**Weller 1**	Birchenall	Glover	2
3	7 H	Cagliari	W 2-1	Wallington	Whitworth	**Nish 1 * (Sjoberg)**	Cross	Manley	Sammels	Farrington	**Weller 1**	Birchenall	Partridge * (Fern)	Glover	3
4	10 H	Atalanta	W 6-0	Shilton	Woollett	Yates	Cross	Manley	**Nish 1**	Tomlin	**Weller 2**	Partridge	**Sammels 1**	**Glover 1 * (Farrington 1)**	4

Note: Jun 4, substitutes Farrington and Fern both played, but players withdrawn not recorded; Jun 10, substitute Sjoberg also played, but player withdrawn not recorded.

TEXACO CUP 1972-73

	Date	Opponents	Result	1	2	3	4	5	6	7	8	9	10	11	
1	Sep 13 H	Dundee United (1 leg 1)	D 1-1	Shilton	Whitworth	Rofe	Woollett	Cross	Sammels	Farrington	Worthington	**Weller 1**	Tomlin	Manley	1
2	27 A	Dundee United (1 leg 2)	D 2-2	Shilton	Whitworth	Rofe	Woollett	Cross	Birchenall	Farrington	Stringfellow * (Partridge)	Weller	**Worthington 1**	**Glover 1**	2
3	Oct 24 H	Norwich City (2 leg 1)	W 2-0	Shilton	Whitworth	Rofe	Sammels	Munro	Woollett	**Farrington 1**	Birchenall	Weller * (Partridge)	**Worthington 1**	Glover	3
4	Nov 8 A	Norwich City (2 leg 2)	L 0-2	Wallington	Whitworth	Rofe	Sammels	Munro	Woollett	Farrington	Birchenall	Manley * (Jopling)	Worthington	Glover	4

Note: Sep 27, won 3-0 on penalties; Nov 8, lost 3-4 on penalties.

TEXACO CUP 1973-74

	Date	Opponents	Result	1	2	3	4	5	6	7	8	9	10	11	
1	Sep 19 A	Ayr United (1 leg 1)	D 1-1	Shilton	Whitworth	Manley	Stringfellow * (Partridge)	Munro	Cross	Weller	Sammels	Worthington	Birchenall	Glover	1
2	Oct 3 H	Ayr United (1 leg 2)	W 2-0	Shilton	Whitworth	Yates	**Stringfellow 1**	Munro	Cross	Weller	Sammels	Worthington	**Birchenall 1**	Glover	2
3	24 H	Dundee United (2 leg 1)	D 1-1	Shilton	Whitworth * (Farrington)	Rofe	Stringfellow	Munro	Woollett	Weller	Sammels	**Worthington 1p**	Birchenall	Glover	3
4	Nov 7 A	Dundee United (2 leg 2)	L 0-1	Shilton	Whitworth	Rofe	Farrington * (Stringfellow)	Munro	Manley	Weller	Sammels	Worthington	Birchenall	Glover	4

Note: Sep 19, McAnespie (og).

F. A. CUP THIRD PLACE PLAY OFF 1973-74

	Date	Opponents	Result	1	2	3	4	5	6	7	8	9	10	11	
1	May 9 H	Burnley	L 0-1	Wallington	Woollett	Rofe	Earle	Munro	Cross	Tomlin	Sammels	Stringfellow	Kilkelly	Glover * (Lee)	1

ANGLO-SCOTTISH TOURNAMENT 1975-76

	Date	Opponents	Result	1	2	3	4	5	6	7	8	9	10	11	
1	Aug 2 A	Hull City	D 1-1	Wallington	Whitworth	Rofe	**Sammels 1**	Blockley	Birchenall	Alderson	Kember	Lee * (Tomlin)	Worthington	Garland	1
2	6 A	Mansfield Town	L 0-2	Wallington	Whitworth	Rofe	Sammels	Blockley	Birchenall	Kember	Glover	Worthington	Garland	Alderson	2
3	9 H	West Bromwich Albion	W 2-1	Wallington	Whitworth	Rofe	Kember	Blockley	Birchenall	Alderson * (Tomlin)	Garland	Worthington	Sammels	**Lee 2**	3

Friendlies

There follows a list of friendly, testimonial, charity and minor cup games played by Fosse / City since 1884. Over the years there have been frequent instances where the club has fielded a team containing a mixture of first-team players and reserves. In such cases we have exercised our judgement as best we are able, so that only friendlies classed as 'first team' are included. Matches played behind closed doors are excluded. We have appended details of goalscorers, where known, for all friendly fixtures since the club commenced competitive football in the Midland League in 1891.

FOSSE IN PRE-LEAGUE DAYS

(Key to venues: V = Victoria Park; B = Belgrave Road; M = Mill Lane; A = away)
(NB: Especially in the case of the initial two venues, it is sometimes impossible to gather whether a given game was officially a 'home' or 'away' fixture. A cumulative record for 1884/5 shows Fosse additionally having played two untraced games: a 0-0 draw and a 0-2 defeat. Where no scoreline is appended to a fixture, we know only that the said fixture was scheduled: either the game was cancelled or, more likely, simply not reported. A summary of results for the first decade, produced in the 1893 club history, is sometimes at odds with the total of individual match reports unearthed in the local press).

01.11.84 Syston Fosse (at Fosse Rd) 5-0
08.11.84 Wyggeston Boys School (V) 1-1
15.11.84 Mill Hill House (V) 1-2
22.11.84 Syston St Peters (A) 2-1
(12-a-side)
29.11.84 Mill Hill House (V) 0-0
03.01.85 Melbourne Hall (V) 2-0
10.01.85 Syston Fosse (A) 1-0
(abandoned: rain)
24.01.85 St Marys (V) 1-0
31.01.85 Mill Hill House (V) 1-1
07.02.85 Syston St Peters (V) 2-0
(12-a-side)
07.03.85 Wyggeston Boys School (V) 0-1
14.03.85 Mill Hill House (V) 2-0
21.03.85 St Marys (V) 1-0

03.10.85 Trinity Band of Hope (V) 6-0
17.10.85 Wyggeston Boys School (V) 4-1
24.10.85 Harborough (2nd Team) (V) 1-1
07.11.85 Mill Hill House (V) 0-1
14.11.85 Belgrave (A) 3-0
21.11.85 St Marys (V) 3-0
30.01.86 Mill Hill House (V) 3-0
06.02.86 Wyggeston Boys School (V) 1-0
13.02.86 Syston Wreake Valley (A) 2-1
20.02.86 Belgrave (V) 1-0
17.04.86 Leicester Town (V) 2-0

16.10.86 Leicester Association (V) 2-1
23.10.86 Barwell (A) 1-1
30.10.86 Leicester Wanderers (V) 0-2
06.11.86 Coalville (A) 0-0
(abandoned: Coalville walk-off)
13.11.86 Wyggeston School Past & Present (V) 5-0
20.11.86 Belgrave (A) 2-0
27.11.86 Leicester Association (V) 0-1
04.12.86 St Marks (V) 2-2
11.12.86 Leicester Wanderers (V) 3-0
22.01.87 Coalville (V) 3-0
29.01.87 Wigston (V) 6-0
05.02.87 Loughborough (A) 1-4
12.02.87 Belgrave (V) 5-0
19.02.87 Barwell (V) 2-0
26.02.87 Notts St Saviours (A) 1-1
05.03.87 Market Harborough (V) 0-1
19.03.87 Wyggeston School Past & Present (V) 9-0
26.03.87 Loughborough (V) 3-0
09.04.87 Mill Hill House Past & Present (V) 1-0

01.10.87 Market Harborough (V) 4-0
08.10.87 Mill Hill House (V) 2-0
15.10.87 Wellingborough (A) 0-3
22.10.87 Notts County Reserves (B) 0-5
05.11.87 Burton Swifts (B) 0-4
12.11.87 Kettering (B) 2-4
19.11.87 Market Harborough (A) 2-2
03.12.87 Leicester Wanderers (B) 1-0
15.12.87 Leicester Banks (V) 4-6
26.12.87 Leicester Association (B)
07.01.88 Notts County Reserves (A) 0-1
14.01.88 Mill Hill House (B) 0-2
26.01.88 Thursday Half-Holiday XI (V)
04.02.88 Leicester Association (V)
11.02.88 Kettering (A) 0-3
03.03.88 Burton Swifts (A) 0-0
10.03.88 Leicester Association (V) 2-0
15.03.88 Leicester Banks (V)
17.03.88 Loughborough (B)
24.03.88 Mill Hill House Past & Present (V)
31.03.88 Leicester Wanderers (V) 1-1
07.04.88 Rushden (B)
21.04.88 Coalville (A) 3-1
05.05.88 Coalville (A) 1-5

16.09.88 Long Eaton Midland (A) 1-4
22.09.88 Nottingham Forest Res. (V) 0-3
29.09.88 Loughborough (A) 0-4
06.10.88 Leicester Teachers (V) 5-0
13.10.88 Coalville (V) 4-0
20.10.88 Shepshed (A) 2-2
27.10.88 Market Harborough (A) 6-0
03.11.88 Kettering (A) 2-1
17.11.88 Loughborough (A) 1-3
24.11.88 Nottingham Forest Res. (A) 1-2
01.12.88 Kettering (V) 0-1
08.12.88 Mill Hill House (A) 3-0
15.12.88 Wellingborough (V) 0-0
22.12.88 Beeston St Johns (V)
29.12.88 Notts County Reserves (A)
05.01.89 Market Harborough (V)
12.01.89 Bulwell United (V) 0-0
19.01.89 Sawley Rangers (A) 3-1
26.01.89 Long Eaton Midland (V) 2-3
02.02.89 Notts County Reserves (V) 1-2
09.02.89 Wellingborough (A)
16.02.89 Notts St Johns (A) 2-2
02.03.89 Sawley Rangers (V)
09.03.89 Leicester Teachers (V) 2-1
16.03.89 Wellingborough (A) 8-2
23.03.89 Shepshed (V) 3-2
30.03.89 Leicester Teachers (V) 2-0
06.04.89 Bulwell United (A) 0-0
13.04.89 Mill Hill House (A) (Leics Children's Hospital Fund) 3-2
20.04.89 Coalville Town (A) 1-0

28.09.89 Bulwell United (A) 0-3
05.10.89 Mill Hill House (M) 3-1
12.10.89 Grantham (A) 0-2
19.10.89 Notts Mapperley (M) 0-2
26.10.89 Leicester Teachers (M) 6-2
02.11.89 Coalville Town (A) 3-1
09.11.89 Market Harborough (M) 9-0
16.11.89 Long Eaton Midland (A) 0-2
23.11.89 Nottingham Forest Res. (M) 0-1
30.11.89 Shepshed (M) (Kettering Charity Cup Rd 1) 6-1
21.12.89 Grantham Rovers (A) 0-3
26.12.89 Stafford Rangers (A) 1-2
11.01.90 Notts County Reserves (M) 1-2

18.01.90 Kettering (A) 2-4
25.01.90 Beeston St Johns (A)
01.02.90 Beeston St Johns (M) 4-0
08.02.90 Kettering (A) (Kettering Charity Cup Rd 3) 1-3
15.02.90 Leicester Wanderers (M)
22.02.90 Kettering (M) (Kettering Charity Cup Rd 3) 2-2
08.03.90 Bulwell United (M) 5-0
15.03.90 Coalville Town (M) 1-1
04.04.90 Gresley Rovers (A)
05.04.90 Notts County Reserves (M) 2-3
08.04.90 Sheffield Montrose (M) 2-0

(NB: Kettering Charity Cup 1889/90: Fosse received bye in Rd 2; protested the result in Rd 3 over the state of Kettering's ground; and gained a replay; but we have no record of a further replay after the 2-2 draw, and presume Fosse withdrew).

06.09.90 Boston Town (A) 7-4
13.09.90 Singers (M) 5-3
20.09.90 Northampton (M) 10-0
25.09.90 Wellingborough GS (A) 4-2
27.09.90 Notts Mapperley (M) 3-0
16.10.90 Long Eaton Athletic (M) 3-2
16.10.90 Nottingham Forest Res. (M) 3-2
18.10.90 Burton Casuals (A) 0-1
25.10.90 Wellingborough GS (M) 4-1
01.11.90 Beeston St Johns (M) 4-1
08.11.90 Notts County Rovers (M) 4-3
15.11.90 Aston Villa Reserves (M) 2-3
24.11.90 Finedon (A) (Kettering Charity Cup Rd 1) 1-0
29.11.90 Singers (A)
06.12.90 Derby County Wanderers (M) 3-1
13.12.90 Loughborough (M) 1-1
20.12.90 Beeston St Johns (A)
26.12.90 Stafford Rangers (A) 1-1
27.12.90 London Casuals (M) 1-0
29.12.90 Loughborough (B) (Charity Match) 1-1
03.01.91 Kettering Town (A)
31.01.91 Leicester Teachers (M) 8-0
07.02.91 Loughborough (A) 1-3
14.02.91 Stafford Rangers (M) 0-2
28.02.91 Notts County Rovers (M) 3-3
07.03.91 Grantham Rovers (A) 2-3
14.03.91 Nottingham Forest Res. (M) 2-3
28.03.91 Notts Olympic (M) 5-0
30.03.91 Burton Wanderers (M) 2-2
31.03.91 Nottingham Forest Res. (M) 1-0
04.04.91 Sheffield Attercliffe (M) 2-3
11.04.90 Long Eaton Athletic (M) 3-0
11.04.91 Kettering Town (M) 3-2 [Mixed team - two fixtures same day]
13.04.91 Leicester Teachers / YMCA Select (M) (YMCA Benefit) 2-1
18.04.91 Stafford Rangers (M) 1-0
25.04.91 Burton Alma (M) 5-1
27.04.91 Notts County (M) 2-2

George Swift scored a rare goal on Boxing Day 1896.

(NB: Apart from the first five friendly fixtures marked (H*) below, which were played at the Aylestone Road Cricket Ground, all home fixtures thereafter took place at Filbert Street.)

05.09.91 Stafford Rangers (A) 0-1
(abandoned after dispute)
07.09.91 Derby County (H*) 1-3
[Atter]
14.09.91 Notts County (H*) 3-4
[Mouel 2, Harry Bailey pen]
19.09.91 Stafford Rangers (H*) 5-2
[Atter 2, Herrod 3]
26.09.91 Singers (H*) 4-1
[Opp og, Bennett 2, Johnson]
24.10.91 Notts Olympic (H*) 6-1
[Webb 3, Herrod, Mouel, Johnson]
31.10.91 Kettering (A) 2-0
[Johnson, Atter]
07.11.91 Nottingham Forest 'A' (H) 1-1
[Atter]
21.11.91 Wellingborough (H) (Kettering Charity Cup Rd1) 6-1
[Webb 4, Opp og, Johnson]
12.12.91 Kettering (A) (Kettering Charity Cup Rd2) 0-5
28.12.91 Notts County Rovers (H) 0-0
16.01.92 Loughborough (A) 1-4
[Nuttall]
20.02.92 Singers (A) 1-3
[Johnson]
27.02.92 Wolverhampton W. Res. (H) 1-3
[Gent]
05.03.92 Kettering (H) 2-2
[Nuttall, Harry Bailey]
26.03.92 Leicestershire XI (H) (Children's Hospital Charity) 4-1
[Johnson, Herbert Bailey 2, Mouel]
31.03.92 Notts St.Johns (H) 3-2
[Franklin, Lisle 2]
07.04.92 Notts Waverley (H) 5-1
[Scorers not known]
18.04.92 Ilford (H) 1-2
[Hufton]
23.04.92 Loughborough (H) 1-2
[Mouel]
25.04.92 Bolton Wanderers (H) 0-2

03.09.92 Singers (H) 10-1
[Slack, Webb 3, Carter 3, Silvester, Dorrell, Nuttall]
10.09.92 Rudge's (H) 5-3
[Webb 2, Lowe 2, Dorrell]
21.09.92 Mansfield Greenhalgh's (A) 0-0
24.09.92 Finedon (H) 6-0
[Slack, Freeman, Webb 3, Lowe]
03.12.92 Derby Town (H) 1-1
(abandoned 83 mins)
[Lowe]
10.12.92 Royal Scots (H) 2-0
[Lowe, Slack]
26.12.92 Casuals (H) 4-1
[Dorrell, Hardy 2, Lowe]
27.12.92 Stafford Rangers (H) 1-0
[Webb]
31.12.92 Oswaldtwistle Rovers (H) 5-1
[Slack, Lord, Lowe 2, Hardy]
11.02.93 Notts County Rovers (H) 7-2
[Taylor, Hardy, Slack 3, England, Atter]
04.04.93 Stoke Swifts (H) 2-2
[Priestman, Eccles og]
05.04.93 Loughborough (H) 1-4
[Dorrell]
15.04.93 Nottingham Forest (H) 1-5
[Webb]
24.04.93 Burton Swifts (H) 0-1
29.04.93 Loughborough (H) 5-1
[Worrall, Slack, Paton, Lowe 2]

02.09.93 Gainsborough Trinity (H) 5-0
[Worrall 3, Dorrell 2]
04.09.93 West Bromwich Albion (H) 3-0
[Hill, Dorrell, Worrall]

16.09.93 Sheffield United (H) 4-1
[Worrall 2, Dorrell, Rickus]
25.09.93 Notts County (H) 1-2
[Dorrell]
09.10.93 Accrington (H) 1-0
[Dorrell]
14.10.93 Northwich Victoria (H) 5-1
[Hill, Edwards 2, Miller, Rickus]
28.10.93 Heanor Town (H) 3-1
[Henrys, Seymour, Herbert Bailey]
11.11.93 Burslem Port Vale (H) 5-0
[Brown 3, Dorrell 2]
26.12.93 Casuals (H) (Harry Bailey Benefit) 6-0
[Brown 5, Miller]
27.12.93 Corinthians (H) 0-1
30.12.93 Kettering (H) (Kettering Charity Cup Q/F) 8-0
[Brown 4, Miller 2, Dorrell, Edwards]
17.02.94 Grantham Rovers (at Kettering) (Kettering Charity Cup S/F) 3-0
[Gawthorne, Slack, Bailey] [Fosse reserve XI]
26.03.94 Newcastle United (H) 2-0
[Hill, Miller]
27.03.94 Stockport County (H) 2-0
[Priestman 2]
28.03.94 Rangers (H) 1-2
[Miller]
31.03.94 Loughborough (A) 1-1
[Dorrell]
02.04.94 Aston Villa (A) (Bass Charity Cup Rd.1) 1-5
[Miller]
07.04.94 Wolverton L&NWR (at Kettering) (Kettering Charity Cup F) 3-1
[Miller 2, Dorrell]
16.04.94 Loughborough (H) 6-0
[McArthur 3, Priestman 2, Dorrell]
21.04.94 Rotherham Town (H) 2-0
[McArthur, Dorrell]
30.04.94 Wolverhampton W. (H) 0-2

03.09.94 Derby County (H) 3-2
[Skea, McArthur, 'scrimmage']
10.09.94 Preston North End (H) 3-1
[Miller 2, Hill]
17.09.94 Sunderland (H) 0-3
24.09.94 Sheffield Wednesday (H) 5-3
[Skea 2 (1 pen), McArthur, 2 'scrimmages']
29.10.94 Rushden (H) 4-1
[Stirling, Miller, Gallacher, Gordon]
24.12.94 Casuals (H) 3-2
[Narraway, Hughes 2]
26.12.94 Corinthians (H) 1-2
[Miller]
19.01.95 Kings Own Scottish Borderers (H) 11-0
[Milliken 2, Gordon 4, McArthur 3, Pickard, Gallacher]
11.02.95 Kettering (H) (Kettering Charity Cup Rd.1) 6-1
[Mablestone og, Gordon 3, Brown, Gallacher]
11.03.95 Loughborough (at Kettering) (Kettering Charity Cup S/F) 3-1
[Brown, Skea, Gallacher]
27.03.95 Aston Villa (at Burton Swifts) (Bass Charity Cup S/F) 2-1
[McArthur 2]
08.04.95 Burton Wanderers (at Kettering) (Kettering Charity Cup F) 0-1
16.04.95 Rangers (H) 1-2
[Hill]
24.04.95 Burton Wanderers (at Burton Swifts) (Bass Charity Cup F) 1-2 aet
[Skea]
25.04.95 Everton (H) 0-5

02.09.95 Nottingham Forest (H) 0-1
16.09.95 Millwall Athletic (H) 4-1
[McArthur, Skea, Trainer, Manson]
23.09.95 Millwall Athletic (A) 1-4
[McArthur]
31.10.95 Nottingham Forest (A) 2-5
[Trainer 2]
25.12.95 Cliftonville Athletic (H) 4-1
[Lynes, McArthur, Walker, Manson]
26.12.95 Corinthians (H) 1-2
[Brown]
28.12.95 Casuals (H) 6-5
(largely Fosse reserve team)
[Hogan 3, Manson, Smithson, Gallacher]
02.01.96 Middlesborough (A) 3-2
[Skea, Manson, McArthur]
13.01.96 Walsall (A) (Wellingborough Charity Cup Rd1) 0-3
15.01.96 Burton Wanderers (A) (Kettering Charity Cup Rd1) 0-1
20.01.96 Burton Swifts (A) (Birmingham Charity Cup Rd1) 1-2 aet
[Lynes]
01.02.96 Fairfield (H) 3-3
[Lynes, Davies, Manson]
18.02.96 Loughborough (H) 2-2
[Manson, Opp og]
14.03.96 Small Heath (H) 3-2
[Manson 2, Gallacher]
16.03.96 Wellingborough (A) 0-1
18.03.96 Loughborough (A) 0-0
25.03.96 Burton Wanderers (A) (Bass Charity Cup S/F) 0-1
18.04.96 Preston North End (H) 0-4
25.04.96 Stoke (H) 1-3
[Manson]

01.09.96 Luton Town (H) (Jimmy Thraves Benefit) 2-0
[Walker, Carnelly]
21.09.96 Aston Villa (H) 2-3
[Carnelly, McMillan]
05.10.96 Luton Town (A) 0-2
10.10.96 Kettering (H) 5-2
[Dorrell, McMillan 2, Walker, Lonie]
15.10.96 Loughborough (H) 4-2
[Freebairn 2, Carnelly 2]
31.10.96 Grantham Rovers (H) (Rushden Charity Cup Rd1) 2-0
[Worthington, Dorrell]
07.12.96 Walsall (A) (Birmingham Charity Cup Rd1) 3-8
[Dorrell, McMillan 2]
26.12.96 Corinthians (H) 3-3
[Dorrell, Swift, McDonald]
30.01.97 Reading (A) 3-4
[Dorrell 2, Freebairn]
04.02.97 Burton Wanderers (H) (Kettering Charity Cup Rd1) 2-2
[McMillan, Trainer]
08.02.97 Burton Wanderers (A) (Kettering Charity Cup Rd1 rep) 0-0
15.02.97 Burton Wanderers (at Kettering) (Kettering Ch. Cup Rd1 rep) 2-1
[Dorrell, Trainer]
09.03.97 Wellingborough (at Rushden) (Rushden Charity Cup S/F) 5-1
[Trainer 2, Freebairn, McMillan, Walker]
11.03.97 Luton Town (at Kettering) (Kettering Charity Cup S/F) 0-3
31.03.97 Loughborough (A) 0-0
03.04.97 Nottingham Forest (H) (Burford Charity Cup S/F) 3-0
[McMillan, Forman og, Dorrell]
20.04.97 Rangers (H) 1-1
[Bamford]
24.04.97 Sheffield Wednesday (H) 1-0
[Carnelly]
28.04.97 Notts County (at Nottm Forest) (Burford Charity Cup F) 2-0
[Dorrell 2]
29.04.97 Rushden (A) (Rushden Charity Cup F) 4-0
[Opp og, Carnelly, Freebairn 2]

01.09.97 Glossop North End (H) 5-0
[Freebairn, McLeod 3, Smith]
09.09.97 Derby County (H) 3-1
[Bamford, Flanagan, Gillies]
13.09.97 Burton Wanderers (H) (Jack Lord Benefit) 5-1
[King, Bamford, Freebairn, Gillies, 'scrimmage']
20.09.97 Nottingham Forest (H) 4-0
[Gillies 2, Smith 2]
25.09.97 Long Eaton Rangers (H) 4-2
[Gillies, Smith 2, Swift pen]
27.09.97 West Bromwich Albion (H) 4-1
[Smith, King, Gillies, Swift]
11.10.97 Rushden (A) (Rushden Charity Cup S/F) 1-0
[Gillies]
30.10.97 Luton Town (H) 5-2
[Freebairn, McMillan, McLeod, Swift pen, Smith]
01.11.97 Wellingborough (at Rushden) (Rushden Charity Cup F) 0-1
27.12.97 Everton (H) 1-1
[King]
28.12.97 Corinthians (H) 1-2
[Brown]
01.01.98 Millwall Athletic (A) 2-3
[Dorrell, 'scrimmage']
17.01.98 Wolverhampton Wanderers (H) (Birmingham Charity Cup Rd2) 1-3
[Freebairn]
24.02.98 Loughborough (H) 4-0
[Keech 3, McLeod]
12.04.98 Burslem Port Vale (H) 1-2
[Keech]
13.04.98 Burton Wanderers (A) (Bass Charity Cup S/F) 1-1
[Watkins]
20.04.98 Burton Wanderers (A) (Bass Charity Cup S/F rep) 0-1
23.04.98 Aston Villa (H) 2-1
[Keech, Coulson]
25.04.98 Notts County (H) (Burford Charity Cup S/F) 2-1
[Rowell, Coulson]
28.04.98 Nottingham Forest (A) (Burford Charity Cup F) 0-1

05.09.98 Southampton (H) (Jimmy Brown Benefit) 1-0
[McMillan]
14.09.98 Southampton (A) 0-1
19.12.98 Burslem Port Vale (A) (Birmingham Charity Cup Rd1) 0-5
28.12.98 Corinthians (H) (Billy Dorrell Benefit) 2-2
[McMillan 2]
14.02.99 Brighton United (H) 6-4
[Coulson 2, Watkins, McMillan 2, Walker pen]
25.03.99 Loughborough (H) 1-2
[Lyon]
06.04.99 Nottingham Forest (H) (Bass Charity Cup S/F) 1-1
[McMillan]
17.04.99 Nottingham Forest (at Burton) (Bass Charity Cup S/F rep) 1-7
[Galbraith]
04.09.99 Nottingham Forest (H) 1-4
[McMillan]
07.10.99 Kaffirs (H) 7-3
[King, Bradshaw, Brown, McMillan 2, Ball, Galbraith]
19.10.99 Everton (H) (Jack Walker Benefit) 1-4
[Bishop]
26.12.99 Corinthians (H) 1-7
[Wood]
15.01.00 Aston Villa (H) (Birmingham Charity Cup Rd1) 2-3
[King, Eaton]
10.02.00 Stoke (H) 2-2
[Brown, McMillan]
17.03.00 West Bromwich Albion (H) 3-1
[Brown, King, Eaton]

03.09.00 Chesterfield (H) (Bass Charity Vase S/F) 0-1
11.10.00 Wolverhampton Wanderers (H) (George Swift Benefit) 1-0
[Kyle]
08.12.00 Hinckley Town (A) 3-2
[Brown, Hamilton, Beadsworth]
24.12.00 Notts County (H) (Johnny McMillan Benefit) 3-4
[McMillan, Dunkley, Rosevear]
26.12.00 Corinthians (H) 2-1
[McMillan 2]
23.02.01 Bristol City (A) 0-1
04.03.01 Northampton Town (A) 6-1
[Kyle 3, Brown 2, Allsopp]
06.04.01 Scottish Amateurs (H) 3-2
[Connachan 2, Brown]
13.04.01 Brighton & Hove Rangers (A) 0-0
20.04.01 Lincoln City (A) 1-2
[Swift pen]

02.09.01 Stourbridge (H) 3-0
[Brown 2, Robinson]
16.09.01 Wellingborough (H) 4-0
[Brown 3, Richards]
25.09.01 Chesterfield (A) (Bass Charity Vase S/F) 2-3
[Dainty, Brown]
01.10.01 Grimsby Town (A) 0-1
08.02.02 Brentford (A) 1-1
[Swift pen]
23.04.02 Ripley (A) 3-1
[FS Benskin 3]
25.10.02 Clapton (A) 1-1
[Belton]
13.12.02 Queens Park Rangers (A) 3-2
[Brown, Roulston, Belton]
28.03.03 Brighton & Hove Albion (A) 4-5
[Belton 2 (1 pen), Pollock pen, Stewart]
25.04.03 Reading (H) 1-0
[E Coulson]
27.04.03 Hinckley Town (A) 1-4
[Peers]

01.09.03 Kettering (H) 1-1
[Evenson]
02.09.03 Reading (A) 1-4
[Blessington]
14.09.03 Notts County (H) 0-2
28.12.03 Clapton (H) (Walter Robinson Benefit) 1-1
[Mountain pen]
01.04.04 Watford (A) [Bell] 1-2
23.04.04 Northern Nomads (at Goodison Park) 3-0
[Evenson 2, Blessington]
05.09.04 Northampton Town (A) 2-1
[Brunton, Durrant]
12.09.04 Luton Town (A) 2-2
[Blessington, Evenson]
19.09.04 Hull City (A) 0-2
25.02.05 Leeds City (A) 5-1
[Blessington 2, Allsopp, Mounteney 2]
25.04.05 Nottingham Forest (H) 1-2
[Mounteney]
29.04.05 Clapton (H) [Durrant] 1-1
03.02.06 West Ham United (A) 0-2
12.03.06 Fulham (A) 2-6
[Durrant, Thomas og]
07.04.06 Sheffield United (H) 2-0
[Bannister, Hubbard]
17.04.06 Notts County (H) 1-1
[Hubbard]
23.04.06 Norwich City (A) 3-3
[Moody 3]
28.04.06 Coventry City (H) 3-1
[Durrant, Hubbard, Bannister]
15.10.06 Luton Town (A) 1-1
[Hubbard]
28.02.07 Luton Town (H) 1-0
[Blessington]
02.03.07 Stockport County (H) 4-0
[Hughes 2, Hubbard, Shanks]

16.09.07 Luton Town (A) 1-5
[Donnelly]
23.09.07 Notts County (H) 6-3
[Humphreys 3, Wilcox,
Durrant, RF Turner]
30.09.07 Burton United (A) 2-1
[Bannister, RW Turner]

05.10.08 Blackburn Rovers (at Peel
Croft, Burton) (Rawdon Colliery
Disaster Fund) 1-3
[Shinton]
12.10.08 Northampton Town (A)
(Dick Murrell Benefit) 0-2
26.04.09 Coventry City (A)
(Bass Charity Vase F) 2-0
[RW Turner, Donnelly]

01.01.10 Portsmouth (A) 1-2
[Hubbard]
25.10.10 Grimsby Town (A) 1-3
[Osborn]

30.12.11 Barrow (A) 1-4
[Hubbard]
12.02.12 Merthyr Tydfil (A) 4-0
[Sparrow 4]
06.03.12 Croydon Common (A) 2-3
[Yenson og, W King]
04.05.12 Leicestershire XI (H)
(Titanic Disaster Fund) 3-3
[Benfield, Mitchell, Noble]

16.09.12 Swansea Town (A) 0-1
01.02.13 Gillingham (A) [Mills 2] 2-0
01.03.13 Barrow (A) [Hubbard] 1-3
18.06.13 Örgryte/IFK Göteborg
Combined XI (Gothenburg) 3-2
[Benfield, Mortimer 2]
21.06.13 Stockholm Select XI (A) 4-0
[Mortimer 3, Waterall]
22.06.13 Swedish International
Federation (Rasunda) 4-2
[Benfield 2, Mortimer, Opp og]
24.06.13 Gefle IF (A) 5-1
[Benfield 2, King, Waterall,
Mortimer]
27.06.13 Swedish International
Federation (Rasunda) 4-2
[Malm og, Mortimer 3]

31.01.14 Northampton Town (A) 1-5
[Douglas]

28.09.14 Swansea Town (A) 0-3
29.09.14 Llanelly (A) 1-2
[Harrold]

25.09.15 Luton Town (A) 2-3
[C Freeman, Hogg]
06.05.16 Birmingham (A) 3-6
[Parsonage, Parker,
1 scorer not known]

17.03.17 Coalville Swifts (A) (VAD
Nursing Assn Benefit Fund) 1-1
[Boyne]
28.04.17 Coalville Swifts (A) (Disabled
Soldiers/Sailors Benefit) 1-2
[Roberts]
05.05.17 Leicestershire Regiment (H) 3-0
[Scorers not known]

09.03.18 Coventry City (A) 2-0
[Dennis, Leach]
01.04.18 Coventry City (H) 8-3
[King 3, Mortimer 4, Price]
04.05.18 Coventry City (H) (National
Football War Fund) 0-3
11.05.18 Combined Nottm Forest/
Notts Co XI (H) (NFWF) 3-2
[Donaldson, Price, Donald]
18.05.18 Coventry City (A) ?-?
09.11.18 Coventry City (A) 2-0
[Scorers not known]
28.04.19 British Expeditionary Force
(France) XI (H) 1-1
[Nock]

LEICESTER CITY

02.10.19 Select XI (H) (Billy Mills
Benefit) 7-2
[Scorers not known]
22.04.20 Nuneaton Town (A) 3-1
[Paterson 2, Walker]

21.09.21 Whitwick Imperial (A) 8-1
[King 4, Paterson 2, Richmond,
C Price]
12.10.21 Moira United (A)
(Ground Opening) 3-1
[Smith 3]
27.04.22 Northampton Town (A) 1-0
(Northampton Hospital Shield)
[Trotter]
04.05.22 Northampton Town (H) 1-1
(Leics Royal Infirmary Benefit)
[Graham]

19.10.22 West Bromwich Albion (H)
(Fred Shinton Benefit) 1-5
['Newman']

01.10.23 Raith Rovers (A)
(Bill Collier Benefit) 1-5
[Chandler]

30.04.25 Airdrieonians (H)
(Leics CCC Benefit) 3-1
[Carr, Duncan, Chandler]
04.05.25 Port Vale (A) 5-3
(Stoke Royal Infirmary Benefit)
[Sharp 2, Chandler 3]

15.03.26 Southampton (A)
(Tommy Allen/Albert Shelley
Benefit) 0-2
08.04.26 Hull City (A)
(Hull Hospital Cup) 2-1
[Chandler 2]
10.04.26 Kettering Town (A) 3-1
[Chandler, Lochhead 2]
20.04.26 Airdrieonians (H)
(Peter Hodge Benefit) 2-0
[Carr, Hine]
26.04.26 Norwich City (A) (Norfolk &
Norwich Hospital Cup) 2-1
[Bamber, Chandler]
01.05.26 Torquay United (A) 2-0
[Lochhead, Chandler]

26.02.27 Plymouth Argyle (A) 4-2
[Duncan, Wadsworth, Hine, Carr]
02.05.27 Norwich City (A) (Norfolk &
Norwich Hospital Cup) 4-1
[Hine, Adcock, Chandler 2]

03.03.28 St Mirren (H) 4-1
[Adcock, Barry, Lochhead, Lane]
11.04.28 Scottish League XI (H)
(Leics CCC Benefit) 7-2
[Hine 3, Lochhead 2, Duncan,
Chandler]
03.05.28 Grimsby Town (A)
(Grimsby Hospital Cup) 5-4 aet
[Hine 2, Chandler, Bishop,
Lochhead]

22.04.29 Birmingham (at Loughborough)
(Hospital Benefit) 5-2
[Chandler 4, Duncan]
29.04.29 Northampton Town (A)
(Northants CCC Benefit) 1-3
[Lochhead]
06.05.29 Grimsby Town (A)
(Grimsby Hospital Cup) 2-1 aet
[Hine 2]

30.04.30 Grimsby Town (A)
(Grimsby Hospital Cup) 2-1
[Chandler, Hine]
10.05.30 Blackpool (A)
(Blackpool Hospital Cup) 3-2
[Barry 2, Duncan]

24.01.31 Bournemouth & Boscombe
Athletic (A) 3-3
[Hine, Langford 2]
14.03.31 Aberdeen (A) 2-2
[Hine, Lochhead]
09.05.31 Blackpool (A)
(Blackpool Hospital Cup) 3-2
[Adcock, Chandler, Lochhead]

02.05.32 Northampton Town (A)
(George Allon Benefit) 3-4
['Newman', Smith 2]
05.05.32 Crook Town (A) 6-4
[Chandler 2, Ritchie, Barry 2,
Smith]

19.09.32 Bristol Rovers (A) 3-1
[Lowery, Ritchie, Heywood]
27.09.32 Grimsby Town (at Spalding)
(Nursing Cup) 7-2
[Heywood pen, Campbell 3,
Lochhead, Barry 2]
28.01.33 Rapid Vienna (H) 1-3
[Paterson]

18.09.33 Yeovil & Petters United (A) 1-0
[Liddle]
20.09.33 Exeter City (A)
(Reg Clarke Benefit) 2-3
[Maw 2]

16.04.34 St.Johnstone (H)
(Leics CCC Benefit) 2-1
[Chandler, Liddle]
26.04.34 Doncaster Rovers (A)
(George Flowers Benefit) 2-1
[Liggins 2]
01.05.34 Shelbourne (A) 3-2
[Gardiner, Lochhead, Liddle]
02.05.34 Linfield (A)
(Harry McCracken Benefit) 1-1
[Paterson]

19.09.34 Tunbridge Wells Rangers (A) 4-1
[Liddle, Gardiner, Paterson,
Maw]
15.04.35 Clapton Orient (A) 2-2
[Muncie, Chandler]
06.05.35 Coventry City (A)
(Jubilee Trust Fund) 3-3
[Liddle 2, McLeod]

30.04.36 Central Amateur League XI
(at Loughborough) 5-1
[Grogan 2, Coutts 2, McNally]

26.04.37 Chesterfield (A)
(Herbert Hamilton Benefit) 4-2
[Dewis, Liddle 2, Stubbs]
04.05.37 Grimsby Town (A)
(Grimsby Hospital Cup) 2-5
[Bowers, Liddle]
12.05.37 Venus Bucharest (A) 0-2
13.05.37 Ripensia Timisoara (A) 1-2
[Dewis]
16.05.37 Hungaria Budapest (A) 3-4
[Smith, Maw, Bowers]
17.05.37 BSK Belgrade (A) 0-3
23.05.37 Bratislava (A) 1-3
[O'Callaghan]

20.08.38 Derby County (H) (FL Jubilee
Benevolent Fund) 4-2
[Dewis 2, Moralee, Liddle]
20.04.39 Rushden (A)
(Rushden Charity Cup) 5-2
[Baines, Grant 2, Tompkin,
Moralee]
27.04.39 Stamford Town (A)
(Hospital Cup) 6-0
[S Smith 2, A Smith 2,
Baines, Muncie]
19.08.39 Derby County (A) (FL Jubilee
Benevolent Fund) 6-4
[Bowers 2, Liddle 2, Stubbs 2]
13.09.39 Army XI (H) 7-2
[Bowers 3, Smith 2, Adam pen,
Liddle]

16.09.39 Aston Villa (H) 3-0
[Coutts pen, Cummings og,
Bowers]
23.09.39 Birmingham (H) 6-4
[Smith, Bowers 2, Dewis 2,
Jayes]
30.09.39 Coventry City (A) 3-3
[Bowers, Dewis]
07.10.39 Sheffield United (H) 2-2
[Dewis, Smith]
14.10.39 Port Vale (H) 2-2
[Jayes, Dewis]
26.12.39 Nottingham Forest (A) 1-3
[Bowers]
01.01.40 Chesterfield (A) 2-7
[Thompson 2]
25.03.40 Sheffield Wednesday (H) 5-2
[Thompson, Bowers 2, Jayes 2]
13.04.40 Chelmsford City (A) 0-1

13.12.41 Czech Army XI (H) 8-1
[Sanderson 3, Jayes 3,
Cheney 2]
25.04.42 Crystal Palace (A) 3-1
[Liddle, Jayes, Barratt]
02.05.42 Birmingham (at Villa Park) 3-0
[Liddle, Jayes, Barratt]
09.05.42 Birmingham (H) 4-2
[Jayes 2, Hernon, Liddle]

19.05.45 Crystal Palace (H) 0-1
26.05.45 Crystal Palace (A) 4-1
[Liddle 2, Revie, Blackman og]

02.03.46 Preston North End (A) 3-2
[Revie 2, Cutting]
11.05.46 Notts County (A) (Bolton
Disaster Relief Fund) 0-5

29.03.47 Arsenal (A) 1-3
[Smith]

22.04.48 Moira & District (A) 4-3
[Hines, Revie, Smith, Hernon]
30.04.48 St Mirren (A) 0-3

05.09.49 Linfield (A) 5-1
[Chisholm 3, Griffiths, Adam]
28.01.50 Luton Town (A) 1-4
[Chisholm]
01.05.50 Exeter City (A) 0-1
(Jimmy Gallagher Testimonial)
03.05.50 Notts County (H)
(Sep Smith Test) 3-0
[Marsh, Lee, Barlow]

27.01.51 Sheffield Wednesday (H) 1-0
[Baldwin]
10.02.51 Reading (A) 2-2
[Brice og, Hines]
03.05.51 Derby County (H)
(Willie Frame Testimonial) 4-3
[Hines 2, Barlow, Halton pen]
14.05.51 FK Austria (H)
(Festival of Britain) 1-2
[Rowley]

21.04.52 Torquay United (A)
(Bill Towers Testimonial) 6-2
[Griffiths 3, Rowley 2,
Worthington]
28.04.52 Portsmouth (H) (Tom Bradshaw
[Leics FA] Testimonial) 4-1
[Rowley 3, Griffiths]
07.05.52 Wisbech Town (A)
(Horace Racey Charity Cup) 5-0
[Hines, Rowley, Worthington,
Dryburgh, Griffiths]
13.05.52 North Holland XI
(Groningen) 1-1
[Scorer not known]
17.05.52 East Holland XI (Nijmegen) 4-1
[Scorers not known]
21.05.52 Utrecht (A) 3-1
[Scorers not known]
24.05.52 PSV Eindhoven (A) 3-2
[Dunne (or Dixon?),
Rowley, Worthington]

Above: With the installation of floodlights in 1957, City embarked on a series of prestige friendlies against foreign opposition. Here Willie Gardiner gets in a header against Brazilian club Canto do Rio in April 1958.

31.01.53 Charlton Athletic (H) 4-3
[Morris, Crawford, Hines 2]
22.04.53 Mansfield Town (A) (Johnny
Grogan/Sid Carter Testimonial)
[Crawford, Rowley] 2-3
29.04.53 Wolverhampton Wanderers (H)
(Ian McGraw Testimonial) 1-2
[Rowley pen]
04.05.53 Wisbech Town (A)
(Horace Racey Charity Cup) 2-1
[Rowley, Littler]

30.11.53 Weymouth (A) 3-1
[Morris, Griffiths, Littler]

29.01.55 Lincoln City (A) 4-3
[Graver 2, Morris, Rowley]
11.05.55 Shelbourne (A) 2-1
(Andy Fitzpatrick Testimonial)
[Thomas, Griffiths]
13.05.55 Cork Athletic (A) 4-1
[Hogg, Thomas, Hines 2]

26.09.55 Penzance (A) 6-2
[Rowley, Gardiner, Hogg 2,
Hines 2]
02.05.56 Tommy Lawton's XI
(at Kettering) (Albert Johnson/
Willie Waddell Benefit) 3-3
[Gardiner 2, Ward]
12.05.56 St Mirren (A)
(Paisley Charity Cup) 3-1
[Rowley 3 (1 pen)]
14.05.56 Inverness Select XI (A) 2-0
[Rowley, Gardiner]

16.02.57 Hibernian (A) 3-2
[McNeill 2, Muir og]
25.04.57 International XI (H)
(Mal Griffiths Testimonial) 2-6
[McDonald, Hines]
29.04.57 Hibernian (H) 1-4
[Hogg]
02.05.57 Chelsea (A) 1-2
(Ken Armstrong Testimonial)
[McNeill]

23.09.57 Aberdeen (A) 1-1
[McDonald]
23.10.57 Borussia Dortmund (H)
(Floodlight Inauguration) 1-0
[Gardiner]
14.11.57 BSK Belgrade (H) 3-2
[McNeill 2, Cunningham pen]

25.01.58 Peterborough United (A) 1-2
[Walsh]
27.01.58 Walsall (A) 3-1
[Hines 3]
28.04.58 Canto do Rio (H) 1-0
[Gardiner]
30.04.58 Kettering Town (A) 2-4
(Geoff Toseland Testimonial)
[McNeill, Hines]
05.05.58 Norwich City (A)
(Norfolk Hospital Cup) 2-3
[McNeill, Hines]
21.05.58 TUS Neuendorf (A) 1-1
[Walsh]

10.08.58 Borussia Dortmund (A) 1-2
[Walsh]
29.10.58 Borussia Dortmund (H) 2-2
[McNeill 2]
26.11.58 Raith Rovers (H) 3-3
[McNeill, Lornie, Leek]
01.05.59 Shrewsbury Town (A) (Crossley/
Wallace/Moloney Benefit) 2-2
[Baillie pen, Wills]

26.10.59 Corby Town (A) (Jack Connors/
Tom Hadden Benefit) 5-0
[Cheesebrough 3, McDonald,
Leek]
28.03.60 Hibernian (H) 0-1
02.05.60 Loughborough Brush (A)
(Stan Hodges Testimonial) 6-0
[Keyworth 2, Riley 3, Walsh]

26.09.60 Dunfermline Athletic (A) 2-3
[Riley, Keyworth]
14.11.60 Peterborough United (A) 2-2
[Cheesebrough, Leek]
21.05.61 Southern Rhodesia
(at Salisbury) 2-0
[Keyworth, Walsh]
25.05.61 Southern Rhodesia
(at Bulawayo) 4-3
[Riley, Walsh, McIlmoyle,
Keyworth]
27.05.61 Durban City (A) 2-0
[King pen, Walsh]
01.06.61 Natal (at Pietermaritzburg) 6-0
[Keyworth 2, Cheesebrough 2,
McIlmoyle, Walsh]
03.06.61 Combined Transvaal XI
(at Johannesburg) 1-1
[King pen]

05.08.61 St Mirren (A)
(Paisley Charity Cup) 1-3
[McIlmoyle]
12.08.61 Walsall (A) 0-1
13.12.61 Past City XI (H) (Arthur
Chandler Testimonial) 8-3
[McIlmoyle, Wills 3,
Cheesebrough, Appleton, Heath,
McDerment]
27.01.62 Rotherham United (A) 1-1
[Madden og]
19.03.62 Oxford United (A) (Johnny
Love/Geoff Denial Benefit) 2-5
[Stringfellow, Heath]
31.03.62 Partick Thistle (H) 2-1
[Walsh, Cheesebrough]
09.05.62 Gibraltar (A) 5-0
[Walsh, Riley, Keyworth 2,
McLintock]
12.05.62 Malaga (A) 1-0
[Keyworth]

11.08.62 Leeds United (A) 4-2
[Riley, Walsh, Stringfellow,
Cross]
13.08.62 Leeds United (H) 2-2
[Cheesebrough 2]

13.08.63 GVAV Groningen (A) 3-2
[McLintock, Norman, Cross]
15.08.63 Blau Wit (A) 3-0
[Riley 2, Stringfellow]
19.08.63 Grimsby Town (A) 1-1
[Stringfellow]
24.01.64 Coventry City (A) 1-0
[Riley]
08.04.64 Poole Town (A)
(Stan Rickaby Testimonial) 2-1
[Roberts, McLintock]
29.04.64 All Star XI (H) 7-3
(Colin Appleton Testimonial)
[Svarc 5, Roberts, Stringfellow]
10.05.64 Ingoldstadt (A) 2-2
[Gibson, Appleton pen]
13.05.64 Lustenau (A) 0-1
15.05.64 LASK Linz (A) 1-2
[McLintock]
18.05.64 Innsbruck (A) 5-2
[Gibson 2, McLintock, Keyworth,
Sweenie]

15.08.64 Shrewsbury Town (A) 4-1
[Riley, Svarc 2, Stringfellow]
17.08.64 Peterborough United (A) 3-2
[Gibson, Hodgson, Roberts]
14.09.64 Rugby Town (A) 7-1
[Svarc 3, Roberts 2, Cross,
Sweenie]
26.10.64 Hannover '96 (H) 5-1
[Goodfellow, Cross 2, Gibson,
McDerment]
11.05.65 GVAV Groningen (A) 1-1
[Goodfellow]
15.05.65 Dresden Select (A) 2-2
[Gibson, Cross]
18.05.65 Hannover '96 (A) 1-0
[Opp og]

06.08.65 Shamrock Rovers (A) 5-2
[Dougan 2, Sweenie 2, Gibson]
09.08.65 Cork Hibernian (A) 5-3
[Sinclair 2, Walker,
Dougan pen, Sweenie]
12.08.65 Limerick (A) 6-1
[Stringfellow 2, Sweenie,
Goodfellow, Dougan, Sinclair]
16.08.65 Northampton Town (H) 6-1
[Sweenie 2, Roberts pen,
Stringfellow, Sinclair, Dougan]
25.10.65 Nuneaton Borough (A)
(Floodlight Inauguration) 1-3
[Sweenie]
02.05.66 Scotland XI (H)
(Alec Dowdells Testimonial) 1-1
[Dougan]

06.08.66 Borussia Mönchengladbach (A) 3-0
[Stringfellow, Roberts, Sinclair]
10.08.66 Gottingen (A) 4-1
[Stringfellow 2, Sinclair 2]
13.08.66 Werder Bremen (A) 3-1
[Stringfellow, Roberts, Sinclair]
21.09.66 PSV Eindhoven (A) 3-1
[Dougan, Goodfellow,
Stringfellow]
12.10.66 Oxford United (A) 3-1
[Sinclair, Roberts, Mackay]
16.02.67 Crystal Palace (A) 1-1
[Goodfellow]
18.02.67 Rangers (H) 1-0
[Dougan]
10.03.67 Derby County (A) 2-1
[Gibson, Rodrigues]
18.04.67 Borussia Dortmund (H) 6-0
[Paul og, Nish, Gibson,
Stringfellow, Goodfellow,
Matthews]
01.05.67 Werder Bremen (H) 2-2
[Sinclair, Sharkey]
20.05.67 Southampton
(in Kuala Lumpur) 3-1
[Sinclair 3]
25.05.67 Asian All Stars (in Penang) 7-0
[Nish 2, Stringfellow 3,
Sharkey, Sjoberg]
30.05.67 Asian All Stars
(in Kuala Lumpur) 3-0
[Goodfellow, Sinclair 2 pens]
03.06.67 Asian All Stars
(in Singapore) 3-0
[Gibson, Sharkey, Sinclair]
05.06.67 Southampton (in Singapore) 2-2
[Sinclair pen, Roberts]

05.08.67 1.FC Kaiserslautern (A) 0-1
10.08.67 Eintracht Braunschweig (A) 2-1
[Nish, Roberts]
11.08.67 VfB Stuttgart (A) 1-0
[Sinclair pen]
11.10.67 Racing Club de Strasbourg (A) 1-2
[Stringfellow]
22.05.68 Zambian Combined FA XI
(at Kitwe) 6-1
[Large 3, Manley, Gibson, Fern]
25.05.68 Zambian International XI
(at Lusaka) 1-0
[Large]
26.05.68 Zambian International XI
(at Ndola) 2-0
[Roberts, Large]

373

29.05.68 English Coaches XI (at Muphilira) 4-1 [Gibson, Glover, Fern, Manley]
02.06.68 Zambian International XI (at Lusaka) 3-2 [Large, Glover, Tewley]
03.06.68 Zambian Combined FA XI (at Livingston) 5-1 [Tewley 2, Potts, Gibson, Fern]

02.08.68 Schalke '04 (A) 1-2 [Clarke]
05.08.68 Walsall (A) 0-1
17.12.68 Borussia Dortmund (A) 0-2
24.05.69 Gibraltar XI (A) 4-3 [Fern 2, Manley, Matthews]

26.07.69 Scunthorpe United (A) 4-0 [Brown 2, Lochhead, Fern]
29.07.69 Rotherham United (A) 1-2 [Brown]
02.08.69 Portsmouth (A) 2-2 [Lochhead, Fern]
02.03.70 Plymouth Argyle XI (A) (David Corbett Testimonial) 4-3 [G Brown 4]

01.08.70 Rotherham United (A) 0-1
04.08.70 Notts County (A) 2-1 [Farrington, Brown]
07.08.70 Eintracht Braunschweig (H) 2-0 [Fern, Sjoberg]
09.08.70 ADO (Den Haag) (A) 0-3
18.11.70 Moscow Dynamo (H) 2-0 [Farrington, Matthews]
03.05.71 Vejle Boldklub (A) 0-3
04.05.71 Skive (A) 1-0 [Stringfellow]
07.05.71 Fredrikshavn (A) 6-1 [Nish 3, Partridge, Cross, Opp og]
11.05.71 Landskrona BoIS (A) 2-0 [Brown, Farrington]
25.05.71 Derby County (H) (John Sjoberg Testimonial) 1-0 [Farrington]

04.08.71 Coventry City (at Nuneaton) 0-0
26.10.71 Peterborough United (A) (Brian Wright/Ollie Conmy Testimonial) 2-5 [Nish, Partridge]
26.04.72 Hannover '96 (H) 5-1 [Partridge 4, Weller]
09.05.72 Olympiakos (A) [Weller] 1-2
29.07.72 Bristol City (A) 1-5 [Partridge]
01.08.72 Port Vale (A) 0-1
05.08.72 FC Groningen (H) 2-2 [Sammels 2]
07.08.72 Walsall (A) (Alan Baker Testimonial) 0-0
10.04.73 Bournemouth (A) (Alan Green Testimonial) 1-2 [Farrington]
09.05.73 PAOK Thessalonikis (A) 2-2 [Sammels, Worthington]
26.05.73 Ipswich Town (in Barbados) 3-2 [Worthington 2, Glover]
29.05.73 Barbados XI (A) 1-0 [Stringfellow]
31.05.73 Ipswich Town (in Barbados) 1-1 [Stringfellow]

29.07.73 GAIS Göteborg (A) (Sir Stanley Rous Cup) 5-2 [Worthington 3, Birchenall, Stringfellow]
01.08.73 Wolverhampton W (in Gothenburg) (Rous Cup) 0-1
11.08.73 Notts County (A) 2-1 [Tomlin, Worthington]
18.08.73 Aston Villa (A) 1-0 [Partridge]
03.05.74 Oxford United (A) (Ken Fish Testimonial) 1-2 [Sammels]

06.05.74 Derby County (H) (Graham Cross Testimonial) 2-2 [Worthington, Glover]
13.05.74 Nottingham Forest (A) (John Winfield Testimonial) 1-1 [Rofe pen]
27.07.74 Hannover SV (A) 2-0 [Earle 2]
01.08.74 FC Groningen (A) 1-3 [Earle]
04.08.74 VVV Venlo (A) 3-1 [Earle, Weller, Birchenall]
10.08.74 Nottingham Forest (A) 3-1 [Birchenall 2, Earle]
30.04.75 Wolverhampton W. (H) (Mike Stringfellow Testimonial) 2-2 [Weller, Wilcox]
05.05.75 Bristol City XI (A) (Cliff Morgan Testimonial) 4-2 [Earle 3, Worthington]
09.05.75 Exeter City (A) (Alan Banks Testimonial) 1-1 [Worthington]
27.05.75 Kuwait (A) 1-2 [Scorer not known]

17.07.75 Trollhatten (A) 1-2 [Worthington]
20.07.75 Örgryte (A) 3-0 [Worthington, Waters, Garland]
23.07.75 IFK Göteborg (A) (Sir Stanley Rous Cup) 2-1 [Worthington, Lee]
26.07.75 Varberg (A) (Barometern Cup) 4-1 [Worthington 3, Kember]
28.07.75 Skovde (A) (Barometern Cup) 4-0 [Worthington 3, Alderson]
28.10.75 Fulham (A) (Steve Earle Testimonial) 2-2 [Earle 2]
12.04.76 Northampton Town (A) (John Clarke Testimonial) 1-1 [Worthington]
26.04.76 Peterborough United (A) (Tommy Robson Testimonial) 2-3 [Scorers not known]
27.04.76 Portsmouth (A) (Malcolm Manley Testimonial) 1-3 [Garland]
13.05.76 Mjondalen (A) 5-0 [Weller, Worthington, Lee, Gould 2]
17.05.76 Odd (A) 4-1 [Lee 3, Weller]
19.05.76 Molde (A) 3-1 [Lee 2 Worthington]
23.05.76 Ski (A) 2-1 [Garland, Earle]
26.07.76 Jönköping (A) (Barometern Cup) 4-2 [Lee 3, Worthington]
28.07.76 Kalmar (A) (Barometern Cup) 0-1
01.08.76 Halmstads BK (A) 0-0
05.08.76 CSKA Sofia (in Valencia) 0-1
06.08.76 Levante UD (A) 2-1 [Weller, Garland]
14.08.76 Charlton Athletic (A) 3-1 [Alderson 2, Worthington]
07.03.77 Kuwait (A) 2-1 [Kember 2]
19.04.77 SK Brann (A) 1-1 [Sims]
25.04.77 Sheffield Wednesday (A) (Mick Prendergast Testimonial) 3-2 [Smith, Welsh, Bicknell]
10.05.77 Chelsea (H) (Alan Woollett Testimonial) 3-0 [Worthington, White, Birchenall]
18.05.77 Kettering Town (A) (Roger Ashby Testimonial) 2-1 [Scorers not known]
21.05.77 Southend United XI (A) (Arthur Rowley Testimonial) 3-3 [Earle, Farmer, Laverick og]

01.08.77 Walsall (A) 1-1 [Serella og]
08.08.77 Gallivare (A) 3-0 [Worthington 2, Earle]
10.08.77 Tottenham Hotspur (in Umeå, Sweden) (Nolia Cup) 1-2 [Armstrong og]
13.08.77 Royal Union Bruxelles (in Umeå, Sweden) (Nolia Cup) 2-1 [Alderson, Earle]
12.09.77 Nottingham Forest (A) (Liam O'Kane Testimonial) 0-0

06.08.78 FC Den Haag (A) 4-0 [Christie 2, Hughes, Goodwin]
08.08.78 FC Amsterdam (A) 1-1 [Christie]
11.08.78 Heerenveen (A) 2-2 [Williams 2]
12.08.78 Volendam (A) 2-0 [Christie, Williams]

17.07.79 Västra Nylland (A) 7-1 [Henderson, Young 4, Byrne, Lee]
19.07.79 IFK Grankulla (A) 1-0 [Goodwin]
22.07.79 Lysekil SF (A) 6-1 [Byrne, Young 4, Wilson]
24.07.79 Göteborgs FF (A) 4-1 [Henderson, Young, O'Neill, Byrne]
26.07.79 Örebro SK (A) 3-2 [Stevens, Lee, Peake]
30.07.79 Halverstorp (A) 13-1 [Young 6, Lee 3, Wilson 2, O'Neill, Wilson]
01.08.79 Halmar (A) 3-0 [Buchanan 2, Smith]
02.08.79 Rydboholm (A) 2-0 [Young 2]
05.09.79 Aberdeen (A) 1-1 [Smith]
17.09.79 Elgin City (A) 1-1 [Lineker]
01.10.79 Hinckley Athletic (A) (Floodlight Inauguration) 1-0 [Goodwin]
22.10.79 Tulsa Roughnecks (H) 1-1 [Young]
06.11.79 Coventry City (H) (Steve Whitworth Testimonial) 3-1 [Weller, Kelly, Henderson]
10.12.79 Hibernian (A) 2-3 [May, Strickland]
15.01.80 Hibernian (H) 0-2
16.02.80 Kilmarnock (A) 1-1 [Strickland]
16.05.80 Nottingham Forest (A) (John Robertson Testimonial) 0-0

02.08.80 Hertha Berlin (A) 1-1 [May]
05.08.80 Karlsruher SC (A) 0-1
06.08.80 Asberg (A) 5-0 [Henderson 2, May, Young, Melrose]
09.08.80 Haarlem (A) 1-0 [May]
11.08.80 Hertha Berlin (H) 2-1 [Young, O'Neill]
03.11.80 Haarlem (H) 3-2 [Peake, Young, Opp og]
24.11.80 Australia (H) 1-2 [Smith pen]
11.02.81 Red Star Belgrade (H) 3-0 [Melrose 3]
07.04.81 Saarbrucken (A) 2-1 [Grewcock, Buchanan]
09.08.81 Hallevarsholm (A) 2-0 [Henderson, Melrose]
10.08.81 Laxarby (A) 7-2 [Lineker 3, Young 3, Lynex]
15.08.81 Gunnilse IS (A) 3-0 [Ramsey, Opp og, Melrose]
19.08.81 Skoglunds (A) 0-1
20.08.81 Oddevold (A) 2-1 [Melrose 2]

25.08.81 Saarbrucken (H) 4-0 [Lineker 4]
12.10.81 Berwick Rangers (A) (Centenary Match) 0-1
20.10.81 Desborough (A) (Floodlight Inauguration) 6-1 [Lynex 4, Smith 2]
19.01.82 Bideford (A) 5-0 [Melrose 3, Young, Williams]
13.08.82 Bideford (A) 2-0 [Lineker 2]
16.08.82 Exeter City (A) 1-1 [Melrose]
18.08.82 Plymouth Argyle (A) 3-2 [Melrose 3]
20.08.82 Swansea City (A) 2-2 [Melrose, Ramsey]
23.08.82 Notts County (H) 2-1 [Melrose, Lineker]
20.10.82 Nottingham Forest (H) (Mark Wallington Testimonial) 0-2
08.03.83 Buckingham Town (A) 5-1 [Lynex, English 3, Jones]
28.03.83 Inverness Caledonian (A) 4-0 [Lineker 2, A Smith 2]
16.05.83 Wolverhampton Wanderers (A) (Geoff Palmer Testimonial) 1-3 [A Smith]

13.08.83 Heart of Midlothian (A) 3-2 [Jones, Lineker 2]
15.08.83 St Johnstone (A) 2-1 [Lineker, Opp og]
19.08.83 Barnsley (A) 0-2

06.08.84 Telford United (A) [Lynex] 1-0
08.08.84 Rangers (A) 2-2 [O'Neill, Lineker]
13.08.84 Aberdeen (H) (LCFC Centenary Match) 1-1 [Lynex pen]
18.08.84 Go Ahead Eagles (A) 4-1 [A Smith 2, Bright, Lineker]
20.08.84 PEC Zwolle (A) 3-2 [Bright 2, Lineker]
03.10.84 Wycombe Wanderers (A) (Centenary Match) 0-0
05.11.84 New Zealand (H) 4-1 [Opp og, Wilson, Lineker, A Smith]
13.11.84 Shepshed Charterhouse (A) 3-0 [Eastoe, Feeley, A Smith]

27.07.85 Newcastle United (Douglas, Isle of Man) 3-2 [Feeley, Wilson, A Smith]
31.07.85 Wigan Athletic (Peel, Isle of Man) 0-2
02.08.85 Blackburn Rovers (Castletown, Isle of Man) 1-2 [A Smith]
05.08.85 Sheffield United (A) 2-0 [Bright, Williams]
10.08.85 Grimsby Town (A) 2-1 [Bright, Lynex]
30.10.85 Hinckley Athletic (A) 1-1 [Lynex pen]
14.02.86 Combined Services (in Cyprus) 8-1 [Sealy 3, McAllister 2, Bright, Osman, Lynex pen]
02.03.86 Dundee United (A) 1-0 [A Smith]
06.05.86 Burton Albion (A) (Neil Warnock Testimonial) 0-1

29.07.86 Vastervik (A) 3-2 [Banks, Bright, Lynex]
30.07.86 Eskilstuna (A) 4-0 [A Smith, McAllister, Banks pen, Walsh]
02.08.86 Skarblacka (A) 4-0 [Bright 2, Mauchlen, Lynex pen]
04.08.86 Boo (A) 7-0 [Wilson, Kelly, Banks 2, Horner, Lynex, Venus]
06.08.86 Trosa (A) 8-1 [Bright 5, McAllister, Kelly, Morgan]

09.08.86 Gloucester City (A) 6-1
[Wilson 2, Bright 2, McAllister, Morgan]

13.08.86 VfB Lubeck (A) 2-0
[Bright, Banks]

15.08.86 TSV Auetal (A) 12-0
[Bright 4, Sealy 2, Lynex 2, McAllister, Banks, Kelly, O'Neill]

16.08.86 Hamburg Select XI (A) 10-0
[Sealy 4, A Smith 2, Wilson, Walsh, Kelly, Banks]

30.09.86 Shepshed Charterhouse (H) 6-0
(County FA Centenary Match)
[A Smith 3, Bright, Feeley, McAllister pen]

17.11.86 Al Itifaq (A) 2-1
[A Smith, Moran]

01.12.86 Leicester City Past XI (H) 1-0
(Tommy Williams Testimonial)
[A Smith]

17.02.87 Iraq (in Doha, Qatar) 2-3
[Kelly, Bunce]

02.03.87 Valencia (A) 1-0
[A Smith]

23.07.87 Laholm (A) 5-1
[Ramsey, Mauchlen, Cusack, McAllister 2]

24.07.87 Solve BK (A) 2-0
[Walsh, Reid]

26.07.87 Glimakra IF (A) 10-0
[McAllister 2, Cusack 4, Reid 2, Russell, Jobling]

28.07.87 Tomelilla IF (A) 3-0
[Moran, James, McAllister]

29.07.87 Farjestadens GIF (A) 0-2

02.08.87 Kavlinge GIF (A) 4-0
[McAllister 2, Ramsey, Wilson]

07.08.87 Mansfield Town (A) 1-1
[McAllister]

09.08.87 Derry City (A) 5-0
[Cusack 2, Moran, Wilson, Russell]

15.04.88 Peterborough United (A) 1-2
(Bill Harvey Testimonial)
[Cusack]

27.04.88 Burton Albion (A) 5-0
(Floodlight Inauguration)
[Cross 3, Newell, Groves]

04.08.88 Ayr United (A) 4-2
[Russell, Newell, McAllister, Quinn]

07.08.88 St Johnstone (A) 2-1
[Cross, Groves]

10.08.88 Kettering Town (A) 2-0
[Cross, Quinn]

15.08.88 Lincoln City (A) 4-1
[Weir, Newell 2, Reid]

19.08.88 Arsenal (H) 1-4
[Quinn]

22.08.88 Cambridge United (A) 1-1
[Cross]

23.01.89 Spalding United (A) 4-2
[Scorers not known]

24.04.89 Trinidad & Tobago
(at Mucurapo) 2-0
[McAllister, Morgan]

26.07.89 Kramfors Alliansen (A) 2-3
[Wilkinson, McAllister]

29.07.89 Solleftea (A) 6-1
[Clarke 2, Puttnam 2, Wilkinson, Groves]

31.07.89 Ljusdals IF (A) 5-0
[Mauchlen, Mills, Spearing, Opp og, Clarke]

02.08.89 Hovsala (A) 1-0
[Puttnam]

03.08.89 Helsinki Select (A) 3-1
[McAllister 2, Wilkinson]

07.08.89 Barnet (A) 1-1
[Reid]

09.08.89 Walsall (A) 1-3
[Mills]

12.08.89 Peterborough United (A) 2-2
[Mills, Russell]

15.08.89 Nottingham Forest (H) 2-2
[Clarke, Mills]

06.11.89 Tottenham Hotspur (H)
(Paul Ramsey Testimonial) 2-5
[North, Worthington pen]

21.11.89 Andover (A)
(Ground Opening) 10-1
[Campbell 4, Moran 3, Reid, Opp og, A Clarke]

23.01.90 Shelbourne (A) 1-3
[Baraclough]

26.01.90 Derry City (A)
(Floodlight Inauguration) 1-2
[Campbell]

06.08.90 Exeter City (A)
(Tony Kellow Testimonial) 2-1
[Peake 2 (1 pen)]

10.08.90 Cambridge United (A)
(Lindsay Smith Testimonial) 1-0
[Baraclough]

13.08.90 Morton (A) 1-1
[Peake pen]

15.08.90 St Mirren (A) 0-0

17.08.90 Motherwell (A) 2-2
[Gavin, Wright]

20.08.90 Coventry City (H) 0-0

06.11.90 Huntingdon United (A)
(Floodlight Inauguration) 4-0
[Kelly 2, Peake, Mills]

14.05.91 Lutterworth Town (A)
(Ground Opening) 9-0
[James 2, Russell, North, Oakes, Wright, Kelly 2, Oldfield]

04.08.91 Monaghan United (A) 0-0

06.08.91 Bray Wanderers (A) 2-0
[Gibson, Oldfield]

08.08.91 Athlone Town (A) 2-1
[Smith 2]

30.07.92 Darlington (A) 5-1
[Ormondroyd, Gee, Mills 2, Smith]

01.08.92 Hartlepool United (A) 3-1
[Lowe, Ormondroyd 2]

04.08.92 Scarborough (A) 1-0
[Oldfield]

06.08.92 Borussia Monchengladbach (H) 1-3
[Smith]

20.10.92 Northampton Town (A)
(Roly Mills Testimonial) 2-0
[Gee, Trotter]

21.07.93 Ex-City All Stars XI 3-2
(at Saffron Lane)
(Nev Hamilton Benefit)
[Oldfield, Gee, Davison]

26.07.93 Verdal (A) 4-1
[Walsh 2, Thompson pen, Ormondroyd]

30.07.93 Rissa (A) 0-0

02.08.93 Oppdal (A) 3-1
[Thompson, Speedie, Oldfield]

03.08.93 Varden/Merajker (A) 3-0
[Speedie, Walsh, Lowe]

04.08.93 Ardal (A) 8-0
[Speedie 4, Opp og, Thompson, Lowe, Gee]

01.08.94 Wycombe Wanderers (A) 1-0
[Lowe]

03.08.94 Walsall (A) 1-2
[Walsh]

05.08.94 York City (A) 2-4
[Lewis, Draper]

06.08.94 Scunthorpe United (A) 3-0
[Joachim, Ormondroyd, Roberts]

09.08.94 Leicester United (A)
(Ian Marsden Testimonial) 5-0
[Gee, Roberts 2, Lowe, Oldfield]

11.08.94 Rushden & Diamonds (A) 4-0
[Agnew 2, Smith, Gee]

13.08.94 Rapid Bucharest (H) 1-3
[Agnew]

19.04.95 International XI (H)
(Gordon Banks Testimonial) 6-6
[Speedie 3, Robins 2, Roberts]

19.07.95 Eider-Oberstein (A) 3-1
[Robins, Parker, Joachim]

21.07.95 Einbacht (A) 2-0
[Philpott, Lowe]

25.07.95 SSV Rentlingen (A) 1-1
[Robins]

29.07.95 1.FC Nurnberg (A) 0-3

05.08.95 Notts County (A) 1-2
[Adamczuk]

24.04.96 Chelsea (H)
(David Speedie Benefit) 0-3

24.07.96 Penzance (A) 4-2
[Robins 2, Harrington, Campbell]

27.07.96 Torpoint (A) 5-0
[Robins 2, Hallam, Izzet, Wilson]

29.07.96 Shepshed Dynamo (A) 2-1
[Wilson, Akeredolu og]

30.07.96 Corby Town XI (A)
(Pat Rayment Testimonial) 4-1
[Robins 2, Harrington 2]

02.08.96 Dundee United (A) 1-2
[Izzet]

05.08.96 PAOK (A) 0-3

07.08.96 Kettering Town (A) 1-2
[Whitlow pen]

09.08.96 Bournemouth (A) 1-1
[Izzet]

11.08.96 Peterborough United (A) 1-1
[Walsh]

28.04.97 Brian Little Select XI (H)
(Steve Walsh Testimonial) 7-3
[Scorers not known]

16.05.97 Port Vale (A)
(Ray Walker Testimonial) 8-6
[Scorers not known]

16.07.97 Penzance (A) 7-1
[Heskey 2, Whitlow pen, Fox, Skeldon, Robins, Izzet]

18.07.97 Torpoint (A) 3-1
[McMahon, Guppy, Heskey]

19.07.97 Torquay United (A) 1-3
[Izzet]

21.07.97 Grantham Town (A) 5-0
[Wilson 4, Skeldon]

22.07.97 Scunthorpe United (A) 4-0
[Claridge, Marshall, Wilson, Robins]

23.07.97 Notts County (A) 2-1
[Oparaku, Savage]

28.07.97 Olympiakos (A) 1-3
[Campbell]

01.08.97 Preston North End (A) 2-0
[McMahon, Marshall]

03.08.97 Northampton Town (A)
(Centenary Match) 2-1
[Heskey, Campbell]

05.08.97 Peterborough United (A) 2-2
[Robins, Campbell]

08.10.97 Gresley Rovers (A)
(Richard Denby Testimonial) 6-1
[Allen 2, Elliott, Wilson, Cottee, Beiersdorfer]

09.11.97 Barrow Town (A)
(Floodlight Inauguration) —-

12.11.97 Wycombe Wanderers (A)
(Dave Carroll Testimonial) 1-2
[Scorer not known]

20.05.98 Tampa Bay Mutiny (A) 0-0

26.05.98 Jacksonville Cyclones (A) 4-2
[Guppy, Cottee, Branston, Fenton]

24.07.98 Finn Harps (A) 4-1
[Heskey 2, Dykes og, Fenton]

26.07.98 Galway United (A) 6-1
[Fenton, Heskey, Oakes, Cottee, Lennon 2 (1 pen)]

01.08.98 Swindon Town (A) 2-1
[Borrows og, Wilson]

03.08.98 Norwich City (A) 1-0
[Cottee]

08.08.98 Rushden & Diamonds (A) 1-0
[Heskey]

10.08.98 Woking (A) 2-0
[Fenton, Otta]

23.03.99 Nottingham Forest XI (A)
(Steve Chettle Testimonial) 2-3
[Cottee, Oakes]

10.05.99 Grimsby Town (A)
(Kevin Jobling Testimonial) 2-3
[Gunnlaugsson 2]

17.05.99 Port Vale (A)
(Neil Aspin Testimonial) 3-5
[Scorers not known]

17.07.99 Kettering Town (A) 3-2
[Savage, Zagorakis (pen), Cottee]

19.07.99 Bournemouth (A) 3-2
[Gunnlaugsson, Heskey, Campbell]

21.07.99 Torquay United (A) 1-2
[Wilson]

24.07.99 Portsmouth (A) 1-2
[Elliott]

26.07.99 Lincoln City (A) 7-2
[Izzet 3, Heskey 2, Marshall, Campbell]

28.07.99 Crystal Palace (A) 1-1
[Cottee]

31.07.99 AEK (Athens) (A) 2-3
[Zagorakis 2 (1 pen)]

01.08.99 Iraklis (in Athens) 3-0
[Walsh, Heskey, Elliott]

16.05.00 Gary Lineker's All Stars (H) 5-3
(Alan Birchenall Testimonial)
[Cottee 2, Zagorakis, Savage, Arphexad (pen)]

28.07.00 Finn Harps (A) 1-0
[Eadie]

29.07.00 Cliftonville (A) 2-0
[Eadie, Savage]

31.07.00 Portadown (A) 1-0
(Derek McKinlay Testimonial)
[Benjamin]

01.08.00 Wycombe Wanderers (A)
(Keith Ryan Testimonial) 3-0
[Akinbiyi, Collymore, Dudfield]

05.08.00 Tranmere Rovers (A) 1-3
[Akinbiyi]

07.08.00 Gillingham (A) 2-1
[Davidson, Izzet pen]

09.08.00 Hereford United (A) 0-1

11.08.00 RKC Waalwijk (A) 0-0

11.05.01 Hinckley United (A) 1-0
[Sturridge]

Above: *City take to the field, literally, to face Monaghan United in August 1991.*

Reserves Seasonal Record

Leicestershire & Northamptonshire League

First fixture: 08.09.1894 v Hugglescote Robin Hoods (A) 3-1 (Priestman, Mellor 2)
Team: Chappell, Thompson, Davis, Bridgford, Lord, Atkins, Pickard, Narroway, Mellor, Priestman, Harlow.

	P	W	D	L	F	A	Pts	
1894/5	20	17	1	2	75	20	35	Champions
1895/6	16	11	3	2	45	14	25	Champions

Leicestershire Senior League

First fixture: 05.09.1896 v Coalville Town (A) (Score / scorers not known)
Team: Howes, Thompson, Bailey, Bevans, Wood, n/k, Wooding, Harris, Manson, Trainer, Bishop.

	P	W	D	L	F	A	Pts	
1896/7	20	14	1	5	63	18	27*	2nd/11

(* 2pts deducted)

United Counties League

First fixture: 11.09.1897 v Sheepbridge Works (H) 4-1
(McMillan 2, Flanagan 2 [1 pen])
Team: Saer, Thompson, Rowell, Lord, Bailey, Cassell, McMillan, Bamford, Gillies, Flanagan, Atkins.

	P	W	D	L	F	A	Pts	
1897/8	14	5	2	7	30	29	12	5th/8

Midland League

First fixture: 10.09.1898 v Wellingborough (H) 1-3 (Dorrell)
Team: Underwood, Thompson, Ballard, Cassell, Lord, Robinson, Fulwood, Shaw, Coulson, Eaton, Dorrell.

	P	W	D	L	F	A	Pts	
1898/9	26	9	2	15	34	58	20	12th/14
1899/00	24	3	3	18	34	74	9	13th/13
1900/1	26	11	1	14	60	64	23	9th/14
1901/2	28	7	5	16	38	70	19	13th/15
1902/3	32	6	4	22	30	87	16	17th/17

Leicestershire Senior League

First fixture: 05.09.1903 v Coalville United (H) (Score / scorers not known)
Team: Haywood, West, Harrison, Watts, Berry, Manship, Coulson, Beer, Gwynne, Belton, Jayes.

	P	W	D	L	F	A	Pts	
1903/4	16	11	2	3	41	21	24	2nd/9
1904/5	20	14	2	4	75	27	30	Champions
1905/6	20	14	2	4	43	21	30	Champions
1906/7	22	19	2	1	101	25	40	Champions

1892/3 Reserve Team (Fosse Rovers)
Back: Brown, Bates, Lisle, Buswell, Davis, Cornell, Machin (Trainer). Middle: DeVille, Gardner, Tomlinson, Mouel. Front: Carter, Vickers.

Midland League

First fixture: 02.09.1907 v Denaby United (H) 1-3 (Hubbard)
Team: Starbuck, Keogh, Godwin, Trueman, King, West, Bracey, Hubbard, Vann, Shanks, Turner.

	P	W	D	L	F	A	Pts	
1907/8	38	17	5	16	72	70	39	8th/20
1908/9	38	13	7	18	87	70	33	13th/20
1909/10	42	13	10	19	76	93	36	18th/22
1910/1	38	11	7	20	62	100	29	18th/20
1911/2	36	17	8	11	90	54	42	4th/19

Central Alliance

First fixture: 02.09.1912 v Shirebrook (H) 10-0 (Straughton 2, Wain, Osborn 4, Mills 2, Lightbody)
Team: Mearns, Beeby, Webber, Burton, Lightbody, Hubbard, Wain, Mills, Straughton, Osborn, W Furr.

	P	W	D	L	F	A	Pts	
1912/3	32	19	5	8	76	38	43	4th/17
1913/4*	30	17	4	9	74	43	36*	5th/16
1914/5	30	8	7	15	44	45	21*	15th/16

(* 2pts deducted)

South Eastern League

First fixture: 01.09.1913 v Peterborough City (H) 2-2 (Mortimer, Waterall)
Team: Bown, Pudan, Berrington, Burton, Webber, Woodward, Hodges, Stoodley, Mortimer, Waterall, Kenyon.

	P	W	D	L	F	A	Pts	
1913/4*	40	8	10	22	56	86	26	19th/21

Central Alliance

First fixture: 30.08.1919 v Shirebrook (A) 0-0. Team not known.

	P	W	D	L	F	A	Pts	
1919/20	30	13	11	6	66	46	37	4th/16
1920/1	34	28	1	5	133	29	57	Champions
1921/2	34	27	4	3	132	19	58	Champions
1922/3	32	24	4	4	107	34	52	Champions

Southern League (Eastern Section)

First fixture: 25.08.1923 v Peterborough & Fletton United (H) 0-2
Team: Davies, Barrett, Brown, Newton, Watson, Moore, T Duncan, Middleton, Waterston, J King, Trotter.

	P	W	D	L	F	A	Pts	
1923/4	30	19	3	8	72	30	41	2nd/16
1924/5*	32	15	7	10	61	45	37	7th/17
1925/6*	34	23	2	9	105	60	48	2nd/18
1926/7*	32	12	5	15	94	72	29	11th/17

East Midlands League

First fixture: 01.09.1924 v Peterborough & Fletton United (A) 0-0
Team: Hebden, Barrett, Brown, H Smith, Heywood, Gouch, Place, Riley, Heathcock, Woodcock, Gibbs.

	P	W	D	L	F	A	Pts	
1924/5*	18	7	4	7	37	25	18	-/10
1925/6*	14	10	0	4	41	16	20	2nd/8

London Combination

First fixture: 28.08.1926 v West Ham Utd Reserves (H) 3-0 (Allen, Gouch, Heathcock)
Team: Godderidge, Brown, Moyes, Findlay, Carrigan, Gibson, Gouch, Allen, Heathcock, Lochhead, Wadsworth.

		P	W	D	L	F	A	Pts	
1926/7*		42	28	5	9	121	61	61	2nd/22
1927/8		42	19	8	15	89	70	46	8th/22
1928/9		42	24	4	14	109	76	52	3rd/22
1929/30		42	20	5	17	111	99	45	8th/22
1930/1	Div.1	42	21	3	18	102	84	45	8th/22
1931/2	Div.1	42	16	9	17	109	103	41	11th/22
1932/3	Div.1	46	18	11	17	101	103	47	8th/24
1933/4		46	18	9	19	91	77	45	12th/24
1934/5		46	25	7	14	88	60	57	4th/24
1935/6		46	17	6	23	79	98	40	18th/24
1936/7		46	17	6	23	69	92	40	16th/24
1937/8		46	17	10	19	79	78	44	13th/24
1938/9		46	18	5	23	84	108	41	17th/24

1939-44:	No Reserve side: Colts XI only
1944/5:	Midland Senior League
1945/6:	Notts & Derbyshire Senior League

Football Combination

First fixture: 31.08.1946 v Brentford Reserves (A) 1-2 (Mercer)
Team: Bradley, J Harrison, Howe, W Harrison, Grogan, Towers, Mercer, Iggleden, Lee, Sutton, Anderson.

		P	W	D	L	F	A	Pts	
1946/7	Sect. B	30	14	5	11	69	54	33	7th/16
1947/8	Sect. B	30	15	5	10	53	33	35	6th/16
1948/9	Sect. B	30	11	5	14	40	40	27	11th/16
1949/50	Sect. A	30	10	10	10	42	37	30	8th/16
1950/1	Sect. A	30	11	6	13	54	57	28	11th/16
1951/2	Sect. A	30	10	7	13	60	64	27	10th/16
1952/3	Div.2	30	20	5	5	86	40	45	2nd/16
1953/4	Div.1	30	15	4	11	76	63	34	8th/16
1954/5	Div.1	30	15	2	13	61	56	32	7th/16
1955/6		42	17	12	13	103	88	46	10th/32
1956/7		42	23	6	13	116	66	52	8th/32
1957/8		42	23	7	12	108	63	53	4th/32
1958/9	Div.1	34	23	5	6	77	41	51	Champions
1959/60	Div.1	34	12	6	16	59	58	30	12th/18
1960/1	Div.1	34	12	3	19	55	83	27	15th/18
1961/2	Sat.Sect.	34	17	5	12	71	63	39	5th/18
1962/3	Sat.Sect.	34	9	8	17	66	91	26	15th/18
1963/4	Div.1	34	18	7	9	84	65	43	3rd/18
1964/5	Div.1	34	11	5	18	60	73	27	15th/18
1965/6	Div.1	34	16	6	11	61	53	40	7th/18
1966/7	Div.1	32	13	8	11	61	45	34	7th/17
1967/8	Div.1	28	10	7	11	47	47	27	9th/15
1968/9		25	9	6	10	35	37	24	11th/26
1969/70		25	13	4	8	51	34	30	8th/26
1970/1		42	16	11	15	53	51	43	12th/22
1971/2		40	18	11	11	71	50	47	5th/21
1972/3		40	12	10	18	45	55	34	14th/21
1973/4		42	20	12	10	56	33	52	4th/22
1974/5		40	14	12	14	54	48	40	10th/21
1975/6		42	13	10	19	56	55	36	16th/22
1976/7		42	14	14	14	71	57	42	12th/22
1977/8		42	24	6	12	74	50	54	5th/22
1978/9		42	8	11	23	47	72	27	19th/22
1979/80		42	17	7	18	66	65	41	12th/22
1980/1		42	18	9	15	71	58	45	10th/22
1981/2		38	10	10	18	47	64	30	15th/20
1982/3		42	11	12	19	65	84	34	18th/22
1983/4		42	18	9	15	96	63	45	11th/22

Central League

First fixture: 28.08.1984 v Scunthorpe United Reserves (H) 6-0 (Banks 2, Rennie, Bright 2, Kelly)
Full team not known; but also included Burnside, Hazell, Bunce & R Jones.

		P	W	D	L	F	A	Pts	
1984/5	Div.2	34	27	6	1	81	20	87	Champions
1985/6	Div.1	34	12	10	12	60	58	46	11th/18
1986/7	Div.1	34	10	7	17	48	65	37	13th/18
1987/8	Div.1	34	14	3	17	61	55	45	12th/18
1988/9	Div.1	34	13	6	15	65	63	45	10th/18
1989/90	Div.1	34	16	8	10	51	48	56	6th/18
1990/1	Div.1	34	7	8	19	41	62	29	18th/18
1991/2	Div.2	34	18	8	8	57	29	62	3rd/18
1992/3	Div.1	34	12	12	10	42	38	48	9th/18
1993/4	Div.1	34	8	7	19	37	57	31	17th/18
1994/5	Div.2	34	20	4	10	72	42	64	5th/18
1995/6	Div.2	34	13	13	8	64	42	52	9th/18
1996/7	Div.1*	24	11	3	10	37	42	36	6th/13
1997/8	Div.1*	24	13	5	6	48	30	44	2nd/13
1998/9	Prem*	24	8	6	10	30	41	30	8th/13

Premier Reserve League – South

First fixture: 16.08.1999 v Arsenal Reserves (H) 2-0 (Wilson 2)
Team: Arphexad, Bacon, McCann, Goodwin, Gilchrist, Fenton [Piper], Wilson [Stewart], Oakes, Marshall [Boateng], Dudfield, Thomas.

	P	W	D	L	F	A	Pts	
1999/2000	24	7	7	10	36	44	28	10th/13
2000/1	24	7	7	10	37	44	28	10th/13

NOTES: *In seasons 1913/14 and 1924-27 inclusive the club fielded reserve sides in two separate League competitions.*
The Central League adopted a four-division format 1996-99.

1958/9 FOOTBALL COMBINATION CHAMPIONS

Apps/Goals:

Bill Calder 27 (7 goals), Ian MacFarlane 27, John Anderson 26, Don Walker 26 (6 goals), Ian Ogilvie 24 (3 goals), Len Chalmers 21, Ian White 20 (3 goals), Tony Knapp 19, Jack Lornie 17 (15 goals), Ian McNeill 15 (6 goals), Gordon Wills 15 (6 goals), Colin Appleton 14, Brian Wright 14 (4 goals), Frank McLintock 13, Howard Riley 11 (6 goals), Derek Hines 8 (1 goal), Brian Punter 8 (1 goal), Barry Reed 8, Ian King 7, Ken Leek 7 (8 goals), Willie Gardiner 6 (2 goals), Oliver Beeby 5, David Cartlidge 5 (2 goals), Bernie Kelly 5 (2 goals), Ken Keyworth 5, Tommy McDonald 4, Tony Lines 3, Dave MacLaren 3, Willie Cunningham 2, John Currie 2 (1 goal), Alan Wright 2 (1 goal), Joe Baillie 1, Alex Bowman 1, Stan Milburn 1, John Sjoberg 1, Rodney Slack 1; (+ 2 own goals).

Jack Lornie top scored for the Combination champions.

FOOTBALL COMBINATION CUP

For a number of postwar seasons, the Combination fare was augmented by a Cup competition, usually run on a group basis prior to its knockout stage. City Reserves won the Football Combination Cup outright in 1947/8, and shared the trophy with Spurs Reserves in 1966/7; they were beaten semi-finalists in 1948/9 and 1953/4.

Combination Cup Final details:

24.04.48   v Bournemouth & Boscombe Athletic 2-1 (Scott [pen], A.Smith / Holland) (Filbert Street; 13,073)
Major, McGregor, Scott, Staples, McArthur, Revie, Dawson, A.Smith, Dewis, Iggleden, Anderson.

29.03.67   (First Leg) v Tottenham Hotspur 1-2 (Svarc / Possee, Bond) (White Hart Lane; 6,500)
Shilton, Potts, Bebbington, Woollett, McDerment, Nish, Matthews, Mackay, Svarc, Sweenie, Tewley.

04.04.67   (Second Leg) v Tottenham Hotspur 1-0 (Sweenie) aet (Filbert Street; 8,804)
Shilton, Potts, Bebbington, Woollett, McDerment, Nish, Matthews, Mackay, Svarc, Sweenie [Fern], Tewley.

OTHER RESERVE HONOURS (with results of Finals):

Leicestershire & Rutland Senior Cup

(Won by Leicester Fosse first XI in 1889/90, 1890/1).

Won by Fosse/City Reserves in:

1894/5 [4-0 v Loughborough Athletic], 1895/6 [2-1 v Hugglescote Robin Hoods], 1907/8 [2-1 v Loughborough Corinthians], 1908/9 [2-1 v Hinckley United], 1911/12 [1-0 v Hinckley United], 1913/14 [2-1 v Holwell Works], 1919/20 [11-2 v Moira United], 1920/1 [3-0 v Loughborough Corinthians], 1923/4 [0-0, 5-1 v Barwell United], 1924/5 [5-2 v Barwell United], 1925/6 [8-1 v Moira United], 1926/7 [3-2 v Hinckley United], 1929/30 [5-3 v Market Harborough Town], 1930/1 [2-0 v Loughborough Corinthians], 1931/2 [5-1 v Market Harborough Town], 1932/3 [3-0 v Loughborough Corinthians], 1934/5 [4-1 v Hinckley United], 1935/6 [5-0 v Leicestershire Nomads], 1936/7 [7-1 v Leicestershire Nomads], 1937/8 [2-0 v Leicestershire Nomads], 1938/9 [1-0 v Ibstock Penistone Rovers], 1945/6 [5-1 v Coalville Town], & 1949/50 [1-1, 2-0 v Brush Sports].

Leicestershire FA Challenge Cup

Won by City Reserves in:

1950/1 [6-2 v Brush Sports], 1951/2 [2-0 v Brush Sports], 1952/3 [6-0 v Brush Sports], 1953/4 [7-1 v Brush Sports], 1954/5 [1-0 v Hinckley Athletic], 1955/6 [4-0 v Hinckley Athletic], 1956/7 [9-0 v Anstey Nomads], 1982/3 [2-1 v Enderby Town], 1988/9 [4-2 v Leicester United], 1990/1 [2-1 v Hinckley Town], 1991/2 [3-0 v Leicester United], 1994/5 [2-2, 4-1 v Hinckley Town], 1995/6 [2-1 v St Andrews], 1997/8 [6-1 v Shepshed Dynamo], 1998/9 [10-1 v Oadby Town] & 1999/2000 [4-0 v Barwell].

Bass Charity Vase

Only intermittently competed for by Leicester, this magnificent trophy was won by Fosse's first XI in 1909 [2-0 v Coventry City]. The Burton-based competition underwent mixed fortunes in terms of the calibre of teams attracted over the next 60 or so years, but settled to become a pre-season invitational tournament in the '70s, and was won by City Reserves in 1977 [Final: 2-0 v Derby County], 1978 [4-3 v Notts County], 1979 [5-1 v Notts County] and 1982 [3-2 v Burton Albion].

During their Midland League and Central Alliance days, the club's Reserve team met several sides against whom their seniors would later compete as equals. Fosse and/or City Reserves therefore appear as opponents in the cumulative senior playing records of the following clubs (seasons or years of meetings in brackets): Chesterfield Town (1898/9; 1909-1912); Doncaster Rovers (1898-1901; 1907-1912); Grimsby Town (1910/11); Huddersfield Town (1909/10); Lincoln City (1908/9); Mansfield Town (1912-14; 1919-21); Northampton Town (1899-1901) & Walsall (1901-1903). Additionally, Fosse Reserves met both Rotherham Town and Rotherham County (later to amalgamate as Rotherham United) between 1907-1912.

Youth and Junior Teams

In the last two seasons prior to WW2, a City third team played in the Midland Midweek League, and this competition revived in 1949, continuing until 1958. A Colts team featured in the wartime Leicestershire Senior League; supplemented from 1941/2 by a Juniors side in the City & Mutual League; then itself becoming the third-string in 1944/5 when the Reserves revived. After the war, City's Colts had a season (1947/8) in the United Counties League (playing all their games away from home); one (1948/9) in the Birmingham League (with Barwell as home ground); and then switched to the Leicestershire Senior League, winning the Championship in 1954/5, 1956/7 and 1957/8; and finishing runners-up to Whitwick Colliery in 1955/6. From 1958 to 1961, City ran both an 'A' and 'B' team: the latter carrying on the Leicestershire Senior League fixtures. The 'A' team came 2nd in the Second Division of the Birmingham & District League in 1958/9, and played the following season in the First Division of that competition. For almost forty years afterwards, City's 'thirds' competed with much success in essentially specialist youth leagues, being founder members of the Midland Intermediate League, and alternating between this set-up and the Midland Youth League, plus their associated Cup competitions, until 1998. At this point, the FA's Charter for Quality came into operation, with City qualifying for Youth Academy status, and entering the FA Premier Academy League at both Under-19 and Under-17 levels.

The City record in the major national knockout competition, the FA Youth Cup, has not been terribly auspicious in the years since its 1952/3 inauguration. In fact, no entry was made until 1956/7, when City seemed to misread the player qualification rules: choosing an all-amateur eleven which beat the oddly-named Square Club (Birmingham) by 3-1 at Melton Road, but then bowed out to West Bromwich Albion in the Second Round by 1-8. No progress beyond the Fourth Round was made until 1982/3, when Luton overcame City in a Kenilworth Road quarter-final by 0-2; but City did reach the semi-finals in 1986/7 with a run that took them past the challenges of Shrewsbury Town, Manchester United, Sheffield United and Chelsea to face Charlton Athletic in a two-legged tie. A 0-4 deficit from the Selhurst Park leg proved too much to make up, however, and City's 2-1 Filbert Street win was not enough to earn them a Final place against Coventry City. A run to the quarter-finals in 1989/90 has been the best effort since then.

First FA Youth Cup line-up:

29.09.1956   v Square Club [Birmingham] (H - Melton Rd) 3-1
Knowles, Siddons, Barnes, Cartlidge, Eaton, Adcock, Burton, Rhoden, Sansome, Powell, Ramsey.

Who's Who

ADAM, Charles

b. Glasgow, 22nd March 1919
d. Kirby Muxloe, Leics, 30th September 1996

Career: Greenhead Thistle; Strathclyde; Sept 1938 CITY; July 1952 Mansfield Town; cs 1955 Corby Town.

City debut (WW2) v Tottenham Hotspur (A) 24.5.41; (postwar) v Chelsea (A) FAC 5.1.46 (scored once)

> City's first postwar scorer in the revived FA Cup, and an ever-present in the club's surprising run to Wembley in 1949, outside-left Charlie spent the bulk of the first half of his fourteen years with the club away from Filbert Street. A Frank Womack signing from Glasgow Junior football, he had to build what footballing experience he could with each of City, Arbroath, Leeds United and QPR as wartime exigencies took him initially into the Building Trades Flying Squad (repairing blitz damage) and then on military service in France and Italy. On returning to the full-time game, though, he soon struck a fine understanding with City spearhead Jack Lee, and built a reputation as a neat, nippy and constructive winger across five Second Division seasons. His veteran game-reading abilities and accurate crossing were then put at the service of the Stags (under the management regimes of ex-Leicester players George Jobey and Stan Mercer) for a further 98 League and Cup games. Charlie's enthusiastic involvement with the game continued past his professional days, however. From 1960 to 1976 he managed the County Youth squad (bringing home the national FA trophy in 1966 with proteges such as David Nish and Rodney Fern); he lent coaching acumen to Blaby Boys Club, the paramount seedbed of local talent; acted as a part-time City scout; and organised umpteen reunion games of old City stars for charity. His son Lee was on City's schoolboy books in 1970, but undertook his apprenticeship with Derby County then left to play successfully for Inglewood Kiev in Perth, Australia, and has recently been managing Corby Town.

Apps: FL 158; FAC 22; WW2 8.
Goals: FL 22; FAC 3.

ADCOCK, Hugh

b. Coalville, Leics, 10th April 1903
d. Coalville, 16th October 1975

Career: Ravenstone United; Aug 1920 Coalville Town; am Apr 1921/pro Sept 1922 Loughborough Corinthians; 1922-trials-Grimsby Town; Feb 1923 CITY; July 1935 Bristol Rovers; Sept 1936 Folkestone; Ibstock Penistone Rovers.

City debut v Hull City (A) 25.8.23

> Having shared a City debut with record-scorer-to-be Arthur Chandler, diminutive-but-direct right-winger Hughie gave equivalent, and equivalently valuable, service across the next dozen campaigns; encompassing those justifiably regarded as the club's halcyon days. For his role in assisting City up to the top flight via the 1925 championship, and then to the Division One runners-up slot four years later, Hughie actually received better recognition than the scorer-in-chief; winning five full England caps and a Football League selection in 1929 and 1930. Three of those international appearances came in the forward-line company of his Coalville-born cousin, Birmingham's Joe Bradford; but most noteworthy is that three also featured Hughie's opposite City flanker, Len Barry, and a further two restored his club partnership with inside-right Ernie Hine. For a player best renowned for his supply-line inventiveness, Hughie also racked up a fair share of hard-struck goals; and for a man of 5ft 4ins he showed an often courageous resilience. A former pit pony driver, originally signed for £200 after he had helped Loughborough take the 1922 County Cup, he was still exhibiting characteristic trickery and pluck when featuring in the final of the same competition 17 years later for Ibstock against City's Reserves. In the interim, he'd made an ironic debut for Bristol Rovers against Notts County (featuring Arthur Chandler in his debut for that club!), and had assisted Folkestone to third place in the Southern League. Just before the war, Hughie was running The Horse & Trumpet at Sileby; afterwards, he worked as a colliery maintenance engineer while managing and training Whitwick Colliery and Coalville Town. Another of his cousins, Bill Bradford, was also a pro with Brighton, Preston and, for twelve years, Walsall.

Apps: FL 434; FAC 26.
Goals: FL 51; FAC 1.

AGNEW, Stephen Mark

b. Shipley, Yorks, 9th November 1965

Career: app 1982/pro Nov 1983 Barnsley; June 1991 Blackburn Rovers; Nov 1992-loan-Portsmouth; Feb 1993 CITY; Jan 1995 Sunderland; July 1998 York City; Sept 1999-trials-Hull City.

City debut v Portsmouth (A) 20.2.93

> A tenacious midfield prompter who invariably turned it on whenever the Tykes faced City, Steve had to overcome serious injury problems (which virtually negated his entire Blackburn stint following a record £750,000 move) before becoming a £250,000 Brian Little capture. The balding linkman was a key contributor to the 1993 Play-Off campaign which saw City fall at the last to Swindon, but missed out through injury on the big day a year later as Derby were toppled at Wembley, despite appearing regularly in the promotion effort. Briefly the side's acting skipper in Gary Mills' absence, he gave a few fine ball-winning exhibitions in front of the back line, but the flair and shooting power City had once so often faced seemed a little muted in their colours. Little offered to let Steve go to Stoke in October 1994, but only shortly thereafter he became the first sale (at £200,000) made by the incoming Mark McGhee; going on to contribute to Sunderland's 1996 First Division championship win, but sharing in York's demotion to the basement only three years later. He once more faced City at Filbert Street in the 2001 FA Cup tie, during his final season with the Minstermen.

Apps: PL/FL 52+4; FAC 2; LC 4+1; PO 2.
Goals: FL 4.

Steve Agnew

AITKEN, Andrew

b. Ayr, 27th April 1877
d. Ponteland, Northumberland, 15th February 1955

Career: Annbank; Ayr FC; 1894 Ayr Parkhouse; July 1895 Newcastle United; Feb 1899-loan-Kilmarnock; Nov 1906 Middlesbrough (p/mgr); Feb 1909 FOSSE (p/mgr from Apr 1909); Apr 1911 Dundee; June 1912 Kilmarnock; Aug 1913 Gateshead Town (p/mgr).

Fosse debut v Liverpool (A) 13.2.09

> A residual sense of 'if only' lingers over Scottish international Andy's time with Fosse: if only the club had signed someone of his acumen and experience earlier in their sole First Division campaign, they may have saved themselves the embarrassment of being such definitive one-season wonders. An integral part of Newcastle's promotion side of 1898, their championship squad in 1905, and their Cup Final elevens of 1905 and 1906, and skipper for many of his 349 senior games on Tyneside, the cultured and creative defender had then directed the tactics of top-flight Boro (featuring the likes of Steve Bloomer and £1,000-man Alf Common) before being recruited late (at a £300 fee) to a seemingly doomed cause at Leicester. The formal designation of player-managership came only after the relegation fate was confirmed; yet Andy's own efforts at the heart of the survival effort were enough to win him back the captaincy of his country even at such a veteran stage. He then led Fosse to creditable 5th and 7th-place finishes in his two full Second Division seasons at the helm, drawing typical admiration from the press: 'Seldom wastes a ball, and shines best as a sixth forward ... Invariably subordinates force to science'. A part-time football columnist himself (for instance in the *Nottingham Football Mail* in 1909/10), Andy applied to return to the Middlesbrough managerial seat in April 1911, before signing for Dundee, where he replaced ex-Fossil Herbert Dainty. On retirement from Kilmarnock, he was dubbed by *The Scottish Referee*, 'A typical Scot; pawky, genial and heady; playing the placing game almost to perfection', and made a final effort to re-enter top-class manage-ment, with an unsuccessful application for the vacant Spurs job. Originally a grocer's delivery boy, and known as 'Daddler' throughout his playing career, Andy later lived in each of Manchester (where he ran a pub and had an informal involvement with the South Manchester club), Stoke and Newcastle, and acted as Northern scout for Arsenal.

***Apps:** FL 64; FAC 7.*
***Goals:** FL 1.*

AKINBIYI, Adeola Peter Oluwatoyin

b. Hackney, 10th October 1974

Career: YT July 1991/pro Feb 1993 Norwich City; Jan 1994-loan-Hereford United; Nov 1994-loan-Brighton & Hove Albion; Jan 1997 Gillingham; May 1998 Bristol City; Sept 1999 Wolverhampton Wanderers; July 2000 CITY.

City debut v Aston Villa (H) 19.8.2000

> Probably overburdened with the status of being the club's current record purchase, at £5m, Ade spent his first City campaign as the object of intense critical scrutiny, yet contrived to maintain a fiercely sympathetic level of support from the majority of the Filbert Street crowd. The muscular striker was always likely to discover the step back up to Premiership action difficult to negotiate after his lower-division scoring spree, and to find himself bereft of an experienced partner up front following the departures of Cottee and Collymore was of scant assistance. But if his confidence occasionally showed signs of wilting – especially when the goal was in his mid-range sights – his willingness to battle never did, even when he was required to play an unfavoured role with his back to goal. The value of his pace was at these times somewhat negated, and a lack of finesse in first-time control over-emphasised. Nonetheless, a double-figure goal return from an initial top-flight term was hardly a mark of failure, and sheer determination to justify both his place and his price-tag seems likely to pay off in the mid-term and vindicate Peter Taylor's investment. Ade made his very first mark on the senior game when appearing as substitute for Darren Eadie in Norwich's UEFA Cup tie against Bayern Munich in November 1993, and had a brief stint under Martin O'Neill's management at Carrow Road before establishing his striking credentials at Priestfield and Ashton Gate (albeit in a relegation term for Bristol City). His transfer value ever escalating, he became a Colin Lee recruit at Wolves (with the £3.2m fee a record between Nationwide clubs), and earned a call-up for Nigeria against Greece, only to be subsequently rejected by then-coach Jo Bonfrere after a misunderstanding about reporting times for the next inter-national. It was presumably a small matter of 56 League goals for three clubs in the previous three seasons, however, that impinged on Peter Taylor's mind when he turned to Ade after missing out on Carl Cort in the 2000 summer sales. Confirming that applied pace runs in the family, Ade's sister Sara was an international hurdler.

***Apps:** (to end 2000/1): PL 33+4; FAC 4; UEFA 2.*
***Goals:** PL 9; FAC 1.*

ALDERSON, Brian Roderick

b. Dundee, 5th May 1950
d. Atlanta, USA, 23rd April 1997

Career: Lochee Harp; July 1970 Coventry City; July 1975 CITY; Mar 1978 New England Tea Men; Oct 1978 Nuneaton Borough; 1979 New England Tea Men; Mar 1980 Atlanta Chiefs; Aug 1983-trials-Leicester United.

City debut v Birmingham City (H) 16.8.75 (scored once)

> A prolific scorer as a utility forward at Highfield Road, forging a striking partnership with Colin Stein and earning himself a Scottish Under-23 call-up, Brian could rarely replicate such incisiveness at Leicester. Jimmy Bloomfield's insistence on margin-alising him on the right flank may have been to blame, when his small but stocky frame seemed to better suit him for close-quarters skirmishing, but Brian was well and truly out of the Filbert Street picture when he joined the remarkable nine-man transatlantic exodus towards the end of the disastrous McLintock-helmed rele-gation season. He remained for four summer terms in the NASL, and eventually settled permanently in the States; sadly being killed in a building-site scaffolding accident.

***Apps:** FL 87+3; FAC 4; LC 4+1.*
***Goals:** FL 9.*

ALLEN, Henry

b. Spondon, Derbyshire, 1879
d. Bulawayo, Rhodesia, 13th September 1939

Career: Alvaston; Oct 1898 Derby County; Dec 1899 FOSSE; May 1900 Derby County; 1900 Alvaston & Boulton; 1901 Rhodesian football.

Fosse debut v New Brighton Tower (A) 16.12.1899

> An inexperienced, 'dainty' teenage outside-left in Derby's defeated Cup Final side of 1899, Harry was released by the Rams after only two subsequent League appearances, and made little impact on Fosse's left flank as a mid-season alternative to Rab King. Reportedly applying for reinstatement as an amateur in April 1900, Harry emigrated to Rhodesia (now Zimbabwe) in June 1901 to become a typical pillar of Empire. Working his way through the hierarchy of the local railway administration, he finished as principal assistant to the general manager, Rhodesia Railways, while involved in boxing (president, Rhodesian ABA), cricket (vice-president Rhodesian Cricket Union), bowls, golf, horseracing and, inevitably, football activities. He captained Southern Rhodesia in the Currie Cup in 1911, represented Mashonaland and Matabeleland, and became vice-president of the Bulawayo & District FA. His amateur dramatic career peaked with his portrayal of Cecil Rhodes in the pageant at the Johannesburg Empire Exhibition. A massively-attended, 'semi-military' funeral for Captain Allen (he had retained his WW1 rank) followed his death after an appendicitis operation.

Apps: FL 13; FAC 1.
Goals: FL 2.

ALLEYNE, Robert Anthony

b. Dudley, West Midlands, 27th September 1968

Career: YT/pro Sept 1986 CITY; Oct 1987-loan-Wrexham; Mar 1988 Chesterfield; Aug 1989 Teilt (Belgium); 1990-trials-Walsall; Mar 1992 Telford United; cs 1992 Sutton Coldfield Town; 1993 Tamworth; cs 1994 Matlock Town.

City debut v West Ham United (A) 1.1.87 (sub)

> A first-teamer before experiencing a single reserve game, Robert had an injury crisis in a relegation-bound squad to thank for his rapid elevation from the youth ranks. Two days after his Upton Park cameo, he contributed from the kick-off, as a left-sided attacker, to the seasonal highlight of a 6-1 home win over Sheffield Wednesday. A key member of City's Youth Cup semi-final team of 1987, he gained extra senior exposure on loan at the Racecourse, but fell victim to David Pleat's initial pruning of the Filbert Street roster. The Belgian Third Division was an unexpected diversion from the Midland scene thereafter, and one that cost him a couple of years out of the game, as his club demanded a hefty fee on his return home, effectively shackling him in those pre-Bosman days. Robert was most recently noted as a fitness consultant at a Matlock health club.

***Apps:** FL 1+2.*

ALLMAN, Messina Wilson (Dick)

b. Burslem, Staffs, 1883
d. Croydon, 1943 (?)

Career: Burslem Higherhave; Apr 1903 Burslem Port Vale; cs 1905 Reading; May 1907 Portsmouth; Nov 1907 Plymouth Argyle; July 1908 Liverpool; cs 1909 Wrexham; cs 1910 Ton Pentre; Aug 1911-trials-FOSSE; Grantham; Nov 1911 FOSSE; June 1912 Croydon Common; cs 1919 Crystal Palace; cs 1920 Maidstone United.

Fosse debut v Barnsley (H) 18.11.11

> The notorious weather-beaten game at Grimsby in January 1912, when Dick was one of six Fossils to leave the field early, spelled the end of a disappointing Leicester stint for this well-travelled inside- or centre-forward, who failed to spark the side to a single victory during his short stay. Apprenticed in the Potteries as an earthenware painter, he'd turned pro with the Valiants (scoring for them against Fosse in April 1905) before starting wandering in earnest. Dick's Southern League experiences peaked with Plymouth's 1908 runners-up placing, and his Anfield lot was a single League game, but he scored the winning goal of the 1910 Welsh Cup Final for Wrexham; and in 1914 he would aid Croydon's ascent from the Southern League's Second Division via the championship. Enlisting in 1915 and serving in France (after guesting once for Watford), he joined Palace on demob as a reserve centre-half, and also fulfilled this role at Maidstone.

***Apps:** FL 7.*
***Goals:** FL 3.*

ALLSOPP, Thomas Charlesworth

b. Leicester, 18th December 1880
d. Norwich, 7th March 1919

Career: Aug 1899 FOSSE; cs 1902 Luton Town; May 1904 FOSSE; cs 1905 Brighton & Hove Albion; May 1907 Norwich City.

Fosse debut v Middlesbrough (A) 16.2.01

> A two-sport man, and twice a Fossil, Tommy stuck, albeit speedily, to the left-wing as a footballer, but was very much an all-rounder in his parallel cricket career. Initially jettisoned after two Filbert Street terms, he built enough of a reputation at Luton to get the call to help revitalise the rock-bottom, just re-elected Fosse; but was soon off for another five campaigns of Southern League fare. Meanwhile, having coached the summer game at Horsham School in 1902, Tommy made his Leicestershire breakthrough between 1903 and 1905 (he was also on the MCC groundstaff at Lord's in the latter year), and went on to Minor Counties success with Norfolk between 1907 and 1912. Tommy survived WW1 service as a Labour Battalion sergeant in France, but succumbed to influenza on his return to his Norwich hostelry.

***Apps:** FL 64; FAC 6.*
***Goals:** FL 6; FAC 1.*

ANDERSON, Andrew L.

b. Glasgow

Career: Ashfield Juniors; cs 1904 St Mirren; May 1908 Newcastle United; May 1912 Third Lanark; July 1914 FOSSE.

Fosse debut v Lincoln City (H) 2.9.14

> Though we've yet to discover whether there were any non-league takers when Third Lanark listed Andrew at £30 in 1913, or simply whether he had a year rusting out of the game before Fosse took him on, there was little doubt that his efforts at outside-left were well short of the mark in turning around the club's re-election-bound fate in the final pre-war season, even in tandem with fellow-Glaswegian George Hastie. The contrast with Andrew's initial English experiences was marked: his role in taking St Mirren to the Scottish Cup Final in 1908 had earned him a £350 move to Tyneside; and a 1909 Championship medal, plus an international trial, had been the immediate rewards.

***Apps:** FL 25; FAC 1.*
***Goals:** FL 1.*

ANDERSON, John

b. Barrhead, Renfrewshire, 8th December 1929

Career: St Charles (Paisley); 1946 Arthurlie; Dec 1948 CITY; July 1960 Peterborough United; July 1961 Nuneaton Borough; Sept 1962 Bedworth Town; Mar 1963 Syston St Peters; Nov 1965 Husbands Bosworth Albion.

City debut v Barnsley (A) 6.4.49

> Not the most physically imposing of goalkeepers, but a wiry and wily last-line exploiting good positioning and reflexes, Johnny had his fine City form, especially in the Second Division championship campaign of 1954, recognised by Scotland to the tune of one full cap, one 'B' team honour, and the status of standby keeper for the World Cup. National Service with the RAMC hampered his Filbert Street progress in the very early 50s (after he had appeared in the only Scottish Junior 'international' ever held at Hampden Park, against the Republic of Ireland in 1948), but was the cause of his regularly appearing in a star-studded Army side behind the likes of John Charles, Tommy Taylor and Bobby Smith; and on demob he became consistent first-choice for City until cracking his wrist against Bristol Rovers in the second of his promotion years, 1956/7; bringing to an end a 106-game run and sidelining him for the championship run-in. A battle with Dave MacLaren for the green jersey thereafter ensued, and an April 1959 selection for the Football Combination side in Amsterdam indexed his residual reputation, but it was the advent of Gordon Banks which marked Johnny as surplus to Filbert Street needs. Sadly, after turning down approaches from Exeter and Chesterfield to join Posh, only a single League Cup appearance spiced a term in reserve as his new club took the Fourth Division by storm.

***Apps:** FL 261; FAC 16.*

ANDERSON, Robert

b. Newton Mearns, Ayrshire, 11th August 1928
d. Leicester, 29th August 2000

Career: Mearns Amateurs; am Aug 1944/pro Jan 1946 CITY; Aug 1949 Coalville Town; Jan 1950-trials-Ipswich Town; 1950 Whitwick Colliery; Sept 1951 Third Lanark; Nov 1951 Kilmarnock; July 1953 Hamilton Academical; Feb 1954 Forres Mechanics (?); 1954 Dumbarton; Aug 1955 Whitwick Colliery.

City debut (WW2) v Brentford (A) 6.9.45; (postwar) v West Ham United (A) 7.9.46 (scored once)

> Pitched into the transitional season of 1945/6 as a teenager, Bobby was a nippy winger who found himself thereafter cast almost exclusively in the role of understudy to the ultra-consistent Mal Griffiths and Charlie Adam. A homeward sojourn from the North Leicestershire coalfields reintroduced him to senior football (most successfully with Killie), but it was to his adopted county that Bobby then returned. In the mid-60s he was coaching District League side Thurmaston Progressive WMC in tandem with ex-City keeper Adam Dickson.

***Apps:** FL 19; WW2 5.*
***Goals:** FL 2.*

ANDREWS, Ian Edmund

b. Nottingham, 1st December 1964

Career: app 1980 Mansfield Town; Sept 1981 CITY; Jan 1984-loan-Middlesbrough; Jan 1984-loan-Swindon Town; July 1988 Celtic; Dec 1988-loan-Leeds United; Dec 1989 Southampton; Aug 1994-loan-Plymouth Argyle; Sept 1994 Bournemouth; Mar 1997-loan-CITY; July 1997-trials-Scarborough; Aug 1997-1998 & Mar 2001-May 2001 CITY.

City debut v Wolverhampton Wanderers (A) 7.5.84

> England Youth and Under-21 honours accrued to goalkeeper Ian at Leicester, but in some respects his 1986 choice as an over-age player for the intermediate national line-up marked an unwelcome turning point in

his career. Taken on by City at youth coach Dave Richardson's insistence while both Nottingham Forest (who'd had him on schoolboy forms) and Mansfield (where he'd started an apprenticeship) dithered, Ian was soon looking likely material to succeed Mark Wallington. His senior bow came with Swindon, and he was soon justifying City's confidence in a First Division context. But the sudden and radical dip in City's form partway through 1986/7 was mirrored in Ian's alarming drop in confidence, and his occasional mishandlings and ill-judged wanderings from his line were soon being ruthlessly exploited. Paul Cooper assumed his senior jersey, but the £300,000 that Celtic paid indexed the apparent certainty that Ian's form would rapidly return. He lost, however, the battle for the No 1 spot with one-time City trialist Pat Bonner, and reserve status then persistently dogged him until he arrived at Dean Court. (Indeed Ian set a record by sitting out the entirety of the 1992/3 season on Southampton's bench, as unused backup to Tim Flowers). A regular with the Cherries for almost two years, Ian then sadly had to seek compassionate leave owing to the serious illness of his wife, to which she tragically succumbed in 1987. Latterly, Ian had been keeping fit with City, and he subsequently re-signed on loan and then on a monthly contract, when there seemed to be no cover for Kasey Keller. In 1998 Ian was appointed as physio to City's Youth Academy sides; but yet again was re-registered as a player towards the end of 2000/1; featuring in the reserves and sitting on the senior bench for both Cup and Premiership fixtures as cover for Simon Royce.

Apps: *FL 126; FAC 7; LC 6.*

ANSTEY, Brendel

b. Bristol, November 1887
d. Wednesbury, Staffs, 9th December 1933

Career: Hanham Athletic; 1910 Bristol Rovers; Feb 1911 Aston Villa; Sept 1919 CITY; July 1920 Mid-Rhondda; Dec 1921 Wednesbury Old Athletic.

City debut v Wolverhampton Wanderers (A) 6.9.19

> A Gloucestershire Intermediate Cup winner with Hanham, but unused at senior level at Eastville, Brendel became a patient understudy to international keeper Sam Hardy at Villa Park, but still managed 45 League outings before WW1. In regionalised football he briefly represented each of Villa, Birmingham and Lincoln City; then he was given a chance at Leicester to replace Herbert Bown between the sticks. Manager Peter Hodge seemed to agree, however, with local critic 'Scrutator' in the *Leicester Mail* about Brendel's "unaccountable hesitation and discomfort with low drives", and soon let him drop to Southern League level in Wales. In December 1921, he took over the Park Inn, Wednesbury, and was still licensee there at the time of his death.

Apps: *FL 7.*

APPLETON, Colin Harry

b. Scarborough, 7th March 1936

Career: 1951 Scarborough; trials Nov 1953/pro Mar 1954 CITY; May 1966 Charlton Athletic; July 1967 Barrow (p/mgr); cs 1969 Scarborough (p/coach; p/mgr).

City debut v Manchester City (H) 4.9.54.

> A Midland League debutant at 16 for Scarborough, and soon recommended to Leicester by former City man Reg Halton, Colin gave further early indications of making the grade when handed a senior blue shirt after only three reserve outings, and when making a substantial contribution to the 1957 Second Division championship effort. National Service then intervened, but with Colin based with the Leicesters at Glen Parva, and regularly repping the Army, he added a fair bit of experience to his burgeoning half-back repertoire. Certainly, from 1959 Colin made the No 6 shirt his own for five seasons in which he missed only a total of eight games. That this spell encompassed two trips to Wembley and a League Cup triumph was no coincidence (Colin skippering City in 1963 and when getting his hands on the club's first national knockout trophy a year later). FA representative honours (including a 1961 tour of New Zealand and the Far East) and a Football League selection were partial reward for his cool and forcefully prompting play, which also brought the occasional selection in the inside-left slot, and further recognition of his value came from a club Testimonial in 1964. A year on, Colin was a first-leg scorer as City reached the Final stage again in just failing to retain the League Cup; and it was only after a dozen years of City service that he moved on, briefly to resume his partnership with Ian King at The Valley. A transition to management was achieved at Holker Street, and developed at Scarborough, where the prodigal returned with remarkable success. Colin's penalty winner in the FA Trophy semi-final saw him through to his first Wembley win (as a right-back) in 1973; and as boss he would twice more lead out his home-town side in this competition at the national stadium. Unsurprisingly, he was gifted another Testimonial in 1982; and snapped up for backroom influence back at League level. A coach at Grimsby, he took the hot seat at each of Hull City (twice), Swansea and Exeter; before stepping towards retirement with Bridlington Town. Colin's younger brother David was a City professional in the early 60s.

Colin Appleton

Apps: *FL 277; FAC 32; LC 20; ECWC 4.*
Goals: *FL 19; LC 2; ECWC 1.*

ARMSTRONG, George

b. Hebburn, Co Durham, 9th August 1944
d. Hemel Hempstead, Herts, 1st November 2000

Career: Hawthorn Leslie; Aug 1961 Arsenal; Sept 1977 CITY; Sept 1978 Stockport County(-1979); cs 1982 Trowbridge Town.

City debut v Nottingham Forest (H) 24.9.77

> Renowned for hardly ever having stopped running effectively during 621 League and Cup games for the Gunners, George was understandably looking somewhat jaded when he found himself recruited to a dispiriting relegation campaign by former Highbury team-mate Frank McLintock. A Geordie terrier whose energetic and pacy wingplay earned him five England Under-23 selections, he was also multiply-bemedalled at club level; having featured in the Fairs Cup win of 1970, the Double side of 1971, and in three runners-up efforts in the FA Cup and League Cup. Such achievements looked extremely distant at Filbert Street, where a midfield role in a regularly chopped and changed line-up did little for his reputation, and where the match-winner in a Cup tie at Hull was his only mark on the scoresheet. Jock Wallace allowed George to leave after giving him a quartet of outings in 1978/9, and he retired as a player the following summer, to move into coaching. Appointments at Aston Villa, Fulham, Enderby Town, Middlesbrough, QPR and Worcester City bracketed a brief return to action for the Alan Birchenall-managed Trowbridge side, and preceded a return 'home' to Highbury, as Arsenal reserve coach, in July 1990. His untimely death followed his collapse at the end of a training session there.

Apps: *FL 14+1; FAC 1; LC 1.*
Goals: *FAC 1.*

ARPHEXAD, Pegguy Michel

b. Les Abymes, Guadeloupe, 18th May 1973

Career: 1987 Brest-Armorique; 1991 RC Lens; Aug 1996-loan-Lille OSC; July 1997-trials-Motherwell; Aug 1997 CITY; July 2000 Liverpool.

City debut v Chelsea (A) 18.10.97

> A goalkeeper who left his Caribbean home at the age of 14 to join Brest's youth set-up, and found himself briefly both there and at Lens apprenticed to future international Bernard Lama, Pegguy had to wait until April 1996 for his First Division debut in France, despite winning seven Under-21 selections, and still possessed only a modicum of top-level experience when he came to Leicester for pre-season trials in friendlies at Preston, Northampton and Shepshed. With City lacking cover for Kasey Keller at that point, free agent Pegguy signed on the deadline day for UEFA Cup registrations, and eventually made his bow at Stamford Bridge after Keller dislocated a finger. An eye-catchingly agile shot-stopping display ensued, with Pegguy beaten only by a last-minute screamer from compatriot Franck Leboeuf; and subsequent performances, earning a contract extension and immense popularity with City fans, justified the Martin O'Neill gamble on his talents. He became a more regular stand-in for the injury-prone Tim Flowers, and starred in several of City's Cup ties in 1999/2000, emerging as the hero of the penalty shoot-outs with each of Fulham and Arsenal, and putting on a faultlessly spectacular display in the Premiership win at Anfield; immediately prompting interest from Liverpool boss Gérard Houllier. The latter then snapped up his compatriot on a Bosman free transfer; though consigned him to bench duties as deputy to Sander Westerveld for almost the whole of his first term – including the victorious Finals of each of the League, FA and UEFA Cups. Pegguy's brother Bruno (at Evry) and his cousin Claude (at Plabennec) have also featured in the French lower leagues.

Apps: *PL 17+4; FAC 3+1; LC 4.*

ASHBY, Henry Radford

b. Derby
d. Australia, ca 1926

Career: Derby Athletic; cs 1896 Burton Swifts; cs 1899 Brighton United; Nov 1899 not known; cs 1901 Burton United; cs 1904 Plymouth Argyle; July 1905 FOSSE.

Fosse debut v Clapton Orient (H) 2.9.05

> A broken leg sustained in tackling Hull City's famous Corinthian amateur, EGD Wright, in March 1907, brought a sad end to the career of this cultured full-back, generally regarded as one of the classiest Fosse had ever fielded to that date. Harry had cost £80 (paid to League club Burton United rather than Southern League Plymouth), and had missed but a single Fosse fixture thereafter, so was a popular beneficiary of compensation raised by the club from both a reserve fixture against Hull in March 1908, and a series of Sacred Concerts at the Palace Theatre the same month. Earlier, Burton Swifts had occasionally experimented with Harry at centre-forward, and he'd notched a hat-trick against Burnley in his first front-line outing; while he'd captained Brighton United in their first eleven Southern League and FA Cup games of 1899/1900 before temporarily disappearing from the game – we strongly suspect for voluntary Boer War service. By 1911, Harry was running a Leicester pub, but emigrated Down Under a year or so later.

Apps: *FL 66; FAC 2.*

ATHERLEY, R.

Career: Anstey Town; Aug 1899-trials-FOSSE; Leicester Imperial; Oct 1901 FOSSE; cs 1902 Leicester Imperial; Dec 1904 Humberstone Victoria; cs 1905 St Andrews.

Fosse debut/only game v Blackpool (A) 28.3.02

> A local centre-forward tried out in the above Good Friday defeat, shortly after Charles Richards and Jimmy Stevenson had been dispensed with on disciplinary grounds, and at a time when seemingly every member of the Imperial forward-line got a senior opportunity with Fosse.

Apps: *FL 1.*

ATHERTON, James

b. Lancashire, ca 1872

Career: South Shore; cs 1894 Blackpool; May 1895 FOSSE; Aug 1896 Kettering; cs 1898 New Brompton (- 1904).

Fosse debut v Burton Wanderers (H) 28.9.1895

> A centre-half understudy to the consistent Jack Walker during his term with Fosse, James had first come to Filbert Street notice as pivot of the South Shore team (from Blackpool) encountered in the FA Cup in 1893/4, and had in the interim helped the other senior Blackpool club to the runners-up spot in the Lancashire League in 1895. Two Midland League campaigns with Kettering ensued, and James completed his tour of senior regional competitions with a fine six-year stint at Southern League New Brompton (forerunners of Gillingham).

Apps: *FL 2.*

ATKINS, Amos

b. Hemington, Leics

Career: Castle Donington; Notts Olympic; Heanor Town; Mar 1892 FOSSE; cs 1892 Mansfield Greenhalgh's; 1893 Castle Donington; Ilkeston Town; cs 1895 Grantham Rovers.

Fosse debut/only game v Derby Junction (A) ML 12.3.1892

> 'Played one, missed one', was the senior Fosse record of this peripatetic outside-left, and it was the game he missed, rather than the above goalless draw, which was most significant. For a month later he failed to show up for the fixture at champions-elect Rotherham Town which saw a ten-man team go down by eleven goals in the club's heaviest-ever Midland League defeat.

Apps: *ML 1.*

ATTER, Charles

Career: Dec 1891 FOSSE.

Fosse debut/only game v Doncaster Rovers (A) ML 26.12 1891

> The younger brother of star winger Jimmy operated on the right flank in the above Boxing Day defeat during the initial Midland League wooden-spoon season. No other senior experience in the game is evident from research of the era, which instead reveals that he was far from a regular even in the Melton eleven of 1894/5.

Apps: *ML 1.*

ATTER, James

b. Stamford, Lincs, 2nd March 1870
d. Melton Mowbray, Leics, 10th February 1950

Career: Mill Hill House; Stamford Town; 1890 FOSSE; Feb 1892 Crouch End; Feb 1893 FOSSE; 1893 Crouch End; 1893 Corinthians; 1893 Melton Town;1893 Aylestone Park Rovers; cs 1895 Melton Town.

Fosse debut (competitive) v Burton Wanderers (H) FAC 4.10.1890

> 'Mr Atter Will Play'. So read the message of the sandwich-board men currying support for the early Fossils, in testimony to the drawing power of their first star. Jimmy, a trainee solicitor (like his father) whose studies often took him to the capital, who qualified in January 1893, and who eventually settled to practice in Melton Mowbray, was a pacy amateur outside-left who simultaneously served on the Fosse committee that secured Midland League football for Leicester. In fact, he was in the club's initial line-ups in both that competition and the FA Cup, and scored the first Fosse goal at Filbert Street when that ground was acquired. As a teenager, after education at Mill Hill and Oakham, Jimmy appeared for Mill Hill House in the first two Finals of the County Cup (1888 and 1889), and as a Fossil took a victor's medal from the fourth decider for this trophy. He represented each of Leicestershire, Middlesex and the London FA in inter-county football fare, as well as the Midland League select side, and won occasional call-ups for the prestigious Corinthians. By 1896, he was on the executive committee of the Leicestershire FA, and in the early years of the twentieth century was president of the District League club, Melton Mowbray FC. Jimmy's sporting prowess didn't stop there, though. As a fine batsman, he starred locally for the Banks, Ivanhoe and Egerton Park cricket teams, and occasionally for the County from 1888-1894, just before they gained first-class recognition. Jimmy served in the Boer War, and lost two sons in WW1. A Freemason and noted chess player, he retired from legal practice in the 30s.

Apps: *FAC 2; ML 24.*
Goals: *ML 6.*

ATTERBURY, Septimus

b. Allestree, Derby, 18th October 1880
d. Osgathorpe, Leics, 13th March 1964

Career: Leicester jnr football; Mar 1898 Loughborough; cs 1899 Barnsley; cs 1901 Wellingborough; Aug 1902 FOSSE; cs 1903 Swindon Town; May 1907 Plymouth Argyle (- 1921).

Fosse debut v Gainsborough Trinity (H) 25.12.02

> A dozen years separated Sep's left-back appearances for Fosse in the League and as a guest in WW1 football, but in a lengthy career it was the then almost unprecedented fourteen years which separated his first and last Plymouth outings which were deemed most noteworthy.

Sep Atterbury

Steadiness was the adjective most often applied to his unostentatious playing style, and steadfastness clearly became his watchword. Given only a couple of chances by the ailing Luffs, and a couple of seasons by fellow Second Division side Barnsley, Sep then moved, essentially sideways, into the Southern League football for which he developed such a taste. His Fosse stint in the latter half of 1902/3 was his only departure from that sphere until Plymouth were elected with their peers into the new Division Three in 1920, by which stage he had totted up a remarkable 435 Southern League appearances with Wellingborough (23), Swindon (118) and the Pilgrims (294), and had won both a championship medal and a representative selection against the Irish League in 1913. Sep was a member of Argyle's first-ever Football League line-up, and as a 40-year-old reserve later that term won a final sentimental selection for the game between the Southern and Welsh Leagues. He immediately assumed the role of Argyle trainer from 1921 to 1937, trained Leicestershire club Holwell Works from November 1937, and joined Chester as trainer in August 1938. Between the wars, he also spent his summers as cricket coach at Loughborough Grammar School, and after WW2 continued to work there as an odd-job man. A committee member of the Players Union in 1911/12, Sep was the only Fossil to be sent off in WW1 football, on Boxing Day 1916 at Barnsley.

***Apps:** FL 21; WW1 50.*
***Goals:** WW1 3.*

AYTON, James

b. Barrhead, Renfrewshire, 15th October 1923
d. Leicester, 25th August 1988

Career: Neilston Victoria; 1944 Third Lanark; Oct 1948 CITY; June 1951 Shrewsbury Town; July 1952 Bedford Town; June 1954 Nuneaton Borough.

City debut v Barnsley (H) 30.10.48

> A Johnny Duncan capture at a record £7,750, inside-left Jimmy was jinxed throughout his City stint, with jaundice sidelining him from the joint 1948/9 struggle against relegation and towards Wembley, and his next term wrecked by successive injuries to jaw and knee. Even on recovering fitness, he found himself in no-win competition with interim signing Arthur Rowley for the No 10 shirt. A £4,000 transfer to the Shrews resulted, but Jimmy's previous Scottish League form was still proving elusive, and he was criticised in the local press there for 'a tendency for temperamental demonstrations towards his team-mates'! Jimmy, who had seen wartime service with the Navy in Ceylon, was by the late 50s installed as sports officer with a Leicester engineering firm.

***Apps:** FL 8.*
***Goals:** FL 1.*

BACON, Ernest Frederick

b. Leicester, 19th February 1896
d. Aylestone, Leics, 9th January 1972

Career: Oxford Street; St Andrews; Aug 1919 CITY; May 1920 Watford; July 1921 Charlton Athletic; May 1923 Nuneaton Town; Dec 1923 Kettering; 1924 Barwell United; 1928 Erith & Belvedere (?); 1929 Callendar Athletic (?).

City debut v Fulham (H) 13.9.19

> Capped as a schoolboy before the war, then seeing military service in Salonika, Ernest made his Filbert Street bow when guesting for Coventry City in a wartime friendly. An early Peter Hodge selection for City at right-half, he didn't quite meet the boss's exacting team-building requirements, and was soon settled in reserve. Ernest featured in Watford's first-ever Football League line-up, but made only sporadic first-eleven appearances for his two Third Division clubs, mainly at right-back. A scorer for City Reserves in their 1920 Senior Cup Final win over Moira United, he also featured in the same local showpiece for Barwell against City in 1925. His final (1925/6) season with Barwell saw them crowned as Senior League champions.

***Apps:** FL 4.*

BAILEY, Herbert

b. Melton Mowbray, Leics

Career: Melton Town; Birmingham St Georges; 1891 Wolverhampton Wanderers; Melton Town; Mar 1892 FOSSE; 1894 Melton Town.

Fosse debut v Gainsborough Trinity (A) ML 19.3.1892

> A brother of Fosse full-back Harry, centre-forward Herbert picked up early experience as a professional with St Georges in the Football Alliance and in one Football League outing for Wolves. He was the only Fossil actually to find the net in the final eight fixtures of the disastrous first Midland League fling, but earned no contract for the following term. Reinstated as an amateur in August 1893, however, he returned for the briefest contribution to the 1893/4 Midland League title-chase, and also that season scored twice for Leicestershire in a 6-1 win over Northants at Wellingborough.

***Apps:** ML 5.*
***Goals:** ML 1.*

BAILEY, Horace Peter

b. Derby, 3rd July 1881
d. Biggleswade, Beds, 1st August 1960

Career: Sept 1899 Derby County; 1901 Crich; Dec 1902 Ripley Athletic; 1905 Leicester Imperial; Jan 1907 FOSSE; Mar 1910 Northern Nomads; Apr 1910 Derby County; Sept 1910 Blackburn Rovers; Nov 1910 Stoke; Feb 1911 Birmingham (- 1913).

Fosse debut v Wolverhampton Wanderers (H) 9.9.07

> 'Bailey negotiates likely-looking shots in a manner which stamps him as being a cut above the ordinary class', opined the *Nottingham Evening Mail;* while the *Leicester Mercury* admiringly credited him with 'an eye like a hawk, and cat-like agility'. Another contemporary view was that 'his resource saves him the trouble of being in a hurry'. Fosse's first England goalkeeper was an amateur (otherwise a rating official for the Midland Railway Company at Derby) whose *annus mirabilis* was undoubtedly 1908. A prime contributor to Fosse's successful promotion effort, Horace was capped that year at both full and amateur level, and additionally picked up a gold medal when appearing for the victorious United Kingdom XI in the football Final of the Olympic Games. A year later, Horace was the blameless but severely embarrassed last-line for relegation-bound Fosse in their record 0-12 defeat at Nottingham Forest, and one of two players to give satisfactorily explanatory evidence at the subsequent League enquiry. His eventual departure from Leicester was solely aimed at helping the Rams over an injury crisis (as were his short-term signings for Blackburn and Stoke), and he was still in good enough form at St Andrews to win further international recognition.

***Apps:** FL 68; FAC 2.*

BAILEY, William Henry

b. Melton Mowbray, Leics, 2nd October 1869
d. Leicester, 19th October 1930

Career: Melton Rovers; Melton Town; Birmingham St Georges; Melton Rovers; 1891 FOSSE (- 1899).

Fosse debut (competitive) v Derby Junction (H) ML 12.9.1891

> A teenage founder-member of the Melton Town club with his brother Herbert, and holder of a Birmingham Senior Cup medal from his St Georges stint, Harry became a Fosse stalwart with several 'firsts' to his name. At left-back in the club's debut games in each of the Midland and Football Leagues, and the scorer of Fosse's first-ever penalty (in a friendly against Notts County two days after his competitive bow), he also became the initial recipient of a Fosse benefit payout: £146 from a Boxing Day 1893 friendly against prestigious touring amateurs, the Casuals. His League days looked to be behind him after January 1897, and he accepted reinstatement as an amateur when taking over the Full Moon pub in Leicester, but when he accompanied Fosse to Walsall in Septeber 1899 he assumed a new role. Godfrey Beardsley reported injured, it was uncertain whether Peter Goudie could arrive in time from Derby, and Harry was accordingly pressed into service as goalkeeper - being beaten only once in a welcome away win! The versatility was characteristic, as Harry was also on Leicestershire CCC's books as a hard-hitting batsman for several years from 1891, and also played cricket for Egerton Park and as a pro in Scotland.

***Apps:** FL 47; FAC 17; ML 61.*

BAILLIE, Joseph

b. Dumfries, 26th February 1929
d. Maryhill, Glasgow, 23rd March 1966

Career: St Roch's; Dec 1945 Celtic; Nov 1954 Wolverhampton Wanderers; June 1956 Bristol City; June 1957 CITY; June 1960 Bradford Park Avenue.

City debut v Preston North End (H) 16.11.57

> Originally a left-half with Celtic, skilled enough to win a Scotland 'B' cap, three Scottish League selections and a Scottish Cup-winners medal (1951), Joe had such a nightmare introduction to English football that he was seriously contemplating early retirement when David Halliday recruited him to the cause of First Division survival and consolidation at Filbert Street, where he held down the left-back spot with cultured coolness for much of his three-season tenure. Only a single League outing (at right-back) had accrued in two years at Molineux, and Bristol City even experimented with Joe up front against City in 1956/7, but Halliday's persuasiveness paid off after Joe was introduced as a half-time substitute in a friendly against BSK Belgrade, then featured from the start two days later in the first League game under floodlights at Filbert Street. Thereafter, he shaded rivalries with both John Ogilvie and Willie Cunningham for the No 3 shirt until the advent of Richie Norman. A slater when he left school, Joe worked, during his Parkhead days, as a Bevin Boy miner in lieu of National Service with the military. His tragic death occurred when his car skidded into the River Kelvin.

***Apps:** FL 75; FAC 5.*

BAINES, Stanley Norman

b. Syston, Leics, 28th July 1920
d. Syston, 12th March 1990

Career: 1934 Syston Methodists; 1936 Syston St Peter's; Aug 1937-trials-CITY; Coalville Town; Nov 1937 CITY; Aug 1939 Northampton Town; Syston Imperial; cs 1947 Hinckley Athletic.

City debut v Preston North End (H) 10.9.38

> One of City's first 'conditional' transfers, lightweight left-winger Stan was bought by Frank Womack from Coalville for £25 down, plus the promise of a further £100 and a friendly fixture after he'd played three First Division games. Noted for his speed when briefly displacing Eric Stubbs in the final pre-war term, he was nonetheless offered free to the Cobblers at season's end, after relegation had been confirmed. Stan, a 5ft 5in 'lively customer', played only a little regional football for Northampton and Watford, and but once in Division Three (South) in 1946/7.

***Apps:** FL 7.*
***Goals:** FL 1.*

BAIRD, John

b. Alexandria, Dunbartonshire, ca 1870
d. Alexandria, 31st July 1905

Career: Vale Athletic; Vale of Leven; 1889 Aston Villa; 1889 Kidderminster Olympic; 1890 Kidderminster; cs 1891 Aston Villa; May 1895 FOSSE; Aug 1896 Clyde; cs 1897 Vale of Leven.

Fosse debut v Burton Swifts (H) 7.9.1895

> Injury-hit during his Fosse season, Jack struggled to win a full-back place from Harry Davy and Harry Bailey. Ironically, he replaced Andrew Whitelaw at Leicester: the man who had taken Jack's spot at Vale of Leven when he'd first journeyed south. Villa initially loaned him out to the Kidderminster Olympic club that took the inaugural championship of the Birmingham & District League, but later with the Villains he would earn an FA Cup consolation medal from the 1892 defeat by West Brom (in the last Final held at Kennington Oval), and an 1894 League championship memento. In June 1896, Jack was reported to be in the summer employ of the Third Lanark chairman, but no subsequent senior appearances are apparent at either that club or Clyde. His death at the age of 34 was attributed to heart disease.

***Apps:** FL 13; FAC 1.*

BALDWIN, James J.

b. Blackburn, 12th January 1922
d. Blackburn, 13th February 1985

CAREER: Mill Hill St Peters; 1945 Blackburn Rovers; Feb 1950 CITY; Apr 1956 Great Yarmouth Town (p/mgr); cs 1957 Yeovil Town (p/mgr - 1960).

City debut v Luton Town (H) 25.2.50

> A £10,000 signing by Norman Bullock, who gave City fine value as forager and prompter from either the right-half or inside-right position across the early 50s, Jimmy had prior experience of both top divisions with his hometown club. He had less happy memories of his November 1951 return to Ewood with City, however: contributing an own-goal equaliser to a 1-2 defeat and suffering a broken cheekbone. A relatively slight, balding figure in the middle-line, Jimmy exhibited shrewdness and stamina rather than flair, but well earned his 1954 Second Division championship medal, and was still as a real veteran quietly directing operations for a Yeovil side on a couple of their traditional giant-killing FA Cup runs.

***Apps:** FL 180; FAC 10.*
***Goals:** FL 4.*

BALL, Aloysius (Alf)

b. Preston, ca 1874

Career: 1893 Preston North End; 1895 Kettering; May 1897 FOSSE; cs 1900 Nelson.

Fosse debut v Luton Town (H) 4.9.1897

> Mr Consistency as an ever-present right-half for the first two of his three Filbert Street seasons, Alf was possibly atoning for having scored one of the Kettering goals which removed Fosse from the FA Cup in 1896/7. Previous to that, he had tasted First Division fare in a handful of games for Proud Preston (in their first-ever season finishing outside the top two). Alf's Fosse debut came in opposition to a Luton side fulfilling their first-ever League fixture.

***Apps:** FL 75; FAC 6.*
***Goals:** FL 3.*

BALLARD, Frank

Career: Long Eaton Rangers; cs 1898 FOSSE; cs 1899 Ilkeston Town.

Fosse debut v Manchester City (A) 15.10.1898

> A luckless understudy to Fosse full-backs Jack Walker and George Swift after being recruited from Midland League football in a joint deal with winger Benny Fulwood, Frank was soon on his way to Ilkeston in the same company after breaking through only once on each defensive flank.

***Apps:** FL 2.*

BAMBER, John

b. Peasley Cross, Lancs, 11th April 1895
d. Thatto Heath, St Helens, Lancs, late August 1971

Career: St Helens Recreational; Alexander Vics; Heywood; St Helens Town; Dec 1915 Liverpool; Feb 1924 CITY; July 1927 Tranmere Rovers; Aug 1930 Prescot Cables.

City debut v Sheffield Wednesday (H) 9.2.24

> Honoured with an England cap, two Football League selections and a place on the 1920 FA tour of South Africa, two-footed wing-half Jack nonetheless emerged from his lengthy Liverpool stint with his career in need of some re-railing. Despite being an Anfield fixture throughout wartime football and for the initial pair of top-flight campaigns afterwards, he suffered the frustration of being sidelined (initially through injury) from the bulk of the two championship seasons that followed. Peter Hodge's lifeline to Filbert Street was welcome then, as Jack grasped the ball-winning left-half spot, earned himself a Second Division champs medal in 1925, achieved an ever-present record in the initial consolidatory term, and became a member of the first City team to perch the club (albeit briefly) on the League's pinnacle. Displaced soon afterwards by Willie Orr's expensive acquisition Sid Bishop, Jack returned to Merseyside to play out his career. His first City goal, in November 1924, was scored from a range of one yard, direct from a referee's dropped ball, after the Fulham goalie had been penalised for lying on the ball too long!

***Apps:** FL 113; FAC 7.*
***Goals:** FL 7.*

BANKS, Gordon

b. Sheffield, 30th December 1938

Career: Millspaugh Steelworks; Rawmarsh Welfare; Millspaugh Steelworks; Sept 1955 Chesterfield; May 1959 CITY; Apr 1967 Stoke City (- 1973); 1971-loan-Hellenic (South Africa); Mar 1977 Fort Lauderdale Strikers; Oct 1977-loan-St.Patrick's Athletic.

City debut v Blackpool (H) 9.9.59

> The 1956 FA Youth Cup Final in which Gordon competed among Chesterfield's other 'unknown' hopefuls was not a Wembley event, but the next 16 years of this remarkable goalkeeper's career would be littered with many such showpiece occasions, including the 1966 World Cup Final victory that sealed his global reputation as No 1. After only 23 Saltergate senior outings, Gordon still represented something of a £7,000 gamble on Matt Gillies' part when acquired for Filbert Street, but his development with City was swift, and his top-flight qualities quickly apparent. There would be no gratuitous flashiness to his game, based as it was on uncanny positioning and body-behind-the-ball solidity, but the essential fall-backs of agility and sharp reflexes were always present and correct, engendering a calming confidence within the box. As City consolidated in Division One, it was clear that defensive security was Gillies' priority, and Gordon the man to provide its backbone. The Wembley dates started with City's jinxed 1961 attempt to disrupt the Spurs Double, and accumulated as Gordon played his way into the England set-up. He had a rare nightmare during the 1963 Cup disappointment against Manchester United, yet he'd almost single-handedly shattered Liverpool dreams at the backs-to-the-wall Hillsborough semi-final stage. The 1964 League Cup win and 1965 near-miss were negotiated away from the national stadium, but 1966 saw the yellow-clad England keeper cavorting joyously round it with the Jules Rimet trophy. A Leicester civic reception and a hero's return to Filbert Street were inevitable moments in the aftermath. Yet there would be a troubled postscript, for a young Peter Shilton had already taken advantage of one of Gordon's international absences to press a prodigy's claim to the master's mantle. By the April of 1967, Gillies was in a quandary: almost certain to lose one of his brilliant keepers, he had to decide which. Banks, it transpired, would go. West Ham honourably dropped their promised first option, and Liverpool came just too late. Gordon was off to the Potteries. Sheer top-level consistency and a truly mature reading of match situations kept him an England regular despite Stoke being no more fashionable a club than City, and his international career reached perhaps its personal pinnacle during the 1970 World Cup, when his twisting reflex deflection of Pele's downward header earned 'save of the century' accolades and literally countless TV re-runs. The award of an OBE followed, while at club level Gordon inspired Stoke to their first-ever Wembley trip, and first-ever trophy, in the League Cup victory of 1972. He was named Footballer of the Year that term, but that October his world fell in when an horrendous car crash cost him the sight of one eye. His own high standards precluded a comeback at League level, but eventually he would return between the sticks in the transatlantic NASL, where he became Goalkeeper of the Year in 1977 for his efforts in Florida, and for one game in the League of Ireland. Comparatively unsuccessful spells coaching at Stoke and Port Vale, and managing at Telford United also marked the closing period of Gordon's direct involvement with the game. Thereafter primarily engaged in the corporate hospitality business, he returned to Filbert Street in 1986 as chairman of a short-lived 'Lifeline' fund-raising initiative, was granted a 1995 Testimonial game there, and had a suite in the Carling Stand named in his honour. In 2001, Gordon auctioned much of his World Cup memorabilia to help secure his family's future.

***Apps:** FL 293; FAC 34; LC 25; ECWC 4.*

BANKS, Ian Frederick

b. Mexborough, Yorks, 9th January 1961

Career: app/pro Jan 1979 Barnsley; June 1983 CITY; Sept 1986 Huddersfield Town; July 1988 Bradford City; Mar 1989 West Bromwich Albion; July 1989 Barnsley; July 1992 Rotherham United; Aug 1994 Darlington; Aug 1995 Emley (- 2000).

City debut v Notts County (H) 27.8.83

> The man whose nerveless penalty goal against Newcastle, in the final game of 1985/6, helped clinch First Division survival for another year, Ian was a stocky but skilful left-sided midfielder with an explosive long-range shot, whose popular Filbert Street nickname was 'Banger'. A Gordon Milne purchase at £100,000 who took a while to settle with City and could sometimes appear under-motivated, he nevertheless as often showed a welcome knack of alternating accurate hard-driven crosses with a shuffle inside for a telling strike. Incoming boss Bryan Hamilton soon allowed Ian to return to Yorkshire, where he played the bulk of his football thereafter. He skippered a relegated Huddersfield side in 1988, but earned several more big-money moves on the Second Division roundabout. In December 1989, warming up as Barnsley substitute at Bournemouth, he was 'sent off' for remarks to a linesman about the vailidity of a goal; and was also red-carded on his Darlington debut. Ian was the captain, and unlikely leading scorer, of the Emley side which beat Lincoln City and severely frightened West Ham in the 1997/8 FA Cup, and only hung up his playing boots when almost 40, to undertake stints as assistant manager at Barnsley and Chesterfield.

***Apps:** FL 78+15; FAC 6; LC 3+1.*
***Goals:** FL 14; LC 1.*

BANNISTER, William

b. Burnley, 1879
d. Leicester, 26th March 1942

Career: Earley; 1899 Burnley; Nov 1901 Bolton Wanderers; Dec 1902 Woolwich Arsenal; May 1904 FOSSE; Aug 1910 Burnley; cs 1912 Crewe Alexandra; 1913 Leicester Imperial.

Fosse debut v Blackpool (A) 3.9.04

> Fosse's skipper in the promotion season of 1907/8, Billy was a towering centre-half who had won two England caps and a pair of Football League selections while with his Lancashire clubs. A £300 purchase from Arsenal, the tough pivot with the attacking bent and mule-like long-range shot gave five seasons' service as a regular, and a final one largely in reserve, when he took a benefit from a Christmas 1909 reserve game against Nottingham Forest, and earned a County Cup-winners medal after playing the Final as emergency goalkeeper. Billy ran pubs in both Burnley and Leicester, and was landlord of the Woolcomber's Arms at the time of his death. His son, also Billy and also a centre-half, had to settle for purely local football in the 20s and 30s, primarily with Mountsorrel Town and Abbey Lane Imperial.

***Apps:** FL 149; FAC 11.*
***Goals:** FL 15; FAC 3.*

BARACLOUGH, Ian Robert

b. Leicester, 4th December 1970

Career: YT July 1987/pro Dec 1988 CITY; Mar 1990-loan-Wigan Athletic; Dec 1990-loan-Grimsby Town; Aug 1991 Grimsby Town; Aug 1992 Lincoln City; May 1994 Mansfield Town; Oct 1995 Notts County; Mar 1998 Queens Park Rangers; June 2001 Notts County

City debut v Charlton Athletic (A) FMC 14.11.89 (sub)

> Though now regarded primarily as a utility defender, Ian initially struggled to make his way through the City ranks as a central striker. Indeed, he and Paul Kitson spearheaded a Football League Youth XI in Moscow in 1989, and he made a reasonable impact at Central League level subsequently. His senior bow at Selhurst Park in City's Zenith Cup exit was a brief affair, and his start in the club's FA Cup defeat at home to Barnsley an understandably difficult one as emergency target-man, but Ian got off the scoring mark on loan at Wigan the same season. An essentially anonymous reserve campaign followed, though, and Brian Little freed him in his initial pruning of the staff. Ian fared little better at Grimsby, but eventually came more into his own as he retreated via midfield to the back line, adding wing-back abilities to his repertoire, and seeing his transfer value rise accordingly. QPR's relegation to Division Two, however, saw him freed back to Meadow Lane in summer 2001.

***Apps:** FAC 1; FMC 0+1.*

BARLOW, Herbert

b. Kilnhurst, Yorks, 22nd July 1916

Career: Silverwood Colliery; July 1935 Barnsley; June 1938 Wolverhampton Wanderers; Feb 1939 Portsmouth; Dec 1949 CITY; June 1952 Colchester United; cs 1954 Crittall's Athletic; cs 1956 Long Melford (p/coach).

City debut v Sheffield Wednesday (H) 17.12.49

> Norman Bullock's first signing for City, Bert gave three seasons of a wily veteran's inside-forward experience to City's Second Division travails of the early 50s. Having developed at Oakwell and earned elevation to top-flight Wolves, he first really hit the headlines in 1939, when he was then deemed surplus to requirements after only three games at Molineux. He moved to Fratton Park on a deferred-payment basis, scored a Cup semi-final goal to secure otherwise struggling Pompey a Wembley appearance, and there netted again to help his underdog team to a 4-1 victory – over Wolves! Ironically, exactly ten years on, Bert and his Pompey mates again had Wembley (and a potential League/Cup double) in sight – when their expectations of a Highbury semi-final walkover were rudely upset by an inspired, giant-killing City side he was to join before the year was out. Bert was mulling an offer of the player-manager's role at Wisbech Town in 1952, when the chance to extend his League career at Colchester came along, and he finished his two-year Layer Road stint as that club's oldest-ever player at the age of 38. Again irony attaches here, for in December 1966 his son Peter became Colchester's youngest-ever first-teamer at 16 (before also serving Workington and Hartlepool).

***Apps:** FL 42; FAC 2.*
***Goals:** FL 9.*

BARLOW, John

b. Prescot, Lancs, 1876

Career: Prescot; cs 1897 Everton; cs 1899 Reading; cs 1901 Tottenham Hotspur; Feb 1903 Reading; May 1903 FOSSE.

Fosse debut v Barnsley (A) 5.9.03

> Signed a week after Fosse faced Reading in a friendly, on a free transfer arrangement as part of the deal which took Tom Simpson to Everton, John was a left-sided forward who found little Filbert Street success in a team freefalling dismally towards its first re-election bid. He'd previously made only a quartet of First Division appearances in two years at Goodison, and then sampled Southern League fare with mixed results at each of Elm Park and White Hart Lane.

***Apps:** FL 22; FAC 5.*
***Goals:** FL 2; FAC 1.*

BARNETT, Charles

b. Derby, ca 1887

Career: 1907 Newark; am Sept 1912/ pro Feb 1913 FOSSE; Sept 1920 Mansfield Town; Oct 1921 Alfreton Town.

Fosse debut v Hull City (A) 26.4.13

> Only seven times in total on a winning side with Fosse before the war, second-choice keeper Charles failed to make a single senior breakthrough in his City season after peace returned. The understudy to both Ronald Brebner and Herbert Bown also briefly assisted Derby County during WW1, and won County Cup medals in each of 1914 and 1920 with Fosse and City Reserves. After initially agreeing to join Ilkeston United in 1920, Charles turned out instead as the regular custodian for Central Alliance runners-up Mansfield.

***Apps:** FL 20; WW1 5.*

BARRATT, Alfred E.

b. Oadby, Leics, ca 1896

Career: Aug 1914 FOSSE.

Fosse debut/only game v Lincoln City (A) 2.4.15

> Better known as a postwar Tigers rugby player (bagging three tries in eight games in 1920), local outside-left Alfred's sole distinction for Fosse was as the last player to make a League debut for them (in a 3-2 win which nonetheless failed to lift the club from the re-election zone), before the upheavals of war and reconstruction.

***Apps:** FL 1.*

BARRATT, Alfred George

b. Weldon, Northants, 13th April 1920

Career: Weldon; July 1938 Northampton Town; Sept 1939 Stewart & Lloyds (Corby); Sept 1946 CITY; July 1950 Grimsby Town; July 1951 Southport (- 1956).

City debut v West Ham United (H) 17.4.48

> Having previously featured for the Cobblers in one League game and one wartime fixture, Alf returned from service with 47th Royal Marine Commandos, and participation in the Normandy D-Day landings, to assume the loyal role of reserve-team stopper for City across four seasons. Ironically, though, he missed the highlight of the period for the second string – the 1947/8 Combination Cup Final against Bournemouth – as he was making his third appearance in a week (and in all) in the senior centre-half berth. One further outing, at No 2, ensued before Alf then suffered the ignominy of a Divsion Two relegation term at Grimsby. He flourished, however, at Southport, skippering them for five years in the Third Division (North), and standing firm at the heart of the meanest defence in the entire League in 1954/5. On retirement from the game, Alf returned to Leicester as a bricklayer.

***Apps:** FL 4.*

BARRETT, William Henry

b. Nuneaton, Warks, July qtr 1893

Career: Stockingford Congregationals; 1911 Bromsgrove Rovers; 1912 Nuneaton Town; Army football; Dec 1918 Hinckley United; Apr 1919 CITY; July 1925 Derby County; Apr 1927 Hinckley United; Sept 1927 Hereford United.

City debut v Wolverhampton Wanderers (H) 30.8.19

> A plucky, speedy right-back with notable first-time tackling power, Billy gave five seasons of excellent service to City's postwar Second Division defence, but was sadly reduced to a covering role in the term they finally gained promotion as champions; and then didn't get so much as a senior look-in as Derby followed them up a year later. As a veteran, however, he assisted Hereford in their final season at Birmingham Combination level. Billy's pair of penalty goals for City came in each of his final FA Cup and Football League games for the club.

***Apps:** FL 143; FAC 9.*
***Goals:** FL 1; FAC 1.*

BARRON, Charles W.

b. Hexham, Northumberland

Career: Durham City; Sept 1914 FOSSE; cs 1919 Scotswood.

Fosse debut v Birmingham (A) 2.1.15

> A right-back who helped at least to stem partially the tide of high-scoring defeats which pointed Fosse towards re-election in their final League season, Charles nonetheless added a minor personal embarrassment to the club record. For the very last goal they conceded at League level was Charles's hapless hack into his own net in attempting to clear a Clapton Orient shot spinning goalward off keeper Charles Barnett – a moment secured for posterity on a grainy Topical Budget newsreel. Charles briefly returned to Filbert Street for a couple of outings in the final wartime season of 1918/19, having 'kept fit playing for a team in the Newcastle area'. (There was never any variation in the spelling of Charles's surname at the time, so we can only assume that the *Mercury* must have been in error in 1922 when repeatedly referring to him as the older brother of newly-signed Northumbrian reserve forward Fred Baron).

***Apps:** FL 16; WW1 6.*

BARRY, Leonard James

b. Sneinton, Notts, 27th October 1901
d. Mapperley, Notts, 17th April 1970

Career: RAF Cranwell; am May 1920/ pro Nov 1923 Notts County; Sept 1927 CITY; Aug 1933 Nottingham Forest.

City debut v Manchester United (H) 1.10.27

> An England amateur international while with the Magpies, and a thorn in City's side when Notts KO'd them from the FA Cup in 1926, Len arrived at Filbert Street for a hefty £3,500 fee as Willie Orr fine-tuned his forces for the successive assaults on the First Division title that saw City finish successively third and second in the table. Len's contributions were immense, with his dribbling skills on the left wing, his interplay with inside partner Arthur Lochhead, his accurate service to Chandler and Hine, and his own willingness to take spectacular cross-shot opportunities gaining him due recognition. Five full England caps accrued in 1928 and 1929 (with City men taking both flanks when

Hughie Adcock twice appeared in the same side). Len was finally slowing a little when Danny Liddle inherited his role for City, and he featured only briefly in Forest's struggling Second Division line-ups.

Apps: *FL 203; FAC 11.*
Goals: *FL 25; FAC 1.*

BAUCHOP, William Fotheringham

b. Alloa, Clackmannan, 18th January 1882
d. USA, 1948

Career: Alloa Athletic; cs 1900 Abercorn; June 1901 East Stirlingshire; Jan 1902 Alloa Athletic; cs 1905 Plymouth Argyle; May 1906 Heart of Midlothian; June 1907 Carlisle United; June 1909 Stockport County; Aug 1911 FOSSE; Aug 1912 Norwich City; cs 1913 Fulham; Jan 1914 Grimsby Town; cs 1914 Alloa Athletic.

Fosse debut v Gainsborough Trinity (A) 2.9.11

> Seemingly over-accustomed to the role of runner-up, Willie even managed to have his entire career somewhat overshadowed by that of his equally peripatetic younger brother, Jimmy (of Alloa, Celtic, Norwich, Crystal Palace, Derby, Spurs, Bradford, Doncaster and Lincoln). A jinking outside-left, Willie took a consolation medal from Hearts' 1907 Scottish Cup Final defeat, and featured in the Carlisle side that finished second in the Lancashire Combination a year later. With Fosse, after signing to partner Frank Rollinson, he was soon displaced by local youngster George Harrison; and his biggest role in Leicester affairs would seem to have been the two crosses he provided for Norwich's first-half goals against Fosse in the embarrassing FA Cup exit of 1912/13. Willie was stuck in the reserves at both Fulham and Grimsby before his final homeward move.

Apps: *FL 18; FAC 3.*
Goals: *FL 1.*

BAXTER, James

b. Glasgow, ca 1904

Career: Parkhead; Aug 1925 CITY; June 1929 Reading; Nov 1930 Torquay United; 1931 not known; cs 1934 Boston United.

City debut v Bury (A) 24.4.26

> A former captain of the Glasgow Junior League XI, and a Scottish Junior Cup winner in 1924 with Parkhead, Jimmy was deemed a 'methodical, hard-working half-back' when spreading his half-dozen senior selections for City across four seasons, at a time when a settled side was proving a genuine First Division force. In fact, a surfeit of reserve football probably set Jimmy back considerably, for, following his coincidental appearance on the City transfer list with two other ex-Parkhead men in Harry Callachan and Dr Tom Gibson, he failed to make the senior side at either Elm Park or Plainmoor.

Apps: *FL 6.*
Goals: *FL 1.*

BEADSWORTH, Arthur

b. Leicester, 1876
d. France, 9th October 1917

Career: Nov 1893 FOSSE; Aug 1894 Leicester YMCA; Jan 1895 Hinckley Town; trials-Notts County & FOSSE; May 1900 FOSSE; cs 1901 Preston North End ; Sept 1901 Coventry City; Oct 1902 Manchester United; cs 1903 Swindon Town; cs 1905 New Brompton; Aug 1906 Burton United; Mar 1907 Hinckley United; cs 1907 Nuneaton Town; Feb 1909 Hinckley United.

Fosse debut v Newton Heath (H) 29.9.1900

> Released as a teenager, but taken on again by Fosse after figuring in Hinckley's County Cup-winning side of 1900, Arthur this time briefly found senior status as a utility forward, with a debut at outside-right and a trio of outings in the inside-left berth. His League registration then passed to Preston, but he spent the entirety of 1901/2 with Coventry in the Birmingham & District League, and then joined the newly-rechristened club against whom he'd made his Fosse debut. A goal on his Manchester United debut at Arsenal proved to be the only one of his entire career, for both he and Burton United were in the final campaign of their League careers when he found himself goalless there after eighteen games. In the interim, his Southern League exploits with Swindon (where he was on the princely sum of £2 per week) and New Brompton had added a more worthy respectability to Arthur's career; though there had been another two-club glitch when it was discovered that he'd signed for Penrith as well as New Brompton. On leaving the game, he entered the boot and shoe trade in Hinckley, but was serving as a sergeant in the Leicesters when he succumbed to gas poisoning on a French WW1 battlefield.

Apps: *FL 4.*

BEARDSLEY, Godfrey Leonard

b. Barrow-on-Soar, Leics, 1879
d. Erpingham, Norfolk, June 1912

Career: Jan 1894 Rossal School; Dec 1896 Loughborough; Feb 1898-loan-Loughborough Corinthians; Sept 1898 FOSSE (-1901); Reigate Priory; Old Rossalians; (1903 Corinthians).

Fosse debut v Woolwich Arsenal (A) 10.9.1898

> Given that amateur goalkeeper 'Goff' interrupted his law studies to turn professional, it was somewhat ironic that the legality of his transfer from the Luffs to the Fosse was such a contentious matter. Fosse were initially accused of poaching, but it was Loughborough's swift about-turn on this matter which caused resignations among their own committee and caught the curiosity of the FA. Eventually, Fosse were fined £50, their secretary William Clark was suspended sine die, but Godfrey was allowed to continue between the sticks. Which he did with some distinction, once saving a thrice-taken penalty at Small Heath in March 1899. On resuming his law practice, he was allowed to revert to amateur status, and indeed assisted the mighty Corinthians occasionally before his early death. His brother Bent Beardsley founded Loughborough Corinthians (for whom Godfrey played one game at left-back in February 1898), and went on to become president of Quorn Methodists, while another brother (initialled HE) represented Fosse against the Corinthians at Christmas 1899; but we remain unsure of any familial connection to former Forest goalkeeper Fred Beardsley, credited with founding the Arsenal club in 1886.

Apps: *FL 69; FAC 7.*

BEBY, John Victor

b. Gillingham, 23rd August 1907
d. Rochester, Kent, 8th April 1976

Career: Cuxton; am Nov 1924 Charlton Athletic; Army football; am Dec 1929/pro Feb 1930 Gillingham; Apr 1930 CITY; June 1932 Ashford Town; Oct 1932 Bristol Rovers; July 1933 Crystal Palace; Mar 1934 Darlington; Mar 1936 Exeter City; cs 1936 Ashington; Oct 1936 Vickers Aviation FC; 1945 Shorts Sports.

City debut v Birmingham (A) 3.5.30

> Reputed on his City debut to be playing in a First Division game before he'd ever actually seen one, goalkeeper Jack had spent a fair spell in the Grenadier Guards, where he had been noted as much for his rugby prowess as for his football abilities. He'd nonetheless appeared in twenty games of Gillingham's re-election zone struggle before being picked up by Willie Orr. His two years with City eventually saw him lose out in a straight tussle with Jim McLaren for the first-team green jumper. During that time he'd also fallen out violently with winger Billy Jackson, when the two argued over dressing-room pegs before a reserve game at Brentford in November 1931; and had put in a transfer request on the grounds that the Leicester climate did not agree with him or his wife! Jack's subsequent exploits were almost as up-and-down. He failed to appear in a League game for Palace, but in his only senior game for them, a Division Three (South) Cup tie against Exeter, he was on the wrong end of a ludicrous 6-11 scoreline. Yet by the end of the same season he was on the winning side in the Final of the Third Division (North) Cup for Darlington! Years after his nominal retirement, Jack returned to assist the Gills in a trio of 1944 wartime fixtures; then embarked on a coaching career which took in spells with AEK Athens and Blida of Algeria, as well as in Germany and India. Later he was mine host at the Cricketers pub in Gillingham.

Apps: *FL 29; FAC 1.*

BEDFORD, George

b. Chesterfield, 12th April 1916
d. Leicester, January 1984

Career: Williamthorpe Colliery; trials-Bradford City & Derby County; Temple Normanton Old Boys; Sept 1934-trials-Chesterfield; trials Dec 1934/pro Jan 1935 CITY; Mar 1941 Northampton Town (-1943); Mar 1947 Stamford Town; July 1947 Hinckley Athletic.

City debut v Barnsley (A) 14.12.35

> Though his limited League record might imply otherwise, by showing two stopgap outings up front as incoming boss Frank Womack negotiated the arrival of Jack Bowers, George was primarily an out-and-out stopper centre-half who proved a stalwart reserve in the late 30s: a fact indexed by his club-record tally of five successive winners' medals from the County Cup, and a runners-up memento from the 1940 Final to boot! There was something of the luckless about George and the first-team, however: even on his debut, he conceded the penalty which provided the first goal of a hat-trick for former City hero Ernie Hine. Turning out during the early war years for each of City, Northampton, Mansfield and Forest, George was the subject of one of the few near-conventional transfers of this time, when City formally exchanged him for Northampton's Stan Frost, but he had to retire on medical advice in October 1943. A postwar non-league comeback did prove possible, however, and George then became coach to Rugby Town in July 1948. He was a nephew of Harry Bedford, the England international spearhead of the early 20s.

Apps: *FL 4; WW2 14.*

BEEBY, Oliver

b. Whetstone, Leics, 2nd October 1934

Career: Cosby United; Enderby Town; Aug 1952 Whitwick Colliery; Mar 1953-trials-Wolverhampton Wanderers; May 1953 CITY; June 1959 Notts County; cs 1961 Oxford United; cs 1962 Burton Albion.

City debut/only game v Doncaster Rovers (A) 5.9.55

Oliver Beeby

> No sooner had he made his City breakthrough (albeit in the dispiriting circumstances of a 2-6 defeat), than right-back Oliver was whisked away for two years of National Service. The Filbert Street career of the former Youth international never recovered from this interruption; and he had little more fortune elsewhere. An unlucky 13 appearances in the Magpies' Division Four promotion campaign of 1960 represented his Meadow Lane lot, while outings in five straight wins of Oxford's 1962 Southern League championship effort were insufficient to earn him a contract on their subsequent election to the League.

Apps: *FL 1.*

BELL, John

b. Dundee, 1877

Career: Dundee Wanderers; Renton; Bacup; cs 1897 Grimsby Town; June 1899 Chesterfield Town; cs 1901 Millwall; May 1903 FOSSE.

Fosse debut v Barnsley (A) 5.9.03

> Joining Fosse shortly after helping prompt Millwall's surprise run to the FA Cup semi-finals, centre-half Jock found his longstanding reputation for constructive playmaking of little account in a Leicester side plummeting towards its first re-election application. Formerly a member of Chesterfield's first-ever League line-up, he was also then a part-time reservist with the Fife & Kincardine Militia.

Apps: *FL 21; FAC 1.*

BELL, William John

b. Backworth, nr Newcastle on Tyne, 1906

Career: Blyth Spartans; Chopwell Institute; Dec 1923 Aston Villa; Aug 1924 Lincoln City; May 1925 Mansfield Town; Feb 1926 CITY; July 1930 Torquay United.

City debut v West Bromwich Albion (A) 27.2.26

> Signed in a joint deal with Mansfield full-back Bert Garner, and elevated straight from the Midland League to the First Division, outside-left Billy was soon vying earnestly with Harold Wadsworth for the senior flank role, and for some time held it on merit until the arrival of Len Barry. He improved on his aggregate City goal tally over the course of a single season under Frank Womack at Torquay, but preferred thereafter to concentrate on the wine and grocery business he had opened near the Plainmoor ground. Billy's father, Jock, was a Rangers goalkeeper back in 1895.

Apps: *FL 41.*
Goals: *FL 5.*

BELL, William John

b. Johnstone, Renfrewshire, 3rd September 1937

Career: Neilston; 1957 Queen's Park; July 1960 Leeds United; Sept 1967 CITY; June 1969 Brighton & Hove Albion (p/coach).

City debut v Everton (H) 30.9.67

> Deemed by Matt Gillies to be a ready-made replacement for Richie Norman, Willie presented a pretty forbidding aspect to the wingers he came up against, but didn't show himself as the most mobile of defenders after his £45,000 purchase. Already twice capped for Scotland as an amateur half-back, he'd added two full international selections to his list of club honours as a left-back with Don Revie's Leeds: a 1964 Second Division championship medal, plus runners-up rewards from the 1965 FA Cup and the 1967 Fairs Cup. Willie assisted City to the Sixth Round of the Cup in his first Filbert Street season, but the relegation struggle that ensued saw him first sidelined from the action, and then from the temporary first-team coaching role he held between the departures of Gillies and Bert Johnson, and new boss Frank O'Farrell's hiring of Malcolm Musgrove. In 1970, Birmingham were fined for giving Willie a coaching contract while Brighton still held his playing registration, but he went on eventually to manage the Blues (1975-77). Lincoln City next employed his managerial talents, but in October 1978 he resigned to join an evangelical religious movement (the Campus Crusade for Christ) in the USA. In 1996 Willie was noted as splitting his energies on a six-monthly basis between coaching football at a Christian university in Virginia, and working with young offenders in the British prison system.

Apps: *FL 49; FAC 6; LC 2.*

BELTON, Thomas

b. Loughborough (?), 1879
d. 1944

Career: Woodhouse United; Loughborough Emmanuel; cs 1901 Whitwick White Cross; June 1902 FOSSE; cs 1904 Coventry City; cs 1905 Loughborough Corinthians; June 1906 Hinckley United; Nov 1907 Mansfield Wesley; 1909 not known; Dec 1911 Loughborough Corinthians.

Fosse debut v Small Heath (H) 6.9.02

> Tom was the eldest of a trio of footballing brothers: George 'Tuzza' Belton was a Fosse trialist in January 1904, who otherwise played at inside-forward for Newark, Loughborough Emmanuel and Loughborough Corinthians; while Jack left the Corinthians to star for many years (1914-28) with Nottingham Forest. First noted himself after scoring the winning goal for Whitwick against Hinckley Town in the 1902 County Cup Final, Tom became a spirited trier at inside-forward in a Fosse side generally lacking that quality as it plumbed the Second Division depths; and proved very much in demand on the Midland non-league circuit.

Apps: *FL 49; FAC 5.*
Goals: *FL 12; FAC 5.*

BENFIELD, Thomas Charles

b. Leicester, 1889
d. France, 19th September 1918

Career: 1905 Leicester Old Boys; Army football; Feb & Oct 1907-trials-FOSSE; Oct 1907 & Jan 1910 Leicester Nomads; pro July 1910 FOSSE; June 1914 Derby County.

Fosse debut v Hull City (H) 12.11.10

> A Leicestershire Regiment soldier who had Filbert Street trials while stationed at Glen Parva, and won Folkestone & Dover Senior League and Cup medals while based at Shorncliffe, Tommy was marked early for a post-demob professional career, especially after he became in 1909 the first Leicestershire man to be selected for

the prestigious annual Army v Navy encounter. With Fosse, he appeared in four of the five forward positions across four seasons, and entered the game's annals as the first player to score a goal at Highbury, when Fosse faced Arsenal there in the inaugural match of September 1913. Tommy's developing marksmanship attracted the newly-relegated Rams (and poverty-stricken Fosse were rarely able to say no to a fee at this time), and in 1914/15 he returned to Filbert Street in a white shirt, scoring twice in a 6-0 away win. His fifteen goals as an ever-present inside-right the following term helped secure his new team the Second Division championship. Tommy, back in khaki, guested briefly for Fosse, Nottingham Forest and Grimsby; but Sergeant Benfield met a cruel end when shot by a German sniper, dying after a battlefield operation. [Incidentally, we offer sincere apologies to all, particularly relatives, for appending an erroneous date of death in earlier drafts of this work].

***Apps:** FL 106; FAC 5; WW1 36.*
***Goals:** FL 23; WW1 9.*

BENJAMIN, Trevor Junior

b. Kettering, 8th February 1979

Career: YT/pro Feb 1997 Cambridge United; July 2000 CITY.

City debut v Sunderland (A) 1.10.2000 (sub)

> Unimaginatively dubbed 'Bruno' at Cambridge, this young juggernaut of a striker was snapped up by Peter Taylor for his clear promise of developing along Heskey-like lines. Avowedly far from the finished footballing article, Trevor did indeed exhibit odd flashes of such potential while being used sparingly in his first Filbert Street season, and it is not difficult to envisage him making a stronger challenge for a regular City selection if he can introduce a touch more swagger to his game. His assertiveness off the pitch was hinted at by the much-publicised bust-up with Stan Collymore at half-time of a reserve game, and his cameo roles in Premiership action confirmed his unwillingness to shirk the physical tussle, but he probably needs to become a little more confidently pro-active in making his powerful physique pay dividends on the park. In mid-season, Trevor suffered the frustration of sitting on the England Under-21 bench in Italy, awaiting a promised second-half call, when fog caused an early abandonment of the game; but he finally won his representative spurs as a second-half sub in the Under-21 clash with Mexico at Filbert Street in May. He'd first tasted League action from the Abbey Stadium bench as a 16-year-old, and gradually moved into a central striker's role there from the left wing, maturing to help fire Cambridge up from Division Three to Two in 1999, and claiming 20 League and 3 Cup goals from the following campaign.

***Apps** (to end 200/1): PL 7+14; FAC 1+2; LC 0+1.*
***Goals:** PL 1.*

BENNETT, A.

Career: Notts Mapperley; cs 1891 FOSSE.

Fosse debut v Derby Junction (H) ML 12.9.1891

> Signed with his club-mate, goal-keeper George Old, to help Fosse make the transition from local friendly fare to their first season of Midland League competition, this centre-forward spent longer on the injury list than in action in his eight months as a professional.

***Apps:** FAC 1; ML 5.*
***Goals:** ML 2.*

BENNETT, John William

b. Liverpool, 29th November 1879

Career: Wavertree; trials-Liverpool; 1898 Wellingborough; cs 1900 Lincoln City; cs 1901 Northampton Town; May 1903 Luton Town; May 1904 FOSSE; Apr 1905 Blackburn Rovers.

Fosse debut v Blackpool (A) 3.9.04

> A right-back who had faced Fosse in the FA Cup for Wellingborough, and had built a decent Southern League reputation despite disciplinary problems having cut short his Second Division spell at Lincoln, Jack joined Fosse's concerted attempt to bounce back from the 1904 re-election reprieve, and impressed so much that he was snatched away by Blackburn before the campaign's end. He deputised once there for international Bob Crompton, but obviously didn't fancy Ewood. Jack refused to return there for pre-season training in August 1905, and let it be known through friends and via the press that he wouldn't be averse to signing again for Fosse, but the club simply couldn't afford to accede to his wishes.

***Apps:** FL 27; FAC 7.*
***Goals:** FL 1.*

BENSKIN, F. Samuel

b. Leicester

Career: Leicester Old Boys; Belgrave Thursday United; Apr 1902 FOSSE; cs 1904 Leicester British United; 1905 South Wigston Albion; 1905 Leicester Old Boys; cs 1906 Leicester British United.

Fosse debut/only game v Burnley (A) 24.1.03 (scored once)

> The more attack-minded half of the amateur Benskin brothers partnership, Sam was 'a capital sprinter' at inside- or outside-left who could justifiably have expected more than the one chance with Fosse at League level. Not only was this game goal-crowned, but his initial senior friendly, at Ripley in April 1902 saw him notch a hat-trick. Both brothers were in the Wigston side which beat Fosse Reserves in the 1905 County Cup Final, while Sam toured Holland the following Christmas with the Amateurs of Leicestershire, under RA Thompson's captaincy.

***Apps:** FL 1.*
***Goals:** FL 1.*

BENSKIN, William Ewart

b. Leicester, 8th April 1880
d. Leicester, 1st June 1956

Career: 1898 Hugglescote Robin Hoods; Wigston Excelsior; Thursday Wanderers; Leicester Old Boys; Apr 1901 FOSSE; Sept 1904 Leicester British United; 1904 South Wigston Albion; July 1906 Northampton Town; Leicester Pilgrims; Jan 1911 Leicester Imperial; Sept 1911 St Johnstone.

Fosse debut v Burslem Port Vale (H) 25.1.02

> Earlier on the Fosse scene than brother Sam, Ewart was a centre- or left-half who got the occasional call-up from the reserves in each of three seasons of fairly undignified Second Division struggle, culminating in the 1904 re-election appeal. 'Benny', saddled at birth with Prime Minister Gladstone's forenames, wrote his name more boldly across the cricketing annals of Leicestershire CCC, having two spells with the club as a fast bowler between 1906 and 1924, and performing the summer game hat-trick on his first-class debut, against Essex at Southend. Still effective postwar, he took four Derbyshire wickets in five balls in August 1921. In the interim, he played as cricket pro with the Perthshire, West of Scotland and Ramsbottom clubs, and represented Scotland against the Australians and South Africa. Indeed, it was his Perthshire stint which led to his belated return to senior football, as trials won him a defensive role in St Johnstone's first-ever season in the Scottish League. Apparently renowned as a practical joker, 'Benny' later worked as an upholsterer at the Royal Infirmary.

***Apps:** FL 11.*

BERRINGTON, W. Albert

b. Ruabon, Denbighshire, ca 1888

Career: Army football; Mar 1913 Aberdare; June 1913 FOSSE.

Fosse debut v Leeds City (H) 7.2.14

> Reputed to have represented Southern Counties, Middlesex, Berks & Bucks and the Household Brigade while serving in the Grenadier Guards, tall left-back Albert was spotted by Fosse during his brief spell of lower-echelon Southern League football in his homeland. (Where, confusingly, the local press gave his name as Alf; where he was briefly tried out at centre-forward; and where he was eloquently described as 'unceremonious'). He played in all five matches of Fosse's 1913 Swedish tour, but thereafter stood in only twice for Sam Currie.

***Apps:** FL 2.*

BERRY, Arthur

b. Leicester (?)
d. Leicester, October 1940

Career: Leicester Imperial; Dec 1900 FOSSE (- 1904).

Fosse debut v New Brighton Tower (H) 16.3.01

> A steady stand-in right-half (and second XI skipper) for Fosse across four generally uninspiring Second Division campaigns, Arthur was one of several such Fossils whose lives and careers beyond the Filbert Street confines unfortunately remain a mystery – even the local press being uninformative when briefly noting his passing.

***Apps:** FL 24.*

BETTS, Herbert

b. Leicester

Career: Belgrave St Michael's; Leicester Imperial; Mar 1901-trials-FOSSE; Mar 1902 FOSSE; cs 1903 Leicester Imperial.

Fosse debut v Preston North End (H) 31.3.02

> Fosse's poverty-stricken alternative to the transfer market at this period was to lean heavily on the foremost of the local clubs, to the extent that a typical Imps line-up of the time would contain up to nine players with past, present or future Fosse connections – some twenty-odd would eventually find their way into senior Fosse line-ups. The case of Herbert was characteristic: featuring at left-half in a home win and home draw before being released back to play alongside his brother Harry, whose own Fosse trials had come at reserve level. (One of the Imps pair was initialled HT, the other HL; but we haven't been able as yet to sort out which was which). In 1904 it was baldly stated in the local press that Herbert 'has left the town'.

***Apps:** FL 2.*

BICKNELL, Stephen John

b. Stockton, nr Rugby, Warks, 28th November 1958

Career: VS Rugby; app July 1975/ pro Nov 1976 CITY; Aug 1978 Torquay United; cs 1979 VS Rugby; Southam United.

City debut v Newcastle United (A) 9.4.77

> Introduced towards the close of Jimmy Bloomfield's frustrating final campaign, as high hopes of European qualification petered out to a background of crowd unrest, Steve was something of an appeasing sop to supporters who'd bemoaned the lack of a conventional left-flank attacker since the departure of Len Glover. The teenager simply wasn't up to the mark, and got no chance subsequently under Frank McLintock to restore his dented confidence. At Plainmoor he was restricted to three substitute appearances, and quickly returned to minor-grade football.

***Apps:** FL 6+1.*

BINNEY, John

Career: Worksop Town; June 1902 FOSSE; cs 1903 Worksop Town; cs 1904 Denaby United; June 1905 Worksop Town.

Fosse debut v Small Heath (H) 6.9.02

> Having impressed in pre-season practice, John was chosen at inside-left for Fosse's first two fixtures of 1902/03, but jettisoned after two heavy defeats to re-establish himself at Midland League level.

***Apps:** FL 2.*

BIRCHENALL, Alan John

b. East Ham, London, 22nd August 1945

Career: Thorneywood Thistle; June 1963 Sheffield United; Nov 1967 Chelsea; June 1970 Crystal Palace; Sept 1971 CITY; Mar 1976-loan-Notts County; Apr 1977-loan-San Jose Earthquakes; Sept 1977 Notts County; Apr 1978 Memphis Rogues; Sept 1978 Blackburn Rovers; Mar 1979 Luton Town; Oct 1979 Hereford United; cs 1980 Trowbridge Town (p/mgr).

City debut v Crystal Palace (H) 2.10.71

> There are probably now more City supporters who've only ever known 'The Birch' as the club's energetically extrovert and good-humoured part-time PR man, via his pre-match and half-time microphone wielding, his programme column and his annual charity run, than those who can match memories with him of his striker-cum-midfielder's impact on Jimmy Bloomfield's side of the 70s. But Alan's occasionally wry re-writing of his legend has real substance behind it, for he was indeed as much a key component of the entertainment package on the Filbert Street pitch in the Weller-Worthington-Glover era as he now is off it. London-born, but Nottingham-raised, Alan entered the First Division as a striking partner to Mick Jones at Bramall Lane, and soon earned the first two of four call-ups to England's Under-23 side; the other pair coming after he'd become an early, expensive Dave Sexton acquisition at Stamford Bridge. Six-figure values were also placed on Alan's moves to Selhurst and Filbert Street (with Bobby Kellard returning to Palace as part of the latter deal), and while repayment wasn't particularly measured in goals (these tended to the seldom-but-spectacular class), it certainly was in 'assists' as Alan matured into a deeper-lying role. Inclining to the nomadic life to see out his playing career, then entering the shoe trade, Alan returned to gee-up Filbert Street in 1983, and subsequently also took over the Griffin pub in Swithland.

Alan Birchenall

***Apps:** FL 156+7; FAC 14; LC 6.*
***Goals:** FL 12; FAC 1; LC 1.*

BISHOP, Matthew

b. Melton Mowbray, Leics, ca 1876
d. Melton Mowbray, 30th September 1947

Career: Melton Town; Aug 1895 FOSSE; cs 1897 Warmley; Feb 1899 FOSSE; cs 1901 Coalville Town; 1903 Melton Town; Oct 1904 South Wigston Albion; cs 1906 Melton Mowbray; Melton WMC.

Fosse debut v Hinckley Town (H) FAC 12.10.1895 (scored once)

> A young outside-left whose progress was initially inhibited by the return of old favourite Billy Dorrell, Matt himself became a twice-signed Fossil, though with even fewer senior selections second time around, when competition came from Alf Watkins, Rab King and Harry Allen. His interim spell with Bristol club Warmley coincided with their elevation to the Southern League's top-flight, with Matt claiming four goals in the decisive Test Matches, and ended when they resigned and wound up partway through 1898/9. Matt was reinstated as an amateur in 1903, and was alongside the Benskin brothers in South Wigston's 1905 County Cup Final victory over Fosse Reserves. After WW1, in which he served with the Lincolnshire Regiment in Russia, he was refereeing in the Melton district, and in the mid-20s was noted as captain of Melton British Legion cricket club. Matt went on to become chairman of the Melton & District Cricket League; was a stalwart of the local WMC's football, cricket, whist and skittles teams; and his various jobs included stints at the local Remount Depot and as a postman. At the time of his death he had been superintendent of Melton's Tuesday Cattle Market for ten years.

***Apps:** FL 13; FAC 6.*
***Goals:** FL 2; FAC 2.*

BISHOP, Sidney Macdonald

b. Stepney, London, 10th February 1900
d. Chelsea, 4th May 1949

Career: Ilford; RAF football; trials-Crystal Palace; May 1920 West Ham United; Nov 1926 CITY; June 1928 Chelsea (- 1933).

City debut v Derby County (A) 6.11.26

> One of the stars of the 1923 'White Horse' Cup Final at Wembley, Sid was a cultured, constructive left-half who skippered West Ham before his purchase by Willie Orr, and fitted effortlessly into City's ascending First Division side. That is, effortlessly in footballing terms, for he was talented and expressive enough to win four England caps and a Football League selection while at Filbert Street. But a catalogue of injuries and illnesses blighted his stay, costing him another two caps (he would have captained his country against Scotland in March 1928 but for eve-of-game sickness), and he found settling outside London a fraught affair. Indeed, it was his request to be allowed to live and train in the capital that led to his record £3,800 sale to Second Division Chelsea. More injuries hit him there (another chance to skipper England against Ireland in 1928/9 also

slipping away; and Sid being sidelined at one point after falling down the steps of a London bus), but he helped the Stamford Bridge side to promotion in 1930. Sid was a Limehouse publican in the late 30s. An Australia-based relative and City supporter asserts that Sid was in fact a nephew of Fosse's Matt Bishop.

Apps: *FL 49; FAC 4.*
Goals: *FL 7.*

BLACK, Adam Hudson

b. Denny, Stirlingshire, 18th February 1898
d. Leicester, 30th August 1981

Career: Mar 1919 Bathgate; Jan 1920 CITY (- 1935).

City debut v Hull City (H) 24.1.20

> No-one in the club's history has appeared in more Football League games for City than full-back Adam, and only Graham Cross outstrips him in the aggregate reckoning of senior outings. Ever-present in four of his sixteen Filbert Street seasons, and missing but a single game in each of three more, Adam could and did play on either flank, before finally settling for the right-back berth – in which position his failure to win a Scottish cap was inexplicable. He represented the Anglo Scots against the Home Scots in March 1923, on the penultimate occasion the international trial was held in this popular format, but was overlooked by the selectors, who were possibly deceived by his relatively slight build and stature. His bravery and resilience had already been proved, however, with the award of the Distinguished Conduct Medal during his wartime service as a corporal in the Argyll & Sutherland Highlanders, and his mobility and technical mastery of the defensive game already noted in his brief Central League spell with Bathgate (with whom he'd just won a Scottish Qualifying Cup winners' medal when Peter Hodge signed him up). Adam would earn a Second Division championship medal in 1925, and would figure classily and consistently in the top echelon for the next decade, until relegation and retirement to concentrate on his Wilberforce Road newsagent's shop. He earned three cash benefits for loyalty from the club; though on the occasion of his first benefit game, against Southampton in April 1925, he blotted his copybook by missing a penalty. Three previous successful spot-kicks had contributed to that year's title progress; while Adam's only other City goal came from a fluke 60-yard free-kick whose flight flummoxed everyone against Sunderland in 1932/3. He hit different headlines in June 1957 when, as a 59-year-old, he took a 17-year-old bride; and finally relinquished his business in 1973. Adam's younger brother Johnny was more of a footballing wanderer: serving Denny Hibs, Sunderland, Nelson, Accrington Stanley, Chesterfield, Luton and Bristol Rovers.

Apps: *FL 528; FAC 29.*
Goals: *FL 4.*

BLACKETT, Joseph

b. Newcastle on Tyne, 1875

Career: Newcastle United; Gateshead; Willington Athletic; June 1896 Loughborough; May 1897 Wolverhampton Wanderers; July 1900 Derby County; Apr 1901 Sunderland; Oct 1901 Middlesbrough; May 1905 Luton Town; July 1906 FOSSE; June 1909 Rochdale (p/mgr); cs 1912 Barrow.

Fosse debut v Burslem Port Vale (A) 1.9.06

> In a post-retirement memoir, Teddy King recalled an instance of the resolve that full-back Joe exhibited across his Fosse career. The rugged defender had been virtually ruled out by injury from the vital 1908 promotion decider at Stoke, and Teddy called up as his deputy; only to find Joe in full kit in the dressing room an hour before kick-off to signify to all his determined desire to play. Though he'd started his League career (breaking through with the Luffs) as an outside-left, and had even played the odd game at centre-forward for Derby, it was in either full-back berth that he forged his real reputation. Having represented the English XI in the Players Union international of March 1900, Joe helped Boro to their first-ever promotion in 1902, and had been chosen as travelling reserve for the Football League game in Belfast in October 1904 before assisting Luton through their first season at Kenilworth Road. He then cost Fosse a £110 cheque to the former club, who held his League registration, rather than to the Southern League Hatters. Stiffening the Leicester back line, Joe experienced both the joy of promotion and the disappointment of first-time demotion before taking the player-manager reins at Spotland. Promoted to the top flight of the Lancashire Combination in 1910 (when also Lancashire Junior Cup winners), and champions in 1911 and 1912 (when also sharing in the Manchester Senior Cup), Rochdale remained unbeaten at home across all three of Joe's campaigns there. A trainer at Reading from 1913, Joe then enlisted for WW1 service in May 1915, as a 40-year-old.

Apps: *FL 78; FAC 3.*

BLAKE, Mark Antony

b. Nottingham, 16th December 1970

Career: YT 1987/pro May 1989 Aston Villa; Jan 1991-loan-Wolverhampton Wanderers; Aug 1993 Portsmouth; Mar 1994 CITY; Aug 1996 Walsall (- 1998); July 1999-trials-Notts County; Aug 1999 Mansfield Town; July 2001 Kidderminster Harriers.

City debut v Notts County (A) 26.3.94

> There was much wry amusement raised amongst City fans when, at a time of rampant transfer market inflation, Brian Little managed to raise the club's record outlay by a matter of £10,000, and make midfielder Mark, for a few months at least, their most expensive purchase ever at £360,000. Mark himself didn't particularly suffer as a consequence, but set about integrating himself into the hectic progress towards the Play-Offs, and featuring as a near-conventional right-back in the glory line-up silencing the Rams at Wembley. In the first, fated Premiership season, Mark re-emerged as a shaven headed snapper, a rare ball-winner in an often overrun midfield area; though he was affected and finally sidelined by asthma towards the end of the term. Thereafter, he could win regular favour with neither Mark McGhee nor Martin O'Neill. Previously capped eight times at Under-21 level without ever fully establishing himself at Villa, Mark had found himself unsettled at Fratton Park after joining Pompey in a part-exchange deal involving Guy Whittingham; and his preference for Midlands-based football continued when he left Filbert Street for Bescot on a free. The 1998/9 season saw Mark inactive at any level, but he returned to the League sphere with the Stags for two basement seasons as a regular.

Apps: *FL/PL 42+7; LC 4; PO 3.*
Goals: *FL/PL 4.*

BLESSINGTON, James

b. Linlithgow, West Lothian, 28th February 1874
d. Newton Abbott, Devon, 18th April 1939

Career: Harp Athletic; Aug 1890 Hibernian; Feb 1891 Leith Hibernians; 1891 Leith Athletic; Aug 1892-loan-St.Bernards; Aug 1892 Celtic; Feb 1898 Preston North End; June 1899 Derby County; Oct 1899 Bristol City; Aug 1900 Luton Town; May 1903 FOSSE (- 1909).

Fosse debut v Barnsley (A) 5.9.03

> Seasoned and skilful, cerebral but tough, inside-forward Jimmy brought to Leicester a 'professorial' influence the Fosse hadn't seen the like of since the days of Jimmy Brown. The son of a quarryman and himself initially apprenticed as a blacksmith, Jimmy was early in his career being described, by *The Scottish Referee*, as 'a neat, dashing, go-ahead forward. His style is stronger than the body that carries it.' Four times capped by Scotland, and five times a member of the Scottish League representative side, he was twice a Scottish Cup Finalist, and contributed to four Celtic champion-ship campaigns before first crossing the border for Deepdale. Having then lit up the forward lines of his two Southern League clubs, Jimmy became an ever-present inside-right (and just about the only bright light) in his first term at Leicester, and then an inspirational prompter as Fosse fought back from their re-election reprieve. Still active, Jimmy additionally assumed the onus of being named the club's first-ever Team Manager in January 1907 – earning, if not actually being publicly granted, much credit for the club's 1908 promotion, and continuing his dual function (especially tutoring and mentoring the reserves) until the arrival of Andy Aitken late in the ensuing First Division campaign. Profiting from a Boxing Day 1908 reserve game against Leeds City as his benefit seemed wholly inadequate reward for his efforts; which even extended to part-time coaching of the Leicester Borough Police XI. From August 1909 to 1911 Jimmy coached Irish club Cliftonville, and returned to Ireland in 1913 as coach to Belfast Celtic. He also acted as an athletics handicapper in Ireland, and in the interim took his first steps in the licensed trade in Leicester. About to take up a further coaching appointment in Germany on the outbreak of war, Jimmy instead joined the Merchant Navy. Postwar, he took an electrician's job in Luton until a recall to football in 1920 as manager of Southern League Abertillery, and then ran a succession of pubs and hotels in the Channel Islands, Exeter, Leicester (the Stag & Pheasant, Humberstone Gate, and the Royal Arms, Welford Road), and Newton Abbot. There he was licensee of the Bradley Arms when he died in hospital; coincidentally on the same day as former Fosse team-mate Jonty Starbuck.

Apps: *FL 100; FAC 12.*
Goals: *FL 18; FAC 3.*

BLOCKLEY, Jeffrey Paul

b. Leicester, 12th September 1949

Career: Midland Athletic; app/pro June 1967 Coventry City; Oct 1972 Arsenal; Jan 1975 CITY; Feb 1978-loan-Derby County; June 1978 Notts County; July 1980 Enderby Town (p/coach); 1981 Gloucester City.

City debut v Chelsea (H) 1.2.75

> Initially overlooked by his home-town club, but something of a saviour for them ten years later, centre-half Jeff had been a team-mate of Peter Shilton (and future Showaddywaddy drummer Romeo Challenger) in the 1965 Schools Trophy-winning Leicester Boys side, yet journeyed to Highfield Road as a junior. Progress through the Sky Blue ranks saw him to the first of ten Under-23 honours, but the cool,

Jeff Blockley

strong and aerially dominant defender received only one full cap, shortly after a £200,000 move to Highbury. There Jeff struggled to regularly depose Frank McLintock, and had a hard time with the fans after finding himself carrying the can for the 1973 Cup semi-final defeat by Sunderland. But what appeared a panicky £100,000 swoop by Jimmy Bloomfield revived fortunes for both player and club, as City escaped an apparently pre-ordained relegation placing largely on the strength of Jeff's defensive solidity and fellow-newcomer Chris Garland's front-line flair. Injuries unfortunately dogged Jeff's City days thereafter, but he remained first choice until the promise of Steve Sims asserted itself, and he fell victim to the chopping and changing of the brief McLintock managerial regime. Jeff returned to the county on retirement, briefly bossing each of Leicester United, Shepshed Charterhouse and Hinckley Athletic in the 80s, and has his own Nuneaton-based engineering supplies business.

Apps: *FL 75+1; FAC 7; LC 2+1.*
Goals: *FL 2.*

BOWERS, John William Anslow

b. Santon, nr. Scunthorpe, 22nd February 1908
d. Lichfield, Staffs, 4th July 1970

Career: Appleby Works; Dec 1927 Scunthorpe United; May 1928 Derby County; Nov 1936 CITY (- 1941).

City debut v Swansea Town (A) 21.11.36 (scored once)

> Starting his remarkable goalscoring career at Midland League Scunthorpe alongside future City team-mate Digger Maw, Jack soon advertised his prowess as a battling, brave marksman when stepping up to score on his Derby debut and add a hat-trick in the next game. In fact by 1934 Jack had been the First Division's top scorer in three of the four previous seasons. He'd notched three goals in two Football League representative matches, and two in his three full internationals, before a serious knee injury brought a hiccup to his record-breaking exploits. Nonetheless, a fit-again Jack already had 12 League goals in the bag for the Rams in 1936/7 when Frank Womack expended £7,500 for his services: initially to be seen as a hedge against relegation from the Second Division. City's exit that term would, however, be upward, with Jack adding no less than 33 goals to his seasonal tally to energise what became City's most unlikely championship campaign of all time. To speak of justified hero-worship from the City fans in this context is almost to understate Jack's transformational impact, and after netting in his first six games for the club (to the tune of twelve goals) he was certainly forgiven his one slip-up: a missed penalty against Blackburn. His strike-rate understandably decreased a little back in the top flight, and he had to settle for being the reserves' top scorer in 1938/9 (adding 19 counters to his first-team double-figures), but when the outbreak of war put an end to Jack's 'official' statistics, he could look back on a career total of 219 goals in only 282 League games, plus 20 from only 22 FA Cup starts. After quitting City and turning out in the odd wartime game for Derby and Forest, Jack did a stint of coaching with Notts County, and in 1945 returned to the Baseball Ground as assistant trainer and physio-therapist. His son John also played, in the 60s, at League level for Derby and Notts County.

Apps: *FL 79; FAC 5; WW2 31.*
Goals: *FL 52; FAC 4; WW2 15.*

BOWN, Herbert Arthur

b. East Ham, London, 3rd May 1893
d. Leicester, 11th February 1959

Career: Squirrel Heath; Roneo Works FC; 1910 Romford Town; trials-West Ham United; Apr 1913 FOSSE; May 1922 Halifax Town; Jan 1925 Hull City.

Fosse debut v Notts County (H) 8.11.13

> The proud keeper when City went a club-record seven successive League games without conceding a goal in 1919/20, Herbert was an unflappable last-line before, during and after WW1. His calm demeanour nonetheless disguised a taste for drama, for his goalscoring ambitions saw him take a couple of Fosse penalties in wartime football, and he similarly got on the scoresheet during two ever-present seasons at The Shay in the Third Division (North), before being listed at a forbidding fee. With no immediate takers, even at a League-reduced price-tag of £350, Herbert retired to his Leicester fish and poultry business, only to be called on to help out Hull for four games in an injury crisis. He had originally joined Fosse after representing Essex as an amateur, and only signed pro after being an ever-present on their first-ever overseas tour, to Sweden in the summer of 1913.

Apps: *FL 143; FAC 11; WW1 112.*
Goals: *WW1 1.*

BRACEY, Frederick Cecil

b. Derby, 20th July 1887
d. Derby, 28th March 1960

Career: Small Heath; Holbrook Swifts; Nov 1905 FOSSE; July 1908 Bradford Park Avenue; Sept 1909 Rochdale (- 1912).

Fosse debut v Hull City (H) 7.12.05

> Perhaps better known as a Derbyshire cricketer, appearing as a bowler from 1906-14, Fred was a two-footed winger who got precious few chances on either wing during his three Filbert Street seasons. His reserve form sufficiently impressed former team-mate Joe Blackett, however, for the latter to take Fred to Rochdale to share in their Lancashire Combination triumphs of 1909-12, after he'd had an interim spell with Park Avenue during their first-ever Division Two campaign. Fred, whose younger brother William was an amateur on the books of each of Bradford and Rochdale, later settled as a Derby greengrocer.

Apps: *FL 10.*

BRADLEY, Gordon

b. Scunthorpe, 20th May 1925

Career: am Scunthorpe United; Sept 1942 CITY; Feb 1950 Notts County; Aug 1958 Cambridge City; 1959 Glentoran.

City debut (WW2) v Derby County (A) 14.11.42; (postwar) v West Bromwich Albion (A) 21.12.46

> City's luckless goalkeeper in the

1949 Cup Final, Gordon edged selection over the younger Leslie Major when Ian McGraw's hand injury removed him from contention, having had an in-and-out couple of seasons since RAF demob in November 1947. Originally joining the wartime City ranks on Digger Maw's recommendation, he also guested for Grimsby, Lincoln, Sheffield United and Notts County while hostilities continued, trading on a reputation for agility and quick reflexes that were a concomitant of his all-round sporting prowess. Gordon was Leicestershire table-tennis champion while at Filbert Street, and played a high standard of professional lawn tennis. During his eight-year stint with the Magpies, Gordon featured in one remarkable game at Leicester in September 1956: being injured during a 6-3 City win, but claiming the final goal from an outfield position. He was appointed coach to the Irish Lawn Tennis Association in the 60s.

Apps: *FL 69; FAC 5; WW2 6.*

BRADSHAW, Thomas Dickinson

b. Hambleton, Lancs, 15th March 1879

Career: Lostock Hall; Apr 1896 Preston North End; Dec 1896 Blackpool; May 1897 Sunderland; Jan 1898 Nottingham Forest; Mar 1899 FOSSE; May 1900 New Brighton Tower; Aug 1901 Swindon Town; Oct 1901 Reading; Aug 1902 Preston North End; cs 1903 Wellingborough; June 1904 Southport Central; Dec 1904 Earlestown; Accrington Stanley; Oct 1905 FOSSE; Feb 1906 Rossendale United; May 1907 Glossop.

Fosse debut v Grimsby Town (H) 3.4.1899

> A nomadic inside- or outside-right who twice signed for Fosse, Tom also acted as cricket professional to Preston CC and briefly as summer-game coach at Harrow School. He'd first tasted League football with Blackpool during their first season at that level (when he scored against Fosse), and made his Division One bow at Roker Park, but he missed selection when Forest won the FA Cup in 1898. His initial move to Leicester was in a joint deal with Billy Wragg, but his temperament hardly aided him in settling. In July 1899 he pleaded guilty to breach of the peace charges after fighting with Preston goalkeeper Jim Trainer in a dispute over a game of bowls (!), and in January 1900 was under Fosse suspension for 'inattention to the training rules', which usually stood as a euphemism for drink-related indiscipline. Eight moves later, Tom returned, having faced Fosse in the interim in the 1903/4 FA Cup. Old habits were still resurfacing, though, as by 1908 he was said to be under suspension by Glossop when arraigned for wife-beating. In 1923, when City visited Bradford City, Tom appeared in their dressing room, described himself haplessly as 'down and out', and departed with the proceeds of a quick whip-round. Then, in December 1924, Tom dropped in once again on the City party at Valley Parade: this time cheerfully relating how he'd used their charity to set himself up successfully as a baker!

Apps: *FL 43; FAC 5.*
Goals: *FL 9; FAC 1.*

BRASH, Archibald

b. Edinburgh

Career: St Mirren; cs 1894 Sheffield Wednesday; cs 1898 Crewe Alexandra; cs 1899 Sheffield Wednesday; June 1900 FOSSE; cs 1901 Aberdeen.

Fosse debut v Stockport County (H) 1.9.1900

> The highlight of Scottish right-winger Archie's stay with Fosse came with a four-goal display against Burton Swifts in December 1900 – only days after Billy Langham had been signed to replace him. His form had certainly not matched his billing, for his Wednesday record had included laying on the first goal in their 1896 FA Cup Final victory, and a decent contribution to their 1900 Second Division championship campaign. The Pittodrie-based club Archie moved on to were one of the three senior Aberdonian non-league sides who would amalgamate in 1903 to form the still-existing Dons.

Apps: *FL 14.*
Goals: *FL 5.*

BREBNER, Ronald Gilchrist

b. Darlington, 23rd September 1881
d. Chiswick, London, 11th November 1914

Career: 1903 Edinburgh University; Elgin City; May 1905 Sunderland; Jan 1906 Rangers; Sept 1906 Darlington; Oct 1906 Chelsea; London Caledonians; 1907 Darlington; 1907 Elgin City; Dec 1907 Pilgrims; Aug 1908 Stockton; Northern Nomads; Feb 1910 Queens Park; Sept 1910 Darlington; Nov 1910 & Apr 1911 English Wanderers; Aug 1911 Huddersfield Town; Aug 1912 Chelsea; May 1913 FOSSE.

Fosse debut v Nottingham Forest (A) 3.9.13

> A lifelong amateur (hence the clutter of clubs and occasional combinations above), goalkeeper Ron won a total of 23 England amateur caps, and additionally emulated the gold-medal achievement of Fosse's Horace Bailey in appearing as last-line in the victorious United Kingdom side at the 1912 Stockholm Olympics. A qualified dentist, he also earned a full England international trial in November 1912, and represented the Amateurs v Professionals in the 1913 Charity Shield match. Having played in all but two of Fosse's first twenty fixtures in 1913/14 (and having picked up his last two caps on the dates of his absences), he was stretchered off the field at Lincoln after a jarring collision with Imps forward George Barrell. Initially, it was believed to be a simple rib injury, but internal complications ensued, and Ron was soon confined to nursing homes in Newcastle and then Chiswick, where his father was Medical Officer of Health; never recovering fully before his death ten months later. Back in October 1908, Ron had saved a trio of York City penalties in a 7-0 Northern League away win for Stockton; he also scored one for Darlington against Jarrow in April 1911. Ron featured in tours to Carlisle and Scotland for the Pilgrims, and to France, Russia and Denmark with English Wanderers.

Apps: *FL 18.*

BRIEN, Anthony James

b. Dublin, 10th February 1969

Career: app/pro Feb 1987 CITY; Dec 1988 Chesterfield; Oct 1993 Rotherham United; June 1995-loan-Sheffield Wednesday; Aug 1995 West Bromwich Albion; Feb 1996-loan-Mansfield Town; Mar 1996-loan-Chester City; July 1996 Hull City; Jan 1998 Stalybridge Celtic; August 1999 Bromsgrove Rovers; 1999 Stourbridge; 1999 Alfreton Town.

City debut v Ipswich Town (H) 30.9.87 (sub).

> A cool central defender in City's Youth Cup semi-final side of 1987, and capped at Youth level by the Republic, Tony kept his composure at senior level when given early outings by Bryan Hamilton in both the right-back and centre-back berths. A contract extension came from new

Tony Brien

boss David Pleat, but Tony was effectively leapfrogged in the Filbert Street shadow squad by Grant Brown. A £90,000 move to Saltergate indexed the 19-year-old's promise, however, and 239 League and Cup games for the Spireites gave them good value, despite relegation in Tony's first term. Rotherham and Hull also got some good senior football out of Tony, though his brief loan to the Owls was for a single Intertoto Cup game. In January 1998 he was sadly forced to retire from the full-time game with an arthritic hip, and managed only three Conference starts thereafter, while training for a commercial pilot's licence. He then attempted a further part-time comeback 18 months later in Midlands football.

Apps: *FL 12+4; FAC 1; LC 1; FMC 3.*
Goals: *FL 1.*

BRIGHT, Mark Abraham

b. Stoke-on-Trent, 6th June 1962

Career: Leek Town; Oct 1981 Port Vale; June 1984 CITY; Nov 1986 Crystal Palace; Sept 1992 Sheffield Wednesday; Dec 1996-loan-Millwall; Jan 1997 FC Sion; Mar 1997 Charlton Athletic (- 1999).

City debut v Newcastle United (H) 25.8.84

> Impressing Gordon Milne with a ten-goal salvo for the Valiants at the end of 1983/4, Mark joined City after the League's transfer tribunal had set an appearance-related fee which would potentially rise to £99,000. Circumstances would dictate that City's outlay, however, would add up to only two-thirds of that amount, for the tall striker found the going rough at Filbert Street. Used extensively as a substitute in his first season, Mark somehow failed to add a first-team strike to his fine Central League record of 28 goals in 27 games, but looked to have broken his hoodoo in style on the opening day of 1985/6, when he both replaced and faced Gary Lineker, and then outshone him with a spectacular brace against Everton. Thereafter, though, overly-critical comparisons with his predecessor, and his targeting with a rare degree of overtly racist hostility at Filbert Street, saw his confidence eroded and his form suffer; so it was a relief when Palace came in for him with a £75,000 offer soon after he had turned down mooted moves to Hull or Walsall. At Selhurst, as a lethal attacking partnership with Ian Wright developed, Mark found himself Second Division top scorer in 1988, part of the Eagles' promotion side of 1989, an FA Cup finalist in 1990, and a Zenith Cup winner a year later. He had already notched his 100th League goal when the Owls invested £875,000 in his unselfish talent, and would finish his initial Hillsborough term with Wembley runners-up medals from both major Cup tourneys. In fact, on the way to the League Cup showcase, Mark scored twice against City in the 1-7 defeat which represents the club's heaviest-ever reverse in that competition. Wednesday received excellent value over four years, though it looked that Mark might be closing his career on an inappropriately discordant note when a financial dispute nullified his Swiss contract before he'd even played there. Yet his return to South London saw him once more as a key element in a promotion campaign, aiding Charlton's Premiership ascent of 1998. Retirement a year later came with Mark wishing to develop his media profile.

Apps: *FL 26+16; FAC 1; LC 3+1.*
Goals: *FL 6.*

BRODIE, Murray

b. Glasgow, 26th September 1950

Career: Cumbernauld United; Nov 1968 CITY; Sept 1970 Aldershot; July 1983 Basingstoke Town.

City debut v Watford (H) 4.10.69 (scored once)

> Given a Second Division break by Frank O'Farrell only eight days after turning nineteen, strongly-built forward Murray then found his entire senior City career compressed into the following eight days. His unexpected, goal-capped debut was followed by another scoring outing in midweek against Middlesbrough, and then an early exit through injury at Preston. Failing to recapture a place upon recovery, he moved on to Aldershot in a joint deal with reserve full-back Jimmy Burt, and established a rather lengthier first-team tenure there. In fact it would be thirteen years before he was deposed, after smashing that club's appearance record - totalling 514 League and Cup outings, and notching 94 goals - and taking a well-earned testimonial.

Apps: *FL 3.*
Goals: *FL 2.*

BROOKS, Joseph Ernest

b. Heanor, Derbyshire, 20th November 1892
d. Heanor, Apr qtr 1975

Career: Langley Heanor; May 1919 Grimsby Town; cs 1920 Shirebrook; June 1921 CITY; cs 1922 Shirebrook; July 1923 Kettering Town.

City debut v Clapton Orient (H) 9.2.22

> Almost 27 when making his three League appearances in a Grimsby side destined to be the first to drop from Division Two to Three, diminutive winger Ernie had essentially lost his best chance of soccer glory to the exigencies of WW1, and there would be no veteran's impact made when Peter Hodge offered him a lifeline back from the Central Alliance to the Second Division. He was on the winning side when making a joint debut with inside-forward Jack King, but failed to impress in three defeats thereafter.

Apps: *FL 4.*

BROWN, Alistair

b. Musselburgh, Midlothian, 12th April 1951

Career: app Oct 1966/pro Apr 1968 CITY; Mar 1972 West Bromwich Albion; May 1981-loan-Portland Timbers; Mar 1983 Crystal Palace; Aug 1983 Walsall; June 1984 Port Vale (-1986).

City debut v Sunderland (H) 5.5.69 (scored twice)

> Introduced for a match-winning teenage dream debut as City's post-Cup Final survival struggle intensified, Ally was a tall, cultured striker whose goals would do much to return City to the top flight two years later. A Scottish Youth cap and an Under-23 trialist, he top-scored in 1970/1, when his goal at Bristol City secured the Division Two championship, and was still at the head of the City goal chart at the end of the following season, by which time he had started his lengthy and prolific spell at The Hawthorns. Ally had got the entire Football League goal record started that term with a 45-second strike at Huddersfield on opening day, but was nonetheless jettisoned for just over £60,000 as Jimmy Bloomfield needed to recoup some of his outlay on the Sammels/Weller/Birchenall combination he'd constructed. With West Brom, Ally struck a useful partnership with namesake Tony Brown as the Baggies themselves experienced relegation and promotion, before tasting their late 70s glory days of European qualification. He retreated into a slightly deeper role as he commenced his later League wanderings; helping Port Vale to a 1986 Fourth Division promotion spot in his final campaign; and finishing his career with a tally of 141 League goals from 495 games. Ally took a pub in Aldridge upon retirement.

Apps: *FL 93+8; FAC 7+2; LC 10+1.*
Goals: *FL 32; FAC 2; LC 1.*

BROWN, Graham Frederick

b. Leicester, 5th November 1950

CAREER: Blaby Boys Club; app June 1967/pro Nov 1968 CITY; cs 1971 Burton Albion; cs 1974 Enderby Town; cs 1975 Oadby Town; cs 1976 Wigston COB; cs 1978 Harborough Town.

City debut/only game v Aston Villa (H) 4.4.70 (sub)

> Having scored all City's four goals in a testimonial friendly at Plymouth in March 1970, young local striker Graham earned rapid promotion to the senior bench, but only tasted action on one of the five occasions he was named substitute, when replacing John Sjoberg during the 1-0 victory over Villa that helped consign the visitors to Division Three. Despite a decent reserve-team scoring rate, Graham was released before the 1971 First Division campaign, to be snapped up by Richie Norman at Burton, and to become top scorer across two Southern League campaigns culminating respectively in promotion and relegation. His subsequent local wanderings were spiced by an appearance in the 1976 County Cup final.

Apps: *FL 0+1.*

BROWN, Grant Ashley

b. Sunderland, 19th November 1969

Career: YT July 1986/pro July 1987 CITY; Aug 1989-loan-Lincoln City; Jan 1990 Lincoln City.

City debut v Bradford City (A) 30.4.88

> A promising graduate of City's 1986/7 FA Youth Cup semi-final side, central defender Grant was given early responsibility by David Pleat at Second Division level. With only two senior games under his belt, Grant was handed the No.6 shirt at the beginning of 1988/9 in preference to experienced summer signing Steve Thompson (ex-Charlton), and seemed to be maturing swiftly as he added poise and pace to his defensive strength. But he started the next term with a loan spell at Lincoln, and Pleat okayed a £60,000 move when the Imps returned with a permanent offer later in the season. By November 1990, Grant was playing under new Lincoln boss Steve Thompson (!), who handed him the captaincy in 1992. He earned a May 2000 testimonial against Middlesbrough, and had just passed the Lincoln record for aggregate appearances (427) when suffering a broken leg in January 2001.

Apps: *FL 14; LC 2.*

BROWN, James

b. Renton, Dunbartonshire, 1870
d. Leicester, 11th January 1924

Career: Renton Union; Renton Thistle; Renton; cs 1890 Aston Villa; Oct 1893 FOSSE; Sept 1899 Loughborough.

Fosse debut v Mansfield Town (H) FAC 4.11.1893

> The first real Scottish influence on the Fosse's formations and fortunes, Jimmy was a moustachio'd 'professor' of the game who gave six seasons of fine service to the club after joining up early in the final Midland League season. A Scottish Cup semi-finalist with Renton in 1889, and a Villa stalwart for three top-flight terms, he initially alternated with Fosse between roles as a wing-half or free-scoring centre-forward, before settling as a playmaking centre-half in the Second Division. The club's first skipper in that sphere, Jimmy was recognised as the most astute of on-field prompters, and served as exemplar for the weighting of Fosse's transfer policy towards the acquisition of Caledonian talent. He took a club benefit from a friendly against Southampton in September 1898, and a year later moved slightly northward to lend his veteran skills to the hard-up Luffs' eventually futile efforts to maintain League status. In 1902 Jimmy became a League referee, having in the interim founded a Leicester travel agency. He died suddenly at his home at 26 Welford Road. [Mystery still surrounds the provenance of the cap - marked 'SFA' - which Jimmy can be seen wearing in several early Fosse team pictures. A mid-30s interview with his son mentions his international status, but no other records do; as all references to Scotland's inside right versus Wales in 1890 are to a Cambuslang player named J Brown, and 'Junior' internationals had yet to start by that date].

***Apps:** FL 116; FAC 23; ML 14.*
***Goals:** FL 4; FAC 3; ML 14.*

BROWN, John Thomas

b. Eastwood, Notts, 15th June 1901
d. Eastwood, 28th January 1977

Career: Kirkby Colliery; Aug 1922 CITY; Aug 1931 Wrexham; July 1934 Nuneaton Town; Sept 1936 Heanor Town.

City debut v Aston Villa (H) 10.10.25

> Belatedly making his City bow in the club's 1000th Football League game, Jack was still regarded primarily as a loyal understudy for either Adam Black's or Reg Osborne's full-back slot until 1928, when he finally made the left-flank defensive role his own during City's most sustained attempt ever for top-flight honours, which eventually brought them the runners-up position behind Sheffield Wednesday. A former Notts miner, he presented a physical and temperamental contrast to his stylish back-line partner Black, but was no less effective against First Division wingers; and his patient clubmanship was also rewarded in 1928/9 with a benefit game. In the summer of 1931 he turned down a mooted move to Bradford City, and transferred to North Wales instead. There, extending his comparative misfortune in terms of honours, he earned runners-up medals from the Welsh Cup Finals of 1932 and 1933, and also assisted Wrexham to what was then their highest-ever League placing – runners-up spot in Division Three (North).

***Apps:** FL 114; FAC 3.*

BROWN, Paul Andrew

b. Birmingham, 19th September 1964

Career: app Aston Villa; Sept 1982 CITY; May 1983 Nuneaton Borough; Stourbridge; Alvechurch; Willenhall Town.

City debut/only game v Notts County (H) FAC 8.1.83

> Called up for a Cup-tie debut after Tommy Williams had suffered his second broken leg, left-back Paul was somewhat overawed by the occasion as Notts raced to a merited three-goal lead, and his subsequent loss of confidence saw him released after only a year on City's books. Originally capped by England Schools at outside-left, Paul was a Villa Park apprentice when making progress to Youth international honours; yet it had been City who'd given him his initial professional contract after he'd impressed in pre-season trials (scoring in the 1982 Final of the Bass Charity Vase competition).

***Apps:** FAC 1.*

BROWN, Thomas

b. Beith, Ayrshire, ca 1880

Career: Glenbuck Cherrypickers; Aug 1899 FOSSE; Dec 1901 Chesterfield Town; cs 1902 Third Lanark; Nov 1902 FOSSE; cs 1903 Portsmouth; Sept 1904 Dundee.

Fosse debut v Woolwich Arsenal (A) 2.9.1899 (scored once)

> Fosse's top scorer for three seasons running, despite the break of almost a year in his service, bustling centre-forward Tommy had his career somewhat overshadowed by that of his brother, Scottish international Sandy (whose clubs included Preston, Portsmouth, Spurs, Middlesbrough and Luton). His first departure from Filbert Street followed an internal suspension for breaches of training discipline, and involved a deal with Chesterfield (against whom he'd already notched a hat-trick, and for whom he scored at a rate of a goal-per-game) for a deferred payment which, in the following summer, they then couldn't afford. His second leave-taking saw him replace his brother at Fratton Park.

***Apps:** FL 72; FAC 5.*
***Goals:** FL 38; FAC 3.*

BRUCE, David

b. Perth, 23rd February 1911
d. Bridge of Earn, Perthshire, 15th September 1976

Career: Perth Thistle; Aug 1930 East Fife; Apr 1931 Dundee East Craigie; trials-Dundee; Aug 1935 CITY; May 1936 Bristol Rovers; Aug 1937 St.Mirren.

City debut/only game v Burnley (A) 25.4.36

> Possibly a victim of his own versatility, David never settled for long in one playing position or, consequently, at one club. A centre-forward when recruited by a relegation-bound East Fife, his return to the Junior ranks had seen him build a fine full-back reputation which was due to earn him a cap at that level when City took him on. First-team selection remained out of reach, however, until brief trials in the Combination forward-line resulted in a call-up at outside right in a 2-2 draw at Turf Moor, only days before David found himself transfer-listed. Moving to Eastville with Tommy Mills, he remained on the wing, and got on the scoresheet twice in a dozen League outings before returning north of the border, where St Mirren also became indecisive as to whether his most effective role was at full-back or centre-forward.

***Apps:** FL 1.*

BRUNTON, Matthew

b. Burnley, 20th April 1878
d. Burnley, 29th December 1962

Career: Army football (South Lancs Regt); Aug 1899 Preston North End; cs 1900 Accrington Stanley; July 1901 Burnley; cs 1902 Accrington Stanley; May 1904 FOSSE; Feb 1905 Nelson; cs 1905 Accrington Stanley; July 1906 Oldham Athletic; cs 1908 Southport Central; Aug 1909 Great Harwood; Oct 1909 Haslingden; Oct 1910 Darwen; Nov 1910 Accrington Stanley.

Fosse debut v Blackpool (A) 3.9.04

> Matt's brief, unsuccessful sojourn as a Fosse centre-forward, taken on after re-election had been achieved, seems a distinct aberration in a career so closely tied to his home county (with even three of the teams he faced as a Leicester man coming from Lancashire). He had played at the highest level with Preston, and had been a Second Division regular for Burnley in 1901/2, but it was in Lancashire Combination football that Matt excelled. Accrington Stanley became, in 1903, the first non-reserve side to win that championship, with Matt claiming 40 goals; he was back with them for their repeat triumph of 1906; and his hat-trick of title medals came a year later on the back of a 23-goal campaign with Oldham, who subsequently gained election to the League. There Matt would appear but once more, before further moves around his favoured Combination. On retirement to the trainer/coach ranks, it was predictable that Accrington and Burnley would become his employers. He was a swimming instructor at Burnley Corporation Baths when WW1 broke out, and suffered a serious leg wound while serving as a sergeant in his second stint with the South Lancashire Regiment; ironically spending his recuperation period in a Leicestershire military hospital.

***Apps:** FL 5; FAC 1.*

BUCHANAN, David

b. Newcastle on Tyne, 23rd June 1962

Career: Loughborough Dynamo; app July 1978/pro June 1979 CITY; Oct 1982-loan-Northampton Town; July 1983 Peterborough United; 1984 North Shields; 1984 Blyth Spartans; July 1986 Sunderland; Sept 1987-loan-York City; Apr 1988-trials-Middlesbrough; May 1988 (Norwegian football); Aug 1988 Blyth Spartans; 1988 Newcastle Blue Star; Bedlington Terriers; Whitley Bay.

City debut v Oldham Athletic (H) 1.1.79 (scored once)

> The youngest player ever to turn out for City in both Football League and FA Cup competitions, David was a New Year's Day beneficiary of Jock Wallace's resolve to rely on his juniors to avert the possibility of the club dropping into Division Three at the end of his first, ship-steadying term at the helm. David's scoring bow (alongside fellow debutants Bobby Smith and Gary Lineker) came at the age of 16 years, 192 days, and his first taste of Cup action five days later (with Andy Peake another teenage newcomer that day), as the slender, light-haired striker justifiably became an immediate crowd favourite. His initially meteoric progress was not maintained however, and a degree of immature impatience set in. August 1981 saw a transfer request from David, followed days later by the setback of breaking his ankle while scoring in the Final of the pre-season Bass Charity Vase competition against Burton Albion; and disenchantment deepened. His appetite for the game never wholly returned during his season with Posh, and he turned his back on senior football for a couple of years to build a career in leisure centre management; but his evident class in part-time Northern League circles brought him both England semi-pro caps to add to his earlier Youth international honours, and an offer from Lawrie McMenemy to return to the big time at Roker. After Sunderland's drop to the Third Division, however, further northeastern roamings followed, but David had definitively retired from action by the age of 28. In June 2001, however, he took the General Manager's job at Crook Town.

***Apps:** FL 24+9; FAC 4+1.*
***Goals:** FL 7; FAC 1.*

BUCKLEY, John William

b. East Kilbride, Lanarkshire, 18th May 1962

Career: Queens Park; May 1978 Celtic; Mar 1983 Partick Thistle; July 1984 Doncaster Rovers; July 1986 Leeds United; Mar 1987-loan-CITY; Oct 1987-loan-Doncaster Rovers; Nov 1987 Rotherham United; Oct 1990 Partick Thistle; July 1991 Scunthorpe United; Feb 1993 Rotherham United; Dec 1994 Buxton.

City debut v Newcastle United (A) 4.4.87 (sub)

> Twice bought by Billy Bremner after showing himself as something of a throwback to the heyday of jinkily dribbling Scottish wingplay, John came to City on extended loan for the fateful run-in to eventual relegation in 1987. His crowd-pleasing, ball-playing cheek was barely trusted, however, and he spent more time on the bench than in action; returning to Leeds when it still looked possible that he might have to face them in the then-operative Play-Off structure of First v Second Division clubs. A second circuit of Yorkshire area clubs ensued as a midfield role beckoned, bracketing a spell back with Partick, the club who'd given him a Scottish League break following brief Celtic run-outs in each of the Glasgow Cup and League Cup. John won a Fourth Division championship medal with the Millers in 1989, and was a Wembley Play-Off loser (alongside Matt Elliott) with the Iron in 1992. He suffered a fractured skull during his fourth game back with Rotherham, and for some time lay in a coma until recovery. John played a little non-league football later, but by the mid-90s was involved in the Millmoor Football in the Community programme.

***Apps:** FL 1+4.*

BULLING, James

b. West Bridgford, Nottingham, 12th February 1909
d. Wrexham, 13th October 1992

Career: am 1926/pro Feb 1928 Nottingham Forest; July 1928 Shirebrook; May 1930 CITY; June 1932 Wrexham; June 1936 Shrewsbury Town.

City debut v Liverpool (A) 15.11.30

> Jimmy belonged to the second generation of Nottinghamshire's footballing Bullings, who also included Chris (Watford), Ted (Spurs) and Harold (Watford & Forest). A wing-half who occasionally deputised for either George Ritchie or Billy Findlay, he had been signed from Shirebrook in a joint deal with reserve full-back Charles Gellatly, but he found his level most comfortably at an interim level, as a Racecourse regular over four Third Division (North) seasons. Jimmy's Wrexham days also saw him pick up a 1933 Welsh Cup runners-up medal (alongside Jack Brown); while, in the company of Jack Liggins, he also aided the Shrews to runners-up spot in the Birmingham & District League. He served in Italy with the Royal Engineers during WW2, then settled to the plumbing trade at Shotton Steelworks.

***Apps:** FL 12.*

BUNCE, Paul Eric

b. Coalville, Leics, 7th January 1967

Career: app July 1983/pro Jan 1985 CITY; Mar 1987 Northampton Town; cs 1988 Weymouth; cs 1989 Burton Albion; Feb 1990 Shepshed Charterhouse; Apr 1992 Hinckley FC; Thringstone.

City debut v Nottingham Forest (H) 11.10.86

> A homegrown teenage wing prospect given a break by Bryan Hamilton, Paul had little time to acclimatise to the senior game in the hurly-burly of City's 1986/7 relegation campaign, and proved no answer to the crying need for attacking width that season, despite making his bow in a heartening home derby win. His only City goal came in a friendly defeat by the Iraqi national team in February 1987, but a month later he became a deadline-day mover to the Cobblers - already Fourth Division championship certs. Paul scored on his full debut, but lasted only just over a year at the County Ground, then returned via Conference and Southern League football to local fare.

***Apps:** FL 5+1.*

BURBECK, Ronald Thomas

b. Leicester, 27th February 1934

Career: Wellington Vics; am 1950/pro May 1952 CITY; Oct 1956 Middlesbrough; Aug 1963 Darlington; July 1964 Hereford United.

City debut v West Ham United (A) 15.9.52

> A goalscoring member of the first Leicestershire team to reach the Final of the County Youth Cup (in 1951, when they lost 1-3 on aggregate to a Middlesex side containing John Hollowbread, Johnny Haynes, Ernie Walley and Tosh Chamberlain), Ron also featured in the final Amateur International trial of that year, and picked up England Youth caps during 1951/2 against Wales and Scotland, and on a Spanish tour. He signed professionally for City during the same week he was notified of his National Service RAF call-up, and stood in once for Tom Dryburgh on the left wing at Upton Park while on leave. Ron's next chance didn't arise until some three and a half years later, but the then-intense competition among Filbert Street flankmen soon saw him on his way northward. His 139-game Ayresome record saw him largely employed as a provider for the prolific Brian Clough and Alan Peacock, but he netted twice in Boro's 6-6 draw at Charlton in 1960/1, which equalled the League record scoreline set previously by City and Arsenal. Ron contributed to Hereford's 1965 Southern League championship alongside future City boss Jock Wallace and former Filbert Street reserve Brian Punter. Additionally, he played cricket for Leicestershire Seconds during the summer of 1958.

***Apps:** FL 3.*

Ron Burbeck

BURGESS, Thomas

b. Leicester

Career: Belgrave St Michael's; Jan 1898-trials-FOSSE; Leicester Imperial; May 1901 FOSSE; cs 1902 Leicester Imperial; cs 1906 Hinckley United; Nuneaton Town; cs 1908 Hinckley United; Jan 1910 Leicester Imperial.

Fosse debut v Stockport County (H) 23.11.01 (scored once)

> In the early years of the century, Leicester Imperial forever seemed a cross between an unofficial nursery and a virtual knacker's yard for local Fosse talent. Outside- or inside-right Tommy's brief attempt to break through into the senior ranks was well behind him by 1906, when he won a County Cup victor's medal during the second of his three spells with the Imps, and regularly featured for them alongside six more sometime Fossils: Norman, Hackett and the two Turners in attack, with Betts and Teddy King backing up.

Apps: *FL 3.*
Goals: *FL 1.*

BURTON, Horace

b. Melton Mowbray, Leics, 28th July 1887
d. Melton Mowbray, 2nd September 1969

Career: Melton Mowbray; Holwell Works; Sept 1910-trials-Nottingham Forest; Oct 1910 FOSSE; 1919 Loughborough Corinthians; cs 1921 Mountsorrel Town; Melton WMC.

Fosse debut v Bradford Park Avenue (A) 1.4.11

> 'A burly bundle to run up against', Horace was a wing-half who loyally served Fosse across five pre-war seasons, often deposing nominally more illustrious or experienced imports, and earning the captaincy by the time of Fosse's final peacetime fixture. He was one of Arsenal's guests in 1963 when they marked the 50th anniversary of the opening of Highbury and the first game there against the Fosse, in which Horace played left-half. During the latter months of WW1, as a Lance-Corporal in the Leicestershire Regiment, he was taken prisoner in Germany, and was involved in an 'escape' which actually took place after peace had been declared, unbeknownst to its participants. Prior to this adventure, Horace had also appeared as a wartime guest for Notts County.

Apps: *FL 78; FAC 4.*
Goals: *FL 1.*

BUSHELL, William

b. Wednesbury, Staffs, 1907

Career: Darlaston; Apr 1926 West Bromwich Albion; 1926 Willenhall; May 1928 CITY; Aug 1931 Walsall.

Debut v Birmingham (H) 17.10.29 (scored once)

> City just pipped Blackburn Rovers to the signature of outside-right Willie, but his Filbert Street years were entirely spent in reserve to Hugh Adcock. Indeed, it was while Hughie was off winning his first England cap that Willie stepped up for the first pair of his rare outings, making one goal and scoring another against Birmingham. His season at Walsall brought him four goals in 31 games, but Willie was soon back in Leicester to work in the insurance business. He signed for George Carr at Nuneaton Town in February 1934, but never actually played.

Apps: *FL 3.*
Goals: *FL 1.*

BUTLER, Richard

b. Shepshed, Leics, 1885

Career: Shepshed Albion; Apr 1905-trials-FOSSE; cs 1906 Nottingham Forest; Oct 1910 FOSSE; Loughborough Corinthians.

Fosse debut v Bolton Wanderers (A) 31.12.10

> Though he first played for Fosse in an April 1905 friendly against Clapton, it was not for another five and a half years that wing-half Dick actually signed for the club. In the interim he'd been a stalwart Forest reserve, gaining but a single senior outing at each of League and FA Cup level during their 1907 Second Division championship term. At Leicester, his two years saw him rivalling Teddy King for a first-team jersey, and as dressing-room joker. By the final pre-war season, Dick was skipper of Loughborough's foremost club.

Apps: *FL 26; FAC 2.*

BYRNE, Patrick Joseph

b. Dublin, 15th May 1956

Career: 1974 Bohemians; Mar 1978 Philadelphia Fury; 1978 Shelbourne; July 1979 CITY; July 1981 Heart of Midlothian; Aug 1983 Shamrock Rovers; cs 1988 Shelbourne (p/mgr).

City debut v Rotherham United (H) LC 11.8.79

> A tenacious midfield contributor to City's 1980 Second Division championship push, Pat offered useful attacking options on the right for Jock Wallace's side, but proved slightly less effective in prompting a struggling top-flight team a season later. Goals at Anfield and White Hart Lane nonetheless highlighted the English phase of his remarkable career. Pat had already won FAI Cup (1976) and League of Ireland championship (1978) medals with Bohs before his NASL stint in the company of Martin Henderson and Alan Lee, and a litany of success followed his move from Filbert Street. He aided Hearts' ascent back to the Scottish Premier League in his second season there, by which time he was commuting weekly from Dublin owing to his wife's inability to settle in Edinburgh; then returned to Irish football with a vengeance. In his first four years as Shamrock's skipper and playmaker, he led them to the championship and FAI Cup Final in 1984 and, remarkably, to the domestic double in each of the next three campaigns. Perhaps even more notably, his final active term as player/manager at Shelbourne, 1991/2, saw him once more in the driving seat of a championship triumph. Pat's playing career brought additional honours: eight full caps for the Republic; the PFA of Ireland's Player of the Year award for 1983/4; and the Personality of the Year award from the Sportswriters Association of Ireland in each of 1984/5 and 1991/2. Meanwhile, his managerial career continues. In 1995/6 he was in the hot seat at St James Gate; and a year later embarked on a spell with Shamrock Rovers that saw him successively titled as general manager, caretaker manager, and secretary/commercial manager. In the 1999 close season, Pat took over as boss of Kilkenny City.

Apps: *FL 31+5; FAC 3; FLC 2.*
Goals: *FL 3.*

CALDER, John

b. Kilbirnie, Ayrshire, 19th October 1913

Career: Mar 1931 Dalry Thistle; July 1931 CITY; Aug 1932 Falkirk; cs 1933 St Johnstone; Sept 1934 Dunfermline Athletic; Dec 1934-trials-Alloa Athletic; Dec 1934 Morton; Feb 1937 Bolton Wanderers; May 1938 Barnsley; 1939 Morton; cs 1941 Albion Rovers; Apr 1942 Morton.

City debut/only game v Grimsby Town (A) 19.9.31

> That City - or at least boss Willie Orr - saw promise in 17-year-old centre-forward Jack was evident, but it took slightly more patience than was extended from Filbert Street for it to come to fruition. Jack had played only two Intermediate games for Dalry before being signed in tandem with clubmate Johnny Campbell, and had only one reserve match under his belt when asked to stand in for Arthur Chandler. This early First Division bow was unfortunately marked by both a 0-3 scoreline and by the City players' close shave in a rail accident en route to Grimsby. Despite such an inauspicious context for a debut, and despite a reserve scoring record of 28 strikes from 23 games, Jack was allowed to rejoin Orr at Falkirk. Success was still slow coming back in Scotland, but a trial game for Alloa v Morton at the end of 1934 changed the picture. Jack was billed as 'Newman', scored, and was immediately snapped up by the visitors! By the end of 1935/6, he was at the head of the Scottish seasonal scoring charts, with his 55 League goals featuring three trebles, a 4, a 5, a 6 and, finally, a record-equalling eight-goal haul from an 11-2 win over Raith. Morton benefitted from another 34 Second Division strikes from Jack the following term (including five on the opening day of the season) before disgruntling their fans by accepting Bolton's £4,000. Jack helped keep the Trotters in the top flight for two years, then assisted Barnsley to the championship of the Third Division (North) in 1939, before returning to Cappielow to resume his prolific ways in wartime football. In October 1936, Jack had been named as reserve to Dave McCulloch for Scotland's meeting with Ireland.

Apps: *FL 1.*

Jack Calder

CALDER, William Carson

b. Glasgow, 28th September 1934

Career: Port Glasgow; Aug 1955 CITY; Apr 1959 Bury; Nov 1963 Oxford United; Nov 1966 Rochdale; cs 1967 Macclesfield Town.

City debut v Everton (H) 23.8.58

> Signed by David Halliday only days before his departure on a National Service posting to Gibraltar, Bill eventually returned to understudy Derek Hogg, and briefly took the latter's No 11 shirt at the opening of 1958/9 before surrendering it in turn to newcomer Gordon Wills. New boss Matt Gillies offered to sell him to Arthur Rowley's Shrewsbury in December 1958, but it was not long anyway before Bill moved on. He became a robust, free-scoring right winger in Bury's 1961 Third Division championship side, and a centre-forward spearhead for Oxford's first-ever promotion campaign in 1965. After aggregating 96 League goals, Bill took some late glory from Macclesfield's 1967/8 FA Cup giant-killing efforts.

Apps: *FL 3.*

CALLACHAN, Harry

b. Madras, India, 9th April 1903
d. Leicester, 11th February 1990

Career: Kirkintilloch Rob Roy; Parkhead; Aug 1925 Celtic; Aug 1925-loan-Alloa Athletic; Aug 1926-loan-Beith; Sept 1927 CITY; Aug 1930 Tunbridge Wells Rangers; Aug 1931 Burton Town; Aug 1932 Wigan Athletic; Aug 1933 Market Harborough Town.

City debut v Newcastle United (A) 7.4.28

> A soldier's son who became Celtic's left-back understudy to international Willie McStay after a £50 move from their Junior neighbours, Harry played but sporadically in the 1926 championship side and that of the following term, and then suffered even more disappointment with City. Reg Osborne and Jack Brown barred the tall defender's way to a first-team spot, though City were clearly in two minds as to his potential value: listing him at the end of 1928/9, only to re-sign him at the start of the next season for another year's reserve football. Harry's subsequent wanderings featured an appearance in the first ever Wigan Athletic line-up, when that club was formed to play in the Cheshire League following the Football League demise of Wigan Borough. His return to Leicester saw him complete 25 years' service with the Dunlop Rubber Co, where at various times his workmates included Roger Heywood and Jim McLaren.

Apps: *FL 3.*

CALVERT, Joseph William Herbert

b. Beighton, Yorks, 3rd February 1907
d. Leicester, 23rd December 1999

Career: Owston Park Rangers; Bullcroft Colliery; 1930 Frickley Colliery; May 1931 Bristol Rovers; May 1932 CITY; Jan 1948 Watford; May 1948 Brush Sports.

City debut v Sheffield United (H) 27.8.32

> A former pit-worker who was 24 before he sampled the senior game, goalkeeper Joe was not about to contemplate any sort of early retirement from it. Indeed, his final outing for City came at the age of 40 years, 313 days; bringing him the enduring status of being the club's oldest player in peacetime football and, after over 15 years' service, one of its most loyal. An ever-present behind an exceptionally leaky defence in his season at Eastville, he came to Leicester as cover for one McLaren (Jim), and soon found himself in reserve to another (Sandy). Joe's pre-war appearances tended to be sporadic, then, although a couple of broken collarbone injuries in the mid-30s cut into his availability. (These were not the only index to the punishment his near-reckless bravery invited: Joe also set a club goalkeeping record by failing to finish no less than five first-team and three reserve games through injury). WW2 also cut into his career, though he aggregated 62 games for City at this time, as well as 19 guest outings for Northampton Town, and numerous RAF representative games in India and Burma; and Joe became the most consistent choice between the City sticks on League soccer's resumption in 1946/7. Eventually he joined the mass transfer-and-loan exodus that took five City players to Watford on the same day; was typically stretchered off on his debut; and was still exhibiting true veteran prowess for his final, Loughborough-based team as they lifted the Leicestershire Senior Cup in May 1949.

Apps: *FL 72; FAC 8; WW2 62.*

CAMPBELL, James

b. Glasgow, 25th November 1918

Career: St Mungo Juveniles; Petershill; June 1939 Celtic; St.Anthony's; Oct 1943 CITY; Oct 1946 Walsall.

City debut (WW2) v West Bromwich Albion (H) 9.10.43; (postwar) v Chelsea (A) FAC 5.1.46

> His prospective Celtic career snatched away on the declaration of war, two-footed winger Jim guested for Aldershot and Chelsea while acting as a military PT instructor, and saw service in France, Belgium and Germany as a paratrooper. City utilised his attacking versatility for three seasons of regional fare, and played him at outside-right in the Stamford Bridge leg of the first postwar FA Cup tie, in the only season the competition operated on a two-leg basis, only to see him carried off with a cut eye and mild concussion. Jim briefly assisted Reading in further wartime games, then was released by City for two terms of Third Division (South) football at Fellows Park.

Apps: *FAC 1; WW2 46.*
Goals: *WW2 11.*

CAMPBELL, John

b. Ardrossan, Ayrshire, 7th March 1910

Career: 1930 Dalry Thistle; July 1931 CITY; Dec 1933 Lincoln City; July 1939 Scunthorpe United; Nov 1946 Lincoln Co-Op.

City debut v Birmingham (H) 17.12.32 (scored once)

> The more senior of the Dalry attacking duo brought to Leicester by Willie Orr, Johnny took longer than Jack Calder to make his first-team breakthrough, but could count himself somewhat unfortunate not to sustain it. For his goals-per-game ratio was pretty impressive – despite local press comment on his 'habit of falling into the offside trap', and a penalty miss in City's first-ever home encounter with continental opposition (a 1-3 defeat by Rapid Vienna in January 1933) – and it was primarily competition from Jim Paterson, and the advent of George Dewis, which restricted his Filbert Street centre-forward chances. Johnny's move to Sincil Bank for £1,250 was the first of three occasions the Imps have upped their record fee for a Leicester man (Andy Graver and Grant Brown would follow), and despite their relegation from the Second Division in 1934, he certainly repaid them handsomely by racing to over a century of League goals before the war – top-scoring for four terms there, and claiming seven hat-tricks along the way. Then, in the three Midland League fixtures Scunthorpe played before 1939's wartime close-down, Johnny renewed his occasional City partnership with Digger Maw, and netted four times. Having maintained his pharmaceutical studies while at Filbert Street, the suitably qualified Johnny eventually became Superintendent Optician for Lincoln Co-Op on leaving the game.

Apps: *FL 21; FAC 1.*
Goals: *FL 12; FAC 2.*

CAMPBELL, Kenneth

b. Cambuslang, Lanarkshire, 6th September 1892
d. Macclesfield, 28th April 1977

Career: Clyde Vale; Rutherglen Glencairn; July 1910 Cambuslang Rangers; May 1911 Liverpool; Apr 1920 Partick Thistle; June 1922 New Brighton; Mar 1923 Stoke; Nov 1925 CITY; Nov 1929 New Brighton.

City debut v Sunderland (H) 14.11.25

> 'Thrilling and courageous ... were his efforts when playing the lone hand with a centre-forward who was in full career for goal'. Scottish international goalkeeper Kenny drew many such plaudits on his 1931 retirement (to open a sports shop in Wallasey), and City supporters joined in. For despite his relative veteran status when arriving to aid First Division consolidation, his reliabilty, modesty and quiet efficiency between the posts had indeed significantly helped the top-flight transition of Peter Hodge's team; and he won a fair share of headlines with City, as when saving penalties from each of Hudspeth and Hughie Gallacher at Newcastle in 1926/7. Capped on eight occasions, and a Scottish League representative, Kenny was a medallist from Cup Finals on both sides of the border – a 1914 loser with Liverpool and a 1921 victor with Partick. His first New Brighton stint was in the Lancashire Combination; the second in Division Three (North). He also guested for Southport during WW1.

Apps: *FL 79; FAC 2.*

CAMPBELL, Kevin Joseph

b. Lambeth, London, 4th February 1970

Career: YT/pro Feb 1988 Arsenal; Jan 1989-loan-Leyton Orient; Nov 1989-loan-CITY; July 1995 Nottingham Forest; July 1998 Trabzonspor; Mar 1999 Everton.

City debut v Leeds United (H) 11.11.89

> A hat-trick hero of Arsenal's 1988 FA Youth Cup triumph, who had made but two brief substitute appearances for the Gunners prior to his loan to Leicester, Kevin soon had City fans reacting with a unique mixture of admiration and envy. The teenage striker's impact on an injury-hit, lightweight front-line was immense, for in embryo were all the spearhead's attributes: challenging strength, ball-shielding ability, aerial skill and phenomenal shooting power amongst them. In a previous three-month loan spell at Brisbane Road, Kevin had claimed nine Division Four goals in 16 games: he was marginally slower off the mark with City, but had become a firm crowd favourite some time before a rather touchingly emotional Filbert

Kevin Campbell

Street farewell. A covetous David Pleat had already extended the loan to the maximum three months, but could do nothing to prise such talent away from Highbury on a permanent basis, despite Kevin's immediate prospect of a return to reserve football. His Arsenal breakthrough eventually followed, with Alan Smith playing the most unselfish of mentors, and the personal honours began accruing: four Under-21 caps, a 1991 championship medal, and winners' gongs from each of the 1993 FA and League Cups and the 1994 European Cup Winners Cup. A slight slump followed, with a £2 million move to Forest only really paying off as they bounced back to the Premiership in his third and final term (a 23-goal campaign), and an exile with Gordon Milne's Turkish outfit turning nightmarish after his club chairman heaped racial insults upon him. A loan to Goodison revived both player and moribund team, with Kevin's nine goals in eight games essentially keeping Everton up; and a permanent contract followed payment of a £3m fee in July 1999. Despite injuries, two double-figure scoring campaigns have ensued.

Apps: *FL 11; FMC 1.*
Goals: *FL 5; FMC 1.*

CAMPBELL, Stuart Pearson

b. Corby, Northants, 4th December 1977

Career: YT July 1994/pro July 1996 CITY; Mar 2000-loan-Birmingham City; Sept 2000 Grimsby Town.

City debut v Scarborough (A) LC 17.9.96 (sub)

> A lightweight midfielder who retained the 'promising' tag for perhaps too long for his own or his management's comfort, Stuart (named after the former Manchester United striker) made a nerveless Premiership start at Old Trafford when deputising for Scott Taylor, and was dubbed City's Young Player of the Year for 1996/7. His progress as a neat and perceptive passer was indexed by the first of numerous Scotland Under-21 call-ups in March 1998, but the apparent ease with which he could be crowded out of the midfield hurly-burly meant he struggled to break free of 'fringe player' status with the club. His St Andrews loan stint brought him only peripheral involvement in Birmingham's Play-Off qualification; and any plans he had to impress the incoming Peter Taylor were short-circuited early with a further loan-out. Yet virtually a season's worth of regular Division One football at Blundell Park proved him an effective operator, alongside Paul Groves, at that level; at which Grimsby eventually survived on a fraught final day. Accordingly, £200,000 changed hands in May 2001 to confer permanency on the deal.

Apps: *PL 12+25; FAC 3+3; LC 2+5; UEFA 0+1.*

CAREY, Brian Patrick

b. Cork, 31st May 1968

Career: Albert Rovers; Sept 1987 Cork City; Sept 1989 Manchester United; Jan 1991-loan-Wrexham; Dec 1991-loan-Wrexham; July 1993 CITY; July 1996 Wrexham.

City debut v Peterborough United (H) 14.8.93

> Called up for his country's Under-21s and then twice capped by Jack Charlton while an Old Trafford reserve, tall central defender Brian never did break into Alex Ferguson's first-team, but he featured in Wrexham's memorable Cup giant-killing of Arsenal during the second of his loan spells at the Racecourse. Brian Little invested £250,000 to add him to the City squad for the third attempt at Play-Off-assisted promotion, but he often struggled to impose himself amidst the plethora of central defensive pairings and trios experimented with that term. A lack of pace and occasionally wayward distribution could count against him, but Brian nonetheless earned a further Republic of Ireland cap in March, then shared in Wembley glory over Derby alongside Jimmy Willis. He was sent off at Wimbledon in his first Premiership game, and requested a transfer from Mark McGhee before returning for a fair run, was then listed and reprieved and, having broken his goalscoring duck against Millwall in his penultimate selection, was finally deposed by Julian Watts as Martin O'Neill imposed his own promotion blend on the side. Wrexham happily stumped up £100,000 for their former talisman, and Brian was Player of the Year for them in 1997/8, when they won the Welsh Invitation Cup. He remains at the Racecourse as a defensive linchpin.

Apps: *FL/PL 51+7; FAC 0+1; LC 3; AIC 1; PO 3.*
Goals: *FL 1.*

CARLIN, William

b. Liverpool, 6th October 1940

Career: May 1958 Liverpool; Aug 1962 Halifax Town; Oct 1964 Carlisle United; Sept 1967 Sheffield United; Aug 1968 Derby County; Oct 1970 CITY; Sept 1971 Notts County; Nov 1973 Cardiff City.

City debut v Birmingham City (A) 20.10.70

> A tiny, all-action midfielder for whom the cliche of 'pocket dynamo' might have been invented, Willie overcame both his physical limitations and early playing disappointments to forge a career that was positively inspirational. City were but one team to benefit from his trademark admixture of guts and skill, but memories of his impact alongside Bobby Kellard in the engine-room of Frank O'Farrell's 1971 promotion side are indelible. Discarded by his hometown club after only a single Anfield outing as a diminutive striker, Willie suffered relegation to the League basement in his first term at The Shay, but soon led Halifax's scoring charts. Then, alongside Frank Large, he helped chivvy Carlisle to the Third Division championship in 1965, before involvement in the Blades' top-flight relegation struggle saw his transition to midfield grafter. Next, Brian Clough's £60,000 imported Willie to Derby's successful Division Two championship campaign of 1969, and his true-grit approach aided their rise to fourth the following term. Willie had already picked up a winners medal from the pre-season Watney Cup when O'Farrell expended a bargain £35,000 to bring him across the East Midlands and exploit both his wiliness and his motivational presence; and it was both a surprise and a disappointment when Jimmy Bloomfield discarded him without so much as a Division One run-out. Willie simply got on with prompting Notts County from Third to Second in 1973 and, under O'Farrell again, sparking another of Cardiff's then-annual Second Division survival acts a year later. Willie has subsequently become a bar owner in Majorca.

Apps: *FL 31; FAC 6.*
Goals: *FL 1.*

CARNELLY, Albert

b. Nottingham, 29th December 1870
d. Nottingham, 18th August 1920

Career: Westminster Amateurs (Nott'm); 1889 Mapperley; 1890 Notts County; 1891 Loughborough; May 1894 Nottingham Forest; May 1896 FOSSE; cs 1897 Bristol City; Sept 1898 Ilkeston Town; Nov 1898 Bristol City; cs 1899 Thames Ironworks; cs 1900 Millwall; cs 1901 IlkestonTown.

Fosse debut v Darwen (H) 5.9.1896

> Fosse were rather familiar with the cry of 'Give it to Nelly' some time before they signed him. Along with Jimmy Thraves, Albert had been in the Notts County side which had faced them in the last game ever at Mill Lane; and he'd scored a Midland League hat-trick against them for the Luffs in 1891/2, in the first senior competitive meeting of the local rivals. He was operating a Division above them in 1894/5, when registering as top-flight Forest's top scorer; but was deemed 'the most inexplicable packet' during his single term as a Fossil. Despite such criticism of his in-and-out form, however, Albert missed but two games that season. He then joined Bristol City (along with Harry Davy) for their first Southern League campaign, and their first since jettisoning their Bristol South End monicker, scoring four times in their first-ever FA Cup tie. Contrastingly, Thames Ironworks were in their final year under that name when Albert assisted them (becoming West Ham United upon his departure). He was reported to have regained amateur status from the FA in August 1903, but it is not known if he ever exercised it.

Apps: *FL 28; FAC 3.*
Goals: *FL 10.*

CARR, Everton Dale

b. Antigua, West Indies, 11th January 1961

Career: app July 1977/pro Jan 1979 CITY; July 1981 Halifax Town; Mar 1983 Rochdale; cs 1983 Nuneaton Borough; July 1987 Weymouth; Oct 1987 Bath City; Nov 1987 Barnet; Jan 1988 Nuneaton Borough; 1988 Oadby Town; 1990 Lutterworth Town; 1991 North Kilworth.

City debut v Fulham (A) 28.4.79 (sub)

> A New Parks schoolboy discovery, Everton was a pacy, harrying full-back given an early break by Jock Wallace as City's Second Division survival became assured at the end of 1978/9. Unfortunate to be sent off in his third game – a venomous, weakly refereed farce at Bramall Lane that marked relegated Sheffield United's farewell to Second Division football – he became an occasional stand-in for Dennis Rofe over the next couple of seasons, but couldn't claim a regular League spot until his move to The Shay. Everton later renewed his occasional City partnership with Willie Gibson at both Nuneaton and Weymouth; and while with the latter was involved in an amusing incident in a Conference game at Maidstone: entering the action as a half-time substitute, and then being booked a full 25 minutes later for not reporting the fact to a referee who'd only belatedly noted the only black player on the pitch!

Apps: *FL 11+1; LC 2.*

CARR, Franz Alexander

b. Preston, 24th September 1966

Career: app 1983 Blackburn Rovers; Aug 1984 Nottingham Forest; Dec 1989-loan-Sheffield Wednesday; Mar 1991-loan-West Ham United; June 1991 Newcastle United; Jan 1993 Sheffield United; Sept 1994 CITY; Feb 1995 Aston Villa; Sept 1996 Reggiana; Oct 1997 Bolton Wanderers; Feb 1998 West Bromwich Albion.

City debut v Wimbledon (A) 10.9.94.

> Pretty much a saga of two contrasting decades, Franz's career was one of massive potential, partly realised in the 80s, but inexplicably betrayed after 1990. An untried teenage reserve at Ewood when Brian

Franz Carr

Clough purchased his traditional wing-play promise, he soon became a key Trentside attacker, exploiting explosive pace and fine dribbling skills, and earning nine England Under-21 caps. Franz was twice in victorious Forest teams at Wembley: coming on as sub to lay on the winning goal against Everton in the 1989 Simod Cup Final, and contributing a year later to the League Cup eclipse of Oldham. Inconsistency was already setting in, however, and dogged his progress thereafter, as Franz tended to drift through his later clubs. The flashes of high excitement were becoming rarities amidst stretches of marginalised anonymity, and this pattern was repeated during a month's loan in the Premiership with City, surprisingly turned into a £100,000 permanent move by Brian Little. Over-intricacy had largely taken the place of directness in Franz's flank-play, and he made only a single appearance in a Mark McGhee line-up before being unloaded back to Little's care in the part-exchange/peace-making deal which more profitably brought Garry Parker to Leicester. It was then a year before Franz made his first Villa start; though ironically his goal against Forest put his new team into the 1996 FA Cup semi-finals. A brief stint in Serie A's relegation zone brought no joy; and Franz would start but one game for his final pair of English clubs, and make no impact from the bench.

Apps: *PL 12+1.*
Goals: *PL 1.*

CARR, George

b. South Bank, nr Middlesbrough, 19th January 1899

Career: Nov 1916 Bradford Park Avenue; June 1919 Middlesbrough; Feb 1924 CITY; Aug 1932 Stockport County; May 1933 Nuneaton Town (p/mgr).

City debut v Coventry City (H) 23.2.24 (scored once)

> A beefy, hard-shooting inside-forward when signed by Peter Hodge – having played First Division football at Ayresome alongside his brothers Willie and England international Jacky – George scored the goal (against Bradford City) which guaranteed City promotion in 1925, and proved a splendid linkman between left-winger Harold Wadsworth and spearhead Arthur Chandler. The broken leg he suffered at Filbert Street against Leeds during the next term was so severe that several spectators nearby fainted, to be revived with salts and water by Duncan and Chandler, but it proved a different sort of turning point in George's career. For after returning with a compen-satory hat-trick against the same opponents, it was not long before he switched with signal success to the pivotal position of centre-half (he had, in fact, played there as a teenager in wartime football for Bradford Park Avenue; at a stage when he also guested for

Chesterfield Municipal). From here George provided the bedrock from which City's best-ever First Division attack launched its two near-miss assaults on the title. Fine clubmanship kept him at Leicester for three more terms in which his services were called on less regularly, and his active senior career ended with a season at Edgeley Park, but he had more than one favour still to grant City. The first was his signing and sale of George Dewis, the next his advocacy of City 'adopting' Middlesbrough Swifts (whence came Don Revie) as their nursery team during WW2, and the last his role as the club's Northeast scout in the early postwar years. In the interim, he had managed Cheltenham Town from May 1935 to March 1937, found himself on a shortlist of two with ex-Fossil Angus Seed for the Barnsley management job during that latter month, and had successively taken over the Zetland Hotel at Marske and the Black Swan in North Ormesby. As a part-time coach to Stockton, he was playing as a permit amateur for their reserves as late as December 1938; and his coaching work both there and at South Bank occupied some of his time after the war. Brother Jacky was an unsuccessful interviewee for the City manager's post taken by Frank Womack in October 1936; while yet another Carr brother – Henry, the eldest – had actually preceded the other three into the Middlesbrough first team in 1911.

***Apps:** FL 179; FAC 13.*
***Goals:** FL 24; FAC 1.*

CARRIGAN, Patrick

b. Cleland, Lanarkshire, 5th July 1898 (?)

Career: Douglas Water Thistle; Oct 1923 CITY; Mar 1930 Sheffield United; Sept 1933-trials-Southend United; Nov 1933 Hinckley United.

City debut v Bury (A) 2.1.24

> In six-and-a-half years on the books, Pat was City's regular first-choice centre-half for only one full season, but his sturdy efforts towards securing the Second Division championship of 1925 were due substantial credit, and likewise his loyalty subsequently as an ever-reliable reserve to the likes of Norman Watson and George Carr. Indeed, it was only the signing of Roger Heywood in 1929 which prompted a transfer request from a frustrated Pat, and a reasonable £1,750 cheque from the top-flight Blades which finally prised him away. When his First Division days were over, Pat actually faced City's reserves during his Southend trial, but it was the Yorkshire club's insistence on a fee which deterred the Shrimpers from signing him. City's seconds were also the opposition when Pat appeared at right-back for Hinckley in the 1935 County Cup Final. The legitimate query over his birthdate arises from the *Mercury's* contemporary report that he was aged only 22 on signing.

***Apps:** FL 75; FAC 7.*
***Goals:** FL 3.*

CARROLL, James (Tony)

b. Glasgow

Career: Strathclyde; Newry Town; cs 1928 Belfast Celtic; June 1931 Shelbourne; cs 1933 Clyde; Feb 1935 CITY; June 1938 Luton Town; Feb 1940 Ayr United.

City debut v Preston North End (A) 23.2.35

> A late recruit by Arthur Lochhead to City's eventually futile attempt to avoid relegation in 1935, Tony was a small, nippy outside-right with an eye for goal (registering 15 in 1935/6 alone), whose more orthodox crossing skills also provided Jack Bowers with many an opening as the club bounced back to the top flight in 1937. Tony's championship medal was not his first: he'd contributed to Belfast Celtic's 116-goal attack as they took the Irish title in 1929, though he missed that year's IFA Cup Final defeat. He was twice a semi-finalist in the equivalent FAI competition with Shelbourne, and had featured in the Scottish First Division as well before joining City. Tony was not the luckiest of players with injuries – missing the early part of the City promotion season with a broken shoulder sustained in a summer car crash in Scotland, and severely injuring his ankle on his Luton debut – but his fortune later changed substantially. For in March 1944, Tony was officially reported lost at sea as a result of enemy action; and he seriously surprised club personnel when he made a postwar visit to Filbert Street, having miraculously survived being marooned on a makeshift raft for some six weeks – losing four stones in weight – before being rescued! Tony then returned to the game for a short spell on New Brighton's training staff under Neil McBain.

***Apps:** FL: 94; FAC 3.*
***Goals:** FL 25; FAC 1.*

CARTER, Alfred Albert

b. ca 1868

Career: Notts Olympic; Notts Jardine; Heanor Town; Aug 1892 FOSSE (- 1893).

Fosse debut v Mansfield Town (A) ML 17.9.1892

> A hat-trick hero in Fosse's first pre-season friendly of 1892/3 (a 10-1 pasting of Singers, the team which spawned Coventry City), centre-forward Alf nonetheless bore the brunt of the local *Mercury's* disdain after the opening Midland League defeat at Mansfield: '... he is scarcely worth his place in the team, and from what transpired in the game on Saturday it could be seen that he was not to be trusted too much with the ball.' Only a trio of further outings at inside-left ensued for the former Midland Alliance teammate of Atkins and Stott.

***Apps:** ML 4.*
***Goals:** ML 1.*

CARTER, Roger

b. Leicestershire

Career: Hugglescote Robin Hoods; Aug 1898-trials-FOSSE; Bristol St George; Whitwick Town; Sept 1899 FOSSE; Whitwick Town; cs 1901 Whitwick White Cross.

Fosse debut/only game v Burslem Port Vale (A) 3.2.1900

> A local keeper whose first senior experience had come in both the Birmingham and District League and the Western League while in brief Bristolian exile, Roger had a decidedly dodgy time with Fosse. His unofficial bow came in the October 1899 friendly with the touring South African side, the Kaffirs, and he managed a clean sheet when deputising for Godfrey Beardsley in Division Two fare at Burslem, but his reserve-team form was reportedly so poor that only a month later, with Beardsley again absent, the Fosse selectors overlooked him and instead chose inside-forward Bertie Lyon as replacement goalie! He had his nightmares, too, with Senior League side Whitwick Town, letting in 16 goals against Aston Villa Reserves in a Walsall Cup tie; but later joined White Cross on their elevation to the Midland League.

***Apps:** FL 1.*

CHALMERS, Leonard Austin

b. Corby, Northants, 4th September 1936

Career: 1953 Corby Town; Jan 1956 CITY; June 1966 Notts County; July 1968 Dunstable Town.

City debut v Birmingham City (A) 26.4.58

> On National Service as a military policeman with the Northamptonshire Regiment at the time of his signing, Len gave over a decade's dedication to the City cause, but remains best remembered for two particular dramatic games. The first was his nervewracking debut, when City needed a point at St Andrews to avoid the drop on the 1957/8 season's final day (and took two with a fine smash'n'grab performance), and the second the 1961 Cup Final, when the crippling injury he suffered in the first half proved to be the turning point. In the interim, Len had switched from wing-half to right-back, a position he made his own for nigh on four seasons until displaced by John Sjoberg. An incisive tackler who was tagged affectionately as 'Chopper' some years before the nickname was revived for Chelsea's Ron Harris, he was in fact only once to get on the wrong side of a referee, when becoming the first (and so far only) City man to be sent off in a League Cup tie – at Charlton in 1962. He made one of his increasingly sporadic senior appearances in the first leg of the Final of that competition at Stamford Bridge in 1965. City's PFA representative, Len was actively involved on the Union executive in the 1961 negotiations to abolish the maximum wage. His two seasons at Meadow Lane saw him in League action for a further 51 games, adding one goal to his tally; while he followed his Dunstable stint with a period coaching Melita Tigers in New South Wales, before returning to settle in Northampton.

***Apps:** FL 171; FAC 20; FLC 9; ECWC 4.*
***Goals:** FL 4.*

CHANDLER, Arthur Clarence Hillier

b. Paddington, 27th November 1895
d. Leicester, 18th June 1984

Career: Hampstead Town; 1919 Handley-Page; am/pro Sept 1920 Queens Park Rangers; June 1923 CITY; June 1935 Notts County.

City debut v Hull City (A) 25.8.23

> Pretty much unrivalled for the title of City's greatest-ever marksman – Channy notched the highest aggregate and by far the most top-flight goals, even if Arthur Rowley had a marginally better goals-per-game ratio – this Cockney centre-forward was an inspired purchase by Peter Hodge, especially as he had but a mere 18 goals already to his credit, had been regarded by QPR primarily as a support player, and on grounds of age alone might have been deemed past his peak. Hard and courageous, but resilient, too – Arthur made a then-record 118 consecutive appearances from the date of his City debut – he bulged nets in both top Divisions with strikes delivered from every angle and distance, and seemingly with every part of his anatomy. Though, curiously, not a single penalty goal figures in his otherwise sure-shot record: the two he took for City were both saved, by Chelsea's Howard Baker in September 1924, and Sheffield Wednesday's Brown in November 1930. Arthur gave immediate notice at Filbert Street of his net-busting intent, scoring five times in the two pre-season practices of 1923 which preceded his official debut. He equalled Fred Shinton's long-standing seasonal scoring record for the club in the 1925 promotion drive, and eclipsed it with 34 goals in each of 1928 and 1929; and equalled Johnny Duncan's record of six goals in a game, when inaugurating the true legend of the six swans flying overhead during the 10-0 pasting of Portsmouth in October 1928. Arthur had less luck, though, in gaining the international recognition his efforts so clearly merited. The selectors first visited Filbert Street to run the rule over him in October 1926, when it was confidently expected he'd notch his 100th City goal against Sunderland: he did so in the first minute, and netted again after six minutes, but was then carried off. A lay-off of over seven weeks with a knee injury followed, and the immediate chance of a cap passed by. Irrepressible, though, Arthur marked his comeback with a five-goal salvo against Villa, after demanding that both his knees be bandaged before the game, so as not to alert defenders to the weaker one. Three times after this he played in the annual England trial (once for the North v South, twice for The Rest v England), and each time he scored; but a single appearance for the Football League – when they met the Scottish League at Filbert Street in 1927, and when for once Channy failed to register a goal – and a place on the 1929 FA tour of South Africa (which brought him a haul of 33 goals from 16 games, including six in the three 'Test Matches') were his only tangible honours. There was a tactical shrewdness to Arthur's game as well: it was his eager suggestion that the end-of-season friendly at Port Vale in May 1925 be played under the revised offside rule to come into force the next term, and he helped himself to a hat-trick from a 5-3 win. At senior level, his final tally of 17 hat-tricks or better is also a club record; as is his aggregate of 173 goals at Filbert Street. He remains the oldest man ever to score for City, and the oldest to play for them in the First Division. A consistently cheery character – whose off-field status within Leicester was indexed by such occasions as when he and popular comedian George Robey ('The Prime Minister of Mirth') were invited to play the first round at the city's first crazy golf course, installed at the Corn Exchange, in October 1930 – Arthur officially hung up his boots after adding half a dozen goals to his haul as a Magpie. But November 1936 saw him return to Filbert Street on the training staff – he would still be playing the odd game at centre-half for the Colts team he managed during 1938/9 – and he remained with the club in one backroom capacity or another – as living testimony to their and the game's best traditions – until September 1969, when persuaded to retire at the age of 73. His 1961/2 Testimonial (City v City Past XI) drew 13,206 to the gate, and a flood of grateful memories from supporters who'd seen him in his prime, though it would not be until the early 90s that the club formally recognised his pivotal role in their history by installing a cabinet of Channy memorabilia in the boardroom. Yet there was nothing in Arthur's early days to point forward to such status: he'd been a bookstall assistant on Paddington station who played the odd Sunday game on Wormwood Scrubs before WW1, when he served with the RGA in France. On his return, he worked as a gardener at a London boarding school, but his part-time football saw him representing the Middlesex Senior League against the Athenian League at Highbury, when he was recommended to QPR by their player – and former wartime Fossil – David Donald. The record books thereafter beckoned. (It should not be forgotten that Channy was a fine club cricketer, too: though the summer-game incident best remembered is that which occurred on 12th August 1937 when Arthur was summoned from Filbert Street to Aylestone Road to act as 12th man for both Leicestershire and Nottinghamshire, and contrived to field for both sides during three spells on the pitch!). His cousin Sid Chandler was the only other footballer in the family: a half-back for Southall, Aston Villa reserves, Preston North End and Reading.

***Apps:** FL 393; FAC 26.*
***Goals:** FL 259; FAC 14.*

CHAPMAN, Vernon William

b. Leicester, 9th May 1921

Career: Aylestone United; Leicester Nomads; Mar 1939 Ibstock Penistone Rovers; Bath City; Mar 1941 CITY; July 1947 Leyton Orient; Aug 1949 Brush Sports; cs 1951 Burton Albion; Tamworth (p/mgr).

City debut (WW2) v Lincoln City (H) 14.4.41 (scored once); (postwar) v Swansea Town (H) 12.4.47

> Initially marked as a teenage rugby prospect (a Wyggeston fly-half), Vernon was first noted by City for his round-ball prowess when he faced the reserves in the 1939 County Cup Final as Ibstock's centre-forward. Signed prior to his departure on RAF service (which involved flight training in Canada), and showing a decent goal-sense in senior regional football, he made an indelible scoring mark with City's colts in September 1941 when netting ten times in a 17-0 demolition of Holwell Works. Yet Vernon was to get but a single opportunity at postwar League level, deputising for Mal Griffiths at outside-right in a 0-1 home defeat barely a month or so before his transfer listing. A £550 fee took him to Brisbane Road, where he notched seven goals from 31 games in the Third Division (South). His transition to management accomplished at Tamworth, Vernon returned to the county for spells as Enderby Town boss in both the early 60s and mid-70s, bracketing a spell as manager/ physiotherapist at Oadby Town. He also acted as physio to a joint Oxford/Cambridge University football XI on a 1969 Japanese tour.

***Apps:** FL 1; WW2 11.*
***Goals:** WW2 6.*

CHARLES, Gary Andrew

b. Newham, London, 13th April 1970

Career: app July 1986/pro Nov 1987 Nottingham Forest; Mar 1989-loan-CITY; July 1993 Derby County; Jan 1995 Aston Villa; Jan 1999 Benfica; Aug 1999 West Ham United; Sept 2000-loan-Birmingham City.

City debut v Birmingham City (H) 25.3.89 (sub)

> A teenage full-back given his initial Trentside break by Brian Clough as an emergency right-winger, Gary joined City on a month's loan as defensive cover when Tony Spearing was facing imminent suspension, but soon earned an extension to the season's end after displaying a surprising amount of mature confidence both on and off the ball. Indeed, his form was sufficiently exciting to gain him and England Under-21 squad call-up after only seven weeks at Filbert Street. Gary eventually won four such honours, and stepped up to full international level on England's 1991 summer tour, by which time he had registered his initial Forest goal in the FA Cup semi-final against West Ham, and earned a runners-up medal from the ensuing Final (when he was the victim of a notorious Paul Gascoigne tackle). He then picked up a victor's medal at Wembley from the ZDS Cup Final of 1992 (after Forest had eliminated City

Gary Charles

at the penultimate stage), but was suffering a severe loss of confidence when involved in Forest's relegation a year later. His first Derby season ended in Play-Off defeat at City's hands, and Gary became a transfer target for Brian Little in October 1994, but no deal transpired until Little had decamped to Villa Park, where he took Gary and Tommy Johnson in a joint £2.9 million deal. A League Cup winner in 1996, Gary then missed the entirety of the next term through injury, and was no longer guaranteed a place on his return. A Graeme Souness purchase for Benfica, he survived there only a little longer than his boss, and joined the Hammers after ludicrously protracted negotiations for £1.2 million. His story since, however, has been something of a two-year nightmare of non-involvement, spiced with the merest handful of senior selections and a drink-drive scrape with the law.

Apps: *FL 5+3.*

CHEATER, J.

b. ca 1882

Career: South Wigston Albion; Jan 1904 FOSSE; cs 1904 South Wigston Albion; South Wigston Primitive Methodists.

Fosse debut v Stockport County (H) 16.1.04

> Signed only days after his selection for a County XI v Lancashire, Cheater was one of three local full-backs called up for Second Division try-outs in the wake of George Mountain's sending off in Fosse's 1903/4 FA Cup exit. However, according to the *Mercury* at the time, he 'did not fulfil the high hopes formed about him', even in a side bound for a re-election bid. He nonetheless took a winners medal from the 1905 County Cup Final when South Wigston (also featuring Matt Bishop and the Benskin brothers) overcame Fosse's second string. It is believed that a contemporary local prospect named Cheater (initial 'P'), who featured for Countesthorpe United and Leicester Imperial, was probably a brother.

Apps: *FL 6.*

CHEESEBROUGH, Albert

b. Burnley, 17th January 1935

Career: Jan 1952 Burnley; June 1959 CITY; July 1963 Port Vale; July 1965 Mansfield Town.

City debut v West Ham United (A) 22.8.59

> A Matt Gillies signing at a not insubstantial fee of £19,775, Albert was a skilful, hard-shooting utility forward who'd made a First Division breakthrough with his hometown club at the age of 17, had won one England Under-23 cap, and had poached a hat-trick off City in November 1957. A left-winger converted to inside-forward at Turf Moor, he was temporarily converted back again by City for what proved his most important matches, standing in for injury victim Gordon Wills in five games of the 1961 FA Cup run, including the Final. Albert also featured as a pacy support striker in almost half the games of the 1962/3 Double-chasing season, but missed out on a second Wembley selection, and was soon off on Third Division travels after Vale invested their record fee of £15,000 in him. Cartilage trouble hindered him there, and a broken leg spelled the end of his Field Mill stint. Albert became a Southport businessman, and at one time a Lancashire scout for Plymouth Argyle. His daughter Susan became an international gymnast.

Apps: *FL 122; FAC 11; LC 4; ECWC 1.*
Goals: *FL 40; FAC 2; LC 1.*

CHENEY, Dennis

b. Coalville, Leics, 30th June 1924

Career: Feb 1939 Coalville Town; am Mar 1940/pro Nov 1941 CITY; Jan 1948-loan-Watford; Oct 1948 Bournemouth & Boscombe Athletic; June 1954 Aldershot; Aug 1956 Dorchester Town.

City debut (WW2) v Mansfield Town (H) 9.11.40; (postwar) v Fulham (H) 30.8.47

> A graduate of the Coalville Boys team who made his wartime City debut as a 16-year-old, top-scored youthfully for the club in 1941/2, and saw active service in Singapore before his 1947 demob, Dennis only twice deputised for Charlie Adam in the No 11 shirt in peacetime. The second occasion was after he'd returned from being the loan component of the famous five-man transfer to Watford, having scored five times in his 18-game Vicarage Road stint, but a permanent move further south soon beckoned. Switched successfully to the centre-forward berth at Dean Court, Dennis ended his senior career with a very respectable 71-goal League aggregate, all scored in Division Three (South).

Apps: *FL 2; WW2 42.*
Goals: WW2 22.

CHISHOLM, Kenneth McTaggart

b. Glasgow, 12th April 1925
d. Chester-le-Street, Co Durham 4th May 1990

Career: Feb 1942 Queens Park; cs 1946 Partick Thistle; Jan 1948 Leeds United; Dec 1948 CITY; Mar 1950 Coventry City; Mar 1952 Cardiff City; Dec 1953 Sunderland; Aug 1956 Workington; Jan 1958 Glentoran (p/mgr); June 1958 Spennymoor United; 1959 Los Angeles Kickers.

City debut (WW2) v Chelsea (H) 12.1.46; (postwar) v Coventry City (H) 1.1.49

> His penchant for dressing-room comedy only rivalled by his instinct for controversy, Ken was a distinctly forceful character in 40s and 50s football, unwilling to let only his on-field skills do his talking for him. A Hampden amateur when called up for bomber pilot service with the RAF, he prefigured his later nomadic tendency with a series of wartime guest outings: for Manchester City in 1943/4, and for each of Leicester, Bradford Park Avenue, Chelsea and Portsmouth in 1945/6, when his form with Queens Park was good enough additionally to earn him a call-up for Scotland's 'Victory International' against Ireland. Thereafter, Ken embraced profession-alism with something of a vengeance. A hefty, bustling inside-forward with fine heading ability and a pile-driving left foot, he eventually arrived at Filbert Street on a permanent contract when Johnny Duncan pushed through the club's first five-figure transfer deal: a cash-plus-player affair which saw Ray Iggleden and a cheque for £11,000 on their way to Elland Road. In his first term, joker-in-the-pack 'Chizzy' helped City to both Wembley and Second Division survival; scoring a semi-final goal and having a potential equaliser disallowed for a marginal offside in the Cup Final, and missing only the last, crucial League game at Cardiff. Some 36 years later, Ken would cause only a muted controversy with his published claim that this match was effectively squared beforehand; though he would figure in further scandal in the interim. He left Leicester in another deal involving a player-exchange, with Jack Marsh joining City from Highfield Road, and his time with both Coventry and Cardiff – he switched from the relegation-bound Bantams to the promotion-bound Bluebirds – was relatively quiet (even if he sub-sequently claimed to have played in another rigged match for the latter against Leeds). Indeed, it was not until he'd left top-flight Sunderland that Ken became centrally involved in the joint League/FA investigation of illegal overpayments at Roker, with his eventual admission of receiving the same accompanied by a letter claiming to have done likewise at each of Partick, Leeds and Leicester. Denials and lack of evidence kept these three clubs out of scrutiny, but Ken was one of several Sunderland men initially banned, then forced to forfeit part of their accrued benefit money. Not long afterwards, Ken left his current club Workington in the lurch when walking out on his contract to take on player-manager duties in Belfast. His colourful playing career eventually finished in Los Angeles, where he was additionally employed as a newspaper ad-man, and where he broke his leg in the penultimate game of a season in which his team became California State champions. He later worked in the insurance business in the North East.

Apps: *FL42; FAC 7; WW2 3.*
Goals: *FL 17; FAC 2; WW2 1.*

CHRISTENSEN, Thomas Anton

b. Aarhus, Denmark, 20th July 1961

Career: AGF (Aarhus); Dec 1979 PSV Eindhoven; 1981 AGF (Aarhus); Vejle BK; Feb 1985 Elche CF; Nov 1985-loan-CITY; Nov 1985-loan-Portsmouth; 1986 Brøndby IF; Aug 1987 Vejle BK; July 1988 Eintracht Braunschweig; 1990 (Danish football - club n/k).

City debut v Southampton (H) 9.11.85 (sub)

> Tommy's was very much a fits-and-starts career, outside of his native Denmark, at least. A compact blond striker who became a teenage fringe player with PSV in Holland, he returned home to be rewarded with one cap: from a four-minute substitute appearance in a June 1983 game v Finland in his home town. Later, unsettled in Spain following Elche's relegation, he came to City on trial and made an immediate first-team impact when coming on for 30 minutes against Southampton and bringing the best out of Peter Shilton. A week later, however, he shared in a generally inept struggle on QPR's artificial pitch. A further three reserve outings, featuring one goal, were still insufficient to make up Gordon Milne's mind for him, but he was unsuccessful in extending Tommy's stay. A four-game spell at Fratton Park then brought two League counters, but was ended by injury. Tommy later re-emerged once more from Danish football to try his luck in the German Second Division ('2 Bundesliga'). He was not, incidentally, the first Dane to figure in a Leicester line-up: a student named Sandval having played centre-forward for the reserves at Brentford in September 1951.

Apps: *FL 1+1.*

CHRISTIE, Trevor John

b. Widdrington, Northumberland, 28th February 1959

Career: app Sept 1975/pro Dec 1976 CITY; June 1979 Notts County; June 1984 Nottingham Forest; Feb 1985 Derby County; Aug 1986 Manchester City; Oct 1986 Walsall; Mar 1989 Mansfield Town; July 1991 Kettering Town; Mar 1992 VS Rugby; cs 1992 Hucknall Town (p/coach); Mar 1995 Arnold Town.

City debut v Wolverhampton Wanderers (H) 25.2.78

> Originally recommended to City by John Farrington's father, then given a senior break by Frank McLintock virtually as a premature 19th birthday present, gangling striker Trevor went on to become City's top scorer during Jock Wallace's first season in charge (albeit with only 8 Second Division goals), but was somewhat inhibited by having to take on so much responsibility so young. His front-running, heading and ball-shielding skills only fully developed following his move to Meadow Lane, where his confidence flowered. A number of his 63 goals for the Magpies helped them into the First Division in 1981, while another three rudely welcomed City back into the top flight on the opening day of 1983/4. Brian Clough invested £165,000 to take Trevor the short distance across the Trent, but soon off-loaded him to Derby, where he missed but one game of the Third Division championship campaign of 1986. Then surprisingly swapped for Mark Lillis, Trevor had only a short stay at Maine Road (though there hitting his 100th aggregate League goal) before joining Walsall and contributing to both their fine 1987 Cup run and their 1988 promotion to Division Two. By then an experienced mentor to the young David Kelly at Fellows Park, Trevor later performed a similar role alongside Steve Wilkinson at Mansfield. Extending the City connections, Trevor also benefitted himself from the midfield promptings of his near-contemporary, Mark Goodwin, at each of Leicester, Notts, Walsall and Hucknall.

Apps: *FL 28+3; LC 1.*
Goals: *FL 8.*

CLARIDGE, Stephen Edward

b. Portsmouth, 10th April 1966

Career: app 1982 Portsmouth; Aug 1984 Fareham Town; Nov 1984 Bournemouth; Oct 1985 Weymouth; July 1988 Basingstoke Town; Aug 1988 Crystal Palace; Oct 1988 Aldershot; Feb 1990 Cambridge United; July 1992 Luton Town; Nov 1992 Cambridge United; Jan 1994 Birmingham City; Mar 1996 CITY; Jan 1998-loan-Portsmouth; Mar 1998 Wolverhampton Wanderers; Aug 1998 Portsmouth (p/mgr Oct 2000-Mar 2001); Mar 2001-loan-Millwall.

City debut v Ipswich Town (A) 3.3.96

> Steve's entertaining autobiography, published in April 1997, took the title 'Tales from the Boot Camps'. By the time of the paperback edition it could well have been retitled 'Fairy Tales from the Blue Camp'. For the narrative of the journeyman footballer discovering autumnal glory with a late surge into the big time had been even more fantastically capped in the interim, as its subject shot his club to their first knock-out trophy in 33 years, and onward into Europe. Steve was already well known as an effective socks-down striker, a willing runner with good back-to-goal control and a decent lower-League strike rate, when Martin O'Neill snapped him up for City from St Andrews. Yet a fee set to rise from £1 million to £1.2 million seemed a lot at the time for a 29-year-old, especially so soon after Julian Joachim had departed for only £1.5 million, and even more so when it was known Steve was suffering from a thyroid problem. Early appearances were inconclusive, if scoreless, but it was Steve's first City strike, the winning goal at Charlton, which saw the 1996 promotion bid revived in earnest, and it was he who would have the last-gasp last laugh that term as his exquisitely 'shinned' extra-time decider flashed past Nigel Martyn to give City a Wembley Play-Off triumph over a club who'd rejected the scorer, untried, back in 1988. His ragamuffin enjoyment in the subsequent Premiership campaign was evident to all, and his foraging skills and marksmanship in no way out of place. But not only did he take top-scorer slot that term, plus the Goal of the Season award for his blinding volley from an Emile Heskey flick against Manchester United, plus the Midland Player of the Year kudos. Steve also managed to hook home the extra-time winner which stunned Middlesbrough at Hillsborough, gave City the League Cup and opened the door to the UEFA Cup. No matter whatsoever that only one further City goal would come from the hero who had deservedly become far too popular to qualify for mere cult status; or even that he played a half-dozen games for hissable villain Mark McGhee after a £400,000 deadline-day move to Molineux. Super Steve's place in City lore is more than secure. The irony of his next transfer, back to hometown Pompey, would not be lost on Steve, for he left Fratton first time around without ever being given a chance. Not making much impact at Dean Court, either, he substantially rebuilt his career in the Conference, took the various disappointments of rejection at Palace and relegation at Aldershot in his stride, then plugged into the upward momentum of a Cambridge side which rose rapidly under the eccentric John Beck from the League basement to the Play-Off portals guarding the new Premiership (where City emphatically denied them entry). Second time around at the Abbey, it was a relegation scenario in which Steve found himself, but he was on the promotion trail again with Birmingham as 1995 saw them installed as champions of the (new) Division Two as well as Wembley winners of the Associate Members Cup. Whether Steve himself – a noted gambler – would have bet on the next chapter turning out as it did is doubtful; certainly not so is the feeling that City took a bumper payout from Martin O'Neill's flutter on the outsider. During season 2000/1, Steve tasted management responsibility himself, briefly helping revive Pompey as player-boss until deposed by Graham Rix; and then shifted base again to add his scoring weight to Millwall's Division Two championship run-in.

Apps: *FL/PL 53+10; FAC 4; LC 8; UEFA 0+1; PO 3.*
Goals: *FL/PL 16; FAC 1; LC 2; PO 1.*

CLARK, William

b. Airdrie, Lanarkshire, ca 1881
d. Bristol, 17th March 1937

Career: 1900 Port Glasgow Athletic; May 1904 Bristol Rovers; May 1908 Sunderland; Oct 1910 Bristol City; Aug 1911 FOSSE.

Fosse debut v Gainsborough Trinity (A) 2.9.11

> 'Has lightsome heels ... brings the ball into quick subjection'. So the *Mercury* summed up the speed and skill of outside-right Willie, but both attributes were soon to be deemed inferior to those of Tommy Benfield as a fine career came to its end. Willie had assisted Port Glasgow to the Scottish League's Second Division championship in 1902 and Bristol Rovers to the Southern League title in 1905 (when playing alongside Dick Pudan and Albert Dunkley). His time at Roker and Ashton Gate was all spent in the top flight, though Bristol City suffered relegation prior to Willie's move to Fosse. He was twice chosen in the Anglo-Scots v Home Scots international trial game: having to cry off in 1906, but playing in the March 1908 fixture. After giving up the game, Willie ran a couple of pubs in Bristol, and was proprietor of the Clifton Wood Wine & Spirits Vaults at the time of his death.

Apps: *FL 6.*
Goals: *FL 1.*

CLARKE, Allan John

b. Willenhall, Staffs, 31st July 1946

Career: app 1961/pro Aug 1963 Walsall; Mar 1966 Fulham; June 1968 CITY; June 1969 Leeds United; June 1978 Barnsley (p/mgr).

City debut v Queens Park Rangers (A) 10.8.68 (scored once)

> An instinctive goalscorer whose transfers both to and from City created new British records (at £150,000 and £165,000 respectively), Allan began his Filbert Street year as a tangible symbol of the club's ambition; soon ingratiated himself to the fans with a hat-trick (against Manchester City) amongst his early goal flow; but increasingly came to look something of a luxury as 1968/9 unexpectedly developed into an earnest relegation struggle. He was clearly a man for the big occasion (scoring the FA Cup semi-final winner against West Brom, then taking the Man of the Match award at Wembley), but his apparently leisurely style seemed at odds with the requirements of a scramble for safety points. The slender striker added one Under-23 cap to his burgeoning representative tally while with City (his admirably consistent marksmanship at both Fellows Park and Craven Cottage having first caught the selectorial eye), but only made the breakthrough to full international honours after being snapped up by Don Revie. Nicknamed 'Sniffer' at Elland Road in recognition of his clinical penalty-area poaching skills, Allan played in three FA Cup Finals for Leeds (scoring their winner in 1972), scored in their 1971 Fairs Cup victory, won a championship medal in 1974 after a trio of League runners-up placings, and was in the side beaten in the 1975 European Cup Final. He led Barnsley out of the Fourth Division in his first term of player-management, then returned to Leeds as boss; subsequently also managing Scunthorpe United, Barnsley again, and Lincoln City. Allan, who actually chose to join City in preference to Manchester United, and has subsequently gone on record with the claim he'd have stayed at Filbert Street had it not been for the mid-season departure of Matt Gillies, now lives in Scunthorpe and works as a rep for a Wakefield plant-hire firm. His brothers Frank (who faced him for QPR on his City debut), Derek, Kelvin and Wayne each also carved out senior football careers, and the latter became another expensive City purchase in June 1989.

Apps: *FL 36; FAC 8; LC 2.*
Goals: *FL 12; FAC 1; LC 3*

CLARKE, Bernard Maurice

b. Leicester, 2nd March 1891

Career: St Peters; Dec 1919 CITY; July 1921 Halifax Town; Sept 1921 Barwell United.

City debut v Clapton Orient (A) 28.8.20

> A right-back who spent much of the first post-WW1 season as an amateur in City's reserves, Bernard then signed professional forms, and found himself almost immediately elevated to deputise for the injured Billy Barrett in the opening trio of fixtures of 1920/1. Bernard himself would miss the bulk of the term on the injury list (October to March), though, and never played League football again, for his move to The Shay, for the first-ever Division Three (North) campaign, simply did not work out.

Apps: *FL 3.*

CLARKE, Malcolm McQueen G.

b. Clydebank, 29th June 1944

Career: Johnstone Burgh; Aug 1964 CITY; Aug 1967 Cardiff City; July 1969 Bristol City; July 1970 Hartlepool; 1972 APIA-Leichardt.

City debut/only game v Leeds United (H) 18.9.65 (sub)

> Dubiously distinguished by having had the shortest-ever first-team career with City, wing-half Malcolm was called on as No 12 in the 89th minute of his sole League game – curiously, as both John Sjoberg and Derek Dougan simultaneously left the field injured – and was reliably reported not to have touched the ball during the remainder of play! Malcolm initially underwent successful trials at Leicester in January 1964, but his signing awaited Johnstone Burgh's exit from the Scottish Junior Cup – a competition they went on to win. His frustrating Filbert Street experience came to an end when he joined Cardiff after a three-month trial, going on to become a scorer in their 1968 Welsh Cup Final win (an aggregate victory over Hereford United) and to aid the Bluebirds' surprising progress to the semi-finals of the European Cup Winners Cup. Given few chances at Ashton Gate, Malcolm then played alongside Nick Sharkey in a re-election campaign at Hartlepool, before trying his luck in Sydney, Australia. His younger brother Colin forged a fine 13-year career with Oxford United.

Apps: *FL 0+1.*

Malcolm Clarke

CLARKE, Patrick

b. Dundalk, ca 1914

Career: Dundalk; May 1934 CITY; July 1938 Bristol City; June 1939 Hull City; 1939 Sligo Rovers; 1945 Leicester Frith (p/coach).

City debut/only game v Manchester City (A) 2.2.35

> Recommended to City by the Leicester-born Dundalk boss Steve Wright, left-back Paddy had anything but the luck of the Irish during his career. His sole League outing with City came when both Adam Black and Sandy Wood were unable to turn out in the above 3-6 defeat, and he had to settle for becoming the Mr Consistency of the Combination over the next three years, with his reserve-team labours bringing him the scant consolation of a haul of four County Cup winners medals. Nonetheless, he came close to a cap when the Irish Free State FA checked with City on his likely availability for their European tour of May 1936, but then omitted him from the final party. He fared little better at Ashton Gate, where a single selection in a Division Three (South) Cup tie against Torquay was his first-team lot; while the outbreak of war stymied his chances at Hull. Eventually, Paddy retrained as a masseur and hospital nurse, and returned as such to Leicester after the war.

Apps: *FL 1.*

CLARKE, Wayne

b. Wolverhampton, 28th February 1961

Career: app/pro Mar 1978 Wolverhampton Wanderers; Aug 1984 Birmingham City; March 1987 Everton; June 1989 CITY; Jan 1990 Manchester City; Oct 1990-loan-Shrewsbury Town; March 1991-loan-Stoke City; Sept 1991-loan-Wolverhampton Wanderers; July 1992 Walsall; Aug 1993 Shrewsbury Town; cs 1995 Telford United (p/mgr).

City debut v Hull City (A) 19.8.89 (scored once)

> The youngest of the five footballing Clarke brothers, Wayne won both schools and youth caps and made a Division One debut for Wolves at the age of 17, going on to experience two relegation campaigns and one promotion while wearing the Old Gold. An £80,000 move to St Andrews saw him become leading scorer in the Blues' 1985 promotion side, but characteristic West Midlands yo-yo-ing had him poaching against Second Division defences again before he was added to Everton's 1987 championship squad to contribute tellingly to the title run-in. Wayne claimed the Wembley winner in the Charity Shield pipe-opener to the 1987/8 season, but was thereafter never quite certain of a first-team striking slot at Goodison against the competition offered by Heath, Sharp and, latterly, Tony Cottee. Following brother Allan to Leicester at a twenty-year remove, as a £250,000 element of the deal which took Mike Newell northward, he showed typical predatory instincts in scoring on his City debut, but instilled something of a sad sense of déja vu in older City watchers who saw his leisurely style as inappropriate to the needs of a David Pleat side struggling to make its Second Division mark, especially as it brought next to no goal dividends. The New Year of 1990 saw Wayne return to fitness after a lengthy injury lay-off, but immediately involved in another part-exchange deal in which Howard Kendall signed him for the second time, and David Oldfield made the opposite journey from Maine Road. Not a great deal of first-team football came his way over the next couple of years, until his revived goal touch shot Walsall to the Third Division Play-Offs in 1993, and assisted Shrewsbury to the title of the same section a year later. His move into the Conference came after he'd amassed an aggregate League tally of 141 goals; though his tenure at Telford lasted only until November 1996.

Apps: *FL 10+1; LC 1.*
Goals: *FL 1; LC 1.*

CLAY, Thomas

b. Leicester, 19th November 1892
d. Southend, 21st February 1949

Career: 1906 Belvoir SS; Aug 1910-trials-Leicester Nomads; Apr 1911 FOSSE; Jan 1914 Tottenham Hotspur; June 1929 Northfleet (p/coach).

Fosse debut v Bradford Park Avenue (A) 25.11.11

> A teenage prodigy as an unflappable full-back in local football circles – he had been skippering Belvoir SS from the age of 13, and led them to the Mutual League Division Two title in 1911 – Tommy rapidly stepped up to first-team action with the Fosse when Billy Henry moved to Manchester City. A cultured thinker and passer of the ball in an age of generally hoof-happy defenders, he shone regularly in a struggling side, and following the epic FA Cup tussles with Spurs in 1914, he and Harry Sparrow were togther snapped up by the victors. At White Hart Lane, Tommy captained the Second Division championship side of 1920, and starred in both the FA Cup-winning team of 1921 and the League runners-up campaign of 1922; became a sure-shot penalty expert and a fine tactical manipulator of the offside trap; and was even chosen for one game as goalkeeper (keeping a clean sheet at Sunderland in March 1921). After playing 351 League and Cup games for Spurs (plus another 107 wartime matches), and sharing in their relegation of 1928, he was entrusted with inspiring the youngsters at their nursery club in, first, the Southern League, then the Kent League. Tommy (who also guested for Notts County during WW1) won four full England caps after 1920, and represented the Football League once, but the oft-repeated claim that he was the first Leicester-born man to play for his country is erroneous – that honour had fallen to Small Heath Alliance goalkeeper Christopher Charles Charsley in 1893. Tommy's active involvement with football closed with spells coaching (from July 1931) at St Albans and (briefly in early 1939) for the Dutch FA. He had a parallel cricket career which had seen him as a Leicestershire trialist in June 1923, and employed as cricket coach at each of Highgate School (1926), St Pauls, West Kensington (1927), Berkhamstead School (1928 & 1929) and St Albans School. In 1932 he ran a pub in the latter town, and from 1934 a sports outfitters' business; though Tommy was working as a builder's labourer at the time of his death.

Apps: *FL 63; FAC 6.*

Tommy Clay

COATSWORTH, Gary

b. Sunderland, 7th October 1968

Career: 1986 Barnsley; cs 1989 Darlington; Oct 1991 CITY; Apr 1995 Spennymoor United; 1996 Nissan (Sunderland).

City debut v Portsmouth (A) 5.11.91 (sub)

> Utterly unceremonious but usually effective, Gary was a tough-tackling, no-frills defender signed initially as cover for broken-leg victim Tony James. He had previously played under Brian Little for Darlington, and had entered Quakers folklore when, in but his third appearance of their 1989/90 Conference campaign, he scored the only goal of their final fixture at Welling to book their return to the League. After only three senior games for City, Gary faced two operations to repair cruciate ligament damage, but came back bravely; marking his 1992/3 return to Oakwell (as City's right-back on the ground where his League career had started) with a joyous two-goal contribution to a 3-2 away win. Where Gary's defensive interventions (also occasionally used to buttress midfield) were often decisive, his distribution could just as often appear clumsy; but City still had reason to be grateful for even this aspect of his play when, in what unfortunately turned out to be his final senior outing, his up-and-under cross from the right led to Steve Walsh's equaliser in the Play-Off Final against Derby. Further injury problems denied Gary any part in the subsequent Premiership struggle, and he was forced to bow out of full-time football early in 1995.

Apps: *FL 27+5; FAC 1; FMC 0+1; AIC 0+1; PO 3.*
Goals: *FL 4.*

COCHRANE, Michael

b. Belfast
d. Belfast, 13th April 1912

Career: Milltown; Distillery; May 1900 FOSSE; Mar 1901 Middlesbrough; cs 1901 Distillery.

Fosse debut v Small Heath (A) 8.9.1900

> Distillery's skipper and a regular Irish international, right-back Mick came to Leicester only two years after a Celtic bid of £200 had failed to land him in Glasgow. An ever-present from the date of his debut to that of his transfer, he also won the last of his eight caps while on Fosse's books (in a team unfortunately humiliated by a 0-11 scoreline in Scotland). During his first stint in hometown football, he had also represented the Irish League on four occasions, as well as featuring alongside ex-Fossil Arthur Worrall in the annual Belfast v Derry fixture, and winning a championship gong in 1899; while on his return, Mick took a runners-up medal from the 1902 Irish Cup Final, when a John Mercer-inspired Linfield beat Distillery 5-1. He managed only half a dozen outings for Boro.

Apps: *FL 27; FAC 1.*

CODD, Thomas H.

Career: Goole Town; Aug 1914 FOSSE.

Fosse debut v Arsenal (A) 26.12.14

> A well-respected outside-left in the Midland League, Tommy had anything but a happy introduction to Second Division football – his first two games both being 0-6 defeats. Nonetheless, he retained his Fosse flank position for most of the remainder of the ignominious final pre-war season, closing his career in a 5-1 victory! The local *Mail* critic couldn't have known, though, the accuracy of his description of Tommy as being 'of the persevering kind'. For, after enlisting in the Footballers Battalion in April 1915, he lost his left eye and suffered shell shock in action at Vimy Ridge on 1st June 1916 (being carried two miles under fire to safety by former Fossil Arthur Mounteney), yet was still happy less than four months later to volunteer to turn out for Fosse at Leeds, when it briefly looked like they would be unable to raise a full team. In fact Tommy did get one game before WW1 ended, for Grimsby Town. Postwar, he became musical director at Harrogate Hydro, then returned to Leicester and a business career in April 1933.

***Apps:** FL 13.*

COLES, Donald Stratton

b. Plymouth, 29th July 1879

Career: Ardingly College; Burgess Hill; Brighton Athletic; Brighton & Hove Rangers; cs 1901 Brighton & Hove Albion; Aug 1902 FOSSE; Dec 1902 Brighton & Hove Albion; 1904 (Sussex amateur football); 1905 St Leonards United.

Fosse debut/only game v Chesterfield (A) 13.9.02

> A slightly late start to the 1902/3 Second Division season saw Fosse choose their first-team for the opening Midland League fixture against Hinckley, and include new right-back Donald. He was the odd man out, however, when the initial League line-up was named; and then found himself heavily criticised (for playing too far forward, and lacking speed of recovery) on his only subsequent senior outing, a 0-5 defeat. His previous experience had come under former Fosse trainer John Jackson in the Southern League's Second Division, and his return to the Goldstone club brought a five-game contribution to their 1903 title-winning effort in that sphere.

***Apps:** FL 1.*

COLLINS, Arthur

b. Leicester, 29th May 1882

Career: Leicester Old Boys; Sept 1901 FOSSE; May 1905 Fulham; cs 1914 Norwich City.

Fosse debut v Blackpool (A) 28.3.02

> An elegantly constructive centre- or left-half in a distinctly struggling Fosse side, Arthur was one of the few individuals of substantial saleable value to have been caught up in the first re-election scare of 1904. Accordingly, after four year's service to his hometown club, there was a queue of suitors for his services. Derby and Southampton were both rejected, but he chose well in pledging himself to Fulham, for a nine-year union. A popular hero dubbed 'Prince Arthur' by the Craven Cottage crowd, he helped his side to two successive Southern League championships (1906 & 1907), and onward into the Second Division. He came close to England honours when playing in the 1906 Professionals v Amateurs international trial, and from 1909 served on the management committee of the Players Union. His Fulham benefit game (against Clapton Orient) came in April 1911, and it was not until the final pre-war season that he transferred back into the Southern League. For the first two terms of WW1 football, Arthur assisted Fosse; then in 1922 he returned to settle locally at Countesthorpe. His father, Tom, was a Fosse director from 1903 until his death in June 1913.

***Apps:** FL 82; FAC 14; WW1 47.*
***Goals:** FL 5.*

COLLYMORE, Stanley Victor

b. Cannock, Staffs, 22nd January 1971

Career: YT Wolverhampton Wanderers; 1989-trials-Walsall; 1989 Stafford Rangers; Jan 1991 Crystal Palace; Nov 1992 Southend United; July 1993 Nottingham Forest; July 1995 Liverpool; May 1997 Aston Villa; July 1999-loan-Fulham; Feb 2000 CITY; Oct 2000 Bradford City; Jan 2001 Real Oviedo (-Mar 2001).

City debut v Watford (A) 12.2.2000

> Rehabilitation was the single concept which was supposed to define Stan's short time at Leicester, but recrimination was the possibly predictable upshot. Initially, the striker with everything to prove on a personal and professional level seemed well-set to put some damning headlines and a hellish descent behind him. Stan clearly re-emphasised the depth of his talent in his first few games with City, evidencing a trojan front-running work-rate and – as highlighted by his home-debut hat-trick against Sunderland – a reawakened goal-hunger. It is idle to speculate how his pleasurably anticipated progress from there would have impacted on City's forward fortunes had he not been so cruelly knocked back by the broken leg he suffered at Derby; but it was the extent of his recovery from that mishap which became a crucial matter of contention between the player and his new manager, Peter Taylor. Convinced of his own fitness, his own worth, and his right to a place in the starting line-up, he nonetheless failed to convince his boss of his ability to put in 90 minutes-worth of effort. With a transfer request on the table, Stan then found himself fined for missing training, on an FA disrepute charge for an incident with Paul Gascoigne during his final senior City outing, involved in a dressing-room bust-up with teammate Trevor Benjamin at half-time in a reserve game, and soon offloaded on a free to Bradford. (Where he quickly set about courting controversy and cult status in equal measure, but was soon doomed to be regarded as an expensive luxury in a side free-falling to relegation. The briefest of stints in the Spanish sun then proved to be the mere prelude to premature retirement). Stan's potent on-field credentials actually took a while to establish in the early 90s, with a Conference spell initially compensating for release from Molineux, then the Mark Bright/Ian Wright combination barring the way to a first-team spot at Palace. But a streak of prolific action from Stan after Colin Murphy had taken him to Roots Hall suddenly escalated his value, and hastened the payment of the first of three seven-figure transfer fees the tall, pacy and skilful attacker would attract. He shot Forest up to the Premiership in 1994 and led their scoring chart in the following term, winning international recognition just before Liverpool made him the most expensive player in Britain at £8.5m. The first controversies of Stan's career erupted in a low-key at Anfield, where dividing lines were drawn by various factions between a goalscorer's natural selfishness and its subordination to team play, and the player's 'loner' tendency was first adduced as a problem. Stan remained a scoresheet regular, however, and picked up a runners-up medal from the 1996 FA Cup Final, before moving closer to his West Midlands base as a Brian Little signing. Injuries, suspensions and off-field disgrace blighted the early part of his Villa stay, however, and his subsequent admission that he was receiving counselling for clinical depression did not bring the most sympathetic of responses from his employers, with new manager John Gregory notably illiberal in his attitude. A brief spell at Craven Cottage shook some of the rustiness from a recovering Stan's game, and eventually Martin O'Neill negotiated a pay-as-you-play deal for the Villa Park outcast. The disproportionate tabloid furore over a prank with a fire extinguisher at City's training camp in La Manga paradoxically seemed to aid Stan's integration at Filbert Street, and his displays until his injury at Pride Park were distinctly happy reminders of both his class and charisma. It was a genuine pity that the self-destruct button was never thereafter far enough out of reach.

***Apps:** PL 7+4; UEFA 0+1.*
***Goals:** PL 5.*

CONNACHAN, James

b. Glasgow, 29th August 1874

Career: Duntocher Hibs; Glasgow Perthshire; Feb 1897 Celtic; Oct 1898 Airdrieonians; Oct 1898 Newton Heath; Feb 1899 Glossop North End; May 1900 FOSSE; Aug 1901 Nottingham Forest; Oct 1901 Morton; Aug 1902 Renton; 1906 Britannia (Winnipeg, Canada); Dec 1907 Dumbarton Harp.

Fosse debut v Stockport County (H) 1.9.1900 (scored once)

> A roving forward tried everywhere in the front line by Fosse except at outside-left, Jamie was hardly prolific, but at least contrived to score against each of his previous English clubs during his single season at Leicester. Originally noted for his speed, he was described a 'a demon in spikes' while with Celtic, for whom he nonetheless made but a single Scottish League start. He certainly didn't let the grass grow under his feet on leaving them: staying for only four days and one game at Airdrie before moving on to Manchester! Jamie then shared in both Glossop's 1899 promotion and the disastrous top-flight campaign that relegated them back a year later. Following his Fosse release, he also left Forest in haste after failing to find a first-team selection.

***Apps:** FL 29.*
***Goals:** FL 6.*

COOPER, Paul David

b. Cannock, Staffs, 21st December 1953

Career: Sutton Coldfield Town; trials-Shrewsbury Town; app/pro July 1971 Birmingham City; Mar 1974 Ipswich Town; July 1987 CITY; Mar 1989 Manchester City; July 1990 Stockport County.

City debut v Crystal Palace (A) 12.9.87

> Having false-started his career as a teenage striker good enough to win Shrewsbury reserve trials, Paul picked up his goalkeeping gloves as the prelude to a twenty-year profession. Not the tallest at his trade, but certainly one of the most agile and quick-witted, he broke into Birmingham's Division Two promotion side of 1972, but was still regarded as reserve cover when embarking on a loan spell with Ipswich which stretched to a thirteen-year stay of over 500 games between the sticks, and incorporated the winning of both FA Cup and UEFA Cup medals, as well as a 1986 testimonial. Happier to stress his all-round stability in the six-yard box over his legendary expertise at penalty-saving (8 stopped out of 10 faced in 1979/80 alone), Paul joined City as an out-of-contract free agent, and soon renewed his old defensive partnership with Russell Osman after displacing the out-of-sorts Ian Andrews. His rapid, accurate distribution proved every bit as noteworthy as his persistent prowess at repelling spot-kicks, and he held the No 1 position in stalwart shot-stopper's fashion after newcomer Martin Hodge's injury at the start of the following season. Only a shaking received in a car crash sidelined him for a few weeks, but when his recovery coincided with Hodge's, David Pleat allowed him to become a deadline-week mover to augment a successful Maine Road promotion challenge. Before an elbow injury enforced his retirement in 1991, Paul had also assisted Stockport's rise from the basement to Division Three.

***Apps:** FL 56; FAC 1; LC 9; FMC 4.*

CORBETT, William R.

b. Falkirk, Stirlingshire, 31st August 1922

Career: Dunipace Thistle; Maryhill; May 1941 Celtic; June 1948 Preston North End; Aug 1949 CITY; July 1950 Yeovil Town; Nov 1951 Dunfermline Athletic; Nov 1952 Morton.

City debut v Bury (A) 1.10.49

> Bought from Deepdale by Johnny Duncan for £7,000's worth of Cup-run profit, to challenge Tom McArthur and Norman Plummer for the centre-half spot, Willie rather prefigured the luckless tone of his Leicester stay on the opening day of 1949/50, when missing a penalty for the reserves against Arsenal. He'd barely made a senior breakthrough when Duncan departed, and was soon listed himself after failing to convince incoming boss Norman Bullock that he could marshall City's defence as well as he had Celtic's in the immediate postwar period. Willie went on to represent the Southern League (against the Cheshire League) during his Yeovil sojourn, then drifted homeward in the Scottish Second Division. This was all a far cry from the stellar start to his career during the war, which had seen the former motor mechanic (a pole-vault champion's son) 'capped' in the 1942 Wembley meeting with England: forming a middle-line with Bill Shankly and Matt Busby, and shackling Tommy Lawton. Willie also guested at this time for Cardiff City, Swansea Town, Southampton and West Ham, where his older brother Norman was a defensive stalwart from 1937 to 1951. Another older brother, David, had also figured in the line-ups of Dundee United, West Ham and Southport in the 30s.

***Apps:** FL 16; FAC 1.*

CORICA, Stephen Christopher

b. Innisfail, Queensland, Australia, 24th March 1973

Career: 1990 Marconi Fairfield (Sydney); July 1995-trials-Hamburger SV; Aug 1995 CITY; Feb 1996 Wolverhampton Wanderers; Mar 2000 Sanfrecce Hiroshima.

City debut v Sunderland (A) 12.8.95 (scored once)

> An EC passport holder on account of his Italian ancestry, midfielder Steve was unaffected by the work-permit wrangles in which City's other 1995 signing from Down Under, Zeljko Kalac, became entangled, and made his competitive debut at Roker barely 24 hours after signing, having impressed on a pre-season tour of Germany. A ninth-minute 20-yarder got his League career off to a spectacular start, and further evidence

Steve Corica

of his abilities as an attack-minded, left-sided support player soon accrued as Steve conveyed a satisfying overall impression of neatness in control and use of the ball. A broken bone in his ankle, suffered at Port Vale, halted progress, and it was a less confident player, showing patchy form, who rejoined his boss Mark McGhee at Molineux for between £1.1-£1.5 million; ironically only a month after a FIFA tribunal, sitting in Paris, had set City's debt to his Australian club at a mere £325,000. Steve's home debut for Wolves came in an emotive 2-3 defeat by City , but he had further serious setbacks (losing virtually the entire 1997/8 campaign to a knee injury) before establishing himself in the Old Gold. In his final Wolves season, before a cut-price move to the J-League, he occasionally found himself partnered in midfield by Scott Taylor, with whom he'd originally shared his City debut. Capped by Australia at every level from youth to full international level, Steve featured in the semi-finals of the 1991 World Youth Championships, was in the Under-21 'Olyroos' squad which reached the semi-finals of the 1992 Barcelona Olympic football tournament, and figured at the 1996 Atlanta Olympics; while his tally of senior caps currently stands at 27, with four international goals to his credit.

***Apps:** FL 16; FAC 2.*
***Goals:** FL 2.*

COTTEE, Anthony Richard

b. West Ham, 11th July 1965

Career: Chase Cross United; app/pro Sept 1982 West Ham United; Aug 1988 Everton; Sept 1994 West Ham United; Oct 1996 Selangor; Aug 1997 CITY; Nov 1997-loan-Birmingham City; Sept 2000 Norwich City; Nov 2000 Barnet (p/mgr); Mar 2001 Millwall; May 2001-trials-Ajax Cape Town.

City debut v Arsenal (H) 27.8.97 (sub)

> Essentially written off as a top-class striking force when tempted to Malaysia for the third year of that country's professional league operation, Tony initially looked like bearing out that judgement in the first few months after Martin O'Neill gambled £500,000 on his veteran predatory skills. But his career then underwent a thorough resurrection, and City continued to reap the considerable benefits for almost three years. In the months until he went on loan to Birmingham, Tony made only a single start in each of the Premiership and the League Cup, and looked like having to settle for fulfilling just one ambition – his brief sub appearance against Atletico Madrid being his long-awaited first taste of European competition. But his return from St Andrews saw him in the starting line-up at Old Trafford, and his winning goal marked the start of a fine upsurge in form, which even West Ham fans had to acknowledge when

he knocked two past them on the final day of 1997/8. Tony was the first-choice partner for Emile Heskey for the following term, ever busy and wily around the box, and ended it as the club's Player of the Year. He earned a contract extension after his two goals had removed Charlton from the League Cup, and his strikes in both legs of the semi-final against Sunderland won City their 1999 Wembley date: when defeat by Spurs rung the only sour note of the season, as Tony was still unable to collect a winner's medal after 17 years in the senior game. A fortnight later, however, his revenge would come when sealing City's Premiership victory at White Hart Lane – and when a statistical quirk of pleasing symmetry would mean he was claiming his 200th League goal against Spurs, as he had done both his very first and his 100th. Though it was rare after that for O'Neill to expect Tony to get through two successive 90-minute stints, it was often the case of the scorer being withdrawn to a hero's accolades; and City's eclipse of Tranmere at Wembley finally earned him that long-coveted memento of knockout success. Having made no secret of his desire to move eventually into management, it was no surprise to find him linked with Steve Walsh in candidature for the Filbert Street job in the summer of 2000; or that he was willing to cut short his subsequent spell at Carrow Road to take on a dual role at Underhill. Unfortunately unable to build on a fine start with the Bees, and despite a decent goalscoring contribution, he was nonetheless removed from his post within months as his side were sucked into the Third Division relegation dogfight, which eventually saw them take a last-day drop into the Conference. His subsequent brief non-contract stint with Millwall ended rather differently (with the Division Two championship won), and landed Tony with a unique record of having appeared in all four divisions within a single season. Tony was only 17 when he made his scoring debut for West Ham, and his hatful of goals for the Hammers (including an aggregate of six against City) helped them to their highest-ever League placing of third in 1986, and soon earned him eight Under-21 call-ups and the first three of his seven full caps. England continued to call on the pint-sized striker after his £2.3m move to Goodison, but he was three times a Wembley loser with Everton, in the FA Cup Final of 1989, and the Full Members Cup Finals of 1989 and 1991. His return to Upton Park kept him in the Premiership with a barely diminished strike-rate, and even if his Selangor sojourn was not a wholly happy experience, he still managed a fourteen-goal return from 23 games there. These included, Tony ended 2000/1 on a grand total of 317 senior competitive goals.

***Apps:** PL 66+19; FAC 3+2; LC 9; UEFA 0+1.*
***Goals:** PL 27; FAC 2; LC 5.*

COULSON, Ernest

Career: Leicester Excelsior; Nov 1898 FOSSE; Jan 1899 Hugglescote Robin Hoods; 1900 Ratby Swifts; Feb 1901 Burton Wanderers; June 1901 Burton United; Oct 1902 Allsopp's Brewery FC; Nov 1902 Chesterfield Town; Apr 1903 FOSSE; Oct 1904 Leicester Imperial.

Fosse debut/only game v Chesterfield (A) 23.1.04

> The outside-right and younger brother of a pair of amateurs with a habit of moving between clubs in tandem, Ernest notched a hat-trick on his Fosse reserve debut; scored the winner in his first senior friendly outing against Reading four-and-a-half years later; and was granted his single shot at League action some seven months after that – in a 0-2 defeat which kept the side anchored to the foot of Division Two.

***Apps:** FL 1.*

COULSON, Henry William

Career: Leicester Excelsior; Jan 1898 FOSSE; Jan 1899 Hugglescote Robin Hoods; 1900 Ratby Swifts; Feb 1901 Burton Wanderers; June 1901 Burton United; Oct 1902 Allsopp's Brewery FC; Nov 1902 Chesterfield Town; Apr 1903 FOSSE; Oct 1904 Leicester Imperial; Syston Robin Hoods.

Fosse debut/only game v Lincoln City (H) 12.2.1898 (scored once)

> Of the nigh-inseperable Coulsons, Harry was the first on the Fosse scene with occasional appearances in the inside-forward berths in friendlies and charity cup games, but could still never improve on his record of a single Second Division selection (when, with Sam Eaton also making a bow alongside him, he opened the scoring in a 3-1 win). Harry was twice sent off playing for Fosse reserves (earning a two month FA suspension in 1899, and also walking in 1904), and the brothers often played together at that level – as indeed they must have done for the second strings of both Burton United and Chesterfield, for neither played even once at League level for either club. Both featured in the 1902 FA Cup exit of a Burton brewery side; while with the Imps they formed a forward line with the Turners and Tommy Burgess.

***Apps:** FL 1.*
***Goals:** FL 1.*

COUTTS, William Farquharson

b. Edinburgh, 26th June 1909d. Leicester, 25th July 1991

Career: Edinburgh Ashton; Dunbar United; Aug 1930 Heart of Midlothian; Feb 1932-loan-Leith Athletic; May 1934 CITY (- 1940).

City debut v Wolverhampton Wanderers (H) 25.8.34 (scored once)

> A Scottish Cup semi-finalist with Hearts in 1932/3, and a one-time Tynecastle team-mate of Archie Gardiner, Billy was (at £950) one of Peter Hodge's last City signings before his death, and won only sporadic favour with either Arthur Lochhead or Frank Womack thereafter. He didn't quite qualify for a Second Division championship medal in 1937, but remained as a usefully tricky inside-forward, or occasional wing-half, throughout the immediate pre-war top-flight days, and on into the first season of wartime football, when he additionally guested for Northampton Town. Billy also turned out for Nottingham Forest at Filbert Street on Christmas Day 1941. He marked the 50th anniversary of his City debut by appearing as a still sprightly guest at the club's Centenary celebrations.

***Apps:** FL 48; FAC 2; WW2 10.*
***Goals:** FL 4.*

COX, William James

b. Blackpool, ca 1881

Career: Rossendale United; Feb 1903 Bury; May 1904 Plymouth Argyle; Aug 1905 FOSSE; Oct 1905 Accrington Stanley; Nov 1905 Oldham Athletic; Jan 1906 Preston North End; May 1906 Dundee; Apr 1907 Heart of Midlothian; Nov 1907 Bradford Park Avenue.

Fosse debut v Clapton Orient (H) 2.9.05

> A younger brother of England international forward Jack Cox (Blackpool & Liverpool), Bill was a centre-forward who best days came, curiously enough, in Scotland. He had a modicum of experience in both Division One and the Southern League (though only one goal in the latter sphere) by the time he came to Leicester, but he was soon discarded after the opening trio of games of 1905/06. He failed to dislodge Matt Brunton at Accrington, featured in only a pair of Lancashire Combination fixtures for Oldham, and never reached the Deepdale first-team. Yet his move to Dundee revivified him: top-scoring with 18 League goals in a term which saw them as runners-up, and being described by *The Scottish Referee* as 'a thoroughly earnest and well-behaved player'. His subsequent term at Park Avenue saw his new (and newly-formed) club operating, incongruously, as by far the most northerly outfit in the Southern League, prior to its election to Division Two.

***Apps:** FL 3.*

CRAWFORD, James Cherrie

b. Bellshill, Lanarkshire, 27th September 1930

Career: (Corby jnr football); Oct 1947 CITY; March 1954 Plymouth Argyle; cs 1956 Peterborough United; cs 1958 Corby Town.

City debut v Grimsby Town (H) 26.12.50

> One of several 'Corby Scots' signed by City over the years (Stuart Campbell being the most recent), ball-playing attacker Jimmy returned from National Service to feature sporadically in four forward positions over a four-season span, but suffered essentially by being regarded as back-up to first Bert Barlow, then Johnny Morris. He unfortunately found himself similarly cast as a utility reserve at Home Park, and made his final appearance in a relegation-bound Plymouth side beaten 5-1 at Filbert Street in February 1956. Thereafter, Jimmy contributed to two successive Midland League championship campaigns for Posh, but even then not as a regular.

***Apps:** FL 10; FAC 1.*
***Goals:** FL 2.*

Jimmy Crawford

CRESSWELL, Richard Paul Wesley

b. Bridlington, Yorks, 20th September 1977

Career: YT/pro Nov 1995 York City; Mar 1997-loan-Mansfield Town; Mar 1999 Sheffield Wednesday; Sept 2000 CITY; Mar 2001 Preston North End.

City debut v Red Star Belgrade (H) UEFA 14.9.2000 (sub)

> Further evidencing Peter Taylor's faith in his former England Under-21 charges, Richard was rescued from the Hillsborough sidelines to challenge for a senior striker's slot with City, but then given precious few opportunities to stake his claim. Blessed with a more confident first touch than several of his rivals for a front-running role, he seemed unable to augment it with any more penetrative skills, and his sole City strike – a powerful header – came in the Cup eclipse of his former York teammates. It was while still with the Minstermen that Richard had earned his representative recognition, and his 16 Division Two goals (plus three Cup strikes) in the first two-thirds of 1998/9 alerted the Owls to his potential, tempting them to a payment of £950,000. Nonetheless, he made only three subsequent starts in the Premiership for Wednesday, who tended to use him more regularly from the bench; and it was a sub's role he soon had to get used to again with City after his £750,000 purchase. The latter was also the fee provisionally agreed on should Preston take up their option of buying Richard after his loan spell at Deepdale, but following their defeat in the Division One Play-Off Final at the Millennium Stadium in Cardiff (to which Richard characteristically contributed only a ten minute cameo), it took until July to conclude a re-negotiated deal at a new figure of £600,000.

***Apps:** PL 3+5; FAC 0+2; LC 1; UEFA 0+2.*
***Goals:** FAC 1.*

CREWS, Alexander N.

b. Plymouth

Career: Green Waves; cs 1910 Plymouth Argyle; am Aug 1912 Chelsea; pro Sept 1912 FOSSE; Sept 1913 Stockport County.

Fosse debut/only game v Grimsby Town (A) 12.10.12

> In a season when Fosse tried no less than six centre-halves, the selection of this Devonian pivot proved (according to the local *Mail*) 'a disappointing experiment', as Alex 'gave tokens of his class only in a few nicely distributed passes' during Fosse's 0-2 defeat. He had previously played twice in the Southern League for his hometown club, but would gain no further experience in senior football.

***Apps:** FL 1.*

CROSS, Graham Frederick

b. Leicester, 15th November 1943

Career: Enderby Town; am May 1959/pro Nov 1960 CITY; Mar 1976-loan-Chesterfield; June 1976 Brighton & Hove Albion; July 1977 Preston North End; Jan 1979 Enderby Town; Mar 1979 Lincoln City; Aug 1979 Enderby Town; cs 1981 Hinckley Athletic (p/mgr).

City debut v Birmingham City (H) 29.4.61 (scored once)

> Falling just short of Adam Black's club record total of League appearances, but bettering his aggregate tally to stand, with 599 senior games for City, as Leicester's most consistent servant ever, Graham also proved himself one of the most versatile over his sixteen seasons. The burly 15-year-old inside-forward who netted on his reserve debut at Brighton, then became City's youngest-ever top-flight scorer, was, on his eighteenth birthday, quite happily entrusted with the centre-half role in City's first gallant European exit in Madrid. It was often said in the 60s that Graham's regular switching of positions cost him an England place (especially in the days when little premium was put on zonal adaptability), but his failure to add senior international honours to his eleven Under-23 caps nonetheless seemed more a case of culpable over-sight on the part of the national team's management. As early as 1962/3, Matt Gillies' tactical interchanging of Graham and Frank McLintock was a match-winning ploy, though a later tendency to shuttle Graham between defence, midfield and the striking line could occasionally be put down to desperate expediency. Eventually, when the twin centre-back game became the norm, it was in defence that Graham settled – if that's the right word, given his relentless energy and enthusiasm. Appearances in two FA Cup Finals and two League Cup Finals, a Second Division championship medal, a Charity Shield win and a 1973 testimonial were the tangible mementos of his City career but, for supporters, other memories of 'The Tank' still jostle: of the cool back-heel that won a Cup replay at Blackburn; of the hat-trick against Forest, consisting of 'one for them, two for us'; of numerous barrelling forays forward, and of countless opposing strikers cowed into frustration by Graham's sturdy shadowing and solid tackle. His football prowess – several times coveted by Brian Clough in his Derby days – certainly cost him a much more successful county cricket career than he actually managed (as, naturally, a Leicestershire all-rounder), but the winter game kept a hold on him for some time following his departure from Filbert Street. He was the ever-present defensive bedrock of Brighton's rise from Third to Second Division in 1977, and an inspiration for Preston's similar promotion a year later. It was wholly unfitting, then, that when he answered Lincoln's emergency call in 1979, even Graham couldn't save them from relegation to the Fourth. Sadly back in the news in February 1993, when briefly jailed for the misuse of Post Office funds, Graham has more recently been employed in the knitwear trade in Hinckley.

***Apps:** FL 495+3; FAC 59; LC 40; ECWC 2.*
***Goals:** FL 29; FAC 6; LC 2.*

CROSS, Nicholas Jeremy Roland

b. Birmingham, 7th February 1961

Career: app 1977/pro Feb 1979 West Bromwich Albion; Aug 1985 Walsall; Jan 1988 CITY; June 1989 Port Vale; July 1994 Hereford United; Aug 1996 Solihull Borough; 1999 Redditch United.

City debut v Reading (A) 30.1.88

> An early £65,000 David Pleat buy to play in support of Mike Newell, Nicky was a a well-balanced, eager bustler of a striker, adept at shielding and turning with the ball in tight positions, and proved tenacious enough to see off the challenge of more expensive newcomer Jimmy Quinn during his second City campaign. A long-term injury cut into his subsequent five-year spell at Vale Park, but he there experienced both relegation and promotion as well as the frustration of missing out on a 1993 Wembley win in the Autoglass Trophy, and he assisted Hereford to Play-Off qualification during his final season as a League player; bowing out with a total of 129 goals in that competition. Initially, Nicky had been a young rival for a West Brom striking position to the likes of Ally Brown and Peter Eastoe, and had then partnered Trevor Christie at Fellows Park as his own goals-per-game ratio shot up in the Third Division and he developed the characteristic penalty-area control and resilience which attracted Pleat's interest. Nicky was still active in West Midlands soccer in 2000/1; a season he also opened as caretaker player/manager at Redditch.

***Apps:** FL 54+4; FAC 1; LC 3+2; FMC 1.*
***Goals:** FL 15; LC 1.*

CUNNINGHAM, Laurence Paul

b. Archway, London, 8th March 1956
d. Madrid, Spain, 15th July 1989

Career: app Aug 1972/pro July 1974 Orient; Mar 1977 West Bromwich Albion; June 1979 Real Madrid; Mar 1983-loan-Manchester United; Aug 1983 Sporting Gijon; cs 1984 Olympique Marseille; Oct 1985-loan-CITY; July 1986 Rayo Vallecano; Aug 1987-trials-Real Betis; Oct 1987 RSC Charleroi; Feb 1988 Wimbledon; July 1988 Rayo Vallecano.

City debut v Manchester United (H) 23.11.85

> A superbly skilful, confidently confrontational winger who amassed six caps at each of Under-21 and full England levels after becoming the first black player to win meaningful national recognition, Laurie made a major teenage impact with Second Division Orient, and had assisted them to an Anglo-Scottish Cup Final victory before being snapped up by Johnny Giles for West Brom at £110,000. His assimilation was near-instant, and he inspired the Baggies to the classy 5-0 win at Filbert Street in May 1977 which effectively prompted Jimmy Bloomfield's resignation. Continued success at the Hawthorns attracted an irresistible near-£1 million offer from Spain, and 'El Negrito' helped Real to the Spanish Double and, successively, the semi-final and Final of the European Cup in his first two years at the Bernabeu, before niggling injuries began to bite into his career, which became increasingly peripatetic. A brief spell at Old Trafford reminded an English public of his abilities, and came close to winning him a 1983 Cup Final place; but it was his later extended loan at Filbert Street under Gordon Milne which had the more import. For, despite further injuries, Laurie was inspirationally instrumental in (just) keeping City in Division One in 1986. Some of his once-electrifying pace had gone, but little of the ball-juggling cockiness, and he genuinely lit up Filbert Street for a while with his bursts of effective footballing extroversion. In the midst of further continental wanderings, he again briefly returned to London, and said a Wembley adieu with a substitute appearance for surprise FA Cup-winners Wimbledon in 1988. Tragically, Laurie was killed in a car crash only weeks after sharing in Rayo Vallecano's promotion to the Primera División.

***Apps:** FL 13+2.*

CUNNINGHAM, William Edward

b. Mallusk, Co Antrim, 20th February 1930

Career: Renfrew Waverley; Tranent Juniors; Ardrossan Winton Rovers; 1948 St Mirren; Nov 1954 CITY; Sept 1960 Dunfermline Athletic.

City debut v Wolverhampton Wanderers (H) 11.12.54

> Twenty-three of Willie's thirty Irish caps were earned while he was with City – making him at the time the club's most capped player – yet ironically many of them were awarded while he was a regular in the Combination XI. Having learned his football in Scotland, become apprenticed as a machine-tool fitter and completed RAF service, he'd broken through as a stylish defender with both St Mirren and the country of his birth when Norman Bullock laid out £4,750 for him to see if he could help reverse failing First Division fortunes. Willie couldn't achieve that, but settled well initially, alternating between the two full-back berths until squeezed out by the Stan Milburn/John Ogilvie partnership which saw City through the 1957 promotion year. He returned for the bulk of the following three top-flight campaigns though, again ironically, only ever played twice for City in the centre-half position he held for Northern Ireland throughout the 1958 World Cup finals. Willie went on to the list at his own request in 1959, but turned down a mooted September move to Bristol City. Then, a year later, he moved house back to Paisley despite having no club. His eventual transfer to Dunfermline (in time to debut in a friendly against City) worked well, however: he played in the 1961 Scottish Cup Final victory, tasted runs in both the Cup Winners Cup and the Fairs Cup, and was manager when the Pars returned to Hampden in 1965, having had a spell coaching under Jock Stein in the interim. He sold Jackie Sinclair to Leicester before moving on for further spells of management at Falkirk (promoted under him in 1970) and St Mirren, and in September 1971 turned down the national team manager's job proffered by the Scottish FA. Willie was a nephew of the Linfield and Irish League representative winger Ed McCormick.

***Apps:** FL 127; FAC 11.*
***Goals:** FL 4.*

CURRIE, Samuel

b. Kilwinning, Ayrshire, 22nd November 1889

Career: 1906 Kilwinning Rangers; trials-St Mirren; May 1909 FOSSE; May 1922 Wigan Borough.

Fosse debut v Birmingham (A) 19.3.10

> Fosse's regular left-back for six seasons before the war (as well as during it), and City's for three campaigns after it, Sam displaced Dick Pudan and went on to forge useful back-line partnerships in hard times with Tommy Clay, Billy Barrett and Adam Black; in each successive case sharing the benefits of his experience with younger players. His signing actually cost Sam a medal, for Fosse swooped between the first, drawn, Final of the 1909 Scottish Junior Cup and its replay, in which Kilwinning triumphed. One of Fosse's several early union activists, Sam played in December 1910 for the Players Union XI against a combined Manchester United/City side – scoring an own goal and being injured badly enough to miss the next five League fixtures! An occasional penalty-taker for Leicester, he received a well-merited club benefit from the November 1919 game with North Shields, and took his veteran defensive skills into the Third Division (North) upon finally leaving City, before accepting the post of player-coach to Wigan's reserves in March 1924. Brother Bob featured for each of Middlesbrough, Morton, Bury, Hearts and Darlington before WW1, while brother Duncan had established himself with Hearts when tragically killed in action on the Somme in 1916.

***Apps:** FL 236; FAC 12; WW1 123.*
***Goals:** FL 4; FAC 2; WW1 7.*

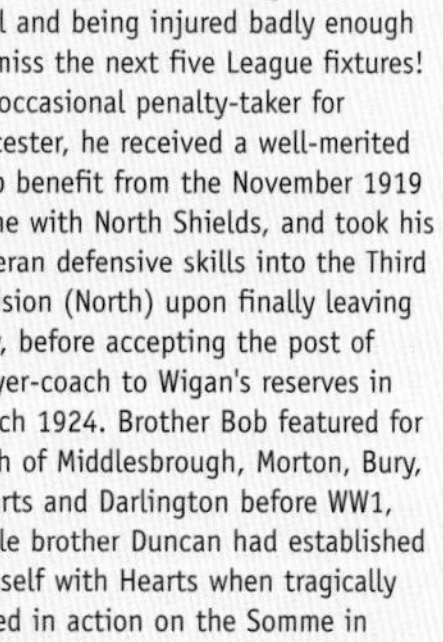

Sam Currie

CURRIE, Walter Robertson

b. Lochgelly, Fife, 5th October 1895

Career: East Fife; 1916 Raith Rovers; Dec 1919 CITY; May 1922 Bristol Rovers; Aug 1923 Clackmannan; 1923 Lochgelly United.

City debut v Stockport County (A) 14.2.20

> One of several players plucked by City from Starks Park as a direct result of return visits by former Raith boss Peter Hodge, Wattie had impressed in wartime football as a skilful wing-half. Yet although he played a fair number of games in front of his unrelated namesake, he could never secure a guaranteed middle-line place over his three seasons at Filbert Street. An ever-present in his sole Third Division (South) campaign at Eastville, Wattie must then have fallen out with them over their imposition of a £250 value on his registration, for he was still appealing unsuccessfully to the League for its reduction in March 1924, after taking his services into the Third and Scond Divisions of Scottish football. (One source indicates credibly that Wattie may have additionally played during WW1 for Cowdenbeath).

***Apps:** FL 32.*
***Goals:** FL 1.*

CUSACK, Nicholas John

b. Maltby, Yorks, 24th December 1965

Career: City of Birmingham Polytechnic; 1986 Long Eaton United; 1987 Alvechurch; June 1987 CITY; July 1988 Peterborough United; Aug 1989 Motherwell; Jan 1992 Darlington; July 1992 Oxford United; Mar 1994-loan-Wycombe Wanderers; Nov 1994 Fulham; Oct 1997 Swansea City.

City debut v Shrewsbury Town (H) 15.8.87

> As a tall, ex-student, central striker signed from Alvechurch, Nick followed rather too closely in Alan Smith's footsteps for lightning to strike twice. Bryan Hamilton blooded him on the opening day of 1987/8, and his reserve form earned him an extension to his contract, but competition from Newell, Cross and Reid limited his chances, and incoming boss David Pleat used him only sparingly as a substitute. Posh, however, were clearly impressed by his spectacular strike against them in a testimonial friendly in April 1988, and the summer saw Nick move to London Road in the part-exchange deal which landed Alan Paris at Leicester. After a term as Posh's top scorer, he made a decent impact on the Scottish Premier League (though sent off three times in his first Fir Park campaign), helped Motherwell to the 1991 Cup Final (but missed out on the showpiece itself), and cost Darlington a club record £95,000 as they fought in vain against relegation in 1992. A further relegation experience followed at Oxford in 1994, but it was as a mature midfielder that Nick finally tasted a promotion campaign, alongside Simon Morgan at Fulham in 1997. Nick followed manager Alan Cork from Craven Cottage to the Vetch, and was skippering the side by the time they ejected West Ham from the FA Cup in 1999, but then suffered Play-Off disappointment the same season. He led them, however, to the switchback experience of the Third Division championship in 2000 and relegation back in 2001.

***Apps:** FL 5+11; FAC 0+1; FMC 1+1.*
***Goals:** FL 1.*

DAINTY, Herbert Charles

b. Geddington, Northants, 2nd June 1879
d. Kettering, 10th September 1957

Career: Kettering; Aug 1899 FOSSE; May 1900 New Brighton Tower; Aug 1901 FOSSE; cs 1902 Northampton Town; May 1903 Notts County; May 1904 Southampton; May 1905 Dundee; May 1911 Bradford Park Avenue; Oct 1913 Ayr United (p/mgr from May 1914); Apr 1915 Dundee Hibernian (p/mgr).

Fosse debut v Luton Town (A) 23.9.1899

> A sturdy and authoritative Northamptonshire pivot, Herbert had two spells as Fosse's centre-half around the turn of the century (for campaigns in which they finished 5th and 14th), and brought the decent fee of £200 into the Filbert Street coffers on each occasion he moved on. His League and Southern League wanderings (including a top-flight spell at Trent Bridge) boosted his reputation, but it was in Scotland that he truly distinguished himself. 'The little Englishman is a player of the untiring order', noted one Caledonian critic; and he twice prompted Dundee to the League runners-up spot before appearing, as one of four Anglos, in their first (and only) Scottish Cup triumph in 1910. He also represented the Scottish League that year, enjoyed a Dens Park testimonial against Celtic, and eventually became something of a Tayside legend. For he returned to that area during WW1 as player-manager (and, for a while in 1922, as chairman) of the local Hibernians – soon to change their name to Dundee United. In April 1925, Herbert became the first British coach in Guayaquil, Ecuador, for the new local Barcelona club; and in July 1927 was on a shortlist of three for the manager's job at Blackpool. From August 1931 he was boss at Kettering; had two years from 1932 as Ipswich Town trainer; and coached for the Northants FA from the mid-30s. Herbert was settled back in Geddington at the time of his death in St Mary's Hospital. A younger brother was a half-back who moved from Geddington to Kettering in 1901, and faced Fosse in the FA Cup in October 1903 for Market Harborough Town.

***Apps:** FL 53; FAC 5.*
***Goals:** FL 3.*

DALY, Gerard Anthony

b. Cabra, Dublin, 30th April 1954

Career: Bohemians; Apr 1973 Manchester United; Mar 1977 Derby County; May 1978 & May 1979-loans-New England Tea Men; Aug 1980 Coventry City; Jan 1983-loan-CITY; July 1984 Birmingham City; Oct 1985 Shrewsbury Town; Mar 1987:Stoke City; July 1988 Doncaster Rovers; Dec 1989 Telford United (p/coach; p/mgr).

City debut v Carlisle United (A) 5.2.83

> The only player to have been capped in a full international while on loan with City, slender midfielder Gerry was in the midst of an inspirational spell for Gordon Milne's promotion-bound side of 1983 when appearing as a substitute for the Republic of Ireland against Spain in Zaragoza. City lost only once before the season's end after Gerry joined the fray from Highfield Road, with the forward line gratefully latching on to his intelligent promptings and judiciously varied distribution, and the midfield well buttressed by his own battling commitment. It was a genuine surprise and disappointment when Milne decided to face subsequent First Division rigours without him, especially as he had originally signed him for Coventry, for £300,000 from a relegated Derby outfit. Gerry's initial prominence had come as a vital midfield cog in Tommy Docherty's mid-70s reconstruction of Manchester United, when relegation and promotion were followed by a 1976 Cup Final outing and top-flight re-establishment; but he later clashed verbally with the volatile manager at both Old Trafford and the Baseball Ground. Gerry figured in a further promotion campaign, with Birmingham two years after leaving Filbert Street, and maintained a classy presence at lower League levels for a while thereafter.

***Apps:** FL 17.*
***Goals:** FL 1.*

DARBY, Ernest W.

Career: 1900 Leicester Nomads; 1904 Clarendon Park Congregational; 1904 Leicester Old Boys; Aug 1906-trials-FOSSE; Sept 1906 Leicester British United; 1906 Clarendon Park Congregational; cs 1907 Leicester Nomads; am Oct 1908/am Apr 1910 FOSSE; Sept 1910-trials-Woolwich Arsenal; Sept 1910 Loughborough Corinthians; Sept 1919 Belvoir SS; Stafford's FC.

Fosse debut v Hull City (A) 14.4.10

> A local amateur goalkeeper who often lent his services to Fosse's reserve team, Ernest was called up for League action at the tail-end of 1909/10, in the absence of both Jonty Starbuck and Horace Bailey, as the club's attempt to bounce straight back to Division One petered out tamely in a nine-game run without victory. The *Mercury* deemed that he could 'pat himself on the back for his performance' in the first of his quartet of senior outings; while trials soon afterwards at Plumstead indicated that not only locals were impressed with his 'keeping. At Christmas 1905, Ernest had toured Holland with the Amateurs of Leicestershire; in February 1908 represented the international-packed Pilgrims against Sheffield; and in April 1909 toured Germany with another amateur combination, The Pirates, accompanied by his long-time club-mate left-half (and future FA Cup Final referee) Tom Crew. Ernest announced his retirement in 1911, for business reasons, but was back between the sticks in postwar action; taking a Mutual League chanmpionship medal with Stafford's in 1923/4. A cricketer for over 30 years with Clarendon Park CC, he was also involved in the summer game's local administration in the late 1930s.

***Apps:** FL 4.*

DAVIDSON, Callum Iain

b. Stirling, 25th June 1976

Career: jnr/pro June 1994 St Johnstone; Feb 1998 Blackburn Rovers; July 2000 CITY.

City debut v Aston Villa (H) 19.8.2000

> The ups and downs of Callum's first campaign with City could almost be measured by the three fixtures against Villa. The £1.3 - 1.6m summer buy made the starting line-up for the seasonal opener, but suffered an injury that day which sidelined him for several games and did little to aid his integration into Peter Taylor's new-look defence. In the Cup game at Villa Park he was sent off in a frenetic first half, but back there on Premiership duty was able to celebrate his first City goal. Such mixed fortunes typified a term in which the Scottish international, usually regarded as a conventional left-back, was also occasionally asked by Taylor to adapt himself to a wing-back role and, a little more happily, a berth in central defence. Nonetheless, Callum added twice to his prior tally of 12 caps during the season. City's fee, incidentally, did not quite match that

paid by Blackburn to St Johnstone, where Callum first established himself in the 1997 promotion campaign that landed the Perth side in the Scottish Premier League. The Ewood side were also top-flight occupants when he signed for £1.7m, but he suffered relegation with them in 1999.

***Apps** (to end 2000/1): PL 25+3; FAC 2; LC 1; UEFA 0+1.*
***Goals:** PL 1.*

DAVIES, Benjamin Edward

b. Middlesbrough, 9th June 1888
d. Middlesbrough, 1970

Career: Middlesbrough United; Shildon; Feb 1911 Middlesbrough; May 1920 Cardiff City; June 1923 CITY; June 1924 Bradford Park Avenue.

City debut v South Shields (A) 8.12.23

> A beanpole 'keeper whose First Division experience at Ayresome was limited by the form of England international Tim Williamson, Ben joined Cardiff for their debut season in League football, and assisted them to promotion and an FA Cup semi-final appearance. A Welsh Cup medallist the following term, he then proved an insurmountable barrier to City in their 1922/3 Cup exit at the hands of the Bluebirds. Another year on, though, and Ben became Leicester's then oldest debutant (at 35 years, 182 days); briefly standing in for George Hebden between the City posts for a trio of unbeaten outings. It transpired they would be his last in the senior game, for Bradford, who had utilised him once as a WW1 guest, never gave him the first-team nod after his formal move to Park Avenue. Ben had also briefly served Hartlepool in the Northern Victory League in 1919.

***Apps:** FL 3.*

DAVIES, Richard

b. Hanley, Staffs, ca 1876

Career: Wrexham; Nov 1894 Manchester City; 1895 Hanley Town; trials Apr 1895/pro May 1895 FOSSE; June 1896 South Shore; cs 1897 Glossop North End; May 1898 Wolverhampton Wanderers; cs 1899 Reading.

Fosse debut v Darwen (A) 21.9.1895

> Given an April 1895 trial in a friendly against Everton, youthful centre-forward Richard was signed on for the following term, but barely allowed time to adapt from the standard of The Combination (where Hanley had just spent their sole season) to that of Division Two, being shuffled across the front-line positions before demotion to the reserves. Second-team football had been his lot at Manchester City; but on leaving Leicester he rebuilt his repute in the Lancashire and Midland Leagues, and got a crack at the First Division with Wolves: scoring on his debut, but only once more in a further ten games. The briefest of spells with Southern League Reading at least completed a record of appearing in different competitive company in each year of his career.

***Apps:** FL 7; FAC 3.*
***Goals:** FL 4.*

DAVIES, Roger

b. Wolverhampton, 25th October 1950

Career: Bridgnorth Town; July 1971 Worcester City; Sept 1971 Derby County; Aug 1972-loan-Preston North End; July 1976 Club Brugge; Dec 1977 CITY; Mar 1979 Tulsa Roughnecks; Sept 1979 Derby County; Mar 1980 Seattle Sounders; Apr 1983 Fort Lauderdale Strikers; Sept 1983-trials-Burnley; Nov 1983 Darlington; Feb 1984 Gresley Rovers (p/co-mgr); Nov 1985 Stapenhill; Tutbury Hawthorn.

City debut v Derby County (H) 10.12.77

> Frank McLintock's City were already in an unholy mess when a club record £250,000 returned Roger from Belgian football to Division One, and it was always going to be difficult for the lanky striker to live up to the hopes his move engendered. He clearly required time to play himself back into the pace and physicality of the English game, and especially of a backs-to-the-wall relegation struggle, but time was a commodity City's predicament (and the crowd's short patience) excluded. Roger could recover neither his goal touch nor general form, and of the four efforts that ironically gave him joint top-scorer status for the term, one was a penalty and another, his first, might less charitably have been credited as a Norwich own goal. Even when Jock Wallace took over at Filbert Street, City fans saw little of the razor-sharpness and awkward unorthodoxy that had marked Roger's first spell at Derby with some spectacular scoring feats (a debut goal in the 1972 Texaco Cup Final; a memorable hat-trick in a televised Cup replay with Spurs; all five against Luton in the Rams' championship campaign of 1974/5) and had earned him England Under-23 recognition. Success had come Roger's way in Belgium, too, with a domestic Double win in 1977 for Club Brugge, and four goals in four games contributing to their subsequent European Cup run. By the time they faced Liverpool at Wembley, however, Roger was embroiled in City's plummet to Division Two. Roger had first been noted in the Bridgnorth team which took the Welsh Amateur Cup on a cross-border raid in 1971, and had been snapped up for the Baseball Ground after seven goals in seven games for Southern League Worcester City. His second spell with Derby also landed him in a relegation campaign; but he had reasonable success in the States, scoring 54 NASL goals and appearing as a substitute in Soccer Bowl 1982, when Seattle lost 0-1 to New York Cosmos. In 1987 Roger earned a winner's medal from the Centenary Final of the Leicestershire Senior Cup, playing for Staffordshire-based Stapenhill.

***Apps:** FL 22+4; FAC 2; LC 0+1.*
***Goals:** FL 6.*

DAVIES, William McIntosh

b. Glasgow, 31st May 1964

Career: Pollok United; 1980 Rangers; 1986 Jönköping; 1987 IF Elfsborg; Oct 1987 St Mirren; July 1990 CITY; Oct 1990 Dunfermline Athletic; Mar 1994 Motherwell.

City debut v Bristol Rovers (H) 25.8.90

> A scurrying, diminutive Scottish midfielder whose £165,000 signing fee represented David Pleat's first outlay from the 'McAllister Million' of the 1990 close season, Billy proved unfortunately unable to settle either on or off the pitch at Leicester, and was homeward bound as soon as City could negotiate a break-even on his transfer. He actually made his City bow in a friendly at Love Street, where he had hitherto been an occasional team-mate of Peter Weir in a struggling Premier Division side, but competitive English fare soon showed him short of the inspirational flair it was hoped he would provide. Billy had initially broken through into Rangers' senior side as a 17-year-old, but his gradual Ibrox progress (including a substitute appearance in the 1983 Scottish Cup Final) was foreshortened by the policy changes of the Graeme Souness regime, and he chanced his arm thereafter in Swedish football: initially alongside his brother John at Jönköping, then in an Elfsborg side relegated from the Allsvenskan in 1987. With Dunfermline in 1991/2 he suffered double disappointment, when relegation from the Premier followed League Cup Final defeat; and Billy also had to settle for a League runners-up placing with Motherwell in 1995. He added youth coaching responsibilities to his Fir Park role in May 1998; and since October of that year has been manager. He signed his brother John in 1999 after the latter had played for Clydebank, Airdrie and Ayr.

***Apps:** FL 5+1.*

Billy Davies

DAVIS, Herbert

b. Bradford, 11th August 1906
d. Yeadon, Yorks, 17th July 1981

Career: Guiseley; Nov 1927 Bradford Park Avenue; Apr 1932 Sunderland; Dec 1936 CITY; June 1937 Crystal Palace.

City debut v Chesterfield (A) 12.12.36

> Rather lost in the slipstream as City rocketed to promotion in 1937, Bert was a 5ft 4in right winger with a fine scoring record who was nonetheless soon displaced at Filbert Street by Tony Carroll, and released when top-flight status was secured. A former mill-hand who assisted Bradford to the championship of the Third Division (North) in his first season as a pro, he had also been a Roker regular right up to the point where Sunderland took the First Division title in 1936 (though sent off twice that term), and had an aggregate League haul of 77 goals, remarkable for an orthodox flank player, before taking City's £7 per week. Bert's involvement in three separate Divisional championship campaigns was notable enough, but he also came close to completing the Football League set; with Third (South) success at Selhurst being missed by one place in 1939. His senior career ended with wartime guest stints with Huddersfield, York and back at Park Avenue.

***Apps:** FL 8; FAC 1.*

DAVIS, William

b. Nantwich, Cheshire, ca 1863
d. Leicester, 21st March 1949

Career: Nantwich; 1889 FOSSE; 1894 Hinckley Town.

Fosse debut (competitive) v Burton Wanderers (H) FAC 4.10.1890

> A defender who arrived from Nantwich along with Albert Vickers, Billy played at left-back in Fosse's first FA Cup tie, and at centre-half in the club's initial Midland League fixture, though then spent the bulk of his Leicester career thereafter turning out for Fosse Rovers. He was, however, a regular representative for Leicestershire in inter-county fare between 1890 and 1895, and featured in Hinckley's side in the 1897 County Cup Final. Local weekly *The Wyvern* dubbed him 'unassuming, but very capable'. Though Jimmy Atter is rightly credited with the first goal at Filbert Street at senior level, it was in fact Billy who had netted the club's initial strike on their new ground some three weeks earlier, when equalising a Paddy Slawson goal for Melton Rovers in a 3-2 reserve-team win on 17th October 1891. Billy settled in Aylestone when his playing days ended, becoming a shoe-hand at the Wheatsheaf Works.

***Apps:** FAC 1; ML 5.*

DAVISON, Robert

b. South Shields, 17th July 1959

Career: Red Duster; Seaham Colliery Welfare; July 1980 Huddersfield Town; Aug 1981 Halifax Town; Dec 1982 Derby County; Nov 1987 Leeds United; Sept 1991-loan-Derby County; Mar 1992-loan-Sheffield United; Aug 1992 CITY; Sept 1993 Sheffield United; Oct 1994 Rotherham United; Nov 1995-loan-Hull City; July 1996 Halifax Town; Nov 1996-loan-Guiseley; May 1997 Guiseley (p/coach; p/mgr from Feb 1998).

City debut v Luton Town (H) 15.8.92

> A reasonably effective stopgap signing by Brian Little after newcomer David Lowe suffered pre-season injury, 33-year-old Bobby proved himself still to be a busily bustling, willing forager until sidelined by the emergence of Julian Joachim and the conversion of Steve Walsh to a central striking role. A former shipyard welder who played as a part-timer until he was 21, he first made a striking impact at Halifax, notching the Shaymen's first hat-trick in nine years, and earning an £80,000 move to Derby after netting against them in the League Cup. His goal in the final fixture of his first Baseball Ground term was the one that frustrated Fulham and saw City promoted in the Cottagers' stead. Bobby later top-scored in each of the successive promotion efforts that saw the Rams rise from Third to First, and made a fair contribution to Leeds' Second Division championship campaign of 1990, though being only a fringe player during their title-winning season of two years later. Bobby initially left Filbert Street for Bramall Lane on a loan deal, but signed up a month later for the Blades' ill-fated Premiership campaign. Further Yorkshire travels then landed him with a second Halifax spell, though this time in the Conference; and he was nearly 40 when deciding to drop his hyphenated title at Northern Premier League Guiseley and concentrate there on management.

***Apps:** FL 21+4; LC 3; AIC 2+1.*
***Goals:** FL 6; LC 1, AIC 2.*

D'AVRAY, Jean Michel

b. Johannesburg, South Africa, 19th February 1962

Career: Rangers (Johannesburg); May 1979 Ipswich Town; Feb 1987-loan-CITY; June 1990 NEC Nijmegen; June 1992 Moroka Swallows (p/coach; p/mgr); Jan 1994 Cape Town Spurs (p/mgr).

City debut v Liverpool (A) 14.2.87

> A tall striker of massive but largely unrealised scoring potential by the time he arrived at Leicester for a brief loan spell, Mich had emerged from Paul Mariner's shadow at Ipswich, yet never convincingly assumed the latter's goal mantle. Naturalised in 1983, he had won two England Under-21 caps despite finding himself a regular occupant of the Portman Road subs' bench; and while with City appeared either ill-briefed as to how to play alongside Alan Smith, or simply unable to adapt to a twin-spearhead role. Mich subsequently reverted to a deeper-lying position

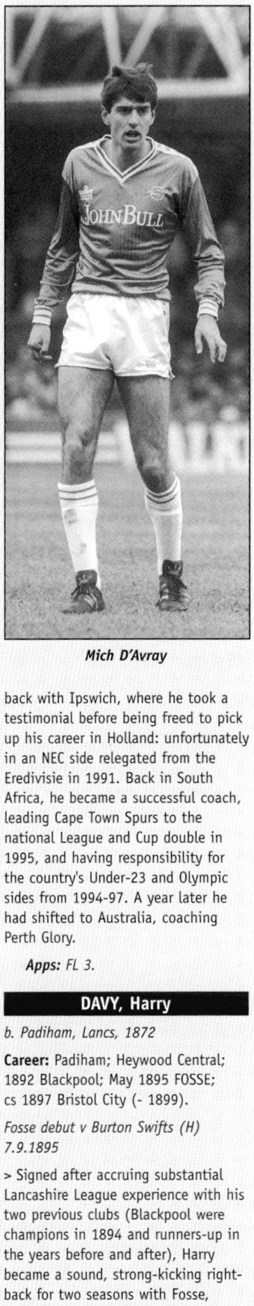

Mich D'Avray

back with Ipswich, where he took a testimonial before being freed to pick up his career in Holland: unfortunately in an NEC side relegated from the Eredivisie in 1991. Back in South Africa, he became a successful coach, leading Cape Town Spurs to the national League and Cup double in 1995, and having responsibility for the country's Under-23 and Olympic sides from 1994-97. A year later he had shifted to Australia, coaching Perth Glory.

***Apps:** FL 3.*

DAVY, Harry

b. Padiham, Lancs, 1872

Career: Padiham; Heywood Central; 1892 Blackpool; May 1895 FOSSE; cs 1897 Bristol City (- 1899).

Fosse debut v Burton Swifts (H) 7.9.1895

> Signed after accruing substantial Lancashire League experience with his two previous clubs (Blackpool were champions in 1894 and runners-up in the years before and after), Harry became a sound, strong-kicking right-back for two seasons with Fosse, welding an ever-present partnership with George Swift in 1896/7. He then joined former team-mate Albert Carnelly and Fossil-to-be Jack Hamilton for Bristol City's inaugural Southern League campaign. His second and final season in the West Country saw Harry twice chosen in goal.

***Apps:** FL 50; FAC 6.*

DAW, Edwin Charles

b. Doncaster, 23rd January 1875
d. Doncaster, 1944

Career: Doncaster Congregationals; Hexthorpe Wanderers; trials-Sheffield United; Nov 1896 Grimsby Town; cs 1897 Barnsley St Peters; cs 1898 Rushden; May 1899 Luton Town; May 1900 FOSSE; cs 1902 New Brompton; cs 1903 not known; Nov 1904 Doncaster Rovers; Nov 1905 Bradford City; May 1906 Oldham Athletic; cs 1907 not known; cs 1909 Merthyr Town; Feb 1910 FOSSE.

Fosse debut v Burton Swifts (A) 1.10.1900

> Six-foot goalkeeper Teddy's two-year stint with Fosse, as a capable, consistent replacement for Godfrey Beardsley, represented the only stay of more than one season in his peripatetic career; though Leicester also figured at other junctures of his

record. Filbert Street had seen his League debut in a 4-2 Fosse win over Grimsby in December 1896, and there too he had suffered FA Cup defeat with Rushden in 1898/9. It was also in Leicester that he would settle for many years after his wanderlust had exhausted itself. Two of his clubs – Midland Leaguers Barnsley and Lancashire Combination champions Oldham – were negotiating their final season before joining the Football League; while Luton temporarily but willingly dropped out of that sphere at the end of his term with them, and Doncaster failed re-election. Twice, also, Teddy found a first-team place beween the sticks barred (at Sheffield United and Bradford City) by the gargantuan frame of Willie Foulke. As a true veteran released by Merthyr, Teddy answered Fosse's emergency recall: he saved a penalty on his first reserve game back, but showed understandable rustiness when conceding six (and being blamed for three) in his senior finale at Stockport. Nonetheless, he still had one last second-string outing in February 1911.

Apps: *FL 56; FAC 2.*

DAWKINS, Derek Anthony

b. Edmonton, London, 29th November 1959

Career: app/pro Oct 1977 CITY; Dec 1978 Mansfield Town; Dec 1981 Bournemouth; July 1983 Torquay United; Feb 1989 Newport County; Sept 1989 Yeovil Town; Nov 1990 Gloucester City.

City debut v Derby County (A) 22.4.78

> Given a run-out at right-back in the three final games of 1977/8 by caretaker boss Ian MacFarlane, as already-relegated City sought a bit of belated pride and some optimistic pointers to the future, Derek was still a teenager when released by Jock Wallace to Field Mill. He subsequently built a lengthy career in the lower divisions; featuring in a relegated Mansfield side (1980), a promoted Bournemouth squad (1982) and, during a 175-game stay at Plainmoor, a basement Torquay team which yo-yoed between re-election applications and the Play-Offs. In fact, it was former team-mate Dave Webb who signed Derek for both his South Coast clubs. His move to Newport came immediately before their winding-up, halfway through their initial Conference campaign, and he played only in their last-ever fixture, a Clubcall Cup tie lost 5-6 to Kidderminster after extra time. In 1991/2, Gloucester City were briefly suspended by the FA when claiming inability to pay off the insurance for the injury which ended Derek's career.

Apps: *FL 3.*

DAWSON, James E.

b. Stoneyburn, West Lothian, 21st December 1927

Career: Polkemmet; May 1946 CITY; June 1949 Portsmouth; Sept 1951 Corby Town; Aug 1952-trials-Third Lanark; Brush Sports; July 1956 Hinckley Athletic.

City debut v Birmingham City (H) 12.9.46

> Not actually signed as a full-time professional by City until his RAF demob in November 1947, Jimmy was primarily groomed in the reserves as an outside-left, but a pair of his infrequent senior outings were in the right-half slot. It was his flank promise that was noticed by League champions Pompey, but his lot there was as understudy to England wingers Jack Froggatt and Peter Harris, and Jimmy made but a single appearance in the title-winning encore.

Apps: *FL 5.*

DELANEY, Damien

b. Cork, 29th July 1981

Career: jnr/pro cs 2000 Cork City; Oct 2000 CITY.

City debut v York City (H) FAC 6.1.2001 (sub)

> The most promising of Peter Taylor's several 'squad' signings of 2000/1, Damien has already impressed with his confident assumption of both left-sided defensive and midfield roles on his limited senior outings, and more than a few observers have already been prepared to compare him in style and stature to a young Graham Cross. A recommendation from Colin Murphy landed the young Irishman at Filbert Street only a couple of months after he'd signed his first part-time professional contract with Cork, whose FAI Youth Cup-winning side of 2000 he'd skippered, and for whom he'd played only a handful of League of Ireland and UEFA Cup games. His cost to City (set between £50,000-£100,000) rose by a £10,000 increment at the moment he made his late entry to the York Cup tie, replacing Robbie Savage; but confirmation that the club had landed a true bargain came with Damien's first starts: in the Villa Park FA Cup game in which he was involved in the lead-up to Arnar Gunnlaugsson's 'Goal of the Season' winner, and at Old Trafford in the backs-to-the-wall Premiership display which lucklessly crumbled only in the final minutes. He was utterly unfortunate not to find himself on the City scoresheet, as well: having almost broken the bar against Middlesbrough at Filbert Street. Damien deservedly picked up Under-21 recognition from the Republic in June. The notion that there might be 'more where he came from' underpinned City's formal development deal with Cork City, and is rather a seductive prospect.

Apps *(to end 2000/1): PL 3+2; FAC 1+1.*

DeVILLE, Thomas

b. ca 1865

Career: Stoke Wanderers; Leicester Town; 1886 FOSSE; Nov 1888 Loughborough; Rotherham Town; Jan 1892 FOSSE.

Fosse debut (competitive) v Long Eaton Rangers (A) ML 23.1.1892

> A veteran of the 'Friendly Fossils' era, Tom actually turned out at right-back in the club's first-ever County Cup tie in 1887, but it was as a goalkeeper that he gained a reputation good enough to take him onto the Midland League transfer roundabout, and it was as a last-line that he returned to find Fosse esconced at Filbert Street. He'd initially left the club, along with skipper Tommy Ashmole, when Fosse lost the tenancy of the Belgrave Road Grounds in 1888 and had to return to the wide open spaces of Victoria Park. His former Rotherham team-mates certainly did him no favours in April 1892, when they put eleven past him as their contribution to his 'goals against' total of 27 in only 10 Midland League fixtures. Another of those goals, put across his own line to the credit of Gainsborough Trinity a month earlier, was the first instance of a Fosse own goal at competitive level.

Apps: *ML 10.*

DEWIS, George Renger

b. Burbage, Leics, 22nd January 1913
d. Hinckley, Leics, 23rd October 1994

Career: Stoke Golding; am Apr 1933/pro Nov 1933 Nuneaton Town; Nov 1933 CITY (- 1950).

City debut v West Bromwich Albion (H) 9.12.33

> City scouts could hardly have been inconspicuous as they logged the centre-forward progress of young George Dewis at Nuneaton. Recent City retiree George Carr was manager at that impecunious club, and got his prodigy to sign a professional form precisely a week before City came in with an offer; which duly had to be upped to £220! The new signing's prowess, based on strength, determination and aerial ability, was used sparingly over his first five seasons, and luck was not always with him. Providentially, his first City strike, at Birmingham a week after his debut, was voided when fog caused the game to be abandoned after 65 minutes; and he was unarguably reaching the peak of his bustling effectiveness when war was declared (as reserve-team top-scorer for three late-30s terms, he won selection for the London Combination and scored twice both home and away in victories over the Central League in 1937). His and the club's loss at this time was instanced by George's wartime playing record: a 62-goal return from the 81 City games he managed to fit in during Army service and between representative matches for Northern Command and guest outings for Chesterfield, Leeds, Sheffield United and Yeovil. At one stage during the winter of 1940/1, he netted in ten successive City games, totalling fifteen goals in that sequence. George's best years were effectively behind him when peacetime football resumed, even if an aggregate 19 goals in 1946/7 represented City's top individual haul. He gave three more seasons' service as a senior player, then became third-team coach in July 1950, though turning out with his young charges in emergencies as late as October 1953. The meticulous care he thereafter lavished on successive waves of City hopefuls deserved high tribute, and appropriately later drew grateful public testimony from the likes of Peter Shilton. Rather like Arthur Chandler, George wouldn't let even his pension-book keep him away from Filbert Street, where he remained as kit-man until 1983.

Apps: *FL 116; FAC 13; WW2 81.*
Goals: *FL 45; FAC 6; WW2 62.*

DICKSON, Adam

b. Hamilton, Lanarkshire, 4th January 1929

Career: Thorniewood United; June 1951 CITY; cs 1955 Peterborough United; Dec 1957 Hinckley Athletic; Jan 1960 Syston St Peters; 1962 Oadby Town; Thurmaston Progressive WMC.

City debut v West Ham United (A) 27.10.51

> A reliable, safe-handling goalkeeper who understudied fellow Scot Johnny Anderson throughout his City career, Adam made an early breakthrough into Second Division fare when Anderson was ordered to play for the Army against Aberdeen. His first five games all brought win bonuses; but his last dozen featured only one victory. Unlucky not to find another League club on his release, Adam was more unfortunate still in failing to win a regular place in a Posh side steaming to the first two of their five successive Midland League championships. He was involved in a Senior League/County Cup double with Oadby in 1964; and a couple of years later was involved with another ex-City man, Bobby Anderson, in the management of District League side Thurmaston; playing his final games for them when over forty.

Apps: *FL 16; FAC 1.*

DILKS, Frank Thomas

b. Lamport, Northants, ca 1881
d. London, 24th June 1937

Career: Daventry Town; cs 1901 Northampton Town; May 1903 Reading; Oct 1903 FOSSE; cs 1904 Wellingborough; cs 1905 Northampton Town.

Fosse debut v Grimsby Town (H) 24.10.03

> Apparently unhappy to be away for long from the Northants/Leicestershire border, outside-left Tommy built a reasonable Southern League reputation in a Cobblers side that also featured Jack Bennett and Herbert Dainty, but then lasted for only a three-game spell in that sphere with Reading. He became the third of eight players tried on the Fosse left flank in the barrel-scraping, rock-bottom season of 1903/04, and fared little better than any other. On finishing his second stint with Northampton, he took over the pub he had grown up in, the Fitzgerald Arms at Naseby; and was later licensee of the nearby Kelmarsh Arms. Tommy's death in a London hospital followed a three-month illness.

Apps: *FL 8; FAC 1.*

DIXON, Arthur

b. Middleton, Lancs, 17th November 1921

Career: Baillieston Juniors; May 1940 Queens Park; cs 1945 Clyde; Sept 1947 Heart of Midlothian; Nov 1949 Northampton Town; Oct 1951 CITY; July 1953 Kettering Town; British Timken.

City debut v Bury (H) 6.10.51

> An English-born, Scottish-raised inside-forward whose Hampden Park scoring record during wartime (88 goals in five years for Queens Park) saw him selected for a Scottish representative line-up before he admitted to his birthplace, Arthur proved himself in English football at the County Ground, but had a luckless stay with Leicester. Only briefly able to displace Fred Worthington from the first-team, he never got another look-in after City signed Johnny Morris. The heading ability that had won him the nickname 'Rubberneck' with the Cobblers was never seen to effect, and his Filbert Street stint remained scoreless. His father, also Arthur, had played for Oldham, St Mirren, Rangers and Cowdenbeath between 1912 and 1929; had managed Dolphin in the League of Ireland; was trainer at each of Rangers, Partick Thistle and Oldham; and acted as spongeman to the Scottish international team in the late 30s. Arthur junior himself assumed masseur/physiotherapist duties at Notts County when Tommy Lawton took over there in 1957.

Apps: *FL 11.*

DOHERTY, John

b. Manchester, 12th March 1935

Career: am 1950/pro Mar 1952 Manchester United; Oct 1957 CITY; July 1958 Rugby Town (p/mgr); Sept 1958 Altrincham.

City debut v Everton (H) 5.10.57

> A genuine 'Busby Babe', given his United League bow at the age of 17, and a four-goal contributor to their 1956 Championship campaign, John eventually found competition for a regular inside-forward spot at Old Trafford unbearably intense. He had scored for United on a rare senior outing only a fortnight before City laid out £6,500 for his transfer, but he was fated never to justify the fee. He was suffering from 'flu on his City debut, and barely tottered through the second half. He scored after 30 seconds at Turf Moor, but the game

John Doherty

still resulted in a 3-7 defeat. While after a dozen games had given cause for pleasure at his integration, the effects of an old knee injury manifested themselves again. John underwent surgery, then contracted scarlet fever; and was then advised on medical grounds to avoid the stresses of League football altogether. Duly freed by City, he became the fourth player that summer (after Froggatt, Morris and Rowley) to dive into player-management; becoming at 23 the youngest boss in the Southern League. After a quartet of defeats, however, and with his wife ill, John resigned and moved back homeward, becoming a car salesman. In the early 80s he was Burnley's chief scout; and in the 90s became chairman of Manchester United's Former Players Association

Apps: *FL 12.*
Goals: *FL 5.*

DONNELLY, James

b. South Bank, nr Middlesbrough, 1882

Career: South Bank; Darlington St.Augustine's; Oct 1902 Sheffield United; May 1907 FOSSE; cs 1910 Darlington (- 1913).

Fosse debut v Leeds City (H) 7.9.07

> A £150 signing who contributed tellingly to Fosse's only promotion campaign from both right-flank forward positions, Jimmy remains best remembered as the scorer of the club's inaugural First Division goal (in the 1-1 home draw with Sheffield Wednesday which opened 1908/09). Indeed, he finished that unfortunate top-flight term as top scorer (with 10), and then turned selfless provider as Fred Shinton raced to his record seasonal goal-haul in 1909/10 – Jimmy's contract for that season showing him to have been one of 573 professionals in England then receiving the maximum wage of £4 per week. He was a member, as was Ronald Brebner, of the Darlington squad which reached the last 16 of the FA Cup in 1911 (beating his former First Division club Sheffield United along the way) and he was still active when the Quakers took the North Eastern League championship in 1913. Fosse were definitely being over-optimistic, though, when still keeping Jimmy's League registration in May 1914, with a £50 fee on his head.

Apps: *FL 74; FAC 2.*
Goals: *FL 26; FAC 1.*

DORRELL, William

b. Coventry, ca 1872
d. Leicester, 14th February 1953

Career: 1889 Singers; cs 1892 FOSSE; Apr 1894 Aston Villa; Mar 1896 FOSSE (- 1899).

Fosse debut v Mansfield Town (A) ML 17.9.1892

> Billy actually made his Fosse bow a fortnight before the competitive debut cited above, in the first friendly of the new season, and contributed a goal to the 10-1 demolition of his former club – the one we now know as Coventry

City. As a Birmingham Junior Cup winner, he'd been a hero there, and was to become one – twice! – with Fosse, despite initially assuming the left-wing spot from the poular Jimmy Atter. Speedy and incisive, he was eventually tempted to Villa after scoring Fosse's last-ever Midland League goal, but with England internationals Smith and Athersmith acting as obstacles to him gaining a regular first-team spot on either wing, Billy's chances at Perry Barr were limited. He nonetheless scored five goals in only 11 First Division appearances, adding a brace in his only FA Cup outing as Villa progressed to the 1895 Final, and was chosen for the Football League against the Irish League. The welcome on his return to Fosse was heartfelt – and Billy obliged his fans by scoring in the first League game of his three-year second spell, during which he turned in a number of scintillating displays on both flanks. He even once tested his pace in a 440-yard challenge race with a visiting American athlete, and won, before the kick-off of the home game with Darwen in February 1898. In December of that year, he took a benefit from the prestigious friendly against the touring Corinthians; and completed his Fosse days with the then club record for goals scored in FA Cup ties. Billy became a Villa scout in the 20s, by which stage his son Arthur was starring both for that club and England; while another son, Billy Jnr (see below), had by then completed a brief City career. He then became a machine parts inspector for Jones & Shipman, and never actually retired; dying at the age of 80 at his Lancashire Street home, to be survived by his third wife.

Apps: *FL 59; FAC 14; ML 43.*
Goals: *FL 20; FAC 11; ML 16.*

DORRELL, William Ernest

b. Leicester, 9th May 1893
d. Leicester, 17th June 1973

Career: 1911 Carey Hall; 1913 Belgrave Primitive Methodists; Dec 1919 CITY; cs 1920 Hinckley United; cs 1921 Coalville Swifts; Aug 1922 Loughborough Corinthians; Sept 1923 Coalville Swifts.

City debut/only game v Rotherham County (H) 6.12.19

> With both George Douglas and Joe Norton unfit prior to this 1-1 draw, Billy Jnr didn't quite grasp the chance to inscribe his family name as indelibly in the City annals as had his father into Fosse's. 'Not energetic enough', opined Scrutator in the *Mail;* while the *Sports Mercury* estimated that he 'did not reveal quite League class'. Happier at a less elevated level of football, he was twice in County Cup-winning sides: for City Reserves in 1920, and for Loughborough Corinthians (where Billy briefly succeeded Hughie Adcock) in 1923.

Apps: *FL 1.*

DOUGAN, Alexander Derek

b. Belfast, 20th January 1938

Career: 1955 Distillery; Aug 1957 Portsmouth; Mar 1959 Blackburn Rovers; July 1961 Aston Villa; June 1963 Peterborough United; May 1965 CITY; Mar 1967 Wolverhampton Wanderers; Dec 1975 Kettering Town (p/chief exec).

City debut v Liverpool (H) 21.8.65

> Reversing the usual dynamic by which a modern 'personality' is constructed, Derek achieved a remarkable about-turn in his career and his image midway through his playing days. A process begun at Peterborough, accelerated at Leicester and completed at Wolves actually provided a rare example of a virtual caricature turning into a genuine character. Despite teenage success in Belfast (an FAI Cup-winner's medal in 1956), and a fairly smooth transition to First Division fare, Derek expended too many of his early energies on the establishment of a rebellious persona as a joker and wilful controversialist – often to the detriment of his football – before he found a mature balance between showmanship and soccer. He'd been to Wembley with Blackburn (in 1960, when he'd netted the two semi-final goals, then posted a transfer request on the morning of the Cup Final) and his status as a Northern Ireland regular seemed assured, but the trajectory of his striking career seemed permanently stalled when Villa let him go to London Road, after he'd amused many with his adoption of a shaven head, and scared more with his propensity for off-field scrapes. Perhaps a spell in the Third Division helped restore a sense of perspective, or perhaps a renewed burst of media interest in 'The Doog' when Posh met Arsenal in the Cup rekindled ambitions. At any rate, Derek took a pay cut to join City back in the top flight, and proceeded to fully justify Matt Gillies' £25,000 gamble as he managed both to put a smile back on City's game and to link with fellow newcomer Jackie Sinclair in a lethal finishing partnership. Brilliant in the air, and with a remarkably sure and subtle first touch for a tall striker, Derek led City's line with unique flair, and lapped up the crowd's adulation – not least on such occasions as when he knocked in a flamboyant hat-trick against former club Villa, or when he led a bemused close marker behind the goal while awaiting a City corner! The Doog's departure was the cause of much ill-feeling between the club and its supporters, centred on the belief that City had merely, unimaginatively, cashed in on the first offer to doubly recoup their investment; and City fans were irked even more when Derek (taking over from Hugh McIlmoyle) made an immediate impact at Molineux, where his goals ensured promotion within a couple of months. Settling with Wolves for 310 senior games and 118 goals over almost eight years, Derek also won with them his sole victor's trophy, for the 1974 League Cup, a year before retirement. Eventually, he finished his senior career with 222 League goals and 43 Irish caps. An articulate chairman of the PFA, a stimulating author and easeful TV pundit, he surprised few with a move into management (albeit with Kettering, where he clashed with the FA over shirt sponsorship before such became the permitted norm, and from where he resigned in 1977 after leading them to third place in the Southern League). In 1982 he led a consortium of businessmen in rescuing and reconstructing Wolves after they had fallen into receivership; but strangely thereafter became lost to the game. Incidentally, of all ex-Leicester players, Derek was the one to have scored most goals against the club: one for Blackburn, four for Villa, and three for Wolves.

Apps: *FL 68; FAC 5; LC 3.*
Goals: *FL 35; FAC 1; LC 5.*

DOUGAN, Maxwell Spalding

b. Stoneyburn, West Lothian, 23rd May 1938

Career: cs 1962 Queens Park; Sept 1963 CITY; Dec 1966 Luton Town; July 1970 Dunstable Town.

City debut v Gillingham (H) LC 27.11.63

> A latecomer to the senior game, centre-half Max bought himself out of the army to play as an amateur for a year at Hampden Park, and his representative career at unpaid level peaked in the FA's Centenary Amateur International Tournament of 1963, with Scotland beating West Germany 5-2 at Roker Park to take the trophy. The strongly-built stopper then trained with City for a couple of months until eligible to sign pro forms, though he was to make his Filbert Street debut as an emergency centre-forward in aiding the club past one hurdle on the way to League Cup glory, and win a half-back place in the first leg of the Final at Stoke. Overall, Max's City chances were severely limited by the consistency of Ian King and John Sjoberg, but it was his occasional experience at full-back which would stand him in good stead for his subsequent years as a rugged, unceremonious No.2 with Luton, who he assisted via the 1968 Fourth Division championship to the verge of Division Two.

Apps: *FL 9; LC 2.*

DOUGLAS, George Harold

b. Forest Gate, London, 18th August 1893
d. Southborough, Kent, 24th January 1979

Career: St Saviours; Forest Gate; Custom House; 1911 Ilford; am May 1912/pro May 1913 FOSSE; Feb 1921 Burnley; May 1922 Oldham Athletic; Aug 1926 Bristol Rovers; July 1928 Tunbridge Wells Rangers (p/mgr); Nov 1930 Dover United.

Fosse debut v Hull City (H) 21.12.12

> A graduate of West Ham schools football who became an outside-right (and occasional goalscoring centre-forward) in the Isthmian League, George was already on the fringe of the England amateur international squad when Jack Bartlett signed him up to the burgeoning ranks of the Filbert Street unpaid. Impressing sufficiently at Second Division level to earn a couple of amateur caps, George then toured Spain with Bromley in May 1913, and returned to put his name on a professional contract with Fosse. He enlisted in the Leicester Royal Horse Artillery in April 1915, and managed only the odd wartime game for Fosse, Arsenal and Norwich City between stints of active service; but was back at Filbert Street in April 1919 for the last match Fosse ever played under that title, albeit in the visiting B.E.F. (France) eleven. George missed a penalty that day, but four months later he scored the very first goal attributed to to Leicester City (in the 1-2 home defeat by Wolves which inaugurated 1919/20). He prowled City's right wing for another season-and-a-half (taking a benefit against Birmingham in September 1920), before becoming a buttress to Burnley's 1920 championship run-in. An apparently colourful off-field life accompanied his post-Leicester wanderings: on the very day of his Burnley bow at Derby, he was summoned in the Police Court at Leicester for alleged desertion of his wife (the case was dismissed a week later), while at Christmas 1922 George appeared on the official missing person's list after Oldham briefly lost touch with him. He eventually retired through injury in 1931; going on to manage a Tunbridge Wells sports shop for 32 years, and then to act for a further decade as a water bailiff on the Medway, walking ten miles daily. When he was at Highbury for the 50th anniversary game with City, George produced his original three-year Fosse contract (one of the first such issued) for £4 per week; unrecorded are his comments on football wages then (1963), though as early as 1935 he'd written to the national press decrying the amounts players were taking from a game from which he'd accrued a relative pittance.

Apps: *FL 127; FAC 6; WW1 3.*
Goals: *FL 10; FAC 1.*

DRAPER, Mark Andrew

b. Long Eaton, Derbyshire, 11th November 1970

Career: YT/pro Dec 1988 Notts County; July 1994 CITY; July 1995 Aston Villa; Jan 2000-loan-Rayo Vallecano; July 2000 Southampton.

City debut v Newcastle United (H) 21.8.94

> It took less than a dozen games into City's initial Premiership misadventure for them to be assailed on all sides by three pieces of consensual wisdom: that they would be relegated, that they had contrived a bargain buy in their new playmaker, and that said quality midfielder would be on his way to a 'big' club either before deadline day or at the end of the season. The correctness of this diagnosis from seemingly every professional observer doesn't detract from it standing as an example of the top-flight myopia afflicting the game's coverage these days; for the skills and strength Mark brought to that arena had for long previously been evident even in the context of Notts County's regular upheavals. A 17-year-old Meadow Lane debutant in 1988, Mark had played himself into a key prompting role when the Magpies achieved successive promotions to the old First Division by 1991. A relegation campaign ensued, then a term when Mark top-scored from the middle line, and a 1994 Wembley appearance in the Anglo-Italian Cup Final; while a trio of England Under-21 selections indexed his progress. Notts valued Mark at £2.5 million when Brian Little bid for him, and it was quite a surprise when a transfer tribunal settled the deal at an initial fee of half that amount (still by some distance a record outlay for City); less so that the player himself negotiated a 'get-out' clause in his contract in the event of City failing to maintain their hard-won new status. A penalty hit over-hastily at Newcastle's Pavel Srinicek clouded Mark's City debut, and presaged a disappointing strike-rate overall for the club, but compensatory pleasures abounded from his mastery of the ball, of the tellingly angled pass, and of the tight turning circle. The close-cropped Midlander may not have exhibited the sheer elegance of a Gary McAllister, but his knack of finding space around a crowded halfway line, and his dribbling skills, stood out regularly. Little called back twice to secure a Villa Park reunion with Mark; having a £3 million bid turned down in March 1995, but succeeding with a £3.25 cheque some four months later. City handed half-a-million to Notts County as their share of the profit, while Mark soon picked up his first major medal from Villa's 1996 League Cup win. Yet his impact in claret-and-blue was essentially muted, and he could find only limited first-team favour after John Gregory succeeded Little in the Villa management role. More recently, he struggled to adapt to Spanish football at the same club as Kasey Keller, and suffered a somewhat anonymous campaign as the Saints said farewell to The Dell.

Apps: *PL 39; FAC 2; LC 2.*
Goals: *PL 5.*

DRYBURGH, Thomas James Douglas

b. Kirkcaldy, Fife, 23rd April 1923

Career: Lochgelly Albert; June 1947 Aldershot; July 1948 Rochdale; Aug 1950 CITY; May 1954 Hull City; July 1955 King's Lynn; Aug 1957 Oldham Athletic; Nov 1957 Rochdale; cs 1958 Kings Lynn.

City debut v Notts County (H) 4.9.50

> A former ice-hockey star with Kirkcaldy Fliers, who won Scottish junior international honours as an outside-left while playing for Lochgelly (Fife County League champions in 1947), Tom then tasted life in both Sections of the Third Division, and was part of the first Rochdale side to win the Lancashire Senior Cup in 1949. Norman Bullock brought him to City for £6,500 to replace Charlie Adam, and Tom became Arthur Rowley's first regular left-wing partner. Maintaining a decent scoring rate himself, he was the first City man to be recorded as netting within ten seconds of the start of a game (against Swansea at home in March 1953), but it was in the following, Second Division championship-winning term that Tom lost his senior No.11 shirt to Peter Small, and he failed thereafter really to recapture his effective dash at League level. It is possible that Tom's second stint with King's Lynn may have been followed by a spell with Morecambe.

Tom Dryburgh

Apps: *FL 95; FAC 4.*
Goals: *FL 29; FAC 1.*

DUDFIELD, Lawrie George

b. Southwark, London, 7th May 1980

Career: 1996 Kettering Town; June 1997 CITY; Sept 2000-loan-Lincoln City; Dec 2000-loan-Chesterfield; June 2001 Hull City.

City debut v Everton (H) 8.4.2000 (sub)

> A tall young striker who played Conference football for the Poppies at the age of 16, Lawrie top-scored for City's youth team in 1997/8 and earned himself a contract renewal that April. His form in City's first term in the Premier Reserve League (South) then won him an elevation to the senior bench, and brief late-season stints against Everton and at Villa Park ensued – with Lawrie inches away from opening his goal account in the latter game. He broadened his experience more substantially during 2000/1 away from Filbert Street, and opened his senior goal account with a trio of strikes for a promotion-bound Chesterfield before his return; but was then a surprise summer departure when attracting Hull's highest-ever fee of £250,000.

Apps: *PL 0+2.*

DUFFY, Christopher Francis

b. Jarrow, Co Durham, 1885

Career: Jarrow; St Mary's College (Hammersmith); Jan 1905 Brentford; Oct 1905 Middlesbrough; Aug 1906 Newcastle United; May 1908 Bury; cs 1913 not known; July 1914 North Shields Athletic; Nov 1914 Bury; Dec 1919 CITY; Aug 1920 Chester-le-Street.

City debut v Bristol City (H) 6.4.20 (scored once)

> A real veteran, settled as a Newcastle schoolteacher by the time Peter Hodge called on his services as a left-sided forward in the initial post-WW1 season, Chris featured in City's reserve side during his Yuletide holiday, and broke into the first team during his Easter break. The pace which had seen him gain repute as, initially, an athletic sprinter, and then as a First Division winger, had predictably though by now deserted him. Chris had made a seven-game contribution to Newcastle's 1907 championship campaign, and had been a regular over six seasons (in two stints) with Bury, scoring against Fosse in both fixtures of the 1908/9 top-flight term. His scholarly pursuits saw him promoted to a headmastership on Tyneside shortly after his retirement from the game.

Apps: *FL 4.*
Goals: *FL 1.*

DUFFY, Michael Kevin

b. Leicester, 12th June 1961

Career: app/pro July 1978 CITY; 1981-trials-Vfb Stuttgart; May 1981 Enderby Town; 1981 Wigston Fields; Birstall United; Nov 1985 Leicester United; Shepshed Charterhouse; Corby Town; Oadby Town (p/mgr); 1991 North Kilworth; Dunton Bassett; July 1992 Oadby Town (p/mgr).

City debut v Notts County (H) 9.9.78

> The first of the several teenagers unexpectedly elevated to a first-team spot as part of Jock Wallace's 1978/9 rejuvenation plan, Mick was a busy inside-forward with a useful youth-team scoring rate, and on his debut netted a neat header that was dubiously disallowed. In the Second Division return fixture with the Magpies he provided the 'assist' for Gary Lineker's first senior goal, and scored himself in the final fixture of that term, at Bramall Lane, when City actually fielded their youngest-ever line-up. Yet Mick was only ever to make one further substitute appearance in the senior game thereafter; and soon had to settle for becoming a stalwart of the local scene. In the mid-90s, he was managing Aylestone Park and working as a day centre officer in Leicester, on activities for people with learning disabilities.

Apps: *FL 7+5.*
Goals: *FL 1.*

DUMBRELL, George

b. Catford, London, 23rd September 1906
d. Gravesend, Kent, March 1990

Career: Botwell Mission; Nunhead; Catford South End; Cray Wanderers; 1927 Dartford; May 1928 Brentford; May 1930 CITY; Nov 1933 Bournemouth & Boscombe Athletic; Aug 1934 Brentford.

City debut v Blackburn Rovers (A) 2.3.31

> A reserve full-back in both of his Griffin Park spells (retiring in 1938 with an aggregate of only 17 League appearances for the Bees), George nonetheless cost City £1,750 when recruited as cover for Reg Osborne, and in fact made fairly light work of bridging the gap in divisional status. Very rarely did he let down City's top-flight defence when being called upon to partner Adam Black, even if his defensive style was deemed somewhat unsophisticated. Brentford themselves had risen to the First Division by the time George next started a game for them; but in the interim his efforts at Dean Court (including his only pair of senior goals) had failed to raise Bournemouth above a re-election placing. Back in his Dartford days, George had first made his name as a goalscoring centre-forward, and had won selection as such for a Kent representative side.

Apps: *FL 37; FAC 2.*

DUNCAN, John

b. Lochgelly, Fife, 14th February 1896
d. Leicester, 14th March 1966

Career: Denbeath Star; Aug 1915 Lochgelly United; 1916 Raith Rovers; July 1922 CITY (- 1930); May 1933 Solus FC.

City debut v Stockport County (A) 26.8.22 (scored twice)

> A strongly-built ball artist; a far-from shot-shy schemer; an inspirational skipper; and a shrewd manager. Attributes all of an indelible City 'great': whether remembered as John, Johnny or 'Tokey'; as a forceful inside-forward, a wing-half playmaker, a besuited boss or a genuinely respected barroom sage. A teenager when scoring a hat-trick on his Eastern League debut for Lochgelly, he came early under the wartime wing of Peter Hodge at Raith, and remained under scrutiny by his countryman as the latter set about rebuilding City as the purists' favourites. Johnny had led the Kirkcaldy club to their highest-ever Scottish League placing (3rd) in 1922 when City finally expended £1,500 to bring him and his brother Tom to Filbert Street, and he would be quickly identified as the creative linchpin of the club's sustained scrap for League honours over the next eight years. By the end of his initial season, he had contributed 20 goals and an almost ever-present record to a campaign in which City missed promotion on goal average – Johnny himself only missing the final, crucial defeat at Bury. After three terms he was handling the Second Division championship trophy with a 30-goal haul, including a successive sextet notched on Christmas Day in the 7-0 pasting of Port Vale. Maintaining influence and incisiveness in the top echelon, Johnny was rewarded with a Scottish cap in October 1925. Yet despite scoring against Wales, he was subsequently overlooked by his country. At club level, his tactical retreat to the middle line stressed his effectiveness as an orchestrator over that of the opportunist, and his intelligent promptings were a key element in City's near-miss assaults on the title in 1928 and 1929. Sadly, a year later Johnny found himself at loggerheads with the City board over their refusal to sanction him running a pub while still on the playing staff; over which point of principle the Turk's Head on Welford Road acquired a genial landlord. City immediately fielded enquiries from Nottingham Forest, Northampton Town, Market Harborough Town, Grantham & Nuneaton; but Johnny himself decided he would only play on loan (and choose his matches) so as to concentrate on his new business, and these terms cooled all interest. In May 1933 he signed for the Leicester Thursday League side, Solus; and in August 1935 became honorary coach to Leicester Nomads; while his pub gained wide renown as a football-talk 'academy'. Johnny became a founder committee-member of the new City Supporters Club in August 1940 and then, in March 1946, it was to Johnny that City turned for a manager to succeed Tom Bromilow and prepare the club for its none-too-easy return to peacetime football. Three years later, it was he who was proudly to lead out his Second Division team for their first-ever appearance at Wembley (even if, only a week before, he had had to defer a call for jury service). But only a matter of months later, in October 1949, Johnny was telling the *Mercury*, 'I have been sacked'. His main argument with the board was over transfer policy – with Johnny declaring that he didn't believe in close season deals when he couldn't judge a player's current form; and that he would thereafter return permanently to his pumps. Something of the man's managerial character is affectionately sketched in Don Revie's 1955 autobiography; but it is in City's cherished reputation down the years as a 'footballing' side wherein resides the best testimony to the influence of Johnny's playing personality. Only one quote is here necessary to support the contention; from the *Sunday Express's* 'Man in the Corner' at the end of the 1928/9 runners-up campaign: "The best football team have been Leicester City, who have approached nearer to the pre-war standard than any other in individuality and constructive clever-ness. I attribute this largely to the influence of their Scottish captain, John Duncan, who has insisted that the way to success was by expert use of the ball rather than by helter skelter methods". A third Duncan brother, Jim, played in the Scottish League for Lochgelly United; their uncle David Bain for Hearts, and cousin Jock Bain for Dunfermline and Dundee United.

Apps: *FL 279; FAC 16.*
Goals: *FL 88; FAC 7.*

DUNCAN, Thomas Grossett

b. Lochgelly, Fife, 1st September 1899
d. Leicester, 9th February 1940

Career: Lochgelly United; 1920 Raith Rovers; July 1922 CITY; Sept 1924 Halifax Town; May 1926 Bristol Rovers; July 1927 Kettering Town.

City debut v Rotherham County (A) 4.9.22

> A right-flank partner to brother Johnny for some time at each of Starks Park and Filbert Street, Tom had nothing like as illustrious a career, but was a bit unfortunate to be in direct competition with Hughie Adcock for the City winger's position. His selection was far from guaranteed, however, with either of his subsequent Third Division clubs; for whom he aggregated only seven goals in 45 League outings. Consolation of sorts came in two championship campaigns for Kettering at the head of the Southern League's Eastern Section. Tom survived a serious stomach illness in Leicester Infirmary in July 1930, but was still fated to an early death a decade later; his bereaved daughter Elsie afterwards marrying Don Revie.

Apps: *FL 41; FAC 1.*
Goals: *FL 6.*

DUNKLEY, Albert E.

b. Northampton, 1877

Career: Earls Barton Wesleyans; Rushden; cs 1897 Northampton Town; May 1900 FOSSE; Feb 1901 Northampton Town; July 1901 New Brompton; May 1903 Blackburn Rovers; cs 1904 Bristol Rovers; Aug 1906 Blackpool; cs 1907 Northampton Town.

Fosse debut v Stockport County (H) 1.9.1900

> A cousin of the contemporaneously more famous amateur Fred Dunkley, outside-left Albert was a member of the first-ever competitive side fielded by Northampton, and top-scorer in their initial Northants League campaign. He had only a brief liaison with Fosse, moving back home almost immediately after surrendering his position to Tommy Allsopp, then inclining to the nomadic life. He had a taste of top-flight fare at Ewood, but his most successful season followed, when he was a key member of Bristol Rovers' 1905 Southern League championship side, alongside future Fossils Willie Clark and Dick Pudan. His 1907 re-signing for the Cobblers was a fated affair: Albert was injured in pre-season and after two cartilage operations retired to become a publican.

Apps: *FL 10; FAC 1.*

DUNNE, James Peter

b. Dublin, 16th March 1935

Career: Sept 1953 CITY; cs 1956 St.Patrick's Athletic; Sept 1959 Peterborough United; cs 1962 Bedford Town; cs 1963 Cambridge United.

City debut v Sheffield Wednesday (A) 16.4.55

> A son of Irish international centre-forward Jimmy (of Sheffield United, Arsenal and Southampton fame), and a cousin of City's Tommy Dunne, Jimmy junior completes the genealogical Irish stew by having a brother named Tommy who won his own cap for the Republic in 1956. This young inside-left, however, must hold some sort of Football League record in having made a statistically neat eight appearances across all four divisions. His City debut came in a relegation-haunted defeat by the only team then lower than Leicester in the First Division chart; and it was unique in that he was the only player selected for his bow at the time City were manager-less, with the board elevating Jimmy after Norman Bullock's resignation. David Halliday also picked Jimmy twice in the Second Division, but he then left the club when to have stayed would have made him liable for two years of National Service. With St Pat's he was an FAI Cup-winner in 1959; with Posh a contributor to their final Midland League championship before election to Division Four. Only one selection followed in the following all-conquering term, then three more at Third Division level, before the Southern League beckoned.

Apps: *FL 4.*

DUNNE, Thomas

b. Dublin, 19th March 1927
d. Fazackerley, Lancs, 23rd January 1988

Career: Johnville; 1944 Ringsend CYMS; Home Farm; St.Patrick's Athletic; 1945 Shamrock Rovers; Nov 1949 CITY; July 1954 Exeter City; Aug 1956 Shrewsbury Town; July 1957 Southport.

City debut v Cardiff City (A) 17.2.51

> A beneficiary of the coaching of uncle Jimmy Dunne senior at Shamrock (where he'd picked up an FAI Cup-winners medal in 1948), wing-half Tommy followed former teammate Tommy Godwin to Filbert Street, but had to wait longer in the wings than did the international 'keeper for a City breakthrough. Tommy contented himself for some time with becoming the sure-shot penalty expert of the Combination side, but finally displaced Johnny King to win a fair run in the senior No.6 shirt in 1953. He lost out himself, however, to newcomer Eddie Russell midway through the 1954 promotion campaign, and was soon Third Division-bound with the Grecians, Shrews and Sandgrounders, accruing a further 61 League outings (and a solitary goal while at Exeter). Though their City careers overlapped by a year, cousins Tommy and Jimmy never played together in senior football. Having run a pub in Southport, Tommy died of throat cancer.

Apps: *FL 33; FAC 1.*

DURRANT, Arthur Francis (Jamie)

b. Luton, ca 1880
d. Luton, 6th April 1927

Career: Luton Stanley; Mar 1898 Luton Town May 1904 FOSSE; Sept 1909 Leyton; cs 1913 Luton Town.

Fosse debut v Blackpool (A) 3.9.04

> The epitome of the orthodox outside-right, rarely wandering from his narrow corridor of operation, but patrolling it with speed and trickery, Jamie gave Fosse five seasons of valuable service, culminating in the rollercoaster experience of successive promotion and relegation. At Luton, where he'd appeared across three Second Division terms and four in the Southern League, he had learned good footballing habits from Jimmy Blessington, who he followed to Filbert Street; while later, as a senior player at Southern League Leyton, he was in turn mentor to the young Charles Buchan, who acknowledged the debt he owed Jamie in his autobiography. It was another contemporary, however, who came up with the rather fanciful description of how Jamie 'ran with amazing speed in a soft-footed manner reminiscent of a wolf'! Jamie was in the Leyton side when they were beaten in front of their all-time record crowd by Fosse in the 1909/10 FA Cup; while his eventual return to Luton was to assist them upwards from their embarrassing status in the Southern League's Second Division. He served in the RNAS during WW1, and played cricket for Bedfordshire afterwards. He ran a confectionary business for a while, then took over a straw-hat manufacturers. At the time of his death after a long illness, aged 47, it transpired that no-one used his given names: while he'd always been known as Jamie while with Fosse, he was invariably referred to as Jack by his family!

Apps: *FL 140; FAC 13.*
Goals: *FL 24; FAC 3.*

EADIE, Darren Malcolm

b. Chippenham, Wilts, 10th June 1975

Career: YT/pro Feb 1993 Norwich City; Dec 1999 CITY.

City debut v Derby County 18.12.99

> A club record signing for City at an initial £3m, after being stalked over a long period by his one-time Carrow Road boss Martin O'Neill, Darren has still yet quite to hit his stride at Filbert Street in an attacking midfield role: showing himself neat on the ball and on the turn, and a willing chaser, but so far lacking consistent penetration in hitting either the by-line or the target. A winger when he first broke through with Norwich, he established himself during the Canaries' 1995 Premiership relegation campaign, and became a left-sided, pacy supporting striker before top-scoring himself with seventeen Division One goals in 1996/7. Darren also scored twice in seven England Under-21 outings, but a catalogue of injuries thereafter impeded – and often still hamper – his progress, and seem to have temporarily taken a little of the edge off his confidence and his telling acceleration. Darren, who proved the man to break City's long-standing Upton Park hoodoo during 2000/1, still has the potential,

Darren Eadie

however, to re-emphasise his class under a manager, in Peter Taylor, who played much the same role in his active days.

Apps *(to end 2000/1): PL 31+9; FAC 3+1; LC 1; UEFA 2.*
Goals: *PL 2.*

EARLE, Stephen John

b. Feltham, Middlesex, 1st November 1945

Career: am July 1961/pro Nov 1963 Fulham; Nov 1973 CITY; Nov 1977-loan-Peterborough United; Mar 1978 Detroit Express; July 1978 Tulsa Roughnecks; Oct 1978 Telford United; Mar 1979 Tulsa Roughnecks; 1981 Wichita.

City debut v Tottenham Hotspur (H) 1.12.73 (scored once)

> A prolific scorer across three Divisions for a yo-yo-ing Fulham (his 98 League goals for them included a vital hat-trick in the 1966 relegation decider at Northampton, and a personal nap-hand at Halifax in September 1969), Steve was also a former striking partner of both Allan Clarke and Frank Large, and was bought by Jimmy Bloomfield for £100,000 to lift some of the City scoring burden from Frank Worthington. After helping City dispose of his former club on the way to the 1974 FA Cup semi-final in his first season, (and having returned to Craven Cottage with City for a belated testimonial game in October 1975), nimble and unselfish front-runner Steve ironically then suffered something of a goal drought himself, and was displaced for a spell by Chris Garland before returning to hit 13 counters in 1976/7. Apparently unfancied by Frank McLintock, Steve was allowed to drift States-ward at a time his experience might have been better harnessed at Filbert Street. [Unchecked as yet, incidentally, is a stray reference to Steve's father having been a player for Airdrie].

Apps: *FL 91+8; FAC 13; LC 3.*
Goals: *FL 20; FAC 6.*

EASTOE, Peter Robert

b. Tamworth, Staffs, 2nd August 1953

Career: June 1971 Wolverhampton Wanderers; Nov 1973 Swindon Town; Mar 1976 Queens Park Rangers; Mar 1979 Everton; Aug 1982 West Bromwich Albion; Oct 1983-loan-CITY; Mar 1984-loan-Huddersfield Town; Aug 1984-loan-Walsall; Oct 1984-loan-CITY; Feb 1985-loan-Wolverhampton Wanderers; July 1985 Sporting Farense; 1986 not known; cs 1988 Atherstone United; 1989 Bridgnorth Town; Nov 1991 Alvechurch (p/mgr).

City debut v Norwich City (A) 19.10.83 (scored once)

> An idiosyncracy of Alan Smith's days with Leicester was that he often made a slow start to the season before his partnership with Gary Lineker would really gel. On two such occasions, Gordon Milne contacted West Brom to borrow their own out-of-favour striker as a temporary alternative. Peter actually made his initial City bow in the home game against Southampton that was abandoned when a torrential downpour flooded the pitch, and showed signs of settling after that false start until suffering a double fracture of his jaw in a match versus Manchester United. Adept at shielding and laying off the ball in attack, Peter had not shown particularly prolific scoring form since his time in Division Three at Swindon, yet his second goal for City – in the first match of his second spell, a 5-0 win over Aston Villa – was the 95th (and last) League strike of his career. He had featured in UEFA Cup action for each of Wolves, QPR and Everton; and with the latter club in 1980/81 had decided both home and away fixtures against City with a single goal. After a total of no less than five loan-outs from the Hawthorns, Peter briefly extended his career in Portugal, then did a circuit of the West Midlands non-league scene which additionally saw him in a short stint as assistant manager at Nuneaton Borough in 1993.

Apps: *FL 11; LC 1.*
Goals: *FL 2.*

EATON, Samuel Llewellyn

b. Derby, 1878

Career: Derby St James; 1895 Derby County; Derby St Lukes; 1897 Hinckley Town; Jan 1898 FOSSE; Aug 1900 Hinckley Town; June 1901 Stockport County; Jan 1902 FOSSE; May 1903 Luton Town; May 1905 Watford; Aug 1906 Earlestown; Oct 1906 Accrington Stanley; Dec 1906 Maidstone United.

Fosse debut v Lincoln City (H) 12.2.1898

> A junior apprentice to Steve Bloomer at Derby, and then a member of a Hinckley side bound for the Leicestershire Senior League championship, Sam shared his teenage Fosse debut with Henry Coulson, then held down a right-sided attacking berth for much of the following two Second Division seasons. The management were clearly in two minds about his likely development when they released him, for he'd no sooner revisited Filbert Street as a Stockport winger than he was re-recruited to the squad, in what was effectively a swap deal involving Arthur Marshall. No real success ensued, however, either with Fosse or subsequently in stints in the Southern League, Lancashire Combination and Kent League. By 1907/08, though, Maidstone had converted Sam into a centre-half.

Apps: *FL 52; FAC 5.*
Goals: *FL 12; FAC 1.*

ECCLES, Peter Edward

b. Dublin, 24th August 1962

Career: St Brendan's (Cabra); 1981 Shamrock Rovers; Aug 1988 Kingsway Olympic; Oct 1988 Dundalk; Oct 1988 CITY; Jan 1989-loan-Stafford Rangers; cs 1989 Dundalk; Oct 1989 Shamrock Rovers; June 1994 Crusaders; Shamrock Rovers; 1996 Athlone Town; 1996 Home Farm Everton.

City debut/only game v Blackburn Rovers (A) 8.4.89

> A tall central defender who had won a fistful of League of Ireland championship and FAI Cup medals in the first of two lengthy spells with Shamrock, and made an international appearance as substitute for the Republic against Uruguay in 1986 (alongside Gerry Daly, David Langan and clubmate Pat Byrne), Peter joined David Pleat's City on a free transfer after returning from a summer stint in Australian football. He received some fine notices for his Central League performances, and played twice at Conference level on loan at Stafford, but when belatedly called up to stand in for the injured Steve Walsh at Ewood was transparently embarrassed by the Second Division pace, and subbed at the interval. Soon back with his beloved Shamrock, Peter appeared in another FAI Cup Final in 1991, and took the club's Player of the Year award in 1993. His active career would seem to have ended with Home Farm's relegation in 1997.

Apps: *FL 1.*

Peter Eccles

EDMUNDS, Paul

b. Doncaster, 2nd December 1957

Career: Troston Welfare; Apr 1979 CITY; May 1981 Bournemouth; cs 1982 Bentley Victoria; Grantham; 1985 Burton Albion; Armthorpe Welfare.

City debut v Sunderland (A) 8.3.80

> Giving up his place in the British squad for the World Student Games in Mexico to sign for City, red-haired right-winger Paul went on to contribute two cracking individual goals as a latecomer to City's 1980 Second Division championship effort, before breaking his wrist at Wrexham (in an incident itself punished by Eddie Kelly's resultant free-kick goal). Jock Wallace thereafter chose him only for the opening defeat of the following top-flight season, and it would be in a promotion campaign for Bournemouth that Paul would next make an impact. There, his 14-game, 2-goal contribution to raising the Cherries from Division Four nonetheless failed to gain him a contract renewal; and for a while he resumed his schoolteaching career while part-timing in the non-league game. He then gained greater repute as manager/coach of the successful women's soccer team, Doncaster Belles, for whom his wife was an occasional player.

Apps: *FL 8.*
Goals: *FL 2.*

EDWARDS, Harry Ross

b. Coventry, 1870

Career: Singers; May 1892 Small Heath; Aug 1893 Ryton Rovers; Oct 1893 FOSSE; Aug 1894 Derby County; 1895 Wolverton L&NWR; Dec 1898 Watford; cs 1899 Bedford Queens (-1902).

Fosse debut v Mansfield Town (H) ML 21.10.1893 (scored once)

> Briefly renewing acquaintance with old Singers teammate Billy Dorrell during Fosse's final Midland League season, but spending much of it in a pay dispute with the club committee, Harry was a constructive inside-right who had joined Small Heath for their initial Second Division campaign, and indeed had scored in their first League fixture. At Derby, he failed to make the First Division eleven, despite turning out as attack leader against Fosse in the opening friendly of 1894/5. Wolverton were still a force in Southern League football when Harry joined them as an attacking centre-half (helping them to promotion in 1896 and keeping them up until 1898), while Watford were in their first season under that name (having previously been known as West Herts).

Apps: *FAC 6; ML 12.*
Goals: *ML 2.*

EDWARDS, Leslie

b. Nuneaton, Warks, Oct qtr 1910

Career: Bradbury's FC (Hinckley); Dec 1930 CITY; May 1932 Folkestone; May 1933 Crystal Palace; May 1936 Newport County; Aug 1938 Hinckley United.

City debut v Blackburn Rovers (A) 12.12.31

> Raised in Earl Shilton, right-half Les had two reserve trials before signing professionally for City, and it did him no harm whatsoever that an enthusiastic advocate of the club's action was the recently retired Johnny Duncan, then penning a regular *Mercury* column. His trio of first-team outings were all in First Division away games, however, and his debut came in a 0-6 thrashing at Ewood. He revived his spirits in Folkestone's FA Cup run of 1932/3 (when they KO'd Norwich and Newport before a narrow defeat by top-flight Huddersfield), and returned to League football at Selhurst; though a cartilage operation kept him out of the picture for the entirety of 1934/5. Les inherited the Newport captaincy for much of 1936/7, and was skipper again at Hinckley until walking out on the club in March 1939. He briefly assisted Reading as a guest during WW2. A Football League ledger from the time of his City days has him erroneously listed as Leonard Edwards.

Apps: *3.*

EDWARDS, Walter Thomas

b. Llanelli, 13th March 1923

Career: Workington; Aug 1946 Fulham; Mar 1948 Southend United; Dec 1948 CITY; cs 1949 Workington; June 1950 Bath City; May 1952 Walsall; cs 1953 Oswestry Town.

City debut v Leeds United (A) 18.12.48 (scored once)

> Outside-left Tommy was one of three City signings in three days (along with goalkeepers Johnny Anderson and Ian McGraw), but the tone of club comment at the time led to speculation whether he had been recruited by Johnny Duncan or by the board. Whatever, he only lasted five months on the books as a hapless pretender to Charlie Adam's No.11 shirt. A former scrum-half for Felinfoel, who took up soccer when posted to pit work in the north, he had played in only two League games and one Cup tie for Fulham, and had notched a single goal in eleven outings for Southend, before his brief City sojourn. Ironically, his brother Ivor, a Devon county rugby player, signed as a Rugby League pro for Salford only a week after Tommy's arrival at Filbert Street; while Tommy's return to Workington coincided with City's signing of an ex-Mansfield and Leeds left-winger named Walter Edwards, who would find even less favour with Leicester. Tommy's eventual return to the League sphere would win him a further dozen appearances as a Saddler.

Apps: *FL 3.*
Goals: *FL 1.*

EGGLESTON, Thomas

b. Consett, Co Durham, 21st February 1920

Career: Medomsley Juniors; am Dec 1936/pro Feb 1937 Derby County; July 1946 CITY; Jan 1948 Watford (- 1953).

City debut v Manchester City (H) 31.8.46

Though wartime Royal Navy service left him short of senior playing experience (he had guested for each of Lincoln, Southampton and Coventry, and was an emergency choice for one of the ties which saw Derby through to the 1946 FA Cup Final), Tommy became City's regular left-half in the first postwar League season after arriving as the less-regarded half of the joint deal which also landed Dave McCulloch at Filbert Street. A tough tackler and sound distributor, he nonetheless lost his battle for selection against Johnny King early in 1947/8, and became part of the remarkable five-man exodus to Vicarage Road, where he was to make 177 appearances in Division Three (South) before his playing days ended. Tommy stayed in the game, however, until his pension book became due: coaching at Brentford, Watford, Sheffield Wednesday and Everton; managing Mansfield Town and Greek clubs Ethnikos and Panahaiki; and acting as physiotherapist to Plymouth Argyle and Ipswich Town. His skills as a masseur were also employed at international level in the cycling world. Tommy settled in eventual retirement in Tockwith, Yorkshire.

Apps: *FL 34.*
Goals: *FL 2.*

ELLIOTT, Matthew Stephen

b. Wandsworth, London, 1st November 1968

Career: Epsom & Ewell; Sept 1988 Charlton Athletic; Mar 1989 Torquay United; Mar 1992 Scunthorpe United; Nov 1993 Oxford United; Jan 1997 CITY.

City debut v Wimbledon (H) 18.1.97

> Strapping centre-back Matt may have cost a club record fee of £1.6m, but he was soon being deemed the sort of rough-diamond bargain that sustained Martin O'Neill's reputation as such a shrewd transfer-market operator. After a near-decade of unspectacular lower-league action, it took less than a year of Premiership experience to elevate Matt to international status, and not much longer to cement his place in City's pantheon of iconic favourites. Ineligible to contribute to the 1997 League Cup run after signing from Oxford, the skinheaded stopper was soon into Man of the Match mode with his alternately resolute and adventurous performances in such games as the Chelsea FA Cup tie and the Premiership win over Wimbledon, and it was his goal in the penultimate game against Sheffield Wednesday that banished all lingering relegation fears that year. There was soon speculation linking him with possible call-ups to any of the English, Irish and Scottish squads, but a grand-maternal connection meant that it was for Scotland that he would appear as the 50th player to be capped while on City's books. A rugged defensive rock, aerially dominant yet almost cockily comfortable on the ball, and a fine marshal of the back-line, he suffered a few isolated disappointments over the next couple of years, with a very rare poor display hastening City's 1998 FA Cup exit at Crystal Palace, a frustrating spell on the Scottish bench throughout the World Cup Finals that summer, a share in the flat performance at Wembley that saw City lose out on the League Cup to Spurs, and a sending-off for Scotland against the Faroe Islands which earned him a five-game international suspension. But all through this period his mastery of a host of stellar Premiership attackers was a consistent boon to City, as became his willingness to switch in emergencies to a striking berth himself, and play his inspirational captain's role from the front. There was no surprise, then, when Matt's City career hit its peak to date with his match-winning, goalscoring efforts in the semi-final and Final of the 2000 League Cup – a trio of headers that more than earned him the right to lift the trophy on the last occasion it would be fought for at the 'old' Wembley. Definitely one of the best bits of news of a turbulent summer of 2000 was that Matt had re-emphasised his commitment to the club and extended his City contract; and he maintained his high repute with both club and country – recognised via the Midlands Player of the Year award for 2000 – until removed from the fray through a rare injury in April 2001. His career originally began in the Isthmian League, and appeared to be heading

nowhere when Charlton let him go after a solitary League Cup outing. But he reached Wembley that same term, when Torquay lost in the Sherpa Van Trophy Final to Bolton, and would rapidly return there twice more: with the Gulls in 1991 for a successful Division Four Play-Off Final, and with Scunthorpe a year later for a defeat at the same stage. Oxford were relegated at the end of his first term with them, but he was their Player of the Year in 1996 when they rose again from Division Two, and was soon to be encouraged to reinvent himself as the ideal top-level defender.

***Apps** (to end 2000/1): PL 161; FAC 15; LC 15+1; UEFA 4.*
***Goals:** PL 22; FAC 2; LC 3.*

ELLISON, Kevin

b. Liverpool, 23rd February 1979

Career: 1996 Southport; 1997 Chorley; Mar 1998 Conwy United; cs 1999 Altrincham; Feb 2001 CITY.

City debut v Manchester United (A) 17.3.2001 (sub)

> A left-sided attacker offered a surprise opportunity to resurrect a career that has false-started on a couple of occasions at non-leage level, Kevin may have only 6 minutes of Premiership action under his belt so far, but seems set to offer a potent challenge for a squad role in the coming year. Though he made a Conference debut as a teenager at Southport, it took detours via the Unibond League, Liverpool Sunday football and the League of Wales to return him to that level with Altrincham, for whom he was the 14-goal top scorer in their 1999/2000 relegation campaign. Unsuccessful trials with each of Everton, Wigan and Manchester City also spiced Kevin's progress, which took a quantum leap with his move to Filbert Street at a fee set to rise in appearance-related instalments from £50,000 to a maximum £100,000.

***Apps** (to end 2000/1): PL 0+1.*

ENGLISH, Thomas Steven

b. Cirencester, Glos, 18th October 1961

Career: app/pro June 1979 Coventry City; Sept 1982 CITY; Aug 1984 Rochdale; Sept 1984 Plymouth Argyle; Nov 1984 Colchester United; cs 1985 Canberra City Olympians; Sept 1985 Colchester United; cs 1987 Wealdstone; cs 1988 Bishops Stortford; Oct 1989 Colchester United; cs 1990 Happy Valley (Hong Kong); Aug 1991 Crawley Town; Oct 1991 Wivenhoe; 1992 Bishops Stortford; Sudbury Town; Harwich & Parkeston.

City debut v Blackburn Rovers (A) 18.9.82

> An England Youth international forward upgraded from his Highfield Road apprenticeship by Gordon Milne, Tom struck an early League scoring partnership with Mark Hateley, and managed a hat-trick against City in March 1981. However, he was dogged with domestic troubles which unfortunately continued to distract him after a controversial move to Filbert Street, when Milne acquired him in a straight swap deal for popular Jim Melrose. Tom's wayward marksmanship failed to impress an accordingly highly critical Leicester crowd, despite his all-round contribution to the 1983 promotion effort, and despite his increasing effectiveness in a more withdrawn midfield role. He became a wanderer upon his release, taking a year to earn a contract of any length, and then developing an on/off relationship with Colchester, where he played alongside his younger brother Tony. In a rare and possibly unique occurrence at Crewe in 1985/6, both brothers were sent off. As true veterans, the siblings were playing together in 2000/1 for Harwich & Parkeston; as was Tommy's 18-year-old son.

***Apps:** FL 29+15; FAC 0+1; LC 2+1.*
***Goals:** FL 3; LC 1.*

ESSOM, Walter

b. Leicester, November 1895
d. Hitchin, Herts, Jan qtr 1966

Career: Carey Hall; 1913 Leicester Imperial; 1919 British United; Aug 1919 CITY; cs 1920 Ashby Town (- 1927).

City debut v Fulham (H) 13.9.19

> A local left-back who briefly stood in for Sam Currie in the home and away fixtures with Fulham in 1919/20, little more than a year after playing representative army football in Le Havre, Walter had originally been a rugby player with the local St Albans club upon leaving Belper Street school, though he'd starred for the Imps before enlisting in 1915. His parents were Ashby hoteliers, and Walter himself took over the stewardship of the Ashby Soldiers & Sailors Institute in 1922. With the local Town side, he took over the captaincy from Shirley Hubbard until the club folded in 1927.

***Apps:** FL 2.*

EUSTACE, Scott Douglas

b. Leicester, 13th June 1975

Career: YT Aug 1991/pro July 1993 CITY; Nov 1994-loan-Shelbourne; June 1995 Mansfield Town; Aug 1998 Chesterfield; Dec 1998 Cambridge United; July 2000 Lincoln City.

City debut/only game v Bristol City (H) 11.12.93 (sub).

> A tall central defender who had come through his traineeship to feature in 21 Central League games prior to his brief breakthrough, Scott was a composed substitute for Gary Coatsworth during a 3-0 home win. He added to his experience with a month in the League of Ireland, but fell victim to Mark McGhee's evident need to whittle down the size of his professional squad when freed to the Stags. A regular at Field Mill over three seasons, he was strangely marginalised at Saltergate, with his only senior game for the Spireites coming as a second-half substitute in their League Cup tie at Filbert Street. Scott thereafter assisted Cambridge both to promotion and Division Two consolidation; broadening his repertoire with occasional shifts into midfield. His brief Lincoln stint, however, was blighted by off-field problems, and his Imps contract was terminated in October 2000 after he'd been put on probation for a kebab-shop affray.

***Apps:** FL 0+1.*

EVANS, Allan James

b. Polbeth, West Lothian, 12th October 1956

Career: Dunfermline United; cs 1973 Dunfermline Athletic; May 1977 Aston Villa; Aug 1989 CITY; May 1990 Victoria Vistas [Vancouver] (p/coach); 1990 Brisbane United (p/coach); March 1991 Darlington; May 1991 CITY (p/coach).

City debut v Hull City (A) 19.8.89

> Given a free transfer by Villa in recognition of his outstanding twelve-year service, Allan initially joined City to steady the back four, but proved every bit as prone to costly errors as his more junior colleagues as David Pleat's team plummeted unexpectedly to the Second Division depths. Essentially, and sadly, it was a case of the central defender appearing to have lost the requisite pace by the time he first donned a blue shirt, and for much of his Filbert Street season

Allan Evans

he had to take on the less demanding task of anchoring the Central League side, before setting himself up for what looked likely to be a playing swansong in Canada and Australia. Allan's surprising return to the League sphere – albeit for only four minutes of competitive action as a Darlington sub – reunited him with one-time Villa teammate Brian Little as the latter helmed the Feethams side to the Division Four championship; and when Little moved to the the City boss's chair, Allan became the first recruit to the coaching staff, as well as a buttressing force for the Reserves' successful promotion bid. In November 1994, caught up in the acrimony surrounding Little's departure, he actually took the caretaker manager's role for a midweek Premiership home win over Arsenal, but resigned two days later and was soon, predictably, back in harness with Little at Villa Park. (As, later, he would be at Stoke). Allan's top-level career had started in unsettling manner back in 1973/4, when, as a 16-year-old amateur, he broke his leg during his Dunfermline debut game against Rangers. He bounced back, however, to star for the Pars as both a centre-back and an out-and-out striker and, following his move southwards, he indeed made his delayed League bow for Villa in the No.7 shirt against Leicester, shortly after a 6-goal reserve-team performance. It was from the pivotal defensive berth, though, that Allan's aerial prowess and speedy covering helped inspire Villa to win both the Championship in 1981 and the European Cup the following year. Picking up four Scotland caps (the last in the World Cup Finals of 1982), he later assumed his club's captaincy, and also experienced successive relegation and promotion capaigns during a West Midlands tenure aggregating 474 games and 62 goals. The only one of the latter total he scored at Second Division level was the winner against City in 1987/8. In July 2000, Allan took over the management of Greenock Morton, but left the crisis-torn, cash-strapped club in January 2001.

***Apps:** FL 14; LC 2.*

EVENSON, Isaac

b. Manchester, 1878
d. Stockport, 3rd April 1936

Career: Tonge; Nov 1898-trials-Glossop North End; Apr 1901 Stockport County; July 1903 FOSSE; July 1905 Clapton Orient; Apr 1907 West Bromwich Albion; May 1908 Plymouth Argyle; Stalybridge Celtic.

Fosse debut v Barnsley (A) 5.9.03

> Two appearances in a promotion-bound Glossop side were hardly accurate auguries for Ike's subsequent Second Division travails: in all three of his Stockport seasons, and his first at each of Fosse and Orient, his club would end the term with an application for re-election! Having top-scored (with 7) at Edgeley Park in 1902/3, Ike was taken on by Fosse as a centre-forward, but settled by preference for the inside-left berth. His 8 goals this time out gifted him the top marksman status, and he stayed to help the duly re-elected club a few rungs up the ladder the following season. In March 1905 he was, along with Bob Pollock, one of two Fossils sent off at Bolton in a match which 8-man Fosse (Archie Hubbard was stretchered off!) won 1-0. His subsequent suspension, carried over to the next campaign, meant he missed Clapton Orient's first-ever League game (at Filbert Street), but his two years in London also saw him taking on caretaker team management duties at his financially ailing club for three months in 1906. Ike was better known as a middle-line schemer on his later travels, which ended when he took over the Windsor Castle Hotel in Stockport. He later became a partner in a cabinet-making business.

***Apps:** FL 42; FAC 10.*
***Goals:** FL 14; FAC 6.*

FARMER, John

b. Biddulph, Staffs, 31st August 1947

Career: Chatterley BC; Jan 1965 Stoke City; July 1972-loan-West Bromwich Albion; Dec 1974-loan-CITY; cs 1976 Northwich Victoria.

City debut v Everton (H) 7.12.74

> Despite managing 163 League games in goal for Stoke and winning himself England Under-23 recognition, John spent much of his Victoria Ground career in the shadow of Gordon Banks, and was just having to come to terms with the start of another spell as understudy – this time to Peter Shilton – when he answered the call to alleviate a City goalkeeping emergency. With Mark Wallington injured and Carl Jayes as yet inexperienced, John was a decidedly classy stopgap, but ironically he was injured himself in his second match (at Middlesbrough), and returned to Stoke just as Wallington embarked on his monumental record of consecutive City appearances. John himself, however, was never to appear at League level again, and retired after assisting Northwich to runners-up spot in the Northern Premier League in 1977. His earlier loan spell had consisted solely of a trio of Albion friendly matches on a Swedish tour. He now manages a crisp factory at Cheadle.

***Apps:** FL 2.*

FARMER, Kevin John

b. Ramsgate, Kent, 24th January 1960

Career: Wigston Fields; app July 1976/pro Oct 1977 CITY; Aug 1979 Northampton Town; cs 1982 Bedworth United; cs 1983 VS Rugby.

City debut/only game v Ipswich Town (A) 17.12.77

> City were anchored to the bottom of the First Division when Frank McLintock thrust seventeen-year-olds Kevin and Mark Goodwin into the limelight at Portman Road, and for the slender striker, raised in Kirby Muxloe, the 0-1 defeat was his sole first-team opportunity. Grandson of a QPR director, Kevin was released by Jock Wallace and went on to play 77 League games and score a dozen times in three seasons with the Cobblers, who he represented at centre-back as well as up front. In the later 80s he was involved at a coaching and managerial level with both Kirby Muxloe and Melton Town.

***Apps:** FL 1.*

FARRINGTON, John Robert

b. Lynemouth, Northumberland, 19th June 1947

Career: app Sept 1963/pro June 1965 Wolverhampton Wanderers; Oct 1969 CITY; Nov 1973 Cardiff City; Oct 1974 Northampton Town; cs 1980 AP Leamington; 1981 Bedworth United; Shepshed Charterhouse; Aug 1982 Earl Shilton Albion.

City debut v Bristol City (H) 18.10.69

> Never quite a Molineux regular after his teenage debut, right-winger John nonetheless laid on his share of converted crosses for Derek Dougan, and impressed Frank O'Farrell sufficiently to prompt a £30,000 move to Filbert Street. He was straight out of the blocks on his City debut, with a pinpoint centre gifting Rodney Fern a goal, and his orthodox flank play immediately became a positive factor in the 1971 Second Division championship campaign. With John on the right and Len Glover on the left, City's quick-break style was based on an attack of genuine width and pace, and the Northumbrian pigeon-fancier's finishing wasn't bad, either; with some of his best goals reserved for the Cup competitions. O'Farrell called back for John when attempting to keep Cardiff out of the Third Division, and the winger managed a valuable League hat-trick, a Welsh Cup Final appearance and a European outing during his short spell at Ninian Park.

John Farmer

Then former City coach Bill Dodgin took him to Northampton, where a 232-game stint as a midfield schemer in Divisions Three and Four ended his 14-year League career. John briefly became manager of the AP Leamington side he was playing for before the club's demise; and in 1992, after a long-term coaching spell, took over the boss's role at Barlestone St Giles. John's father Bob acted as a part-time scout for City in the North-East: most notably discovering Trevor Christie.

Apps: *FL 115+3; FAC 16; LC 9+2.*
Goals: *FL 18; FAC 6; LC 3.*

FEELEY, Andrew James

b. Hereford, 30th September 1961

Career: app 1978/pro Aug 1979 Hereford United; Mar 1980-loan-Chelsea; 1980 Moorfields; 1980 Trowbridge Town; Jan 1984 CITY; July 1987 Brentford; June 1989 Bury; Aug 1991 Atherton Laburnam Rovers; Nov 1991 Northwich Victoria; cs 1992 Atherton Laburnam Rovers.

City debut v Manchester United (A) 10.3.84

> When 17-year-old Andy led out Hereford against York on 18th August 1979, he entered the record books as the youngest ever captain of a Football League team. He already had 26 games as a midfielder under his belt, but a combination of injury and disciplinary problems meant that he'd only make 29 further senior appearances before being jettisoned to the non-league wastelands. In fact, for a while he played only in Herefordshire Sunday football, until resurrecting his career and shrugging off his tearaway reputation with Trowbridge in each of the Southern and Alliance Premier Leagues. Alan Birchenall was briefly his boss there, and was not slow to recommend Andy to Gordon Milne. Nor was Andy slow to grasp his second chance, with his Old Trafford baptism illuminated by the tigerish tackling and committed attitude that soon had him installed as a popular regular at right-back. Tattooed and slightly tubbier than the First Division norm, he was no respecter of the opposition's pedigree, and his uncomplicated application and spirit would have been priceless to City's cause in the relegation campaign of 1986/7 if he had not been sidelined by injury at a crucial stage. Upon refusing new contract terms, he moved to Griffin Park as a free agent, and completed a couple of years in Division Three with each of the Bees and the Shakers; netting for the latter the fourth and fifth goals of his career some ten years after the first three. In both 1993 and 1994, while working as a prison officer in a unit for the criminally insane, Andy was a key member of the Atherton LR side which took successive NorthWest Counties League championships.

Apps: *FL 74+2; FAC 6; LC 4.*

FENTON, Graham Anthony

b. Wallsend, 22nd May 1974

Career: YT/pro Feb 1992 Aston Villa; Jan 1994-loan-West Bromwich Albion; Nov 1995 Blackburn Rovers; Aug 1997 CITY; Mar 2000 Walsall; July 2000-trials-Barnsley; Aug 2000 Stoke City; Sept 2000 St Mirren.

City debut v Liverpool (A) 13.8.97 (sub; scored once)

One of the very few ill-fated transfer deals of the Martin O'Neill regime landed once-promising striker Graham at Leicester for a cool £1.1m outlay which the player rarely looked like justifying. A close-range finish on his debut as a substitute at Anfield was very much a false dawn, with the burly striker appearing increasingly cumbersome, and losing faith in both his control and pace, as his Filbert Street stay mutated into a matter of ever-diminishing opportunities. Graham seemed almost resigned to disappointment: he'd failed to win a regular place at Villa despite a Wembley outing for their 1994 League Cup-winning side during his breakthrough season (and despite England Under-21 recognition), while his £1.5m move to Ewood was blighted by hamstring problems. His most famous moment there was when his two goals as a sub against Newcastle did much to deprive his home-town team of the 1996 Premiership title; though his seventh and last Blackburn strike actually came against City during the following term. Several clubs offered Graham the chance to join them on loan after he'd become pretty much a reserve-team fixture at Leicester (including, in January 1999, Greek outfit PAOK), but he declined all moves until City agreed to cancel his contract altogether; at which point he joined Mark Robins in a futile attempt to keep the Saddlers afloat in Division Two. Another downbeat season followed in 2000/1, with a scoreless sojourn at Stoke, and a Scottish Premier relegation fate awaiting at Love Street.

Apps: *PL 13+21; FAC 0+4; LC 2+5; UEFA 0+2.*
Goals: *PL 3; LC 2.*

FENWICK, Terence William

b. Seaham, Co Durham, 17th November 1959

Career: app/pro Dec 1976 Crystal Palace; Dec 1980 Queens Park Rangers; Dec 1987 Tottenham Hotspur; Oct 1990-loan-CITY; Aug 1993 Swindon Town; Feb 1995 Portsmouth (p/mgr).

City debut v Ipswich Town (H) 27.10.90

> Out of the Spurs side for a year after breaking a leg, experienced defender Terry was loaned to City both to prove his match fitness and to shore up a regularly crumbling Second Division rearguard, and stayed for two months in hardly more secure centre-back pairings with Steve Walsh or Tony James, as the 'Pleat Out' cries grew more insistent, before recall to White Hart Lane. Ironically, he was to break his ankle only weeks later during the warm-up for a Cup tie at Portsmouth; and on recovery from that setback was then jailed for motoring offences. Such misfortune, which continued when he became part of Swindon's relegation-bound Premiership squad, was in contrast to his earlier years in the game, and his virtual lucky mascot status for Terry Venables. The latter nurtured his early career at Selhurst, then bought him expensively for each of QPR and Spurs. As a teenager, Terry scored the winning goal in each of the FA Youth Cup Finals of 1977 and 1978; and his later honours list was substantial: playing in Division Two championship sides at both Palace and QPR (where he partnered Bob Hazell and backed up Tony Sealy); featuring in defeated Rangers sides at Wembley in each of the FA Cup (when he scored in the first drawn game of 1982) and League Cup; and being capped 20 times at full England level following Youth and Under-21 representation. Terry's move into management came when Jim Smith departed Fratton Park in the wake of City's FA Cup win over Pompey, and led to further liaisons with Venables, who controversially became his chairman until both men were ousted in January 1998. Terry then became a Palace coach under his mentor's short-lived 'second coming' Selhurst regime.

Apps: *FL 8; FMC 1.*
Goals: *FL 1.*

FERN, Rodney Alan

b. Burton-on-Trent, 13th December 1948

Career: Measham Social Welfare; Dec 1966 CITY; June 1972 Luton Town; Jan 1973-loan-Coventry City; July 1975 Chesterfield; June 1979 Rotherham United (- 1983).

City debut v Leeds United (H) 3.2.68

> Sharing much the same football background as David Nish, Rodney worked as a Coal Board clerk while on City's amateur roster, but was piling up the honours as he awaited his professional contract: 1966 bringing winners medals with Leicestershire in the FA County Youth Cup and with Measham in the Senior Cup. A winger then, he soon developed as a distinctly versatile and unorthodox forward. He had an early taste of a big crowd hailing him with the 'Rod-neeeee' chant borrowed from QPR (and usually directed at Rodney Marsh) when coming on as sub in the Filbert Street leg of the Combination Cup Final of 1967; and then appeared anything but overawed when promoted to First Division football by coach Bert Johnson (acting as caretaker manager during Matt Gillies' sick leave). Forming an unlikely-looking but highly effective striking partnership with the marauding Frank Large, he was soon into his stride. In only his third game, it was Rodney's 44th-minute goal which prompted City's hoodoo-breaking FA Cup fightback against Manchester City (when a 0-2 deficit was turned into 4-3 victory on a night of unforgettably pulsating drama); and indeed it was the Cup which regularly brought the best out of him. The 6th Round winner at Mansfield helped City towards Wembley in 1969, while his headed 'goal' at Highbury in 1971 might have opened the way to another medal opportunity had it not been so controversially disallowed by Jim Finney. Rodney became City's top scorer in 1969/70 (when he got off the mark with a spectacular overhead kick in the opening fixture against Birmingham), and his popularity with the Leicester crowd seemed to increase further as his game became an unpredictable patchwork of deadly marksmanship, creative inspiration and almost endearing clumsiness, but it was a superb performance as a deeper-lying playmaker in the crucial Easter game at Luton in the next promotion campaign which probably earned him his £45,000 move to Kenilworth Road just over a year later. There his contribution to the Hatters' 1974 promotion to the top-flight was fairly peripheral, but at Chesterfield Rodney's goal ratio picked up appreciably, and he had become a truly wily veteran (replete with balding pate) by the time he inspired Rotherham first to embarrass City in the 1979/80 League Cup and then to take the Third Division championship in 1981. Retirement came after he'd aggregated 125 League goals; Rodney initially running a pub in Lount, but more recently establishing himself as a coal merchant back in Measham.

Rodney Fern

Apps: *FL 133+19; FAC 22+1; LC 12.*
Goals: *FL 32; FAC 5; LC 3.*

FINCHAM, Gordon Richard

b. Peterborough, 8th January 1935

Career: Soke YC; Phorpres Sports; Nov 1952 CITY; June 1958 Plymouth Argyle; July 1963 Luton Town; 1965 Port Elizabeth City (p/coach).

City debut v Rotherham United (A) 6.4.53

> An office boy at the London Brick Co before signing pro for City, Gordon was rated by good judges as one of the most promising centre-halves the club had possessed, but developed as one of the unluckiest. His debut as understudy for Matt Gillies came while he was still on National Service with the Army Catering Corps at Aldershot, and he was restricted to a two-game contribution to the 1954 Second Division championship effort by both military duties and military football calls. Next properly blooded in a campaign of top-flight struggle, and given the status of a regular selection in 1955/6, Gordon was then stricken by injuries which denied him all but a single game over the next two seasons. With Ian King and Tony Knapp vaulting over him in the senior reckoning, he rebuilt his career at Home Park, where Plymouth took the Third Division championship in his initial term, and where he often played alongside former Filbert Street colleagues John Newman and Dave MacLaren. Luton's relegation to the League basement signalled the end of Gordon's first-class career, and presaged his emigration to South Africa.

Apps: *FL 50; FAC 4.*

FINDLAY, William

b. Wishaw, Lanarkshire, 17th February 1900
d. Braunstone, Leicester, 11th June 1949

Career: Preston Grange Athletic; 1922 Musselburgh Bruntonians; cs 1923 Third Lanark; Aug 1924 Liverpool; May 1925 CITY; June 1932 Watford.

City debut v Newcastle United (A) 19.9.25

> An unassuming, loyal Scottish wing-half who provided valuable cover for City over seven First Division seasons, playing in a third of all League fixtures over that period, Billy doggedly refused to be overawed at the prospect of standing in for the likes of internationals Johnny Duncan, Jack Bamber or Sid Bishop. A member of Musselburgh's Scottish Junior Cup Final side of 1923 (from which City signed matchwinner Archie Waterston directly), and a Junior 'cap' at that point, Billy stepped up to top-flight Scottish soccer with 26 outings at Cathkin Park, but was unable to make a League breakthrough at Anfield, even though featuring in Liverpool's prestige friendly against the touring South African International XI in October 1924. Even though it essentially confirmed him as a City fringe player, there was prestige, too, in Billy's selection for the London Combination against the London League at Highbury in March 1927, alongside George Carr. A four-year playing regular for Watford (skippering them against City in the 1936 FA Cup tie), Billy then took over the manager's reins at Vicarage Road for just short of a decade. A qualified physiotherapist, and an elder of the Presbyterian Church, he was manager of Edgware Town at the time of his death. His brother Andrew, a winger, signed for City in October 1927 after lengthy military service in India, but got no senior opportunity before moving on for brief spells with Market Harborough Town and Hinckley United.

Apps: *FL 100; FAC 4.*

FITZPATRICK, Gary Gerard

b. Birmingham, 5th August 1971

Career: YT 1988/pro Jan 1990 CITY; cs 1991 VS Rugby; Mar 1993 Moor Green; May 1993 Rannberg; Oct 1993 Hednesford Town; Jan 1999 Telford United.

City debut/only game v Sheffield United (H) 5.5.90 (sub)

> A 15-goal haul for the youth team during 1989/90 won winger Gary a final-game elevation to the senior bench, and a brief appearance alongside cousin David Kelly in a game that had already turned into a Blades promotion party. The following term the Irish Youth cap was unable to maintain his progress in a struggling Central League side, and was released in the initial clear-out following City's last gasp escape from relegation to the Third. Gary made an immediate impact at Rugby, scoring the winner against a Manchester United XI in a pre-season testimonial game; but subsequent interest from League scouts failed to produce a solid offer. Subsequent West Midlands wanderings, spiced with a summer stint in Swedish football, revealed Gary as a class midfielder, who in 1995 assisted Hednesford up into the Conference (scoring the last goal at their old Cross Keys ground), in 1998 was named their Player of the Year, and later cost Telford their record (undisclosed, five figure) transfer fee. He was still at The Buck's Head, alongside Kevin Jobling, during 2000/1.

Apps: *FL 0+1.*

FITZPATRICK, Paul James

b. Liverpool, 5th October 1965

Career: Tranmere Rovers (non-contract); Liverpool (n/c); Preston North End (n/c); Mar 1985 Bolton Wanderers; Aug 1986 Bristol City; Oct 1988 Carlisle United; Dec 1988-loan-Preston North End; June 1991 CITY; Jan 1993 Birmingham City; Mar 1993-loan-Bury; July 1993-trials-Shrewsbury Town; Sept 1993 Hamilton Academical; Feb 1994 Northampton Town; 1994 (Hong Kong football); Dec 1994 Rushden & Diamonds; Jan 1995 Leicester United; 1995 Forest Green Rovers; 1995 Racing Club Warwick; Jan 1996 Corby Town (p/mgr cs 1996-Nov 1996); Aug 1997 Forest Green Rovers; Sept 1997 Oadby Town; Nov 1997 Gresley Rovers (p/asst mgr); Mar 1999 Kings Lynn; Aug 1999 Workington.

City debut v Swindon Town (A) 17.8.91

> A distinctly versatile performer whose 6ft 4in presence was valued in various positional roles, Paul made his belated League bow as a Bolton full-back in May 1985, had spells both in midfield and as a target-man at Ashton Gate, and shone defensively for Carlisle. Brian Little's first purchase for City at a modest £40,000, Paul continued to have his adaptability exploited for tactical ends, being principally utilised as a sweeper or third centre-back, but demonstrating a cool ease on the ball when moving forward. Several of his interventions in the opposition box bore goalscoring fruit, and his extra-time diving header at a sodden Meadow Lane in the ZDS Cup remains especially memorable. Barely given a break in 1992/3, however, when

competition for rearguard shirts was fierce, Paul took a free transfer to St Andrews to bid – in vain, as it turned out – for regular first-team football. In fact there would only be a further 37 senior outings to come in total for the Blues, Shakers, Accies and Cobblers, before a five-year wander in non-league circles which saw Paul briefly in sole charge at Corby, and assisting Gary Birtles at Gresley.

Apps: *FL 21+6; FAC 1; LC 2; FMC 3+2; AIC 0+1.*
Goals: *FL 4; FMC 1.*

FLANAGAN, William

b. Birmingham, ca 1876

Career: Smethwick Carriage Works; Oldbury Town; Aston Villa; Oct 1896 Burton Wanderers; Aug 1897 FOSSE; Feb 1898 not known; Sept 1899 Glentoran; Oct 1900 Morton; 1901 Port Glasgow Athletic.

Fosse debut v Burton Swifts (A) 27.11.1897

> A one-time Villa reserve inside-forward, who had scored only once in nine Second Division games at Derby Turn, during Burton Wanderers' final season in the League, William got even fewer chances to impress after joining Fosse, who freed him in February 1898. A sojourn in Belfast boosted his reputation a little, but only a handful of Scottish League appearances on Clydeside ensued.

Apps: *FL 4.*

FLETCHER, Thomas

b. Heanor, Derbyshire, 15th June 1881
d. Derby, 29th September 1954

Career: Hill's Ivanhoe; Dec 1898-trials-FOSSE; Derby Nomads; Apr 1902 FOSSE; Derby Nomads; Nov 1904 Derby County; cs 1907 Derby Thornhill.

Fosse debut v Doncaster Rovers (A) 12.4.02 (scored once)

> One of three footballing sons of a Derby alderman (of whom JT was a Fosse reserve from September 1898, and Fred a former Derby and Notts County winger), amateur forward Tom first turned out for Fosse in Billy Dorrell's testimonial friendly against the Corinthians at Christmas 1898 and, having helped Hill's Ivanhoe to the Amateur Cup semi-finals in 1901/2, returned to Filbert Streeet to make sporadic senior appearances at either inside- or outside-left over the course of three League campaigns. Later, with the Rams, he would amass a total of 33 First Division outings (scoring eight times), and would take part in the 1905 tour of the USA and Canada undertaken by the amateur combination, the Pilgrims, under Fred Milnes' captaincy. Tom also appeared as a fine cricketing all-rounder for Derbyshire CCC against the West Indies.

Apps: *FL 5.*
Goals: *FL 2.*

FLINT, James

b. Northants, 1870 (?)
d. Syston, Leics, 24th November 1932

Career: St Matthews; Leicester Teachers; Sept 1890 FOSSE; 1891 Leicester Invicta; 1892 Leicester YMCA.

Fosse debut (competitive) v Burton Wanderers (H) FAC 4.10.1890

> Raised on a Northamptonshire farm by an uncle, Jimmy developed into one of the amateur pioneers of Fosse's pre-League days. He was at outside-right in the club's initial foray into the FA Cup, and in the 1891 County Cup-winning side, but made only the odd appearance in friendly matches following Fosse's elevation to the Midland League.

Apps: *FAC 1.*

FLOWERS, Timothy David

b. Kenilworth, Warks, 3rd February 1967

Career: app/pro Aug 1984 Wolverhampton Wanderers; June 1986 Southampton; Mar 1987-loan-Swindon Town; Nov 1987-loan-Swindon Town; Nov 1993 Blackburn Rovers; July 1999 CITY.

City debut v Arsenal (A) 7.8.99

> A confident, commanding international 'keeper who has by and large maintained a calming influence on City's Premiership defence since succeeding Kasey Keller, Tim had his first two Filbert Street terms increasingly disrupted by illness and injury, but built quite a rapport with the fans on the back of some fine shot-stopping displays and his determination to share his final-whistle glee. His accumulated reputation is sometimes sufficient to give pause to an opponent and make him consider other options, as is his refusal to commit himself too early, and each of his speed from his line, his rapid recovery after going to ground and his general positioning index the depth of his experience: duly rewarded with a League Cup winner's medal in 2000. It is sheer ill-fate that a premature arthritic condition affecting his hip and back threatens to cut severely into Tim's future availability for, fit and on-song, he can be inspirational, and his performance at Newcastle in late 2000/1 proved that there was no diminution of his skill. City's final Premiership fixture, at Leeds, represented his 500th League game. Tim didn't have the easiest introduction to the senior game: his first two seasons with Wolves saw them successively relegated from Division Two to Four. But he was taken on at The Dell, initially as understudy to Peter Shilton, and then kept Ian Andrews sidelined as he began to claim the No 1 jersey for himself, and to receive Under-21 recognition. A Wembley visit in the Full Members Cup Final of 1992 was the nearest he came to a club honour with the Saints, though he graduated to the full England side a year later, and was then whisked to Ewood for £2.4m. His imposing last-line presence assisted Blackburn to runners-up spot in 1994, and to the Premiership title the following term, and he added nine caps to his tally. But he had begun to come under pressure for his club place from Shay Given and John Filan by the time of Rovers' relegation in 1999, and Martin O'Neill snapped him up for an appearance-related fee that has risen from £1.1m to £1.4m.

Apps *(to end 2000/1): PL 51; FAC 2; LC 5+1, UEFA 2.*

FORD, Gary

b. York, 8th February 1961

Career: Leeman United; app June 1977/pro Feb 1979 York City; June 1987 CITY; Dec 1987 Port Vale; Mar 1990-loan-Walsall; Mar 1991 Mansfield Town; Aug 1993 Lillestrom; Nov 1993 Telford United; Jan 1995 Tromso IL; Harstad IL; Sept 1995 Hartlepool United; Oct 1996 York Railway Institute.

City debut v Shrewsbury Town (H) 15.8.87

> Originally on schoolboy forms with Hull City, Gary was nonetheless a veteran of 426 senior games for his home-town club (and a prime factor in their rise in fortunes from re-election in 1981 to the Fourth Division championship in 1984) when the wide midfielder was bought by Bryan Hamilton for £25,000. Asked to play as an out-and-out right winger for City, he knuckled down to the task

Gary Ford

with energy and enthusiasm, despite an early injury setback, but his natural tendency to drift inside with the ball evidenced his discomfort at being isolated on the flank. Gary became the first departure of the David Pleat regime, becoming immediately involved in Vale's 1988 FA Cup giant-killing of Spurs and, a year later, their promotion to Division Two. Further injury problems then sidelined Gary for some months, though he eventually proved his fitness in a relegation-bound Saddlers side; and experienced a rollercoaster trio of campaigns at Field Mill, with two relegations flanking a promotion, before tasting Norwegian football. Incidentally, Gary's trio of strikes for City included the club's first-ever in the little-mourned Full Members (then Simod-sponsored) Cup, the winner against Huddersfield Town.

Apps: *FL 15+1; LC 1+1; FMC 2.*
Goals: *FL 2; FMC 1.*

FOSTER, James

Career: 1897 Reading; cs 1899 Northampton Town; May 1900 FOSSE; May 1901 Kettering.

Fosse debut v Stockport County (H) 1.9.1900

> A half-back signed after three years of Southern and Midland League experience, and originally slated to replace Herbert Dainty, James was allowed to move on when Dainty returned to the club. 'A heavy but smart player' was the description he drew during his Kettering stint. His Fosse debut (shared with fellow newcomers Brash, Mills, Kyle, Connachan and Dunkley) was in the 2-2 draw that marked Stockport's first fixture as a League club.

Apps: *FL 20; FAC 1.*

FRAME, William Lammie

b. Carluke, Lanarkshire, 7th May 1912
d. Nottingham, 9th September 1992

Career: Overton Athletic; Shawfield Juniors; Oct 1933 CITY; July 1950 Rugby Town (p/coach).

City debut v Tottenham Hotspur (A) 6.10.34

> Signed from Glaswegian junior football at the same time as Johnny Grogan, right-back Willie was pitched precisely one year later into First Division action at White Hart Lane, and haplessly conceded an own goal in the 89th minute of the 2-2 draw. The hardy Scot was quick to recover from this potentially unnerving experience, though, becoming a regular in time to gain a medal from City's 1937 Division Two championship campaign, and eventually giving almost 17 years' service to the Filbert Street cause (though without once scoring at the right end). Willie featured in more games in WW2 competitions than any other City player, and was still an automatic choice when a Christmas injury sadly robbed him of the chance to play a major role in City's 1949 Wembley progress. Having opened his City record eventfully, Willie just had to bookend it in memorable style, missing a penalty in the May 1950 replayed Final of the County Cup, in which City reserves nonetheless beat Brush Sports. A year on, 10,572 turned out for Willie's belated testimonial game, with City beating Derby 4-3. He left Rugby in January 1953, and thereafter ran the Griffin Inn in Belgrave Gate.

Apps: *FL 220; FAC 19; WW2 220.*

FREEBAIRN, William

b. Stirlingshire, ca.1875
d. Glasgow, 19th November 1900

Career: 1893 Partick Thistle; cs 1895 Abercorn; May 1896 FOSSE; cs 1898 East Stirlingshire; cs 1899 Partick Thistle.

Fosse debut v Darwen (H) 5.9.1896 (scored once)

> Willie joined Fosse after helping Paisley-based Abercorn to the championship of the Scottish Second Division, and soon made the outside-right spot his own. Discipline was clearly not his strongest suit, though: he became the first Fossil to be sent off in League football, after insulting a linesman at Lincoln in April 1897, was then one of six players suspended by the club for unspecified (but probably drink-related) offences in February 1898. He never played for Fosse again, but returned north for both triumph and tragedy. Having assisted East Stirling to the Scottish Qualifying Cup in 1898/9, he linked again with David Proudfoot to prompt Partick to the Division Two title the following term. Sadly, though, he fell ill partway through the next top-flight campaign, and died after an operation in Glasgow's Great Western Infirmary, only days before he was due to be married. A 16-verse poetic 'parting tribute' was soon published to mark Willie's passing into Partick legend. His brother Archie also played for Partick, and had a lengthy career as a half-back and skipper at Bolton.

Apps: *FL 44; FAC 4.*
Goals: *FL 14; FAC 3.*

FREEMAN, Levi

b. Grantham, Lincs, ca 1871
d. Grantham, 3rd September 1939

Career: 1884 Grantham Rovers; Hyde; 1891 Kettering; cs 1892 FOSSE; cs 1893 Grantham Rovers; Gainsborough Trinity; cs 1899 Grantham Avenue.

Fosse debut v Mansfield Town (A) ML 17.9.1892

> A Grantham first-teamer from the age of 13, Levi became eight years later the rather diminutive (5ft 4in) Fosse inside-left for the early months of the second Midland League season; and, until injury sidelined him, fared well enough in a front line whose average height was only 5ft 6in!

Apps: *FAC 4; ML 10.*
Goals: *FAC 2; ML 5.*

FRETTINGHAM, John Henry Abel

b. Nottingham, 1871
d. Derbyshire, 17th May 1904

Career: Beeston St Johns; 1891 Stapleford; Basford; Newark; 1892 & Apr 1893-trials-Nottingham Forest; Dec 1892 & Apr 1893-trials-FOSSE; cs 1893 Long Eaton Rangers; cs 1894 Lincoln City; June 1896 New Brompton (- 1904).

Fosse debut/only game v Wednesbury Old Athletic (A) ML 24.12.1892

> Inside-left Jack really knew how to exploit his early amateur status to get a regular game: he'd already featured for each of Stapleford, Basford, Newark, Forest and Fosse in the early part of 1892/3, but decided to repeat part of his roundabout tour in style during April: on All Fools' Day he scored for Newark against Fosse in a 3-3 Midland League draw, a week later figured for Forest in a friendly at Sheffield Wednesday, and a further week on was in Fosse's friendly line-up at home to Forest! Jack turned professional that summer, and gradually lost his wanderlust, playing alongside Kiddy Lowe at Long Eaton, starring in Second Division football for the Imps, and eventually settling for a then-remarkable seven-year spell with Southern Leaguers New Brompton. He was reinstated as an amateur in 1903, and took over a wine and spirit business in New Brompton. Tragically, though, it was a football injury which ended his life: receiving an ankle wound during an April 1904 representative game between the South Eastern League and the War Office, he was apparently recovering at his mother's house when he succumbed to blood poisoning.

Apps: *ML 1.*

FRIAR, John Paul

b. Govan, Glasgow, 6th June 1963

Career: Woodhill BC; Celtic BC; app 1979/pro June 1980 CITY; Feb 1983 Rotherham United; Nov 1983-loan-Motherwell; July 1984 Charlton Athletic; Mar 1986-loan-Northampton Town; cs 1986 Aldershot; June 1987 Dover Athletic; Nov 1987 Welling United; Dec 1987 Dartford; 1988 Crawley Town; 1988 Aylesbury United; 1988 Enfield; 1989 Fisher Athletic; Aug 1990 Spalding United; Sept 1990 Fisher Athletic; Oct 1991 Partick Thistle; Feb 1992 East Stirlingshire; Nov 1993 Albion Rovers.

City debut v Leeds United (H) 17.1.81

> City had a problem in adequately filling their left-back spot for several years after the departure of Dennis Rofe; and it was as unsurprising that Jock Wallace should turn to teenage talent in seeking a solution as it was that Gordon Milne would attempt conversions of seemingly half his midfield to the role. Seventeen-year-old Paul was recently capped at Scottish Youth level when making his bow, and soon proved himself a competent enough tackler, willing to mix it with heftier and more experienced opponents, as well as being pacy on the overlap; though his crossing control was poor. Over three seasons, however, he was involved in a three-way tussle for the senior No.3 shirt with Willie Gibson and Norman Leet, only to lose out comprehensively to a re-positioned Bobby Smith halfway through the 1983 promotion campaign, and find himself, by the end of that term, taking the opposite route out of Division Two with Rotherham. Three years later, Paul was out of favour at Charlton as they rose to Division One, but he helped Aldershot win promotion via the Play-Offs from Division Four in 1987, before surprisingly being released. After various non-league travels in southern England, Paul then tasted life briefly in all three lower divisions of Scottish football.

Apps: *FL 56+2; FAC 6; LC 2.*

FROGGATT, John

b. Sheffield, 17th November 1922
d. Worthing, Sussex, 17th February 1993

Career: Vospers; RAF football; Sept 1945 Portsmouth; Mar 1954 CITY; Nov 1957 Kettering Town (p/coach; p/mgr).

City debut v Bury (H) 6.3.54

> Multiply capped by England at both outside-left and centre-half, the masterfully versatile, always ebullient Jack had twice picked up

Championship medals with Pompey and became, after Bert Barlow, the second of the beaten Portsmouth semi-finalists of 1949 to find his way to the Filbert Street home of that game's victors. The transfer itself was something of a shock, as Jack had turned down a mooted move to Arsenal in only the previous September; but the entailed drop in status always looked temporary, for he became the final link – a virtual insurance policy against run-in jitters – in the 1954 promotion side. And relegation a year later did nothing to dampen his commitment to City as he shifted effortlessly and effectively between half-back and forward lines, until finally settling as the ever-present centre-half and captain of the 1957 Second Division championship side. Utterly dominant in the air, Jack also leant on his attacking experience to become a superb distributor of the ball from the back. Seeing off competition from Southend United, Kettering paid £6,000 to take him from the top-flight to the Southern League, and he stayed with them until 1963, having been player/manager from 1958-61, for successive relegation and promotion terms. At that time a partner in a Kettering electrical shop, he subsequently entered the licensed trade back in Portsmouth. Jack's father Frank was a Sheffield Wednesday, Notts County and Chesterfield player in the 20s; while his second cousin, Wednesday's Redfern Froggatt, played four times at Jack's side for England in 1952/3.

Apps: *FL 143; FAC 5.*
Goals: *FL 18.*

FULWOOD, Benjamin

b. Long Eaton, Derbyshire

Career: Long Eaton Rangers; Aug 1898 FOSSE; cs 1899 Ilkeston Town; Long Eaton St Helens.

Fosse debut v Gainsborough Trinity (H) 8.10.1898

> A young outside-left who contributed to Fosse's near-miss promotion effort of 1898/9, vying for the flank position with Welsh international Alf Watkins, and occasionally partnering him, Bennie then moved to Ilkeston jointly with Frank Ballard. He was from a remarkable Long Eaton family of sportsmen, which could – and did – raise a full cricket XI, plus umpire, from within its own ranks; though the plethora of Fulwoods makes nigh-impossible the task of comprehensively mapping their footballing careers. Bennie was possibly with Castle Donington in 1901, definitely back in his home town by 1904/5, and probably the Long Eaton administrator who joined the Management Committee of the Central Alliance in June 1922; but as for the identity of a brother of his who underwent Fosse reserve trials in 1906...??

Apps: *FL 11; FAC 2.*
Goals: *FL 3; FAC 2.*

FURR, Harold Frederick

b. Hitchin, Herts, 23rd January 1887
d. Hitchin, 23rd November 1971.

Career: Hitchin St Johns; Hitchin Town; cs 1906 Hitchin Union Jack; cs 1907 Hitchin Blue Cross Brigade; 1907 Hitchin Town; cs 1908 Croydon Common; Oct 1911 Brentford; Mar 1912 Croydon Common; May 1912 FOSSE.

Fosse debut v Huddersfield Town (A) 28.9.12

> Goalkeeper Harold had previously played for Fosse manager Jack Bartlett at Croydon, and had briefly stood in for ex-Fossil Archie Ling at Brentford, when recruited as cover for Fred Mearns. Neither his Southern League nor Division Two experiences were of the happiest, though, for he'd shared in Croydon's 1910 relegation, bowed out of Griffin Park on the sharp end of a 0-9 pasting by Coventry, and found himself leaking goals with Fosse at an average rate of over three per game. A former Hertforshire representative, he came from another seriously soccer-centred family. Brother Willie followed him to Filbert Street within weeks; brother George turned out for Watford, Manchester City and Croydon Common; brother Vic also played once for Watford; one sister married footballer Billy Grimes (Watford, Glossop, Bradford City and Derby), and another wed the Spurs, Crystal Palace and Sunderland centre-forward George Payne.

Apps: *FL 8.*

FURR, William Stanley

b. Hitchin, Herts, Oct qtr 1891

Career: Hitchin Town; Dec 1911-trials-Everton; Jan 1912 Brentford; July 1912 FOSSE; Aug 1913-trials-Luton Town; 1913 not known; 1919 Luton Town.

Fosse debut/only game v Huddersfield Town (A) 28.9.12

> Winger Willie's Division Two baptism came in the same game as brother Harold's, but led to no further chances at Filbert Street. Chosen on the right flank despite being deemed an outside-left speed merchant (a former Hertfordshire 220-yards sprint champion), he was summed up as 'raw' by the local *Mail.* He had played but twice in the Southern League with Brentford, and would do so only once – after WW1 – with Luton.

Apps: *FL 1.*

GALBRAITH, Thomas D.

b. Vale of Leven, Dunbartonshire

Career: May 1896 Renton; Nov 1896 Vale of Leven; Jan 1898 Sunderland; Aug 1898 FOSSE; cs 1900 Vale of Leven.

Fosse debut v Lincoln City (H) 3.9.1898

> Whilst he only contributed fleetingly to the Sunderland campaign that saw them occupying the Division One runners-up spot in 1898, Tommy became a free-scoring right-winger for the Fosse team that just failed to attain promotion in 1899. However, his goal-touch deserted him the following term, despite a shift to the inside-right berth; and his frustratingly near-miss-strewn career later saw him in the Vale of Leven side beaten in the semi-final of the 1902/3 Scottish Qualifying Cup.

Apps: *FL 62; FAC 6.*
Goals: *FL 17; FAC 1.*

GALLACHER, Hugh M.

b. Girvan, Ayrshire, 11th May 1870

Career: Maybole; May 1889 Celtic; Sept 1890 Preston North End; Jan 1893 Sheffield United; Aug 1894 FOSSE; cs 1896 Rossendale United; Nelson; July 1897 New Brompton.

Fosse debut v Rotherham Town (H) 8.9.1894 (scored once)

> A fine outside-left with a fairly colourful career, Hugh played and scored in Celtic's first-ever Scottish League game (lost 1-4 in August 1890), only to find appearance, goal and game struck from the records when opponents Renton were removed from the League couple of months later. One further outing as a Celt, however, was enough to convince Preston to buy him. North End were just losing their 'Invincibles' tag, but Hugh top-scored as they took second place in 1891, was ever-present as they finished runners-up again in 1892, and was halfway through another near-miss assault on the title when switching to Bramall Lane to assist the Blades promotion-wards. He played in the first Sheffield derby at League level, scored against Fosse in a September 1893 friendly, and became known at that time for the eccentricity of chewing his way through an ounce of 'twist' tobacco per game. With Fosse he regularly patrolled the left flank over the first two seasons in the Second Division, but found his days numbered when Billy Dorrell returned from Aston Villa and he began to experience weight problems. Jeered as 'Fatty' at Nottingham, he prompted the local paper to note that 'during the last month or so he has put on flesh to a remarkable extent'. Three further seasons of decent standard football in the Lancashire and Southern Leagues nonetheless followed, and at New Brompton Hugh briefly renewed his partnership with fellow ex-Fossil David Skea.

Apps: *FL 47; FAC 7.*
Goals: *FL 11; FAC 4.*

GALLOWAY, Michael

b. Oswestry, Monmouthshire, 30th May 1965

Career: am 1981 Berwick Rangers; pro June 1983 Mansfield Town; Jan 1986 Halifax Town; Nov 1987 Heart of Midlothian; June 1989 Celtic; Feb 1995 & July 1995-loans-CITY.

City debut v West Ham United (H) 4.2.95

> Reputedly turned down by City as a 16-year-old prospect on the grounds of size, Mike had a convoluted, turbulent and near-tragic time with the club some 14 years later. Mark McGhee negotiated a month's loan for the player in January 1995, but a hamstring injury during his first training session put the deal on hold. Returning, Mike was then booked in each of his first trio of City outings, but impressed with his strength and energetic commitment as either a midfielder or right-back, and exhibited a refreshing accuracy with his crossing, especially in the Premiership fightback thrillers at Aston Villa and Coventry. However, no sooner had City re-registered Mike's temporary contract, with the intention of paying £200,000 at season's end if the loan extension proved successful, than he was sidelined again by injury. McGhee checked on the player's fitness again before 1995/6, but was still only offering an extended loan deal when Mike tired of the saga. Portsmouth came in with their own loan offer, but before Mike could take it up, he was seriously injured in an horrific car crash at Dunton Bassett, and lay critically ill in a Leicester hospital for some time before pulling through. Mike's marriage in Glasgow in November 1995 happily signalled his recovery, but his only football involvement since has been as manager of Junior side Tranent for most of 1996/7. Mike's early career was pretty much a showcase for his on-field versatility: primarily regarded as a defensive midfielder, he had already essayed excursions to the roles of full-back and striker in the lower reaches of the Football League before his move to Hearts, where he became noted as something of a talismanic goalscoring presence in European competition. A £500,000 switch to Parkhead ensued, as did the winning of a couple of Scottish Under-21 caps during 1989/90 (as an over-age player, qualifying as the son of a Scottish soldier). Mike was elevated to senior international status in October 1991, when Scotland faced Romania in Bucharest, while at club level he featured as substitute in Celtic's 1990 Cup Final defeat (on penalties) by Aberdeen, and in the starting line-up for the 1994/5 League Cup Final against Raith, again lost on spot-kicks.

Apps: *PL 4+1; FAC 1.*

Mike Galloway

GARDINER, Archibald

b. Penicuik, Mid Lothian, 17th March 1913

Career: Burnbank; Penicuik Athletic; trials-Clapton Orient; May 1931 Heart of Midlothian; Feb 1934 CITY; Oct 1934 Wrexham; Aug 1936 Hamilton Academical; May 1937-trials-Olympique Lillois; Aug 1937 Brideville; Nov 1937-trials-Morton; Dec 1937 Inverness Thistle.

City debut v Portsmouth (A) 21.2.34 (scored four)

> Archie's was a career marked by headline-grabbing dynamism, and a life scarred by smaller-print disgrace. The instant impact which the young centre-forward made on his transfer south is unlikely ever to be equalled or bettered in City annals: a four-goal debut in a 5-3 away win (his first strike coming after 90 seconds), followed two games later by a home hat-trick against champions-to-be Arsenal! Another two matches down the line, Archie was in City's first-ever FA Cup semi-final team, yet after only three outings the following term, he was allowed to move on, as the first sale of Arthur Lochhead's management. The turnaround in fortunes was remarkable, yet Archie was not entirely new to disappointment, having for some time understudied the Scottish international goalscoring legend Barney Battles at Tynecastle, and dropped back into Hearts' reserves, no matter how successful, whenever the senior man returned to the side. With the senior centre-forward at Leicester being the veteran Arthur Chandler, there was certainly an element of 'as you were'. Perhaps predictably, Archie managed to mark his Wrexham home debut with a hat-trick, but his goalscoring record at the Racecourse soon tailed off; and by the end of his first term with the Accies he was listed at a £200 asking price. Wanderings in France, Ireland and Scotland failed to earn Archie a contract, and ignominy was just around the corner. He had already served a Borstal sentence in 1929 for theft, before his professional career took off, and now returned to crime, being fined at Birmingham Police Court in March 1938 for theft from his lodgings; and then jailed in Manchester two months later for intent to commit a felony and assaulting two police officers. Archie's father Harry was a former Renton, Bolton and Rangers centre-half who had represented the Football League in their first (1892) clash with the Scottish League, despite being Scottish-born himself; while two older brothers had been on the books of Motherwell and Hamilton.

Apps: *FL 18; FAC 1.*
Goals: *FL 11.*

GARDINER, William Silcock

b. Larbert, Stirlingshire, 15th August 1929

Career: Smith & Wellstood (Falkirk); Bo'ness United; Nov 1950 Rangers; Aug 1955 CITY; Nov 1958 Reading; 1960 Sudbury Town.

City debut v Doncaster Rovers (A) 5.9.55 (scored once)

> Another prolific scorer who spent much of his early career in Scottish reserve football (nonetheless claiming one Scotland 'B' cap; and making a two-game, two-goal contribution to Rangers' 1953 championship triumph), Willie moved from Ibrox for £4,000 to become the first of David Halliday's numerous Caledonian captures. Installed alongside Arthur Rowley, he performed the almost unthinkable feat of outgunning his new partner in his first term: averaging exactly a goal per game to end up with 34 Second Division strikes and one in the Cup. The tall, fair-haired centre-forward (who certainly made up in crash-bang effectiveness what he lacked in elegance) lost his place to Derek Hines during the 1957 promotion campaign (settling for becoming the reserves' 18-goal top scorer), but returned to help City survive their first fraught season back in Division One. Willie declined the option of a move to Lincoln City in March 1958, but then had his Elm Park stay utterly ruined when fracturing each leg in turn.

Apps: *FL 69; FAC 2.*
Goals: *FL 48; FAC 1.*

GARDNER, Frank

b. 1866
d. Leicester, 8th December 1943

Career: 1884 FOSSE (- 1891).

Fosse debut (competitive) v Doncaster Rovers (A) ML 26.12.1891

> A genuine founding father of the Fosse (at the age of 18!), Frank was elected secretary and treasurer at the formative meeting of the club in the spring of 1884, and played as a half-back in the very first friendly fixture (on 1st November 1884, versus Syston Fosse). He was also a leading agitator for the formation of the Leicestershire FA (October 1886), which honoured him with its presidency soon afterwards. Appropriately, Frank was a scorer in the Final when Fosse secured that body's Senior Cup for the first time in 1890 (with a replay win over Coalville Town), but he was primarily concentrating on his secretarial duties (conducting the club's business from 41 Hinckley Road) by the time he was called upon to make up the Fosse's Midland League eleven on their Boxing Day 1891 jaunt to Doncaster. A company secretary by profession, Frank was also chairman and treasurer of the Leicester & District League from 1895, a referee at both Midland and Football League levels from 1898, and chair of the Rolleston Charity Cup competition from 1900. Strangely, he declined a 1905 offer to join the Fosse board; but in 1913 chaired George Johnson's testimonial committe to re-emphasise his commitment to the club. Aside from brief spells on business in Ireland during the early 30s, Frank spent all his working life in Leicester.

Apps: *ML 1.*

GARLAND, Christopher Stephen

b. Bristol, 24th April 1949

Career: app/pro May 1966 Bristol City; Aug 1971 Chelsea; Mar 1975 CITY; Nov 1976 Bristol City; cs 1983 Minehead (p/mgr).

City debut v Coventry City (A) 15.3.75

> A teenage local hero at Ashton Gate, blond striker Chris had won one England Under-23 cap when Chelsea laid out a six-figure fee for him, and he appeared for the Blues in their 1972 League Cup Final defeat by Stoke. His £95,000 move to City had an inspirational effect on a struggling side, and his eight goals in ten games at the end of 1974/5 (in tandem with fellow newcomer Jeff Blockley's strengthening of the back line) did much to avert the very real threat of relegation. Sent off in the opening game of the following campaign (when a 9-man City twice equalised to secure an unlikely 3-3 draw against Birmingham), Chris bounced back in a hard-working support role to Frank Worthington, and had only just lost his place during Jimmy Bloomfield's final season when Bristol City's offer to take him home for £110,000 was accepted. Injuries dogged his second spell there, and indeed his contract was twice cancelled (once with his complicity to aid the club from the brink of bankruptcy and closure), as the Robins slid from First to Fourth, but Chris refused to retire, and took his career tally of League and Cup goals to 103 with a final strike in 1982/3. In 1992, it was revealed that Chris was suffering from Parkinson's Disease, and many of his former playing colleagues rallied round for a series of testimonial events hosted by Minehead FC; while Bristol City played Manchester United on his behalf in May 1993.

Apps: *FL 52+3; FAC 3; LC 5.*
Goals: *FL 15; FAC 3; LC 1.*

Chris Garland

GARRATY, William

b. Saltley, Birmingham, 6th October 1878
d. Birmingham, 6th May 1931

Career: Highfield Villa; Aston Shakespeare; cs 1897 Aston Villa; Sept 1908 FOSSE; Oct 1908 West Bromwich Albion; Nov 1910 Lincoln City.

Fosse debut v Bristol City (H) 12.9.08

> A veteran goalscoring centre-forward who had been capped for England against Wales in 1903, and won both Championship (1900) and FA Cup (1905) medals during his 259-game, 112-goal stay with Villa, Billy remained with Fosse only a contrasting matter of some seven weeks after signing to augment their First Division forces. He was hardly over the hill, though – his twenty goals for West Brom over the next couple of years evidenced that – and the wisdom of Fosse letting him go (at £270, representing a quick £20 profit) has to be questioned in view of their subsequent nosedive to relegation. They had lost only once with Billy in the side, despite his own inability to get on the scoresheet. Back in the early days of his senior career, Billy took part in the notorious ten-and-a-half minute match between Sheffield Wednesday and Villa – the Football League had demanded that a game abandoned in November 1898 had to be completed almost four months later, and Billy, who wasn't in the side for the first 79 minutes, had made his breakthrough in the interim! In later life, he was a driver for Ansells Brewery back in Birmingham.

Apps: *FL 6.*

GARVEY, James

b. Paisley, 4th June 1919

Career: Corby Town; am Dec 1937 Queens Park Rangers; Stewart & Lloyds; May 1939 Northampton Town; June 1946 CITY; July 1950 Corby Town; Oct 1955 Hinckley Athletic.

City debut v Burnley (H) 24.5.47

> Having had his League debut for the Cobblers expunged from official records after the abandonment of the 1939/40 season, and having reputedly assisted Brentford reserves during 1945/6, while stationed on the Isle of Wight with his Royal Artillery unit, Jim was decidedly short of senior footballing experience when Johnny Duncan took him on for postwar Second Division duty. The Scottish left-half or inside-left was valued for his constructive approach work, but niggling knee injuries held him back whenever he looked about to make a sustained first-team breakthrough. His final senior outing was in the crucial last game of 1948/9 at Cardiff, when the point gained kept City out of Division Three. Jim did well, though, with Corby in their heyday: sharing in United Counties League championships in 1951 and 1952, and a year later helping them to runners-up spot in their inaugural Midland League campaign.

Apps: *FL 15; FAC 1.*

GAVIN, Patrick John

b. Hammersmith, 5th June 1967

Career: Hanwell Town; Mar 1989 Gillingham; June 1989 CITY; Sept 1989-loan-Gillingham; Mar 1991 Peterborough United; Mar 1992-loan-Kettering Town; Aug 1992-loan-Kettering Town; Nov 1992-loan-Boston United; Feb 1993 Northampton Town; cs 1993 Wigan Athletic; July 1995-trials-Crewe Alexandra; 1995 Hayes; 1995 Aylesbury United; 1995 Harrow Borough; Dec 1995 Farnborough Town; cs 1997 Harrow Borough.

City debut v Charlton Athletic (A) 13.10.90 (sub)

> The subject of heated dispute between the Gills and City when signing on at Filbert Street – David Pleat averred he was a free agent, while the Kent club (for whom he'd scored seven goals in thirteen Third Division outings) claimed he was under contract to them – tall young striker Pat was initially barred from training with either club until his registration details had been ironed out. An immediate compromise saw Pat loaned back to Priestfield for a year, but he failed to consolidate his initial impact, and added but a single strike to his record that term. The former postman fronted City's attack in the Scottish pre-season friendlies of 1990 (scoring at Motherwell), but his total Second Division experience with Leicester then amounted to only 83 minutes in three games before he became a £15,000 deadline-day mover to London Road. Six strikes immediately helped Posh to promotion from the basement, but Pat was out on Conference loan when they went up again the following season, and was not to hit the headlines again until his final game for Northampton. The Cobblers had to win their game at Shrewsbury to retain League status, and substitute Pat's two goals obliged, though his contract was cancelled only days later. He then saw more first-team action with Wigan than with any of his previous clubs, but only as a prelude to a lengthy career in southern non-league football; latterly with Alan Paris at Harrow.

Apps: *FL 1+2.*

GEE, Philip John

b. Pelsall, Staffs, 19th December 1964

Career: Riley Sports; July 1985 Gresley Rovers; Sept 1985 Derby County; Mar 1992 CITY; Jan 1995-loan-Plymouth Argyle; Jan 1997 Hednesford Town; Mar 1997 Shepshed Dynamo.

City debut v Portsmouth (H) 11.3.92

> Originally recommended to Derby by David Nish, in his capacity at the time of Gresley chairman, Phil made a significant goalscoring contribution to the Rams' 1987 Second Division championship campaign, but was soon thereafter regarded more as a useful squad player than a first-choice striker. He joined City, along with teammate Ian Ormondroyd, as the £200,000 makeweight in the Paul Kitson package deal, and got off the scoring mark with a magnificent long-range strike at Tranmere, but his efforts in City's qualification for their first Play-Off experience weren't enough to win him the nod over Kevin Russell when the season's-end thrillers were played (though he did figure as a substitute against Blackburn at Wembley). A remarkable performance at Filbert Street against his former Derby side (when he scored twice and hit a post with a spectacular shot during a 3-2 win) was one of the few highlights of the following term, as Phil gradually faded from Brian Little's first-team plans; though isolated games when the front-runner played in a wider role, and operated a shoot-on-sight policy, more happily studded his City record. His last-gasp drive against QPR won City their first-ever Premiership point, but Phil got very few chances under Mark McGhee, who would have sold him at the end of his Home Park loan period had Argyle been able to raise the requested £75,000. Listed in May 1995, Phil was freed a year later, with knee problems preventing him playing thereafter. Since 1988, he has done some scouting for Wolves.

Apps: *FL/PL 35+18; LC 2+3; AIC 3; PO 2+1.*
Goals: *FL/PL 9; AIC 4..*

GIBSON, Colin John

b. Bridport, Dorset, 6th April 1960

Career: app July 1976/pro Aug 1978 Aston Villa; Nov 1985 Manchester United; Sept 1990-loan-Port Vale; Dec 1990 CITY; Aug 1994 Blackpool; Sept 1994 Walsall.

City debut v Watford (H) 23.12.90

> Primarily a left-back at Villa, where he won numerous honours in the early years of a subsequently injury-marred career, Colin was also utilised by City in more advanced midfield positions, but had perhaps suffered one too many knocks by the veteran stage to be fully convincing in the increasingly fashionable, but highly demanding, wing-back role. Nonetheless, his contributions to City's efforts to raise themselves back to the top flight were patently wholehearted, and it was rather fitting that his final game in a Leicester shirt should have been the promotion-clinching Play-Off victory over Derby. David Pleat's final City purchase at £100,000, Colin showed as much grit as class over his three-and-a-half seasons at Filbert Street, where he was often sidelined by the knee injuries which had first flared at Old Trafford, and enlivened several games with a vicious long-range shot. During 1992/3 he set two minor club records, by becoming the first City substitute to be himself substituted (coming on for Michael Trotter at Watford, and limping off to be replaced by Colin Gordon), and the first City substitute to be sent off (at Luton); and he was actually placed on the free transfer list at the end of that term. Yet he renegotiated a one-year contract with Brian Little and ended his City days with a Wembley winner's memento and a broad, gap-toothed grin. Eighteen years earlier, he had accepted a Villa apprenticeship despite having been on schoolboy forms with Portsmouth, and went on to taste rapid success. An FA Youth Cup Finalist in 1978, he was a regular in Villa's 1981 Championship side, and played in the European Super Cup team of 1983; though he sat out the 1982 European Cup Final as an unused substitute. Colin also won one cap at each of England Under-21 and 'B' levels while with Villa; and figured in Manchester United's title runners-up squad of 1988. In 1995 he played a substantial role in Walsall's promotion to Division Two; but then retired from the game. For the past couple of years, Colin has been involved in the Filbert Street matchday hospitality set-up.

Apps: *FL 50+9; FAC 1+1; LC 4; FMC 2; AIC 1; PO 4+1.*
Goals: *FL 4.*

GIBSON, David Wedderburn

b. Winchburgh, West Lothian, 23rd September 1938

Career: Livingston United; 1955 Hibernian; Jan 1962 CITY; Sept 1970 Aston Villa; Jan 1972 Exeter City (- 1974).

City debut v Fulham (H) 3.2.62

> One of the very finest ball-players to have graced Filbert Street since the war, Davie had still to complete his National Service when Matt Gillies paid Hibs a bargain £25,000 for his signature. He was expecting a near-immediate posting to Aden with the Kings Own Scottish Borderers, but had that postponed when selected for all that season's showpiece Army representative games. Turning full-time to City's cause after his August 1962 demob, however, he forged an unforgettable early partnership with Mike Stringfellow on the left flank of the attack. His elegant control and visionary passing skills were major prompts to City's Wembley visits in 1963 and 1969; and Davie himself found the net with pleasing regularity, scoring in both legs of the 1964 League Cup Final victory over Stoke, and knocking in three goals in his seven full Scottish international appearances of the early 60s. His artistry – always marbled with a tough resilience – was barely on the wane when he left to give a veteran's course in midfield style at Villa and Exeter, and while with the former club he returned to Wembley, albeit as unused substitute for the 1971 League Cup Final. Davie remained settled in Leicestershire after bowing out from the playing ranks, working in the postal service and helping his wife run a residential home for the elderly.

Apps: *FL 274+6; FAC 29; LC 30.*
Goals: *FL 41; FAC 5; LC 7.*

GIBSON, George Eardley

b. Biddulph, Staffs, 29th August 1912
d. Blackburn, 30th December 1990

Career: Kidderminster Harriers; trials-Stoke City; Nov 1931 Frickley Colliery; Apr 1932 Sunderland; Nov 1934 CITY; July 1935 US Valenciennes; Jan 1936 Distillery; cs 1936 RC Roubaix; Dec 1936 Shelbourne; June 1937 Workington; May 1938 Bradford City.

City debut v Stoke City (H) 10.11.34

> Arthur Lochhead's first signing, when City were searching for both short- and long-term replacements for Arthur Chandler, and had just released Archie Gardiner, George was brought down from Roker to hold a briefer purchase than most on the old goalgetter's centre-forward shirt, playing only in two heavy defeats within ten days of his arrival. A young bustler of the vintage brylcreem-and-centre-parting style, he had indeed played only twice previously in Division One for Sunderland (though he'd netted twice in their first-ever floodlit game, an away friendly against Racing Club de Paris), and would eventually taste League fare only three more times in a brief run-out at Valley Parade in 1938. In the interim, though, he had quite an adventuresome time out of the country. Playing alongside former Chelsea and England defender Peter O'Dowd for Valenciennes in the French top flight, he was deemed a great success until wild allegations arose that the two Englishmen had been bribed to 'throw' a match with Lille that resulted in a 1-5 defeat. In clearing his name with the French FA, George actually received 5,000 francs compensation for loss of engagement; but his contractual difficulties were far from over. Signing for the next term with Roubaix, he walked out in October 1936 when the franc was devalued, and this time ended up owing a 500 franc fine to the FFF! The Players Union offered to pay it, but George was adamant that his club were in the wrong, and once more set off for Ireland, outside the jurisdiction of an FA/FFF agreement. He was living in Great Harwood at the time of his death in the East Lancs Hospice.

Apps: *FL 2.*

GIBSON, Dr Thomas Maitland

b. Dennistoun, Glasgow, ca 1905

Career: Parkhead; May 1926 CITY; Oct 1929 Ashby White Rose; Dec 1929 Burton Town; Ashby Town.

City debut v West Ham United (A) 12.3.28

> The only General Practitioner to have turned out for City in League football, 'Doctor Tom' was an inside-forward who occasionally filled in for Ernie Hine or Arthur Lochhead – though his limited senior career consisted entirely of away matches, and he was never on a winning City side at League level (his only goal coming in a 3-6 Anfield defeat). A Junior international in March 1926, Tom was still a medical student when he signed (a few days after Peter Hodge, who had set up the deal, left for Manchester City), qualified through September exams for eventual practice in Leicester and Ashby, and had a delayed, but eventful debut for City reserves against Clapton Orient in October, when he scored in the first minute and was removed to the Infirmary half-an-hour later, suffering from serious concussion. Upon his 1929 release, Tom was refused permission, as an ex-pro, to play for Ashby White Rose in the Coalville & District League (though having one outing for their seconds), and so joined Burton. He became president of Mountsorrel Amateurs in the early 30s, and was still taking part in the then-annual Doctors v Parsons charity fixture at Filbert Street in April 1939. (He should not be confused with the Thomas Gibson who was an amateur trialist with City in both August 1920 and March 1922, and also represented Ashby Town, Loughborough Corinthians, Barwell United and Nuneaton Town).

Apps: *FL 4.*
Goals: *FL 1.*

GIBSON, William

b. Lanark, 24th June 1959

Career: Easthouses BC; Mar 1979 CITY; Oct 1982 Nuneaton Borough; cs 1987 Weymouth; 1997 Portland United.

City debut v Ipswich Town (H) 16.8.80

> Left-back Willie impressed Jock Wallace on a 1980 close-season tour of Germany and Holland and surprisingly found himself pitched into City's opening game on their First Division return, holding his place for half of that season of struggle against the drop. He lost out, though, in the three-cornered fight for the No.3 shirt with Paul Friar and Norman Leet early in the next campaign, and was soon to drop out of League football. He spent five years at the top of the non-league pyramid with Nuneaton, and then a monumental decade with Weymouth in both Conference and Southern League, becoming skipper and earning a 1995 testimonial game.

***Apps:** FL 28; FAC 1; LC 3.*

GILCHRIST, Philip Alexander

b. Stockton on Tees, 25th August 1973

Career: YT/pro Dec 1990 Nottingham Forest; Jan 1992 Middlesbrough; Nov 1992 Hartlepool United; Feb 1995 Oxford United; Aug 1999 CITY; Mar 2001 West Bromwich Albion.

City debut v Coventry City (H) 11.8.99 (sub)

> Bought for £500,000 after Steve Walsh had suffered injury on the season's opening day at Highbury, central defender Phil was granted by Martin O'Neill the opportunity to recreate his old Manor Ground central defensive partnership with Matt Elliott. At first, it appeared that the pace of the Premiership might be too much for him, especially when twice caught out with slow reactions for Spurs goals at White Hart Lane, but he had surmounted a steep learning curve by the end of the 1999/2000 campaign, and fully deserved the icing on the cake of a goal at Anfield for the way he'd tightened his rearguard game, honed his concentration, and begun timing his tackles to perfection. He didn't disappoint when called upon by Peter Taylor, either, so it was some surprise when the most expensive deal of the 2001 deadline day, recouping City's outlay, took him to The Hawthorns. There, he and Russell Hoult assisted the Baggies to the Play-Off semi-finals. Never a first-teamer with either Forest or Boro, Phil suffered relegation to Division Three in his second term with Hartlepool, but matured into a steady defender at Oxford, where he formed a formidable barrier with Elliott in the 1996 side promoted to Division One, and took the Player of the Year award in 1999 despite his poverty-stricken club's slide back. He was also noted at Oxford as a long-throw expert but, strangely, City never utilised this aspect of his game.

***Apps:** PL 23+16; FAC 4+1; LC 6+1.*
***Goals:** PL 1.*

GILL, Ernest Harry

b. Mountsorrel, Leics, 1877
d. Hull, 1950

Career: Poole White Star; Bridgewater; trials-Bristol City; Sept 1899-trials-Grimsby Town; Mar 1900 Southampton; 1900 Freemantle; Apr 1901 FOSSE; cs 1902 Melton Amateurs; 1903 Excelsior Thursday.

Fosse debut/only game v Gainsborough Trinity (A) 26.10.01

> Playing his cricket as a professional and his football as an amateur, Ernest never quite established a major reputation at either sport. Despite his county birth, his early experiences with the winter game were in Dorset, Somerset and Hampshire, peaking with a single Southern League outing for the Saints. The summer of 1901 saw his return to Leicestershire to sign for both Fosse as a full-back and the County as a right-arm fast-medium bowler. Ernest impressed in a couple of Fosse friendlies, and replaced George Swift at left-back in the above match, only to have his senior career abruptly terminated by a broken leg suffered in a reserve fixture at Ilkeston. He did return, however, to Filbert Street to help out the reserves as either goalkeeper or right-back during 1903/4. His cricketing career then reasserted itself with his appointment as pro to Swansea CC in 1904. Ernest's brother George also played County cricket for both Somerset and Leicestershire.

***Apps:** FL 1.*

GILLIES, Alexander

Career: Lochgelly United; Oct 1895 Bolton Wanderers; Feb 1896 Manchester City; Aug 1896 Heart of Midlothian; Feb 1897 Sheffield Wednesday; Aug 1897 FOSSE; cs 1898 Lochgelly United.

Fosse debut v Grimsby Town (A) 18.9.1897

> With five clubs in less than three years away from his Lochgelly home, Sandy was a Scottish inside-forward well and truly bitten by the wandering bug. He briefly deposed Johnny McMillan at Leicester, largely on the valid strength of his feat of scoring at least once in each of his six Fosse friendly games; yet he contrived to extend throughout his Filbert Street stay an unenviable record of failing to notch a single goal for any of his Football League clubs in that competition. Sandy became one of several Fossils whose services were dispensed with as a disciplinary measure in February 1898, and he returned to Lochgelly, where he was in the side which won the 1899/1900 East of Scotland Consolation Cup, just as he had been back in 1894/5.

***Apps:** FL 4.*

GILLIES, Matthew Muirhead

b. Loganlea, West Lothian, 12th August 1921
d. Nottingham, 24th December 1998

Career: Winchburgh; am Motherwell; RAF football; Oct 1942 Bolton Wanderers; Jan 1952 CITY.

City debut v Doncaster Rovers (H) 26.1.52

> A medical student before the war, Matt was on RAF service when signing for Bolton, and also guested at centre-half for Arsenal, Chester, QPR and Chelsea. Established as the Trotters' First Division captain and defensive linchpin for 145 League games after hostilities ceased, he signed for Norman Bullock for £9,500 to bolster City's rearguard, and became the regular pivot, thoughtful but solid, in the 1954 Second Division championship side, before giving way to the re-positioned Jack Froggatt partway through the hapless top-flight campaign which followed. Despite his steadying on-field influence as a senior pro, however, it soon became obvious that it was beyond the playing arena that Matt would make his more significant mark. He had already received coaching offers from Italy when it was announced in April 1956 that he would take up tracksuit duties at Filbert Street, and in November 1958, on David Halliday's resignation, he assumed the role of acting manager of the relegation-threatened club. An immediate upswing in results then prompted confirmation of Matt's assumption of full managerial control in January 1959. Thereafter, he was to direct City's generally upbeat fortunes for a decade spent entirely in the top echelon, twice leading his team out for Wembley Cup Finals, twice taking them to the League Cup Final, and thoroughly earning for himself a reputation as both a shrewd market operator and a good judge of character. Matt became a local Justice of the Peace while still in office at Filbert Street, though his primary commitment to his club's continuing honours-chase even led to him suffering a lengthy spell of stress-related ill-health towards the end of his regime, making something of a nonsense of the occasionally-voiced criticism that he was somehow 'too gentlemanly' for the purported rat-race of modern football. While his own transfer dealings brought in such giants as Banks, and such ideal pairings as Gibson and Stringfellow, or Dougan and Sinclair, and he ushered City's record outlay upwards through the six-figure mark, he was every bit as keen to pass the lion's share of credit for City's tactical innovations of the 60s to his trusty coach Bert Johnson. Accordingly, it was little surprise to anyone – least of all, one presumes, to the board – when he immediately resigned in the wake of Johnson's sacking in November 1968, during the first campaign to threaten demotion since his first in office. What did surprise many was that he then took another managerial post, at a largely unresponsive Nottingham Forest, where the main long-term repercussion of his tenure was the signing of a young Martin O'Neill. Yet even an apparent 'defection' to City's local rivals failed to diminish Matt's standing for those in Leicester who recognised his crucial contribution to the process of turning a club with a longstanding 'yo-yo' reputation into one with a sustained 'First Division' image. From 1972, Matt acted as a director of a Sharnford-based specialist engineering firm run by the son of City's famous Scottish scout, Walter McLean; but he returned to Nottingham in retirement. His passing there was marked by a perfectly-observed minute's silence before City's Christmas 1998 game with Blackburn.

***Apps:** FL 103; FAC 8.*

GLOVER, Edward Lee

b. Kettering, Northants, 24th April 1970

Career: YT 1986/pro May 1987 Nottingham Forest; Sept 1989-loan-CITY; Jan 1990-loan-Barnsley; Sept 1991-loan-Luton Town; Aug 1994 Port Vale; Aug 1996 Rotherham United; Mar 1997-loan-Huddersfield Town; July 2000 Macclesfield Town.

City debut v Bradford City (A) 16.9.89

> A 16-year-old League Cup debutant for Forest, and a scorer on his First Division bow a season later, Lee soon won Scottish Under-21 recognition as Brian Clough kept faith in his young striker, but long-term injury then removed him from senior contention until David Pleat brought him on loan to Filbert Street. Wayne Clarke and Kevin Russell were sidelined, and Tommy Wright facing imminent suspension, when Lee arrived to form a teenage spearhead with Paul Kitson, and at least marked an otherwise in-and-out month's stay with the decisive goal of City's belated first win of the season, against Brighton. Lee then had the ill-luck to break his leg in a Forest reserve game shortly after his Oakwell loan stint, but he was back to take a runners-up medal from the 1991 FA Cup Final defeat by Spurs. He was an unused sub for Forest's two Wembley visits of 1992 (in the ZDS and League Cup Finals), and part of their relegated squad of 1993, then back beneath the Twin Towers with Port Vale in 1996 for an Anglo-Italian

Lee Glover

Cup Final disappointment against Genoa. He became Rotherham's joint record signing at £150,000, suffered relegation with them in his first term, rediscovered his scoring touch over the next two basement campaigns, and returned from serious injury to score a penalty with the last kick of their 2000 promotion season. Lee's goal tally finally crept over the 50 mark midway through 2000/1, with the fourth of his eight strikes for Macclesfield.

***Apps:** FL 3+2.*
***Goals:** FL 1.*

GLOVER, Leonard

b. Kennington, London, 31st January 1944

Career: am May 1959/pro May 1962 Charlton Athletic; Nov 1967 CITY; Apr 1976 Tampa Bay Rowdies; Nov 1976 Kettering Town; Mar 1977 Tampa Bay Rowdies; Sept 1977 Kettering Town; Aug 1978 Earl Shilton Albion (p/mgr); 1979 Shepshed Charterhouse (p/coach); 1994 Harlow Town (p/mgr).

City debut v Arsenal (H) 18.11.67

> A series of niggling injuries marred both the beginning and end of Lenny's City career, but in the interim seasons his left-wing skills and pace bemused many an opposing full-back; and it was a genuine tribute to both his ability and personality that he became such a firm favourite of the usually highly-critical Popular Side terrace support, whose anticipatory roar whenever Lenny received the ball must have unnerved many an adversary. He had first faced City as a Charlton teenager in 1962/3, when his replay winner ejected City from the League Cup, and the £80,000 fee Matt Gillies paid for him five years later represented at the time an English record for a winger. Lenny's goals saw City through the first two rounds of their 1969 Cup run to Wembley (though his fitness to start the Final came down to a gamble), and two years later he regularly ripped open Second Division defences as Frank O'Farrell's City sped to promotion. Back in the top flight he laid on many of Frank Worthington's goals, and when Jimmy Bloomfield's entertaining 'nearly' team reached the Cup semi-finals in 1974, Lenny claimed the equalising (if eventually only consolatory) goal in the replay against Liverpool. After returning from America the first time, registration difficulties meant Lenny had to turn down approaches from each of Notts County, Blackpool and Colchester; while his second Kettering spell featured an odd swansong to FA Cup football – he played in a First Round victory over Tilbury, but had his eligibility queried officially by the losers, who went on to triumph in a replay ordered by the FA. Retiring to the role of publican (for some time running the Kings Head at Smeeton Westerby), Lenny made a surprise return to football in the summer of 1994, when taking on the manager's role at Harlow Town; and in fact registered himself as a player in mid-season, making a brief active comeback in January 1995 as the first 50-year-old to appear in the Diadora League, shortly before resigning.

***Apps:** FL 245+7; FAC 35+1; LC 17.*
***Goals:** FL 38; FAC 8; LC 2.*

GODDERIDGE, Albert Edward

b. Tamworth, Staffs, 29th May 1902
d. Lichfield, Staffs, Apr qtr 1976

Career: Two Gates; trials-Aston Villa & Preston North End; May 1922 CITY; June 1927 Barnsley; Aug 1929 Newark Town; Nov 1930 Hinckley United; 1932 Nuneaton Town; cs 1933 Tamworth.

City debut v Fulham (H) 29.3.24

> A former collier who graduated from the backwaters of Trent Valley League football to wrest the City first-team goalie's jersey from George Hebden, Albert became the sturdy last line of defence in the successful promotion push of 1925, but found himself back in the reserves after the squad charged with consolidating top-flight status had been augmented by the vastly experienced Kenny Campbell. Then, at Oakwell, he again had to knuckle down primarily to an understudy's role; this time to the consistent Tommy Gale. Albert used to harbour goalscoring ambitions with City's seconds: he took two penalties in the record 22-0 victory over Ibstock in the 1923/4 County Cup, netting once while still wearing his cap, and also missed a spot-kick against Reading in the London Combination in 1926/7. His brother George was a prolific forward who played alongside Albert with Hinckley from November 1931 (and also served Atherstone Town, Nuneaton Town and Coalville Town).

***Apps:** FL 50; FAC 6.*

GODWIN, Thomas Fergus

b. Dublin, 20th August 1927
d. Bournemouth, 27th August 1996

Career: Home Farm; Shamrock Rovers; Sept 1949 CITY; Dec 1951-loan-Carlisle United; June 1952 Bournemouth & Boscombe Athletic; June 1963 Dorchester Town.

City debut v Swansea Town (H) 26.11.49

> Signed by Johnny Duncan only days after starring for the Republic of Ireland in a shock 2-0 win over England at Goodison Park, Tommy then made his debut under the new management of Norman Bullock, and found his last-line position constantly pressured thereafter by the claims of Scottish international-to-be Johnny Anderson. Fitting the traditional mould of City's capped keepers, Tommy made a virtue of unspectacular soundness: he was a master of the high ball and no mean shot-stopper. He added four international call-ups while with City to the five he'd received with Shamrock, where he'd been sidelined for some time with a broken leg received in a 1948 FAI Cup semi-final; and he would go on to add four more caps to his collection after moving to Bournemouth. Tommy was on the City list at his own request when Carlisle tried him out in a friendly against Northampton, but he chose to move south rather than north, and settled at Dean Court for a total of 357 Third Division starts over ten seasons. He took a testimonial there in 1962 against West Ham; and after his playing days were over worked as a parks supervisor for Bournemouth Corporation.

***Apps:** FL 45; FAC 1.*

GOLDIE, William Glover

b. Hurlford, Ayrshire, 22nd January 1878

Career: 1895 Hurlford Thistle; 1897 Clyde; Mar 1898 Liverpool ; Dec 1903 Fulham; Aug 1908 FOSSE; Sept 1911 Leicester Imperial.

Fosse debut v Sheffield Wednesday (H) 1.9.08

> 'Bustle and noise would be impossible to a footballer of his stamp... The delicate and far more deadly rapier is his weapon, and he wields it with a master's hand. Goldie is essentially 'class". Old Fossil in the *Mercury* was not alone in his praise for experienced left-half Billy – another critic dubbed him 'thoroughly reliable under all circumstances' – and the Scot's performances for Fosse over three seasons justified it, with both his tough tackling and slide-rule passing drawing admiring comment as he came to the end of an eventful senior career. Billy had followed his elder brother, full-back Archie, from Clyde to Anfield, and there, in the middle of one spell of 119 consecutive appearances, became an ever-present in Liverpool's first Championship-winning side of 1901. He then helped Fulham to the Southern League title in each of 1906 and 1907, and into the Second Division the following year, before joining Fosse for their first, fated tilt at top-flight football. Billy took a local pub on retirement; though how his patrons coped with his notoriously near-impenetrable Scottish accent is unrecorded: an FA disciplinary committee had once felt the need to employ an interpreter in dealing with him during his Liverpool days! Billy's younger brother John became the third of the family to build a career in England, serving Fulham, Glossop and Bury, but was later disgraced in a bribery scandal after moving to Kilmarnock.

***Apps:** FL 82; FAC 6.*
***Goals:** FL 1.*

GOODFELLOW, James Boyd

b. Edinburgh, 30th July 1938

Career: Tranent; 1957 Third Lanark; May 1963 CITY; Mar 1968 Mansfield Town; July 1971 Weymouth; Durban City; Nuneaton Borough; AP Leamington.

City debut v Stoke City (A) 7.9.63

> A nippy, neatly-balanced 'cruiserweight' striker picked up on a free transfer from Thirds when economy measures dictated that the ill-fated Glasgow club divest itself of a superbly skilful forward line, Jimmy gave excellent inside-forward support to City's mid-60s attack, and notched several useful and memorable goals – including one in the first leg of the 1965 League Cup Final, and an 18-yard header in one sweet home win over Forest. He enters the club record-book indelibly, however, for his 35th (and shortest) League appearance for City – when he replaced the injured Graham Cross after 80 minutes of the home game against Liverpool in August 1965 to become Leicester's first-ever official No.12. At Field Mill, Jimmy renewed an effective partnership with Nick Sharkey that had first been forged in City's Combination side, and was a stylish prompter of the Stags' 1969 Cup run which City halted in the Sixth Round. Previously, he'd helped Thirds to a Scottish Cup semi-final replay in 1959, and had been (usually on the right wing) an integral part of their team which topped 100 League goals in 1961. A year later he'd won his only representative honour, with selection for the Scottish League against Scotland. Jimmy, whose grandfather George Goodfellow was Hearts' left-back in their 1891 Scottish Cup Final victory and later trainer at Raith Rovers, settled after retirement as a county-based electrician.

***Apps:** FL 96+2; FAC 9; LC 14.*
***Goals:** FL 26; FAC 3; LC 7.*

GOODWIN, Mark Adrian

b. Sheffield, 23rd February 1960

Career: app July 1976/pro Oct 1977 CITY; Mar 1981 Notts County; July 1987 Walsall; cs 1990 Kettering Town; cs 1991 Eastwood Town (p/coach; p/mgr); 1992 Arnold Town (p/coach); cs 1994 Hucknall Town.

City debut v Ipswich Town (A) 17.12.77

> The sheer ebullience 17-year-old blond midfielder Mark brought to the seemingly leg-weary City side shuffling towards relegation under Frank McLintock was a rare bright spot of 1977/8, and was a virtue sufficient to assure him of a squad position under the more explicitly youth-oriented regime of Jock Wallace over the next fewyears. Occasionally looking a little overwhelmed by the physical rigours of Second Division struggle, Mark was often used on the sub's bench, but his varied experience as ball-winner, distributor and full-back made him a suitably versatile understudy for most eventualities, and he picked up a medal from City's 1980 Division Two championship campaign after weighing in with a quartet of goals. He moved to Meadow Lane as the last link in County's promotion-winning team of 1981, alongside Trevor Christie (also featuring in that term's Anglo-Scottish Cup Final), and passed the 200 mark in League appearances for the Magpies early in 1986/7, having also suffered relegation twice, before once more rejoining Christie at Fellows Park for, successively, one promotion and two more demotions. In 1994 he and Christie were together again, for the fourth time, at Hucknall.

***Apps:** FL 69+22; FAC 4+1; LC 3.*
***Goals:** FL 8.*

Mark Goodwin

GOODWIN, Thomas Neil

b. Leicester, 8th November 1979

Career: YT July 1996/pro July 1998 CITY; Dec 2000-trials-Barnet; Apr 2001-trials-Peterborough United.

City debut/only game v West Ham United (H) 22.1.2000

> First entering the senior picture with City during their heavy pre-season schedule of 1999, sturdy young right-back Tommy won a Premiership break in the injury-hit side which lost at home to the Hammers, as the club tried to patch up its wounded for the impending League Cup semi-finals, and still found itself applauded from the Filbert Street pitch. It was, though, hardly the context in which to judge the defensive debutant, who sadly received no further chances to shine in a more settled line-up, and less than a year later found himself attempting to impress in reserve football at each of Underhill and London Road, prior to his City release.

***Apps:** PL 1.*

GORDON, Colin Kenneth

b. Stourbridge, Worcs, 17th January 1963

Career: Lye Town; Stourbridge; 1981 Worcester City; 1982 Oldbury United; Nov 1984 Swindon Town; July 1986 Wimbledon; Feb 1987-loan-Gillingham; July 1987 Reading; Mar 1988-loan-Bristol City; Oct 1988 Fulham; June 1989 Birmingham City; Sept 1990-loan-Hereford United; Dec 1990-loan-Walsall; Jan 1991-loan-Bristol Rovers; July 1991 CITY; Jan 1993 Kidderminster Harriers (p/coach); 1993-loan-Gloucester City; cs 1994 Stourbridge (p/mgr).

City debut v Bristol City (H) 7.9.91 (sub)

> A tall, heftily bustling striker who made a fine scoring impact on his belated introduction to the League scene at Swindon, Colin thereafter found his further wanderings a fairly frustrating affair. His promise had prompted four transfers worth £80,000 or more; but disappointing delivery had also led to five loan-outs before Brian Little took Colin on as a free agent during his initial City team-building spree. Always deemed a short-term acquisition, 'Flash' nonetheless proved a useful Second Division target man, even if usually happier when the ball was in the air (efforts with either foot seeming to have a maked affinity for hitting woodwork). Colin's otherwise unremarkable St Andrews sojourn was once disrupted by a possibly unique injury: he contracted blood poisoning after being accidentally bitten on the arm by a Swansea player. His management role at his home-town club came to an end in mid-1995/6.

***Apps:** FL 18+6; FAC 1; LC 1; FMC 4+1; AIC 0+1.*
***Goals:** FL 5; FMC 2.*

GORDON, Robert

b. Leith, Edinburgh, 1873

Career: 1889 Leith Rangers; Leith Athletic; 1890 Heart of Midlothian; 1891 Middlesbrough Ironopolis; July 1893 Heart of Midlothian; May 1894 Aston Villa; Oct 1894 FOSSE; June 1895 Woolwich Arsenal; cs 1896 Reading.

Fosse debut v Kimberley (H) FAC 3.11.1894 (scored twice)

> A well-built bustler of a centre-forward, but none too speedy – the *Daily Post* rather harshly described him as 'cumbrous' – Bob was the fifth attack-leader tried by Fosse within the first two months of their initial League season, and the fifth former Ironopolis player to appear in their ranks that term. He'd already notched two goals in four First Division games for Villa that season (plus one against the Football League, in a game played as a benefit for League founder William McGregor), and arrived to form a prolific inside trio with David Skea and Billy McArthur before taking his shooting boots to Plumstead for a £30 fee. In February 1897, Bob (who'd helped Ironopolis to Northern League championships in both 1892 and 1893) represented the Southern League against the London FA, scoring twice.

***Apps:** FL 21; FAC 4.*
***Goals:** FL 12; FAC 2.*

GORMAN, James

b. Middlesbrough, 1882

Career: Middlesbrough St Marys; Newport Celtic; South Bank; 1904 Darlington St.Augustine's; 1905 Darlington; Mar 1906 Liverpool; May 1908 FOSSE; July 1910 Hartlepools United.

Fosse debut v Manchester City (A) 3.10.08

> Fosse's first signing after promotion had been assured, Jimmy was a highly-rated centre-half ('zealous and untiring') whose Anfield role had been primarily to understudy Scottish international Alec Raisbeck. He suffered terrible ill-fortune at Leicester, however – having his knee so badly injured on his debut that he was unable to return until the club's relegation fate had been already sealed. To rub salt into the wound, the second match of his comeback, and his final senior Fosse outing, was the ignominious 0-12 defeat by Forest. Jimmy's two-year spell with Hartlepools was also interrupted by the need for a cartilage operation.

***Apps:** FL 3.*

GOUDIE, Peter A.

b. Derby

Career: Derby Nomads; am Jan 1899/pro May 1899 FOSSE; Derby Nomads.

Fosse debut/only game v Luton Town (A) 14.1.99

> An amateur goalkeeper – in fact a reporter on a Derby newspaper by profession – Peter stood in for Godfrey Beardsley in the above match, after having faced the Corinthians in a friendly three weeks previously. There can't have been many players who've made their senior bow in a 6-1 away win and never been selected again (especially after subsequently accepting a pro contract), but Peter was one such. (Incidentally, crowd disturbances at this game – including attempts to assault referee Kingswell – led to Kenilworth Road being closed for a fortnight). Peter's journalistic career certainly flourished more than his football: he became the Paris editor for the *Daily Mail* and, in 1922, a director of Harmsworth Publications.

***Apps:** FL 1.*

GOULD, William

b. Burton-on-Trent, ca 1885

Career: 1903 Burton United; June 1905 FOSSE; May 1906 Bristol Rovers; May 1907 Glossop; Sept 1908 Bradford City; May 1909 Manchester City; 1911 Tranmere Rovers (- 1914).

Fosse debut v Leeds City (H) 16.9.05

> A teenage scorer of one of the goals which removed Fosse from the 1903/4 FA Cup (before he had even made a League debut), Willie developed into the Peel Croft club's top marksman in the following term. But at Leicester he had to vie for his favoured inside-left spot with a fellow newcomer, the more experienced Harry Moody, and was soon sidelined when he failed to deliver regularly in the finishing stakes. He became an ever-present on the Southern League left-wing at Eastville, and remained a useful flank player for his subsequent League clubs. His first half-dozen Manchester City appearances were in the Division Two championship-clinching games of 1910; and Willie aided Tranmere both to Lancashire Combination promotion in 1912, and to its top-flight championship in 1914.

***Apps:** FL 6.*
***Goals:** FL 1.*

GRAHAM, Harry

b. Edinburgh, 16th December 1887

Career: Granton Oakvale; Nov 1908 St Bernards; Apr 1910 Bradford City; Oct 1911 Birmingham; Sept 1912 Raith Rovers; cs 1913 Heart of Midlothian; Dec 1920 CITY; Nov 1924 St Bernards; cs 1925 Reading.

City debut v Stoke (H) 25.12.20

> After winning Scottish Junior recognition in 1908, and featuring alongside Harry Simpson for the Edinburgh-based St Bernards, inside-forward Harry experienced a fairly uneventful first stint in English football, but then earned both a runners-up medal and a move back to the northern capital from Raith's Scottish Cup Final appearance of 1913. Starring for the Jam Tarts on both sides of WW1, he was chosen to represent the Scottish League in October 1914. A qualified dentist, he was exempt from military call-up, but volunteered and fought with the Gloucestershire Regiment and the Royal Engineers before returning to football action: latterly alongside Arthur Lochhead at Tynecastle. Fairly prolific in his pre-war years, Harry was more of a quality creative operator by the time he reached Filbert Street, and prompted Jock Paterson to a hat-trick in his City debut game; then held his place in an otherwise regularly changing Second Division front line until the arrival of George Carr. It was slightly ironic that he should initially return to St Bernards – that club had attempted years before to block his move from Birmingham to Raith by claiming still to possess Harry's Scottish registration, and that they were due a fee for it. Nine of Harry's last dozen senior games at Elm Park were in Reading's 1926 Division Three (South) championship campaign. He was still in a dentistry practice in Edinburgh for some time after WW2. His brother David was also at one time on Hearts' books.

***Apps:** FL 110; FAC 6.*
***Goals:** FL 14; FAC 2.*

GRANT, Alexander Frank

b. Peasedown St John, Somerset, 11th August 1916

Career: am Doncaster Rovers; am Sheffield United; Aug 1937 Bury; May 1938 Aldershot; Dec 1941 CITY; Nov 1946 Derby County; Nov 1948 Newport County; Aug 1949 Leeds United; Mar 1950 York City; July 1950 Worksop Town; July 1953 Corby Town.

City debut (WW2) v Walsall (H) 15.11.41; (postwar) v Manchester City (H) 31.8.46

> A dependable reserve keeper for most of his clubs, Alick was probably at his peak during the war years, when he guested for Aldershot, Forest, Derby, Notts County, Southport and Mansfield, and represented Western Command, as well as turning out regularly for City. Indeed, his trio of guest appearances for Derby included both legs of the 1944/5 Midland Cup Final against Villa. Alick unfortunately had to pick the ball out of the net seven times in City's first two postwar League games, and soon moved 'officially' to the Baseball Ground. Both there and at Newport (where he was signed for the second time by Tom Bromilow, and where he was regarded as the Brynmawr-born intellectual) he had a contracted wage of only three pence per week, in order that he could claim a full government family allowance while training as a teacher at Loughborough Colleges. Alick eventually became another ex-City man to taste football in all four divisions (1, 2, 3S and 3N).

***Apps:** FL 2; WW2 97.*

GRAVER, Andrew Martin

b. Craghead, Co Durham, 12th September 1927

Career: Willington; 1947 Annfield Plain; Sept 1947 Newcastle United; Sept 1950 Lincoln City; Dec 1954 CITY; July 1955 Lincoln City; Nov 1955 Stoke City; Sept 1957 Boston United; Oct 1958 Lincoln City; July 1961 Skegness Town; July 1962 Ilkeston Town.

City debut v Chelsea (A) 18.12.54 (scored once)

> Centre-forward Andy's Tyneside status as understudy to Jackie Milburn allowed him but a single shot at League football with his local club, but he soon made up for lost time at Sincil Bank, notching 106 goals in 172 games during his first spell there, including six in one game against Crewe as Lincoln raced to the 1952 championship of Division Three (North). That season he also won a call-up to the England 'B' side to face Holland, but had to withdraw through injury. City paid a club record fee in the hope that Andy's goal touch would keep them in Division One, but despite scoring in his first two games, he failed to spark alongside Arthur Rowley, and returned to Lincoln during the close season, after Derek Hines had reclaimed the City No.9 shirt. Press rumours of the time intimated that City had lost heavily on the deals, but in fact Andy's moves both constituted club records (in the same way that Allan Clarke's and Mark Draper's would later): arriving for £27,000 plus Eric Littler (valued at £600), and departing for £26,000. A further onward move, however, was definitely to City's detriment, for having joined the Stoke club who'd first bid for him in March 1955, Andy scored for them the goal which sealed City's 1956 Cup exit. By the time Andy had completed his third spell with the Imps, he had created (and still holds) that club's aggregate scoring record of 143 League goals; and he later briefly served them as youth coach and scout, while working as a financial consultant. Unsurprisingly, he was one of the first two men inducted to Lincoln's Hall of Fame in 1996. His father, Fred, had played as a forward in the 20s for Grimsby, Leeds and Southend; while brother Alf was a Lincoln reserve.

***Apps:** FL 11; FAC 1.*
***Goals:** FL 3.*

GRAYSON, Simon Nicholas

b. Ripon, Yorks, 16th December 1969

Career: YT 1986/pro June 1988 Leeds United; Mar 1992 CITY; June 1997 Aston Villa; July 1999 Blackburn Rovers; Aug 2000-loan-Sheffield Wednesday; Jan 2001-loan-Stockport County.

City debut v Ipswich Town (A) 14.3.92

> The first City skipper to gleefully lift a trophy at Wembley, Simon was acting captain on the day Derby were vanquished in the 1994 Play-Off Final, shortly before being named as the supporters' choice for Player of the Year. One of the trio of central defenders initially fielded for that game, yet also the man whose first-time cross from the right led to Steve Walsh's winning goal, Simon had previously starred in midfield and at right-back since his move from Leeds, and his dogged tenacity in each of those positions was a prominent feature of his Filbert Street game. A useful anchorman in his early performances, which included the first Wembley Play-Off encounter with Blackburn, he then settled to more overtly defensive roles. Severely embarrassed by occasional defects in technique and concentration during City's initial Premiership misadventure, he had comprehensively overcome these by the time the club rejoined the elite, and picked up his second Player of the Year award for a superb 1996/7, when he was also in the victorious League Cup line-up. Simon was apparently renegotiating his City contract when prised away to Villa Park by Brian Little for a fee eventually agreed at £1.35m; and two years later rejected the chance to return to Filbert Street, opting instead for an Ewood move that unfortunately soon soured. Before his £50,000 arrival at City, his senior experience amounted to only a pair of Second Division outings (and one in the Full Members Cup) in 1987/8, when still a Leeds trainee. Simon, whose brother Paul has played county cricket for Yorkshire and Essex, is the co-owner of the Churchgate bar, Undecided.

***Apps:** FL/PL 175+13; FAC 9; LC 16+2; AIC 4; PO 9+1.*
***Goals:** FL 4; LC 2.*

GREATOREX, George Arthur

b. Huthwaite, Notts, 4th December 1899
d. Huthwaite, Oct qtr 1964

Career: 1919 Sutton Junction; trials-Derby County; May 1921 CITY; May 1922 Mansfield Town; cs 1923 Sutton Town; Feb 1926 Frickley Colliery; June 1928 Scarborough; cs 1929 Shirebrook.

City debut v Bradford Park Avenue (A) 27.8.21

> An inside-right who had impressed City while playing Central Alliance football against the reserves, and started the 1921/2 season in support of Jock Paterson, George scored in his first two home appearances. Only 5ft 5in tall, yet sturdily built, he was quickly dubbed 'Baby' by the Leicester crowd, but soon faded from the picture as Peter Hodge sought a promotion-worthy combination. His move to Mansfield brought him a 22-goal Midland League haul in the same side as Bob Villiers; though he also appeared in the half-back line with Sutton.

***Apps:** FL 11.*
***Goals:** FL 2*

GREENHALGH, Brian Arthur

b. Chesterfield, 20th February 1947

Career: app July 1964/pro Feb 1965 Preston North End; Sept 1967 Aston Villa; Feb 1969 CITY; June 1969 Huddersfield Town; July 1971 Cambridge United; Feb 1974 Bournemouth; Aug 1974-loan-Torquay United; Mar 1975 Watford; July 1976 Dartford; Sept 1977 Bedford Town; cs 1979 Hitchin Town; Wealdstone; Staines Town; Carshalton Athletic (p/mgr).

City debut v Coventry City (A) 1.4.69 (sub)

> It was difficult to gauge Frank O'Farrell's motives in bringing striker Brian to Filbert Street as his first signing. The demands of an ever-worsening relegation struggle surely precluded long-term planning, yet the inside-forward was to get very few chances to contribute to the immediate crisis: even if his debut came in the ultra-tense Highfield Road game on which the club's Division One fortunes really hinged. The game with rivals-in-distress Coventry was in its late stages when substitute Brian was brought down in the Coventry box, but the referee reversed his initial penalty decision, awarding the Sky Blues a free kick instead, from which they constructed the only goal of the night against a City side still to regroup. None of Brian's other three City outings brought a win bonus, either. He moved on to play five times alongside Frank Worthington in Huddersfield's 1970 Division Two championship campaign, and ten times in the top flight thereafter; then at Cambridge rediscovered a goal touch that had been utterly dormant since his Villa days, helping them out of Division Four in 1973. Two years later, he was relegated back to the basement with Watford, and later commenced a series of non-league travels, which took in a scoring contribution to Dartford's 1977 Southern League Cup win, and culminated in coaching spells with Maidenhead United and Chesham United. Born in Chesterfield but raised in Southport, Brian had made a fine teenage impact at Preston (five goals in his first seven games), and had partnered Brian Godfrey from Deepdale to Villa Park. In November 1990, he was appointed as chief scout at Everton; and in October 1999 to the same position at Watford.

Brian Greenhalgh

***Apps:** FL 2+2.*

GREW, Mark Stuart

b. Bilston, Staffs, 15th February 1958

Career: app 1975/pro June 1976 West Bromwich Albion; Dec 1978-loan-Wigan Athletic; Mar 1979-loan-Notts County; July 1983 CITY; Oct 1983-loan-Oldham Athletic; Mar 1984 Ipswich Town; Sept 1985-loan-Fulham; Jan 1986-loan-West Bromwich Albion; Mar 1986-loan-Derby County; June 1986 Port Vale; Oct 1990-loan-Blackburn Rovers; July 1992 Cardiff City; cs 1994 Stafford Rangers; Sept 1994 Hednesford Town.

City debut v Notts County (H) 27.8.83

> When City laid out £60,000 for goalkeeper Mark while Mark Wallington was briefly in contractual dispute, the newcomer had just completed eight years at the Hawthorns, during which he had patiently amassed a record of only 33 League starts. Mark's West Brom debut had, in fact, been a real oddity for the time: coming on as substitute keeper in a 1978/9 UEFA Cup tie against Galatasaray. At Filbert Street, he had an unnerving introduction, conceding a Trevor Christie hat-trick on his debut; being beaten by a succession of long-range power shots as City struggled to find their First Division feet; and giving way to Wallington after five straight defeats and a 14-goal deficit. Mark fared little better at Portman Road, in the shadow of Paul Cooper, but seemed set fair to establish some sort of record for the number of loan deals he had been involved in. He suffered a severe knee injury early in his Port Vale career, but returned to perform heroically in both their 1988 Cup run and their 1989 Division Three promotion campaign, going on to complete over 200 League and Cup games for them until being freed following relegation in 1992. At Cardiff, Mark was involved in the (new) Division Three championship term of 1993, and was briefly a rival with Gavin Ward for the first-team jersey. He returned to Vale Park to join the coaching staff in December 1994, and was John Rudge's assistant manager there from June 1999.

***Apps:** FL 5.*

GREWCOCK, Neil

b. Leicester, 26th April 1962

Career: Leicester Beavers; app June 1978/pro June 1979 CITY; Mar 1982 Gillingham; June 1983 Shepshed Charterhouse; Aug 1984 Burnley; Aug 1991-trials-Cardiff City; 1991 Burnley Bank Hall.

City debut v Cardiff City (H) 3.3.79 (scored once)

> Still a 16-year-old apprentice when gifted a goal-crowned League baptism by Jock Wallace, Neil then had to bide his time for another crack at senior action, having one short spell on either wing near the beginning and end of the 1980/1 First Division campaign. Short but stocky, he didn't quite develop the pace necessary to maintain a conventional flank position, and drifted into a midfield role with Gillingham. Neil then returned to Leicestershire with his League career seemingly at a premature end, but was offered a lifeline back by John Bond, which he grasped eagerly. He suffered relegation to the Fourth Division in his first Turf Moor season, but his performances were a rare bright element of Burnley's near-disastrous 1987 cliffhanger, when his goal in the final fixture helped ward off the prospect of the old club dropping into Conference football. When finally freed, Neil had amassed 202 League appearances and 27 goals for the Clarets. A brief trial in Wales with his former City reserve boss, Eddie May, did not pay off, but 1991/2 still saw Neil amongst the silverware, as Burnley Bank Hall took the West Lancs League title and won its cup competition.

***Apps:** FL 7+1; LC 0+1.*
***Goals:** FL 1.*

GRIEVE, Robert B.

b. Greenock, Renfrewshire, 28th March 1884

Career: 1902 Morton; Aug 1906 Manchester City; Nov 1909 Accrington Stanley; am Dec 1910 FOSSE; Mar 1911 Accrington Stanley; Sept 1911 Southport Central; Oct 1911 Accrington Stanley.

Fosse debut v Wolverhampton Wanderers (H) 7.1.11 (scored twice)

> An amateur throughout his career, unwilling to jeopardise a good business post, Scottish centre-forward Bob had notched 17 goals in the Scottish First Division and 18 in the English top flight before he stepped up once more from Lancashire Combination fare to join Second Division Fosse and replace the departed Jack Hall. He had the misfortune, however, to sign on at Filbert Street less than a month before old hero Fred Shinton returned from Bolton, and his first-team tenure was accordingly short. It was marked, though, by one oddity which points to the idiosyncracy of then-prevailing registration rules: only a week after his Fosse debut (when his first headed goal had arrived after only three minutes), he played for Accrington in their First Round FA Cup tie against the same opposition, Wolves! Bob's main claim to fame while playing for his local club had been a four-goal haul from Morton's 1906 Renfrewshire Cup Final win over Arthurlie. It is also likely (though as yet unconfirmed) that he briefly assisted Port Glasgow Athletic during 1907/08.

***Apps:** FL 4.*
***Goals:** FL 2.*

GRIFFITHS, William Malwyn

b. Merthyr Tydfil, 8th March 1919
d. Wigston, Leics, 5th April 1969

Career: Merthyr Thursday; am Sept 1935/pro Feb 1937 Arsenal; May 1936-loan-Margate; Sept 1938 CITY; June 1956 Burton Albion.

City debut v Bolton Wanderers (H) 24.9.38

> Plucked from Welsh junior football by Arsenal, and then loaned out to their own 'nursery' club for experience, right-winger Mal made his senior Highbury bow against City in February 1938, and contributed five goals in nine appearances as the Gunners raced to the First Division title that year. Rivalries for first-team shirts at Arsenal were fierce, however, and only a bargain £750 transfer to City opened the door to a regular position – one Mal was still holding some 18 years later. He 'lost' one League appearance and one goal when the 1939/40 season was abandoned after only three rounds of fixtures; and after he had become the first City player to be automatically conscripted (into the Welsh Regiment), City somehow contrived to lose touch with Mal himself during the war. Given the list of clubs for whom he guested (Cardiff, Fulham, Aldershot, Chelsea, Bournemouth, Southampton, Brighton and Aberaman) this was perhaps not so surprising, but when Johnny Duncan took over the managerial reins at Filbert Street, he had to despatch director Leslie Green to Wales to persuade Mal to resume his full-time City career. Thereafter, though, Mal's consistency made him the one automatic choice in an ever-changing City front line, and his steady goalscoring record peaked at two crucial times: when he added to his six counters on City's 1949 Cup run the club's first-ever goal at Wembley, and when he notched his own best seasonal League total of eleven during the 1954 Division Two championship effort. City played an invited International XI at the end of their next promotion campaign in a testimonial match for Mal, who had represented his own country eleven times (scoring twice) between 1947 and 1954. Sixth on the all-time City list for League appearances, he has been out-scored by only one specialist winger (Mike Stringfellow). He retired after a season in the Birmingham League at Wellington Street to run the Queen's Head in Wigston Magna.

***Apps:** FL 373; FAC 36; WW2 11.*
***Goals:** FL 66; FAC 10; WW2 3.*

GROGAN, John

b. Paisley, Renfrewshire, 30th October 1915
d. Thurcaston, Leics, 2nd April 1976

Career: St Mirren Boys Guild; Paisley Carlisle; trials-Partick Thistle, St Mirren & Celtic; Shawfield; Oct 1933 CITY; Sept 1947 Mansfield Town; Aug 1952 Bentley Engineering FC (p/mgr).

City debut v Newcastle United (A) 19.10.35

> Signed in a joint deal with Willie Frame, Johnny was Sep Smith's trusty understudy at right-half during the four up-and-down seasons before the war, and then had to vie with the same player for the centre-half shirt when League competition resumed. Despite his ten-game contribution to the 1937 Second Division championship campaign, his reserve status was confirmed (albeit in flattering terms) by his record in London Combination representative matches: after playing in front of 40,000 in Brussels in the annual game against Diables Rouges (the Belgian international trial side) some seven months before making his senior City bow, he won a further three selections

in this fixture, and six in all up to February 1939. It's fair to say that Johnny was robbed of his best footballing years by the war, during which he served in the RAF and guested for Northampton, Crystal Palace, Swansea, Luton and Grimsby; but City were wrong if they thought he was close to retirement when they let him go to Field Mill. Johnny kept going there for five years and 217 League and Cup appearances, being an ever-present when the Stags took runners-up spot in the Third Division (North) in 1951, but remained goalless throughout his peacetime career. He was honoured with a shared Mansfield testimonial game against City in April 1953, by which time he was back in Leicestershire local football; and on leaving Bentley's became manager of Midland Athletic.

Apps: *FL 46; FAC 6; WW2 38.*

GROSVENOR, Percy

b. Dudley, 17th March 1911

Career: Dudley Works; am Birmingham; trials-West Bromwich Albion; Jan 1933 Evesham Town; Feb 1933 CITY (- 1940).

City debut v Aston Villa (H) 30.12.33

> A left-half passed over by his local West Midlands clubs, Percy was taken on by Peter Hodge as a likely understudy to George Ritchie and, having made his breakthrough, went thirteen League and Cup games before appearing in a beaten City side – that being in the club's first-ever FA Cup semi-final side of 1934. Thereafter he went on indeed to inherit Ritchie's shirt as a regular from 1935/6 to the outbreak of war, showing fight and finesse in City's up-and-down travails of the time, and taking a medal from the 1937 Second Division championship campaign (when his sole City goal came in an away win at Barnsley). Percy, who also guested for Northampton during his final active season (1939/40) came from a real footballing family: his father Syd had been a Wolves full-back in 1904/5 and also played for Crewe, Walsall and Worcester City; his brother Tom was an England international whose career took in stints with Birmingham, Sheffield Wednesday and Bolton; and younger brother Clifford joined the City reserve roster in August 1937. At the time of publication of 'The Foxes Alphabet' (1995), Percy wrote generously to the authors from his West Midlands home: if, as we hope, he is still well enough to read this tome, it is likely that he just shades from Sep Smith the status of City's oldest surviving ex-player.

Apps: *FL 168; FAC 12; WW2 6.*
Goals: *FL 1.*

GROVES, Paul

b. Derby, 28th February 1966

Career: Belper Town; Nov 1986 Burton Albion; Apr 1988 CITY; Aug 1989-loan-Lincoln City; Jan 1990 Blackpool; Aug 1992 Grimsby Town; May 1996 West Bromwich Albion; July 1997 Grimsby Town (p/coach from July 2001).

City debut v Huddersfield Town (H) 2.5.88 (sub; scored once)

> A former part-timer with Burton, whom he helped to the Wembley Final of the FA Trophy in 1987 (also scoring their consolation goal in a replay defeat), Paul was offered the chance to drop his bricklaying day-job when signed by David Pleat after the 1988 transfer deadline. The strongly-built attacking midfielder cost £12,000 and the promise of a visit from City to play a friendly under Burton's new floodlights, and Pleat received Football League sanction to name him amongst the thirteen players for the season's penultimate game, against an already relegated Huddersfield. Paul's fine header then made him the first City substitute to score on his debut; while another headed goal, in the League Cup replay at Nottingham Forest, proved the high point of his first full season as a City squad player. Overall, though, his impact at senior level was muted, and an onward transfer looked likely from the moment City offered him the chance to move to Peterborough in March 1989. Though he declined, Paul soon accompanied Grant Brown on loan at Sincil Bank (scoring once in a ten-game spell), then eventually signed up at Bloomfield Road for a £60,000 fee. He revisited Wembley in 1991, when Blackpool failed at the final Fourth Division Play-Off hurdle despite Paul's opening goal, but finally appeared on a winning side at the Stadium a year later when the Seasiders sealed promotion under his captaincy. He then set about creating a remarkable record of consistency at Grimsby – not missing a game at all during his initial four-year stay, nor during the first two years after his return. In the interim, he'd followed manager Alan Buckley to the Hawthorns and back. Paul's powerful prompting for the Mariners won him selection in the PFA Second Division XI at the end of 1997/8 (when two further Wembley visits saw his team take the Associate Members Cup and win promotion by Play-Off); he was their supporters' Player of the Year in 1999; and his goal in the final fixture of 2001 kept them in Division One. Back at Filbert Street with Grimsby in March 1993, Paul's misplaced header saw him become the first ex-City player ever to notch an own goal to the credit of his old club at competitive level.

Apps: *FL 7+9; FAC 0+1; LC 1; FMC 0+1.*
Goals: *FL 1; LC 1.*

GUNNLAUGSSON, Arnar Bergmann

b. Akranes, Iceland, 6th March 1973

Career: 1990 ÍA Akranes; 1992 Feyenoord; 1994 1.FC Nürnberg; Aug 1995 ÍA Akranes; 1995 FC Sochaux-Montbéliard; May 1997 ÍA Akranes; Aug 1997 Bolton Wanderers; Feb 1999 CITY; Mar 2000-loan-Stoke City.

City debut v Sheffield Wednesday (H) 6.2.99 (sub)

> When 'Arnie' hit his stunning strike to win the 2000/1 home encounter with Derby County, a minute after coming on as sub, he well and truly broke a jinx. For so long it had appeared that he was enigmatically fated not to score for City in the Premiership, as he'd extended at Filbert Street a curious record of remaining goalless in the top flight of any nation's league except that of his native Iceland, where he headed the country's goal chart in each of 1992 and 1995. Arnar never got off the mark in nine outings for Dutch champions Feyenoord, and failed to net a Premiership goal for Bolton, though he never had any trouble getting on the scoresheet at Second

Arnar Gunnlaugsson

Division level in either Germany or France, in the lower divisions here with Bolton or Stoke, or in international football. The mobile striker was a welcome £2m signing for City, with 14 goals already to his credit in 1998/9, but his determined propensity for dribbling at defenders too often led directly to a dead end, and his fierce shooting lacked sufficient accuracy. While he was reduced, largely through injury, to a fringe role in the following term, he at least set one record for reliability: he was the only City player to score in all three of the victorious penalty shoot-outs of 1999/2000, each time being the first to step up for the responsibility. Arnar's loan spell at Stoke (a virtual Icelandic colony itself at present) saw him feature in both the Potters' Auto Windscreens Shield triumph at Wembley and in their Play-Off semi-final disappointment at the hands of Peter Taylor's Gillingham. His belated breakthrough onto the City scoresheet was followed by a further luckless sidelining – thanks to appendicitis – but his seasonal record of four 'supersub' strikes was to land him the 2001 Goal of the Season award for the spectacular shot that removed Villa from the FA Cup, and heralded much vocal encouragement to Peter Taylor to grant him more than mere cameo opportunities. His identical twin brother Bjarki, also an international, has played across Europe for each of ÍA, Feyenoord, Waldhof Mannheim, Molde, SK Brann and KR Reykjavik, and is currently with Preston North End.

Apps *(to end 2000/1): PL 10+18; FAC 2+4; LC 1+2; UEFA 0+1.*
Goals: *PL 3; FAC 1.*

GUPPY, Stephen Andrew

b. Winchester, Hants, 29th March 1969

Career: Colden Common; 1988-trials-Southampton; Aug 1989 Wycombe Wanderers; 1991-trials-Charlton Athletic; Aug 1994 Newcastle United; Nov 1994 Port Vale; Feb 1997 CITY.

City debut v Wimbledon (A) 1.3.97

> It could hardly have been much of a surprise to hitherto orthodox winger Steve that he would be asked to play in an unaccustomed left wing-back role on his City debut (and pretty much ever since), such had been the twists and turns of a career that even now continues to make the term 'eventful' look wholly inadequate. Rejected as a teenager by Southampton, he linked up with Conference side Wycombe and would soon come under the influence of Martin O'Neill as that club accomplished its move from Loakes Park to Adams Park and embarked on a period of sustained success: winning the FA Trophy in 1991, the Bob Lord Trophy in 1992, the Conference championship and Trophy double in 1993, and promotion to Division Two via the Play-Offs in 1994. Steve picked up England semi-professional recognition while still playing at the pinnacle of the non-league Pyramid, and a £150,000 move to Kevin Keegan's Newcastle after proving himself in League fare. But he would play only a matter of minutes as a League Cup substitute while on Tyneside, and had to rebuild his confidence at Vale Park after a £225,000 switch. His fourth trip to Wembley brought him a runners-up medal from the Anglo-Italian Cup Final of 1995/6, and he'd clearly developed an insatiable taste for knockout football: playing one FA Cup tie for Vale against Everton after running two miles to the ground from his traffic-jammed car! His First Division form suggested to O'Neill that a reunion would be profitable, and after City had a joint bid for Steve and midfielder Jon McCarthy turned down, the manager persisted until netting his main target for a fee rising to £950,000. The tactical conversion of Steve's flank play to encompass additional defensive duties was initially a matter of need, but soon became one of choice; and he was quickly on course for recognition as one of the Premiership's most effective left-sided providers. He won call-ups for England 'B' and as an over-age choice for the Under-21s, and notched another couple of milestones in 1998/9. As the only Premiership player to start and complete every game, he also topped the Opta statistical index for the highest number of crosses delivered – though there was still some debate among City regulars as to just how many of them had been accurate. At the same time, he was assuming a useful knack for curled shots into the far corner from the edge of the box. Eventually, former boss Keegan had to give Steve his full international opportunity, making him only the second player after Alan Smith to have completed the rise from the England semi-pro eleven to the senior representative side. His first serious injury unfortunately then halted his progress, but even as he struggled to regain form towards the end of 1999/2000, Steve re-emphasised his value with the two Wembley corner-kicks that Matt Elliott converted for League Cup glory. Argument accordingly still rages amongst City fans over the wisdom or otherwise of Peter Taylor in only calling upon him sporadically.

Apps *(to end 2000/1): PL 133+13; FAC 9; LC 15; UEFA 4.*
Goals: *PL 9; FAC 1.*

GURRY, John William

b. Barking, Essex, 17th July 1907
d. Leicester, 1st October 1983

Career: Nov 1929 Barking Town; am Dec 1929 West Ham United; Mar 1930 CITY; July 1935 Southampton; June 1936 Chester.

City debut v Leeds United (A) 12.11.32

> One of the more luckless aspirants of his era, Jack found the consistency of Sep Smith not the only barrier to his quest for a senior City shirt at either right-half or inside-forward. He'd only been tempted out of Athenian League football for a matter of months (partly with the fall-back lure of a job in the Leicester hosiery trade) when he broke his leg in a game with Crystal Palace reserves in October 1930, and it was a year later (for the November 1931 home game with Sheffield United) that he was first named to replace Ernie Hine up front – only to contract 'flu the day before the match. 1932/3 was his best season at First Division level, though the following term saw him claim top scorer status for the reserves with 15 strikes (after scoring only 30 seconds into the season on the way to an opening-game hat-trick). Jack remained goalless at senior level in nine games with the Saints; but finally got on the scoresheet on one occasion in his year at Chester: with a hat-trick in a 7-3 win over Lincoln.

Apps: *FL 23.*

GWYNNE, Ernest

Career: Aug 1903 FOSSE.

Fosse debut/only game v Woolwich Arsenal (A) 26.10.03

A youthful centre-forward from junior football in the Birmingham area, Ernest could have asked for better luck in making his sole first-team appearance for Fosse – he was up against international centre-half and future Fossil Billy Bannister, and the above match ended in a 0-8 defeat.

Apps: *FL 1.*

HACKETT, A.

Career: Leicester Imperial; Sept 1901 FOSSE; cs 1902 Leicester Imperial; cs 1910 Hinckley United.

Fosse debut v West Bromwich Albion (A) 6.1.02

> 'Glimpses of good football' could be discerned by the *Mercury* reporter in this local inside-left's debut performance, but two away defeats were the extent of his senior Fosse experience after he'd been taken on as a pro following the pre-season trial games of August 1901. He was in the Imps' Senior Cup-winning side of 1906, and in Hinckley's side beaten by the Imps in the Final of 1911. It is possible that he started his career with Market Harborough Town.

Apps: *FL 2.*

HADLEY, Arthur

b. Reading, 1877

Career: cs 1895 Reading; cs 1898 Notts County; June 1902 FOSSE; cs 1904 not known; Apr 1905 FOSSE; cs 1905 not known; Dec 1906 Notts County.

Fosse debut v Small Heath (H) 6.9.02

> A goalscoring outside-right in both the Southern and Football Leagues, Arthur was a member of the first Reading side to play at Elm Park, and assisted the Magpies to third place in Division One in 1901 (the second time they'd reached their highest-ever position). His goal supply, however, rather dried up as Fosse slithered towards the Second Division basement, even if Arthur was a popularly regarded provider. He was released before the vote to re-elect Fosse in 1904, but returned for a five-game stint in April 1905 before succumbing to knee injuries. He failed to make the Meadow Lane senior team in his second spell there.

Apps: *FL 64; FAC 7.*
Goals: *FL 4; FAC 3.*

HAIG, Paul

b. Nottingham

Career: Mapperley; cs 1907 Eastwood Rangers; cs 1908 Mansfield Mechanics; Feb 1911 FOSSE; cs 1911 Mansfield Mechanics; Jan 1912 Stanton Hill Victoria; cs 1912 Eastwood Rangers; Aug 1913 Notts County; Nov 1913 Mansfield Town; cs 1914 Loughborough Corinthians.

Fosse debut v Huddersfield Town (H) 25.2.11

> His name often rendered as Haigh in contemporary papers, Paul was an outside-left who briefly stepped up from Notts & Derbyshire League football at a fee of £25, and quickly dropped down again to the Central Alliance. In the interim, he made little impact as Syd Owen's replacement in a Fosse side which struggled to 15th place in Division Two. In the midst of further East Midlands wanderings, he later got a single League outing for the Magpies.

Apps: *FL 12.*
Goals: *FL 2.*

HAINES, John Thomas William

b. Wickhamford, Worcs, 24th April 1920
d. Evesham, Worcs, 16th March 1987

Career: Evesham Town; Cheltenham Town; Nov 1937 Liverpool; June 1939 Swansea Town; July 1947 CITY; Mar 1948 West Bromwich Albion; Dec 1949 Bradford Park Avenue; Oct 1953 Rochdale; July 1955 Chester; cs 1957 Wellington Town; cs 1958 Kidderminster Harriers; Oct 1958 Evesham Town.

City debut v Leeds United (A) 23.8.47

> His early career stymied by the outbreak of war, Jack made his long-

delayed League debut with Swansea in 1946/7 (after having guested for Worcester City, Bradford Park Avenue, Doncaster, Lincoln, Wrexham and Notts County) and, aside from netting twice for the relegation-bound Swans against City, impressed Johnny Duncan as a forceful linkman. The City manager seemed, however, unsure of how best to utilise Jack at Filbert Street – handing him shirts numbered 4, 6, 8, 9 and 10 in his limited Second Division spell in blue, before swapping him for West Brom's Peter McKennan. Jack was used exclusively in the forward line at The Hawthorns, and soon won an England cap, scoring twice against Switzerland. Albion were promoted back to the top flight in 1949, but Jack was tasting more bitter fortunes only a year later, when dropping with Bradford from the Second to the Third Division (North). Harry Catterick paid a club record of £2,000 to take Jack to Spotland as he continued to play out his rather erratic career in the League's lower echelons. He returned to his Wickhamford birthplace after retirement, and worked for a local engineering company.

***Apps:** FL 12; FAC 3.*
***Goals:** FL 3; FAC 1.*

HALES, A.

Career: am Jan 1902 FOSSE; Leicester Old Boys.

Fosse debut/only game v Burnley (H) 27.9.02

> A young outside-left whose appearance in the above 2-1 victory was very much a flicker in footballing obscurity. Only one other fact on this Fossil has emerged from research: in 1933, he was appointed by Dunlop as their East Midlands sales manager.

***Apps:** FL 1.*

HALL, Benjamin

b. Ecclesfield, Yorks, 6th March 1879
d. 1963

Career: Jan 1900 Grimsby Town; Aug 1903 Derby County; Aug 1911 FOSSE; cs 1912 Hyde; 1912 Heywood United (p/coach); May 1913 South Shields.

Fosse debut v Gainsborough Trinity (A) 2.9.11

> At his peak 'a businesslike artiste', Ben made a teenage debut for Grimsby against Fosse in January 1901, scoring once in his side's 4-1 win on their way to the Second Division championship. An inside-right with the Mariners, he was taken on by Derby to replace the charismatic Archie Goodall at centre-half, when that role was effectively the midfield linchpin of the side, and skill and vision were more important requisites than brawn. He made 245 League appearances for the Rams (scoring 11 times), but had lost a lot of his pace by the time he joined Fosse, and could not for long hold off the challenge of the younger Percy Hanger for the pivot's position. Having then assisted South Shields to the championship of the North Eastern League in both 1914 and 1915, he did, though, make a veritable veteran's comeback to Filbert Street during WW1; often assisting Fosse, but also regularly making up the numbers for the visitors: Grimsby (twice), Forest, Huddersfield and Lincoln amongst them. He also turned out five times for Derby during this period. Ben briefly took trainer/coach roles at Huddersfield and Grimsby during 1919/20, before becoming Bristol Rovers manager in May 1920. He later scouted for Huddersfield, managed Loughborough Corinthians (May 1929-Jan 1931), brefly contributed a column on local football to the *Leicester Mail*, took up an appointment as Leicestershire FA coach in 1935, and was still involved in the game, scouting for Southend United, after WW2. He had three brothers who also played League football: Ellis (Hull, Hastings & St Leonards, Stoke, Huddersfield, Hamilton Academical, Millwall, Halifax); Fretwell (South Shields, Goole Town, Norwich, Brighton, Halifax, Torquay, Peterborough & Fletton United); and Harry (Huddersfield). Additionally, Ben's son Gordon was a Derby reserve in January 1931.

***Apps:** FL 14; WW1 30.*

HALL, John Henry

b. Hucknall, Notts, 3rd July 1883
d. Birmingham, 20th February 1949

Career: Newstead Byron; 1902 Newark; trials-Nottingham Forest; Oct 1904 Stoke; May 1906 Brighton & Hove Albion; Apr 1908 Middlesbrough; June 1910 FOSSE; Dec 1910 Birmingham; 1915 Hucknall Town.

Fosse debut v Bolton Wanderers (H) 3.9.10 (scored twice)

> Even as late in Jack's impressive career as 1914, the *Nottingham Evening Mail* was describing him as 'a hustling, never-apply-the-brake centre'; this effective playing style having brought him an aggregate senior tally of 138 goals. The top scorer for each of his clubs from 1905/6 onwards (outshooting even Steve Bloomer during his two years at Ayresome, and netting a hat-trick against City in 1909), Jack – signed for the second time by Andy Aitken – had only a short spell as leader of Fosse's attack before the directorate accepted a 'substantial' bid from Birmingham for his services. He had certainly engendered high expectations among the Filbert Street faithful: in the four public trial matches of August 1910, he scored eleven goals, including three hat-tricks! Jack also rewarded Birmingham with a goal in each of his first six Second Division games; then netted twice for them against Fosse in each of the following two terms. Originally, he had cost Newark £25 and garnered them £250 from Stoke, and he was still on the latter's retained list when 'Boro signed him – earning themselves a £100 fine for their oversight. A coach at St Andrews from February 1922, Jack then settled as landlord of the Small Heath Tavern until his death.

***Apps:** FL 15.*
***Goals:** FL 5.*

HALTON, Reginald Lloyd

b. Leek, Staffordshire, 11th July 1916
d. Buxton, Derbyshire, March 1988

Career: Cheddington Hospital FC; Aug 1934 Buxton; Oct 1936 Manchester United; June 1937 Notts County; Nov 1937 Bury; Dec 1948 Chesterfield; Sept 1950 CITY; Feb 1953 Scarborough (p/mgr); Jan 1954 Goole Town; May 1954 Symingtons (p/coach); Oct 1954 Brush Sports.

City debut v Cardiff City (H) 30.9.50

> Starting his career as an outside-left at Old Trafford, Reg soon settled down as a constructive left-half at Gigg Lane, and may well have developed to international level if the war had not interrupted his career. As it was, he guested for Rochdale, York, Fulham, Aldershot, Millwall, Southampton and Portsmouth, and also played perhaps his most memorable match before League football resumed – in the Arsenal side which met Moscow Dynamo in a fogbound classic of propaganda and prestige in November 1945. Reg was 34 when former Bury boss Norman Bullock signed him for the second time (in part-exchange for Jack Marsh) to add experience to City's middle line, and he gave two seasons' staunch Second Division service before taking the reins (and a centre-forward role!) at Midland League Scarborough, where he also had a cricket pro's contract, and from where he sent the young Colin Appleton to Filbert Street. Reg, who had been elected to the Management Committee of the Players' Union shortly after joining City, and whose probity had led him to resign from Scarborough after conviction for a minor motoring offence, had always had an extra cricketing string to his sporting bow: having had trials with both Lancashire and Worcestershire, he played for Leek, for Staffordshire in Minor Counties competition, for Horwich RMI, for Leicestershire Seconds in 1951, and for Scarborough CC. In September 1955 he was appointed groundsman to the Poloc CC, in Pollokshaws, Glasgow.

***Apps:** FL 64; FAC 3.*
***Goals:** FL 3.*

HAMILL, Stewart Peter

b. Glasgow, 22nd January 1960

Career: Anniesland United; Possil YM; Pollok; Sept 1980 CITY; Mar 1982-loan-Scunthorpe United; Sept 1982 Kettering Town; Aug 1983 Nuneaton Borough; Mar 1986 Northampton Town; cs 1986 Altrincham; Mar 1987 Scarborough; cs 1988 Boston United; 1990 not known; Aug 1992 Lutterworth Town; Houghton Rangers.

City debut v Manchester City (H) 8.11.80.

> Winger or midfielder Stewart made a rapid rise from part-time Scottish junior football – and a job as a Co-Op van driver – to the First Division, and held his place in Jock Wallace's young side for eight games. Returning for the second and third matches of the 1981/2 Second Division campaign, he was unlucky not to claim further selection, for he scored the winning goal in each! Scunthorpe decided against taking up their option on Stewart's signature after his four-game loan spell, and he dropped into non-league football. Nuneaton were twice runners-up in the Alliance Premier League with Stewart as a regular, and it was former Borough boss Graham Carr who gave him a brief chance to return to the League fray at Northampton, for whom he scored a mere 35 seconds into his debut at Tranmere. Stewart's third and final sample of Fourth Division fare came with Scarborough – having assisted them to becoming the first side automatically promoted from the top of the non-league pyramid, he stayed another season and was part of their first-ever League line-up.

***Apps:** FL 10.*
***Goals:** FL 2.*

HAMILTON, John

b. Ayrshire, 1872

Career: 1891 Ayr; June 1894 Wolverhampton Wanderers; Aug 1895 Loughborough; May 1897 Bristol City; Sept 1900 FOSSE; June 1901 Watford; May 1902 Wellingborough; cs 1903 Fulham.

Fosse debut v Grimsby Town (H) 15.9.1900

> 'He is endowed with any amount of pluck and endurance, is a champion tackler, and feeds his forwards with wonderful tact and judgement'. The testimonial to Jack dates from his veteran years, though similar commentaries attended most of his playing career after he left Ayr, reportedly 'as a consequence of the dullness of trade'. An early victim of serious injury at Wolves, he became the ever-present left-half in the Luffs' inaugural League season, and skipper of Bristol City in the last of his three Southern League campaigns at Ashton Gate, where his teammates had included Harry Davy, Albert Carnelly, Billy Langham and Jimmy Stevenson. With Fosse he took the pivot's role for the bulk of a mid-table Second Division term; then assumed the captaincy at Watford. After a single active season at Craven Cottage, he remained on the Fulham training staff until 1910, then returned to Ashton Gate as assistant trainer and, during WW1, as manager. In the summer of 1906, Jack broke new ground as the first professional coach to be employed in Brazil, by the CS Paulistano club; and was reputed thereafter to have always sworn at his (English) players in Spanish!

***Apps:** FL 28; FAC 1.*

HAMILTON, Neville Roy

b. Leicester, 19th April 1960

Career: Leicester Beavers; app Nov 1976/pro Oct 1977 CITY; Jan 1979 Mansfield Town; Aug 1981 Rochdale; cs 1984 Wolverhampton Wanderers.

City debut v Manchester United (A) 27.12.77

> Blooded as a 17-year-old at Old Trafford by Frank McLintock, midfielder Nev was then given a trio of top-flight outings by caretaker boss Ian MacFarlane after City's 1977/8 relegation fate had already been confirmed. He was not to win favour, however, under Jock Wallace, and joined the Stags for £25,000. He experienced relegation at Field Mill in 1980, but remained a Fourth Division regular both there and at Spotland until Tommy Docherty took him to Molineux for a shot at Second Division football. Yet Nev was never to kick a ball in anger again, for he suffered a heart attack during pre-season training with Wolves, and took medical advice to end his playing career. More happily, after recovery, he qualified as a full FA coach in August 1986, spent a while coaching Leicester United and, in the summer of 1989, returned to Filbert Street as Community Development Officer. The beneficiary of a Saffron Lane friendly against an Ex-City All-Stars XI in July 1993, Nev was an Assistant Manager of City's Youth Academy set-up until its shake-up in 2000/1.

***Apps:** FL 4.*

Nev Hamilton

HAMMOND, Walter Henry

b. Chorlton, Lancs, 1868
d. Bolton, 28th December 1921

Career: Edgehill; 1889 Everton; June 1891 Sheffield United; cs 1897 New Brighton Tower; May 1900 FOSSE.

Fosse debut v Nottingham Forest (A) FAC 9.2.01

> A high-scoring veteran centre-forward whose Filbert Street season seemed to be jinxed, Harry had no sooner signed for Fosse than he was hospitalised with typhoid fever and, after recuperating in Sheffield and Southport, returned some five months later to lead a side in the middle of an eleven-game run without a win. His belated debut game, a 1-5 defeat, was the only occasion that Leicester and Forest have been drawn together in the FA Cup; and the quartet of League outings that followed were to be the last of Harry's career. Previously, he had been a prolific marksman for the Blades, who he joined for their final term of Northern League football; for whom he scored a hat-trick in their first-ever Division Two fixture; and who he led to immediate promotion. Chosen once to represent the Football League in 1894, Harry then prompted the newly-formed New Brighton Tower to the 1898 championship of the Lancashire League, and led them, too, into the Second Division. Perhaps predictably, he netted in the Towerites first-ever League game; scored in each fixture against Fosse in 1898/9; and remained his club's top scorer a year later despite spending much of the campaign in the centre-half berth. One amusing anecdote attaches to Harry from his Sheffield days: in becoming the first Blade to be sent off at League level, during a 4-0 win at Crewe in April 1893, he so incensed the home crowd that a panicky flight from the ground seemed to him the wisest option – and accordingly he was later discovered by teammates hiding on Crewe station, with just a coat over his playing kit! Harry ran a couple of pubs in Bolton after his playing swansong at Leicester, and died while playing billiards at a local club.

***Apps:** FL 4; FAC 1.*
***Goals:** FL 1.*

HANGER, Percy

b. Kettering, Northants ca 1889

Career: Kettering St Mary's; Dec 1908-trials-FOSSE; Kettering; Apr 1910 FOSSE; cs 1913 Kettering.

Fosse debut v.Burnley (H) 23.4.10

> 'Hanger's phenomenal activity, seldom degenerating into exuberance, needs to be supplemented by sounder judgement in attack'. Such was the mixed view of the pseudonymous critic Pen Alty in the local *Mail* on Fosse's energetic centre-half, who understudied each of Andy Aitken and Ben Hall before winning himself a regular Second Division selection. Percy, who was still playing for Kettering during 1920/1, was a member of a noted Northants footballing family, of whom brother Harry was a half-back with Bradford City and Crystal Palace from 1906 until his death in WW1 action.

***Apps:** FL 54; FAC 3.*
***Goals:** FAC 1.*

HARDY, Walter

b. Stapleford, Notts

Career: Long Eaton Athletic; Aug 1892 Long Eaton Rangers; Dec 1892 FOSSE.

Fosse debut v Wednesbury Old Athletic (A) ML 24.12.1892 (scored once)

> Described in the local press as a former professional who had regained amateur status with Long Eaton, Walter appeared at either outside- or inside-right in eleven consecutive Midland League games for Fosse during their second season in that competition. He additionally claimed four goals from four friendly outings. Attempts to pin down details of his previous or subsequent career founder on the plethora of Hardy's then active in East Midlands football; though we strongly suspect he may have been with Whitwick White Cross around the turn of the century.

***Apps:** ML 11.*
***Goals:** ML 2.*

HARPER, Ernest

b. Hugglescote, Leics

Career: Coalville United; Dec 1900 Coalville Town; Coalville Wednesday; 1903 Hugglescote United; Coalville Town; am Aug 1904 FOSSE; am Mar 1905 Derby County; cs 1905 Hugglescote United.

Fosse debut/only game v Burton United (A) 21.1.05

> A left-back elevated from the reserves for Fosse's first away win of 1904/5, Ernest was judged 'not particularly sound' by the *Mercury*, and won no further selections against the heavy competition of Bennett, Oakes, Robinson and Pollock. Never a Rams first-teamer, Ernest did guest for Clapton against Fosse in an April 1905 friendly, and captained the county amateur XI against Notts in January 1906. During 1903/4, prior to them both joining Fosse, he and Jack Sheffield alternated sporting codes on an almost weekly basis: representing both Coalville Town and Coalville Rugby Club. In fact, Ernest skippered the latter during that term.

Apps: *FL 1.*

HARPER, William E.

b. Nechells, Birmingham, 1876
d. Weston-super-Mare, 1944

Career: Smethwick Wesleyan Rovers; Oct 1899 West Bromwich Albion; Sept 1903 FOSSE.

Fosse debut v Chesterfield Town (H) 26.9.03

> Another Fossil who failed to appear on a winning side (unsurprisingly, in the season Fosse first had to go to the re-election vote), Billy was a tall, speedy outside-left with a modicum of previous League experience at The Hawthorns. He'd featured seven times, scoring once, in their promoted line-up of 1902, but had only one top-flight outing the following year. He had represented 'England' in 1899 in the little-known series of Junior international matches against Scotland – as there was no precise equivalent south of the border to Scottish Junior football (a non-league grade which still exists, and confusingly has nothing to do with the age of the players), the 'national' representative side was then drawn almost wholly from minor West Midlands clubs.

Apps: *FL 4.*

HARRIS, W.H.

Career: Leicester Teachers; 1890 Loughborough; Jan 1892 FOSSE; Cumberland Rangers (Leicester).

Fosse debut/only game v Rotherham Town (H) ML 9.1.1892

> The amateur goalkeeper in Fosse's best win of their (otherwise dispiriting) inaugural Midland League campaign – and that by 4-1 against the champions-to-be – Harris won subsequent selection only in three friendlies that term. While serving as a Fosse committee man during 1896/7, however, he did twice turn out in emergencies for the reserves. He became at various times president and secretary of the Leicester Senior League; and he was opening the batting for Leicester CC in 1911.

Apps: *ML 1.*

HARRISON, Albert

b. Leigh, Lancs, 15th February 1904

Career: West Leigh; am cs 1921 Wigan Borough; cs 1923 Atherton Colliery; 1925 Chorley; Mar 1927 Nottingham Forest; Dec 1929 CITY; May 1931 Dundalk; Aug 1932 Drumcondra; July 1933 Wigan Athletic; Dec 1933 Lugano (p/coach).

City debut v Derby County (H) 7.12.29

> A tall blond centre-half who took over the pivotal berth from George Carr, Albert possessed 77 games' worth of Second Division experience, and had been chosen the summer previously for the FA team touring South Africa, when he'd played in one 'Test Match' behind Arthur Chandler. His move from Trentside to top-flight football was not a wholly successful affair, though, and he effectively carried the can for a 2-8 mauling at Grimsby in November 1930; thereafter finding himself displaced by the up-and-coming Roger Heywood – one of his successors at Chorley. Signed by Leicester-born manager Steve Wright at Dundalk, he was invariably known as 'Snowy' during his years in Ireland. Albert then left Cheshire League fare to taste Swiss football halfway through the inaugural season of the National League there; leading Lugano to a 3rd place finish.

Apps: *FL 32; FAC 1.*
Goals: *FL 1.*

HARRISON, Derek

b. Littlethorpe, Leics, 9th February 1950

Career: Blaby Boys Club; app Aug 1965/pro Feb 1967 CITY; Feb 1971 Torquay United; June 1975 Colchester United; cs 1976 Dawlish; Aug 1977 Salisbury.

City debut v Bristol City (H) LC 10.9.69

> A commanding centre-half and skipper for City reserves, Derek was unfortunate to be understudying the consistent John Sjoberg for the bulk of his Filbert Street career, and to have the more versatile Malcolm Manley to contend with when rare senior opportunities arose. Derek's two League Cup appearances came 13 months apart, and with his chances in Frank O'Farrell's promotion-bound side clearly limited, he moved (after a loan spell) to his boss's old stamping ground at Plainmoor to tot up 128 League games in Divisions Three and Four. Bobby Roberts then took on Derek at Layer Road, but his impact there in a relegation campaign was muted.

Apps: *LC 2.*

Derek Harrison

HARRISON, George

b. Church Gresley, Derbyshire, 18th July 1892
d. Church Gresley, 12th February 1939

Career: Gresley Rovers; Feb 1911 FOSSE; Apr 1913 Everton; Dec 1923 Preston North End; Nov 1931 Blackpool.

Fosse debut v Leeds City (H) 22.4.11

> A hefty, direct outside-left who soon showed with Fosse that he was worthy of a much higher grade of football, George was ever-present in 1912/13 and then signed for Everton two days after the final fixture. At Goodison he won a Championship medal in 1915, and his continuing reliability as both a provider of quality crosses and a vicious finisher earned him two full England caps after the war; during which he served with the Scots Guards, returned to Leicester for a handul of regional games, and also guested for West Ham. Occasionally known by the nickname of 'Jud', George had such a strong shot that he always claimed he hit penalties straight at the 'keeper, knowing the latter would take evasive action! His stamina was almost as remarkable as his touchline skill, and he was nearly forty when he retired from First Division football, on the frustrating figure of 99 League goals from 526 games. Initially he ran a pub in Preston, but George was licensee of the Rising Sun back in his native village when he committed suicide, slitting his throat when in failing health. His son, also George and also a winger, signed professional forms for City in October 1931, but failed to break through to senior level; while a nephew was Preston and Newcastle goalkeeper Jack Fairbrother.

Apps: *FL 59; FAC 1; WW1 5.*
Goals: *FL 9; WW1 2.*

HARRISON, James Charles

b. Leicester, 12th February 1921

Career: Wellington Victoria; Dec 1940 CITY; July 1949 Aston Villa; July 1951 Coventry City; July 1953 Corby Town; Hinckley Athletic.

City debut (WW2) v Notts County (H) 7.12.40; (postwar) v Fulham (A) 21.9.46 (scored once)

> A local signing during WW2, Jimmy served in the forces in India and Burma and guested for both Brentford and Reading before making his League bow for City as a centre-forward; a position to which he occasionally reverted in emergencies from his more regular slot at full-back. His bulk and enthusiasm appeared to suit him for forward forays, but the fact that Jimmy had only ever added one other first-team counter to his debut goal made his selection in the No 9 shirt for City's first Wembley Final something of a desperate gamble; albeit one partly dictated by circumstance. The crucial face-saving and status-saving game at Cardiff a week after the Cup Final was Jimmy's last for City, for Villa stepped in with a £12,000 bid during the close season, and relieved Jimmy from the terrace barracking he'd been receiving at Filbert Street. (His impending marriage to chairman Len Shipman's daughter, giving rise to accusations of favouritism, had brought that about). He was only, however, to make eight First Division starts for Villa (scoring once), before moving on again to Highfield Road, where a team with an average age of 31 dropped from the Second to the Third Division (South), yet still thrashed City in the FA Cup in 1952. Jimmy broke his ankle while skippering Hinckley from the centre-half berth in 1956/7. He later settled to run a successful haulage business from a Wigston base. Jimmy's younger brother Jack was a City reserve full-back at the end of 1947/8, spent two years in Villa's second team, and became from 1950-57 a 245-game stalwart for Colchester United.

Apps: *FL 81; FAC 11; WW2 15.*
Goals: *FL 1; FAC 1; WW2 3.*

HARRISON, Walter Edward

b. Coalville, Leics, 16th January 1923
d. Leicester, 1979

Career: Coalville Town; Navy football; am June 1945/pro Aug 1945 CITY; Dec 1950 Chesterfield; cs 1953 Corby Town; cs 1955 Grantham Town; Nov 1957 Hinckley Athletic (- 1961).

City debut (WW2) v Millwall (H) 2.2.46 (scored once); (postwar) v West Ham United (A) 7.9.46

> A tall, wiry right-half who had guested for Kilmarnock (11 games, 4 goals) while on wartime Navy service, Walter soon gained the nickname 'Spider' from the Filbert Street fans, and had his intelligent prompting recognised with two England 'B' caps in May 1949, immediately after helping City to Wembley and picking up a consolation medal alongside his unrelated namesake Jimmy. Walter excelled at the wall-pass, give-and-go game, but was long best remembered for a 50-yard dribble past five men that ended with him scoring a Cup goal against Sheffield Wednesday in 1948. Chesterfield recruited him, for £8,500, to their unsuccessful fight against relegation from the Second Division in 1951, but he went on to make 74 League appearances for the Saltergate side (for whom he netted eight penalties in 1951/2 alone). Curiously, Walter had twice previously finished City games against the Spireites in goal: as City's favoured stand-in, he had to take over the green jersey three times in all between November 1947 and September 1948, replacing Joe Calvert, Gordon Bradley and Les Major after each had suffered injuries. He skippered Hinckley to victory in the 1958 County Challenge Cup Final, when they beat Brush Sports 2-1 on the first occasion City reserves had neither entered nor won, and later acted as trainer to Friar Lane Old Boys. Qualified in childcare work with handicapped kids, Walter became a Welfare Officer for Leicester Education Department.

Apps: *FL 125; FAC 18; WW2 2.*
Goals: *FL 3; FAC 2; WW2 1.*

HARROLD, James George William

b. Poplar, London, 26th March 1892
d. Epsom, Surrey, 7th October 1950

Career: 1908 Custom House; am Jan 1912 Huddersfield Town; am 1912 West Ham United; am Feb 1913/pro cs 1913 FOSSE; July 1923 Millwall; Aug 1925 Clapton Orient.

Fosse debut v Grimsby Town (H) 15.2.13

> Fosse were in such a hurry to field Essex and England amateur centre-half Jimmy that they were subsequently fined two guineas by the FA for selecting him before the completion of registration formalities (one week after he'd first appeared for his country, and scored, in Wales; and less than a fortnight before he won his only other cap, in Paris). The tall Londoner – 'by nature an intervener, a despoiler' according to the Nottingham Evening Mail – blessed with brilliant heading ability and a seemingly telescopic tackle, soon proved worthy of conversion to the professional ranks, and went on to give a decade's worth of superb service on both sides of WW1; during which he served as a First Class Air Mechanic. Jimmy took a benefit from the home game with Blackpool in December 1920, and received £500 from a £1,000 transfer fee as accrued share of his next benefit when moving on to The Den. He'd been baited by a section of the City crowd before asking to be listed, and ill-luck with injuries stymied the close of his senior football career at both Millwall and Orient; but he'd made his County Championship debut with Essex in the same month as his move back to the capital, and continued to play occasional first-class cricket until 1929, while also assisting South West Ham CC in the club game. By that stage he had a tobacconist's business in Stratford. In 1941, Jimmy was a visitor to Filbert Street shortly after being bombed out of his London home.

Apps: *FL 206; FAC 12; WW1 13.*
Goals: *FL 7.*

HARROLD, Sidney

b. Stourbridge, Worcs, 5th June 1895

Career: Willenhall; Stourbridge; Wednesbury; Feb 1919 FOSSE; May 1920 Nottingham Forest; June 1922 Accrington Stanley.

Fosse debut (WW1) v Nottingham Forest (A) 11.1.19; (postwar) v Wolverhampton Wanderers (H) 30.8.19

> Unrelated to Jimmy, Sid was an outside-left who joined Fosse during the final season of WW1 football, and appeared in the side for City's first League outing after reconstruction, but who found himself out of favour with Peter Hodge before the term was over. The last thirteen of his fifty starts for Forest came in their Division Two championship campaign of 1922, but a broken ankle suffered during his sixth game for Accrington brought his career to a sadly premature end. A combined City/Forest XI (featuring Newton, Thomson, Adcock, King and Tompkin) played a Northern selection at Peel Park in a benefit game for Sid in May 1923; while the latter became in turn a cricket pro and a Wednesbury licensee. He was not the winger with Bilston United and Burton Town at this time with whom he has elsewhere been confused.

Apps: *FL 18; WW1 16.*
Goals: *FL 2; WW1 2.*

HASTIE, George

b. Glasgow

Career: Govan Glentoran; July 1906 Ashfield; June 1909 Kilmarnock; June 1910 Bristol Rovers; cs 1911 Bath City; Nov 1911 Kilmarnock; Aug 1912 St Johnstone; Nov 1912 Abercorn; July 1914 FOSSE; Oct 1915 Belfast United; Abercorn; cs 1919 Belfast Celtic; Abercorn; Sept 1920 Johnstone.

Fosse debut v Lincoln City (H) 2.9.14

> A Scottish inside-left caught up with understandable bewilderment in Fosse's plummet to the Second Division re-election zone in the war-shadowed season of 1914/15, when he was even experimented with at centre-half, George was still officially on City's transfer list in August 1919, at which point the Football League granted him a rather academic free transfer. A Junior international in 1906/07, and a Scottish Qualifying Cup winner with Abercorn in 1912/13, he'd played in both echelons of Scottish League football, as well as in the Southern and Western Leagues at Eastville and Twerton Park, prior to his Second Division bow; and after the war would contribute very briefly to Belfast Celtic's 1919/20 Irish championship campaign.

Apps: *FL 17; FAC 1.*
Goals: *FL 1.*

HAZELL, Robert Joseph

b. Kingston, Jamaica, 14th June 1959

Career: app/pro May 1977 Wolverhampton Wanderers; Sept 1979 Queens Park Rangers; Sept 1983 CITY; May 1985-loan-Kilfa AIK; Sept 1985-loan-Wolverhampton Wanderers; Aug 1986-trials-Luton Town; Oct 1986-trials-Leeds United; Nov 1986 Reading; Dec 1986 Port Vale (- 1989).

City debut v Birmingham City (A) 1.10.83

> A valuable and immensely popular contributor to City's First Division survival struggles of the mid-80s, Bob came to Leicester after the upward trajectory of his career seemed temporarily to have stalled at Loftus Road. England honours at Youth, Under-21 and 'B' levels had come the way of the big central defender, and he had starred for Rangers in the 1982 FA Cup Final against Spurs and in the following term's Second Division

championship campaign. His disciplinary record was far from unsullied, however, and Filbert Street regulars had already witnessed one of his dismissals after a clash with Mark Goodwin. There was general approval, though, when Gordon Milne signed Bob for £100,000 to play alongside John O'Neill, and subsequent delight in the way he combined an intimidatory presence with some almost delicate ball skills, as well as relish at the sight of him strolling forward with the ball while opponents hesitated over the wisdom of trying to tackle him. Unfortunately, off the field, Bob soon had disagreements with Milne over both training and tactics, and never played again for the first team after being substituted at Forest in November 1984. A series of injuries then set him back severely, with a ruptured achilles tendon received in the opening game of a loan spell back at Molineux keeping him sidelined for nine months. After City gave him a free in 1986, Bob had a month's trial at Luton again invalidated by injury, but proved his fitness on a non-contract basis at Reading (after being sent off on his debut!), and then signed up with Vale for just over two more years of Division Three football, culminating in their 1989 promotion campaign.

Apps: *FL 41; FAC 1; LC 4.*
Goals: *FL 2.*

HEATH, Richard Terence

b. Leicester, 17th November 1943

Career: app/pro Nov 1961 CITY; May 1964 Hull City; Mar 1968 Scunthorpe United; Feb 1973 Lincoln City.

City debut v West Ham United (H) 10.11.62

> A teenage inside-forward with a decent reserve-team scoring record, Terry briefly emerged as a valuable squad member when City mounted their attempt on the Double in 1962/3, with one of his goals proving decisive in separating Leicester and Manchester United at Filbert Street after hat-tricks from Keyworth and Law had cancelled each other out. A first-team place was more elusive the following season, but Terry left the club on a high note, playing in the first leg of the League Cup Final at Stoke. Gradually withdrawing to a scheming role with his subsequent clubs, he assisted Hull to the Third Division championship of 1966 (when also scoring twice in a Cup giant-killing of Nottingham Forest), and Scunthorpe to promotion from the basement in 1972. Playing a number of his Old Showground games alongside Kevin Keegan, Terry netted 49 goals in his five years there. His career unfortunately ended through injury after two knee operations in a year and, as a technicality precluded compensation being paid, Lincoln very honourably held a testimonial match against Ipswich on Terry's behalf in March 1976. He was last heard of as proprietor of a Newquay guest house.

Apps: *FL 8; LC 1.*
Goals: *FL 2.*

HEATHCOCK, Joseph Bert

b. Cradley Heath, 5th December 1903
d. Cradley Heath, 21st May 1990

Career: Cradley Heath; Sept 1923 Leamington Town; Oct 1923 CITY; June 1928 Nottingham Forest; June 1930 Cradley Heath; Sept 1931 Hereford United; June 1932 Nuneaton Town.

City debut/only game v Sheffield United (A) 19.3.27 (scored twice)

> Having waited so patiently to make his senior centre-forward breakthrough in place of Arthur Chandler (that day representing the Football League against the Scottish League at Filbert

Bert Heathcock

Street), it was bleakly ironic that Bert should be badly injured while scoring his second goal of the match on his Bramall Lane debut. Immediately stretchered off, he required a cartilage operation, and was never in Filbert Street contention again. His opportunities after a £150 move to Forest were limited, too, even though two spectacular scoring bursts in his first season there brought him a 14-goal haul from only 16 games! City had originally snapped Bert up after he'd had only three Birmingham Combination outings for Leamington (netting eight times!), and he'd cemented his reserve reputation within months when notching nine of City's record 22 goals against Ibstock Colliery in the Senior Cup. Eventually returning to the non-league sphere, Bert helped Cradley Heath to the Birmingham League championship in 1931, and hit 16 counters in his first nine games for Hereford in that competition.

Apps: *FL 1.*
Goals: *FL 2.*

HEBBERD, Trevor Neil

b. New Alresford, Hampshire, 19th June 1958

Career: Alresford; app Sept 1974/ pro July 1976 Southampton; Mar 1981-loan-Washington Diplomats; Sept 1981-loan-Bolton Wanderers; Nov 1981-loan-CITY; Mar 1982 Oxford United; Aug 1988 Derby County; Sept 1991 Portsmouth; Nov 1991 Chesterfield; cs 1994 Lincoln City; cs 1995 Grantham Town.

City debut v Cambridge United (H) 28.11.81 (scored once)

> Still in his teens when assisting Southampton's rise to the top flight, Trevor thereafter suffered for his own versatility at The Dell, often being the man to drop out to accommodate one of Lawrie McMenemy's pricy imports, and regularly warming the bench before coming on as striker, wideman or midfield prompter. He faced City while on loan at Burnden Park, then weeks later Jock Wallace borrowed Trevor for a closer look, but his elegant, deceptively casual style on the left of midfield failed to impress the boss despite him never being in a losing City line-up. At Oxford, alongside ex-City reserve Malcolm Shotton, he became a major motive force in the team which won successive divisional championships in 1984 and 1985 to establish itself in the top echelon, and scored the opening goal at Wembley as the U's captured the 1986 League Cup. Trevor also took the 'Man of the Match' award from that game. He left each of the Manor and Baseball Grounds following relegation campaigns, was uncharacteristically sent off on his initial Chesterfield start, developed into an occasional sweeper at Saltergate, and was still active during 1994/5 in a Lincoln side that sometimes also contained ex-City men Grant Brown, Nicky Platnauer and

Trevor Hebberd

David Puttnam, plus on-loan 'keeper Russell Hoult.

Apps: *FL 4.*
Goals: *FL 1.*

HEBDEN, George Horace Robert

b. West Ham, 2nd June 1900
d. Leicester, 16th August 1973

Career: Clapton; Barking Town; May 1920 CITY; May 1925 Queens Park Rangers; July 1927 Gillingham; Nov 1929 Queens Park Rangers.

City debut v Hull City (H) 9.4.21

> The hero of the goalless May 1914 schoolboy international at Hampden Park, goalkeeper George had his football future severely jeopardised by teenage war service in the Navy and merchant marine (reportedly being torpedoed four times), but survived to assist Barking to the Final of the London Amateur Cup in 1920, and arrived at Filbert Street to understudy fellow East Ender Herbert Bown. By 1922 he had made the first-team position his own with a string of instinctively fearless performances (occasionally criticised for bordering on the reckless), yet himself came under pressure from the calmer Albert Godderidge right from the start of the 1924/5 promotion season. Playing for the reserves against Grantham in October 1921, George had contrived to get himself simultaneously stretchered off and sent off; while, more soberingly, he had to appear as a witness at the November 1924 inquest on the Fulham forward Harvey Arthur Darvill, with whom he'd collided a few weeks previously, and who'd died of undiagnosed internal injuries after completing an interim pair of Division Two games. George never played senior football for City again after that experience, though he did tot up a further 130 games for his two Division Three (South) clubs. On retirement, he initially ran his own garage business in Ilford while coaching part-time at Leytonstone; but City had to come to his aid financially in January 1938, after a fall from a ladder the previous March had left him incapacitated with serious spinal injuries. George had been back in Leicester (as a staunch member of the Wilberforce Road Conservative Club) for some time before his death.

Apps: *FL 101; FAC 3.*

HEDLEY, George Thomas

b. Co Durham, 1882
d. 1937

Career: West Stanley; cs 1905 Middlesbrough; Chester-le-Street; Jan 1906 Heart of Midlothian; Mar 1906 Hull City; Apr 1908 FOSSE; cs 1909 Luton Town; cs 1910 Hartlepools United; Dec 1912 Jarrow Caledonians.

Fosse debut v Fulham (A) 4.4.08

> 'A back neat and polished', according to the *Mercury*, 'Tot' was bought for £275 to boost Fosse's defensive strength during the final promotion push of 1908. The regular right-back in the torrid First Division campaign which followed, he was the only player besides Jim Gorman and Bob Pollock to make his final appearance in the infamous 0-12 drubbing by Forest, which he later helped explain away to the satisfaction of the League's commission of enquiry. Previously, 'Tot' had featured in each of Division One (three 'Boro outings), the top-flight and Cup in Scotland (a trio of games for Hearts) and Division Two (eleven Hull starts) during his very first season in the senior game. A regular for the Tigers thereafter until his Filbert Street move, he notched a rare goal for them in a March 1907 1-1 draw against Fosse. Despite the ruffling he received at Leicester, he was still noted for his coolness in clearing his lines in both Southern and North Eastern League company.

Apps: *FL 35; FAC 3.*
Goals: *FL 1.*

HENDERSON, John Neil

b. Dumfries, ca 1874
d. Maxwelltown, Dumfries, 30th August 1930

Career: 1890 5th Kirkudbright Rifle Volunteers; Dec 1895 Celtic; May 1897 Victoria United (Aberdeen); May 1898 Lincoln City; Dec 1900 FOSSE; Mar 1901 Small Heath; Sept 1902 Maxwelltown Volunteers; Aug 1905 Carlisle United; 1906 Maxwelltown Volunteers (from 1908 known as 5th Kings Own Scottish Borderers); Sept 1910 Annan United; Nov 1910 Nithsdale Wanderers.

Fosse debut v Woolwich Arsenal (H) 15.12.1900

> In a stay of just over three months at Filbert Street, Jock played five times at outside-left and eight times at inside-right, but failed to perk up a fairly goal-shy Fosse front line. Perhaps surprisingly, Small Heath still saw him as a likely candidate to buttress their squad in the successful run-in to promotion in 1901, though he only managed four games for them alongside Johnny McMillan. Jock's chances at Celtic had been equally limited at the start of his senior career, but mixed experiences there saw him win selection in the annual Glasgow v Sheffield fixture of 1896, and partner Jimmy Blessington in the infamous 1897 Cup defeat by little Arthurlie, before which many of the Celtic regulars declared themselves 'on strike'. The Aberdonian side Victoria United were champions of the Scottish Northern League at the end of Jock's term there, and he became a Second Division regular with the Imps. In 1905, he was a member of Carlisle United's first-ever Lancashire Combination line-up. Some obituary notes add Notts County and Arsenal to Jock's list of clubs, but it is certain that the latter reference, at least, had crept in from the career details of his older brother James, who had also started playing with the 5th KRV, and was a member of Woolwich Arsenal's inaugural Football League side. Jock himself was a Dumfries tobacconist at the time of his death.

Apps: *FL 13.*

HENDERSON, William Martin Melville

b. Kirkcaldy, Fife, 3rd May 1956

Career: 1973 Rangers; Oct 1977-loan-Hibernian; Apr 1978 Philadelphia Fury; Oct 1978 CITY; Sept 1981 Chesterfield; Oct 1983 Port Vale (- 1984); Sept 1989 Spalding United; Feb 1991 Leicester United; Mar 1991 Spalding United (p/mgr); cs 1991 Bourne Town (p/coach); 1992 Spalding United.

City debut v Charlton Athletic (H) 14.10.78 (sub)

> Bursting into Rangers' Treble-winning team of 1975/6 as a teenage striker, and one of the few non-internationals in Jock Wallace's Ibrox squad, Martin missed out only on the League Cup portion of that success, to which he contributed ten League and three Cup goals. Yet he was utterly unable to consolidate his impact or add to his medal tally thereafter, and was rebuilding his career in the NASL when Wallace called upon him to add comparative experience to City's youthful Second Division front line. An ever-willing target man, but occasionally clumsy, and far from prolific, Martin found his most useful role with City was as foil to Alan Young, his one-time Kirkcaldy schoolboy partner, in the 1979/80 promotion campaign. His goal ratio improved at Saltergate, though he experienced successive relegations from Division Three with both the Spireites in 1983 and Vale in 1984, when he had briefly partnered Mark Bright. Martin was then involved in a contract dispute which ended his senior career, and a criminal fraud case which temporarily curtailed his freedom. His rehabilitation included a part-time involvement in the non-league game, and work in sales development within the brewery trade.

Apps: *FL 79+12; FAC 5; LC 3+1.*
Goals: *FL 12; FAC 4.*

HENRY, William Armstrong

b. Glasgow, 6th September 1884

Career: Blantyre Victoria; cs 1906 Rangers; cs 1908 Falkirk; June 1909 FOSSE; Nov 1911 Manchester City; July 1920 St Bernards.

Fosse debut v Wolverhampton Wanderers (H) 1.9.09

> 'Fleet, with a frame of iron, splendid tackler, beautiful kick...'. The *Mercury's* shorthand encomium to right-back Billy was wholly justified, for he raised for Fosse their highest-ever incoming transfer fee of £1,000. Missing only a single game during his Filbert Street spell of over two seasons, he matched consistency to evident class, and came very close to a Scottish cap, appearing for the Anglo-Scots against the Home Scots in the international trial of March 1911. His back-line partnerships with, successively, Dick Pudan and Sam Currie considerably tightened a Fosse defence still smarting from its First Division muggings, and made inevitable the profitable elevation to top-flight football his Manchester move entailed. At Hyde Road he made 143 League appearances on either side of WW1, many of them in front of former Fosse 'keeper Walter Smith. Billy's single League goal was a 40-yard matchwinner at Meadow Lane on the opening day of 1912/13. Strangely, he was living and running a business in Birmingham during some of his time with Manchester City. He gained one 'unofficial' honour during the war, when Scotland met England at Goodison Park in a 'Grand Military International' in May 1916; after a season in which Billy had also guested for Southampton.

Apps: *FL 89; FAC 7.*

HENRYS, Arthur

b. Nottingham, 1867
d. Nottingham (?), 30th June 1922

Career: Notts Rovers; Notts St Johns; Notts Jardines; Nottingham Forest; cs 1890 Gainsborough Trinity; cs 1891 Newton Heath; Aug 1892 Notts Jardines; Oct 1892 Newton Heath; Mar 1893 FOSSE; June 1896 Notts County.

Fosse debut v Newark (A) ML 1.4.1893

> A member of Gainsborough's 1891 Midland League championship side, and an outside-left in his first season with the team who finished runners-up in the Football Alliance and would later be known as Manchester United, Arthur converted to defensive roles as he played at three different levels over the next three campaigns. He made three First Division appearances for the Heathens in 1892/3 before his move to Leicester; becoming the regular Fosse centre-half (and captain) in the Midland League; and taking the left-half berth in the inaugural Second Division term. Despite his team-leading responsibility, Arthur was several times suspended by the Fosse committee: on the last such occasion the writer Custodian in local magazine The Wyvern commented, 'The reason for this is the old, old tale - a too fervent longing for the fascinating alcoholic nectar'. After his move homeward, Arthur would make only seven starts in the Magpies' Second Division championship side of 1896/7.

***Apps:** FL 37; FAC 14; ML 23.*
***Goals:** FL 1; ML 1.*

HERNON, James

b. Cleland, Lanarkshire, 6th December 1924

Career: Mossvale Strollers; Apr 1942 CITY; Sept 1948 Bolton Wanderers; Aug 1951 Grimsby Town; July 1954 Watford; July 1956 Hastings United.

City debut (WW2) v Northampton Town (A) 16.5.42; (postwar) v Fulham (H) 7.6.47

> A teenage signing from Paisley junior football during the war (when his City record was supplemented by a guest spell with Partick Thistle), Jimmy had to wait until his Army demob in 1947 for a League bow, on the only occasion City's official fixture programme has stretched into June. A slim inside-forward who seriously challenged Don Revie for the scheming role at Filbert Street during the following term, he then put in a transfer request. City would initially only consider a player exchange deal, and a rebellious Jimmy was considering offers to play non-league football with either Dartford or Hinckley Athletic when First Division Bolton handed over a record incoming fee of £14,750 to whisk him to Burnden, where his younger brother John was on amateur forms. Never assured of automatic selection there, partly because the subtleties of his style could often be nullified by close physical attention, he ironically did better in the supposedly 'harder' context of Third Division football with the Mariners (runners-up in the Northern Section in 1952) and the Hornets. Former City boss Johnny Duncan later wrote, resignedly, 'I did my best for Jimmy Hernon. I put him on sherry and egg. His ball-control was brilliant, but he was a featherweight'.

***Apps:** FL 31; FAC 3; WW2 25.*
***Goals:** FL 7; WW2 2.*

HERROD, E. Robert

Career: Derby St Luke's; Sept 1890 Doncaster Rovers; cs 1891 FOSSE; Jan 1892 Rotherham Town; 1892 Derby Town.

Fosse debut v Derby Junction (H) ML 12.9.1891

> Originally a teammate of Jack Lord's at Derby St Luke's, and the top-scoring winger in Doncaster's initial competitive fixtures in the Midland Alliance, Bob took the outside-right position in Fosse's first Midland League game but, despite a shift to the inside-right berth, faded from the scene shortly after the club's move from Aylestone Road to Filbert Street. He still impacted on that transitional term, though, as a member of the Rotherham side that handed out the record 0-11 beating to Fosse on its way to the championship.

***Apps:** FAC 1; ML 7.*
***Goals:** FAC 1.*

HESKEY, Emile William Ivanhoe

b. Leicester, 11th January 1978

Career: YT July 1994/pro Oct 1995 CITY; Mar 2000 Liverpool.

City debut v Queens Park Rangers (A) 8.3.95

> One of the most enigmatic talents City have ever possessed, Emile is even now, after apparently well justifying a record £11m transfer, a focus for widely conflicting opinions. Maddeningly inconsistent; a scorer of great goals rather than a great goalscorer; an immensely powerful brick outhouse of a man who can nonetheless crumple under the lightest of challenges; a shy individual whose flashes of on-field arrogance can illuminate any game, in any company. A local lad who shared Gary Lineker's scholastic background, Emile made the quicker impact, with four selections for England's Under-16 schools side before taking a YT contract at Filbert Street. He was still a first-year trainee when thrust into an injury-hit and 'flu-stricken City side at Loftus Road as the club's youngest Premiership player to date, but signed pro after a kick-off to the 1995/6 season which saw him notch eight goals in the opening pair of youth-team fixtures, score once for the reserves, and come on at Norwich to claim a late winner that kept City at the top of the table. It would be by the Play-Off route that City would rise that term, with the hefty striker becoming a regular after Martin O'Neill's arrival, and only missing his initial Under-21 selection because of the Wembley date. The Premiership campaign of 1996/7 brought Emile his best-ever tally of City goals (his aggregate dozen including the late, scrambled Wembley equaliser against Middlesbrough which was the prelude to League Cup glory), his delayed Under-21 call-up, and runner-up position to David Beckham in the PFA's Young Player of the Year voting. Full England squad duties and a 'B' cap came his way the following season, along with early 'Goal of the Month' acclaim, but so did criticism for a lengthy goal-drought, and a perceived dip in confidence when asked to play alongside a variety of striking partners. In fact, it was Tony Cottee's establishment alongside Emile that sparked his own late scoring burst to the top of the City goal-chart. A more purposeful start to 1998/9 reactivated transfer rumours, but he signed a new two-year contract, and then ironically began to suffer injury problems, especially with his back. He failed to net after December, and made little impact in the League Cup Final defeat against Spurs. Nonetheless, the value of the predictably-nicknamed 'Bruno' to City was immense, with his very presence usually attracting double-marking, his sheer pace useful for the get-out ball, and his ability to run at defenders either centrally or from the flanks an effectively varied ploy. As 1999/2000 got underway, O'Neill's estimation of such worth was replicated by national boss Kevin Keegan. A series of England substitute outings for Emile heralded a first start which earned man-of-the-match plaudits against Argentina. Days later, he would pick up his second League Cup winner's medal with City; and a fortnight on, after Filbert Street appetites had been tantalisingly whetted by the prospect of a Collymore/Heskey strike force, he would sign for Liverpool as the third most expensive acquisition ever by a British club. The Anfield jury may still have been out by the end of that term, but Emile would definitely have won a majority verdict among City fans that the goods were in first-class order. A verdict that most Reds would share after Emile's startlingly effective return from 2000/1: 22 goals overall (including the Anfield winner against City); winner's medals from the Finals of each of the FA, League and UEFA Cups; and an established slot in Sven Goran Eriksson's national side.

***Apps:** PL/FL 143+11; FAC 11; LC 25+2; UEFA 2; PO 3.*
***Goals:** PL/FL 40; LC 6.*

Emile Heskey

HEYES, George

b. Bolton, 16th November 1937

Career: Apr 1956 Rochdale; July 1960 CITY; Sept 1965 Swansea Town; July 1969 Barrow; June 1970 Bedford United; Hereford United.

City debut v West Bromwich Albion (A) 11.3.61

> A reliably unflappable stand-in for Gordon Banks over six seasons, whenever the England keeper was either injured or absent on international duty, George had his lengthiest first-team run at the start of 1965/6, under distinctly ironic circumstances. With 16-year-old Peter Shilton then pushing the loyal understudy even for his Combination place, George was to be 'put in the shop window' with a second-half appearance, in front of the watching Swansea management, in a pre-season Filbert Street friendly against Northampton. However, Banks suffered a broken wrist after 17 minutes, and George was required not only to substitute, but to fill in for the first nine League matches. He then immediately completed a move to the Vetch, and ended a busy season with 48 League games under his belt: more than would have been possible as an ever-present with a single club! A Welsh Cup winner's medal also came George's way that term, and he would leave Swansea with a runners-up memento from the same competition three years later, before completing his League career at Holker Street. He had started his senior career as a part-timer in a relegated Rochdale side, also working for the Post Office; and he would pass on useful experience to his son Darren, an England schoolboy keeper who faced City for Scunthorpe in the 1987/8 League Cup. George is now back in Leicester, working as a security guard.

***Apps:** FL 25; LC 2.*

HEYWOOD, Roger

b. Chorley, Lancs, 4th May 1909
d. Leicester, 30th December 1985

Career: Chorley St James; 1927 Chorley; Nov 1929 CITY; WW2 Corby Town.

City debut v Birmingham (A) 3.5.30

> Bought for a bargain £575 from the club which had taken the Lancashire Combination title for two seasons running, Roger was a towering stopper centre-half who gave lengthy service to City after the most unpromising of starts: when on his debut he conceded a hat-trick by Leicestershire-born centre-forward Joe Bradford. The bulk of his appearances came in City's early-30s years of First Division struggle, when he was regarded as coolness personified (being used to advertise Fox's Glacier Mints at the time of the 1934 FA Cup semi-final!), and it was somewhat sadly ironic that he should play little part in the 1937 Second Division championship effort, yet have his own fortunes revive (in a wing-half slot) during the final pre-war relegation campaign. City and Northampton shared Roger's services during the first year of regional football, and he officially retired in 1941 to coach the club's Colts, though his final game in blue was in the April 1946 County Cup Final win over Coalville, when he was on leave from the East Yorkshire Regiment. A cousin of Arsenal and England goalkeeper Frank Moss, and a summer exponent of League cricket in Lancashire, Roger later worked at Dunlops in Leicester.

***Apps:** FL 228; FAC 12; WW2 41.*
***Goals:** FL 2; WW2 2.*

HIBBERD, John Turner

Career: Oct 1895 FOSSE

Fosse debut/only game v Hucknall St Johns (H) FAC 2.11.1895 (scored once)

> One of the several instances of a 'blink-and-you-missed-it' senior Fosse career – there's not even a record of this inside-right featuring in any of the club's then-numerous friendly fixtures to supplement the above appearance against an obscure Nottinghamshire team of Cup hopefuls. John did, however, notch the Fosse Rovers' winning goal in the Leicestershire Senior Cup Final of 1896; and had represented the county a year previously.

***Apps:** FAC 1.*
***Goals:** FAC 1.*

HILL, Colin Frederick

b. Uxbridge, 12th November 1963

Career: Glebe Athletic; Park Lane; Hillingdon; am Dec 1979/pro Aug 1981 Arsenal; Jan 1986-loan-Brighton & Hove Albion; cs 1986 CS Maritimo; Oct 1987 Colchester United; Aug 1989 Sheffield United; Mar 1992 CITY; July 1997 Trelleborgs FF; Nov 1997 Northampton Town.

City debut v Tranmere Rovers (A) 27.3.92

> A widely-experienced central defender who played in the Wembley defeat by Blackburn Rovers while still on loan with City – his £200,000 transfer not being negotiated until two months later – Colin went on to pick up the club's Player of the Year trophy following an ever-present 1992/3, but was sidelined by injury from completing a hat-trick of successive Play-Off appearances in 1994. A cool head, a strong tackle and fine anticipation were features of Colin's game under Brian Little, and deservedly earned him the captaincy under Mark McGhee, but Martin O'Neill seemed less sure of the veteran's mobility after he assumed the reins. He went on the list at his own request in September 1996, but bade a farewell to both City and his first club Arsenal when skippering the side at Highbury in April 1997 – only to be stretchered off after a collision with Kasey Keller. His three months in Sweden helped Trelleborgs avoid relegation; but that was Northampton's fate in 1999, a year after Colin had helped them to Wembley in the Play-Offs (and had returned to Filbert Street in the FA Cup). His initial League breakthrough had come back in 1983/4, when he

Colin Hill

appeared at both centre- and right-back for the Gunners, but, deposed by expensive newcomers, he chose to broaden his repertoire further while playing Portuguese First Division football from the offshore base of Funchal, Madeira – and ended up as his club's 1987 top-scorer. The contrast of Division Four fare as a Layer Road defender followed, but Colin was soon winning his first half-dozen caps for Northern Ireland after moving to Bramall Lane and assisting the Blades' 1990 promotion to the top flight. For some time, despite his form for City, Colin seemed unable to add to his representative record, but after three successive call-ups from Bryan Hamilton were negated by injury, he returned to the green as an international regular in Spring 1995. Since hanging up his boots, he has been employed on City's sales and marketing staff.

Apps: *FL/PL 140+5; FAC 8; LC 10+2; AIC 3; PO 6+1.*
Goals: *LC 1.*

HILL, John

b. Kirkcaldy, Fife, 1871

Career: Leith Rangers; Leith Athletic; 1892 Middlesbrough Ironopolis; May 1893 FOSSE; cs 1895 Glossop North End; Oct 1897 West Herts (- 1901).

Fosse debut v Burton Wanderers (H) ML 9.9.1893

> A 'fast and tricky' teammate of McArthur and Seymour in the Ironopolis team which reached the quarter-finals of the FA Cup in 1893, outside-right Jacky moved to Leicester with the latter for what proved to be the final season of Midland League competition, and was soon joined by the former. When Archie Hughes and Bob Gordon then later reunited with their former fellows, it meant five ex-Nops (all Scotsmen) were assisting Fosse in their initial assault on the Second Division. A Scottish Junior international (1891), Jacky helped prompt Glossop in 1897 to the same Midland League runners-up slot that Fosse had occupied three years previously, then moved to the newly professionalised outfit which changed its name to Watford in 1898, and won promotion to the top level of the Southern League in 1900. He became a director of the Hornets in 1909, when running a newsagent/ tobacconist business in Watford High Street.

Apps: *FL 20; FAC 13; ML 20.*
Goals: *FL 2; FAC 7; ML 7.*

HILL, Ricky Anthony

b. Hammersmith, London, 5th March 1959

Career: app 1975/pro May 1976 Luton Town; June 1989 Le Havre AC; Aug 1990 CITY; Sept 1991-trials-Oxford United; 1991 Tampa Bay Rowdies; Nov 1992 Hitchin Town; cs 1993 Chertsey Town.

City debut v Bristol Rovers (H) 25.8.90 (sub)

> Rescuing his former Luton playmaker from the French Second Division may have struck some as a mere act of sentiment on David Pleat's part, but a City midfield just stripped of the talent of Gary McAllister was clearly in need of added touches of class when the £100,000 deal went through to bring Ricky to Filbert Street. Unfortunately, sporadic flashes of sweet skill were all Ricky could bring to City's anti-relegation battle, in which he was so often harried into ineffectuality by pace-and-power merchants whom he'd have made mugs out of a few years earlier. It was sadly characteristic of Ricky's year with Leicester that the most overt tribute he received – a virtual standing ovation from Plymouth supporters at Home Park, genuinely marvelling at his silky contributions to the game – came during and after another City defeat; while a groin injury curtailed his involvement in the climactic months of the 'Great Escape' under Gordon Lee. Such disappointments were a far cry from his prime years at Kenilworth Road, where he made an immediate impact as a 17-year-old scoring substitute in April 1976, and went on to develop into the powerful creative linchpin of Pleat's side; eventually amassing 507 senior Luton appearances and scoring 65 goals. At club level his honours came from a Division Two championship in 1982 and from the Hatters' League Cup Final victory over Arsenal in 1988, while Ricky could count himself unlucky to have won only three caps for England in the mid-80s. His year in France saw Le Havre fail in their promotion bid; while he added to his cosmopolitan experience with two later stints in the USA: playing and coaching under Rodney Marsh shortly after Brian Little released him, and in 1996 returning to Florida to coach Cocoa Beach Express. David Pleat then renewed partnership twice with Ricky, adding him to the coaching staff both at Hillsborough and (from July 1999) at White Hart Lane. In July 2000, though, he struck out on his own in management, back at Luton; only to find his tenure lasting merely until mid-November.

Apps: *FL 19+7; FAC 1; LC 0+2; FMC 1.*

HINE, Ernest William

b. Smithy Cross, Yorks, 9th April 1901
d. Meltham, Yorks, 15th April 1974

Career: New Mills; Staincross Station; Apr 1921 Barnsley; Jan 1926 CITY; May 1932 Huddersfield Town; Feb 1933 Manchester United; Dec 1934 Barnsley.

City debut v Burnley (H) 16.1.26 (scored twice)

> Eventually notching more than 300 senior goals (286 in the League) over a 17-year career span, former miner Ernie was another prolific marksman to announce his intentions early – scoring on his Barnsley debut in a Cup replay at Norwich; averaging the classic ratio of a goal every two games in his initial Oakwell stint; then hitting two in his first game in City colours (although also missing a penalty that day!) after a £3,000 elevation from Second to First Division football. An automatic selection at inside-right thereafter, he became the only one of City's trio of all-time top scorers to receive halfway decent recognition of his sharpshooting prowess: graduating from Football League honours (5 games; 2 goals) to international trials (4 games and 2 goals in the England v The Rest series) to the full England eleven (6 caps; 4 goals). He celebrated the announcement of his initial selection for the national side by claiming a hat-trick from the record 10-0 win over Portsmouth in 1928/9, when his 32 strikes in 35 outings saw City to runners-up spot in the First Division; and he topped the 30-goal mark again two years later, when his ferocious Boxing Day goal against Sunderland actually broke the net. A place on the FA Tour of Canada was his reward in the summer of 1931, and Ernie was still severely embarrassing top flight defences twelve months on when City surprisingly allowed him to move for £4,000 back to Yorkshire. His first goal for the Terriers actually came against City, but neither at Leeds Road nor Old Trafford could Ernie quite recapture his deadly touch. It took a transfer back 'home' to Oakwell for the veteran to settle back into his old scoring habits – which included a hat-trick against City in a 3-3 draw in December 1935, and another counter in the following term's repeat fixture. Promoted to the Barnsley player/coach role in December 1937 (under former Fossil Angus Seed), Ernie hung up his boots shortly afterwards; though his aggregate of 123 League goals for the Tykes remains that club's record individual tally to this day.

Apps: *FL 247; FAC 12.*
Goals: *FL 148; FAC 8.*

HINES, Derek Jabez

b. Woodville, Derbyshire, 8th February 1931

Career: Moira United; 1946-trials-Southend United; am 1946 Derby County; am June 1947/pro Mar 1948 CITY; Nov 1961 Shrewsbury Town; cs 1964 Rugby Town.

City debut v Tottenham Hotspur (A) 27.3.48

> A genuine teenage prodigy who turned into the fourth highest scorer in City's history, centre-forward Derek was tried out in Southend's reserve team at the age of 15, but luckily given an early League baptism by City, who then nursed him gradually into regular first-team football while he was still eligible for England Youth selection. In fact, Derek played and scored in the first-ever international Youth side (in a 4-2 win against Scotland at Doncaster in October 1947), and for City had seven Second Division goals under his belt before he was seventeen-and-a-half. His substantial breakthrough would come, however, in tandem with Arthur Rowley from 1950 onwards. The Gunner's shift to inside-left allowed Derek to assume the No 9 shirt, and if his own scoring rate was somewhat eclipsed by that of Rowley, he proved a wonderful forager in the more advanced spearhead role, opening up spaces for his more prolific teammate to exploit; and earning the role of first reserve to the England 'B' side to face Holland in March 1952. An Army call-up two months later was deferred until Derek completed his apprenticeship as a bricklayer, but when activated handed the striker a punishing schedule, for a plethora of prestigious representative games had to be fitted into the gaps between City outings. After contributing 19 goals to City's 1954 Second Division championship, he played and scored for Young England v England in the then-annual eve-of-Cup Final game, but (the following year's repeat fixture apart), was subsequently passed over by the selectors. While his value to the club was re-emphasised by his 14-goal tally in the 1957 Division Two championship campaign, and he became the last City player to net four times in a League game (in a 6-3 home win over Aston Villa in November 1958), Derek did suffer in one sense from bad timing with Leicester: missing out on trips to Wembley because he was regarded as a lucky mascot reserve in 1949 and a veteran calming influence on the 1961 squad. Not long after answering Rowley's invitation for a brief reunion at Gay Meadow, and Jimmy Walsh's for a similar re-pairing at Rugby, he returned to Filbert Street as youth team coach. In the 70s, Derek was running a store and sub-post office at Blackfordby.

Apps: *FL 299; FAC 18.*
Goals: *FL 116; FAC 1.*

HODGE, Martin John

b. Southport, 4th February 1959

Career: app Sept 1975/pro Feb 1977 Plymouth Argyle; July 1979 Everton; Dec 1981-loan-Preston North End; July 1982-loan-Oldham Athletic; Jan 1983-loan-Gillingham; Feb 1983-loan-Preston North End; Aug 1983 Sheffield Wednesday; Aug 1988 CITY; Aug 1991 Hartlepool United; July 1993 Rochdale; Aug 1994 Plymouth Argyle.

City debut v West Bromwich Albion (H) 27.8.88

> Aggravating a stomach muscle injury on his City debut, only two days after signing for David Pleat at £200,000, goalkeeper Martin was sidelined for several months, and struggled thereafter to recapture the sort of consistency that had initially prompted City's interest, despite ever-present status in 1989/90. Perhaps most noteworthy for his courageous mastery of one-on-one situations (at which he was given rather over-much practice), Martin had by far his best spell for the club in analogous last-ditch circumstances, during the final eight instalments of the 1991 Second Division survival drama, when last-line inspiration was most needed, and when some of his saves definitely kept crisis from turning to catastrophe. City rather ungratefully embarrassed Martin on a couple of occasions thereafter: with Ian Ormondroyd chipping him from 35 yards in a Victoria Ground friendly in 1992, and six of the best being put past him at Spotland in the League Cup tie of 1993/4. He was at the veteran stage by then, and retired to the Argyle coaching ranks after a relegation campaign with Peter Shilton's Plymouth, with his career having aggregated 520 League starts, and 95 in Cup competitions. That career had started at Home Park, too, and had first hit the headlines when detouring with a big-money move to Goodison, but it was Martin's five-year tenure between the posts at Hillsborough which provided its backbone. Wednesday were promoted to the top flight at the end of his first ever-present term, and he went on to re-set the Owls' record for consecutive appearances with an unbroken run of 214 League and Cup outings; during which he had a spell as skipper, and was noted almost as much for the contribution of his kicking to their then-favoured long-ball game as for his penalty-area command.

Apps: *FL 75; FAC 1; LC 4; FMC 1.*

HODGKINSON, Albert Victor

b. Pembroke Dock, Pembrokeshire, 10th August 1884
d. Shardlow, Derbyshire, 25th November 1939

Career: Old Normanton; Derby County; cs 1902 Hinckley Town; May 1903 Derby County; Nov 1903 Grimsby Town; May 1904 Plymouth Argyle; May 1905 FOSSE; June 1906 Bury; May 1907 Southampton; cs 1909 Croydon Common; Feb1911 Southend United; Nov 1911 Ilkeston United.

Fosse debut v Clapton Orient (H) 2.9.05

> Not yet 21 when Fosse became his fourth senior club (after prolonged haggling with Grimsby over his League registration had been settled with a £50 fee), Albert was a clever but 'mercurial' Welsh winger who suffered somewhat at Leicester from the club's inability to settle on a regular inside-left partner for him. He had failed to win a first-team breakthrough at Derby, where his brother William made a brief impact at centre-forward, but left both Second Division Grimsby and Southern League Argyle with identical seasonal records of four goals in 16 starts. The appearance tally doubled with Fosse, but the goal tally didn't keep pace during a campaign which saw the club fringeing the promotion race until a late tail-off to 7th place. Albert's value had nonetheless soared to £165 as a prelude to his First Division bow with Bury. Confusingly for researchers, he took over the outside-left berth there directly from another Hodgkinson (Joseph, transferred to Crystal Palace); but at least the Welsh selectors knew they had the right man when awarding him a cap against Ireland after he'd helped Southampton to the FA Cup semi-finals in his initial season at The Dell. He then experienced Southern League relegation terms at both Croydon and Southend. Albert was also at one time a noted baseball player, and on retirement ran the Rose & Crown at Chellaston in Derbyshire. His father had been a military musket instructor, who moved to Derby when Albert was only three.

Apps: *FL 33; FAC 1.*
Goals: *FL 5.*

HODGSON, William

b. Glasgow, 9th July 1935

Career: Dunoon Athletic; cs 1954 St Johnstone; Sept 1956-loan-Guildford City; May 1957 Sheffield United; Sept 1963 CITY; June 1965 Derby County; Sept 1967 Rotherham United; Dec 1967 York City (p/coach) (- 1970); Sept 1971 Hamilton Academical (p/coach).

City debut v Bolton Wanderers (A) 14.9.63

> A diminutive, enthusiastically industrious and virtually tireless utility forward who wore four different attacker's shirts at Filbert Street, but made most of his appearances in Howard Riley's right-wing stead, Billy had been an old adversary of City's during his Bramall Lane days, playing against them in the FA Cup semi-final marathon of 1961, and thereafter in Division One. He gained further semi-final experience at Leicester, in the League Cup campaigns of 1964 and 1965, missing out on a winner's tankard in the first season, but taking a runners-up memento from the Finals against Chelsea. Billy also scored the first City goal to be featured on 'Match of the Day', when that programme televised the 3-2 home win over Nottingham Forest in October 1964. He became a Baseball Ground

Billy Hodgson

regular at outside-left, and a veteran inspiration to York, where he also put his full FA coaching qualification to use, and where he was caretaker-manager from August to October 1968. He retired to become a Blades coach in summer 1970, but on returning homeward to his original trade as a cooper, Billy played a few Scottish League games as a part-timer for Hamilton. In 1983, he was noted as manager of Scottish Junior team Irvine Victoria, and was reported to be coaching abroad in in the late 90s.

Apps: *FL 46; FAC 5; LC 13.*
Goals: *FL 10; LC 5.*

HOGG, Charles

b. Leicester

Career: Knighton SS; St Andrews; am Feb 1915/pro Apr 1915 FOSSE; cs 1920 Whitwick Imperial; 1921 J Pick & Sons FC

Fosse debut v Blackpool (H) 27.2.15 (scored once)

> In a complaint to the Leicestershire FA, the management of local club St Andrews claimed that their team were actually getting stripped for a Mutual League game before realising that Fosse had spirited away Charlie, their top scorer, for a Filbert Street trial. Apologies ensued, by which time this two-footed inside-forward had made a goal-graced League bow as an amateur. Then, two months later, he became the last player to sign as a Fosse professional before the WW1 break. Charlie continued to turn out during the first campaign in the wartime Midland Section, and had a few games for City reserves in 1919/20.

Apps: *FL 7; WW1 13.*
Goals: *FL 2; WW1 4.*

HOGG, Derek

b. Stockton Heath, Lancs, 4th November 1930

Career: Lostock Hall; am Preston North End; Eccleston; Aug 1952 Chorley; Oct 1952 CITY; Apr 1958 West Bromwich Albion; Oct 1960 Cardiff City; July 1962 Kettering Town (-1965).

City debut v Leeds United (H) 14.2.53

> A former clerk with a Preston-based firm of shipbreakers, who was on North End's books either side of service in Egypt with the Royal Corps of Signals, Derek was signed by City from Lancashire Combination football as a potential right-wing successor to Mal Griffiths. However, he claimed a regular first-team spot only after switching to the left flank at the start of the 1954/5 First Division season. By October 1955 his usually effective (if occasionally over-elaborate) close-dribbling style had earned him a call-up for the Football League against the Scottish League, but heavy local press advocacy (and further representative experience for the FA XI against The Army) failed to win him the nod over Blackpool's Bill Perry for the England No 11 shirt. A run of 104 consecutive City games ended during the 1956/7 Second Division championship season, but he was a key component both in that triumph (in left-sided partnership with Arthur Rowley) and the consolidatory struggle that followed. Having, though, asked for a transfer in March 1958 to further his international ambitions, Derek was allowed to move to The Hawthorns for £20,000 two days after Division One status had been assured at St Andrews. His confidence never wavered there, but the England call never materialised. Derek's Cardiff debut brought him a goal against City; and he made almost a hundred Southern League appearances for the Poppies. In the early 70s, he was running a pub in Osgathorpe, but is believed to have later settled in Lincolnshire.

Apps: *FL 161; FAC 4.*
Goals: *FL 26.*

HOLDEN, Steven Anthony

b. Luton, 4th September 1972

Career: YT 1989/pro Mar 1991 CITY; Oct 1992-loan-Carlisle United; Feb 1993 Carlisle United; Nov 1993 Kettering Town; Jan 1996 Rushden & Diamonds; cs 1997 Stevenage Borough; Mar 1998 Cambridge City.

City debut/only game v Derby County (H) 22.2.92

> A highly regarded prospect as a teenage central defender, Steve had ironically just run into a reserve-team scoring seam before his call-up into the senior back line. A local derby, with promotion rivalry adding to the pressures, represented a fiery baptism; and in fact the 1-2 defeat represented Steve's only real chance to impress at Filbert Street. The depth of experience in Brian Little's squad effectively stymied Steve's development, and he moved for a nominal fee to Brunton Park shortly after completing a successful loan spell there. A further loan move, to Kettering, was oddly marked by a mistaken call-up into the England semi-pro international squad in January 1994, but this was regularised when Steve then signed permanently for the Poppies, and led to further selections at that international level. He aided Rushden's ascent to the Conference via the Southern League title of 1996.

Apps: *FL 1.*

HOLDING, William

Career: Castle Donington; Feb 1909 FOSSE.

Fosse debut v Sheffield United (A) 27.2.09

> Pitched into Fosse's struggling First Division side only a fortnight after scoring on his reserve debut, this inexperienced outside-right contrived to impress sufficiently to be retained for 1909/10, despite being one of the hapless victims of the record 0-12 slaughter on Trentside. William played but a single Division Two game thereafter; yet could be described by the Mercury as 'the india-rubber wonder' after a 1910 reserve outing!

Apps: *FL 3.*

HOLMES, James Paul

b. Dublin, 11th November 1953

Career: St.John Bosco BC; pro Nov 1970 Coventry City; Mar 1977 Tottenham Hotspur; Mar 1981 Vancouver Whitecaps; Oct 1982-trials-CITY; Feb 1983-trials-Brentford; Mar 1983 Torquay United; Nov 1983 Peterborough United; Dec 1985 Nuneaton Borough (p/mgr); 1987 Leicester United; 1987 Hitchin Town (p/mgr); Aug 1988 Northampton Town (asst.coach); 1989 Bedworth United (p/co-mgr).

City debut v Sheffield Wednesday (H) 30.10.82

> The Republic of Ireland's youngest-ever international (at 17 years, 200 days), skilful full-back Jimmy showed precocious class at Highfield Road, playing in the 1970 Youth Cup Final and winning the first of thirty full caps before making his League bow against Leicester in December 1971; then going on to attract numerous bids until Gordon Milne accepted a six-figure fee from struggling Spurs. Jimmy couldn't stop the White Hart Lane side going down at the end of his first term, but became a stalwart of the promotion campaign which followed in 1978. A horrific leg-break suffered in an international in Bulgaria threatened to bring Jimmy's career to a premature end, but after almost two years out of the game he returned to the fray alongside Johnny Giles in Canada. Milne gave his former charge a brief non-contract trial with City, when the Second Division pace seemed too much for him, though Jimmy thereafter managed a total of 78 more League games as he gradually accomplished a transition to coaching and non-league managerial roles; and he received a Dublin testimonial game from the Republic's FA in August 1985. His final backroom club affiliation was with Coventry Sporting in the early 90s, and he then joined the West Midlands Police.

Apps: *FL 2.*

HOOPER, Harold

b. Aston, Birmingham, 18th August 1900
d. Leicester, 4th February 1963

Career: Brierley Hill Alliance; May 1921 Southampton; May 1924 CITY; Aug 1926 Queens Park Rangers.

City debut v Manchester United (A) 30.8.24

> A dour, resolute defender who arrived in an exchange deal which saw Fred Price and Dennis Jones departing for The Dell, Harry had been a fringe first-teamer when the Saints took the Division Three (South) championship in 1922, and maintained stand-in status for the two years following. He won his personal duel with Reg Osborne for the City left-back berth for the larger part of the 1925 promotion season, but couldn't keep his rival out for long once the ensuing First Division campaign got under way. Harry – who was a cousin of England centre-half Charlie Roberts – was restricted to Southern Section fare only during his season with QPR: his new club having forgotten to enter the FA Cup for 1926/7! He died in the Towers Hospital, and when the authorities' press appeal for relatives to come forward failed, Leicester City bore the costs of his funeral.

Apps: *FL 33; FAC 6.*

HOOPER, Michael Dudley

b. Bristol, 10th February 1964

Career: Mangotsfield United; Nov 1983 Bristol City; Feb 1985 Wrexham; Oct 1985 Liverpool; Sept 1990-loan-CITY; Sept 1993 Newcastle United; Nov 1995-loan-Sunderland.

City debut v Sheffield Wednesday (H) 22.9.90

> Despite being beaten ten times in his first two City games, Mike soon joined the line of short-term loan signings (after Gary Charles and Kevin Campbell) to prompt the Filbert Street crowd into futile 'Sign him up' chants; and found his initial one-month stay being twice extended as he continued to impress behind a sieve-like Second Division defence. Having arrived in Leicester as part of a rare loan-exchange deal (with Carl Muggleton temporarily switching to Anfield), the red-haired 'keeper managed to temper City's embarrassments by keeping the score down substantially in a couple of virtual whitewashes, and also managed the first clean sheets of the near-disastrous 1990/1 League campaign. An agile shot-stopper, he also brought to his role the sort of outfield sweeper's vision and covering speed most often associated with his Liverpool mentor, Bruce Grobbelaar. As a teenager, Mike had played but once in each of the Associate Members Cup, Division Three and FA Cup for his hometown team before a loan move to the Racecourse was made permanent in July 1985; and his form in North Wales soon attracted the attention of new Anfield boss Kenny Dalglish. A Wembley substitute appearance in the 1986 Charity Shield marked his Liverpool bow, but only 30 League outings in Grobbelaar's stead had followed by the time of his Leicester stint. Mike was later stricken by injury shortly after winning a regular Reds selection, and with Newcastle generally played second string to one-time City trialist Pavel Srinicek. He substituted for the latter at Filbert Street after 85 minutes of City's first-ever Premiership fixture, and conceded City's first goal at that level by way of Julian Joachim's last-minute consolation strike. The former Swansea University student was freed by the Magpies in 1996, quit the game entirely on account of his back injuries, and took up teaching in Northumberland.

Mike Hooper

Apps: *FL 14; FMC 1.*

HORNER, Philip Matthew

b. Leeds, 10th November 1966

Career: app 1983/pro Nov 1984 CITY; Mar 1986-loan-Rotherham United; July 1988 Halifax Town; Sept 1990 Blackpool; Nov 1995-loan-Southport; cs 1996 Southport; July 1999 Lancaster City.

City debut v Sheffield Wednesday (H) 3.1.87 (sub)

> A tall reserve striker for over two seasons, capped at England Youth level and also used upfront while on loan at Millmoor, Phil was experimentally transformed into a central defender just before his emergency elevation to the first-team bench, and colly slotted into that position as sub for John O'Neill in City's 6-1 thrashing of the Owls. A couple of his subsequent senior run-outs proved, however, to be nightmarish affairs in defensive terms, and Phil failed to make David Pleat's first retained list in 1988. He initially took the No 3 shirt at The Shay, was also noted there as a sweeper, and moved to play alongside Paul Groves for the Seasiders. Blackpool were promoted from the basement via the 1992 Play-Offs, and Phil was back at Wembley six years later, when Southport were beaten 0-1 by Cheltenham in the FA Trophy Final.

Apps: *FL 7+3; FAC 0+1; LC 1.*

HOUGHAM, H.

Career: South Wigston Albion; Apr 1904 FOSSE; 1904 South Wigston Albion; South Wigston Imperial.

Fosse debut v Bradford City (H) 16.4.04

> A local trialist who played at outside-left in Fosse's final two defeats of the dismal 1903/4 re-election campaign, but failed to break through again to senior level after briefly being retained for the following season. Another left-winger with the same name and initial - possibly his son - moved from South Wigston Imperial to Hinckley United in September 1927.

Apps: *FL 2.*

HOUGHTON, William Gascoigne

b. Hemsworth, Yorks, 20th February 1939

Career: Aug 1957 Barnsley; July 1964 Watford; June 1966 Ipswich Town; July 1969 CITY; Jan 1970 Rotherham United (- 1974).

City debut v Birmingham City (H) 9.8.69

> A vastly experienced defender, Billy had the shortest spell of his 507-game League career at Filbert Street, joining Frank O'Farrell's Second Division team as a motorway commuter after moving house from Ipswich back to his native Barnsley, and briefly holding down the left-back berth as City tried moving David Nish into a more advanced role. He had been a schoolboy prodigy and an England Youth international left-half while at Oakwell, and in 1968 had won a Second Division championship medal as a Portman Road No 3, but he was hard pressed with City to keep out Alan Woollett, and a small fee took him back to Yorkshire to play as well as reside. When Billy turned out for Rotherham's newly-relegated side in 1973/4, he completed his 'set' of having played in all four divisions.

Apps: *FL 6+1; LC 3.*

HOULT, Russell

b. Ashby de la Zouch, Leics, 22nd November 1972

Career: Thringstone; Shepshed Amateurs; YT July 1989/pro Mar 1991 CITY; Aug 1991-loan-Lincoln City; Dec 1991-loan-Cheltenham Town; Mar 1992-loan-Blackpool; July 1993-loan-Kettering Town; Nov 1993-loan-Bolton Wanderers; Aug 1994-loan-Lincoln City; Feb 1995-loan-Derby County; July 1995 Derby County; Jan 2000 Portsmouth; Jan 2001 West Bromwich Albion.

City debut v Wolverhampton Wanderers (H) 13.9.92

> City's Young Player of the Year in 1991, Russell burst into the limelight on the occasion of City's first-ever League game to be televised live. Carl Muggleton slipped a disc during the warm-up kick-in, and Russell had to be summoned from the stand for an emergency debut between the sticks. Immediately (owing to his non-standard pre-match meal) dubbed 'The Hot Dog Kid', he went on to perform immaculately against Wolves; keeping a clean sheet and earning the Man of the Match plaudits. He conceded only one goal in his first five League starts, then was rested after the 1-7 League Cup massacre at Hillsborough; yet he soon returned with confidence intact, and earned particular admiration for sound handling and his extensive reach. Nonetheless, his 14 games of 1992/3 would be his only senior experience with Leicester, even if several of the clubs he was loaned to would happily have signed him. He conceded only one penalty goal in eight Conference games at Kettering before breaking a bone in his hand; and the reputation he built during his temporary Derby stint under Roy McFarland was such to tempt incoming Rams boss Jim Smith to make Russell his first capture at £200,000. He was first choice in the Baseball Ground side promoted to the Premiership in 1996, but after the 1997 move to Pride Park suffered intense competition from Mart Poom, and a Pompey loan became a permanent move in March 2000. A further shift saw Russell and Phil Gilchrist assist West Brom to the Division One Play-Offs in 2001.

Apps: *FL 10; LC 3; AIC 1.*

HOWE, Herbert Alexander

b. Rugby, Warks, 1st April 1916
d. Rugby, 14th June 1972

Career: Braunston; Rugby Town; Aug 1935-trials-CITY; Aug 1935 Market Harborough Town; Sept 1935 Leicester Nomads; trials Oct 1936/pro Feb 1937 CITY; July 1947 Notts County; 1949 Rugby Town (p/coach); Aug 1953 Hinckley Athletic (p/mgr from Sept 1954).

City debut v Wolverhampton Wanderers (H) 4.5.39

> First noted locally as an inside-left, and then forced to mark time in WW2 regional football between his senior City debut at left-half and his immediate postwar stint at left-back, Bert was effectively robbed of the opportunity to fulfil his evident potential at Filbert Street; and pretty much acknowledged as much himself when insisting on part-timer status – mixing his football with a draughtsman's post at BTH in Rugby. Yet he had compiled a wartime appearance total for City bettered only by Willie Frame and Sep Smith, and had also managed eleven guest outings for Northampton in that time. Twice in 1946/7, Bert (or 'Dapper', as he was nicknamed) had to take over the injured Joe Calvert's goalkeeping jersey, but such gameness was no barrier to Johnny Duncan allowing him to drop into the Third Division. Ironically the larger part of his 52-game spell at Meadow Lane was played out before huge crowds and in the full glare of media attention, attracted by the presence of his new teammate Tommy Lawton. A broken leg suffered at Swindon brought an end to his Magpie days, but first Rugby and then Hinckley profited from his veteran influence. With the latter, he faced City's reserves in both the 1955 and 1956 County Challenge Cup Finals; took the trainer's role the following term; and was caretaker manager in early 1959.

Apps: *FL 28; FAC 3; WW2 209.*
Goals: *WW2 7.*

HOWES, Arthur

b. Leicester, ca 1876

Career: Leicester Waverley; Sept 1896 FOSSE; Mar 1898-trials-Lincoln City; Mar 1898 Reading; Sept 1898 FOSSE; cs 1899 Brighton United; cs 1900 Dundee; cs 1902 Brighton & Hove Albion; Nov 1904 Queens Park Rangers.

Fosse debut v Blackpool (A) 27.2.1897

> An alert and agile goalkeeper who successively understudied Jimmy Thraves and Charlie Saer, Arthur was released by Fosse in February 1898, but returned within months when it looked as if their interim illicit acquisitions, Billy Rowley and Godfrey Beardsley, might be barred from playing. He would only turn out thrice afterwards, but his final game was in the home victory over Barnsley in January 1899 which put the club on top of the Second Division table for the first time ever (though they were to fall away to 3rd by season's end). Arthur's next club were wound up before completing their Southern League fixtures, and he became one of the substantial number of English players (Herbert Dainty and Charles Webb amongst them) to assist Dundee – a club seemingly intent on single-handedly reversing the usual cross-border flow of football talent around the turn of the century. The lure of the South Coast sea air then exerted itself for a second time (with Brighton's second attempt at a professional club now esconced at the Goldstone Ground), before Arthur took cap and gloves to QPR's imposing-sounding home of the time: the Agricultural Society Grounds, Park Royal. Arthur was subsequently heard of only for a bit of early football entrepreneurism back in Leicester: the *Mercury* reported in 1908 that he had 'rented a piece of ground opposite the stand entrance for the storage of cycles during the coming season'.

Apps: *FL 15; FAC 1.*

HUBBARD, Archibald

b. Leicester, 7th February 1883
d. Gloucester, 24th September 1967

Career: South Wigston Albion; Oct 1901 Humberstone Victoria; cs 1902 Leicester Imperial; cs 1903 St Andrews; trials Apr 1904/pro Aug 1904 FOSSE; May 1907 Fulham; Jan 1908 Watford; May 1909 Norwich City; Nov 1910 Grimsby Town; Aug 1912 Lincoln City; Sept 1913 Leicester Imperial.

Fosse debut v Gresley Rovers (H) FAC 12.11.04 (scored twice)

> Invariably but inexplicably known as 'Ranji' throughout his Fosse career, Archie was switched regularly around the central attacking positions before settling into the centre-forward berth he was to occupy until the advent of the apparently unrelated Shirley Hubbard. A crowd favourite for his dashing enthusiasm, he top-scored in 1906, and figured regularly in the side which managed a third-place finish a year later. Archie went on to feature in Fulham's first-ever League line-up (alongside ex-Fossil Arthur Collins and Fossils-to-be Billy Goldie and Fred Threlfall); led the goal charts at Southern League Watford in 1909; assisted Grimsby to the championship of the Midland League in 1911; again took the highest-scorer laurels for the Mariners on their re-admission to the Second Division; and finally assisted Lincoln's re-integration to League football after they, too, had spent a season outside that sphere.

Apps: *FL 58; FAC 2.*
Goals: *FL 21; FAC 2.*

HUBBARD, Shirley

b. Leicester, 18th February 1885
d. Houghton-on-the-Hill, Leics, 22nd February 1963

Career: St.Andrews; Army football (1903 17th Regimental District); Leicester Imperial; Feb 1907 FOSSE; May 1913 Darlington; 1914 South Shields; cs 1919 CITY; cs 1920 Ashby Town (p/coach).

Fosse debut v Burton United (A) 29.3.07

> Still a serving soldier in the Leicestershire Regiment when he made his League bow with Fosse in place of namesake Archie, Shirley was bought out of the Army by the club during the following summer. His experience in military football had seen him playing in each of the Leicestershire and Kent Leagues as well as, most recently, at Poona, Bombay and Madras; but his transition to the exigencies of Second Division centre-forward play was near-immediate. The two Hubbards, who also shared two Leicester junior clubs but apparently no close kinship, played together only once (when both scored against Lincoln in the final fixture of 1906/7); and Archie was but the first of several rivals Shirley would see off over the next six years, as he successively sampled promotion, relegation and Division Two struggle from the sharp end. On Christmas Day 1912, while his benefit match (a reserve fixture against Long Eaton St Helens) was taking place at Filbert Street, Shirley was being led off the Clapton Orient pitch with a broken collarbone; characteristically, though, he was back in senior action before the season was out. He joined Donnelly, Turner and Trueman at Darlington, but switched clubs partway through 1913/14, going on to score 12 times in only eight games to help South Shields to the North Eastern League championship. If the Fosse directorate had been content to let him leave in 1913, however, they were glad to receive the assistance of Sergeant Hubbard (back in WW1 khaki from November 1914) for a few wartime games – he also guested once for Port Vale – and Shirley's five goals in 1918/19 were enough to earn him a veteran's contract for Leicester City's inaugural League season, when he capped his brief comeback with a goal in the new club's first away win. He skippered Ashby from the centre-half position until retirement in 1922, and was then lost to the game for some time. In 1930, he was described as a dyer's labourer when involved as the victim of a stabbing incident, but within months had been taken on as trainer to Loughborough Corinthians, where his old Fosse and South Shields teammate Ben Hall was manager. Shirley penned a *Sports Mercury* column on local football in 1931 and, in December 1932, when Ernest Nixon was ill, took charge of City's reserves. He returned to the club again in 1938 as trainer to the Colts, but was a part-time scout for Birmingham City just after WW2. Shirley was the only member of the 1908 promotion side able to attend City's 1954 Division Two championship celebration at the Bell Hotel.

Apps: *FL 140; FAC 14; WW1 17.*
Goals: *FL 36; FAC 3; WW1 5.*

HUFTON, Samuel

Career: Notts Mapperley; Ilkeston Town; 1891 FOSSE; 1892 Ilkeston Town.

Debut (competitive) v Small Heath (H) FAC 3.10.1891

> Fosse's centre-forward in the final game played at Mill Lane (the April 1891 friendly with beaten Cup Finalists Notts County), Sammy re-emerged as the hapless pivot in the 2-6 FA Cup exit at Aylestone Road (when Leicester fell to comparative 'giants' from the Football Alliance), then interchanged twixt forward and half-back lines as the club established itself both at Filbert Street and the foot of the Midland League table. He was later a fairly regular scorer for Ilkeston.

Apps: *FAC 1; ML 16.*
Goals: *ML 1.*

HUGHES, Archibald

b. Arthurlie, Renfrewshire, ca 1871

Career: Barrhead; Arthurlie; cs 1892 Middlesbrough Ironopolis; cs 1893 Bolton Wanderers ; Aug 1894 FOSSE; cs 1895 Glossop North End.

Fosse debut v Grimsby Town (A) 1.9.1894

> Preparing for their first tilt at League football, Fosse signed Archie to assume their 'playmaker' role and, according to the custom of the day, handed him either the centre-half or inside-forward berth from which to direct midfield operations. One of the quintet of ex-Nops at Leicester during 1894/5, he had helped the Middlesbrough club to the Northern League championship in 1893, and assisted First Division Bolton to the FA Cup Final a year later, only to spend all but the first five minutes of their defeat by Notts County as a limping passenger. His track record with Fosse was interrupted, however, for different reasons, as Archie twice found himself suspended by the committee for breaches of training discipline, and his services dispensed with at season's end.

Apps: *FL 18; FAC 3.*
Goals: *FL 2.*

HUGHES, Bernard

Career: Humberstone Victoria; Aug 1904 FOSSE; Leicester Nomads.

Fosse debut/only game v Hull City (A) 14.4.06

> Initially signed as an amateur right-back, but utilised at left-half when the reserves lost the 1905 County Cup Final to South Wigston Albion, Bernard gained a professional contract as cover for the latter position after impressing in the three trial matches of August 1905 (in the second of which he had to take over in goal). He got, though, only a single chance to deputise for William Morgan at senior level, in the above goalless draw. Regaining amateur status to play for the local Nomads, Bernard was still turning out occasionally for Fosse's second string as late as 1910, at which point his selection as emergency goalkeeper was said to mean he'd represented them in all eleven positions.

Apps: *FL 1.*

HUGHES, William

b. Coatbridge, Lanarkshire, 30th December 1948

Career: Coatbridge Jnrs; Dec 1965 Sunderland; Aug 1977 Derby County; Dec 1977 CITY; Sept 1979-loan-Carlisle United; Apr 1980 San Jose Earthquakes; July 1980 Enderby Town; Corby Town.

City debut v Middlesbrough (H) 26.12.77

> Despite totting up the years at Roker as a valuably versatile forward, Billy had his most modest achievements overshadowed for a long time by those of his brother, Celtic's John 'Yogi' Hughes; but eventually righted that particular imbalance when making a sizeable contribution to Sunderland's underdog FA Cup-winning side of 1973: scoring four times en route to Wembley, and taking the corner which led to the decisive goal in the Final. The strongly built striker, trading on a direct-running, hard-shooting, but often subtle style, completed eleven seasons on Wearside (including the relegation terms of 1970 and 1977, and the Second Division championship campaign of 1976), earning one cap as a Scotland substitute in 1975, plus a Roker testimonial game. He was just hitting his scoring stride at Derby when Frank McLintock tempted him to help dig City out of the relegation mire, but Billy understandably wasn't up to that particular task as his strike partners changed almost weekly; though he remained a comparatively grizzled-looking foil to Jock Wallace's youngsters during the following term. He played only once in the NASL, and failed to settle long in Midlands non-league football, moving into the pub trade in Derby before becoming clubhouse manager and steward at a Darlington golf club. Back in January 1973, Billy and John played one game together for Sunderland, when the latter sustained the injury which ended his career; while a third Hughes brother, Pat, played for St Mirren and Darlington.

Apps: *FL 36+1; FAC 1; LC 1.*
Goals: *FL 5.*

HUMPHREYS, Percy

b. Cambridge, 3rd December 1880
d. Stepney, London, 13th April 1959

Career: Cambridge St.Mary's; cs 1900 Queens Park Rangers; July 1901 Notts County; June 1907 FOSSE; Feb 1908 Chelsea; Dec 1909 Tottenham Hotspur; Oct 1911 FOSSE; cs 1912 Hartlepools United (p/mgr); Nov 1914 Norwich City.

Fosse debut v Leeds City (H) 7.9.07

'His dribbling is of the deceptive order'; 'his sudden dashes for goal are not unlike those meteoric spurts which characterise Bloomer's play'. Such testimonials helped elevate centre-forward Percy to both the Football League and full England sides of 1903 against their Scottish counterparts, partway through a six-year, 66-goal First Division spell for the Magpies. He then stepped down a level to join Fosse, and showed magnificent goalscoring class, making a whirlwind contribution of 19 goals in 26 starts to set the club fair on its way to a first-ever promotion. Fosse were overjoyed at his success, but less so when he was spirited away to Stamford Bridge. Percy had cost them £600 (double the previous club record fee), but Chelsea only had to pay £350 to return him to the top flight: for four months from New Year's Day 1908, the Football League operated a transfer ceiling at that amount, before such iniquities forced them to return to the 'free market'. His scoring ratio dropped a little with Chelsea, then perked up again with Spurs, but when Percy returned for a second Filbert Street stint, it was unfortunately to join a mediocre side which the veteran proved unable to lift. His departure into North Eastern League player-management also cost Fosse dear; as they failed to recoup a penny of the £500 they'd invested in Percy this time, despite keeping his League registration until November 1914. At the time war was declared, he was about to take up a three-year appointment as player/coach with a Swiss club, but immediately returned home to bid a three-game adieu to the senior game with Southern League Norwich. Postwar, however, he did make some impact on continental soccer: a press snippet of November 1921 reported his return from coaching in Italy. Percy's death was deemed a suicide.

Apps: *FL 40; FAC 4.*
Goals: *FL 21; FAC 4.*

HUTCHINS, Donald

b. Middlesbrough, 8th May 1948

Career: Stockton Juniors; Feb 1966 CITY; July 1969 Plymouth Argyle; July 1972 Blackburn Rovers; June 1974 Bradford City; 1981 Scarborough.

City debut v Burnley (A) 15.4.68

> A compact orthodox outside-left who had the thankless task of understudying both Len Glover and Mike Stringfellow, Don was given his breakthrough by Matt Gillies, but received only one opportunity to impress incoming boss Frank O'Farrell, who accepted £6,000 for him at the end of his first term in charge. Don's natural pace and exuberant skills came to the fore, however, in the Third Division at both Home Park and Ewood, and were recognised by his peers in 1976, when his form at Valley Parade won him a place in the PFA's Fourth Division team of the year.

Don Hutchins

He was a popular prompter of Bradford City's promotion in 1977, and remained with them after their instant relegation back to the basement, eventually claiming 52 of his aggregate 81 League and Cup goals came for the Bantams. On leaving football, Don became a sales manager for a paint company.

Apps: *FL 4.*

HYETT, James

Career: Stapleford Town; Jan 1905 FOSSE.

Fosse debut/only game v Liverpool (H) 28.1.05

> Without so much as a reserve outing before his Second Division bow in a 0-3 home defeat by the champions-to-be, centre-forward James faced the Reds' international stopper Alex Raisbeck and, according to the *Mercury*, was 'never really prominent'. He did claim four goals the following week from the reserve fixture with Coalville United, but disappeared from Filbert Street altogether after a month.

Apps: *FL 1.*

IGGLEDEN, Horatio

b. Hull, 17th March 1925

Career: am July 1941/pro Mar 1942 CITY; Dec 1948 Leeds United; July 1955 Exeter City; Aug 1956 Goole Town.

City debut (WW2) v Wolverhampton Wanderers (H) 4.10.41; (postwar) v Luton Town (A) 5.10.46

> A 16-year-old Hull dock worker when recruited by City and handed an early senior debut, Ray also guested once for Grimsby Town during 1941/2, and signed professional forms at Filbert Street on his 17th birthday before departing for Royal Marine service. A versatile forward who returned to make sporadic first-team appearances in four attacking positions, he was still looked upon as a fine goalscoring prospect when involved in the part-exchange deal which brought Ken Chisholm to Leicester. Ray's pace and shooting power brought him exactly 50 League and Cup goals at Elland Road, including a hat-trick against City in January 1954, by which time he was the regular inside-left partner to the great John Charles.

Apps: *FL 11; WW2 6.*
Goals: *FL 2.*

IMPEY, Andrew Rodney

b. Hammersmith, London, 13th September 1971

Career: Yeading; June 1990 Queens Park Rangers; Sept 1997 West Ham United; Nov 1998 CITY.

City debut v Coventry City (A) 28.11.98

> A fleet winger, who in three years rose from Yeading's FA Vase-winning side to England's Under-21 line-up, Andrew added a touch of useful unpredictability to QPR's Premiership side of the early 90s, and attracted a fee of £1.3m when crossing London from west to east. The Hammers eased him into a wing-back role, but he was never quite assured of senior selection at Upton Park, even though manager Harry Redknapp remonstrated bitterly when Andrew was sold on to Martin O'Neill's City for £1.6m without his prior knowledge or approval. A fine debut performance raised Filbert Street expectations, but Andrew's integration into the City style proved a longer-term project. While there can be no doubting his class and touchline skills when on song – or the efficacy of his prompting, as seen when laying on an inch-perfect ball for Tony Cottee to convert at Newcastle in 1999/2000 – there have also been times when he has appeared ponderous and indecisive, with even his close control going awry. A move further forward in Peter Taylor's 4-4-2 system looked far better suited to his more flamboyant talents, and the upsurge in consistent form won him a contract extension before the end of 2000/1.

Apps *(to end 2000/1): PL 74+6; FAC 6+1; LC 5+2; UEFA 2.*
Goals: *PL 2.*

Andrew Impey

IZZET, Mustafa Kemal

b. Mile End, London, 31st October 1974

Career: YT/pro May 1993 Chelsea; Mar 1996 CITY.

City debut v Sheffield United (H) 30.3.96 (sub)

> Unblooded by Chelsea, and utterly unknown elsewhere at the time Martin O'Neill made him a deadline-day loanee, midfielder Muzzy took next to no time to make his mark as City's promotion drive took off steeply following the nadir of his debut day defeat. Slotting in alongside Neil Lennon and demonstrating some neat close control and nifty right-foot trickery, he earned an extension to his temporary contract, scored the goal at Watford that ensured Play-Off qualification, was brought down at Wembley for the equalising penalty against Crystal Palace, and was then signed permanently in July for a fee rising to £800,000 (plus a sell-on clause). Ever since, he has been a genuine jewel in City's proud, critic-confounding Premiership odyssey; matching a bubbly, buzzing enthusiasm to maturing talent as a quick-witted, attack-minded linkman, exhibiting occasional right-wing by-line magic, and increasing the frequency of his spectacular scoring strikes. Muzzy impressed in all three of the League Cup Finals of the past four years, uncomplainingly assumed front-running duties in emergencies, took over penalty responsibilities in 1999, became the first City man to win the Carling Player of the Month award (September 1999), and around that time scored in five successive

Muzzy Izzet

Premiership home games. In 1998 O'Neill was vocal in his surprise that no England call-up had come Muzzy's way, and the Londoner eventually tired of waiting for such a merited honour. He had previously been courted by Turkey (on account of his Turkish Cypriot paternity), and had shown interest until learning he'd have to undergo military service to qualify; but when that condition was removed, Muzzy took out Turkish citizenship in early 2000, and duly made his international debut against Sweden in the European Championship Finals (only to bow out after 58 minutes following a vicious foul by Sweden's Johan Mjällby). The departure of Neil Lennon thrust extra responsibility on Muzzy during 2000/1, but he remained the source (and likely cutting edge) of much of City's forward momentum until an injury suffered in the Wycombe Cup humiliation curtailed his season. His younger brother Kemal for some time fringed Charlton Athletic's first team, and has now made his League bow with Colchester United.

Apps *(to end 2000/1): FL/PL 168+2; FAC 12; LC 19+1; PO 3; UEFA 4.*
Goals: *FL/PL 28; FAC 4; LC 3; UEFA 1.*

JACKSON, Ronald

b. Crook, Co Durham, 15th October 1919
d. Althorpe, Lincs, 28th February 1980

Career: Sept 1945 Wrexham; Dec 1949 CITY; July 1955 Kettering Town; Aug 1957 Rugby Town.

City debut v Hull City (A) 24.12.49

> Norman Bullock's second signing (at a cost of £9,000), Ron was a left-back noted for his positional sense, speed in recovery and a remarkable heading ability for a man only 5ft 7ins tall. A games master at a Leicester school (he had been a science teacher in Wrexham, following his stationing there as a PT instructor), he twice broke his nose in action during his initial Filbert Street term. Ron appeared to be on his way out of the senior reckoning after a lengthy contract dispute in 1952, but returned to hold down his place as an ever-present in the 1954 Second Division championship campaign. The highlight of that particular season for Ron, though, was in the first game of the Cup quarter-final marathon against Preston, when he outplayed Tom Finney and still managed to score his only City goal: albeit a rather flukey free-kick from close to the half-way line! By the early 60s, Ron was manager of the Leicestershire Schools FA XI.

Apps: *FL 161; FAC 12.*
Goals: *FAC 1.*

JACKSON, William

b. Farnworth, Lancs, 5th July 1902
d. Blackpool, Oct qtr 1974

Career: Leyland; 1922 Altrincham; cs 1923 Darwen; May 1924 Sunderland; Sept 1925 Leeds United; May 1927 West Ham United; Feb 1928 Chelsea; Apr 1931 CITY; May 1932 Bristol Rovers; cs 1934 Cardiff City; Jan 1935 Watford; cs 1935 Chorley; Sept 1936 Netherfield.

City debut v Liverpool (H) 12.9.31

> Already inured to a degree of frustration in his stop-start career, two-footed winger Billy pretty much overdosed on it at Leicester. Chosen for an end-of-season debut at Birmingham only days after signing, he had to withdraw on the death of his father; breaking through to take an understudy's opportunity to replace Hughie Adcock at outside-right, he was injured on his debut; returning, he had his only City goal chalked off the record when the home game with Portsmouth in December 1931 was abandoned; and he then completed his senior Filbert Street career in a trio of defeats over Christmas and New Year, culminating in the 3-8 home defeat by Aston Villa which still remains the sole instance of such a scoreline in favour of the away team in League history. There was perhaps little wonder that a trivial dressing-room argument with 'keeper Jack Beby, before a City reserve game at Brentford, escalated into a fight for which Billy was fined £5 by the management! Previously, Billy had failed to win first-team selection at Roker, had fallen out of First Division favour at Leeds, had been jettisoned by West Ham after only two games, and had been regarded primarily as a reserve at Stamford Bridge as they returned to the top flight in 1930. After leaving City, he found a few more opportunities in Division Three (South), making a two-goal start at Eastville, and ending his League days with a quartet of Watford games alongside ex-City men Jim McLaren, Billy Findlay and Billy Lane. His brother Robert was a Bury reserve.

Apps: *FL 4.*

JAKEMAN, Leslie (Mick)

b. Nuneaton, Warks, 14th March 1930

Career: Atherstone Town; am June 1947 Derby County; cs 1949 Hinckley Athletic; May 1951 CITY; Feb 1955-trials-Coventry City; Mar 1955 Nuneaton Borough; 1955 Lockheed Leamington; Sept 1956 Hinckley Athletic; 1957 Nuneaton Borough.

City debut/only game v Burnley (A) 6.9.54

> Popularly known as Mick, this versatile wing-half or inside-forward caused quite a stir with his sole senior outing. Originally signing for City while stationed on RAF service in Essex, he returned from Egypt in March 1953 to take up a berth in the Filbert Street 'stiffs', and was unfortunate enough to break his leg that October. On recovery, however, he won a surprise First Division selection in the No 4 shirt for a 1-3 Turf Moor defeat (when he 'could not work up to the standard of mobility required'). Hard-up Hinckley at this point asked City for a fee for their former player and, finding their request denied, initiated an FA probe which resulted in a 15-guinea fine for Leicester, for having illegitimately signed Mick over three years earlier, and the cancellation of the player's registration. The luckless Mick then failed to win either a first-team selection or a contract at Highfield Road.

Apps: *FL 1.*

JAMES, Anthony Craig

b. Sheffield, 27th June 1967

Career: Sheffield FC; 1988 Gainsborough Trinity; Aug 1988 Lincoln City; Aug 1989 CITY; July 1994 Hereford United; Aug 1996 Plymouth Argyle.

City debut v Watford (A) 2.9.89 (sub)

> Though too much of his City career was a matter of injury-induced frustration, Tony will never be forgotten for his heroics of 1990/1, when his close-range conversion of a left-wing corner against Oxford United proved decisive in keeping a severely relegation-threatened City in Division Two, and essentially marked the upward turn the club's fortunes would take in the 90s. On that same joyous May day, he deservedly received the fans' Player of the Year award, though primarily for his defensive contributions. A 6ft 3in gentle giant, blessed with a telescopic tackle and a prodigious long throw, Tony had made a rapid rise from Sheffield amateur football, playing only three times for Gainsborough before joining Lincoln for £6,000 on their return to the League, and learning his centre-back trade in front of Mark Wallington. He cost City £150,000 when David Pleat swooped for him after the first game of 1989/90, and soon became an immensely popular addition to a hard-pressed back line, compensating for a lack of finesse with total enthusiastic commitment, and regularly creating havoc in opposing penalty areas either with his bustling presence or missile-like throw-ins. A double fracture of the leg during a home win over Wolves in October 1991 was the first of several injuries to mar Tony's progress after his golden goal, and despite a Wembley appearance in the 1992 Play-Off Final, he never managed a lengthy first-team run thereafter. He helped Hereford to the Division Three Play-Offs in 1996, but suffered again at both Edgar Street and Home Park with injuries that ended his career at the age of 30. Tony's cousin Scott James was a youth trainee with City for two years from 1993.

Apps: *FL 79+28; FAC 2; LC 6; FMC 0+1; PO 3.*
Goals: *FL 10; FAC 1.*

JAMES, Robert Mark

b. Gorseinon, West Glamorgan, 23rd March 1957
d. Llanelli, Dyfed, 18th February 1998

Career: trials - Cardiff City & Arsenal; app Mar 1973/pro Apr 1974 Swansea City; July 1983 Stoke City; Oct 1984 Queens Park Rangers; June 1987 CITY; Jan 1988 Swansea City; Aug 1990 Bradford City; Aug 1992 Cardiff City; Oct 1993 Merthyr Tydfil (p/mgr); Sept 1994 Barry Town; Aug 1996 Weston-Super-Mare; cs 1997 Llanelli (p/mgr).

City debut v Shrewsbury Town (H) 15.8.87

> Only Peter Shilton, Tommy Hutchison, Tony Ford and Terry Paine have bettered the total of 782 League appearances which Robbie amassed across 22 seasons, yet his City stint barely registered on his record, and Leicester were the only one of his clubs whose score-sheet he did not grace. A 16-year-old apprentice when he made his Vetch Field debut, he went on to play in all four divisions in ascending order as the Swans rocketed upwards into the elite, knocking in 110 senior goals for them as he matured from a hefty front-runner into a powerful Welsh international midfielder. On the Swans' relegation, he remained in Division One for another four seasons, as sizeable fees took him via Stoke to QPR, and appeared for the latter in the League Cup Final of 1986. He also switched to a full-back slot at Loftus Road, but

there reminded City of his long-range shooting prowess during their 1987 FA Cup exit. Bryan Hamilton saw in Robbie the sort of experienced campaigner who could help settle a predominantly youthful Second Division defence, but many of his efforts were negated by a lack of pace, and some of the vigour seemed to leave his game after Wales were eliminated from the European Championships. A couple of lack-lustre performances in front of new boss David Pleat resulted in a rapid departure for Robbie, but he immediately assumed the captaincy back at his beloved Swansea, leading them once more to promotion from Division Four via the 1988 Play-Offs, and scoring in their Welsh Cup Final win of 1989. He missed only three League games in two seasons at Valley Parade, then with Cardiff celebrated both the 1993 Third Division championship and another Welsh Cup winner's medal – his fifth! Robbie's move to Merthyr prompted the first instance of the FA of Wales convening a transfer tribunal to settle the £10,000 fee, and he remained in non-league circles until his premature death, when he collapsed and died on the pitch while playing for Llanelli against Porthcawl. A year later, Brains Brewery renamed one of their Llanelli pubs as 'The Robbie James' in honour of the 47 times capped stalwart.

***Apps:** FL 21+2; LC 4; FMC 1.*

JARVIE, John

b. Old Monkland, Lanarkshire, 19th October 1900
d. Leicester, 30th January 1985

Career: Bellshill Athletic; June 1923 Third Lanark; Aug 1925 CITY; Oct 1926 Portsmouth; Mar 1928 Southend United; Aug 1929-trials-Watford; Aug 1929 Norwich City; Aug 1930 Chester; Aug 1931 Shrewsbury Town.

City debut v Manchester United (A) 16.9.25

> Joining newly-promoted City on Third Lanark's relegation from the Scottish top flight, John impressed City as a likely goalkeeping deputy to Albert Godderidge, and in fact got an early first-team run as the side started its Division One campaign rather shakily. Notable agility and clean handling partly compensated for his lack of height, but John was unable to stem a rising goal-deficit column, and was edged out defintively by the arrival at Filbert Street of his experienced international compatriot, Kenny Campbell. John became an emergency signing for promotion-bound Pompey, arriving at Fratton 15 minutes before his debut. A week later he conceded seven Middlesbrough goals and, on his sole First Division outing for them in the next term, eight at Liverpool. A lot of his time at Southend was also spent in reserve, but he was an ever-present for Norwich before leaving them for non-league fare. John assisted Chester to runners-up spot in the Cheshire County League and took a Cheshire Senior Cup-winner's medal, but he also sustained a broken leg there; while broken ribs suffered in Shrewsbury's Birmingham League cause convinced him to retire from the game. Between 1935 and 1965, John was employed as a refuse collector at the Jarvis Street depot of the Leicester City Cleansing Department.

***Apps:** FL 5.*

JAYES, Brian

b. Leicester, 13th December 1932
d. Leicester, 12th January 1978

Career: am/pro July 1954 CITY; July 1956 Mansfield Town; July 1960 Ramsgate; Wisbech Town; cs 1963 Rugby Town; Humberstone United; Retail Markets FC.

City debut v Nottingham Forest (A) 31.8.55

> Returning from Army service in Singapore in November 1953, Brian took up his amateur contract at Filbert Street, and then signed pro on the same day as his Argyle Street neighbour, Ken Mellor. Bad timing rather afflicted the right half on his first-team breakthrough, though. The injury crisis that offered him a Second Division bow was in fact quite widespread, and a depleted City side shipped 15 goals in the three away defeats in which he played near the beginning of 1955/6. Brian subsequently became a regular at Field Mill, however, totalling 115 League games despite breaking his leg in November 1958. Sadly, he collapsed and died while playing for Retail Markets in the Leicester Thursday League at the age of 45.

***Apps:** FL 3.*

JAYES, Carl Geoffrey

b. Leicester, 15th March 1954

Career: app Mar 1969/pro July 1971 CITY; Aug 1973-loan-Peterborough United; Nov 1977 Northampton Town; cs 1980 AP Leamington.

City debut v Orient (H) FAC 5.2.72

> Capped seven times for England schoolboys, and an occasional City reserve-team goalkeeper while still at school, Carl looked set to eventually follow Peter Shilton's route to the top. His unexpected debut was a nightmare, however, as City found themselves in the position of felled giants at the Fourth Round stage of the Cup, with Carl dropping an innocuous ball into the net for Orient's second goal. He waited patiently for two-and-a-half years for another chance, briefly but efficiently deputising for Mark Wallington in the First Division just prior to that keeper embarking on his record marathon run of consecutive appearances. Carl was pretty much a regular for the Cobblers until accompanying John Farrington to Leamington, and after a year there hung up his boots to become a policeman.

***Apps:** FL 5; FAC 1.*

JELLY, Horace Edward

b. Leicester, 28th August 1921
d. Leicester, 16th January 2000

Career: Newarke Athletic; Belgrave United; Navy football; am Jan 1944/pro May 1946 CITY; Aug 1951 Plymouth Argyle.

City debut v Southampton (A) 26.5.47

> A teenage right-winger who converted to full-back while on wartime Navy service, Ted first signed for City while on leave and became a professional when demobbed. Very much a reserve for the first two postwar seasons, he timed his New Year's Day re-entry perfectly in 1949, holding his place in the No 2 shirt throughout the glory run to Wembley after taking over from the injured Willie Frame. A regular in the following campaign, Ted lost out when City signed Arthur Lever, and spent an infuriatingly unlucky time at Plymouth: waiting eighteen months for his first-team debut as the Pilgrims won promotion to Division Two, then having his 13-game record curtailed by a cartilage injury. Ted held an FA coaching badge, but when in 1954 he couldn't find a senior club with whom to exploit it, turned his energies to a thriving electrical and television business back in Leicester. A mooted playing comeback with Hinckley Athletic in March 1955 was stymied by registration problems. In the 90s, Ted had a part-time role leading guided tours of Filbert Street.

***Apps:** FL 56; FAC 9.*
***Goals:** FL 1.*

JOACHIM, Julian Kevin

b. Peterborough, 20th September 1974

Career: Boston Town; YT July 1991/pro Sept 1992 CITY; Feb 1996 Aston Villa; July 2001 Coventry City.

City debut v Barnsley (H) 3.10.92

> The brilliant 'Crown Jules' of the Brian Little era, whose youthful impact set a standard he has since struggled to maintain, Julian fully justified the hero-worship he initially received at Filbert Street with the sense of electrifying excitement he brought to City's attacking options. Signed professionally only two months into the second year of his trainee contract, having scored ten times in the first five youth games, plus the reserves' only goal to that date, he made an early senior bow, too, following injuries to David Lowe and Phil Gee. His first goal came three days later, in a League Cup tie in the city of his birth, and by the end of 1992/3 Julian's was a name noted nationally. For heading the list of his several spectacular strikes was the individualist goal against Barnsley in City's FA Cup exit which took the BBC's Goal of the Month award and was runner-up in the Goal of the Season rating; while further evidence of his scintillating pace, forceful strength and controlled direct dribbling skills had amassed almost weekly. Another solo rampage from the half-way line led to the goal advantage over Portsmouth which eventually saw City into the Play-Off Final at Wembley, where Julian led the frustrated fightback against Swindon. His progress was maintained in the following successful promotion campaign, when he came on as a sub and prompted the move which led to Steve Walsh's winning Wembley goal against Derby; and he had claimed both City's first Premiership goal (against Newcastle) and a sparkling double in the initial victory over Spurs before a serious (and initially mis-diagnosed) foot injury saw him sidelined for the bulk of the season. Rumours of off-field distractions arose at this point, as Julian strained to regain form following recovery, though he was beginning to look sharper just before what seemed a cut-price £1.5m move to Little's Villa. He found the going tough there, too, until finding a regular role, and a rich scoring seam, during 1998/9, when he was voted the Villains' Player of the Year. Nonetheless, his contribution to the Cup Final a year later was confined to a sub's cameo in the last dozen minutes; and even in 2000/1 he could never be quite sure of John Gregory's favour. Julian's representative career to some extent mirrors that at club level. He helped England to third place in the 1993 World Youth Championship, and to victory in the European Under-18 Championships a few months later, and won the first of his nine Under-21 caps in March 1994; it was these early honours, however, which ruled him frustratingly ineligible when called up to represent St Vincent in the World Cup qualifiers of April 2000.

Julian Joachim shadowed by Des Linton

***Apps:** FL/PL 77+22; FAC 4+1; LC 7+2; PO 4+2.*
***Goals:** FL/PL 25; FAC 1; LC 3; PO 2.*

JOBEY, George

b. Heddon, Northumberland, 1885
d. Chaddesden, Derby, 9th May 1962

Career: Morpeth Harriers; Apr 1906 Newcastle United; May 1913 Arsenal; June 1914 Bradford Park Avenue; Aug 1919 Hartlepools United; Sept 1919 CITY; May 1920 Northampton Town.

City debut v Wolverhampton Wanderers (A) 6.9.19

> A robust half-back and occasional centre-forward for his local League club (to whose Championship campaigns of 1907 and 1909 he contributed briefly), George took the latter position when earning a runners-up medal from the 1911 Cup Final, and when he made his Arsenal debut (against Fosse) in the first game at Highbury – an occasion he also marked by scoring the equaliser, by being carried off injured, and by making an undignified exit from the half-built stadium on a milk cart! He returned to the top flight at Bradford, then briefly assisted each of Park Avenue, Hamilton Academical and Arsenal while on leave from wartime service with the Royal Garrison Artillery. George signed for City on his demob, but actually turned out in the North Eastern League for Hartlepools a week before his Leicester debut. After three goalless games up front, he was switched by Peter Hodge to his old right-half berth, but his waning pace told against him, and he was not retained at the end of his first term. It was initially announced that George had assumed the player/manager role at Ebbw Vale, but he disappointed the Welshmen by electing to continue his active career for two seasons at Northampton. In 1922, he became manager of Wolves (and simultaneously held the licence of The Fox & Goose in nearby Penn), and from 1925 to 1941 was the boss at Derby County. Renowned there as a disciplinarian who bought big, George got the Rams promotion in 1926, and took them to ther Championship runners-up spot twice in the 30s, but he was eventually suspended by a joint FA/League commission for alleged complicity in the over-payment of bonuses and signing-on fees. When his ban was finally lifted, George took charge at Mansfield Town for 1952/3, but reportedly his heart was no longer in the game.

***Apps:** FL 30; FAC 4.*

JOBLING, Kevin Andrew

b. Sunderland, 1st January 1968

Career: app July 1984/pro Jan 1986 CITY; Feb 1988 Grimsby Town; Jan 1994-loan-Scunthorpe United; July 1998 Shrewsbury Town; cs 2000 Telford United (p/asst mgr).

City debut v Newcastle United (A) 4.4.87

> A tidy teenage midfielder who seemed to lack the necessary confidence to express himself with more flair on his intermittent senior opportunities with City, Kevin was one of several youngsters to be given a break by Bryan Hamilton and then quickly to be assessed as not meeting David Pleat's standards. Perhaps unfortunately, Kevin reserved his most forceful display for the Simod Cup tie against Carlton at Selhurst Park in 1987/8, when his match-winning two-goal performance was watched by hardly more spectators than he was used to playing before in City's reserves. It was Bobby Roberts who snapped up his signature in part-exchange when City moved for Phil Turner, but Kevin couldn't keep Grimsby from slipping into Division Four at season's end. He did, however, assist them to successive promotions in 1990 and 1991, from a nominal left-back berth; suffered relegation again in 1997; then, during their further promotion campaign of 1997/8, claimed the equaliser against City which led to League Cup collapse, and appeared as Wembley sub in the Mariners' Associate Members Cup victory. In May 1999, a year after Kevin moved to Gay Meadow, having aggregated 331 senior games at Blundell Park, Grimsby met City in a belated testimonial game for him.

***Apps:** FL 4+5; FAC 0+1; FMC 3.*
***Goals:** FMC 2.*

JOHNSON, Edward A.

b. Leicester

Career: ca 1886 FOSSE; 1892 Leicester YMCA.

Fosse debut (competitive) v Burton Wanderers (H) FAC 4.10.1890

> One of the four sons of Fosse treasurer and benefactor Joseph Johnson who played for the club as amateurs in its pioneering days, Teddy was the only one to last into the era of official competitive football and, with Harry Webb, one of only two Fossils to play in the inaugural fixtures at both Mill Lane and Filbert Street. The inside-left in Fosse's first two FA Cup defeats, he was also a regular in the initial Midland League season, but found the demands of the club's new, increasingly professionalised station a little too much for him. As a club committee man, he occasionally acted as linesman in Fosse's early Football League fixtures, before neutrals were employed for the role. By the mid-20s, he had his own shoe manufacturing firm, EA Johnson & Co of Ash Street, Leicester. Of the other Johnsons, William had been the club's first captain in 1884, Hilton had been a two-goal scorer in the first fixture, and Joseph junior had also been a stalwart.

***Apps:** FAC 2; ML 18.*
***Goals:** ML 1.*

JOHNSON, James

b. Nottingham

Career: Notts St James; 1886 FOSSE; 1892 Leicester YMCA.

Fosse debut (competitive) v Burton Wanderers (H) FAC 4.10.1890

> Previously erroneously identified as another of the Fosse's Johnson brothers, Jimmy was an 'outsider' who nonetheless took over the club captaincy in 1889, led his men into their first FA Cup foray (played at Mill Lane), and was also involved in the first two County Cup-winning sides. He was thus the first Fossil to raise a trophy of any description following the 4-0 replay win over Coalville at Loughborough in April 1890. He was still living on the Narborough Road in the mid-30s.

***Apps:** FAC 1.*

JOHNSON, Robert Simon

b. Bedford, 22nd February 1962

Career: Bedford Town; app/pro 1980 Luton Town; Aug 1983-loan-Lincoln City; Aug 1989 CITY; Aug 1991 Barnet; Nov 1991 Hitchin Town; cs 1994 Bedford Town; 1997 Baldock Town.

City debut v Hull City (A) 19.8.89

> A junior full-back under David Pleat at Luton, Rob made his League bow while on loan at Lincoln (filling in for Worcestershire cricketer Phil Neale), but then had his senior development back at Kenilworth Road interrupted by a serious knee injury. One of his subsequent stints as a Hatters regular

encompassed a starring role in their 1988 League Cup Final win over Arsenal, though Rob was being regarded primarily as a back-up squad player when reunited with his former manager at Leicester in the eve-of-season part-exchange deal which took Mick Kennedy down the M1. Such was to become his lot at Filbert Street, too, after early experience on both flanks of City's rather porous Second Division defence had left him looking a little rattled. Rob failed to impress in a handful of midfield outings, either; though a fortnight after being freed by Brian Little he made a last claim to fame as a member of Barnet's first-ever League line-up. He renewed acquaintance with Ricky Hill for one term at Hitchin.

Apps: *FL 19+6; LC 1; FMC 1.*

JOHNSTON, James C.

b. Aberdeen, 12th April 1923

Career: Peterhead; Feb 1947 CITY; May 1950 Reading; Mar 1953 Swindon Town; June 1955 Merthyr Tydfil (p/mgr); July 1956 Rugby Town.

City debut v Brentford (A) 15.9.48

> A wiry, tough-tackling left-half signed by Johnny Duncan from the Highland League after trials, Jimmy found his first-team breakthrough delayed by a niggling foot injury, and was then edged out of the Wembley reckoning by Johnny King's consistency. The pair vied for the senior No 6 shirt throughout the following 1949/50 season, but Norman Bullock allowed Ted Drake to take Jimmy to Elm Park, where he became a defensive fixture for three seasons. His 194 Division Three (South) outings for Reading and Swindon remained (as had his City stint) goalless. Jimmy retired from the playing ranks in 1957, and took the trainer/coach role at Enderby Town.

Apps: *FL 35; FAC 1.*

JONES, David Owen

b. Cardiff, 28th October 1910
d. Oadby, Leics, 20th May 1971

Career: Ely United; 1929 Ebbw Vale; 1929-trials-Charlton Athletic; cs 1930 Millwall; Aug 1931 Clapton Orient; May 1933 CITY; Oct 1947 Mansfield Town; July 1949 Hinckley Athletic (p/mgr).

City debut v Aston Villa (A) 26.8.33

> A bargain buy from penurious Orient at only £200, and initially signed to partner Adam Black, Dai was an outstanding full-back who soon walked into the Welsh international side, and won a total of seven caps. An ever-present in the 1937 Second Division championship campaign, he went on to play throughout the war years for City, Notts County, West Ham, Mansfield and Wolves, and was still a Filbert Street regular for the first postwar season, in which he notched the opening goal (with a lobbed free-kick that almost apologetically entered the West Ham net in the third fixture). Almost 37 years old when he moved to Field Mill, Dai still stamped his authoritative class on another 74 League games before dropping down to Birmingham Combination level; and indeed held the record of being the Stags' oldest player until Tony Ford assumed that status in the late 90s. Rather redundantly, Dai was banned from football some three years after stopping playing for Hinckley, as a court case had brought to light his receipt of an illegal £150 signing-on fee from Mansfield. By that stage he was a partner in the local firm of Day & Jones (Leather Factors), and was still working as a shoe-sales executive at the time of his death. A sawyer at the time he played for Ebbw Vale, Dai had joined his brother Vincent at Millwall, but had had to wait until his move to Orient for a League blooding. When Dai married in Leicester in May 1936, he had to call up the club's assistant secretary George Smith to act as a stand-in best man, as his fellow Welsh international Freddie Warren, due to do the honours, was that very day transferred from Middlesbrough to Hearts.

Apps: *FL 226; FAC 12; WW2 54.*
Goals: *FL 4; WW2 2.*

JONES, Dennis

b. Bolsover, Derbyshire, 14th May 1894
d. Bolsover, 12th December 1961

Career: cs 1913 Shirebrook; June 1921 CITY; May 1924 Southampton; June 1925 Mansfield Town; Aug 1926 Shirebrook; Aug 1927 Sutton Town; Aug 1928 Wombwell.

City debut v Barnsley (H) 5.11.21

> A centre-half for his local Central Alliance club, Dennis made the bulk of his City appearances on the right of the middle line, deposing the veteran Teddy King and holding the position until Billy Newton arrived, then going south as part of the deal which brought Harry Hooper to Filbert Street. He had only seven Second Division outings for the Saints, though, before comencing a ramble round the Midland League with a season at runners-up Mansfield. Dennis ran a Bolsover newsagents store before the war, and acted as an insurance agent later, but remained in the football world as a scout for both City and the Stags, whose assistant trainer he became from 1949 to 1953.

Apps: *FL 64; FAC 3.*
Goals: *FL 2.*

JONES, Matthew Graham

b. Llanelli, 1st September 1980

Career: YT/pro Sept 1997 Leeds United; Dec 2000 CITY.

City debut v Charlton Athletic (H) 16.12.2000

> Quite possibly unaware at first of the magnitude of the task he was taking on with City – that of effectively replacing Neil Lennon at the hub of the midfield engine-room – Matthew had a somewhat unsteady start to his City career, with suspension and injury cutting across his progress after a move from Elland Road valued at an initial £3m. Immediately revealing elements of a functionally tidy short-passing game and a willingness to dig in, he has nonetheless yet quite to replicate the perpetual-motion aspect of his predecessor's style, and may need to work on his stamina for the necessarily non-stop shuttle-work either side of the halfway line. It was perhaps telling that when the 'Lennon' pressure was off, Matthew received fine notices for his work with Wales; and time is very much on his side, especially if he can form a balanced unit with Robbie Savage for both club and country. A Youth Cup winner with Leeds in 1997, he made their first team during 1998/9, but remained essentially a fringe player both in domestic and European football until David O'Leary and Peter Taylor agreed on his transfer.

Apps *(to end 2000/1): PL 10+1; FAC 3.*

JONES, Richard

b. Wales, ca 1875

Career: Hanley Swifts; Jan 1896 South Shore; May 1897 FOSSE; Aug 1901 Burton United; Sept 1902 Royston United; 1904 Leeds City.

Fosse debut v Luton Town (H) 4.9.1897

> For years football record books (including, unfortunately, the first version of this one) conflated the personal details and careers of two separate Welsh international players: the Wrexham-born, Everton and Manchester City defender Robert Samuel Jones, and Fosse's Dick Jones. Thanks to the excellent sleuthing of Welsh historian Ian Garland, we can now at least identify the Fossil capped for Wales against Scotland in March 1898 (alongside clubmate Alfred Watkins) by his given name, though we are still unable to place the birth credentials of a man thereafter raised in the Staffordshire area. Dick had well earned his country's recognition with some stalwart Second Division displays at left-half; and when Fosse just missed out on promotion a year later, he was absent only once from a steadfast defence. He had disciplinary problems at Burton (earning a year-long club suspension for some unspecified misdemeanour), and then reappeared in junior football in Yorkshire. But later, when the newly-formed Leeds City embarked on a series of high-class friendlies as a means of angling for League election, the now-veteran Dick was in their side which faced Fosse at Elland Road. Back in September 1898, Dick had suffered one of the oddest injuries ever received by a Leicester player: being hurt by an exploding ginger beer bottle in the dressing room!

Apps: *FL 104; FAC 9.*
Goals: *FL 1.*

JONES, Robert

b. Coventry, 17th November 1964

Career: app June 1981 Manchester City; Sept 1982 CITY; Aug 1986 Walsall; cs 1987 Kidderminster Harriers; Nov 1989 Burton Albion; July 1991 VS Rugby; Oct 1991 Burton Albion; Aug 1993 Ravenstone.

City debut v Oldham Athletic (A) 7.5.83 (scored once)

> An England schoolboy international who failed to win a contract at Maine Road, Robbie then took advantage of parental links to become the possessor of Welsh youth caps shortly after arriving at Filbert Street as a professional. He made a stunning impact when standing in for Gary Lineker in the crucial promotion tussle at Boundary Park, scoring the opener as City grabbed an invaluable win. When he next scored to help City to their belated opening point in the First Division during the next term (against Stoke in the seventh fixture), a rosy future looked assured for the young striker; but despite his close control, willing running and impressive reserve-team scoring ratio, Robbie's diminutive stature eventually counted against him at the highest level, and he was freed by Gordon Milne in 1986. He got few chances as a Saddler, but appeared for Kidderminster in the 1989 Welsh Cup Final (lost 0-5 to a Robbie James-led Swansea) before moving to Burton jointly with former City reserve Jon Pearson in the Brewers' then-record purchase deal.

Apps: *FL 12+3; LC 2.*
Goals: *FL 3.*

JOPLING, Joseph

b. South Shields, 21st April 1951

Career: Horton Westhoe; trials-Sunderland; Aug 1969 Aldershot; Sept 1970 CITY; Jan 1974-loan-Torquay United; Mar 1974 Aldershot (- 1984).

City debut v Sunderland (H) 10.10.70

> A teenage regular in his first term with the Shots, full-back Joe was regarded by Frank O'Farrell as very much an investment for the future when he arrived in a deal which sent a £30,000 cheque plus Murray Brodie and Jimmy Burt south. He made an early bow in place of David Nish, but got minimal opportunity to impress Jimmy Bloomfield over the next three seasons, and eventually returned to Aldershot to stay. By the time Joe retired, he had proved his all-round defensive versatility at the Recreation Ground in an aggregate of 421 League and Cup games.

Apps: *FL 2+1.*

KALAC, Zeljko

b. Sydney, Australia, 16th December 1972

Career: Sydney United; July 1995 CITY; Aug 1996 Sydney United; cs 1998 Roda JC.

City debut v West Bromwich Albion (A) 5.11.95

> The protracted saga of giant goalkeeper Zeljko's registration tribulations utterly dwarfed his on-field contributions to English football, yet ironically his City appearances are now almost part of club folklore. The Australian international of Croatian descent had already interested both Norwich and Leeds before Mark McGhee expended £760,000 to make him Australia's most expensive export, shortly after the departures of both Russell Hoult and Gavin Ward. However, a work permit was denied on application in August, and not granted on appeal until October. The 6ft 7in 'Spider' then made his bow in the same Hawthorns game as Pontus Kåmark, looking a little nervy as West Brom fought back with two late goals from an 0-3 deficit. Days later, in the home League Cup game against Bolton, a veritable nightmare ensued, as City's battling performance was negated by three elementary errors by the 'keeper, who took the blame for all three goals. McGhee surprisingly bid for Zeljko after his shift to the Molineux managerial chair, and a £1.1m joint move with fellow-Aussie Steve Corica was announced in February 1996. Wolves then reneged on part of the deal, delaying their application for a new work permit, and a bewildered Zeljko returned to Filbert Street a month later (Wolves having eventually pay £250,000 damages to City for breach of contract). The twist in Zeljko's tale was to come however at the literal end of the season. With the Play-Off Final against Crystal Palace almost completing its extra-time period, and a penalty shoot-out looking imminent, Martin O'Neill decided to substitute Zeljko for Kevin Poole. Palace were seemingly distracted by this radical move, and Steve Claridge's last-gasp winner obviated the need for the 'keeper to be brought into any action at all. He returned to Australia when his work permit was predictably not renewed, and then went frustratingly through the red-tape rigmarole again a year later, when Terry Venables attempted to sign him for Portsmouth, having had charge of him in the interim with the Socceroos. Zeljko has subsequently played with success in the Dutch League in Kerkrade, and was in the Roda JC team which won the Dutch Cup in May 2000.

Apps: *FL 1; LC 1; PO 0+1.*

Zeljko Kalac

KÅMARK, Pontus Sven

b. Västerås, Sweden, 5th April 1969

Career: Skiljebo SK; 1985 Västerås SK; 1989 IFK Göteborg; Sept 1995 CITY; July 1999 AIK; Dec 2000 IFK Göteborg.

City debut v West Bromwich Albion (A) 5.11.95

> His surname invariably anglicised to Kaamark while with Leicester, Swedish defender Pontus suffered appalling ill-luck on his arrival at Filbert Street, but established himself as a focus of all-round respect before his departure. Signed, by Mark McGhee for £840,000, on the pitch prior to a home defeat by Southend, but not due to join up with his new club until IFK had completed their Allsvenskan title-winning campaign a month later, he was already the holder of 28 caps, had appeared four times for third-placed Sweden in the 1994 World Cup Finals, and had figured in four previous Championship wins for IFK, plus one Cup victory. His City debut came in the game at The Hawthorns in which McGhee's Leicester had probably their finest 45 minutes of flowing football, going 3-0 up at half-time before late jitters set in; and Pontus settled well at right-back, even if, in hitting the post with a spectacular long-range shot, he gave a distinctly false portent of likely attacking potency! Just days later, however, he was stretchered out of the home League Cup encounter with Bolton with ligament damage, and broke down in the first minute of his reserve comeback at Grimsby the following January, requiring major knee surgery. It was over a year later that Pontus rejoined Martin O'Neill's Premiership squad, and still injuries bit into his record, including a broken arm suffered in the FA Cup win over Norwich. His defensive coolness, reading of the game and neat distribution nonetheless shone through, and O'Neill didn't hesitate to call on him to do a man-marking job on the dangerous Juninho in both League Cup Final games of 1997, even if Pontus himself was quoted as expressing qualms about the morality of such a role. He returned to the Swedish international team in April 1997, and cemented his place with both them and City for the next year. Multi-lingual (he studied Arabic while in Leicester, as well as taking a university course in marketing), and tee-total, he became regarded as the intellectual of the club, but his personality inspired wide popularity. Pontus began to hint early in 1999 that he'd move that summer on a Bosman transfer back to Sweden to be closer to his young daughter, but the level of his City commitment never dropped until his departure for Stockholm. Sadly, an injury received while representing his country against Denmark in April 2000 ruled him out of both AIK's Cup Final appearance and Sweden's European Championship squad, though it propelled him into developing a parallel part-time media career. Fit once more, he clashed publicly with AIK boss Stuart Baxter, and returned to Gothenburg.

Apps: *FL/PL 60+5; FAC 4; LC 5+1; UEFA 2.*

KEECH, William

b. Irthlingborough, Northants, 1872

Career: 1890 Wellingborough; Sept 1891 Finedon; Kettering Hawks; Irthlingborough Wanderers; Aug 1894 Kettering; Sept 1894 Barnsley St Peters; Oct 1895 Liverpool; cs 1896 Barnsley; cs 1897 Blackpool; Feb 1898 FOSSE; Feb 1899 Loughborough; Aug 1899 Queens Park Rangers; cs 1902 Brentford; cs 1904 Kensal Rise United.

Fosse debut v Walsall (A) 26.2.1898

> A hat-trick in a friendly against old rivals Loughborough two days before his League debut immediately endeared centre-forward William to the Fosse followers. But after leading the attack for the rest of 1897/8 and the beginning of the next season, he struggled to find a first-team berth, and ironically became one more hand to the pumps for the terminally floundering Luffs. A former Northants county player, who assisted Barnsley into the Midland League and played half-a-dozen games in Liverpool's Second Division championship side of 1896, William was as well regarded as a wing-half as he was a spearhead, and it was in the middle-line that he would feature in Southern League fare for his London clubs, the newly professionalised QPR and the lowly Bees. An 1899 profile credited him with honours as both a skater and a boxer; and also alluded mysteriously to William holding the gold medal of the Royal Humane Society. There were two Keech's in the Irthlingborough side which reached the First Round Proper of the FA Cup in 1906/7, but they are presumed to have been younger brothers. William himself was on the training staff back at QPR just prior to WW1.

Apps: *FL 15.*
Goals: *FL 5.*

KEELEY, Ernest

b. Ellesmere Port, Cheshire, 1st October 1908
d. Little Sutton, Cheshire, 24th May 1974

Career: Ellesmere Port Town; 1929-trials-Everton; Aug 1931 Chester; Feb 1932 CITY.

City debut v West Ham United (H) 18.2.32

> A product of Cheshire junior football, lanky wing-half Ernie was signed up in time to play in Chester's first-ever League side, and had started but 22 senior games after this elevation before City gave him the chance to sample First Division fare. Chairman WH Squires completed the £2,500 formalities the day after Peter Hodge had confirmed he would return to the City manager's role. Looked upon as a longer-term contender for the problematic right-half slot, Ernie unfortunately never got much chance to lay claim to it. On only his fourth City outing, while playing inside-right to debutant winger Idris Miles against Everton, he badly injured his knee; which promptly 'went' again after only ten minutes of the following term's pre-season Blues v Reds game, and enforced his retirement from the game. He initially went into the insurance business, though also qualifying as a referee with the Chester & Runcorn FA by 1936. Ernie's father Bill was Chester's goalie from 1906-1910, and in their 1908 Welsh Cup-winning team; while his ill-fated younger brother Arthur played as a forward for Chester, Wolves, Bournemouth and Portsmouth before being killed in WW2 action.

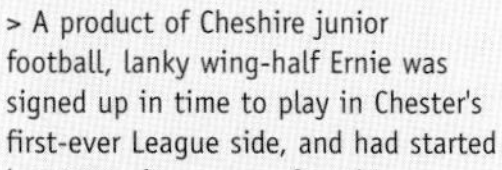

Ernie Keeley

Apps: *FL 4.*

KELLARD, Robert Sydney William

b. Edmonton, London, 1st March 1943

Career: am 1958/pro Mar 1960 Southend United; Sept 1963 Crystal Palace; Nov 1965 Ipswich Town; Mar 1966 Portsmouth; July 1968 Bristol City; Aug 1970 CITY; Sept 1971 Crystal Palace; Dec 1972 Portsmouth; Jan 1975-loan-Hereford United; summer 1975 Durban City; Sept 1975 Torquay United; Nov 1975 Chelmsford City; Grays Athletic.

City debut v Cardiff City (H) 15.8.70

> A combative midfielder with an alert brain to complement his ball-winning skills, Bobby was the mainspring of Frank O'Farrell's 1971 promotion side, and as soon as he linked with the similarly industrious and inspirational Willie Carlin, the club's upward ambitions achieved an undeniable momentum. Chipping in with some valuable goals on the way to that championship, Bobby was thereafter unfortunate not to consolidate his First Division career with City; but new boss Jimmy Bloomfield soon had him crossing paths with Alan Birchenall as the club's tactical emphasis changed. His League bow had arrived at the age of 16, and England youth caps had come Bobby's way before he embarked from Roots Hall on a round of southern travels; and the alacrity with which former clubs Palace and Pompey welcomed the mature player back for second spells with them was additional testimony to the value placed on his tenacious talent. Strangely, in a seventeen-year playing career encompassing all four of the League's levels, he was to win a medal only with City, the most northerly club he assisted. He'd been part of the Palace side promoted from Division Three in 1964, and wouldn't taste a relegation campaign until Chelmsford dropped out of the Southern League Premier in 1977, when he'd been playing alongside Jimmy Greaves. On leaving football, Bobby entered the antiques business, but was tempted back into two further dalliances with the game: in 1994 taking the assistant manager's role to Len Glover at Harlow Town (where his son played), and later bossing Basildon United.

Apps: *FL 48; FAC 6; LC 6.*
Goals: *FL 8.*

KELLER, Kasey C

b. Olympia, Washington, USA, 27th November 1969

Career: University of Portland; Feb 1992 Millwall; Aug 1996 CITY; July 1999 Rayo Vallecano.

City debut v Sunderland (A) 17.8.96

> An exemplar of the fact that the strength of football in the States lay in the college game during the period between the demise of the NASL and the start of Major League Soccer, goalkeeper Kasey helped the USA to the semi-finals of the 1989 World Youth Championship, and had won five full caps before joining Millwall. Four full seasons in the (new) First Division, at both old and new Dens, saw him acclimatised to the English game at its most frenetic, but the Lions' relegation (and a useful Olympic tournament) advertised his availability, and Martin O'Neill stepped in to pay an appearance-related £900,000 fee and insert Kasey as first-choice at City as they returned to establish themselves in the Premiership. A brilliant and spectacular shot-stopper, if occasionally a little indecisive on crosses, Kasey became only the second American (after Sheffield Wednesday's John Harkes) to appear in a major domestic Final at Wembley, and his heroics in the Hillsborough replay of the League Cup Final against Middlesbrough well earned him his medal. A laid-back character, bespectacled off the pitch, and a frequent transatlantic flyer on account of his numerous international calls, he was named the US Soccer Federation's Player of the Year in 1997, and made two appearances in the following year's World Cup Finals in France. He took a runners-up medal from the 1999 League Cup Final against Spurs, but had already by then made known his desire to move to the continent upon the expiry of his contract. Kasey helped prompt his unfashionable Madrid-based club to unlikely heights in the Primera early in 1999/2000, but they were unable to sustain their effort. (His middle initial, incidentally, is merely ornamental).

Apps: *PL 99; FAC 8; LC 16; UEFA 2.*

KELLY, Bernard

b. Carfin, Lanarkshire, 21st October 1932

Career: Law Hearts; 1951 Muirkirk Juniors; Oct 1951 Raith Rovers; July 1958 CITY; Apr 1959 Nottingham Forest; Sept 1959 Aberdeen; Aug 1960 Raith Rovers.

City debut v Arsenal (A) 30.8.58

> A hefty goalscoring inside-forward who developed a formidable reputation at Starks Park and garnered due recognition in 1957 at Scotland 'B' and Scottish League levels, Bernie came south (as David Halliday just pipped Forest to his signature) with a record of 92 League and Cup goals from 207 Raith outings. A cousin of Blackpool's Scottish international Hugh Kelly, he was soon on the goal trail again at Filbert Street in the First Division, sniping successfully alongside Jimmy Walsh during a typically entrenched rearguard campaign for the club, but sadly failing to settle off the pitch. A friendly against Raith had been part of the transfer package, but Bernie missed it when both he and his wife were hospitalised with facial injuries received in a car crash on the A1 as they returned from their wedding in Scotland. Forest then belatedly and briefly got their man, but two League starts, plus one in the Charity Shield, did nothing to ameliorate the Kellys' homesickness. Unfortunately, a return to the top flight in Scotland did nothing to ameliorate Bernie's rapidly fading form, either, and he had left the senior game by 1961. He was last heard of working in a solar heating business in Canada.

Apps: *FL 24; FAC 3.*
Goals: *FL 13; FAC 2.*

KELLY, David Thomas

b. Birmingham, 25th November 1965

Career: Alvechurch; trials-Wolverhampton Wanderers; Dec 1983 Walsall; Aug 1988 West Ham United; Mar 1990 CITY; Dec 1991 Newcastle United; June 1993 Wolverhampton Wanderers; Sept 1995 Sunderland; July 1997 Tranmere Rovers; July 2000 Sheffield United; July 2001 Motherwell.

City debut v Plymouth Argyle (H) 24.3.90

David Kelly

> Top scorer for City in his only full campaign – albeit that of the near-disastrous flirtation with the drop to the Third Division – David substantially rehabilitated himself as a fine finisher and supporting attacker during a Filbert Street tenure that promised to last somewhat longer than it did. A £300,000 deadline-week mover from Upton Park, where his goal touch had deserted him during the Hammers' relegation from the top flight, the compact Brummie-Irishman soon re-aligned his sights at Leicester, and offered reminders of his predatory instinct at every opportunity to Republic boss Jack Charlton, who capped him seven times during his City stint, but whose over-reliance on beanpole target men nonetheless left David sidelined during the 1990 World Cup Finals. David's nippiness, control and occasionally impish cheek within the six-yard box gave a contrasting focus to City's attack, and a hat-trick in the 5-4 win over future club Newcastle was a highlight of the doom-threatened season which followed; though strangely only two strikes from David followed the mid-campaign change of management from Pleat to Gordon Lee. He was still the man in possession of the spearhead role throughout the first weeks of Brian Little's regime, but a clash with the manager led to his listing, and a move to Tyneside only days after he'd rejected Sunderland's advances. David had actually overcome childhood disability to build his footballing career, but was working at Cadbury's and part-timing for Alvechurch at the time he was given his professional break at Fellows Park. In partnership with Nicky Cross and Trevor Christie, he helped shoot the Saddlers into Division Two. A hat-trick on his international debut ensued, as did the big-money move to West Ham which turned into something of a nightmare thanks to a cruelly barracking crowd. In May 1993, David registered yet another hat-trick – in a 7-1 win over City which confirmed him as top scorer for Division One champions Newcastle, and which proved to be his last game on Tyneside prior to a £750,000 return to the Midlands. With Wolves he remained a thorn in City's side, and his diving header removed his old club from the 1995 FA Cup at the Fifth Round stage. Three days previously, David had scored for his country against England in the notorious abandoned international at a riot-torn Lansdowne Road. He was sidelined by injury from much of Sunderland's 1996 First Division championship campaign, and took a less effective midfield role as they fell from the Premiership a year later; but he laced his scoring boots back on with Tranmere, and skippered his side against City at Wembley in 2000, when his well-taken equalising goal briefly threatened the Leicester victory. David left Bramall Lane with an aggregate 245 senior goals to his credit to sign for former City team-mate Billy Davies.

Apps: *FL 63+3; FAC 1; LC 6; FMC 2.*
Goals: *FL 22; LC 2; FMC 1.*

KELLY, Edward Patrick

b. Glasgow, 7th February 1951

Career: Possilpark YMCA; app 1966/pro Feb 1968 Arsenal; Sept 1976 Queens Park Rangers; July 1977 CITY; July 1980 Notts County; Aug 1981 Bournemouth; Dec 1981 CITY; Mar 1983 Kettering Town; 1984 Melton Town; Oct 1984 Torquay United; 1986 Saltash United.

City debut v Manchester City (A) 20.8.77

> Frank McLintock's first and probably most valuable signing at £50,000, Eddie was a former teammate of his new boss during the Highbury glory years as well as at Loftus Road. A midfielder with a fine 'engine', he didn't claim that many Arsenal goals, but they tended to be notable: one during the Fairs Cup Final win of 1970, several during the following Double season (including the first ever registered by a substitute in an FA Cup Final), one on his Scotland Under-23 debut, and one which removed City from the Cup in 1973. His compact, chivvying style was somewhat overwhelmed in City's 1978 plummet, but he reacted well to the responsibility of becoming the mature anchorman to Jock Wallace's young promotion side, and it was a genuine surprise when greater efforts weren't made to retain his services in 1980, when his contract expired. Eddie's immediate success in inspiring the Magpies to swap divisions with City seemed a sad irony to Leicester supporters, but it wasn't in fact long before Wallace called him back to the Second Division fray, for City once more to lean a little on his wily experience. In 1984 David Webb (a QPR and City clubmate, and his interim boss at Bournemouth) also signed him for a second time, and after two basement terms at Plainmoor Eddie settled for some time in the Devon area, working in the double-glazing business, and part-timing successively as coach to Torquay Amateurs Combined 89, and manager to each of NT Paignton and Barnstaple Town. Most recently, however, he has found a role as a part-time junior coach with Halifax Town.

Apps: *FL 119; FAC 8+1; LC 5.*
Goals: *FL 3.*

KELLY, Robert Anthony

b. Birmingham, 21st December 1964

Career: app Oct 1981/pro Dec 1982 CITY; Dec 1984-loan-Tranmere Rovers; Feb 1987 Wolverhampton Wanderers; cs 1990 Burton Albion.

City debut v Sunderland (H) 12.5.84

> A Brummie midfielder whose parentage qualified him to play youth international football for the Republic of Ireland, Robert clearly possessed useful ball skills, but occasionally appeared less well equipped for the robust physical challenge of top-class football. A loan spell with Bryan Hamilton's Tranmere (two goals in five games) seemed to signal City's willingness to jettison him after only a single first-team run-out, but Robert made Gordon Milne's opening line-up of 1985/6, and was also a squad member under Hamilton the following season, distinguishing himself with a neatly chipped goal against Manchester United. With his Filbert Street development at something of a standstill, though, the club accepted Wolves' £30,000 bid for Robert. He helped steer the Molineux side into the 1987 Third/Fourth Division Play-Offs, but then sustained a back injury serious enough to keep him out of the successful promotion sides of the next two seasons, and which enforced his departure from the League game in 1990. Two years later, however, Robert

returned to run Wolves' School of Excellence, and his highly-rated youth coaching abilities have subsequently been utilised by each of Watford and Blackburn Rovers.

Apps: *FL 17+7; LC 1+2.*
Goals: *FL 1.*

KEMBER, Stephen Dennis

b. Croydon, 8th December 1948

Career: app July 1965/pro Dec 1965 Crystal Palace; Sept 1971 Chelsea; July 1975 CITY; Apr 1978-loan-Vancouver Whitecaps; Oct 1978 Crystal Palace; Mar 1980 Vancouver Whitecaps.

City debut v Birmingham City (H) 16.8.75

> A tigerish midfielder who made an early impression as a Selhurst teenager, and was part of the first Palace side to reach Division One (in 1969), Steve moved to Chelsea for a club-record £170,000 just as Dave Sexton's side were going into decline. By the time he arrived at Filbert Street for £80,000, on the heels of Chelsea's eventual relegation, Steve had already totted up nearly 350 League games (and had won three England Under-23 caps), but there was no sign of tiredness in his play as he chased and prompted among his fellow London exiles with City. The 1977/8 debacle took much out of him, though, and Steve didn't last long into the Jock Wallace regime. A £50,000 return to Selhurst was the prelude to two more playing seasons and then successive stints as youth coach and caretaker manager. In the late 80s, while running a Croydon wine bar which unfortunately temporarily bankrupted him, Steve took on the management of non-league Whyteleaf; then in 1995 was back once more with Palace, this time for stints as reserve team coach and chief scout. Virtually wedded to Selhurst, he was called upon as caretaker boss once more in April 2001, overseeing two victories that earned Palace an unlikely relegation reprieve.

Apps: *FL 115+2; FAC 5; LC 6.*
Goals: *FL 6.*

KENNEDY, Michael Francis Martin

b. Salford, Lancs, 9th April 1961

Career: app 1977/pro Jan 1979 Halifax Town; Aug 1980 Huddersfield Town; Aug 1982 Middlesbrough; June 1984 Portsmouth; Jan 1988 Bradford City; Mar 1989 CITY; Aug 1989 Luton Town; Aug 1990 Stoke City; Aug 1992 Chesterfield; cs 1993 Wigan Athletic.

City debut v Plymouth Argyle (A) 18.3.89

> Having brought Halifax their then-record incoming fee of £50,000 as a teenage midfielder, Mick developed his ball-winning skills in several hard-knocks schools throughout the 80s; drawing admiration from many for his drive and commitment (and winning two caps for the Republic of Ireland in May 1986), but also attracting censure during his Pompey days for some ill-judged verbal revelling in his hard-man image. He added steel to Portsmouth's rise to Division One in 1987, and to Bradford City's progress to the Play-Offs a year later, and became a David Pleat acquisition just before the 1989 transfer deadline, in a £250,000-rated swap with Jimmy Quinn. Immediately assuming Paul Ramsey's anchoring role, he unfortunately showed neither a great deal of creativity nor mobility to match his combativeness, and Mick was on his way again on the eve of the following season, in a part exchange deal which brought Rob Johnson and some £150,000 to City.

Apps: *FL 9.*

KEOGH, George A.

b. Leicester

Career: 1901 St Andrews; Sept 1905 Leicester Imperial; Oct 1905 FOSSE; Sept 1907 Leicester Imperial; cs 1908 Hinckley United; Sept 1910 Leicester Imperial; cs 1913 Aylestone Park Adult School.

Fosse debut/only game v Leeds City (A) 20.1.06

> A local left-back who showed promise in trial and friendly games, but got only a single crack at senior level, replacing the injured Billy Oakes in a 1-4 defeat at Elland Road. George was in the Hinckley side beaten by Fosse reserves in the County Cup Final of 1909; and was still turning out for Aylestone Park AS after WW1.

Apps: *FL 1.*

KERR, Paul Andrew

b. Portsmouth, 9th June 1964

Career: app June 1980/pro May 1982 Aston Villa; Jan 1987 Middlesbrough; Mar 1991 Millwall; July 1992 Port Vale; Mar 1994-loan-CITY; Nov 1994 Wycombe Wanderers; Mar 1995 Waterlooville.

City debut v Portsmouth (H) 30.3.94 (sub)

> Brian Little's 1994 deadline-day exchange of loanees with Port Vale worked rather well for both clubs, for attacking midfielder Paul contributed impressively to City's run-in to Play-Off qualification, and David Lowe added a five-goal punch to the Valiants' own succesful promotion quest from the division below. A cool penalty conversion at Roker and the decisive goal at Fratton Park were the most tangible elements of Paul's brief stay in City blue (probably prompted by the time player and manager spent together at Ayresome), but he definitely buttressed a side relying heavily on reserve strength to maintain its promotion-bound momentum. He had made his League bow as a Villa substitute at Filbert Street in April 1984, and, after involvement in two elevations and a relegation with Boro (netting twice against City in 1990), coincidentally also made his Millwall debut at the same ground; going on to score for the Lions at Leicester during the following term. Indeed, for a deep-lying player, Paul always maintained a decent strike-rate, claiming one for Vale at Wembley in their 1993 Autoglass Trophy Final win, and notching one as a Wycombe substitute on his very last League outing.

Apps: *FL 4+3.*
Goals: *FL 2.*

KEYWORTH, Kenneth

b. Rotherham, 24th February 1934
d. Rotherham, 7th January 2000

Career: am Wolverhampton Wanderers; Jan 1952 Rotherham United; May 1958 CITY; Dec 1964 Coventry City; Aug 1965 Swindon Town.

City debut v Everton (H) 23.8.58

Ken Keyworth

> 'Fearless, well-nigh indestructible, and an important component of the feistily effective Leicester combination assembled by Matt Gillies in the early 60s ... a durable all-rounder renowned for his selflessness.' The fulsome obituary carried by *The Independent* on Ken's death was a well-merited tribute to both his playing abilities and Yorkshire grit, each of which became evident and ever more valuable over the seven seasons of unflashy commitment the left-half turned centre-forward gave to First Division City. Ken almost joined Wolves as a junior, but became a home-town Millmoor regular in the middle line after finishing his RAF National Service; scoring his first-ever League goal against City in 1955/6, and representing a Sheffield Select XI against England 'B'. He cost City a bargain £9,000 and soon showed the rugged resolution and forcefulness which would encourage Gillies and Bert Johnson to experiment with him as an attacking spearhead. Ken wore the No 10 shirt in the 1961 Cup Final (but had to play a withdrawn role following Len Chalmers' injury), and the No 9 two years later, when his superb, brave diving header proved City's only moment of Wembley glory against Manchester United – the team he'd claimed a six-minute hat-trick off only weeks previously. Ken was still City's central striker in both legs of the 1964 League Cup Final triumph, but injuries received in a car crash blunted his effectiveness thereafter. His free-transfer move to Jimmy Hill's Coventry was ironically completed on the day City routed them 8-1 at Highfield Road on the way to another League Cup Final; and Ken was a success with neither Sky Blues nor Swindon. He returned to his Rotherham roots to work in turn as a quantity surveyor at a steelworks, then as an office manager for a building company, but two heart attacks and by-pass surgery forced him into early retirement.

Apps: *FL 177; FAC 23; LC 11; ECWC 4.*
Goals: *FL 62; FAC 7; LC 4; ECWC 3.*

KING, Edwin

b. Leicester, 7th July 1884
d. Braunstone, Leicester, 7th July 1952

Career: Aylestone Swifts; cs 1903 St Andrews; cs 1905 Leicester Imperial; May 1906 FOSSE (- 1924).

Fosse debut v West Bromwich Albion (A) 6.4.07

> Having played for Leicester Boys in 1897 while attending Hazel Street school, having undergone a lengthy apprenticeship in local football culminating in a County Cup win with the Imps in 1906, therefore having come comparatively late to the senior game, and having held down for some time a parallel job in the leather trade, it was amazing that Teddy found the stamina to complete eighteen playing seasons with Fosse and City. Equally remarkable were his patience and versatility: by 1910, he had only 15 first-team outings under his belt, yet by WW1 he had played in seven different positions. Usually a wholehearted worrier of a half-back, he shifted to the centre-forward berth during 1914/15, when his ten goals made him second-top scorer, and would basically fit in reliably wherever asked. His veteran utility-man status was just as valuable to City after the war, for three seasons in the Second Division and a further two with the reserves, and then Teddy retired to a purely coaching role when just about to turn 40. He was past that age, though, when finally breaking through in summer 1925 for a couple of games of County Championship cricket with Leicestershire, whose Second XI wicket-keeper he had been since the war. Teddy, who took a club benefit from the League encounter with Stockport County in February 1920, made two further incidental entries in City annals: in September 1919 at Craven Cottage he became the first player for the reconstructed club to be sent off (along with Fulham's Johnny McIntyre), and in January 1921 the first to register an own goal against the 'new' club (contributing to the 3-7 home FA Cup defeat by Burnley). His reminiscences were serialised in the *Sports Mercury* in May 1932, including monetary memories of a 7s 6d wage for 1906/7, and a rise to £1 the following term; and a possibly embellished yarn of playing in the 1914/15 Cup defeat at Swansea with £22 in sovereigns (the team's weekly wages) stuffed in his boots! A member of Kirby Muxloe Golf Club and a keen angler, Teddy died on his 68th birthday.

Apps: *FL 227; FAC 9; WW1 121.*
Goals: *FL 26; WW1 24.*

KING, George

b. Coalville, Leics

Career: Coalville Town; Aug 1909 FOSSE; cs 1911 Mansfield Mechanics; cs 1912 Mansfield Town (- 1915).

Fosse debut/only game v Gainsborough Trinity (H) 10.12.10

> A reserve left-back for two seasons with Fosse, George was described as possessing a 'pretty style' but appearing 'fragile' when making his sole League appearance in a 1-0 Filbert Street victory while Sam Currie was sidelined by the injury he'd picked up in a Players Union representative game. George's original contract, still on the club's files, gives weight to the development of the footballing pay structure mentioned above in the entry for Teddy King: the weekly wage had apparently risen to £1 7s 6d by 1909, but would not be paid at all after April 1910 if George's registration wasn't retained. A year after that, it wasn't, and he switched clubs with John Thorpe.

Apps: *FL 1.*

KING, Harry Edward

b. Evesham, Worcs

Career: Evesham Star; Army football; Worcester City; Nov 1907 Birmingham; cs 1910 Crewe Alexandra; June 1911 Northampton Town; Apr 1914 Arsenal; Oct 1919 CITY; Sept 1920 Brentford; cs 1921 Stourbridge.

City debut v Huddersfield Town (A) 18.10.19

> A free-scoring centre-forward before the war, Harry arrived at Filbert Street in a package deal with forward partner Billy Spittle, but though both ex-Gunners scored on their home debut, neither really settled with City. Harry was not quite a spent force, as his top-scorer status with Brentford in 1920/1, their first-ever League season, testified; though he did soon retire, having also claimed the Bees' first hat-trick at that level. A Grenadier Guardsman before he joined Worcester, he got an unpromising baptism with a relegation-bound Birmingham (in a 0-8 defeat at Newcastle), and played only a marginal role two years later when they finished in the Second Division re-election zone. But he developed a fine strike rate in the Birmingham League with Crewe, and notched 67 goals in only 99 Southern League games for the Cobblers. Harry then continued to hit the net regularly at Highbury, where his tally included a four-goal haul from the last fixture Arsenal ever played in the Second Division, before signing up again to the colours and seeing WW1 service in Italy with the Royal Garrison Artillery.

Apps: *FL 8.*
Goals: *FL 1.*

KING, J.

Career: Feb 1892 FOSSE.

Fosse debut v Gainsborough Trinity (H) ML 13.2.1892

> Very much a Midland League mystery man: a forward whose outings in the above home defeat and the rearranged April fixture at Port Vale were utterly isolated (and unremarked upon) appearances. He played in none of the 21 senior friendlies of the 1891/2 term.

Apps: *ML 2.*

KING, John

b. Birmingham, ca 1901

Career: Hockley St Georges; Feb 1921 Hinckley United; Jan 1922 CITY; July 1924 Halifax Town; Sept 1925 Nuneaton Town; cs 1926 Kidderminster Harriers; Dec 1926 Hinckley United.

City debut v Clapton Orient (H) 9.2.22

> Hinckley's top scorer at the time of his £140 purchase, Jack claimed a hat-trick from his first City reserve game (a 15-0 whitewash of Sutton Junction), and managed a respectable goal ratio on his sporadic senior appearances during 1921/2 and 1923/4, after sharing a debut with Ernie Brooks. But Harry Graham's classy consistency was the main barrier to his progress, and he moved to The Shay in a joint deal with Tommy Duncan. Strangely, Jack lasted only one term with Halifax in the Third Division (North), despite five goals in twelve starts.

Apps: *FL 7.*
Goals: *FL 4.*

KING, John Aitken (Ian)

b. Loanhead, Midlothian, 27th May 1937

Career: Broughton Star; Arniston Rangers; June 1957 CITY; Mar 1966 Charlton Athletic; Mar 1968 Burton Albion (p/mgr); Mar 1970 Ibstock Penistone Rovers; 1970 Enderby Town (p/coach).

City debut v Sheffield Wednesday (A) 11.9.57

> A Scottish schoolboy international surprisingly released from a provisional contract with Hearts, centre-half Ian came down to Leicester as a part-timer (also being found work at Desford Colliery), but broke through into First Division football under David Halliday after only three reserve outings. It would take over three seasons, though, for him eventually to win a fascinating personal duel with England prospect Tony Knapp for the City No 5 berth under Matt Gillies. Notably strong in the air, and also a composed distributor who spread the ball forward with some poise and vision, he was the rugged pivot in all four of City's early 60s Cup Finals (missing only the second leg of the League Cup Final against Chelsea). When Ian finally surrendered his position to John Sjoberg, he soon found himself in familiar company at The Valley, playing alongside Colin Appleton again, before returning to the East Midlands. He resigned his Burton post at Christmas 1969, spent some time away from the game until undertaking coaching stints abroad (in Riyadh, Saudi Arabia, from October 1977; and later in Canada), and was briefly manager of Thringstone after November 1986. Running a dry-cleaning operation in his Burton days, he has more recently been involved in a transport business, and in 2000 commenced a part-time job in City's matchday hospitality set-up.

Apps: *FL 244; FAC 27; LC 22; ECWC 4.*
Goals: *FL 6; LC 1.*

KING, John Charles

b. Great Gidding, Hunts, 5th November 1926

Career: am Sept 1943/pro Sept 1944 CITY; July 1955 Kettering Town.

City debut (WW2) v Nottingham Forest (H) 26.2.44; (postwar) v Manchester City (H) 31.8.46

> Signed as a part-timer during the war after impressing in Peterborough schools football (and invariably then known to the local press as 'Boy' King), Johnny was a left-half and occasional inside-forward who maintained the unusual dual professions of footballer and farmer throughout his career. The youngest and smallest player of the 1949 Cup Final team, he couldn't have been further from the rustic stereotype, for his wiry physique was driven by a shrewd footballing intelligence which served City well for the bulk of nine postwar seasons. Johnny actually came close to missing the dramas of 1948/9, undergoing an operation for appendicitis that August, but his consistent form upon recovery was well noted in high places: after representing an FA XI in Cornwall (a jubilee game for the Cornish FA), he was chosen in October 1949 for the FA against the RAF – a fixture then deemed an unofficial international trial. Two cartilage operations in 1953 sidelined Johnny completely from the Second Division championship campaign of 1954, but at least he managed one game in the top flight the following season before moving to Kettering only a matter of days after Ron Jackson. Johnny is still a regular Carling Stand spectator at Filbert Street.

***Apps:** FL 197; FAC 21; WW2 40.*
***Goals:** FL 5; WW2 2.*

KING, Robert

Career: 1893 Wishaw Thistle; 1895 Airdrieonians; Aug 1897 FOSSE; Apr 1900 Glossop; Aug 1901 FOSSE; cs 1902 Hamilton Academical; cs 1904 Dykehead.

Fosse debut v Small Heath (A) 11.9.1897

> A versatile forward in both his spells with Fosse, Rab alternated primarily between the outside-left and centre-forward positions, and was top scorer in the term before he first moved on to Second Division rivals Glossop (in fact a year after the rejection of a Liverpool bid). His meagre return of only two goals for the Peak District side included one against Fosse, though he was under suspension by his club at the time of the return fixture. Fosse had no qualms about re-signing Rab, however, and he played through 1901/2 as an ever-present. His older brother Alex was a near-contemporaneous Hearts and Celtic hero.

***Apps:** FL 115; FAC 9.*
***Goals:** FL 34; FAC 5.*

KING, William

Career: Hull City; Sept 1911 FOSSE; June 1912 Goole Town; Sept 1913 Mexborough Town; Jan 1914 Goole Town.

Fosse debut v Nottingham Forest (A) 16.9.11

> A young Hull reserve centre-forward who notched five goals in a Midland League fixture against Fosse's stiffs in 1910/11, but never got a senior break on Humberside, Willie brought enthusiasm and pluck to his shot at Division Two glory with Fosse, when Shirley Hubbard and Fred Osborn usually shared the spearhead role, but when the *Daily Post's* critic concluded that 'his only defect was lack of weight'. He joined Goole as they prepared for their first season in the Midland League.

***Apps:** FL 7; FAC 1.*
***Goals:** FL 4.*

KIRKMAN, Norman

b. Bolton, 6th June 1920
d. Bolton, 17th November 1995

Career: May 1939 Burnley; Sept 1946 Rochdale; Dec 1947 Chesterfield; Aug 1949 CITY; July 1950 Southampton; Mar 1952 Exeter City (p/mgr).

City debut v Hull City (H) 27.8.49

> Freed by Burnley without playing a peacetime League game (though his WW2 Turf Moor record was supplemented by guest outings with Rochdale, Brighton, Fulham, Manchester United and Bradford City, between duties as an RAF navigator), Norman became a sought-after full-back at Spotland, and earned his club its then-record fee from Second Division Chesterfield, who partnered him with Stan Milburn. Johnny Duncan paid £8,500 from the Cup-run profits to bring him to Leicester but, after breaking his nose during his debut game and failing to hang on to the No 3 shirt for long, he was soon asking new manager Norman Bullock for a transfer. Two seasons at The Dell saw a similar in-and-out scenario develop (at a time when Norman had become a practising freemason), and he picked himself for only eleven games at Exeter, scoring his first-ever goal in his penultimate game after deciding to have a crack at the centre-forward slot against Torquay. His year as boss of the Grecians was followed by a two-year stint in the manager's chair at Bradford Park Avenue and, in 1965, an unsuccessful 14-game spell in charge at Northwich Victoria.

***Apps:** FL 12.*

KITSON, Paul

b. Murton, Co Durham, 9th January 1971

Career: YT July 1987 CITY; Mar 1988-loan-VS Rugby; pro Dec 1988 CITY; Mar 1992 Derby County; Sept 1994 Newcastle United; Feb 1997 West Ham United; Mar 2000-loan-Charlton Athletic/Sept 2000-loan-Crystal Palace.

City debut v West Bromwich Albion (H) 9.9.89 (sub)

> Rather prematurely and innacurately dubbed 'the second Lineker' during his brief stint of effective striking form with City's Second Division side, Paul became the subject of City's record outgoing transfer deal when moving to promotion rivals Derby at a cash-plus-players valuation of £1.35m. The slender but extremely pacy young striker had won early representative recognition with the League's Youth XI in Moscow in 1989, and when David Pleat elevated him to the first team at Leicester, he soon notched a League Cup counter at Selhurst Park. Yet his club progress thereafter was erratic, and it was essentially his scoring impact for England's victorious Under-21 side in the 1991 Toulon tournament that recommended him for a regular place in Brian Little's starting line-up. A burst of quicksilver front-running performances, and a clutch of well-struck goals, then catapulted Paul into the transfer-gossip columns; and the attention clearly revealed unsettling temperamental flaws. The apparent dip in his motivation meant that the 'controversy' attending his departure was somewhat artificial, and despite a fair scoring rate he proved unable to lift an expensively-assembled Rams outfit to their top-flight goal. A £2.25m fee added him to Kevin Keegan's Premiership squad on Tyneside, and a further inflated £2.3m move landed him at Upton Park to help, in tandem with John Hartson, revive a relegation-threatened Hammers; but initial success at both clubs was not sustained, and a sense of distinct underachievement still clings to Paul's career.

***Apps:** FL 39+11; FAC 1+1; LC 5; FMC 5.*
***Goals:** FL 6; FAC 1; LC 3; FMC 1.*

KNAPP, Anthony

b. Newstead, Notts, 13th October 1936

Career: Newstead Colliery; am Nottingham Forest; Bentinck Methodists; Dec 1953 CITY; Aug 1961 Southampton; Aug 1967 Coventry City; Mar 1968 Los Angeles Wolves; Mar 1969 Bristol City; Oct 1969 Tranmere Rovers; July 1971 Poole Town (p/mgr).

City debut v Stoke City (A) 11.2.56

> A classy young centre-half who made rapid strides in Matt Gillies' First Division side after 1958, Tony was unfortunate to find himself involved in a straight fight for the senior No 5 shirt with the equally proficient Ian King, and eventually to lose out after injury handed his rival the upper hand during the 1960/1 campaign. Already having represented the Football League against the Scottish League in March 1960, Tony found himself in a 14-man England squad early the next season when he couldn't even win back his place in City's first team, and the term 'travelling reserve' for the national side took on a bleak irony for him. As King held down the pivotal run for City's march to Wembley, Tony was turning down an agreed £30,000 deadline move to Chelsea, and then spent the summer weighing the relative options of bids from Liverpool and Southampton, joining the latter for City's then-record incoming fee of £27,500. In the course of a 233-game League career with the Saints, Tony's only honour was to help that club into Division One for the first time in 1966, and his involvement in their initial top-flight campaign was mirrored a year later when he became an emergency purchase for Coventry, who'd lost broken-leg victim George Curtis only two games into their first-ever season among the elite. His transition to a managerial role came at Poole, but it was abroad that he would make his biggest impact behind the scenes: managing the Icelandic national side (from 1974-77 and 1984-85) as well as four leading Norwegian clubs (Viking Stavanger, Fredrikstad, Vidar Stavanger and Brann Bergen).

***Apps:** FL 86; FAC 4; LC 2.*

KRUSE, Patrick Karl

b. Arlesey, Beds, 30th November 1953

Career: Arlesey Town; app June 1970/pro Feb 1972 CITY; Sept 1974-loan-Mansfield Town; Mar 1975 Torquay United; Mar 1977 Brentford; Feb 1982-loan-Northampton Town; May 1982 Barnet.

City debut v Tottenham Hotspur (A) 27.4.74

> A role as stand-in centre-half for Malcolm Munro for the last two games of 1973/4 was the extent of Pat's senior record with City, but he indexed his neat defensive abilities with over 300 League and Cup starts for his subsequent clubs. His six-game loan at Field Mill brought him his first goal during an unbeaten run which aided the Stags' progress to that term's Fourth Division championship, and his move to Plainmoor saw him succeed Derek Harrison in the Torquay rearguard. Then, towards the end of his spell there, Pat put himself unwillingly but almost indelibly into the record books by notching the fastest-ever own goal in League history (on Cambridge's behalf in January 1977, only six seconds after kick-off). Former City coach Bill Dodgin took him to Griffin Park for a steady spell which encompassed Brentford's ascent from Division Four in 1978, and it was unfortunate that his accumulated experience couldn't help lift Northampton from the re-election zone during the extended loan spell at the County Ground which brought his League career to a close.

***Apps:** FL 2.*

KYLE, Peter

b. Cadder, Lanarkshire, 21st December 1878
d. Glasgow, 19th January 1957

Career: Linton Villa; Parkhead; Oct 1898 Clyde; cs 1899 Liverpool; May 1900 FOSSE; Oct 1901 West Ham United; Dec 1901 Kettering; Oct 1902 Aberdeen; Jan 1903 Cowdenbeath; Apr 1904 Port Glasgow Athletic; Nov 1904 Royal Albert; Apr 1905 Larkhall Thistle; May 1905 Tottenham Hotspur; Apr 1906 Woolwich Arsenal; Mar 1908 Aston Villa; Oct 1908 Sheffield United; Aug 1909 Royal Albert; Nov 1909 Watford; cs 1910 Royal Albert.

Fosse debut v Stockport County (H) 1.9.1900

> A merry wanderer of an inside-forward – overly merry for most of his English clubs, as several suspended or sacked him for alcohol-induced breaches of discipline – Peter proves yet another researcher's nightmare. With official transfer recognition at the time in place only between the Football and Scottish Leagues, it comes as no surprise to find Peter's registration being misleadingly swapped between Fosse and Port Glasgow some three years after he left Leicester – and when he had played for a couple of Southern League sides plus a pair of Scottish non-league clubs in the interim. (Indeed, a profile in *The Scottish Referee* fuelled further confusions by conflating his career with that of Hearts and Rangers forward Archie Kyle; and leaves uncertain which player actually gloried in the nickname of 'Pinny'). Peter's Anfield record amounted to only five barren League and Cup games, and his term as a Filbert Street regular was hardly a free-scoring affair, yet his creative reputation remained high. Kettering took him on in a straight exchange deal with West Ham for Welsh international Bill Jones, but it was only on his return to London four years later that he began to really justify his status, even if Spurs had to suspend him in March 1906. Indeed, his form for First Division Arsenal (Cup semi-finalists in 1907) got him to the verge of an international call-up, with an appearance for the Anglo-Scots in the March 1907 trial. Characteristically, though, it was noted at Sheffield United that 'training wasn't Kyle's strong point', and it was 'disgraceful conduct' which earned him his leaving papers at Watford.

***Apps:** FL 31; FAC 1.*
***Goals:** FL 3; FAC 1.*

LANE, William Harry Charles

b. Tottenham, 23rd October 1904
d. Chelmsford, Essex, 10th November 1985

Career: Gnome Athletic; Park Avondale; Nov 1923 Summerstown; Jan 1924 Barnet; Northfleet United; May 1924 Tottenham Hotspur; Nov 1926 CITY; May 1928 Reading; May 1929 Brentford; May 1932 Watford; Jan 1936 Bristol City; July 1937 Clapton Orient; cs 1938 Gravesend United.

City debut v Derby County (A) 6.11.26 (scored once)

> Signed for £2,250 after showing early goalscoring potential with Spurs, and indeed netting against City two months before his move, Billy spent an almost inevitably frustrating couple of seasons at Leicester as understudy to Arthur Chandler; scoring in the first two of his extremely limited outings in the First Division centre-forward berth, but never actually appearing in a winning City side. His chances at Reading, too, were few; but he found his ideal environment in Division Three (South), serving four clubs and amassing a 159-goal record in 272 games at that level, including a three-minute hat-trick for Watford against Clapton Orient in December 1933. Tangible rewards failed to accrue for Billy, however: Brentford were divisional runners-up in 1930, and Watford were beaten finalists in the Third Division (South) Cup in 1935. Billy went on to serve a postwar managerial apprenticeship as assistant at Brentford and, from 1947-50, in charge at Guildford City; and was directing the fortunes of Brighton & Hove Albion (1951-61) at the time they won promotion to Division Two in 1958. He later managed Gravesend & Northfleet, and scouted for Arsenal and Brighton. Watford's Centenary history mentions Billy's cunning habits of talking non-stop on the pitch, and instructing his wingers always to aim their first couple of crosses a little nearer the 'keeper than usual, to let him know Billy was around; while it quotes from an interview with him in later life about his hat-trick record: "I doubt [it] will ever be beaten. Modern players spend too much time hugging and kissing to ever get around to hitting three goals in three minutes". Billy's emigré parents had anglicised their name from Löhn on settling in London.

***Apps:** FL 5.*
***Goals:** FL 2.*

LANG, John

b. Kilbirnie, Ayrshire, 16th August 1882

Career: Govan; Co-Operative United (Glasgow); cs 1902 Barnsley; Feb 1903 Sheffield United; Sept 1909 FOSSE; cs 1910 Denaby United.

Fosse debut v Lincoln City (A) 18.9.09

> The right-wing partner of Jimmy Donnelly for several of his early First Division seasons with the Blades, Johnny was a candidate for full international honours when chosen for the Anglo-Scots against the Home Scots in March 1905, having previously won Junior recognition in each of 1901 and 1902. He briefly resumed his old Bramall Lane liaison at Filbert Street, though as often as not the former teammates were in direct competition for the outside-right spot during Fosse's highest-scoring campaign (when 79 goals helped them to 5th place in Division Two). Johnny's transfer itself was a far from straightforward affair: not only was the £75 fee to rise by another £25 should he be retained for a second season; but Fosse's original cheque for the lower amount actually bounced on first presentation!

***Apps:** FL 17.*
***Goals:** FL 2.*

LANGAN, David Francis

b. Dublin, 15th February 1957

Career: Cherry Orchard; app June 1974/pro Feb 1975 Derby County; July 1980 Birmingham City; July 1984 Oxford United; Oct 1987-loan-CITY; Nov 1987 Bournemouth; July 1988 Peterborough United; 1989 Ramsey Town; 1989 Holbeach United; Aug 1990 Rothwell Town; 1990 Mirlees Blackstone.

City debut v Hull City (H) 24.10.87

> The regular right-back choice for the Republic of Ireland over almost a

decade, David won 25 caps while playing First Division football for each of the Rams and Blues: leaving the former on their 1980 relegation to sign at the latter's then-record fee of £350,000. He was a stalwart of Oxford's Division Two championship side of 1985, and assisted them to their Wembley League Cup Final win a year later. A tenacious tackler with an adventurous streak, he briefly added his experience to Bryan Hamilton's struggling side, but Oxford's demand for a transfer fee precluded a permanent move to Filbert Street. Within days of his loan spell coming to an end, Second Division rivals Bournemouth invested £25,000 in his defensive acumen. Though David continued to play on for several years, he has paid a heavy price for football's physical demands: in the late 90s he was registered disabled with serious back problems, and was working as a porter at Peterborough Town Hall.

***Apps:** FL 5.*

LANGFORD, Walter

b. Wolverhampton, 24th March 1905
d. Wolverhampton, 6th January 1976

Career: cs 1924 Sunbeam Motor Works FC; cs 1925 Wellington Town; May 1928 CITY; Aug 1933 Queens Park Rangers; July 1935 Wellington Town.

City debut v Newcastle United (H) 2.2.29

> Even positional versatility was not sufficient to save Walter from becoming another of the several City reserves of decent class left champing frustratedly at the bit during the club's First Division heyday of the late 20s. He'd top-scored with 36 goals as Wellington finished 1927/8 in the Birmingham League runners-up slot, and while he settled for some time with City to the thankless task of understudying Arthur Lochhead's inside-left spot, he was not averse to grabbing the occasional first-team opportunity at wing-half. Eventually, Mick O'Brien took Walter to QPR, but he won only a dozen selections there over two seasons. Walter's debut game for City may have signposted his fate of usually being overshadowed: making his record-breaking and much more highly-publicised bow for the opposition was Andy Cunningham, who became that day the oldest-ever Football League debutant following his move from Rangers.

***Apps:** FL 13; FAC 2.*
***Goals:** FL 5; FAC 1.*

LANGHAM, William

b. Nottingham, 1876

Career: Stapleford; Mar 1894-trials-FOSSE; Hucknall Portland; 1894 South Shore; cs 1896 Notts County; cs 1898 Bristol City; Nov 1900 FOSSE; cs 1901 Doncaster Rovers; May 1903 Gainsborough Trinity; cs 1906 Doncaster Rovers; Mar 1907 Lincoln City (- 1910).

Fosse debut v Woolwich Arsenal (H) 15.12.1900

> Fosse definitely seemed to have missed a trick when they failed to sign young outside-right Billy after his 1894 friendly outings against Stockport, Rangers and Loughborough; and it took them six years to acknowledge it. In the interim Billy had helped Notts County to the Second Division championship in 1897 (and through the Test Matches which then determined whether they'd be promoted or not!), and Bristol City to runners-up spot in the Southern League in 1899. Yet he never quite settled with Fosse after deposing Archie Brash, and his goal return especially was poor by his own standards. Billy next moved on for a strange experience at Doncaster: playing in their first Midland League fixture of 1901/2, only to find his new club then hurriedly elected to Division Two alongside Fosse a week later! His later stint at Lincoln also involved a shuffle between competitions: the Imps failed the re-election vote in 1908, but got back to Division Two a year later after taking the Midland League championship, with Billy – now a centre-forward – top-scoring in each campaign. Billy, who had represented Lincolnshire v Norfolk in January 1905, and actually claimed five goals against Fosse during his career, became trainer and groundsman at Sincil Bank in 1920; and later ran a Gainsborough pub.

***Apps:** FL 14; FAC 1.*
***Goals:** FL 2.*

LARGE, Frank

b. Leeds, 26th January 1940

Career: British Railways (Halifax); June 1959 Halifax Town; June 1962 Queens Park Rangers; Feb 1963 Northampton Town; Mar 1964 Swindon Town; Sept 1964 Carlisle United; Dec 1965 Oldham Athletic; Dec 1966 Northampton Town; Nov 1967 CITY; June 1968 Fulham; Aug 1969 Northampton Town; Nov 1972 Chesterfield; Apr 1974 Baltimore Comets; Sept 1974 Kettering Town.

City debut v Manchester City (A) 11.11.67

> If he didn't start working life on the railways with an expert knowledge of English geography, Frank must certainly have developed one as his footballing career took in all points of the national compass. One of the old have-boots-will-travel brigade, he was an almost anachronistically effective bustler of a centre-forward who could terrify goalkeepers with nothing more than a smile in their direction. Given his exclusively lower-level track record, it looked a rather desperate measure for City to offer Frank his first break in the top flight, but the two-thirds of a season he spent leading the Filbert Street attack remain utterly memorable – for his bravery, his unselfish lay-offs, his aerial power, and his sheer infectious delight that First Division defences were as susceptible to his barnstorming style as had been those he'd been accustomed to embarrassing. When City included Frank in the package deal which secured Allan Clarke, there was a distinct sense of loss to set against the excitement of a record buy; and the club's history might have been a lot different if Frank had been around for the relegation battles of 1969. (Matt Gillies did, in fact, bid to recapture Frank, but Fulham quoted an inflated fee). As it was, he was soon back at the County Ground for a third spell with the Cobblers. He'd won Third Division championship medals both there in 1963 and at Carlisle in 1965, but divisional changes figured almost as much in Frank's record as did club changes: he also suffered relegation from the Second with each of Northampton in 1967 and Fulham in 1969. He had 209 League goals under his belt before flying off for a taste of Stateside soccer, and even in his last active term with Kettering was involved in a Cup giant-killing of Swansea. Frank later moved to a cottage in Liscarney, County Mayo, running a B&B operation and working as a gamekeeper and handyman on a neighbouring estate.

***Apps:** FL 26; FAC 6.*
***Goals:** FL 8; FAC 3.*

LAWRENCE, James Hubert

b. Balham, London, 8th March 1970

Career: Cowes; Oct 1993 Sunderland; Mar 1994 Doncaster Rovers; Jan 1995 CITY; June 1997 Bradford City.

City debut v Crystal Palace (A) 14.1.95

> A late starter in the professional game, after serving two years in Parkhurst prison for his part in an armed robbery, Jamie was given a rehabilitative break at Roker after starring in Wessex League football on the Isle of Wight. A handful of senior games and a managerial change later, he moved for £20,000 to Belle Vue, where his form and flair on the wing encouraged Mark McGhee to make Jamie his initial City recruit (at an appearance-related fee rising to £175,000). He picked up some useful Premiership experience while alternating between the bench and the starting line-up, memorably laying on the debut goal for Mark Robins which brought that term's only away win at a rain-sodden Maine Road, and his pacy dribbling lent him as much eye-catching distinction as his 'pineapple' of piled-up dreadlocks. His occasional lack of concentration, and a habit of sometimes going walkabout from training, did not wholly endear Jamie to Martin O'Neill, and he was listed in May 1996. But another year's contract was eventually forthcoming, and brave diving headers from Jamie in both legs of the League Cup campaign opener against Scarborough were good justification of his squad role, which also saw him substitute for Mike Whitlow in extra-time of the Final replay at Hillsborough. He moved northwards to Valley Parade for £60,000, curiously after failing to agree a move of his home base from London to Leicester, and played key functions in each of Bradford's 1999 promotion and 2000 Premiership survival seasons. A mixed 2000/1 saw him experiencing a long relegation slog with the Bantams, but winning his first full caps for Jamaica.

***Apps:** PL/FL 21+26; FAC 1+1; LC 3+4.*
***Goals:** PL 1; LC 2.*

LEE, Alan Robert

b. Wegberg, West Germany, 19th June 1960

Career: 1975 Rangers; Apr 1978 Philadelphia Fury; Jan 1979 CITY; cs 1981 Kidderminster Harriers.

City debut v Fulham (A) 28.4.79

> A tall, sandy-haired winger, born on an RAF base in Germany but raised in Scotland, Alan had been a youth team player under Jock Wallace at Ibrox, and became the third City signing from Philadelphia within a year, following Pat Byrne and Martin Henderson to Filbert Street after a half-dozen NASL selections. Unfortunately, he made minimal impact on his Second Division outings for City, at the end of 1978/9 and the opening of the next season, as a left-sided attacker; though his third start, at Bramall Lane in May 1979, at least lent him the distinction of appearing in the youngest-ever City line-up

***Apps:** FL 6.*

LEE, Albert George

Career: Oxford Victoria (Leicester); Aug 1904 FOSSE; 1906 Thursday Excelsior; cs 1907 Leicester Imperial; Oct 1908 Leicester Nomads; Thursday Excelsior.

Fosse debut/only game v Lincoln City (A) 18.3.05

> 'Far from being a success, especially when near goal'. Albert was the deputy inside-left for Arthur Mounteney in the above 1-5 defeat, and the judgement of the *Mercury* on this young local amateur seemed to be shared by the management. He was at centre-forward for the reserves a month later when they lost the 1905 County Cup Final to South Wigston Albion, but his only other senior outing was in a friendly against Coventry City a year after that.

***Apps:** FL 1.*

LEE, John

b. Sileby, Leics, 4th November 1920
d. Loughborough, Leics, 15th January 1995

Career: Quorn Methodists; am Dec 1940/pro Feb 1941 CITY; June 1950 Derby County; Nov 1954 Coventry City.

City debut (WW2) v Northampton Town (H) 25.12.40 (scored once); (postwar) v Luton Town (A) 5.10.46 (scored twice)

> Very much a natural candidate to sign for Leicester after his two goals at Filbert Street had helped Quorn beat City's Colts in the 1940 County Cup Final, Jack gave confirmation of his scoring prowess in wartime regional fare before departing for RAF service in India (and forces football alongside Joe Calvert). On his return, he soon set about establishing himself as the club's main marksman of the decade, and overcame a couple of serious injury setbacks to show international-class striking form; though it wasn't until he became a Derby player that he actually gained his England cap, scoring in a 4-1 win in Belfast in 1950. Lethal with both head and feet, and selfless at bringing his fellow forwards into play, Jack had a profound effect on City's fortunes: never more so than when heading the goal at Cardiff which averted 1949 relegation to the Third Division. It was that term's FA Cup heroics which were to loom largest in memories of Jack's predatory effectiveness, though: he returned to the Kenilworth Road scene of his postwar scoring debut to notch four in the 5-5 draw, and in total contributed twice that number of goals to the Wembley run. The injury-induced reshufflewhich saw Jack moved to the inside-right berth for the Final was, sadly if predictably, counter-productive. His popularity was such that there was prolonged uproar when City accepted Derby's £16,000 bid, even if hindsight suggests that City got the better of that day's dealings in the long term, with Arthur Rowley arriving as replacement on the same date. Jack had a fine initial First Division campaign for the Rams, but soon suffered more injuries which restricted his appearances thereafter – indeed, he would face four cartilage operations in total throughout his career. On official retirement from the game (in November 1955), he had tallied 136 League goals in 232 games; and went on to act as groundsman at the BTH sports ground in Rugby. He had also been a Leicestershire cricketer, whose first County Championship selection in 1947 curiously proved to be the only one – despite him taking a wicket with the first ball he bowled! Jack's younger brother Billy played several games at left-half for City's A team during 1950/1.

***Apps:** FL 123; FAC 14; WW2 26.*
***Goals:** FL 74; FAC 10; WW2 13.*

LEE, Robert Gordon

b. Melton Mowbray, Leics, 2nd February 1953

Career: Blaby Boys Club; app July 1971/pro Feb 1972 CITY; Aug 1974-loan-Doncaster Rovers; Sept 1976 Sunderland; Aug 1980 Bristol Rovers; July 1981 Carlisle United; Mar 1983 Southampton; 1983 (Hong Kong); Aug 1983 Darlington; 1984 (Hong Kong); 1984 Boston United.

City debut v Derby County (A) 18.3.72 (sub)

> A relatively slow starter in senior football, with only one-and-a-bit City outings in almost three years, and painful memories of an embarrassingly missed 'sitter' on his brief Baseball Ground bow, rangy striker Bob might have been forgiven for believing he was on his way out of Filbert Street when loaned to Doncaster at the beginning of 1974/5. But a decent run of League football re-invigorated his play, and a two-goal City comeback at Loftus Road on Boxing Day 1974 eased him into a regular support role to Frank Worthington and Chris Garland. In fact, Bob himself headed City's scoring list the following term, as he began to make his powerful physique pay dividends in opposing penalty areas, but he was soon off to Roker in a £200,000 deal after Sunderland had failed to land Worthington. His thirteen goals failed

Jack Lee (centre) pictured during the 1949 FA Cup semi-final win over Portsmouth at Highbury.

to keep his new club in the First Division that term, but he remained a regular striking choice until shortly after Steve Whitworth joined him as a Rokerite; his final goal in red-and-white coming at Filbert Street in 1979/80. In 1981 Bob was in an Eastville outfit relegated from Division Two, but he helped Carlisle back up to that level a year later. He would have few League outings after appearing as sub at Filbert Street the following September, when City humiliated the Cumbrians by 6-0, but one of his proudest achievements would come in the non-league game, with his two goals in the semi-final of the FA Trophy taking his Boston United side to Wembley in 1985. That year Bob took over a Loughborough pub.

Apps: *FL 55+8; FAC 3+1; LC 4.*
Goals: *FL 17; FAC 2.*

LEECH, William

b. Newcastle-under-Lyme, Staffs, 15th July 1875
d. Leicester, 24th November 1934

Career: Newcastle White Star; Newcastle Swifts; cs 1898 Tottenham Hotspur; June 1899 Burslem Port Vale; May 1900 Stoke; cs 1903 Plymouth Argyle; July 1906 FOSSE (- 1914).

Fosse debut v Burslem Port Vale (A) 1.9.06

> A defensive half-back by the time he came to Leicester, Billy had initially moved from the Potteries to London as a goalscoring winger, but was soon homeward bound. His Vale debut came at Filbert Street (while later he'd conversely make his Fosse bow at Burslem), and he featured for them in each of the Birmingham and Staffordshire Cup Finals as well as the Second Division, before stepping up to a Stoke side exercising successful top-flight brinksmanship. 1902/3 was a 'lost' term for Billy, but he then became one of the first professionals engaged by the newly-formed Plymouth Argyle, and showed admirable consistency across three seasons of Southern League football before Fosse paid £40 for the 31-year-old's experience. Missing only two League games in his first season in Fosse's right-half berth, he became an ever-present in the 1908 promotion campaign (when a little grudgingly described by the Nottingham Post as 'a bit prone to wander, but feeds his forwards well'). Thereafter, his senior selections were more sporadic as Arthur Randle usurped his position, and his main role was coaxing along the reserves. Billy was named assistant trainer in the 1910 close season, and took over Harley Thompson's duties upon the latter's suspension in January 1912, but he was relieved of the post in May 1914, just after he'd played a reserve-team swansong in their County Cup Final win over Holwell Works. Only a month later, a letter to the local Mail from concerned supporters suggested a benefit game for Billy, as interim family problems had left him utterly without means. His son Jack, initially an inside-right with Hugglescote Imperial, signed amateur forms for City on leaving the RAF in August 1926, but failed to make the grade.

Apps: *FL 84; FAC 3.*
Goals: *FL 3.*

LEEK, Kenneth

b. Ynysybwl, nr Pontypridd, 26th July 1935

Career: Ynysybwl; Pontypridd YC; Aug 1952 Northampton Town; Apr 1958 CITY; June 1961-guest- Montreal Concordia; June 1961 Newcastle United; Nov 1961 Birmingham City; Dec 1964 Northampton Town; Nov 1965 Bradford City; Aug 1968 Rhyl; Sept 1968 Merthyr Tydfil; 1970 Ton Pentre.

City debut v Everton (H) 23.8.58 (scored once)

> A fine, skilful and mobile centre-forward, ironically remembered best at Leicester for the game he didn't play, Ken may well have developed a truly stellar career if the blow of being dropped on the eve of the 1961 Cup Final hadn't hit him so hard. Employed at Lady Windsor Colliery prior to joining the Cobblers in Division Three (South), he had come to prominence as a scorer in their 1958 Cup giant-killing of Arsenal, and also netted on his Under-23 debut for Wales against England. Initially joining City in the top flight as an inside- or outside-left (inheriting the recently-departed Arthur Rowley's shirt on his debut), Ken was soon vying with Derek Hines for the spearhead role, winning the first half-dozen of his eventual 17 full Welsh caps, and accelerating his chance-taking ratio – to the point where he had scored in every round of the 1961 FA Cup before Matt Gillies inexplicably and controversially left him out of the Wembley line-up. A move was inevitable after that, and Ken spent the summer guesting in the American International Soccer League before transferring to Tyneside. Only a matter of months later, Birmingham restored him to the First Division stage, and in 1963 he became a key member of their League Cup-winning side: scoring twice in the Final against Villa, after netting six times in earlier rounds. A return to the County Ground saw Ken assisting Northampton up into Division One, but a year later he was embroiled in the re-election zone with Bradford City after costing them their record £10,000. By the time he left Valley Parade, he had totted up 145 League goals. Ken later settled in the Daventry area, working for Ford Motors; and it was good to see that during City's Centenary Celebrations of 1984, he and Matt Gillies had adopted a mature forgive-and-forget rapport.

Apps: *FL 93; FAC 17; LC 1.*
Goals: *FL 34; FAC 9.*

LEET, Norman David

b. Leicester, 13th March 1962

Career: Shepshed Charterhouse; June 1980 CITY; Feb 1983 Shepshed Charterhouse; Oadby Town; British Shoe.

City debut v Norwich City (A) 2.5.81

> A sturdily-built, no-frills defender who had been an England schoolboy international at centre-half, Norman came into senior contention for the game in which already-relegated City contrived to take Norwich down with them. He subsequently held the left-back spot for a couple of spells during 1981/2 under Jock Wallace, but barely recovered from the embarrassment of conceding an own goal in a home defeat by Norwich, and got only a single chance to impress Gordon Milne after the summer's managerial change. Sadly, a combination of injury and employment difficulties then denied Norman even a decent part-time career in senior football.

Apps: *FL 19; LC 3.*

LEGGE, A.

b. London

Career: Custom House; July 1914 FOSSE; cs 1915 Croydon Common; Jan 1918 Millwall; Aug 1920 Charlton Athletic.

Fosse debut v Glossop (A) 13.3.15

> A reserve centre-forward who followed Jim Harrold's path from London League football to the Fosse – though who remarkably made all four of his moves in tandem with Harold Wise – he became the sixth selection as attack leader during the club's final, dismal pre-war season. The *Mail* critic couldn't understand his brief elevation, deeming him 'much too slight and slim ... lacks the necessary vim', yet he was also tried out at centre-half in the reserves. Legge's forename remains a mystery to us: a local press mention initialised him as above, the *Croydon Advertiser* introduced him as Private J Legge for his December 1915 debut with the Robins, and Charlton's historian Colin Cameron has him tagged with the initial T. In netting Charlton's first-ever Southern League goal, he also appeared to have claimed his own initial counter in senior football, but he left The Valley after four games and four goals in that competition.

Apps: *FL 2.*

LEIGHTON, John

b. (Scotland)

Career: Hibernian; July 1896 FOSSE.

Fosse debut v Darwen (H) 5.9.1896

> With only one prior outing in the top-flight of Scottish football to his name, Jock vied with Jack Lord for the left-half spot during his Fosse season, and almost invariably completed an all-Caledonian middle line (with Jimmy Brown and either Jack Walker or David Proudfoot) whenever he appeared. He was reported as returning north of the border in 1897, but no record of him playing subsequently at Scottish League level is apparent.

Apps: *FL 14.*

LENHART, Sascha David Daniel

b. Köln, West Germany, 16th December 1973

Career: 1.FC Köln; cs 1995 Royal Antwerp; Sept 1996 CITY; cs 1998 Wuppertaler SV.

City debut/only game v Scarborough (H) LC 25.9.96 (sub)

> A free-agent trialist under the post-Bosman conditions of the European transfer market, diminutive left-winger Sascha had made ten appearances in the Belgian First Division before a trial period of two reserve games saw him win from Martin O'Neill a month-long contract at Filbert Street. Substituting for Jamie Lawrence after the latter suffered a head injury in scoring against Scarborough, he was for some time starved of possession, but did not impress overly when finally brought into the game. This marginal contribution to a Wembley run was his sole senior experience with City, for he broke a bone in his foot in an ensuing reserve fixture with Middlesbrough and, despite returning after recuperation in Germany, was not retained. Sascha then seems to have had a year out of the game altogether, reappearing in a German Regionalliga team to score three times in 29 outings before his club was demoted in 1999 to the Oberliga on financial grounds.

Apps: *LC 0+1.*

LENNON, Neil Francis

b. Lurgan, N Ireland, 25 June 1971

Career: YT/pro Aug 1989 Manchester City; Aug 1990 Crewe Alexandra; Feb 1996 CITY; Dec 2000 Celtic.

City debut v Reading (A) 24.2.96 (sub)

> The influential embodiment of both the actual and the widely mis-perceived strengths of Martin O'Neill's City phenomenon, Neil often had his talent undervalued as commentators concentrated all too exclusively on his prodigious workrate and unquenchable commitment. His midfield dynamism extended well beyond heel-snapping, ball-winning persistence and into shrewd constructive prompting, and his 'Kray Twin' partnership with Muzzy Izzet was a much more finely balanced matter of complementary skills than the enforcer/extrovert cliché would admit. Nonetheless, Neil's apparent revelry in against-the-odds situations with City rather reflected the early trajectory of his career. Rejected by Manchester City despite a debut at 17 and a role in their Youth Cup Final team alongside Ashley Ward and Gerry Taggart, he became a protegé of Dario Gradi at Gresty Road, but still had a couple of setbacks to overcome. Crewe were relegated in 1991, at the end of his first season there, and Neil was to miss the entirety of the next campaign after a back injury left him virtually immobilised in an upper-body plaster-cast for almost a year. Re-establishing himself, the red-haired terrier then assisted his team to promotion in 1994, and to the Division Two Play-Offs a year later. Neil became O'Neill's first purchase for City at £750,000, only a week after he'd turned down an offer from Coventry, and had a turbulent time on the promotion trail: coming on for his Elm Park debut, he laid on a Neil Lewis goal and conceded a penalty equaliser within the space of three minutes, then was sent off at Oldham and notched an own goal at Tranmere. He was a prime contender for Man of the Match honours at Wembley, with his tackling back and perpetual motion a major inspiration to victory over Crystal Palace; and he carried that impressive form into the Premiership with utter consistency. After picking up his first League Cup medal, he played through the later stages of 1996/7 with a broken toe; and only a one-game suspension stymied his shot at ever-present status in 1998. Neil was absent only once in the following term, too, and well merited his selection as the Midland Sportswriters' Player of the Year for 1999. In October of that year he first assumed the captaincy of the Northern Ireland side in which he'd become a first-choice fixture, and he returned from a rare injury to chivvy City to Wembley glory again in 2000. He spent the summer of 2000 mulling a potential move to rejoin O'Neill at Celtic, and despite re-committing to City when they ameliorated an already lucrative contract, he was unable just a few months later to resist the traditional Catholic lure of Parkhead; garnering for City a £5m profit. And garnering for himself both the kudos often denied him down south, and victor's mementos from a magnificent domestic Treble.

Apps: *FL/PL 169+1; FAC 8; LC 23; UEFA 4; PO 3.*
Goals: *FL/PL 6; LC 3.*

LEVER, Arthur Richard

b. Cardiff, 25th March 1920

Career: Machine Products; Cardiff Corinthians; cs 1943 Cardiff City; Sept 1950 CITY; July 1954 Newport County; Sept 1957 Barry Town.

City debut v Sheffield United (H) 9.9.50

> Always popularly known as 'Buller', right-back Arthur was an ever-present member of the Cardiff side which took the Division Three (South) title in 1947, and which was soon knocking on the door of the First. A club record buy at £15,000, Arthur was entrusted by Norman Bullock with the team captaincy, and exhibited a cool defensive acumen, though for his last two seasons he had to fight hard with Stan Milburn for the senior No 2 berth. He was experimented with at centre-forward in the final game of 1952/3, but was back in his usual position for the first half of the ensuing Division Two championship term, though being sidelined for the celebrations. Arthur won his sole Welsh cap in October 1952, against Scotland, and later returned to his homeland; assisting Newport for three years, but Barry only briefly. On retirement from the game, he worked as a market gardener.

Arthur Lever

Apps: *FL 119; FAC 5.*

LEWIS, Albert Edward Talbot

b. Bedminster, Bristol, 20th January 1877
d. Bristol, 22nd February 1956

Career: Jan 1896 Bedminster; cs 1897 Bristol City; cs 1898 Everton; 1899 Bristol City; Aug 1901 Walsall; May 1902 Sheffield United; June 1904 Sunderland; May 1905 Luton Town; Aug 1906 FOSSE; Oct 1907 Bristol City (- 1908).

Fosse debut v Burslem Port Vale (A) 1.9.06

> Usually known simply as Tal, this tall, athletic goalkeeper proved an unexpected bargain for Fosse. The departure of the brilliant Walter Smith had just brought Fosse a £600 cheque when they paid Sunderland £25 for his replacement's League registration, and Tal went on to give ever-present service throughout a fine, near-miss season in which Fosse finished in 3rd place in the Second Division. This represented a career-best unbroken run of first-class games for the footballer/cricketer, but he could not thereafter resist the lure of First Division fare back in his home town (when an alternative offer came in the form of the player/manager role at Lancashire Combination side Carlisle United). He nonetheless retired from the winter game a year later, to concentrate on his parallel activities as a Somerset batsman (208 matches in the fifteen pre-war seasons), going on to score one double-century championship innings, and coaching in India in 1920. Until the turn of the century, the majority of Tal's outings in senior football had been as a full-back (scoring once in the Western League with Bedminster), but his conversion to the last line of defence had seen him engaged in the Midland League with Walsall and Division One at each of Bramall Lane and Roker Park. He was a capable deputy to man-mountain Willie Foulke with the Blades, and briefly succeeded Scottish international Ned Doig at Sunderland, where he'd arrived in a joint transfer with Alf Common, but he was sidelined entirely during his nominal year with Southern League Luton. Tal, who was also noted for his billiards skills, died in Southmead Hospital, Bristol.

Apps: *FL 38; FAC 1.*

LEWIS, George

b. Chasetown, Staffs, 1876

Career: Nov 1894 Walsall Town Swifts; Feb 1897 Wellingborough; Jan 1898 Notts County; cs 1902 Bristol City; cs 1903 Stourbridge; Oct 1903 FOSSE.

Fosse debut v Burnley (H) 10.10.03

> A left-back who had accumulated a fair amount of top flight experience from his Magpies days (129 starts),

George came to Leicester from their Division Two Ashton Gate rivals by way of a brief detour into the Birmingham League. He contested his usual defensive berth with Walter Robinson, but showed few signs of being able to reverse the team's precipitous drop into the re-election zone, and rather too obvious signs of advancing age. His Walsall stint had consisted of two Second Division campaigns bracketing a season in the Midland League, and it was at the latter level that he served Wellingborough. As an aside relevant to changing trends in football fashion, George was invariably photographed in team groups with his hands in his shorts pockets.

Apps: *FL 10; FAC 5.*

LEWIS, Karl Junior

b. Wembley, Middlesex, 9th October 1973

Career: YT/pro July 1992 Fulham; cs 1993 Dover Athletic; Aug 1996 Hayes; Oct 1996 Hendon; Aug 1999 Gillingham; Jan 2001 CITY.

City debut v Southampton (A) 31.1.2001

> A spidery defensive midfielder, well used to playing a contained get-and-give holding role, but showing occasionally flamboyant passing touches with his left foot, Junior joined City on loan for his third stint under Peter Taylor's management, and earned himself a permanent move in March 2001 (at a fee that may rise to £150,000) after adapting to Premiership football with apparent ease. Originally released by Fulham after only seven games and one year of a teenage professional contract as a striker, he rebuilt his confidence with a part-time career in Conference and Isthmian League circles (first encountering Taylor at Dover, where he occasionally played as sweeper), and was then called upon by Taylor to take his leggy box-to-box skills to Priestfield, for a season that ended with Junior celebrating promotion to Division One via the Wembley Play-Off Final.

Apps *(to end 2000/1): PL 15.*

LEWIS, Neil Anthony

b. Wolverhampton, 28th June 1974

Career: YT July 1990/pro July 1992 CITY; June 1997 Peterborough United.

City debut v Wolverhampton Wanderers (H) 13.9.92 (sub)

> An orthodox left-winger throughout his trainee period, Neil subbed for Richard Smith and slotted in at left-back in the above game, and subsequently underwent conversion to that role on a semi-permanent basis. Despite the occasional run-out in a wide midfield berth, it was as a newly-defined wing-back that he made most impact, albeit with maddening inconsistency. At times his positioning and concentration could be suspect, yet at others he would simply 'pocket' an opponent and give full rein to his attacking flair down the flank. At Millwall during the 1993/4 promotion season, Neil left the field temporarily, believing he had been sent off; while the only genuine blot on his disciplinary record was an excusable dismissal against Forest in the Premiership for an instinctive handball on the line. Yet it was to be the repercussions of his off-field temperament which closed his City career, for in February 1997 Neil received a six-month prison sentence for a nightclub affray and wounding incident. On release, he signed a three-year deal with Posh, but only saw out the first season of it.

Apps: *FL/PL 53+14; FAC 2; LC 6+1; AIC 2.*
Goals: *FL 1.*

LEWIS, R.

Career: Mar 1892 FOSSE.

Fosse debut v Derby Junction (A) ML 12.3.1892

> A still-untraced centre-half who made his debut in the same goalless Midland League game as Lisle and Atkins, and officially 'lost' a quarter of his appearance total when the April 1892 fixture at Port Vale (refereed by a spectator) was declared void, and eventually replayed without him. His final selection was for the 0-11 thrashing administered by Rotherham Town to a 10-man Fosse.

Apps: *ML 3.*

LEWIS, William Jasper

b. Bordesley Green, Birmingham, 1871

Career: Windsor Street Gasworks; Feb 1894 Small Heath; cs 1896 Nechells; Stourbridge; May 1902 FOSSE; cs 1903 Stourbridge.

Fosse debut v Small Heath (H) 6.9.02 (scored once)

> All five members of the Fosse front line were making their club debuts when this veteran centre-forward made his scoring bow against his former team, and he was one of only three who saw out the season, albeit at inside-right and with a fairly dismal goalscoring record. Eight years previously, Bill had scored on his Division One debut for Small Heath, and a year later on his FA Cup bow for them, yet he left them with a record of only three senior outings in total! He reputedly notched 35 goals for Birmingham League runners-up Stourbridge in the season before joining Fosse; and at least his enthusiasm couldn't be faulted. In October 1914, he was among the 'old pros' taken on by Worcester City to replace their players 'striking' after being denied even expenses following the outbreak of WW1 – representing himself as in his early 30s, when he was actually 43. Bill didn't make their first team, but did turn out for their reserves.

Apps: *FL 30; FAC 1.*
Goals: *FL 3.*

LIDDLE, Daniel Hamilton Sneddon

b. Bo'ness, West Lothian, 19th February 1912
d. Wigston, Leics, 9th June 1982

Career: Bo'ness; Wallyford Bluebell; April 1929 East Fife; May 1932 CITY; July 1946 Mansfield Town; Mar 1947 Stamford Town; Sept 1947 Hinckley Athletic; 1950 South Wigston WMC (p/coach).

City debut v Sheffield United (H) 27.8.32

> A small, tricky left-winger with a fair eye for goal, Danny helped East Fife into the Scottish top flight in 1930, and became his club's first-ever player to be capped for his country, turning out three times for Scotland in May 1931 despite the Fifers' immediate relegation. He arrived at Filbert Street a year later in a joint transfer with Ted Lowery, proving himself a remarkably consistent performer – and occasionally an electrifying one – up to and through the war, and twice taking the top scorer's laurels in the years of First Division struggle. He switched to the inside-left berth to accommodate Eric Stubbs during the Division Two championship campaign, and alternated between his old flank position and the left-half role for the bulk of his wartime football, which also saw him assisting Northampton, Notts County, Mansfield and Leicester City Police. After nominally retiring in 1946, Danny returned for a final taste of League fare with the Stags, and was over 39 when finally hanging up his boots after emergency service in the Mutual League. He had originally delayed turning professional with East Fife until completing his carpentry apprenticeship, but his post-football career in Leicester encompassed jobs with both Armstrong-Siddeley and Bentley Engineering.

Apps: *FL 255; FAC 19; WW2 115.*
Goals: *FL 64; FAC 7; WW2 21.*

LIGGINS, John Granville

b. Altrincham, Cheshire, 26th March 1906
d. Hyde, Cheshire, 22nd February 1976

Career: Rotherham YMCA; am 1930 Rotherham United; cs 1932 Mossley; cs 1933 Hyde United; Dec 1933 CITY; Nov 1935 Burnley; cs 1936 Shrewsbury Town; Jan 1937 (poss Wigan Athletic); cs 1938 Worksop Town; Sept 1938 Bridlington Town.

City debut v Leeds United (H) 24.11.34 (scored once)

> Another pretender to the mantle of the ageing Arthur Chandler, Jack was doubly unfortunate to receive only limited opportunities. Having previously worked with his father in Rotherham as a railway engineer, he'd turned pro in the Cheshire League and mightily impressed City with his scoring rate at Hyde – 39 goals in only 20 starts! A fee of £780 from Peter Hodge landed him at Filbert Street, but after opening the scoring on his Christmas Day reserve debut, Jack promptly broke his collarbone. It would be almost a year later that Arthur Lochhead handed him his senior break, a week after a four-goal performance for the second team, and a scrambled 9th minute winner justified the selection. But to be fighting for his place with older heads in a relegation-bound team wasn't an ideal situation, and his days were clearly numbered from the moment City converted Fred Sharman to the spearhead role, with young George Dewis next in line for selection. Accordingly, City accepted a £640 cheque from Burnley, only for Jack to walk into another difficult scenario there, with the 16-year-old Tommy Lawton pressing irresistible claims to the first-team leader's role. Most of Jack's post-football life was spent as an engineer for the Senior Service company in Hyde.

Apps: *FL 8.*
Goals: *FL 5.*

LIGHTBODY, Thomas

b. Motherwell, Lanarkshire

Career: Law Volunteers (Motherwell); Dec 1911 FOSSE; cs 1913 Peebles Rovers.

Fosse debut v Clapton Orient (H) 9.4.12

> 'Belies his name, for he turns the scale at nearly twelve and a half stone', remarked the *Nottingham Post Football Guide* of 1912 of this young Scottish centre-half. Tom found himself understudying Percy Hanger at Leicester, and moved on after Jimmy Harrold had arrived to claim the regular pivotal role, having at least had the satisfaction of contributing to a trio of home wins, as well as to the reserves' 1912 County Cup Final victory over Hinckley United.

Apps: *FL 3.*

LINEKER, Gary Winston

b. Leicester, 30th November 1960

Career: app July 1977/pro Dec 1978 CITY; June 1985 Everton; July 1986 Barcelona; June 1989 Tottenham Hotspur; June 1992 Nagoya Grampus Eight.

City debut v Oldham Athletic (H) 1.1.79

> Although eventually and justifiably regarded as one of the world's foremost strikers, Gary made rather a stuttering start to his first-team career with City. Outshone on his initial appearance as an 18-year-old by the two-years-younger David Buchanan, after being handed a New Year's Day breakthrough by Jock Wallace, he continued to work at his game as a squad player in the rollercoaster years of 1980 and 1981, while City in turn struggled to harness his remarkable pace to a coherent tactical role. Indeed, Gary was often played wide in his early days, until his alert goal-poaching habit began truly to blossom during the Second Division term of 1981/2. There were still distinct gaps in his footballing repertoire when City fought their way back to the top flight in 1983, but, forming with Alan Smith and Steve Lynex a potent triangular threat of real variety, Gary gradually refined his ball-holding and control skills. Leading the Filbert Street scoring list for four seasons running on quick-witted predatory instinct, he became an inevitable England choice up front despite City's lowly status in Division One. Equally inevitable, perhaps, was a move; and it was to reigning champions Everton that Gary went in return for an £800,000 cheque. Thirty League goals, ten more in the Cups (including one at Wembley in the FA Cup Final), and both versions of the Footballer of the Year award made up Gary's individual tally from his Goodison season, when he also emerged as an unexpectedly fine header of the ball; though the Toffees finished as runners-up to Liverpool in both major domestic competitions. His value escalated dramatically again, though, following his summer exploits in the 1986 World Cup, when his hat-trick against Poland made him a national hero and his total of six goals won him the competition's Golden Boot award as top scorer. Terry Venables' Barcelona laid out some £2.75m in pesetas for Gary's now globally-famous talent, with City benefitting from a negotiated percentage of Everton's profit (amounting to £250,000), and the quicksilver striker maintained his fine scoring record at both club and international level, though neither of his partnerships with fellow-exiles Mark Hughes or Steve Archibald could quite prompt Barcelona higher than second place in the Spanish League in 1987. Gary picked up his first-ever winner's medal from the 1988 Spanish Cup Final, but took the first real knock to his modestly-handled prestige when, suffering from the onset of hepatitis, he shared in England's poor showing in that summer's European Championships. Perhaps ironically, his rehabilitation at Barcelona under Johan Cruyff's management entailed a return to virtually orthodox wing play; with his cross from the right providing the opening goal in the Catalans' European Cup Winners Cup Final victory of 1989. A comeback to characteristic scoring form for England, and a second signing for Terry Venables, then heralded Gary's return to the Football League and, immediately, to the head of the First Division marksmanship list. The 1990 World Cup saw him claim another four goals as England's campaign reached a semi-final penalty shoot-out before derailing, and Gary picked up the individual FIFA Fair Play award. He earned an FA Cup winner's medal with Spurs in 1991, despite failing with a penalty against Nottingham Forest; and eventually another unsuccessful spot-kick (against Brazil) proved crucial in leaving his international tally at 48 – one short of Bobby Charlton's England record – when Graham Taylor controversially closed his occasional captain's representative career in 1992 on the 80-cap mark. Gary was named Footballer of the Year again in 1992 by the FWA, by which time he had announced his intention to move to Japan to assist in the 1993 launch of the J-League. His ambassadorial role there was superbly handled, but unfortunately a series of foot and toe injuries marred his on-field contributions to the Grampus Eight cause (including a spell under former City boss Gordon Milne), and Gary announced his retirement from the game in November 1994. A distinctly high-profile media career awaited, culminating in recent ubiquity as 'Match of the Day' presenter, 'They Think It's All Over' panellist, and advertising icon for Walkers Crisps. Previous extra-curricular activities included the co-authorship of a well-received, football-themed novel in Spain, a role as co-creator of the less successful ITV drama series 'All in the Game', and inspirational status for the long-running play 'An Evening With Gary Lineker'. In his heyday also a fair cricketer, he was honoured as a Freeman of the City of Leicester in April 1995. His grandfather Harold had played at Filbert Street in March 1925, at outside-right for Leicester Boys against West Ham; and the family name goes further back into club history, as a T Lineker, formerly with Leicester Teachers, appeared as a Fosse amateur in 1890/1.

Apps: *FL 187+7; FAC 13; LC 9.*
Goals: *FL 95; FAC 6; LC 2.*

LING, Arthur Samuel (Archie)

b. Cambridge

Career: Albert Institute (Cambridge); June 1902 FOSSE; May 1905 Swindon Town; cs 1909 Brentford (- 1913).

Fosse debut v Small Heath (H) 6.9.02

> Signed from the champions of the Cambridgeshire Senior League, Archie became the regular goalkeeper, gamely obdurate but over-exposed behind a flimsy defence, during two lowly seasons of Second Division struggle with Fosse. Released before the re-election vote went Fosse's way, he nonetheless loyally returned in December 1904 to deputise for the injured Walter Smith, then built a decent career in the Southern League. Though he came close to joining Norwich in 1907, he completed four terms at Swindon, culminating in him attaining ever-present status when they finished runners-up in 1909; and he was a three-season regular at Brentford, where a flair for drama marked his stay. In the first three games of 1910/11, he saved a penalty taken by Exeter's goalie, and then notched a successful spot-kick himself against each of Swindon and Bristol Rovers! Archie also played a reasonable standard of Minor Counties cricket for Cambridgeshire.

Apps: *FL 59; FAC 7.*

LINTON, Desmond Martin

b. Birmingham, 5th September 1971

Career: YT 1988/pro Jan 1990 CITY; Oct 1991 Luton Town; Mar 1997 Peterborough United; Mar 1999-loan-Swindon Town; 1999 Cambridge City.

City debut v Portsmouth (H) 14.4.90 (sub)

> A leggy young defender who could perform with equal distinction on the flanks or in the centre of the back line, Des was marked early for senior progress, winning several friendly-game run-outs prior to his League debut, and earning the club's Young Player of the Year award for 1990. Gradually developing his reputation as a reliable cover player under the aegis of each of David Pleat, Gordon Lee and Brian Little, Des was a surprise departure (in the company of Scott Oakes) when Little and Pleat

engineered the exchange deal which saw Steve Thompson arrive at Filbert Street. He was unfortunate to suffer a long-term injury only a few games into his Luton career, but had one-and-a-half seasons as a regular and three subsequently as a squad player while the Hatters slid down two divisions. A teammate of Jimmy Quinn's (and briefly of Neil Lewis's) at Peterborough, Des failed to win a contract at Swindon after Quinn recruited him there on loan.

***Apps:** FL 6+5; LC 0+1; FMC 1.*

LISLE, C.R.

Career: 1890 FOSSE

Fosse debut/only game v Derby Junction (A) ML 12.3.1892

> An occasional Fosse reserve in 1890/1, before the club commenced regular competitive action, this one-shot Midland Leaguer retained his tenuous association for a second term, playing on the right wing in the above goalless draw, scoring twice in a subsequent friendly against Notts St Johns, and featuring in the Fosse second string which fell to Hugglescote Robin Hoods in the County Cup Final replay of April 1892. He also had one outing for the Fosse Rovers in January 1894. Otherwise, a shroud of anonymity obscures discovery of his forename or his other club affiliations.

***Apps:** ML 1.*

LITTLER, Joseph Eric

b. St Helens, Lancs, 14th April 1929

Career: 1946 St Helens Town; 1950 Stubshaw Cross; May 1951 CITY; Dec 1954 Lincoln City; June 1955 Wrexham; Dec 1955 Crewe Alexandra; Aug 1956 Chorley; cs 1960 Fleetwood; 1960 Prescot Cables; 1961 Sutton Parish.

City debut v Notts County (H) 26.4.52 (scored once)

> Plucked from the lower reaches of Lancashire Combination football by Norman Bullock, Eric was a stubborn trier of a centre-forward who made sporadic appearances over the course of four seasons as deputy to Derek Hines, then moved on, after a single First Division run-out, in part-exchange for Andy Graver. His inability to command a regular senior berth (despite notching 39 reserve goals in 1952/3, and 31 a season later) was unfortunately repeated with his three subsequent clubs, and Eric aggregated only 28 League appearances and five goals after leaving Filbert Street. Yet he smashed Chorley's scoring record in 1957/8 with a 51-strike tally from Lancashire Combination and Cup games, and eventually left them as 1960 champions of that league. Later a committee member at St Helens Town, Eric worked successively in a glassworks and as a taxi driver on his home turf. His younger brother Bill had a trial in City's A team forward line in September 1952.

***Apps:** FL 5; FAC 1.*
***Goals:** FL 2.*

LOCHHEAD, Andrew Lorimar

b. Milngavie, Dunbartonshire, 9th March 1941

Career: Renfrew Juniors; Dec 1958 Burnley; Oct 1968 CITY; Feb 1970 Aston Villa; Aug 1973 Oldham Athletic; Apr 1974-loan-Denver Dynamos.

City debut v Newcastle United (A) 2.11.68

> A six-foot, bullet-domed central striker who made his First Division mark as a superb header of the ball, Andy won a Scotland Under-23 cap in 1963, and twice notched five in a game for Burnley in amassing a 128-

Andy Lochhead

goal aggregate in League and Cup fare at Turf Moor. Though he'd once totally frustrated a City attack when serving as a stand-in centre-half for the Clarets at Filbert Street, it was definitely his goal touch that the soon-to-depart Matt Gillies coveted, and for which he paid £80,000. Andy was immediately partnered with Allan Clarke, and shared in the contrasting fortunes of the 1968/9 experience, as relegation-bound City fought their way to Wembley. Andy gloried in the headed Fifth Round winner at Anfield, but rather muffed his chance of Cup Final heroism with a miscued shot over the bar from a good position. He started the following season with an excitingly quickfire goal spree, but couldn't quite maintain the momentum Frank O'Farrell required in attempting to plot a one-term return to the top flight; and in fact Andy was to leave the Second Division scene by the trapdoor route that term after his move to Villa Park. He assisted Villa to the League Cup Final in 1971, though, and top-scored for their Third Division championship side a year later, and only left after succumbing to rivalry from both Allan Evans and Brian Little. Oldham, too, took the Division Three title with Andy as a key contributor, and he was to remain for a while at Boundary Park as a coach. Andy also managed Padiham, before becoming successively a licensee and a bowling club steward in the Burnley area, and a customer relations officer for an Oldham water-meter firm.

***Apps:** FL 40+4; FAC 12+1; LC 6.*
***Goals:** FL 12; FAC 3; LC 4.*

LOCHHEAD, Arthur William

b. Busby, Lanarkshire, 8th December 1897
d. Edinburgh, 30th December 1966

Career: Army football; 1917 Heart of Midlothian; Jan 1919-loan-Clyde; June 1921 Manchester United; Oct 1925 CITY (- 1934).

City debut v West Bromwich Albion (H) 17.10.25 (scored twice)

> Exhibiting in embryo the confidence that would later allow him to strut his way through many a City game, Arthur demanded a trial with Hearts after he'd returned from WW1 service in France and India with the Royal Garrison Artillery, had watched a Tynecastle reserve match, and had become convinced he could do better. Duly recruited, he was soon top-scoring from the inside-left berth alongside Harry Graham, and meriting an international trial in the Home Scots v Anglo-Scots fixture of March 1920. Then captured by Manchester United in exchange for Scotland forward Tom Miller, he went on to build a reputation as both marksman and playmaker, while training in the evenings at Old Trafford and studying for teaching qualifications during the day. United were relegated in 1922, but Arthur saw them up again in 1925; in the interim scoring three times against City in 1923/4. He then became a key Peter Hodge signing, at a club record £3,300 fee, with the intention of adding his guile in both scoring and scheming departments to City's initial attempts at First Division consolidation. Arthur duly delivered – and an index of his influential class at inside-left was that eight years on from his first international trial, he was chosen to represent the Anglos in the equivalent fixture, while helping City to their highest-ever top-flight finishes. His nine years' active service combined a forceful physicality with a tactician's subtlety and stealth, and it was the latter quality that recommended Arthur to the City board when they convinced the veteran to take over the managerial reins – precisely on the ninth anniversary of his City debut – following the death of Peter Hodge. It was widely appreciated, however, that a side whose central figures had all aged together would struggle to retain their First Division status, and relegation did indeed ensue in 1935 despite Arthur's attempts to turn over and rejuvenate the playing staff. His side finished a respectable seventh in the Second Division a year later, but that summer a simmering row surfaced, with criticisms at the shareholders' meeting exposing a split on the board over the level of autonomy the manager should have. Only two games into the new season, and following a 5-0 win, Arthur resigned; and two months later returned to Edinburgh. He was considered a front-runner for the managerial vacancy at Hearts in early 1937, but didn't land the job, and is believed to have had no further football connections thereafter. During his playing days with City, he and his brother had run a wireless and music shop in Loseby Lane, and it is uncertain whether Arthur ever exploited his teaching certificates: by the middle of 1938 he was running the Border Hotel at Yetholm near Kelso.

***Apps:** FL 303; FAC 17.*
***Goals:** FL 106; FAC 8.*

LONIE, Thomas

b. Dundee, ca 1872

Career: Dundee Harp; cs 1893 Johnstone Wanderers; Jan 1894 Notts County; July 1894 Darwen; 1894 Dundee Wanderers; Apr 1895 Dundee; Oct 1895 Stoke; June 1896 FOSSE.

Fosse debut v Darwen (H) 5.9.1896 (scored once)

> One local pressman deemed Tom to look overweight on his Filbert Street arrival; another rather self-contradictorily described him as 'a plodding player', yet 'at home in a vigorous contest'. Whatever, the new centre-forward lasted but two months in the Fosse first team and less than another in the reserves, with his piqued absence from a second-string line-up leading to his 'defection' and return to Scotland in November. He'd claimed a hat-trick from the second public trial of 1896, and had netted in both League fixtures against his former Darwen clubmates, but his limited pedigree (a smattering of top flight football both north and south of the border with Dundee and Stoke) stood him in no great stead at Leicester.

***Apps:** FL 7.*
***Goals:** FL 2.*

LORD, Jack

b. Derby, ca 1870
d. 26th November 1934

Career: 1885 Derby St Luke's; 1890 Derby Junction; cs 1891 FOSSE (-1897).

Fosse debut v Derby Junction (H) ML 12.9.1891

> A recruit for Fosse's first Midland League fixture – against his previous employers – right-half Jack became the club's first ever-present player in negotiating the entirety of that difficult campaign, and stayed to serve across all three terms in that competition, plus the first three in the Second Division, while also turning out in the centre and on the left of the middle line. Invariably described as a dogged, rather than spectacular player, he was esteemed as a loyal and ever-enthusiastic clubman, often skippered the Fosse Rovers, and took a benefit worth £50 from a friendly against Burton Wanderers in September 1897.

***Apps:** FL 29; FAC 16; ML 56.*
***Goals:** FL 2; FAC 2; ML 3.*

LORNIE, John

b. Aberdeen, 2nd March 1939

Career: Banks O'Dee; Mar 1958 CITY; June 1961 Luton Town; June 1963 Carlisle United; June 1964 Tranmere Rovers; Sept 1966 Ross County.

City debut v West Bromwich Albion (A) 7.2.59 (scored once)

> A Scottish schoolboy international and holder of a winner's medal from the 1957 Scottish Junior Cup Final (when Banks O'Dee beat Kilsyth Rangers 1-0 in front of almost 31,000 at Hampden), Jack spent three seasons at Filbert Street as reserve centre-forward, getting few chances to shine at senior level despite claiming a goal from each of his first two First Division outings. His limited glory, then, came from scoring twice at White Hart Lane in the final-fixture 2-1 win which secured the 1959 Football Combination championship for City (for the only time), and gave him top-marksman status for the reserves with 15 strikes from 17 appearances. Jack led the second-string scoring list again in 1959/60, but was nudged aside by Hugh McIlmoyle a year later, and his departure meant he'd failed to appear on a winning City side at first-team level. A fairly uneventful Kenilworth Road stay was followed by only a four-game stint at Carlisle, where ironically he played on the wing in support of McIlmoyle! Subsequently, a faint mark on the record book came when Jack became Tranmere's first-ever substitute. His brother Jim was the St Mirren goalkeeper in the 1955 Scottish League Cup Final, while his grandfather, James Lamb, had long before found goalkeeping fame of the wrong sort – as the Bon Accord last-line beaten a record 36 times by the Arbroath forwards in the notorious Scottish Cup tie of 1885.

***Apps:** FL 8; LC 1.*
***Goals:** FL 3.*

LOVATT, Harold Albert

b. Audley, Staffs, 18th August 1905
d. Halmerend, Stoke-on-Trent, 11th November 1984

Career: Wood Lane United; Red Street St Chads; trials-Sunderland & Stoke; Mar 1924 Port Vale; July 1924 Preston North End; Sept 1925 Crewe Alexandra; Mar 1926 Bradford City; Nov 1926 Wrexham; Aug 1927 Scarborough; May 1928 CITY; Dec 1930 Notts County; Nov 1931 Northampton Town; July 1932 Macclesfield Town; Nov 1934 Stafford Rangers; July 1936 Winsford United.

City debut v Cardiff City (H) 21.2.29 (scored once)

> Centre-forward Harry could hardly have done more to lay claim to a first-team berth at City. At the time of his debut, he had netted 33 times in only 19 reserve games, and indeed finished the 1928/9 term with 43 from 26. At one stage he scored hat-tricks in three successive Combination games, and claimed nine triples in total that term for the stiffs; then adding another in the first team's final fixture. Such superb form (confirmed months later when he walloped a second senior hat-trick past Bolton) would have had him walking into many a team, but City were now at the pinnacle of their First Division fame, and it was Arthur Chandler whose ultra-consistent spearhead prowess had contributed so much to their rise. Harry's second-team goalgetting continued (with another 31 strikes) before he moved to assist Notts County's run-in to the Third Division (South) championship. Yet he would settle with neither Magpies nor Cobblers, and took to the non-league game when he felt Northampton had over-priced him on their 1932 transfer list – putting him in limbo until officially freed in 1934. His career had started in earnest only with a goal-rush at Crewe (after youthful reserve stints in the Potteries and at Deepdale), but it was his prolific form with Midland League runners-up Scarborough that had tempted Willie Orr to take him on at Leicester.

***Apps:** FL 10.*
***Goals:** FL 9.*

LOWE, David Anthony

b. Liverpool, 30th August 1965

Career: app Aug 1982/pro June 1983 Wigan Athletic; June 1987 Ipswich Town; Mar 1992-loan-Port Vale; July 1992 CITY; Feb 1994-loan-Port Vale; Mar 1996 Wigan Athletic; June 1999 Wrexham; Jan 2000-loan-Rushden & Diamonds.

City debut v Brentford (H) 19.9.92 (sub)

> A Liverpudlian striker who made his breathrough at Wigan in October 1982, while still an apprentice, David was a teammate of Steve Walsh and Mike Newell in the 1985 Freight/Rover Trophy win, scoring the Latics' final goal in a 3-1 win over Brentford. He top-scored in his initial Ipswich campaign, and won two England Under-21 caps while at Portman Road, but had merely a peripheral role by the time of the East Anglians' 1992 Second Division championship win. A £200,000 Brian Little purchase, he shattered his cheekbone in a home pre-season friendly against Borussia Mönchengladbach, but settled well after his delayed debut as a useful penalty-box predator, who played well with his back to goal and often profitably dragged defensive cover wide. David nonetheless missed out on the Play-Offs of 1993, and made no impact whatsoever in his second Filbert Street term, but substantially aided Port Vale's promotion after he and Paul Kerr had been temporarily swapped. His Premiership experiences were decidedly mixed: scoring and

David Lowe

then being sent off with Vinnie Jones at Wimbledon, and a week later coming on as sub against Spurs to curl in the strike eventually voted by the supporters as Goal of the Season. That term's 4-4 draw at Villa Park was also memorable for both fans and player: David's second strike after coming on from the bench to lead the three-goal fightback was in fact his 100th at League level. Though Mark McGhee occasionally asked David to play much deeper than usual to some effect, he failed to convince Martin O'Neill that he had a role in the new scheme of things. Partway through 1997/8, David took over the mantle of being Wigan's all-time aggregate top League scorer, and Latics fans voted him that term's Player of the Year. He later failed to settle at the Racecourse, and a negative medical judgement when he was about to sign permanently for Rushden spelt the end of his active career; though he is now engaged as a regional coach by the PFA.

***Apps:** FL/PL 68+26; FAC 2+2; LC 4+3; AIC 3.*
***Goals:** FL/PL 22; LC 1.*

LOWE, William

b. ca 1870

Career: Long Eaton Midland; 1886 Long Eaton Rangers; Notts Rangers; Oct 1890 Loughborough; cs 1892 FOSSE; cs 1893 Long Eaton Rangers; cs 1895 Loughborough.

Fosse debut v Mansfield Town (A) ML 17.9.1892 (scored once).

> Retaining throughout his Fosse spell the nickname of 'Kiddy' which presumably had first adhered when, as a 16-year-old, he'd helped Long Eaton Rangers win the Birmingham Senior Cup, this right-sided attacker was actually, at 5ft 10in, the tallest Fosse forward of his era. Kiddy had scored for the Luffs in both their initial seasons in the Midland Alliance and Midland League (once, indeed, in the first senior competitive fixture between Loughborough and the Fosse), then got a curious baptism after his transfer of allegiance. He played the first 35 minutes of his debut game in goal, with Jimmy Thraves arriving on a late train at Mansfield, then scored Fosse's consolation goal after being relieved. A nippy player (as befitted a successful amateur sprinter), he maintained a healthy enough goal rate with Fosse, but was allowed homeward to sign for a Long Eaton side who were now Midland League rivals. Shortly afterwards, he wrote to the Leicester press, offering a £20 reward to anyone identifying the 'slanderer' who'd started the rumour that he'd just been jailed for theft! Back with the Luffs in 1895, Kiddy was to make the first of a total of only three Football League starts at Filbert Street in October.

***Apps:** FAC 4; ML 20.*
***Goals:** FAC 2; ML 9.*

LOWERY, Edward

b. Walker-on-Tyne, Oct qtr 1907
d. 16th September 2000

Career: Walker Park; Usworth Colliery; Dec 1930 East Fife; May 1932 CITY; 1934-loan-Yeovil & Petters United; July 1934 Torquay United; cs 1936 Darlington; June 1937 Frickley Colliery (- 1939).

City debut v Sheffield United (H) 27.8.32

> A Geordie inside-right who had learnt the graces of Scottish style before arriving at Filbert Street in the company of Danny Liddle, Ted was City's first-choice schemer for the opening ten First Division games of 1932/3, and looking every inch another of Peter Hodge's astutely effective cross-border purchases, when successive illness and injuries completely ruined his progress. To the extent, in fact, that with Arthur Maw having assumed his position, he would soon be able to parade his talents only in a Third Division context. Even then, only eleven goals in 36 League outings at Plainmoor, and a re-election campaign at Feethams, ensued.

***Apps:** FL 14.*
***Goals:** FL 1.*

LYNES, James

b. Cheltenham, Glos, ca 1869

Career: Nov 1895 FOSSE; May 1896 Lincoln City.

Fosse debut v Hucknall St.Johns (H) FAC 2.11.1895

> Signed from an unnamed junior club in the Birmingham area, James rejoiced in the nickname of 'Trilby', and made intermittent appearances during 1895/6 at both outside-right and centre-forward, where he was regarded as less skilful than Harry Trainer, but a better and weightier bustler than his Welsh international rival. For some unfathomed reason, he adopted his forename as a pseudonymous surname on each of his first three Fosse outings – a friendly at Nottingham Forest, the above Cup tie and a League game at Anfield. At Lincoln, in a re-election-bound side, he claimed four Second Division goals, the last proving to be the winner against Fosse. A cricketer in Birmingham and the South-West before his name appeared in senior football (playing for Yardley, Liskeard, Plymouth Garrison and Devon side Ivy Bridge), he also assisted Lincoln Lindum at the summer game, and we suspect strongly that he was much later the man who held the cricket pro job at each of Warrington (1904) and Bacup (1905 & 1906); with, just possibly, a similar stint in Halifax in the interim.

***Apps:** FL 7; FAC 3.*
***Goals:** FL 3.*

LYNEX, Stephen Charles

b. West Bromwich, 23rd January 1958

Career: Sandwell Rangers; app July 1974/pro Jan 1976 West Bromwich Albion; cs 1977-trials-Sligo Rovers; Aug 1977 Shamrock Rovers; Apr 1979 Birmingham City; Feb 1981 CITY; Oct 1986-loan-Birmingham City; Mar 1987 West Bromwich Albion; cs 1988 Cardiff City; Mar 1990-loan-Telford United; Aug 1990 Trafford Park; Feb 1991 Telford United; Mar 1991 Mitchells & Butlers; Ansells.

City debut v Sunderland (A) 14.2.81

> Despite having only a limited League career at St Andrews, where he rapidly gained a reputation as a 'super-sub', Steve also had two cup-winning medals to his name by the time Jock Wallace paid £60,000 to bring him to Leicester – from West Brom's FA Youth Cup victory of 1976, and from Shamrock's FAI Cup win in 1978. In fact, the speedy winger's confidence-building sojourn in Irish football got off to a uniquely unpromising start – with a gunman offering Steve a persuasive reason not to prolong his trial period with Sligo – but Johnny Giles soon gave him a second chance after having been responsible for freeing him from The Hawthorns only weeks earlier. Later he developed quickly at Filbert Street with regular first-team football, playing an ever-more influential role as City reached the FA Cup semi-finals in 1982, and were promoted under Gordon Milne a year later. Assuming the role of penalty-taker, Steve claimed a good proportion (23) of his respectable goal tally from the spot, and held up effectively his side of the Lynex-Lineker-Smith striking triangle in the top flight. For much of his City days the only orthodox winger on the club's books (and Player of the Season in 1983/4), Steve suffered occasionally from either instructions or an inclination to assume all-round midfield responsibilities, and sometimes looked reticent to play to his pacy dribbling strengths; but the sight of him taking on his marker close to either touchline or by-line, and leaving him flailing, brightened many an early-80s afternoon. However, a combined loss of form and, apparently, motivation led to a marked drop in Steve's valuation: he moved back to his hometown club for a merely nominal fee only a year after City had held out for a six-figure price from the Baggies. Steve hit the headlines again in 1994 in unfortunate circumstances when, as a West Midlands licensee, he was burned in a Fireworks Night bonfire explosion which proved fatal for one child; though more happily he was on view at Wembley in 1998, in action for the Birmingham-based Club Sporting in the Umbro Veterans Cup.

***Apps:** FL 200+13; FAC 12; LC 14+1.*
***Goals:** FL 57; FAC 1; LC 2.*

LYON, Herbert Ernest Saxon Bertie Cordey

b. Mosbrough, Derbyshire, 1877

Career: Sept 1895 Overseal Town; Aug 1898 Gresley Rovers; Jan 1899 FOSSE; June 1900 Nelson; June 1901 Watford; May 1902 Reading; cs 1903 West Ham United; May 1904 Brighton & Hove Albion; May 1905 Swindon Town; May 1906 Carlisle United; cs 1907 Swindon Town; June 1908 Blackpool; cs 1909 Walsall; cs 1910 Tredegar.

Fosse debut v Luton Town (A) 14.1.1899 (scored once)

> Primarily an inside-forward, Bertie makes the Leicester record books as the only outfield player actually selected in advance by the club to play a full first-class game as goalkeeper – and he kept a clean sheet against Bolton Wanderers in March 1900, after only three reserve outings between the sticks, before resuming his attacking duties. Otherwise he's renowned for his mouthful of Christian names (almost certainly self-adopted, including the affected corruption of 'coeur-de-lion'), and for his habit, post-Fosse, of switching clubs (and often competitions) on an annual basis. Fosse actually picked up £35 from Blackpool for his League registration eight years after he'd left the club (in a joint transfer with Alf Ball), and after he'd experienced a year in the Lancashire League, five seasons of moderate scoring with five Southern League clubs, a Lancashire Combination Division Two title campaign with Carlisle, and a second bite at Swindon. Even after leaving Bloomfield Road, though, Bertie hadn't quite finished his travels; packing into his footballing itinerary a Birmingham League term with Walsall, and a championship season in the South Wales League.

***Apps:** FL 15; FAC 1.*
***Goals:** FL 5; FAC 2.*

MABBOTT, John

Career (Probable): Mellors Ltd FC; 1889 Nottingham Forest; 1891 Newark; Feb 1892 Grantham Town; 1892 Kettering; Apr 1892 FOSSE; Notts County; Nov 1892 FOSSE; Mar 1893 Notts County; 1894 Newark; 1895 Mansfield; 1897 Long Eaton Rangers; Oct 1901 Whitwick White Cross.

Fosse debut v Doncaster Rovers (H) ML 30.4.1892

> The tentative nature of the career path we've assigned above to this inside-right illustrates the difficulties of properly researching amateur players of Fosse's Midland League era. Both previous versions of this Who's Who project have carried the initial 'C' for the Fossil who played in friendlies against Loughborough and Bolton Wanderers prior to the above game, and who returned once in the following season to score in the home Midland League fixture with Grantham Rovers. But this partial and inadequate identification was based on only a single Leicester press source, while all other (circumstantial) evidence points to 'our' man being the John Mabbott who briefly turned out for each of the above clubs: for instance for Forest's reserves against Fosse in November 1889, and for Notts County in a friendly against Fosse in October 1893. For the latter club, John also started one game in each of the League's divisions. The *Saturday Herald* columnist at least put his finger on Fosse's unwillingness to offer a contract to the forward: 'He plays the proper game wonderfully well, but he is a mere midget'.

***Apps:** ML 2.*
***Goals:** ML 1.*

McALLISTER, Gary

b. Motherwell, 25th December 1964

Career: Fir Park BC; Sept 1981 Motherwell; Aug 1985 CITY; June 1990 Leeds United; July 1996 Coventry City; July 2000 Liverpool.

City debut v Ipswich Town (H) 28.9.85

> Soon dispelling notions that he was any sort of 'makeweight' in the joint £250,000 deal that landed him with more experienced teammate Ali Mauchlen at Filbert Street, attacking midfielder Gary very soon displayed a refreshingly mature regard for the value of accurate passing to feet, and rapidly gained confidence to express a pleasingly ambitious range of skills on the ball as he adapted to First Division football. His initial experiences had come in a relegated Motherwell side, but he'd significantly aided their immediate return to the Scottish Premier Division as champions in 1985, when he'd also scored in the Cup semi-final against Celtic. He would face a further relegation term in 1987 with City, though his own form was such as to justifiably attract the attention of international boss Andy Roxburgh. Unfortunately, a scoring outing for Scotland 'B' against France in April 1987 also brought the injury which sidelined him from the last three vital games prior to the drop being confirmed. Given by Bryan Hamilton the rather back-handed compliment of being expected to function effectively in a variety of midfield and forward roles, Gary found his form suffering for a while, but he perked up under David Pleat's guidance, and his elegant playmaking abilities were soon drawing covetous glances from several clubs of higher status. A distinctly erratic successor to Steve Lynex as City's regular penalty taker, he nonetheless boosted his goal tally to very respectable levels with a number of blindingly executed strikes from less favourable positions. The only ever-present player in 1988/9, Gary remained the nub of constant transfer speculation throughout the following term, but memorably turned down a mooted £1.15m move to Nottingham Forest when unimpressed by Brian Clough's rude manner at interview. With his contract ended, though, and a trio of full international selections having made him a shoe-in for Scotland's 1990 World Cup squad, he signed for Leeds in a move which brought City, via a tribunal decision, their first seven-figure fee. Gary's sinuous prompting alongside Gordon Strachan was a major element in the Elland Road side's 1992 League title win, and he assumed the captaincy of both club and country. A couple of setbacks lay in wait at Wembley in 1996, when Leeds fell to Aston Villa at the Final hurdle in the League Cup, and when Gary missed a crucial penalty for Scotland against England in the Euro 96 tournament. But he was valued at £3m in moving to Highfield Road, and was soon reunited there with Strachan. Gary led Scotland through the qualifying process for the 1998 World Cup, but a knee injury first suffered in a Premiership game against City developed complications, and forced him to miss out on the Finals. Unfortunately, on his return to the national side in 1999, he became a target for mindless barracking, and decided to end his representative career on a total of 57 caps. He had a fine, high-scoring campaign at Coventry in 1999/2000, passing the personal landmark of 100 League goals, and then agreed to an approach from Gérard Houllier to take a free Bosman transfer to Anfield, and add his vast experience and undiminished appetite for the game to Liverpool's youthful midfield. With results that turned out to be mutually joyous, as an apparently rejuvenated Gary collected a late-season hatful of goals in prompting the Reds to their unique hat-trick of Cup wins (League, FA and UEFA), and deservedly took the Man of the Match award from the latter Final against Alaves – a goal-feast to which he contributed one cool penalty and two crucial assists.

***Apps:** FL 199+2; FAC 5; LC 14+1; FMC 4.*
***Goals:** FL 46; FAC 2; LC 3.*

McARTHUR, Thomas

b. Neilston, Renfrewshire, 23rd April 1925
d. Enderby, Leics, 19th April 1994

Career: Neilston Thistle; Neilston Victoria; Jan 1947 CITY; Jan 1954 Plymouth Argyle; July 1955 Brush Sports; Sept 1957 Enderby Town.

City debut v Chesterfield (A) 17.5.47

> A tall, tough, former Scots Guardsman, centre-half Tom won just under a century of first-team selections across eight Second Division seasons, commanding the position only during 1950/1, yet loyally and reliably understudying Sep Smith, Norman Plummer and Matt Gillies in succession while skippering the reserves (and lifting the Combination Cup in 1948). Rejecting a mooted move to Bury in November 1953, Tom then appeared only once more for City, being given a rare runaround in a 1-7 defeat at Leeds, and immediately headed south to Home Park. Unfortunately, he was to make only two League starts for Argyle, the first of them in a 4-8 pasting at Goodison Park, and he soon returned to the county to settle in the Narborough area.

***Apps:** FL 97; FAC 2.*

Tom McArthur

McARTHUR, William

b. Neilston, Renfrewshire, 17th August 1870

Career: 1889 Renton Union; 1890 Sunderland Albion; 1890 Middlesbrough Ironopolis; cs 1893 Bolton Wanderers; Apr 1894 FOSSE; Sept 1896 Dundee; May 1898 Brighton United; (Apr 1900 Army service); 1901 Worthing (-1909).

Fosse debut v Grantham Rovers (A) ML 28.4.1894

> A regular member of the Ironopolis side which won the Northern League championship three years running, centre- or inside-forward Willie was elevated to Division One fare at Bolton, but sidelined from the Trotters' FA Cup Final side of 1894, and joined Fosse in time to play in their final fixture in the Midland League. In fact, a fortnight earlier, he won over Leicester supporters with a hat-trick performance in a friendly against old rivals Loughborough, and there was no doubt that he would be re-registered for the club's first assault on the Second Division. That term he finished as second-top scorer to David Skea, and notched four goals in Fosse's record 13-0 FA Cup win over Notts Olympic. He himself took the laurels as the club's highest marksman the following season, but then followed club trainer Joe Newton to Tayside. Willie appeared in a Scottish Cup semi-final in 1898, then became one of seven Dundee men recruited by the newly-formed Brighton United for Southern League competition (under another ex-Fosse trainer, John Jackson). This club wound up in March 1900, however, and Willie signed up with the Royal Sussex Regiment for Boer War action; settling for amateur football on the South Coast after his return.

***Apps:** FL 55; FAC 10; ML 1.*
***Goals:** FL 27; FAC 9.*

MACAULEY, James Lowry

b. Portarlington, Queens County, Ireland, 1889
d. Preston, 8th October 1945

Career: Cloughfern; 1907 Cliftonville Olympic; Sept 1907 Cliftonville; am Oct 1910 Rangers; am Oct 1910/pro Mar 1911 Huddersfield Town; Nov 1913 Preston North End; 1918-loan-Belfast Celtic; July 1919 CITY; June 1920 Grimsby Town; cs 1921 Lancaster Town; cs 1923 Morecambe (- 1927).

City debut v Wolverhampton Wanderers (H) 30.8.19

> For some time remaining an amateur, and soon capped at that level by Ireland after previous Junior recognition, inside-left Jim exploited his unpaid status to set what is surely a record: in the space of three weeks in October 1910 he turned out in the Scottish League for Rangers, in the Irish League for Cliftonville, and in the Football League for Huddersfield! The latter club were actually fined ten guineas for mis-registering him, but manager Dick Pudan (between his two stints as a Fossil) eventually persuaded Jim to turn professional some three years after he'd rejected that opportunity with Sunderland. He won six full Irish caps while settled in Yorkshire (adding to his previous five selections for the Irish League representative side), then switched to Deepdale in a vain attempt to help avert Preston's relegation. He and Fred Osborn shot them back to promotion again in 1915, but it was with Second Division City that Jim would resume his postwar career, bringing experience and artistry to bear on the forward line when not hampered by a knee injury. A year later, he scored the opening goal for Grimsby in the newly-established Third Division, to which they had become the first-ever club to be relegated. Jim settled in Fulwood following his retirement, and died in Preston Royal Infirmary.

***Apps:** FL 19; FAC 4.*
***Goals:** FL 2.*

McCULLOCH, David

b. Hamilton, Lanarkshire, 5th October 1911
d. Hamilton, May 1979.

Career: Hamilton Amateurs; Shotts United; 1932 Third Lanark; June 1934 Heart of Midlothian; Nov 1935 Brentford; Oct 1938 Derby County; July 1946 CITY; Dec 1946 Bath City; Aug 1949 Waterford (p/coach); July 1951 Alloa Athletic (p/mgr)(- 1952).

City debut v Manchester City (H) 31.8.46

> Unfortunately looking well past his best when briefly turning out for City in the first postwar League season, Dave had been a centre-forward in the classic mould throughout the 30s, leading the Scottish scorers' list in 1934/5 with 38 goals, and winning his first representative honours while averaging a goal per game at Tynecastle (as indeed he did in his initial First Division term at Griffin Park). He scored in his only inter-League game, then added three goals while winning seven full Scottish caps; and also played in one wartime international at a time when he was regularly guesting for the likes of Falkirk, Aldershot, Bath City, Chelsea, Bournemouth, Swansea Town and Brentford. The latter club had originally paid £6,000 for Dave's all-action foraging and aerial ability, and got 85 goals in return, out of his pre-war total of 178. He had been Derby's record signing at £9,500, but joined City with Tom Eggleston for a joint fee of £3,100. As a real veteran, Dave led the League of Ireland scoring chart at the end of his first season with Waterford, and in later years worked for Rolls Royce at East Kilbride.

***Apps:** FL 4.*
***Goals:** FL 2.*

McDERMENT, William Stirling

b. Paisley, Renfrewshire, 5th January 1943

Career: Johnstone Burgh; May 1961 CITY; July 1967 Luton Town; May 1969 Notts County; 1970 Morton; Feb 1972 Lockheed Leamington.

City debut v Aston Villa (A) 15.5.63

> A reliable reserve wing-half who made sporadic appearances across five First Division seasons in the mid-60s, Billy could never quite lay claim to a regular senior berth, and perhaps the closest he came to a moment of Filbert Street glory was in getting one hand on the Football Combination Cup in 1967 as skipper of the reserves side which shared that trophy with Spurs. Curiously, City won only one League game with Billy in the line-up, yet he was never in a defeated Leicester side in Cup football. At the time of his signing, as another coup by north-of-the-border scout Walter McLean, it was stated that he was the first Scottish Junior ever to have appeared in a senior amateur international. Billy contributed alongside Max Dougan to Luton's Fourth Division championship triumph of 1968, and had a decent run in the top flight in Scotland after failing to settle at Meadow Lane.

***Apps:** FL 20+3; FAC 2; LC 5.*
***Goals:** FL 1.*

McDONALD, David

b. Dundee

Career: Dundee Wanderers; cs 1895 Dundee; cs 1896 Everton; Oct 1896 FOSSE; cs 1897 Dundee; Feb 1898 Millwall; cs 1898 Dundee Wanderers; cs 1899 Dundee (- 1901).

Fosse debut v Lincoln City (H) 7.11.1896

> Unable to make a Goodison Park breakthrough, inside-right Davie was signed by Fosse as an instant early-season replacement for his former Dundee teammate, Tom Lonie, but lost his goal touch after an early burst of deadly finishing. He had been Dundee's top scorer in the Scottish First Division in the previous term (albeit with a mere six counters), but his impact as a whole in England was muted, with a later Millwall record of only one goal in two Southern League outings.

***Apps:** FL 16; FAC 2.*
***Goals:** FL 7.*

MACDONALD, Kevin Duncan

b. Inverness, 22nd November 1960

Career: Inverness Caledonian; May 1980 CITY; Nov 1984 Liverpool; Dec 1987-loan-CITY; Nov 1988-loan-Rangers; July 1989 Coventry City; Mar 1991-loan-Cardiff City; Aug 1991 Walsall.

City debut v Norwich City (H) 29.11.80 (sub)

> Striding into the First Division after only two seasons of Highland League football, midfielder Kevin impressed immediately with his combativeness and almost cocky confidence. The latter attribute stuck with him throughout his City career, from the moment he stepped up to convert a crucial penalty in his first full home game, and was later evidenced by some memorably cool defensive work (including a number of heart-stopping back-headers to Mark Wallington) when he filled in at centre-back for Larry May during the 1983 promotion run-in. An ever-present that term, he retained consistency back in the First Division and, after mastering his occasionally fiery temper (he was the first City player to be twice sent off), he proved a genuinely classy operator, with only a marginal lack of pace detracting from his repertoire of control, vision and ball-winning ability. A £400,000 cheque took him to Anfield, where injuries cruelly hampered his progress in a formidably strong squad. Even so, he collected an FA Cup winner's medal to gild the Double year of 1986, before a broken leg once more heralded a long lay-off. Kevin had still to return to the senior Liverpool line-up when he came back to Filbert Street for a loan spell under caretaker manager Peter Morris, and unfortunately showed every sign of rustiness in the three defeats in which he played. On full recovery, he remained for a while in top-flight contention at Coventry, then turned down a proffered player/coach role at Cardiff before moving to Bescot Stadium. Kevin retired after Walsall's 1993 Play-Off exit, and rejoined City that summer as a youth coach. In December 1994, in the wake of Brian Little's departure, he and Tony McAndrew jointly assumed the club's caretaker management role for three Premiership fixtures; but both men resigned in January 1995. Kevin later rejoined Little at Villa Park, where he remains on the coaching staff under John Gregory.

Kevin MacDonald

***Apps:** FL 136+5; FAC 4; LC 10.*
***Goals:** FL 8.*

McDONALD, Thomas

b. Hill of Beath, Fife, 24th May 1930

Career: Pitreavie Rovers; Inverkeithing; Hill of Beath; Rosyth Recreation; 1947 Hibernian; Apr 1954 Wolverhampton Wanderers; July 1956 CITY; July 1960 Dunfermline Athletic; Dec 1962 Raith Rovers; July 1963 Queen of the South; Dec 1963 Stirling Albion.

City debut v Doncaster Rovers (H) 18.8.56 (scored twice)

> Still on National Service with the Black Watch when he made his Easter Road debut, Tommy was initially understudy to, and then the replacement for, the great Gordon Smith. The outside-right figured in a League runners-up side and two title-winning squads between 1950 and 1952, and earned a Scotland 'B' cap in the same March 1954 game against England as City's Johnny Anderson, but his move to reigning English champions Wolves saw him stuck in the Molineux reserves for much of his stay. David Halliday paid £6,000 to bring the tricky and pacy flanker to Filbert Street, and he got the 1956/7 promotion campaign off to a flying start; though eventually missing out on the run-in. For three seasons thereafter he vied with Howard Riley for the No 7 shirt, winning his highest number of selections and claiming his best seasonal goal tally just prior to returning to Scotland. Ill-luck dogged Tommy there, especially when he went down with appendicitis virtually on the eve of the 1961 Scottish Cup Final, though he subsequently played in European competition for Dunfermline along with Willie Cunningham, and passed on more than a few tips to the young Jackie Sinclair.

***Apps:** FL 113; FAC 5.*
***Goals:** FL 27; FAC 2.*

MACFARLANE, Ian

b. Lanark, 26th January 1933

Career: Douglas Water Thistle; May 1954 Aberdeen; Aug 1956 Chelsea; May 1958 CITY; July 1959 Bath City (-1967).

City debut/only game v Luton Town (H) 4.10.58

> Signed for the second time by former Aberdeen boss David Halliday, almost four years to the day after he'd first elevated him to the senior game, Ian was a tough, hefty full-back who probably set the Doug Rougvie mould at both Pittodrie and Stamford Bridge. City's £9,000 investment was hardly repaid, though, with Ian only filling in once at right-back while Willie Cunningham was away representing Northern Ireland against England, and local scribe Billy King in the *Mail* deeming him 'easily beaten ... as though completely out of touch with the requirements of this class of football'. He then moved on to partner Tony Book in Bath's Southern League championship side of 1960, and remained almost eight years at Twerton Park, making around 300 appearances. Perhaps inspired by his encounters there with Malcolm Allison, Ian then embarked on a successful coaching career, which saw him return to Leicester as assistant manager to both Frank McLintock and Jock Wallace, with an interim caretaker spell in charge of City's already-relegated side at the end of 1977/8. Previously he had fulfilled second-in-command duties at each of Middlesbrough, Manchester City and Sunderland, and had held the managerial reins at Carlisle; though he almost invariably tended to be associated with highly-motivated but essentially dour sides. After Leaving Filbert Street again, he had a spell as manager of Yeovil Town, and was later chief scout for Leeds.

***Apps:** FL 1.*

McFARLANE, Peter

b. Motherwell

Career: Carfin; 1894 Motherwell; Dec 1894 FOSSE.

Fosse debut/only game v Crewe Alexandra (A) 12.1.1895

> A 'sturdy' left-back who matched his single Scottish League appearance for Motherwell with one senior selection south of the border (a 2-2 draw at Gresty Road), Peter was described as 'too prone to dribble' in an era when the back-line positions were dominated by big kickers specialising in first-time clearances. He was listed as available for a £10 fee at the end of his Fosse term (after scoring once in a United Counties League outing), but we can find no evidence of any club paying it. Nonetheless, circumstantial evidence points to the possibility of Peter having assisted Falkirk from 1896.

***Apps:** FL 1.*

McGRAW, Ian

b. Glasgow, 30th August 1926

Career: Army football; Rutherglen Glencairn; cs 1948 Arbroath; Dec 1948 CITY; 1952 Belgrave WMC (coach only); Jan 1954 Corby Town.

City debut v Tottenham Hotspur (H) 25.12.48

> Ian's was a tragically truncated City career following his £4,200 signing by Johnny Duncan. The easefully authoritative young Scottish 'keeper had really endeared himself to City supporters with his performances in the 1949 Cup run, and had helped rebuff hot favourites Portsmouth in the semi-final, when he was seriously injured a week later in a rough-house League game with Grimsby. A broken little finger not only kept Ian out of the Wembley line-up, but also developed complications which led to the necessity of the digit's amputation. At that stage, he had made eight appearances in each of the League and Cup competitions, and even though he bravely returned for another five senior games in 1950/1 despite his handicap, he remained ill-starred. A spinal injury sustained in a reserve game against Cardiff in October 1950 interrupted his comeback, he faced direct competition from internationals Tommy Godwin and Johnny Anderson, and even after he'd had the odd game at centre-half for the A team in 1951/2, he had to undergo an appendix operation that March. The former Scots Guardsman at least received two minor consolations: in July 1949 the FA granted him an FA Cup runners-up medal, and in April 1953 City played a testimonial game for Ian against Wolves.

***Apps:** FL 13; FAC 8.*

McGREGOR, William

b. Paisley, Lanarkshire, 1st December 1923

Career: Mossvale YMCA; am 1946/pro April 1947 CITY; Sept 1953 Mansfield Town; Aug 1956 Corby Town (- 1958).

City debut v Tottenham Hotspur (A) 27.3.48

> A spirited, compact, quick-tackling reserve right-back for six seasons at Filbert Street, Willie picked up a medal from the 1948 Combination Cup win

but, with Willie Frame, Ted Jelly and Arthur Lever successively holding down the senior No 2 position, got few chances to shine in the Second Division before joining the colony of ex-City men at Field Mill. The £2,500 fee which took him to Mansfield not only equalled that club's record outlay, but was also their first HP deal (payable over 12 months), and Willie justified it with 119 League appearances over three seasons in the Third Division (North).

***Apps:** FL 9; FAC 1.*

McILMOYLE, Hugh

b. Cambuslang, Lanarkshire, 29th January 1940

Career: Port Glasgow Juniors; Aug 1959 CITY; July 1962 Rotherham United; Mar 1963 Carlisle United; Oct 1964 Wolverhampton Wanderers; Mar 1967 Bristol City; Sept 1967 Carlisle United; Sept 1969 Middlesbrough; July 1971 Preston North End; cs 1973 Morton; July 1974 Carlisle United; cs 1975 Morton (p/coach).

City debut v West Ham United (H) 3.4.61 (scored once)

> The centre of a major City controversy when chosen by Matt Gillies in Ken Leek's No 9 shirt for the 1961 FA Cup Final, after having played only seven League games, Hugh was in no way overawed by the Wembley occasion, assuming an intelligent deep-lying role and looking City's most dangerous forward on the day. Hugh, who had started his working life as a ship's painter in the Greenock yards, was not quite without pedigree: those seven games had seen him score four times, and his status as the reserve-team's top marksman (19 in 20 starts) had been built on hat-trick Combination performances against each of Spurs and Arsenal. But the shadow of that shock Cup selection fell heavily over him in the following term, and he struggled to maintain the role of Leek's successor when coming under intense scrutiny from a sceptical crowd. Again he top-scored for the second team (with 14), but was allowed to move on at season's end. The sense of too much responsibility having been heaped too soon upon the slender youngster was borne out by his future development into a fine and versatile servant for a host of other clubs. In the first of three spells with Carlisle, Hugh topped the Football League scoring charts with a 39-goal contribution to the Cumbrians' 1964 rise from the Fourth Division, and he assisted them partway to the championship of Division Three a year later, though he was actually suffering relegation from the First with Wolves as Brunton Park celebrations broke out. Again at Molineux, Hugh moved on before the completion of a promotion campaign, with Derek Dougan displacing him for the run-in to elevation in 1967. Subsequent moves attracted some hefty transfer fees, with Hugh's heading abilities in particular being much in demand, and he matured into a perceptive attacking midfielder, bowing out of the senior game with a career aggregate of exactly 200 League and Cup goals in England and Scotland. In 1976, Hugh returned to Leicester to work for Walkers Crisps, and briefly coached at Roundhill Community College.

***Apps:** FL 20; FAC 1; ECWC 1.*
***Goals:** FL 5; ECWC 1.*

MACKAY, Robert

b. Harthill, Lanarkshire, 6th May 1948

Career: Whitburn Bluebells; Harthill Juniors; Apr 1965 CITY; 1970 Burton Albion; cs 1970 Boston United; cs 1971 Kidderminster Harriers; Enderby Town; Atherstone Town; 1974 Nuneaton Borough; Aug 1975 Worcester City; Oct 1975 Tamworth; Bedworth Town; Nov 1976 New Parks Social; cs 1979 Enderby Town.

Bobby Mackay

City debut v Manchester City (H) 21.8.68

> A versatile defensive midfielder who looked set for a decent run in City's first team, Bobby suffered a definitive knock to his progress in the first game he played for new manager Frank O'Farrell: being stretchered off in the Third Round FA Cup tie at Barnsley as City embarked on their 1969 Wembley run. Only one League Cup outing followed his cartilage operation, and Bobby's senior career came to a premature end. He was in a Burton side relegated from the Southern League's top flight; scored a Cup giant-killing winner for Boston against Fourth Division Southport; and at Kidderminster briefly teamed up again with former City reserves John and Jim Flannagan. He was a member, with Bob Newton, of Nuneaton's Southern League squad of 1974/5, pipped to the title by Wimbledon.

***Apps:** FL 6+1; FAC 1; LC 1+1.*
***Goals:** FL 1.*

McKENNA, James Peter

b. Blackpool, 18th April 1910
d. Blackpool, 27th August 1986

Career: am Port Vale; Oct 1929 Great Harwood; Feb 1930 CITY; cs 1932 Bath City; June 1933 Nuneaton Town; Aug 1935 Market Harborough Town.

City debut/only game v Birmingham (H) 26.3.32

> The third-choice City 'keeper behind Jim McLaren and Jack Beby, Jim got but the one chance to exhibit his prowess at senior level, in the above 3-1 home win. He might have known his Filbert Street luck would be out: he was stretchered off unconscious on his February 1930 reserve-team debut. Bath won the championship of the Southern League's Western Division in 1933, but we have no confirmation of the scale of Jim's contribution; he was then signed by George Carr at Nuneaton. At this point he also acted as honorary secretary to the Thursday League club Solus, with whom Johnny Duncan also had an off-field association; spent his summers as wicketkeeper for City League outfit Hill Street Guild; and was engaged as a joiner in Leicester's slum clearance programme. Though he turned down terms offered by Lancaster City in 1935 to remain on the local scene, Jim was set up in business in Blackpool by 1937.

***Apps:** FL 1.*

McKENNAN, Peter Stewart

b. Airdrie, Lanarkshire, 16th July 1918
d. Dundonald, Ayrshire, 28th September 1991

Career: Whitburn Juniors; July 1935 Partick Thistle; Oct 1947 West Bromwich Albion; Mar 1948 CITY; Sept 1948 Brentford; May 1949 Middlesbrough; July 1951 Oldham Athletic; July 1954 Coleraine (p/coach).

City debut v Cardiff City (A) 13.3.48

> A fascinating and colourful character who barely settled at Filbert Street at all, inside-forward Peter was known throughout his career by the nickname 'Ma Ba' ('My Ball'), after his habitually confident on-field shout for possession. A virtual legend at Firhill for both his talent and his temperament, he won two Scottish League representative selections before the war, and in December 1938 was fined in Kilmarnock Sheriff Court for assaulting – and knocking out – the Killie defender Milloy after a game two months previously. Peter served in the Royal Welch Fusiliers during WW2, and was promoted to sergeant-major while in France, but he also packed in a fair amount of 'guesting': for Wrexham, West Brom, Chelsea and Brentford, as well as in Belfast throughout 1940/1 for Glentoran. There he also picked up two selections for the Northern Ireland Regional League against the League of Ireland, scoring five times. After a notably short stint with West Brom, Peter came to Leicester as the more highly-valued component of the part-exchange deal that took Jack Haines to The Hawthorns, but clashed with Johnny Duncan and left within a month of the new season starting, signing for Brentford on the day City beat them in a Second Division encounter at Griffin Park. The move threatened to rebound on City as the 1949 Cup run developed, for a week before City had to meet the Bees again, on Sixth Round business, Peter knocked in five goals for them in an 8-2 mauling of Bury. He was kept quiet on the big day, however. His four-clubs-in-two-seasons meanderings slowed in the First Division at Ayresome (where he scored the only goal in a derby game against Newcastle that attracted that ground's highest-ever attendance of 53,802); and as a veteran he inspired Oldham to the 1953 Division Three (North) title, while his career-closing stint at Coleraine was beset by disciplinary problems which attracted a three-month suspension. When his career was over, he worked for a while in North-East shipyards, and became purchasing manager for John Brown Construction in Persia (now Iran).

***Apps:** FL 18.*
***Goals:** FL 7.*

MACKIE, Robert

b. Dalry, Ayrshire, August 1882

Career: Cowie Wanderers; Stenhousemuir; May 1904 Heart of Midlothian; Aug 1905 Chelsea; Nov 1907 FOSSE; cs 1909 Darlington; Aug 1910 Airdrieonians.

Fosse debut v Derby County (H) 23.11.07

> 'Ungainly but obstinate' was full-back Bob according to one Leicester critic, while a counterpart on the *Mercury* painted a similar picture: 'Inclined to be shambling in style but, my word, he teaches those right wing men to be careful'. Bob had played but a single game as a Junior before Stenhousemuir tempted him into the professional ranks, and a year later he was in the Scottish First Division with Hearts. Chelsea then signed him for their first-ever League campaign, though he played only a minor role in their 1907 promotion. At a cost of £300, however, he became a vital defensive cog in Fosse's own promotion effort, before suffering along with his teammates some of the First Division embarrassments of 1908/9. Eventually settling at Broomfield for five years, he received an Airdrie benefit from a game against Albion Rovers in 1914. That year, also, he turned out in goal in a friendly at Birmingham: he had previously done so for Chelsea when chosen to replace Willie Foulke in an FA Cup preliminary tie against Southern United in October 1905.

***Apps:** FL 33; FAC 3.*

McKINLAY, William

b. Glasgow, 22nd April 1969

Career: Hamilton Thistle; June 1985 Dundee United; Oct 1995 Blackburn Rovers; Oct 2000-loan-CITY; Nov 2000 Bradford City.

City debut/only game v Crystal Palace (H) LC 1.11.2000

> An experienced midfielder brought to Filbert Street by Peter Taylor on what was intended to be a three-month loan, Billy made an uninspiring debut as City embarrassed themselves severely on the occasion of their first defence of the Worthington Cup, and soon had his temporary stay further curtailed when he became the first signing of the Jim Jeffries regime at Valley Parade. To cap something of a nightmare season, the Bantams were early booked for relegation, with Billy's occasional engine-room bite insufficient to turn around their fortunes, or indeed to secure for himself a contract extension. Himself marked early for progress in the game, Billy successively won Schools, Youth, Under-21 and B caps for Scotland, going on to earn 29 full international selections; but was not always so fortunate at club level: appearing as a sub in both of Dundee United's losing Cup Finals of 1988 and 1991, and missing out when they finally raised the trophy in 1994. Never a prolific scorer, he nonetheless said farewell to Tannadice with a hat-trick in the Tayside derby. His integration at Ewood wasn't helped when he soon picked up a disproportionate number of bookings; a groin injury then kept him out for a year; and his failure to find favour with incoming boss Graeme Souness comprehensively marked his cards.

***Apps:** LC 1.*

MACKLEWORTH, Colin

b. Bow, London, 24th March 1947

Career: app 1962/pro Apr 1964 West Ham United; Nov 1967 CITY; cs 1971 Kettering Town; Metropolitan Police; Clapton.

City debut v Rotherham United (A) FAC 9.3.68

> A cool and capable reserve 'keeper for both his League clubs, Colin won a Youth Cup medal with the Hammers in 1963, but only turned out three times in Division One during 1966/7. Brought to Filbert Street as cover for Peter Shilton, he faced a high-pressure debut in the drawn Fifth Round Cup tie at Millmoor, and also saw City through the replay before making his League bow. For another three seasons Colin bore the frustrations of experiencing regular Combination football and distinctly rare senior opportunities, but at least he tasted some success at Kettering, as they won promotion under Ron Atkinson in 1972, and the Southern League championship a year later. Colin subsequently joined the police force.

***Apps:** FL 6; FAC 3.*

McLAREN, Alexander

b. Tibbermore, Perth, 25th December 1910
d. Perth, 5th February 1960

Career: Tulloch; am Apr 1927/pro Dec 1927 St Johnstone; Feb 1933 CITY; Oct 1940 Morton; Oct 1945 St Johnstone.

City debut v Everton (A) 8.3.33

Taking over the City green jersey from unrelated namesake Jim, former blacksmith and Scottish international 'keeper Sandy must have wondered what had hit him on his debut, as a Dixie Dean hat-trick accounted for only half the Everton goals which flew past him that afternoon. Nonetheless, he went for 102 consecutive games between the City sticks from that date, and was still very much the first-choice custodian when war brought a halt to League football over six years later. Noted particularly for his unflappability and the prodigious strength of his punch, Sandy was unfortunate not to add to his tally of five caps while with City (he'd remarkably won the first at the age of 18), and took a Second Division championship medal in 1937 as the only tangible honour from a superb Filbert Street career. Sandy spent the first year of the war as a Leicester taxi driver, moved homewards to represent Morton and (as a guest) Airdrie during 1940/1, and joined the Navy in May 1941, later seeing service in the Middle East. Postwar, he returned briefly to St Johnstone for an eight-game adieu to football, then commenced work as a security policeman for the Admiralty at Almondvale. Sandy died at the age of 49 from bronchial pneumonia. One of his sons, also known as Sandy, was a Dundee United goalkeeper in the mid-50s.

***Apps:** FL 239; FAC 17; WW2 30.*

MacLAREN, David

b. Auchterarder, Perthshire, 12th June 1934

Career: 1948 Comrie Athletic; St Johnstone Juniors; RAF football; Feb 1956 Dundee; Jan 1957 CITY; May 1960 Plymouth Argyle; Jan 1965 Wolverhampton Wanderers; Sept 1966 Southampton; July 1967 Worcester City.

City debut v Notts County (A) 2.2.57

> Though unrelated to either of City's other goalkeeping McLarens, Dave was clearly destined by kinship for fame as a custodian: brothers Jimmy and Roy both kept goal in League football (the former for Berwick, Chester and Carlisle; the latter for St Johnstone, Bury and Sheffield Wednesday) and another brother, Monty, was a Liverpool reserve. He followed a roundabout route, however, as RAF service took him to Malaya, where he was adjudged 'Sportsman of the Year' in 1954; and it was there that he actually signed his Dundee forms. As cover to Bill Brown (later of Spurs fame), Dave had made but a single Scottish League appearance when he became an emergency buy for City after Johnny Anderson suffered injury partway through the 1957 Second Division championship campaign. Thereafter he just shaded the rivalry for the green jersey, in a side struggling desperately but successfully to consolidate in the First Division, until the advent of Gordon Banks. Dave's alertness and agility next found a Home Park context (in the company of Johnny Newman) until he was prised away to Molineux to join Wolves' futile attempt to maintain top-flight status in 1965. He was still, however, deemed the man to shore up Southampton's defence during their first-ever Division One season, and he assisted Worcester City to the Southern League title in 1968. Dave became a coach in Malaysia in 1970, and took over the national side there in 1972; then managed Hakoah in the New South Wales Federation before assuming control of Australia's international eleven in June 1975.

***Apps:** FL 85; FAC 5.*

McLAREN, James

b. Falkirk, Stirlingshire, 12th July 1897
d. Leicester, 16th November 1975

Career: Bonnybridge Heatherbell; 1920 Stenhousemuir; May 1922 Bradford City; May 1927 CITY; Oct 1933 Watford.

City debut v Newcastle United (H) 7.5.27

> The son of a former Scottish champion racing cyclist, Jim had been, in 1911, the goalkeeper in the first schoolboy international played by Scotland, and the lad from Larbert Central School had then distinguished himself with a penalty save against the English. After WW1 service in France with the Argyll & Sutherland Highlanders, he helped Stenhousemuir into, and through, their first season in the Scottish League, then built a good reputation in a struggling Bradford City side which was eventually relegated from Division Two in 1927 – his transfer to City helping to relieve some of the financial embarrassment the Valley Parade outfit were then suffering. At Leicester, Jim displaced fellow-countryman Kenny Campbell as City mounted their most convincing assaults on the First Division title, and held his key position for all but a few games until succeeded in turn by namesake Sandy: like himself, a 'keeper not averse to using a hefty frame to full advantage when advancing from his line. By the time he retired from Vicarage Road in 1939 (after twice featuring in the Final of the Third Division South Cup), Jim had amassed a career total of 519 League games, and had become only the second player in League history to receive five-year benefit payments from three separate clubs. In fact he holds the record as the oldest player to turn out for Watford (at 41 years, 172 days): a feat he shades by a mere matter of months from another former City 'keeper, Joe Calvert. Jim won no official senior representative honours, but in April of each of 1931, 1932 and 1933 he took part in a little-noted series of well-supported games at Newcastle, which revived the old Anglo-Scots v Home Scots format in aid of Northumberland miners' charities.

***Apps:** FL 170; FAC 10.*

McLEOD, Roderick

b. Kilsyth, Stirlingshire, February 1872
d. Lambeth, London, 20th December 1931

Career: Westburn; Partick Thistle; Jan 1891 West Bromwich Albion; Aug 1897 FOSSE; May 1898 Brighton United; Apr 1899 Southampton; Aug 1900 Brentford.

Fosse debut v Luton Town (H) 4.9.1897

> A classy inside-forward whose successful stint with West Brom had brought him 50 League goals at virtually a one-in-three ratio, and who had twice faced Aston Villa in the FA Cup Final (as a winner in 1892, and a loser three years later), Roddie became Fosse's leading marksman in his only Second Division season, but was soon to join the Southern League roundabout onto which so many early players leapt from Leicester. In this instance, he accompanied trainer John Jackson, and appeared for Brighton alongside ex-Fossils Willie McArthur and Peter McWhirter; but he had moved to champions-elect Southampton before the term was out. He departed from The Dell in pique after being omitted from their 1900 Cup Final team, and assisted Brentford to promotion from the Southern League's Second Division a year later, when scoring at a goal-a-game rate. In March 1911, a press report

Roddie McLeod

remarked that he had 'fallen on evil days', and that an appeal was being made to find Roddie employment as a warehouseman or storekeeper.

***Apps:** FL 28; FAC 1.*
***Goals:** FL 13; FAC 1.*

McLINTOCK, Francis

b. Glasgow, 28th December 1939

Career: Shawfield Juniors; Jan 1957 CITY; Oct 1964 Arsenal; June 1973 Queens Park Rangers.

City debut v Blackpool (A) 14.9.59

> Brought down from the Gorbals and nurtured at Filbert Street as a probing wing-half, Frank possessed the rare combination of toughness and elegance, constantly added constructive variety and vision to his play, and soon became a key element in City's then-revolutionary midfield strategies of the early 60s. Whether switching right-half and inside-right roles in mid-match with Graham Cross or creating crossfield magic with Davie Gibson, he oozed footballing class; and it was a surprise neither when he graduated to full international honours with Scotland, nor when Billy Wright's Arsenal eventually paid City their then-record incoming fee of £80,000 for his services. Frank actually took some time to settle at Highbury, and extended his apparent Wembley hoodoo in the late 60s (following heartbreak FA Cup Final defeats with City in 1961 and 1963 with a pair of losing League Cup Final appearances for Arsenal in 1968 and 1969) even after shifting to a central defensive role. Then, though, he experienced a couple of years of genuine glory: skippering the Gunners to their 1970 Fairs Cup win, and to the domestic Double a year later, as well as picking up both the 1971 Footballer of the Year award and a CBE, and re-establishing himself as an influential international. Though Frank then collected his fifth Wembley runners-up medal from the 1972 FA Cup Final, it was not long before Arsenal erred in writing off their asset too early and cheaply. Becoming a Loftus Road defensive regular across four more seasons, he led QPR in a near-miss title bid in 1976, and on a decent UEFA Cup run the following term. Yet even after 609 games in the First Division had lent Frank a reputation for on-field generalship, he had no backroom experience at all when City riskily, and unwisely as it worked out, turned to their former player as the managerial successor to Jimmy Bloomfield. Even with Ian MacFarlane installed as his assistant, Frank seemed unable either to motivate his inherited squad or transmit effectively any new tactical thinking. He jettisoned the talismanic Frank Worthington, too many of his transfer-market dealings bore the stamp of quick-fix desperation, and any pretence that City might escape their rapidly-signposted relegation fate was dropped at an early stage of his stewardship. Frank's unwillingness to commit to living again in Leicester (or to leaving behind his London business interests) hardly helped his cause, and he deserted his broken-backed City team in April 1978. Subsequently, he has acted as adviser to the dire soccer-themed movie 'Yesterday's Hero', as youth coach at QPR, manager at Brentford, assistant boss at Millwall, part-time players' agent, and media pundit.

***Apps:** FL 168; FAC 20; LC 11; ECWC 1.*
***Goals:** FL 25; LC 3.*

McMAHON, Samuel Keiron

b. Newark, Notts, 10th February 1976

Career: YT July 1992/pro July 1994 CITY; Jan 1997-loan-Kettering Town; Jan 1999 Cambridge United; cs 1999 Stevenage Borough.

City debut v Wimbledon (H) 1.4.95 (sub)

> First noticed for his energetic probing during City's 1994 schedule of pre-season friendlies, Sam developed his high promise as an attack-minded midfielder in the Central League and earned himself the club's Young Player of the Year award in 1995. By then he'd made a brief Premiership bow, subbing for Nicky Mohan with pleasing impact in a farcically see-saw 3-4 defeat by the Dons; but his subsequent City career was then also a fitful affair of occasional entrances from the bench, with only one starting selection to his record. Sam scored at Port Vale after replacing broken-bone victim Steve Corica, but was himself badly injury-hit during 1996/7, then suspended following a dismissal during his Conference loan spell. Neither his skills nor workrate thereafter matched Martin O'Neill's standards, and Sam, when freed, failed to win a long-term contract as Third Division leaders Cambridge achieved their promotion goal. In the early weeks of 2000/1 he was called up for an FA XI for one of a series of trials for the England semi-professional squad, but lucklessly found the game postponed.

***Apps:** PL/FL 1+4; LC 0+2.*
***Goals:** FL 1.*

McMILLAN, John Stuart

b. Port Glasgow, Renfrewshire, 16th February 1871
d. Birkdale, Lancs, 3rd November 1941

Career: Port Glasgow Athletic; cs 1890 St Bernards; Nov 1890 Derby County; May 1896 FOSSE; Jan 1901 Small Heath; May 1903 Bradford City; May 1906 Glossop (p/mgr).

Fosse debut v Darwen (H) 5.9.1896 (scored once)

> A prodigy in pre-league football with his hometown Clydeside club, appearing regularly from the age of 14, Johnny was only 16 when claiming eight goals from the Scottish Cup campaign of 1887/8, and still in his teens when embroiled in a bitter row over professionalism at the Edinburgh-based St Bernards, which saw him depart from the suspended club after only one game in their colours. The powerful inside-forward then gave fine service to Derby, scoring 50 League and Cup goals over six seasons (including the late winner in the Test Match against Notts County at Filbert Street which retained top-flight status for the Rams in 1895). At Leicester, the versatile Scot led by example, maintaining a high scoring ratio while demonstrating a rare degree of creative flair, and prompting the club to its first serious promotion challenge in 1899, when Fosse finished 3rd. He took a club benefit from a friendly with Notts County in December 1900, and moved to Small Heath only a month later, to notch thirteen goals in thirteen games and help them secure promotion. Johnny would experience relegation and promotion again in Birmingham over the next two terms, and was then handed the role of captaining Bradford City for their inaugural League season (when still being described as 'an agile player with excellent command over the ball'). His transition to backroom roles started at Glossop and with a spell as Birmingham trainer from 1909, and resumed after WW1 with two seasons in charge of Gillingham following their 1920 election to the League (though there is an unconfirmed hint that Johnny may have closed his playing career with a few games for Abercorn from January 1910). He was later landlord of the Normanton Hotel in Derby. His Leicester-born son, Stuart, was also a player with Derby, Wolves, Chelsea, Gillingham, Clapton Orient and Bradford City, and managed Derby to their 1946 FA Cup triumph.

***Apps:** FL 122; FAC 9.*
***Goals:** FL 43; FAC 5.*

McNALLY, Owen

b. Denny, Stirlingshire, 20th June 1906

Career: Denny Hibs; Feb 1927 Celtic; Aug 1927-loan-Arthurlie; Feb 1929-loan-Hamilton Academical; Sept 1930 Bray Unknowns; cs 1931 Cardiff City; cs 1932 Bray Unknowns; cs 1933 Lausanne-Sports; Feb 1935 Sligo Rovers; cs 1935 Distillery; Jan 1936 CITY; Aug 1937 Racing Club de Calais; Nov 1938 Shamrock Rovers.

City debut v Nottingham Forest (A) 30.1.36

> Born in the same Scottish town as Adam Black, centre-forward Owen was certainly possessed of rather more wanderlust than his eminently settled City predecessor. A frustrated reserve to record scorer Jimmy McGrory at Celtic (totalling but a dozen League games and a trio of goals for the Bhoys), he clearly determined to make his own mark in the game's annals, and grasped his first opportunity of a loan out to Second Division Arthurlie somewhat greedily. In only his seventh start, he notched eight goals in a 10-0 win over Armadale in October 1927, and finished that term with 30 successes in 30 games. Then, on his Celtic release, he started collecting clubs and countries in almost equal proportion. The trek from Scotland through Ireland, Wales and Switzerland (under the coaching of the legendary Jimmy Hogan) might have satisfied many a footballing mercenary, but the 5ft 7 in Owen maintained his rolling-stone status for some years yet; playing again on both sides of the Irish border, and gathering the significant 'moss' of a scoring performance for the Irish League at Blackpool in September 1935, on the first occasion that representative side had conquered the Football League since the series of regular meetings started in 1894. Shortly thereafter, signing for £1,000, Owen had a spirited bash at solving City's centre-forward problem, at that time being wrestled with by converted centre-half Fred Sharman, but soon to be comprehensively resolved by the advent of Jack Bowers. Accordingly, nothing daunted, Owen simply got out his pasport once again... He closed his career as the 14-goal leading scorer for League of Ireland champions Shamrock in 1938/9.

***Apps:** FL 16; FAC 1.*
***Goals:** FL 7; FAC 1.*

McNEILL, Ian McKeand

b. Baillieston, Glasgow, 24th February 1932

Career: Bridgeton Waverley; 1950 Aberdeen; Mar 1956 CITY; Mar 1959 Brighton & Hove Albion; July 1962 Southend United; July 1964 Dover; cs 1965 Ross County (p/coach).

City debut v Sheffield Wednesday (H) 2.4.56

> The holder of five Scottish Youth caps, whose National Service in Kenya restricted him to a mere ten senior starts in almost six seasons at Pittodrie, inside-forward Ian was signed jointly with Joe O'Neil from City boss David Halliday's former club, and soon made a rather more substantial impact at Filbert Street. In contributing 18 goals to the 1957 Second Division championship campaign (including the 10-second strike on Trentside which crucially disheartened promotion rivals Forest), he presented a nippily darting, and highly effective, contrast and complement to the styles of scorer-in-chief Arthur Rowley and target-man Derek Hines. He found goals, and a regular place, somewhat harder to come by in the top flight against the challenges of John Doherty, Jimmy Walsh and Bernie Kelly, but it was nonetheless Ian's invaluable strike at

St Andrews in the final fixture of 1957/8 which ensured City would not take an immediate drop back. Then the subject of a deadline-day deal which saw him sign for Brighton boss and ex-City man Billy Lane on St Pancras station, he gradually adopted a deeper-lying schemer's role in a decent South Coast stint with both Seagulls and Shrimpers. Ian entered management with Ross County (prompting them to their first-ever Highland League championship in 1967); took over at Wigan Athletic in 1968 to lead them into the newly-formed Northern Premier League (and actually made a substitute appearance for them that term); had further backroom stints at Salisbury and Ross County (winners of the Scottish Qualifying Cup); and then returned to Wigan to plot and then oversee their elevation to Division Four football in 1978. Subsequently, he has bossed Northwich Victoria, been assistant manager at Chelsea, held the reins at Shrewsbury, acted as No 2 at Millwall, and assumed the chief scout's role at Bolton (from 1995) and Leeds (from 1997).

Apps: *FL 72; FAC 4.*
Goals: *FL 26; FAC 1.*

McWHIRTER, Douglas S.

b. Erith, Kent, 13th August 1886
d. Plumstead, London, 14th October 1966

Career: Bromley; Mar 1912 FOSSE; July 1914 Southend United.

Fosse debut v Bradford Park Avenue (H) 30.3.12

> 'A regular Trojan for work, quietly but firmly putting a spoke in the wheels of the opposing left wing, and a fine feeder of the forwards': the local *Mail* clearly implied that right-half Douglas was one of the few stars of Fosse's pre-war years of steep Second Division decline. He was a newly-capped amateur international when Jack Bartlett signed him, and went on to accrue mementos of three more England appearances at that level, plus an Olympic football Final victor's medal from the United Kingdom's eclipse of Denmark in Stockholm in July 1912. He additionally already held a winner's medal from Bromley's 1911 FA Amateur Cup Final encounter with Bishop Auckland, and he would also assist Bromley again in a Cup tie in March 1913, before Fosse persuaded him to sign professionally that summer. He played a supplementary quartet of Southern League games for Southend with that status, and was later refused reinstatement as an amateur by a rather narrow-minded FA in 1921.

Apps: *FL 58; FAC 2.*
Goals: *FL 2.*

McWHIRTER, Peter

b. Glasgow, 23rd June 1871
d. 1943

Career: 1887 Toronto Scottish; Chicago Thistles; Dec 1893 Morton; 1894 Clyde; Oct 1895 FOSSE; Aug 1896 Freemantle; cs 1897 Warmley; cs 1898 Brighton United; Aug 1899 FOSSE.

Fosse debut v Darwen (H) 26.10.1895

> An outside-right who'd had six years in North American football, and a six-game record with Morton, Peter was plucked from Clyde's reserve team for Fosse's second assault on Division Two, but only briefly held his position in mid-season. After joining the Southampton-based Southern League club Freemantle, he was next heard of sailing for Canada in December 1896 to rejoin his emigrant family, but he was soon back again to link up with former Fosse inside-forward partners David Manson and Willie McArthur at promotion-bound Warmley and newly-formed Brighton respectively. Peter's second stint with Fosse was then played out entirely in the reserves, and spiced only with an outing in Jack Walker's benefit friendly against Everton.

Apps: *FL 17; FAC 1.*
Goals: *FL 1.*

MADDEN, Lawrence David

b. Bethnal Green, London, 28th September 1955

Career: am 1973 Arsenal; Manchester University; am Mar 1975 Mansfield Town; 1976 Boston United; 1977-trials-Tottenham Hotspur; Dec 1977 Charlton Athletic; Mar 1982 Millwall; Aug 1983 Sheffield Wednesday; Jan 1991-loan-CITY; July 1991-trials-Derby County; Aug 1991 Wolverhampton Wanderers; Sept 1993 Darlington; Oct 1993 Chesterfield; Mar 1996 Emley.

City debut v West Ham United (A) 19.1.91

> David Pleat's final signing, veteran defender Lawrie arrived on loan to cover for Steve Walsh's absence through suspension; became City's (then) oldest postwar debutant at the age of 35; saw Pleat depart ten days later; was rendered idle for two snowed-off games; and then declined the offer of a month's extension to his stay at crisis-racked Filbert Street. By this time very much a member of Wednesday's shadow squad (having received a profitable testimonial from an Owls/Blades friendly in August 1990), the Londoner had already experienced a lengthy career notable for its stop-start elements. A youth-level Highbury teammate of the likes of Brady, Stapleton and Rostron, Lawrie turned down Arsenal's offer of professional terms to take a full-time degree course in Economics & Social Sciences, but impressed so much in university football that he made a League breakthrough as a non-contract player at Field Mill, playing in the final seven games of Mansfield's Division Four championship campaign of 1975. A spell under Howard Wilkinson at Boston was followed by trials at The Valley, and Lawrie's professional career then got underway in earnest. Charlton slipped from Division Two to Three and rose back again during his time there as a sturdy central defender (sent off at Filbert Street in 1980) and, following a comparatively uneventful spell at The Den (when he nonetheless picked up a winner's medal from the Football League Trophy Final against Lincoln),

Lawrie Madden

he joined Wilkinson's Owls on a free in time to help them up to the top flight in 1984. While contributing to keeping them in Division One until 1990, he briefly formed a defensive partnership with Larry May, and also returned to university on a part-time basis to earn an MA degree in Leisure Management in 1988. Following his stopover at Leicester, Lawrie appeared as a Wembley substitute in Wednesday's League Cup Final win over Manchester United, then moved to Molineux and remarkably earned Player of the year kudos from the Wolves fans in 1992. Less happily, he was sent off on his Chesterfield debut, but was still an occasional contributor to their Play-Off qualification in 1994/5 (featuring in his 500th League game during that term) and played his last game for them when only a month short of his 40th birthday. At that time a *Sheffield Star* columnist, he has subsequently consolidated a career in the media.

Apps: *FL 3.*

MAJOR, Leslie Dennis

b. Yeovil, Somerset, 25th January 1926

Career: Loughborough Corinthians; Brush Sports; am June 1943/pro Dec 1944 CITY; May 1949 Plymouth Argyle (- 1957).

City debut (WW2) v Aston Villa (H) 18.12.43; (postwar) v Plymouth Argyle (H) 25.8.47

> Trained as a PT instructor at Loughborough, Les was the Brush goalkeeper when they beat City's second string in the 1942 County Cup Final, and managed a few outings in wartime football for each of City and Notts County. Then engaged on RAF duties as both a corporal and representative footballer, he became the last City first-teamer to be demobbed (in February 1948), after already having had a decent run of fifteen Second Division games as stand-in for Joe Calvert while still nominally in uniform. Les was also pitched into the anti-relegation scuffles of 1949, but was overlooked for the 'keeper's job at Wembley that year. Almost immediately, he moved to Home Park for £1,800 and played 75 times for the Pilgrims across seven seasons, during which they were twice relegated from Division Two and involved in a Division Three (South) championship campaign, before injury cut short his career and enforced retirement in February 1957. Les then became steward of Newbold Verdon WMC, and Ashby Ivanhoe made attempts to sign him up for local football that October, though we have no evidence that they succeeded. He currently resides in Swadlincote.

Apps: *FL 26; WW2 28.*

MANCINI, Roberto

b. Jesi, Ancona, Italy, 27th November 1964

Career: 1980 Bologna; cs 1982 Sampdoria; cs 1997 Lazio; Jan 2001-loan-CITY.

City debut v Arsenal (H) 20.1.2001

> Finishing off an absolutely magisterial career with an (all-too) short-term contract at Filbert Street, almost twenty years after he'd first hit the global headlines as the world's most expensive teenager, Roberto exuded veteran class for City, but was to find that getting his temporary teammates onto the same quick-thinking wavelength was no easy task. His first start – granting him the record as City's eldest debutant – introduced him to the Premiership at its most frenetic, with 10-man City holding out against the Gunners for a scoreless draw, and moral victory, after Matthew Jones's dismissal; and acclimatisation to an alien game was further problematised when the following week's Cup tie at Villa Park also turned into a 100-mph blood-and-thunder affair. But Roberto's quiet and skilful chivvying showed greater influence over the next two fixtures (even if he showed total disdain for any heading challenge outside the box), and what turned out to be his final game in England produced from him in the second 45 minutes at Goodison Park a perfect cameo of his art as a deep-lying forward. As City contrived to not-quite come back against an Everton side to whom they'd meekly ceded the first half, his flicks, feints and ability to perfectly weight a forward ball were a delight to watch; and it was sheer frustrating bad timing from a Leicester point of view that he should rush back immediately afterwards to fill the suddenly vacant Fiorentina coaching role. It was Sampdoria who paid the £1m to Bologna to first index Roberto's exalted status, and he would faithfully give them 15 years service in Serie A, forging a fine partnership with Gianluca Vialli for part of that time, and leading them to the championship in 1991. He also played for them in six Italian Cup Finals (four won), in their Cup Winners Cup victory of 1990, and in the European Cup Final of 1992. This honours list was then augmented, after a free move to Lazio to re-unite with manager Sven-Goran Eriksson, with an Italian Cup win and a UEFA Cup Final in 1998, a Cup Winners Cup triumph in 1999, and the Italian Double in 2000; at which point his career record from Serie A games alone closed on 541 appearances and 156 goals. He had won 36 Italian caps after 27 Under-21 and Olympic honours, and retired to assist as a coach Eriksson's attempt to repeat Lazio's 'Scudetto'. But when links were forged between Eriksson and Peter Taylor around the England manager's post, the former suggested that his lieutenant was still fit enough to do a job for City – a sound judgement, as it transpired.

Apps: *PL 3+1; FAC 1.*

MANDY, Leonard Aubrey

b. Transvaal, South Africa, ca 1906
d. Brakpan, South Africa, 26th September 1957

Career: State Mines Club (Transvaal); Oct 1929 CITY; Jan 1930 State Mines Club.

City debut v Grimsby Town (H) 26.12.29

> A 6ft 1in, 14st South African trialist goalkeeper, Aubrey arrived to quite a fanfare in a less cosmopolitan era. Met off the SS Windsor Castle at Southampton by Arthur Chandler, he'd signed a short-term amateur contract for City on the recommendation of Chandler and Reg Osborne, who'd faced him, representing both Transvaal and his national side, the previous summer on the FA XI tour; and high expectations were maintained after he'd saved a penalty on his Filbert Street reserve debut against Crystal Palace. Then standing in for Jim McLaren for a Boxing Day first-team bow, he kept a clean sheet against the Mariners, but saw in the New Year with seven Sheffield United goals whistling past him. He then left for home a few weeks later, citing his 'indifference' to the professional game, but having made a friendly impression. At one stage an official in the gold-mining industry, he returned to a post in the motor trade, but later built up his own Mandy Engineering Works. For some time retaining the captaincy of the State Mines club, Aubrey also continued to represent both Transvaal and Eastern Transvaal. At the time of his retirement from football in March 1936, a Reuters report from Johannesburg described him as a motor-racing enthusiast and fine polo player; while his obituary in the *Rand Daily Mail* logged him as a 'well-known East Rand industrialist' and charity benefactor.

Apps: *FL 3.*

MANLEY, Malcolm Richardson

b. Johnstone, Renfrewshire, 1st December 1949

Career: Johnstone Burgh; Jan 1967 CITY; Dec 1973 Portsmouth (-1975); Jan 1976 Barlestone St Giles; July 1977 South Melbourne Hellas.

City debut v Southampton (H) 20.4.68

> The final discovery of City's near-legendary Scottish scout Walter McLean, Malcolm had faced Peter Shilton in a Wembley schools international before gaining experience and stature in Junior football, and was honoured by Scotland Youth shortly after his arrival at Filbert Street. Equally adept at the centre of the back four, or playing just in front of it (and even once utilised as a scoring spearhead), he had his youthful versatility often traded into a position on the City sub's bench – from where he joined the action in three crucial Cup ties in 1969, including the Wembley Final. When he did make the starting line-up on a more regular basis, Malcolm was living testimony to the growing redundancy of the conventional shirt numbering system, and some of his most useful defensive contributions to the 1971 promotion effort came when he was wearing a No 11. For a couple of First Division seasons he vied strongly with John Sjoberg and Alan Woollett for a pivotal berth, then lost his hard-won place with the advent of Malcolm Munro. A £50,000 move to Fratton Park looked promising, but a serious injury cut short Malcolm's career after only sixteen senior games for Pompey. Eventually, in April 1976, Portsmouth and City played a testimonial friendly on his behalf; though Malcolm had sufficiently recovered a year later to try his luck in Australia.

Apps: *FL 109+11; FAC 1+4; LC 11.*
Goals: *FL 5; LC 1.*

MANSHIP, E.

b. Leicester

Career: Latimer; Dec 1902 FOSSE; 1903 Humberstone Victoria; Clarence Hall.

Fosse debut/only game v Burton United (H) 28.2.03

> A local amateur inside-left who captained the Latimer club, and represented the Town League's select side in April 1903. Overall, though, that year didn't bring him the best of fortune. He was deemed unimpressive on his sole senior outing for Fosse (a 0-1 home defeat), and his moment of minor glory for the reserves – the equalising goal in the drawn first game of the County Cup Final – counted for nothing when a dispute over replay dates led to opponents Whitwick White Cross being awarded a walkover. Then, in October 1903, Latimer folded.

Apps: *FL 1.*

MANSON, David Garrioch

b. Glasgow, 20th September 1871.

Career: 1891 Ayr; 1893 Thistle; cs 1894 Rotherham Town; May 1895 FOSSE; Oct 1896 Lincoln City; cs 1897 Warmley; Feb 1899 Gravesend United; cs 1900 Coalville Town.

Fosse debut v Burton Swifts (H) 7.9.1895

> 'Scientific at times, but always slow', was the parting judgement on red-headed forward David of Custodian in *The Wyvern*. Initially tried by Fosse at outside-right, David met with more

success in the inside position and was re-signed for the 1896/7 season. After only one senior game that term, however, he was suspended as an internal disciplinary measure by the committee, and swiftly packed his bags – only to find himself plunged briefly into the midst of a Lincoln run of twelve successive defeats which landed them bottom of the heap. Alongside Matt Bishop and Peter McWhirter as the Bristol-based Warmley fought for promotion from the Southern League's Second Division, David claimed three of the Test Match goals which achieved that feat, and was still with them when they folded in mid-season less than a year later. Much earlier, David's Scottish League bow had come with the West of Glasgow club Thistle, who came bottom of Division Two in their only tilt at that competition.

Apps: *FL 24; FAC 1.*
Goals: *FL 8; FAC 1.*

MARSH, John Kirk

b. Mansfield, 8th October 1922
d. Mansfield, 5th December 1997

Career: Mansfield BC; Aug 1942 Notts County; Oct 1948 Coventry City; Mar 1950 CITY; Sept 1950 Chesterfield; Aug 1951 Worksop Town; cs 1955 Ilkeston Town.

City debut v Sheffield United (A) 18.3.50

> One of three City acquisitions on the same transfer-deadline day, Jack figured in the part-exchange deal that took Ken Chisholm to Highfield Road, and made his bow in a reconstructed City front line that also included Peter Small and Ian Wilson for the first time. Luckless in front of goal by the end of 1949/50, the inside-left started the following season with a couple of double strikes, but then had to drop out to accommodate Arthur Rowley's momentous shift from No 9 to No 10. Leaving as he had arrived, in a part-exchange transaction – this time involving Reg Halton – Jack proved unable to save Chesterfield from relegation at the end of that term, and drifted away from the League game; never really having been able to recapture the brief burst of scoring form he had found alongside the inspirational Tommy Lawton at Meadow Lane. Jack, who'd been posted with the RAF to Sudan during the war, found post-football careers as a National Coal Board administrator and a hospital storekeeper, and was a long-time Forest season-ticket holder.

Apps: *FL 14.*
Goals: *FL 4.*

MARSHALL, Arthur George

b. Liverpool, 1881

Career: Everton; cs 1898 Chester; cs 1899 not known; cs 1900 Crewe Alexandra; May 1901 FOSSE; Jan 1902 Stockport County; May 1902 Manchester United; May 1903 Portsmouth; cs 1904 Hull City; cs 1905 Chester.

Fosse debut v Woolwich Arsenal (A) 7.9.01

> Topping and tailing his senior career with stints in The Combination with Chester, the first of which he played at centre-half, Arthur seemed to suffer from indecision thereafter as to whether he was best suited as a full-back or inside-left! Fosse used him exclusively in the front line, and he was building a fair reputation until Jimmy Stevenson joined the club, at which point Arthur immediately found himself involved in a swap deal with Stockport that returned Sam Eaton to Filbert Street. One of his two goals at Edgeley then came in a rare victory over Fosse in March, but Arthur was also utilised at full-back as his new club bottomed out in the re-election zone. It was as a back-line player that United then signed him, though they only selected him for six Second Division games; and he appeared but once as right-back in a Pompey Southern League line-up. The newly-formed Hull City publicised Arthur's signing as they embarked on a series of friendlies for the season prior to their League election, but there is no record of him actually turning out for them.

Apps: *FL 15; FAC 1.*
Goals: *FL 5.*

MARSHALL, Ian Paul

b. Liverpool, 20th March 1966

Career: app/pro Mar 1984 Everton; Mar 1988 Oldham Athletic; Aug 1993 Ipswich Town; Aug 1996 CITY; June 2000-trials-San Jose Earthquakes; July 2000-trials-Stoke City; Aug 2000-trials-Queens Park Rangers; Aug 2000 Bolton Wanderers.

City debut v Sheffield Wednesday (A) 2.9.96 (sub)

> A burly Scouser who, with City, could appear deceptively slow and shambling until he caught sight of the merest chink of a chance, when he could be a deadly finisher, Ian has had a career of switching between roles as a spearhead and in central defence; and in fact Leicester exploited his prowess at both ends of the park in turning him into an unlikely cult hero. A youthful stopper when making his Goodison debut behind Gary Lineker, he contributed only briefly to Everton's second-placed and title-winning campaigns of 1986 and 1987, and moved on to Boundary Park with only a Charity Shield memento to his name. Ian missed out on Oldham's 1990 League Cup Final appearance, but notched seventeen goals from his new attacking berth when they took the Second Division championship a year later. He helped keep the unfashionable Latics in the top flight, but dropped down from the Premiership after his second term with Ipswich. His most prolific season followed, and included goals in both the home and away fixtures against City, and it was as a front-runner that Martin O'Neill took him on as support for Steve Claridge and Emile Heskey at a fee rising to £890,000. Ironically, his first extended run for City would be as defensive deputy for Steve Walsh, but he was soon back in the firing line with a 21-minute hat-trick against Derby, even if his ineligibility for the 1997 League Cup run gave him a disruptively in-and-out status. It was Ian's close-range clump which put City ahead in Madrid, and his stretchering-off which encouraged Atletico back into the game; and in fact he additionally opened City's account in each of the Premiership, the League Cup and the FA Cup during 1997/8. Persistent injury problems asserted themselves a year later, but Ian still showed his liking for Merseyside returns: he'd netted Goodison equalisers in each of the previous two years, and now added a last-minute Anfield winner to his portfolio. A week earlier, his bustling aerial threat had memorably reduced Chelsea's 'sophisticated' defence to sheer panic. He came on from the bench in both League Cup Finals of 1999 and 2000, and it was his two-goal inspiration for the quarter-final comeback against Fulham which did much to keep City on the Wembley track in the latter year. He was to become something of a talisman for Bolton, too, after his free move, contributing both goals and guile as a vital squad player in their 2001 elevation to the Premiership via the Play-Offs, and earning the offer of an extended contract.

Apps: *PL 49+34; FAC 6+2; LC 4+2; UEFA 2.*
Goals: *PL 18; FAC 3; LC 4; UEFA 1.*

MARSHALL, Lee Keith

b. Islington, London, 21st January 1979

Career: 1995 Enfield; Mar 1997 Norwich City; Mar 2001 CITY.

City debut v Charlton Athletic (A) 1.4.2001

> Another City import previously capped at Under-21 level by Peter Taylor, Lee had the misfortune to make his City bow in one of the most abject collective performances of the 2000/1 season, and just after the club's record-breaking run of consecutive defeats had got underway. Initially playing in a rather ill-defined midfield role, with little evident confidence, then detouring via an emergency central-defensive outing at Newcastle, Lee finally settled in the right-back slot for the final two fixtures: at last tasting victory (over Spurs), but then gifting Leeds their first goal in further final-match defeat. Such circumstances wholly preclude judgement on the tall Londoner, who arrived for £600,000 with a fine First Division reputation from Carrow Road. Norwich originally recruited him as a right-back but, after he'd recovered from a broken leg suffered on only his second senior outing, he figured more often as an attacking midfielder for them, though seeing through a stint exploiting his play-anywhere utility under Bryan Hamilton's management there.

Apps *(to end 2000/1): PL 7+2.*

MATTHEWS, Paul William

b. Leicester, 30th September 1946

Career: app Aug 1963/pro Aug 1964 CITY; Sept 1972-loan-Southend United; Dec 1972 Mansfield Town; Oct 1977 Rotherham United; Mar 1979-loan-Northampton Town; July 1979 Enderby Town; Heanor Town; Oadby Town.

City debut v Aston Villa (H) 19.4.65

> A former County schools rugby player, Paul was deceptively frail-looking with the round ball at his feet, but patiently chiselled out a resilient career. He originally developed at Filbert Street as an orthodox outside-right, and stood in several times for Jackie Sinclair before seeming to drop out of the senior reckoning for a year or so. He returned to the fray, however, in City's desperate late attempts to beat the drop in 1969, and came closest to establishing a regular first-team slot in midfield during the following season, when Frank O'Farrell asked him to assume the nigh-impossible task of replacing Davie Gibson. After another couple of potentially dispiriting years in the background, Paul then had his more mature playmaking skills better appreciated at Field Mill, where in the course of a 124-game stay he helped prompt the Stags from the Fourth to the Second Division via two championship campaigns. He took a County Cup winner's medal from the 1981 Final when Oadby vanquished Earl Shilton Albion.

Apps: *FL 56+5; FAC 4; LC 6+3.*
Goals: *FL 5.*

MAUCHLEN, Alister Henry

b. Kilwinning, Ayrshire, 29th June 1960

Career: Irvine Meadow; Aug 1978 Kilmarnock; Oct 1982 Motherwell; Aug 1985 CITY; Mar 1992-loan-Leeds United; July 1992 Heart of Midlothian; Oct 1993 Glenavon; cs 1995 Ballymena United; Aug 1996 Leicester United (p/coach); Aug 1996 Corby Town; 1996 VS Rugby; Nov 1996 Hinckley Town (p/coach; p/mgr); cs 1997 Oadby Town (p/mgr).

City debut v Oxford United (A) 24.8.85 (sub)

> A terrier-like, ball-winning midfielder, Ali was twice in Kilmarnock sides promoted to the Scottish Premier Division, won with them the pre-season Tennant-Caledonian Cup in 1979, and became a Jock Wallace purchase for Motherwell. There, with Gary McAllister, he became a key member of the First Division championship team of 1985, when 'Well also took Celtic to a replay in the Scottish Cup semi-final. The pair moved together to Filbert Street for £250,000, and neither looked out of place in the English top flight, with Ali settling to the more defensively-inclined role, and linking well with Ian Wilson in a neat, if diminutive, partnership. His goal against Newcastle in the final game of 1985/6 helped keep City up, and he shed a lot of honest sweat in toiling vainly to repeat the feat a year later. Bryan Hamilton had tried him a few times as an emergency full-back, and Ali settled in that position when David Pleat arrived; or at least used it as a starting block for his forays forward. Very much a crowd favourite for his intense commitment, Ali took on player/coach responsibilities under Gordon Lee (figuring in the last-ditch relegation reprieve game against Oxford United), but returned to the ranks on Brian Little's appointment, a little miffed that his backroom services had been curtailed. His loan spell at Leeds was an in-reserve insurance policy for their Championship run-in of 1992, and he didn't actually get a senior game again until being freed to Hearts. Later, on a seven-month loan stint in Ireland, Ali helped inspire Glenavon to within one game of what would have been their first title triumph in 34 years; then, a few months into the next season, after a full transfer, briefly assumed their caretaker managership. Back in Leicestershire, he had a couple of bizarre experiences. Leicester United folded only a matter of days after Ali's recruitment (leaving him as the scorer of their last-ever Southern League goal), while he was the manager to lose out when Hinckley Town and Athletic merged in 1997. He did, however, lead Oadby to the Senior League title in 1999, before reverting solely to the playing ranks for their inaugural, championship-winning season in the Midland Alliance. Ali's teenage son Iain briefly played with him at Oadby following his release from Dundee United.

Apps: *FL 228+11; FAC 6+1; LC 17+1; FMC 9.*
Goals: *FL 11; LC 1.*

MAW, Arthur

b. Frodingham, nr Scunthorpe, 29th December 1909
d. Scunthorpe, 20th April 1964

Career: Frodingham Athletic; 1927 Scunthorpe United; Mar 1929 Notts County; July 1932 CITY; July 1939 Scunthorpe United.

City debut v Wolverhampton Wanderers (H) 7.1.33

> An apprentice fitter who entered senior football as a teenage goalscoring inside-forward at Midland League Scunthorpe, alongside Jack Bowers, Arthur developed his game at Meadow Lane in a side relegated from Division Two in 1930 and promoted back by way of a Third Division (South) championship win a year later. Always popularly known as 'Digger', he chose to accept City's transfer offer in preference to that tabled by Racing Club de Paris, and got off to a fine start at Filbert Street, topping the 1932/3 scoring chart with 14 goals from only 18 games, and maintaining his First Division form in the early months of the following term at such a level that he was chosen as travelling reserve for both the Football League against the

Paul Matthews

Irish League and England's full international in Belfast in October. It was poor reward for his consistently dangerous efforts during City's mid-30s struggles (top scorer again in 1936) that he should miss out on the Second Division championship medals in 1937, his leanest season; but Arthur bounced back to commit his foraging skills to the club until the summer before the outbreak of war, once more linking usefully on occasions with Bowers. He played again for Scunthorpe in the three Midland League games possible before the season's abandonment, and also briefly guested for Grimsby during hostilities. Arthur later spent 20 years as a bookmaker, and died in his own betting shop.

***Apps:** FL 179; FAC 10.*
***Goals:** FL 58; FAC 6.*

MAY, Lawrence Charles

b. Sutton Coldfield, 26th December 1958

Career: Warren FC; app July 1975/pro Sept 1976 CITY; Apr 1978-loan-New England Tea Men; Aug 1983 Barnsley; Feb 1987 Sheffield Wednesday; Sept 1988 Brighton & Hove Albion.

City debut v Bristol City (H) 26.3.77

> Given the briefest of teenage opportunities by each of Jimmy Bloomfield and Frank McLintock, Larry began to exhibit his central defensive skills and strength most forcefully under Jock Wallace's management; supplying the pace in a fine partnership with John O'Neill, and getting forward to claim some vital goals in the promotion seasons of 1980 (including the championship clincher at Brisbane Road) and 1983, and on the Cup semi-final trail of 1982. Larry's aerial prowess and acute reading of the game were much appreciated by a Leicester crowd that was accordingly somewhat baffled when Gordon Milne accepted £110,000 from Barnsley for his talents on the very eve of 1983/4. Three and a half years and 122 League games later, Larry's transfer value had almost doubled as the Owls swooped to restore him to the First Division stage (and an occasional teaming with Lawrie Madden), and the price was again high when the newly-promoted Seagulls took on Larry to plug their leaky Second Division defence. Sadly, a recurrent knee injury enforcdd Larry's premature retirement in September 1989, and his stint as cash-strapped Brighton's reserve coach ended in redundancy in November 1993; though he then stayed in Sussex as coach top local club Ringmer. He was youth coach at Portsmouth from 1995-97, and has since headed Crawley Town's Football in the Community scheme.

***Apps:** FL 180+7; FAC 12; LC 8.*
***Goals:** FL 12; FAC 3.*

MEARNS, Frederick Charles

b. Sunderland, 31st March 1879
d. Sunderland, 21st January 1931

Career: Selbourne; Jan 1901 Sunderland; May 1902 Kettering; Mar 1903 Tottenham Hotspur; May 1904 Bradford City; cs 1905 Grays United; Dec 1905 Southern United; Mar 1906 Barrow; May 1906 Bury cs 1908 Hartlepools United; cs 1909 Barnsley; Jan 1911 FOSSE; cs 1913 Newcastle City; Oct 1919 Sunderland West End.

Fosse debut v Glossop (H) 11.2.11

> A well-travelled goalkeeper who started his senior career as understudy to the long-serving Scottish international Ned Doig at Roker Park, Fred had sampled the game at numerous levels before joining Fosse in an exchange deal which took forward George Travers to Barnsley – with whom Fred had recently become the first 'keeper ever to be beaten by a Cup Final penalty. Kettering and Spurs were of equal Southern League status when he assisted them between the sticks (reputedly saving 19 penalties during his Kettering season!); Bradford City utilised him at Second Division level; both Grays and the Nunhead-based Southern United were in the Southern League's lower echelon, and Barrow in the Lancashire Combination; he returned to occasional First Division fare at Bury; and played in newly-forrmed Hartlepools' inaugural term in the North Eastern League. He was then to be found as Barnsley's last line in both games of the 1910 FA Cup Final, when Newcastle's Albert Shepherd settled the replay with the aid of a record-setting goal from the spot. Fred gave Fosse fine service as a hefty custodian for two and a half years, then moved back for a final time into the North Eastern League. He later acted as trainer to Durham City, but was working as a joiner when he died following a building-site accident. A 1903 testimony read, 'A cool, calculating and level-headed player, wonderfully active, and clears low shots with ease'; but it was Leicester's *Mail* which later had the more colourful description, marvelling that Fred 'carries a left-hand punch that Jack Johnson might envy'.

***Apps:** FL 68; FAC 2.*

MEEK, George

b. Glasgow, 15th February 1934

Career: Thorniewood United;1951 Hamilton Academical; Aug 1952 Leeds United; Jan 1954-loan-Walsall; July 1960 CITY; July 1961 Walsall; Mar 1965 Dudley Town (p/mgr); Rushall Olympic.

City debut v Blackpool (H) 20.8.60

> Almost invariably described by contemporary commentators as a 'big-hearted little 'un', George wasn't one to let his limited stature in any way diminish his effectiveness as a darting winger, and he was a regular thorn in City's flesh for Leeds throughout the 50s in both the Second and First Divisions. Indeed, when he notched Leeds' opener in a 3-3 draw at Filbert Street in February 1953, it was not only his first strike for that club, but also the 3000th League goal conceded by Leicester. Thoroughly experienced by the time Matt Gillies bought him as a replacement for Tommy McDonald and rival for Howard Riley, he suffered from quinsy shortly after arrival, and struggled to make an impact; later filling in for a while for Gordon Wills on the left flank, but never really in contention for an FA Cup Final selection. A second spell at Fellows Park then beckoned, stretching four seasons; and an even longer stint in West Midlands non-league football, where George was active until the age of 50, latterly 'guesting' for Wolves Old Boys in veterans' football. George, who'd done his National Service in the Royal Armoured Corps, was for some time involved in a Black Country engineering business, but was last heard of in 1992 as a Walsall postman.

***Apps:** FL 13.*

George Meek

MELROSE, James Millsop

b. Glasgow, 7th October 1958

Career: Eastercraigs; 1975 Partick Thistle; July 1980 CITY; Sept 1982 Coventry City; Aug 1983 Celtic; Sept 1984-loan-Wolverhampton Wanderers; Nov 1984 Manchester City; Mar 1986 Charlton Athletic; Sept 1987 Leeds United; Feb 1988 Shrewsbury Town; Aug 1990 Macclesfield Town; Oct 1990 Curzon Ashton; 1991 Halesowen Harriers.

City debut v Ipswich Town (H) 16.8.80

> Capped eight times at Scotland Under-21 level, and a scorer for the Scottish League against the Irish League in March 1980, Jimmy developed a nippy striking profile in the Premier Division at Firhill, and became City's third £250,000 buy when Jock Wallace judged him a likely foil for target man Alan Young. He initially struggled to adapt to the pace of the First Division – as did many of his youthful teammates in 1980/1 – but picked up a few useful goals as City belatedly battled against their relegation fate, and signed off his first term with a cheeky hat-trick at Norwich which doomed the Canaries as well. Jimmy developed into a crowd favourite during the next season, and many were critical that his enforced role as 'super-sub' kept him for too long out of the important action (such as the FA Cup semi-final against Spurs); while almost all were vocal in their condemnation of the exchange deal involving Tommy English which Gordon Milne engineered early in his Filbert Street tenure. Maintaining a decent scoring record, Jimmy nonetheless became something of a wanderer. At Celtic he made delayed appearances from the bench in the Finals of both Scottish knockout competitions of 1984, and he assisted both Manchester City and Charlton up into the First Division. Indeed, his goals for the latter in the 1987 promotion/relegation Play-Offs did a lot to keep them there. While at Shrewsbury (initially on loan), Jimmy was the victim of an on-field assault by Swindon's Chris Kamara that eventually saw the aggressor become the first to face legal prosecution for such an act. Jimmy, who closed his career on a frustrating aggregate of 99 League goals, became a registered players' agent, then returned to Filbert Street in November 1996 as Chief Scout.

***Apps:** FL 57+15; FAC 2+6; LC 6.*
***Goals:** FL 21; FAC 4; LC 1.*

MERCER, John Thompson

b. Belfast, ca 1877

Career: Linfield Swifts; trials-Preston North End; Distillery; May 1899 Brighton United; Feb 1900 FOSSE; cs 1900 Linfield; Feb 1903 Distillery; Oct 1903 Derby County; cs 1905 Distillery; cs 1906 Colne; Sept 1908 Distillery.

Fosse debut v Chesterfield 24.2.1900

> A 'dashing' Irish international outside-right (capped four times before first sampling English football, and a further seven after leaving Fosse), Johnny had impressed in Brighton United's terminally-struggling Southern League line-up, but failed to bolster Fosse's still-viable promotion prospects after his mid-season arrival. Having already been part of Distillery's Irish League championship side of 1899, he returned to Belfast for further glory, participating in Double triumphs with Linfield in 1902 and with Distillery a year later. Derby were encouraged to give him another chance on this side of the water, but a more experienced Johnny was only a little more successful with the Rams in Division One (scoring once in 26 outings), though he did assist them to the 1904 FA Cup semi-finals. A further pair of back-and-forth moves then landed him in the Lancashire Combination with newly-promoted Colne. Johnny was later heavily involved in Irish football administration, with boardroom stints at each of Glentoran and Distillery, patronage of Belfast United, and a spell as President of the Irish League in 1941/2; though by this stage he was familiarly known as Toby.

***Apps:** FL 9.*
***Goals:** FL 2.*

MERCER, Stanley

b. Birkenhead, 11th September 1919

Career: Blackpool Services; am Jan 1944 Blackpool; am July 1944/pro Nov 1944 CITY; Jan 1947 Accrington Stanley; Oct 1948 Mansfield Town.

City debut (WW2) v Walsall (A) 16.9.44 (scored once); (postwar) v Chelsea (A) FAC 5.1.46

> A handily aggressive centre-forward with a decent wartime strike rate for City, Stan also guested for Accrington (for whom he scored a hat-trick to celebrate signing his professional contract with Leicester!), Arsenal and Manchester United while serving as a PT instructor in the RAF, and represented the latter's stellar team against Portugal in Lisbon. Despite top-scoring in the transitional 1945/6 season, he hardly got a break at Filbert Street when peace returned: Jack Lee was staking his claims to the No 9 shirt, and Stan had the handicap of training in the north and only visiting Leicester on matchdays. His wife was suffering a lengthy illness at their Lytham St Anne's home, and Stan soon transferred to Accrington for £750 to be closer to her. Three seasons of double-figure scoring in the Third Division (North) ensued, but a knee injury curtailed his Field Mill career. Stan stayed on as Mansfield trainer and then, between 1953 and 1955, occupied the manager's chair there in succession to George Jobey. Subsequently, he moved back to Lytham and worked as an administrator in the Premium Bonds office until his retirement.

***Apps:** FL 1; FAC 2; WW2 27.*
***Goals:** WW2 13.*

MESSER, Robert

b. Edinburgh, ca 1889

Career: Broxburn Shamrock; Kings Park; Bo'ness; May 1910 FOSSE; cs 1911 not known; cs 1912 Broxburn United.

Fosse debut v Clapton Orient (A) 24.9.10

> An Andy Aitken signing, this tall young Scottish outside-right was one of no less than nine players tried in that problematic position in 1910/11, and not a conspicuous success. Robert had a year earlier assisted Bo'ness to the championship of the Scottish Central League; and would return to that competition with the newly-amalgamated Broxburn United. We still await confirmation that it was this man who was killed in action on 16th October 1918, while serving as a private in the King's Own Scottish Borderers.

***Apps:** FL 2.*

MIDDLETON, Francis

b. Whitwick, Leics, ca 1881

Career: 1896 Whitwick White Cross; Nov 1901 Derby County; Aug 1906 FOSSE; cs 1909 Whitwick Imperial.

Fosse debut v Burslem Port Vale (A) 1.9.06 (scored once)

> An outstanding outside-left whose top-class potential was first signalled when Derby paid £100 to his local Midland League club for his signature, Frank stepped straight into the Rams' First Division front line alongside the near-legendary likes of Steve Bloomer. After 65 League games, he had confirmed his chief role to be as a provider, having scored only three goals; yet upon moving to Leicester for £75 he notched one counter in each of his first four games before suffering injury. Frank contributed some fine wing performances in the first half of Fosse's promotion season – being described as 'light, but a flier on the sinister flank', and 'a capital hand at centring' – but was sorely distressed by the death of one of his young children in January 1908, and dropped out of contention soon after. He was subsequently noted as raising a charity cricket XI in Whitwick in 1923, while running the White Horse Inn there. Of his sons, Aubrey was a winger with Whitwick Imperial and Stapleford's Works in the mid-20s, while Harold later played local football for Whitwick Imperial, Loughborough Corinthians, Whitwick Holy Cross and Whitwick White Cross, and in September 1934 undertook a month's trial with Racing Club de Calais.

***Apps:** FL 49; FAC 3.*
***Goals:** FL 10.*

MIDDLETON, John

b. Sunderland, 19th April 1898
d. Aldershot, 16th January 1974

Career: Herrington Swifts; Lambton Star; May 1922 CITY; May 1925 Queens Park Rangers; Aug 1927 Aldershot (- 1937).

City debut v Bury (H) 28.4.23

> Elevated from Wearside League football to become a reserve inside-right at Filbert Street, Jack made his debut in dramatic circumstances when, with two games of the 1922/3 season remaining, both against Bury, City could still look forward to the possibility of promotion. Unfortunately a home win was followed by Gigg Lane defeat, and goal average kept City down. Thereafter an occasional deputy for Johnny Duncan, Jack was understandably unable to consolidate a senior slot, though he was a scorer for the reserves in their 1924 County Cup Final replay win, by 5-1 over Barwell United. With QPR, he sometimes shared selections with former City men George Hebden and Hugh Richmond, while himself converting to a wing-half role; and he then had a magnificent Aldershot career, over five Southern League seasons and five more in the Third Division (South). An Angus Seed signing there, he was left-half in the Shots' first-ever League line-up, took player/coach responsibilities from August 1935, and retired to the trainer's role in 1937. He played once as an emergency selection in goal during 1930/1, and did so three times again in wartime football at the age of 43.

***Apps:** FL 12; FAC 1.*
***Goals:** FL 3.*

MILBURN, Stanley

b. Ashington, Northumberland, 22nd October 1926

Career: Ashington; Jan 1947 Chesterfield; Feb 1952 CITY; Jan 1959 Rochdale; cs 1965 Spotland Methodists; TBA (Rochdale).

City debut v Sheffield United (A) 22.3.52

> A member of the remarkable Geordie footballing dynasty of Milburns and Charltons, Stan followed three of his brothers in exhibiting an affinity for

the full-back position, and made his Chesterfield debut in back-line partnership with brother George. He took little time, as a clean-tackling Second Division regular, in impressing the various national selection panels who, in 1950, successively honoured him with one England 'B' cap, two Football League representative appearances, and a place on the FA XI tour of Canada. Norman Bullock expended £10,000 in bringing Stan to Leicester, where his sterling defensive work was a feature for seven seasons, including the Second Division championship campaigns of 1954 and 1957. He was an ever-present in the latter term, scoring his only City goal in a 5-4 win at Bury, and keeping Irish international Willie Cunningham sidelined. Then, after bowing out of the First Division fray at an age when many players would be contemplating retirement, Stan took his boundless enthusiasm to Rochdale, playing on for seven more seasons, top-scoring for them in 1959/60 when briefly converted to the centre-forward role, skippering them to the 1962 League Cup Final, and completing his first-class career with an aggregeate of 589 League games. Characteristically, though, Stan was still turning out in local football in Rochdale in the early 80s, while working as a warehouseman. Of his two indelible entries in the game's records, one was a matter of embarrassment, the other of pride: the first was his part in the shared own-goal incident at Chelsea in 1954; the second the fact that he was the first postwar player to earn loyalty benefits from three separate clubs.

***Apps:** FL 173; FAC 10.*
***Goals:** FL 1.*

MILES, Idris

b. Neath, Glamorgan, 2nd August 1908
d. Dudley, West Midlands, Oct qtr 1983

Career: Radnor Road FC; Nov 1930 Cardiff City; May 1932 Yeovil & Petters United; Oct 1932 CITY; May 1934 Clapton Orient; cs 1937 Exeter City; Yeovil & Petters United; July 1938 Worcester City.

City debut v Everton (H) 22.10.32 (scored once)

> Only 5ft 4 in tall, Idris was even smaller than the pocket dynamo for whom he briefly deputised at Filbert Street. Assuming Hughie Adcock's right flank position for a run of seven First Division games, he was then unlucky enough to twice break his collarbone in the course of his first City year, and failed to win a recall on recovery. He moved on in the part-exchange deal with Orient that brought fellow-Welshman Tommy Mills to Leicester (and which re-united Idris with his former Yeovil boss, David Pratt), and for the club then playing at Lea Bridge Speedway he totted up 73 League starts across three seasons, scoring six times. He was goalless after ten outings for Exeter, and then returned to Southern League football. Originally released by Cardiff after only three Second Division games, Idris had also played baseball in Wales. In August 1935, his younger brother Leslie joined City from Ashford as an inside-left, but moved on untried a year later to Barry Town.

***Apps:** FL 7.*
***Goals:** FL 1.*

MILLER, Charles

b. Glasgow, 18th March 1976

Career: Rangers Boys Club; July 1992 Rangers; Mar 1999-loan-CITY; Sept 1999 Watford; Nov 2000 Dundee United.

City debut v Aston Villa (H) 6.4.99 (sub)

> Scotland's Young Player of the Year in 1995, and eight times capped at Under-21 level, Charlie became a prime example of the marginalisation of native talent as Rangers became an ever more cosmopolitan team in pursuit of European credibility. Though he contributed to five domestic title wins for the Ibrox team, the attacking midfielder had been reduced largely to cameo appearances from the bench by the time Martin O'Neill offered him a loan spell at Filbert Street, with the possibility of signing permanently at the end of the term. Charlie started in a familiar sub's role, replacing Arnar Gunnlaugsson as City pulled back a two-goal deficit against Villa to gain a Premiership point, but when unfortunately injured only 20 minutes into his first game as a starter, against Newcastle, and sidelined for the rest of his stay, he had yet to exhibit much in the way of flair or generate much excitement. City dropped the option on his purchase, and he subsequently failed to shine in Watford's Premiership misadventure when Graham Taylor took him on following trials. Yet his efforts as both prompter and scorer in a relegation-threatened Dundee United line-up only a year later were impressive enough to earn him a nod from Craig Brown, and he won his first full cap in the April 2001 friendly in Poland.

***Apps:** PL 1+3.*

MILLER, William Thomas

b. Burton-on-Trent, 15th August 1868
d. Derby, 20th February 1950

Career: 1888 Derby Junction; cs 1891 Burton Wanderers; cs 1893 FOSSE; cs 1895 Kettering; cs 1899 Northampton Town; cs 1901 Bedford Queens; Feb 1902 Northampton Town.

Fosse debut v Burton Wanderers (H) ML 9.9.1893.

> An inside- or centre-forward with a fine Midland League record, 'Tout' was an impressive ever-present for Fosse in their final, runners-up campaign in that competition, and was retained for the first shot at the Second Division. His goal-tally at that level ought to have been higher: he missed the first League penalty awarded to Fosse, against Newcastle in October 1894, when it would have secured him a hat-trick! (He had, though, back on 1st September 1891, on the very day the penalty kick was introduced to the game, netted one for Burton Wanderers against Great Bridge Unity). A former iron turner, 'Tout' had played two Midland League seasons for each of Derby Junction and Burton, assisting the latter to the same second-place finish in 1893 he would experience a year later with Fosse. Upon moving back to that sphere, he would go one better and prompt Kettering to the 1896 title. The Cobblers, too, were Midland League members during his initial spell with them, and he returned for one final game in their colours after they switched to the Southern League. In the interim, 'Tout' had played alongside Harry Edwards in the Bedford Queens side eliminated from the FA Cup by Luton Town. In later life he worked as both a timber loader and bricklayer.

***Apps:** FL 10; FAC 9; ML 20.*
***Goals:** FL 2; FAC 5; ML 7.*

MILLS, Andrew

b. Knighton, Radnorshire, 15th December 1877

Career: Knighton; cs 1897 Blackburn Rovers; cs 1898 Swindon Town; cs 1899 Brighton United; May 1900 FOSSE; cs 1903 not known; Aug 1905-trials-Shrewsbury Town.

Fosse debut v Stockport County (H) 1.9.1900

> A versatile defender who settled best in Fosse's right-back berth, in partnerships with old hands George Swift or Walter Robinson, Andy ironically came closest to international recognition just as he was fading from the first-team picture at Leicester. In fact he was stretchered out of the Welsh trial game of February 1903 and subsequently made only one further Fosse appearance. Two of Andy's goals were penalties; the other a lofted shot from his own half, against Burnley in September 1902. He had originally joined Fosse upon Brighton United's liquidation, and had previously played in two top-flight fixtures, plus one Test Match, for Blackburn in a season when they should have been relegated, but won a reprieve when the number of clubs in the First Division was extended.

***Apps:** FL 64, FAC 3.*
***Goals:** FL 3.*

MILLS, Gary Roland

b. Northampton, 11th November 1961

Career: app/pro Nov 1978 Nottingham Forest; Mar 1982-loan-Seattle Sounders; Oct 1982-loan-Derby County; Apr 1983-loan-Seattle Sounders; Aug 1987 Notts County; Mar 1989 CITY; Sept 1994 Notts County; Sept 1996 Grantham Town (p/mgr); Aug 1998 Gresley Rovers; Sept 1998 King's Lynn (p/mgr from Oct 1998); Nov 2000 Boston United; Jan 2001 Tamworth (p/mgr).

City debut v Walsall (H) 4.3.89

> The son of former Northampton Town stalwart Roly Mills, Gary was a schoolboy star at both rugby and soccer, whose choice to pursue the latter sport was almost instantly rewarded with a first-team berth at Forest. His prodigious impact on Trentside saw him playing in both the First Division and Europe while still only 16; earning a winner's medal from Forest's second European Cup triumph in 1980 while still a teenager; and picking up two England Under-21 caps to add to his youth international honours. The attacking midfielder later fell foul, however, of the League's attempts to tighten up registration regulations regarding loan and transfer deals with American clubs in the NASL (where Gary played in the culminating showpiece Soccer Bowl of 1982, when Seattle finally bowed to New York Cosmos). A combination of such difficulties and injury problems kept him out of the City Ground limelight for some time, and he had been somewhat eclipsed by a new generation of Brian Clough discoveries by the time he crossed the river to Meadow Lane. His consistency with the Magpies as a wide player encouraged David Pleat to view him as a likely replacement for Peter Weir at Filbert Street, and he arrived in a part-exchange deal involving Phil Turner. After a brief acclimatisation, Gary settled to a key role on City's right, getting forward effectively from either a middle-line or attacking full-back slot, and exciting with both his trademark diagonal dribbles and fine crossing control. Reliability as well as flair marked his mature game, and Gary won the club's Player of the Year award at the end of each of the 1989/90 and 1991/2 campaigns. In the interim, he successively assumed the team and club captaincies, and for a time shouldered penalty-taking duties (utilising no run-up); while his ever-present seasonal tally of 61 appearances in 1991/2 set a new club record. A slight lapse in form and a series of injuries bit into Gary's last two terms with City, but he skippered the side at Wembley in 1993 and was a popular choice to lead out the team, in Brian Little's stead, before the 1994 Play-Off Final, with his local radio commentary reaction to Steve Walsh's winner that day entering Leicester folklore. Unfortunately, Gary's £50,000 departure from City's Premiership struggle only led him into an analogous position with Notts County, duly relegated from Division One in 1995; though he made another playing appearance at Wembley in the Magpies' Anglo-Italian Cup victory over Ascoli that March. A combined City and Derby XI met a Forest/County combination in a Meadow Lane benefit match for Gary in April 1997, and a year later he took his Grantham side to the championship of the Southern League Midland Division, only to depart on the arrival of a new chairman. Gary then built up a fair colony of ex-City men at King's Lynn, after taking over the reins there from Tony Spearing, and is continuing his managerial apprenticeship at Tamworth.

***Apps:** FL/PL 195+5; FAC 7; LC 9+1; FMC 7; AIC 2; PO 6.*
***Goals:** FL 16; LC 1.*

MILLS, Thomas James

b. Ton Pentre, Glamorgan, 28th December 1911
d. Bristol, 15th May 1979

Career: Ton Pentre BC; Trocadero Restaurant FC; Sept 1929 Clapton Orient; May 1934 CITY; May 1936 Bristol Rovers.

City debut v Everton (H) 3.9.34 (scored once)

> 'The little Welshman is game to the core, as well as skilful.' The *Mercury's* assessment of Tommy wasn't necessarily shared by manager Arthur Lochhead, who inherited the creative inside-forward as one of Peter Hodge's final captures, gave him only limited opportunities in a relegation-bound City side, and barely chose him at all in the Second Division. Though capped as a schoolboy, Tommy had initially believed any chance of a football career had gone, until Orient spotted him playing for the Sunday staff team of a London hotel, where he was working as a burnisher after he'd been laid off from the mines. He won two full caps while on their books (scoring one of the goals for a Welsh team victorious over England at Newcastle in November 1933), and added a couple more while at Filbert Street, having arrived in a part-exchange deal involving Idris Miles. He moved to Eastville in a joint £575 deal with David Bruce, and revived his career to the extent of accruing 99 League games for Rovers before the outbeak of war. Nominally retiring in 1939, he nonetheless turned out in local Bristolian football for the Kleen-e-ze FC, and assisted Rovers during 1945/6, when notching two FA Cup goals. Subsequent trials with Notts County did not, however, herald an extended return to the senior game. Tommy's eventual demise came as the result of being knocked down by a lorry.

***Apps:** FL 17; FAC 1.*
***Goals:** FL 5.*

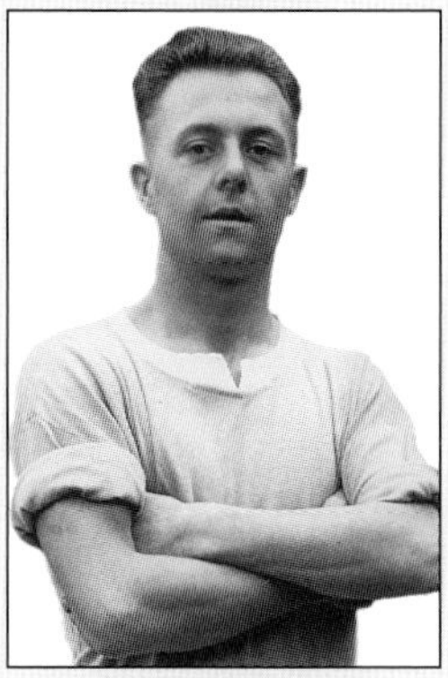

Tommy Mills

MILLS, William

b. Hackney, London, 1891

Career: Barnet Alston; Vicar of Wakefield FC; Dec 1911 FOSSE (-1918).

Fosse debut v Stockport County (H) 16.12.11 (scored once)

> An energetic inside-forward who cost Fosse a £5 signing-on fee from London junior football, Billy clearly enthused Pen Alty in the local *Mail* to a bit of hyperbole: 'Just the Kutest Kockney Kid that ever donned the studded leathers'. Billy felt the wrath of the game's hidebound establishment almost as soon as he arrived at Filbert Street – receiving a draconian two month suspension for the heinous offence of having played Sunday football in London after registering with Leicester. Thankfully not overly discouraged by such pettiness, he continued to assist Fosse regularly until the outbreak of war (being top scorer in the disastrous 1914/15 re-election season) and very occasionally, while on leave, during it. Sadly, he suffered serious wounds – losing a foot after an aerial bombardment – in the conflict in France; and City played a benefit friendly on his behalf in October 1919, against a Select XI, which raised just over £100. Billy was still living in Eyres Monsell in the early 60s, and attended the Highbury 50th anniversary celebrations along with old teammates Horace Burton and George Douglas.

***Apps:** FL 77; FAC 2; WW1 2.*
***Goals:** FL 20; FAC 1; WW1 1.*

MILNES, Frederick Houghton

b. Wortley, Yorks, 25th January 1878
d. Leeds, 1st July 1946

Career: Sheffield Wycliffe; Sheffield Club; May 1902: Sheffield United; Oct 1904: West Ham United; 1905 Pilgrims; Dec 1905: Tottenham Hotspur; Jan 1906: West Ham United; Mar 1906: Manchester United; 1906: Reading; Feb 1907:FOSSE; Oct 1907: Northern Nomads; Ilford; Sept 1908: Norwich City; Sheffield Club.

Fosse debut/only game v Lincoln City (A) 27.4.07

> A classy amateur international right-back (capped in the 15-0 cakewalk over France in Paris in November 1906), Fred's primary allegiance was to the long-established Sheffield Club – for whom he scored a penalty in their 1904 FA Amateur Cup Final win over Ealing – and the primary cause of his fame was his devotion to selling the game to the States. Always ready to lend his assistance on a non-contract basis to almost any club who asked, he'd played a dozen First Division games for the Blades (sharing a debut with Jimmy Donnelly), had outings in the Southern League with Reading and West Ham, played two FA Cup ties with the latter, featured in Spurs' Western League side, and would go on to bolster Norwich's United League line-up. Additionally, he'd won selections for the combined Sheffield team in their then-annual inter-city prestige matches against Glasgow. For Fosse he only turned out in a home friendly against Stockport and in the above League match, yet the local press reaction to his appearance was little short of ecstatic. Fred also played at Filbert Street in 1907 as captain of the Pilgrims, a high-status amateur combination playing a Leicestershire XI in preparation for one of a number of tours they made to the US and Canada to propagandise on behalf of the soccer cause. The first such jaunt, in 1905, brought Fred face-to-face with Teddy Roosevelt at the White House, at a time the President was keen on replacing the increasingly violent gridiron game with soccer in colleges; and the

itinerary for the international-heavy squad was extended to include Argentina in 1909. In December 1912, the *Nottingham Evening Mail* noted that, 'Fred Milnes, the erstwhile Sheffield back, is again delighting American crowds with his skill'.

Apps: *FL 1.*

MITCHELL, J.

Career: Royal Field Artillery; trials Apr 1912, Mar 1913 & Apr 1914 FOSSE.

Fosse debut/only game v Leeds City (H) 27.4.12

> A serving bombardier (in the 47th Brigade, RFA) who occasionally turned out for Fosse reserves when stationed nearby, Mitchell was given a senior break at left-half (along with fellow-squaddie William Sharpley) in the final League fixture of 1911/12, when described by the *Mercury* as 'hesitant'. A week later, he at least managed to get on the scoresheet in the friendly played for the Titanic Disaster Fund, a 3-3 draw against a Leicestershire XI; and two years later figured for the Fosse reserves in the County Cup Final victory over Holwell Works. Something of an all-rounder, he also played for Aldershot Command against Southampton, and had represented the Irish Army at both rugby and hockey. During WW1, he wrote as Lieutenant Mitchell to Fosse secretary Harry Linney, asking for footballs to be forwarded to his battery at the front.

Apps: *FL 1.*

MITTEN, John

b. Manchester, 30th March 1941

Career: am 1957 Mansfield Town; am 1958/pro Sept 1960 Newcastle United; Sept 1961 CITY; Apr 1963 Manchester United [-]; Aug 1963 Coventry City; Jan 1967 Plymouth Argyle; July 1968 Exeter City; Aug 1971 Bath City; Trowbridge Town; Sidmouth Town (p/mgr); 1978 Tiverton Town

City debut v West Ham United (A) 30.9.61

> A son of former Manchester United and Fulham player – and Bogota rebel – Charlie Mitten, and honoured himself by England at both schoolboy and youth levels, John was managed and blooded by his father at both Mansfield and Newcastle; and hardly endeared himself to a Geordie crowd already whispering of nepotism when he missed a penalty on his Magpies debut as a 17-year-old. He came to Leicester initially on trial, being signed permanently only after his first-team debut at outside-left, and going on to play in four senior competitions in a four-month spell, including both legs of the Cup Winners Cup tie against Atletico Madrid. The arrival of Mike Stringfellow comprehensively blocked John's City progress and, after he'd turned down a firm bid from Ipswich, he could get no further at Old Trafford than the reserve side. By this stage, John's parallel career as a Leicestershire wicket-keeper was also winding down, after 14 first-class matches between 1961 and 1963. Eventually, he joined Jimmy Hill's Sky Blue revival at Coventry, then had his most consistent spell as a useful midfield operator in the West Country. His younger brother, Charlie junior, was also on the books of four League clubs, yet made but a single League appearance: for Halifax in 1965; while his son, Paul, was an unsuccessful Manchester United trainee in the mid-90s.

Apps: *FL 12; FAC 1; LC 1; ECWC 2.*
Goals: *LC 1.*

John Mitten

MOHAN, Nicholas Martin

b. Middlesbrough, 6th October 1970

Career: Acklam Steelworks; trials-Charlton Athletic; YT/pro Nov 1987 Middlesbrough; Sept 1992-loan-Hull City; July 1994 CITY; July 1995 Bradford City; Aug 1997 Wycombe Wanderers; Mar 1999 Stoke City; July 2001 Hull City.

City debut v Newcastle United (H) 21.8.94

> Primarily a central defender, but also utilised occasionally at right-back by his hometown club, Nicky made his teenage Boro debut during their 1988/9 slide from Division One, and experienced promotion and relegation again during his stint as an Ayresome squad player. He clearly impressed former Boro coach Brian Little during this period, though, for the City boss made strenuous attempts to sign him before the 1994 deadline day and, having failed, went back with £300,000 for the player after promotion had been sealed. Nicky's immediate impact with City could have been happier: he netted a Filbert Street own goal within two minutes of the start of the pre-season showpiece game against Rapid Bucharest! Indeed, his entire Premiership experience could only be judged a disappointment, with a sending-off at Forest interrupting his acclimatisation, and only intermittent selections at the heart of City's shaky five-man defensive line preceding his placing on the open-to-offers list in May 1995. He helped Bradford City to promotion by the Play-Off route in his first Second Division term after a £225,000 transfer, and two moves later found himself briefly back with Little at the Britannia Stadium until the latter's departure. Stoke took the Auto Windscreens Shield at Wembley in 2000 with Nicky, Gavin Ward and Arnar Gunnlaugsson in the side, and Carl Muggleton on the bench, but faced Play-Off frustration in each of 2000 and 2001.

Apps: *PL 23; FAC 1; LC 2.*

Nicky Mohan

MOODY, Herbert B.

b. Luton, 1880

Career: Luton Stanley; cs 1901 Luton Town; Aug 1905 FOSSE; cs 1907 Luton Town; June 1912 Millwall (- 1920).

Fosse debut v Clapton Orient (H) 2.9.05 (scored once)

> That this clever inside- or centre-forward still had his best days in front of him when leaving Leicester is conventional wisdom bulwarked by this *Mercury* opinion from 1912: "A nice gentlemanly footballer... Moody is nowadays a regular and confirmed baiter of goalkeepers, but when he used to shoot for Fosse, imps of mischief, invisible Ariels, seemed abroad to turn his best-intentioned drives astray'. Seemingly alternately known as Bert or Harry, and generally thought as good at creating chances as taking them, he did indeed have more prolific days ahead after his two years in an improving Fosse side building towards its promotion challenge. In both his first spell with Luton and his Fosse days, he benefitted from the tutelage of Jimmy Blessington, and was also able to exploit at Filbert Street his familiarity with Jamie Durrant's style and strengths. His debut goal was the first conceded at League level by Clapton Orient, playing their initial game in the competition at Filbert Street, and drawing 2-2. He was chosen six times for the Southern League representative side between 1910 and the outbreak of war, and had scored 122 goals from 345 games in that sphere when he closed his Millwall career just as that club were about to become founder-members of the new Division Three.

Apps: *FL 54; FAC 1.*
Goals: *FL 11; FAC 1.*

MORALEE, Matthew

b. Mexborough, Yorks, 21st February 1912
d. Doncaster, September 1991

Career: Ormsby United; 1929 Denaby United; cs 1930 Gainsborough Trinity; Feb 1931 Grimsby Town; Oct 1936 Aston Villa; Nov 1937 CITY; July 1939 Shrewsbury Town.

City debut v Preston North End (H) 13.11.37

> An intelligent, prompting inside-forward who never quite bore out his initial promise, Matt came to Leicester effectively a year late. His Grimsby boss Frank Womack, accepting the Filbert Street managerial vacancy, proposed bringing Matt with him, but only a day later was ordered by his old directorate to oversee the player's sale to Villa (then suffering the ignominy of their first-ever season in Division Two). In fact, Matt got few breaks as Villa failed to rebound immediately, and when he did belatedly reunite with Womack, it was primarily a hectic, eventually unsuccessful battle to help keep City in Division One that he joined. Despite a few sparkling displays, he was released into Midland League football on the eve of war. Appearances as a guest player for Grimsby, Doncaster, Bradford City and Rotherham followed, before Matt saw out his active career back at Denaby.

Apps: *FL 38; FAC 5.*
Goals: *FL 6.*

MORAN, Edward

b. Cleland, Lanarkshire, 20th July 1930

Career: Cleland BC; Coltness; Sept 1947 CITY; Oct 1951 Stockport County; Feb 1957 Rochdale; Sept 1958 Crewe Alexandra; Aug 1959 Flint Town United; 1963 Glossop (p/coach).

City debut v Grimsby Town (H) 2.4.49

> Another of the skilful young Scots snapped up in Johnny Duncan's regular cross-border raids of the immediate postwar years (reputedly from under the nose of Manchester United), Eddie was a ball-playing inside-right who was initially noted for coming unscathed through his teenage debut game – a veritable battle with Grimsby in which eight City men suffered injuries of varying severity. A brief run in Bert Barlow's shirt in 1950/1 was the pinnacle of Eddie's senior career at Leicester but, after a return home in summer 1951 and a protracted dispute over City's transfer valuation (eventually knocked down by two-thirds to a Stockport record of £5,000), the schemer also found his shooting boots at Edgeley Park, knocking in 47 goals in 117 League and Cup games, and then remaining in the North West to see out his senior playing days. Eddie, the elder brother of Jimmy (see below), settled in Stockport to work for British Aerospace, Shell and a games machine company amongst others.

Apps: *FL 8.*
Goals: *FL 1.*

MORAN, James

b. Cleland, Lanarkshire, 6th March 1935

Career: Wishaw Juniors; Dec 1955 CITY; Nov 1957 Norwich City; Jan 1961 Northampton Town; Aug 1962 Darlington; July 1963 Workington; May 1966 Lowestoft Town (p/coach).

City debut v Leyton Orient (A) 19.4.57 (scored once)

> Jimmy's City career was short but relatively sweet – his League bow coming in the 5-1 victory at Brisbane Road which clinched the Second Division championship of 1957. There seemed little chance of the inside-right deposing Ian McNeill for long, however, and his transfer to Norwich looked merely a wise career move until the Canaries introduced a note of teasing mystery to the proceedings – playing Jimmy in a floodlit friendly against Aberdeen under the pseudonym 'Johnstone' before actually signing him. He contributed a handful of goals to promotion campaigns at each of Norwich (Three to Two in 1960) and Northampton (Four to Three a year later), and was an ever-present in Workington's rise from the basement in 1964, in the midst of a century of League outings for the Reds. Then returning to East Anglia, he hit big trouble in April 1972, being fined £50 and given a suspended six-month jail term for assaulting a referee in an Eastern Counties League game for Lowestoft, and being handed a sine die FA suspension a month later. When this was eventually revoked, Jimmy had spells as boss of Great Yarmouth Town and local side Coltishall HV. Both of City's Moran brothers finished their senior careers with aggregate tallies of just over 50 League goals; while a third brother, John, made only two League appearances for Derby in 1954, before a homeward move to St Mirren.

Apps: *FL 3.*
Goals: *FL 1.*

MORAN, Joseph

Career: Aston Villa; cs 1903 Doncaster Rovers; trials Aug 1904/pro Oct 1904 FOSSE.

Fosse debut/only game v Lincoln City (H) 19.11.04

> Discarded by Doncaster on their re-election to the Second Division (despite a 12-goal haul from their 1903/4 Midland League campaign), this left-winger proved an unimpressive one-off deputy for Tommy Allsopp on Fosse's flank in a 0-1 home defeat. Joe had previously failed to make the Villa first team at all.

Apps: *FL 1.*

MORAN, Paul

b. Enfield, London, 22nd May 1968

Career: YT July 1984/pro July 1985 Tottenham Hotspur; Jan 1989-loan-Portsmouth; Nov 1989-loan-CITY; Feb 1991-loan-Newcastle United; Mar 1991-loan-Southend United; Sept 1992-loan-Cambridge United; cs 1994 Peterborough United; Feb 1996 Enfield; 2000 Hertford Town.

City debut v Sheffield United (A) 4.11.89

> Suffering an eventual eight seasons of intense frustration at Spurs after being handed an early senior bow by David Pleat, Paul was an attacking midfielder and sometime striker whose promise seemed to wither visibly after he'd returned to the White Hart Lane second string following his upbeat stint at Leicester. Initially borrowed by Pleat for a month, a week after he'd laid on a Gary Lineker goal at Old Trafford, Paul made an impressive front-running debut, marred only by penalty-area profligacy, and then settled alongside fellow loan striker Kevin Campbell to boost City into a fine run of results that catapulted them from the Second Division basement towards a more respectable ranking. He was recalled by Spurs only after Pleat had earnestly negotiated to secure his services for a third month, and behind him too at Leicester was a hat-trick performance from a 10-1 friendly win at Andover. He looked pacy, with a neat and often flamboyant touch on the ball, but such qualities were rarely in evidence from then on. Only once did Paul start a Spurs first-team game over the next four years, and his further loan-outs were hardly inspiring: half a game for Newcastle, a single Southend outing, and no selections at all at Cambridge. He made little impact with Posh, either; before contenting himself with local non-league football.

Apps: *FL 10.*
Goals: *FL 2.*

MORAN, Steven James

b. Croydon, 10th January 1961

Career: app/pro Aug 1979 Southampton; Sept 1986 CITY; Nov 1987 Reading; Aug 1991 Exeter City; cs 1993 Hull City.

City debut v Sheffield Wednesday (A) 13.9.86 (scored once)

> Bought for £300,000 to help consolidate City's seemingly well-established First Division position, record signing Steve unfortunately extended a dismally ironic sequence: his immediate predecessors with the 'most expensive purchase' tag, Allan Clarke and Roger Davies, had each arrived for relegation seasons, and Bryan Hamilton's team duly made the drop in 1987 despite Steve's goals. In fact Steve's City spell has to be adjudged a disappointment overall, for only in sporadic flashes did Filbert Street fans witness the incisive opportunism which had established him at The Dell and won him England Under-21 selection, and he proved unable to strike up an effective partnership with any of the club's other frontmen, as he had previously for the Saints with Mike Channon and Kevin Keegan. Lawrie McMenemy had spotted Steve as a schoolboy, offering him a new pair of boots if he collected a second-half hat-trick in a Sunday junior game, duly coughing up when the feat was achieved, and signing him shortly afterwards. He made a scoring substitute's debut for Southampton, and his mercurial progress thereafter (including a 21-goal haul from the runners-up campaign of 1984) was hampered only by a couple of lengthy spells on the treatment table. It was, however, inconsistency rather than injury which

prompted his in-and-out status at Leicester (where a debut header at Hillsborough, and a hat-trick in the return fixture with Wednesday stand out most sharply in the memory), and even after a £200,000 move to Reading (a record for that club, too) Steve's frustrations continued: he was cup-tied and therefore sidelined as the Royals took the Simod Cup at Wembley, and was then unable to stop them sliding into Division Three at the end of his first term. The first of his five goals for last port-of-call Hull was his 150th at League level.

Apps: *FL 35+8; FAC 1; LC 5+2; FMC 0+1.*
Goals: *FL 14; LC 3.*

MORGAN, Simon Charles

b. Birmingham, 5th September 1966

Career: app July 1983/pro Nov 1984 CITY; Oct 1990 Fulham; June 2001 Brighton & Hove Albion.

City debut v Coventry City (A) 6.10.85

> A left-back of seemingly unbounded promise when he joined the City defensive ranks as a teenager, Simon settled quickly to his responsibilities in a struggling side, showing the sort of style and spirit which made Under-21 honours for his country an inevitability. Both his anticipation and his tackling skills marked the fair-haired Brummie as the first apparently specialist No 3 to hold a regular City place since Dennis Rife, but squad-system exigencies soon saw his mettle being tested in roles all across the back four (and even behind it, in Bryan Hamilton's short-lived tactical experiments utilising a sweeper). A degree of inconsistency then was an understandable concomitant, and Simon also suffered lengthy injury problems in each of 1987/8 and 1989/90, but his value as a utilitarian defender was buttressed by his unquenchable enthusiasm, and it was surprising that he should be offloaded (for £100,000) at precisely the time his motivational qualities might have been deemed most useful to City's Second Division survival campaign. Only later did it emerge that David Pleat had rather cruelly misjudged Simon as 'too small for a centre-half, not quick enough to be a full-back and not skilful enough to be a midfield player'; a verdict given the lie by his subsequent decade of achievement at Craven Cottage, where he enjoyed his Testimonial year in 2000, culminating in a game against Spurs. Soon elevated to the Fulham captaincy and status of crowd favourite, Simon battled through the poverty years at the club before its upturn in fortune, occasionally pushing up into a goalscoring midfield role. He celebrated their 1997 promotion by writing and publishing a diary of the season, which was actually launched at Harrods following the interim takeover of the the club by multi-millionaire Mohamed Al Fayed; and Simon was still integral to the sides which took the Division Two championship under Kevin Keegan and then consolidated in Division One.

Apps: *FL 147+13; FAC 4+1; LC 14; FMC 3.*
Goals: *FL 3; LC 1.*

Simon Morgan

MORGAN, William

b. Horwich, Lancs

Career: Horwich; 1896 Newton Heath; Mar 1903 Bolton Wanderers; July 1903 Watford; Aug 1904 FOSSE; cs 1906 New Brompton; cs 1907 not known; Sept 1910 Newton Heath Athletic.

Fosse debut v Blackpool (A) 3.9.04

> A long-serving stalwart of the Manchester club which had been officially re-christened as United before he left them, but only a marginal contributor to Bolton's relegation slide, Billy was retrieved for League football by Fosse from Watford's unbeaten Southern League Second Division championship side, to give two seasons' worth of consistent, grafting effort at either right-half or centre-forward. His veteran skills in each of these roles then had their final senior outings in a lowly Southern League term for the club later to be known as Gillingham.

Apps: *FL 66; FAC 7.*
Goals: *FL 9; FAC 3.*

MORRIS, John

b. Radcliffe, Lancs, 27th September 1923

Career: Mujacs; am Aug 1939/pro Mar 1941 Manchester United; Mar 1949 Derby County; Oct 1952 CITY; May 1958 Corby Town (p/mgr); July 1961 Kettering Town.

City debut v Plymouth Argyle (H) 4.10.52

> A teenage revelation in wartime football at Old Trafford (and a guest for each of Bolton, Wrexham and Charlton before call-up to a Royal Armoured Corps tank crew), Johnny was a strong, skilful inside-forward, blessed with a thunderbolt shot, who returned to peacetime football with equivalent impact. He contributed to United's three successive runners-up placings in Division One, helped engineer their 1948 FA Cup Final victory, won the first of his five Football League representative selections, and then attracted a British record fee of £24,500 from Derby after he'd disagreed with Matt Busby over tactics. His form with the Rams won him three England caps (and three international goals to go with them), and his capture by Second Division City (at a club record of £21,500) was regarded with some surprise. A regular at inside-right for four seasons (with a Division two championship medal from 1954), Johnny then switched to right-half, and was an ever-present inspiration to the next table-topping promotion side of 1957. An obviously strong-willed character both on and off the pitch, his relations with the club management were not always the most cordial (he was fined and briefly suspended for his part in the incidents which led to the sacking of Norman Bullock), but Johnny's most notorious brush with authority came when he managed to get himself sent off for insulting the referee during City's public practice match in August 1957, and picked up a 14-day suspension to interrupt the early part of his final Filbert Street season. Following his successful Southern League days, which he finished in renewed partnership with Jack Froggatt at Kettering, he also managed both Great Harwood (Lancashire Combination) and Oswestry Town (Cheshire League) before the 60s were out. Subsequently a salesman for a tyre company until retirement in the North West, he remains a keen golfer. A nephew of Sheffield Wednesday and Preston star Eddie Quigley, Johnny also had a footballing younger brother, Billy, who was on the books at Bury and Derby before a brief League breakthrough with Rochdale, and was later signed by Johnny at Corby.

Apps: *FL 206; FAC 14.*
Goals: *FL 33; FAC 1.*

MORTIMER, Francis Ernest (Fred)

b. Draycott, Derbyshire, ca 1891

Career: Grenadier Guards; 1912 Crystal Palace; May 1913 FOSSE; May 1914 Swansea Town; Sept 1919 Bowmar's Athletic; cs 1920 Rugby Town; cs 1921 Coalville Swifts; Oct 1923 Aylestone St James; 1924 Aylestone WMC.

Fosse debut v Birmingham (A) 20.9.13

> Reputed to have scored 125 goals in three seasons of regimental football, Fred made but a single, scoreless Southern League appearance for Palace after returning to civvy street. The summer of 1913 was pivotal to his future, however, for he first underwent cricket trials with Surrey, and then accompanied Fosse on their Swedish tour, notching ten goals in his five games at centre-forward. A contract was inevitably forthcoming, though Fred started the term as second choice behind Harry Sparrow, and after breaking through was unable as consistently to lift a struggling Second Division side. He hit a hat-trick on his home debut (against Bristol City), but overall shared in a shot-shy campaign at senior level. For the reserves, his 29-goal tally for 1913/14 included the winner in the County Cup Final defeat of Holwell Works. Fred followed manager Jack Bartlett to Swansea, in the lower tier of the Southern League, but was not in the Swans side which humbled Fosse in the FA Cup the following December, having already been recalled for wartime service with the Grenadier Guards. He made brief Filbert Street comebacks before and after receiving a serious arm wound, and later opened a sports outfitter's business on the Hinckley Road, which sadly bankrupted him in December 1924. That summer he'd been playing his cricket for the City of Leicester WMC.

Apps: *FL 22; FAC 2; WW1 14.*
Goals: *FL 8; FAC 1; WW1 5.*

MOUEL, Ernest Alfred

b. Cambridge, ca 1872

Career: Cambridge Swifts; Cambridge Rovers; Aug 1891 FOSSE; cs 1892 not known; Stoke; Oct 1894 Barnsley St Peters.

Fosse debut v Loughborough (A) ML 14.11.1891 (scored once)

> A Cambridge county representative at soccer from the age of 16, Ernest came to Leicestershire as a cricket professional in 1890 (he was loaned in this respect to Ashby-de-la-Zouch CC in 1892), and signed amateur forms for Fosse shortly afterwards. His single campaign was Fosse's first in the Midland League, and his goal-every-three-games return from the right wing made him second-top scorer. Curiously nicknamed 'The Doctor' by his teammates, he followed his cricketing career into Staffordshire (where we lose touch with his winter game allegiances apart from his brief reserve stint at Stoke), and was based in Fenton at the time he signed for Barnsley (then still a Sheffield League club) to play alongside Billy Keech.

Apps: *ML 15.*
Goals: *ML 5.*

MOUNTAIN, George

b. Grimsby, 1874
d. Grimsby, 10th July 1936

Career: 1889 Grimsby White Star; Waltham Hornets; Aug 1895 Grimsby Town; Grimsby All Saints; Sept 1897 Grimsby Town; May 1903 FOSSE; cs 1904 Grimsby Rangers.

Fosse debut v Barnsley (A) 5.9.03

> Almost lost to the game when, after a single Division Two outing for Grimsby, he put to sea as an engineer on a steamship bound for South America, George returned to feature in over 150 more Mariners matches. A hearty play-anywhere type who eventually settled to the right-back berth, he gloried in the nickname 'Bodge', and assisted his hometown team to the Second Division championship in 1901. He earned a club benefit from a game against Lincoln City, and only departed the trawler town on Grimsby's relegation in 1903. Thoughts of frying pans and fires must have crossed his mind, however, as Fosse slumped into the re-election mire, and for all his fighting spirit (literally expressed in the FA Cup defeat by Burton United, when he was sent off – not for the first time in his career), 'Bodge' was unable to effect a turnaround in their fortunes. 'As a tackler, few can beat him, but he plays with in-and-out judgement', commented a critic at the time of his move to Leicester, whose cheque for his transfer would have been passed on directly to the player if the FA hadn't forbidden this fine Grimsby gesture. A publican at the King's Head in Waltham after retirement from the game, he made a single significant mark on the Fosse scoresheet: his own goal conceded in December 1899 made him the first player to have scored for Leicester before actually joining the club, and the only one until Frank Sinclair arrived almost a century later.

Apps: *FL 26; FAC 4.*

MOUNTENEY, Arthur

b. Belgrave, Leicester, 11th February 1883
d. Leicester, 31st May 1933

Career: Belgrave Nonconformists; cs 1903 Leicester Imperial; Nov 1903 FOSSE; Apr 1905 Birmingham; Apr 1909 Preston North End; July 1911 Grimsby Town; Dec 1912 Portsmouth; cs 1914 Balmoral United; Nov 1914 Hinckley United.

Fosse debut v Bolton Wanderers (H) 30.1.04

> Joining Fosse when they were at their lowest ebb, 'Pecker' was one of the young local forward prospects on whom the club pinned hopes of a revival, and he didn't let them down, winning a regular place shortly after the start of 1904/5 and ending that term as top scorer. It was, though, his FA Cup hat-trick which, simultaneously destroying West Brom and alerting top-flight clubs to his potential, made it certain that Fosse couldn't hope to hang on to him. Small Heath changed their title to Birmingham in the summer they signed 'Pecker', and there he continued to develop into a coolly precise all-round forward, albeit one with an easy-going off-field nature. Birmingham were relegated in 1908, but Preston soon restored him to the First Division arena. At Grimsby he drew the comment, 'Physically the biggest forward in class football ... he has brains with his brawn, though', and there were many ready to ascribe his calculating approach to tactics to his ancestry. His father, Arthur senior, had played cricket for Leicestershire between 1884 and 1891, and 'Pecker' himself would soon star for the county side, playing as a batsman in 144 first-class matches between 1911 and 1924, and claiming six postwar centuries. In the interim, as was recalled by Tommy Codd at the time of his death from pneumonia, 'Pecker' had shown heroism while serving the Footballer's Batallion of the Middlesex Regiment, and had saved Codd's life at Vimy Ridge in June 1916. Later an assistant groundsman for Leicestershire, he also had a spell as cricket coach at Stoneygate School.

Apps: *FL 30; FAC 4.*
Goals: *FL 11; FAC 10.*

MOYES, David

b. Cowdenbeath, Fife, ca 1900

Career: Cardwell; Kingseat Juniors; Sept 1919-trials-CITY; Hearts o'Beath; Dec 1919 Raith Rovers; Aug 1926 CITY; Aug 1927 Cowdenbeath; June 1930 East Fife; 1933 Rosyth Dockyard Recreation.

City debut v Liverpool (A) 23.10.26

> Unsuccessful in his initial brief try-out for Peter Hodge, left-back Davie then built a substantial career and reputation with the manager's old club. A stalwart of the Raith side (also including the Duncan brothers) which finished third in the Scottish First Division in 1922, he amassed a 235-game senior record for the Starks Park outfit, and was the beneficiary of a Raith v Darlington friendly in April 1925. He was also involved in the shipwreck that got Raith's 1923 summer programme of friendlies in the Canary Islands off to a frightening start! Ironically becoming the very first signing for incoming boss Willie Orr, Davie then spent most of his Filbert Street term in the shadow of Reg Osborne, failed to appear in a winning City side in the First Division, and, not wishing to serve a belated reserve-team apprenticeship, was glad to return homeward to the east of Scotland to extend his senior career (eventually playing alongside Danny Liddle and Ted Lowery at East Fife).

Apps: *FL 3.*

MUGGLETON, Carl David

b. Leicester, 13th September 1968

Career: app 1985/pro Sept 1986 CITY; Sept 1987-loan-Chesterfield; Feb 1988-loan-Blackpool; Oct 1988-loan-Hartlepool United; Mar 1990-loan-Stockport County; Sept 1990-loan-Liverpool; Aug 1993-loan-Stoke City; Nov 1993-loan-Sheffield United; Jan 1994 Celtic; July 1994 Stoke City; Nov 1995-loan-Rotherham United; Mar 1996-loan-Sheffield United; Sept 1999-loan-Mansfield Town; Dec 1999-loan-Chesterfield; Mar 2001-loan-Cardiff City; July 2001 Cheltenham Town.

City debut v West Bromwich Albion (A) 21.1.89

> A nerveless, sure-handed goalkeeper who strangely seemed often to impress opposition managers more than his own, Carl never quite commanded possession of the City No 1 jersey in a way that would have borne out his immense promise with this hometown club. Initially denied senior experience by Ian Andrews and Paul Cooper, he eagerly grasped several on-loan opportunities to prove his early worth at League level and boost confidence (his Chesterfield stint literally ending with a last-minute penalty save at Fulham), before calmly stepping up for his senior City bow at The Hawthorns. Martin Hodge was the next experienced man to keep Carl sidelined, but summer 1990 saw him nonetheless called up for an England Under-21 cap against France in Toulon. He was involved in a rare loan-exchange deal (with Mike Hooper) to taste Kenny Dalglish's Anfield set-up, and on his return became the first City 'keeper to be sent off: a victim of the new

'professional foul' rules when conceding a penalty to Charlton in March 1991. The following season he had a new rival for senior selection in Kevin Poole, but it was Carl who ended the term in relative glory, capping a fine Wembley display in the Play-Off Final against Blackburn by saving Mike Newell's second penalty. Injury-hit during the following campaign, Carl later found himself to be one of four League-experienced 'keepers on the books, and the one deemed most dispensable by Brian Little. A loan spell with Lou Macari's Stoke was followed by a surprisingly modest £150,000 move to Macari's Celtic; but a further Parkhead change of management then saw Carl return to the Potteries at a £200,000 fee. Mixed fortunes followed (including a brief substitute appearance as an outfield player for Sheffield United at Reading; a relegation term for Stoke in 1998; and a brief reunion with Brian Little), but he remained a keen contender with Gavin Ward for first-choice status at the Britannia Stadium until his release in 2001.

Apps: *FL 46; FAC 3; FMC 1; AIC 1; PO 3.*

MUNCIE, William Paul

b. Carluke, Lanarkshire, 28th August 1911
d. Leicester, 29th January 1992

Career: Carluke; cs 1934 Shettleston; Aug 1934 CITY; May 1938 Southend United; Aug 1939 Nuneaton Borough; Nov 1939 Hinckley United; Mar 1944 CITY; Oct 1946 Crewe Alexandra; Sept 1947 Sphinx FC (Coventry).

City debut v Middlesbrough (A) 20.10.34

> Reportedly having scored 52 goals for Carluke in 1933/4, Willie had notched four in only three outings for Shettleston when he became Peter Hodge's final signing, only days before the manager's death. Thereafter becoming a reliable stand-in winger on either flank for City, he was unfortunate to be stuck in the queues behind Hughie Adcock and Tony Carroll for the right-wing berth, and Danny Liddle and Eric Stubbs for that on the left. Willie's best term was 1936/7, and his appearance in a third of that championship term's games earned him a senior medal to go with his quartet of winner's mementos from the reserves' successive County Cup triumphs of the 30s. Willie scored on his Southend debut, but was back in the Midlands when war was declared. The first of several wartime returns to Filbert Street was made as a guest member of the Forest side beaten at Christmas 1941 in the game that secured the Southern Regional title for City, and Northampton also fielded him before duties as an Army PT instructor took him to Ireland in 1943, when he enjoyed the odd game for Derry City. A veteran's return to League football at Crewe did not work out, and Willie regained amateur status in 1947 to play for a Coventry works team. His son Ian was a teenage centre-forward trialist for Northampton Town in October 1955.

Apps: *FL 42; FAC 1; WW2 2.*
Goals: *FL 11; WW2 1.*

MUNRO, Malcolm George

b. Melton Mowbray, Leics, 21st May 1953

Career: app July 1968/pro May 1970 CITY (- 1975).

City debut v Ipswich Town (A) 11.9.71

> Portman Road was a ground of mixed memories for young centre-back Malcolm. He broke his cheekbone on his debut there, and, on the day he made his breakthrough to become a regular City choice, in the opening fixture of 1973/4, he netted an own goal. Thereafter, though, he didn't look back for eighteen months or so, welding a rigid partnership with Graham Cross that helped secure City's progress to the FA Cup semi-final (and even scoring his sole League goal, at the right end, in the return fixture with Ipswich). The defensive bond wasn't quite so solid during the following First Division term, but the slender and speedy Malcolm was definitely over-hasty and rather immature in his response to losing his place to Jeff Blockley: walking out on his contract and emigrating to Canada to work as a truck driver. City retained his registration until July 1980, when it became patently obvious he wouldn't return. He remains perhaps best remembered for the goal-line clearance which saved City from going 0-3 down to Leatherhead in the 1975 Cup tie.

Apps: *FL 69+1; FAC 9; LC 5.*
Goals: *FL 1; LC 1.*

MURDOCH, James

b. unknown
d. Glasgow, May 1927

Career: 1888 FOSSE.

Fosse debut (competitive) v Burton Wanderers (H) FAC 4.10.1890

> The Victorian equivalent of a midfield playmaker, Jimmy was a Fosse pioneer who lined up in the first County Cup-winning side of 1890 in the pivotal centre-half position, and scored a long-distance fourth goal in the Final replay against Coalville. He was then to assume the inside-right berth both when Fosse retained that trophy a year later and when they made their first-ever entrance into the FA Cup. Jimmy was in business in Glasgow at the time of his death.

Apps: *FAC 1.*

NEWELL, Michael Colin

b. Liverpool, 27th January 1965

Career: am Liverpool; Sept 1983 Crewe Alexandra; Dec 1983 Wigan Athletic; Jan 1986 Luton Town; Sept 1987 CITY; June 1989 Everton; Nov 1991 Blackburn Rovers; July 1996 Birmingham City; Dec 1996-loan-West Ham United; Mar 1997-loan-Bradford City; July 1997 Aberdeen; Mar 1999 Crewe Alexandra; June 1999 Doncaster Rovers (p/coach); Feb 2000 Blackpool.

City debut v Oldham Athletic (H) 16.9.87 (scored once)

> Under Bryan Hamilton's management when he scored for Wigan at Wembley in their 1985 Freight/Rover Trophy victory, Mike became an expensive David Pleat signing at Luton, and forged a useful striking partnership with Mick Harford that saw him elevated to Under-21 honours. He netted Luton's winner against City in 1986/7, then played again for both former managers within a matter of months of swapping the dubious delights of Kenilworth Road's artificial turf for the Filbert Street sward in a club record £350,000 deal. He rapidly headed himself into the good graces of City fans, but then succumbed to a bout of the inertia which spread itself alarmingly over the struggling Second Division side, and prompted the managerial switch. Mike experienced continuing spells of frustration in front of goal even after Pleat's initially reinvigorating arrival, and twice let his temper boil over to earn dismissals; but when allying his remarkable ball control and mobility to an admirable work-rate, he was awarded the City captaincy midway through 1988/9: a season he finished as top scorer, with flashes of form that earned him a highly-valued move to Goodison. He made a scoring bow as a substitute for England 'B', and took a runners-up medal from the Full Members Cup Final in 1991 as an Evertonian, before becoming a £1.1m Kenny Dalglish capture at Ewood. Mike's first Wembley penalty for Blackburn in the 1992 Play-Off Final (his second was saved by Carl Muggleton) denied City entry to the inaugural season of the Premiership; and he helped establish big-spending Rovers at that level before being sidelined by injury and the Shearer/Sutton combination for most of the 1995 championship campaign. An unhappy spell at St Andrews ensued, being most notable for its March 1999 sequel, when Mike accepted an out-of-court settlement from three parties, including Blues boss David Sullivan, having sued for libel when a proposed move to Bolton fell through. Brought back to League fare from the Conference by Blackpool, Mike ended the 2000/1 season on an aggregate tally of 116 League and 49 Cup goals.

Apps: *FL 81; FAC 2; LC 9; FMC 4.*
Goals: *FL 21; LC 5.*

NEWMAN, John Henry George

b. Hereford, 13th December 1933

Career: jnr Hereford United; St Andrews Athletic; Mar 1951 Birmingham City; Nov 1957 CITY; Jan 1960 Plymouth Argyle; Oct 1967 Exeter City (p/mgr from Apr 1969).

City debut v Burnley (A) 9.11.57

> Primarily regarded as a stand-in centre-half at St Andrews, Johnny nonetheless made a fair contribution to Birmingham's 1955 Second Division championship effort, and became an emergency choice for them at right-half in their FA Cup Final defeat by Manchester City a year later. He nonetheless stepped straight into the pivot's role at Leicester as City fought to establish themselves back in the top division, and must have quickly doubted the wisdom of his £12,000 move as he stood at the centre of a defence which shipped 29 goals in his first eight games, including seven on his debut! He gratefully handed back the No 5 shirt to Ian King following that little whirlwind, but after helping secure top-flight survival in the April 1958 crunch match back at his old St Andrews stamping ground, Johnny became immovable from the right-half berth throughout the whole of the next term, until finally giving way to the promise of Frank McLintock in September 1959. He then amassed well over 300 League and Cup appearances for Plymouth, where he initially teamed with Gordon Fincham, soon became skipper, and faced City in the League Cup semi-finals of 1965. Johnny's transition to backroom roles came at Exeter, where his managerial stint stretched to December 1976. He subsequently bossed Grimsby Town, Derby County and Hereford United, held assistant roles at York City, Notts County and Burton Albion; and was chief scout at Mansfield Town. It was at Plymouth in November 1964 that he fuelled countless 'fancy that' snippets in the press by actually passing a penalty kick a few feet forward for teammate Mike Trebilcock to score. Back in 1953, while on a National Service posting, Johnny had somehow contrived to represent 'Wales' versus Scotland in the Junior International series.

Apps: *FL 61; FAC 4.*
Goals: *FL 2.*

NEWTON, Robert Arthur

b. Earl Shilton, Leics, 19th January 1946

Career: app Dec 1962/pro Aug 1963 CITY; July 1965 Bradford City; cs 1966 Wellington Town; cs 1968 Tamworth; Nuneaton Borough; 1976 Worcester City; cs 1977 Tamworth.

City debut v Aldershot (H) LC 25.9.63 (scored once)

Bob Newton

> City's youngest-ever League Cup scorer, Bob was a rangy outside-left who briefly understudied Mike Stringfellow, and took his only real Filbert Street consolation from his debut-making contribution to the eventually-successful trophy hunt of 1963/4 (on the only occasion City ever met the Shots). A season at Valley Parade (also marked by a debut goal, and by an occasional partnership with Ken Leek) closed his brief League career at the age of 20; and by the time Bob appeared in Tamworth's FA Cup runs of the late 60s and early 70s, he had been converted to a full-back role. He was alongside Bobby Mackay in Nuneaton's 1974/5 side, pipped to the Southern League championship by Wimbledon.

Apps: *FL 2; LC 1.*
Goals: *LC 1.*

NEWTON, William

b. Quebec, Co Durham, 6th August 1898
d. Stockport, 29th April 1973

Career: Hartford Colliery; Blyth Spartans; cs 1919 Newcastle United; July 1920 Cardiff City; May 1922 CITY; May 1926 Grimsby Town; July 1927 Stockport County; July 1931 Hull City.

City debut v Bradford City (A) 13.10.23

> A tough-tackling Geordie whose senior career got off to a slow start, Billy showed remarkable stamina in remaining involved in football until past pensionable age, returning to Edgeley Park in 1932 for a 33-year stint on Stockport's coaching and training staff. He could hardly have looked forward to such a lengthy professional life when Newcastle released him without a senior game to his name (having converted him from a Blyth centre-forward to the middle line). But he made sufficient sporadic wing-half appearances in Cardiff's first two seasons in the League to attract Peter Hodge's attention. Nonetheless, Billy was fated to a frustrating first term at Filbert Street, with a rare record: as an ever-present in the reserves' Central Alliance campaign of 1922/3. Having displaced Dennis Jones from the right-half berth, however, he held it for three seasons, which encompassed the 1925 Division Two championship win and ensuing consolidation in the top flight. Thereafter, though Grimsby and Hull each got a season's commitment out of him, Billy devoted his considerable enthusiasm to Stockport on an almost lifelong basis.

Apps: *FL 87; FAC 8.*
Goals: *FL 1.*

NISH, David John

b. Burton-on-Trent, 26th September 1947

Career: Measham Social Welfare; am/pro July 1966 CITY; Aug 1972 Derby County; Feb 1979 Tulsa Roughnecks; Mar 1980 Seattle Sounders; 1981 Shepshed Charterhouse; June 1982 Gresley Rovers (p/mgr); Stapenhill.

City debut v Stoke City (H) 3.12.66 (scored once)

> A true teenage prodigy, David made his first appearance in City's A team at the age of 15 in April 1963, but determined to see through his schooling at Ashby Grammar. Before leaving, he had a remarkable 1965/6 season: winning England youth caps, helping Leicestershire to victory in the FA County Youth Cup, assisting Measham through the early rounds of the County Cup on their way to its capture, and three times being chosen as City's first-team substitute. Then turning professional, he exhibited amazing versatility over his first few seasons in City's senior squad, appearing as a creative midfielder and a defensive wing-half before settling as an attacking left-back. By this time his natural ease and cool authority had identified him as ideal material for the team captaincy, and when City got to Wembley in 1969, David became the youngest-ever Cup Final skipper at 21. Rarely missing a game (or a penalty: he notched fourteen successful spot-kicks until Kevin Keelan saved from him at Norwich in November 1970), he amassed ten England Under-23 caps and several Football League honours in recognition of his elegant effectiveness, and led City back to the top flight in 1971. An ever-present First Division campaign ensued, but the next term had barely started when reigning champions Derby came in with a British record fee of £225,000 to take him to the Baseball Ground. Five full caps and a League championship medal (1975) deservedly came David's way, but he subsequently suffered a series of knee injury problems and left for the less demanding sphere of the NASL when he felt he was slipping from his own high standards of performance. A testimonial game between current Rams and their title-winning predecessors in December 1979 was Derby's fitting adieu to him, yet he completed three seasons in the States, then once more graced local football: celebrating a County Cup triumph with Shepshed in 1982. He rejoined former Derby teammates Bruce Rioch and Colin Todd on the coaching staff at Middlesbrough in 1988, then, twenty-five years after his professional signing, returned to Filbert Street as Youth Development Officer. David was, for two games in December 1995, part of the caretaker management team at the club following Mark McGhee's walkout, and otherwise continued his coaching under several rubrics until very recently: in summer 2000 briefly swapping the title of Youth Academy Director for that of Head of Youth Coaching.

Apps: *FL 228; FAC 28; LC 16.*
Goals: *FL 25; FAC 4; LC 2.*

NOBLE, Robert

b. Buckhaven, Fife, 29th September 1891
d. Newcastle on Tyne, 1st May 1976

Career: 1908 Bromley; am May 1910 Aston Villa; am Nov 1910 Queens Park Rangers; May 1912 FOSSE; Nov 1912 Millwall; 1921 London Caledonians.

Fosse debut v Nottingham Forest (H) 7.9.12

> A Scottish-born civil servant who played as an amateur in England from the age of 17, Bob was a teammate of Douglas McWhirter in Bromley's Amateur Cup-winning side of 1911, and represented both London and Kent, though neither of his alliances with Villa nor QPR brought him senior selections. Jack Bartlett, as ever, showed more faith in the adaptability of the London amateur, initially giving

him a scoring trial in the Titanic Disaster Fund friendly of May 1912, but even he was unimpressed by Bob's form at inside-forward in the early weeks of 1912/13, while the local press were more concerned with his fitness, deeming him 'not sufficiently robust to stand the hard battles of Second Division football'. Bob was presumably happier anyway to assist Millwall in the Southern League to cut down on travel from his capital base, and he gave both them and London Caledonians lengthy service. With the former he turned out one last time at League level following their Third Division election in 1920, and with the latter experienced a second Amateur Cup Final triumph in 1923. Bob was back at Filbert Street in December 1926, playing alongside Jack Roxburgh for Scotland in the amateur Auld Enemy international, and scoring once in their 4-1 win. Caledonians reached an advanced stage of the FA Cup in both 1927 and 1928, and Bob as a veritable veteran netted against each of Luton and Crewe in those years.

Apps: *FL 4.*

NORMAN, Alfred

Career: Oxford Victoria (Leicester); 1902 St Andrews; cs 1905 Leicester Imperial; Aug 1906 FOSSE ; cs 1907 Leicester Imperial.

Fosse debut v Bradford City (A) 24.11.06

> Nicknamed 'Stuts', this local outside-right twice deputised for Jamie Durrant at League level (scoring in a 3-0 home win over Lincoln City), and once in a friendly against Luton. Alfred had twice netted for the Imps in their 1906 County Cup Final win over Market Harborough; and before that had played on the opposite flank for St Andrews to his brother Alexander.

Apps: *FL 2.*
Goals: *FL 1.*

NORMAN, Richard

b. Newcastle on Tyne, 5th September 1935

Career: Throckley Juniors; Ferryhill Athletic; cs 1958 Horden Colliery Welfare; Nov 1958 CITY; June 1968 Peterborough United; July 1969 Burton Albion (p/mgr from Dec 1969 - 1973).

City debut v Newcastle United (A) 23.1.60

> A steady, unflamboyant Geordie left-back, overlooked by his hometown League club despite starring for Ferryhill's Northern League championship team of 1958, Richie arrived at Filbert Street just as manager David Halliday departed, and then had to complete his National Service in the Royal Signals Corps. Matt Gillies gave him a run-out in the Southern Professional Floodlit Cup tie at Arsenal in November 1959, and a League bow back on Tyneside a couple of months later, and Richie needed but a few more chances to deputise for Willie Cunningham before developing an unshakeable grip on City's No 3 shirt. From 18th April 1960 to the end of February 1964 he never missed a match, shattering the then-standing City record for consecutive League and Cup appearances, and matching consistency to fitness through 194 games, including two FA Cup Finals and City's brief European adventure. Richie wasn't to miss many games over the next four seasons, either; playing in both 60s League Cup Finals, and leaving an abiding impression of cheerful sportsmanship. After a brief stint with Posh, Richie joined Ian King at Burton, then succeeded him as player/manager there, and later assumed coaching, training and physiotherapy duties at Derby County, Northampton Town, Kettering Town, Northamptonshire CCC and Nuneaton Borough.

Apps: *FL 303; FAC 30; LC 28; ECWC 4.*
Goals: *FL 2; LC 3.*

Richie Norman

NORTH, Marc Victor

b. Ware, Herts, 25th September 1966

Career: app/pro Mar 1984 Luton Town; Mar 1985-loan-Lincoln City; Jan 1987-loan-Scunthorpe United; Mar 1987-loan-Birmingham City; Aug 1987 Grimsby Town; Mar 1989 CITY; July 1991-trials-Luton Town; Sept 1991-trials-Grimsby Town; Oct 1991 Leicester United; Nov 1991 Whetstone United; Jan 1992 Shepshed Albion; Jan 1992-trials-Walsall; Mar 1992 Boston United; Mar 1992 Kettering Town; Aug 1992 St Andrews; Dec 1993 Desborough Town; Jan 1994 St Andrews; Oct 1994 Corby Town; Nov 1995 Leicester United.

City debut v Birmingham City (H) 25.3.89 (sub)

> Initially signed as a teenage goalkeeper by David Pleat at Luton, and later taken on as a striker at Blundell Park by Bobby Roberts, Marc rejoined both at Filbert Street as a £100,000 deadline-day signing, just a couple of months after hitting the goalscoring headlines in Grimsby's giant-killing Cup run. Marc had, in fact, taken his transition from last-liner to front man in stages: making his League bow as a defender while on loan at Lincoln, before briefly partnering Mike Newell at Kenilworth Road. With City, Marc again found opportunities in each position (twice, in fact, taking over as an emergency goalkeeper in mid-match) but became something of a victim of his own versatility after a luckless introduction. His first Leicester start, against Crystal Palace, saw him open the scoring with a fine header, then exit with a broken shin; while throughout the following two seasons he was unsettlingly experimented with as sweeper, full-back, central defender, midfielder and target-man. Marc's final game was in the status-saving nailbiter against Oxford, but he was then offloaded as Brian Little set about slashing the club's wage bill. Unfortunately, neither a Scottish pre-season tour with Pleat's Luton nor another nostalgic return to Grimsby earned him a further League contract, and he incredibly spent brief spells at no less than eight clubs in 1991/2 alone. Marc's brother Stacey also came up through the Luton ranks, later playing at centre-back for West Brom and Fulham.

Apps: *FL 51+20; LC 0+2; FMC 1.*
Goals: *FL 9.*

NORTON, Joseph Patrick

b. Leicester, 1890

Career: Avondale; cs 1908 Leicester British United; (cs 1910 Leicester Imperial); cs 1910 Atherstone Town; trials Jan 1911/pro cs 1911 Stockport County; cs 1912 Atherstone Town; cs 1913 Nuneaton Town; Dec 1913 Manchester United; July 1919 CITY; May 1920 Bristol Rovers; cs 1922 Swindon Town; June 1923 Kettering Town; Sept 1924 Atherstone Town; Nov 1924 Hinckley United; Feb 1925 Ashby Town.

Fosse debut (WW1) v Coventry City (A) 15.3.19; (postwar) v Tottenham Hotspur (A) 1.9.19

> There were a couple of eccentricities in the busy transfer record of this mustard-keen little forward: he signed for the local Imps in 1910 but didn't actually play before accepting Atherstone's counter-offer, and when he moved from Nuneaton to Old Trafford in 1913, the deal consisted of a £195 payment plus the promise of a friendly fixture: the latter eventually took place in September 1919! An elusive winger who was never the most prolific of scorers, Joe actually opened his League account with a Stockport equaliser at Filbert Street, at a time when claims were being advanced for him as the lightest man in senior football: he weighed precisely 8st 4lbs when signing for County. His second spell in the North West saw him as a First Division regular with United on the eve of war, and he guested regularly for Nottingham Forest before joining up with the Leicestershire Regiment. On his return from the front, Joe briefly assisted Forest, United and Fosse, then signed for the reconstructed City prior to their first League season. Happily working either flank after his debut as an emergency centre-forward, Joe nonetheless seemed to carry a jinx throughout his Filbert Street season – in only three of the dozen games he played did City score at all. Ironically, at Eastville, one of his own rare goals helped Rovers to their first-ever League win. Joe later re-settled in the Belgrave area, and worked for the City Corporation.

Apps: *FL 11; FAC 1; WW1 7.*

NUTTALL, Ernest Albert

b. Leicester, 1st February 1871
d. Barnes, Middlesex, 12th February 1920

Career: Syston Wreake Valley; Mill Hill House; Repton School; 1889 FOSSE; 1894 Crouch End.

Fosse debut (competitive) v Burton Wanderers (H) FAC 4.10.1890

> An amateur wing-half signed during Fosse's final season of friendly fare, law student 'Snooks' went on to be elected captain for the club's initial assaults on the Midland League, having previously skippered the Leicestershire FA side for three seasons in inter-county encounters. At right-half in the inaugural foray into the FA Cup in 1890, he was on the left of the middle line when claiming the club's first-ever FA Cup goal a year later, against Small Heath. He was also in the County Cup-winning side of 1891, and was still turning out in the occasional Fosse friendly in 1893/4 as the club embraced professionalism ever more firmly. Much of his career ran in parallel with that of fellow solicitor-to-be Jimmy Atter: the pair were together in each of Mill Hill House's County Cup Final side of 1889 (beaten by Loughborough) and Crouch End's London Senior Cup run (to the semi-finals) in 1894. 'Snooks' thereafter took up his legal practice in London, but volunteered for WW1 service at an advanced age. Sent home ill from Russia, he later died of tuberculosis. Back in 1889, 'Snooks' had also been a founder-member, along with fellow Fossil SWR Stretton, of Leicester Hockey Club.

Apps: *FAC 3; ML 35.*
Goals: *FAC 1; ML 2.*

OAKES, Scott John

b. Leicester, 5th August 1972

Career: YT Aug 1988/pro May 1990 CITY; Oct 1991 Luton Town; July 1996 Sheffield Wednesday; July 2000-trials-Burnley; Aug 2000-trials-Peterborough United; Aug 2000 Cambridge United; July 2001 Leyton Orient.

City debut v Plymouth Argyle (A) 17.10.89 (sub)

> The first of the sons of Showaddywaddy rocker Trevor Oakes to play for City, Scott was still a 17-year-old trainee winger when pitched late into the fray at Home Park as David Pleat's team vainly attempted to pull back a three-goal deficit. Steadily nurtured into the professional ranks, he was tried out both at full-back and as sweeper on City's pre-season tour of Scotland in 1990, and it was in the right-back berth that Scott made a promising breakthrough into Brian Little's line-up a year or so later; though it was to be only a matter of days after his first League start (at Newcastle) that Scott would rejoin Pleat as part of the Steve Thompson exchange package. At Kenilworth Road, he was rapidly lauded as the mature-beyond-his-years playmaker of Luton's anti-relegation struggle, but a cartilage injury then sidelined him until his club's fate was virtually sealed. He got one brief shot at England Under-21 football in the summer of 1993, and his steadily rising goal tally from midfield included a hat-trick against West Ham that saw the Hatters into the FA Cup semi-finals of 1994. Luton suffered a further drop in 1996, though, and Pleat swooped again on behalf of the Owls to sign Scott for £425,000. His Hillsborough career unrolled as a disappointing affair of limited opportunities, however, and another injury completely ruined Scott's 1999/2000 season, keeping him out of action until the last couple of reserve fixtures. Trials at Cambridge proved his return to fitness, and he accepted non-contract terms there in October 2000. But, following a managerial change, he was released in the summer.

Apps: *FL 1+2; FMC 1.*

OAKES, Stefan Trevor

b. Leicester, 6th September 1978

Career: YT 1995/pro July 1997 CITY.

City debut v Chelsea (H) 21.11.98 (sub)

> Named City's Young Player of the Year for 1999 after only a modicum of Premiership experience, Stef had already given glimpses of the strongest aspects of his attacking midfielder's armoury: a sweet left foot, and the intelligence to know when to use it. Scott's younger brother in fact made his bow when City were chasing the game against Chelsea, and was forced to sit in defence as Steve Walsh rampaged up front, but most of his subsequent outings have exploited his ability to spray passes from just inside the halfway line. Also of definite occasional use to City are his free-kicks, whipped in left-footed from the right wing; though he may have to toughen up in one-on-one challenges to find himself more time and space as opponents get used to his favoured distribution options and angles. Stef opened his scoring account in the League Cup tie with Crystal Palace on a night he should have had a hat-trick (missing, as well as converting, one penalty), and thereafter kept his place in the 2000 Wembley run, climaxing his first term as a regular squad member with a winner's medal from the Final victory over Tranmere. 2000/1, however, proved to be something of a disappointing campaign in terms of Stef's anticipated progress, with rather too many over-casual performances diluting his claim to regular selection.

Apps *(to end 2000/1): PL 22+16; FAC 4+2; LC 7.*
Goals: *PL 1; LC 2.*

OAKES, WIlliam Henry

b. Barking, Essex, ca 1882
d. Leyton, 8th September 1927

Career: Barking Lads Institute; Barking; Clapton; Feb 1904 West Ham United; May 1904 FOSSE (- 1907).

Fosse debut v Blackpool (A) 3.9.04

> A well-regarded full-back, noted for the length and accuracy of his clearances, Billy signed for Fosse after fourteen Southern League outings for West Ham, just prior to that club's move to Upton Park. He had three rather injury-hit seasons at Leicester, contesting the left-back berth with Walter Robinson and Bob Pollock, but being displaced by Joe Blackett for all but one game of the 3rd-place campaign of 1906/7. Billy's parents ran the Ship Inn in Barking, and he followed their trade by taking the licence of the Antelope Hotel in Church Road, Leyton, before becoming a partner in the contracting company Sanders & Oakes.

Apps: *FL 40; FAC 1.*

O'BRIEN, Michael Terence

b. Kilcock, Dublin, 10th August 1893
d. Uxbridge, Middlesex, 21st September 1940

Career: Walker Celtic; Wallsend; Blyth Spartans; Newcastle East End; Celtic; Alloa Athletic; Dec 1914 Brentford; Aug 1919 Norwich City; Dec 1919 South Shields; May 1920 Queens Park Rangers; Mar 1922 CITY; June 1924 Hull City; May 1926 Brooklyn Wanderers; Dec 1926 Derby County; June 1928 Walsall; May 1929 Norwich City; June 1931 Watford.

City debut v Notts County (H) 18.3.22

> Mick was a virtually legendary figure in inter-war football, whose itchy feet and love of the blarney could scarcely disguise a genuine talent for classical centre-half play. One of his claims was that he'd never kicked a football until the age of 18, when his family moved from Ireland to the North East, and shortly before he joined the Army. Nonetheless, he quickly became a footballing mercenary before the outbreak of war, served during the hostilities in each of the Navy (seeing action at the Battle of Jutland) and the Royal Flying Corps, and then resumed his soccer wanderings in 1919. After almost two seasons easing QPR into the League, and having won both his first Irish cap and selection for the Football League against the Army (November 1921), Mick brought his 6ft 1in presence and his outsize personality to Leicester. A further four international appearances came his way as firstly he played alongside Jimmy Harrold in a daunting defensive pairing, then usurped his partner's pivotal role. He was denied a further cap, in February 1923, when City prioritised their promotion effort over his release, but unfortunately Mick missed out on the frustrating run-in to a 3rd-place finish after suffering a broken toe. A year later, however, the *Sunday Post* had no sooner declared of his game that he 'had brains behind his boots – he eschewed the haphazard', than he had a bust-up with the board in a Blackpool hotel and found himself listed. After the League reduced City's asking fee from £2,000 to £750, Mick joined Second

Division rivals Hull, and his only goal for the Tigers came in the 1-1 FA Cup draw againsrt City in February 1925. That year he was summoned at Leicester Police Court for non-payment of rates on his Thurmaston house; but he seemed to have put such monetary worries behind him when essaying an inquisitive taste of early Stateside soccer, with Brooklyn Wanderers offering a tempting five-year contract at £16 per week. After a mere seven games, disillusion brought him back to Derby, for his only sustained stint of reserve-team football; then three more moves aroound Division Three (South) helped boost his final tally of caps to ten for Ireland, plus four as the Free State's skipper. Mick tried his hand at poultry farming while with Derby, and had a tobacconist's business at Norwich, but on hanging up his boots moved straight into management: at QPR for two years from 1933, as assistant at Brentford for a season, and then in control at Ipswich Town for their first, championship-winning Southern League campaign (1936/7). He was an FA coach in Middlesex at the time of his death.

Apps: *FL 65; FAC 2.*
Goals: *FL 6.*

O'CALLAGHAN, Eugene

b. Ebbw Vale, Monmouthshire, 6th October 1906
d. London, 4th July 1956

Career: Victoria United; Ebbw Vale Corries; am 1924 Tottenham Hotspur; loan-Barnet; loan-Northfleet United; pro Dec 1926 Tottenham Hotspur; Mar 1935 CITY; Oct 1937 Fulham.

City debut v Middlesbrough (H) 2.3.35

> An outstanding Welsh international inside-right who earned eleven caps while scoring 98 League and Cup goals for Spurs, the inevitably-nicknamed 'Taffy' first came to City's attention when upsetting the bulk of the all-time record Filbert Street crowd of 47,298 with his match-winning performance for the Londoners in the 1928 FA Cup tie. Spurs would be relegated that term, and promoted again in 1933, but they were booked for a further demotion when he joined Arthur Lochhead's City in an eventually futile attempt to help stop his new club accompanying them. Gene knuckled down to the task of prompting (and skippering) City back up again – turning down a final cap in October 1935 to lead a 6-0 Second Division eclipse of Doncaster – and well earned his 1937 championship medal as second-top scorer behind Jack Bowers. He would play but once more in the top flight before returning to the capital with Fulham, on whose books he remained throughout the war years (when also featuring in guest outings for Spurs, Aldershot and Brentford); and he acted as reserve-team trainer at Craven Cottage for the decade before his death. Gene also trained the Indian soccer team at the 1948 Olympic Games.

Apps: *FL 84; FAC 5.*
Goals: *FL 30; FAC 1.*

OGILVIE, John Forrest

b. Motherwell, Lanarkshire, 28th October 1928

Career: Thorniewood United; 1947 Hibernian; Aug 1955-trials-Sheffield United; Oct 1955 CITY; Jan 1960 Mansfield Town; Oct 1962 Bedworth Town.

City debut v Swansea Town (H) 12.11.55

> Denied his true share of the glory as a valuable defensive member of Hibernian's 1951 Scottish championship squad – he took a runners-up medal from that term's League Cup Final and then broke a leg

John Ogilvie

after 15 minutes of the Scottish Cup semi-final – John found it difficult subsequently to maintain the progress of his Easter Road career, and was freed in 1955. Bramall Lane briefly beckoned, but it was David Halliday who offered John a firm contract, and the left-back settled into sound partnerships with, first, Willie Cunningham, and then, throughout the 1957 Second Division title campaign, with Stan Milburn. In the years of top-flight consolidation, Ogie's place was not so secure, but even with an in-and-out senior record and a series of injuries, he remained the chief dressing-room joker and morale-booster among the club's large Scottish contingent. His two penalty goals ironically came in his last two senior City games, while his only appearance on the Mansfield scoresheet also came with a spot-kick – on the occasion of his final selection! John, who'd turned down a mooted move to Wrexham before signing up at Field Mill, returned to Leicester to work successively in the knitwear and printing trades, remaining active behind the scenes in local soccer, earning his preliminary FA coaching badge in 1975, and for some time in the 80s and 90s helping manage Alan Birchenall's charity-supporting team of self-avowedly geriatric ex-City players.

Apps: *FL 82; FAC 3.*
Goals: *FL 2.*

OLD, George

Career: Notts Mapperley; Mar 1891 FOSSE; cs 1892 Ruddington.

Fosse debut v Derby Junction (H) ML 12.9.1891

> Fosse's goalkeeper in the final friendly game at Mill Lane and the first competitive fixture in the Midland League, George saw the club through its brief tenancy of the Aylestone Road cricket ground (including the 1891/2 FA Cup exit to Small Heath) and its first few games at Filbert Street, but lost his place at Christmas 1891 and drifted away; returning only to face Fosse Rovers the following term for a minor Nottinghamshire team.

Apps: *FAC 1; ML 7.*

OLDFIELD, David Charles

b. Perth, Australia, 30th May 1968

Career: Almondsbury Rangers; app 1984/pro June 1986 Luton Town; Mar 1989 Manchester City; Jan 1990 CITY; Feb 1995-loan-Millwall; July 1995 Luton Town; June 1998 Stoke City; Mar 2000 Peterborough United.

City debut v Newcastle United (A) 13.1.90

> Nicknamed 'Skippy' by the Filbert Street crowd on account of his Australian birth (though he'd grown up in England from the age of four), David started his City career as a gangly, awkwardly unorthodox front-runner, and gradually retreated into a deeper-lying role. His persistently individualistic dribbling style, often involving abrupt changes of direction and a step-over speciality, many times saw him dubbed 'coltish'; though scrappy distribution occasionally spoiled his energetic approach work, and his finishing could be as wildly erratic as it was sometimes lethally spectacular. Like Marc North and Rob Johnson, a product of the David Pleat / John Moore youth set-up at Kenilworth Road, David made his initial Luton impact with a goal at Anfield, and had won one England Under-21 cap prior to his £600,000 move to boost Manchester City's promotion bid. Introduced on the pitch to the Maine Road crowd immediately before they beat City 4-2, he made his biggest mark there in the following season: scoring twice in the 5-1 local derby slaughter of United. Then involved in the part-exchange deal in which Wayne Clarke departed for Manchester, David made his bow in a typically crazy Leicester performance at St James' Park, which saw City 4-2 up with just 13 minutes left, only to lose 4-5 to a Mark McGhee-inspired Magpies side. Never a wholly consistent goalscorer thereafter, he nonetheless had a knack of opening up opposing defences to teammates' benefit with his unpredictable meanderings and willing support play, and won fairly regular selections from each of Pleat, Gordon Lee and Brian Little; though the Swindon Town defeat was the only one of City's three successive Wembley Play-Off dates in which David appeared. McGhee, too, gave him a break while assessing his Filbert Street inheritance, but sold him back to Luton for £150,000 after he'd had an unlikely loan spell with the Lions: he'd been sent off on his previous outing at the New Den. The Hatters suffered relegation to Division Two in 1996, but David was named as their 1998 Player of the Year before becoming an early Little signing at Stoke. He assisted Posh to promotion via the 2000 Play-Off Final victory over Darlington, and retains 'old head' status in Barry Fry's squad.

Apps: *FL/PL 163+25; FAC 7; LC 10+2; FMC 5+1; AIC 3; PO 3+2.*
Goals: *FL/PL 26; FAC 3; LC 1; FMC 1; AIC 1.*

O'NEIL, Joseph

b. Glasgow, 15th August 1931

Career: Bridgeton Waverley; 1950 Aberdeen; Nov 1952-loan-Southend United; Mar 1956 CITY; Oct 1957 Northampton Town; July 1959 Bath City; May 1961 Weston-super-Mare (p/mgr).

City debut v Manchester United (H) 24.8.57

> Never a Pittodrie regular, Joe nonetheless drew startled admiration from Dons followers for one particular show of bravery, bordering on recklessness. Three weeks before the 1954 Scottish Cup semi-final against Rangers, he suffered a depressed skull fracture – yet played on the big day and contributed a hat-trick to Aberdeen's 6-0 win. Further injury problems then unfortunately ruled the tall forward out of the Hampden Final line-up; though he contributed as a squad player to the championship triumph of 1955. He accompanied clubmate Ian McNeill to Filbert Street, to renew acquaintance with former Dons boss David Halliday, but had to wait almost eighteen months for his first-team bow. Indeed, he was still unblooded at senior level for City when he asked for a transfer late in the 1956/7 campaign, and guested for Coventry City in a March friendly against Akademisk Boldklub. No deal ensued, and with Colin Appleton, Pat Ward and Eddie Russell all injured for the opening First Division fixture of the following season, Joe won selection at left-half. City's shaky start hardly helped his integration, despite his impact on the scoresheet, and he soon moved to the County Ground. A two-goal Cobblers debut at centre-forward preceded another shift back to the middle line, then he re-united at Bath with another ex-Aberdonian, Ian MacFarlane. The pair figured strongly in the non-leaguers' 1959/60 Cup run: with Joe getting sent off in the First Round win over Millwall, scoring the only goal of the Round Two clash with Notts County, and then sharing in the 0-1 defeat by Ian McNeill's Brighton in front of the all-time Twerton Park record crowd of 18,020. The lengthy stint with Southend early in his career was a consequence of his National Service posting at nearby Shoeburyness: he was actually withdrawn from one first-team fixture there to fill sandbags in the wake of severe Essex flooding. In December 1971, Joe returned to Bath as manager.

Apps: *FL 5.*
Goals: *FL 2.*

O'NEILL, John Patrick

b. Derry, 11th March 1958

Career: Derry BC; non-contract Mar 1976/pro Feb 1979 CITY; July 1987 Queens Park Rangers; Dec 1987 Norwich City.

City debut v Burnley (A) 19.8.78

> John was still a Loughborough undergraduate, playing for City on a non-contract basis while completing his economics studies, when Jock Wallace gave him an unexpected first-team nod for the opening game of 1978/9 at Turf Moor. The gamble soon paid off, for John quickly developed into a cool, polished central defender. Already capped at Under-21 level for Northern Ireland prior to his League bow, he soon began adding full caps to his record on a regular basis, as his fine reading of the game brought him the added responsibility of the City captaincy. Occasionally criticised for an apparently over-casual on-field approach, and sometimes embarrassed by a relative lack of pace, John nonetheless saved Leicester many a goal against with his intelligent interventions, and the experience gained in two World Cup campaigns for his country stood City's defence in good stead during the up and down struggles of the early 80s, which saw him feature in two promotion campaigns alongside Larry May. In 1986, he surpassed Gordon Banks' record as the most-capped City player (eventually representing his country 39 times), but a year later was allowed to move on to Loftus Road for £150,000. As QPR enjoyed a brief flurry of First Division success, John was restricted to only two League selections, but then hit far worse fortune: suffering a crippling knee injury after only 34 minutes of his Norwich debut at Wimbledon, and some months later having to concede his career had come to a sadly premature end. Norwich very honourably hosted a testimonial match against City on his behalf in May 1989, and John's subsequent involvement in the game amounted only to a two-year spell as manager of League of Ireland side Finn Harps from February 1990. Having then concentrated on a wine and spirits business in Derry, he hit the headlines in October 1994 with a High Court action for negligence against John Fashanu and Wimbledon FC (arising from the tackle that put him out of the game), which terminated with an out-of-court settlement of £70,000 in John's favour.

Apps: *FL 313; FAC 19; LC 13.*
Goals: *FL 10; FAC 1; LC 1.*

ORMONDROYD, Ian

b. Bradford, 22nd September 1964

Career: Manningham Mills; Thackley; Sept 1985 Bradford City; Mar 1987-loan-Oldham Athletic; Feb 1989 Aston Villa; Sept 1991 Derby County; Mar 1992 CITY; Jan 1995-loan-Hull City; July 1995 Bradford City; Sept 1996 Oldham Athletic; Sept 1997 Scunthorpe United.

City debut v Portsmouth (H) 11.3.92

> A 6ft 4in attacker who seemed to polarise the opinions of home crowds wherever he played, Ian could easily be represented as a bundle of contradictions. Probably more effective on the ground than in the air, where he sometimes struggled to exploit a natural advantage, he would as happily play wide on the left as in a central striking role, while his undoubtedly high work-rate and general unselfishness was too often undermined by an ungainly awkwardness on the ball. His ups-and-downs with City were hardly accompanied by a significant goal touch overall, but Ian was a crucial scorer in each of the three Play-Off semi-finals the club was involved in from 1992-94, and it was his parried header which led to Steve Walsh's winner in the Final against Derby. It was subsequently ironic that Ian's only Premiership goal for City, in the home victory over Arsenal, should belatedly have been scrubbed off when the League panel re-assigned it as a Gunners' own goal. A late entrant to the senior game, Ian made unsuccessful Play-Off appearances for each of Bradford and Oldham before his £650,000 move to join Graham Taylor at Villa Park. He shared in Villa's 1990 First Division runners-up campaign, but his price had fallen to £300,000 when he signed for Derby after a loan spell. He netted in both 1991/2 fixtures for the Rams against City prior to his involvement in the deal which took Paul Kitson to the Baseball Ground, and in which his own value was estimated at a club record-equalling £350,000. Ian rediscovered a dormant scoring flair when Mark McGhee loaned him out to Hull, but he was allowed to return to Valley Parade as part of the £475,000 package that also sent both Gavin Ward and Nicky Mohan northwards. He assisted Bradford upwards via the Play-Offs in 1996, then notched the last of his 62 League goals whilst at Oldham, before retiring in 1998. Ian has since headed Bradford's Football in the Community programme.

Apps: *FL/PL 67+10; FAC 1+1; LC 6; AIC 4; PO 7.*
Goals: *FL 7; LC 2; PO 3.*

OSBORN, Frederick

b. Leicester, 10th November 1889
d. Leicester, 11th October 1954

Career: Avondale; cs 1909 Hinckley United; Apr 1910 FOSSE; May 1913 Preston North End; Jan 1921 Nuneaton Town.

Fosse debut v Huddersfield Town (A) 22.10.10

> Forty-five goals for Hinckley in 1909/10, when they headed the Leicestershire Senior League and took the County Cup (with Fred scoring twice in the Final), were sufficient recommendation for this local inside- or centre-forward to be snapped up by Fosse, and his progress over three Second Division terms thereafter was inexorable, both in terms of marksmanship and increasing consistency of selection. First Division Preston expended £250 on his talent, but must have had early doubts over the wisdom of their outlay: Fred went a dozen games without scoring, but then got off the mark with the first of his three hat-tricks that term, and finished top scorer in what was, in fact, a relegation term. However, in harness with Jim Macauley, he shot them back to promotion in the war-shadowed 1914/15 season, when he netted in both home and away fixtures against Fosse. Fred managed some wartime football for Hull City between military excursions to the front in France, and survived a bullet through the thigh while serving as a driver with the Royal Field Artillery in November 1918. He returned to Deepdale for the resumption of League football, but ironically it was the form of Fosse's wartime discovery Tommy Roberts, transferred to Preston in 1919 and destined to win England honours, which kept him sidelined for much of this period. Another of Leicester's amazingly numerous breed of footballer/cricketers, Fred was also a stylish batsman for the County before the war; and for some unfathomable reason rejoiced in the nickname 'Spoe'. His brother George, also formerly a Hinckley United player, guested for each of Fosse and Hull during WW1.

Apps: *FL 67; FAC 4.*
Goals: *FL 28; FAC 2.*

OSBORNE, John

b. Renfrew, 14th October 1919
d. Leicester, 19th September 1981

Career: 1938 Linwood Thistle; Sept 1938 CITY; Jan 1948 Watford; Aug 1949 Brush Sports; July 1950 Rugby Town; Aug 1953 Jones & Shipman.

City debut (WW2) v Manchester City (H) 26.8.39; (postwar) v Chelsea (A) FAC 5.1.46

> A right-half who arrived at Filbert Street from Scottish Junior football on the same day as Charlie Adam, Johnny made his first-team breakthrough on the opening day of the abandoned 1939/40 season, and thus had his only League appearance for City expunged from all official records. He managed the odd wartime outing for St Mirren and Dundee United, but was severely wounded in the arm and side while serving in France, and didn't return to Leicester until the transitional season of 1945/6, when he was back in the No 4 shirt for both legs of the FA Cup tie with Chelsea. Thereafter a reserve-team regular, Johnny later became a component of the extraordinary five-man, £4,750 transfer deal with Watford, for whom he scored 13 times in 35 senior outings. He was still turning out for Jones & Shipman in the early 60's.

Apps: *FAC 2; WW2 13.*
Goals: *WW2 1.*

OSBORNE, Reginald

b. Wynberg, Cape Town, South Africa, 23rd July 1898
d. Hounslow, Middlesex, Apr qtr 1977

Career: Army football (RAMC); 1922 Bromley; Feb 1923 CITY; Nov 1933 Folkestone.

City debut v Fulham (H) 2.4.23

> The son of an army major, who moved his family to Hampshire in 1909, Reg himself spent a ten-year stint in the RAMC after joining up aged 14. He experienced both WW1 service and representative football in Italy, then in 1921 attracted City's attention when he twice played as a stylish left-back at Filbert Street: for RAMC (Aldershot) against the Inniskillen Dragoons in an Army FA Cup tie in February, and in the England v Ireland amateur international in November. His 1922 demob brought City and Everton into competition for his professional signature, and after two games for Bromley, Reg took up a position with the Watling Street Boot Company in Atherstone, obtained for him by the club, while he saw out the then-mandatory year before he could officially commence a full-time football career. His City debut, preparatory to him becoming a regular back-line partner for Adam Black, pitched him into direct opposition to his brother Frank, Fulham's England winger, and it was only four years before Reg himself stepped up to full international status. Actually capped only once, in a home defeat by Wales, he also toured the land of his birth with an FA party (in Arthur Chandler's company) in 1929, when injury unfortunately kept him out of the 'Test Matches' with South Africa's national XI. Nevertheless, he came under pressure for his senior jersey at Leicester on several occasions (from the likes of Harry Hooper and Jack Brown), and there was much to commend in the loyalty which kept him with City for more than a decade. Both his goals were penalties and both were scored against Sunderland in 1931/2; though it was one Reg missed almost seven years earlier that threatened briefly to be his biggest embarrassment, for he failed from the spot in the game against Bradford City which, thanks to George Carr's later strike, sealed City's promotion in 1925. Reg was living in Kingston-on-Thames when he played a season with Folkestone which brought them the Kent Senior Cup and Kent Senior Shield, while in the mid-60s he was co-manager of a pub just outside Stamford Bridge. A third Osborne brother, Harold, appeared once at League level for Norwich City.

Apps: *FL 240; FAC 9.*
Goals: *FL 2.*

OSMAN, Russell Charles

b. Repton, Derbyshire, 14th February 1959

Career: app July 1975/pro Mar 1976 Ipswich Town; July 1985 CITY; June 1988 Southampton; Oct 1991 Bristol City; Jan 1995 Sudbury Town; Mar 1995 Plymouth Argyle (p/coach); Sept 1995 Brighton & Hove Albion; Feb 1996 Cardiff City.

City debut v Everton (H) 17.8.85

> The son of Rex Osman, a Derby County reserve half-back of the 50s, Russell made great strides as an Ipswich youngster, winning an FA Youth Cup-winner's medal in 1975 and only just missing out on a place in the 1978 FA Cup side. Established at club and eventually England level in a resolute centre-back partnership with Terry Butcher, he was also a member of Bobby Robson's victorious UEFA Cup team of 1981, but his once meteoric progress, founded equally on strength and skill, appeared to have halted during his later years at Portman Road. Russell cost Gordon Milne a £240,000 fee when arriving to stiffen City's First Division defence, and expressed the hope that he'd hit high enough form to start adding to his tally of eleven full caps (which had been preceded by seven Under-21 call-ups). The latter goal failed to materialise, but Russell's energetic and intelligent efforts to keep City in the top flight could hardly be faulted, even when they did take the drop in 1987. He assumed the captaincy from the start of the following term, and his coolness and comfort on the ball stood out pleasingly against a Second Division backdrop, but his retention of higher ambitions led to him moving to The Dell on the expiry of his contract. He played on for over three seasons at the highest level, and then led the Bristol City side which removed City from the FA Cup in 1992. He assumed player/manager duties at Ashton Gate from January 1993 to November 1994, briefly tasted non-league football, then joined Plymouth as reserve-team player/coach. Within days, he was elevated to the post of 'football adviser' to the managerless, relegation-haunted club, and even had to name himself as substitute goalkeeper for the final fixtures of 1994/5. Russell was playing for Brighton when he applied for the City manager's job a day after Mark McGhee's walkout, but his next backroom appointment, after closing his playing career at Ninian Park, was to be as Cardiff manager from November 1996 to January 1998. In May that year, he took over youth coaching responsibilities at Bristol City.

Apps: *FL 108; FAC 2; LC 8; FMC 2.*
Goals: *FL 8.*

OSVOLD, Kjetil

b. Aalesund, Norway, 5th June 1961

Career: IK Start; Lillestrøm SK; Nov 1986-trials-Nottingham Forest; Apr 1987 Nottingham Forest; Dec 1987-loan-CITY; Apr 1988 Djurgardens IF; Apr 1989 PAOK; Nov 1989-loan-Admira Wacker; Apr 1990 Lillestrøm SK.

City debut v Middlesbrough (H) 5.12.87

> One of Bryan Hamilton's last acts as City manager was to bring Norwegian international Kjetil to Filbert Street on loan, but the blond midfielder looked as unhappy in the then-persistent problem position on the left flank as had most recent candidates, especially as his time in a blue shirt coincided with City's seven-game Second Division goal-drought. A few months earlier, Brian Clough had paid £100,000 for 'Ossie', whose 37-game international career had previously peaked when he claimed the winning goal for Norway against Argentina; but the Forest boss gave him few first-team opportunities, and soon accepted £70,000 from Sweden for his unsettled import. Further moves to Greece and Austria quickly followed, before a return to the club with whom he'd won Norwegian Cup and Championship medals in 1985 and 1986. Kjetil was briefly senior coach at Lillestrøm in 1995.

Apps: *FL 3+1.*

Kjetil Osvold

OWEN, Alfred Sydney

b. Newcastle-under-Lyme, Staffs, ca 1885
d. Blackpool, 22nd August 1925

Career: North Stafford Nomads; Newcastle Town; Northern Nomads; Jan 1907 Stoke; July 1907 Stockport County; Oct 1907 Port Vale; Apr 1908 Stoke; Sept 1908 Port Vale; Sept 1908 FOSSE; (Mar 1910 Northern Nomads); (Nov 1910 & cs 1911 English Wanderers); July 1911 Blackpool; Nov 1912 Stoke.

Fosse debut v Nottingham Forest (H) 7.11.08

> A noted amateur who transferred allegiance to Leicester just before completing his chartered accountancy examinations, and shortly after Stoke had resigned from the Football League, Syd was one of the few individual successes of Fosse's relegation-bound team of 1909, and continued to turn out for the club as a forceful inside- or outside-left over the next two seasons whenever business commitments – or his numerous amateur international call-ups – would permit. Originally he had been a full-back at Stoke, but took to the advanced role so well that he was chosen for the senior England trial match of January 1910, scoring once in the Whites v Stripes fixture at Anfield, but only winning the named reserve's role for the March game against Wales. It was in 1910, too, that Syd was elected to the post of secretary to the Players Union (rising from the role of membership auditor to the position ex-Fossil Charlie Saer had held 12 years previously), but his tenure would end in controversy following the union's 1912 defeat in the courts in an ill-fated legal challenge to the League's retain and transfer system ('The Kingaby Case'). An intemperate response, by way of a letter to the press assigning qualities of stupidity and vindictiveness to the FA, led to a refusal on the part of the football authorities to recognise Syd's office at all, and he resigned in February 1913 to take up a commercial appointment in Budapest. He had already played in that city with the amateur combination English Wanderers, whose itinerary featured a French tour in November 1910, a trio of games in Budapest in the following Easter, and a tour of Sweden, Russia and Denmark later that summer. Syd played once during WW1 for Watford, was reported in November 1915 as having been wounded in action in France, and at various times served in the North Staffords, the Grenadier Guards and the Northamptonshire Regiment before being invalided out of the army shortly before the armistice. At this stage, he briefly took up the secretarial reins at Port Vale, but soon returned to business matters in Czechoslovakia. His brother, WA Owen, was briefly on Manchester City's amateur roster from March 1911.

Apps: *FL 43; FAC 8.*
Goals: *FL 12; FAC 1.*

OWEN, James

b. ca 1868

Career: Rushden; Dec 1891 FOSSE (- 1893).

Fosse debut v Wednesbury Old Athletic (A) ML 5.12.1891

> A 5ft 4in right-back partner to Harry Bailey during the first two Midland League seasons, James was a former Northamptonshire county representative, having played against the touring Canadian team in October 1888, when the visitors won 3-2. He was also a well-known amateur runner, holding a host of athletics prizes. The columnist Half-Back in the local *Saturday Herald* averred that 'he kicks well and with capital judgement'.

Apps: *FAC 4; ML 18.*

PARIS, Alan David

b. Slough, Berkshire, 15th August 1964

Career: Slough Town; Nov 1982 Watford; Aug 1985 Peterborough United; July 1988 CITY; Jan 1991 Notts County; cs 1994 Slough Town (p/coach); Mar 1996 Stevenage Borough; Dec 1996 Harrow Borough (p/coach; p/mgr); cs 2000 Boreham Wood (p/coach).

City debut v Portsmouth (A) 29.8.88

> Never a first-teamer at Watford, Alan built himself a fine reputation as

a footballing full-back with Posh, and joined David Pleat's Second Division squad in the deal which took Nick Cusack to London Road. It was as a central defender that he made his initial Filbert Street mark, however; allying pace and determination to an evident relish for playing his way out of trouble whenever possible, and winning over an initially sceptical crowd, which was soon hailing him with his dressing-room nickname of 'Delbert'. Inconsistency, and a tendency to self-effacement, though, afflicted Alan after he had picked up the fans' Player of the Year trophy in 1989, and sporadic lapses of concentration and confidence on his part invariably, if unluckily, seemed to cost his side dearly. An £80,000 fee from higher-placed Second Division rivals confirmed his reservoir of ability, however, and within months he had helped the Magpies into the top flight via the Wembley Play-Off Final. Injury then cruelly cut short Alan's Meadow Lane career, leaving two wholly blank seasons on his record. In 1994 he returned to Slough as both player and youth-team coach, aiding their ascent from the Isthmian League to the Conference; then joined Stevenage for the culmination of their Conference title campaign of 1996, when they were only denied entry to the League on the ground-grading rules. Alan assumed player/manager duties at Harrow partway through his second term with them, and at one stage numbered Pat Gavin amongst his charges there.

***Apps:** FL 80+8; FAC 2; LC 7+2; FMC 3.*
***Goals:** FL 3; FAC 1; LC 1.*

PARKER, Garry Stuart

b. Oxford, 7th September 1965

Career: app/pro May 1983 Luton Town; Feb 1986 Hull City; Mar 1988 Nottingham Forest; Nov 1991 Aston Villa; Feb 1995 CITY (- 1999).

City debut v Wolverhampton Wanderers (A) FAC 18.2.95

> Central to the transfer deal with which City and Villa effectively settled their financial and legalistic differences over the Brian Little 'poaching' affair, experienced midfielder Garry featured in City's Fifth Round FA Cup exit at Molineux, then made his Premiership bow back at Villa Park in the sweet-tasting 4-4 draw which City contrived from a 1-4 deficit. Initially fielded in a holding role in front of the back line (allowing Mark Draper a licence to advance more, while maintaining for the side some passing vision from deep), Garry soon exhibited his classy reading of the game, if appearing reluctant to trust to his pace. By the end of the relegation term, however, he was visibly relaxing into his middle-line role, and getting forward himself with greater purpose: a development which culminated in a wonderfully individualistic goal at The Dell in the final fixture. Assuming the City captaincy from the start of 1995/6, and leading by example, Garry was then stripped of the honour in March after a row with the recently-appointed Martin O'Neill led to him missing a game at Oldham. Thereafter, he was briefly marginalised until a dramatic return in the second leg of the Play-Off semi-final at Stoke, when he notched the winner immediately after half-time. Then going on to coolly slot home the penalty equaliser in the Final against Crystal Palace, he took both the Wembley Man of the Match and City Player of the Year awards. Much admired for his commitment in playing through a crucial segment of the ensuing Premiership campaign while his prematurely-born daughter was in intensive care, Garry further developed

Garry Parker

his role as the centre-circle fulcrum of City's game-plan as the League Cup was added to the achievement of top-level consolidation. His ludicrous dismissal for taking a free kick too quickly was the turning point of City's UEFA Cup exit in September 1997, and more daft disciplinary trouble came his way five months later, when Garry was fined £750 by the FA for having harangued a referee while acting as linesman for his local Oxfordshire Sunday side. As his selections then became more sporadic, Colin Lee had a December 1998 bid to take Garry to Wolves as a player/coach spurned by O'Neill, and in summer 1999 he was instead added to the Filbert Street coaching staff; graduating to reserve-team manager under Peter Taylor in 2000. Some seventeen years previously, his senior career had started under David Pleat at Luton, but it was in an influential stint at Boothferry Park that he first attracted representative interest, eventually earning six Under-21 caps. A Brian Clough swoop followed; as did a quartet of Wembley appearances in a Forest shirt. Garry scored twice in the 1989 Simod Cup Final victory over Everton; took winner's medals from each of the League Cup Finals of 1989 and 1990; and was in the 1991 side beaten in the FA Cup showpiece by Spurs. His Villa days were comparatively uneventful, though he was a regular in the 1992/3 team which finished as the Premiership's inaugural runners-up.

***Apps:** PL/FL 89+25; FAC 9+2; LC 16+1; UEFA 2; PO 2+1.*
***Goals:** PL/FL 10; FAC 2; LC 2; PO 2.*

PARKER, John Francis

b. Ellistown, Leics, 16th January 1896
d. Burton on Trent, 2nd November 1973

Career: Newhall UM; Midway Athletic; Army football; Newhall Swifts; trials Feb 1919/pro Sept 1919 CITY; May 1920 Norwich City; Feb 1921 Gresley Rovers; cs 1921 Burton All Saints; 1922 Gresley Rovers; Newhall United; Aug 1924-trials-Burton Town; Newhall Swifts.

City debut v Fulham (A) 20.9.19

> A centre-forward understudy to Harry King and Jock Paterson for most of his season on City's books, Jack best distinguished himself in the reserve side, scoring six in the 11-2 County Cup Final victory over Moira Athletic. It was felt that his compact build counted against him at senior level, yet his only Second Division goal for City came when he bundled both Port Vale 'keeper Bourne and the ball into the net. After a £50 move, he led Norwich's attack in their inaugural Football League game, but managed only two goals in a dozen outings for the Canaries. Jack, who'd spent three and a half years in France with the Royal Field Artillery, was originally chosen for a wartime Fosse fixture at Coventry in March 1919, but missed his train connection and the game. He was later a painter and decorator in Swadlincote.

***Apps:** FL 5.*
***Goals:** FL 1.*

PARRY, Maurice Pryce

b. Trefonen, nr Oswestry, ca 1879
d. Bootle, Lancs, 24th March 1935

Career: 1895 Oswestry United; Sept 1897-trials-Nottingham Forest; 1897 Long Eaton Rangers; Aug 1898 FOSSE; Feb 1899 Loughborough; May 1899 Brighton United; cs 1900 Liverpool; May 1909 Partick Thistle; Feb 1911 (South Africa); Sept 1913 Oswestry United.

Fosse debut/only game v Woolwich Arsenal (A) 10.9.1898

> A half-back from a footballing family (his younger brother Tom would win Welsh caps while remaining an amateur with Oswestry, where another Parry, Charlie, was the goalkeeper), Maurice was initially more interested in completing his engineering apprenticeship than in pursuing a professional career. Deemed 'lackadaisical' on the occasion of his Forest trial, he followed his trade to Leicester, and joined Fosse almost as an afterthought. He stepped up but once to Second Division fare, when deputising for his countryman Dick Jones in a 0-4 defeat at Plumstead, before being allowed to assist the ailing Luffs. He became a Southern League regular at Brighton before his club disbanded, then embarked on a fine nine-year career at Anfield, making 207 League appearances as a tough and persistent ball-winner, and winning championship medals from both top divisions (in 1905 and 1906) as well as sixteen Welsh caps. Maurice, an organ-playing advocate of teetotalism, later became a member of the first Partick team to play at Firhill. He then honed his coaching skills in South Africa, By October 1914, he was a 'military instructor' and temporary sergeant with the Montgomeryshire Yeomanry, and sadly suffered the affects of gassing during the conflict. Nonetheless, he managed Rotherham County from 1921-23, and was later a coach at Liverpool, Barcelona, Dusseldorf, Frankfurt, Cologne, in Czechoslovakia and in Jersey before his death from chronic bronchitis. His son Frank played as a winger for Everton, Grimsby, Accrington Stanley and Nelson in the 20s.

***Apps:** FL 1.*

PARTRIDGE, Malcolm

b. Calow, Chesterfield, 28th August 1950

Career: app/pro Sept 1968 Mansfield Town; Sept 1970 CITY; Jan 1972-loan-Charlton Athletic; Mar 1975 Grimsby Town; July 1979 Scunthorpe United; Mar 1982 Skegness Town.

City debut v Charlton Athletic (A) 19.9.70 (scored once)

> A tall striker who impressed Frank O'Farrell as a teenage goalscorer at Field Mill (where he had made his debut in the first game Nick Sharkey and Jimmy Goodfellow played for the Stags), Malcolm got 1970/71 off to a flying, six goals in seven games start, and then cost £50,000 when introduced to City's promotion chase. He was just settling alongside Ally Brown when a broken arm, suffered at Birmingham, interrupted his progress, and thereafter he struggled to hold down a regular senior place, despite a palpable willingness to draw markers all across the field, a useful habit of scoring in Cup ties, and a memorable four-goal performance in an April 1972 friendly against Hannover '96. Very much a fringe member of Jimmy Bloomfield's First Division squad, Malcolm nevertheless worked hard on developing other aspects of his game, and at both Grimsby (in 138 League games) and Scunthorpe (in 97) he was successful as a deeper-lying attacker. His Leicester-born son Scott was throughout the 90s a peripatetic striker with Bradford City, Bristol City, Torquay, Plymouth, Scarborough, Cardiff and Brentford.

***Apps:** FL 25+11; FAC 3+1; LC 1+2.*
***Goals:** FL 4; FAC 3; LC 1.*

PATERSON, James

b. Stirling, 1907

Career: Causewayhead FC; Camelon Juniors; Jan 1927 Everton; cs 1927 St Johnstone; cs 1930 Cowdenbeath; May 1932 CITY; July 1935 Reading; July 1938 Clapton Orient.

City debut v Sheffield United (H) 27.8.32 (scored once)

> Signed by Peter Hodge on the same cross-border buying spree which landed Danny Liddle and Ted Lowery at Leicester, centre-forward Jim had, a year earlier, played in the same three Scottish international line-ups as Liddle. A comparatively lightweight attack-leader, but blessed with great pace and bravery, he could never quite shake off the challenge of the veteran Arthur Chandler for a regular City berth, though he hits the record book for scoring the club's first goal against continental opposition at Filbert Street (in the 1933 friendly defeat by Rapid Vienna). City also utilised him in the inside-forward positions, and it was at inside-left that he subsequently settled in Division Three (South). His 44-goal aggregate in English football did not approach, however, his two-season tally of over fifty with Cowdenbeath. Jim had briefly understudied Dixie Dean at Goodison before rebuilding his confidence in Perth, and going on at Central Park (where nicknamed 'Darky') to secure his position as Cowden's most-capped player.

***Apps:** FL 48; FAC 1.*
***Goals:** FL 17; FAC 1.*

PATERSON, John William

b. Dundee, 14th December 1896

Career: Dundee Arnott; Dundee North End; Army football; Fort Hill; Apr 1919 Dundee; Dec 1919 CITY; Mar 1922 Sunderland; Oct 1924 Preston North End; Sept 1925 Mid-Rhondda; Jan 1926 Queens Park Rangers; July 1928 Mansfield Town; Oct 1928 Montrose.

City debut v Stoke (H) 20.12.19 (scored once)

> Five times wounded while serving with the Black Watch in France, Jock proved his fitness with Dundee, but had appeared only once in their Scottish First Division side when Peter Hodge shrewdly moved in to secure him for the City centre-forward berth. Soon among the goals at Filbert Street, he hit the reconstructed club's first hat-trick (against Lincoln in March 1920) a week before scoring for the Anglo-Scots in the international

Jock Paterson

trial, and was then chosen by Scotland to face England the following month. Top scorer in each of his three terms with City, when described as 'one of the few forwards who can go through a modern defence on his own', Jock attracted an irresistible £3,790 bid from Sunderland, and subsequently led the Roker team to second and third places in the First Division with a perfect goal-every-other-game record. Strangely, he then proved an utterly ineffectual replacement for Tommy Roberts at Deepdale; remaining scoreless in 17 League outings as Preston took the drop. Transfer-listed at £750, he dropped into the Southern League in Wales to keep active, then declined a move to Raith Rovers after Preston had offered him in part-exchange for Alex James. Eventually QPR negotiated a cut-price return to the League for Jock, though some poor fortune for Rangers culminated in him suffering a broken leg in February 1927. Only brief stints in the Midland League and Scottish Alliance ensued. Jock was reported as both hospitalised and unemployed in Dundee in the early years of the Depression, but he later found a shipyard post and was still living in that city in 1956, when travelling down to watch a Liverpool v Leicester fixture at Anfield.

***Apps:** FL 81; FAC 8.*
***Goals:** FL 34; FAC 3.*

PATERSON, Thomas

b. Lochore, Fife, 3rd April 1927

Career: Raith Athletic; Lochore Welfare; Jan 1946 Raith Rovers; July 1946 Lochgelly Albert; Mar 1948 CITY; June 1950 Newcastle United; July 1952 Watford; July 1955 Berwick Rangers.

City debut v Brentford (A) 15.9.48 (scored once)

> Tom had a few outings for Raith in wartime football, but had reverted to the Junior ranks when Johnny Duncan spotted him on a trip home, figuring in the front line of the Fife County League champions. A play-anywhere forward with an expressed preference for the inside-right spot (which he briefly inherited from Peter McKennan), Tom effectively had to settle with City for becoming Charlie Adam's understudy for the No 11 shirt. He got only two chances to impress on Tyneside after a £2,500 move, but made 45 League appearances (scoring 7 goals) for Watford before assisting Berwick in their first assault on the Scottish 'B' Division. Knee injuries ended his career at Shielfield in 1957, and he later settled in Gateshead. (Tom should not be confused with his later City namesake, who left Filbert Street without a senior outing to his name, but played League football in the 70s for Middlesbrough, Bournemouth and Darlington).

***Apps:** FL 17.*
***Goals:** FL 4.*

PEAKE, Andrew Michael

b. Market Harborough, Leics, 1st November 1961

Career: app July 1978/pro Jan 1979 CITY; Aug 1985 Grimsby Town; Sept 1986 Charlton Athletic; Nov 1991 Middlesbrough; Oct 1994 Leicestershire Constabulary FC.

City debut v Norwich City (H) FAC 6.1.79

> Another teenager given a deep-end dunking by Jock Wallace (less than a week after he'd blooded Gary Lineker and David Buchanan), midfielder Andy performed with remarkable maturity on his televised Cup debut and proceeded to establish himself as an exciting linkman of prodigious promise. His record of thirteen England Youth selections included an

Andy Peake

appearance in the Final of the UEFA Youth tournament of 1980 (a 2-1 victory over Poland), and his single Under-21 cap would come against the same opposition during 1981/2. In the meantime, even though injuries and City's desire not to rush his development occasionally kept him out of the limelight, Andy had earned a Second Division championship medal and suffered the ensuing drop back. His inventive playmaking and mastery of the accurately flighted and weighted long ball could rarely be suppressed, and his knack of scoring spectacular long-range goals was a valuable feature of City's attacking options in the early 80s. It was regrettable that Andy's departure (for £110,000) seemed to set the seal on growing suspicions that he had failed quite to live up to his immense early potential, but at least he was back in top-flight football within a year, battling to help keep Charlton there in a Play-Off cliffhanger. His mature linchpin role at The Valley was later acknowledged and honoured when manager Lennie Lawrence signed him a second time for promotion-bound Middlesbrough. Andy played through the Premiership's inaugural season, and for one more term at a level lower, then in July 1994, when far from a spent footballing force, retired to join the police force.

Apps: *FL 141+6; FAC 9; LC 5+1.*
Goals: *FL 13.*

PEAKE, Jason William

b. Leicester, 29th September 1971

Career: YT 1988/pro Jan 1990 CITY; Feb 1992-loan-Hartlepool United; July 1992-trials-Newcastle United; Aug 1992 Halifax Town; Mar 1994 Rochdale; Aug 1996 Brighton & Hove Albion; Aug 1997-trials-Northampton Town; Oct 1997 Bury; July 1998 Rochdale; July 2000 Plymouth Argyle; Dec 2000 Nuneaton Borough.

City debut v Charlton Athletic (A) FMC 14.11.89

> Heavily tipped to inherit Gary McAllister's midfield mantle at Leicester, young Jason appeared well on course for development into an elegant playmaker as his precocious form elevated him successively into England squads at each of Under-18 and Under-19 level. Sporadic senior selections also seemed encouraging pointers to the local lad's future – a lively willingness to take venomous potshots spicing his neat passing game, and a wind-assisted free-kick winner against Barnsley boosting his confidence – but an enigmatic 'standstill' season followed Brian Little's arrival, and summer 1992 saw Jason released on a free. Unfortunately, summer 1993 then saw him reflecting on a term in which the Shaymen lost their Football League status; though his starring Conference performances soon earned him a return to Division Three. Increasingly highly regarded at Spotland, Jason moved to Brighton for a tribunal-set fee designed to rise from £80,000 to £120,000 on an appearance-related basis, but he was released after the cash-strapped Seagulls had paid but £95,000. He briefly detoured via Gigg Lane, then re-assumed an influential role in the Rochdale middle line. A short spell as a Pilgrim ensued, until a return to the Midlands saw his creative contributions at Conference level win him a permanent contract at Nuneaton after an initial loan period.

Apps: *FL 4+4; FMC 1+1.*
Goals: *FL 1.*

PEERS, Samuel

b. Coventry (?)

Career: 1897 Rudge Whitworth; Lord Street; Sept 1900 Foleshill Great Heath; Apr 1901 Coventry City; Apr 1902 FOSSE ; Nov 1903 Swindon Town; cs 1904 Coventry City.

Fosse debut v Lincoln City (H) 19.4.02

A trialist centre-half form the Birmingham and District League (at that time Coventry's station), Sam impressed sufficiently in his debut game to win a contract for the following season. He vied with Arthur Collins for the position of attack-minded pivot, and then demonstrated his versatility by briefly challenging for Fosse's outside-left berth. Surviving Swindon Town account books show him earning the princely sum of £1 15s per week during his Southern League season there.

Apps: *FL 14; FAC 2.*
Goals: *FL 1.*

PEPPER, William

Career: Sheppey United; Jan 1913 FOSSE; July 1913 Gillingham.

Fosse debut/only game v Leeds City (A) 8.2.13

> A young trialist goalkeeper plucked from the Kent League, Bill kept a clean sheet in a senior friendly at Gillingham, and a week later was given the chance to deputise for Fred Mearns at League level, when unfortunately five goals whistled past him at Elland Road. His subsequent Southern League career with the Gills was equally brief – consisting of but a single outing in a 4-2 home win over Southend.

Apps: *FL 1.*

PERKINS, George H.

Career: Market Harborough Town; May 1904 FOSSE; Hinckley United; Market Harborough Excelsior; 1907 Market Harborough Town.

Fosse debut/only game v Lincoln City (H) 19.11.04

> In signing this young 'keeper, Fosse might well have been trying to console him for recent embarrassments at their hands – he had been the hapless Harborough last-line who'd conceded ten goals when the Fossils removed his team from the FA Cup in October 1903, and Fosse reserves had put five past him in January 1904. His Filbert Street role was to understudy the consistent Walter Smith, and he rather botched his sole opportunity at senior level, being at fault for the only goal of the game. We are unsure of George's family background, but suspect he may have been related to the Wellingborough-born 'keeper Bill Perkins, who played for Kettering, Luton, Liverpool and Northampton at this time; and/or possibly to another goalkeeping Perkins, who featured for nearby Rothwell in 1901.

Apps: *FL 1.*

PERRY, Richard

Career: 1889 FOSSE; 1892 Singers (Coventry); cs 1893 Hinckley Town.

Fosse debut (competitive) v Burton Wanderers (H) FAC 4.10.1890

> A Fossil from 1889 onwards, Dick played (and was injured) in the first, drawn Final of the 1890 County Cup, was a medallist from the following year's victory in the same competition, and figured at centre-half when the club made its FA Cup bow in the interim. He also managed a handful of games during the initial Midland League campaign; before swapping clubs with Billy Dorrell.

Apps: *FAC 1; ML 5.*

PHILP, John Bain

b. Kelty, Fife, 5th September 1911

Career: Kelty Boys; Inverkeithing; May 1932 CITY; July 1934 Rhyl Athletic; Nov 1934 Alloa Athletic; Nov 1935 Raith Rovers; cs 1937 Glenavon.

City debut/only game v Tottenham Hotspur (H) 9.9.33

> Jack became another addition to the club's solo appearance ranks when Sep Smith was taken ill shortly before the above game, and the reserve team had already set off for Northampton. He 'never settled down' at right-half in the 1-3 home defeat; and was on his way during the next summer to play Birmingham & District League football with his Welsh club (the notion then of the Second City's 'district' being somewhat flexible). A homeward return to the Scottish Second Division followed, with Jack playing as centre-half or left-back in a Raith side bound for a 1936 re-election appeal, alongside a forward named Hector Philp whose kinship we have yet to confirm. His final League selection came in the 2-11 defeat by Morton in which Jack Calder scored eight times, and he would later taste Irish League fare to complete his tour of the home nations.

Apps: *FL 1.*

Jack Philp

PHILPOTT, Lee

b. Barnet, 21st February 1970

Career: Cambridge Crusaders; YT 1987/pro July 1988 Peterborough United; May 1989 Cambridge United; Nov 1992 CITY; Mar 1996 Blackpool; July 1998 Lincoln City; July 2000 Hull City.

City debut v Bristol Rovers (H) 28.11.92

> One of the flank players expected to hare after the long balls from the back which were Cambridge's trademark tactic as they rose via successive promotions from the League's basement to the upper reaches of the Second Division, Lee was himself the object of a long chase by Brian Little. Having featured alongside Steve Claridge in the side demolished in the 1992 Play-Off semi-finals by City, he eventually signed for an appearance-related fee rising to a record-equalling £350,000, in time to watch a 2-2 Filbert Street draw between his old and new clubs. He was soon noted for the quality of his crosses, but as often berated for not delivering enough of them. After his finest moments as provider in the 1993 Play-Off Final comeback against Swindon, Lee virtually defined inconsistency, whether employed as a mazy winger, in midfield or at left-back, and could appear under-motivated on occasion. His sometimes peripheral on-field involvement, and alternating generation of excitement and frustration, has been reflected in his subsequently erratic selection record with both the Seasiders and Imps; but Little made him an early recruit at Boothferry Park, and he featured strongly in the Tigers' 2000/1 rise from near-extinction to the Play-Offs.

Apps: *FL/PL 57+18; FAC 6+2; LC 2+1; AIC 2; PO 2+1.*
Goals: *FL 3.*

PICKARD, John W.

b. Syston, Leics

Career: 1891 Syston Swifts; am 1894/pro Sept 1895 FOSSE.

Fosse debut v Loughborough (H) 5.10.1895

> A young local outside-right who got few chances to shine at senior level with Fosse, John made his actual first-team bow in the subsidiary United Counties League programme of 1894/5, against Notts County. His Division Two breakthrough came in the club's first League encounter with their old local rivals, the newly-elected Luffs, but apparently the 5-0 scoreline then, and that of 4-0 a week later in an FA Cup romp against Hinckley Town, satisfied more than did the lad's performances. He would feature only once more on the first-eleven teamsheet, for the Christmas friendly against the club's first Irish guests, Cliftonville; while his record for the reserves in the County Cup saw him score in the 1895 Final and pick up a second winner's medal a year later.

Apps: *FL 1; FAC 1.*

PILKINGTON, Saville H.

b. Hathern, Leics (?)

Career: Hathern; Aug 1913 Loughborough Corinthians; Dec 1913 FOSSE.

Fosse debut/only game v Birmingham (H) 17.1.14

> An outside-left taken on trial from the reigning champions of the Leicestershire Senior League, Saville played only in the above goalless League game and in an embarrassing 1-5 friendly defeat at Northampton a fortnight later. It is believed he may have briefly resumed his career with Loughborough after the war.

Apps: *FL 1.*

PLATNAUER, Nicholas Robert

b. Leicester, 10th June 1961

Career: app Northampton Town; Bedford Town; Aug 1982 Bristol Rovers; Aug 1983 Coventry City; Dec 1984 Birmingham City; Jan 1986-loan-Reading; Sept 1986 Cardiff City; Aug 1989 Notts County; Jan 1991-loan-Port Vale; July 1991 CITY; Mar 1993 Scunthorpe United; July 1993-trials-Kettering Town; Aug 1993 Mansfield Town; Feb 1994 Lincoln City; Sept 1995 Bedworth United; Aug 1997 Hinckley United.

City debut v Swindon Town (A) 17.8.91

> A multi-club veteran before he joined his hometown club as a free agent, Nicky was fondly regarded as 'a supporter in a City shirt' during his stint as a left-back for Brian Little. Not by then the paciest of coverers, he nonetheless exuded an effective enthusiasm and commitment during the near-miss promotion drive of 1992, while both his positional play and distribution were ultra-reliable. Originally a forward with Bedford's 1981 Southern League Cup-winners (a year before the Eagles' demise on the loss of their ground), Nicky was then signed by Bobby Gould for each of his first two League clubs, featured in all four divisions within five years, and on further travels converted through midfield roles to his eventual No 3 berth. He was in both promoted and relegated sides at St Andrews, earned a winner's medal from the Welsh Cup Final of 1988 as a member of the Bluebirds side also promoted that year, and assisted Notts County out of Division Three via the 1990 Play--Offs. A day after leaving City, Nicky scored on his Glanford Park debut, and remained a Division Three stalwart for another two and a half years. Nicky had his own sandwich business in Leicester in the late 90s, and in 2000 took over the management of Rothwell Town. He also coaches the Under-14 age group at City's Academy.

Apps: *FL 32+3; LC 4+1; FMC 2.*

PLUMMER, Norman Leonard

b. Leicester, 12th January 1924
d. Leicester, 25th October 1999

Career: ATC (Leicester Wing); am July 1942/pro Nov 1942 CITY; July 1952 Mansfield Town; Aug 1956 Kettering Town.

City debut (WW2) v Coventry City (A) 3.11.42 (scored once); (postwar) v Brentford (A) 25.12.47

> A play-anywhere enthusiast after his teenage wartime signing, Norman was soon whisked off to Canada for RAF training as a Flying Officer, and saw service in Singapore before returning to Filbert Street. His first and last senior City appearances were made in the centre-forward berth, but it was his interim adherence to the central defensive role which was to make his name. He inherited the team captaincy from the veteran Sep Smith early in the 1948/9 campaign of radical contrasts, getting plenty of hard work in City's desperate struggle to avoid the drop into Division Three, and taking appropriate plaudits for the qualities of undemonstrative leadership which saw the club through to Wembley. Strangely enough, Norman was soon having to fight for his pivotal place with the likes of Tom McArthur and Bill Corbett, and eventually followed the well-worn path from Filbert Street to Field Mill (as a George Jobey signing) shortly after Matt Gillies had arrived to assume the City No 5 shirt. He made 166 appearances in the Third Division (North) for the Stags, scoring five times in 1953/4 when briefly re-converted to a spearhead role, then became the rock anchor of Tommy Lawton's Kettering side which took the Southern League title in 1957. Norman was later involved in a Leicester haberdashery business for many years, before his death from cancer in the LOROS hospice.

Apps: *FL 66; FAC 9; WW2 24.*
Goals: *FL 1; WW2 6.*

POLLOCK, Robert

b. Wishaw, Lanarkshire, 1880

Career: Wishaw Thistle; 1898 Third Lanark; Jan 1900 Bristol City; cs 1900 Kettering; cs 1901 Notts County; Sept 1902 FOSSE; Sept 1909 Leyton; cs 1910 Leicester Imperial (- 1915).

Fosse debut v Preston North End (A) 4.10.02

> Versatile defender Bob had a rather stuttering start in senior football, but settled admirably with Fosse to

display resilience and no little quality over seven seasons: becoming the only man aside from Jimmy Blessington to appear for the club both in the re-election campaign of 1903/4 and the Division One adventure of 1908/9. A Scottish Junior international in 1898, but never a first-teamer at either Third Lanark or Notts County, he had first tasted Southern League fare at Ashton Gate, and was alongside Arthur Roulston and Charles Webb in the Kettering side which reached Round Two (the equivalent of today's Fifth Round) of the FA Cup in 1900/1. At Leicester, having signed for £50, Bob favoured the wing-half positions and the passing game, building long runs of appearances on either flank, but would slot into a full-back role whenever the necessity arose. As the *Mercury* had it, "He has never been seen flurried yet". It was fitting that his benefit match – against Grimsby in February 1908, on the first occasion the profits from a League game had been set aside for such a purpose by Fosse – should have come in a season which climaxed in the promotion he had laboured so hard to secure. His total of senior appearances constituted a Fosse record; as, incidentally, did his aggregate haul of fourteen successful penalties. Bob moved to Leyton along with Tommy Shanks, and a year later turned down an offer to join Croydon Common from the former Leyton boss Sandy Tait, preferring local fare in Leicester. In April 1913, he was sentenced to 21 days' hard labour for neglecting his wife and children, counter-claiming that he'd been thrown out of the family home and had been seeking work in Grimsby.

***Apps:** FL 211; FAC 19.*
***Goals:** FL 14; FAC 5.*

POOLE, Kevin

b. Bromsgrove, Worcs, 21st July 1963

Career: app/pro June 1981 Aston Villa; Nov 1984-loan-Northampton Town; Aug 1987 Middlesbrough; Mar 1991-loan-Hartlepool United; July 1991 CITY; Aug 1997 Birmingham City.

City debut v Swindon Town (A) 17.8.91

> A decade as a professional had seen 'keeper Kevin amass only 89 League and Cup appearances before his one-time Boro coach Brian Little expended £40,000 to add him to the Filbert Street roster a day after his 28th birthday. Yet he stepped straight between the sticks for City with Carl Muggleton carrying over a suspension, and missed only four League outings over his first season. He subsequently won the lion's share of senior selection over Muggleton, Russell Hoult and Gavin Ward, and missed only two games of the promotion campaign of 1996. Kevin featured in two of the Wembley Play-Off visits, being involved in conceding the controversial decisive penalty against Swindon, and seeing out 119 minutes of the victory over Crystal Palace before the beneficial distraction caused when he was replaced by Zeljko Kalac. In the following Premiership term, however, he got a look-in only when newcomer Kasey Keller was away on USA international duty. Not the tallest of last-liners (and occasionally exposed for his concomitant lack of reach), Kevin was nonetheless a fine reflex shot-stopper, and peppered his City progress with some outstanding performances. One of these, at Tottenham in 1994/5, virtually ensured he would win the club's Player of the Year award; and he contributed to multiple morning-after quips as reports spread that he'd dropped the memento in question! His Birmingham debut was delayed until the final fixture of 1997/8, but the following term saw him as a St Andrews regular (beaten four times by City in an FA Cup tie), as he remained until sidelined by injury partway through 1999/2000.

***Apps:** FL/PL 163; FAC 8; LC 10; FMC 5; AIC 1; PO 6.*

POTTS, Brian

b. Sunderland, 3rd September 1948

Career: app Aug 1964/pro Sept 1965 CITY; July 1969 Peterborough United; 1971 Hereford United; July 1971 South Shields.

City debut v Newcastle United (A) 3.4.68 (sub)

> A teenage member of City reserves' Combination Cup-winning side of 1967, Brian finally got a substantial first-team chance during the last months of Matt Gillies' managerial tenure at Leicester, filling in for Peter Rodrigues in the right-back spot as City unfortunately began their slide into the relegation zone. Indeed, collective form was such that he finished a game on the winning side only once. He won no selections under Frank O'Farrell, and the latter released Brian at the end of the term. He became a near ever-present in Posh's Fourth Division side during 1969/70, but was allowed to move on early in the next campaign, only to find himself returning briefly to Filbert Street as a member of John Charles' Hereford line-up, there contesting the FA Trophy semi-final against Hillingdon in April 1971.

***Apps:** FL 9+1; LC 1.*

PRICE, Ernest Clifford

b. Market Bosworth, Leics, 13th June 1900

Career: Ibstock Albion; Coalville Swifts; am Jan 1917 FOSSE; Nov 1919-loan-Coalville Swifts; pro Oct 1920 CITY; June 1922 Halifax Town; Dec 1923 Southampton; June 1926 Nottingham Forest; Oct 1928 Loughborough Corinthians; cs 1929 Nuneaton Town; Feb 1932 Gresley Rovers; Oct 1933 Snibston United.

Fosse debut (WW1) v Notts County (H) 13.1.17; (postwar) v Tottenham Hotspur (H) 11.9.19 (scored twice)

> Fosse's leading marksman in wartime competition, Cliff hit three counters in his first two senior games for City, and was finally persuaded by Peter Hodge to sign professionally just over a year later. The local inside-left didn't find it easy, however, to compete for a first-team slot with imports like Jim Macauley and Harry Graham, and eventually moved on to make his mark elsewhere: as a goalscorer in Division Three (North), and as a more studious contributor to the attacks of Second Division Saints and Forest. Cliff, the youngest of eleven children, had been a teenage collier during WW1, and was sent back to pit work only four days after enlisting for active service in the summer of 1918. Twenty years later, he was noted as cricket captain of Hugglescote Albion CC. His brother Tom played at centre-forward for Lincoln City in 1902/3; and his nephews Fred (see below) and Jack were also on the Filbert Street books.

***Apps:** FL 28; WW1 75.*
***Goals:** FL 8; WW1 33.*

PRICE, Frederick Thomas

b. Ibstock, Leics, 24th October 1901
d. Coalville, Leics, 16th November 1985

Career: Coalville Swifts; cs 1920 Whitwick Imperial; am Feb 1921/ pro May 1921 CITY; May 1924 Southampton; May 1925 Wolverhampton Wanderers; cs 1927 Chesterfield; cs 1928 Burton Town; Sept 1929 Nuneaton Town; Midland Red Sports (Coalville).

City debut v South Shields (H) 26.2.23

> A clever outside-left, Fred was unfortunate to find himself third in line for the City first-team shirt behind Sandy Trotter and Percy Tompkin, and moved to The Dell, along with Dennis Jones, as part of the deal which brought Harry Hooper to Leicester, having figured in four Second Division victories. By far his most consistent campaign thereafter – and, with 8 goals, his highest-scoring – was his first term with Wolves after a £250 transfer. He scored four goals on his Nuneaton debut in an FA Cup qualifier, and was playing Thursday League football in the early 30s when working on the buses. Fred's father Tom had been a forward who moved from Midland Leaguers Whitwick White Cross to Second Division Lincoln in February 1903; his brother Jack played as a full-back for City reserves, Bristol Rovers, Swindon and Torquay; while Cliff (see above) was his uncle and, briefly, his inside-forward partner at both Southampton and Nuneaton. Fred was also on the Leicestershire CCC ground staff in 1923.

***Apps:** FL 4.*

PRIESTMAN, James (Derrick)

b. Melton Mowbray, Leics, ca 1872

Career: Melton Rovers; Melton Town; Mar 1893 FOSSE; cs 1895 Melton Town.

Fosse debut v Long Eaton Rangers (A) ML 11.3.1893

> A versatile reserve forward who turned out occasionally in all the front-line positions for Fosse across the final pair of Midland league seasons and the first in the Second Division, James declined an 1894 offer to join Sheffield United to remain with his local club. He took the outside-left berth in the opening League fixture after a mix-up over new signing Hugh Gallacher's registration – and Grimsby 'keeper Whitehouse later admitted that one of his shots had been clawed back from over the line, unseen by the referee, during the 3-4 defeat. He was also a goalscoring representative for Leicestershire in inter-county fare.

***Apps:** FL 8; ML 7.*
***Goals:** FL 2; ML 3.*

PRINDIVILLE, Steven Alan

b. Harlow, Essex, 26th December 1968

Career: YT July 1985/pro Jan 1987 CITY; June 1988 Chesterfield; June 1989 Mansfield Town; July 1991 Hinckley Town; Sept 1991 Leicester United; Sept 1991 East Bengal; Feb 1992 Leicester United; Feb 1992 Doncaster Rovers; Jan 1994-trials-Wycombe Wanderers; Feb 1994 Halifax Town; Oct 1995 Dagenham & Redbridge; cs 1996 Kidderminster Harriers; cs 1998 Nuneaton Borough.

City debut v Shrewsbury Town (A) 16.1.88 (sub)

> A scorer in City's FA Youth Cup semi-final defeat against Charlton in 1987, full-back Steve made a brief step up to senior level during the early days of David Pleat's management, and looked confidently adventurous in his Simod Cup start against Stoke, but was freed in the summer of 1988. At Saltergate he was for one season a Third Division regular, linking again at various times with Robert Alleyne and Tony Brien, but relegation saw him move on to Field Mill, and briefly renew on-field acquaintance with Steve Wilkinson, another Filbert Street youth-squad contemporary. A short return to local football was rather exotically spiced with a three-month playing contract in India, during which Steve played in both the Durand Cup Final and in the quarter-finals of the Asian Cup Winners Cup for his Calcutta-based side; and then a non-contract spell at Belle Vue developed into a near two-year engagement. At the end of 1994/5, Steve was named as Conference side Halifax's Player of the Year, and in continuing to play at that level, he won his first cap as an England semi-professional international in April 1997. Steve became a part-time coach at City's School of Excellence in that year, and in 1999 assisted Nuneaton to the Southern League championship, and back into the Conference.

***Apps:** FL 0+1; FMC 1.*

PRIOR, Spencer Justin

b. Rochford, Essex, 22nd April 1971

Career: YT July 1987/pro May 1989 Southend United; June 1993 Norwich City; Aug 1996 CITY; Aug 1998 Derby County; Mar 2000 Manchester City; June 2001 Cardiff City.

City debut v Sunderland (A) 17.8.96

> A centre-back blooded at Southend by Dave Webb, and briefly managed at Norwich by Martin O'Neill, Spencer rejoined the latter at Filbert Street for a fee that rose to £600,000 as he established himself in City's Premiership defence. Initially installed alongside Steve Walsh in a partnership that carried City to League Cup victory over Middlesbrough, he also linked effectively and intimidatingly in a skinhead duo with Matt Elliott, and took occasional excursions to the right-back berth if Pontus Kåmark was being utilised in a man-marking role. Excellent skills in the air, and a quick eye for an interception were hallmarks of his defensive solidity, and it was some surprise when O'Neill took on Frank Sinclair and Gerry Taggart as a prelude to allowing the popular Spencer to move to Pride Park (for £700,000). Equivalent eyebrow-raising went on when the inspirational cornerstone of the Rams' erratic defence then took a £500,000 shift to Maine Road, but Spencer simply got on with proving the last piece in Manchester City's promotion jigsaw, knocking in three vital goals on their run-in to a Premiership return. Spencer had previously been involved in one demotion and two successive elevations at Southend, and also had figured in a fall from the top flight at Norwich (where he was Player of the Year in 1996); so it was little surprise to find him taking the trapdoor from the Premiership again in 2001 – at which point a further £700,000 changed hands to take him to Ninian Park.

***Apps:** PL 61+3; FAC 5; LC 7; UEFA 2.*

PROCTOR, James F.

b. London, ca 1892

Career: Custom House; Apr 1911 Huddersfield Town; Nov 1912 FOSSE.

Fosse debut v Fulham (H) 30.11.12

> Briefly one of Dick Pudan's charges during his stint as manager at Leeds Road, this inside-forward then played a few games in front of his former boss when the latter resumed his playing career with Fosse. James had also been a former amateur teammate of Jim Harrold, but made nothing like the same impact at Leicester. However, his sole League goal (a consolation in a 1-5 defeat at Birmingham in January 1913) was the club's 1000th in the competition. His other Fosse counter had come two days earlier, and was even less consoling: lending no respectability whatsoever to the 1-4 scoreline suffered in the home Cup defeat by Southern League Norwich City.

***Apps:** FL 7; FAC 1.*
***Goals:** FL 1; FAC 1.*

Norman Proctor

PROCTOR, Norman

b. Blaydon, Northumberland, 11th May 1896
d. Winlaton Mill, Co Durham, 27th February 1947

Career: Spen Black & White; Scotswood; Blyth Spartans; May 1922 Rotherham County; June 1923 West Ham United; June 1924 CITY; May 1925 Tranmere Rovers; Sept 1927 Halifax Town; cs 1931 Workington; Oct 1933 Newbiggin West End.

City debut v Manchester United (A) 30.8.24

> A deep-lying, scheming inside-forward who first came to notice in the prewar County Durham schools side, Norman developed in the North Eastern League, and was introduced to Second Division football by ex-Fossil Maurice Parry. He experienced an unexpected elevation in status a year later, for as Rotherham County exited the second tier by way of the relegation trapdoor, he was taken on for top-flight football by promoted West Ham (against whom, in fact, he'd claimed his sole Millmoor goal). He only managed seven First Division starts for the Hammers, though, and then had an even shorter senior run at Filbert Street, definitively losing his place after four of the first five fixtures of 1924/5 had seen City scoreless – and this in a campaign they would end promoted as champions. Norman's best season in scoring terms would come with a dozen League and Cup goals in his initial Tranmere term, and his most sustained spell of first-team football with 126 League appearances for the Shaymen.

***Apps:** FL 5.*

PROUDFOOT, David

b. Dunfermline, Fife, 1872

Career: Whiteinch Juniors; 1893 Partick Thistle; Dec 1896 FOSSE; cs 1898 Bedminster; cs 1899 Partick Thistle.

Fosse debut v Grimsby Town (H) 5.12.1896

> A former shipyard apprentice in Glasgow, David was a skilful centre-half from a footballing family – his brother John also trekked south from Partick to play for Blackburn, Everton and Watford, and returned to assist Hamilton Academical – but demonstrated suspect temperament with Fosse. After losing his place to Jimmy Brown during his second Filbert Street term, he became one of six Fossils suspended by the club on disciplinary grounds in February 1898, and never featured again in Leicester colours. His only goal in English football was scored on his Southern League debut for Bedminster against Spurs; but he was soon reunited with Willie Freebairn in Partick's 1900 title-winning campaign in the Scottish Second Division.

***Apps:** FL 25; FAC 2.*

PUDAN, Albert Ernest (Dick)

b. West Ham, London
d. Clacton, Essex, early January 1957

Career: Clapton; cs 1900 West Ham United; cs 1902 Bristol Rovers; July 1907 Newcastle United; May 1909 FOSSE; Sept 1910 Huddersfield Town (p/mgr; sec/mgr from Nov 1910); Nov 1912 FOSSE.

Fosse debut v Wolverhampton Wanderers (H) 1.9.09

> Universally known throughout his career as Dick, this extremely cultured left-back stood out in an age of hefty back-line hoofers by dint of his thoughtful and constructive approach to the game. He joined West Ham as an amateur for their initial Southern League season under that name, and won a championship medal in that sphere in 1905 while totting up 116 appearances for Bristol Rovers. Dick also took an FA Cup runners-up medal from Newcastle's 1908 Final defeat by Wolves, but had only a marginal part to play in the Magpies' Division One title win of the following year. His Fosse full-back partnership with Billy Henry was the classiest the club had fielded to that point, and Dick became the team's sure-shot penalty taker. However, the newly-elected Huddersfield offered him an early chance to preach tactics, and a £460 fee took Dick to Leeds Road. It was initially intended that the appointment would be of a player/manager, but he selected himself only for a single West Riding Cup outing, and was soon re-confirmed as secretary/manager. He directed their fortunes from the sidelines for two seasons, then returned to Leicester to don his boots again, deputise for Sam Currie, and act as an occasional on-field mentor to the young Tommy Clay. When the club was reconstructed as Leicester City in 1919, Dick – described on registration documents as a hosiery manufacturer – was among the new directors; though as he had been a professional player, it took until March 1921 for the FA to sanction his appointment in that capacity. He remained on the board until February 1940, and between 1929 and 1931 took the chair; the only former player so to serve the club. Despite being dogged by long-term illness, Dick was also regarded in some influential quarters as a valid candidate for the City managerial vacancy in June 1939, prior to the appointment of Tom Bromilow. He spent his retirement in the sea air at Clacton.

***Apps:** FL 46; FAC 5.*
***Goals:** FL 7.*

PUTTNAM, David Paul

b. Leicester, 3rd February 1967

Career: Kirby Muxloe; 1986 Leicester United; Feb 1989 CITY; Jan 1990 Lincoln City; Oct 1995 Gillingham; Mar 1997-loan-Yeovil Town; Aug 1997 Swansea City; 1997 Gresley Rovers; Dec 1997 Anstey Nomads; 1998 Barry Town; 1998 Gresley Rovers; cs 1998 King's Lynn.

City debut v Barnsley (H) 11.4.89 (sub)

> The only player City ever signed from their Southern League neighbours after the latter's name-change and move from Enderby to Blaby, David scored one goal and made two more in his first Central League try-out, and was soon taken on by David Pleat as a likely contender to fill the left-wing gap occasioned by Peter Weir's return to Scotland. His willingness to take on his full-back for pace and skill provided some optimistic pointers from the tail-end of 1988/9, but David failed to consolidate his progress during the following term. He rejected a mooted move to Carlisle, but soon signed on at Sincil Bank for £40,000 after impressing during a two-month loan spell. Lincoln's Player of the Year in 1993, he assisted Gillingham up from the basement in 1996, and helped return Yeovil to the Conference a year later. More recently, David figured in Gary Mills' King's Lynn side, for whom he top-scored in 1999/2000.

***Apps:** FL 4+3; LC 0+1.*

PYNEGAR, Albert

b. Eastwood, Notts, 24th September 1895
d. Basford, Notts, 26th March 1978

Career: Awsworth Amateurs; Eastwood Rangers; 1913 Sutton Town; May 1920 CITY; Jan 1924 Coventry City; July 1925 Oldham Athletic; Jan 1929 Port Vale; Oct 1930 Chesterfield; Aug 1932 Rotherham United; Apr 1934 Sutton Town.

City debut v Bury (H) 2.9.20 (scored twice)

> The *Mercury Annual* thumbnailed the appeal and value of centre-forward Albert in his City days, lauding how he put 'a rugged ferocity into his shooting that might well make goalkeepers turn pale'. Almost 25 before he made his League bow, but rapidly regarded as a veritable goal machine, he was distinctly unfortunate to be edged out of the senior reckoning so often with City by Jock Paterson, George Waite and Arthur Chandler. He could hardly be faulted for the vigour with which he pressed his claims, though: swapping Central Alliance football with Sutton for record-breaking action in the same league with City reserves, he scored six times on his debut and finished 1920/1 with 49 goals from only 25 outings, to add to his six counters for the first team. A bustler who actually preferred the inside-forward positions to the leader's role, Albert indexed his goal knack again in 1922/3, with eleven goals from only fourteen Second Division starts, yet still wasn't assured of a regular place. At Coventry, he was top scorer in a relegated team in 1925; he twice topped Oldham's Second Division goal charts; and came close to keeping Port Vale up in 1929. A year later he shot Vale to the championship of Division Three (North), and did precisely the same thing again for Chesterfield in the following term. By the time he left Millmoor, as a balding 38-year-old, he had amassed 174 League goals in 366 games. Albert paid a sentimental visit to Filbert Street in September 1964 to look up 'Channy', his old rival and successor.

***Apps:** FL 44; FAC 4.*
***Goals:** FL 20; FAC 1.*

QUINN, James Martin

b. Belfast, 18th November 1959

Career: Whitchurch Alport; Oswestry Town; Dec 1981 Swindon Town; Aug 1984 Blackburn Rovers; Dec 1986 Swindon Town; June 1988 CITY; Mar 1989 Bradford City; Dec 1989 West Ham United; July 1991 Bournemouth; July 1992 Reading (joint mgr from Dec 1994); July 1997 Peterborough United; Oct 1998 Swindon Town (p/mgr); Cirencester; Nantwich Town; Sept 2000 Northwich Victoria; Oct 2000 Hereford United; Nov 2000 Highworth Town; Jan 2001 Hayes.

City debut v West Bromwich Albion (H) 27.8.88 (sub)

> Often an international teammate of John O'Neill and Paul Ramsey, Jimmy had collected 19 Northern Ireland caps as a striker by the time City signed him for a tribunal-set fee of £210,000, and would add a further four selections for his country as a Leicester player. A relatively late entrant to senior football, he had quickly built a reputation as an elegant front-runner, and had helped Swindon up into Division Two, but it was not until the 1987/8 season, when he played alongside hefty target-man Dave Bamber, that he revealed a really prolific predatory knack. Three goals against City had featured in his sizeable haul that term but, having arrived at Filbert Street, he proved unable to convince David Pleat that he merited a regular spearhead role ahead of either Nicky Cross or Mike Newell. Jimmy accordingly suffered much frustration on the subs' bench during his short City spell (despite three times coming on and scoring); was able only to offer tantalising glimpses of his aerial power and dead-ball accuracy; and soon had to accept that he was something of a tactical fish out of water with Leicester. He moved on to Valley Parade in the ill-advised exchange which brought Mick Kennedy in the opposite direction, and perhaps predictably punished City with Bradford's late winner against them a month later; repeating the dose during the next season. He reunited with former Swindon boss Lou Macari at Upton Park, and contributed significantly to the Hammers' 1991 promotion. At Reading he led the Division Two championship campaign of 1994 from the front, as the League's 35-goal top marksman, and in the following December, when Mark McGhee decamped to Leicester, Jimmy assumed the Royals' joint player/manager role with Mick Gooding. In fact he led his side to Wembley and the Play-Off brink of the Premiership (scoring the final goal in a 3-4 thriller shaded by Bolton). By the time he left Posh for another managerial challenge at Swindon (which ended with dismissal in May 2000 after relegation was confirmed), Jimmy had accumulated 210 League goals, 64 in the Cups, and a dozen international strikes which leave him in joint second place in the all-time Northern Ireland scorers' chart. His unsated appetite for the game was re-confirmed, though, by his non-league, non-contract travels during 2000/1, which ended with him settling at Hayes and scoring the goals which prompted their Conference survival effort, before being appointed Northwich Victoria manager in July 2001.

***Apps:** FL 13+18; FAC 0+1; LC 2+1; FMC 0+1.*
***Goals:** FL 6.*

Paul Ramsey

RAMSEY, Paul Christopher

b. Derry, 3rd September 1962

Career: Derry Athletic YC; app 1979/ pro Apr 1980 CITY; Aug 1991 Cardiff City; Aug 1993 St Johnstone; Nov 1994-loan-Cardiff City; 1995 Barry Town; Oct 1995-trials-Mansfield Town; Nov 1995 Telford United; Nov 1995 Torquay United; Oct 1996 Merthyr Tydfil; 1997 TPV (Finland); 1997 Rothwell Town; Feb 1998 Grantham Town; cs 1998 King's Lynn.

City debut v Arsenal (H) 7.3.81 (sub)

> One of many latter-day City midfielders also utilised extensively as a full-back, Paul developed his ball-winning skills during the club's Second Division stint of the early 80s; wearing the No 2 shirt throughout the 1983 promotion campaign, and timing his first goal – in the crucial victory at Oldham – to perfection. He won the first of fourteen Northern Ireland caps in September 1983, though injuries and spells of in-and-out form occasionally left him sidelined from both domestic and international action. Probably strongest in a man-marking role, and least effective as the fulcrum of a passing game, Paul nonetheless claimed the City supporters' Goal of the Season award for a precise piece of opportunism against QPR in 1986/7. He was handed the team captaincy on the arrival of manager David Pleat, and granted a testimonial in 1989 (with Spurs in opposition), yet City were ready to offload him in a mooted exchange deal with Walsall's Craig Shakespeare before that year's transfer deadline. Paul opted to stay and fight for his place, and indeed re-asserted himself as a middle-line grafter as City began compensating for their disastrous start to the 1989/90 Second Division campaign, with his two-goal 'super-sub' intervention in a 4-3 win over Leeds marking a vital turning point. Two dismissals somewhat marred his final season at Filbert Street, and he moved on, when it became clear he would not figure regularly in Brian Little's plans, to rejoin his one-time City reserve coach, Eddie May, at Ninian Park. Two Welsh Cup-winners medals and a Third Division championship gong (as skipper) accrued from his initial Cardiff spell; and Paul would have returned to Wales in October 1993 after failing to settle in Perth, had not the Football League invoked a rule forbidding a transfer back within twelve months. Rules tripped him up again when, a year later, he rejoined the Bluebirds on loan, for he was ineligible to turn out against Ebbw Vale in the Welsh Cup, and his team were on the point of being unceremoniously dumped from the 1994/5 competition until legal action won them reinstatement. Paul said farewell to League football with another stint under Eddie May, at Plainmoor; and in 1998 assisted Gary Mills' Grantham to the championship of the Southern League's Midland Division.

***Apps:** FL 278+12; FAC 9+1; LC 19; FMC 2+1.*
***Goals:** FL 13; FAC 1; LC 1.*

RANDLE, Arthur John

b. West Bromwich, 3rd December 1880
d. West Bromwich, 29th September 1913

Career: Lyng Rovers; Oldbury Town; Darlaston; cs 1901 West Bromwich Albion; May 1908 FOSSE.

Fosse debut v Sheffield Wednesday (H) 1.9.08

> An experienced wing-half who had made 132 League appearances during his seven-year stint as a Throstle (having shared a debut with Billy Harper), Arthur signed on for Fosse's fateful First Division bow, and shook off the disappointments of that campaign to complete five years' service as a defensive linchpin in the right-half berth. Ironically, one of his only pair of Fosse goals was notched against West Brom. When Fosse released him in 1913, he became licensee of The Golden Cup back in his home town, but within months succumbed to cancer at the age of 32. All proceeds from the South Eastern League game between the reserves of Fosse and Brentford were donated to Arthur's widow. Arthur was another West Midlander to have been selected early in his career to face the Scottish Junior international team; his hobby during his playing years was beekeeping.

***Apps:** FL 123; FAC 10.*
***Goals:** FL 2.*

RANTANEN, Jari Juhani

b. Helsinki, Finland, 31st December 1961

Career: HJK; Estoril; Beerschot VAV; HJK; 1986 IFK Göteborg; Aug 1987 CITY; Dec 1988-loan-Os Belenenses; July 1989 HJK; 1993 FinnPa; July 1996 HJK; 1997 FinnPa; 1998 PK-35.

City debut v Crystal Palace (A) 12.9.87

> A peripatetic international striker whose goal earned Finland a draw

against England in 1985, and who had gained wide experience in Portuguese, Belgian and Swedish football, Jari joined City for £50,000 after a week's training-ground trial, and despite the fact that Bryan Hamilton had never seen him play a senior game. He had been omitted from IFK's UEFA Cup Final side despite heading their scoring list in the competition, and the move to England initially reinvigorated his career, with City fams soon overcoming their incredulity about the circumstances of his signing to hail 'The Mighty Finn'. A handful of bustling, goalscoring appearances also indicated that the hefty front man possessed a fair amount of vision and finesse on the ball, but an ankle injury and subsequent loss of confidence denied Jari the chance to develop his initially promising partnership with Mike Newell, which was never renewed again by David Pleat. The latter's attempts to offload Jari were for a long time frustrated – the terms of his work permit precluded sale or loan to another British club, while the demands of the player's agent scuppered a proposed deal with Bundesliga club Köln. Jari had been out of first-team action for almost a year prior to his unsuccessful trial spell in Lisbon, but continued to add caps to his tally throughout this unhappy period on Leicester's books. The award of another year's contract to Jari, after he had done much to keep the reserves in the top flight of the Central League in 1989, was soon revealed to be a method of ensuring City of a fee (£45,000 in fact) when he did indeed move on. Jari shared in HJK's 1990 Finnish title win, but was sent off in the second leg of the championship play-offs. In 1994, he suffered a fractured skull after colliding with a goalkeeper, but bounced back as a veteran to make a substitute appearance in HJK's 1996 Finnish Cup triumph. His manager at FinnPa, Martti Kuusela, joked in 1997 that 'the last time I saw Jari in this good shape was after the Second World War'; while Jari finally hung up his boots to join the FinnPa coaching staff in 1998.

***Apps:** FL 10+3; LC 2+1; FMC 2+1.*
***Goals:** FL 3; LC 1.*

REED, Kevin David

b. Leicester, 22nd September 1960

Career: Syston Youth; app July 1977/pro May 1978 CITY.

City debut/only game v Wrexham (H) 22.11.78 (sub)

> Having joined City straight from school in Quorn, diminutive winger Kevin made his solitary senior appearance under faintly farcical circumstances. Larry May's car broke down on the way to an evening match, nominated substitute Peter Welsh stepped into the vacant defensive berth, and Kevin was plucked from the stand to wear the No 12 shirt despite having only one reserve game's experience to his credit at the time. The inevitable happened when Trevor Christie suffered injury, and Kevin almost made his bow a scoring one when hitting the Wrexham bar with his first shot. Never again in contention, though, he was released in July 1979.

***Apps:** FL 0+1.*

REEDAY, Maurice J.

b. Darwen, Lancs, 28th August 1909

Career: 1929 Darwen; trials-Blackburn Rovers & Burnley; May 1934 Blackpool; May 1936 Accrington Stanley; Mar 1937 CITY (- 1944).

City debut v Arsenal (H) 11.9.37

> The full-back always popularly known as 'the man Stanley Matthews couldn't beat', Maurice was given confirmatory credit as such by his frustrated victim, who never relished the ultra-tight marking that was Maurice's trademark. 'He was a grand player. I'd say, "Haven't you got a home to go to, Maurice"? And he'd say "Sure I have, but it won't burn down 'til the end of this 90 minutes, Stan"'. Though he had never made a senior breakthrough at Bloomfield Road, Maurice showed sufficient promise in his 28 League and Cup games at Accrington to tempt a £900 bid from Frank Womack, and in the final two pre-war First Division seasons regularly displaced either Dai Jones or Willie Frame in showing that his defensive capabilities could be adapted to either flank. Another player to 'lose' three appearances from the abandoned 1939/40 season, Maurice virtually ended his career as a guest player back in Lancashire, for Accrington, Blackburn and Burnley; though he also had a few last games for non-league Darwen after rejoining them as coach in October 1947.

***Apps:** FL 74; FAC 5; WW2 4.*
***Goals:** FL 2.*

REID, Paul Robert

b. Warley, Worcs, 19th January 1968

Career: app July 1984/pro Jan 1986 CITY; Mar 1992-loan-Bradford City; July 1992 Bradford City; May 1994 Huddersfield Town; Mar 1997 Oldham Athletic; July 1999 Bury.

City debut v Southampton (A) 7.3.87

> A competitive, nimble teenage striker when his promise was first recognised by Bryan Hamilton, Paul found his career given a major boost when David Pleat decided to play him as a left-footed right-winger. He thrived initially on this unorthodox tactical switch, especially when able to exploit his penchant for cutting inside and across a defence before unleashing a powerful shot, but the predictability of the manoeuvre eventually diminished its effectiveness. A distinct lull in Paul's progress was barely disguised by his later assumption of alternative roles in midfield and at full-back; though he could for a while be relied upon for a sprinkling of spectacular goals, such as the brilliant solo effort at Blackburn which won the 1988 Goal of the Season award from the supporters. Two disastrous back passes, each costing important goals, ended Paul's spell as a City defender, and he reverted to wide midfield play once more in Yorkshire. Heavily involved in Huddersfield's 1995 promotion to Division One, he proved unable to avert Oldham's descent from that level two years later; and for some years played under the shadow of a legal suit brought by Crystal Palace's Darren Pitcher, who'd suffered serious injury in a tackle by Paul. His first goal for Bury was his 50th in League football; and he remains an influentially hard-working force at Gigg Lane.

***Apps:** FL 140+22; FAC 5+1; LC 13; FMC 6+2.*
***Goals:** FL 21; LC 4.*

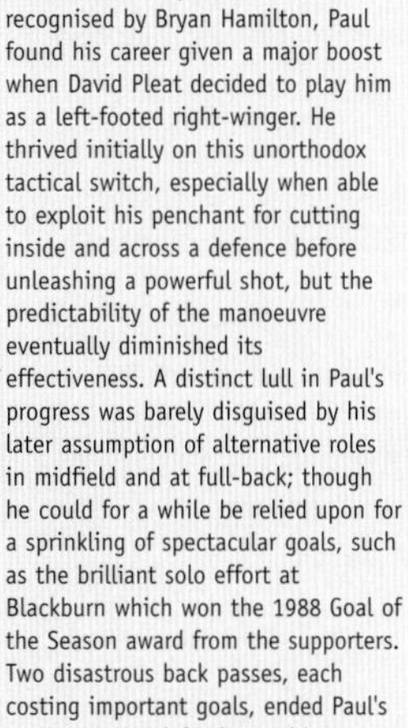

Paul Reid

RENNIE, David

b. Edinburgh, 29th August 1964

Career: app July 1980/pro May 1982 CITY; Jan 1986 Leeds United; July 1989 Bristol City; Feb 1992 Birmingham City; Mar 1993 Coventry City; Aug 1996 Northampton Town; Dec 1997 Peterborough United; cs 1999 Boston United/Sept 2000 Burton Albion.

City debut v West Bromwich Albion (A) 3.9.83

> Scotland's skipper when they triumphed in the European Youth championships of 1982 (beating Czechoslovakia 3-1 in the Helsinki Final), David looked set for a long Filbert Street career as a coolly elegant defender in the Alan Hansen mould. But City's constant need for experience at the back in their First Division rearguard campaigns allowed scant opportunity for him to play himself into the side in his favoured position, and a series of lacklustre performances when David was experimentally shoe-horned into midfield or full-back roles did little to aid his confidence. His only goal for City, though, was a landmark: his header against Coventry during Filbert Street's first-ever Sunday fixture in December 1984 being the club's 5,000th in the League. Traded to Elland Road for £45,000, David initially had to get used once more to having his versatility exploited for tactical purposes, though he popped up with Leeds' first goal in their 1987 FA Cup semi-final defeat before successfully claiming central defensive responsibilities there. His move to Ashton Gate involved a £175,000 fee, duly paid off in contributions to Bristol City's Third Division promotion season of 1989/90, but he only briefly partnered Russell Osman for that club before moving on to aid Birmingham's equivalent elevation in 1992. David supplemented the under-pressure Premiership back line at Highfield Road, then stiffened the Cobblers challenge that ended in promotion via the 1997 Division Three Play-Offs. In 2000, he skippered Boston to the Southern League championship, and back up into the Conference.

***Apps:** FL 21; LC 2.*
***Goals:** FL 1.*

REVIE, Donald George

b. Middlesbrough, 10th July 1927
d. Edinburgh, 26th May 1989

Career: Middlesbrough Swifts; am July 1944/pro Aug 1944 CITY; Nov 1949 Hull City; Oct 1951 Manchester City; Nov 1956 Sunderland; Nov 1958 Leeds United.

City debut (WW2) v Wolverhampton Wanderers (H) 26.8.44; (postwar) v Manchester City (H) 31.8.46

> Though the controversies of his managerial career seem to have set the tone of posterity's overly harsh judgement on him, Don was no stranger to acrimony even in his early days at Leicester. A teenage signing from City's short-lived North Eastern 'nursery' club, who was taken under Sep Smith's wing and taught the basics of constructive inside-forward play, Don was an early victim of the City crowd's occasional propensity for giving 'stick' to their own players, with his thoughtful style initially deemed ponderous by spectators wanting the ball delivered into the box rather more speedily. (That said, he laid on two George Dewis goals on his wartime debut as a 17-year-old, the first after only three minutes, to signpost his alertness). A broken ankle in November 1947 interrupted his still self-confident playmaking progress, but he turned City hero with his efforts in the 1949 FA Cup run, culminating with his two semi-final goals against Portsmouth. It was a hefty blow to both player and club that he had to miss out on the Wembley showpiece after broken blood vessels in his nose almost cost him his life (even if the FA granted him a runners-up medal a few months after the Final), and he agitated for a move shortly afterwards. A £20,000 fee took Don to Hull, to learn more of the game's finer points alongside player/manager Raich Carter (and, as emergency goalkeeper, to concede an Arthur Rowley special in October 1950); and then at Maine Road he hit the headlines as the tactical architect of the so-called 'Revie Plan', which represented a domestic response to recently rubbed-in lessons from the Hungarians. He played as a deep-lying centre-forward in both the 1955 and 1956 Cup Finals, picked up the Footballer of the Year award for 1955, and won recognition at both Football League (two games; six goals) and full England levels (six caps; four goals). He had rather less playing success at either Roker or Elland Road, where both his clubs suffered relegation from the top flight – while Don was twice winning the PFA's golf championship – but he assumed the Leeds player/manager's role in March 1961, dropped the on-field responsibility in May 1963, and thereafter led his uncompromising side through a lengthy catalogue of successes and near-misses in League, Cup and European competitions. He took the England manager's reins in 1974; was honoured with the OBE; shouldered much criticism for his safety-first tactical approach and his legendary dossiers on the national side's opposition; and was then accused of everything short of treason when secretly negotiating himself a more highly-paid coaching job in the United Arab Emirates from July 1977. Sadly, while the derogatory nickname of 'Don Readies' still hung over him, the last few years of his life were blighted by motor neurone disease.

***Apps:** FL 96; FAC 14; WW2 33.*
***Goals:** FL 25; FAC 4; WW2 4.*

REYNOLDS, Walter

b. Leicester

Career: All Souls FC; 1908 Belvoir SS; am Oct 1912/pro Dec 1912 FOSSE; cs 1913 Leicester Imperial; Aug 1915 Nottingham Forest; 1919 Eccles United; Feb 1921 Whitwick Imperial; Barwell United.

Fosse debut/only game v Birmingham (A) 18.1.13

> An outside-right from the same local Mutual League club as Tommy Clay, Walter understudied Tommy Benfield and George Douglas for a few months, and made his sole senior appearance in a 1-5 defeat at St Andrews. He scored for Forest in the only wartime game he played for them, and when peace returned he experienced a little Lancashire Combination football, but then returned to reside in Loughborough.

***Apps:** FL 1.*

RICHARDS, Charles Henry

b. Burton-on-Trent, 9th August 1875

Career: Gresley Rovers; Newstead Byron; July 1895 Notts County; Jan 1896 Nottingham Forest; Jan 1899 Grimsby Town; June 1901 FOSSE; Aug 1902 Manchester United; Mar 1903 Doncaster Rovers.

Fosse debut v Woolwich Arsenal (A) 7.9.01

> Though he featured in Fosse's most goal-shy attack ever (1901/2 saw them collectively notch only 38 goals from 34 fixtures), stocky inside-right Charles had a fair scoring record behind him. He'd won an England cap in March 1898 (replacing Steve Bloomer against Ireland), helped Forest to FA Cup Final victory over Derby a month later, figured in the side that beat Fosse in the Burford Charity Cup Final a couple of weeks after that, and had claimed 42 Second Division goals in 80 outings for Grimsby. He came to Filbert Street immediately after the Mariners had claimed the championship, but, having missed only a single game since the season's opening day, was dismissed in March 1902, along with Jimmy Stevenson, for unspecified misdemeanours. He would later notch the first League goal scored by the newly-rechristened Manchester United under that name, but failed in his late bid to save Doncaster from an unsuccessful re-election application. A brother of Charles' briefly appeared in the forward lines of both Derby and Sheffield Wednesday in 1898/9. (Our previous speculative references to Charles as a printer and publisher, incidentally, were erroneous, and arose from a confusion over a Nottingham namesake more famous as a cricket historian).

***Apps:** FL 25; FAC 1.*
***Goals:** FL 5.*

RICHARDS, Percy

b. Merthyr Tydfil, 1908

Career: Merthyr Vale; Aug 1925 Cardiff City; May 1928 Tranmere Rovers; Sept 1929 Newport County; Aug 1930 Merthyr Town; Jan 1931 CITY; May 1932 Coventry City; Apr 1934 Bath City; July 1936 Brierley Hill Alliance; Oct 1936 Kidderminster Harriers; July 1937 Hereford United.

City debut v Arsenal (H) 5.2.31

> A Welsh outside-left who understudied Len Barry during his City days, and experienced distinct ups and downs: his first two senior outings were in a 2-7 defeat and a 6-0 victory! Percy had made a First Division bow as an 18-year-old for Cardiff, but seemed to have betrayed early promise when finding himself back in the Welsh League with Merthyr. However, his hard-up club came to Filbert Street in January 1931 for a friendly against City's reserves arranged explicitly as a 'shop window' for their saleable talent, and nine days later Willie Orr offered Percy another top-flight opportunity. A Highfield Road record of 46 League games (seven goals) followed his release.

***Apps:** FL 10.*
***Goals:** FL 2.*

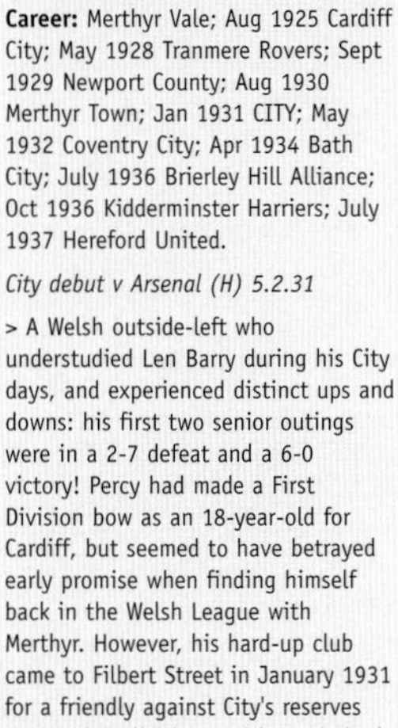

Percy Richards

RICHARDSON, David

b. Billingham, 11th March 1932

Career: Nov 1949 CITY; June 1955 Grimsby Town; June 1960 Swindon Town; July 1961 Barrow; Oadby Town.

City debut v Newcastle United (H) 18.9.54

> Recruited from Teesside junior football, and then soon lost to National Service, Dave developed into a versatile left-sided reserve defender who had the misfortune to get his belated senior break – in a 3-2 home win followed by a remarkable 4-6 defeat at The Hawthorns – while Eddie Russell was still firm favourite for the No 6 shirt, and just after Colin Appleton had given notice of his claim on the same position. In his first term at Grimsby, for whom he eventually totalled 175 League games, Dave helped the Mariners to the championship of Division Three (North), but he also took the drop with them in 1959. His Swindon stint was spent entirely in reserve, and he returned to Leicestershire after seeing out his Holker Street days in the Fourth Division. Despite the coincidence of name and north-eastern origins, he should not be confused with City's youth coach of the 80s.

***Apps:** FL 2.*

RICHMOND, Hugh

b. Kilmarnock, 9th March 1893

Career: 1911 Kilbirnie Ladeside; July 1913 Kilmarnock; May 1914 Galston; Aug 1916 Arthurlie; Mar 1919 FOSSE; Jan 1920-loan-Nuneaton Town; May 1922 Coventry City; May 1925 Queens Park Rangers; July 1926 Blyth Spartans (p/coach); Aug 1929 Spennymoor United.

Fosse debut (WW1) v Notts County (H) 22.3.19 (scored twice); City debut (postwar) v Wolverhampton Wanderers (H) 30.8.19

> A former Seaforth Highlander, signed on a recommendation from regular WW1 Fosse guest Alec Donaldson, who had played alongside him at Arthurlie, Hugh was initially regarded as a goalscoring inside-forward – and in fact claimed the strike at Molineux that belatedly earned the reconstructed City their initial Second Division point – but soon demonstrated a natural facility at centre-half, too. Unfortunately, in settling to the latter role, he then had to play second fiddle to Jimmy Harrold for the bulk of his stay. After returning from a loan spell in the Birmingham League, he married Teddy King's niece, and skippered the City reserve team in the Central Alliance. Hugh had more luck at Coventry, where his aerial ability earned him the nickname 'Rubberneck', as well as a 19-goal return from 67 League and Cup games – including a consolation against City in 1924/5, when the Bantams were relegated. In his QPR season, he once more played in front of George Hebden, and briefly alongside Jack Middleton.

***Apps:** FL 24; WW1 5.*
***Goals:** FL 2; WW1 4.*

RICKUS, Jack

Career: Singers (Coventry); trials-West Bromwich Albion; cs 1893 FOSSE; cs 1894 Hinckley Town; 1896 Gravesend United.

Fosse debut v Long Eaton Rangers (H) ML 23.9.1893

> Handed his Midland League opportunity with Fosse a week after scoring in a 4-1 friendly win over Sheffield United, Jack completed but a trio of scoreless games at inside-forward for the seniors. For two years thereafter he became an opponent of Fosse's second string in the original Leicestershire and Northamptonshire League, then tasted Southern League fare at Gravesend. Jack may well have had other clubs in the the three years after 1897, as he did not reappear in Gravesend's line-up until 1900/1.

***Apps:** ML 3.*

RIDLEY, Fred

b. London, ca 1888

Career: Oct 1906 Barnet Alston; June 1913 FOSSE.

Fosse debut/only game v Birmingham (A) 20.9.13

> One of several outside-lefts tried out following the departure of George Harrison, this experienced amateur had been a regular when Barnet Alston (forerunners of the current League club) won the London League championship in 1907, and had represented both the Hertfordshire and London FAs. Jack Bartlett gave Fred but a single League outing, however, in a 0-1 defeat at St Andrews.

***Apps:** FL 1.*

RIDLEY, John

b. Consett, Co Durham, 27th April 1952

Career: Sheffield University; pro Aug 1973 Port Vale; Apr 1978-loan-Fort Lauderdale Strikers; Oct 1978 CITY; Aug 1979 Chesterfield; Aug 1982 Port Vale; Aug 1985 Stafford Rangers (p/coach); Jan 1989 Matlock Town (p/coach); Newcastle Town (p/coach); Eastwood Hanley (p/mgr); Rists United; Silverdale Athletic.

City debut v Bristol Rovers (H) 28.10.78

> Signed by Jock Wallace to stiffen the City midfield during the manager's first, crucial 'holding' season in the Second Division, John performed his short-term function well, with some gritty displays in front of the back four, and exercised a useful calming influence on the predominantly younger players around him. Subsequently, he helped Chesterfield take the Anglo-Scottish Cup in 1981, was a valuable member of Port Vale's Division Four promotion side of 1983, and led Stafford to Bob Lord Trophy success in 1986. Originally a Gordon Lee signing at Vale Park, John had also had a brief Stateside spell playing in front of Gordon Banks. He extended his playing career in minor Staffordshire football while working as a maths teacher in Stoke.

***Apps:** FL 17+7; FAC 2.*

John Ridley

RILEY, Howard

b. Wigston, Leics, 18th August 1938

Career: Wigston COB; Aug 1955 CITY; Dec 1965 Walsall; Apr 1967 Atlanta Chiefs; July 1968 Barrow; July 1969 Rugby Town; cs 1970 Burton Albion; cs 1972 Ibstock Penistone Rovers (p/mgr); cs 1974 Midland Athletic; cs 1975 Wigston COB; cs 1978 Wigston Town (p/mgr).

City debut v Nottingham Forest (H) 22.8.55

> A first-teamer within weeks of leaving Kibworth School, and only four days after his seventeenth birthday, Howard put down his name as a serious claimant to the City outside-right birth even before being whisked off for National Service. Already honoured at England Youth level, he would graduate to Under-23 recognition while still a Private in the Royal Leicestershire Regiment, as well as representing the senior Army side in a handful of prestige fixtures. Indeed, on the day of his Under-23 debut (when he'd face Ken Leek in the Welsh opposition), he had also been chosen for an Army Cup game with his regiment and for the Army against Hearts! Ironically, on demob in July 1959, Howard faced his leanest City term, as Tommy McDonald shaded the competition for the No 7 shirt in 1959/60, but the energetic flank play that had earned him the crowd's nickname of 'Puffer', and his penchant for the angled thunderbolt shot, soon saw him restored to both club and Under-23 sides. He was the only county-born player in the 1961 Cup Final team, and maintained his place as an orthodox speedy winger for both the 1963 Wembley return and the 1964 League Cup Final against Stoke, when he drove home the decisive goal. By this time he was a part-timer by choice, as he'd commenced a three-year training course at Saltley to become a PE teacher, and his move to Fellows Park took him closer to his college base. Following a brief stint in the FIFA-outlawed National Professional Soccer League in America, Howard had to sit out what was effectively a year's suspension, then ended his League days with Colin Appleton at Holker Street, and his senior non-league career with Richie Norman at Burton. He remained active in local soccer for years afterwards, however, winning a County Junior Cup-winner's medal in 1976 with Midland Athletic, and later serving as manager of Wigston Town. Howard retired from teaching in 1995, after undergoing a hip replacement operation, and returned to Filbert Street in 1999 as Education & Welfare Officer for City's Youth Academy. His sporting prowess was clearly in the Riley genes: his grandfather Edwin and father Harold had both been Leicestershire County cricketers, and the latter had been a City reserve in 1925 (before playing for the likes of Worcester City, Brierley Hill Alliance, Loughborough Corinthians, Nuneaton Town, Hinckley Town and Atherstone Town). Brother Bob was a City reserve in the 60s, who would move on to play one League Cup game for Luton; and a third brother, Jim, featured briefly in City A and B teams during 1960/1, before serving Wigston Fields.

***Apps:** FL 193; FAC 24; LC 12; ECWC 4.*
***Goals:** FL 38; FAC 5; LC 4.*

RITCHIE, George Thompson

b. Maryhill, Glasgow, 16th January 1904
d. Leicester, 10th September 1978

Career: Maryhill; Feb 1923 Blackburn Rovers; cs 1923 Royal Albert; cs 1924 Falkirk; Sept 1928 CITY; Aug 1937 Colchester United.

City debut v Burnley (H) 29.9.28

> 'Cool of head and thick of thigh, Ritchie is a player who gets there in a manner most unobtrusive, but nonetheless *there*...'. Classy left-half George was signed by Willie Orr shortly after he'd starred (and scored) for a Scottish League XI in a Filbert Street friendly for the benefit of Leicestershire CCC, and soon took a grip on the City position vacated by Sid Bishop, forming a fine triangular link on the left flank with Arthur Lochhead and Len Barry as the club rose to runners-up spot in the First Division. Eight seasons of poised performances followed, with George assuming the captaincy on Johnny Duncan's departure, and holding it until his place was put under pressure by Percy Grosvenor. The promotion campaign of 1937 was his last with City but, ignoring offers from Motherwell and Derby, he joined the newly-formed Colchester United and skippered them to the Southern League Cup and championship in successive seasons. Appointed assistant coach at Ipswich Town on the eve of WW2, George was then to be found on the backroom staff at Filbert Street between 1946 and 1950, and coaching Leicester Nomads on a part-time basis for a while thereafter. Originally, his career had got off to something of a false start at Ewood, from where he was released after two outings at centre-forward. He'd featured in the first of three seasons in the ill-fated Scottish Third Division for the Larkhall-based Royal Albert, then developed his middle-line mastery in the top flight at Falkirk.

***Apps:** FL 247; FAC 14.*
***Goals:** FL 12; FAC 1.*

ROBERTS, Iwan Wyn

b. Bangor, Caernarvonshire, 26th June 1968

Career: app May 1985/pro July 1986 Watford; Aug 1990 Huddersfield Town; Nov 1993 CITY; July 1996 Wolverhampton Wanderers; July 1997 Norwich City.

City debut v Wolverhampton Wanderers (H) 27.11.93 (scored twice)

> "Iwan is a Welshman..." (as the Kop song had it), indeed. Watford enticed him to join them from school precisely because they had a Welsh-speaking coach in Tom Walley; while Iwan has remained in demand for media work in his native tongue as one of the few contemporary internationals able so to converse. Initially developing as a gangling teenage striker at Vicarage Road, Iwan memorably scored his first goal for the Hornets as a substitute against Manchester United, and won his first cap against Holland in 1989. Further national call-ups, though, were delayed until he'd settled as a Terriers regular following a £275,000 move (then Huddersfield's record outlay). Iwan's decent strike rate brought him to Brian Little's attention, but it took months of rumour – and a misfiring City experiment to play without a target man following Steve Walsh's injury – before £300,000 landed him at Filbert Street. Iwan's fine two-goal debut rescued a home point, and his scoring touch soon lent credibility and substance to City's 1994 promotion drive. A 12-minute hat-trick in a 3-3 draw with Derby sealed his place in City folklore (and song!), and both his shooting and heading power recommended that Little should gamble on his return from injury to share the sharp end of the attack against the Rams in the Wembley Play-Off Final. Iwan made less impact during the following Premiership season, with his first touch often letting him down, but was always a willing workhorse, and once more ended up as leading scorer. He would again in the 1996 bounce-back campaign, when his final City strike, the winner at Crystal Palace, was also his 100th at League level. A rib injury ruled him out of the Play-Offs that term, and Iwan then rejected Martin O'Neill's offer of a two-year extension to his contract, instead rejoining Mark McGhee at Molineux for a £1m-plus fee, and for a term ending in characteristic Play-Off frustration for Wolves. Following another seven-figure transfer and a slow start, Iwan has regained his reputation for consistent First Division marksmanship at Carrow Road, and in May 2000 earned a recall to Mark Hughes' Welsh line-up after several years out of the national reckoning. At the end of 2000/1, his aggregate tally of League goals stands at 168.

***Apps:** FL/PL 92+8; FAC 5; LC 5; PO 1.*
***Goals:** FL/PL 41; FAC 2; LC 1.*

ROBERTS, Jeremy

b. Middlesbrough, 24th November 1966

Career: YT 1983 Hartlepool United; June 1984 CITY; Oct 1986 Luton Town; Mar 1987 Darlington; Sept 1988 Brentford; Oct 1988-loan-Maidenhead; cs 1989 Gillingham; 1989 Whitby Town.

City debut v West Bromwich Albion (H) 12.10.85

> A non-contract trainee at Hartlepool, goalkeeper Jerry made his senior bow as a 16-year-old in an FA Cup tie at Rotherham, and subsequently played in the replay and one Fourth Division game before being released. He followed Ian Andrews into the England Youth team's yellow jersey shortly after arriving at Filbert Street, and understudied his international predecessor for the first-team custodianship after Mark Wallington moved on; standing in for one draw and two defeats during the 1985/6 First Division campaign. His contract was cancelled by mutual consent, however, in October 1986, and Jerry returned to the North East to resume his League career after a spell in Luton's reserves. The Quakers were relegated in 1987, but his form in the Fourth Division was good enough to win him an elevation to Brentford, where he briefly featured in the same defence as Andy Feeley. Jerry would win no breakthrough at all with the Gills, however, and his senior career closed when he was only 23.

***Apps:** FL 3.*

ROBERTS, Robert

b. Edinburgh, 2nd September 1940

Career: Edinburgh Norton; 1958 Motherwell; Sept 1963 CITY; Sept 1970 Mansfield Town; cs 1972 Coventry City (coach); Mar 1973 Colchester United (p/coach; mgr); June 1982 Wrexham (mgr).

City debut v Fulham (H) 21.9.63

> City's record signing at the time, Bobby cost £41,000 as Matt Gillies outbid Ipswich Town for his services. Primarily an attacking linkman, he claimed Motherwell's consolation goal against Rangers in the 1962 Scottish Cup semi-final (having knocked out the Gers with a two-goal show the previous season), and had one selection for each of the Scottish League and the Under 23s to his name before initially struggling to meet high expectations at Filbert Street. In mitigation, he was successively and bewilderingly employed by City at left-half, inside-right and centre-forward, and he missed out on the 1964 League Cup Final despite having scored in both legs of the semi-final classic against West Ham. Bobby really clicked, however, when he inherited Frank McLintock's No 4 shirt, rolling up his sleeves both literally and figuratively to become City's midfield anchorman throughout the mid- and late-60s, and finally gaining a modicum of reward as an ever-present in the 1969 Cup run. Much valued for his 100% effort and skilful prompting, Bobby could be relied upon also to

place at least one thunderbolt shot high over the bar in each match: a trait that became almost ritualistic. He later gave two seasons and 80 games of middle-line endeavour to Mansfield, and twice returned to the League fray when coaching at Colchester, where he assumed his first managerial role in June 1975 and met much success. Subsequently, as boss at Wrexham, Bobby was forced to make one last return to on-field action – playing at the age of 43 in a Welsh Cup tie against Worcester City as a goalkeeper (in a 1-1 draw that was a prelude to European qualification)! His dubious credentials for this extended no further than his temporary stand-in role following Peter Shilton's injury at Old Trafford in 1967, and a prior net-guarding stint behind Ian St John in a trophy-winning Motherwell 5-a-side team. On leaving the Racecourse Ground, Bobby coached the Al Shabar side in Kuwait, managed Grimsby Town during their 1987/8 relegation season, and returned to Filbert Street in June 1988 for a three-year spell on the City coaching staff. In 1992, he was again coaching in Kuwait, and since 1995 has been chief scout for Derby County.

***Apps:** FL 224+5; FAC 30; LC 21+1.*
***Goals:** FL 26; FAC 4; LC 6.*

ROBERTSON, Archibald Lamond

b. Paisley, Renfrewshire, 27th September 1947

Career: Drumchapel; Benburb; pro Sept 1966 Burnley; June 1968 Bury; Feb 1969 Halifax Town; Dec 1972 Brighton & Hove Albion; May 1974 Exeter City; Apr 1976-loan-Chicago Sting; Sept 1977 CITY; Aug 1978 Peterborough United; Jan 1979 Bradford City; July 1981 Northwich Victoria (p/mgr); Oct 1981 Darwen.

City debut v Arsenal (A) 17.9.77

> Never a first-teamer at Turf Moor, midfielder Lammie got his League break with Bury and helped Halifax clinch their first-ever promotion in 1969. He dropped from Division Two to Three in his first season at Brighton, but prompted Exeter to rise from the basement in 1977. His aggregate appearance record to the date of his £8,000 signing by Frank McLintock therefore consisted only of 21 Second Division games and 314 in the two lowest echelons, so it would have been little surprise if he found adapting to the top flight a difficult proposition. But with McLintock switching the shape and personnel of his relegation-bound line-up on a near-weekly basis, Lammie had even less chance of establishing himself, and faced a sceptical crowd who'd got hold of the rumour that McLintock had originally bid for his Exeter teammate, Alan Beer, and hadn't wanted to come away empty-handed. Accordingly, his occasionally delicate ball skills were exhibited largely in a reserve-team context until he resumed his travels, never having appeared in a winning City side.

***Apps:** FL 6+1.*

Lammie Robertson

ROBERTSON, Hugh

b. Newmains, Lanarkshire

Career: Partick Thistle (?); cs 1890 (?) Everton; cs 1894 Millwall Athletic; June 1895 Burnley; June 1897 Lincoln City; May 1899 Millwall; cs 1900 Dundee; Nov 1900-trials-FOSSE.

Fosse debut v Burton Swifts (H) 1.12.1900 (scored once)

> An experienced Scottish centre-forward deemed not to fit the bill for Fosse at the end of his month's trial, Hugh returned to Dens Park to play out the remainder of 1900/1 in front of Arthur Howes in a Dundee second string which won that term's Northern League title. Previously, he'd contributed to Millwall's Southern League championship win of 1895, top-scored for First Division Burnley in 1896 and gone down with them via the Test Match system a year later, and been an ever-present across two terms at Lincoln on either side of their 1898 re-election, when he was described as 'a fine, well-built player with plenty of devil and dash'. Though doubt persists, it would appear that Hugh had never figured in Everton's first-team, even though he'd been on their books prior to his first Millwall move: he's elsewhere been credited with appearances made by a contemporary half-back named Hope Robertson whose career had an Everton - Bootle - Partick Thistle progression; though there was an H Robertson (still to be definitively identified) who featured three times in the Everton forward-line in their title-wining campaign of 1890/1, when they were still playing at Anfield.

***Apps:** FL 5.*
***Goals:** FL 1.*

ROBINS, Mark Gordon

b. Ashton-under-Lyme, 22nd December 1969

Career: YT July 1986/pro Dec 1986 Manchester United; Aug 1992 Norwich City; Jan 1995 CITY; Oct 1996-loan-FC København; Aug 1997-loan-Reading; Jan 1988 CD Orense; Aug 1988 Panionios; Mar 1999-loan-Manchester City; Aug 1999 Walsall; cs 2000 Rotherham United.

City debut v Manchester City (A) 25.1.95 (scored once)

> Mark McGhee's second capture for a City side rock-bottom of the Premiership, and the club's second £1m import, nippy striker Mark scored the debut header at a waterlogged Maine Road which secured that term's only away win, and signed off the season with a fine last-minute equaliser at The Dell. In the interim, he'd shown some characteristic mobility around the edge of the box, and a few more glimpses of a predatory nature within it, though his confidence seemed affected by the generally downbeat context in which relegation-booked City were performing. He came under pressure for his place from David Lowe near the start of the next season, and struggled to recapture an elusive spark on a 90-minute basis under Martin O'Neill, although appearing as a Wembley sub in the Play-Off Final victory over Crystal Palace. He would also belatedly enter the Wembley action in the following year's League Cup Final, when hooking over the cross for Emile Heskey's late equaliser, and subbed again in extra time in the Hillsborough replay triumph. In the interim, Mark had played in Copenhagen (scoring four times in six Danish League games after netting on his debut against Brøndby) while listed at his own request; and his continental travels would continue after his City release: initially in a mid-table Spanish Second Division campaign. Mark later returned to Manchester after his Greek side's interest in the Cup Winners Cup ended, but only two substitute outings ensued. He spent 1999/2000 embroiled in Walsall's eventually futile fight against relegation, latterly alongside Graham Fenton, and started the new season in place of Lee Glover at Millmoor; going on to claim a career-best 24-strike haul to fire Rotherham to automatic promotion. Originally a graduate of the FA's School of Excellence at Lilleshall, Mark was a prolific reserve scorer at Old Trafford whose Third Round FA Cup winner against Nottingham Forest in 1990 is widely credited with saving Alex Ferguson's managerial job. It was followed by the extra-time goal which separated United and Oldham in the semi-final, and a first Wembley appearance from the bench in the drawn Final against Crystal Palace which ensued. However, despite a fine haul of representative honours (following up England Youth caps with six appearances for the Under-21 side, and a personal five-goal tally from one such game against France), Mark was far too regularly confined to sub's duties with United, making 42 late entries into League and Cup action, yet only 27 starts. Determined to move on, he declined an offer from Dynamo Dresden, but £800,000 took him to Carrow Road, and his 15 goals in 1992/3 helped the Canaries into Europe. Mark was injured in the famous away win over Bayern Munich, and two subsequent knee operations ruined much of the rest of his Premiership stint at Norwich.

***Apps:** PL/FL 40+16; FAC 4+2; LC 5+4; PO 1+1.*
***Goals:** PL/FL 12; LC 5.*

ROBINSON, Walter L.

b. Irthlingborough, Northants

Career: 1894 Finedon; Irthlingborough Town; Aug 1898 FOSSE; Aug 1905 Burton United (- 1909).

Fosse debut v Newton Heath (H) 17.12.1898

> A dogged, hard-tackling defender, Walter inherited the Fosse pivot's role from Jimmy Brown and over seven Second Division seasons turned out in all five full- and half-back positions, battling his way back past countless interim signings after several times appearing to have dropped out of the senior reckoning. His loyalty was rewarded, and his popularity acknowledged, with a benefit game in 1903 (a Christmas friendly against Clapton), and his fighting spirit was recognised by Burton United, who he skippered through their last two seasons in the Football League, and whose player/manager he became in the summer of 1908, for their second and penultimate term in the Birmingham League. We assume him to have been from a footballing family: Irthlingborough (long-ago precursors of Rushden & Diamonds) fielded two other centre-halves named Robinson in 1900 and 1901.

***Apps:** FL 177; FAC 17.*
***Goals:** FL 3.*

ROBSON, Keith

b. Hetton-le-Hole, Co Durham, 15th November 1953

Career: May 1971 Newcastle United; Sept 1974 West Ham United; May 1977-loan-Team Hawaii; Aug 1977 Cardiff City; Feb 1978 Norwich City; Sept 1981 CITY; Mar 1983-loan-Carlisle United; Sept 1983 (Hong Kong); Wroxham; Norwich Busmen; Corinthians; Wroxham.

City debut v Derby County (A) 12.9.81

> The luckless understudy to Malcolm MacDonald on Tyneside, Keith exhibited some of his rival's bustling aggression, and, after a £60,000 move to Upton Park, some of his goal touch, too. Yet he could never quite be sure of selection by the Hammers: missing out on the 1975 FA Cup Final despite a double-figure haul of goals from his first season. He did, however, claim one of the consolation goals in the 1976 European Cup Winners Cup Final defeat by Anderlecht, and briefly formed a forward partnership with his near-namesake, 'Pop'. Two transfers later, via a lowly Second Division campaign at Ninian Park and a sojourn back in the top flight at Carrow Road, Jock Wallace bought him for a small fee to inject some extra experience and weight into City's youthful promotion challenge, but Keith seemed slightly off the pace, and his first-team tenure as a left-sided attacker was brief. A resurrection of the dual-Robson spearhead with 'Pop' at Carlisle did not lead to a contract, and he returned to East Anglia after a brief taste of Hong Kong football, remaing active for some time in local fare in the Norwich area. Keith's semi-idyllic summer of 1977 had come about when four Hammers assisted Team Hawaii in their only North American Soccer League campaign: the club franchise had simply shifted from San Antonio to mid-Pacific, and gates at the Aloha Stadium, Honolulu, ranged from 1,800 up to almost 13,000.

***Apps:** FL 8+1; FAC 1+1; LC 1.*
***Goals:** LC 1.*

RODRIGUES, Peter Joseph

b. Cardiff, 21st January 1944

Career: May 1961 Cardiff City; Dec 1965 CITY; Oct 1970 Sheffield Wednesday; July 1975 Southampton; 1977 Romsey Town.

City debut v Stoke City (H) 1.1.66

> At his peak the undisputed master of the sliding tackle, Peter was already an established Welsh international right-back, with additional experience in Cardiff's early forays into the Cup Winners Cup, when he became a New Year's Eve signing for City at their new record fee of £42,500. Thereafter, his pace, overlapping inclinations and that trademark method of dispossessing his winger brought a new dimension to received notions of Filbert Street full-back play, and his City career would surely have stretched much further had it not been for the exciting emergence of Steve Whitworth. Injury kept him out of the first half of City's 1968/9 season of contrasts, but Peter showed extra grit in the relegation dogfight that followed, and it was only a minor blemish on his record when he was guilty of missing a close-range chance against Manchester City in that term's FA Cup Final. He nonetheless definitively obliterated that particular Wembley memory when, after being freed by the Division Three-bound Owls and having won the last of his 40 caps, he skippered underdogs Southampton to Cup victory over Manchester United in 1976. Retiring a year later, Peter has subsequently busied himself as the landlord of pubs in Hampshire and Carmarthen, and with coaching such local southern outfits as Telephone Sports, Braishfield, Romsey Town and Blacfield & Langley, as well as holidaying schoolkids at Tenby Soccer Schools.

***Apps:** FL 139+1; FAC 18+1; LC 11+1.*
***Goals:** FL 6.*

ROFE, Dennis

b. Epping, Essex, 1st June 1950

Career: app Sept 1965/pro Feb 1968 Orient; Aug 1972 CITY; Feb 1980 Chelsea; July 1982 Southampton.

City debut v Coventry City (H) 26.8.72

> Lined up to rejoin his former manager Jimmy Bloomfield at Leicester on the very day David Nish left, Dennis cost precisely half the £250,000 fee City received. Comparisons between the two left-backs, if invidious, were inevitable, but sound judgement saw that what City had lost in sheer elegance, they'd gained in cheery enthusiasm and whole-hearted vigour. Dennis justifiably became a fixture in City's No 3 shirt, quick into the tackle and quick to augment the attack, and was unlucky to win only one Under-23 cap. The dressing-room joker among City's Cockney colony of the mid-70s (and known there as 'Sid' on account of a purported resemblance to Sid James), he faced his on-field responsibilities with determined seriousness, took the team captaincy when Frank McLintock arrived, and remained an undaunted, if diminutive, pillar of strength for Jock Wallace. The majority of his small tally of goals remain utterly memorable: a last-minute solo waltz from the halfway line to clinch a 4-3 away win at St Andrews; a flukey free-kick from his own half that floated over QPR's Phil Parkes; and a pair of hot shots at Swansea that hit, and almost broke, the same stanchion. Later, Dennis unfortunately misjudged the relative promotion potentials of City and Chelsea when leaving for Stamford Bridge, but returned to the top flight at The Dell, where he extended his stay as coach until 1991. Then joining Bristol Rovers in a similar capacity, he found himself quickly elevated (for a 14-month stint) to the manager's role; and then coached at Stoke City before returning to Southampton in July 1995, where he remains in charge of the reserves. Way back at the start of his career, he had been converted from an inside-forward to the full-back slot by Orient boss and former wartime City goalkeeper Dick Graham; his Orient debut was as a scoring substitute at Eastville in April 1968, and he missed but a single game in the Division Three championship effort of 1970 under Bloomfield.

***Apps:** FL 290; FAC 22; LC 12.*
***Goals:** FL 6.*

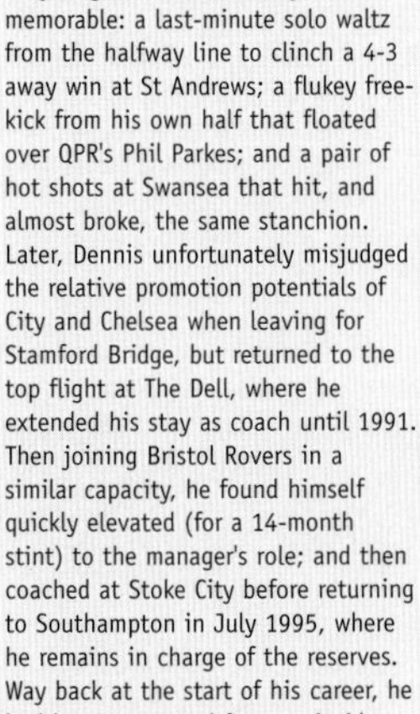

Dennis Rofe

ROLLING, Franck Jacques

b. Colmar, France, 23rd August 1968

Career: Colmar; RC Strasbourg; cs 1992 FC Pau; Aug 1994 Ayr United; Sept 1995 CITY; July 1997 Bournemouth; Sept 1998-trials-Gillingham; Oct 1998-trials-Wycombe Wanderers; Feb 1999 SK Vorwärts Steyr.

City debut v Norwich City (A) 30.9.95

> Initially secured from Ayr on a month's loan, French defender Franck made a superbly assured debut in place of Jimmy Willis in a Carrow Road victory which maintained City's early leadership of Division One, and earned himself a £100,000 transfer. A central defender (or full-back) who sometimes appeared happier in possession of the ball than in winning it, he based his game more on anticipatory intervention than physical contact, and for a while accommodated himself ideally to Mark McGhee's short-passing tactical preferences. He won few selections under Martin O'Neill, however, with the new boss apparently unconvinced by his tackling skills; and it was not until the retention of Premiership status had been confirmed that the popular Franck was given a farewell senior run-out in the final fixture of 1996/7 at Ewood Park. Released to Bournemouth, he showed an unexpected goalscoring penchant for the Cherries, and netted in each leg of the Auto Windscreens Trophy Southern Final to book them a Wembley spot, though Franck remained an unused substitute on the big day. He suffered a head injury on his only Gillingham outing, and failed to impress Wycombe before a return to the continent. Vorwärts were already near-certs for relegation from the Austrian Bundesliga when Franck joined them, however; and actually went bankrupt midway through the following campaign. Originally sidelined at Strasbourg by Franck Leboeuf, he had been rescued from the French equivalent of Third Division football by Ayr manager (and former Strasbourg teammate) Simon Stainrod, and replaced Malcolm Shotton at Somerset Park.

***Apps:** FL/PL 18; FAC 0+1; LC 5.*

ROLLINSON, Frank

b. Heeley, Sheffield

Career: Heeley; 1906 Sheffield Wednesday; Aug 1911 FOSSE; Feb 1912 Portsmouth; Sept 1913 Luton Town.

Fosse debut v Gainsborough Trinity (A) 2.9.11

> An inside-left who'd registered a 15-goal First Division tally for the Owls on his sporadic selections, Frank rather lost his scoring touch at Leicester and, after leaving the field in the notorious weather-beaten match at Grimsby in January 1912, which ended with only five Fossils on the pitch, and stretched the Second Division run to ten games without a win, he promptly departed for pastures new. He helped both of his subsequent Southern League clubs to promotion, and got back to some serious scoring form at Luton, with 34 league and cup goals across two pre-war seasons.

***Apps:** FL 17.*
***Goals:** FL 2.*

ROSEVEAR, C.

b. Leicester

Career: Leicester Imperial; Mar 1900 FOSSE; cs 1902 Leicester Imperial; Leicester Olympic.

Fosse debut v Newton Heath (A) 29.3.02

> One of three local centre-forwards tried out at the tail end of the goal-drought season of 1901/2, Rosevear had earlier entered the Fosse record books as the club's first (albeit unofficial) substitute, when replacing the injured Billy Wragg during Johnny McMillan's benefit friendly against Notts County on Christmas Eve 1900, and scoring the third goal. An amateur, he remained active in Thursday League football long after leaving the Imps. His son Jimmy played for Leicester Boys, became a League referee, was elected President of the City League and, in the 70s, acted as City's Press Steward.

***Apps:** FL 3.*

ROULSTON, Arthur

b. Castle Donington, Leics

Career: Castle Donington; Jan 1896 Loughborough; cs 1900 Kettering; May 1901 FOSSE; cs 1903 Whitwick White Cross; cs 1904 Ilkeston United; 1906 Long Eaton Rangers.

Fosse debut v Woolwich Arsenal (A) 7.9.01

> The only player to serve the luckless Luffs in each of their five seasons in the Football League (and their record-holder for most appearances – 123 – in that competition), Arthur made his breakthrough as a winger, but soon converted to the left-half position he would hold until the end of his career. Also occasionally known as Tim, he aided Kettering's decent Cup run of 1900/1, and then joined Fosse as a consistently sound and steady defender, ever-present throughout two fairly nondescript Second Division seasons which ended in placings of 14th and 15th. Whitwick were in their final season at Midland League level when he represented them, and he became one of five White Cross players to transfer together to Ilkeston. His brother Walter was a Derby County left-half.

***Apps:** FL 68; FAC 3.*
***Goals:** FL 1.*

ROWELL, Thomas

b. Birtley, Co Durham, ca 1875

Career: Hedley Harriers; Dipton Wanderers; Birtley; Aug 1897 FOSSE.

Fosse debut v Walsall (H) 16.10.1897

> A tough right-back from Northern Alliance football (and the Durham county team), Tom briefly covered absences in four different defensive positions during his single Fosse season after finding Jack Walker virtually immovable from his favoured berth. Like many fringe players of his era, he fared better in the club's then-heavy programme of friendlies and minor cup games, playing in eleven of the season's twenty such matches, and scoring once in the Burford Cup semi-final victory over Notts County. Fosse offered to re-sign him for another term, but he was said to have taken a job in the North East away from football in 1898.

***Apps:** FL 5.*

ROWETT, Gary

b. Bromsgrove, West Midlands, 6th March 1974

Career: YT/pro Sept 1991 Cambridge United; May 1994 Everton; Jan 1995-loan-Blackpool; July 1995 Derby County; Aug 1998 Birmingham City; July 2000 CITY.

City debut v Aston Villa (H) 19.8.2000

> Ever-present in both League and Cup football during 2000/1, and a virtual model of consistency, Gary was Peter Taylor's first signing for the club, and for three weeks his initial £3m purchase price stood as equalling the club record. He has looked comfortably Premiership class at either right-back, or on the right side of central defence, ever since, though he maintains an utterly undemonstrative presence that threw his only two serious slips of the season (leading to goals conceded at Spurs and Ipswich) into stark relief. He began to assert himself more in the opposition box as the season wore on, too (especially after his perfectly-timed winner against Chelsea), and he cancelled his Tottenham error with the opening goal of the return game that ended City's win-drought. Incisively clean-tackling when required, Gary as often snuffs out danger through anticipation, and shows a confident control befitting a former midfielder. It was in the centre of the park that he first came to prominence at the Abbey Stadium, and earned a £200,000 move to Goodison. Things didn't work out well for Gary there, though, and he was soon involved in Derby's 1996 elevation to the Premiership as he completed his retreat to defensive duties. It was quite a surprise to see him drop back into First Division fare at St Andrews, but for his evident ease and effectiveness he was voted into the PFA's divisional team of the year at the end of both his seasons there.

***Apps** (to end 2000/1): PL 38; FAC 4; LC 1; UEFA 2.*
***Goals:** PL 2, FAC 1.*

Arthur Rowley

ROWLEY, George Arthur

b. Wolverhampton, 21st April 1926

Career: Blackhall St Lukes; am Wolverhampton Wanderers; Apr 1944 West Bromwich Albion; Dec 1948 Fulham; June 1950 CITY; June 1958 Shrewsbury Town (p/mgr).

City debut v Bury (A) 19.8.50 (scored once)

> The most prolific marksman the Football League has ever known, and second only to Arthur Chandler in City's aggregate scoring stakes, Arthur clearly gave early promise of feats to come despite Wolves' failure to sign him on professional forms. A son of a former Worcester City goalkeeper, he made his senior debut, alongside his brother Jack and only five days after his 15th birthday, in a wartime Manchester United fixture at Anfield; and also turned out as a guest player for Lincoln, Middlesbrough and Brighton before undertaking military service in Germany and Palestine with the Duke of Cornwall's Light Infantry. His introduction to League combat, however, was initially a slow process at The Hawthorns (his 24 appearances including one 60-minute stint as an emergency stand-in goalkeeper against City in February 1948, and bringing him only four goals); and it wasn't until Arthur reached Craven Cottage, and gunned Fulham into the First Division in 1949, that his reputation began to rise. There was still much disquiet among City fans, though, when Arthur arrived as an instant, cheaper replacement for the well-liked Jack Lee; and it took a shift from the nominal spearhead role to the No 10 berth to set off the powerful forward's rampage through the record books. The imminent event of the first of his sixteen Leicester hat-tricks, and an initial campaign total of 28 goals, rather smoothed his integration; and his smashing of Channy's seasonal scoring record with 38 the following term duly conferred heroic status upon him. Arthur went one goal better in 1953, rifled home 30 in the 1954 promotion success, 23 more in the First Division, then was actually toppled from the peak of the club's goal charts by Willie Gardiner's 34 (Arthur following with 29). The Second Division championship year of 1957 was a matter of numerous club records for City, so Arthur just had to help himself to one which would last: 44 strikes in an ever-present season. A haul of only(!) 20 counters back in the top flight was considered such a lapse from his standards that the club then rather crazily allowed Arthur to slip away to Shrewsbury, there to continue his path towards a career total of 434 League goals from 619 games (first surpassing Dixie Dean's English benchmark, then Jimmy McGrory's British record). At the risk of representing the burly, lion-hearted inside-left as a merely statistical construct, several other landmarks should nonetheless be noted. His first 100 goals for City came in only 122 games; his first 200 overall came in the same month as brother Jack achieved that tally; his 200th City goal came on the same Gigg Lane ground as his first. (Indeed, Bury were by far his favourite victims: he'd already scored one for West Brom and four in one game for Fulham against them before adding 15 for City). He was the entire League's top individual marksman in both 1953 and 1957, and holds the City record for most penalties converted (41 out of 49 taken in League and Cup). Arthur scored in all four Divisions (50 in One; 232 in Two; 114 in Three; and 38 in the basement, from which he lifted the Shrews at the first attempt); and predictably netted on his final Filbert Street appearance with Shrewsbury's reserves in February 1963. That he never added full England honours to his representative record was a clear injustice (especially as the less prolific Jack won six caps); and even then his selections at lower levels were somewhat derisory. He netted a twisting header from a Bryan Douglas cross for England 'B' against Switzerland in 1955/6, and replaced original choice Denis Viollet for the Football League against the Irish League in the following October. A week previously had come his most ironic selection: a two-goal performance for the Football Combination, in a 6-0 win against a Dutch XI in Amsterdam, at a time when he had still to appear even once in City's reserves! It would be February 1958 before Arthur would indeed first find himself demoted by David Halliday (his Combination record eventually totalling 6 games and 5 goals), and a month later that he would turn down the chance to join Lincoln City, before being controversially listed in May and shifting to Gay Meadow. Left behind was the inescapable inference that City would be highly unlikely ever again to see a forward with quite such an appetite for hitting the back of the net. Arthur's managerial career after hanging up his shooting boots was comparatively unremarkable, taking him from Shrewsbury to spells with Sheffield United, Southend United and Oswestry Town; and it was sad that his second, belated testimonial game in 1977 was such a low-key affair between Southend and City. (Twelve years earlier the celebratory participants had been Shrewsbury and Wolves, and these two clubs would meet again for Arthur's benefit in May 1995, when a Filbert Street collection also helped towards the financing of a knee operation). But nothing could dim the Leicester folk memory of 'The Gunner' on a one-man stampede past helplessly flailing defenders, bringing his thunderbolt left peg into lethal action, and giving the Goalkeepers' Union a collective backache. A district manager for Vernons Pools after his football ties were severed, Arthur lives in retirement in Shrewsbury.

***Apps:** FL 303; FAC 18.*
***Goals:** FL 251; FAC 14.*

ROWLEY, William Spencer

b. Hanley, Staffs, 1865
d. USA, ca 1939

Career: Hanley Orion; 1883 Stoke; Apr 1884 Burslem Port Vale; Aug 1886 Stoke; Aug 1898 FOSSE.

Fosse debut/only game v Lincoln City (H) 3.9.1898

> Fosse just couldn't escape controversy with their newly-signed goalkeeping choices for the start of the 1898/9 season. Not only did the 'poaching' of Godfrey Beardsley land them in deep trouble, but their engagement of this former England and Football League custodian also had them carpeted before the football establishment. At issue was Billy's status as an amateur player and Stoke secretary: in negotiating his own move to Leicester he had accepted a signing-on fee before playing in the opening Second Division fixture. A month later, Fosse faced an FA fine of £10, while both Billy and Fosse secretary/manager William Clark received twelve-month suspensions from the game for such unethical practice. Curiously, there had been legalistic shenanigans when Stoke re-signed Billy back in 1886, with Port Vale winning a courtroom argument that their already-illustrious 'keeper had been 'seduced' by their bitter local rivals, and accepting a player-plus-cash deal in compensation. Twice capped after seeing Stoke into the Football League, and described as 'one of the cleverest men who ever stood between the posts ... always judicious and wonderfully cool', he was nevertheless actually the first goalie to concede ten goals in a League game (against Preston on the opening day of 1889/90). He missed a large part of Stoke's Football Alliance championship campaign of 1890/1 after breaking his breastbone, but returned to play on consistently in the League's top flight, reverting to the unpaid ranks after taking on the club's secretarial duties. After his Fosse move had soured so spectacularly, Billy was successively a postman and a licensee in the Potteries, then emigrated to the USA.

***Apps:** FL 1.*

ROWSON, Samuel

b. Stafford (?)

Career: Leicester Wanderers; 1890 FOSSE; 1892 Leicester YMCA.

Fosse debut (competitive) v Burton Wanderers (H) FAC 4.10.1890

> Another of the youthful Ancients (as Fosse were ironically nicknamed in their early years) to date his allegiance to pre-league days, Sammy was a right-back who turned out in each of the club's first two ill-fated stabs at FA Cup glory, then faded from the scene during the initial Midland League campaign. He did, though, play in both of Fosse's County Cup-winning teams of 1890 and 1891, and represented Leicestershire against the Birmingham FA in 1890. Sammy was still a Leicester resident in 1926.

***Apps:** FAC 2; ML 6.*

ROXBURGH, Andrew

b. Granton, Edinburgh, 1900

Career: Rugby Town; June 1920 CITY (- 1922); 1925 Rugby Town; Oct 1926 Leicester Nomads; Rugby Town.

City debut v Clapton Orient (A) 28.8.20

> The elder of two Scottish-born brothers, raised in Rugby after 1908, who contemporaneously assisted City as amateurs, Andy was a ball-playing inside-forward, 'sturdy and resolute', who actually gave up the game after his second Filbert Street season. Instead, for three years, he preferred the oval-ball game and, from October 1922, as a Tigers fly-half, followed Alfred Barratt in becoming the second and last man to have featured at peacetime first-team level for both Leicester's senior football clubs. Andy also won county representative honours in a Warwickshire XV while playing for Old Laurentians, though curiously it was a knee injury suffered in a rugby game which decided his return to soccer, and a decade's further active involvement in the local amateur game from a Kirby Muxloe base. In 1936, he was noted as treasurer of both Leicester Nomads and of the competition they then played in, the Central Amateur League, and was still in post with the latter organisation in the early postwar years.

***Apps:** FL 19.*
***Goals:** FL 2.*

ROXBURGH, John A.

b. Granton, Edinburgh, 10th November 1901

Career: Rugby Town; June 1920 CITY; Oct 1922 Aston Villa; Feb 1924 Stoke; Aug 1925 Sheffield United; Sheffield FC; Apr 1928 Leicester Nomads.

City debut v West Ham United (H) 9.10.20

> Initially more single-minded about a senior soccer career than brother Andy (though himself also turning out at rugby for Old Laurentians in January 1921, when otherwise a regular right-wing Second Division choice for City), Jack was deemed 'fast and clever, and an ornament to the game both on and off the field'. Still in his teens when making his City bow, he soon deposed George Douglas, and was developing as a speedy, jinky flank player (featuring five times alongside his brother) until he suffered an industrial accident at his BTH Engineering workplace in Rugby, where a heavy trolley ran over both his feet, and cost him over six months' football. Jack proved his fitness in the first half-dozen games of 1922/3, then switched allegiance to First Division Villa, and would feature on the scoresheet of each of his League clubs from then on, including a goal on his Blades debut. While working at the Brightside Foundry in Sheffield in 1926, Jack's footballing prowess won national attention. In March, he was selected by England for the amateur international against Wales, having to drop out when his birthplace was made known to the FA, but when Scotland's amateurs beat England 4-1 at Filbert Street in December, Jack was in the line-up alongside former Fossil Bob Noble. By 1967, Jack was settled in retirement in Kenilworth. A third Roxburgh sibling, Walter, played in City's pre-season trials of 1921, and for the Tigers in 1924.

***Apps:** FL 48; FAC 2.*
***Goals:** FL 2; FAC 1.*

ROYCE, Simon Ernest

b. Forest Gate, London, 9th September 1971

Career: Heybridge Swifts; Oct 1991 Southend United; July 1998 Charlton Athletic; July 2000 CITY.

City debut v Crystal Palace (H) LC 1.11.2000

> The only free agent recruited during Peter Taylor's initial signing spree, Simon was realistic enough to know that he was essentially swapping bench duties at The Valley for those at Filbert Street. Replacing Pegguy Arphexad as cover for Tim Flowers, the keeper had previously come briefly under Taylor's management at Southend (where he was first-choice only in his final three seasons), and hadn't actually played a senior game since the potentially dispiriting experience of figuring in three successive relegation campaigns (at Roots Hall in 1997 and 1998, and – for eight games – in Charlton's 1999 drop from the Premiership). He wasn't to have the happiest introduction to City action, either: helplessly conceding a close-range header and two long-distance screamers as Palace humiliated the weakened Worthington Cup holders in their first defence of the trophy. With Flowers proving increasingly injury-prone, however, plenty of chances to prove a distinctly above-average shot-stopping ability would arise, and Simon showed himself no mean slouch in the air, either, as he saw rather more first-team action than anticipated and eased his way into the crowd's ironic affections as 'England's No 2'. Indeed, a genuine rivalry for the place between the senior sticks was developing by season's end. Simon could also look back wryly on two particular games: at Villa Park when the linesman was the only person in the stadium to believe he'd carried a Dion Dublin header over his own line while saving it, and at Charlton where he revived an obvious rapport with the home crowd, only to be beaten in front of them by Shaun Bartlett's viciously volleyed (and umpteen times replayed) 'Goal of the Season'.

***Apps** (to end 2000/1): PL 16+3; FAC 4; LC 1.*

RUSSELL, Andrew

b. Airdrie, Lanarkshire, 1904

Career: Harthill Athletic; cs 1924 Airdrieonians; Dec 1927 CITY; Sept 1928 Falkirk; 1930 Morton; July 1931 Queen of the South; July 1934 Coleraine.

City debut/only game v Birmingham (H) 14.4.28

> Signed by Willie Orr for both Airdrie and City, Andy had completed an engineering apprenticeship while at Broomfield Park, and first appeared at Filbert Street in an April 1925 friendly. His southerly move was intended to bolster City's reserve half-back strength during the push for the First Division title, and indeed he got but a single chance to deputise for Billy Findlay, in a 3-0 home win. Soon he was heading back over the border (in the company of fellow second-teamer George Wyness) in the part-exchange deal that landed George Ritchie at Leicester. As a later regular for Queen of the South, Andy assisted them to their first-ever promotion in 1933, and to their highest-ever Division One placing of fourth a year later, before trying his luck in Ireland.

***Apps:** FL 1.*

RUSSELL, Edward Thomas

b. Cranwell, Lincs, 15th July 1928

Career: St Chad's College; Apr 1946 Wolverhampton Wanderers; Dec 1951 Middlesbrough; Oct 1953 CITY; Aug 1958 Notts County.

City debut v Notts County (A) 14.11.53

> One of several City players over the years to have simultaneously followed a schoolteaching career, Eddie was a tall left-half, hard-tackling yet constructive. A fine contributor to the 1954 Second Division championship effort, he became the regular No 6 in the ensuing top flight campaign, but was utterly out of the first-team picture by the time of the 1957 title win, only to bounce back yet again in the First Division consolidation term. His first City goal was a tribute to his spirit (if not necessarily his sense): Eddie had been unconscious for 35 minutes after a clash of heads with Dave Sexton, when he returned to net the winner against West Ham in December 1953, and then collapsed again after the final whistle! A teacher at Guthlaxton until 1963,

Eddie Russell

when he took up an industrial career, he recommended Alan Woollett to City. Originally the understudy to Billy Wright at Molineux after completing his RAF service, Eddie had worn the Old Gold in the 1949 Charity Shield match, and toured Canada with the FA party in 1950. He had a bust-up with Middlesbrough when enrolling for a two-year PE teacher's course at Loughborough, and was blocked from turning out with Brush Sports before Norman Bullock's £8,000 City cheque broke the impasse. Eddie's son Paul was a surfing champion in the late 70s and early 80s.

***Apps:** FL 90; FAC 11.*
***Goals:** FL 5.*

RUSSELL, Kevin John

b. Portsmouth, 6th December 1966

Career: app 1983 Brighton & Hove Albion; Oct 1985 Portsmouth; July 1987 Wrexham; June 1989 CITY; Sept 1990-loan-Peterborough United; Jan 1991-loan-Cardiff City; Nov 1991-loan-Hereford United; Jan 1992-loan-Stoke City; June 1992 Stoke City; June 1993 Burnley; Mar 1994 Bournemouth; Feb 1995 Notts County; July 1995 Wrexham.

City debut v Hull City (A) 19.8.89

> A major Filbert Street cult hero for his inspirational interventions in the closing stages of two contrasting Second Division campaigns, 'Rooster' in fact had to quarry his limited chances to shine from what was otherwise a mass of ill-fortune at Leicester. Fitness problems hit the prematurely-balding but extremely pacy frontman almost as soon as he arrived, and even when loaned out Kevin fared little better: his Posh period embraced a severe shaking in a car crash and ended with a stress fracture, while Cardiff faced winding-up proceedings during his spell there. Eventually, Gordon Lee brought Kevin back from the wilderness as City strove to stay up in 1991, and his impact (and goals) over the final thirteen games proved crucial to the last-gasp escape. The advent of Brian Little's reshaped line-up meant that once more Kevin dropped out of the picture, but his late-season return (in a slightly deeper-lying role) again turned out to be a substantial fillip to City's ambitions, this time ending in Play-Off qualification. Kevin's willingness to chase and to run at defenders with the ball marked him out for many, but his keenness to make himself available to hemmed-in providers was every bit as useful. Accordingly, there was genuine regret when the out-of-contract player chose to move on to Stoke, closer to the Wrexham base he had maintained as a hedge against Filbert Street uncertainties. Kevin's last games for both Wrexham and City, therefore, turned out to be in Play-Off Finals, for David Pleat had originally laid out £175,000 to the Welsh club after their defeat at Orient in the 1989 two-legged version, and after Kevin had scored 50 goals in just two seasons for the Robins (including one spell of netting in ten successive games). He'd started his career as a midfielder, released from his Brighton apprenticeship without a senior chance (despite England Youth recognition), but laid the basis of his striking career with his hometown club, intermittently deputising for Paul Mariner before the lure of regular first-team fare drew him to the Racecourse Ground. A roundabout of post-Leicester transfers (which landed Kevin a star role in Stoke's Division Two championship side of 1993, and a cameo in Notts County's 1995 drop from the First alongside Gary Mills and Phil Turner) eventually led him back to North Wales, where he resumed a midfield role, and where his 1997 giant-killing goal against West Ham has been the highlight of a six-year stint to date.

***Apps:** FL 24+19; FAC 1; LC 0+1; FMC 2; PO 3.*
***Goals:** FL 10; PO 2.*

RUSSELL, Martin Christopher

b. Dublin, 27th April 1967

Career: Belvedere YC; May 1984 Manchester United; Oct 1986-loan-Birmingham City; Jan 1987-loan-Norwich City; Mar 1987 CITY; Feb 1989 Scarborough; Mar 1990 Middlesbrough; Aug 1991 Portadown; cs 1998 St Patrick's Athletic.

City debut v West Ham United (H) 18.4.87

> Honoured at Under-21 level by the Republic of Ireland both before and after his £25,000 move to Filbert Street, Martin built a fair reputation in the Old Trafford reserves as an attacking midfielder, but left United without a senior game to his credit. In fact, his only League experience had come during his short St Andrews loan spell, and it hadn't really equipped him with sufficient assertiveness for the left-flank role which Bryan Hamilton initially asked him to fill for City's relegation-bound side. Martin's neat footwork and silky changes of direction were put briefly to better use in the midfield department of David Pleat's Second Division squad, though a tendency to get too easily hustled out of his stride still limited his senior chances. The valuation of his outward move at £105,000 raised a few eyebrows, and represented by some margin Scarborough's record fee, but it was soon overtaken by the amount paid by Colin Todd to take Martin to Ayresome. He still failed to become a Second Division regular, but success awaited him on both sides of the Irish border thereafter. Playing for Northern Ireland champions Portadown, and taking them to within a single place of repeating their title win in 1992, Martin won a call up to the Republic's 'B' side, and found himself named the Irish PFA's Player of the Year. He featured in Portadown's Irish League championship win in 1996; prompted St Pat's to the League of Ireland title in 1999; and was still exhibiting mature, leisurely class in the latter club's capture of the Eircom League Cup in 2000/1.

***Apps:** FL 13+7; LC 3+1; FMC 1.*

RUSSELL, William

Career: West Norwood; Dec 1913 FOSSE.

Fosse debut v Huddersfield Town (A) 20.12.13

> An amateur outside-right, noted as 'a sprinter' at the time of his signing

by Jack Bartlett, William was elevated from Isthmian League football to cover briefly for George Douglas, but found himself on the losing side in every Fosse game after his debut two-pointer. He had also played representative matches for both Surrey and London, and in fact turned out for London against Southern Counties on New Year's Day 1914, when Fosse were without a game.

Apps: *FL 5.*

SAER, Charles

b. St Clears, Carmarthenshire, 1871
d. Blackpool, 27th November 1958

Career: Fleetwood Rangers; Feb 1897 Blackburn Rovers; Sept 1897 FOSSE; cs 1898 Stockport County.

Fosse debut v Grimsby Town (A) 18.9.97

> A cheerfully charismatic but ultra-competent goalkeeper, Charlie earned much due credit for helping Fosse to create their best defensive record during his single season with the club; but not, apparently, all his pay – for he was said to be still in dispute with Fosse over back wages when injury cut short his subsequent Lancashire League career after only two games. In fact, shortly after joining Stockport, Charlie became centrally involved in early activism among professional players, being voted secretary of the first Players Union during 1898, and leading the initial attempt to reform the transfer system. His scheme for tying transfer fees to wages met with haughty disdain from both the League and the FA, however, and Charlie soon resigned to concentrate on his parallel career as a schoolteacher in Fleetwood. He'd been born the sixth of eleven children on a small Welsh farm, moved to Leominster on the death of his father, and qualified for, and from, Bangor Teacher Training College. He took his first teaching post in Fleetwood in 1892, and was a headmaster by the time WW1 broke out. Charlie was wounded in France after reaching the rank of Captain, then worked at the Woolwich Arsenal, testing rifles and ammunition. By the time he watched City's Cup-tie at Deepdale in 1938, he was Mayor of Fleetwood; and he received the OBE in 1947 for his public service work, such as his chairmanship of the Fylde Water Board. A new County Primary school in Fleetwood was named after him in October 1958, a month before he died following an operation at Blackpool Victoria Hospital.

Apps: *FL 28; FAC 1.*

SALMONS, Geoffrey

b. Mexborough, Yorks, 14th January 1948

Career: app/pro Feb 1966 Sheffield United; July 1974 Stoke City; Sept 1977-loan-Sheffield United; Oct 1977 CITY; Aug 1978 Chesterfield; cs 1982 Gainsborough Trinity.

City debut v Coventry City (H) 15.10.77

> Starting his League career in the same line-up as Alan Birchenall and Willie Carlin, Geoff developed as the more steely component of a Tony Currie-graced midfield in the Blades side which was promoted behind City in 1971. His much regretted sale came about when Stoke's £180,000 fee covered an equivalent trading loss by his club, at the time it was attempting to finance Bramall Lane's conversion from its cricket-ground configuration. Geoff maintained his top-flight progress in the Potters' elegant engine room until their relegation in 1977, when he commenced successive loan spells at each of Bramall Lane and Filbert Street, where his thrusting displays in Frank McLintock's struggling side soon earned him a £40,000 transfer. Though it was an all-too-typical reflection on a disastrous season that Geoff's four goals made him the club's joint top scorer, it was perhaps surprising that Jock Wallace deemed him surplus to City's revivalist requirements at the start of the following term. The fact that he was simultaneously running a Mexborough pub may have influenced the decision, but Chesterfield got three fine seasons out of him before injury struck, and he starred alongside John Ridley in the Spireites team which became the last winners of the Anglo-Scottish Cup in 1981. Subsequently, Geoff has run a string of pubs, restaurants and function venues around Yorkshire, most recently near Swinton.

Apps: *FL 25+1; FAC 2.*
Goals: *FL 4.*

SAMMELS, Jonathan Charles

b. Ipswich, 23rd July 1945

Career: app Jan 1961/pro Aug 1962 Arsenal; July 1971 CITY; Jan 1978 Vancouver Whitecaps; Jan 1979 Nuneaton Borough; 1979 Vancouver Whitecaps; 1979 Nuneaton Borough (p/coach); Aug 1982 Trowbridge Town.

City debut v Huddersfield Town (A) 14.8.71

> Though having gained immense top-level experience at Highbury, and having shared in some of Arsenal's greatest glory days, Jon had also suffered a rare measure of disappointment before arriving at Leicester for £100,000 as Jimmy Bloomfield's first purchase. To set against his winning of one Football League selection and nine Under-23 caps, his pair of Wembley League Cup Final trips had both ended in defeat, while his winning goal in Arsenal's 1970 Fairs Cup Final triumph had seemed to herald a brighter fate than being sidelined for much of the ensuing Double season. The elegant midfielder soon shrugged off any ill-effects on his morale, however, as he set about helping re-establish City as a First Division force, and in fact, in his first senior outing, prompting them to capture the FA Charity Shield. Adept at slowing the pace of a game, Jon didn't always endear himself to an impatient crowd, but he was blessed with a sharp eye for a telling long pass and could unleash a fair long-distance shot, even if the wait between his 49th and 50th League goals stretched lucklessly over fifteen months! He also showed a willingness to play guinea-pig at the centre of some of Bloomfield's more extrovert tactical experiments – such as the so-called 'S Plan', with Jon briefly cast in a Beckenbauer-like sweeper's role. His consistency over six and a half seasons in the top flight was admirable, and it was notable that the team's precipitate decline in 1977/8 coincided with the waning influence of Jon on the City attack. After decent spells in the NASL and in senior non-league football (completing his Nuneaton stint with the championship of the Southern League's Midland Division in 1982), Jon settled in the county to run a driving school from a Countesthorpe base.

Apps: *FL 236+5; FAC 17+1; LC 12.*
Goals: *FL 21; FAC 1; LC 3.*

SANDERCOCK, Kenneth Leslie

b. Plymouth, 31st January 1951

Career: Plymstock United; app/pro Jan 1969 Torquay United; Nov 1969 CITY; Nov 1971 Torquay United; Feb 1975 Yeovil Town.

City debut v Blackpool (A) 8.11.69 (sub)

> Blooded as a teenage midfielder at Plainmoor by Frank O'Farrell, and also given early experience in the right-

Ken Sandercock

back position, Ken followed his former boss to Filbert Street and quickly found a senior squad place for his compact skills and tenacity. His Bloomfield Road bow as substitute gave him more time to impress than did his first starting selection, however, as he was carried off only moments into the next game at Bolton. Thereafter, Ken alternated for a while between the bench and the half-back line, but was unable to win a look-in during the following term's promotion push. Eventually returning to Torquay after failing to impress incoming boss Jimmy Bloomfield, he revived his South Coast career alongside his brother Phil.

Apps: *FL 5+5.*

SAVAGE, Robert William

b. Wrexham, 18th October 1974

Career: YT/pro July 1993 Manchester United; July 1994 Crewe Alexandra; July 1997 CITY.

City debut v Aston Villa (H) 9.8.97 (sub)

> The high-energy epitome of City's recent never-say-die attitude, Robbie was both one of the most effective and one of the most under-rated components of the Martin O'Neill combination, and has finally begun to attract wider acknowledgement of his genuine footballing talents as he has assumed greater responsibility under Peter Taylor. Whether scampering around midfield or breaking forward from the right wing-back berth he has occasionally occupied, he brings a bright intensity to his harrying, ball-winning role, and will run all day after the most hopeless-seeming cause. Often revelling in being the target of abuse from opposition supporters, he's in the past also borne a lot of criticism for a purportedly loose-cannon, headless-chicken style; but such characterisations rather overlook his inspirational abilities to work as well off the ball as on it, or even to turn his reputation as a distracting 'wind-up merchant' to his side's advantage. Twice a Youth Cup Finalist as a trainee striker with United, Robbie left Old Trafford untried at senior level, to become briefly a teammate of Neil Lennon at Crewe, and to convert to an attacking midfield position. He was a regular in the promotion-bound Division Two side of 1997, but was left out of the Play-Off games after failing to sign a new contract. Thereafter, he chose Leicester's bid over those of Crystal Palace, Coventry and Hearts, and a fee rising to £650,000 landed him in the Premiership. Already a Welsh international, he played his first World Cup qualifier (scoring in a 4-6 defeat in Turkey) shortly afterwards, though City initially asked him to play primarily as a wing-back. But the League Cup run of 1999 was to re-define both his role and reputation. His gee-up introduction to the second leg of the semi-final against Sunderland was a turning point in convincing O'Neill that he could handle central midfield responsibilities; while the controversies of the Final would prompt hysterical over-reaction to his all-action mix-it-up performance, with certain Spurs players attempting to goad him to retaliation after he'd reacted late to the blow from Justin Edinburgh that had earned the latter his dismissal, and the London press subsequently crucifying him in print. Robbie's short-term response was, typically, to flamboyantly prompt City to victory at White Hart Lane in the very next fixture; while, in the longer term, he simply applied his determinedly non-stop chivvying to ensuring a triumphant Wembley return a year later. His goal-capped outing at Newcastle in April 2000 first prompted a few hitherto hostile journalists to admit that their favourite bête noir could play a bit, and his crucial contributions to City's 2000/1 cause – gleefully capped by his penalty goal against old adversaries Tottenham, and rewarded with his club Player of the Year award – forced more into admitting admiration.

Apps *(to end 2000/1): PL 125+12; FAC 11; LC 13+2; UEFA 2+1.*
Goals: *PL 8; FAC 1.*

SCOTT, Alexander MacNaughton

b. Kingsbarns, Fife, 17th November 1922
d. Glenrothes, Fife, 27th August 1995

Career: Lochgelly Albert; Mar 1947 CITY; Jan 1950 Carlisle United; July 1956 South Shields.

City debut v Fulham (A) 3.1.48

> A strongly-built inside- or outside-left when spotted by Johnny Duncan on a hometown return, Sandy signed an agreement to join City in November 1946, but it was contingent on Lochgelly Albert's exit from the Scottish Junior Cup: almost five months later! He was soon converted to left-back by Duncan, and then went through his forward-to-defender transformation all over again in the course of City's 1949 FA Cup run, when he stood in successively for Ken Chisholm and Jimmy Harrison, and was a notable rearguard success in the Highbury semi-final against Portsmouth. In the interim, he had been a scorer in the 1948 Combination Cup Final victory over Bournemouth. New manager Norman Bullock let him go for £1,500 halfway through 1949/50, though, after signing Ron Jackson for the No 3 berth, and it was left to Bill Shankly to recognise Sandy's fighting qualities by taking him to Brunton Park, where he totted up exactly 200 Third Division (North) appearances in six years before joining North Eastern League high-fliers South Shields.

Apps: *FL 31; FAC 10.*
Goals: *FL 1.*

SCOTT, Geoffrey Samuel

b. Birmingham, 31st October 1956

Career: app Aston Villa; Kings Heath; Solihull Borough; Highgate United; Apr 1977 Stoke City; Feb 1980 CITY; Feb 1982 Birmingham City; Oct 1982 Charlton Athletic; Aug 1984 Middlesbrough; Sept 1984 Northampton Town; July 1985 Cambridge United.

City debut v Swansea City (H) 20.2.80

> The regular left-back in Stoke's 1979 promotion side, Geoff replaced the departed Dennis Rofe for the run-in to City's Second Division championship the following season. His form, though, was far from convincing, and it was as an emergency central defender that he played his best games for City in their subsequent attempts to retain top-flight status. Almost exclusively a left-footed player, Geoff could occasionally appear ungainly, but his new-found effectiveness in the middle of the back line, partnering John O'Neill or Larry May, earned him a £50,000 move back into the First Division with Birmingham. Later, serious injury marred his Charlton spell after only two games, and threatened his career, finally forcing him to retire halfway through his first term as Cambridge skipper. Geoff, whose cousin Keith Masefield had also been an unsuccessful Villa apprentice (but had then made his name in Holland with Haarlem), eventually returned to Midland Combination outfit Highgate United as manager.

Apps: *FL 39; FAC 2; LC 3.*

SEALY, Anthony John

b. Hackney, London, 7th May 1959

Career: app/pro May 1977 Southampton; Mar 1979 Crystal Palace; Feb 1980-loan-Port Vale; Mar 1981 Queens Park Rangers; Feb 1982-loan-Port Vale; Dec 1983-loan-Fulham; cs 1984 Fulham; Sept 1985 CITY; Feb 1987-loan-Bournemouth; July 1987 Sporting Clube de Portugal; Aug 1988 SC Braga; Mar 1989 Brentford; Aug 1989 Bristol Rovers; May 1991 MyPa Myllykosken; Oct 1991 Brentford; Aug 1992-trials-Merthyr Tydfil; Sept 1992 Michelotti (Hong Kong); July 1993 Eastern (Hong Kong); Aug 1995 Hong Kong FC.

City debut v Birmingham City (A) 21.9.85 (scored once)

> A distinctly well-travelled striker when he joined Gordon Milne's City side as a rival to Mark Bright, Tony became even more so after his departure, numbering Portugal, Finland and Hong Kong among his ports of call. He also collected, as a concomitant of his multiplicity of moves, an all-time record to go with his cabinet-full of medals: winning championship mementos with each of QPR (Division Two, 1983), Bournemouth (Division Three, 1987), Bristol Rovers (Division Three, 1990), MyPa (Finnish Second Division, 1991) and Brentford (Division Three, 1992), and also appearing briefly in Crystal Palace's Second Division championship side of 1979. [His nearest rivals, with title-winning medals from four different clubs each, are Jimmy Ross (1889-99) and Trevor Steven (1982-1992)]. Ironically, perhaps, Tony often found in the first half of his career that, despite his neat and speedy front-running style, his lack of height and weight often made him a likely candidate to step down from the frontline, at least to the sub's bench. Indeed, for City, as much as his other clubs, it was in short bursts of energetic and enthusiastic harrying that he proved most effective. Starting out as a contemporary of Trevor Hebberd at The Dell, Tony made an appearance as No 12 in the Saints' 1979 League Cup Final defeat, then twice had to take temporary Vale Park detours from his metropolitan odyssey to kick-start his scoring form. At Filbert Street, during his second term, he struggled to find a role in the shifting patterns Bryan Hamilton vainly attempted to impose on City's play, but was soon whisked to Lisbon by Keith Burkinshaw to form a useful striking partnership with the Brazilian Cascavel. Tony bounced back from twice breaking his fibula while with Bristol Rovers, and trained for qualification as a physiotherapist while playing out the twilight of his career in Hong Kong, where he also undertook media work.

Apps: *FL 28+11; LC 2+2.*
Goals: *FL 7.*

SEED, Angus Cameron

b. Whitburn, Co Durham, 6th February 1893
d. Barnsley, 7th March 1953

Career: Whitburn; July 1912 South Shields; Seaham Harbour; Dec 1913-trials-Everton; Jan 1914 FOSSE; July 1914 Reading; Nov 1916 St Bernards; Dec 1919 Mid-Rhondda; cs 1921 Ebbw Vale; Broxburn United; cs 1923 Workington.

Fosse debut v Glossop (H) 21.2.14

> Briefly tried out as a right-back replacement for the Tottenham-bound Tommy Clay, Angus took his Fosse consolation from the reserves' County Cup Final win of 1914, and won far greater glory on the WW1 battlefields of Vimy Ridge, when decorated with the Military Medal for valorous conduct while serving with the Footballers' Battalion. But on the whole he had his playing career fairly comprehensively overshadowed by that of his younger brother Jimmy. The latter was alongside Angus in 1919 when Mid-Rhondda (a side glorying in the nickname of the Mushrooms) began their push towards the title of the Southern League's Second Division, then went on to win England caps as a Spurs inside-forward, and to skipper the Sheffield Wednesday side which pipped City to the First Division title in 1929. Angus, meanwhile, completed his active career in the Scottish Second Division and the North Eastern League, eventually graduating to the trainer/coach role at Workington. He became Aldershot's first manager in 1927 and stayed for a decade, leading them into the Football League in 1932. He then pipped George Carr for the Barnsley managerial vacancy in February 1937, and remained in charge at Oakwell for 16 years until his death in office. Yet even then, brother Jimmy's record took a higher proportion of the limelight: after a stint bossing Clapton Orient, the latter managed Charlton Athletic for 23 years to 1956. A third Seed brother, Charles, signed for Sunderland in May 1914, but made no senior breakthrough.

***Apps:** FL 3.*

SEYMOUR, Thomas

b. Ahoghill, Antrim, 7th June 1866
d. Barrhead, Renfrewshire, 12th May 1951

Career: 1886 Arthurlie; Dec 1889 Middlesbrough Ironopolis; Aug 1893 FOSSE; cs 1895 Arthurlie.

Fosse debut v Burton Wanderers (H) ML 9.9.1893

> When the 'Nops' were formed as the first professional club on Teesside, Tom was netted in the customary initial trawl of Scottish talent, and scored their first-ever goal in their introductory fixture, a December 1889 friendly against Gainsborough Trinity. Within a year and a half, Ironopolis were Northern League champions, and when Tom notched a hat-trick for them in the final fixture of 1892/3, it was to seal a third successive title win. So his release on the eve of their election to the Football League was a surprise, as was Fosse's capture of a classy, forceful right-half for their final, runners-up campaign in the Midland League. Fosse were only too keen to retain Tom's services for their own elevation to the Second Division, and it was ironic that Middlesbrough had dropped out of that sphere after only one term, while Fosse fought their opening campaign with five ex-Nops in their line-up. Sadly, though, Tom was badly injured at Burton in February 1895, and thereafter made his recuperative return to Scotland permanent. Tom, whose family moved from Ireland to Scotland in about 1869, and who initially worked in the calico printing trade, represented Renfrewshire both before and after his English experience; was a runner-up in the Renfrewshire Cup Final of 1887 (a riot-interrupted game against Abercorn); and a beaten finalist again in the Scottish Qualifying Cup of 1898/9 when, as captain, he scored Arthurlie's consolation against East Stirlingshire. He had retired, however, prior to Arthurlie's 1901 election to the Scottish League.

***Apps:** FL 19; FAC 13; ML 20.*
***Goals:** FL 1; FAC 1; ML 1.*

SHANKS, Thomas

b. New Ross, Co Wexford, Ireland, 1880

Career: Derby West End; Derby Fosse; Apr 1898 Derby County; Oct 1901 Brentford; Dec 1902 Woolwich Arsenal; May 1904 Brentford; Oct 1906 FOSSE; cs 1909 Leyton; cs 1912 York City.

Fosse debut v Clapton Orient (A) 13.10.06

> An Irishman raised in Derby from the age of two, Tommy played his first League football alongside Steve Bloomer for the Rams, and, between his Southern League spells with Brentford, helped shoot Arsenal into Division One in 1904. As top scorer and penalty expert that term, he notched a hat-trick for the Gunners in their 8-0 eclipse of Fosse. The inside-forward came to Leicester after an arrangement had been made to pay £100 to each of Arsenal and Brentford, and helped prompt Fosse to third place in the Second Division in his first term, with the *Mercury* noting that he 'shoots like a horse kicking'. He is best remembered though, as the effective schemer of their promotion bid in the following season, and scorer of the crucial goal at Stoke in April 1908 that guaranteed their first-ever elevation. Less successful in the top flight (as all his teammates were), Tommy returned to Southern League fare in the company of Bob Pollock, and also figured in the same Leyton line-up as Jamie Durrant. He closed his career with the first professional York City side, which competed in the Midland League for three years before folding.

***Apps:** FL 57; FAC 2.*
***Goals:** FL 16.*

SHARKEY, Dominic

b. Helensburgh, Dunbartonshire, 4th May 1943

Career: Drumchapel Amateurs; am May 1958]/pro May 1960 Sunderland; Oct 1966 CITY; Mar 1968 Mansfield Town; July 1970 Hartlepool; cs 1972 South Shields.

City debut v Manchester United (H) 30.11.66

> A diminutive striker who made a Roker debut at the age of 16, inherited Brian Clough's No 9 shirt, and helped shoot Sunderland back into Division One in 1964, Nick also earned for himself a pair of Scotland Under-23 selections as he bettered the classic goal-every-two-games marksmanship ratio. Matt Gillies brought him to Filbert Street with a view to taking some of the central attacking burden off Derek Dougan, but the pair played together only once, and it was almost the end of the 1966/7 campaign before Nick grabbed another chance with characteristic goal flair. He soon lost his place the following term, though, and it was his prolific reserve-team partnership with Jimmy Goodfellow, later continued at League level after both had moved to Field Mill, which most memorably marked his City career. Having closed his playing days back in the North East, with 101 League and Cup goals to his credit, Nick remains Sunderland-based, as a sales rep for a leisure company.

Nick Sharkey

***Apps:** FL 6.*
***Goals:** FL 5.*

SHARMAN, Frederick

b. Loughborough, 23rd November 1912
d. Loughborough, 19th June 1960

Career: Loughborough Red Triangle; Brush Sports; Feb 1932 Loughborough Corinthians; May 1933 CITY; 1944 Brush Sports (p/mgr July 1950-cs 1951).

City debut v Liverpool (H) 1.2.34

> The youngest of four brothers who all represented Loughborough Corinthians, and whose father had been a Notts County goalkeeper in 1899, Fred was spotted playing against City's reserves in the County Cup Final of 1933, and became a versatile and muscular stalwart of the club's up-and-down struggles of the pre-war era. Primarily a defender, standing in for and then displacing Roger Heywood as a First Division centre-half, he also took the right-back spot from time to time, and had a lengthy spell at centre-forward in 1935/6, with no mean success as a bustling goalscorer. Fred won a Second Division championship medal as pivot in 1937, when ever-present from the second fixture onwards, and was still going strong when war broke out, making a further 54 appearances for City (and 22 for Notts County) before taking charge of the reserve team for 1944/5 and rejoining Brush Sports. He resumed his job as a fitter in the turbine unit at Brush, and when the works team appeared in the First Round of the FA Cup in 1946/7 (losing 1-6 to Southend United), they were the first Leicestershire side other than City to have reached the Competition Proper since the original Loughborough club in 1892/3. Fred had two years away from football after his player/manager stint, but picked up the Brush managerial reins again in 1953.

***Apps:** FL 190; FAC 10; WW2 54.*
***Goals:** FL 18; WW2 1.*

SHARP, Buchanan

b. Alexandria, Dunbartonshire, 2nd November 1894
d. Bolton, 11th January 1956

Career: Vale of Leven Jnrs; Nov 1919 Chelsea; Mar 1923 Tottenham Hotspur; Jan 1925 CITY; June 1926 Nelson; Oct 1928 Southport.

City debut v Coventry City (H) 24.1.25 (scored once)

> Familiarly known as Kenny, this tricky inside-forward was just getting into his First Division goalscoring stride at Stamford Bridge when Spurs swooped for his signature, but then had his progress stymied when consigned to a reserve role at White Hart Lane, where he received only a trio of senior selections. Peter Hodge added him to the City squad pressing for promotion as a back-up to Johnny Duncan, and then saw him as a potential replacement for broken-leg victim George Carr in the top flight, though the signing of Arthur Lochhead soon sidelined him once more. Kenny moved on to complete his League career in Lancashire, netting 22 goals in his first season with Nelson in the Third Division (North), and having a spell as caretaker manager there from March 1928. The most intriguing aspect of Kenny's City stay occurred over the wekend following his scoring debut: for the Leicester rumour machine sent wildfire whispers through the clubs and pubs that Kenny had been killed in a motorcycle accident on his way home, and it took an official City denial on the Monday to quash the idea. His actual demise came over thirty years later, while he was working as a machinist at De Havilland's in Bolton.

Buchanan Sharp

***Apps:** FL 12.*
***Goals:** FL 2.*

SHARP, W.A.

b. Leicester

Career: Leicester Imperial; am Apr 1902 FOSSE; cs 1903 Leicester Old Boys.

Fosse debut/only game v Chesterfield (H) 10.1.03

> A local amateur outside-right, whose sole senior run-out drew from 'Observer' in the *Daily Post* a rather damning assessment: 'a total failure' and 'very weak' being his observations on the former Imp following a dispiriting 0-2 home defeat. A brief profile of the Old Boys team later identified him as being better known as a local swimming champion.

***Apps:** FL 1.*

SHARPLEY, William

b. Bow, London
d. France, 1st July 1916

Career: Army football; Mar 1912-trials-FOSSE.

Fosse debut/only game v Leeds City (H) 27.4.12

> An Army corporal given the briefest of League breaks in the final game of the 1911/12 season, at left-back behind fellow squaddie Mitchell, William was stated by the *Mercury* to have made 'an auspicious debut' in a 2-1 win which lifted Fosse to 10th in the table. An Aldershot drill instructor, he still had two years to serve in the Essex Regiment at this time, though of course he remained in the service upon the declaration of war, rising to the rank of sergeant and winning the Distinguished Conduct Medal before falling in action.

***Apps:** FL 1.*

SHAW, H.

Career: London Road; Aug 1893 FOSSE.

Fosse debut/only game v Burton Wanderers (H) ML 9.9.1893

> A local inside-left who played under the pseudonym 'Archer' in pre-season trial games, then hid his talent in his only Midland League outing – the 1-2 home defeat on the opening day of 1893/4 which nonetheless effectively made the difference between Fosse and Burton taking that campaign's championship. He was released in October 1893 after poor displays in the reserves.

***Apps:** ML 1.*

SHEARD, Frank

b. Spilsby, Lincs, 29th January 1922
d. Leicester, 11th July 1990

Career: Skegness Town; am Nov 1940/pro Aug 1941 CITY; May 1946 Southend United; June1956 Gravesend & Northfleet.

City debut (WW2) v Mansfield Town (A) 22.3.41; (postwar) v Chelsea (A) FAC 5.1.46

> A hefty young centre-half signed on during the second season of wartime football, whilst working as a 'Bevin Boy' at Whitwick Colliery, Frank also saw service as an RAF policeman, and held the senior pivot's position for both legs of City's first postwar FA Cup tie. Released to Southend before the Football League resumption, totting up 180 games over seven seasons, he gained a reputation for the classic virtues of a stopper: uncompromising robustness and bravery.

***Apps:** FAC 2; WW2 84.*
***Goals:** WW2 2.*

SHEFFIELD, John Davenport

b. Coalville, Leics, ca 1879
d. Neuve Chapelle, France, 10th March 1915

Career: 1897 Coalville Albion; Apr 1900 Whitwick White Cross; Aug 1900 Coalville Town; Coalville Wednesday; Oct 1902 Burton United; cs 1903 Coalville Town; am July 1904 FOSSE; Aug 1905 Loughborough Corinthians; 1905 Ibstock Albion; cs 1906 Coalville Excelsior; cs 1908 Ibstock Albion; Coalville Wednesday; cs 1910 Coalville Town; cs 1912 Coalville Swifts.

Fosse debut v Liverpool (A) 1.10.04

> As his list of clubs in the North Leicestershire area testifies, amateur outside-right Jack clearly didn't fancy taking his football talents far from home (his father William ran the Railway Hotel, Coalville, and was President of Coalville Town FC). Yet he also managed to fit a spell of far-flung Boer War service into the above chronology (as a corporal in the Leicester Volunteer Battalion, in South Africa in 1901 and 1902). He totalled a dozen Second Division outings for the Brewers in front of Harry Ashby (and his goal earned them a Cup replay against Manchester United), but was effectively debarred from much extending his experience at that level with Fosse by the consistency of Jamie Durrant. Jack took runners-up medals from the County Cup Finals of 1904 (with Coalville Town) and 1905 (with Fosse reserves), and represented Leicestershire against Lancashire in January 1904 and February 1905. Curiously, in the season before he signed for Fosse, he divided his Saturdays between appearances for Coalville Town and Coalville Rugby Club, starring for the latter as a speedy three-quarter. Tragically, Jack's second stint in his country's colours – as a Leicestershire Regiment corporal – heralded his death from a head wound in the WW1 trenches.

***Apps:** FL 2.*

SHEPHERD, John

Career: Apr 1912 FOSSE.

Fosse debut/only game v Stockport County (A) 20.4.12

> A trialist inside-left of so-far untraced origin; though John was stated at the time of arrival to be 'well recommended from the South' (as were so many of Jack Bartlett's acquisitions from the London amateur scene). This particular recommendation clearly proved resistible, anyway, despite Fosse registering their first-ever away win over Stockport on the occasion of his sole outing.

***Apps:** FL 1.*

SHILTON, Peter Leslie

b. Leicester, 18th September 1949

Career: Blaby Boys Club; app June 1965/pro Sept 1966 CITY; Nov 1974 Stoke City; Sept 1977 Nottingham Forest; Aug 1982 Southampton; June 1987 Derby County; Mar 1992 Plymouth Argyle (p/mgr); Feb 1995 Wimbledon; Mar 1995 Bolton Wanderers; June 1995 Coventry City; Jan 1996 West Ham United; Nov 1996 Leyton Orient.

City debut v Everton (H) 4.5.66

> It's almost the case that however far back into Peter's superb goalkeeping career one delves for perspective, one could have safely predicted the heights it would reach. A schoolboy prodigy, his dedication to working on the practice and psychology of his destined profession (and even on building an appropriate physique for it) was evident while he was helping Leicester Boys to their 1965 Trophy win, and picking up his first international recognition with England Schools. At Filbert Street, there was immediate acknowledgement of Peter's precocious talent, plus devoted encouragement from the likes of veteran coach George Dewis, and he became City's youngest-ever First Division debutant at 16, when characteristically keeping a clean sheet against Cup-winners-to-be Everton. Barely another year had elapsed before a queue of top clubs was forming, ready to snatch Peter (now an automatic choice for England Youth) from the Filbert Street shadow of Gordon Banks, and an unenviable choice soon faced Matt Gillies over which of his top-rank 'keepers to part with. He elected to invest in the younger man's ability and ambition, and it was not too long before his judgement was substantiated by Peter's assumption of Banks's place in the international arena. In the interim, City experienced a Cup Final, a relegation and a promotion (with Peter's shot-stopping solidity, aerial agility, uncanny sense of positioning and absolute command of his area as major factors in the club creating its best-ever defensive record during 1970/1, when he kept a record 23 clean sheets). Rarely out of the public eye – his adoption of an all-white playing kit, his 50% penalty-save record, and his long-distance scoring success at Southampton at various times ensuring that – Peter was inevitably now adding full international mementos to his thirteen Under-23 caps, but also becoming less than enchanted with City's trophy-winning prospects. Jimmy Bloomfield eventually accepted a £325,000 cheque from Stoke for the unsettled star, and the move ironically threatened to rebound on Peter as the Potters themselves struggled, and he found himself only sharing the yellow jersey of England with Ray Clemence. But when Stoke dropped into Division Two, Peter was the subject of a typically shrewd bit of Brian Clough business, and in five years of almost uninterrupted success in domestic and European competitions with Forest, he once more re-established himself as the country's undisputed No 1. Maintaining his impeccable, highly self-critical standards at The Dell (after another £325,000 move), Peter became the most-capped England 'keeper of all time, skippering the national side on occasion, and earning the civil honour of the MBE in 1986. Then, following a final big-money transfer to the Baseball Ground, he set about creating a further series of career landmarks: passing Terry Paine's all-time record for the highest number of League appearanes with his 825th such game in April 1988, and overtaking Bobby Moore's record haul of England caps with his 109th selection against Denmark in June 1989. In July 1990, Peter finally retired from the international scene with a then world record 125 caps to his name, bowing out at the very top of his profession, having kept 67 international clean sheets, and played in a record 37 World Cup games. He was up-graded to an OBE in 1991, and later took the plunge into management. Initially successful as Argyle's player/manager (though content to sideline himself from action on the 995 League games mark), Peter soon proved unable to juggle the pressures of a relegation scrap with those of his well-publicised personal financial difficulties. He resigned from Home Park in January 1995, after being suspended by his chairman; but not before giving a League debut to his 16-year-old son Sam (who has since served as a winger with Coventry, Hartlepool and Kidderminster). He then signed on a non-contract basis as goalkeeping cover at each of Selhurst, Burnden, Highfield Road and Upton Park, aiding Bolton's promotion to the Premiership with a fine Play-Off semi-final performance at Molineux. Peter would have stepped straight into Cambridge United's first team in October 1996 if he hadn't been recalled at the last minute by West Ham to sit on their bench for a game against City, but he finally got his chance to pass the remarkable four-figure milestone in League games while with Orient, ending his playing career after 1,005 such outings, and 1,391 senior games in aggregate. (Another index to the longevity of his career has him as the joint record-holder, with Ian Callaghan, of the highest number of FA Cup appearances ever: 88 after the minor embarrassment of Orient's giantkilling by Stevenage). For almost three years from August 1997, Peter was engaged as goalkeeping coach at Middlesbrough. His uncle, Fred Shilton, was a City reserve 'keeper in the mid-30s, on secondment from Leicester Nomads. Strangely, two of his original Blaby Boys teammates both made League debuts as 16-year-olds before he did: Bobby Vincent and David Needham each making Notts County bows a matter of weeks earlier.

***Apps:** FL 286; FAC 33; LC 20.*
***Goals:** FL 1.*

SHINTON, Frederick

b. Wednesbury, Staffs, March 1883
d. Wednesbury, 11th April 1923

Career: Hawthorn Villa; Moxley White Star; Wednesbury Old Athletic; Hednesford Town; Apr 1905 West Bromwich Albion; Nov 1907 FOSSE; June 1910 Bolton Wanderers; Jan 1911 FOSSE.

Fosse debut v Lincoln City (A) 30.11.07 (scored once)

> Fosse decidedly got the best of the bargain from the part-exchange deal which took Harry Wilcox and £125 to The Hawthorns and brought inside-forward Fred to Leicester part-way through what turned out to be the club's first promotion season; for the latter went on to become Fosse's first true goalscoring hero since David Skea. His strike rate at West Brom was already mightily impressive (46 goals from 64 Second Division outings), and ten strikes towards the promotion taget did much to endear the enthusiastic bustler to his new supporters. Strangely, Fred got fewer chances to enliven Fosse's struggling front line in the top flight, but when they tried to bounce straight back up again in 1909/10, Fred weighed in with a 32-goal haul from the centre-forward berth that remained a club record until the days of Arthur Chandler, and saw him share the League's leading marksman laurels with Hull City's Jack Smith. Dubbed by the *Mercury* as 'the opportunist incarnate, always on the qui vive for an opening', his brave, almost reckless style of headlong assault earned him the Filbert Street nickname 'Nutty', and it was often remarked what an attraction he was to Fosse's fairly substantial female support. A highlight of his best term was a five-minute hat-trick against Oldham in November 1909. A brief, unhappy spell with a promotion-bound Bolton side interrupted Fred's progress and seemed to take the gloss off his game, for despite a scoring comeback with Fosse, he failed to earn a new contract in 1911. Nonetheless, he was the only Fossil ever to break the 50-goal barrier. In November 1922, City and West Brom fielded what were largely reserve teams in a hastily-arranged benefit game for Fred, when he was totally incapacitated by ill-health and responsible for his wife and six children, but he died of consumption five months later. One of his brothers scored for Wolves on his only League outing in 1909, while another, Arthur, signed for City in 1919, but failed to make the grade prior to a move to Hinckley United.

***Apps:** FL 92; FAC 9.*
***Goals:** FL 55; FAC 3.*

SILVESTER, Edward Ernest

b. ca 1869

Career: 1889 Kidderminster Harriers; West Bromwich Albion; Dec 1891 Walsall Town Swifts; cs 1892 FOSSE.

Fosse debut v Mansfield Town (A) ML 17.9.1892

> A centre-half taken on to add creative wit to Fosse's middle line after the embarrassments of the initial Midalnd League season, and handed the captaincy in Snooks Nuttall's absence, Edward had previously graduated from assisting the Harriers to victory in the Kidderminster Weavers' Cup, through a reserve stint at West Brom, to a 13-game Football Alliance record with Walsall. He at least aided Fosse to a respectable 4th-place finish, and scored himself in the club's record Midland League victory, 7-1 over Newark, but was not retained on the expiry of his contract. (Several sources render Edward's surname as Sylvester; the local press in Leicester rather unhelpfully alternated the spellings during his stay).

***Apps:** FAC 4; ML 11.*
***Goals:** ML 1.*

SIMMS, Samuel

b. Atherton, Lancs, Jan qtr 1888
d. Swindon, 25th May 1952

Career: Tyldesley College; cs 1910 Ton Pentre; Atherton; Dec 1912 Everton; June 1913 Swindon Town; June 1914 FOSSE; cs 1919 Swindon Town; June 1921 Gillingham.

Fosse debut v Lincoln City (H) 2.9.14 (scored twice)

> The top scorer for Lancashire Combination Division Two leaders Atherton at the time he signed up at Goodison, Sam became essentially a reserve centre-forward for his first two senior clubs. A debut scorer for Everton, he played but once more in the First Division, and deputised only three times in Swindon's Southern League championship season of 1914. He got off on the right foot for Fosse, but then had to vie with near-namesake Stephen Sims for a regular forward berth (eventually making emergency excursions to left-back and centre-half) in what proved the worst season ever for the club, ending in rock-bottom position and the eve-of-war re-elecion appeal. Having guested briefly for Stockport County alongside Tom Waterall in 1916, Sam retreated to the right-half berth with Swindon and the Gills after the war. He died within sight of his retirement from Swindon Railway Works.

***Apps:** FL 16; FAC 1.*
***Goals:** FL 5.*

SIMPSON, Frank L.

Career: Syston Victoria; Oct 1902-trials-FOSSE; Leicester Imperial; am Aug 1903 FOSSE; Humberstone Victoria; cs 1904 Leicester Imperial; Syston Victoria; Thursday Excelsior; 1905 Melton Mowbray; cs 1907 Leicester Nomads; Wand's United; cs 1909 Hinckley United.

Fosse debut v Burton United (at Derby) FAC 7.12.03

> A local amateur outside-left who had to overcome a dispiriting setback on his club debut – he broke his collarbone in a rough-house reserve match against Whitwick White Cross; an incident that precipitated a near-riot at Filbert Street, and a month's FA suspension for Fosse director Tom Collins on account of his incautious comments and behaviour. Familiarly known as Sandy, he eventually had only a brief brush with the senior game after his bow in a Cup second replay, and was later alongside ex-Fossil Ernest Vickerstaffe in helping found Leicester Nomads as the town's first-class amateur combination. In 1910 he was noted as residing in Exeter, but appears to have had no connection with the Grecians, who by then were a professional outfit.

***Apps:** FL 2; FAC 1.*

SIMPSON, Henry C.

b. Aberdeenshire, ca 1889

Career: Peterhead; Oct 1907 St Bernards; Mar 1910 FOSSE; June 1910 Raith Rovers; Oct 1910 Ayr United (- 1913).

Fosse debut v Oldham Athletic (A) 2.4.10

> A member of St Bernards' 1907/8 Qualifying Cup-winning side, and well experienced in Scottish Second Division football (playing alongside Harry Graham on occasion), Harry joined Fosse as an inside-right partner to Fred Shinton just at the unfortunate point when their efforts to bounce straight back into Division One were beginning to founder, leaving them a frustrated 5th at the end of 1909/10. In fact the tiny forward failed to appear in a winning Fosse side during his brief stay, and returned to Scotland for a fee of £45. His old Edinburgh club were favourites to sign him, but Raith nipped in before quickly passing him on again to Ayr, where success awaited. The Somerset Park outfit were runners-up in the Second Division in 1911, and took the championship in each of the following two campaigns with Harry amongst their leading scorers. Promotion was not then automatic in Scotland, but Ayr did at least find themselves in an extended Division One in 1913.

***Apps:** FL 7.*
***Goals:** FL 1.*

SIMPSON, Thomas

b. Keyworth, Notts, 13th August 1879
d. Oldham, 19th December 1961

Career: Mar 1900 Notts County; Oct 1902 FOSSE; May 1903 Everton; Sept 1904 Nelson.

Fosse debut v Barnsley (A) 18.10.02

> An outside-left who really only came into his own while at Leicester, Tom had totted up only seven First Division appearances in three years for the Magpies prior to his Fosse stint, and would play but one senior game for the Toffees while understudying the noted amateur and England international, Harold Hardman. Yet his left-wing thrusts and his brief scoring burst did much to save Fosse from the embarrassment of a re-election application in 1903 (albeit for only one year), and earned him at least the promise of an elevation from the League's basement to its heights as the object of a deal that landed John Barlow and £175 at Filbert Street. His goal tally with Fosse should have been one higher: for during a 3-1 Fosse win at Burnley in January 1903, his goalbound shot was stopped on the line by a stray dog! Tom, also a Notinghamshire county cricketer, later put down footballing roots in Nelson's Lancashire Combination side for several seasons.

***Apps:** FL 27; FAC 1.*
***Goals:** FL 5.*

SIMS, Stephen

b. Bedminster, Bristol, 11th December 1895
d. Weston-super-Mare, Jan qtr 1973

Career: Bath City; July 1914 FOSSE; July 1919 Bristol Rovers; July 1922 Burnley; July 1924 Weymouth; Sept 1925 Bristol City; Sept 1926 Bristol Rovers' July 1927 Newport County.

Fosse debut v Lincoln City (H) 2.9.14

> A prolific scorer for 1914 Western League runners-up Bath, Stephen unfortunately proved to be another of Louis Ford's signings for the final pre-war League season who could do little to halt the Fosse's dire decline, despite his clear promise as a 19-year-old inside-forward. Going on to serve in the wartime Royal Field Artillery, he played representative football for the BEF (Egypt) XI in 1919, and signed up for what proved to be Bristol Rovers' final season in the Southern League before the formation of Division Three. He skippered them in their opening League game from the centre-forward berth, but soon was playing as often at centre-half, and cost Burnley £2,000 to add him to their First Division fringe squad. Then fading from the senior picture, Stephen was rescued from the Ashton Gate reserves by their Eastville neighbours, who were promptly fined for playing him again without properly re-registering him. After a short stint in Wales, he became a Bristol publican.

***Apps:** FL 11.*
***Goals:** FL 2.*

SIMS, Steven Frank

b. Lincoln, 2nd July 1957

Career: Lincoln United; app Aug 1973/pro July 1974 CITY; Dec 1978 Watford; Sept 1984 Notts County; Oct 1986 Watford; June 1987 Aston Villa; June 1990 Burton Albion; Oct 1990 Lincoln City; Feb 1991-trials-Bournemouth; 1991 Boston FC; 1991 Stafford Rangers; Dec 1991 Shepshed Albion.

City debut v Manchester City (A) 20.8.75

> Like Fred Sharman before him and Russell Osman more recently, Steve was a City centre-half with a footballing father: in his case, Frank, a good Lincoln City clubman for seven

Steve Sims

years in the 50s. After a rapid rise through the City junior ranks, Steve made his League bow as replacement for the injured Jeff Blockley, and established himself during the last year of Jimmy Bloomfield's management as a central defender of some class, whose evident brawn and aerial power were simply highly useful adjuncts to his astute intelligence. He became an England Under-21 regular (ten caps; one goal) and appeared once for England 'B', and even came out of the 1978 relegation farrago with some credit. Yet he didn't last long into the Jock Wallace era. An agreed move to Derby was cancelled in November 1978 on undisclosed 'medical grounds', but only a month later Watford paid £175,000, a then record outlay by a Third Division club, to take him to Vicarage Road, and give him a pivotal role in their meteoric ascent of the League ladder. As an unfussily effective exponent of their long-ball tactics, Steve eventually had two seasons in the top flight with the Hornets (runners-up in 1983), plus a taste of European competition, until transferring to Meadow Lane after a series of injuries. He experienced relegation to the Third with the Magpies at the end of his first term, but was soon reunited with his former manager and mentor, Graham Taylor, both in the First Division with Watford and in Villa's successful 1988 promotion drive. Steve then remained in Birmingham as head of Villa's Football in the Community scheme, and part-timed for various non-league outfits after breaking his jaw five games into a non-contract spell with his hometown Red Imps. In 1994, he joined Coventry's youth coaching staff, and in October 1996 returned to Filbert Street for a four-year stint working as Youth Development Officer alongside David Nish.

Apps: *FL 78+1; FAC 3; LC 5.*
Goals: *FL 3.*

SINCLAIR, Frank Mohammed

b. Lambeth, London, 3rd December 1971

Career: YT/pro May 1990 Chelsea; Dec 1991-loan-West Bromwich Albion; Aug 1998 CITY.

City debut v Manchester United (A) 15.8.98

> A strong, pacy defender who has usually taken the right-sided berth in a City back-three formation, Frank was an eve-of-season buy just over 24 hours before turning out impressively at Old Trafford, costing Martin O'Neill a club record fee rising in instalments from £2.05m to £2.55m. Tough in the challenge both on the floor and in the air, he nonetheless reads the game well, and has developed an admirable degree of defensive consistency. Rising through the ranks as a Chelsea teenager to become a regular at right- or centre-back after 1992, he'd already faced one setback when receiving a lengthy suspension for making contact with a referee while on loan at The Hawthorns, and though he played three times at Wembley for Chelsea, he was gradually marginalised by the massive influx of foreign talent installed at Stamford Bridge by managers Ruud Gullit and Gianluca Vialli. An FA Cup runner-up in 1994 and a winner in 1997, he also tasted victory in the 1998 League Cup Final, but missed out on the European Cup Winners Cup Final months later. Called up by Jamaica before the World Cup Finals of that summer – thereby becoming one of the so-called UB40 element of the Reggae Boyz – Frank figured in all three games they contested in France (and has continued since to collect Caribbean caps). His first City season saw him unfortunate not to score past his old Chelsea mates at Filbert Street, unluckily sent off at Coventry, notching his first goal in the FA Cup win over Birmingham, and then peremptorily dropped from the squad the day before the League Cup Final against Spurs, for a timekeeping breach of club discipline. There would be no sulking from Frank, however, and he would show undiminished commitment throughout the following term of Premiership contention and League Cup triumph; a quality just as evident when he returned from a lengthy injury lay-off partway through 2000/1.

Apps *(to end 2000/1): PL 78+4; FAC 6; LC 14.*
Goals: *PL 1; FAC 1.*

SINCLAIR, Harvey Patrick (Harry)

b. Bournemouth, 30th November 1933

Career: am Bournemouth & Boscombe Athletic; Dec 1950 Fulham; cs 1954 Cambridge United; Aug 1956 CITY; July 1957 Yeovil Town; Aug 1958-trials-Watford; Sept 1958 Bristol Rovers; July 1959 Fulham.

City debut/only game v Grimsby Town (H) 26.1.57

> More familarly known as Harry, this luckless goalkeeper must have been heartily sick of reserve-team football by the time he finished his wanderings. On Fulham's books before and during his National Service, he couldn't even win a regular Eastern Counties League selection at Cambridge. His City break came about when Johnny Anderson cracked his wrist, and days before Dave MacLaren arrived to see out the rest of the 1957 Second Division championship campaign. The 4-3 home win was crucial however, and Harry got a reasonable press after recovering from conceding a John Ogilvie own goal. He played under Jimmy Baldwin's management at Yeovil, and made his second, and last, League appearance for Bristol Rovers, two days after signing for them, in a 2-3 defeat at Derby.

Apps: *FL 1.*

SINCLAIR, John Evens Wright

b. Culross, Fife, 21st July 1943

Career: Blairhall Colliery; cs 1960 Dunfermline Athletic; May 1965 CITY; Dec 1967 Newcastle United; Dec 1969 Sheffield Wednesday; Mar 1973-loan-Chesterfield; cs 1973 Durban (SA); Aug 1973 Dunfermline Athletic; cs 1975 Stenhousemuir.

City debut v Liverpool (H) 21.8.65 (scored once)

> A Jock Stein signing for Dunfermline, where he had Tommy McDonald as an on-field mentor and rival, Jackie was a nippy, goalscoring winger who had already come close to glory in both European competition and the 1965 Scottish Cup Final when Matt Gillies brought him to Filbert Street for £25,000 to forge an instantly successful little-and-large striking partnership with Derek Dougan. The adjective 'dynamic' seemed coined for Jackie as he adapted his killing pace and shooting instincts to service on either flank, and it was no surprise that he won a full Scotland cap at the end of his first City season (making up for the disappointment of having been chosen for a postponed Scottish League representative game while with the Pars). After two years in the First Division, Jackie was still bettering the classic striker's average of a goal-every-other-game, and indicating moreover that he really knew when to cross and when to cut inside. And if his scoring ratio dropped slightly during 1967/8, there was every sign of him being jettisoned with undue haste at the wave of a Newcastle cheque for £67,500. He met less overall success on Tyneside, despite contributing crucially to the Geordies' 1969 Fairs Cup triumph, and was eventually exchanged for Sheffield Wednesday's David Ford, linking up again at Hillsborough with former City teammate Peter Rodrigues. Later Jackie found his way back to East End Park, and ended his senior career at Ochilview with an aggregate of 115 League goals from both sides of the border. His older brother Willie played for Falkirk, Huddersfield, Tranmere and Halifax; his uncle was Tommy Wright, Sunderland's Scottish international of the 50s; his cousin was City's 90s winger, Tommy Wright; and his son Chris played for Dunfermline in the Scottish League Cup Final of October 1991. In the late 90s, Jackie himself was assistant steward at Dunfermline Golf Club.

Apps: *FL 103; FAC 5; LC 5.*
Goals: *FL 50; FAC 2; LC 1.*

SJOBERG, John

b. Aberdeen, 12th June 1941

Career: Banks O'Dee; Aug 1958 CITY; June 1973 Rotherham United.

City debut v Cardiff City (A) 28.10.60

> A teenage centre-half when he followed Jack Lornie's route to Filbert Street, John made his initial impact for City's first team as a right-back, eventually taking over from Len Chalmers just prior to the start of the 1963 Cup run, and climaxing his first season as a regular choice with a Wembley appearance against Manchester United. He was a stalwart of the League Cup campaigns of the next two years (scoring the decisive semi-final goal at Home Park in 1965), and was still shuttling between the No 2 and No 5 berths with effective ease until the arrival of Peter Rodrigues to hold down the former position. Barring an unluckily aberrant performance at West Brom in April 1966, when he became the only Leicester player ever to score two own goals in one game, John settled thereafter to a memorable central defensive partnership with Graham Cross, displaying a craggy consistency and imposing his aerial mastery on many a First Division game. This quality tempted Matt Gillies into giving him one spell at centre-forward during 1967/8, but John's back-four abilities were more vital to City's strength and shape, and it was notable that the club's 1969 relegation occurred in a season when niggling injuries severely limited his appearances, and indeed kept him out of the FA Cup Final line-up after he failed a fitness test. Two years later, he was a key member of the defensively miserly Second Division championship side, and took his testimonial game against Derby after the title had been secured, attracting a best-ever Filbert Street crowd for such an event of around 24,000. During his latter Leicester days, he had started a printing business, and it was to this that John returned after a very brief spell of six Division Four starts (plus a scoring League Cup outing) at Millmoor.

Apps: *FL 334+1; FAC 44; LC 34.*
Goals: *FL 15; FAC 1; LC 3.*

SKEA, David Frederick

b. Arbroath, 1871

Career: 1888 Arbroath; cs 1892 Aston Villa; Apr 1893 Dundee Thistle; July 1893 Darwen; Dec 1893 Bury; Aug 1894 FOSSE; cs 1896 Swindon Town; Dec 1896 New Brompton; cs 1898 Cowes.

Fosse debut v Grimsby Town (A) 1.9.1894 (scored twice)

> A skilful hotshot of an inside-left to whom a number of the club's Football League 'firsts' attach, David notched Fosse's initial goal in the competition, and claimed each of the first hat-tricks and successful penalties for Leicester at this level. Unsurprisingly his marksmanship granted him the honour of being the Fosse's first seasonal top scorer (with a creditable 23 goals from a maximum 30 games), and his tally stood as a record until Fred Shinton's goal-rush in 1909/10. In addition, his feat of scoring in each of the first four fixtures of the campaign has never been beaten, even if equalled by Frank Middleton (1906/7), Tommy Benfield (1913/14), Mike Stringfellow (1962/3) and Andy Lochhead (1969/70). Clearly, David suffered closer attention from Second Division defences in his second term, and his goal rate dropped accordingly; but that he could still accept limited opportunities with a rare alacrity was indexed by his subsequent record with Swindon, where he netted five goals in six starts before being dismissed when arriving for training 'in an intoxicated condition'. He continued his Southern League wanderings at New Brompton and Cowes, who headed the Second Division of that sphere in 1899, but lost out on promotion in a Test Match. David's original bow in English football (after an international trial during 1890/1) had been a scoring one, but one game and one goal represented the full extent of his senior Villa career, and a single First Division outing for Darwen was his injury-hit lot there. He proved his fitness at Bury, though, with seven goals in nine games contributing to their runners-up placing in the Lancashire League.

Apps: *FL 45; FAC 7.*
Goals: *FL 29; FAC 8.*

SLACK, Alfred

b. ca 1871

Career: Mansfield Greenhalgh's; cs 1890 Mansfield Town; cs 1892 FOSSE; 1894 not known; Sept 1897 Mansfield Wesleyans.

Fosse debut v Mansfield Town (A) ML 17.9.1892

> Fosse's top-scoring, ever-present centre-forward during 1892/3, but an irregular reserve the following season, Alf claimed the club's first Midland League hat-trick, during the 7-1 demolition of Newark which constituted the best win in that competition. His second personal triple came in the 6-0 win over Derby Junction that same season which was later declared void (the scheduled away fixture having been played at Filbert Street), and was thus stricken from the record. The original Mansfield Town club, from whom he joined Fosse and against whom he made his debut, had headed the Nottinghamshire League in 1891 and finished as Midland Alliance runners-up in 1892 with Alf in their side, and he had also taken two winner's medals from the Mansfield Charity Cup; while the Wesleyans team for whom he scored in their inaugural game were the actual forerunners of today's Mansfield Town club. Alf's hat-trick propensity also followed him into representative football – he netted half of Leicestershire's goals in the 6-1 win over Northants in January 1894.

Apps: *FAC 4; ML 26.*
Goals: *FAC 1; ML 11.*

SLACK, Rodney

b. Farcet, nr Peterborough, 11th April 1940

Career: Fletton YC; Sept 1958 CITY; Mar 1961 Queens Park Rangers; July 1962 Cambridge United; 1970 Soham Town; 1971 Bury Town; Histon.

City debut v Mansfield Town (H) LC 12.10.60

> The occasion of City's first-ever League Cup tie was almost a major embarrassment: both Gordon Banks and George Heyes were ruled out by injury, and third-teamer Rodney was himself undergoing treatment for a dislocated finger, so when Matt Gillies announced his line-up a day before

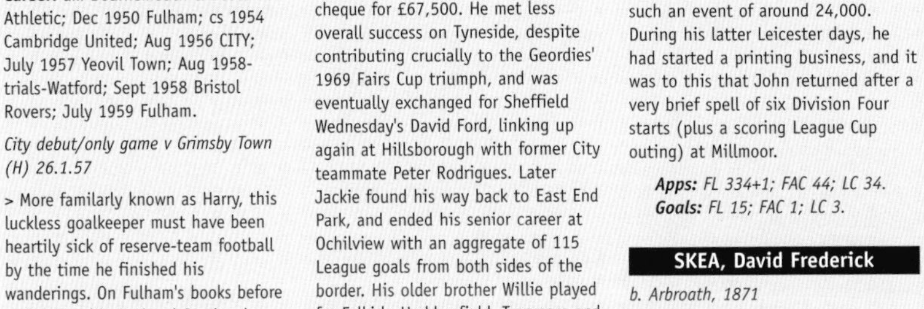

'Harry' Sinclair

Rodney Slack

the game, the goalkeeping spot was given as being a last-minute choice between Rodney and centre-half Tony Knapp. Luckily the young specialist declared himself fit enough, and kept a clean sheet against the Stags in what would prove his only senior start. In fact, he'd actually managed a shut-out, too, a year previously against Charlton Athletic, in the club's initial game in the Southern Professional Floodlit Cup – an invitational forerunner of the League Cup in which City played but one term, going out at the second hurdle at Highbury. Rodney's spell with QPR resulted in only one League appearance (in a 1-1 draw at Halifax), but he served Cambridge consistently well in their Southern League battles. Runners-up in 1963, they took the Cup in 1965, the Double in 1969, and the championship again a year later; and Rodney finally left them on the eve of their election to the League.

Apps: *LC 1.*

SMALL, Peter Victor

b. Horsham, Sussex, 23rd October 1924

Career: Army football; Troisdorf; Neumunster; Horsham Town; Aug 1947 Luton Town; Mar 1950 CITY; Sept 1954 Nottingham Forest; July 1957 Brighton & Hove Albion.

City debut v Sheffield United (A) 18.3.50

> Serving with the RASC in Germany at the end of the war, Peter exercised his flourishing football skills with a couple of local sides, and returned home for a rapid elevation to Division Two fare at Kenilworth Road. Nicknamed 'The Horsham Flier', he was a compact, strong and pacy winger who faced City in the epic high-scoring Cup ties of 1949, and cost Norman Bullock a £6,000 fee to install him as a reliable deputy to the evergreen Mal Griffiths. It was only during the 1954 promotion season, when he starred mainly on the left flank and contributed the bulk of his City goals, that he was finally able to make a substantial breakthrough, and even this run was curtailed by the pressing claims of young Derek Hogg. Peter was somewhat luckier in his three years on Trentside (87 appearances; 20 goals), and was a valuable squad member for Forest when they accompanied City back into the First Division in 1957. The following term, as a Billy Lane signing, he contributed three goals in eight outings towards Brighton's Division Three championship-winning effort, and for a while remained at the Goldstone Ground on the coaching staff. Living in retirement in Elsworth, Cambridgeshire, Peter was sadly stricken with Parkinson's Disease in the late 90s.

Apps: *FL 65; FAC 7.*
Goals: *FL 16; FAC 4.*

SMITH, Alan Martin

b. Birmingham, 21st November 1962

Career: 1980 Alvechurch; June 1982 CITY; May 1987 Arsenal.

City debut v Charlton Athletic (H) 28.8.82

> Capped by England at semi-pro level while playing as a left-sided striker for Alvechurch's successful Southern League side (Midland Division champions in 1981), Alan became the final signing of the Jock Wallace era at City, and a bargain inheritance for Gordon Milne, who immediately paired the tall, elegant striker with Gary Lineker. Though the latter initially hogged the headlines for his scoring exploits as City returned to the First Division and set about their battle for consolidation, Alan soon proved an unselfish foil, creating numerous chances with his excellent ball control and vision, and snapping up a fair quotient himself. Displaying a rare combination of stylishness and ready willingness to chase and harry, and posing an effective striking threat both in the air and on the ground, Alan also stood out for that even rarer commodity of sportsmanship: for while neither his bravery nor commitment could be questioned, his record of a single booking over five seasons was positively remarkable in a context of so much 'professional' niggling. On Lineker's departure, Alan determinedly shouldered the responsibility as City's primary goalgetter, and after he finally shrugged off his reputation as a sluggish seasonal starter in 1986/7, there was as much inevitability in the upsurge of million-pound transfer rumours as there was credit in the player's modestly-expressed desire to honour his Leicester contract. Indeed, when his £800,000 move to Highbury was finally negotiated in March 1987, he agreed on an instant loan-back to Leicester, to aid their eventually futile fight to stay in the top rank. This was the spell which ironically and confusingly saw him facing his new club for his old as an introduction to his new fans. Alan's initial season with the Gunners brought mixed fortunes under intense critical scrutiny, though he scored one of their consolation goals in the Littlewoods Cup Final of 1988 and finished as their leading marksman; but it was his goal-burst at the start of 1988/9 which fully established him as a Highbury favourite and elevated him into the England squad. His first cap heralded a brief international renewal of his old Filbert Street partnership with Lineker; and he closed the term by scoring one goal and making the other in the dramatic Anfield title decider, which gave Arsenal the championship by the narrowest of margins. His 23 First Division strikes also earned Alan the Golden Boot for 1989. He similarly led the Highbury scoring list in the 1991 championship triumph; with England again was noted as the innocent party in the controversy surrounding Lineker's final international substitution; shared in Arsenal's 1993 FA Cup win; and then volleyed the winning goal in the 1994 European Cup Winners Cup Final against Parma. A knee injury wrecked his 1994/5 campaign, and medical advice sadly led to his retirement, at the age of only 32, in July 1995; at a point where he had amassed an aggregate total of 199 League and Cup goals, plus two for England and four for England 'B'. St Albans City tried to tempt him into part-time action but, his Highbury benefit match against Sampdoria aside, he has subsequently concentrated on a career in journalism and media punditry.

Apps: *FL 190+10; FAC 8; LC 8+1.*
Goals: *FL 76; FAC 4; LC 4.*

SMITH, Arthur Eric

b. Whetstone, Leics, 5th September 1921

Career: Whetstone Athletic; am 1939 Wolverhampton Wanderers; am Nov 1940/pro Feb 1941 CITY; June 1948 West Bromwich Albion; Aug 1952 Plymouth Argyle; June 1954 Crewe Alexandra.

City debut (WW2) v Walsall (H) 30.11.40; (postwar) v Brentford (A) FAC 25.1.47

> Four of the seven Smith brothers of Whetstone were associated with City, though only Arthur made it as far as the League XI. (Jack and Ken were both reserves – the former going on to become a long-term Northampton Town stalwart – while Ray was for a while on the amateur roster). City were in fact fined for fielding the local inside-left for his wartime debut, as his amateur registration was still nominally held by the then-inoperative Wolves, but he went on to impress with some convincingly crafty and prolific performances in regional fare, and added experience with both Linfield and Derry City while stationed in Ireland as a PT instructor with the Royal Inniskilling Fusiliers. Less happily, Arthur broke his jaw in three places while playing for Derry against Glentoran on Christmas Day 1943. Demobbed in November 1946, he created a minor embarrassment for City, who'd forgotten to re-register him as their player, but was soon to start his senior career with a probably unique run: he figured in four FA Cup ties before his League bow. Arthur nonetheless found his first-team chances limited by the partnership of George Dewis and Jack Lee, and his winning goal for the reserves in the 1948 Combination Cup Final provided possibly the highlight of his Filbert Street career. At The Hawthorns, a rather delicate situation ensued: Arthur had to vie with Jack Haines for a place in the starting line-up at the same time he was lodging with the ex-City man and his family! He briefly contributed to the Throstles' 1949 promotion campaign, and played three seasons in the top flight before closing his League days at Home Park and Gresty Road.

Apps: *FL 17; FAC 5; WW2 74.*
Goals: *FL 3; FAC 2; WW2 32.*

SMITH, Arthur Hoyle

b. Bury, 8th May 1915

Career: Bury Co-Op FC; May 1934 Bury; May 1938 CITY.

City debut v Stoke City (H) 27.8.38

> A right-winger signed on a free transfer on the eve of the final pre-war League season, Arthur soon lost his place to newcomer Mal Griffiths, and barely got a look-in thereafter. He claimed two goals in the opening match of 1939/40, but promptly 'lost' them from official records when that campaign was abandoned, and very soon he disappeared from senior football entirely, with City frankly admitting in 1942 that they had no idea of his whereabouts; a position they were still in when they formally freed him in 1946. Arthur had previously won only four Second Division selections at Gigg Lane in the first season after his teenage signing, and had scored for Bury in the 1935 Final of the Lancashire Senior Cup.

Apps: *FL 8; WW2 2.*
Goals: *WW2 2.*

SMITH, Dean

b. Leicester, 28th November 1958

Career: app Apr 1975/pro Dec 1976 CITY; Apr 1978-loan-Houston Hurricane; Oct 1978 Brentford; Feb 1981 Nuneaton Borough; 1982 Enderby Town/Leicester United; Feb

Dean Smith

1984 Corby Town; Shepshed Charterhouse; St Andrews; Aug 1990 Houghton Rangers; 1992 Lutterworth Town; Hinckley Town; Thurnby Rangers; Oadby Town.

City debut v Everton (H) 10.9.77 (sub)

> Along with Derek Dawkins, Nev Hamilton and Kevin Farmer, Dean was another of the City teenagers unlucky enough to be thrown into the deep mire of the 1977/8 relegation farce, and then find themselves at odds with, or superfluous to the plans of, incoming manager Jock Wallace. Dean was a strong, combative and mobile striker who got off the scoring mark in a home defeat by Manchester United, and netted six times in his NASL summer with Houston (in company with Peter Welsh). But his high promise seemed to dissipate after a £20,000 move to Griffin Park and two-and-a-half seasons of Third Division football with the Bees, which brought him a 15-goal haul from 54 League games (many played alongside Pat Kruse); and he returned to become a stalwart of the Leicestershire and district non-league arena.

Apps: *FL 8+2.*
Goals: *FL 1.*

SMITH, Eric Thomas Henry

b. Tamworth, Staffs, 3rd November 1921

Career: Castle Bromwich; am 1942/pro 1945 CITY; Jan 1947 Bath City.

City debut (WW2) v Newport County (A) 3.11.45; (postwar) v Manchester City (H) 31.8.46

> A centre-half whose promise, shown during the transitional season of 1945/6, tempted City into releasing Frank Sheard on the resumption of peacetime football. Eric held the No 5 berth for the initial postwar quintet of Second Division fixtures, but soon followed the equally disappointing Dave McCulloch to Bath. A year before his City debut, Eric had been loaned to a short-handed Walsall for a Filbert Street encounter.

Apps: *FL 5; WW2 13.*

SMITH, George H.

b. Sheffield, 2nd September 1872

Career: Westminster Amateurs (Nott'm); Mapperley; Sneinton Institute; Bulwell; Hinckley Athletic; Dec 1892 FOSSE; Aug 1895-trials-Preston North End; Aug 1895 Ilkeston Town.

Fosse debut v Grantham Rovers (H) ML 26.11.1892

> A sure-footed stalwart right-back for Fosse in the last two Midland League seasons, plus the initial campaign in the Second Division, George failed to earn a Deepdale contract after his release (perhaps mercifully for Preston historians, as North End already had three Smiths in their senior line-up), and returned to Midland League fare. For some unfathomable reason, his first Fosse appearance saw him adopting the pseudonym 'Thompson': surely one of very few instances of a man named Smith seeking anonymity!

Apps: *FL 24; FAC 12; ML 36.*

SMITH, Harry

Career: Worcester Rovers; Dec 1887 Kidderminster Olympic; cs 1890 Kidderminster FC; cs 1891 Kidderminster Harriers; cs 1893 Berwick Rangers; Aug 1897:FOSSE; cs 1898 Bedminster (p/mgr).

Fosse debut v Luton Town (H) 4.9.1897

> Harry led the Fosse attack during the early stages of 1897/8 without conspicuous success, after joining as a veteran from the Birmingham & District League club who would later become Worcester City (i.e. not the current Scottish League club of that name). Elevated to team management at his subsequent Southern League club, he decided against picking himself for any senior game with the Bristol-based outfit.

Apps: *FL 15.*
Goals: *FL 4.*

SMITH, Isaac

b. Wednesbury, Staffs

Career: Wednesbury Old Athletic; Darlaston; Oldbury Town; June 1919 CITY.

City debut (WW1) v Notts County (H) 22.3.19; (postwar) v Wolverhampton Wanderers (H) 30.8.19

> A young left-half who failed to live up to the demands of post-WW1 League football, Ike at least makes the record books as a member of Leicester City's first side to play under that title. He had previously featured in half a dozen wartime games for Fosse during 1918/19, when so much of the club's player recruitment drive was focused on the West Midlands.

Apps: *FL 2; WW1 6.*

SMITH, Richard Geoffrey

b. Lutterworth, Leics, 3rd October 1970

Career: Oadby Town; YT 1987/pro Dec 1988 CITY; Sept 1989-loan-Cambridge United; Dec 1990-loan-Nuneaton Borough; Sept 1995-loan-Grimsby Town; Mar 1996 Grimsby Town.

City debut v Oldham Athletic 3.4.90 (sub)

> Before the emergence of Emile Heskey in the second half of the decade, Richard was one of very few locally-born players to have held anything like a regular senior spot with City during the 90s. Nonetheless, he had to endure an anxious wait before getting the opportunity to consolidate his promise. The centre-back got a League bow while on loan with Cambridge, then sat for a long time unused on the City bench, and it took ten months and an interim spell of Southern League action to elapse between his first substitute appearance and his first start – in the home defeat by Blackburn that proved to be David Pleat's last in charge at Leicester! Gordon Lee barely called on Richard at all, but Brian Little eased the tall defender into regular contention, and he responded with some classy performances under pressure. He hit his first (ands so far only) League goal just after Christmas 1991, and precisely seven days later volleyed home from long range at the far post the late winner against Crystal Palace which secured for City their first FA Cup victory in seven years. Richard missed only two games in 1992/3; took over Tony James' long-throw role; did a stint as stand-in goalkeeper for the injured Carl Muggleton in a crucial home win over

Oxford; and was in the Wembley side which suffered Play-Off frustration at the hands of Swindon Town. Injuries then cut severely into Richard's progress, and his senior breaks became more intermittent as his pace and concentration seemed to slip a notch. Occasional excursions to full-back did little to build or inspire confidence, and Richard failed to impress either Mark McGhee or Martin O'Neill, who gave him two outings between his temporary and permanent moves to Blundell Park. A £50,000 fee landed him in a Grimsby side relegated from Division One in 1997, and he missed the ensuing promotion year entirely owing to an achilles injury before returning successfully to the Mariners' line-up.

Apps: *FL/PL 82+16; FAC 6; LC 4; FMC 5; AIC 4; PO 3.*
Goals: *FL 1; FAC 1.*

SMITH, Robert Nisbet

b. Dalkeith, Midlothian, 21st December 1953

Career: Musselburgh Victoria; 1970 Hibernian; Dec 1978 CITY; Feb 1982-loan-Peterborough United; Nov 1982-loan-Hibernian; Oct 1986 Hibernian; Sept 1987 Dunfermline Athletic; cs 1989 Partick Thistle; Aug 1990 Berwick Rangers.

City debut v Oldham Athletic (H) 1.1.79 (scored once)

> Basically an attacking midfielder, Bobby had proven his versatility at Easter Road by leading Hibs' seasonal scoring list and then converting to left-back in the course of a year, and Jock Wallace chased his signature for some six months before an £85,000 deal was struck, in time for Bobby to share a New Year's Day League bow with Gary Lineker and David Buchanan. He settled well at Filbert Street as an aggressive prompter, opportunist and penalty expert, and was second-top scorer in the 1980 promotion campaign. Yet a lean spell followed, when City seemed willing to offload Bobby at the end of either of his loan-outs, and it was at full-back that he surprisingly re-established himself, contributing to the 1983 promotion effort, and holding his place in Gordon Milne's First Division line-ups for much of the next three seasons. Eventually, another Easter Road loan did lead to Bobby rejoining his first club on a free transfer; though Hibs pocketed a decent fee when he shifted Premier Division bases. Dunfermline made a presentation to Bobby midway through their 1988/9 promotion season to mark his 500th senior game, and he raised that tally by 66 before retiring from Berwick to run a pub back in Dalkeith.

Apps: *FL 175+6; FAC 10; LC 8+1.*
Goals: *FL 21; FAC 1.*

SMITH, Septimus Charles

b. Whitburn, Co Durham, 13th March 1912

Career: Whitburn; am 1928/pro Apr 1929 CITY (- 1949).

City debut v Huddersfield Town (A) 31.8.29

> Still many veteran followers' notion of the best all-round City player ever, Sep was unarguably one of the club's most loyal servants, ending his magnificent twenty-year playing span with an all-too-brief spell as coach. As his name implies, he was the seventh son of a fanatical footballing family, of whom five played at League level; with Tom also turning out for Leicester, Joe moving from City reserves to Watford, and Jack and Willie both spending the bulk of lengthy careers at Portsmouth. In fact, Sep would face the latter pair of siblings in the 1934 FA Cup semi-final at St Andrews, while Jack would precede him into the England team. Sep himself was first noticed on the national stage, starring for England Schoolboys in 1926 after playing in the North/South trial at Filbert Street in March of that year, and was eagerly snapped up at the age of 16 by Willie Orr as a creative inside-forward. His debut was somewhat premature, with the local press deeming him 'unable to pull his weight' when he covered for a sick Arthur Lochhead, but, as he filled out, he was soon exhibiting a fair poaching prowess to supplement his cool distributive skills, and top-scored for the reserves in 1930/1, with 19 London Combination goals to add to his pair of First Division counters. Yet it would be in a deeper, right-half role that he would truly blossom during the club's turbulent times of the mid-30s, and provide the energy that his ageing teammates of that time could no longer supply in such measure. The widespread respect afforded Sep was not, however, reflected in the derisory-looking tally of representative honours he accrued: only one full cap, one appearance as second-half substitute in the 1935 Jubilee international against Scotland, and one game for the Football League. There was a sign here that his versatility may have militated against better recognition, for two years later, during 1937/8, Sep was named as travelling reserve for representative sides on no less than five occasions (twice for the Football League, once for the international trial, and twice more for full internationals). For club honours, too, Sep had to make do with only meagre reward for his inspirational captaincy, by way of a Second Division championship medal in 1937. He managed a City appearance record during WW2 that was second only to Willie Frame's, despite sitting out a year's suspension, and was still holding together City's postwar efforts as a veritable veteran of a pivot. Indeed, having taken the likes of young Don Revie under his tutelary wing, and aided Johnny Duncan's tactical preparations for City's 1949 Wembley run, he was many fans' choice to take Revie's place in the FA Cup Final – a move that would have obviated the need to shift Jack Lee from the spearhead role, and gamble on full-back Jimmy Harrison at No 9. As it was, he saved his last on-field hurrah for the crucially drawn last-match tussle at Cardiff. Duncan was happy to keep Sep on the backroom staff for 1949/50, and a testimonial fund was opened that year which brought him about £2,100, but after Norman Bullock had taken over the manager's job, Sep's ties with Filbert Street were somewhat brutally severed.

Apps: *FL 350; FAC 23; WW2 213.*
Goals: *FL 35; FAC 2; WW2 48.*

Sep Smith

SMITH, Thomas Gable

b. Whitburn, Co Durham, 18th October 1900
d. Whitburn, 21st February 1934

Career: Marsden Villa; Whitburn; May 1919 South Shields; Dec 1919 CITY; Jan 1924 Manchester United; June 1927 Northampton Town; May 1930 Norwich City; Feb 1931 Whitburn.

City debut v Stoke (H) 20.12.19

> Another of the Whitburn clan of footballing Smiths, Tom was the first on the Filbert Street scene, and the first to sew confusion about his record: being signed by Peter Hodge from South Shields a matter of days after that club had beaten City with goals from brother Jack and the wholly unrelated George Smith, but not himself having featured at senior level for the Tyneside club. Essentially an inside-forward – 'a nice blend of the clever and the forceful' – Tom's attacking versatility ironically militated against him holding down a regular first team berth with City across the first five postwar seasons. Nicknamed 'Tosser', he turned out in each of the forward positions except outside-left as City sought a promotion-worthy blend, yet he had to move to Old Trafford to win a rise in status, as United accompanied City out of the lower sphere in 1925. Indeed, Tom's United debut in the inside-right slot he held for 83 League matches (scoring 12 goals) was against City; and he also appeared in that berth in the all-Mancunian FA Cup semi-final of 1926. Then, in his first term as a Cobbler, he experienced the frustration of a runners-up campaign in Division Three (South), and eventually finished his League career with a single game at Norwich. At this time he maintained an interest in a dairy business in Manchester. It was widely (but erroneously) credited in Leicester that it had been during the reception following a Northampton v City friendly in 1929 that Tom had 'sold' Willie Orr on the idea of signing young Sep – who actually put his name to professional forms a few weeks earlier – but at least he was able to see the 'babe' of the family become a First Division regular before his own tragically early death. Tom also had a few outings for Durham in Minor Counties cricket. (There is a still unconfirmed possibility that Tom also had one WW1 outing at right-back for Fosse, as we believe that he was at one stage stationed at Clipstone Camp near Mansfield, the town stated to be the base of a January 1919 guest player initialled T Smith).

Apps: *FL 72; FAC 9.*
Goals: *FL 12; FAC 3.*

SMITH, Wallace

b. Allerton, Yorks, 1883
d. Worksop, Notts, 3rd July 1917

Career: Rothwell; 1901 Kettering Town; cs 1904 Northampton Town; May 1905 Bradford City; Jan 1909 FOSSE; Mar 1909 Hull City; cs 1912 Worksop Town.

Fosse debut v Bristol City (A) 9.1.09

> The first of six Leicester forwards to cost club record fees either before or during relegation seasons (Andy Graver, Allan Clarke, Roger Davies, Steve Moran and Mark Draper would follow), Wally was a £625 flop for Fosse. His failure either to shine or to score in his stay of under two months, however, was uncharacteristic – even if it extended a barren First Division sequence to 21 games – and Hull were convinced they'd got a bargain when he rapidly moved on for £500. Wally's initial senior experience had come in the Southern League with two Northamptonshire clubs (he faced Fosse in the 1904/5 FA Cup tie against the Cobblers), but his most consistent goal-poaching days would come in the Second Division, as instanced by his hat-trick against Fosse in March 1906. He won a championship medal with the Bantams in 1908, when they just pipped Fosse for the title, and after featuring in each of the inside- and centre-forward positions with Fosse in five defeats and a scoreless draw, picked up his goal habit again at Hull, where injury curtailed his stay in early 1912. He still made one further Filbert Street appearance, though: as emergency linesman for the first half of the Fosse v Hull fixture of March 1912, when the appointed whistler arrived late. Wally had become a Worksop licensee when he died, aged only 33.

Apps: *FL 5; FAC 1.*

SMITH, Walter Ernest

b. Leicester, 25th March 1884
d. Melton Mowbray, Leics, 6th February 1972

Career: Shaftesbury SS; Forest Rovers; 1899 Crafton Swifts; cs 1903 Leicester Imperial; am Feb 1904/pro May 1904 FOSSE; May 1906 Manchester City; Oct 1920 Port Vale; cs 1922 Plymouth Argyle; Jan 1923 Grimsby Town.

Fosse debut v Bristol City (H) 25.2.04

> The first of Leicester's star-quality goalkeepers to be generally recognised as such, Walter joined Fosse as an amateur when they were at their lowest ebb in playing terms, but signed professional forms even before the result of the re-election vote was known, and substantially helped restore defensive confidence to lift them quite a few notches up the Second Division table over the next two years. Rapidly gaining repute as the Division's best 'keeper for his agility and resilience – with his lack of height (5ft 8ins) proving no handicap, but his hefty frame presenting an awkward barrier to rampaging, charge-happy forwards – he missed only three games as a Fosse pro, and saved two penalties at Anfield during Fosse's 1906 FA Cup exit (when Billy Bannister also missed a spot-kick during the 1-2 defeat). His departure for top-flight fare at Hyde Road, for a record £600, caused uproar in Leicester, and chairman WH Squires had to read to a public meeting the letter from the bank demanding that the Fosse board accept Manchester City's offer, in order to reduce the club's overdraft. For the Mancunians, Walter totted up 233 League games (all but three in the First Division), while being noted in 1907 by the *Athletic News* as 'the only first-class goalkeeper in the country who disdains training' – preferring to develop his Leicester plumbing business. He was honoured for the Football League against the Scottish League in 1915, but the war robbed him of his chance of a full cap, and also saw him guesting for Fosse and Fulham. Though only a reserve at Plymouth, he was still exhibiting a clean pair of hands at Grimsby when aged 39. There was only one (temporary) blot on Walter's record: he was actually arrested on the very morning of his Port Vale debut at South Shields, accused of indecently assaulting a chambermaid at the town's Regent Hotel, then bailed in time to play, nervily, in front of a crowd augmented by a watching detective! He was acquitted by a jury at Durham Assizes soon afterwards. Something of an all-round sportsman himself (a schoolboy rugby star, and a wicket-keeper for both Leicester Temperance CC and the County seconds), this non-smoking tee-totaller had a son, Walter Alfred, who captained Combined Universities at both rugby and cricket, also played both sports for Leicestershire, and regularly featured in the Tigers XV.

Apps: *FL 79; FAC 8; WW1 24.*

SOO, Frank [Hong Soo]

b. Buxton, Derbyshire, 8th March 1914
d. Cheadle, Cheshire, 25th January 1991

Career: West Derby BC; 1932 Prescot Cables; Jan 1933 Stoke City; Sept 1945 CITY; July 1946 Luton Town; Aug 1948 Chelmsford City.

City debut (WW2) v Plymouth Argyle (H) 29.9.45; (postwar) v Chelsea (A) FAC 5.1.46

> The first player of Chinese extraction to play League football when he made his First Division breakthrough with Stoke, Frank was a son of a laundryman (based in Liverpool from 1918) and an English mother. A midfield ball-artist whose skills both complemented and contrasted with those of his great pre-war teammate, Stanley Matthews, he was on the verge of full international recognition in 1939. In fact, he won a total of eight wartime and Victory caps for England, the last (against Wales in October 1945) being gained shortly after he signed for an all-too-brief spell on City's books. Frank also played in numerous RAF and FA representative games during WW2, and guested for each of Newcastle, Blackburn, Everton, Millwall, Chelsea, Brentford, Reading, Shrewsbury, Port Vale, Crewe, and Burnley, but it was to join his former Stoke boss Tom Mather that he accepted a £4,600 move to less fashionable City a few games into the transitional postwar campaign. Frank impressed City supporters immensely with his craft and trickery at either left-half or inside-left, but RAF duties and representative calls (and an unsanctioned guest outing for Port Vale) cut into his availability, and he failed to settle to the prospect of a

Frank Soo (left) with Sep Smith

new regime after Mather left, so the club rather gratefully recouped £3,000 of its outlay in banking Luton's cheque for his services. After two Second Division terms at Kenilworth Road, and a Southern League runners-up season with Chelmsford in 1949, Frank spent much time coaching abroad, but spiced his travels with spells as manager of both Scunthorpe United (1959-60) and St Albans City. In Italy, he was with Padova; in Sweden with Eskilstunas, Örebro, Djurgårdens, Oddevold, Köpings IS, AIK, IFK and Hoganas; in Denmark with AB København amongst others; and in 1963 had charge of the Israeli national side. His younger brother Ken was a forward with Sutton Town in the Central Alliance, and a Portsmouth trialist in February 1952.

Apps: *FAC 2; WW2 14.*
Goals: *WW2 3.*

SPARROW, F. Henry

b. Faversham, Kent, 13th June 1889
d. Dunholme, Lincs, 13th June 1973 (?)

Career: Faversham Thursday; Dec 1909 Portsmouth; Oct 1910 Sittingbourne; Oct 1911 Croydon Common; Feb 1912 FOSSE; Jan 1914 Tottenham Hotspur; cs 1919 Margate.

Fosse debut v Bristol City (A) 10.2.12 (scored once)

> 'Has an excellent idea where the net lies'. Harry actually failed to follow this idea through while with Pompey, for whom he remained scoreless after five Southern League outings, but clearly earned the encomium later. He aligned his sights in the Kent League, with a 37-goal campaign for Sittingbourne, and then continued to show eager marksmanship with Jack Bartlett's Croydon Common. He was Cup-tied when Fosse met the latter in 1912, but nonetheless switched clubs for £90 immediately afterwards, while, ironically, he would eventually leave Leicester, along with Tommy Clay, to join Spurs the day after they'd secured a Cup replay win over Fosse. Bartlett reunited with Harry at Filbert Street only a month after selling him, and oversaw his immediate rise to the top of the Fosse scoring chart. Harry maintained an excellent goal ratio in a struggling side, linking well with Fred Osborn, until whisked off to White Hart Lane, where he got fewer First Division chances to shine despite a two-goal debut. Two days after Harry's Fosse debut, noted above, he scored all four goals in a friendly at Merthyr.

Apps: *FL 48; FAC 3.*
Goals: *FL 29.*

SPEARING, Anthony

b. Romford, Essex, 7th October 1964

Career: Oulton Broad Eagles; app/pro Oct 1982 Norwich City; Nov 1984-loan-Stoke City; Feb 1985-loan-Oxford United; July 1988 CITY; June 1991 Plymouth Argyle; Jan 1993 Peterborough United; cs 1997 King's Lynn.

City debut v West Bromwich Albion (H) 27.8.88

> A former England Youth skipper and a graduate of Norwich's 1983 FA Youth Cup win, Tony had become a Carrow Road regular at left-back in the First Division (despite a debut own goal, and a broken leg suffered shortly afterwards), and surprised many observers when electing to step down a grade to join City for £100,000 and challenge Simon Morgan for the No 3 shirt. Initially exhibiting tenacious tackling and jockeying skills, and an infectious cheeriness, he became a regular choice for one season only, after which injuries, inconsistencies and occasional impetuosity saw him follow a stop-start course across two more years of lowly Second Division football. Indeed, David Pleat put him on the open-to-offers list at the end of the 1988/9 campaign, only to reinstate him later that summer. But a year on there was no new contract forthcoming from the club, and Tony moved to Home Park as a free agent. He then suffered relegation campaigns with Plymouth in 1992 and Posh in 1994, but had notched up over 300 League outings in total by the time he left London Road. Tony had a brief stint as player/manager at King's Lynn from the start of 1998/9, bridging the gap between the regimes of Peter Morris and Gary Mills; continued to play under the latter; and assumed the reins again midway through 2000/1.

Apps: *FL 71+2; FAC 1; LC 2+1; FMC 2.*
Goals: *FL 1.*

SPEEDIE, David Robert

b. Glenrothes, Fife, 20th February 1960

Career: app July 1977/pro Feb 1978 Barnsley; June 1980 Darlington; June 1982 Chelsea; July 1987 Coventry City; Feb 1991 Liverpool; Aug 1991 Blackburn Rovers; July 1992 Southampton; Oct 1992-loan-Birmingham City; Jan 1993-loan-West Bromwich Albion; Mar 1993-loan-West Ham United; July 1993 CITY; Aug 1995 Crawley Town; Mar 1996 Atherstone United; Aug 1996 Hendon; Sept 1996 Stamford; Jan 1997 Kirby Muxloe; Mar 1997 Guiseley; Oct 1997 Crook Town.

City debut v Peterborough United (H) 14.8.93

> A demonised hate-figure to City fans at one juncture of his regularly controversial career, David had become something of a cult hero to the Filbert Street faithful by the time his senior playing days were sadly curtailed by injury. The man whose graceless 'dive' at Wembley in 1992 had apparently cheated Leicester out of promotion-via-Play-Off to the inaugural Premiership campaign, whose two goals for West Ham a year later did much to derail another upward push, and whose free-transfer signing by Brian Little was therefore instantly judged a potential PR disaster, ended up with the scorer's credit for giving the club their third-time-lucky chance at Wembley glory in 1994. Whether or not he actually got a subsequently-claimed touch to the ball which decisively nestled in the back of the Tranmere net, late in the Play-Off semi-final second leg, that and his (rather unfair) dismissal moments afterwards proved to be his last acts in a senior City shirt, for suspension sidelined David at Wembley, and a summer knee injury prompted an enforced retirement in January 1995. City thus had the final League season from this former Scottish international striker, and one in which his full repertoire was demonstrably still in play: a bustling predatory sense at close range, a speciality of controlled chip shots, a ready willingness to forage deep, a fine heading ability for a small man, and a distinctly volatile temperament. Scots-born, but Yorkshire-raised, this former Brodsworth Colliery miner was initially a midfielder at Oakwell (where he was overshadowed by Ian Banks), but graduated at Feethams to a secondary striker's role (one which he would most memorably incarnate while playing off Kerry Dixon at Chelsea). David's first five caps came while he was a Stamford Bridge regular, and a Wembley hat-trick (from the 1986 Full Members Cup victory over Manchester City) was another highlight of his Blues stint, while he won another handful of Scotland selections while at Highfield Road. His 100th Leage goal came on his Liverpool debut, and in total 48 more accrued to his career credit, plus 26 in other senior games. Sadly, but predictably, David became something of a target for referees during his later non-league wanderings.

Apps: *FL 37; FAC 1; LC 3; PO 0+1.*
Goals: *FL 12; LC 1; PO 1.*

David Speedie

SPITTLE, William Arthur

b. Southfields, London, Apr qtr 1893

Career: Southfields Juniors; Sept 1912 Woolwich Arsenal; Oct 1919 CITY; May 1921 Nuneaton Town; Jan 1922 Tamworth Castle; Dec 1925-trials-Brentford.

City debut v Huddersfield Town (A) 18.10.19

> Partnering Harry King in a joint move from Highbury that was hardly Peter Hodge's best bit of business as City boss, Billy was a scheming inside-right whose Arsenal career had effectively peaked in the final season of WW1 football, despite him having been wounded on active service in France with the Footballers' Battalion (17th Middlesex Regiment). He'd had half a dozen outings in the Gunners' relegated side of 1912/13, but had then only made one Second Division start in the following term, and become resigned to reserve-team football. His integration at Filbert Street was hampered by the need for a cartilage operation soon after his arrival, and both Tom Smith and Albert Pynegar proved strong competition to him in the following season. Billy moved with WW1 Fossil Jimmy Nock from Nuneaton to Tamworth after a seven-goal start to 1921/2, but his regular club affiliation at the time he briefly featured in Brentford's reserves is unknown to us.

Apps: *FL 26.*
Goals: *FL 3.*

SPRIGGS, Frank

b. Leicester, ca 1882

Career: Leicester Old Boys; cs 1901 Leicester Imperial; Mar 1902 FOSSE; 1903 Oxford Victoria (Leicester); Apr 1904 Leicester Imperial; cs 1905 Hitchin Town; Dec 1907 New Brompton; cs 1908 not known; Aug 1909 FOSSE; July 1910 Merthyr Town; cs 1911 Rochdale; Oct 1911 Heywood United; cs 1912 Ilkeston United; cs 1913 Mansfield Town; Feb 1914 Leicester Imperial.

Fosse debut v Lincoln City (H) 19.4.02 (scored twice)

> A mystery solved, and a unified, near-complete career trajectory at last for this twice-signed Fossil who we'd assigned with a split personality in both previously published drafts of this work. Centre-forward Frank was a member of the same Leicester Boys side as Tommy Allsopp and Nigger Trueman, and made quite an impact for Fosse in the final game of 1901/2, yet thereafter got but a single outing in the following term, in a near-embarrassing Cup tie at Irthlingborough. After further experience at local level, he had two and a half seasons in the South Eastern League, and a brief elevation to the Southern League at New Brompton. His 'missing' season was almost certainly spent outside Leicestershire, but must presumably have alerted Fosse to his growing maturity; though again he was restricted to a single seasonal senior selection, partnering Fred Shinton in a 1-0 away win at Blackpool. He top-scored that term for the reserves, with 14 Midland League goals and six more in the County Cup, but soon found himself involved in a near-miss promotion struggle with Southern League Merthyr, for whom he claimed five goals in an eleven-goal thrashing of Salisbury City. In spite of a two-goal debut, he was only briefly utilised by former Fossil Joe Blackett at Rochdale, then faced that club on his Lancashire Combination debut for Heywood. To complete his League-hopping career, Frank appeared for each of Ilkeston, Mansfield and the Imps in the Central Alliance.

Apps: *FL 2; FAC 1.*
Goals: *FL 2.*

STAPLES, John William

Career: Castle Donington; Nov 1901 Whitwick White Cross; May 1902 FOSSE; cs 1903 Whitwick White Cross; cs 1904 Ilkeston United; Castle Donington Town.

Fosse debut v Small Heath (H) 6.9.02

> An outside-left who took over Frank Middleton's Midland League berth at Whitwick when the latter signed for Derby, John was the subject of a technically illegal transfer approach by Fosse in April 1902, which cost the club a £10 fine at just the point they were deciding he wouldn't fit the Second Division bill. After four defeats in his handful of senior outings, he lost his place to Tom Simpson, and his subsequent season in the reserves culminated ironically in two drawn County Cup Final games against Whitwick, after which Fosse refused to agree a further replay date, and the cup and medals were awarded to their opponents.

Apps: *FL 5.*

STARBUCK, Jonathan

b. Measham, Leics, 1884
d. Burton-on-Trent, 18th April 1939

Career: Measham United; cs 1905 Burton United; June 1907 FOSSE; cs 1912 Ilkeston United; Burton All Saints.

Fosse debut v Leeds City (H) 7.9.07

> The skipper of Measham United at the time he represented Leicestershire against Lancashire in February 1905 (along with Jack Sheffield, Bob Thompson and Billy Turner), goalkeeper Jonty missed only two games for Burton United in their last two campaigns as a League club, and gave five seasons of loyal service to Fosse despite regularly being cast in the role of reserve to Horace Bailey and Fred Mearns. His safe handling saw Fosse through several tricky encounters on the way to promotion in 1908, and he was hardly to blame

for either their immediate return to the lower Division or any failure to bounce back. Jonty moved on to Central Alliance football after leaving Leicester; and at the time of his death – on the same day as Jimmy Blessington – he was licensee of the Plough Inn at Burton.

Apps: *FL 77; FAC 12.*

STARKEY, Arthur E.

b. Coalville

Career: Hugglescote St Johns; 1904 Gresley Rovers; 1905 Coalville Amateurs; Dec 1906 Coalville Town; cs 1907 Hugglescote United; cs 1908 Coalville Swifts; cs 1909 Shepshed Albion; Feb 1911 FOSSE; July 1912 Whitwick Imperial; cs 1913 Coalville Town; Ibstock Albion; cs 1914 Coalville Swifts; cs 1919 Shepshed Albion; Sept 1920 Coalville Swifts.

Fosse debut v Fulham (H) 25.3.11

> A local outside-right who had an extended first-team trial at the end of 1910/11, inheriting Fred Threlfall's role, Arthur failed to win a contract for the next campaign and returned to local fare in the north of the county. He did briefly reappear, though, in March 1917 for a single wartime outing in Fosse colours against Nottingham Forest, and in the following month assisted Notts County against Fosse at Filbert Street. He was noted in 1928 as a cricketer for Snibston Colliery CC.

Apps: *FL 8; WW1 1.*

STEPHENSON, Roy

b. Crook, Co Durham, 27th May 1932

Career: Sunnyside Juniors; Crook Town; June 1949 Burnley; Sept 1956 Rotherham United; Nov 1957 Blackburn Rovers; Mar 1959 CITY; July 1960 Ipswich Town; June 1965 Lowestoft Town.

City debut v Chelsea (H) 14.3.59

> Although he had racked up a fair number of top-flight games at Turf Moor as a utility forward, occasionally in partnership with Albert Cheesebrough, and had recently contributed to Blackburn's 1958 promotion to Division One, Roy appeared to be facing something of a late career crisis when he found himself sidelined for all but two games of his second Leicester season. Matt Gillies, in his first managerial deal, had paid £8,000 to add Roy's prompting skills to City's successful attempt to ward off relegation in 1959, but he was then edged out of the reckoning for his favoured No 7 shirt by Tommy McDonald and Howard Riley. One move, though, revived Roy's enthusiasm and effectivenes at a stroke; with Alf Ramsey taking him on as the right-wing provider for the Ray Crawford/Ted Phillips goal combine which sensationally saw Ipswich to successive Divison Two and One championships, and into the European Cup. Formerly an Under-18 cricketer for Durham, Roy qualified as a mining engineer at night school.

Apps: *FL 12.*

STEVENS, Gregor Mackenzie

b. Glasgow, 13th January 1955

Career: Baillieston Juniors; 1974 Motherwell; May 1979 CITY; Sept 1979 Rangers; Jan 1984-loan-Heart of Midlothian; cs 1984 Motherwell; Nov 1984 Partick Thistle; Aug 1986 Brechin City; Oct 1989 Dumbarton.

City debut v Rotherham United (H) LC 11.8.79

> All too evidently ill-at-ease with English football, Gregor struggled through only a handful of shaky performances as a City central defender, and conceded a needless penalty in his final outing against Luton, before Jock Wallace somehow shrewdly contrived to recoup his £125,000 investment in a second cross-border deal. Gregor had begun his Motherwell career as a midfielder, but had developed as a tough-tackling sweeper to win Scottish League and Under-21 honours; though he was definitely to overdo the toughness when he got to Ibrox, where he revelled in the nickname 'Igor' and, in February 1982, received a shaming six-month suspension after his fifth sending-off in two years. He also picked up a trio of medals – as a beaten Scottish Cup Finalist in 1980, as a winner in the same competition a year later, and from the Scottish League Cup Final triumph of 1981/2 – but, sadly was still showing the less salubrious side of his playing nature even as an 'old head'. Ordered to an early bath on the very first day of 1989/90, he was then dismissed again weeks later on his Dumbarton debut.

Apps: *FL 4; LC 2.*

STEVENSON, James

b. Paisley, Renfrewshire, 1876

Career: Ashfield; cs 1894 Clyde; Jan 1895 Derby County; Oct 1898 Newcastle United; cs 1900 Bristol City; Sept 1901 Grimsby Town; Jan 1902 FOSSE; Oct 1902 Clyde.

Fosse debut v Burton United (A) 18.1.02

> A Cup Finalist with Derby in 1898, when described as 'a wizard of the leather', Jimmy was a noted dribbler as an inside-left, as well as a fair marksman (31 First Division goals in 73 games for the Rams), and fetched the handsome transfer fee of £225 from newly-promoted Newcastle. He began his wanderings as his goal touch waned, however, and his brief spell at Leicester – which brought only one win from his seven outings – ended in acrimony, with Jimmy one of several Fosse players suspended as an internal disciplinary measure within two months of signing on. A near-miss career all-round, with Jimmy having featured in runners-up sides in the First Division in 1896 and the Southern League in 1901, as well as in Derby's FA Cup disappointment, ended when he went into business in Glasgow. A Derby history asserts that he was killed during WW1.

Apps: *FL 7.*
Goals: *FL 1.*

STEWART, Alexander

b. Greenock, Renfrewshire, 1869

Career: Morton; Dec 1889 Burnley; Dec 1892 Everton; cs 1893 Nottingham Forest; Mar 1897 Notts County; cs 1898 Bedminster; cs 1899 Northampton Town; Aug 1901 Burnley; Aug 1902 FOSSE (trainer).

Fosse debut v Glossop (A) 10.4.03 (scored once)

> The scorer of both Burnley's goals when they beat FA Cup-holders Blackburn in the 1890 Final of the prestigious Lancashire Cup, an Evertonian FA Cup finalist in 1893 as a wing-half, and the last link in Notts County's promotion line-up of 1897, Alick had an eventful and pretty successful playing career which was supposed to have closed when he signed on as Fosse's trainer in 1902. Yet injury crises conspired to force him to don his boots again in the above match, and his goal from inside-left pointed the way to a welcome away win that did much to avert the threat of an enforced application for re-election. Alick also turned out in three Fosse friendly fixtures to demonstrate his own fitness to his charges, and remained at Filbert Street until 1905.

Apps: *FL 1.*
Goals: *FL 1.*

Jordan Stewart

STEWART, Jordan Barrington

b. Birmingham, 3rd May 1982

Career: assoc sch Aston Villa; academy July 1998/pro Mar 2000 CITY; Mar 2000-loan-Bristol Rovers.

City debut v West Ham United (H) 22.1.2000 (sub)

> A second-year academy trainee with reserve experience in both midfield and defence, Jordan graduated to the senior bench in early 2000 as City's resources were stretched to the limit. Twice called on with an injury-hit City chasing the game, he showed glimpses of a confident skill against the Hammers, and a promising refusal to be overawed by a stellar Chelsea opposition in the FA Cup exit; and was then loaned out for extra experience in Division Two, making his first senior start in the Pirates' clash with Millwall at The Den. Jordan was sidelined by a back injury for much of the 2000/1 campaign, but before its end had returned to win deserved England Under-18 recognition and pick up City's 'Young Player of the Year' award.

Apps *(to end 2000/1): PL 0+1; FAC 0+1.*

STIRLING, James

Career: Third Lanark; Oct 1894 FOSSE; cs 1895 Partick Thistle.

Fosse debut v Newton Heath (A) 27.10.1894

> A utility forward, James could never command a regular berth during Fosse's initial Second Division campaign, despite never being in a beaten side, and scoring in his final senior game. He'd been signed in a joint deal with Thirds' inside-forward James Milliken, whose own Fosse career was restricted to friendlies and games in the supplementary United Counties League competition, in which Stirling also managed a record of four games and one goal. The latter was also a scorer in the County Cup Final win of 1895 (a 4-0 defeat of Loughborough's second string), but even thereafter he made little impact with Partick, playing only twice in the Scottish Second Division.

Apps: *FL 4.*
Goals: *FL 1.*

STOODLEY, Claude Henry

b. Plumstead, London, ca 1891

Career: trials-Clapton Orient & Chelsea; Aug 1911 Walthamstow Grange; Mar 1912 Glossop; Aug 1913 FOSSE; May 1914 Merthyr Town.

Fosse debut v Birmingham (A) 20.9.13

> Hardly a prolific scorer during his Fosse season at inside-right, Claude must have rather startled himself by belatedly opening his goal acount with a hat-trick in the classic 5-5 FA Cup-tie draw with Spurs. This was very much his only moment of glory, however, as Fosse bowed out of the knock-out competition in the replay and then barely kept their heads above the re-election zone. He nonetheless played on pluckily after the death of his wife in March 1914. Claude was later a Southern League debut scorer for Merthyr, and his goals set them up for an FA Cup meeting with Arsenal, decided by a Harry King hat-trick.

Apps: *FL 25; FAC 2.*
Goals: *FL 3; FAC 3.*

STOTT, J.

Career: Heanor Town; 1892 Kettering; Feb 1893 FOSSE; 1893 Kettering; cs 1894 Heanor Town.

Fosse debut/only game v Burton Wanderers (A) ML 25.2.1893

> A trialist centre-forward who got a comprehensive thumbs-down signal from the local press after his sole Midland League outing for Fosse (a 0-3 defeat): he 'failed to shine' and 'might easily be improved upon' according to two commentators. Jettisoned after a few further reserve outings, he was a former Heanor teammate of Amos Atkins and Alf Carter in the Midland Alliance, and ended up back at that club.

Apps: *ML 1.*

STRAUGHTON, James H.

b. Workington, ca 1889

Career: Army football; Sept 1912 FOSSE; Aug 1914 Pontypridd; Jan 1915 Leicester Imperial; Aug 1919-trials-Nuneaton Town; 1919 Flimby Rangers.

Fosse debut v Wolverhampton Wanderers (H) 16.11.12

> A Cumbrian centre-forward whose football prowess was noted while he was soldiering in the Border Regiment, James turned out to be something of a goal-shy attack leader for Fosse, and was regarded as very much third choice behind Harry Sparrow and Fred Mortimer. Indeed, the whole team failed to score on the five occasions he played during 1913/14, when he was also experimented with as a right back in both reserve and senior sides. He was back in his country's colours in late 1914, but for a while maintained a Leicester base, and featured in a wartime Lincoln City line-up at Filbert Street in September 1918. His brother Joe also had a few games for Fosse reserves in 1912/13 before joining Workington Central, then died only months later in an industrial accident.

Apps: *FL 15.*
Goals: *FL 2.*

STRICKLAND, Derek

b. Stoneyburn, West Lothian, 7th November 1959

Career: 1976 Rangers; Sept 1979 CITY; May 1981 Heart of Midlothian; 1982-trials-Motherwell; Feb 1983 East Stirlingshire; 1984 Stoneyburn Juniors.

City debut v Fulham (H) 22.9.79 (sub)

> A Scottish schoolboy international, and a youth-team winger at Ibrox under Jock Wallace, Derek came to Filbert Street as part of the deal which returned Gregor Stevens north of the border. He'd played but once in each of the Scottish Premier and the Scottish League Cup for Rangers (though he'd scored in a Glasgow Cup Final victory over Celtic in 1979), and found his City opportunities limited, but acted as a virtual lucky mascot for the promotion-bound side of 1980: scoring against Wrexham on his first start, never appearing in a losing side, and contributing the only goal of a crucial win at Notts County. Unused in the ensuing top-flight term, Derek moved to Hearts alongside Pat Byrne, but managed only one substitute appearance for the Tynecastle club's first team; and failed to score in fifteen outings for East Stirling. He remained active in Scottish non-league football, however, being noted in the mid-90s as manager at each of Bonnyrigg Rose and Whitburn Juniors.

Apps: *FL 4+3.*
Goals: *FL 2.*

STRINGFELLOW, Michael David

b. Kirkby in Ashfield, Notts, 27th January 1943

Career: am Aug 1959/pro Feb 1960 Mansfield Town; Jan 1962 CITY; Aug 1975 Nuneaton Borough.

City debut v Everton (A) 20.1.62

> To attempt to characterise Mike's fourteen seasons with City is to risk an unfortunately not overly glib analogy with the footballing cliché, 'It's a game of two halves'. For seven years after his £25,000 move from Mansfield the lanky outside-left was one of the most feared attackers in the country, forming a lethal left-wing partnership with Davie Gibson and racking up a very healthy goal tally. He was also taking a disproportionate amount of 'stick', though, from defenders otherwise at a loss to curb his pace and strength; and the legacy was a further seven years of courageous struggle and determination as Mike fought to overcome a succession of near-crippling injuries (and a sometimes sadly unsympathetic crowd) to continue to give his all for City. Mike had developed at Field Mill under Raich Carter, making his League bow at 17 alongside Ken Wagstaffe, playing at Filbert Street in the inaugural Football League Cup tie, and soon impressing Matt Gillies as a likely successor to Gordon Wills. City bids were rebuffed in each of September and November 1961 before the transfer went through at the third attempt, days after City had limply bowed out of the Cup at Stoke. Mike still hadn't disturbed the scoresheet after his dozen outings of 1961/2, but he kicked off the following term with goals in each of the opening quartet of fixtures, totalling six before August was out, and 19 in League and Cup by the season's end, including the looping header past Liverpool's Tommy Lawrence which assured City of a 1963 Wembley Cup Final appearance. For five campaigns thereafter his seasonal goal tally never dropped below double figures, while the number of strikes attributable to his crosses was countless. Mike was the opening scorer of the 1964 League Cup Final second leg against Stoke, took a runners-up memento from the next year's Final, and is still, with eight goals, City's aggregate leading scorer in that competition. Injury problems (which had previously cost Mike an England Under-23 cap) really began to bite, however, during the 1968/9 relegation/Cup Final campaign, and a catalogue of operations, comebacks, breakdowns and sheer frustrations ensued. Yet all this time even a semi-fit 'Stringy' was a valuable squad member, and his April 1975 testimonial game against Wolves was barely adequate recognition of the club's debt to his early excellence and later against-the-odds example. He remains only the second player after Arthur Chandler to figure in the club's top-ten records for both appearances and goalscoring. Mike's eight-game spell with Nuneaton was another injury-curtailed knockback, and he subsequently ran pubs in Narborough and Littlethorpe before moving into the newsagents business, latterly in

Enderby. His nephew, Ian, began a senior footballing career with Mansfield in 1986.

Apps: *FL 292+23; FAC 26+2; LC 26+1.*
Goals: *FL 82; FAC 7; LC 8.*

STUBBS, Philip Eric Gordon

b. Chester, 10th September 1912

Career: Winsford United; Nantwich; Jan 1934 Bolton Wanderers; Sept 1934 Wrexham; June 1935 Nottingham Forest; Nov 1936 CITY; Dec 1945 Chester.

City debut v Southampton (H) 14.11.36

> Something of a prototype for Mike Stringfellow in terms of physical stature and playing style, Eric was also a forceful outside-left who had a dramatic impact on City's fortunes on arrival. Again it was a matter of a constructed partnership perfectly clicking, for where Mike preceded Davie Gibson into the City side by a week, so Eric had become Frank Womack's first major signing a week before Jack Bowers joined the club, and the powerful pair set about transforming a dangerously mundane Second Division season into an excitingly convincing championship win. Eric's orthodox flank play was a feature for much of the following two top-flight campaigns, although he was also tried out as a full-back in the reserves, and it was at No 2 where he would end his senior playing days in both legs of Chester's 1945/6 FA Cup exit to Liverpool. In the interim, there had been a six-year gap between the penultimate and the last of his City outings, and he'd managed only a few wartime appearances for Wrexham (where he'd originally made his League bow) and Chester while working as a Cheshire fruit farmer. In 1946 he was named as trainer to Chester's reserve side.

Apps: *FL 74; FAC 4; WW2 4.*
Goals: *FL 14; FAC 1; WW2 1.*

STURRIDGE, Dean Constantine

b. Birmingham, 27th July 1973

Career: YT/pro July 1991 Derby County; Dec 1994-loan-Torquay United; Jan 2001 CITY.

City debut v Arsenal (H) 20.1.2001

> Once a Martin O'Neill target at a reputed £3.5m valuation, Dean finally landed at Leicester for 10% of that cost; laid out by Peter Taylor as he sought an experienced partner for Ade Akinbiyi. The cut-price deal (which may eventually rise to £400,000) was accounted for by the nippy striker's contract being about to expire at the end of the term, though Derby's longest-serving player was also by then something of a fringe player in the Pride Park squad; and had, in fact, scored twice for the Rams reserves against City's seconds only days previously. It was probably something of a culture-clash shock for Dean to find himself lining up for his City debut alongside Roberto Mancini rather than Akinbiyi, but it was not long before the old-style little-and-large partnership was in harness for City, or before Dean started to re-emphasise his quick-witted opportunism with a spell of three goals in three games, plus one in the long-awaited victory over Spurs. That one just had to come, to level up the number of strikes for City with those he'd claimed against the club for Derby over the years. He'd started out as a Baseball Ground youngster, with teenage experience in both the old Second Division and the 'new' First, though it had taken a loan-out in the South West to spark his goalscoring instincts, which then saw him claim a career-best 20 strikes in Derby's 1996 rise to the Premiership (in the same side as Gary Rowett), and justify his status as a top-flight regular for the next few seasons. Dean is the younger brother of Simon Sturridge, whose own striking career took off at Birmingham City and also saw him through travels to Stoke, Blackpool, Northampton and Shrewsbury.

Apps *(to end 2000/1): PL 12+1; FAC 2.*
Goals: *PL 3; FAC 1.*

SUMMERS, John Lawrence

b. Manchester, 8th February 1915
d. Southampton, 12th April 1991

Career: 1931 Manchester North End; Feb 1932-trials-Burnley; Fleetwood; 1932-trials-Preston North End; June 1933 Tunbridge Wells Rangers; Apr 1934 CITY; May 1935 Derby County; Oct 1936 Southampton; 1938 Southampton Police.

City debut v Chelsea (A) 1.9.34 (scored once)

> A young right-winger who was given two spells during City's 1935 relegation season to lay claim to the place of the ageing Hughie Adcock, Jack much impressed George Jobey with a goalscoring performance against the latter's Derby side, and moved on a few months later to learn more of the tricks of his trade in the shadow of another international, Sammy Crooks, at the Baseball Ground. Despite Jack receiving only two call-ups as the Rams took runners-up place in the 1936 title race, such high-class tutelage at least paid a modicum of a dividend at The Dell, where he notched seven Second Division goals in 31 outings following a £250 transfer partly underwritten by the Saints Supporters Club. Jack retired prematurely from the professional game in 1938 to join the police force, but continued to represent his constabulary side until 1954, and eventually rose to the rank of Chief Inspector.

Apps: *FL 11.*
Goals: *FL 2.*

Jack Summers

SVARC, Robert Louis

b. Leicester, 8th February 1946

Career: app Oct 1961/pro Mar 1963 CITY; Dec 1968 Lincoln City; Sept 1970-loan-Barrow; Oct 1971 Boston United; Dec 1972 Colchester United; Oct 1975 Blackburn Rovers; Sept 1977-loan-Watford.

City debut v Peterborough United (H) LC 23.9.64

> A free-scoring reserve striker of Czech descent, Bobby first took the Filbert Street spotlight when netting five goals in Colin Appleton's April 1964 testimonial game. He got a brief run at centre-forward in Ken Keyworth's stead in the following term, but then had to wait another three seasons for his next few opportunities to impress at senior level. A tough, compact forager rather than a target man, he always looked likelier to make the grade in a lower echelon, although it took him a while to kick-start his career at Lincoln: the Imps actually recalled him from a Barrow loan to score against the latter in the FA Cup. Boston were Northern Premier League high fliers while Bobby was there, and he became something of a talisman for manager Jim Smith, who subsequently signed him again for each of Colchester and Blackburn. With the U's, who he assisted to promotion from Division Four in 1974, he registered 60 strikes from 116 League games, and eventually finished his career only three goals short of his League century, after suffering injury in his sole game for Watford. A Jehovah's Witness, Bobby went into the burglar alarm business in the Blackburn area.

Apps: *FL 13; FAC 1; LC 4.*
Goals: *FL 2.*

SWEENIE, Thomas Thornton

b. Paisley, Renfrewshire, 15th July 1945

Career: Johnstone Burgh; June 1963 CITY; July 1968-trials-Arsenal; Aug 1968-trials-Huddersfield Town; Oct 1968 York City; June 1969 Burton Albion; cs 1970 Lockheed Leamington; Bedworth Town; Shepshed Charterhouse; Sept 1977 Enderby Town.

City debut v Gillingham (H) LC 27.11.63

Tom Sweenie

> A teenage inside-forward of unbounded promise, possessing a firecracker left-foot shot which at one point drew earnest, if exaggerated, comparisons with Puskas from the football press, Tom sadly had his top-class career cut short by injury. Having pipped Liverpool to his signature, Matt Gillies was determined to nurture Tom's potential slowly, but after his senior bow in City's only competitive meeting with the Gills he made an explosive First Division entrance with a two-goal show at Blackpool. He won two League Cup tankards (appearing in the second-leg victory over Stoke in 1964, and in the Stamford Bridge leg of the following year's Final), and also put himself into the City records as their first-ever scoring substitute (against Blackburn in April 1966). He was additionally the second-leg scorer who levelled the aggregate in the Final against Spurs when City's reserves took a share of the Combination Cup in 1967. By this time, however, he was suffering the after-effects of serious damage to his knee caused by a bad tackle at Forest in February 1967, which would eventually lead to his withdrawal from senior football. He was offered a short-term contract by Arsenal but, in search of greater security, tested his fitness with Billy Hodgson's York, scoring on his debut there but sadly having to acknowledge he could no longer bear the stresses of the full-time game. He later set up a carpet-fitting business in the county.

Apps: *FL 50+1; FAC 1; LC 4.*
Goals: *FL 11; FAC 1.*

SWIFT, George Harold

b. Oakengates, Shropshire, 3rd February 1870

Career: 1885 St.Georges Swifts; 1886 Wellington Town; 1886 Wellington St.Georges; 1887-trials-Stoke; 1889 Crewe Alexandra; cs 1891 Wolverhampton Wanderers; cs 1894 Loughborough; Aug 1896 FOSSE; June 1902 Notts County; cs 1904 Leeds City (trainer).

Fosse debut v Darwen (H) 5.9.1896

> A fine left-back who showed early promise in Shropshire football, played in the Football Alliance for Crewe, and stepped up to the top flight with Wolves, George appeared for the latter club in the Cup Final of 1893 (when they beat Everton 1-0), then became the only Loughborough player ever to win a senior representative honour when selected for the Football League against the Irish League in 1895. His move to Filbert Street, while legitimate, was the cause of a major row between the city and county neighbours over the fee, on which the League authorities refused to arbitrate. George proved an inspirationally consistent captain for Fosse, being ever-present in four of his six seasons, and almost leading them into the First Division in 1899, when they finished third. His goals tended to be either penalties or spectacularly long-range efforts: he scored from the halfway line against Walsall in March 1901, and was not much closer to goal when he won the home encounter with Blackpool a year later with a shot past the visitors' secretary, Tom Barcroft, who was forced to play between the sticks that afternoon and remained otherwise unbeaten. George took a well-earned benefit from an October 1900 friendly against Wolves, and eventually moved on to Meadow Lane, where the promise of the trainer's role awaited his eventual retirement. He next took on the trainer's duties at newly-founded Leeds City, yet had to don playing kit once more in an emergency when Leeds played at Chelsea in March 1906. George became manager of Chesterfield Town in 1907, remained there after they dropped out of the League, and took them to the 1910 Midland League championship; then subsequently bossed Southampton. He had attained a senior position in an insurance business in Southampton by the late 20s, but at the time City reached the Cup Final in 1949, a press snippet identified George as a Wembley resident, having just celebrated his golden wedding anniversary.

Apps: *FL 186; FAC 14.*
Goals: *FL 4; FAC 2.*

TAGGART, Gerald Paul

b. Belfast, 18th October 1970

Career: YT/pro July 1989 Manchester City; Jan 1990 Barnsley; Aug 1995 Bolton Wanderers; July 1998 CITY.

City debut v Manchester United (A) 15.8.98 (sub)

> A former teammate of Neil Lennon in both Manchester City's FA Youth Cup Final side of 1989 and in the Northern Ireland line-up, Gerry inherited the national team captaincy from his Leicester club colleague in April 2000. The revival in his career during 1999/2000 made that honour almost a due formality, for a return to full fitness and a renewal of confidence had easily banished memories of a first Filbert Street term in which he'd visibly lacked both attributes, had generally struggled, and had experienced a couple of nightmarish defensive displays. Instead, he treated City fans to a regular helping of almost swaggering centre-back dominance alongside Matt Elliott, and earned immense popularity on the back of an adventurous attacking streak, eventually lifting the Player of the Year award. It was form he largely maintained throughout 2000/1, as well, though injuries latterly disrupted his consistency. A left-back at the time he became a teenage Maine Road escapee, he joined Barnsley only days after they'd KO'd City from the 1990 FA Cup, and scored on his debut for them. Converting to central defence at Oakwell and winning his first Irish call-ups, he matured rapidly and craggily, and attracted a £1.5m move to Bolton. Hit by injuries and suspensions, he was unable to help the Trotters maintain Premiership status, but was then the rock on which they built their Division One championship triumph of the following year. The Reebok rollercoaster continued, however, with a second relegation in two years, and Gerry was a marginalised figure there in the final year of his contract. Martin O'Neill captured him on a free transfer under the new Bosman-influenced rules, and Gerry scored on the occasion of his first start for City (against Chesterfield in the League Cup). A broken toe then hindered his acclimatisation, and his form touched bottom in the home defeat by Manchester United. But he called on reserves of determination, and turned around his City career emphatically to command a regular back-three role in the next season. For a long time Gerry was stranded on a total of 45 caps for his country – he was vindictively ostracised for two years by Lawrie McMenemy for a minor disciplinary infraction – but Sammy McIlroy immediately called him up on assuming the Irish management; eventually handing him the captain's armband for a second time to celebrate his 50th international outing.

Apps *(to end 2000/1): PL 63+7; FAC 8+1; LC 12+2; UEFA 2.*
Goals: *PL 8; LC 2; UEFA 1.*

TAYLOR, H. Albert (Dick)

b. Earl Shilton, Leics, 24th October 1891

Career: 1910 Earl Shilton Town; Earl Shilton Victor; cs 1913 Earl Shilton Town; Jan 1914 FOSSE; Aug 1919 Nuneaton Town; 1923 Hinckley United.

Fosse debut v Huddersfield Town (H) 19.9.14

> A local left-back ('a sturdily-built youth') who recovered from a shaky debut standing in for Billy Troughear (the *Mail* regarded him as 'erratic' and 'reckless'), Dick subsequently deputised a little more calmly for Sam Currie during the irredeemably downbeat 1914/15 campaign. He also had the unfortunate experience of seeing three Derby County goals whizzing past him in fifteen minutes after he'd replaced the injured Herbert Bown between the sticks during that term's 0-6 Filbert Street defeat by the Rams. In April 1917, he suffered six wounds to an arm and both legs in fighting at Arras, and was taken prisoner by the Germans, but he recovered to become the acknowledged star of Nuneaton's postwar defence. Dick was then a veteran calming influence on the Tin Hatters, too, though an eye injury caused him to miss the 1927 County Cup Final against City's reserves. He took the position of Hinckley trainer in 1928, but was still playing regularly that term.

Apps: *FL 14.*

TAYLOR, Henry

b. Birmingham, ca 1870

Career: Saltley Gasworks FC; Warwick County; Small Heath; cs 1891 FOSSE; cs 1894 Hinckley Town.

Fosse debut v Long Eaton Rangers (A) ML 23.1.1892

> A versatile reserve defender for Fosse in both the first and third Midland League campaigns, Harry was an interim ever-present (mainly at right-half) in 1892/3. He had previously failed to make a senior breakthrough at Small Heath, then playing at Football Alliance level, but had nonetheless represented Warwickshire in inter-county fare. Suspicions remain that he may subsequently have served Singers and their Coventry City successors from 1895-99, though their Harry Taylor played excusively as a forward.

***Apps:** FAC 4; ML 30.*
***Goals:** ML 1*

TAYLOR, Scott Dean

b. Portsmouth, 28th November 1970

Career: YT/pro June 1989 Reading; July 1995 CITY; Sept 1999 Wolverhampton Wanderers.

City debut v Sunderland (A) 12.8.95

> Reunited with former Reading boss Mark McGhee at a cost to City of £500,000, Scott made a quiet start to his First Division term, but was soon getting forward effectively in what was almost an old-fashioned inside-forward role, and finding his passing range as he, Garry Parker and Steve Corica initially shared midfield duties. Noteworthy as a jinky dribbler, he was nonetheless an erratic finisher, but his energetic support play did much to prompt City to their fourth Play-Off Final in five years: a day Scott celebrated in advance with a blond dye-job to his hair. Less than a year later, he would return to Wembley with City, as a substitute in the drawn League Cup Final against Middlesbrough, but it would prove his penultimate outing in blue, as a knee operation awaited. Back in time for pre-season training, Scott then agonisingly ruptured his patella tendon at Belvoir Drive. A year out of the game was the initial diagnosis, but a further operation in November stretched his actual absence to two full seasons. It was assumed he'd take medical retirement in 1999, but Wolves boss (and former Reading and City coach) Colin Lee gave him a Molineux trial period, a brief link-up again with Corica, and then a full contract. Sadly, however, this had to be terminated in 2001, after a further breakdown quashed all hopes of a career extension. Scott had made his original Reading bow in September 1988 while still a trainee, and often played at Elm Park as an orthodox winger as he totted up a League record of 207 appearances and 24 goals, assisting them to the Division Two championship of 1994, and the verge of the Premiership a year later, when he closed his Royals career in the 3-4 Wembley Play-Off Final defeat by Bolton.

***Apps:** FL/PL 59+5; FAC 2+1; LC 7+3; PO 3.*
***Goals:** FL 6.*

TEARSE, David James

b. Newcastle on Tyne, 7th August 1951

Career: North Kenton Boys Club; May 1969 CITY; Nov 1971 Torquay United; Jan 1975-loan-Reading; July 1975 Atherstone Town (- 1977).

City debut v Preston North End (A) 11.10.69 (sub)

> A teenage Geordie striker given an early chance by Frank O'Farrell, David played his first full game for City as an emergency right-back at Ewood Park, and then had a brief run in competition with Ally Brown and Murray Brodie as a candidate for Andy Lochhead's target-man role. After two further isolated appearances, he made an early departure when Jimmy Bloomfield started applying the chequebook to rebuilding his First Division forward line. David, whose £15,000 fee was a Torquay record, was unable to save his new club from relegation to the basement in 1972, but scored 23 times in 77 League starts across four seasons at Plainmoor.

David Tearse

***Apps:** FL 7+1; FAC 1+2; LC 0+1.*
***Goals:** FL 1.*

TEWLEY, Alan Bernard

b. Leicester, 22nd January 1945

Career: app 1960/pro July 1962 CITY; Aug 1964-loan-Rugby Town; Nov 1969 Bradford Park Avenue; Oct 1970 Crewe Alexandra; Nov 1972 Bedford Town; cs 1973 Boston United; Wigston Town.

City debut v Newcastle United (H) 6.5.67 (sub)

> A patient reserve winger, effective on either flank, and possessing a fair eye for goal, David spent a four-month loan with Jimmy Walsh's Rugby Town in the company of fellow City youngster Mick Balmer, and his distinctly belated senior breakthrough marked his status as the reserves' leading marksman of 1966/7, with 21 goals and a Combination Cup Final medal. He scored on his initial first-team start (in the 5-1 win at The Dell in October 1967 that represented City's only victory on that ground in the twentieth century), and earned City three points with his next two strikes, but he suffered badly from the shift in tactical thinking that saw the employment of even one orthodox flanker as something of a luxury; for City soon had Len Glover operating on the left and Rodney Fern emerging as a versatile attacker in the No 7 shirt. After having been released following only a pair of brief substitute run-outs under Frank O'Farrell, Alan's sense of a rather cruel fate must have been compounded when Park Avenue failed their re-election plea in 1970: he played in both their last-ever League game and their first at Northern Premier level. Crewe at least won the vote to maintain their Division Four status in 1972, and Boston took the championship of the Northern Premier League in 1974. That term they also came mighty close to embarrassing Derby in the Cup's Third Round, leaving the Baseball Ground with a scoreless draw after Alan's header had hit the post and run along the line before being cleared.

***Apps:** FL 15+3; LC 1+1.*
***Goals:** FL 5.*

THOMAS, Barrie Ernest

b. Measham, Leics, 19th May 1937

Career: Measham Imperial; am Nov 1953/pro July 1954 CITY; June 1957 Mansfield Town; Sept 1959 Scunthorpe United; Jan 1962 Newcastle United; Nov 1964 Scunthorpe United; Nov 1966 Barnsley; cs 1968 Measham Social Welfare (p/mgr).

City debut v Sheffield United (A) 25.12.54

> A precocious former pit-boy who made a First Division breakthrough at 17 as deputy for Johnny Morris, became an England Youth international, and signed off the 1954/5 season with a hat-trick against Bolton, Barrie was clearly jettisoned inadvisedly early by City after his return from National Service, for he went on to build a substantial striking reputation until injury curtailed his career in 1968. There were few frills to his game, but a brave, direct style brought him a phenomenal haul of League goals, and won him a call-up to England's pre-World Cup training squad in 1962. Following his stunted City spell, he was first noticed claiming 48 goals from only 72 centre-forward games with the Stags, then accelerating his ratio even further to grab 67 in 91 outings for Second Division Scunthorpe. A fee of over £40,000 took him to Tyneside (48 goals from 73 starts), and half that amount constituted Scunthorpe's transfer record when he returned there. A nagging knee problem brought his exploits to a halt at Oakwell with a career League aggregate of 210 goals from 335 games, after he'd put the Tykes well on course for promotion from Division Four, and Barnsley met Newcastle in a testimonial for Barrie in November 1968, by which time he was back in the Leicestershire Senior League.

***Apps:** FL 7.*
***Goals:** FL 3.*

THOMAS, Danny Justin

b. Leamington Spa, Warks, 1st May 1981

Career: YT 1997 Nottingham Forest; YT Aug 1998/pro Dec 1999 CITY.

City debut v Newcastle United (H) 28.12.99 (sub)

> City's last debutant of the twentieth century, left-winger Danny substituted for Tony Cottee during the club's final game of the millennium, when they were 0-2 down to the Magpies, but couldn't quite prompt them to a point-saving comeback. The youngster, whose traineeship had been split between Forest and City, had won two previous nominations to the bench that month, and would go on to give two more short displays of promise in the Premiership as Martin O'Neill offered encouragement to Danny, Jordan Stewart, Tommy Goodwin and Lawrie Dudfield. In company with the other three, Danny has not been afforded a similar boost from Peter Taylor.

Danny Thomas

***Apps** (to end 2000/1): PL 0+3.*

THOMPSON, Robert

b. Bells Close, Newcastle, 27th February 1890
d. Liverpool, 1958

Career: Blaydon; Swalwell; 1909 Scotswood; May 1911 FOSSE; Apr 1913 Everton; June1921 Millwall; cs 1922 Tranmere Rovers.

Fosse debut v Nottingham Forest (A) 16.9.11

> 'The young Hercules from Scotswood', according to the local *Mail*, full-back Bob was elevated from Northern Alliance football and vied with both Tommy Clay and Sam Currie for a first-team berth during his two Leicester seasons, then being snapped up by Everton along with winger George Harrison in a joint £750 transfer deal. He shared in the 1914/15 First Division campaign that brought the Goodison side the title it would hold for four more years, and made slightly more Evertonian wartime appearances than his 83-game record on either side of the conflict. Five League goals eventually accrued to Bob's career record: all coming for Tranmere in his final active season.

***Apps:** FL 27; FAC 1.*

THOMPSON, Robert Arthur

b. Derby, ca 1876

Career: 1894 FOSSE; Leicester Banks; South Wigston Albion.

Fosse debut v Burslem Port Vale (H) 23.3.1895

> 'Represents the best and cleanest type of amateurism', was the *Mercury's* verdict on right-back Bob, who remained affliated to Fosse until 1900, and seemed happier to skipper the Fosse Rovers (or simply the reserves, as they became) than to press any claims to a senior role, though he tended to turn out in prestigious friendly fixtures, especially if the opposition were amateurs. Having his own boot and shoe business in Belgrave allowed Bob to treat his football as such a diversion, but he was regarded as good enough to skipper Leicestershire in inter-county fare in most years from 1895 to 1905, and committed enough to play regular Thursday League football as well. He partnered and mentored Fossil-to-be Cheater in the South Wigston back line, and led a team of Leicestershire Amateurs on a tour of Holland in December 1905. Bob was also the skipper of Leicester Town Cricket Club in 1903. He was a London-based businessman in the 20s. (Previous confusions having now been overcome satisfactorily, we can note that a once-credited Midland League outing for Bob in 1892 was in fact a case of his surname being utilised pseudonymously by George Smith; and add that the full-back also named Arthur Thompson who signed from Castle Donington in April 1899 never actually played at senior level for Fosse).

***Apps:** FL 4.*

THOMPSON, Stephen James

b. Oldham, 2nd November 1964

Career: Poulton Victoria; app/pro Nov 1982 Bolton Wanderers; Sept 1991 Luton Town; Oct 1991 CITY; Feb 1995 Burnley; July 1997 Rotherham United; cs 2000 Halifax Town; July 2001 Leigh RMI.

City debut v Oxford United (A) 26.10.90 (sub; scored once)

> The creative fulcrum of Brian Little's persistent promotion seekers, midfielder Steve was nearly lost to City entirely, for David Pleat beat Little to the Bolton playmaker's signature, only to use him, six weeks and five League starts later, as barter material in the transfer of Scott Oakes and Des Linton to top-flight Luton. Previously a fixture for almost nine years in the Burnden Park midfield (totalling 422 League and Cup games there), Steve had played in all three lower Divisions (twice suffering relegation, and enjoying a 1988 promotion from the basement), and had three times turned out at Wembley for the Trotters (on the losing side in the 1986 Freight / Rover Final and the 1991 Play-Offs, and as a victor in the 1989 Sherpa Van Trophy). After a 45-minute City debut at the Manor Ground, which featured one peach of a through-ball for Paul Kitson and an amazing chipped goal (his 50th in the League) as welcome auguries of his vision, Steve soon settled as the distributive hub of the Filbert Street middle line, and would return thrice to Wembley with the club in successive Play-Off Finals: coolly sliding home the third comeback goal against Swindon, and coming on as sub in the climactic victory over Derby. Sadly, Steve did not shine quite so brightly in the Premiership: record signing Mark Draper inherited his key prompting role; he wasted two important penalties after a valuable run of nine without a miss; and looked generally below the pace, even if his passing accuracy was still a joy to behold. Steve had talks with Port Vale in February 1995, but a week later joined struggling Burnley for £200,000, only to go down to Division Two with them at season's end. His mature match-reading skills, and rediscovered scoring touch, helped Rotherham into the Play-Offs in 1999, and to automatic promotion in 2000 before the expiry of his contract.

***Apps:** FL/PL 121+6; FAC 8; LC 6; FMC 3+1; AIC 2; PO 6+2.*
***Goals:** FL 18; FAC 1; LC 2; FMC 1; PO 3.*

THOMSON, David Laing

b. Bothkennar, 2nd February 1938

Career: Bo'ness United; cs 1959 Dunfermline Athletic; Aug 1961: CITY; cs 1963 Queen of the South; (Scottish Junior football - club n/k); Nov 1965-trials-Bradford Park Avenue; Aug 1967 Berwick Rangers.

City debut/only game v Tottenham Hotspur (H) 30.4.62 (scored once)

> The hero of Dunfermline's 1961 Scottish Cup triumph – as an unexpected selection for the Final replay against Celtic, he scored the first goal with a diving header – David had in fact made his Pars debut in a friendly against City in September 1960 (when he scored once, and Tommy McDonald twice, in a 3-2 win for the hosts). He cost Matt Gillies £10,000 when snapped up as a possible replacement for Ken Leek, but in two seasons managed only one senior outing (and that at inside-left, marked by a bullet header from a Len Chalmers free-kick) while the City No 9 shirt was being swapped around with some abandon. He recovered well from an October 1962 cartilage operation, but did not stay long at a relegation-bound Queen of the South after sharing a debut there with Tommy McDonald. David's subsequent fortunes in Scottish Junior football remain a mystery to us, but they were enough to persuade Jock Wallace to give him a final senior opportunity at Berwick, where he scored twice on each of his League and League Cup debuts, but soon disappeared from the picture.

***Apps:** FL 1.*
***Goals:** FL 1.*

THOMSON, William

b. Glasgow, ca 1894

Career: Blantyre Victoria; Parkhead; cs 1912 Clyde; Sept 1914 FOSSE; 1915 Arthurlie; Johnstone; cs 1919 CITY; Oct 1924 Bristol Rovers.

Fosse debut v Grimsby Town (A) 12.9.14

> By the time he left for Eastville, Billy was the last of the pre-war Fossils still to be active for the reconstructed City. Having originally signed from Shawfield as a tough wing-half, and suffered Fosse's plunge to the nadir of their fortunes, he returned from Scotland (and wartime work on naval repairs) for City's reinvigorated assault on the Second Division, and became a strong defensive anchor for Peter Hodge's predominantly attack-minded team-building efforts, partnering Jimmy Harrold and Mick O'Brien in succession until displaced by Jack Bamber. He took his City benefit from the game against Oldham in December 1923. Billy's single season with Bristol Rovers brought him a further 25 League and Cup selections (plus a sending-off in the Ashton Gate League derby); then in November 1925 he took up the position of coach at Highland League club Inverness Citadel.

***Apps:** FL 197; FAC 12.*
***Goals:** FL 3.*

THORNTON, William

b. Aston, Birmingham

Career: Bathurst Works; May 1919 CITY; cs 1920 Wellington Town.

City debut v Wolverhampton Wanderers (H) 30.8.19

> Signed from a Birmingham factory team in time for City's first match under their new title, but dropped immediately after that 1-2 home defeat, William was an inside-right who also failed subsequently to satisfy Peter Hodge's rigorous standards, and apparently exasperated some onlookers with his failure to exploit his potential. The columnist Scrutator in the *Mail* deemed him 'a mystery as far as form in the first team is concerned'. His departure after one season took him into Wellington's Birmingham & District League championship side.

***Apps:** FL 11.*
***Goals:** FL 2.*

THORPE, Harold Cheetham

b. New Whittington, Chesterfield, 1880
d. New Whittington, 16th September 1908

Career: Poolsbrook United; Jan 1901 Chesterfield Town; May 1903 Woolwich Arsenal; cs 1904 Fulham; Aug 1907 FOSSE.

Fosse debut v Leeds City (H) 7.9.07

> 'A gem of a back; daring, cool and clever', Harry had built up a solid body of top-class experience before joining Fosse. A £20 signing for Second Division football with his hometown club, he'd assisted Arsenal to promotion from that sphere in 1904 and helped Fulham to a pair of Southern League title wins in 1906 and 1907. After costing a sizeable £300, his skilful and powerful defensive qualities were a major boost to Fosse's successful promotion effort of the following term, but Harry sadly failed to finish the season, having contracted a debilitating strain of influenza after a game at Glossop in March 1908. Tragically, he never recovered, and died at his family home within months, with several Fosse players acting as pall-bearers at his funeral. Harry's fatal illness also deprived him of the chance to take up Derbyshire's offer to him to play county cricket in the summer of 1908. His younger brother Frank was a Staveley Town inside-left who played once at League level for Chesterfield in December 1911.

***Apps:** FL 26; FAC 2.*

THORPE, John

b. Skegby, Mansfield, ca 1892

Career: Stanton Hill Victoria; cs 1909 Mansfield Mechanics; May 1911 FOSSE; Mar 1912 Mansfield Mechanics; cs 1913 Sutton Town; July 1914 Shirebrook.

Fosse debut v Huddersfield Town (H) 21.10.11

> A young right-half who failed to make the transition from Notts & Derbyshire League football (in which the Mechs were title-holders in the two previous years) to the demands of Second Division fare, John appeared only in a couple of Fosse defeats when deputising for Arthur Randle. He'd arrived at Leicester in a straight swap for George King, but the two would play together for the Mechs in the new Central Alliance before the season was out.

***Apps:** FL 2.*

THRAVES, James

b. Stapleford, Notts, 1869
d. Bramcote, Notts, 29th May 1936

Career: Notts St Johns; 1889 Notts County; cs 1892 FOSSE; Sept 1897 Long Eaton Rangers.

Fosse debut v Mansfield Town (A) ML 17.9.1892

> Notts County's FA Cup Final goalkeeper in 1891, at a time when he had only two previous League games and four Cup outings to his credit, Jimmy even ended his stint with the Magpies having played in more Cup combat than First Division fare! He was the 'keeper who faced Fosse in the April 1891 friendly that was the last game played at Mill Lane, and earlier that year had played a key role in inspiring the introduction of the penalty kick for the following season. In the Magpies' Cup-tie with Stoke in February, he had been beaten by a shot which defender Jack Hendry fisted away from the line, then spread himself immediately in front of the ball at the ensuing free-kick, smothering it at the instant it was kicked. This obvious injustice, in a game Stoke lost 0-1, sealed the case for the penalty kick only a year after the FA had rejected out of hand the same proposed change to the Laws. With Fosse, Jimmy got off on the wrong foot, missing a train connection and turning up 35 minutes late for his Midland League debut at Mansfield; but rather compensated by being an ever-present between the sticks for the next four and a half seasons, making 148 consecutive appearances. A measure of his ability as much as his consistency was that his frustrated understudy during the first League season, former Buxton 'keeper Tom Chappell, was good enough to win an eventual move to Manchester City; while the man in his shadow during 1895/6, ex-Arbroath goalie William Strachan, even took to playing the odd reserve and friendly game in the half-back line to try to win a senior breakthrough. Goalkeeping in those days was primarily an art of first-time clearances, with any custodian foolish enough to hold onto the ball liable to rough handling, but Jimmy was an early master. Just to emphasise the 'whole different ball game' nature of Victorian football, however, one could instance the fact that Jimmy actually played throughout the eventually-abandoned Midland League fixture against Doncaster at a snowbound Filbert Street in November 1893 wearing his overcoat. For a couple of years he also pursued a unique parallel career as Fosse groundsman. He benefited from a friendly against Luton in September 1896, and played his last competitive Fosse game in the 1897 Burford Cup Final victory over Notts County, who he rejoined in the 20s for an eleven-year stint as director. At that time, having graduated through his father's road contracting company to form his own, he was a successful Stapleford businessman. Before WW1 he had also captained Stapleford Town Cricket Club.

***Apps:** FL 80; FAC 24; ML 44.*

THRELFALL, Frederick

b. Preston, 1879

Career: June 1898 Manchester City; cs 1905 Fulham; July 1909 FOSSE.

Fosse debut v Wolverhampton Wanderers (H) 1.9.09 (scored once)

> A deft, speedy winger whose Manchester City mentor was the great Billy Meredith, Fred had an eventful time in the early years of the century, experiencing relegation in 1902, winning a Second Division championship medal in 1903, and contributing to the top-flight runners-up campaign which ensued. He was also one of the few 'innocents' on the Hyde Road payroll when the FA uncovered a mesh of financial irregularities there and slapped massive fines and suspensions on a majority of the players and management, almost causing the club to fold. His move to Craven Cottage brought him immediate success, as Fulham raced to the Southern League championship in both 1906 and 1907, and won election to the League. Fred played in the Professionals v Amateurs international trial (alongside Arthur Collins) in 1906, and for the South v North a year later, and he was regarded as a prize capture by Fosse as they attempted to bounce straight back into Division One. He turned in some scintillating displays on either flank until February 1911 (his goal at Leyton putting the club into the FA Cup quarter-finals for the first time in 1910), and off the field was a member of the management committee of the Players Union. In August 1911 he took over coaching duties at Irish club Cliftonville from Jimmy Blessington, but in October that year was noted as winning a prestigious bowls tournament in Blackpool. It is believed that Wilfred Threlfall, a Birmingham and Bournemouth winger of the 20s, was his son.

***Apps:** FL 50; FAC 6.*
***Goals:** FL 6; FAC 4.*

Fred Threlfall

TIMSON, David Youles

b. Syston, Leics, 24th August 1947

CAREER: Blaby Boys Club; app Dec 1962/pro Sept 1964 CITY; Aug 1967 Newport County; Nov 1968 Oadby Town; Jan 1976 Enderby Town.

City debut v Blackpool (H) 11.4.64

> A Leicester Boys goalkeeper who made his A team debut for City when just turned 15, David was still a Filbert Street apprentice when making his first-team bow. Indeed, until Peter Shilton broke his record two years later, he was the youngest peacetime City debutant, having made a single stand-in appearance at the age of 16 (in a 2-3 home defeat) when Gordon Banks was on England duty and regular reserve George Heyes was injured. Ironically, David was not to don the senior green jersey again until Shilton had become the established No 1; playing in the final two games of 1966/7 (both home wins) while Shilton was away with England Youth. He managed 27 League and Cup starts at Somerton Park, then returned to local football, winning a Senior League championship medal with Oadby in 1973.

***Apps:** FL 3.*

TOMLIN, David

b. Nuneaton, Warks, 9th February 1953

Career: app Aug 1970/pro Oct 1971 CITY; Apr 1977 Torquay United; Aug 1978 Aldershot; June 1981 Andover; Godalming.

City debut v Huddersfield Town (H) 16.10.71

> A young winger who persistently fringed Jimmy Bloomfield's squads of the early 70s, and regularly warmed the City sub's bench, David is chiefly remembered for one inspired performance in his first season, when he ran England full-back Terry Cooper ragged in a home game against Leeds. It was the sort of form David could not maintain consistently, however, and his role became that of occasional stand-in for Len Glover. He managed 39 League and Cup games at Torquay and 35 at Aldershot, scoring twice in the Fourth Division for each club.

***Apps:** FL 19+7; FAC 1+2; LC 1.*
***Goals:** FL 2.*

TOMPKIN, Maurice

b. Countesthorpe, Leics, 17th February 1919
d. Leicester, 27th September 1956

Career: Countesthorpe United; trials Feb 1938/pro Mar 1938 CITY; Nov 1945 Bury; Sept 1946 Huddersfield Town; Oct 1947 Kettering Town.

City debut/only game v Birmingham (H) 7.5.38

> The son of former City winger Percy, and an outside-right himself, Maurice made a teenage Filbert Street debut in a 1-4 defeat which maintained Birmingham's First Division status, and weeks later made his bow in the County Cricket Championship with Leicestershire. But service with the RAMC in India meant that he played no more senior football until appearing in 24 games for Bury during the transitional 1945/6 season, and going on to feature in ten top-flight games for Huddersfield. His cricket definitely took precedence though, and he starred as a stylish and prolific batsman until his death, amassing 29 centuries amongst his 18,590 runs. Maurice toured Pakistan with the MCC in the winter of 1955/6, and played his final Leicestershire campaign when plagued with back pain, only to die a week after the operation intended to ameliorate it.

***Apps:** FL 1.*

Maurice Tompkin

TOMPKIN, Percy Lord

b. Salford, Lancs, 28th January 1894
d. Countesthorpe, Leics, 25th February 1948

Career: Countesthorpe United; cs 1912 Leicester Imperial; Oct 1912 Sutton Junction; Apr 1913-trials-FOSSE; May 1913 Hinckley United; cs 1914 Nuneaton Town; Army football; July 1919 Huddersfield Town; June 1920 CITY; July 1925 Nuneaton Town.

City debut v Bury (H) 2.9.20 (scored once)

> 'A spirited flyer on the wing, he is a real top-notcher when at his best'. The *Mercury* so described the senior member of the Tompkin family duo, who rejoiced in the non-derogatory nickname of 'Fairy', and battled for four Second Division seasons with Sandy Trotter for the City outside-left berth, with honours roughly even between them until both were eclipsed by the advent of Harold Wadsworth. In fact, Percy twice broke his arm in 1924, and never won back his place thereafter. He had previously played but a single League game for the powerful Terriers outfit which in 1919/20 both won promotion and reached the Cup Final, only months after almost folding. By the time son Maurice signed for City, Percy was established as a Countesthorpe hosiery manufacturer.

***Apps:** FL 87; FAC 3.*
***Goals:** FL 4.*

TOWERS, William Harry

b. Leicester, 13th July 1920

Career: Bentley Engineering Co FC; am Mar 1940/pro Jan 1945 CITY; Oct 1946 Torquay United; Sept 1956 Minehead.

City debut (WW2) v Coventry City (H) 7.9.40; (postwar) v Chelsea (A) FAC 5.1.46

> A local left-half who played a handful of Regional League games for City in 1940/1 before seeing service with the Fleet Air Arm, Bill eventually proved himself worthy of a professional contract from wartime boss Tom Bromilow. Having twice faced Chelsea in the FA Cup during 1945/6, he briefly shared in the return to Second Division football under Johnny Duncan, but was soon allowed to rejoin former City coach Jack Butler, by then managing at Plainmoor. Bill stayed with Torquay for ten years in Division Three (South), making 274 League appearances, prompting City 's visit for his 1952 benefit match, and spending some of his summers as a Devon lifeguard.

***Apps:** FL 4; FAC 2; WW2 44.*
***Goals:** WW2 2.*

TRAINER, Harry

b. Wrexham, 1872
d. Wrexham, 1924

Career: 1890 Wrexham Victoria; 1891 Wrexham Grosvenor; 1893 Westminster Rovers; cs 1894 Wrexham; Feb 1895-trials-West Bromwich Albion; May 1895 FOSSE; cs 1897 Sheppey United; cs 1899 Wrexham.

Fosse debut v Burton Swifts (H) 7.9.1895

> International centre-forward Harry first cropped up in the Fosse annals in November 1894, when the club received an FA censure for illegally approaching and registering him. But they got their man eventually, after he had led Wales in all three home internationals of March 1895 (scoring twice against Ireland), had spearheaded Wrexham to the Welsh League title, and had picked up his second successive Welsh Cup runners-up medal. The diminutive Harry nonetheless proved an inconsistent marksman in the Second Division, and a nap-hand of goals in an 8-0 demolition of Rotherham Town provided precisely half his first seasonal League tally. Unable thereafter to command a regular attacking role, he moved on for a couple of seasons at Sheppey, then enjoying an elevated status in the Southern League's top echelon, and bowed out of the game when 'knee failure' aborted his second Wrexham stint. He was a cousin of the oft-capped Preston and Wales 'keeper Jim Trainer.

***Apps:** FL 31; FAC 4.*
***Goals:** FL 12; FAC 4.*

TRAVERS, James Edward (George)

b. Newtown, Birmingham, 4th November 1888 (?)
d. Smethwick, Worcs, 31st August 1946 (?)

Career: 1904 Bilston United; 1905 Rowley United; July 1906 Wolverhampton Wanderers; Aug 1907 Birmingham; Dec 1908 Aston Villa; May 1909 Queens Park Rangers; Aug 1910 FOSSE; Jan 1911 Barnsley; Feb 1914 Manchester United; Army football; cs 1919 Swindon Town; June 1920 Millwall; Oct 1920 Norwich City; June 1921 Gillingham; 1922 Nuneaton Town; Nov 1922 Cradley St Lukes; 1929 Bilston United.

Fosse debut v Bolton Wanderers (H) 3.9.10 (scored twice)

> The son of a music-hall comedian, and essentially a youthful reserve for his West Midlands clubs, inside-forward George was best-known prior to his brief Fosse spell for having notched a hat-trick on his Villa debut against Bury on Boxing Day 1908. As deputy to future England international Harry Hampton, though, he found few chances at Villa Park and, curiously, it was his Southern League record at QPR (of only seven goals in 34 games) which recommended him to Leicester player/manager Andy Aitken. George was lucky to be around for this move, as he'd briefly been put on the critical list when hospitalised following a collision with a teammate in a QPR v Leyton encounter, but he found little fortune at Filbert Street as Fosse slumped to mid-table after winning six of the first nine fixtures of 1910/11, and was soon involved in a straight swap with Barnsley 'keeper Fred Mearns. He went on to appear in the Tykes' victorious 1912 FA Cup Final team, losing his medal that July but having it returned anonymously by post. George switched to Division One fare at Old Trafford before the war, then briefly guested for Spurs before seeing Army service in Salonika. On demob, he notched a dozen Southern League goals for Swindon; appeared in Millwall's first-ever League line-up; and scored the goal which gave Norwich their belated first-ever League win. A colourful off-field and post-football life culminated in a Gillingham jail sentence in 1933.

***Apps:** FL 12.*
***Goals:** FL 5.*

TROTTER, Alexander E.

b. Jarrow, Co Durham

Career: 1912 Jarrow Croft; Dec 1916 Leeds City; Apr 1917 Raith Rovers; Dumbarton; Ashington; June 1920 CITY; May 1924 South Shields; May 1927 Port Vale; July 1928 Manchester Central; Oct 1929 Bedlington United.

City debut v Bury (H) 2.9.20 (scored once)

> Essentially an outside-left, Sandy made his City bow in the centre-forward berth after stepping up from North Eastern League football, and managed quite a few more games as makeshift leader while attempting to shrug off Percy Tompkin's challenge for the flank position. He exhibited flair and forcefulness in City's attempts to rise from the Second Division – the *Mercury* admiringly noting that he could 'put in all the dash that is wanted when concentrating on the main chance' – but by the time they achieved that feat, Sandy was in the middle of a consistent three-year spell with South Shields, then still to experience the rapid decline that presaged their later lock, stock and barrel uprooting to Gateshead. His Port Vale season took him back to a club for whom he'd 'guested' in an October 1922 benefit friendly, and he then joined the ambitious, newly-formed Manchester Central club which occupied Belle Vue stadium and was entering on the first of its three years in the Lancashire Combination. Sandy's wartime experience prior to joining City was not only on Northern and Scottish football fields: he also lost a finger in military action.

***Apps:** FL 96; FAC 4.*
***Goals:** FL 10; FAC 1.*

TROTTER, Michael

b. Hartlepool, 27th October 1969

Career: YT/pro Nov 1987 Middlesbrough; Nov 1988-loan-Doncaster Rovers; June 1990 Darlington; Dec 1991 CITY; Nov 1993 Chesterfield; 1994-trials-Walsall; Aug 1994 Frankwell (Hong Kong); Dec 1994 Buxton; Jan 1995 Halifax Town; Dec 1996 VS Rugby; Jan 1998 King's Lynn; Feb 1998 Hinckley United; 2000 North Ferriby United.

City debut v Bristol Rovers (A) 1.1.92 (sub)

> Coached by Brian Little at Ayresome, where he failed to make a senior breakthrough, and then a member of Little's 1991 Division Four championship team at Feethams, defensive midfielder Michael was given a third chance to impress his mentor when brought to City as something of a wild card in the Jimmy Willis purchase deal. But his sporadic senior appearances tended to emphasise willingness and workrate rather than technical acumen, and a limited future in the Central League seemed to beckon until a loan spell at Saltergate (marked by a debut goal) developed into a further free transfer. For a while a Conference regular at Halifax, Michael then returned to Filbert Street as a part-time coach at City's school of excellence, and later held the post of Community Football Development Officer until late 1999.

***Apps:** FL 1+2; LC 1; AIC 0+1.*

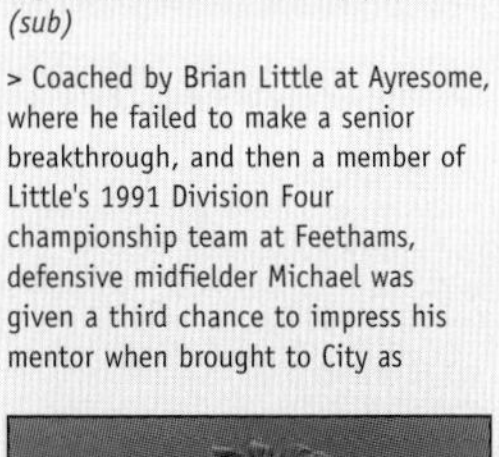

Michael Trotter

TROUGHEAR, William

b. Workington, 1885
d. Whitehaven, Cumberland, 15th October 1955

Career: Workington Marsh Mission; May 1907 Workington; May 1909 Sunderland; May 1914 FOSSE; cs 1919 Flimby Rangers; 1922 Workington.

Fosse debut v Lincoln City (H) 2.9.14

> Right-back Billy made exactly a century of League appearances for Sunderland, but only the final six of them had been in the year of their 1912/13 First Division title win. An England trialist in 1910/11 (Whites v Stripes), he was approaching the veteran stage when he brought his dour defensive qualities to Leicester, and proved no better equipped than his teammates to stem the tide of humiliating results which left Fosse clutching at the re-election straw before the abandonment of League football. After wartime munitions work, and guest appearances for Preston North End, Billy played out most of his postwar career in the North West Cumberland League, in the company of another former Fossil, James Straughton. A steel worker after quitting the game, he collapsed and died on a bus between his Mirehouse home and Whitehaven.

***Apps:** FL 15; FAC 1.*

TRUEMAN, Albert Harry

b. Leicester, Apr qtr 1882
d. Leicester, 24th February 1961

Career: Wigston Excelsior; Grasmere Swifts; am Aug 1899 FOSSE; cs 1901 Coalville Town; cs 1902 Hinckley Town; 1903 Coalville Town; Sept 1904 St Andrews; Mar 1905 FOSSE; May 1908 Southampton; Mar 1911 Sheffield United; cs 1913 Darlington; Sept 1914 Leicester Imperial.

Fosse debut v Clapton Orient (H) 2.9.05

> Inexplicably known to all and sundry throughout his career as 'Nigger', this local left-half was on Fosse's books as an amateur from an early age, represented the county at juvenile level, and played in benefit friendlies for both George Swift and Johnny McMillan during 1900/1, but he would be allowed to gain wider experience in localised fare before settling to a regular challenging role as a Filbert Street professional. Harry wrestled for three seasons with Bob Pollock for a first-team place, and also patiently captained the reserves as Fosse headed for promotion. He flourished with Southampton, though, winning representative honours for the Southern League and scoring the winning goal for that combination when they beat the Football League in November 1910 at White Hart Lane, on the way to a clean sweep of that season's Inter-League tourney. He racked up a 55-game First Division record at Bramall Lane, and played alongside Jimmy Donnelly, Bob Turner and Shirley Hubbard in the North Eastern League at Darlington. Harry made a nostalgic return to Filbert Street in September 1916, when persuaded from the stand to make up the numbers in a wartime Fosse game against Grimsby; and it is believed that he may well have later briefly assisted Clydebank in the immediate postwar period.

Harry Trueman

***Apps:** FL 43; FAC 1; WW1 1.*
***Goals:** FL 2.*

TURNER, Philip

b. Sheffield, 12th February 1962

Career: Sheffield Rangers; app July 1978/pro Feb 1980 Lincoln City; Aug 1986 Grimsby Town; Feb 1988 CITY; Mar 1989 Notts County (- 1996).

City debut v Blackburn Rovers (A) 19.3.88 (sub)

> Arriving in the part-exchange deal that took Kevin Jobling to Blundell Park, and departing in the two-way transaction that brought Gary Mills to Leicester, Phil also found in the interim his tactical role in David Pleat's Second Division side being swapped around on a fairly regular basis. Stints at full-back, in midfield and as an auxiliary winger hardly allowed him to settle, but his neat and busy skills on the ball were unfortunately supplemented neither by exceptional pace nor a great deal of penetration – though a magnificent 30-yard strike against Blackburn at Filbert Street, bringing him his first City goal, will live long in the memory. Phil had previously totted up 239 League appearances for Lincoln (promoted from Division Four in 1981), and built a fine reputation for cultured playmaking in his season and a half in a downwardly-mobile Grimsby side. He later skippered the Magpies back into the First Division via Wembley victories in both the 1990 and 1991 Play-Offs; appeared twice more at the national stadium in Anglo-Italian Cup Finals in 1994 (as a runner-up) and 1995 (as a victor); and suffered two Meadow Lane relegation terms in 1992 and 1995. He closed his career with an impressive aggregate of 694 competitive appearances and 52 goals.

***Apps:** FL 18+6; FAC 1; LC 1+1.*
***Goals:** FL 2.*

TURNER, Richard William

b. Leicester, ca 1884

Career: Leicester Imperial; trials Apr 1905/pro Feb 1906 FOSSE; Aug 1910 Portsmouth; Aug 1911 Leyton.

Fosse debut v Bradford City (H) 24.3.06

> Mistakenly identified as brothers in previously published drafts of this project, Billy and Bob Turner were in fact unrelated by anything stronger than an early rivalry for a Fosse first-team spot, after both had played for the local Imps and represented the county XI. Inside-left Billy was the first to make his senior bow, but then had to spend a rather longer apprenticeship in the reserves, barely getting a look-in until his near-namesake moved on. Indeed, the only occasion in which the pair turned out together (after their joint introduction as trialists in an April 1905 friendly against Forest), was when they formed the left-flank in a 2-2 draw at Chesterfield in the promotion season of 1907/8. Billy was a county representative as an Imp even before he came to Fosse's attention; and when he'd completed his five-year Filbert Street stint he had the choice of moves to either Partick Thistle or Portsmouth at a £25 fee. He lucklessly chose the Southern League route for what turned out to be a relegation season for Pompey, and he played only twice the following term for Leyton. Billy returned to Leicester upon ceasing playing and successively ran two pubs: The Rifle Volunteer in Wharf Street and, from 1923, the Granby Hotel in Morton Road.

***Apps:** FL 14.*
***Goals:** FL 3.*

TURNER, Robert Frewen

b. Leicester, 15th July 1885
d. Darlington, 15th February 1959

Career: Grasmere Swifts; St Andrews; St Marks; 1904 Leicester Imperial; trials Mar 1905/pro May 1906 FOSSE; Apr 1909 Everton; July 1911 Preston North End; cs 1912 Darlington; June 1914 Coventry City; Dec 1919 Durham City.

Fosse debut v Barnsley (H) 22.9.06

> The younger and more successful of the rival Turners, Bob – or 'Leggy' as he was usually known – also led the more colourful career. Not only was he a speedy outside-left with Fosse, good enough to take over from Frank Middleton halfway through the 1908 promotion season and hold his place in the top flight, but he also emulated his father Frew as a cricketing all-rounder for Leicestershire (1909-11). His club record £700 transfer to Everton, when Fosse's relegation fate was already settled, was a truly controversial affair, with Bob's new club reporting him to the FA for demanding an illicit £100 signing-on fee, and Bob finding himself suddenly somewhat worse off after a then-massive £50 fine. Undaunted, however, he made a scoring Goodison debut in the Liverpool derby and set about making final preparations for his impending marriage. This union – to Jimmy Blessington's sister-in-law, with Bob Pollock as best man – was the notoriously celebrated affair attended by most of the Fosse team on the eve of their record 0-12 defeat at Nottingham Forest. As if Bob hadn't wrought enough havoc for one month, he then assisted Everton to a 4-2 win over a rather more sober Fosse only three days later. His later efforts for a relegated Preston side, for North Eastern League champions Darlington, and for Coventry in the Southern League's Second Division inevitably seem almost mundane in comparison. Bob starred for Darlington Cricket Club after the war, while working there as a driller, but he was almost crippled by arthritis in later life. Right back at the start of his career, he's scored for the Imps in their County Cup Final win of 1906. His son Bobby (actually also christened Robert Frewen) played League football for Southport, Carlisle United and York City in the early 30s.

***Apps:** FL 56; FAC 3.*
***Goals:** FL 7; FAC 1.*

ULLATHORNE, Robert

b. Wakefield, Yorks, 11th October 1971

Career: YT/pro July 1990 Norwich City; July 1996 CA Osasuna; Feb 1997 CITY (- 1999); Sept 2000-trials-Newcastle United; Nov 2000 Sheffield United.

City debut v Wimbledon (H) LC 18.2.97

> A left-sided defender or midfielder

honoured at England Youth level while establishing himself at Carrow Road, Rob was briefly under Martin O'Neill's management there before sampling Spanish Second Division fare. His integration in Pamplona was proceeding well (certainly better than that of the quick-to-return Jamie Pollock, Osasuna's other English signing), but O'Neill tempted him back with the prospect of Premiership football at Filbert Street, and expended a split transfer fee – of around £500,000 to Osasuna and £100,000 to Norwich. Injuries and suspensions were stretching City's squad as they prepared for the first leg of their League Cup semi-final against Wimbledon, and there was therefore a sad irony that Rob would last only 11 minutes into his debut, being stretchered off with a broken ankle after making a non-contact interception. It would not be until the following December that he was fit to return, and his contributions for the rest of 1997/8 were indeed fitful, though they included a tasty strike at Ewood Park as City sought respectability in a 3-5 scoreline after a disastrous first half, and a dismissal at Bolton. Surprisingly, it was in central defence, alongside either Steve Walsh or Matt Elliott, that Rob made his mark in 1998/9, with his covering pace and positional sense more than compensating for his lack of inches. He was denied the Man of the Match award from the disappointing League Cup Final against Spurs – clearly earned for his man-marking job on David Ginola, and for contributing City's only goalworthy shot – when the vote was suddenly switched to late scorer Allan Neilsen; and weeks later suffered much more cruel luck, breaking his leg in two places in a collision with Kasey Keller as both men attempted to prevent a Gianfranco Zola goal for Chelsea at Stamford Bridge. Despite his injury and out-of-commission status, Rob rather perversely refused new City contract offers in June and July 1999. He was said to be training at Huddersfield in October of that year, and briefly figured in the St James's Park reserve side almost twelve months after that, but played no further senior football before December 2000, after which he became a Blades regular.

***Apps:** FL 28+3; FAC 2; LC 8+1.*
***Goals:** FL 1; FAC 1.*

VENUS, Mark

b. Hartlepool, 6th April 1967

Career: YT cs 1984/pro Mar 1985 Hartlepool United; Aug 1985 CITY; Mar 1988 Wolverhampton Wanderers; July 1997 Ipswich Town.

City debut v Aston Villa (A) 31.3.86

> Recruited as a trainee by his hometown club after he'd spurned approaches by Barnsley and Coventry, left-back Mark made four League appearances as a non-contract player, and came to Leicester as a free agent when 'Pool wanted him to continue on that basis. Reserve-team Player of the Year by the end of his first season, Mark had also made a single appearance in Simon Morgan's stead prior to finding himself the regular senior No 3 from the start of 1986/7. Though he understandably betrayed occasional defensive näiveté in City's First Division struggles, he also demonstrated commendable accuracy with his crosses from advanced positions, and laid on several of the goals which lifted the club to a then-unaccustomed mid-table slot. With relegation on the cards thereafter, though, he suffered as something of a regular scapegoat for a frustrated crowd, yet stuck doggedly to his game; and had won over many of his detractors by the time he netted his

Mark Venus

single goal for City: a memorable last-minute volley that won the home game against Swindon in 1987/8. David Pleat allowed Mark to move on to Molineux for £40,000, for Wolves' run-in to the Division Four championship, and he became a regular the following term when they took the Third Division title, soon afterwards assuming their captaincy, and occasionally moving forward into a middle line role. He then suffered a rare degree of Play-Off frustration, with semi-final exits for Wolves in 1995 (when Mark scored past Peter Shilton in the Bolton goal) and, after he'd been involved in a part-exchange with Steve Sedgley, for Ipswich in each of 1998 and 1999. The final domestic game of 1999/2000 then at last saw Mark and his East Anglian team promoted to the Premiership via their Wembley win, and embark on the remarkable term which ended with them securing UEFA Cup qualification.

***Apps:** FL 58+3; FAC 2; LC 3; FMC 2+1.*
***Goals:** FL 1.*

VICKERS, George Albert

b. Nantwich, Cheshire, ca 1866
d. Leicester, 19th August 1946

Career: Nantwich; 1889 FOSSE.

Fosse debut (competitive) v Loughborough (A) ML 14.11.1891

> Left-half throughout Fosse's initial County Cup-winning run of 1889/90, Albert arrived from Nantwich with Billy Davis, taking the professional plunge some two years before the club's Midland League era – for five shillings per match! He was in the first senior Fosse side to play at Filbert Street (by which stage his earnings had risen to 7s 6d), and was still turning out in occasional senior friendly fixtures in 1892/3. He was employed for many years thereafter at the Wheatsheaf Works.

***Apps:** ML 4.*

VICKERSTAFFE, Ernest B.

b. Hanley, Staffs, ca 1884
d. Liverpool, November 1935

Career: 1900 Cheltenham Town; 1901 Eastville Athletic; 1902-trials-Bristol City; Sept 1902 Leicester Old Boys; Nov 1902 FOSSE; Leicester Old Boys; cs 1907 Leicester Nomads; cs 1909 Hinckley United.

Fosse debut/only game v Burslem Port Vale (A) 27.2.04

> Educated at Granby Road school, and a centre-forward for Leicester Boys, Ernest showed a keen homing instinct after his brief forays in West Country football, and developed into a well-respected amateur full-back. His affiliation with Fosse reserves stretched from 1902 to 1913, but his senior record was, cruelly, of the briefest order; for he broke his leg in two places during a 2-6 Second Division defeat in the Potteries. Ernest was a county representative in 1904, played four times in County Cup Finals (with Fosse in 1905 and 1909, and with Hinckley in 1910 and 1911), and was co-founder and captain of Leicester Nomads. He also played local cricket as a batsman for St Peter's.

***Apps:** FL 1.*

VILLIERS, Henry George (Bob)

b. Faversham, Kent, 29th June 1892
d. Leicester, 28th August 1972

Career: Bedford Town; Army football; cs 1919 Rugby Town; July 1920 CITY; Dec 1921 Hinckley United; cs 1922 Mansfield Town; July 1923 Nuneaton Town; Oct 1923 Rugby Town; Oct 1926 Hinckley United.

Fosse debut v Clapton Orient (A) 28.8.20

> Having completed wartime service with the Hussars, and returned to football in the Birmingham Combination, Bob was a wing-half in whom high hopes were invested at the start of 1920/1. He was nonetheless released after one and a half seasons of understudying Teddy King and Billy Thomson, having made considerably less impact than his former Rugby teammates, the Roxburghs. Mansfield finished tenth in the Midland League with Bob alongside George Greatorex in their side, and he scored once for them in the FA Cup in a total of 35 outings. His impact on Hinckley United was remarkable: they embarked on a run of 24 successive victories in league and cup football from the date of his debut, taking the Birmingham Combination title for 1926/7, but losing to City's seconds in the Senior Cup Final just after their run ended. Bob was later a partner in the Leicester printing firm of AT Shelley & Co until retirement in 1965

***Apps:** FL 5.*

VINCETT, John Herbert

b. Hastings, Sussex, 24th May 1883
d. Lambeth, London, 28th December 1953

Career: Hastings Rovers; Old Hastonians; St Leonards; Hastings; cs 1905 St Leonards United; Aug 1907 Grimsby Town; July 1908 FOSSE; Jan 1909 Barnsley; cs 1909 Hastings & St Leonards; Oct 1910 Tottenham Hotspur.

Fosse debut: 12.12.08 v Manchester United (A).

> Declared to be a professional in October 1905, when St Leonards United were fined for excess payments, and three of their players received month-long suspensions, John was a tall, weighty full-back who was still with his hometown Southern League club (renamed Hastings & St Leonards in 1906) when they reached the First Round Proper of the FA Cup, and lost 1-3 to Norwich. He became a regular, noted for his powerful, lengthy kicking, in his Second Division term with the Mariners, but his essentially unsophisticated style was soon deemed not to be up to the First Division standard after his £100 transfer. Indeed, the 2-4 defeat at Old Trafford that marked his sole Fosse outing was to prove his last at League level. Barnsley failed to select him in a senior line-up, and he thereafter made a rather radical revision to his game in the attempt to win further recognition. He completed Spurs trials, and subsequently signed, as a goalkeeper; having switched positions during the previous term when, according to the *Mercury*, he 'got too big and slow'. He failed, however, to make the White Hart Lane first team. Nonetheless, for twelve summers from 1907, John was a professional medium-pace bowler with Sussex, and also turned out twice for Surrey in 1921.

***Apps:** FL 1.*

WADDLE, Alan Robert

b. Wallsend, Northumberland, 9th June 1954

Career: Nov 1971 Halifax Town; July 1973 Liverpool; Sept 1977 CITY; May 1978 Swansea City; Dec 1980 Newport County; July 1982 Gloucester City; Aug 1982 Mansfield Town; Dec 1982 (Hong Kong); Aug 1983 Hartlepool United; Oct 1983 Peterborough United; Jan 1985 Hartlepool United; Mar 1985 Swansea City; cs 1986 Barry Town; Dec 1986 Wakrah Sports (Qatar); Feb 1987 Barry Town; Jan 1988 Llanelli; Port Talbot; Maesteg Park; Nov 1989 Bridgend Town; Dec 1989 Llanelli.

City debut v Nottingham Forest (H) 24.9.77

> A tall striker who had only scored four goals in 40 games when added to the Anfield investment collection for £45,000, Alan failed to make the grade on Merseyside despite scoring the winning goal in his first Goodison derby, and had become resigned to Central League football when Frank McLintock asked him to help turn around City's atrocious start to the 1977/8 season. Within a couple of months, though, it was evident that neither Alan's confidence nor mobility were up to the task at hand; and it was only during his first spell at Swansea, under John Toshack, that he began to score with any regularity. He assisted the Swans up to the Second Division (during their whirlwind rise from Fourth to First), then cost Newport their all-time record outlay of £80,000. Alan's subsequent wanderings in the Fourth Division brought mixed fortunes; perhaps best summed up in his experience in the Mansfield v Crewe fixture of October 1982, when he scored for both sides and was then sent off! His return to the Vetch sparked a successful fightback against relegation from Division Three on the part of the Swans, and though Alan joined Barry Town for the 1986/7 season (which they ended as Welsh League champions), he also held a post running Swansea's commercial operations. He is a cousin of England international Chris Waddle.

***Apps:** FL 11.*
***Goals:** FL 1.*

Alan Waddle

WADSWORTH, Harold

b. Bootle, Lancs, 1st October 1898
d. Chesterfield, 2nd November 1975

Career: Bootle St Matthews; Tranmere Rovers; Jan 1918 Liverpool; Jun 1924 CITY; Apr 1927 Nottingham Forest; June 1928 Millwall (- 1931); Dec 1934 Cray Wanderers.

City debut v Manchester United (A) 30.8.24

> Harold joined his older brother, long-serving centre-half Walter, at Anfield for the final seasons of WW1 football, and soon etched a reputation as a raiding winger, but was then demoted to reserve status for the bulk of both Liverpool championship seasons of 1922 and 1923. The move to Filbert Street, however, brought him immediate recompense (albeit in a lower key), as his ever-present record on City's left wing immeasurably aided the 1925 Second Division title success, and his continuing consistency as partner to George Carr or Arthur Lochhead contributed sturdily to First Division consolidation. Harold's rather lowly goal ratio picked up appreciably during his Forest season (10 in 35 League and Cup games), and he then helped establish newly-promoted Millwall as a Second Division force over the following three campaigns. Harold was an antique dealer in New Cross when he decided on a brief Kent League comeback.

***Apps:** FL 98; FAC 8.*
***Goals:** FL 7.*

WAITE, George H.

b. Bradford, 1st March 1894
d. Bradford, 17th June 1972

Career: Royal Artillery; June 1915 Bradford Park Avenue; May 1920 Raith Rovers; Jan 1921 Clydebank; cs 1921 Pontypridd; May 1922 CITY; Mar 1923 Clapton Orient; July 1926 Hartlepools United; July 1927 York City.

City debut v Sheffield Wednesday (A) 6.5.22

> Re-emerging from WW1 service in Salonika, centre-forward George got the First Division ball rolling for Park Avenue, but won only half a dozen selections for his hometown club before briefly becoming a teammate of Davie Moyes and the Duncan brothers at Raith. There he claimed 11 Scottish League goals in a rapid burst, but detoured prolifically through the Southern League's Welsh Section before Peter Hodge caught up with him. An attack leader who relied more on speed than brawny bustling (he'd sprinted his way to the winning tape in two professional 60-yard handicaps), George attempted to fill Jock Paterson's boots at Filbert Street, but was always aware of the tactically-contrasting challenge of Albert Pynegar for City's chief scoring mantle. Later in his career, he set aside the marksman's role for that of provider, accomplishing a shift towards the right-wing position across three Second Division seasons at Orient, a Division Three (North) term at Hartlepools, and a Midland League campaign with York.

***Apps:** FL 28; FAC 2.*
***Goals:** FL 12.*

WALKER, Charles J.

b. Leicester, 1870

Career: 1889 FOSSE; Mar 1892 Leicester Hornets; Leicester YMCA.

Fosse debut (competitive) v Burton Wanderers (H) FAC 4.10.1890

> One of the Fosse pioneers from the pre-Midland League days, Charlie was the goalkeeper in both the first victorious County Cup Campaign and the club's initial FA Cup encounter. He

was also the embarrassed centre of the 'lost in the fog' incident, when belatedly discovered still guarding his goal some time after the end of a mist-enshrouded Fosse v Loughborough friendly in December 1890. Charlie's three first-class games, all defeats, resulted in him conceding eleven goals, but he was still rated highly enough to play for the county amateur XI in 1893/4, when assisting the local YMCA. By December 1938, he was in charge of the indoor bowling greens in Herbert Avenue, Belgrave.

Apps: *FAC 1; ML 2.*

WALKER, David

b. Walsall, 1884
d. Walsall, 31st October 1935

Career: Walsall White Star; Birchfield Villa; 1904 Wolverhampton Wanderers; cs 1905 Bristol Rovers; Apr 1907 West Bromwich Albion; May 1908 FOSSE; June 1911 Bristol Rovers; 1912 Willenhall Swifts; Dec 1913 Walsall.

Fosse debut v Sheffield Wednesday (H) 1.9.08

> A boxer before he turned professional footballer – 'a clever, hard-hitting lightweight' – Davie possessed the nickname 'Solly' amongst his playing colleagues. He briefly tasted top-flight fare at Molineux, scored 25 Southern League goals during his first Eastville spell, and claimed 15 strikes in his Second Division season with West Brom before Fosse paid £700 to bring him and Hawthorns teammate Arthur Randle to Leicester for their inaugural, ill-fated First Division campaign. Davie held one of the three inside-forward positions for almost three seasons, without quite replicating the scoring form his previous record had suggested, and it was ironic that his third Fosse term (during which he became the first Fossil to be sent off at Filbert Street, after scoring in a rough encounter with Clapton Orient) should prove both his least prolific and the one in which he took the leading scorer's laurels! Davie's later travels took him back via the Southern League to his home patch, where Willenhall and Walsall were then on par status in the Birmingham & District League. He'd suffered heart problems at Eastville in 1912, and was running a Birmingham pub when assisting the latter two clubs. Upon his death, City director LH Burridge recalled him as 'a little chap, but a tremendous worker'. One of Davie's brothers, William, made a single scoring appearance for West Brom in 1910/11 and was also at Walsall in 1914/15, while another, George, played over a hundred Southern League games for Bristol Rovers after a 1912 move from Willenhall. His son, Dave, was a Brighton wing-half throughout the 30s, after kicking off his career at Walsall.

Apps: *FL 73; FAC 9.*
Goals: *FL 27; FAC 2.*

WALKER, David Clive Allan

b. Watford, 24th October 1945

Career: app Sept 1961/pro Nov 1962 CITY; Oct 1966 Northampton Town; July 1969 Mansfield Town; July 1975 Chelmsford City; Gravesend & Northfleet.

City debut v Aston Villa (A) 18.4.64

> A left-half for England Schools in 1961, Clive developed at Filbert Street as a youthful, quick-tackling right-back understudy to Len Chalmers and John Sjoberg, and won a League Cup runners-up tankard from the second leg of the 1965 Final against Chelsea. His limited first-team prospects were comprehensively stymied, however, by the arrival of Peter Rodrigues, and he had to take the well-worn trails to both the County Ground and Field Mill to really establish his League-level reputation. He turned out in 72 games (largely in the left-back berth) during the Cobblers' vertiginous plummet to the Fourth Division, but made sufficient impression as an influentially cool strategist to be later recalled for successive spells as coach, manager (twice) and assistant manager after a lengthy interim 229-game stint with Mansfield. His backroom career continued at Maidstone United, with elevation from the assistant's role to the manager's chair in January 1992, but he was a helpless onlooker, with only two registered players to manage, when the Stones folded on the eve of the following season. Thereafter he became assistant boss at Kettering, Weymouth, Dagenham & Redbridge and Dover Athletic in turn. In fact three of his posts as No 2 have been in support of his old Cobblers teammate Graham Carr.

Apps: *FL 17; LC 1.*

WALKER, Donald Hunter

b. Edinburgh, 10th September 1935

Career: Broughton Star; Sept 1955 Tranent Juniors; Nov 1955 CITY; Oct 1959 Middlesbrough; Sept 1963 Grimsby Town; July 1964-trials-Workington; Nov 1964 Rugby Town (- 1970).

City debut v Nottingham Forest (H) 19.10.57

> Initially a part-timer with David Halliday's City, who found him an accountancy job locally, Don helped them re-establish themselves in the First Division with a series of elegant playmaking midfield performances at both wing-half and inside-forward, but his claim to his favoured No 6 shirt soon crumbled against the vigorous competition of the more forceful Ken Keyworth and Colin Appleton. His occasionally fastidious style subsequently failed to guarantee him first-team football at Ayresome (where he signed after a month's trial, and eventually spent over a year on the transfer list), and sadly he broke a leg after only fifteen games of Grimsby's 1964 Division Two relegation campaign. Jimmy Walsh signed Don for Rugby Town, and he completed 223 Southern League games there in six years, encompassing a caretaker manager stint during 1966/7. He came from a footballing family: father John won four Irish League titles and two Irish Cup medals at Belfast Celtic in the 30s; uncle Tommy was the Hearts, Chelsea and Scotland star; and brother Andrew briefly a Southampton reserve in the mid-50s.

Apps: *FL 32; FAC 2.*
Goals: *FL 1.*

Don Walker

WALKER, Ernest Edwin

b. Wigston, Leics, 24th November 1889
d. Leicester, 2nd May 1958

Career: South Wigston Albion; 1908 Army football (17th Regimental District XI); Apr 1909-trials-FOSSE; Dec 1912 Holwell Works; Army football; May 1919 Hinckley United; Oct 1919 CITY; July 1924 Hinckley United.

City debut v Huddersfield Town (A) 18.10.19

> The son of a soldier, and actually born at Glen Parva barracks, Ernie could have harboured little doubt that he would initially incline to the military life. But for quite some time he wavered over his preferred sport, for his initial peacetime engagement in the Leicestershire Regiment also saw him selected as a wing-threequarter in the annual Army v Navy rugby game, and take a winner's plaudits from the 1912 Army Cup Final against the Royal Welsh Regiment's XV. By this stage, he had already undergone Fosse reserve trials and had represented the county at football in 1909, but it would be ten years, and an interim WW1 spell in khaki, before he signed up on a permanent basis at Filbert Street, at a fee of £80. Always known as 'Hookey', he soon totted up over thirty games as a powerful inside-forward or outside-left for City, but was then briefly recalled to uniform for a third time in April 1921. Strangely, on his return, he re-emerged as a left-back challenger to Adam Black, and won a further forty selections as an out-and-out defender. A South Wigston resident, he worked for Constone Ltd after his football days and (though sadly partially disabled) returned to Filbert Street in later life as a gateman.

Apps: *FL 64; FAC 9.*
Goals: *FL 3; FAC 2.*

WALKER, John

b. Alexandria, Dunbartonshire, ca 1869

Career: Vale of Leven; 1889 Grimsby Town; cs 1893 Everton; Oct 1894 Manchester City; May 1895 FOSSE.

Fosse debut v Burton Swifts (H) 7.9.1895

> A versatile Scottish defender who joined Grimsby during their Football Alliance days and stayed with them when they became one of eight clubs from that combination to help form the Football League's Second Division, Jack scored on his top-flight debut for Everton, but played only a further two games for them at centre-half before joining the newly-formed Manchester City (that club being reconstructed from the debris of Ardwick, and elected alongside Fosse to Division Two). Moving on again to Filbert Street, Jack settled as an ever-present defensive pivot in his first term, and indeed missed very few games over four seasons – the latter two at right-back – until he suffered a broken shin in an April 1899 fixture against Grimsby which ended his career. He was awarded a benefit friendly against Everton in October of that year, which not only raised about £75, but also a storm of protest about Fosse's unpublicised decision to field an under-strength side, by all accounts flattered by only a 1-4 reverse.

Apps: *FL 113; FAC 12.*
Goals: *FL 1.*

WALKER, Joseph Nicol

b. Aberdeen, 29th September 1962

Career: Elgin City; 1979-loan-Keith; 1980-loan-Inverness Caledonian; July 1980 CITY; Jan 1983 Motherwell; Dec 1983 Rangers; Dec 1986-loan-Falkirk; Dec 1987-loan-Dunfermline Athletic; Aug 1989 Heart of Midlothian; Feb 1992-loan-Burnley; Dec 1994 Partick

Nicky Walker

Thistle; Aug 1996 Aberdeen; Oct 1997 Ross County.

City debut v Chelsea (A) 9.3.82

> Along with Ian Wilson and Kevin MacDonald, another Jock Wallace recruit from Highland League football, tall goalkeeper Nicky had once toured Holland in the same Caley youth side as MacDonald, and was soon winning Scottish caps at that level after his move to Filbert Street. He briefly stepped up for First Division action after Mark Wallington's record-breaking run of consecutive appearances came to an end through injury, and impressed with his confidence and clean handling after a shaky start at Stamford Bridge. He would then twice more sign for Wallace, at Fir Park and Ibrox, and became a regular for Rangers until displaced by England international Chris Woods, winning a Scottish League Cup-winner's medal in 1987/8, and contributing briefly to title wins in 1987 and 1989. Nicky then competed with Henry Smith for the No 1 jersey at Hearts, winning a surprise Scotland call-up in March 1993, at the age of 30, for a cap from a home encounter with Germany. Three 'B' international selections followed, and one more full cap and, despite Partick's 1996 relegation, Nicky was in the national squad for that summer's European Championship tournament. Later, having extended his Premier record at Pittodrie after a £60,000 switch, and translated his Ross County loan into a permanent move, he skippered them to the Division Three title in 1999, and to further promotion a year later. Nicky is a member of the famous shortbread manufacturing family.

Apps: *FL 6.*

WALLINGTON, Francis Mark

b. Sleaford, Lincs, 17th September 1952

Career: Heckington United; am cs 1971/pro Oct 1971 Walsall; Mar 1972 CITY; July 1985 Derby County; Aug 1988 Lincoln City (- 1991); Sept 1994 Grantham.

City debut v West Ham United (H) 11.3.72

> Faced with the initially daunting and thankless task of succeeding Gordon Banks and Peter Shilton between the City posts, Mark more than made up for a comparative lack of charismatic flair by dint of a dogged consistency and willingness to work at the raw edges of his game; eventually building a monumental club record for consecutive appearances as testament to his awesome reliability. He was very much a goalkeeping tyro when bought for £30,000 by Jimmy Bloomfield as cover for Shilton, having made only eleven League appearances as a Fellows Park discovery, but having impressed mightily with a spectacular televised performance in a Cup-tie at Everton. Indeed, for several seasons he continued to learn his trade while almost exclusively in the England 'keeper's shadow, only stepping up for an extended senior run at the beginning of 1974/5 when Shilton's determination to move was becoming irresistible. It was ironic that Mark should suffer injury only weeks after his predecessor's sale to Stoke, for his return to the fray in the Third Round FA Cup-tie with Oxford in January 1975 became the start of a run in which he was never again absent until March 1982: a spell of 294 League games, 22 FA Cup encounters and 15 League Cup ties (331 senior games in all). During this time he added two England Under-23 caps to his haul of schools and amateur youth honours, experienced two relegation seasons and one Second Division championship, and become one of the select band of goalkeeper-captains in League football; while one of the more remarkable aspects of his unbroken sequence of appearances was that he'd actually ben prevented from training for several years in the middle of his career by a skin affliction. Even after a sickening collision with Shrewsbury's Chic Bates had sidelined Mark for the first time in years, he came back to tot up another invaluable ever-present contribution to City's 1983 promotion campaign (picking up a deserved testimonial on the way), to see off the imported challenge of Mark Grew whilst briefly in contract dispute with the club, and finally to be displaced from the City six-yard box only by the youthful promise of Ian Andrews. Mutterings about the veteran's purported loss of sharpness – prompted as much by superficial judgements about thinning hair and a widening girth as by genuine signs of creakiness – were still proven somewhat premature, though, as his rearguard experience materially assisted new club Derby from the Third to the First Division in the two years following his £25,000 transfer. It was hardly apt reward, then, when Mark subsequently found himself stuck in reserve behind Peter Shilton at the Baseball Ground. A return to his native county coincided with the Red Imps' return to League football, following their one-year exile in the Conference; and retirement, three years later, only came after a career aggregate of 577 League games. Mark briefly acted as a specialist goalkeeping coach at Everton; then took up a coaching appointment with the Lincolnshire FA. A week after his 42nd birthday, he answered an emergency call to turn out in the Southern League for Grantham, and then acted as assistant manager there. Now a teacher in Sleaford, he is also goalkeeping coach to the England Schools Under-18 squad.

Apps: *FL 412; FAC 25; LC 23.*

WALSH, James

b. Blairhall, Fife, 3rd December 1930

Career: Blairhall Boys Club; Valleyfield Colliery; Bo'ness United; Oct 1949 Celtic; Nov 1956 CITY; July 1964 Rugby Town (p/mgr).

City debut v Fulham (H) 23.3.57

> A scorer in the Finals of both the 1953 Coronation Cup and the 1955 Scottish Cup, a title-winner in the interim year, and capped once for Scotland Under-23 against England, Jimmy was yet never quite assured of his inside-forward place for Celtic at a time when the likes of Fernie, Tully, Mochan and Bobby Collins were also in front-line contention. He became the subject of one of David Halliday's regular cross-border transfer raids, but played only his debut game in the 1957 Second Division championship effort, reserving his striking energies

Jimmy Walsh

for the next six years of top-flight combat, during which he was twice City's top scorer. Jimmy claimed a hat-trick against Mansfield in the club's first-ever League Cup tie (indeed, the first registered anywhere in that competition), and later that season led his team out at Wembley as skipper, having contributed the breakthrough goal in the drawn-out FA Cup semi-final series against Sheffield United. Another scoring milestone was Jimmy's opening of City's account in European competition, but his quick-witted, darting elegance was later offset by a diminishing effectiveness in front of goal, and through a combination of problems with injuries and eyesight (Jimmy was one of the first footballers to play regularly in contact lenses), he had lost his place by the time the 1963 Wembley return was achieved. In fact, he was considered for the Mansfield Town player-manager vacancy in that February, but it would be over a year later that he assumed that hyphenate role at Rugby. On hanging up his boots, Jimmy moved into a newsagent's business in Leicester city centre.

***Apps:** FL 176; FAC 18; LC 4; ECWC 1.*
***Goals:** FL 80; FAC 5; LC 5; ECWC 2.*

WALSH, Steven

b. Fulwood, Lancs, 3rd November 1964

Career: app/pro Sept 1982 Wigan Athletic; June 1986 CITY; Sept 2000 Norwich City.

City debut v Luton Town (H) 23.8.86.

> By far the longest-serving player on the City staff in the last quarter-century, Steve also proved himself one of the most enigmatic across his fourteen years at Filbert Street; and for many younger supporters he became the never-say-die embodiment of the history of Leicester City. As such his career is almost impossible to synopsise, for he was an intrinsic feature of almost every low- and highlight of this ultra-eventful era for the club, and one risks merely ticking off his presence in, or influence on, every turning point of the period. There is also the problem of deciding precisely *which* Steve Walsh to attempt to describe. The rugged stopper or the swashbuckling striker? The coolly commanding captain or the reckless recipient of nine red cards? The red rag to Steve Bull, or the man who led the Rams to slaughter...? Having already topped 150 senior games for Wigan and taken a Wembley winner's medal from the 1985 Freight/ Rover Trophy Final, Steve followed former boss Bryan Hamilton to Leicester as the latter's initial purchase, justifying his £100,000 fee by deposing the unsettled John O'Neill in the First Division line-up. But even in his first term he was alternating the promise of becoming an aerially dominant defensive influence with moments of naive impetuosity which cost his relegation-bound side dearly. Steve's first Second Division game for City ended with his (second) dismissal, for a vicious assault on Shrewsbury's David Geddis which eventually earned him an eleven-game ban; but he returned with an apparently much more mature outlook, developing his defensive timing and positioning, and began to show himself additionally as a useful goalscorer. Indeed, Steve took the Player of the Year award in 1988 to index his rehabilitation, but ill-luck with injuries hampered his progress the following term. He remained at the heart of the back-line formations of each of David Pleat, Gordon Lee and Brian Little (skippering the side under the latter boss despite three dismissals in 1990/1 and two more in 1992/3), until Little then gambled on shifting him forward into a muscular target-man role, to which he adapted with enthusiasm and no little effectiveness. Steve became the 15-goal top marksman of 1993 (at one point scoring in five successive victories) as a second Play-Off Final came into view, and he contributed an additional Wembley goal to the exciting fightback against Swindon, to help ease memories of the penalty he'd unluckily conceded against Blackburn's David Speedie the year before. It was a further year on at Wembley, though, that Steve's first pinnacle of glory would be reached, with the two goals against Derby that finally lifted City into the Premiership coming after he'd missed the bulk of the season following a horrendous cruciate ligament injury at Middlesbrough. Further knee problems completely ruined the next top-flight campaign for Steve, but he was restored to the side and the captaincy in time for the 1996 Play-Off triumph over Crystal Palace. His testimonial season followed: featuring a missed penalty at White Hart Lane, an eighth dismissal at Upton Park, and a pair of headed knock-down assists for both City's League Cup Final equaliser against Middlesbrough at Wembley and the winning goal in the Hillsborough replay. His 50th League goal for City was a matchwinner at Leeds, but a hamstring injury suffered in the same game sidelined him from the crucial second-leg UEFA Cup-tie against Atletico Madrid. Indeed, nagging injuries were to cut severely into Steve's appearance record over the next couple of seasons (when, incidentally, his remarkable Highbury up-and-under own goal put him out front in City's records for the most such embarrassments); though he was again fit to skipper City in the 1999 League Cup Final, even if his waning pace may have been exploited in the lead-up to Spurs' late winner. A week later, he was the subject of rejected deadline-day transfer overtures from Aston Villa, and he maintained sterling Premiership value for City whenever called upon during 1999/2000. His spirit and commitment never wavered either, and were epitomised in the League Cup tie with Fulham, when he redeemed uncharacteristic errors by rampaging up-front to set up a goal for Ian Marshall and then blast home an unstoppable equaliser himself. Steve put himself forward for the City managerial vacancy after Martin O'Neill's departure, and only left Filbert Street after being deemed some way down Peter Taylor's pecking order for central defenders. Briefly re-uniting with Bryan Hamilton at Carrow Road after following Tony Cottee there, however, he soon had to accept that a career's worth of injuries had taken their cumulative toll, and he soon retired from the full-time game. With no senior backroom role on offer in the short term, he signed forms for Gary Mills as cover at Tamworth, but has since utilised his immense experience running a series of soccer schools in Leicestershire.

***Apps:** FL/PL 352+17; FAC 16+1; LC 39+1; FMC 10; AIC 1; UEFA 1; PO 11.*
***Goals:** FL/PL 53; FAC 1; LC 4; FMC 1; PO 3.*

WALTERS, Victor

Career: 1911 Walthamstow Grange; Feb 1913 Gravesend; Oct 1913 FOSSE; Oct 1914 Abertillery.

Fosse debut v Huddersfield Town (A) 20.12.13

> Fosse manager Jack Bartlett's partiality for for players with London or South-Eastern credentials was even more pronounced than that later exhibited by City counterpart Jimmy Bloomfield. Amongst them, no less than four former Walthamstow Grange players found their way to Filbert Street, with Victor following Claude Stoodley and preceding reserves Ted Leahy and Herbert Marsh. This amateur left-winger, a Kent Senior Cup finalist in 1913 with Gravesend, fared little better than many of his out-of-their-depth contemporaries, however, and then joined a hard-up Abertillery club who were one of three Welsh outfits to resign from the Southern League partway through 1914/15. A slight doubt remains over his forename: while League registration documents have him as Victor, the *Mercury* welcomed him as Vivian around the date of his signing.

***Apps:** FL 11.*
***Goals:** FL 2.*

WARD, Ashley Stuart

b. Middleton, Lancs, 24th November 1970

Career: Cheadle Town; YT/pro Aug 1989 Manchester City; Jan 1991-loan-Wrexham; July 1991 CITY; Nov 1992-loan-Blackpool; Dec 1992 Crewe Alexandra; Dec 1994 Norwich City; Mar 1996 Derby County; Sept 1997 Barnsley; Dec 1998 Blackburn Rovers; Aug 2000 Bradford City.

City debut v Swindon Town (A) 17.8.91

> A highly-regarded graduate of the Maine Road youth set-up, when a contemporary of Neil Lennon and Gerry Taggart, Ashley overcame early injury worries and scored twice on his Wrexham debut. The most expensive (at £80,000) of Brian Little's first batch of City purchases, the tall striker also proved the most luckless, with a severe lack of confidence seeming to infect his scoreless senior outings, and he had to content himself with heading the marksmanship list for the promoted Central League side during his only full term with the club. He netted again on his Blackpool bow; then only weeks later became the subject of Crewe's record transfer payment as City recouped their original outlay. Sent off partway through his Alex debut, he nonetheless assisted them to the 1993 Wembley Play-Off Final (where his own successful spot-kick was insufficient to see them through a shoot-out against York), and to automatic promotion a year later. His move to Carrow Road raised an eventual £500,000, and he notched two goals against Chelsea on his Premiership introduction. But this level of football was to prove distinctly ill-fated for Ashley as, despite his development into a sturdy handful of a front-runner, with tenacious ball-holding skills and a decent scoring ratio, he has suffered relegation campaigns from the top flight with each of Norwich, Barnsley, Blackburn and Bradford. Back in November 1998, Martin O'Neill bid what would have been a club record of £3.5m in an unsuccessful attempt to return Ashley to Filbert Street, but Blackburn actually paid a million on top of that to sign him a month later.

***Apps:** FL 2+8; FAC 0+1; LC 2+1; FMC 0+1.*

WARD, Gavin John

b. Sutton Coldfield, 30th June 1970

Career: app 1987 Aston Villa; Sept 1988 Shrewsbury Town; Sept 1989-trials-West Bromwich Albion; Oct 1989 Cardiff City; July 1993 CITY; July 1995 Bradford City; Mar 1996 Bolton Wanderers; Aug 1998-loan-Burnley; Feb 1999 Stoke City.

City debut v Peterborough United (H) 14.8.93

> A 6ft 4in 'keeper who made his belated senior breakthrough with Cardiff, and later displaced Mark Grew to help seal the 1993 Division Three title (under Eddie May's management, and alongside Paul Ramsey and Robbie James), Gavin was a Brian Little purchase at an appearance-related fee of between £175,000 and £250,000. Kept busy during a debut game that City were fortunate to win (the first fixture played in the eerie atmosphere of a three-sided Filbert Street, while the Carling Stand was still under construction), and exhibiting fine agility to add to his natural shot-stopping advantage of reach, he held the first-team jersey on merit for much of the 1994 promotion season, though occasionally showing poor judgement on when to leave his line for high balls. His performance in the Prenton Park leg of the Play-Off semi-finals was inspirational, and a Wembley selection against Derby his reward. Gavin started the initial Premiership term in possession, but was then sidelined by Kevin Poole for the majority of the campaign; during which he became the first substitute goalkeeper used by City, replacing the groggy Poole at half-time in the FA Cup exit at Molineux. Mark McGhee was unconvinced of Gavin's all-round reliability, and the 'keeper became one of a trio of City men to switch to Valley Parade in the following summer. He made a £400,000 deadline-day move to Bolton in a futile attempt to help them retain Premiership status, then yo-yoed at the Reebok Stadium over the next two terms as only a sporadic choice. At Stoke he rejoined Brian Little and has finally shaded a rivalry with Carl Muggleton for the first-team spot, which he held during their Play-Off disappointments of 2000 and 2001.

***Apps:** FL/PL 38; FAC 0+1; LC 3; AIC 1; PO 3.*

WARD, Patrick

b. Dumbarton, 28th December 1926

Career: Renton Guild; Glasgow Perthshire; 1948 Hibernian; Sept 1955 CITY; June 1958 Crewe Alexandra; Nov 1959 Corby Town; Sept 1960 Rugby Town.

City debut v Fulham (A) 22.10.55

> Returning from National Service with the King's Own Scottish Borderers in Egypt and Palestine, Pat won an occasional centre-half role in the massively successful Easter Road line-up of the early 50s, and became one of David Halliday's early purchases at £3,500 as City regrouped for a fresh assault on the Second Division. The sturdy, fair-haired defender took the City No 6 shirt from Eddie Russell, and for some time thwarted the first-team progress of the teenaged Colin Appleton; yet after contributing some fine tight-marking performances to the 1957 championship success, Pat received only an isolated trio of opportunities to impress at the top level in England. His stay at Gresty Road brought him 31 Fourth Division outings, and a goal from the last of them; but he refused to re-sign for Crewe and trained at Filbert Street for the early months of 1959/60, before settling for non-league fare.

***Apps:** FL 57; FAC 1.*

Gavin Ward

WARNER, Reginald Owen

b. Anstey, Leics, 1st March 1931

Career: Anstey Methodists; Anstey Nomads; Apr 1949 CITY; Mar 1955 Mansfield Town; June 1957 Hinckley Athletic.

City debut v Swansea Town (A) 8.11.52

> Still a teenager on RAF service at the time of his December 1950 bow in City's reserves, Reg made his senior City debut at left-half on the same Vetch Field ground where he'd represented England Youth as a centre-forward. Indeed, it would be as a two-footed wing-half that he would struggle to fulfil his potential at Filbert Street, but he won only a few chances to deputise for Johnny King or Jimmy Baldwin before hitting the well-worn Field Mill trail for a run of 33 games in the Third Division (North), several of them at centre-half. A pre-season cartilage injury then precluded Reg from ever actually turning out for Hinckley, and he officially retired in April 1958.

***Apps:** FL 7; FAC 1.*

WARREN, George

b. Burton on Trent
d. France, 16th May 1917

Career: Rangemoor Albion; Aug 1898 Burton Swifts; cs 1899 Sheppey United; cs 1900 Hinckley Town; Dec 1903 FOSSE; Sept 1904 Gresley Rovers; cs 1905 Hinckley United; cs 1906 Nuneaton Town; cs 1907 Coventry City; cs 1911 Willenhall Swifts; Oct 1911 Stockport County; cs 1912 Nuneaton Town; Sept 1913 Hinckley United.

Fosse debut v Glossop (H) 12.12.03

> As would the on-loan Peter Eastoe precisely eighty years later, George had the curiously frustrating experience of making his club debut in a match which was abandoned: in this centre-forward's case the disappointment was doubled by the fact that he'd already notched a goal in the fog-halted away fixture against Manchester United in December 1903. He was, however, to hold his line-leading position for much of the rest of the humbling 1903/4 season, despite emerging victorious on only five occasions for the re-election-bound side. George had previously had two games in Division Two with Burton Swifts, a handful of outings in the Southern League at Sheppey, and a trio of Midland League seasons at Hinckley, for whom he faced Fosse's second string in the 1901 County Cup Final. He would oppose the senior Fosse side for Gresley in the 1904/5 FA Cup, and later become quite a prolific stalwart at Coventry, where he picked up the nickname 'Tubby', and served in their final Birmingham League season, plus their first three terms in the Southern League. George would eventually make a brief, three-game return to Second Division fare at Edgeley Park. He was serving with the York & Lancaster Regiment when killed in WW1 action.

***Apps:** FL 21.*
***Goals:** FL 7.*

WATERALL, Thomas

b. Radford, Nottingham, 24th October 1884
d. Nottingham, 8th November 1951

Career: 1904 Radford Institute; Apr 1906 Notts County; June 1908 Bradford Park Avenue; cs 1910 Mansfield Mechanics; July 1913 FOSSE; July 1914 Watford; July 1921 Gillingham; May 1922 Sheppey United; Sittingbourne.

Fosse debut v Nottingham Forest (A) 3.9.13 (scored once)

> A former miner, and a £10 signing for Fosse over four years after he'd last played League football, Tom was an outside-left who kept bouncing back into first-team contention in 1913/14 despite manager Jack Bartlett's several attempts to replace him with southern talent. Persistence and stamina were clearly high on his list of attributes: on Christmas Day he played in the morning for the reserves against Leicester Imperial, and in the afternoon for the seniors against Blackpool. Tom was one of a trio of brothers to play as top-level forwards, with Ike following him into the Notts County side and later moving to Millwall, and Albert leaving Meadow Lane to build a substantial reputation with Stockport County. Tom himself found his moment of glory in the final pre-war season of Southern League football, assisting Watford to the championship; and he was still there, alongside Ernest Bacon, in the Hornets' first-ever Football League line-up in 1920. In the interim, he had made 87 wartime appearances for Stockport in the company of brother Albert. Between the wars, he ran a pub in Sheerness, then returned to Nottingham during WW2 as licensee of the Old Cricket Players in Hyson Green.

***Apps:** FL 31; FAC 2.*
***Goals:** FL 6.*

WATERS, Joseph John Wary

b. Limerick, 20th September 1953

Career: app Apr 1969/pro Sept 1970 CITY; Jan 1976 Grimsby Town; cs 1984 Tacoma Stars.

City debut v Queens Park Rangers (A) FAC 9.3.74 (scored twice)

> Joe's explosive entry into the City annals – joining the 1974 Cup fray as a last-minute replacement for Alan Birchenall, and ensuring the club a semi-final place with two cracking goals past Phil Parkes before a national television audience – perhaps inevitably overshadowed all his subsequent efforts on Leicester's behalf. The chunky little midfielder, already capped at schools and youth level, earned himself a near-immediate call-up to the full Republic of Ireland squad for a South American tour, and then showed himself to be an astute and energetic prompter on his sporadic returns to the City first team after Birchenall's recovery. But Jimmy Bloomfield's side was at its most settled when Joe seemed ready for regular senior football, and the apparent backslide to Blundell Park was in fact a shrewd move. In eight years with Grimsby, Joe established himself as an inspirational skipper, eventually leading his team from the basement depths to Division Two during a near five-year run as an ever-present (his 226 consecutive League games setting the Mariners' record). The fact that he was limited to a mere couple of international caps (in 1976 and 1979) was primarily due to the competing claims of Johnny Giles and Liam Brady, for his competitiveness and class were well worthy of better reward. In 357 League games for Grimsby he claimed 65 goals, before moving into a player-coach role in the States in 1984. Eight years later Joe was still there, assisting Keith Weller with Tacoma Stars in the Major Soccer League.

***Apps:** FL 11+2; FAC 2; LC 1.*
***Goals:** FL 1; FAC 2.*

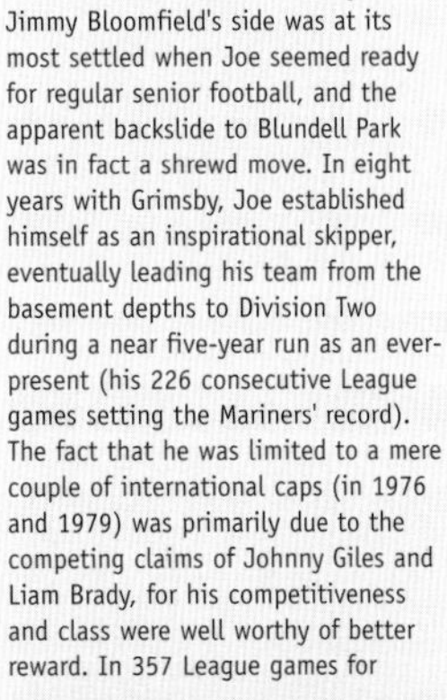

Joe Waters

WATKIN, Frank H.

b. Newark

Career: Newark Castle Rovers; trials-Leeds City; Oct 1910 FOSSE; 1911 not known; Aug 1912 Notts County; Oct 1912 Scunthorpe & Lindsey United.

Fosse debut v Clapton Orient (H) 28.1.11

> A left-wing understudy to Sydney Owen, Frank had no sooner laid claim to the amateur international's flank position than he was himself displaced by a fellow capture from Nottinghamshire junior football, Paul Haig. He played no senior football for the Magpies, and failed to score for Scunthorpe in their inaugural Midland League season.

***Apps:** FL 4.*
***Goals:** FL 1.*

WATKINS, Alfred Ernest

b. Llanwnnog, Montgomeryshire, June 1878
d. Barking, Essex, 7th December 1957

Career: Caersws; 1895 Oswestry United; Oct 1897 FOSSE; Apr 1899 Aston Villa; Feb 1901 Grimsby Town; cs 1901 Millwall; cs 1906 Southend United.

Fosse debut v Darwen (H) 5.2.1898

> A former Oswestry teammate of Maurice Parry, Alfred holds jointly with Dick Jones the record of being the first player to win a full cap while on Leicester's books – even though, by the time of the Welsh encounter with Scotland on 19th March 1898, he had played only a single senior game for Fosse! Indeed, when the close season came round, his appearances for club and country evened out at two apiece. At least the inside- or outside-left became a Fosse regular in the near-miss promotion effort of 1898/9, showing a useful goal touch, turning down further Welsh honours to help the League cause, and attracting an unrefusable £75 offer from Villa at season's end. With the First Division giants, however, his internationals-to-League-games ratio looked even more disproportionate – Alfred twice more representing Wales, but only once turning out for Villa's seniors. He contributed five goals to Grimsby's Second Division championship campaign of 1901; was in Millwall's 1903 FA Cup semi-final team (having got them that far with a 40-yard strike against Everton in the previous round, and by then lined up in the company of a different Welsh international Dick Jones); gained the last of his five caps in 1904, playing alongside his brother Walter Martin Watkins (of Stoke, Villa and Sunderland fame); and in September 1906 was in the newly-formed Southend United's first-ever competitive selection. After leaving the game, Alfred was an assistant station-master, and then a cemetery caretaker. He died in a fire at his home.

***Apps:** FL 31; FAC 4.*
***Goals:** FL 12; FAC 2.*

WATKINS, Alfred W.

b. ca 1882

Career: 1901 Accrington Stanley; 1903 Nelson; May 1904 FOSSE; Nov 1904 Blackburn Rovers; Nelson.

Fosse debut v Blackpool (A) 3.9.04

> An inside-right who arrived at Leicester in the same recruiting drive as Matt Brunton, with whom he'd formed a title-winning spearhead at Accrington two years previously, Alf had a decent Lancashire Combination scoring record behind him, but lasted even less time in the Fosse front line than his former partner. His only Fosse strikes came in a 10-1 FA Cup mauling of little Linby Church; and he failed to make the first team at all at Ewood after his early departure.

***Apps:** FL 4; FAC 1.*
***Goals:** FAC 2.*

WATSON, Norman

b. Chester-le-Street, Co Durham, 21st December 1899

Career: Southwick; Chester-le-Street; May 1922 CITY; June 1932 Notts County; cs 1933 Workington; Aug 1934 Wigan Athletic.

Debut v Manchester United (H) 14.4.23

> A sturdy, muscularly defensive half-back who exhibited versatility and patience in equal measure when sporadically backing up City's early-20s promotion efforts, Norman was rewarded with a lengthy run in the pivot's role as soon as Division One was reached, and thereafter shuttled left and right across the middle line (with odd excursions to outside-right and full-back) for another seven top-flight seasons as a semi-regular. Ironically, his only League goal came in a 2-8 defeat at Grimsby in November 1930. Eventually moving to Meadow Lane as a veteran, he made only five Second Division starts before being hit by illness, but showed characteristic steel in non-league football. Norman skippered North Eastern Leaguers Workington to the FA Cup Fourth Round in 1934 (the furthest that club ever reached before, during or after their Football League tenure), then was both captain and penalty-kick expert as Wigan took the Cheshire League championship two years running. Norman spent many of his summers playing for the Hendon Cricket Club in Sunderland.

***Apps:** FL 173; FAC 5.*
***Goals:** FL 1.*

WATTS, Julian David

b. Sheffield, 17th March 1971

Career: Frecheville CA; July 1990 Rotherham United; Mar 1992 Sheffield Wednesday; Dec 1992-loan-Shrewsbury Town; Mar 1996 CITY; Aug 1997-loan-Crewe Alexandra; Feb 1998-loan-Huddersfield Town; July 1998 Bristol City; Dec 1998-loan-Lincoln City; Mar 1999-loan-Blackpool; cs 1999 Luton Town.

City debut v.Sheffield United (H) 30.3.96

> A tall centre-back whose Millmoor introduction to League football consisted of successive relegation and promotion campaigns, Julian became an £80,000 Wednesday signing, but totalled only 20 Owls appearances in four competitions over four years. A deadline signing by Martin O'Neill to bolster the City defence in the closing stages of the 1996 promotion-hunt, whose fee was later set at £210,000 by a transfer tribunal, he slotted in effectively alongside Steve Walsh as the Play-Offs were successfully negotiated, and had a decent first Premiership term in various defensive combinations with Walsh and newcomers Spencer Prior and Matt Elliott. However, his mistake led to Wimbledon's goal in the League Cup semi-final, and his place was never thereafter secure. Julian became the odd man out during the next campaign, recalled from his Gresty Road loan spell to play in the home UEFA Cup-tie against Atletico Madrid, and then brought back again from Huddersfield for a sub's role at Selhurst Park; but he failed to start a single Premiership game in the final year of his contract. He took a Bosman free transfer to Ashton Gate, but soon fell out of favour there as relegation loomed; then doubled his career tally of League goals with four for Luton in 1999/2000. Three more followed last season, but were nothing like enough to spur the Hatters to Division Two survival.

***Apps:** FL/PL 31+7; FAC 2+1; LC 6+1; UEFA 1; PO 3.*
***Goals:** PL 1.*

Julian Watts

WEBB, Charles

b. Higham Ferrers, Northants, 4th March 1879
d. Wellingborough, Northants, 31st January 1935

Career: Higham Ferrers; 1898 Rushden; cs 1900 Kettering; May 1901 FOSSE; May 1902 Wellingborough; cs 1903 Kettering; May 1904 Southampton; July 1905 Dundee; Mar 1908 Manchester City; June 1909 Airdrieonians.

Fosse debut v Woolwich Arsenal (A) 7.9.01

> The regular outside-right in Fosse's somewhat goal-shy attack of 1901/2, Charles exhibited a marked affinity for playing alongside that other Northamptonshire-born soccer wanderer, Herbert Dainty – the pair appearing together for both Southampton and Dundee as well as for Fosse. His second Scottish League term saw Dundee as runners-up, then he faced Fosse in the First Division in October 1908, though in a Manchester City side booked for the same relegation frame as Leicester that season. Originally a harness-maker by trade, Charles became a Rushden bakery manager upon retirement from the game.

***Apps:** FL 32; FAC 1.*
***Goals:** FL 3.*

WEBB, David James

b. East Ham, London, 9th April 1946

Career: am West Ham United; May 1963 Leyton Orient; Mar 1966 Southampton; Feb 1968 Chelsea; July 1974 Queens Park Rangers; Sept 1977 CITY; Dec 1978 Derby County; May 1980 Bournemouth (p/coach; then mgr); Feb 1984 Torquay United (p/mgr).

City debut v Wolverhampton Wanderers (A) 1.10.77

> Best remembered as a chunkily piratical figure at the heart of Chelsea's defence, whose occasional forward rampages brought about such

David Webb

magic moments as the winning goal in the replayed 1970 FA Cup Final against Leeds, and whose try-anything enthusiasm even saw him chosen as goalkeeper for a League game against Ipswich in December 1971, Dave started his lengthy career as a crew-cut full-back at Brisbane Road and The Dell, and only later developed into such a swashbuckling stopper. Dave's first move helped seal Southampton's 1966 promotion to the top flight, but most of his club honours accrued while he was on the Stamford Bridge books, including a victor's medal from the 1971 Cup Winners Cup Final. A six-figure transfer to Loftus Road saw him partnering Frank McLintock at the back as QPR came within a whisker of championship success, and the pair were reunited at Filbert Street as manager McLintock attempted to shore up City's hard-pressed defence with Dave's combative experience. The disappointment of relegation was part of his lot at both Leicester and Derby, but Dave was back on the promotion trail at Bournemouth during his first stint of management. His final appearances as a player came at Torquay, some time after his nominal retirement and before his brief elevation to Managing Director, and he subsequently occupied the managerial chairs at Southend (taking his charges from Division Four to Two in successive seasons in the early 90s), Chelsea and Brentford. While still in office at Griffin Park in August 1997, Dave was part of a three-man consortium which took over ownership of the club, but he sold his controlling interest to Ron Noades less than a year later. He became a consultant to Yeovil Town in February 2000, was named as manager shortly afterwards, but deserted their near-miss Conference championship chase in October 2000 to take over once more at Southend, where he numbered his son Daniel amongst his senior squad.

Apps: *FL 32+1; FAC 2.*

WEBB, Harry

b. ca 1870

Career: Stafford Wanderers; Stafford Rangers; Oct 1888 FOSSE (- 1893).

Fosse debut (competitive) v Burton Wanderers (H) FAC 4.10.1890

> Fosse's first professional player, initially engaged at the princely sum of 2s 6d per week, Harry was a versatile forward who drew particular plaudits for his heading prowess (despite standing less than 5ft 4in tall), and remained a loyal leading attacker for the club until the end of the second Midland League season. He scored six times on his County Cup debut in November 1888 (against Syston Wreake Valley on Victoria Park), and was a scorer in the Final when Fosse won that trophy for the second time in 1891. In the interim, he'd netted the club's first goal at Mill Lane (in a 3-1 friendly win over Mill Hill House in October 1889), and he would go to claim with Billy Dorrell one of the first Fosse hat-tricks in the FA Cup: from the 7-0 win over Rushden in October 1892 which was Fosse's first game in the competition actually to take place at Filbert Street. Previously, Harry had picked up a winner's medal from the Staffordshire Junior Cup, and featured in the Final of the Senior Cup in that county. He had also appeared in court there during 1884, for playing street football with rolled-up paper as a ball 'to the annoyance of foot passengers', and was levied the costs of the case. A South Wigston-based granddaughter of Harry wrote to the *Mercury* a few years back, mentioning that he'd always been known to the family as 'Hedder' (or should that have been 'Header'?), and that he'd fathered eleven children.

Apps: *FAC 6; ML 26.*
Goals: *FAC 5; ML 8.*

WEBB, William

b. Mexborough, Yorks, 7th March 1932

Career: am Hull City; Wath Athletic; trials-Wolverhampton Wanderers; May 1951 Rochdale; June 1951 CITY; June 1957 Stockport County; July 1963 Hyde United.

City debut v Sheffield Wednesday (A) 27.8.51

> A teenage first-teamer at Leicester within months of his surprise £1,250 elevation from Rochdale (where he played only in a Festival of Britain friendly against Bohemians in his extremely brief stay), Bill assumed Ron Jackson's No 3 shirt for what proved to be the longest run of appearances in his six-year City sojourn. Bill's early progress was enough to win him selection for the FA XI that faced the Army (with Johnny Anderson in goal) at Highbury in November 1951, but his own National Service soon beckoned, and in the following year's equivalent fixture, at Elland Road, he was alongside Derek Hines in the military side. Regular representative fare followed, yet after his demob Bill could never quite shake the tag of reliable stand-in at Filbert Street. His main asset was his pace, and a couple of his intermittent senior run-outs were in the outside-left berth, but it was back in defence that Bill later clocked up 234 League games in an admirably consistent Stockport stint (which incidentally still left him goalless). An unfortunate coda to his Edgeley Park service was that he received less than £100 from a shared testimonial game there in 1964.

Apps: *FL 47; FAC 2.*

WEBB, William George

b. Shettleston, Glasgow, 12th July 1906

Career: Cambuslang Rangers; Sept 1925 CITY; July 1927 St.Johnstone; May 1930 Bournemouth and Boscombe Athletic; May 1933 Ramsgate; Guildford City; Third Lanark; 1936 Bo'ness; Aug 1937 Hinckley United.

City debut/only game v Bolton Wanderers (A) 6.2.26

> Born in Scotland of English parents, Willie spent most of his professional career shuttling across the Tweed. The young outside-left was unlucky enough to find himself third in line for a City first-team berth behind Harold Wadsworth and Billy Bell (and to suffer an injury during his sole senior appearance), so had to move to Perth for an effective re-launch of his career (though presumably fearing déja vu when fracturing his collarbone on his St Johnstone debut against Hamilton). He then managed three seasons in the Third Division (South) at Dean Court after a further cross-border move, scoring seven times in 57 League outings. While back in Glasgow with Third Lanark, Willie sadly lost two young sons, and he returned to Leicester again in March 1937 with his locally-born wife.

Apps: *FL 1.*

WEBSTER, Francis R.

Career: cs 1905 Shepshed Albion; Feb 1907 & Feb 1908-trials-FOSSE; Oct 1908 FOSSE; Oct 1909 Everton; Sept 1910 Long Eaton St Helens.

Fosse debut v Manchester United (A) 12.12.08

> Initially a half-back partner to Dick Butler at Shepshed, Francis understandably struggled to make the quickfire transition from the Leicestershire Senior League to the First Division when flung into the midst of Fosse's fateful season of top-flight football. He briefly held the pressurised pivotal role – for three draws and four defeats – after England international Billy Bannister and before Scottish cap Andy Aitken, but he clearly did enough in only his second outing against Everton to later persuade the Toffees to invest £50 in re-uniting him with Leggy Turner. He nonetheless failed to make the Goodison first team in his year there.

Apps: *FL 7; FAC 3.*

WEIR, Peter Russell

b. Johnstone, Renfrewshire, 18th January 1958

Career: Neilston Juniors; 1978 St.Mirren; May 1981 Aberdeen; Jan 1988 CITY; Nov 1988 St Mirren; June 1990 Ayr United.

City debut v Shrewsbury Town (A) 16.1.88

> A tall, deceptively shuffling left-flank forward with notable dead-ball skills and crossing acumen, Peter was in the St Mirren side which won the Anglo-Scottish Cup in 1980, won the first four of his six Scottish caps while dazzling the Love Street faithful, and was soon involved in a part-exchange deal which valued him at £330,000 and set a new transfer record between two Scottish clubs. With the Dons he hit occasionally devastating form and shared in most of the glories of their 80s renaissance, earning medals from two Premier Division championships, three Scotish Cup Final victories, and the classic European Cup Winners Cup triumph over Real Madrid in 1983. He'd also made a late sub's entry to the Scottish League Cup Final of 1987/8 not long before becoming, at £70,000, David Pleat's first City signing – a week before his 30th birthday. Peter quickly slotted into a re-organised Second Division midfield, linking elegantly with Gary McAllister and occasionally delighting those nostalgic for the intricacies of the touchline dribbling art. Unfortunately, Peter's family found it difficult to settle; but his £135,000 homeward

Peter Weir

move was profitable recognition of the significance of his role in City's brief, but vital, revival. He retired in 1992 with an ankle injury, after performing player-coach duties at Ayr and figuring in the Scottish Centenary Cup Final of 1991. In October 1997, Peter joined the coaching staff at Greenock Morton, and was briefly caretaker manager of that troubled club from January 2000.

Apps: *FL 26+2; LC 1; FMC 1.*
Goals: *FL 2.*

WELLER, Keith

b. Islington, London, 11th June 1946

Career: pro Jan 1964 Tottenham Hotspur; June 1967 Millwall; May 1970 Chelsea; Sept 1971 CITY; Apr 1978-loan-New England Tea Men; Feb 1979 New England Tea Men; 1979 Enderby Town; July 1980 Fort Lauderdale Strikers; Sept 1980 Enderby Town; Mar 1981 Fort Lauderdale Strikers; 1984 Fort Lauderdale Sun (p/coach); South Florida Sun (p/coach); 1986 Houston Dynamo (p/coach); Dallas Sidekicks (p/coach); San Diego Sockers (p/coach); 1990 Tacoma Stars (p/coach).

City debut v Crystal Palace (H) 2.10.71

> A marvellously talented, sometimes temperamental individualist who lent £100,000 worth of forceful right-flank panache to Jimmy Bloomfield's elegant teams of the early- and mid-70s, Keith could usually be relied upon to deliver a tellingly spectacular contribution to the most mundane of games. City fans were treated to regular displays of both his midfield and striking skills, while national television audiences also gasped at some of his exploits: a mazy Goal of the Season at Luton (and a long-range own goal on the same ground a year later!), a thunderbolt volley against Newcastle, and Keith's final City strike – when he dazzled Norwich defenders with both his footwork and his white tights – chief among them. He won four England caps (scoring once with a rare header) and once represented the Football League while with City, but suffered at club level as an influential component of a side of maddeningly under-achieving entertainers. His occasional frustrations peaked in the notorious incident when he refused to take the field for the second half of a League game with Ipswich in December 1974, and his last couple of Filbert Street seasons were marred by knee injuries that sadly cut short his top-class career, but memories of his cool brilliance and ball artistry predominate. He'd made his teenage Tottenham bow in a 7-4 win over Wolves, and faced City in the 1967 Combination Cup Final, but remained under-appreciated until re-forming a deadly forward pairing with fellow Spurs reject Derek Possee at The Den. He featured in the Young England v England fixture in 1969, and that summer scored eleven times in eleven games for the FA XI touring New Zealand and the Far East. What remained his sole club honour came two years later, in Chelsea's capture of the European Cup Winners Cup. After first tasting NASL football on loan from City, Keith later settled in Stateside football for longer than most, moving into club management and coaching roles in both the conventional and indoor games, and forming an early-90s partnership with Joe Waters at Tacoma Stars. He retired in 1993, remaining in Seattle and driving an outside-broadcast rig for a local TV station; but was noted again in 1995 coaching Sacramento Knights. Keith's younger brother Phil was on City's books from 1973 to 1975.

Apps: *FL 260+2; FAC 24; LC 11.*
Goals: *FL 37; FAC 3; LC 3.*

Peter Welsh

WELSH, Peter Martin

b. Coatbridge, Lanarkshire, 19th July 1959

Career: Caldervale YC; Aug 1976 CITY; Apr 1978-loan-Houston Hurricane; July 1982 Hibernian; Nov 1983 Falkirk; Mar 1984 Alloa Athletic; 1984/85-trials-Charlton Athletic, Port Vale & Northampton Town; Wigston Town; Lutterworth Town; cs 1990 Houghton Rangers (p/mgr); cs 1992 Lutterworth Town; Nov 1992 North Kilworth (p/mgr); Sept 1993 Anstey Nomads; Oct 1993 Houghton Rangers.

City debut v Tottenham Hotspur (A) 14.5.77

> Blooded as a teenage midfielder in Jimmy Bloomfield's penultimate game in charge at City, Peter had to wait patiently for a call-up from Jock Wallace for further League experience – by which time he'd notched the only hat-trick in Houston's three-year NASL history. A versatile reserve, he employed his strong build best in defensive situations, filling in at various stages in all the back-four positions, yet could also move forward with effective purpose, making him a useful choice for the sub's bench. A late burst of goalscoring unfortunately failed to gain City the promotion that appeared to be in their hands in 1982, and Peter then found himself embroiled in the acrimony surrounding Wallace's shift to Motherwell. The defecting manager was determined to take Peter with him, and the player commenced training at Fir Park, but the City board, still seeking compensation for the alleged poaching, refused to sanction the move. Instead, Peter kicked off the next term with Hibs, but his experiences in Scottish football were not of the happiest, comprising only a total of thirty games for his three clubs before and after he'd torn knee ligaments. The after-effects of this injury then stymied his attempts at a League comeback, but he returned to Leicester and became a well-known figure in local Senior League circles, while working in the glazing trade. In 1995 Peter became manager of Narborough & Littlethorpe, and in 1997 was boss of Leicester YMCA. He is currently on the roster of former City players conducting tours of the ground and assisting with corporate hospitality.

Apps: *FL 24+17.*
Goals: *FL 4.*

WESLEY, George Thomas

Career: Army football; 1906 Leicester Imperial; Jan 1907-trials-FOSSE.

Fosse debut/only game v Barnsley (A) 26.1.07

> Midway through the 1906/7 season, the Fosse board were coming under severe public pressure to enhance their forward line but, with some

validity, were making their habitual plea of ongoing poverty. Outbid by Forest for Notts County's Welsh international spearhead Arthur Green, they turned to this 'muscular' soldier – an amateur still formally attached to the officers' mess at Portsmouth, who'd just scored four in a game for the local Imps – instead. A 'patchy' performance in a 2-2 draw at Oakwell proved to be his sole senior selection, and he failed to score a fortnight later on his first outing for the reserves – in an 8-0 win! He continued to turn out sporadically for the Imps in 1907/8.

Apps: *FL 1.*

WEST, Alfred

b. Enderby, Leics, June 1879

Career: Enderby; Jan 1903 FOSSE; Earl Shilton United; Enderby Granite; cs 1911 Enderby Town.

Fosse debut v Bristol City (H) 25.2.04

> One of seven brothers who were all Enderby cricketers, and most of whom played local soccer as well, Alf was a full-back elevated from the District League, whose individual potential was somewhat overwhelmed by the collective malaise of a Fosse side bound for the re-election zone. His trio of home games produced a win, a defeat and a draw. Both Alf and Jack (see below) were on the committee of Enderby Town in the mid-20s, and in 1929 both were said to hold eight South Leicestershire Cricket League medals.

Apps: *FL 3.*

WEST, James (Jack)

b. Enderby, Leics

Career: Enderby Granite; am Aug 1908/pro Oct 1908 FOSSE; Aug 1910 Leyton; Sept 1912 Enderby Town.

Fosse debut v Notts County (A) 9.4.09

> A younger brother of Alf, Jack (also known as 'Jacobus') was an outside-left who inherited the First Division flank position after the departure of Leggy Turner. Unable to hold his place against the imported challenge of Fred Threlfall, however, he made less than a handful of starts the following season, and re-united with Jamie Durrant and Tommy Shanks (and later Billy Turner) at Southern League Leyton. He served in the Royal Engineers during WW1, and returned to skipper Enderby Town throughout the early 20s (when also a local billiards champion), later serving on their committee and becoming their President by the end of the 30s. In 1953, when still landlord of the New Inn at Enderby, Jack wrote to the *Mail* to mention that he still possessed a medal given on the occasion of his first game for Fosse's seniors, and the only game they played under floodlights, the October 1908 friendly against Blackburn, played at Burton-on-Trent.

Apps: *FL 10.*
Goals: *FL 2.*

WHITE, Eric Winston

b. Leicester, 26th October 1958

Career: Wadkins FC; app July 1975/pro Oct 1976 CITY; Mar 1979 Hereford United; Apr 1983 Hong Kong Rangers; Sept 1983 Chesterfield; Oct 1983 Port Vale; Nov 1983 Stockport County; Dec 1983 Bury; Oct 1986-loan-Rochdale; Mar 1987 Colchester United; Oct 1988 Burnley; Mar 1991 West Bromwich Albion; Oct 1992 Bury; Jan 1993 Doncaster Rovers; Feb 1993 Carlisle United; Mar 1993 Wigan Athletic.

City debut v Stoke City (A) 19.3.77

> A speedy orthodox winger whose dozen City City games encompassed selection by three different managers and gave notice of genuine potential, Winston exhibited remarkable resilience in extending his League career past several stiff setbacks, and joining the leading rank of multi-club movers. General upheavals at Filbert Street meant he had few chances to consolidate the promise of a debut in which he laid on Frank Worthington's winning goal, though a fine performance at Anfield shone through the relegation-haunted gloom of the following season, a year before Jock Wallace accepted Hereford's £15,000 bid. Winston faced City in the FA Cup in 1982, and had played in the Welsh Cup Final a year previously, but three of his Edgar Street seasons ended in re-election applications. Freed for a summer of Far East football, he fixed himself up with a series of trials on his return; the fourth of which paid off in the form of a contract offer from Bury. He was ever-present in the Shakers' successful 1985 promotion push from Division Four; later strengthened the Colchester squad who narrowly failed to repeat that feat via the Play-Offs in 1987; and was still deemed worth a five-figure fee when moving on to Turf Moor with over 400 senior games already under his belt. Winston's mature midfield displays there eventually attracted a £35,000 bid from struggling West Brom, returning him to the Second Division sphere over twelve years after his last City outing at that level. His goal in City's Hawthorns defeat a few weeks later threatened to help seal his hometown club's relegation to the Third, but after final-game traumas it was in fact Albion who made the drop in Leicester's stead. Four more stops on the roundabout followed, before Winston called it a day after 610 League and Cup appearances and 73 goals. In 1998, he was running a restaurant near Burnley.

Apps: *FL 10+2.*
Goals: *FL 1.*

WHITE, Ian Samuel

b. Glasgow, 20th December 1935

Career: Port Glasgow Hibs; trials-Wolverhampton Wanderers; St Anthony's; Petershill; Apr 1956 Celtic; July 1958 CITY; June 1962 Southampton; July 1967 Hillingdon Borough; June 1968 Portals (p/mgr).

City debut v Sheffield Wednesday (H) 7.11.59

> Never given a senior break by Celtic, despite a fine playing record in Junior football, Ian initially found himself similarly stuck in City's reserve team, albeit the 1959 Combination championship side, while Johnny Newman hung on to the First Division No 4 shirt. Then, even though he grasped every opportunity to display his wing-half skills, the unassuming redhead was unfortunate enough to be vying for his place with the younger and more flamboyantly talented Frank McLintock. Ian played through City's European adventure of 1961/2, and the club turned down a Chelsea bid for him that February, but he was shortly afterwards allowed to shift to The Dell and there resume his occasional middle-line partnership with Tony Knapp. He contributed to the Saints' 1966 promotion to the top flight, and settled on the South Coast after quitting the game, later running a sports goods shop in Southampton, but also undertaking a spell of coaching in Saudi Arabia in the late 70s. Ian's early career had peaked with a victor's medal from the Scottish Junior Cup Final of 1956, when Petershill beat Lugar Boswell Thistle in front of a Hampden crowd of 64,702.

Apps: *FL 47; FAC 3; ECWC 4.*
Goals: *FL 1.*

WHITEHEAD, Harry

b. Barlestone, Leics, 19th September 1874
d. Leicester, 14th September 1944

Career: Barlestone; Aug 1896 Loughborough; cs 1897 Hinckley Town; May 1902 FOSSE; cs 1903 Hinckley Town.

Fosse debut v Small Heath (H) 6.9.02

> Harry's trio of right-back appearances for Fosse – each in a losing side, as had been his pair of Second Division outings for the Luffs – were rather emphatically overshadowed by his cricketing record of 380 first-class matches for Leicestershire between 1898 and 1922. His prowess as an opening batsman and medium-pace bowler was recognised by selection for the Players v Gentlemen fixture at The Oval in 1907, and it was the opinion of County historian EE Snow that only Harry's 'lighthearted' and somewhat 'impetuous' approach to the game prevented him gaining higher honours. He scored fourteen centuries in amassing a total of over 15,000 runs, and took over 100 wickets for Leicestershire, sharing with Cis Wood the club's record opening stand of 380 (against Worcestershire in 1906). Aside from his brief Football League experience, Harry took winning medals from the County Cup Finals of each of 1900 and 1901 with Hinckley. Between the wars, he was licensee of the Hastings Arms at Ibstock.

Apps: *FL 3.*

WHITELAW, Andrew

b. Jamestown, Dunbartonshire, 19th May 1865
d. Mansfield, 2nd January 1938

Career: Vale of Leven; cs 1891 Notts County; cs 1893 Heanor Town; Aug 1894 FOSSE; cs 1895 Heanor Town; cs 1897 Ilkeston Town.

Fosse debut v Rotherham Town (H) 8.9.1894

> A rather more mobile exponent of full-back play than many of his hefty peers, and apparently more thoughtful about his distribution, Andrew was twice capped for Scotland, in 1887 and 1890, while with noteworthy Scottish Cup battlers Vale of Leven. He was at left-back when, in the years he won international selection, they reached the semi-finals and a Final replay respectively, and he remained with them when they became founder members of the Scottish League in 1890/1. Andrew's two years in the English top flight with Notts ended in relegation after the 1893 Test Match, and he then chose Midland League fare over the lure of a homeward move to the newly-formed Dundee. Fosse returned him to the League sphere for their first tilt at the Second Division, but he never quite subdued the challenge of Harry Bailey for his defensive berth, and returned to Heanor. Originally connected with the linen printing trade in Scotland, he became an asphalter in the Mansfield area when his playing days were over.

Apps: *FL 16; FAC 5.*

WHITFIELD, Norman

b. Prudhoe, Northumberland, 3rd April 1896
d. 1970

Career: Prudhoe Celtic Juniors; 1912 Jarrow Croft; May 1913 FOSSE; cs 1920 Hednesford Town; May 1922 Chesterfield; Dec 1927 Worcester City; cs 1928 Nuneaton Town; Sept 1930 Hinckley United.

Fosse debut v Stockport County (A) 28.2.14

> A Geordie inside-forward signed as a mere 17-year-old – and as such probably Fosse's youngest debutant – Norman had nonetheless notched 23 North Eastern League goals for Jarrow Croft during the previous season. He got his initial Second Division break in the week Claude Stoodley lost his wife, and showed genuine promise in the difficult circumstances of the immediate pre-war period, also figuring in the reserves' County Cup Final victory of 1914. After a couple of wartime outings for Fosse, and three for Hull City, Norman served with the Royal Garrison Artillery in France, surviving being twice wounded and hospitalised to return to Filbert Street in April 1919. Playing in Fosse's final five regional fixtures, he laid a claim to a contract with the reconstructed club, though Peter Hodge used him sparingly in City's front line during 1919/20, before releasing him into the Birmingham League. His scoring form there earned him a recall to the Third Division (North) at Saltergate, and he finally bore out his striking potential with a Spireites record of 60 League goals in 120 games as an 'uncomplicated' attack leader. Norman later skippered Nuneaton.

Apps: *FL 24; WW1 7.*
Goals: *FL 6.*

WHITLOW, Michael William

b. Northwich, Cheshire, 13th January 1968

Career: Rudheath YC; app 1985 Bolton Wanderers; 1987 Witton Albion; trials-Sheffield Wednesday; Nov 1988 Leeds United; Mar 1992 CITY; Sept 1997 Bolton Wanderers.

City debut v Middlesbrough (H) 1.4.92

> The only ever-present in City's twelve-game series of Play-Off ties in the 90s, Mike had added an aggressive bite to the left flank of the City defence ever since he arrived from Elland Road for £250,000 a fortnight after Simon Grayson. Strong in the tackle and in the air, if sometimes a little too markedly one-footed, he was also forceful in assisting the attack, and usually among the first to volunteer for shot-worthy free-kick duties, claiming the majority of his goals from thunderously-struck dead-ball opportunities. His defensive capabilities and intimidating cragginess just occasionally saw Mike drafted into the centre of the back line, yet he seemed happier the closer to the left touchline he could operate. Mike suffered injury problems in both his first two Premiership campaigns, and had been sidelined for almost five months when returning to play soundly in the 1997 League Cup Final and replay. But by that stage City had signed Steve Guppy to fill a left-wing-back role, and Mike was thereafter surplus to Martin O'Neill's tactical plans. He moved to the Reebok Stadium (and to the club who'd freed him untried following his apprenticeship) for £500,000 only days after sitting on the City bench in Madrid, but proved unable to secure Premiership survival for Bolton in 1998 or, indeed, to help them beyond the Play-Off semi-final stage of an effort to return in 2000 (when sent off at Ipswich). He was, though, still a valuable Trotters squad player when elevation via the Play-Offs was finally achieved in 2001; coming on as a very late sub in the victory over Preston at the Millennium Stadium. Mike had originally been treated as something of a utility man by Leeds before settling to the No 3 berth, but took a medal from their Second Division title win in 1990, and had only just failed to make sufficient appearances in their Championship side of 1992, before signing for Brian Little, to earn another.

Apps: *FL/PL 141+6; FAC 6; LC 12; AIC 2; PO 12.*
Goals: *FL/PL 8; LC 1.*

WHITWORTH, Stephen

b. Ellistown, Leics, 20th March 1952

Career: app July 1968/pro May 1969 CITY; Mar 1979 Sunderland; Oct 1981 Bolton Wanderers; July 1983 Mansfield Town; cs 1985 Barnet (- 1989).

City debut v Bristol City (H) 2.9.70

> An immaculately cool and perceptive right-back, perfectly suited in his adventurous adaptability to a game in which tactical developments meant he was only rarely in direct opposition to an orthodox winger, Steve won his first-team spurs as an early-season stand-in for the injured Peter Rodrigues in Frank O'Farrell's promotion-bound side, and missed only three games throughout the entire six-year span of Jimmy Bloomfield's managerial reign. His

Steve Whitworth

consistently classy performances (one run of 198 consecutive games at the time creating a club record) made international call-ups look inevitable, and Steve duly won seven full caps to add to six at Under-23 level and complete his English representative set, following national schools and youth selections. A temporary loss of form during his testimonial season preceded Steve's £120,000 move to Roker, but the carrot-haired defender continued to display his pace and tackling ability at League level for another six years, and also finally laid to rest the idiosyncratic jinx that may have earned him one of the most unwanted records in football. For while Steve's close-range goal against Liverpool had won for City the FA Charity Shield in 1971, and he had also got on the scoresheet for England Under-23s, he had never registered a strike in League or Cup football until converting a penalty for Mansfield against Hereford in March 1985 – in his 570th League game, and over fourteen and a half years after his debut! The irony here is that it was as a persistently overlapping auxiliary attacker that Steve had first made his name! He matched his City experiences of each of promotion and relegation with campaigns ending in elevation at Sunderland (to Division One in 1980) and demotion at Bolton (to Division Three in 1983), and was player/coach at Barnet in the 1987 near-miss attempt to become the first club automatically promoted from the Conference to the Fourth Division.

Apps: *FL 352+1; FAC 29; LC 18.*

WIGGINS, Joseph Albert

b. Alperton, Middlesex, Apr qtr 1909

Career: Hanwell Town; Grays-Thurrock; May 1927 Brentford; May 1928 CITY; July 1934 Gillingham; July 1935 Rochdale; May 1936 Oldham Athletic; Feb 1937 Stalybridge Celtic; Apr 1937 Hurst.

City debut v Liverpool (H) 21.3.31

> A promising Griffin Park reserve who had scored twice in his four League outings for Brentford, Joe was recruited at £1,400 by Willie Orr as centre-forward cover for Arthur Chandler. But he spent a frustrating six years at Filbert Street, never getting on the senior scoresheet despite, for instance, top-scoring for the reserves in 1929/30 with 42 goals in 31 Combination and County Cup games, and he finally converted to the left-back berth in an attempt to win a First Division place. It was at right-back that Gillingham then employed him, while Rochdale got 14 goals out of Joe as he led their goal chart during his single Spotland season. He was one of twelve children.

Apps: *FL 9.*

WILCOX, Harry Melbourne

b. Dalston, London, 17th January 1878
d. Plymouth, 21st July 1937

Career: Bromsgrove Rovers; Oct 1897-trials-West Herts; Aug 1898 Small Heath; July 1900 Watford; cs 1901 Preston North End; cs 1905 Plymouth Argyle; May 1906 FOSSE; Nov 1907 West Bromwich Albion; July 1908 Plymouth Argyle (- 1920).

Fosse debut v Burslem Port Vale (A) 1.9.06 (scored once)

> Fosse's 14-goal top-scorer in 1906/7, when utilised mainly at centre-forward, Harry had first boosted his journeyman reputation by making his mark as a prolific inside-right and penalty expert at Deepdale: 15 of his 42 League goals there were from the spot, and two of those were scored on his Preston debut – against Fosse. He won a Second Division championship medal in 1904, then detoured via Plymouth to sign up at

Harry Wilcox

Filbert Street for £75 (paid to Preston). He missed out on a further promotion success during his second term when contenders Fosse and West Brom agreed to exchange attackers; with Fred Shinton arriving as the bargain half of the deal, to score twice as many goals for the elevated Fosse as Harry did for fifth-placed Albion. Harry's final move took him back to Southern League Plymouth, where he converted into a masterful centre-half and went on to complete a club aggregate of 325 games (and a career total of 116 goals in 513 senior appearances) before retirement in 1920; saying his Argyle first-team farewell when aged almost 42. He captained the Pilgrims' title-winning side of 1913, and won representative selection for the Southern League against the Irish League in 1911, playing alongside fellow ex-Fossils Trueman and Moody and scoring the opening goal of a 4-0 win.

Apps: *FL 44; FAC 1.*
Goals: *FL 16.*

WILDE, A.

Career: Feb 1903 FOSSE

Fosse debut/only game v Stockport County (H) 26.3.03

> The eighth of nine occupants of the Fosse inside-left berth during 1902/3, this player sets a genuine research poser. We've previously identified him as Arthur Wild, but circumstantial evidence now points to his name having been Archie Wilde, and to his career path being traceable from Wigston Excelsior, to a spell with Market Harborough starting in 1901 (and partly played in the company of Cis Wood), then returning via his one-shot Fosse stint to Wigston (where he was skipper by 1905/6).

Apps: *FL 1.*

WILKINS E.

Career: Apr 1892 FOSSE.

Fosse debut/only game v Doncaster Rovers (A) ML 30.4.1892

> Another one-game Fossil of debatable origin. One Leicester paper identified him as 'an Essex County player' when he appeared at centre-forward in the final, goalless fixture of Fosse's first Midland League season. But it transpires as being much more likely that the county he represented as an amateur was Middlesex, that his club was Crouch End, and that he'd therefore probably been recommended for a trial by Jimmy Atter.

Apps: *ML 1.*

WILKINSON, Stephen John

b. Lincoln, 1st September 1968

Career: app July 1985/pro Sept 1986 CITY; Aug 1988-loan-Rochdale; Sept 1988-loan-Crewe Alexandra; Sept 1989 Mansfield Town; June 1995 Preston North End; July 1997 Chesterfield; July 2000 Kettering Town; 2000 Spalding United.

City debut v Manchester City (H) 28.3.87 (sub)

> Working his way through the City ranks as a prolific teenage goalscorer, Steve topped the reserves' Central League scoring charts in each of 1987/8 and 1988/9, but had less luck in front of goal on his sporadic senior breakthroughs. He reached the City bench under Bryan Hamilton, was granted his first start by caretaker boss Peter Morris, and briefly figured as a David Pleat selection, but his promise was deemed not to match that of the younger Paul Kitson, and he was allowed to move to Field Mill for an £80,000 fee. There, in a lowly Stags side, he nonetheless equalled the Third Division scoring record (shared by Barrie Thomas and Steve Earle amongst others) with a nap-hand return from a 5-2 win over Birmingham during his first campaign. Relegation for Mansfield followed in 1991, despite Steve forming a twin spearhead with the veteran Trevor Christie, and Divisional yo-yoing continued over the next two terms. An unsuccessful Play-Off attempt to rise again in 1995 saw Steve's move to Deepdale as a sequel, and he immediately assisted Preston to the Division Three title. Injury-hit during the next term, he uniquely doubled up as editor of Preston's matchday programme. His first goal for Chesterfield was his 100th in the League, but a declining strike-rate over the next three years saw him freed from Saltergate in summer 2000. Steve is currently a part-time coach with the City Academy's under-11 group.

Apps: *FL 5+4; FAC 1.*
Goals: *FL 1.*

WILLIAMS, Darren

b. Birmingham, 15th December 1968

Career: app July 1985/pro Dec 1986 CITY; Nov 1989-loan-Lincoln City; Mar 1990-loan-Lincoln City; Sept 1990-loan-Chesterfield; Dec 1990 Worcester City; Mar 1992 Tamworth; cs 1993 Brierley Hill; Hinckley Athletic; Oct 1993 Redditch United.

City debut v Hull City (A) 4.10.88 (scored once)

> A lightweight midfielder, originally acquired by way of youth coach Dave Richardson's extensive Brummie scouting network (which also landed the likes of Simon Morgan, Paul Reid and Robert Alleyne at Filbert Street), Darren became perhaps better known for his punishing personal fitness regime than for his on-field impact. He got off on the right foot with a debut scoring strike at Boothferry Park, but a tidy, workmanlike application was more evident in his subsequent Division Two outings than a distinguishing spark. He was experimented with in wing and full-back berths in the Central League, and thrice loaned out for Division Four action, but Darren's mature self-assessment for once made appear genuine the phrase 'by mutual consent' when his City registration was cancelled upon his return from Saltergate. At that stage he evinced an ambition to qualify as an HGV driver, and for a while performed with distinction as a part-timer on the West Midlands non-league scene.

Apps: *FL 7+3; LC 3; FMC 1.*
Goals: *FL 2.*

WILLIAMS, Thomas Edward

b. Winchburgh, West Lothian, 18th December 1957

Career: app July 1974/pro Dec 1975 CITY; July 1986 Birmingham City; July 1988 Grimsby Town; Aug 1990 Leicester Constabulary FC.

City debut v Chelsea (A) 5.10.77

> Born in Scotland but raised in Leicester, Tommy often had to call upon his reserves of native grit to see him through a lengthy spell as one of the club's most versatile yet most ill-fated players of recent years. Pitched into the senior game in the midst of the 1977/8 relegation struggle, and asked by Frank McLintock to play in central defence, at full-back and in midfield during his first few months as a first-teamer, Tommy responded with boundless enthusiasm and no little skill, going on to establish himself as a regular utility player under Jock Wallace, and eventually settling to the right-back role. Having experienced a Second Division championship campaign and a second relegation term, Tommy was at the heart of City's bid to achieve a promotion/Cup double in 1982 when he suffered a broken leg during the Villa Park semi-final against Spurs, and the cost to the club was inestimable as both targets disappeared in his absence. Worse, however, was to follow, for after a comeback of only four senior games, Tommy broke the same leg again in training, and faced another gruelling period of recovery. It was characteristic that he bounced back into First Division football with full-blooded fervour, and his efforts in a centre-back role in 1984/5 did much to secure City's continued top-flight status. Despite Tommy's move to St Andrews, he enjoyed a deservedly profitable Filbert Street testimonial match in December 1986. He returned to Leicester to join the police force upon retirement from the game.

Apps: *FL 236+5; FAC 18; LC 12.*
Goals: *FL 10.*

WILLIAMSON, Brian William

b. Blyth, Northumberland, 6th October 1939

Career: Seaton Delaval; Oct 1958 Gateshead; July 1960 Crewe Alexandra; Dec 1962 Leeds United; Feb 1966 Nottingham Forest; Aug 1967-loan-CITY; Dec 1968 Fulham.

City debut v Sheffield Wednesday (H) 30.8.67

> Borrowed by City from Forest after Peter Shilton had suffered an injury at Old Trafford and the club were caught without senior cover, Brian was an experienced 'keeper who had nonetheless spent some five years in the reserve teams at both Elland Road and the City Ground, understudying Gary Sprake and Peter Grummitt. He didn't endear himself to City supporters with his habit of punching almost every aerial ball, but otherwise performed adequately during his short spell between the Filbert Street sticks, to which he returned in the following May as the Forest goalie past whom City uncharitably, but satisfyingly, netted four. Earlier Brian had racked up 55 League games for Gateshead immediately before they failed the re-election vote, and 57 more in Division Four for Crewe before Don Revie signed him; while later he would manage only a dozen outings for Fulham (relegated from Division Two in 1969) before retiring to go into the security business.

Apps: *FL 6; LC 1.*

WILLIAMSON, William M.

b. Longton, Staffs, ca 1887

Career: Stoke Nomads; Sept 1905 Stoke; cs 1908 Crewe Alexandra; May 1910 FOSSE; June 1911 Stoke; Oct 1911 Wellington Town.

Fosse debut v Barnsley (H) 27.12.10

> An outside-right who barely got a look-in over Fred Threlfall's shoulder during his Fosse season. At Stoke, where his father was a director, Billy briefly figured in the team relegated from Division One in 1907, and played

Brian Williamson (left) with Peter Shilton

a couple of his subsequent handful of games alongside Syd Owen. He became a regular at Crewe as they twice took the runners-up spot in the Birmingham & District League, and was soon back in that sphere, with Wellington, after leaving Filbert Street. [He should not be confused with the Fosse reserve 'keeper Billy 'Beechy' Williamson (1882-1962), who served Whitwick White Cross and Leicester Imperial before his 1905 signing, and later completed a lengthy stint with Coalville Town].

Apps: FL 2.

WILLIS, James Anthony

b. Liverpool, 12th July 1968

Career: YT 1985 Blackburn Rovers; Aug 1986 Halifax Town; Dec 1987 Stockport County; Mar 1988 Darlington; Dec 1991 CITY; Mar 1992- loan-Bradford City.

City debut v Bristol Rovers (A) 1.1.92

> Originally a teenage forward, but denied a senior outing until he arrived at Stockport for a defensive debut behind Frank Worthington, Jimmy then played for Brian Little at Darlington as they first suffered relegation to the Conference, then shot through two successive championship campaigns. Little added him to the City squad in a £200,000 deal (which also landed free-transfer man Michael Trotter at Filbert Street), but the tall centre-back's gradual integration to the Play-Off-bound side was comprehensively derailed by a nightmare performance in the first half of a home defeat by Watford, and only days later Jimmy was off to Valley Parade to rebuild his confidence. He was a debut scorer for the Bantams, and well-regarded by their fans, but he spent the whole of the following term in City's reserves, and his October 1993 comeback was stymied by injury. Nonetheless, two operations later, he returned to the fray to perform heroically in the run-in to promotion, deservedly winning the Man of the Match award from the Play-Off Final victory over Derby. In the Premiership, too, Jimmy proved the most consistent and reliable defender in the City ranks; undaunted even by conceding own goals in successive fixtures against QPR and Wimbledon, or his ludicrous dismissal in the home game with Coventry. His tackling showed as much finesse in its timing as it did bite, and he showed exemplary commitment. He soon, however, became unsettled domestically (living in a caravan in Leicestershire while his family

Jimmy Willis

remained on Merseyside), and got only a brief chance to impress Martin O'Neill after the latter took over from Mark McGhee. A mooted £125,000 move to Burnley in March 1996 fell through, then further injury problems enforced Jimmy's retirement in the following November. He is now a Liverpool cab driver. His brother Paul also had a brief career with Halifax and Darlington, and a younger sibling, Scott, is currently associated with Mansfield Town.

Apps: FL/PL 58+2; FAC 4; LC 4+1; FMC 1+1; AIC 1;PO 3.
Goals: FL/PL 3.

WILLS, Gordon Francis

b. West Bromwich, 24th April 1934

Career: am West Bromwich Albion; Dec 1951 Wolverhampton Wanderers; Aug 1953 Notts County; May 1958 CITY; June 1962 Walsall; cs 1964 Sankeys; cs 1965 Dudley Town.

City debut v Arsenal (A) 30.8.58

> An RAF National Serviceman who had been unable to progress beyond the reserve ranks at Molineux, Gordon became an established Second Division forward at Meadow Lane (playing everywhere but in the inside-left berth), and first impacted on the Filbert Street scene in September 1956 when, during a 6-3 home win, he notched the visitors' first goal, then found himself standing-in between the posts while injured goalie Gordon Bradley himself netted the third. Matt Gillies plucked him from the relegated Magpies side for £9,000 and installed him on City's top-flight left flank. The tall, brave winger helped City through the panics which attended their consolidatory seasons back in Division One, and contributed a lot to the 1961 Cup run with his willingness to augment the attacking spearhead as well as maintain pressure on his full-back. Occasionally injury-prone, Gordon picked up a severe knock in the first, drawn semi-final against Sheffield United, yet insisted on continuing until the whistle despite the eventually-realised danger that he would miss the Final. The advent of Mike Stringfellow spelled the end of Gordon's days with City, though the move to Fellows Park hardly inconvenienced him: he and his wife already ran a grocery business in Walsall. The residual toll of his injuries, however, restricted him to only one term in each of the Second and Third Divisions with the Saddlers.

Apps: FL 111; FAC 10; LC 3; ECWC 4.
Goals: FL 30; FAC 2; ECWC 1.

WILSON, Ian Grieve

b. Kennoway, Fife, 11th February 1923

Career: Sept 1946 Forfar Athletic; Nov 1946 Preston North End; June 1948 Burnley; Mar 1950 CITY; Oct 1951 Chesterfield; May 1953 Rotherham United; July 1956 Boston United; 1957 Vancouver St Andrews; 1960 North Shore United (Vancouver).

City debut v Sheffield United (A) 18.3.50

> One of the objects of Norman Bullock's pre-deadline spending spree of March 1950 (along with Jack Marsh and Peter Small), £7,000 buy Ian was a calculating outside-left who had never quite borne out at First Division level the promise Preston had discerned during his brief introduction to the senior game in Scotland, despite scoring in each of his first four games for them while occupying the opposite flank to Tom Finney. His Turf Moor record was more notable for the way his goals had won them a last-gasp Central League championship than for first-team exploits; and he was soon deemed below par at Leicester, too: succumbing to the joint

challenge of veteran No 11 Charlie Adam and newcomer Tom Dryburgh. Ian got back some of his goalscoring confidence in the Third Division (North) at Saltergate, and became a great favourite at Millmoor. He twice scored against City in Rotherham colours, and he contributed four goals to the final game of 1954/5 in a bold attempt to push the Millers to the double-figure score they required to gain promotion to Division One on goal average – in fact they beat Liverpool 6-1 and stayed down. Ian emigrated to Canada in April 1957, and continued playing and coaching there into the mid-60s. A Chesterfield history mentions his somewhat eccentric hobby of collecting wishbones.

Apps: FL 12.
Goals: FL 2.

WILSON, Ian William

b. Aberdeen, 27th March 1958

Career: jnr Aberdeen; jnr Dundee; Elgin City; Apr 1979 CITY; Sept 1987 Everton; Aug 1989 Besiktas; Feb 1991 Derby County; Aug 1991 Bury (p/coach); Aug 1992 Wigan Athletic; Nov 1992 Peterhead.

City debut v RotherhamUnited (H) LC 11.8.79

> Blending constructive and combative play in the middle of the park, Ian caught Jock Wallace's eye in Highland League football, and arrived for a £30,000 fee, which he repaid many times over with his influential prompting and playmaking skills. A key member of both Wallace's and Gordon Milne's promotion sides, Ian impressed most in the latter, adopting an advanced role which saw him coming late into the box behind Gary Lineker and Alan Smith and claiming a fair tally of eight goals, including the crucial winner at Craven Cottage. He fell victim to the then-prevalent City habit of selecting midfielders in full-back positions during the next two seasons, digging in well but appearing cramped by defensive discipline, but then re-emerged as a mature motivator and anchor-man, long forgiven for his unfortunate own-goal contribution to City's 1982 FA Cup semi-final defeat. Belated but deserved international recognition came Ian's way at the age of 29, when he followed his call-up at 'B' level in April 1987 with two Scottish caps a month later; but the combined experience of this personal elevation and City's relegation unsettled him, and a transfer became inevitable. Nonetheless, Ian saved one of his finest performances for his final Filbert Street game: scoring once and laying on two more goals against Plymouth on the day before his £300,000 move to Goodison. While there he won three further international selections, and picked up an FA Cup runners-up medal as a Wembley substitute for Everton in 1989. He then rejoined Gordon Milne in Turkey, where he qualified for both

League and Cup medals as Besiktas achieved the domestic Double for the first time ever in 1990 (though Ian, returning from injury, actually sat out the Cup Final against Trabzonspor as an unused substitute). Unfortunately, on his return to England, Ian could turn around the relegation-bound fortunes of neither the Rams nor the Shakers, and a non-contract spell with Bryan Hamilton's Wigan then pointed him to a full-circle move back into Highland League fare, and soon an assumption of managerial status himself. Ian was then to become assistant to Gordon Milne at each of Nagoya Grampus Eight in Japan (February 1994) and Bursaspor in Turkey (May 1996), prior to a resumption at Peterhead in November 1997; taking his team into the Scottish League in 2000.

Apps: FL 276+9; FAC 15; LC 18.
Goals: FL 17; FAC 1; LC 1.

WILSON, Stuart Kevin

b. Leicester, 16th September 1977

Career: YT 1994/pro July 1996 CITY; Mar 2000-loan-Sheffield United; Dec 2000 Cambridge United.

City debut v Southend United (H) FAC 15.1.97 (sub)

> When he came off the bench to join fellow 19-year-olds Stuart Campbell and Emile Heskey in the Third Round victory over the Shrimpers, little could Stuart have imagined that he'd face twenty one more late entries to City action before being named in a starting line-up. The attacking midfielder was most effective as virtually an orthodox right-winger, always willing to attempt to tie his full-back into knots and deliver a dangerous ball into the box, but Martin O'Neill seemed perhaps over-obsessed with Stuart's slight stature, justifying his joking description of the player as 'six... but big for his age' with a reluctance to pitch him into Premiership action until the introduction of an alternative attacking spark was essential. He'd already netted three times as a substitute (twice in separate matches at Ewood Park) when eventually given the starting nod at Chesterfield in the League Cup in 1998/9, and he predictably celebrated with another goal; but he barely had a look-in thereafter. Stuart's input with the Blades was minimal, and a summer 2001 release followed his not-much-more successful stint at Cambridge.

Apps: PL 1+21; FAC 0+4; LC 1+7.
Goals: PL 3; LC 1.

WILSON, W.T.

Career: Alfreton; Aug 1901: FOSSE; Nov 1903 Whitwick White Cross; Heanor United.

Fosse debut v Barnsley (H) 14.9.01

> A notably tall reserve goalkeeper for Fosse for two seasons, understudying Teddy Daw and Archie Ling in succession. He kept a clean sheet on his debut, was on the losing side only once, and conceded only seven Second Division goals in total, before replacing the Sheffield Wednesday-bound 'keeper RT Jarvis at Whitwick during that club's final Midland League campaign.

Apps: FL 5.

WINTER, R.E.

Career: Notts County Rovers; Nottingham Forest; Apr 1892-trial-FOSSE; cs 1892 Newark.

Fosse debut/only game v Burslem Port Vale (H) ML 19.4.1892

> One of Fosse's Midland League amateur trialists, Winter took the left-flank spot in the above match and in two subsequent friendlies against

Gordon Wills

Loughborough and Bolton Wanderers: all ended in home defeats. Back in October 1890, he had scored for Forest's second string in a Mill Lane friendly against Fosse.

Apps: *ML 1.*

WISE, Harold A.

b. London

Career: Custom House; July 1914 FOSSE; Aug 1915 Croydon Common; Jan 1918 Millwall; cs 1919 Charlton Athletic.

Fosse debut v Huddersfield Town (A) 21.9.14

> Docklands amateurs Custom House were another of Jack Bartlett's favourite London League 'feeder' clubs for Fosse, but few of his other recruits came close to matching Jimmy Harrold's impact at Leicester, and this teenage inside-forward was no exception. Harold's patent inexperience was less than useful to Fosse's scrambling necessity to haul themselves out of the re-election zone, and only one victory accrued with him in the side. Every move Harold made was in tandem with centre-forward Legge, but neither found much success, and both had been jettisoned by Charlton prior to their election to the League, despite appearing in their first-ever professional line-up.

Apps: *FL 11.*
Goals: *FL 1.*

WOOD, A. (Benny)

Career: Finedon; Nov 1891 FOSSE.

Fosse debut v Loughborough (H) ML 28.11.1891

> A Northamptonshire left-back given a brief trial during Fosse's initial Midland League season, in the above home defeat and the following game, the only away win of that embarrassing term, 4-3 at Wednesbury Old Athletic. Though we have yet to discover his given name, he was invariably known as Benny. In the September 1891 trials for his county XI, he vied for his defensive berth with Rushden's James Owen, who would soon follow him into the Fosse team with rather more success.

Apps: *ML 2.*

WOOD, Alexander Lochian

b. Lochgelly, Fife, 12th June 1907
d. Gary, Indiana, USA, 20th July 1987

Career: Gary Soccer Club; 1923 Chicago Bricklayers; 1929 Holley Carburetors FC (Detroit); Nov 1930 Brooklyn Wanderers; Feb 1933 CITY; May 1936 Nottingham Forest; cs 1937 Colchester United; cs 1938 Chelmsford City.

City debut v Blackpool (H) 30.3.33

> A distinctly well-travelled left-back, Sandy had won a Scottish schoolboy cap (against Wales in May 1921) just before his family sailed to try their fortune in the United States; settling in Gary, Indiana. He became a naturalised American (1922) and, having starred in such Stateside soccer showpieces as the 1928 US Open Cup Final (when Chicago Bricklayers lost on aggregate to New York Nationals), was chosen to appear in each of the three games the USA played in reaching the semi-final of the inaugural World Cup in Uruguay in 1930. Having eventually earned four caps in total for his adopted country, and appeared in Brooklyn Wanderers' second-placed side in the American Soccer League of 1931, Sandy found full-time work difficult to obtain in Depression-hit America, and sailed for England. After trials for City, he signed League forms – only to become entangled in the combined red tape of the FA and the Home Office. For some time Sandy had to turn out as an amateur on a short-term permit; but was then officially repatriated. For just over three seasons at Filbert Street he vied principally with Dai Jones for the left-back berth, assisting City to their first-ever Cup semi-final in 1934 – when he broke his nose in a touchline collision with a photographer, but carried on playing. He also broke his collarbone at Hillsborough during City's relegation campaign a year later, and eventually moved on to Trentside for a £750 fee. Sandy was later a member of Colchester United's newly-formed professional side (who won the Southern League Cup in their first term), and he earned inter-league representative selection alongside club-mate George Ritchie. With Chelmsford at the same level, he featured in a Cup run to Round Four that saw them eclipse Darlington and Southampton en route. He briefly worked in a Marconi Radio plant on the outbreak of war, then sailed once more for the States in October 1939; settling back in Gary, and working for the US Steel Corporation (where he helped start up a soccer club) until retirement in 1970. Four years before that, he assisted his son William in inaugurating a youth soccer league in Northwest Indiana. His sister Etta was a champion swimmer, while his niece Jean Stunyo was an Olympic silver-medallist diver. His father had been a Motherwell inside-forward in 1905.

Apps: *FL 52; FAC 5.*

WOOD, Cecil John Burdett

b. Northampton, 21st November 1875
d. Leicester, 5th June 1960

Career: Sept 1893 Leicester YMCA; Market Harborough; Oct 1896 FOSSE; Market Harborough; Leicester Banks; Leicester Amateurs.

Fosse debut v Walsall (A) 20.3.1897 (scored once)

> Yet another Fossil better known for his prowess at the summer game, 'Cis' was a Leicestershire stalwart between 1896 and 1923, captaining the County in 1914, 1919 and 1920, by which stage he'd also played for London County (opening the batting with WG Grace) and, four times, for the Gentlemen v Players. He carried his bat through an innings on 17 occasions, including the time he managed the feat in both innings in a 1911 game against Yorkshire, and aggregated 34 centuries. He also, in later life, had a spell as secretary to the club during WW2. Next to all this, his amateur football exploits seem rather a sideshow, with his second and third senior Fosse appearances (at inside-right and right-half respectively) being made some three years apart. Yet 'Cis' also scored in the annual Christmas fixture against the powerful Corinthians in 1899, spiced his reserve record with an occasional appearance as goalkeeper, and sometimes acted as trainer/supervisor to Fosse's second string. He also maintained a lengthy career in local Thursday League football. Educated at Wellingborough Grammar School, 'Cis' became after his sporting days a partner in a Leicester firm of coal merchants.

Apps: *FL 3.*
Goals: *FL 1.*

Sandy Wood

WOODVINE, Albert

b. Kirk Sandall, Yorks, 16th June 1917
d. 1972

Career: Pilkington Recreational; Nov 1937 CITY.

City debut v Brentford (A) 5.2.38

> Signed by Frank Womack and called up for senior action only three weeks later, young outside-right Albert had to cry off when an injury confined him to his home near Doncaster. Still working at the local glass factory when he finally made his belated bow in the First Division in a Griffin Park draw, he thereafter had his City prospects wrecked by the coincidence of a broken leg and the outbreak of war. He did return to Filbert Street in September 1944 from an RAF posting in South Africa, and made a brief comeback in regional football, but was freed in 1946.

Apps: *FL 1; WW2 4.*

WOODWARD, Maurice

b. Enderby, Leics, 12th October 1891

Career: Enderby Granite; Enderby Town; Aug 1912 FOSSE; July 1914 Southend United; Apr 1920 Wolverhampton Wanderers; cs 1922 Bristol Rovers.

Fosse debut v Stockport County (A) 28.2.14

> A young local wing-half who shared his Fosse debut with Norman Whitfield, Maurice was unfortunate to be carried off with an ankle injury after only 50 minutes, and then to win subsequent selection only in a home defeat days before his contract expired. His experiences were happier in the Southern League on either side of WW1 – when he was an early volunteer for the Footballers' Battalion of the Middlesex Regiment, and later joined the Army Gymnastic Staff, attached to the King's Own Regiment – and his Southend form earned him a £700 move to Molineux. Maurice represented Wolves at right-back in their 1921 Cup Final defeat by Spurs, and that summer, while living in Nuneaton, played cricket alongside Billy Barrett for Chilvers Coton CC. Only an occasional Second Division choice thereafter, he was in the Central League selection which faced the Southern League in March 1922. He was later kept out of the senior side at Eastville by ex-City man Walter Currie.

Apps: *FL 2.*

WOOLLETT, Alan Howard

b. Wigston, Leics, 4th March 1947

Career: app July 1963/pro Aug 1964 CITY; July 1978 Northampton Town; July 1979 Corby Town (p/coach); cs 1980 Oadby Town.

City debut v Sheffield United (H) 22.4.67 (sub)

> All too often in his early days the scapegoat of an impatient City crowd, Alan was a tenacious central defender and a resilient character, belying his almost diffident appearance with a steely determination both in tackling opponents and in building a more amicable rapport with his vociferous critics. A single off-colour game, albeit in a vital Sixth Round Cup-tie with Everton in 1968, set the crowd on Alan's back (and some even went so far as to blame him for Manchester City's goal in the 1969 Cup Final, when he stood in for injury victim John Sjoberg), yet subsequently there were countless occasions when Alan earned much more than grudging cheers for his sterling back-line performances. He contributed only briefly to Frank O'Farrell's Second Division title-winning side of 1971, and during the course of several of the Jimmy Bloomfield seasons looked likely to have to settle for a role on the fringes of the first-team squad, but each time he bounced back, and was probably at his peak some nine years after his debut, when regularly partnering Jeff Blockley during 1975/6. The loyal clubman, originally recommended by his Guthlaxton teacher, former City wing-half Eddie Russell, took a deserved testimonial in May 1977, but it was somewhat symptomatic of his luck that the friendly against Chelsea should take place at a time of poor home form and the height of the vocal 'Bloomfield Out' unrest. After the ensuing turmoil of the McLintock campaign, Alan closed his League career with a year at Northampton, in the familiar company of coach Clive Walker and on-loan Paul Matthews. He is now a Gartree prison officer.

Apps: *FL 213+15; FAC 15; LC 17.*

Alan Woollett

WOOLLISCROFT, Arthur

b. Salford, Lancs, 17th February 1904
d. Salford, 1977

Career: Salford; Manchester Docks; Sept 1926 Manchester City; cs 1928 Caernarvon Athletic; Mar 1929 CITY; Jan 1930 Watford; Sept 1933 Newport County; July 1934 Northwich Victoria.

City debut/only game v Sheffield Wednesday (A) 2.11.29

> Unable to make a Second Division breakthrough at Maine Road, when simultaneously employed as a cargo hand on the Manchester Ship Canal, inside-right Arthur nonetheless followed his manager, David Ashworth, into the Welsh National League. Playing there alongside former City reserve Chris Hackett, he had already notched 24 goals in 18 outings when City paid £400 for him (denying him the honour of representing the Welsh League against the Cheshire League a week later). Ironically, his only senior selection for City came when he deputised for Ernie Hine – absent on duty for the Football League against the Scottish League! Arthur then netted sixteen League and Cup goals for Watford in three and a half seasons, but claimed only one Welsh Cup counter from his Somerton Park campaign before dropping into the Cheshire County League.

Apps: *FL 1.*

WOOLRIDGE, John

Career: Hanley Swifts; May 1900 FOSSE.

Fosse debut v Small Heath (A) 8.9.1900

> An outside-left from the Potteries given a brief run-out in place of Albert Dunkley, John made appearances in Birmingham, Burton and Glossop, but was jettisoned without playing before a home crowd.

Apps: *FL 3.*

WORRALL, Arthur

b. Wolverhampton, 8th September 1870

Career: Goldthorne Villa; Aug 1889 Wolverhampton Wanderers; cs 1891 Burton Swifts; Apr 1893 FOSSE; Jan 1894 Woolwich Arsenal; cs 1894 Nelson; cs 1897 Stockport County; Dec 1898 Crewe Alexandra; Mar 1899 Barnsley; July 1899 Distillery; cs 1901 Kettering.

Fosse debut v Mansfield Town (H) ML 22.4.1893 (scored once)

> A scoring debut on trial was enough to convince Fosse to sign Arthur for the forthcoming (and final) Midland League campaign, and this prolific centre-forward made a whirlwind start to 1893/4, when his competitive goal tally within five weeks of the start of the season was supplemented by six goals from four friendlies. He was then injured, and thereafter lengthily suspended by the club for 'conducting himself in an objectionable manner'. He was rescued from this impasse by Arsenal paying Burton Swifts for his signature and League registration, but

the Plumstead outfit didn't keep him beyond the end of the term. Almost five seasons of Lancashire League football followed for Arthur, as he shot Nelson to the title in 1896, and scored on his debut for each of Stockport and Crewe. Barnsley then took him on for another stint of Second Division fare, which uncharacteristically proved goalless. They listed him at £100, thus deterring a bid from Wolves to return him to his hometown club, but Arthur circumvented the transfer rules by undertaking a shift to the Irish League. He would play alongside future Fossil Mick Cochrane for Distillery, for Belfast v Derry, and in the first of his pair of inter-league representative games, against the Scots in February 1900 and the Football League in the following November, when he scored once in a 2-4 defeat. Arthur then joined Kettering, but had a barren spell in front of goal in his half-dozen Southern League outings and six of his seven FA Cup ties; only marking the scoresheet with a hat-trick in a replay against Hinckley Town played at Nottingham Forest. Shades of his Leicester days, he was then suspended for unspecified 'irregularities'. Back at the start of his career, Arthur had made a scoring debut for Wolves before helping them to the 1890 Cup semi-finals, and had played in both the Football Alliance and the Second Division for Burton. In 1897/8 he was in the Stockport side which beat Manchester City in the Manchester Cup Final.

Apps: ML 4.
Goals: ML 3.

WORTHINGTON, Frank Stewart

b. Halifax, 23rd November 1948

Career: app/pro Nov 1966 Huddersfield Town; Aug 1972 CITY; Sept 1977 Bolton Wanderers; May 1979-loan-Philadelphia Fury; Nov 1979 Birmingham City; cs 1980-loan-Mjällby AIF; Apr 1981-loan-Tampa Bay Rowdies; Mar 1982 Leeds United; Dec 1982 Sunderland; June 1983 Southampton; May 1984 Brighton & Hove Albion; July 1985 Tranmere Rovers (p/mgr); Feb 1987 Preston North End; Nov 1987 Stockport County; Apr 1988 Cape Town Spurs; Oct 1988 Chorley; Dec 1988 Stalybridge Celtic; Feb 1989 Galway United; Sept 1989 Weymouth; Oct 1989 Radcliffe Borough; Nov 1989 Guiseley (p/coach); 1990 Preston North End (p/t coach); Sept 1990 Hinckley Town (p/mgr); 1991 Cemaes Bay; Aug 1991 Halifax Town (p/coach).

City debut v Manchester United (A) 23.8.72 (scored once)

> At a time when the concepts of 'personality' and 'charisma' first underwent their continuing devaluation in the hands of a 'build 'em up; shoot 'em down' media machine, and when sports commentators in particular seemed desperate to assign 'character' status to any number of average workhorses, Frank remained an original: mainly because his outsize image was always harnessed to an outsize talent. Off-field flamboyance always had its footballing concomitant as Frank's consistent practice of the attacking arts graced the League sphere for over two decades, and one has to reach for a paradoxical construct to try to sum up his striker's impact for City and his numerous other clubs: something like 'casually lethal' might do the trick. The elegant thrust, alternately subtle and spectacular, was an integral part of his repertoire – along with the incisive flick, the arrogant ball control and the deceptively lazy stride – from the time he helped Huddersfield into the First Division in 1970. City made an early move for 'Wortho' as the

Terriers began to slide, but an England Under-23 tour intervened, pushing up the likely fee and alerting Liverpool to Frank's potential availability. A failed medical test quashed Anfield interest, though, and Jimmy Bloomfield jumped at the second chance, watching with glee as his six-figure investment accrued compound interest over five seasons of entertaining 'total football' (or thereabouts) from City and of quality striking from his flair-dripping capture. Frank was a popular choice for the national side, winning eight caps (and scoring twice) for England while at his most prolific with City, yet his best single season as a scorer came at Burnden, after Frank McLintock had unforgiveably allowed him to slip away, when he headed the 1979 First Division list with 24. His St Andrews debut came against City, in a season the Blues accompanied Leicester back to the First Division, and then in the 80s Frank's wanderings began in earnest, with his disdain for the predictable spicing the rather bland tactical recipes of a host of aspiring clubs, and the personal 200-goal milestone being easily surpassed. Leeds went down in 1982 despite his efforts, while Southampton

were top-flight runners-up two years later with Frank's wiles paramount amongst their armoury. He briefly shouldered managerial responsibility, too, at Prenton Park until balance-sheet politics edged him onwards into Preston's 1987 promotion run-in; and Frank left Stockport for South Africa with the record of having scored in 21 successive League seasons. Even in his later gun-for-hire days, he got to within one game of Wembley again with Guiseley in the FA Vase in 1990. The PFA backed his 1991/2 benefit season, which included games at St Andrews, Leeds Road and Filbert Street; while the Elvis obsession has entered popular legend, and the contents of the idiosyncratic autobiography, 'One Hump or Two?', have further fed the folkloric memory. Frank's father Eric played during WW2 for Halifax Town and Lincoln City; brothers Dave and Bob each had lengthy League careers after launching off from Halifax as hefty defenders (the former largely with Grimsby, and the latter primarily with Notts County); and nephew Gary became another peripatetic striker, most notably with Wrexham and Wigan Athletic. Frank himself remains in the

all-time top fifteen of Football League appearance makers: his 757 outings yielding 257 goals.

Apps: FL 209+1; FAC 18; LC 10+1.
Goals: FL 72; FAC 4; LC 2.

WORTHINGTON, Frederick

b. Manchester, 6th January 1924
d. December 1995

Career: July 1947 Bury; Mar 1951 CITY; July 1955 Exeter City; July 1956 Oldham Athletic; cs 1957 Chorley (p/coach); June 1958 Mossley; Ashton.

City debut v Leeds United (A) 31.3.51

> Belatedly following manager Norman Bullock from Gigg Lane to complete a City inside trio with Hines and Rowley (and to link up again with other former Bury acquaintances in Reg Halton and trainer David Jones), Fred became the thoughtful, deeper-lying prompter of the forward line for some eighteen months, until the arrival of the classier Johnny Morris consigned him thereafter to a regular diet of reserve football. As something of a veteran following his brief contribution to City's 1954/5 First Division campaign, he subsequently

found his opportunities limited in each of his seasons at Exeter (figuring in an ex-City enclave alongside Dick Walton, Tommy Dunne and Ray Iggleden) and Oldham. A broken ankle, sustained while playing Lancashire Combination football for Ashton, ended Fred's career in March 1961.

Apps: FL 55; FAC 2.
Goals: FL 9.

WRAGG, William

b. Radford, Notts, ca 1875 (?)

Career: 1891 Notts Olympic; Sutton-in-Ashfield; Newstead Byron; Mar 1895 Hucknall Portland; May 1896 Nottingham Forest; Mar 1899 FOSSE; Jan 1901 Small Heath; Aug 1901 Watford; Aug 1902 Hinckley Town; Aug 1903 Chesterfield Town; cs 1904 Accrington Stanley; Sept 1905 Brighton & Hove Albion. [poss: July 1906 Wombwell Main; Jan 1907 Grantham Avenue; Apr 1907 Wombwell Main].

Fosse debut v Blackpool (A) 1.4.1899

> The left-half in Forest's FA Cup-winning side of 1898 (and creator of the first goal of the Final against Derby), Billy joined Fosse in a joint deal with Tom Bradshaw just as they were about to suffer the disappointment of missing promotion by one place and one point. Fosse used his versatile talents primarily in the right-back berth, but before he moved on he had served in all of the five defensive positions, and proved himself a real hotshot of a free-kick specialist. He made only a single appearance in Birmingham's 1901 promotion push, but had got on their scoresheet with a Fosse own goal a season previously. Despite his subsequent football wanderings, Billy maintained a Leicester base for some time, and was noted in the summer of 1902 as opening batsman for the local Town League side Roslyn. He eventually revealed a further string to his bow, as music-hall handbills dating from 1908 to 1910 indicate. For not only did Billy tread the theatrical boards with three other former pro's in Fred Karno's Colossal Production 'The Football Match (A Struggle for Supremacy between Midnight Wanderers and Middleton Pie-cans)', but he did so in the co-starring company of no less than Charlie Chaplin and Stan Laurel, in their pre-Hollywood days! In fact, he put his boots back on in relative earnest when this show reached Leicester's Palace Theatre in October 1910, and the company team took on Leicester Imperial.

Apps: FL 49; FAC 4.
Goals: FL 5.

WRIGHT, Joseph

b. Gateshead, 1907
d. Newton Abbott, Devon, 20th November 1936

Career: Birtley; Apr 1929 CITY; July 1930 Torquay United; July 1932 Brighton & Hove Albion.

City debut v Manchester United (H) 2.9.29

> A Geordie goalkeeper who made a remarkably rapid rise from the Second Division of the North Eastern League into the top flight, Joe became Jim McLaren's 'occasionally impetuous' stand-in during the early days of the 1929/30 season, and accumulated an unexpected amount of experience. Much of it, however, was backbending, despite City's reasonable League position. He was the first City 'keeper to face a penalty (by Newcastle's Hughie Gallacher) under the revised (and still current) ruling that kept the custodian on his line; while his final game was the exhilarating 6-6 draw with Cup Finalists Arsenal. Joe missed

only one game in his first term at Torquay, then remarkably kept his place (and his nerve) after conceding 24 goals in the first four games of 1931/2, including ten to Fulham. He won only fourteen selections over two years at Brighton, and ill-health cut short his career. Only a year after taking over a Torquay hotel, he died at the age of 29.

Apps: FL 15.

WRIGHT, Thomas Elliott

b. Dunfermline, Fife, 10th January 1966

Career: Hutchisonvale; app Apr 1982/ pro Jan 1983 Leeds United; Oct 1986 Oldham Athletic; Aug 1989 CITY; July 1992 Middlesbrough; July 1995 Bradford City; Aug 1997 Oldham Athletic; Dec 1997 St Johnstone; Mar 1998 Livingston; Aug 1998 Doncaster Rovers; 2000 King's Lynn.

City debut v Hull City (A) 19.8.89

> The son of a Scottish international forward (also Tommy), and a cousin of former City favourite Jackie Sinclair, Tommy earned an Under-21 squad call-up shortly after breaking through as a nippy teenage striker at Elland Road.

But he had to wait for his first Scottish cap at that level until after his £80,000 move to Boundary Park, where he made his mark playing wide on the left; especially enjoying the discomfiture of visiting defenders uncertain of how to deal with the combination of his pace and the 'plastic' home pitch. With City he revelled in (and occasionally suffered) the reception accorded many orthodox wingers, effectively polarising terrace opinion during his three-year Second Division stint. Certainly, there were infuriating aspects to Tommy's game, with the ratio of useful to wasted crosses (often delivered head-down) coming in for most criticism. But the scampering flair of his flank play engendered high excitement levels on a fairly regular basis, and he certainly hit a decent quota of telling strikes, eventually becoming top scorer in his final Filbert Street season (and setting the incidental club record of five goals from the unmourned Full Members Cup competition). Indeed, his exploits by then had made him something of a cult hero to sections of the crowd, and his last home game, in the Play-Off demolition of Cambridge, was a true virtuoso performance, worthy of

attracting the sort of Premiership attention that soon led to his £650,000 move northwards. Boro, however, were relegated in 1993, and Tommy lost first-choice status soon afterwards. He assisted Bradford City from Division Two to One in 1996 and, after returning from a two-club stint in Scotland, was taken on by his old Leeds teammate Ian Snodin for two seasons of Conference football at Doncaster. Tommy then served Gary Mills at King's Lynn, and has more recently become assistant manager there to Tony Spearing.

Apps: FL 122+7; FAC 4; LC 7+1; FMC 7; PO 3.
Goals: FL 22; FMC 5; PO 2.

WRIGHT, William John

b. Blackpool, 4th March 1931

Career: May 1950 Blackpool; Aug 1955 CITY; July 1958 Newcastle United; Aug 1959 Plymouth Argyle; Aug 1961 Millwall; July 1962 Tonbridge.

City debut v Barnsley (H) 10.9.55

> Understandably frustrated as understudy to Stanley Matthews at Bloomfield Road, where he had

managed only fourteen League games and two goals over four seasons, Billy then found his high hopes of a regular place with City (after a £1,500 move) soon looking bleak against the challenge of the club's mid-50s super-abundance of wingers. Indeed, after his early debut he played out the bulk of 1955/6 as centre-forward for the reserves, top-scoring with 28 counters from 31 outings. He could hardly be accused of not grasping the main chance when it presented itself, though: entering the 1956/7 promotion fray on Christmas Day, and contributing ten goals to the championship success from seventeen games on either flank. It was somewhat surprising that Billy didn't start the following campaign as an automatic choice; less so, in this light, that Newcastle soon jumped in with £7,500 for his signature. He suffered cruelly from injuries while on Tyneside, though, and moved south with a record of only five games; three goals. At Home Park, he enjoyed the company of Dave MacLaren, Gordon Fincham and John Newman, but his spell at The Den ended a League career marked more by might-have-beens and if-onlys than by potential fulfilled. Billy was still with Tonbridge when they won the Kent Senior Cup in 1965.

Apps: FL 27; FAC 2.
Goals: FL 10.

YATES, Stephen

b. Measham, Leics, 8th December 1953

Career: Measham Social Welfare; app July 1970/pro Mar 1972 CITY; Nov 1977 Southend United; Dec 1983 Doncaster Rovers; Feb 1985-loan-Darlington; Mar 1985-loan-Chesterfield; Aug 1985 Stockport County; Sept 1985-trials-Burnley; Oct 1985 Shepshed Charterhouse.

City debut v Newcastle United (A) 23.3.74 (sub)

> A second cousin of David Nish who had shown all-round sporting ability as a schoolboy – representing England at cricket, and holding the national record for discus-throwing – Steve was a heftily-built left-back who made the majority of his City appearances as a competent stand-in for Dennis Rofe, but stood little chance of displacing the ebullient No 3 on a regular basis. Filbert Street supporters had already twice had sight of Steve's teenage talent before his League bow, against Atalanta in the Anglo-Italian Tournament of 1972, and against Ayr United in the Texaco Cup; while his first start came at the Baseball Ground in October 1974, when Nish was at left-back for the Rams. With Southend, he gradually converted to a central defensive role during the course of a 254-game League and Cup stint which encompassed promotion in 1978, relegation in 1980, and a Division Four title-win in 1981, to which he contributed immense solidity. At left-back again, Steve also assisted Doncaster from the League basement in 1984.

Apps: FL 12+7; FAC 1; LC 1.

YOUNG, Alexander Forbes (Alan)

b. Kirkcaldy, Fife, 26th October 1955

Career: Kirkcaldy YMCA; July 1974 Oldham Athletic; May 1979 CITY; Aug 1982 Sheffield United; Aug 1983 Brighton & Hove Albion; Sept 1984 Notts County; Aug 1986 Rochdale; Mar 1988 Shepshed Charterhouse (p/coach); 1989 Lutterworth Town.

City debut v Rotherham United (H) LC 11.8.79 (scored once)

> Scorer of the hat-trick by which Oldham removed City from the FA Cup in 1979, Alan became one of the first players to be transferred under the new freedom-of-contract regulations

Alan Young

and have his transfer fee set by an independent tribunal. The £250,000 move upset the Latics while still equalling City's then-record outlay, but appeared more of a bargain as Alan led the club's charge towards Division One with a fair goalscoring verve and no little delicacy of skill for a forward so apparently forceful. His scoring touch deserted him somewhat thereafter, though, and it occasionally looked as if he was more intent on back-chatting his way through a game than with knuckling down to playing it. Fitness problems also marred the picture, though Jock Wallace stood by Alan despite the striking challenge of Jim Melrose, and it was not until the very eve of 1982/3, by which time Gordon Milne had taken over, that Alan was on his way to Bramall Lane for £200,000. His subsequent travels saw him maintain a one-in-three scoring ratio until he reached Spotland, but his spells on the treatment table, especially for a nagging back ailment, were becoming more frequent, and severely limited his contribution to Rochdale's Fouth Division struggles. Retiring from the full-time game on an aggregate of 107 League and Cup goals, Alan returned to Leicestershire as player-coach at Shepshed, and to help run the indoor cricket and soccer centre at Thurmaston, and was later organiser of Notts County's Football in the Community scheme. He then took on youth coaching duties at Meadow Lane, and in 1998 became Chesterfield's youth development officer.

Apps: FL 102+2; FAC 10; LC 5.
Goals: FL 26; FAC 2; LC 1.

YOUNG, Archibald W.

b. Twechar, Dunbartonshire, ca 1909

Career: Kilsyth Rangers; Dunipace; Mar 1931-trials-Preston North End; Aug 1931 Dunfermline Athletic; Apr 1932 CITY; July 1935 Bristol Rovers; June 1936 Exeter City; May 1937 Gillingham; Sept 1938 Rochdale.

City debut v Arsenal (A) 29.10.32

Tommy Wright

> Peter Hodge's first signing upon his return to Filbert Street, colliery manager's son Archie was a creative inside-left or left-half who didn't have the happiest of times in English football, but showed an admirable durability. His introduction may have been a portent: his debut saw him standing in for Arthur Lochhead in a crushing 2-8 defeat by Herbert Chapman's champions-to-be at Highbury, and when he returned to that ground at centre-half with the reserves two months later, they lost 1-10. Archie proved a useful deputy across three First Division seasons, though, then moved on following City's 1935 relegation. He turned down the opportunity to accompany George Gibson to Valenciennes, but his subsequent Division Three wanderings still left him goalless after 64 further outings. Further embarrassments were in store, too, for Archie was in the Bristol Rovers side beaten 0-12 at Luton in April 1936 (when Joe Payne claimed his League record ten goals), Gillingham failed the re-election vote at the end of his Priesfield season, and he won only a single selection at Spotland.

Apps: FL 14; FAC 1.

ZAGORAKIS, Theodoros

b. Kavala, Greece, 17th October 1971

Career: 1990 PAOK; Feb 1998 CITY; July 2000 AEK.

City debut v Leeds United (H) 7.2.98 (sub)

> Greece's 1997 Player of the Year, and a midfield fixture in every national team line-up after their 1994 World Cup embarrassment, assuming the captaincy, Theo also impressed City with his part in PAOK's eclipse of Arsenal in the 1997/8 UEFA Cup, and arrived for a week's trial in January 1998. Initial transfer overtures wavered over the appearance of two different agents claiming to represent him, but the deal was eventually settled at a cost of £250,000 (despite being widely reported as three times that figure). Martin O'Neill eased him into Premiership football, and the skilful Theo visibly strengthened as some of the effective combativeness of the likes of Neil Lennon and Robbie

Savage rubbed off on him, though he never quite found the extra half-yard of pace that could have made him outstanding, and would occasionally drift inside if given a wider midfield role. His thunderbolt shot at White Hart Lane, on only his second substitute appearance, was fumbled for a scoring follow-up by Tony Cottee; his excellent diagonal ball led to a Goodison Park equaliser; and his first City goal formally confirmed Barnsley's relegation. His second, a more spectacular long-ranger, was unfortunately overshadowed by a Manchester United goal-rush at the other end. Theo was a last-minute sub in the 1999 League Cup Final, but hadn't touched the ball when Allan Nielsen's header cancelled the need for extra-time; and increasingly thereafter his City contributions tended to come after call-ons from the bench. He played a part in every League Cup tie of 1999/2000 up until the Final, most memorably when taking over in goal at Selhurst Park after both Pegguy Arphexad and Tim Flowers had suffered injuries, but declared well in advance his intention to return to Greece on the expiry of his contract. Always popular, Theo left with a fine send-off from the Filbert Street crowd. He continued to lead his country's international side after resuming his career in Athens, though in April 2001 was temporarily sidelined from all action after initially testing positive for use of a banned steroid.

Apps: PL 34+16; FAC 5+1; LC 6+6.
Goals: PL 3.

Theo Zagorakis

AN UPDATE ON THE NEARLY MEN

Pressure of space in this volume unfortunately precludes publication of a section - much expanded from that contained in the original 'Of Fossils & Foxes' and 'The Foxes Alphabet' - on those Fosse and City's reserves and triallists over the years who have (statistically at least) made a greater mark at other senior clubs. However, any researcher engaged on either club or family history projects who may wish to delve into the details we hold on such players (which range from the cursory to the comprehensive), or indeed any others with Leicester connections, is welcome to contact the authors via the publishers with a view to correspondence. The list of Leicester's 'Nearly Men' now includes:

Alec Acton	Herbert Galloway	J Narraway
Dariusz Adamczuk	Alan Gammie	David Needham
David Agnew	Bert Garner	Gary Neil
John Allen	Jason Garwood	Iain Nicolson
Johnny Allen	Mark Gayle	Gordon Nisbet
Lee Allen	Andy Geddes	George Norton
David Appleton	Paul Geddes	Michael Oakes
Ken Armstrong	Charles Gellatly	Paul O'Connor
Des Arnold	George Gibbs	Billy Odell
Ernie Ashe	Michael Gilkes	Leif Olsson
Tommy Ashmole	Archie Gourlay	Mobi Oparaku
Ewart Astill	Adie Green	Pat O'Toole
Philip Aston	Bobby Greig	Walter Otta
Bob Atkins	George Gummer	Fernando Pasquinelli
Geoff Aunger	Karl Gustafsson	Tom Paterson
Mick Balmer	Chris Hackett	Jess Payne
Arthur Leonard Bamford	Andy Halliwell	Lee Payne
Willie Barbour	Steve Hamilton	Jon Pearson
Fred Baron	Fergal Harkin	Ernest 'Dick' Pegg
Harry Bates	Justin Harrington	Petur Petursson
Peter Bebbington	Jack Harrison	Brendan Phillips
Dietmar Beiersdorfer	Nigel Hart	Ernest Pinkney
Colin Bell	Tom Hartley	Dave Platt
Les Berry	Willie Hay	Gary Plumley
Brian Billington	Hugh Hearty	Stefan Postma
Jimmy Blair	Peter Heathcote	Neil Poutch
Pat Bonner	Pedro Henriques	Rodney Pratt
Samuel Bosworth	Michael Higginbottom	Jimmy Prew
Ken Brandon	Stanley High	Jack Price
Guy Branston	Ian Hill	Gordon Priestley
Doug Brews	Richard Hill	Brian Punter
Bobby Bruce	James Hobson	Sean Rafter
Maurice Buchanan	John Hodges	Richard Reader
Reg Buck	William Hogan	Barry Reed
Robin Bullock	George Holdham	Peter Reeves
John Bunting	Mick Hollis	Bob Riley
Roy Burns	Alan Hoult	Harold Riley
Scott Burnside	Pieter Huistra	William Roberts
Jimmy Burt	Steve Humphries	Joe Rowan
Bernard Cairney	David Huss	Peter Rushworth
John Cairns	Mark Hutchinson	Alan Russell
Donald Cameron	Gary Hyde	Håkan Sandberg
Lars-Gunnar Carlstrand	Godfrey Ingram	Keith Scott
Steve Carr	Peter Jackson	Dean Sewell
Raich Carter	Graeme Jaffa	Malcolm Shotton
David Cartlidge	Tom Jayes	Kevin Sheldon
Mervyn Cawston	Andy Jeffrey	Stuart Slater
Felice Centofanti	Fred Jenkins	Albert Smith
Peter Chamberlain	William Thomas Johnson	Arthur Smith
Thomas Chappell	David Johnston	Joe Smith
Malcolm Christie	Syd Kearney	Adam Sollitt
Kim Christofte	Francis Keith	C Squire
Trevor Churchill	Tom Kilkelly	Pavel Srnicek
Andy Clarke	Vladimir Kinder	John Stalker
Willie Clarke	David Kirk	Billy Steel
Richard Clay	Markus Kranz	Ian Stewart
Barry Cliff	William Lavery	Bill Strachan
Robert Codner	Ted Leahy	Samuel Sudbury
Steve Convey	Tony Lee	Olivier Suray
Robert Cooper	Mark Lillis	Arni Sveinsson
Frank Coster	Tony Lines	Gerry Sweeney
Billy Coventry	Gordon Livie	Jimmy Taylor
Paul Crawford	Matt Lochhead	Robin Taylor
Tom Crew	Ralph Lockwood	Steve Thompson
Jack Crisp	Fred Lohse	Tony Thorpe
Paul Culpin	John Loughlan	Aaron Tighe
William Cummings	Tony Loughlan	George Torrance
John Currie	Desmond Lyttle	John Traynor
Damien Davey	Jack McAlpin	Bill Tuckley
Harry J Davies	Gerard McCaffrey	Harry Turner
Stjepan Deveric	Owen McGee	George Tweed
John Edward Dickinson	Ray McGuiness	Herbert Tyler
Jimmy Dickson	Edwin Rolland MacLachlan	Ted Udall
Ivan Djuric	John McLeod	Bernard William Vann
Gavin Drummond	Dixie McNeil	Percy Vials
Stan Duff	John Hamilton McNeill	Ron Viner
Ken Dunleavy	Pat McShane	Fred Wain
Edwin Dutton	George Maddison	Abraham Wales
Tommy Dutton	Dick Marshall	Ralph Ward
Walter Edwards	Keith Mason	Archie Waterston
Helge Ekroth	Ken Mellor	C Watts
Lee Ellison	Leslie Miles	Derek Watts
Alexander Farmer	Branko Miljus	Robert Weil
Des Farrow	Jimmy Miller	Alan Weldrick
Bobby Ferguson	James Milliken	John Whibley
Alan William Fettis	Yorgos Mirtsos	John White
Mike Ford	J F Mitchell	Martin Williams
David Forrest	Dean Mooney	Paul Williams
Mark Forster	Christian Moore	Jimmy Wilson
Mike Foster	Paul Moss	Ron Worrall
Søren Frederiksen	Bob Mullaney	Brian Wright
Walter Frisby	Jon Narbett	George Wyness

SUMMER 2001 STOP PRESS

Dennis Wise

Ian Walker

Although the time period covered by this volume formally expired at the end of the 2000/1 season, the work involved in the final preparation and checking meant that we did not actually go to press until the pre-season campaign for 2001/2 was getting underway.

As usual, the summer of 2001 was a hive of off-field activity and we have endeavoured to capture close-season moves within the Who's Who section wherever possible. Equally, the final international fixtures of 2000/1, involving Jamaica and the United States in World Cup qualifiers, did not end until 30th June, and the ramifications of these fixtures are reflected in the internationals section.

At Filbert Street, the summer was also a busy time, with a consortium involving former Directors showing interest in purchasing the club; the foundations being laid for the new stadium at Freeman's Wharf; and Peter Taylor targeting three players with Premiership experience to strengthen his first-team squad.

Although their role in the Foxes' history will not be chronicled until future editions, two former England internationals and one Under-21 cap had been added to the club roster as this volume went to print.

Dennis Wise (b. Kensington, 16.12.1966) became City's seventeenth million pound signing in June 2001, when a fee of £1,600,000 tempted him out of the capital for the first time in a sixteen-year career that has seen him pick up winners' medals in the FA Cup (Wimbledon 1988, Chelsea 1997, 2000), the League Cup and the European Cup-Winners Cup (both Chelsea 1998), as well as 21 England caps. Also capped at B and Under-21 level, Dennis is earmarked for the 'Neil Lennon' role in City's midfield and his fee will rise by a further £400,000 if he eventually totals 40 appearances for the club.

Ian Walker (b. Watford, 31.10.1971) is another formerly London-based ex-England international (3 caps) signed by Taylor. Apart from a three-match loan spell at Oxford in 1990, Ian has played all his senior football for Tottenham Hotspur, to whom the Foxes paid an initial fee of £2.5 million in July 2001, and arrives at Filbert Street to provide competition to Tim Flowers and Simon Royce for the goalkeeper's jersey.

As for Taylor's third signing, it looked for a while as though Coventry City's Welsh international striker, John Hartson, might be the man, but just as we closed this chapter, City announced that **Jamie Scowcroft** (b. Bury St Edmunds, 15.11.1975) had joined the club from Ipswich Town for an undisclosed fee. Scowcroft is another player that manager Peter Taylor has previously worked with in the England Under-21 squad and will be used to re-inforce the front line.

WORLD WAR ONE PLAYERS

> **A Armstrong** is alphabetically the first of the several mystery men amongst Fosse's WW1 roster of one-shot players; though there is some circumstantial evidence to suggest the outside-right who faced Bradford Park Avenue in April 1919 (in Fosse's penultimate wartime fixture) was a pre-war Loughborough Corinthians winger. (1 app)

> **Tom Bailey** was a Gresley Rovers right-half who turned out for Fosse in each of the wartime seasons except 1917/18. His own goal settled the game with Stoke in April 1916: perhaps appropriately, as he'd spent three Southern League seasons with that club before the war. This Overseal-born player had also been on Derby's books as an amateur during 1907/08. (36 apps; 1 goal)

> Four otherwise totally unknown players assisted Fosse at Grimsby Town in October 1918 (not an unusual occurrence at that ground during the war, with rail connections often disrupted): inside-left **J Barber** was one, though he did not join the fray until Fosse had completed 40 minutes with only 10 men. (1 app)

> **Joe Barratt** (Josiah; b. Bulkington, 21.2.1895; d. Coventry, April 1968) was an outside-right with Nuneaton Town at the time he guested for Fosse in 1916/17. While hostilities (and service with the 3rd Royal Berkshire Regiment) continued, he also guested once for Birmingham, and occasionally for Coventry City in friendlies. In May 1919, Joe signed for Southampton (playing in their first-ever Football League game in 1920), and in February 1922 transferred to Birmingham. He moved to Pontypridd in June 1923, Lincoln City in June 1924, and Bristol Rovers in May 1926; later becoming a Coventry youth coach. His son Harry was a City guest during WW2. (4 apps)

> A Bradford Park Avenue reserve, who never played for them in League football before or after his seven wartime games, **G Barrett** was picked up by an understrength Fosse on their way to Sheffield United in February 1918, and played at outside-right in a 2-6 defeat. (1 app)

> Private **C H Barrow**, 'a Leicester lad stationed near Hull', was fielded at outside-right in a 1-2 defeat at Hull in March 1917. He'd almost certainly represented Ivanhoe United & Victoria Road Institute in pre-war local circles, and Unity BC afterwards. (1 app)

> Balmoral United right-half **T Bee** made his sole Fosse appearance at Barnsley in a 0-5 defeat in December 1916. (1 app)

> Corporal **F Bennett** was reputed to be on the books of Queens Park Rangers when selected for Fosse at inside-right in the December 1916 home game with Leeds City; but no records exist of him playing any peacetime or wartime games for them. (1 app)

> Chelsea right-back **Walter Bettridge** (b. Oakthorpe, 1886; d. Measham, 23.12.1931) was in Fosse's initial WW1 line-up and was an ever-present until November 1915 while working in Leicester's cold storage factory; afterwards joining up with the Flying Corps. A former Oakthorpe Albion, Measham United and Worksop Town player, he'd signed for Chelsea from Burton United in May 1909, and served them in 224 League games on either side of the war until a November 1922 move to Gillingham. He later played for Newhall Swifts, and was running the Bird in Hand Hotel at Measham at the time of his death. (9 apps)

> Inside-right **Walter Smith Bird** (b. Hugglescote, 1891; d. Coalville, 2.3.1965), who was a Fosse regular for a year from March 1917, had previously gained a little League experience as an amateur with Notts County, following an April 1913 move from Coalville Swifts. Originally with Ellistown St Christophers and Hugglescote United, he also guested for Notts County during WW1, and saw active service in Salonika and India. Coalville once more transferred his registration to a League club in February 1920, when he joined Grimsby Town, and subsequent senior moves saw him at Bristol Rovers (May 1920; figuring in their first League line-up, and also registering their first hat-trick at that level), Dundee (June 1921), Hearts (January 1924; as a hat-trick debutant), Kilmarnock (June 1924) and Loughborough Corinthians (August 1925). (22 apps; 8 goals)

> Borrowed from home club Sheffield United in February 1919 after Herbert Bown had missed his train, goalkeeper **Ernest Blackwell** (b. Sheffield, 19.7.1894; d. Sheffield, 16.10.1964) had joined the Blades in May 1914 from Scunthorpe & Lindsey United, and continued to serve them until retirement through injury and illness in November 1924. He also assisted Sheffield Wednesday in one WW1 game. England keeper Sam Hardy was his cousin, while his brother Harry was a long-serving Aberdeen goalie in the 20s. (1 app)

> Chosen at inside-right for Fosse's 0-5 defeat at Barnsley in December 1916, **C Botterill**, from an unnamed local Leicester club, won no subsequent senior chances. By 1922, he was with Coalville-based Senior League side Stableford's Works. (1 app)

> Another local one-shot during this period was **V H Bowden**, the Balmoral United right winger, who featured in a 0-4 defeat at Leeds City in January 1918. (1 app)

> Born in Leeds (October 1891), but raised in New Zealand, **Reginald Boyne** joined Aston Villa in December 1913, and played eight times in Division One before the outbreak of war. While working at Loughborough Brush, he became a Fosse regular during 1916/17, despite a less-than-prolific scoring record for a centre- or inside-forward, but found his shooting boots for Brentford after his 1919 signing from Brush Works, and claimed the Bees' first-ever League goal a year later. He also made a single WW1 appearance for Notts County. (23 apps; 2 goals)

> Chelsea inside-right **Harry Brittain** (Harold Pemberton; b. Derby, 1894) had a couple of Fosse outings in March 1919. Originally signed from Ilkeston United in December 1913, he left Stamford Bridge in 1920 and emigrated to the United States, playing there for Bethlemen Steel (May 1920), Philadelphia (September 1921), Fall River Marksmen (October 1922), New Bedford Whalers (September 1926) and Boston Fall River (March 1927). (2 apps)

> Oadby man **F R Broadley** played at outside-right for Fosse against Rotherham County in October 1916, and was excused his unremarkable performance by the *Daily Post* reporter on the unlikely grounds that he was 'playing his first Association game'! However, he had been an occasional Tigers player between 1911-15, scoring 8 tries in 13 games as a wing-threequarter; and, in correspondence with the local press in 1939, claimed to have played cricket for the County Seconds as well. (1 app)

> **A Brown,** who turned out at outside-right in the January 1917 away game with Rotherham County, was a Gresley Rovers player who had previously served Shirebrook. (1 app)

> A Bradford Park Avenue amateur, **Tommy Brown** (b. Sheffield, 27.3.1897) was picked up by a depleted Fosse on their way to play Sheffield United in February 1918, and played at centre-half in a 2-6 defeat. Postwar, he played 19 games in the top two Divisions for Avenue, before joining Rotherham Town in May 1923. (1 app)

> Coalville Swifts winger **Tommy Brownlow** took the left flank for Fosse against Notts County and Bradford City on successive afternoons at Easter 1917. Before the war, he'd played with Coalville Town, Coalville PSA & Gresley Rovers; during it he had a brief stint in the Machine Gun Corps before returning to work at Snibston Colliery; afterwards he featured for Coalville Town (in two further spells), Shepshed Albion, Stableford's Works, Whitwick Imperial and Gresley Rovers. (2 apps)

> Sgt-Major **J E C Buckley** volunteered from his local Army camp to turn out for a distinctly under-strength Fosse when they nonetheless ground out a 1-1 draw at Grimsby in December 1917. (1 app)

> In the same game, which featured a pair of off-duty soldiers and an on-leave sailor in Fosse's makeshift line-up, an otherwise unknown player named **Burton** held the right-half position. (1 app)

> A winger from the Birmingham area, **E Burton** first took the Fosse right flank on a trial basis in the March 1917 game at Nottingham Forest, and appeared once more a year later for the final fixture of 1917/18 at Birmingham. (2 apps)

> A son of the Chelsea (and former Lincoln City) manager of the same name, **David Calderhead** (b. Dumfries, ca.1891) was a centre-half who had signed on at Stamford Bridge directly from Lincoln schools football in September 1907, and had not left the paternal orbit until transferring to Motherwell in April 1914. He was in Fosse's initial WW1 line-up in September 1915, staying for three months, and also guested for Notts County and, once more, Chelsea. Postwar, David signed for Clapton Orient in 1919, and then himself became manager at Lincoln from 1921-24. He was later licensee of the Newmarket Hotel in Sincil Street, Lincoln. (8 apps)

> A free-scoring centre-forward in the pre-war years (and again as a veteran afterwards), **James Cantrell** (b.Sheepbridge, 7.5.1882; d. Basford, 31.7.1960) played for Fosse in the home defeat by Bradford City on Easter Tuesday 1917, having scored against them for Notts County in each of the previous Saturday and Monday holiday games. Having learned his football with Bulwell Red Rose, Bulwell White Star and Hucknall Constitutionals, Jimmy had joined Aston Villa in July 1904, moved to Notts County in March 1908, and to Tottenham Hotspur in October 1912. Most of his WW1 football was played back at Meadow Lane, but he continued with Spurs after the war, earning a 1921 FA Cup-winners medal, until released to Sutton United in October 1923. (1 app)

Jesse Pennington

> Barnsley's young centre-forward **G Chapman** was borrowed by Fosse (along with teammate Jack Gittins) to make up the numbers for their fixture at Leeds City in January 1918. (1 app)

> Otherwise unidentified by the local press at the time, **W Clarke** featured on Fosse's left flank at Bradford Park Avenue in February 1917. (1 app)

> **T Cope**, a friend of regular guest Richard Gibson's from a Birmingham junior team, played ('ineffectively') at outside-left for Fosse at Bradford Park Avenue in October 1915; having been called in after George Harrison missed his train. (1 app)

> **Frank R Crowe** (b. Birmingham, 1893), an inside-forward who made 14 wartime appearances for Birmingham following his April 1917 signing from Apollo Works FC, assisted Fosse against his own club in April 1918, and played three times for Aston Villa a year later. Curiously, after an August 1919 move to Coventry City, both his League appearances for his new team were as a 'vigorous' wing-half against Leicester. Frank then moved on to Merthyr Town in 1920, to Chesterfield in May 1922, Rochdale in June 1923, and back to Merthyr in 1924; finishing his career with Penrhiwceiber after 1925. (1 app)

> Another Brummie from junior football tried out by Fosse was **J Crutchley**, who played in two November 1916 defeats at right-half. (2 apps)

> Chesterfield Town and former Derby County reserve full-back **Percy H Cullin** featured in a 1-5 defeat at Notts County in October 1916, and also guested for Nottingham Forest in this period. (1 app)

> Another of the many to briefly swap military khaki for Fosse's blue and white stripes was Sapper **Dalton**, fielded at outside-right at Hull City in December 1917. (1 app)

> A former Birmingham St Georges and Evesham player, **Arthur George Davis** (b. Birmingham, ca 1900) had an extended trial with Fosse at inside-right in December 1918 and January 1919, and also played wartime football for Coventry City and Aston Villa. It was the latter club, however, which signed him up for peacetime action (in July 1919), and his subsequent career took him on to Queens Park Rangers (May 1922), Notts County (February 1924) – where he formed a left-wing partnership with Len Barry – and Crystal Palace (May 1928). He ended his playing days with Kidderminster Harriers after a 1929 move. (6 apps; 4 goals)

> A previous occupant of the inside-right berth in that final WW1 season was Asfordby's **George Davis**, a scorer on his October 1918 debut in a 5-3 home win over Grimsby Town. (3 apps; 1 goal)

> Lieutenant **Day** of the Leicestershire Regiment featured as Fosse's right back at Hull in March 1917, and then skippered his regimental team against Fosse in a friendly two months later. Two possible identifications of this player seem worthy of consideration: he may either have been AG Day, formerly of Leicester Nomads, Whitwick Imperial and Loughborough Corinthians, or Harold Lindsay Vernon Day (b. Darjeeling, 12.8.1898; d. Hadley Wood, Herts, 15.6.1972), who became a Tigers and England wing threequarter and a Hampshire county cricketer. (1 app)

> Though he made a pair of consecutive forward appearances for Fosse in November 1916, **T Day** was confusingly described in successive weeks as hailing from a junior Birmingham club, and as 'a local man living in Derby'. We have very speculatively identified him as TE Day, who played before the war for Atherstone Town, after it for Nuneaton Town, and also briefly guested for Millwall. (2 apps)

> Local winger **George Thomas Dennis** (b. Moira, 12.9.1897; d. Burton-on-Trent, 13.10.1969) made his Fosse bow in friendly games in March 1917, but didn't break through to competitive wartime football until December 1918. His roster of junior clubs included Stanton, Coalville Swifts and Newhall Swifts; while his career took off in the League sphere when peace returned. George took the opposite Nottingham Forest flank to Sid Harrold from February 1921; moved to Luton Town (where he claimed 42 goals) in the 1924 close season; to Norwich City in May 1929; and to Bristol Rovers for the 1930/1 season, throughout which he played at left-back. At both Kenilworth Road and Eastville, he was regarded as a penalty expert. (5 apps; 1 goal)

> Borrowed by Fosse from home club Coventry City in March 1919, when Jack Parker failed to turn up, inside-left **Harry Dobson** (b. Newcastle, ca 1891) had joined Coventry in May 1913 from North Shields Athletic and starred in their pre-war Southern League line-up. Within months of his Fosse outing, 'Dobbin' was on his way to Newport County, and in February 1922 moved to Southend United for a three-year stint, before finishing his career with Rugby Town. (1 app)

> A Fosse regular on the left wing throughout 1917/18, and again at the start of the following season, **David Morgan Donald** (b. Coatbridge, 21.7.1885; d. Derby, 19.1.1932) had begun his career with Albion Rovers (July 1905) before successive moves to Bradford Park Avenue (June 1908), Derby County (March 1910), Chesterfield Town (June 1912), Watford (June 1913), Queens Park Rangers (1914), Ilkeston United (cs 1921), Coalville Swifts (Dec 1921) and Hamilton Academical (July 1922). He also assisted Derby again during WW1; while he was allegedly the man who recommended that QPR sign Arthur Chandler. (42 apps; 3 goals)

> Raised in Leicester from the age of 10, **Alec Donaldson** (Alexander Pollock; b. Barrhead, 4.12.1892) played local football for Belgrave Primitive Methodists, Balmoral United and Ripley Athletic, and had trials with Sheffield United in March 1911, but was snapped up by Bolton Wanderers in December of that year, and went on to win six Scottish caps and appear in an additional trio of Victory internationals. The skilful outside-right was brought back to Leicester by wartime munitions factory

work and turned out for Fosse in every WW1 season but 1916/17. He also assisted Arthurlie during this period, then picked up his Burnden Park career until a March 1922 move to Sunderland. Alec signed for Manchester City in May 1923, then later served Chorley and Ashton National. While with Fosse, he once scored direct from a corner, but before such skill (or fortune!) was recognised by the laws of the game. (51 apps; 6 goals)

> A youthful Bradford City reserve full-back, **George Draycott** (b. Newhall) was working at Church Gresley when given a break by Fosse in December 1916, and went on to give consistent service until the end of the following season. Tragically, though, he was killed in action with the Lincolnshire Regiment in France on 18.9.1918. He'd originally signed for Bradford from Gresley Rovers in March 1913, after playing a trial for them at Filbert Street in George Johnson's testimonial game. (44 apps)

> Twice borrowed by Fosse from their Lincoln City hosts, in November 1915 and February 1917, left-sided defender **John Dunne** (b. Donnybrook, ca 1890; d. 1974) had been at Sincil Bank since June 1914, when he signed from Shelbourne. With that club he had won an Irish Cup-winner's medal in 1911, and in 1913 had represented the Irish League against the Scottish League. John also played wartime football for Rustons Aircraftmen and RAF Cranwell, and his postwar moves took in Mid-Rhondda (June 1919), Boston Town (1921) and Horncastle Town. (2 apps)

> A guesting Fossil for a year from December 1915, **Harold Edgley** (b. Crewe, 1892; d. Birmingham, 1966) was an Aston Villa outside-left who'd signed up from Whitchurch in February 1911, and had briefly been loaned to Stourbridge during 1913. He additionally assisted Birmingham, West Brom, Chesterfield Town, Lincoln and Port Vale during WW1 before resuming his Villa Park career, which hit its nadir when Harold broke his leg a week before the 1920 FA Cup Final, after he had played in every round and scored the semi-final winner. He moved on to Queens Park Rangers in June 1921, and signed for Stockport County in August 1923; then had the misfortune to break his leg again on his Worcester City debut in August 1924. Harold subsequently acted as a Notts County director. (32 apps; 2 goals)

> **N Edwards** was 'a Birmingham lad' given a trial at outside-left by Fosse on the same day as Tommy Roberts, in a 3-2 away win over Notts County in April 1917. (1 app)

> Another unheralded – and unsuccessful – right wing triallist was **A Ellis**, who faced Nottingham Forest in a 1-0 home win in March 1918. (1 app)

> One of the quartet of unknowns recruited by Fosse at Grimsby in October 1918 was outside-left **A Faulconer**. The emergency was created when four selected men (Davis, Donald, Price and Underwood) all missed the train. (1 app)

> A local journalist on Bradford City's books as an amateur, **E Fearnley** was twice borrowed by Fosse for away games at Bradford Park Avenue, playing at inside-right in February and December 1917. He also assisted Park Avenue themselves, plus Notts County, Hull City, Bury and Huddersfield Town, during the war years. (2 apps)

> On leave from service as a stoker on a minesweeper, **G A Foreman** volunteered to make up Fosse's depleted numbers at Grimsby in December 1917, and took the right-wing berth in the 1-1 draw. (1 app)

> A former Leeds City reserve, **N Fox** was recruited at the last minute by Fosse to complete their weakened eleven at Leeds in January 1916; forming an eccentric right-wing partnership with long-retired ex-Burnley goalkeeper Billy Green! (1 app)

> At inside-left in Fosse's first fistful of WW1 fixtures was **Charlie Freeman** (Charles Redfern; b. Overseal, 22.8.1887; d. Fulham, 17.3.1956), who had graduated via Overseal Swifts and Burton United to Chelsea in 1907, and had scored 22 goals in 95 League games for them before war broke out. He added 21 wartime goals to his Stamford Bridge haul before a move to Gillingham in June 1921, then joined Maidstone United in June 1923. On ceasing playing, Charlie returned to Chelsea for the rest of his working life: initially as trainer, then as groundsman until 1953. (5 apps)

> Alongside his near-namesake in Fosse's inaugural wartime line-up was **Neddy Freeman** (Edwin; b. Northampton, 1886; d. Northampton, 7.12.1945), a centre-forward who served his home-town club from 1906 to 1921 (and nearly made the County Ground a full-time workplace, appearing there additionally as an occasional Northants cricketer between 1908 and 1920). Neddy stuck with Fosse until November 1917, and also turned out for Spurs later in the war. (35 apps; 10 goals)

> Corporal **Billy George** (William Samuel; b. Aston, 1895; d. Selly Oak, 29.9.1962), who had been playing for Austin Motor Works, and had made one friendly appearance for Aston Villa during 1916/17, assisted Fosse at right-half at Coventry in March 1919. For the 1919/20 season, he was on Merthyr Town's books, then transferred to Sunderland in August 1920, but only made two First Division appearances prior to joining Shildon in the following close season. He later played with each of Burton All Saints and Birmingham Trams. (1 app)

> An outside- or inside-right who had been on Birmingham's books since signing from North London club Sultan FC in September 1911, **Richard Samuel Gibson** (b. Holborn, 1889) made most of his Fosse wartime appearances during 1915/16, when his own club had shut down; though he later briefly reappeared in January 1919 when an army Private stationed at Bradford. After the war, he remained at St Andrews until a £250 move in June 1921 to Manchester United. (19 apps; 7 goals)

> A Barnsley full-back from 1914, when signed from Bentley Colliery, to October 1926, when he moved to Chesterfield, (and then to Wombwell Town), **Jack Gittins** (John Henry; b. Stanton Hill, 11.11.1893; d. Bentley, 8.10.1956) amassed a 259-game peacetime record for the Tykes. He was borrowed by Fosse in January 1918 as an emergency fill-in for the game at Leeds City. (1 app)

> On trial from a Mansfield club in January 1917 was **J W Goddard**, who featured as a right-sided forward in successive games at Grimsby and at home to Notts County. Before the war he'd been a Mansfield Mechanics reserve; postwar he assisted Hucknall Byron and Mansfield Town reserves. (2 apps)

> The unrelated **Sidney H Goddard**, a Leicester Imperial forward since 1910, made sporadic entries into the Fosse line-up in the first three wartime seasons, but never in a winning side. (4 apps)

> A familiar tale: "With Vlaminck having to go to London for medical examination, King down with influenza, Donald unfit, Bailey unable to play, and Nottingham out of bounds to soldiers, Fosse had to make drastic changes ..." for their game at Notts County in November 1918. One otherwise unidentified draftee was inside-right **Green**. (1 app)

> Coaxed from the crowd awaiting the game at Leeds City in January 1916, **Billy Green** (William John; b. Gravesend, 1882) was given the Fosse right wing berth for the day – despite the fact that he was a long-retired goalkeeper! Billy had started his career with Gravesend, moved to Brentford in 1901, and to Burnley in 1903. After 147 League games between their sticks, he transferred for the last time in December 1908 to Bradford Park Avenue, last playing in 1910. (1 app)

> Uncommented upon by the local press despite his trio of Fosse outings during March and April 1917 was full-back **G Hampton**, who we presume to have been a local trialist. (3 apps)

> Fosse were still picking up obscure talent to make up their numbers at Leeds in September 1916, when local lad **H Hawden** featured at outside-right. (1 app)

> Chesterfield Town left-half **Henry Crookes Hibbert** was another emergency stand-in for Fosse, at Sheffield United in April 1916. He had started his career with Hathersage, and moved on to Sheffield Wednesday (cs 1907), Stockport County (March 1908), Lincoln City (July 1909), Rotherham County (cs 1911), and Sheffield United (April 1913); in each case predominantly as a reserve player. He also guested for Rotherham and Lincoln during WW1. (1 app)

> Fosse's centre-forward at Nottingham Forest in January 1919 was **Leonard G Hopkins**, who also guested for Coventry City during WW1, but who had been on Cardiff City's books since a November 1913 move from Brierley Hill Alliance. (1 app)

> Overseal outside-left **George W Jordan** was deemed 'not clever enough' by the local *Post* after his Fosse outing at Bradford City in October 1918. He was useful enough, however, to be borrowed by the Bantams when they paid the return visit to Filbert Street a week later. A City trialist in August 1919, he then joined Coalville Swifts, Ashby Town (1920), Whitwick Imperial (1921; returning there after a brief stint with Nuneaton Town), Burton Town (1925), Wellington Town and Gresley Rovers (1928), while working at the coalface in Moira. (1 app)

> A youngster on Aston Villa's books who failed to break through to their senior side in either wartime or peacetime football, **J H Joyce** turned out at inside-right for Fosse at Huddersfield Town in October 1916. It is believed that he was with Tamworth Castle in 1919/20.(1 app)

> Fosse's centre-forward in home and away fixtures with Leeds City in 1918/19 was **Frank Bernard Kirrage** (b. Bromley, 3.3.1893; d. Fiskerton, 25.1.1933), who also guested for Blackpool as well as making a wartime breakthrough with his own club, Nottingham Forest. He failed, though, to make more than a single subsequent League appearance for Forest (who he had originally joined after stints with Mapperley and Bulwell), and moved on to Ilkeston United in 1920. (2 apps; 1 goal)

> **J W Lambert** was the outside-right of local club Belvoir SS when given a Fosse trial at Lincoln City in November 1915. (1 app)

> **Harry William Lane** (b. Stoney Stanton, 23.10.1894) was a part-time player and schoolmaster before the war but had still to make a League bow when Fosse gave him a senior break in December 1915, playing him in both wing-half spots as well as at inside-right and centre-forward. The former Stoney Stanton Swifts and Hinckley United (Dec 1911) player had spent 1912/13 on Forest's books and the following term with Notts County, but was by then with Sutton Town. Only days after his final Fosse outing in January 1916, Harry signed up with the Royal Flying Corps. Finally, after the war, he made a minor splash in London football: with West Ham United from May 1919, Charlton Athletic from May 1921, and Queens Park Rangers from June 1922. His Fosse debut match lasted only 73 minutes due to bad weather, and was played without a half-time break. (4 apps; 1 goal)

> A Fosse stalwart at left-half throughout the entire WW1 period, despite never officially switching his registration from Aston Villa, **Jimmy Leach** (James McIntyre; b. Spennymoor, 1890) had originally signed up at Villa Park in August 1912 from North-Eastern football, and remained there until a July 1922 move to Queens Park Rangers, who he represented only once before succumbing to a serious knee injury. He also guested briefly for Chesterfield Town and Lincoln City. (102 apps; 1 goal)

> Fosse's inside-right in a handful of successive games from September 1916, **Syd Leigh** (Alfred Sydney; b. Shardlow, 1893) had been a Derby County signing from local club Osmaston in June 1914, but he managed only a couple of League games for the Rams before joining Bristol Rovers in July 1920, and going on to become that club's top scorer in each of their first two seasons in the League. He also guested for Bradford City and Hull City during WW1. (5 apps; 2 goals)

> Another Ram to assist Fosse was **Harry Leonard** (Henry Doxford; b. Sunderland, 1886; d. Derby, 3.11.1951), who took the centre-forward shirt in the home defeat by Nottingham Forest in January 1919. He'd joined Newcastle United from Sunderland North End in November 1907, then transferred to Grimsby Town in May 1908, Middlesbrough in March 1911, and Derby in October 1911. After 72 League goals in 144 games (and another 25 in 34 wartime appearances) for Derby, Harry moved to Manchester United in September 1920, and Heanor Town in June 1921. He also had one wartime guest outing for Notts County. (1 app)

> **A Leyland** guested at right-half for Fosse at Lincoln City in February 1917, and played a single game for Lincoln at left-half a week later. (1 app)

> Balmoral United centre-forward **Jimmy Longland** (who'd also served Belgrave Athletic and Hinckley United before the war) got a couple of isolated run-outs for Fosse in heavy defeats – 0-5 at Barnsley on Boxing Day 1916, and 2-4 at home to Leeds City in January 1918. The next month he was lent to Barnsley when they arrived at Filbert Street a man short: Fosse won 5-1! Postwar, he played for Atherstone Town, Stableford & Co (Coalville) and Barwell United. (2 apps)

> **W R Lowe** was the mystery-man at left back when Fosse recruited four unknowns to their depleted ranks at Grimsby in October 1918. (1 app)

> Described simply as 'a Birmingham youth', **J Machin** took the Fosse inside-left position in the 2-1 home win over Sheffield United in February 1919. (1 app)

> **E Marriott** of Pinxton, a former Sutton Junction player, made a quartet of appearances as Fosse's outside-left from December 1916. (4 apps)

> A Huddersfield Town reserve, **R May** was borrowed by Fosse to complete their line-up at Barnsley in December 1918, playing right-half in a 2-3 defeat. (1 app)

> A veteran whose first-class career was behind him, **Charles J H Millington** (b. Lincoln, 25.4.1884; d. Lincoln, 13.6.1955) assisted Fosse to a goalless draw at Birmingham in December 1917, taking the inside-right berth. His pre-war wanderings had taken him from Grantham to Ripley Athletic (Jan 1905), Aston Villa (Sept 1905), Fulham (Oct 1907), Birmingham (cs 1909), Wellington Town (1912), Brierley Hill (March 1913) and Stourbridge (April 1914). (1 app)

> Seaman **H Minney**, a local player with Victoria Athletic and Standard Engineering Co FC, featured on the right wing in Fosse's December 1918 home defeat by Bradford Park Avenue. He was an unsuccessful City trialist in August 1919, after which he turned out for Toone & Wells FC. (1 app)

> **W Montgomery**, an inside-forward from Birmingham works team Bellis & Morcom, spent three weeks as a Fossil in March 1916, scoring on his debut in a 5-2 away win at Derby. (3 apps; 1 goal)

> Whitwick Imperial right winger **Andy Moore** (previously with Coalville Swifts) had his sole Fosse outing on the opening day of season 1917/18, in a 1-2 defeat at Notts County. (1 app)

> **T Morrell**, from Birmingham Suburban League side Redditch, was Fosse's inside-right trialist in a 2-2 home draw with Barnsley in February 1916. Back in 1912, he'd played in the annual 'international' between a Birmingham area XI and Scotland's Junior selection. (1 app)

> Drafted in as cover for the recently-bereaved Sam Currie in the home game with Hull City in February 1919, Coalville Swifts and former Hugglescote St Johns right-back **E Mugglestone** earned from the local *Post* the archaically unselfconscious comment that he 'worked like a nigger', but that his performance was 'rather ragged'. We believe him to have been Emanuel Mugglestone (b. Donington), who signed for Gresley Rovers in August 1919, switched to outside-right, played several games as a pro for City reserves during 1920/1, joined Burton All Saints in 1921, Coalville Swifts again in 1922, Ibstock Colliery a year later, and Stableford's Works in February 1925. (1 app)

> Shirebrook outside-left **E Mullins** assisted Fosse at Nottingham Forest in March 1917, and also turned out in four games for Forest the following term, including their fixture at Filbert Street. (1 app)

> **T Murray** was drafted into the Fosse team at outside-left when they arrived at Bradford Park Avenue in December 1917 extremely late and three men short. Indeed, the game kicked off with only eight Fossils on the pitch, and was severely foreshortened, so Murray's sole appearance lasted less than 52 minutes. (1 app)

> On the verge of a promising Aston Villa career when war called a halt to League football, **Harry Nash** (Harold Edward; b. Fishponds, Bristol, 10.4.1892) had scored a hat-trick on his debut against Liverpool only two months after his February 1915 signing from Pontypridd. During the following term, however, he was playing for Bellis & Morcom in the

Birmingham Suburban League; and a year later (from February 1917) guesting for Fosse. He failed to settle with Villa after the war, moving on to Coventry City in July 1920, to Cardiff City in February 1921, and Merthyr Town in May 1923; later finishing his career with Aberbargoed and Ystradmynach. He also made one WW1 appearance for Lincoln City, alongside Harold Edgley, on day they fulfilled two outstanding fixtures simultaneously. (4 apps)

> Only once during WW1 did Fosse resort to using in their line-up that most transparent of pseudonyms, **A Newman**. The identity of the outside-right in the home game with Lincoln City in October 1916 will ever remain a mystery: there is no mention of him in any of the local press reports; and the fact that Football League records credit Tommy Benfield with this appearance would seem misleading: Benfield played both before and after under his own name and military rank, and would certainly have been recognised in a home game if subterfuge were intended. (1 app)

> Stourbridge-born **Jimmy Nock** first underwent Fosse trials in November 1913, when playing for Daimler Motor Works FC, and first figured in senior wartime football with Millwall, who signed him in October 1915 from his home-town club. A prolific centre-forward, he returned to the Midlands in 1919, and featured in Fosse's last eleven regional games, as well as scoring the last goal the club ever registered under that name (in a 1-1 friendly draw with the BEF [France] XI), before being resurrected as Leicester City. Nonetheless, Jimmy failed to gain a Filbert Street contract, and signed instead for Merthyr Town in May 1919. He subsequently joined Nuneaton Town (cs 1920), Tamworth Castle (Jan 1922), Cradley Heath (cs 1923), Burton Town (cs 1924) and Worcester City (Aug 1925). In previous drafts of this work, we have conflated his career with that of Jack Nock, another Cradley Heath forward who later played League football for Cardiff and Wrexham, and served Flint Town and Oswestry; while we have yet to ascertain which of these men (if either) was with Cannock Town in 1929/30. (11 apps; 5 goals)

> A brother of pre-war Fossil Fred, Lieutenant **George Osborn** was a former Hinckley United, Leicester Imperial and Leicester Nomads player who featured at inside-right in a trio of Fosse games in December 1917 and January 1918. He also assisted Hull City during WW1. A military gymnastic instructor at Aldershot in pre-war days, he rejoined Hinckley on his October 1919 demob, and had become, by 1932, a Leicester schools PT inspector. (3 apps)

> Fosse's inside-right in the home and away fixtures with Nottingham Forest in April 1919 was **Fred Osborne** (b. Birmingham, ca 1893), a Worcester City forward who also assisted Lincoln City, Coventry City & Birmingham during WW1, and played postwar for Brighton & Hove Albion, Weymouth and Pontypridd. (2 apps)

> Borrowed from home-team Hull City to face them as Fosse's centre-forward in March 1917, **Arthur Pace** (b. Newcastle, 1885; d. Hull, 1968) was a former wing-half who had initially signed for the Tigers from Hebburn Argyle in November 1907, and had subsequently moved to Rotherham Town (cs 1910) and Croydon Common (September 1911) before returning on the outbreak of war. He also assisted Sheffield United, Lincoln City and Southport Central during WW1. (1 app)

> Another to face his own club in Fosse colours was **George Padley** (b. Grimsby, 1882; d. 2.11.1965), a forward better known by his nickname, 'Punch'. Fosse were several men short when arriving at Grimsby in January 1917, and shocked the home team by romping home 3-1 winners with a distinctly makeshift line-up: Padley claiming one of the goals. Having first signed for Grimsby Town in 1904 from Grimsby St Johns, and been introduced to League fare against Fosse in April 1905, he had made his final League appearance in 1906, spending the interim years until the war largely with Worksop Town. 'Punch' was also a Lincolnshire cricketer, and was still playing local Grimsby soccer with Charlton's in 1919/20. (1 app; 1 goal)

> No details at all adhered to the right-half appearance of **G H Parker** in the September 1918 home win over Rotherham County: but it is assumed that he was George H Parker, a Fosse reserve in 14/15, who played postwar for Westleigh BC and Loughborough Corinthians. (1 app)

> Few more bits of background information were forthcoming when Private **P Parker** featured at centre-forward in a handful of Fosse games in April 1916, beyond the fact that he'd recently impressed in an otherwise unrecorded friendly for the Pioneers against Fosse. (5 apps; 2 goals)

> **Harry Parsonage**, who'd tasted League fare with Wolverhampton Wanderers between 1911 and 1913, moved into the Birmingham League with Shrewsbury Town, and would feature postwar at that level with Walsall and Worcester City, was a regular forward for Fosse during their generally goal-shy 1916/17 campaign. (17 apps; 5 goals)

> **A Peel**, a right-back from 'a Northern club', 'made a moderate start' (according to the *Post*) in a goalless home draw with Leeds City in February 1919, but never played again. (1 app)

> A rather more famous full-back, who featured for Fosse in the Christmas Day and Boxing Day games against Birmingham in 1918, was **Jesse Pennington** (b. West Bromwich, 23.8.1883; d. Stourbridge, 5.9.1970). The eventual winner of 25 England caps between 1907 and 1920, he had signed for West Bromwich Albion from Dudley Town in March 1903, and remained, in peacetime at least, a one-club man until retirement in 1922. During WW1, however, his services were also lent to Birmingham, Coventry City, Lincoln City, Notts County, Manchester United and Oldbury Town. (2 apps)

> A local given a chance after a Fosse trial game against Belvoir SS, inside-right **Cecil Harry Phipps** (b. Leicester, 25.10.1896; d. Leicester, 24.9.1968) faced Coventry City away in March 1919, played in the final Fosse friendly against the BEF (France) XI the following month, and was offered an amateur contract by City for 1919/20. A month later, however, he featured in West Ham's first team for a single game and, after interim service with Coalville Swifts and City reserves, turned up in an August 1921 trial for Halifax Town, which led to him appearing at outside-left in that club's first-ever League line-up. Further stints with Coalville Swifts, Loughborough Corinthians (1922/3), Whitwick Imperial (1923/4), Burton All Saints (Dec 1924), Shepshed Albion (1925), Holy Trinity Pilots (1927) and Municipal Offices FC (1929) followed. His brother, Ernest Horace Phipps, was a City reserve centre-half in 1919/20, between spells with Hinckley United, and before uniting with Harry at Coalville Swifts. (1 app)

> One of the players recruited at the ground when Fosse arrived three men short at Bradford Park Avenue in December 1917, **S Pollard** took the outside-right position. He also played a single WW1 game for Park Avenue on the left wing. (1 app)

> A former Southern League representative player, **Harry Pullen** (b. Wellingborough, 1888) featured at right-back for Fosse at Lincoln City in November 1915. He'd joined Queens Park Rangers from Kettering in June 1910, and amassed a 187-game record in the Southern League before a transfer to Newport County exactly ten years later. A further move, to Hartlepools United in June 1921, was stymied when Harry contracted appendicitis. (1 app)

> A wartime player for Notts County, **B Pykett** (possibly Bernard Arthur) was another to answer Fosse's emergency call for the game at Grimsby Town in January 1917, when he held the centre-forward spot. He'd featured before the war for Ilkeston United. (1 app)

> Formerly a winger with Blackpool, Colne, Sunderland (April 1910), Chelsea (May 1911), Dundee (March 1913) and Swansea Town, **Bill Read** (William Henry; b. Blackpool, 1885) figured on Fosse's right flank at Hull City in March 1919, in one of eleven jerseys borrowed from the home club after Fosse's kit skip went astray, shortly after his demob from three years' Navy service. He featured only briefly postwar for Chesterfield Municipal, and was settled in Leicester as a picture-frame maker by April 1920. (1 app)

> A centre-forward named **Roach** was one of Fosse's otherwise anonymous foursome of temporary recruits at Grimsby in October 1918. He may conceivably have been a Whitwick Imperial player. (1 app)

> The only genuine Fosse discovery of the WW1 era to go on to full international honours was future England centre-forward **Tommy Roberts** (William Thomas; b. Handsworth, 29.11.1898; d. Preston, 13.10.1965). Previously experienced only in Birmingham-area junior football (with Kentish Rovers, Boyce Engineers, Lord Street and Soho Villa), Tommy threw in his lot with Fosse in April 1917, and soon hit the goal trail. Disappointingly, in late 1918 his war work enforced a change of residence to Lancashire, and Southport Vulcan utilised his playing services for much of the final WW1 season; while Preston North End leapt in for his professional signature in the following close season. He was twice capped in 1924, and moved to Burnley in October of that year (where he suffered a broken pelvis), but was back for a second stint at Preston from July 1926. He additionally had a brief spell with Tottenham Hotspur (May 1928), then finished his career back in Lancashire with Dick, Kerr's FC (August 1929) and Chorley (October 1930). He entered the record books as the first player to notch 200 League goals after WW1. (32 apps; 24 goals)

> Left-half **Joseph Roulson** (b. Sheffield, 7.10.1891) was on Birmingham's books (having signed from Cammell Laird FC in August 1912) at the time of his single Fosse outing, but was playing much of his wartime football in his home town. He guested occasionally for Sheffield Wednesday, but it was at Bramall Lane that Fosse borrowed him for their December 1916 meeting with United. Birmingham eventually transferred Joe to Swansea Town in August 1922, and he moved again in August 1924 to Clapton Orient. (1 app)

> Corporal **Henry Sarson** was a bandsman in the Leicestershire Regiment when he appeared as a right-sided forward for Fosse in February and March 1918. (4 apps; 1 goal)

> Sheffield-born Chesterfield Town winger **George W Sharpe** (formerly with Rotherham Town) helped out Fosse at Sheffield United in April 1916, and then appeared several times the following season after a December outing for Fosse against his own team. (9 apps; 1 goal)

> A single pre-war League outing for Aston Villa (plus a trio of wartime games) was the sole top-level experience of **Herbert Horace Smart** when he took Fosse's spearhead role in the February 1919 home win over Sheffield United. He'd originally signed up at Villa Park from Bilston United in January 1914; and went on to record a few postwar appearances for Wolves after a December 1919 move. (1 app)

> Borrowed from Rotherham County when Fosse faced them in November 1917, and positioned on the right wing, **Jack Smelt** (John William; b. Rotherham) was a versatile clubman who even occasionally turned out in goal for the team which also regularly featured his brother Len at full-back. Previously experienced with Mansfield Mechanics and Chesterfield Town before his Millmoor stint, Jack later served Portsmouth (both as goalkeeper and forward from October 1919), Sheffield Wednesday (from January 1921) and Barrow (from 1922). He also guested for Leeds City, Lincoln City and Bradford City during WW1. Two further Smelt brothers, Tom and Alfred, also figured in League football around this time. (1 app)

> Whitwick Imperial right-half **F Smith** appeared in a trio of Fosse defeats from December 1916. (3 apps)

> Recently demobbed, and reputed to have once been a junior on Notts County's books, **George R Smith** settled into Fosse's right-back position for three months at the tail end of 1918/19. (9 apps)

> **S Smith** had a handful of outings at outside-right and right-half after December 1916, when his local club was Newhall Swifts; and added a further right-wing selection in October 1918, when identified as a Stanton player. (6 apps; 1 goal)

> **T Smith** was a Mansfield defender, recommended by former Army football colleague Charlie Storer, who got a Fosse break at right-back in a 2-4 defeat at Leeds City in January 1919. [See also the note on City's Tom Smith]. (1 app)

> A trialist right winger from Birmingham junior football, **J Southwell** played in the home defeat by Hull City in November 1916. (1 app)

> The surprise 3-1 win at Grimsby achieved by Fosse's patchwork eleven in January 1917 was materially aided by a goalscoring contribution from **Colin Stainsby**, borrowed on the day from the home club (who used him themselves only under wartime conditions). Fosse also had to borrow a magenta strip on this day, with their own lost in transit. (1 app; 1 goal)

> Former Balmoral United, Atherstone and Hinckley United forward **Mick (A M) Stanton** figured in Fosse's front line in both home and away fixtures with Sheffield United in February 1919, scoring in the initial home win. Postwar, he served Hinckley and Barwell United. (2 apps; 1 goal)

> Mexborough right-back **J Stern** was a late addition to the Fosse line-up at Barnsley in December 1916 which went down 0-5. (1 app)

> A centre-forward turned centre-half who had moved from Gresley Rovers to Bradford City in February 1913, **Charles Storer** (b. Ibstock, 29.3.1891) spent much of the war back in Leicestershire when not on Army service, and became a regular for both Fosse and Coalville Swifts from late 1916, usually in the pivotal position. By the time Bradford City let him move on to Hartlepools United in September 1924, Charlie had amassed a record of 208 League appearances (13 goals) for them. He had started his career with Ibstock Albion. (71 apps; 2 goals)

> **Sid Storer** was Charlie's brother, a Coalville Swifts right-half, who made exactly half of his sporadic Fosse appearances between January 1917 and January 1918 in Charlie's company. Having had a pre-war spell with Long Eaton Rangers, he later played for Gresley Rovers (from cs 1919), Coalville again and Ibstock Colliery (where he featured haplessly in the 0-22 Senior Cup slaughter by City Reserves in 1924). (8 apps)

> One of two youths borrowed for the first game of the 1916/17 season at Elland Road was Leeds City reserve **Ernest F Sturdy**, who managed a goal for Fosse in the 2-2 draw, yet never forced his way into the reckoning for his own club. (1 app; 1 goal)

> **Aaron Swain**, the Coalville Swifts right winger and a native of Swannington, signed amateur forms for Fosse in April 1917, but faded from the first-team picture after his final game the following September. He played with Shepshed Albion from 1920 to November 1921, then rejoined Coalville Swifts, moved to Loughborough Corinthians in 1924, and later assisted Shepshed Albion again. His father George was a noted referee and football administrator in the Coalville district. (9 apps; 2 goals)

> Loughborough Corinthians forward and army signaller **Bert Thurman** (Albert C; b. Hathern) filled in for Fosse at inside-left in their away game with Sheffield Wednesday in November 1916. The previous January he had guested for Notts County, while his pre-war experience had come with Hathern, Shepshed Albion, Long Eaton and the Corries – for whom he was left-back and skipper by 1925/6. (1 app)

> Left-sided half-back or forward **W Timmins** was borrowed from Nottingham Forest for the City Ground fixture in December 1916. He made 27 wartime appearances for Forest and 24 for Notts County after 8 for Derby County; though it remains unclear at present if he was the same player of this surname who turned out during WW1 for Lincoln City and Chesterfield. Postwar, however, he represented both Heanor Town and Sutton Junction. (1 app)

> Previously a one-shot wartime player for Notts County, **A Turner** was Fosse's inside-left in their game at Birmingham on Christmas Day 1917. It is conceivable that he was a younger brother of 'Leggy' Turner, who had played pre-war for Whitwick Imperial. (1 app)

> Originally a pre-war reserve, unlucky enough to have broken his leg before gaining a senior try-out, **Joe Tyler** held the army rank of sergeant when belatedly handed the Fosse inside-right berth at Barnsley in February 1918. Only recently recovered from a long bout of trench fever, he was nonetheless deemed to look overweight by the *Post's* match reporter. (1 app)

> A right-back who signed on for Fosse prior to the final WW1 season of 1918/19, **J 'Gent' Underwood** became a regular only until the following

Tommy Roberts

Charlie Storer

January, and failed to win a peacetime contract. Pre-war, he'd served Coalville Rangers, Coalville PSA, Ellistown St Christophers and Coalville Swifts, and he rejoined the latter for a lengthy postwar stint. In the early 30s, he was working at New Lount Colliery.
(21 apps)

> Wounded in 1914, Belgian soldier **Honoré Vlaminck** (b. 29.1.1887; d. Sept 1974) recuperated in Leicester with a number of his compatriots, and was well enough to turn out for Leicester Imperial from March 1915. Fosse gave him a chance at a higher level in November 1918, just before his repatriation, and he showed signs of real class in the centre-forward shirt. In his second game, a 7-3 home win over Sheffield Wednesday, he claimed two scoring headers and missed a penalty, and he was also on the mark against Huddersfield a fortnight later. Back in Brussels (where he was nicknamed 'Snoteke') he played for Daring (champions in 1921) and won four full caps for Belgium between 1919 and 1923, scoring twice. (4 apps; 3 goals)

> Sergeant-Major **L Wale** of the Leicestershire Regiment was one of several military volunteers from a Humberside camp to help Fosse fulfil their fixture at Grimsby in December 1917; taking the centre-half role in a 1-1 draw. A career soldier, he had attained by 1932 the rank of Captain, and was based in Londonderry.
(1 app)

> Gunner **James Harry Walker** (b. Wirksworth, 1891; d. 1934) was guesting regularly for Notts County at left-back when he joined Meadow Lane teammate Jimmy Cantrell in assisting Fosse in their home game against Bradford City in April 1917. Originally a forward, who had graduated from Clay Cross to Derby County and played left-half in their 1914/15 Second Division championship side, Harry later signed officially for Notts County (June 1920), then successively for Fulham, Reading, Aberdare Athletic, Bournemouth & Boscombe Athletic and Chesterfield. (1 app)

> Fosse's top scorer in 1915/16 - when his own club, Birmingham, were not playing competitive football - centre-forward **Billy Walker** (William Baird; b. New Cumnock, 5.5.1893) also claimed Fosse's first two hat-tricks of the wartime period from home games with Leeds City and Hull City. Having started his career in his native Scotland with New Cumnock and Lugar Boswell, Billy had a spell with Bradford City between August 1911 and March 1913, then returned north to minor Ayrshire club Lanemark. Birmingham reintroduced him to the League game in November 1913 and held his registration until the close season of 1919, when he transferred to Coventry City. A year later he moved to Merthyr Town, claiming that club's first-ever League goal; then transferred successively to Bristol City (October 1922; helping seal their Third Division South championship)

and Sheffield Wednesday (October 1923) before taking the player-manager's role at Weymouth from 1924. During WW1 Billy also turned out briefly for Aston Villa and Bradford City, scoring against Fosse for the latter in April 1917, when serving as a Sapper in the Royal Engineers. (26 apps; 13 goals)

> Graduating from Belgrave St Peter's Mission to become the pre-war full-back partner to Walter Essom with Leicester Imperial, **Bert Waterfield** had just become an army Private when Fosse briefly utilised his services in April 1916. Soon, after only a month at the front in France and a promotion to Lance-Corporal in the London Regiment, he was dead, killed in action on 27.7.1916, aged 23.
(2 apps)

> **J Watson**, a right-back from a Nottingham works team, played in Fosse's last competitive WW1 fixture, a 2-4 home defeat by Birmingham in April 1919. (1 app)

> Despite playing in every game of Fosse's June 1913 tour of Sweden, Croydon-born centre-half **George A Webber** never got another senior outing in his year at Filbert Street; and it was only under wartime conditions that he played competitive football for Fosse. A 1912 signing by Southern League Croydon Common from Croydon Gas Co FC, he had followed his former manager Jack Bartlett to Leicester, and moved on with his boss in 1914 to Swansea Town. At the start of the following season, George was back with Croydon Common (soon to fold), and then featured with Balmoral United in local Leicester circles when on Navy leave. Strangely, of his sporadic Fosse appearances between April 1916 and April 1917, two were on the left wing. In August 1919, George was on trial with Atherstone Town, and from 1920 played with Senior League side Stableford's. (4 apps)

> 'A local youth' with some wartime experience with Barnsley, **A Whiteman** was borrowed by Fosse to play as their right-half in the February 1918 game at Oakwell.
(1 app)

> A Rotherham soldier already honoured with the DCM, Private **G W Whitworth** assisted Fosse at inside-left against his own club in the clash with Rotherham County in January 1917. (1 app)

> Lance-Corporal **A Willmott** made up the Fosse numbers at Lincoln City in February 1917, playing on the right wing in a 0-1 defeat. (1 app)

> Recommended to Fosse by then-regular guest George Sharpe, Sheffield-based inside-right **G Willoughby** was tried out in the match at Hull City in March 1917, when Fosse's goal in a 1-2 defeat came from goalkeeper Herbert Bown's penalty kick. (1 app)

List of Subscribers

No.	Name / Home Town	Fav. LCFC player	Fav. LCFC game
1	Sir Rodney Walker, Wakefield	N/A	N/A
2	John Elsom, Leicester	N/A	N/A
3	Steve Kind, Leicester	N/A	N/A
4	Greg Clarke, Leicester	N/A	N/A
5	Bill Shooter, Leicester	N/A	N/A
6	Martin George, Peterborough	N/A	N/A
7	Ken Brigstock, Kettering	N/A	N/A
8	Terry Shipman, Newtown Linford	N/A	N/A
9	Charles Rayner, Broughton Astley	N/A	N/A
10	Jonathan Waltho, Rothley	N/A	N/A
11	Alan Birchenall, Mountsorrel	N/A	N/A
12	Val Samuels, Leicester	N/A	N/A
13	Ben Swift, Birstall	N/A	N/A
14	Roger Mason, Leicester	N/A	N/A
15	Ray King, Leicester	N/A	N/A
16	Jack Neale, Broughton Astley	N/A	N/A
17	Bev Parrot, Barlestone	N/A	N/A
18	Marie Morgan, Leicester	N/A	N/A
19	John Bennett, Hinckley	N/A	N/A
20	Mel Plummer, Leicester	N/A	N/A
21	Trevor Jolley, Bury St Edmunds	David Gibson	Crystal Palace
22	Simon Mitchell, Wigston - Leicester	Steve Walsh	v' Oxford to stay up
23	Dave & Peter Johnson, Markfield, Leicester	Keith Weller	Crystal Palace Play Off Final
24	Peter Sharp, Humberstone - Leicester	Gary Lineker	Shrewsbury 1982 Cup
25	David Steel, Worcester	Steve Walsh	90-91 Oxford Home
26	Derek Carruthers, Burbage	Steve Walsh	N/A
27	Adrian Morton, Inverness	Steve Walsh	Play Off Final 1996
28	Stephen Taylor, Leicester	Tommy Wright	At home to Liverpool 1972 (3-2)
29	Robert O'Donnell, Market Harborough	Steve Walsh	Derby Play Off Final
30	Mark Smith, Leicester	Frank Worthington	Shrewsbury FA Cup
31	Les Newbold, Telford - Shropshire	Frank Worthington	Luton Away FA Cup 1974
32	David R Leake, Countesthorpe	Arthur Rowley	Worthington Cup Final 2000
33	Chris McMinn, Leicester	Steve Walsh	Derby Away April 1998
34	Terry Bell, North Kilworth	Frank Worthington	Derby Play Off Final
35	John Checketts, Melton Mowbray	Steve Walsh	Arsenal 1997 (3-3)
36	Anne Newbery, Reading	Gerry Taggart	Derby Play Off Final
37	Ian & Ashley Davidson, Worcester	Frank Worthington	Man City 1968 (4-3)
38	Nigel Peter Wilby, Leicester	Peter Shilton	Man City 1968 FA Cup 4th Rd Rep.
39	Phil Abbott, Nottingham	Steve Claridge	Crystal Palace Play Off Final
40	Stewart Green, Stamford	Steve Walsh	Crystal Palace - Wembley
41	Chris Griffin, Holmes Chapel	Matt Elliott	Crystal Palace Play Off Final
42	Mark Leonard, Leicester	Steve Walsh	Crystal Palace Play Off Final
43	Carl Buck, Leicester	Steve Walsh	Crystal Palace Play Off Final
44	Stafford Buck, Leicester	Steve Walsh	Derby Play Off Final
45	Chris Jinks, Leicester	Lenny Glover	Shrewsbury 1982 Cup
46	David Jinks, Leicester	Arthur Rowley	Luton Away 1949
47	Martin Miller, Leicester	Gary McAllister	Crystal Palace Play Off Final
48	Penelope Duranti, Burbage - Hinckley	Keith Weller	Crystal Palace Play Off Final
49	Bigman, Leicester	Frank Worthington	Liverpool
50	P & J Kinal, Oakham	Gordon Banks	Hillsborough - Coca Cola Cup Final
51	Andrew Hall, Peterborough	Steve Walsh	Cambridge Play Off 1992
52	Nigel Wattam, Bourne - Lincolnshire	Frank Worthington	Derby Play Off Final
53	Alan Bannister, Braunstone - Leicester	Graham Cross	Crystal Palace Play Off Final
54	Graeme Norris, Rothwell - Northants	Steve Walsh	LGE Cup Final Replay 1997
55	Arthur J Guest, Wigston - Leicester	Keith Weller	Manchester City FA Cup 1967
56	Lance Tomlyn, Northampton	Keith Weller	Shrewsbury FA Cup
57	John Lawton, Shenton	Steve Claridge	Hillsborough - Coca Cola Cup Final
58	Rob Twycross, Leicester	Keith Weller	Derby Play Off Final
59	The Fox Fanzine, Leicester	Keith Weller	League Cup Replay 1997
60	Andy Buckingham, Leicester	Steve Walsh	Oxford 90/91
61	Timothy Mawby, Leicester	Steve Walsh	Manchester City FA Cup 1968
62	Mike & Russ Loasby, Leicester	N/A	N/A
63	Graeme Burton, Kent	Steve Claridge	Wembley 1996
64	Andy Young, Teignmouth	Lenny Glover	Coca Cola Cup Final 1997
65	Nick Bilson, Hinckley, Leics	Keith Weller	Liverpool - 1972
66	Jim Purdie, London	David Gibson	Derby Play Off Final
67	Ian Sharman, Burbage	Steve Walsh	Derby Play Off Final
68	Paul Lovelock, Leicester	Gary Lineker	Sunderland 2000
69	Mark Mee, Desford, Leics	Muzzy Izzet	Watford 1996
70	John May, Stevenage	Steve Walsh	Replay League Cup Final 1997
71	David York, Wisbech, Cambridgeshire	Gary Lineker	Derby Play Off Final
72	David Thompson, Frederick of Andover	Allan Clarke	Nottingham Forest 1968/69
73	Ian Harris, Scraptoft	Julian Joachim	Wembley - City 2 Derby 1
74	Geoff Wheelton, Blaby	Lenny Glover	Manchester City 1968
75	Tim English, Leicester	Steve Walsh	Crystal Palace Play Off Final
76	Ken Herts, Batley	Gary Lineker	Crystal Palace Play Off Final
77	Doug Kemp, Wellingborough	Lenny Glover	Derby Wembley 1994
78	Martyn Wilson, London	Keith Weller	Coca Cola Cup Final 1997
79	Jeremy Wakefield, Leicester	Frank Worthington	Crystal Palace Play Off Final
80	David Fearn, Rugby	Keith Weller	Coventry 1984
81	Peter Smith, Leicester	Keith Weller	Coca Cola Cup Final Replay - Mboro
82	Gerard Boland, Aylesbury, Bucks	Gary Lineker	Derby Play Off Final
83	John Preston, Huncote - Leicester	Steve Walsh	Cambridge Play Off 1992
84	Cindy Desborough, Desborough	Steve Walsh	Tottenham Hotspur 2001
85	Alan Cox, Burbage - Hinckley	Malwyn Griffiths	FL Cup 1996 - 1997
86	Geoff Hawes, Loughborough	Frank Worthington	FA Cup 1968 - Manchester City
87	Graham Prosser, Leicester	Steve Walsh	Aston Villa 1994/1995
88	Peter Taylorson, Walthamstow, London	Jackie Sinclair	Crystal Palace Play Off Final
89	Andrew York, Leicester	Gary Lineker	Liverpool - 1984

WORLD WAR TWO PLAYERS

The most exotic of City's WW2 guests, **Emilio Gomez Aldecoa** (b. Bilbao, 30.11.1922; d. Spain, Sept 1999) was a refugee from the Spanish Civil War who signed for Wolves in 1943 (scoring for them against City in September 1944), guested in City's front line in four games during September and October 1945, then transferred to Coventry City, where he continued to play in postwar League football. Eventually returning to Spain in 1947 to join Athletic Bilbao, he later played for Valladolid and Barcelona, featuring in the latter's 1951/2 double-winning side. Emilio also won one Spanish cap (as substitute against the Republic of Ireland in May 1948). He was on the Barcelona coaching staff in the 50s, was briefly chief coach at Birmingham City under Gil Merrick from 1960, and managed each of Gerona, CD Condal and Real Valladolid. (4 apps; 1 goal)

> Primarily remembered for scoring in Walsall's celebrated 1933 giantkilling of Arsenal, **Gilbert Arthur Alsop** (b. Frampton Cotterell, 22.9.1908, d. Walsall, 16.4.1992) turned out eight times for City during 1943/4, though only twice in his accustomed centre-forward role. Gilbert joined Coventry City in December 1929 from Bath City, moved to Walsall in October 1931, to West Brom in November 1935, to Ipswich Town in June 1937, and back to Walsall in November 1938, playing until 1947. Of his 157 League goals, 151 were for the Saddlers; but his 106 wartime goals were accrued for a host of clubs, including Coventry, Bristol Rovers, Mansfield, Luton and Northampton. On Walsall's groundstaff for twenty years after his playing retirement, Gilbert had the honour of having a stand at the new Bescot Stadium named after him. (8 apps; 3 goals)

> **Tom Ansell** was an 18-year-old amateur whose sole City appearance was at outside-left away to Northampton in February 1940. His local clubs had been Humberstone St Mary's and Petronians. (1 app)

> **Derek O Ashton** (b. Worksop, 4.7.1922) had already figured on the City scoresheet (with an own goal for Wolves in March 1945) by the time he became a City guest (the only such in Johnny Duncan's first managerial selection) at right-back in the home game with Coventry in March 1946. Derek never made a peacetime appearance for Wolves, who he joined in 1941, but got eight League outings for Aston Villa after a May 1946 transfer, and before a 1949 move to Wellington Town. (1 app)

> When both Sep Smith and Fred Kilshaw missed their train to join City's party at Charlton Athletic in September 1945, **Arthur Attwood** was recruited as an emergency guest at outside-right. An old RAF colleague of Dai Jones, who had intended spectating, Arthur was also reported to have been an old Bristol Rovers player: if so, he was definitely at the veteran stage, as records show Arthur Albert Attwood (b. Walsall, 1.12.1901; d. Hove, 6.12.1974) to have retired almost ten years previously after a career at centre-forward which had taken in Walsall (January 1928), Everton (March 1929), Bristol Rovers (May 1930), Brighton & Hove Albion (November 1931) and Northfleet (August 1935). (1 app)

> A City Colt during 1941/2, signed as an amateur after being spotted in Hinckley ATC football, **William P Barnes** played twice at left-half in home and away fixtures against Bristol City in May 1942. (2 apps)

> A City regular on the right wing during 1941/2 and 1942/3, **Harry Barratt** (b. Headington, 25.12.1918, d. Coventry, 23.9.1989) was the son of Fosse's WW1 player Josiah Barratt. On Coventry City's books from December 1935 (when signed from Herbert's Athletic) to 1952, Harry was a sergeant in the Royal Warwickshire Regiment during the retreat from Dunkirk, then engaged in industrial war work. He also guested for Nottingham Forest and Walsall. After cutting his football links following spells as manager of Rugby Town, Snowdown Colliery, Gillingham (1957-62) and Tunbridge Wells, and an interim stint as Coventry's chief scout, Harry became national coach and secretary to the British Crown Green Bowls Association. (45 apps; 16 goals)

> One of two guests in City's first competitive WW2 game, Northampton's **Bill Barron** (William; b. Herrington, 26.10.1917) scored the final goal in a 6-1 win over Walsall from the outside-left position, and continued to feature occasionally throughout 1939/40. An October 1937 Charlton Athletic signing from Annfield Plain (after having been an unsuccessful Wolves trialist in November 1936), Bill moved to Northampton in May 1938, and stayed thirteen years before joining Kettering. A pre-war cricketer for Durham, he turned out in the County Championship afterwards for Lancashire and Northants. His son Roger was a Cobblers goalkeeper in the 60s. (7 apps; 1 goal)

> Nottingham Forest centre-half **Bill Baxter** (William Amelius; b. Nottingham, 6.9.1917; d. Nottingham, 21.2.1992) assisted City twice in March 1945, in home and away Cup games against Derby, and also guested for Notts County, Mansfield and Derby during the war. A professional with Forest from December 1936, Bill crossed the Trent to Meadow Lane in October 1946, and finished his career with Grantham after a 1954 move. (2 apps)

> Briefly stationed at Old Dalby, at the RAOC's Central Ordnance Depot (and playing Leicestershire Senior League football for his unit), Scottish international full-back **Andy Beattie** (b. Kintore, 11.8.1913, d. Nottingham, 20.9.1983) was recruited for a quartet of City games in December 1939 and January 1940. A Preston North End signing from Inverurie Loco in March 1935, Andy had appeared in two Wembley Cup Finals and won seven caps before the war, and retired in 1947 as essentially a one-club man. During WW2, however, he also guested for Notts County, Aldershot, Northampton, Derby, Manchester City, Clapton Orient, and Bradford City, and played four wartime internationals; while on retirement he commenced a managerial merry-go-round which encompassed stints with Barrow, Stockport, Huddersfield, Carlisle, Nottingham Forest, Plymouth and Wolves; as well as two spells as boss of Scotland's international team, and other backroom roles at Notts County and Sheffield United. Andy had scored an own goal for City to settle the home game with Preston in November 1937. (4 apps)

> Noted for his all-action enthusiasm at full-back, Arbroath stalwart **Attilio Becci** guested for City during 1943/4. A 1932 signing for his Scottish club, where he was familiarly known as 'Teel', he also turned out for Notts County during WW2, and represented a high-quality British Army XI in Naples in 1945. (8 apps)

> **Mick Betteridge** (Raymond Michael; b. Redditch, 11.8.1924) was a Loughborough College student when he made his sole City appearance (as inside-right at Aston Villa in December 1942), and had previously played for Leicester Nomads. It was some time later, however, before he made his senior mark, signing for West Bromwich Albion in November 1948, for Swindon Town in January 1951, and for Chester in March 1954. With the latter club he was a Welsh Cup medallist as runner-up in the 1954 Final. (1 app)

> Struggling to raise eleven men for the final fixture of 1942/3, at Stoke, City borrowed amateur winger **William J Birks** from the then-inactive Port Vale to help make up the side. He made but a trio of wartime appearances for Vale in 44/5, and then faded into obscurity. (1 app)

> An 18-year-old amateur on Arsenal's books when he burst into City's seniors in October 1943, **Norman H Bowden** (b. Glossop, ca.1925) made such an immediate impact that the Gunners took the insurance-policy step of signing him professionally the next month. The prolific centre-forward had his City stint (in which he was 1943/4's top scorer) interrupted by RAF aircrew training in Florida, and before the war was out had survived baling out of his burning aircraft at 10,000 feet. Norman also guested for Burnley, Wolves, Blackburn and Manchester United, yet strangely made no peacetime League appearances for Arsenal or anyone else; and this in spite of representing the Army XI against the FA XI in in 1946/7, the first of such games to virtually constitute international trials. (23 apps; 14 goals)

> 'Sailor' **Bert Brown** (Robert Albert John; b. Great Yarmouth, 7.11.1915) was known as such because of his rolling gait, for he served with the Auxiliary Police and then the RAF during the war. His single City outing (as inside-right in a defeat at West Brom in October 1944) was but one of many guest appearances for the Charlton schemer, who also turned out briefly for Wolves, Manchester City, Millwall, Luton, Newcastle, West Ham, Chelsea, Aldershot, York, Huddersfield and East Fife during wartime. Previously, he had signed on at The Valley from Gorleston in August 1934. He had toured South Africa with the FA in 1939, and won seven wartime caps for England, but moved on to Forest in May 1946, to Aston Villa in October 1947, and back to Gorleston (as player-manager) in June 1949. (1 app)

> **J H Browne** was a military policeman and unblooded Aston Villa junior when he turned out at inside-left for City at home to Stoke in April 1943. (1 app)

> A Scottish League representative while on Celtic's books (signed January 1932 from Grange Rovers), **Willie Buchan** (William Ralston Murray; b. Grangemouth, 17.10.1914) had been since November 1937 a Blackpool inside-forward, when he made a quintet of City appearances from March 1942. Also winning one Scottish wartime cap, Willie similarly turned out during the hostilities for Manchester United, Aberaman, Bristol City, Fulham, Bath City, Hamilton Academical and Stenhousemuir. Postwar, he moved to Hull City in January 1948, to Gateshead in November 1949, to Coleraine (as player-manager) in July 1953, and to East Stirling in January 1954. (5 apps; 2 goals)

Bob Iverson

> A teenaged Wigston winger, **Maurice C Buckby** had already had one 1943/4 outing for the youth-oriented Wolves when he signed amateur forms for City in December 1944, going on to play one game on either flank for City in the two months thereafter. (2 apps)

> Aptly christened, **Charles Guest Bulger** (b. Manchester, 19.1.1915, d. Ipswich, 18.6.1976) was a Walsall forward who turned out once for City in April 1942, and several times in 1943/4, usually at outside-left. Signed by Birmingham from Congleton Town in May 1934, he had moved to Lincoln City in June 1935, and to Fellows Park in May 1936. He played no senior football postwar; though was reported to be coaching in Trinidad in 1947. (10 apps; 1 goal)

> A Leicestershire talent City had missed, **Ken Burditt** (Frederick Charles Kendall; b. Ibstock, 12.11.1906, d. Ibstock, 27.10.1977) was at the end of his career when called up for a quartet of inside-forward outings in 1940/1, and one as emergency centre-half in the final game of 1942/3. A product of Ibstock Penistone Rovers and Gresley Rovers, Ken had joined Norwich City in November 1930, Millwall in August 1936, Notts County in January 1938, and Southern League Colchester United in May 1939. The war years also saw him turning out for Ibstock Colliery and Pegsons (and once, at Filbert Street, for an under-strength Spurs), before he became player-manager back at Ibstock PR. Ken's brother Les had been a City trialist in March 1933; while his brother George played League football for Millwall, Forest and Wrexham. (5 apps)

> Sergeant **Willie Carver**, a forward experienced with both Arbroath (who he helped to promotion in 1935) and East Fife, was based in Leicester as a PT instructor, and playing for his unit, 23rd PTC, in the Senior League, when chosen by City at inside-left for their trip to Notts County in October 1942. He scored in a 1-1 draw. (1 app; 1 goal)

> A Lincoln-born teenager promoted from the Colts after a hat-trick display, **George Chapman** made a couple of senior appearances at centre-forward (home and away to Birmingham) in September 1943. (2 apps)

> Goalkeeper **Arthur Chesters** (b. Salford, 14.2.1910) assisted City's run in the 1940/1 League War Cup – eventually to end at the semi-final stage. A pre-war mover between Sedgley Park, Manchester United (May 1929), Exeter City (July 1933) and Crystal Palace (April 1937), Arthur had featured in The Grecians' FA Cup giant-killing of City in 1937, and had been under City boss Tom Bromilow's management at Palace. He additionally guested during the war for Brighton and Fulham, and transferred from Palace to Rochdale in October 1945. (4 apps)

> A wartime member of the National Fire Service, Lincoln winger **Joseph Clare** (b. Westhoughton, 4.2.1910, d. Christchurch, 23.9.1987) guested for City at outside-left at Derby in March 1945, and also briefly lent his skills to Nottingham Forest. His pre-war career path led from Westhoughton Town to Manchester City (August 1930), Wigan Borough (August 1931), Westhoughton again (October 1931), Accrington Stanley (November 1933), Arsenal (December 1934), Margate (1935, on loan), Norwich City (May 1936), and to Lincoln (June 1937), where he was top scorer in 1938/9. Joe was later on the Bournemouth coaching staff from 1946-1960; then worked for that town's Water Company. (1 app)

> A former Leicester Schools full-back who started his senior career with Countesthorpe United and Leicester Thursday League side Solus, **William Arthur Cobley** (b. Countesthorpe, 31.12.1913; d. Leicester, April 1989) had left Nuneaton Town for Aston Villa in September 1935 (on the recommendation of former Fossil and Villain Billy Dorrell), and made 45 League appearances during his three years there. Back with Solus on the outbreak of war, William served in the RAF, and then worked and played for Mellor Bromleys until City called on him during September and October 1944. He also guested for Northampton and Fulham, and in 1946 signed for Notts County, but played no senior football for them. (3 apps)

> Primarily a centre-half, but the scorer of eight goals in one wartime game between Coventry and West Brom, **Thomas Crawley** (b. Blantyre, 10.11.1911) also played one of his four City games in March and April 1942 at centre-forward. Having started his career with Blantyre Victoria, he successively signed for Hamilton Academical (cs 1932), Motherwell (March 1934) and Preston North End (May 1935) before starting an eleven-year stint with Coventry in February 1936. (4 apps)

> Signed on amateur forms by City in May 1941, young Welshman **David L Cronin** continued to turn out at outside-right for BTH Sports (Rugby) until getting a senior Filbert Street call-up in September 1943. He continued to win sporadic selections until August 1945. (18 apps; 4 goals)

> Burnley reserve **Ben Crossland** never got a chance in peacetime League football, but his outside-left outing for City at Stoke in March 1944 was supplemented by extra wartime appearances for Blackburn, Luton and Southampton, as well as back at Turf Moor. (1 app)

> **Edwin Cunningham** (b. Jarrow, 20.9.1919) was a pre-war Luton Town junior who had officially moved to Bristol City by the time City recruited him from the Luton crowd to play on the right wing in October 1940, on a day when four selected players missed the train. Also a wartime guest for Brentford, he made but a single postwar League appearance for Bristol City. (1 app)

> The outbreak of war stymied the Norwich City career of **Fred Cutting** (Frederick Charles; b. North Walsham, 4.12.1921; d. 1997), who had signed professionally only months previously and had yet to make his debut. Apparently having guested for a so-far unidentified Scottish League club while on Army posting (and having earned the Military Medal), he was recruited by City in January 1946, but released after a trio of forward outings. Fred spent the next term in Norwich's reserves, then joined

Colchester United who, as a Southern League club, reached the last 16 in the 1948 FA Cup with his inside-left assistance. Fred was still in the side on its election to the League in 1950, then joined Great Yarmouth Town in 1952. (3 apps)

> Unfortunately badly injured during his only City game – at Nottingham Forest in February 1944 – **Davie Davidson** (David Blyth Logie; b. Lanark, 25.3.1920; d. Hackney, 1954) was a left- or centre-half who had joined Bradford Park Avenue in May 1938 from Douglas Water Thistle, but had to wait for postwar football for his League debut. He became a Leyton Orient stalwart after January 1947, until joining Headington (now Oxford) United in April 1950 for the finale of their inaugural professional campaign in the Southern League. He also figured in wartime football for Notts County. (1 app)

> Forest centre-half **Bob Davies** (Robert Griffith; b. Blaenau Ffestiniog, 19.10.1913, d. Nottingham, 10.5.1978) had decidedly mixed fortunes during the war: having luckily survived an incident of his 'chute failing to open while acting as a parachute instructor in 1941, he recovered sufficiently from having both legs in plaster to add to his Welsh wartime cap tally. A Forest signing from his home-town club when he was on the verge of amateur international honours in November 1936, he remained at the City Ground as a player until 1947, and on the training staff until 1974, after an interim spell as Walsall's physio. During wartime, however, he also turned out for Blackpool, Rochdale, Wrexham, Notts County and Leicester - assisting in home and away fixtures against Portsmouth in October 1945. (2 apps)

> Aberdonian **Percy Dickie** (b. 11.12.1907) became a City regular at wing-half or inside-forward for 15 months from the opening game of 1943/4, becoming City's oldest scorer in WW2 football, and additionally made wartime appearances for Lincoln City, Manchester City, Walsall and Bradford PA. He was officially a Blackburn Rovers player; having signed on at Ewood in September 1937 following stints with Aberdeen, Mugiemoss and St Johnstone. Postwar, he coached Peterhead to three Highland League titles between 1947 and 1950. (31 apps; 1 goal)

> On Manchester United's books during wartime, but never a League player for them, **Stuart Dimond** (b. Chorlton, 3.1.1920) became a typically peripatetic centre-forward in regionalised football, briefly turning out for Notts County, Newcastle United, Stockport County and both Bradford clubs as well as for City (at inside-left in home and away games with Villa in December 1943). Eventually he got a November 1945 move to Bradford City, but experienced only nine League outings before a January 1948 step-down to Winsford United. (2 apps)

> Selby-born outside-left **David N Douglas** was in the RAF when signed by City in October 1944. He got only a trio of chances at senior level (plus two guest outings for Wrexham during the same season), and was formally freed in May 1946. (3 apps; 1 goal)

> A defeat at Walsall in November 1941 marked the sole City appearance of England centre-forward **Ted Drake** (Edward Joseph; b. Southampton, 16.8.1912). A Hampshire cricketer and prolific Southampton striker from 1931, Ted had joined Arsenal in March 1934 for a sizeable £6,500 fee, and won two Championship medals on either side of a Cup-winning performance in 1936. His seven-goal haul from a 1935 game at Aston Villa remains a top-flight record; and his 42 strikes in 1934/5 a Highbury benchmark. An RAF Flight Lieutenant during the war, he also guested for West Ham, Fulham and Portsmouth before injury ended his playing career; later he took managerial responsibilities at Reading and Chelsea, an assistant's post at Barcelona, and a director's role at Fulham. (1 app)

> A tricky, speedy outside-right who had two spells as a City guest during 1942/3 and 1944/5, **Maurice Dunkley** (Maurice Edward Frank; b. Kettering, 19.2.1914, d. Rutland, 27.12.1989) also served both Kettering Town and Northampton Town twice; each side of a stint with Manchester City that started in March 1938 and ended in 1947. Also a pre-war Northants cricketer, Maurice turned out additionally during the war for West Ham, Millwall, West Brom and Walsall; and finished his career with Corby Town after 1950. (20 apps; 4 goals)

> A City guest at inside-forward for three months from November 1939, **Harry Eastham** (Henry; b. Blackpool, 30.6.1917; d. Middlesbrough, Sept 1998) was a former Bloomfield Road discovery (am September 1933, pro May 1934) who had signed for Liverpool in February 1936, and would go on to win a Championship medal with them in 1946/7, before moving on to Tranmere Rovers (May 1948) and Accrington Stanley (July 1953). His wartime wanderings would also take him briefly to the assistance of each of New Brighton, Leeds, Southport, Brighton, Bolton, Newcastle and Irish club Distillery. (6 apps)

> One of two guests making their sole City appearances in the club's final game of wartime football, at home to Brentford on 4.5.46, **George Robert Edwards** (b. Great Yarmouth, 1.4.1918; d. Hockley Heath, 21.1.1993) was in fact Aston Villa's top scorer during WW2. He'd joined Norwich City as a professional in April 1936 and moved to Villa Park in June 1938, and would stay until 1951, when linking up with Bilston United. Birmingham, Worcester City, Norwich, Notts County, Northampton, Forest, Wrexham and Walsall also utilised his services during the war. (1 app)

> **Bryn Elliott** (Bernard Harry; b. Beeston, 3.5.1925) was a Forest reserve at the time he made his trio of City appearances in March and May 1945: each of them in cup ties against Derby! The wing-half had signed on at the City Ground in October 1942, and made a post-war League bow prior to being released to Boston United in 1948. In October 1949, however, Southampton restored Bryn to the League sphere, and he turned out in 235 games for them at that level before a July 1959 move to Poole Town. In September 1952 he got on the City scoresheet with an own goal at The Dell. (3 apps)

> City were only one step from Wembley when they drafted in Liverpool's **William Fagan** (b. Musselburgh, 20.2.1917; d. Wellingborough, 29.2.1992) at inside-left to face Arsenal in the second leg of the 1941 War Cup semi-final, though it proved one step too far, with a 1-2 home reverse sealing aggregate defeat. Willie, who won wartime caps for Scotland, began his career with Wellesley Juniors before signing for Celtic in 1934, and moving south to Preston North End in October 1936. He served at Anfield from October 1937 to January 1952, amassing 161 League appearances, then wound down with Distillery and, as player-manager from July 1952, Weymouth. He later became a prison officer. (1 app)

No.	Name / Home Town	Fav. LCFC player	Fav. LCFC game
90	Simon Kimber, Cosby, Leicester	Gary Lineker	Crystal Palace Play Off Final
91	Henryk Cynkar, Leicester	Frank Worthington	Derby Play Off Final
92	Carl Hunt, Leicester	Frank Worthington	Manchester City FA Cup 1968
93	Ernest Hunt, Sunderland	Keith Weller	Manchester City 1958
94	Kelvin Knight, Earl Shilton	Frank Worthington	Cambridge
95	David Miles, South Wigston	Michael Stringfellow	Oxford 1991
96	Robert Howling, Rugby, Warks	Frank Worthington	Crystal Palace Play Off Final
97	Tim Edson, Oadby - Leicester	David Gibson	Man City FA Cup Replay 1968
98	Barry Crouch, Leicester	David Gibson	Crystal Palace Play Off Final
99	Stephen Walker, Leicester	Mark Wallington	Tranmere Rovers 2000
100	Richard Preston, Trowbridge, Wilts	David Gibson	League Cup Final 1964
101	Martin Letts, Northampton	N/A	N/A
102	Don Kendall, Leicester	Keith Weller	Portsmouth 1949 Cup Semi Final
103	Keith Clayson, South Wigston, Leicester	Keith Weller	Manchester City FA Cup 1943
104	Andrew Buncher, Oadby	Alan Smith	Swindon
105	Dave Howard, Leicester	Gary Lineker	Wimbledon 1997
106	Tony Smith, Wigston - Leicester	Steve Walsh	Derby Play Off Final
107	Stanley Fairbrother, Leicester	Steve Walsh	Cambridge 1992
108	Thomas Creighton, Narborough, Leicester	Steve Walsh	Shrewsbury 1982
109	Richard Purser, Dorridge	Frank Worthington	Luton Cup 1974
110	Richie Tyley, Godalming - Surrey	Gary McAllister	Oxford Utd 1991
111	Brian Wood, New Zealand	Arthur Rowley	Everton 1963
112	Nick Green, Leicester	Gary Lineker	Coca Cola Cup Final Replay 1997
113	John Keightley, Melton Mowbray	Johnny Morris	Any win over Liverpool
114	Phil Barker, Northampton	Lenny Glover	Crystal Palace Play Off Final
115	John McMenamin, Ashby De La Zouch	Keith Weller	Derby 1994
116	Bob Butlin, Market Harborough	Keith Weller	Crystal Palace 1996
117	John Rabone, Tokyo	Frank Worthington	Crystal Palace Play Off Final
118	Wayne Greet, Leicester	Gary Lineker	Portsmouth 1949 Cup Semi Final
119	James Johnson, Bedford	Neil Lennon	1996 Play Off Final
120	Maureen Holland, Leicester	N/A	N/A
121	Neil Williamson, Braunstone	Frank Worthington	Derby 1998
122	James Connor, Watford	Frank Worthington	Crystal Palace - Wembley 1996
123	Ken Morbey, Leicester	Steve Walsh	Derby Play Off Final
124	Derek Newton, Wisbech	Frank Worthington	Liverpool 1972
125	Chris Elliott, Syston	Gary McAllister	Shrewsbury 6th Round FA Cup
126	Phil & Steve Brown, Leicester Forest East	Gary Lineker	Middlesbrough Cup win
127	Stephen Goodchild, Rugby, Warwickshire	Peter Shilton	Crystal Palace Final
128	Melvin Carr, Leicester	Dave Maclaren	Burnley 1961/62
129	Kevin Bunney, Loughborough	Steve Walsh	The "Last" win!
130	Peter Wren, Blaby - Leicester	Keith Weller	Liverpool 1972
131	Pete Campbell, Leicester	Lenny Glover	Liverpool 1972
132	Mike Wilbur, Burbage - Hinckley	Lenny Glover	Shrewsbury 1982
133	Dave Smith, Kent	Gary Lineker	Tranmere Rovers 2000
134	Richard Pyatt, Leicester	Steve Walsh	Shrewsbury 6th Round FA Cup
135	Bev Martin, Leicester	Steve Walsh	Arsenal
136	Neil Austin, Leicester	Lenny Glover	Derby Play Off Final
137	Kathy & Steve Lord, Leicester	Steve Claridge	Middlesbrough Replay
138	Kevin Barnes, Wigston - Leicester	Gary Lineker	Shrewsbury
139	James Stewart, Leicester	Pontus Kåmark	Shrewsbury FA Cup 1981
140	Peter Naylor, Melton Mowbray	Arthur Rowley	Middlesbrough Replay
141	Steve Marriott, Leicester	Steve Walsh	Derby Play Off Final
142	Bill Bell, Ailsworth - Peterborough	Arthur Rowley	Crystal Palace Play Off Final
143	Stephen Matthews, Calverton, Nott'm	Frank Worthington	1995/1996 Play Off Final
144	Richard Ford, Yorkshire	Muzzy Izzet	Crystal Palace Play Off Final
145	Paul Preston, Huncote	Steve Walsh	
146	Steve Hitchcox, Banbury	Steve Walsh	Cambridge 1992
147	Nigel Lewis, Leicester	Emile Heskey	Crystal Palace Play Off Final
148	Chris Robinson, Burbage, Hinckley	Norman Leet	Coventry
149	Malcolm Clapham, Wigston, Leicester	David Gibson	League Cup Final Replay 1997
150	Nick Jones, Leicester	Keith Weller	Crystal Palace Play Off Final
151	Ryan Murrant, Corby	Gary Lineker	Oxford 1991
152	Steven Buckley, Penn, High Wycombe	Steve Walsh	Crystal Palace Play Off Final
153	Bryan Fisher, Amersham	Lenny Glover	Arsenal 1966
154	Gilbert Ivens, Rugby, Warwickshire	Frank Worthington	Crystal Palace Play Off Final
155	Jon Keen, Sandhurst, Berkshire	N/A	Crystal Palace Play Off Final
156	David Ingall, Leicester	Robbie Savage	Spurs 2001
157	Robert Freeman, Ellistown	Keith Weller	Derby County - Wembley 1994
158	Ian King, Stoney Stanton, Leics	Frank Worthington	Derby County - Wembley 1994
159	Frank Luce, Rothley	Arthur Rowley	Hillsborough Cup Win
160	Matthew Hearne, Leicester	Frank Worthington	Middlesbrough Cup Replay 1997
161	Peter Belton, Hitchin	Arthur Rowley	Nottingham Forest 1957
162	David Dennison, Cubley - Penistone	Jimmy Baldwin	Manchester United 1963
163	Guy Paul Dickinson, Daventry	Muzzy Izzet	Crystal Palace Play Off Final
164	Miroslaw Olszewski, Leicester	Keith Weller	Shrewsbury Town FA Cup
165	Ann Betts, Leicester	Kevin Russell	Derby Play Off Final
166	Dr John Batterbee, Holme Next The Sea	Arthur Rowley	Portsmouth 1949 Cup Semi Final
167	Simon Batterbee, Oswego - USA	Gary Lineker	Tranmere Rovers 2000
168	Annalise Tridgell, Seaford, Sussex	Steve Walsh	Derby County - Wembley 1994
169	Christopher Batterbee, Brighton, Sussex	Gary Lineker	Tranmere Rovers 2000
170	Paul & Jake Leatherland, Syston	David Gibson	Coca Cola Cup Final Replay
171	Benjamin Smith, Wigston, Leicester	Ian Ormondroyd	Swindon Play Off Final 1992/93
172	Ian Smith, Corby	Frank Worthington	Man City Cup Replay 1967/68
173	Peter Carnall, Leicester	Steve Walsh	Shrewsbury
174	Robert Rylott, Queniborough, Leicester	Mark Wallington	Middlesbrough League Cup
175	Simon Viccars, Essex	N/A	N/A
176	Jeremy Richards, Kendal - Cumbria	Steve Claridge	Crystal Palace Play Off Final
177	Graham Ginetta, Leicester	Derek Dougan	Cambridge 1992
178	Stanley Whitehouse, Leicester	Gordon Banks	West Ham United 1966
179	Stephen Whitehouse, Leicester	N/A	Man City Cup Replay 1967/68
180	David Ward, North Kilworth	Frank Worthington	Ipswich 1973/1974
181	Clive Spencer, Hamilton, Leicester	Gary McAllister	Crystal Palace Play Off Final
182	Geoffrey Hull, Wakefield	Keith Weller	Worthington Cup Final 2000
183	Geoff Hercock, Monmouth	Lenny Glover	Crystal Palace Play Off Final

> **Kenneth Flint** (b. Selston, 12.11.1923) first had his promise noted by City as a 19-year-old left-winger during 1942/3, and played a few wartime games for Notts County the following term, but his professional career was very much a slow-burn affair until 1950. His first postwar club was Bedford Town, who sold Ken to Tottenham Hotspur in July 1947; but his senior record of one goal in five Spurs matches was then dwarfed by his service to Aldershot, amounting to 70 goals in 324 games. He started season 1958/9 with Leyton Orient, then joined Bath City in October. (4 apps)

> February 1941 was a busy month for **Walter L Foster** (b. Coalville, 1920; d. Leicester, Dec 1992). The former North End United, Coalville Town and Western Athletic outside-left signed as a City amateur, played once for the Colts, made his senior debut a week later (scoring in a 3-3 home draw with Birmingham) and two days later joined the Navy. Becoming a Chief Petty Officer, and playing in the odd friendly game for Plymouth Argyle during 1944/5, he returned to Filbert Street to sign pro forms in December 1945, showed further goalscoring ability, but was freed in the following May; later serving Brush Sports (1946), Kettering Town, Burton Albion (1951), Tamworth, Whitwick Colliery and Newfoundpool WMC. (10 apps; 5 goals)

> Signed as an amateur in August 1938, **Billy Freer** (William Henry; b. Syston, 1920) additionally played for Syston St Peters, Syston Imperial and Leicestershire Nomads, and got but one chance to shine in senior wartime football with City, at outside-left in the May 1941 home defeat against Spurs. During 1942/3, though, Billy assisted Bath City in the Football League West. (1 app)

> Better remembered now as a manager (in two spells at Coventry City, but also with Port Vale, Rugby Town, Hinckley Athletic and Stafford Rangers), **Billy Frith** (b. Sheffield, 9.6.1912; d. Kenilworth, 1996) was a defensive half-back who'd begun his playing career in 1929 with Worksop Town, and moved successively to Mansfield Town (April 1930), Chesterfield (May 1931) and Coventry (May 1932). City regularly utilised his experience between January 1941 and May 1942, while Coventry's Highfield Road was out of commission owing to bomb damage. His father, also known as Billy, had played for Rotherham, Luton and South Shields, while his grandfather Paul had acted as trainer to both Middlesbrough and Sheffield Wednesday. Billy himself followed a schoolteaching career until 1977, and was still a Chesterfield scout into the 1980s. (42 apps)

> **Stanley D Frost** (b. Northampton, 19.10.1922) had made but a single wartime appearance for the Cobblers before being involved in one of the few permanent transfer deals City undertook during the war, albeit a straight exchange for George Bedford in March 1941. The outside-right then made isolated City appearances across each season until 1944/5 (his last such coming while on leave from Germany), and was retained for postwar football; only to be offloaded, untried at League level, back to Northampton in January 1947. Stan later assisted Rugby Town. (12 apps; 2 goals)

> Capped once by Scotland in 1935, while in the middle of a 101-goal stint at Sunderland (signed from Bridge of Weir in September 1928), inside-forward **Patsy Gallacher** (Patrick; b. Bridge of Weir, 21.8.1909; d. Greenock, 4.1.1992) joined Stoke City in November 1938 and almost immediately hit injury trouble, but was still on their books when briefly guesting for City (in two goalless draws in September 1942), as well as for Newcastle United, Crewe Alexandra, Dundee United and several other clubs. He also later became Weymouth player/manager. (2 apps)

> A degree of mystery still surrounds the club affiliations of the **C Gardiner** who briefly assisted City in October and December 1942. The inside-forward, who scored on his debut in an away win at Mansfield, was serving (and playing) with COD (Old Dalby) at the time, when he was variously described as being on Portsmouth's books, an ex-Forest player, and a Montrose man! [Charlie Gardiner (b. Glasgow, 17.3.1913; d. North Africa, 1943), a forward whom Nottingham Forest signed from Roselea in 1935, and who subsequently served Mansfield Town in 1938/9, before moving to Montrose on the eve of war, seems the most plausible suspect.] (2 apps; 1 goal)

> **Jimmy Gemmell** (b. Sunderland, 17.11.1911; d. Birmingham, 11.5.1992) first played at Filbert Street in the same schoolboy international trial side as Sep Smith, but was very much a Bury stalwart by the time he returned, having joined the Gigg Lane side from West Stanley in March 1930, and having notched 255 League games for them at either full-back or centre-half. While temporarily based in Hinckley, Jim became a City regular between November 1942 and September 1944, and also assisted Rochdale, Manchester United and Southport during the war, signing officially for the latter club as player/coach in August 1945. Later on the training staffs of both Lincoln City and Coventry City, he was the son of a former Clyde, Sunderland, Stoke, Leeds City and Third Lanark player (also Jimmy). (53 apps)

> A two-footed winger, **Billy Goffin** (William Charles; b. Tamworth, 12.12.1920; d. Tamworth, 15.9.1987) had joined Aston Villa from his home-town club in December 1937, but was still awaiting a League blooding at the time he guested for City (from January 1944). He similarly built wartime experience with Birmingham, Forest and Swansea before his 156-game, 36-goal Villa Park record began in earnest. Billy then spent 1954/5 with Walsall before returning to Tamworth. (5 apps)

> City really called on the veterans for their September 1945 fixture at Charlton, when Sep Smith and Fred Kilshaw missed their trains. Arthur Attwood was one such hastily recruited, and the other was **Jim Graham** (James Arthur; b. Rothwell, 13.1.1911; d. Bath, 28.11.1987), who had last played League football in 1937, and had merely one emergency appearance for Charlton during 1944/5 as subsequent recommendation! He was, however, City goalkeeper Dick's older brother, and he lasted the 90 minutes at right-half. As a forward, he had joined Nottingham Forest from Desborough Town in 1932, and moved to York City in 1935. (1 app)

> Though he later proved himself a fine goalkeeper in both City's wartime side and Crystal Palace's postwar League teams, **Dick Graham** (Richard Douglas; b. Corby, 6.5.1922) had a torrid introduction to netminding at Filbert Street. Signed in December 1941 (after representing Corby Town and Northampton Town's juniors), Dick was within days lent to Norwich City for their game against City, and conceded five goals before being stretchered off during a 6-1 win. The following May, he was similarly lent to Bristol City, and again conceded five, while two days after that he was at last on City's side for the fixture with Northampton: a 1-4 home defeat! It was April 1945 before he reclaimed a City place (having guested for Southport, Notts County and Crewe in the interim), but competition for the green jersey was fierce, and Dick moved permanently to Selhurst Park in December 1945. After retirement, he built a lengthy off-field career: as coach to West Brom, then as manager of Palace, Leyton Orient, Walsall, Colchester and Wimbledon. (18 apps)

> Originally signed as an amateur from Belgrave St Michaels in October 1938, and professionally the following January, centre forward **Ron Grant** (Ronald Angus) spent much of his war on Navy service (being rescued when the cruiser 'Fiji' was sunk off Crete), and was usually restricted to Colts or Reserve appearances when home on leave. He did make a senior bow, however, on Christmas Day 1943 in an away match against Aston Villa. He had a fine record in Leicestershire Senior Cup Finals: scoring twice for City in the 5-1 defeat of Coalville in 1945/6; a hat-trick against City for Brush Sports a year later; and two more in Brush's 1948 win over Whitwick. He later served Hinckley Athletic and Leicester Nomads in the early 50s, and may have had a short interim spell with Kidderminster Harriers. (1 app)

> The only WW2 City guest to masquerade (initially) under the name of 'Newman', Preston's **Willie Hamilton** (b. Hamilton, 1.9.1918) played in four victories off the reel during February and March 1943. Having signed on at Deepdale in September 1937 from Blantyre Victoria, left-half Willie stayed until 1948, when joining Queen of the South. He also guested for Bury, Arsenal, Fulham, Millwall and Oldham. (4 apps)

> **Norman Hanford** signed for City from Quorn Methodists in August 1944, and was briefly tried in each full-back berth in March 1945. As a City reserve, he was successively a Senior Cup winner and runner-up in 1946 and 1947, before release the following year; and while with Brush Sports he earned another loser's medal in 1950. He joined Bentley Engineering FC in December 1954. (2 apps)

> One of four Aston Villa players to assist City during 1939/40, **Fred Haycock** (Frederick Joseph; b. Bootle, 19.4.1912; d. Great Barr, 10.4.1989) was an inside-left who'd started his senior career in Ireland, with Waterford, in 1928; joined Prescot Cables in 1932; and signed on at Villa Park in February 1934. He was certainly a traveller for the rest of the war; additionally guesting for Plymouth, Liverpool, Wolves, Northampton, Notts County, Forest, Walsall and Kidderminster Harriers before signing for Wrexham in December 1945, and Stourbridge in 1947. He later managed Sutton Coldfield Town; and worked for ICI in Birmingham. (13 apps; 3 goals)

> The scorer of City's final goal in WW2 competition was **Wilfred Heathcote** (b. Hemsworth, 29.6.1911; d. Lambeth, 15.6.1991), one of three guests appearing in the 1-3 home defeat by Brentford in May 1946. An Army sergeant, and very much a late entrant to senior football in early 1943, Wilf was best known for scoring 89 goals in 100 wartime appearances for Queens Park Rangers, though he could only manage a single score in five games thereafter, and only briefly served Millwall from December 1946. Millwall had also been one of the other clubs he guested for, as had Wolves, Reading and Southampton. (1 app; 1 goal)

> **Jock Hillard** (John Gordon, b. Aberdeen, 3.9.1916) was an amateur with Leicester Nomads and Coalville Town (and a Sheffield Wednesday trialist) prior to signing for City in a joint deal with Stan Baines in November 1937. He made little immediate progress, however, and was released to Grimsby Town in October 1938. He featured in the early wartime teams of both Grimsby and Mansfield Town, and was also with Anstey Methodists during 1940/1, but re-signed for City during 1942/3; making appearances in both wing berths as well as at left-half, and additionally guesting for Northampton that term. During 1944/5 he guested for Lovell's Athletic in the Football League West; then in September 1946 City transferred him to Torquay United for a six-game League career. (8 apps)

> Seven times capped for England as a Villa player after joining them from Boston United in August 1927, **William Eric Houghton** (b. Billingsborough, 29.6.1910; d. Birmingham, 1.5.1996) amassed a Villa Park peacetime career record of 360 games and 160 goals, while also representing Warwickshire as a cricketer. City borrowed his left-wing services between March and June 1940, and he also turned out during wartime for Coventry, Hereford United, Brentford, Forest and Notts County; eventually being transferred to Meadow Lane in December 1946. He retired in 1949 straight into the Notts manager's chair, and later managed Villa and Rugby Town. He additionally scouted for Forest and Walsall, became general secretary of the Fellows Park club, and served as a Villa director in the 70s. In December 1942, Eric scored a hat-trick against City. (15 apps; 2 goals)

> A left-back turned left-winger who never got a break in League football before or after the war, Sergeant **Leonard Hubble** was a Newcastle United reserve signed from Horden Colliery, who briefly turned out for City during November and December 1944. Elsewhere, he got two WW2 outings for the Magpies, one for Middlesbrough, and a trio for Charlton Athletic, scoring once. (3 apps)

> A young outside- or inside-right when captured by City on amateur forms from BTH (Rugby) in October 1942, **Gwyn Hughes** (Thomas Gwynfor; b. Blaenau Ffestiniog, 7.5.1922; d. Northampton, 14.3.1999) had converted to a wing-half role by the time he signed for Northampton Town in August 1944, though he still scored against City in November of that year. He stayed with the Cobblers until a May 1956 move to Bedford Town, having played 281 postwar games, scoring 26 times; and finished his career with St Neots. (10 apps; 1 goal)

> A City guest at inside-left from December 1944 to May 1945, Preston North End's **Harry Iddon** (b. Preston, 20.2.1921) never made the senior grade with his home-town club. For someone whose postwar career (with Barrow from October 1946, Southport from June 1947 and Morecambe from 1949) was so essentially modest, however, he was much in demand during wartime, with Manchester City, Wolves, Aldershot, Reading, York, Chester, Chesterfield and Notts County the other clubs to utilise his temporary services. He became a plumber, plasterer and roofer in Preston after injury shortened his playing career. (11 apps; 2 goals)

> Another of City's 1939/40 Villains, **Bob Iverson** (Robert Thomas James, b. Folkestone, 17.10.1910; d. Birmingham, 19.6.1953) was a left-half who had first been noted by Spurs while playing for Folkestone, and had signed on at White Hart Lane in May 1932, but didn't make a League breakthrough until switching to Lincoln City in September 1933. His travels thereafter took him via Wolves (February 1935) to Villa Park (December 1936), where he would remain as a player until 1949, before becoming coach to their juniors. During the war, Bob also assisted Birmingham, Forest, Notts County, Northampton and Sutton Town. (11 apps)

> A genuine prodigy - an England schoolboy international for two years running, and a 14-year-old scorer in City's senior pre-season public practice game in 1938 - **Gordon Jayes** (Alfred Gordon; b. Leicester, 26.9.1923; d. Leicester, 26.3.1997) had his footballing development almost totally wrecked by the war's intervention. Signed as an amateur in June 1938, he also played for both Lansdowne Institute and Nuneaton Borough in 1939; then made his competitive City debut (as inside-right at West Brom on 11.11.1939) at the age of 16 years, 46 days. Soon afterwards he was declared by the Football League investigation of City's books to be a professional (despite not being eligible to sign pro forms until his 17th birthday), and suspended until a successful appeal. Gordon later signed up as an Army PT instructor, and in fact played his last senior City game in February 1944, when still only twenty. In October 1946, he was allowed to join Notts County, for whom he scored 7 times in 27 League games. Back in local circles, Gordon moved between Nuneaton Borough and Hinckley Athletic in February 1951, and to Barwell in 1952. He was later involved in running the Hazel Street Youth Club. (59 apps; 22 goals)

> A pre-war England international, capped five times in 1936/7, **Joe Johnson** (Joseph Alfred; b. Grimsby, 4.4.1911; d. West Bromwich, 8.8.1983) turned out just once for City, on the left wing at Wolves in November 1945. He'd moved from Scunthorpe United to Bristol City in May 1931, to Tom Mather's Stoke City in April 1932, and to West Brom in November 1937. As a Baggie, he also guested during wartime for Crewe, Walsall, Notts County and Northampton; then dropped into non-league football in 1946 with Northwich Victoria and Hereford United. (1 app)

> **Harry Johnston** (b. Droylsden, 26.9.1919; d. Blackpool, 12.10.1973) was essentially a one-club player, starring for Blackpool from June 1935 to 1955, but briefly assisted both Reading and City during the war. Now remembered as much for having been Stanley Matthews' skipper in the 1953 Cup Final as for his ten England caps at half-back, Harry made (or, more accurately, delayed) his Leicester bow under faintly farcical circumstances: he'd no sooner promised to turn out, on leave, for City against Stoke at home in September 1940, than he discovered his fiancée had arranged his wedding for that very day. Nonetheless, he was in the City team for the following week's return fixture at the Victoria Ground! Harry later managed Reading for eight years, and was twice caretaker boss at Blackpool. (4 apps)

> A Hearts discovery, left-sided forward **Tom Johnston** (Thomas Deans; b. Berwick-on-Tweed, 30.12.1918) played almost all his senior football in the Midlands. He signed for Northampton Town from Peterborough United in 1942, joined City in February 1943, and was on Forest's books later that year. He also guested for Derby and City during this period, and in August 1948 his transfer from the City Ground only took him across the Trent to Notts

County. Tom later coached Heanor and Birmingham City – and in Finland – before going on to manage both Rotherham United and Grimsby Town. (12 apps; 3 goals)

> Eleven times capped by Wales before the war, and a wartime international on five occasions, **Les Jones** (Leslie Jenkin; b. Aberdare, 1.7.1911; d. Llanfyrnach, 11.1.1981) was a much travelled inside-forward or wing-half who made an isolated guest appearance for City in October 1941, and then returned as a regular between March and December 1944. His career had started with Aberdare Athletic before an August 1929 signing for Cardiff City, and he had gone on to star for Coventry City (from January 1934) and Arsenal (from November 1937). During WW2 he also guested for West Ham, Coventry, Forest, Fulham, Notts County, Lincoln, Manchester City, Southampton, Swansea, Mansfield and Colchester; then was released in June 1946 to become player-coach at Swansea. For 1947/8 he was player-manager of Barry Town, and the following term wound down his playing career at Brighton. Les was later manager of Scunthorpe United for their initial, 1950/51 Football League season. (18 apps; 2 goals)

> **Leslie O Jones** was a City player for little more than a year after his March 1943 signing. A local left-half, he hobbled on the wing as a passenger throughout most of his debut at Derby that month, and got only sporadic chances afterwards, despite switching role to the forward flank position. The *Mercury* later clouded his identity by claiming that a Barry Town player in the 1951 Welsh amateur international side, playing England at Filbert Street, was an ex-City guest. If so, Leslie also had a postwar stint with Millwall. (3 apps)

> A former Rugby Union player with Caerau, **Ralph Jones** (b. Maesteg, 19.5.1921; d. Bridgend, 18.1.1997) was a City signing as an amateur in May 1944 and as a pro in the following December. A couple of February 1945 outings at wing-half (in successive 4-1 wins over Notts County) were his only City chances, however, and he was released to Newport County in May 1946. Nineteen League games later, in December 1947, he became a Bristol Rovers player, but injuries there led to him dropping down to non-league level with Bath City in 1951 and Trowbridge Town from 1955-57. At this point of his career, Ralph was also noted as an operatic baritone at Glyndebourne. One obituary note states that he served in Korea with REME. (2 apps)

> **Tommy Jones** was on Derby's books at the time he guested for City, as outside-right in a handful of fixtures during September and October 1944, and he totted up 33 wartime appearances for the Rams. Yet he got a League chance at neither the Baseball Ground nor after a 1948 move to Rochdale. He may have turned out for Brush Sports during 1946/7. (5 apps)

> An amateur signing for both Coventry and City during the war, Desborough Town's **Don Kelly** (Donald Joseph; b. Market Harborough, 2.7.1922) managed a quartet of outings for each club, mainly in the centre-forward berth: in fact his scoring debut for City came in a November 1944 game at Highfield Road! After the war, he had a brief League career with Torquay United, scoring three goals in five games while posted in Plymouth as an RAF PT instructor, before returning in September 1948 to Harborough to play for Symington's FC. A year later Don signed for Stafford Rangers; and

Jimmy Mullen

then moved via Symington's again to Rugby Town. (4 apps; 1 goal)

> Another to serve both City and Coventry at this time was **Jack Kendall** (John T; b. Rugby), a young left-half who signed on at Filbert Street in January 1942, and shifted allegiance to Highfield Road in 1944. (6 apps)

> Like several of his Army comrades stationed at the Central Ordnance Depot in Old Dalby, **Fred Kilshaw** (b. Wrexham, 24.8.1916) already had a League club connection before his call-up. In his case, he'd been an Everton junior; but it was his exploits with his unit team in the Leicestershire Senior League and Senior Cup which brought him to City's attention. Fred appeared in each of the 1943, 1944 and 1945 Finals of the Senior Cup: and scored twice against City's Colts in the 1944 Final, only a week after his City debut. By the time of the 1945 Final, Sgt Kilshaw was in fact a City professional, having signed in January. Released in July 1946, he joined Third Division New Brighton, scoring once in eight games, and then moved to Prescot Cables. He also appeared once for Nottingham Forest during the war. (6 apps; 1 goal)

> One of two guests from Northampton Town in City's first competitive WW2 fixture, in October 1939, **Bobby King** (Frederick A Robert; b. Hardingstone, 19.9.1919) notched the first goal in a 6-1 victory over Walsall. A month later he became the first player in England to be conventionally transferred under wartime conditions, signing for Wolves, and a further month later scored for them against City! Bobby also guested for Manchester City during the war. He was transferred back to Northampton in December 1947, and joined Rushden in 1950. (2 apps; 1 goal)

> **Sid King** (Sidney Harvey; b. Bordesley Green, 1914) was reserve goalkeeper at Birmingham to Gil Merrick, having joined the Blues from Cradley Heath in October 1936. He assisted City in a quartet of games during March 1943, and also lent his wartime services to Coventry and Northampton. Two FA Cup appearances in 1945/6 constituted the entirety of his 'official' Birmingham record, and he joined Hereford United in 1946. (4 apps)

> A Scottish amateur international who had moved from Queens Park to Liverpool in April 1938, **Bill Kinghorn** (William John Darroch; b. Strathblane, 27.2.1912) briefly guested for City at outside-left in December 1939, and also turned out during wartime for Brighton, Newcastle, Blackburn, Manchester City, Leeds and Burnley. He was released from Anfield in 1946. (2 apps; 1 goal)

No.	Name / Home Town	Fav. LCFC player	Fav. LCFC game
184	Lester Wellington, Bude	Steve Walsh	Crystal Palace Play Off Final
185	David Richens, Leicester	Frank Worthington	Crystal Palace Play Off Final
186	Mark Stocker, Corning - New York	Frank Worthington	Derby Play Off Final
187	Chris Andrews, Drayton - Oxfordshire	Steve Walsh	FA Cup Semi-Final 1973/74
188	Wendy Bennett, Sydney	Mark Wallington	Shrewsbury FA Cup 1981
189	Gerald Hutchinson, Leicester	Frank Worthington	Man City Cup Replay 1967/68
190	Millicent Tuttle, Oadby, Leicester	Steve Walsh	Worthington Cup 5th rnd v Fulham
191	Trevor King, Leicester	Rodney Fern	Shrewsbury FA Cup 1981
192	Clare Knight, Evington, Leicester	Gary Lineker	Crystal Palace Play Off Final
193	Kelvin Brant, Leicester	Gordon Banks	QPR FA Cup 1974
194	Tom Rodwell, Flaunden	Arthur Rowley	Crystal Palace Play Off Final
195	Peter Griffin, Hong Kong	Matt Elliott	Tranmere Rovers 2000
196	Stuart Ettridge, Leicester	Steve Walsh	Derby Play Off Final
197	Doreen Dale, Wigston Magna, Leicester	Pontus Kåmark	Middlesbrough Replay 1997
198	Richard Dale, Peterborough	David Gibson	Tranmere Rovers 2000
199	Alexander Ward, Leicester	Gary Lineker	Derby Play Off Final
200	Andrew Dayman, London Green, Rugeley	Steve Walsh	Play Off Final 1996
201	Tom Matthews, Leicester	Andy Peake	Crystal Palace Play Off Final
202	Grahame Woodroffe, Loughborough	Frank Worthington	Derby Play Off Final
203	Charles Osborne, Hinckley	Steve Walsh	Derby Play Off Final
204	Andy White, Barrow In Furness	Gary Lineker	Derby Play Off Final
205	Gary Hurst, Portishead	Frank Worthington	Division 1 Play Offs - 1994
206	David Lymb, Leicester	Keith Weller	Shrewsbury Town FA Cup
207	Victoria Finley, London	Steve Guppy	Tranmere Rovers 2000
208	David Squires, London	Frank Worthington	Crystal Palace Play Off Final
209	Rhys Austin, Quedgeley, Gloucester	Ian Andrews	Crystal Palace Play Off Final
210	Ben Craig, Burbage	Tony Cottee	Tranmere Rovers 2000
211	Edward Holmes, Glen Parva, Leicester	Gary Lineker	Derby Play Off Final
212	Robert Newton, Wisbech	Frank Worthington	Coca Cola Cup Final 1997
213	David Humberston, Leicester	Keith Weller	Cambridge Play Off 1992
214	Sammi Gregory, Markfield, Leicester	N/A	N/A
215	Martin Stapleton, Skegness	Steve Walsh	Crystal Palace Play Off Final
216	Adrian Calvert, Leicester	Paul Cooper	Crystal Palace Play Off Final
217	Colin Granby, Haworth, West Yorkshire	Keith Weller	Shrewsbury Cup
218	Andrew Tailby, Oundle	Frank Worthington	Sheffield United FA Cup 1976
219	Thomas Mawson, Rugby, Warwickshire	Steve Walsh	Shrewsbury Cup
220	Mark Daulby, Market Harborough	Emile Heskey	Derby Play Off Final
221	Andrew Sivell, Loughborough	Tim Flowers	Derby Play Off Final
222	Christopher Wellman, Littlehampton	Frank Worthington	Crystal Palace Play Off Final
223	Gordon Quick, Anstey - Leicester	Gary Lineker	M'boro Coca Cola Cup Replay 1997
224	Paul Evans, Leicester	Gordon Banks	Shrewsbury FA Cup 1981
225	Paul Smith, Ibstock	Steve Walsh	Derby Play Off Final
226	John Noon, Leicester	Keith Weller	Derby Play Off Final
227	Rikki Lewin, Clarendon Park - Leicester	Steve Claridge	Fulham 1983
228	Paul Russell, Market Harborough	Gary Mills	Derby Play Off Final
229	Ian Baker, Cheltenham	Steve Walsh	Shrewsbury FA Cup 1981
230	Steph Jastrzebski, Elmesthorpe	Gary Lineker	Shrewsbury 1982
231	Joe Scranage, Oadby, Leics	Muzzy Izzet	Worthington Cup v Tranmere
232	Alan Jelley, Glenfield - Leicester	Frank Worthington	Man City Cup Replay 1968
233	Steven R Botting, Stanton Under Bardon	Frank Worthington	Man City Cup Replay 1968
234	Mark Collins, Leicester	Frank Worthington	1996 Play Off Final
235	Will Anthill, Loughborough	Frank Worthington	Man City Cup Replay - 1968
236	Martin Spencer, Desborough	Frank Worthington	Cambridge Play Off Semi Final
237	Joseph Anstee, Hanwell, London	Matt Elliott	Crystal Palace Play Off Final
238	Michael Bremridge, Coalville, Leics	Frank Worthington	Derby Play Off Final
239	Sam Richard Heathcote, Ibstock	Simon Grayson	Cambridge Play Off 1992
240	Simo Pirjo Haavisto, Helsinki, Finland	Gordon Banks	All Live Visits
241	Ann Ford, Leicester	Ken Leek	Man City 1968
242	Phil Arnold, Winchmore Hill, London	Steve Walsh	Derby Play Off Final
243	Philip Harrison, Leicester	Gary Lineker	Shrewsbury FA Cup QF
244	Kevin Heircock, Leicester	Jim Melrose	Crystal Palace Play Off Final
245	Michael Toplis, Meadows, Nottingham	Gordon Banks	Man City FA Cup Final
246	Daniel Bale, Market Harborough	Muzzy Izzet	Crystal Palace Play Off Final
247	Serbia Football Club, Evington	Steve Walsh	Crystal Palace Play Off Final
248	David McGregor, Rugby, Warwickshire	Frank Worthington	Liverpool 1972
249	Michael Knight, St Annes on Sea	Frank Worthington	Liverpool 1972
250	Jamie Preston, Leicester	Steve Walsh	Crystal Palace Play Off Final
251	Christopher Hayes, Stocking Farm	Emile Heskey	Liverpool 2001
252	David Smith, Leicester	Keith Weller	Shrewsbury 1982
253	David Chapman, Wigsthorpe, Northants	Steve Walsh	Crystal Palace Play Off Final
254	John Campbell, Boxford, Suffolk	David Gibson	Everton 1963
255	Philip Clarke, Shepshed	Garry Parker	Crystal Palace Play Off Final
256	Trevor Kilburn, Weston Super Mare	Frank Worthington	Worthington Cup Final 2000
257	Nathan Fletcher, Warwick	Gary Lineker	Tranmere Rovers 2000
258	Mark Fish, Leicester	Jim Melrose	Shrewsbury 1982
259	Keith Laker, Whitehall - Hampshire	Frank Worthington	West Ham 1966
260	Thomas Beavin, Hinckley	Steve Walsh	Crystal Palace Play Off Final
261	Steven Calvert, Reading	Steve Walsh	Derby Play Off Final
262	Roger Chamberlain, Birmingham	Rodney Fern	Crystal Palace Play Off Final
263	John Spiers, Sheffield	Sep Smith	N/A
264	Paul Hatton, Milton Ernest - Bedford	Frank Worthington	M'boro Coca Cola Cup Replay 1997
265	Philip Bird, Thorpe Le Soken	Frank Worthington	Coca Cola Cup Final 1997
266	Ron & Gary Johnson, Wellingborough	Gary Lineker	Madrid 1997
267	Steve Parker, Leicester	Matt Elliott	Oxford 1991
268	Alan Wardle, Nottingham	Frank McLintock	Crystal Palace Play Off Final
269	Tony Asher, St Albans	Steve Walsh	M'boro Coca Cola Cup Replay 1997
270	Keith Morley, Leicester	Keith Weller	Manchester City 1968
271	Sophie Brookes, Coalville, Leics	Steve Claridge	Arsenal 1997/1998
272	Gary Sherrard, Cramlington, Northumberland	N/A	N/A
273	N/A, N/A	N/A	N/A
274	The Robbie Savage Fan Club, Leicester	David Nish	Shrewsbury FA Cup
275	Laurence Ford, Birmingham	Jackie Sinclair	Fulham 1965/1966
276	Richard Edwards, Canterbury	Steve Claridge	Crystal Palace Play Off Final
277	David Wallwork, Watnall - Notts	Gary McAllister	Cambridge Play Off 1992

> Outside-right **Jack Kirkaldie** (John; b. Coventry, 2.8.1917; d. Coventry, July 1985) started his career with Nuneaton Town, and moved successively to Southend United (February 1936), West Ham United (February 1937) and Doncaster Rovers (April 1939, staying until 1948). He assisted City during August and September 1942, and similarly guested for Port Vale two years later. Following his Football League days, he assisted each of Bedworth United and Rugby Town. (3 apps)

> There was a remarkable disparity in the peacetime and wartime scoring records of **Herbert Knott** (b. Goole, 5.12.1914). A Walsall signing in August 1937, he had managed but two strikes for the Saddlers, and a loan spell at Stourbridge, before being offloaded to Brierley Hill in the summer of 1939. Postwar, he would notch but a solitary goal for Hull City, then join Hinckley Athletic. In the interim, however, he was very much an in-demand wanderer, totalling 67 goals in 80 games for a host of clubs, with City included in a list that stretched across Derby, Sheffield United, Lincoln, Notts County, York, Millwall, Hull, Forest, Halifax, Norwich, and Bradford Park Avenue. A sergeant at the time of his City stint (from January to March 1944), he claimed a hat-trick from an away win at Stoke in the Midland Cup as the highlight of his stay. (8 apps; 6 goals)

> Also claiming a City hat-trick during a guest stint was **Tommy Lawton** (b. Bolton, 6.10.1919; d. Nottingham, 6.11.1996), who scored in each of his trio of games during November and December 1939, but was on the losing side at Walsall with his threesome. The scoring prodigy who had been nurtured at Burnley by City boss Tom Bromilow (he'd signed as a 15-year-old amateur from Rossendale United in May 1935), and by then was an Everton and England star (transferred to Goodison in January 1937), Tommy also guested for Chelsea, Aldershot, Millwall, Notts County, Charlton and Morton. In November 1945 he signed for Chelsea, and exactly two years later for Notts County, before moving to Brentford (March 1952), Arsenal (September 1953) and Kettering Town (February 1956, as player-manager). Tommy's peacetime England record was 22 goals and 23 caps, while his return from 22 wartime and victory internationals was 24 goals. He later managed Notts County. (3 apps; 5 goals)

> Six-footer **Bill Leitch**, signed from Wishaw High School by Motherwell in May 1942, was regarded primarily as a reserve centre-half by the Fir Park club. Yet he was mainly played by City, during the January to April 1945 period, at centre-forward; claiming a hat-trick on his debut in an 8-3 win over Mansfield Town, and finishing 1944/5 as the club's joint top scorer. (12 apps; 12 goals)

> An 18-year-old on Rangers' books, **W J Letters** partnered his fellow Scottish amateur, Ken Chisholm, at outside-left in a home defeat by Southampton in February 1946. (1 app)

> **Glyn Lewis** (Glyndwr; b. Abertillery, 3.7.1921; d. 1992) was in the RAF when signing for Crystal Palace in 1941, and continued to play at Selhurst until a July 1948 move to Bristol City. He briefly assisted both City (at inside-left at Derby in March 1943) and Lincoln City during WW2. (1 app)

> Though he didn't make a League breakthrough until 1947/8, **Maurice Lindley** (William Maurice; b. Keighley, 5.12.1915) had joined Everton from his home-town club in February 1936. He did make wartime appearances at Goodison, however, as well as guest outings for Bradford City, Leeds, Walsall, Bournemouth and City (at left-half in January 1945). After retiring in 1952, he became manager of Swindon Town and Barry Town, and then a long-serving Leeds coach. (2 apps)

> **George Little** (b. Newcastle, 30.6.1915) was an August 1936 signing for Doncaster Rovers from Throckley Welfare. He guested at outside-right for City from November 1943 to April 1944, and similarly assisted York City, Aldershot, Brentford, QPR and Chelsea. Rovers transferred him to York in December 1947 and it is believed he subsequently assisted Scunthorpe United, Frickley Colliery and Worksop Town. (11 apps; 1 goal)

> A trialist from Highfields United, **Stanley Logan** was chosen at inside-left for the final game of the 1939/40 season, against Northampton at home, and scored after 30 seconds in a 2-0 win. It proved to be his only outing, and he was back in local football with Wellington Vics the following term. (1 app; 1 goal)

> Another unsuccessful amateur trialist, this time from Nottinghamshire, was RAF Warrant Officer **Danny Long**, who took the outside-left berth at Northampton in November 1944. A month later, he was in the makeshift Nottingham Forest side beaten 1-9 on the same ground. Danny had also appeared three times for Notts County earlier in 1944/5. He was a Forest scout in the late 50s. (1 app)

> Borrowed from the home team to complete the City line-up at Stoke for the final game of 1942/3 was **Eric Longland**, who made the odd appearance for the Potters during wartime, but never got a League break. (1 app)

> Tamworth-born **Tim Lycett** was a City signing in August 1943 from a Castle Bromwich works team, and turned out at inside-left in several games during 1943/4 and 1945/6. In the interim season, he was a four-game guest for Walsall. Tim scored twice for City in the 1946 Senior Cup Final win over Coalville, but was not retained thereafter. (19 apps; 4 goals)

> A left-winger whose City appearances came during February and March 1941, in the War Cup, **Colin Charles Lyman** (b. Northampton, 9.3.1914; d. Cambridge, 9.5.1986) had started his career with Rushden before signing amateur forms for Southend United in July 1933. He moved to Northampton in July 1934, and to Spurs in June 1937. His wartime services were spread between City, Port Vale, Derby, Chesterfield, Forest, Northampton, Notts County, Aldershot and Coventry; then Spurs released him to Port Vale in May 1946. Forest signed Colin in October 1946 (when he scored on his debut against City), and let him go to Notts County in August 1947. After 1948 he was successively player-manager of Nuneaton Borough and (from Jan 1951) Long Eaton Town. (4 apps)

> A COD (Old Dalby) player reputed to be attached to Third Lanark, **A McAskill** twice turned out at outside-right for City during October and November 1942. He additionally represented the Northern Command military select side with COD teammate Gardiner. (2 apps)

> Topping and tailing his playing career with stints for Worksop Town, **Bob McCall** (Robert Henry; b. Whitwell, 29.12.1915) was a Nottingham Forest full-back (February 1935 to 1952, when he returned to Worksop Town) who aided City in home and away fixtures against Derby in March 1945, and also played wartime games for Mansfield and Lincoln. (2 apps)

> **James McCormick** (b. Rotherham, 26.4.1912; d. Marbella, 4.1.1968) was on Spurs' books during the WW2 period, but additionally fitted in guest appearances for each of Fulham, Crystal Palace, Lincoln, Southend, Derby, Birmingham, Bolton, Reading, Liverpool, Crewe, West Brom, Chelmsford City, Chester, Shrewsbury, Rochdale, Tranmere, Walsall and Leicester (March/April 1943). A local signing by Rotherham United in March 1931, the versatile forward had joined Chesterfield in August 1932 (in a swap with Albert Pynegar), and Spurs in March 1933 (scoring a Filbert Street hat-trick against City the following term). Postwar, he transferred to Fulham in May 1946, to Lincoln in August 1947 (champions of Div 3N in 1948), and to Palace in February 1949. His subsequent coaching career took him to Norway, Malta (Sliema Wanderers), Turkey, Wycombe Wanderers and Sheffield United; and he was York City manager in 1953/4. Later a Hertfordshire licensee, he had run a North London sports outfitters during his playing career. (3 apps)

> Motherwell's **John McInally** briefly appeared in City colours at inside-right for a pair of away fixtures in London (at Fulham and Tottenham) in September 1945. (2 apps)

> An NCO in the Military Police, **Bobby McNeil** was a Hamilton Academical player (as had been his father Bob, better known as an inter-war Chelsea star) when he turned out at outside-right for City in the first game of 1943/4, away to Mansfield Town. (1 app)

> Signed by City as an 18-year-old amateur in December 1940, and given a break during 1941/2, **Reg Mansfield** (Reginald Frederick) had previously played for Gresley Rovers. Later in the war, he was noted (with the rank of Lance Corporal) in the COD (Old Dalby) side in the 1944 Senior Cup Final. Johnny Duncan briefly had Reg on a professional contract at City from January 1947. (4 apps)

> A pair of isolated inside-left appearances (in April 1944 and October 1945) marked local lad **William Middleton's** contribution to City's wartime efforts. More often he was to be found in the playing ranks of Pegson's Athletic, and he also served Whitwick Colliery. (2 apps)

> Reportedly 'overwhelmed' on his sole City outing, at centre-half in a 2-5 defeat at Stoke in December 1944, **Jack Morby** (John H; b. Wednesfield, August 1920) had been a year earlier a wartime Aston Villa recruit from Hednesford Town. Though he also guested for Notts County, Portsmouth and Wolves, and played in three FA Cup ties for Villa in 1945/6, he was released in 1947 to Worcester City, and joined Kidderminster Harriers in 1950. (1 app)

> Geordie goalkeeper **Bill Morgan** (William; b. Ryton-on-Tyne, 1914; d. Coventry, February 1993) had joined Coventry City from Chopwell Institute in March 1932 (having a month previously been on amateur forms at Wolves), and built a pre-war record of 150 League games. He guested for Northampton and both Nottingham clubs as well as turning out for City for much of 1941/2, but it was at Filbert Street in September 1942, playing for Coventry against City, that he suffered the severe shoulder injury which eventually enforced his retirement. (17 apps)

> An RAF representative and a Derby County signing from Ross County in October 1944, **Angus Cameron Morrison** (b. Dingwall, 26.4.1924) assisted City at outside-left in home and away fixtures with Aston Villa in April 1945; a month in which he also guested for Stockport County. Postwar, he totalled 95 League goals in 329 games with Derby, Preston North End (November 1948) and Millwall (October 1957), and won one Scotland 'B' cap. In June 1958, he became player/manager of Nuneaton Borough, and later performed similar functions with Belper Town. (2 apps)

> Working at, and playing for, Morris Motors (Coventry), **Alex Morton** signed amateur forms for City in February 1944, and made his sole appearance three days later, on the right wing against Sheffield Wednesday at Filbert Street. He also featured once in a Coventry City line-up the following season, but that seems to have been the extent of his senior experience. Back in February 1938, he'd had one game at centre-forward for Hinckley United. (1 app)

> **Jimmy Mullen** (James; b. Newcastle, 6.1.1923; d. Wolverhampton, October 1987) had barely turned 16 when he made his League debut for Wolves in February 1939, and had to wait another 11 months before being able to sign professionally for the Molineux club. In 1940/1, when Wolves did not compete at all in regional competition, he and Billy Wright became regular guests for City; both having major roles in the capture of the Midland Cup, and indeed both scoring in the Final win over Walsall. Apart from other brief guest stints with Newcastle, Darlington, Middlesbrough, Walsall and Reading, the left-winger then returned to Wolves for the remainder of his career, which stretched to 1960, and brought him 98 League goals from 445 games, as well as eleven England caps. (25 apps; 15 goals)

> Very much a wanderer, **Ambrose 'Jock' Mulraney** (b. Wishaw, 18.5.1916) was as active before and after the war in terms of his club connections as he was during it. Starting in Scottish junior football with Wishaw White Rose and Carluke Rovers, he had trials or reserve spells with each of Hearts, Celtic, Hamilton, Sligo Rovers, Blackpool, and Clapton Orient in a three-year spell from 1933-36. He briefly settled at Dartford, then joined Ipswich Town in November 1936, featuring in that club's initial League season two years later. During the war, he guested for Birmingham, Manchester City, Charlton, Northampton, Clapton Orient, Brentford, Wolves, Brighton, Norwich, Blackburn and Sheffield Wednesday; as well as once, in November 1941, for City (at inside-right at Northampton). Then Jock was on the move 'officially' again: to Birmingham (September 1945), Shrewsbury Town (July 1947), Kidderminster Harriers (July 1948), Aston Villa (September 1948) and Cradley Heath (August 1949, as player-manager). He later managed Brierley Hill from 1952-54. (1 app)

> Initially added to City's amateur roster in February 1937 after starring for Barrow Old Boys, inside-forward **Tom North** (Thomas Williamson; b. Barrow on Soar, 31.10.1919; d. 1996) boosted his local reputation with County Cup Final appearances for Leicester Nomads (against City in 1937) and Brush Sports (with a hat-trick performance in 1941). He rejoined City in July 1943, but got only one selection, at Birmingham in September of that year. In December 1944, Nottingham Forest signed Tom in time to make his debut against City, and he went on to score eleven times in 46 wartime games for them, though only appearing once after the resumption of League football. Tom signed for Gainsborough Trinity in November 1946, and later served both Rugby Town and Barrow Old Boys. (1 app)

> A goalkeeper with Gresley Rovers, Melton Thursday and Holwell Works, **Harry Parker** signed forms for City in September 1941, as cover for Joe Calvert, but conceded six goals in home and away fixtures with West Bromwich Albion that month. His father Arthur had been a reserve goalkeeper on Fosse's books just before WW1. (2 apps)

> Capped by Scotland in 1938, and with a typical medal haul (two League championships, one Scottish Cup) under his belt after signing for Celtic from Dunipace Juniors in March 1932, **George Denholm Paterson** (b. Denny, 26.9.1914; d. New Zealand, 1985) was a fine left-half who substantially lifted City's efforts between April 1941 and October 1942. He also guested for Arsenal, Wolves, Tranmere, Shrewsbury and Blackpool, represented the RAF, and played in three Victory internationals. In October 1946 he transferred from Parkhead to Brentford, and ended his playing career with Yeovil Town from October 1949. George was briefly manager of Stirling Albion from October 1951. (32 apps; 2 goals)

> Described as 'a North Wales lad' (and by one source as an ex-Rhyl Athletic player), **George Pearce** was an RAF sergeant stationed at Market Harborough when he turned out at left-half for City at Newport in October 1945, and was unfortunately injured on this debut. He had played one wartime game for Walsall previously. (1 app)

> A pre-war Plymouth Argyle amateur, **Russell George Thomas Phillips** (b. Exeter, 22.6.1916) was an Army corporal when registered at Filbert Street in March 1943. He turned out occasionally for City at inside-forward until September 1944, then switched allegiance to Millwall (for whom he scored in a 1945/6 FA Cup tie) and Torquay United, who he continued to represent into the first postwar League season. (18 apps; 7 goals)

> A former Stourbridge forward, rediscovered as an army sergeant playing in Nottinghamshire football for RAOC Chilwell, **Doug Pimbley** (Douglas William; b. Kings Norton, 19.6.1917) had played two wartime games for Manchester City when City signed him in December 1945. A debut scorer against West Brom that month, he stayed only until the end of that 'transitional' term, also guesting twice for Forest; then signed professionally for Birmingham City in July 1946, and moved to Notts County in March 1948. (8 apps; 4 goals)

> Also a Stourbridge product, but on Stoke City's books since 1938, **Wallace Poulton** had been playing Leicestershire Senior League football for RAF (Melton) when he won his sole City selection, at outside left in a home game with Forest in October 1945. He made no peacetime appearances for Stoke. (1 app)

> An occasional City guest on either wing during 1939/40, **Jack Pritchard** (Harvey John; b. Meriden, 30.1.1918; d Beccles, May 2000) was an August 1935 signing by Coventry City from Exhall Colliery, who had moved to Crystal Palace in June 1937, and on to Manchester City in March 1938. He additionally guested for Northampton, Coventry, Aldershot and West Ham during the war years; then left Maine Road for Southend United in February 1947, and finished his career with Folkestone from August 1952. He later trained both Folkestone and Chelmsford City. (10 apps; 1 goal)

> A local goalkeeper who had represented Leicester Boys in 1928,

Arthur Queenborough twice stood in for Sandy McLaren during May 1940; having signed three months previously from Wigston COB. (2 apps)

> **'Tex' Rickards** (Charles Thomas; b. Giltbrook, 19.2.1915; d. Peterborough, 10.7.1980) was a versatile forward who guested once for City in March 1944, and more regularly from September to December of that year; notching one hat-trick against Port Vale. Originally a Notts County signing in September 1933 from local works team Johnson & Barnes, he had transferred to Cardiff City for a season from May 1938. He joined Midland Leaguers Scunthorpe United the following summer, then played regularly for Mansfield Town from the earliest days of wartime football, and additionally guested for Notts County, Crewe Alexandra, Stockport County, Derby County and Chesterfield. In 1946 he commenced a three-season stint with Peterborough United. (13 apps; 7 goals)

> An inside-left or left-half, **Dick Riley** (Richard J; b. Northampton) signed for City as an amateur in December 1944, and professionally a month later, but his final senior game came only a year afterwards. He was never on a winning City side. (5 apps)

> A Wolves teenager who guested for City on the left wing at Coventry in September 1943, and also briefly assisted Notts County, **Douglas Gordon Roberts** (b. Foleshill, 30.5.1925) signed for Northampton Town in August 1944, and subsequently served Brighton & Hove Albion (from March 1949), Accrington Stanley (from July 1951), Rugby Town (from 1952) and Cheltenham Town. He later became an engineering draughtsman at British Timken in Northampton. (1 app)

> The scorer of 75 pre-war goals for both Bradford clubs, **Jimmy Robertson** (James Henry; b. Berwick, 22.3.1913; d. Bradford, 1973) was a wartime guest for both Nottingham Forest and Mansfield Town, and it was at the latter's ground in October 1942 that he volunteered to turn out at left-half for a reshuffled City when George Dewis didn't arrive in time. Bradford Park Avenue had signed Jimmy from Welbeck Colliery in August 1932, and he had crossed the city to Valley Parade in February 1938. (1 app)

> Manchester City prospect **Peter Robinson** (b. Manchester, 29.1.1922; d. Sept 2000) had a host of wartime opportunities to develop his game at, and away from, Maine Road, with guest outings for Manchester United, QPR, Luton, Aldershot, Clapton Orient and Crystal Palace, as well as for City. Though primarily a full-back, he turned out at left-half in a pair of London away games for City in September 1945. His postwar travels took him to Chesterfield, Buxton, Notts County and King's Lynn, and he then managed Macclesfield Town and Hyde United. Peter was later youth coach at both Manchester City and Preston. (2 apps)

> A Geordie from Hexham who had played pre-war for Hexham United and Durham University, **Alan Rochester** made a May 1940 debut for City, and signed for the club in November of that year, going on to make sporadic appearances at outside-right or right-half across the first four wartime seasons, latterly when on leave from aircraft-carrier services with the Fleet Air Arm. (27 apps)

> A December 1940 signing from Gresley Rovers, **Robert George Roome** got but a single senior chance: at outside-left in a home win over Forest in June 1941. He'd originally joined Gresley from Woodville in May 1939. (1 app)

> A former Airdrieonians wing-half whose 85 wartime games for Chelsea after a 1942 signing included two Wembley appearances in the League (South) Cup, **Robert Inglis Russell** (b. Aberdour, 27.12.1919) guested once at left-half for City, at Brentford in September 1945, and also for Crystal Palace. Postwar, he played only twice more for Chelsea, and twice for Notts County after an August 1948 move. The following October, he returned to London, with Leyton Orient, but failed to gain a first-team place. (1 app)

> **Bill Rutherford** was a Londoner on Army service locally when signed as an amateur in April 1943. He made a scoring bow at Northampton that month, but a week later had finished his senior career. (2 apps; 1 goal)

> Described as a 'diminutive livewire', **Don Sanderson** cost City a 10s 6d fine from the League when they belatedly registered him four days after his February 1941 scoring debut against Lincoln City. A former Coalville Boys teammate of Dennis Cheney, then a Hugglescote United and Coalville Town centre-forward, Don notched 31 goals for the Colts in 1940/1, and continued to play the occasional first-team game until December 1944. He was also lent to Luton Town at Filbert Street in October 1941, scoring the opening goal for them in a game City eventually won 7-2. After the war, Don briefly assisted Whitwick Colliery, and signed amateur forms for West Bromwich Albion in November 1946. (22 apps; 9 goals)

> A 20-year-old bricklayer from Fleckney, **Fred Sansome** signed for City in April 1940 from Oadby Imperial, having previously served Wigston Imperial, and had a brief run as senior outside-right. (4 apps)

> An Aston Villa centre-forward who had claimed a hat-trick from his pre-war debut, **Frank Shell** (Francis Henry; b. Hackney, 2.1.1912; d. Axminster, July 1988) turned out at inside-left for City at Northampton in November 1939. A former amateur with Barking and Ford Sports (Dagenham), he had joined Villa in May 1937, and he also guested for Northampton, Walsall and Notts County during the war. From September 1946 he was briefly a Birmingham City reserve, soon released to Hereford United, though he spent 1947/8 with Mansfield Town. (1 app)

> A Bolton Wanderers first-teamer in the final pre-war season, after signing in June 1937 from Shettleston, **Tommy Sinclair** (Thomas McKenzie; b. 13.10.1921) additionally assisted Norwich City, Reading, Gainsborough Trinity, Chesterfield, Aldershot and City (on the right wing at Brentford in September 1945) during the war years. Subsequently, from 1946, Aldershot picked up his League registration, before moves to Brentford (August 1950) and Bradford City (August 1951). (1 app)

> The winner in the 1940 War Cup Final was one of 80 wartime goals centre-forward **Sam Small** (Samuel John; b. Birmingham, 15.5.1912) scored for West Ham United, to add to his 39-goal League record. A Birmingham signing from Bromsgrove Rovers in March 1934, he had moved to Upton Park in January 1937, and would stay until a March 1948 transfer to Brighton. As well as his City outing, in a home defeat by Fulham in September 1945, Sam guested for Birmingham and Coventry. (1 app)

> Dundee United winger **Ian S Smart** had his only City outing on the left flank at Walsall in September 1944. Originally with Dundee Violet, he served the Tannadice club until 1952, while also following a schoolteaching career. (1 app)

No.	Name / Home Town	Fav. LCFC player	Fav. LCFC game
278	Martyn Braham, Market Harborough	Gary Lineker	Derby Play Off Final
279	Roy G Jones, Market Bosworth	Keith Weller	Derby Play Off Final
280	Thomas Ormonde, Emmer Green, Reading	Steve Claridge	Crystal Palace Play Off Final
281	Richard Clarke, Dar-Es-Salaam, Tanzania	Steve Walsh	Derby Play Off Final
282	Chris Wigginton, Bogota, Colombia	Steve Walsh	Shrewsbury FA Cup
283	Malcolm Major, Wokingham	Frank Worthington	Crystal Palace Play Off Final
284	Kevin Wells, Harlow	Steve Walsh	Shrewsbury FA Cup
285	Ian Gilbert, Wigston	Steve Walsh	Crystal Palace Play Off Final
286	John Casey, Leicester	Gary Lineker	Shrewsbury FA Cup
287	Cheryl Ann Boulton, Leicester	Steve Claridge	M'boro Coca Cola Cup Replay 1997
288	Julie Kirk, Melton Mowbray	Len Glover	Liverpool 1972
289	Adrian Wood, Duston - Northampton	Ian Wilson	Liverpool 1984
290	Toby Coles, Hinckley	Steve Walsh	Derby Play Off Final - 1994
291	Barry Thompson, Wigston	Gordon Banks	Tranmere Rovers 2000
292	Corinna Fincham, Wigston	David Oldfield	Shrewsbury FA Cup
293	Joe Schmidt, Luxembourg	Keith Weller	Shrewsbury FA Cup
294	Andrew Barwell, Leicester	Keith Weller	Arsenal 1997
295	Stephen Baum, Cosby, Leics	Keith Weller	Manchester City Cup Replay 1968
296	John Eales, Stoney Stanton	Gary Lineker	Crystal Palace Play Off Final
297	Martyn Oldershaw, Leicester	Frank Worthington	Crystal Palace Play Off Final
298	Paul Tyler, Leicester	Neil Lennon	Away win at Liverpool - 1980 (2-0)
299	Ian Stringer, Luton	Steve Claridge	Crystal Palace Play Off Final
300	Paul Stringer, Epsom	Gary Lineker	M'boro Coca Cola Cup Replay 1997
301	Stephen Wilkinson, Hinckley	Gordon Banks	Wembley 2000
302	Matthew Davis, Wigston - Leicester	Gary Lineker	M'boro Coca Cola Cup Replay 1997
303	Brian Austick, Leicester	Jimmy Hernon	Derby Play Off Final
304	Joe Kenney, Enderby	Sep Smith	Tranmere Rovers 2000
305	Jean Wilby, Hinckley	Arthur Rowley	Manchester United 1961
306	Craig Carver, Leicester	Steve Walsh	Derby Play Off Final
307	John Roberts, Leicester	Larry May	Crystal Palace Play Off Final
308	Rob McCoy, Leicester	Keith Weller	Wembley 1994
309	Marcus Muggleton, Market Harborough	Steve Walsh	Derby Play Off Final - 1994
310	Robert Ferguson, Syston, Leics	Frank Large	ManCity 4th Round FA Cup - 1968
311	Roy Bent, Leicester	N/A	N/A
312	Iain Sturch, Birmingham	Steve Walsh	N/A,
313	Alan & Kay Mayes, Leicester	Steve Walsh	Derby Play Off Final - 1994
314	Roman Scuplak, Leicester	Keith Weller	Shrewsbury FA Cup Final
315	Andy Sibson, Rothley	Len Glover	Crystal Palace Play Off Final
316	Tony Kirby, Great Yarmouth	Frank Worthington	Leicester v Norwich 1995 - 3-2
317	John Wilson, Peggs Green	Derek Dougan	Leicester v Man Utd 1963 - 4-3
318	Andrew J Mellor, Upminster	Larry May	Swindon Town 1993
319	Brett Wain, Oadby	Steve Walsh	Derby Play Off Final - 1994
320	John Cumming, County Durham	Keith Weller	M'boro Coca Cola Cup Replay 1997
321	Liam McCarthy, Leicester	Steve Walsh	Away win at Derby (4 - 0)
322	Shane Hull, Norwich	Frank Worthington	Liverpool 1972
323	Syd Lee, Contin - By Strathpeffer	David Gibson	Man City FA Cup Replay - 1968
324	Catherine Bull, Oadby	Gary Lineker	N/A
325	Ian Burns, Lutterworth	Gordon Banks	Nottingham Forest
326	Garry Stokes, Leicester	Steve Walsh	Shrewsbury FA Cup Final
327	Martin Orme, Leicester	Len Glover	Middlesbrough 1997
328	Frank Pattinson, Cheshire	Keith Weller	Man City FA Cup Replay - 1968
329	Paul Wisdish, Groby	Frank Worthington	Crystal Palace Play Off Final
330	Tim Burke, Leicester	Arthur Chandler	Arsenal 1997
331	Keith Faulkes, Thurmaston	Frank Worthington	Man City FA Cup Replay - 1968
332	Raj Kumar, Evington	Ian Ormondroyd	Derby Play Off Final
333	James Colford, East Goscote	Robbie Savage	M'boro Coca Cola Cup Replay 1997
334	Ian P Morris, Leicester	Gary Lineker	Man City 1998
335	Phil Passingham, Market Harborough	Steve Walsh	Derby Play Off Final
336	Andrew Iwaszko, Leicester	Mark Wallington	Shrewsbury FA Cup Final
337	Allan Geary, Coalville	Frank Worthington	Derby Play Off Final
338	Danny Hughes, Wigston, Leicester	Alan Young	Middlesbrough 1987
339	Dave Reed, Huncote	Frank Worthington	
340	Gerald Gilbert, Buxton	Steve Walsh	Derby Play Off Final
341	Stuart Conopo, Northampton	Steve Walsh	Derby Play Off Final
342	Eamonn Harrigan, Leicester	Steve Walsh	Derby Play Off Final
343	Jon Hockin, Leicester	Steve Walsh	Blackburn 1992
344	Martin Adcock, Leicester	N/A	N/A
345	Charles Myring, Leicester	N/A	N/A
346	Andrew Blyth, Whitwick	Steve Lynx	Cambridge Play Off (City win 5-0)
347	Roger Ivor Reed, Syston, Leics	Steve Walsh	Cambridge Play Off 1991
348	David Marson, Ratby - Leics	Gary Lineker	N/A
349	Jonathan Pearson, Leicester	Steve Walsh	Shrewsbury FA Cup Final
350	Ernest Derry, Leicester	Steve Walsh	Derby Play Off Final - 1994
351	John Chapman, Leicester	Gary Lineker	LCFC v Man City (8-4)
352	Douglas Hird, Leicester	David Gibson	Man City FA Cup - 1968
353	Pam Hale, Leicester	Steve Walsh	Crystal Palace Play Off Final
354	Graham Dutton, Desborough	Keith Weller	Arsenal 1997
355	Patricia Ray, Leicester	Gary Lineker	Gary's All Stars - 2000
356	Chris Rouse, Leicester	Frank Worthington	Derby Play Off Final
357	Anne Woolley, Whitwick	Keith Weller	Crystal Palace Play Off Final
358	Peter Sowler, Leicester	Steve Walsh	Swindon Play Off Final
359	Louise J Davies, Leicester	Gordon Banks	Tranmere Rovers 2000
360	Ron Wright, Wootton, Beds	Keith Weller	Cambridge Play Off Semi Final
361	Michael Mills, Leicester	Steve Walsh	Man City Replay - 1968
362	John Page, Leicester	Keith Weller	Man City Cup Replay - 1968
363	John Davies, Hathern, Loughborough	Frank Worthington	Shrewsbury FA Cup Final
364	Mike Flude, Leicester	Keith Weller	N/A
365	Paul Bradshaw, Blaby - Leicester	Gary Lineker	Shrewsbury FA Cup 6th Round
366	Anthony Sharman, Wigston - Leicester	Len Glover	Shrewsbury 1982 Quarter Final
367	Chris Jacques, Billericay - Essex	Steve Walsh	Derby Play Off Final
368	Anthony Trown, Coalville	Mark Wallington	Shrewsbury 1982
369	Richard Pepper, Leicester	Frank Worthington	FA Cup Quarter Final 1982
370	Peter Easthope, Syston - Leics	Frank Worthington	City v Shrewsbury
371	Lee Morton, Leicester	David Gibson	Shrewsbury FA Cup

> Also a one-shot winger was **Charlie Smith** (Charles James; b. Cardiff, 26.8.1915; d. 1984), who appeared at outside-right for City at Derby in February 1945. A pre-war player with Exeter City (August 1936), and under David Halliday at both Yeovil & Petters United (1937) and Aberdeen (January 1938), he also guested for Watford, York City and Charlton, then briefly served Torquay United from 1946. (1 app)

> At one stage during the war, City actually had no less than nine players with the surname 'Smith' simultaneously on their books. One of that ilk was **John D Smith**, an April 1940 signing from Fairfax United who became an occasional senior choice at inside-right until 1942/3. He guested once for Forest in that term, and once for Southampton a season later, and also assisted Portsmouth's reserves. (18 apps; 3 goals)

> **Leslie G Smith** was a local signing in August 1940 who made a quartet of inside-forward appearances in the following campaign. He was unfortunately later a prisoner-of-war in Japanese hands. (4 apps)

> The better-known **Les Smith** (Leslie George Frederick; b. Ealing, 13.5.1918; d. 1995) had become an England international a couple of years before he briefly assisted City in October 1941, scoring on his debut against Luton, at a time when he was taking refereeing exams at Loughborough. An inside-left whose teenage talent developed with Petersham, Wimbledon and Hayes, he signed for Brentford in March 1936. He won further wartime caps while on RAF service; also guested for Chelsea and Fulham; and played in one Victory international after moving officially to Aston Villa in October 1945. In June 1952 he rejoined Brentford, and in August 1953 became player-manager at Kidderminster Harriers. (2 apps; 1 goal)

> A versatile defender for City from October to December 1942, and also briefly a wartime guest for Falkirk, **John Snape** (b. Birmingham, 2.7.1917) was a Coventry City stalwart from 1935 to 1951. He'd previously been spotted with Shirley Town and Solihull Town, and would afterwards serve Bedworth Town. (6 apps)

> **Terry Sparrow** was a young defender signed as an amateur in February 1942 after a few outings with Bristol City's 'A' team. Joining the professional ranks in March 1944, he filled in once at right-half and once at right-back before the end of 1943/4. Terry also turned out twice for Notts County during the following term. (2 apps)

> Just turned 17 when appearing as a stand-in left back in a 5-4 win at West Brom in December 1940, **Terry Springthorpe** (Terence Alfred; b. Draycott, 4.12.1923) had already faced City as a 15-year-old for Wolves during the previous season. A 1939 Molineux signing from Sedgeley Rovers, who also guested for Cardiff and Wrexham during the war, he would make a League bow in the Old Gold in 1947/8, and oppose City again in the 1949 FA Cup Final. A December 1950 transfer to Coventry City didn't work out happily, and in 1951 Terry emigrated to the States; though he didn't give up football, for he featured in the USA team against England in June 1953. (1 app)

> A former captain of Leicester Boys, and an England schools international, **Len Staples** (Leonard Eric; b. Leicester, 23.1.1926) got a few chances as a 17-year-old amateur forward with City in the final game of 1942/3 and the early months of 1943/4, but spent most of his war on Navy service, occasionally representing the Mediterranean Fleet XI. He was a Torquay United trialist during 1946/7, but signed professional forms for City in July 1947, by which time he was regarded as a right-half. Lucklessly, he was the only member of the 1948 Combination Cup-wining side not to taste first-team action with City, but he built a fine 164-game record as a Newport County full-back after an August 1949 move (when signed again by Tom Bromilow). In July 1957, Len signed for Weymouth, in June 1958 for Nuneaton Borough, and in October 1959 for Midland Athletic. (5 apps; 1 goal)

> An outside left who had wandered far and wide before the war, **Ernest Steele** (b. Middleton, 18.6.1908; d. Farnworth, 1972) finished his career as a City guest, forced to retire through injury after a quintet of appearances between November 1942 and January 1943: a period which also saw him hit by the death of his wife. A Rochdale professional from August 1931, he moved exactly a year later to Oldham Athletic, in May 1933 to Torquay United, in October 1934 to Notts County, in July 1936 to Bath City, and in December 1936 to Millwall. Tom Bromilow signed him for Crystal Palace in September 1938, and he moved back to Rochdale on the eve of war. Also a wartime guest for Chesterfield, Stockport and Palace, he was playing in Army football when re-signed by Bromilow. (5 apps; 1 goal)

> On three occasions in the same City line-up was the unrelated **Freddie Steele** (Frederick Charles; b. Hanley, 6.5.1916; d. Newcastle-under-Lyme, 23.4.1976), who averaged a goal-a-game for City across two guest stints, in 1940/1 and 1942/3. A six-cap England international centre-forward who had signed for Stoke City in 1931 from Downings Tileries, Freddie eventually totalled 140 League goals and 88 wartime counters for the Potteries club; the latter haul remarkable for a man who also guested for Fulham, Doncaster, Leeds, Northampton, Forest, Bradford Park Avenue, Notts County and Sheffield United. In June 1949 he became player-manager at Mansfield Town, and performed similar dual duties for Port Vale from December 1951. He concentrated on managerial duties for the Valiants from 1953 to 1957, and had a further spell as their boss from 1962 to 1965. (18 apps; 18 goals)

> A creative inside-forward who'd signed for Blackburn Rovers in 1942, **Harry Stephan** (Harold William; b. Farnworth, 24.2.1924) guested briefly for City during the winter of 1944/5, and also turned out in wartime football for Bolton Wanderers. He made 13 postwar appearances at Ewood, but following unsuccessful trials with Accrington Stanley in September 1948, soon dropped into the non-league sphere with Mossley. (4 apps; 1 goal)

> Unfortunately unblessed with so much as an identifying initial by any of the local press at the time, centre forward **Steward** featured in a goalless draw at Mansfield in September 1943, a week after claiming five goals from the Colts' 15-1 Senior League win at Melton. (1 app)

> Two months later, Third Lanark's **A Sutton** wore the City spearhead's shirt at Derby. A Military Policeman, he had been assisting the Colts from the beginning of 1943/4. (1 app)

> Another from that same Colts team was **Len Sutton**, a former Quorn Methodists team-mate of Jack Lee; though his only centre-forward outing for City came shortly after his military demob, when he led the line in a 1-7 home defeat by Chelsea in January 1946. Postwar, after a season switching twixt City's reserves and Coalville Town, he continued faithfully to serve Quorn for over 20 years, taking over as manager in 1959, yet still turning out gamely on occasion in 1968/9. (1 app)

> Blackpool's **Fred Tapping** (Frederick Harold; b. Derby, 29.7.1921) numbered City amongst several Midlands clubs for whom he guested. His City spell was at right-half or inside-right between March and May 1945, and he also had wartime outings for Derby, Chesterfield, Mansfield and Notts County. He left Bloomfield Road for Chesterfield in November 1947, and in 1949 found himself in the initial Southern League line-up of the newly-professionalised Headington United (now Oxford United). He closed his career with a stint at Gresley Rovers. (7 apps; 2 goals)

> **George Thomas Taylor** (b. Walsall, 1908) was at the veteran stage when he briefly assisted City in March 1942 – indeed the Coventry City winger retired from the game entirely a year later. A former England schoolboy international, George had joined Notts County from Stourbridge back in May 1925, transferring to Bolton Wanderers in December 1933, and to Coventry in September 1937. He additionally returned to each of his previous clubs as a wartime guest. (2 apps; 1 goal)

> A corporal in the RAF when he turned out at inside-left for City in March and April 1945, **Ron Thompson** (b. Sheffield, 24.12.1921) had been a 1942 Sheffield Wednesday signing from Wadsley Colliery. He remained at Hillsborough until a May 1947 move to Rotherham United, then joined York City in June 1949, and Gainsborough Trinity a year later. (3 apps)

> Doncaster-born 18-year-old **Tommy Thompson** became Tom Bromilow's first signing as City manager when he joined from Tunbridge Wells Rangers in August 1939. The young outside-right got a fair bit of senior experience in the initial season of wartime football, but was soon posted to Ireland with his Army unit. There he represented the Army in Ulster XI and guested regularly for Linfield: in fact scoring twice in their 1942 Irish Cup Final win over Glentoran. He managed a couple more appearances for City in December 1942, but was unheard of again at Filbert Street until officially freed in May 1946. Meanwhile, Tommy had taken an Ulster bride and settled in Carrickfergus, and continued his playing career with Linfield in 46/7. Remarkably, he played in three more IFA Cup Final triumphs (in 1948, 1950 and 1953), and scored in each; and was nine times an Irish League representative. (17 apps; 1 goal)

> Offering his services to City along with Mullen and Wright when Wolves ceased operations for the 1940/41 season, **Dennis Thornhill** (b. Draycott, 5.7.1923; d. Southend, Aug 1992) had only a short spell as senior left-half at the beginning of that term. He failed to make a postwar breakthrough at Molineux, and was unfortunate to have his career cut short by injury after only eleven games for Southend United, following a March 1948 move. (3 apps)

> A former member of the *Leicester Evening Mail* staff, who had played occasionally for City's Colts during 1941/2, **Harry Walton** (b. Manchester, 1.4.1924) signed professional forms in September 1942: ironically only two days after his sole senior outing in a goalless draw with West Brom. Harry made one postwar Third Division appearance at left-half for Southend United in October 1946, and later served Coalville Town, Nuneaton Borough, Atherstone United, Whitwick Colliery and City League side St Margaret's Works. (1 app)

> Primarily a right-back, but occasionally utilised at centre-forward, **Dick Walton** (Richard; b. Hull, 12.9.1924) signed as an amateur for City in June 1942, and stepped up to the senior ranks in January 1943, when part-way through a run of 25 consecutive appearances. The following term, he was also a guest for Chester, Middlesbrough and Third Lanark. Dick was discharged from the Army in early 1944, but immediately signed up with the Palestine Police for the duration of the war. City released his registration to Leyton Orient in July 1948, and he moved to Exeter City in December 1951. After 199 League games for these two clubs, he joined Tonbridge in 1956. (31 apps)

> Gresley Rovers 'keeper **Eric Ward** was a local stand-in for Joe Calvert against Spurs in May 1941, and earned praise despite a 1-2 home defeat. In December 1938, he'd left HR Mansfield Sports to sign forms for Blackpool, but made no senior breakthrough there. Later with Pegsons Athletic, he also represented the Combined Services locally, and was with Coalville Town from 1945/6. (1 app)

> Forward **John H Wattie** was climbing the status ladder of Scottish football when war broke out, having moved from Inverurie Loco Works to Forfar in the 1937 close season, and having signed for Dundee two years later. He came to City's notice (rather inevitably) in 1942/3, when playing locally for COD (Old Dalby) and breaking scoring records with ease: in fact he scored a hat-trick or better in seven successive Senior League games from September to November that season. Nonetheless, Nottingham Forest were the first club to introduce him to senior regional fare, at the start of 1943/4. His City outings came in successive matches in April 1944 (in the outside-left berth), and a week after the third, he helped COD beat City in the Final of the Senior Cup. John, a minister's son, was still on Dundee's initial postwar roll-call, but his subsequent moves are unknown to us. (3 apps; 1 goal)

> **Ray Watts** was described as a 20-year-old Chesterfield lad, working as an engineer, when signing for City in April 1945. He had a single outing in each full-back spot during the 'transitional' season of 1945/6. (2 apps)

> A pre-war Scottish schoolboy international, playing in junior football prior to joining the RAF in 1940, **Andy Weatherston** had attained the rank of Flight Lieutenant by the time he joined City (am in cs 1945, pro in December 1945). His subsequent trio of senior games came on the left wing; but he won his 1946 County Cup medal as Don Revie's right flank partner. We are unable to confirm whether Andy forged a postwar career in Scottish football. (3 apps)

> Playing in borrowed boots a couple of sizes too small, **Fred Wilson** (Frederick Charles; b. Nottingham, 10.11.1918; d. January 1994) gamely helped City out in October 1940 when they arrived at Luton minus Mullen and Wright. A tall centre-half, ironically nicknamed 'Shorty', he was a former Wolves reserve who had joined Bournemouth & Boscombe Athletic in 1937, and who went on to serve the Cherries until a June 1951 move to Weymouth. Fred also guested for Brighton and Crystal Palace during WW2. (1 app)

> A local miner who had been assisting Derby County's Colts, **Eric Windle** (one source gives his forename as Ronald) was drafted into City's under-strength line-up at the Baseball Ground in April 1944, and scored from the inside-left berth in a 2-0 victory. He also had a couple of run-outs with City Reserves at the beginning of 1944/5. However, if indeed he was usually known as Ron, then it is likely that he additionally appeared in wartime for Huddersfield Town and Notts County, and postwar for Gainsborough Trinity. (1 app; 1 goal)

> Capped by Wales both during and after the war, **Doug Witcomb** (Douglas Frederick; b. Ebbw Vale, 18.4.1918) made a single guest appearance for City at inside-left at Spurs in May 1941. He'd actually started his senior career as a Spurs amateur in the mid-30s, but found himself farmed out to Northfleet and Enfield before moving to West Bromwich Albion in October 1937 and establishing himself. Wrexham, Newport County, Swansea Town, Lovells Athletic and Grimsby Town also benefitted from Doug's wartime services; while postwar he moved to Sheffield Wednesday (March 1947), Newport (November 1953), Llandudno Town (August 1954) and, in October 1955, to Redditch. (1 app)

> **Dennis Wright** (b. Chesterfield, 19.12.1919; d. Chesterfield, July 1993) was a reserve goalkeeper for Mansfield Town (signed in March 1939 from Clay Lane Rangers) when he was recruited by City to make up the numbers at Field Mill in November 1940, and surprisingly claimed both goals from the right wing berth in a 2-4 defeat. Dennis also assisted Glentoran while on military service in Ireland, but didn't make Mansfield's senior line-up until peacetime football returned. He went on to play 380 League games for the Stags, and later became their groundsman. (1 app; 2 goals)

> While everyone now remembers **Billy Wright** (William Ambrose; b. Ironbridge, 6.2.1924; d. Barnet, 3.9.1994) as the man who won 105 England caps as a centre-half, it was as a teenage forward that City fans first knew him. A 15-year-old when he opposed City for Wolves during 1939/40, he came to Filbert Street less than a year later (upon Wolves' playing shutdown) to star throughout 1940/1 primarily as a goalscoring right winger. He netted in the Midland Cup Final win over Walsall, and also helped City to within one step of Wembley in the League War Cup. He would, of course, later skipper Wolves to FA Cup victory over City in 1949: he had signed initially as an amateur for them in June 1938 (from Cradley Heath), and only as a pro in February 1941 (part-way through his Leicester sojourn), and would serve them through three Championship campaigns until retirement in 1959. A spell managing Arsenal and a later career in television would follow, and the civil honour of a CBE also accrued to this legendary sporting gentleman. Billy also had the odd outing for Notts County during WW2. (33 apps; 12 goals)

> **Harold Wyles** (b. Melton Mowbray, 28.10.1922) first signed for City as an amateur in August 1939, made his debut in April 1941, and signed professional forms a year later. Usually a full-back or centre-half (who also enjoyed occasional excursions to centre-forward), he continued to split his playing time between City and his RAOC unit team, COD (Old Dalby), who he represented in successive Senior Cup Finals from 1942-44, and once guested for Nottingham Forest during 1943/4. In February 1948, Harold moved from City to Gateshead, going on to play 235 League games for them, scoring seven times. (24 apps)

MANAGERS

1884 - 1892	FRANK GARDNER
1892 - 1894	ERNEST MARSON
1894 - Nov 1895	J LEE
Nov 1895 - July 1897	HENRY JACKSON
July 1897 - Sept 1898	WILLIAM CLARK
Sept 1898 - Jan 1912	GEORGE JOHNSON
Mar 1912 - Feb 1914	JACK BARTLETT
Mar 1914 - Jan 1915	LOUIS FORD
Jan 1915 - Sept 1919	HARRY LINNEY
Sept 1919 - May 1926	PETER HODGE
July 1926 - Jan 1932	WILLIE ORR
Mar 1932 - Aug 1934	PETER HODGE
Oct 1934 - Oct 1936	ARTHUR LOCHHEAD
Oct 1936 - May 1939	FRANK WOMACK
July 1939 - May 1945	TOM BROMILOW
June 1945 - Mar 1946	TOM MATHER
Mar 1946 - Oct 1949	JOHN DUNCAN
Dec 1949 - Feb 1955	NORMAN BULLOCK
June 1955 - Nov 1958	DAVID HALLIDAY
Nov 1958 - Nov 1968	MATT GILLIES
Dec 1968 - June 1971	FRANK O'FARRELL
July 1971 - May 1977	JIMMY BLOOMFIELD
July 1977 - Apr 1978	FRANK McLINTOCK
June 1978 - July 1982	JOCK WALLACE
Aug 1982 - May 1987	GORDON MILNE
June 1986 - Dec 1987	BRYAN HAMILTON
Dec 1987 - Jan 1991	DAVID PLEAT
Jan 1991 - May 1991	GORDON LEE
May 1991 - Nov 1994	BRIAN LITTLE
Dec 1994 - Dec 1995	MARK McGHEE
Dec 1995 - June 2000	MARTIN O'NEILL
June 2000 -	PETER TAYLOR

All incumbents prior to the appointment of Arthur Lochhead bore the title Secretary/Manager, and all up to Willie Orr carried out those joint responsibilities alone.

> During George Johnson's tenure, Fosse gave player **Jimmy Blessington** the title of Team Manager between January 1907 and April 1909, and **Andy Aitken** the title of Player/Manager from April 1909 to May 1911.

> Fosse director **S Scattergood** was honorary secretary for the brief period between the departure of George Johnson and the arrival of Jack Bartlett; and fellow board member **James M Hawkes** did similar duty between Bartlett's departure and Louis Ford's appointment.

> The City board failed to make a managerial appointment between February and June 1955, and undertook executive decisions, and team selection, collectively.

> Head coach **Bert Johnson** was acting manager for several months during 1967/8 while Matt Gillies was on medically-prescribed leave of absence.

> Former assistant manager **Ian MacFarlane** took over in a caretaker role to complete the 1977/8 season following Frank McLintock's resignation.

> From June 1986 to May 1987, Gordon Milne was designated as General Manager and Bryan Hamilton as Team Manager.

> Coach **Peter Morris** was briefly caretaker boss between the Bryan Hamilton and David Pleat regimes.

> Following the departure of Brian Little, the caretaker role was in the hands of coach **Allan Evans** for one game, and then passed to the youth-team coaching partnership of **Kevin MacDonald** and **Tony McAndrew** for three more Premiership fixtures.

> Upon Mark McGhee's defection,

David Nish led a four-man temporary management unit, along with coach **Chris Turner** and senior players **Garry Parker** and **Steve Walsh**, for two First Division games.

BARTLETT, John William
> Born in Forest Gate, London, in 1878, Jack Bartlett had joined junior minnows Croydon Common as a player in 1898, and took the role of secretary/manager there in 1903. Something of a visionary, he proposed in 1907 setting up an entirely new professional club, to be called Croydon Town, but then settled instead for professionalising the existing club on its election to the Southern League that summer. The Robins would have moderate success in that sphere until their disbandment during the First World War, with Jack at their helm until Fosse tempted him to the Midlands a few months after the two clubs had twice met in the FA Cup during 1911/12.

With a cash-strapped Fosse he was mainly noted for a policy of recruiting a motley collection of southern-based amateur players to supplement the local youngsters; and indeed helped build some useful publicity (if not a successful combination) out of what was dubbed, on the eve of 1913/14, 'the £105 team' - this being the aggregate cost of the three players in the senior squad for whom any fee had been paid at all! Fosse's precarious playing position (they would escape that term's re-election zone only on goal average) combined with a rap from authority (for employing an agent, and through him making an illegal approach to yet another London-based amateur) to prompt Jack's resignation in February 1914. He turned down a coaching opportunity in Germany, and took over as Swansea Town manager in May 1914, piloting the lowly Southern League Swans to FA Cup victory over Fosse during the next season.

No.	Name / Home Town	Fav. LCFC player	Fav. LCFC game
372	Michael Downie, Leicester	Steve Claridge	Cup Win at Wembley
373	James Jackson, Leicester	Gary Lineker	Crystal Palace Play Off Final
374	Per Persson, Sweden	Mark Wallington	Shrewsbury FA Cup 1982
375	Chris Walker, North Wales	Gary McAllister	Cambridge Play Off
376	Nicholas Hill, Newcastle under Lyme	David Gibson	Huddersfield 1956
377	John Greatorex, Leicester	Gary Lineker	Tranmere Rovers at Wembley
378	John Cawley, Leicester	Keith Weller	Shrewsbury FA Cup Round 6 1982
379	Paul Towers, Stamford	Gary Lineker	Shrewsbury 1982
380	Richard M Holmes, Ashby De La Zouch	Steve Walsh	Crystal Palace Play Off Final
381	Ian Trevor Hooper, Dagenham	Len Glover	Crystal Palace Play Off Final
382	Roman Rataj, London	Gary Lineker	Shrewsbury 1982
383	Chris Swistak, Brinsley - Notts	Gary Lineker	Shrewsbury - 5-2
384	David Middleton, Coalville - Leics	Frank Worthington	Crystal Palace Play Off Final
385	Tom Engel, Leicester	Ian Wilson	Away win at Liverpool - 1984 (2-1)
386	Antony Kavanagh, Marston Trussell	Steve Walsh	Cambridge Play Off Semi Final
387	Richard Hart, Weymouth	Derek Dougan	Man City FA Cup - (4-3)
388	David Hart, Weymouth	Simon Morgan	Crystal Palace Play Off Final
389	Kieron Grace, Bletchley	Steve Claridge	Middlesbrough 1997 Cup
390	Richard Prew, Bedford	Frank Worthington	Leicester V Leeds 1992 (4-3)
391	Mark Hayward, Burbage	Steve Walsh	Derby at Wembley
392	Brian Leitch, Edinburgh	Steve Walsh	Play Off Vs Derby
393	Michael Moczul, Corby	Tony Cottee	Leicester V Leeds 2000
394	Kevin Wesson, Twickenham	Frank Worthington	Shrewsbury 1982
395	Paul Tompkins, Kettering	Steve Walsh	Leicester V Brentford 1984 (4-2)
396	Michael Parker, Leicester	Frank Worthington	QPR FA Cup Quarter Final - 1974
397	Gary Patrick, Leicestershire	Gary Lineker	Leicester V Cambridge (5-0)
398	David Dewsbury, Leicester	Frank Worthington	Derby at Wembley
399	Richard Gibson, Shepshed	Steve Walsh	Derby 1994
400	Ben Scanlan, Loughborough	Steve Walsh	Derby 0 - Leicester 4
401	Cyril Sharman, N/A	N/A	N/A
402	Richard Bramley, Bristol	Gary Lineker	Shrewsbury 1982
403	Tony T Pearce, Leicester	Keith Weller	Shrewsbury 1982
404	Richard Hall, Peterborough	Steve Walsh	Leicester V Cambridge (5-0)
405	Richard Smith, Bury, Lancs	Muzzy Izzet	Derby at Wembley
406	Mick Smith, Wigston Magna	Gary Coatsworth	Man City 1968 Cup Replay
407	Kevin Lewis, Leicester	Frank Worthington	Crystal Palace Play Off Final
408	Barry Allen, Rothwell - Northants	Frank Worthington	Liverpool 1972
409	Steve & Kate Sharpe, Ashby De La Zouch	N/A	Derby Play Off Final
410	Jeff Anderson, Birstall	Frank Worthington	Derby - Wembley 1994
411	Adrian Hyde, Telford	Keith Weller	Man City FA Cup 1967/68
412	Shaun Goodwin, Syston	Pontus Kåmark	Tranmere Rovers
413	Oliver Keene, Leicester	Gary Lineker	Tranmere Rovers 2000
414	David Barker, Somerby	Frank Worthington	N/A
415	David White, Coalville	Gary Lineker	Derby Play Off Final - 1994
416	Barry Orton, Leicester	Keith Weller	Luton Cup Tie
417	Allan Thraves, London	Jimmy Walsh	Derby County Play Off
418	N/A, N/A	N/A	N/A
419	Richard Willcocks, Sileby	Frank Worthington	1997 Coca Cola Cup Final Replay
420	Mark Holmes, Leicester	Gary Lineker	Middlesbrough Coca Cola Cup Replay
421	Peter Berry, Leamington Spa	Keith Weller	Shrewsbury FA Cup (5-2)
422	Ian Andrew Shuter, Northampton	Keith Weller	Liverpool Away - 1998
423	Alistair Marvell, Leicester	Tommy Wright	Crystal Palace Play Off Final
424	Paul Sharman, Kettering	Steve Walsh	Arsenal 1997 (3-3)
425	Nigel I Spiers, Leicester	Julian Joachim/David Nish	Leyton Orient 1962
426	Jean Allsopp, Derby	Robbie Savage	Cup Final 2000
427	Donald Martin, Bleasby - Notts	Keith Weller	Man City FA Cup 1967/68
428	Stephen Martin, Bleasby - Notts	Steve Walsh	Crystal Palace Play Off Final
429	Brian Smith, Leicester		Middlesbrough Coca Cola Cup Replay
430	Tony Randell, Sileby	Arthur Rowley	Grimsby 1949
431	Anna Stead, Leicester	Frank Worthington	Derby Play Off Final
432	Findley Neale, Glenfield	Neil Lennon	Shrewsbury 1982
433	Diane Brandrick, Leicester	Matt Elliott	Coca Cola Cup Final
434	Carl Oughton, Brent Knoll - Somerset	Peter Shilton	Shrewsbury FA Cup Quarter Final
435	Paul Dale, Desford - Leics	Robbie Savage	Arsenal 1997
436	Graham West, Ruschlikon - Switzerland	Keith Weller	Swindon 1993
437	Malcolm Sansome, Market Harborough	Frank Worthington	Tranmere Cup Final
438	Chris Atkins, Burbage	Steve Walsh	Derby Play Off Final
439	Richard Whittington, Leicester	Frank Worthington	Shrewsbury FA Cup 1982
440	Linda Kirman, Leicester	Tommy Wright	Derby at Wembley
441	Brian Flower, Hinckley	Frank Worthington	Shrewsbury FA Cup
442	Angela Brown, Syston	Gordon Banks	Derby at Wembley 1994
443	Fred Walker, Leicester	Dave Gibson	Cambridge - May 1992
444	Kay Walker, Leicester	Russell Osman	Derby - May 1994
445	Ian Walker, Leicester	Gary Lineker	Derby - May 1994
446	Helen Zealand, Sleaford	Muzzy Izzet	Play Off Final - 1996
447	Stephen Bowe, London	Tommy Wright	Cambridge - May 1992
448	Barrie Underwood, Rugby, Warwicks	Frank Worthington	Shrewsbury - 1982
449	Dave Sox, Sonning Common	Malcolm Clarke	The Next One
450	Raymond J Upton, Wigston Magna	Johnny Morris	Semi Final V Portsmouth.
451	Michael Hryniszak, Leicester	Keith Weller	Crystal Palace Play Off Final
452	Scott Ferrar, Leicester	Emile Heskey	Derby (4-0)
453	Graham Jordison, Clitheroe	Gary Lineker	Crystal Palace Play Off Final
454	Ian Hafford, Leicester	Mike Stringfellow	Stoke City League Cup Final 1964
455	Anthony R Owen, Broughton Astley	Gary Lineker	Derby Play Off Final
456	Andy Wells, London - SE4	Keith Weller	Shrewsbury - 1982
457	Bob Wells, Loughborough	Jon Sammels	West Ham - 1966
458	Mick Horn, Clifton Campville	Steve Walsh	Arsenal - 1998
459	David Bryans, Loughborough	Gary Lineker	Leicester v Arsenal (3-3)
460	Stuart Collings, Leicester	Steve Lynex	Man City FA Cup Replay 1967/68
461	Stuart Coe, Leicester	Steve Walsh	Derby Play Off Final - 1994
462	Barry Hudson, Sileby	Steve Walsh	M'boro Coca Cola Cup Replay
463	Iain Jones, Leicester	Frank Worthington	1997 League Cup at Sheffield
464	Martin Boot, Leicester	Frank Worthington	Tranmere - 2000
465	Brian Bale, Woodville	Frank Worthington	Derby County - Wembley 1994

BLOOMFIELD, James Henry
> If, under David Halliday and Matt Gillies, the predominant dressing-room accent was Scottish, then under Jimmy it became Cockney. Expensive exiles from London clubs abounded as Jimmy waved the City cheque-book around with effective abandon and built a superbly entertaining First Division side in the early and mid-70s. Leicester at that time were essentially a 'nearly' team: always threatening to gain a place in European competition yet, somehow, finding 7th to be their highest end-of-season ranking, and a semi-final replay defeat their best FA Cup performance. Jimmy's oft-expressed penchant for attacking football was nonetheless interpreted with some intriguing and genuinely aesthetic variations by his adventurous teams, and regular (if inconsistent) displays of pace and improvisatory skill were almost ample compensation for the lack of success in the eyes of City fans – who turned on him only when his side failed to fulfil for the sixth time the high expectations he'd engendered. His man-management abilities were always going to be tested by the blend of quicksilver, maverick and occasionally temperamental stars under his wing at Filbert Street, but Jimmy usually coped admirably; and while his occasional tactical experiments were usually progressively intended, he generally seemed less inclined to impose rigid formations than to invest in sheer flair. Curiously, he only ever selected four non-Englishmen during his time at Leicester (Sjoberg, Manley, Waters and Alderson), and the last-named was the only one he purchased.

Jimmy (b. Kensington, 15.2.1934; d. London, 3.4.1983) started his playing career as a constructive inside-forward with Hayes, and went on to give fine service between 1952 and 1969 with Brentford (twice), Arsenal, Birmingham City, West Ham, Plymouth Argyle and Orient, amassing 496 League appearances and claiming 93 goals; and even managed to play in two Fairs Cup Finals (for London and Birmingham). Graduating to the managerial office at Orient in 1969, he pointed his team to the Third Division championship, and a year later found himself preparing Leicester for their FA Charity Shield win and their return to the top flight. Following his Filbert Street tenure, Jimmy returned to Orient as boss, but ill-health forced him to retire prematurely, and he was acting as a part-time Luton Town scout at the time of his tragically early death.

BROMILOW, Thomas George
> Tom prepared newly-relegated City for a Second Division campaign throughout the overcast summer of 1939, saw the official season abandoned after only three games on the outbreak of war, and stayed at the helm throughout the difficult days of regionalised wartime competition until May 1945. To him fell the twin tasks of keeping the club going as a morale booster on the home front, and coping with the vicissitudes of fielding eleven recognised footballers each week; and it was to his credit that sufficient attractive 'guest' players (with a vital supporting cast of old hands and youthful colts) turned out in the blue and white during that period to fulfil both functions. Given also that the spine of his team (plus a majority of his Board!) was subject to a year's suspension from the start of 1940/1 for the previous regime's financial misdemeanours, Tom earns a fair share of retrospective kudos for keeping the club alive through one of its darkest hours.

Tom (b. Liverpool, 7.10.1894; d. Nuneaton, 4.3.1959) had an eleven-year, 341-game playing career as a constructive left-half at Anfield during the immediate post-WW1 seasons, and was recognised as the on-field brains behind Liverpool's championship wins of 1922 and 1923. He won five England caps and represented the Football League on six occasions, then turned to management: at Burnley (where he discovered Tommy Lawton), in Holland, and then twice at Crystal Palace. Tom joined City from Selhurst, and left them for Newport County, where he remained until resigning in January 1950. He was back at Filbert Street from the following July as chief scout, and also did some coaching with the A-team. He was returning from a talent-spotting mission for City at a Welsh Cup tie when he died suddenly. His son George was an England amateur international who played League football for Southport in the mid-50s.

BULLOCK, Norman
> The man who bought Arthur Rowley, and who pointed City to their first postwar promotion, as champions in 1954 – right on course for the five-year plan of progress he'd initially delineated to his Board and the press – Norman rather lost ontrol of his charges as the First Division adventure turned sour, and was hastily ushered out of his post in February 1955.

It was in September 1920 when a £10 signing-on fee to Sedgely Park landed young centre-forward Norman (b. Monkton, Manchester, 8.9.1900; d. Bushby, 27.10.1970) at Bury, and eighteen years before he left the Gigg Lane club whose League appearance record (506 games) he still holds, and whose aggregate scoring record he held until the 1980s, with 124 goals. Three times capped by England, he led the Shakers to promotion in 1924, and to 4th position in Division One two years later; briefly held the player/manager's dual responsibility; and then opted for management as a full-time activity in June 1935. His bid for complete control over the team, however, brought him into conflict with certain old-school Bury directors in 1938, and he promptly shifted allegiance to Chesterfield.

Norman had nonetheless been back with Bury for four years when he succeeded John Duncan at Leicester in the first week of December 1949, and he soon created something of a whirlwind of activity on the arrivals and departures front as he re-ordered both the playing and backroom staffs. His scouting net was cast wide (Matt Gillies, Johnny Morris and Jack Froggatt were among his other successful purchases after Rowley; Andy Graver the last of several conspicuously less so), but his style of man-management was becoming worrying to the Board, who had already given him notice that his contract would be terminated at the end of 1954/5, when incidents of indiscipline at a Whitley Bay hotel brought matters to a premature head. Norman's accordingly rolled. An analytical chemist before his football career commenced, he ran a printing business in Leicester following his adieu to the club and the game. His son Robin was a City A team outside-left in 1950/1, and a reserve from April 1952 to 1955, subsequently playing for Grantham Town and Brush Sports.

CLARK, William D
> A former Burton Wanderers centre-half, who became successively a club committee man and then secretary/manager of the Bungs, Billy headed the Midland League executive in 1891/2 and was also a referee, taking charge of Fosse's first-ever Midland League game against Derby Junction that season. He'd held a backroom position at Derby County for two years before being appointed to the Fosse post when the club became a Limited Company in 1897, and thereafter evinced both an eye for gimmickry and a rather more worrying blind eye for League and FA rules. He arranged baseball games at Filbert Street, plus a series of 100-yard handicap races for footballers; and even pitched the club's champion sprinter, Billy Dorrell, into a 440-yard challenge with a visiting American athlete prior to the kick-off of the February 1898 home game with Darwen. He saw no less than six of his players given their cards by the Fosse directorate that same month for undisclosed (but almost certainly alcohol-related) disciplinary reasons, but the culmination of his own slightly anarchic approach to authority would come at the start of the following season. After being found guilty of poaching Loughborough 'keeper Godfrey Beardsley, and conspiring with Billy Rowley, Stoke's secretary and former goalie, to pay the latter (a re-registered amateur) a signing-on fee to play for Fosse, he got himself fined and suspended indefinitely from all football involvement by the FA. When his ban was eventually rescinded, at his second petitioning, Billy found himself back in Burton, with the reins of the amalgamated United, between 1901 and 1904. He was still dogged by controversy, though: in February 1905, he sued Burton United for outstanding wages and expenses. Their retort was that they'd sacked him for transferring a player to Bristol Rovers (who, as a Southern League team, needed to pay no fee) instead of to fellow League club Bristol City (who'd have had to pay)!

DUNCAN, John
> See main players' index.

FORD, Louis
> A real veteran of football administration by the time he found himself floundering at Leicester during 1914/15, when Fosse were poverty-stricken in both financial and playing terms, Louis was a remnant of a far more gentlemanly era of the game, and ill-suited to the maelstrom of conflict infecting the club and football as a whole as Britain went to war. Wednesbury-born, he was an amateur player with Great Bridge Unity, becoming their secretary in 1885. He became honorary financial secretary of West Bromwich Albion from 1887, their general secretary/manager from 1890-92, and then a director until 1896. In that year he joined Walsall as secretary, and by 1900 was acting as a League referee. He was on the Football League Management committee from its inception, serving as Vice-President between 1894-97, and was also an FA Councillor from 1890-93. With this notable background, albeit distant, it was somewhat ironic that Louis would resign his Fosse post as a direct result of a League commission's report on the 'difficulties' between the club's executive and its players. Postwar, he was noted as chairman of Walsall Sports Club in the mid-20s. He had much earlier distinguished himself, at the very foundation of League football in 1888, by proposing the motion that only victories should count towards the League table, and opposing the granting of one point for a draw!

GARDNER, Frank
> See main players' index.

GILLIES, Matthew Muirhead
> See main players' index.

HALLIDAY, David
> Stirring a few more Scots into the playing blend inherited from Norman Bullock, and keeping a much firmer grip on them, David took two seasons to get City back into the top flight after their tumble in 1955 – and his championship-winning side of 1957 proved a record-breaking one as well, as they piled on the goals and considerably heightened the Filbert Street entertainment quotient. That David clearly cared more to see his team going forward than defending with any particularly rigorous security was a trait which, perhaps inevitably, would lead to his downfall when First Division attacks began exploiting the gaps his tactical plans simply didn't cover.

The origins of his attacking inclinations are not hard to pin down. As a player, David (b. Dumfries, 11.12.1897; d. Aberdeen, January 1970) was a centre-forward who scorched his way goalwards with admirable regularity. His football in the immediate post-WW1 era was played with Queen of the South, St Mirren and Dundee, and he won selection for the Scottish League against the Football league in 1924. Then he came south of the border, claiming 153 League goals for Sunderland at a rate of only a little under one-per-game, and earning a £6,000 move to Arsenal. He could not, however, maintain a regular place at Highbury, and exactly half his League goals as a Gunner came in one match against City: the remarkable 6-6 Filbert Street draw of 1930 in which he netted four, and which proved to be his final outing before a transfer to Manchester City. For them he notched 47 goals, and for Clapton Orient a further 33, until taking the player/manager post at Yeovil & Petters United in 1935. He became boss at Aberdeen in January 1938, and had just led them to a first-ever Scottish title when taking the Leicester job in July 1955.

Several of his former Pittodrie charges joined him at Filbert Street over the next few years and he also introduced surprise packages like Willie Gardiner to the City scene as no less than 19 of his 31 recruits for City turned out to be Scots. David took much due credit for his marshalling of the 1957 promotion side, and at least ensured last-gasp First Division survival the following term (with bold team changes securing an essential final-game result at Birmingham); but his days were numbered as soon as 1958/9 started shaping as a similar uphill struggle. He left 'by mutual agreement' in the first week of November, only two days after receiving a vote of confidence from new chairman Tom Bloor, and had soon taken over the running of an Aberdeen hotel. David's brother William was with Queen of the South, Newcastle and Third Lanark in the 20s; his brother John with Lincoln City and Doncaster Rovers in the 30s.

HAMILTON, Bryan
> Brought in by City to work in tandem with Gordon Milne and attempt to reverse the mid-80s pattern of First Division brinksmanship, Bryan got off to a fine start as his infectious enthusiasm caught the imagination of both the Leicester crowd and, unfortunately less sustainedly, his playing staff. His initial months in the Team Manager's post saw City move into the top half of the Division One table for the first time in a decade, yet by the end of that switchback 1986/7 campaign the club found itself relegated; and Bryan, then working solo, proved unable to halt a slide that threatened to lead to the ignominy of the Third Division. Twice he broke the club transfer record, in signing Steve Moran and Mike Newell, but there was otherwise little conviction evident in either his team-building dealings or his attempts at morale-raising motivation.

Bryan Hamilton

Bryan (b. Belfast, 21.12.1946) started his playing career with Distillery, and earned the first of his 50 Northern Ireland caps while starring for Linfield, before Ipswich Town won the race for his in-demand attacking midfield services in August 1971. Over four years and 153 League games later, Everton paid a substantial fee to take him to Goodison, and he appeared in the 1977 League Cup Final before moving on to Millwall and Swindon Town. Contemplating retirement at this stage, and having a brief spell in New Zealand with Christchurch United, he then took the player/manager's role at Tranmere Rovers, and clocked up another 109 League games before hanging up his boots. Working on the proverbial shoestring, Bryan saw through several crises at Prenton Park before leaving in February 1985 to take the reins at Wigan Athletic. A Freight/Rover Trophy win at Wembley was the highlight of his stay there, and in June 1986, after impressing on a World Cup TV panel with his easy manner and analytical shrewdness, he topped the shortlist for the City manager's position.

Questions over the precise division of responsibilities between the new man and General Manager Gordon Milne were temporarily shelved as City made their best start to a campaign for years, but the rapport Bryan built with the fans was not matched by that with his players as City tumbled. He survived a boardroom vote of confidence following relegation and Milne's departure, but thereafter dissension in the dressing-room soon became evident, and there was visible distaste from several players over the positional and tactical roles they were being asked to perform. City were in desperate straits when, unsurprisingly, the axe fell on Bryan in December 1987. Shortly afterwards, he seemed to have tacitly admitted his limitations as a track-suited boss when returning to Wigan as chief executive, but he later re-assumed control of team matters at Springfield Park until March 1993. Eleven months out of the game followed, until Bryan was chosen to succeed Billy Bingham as Northern Ireland's national manager: a post he held until October 1997. He then joined the Ipswich coaching staff, and became Director of Football at Norwich City in June 1998, first working with, and then succeeding, Bruce Rioch, until resigning in December 2000.

HODGE, Peter

> Rightly regarded as the primary architect of City's rise to First Division respectability in the 20s, Peter clearly commanded greater respect from his Board than his Fosse predecessors had done in the same nominal joint role of secretary/manager, and equally clearly exercised a greater degree of autonomy in his involvement with matters of recruitment, selection and tactics. Though he was not actually at the helm for the pinnacle years of City's championship pursuit, he had gradually built up many of the systems and much of the side which saw the club go so close to its grail.

Born in Leith (ca 1871), but soon making his home in Dunfermline, Peter entered football administration with a local juvenile team in 1890, then became secretary of Dunfermline Juniors, who he took to the Final of the Scottish Junior Cup in 1897. At about this time he commenced a ten-year stint of refereeing in the Scottish League, in 1906 became the honorary secretary (or 'quill-driver') of Dunfermline Athletic, and was given life membership of the Scottish Junior FA after eight years on its Council. Raith Rovers appointed him as their first manager in April 1907, and he remained at Starks Park until October 1912, when an ambitious director ousted him only two years after he'd taken Raith into the top flight, and despite an encomium from *The Scottish Referee* which characterised him as 'genial, pawky and far-seeing; sagacious in council and resolute in action'. In June 1914 he took over at Stoke, and led them to the top of the Southern League's Second Division. They promptly applied for election back to the League, and were successful runners-up to Fosse in the voting, though the wartime break meant that they then could not take their place until 1919. By this time, Peter was back in Scotland, initially working in the Army Pay Office in Perth, then, once more, as manager of Raith, who he rebuilt towards peacetime football from October 1916 onwards.

After the reconstruction of Leicester City, the new Board began negotiations for Peter to take over at Filbert Street almost immediately, and the formalities were undergone during the first two weeks of September 1919. Not surprisingly, the new boss returned north of the border for a fair proportion of his key signings; several of whom (like the Duncan brothers) had experienced his guidance at Raith. Peter experimented and dabbled shrewdly in the bargain end of the market (for Arthur Chandler, for instance) with a single-minded aim to get City into Division One; yet his appreciation of the finer points of football artistry never left him. He finally turned out a side of Second Division champions in 1925, and altered it only slightly into one which consolidated its new, elevated status. Then, however, in May 1926, Peter was tempted away by Manchester City, who had reached the previous term's FA Cup Final, but had also been relegated. His new charges missed out by one place on an instant return, but were promoted as champions next time out, and Peter also led them to a third-place finish in the top flight during a Maine Road stint further distinguished by his signing of the young Matt Busby. Yet, in 1932, he proved unable to resist an SOS call from Filbert Street, where City were perilously close to the drop.

Peter Hodge

He confirmed his return in mid-February, but could not leave Manchester City until their own fate was decided, and ultimately took over again at Leicester at the end of March, after Manchester City's FA Cup exit at the semi-final stage. The stars of City's recent heyday were now ageing, and replacements of a similar calibre were hard to come by on a limited budget. Peter nonetheless helped them stay up by the skin of their teeth in 1932 and 1933, lifted them two places to 17th in 1934, and also gave Leicester its first taste of an FA Cup semi-final during that latter term. Tragically, however, he suffered illness during preparations for 1934/5, and died in Perth, on a visit to his mother, on 18th August. A typical obituary deemed him to have 'worked perhaps in a quieter and less flamboyant manner than Mr Chapman, of Arsenal fame, but his eye for a footballer was not a whit less keen'.

JACKSON, Henry S

> 'Swin' Jackson was a hard-working pioneer of West Bromwich Albion's rise to prominence. A clerk to the local magistrates, and a Staffordshire cricketer, he chaired the West Brom committee from 1885-88, was on their initial Board of Directors from 1891-93, and was their general secretary from 1892-94. As the Fosse figurehead he was also the servant to a committee (one damningly described as 'hamstrung by cliques'), for it was not until the end of his second term at Filbert Street that the club took the step of becoming a Limited Company, after he'd only nominally presided over two fairly nondescript Second Division campaigns. 'Swin' then became secretary to Luton Town, and later emigrated to Canada, where he became a parish registrar and postmaster.

JOHNSON, George

> The longest-serving of Fosse's secretary/managers, George had originally been a rugby follower, and a former honorary secretary of the Leicester branch of the National Cyclists' Union. Even his initial attachment to the Fosse came about obliquely via other sporting interests, for he had run their then-annual fund-raising Sports Days for a few years before he took on the task of steadying Fosse's football fortunes (and restoring their administrative respectability) after the damaging scrapes of the Billy Clark management. George clearly left the bulk of responsibility for on-field matters to his trainers and senior pros (and Fosse experimented during his near 14-year tenure with both Jimmy Blessington and Andy Aitken in player/manager roles); while team selection was still then seen essentially as the jealously-guarded province of the directorate. The respect in which he was held within the game, however, was iinstanced when, upon George's retirement to concentrate on a printing business partnership, Bradford City and a Steve Bloomer XI met in a Filbert Street friendly for his

No.	Name / Home Town	Fav. LCFC player	Fav. LCFC game
466	Tony Fezz Hart, Measham	Frank Worthington	Derby County - Wembley 1994
467	Robert Brewin, Leicester	Keith Weller	Man City FA Cup Replay 1967/68
468	David Lenton, Blaby	Frank Worthington	Shrewsbury FA Cup Q/F 1982
469	N/A	N/A	N/A
470	Simon Aldis, London	Steve Walsh	Derby County Play Off Final
471	Matthew Norman, Wigston - Leicester	Gary Lineker	Liverpool (3-3)
472	Roger Hawes, Loughborough	Gordon Banks	1963 Semi Final
473	Christopher Lewitt, Leicester	Graham Cross	Man City FA Cup 1967/68
474	Martin Whitmore, Kenilworth	Emile Heskey	Derby Play Off Final
475	Gary Stone, Thurmaston	Gary Lineker	Shrewsbury FA Cup Q/F 1982
476	David Reilly, Leicester	Steve Walsh	Cambridge - May 1992
477	Geoff Jones, Leicester	Sep Smith	Arsenal 1997
478	Eric Cox, Stafford	N/A	N/A
479	Kevin Durkin, Leicester	Lenny Glover	Manchester City 1968
480	Ollie Coker, Desborough	Steve Walsh	Arsenal 1997
481	Michael Race, Warwickshire	N/A	N/A
482	Peter Humphrey, Leicester	Gordon Banks	Manchester United 1961
483	Andrew Mayneord, Alcester	Peter Shilton	Crystal Palace @ Wembley
484	Robert Smith, Loughborough	Frank Worthington	Crystal Palace Play Off Final
485	Tony Worn, Quorn - Loughborough	Steve Walsh	Shrewsbury Cup 1982
486	Russell Woodward, Coalville	Gary Lineker	Derby Play Off Final
487	Gary Branston, Leicester	Steve Walsh	Derby Play Off Final
488	Gordon Riley, London - Holland Park	Arthur Rowley	Manchester United
489	David Moss, Melton Mowbray	N/A	N/A
490	Geoffrey Brown, Syston - Leicester	Gary Lineker	Manchester City
491	Steve Radwan, London	Frank Worthington	Play Off Final 1994
492	Richard Taylor, Leicester	Jack Froggatt	Manchester City 1968
493	Richard Rogers, Leicestershire	Gary Lineker	Tranmere Cup Final
494	Pete Rosen, Leicester	N/A	N/A
495	Nellie Moore, Castle Donington	Steve Walsh	Worthington Cup
496	Marc Gunby, Walthamstow - London	Frank Worthington	Shrewsbury FA Cup Tie
497	Brain Stanforth, Kettering	Gordon Banks	Wembley
498	Ben Roskrow, Abbots Langley	Frank Worthington	Shrewsbury FA Cup 1981
499	Gary Edwards, Oswestry	Frank Worthington	Shrewsbury FA Cup 1982
500	Paul Lees, Australia	N/A	N/A
501	Rob Gahan, Broughton Astley	David Gibson	Derby Play Off Final
502	David Layhe, Worksop	Gary Lineker	League Cup Final Replay
503	Chris Denny, Northampton	Robbie Savage	Worthington Cup Final 2000
504	Martyn Bailey, Enderby	Muzzy Izzet	Cambridge Play Offs
505	Maurice Allen, Leicester	Frank Worthington	Play Off Final 1994
506	Andrew King, Leicester	Frank Worthington	M'boro Coca Cola Cup Replay
507	Mark Joe Stratford, Rugby	Frank Worthington	Crystal Palace Play Off Final
508	Peter Ross, Leicester	Keith Weller	Crystal Palace Play Off Final
509	Chris Walker, Sheffield	Keith Weller	Derby County Play Off Final
510	Andrew Price, Hinckley	Mike Whitlow	Shrewsbury FA Cup 1/4 Final
511	Richard Moody, London	Gordon Banks	Arsenal 1961
512	Malcolm Kisby, Leicester	Mal Griffiths	Crystal Palace Play Off Final
513	Terence Robinson, Leicester	Arthur Rowley	Crystal Palace Play Off Final
514	Mark Young, Leicester	Steve Walsh	Derby Play Off Final
515	David Pitcher, Market Harborough	Keith Weller	Shrewsbury FA Cup Q/F 1982
516	Rob Norman, Leicester	Rodney Fern	Wimbledon Play Off Final
517	Christopher Redway, Leicester	Keith Weller	Coca Cola Cup Final 1997
518	Clive Gunby, Orpington	Steve Walsh	Crystal Palace Play Off Final
519	Andrew Clarke, Leicester	Gary Lineker	Derby 1998
520	Chris Lymn, Leicester	Gary Lineker	League Cup Final 96/97
521	Iain Matthews, Leicester	Steve Walsh	Coca Cola Cup Final 1997
522	Peter Nunwa, London	Keith Weller	Derby 1994
523	Reid Anderson, Halifax, West Yorks	David Nish	Manchester City FA Cup 1968
524	David Arch, Bourne, Lincs	Frank Worthington	Southampton 1998
525	Lee Middleton, Leicester	Gary Lineker	Shrewsbury FA Cup 1982
526	Phil Preston, Swannington	Arthur Rowley	Cambridge Play Offs 1992
527	Andrew Gale, Leicester	Matt Elliott	Derby Play Off Final
528	Dominic Manning, Newmarket	Muzzy Izzet	Sunderland 2000
529	Chris Harrison, Earl Shilton	Frank Worthington	Shrewsbury FA Cup 6th Round
530	Brian R M Playfair, Motherwell, Scotland	David Gibson	Derby at Wembley
531	Melvyn Bailey, Leicester	Frank Worthington	Atletico Madrid - Away 1997
532	David Smith, Mountsorrel	Steve Walsh	N/A
533	Steve Scott, Leicester	Larry May	Crystal Palace Play Off Final
534	Robert Rylott, N/A	N/A	N/A
535	Richard Pye, Leicester	Steve Walsh	Middlesbrough Cup Replay 1997
536	Paul Marcus, Camberley - Surrey	Gary Lineker	Tranmere Cup Final
537	Julia Ball, Stevenage	Steve Claridge	Play Off Final 1995
538	Simon Cruickshank, Corby	Gary Lineker	Shrewsbury
539	Mick Bucknall, Burton Upon Trent	Gordon Banks	Derby 0 Leicester 4
540	Adrian Berridge, Oakham	N/A	N/A
541	Ian Cole, Market Harborough	Mark Wallington	M'boro Coca Cola Cup Replay
542	Gordon Cole, Market Harborough	Don Revie	Wolves 1963
543	Michael Turner, Narborough - Leicester	Keith Weller	Shrewsbury FA Cup 1982
544	Richard Santy, Leicester	Steve Walsh	Derby Play Off Final
545	Andrew Waterfield, Glasgow	Frank Worthington	Middlesbrough League Cup
546	Neddy Needham, Greenhill, Coalville	Frank Worthington	Middlesbrough Replay
547	Kathryn Thompson, Letchworth	David Nish	Shrewsbury FA Cup
548	Jonathan Bailey, Shepshed	Keith Weller	Liverpool 1984
549	Geoff Owen, Market Harborough	Peter Shilton	Worthington Cup Final 2000
550	Chris Spencer, Markfield, Leicester	Steve Walsh	Shrewsbury FA Cup 1/4 Final
551	Andy Pateman, Leicester	Steve Walsh	Shrewsbury FA Cup
552	Scott Tranmer, Catterick, N. Yorks,	Steve Guppy	Worthington Cup Final 2000
553	Martyn Webb, Princes Risborough	Frank Worthington	Shrewsbury FA Cup
554	Mark Norman, Great Glen	Gary Lineker	Sunderland 2000
555	John McKinnen, Leicester	Gary McAllister	Arsenal 1997
556	John Patrick, Leicester	N/A	N/A
557	Ian Franklin, N/A	N/A	N/A
558	Ray Garner, Wigston, Leicester	Robbie Savage	Tottenham 2001
559	Preston Family, Kenilworth	Steve Walsh	Oxford 1991

Gordon Lee

benefit in March 1913. George was also penning a column for the *Mercury* at this time under the byline of 'Old Official', and first mentioned here the crying need for the club's reconstruction as early as March 1914. He published his reminiscences of the Fosse era in the *Leicester Sports Mail* from October 1927 onwards.

LEE, Gordon Francis

> A short-term appointment with a far-reaching effect on the club, Gordon presided over the 'Great Escape' of 1991, when the final day's results at Filbert Street and Twerton Park combined to keep City out of Division Three, and bought time for the subsequent assaults on top-flight status. David Pleat's coach since January 1988, Gordon was handed a caretaker role in January 1991, was named as manager in March, was replaced by Brian Little at the end of May, and departed a week later. He bought no-one, and gave no player a debut: but he gave a distinctly demoralised team a sufficient extra boost in self-belief, and enough extra space for self-expression, to get them to halt what could so easily have been the most damaging decline in the club's entire history – right on the precipice.

Gordon (b. Cannock, 13.7.1934) was for eleven years and 118 League games an Aston Villa defender, and featured in the League Cup Finals of 1961 and 1963. He took a player/coach role at Shrewsbury Town in July 1966 (briefly guiding winger David Pleat a year later), and commenced his managerial career with Port Vale in June 1968, taking them to the Third Division title in 1971. His one term at Blackburn Rovers (1974/5) also ended in promotion to Division Two; while Newcastle United reached the League Cup Final under his management in the following season. One year on, and it was Everton he was leading out at Wembley in the same competition; and Gordon remained at Goodison until 1981. He was Preston North End boss from 1981-83, then coached and managed abroad in climes as disparate as those of Saudi Arabia and Iceland. Indeed, he had been managing KR Reykjavik when reunited with Pleat at Filbert Street. On leaving Leicester, he stated with dignity that he'd never had to apply for a job in football in his life, and wasn't then about to start.

LEE, J

> Frustratingly, and rather ludicrously, we have still been unable to discover any biographical details whatsoever for the first 'professional' secretary/manager Fosse ever appointed from beyond the ranks of their own committee, and the man who oversaw the club's crucial first campaign in the Football League. We know he had the respect of his players, who clubbed together to buy him a commemorative gold medal on his departure; but no amount of scouring the local and sporting press of the time has brought forth even so much as a forename for the gentleman, and no hint of his background beyond the fact that he was still a Leicester resident, and a keen bowls player, in 1930.

LINNEY, Harry

> In managerial terms, Leicester-born Harry was almost as much an unknown quantity. He was the Fosse director who took over the secretary/manager's role on Louis Ford's departure, and led the successful petition to the League for re-election to Division Two at the end of 1914/15; only to find that his nominal *pro tem* appointment actually stretched four years, throughout the entire period of WW1 football. On the club's 1919 reconstruction, Harry – self-described on registration documents as a cotton manufacturer – became a founder director of Leicester City and gladly gave up his figurehead responsibilities to Peter Hodge. He was still on the City board when he died of diabetes complications on 15th March 1924, reportedly at the age of only 41. At this point, he was described as a financier and partner in the Leicester firm of Arthur Geary & Co.

LITTLE, Brian

> The boss whose Blue Army thrice stormed Wembley in search of promotion-by-Play-Off, and who finally gave City their first taste of Premiership football, Brian deadpanned his way through an incredibly turbulent period of club history to infuse Filbert Street with a reawakened sense of progressivism, and the feelings of betrayal felt by supporters on his defection to Aston Villa were genuine. So too, though, were some unanswered questions about his tenure, or more specifically about the contradictions of his success. How many City managers would still have been in post to savour the third-time-lucky glory of the elevating win over Derby if they'd previously finished Second Division campaigns with placings of 4th, 6th and 4th and there had been no Play-Off safety net? Which other managers would have seemed so reticent to buttress their squads with players they hadn't previously coached or managed? Which would have so often watched their admittedly classy midfield swamped in numbers for the sake of fielding a flat back-five? On the other hand, was it luck or judgement which oversaw the emergence of Julian Joachim, the conversion of Steve Walsh and the eventually or immediately justified acquisitions of Jimmy Willis or Mark Draper? And was it just wretched fortune with injuries (Speedie, Walsh, Joachim) that derailed his Premiership challenge? Or could it simply be that disappointment at his departure (inevitable under the circumstances of his Villa background) tended to retrospectively diminish his substantial achievements in restoring a proud spine to the club?

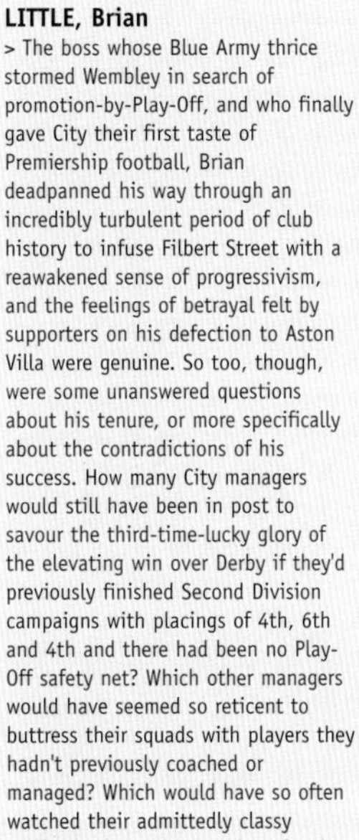

Brian Little

Brian (b. Durham, 25.11.1953) was a Villa Park apprentice from July 1969, and then had ten years there as a pro from March 1971 until his injury-enforced premature retirement from the striking line. He'd been in Villa's Youth Cup-winning side of 1972, their League Cup-winning teams of 1975 and 1977, and had top-scored in their 1975 promotion campaign. His England career had unluckily amounted to only one outing as an 80th-minute substitute against Wales in May 1975, but it was greater mischance that knee injuries effectively wrecked his advancement only a few years later, when he was stuck on a career aggregate of 82 senior goals. He became a coach with Wolves in January 1986, and managed them from August to October of that year before being unceremoniously dumped when they recruited Graham Turner. He then coached Middlesbrough's reserve and youth teams before becoming boss at Darlington in February 1989. Brian couldn't save the Quakers from relegation to the Conference a matter of months later, but chivvied them straight back into the League in 1990, and to the Division Four championship in 1991; at which point City chairman Martin George tempted him to Filbert Street.

For some months after Brian's move back to Villa Park, it looked like his new charges might accompany City in the Premiership drop zone, but they survived, and he was soon flourishing Doug Ellis's cheque-book with some fervour (at the likes of Draper and Joachim amongst others) as he led them to top-five finishes and the capture of the League Cup in 1996. He resigned, however, in February 1998, and in the short time since has held the reins at each of Stoke City, West Bromwich Albion and Hull City. Brian's brother Alan was also in club management, most recently with Southend United, after six years bossing York City, and a playing career in the 70s and 80s with Villa, Southend, Barnsley, Doncaster, Torquay and Halifax.

LOCHHEAD, Arthur William

> See main players' index.

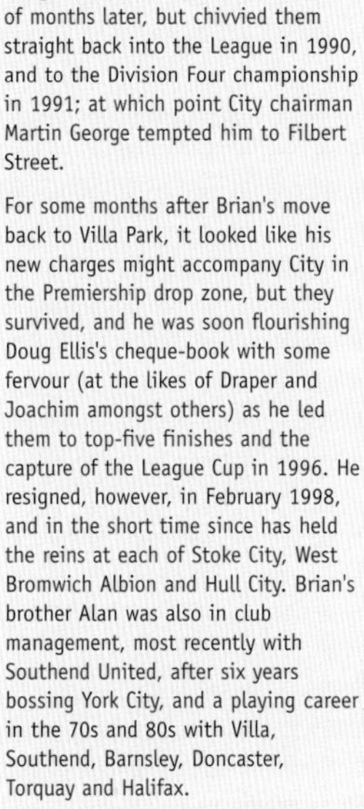

Arthur Lochhead

Mark McGhee

McGHEE, Mark Edward

> There were three main factors contributing to the widespread demonisation of Mark McGhee on his defection to Wolves. The first was the disappointment that City had lost a good young manager for the second time in twelve months; the second that he so publicly deemed comatose giants Wolves a more likely vehicle to express his own ambitions. The third, to give him his due, was that he was betraying exceptionally high hopes he himself had engendered among City's support in his year at the helm. While it's hard to take a perspective on Mark's management that isn't skewed by recall of the acrimony surrounding both his coming and going, it ought to be noted that he had something of a positive effect in the interim. Arriving from Reading with a reputation for favouring a purist passing game, but inheriting a side ill-equipped for instant tactical transformation, engaged as they were in mid-fall from the Premiership, he spent his first few months inspiring the odd bit of backs-to-the-wall revivalism, and fine-tuning for the future. The midfield (and getting City to play through it) was his priority area, with loan acquisition Mike Galloway's drive and Garry Parker's vision the initial introductions here, and his summer rebuilding also added Scott Taylor and Steve Corica to this key unit. The first Manager of the Month award of 1995/6 was outside acknowledgement of his success in remoulding the side, and establishing it on top of Division One after the first month of the campaign; while the first half of the November game at West Brom (on the day Pontus Kåmark and Zeljko Kalac were introduced) was the exemplar of his favoured style, and 45 minutes of the most fluent football seen from City in many a day. There were, of course, games in which the weaving of endless short-passing patterns was an inappropriate response to circumstances, and hence inconsistency was becoming a keynote, but it would have been intriguing to see Mark think his way round the need for more improvisation. His moonlight flit to Molineux scuppered such a prospect, and his subsequent inability to rouse Wolves to anywhere near convincing promotion pretense, despite his scattering of copious amounts of Sir Jack Hayward's cash, perhaps emphasised an enduring flaw in his game-plan. At any rate, after three years of under-achievement there, he was discarded in 1998; and found work only as a Coventry City scout until taking over at Millwall in September 2000, where he built a Second Division championship-winning side.

Mark (b. Glasgow, 20.5.1957) was a teenage Bristol City apprentice who had to move to Morton in 1975 for his first senior action. A sturdy but skilful striker, he had the first of two spells with Newcastle United from December 1977 to March 1979, then signed up at Aberdeen for five glory years in both Scottish and European football. In May 1984 he joined Hamburger SV for a 30-game, 7-goal Bundesliga stint, then returned to another major medal-haul with Celtic. In August 1989 Mark was back at St James's Park, and in May 1991 took over as player/manager at Reading; only hanging up his boots in May 1993, a year before the Division Two championship was secured. Mark's four Scottish caps were won in 1983/4, and he closed his active career on a tally of 170 senior goals.

McLINTOCK, Francis

> See main players' index.

MARSON, Ernest A

> An occasional goalkeeper for Fosse's second string in 1890/1, Ernest was elected from the club committee to succeed inaugural secretary Frank Gardner, and saw Fosse through the second and third Midland League campaigns before his honorary position became professionalised with the appointment of J Lee. Also a founder committee member of the Leicestershire FA, Ernest later acted as a League referee, and became a Fosse director following their assumption of Limited Company status in 1897. He resigned from the board in September 1898, however, in the wake of the Rowley and Beardsley affairs; and poor health forced a step down from County FA duties in 1903. He travelled in both the USA and South Africa to try to ameliorate problems with his lungs, but died in November 1912.

MATHER, Thomas

> City's boss for most of the transitional postwar season of 1945/6, Tom never so much as selected a team for League duty, was frustrated (predominantly by financial constraints) in attempting to rebuild a City side in the stylish image of his pre-war club teams, and resigned after only nine months in March 1946. His signing of classy playmaker Frank Soo indicated the sort of football he would wish a postwar City to play; but it was John Duncan who would lead the club into resumed Second Division combat.

Tom (b. Chorley, 1888; d. Stoke on Trent, 29.3.1957) had entered football administration in 1910, as secretary of Bolton Wanderers, and remained in post there throughout WW1, despite an interim spell in the Navy. A brief stint in the Manchester City office preceded his appointment as Southend United manager in May 1920, upon the mass election of Southern League clubs into the new Division Three, and

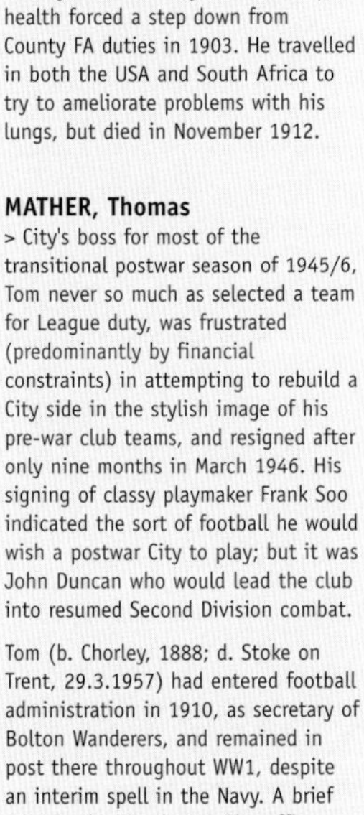

Tom Mather

he stayed at their then home, the Kursaal, until January 1922. Tom assumed the managerial position at Stoke in October 1923 (there giving Stanley Matthews his senior break); and was in charge of Newcastle United from June 1935 to the outbreak of WW2, during one of their Second Division slump periods. After leaving Leicester, he helmed Kilmarnock for part of 1947/8, but resigned in February for domestic reasons, returning to the Potteries to work in the catering industry.

MILNE, Gordon

> Decidedly less charismatic than his predecessor Jock Wallace, Gordon quietly edged City into the promotion frame at the end of his first campaign in charge, and somehow contrived to keep them in the top flight against the odds for three seasons, before closing the Leicester chapter of his career with a year as General Manager, working in harness with new team boss Bryan Hamilton. Gordon's public image throughout his stay was of a man whose first priority was to perform the increasingly difficult task of balancing the City books. His essentially safety-first approach to club management may well have been the most appropriate response to the shifting economic structure of modern top-flight football; but it also appeared to many supporters that perhaps Gordon gained rather more respect from the boardroom than he did from the dressing room, and certainly more than he did from the terraces. Nonetheless, he marshalled his on-field resources with relative success (prompting a winning consistency from inherited assets like Gary Lineker, and exploiting the versatility of others like Kevin MacDonald and Ian Wilson), and rode with dignity the storms of criticism which attended decisions like the Melrose/English swap, the failure to retain Gerry Daly, or the attempted conversion to full-back of seemingly the entire midfield complement.

A man with football in his blood, Gordon (b. Preston, 29.3.1937) started his senior playing career at Morecambe, but soon signed up at Deepdale, where his father Jimmy had been a pre-war star and was then manager. After 81 League games for Preston as a right-half, he moved to Anfield and took a regular berth in Bill Shankly's first great Liverpool side, helping them to promotion and on to two League championships, winning 14 England caps, and only moving on to Blackpool in 1967 after 236 League outings (18 goals). He became player/manager at Wigan Athletic in 1970, taking the Northern Premier League title a year later, and was additionally appointed England Youth coach prior to joining Coventry City in June 1972. Initially he partnered Joe Mercer there, then had a solo spell in charge, and was named chief executive when Dave Sexton arrived to assume team manager duties. He was as well used, therefore, to the system of dual responsibility which operated for the first time at Leicester in his final season, as he was to keeping a club of limited means in the First Division.

Some two months after his City contract expired in May 1987, Gordon surprised many by accepting an offer to manage Besiktas, but he had remarkable success there in becoming the longest-serving foreign coach of all time in Turkish football. League runners-up in 1988, Cup-winners in 1989, Double-winners in 1990 (with Ian Wilson in their line-up), they took further titles in the next two terms and then finished second on goal difference in 1993. Gordon left Ankara in November 1993, and next took an even more far-flung posting: managing Nagoya Grampus Eight in the J-League throughout most of 1994 (with Ian Wilson as coach) before departing at the same time as Gary Lineker. In June 1995 Gordon was appointed chief executive of the League Managers' Association, but was then twice tempted back to Turkey, with Bursaspor for 1996/7 and Trabzonspor for 1998/9. In November 1999 he joined the Newcastle United coaching staff under Bobby Robson.

O'FARRELL, Frank

> Narrowly winning the Board's vote over Allan Brown of Luton as City quickly sought a successor to Matt Gillies, Frank took over a relegation-bound team, yet led them to Wembley as a distinctly consoling diversion. The softly-spoken Irishman then remoulded the club for a rapid return to the top flight, achieved after two seasons on the basis of intelligent pragmatism (and a quick-break counter-attacking style, grounded in defensive frugality), when his management methods even justified the close, near-academic scrutiny of a series of educational documentary TV programmes. Perhaps unfortunately for a City set-up just about to re-engage with First Division requirements, Manchester United may have watched the latter, for they spirited Frank away with the proverbial offer he couldn't refuse.

Frank (b. Cork, 9.10.1927) was introduced to English football by West Ham United, who signed him as a wing-half from Cork United in January 1948. He soon became a Republic of Ireland international and, presciently, joined the unofficial Hammers 'Academy' then being informally tutored by teammate Malcolm Allison, along with other such future managerial luminaries as Noel Cantwell, John Bond and Ken Brown. After 197 League games, Frank moved on in November 1956 to Preston North End for 118 more, and then assumed the player/manager's role at Weymouth, who he eventually helmed to the Southern League title in 1965. Torquay United then stepped in to install Frank in their manager's chair, and it was from success at Plainmoor that he moved to Leicester. Several of his early City purchases were of questionable short-term value, but the signings of Bobby Kellard and Willie Carlin to energise and motivate the push to the 1971 Second Division championship were masterstrokes.

Frank and his coach Malcolm Musgrove (another ex-Hammer) were less happily employed at Old Trafford, where the shadow of Matt Busby and the insistence on instant success from a team in transition weighed heavily upon them, and moved on again after a year. Frank later took over at Cardiff for a crucial five months of anti-relegation struggle during 1973/4, had a spell coaching in Iran, and returned to Torquay for a further couple of management stints in the late 70s and early 80s.

O'NEILL, Martin Hugh Michael

> Receiving ever-mounting acclaim for his remarkable achievements with City, to the extent of near-deification from sections of the crowd, Martin increasingly imposed his personality on the team and the club as a whole, and accordingly wielded more influence on its direction and development than any of his predecessors. The record of playing success under his management was unparalleled, while his impact on boardroom politics and the entire structure of the club was unprecedented. Promotion, four top-ten Premiership finishes, and three League Cup Finals were the high-

No.	Name / Home Town	Fav. LCFC player	Fav. LCFC game
560	Richard Scotton, Rugby	Alan Woollett	Atletico Madrid - Away 1997
561	Stephen Ross, Leicester	Keith Weller	Shrewsbury FA Cup
562	Adrian Sergent, Leicester	Keith Weller	Liverpool
563	Ian Gelling, Leicester	Steve Walsh	N/A
564	Eileen Davis, Ratby - Leicester	Steve Walsh	Derby Play Off Final
565	Gary Murphy, Ratby - Leicester	Frank Worthington	Derby Play Off Final
566	Steve Harrison, Leicester	Steve Walsh	Shrewsbury FA Cup 1982
567	David Riddle, Melton Mowbray	Gary Lineker	Derby @ Wembley
568	Graham Johnson, Leicester	Arthur Rowley	Watford 1996
569	Paul Gary Ward, Leicester	Lenny Glover	Worthington Cup Final 2000
570	Bob & Penny McKnight, Ely, Cambs	Rodney Fern	Arsenal
571	Nigel Hancock, Leicester	Keith Weller	Hillsborough 1998 Cup
572	Andrew Knight, Raunds	Frank Worthington	Middlesbrough Cup Final Replay
573	Neil Kellett, Markfield	Frank Worthington	Shrewsbury Town FA Cup 1982
574	Mark Hoult, Ashby De La Zouch	Steve Walsh	Derby Play Off Final
575	Ian Stuart Matthams, Loughborough	Steve Walsh	Derby Play Off Final
576	Robert Hutchinson, Loughborough	Keith Weller	Liverpool 1972
577	Remesh Patel, Leicester	Steve Walsh	Shrewsbury Town FA Cup
578	Michael Iliffe, Eccleshall - Stafford	Muzzy Izzet	Middlesbrough @ Wembley
579	Paul Lymn, Leicester	Ali Mauchlen	Derby @ Wembley
580	Gary Beesley, Coalville, Leics	Keith Weller	Southampton 1966
581	John Hamilton, Leicester	Frank Worthington	Worthington Cup Final 2000
582	Paul Gudgeon, Broughton Astley	Mark Wallington	Shrewsbury FA Cup Q/F 1982
583	Steven Smith, Wigston, Leicester	Muzzy Izzet	N/A
584	Neil & Eleanor Jones, Sevenoaks	Robbie Savage	Bradford 1999 / 2000
585	Leicestershire County Libraries	N/A	N/A
586	Darren King, Leicester	Steve Walsh	Cambridge Utd Play Off Semi Final
587	Jim Knox, Bedford	Matt Elliott	Worthington Cup Final 2000
588	Adam & Jade Clarke, Glen Parva, Leicester	David Gibson	Man City FA Cup 1968
589	John Harris, Leicester	David Gibson	Derby Play Off Final
590	Derek Pearson, Leicester	Jimmy Goodfellow	Manchester City 1957
591	Barry Gregory, Leicester	Arthur Rowley	N/A
592	James Coe, Leicester	Steve Walsh	Cambridge
593	Ben Fletcher, London	Gary Lineker	Crystal Palace Play Off Final
594	Alan Worth, Swadlincote, Derbys	N/A	N/A
595	Malc Anderson, Leicester	Gordon Banks	Manchester City 1968
596	Paul Stacey, Thatcham, Berks	Steve Walsh	Orient Away
597	Simon Lane, Leicester	Lenny Glover	Derby Play Off Final
598	David Barradell, Sandiacre - Nottingham	Steve Walsh	Derby Play Off Final
599	Chris Barradell, Sandiacre - Nottingham	Steve Walsh	Arsenal 1997
600	Stuart Halsey, Moira	Muzzy Izzet	Crystal Palace @ Wembley 1996
601	Mick Harvey, Thurmaston, Leicester	Keith Weller	Derby Play Off Final
602	Glyn Jones, Cardiff	Gary Lineker	Coca Cola Cup Final 1997
603	Roger Brown, Wakefield	Frank Worthington	Man City FA Cup Replay 1967
604	Michael Scotney, Leicester	Keith Weller	FA Cup Semi Final 1969
605	Kevin Thorpe, Melton Mowbray	Frank Worthington	N/A
606	Daran Taylor, Portsmouth	Muzzy Izzet	Worthington Cup Final 2000
607	Nicholas Harris, Hereford	Gordon Banks	West Ham Away 1963 / 1964
608	Darren Henderson, Leicester	Gary McAllister	Arsenal 1998
609	Stephen Gretton	N/A	N/A
610	Mark Robinson, Thringstone	Keith Weller	Cambridge Play Off 1992
611	Richard Codd, Leicester	Steve Walsh	Crystal Palace 1996
612	Nicholas Early, Leicester	Keith Weller	Liverpool 1973
613	Nick Blackburn, Shepshed	Paul Matthews	Crystal Palace Play Off Final
614	Pete Mackintosh, Leicester	Gary Lineker	Shrewsbury Town
615	Steve Tutty, Staines	N/A	Crystal Palace Play Off Final
616	David Finch, Leicester	Steve Walsh	West Ham 1966
617	Keith Arnold, Leicester	Arthur Rowley	Pompey 1949
618	Mark Chawner, Leicester	Steve Walsh	Derby Play Off Final
619	David Payne, Blackpool	Steve Walsh	Cambridge Play Off 1992
620	Ian Morton, Loughborough	Steve Walsh	Derby Play Off Final
621	Dave Goodacre, Leicester	Graham Cross	Manchester United Away 1998
622	Julie Waterton	N/A	N/A
623	Darrell Quinn, Leicester	Steve Walsh	Middlesbrough League Cup
624	Ian Chester, Alcester	Frank Worthington	Derby Play Off Final
625	Steve Poole, Wigston	Keith Weller	Crystal Palace Play Off Final
626	Richard Ansell, London	Keith Weller	Shrewsbury FA Cup Q/F 1982
627	Justin Farmer, Hinckley	Gary Lineker	Shrewsbury FA Cup
628	Daniel Cotterell, Hinckley	N/A	N/A
629	Graham Parker, Market Overton, Oakham	Steve Walsh	Manchester City FA Cup 1968
630	Alan Hillyard, Coalville	Frank Worthington	Manchester United 1963
631	David Monk, Market Harborough	Steve Walsh	Crystal Palace Play Off Final
632	Andrew Cope, Leicester	Steve Walsh	Crystal Palace Play Off Final
633	Adrian Cormicle, Hinckley	Steve Walsh	Crystal Palace Play Off Final
634	Steve Walker, Norwich	Steve Walsh	Shrewsbury FA Cup
635	Priten Nalinkumar Pancholi, Leicester	Frank Worthington	Shrewsbury FA Cup
636	Paul Soady, Brackley	Graham Cross	Oxford 1991
637	Matthew Soady, Brackley	Steve Walsh	Derby Away 1998
638	Daniel Soady, Brackley	Neil Lennon	Crystal Palace @ Wembley 1996
639	Andy Taylor, Spalding	Steve Walsh	Derby Play Off Final
640	John Sleath, Loughborough	Frank Worthington	Coca Cola Cup Final Replay
641	Ian Allard, Loughborough	Keith Weller	Coca Cola Cup Final Replay
642	Robert Jones, Shepshed	Robbie Savage	Derby Play Off Final
643	John Rayns, Cheltenham	Keith Weller	Shrewsbury 1/4 Final
644	David Rayns, London	Keith Weller	Shrewsbury 1/4 Final
645	Elizabeth Rayns, London	Robbie Savage	Tranmere Final 2000
646	Richard Rayns, Aldershot	Sep Smith	Spurs Home 1937
647	Lauren Rayns, London	Steve Claridge	Tranmere Final 2000
648	Roger Watson, Leicester	Iwan Roberts	Crystal Palace Play Off Final
649	Andrew Bailey, Market Bosworth	Muzzy Izzet	Watford 1992 / 1993
650	Andrew Gubbins, Market Harborough	Steve Walsh	Sunderland 2000
651	Robert J Kelly, Stoney Stanton	Emile Heskey	Crystal Palace Play Off Final
652	Malcolm Hawes, Loughborough	Gary Lineker	Crystal Palace Play Off Final
653	Edward Thomas, Leicester	Gary Lineker	Shrewsbury FA Cup

Martin O'Neill

profile landmarks of his regime; an insistence on the primacy of the football operation in the new corporate culture of the club his hopefully enduring legacy. That there were unpromising beginnings to this particular revolution is undeniable: it was a toss-up as to whether Martin or ex-Norwich and Everton boss Mike Walker would be appointed to succeed Mark McGhee at Filbert Street; he would clash early with popular skipper Garry Parker; and he would remain scarred to the end of his reign by memories of the vitriol hurled at him by an impatient City crowd during a dire performance against Sheffield United a couple of months into his tenure. But there would be barely a murmur of dissent about the increasingly charismatic manager thereafter, especially after his first four signings (Lennon, Claridge, Watts and Izzet), plus a pacified Parker, so crucially contributed to promotion via the dramatic Play-Off victory over Crystal Palace. There was to be no naivete to the club's second assault on Premiership consolidation, and Martin's ability to get the best out of players like Simon Grayson (previously embarrassed at that grade) was as notable a success as his gradual purchasing policy. He seemed initially happy to have City's surprise-packet progress ascribed almost solely to high workrate and team spirit, as so many credulous opponents were beaten by unheralded class, though it irked somewhat when this old chestnut was still being wheeled out several years later to explain City's sustained record of punching above their perceived weight. Long-awaited silverware was won at Hillsborough, and the even longer-awaited return to European football achieved; and two years later the same feat was negotiated, on this occasion via a first-time Wembley win in the League Cup. Other highlights, in both knockout fare and Premiership combat, abounded, with Martin's public image ever becoming more outsized owing to his oft-televised jack-in-the-box routine of touchline involvement, his knowingly quotable Irish-isms, and his re-commitment to the City job after lengthy waverings over approaches from each of Everton and Leeds. A worthy Manager of the Month in each of September 1997 and October 1998, he seemed keen not to be seen as a clone of his early mentor, Brian Clough, but equally determined to create an equivalently individualist persona of an eccentric football sage. He was never to disguise his shrewdness, however: whether in bargain transfer-market dealing, in rehabilitating or revivifyiing wayward or supposedly spent talent, or in exploiting his popularity to resolve the sport and commerce split at the club in his preferred direction. It now remains to be seen whether such qualities, and quirks, are viably operable within rather different parameters at Celtic; but early evidence is utterly positive.

Martin (b. Kilrea, 1.3.1952) started his playing career with Distillery (scoring twice in their 1971 IFA Cup Final victory), and was signed while still a teenager by Matt Gillies at Nottingham Forest. He remained there for a decade, playing a key role as an attacking midfielder in the glory years at home and in Europe under Brian Clough, then spent a while wandering: twice to Norwich, and also to Manchester City and Notts County. He won 64 caps, scored eight international goals, and became the first Catholic to captain Northern Ireland. Martin started the learning curve of his managerial career modestly, with Grantham Town in 1987, and moved to Shepshed Charterhouse in 1989. He was then tempted to Conference side Wycombe Wanderers in February 1990 to bring them massive success: the FA Trophy in both 1991 and 1993, the Conference title in 1993, and promotion to Division Two a year later. He resisted several elevatory approaches until joining Norwich in June 1995, but was soon in an antagonistic relationship with his chairman there, and resigned on the morning of their Filbert Street fixture against City in the following November; being installed as City boss three days later.

ORR, William

> The man who inherited Peter Hodge's First Division side, Willie polished and fine-tuned it to the extent that it sat for two seasons proudly, if slightly frustratedly, in its highest-ever top-flight placings: third in 1927/8 and second (to Sheffield Wednesday) in the following campaign. He maintained Hodge's insistence on stylish football, and his only real fault was in not strategically rejuvenating a side whose key members were ageing collectively.

Willie (b. Shotts, Lanarkshire, 20.6.1873; d. 26.2.1946) was in his playing days a fine defender with Airdrieonians, Preston North End and, for ten years from 1897, with Celtic. He earned three full Scottish caps, four Scottish League championship medals, and five Scottish Cup medals: three as a winner. In 1909 he became a director back at Airdrie, and served as such until November 1921, when he took over the manager's chair there; having already acted as a selector for Scotland. He nurtured the career of Hughie Gallacher, while his side were First Division runners-up on four occasions and took the Scottish Cup in 1924. At Filbert Street, Jim McLaren, Sid Bishop and Len Barry were among his purchases to contribute much to the championship pursuit, while Sep Smith was a later junior recruit. There was a staleness, however, to the side which struggled through the first part of 1931/2, and even though the opening round of the FA Cup had just been negotiated, a run of six successive First Division defeats prompted a mid-January resignation. Willie was adamant that he and the board were 'parting good friends. It is simply and solely a question of viewpoint'.

He soon found new employment as secretary/manager of Falkirk, but sadly it was not long before he faced disgrace. For in April 1935 the Scottish League banned him for life after he had been charged with bribery, and found guilty of paying £3 to Ayr United player Robert Russell to miss a crucial relegation fixture against Falkirk. (The game in question was ordered to be replayed). Though the suspension was actually lifted as early as February 1937, Willie was by then a traffic superintendant for a bus company in Crieff, and evinced no desire to return to football.

Willie Orr

PLEAT, David John

> Both City and David Pleat were at a low ebb when the latter succeeded Bryan Hamilton at Filbert Street. City were nudging the bottom of the Second Division, and were in the midst of their record run of seven League games without a goal, while David was still suffering from the fall-out following a tabloid smear campaign which had led to his departure from Tottenham. By the end of his first term, though, both club and boss were very much rehabilitated, for David had rapidly turned around both tactics and fortunes, and soon had his team playing the most attractive football seen from a Leicester side in some time. Unfortunately, however, there was to be no sustaining this progressive momentum, and there would be more posturing than poise exhibited in the Second Division scrabblings of the next few years. Indeed, as David became ever better known for his media-friendly punditry, it became intensely frustrating for the fans to observe such an evident mismatch between tactics and skills as spoken about, and as inconsistently expressed on the pitch. It may have been true that David was as irked as the Filbert Street support by the comparative paucity of financial resources at his disposal, but whether he confused his players or merely overburdened them with tactical formulae, he could not seem to imbue much cohesive spirit in his selections, who invariably looked particularly forlorn in away matches for the greater part of his stay. When he was allowed to spend, his transfer record was patchy, too; with the likes of Peter Weir, Gary Mills, Tommy Wright and David Kelly settling in the bonus column, but being somewhat outnumbered by those contributing little to the cause. Ultimately, by the time of David's sacking in January 1991, City were pretty much back where they were at the time he arrived, and once more in danger of the unthinkable drop into Division Three.

David (b. Nottingham, 15.1.1945) won England honours at schools and youth level as a speedy winger, but found it hard to sustain a precocious first-team challenge at Nottingham Forest, and moved on while still only 19 to Luton Town. There, a series of injuries cut down his reliance on sheer pace, and forced him into a more studiously constructive game, which served him well through subsequent moves to Shrewsbury Town, Exeter City and Peterborough United. David became player/manager at Nuneaton Borough for a spell, then took on a succession of backroom jobs with Luton, which saw him rise through the coaching heirarchy into the manager's chair in early 1978. He returned the Hatters to the top flight in 1982, kept them there the following term (when his delight at a last-gasp reprieve was evident to the TV-watching millions who saw his celebratory jig across the Maine Road pitch), and had them established as an entertaining playing force when he left to meet the challenge of raising Spurs to the heights coveted by their ambitious board. David introduced the paradoxically attack-minded five-man midfield, and saw Tottenham to the 1987 FA Cup Final, but his future became unsure when press agitation mounted for the return of Terry Venables, and the coincidental appearance of tabloid allegations about David's private life effectively enforced his resignation.

On exiting Filbert Street, he rejoined Luton as manager in June 1991, gave senior chances there to a number of his former City juniors, and was almost tempted back to White Hart Lane in November 1994. In fact, it would be after an interim management period at Sheffield Wednesday (June 1995 - November 1997) that he would rejoin Spurs as Director of Football, initially working alongside Christian Gross and then with George Graham.

David Pleat

TAYLOR, Peter John

> Perhaps inevitably, almost every action of current manager Peter has been debated and questioned in the Carling, the Kop and every other corner of Filbert Street's fan base. He must himself have been aware that he was virtually on 'probation' when assuming his job in succession to Martin O'Neill, and that this particular hot seat would be hotter than most. The notion of 'a hard act to follow' virtually defined the role he stepped into; and no matter how different his approach, his attitude or his achievement, comparisons would be made; and the notorious impatience of some of City's support negotiated. Given the uniquely broken-backed nature of Leicester's 2000/1 campaign, that particularly opinionated and vocal jury is still out; deadlocked over matters of recruitment policy, tactics and motivation. That Peter has also been devoting some of his energies to the England coaching set-up has additionally raised queries as to divided loyalties, but these appear fairly flimsy; what substance they have revolving around simplistic suspicions of how frustrating it must be to work part-time with 'the best' and more regularly with 'the rest'. Peter's role at Belvoir Drive is certainly more hands-on than his predecessor's, so he is bound to be more closely identified with what seemed a more negative tactical approach creeping into City's game; and while his bargain-hunting instincts are superficially similar, he has yet to strike the essential balance between youth and experience amongst his purchases. The learning curve of an initial introduction to the world of the Premiership is, however, a steep one, and Peter has probably heeded more useful lessons from the seasonal downslide than from the heady early experience of hitting its heights.

Peter Taylor

Peter (b. Southend, 3.1.1953) entered the game as a teenage winger at his home-town club, moving on to Crystal Palace in October 1973 and winning England recognition while still playing in the old Third Division. Four years with Spurs from September 1976 followed, until Orient became his third metropolitan club. A loan spell with Oldham, two stints with Maidstone, and one with Exeter closed his League career, but Peter remained active for years thereafter, with contracts as player, player/coach or player/manager at Heybridge Swifts, Chelmsford City, Dartford, Enfield and Harlow. He became assistant boss at Watford in 1991, managed Southend for a while from December 1993 and then remained in charge of their youth team, and was bossing Dover Athletic (from November 1995) when called upon by Glenn Hoddle to take charge of England's Under-21 squad. Three successful years in this role came to an acrimonious end when Howard Wilkinson was parachuted into the post, but Peter's subsequent assumption of the Gillingham managerial job in 1999 furthered his reputation, with the Gills winning a first-ever promotion to Division One via the Play-Offs; making him an early favourite for City chairman John Elsom's shortlist.

WALLACE, John Martin Bokas

> Deserving of heartfelt thanks for taking a dispirited club by the scruff of the neck, shaking it back to self-respect and infusing its representative teams with a battling swagger, Jock quickly built his own potent mythology at Leicester; but in many ways became unproductively trapped within it before he left. It might justifiably be argued that his feat in stopping the side falling into Division Three in 1978/9 (which seemed likely, given the downward momentum of the Frank McLintock disaster) was a greater triumph than the Second Division championship success he prompted the following season; and there is a case to be made for his embarrassment when City dropped straight back being primarily a consequence of the club's belt-tightening priorities starving him of cash. But in that top-flight term, and the subsequently blown attempt to bounce straight back up again, the conflicting strengths and weaknesses of the patented Wallace approach became more and more obvious. A great motivator, a shrewd judge of a player's hunger and commitment, and always one to encourage youthful talent, Jock revelled in the braveheart approach to the game. Yet he could nonetheless often appear a rather naive tactician; and it did not help overmuch on this score that his assistant, Ian MacFarlane, seemed hewn from the same craggy rock. The abiding memory of the latter years of the Wallace regime, which would end

Jock Wallace

in legalistic acrimony when Jock broke his contract to join Motherwell in August 1982, was of Jock and Ian rising together from the City bench, snarling and shaking their fists to demand more frenetic effort, rather than conveying any more subtle shift in playing pattern.

Jock (b. Wallyford, 6.9.1935; d. Basingstoke, 24.7.1996) was the son of a goalkeeper, also Jock, who played for Raith Rovers, Blackpool and Derby County on either side of WW2. He began his own peripatetic goalkeeping career while on National Service, performing for a motley collection of clubs during and after army action as a jungle fighter. Initially a young amateur with Blackpool, he joined Workington in 1952, and then played for Ashton United and Airdrieonians until joining West Bromwich Albion in 1959. After 69 League games at The Hawthorns, Jock moved on again, to Bedford Town in 1962, to Hereford United for their Southern League title-winning season of 1964/5 and, as player/manager, to Berwick Rangers, where he appeared in the celebrated giant-killing of their Glasgow namesakes. He had a spell coaching at Hearts, and two years as assistant to Willie Waddell at Ibrox, culminating in European Cup Winners Cup triumph just before his own assumption of the manager's chair in July 1972. Further remarkable success for Rangers ensued, with the pinnacles of Jock's career coming in 1976 and 1978, when the domestic Treble was clinched. Almost deified by the Ibrox faithful, Jock genuinely shocked British football when joining City, where the contrast in recent fortunes could not have been more extreme. Instituting a famously rigorous fitness-training routine (incorporating use of the sandhill), savagely reducing the average age of his senior squad, and taking a hands-on approach to public relations, he made an instant impact. And it is well worth reiterating that, although Jock left City in the same nominal Second Division grade as when he arrived, his gruffly populist, up-and-at-'em orientation had in the interim given the club back its pride.

The row over Jock's 'poaching' by Motherwell had barely died down when he left Fir Park to return to Ibrox. Success in his second spell at his spiritual home was, however, harder to come by, and in April 1986 he again bade farewell to Glasgow. A couple of months later Jock was somewhat incongruously installed as boss at Spanish League club Sevilla, but soon found himself out of his element. He then remained in semi-retirement in Spain until answering an SOS to return to management in January 1989, with Fourth Division back-markers Colchester United. Predictably, he roused them to clear survival before resigning in the following December. He briefly accepted a seat on the Layer Road board, but in February 1990 announced he was suffering from Parkinson's Disease and was retiring from football. Still living in Fuengerola, Jock returned to Filbert Street in November 1994 for a star-studded testimonial dinner, but he died on a visit to relatives less than two years later.

WOMACK, Frank

> Remembered mainly for his startling success in turning around City's fortunes in his first season at the helm with one decisive flurry of transfer-maket activity, Frank pushed the club from the Second Division depths to its 1937 championship within a matter of months on the heels of his purchases of Eric Stubbs and, especially, Jack Bowers.

A Sheffielder by upbringing, and originally apprenticed in the cutlery business, Frank (b. Wortley, 16.9.1888; d. Caistor, 8.10.1968) spent the entirety of a 515-game, 20-year playing career as a Birmingham full-back, and figured in an England trial match in 1913. He won his managerial spurs with Worcester City, taking them to the Birmingham League title in 1929, and then bossed Torquay United (1929-32) and Grimsby Town (1932-36). The Mariners headed the Second Division in 1934, and were sitting 5th in Division One at the time he succeeded Arthur Lochhead at Leicester (21st in Division Two), lifting the latter to instant glory. Frank's perception in recognising what it took to get out of Division Two, however, did not extend to any brilliant insights as to how to keep City in the top flight thereafter, and he resigned in May 1939 after the club tumbled back down again on the eve of war. A sad postscript to his Filbert Street career was provided in 1940 by the FA, who handed him a one year suspension from the game after implicating him in the payment irregularities then found in City's pre-war books; but Frank bounced back to take charge of Notts County from July 1942 to March 1944, and of Oldham Athletic from February 1945 until April 1947. In 1951, he returned for a brief spell as caretaker manager at Grimsby, and in 1959 was noted as a Huddersfield Town scout.

No.	Name / Home Town	Fav. LCFC player	Fav. LCFC game
654	Jim Thomas, Perth - Australia	Steve Walsh	Manchester City 1968
655	John Blake, Littlethorpe	Steve Walsh	Coca Cola Cup Final Replay
656	Linda & Robert Wortley, Leicester	Steve Walsh	Derby Play Off Final
657	Daryll Ball, Leicester	Gary Lineker	Middlesbrough
658	Dave Smith, Barrow Upon Soar	Steve Walsh	Crystal Palace Play Off Final
659	Karen Bevans, Seagrave	Gary Parker	Sunderland 2000
660	Nigel Horsley, Hinckley	Gordon Banks	Sunderland 2000
661	Richard Rawlinson, Wigston - Leicester	Muzzy Izzet	Hillsborough 1997
662	Antony Rawlinson, Wigston - Leicester	Lenny Glover	Cambridge 1992
663	Martin Gwilliam, Leicester	Lenny Glover	Manchester City FA Cup 1968
664	Jonathan Hinsley, Leicester	Steve Walsh	Coca Cola Cup Final Replay
665	Ketil Figenschou, Trondheim - Norway	Frank Worthington	Norwich 1974
666	Karen Crossley, Whetstone	Steve Claridge	Play Off Final 1996
667	John Lockton, Leicester	Keith Weller	Manchester United 1960's
668	Matt Stevens, Leicester	Steve Claridge	Promotion Play Off
669	William Reed	N/A	N/A
670	Brian Moore, Leicester	David Gibson	Manchester City 1968
671	Robert Laidler, Leicester	Gary McAllister	Fulham 1963
672	James Smith, Wigston	Theo Zagorakis	Swindon Play Off Final
673	Peter & Dean Read, Wigston Fields, Leicester	Frank Worthington	Derby Play Off Final
674	Andrew Braimbridge, Leicester	Steve Walsh	Swindon Play Off Final
675	David Braimbridge, Leicester	Keith Weller	Shrewsbury FA Cup 6th Round 1982
676	Christopher Robson, Letchworth	N/A	N/A
677	Richard Day, Rutland	Frank Worthington	Manchester United 1963
678	Brian Carter, Neasden	Gordon Banks	Burnley
679	Ashley Carter, Loughborough	Frank Worthington	Worthington Cup Final 2000
680	Helen Howkins, Leicester	Muzzy Izzet	Crystal Palace @ Wembley 1996
681	Adrian Howkins, Leicester	David Gibson	Arsenal 1997 / 1998
682	Carl Harrison, Quorn - Loughborough	Steve Walsh	Wolves
683	Roy Sutton, Bournemouth - Dorset	Frank Worthington	Coca Cola Cup Replay 1997
684	Stewart Osborne, Northampton	Frank Worthington	Manchester City 1968
685	Eric Wakefield, Romford	Gordon Banks	Tranmere Final 2000
686	Mike Ward, Leicester	Frank Worthington	Manchester City 1968
687	Trevor Bray, Sapcote	Steve Walsh	Tranmere Final 2000
688	Ian Dunk, Leicester	Steve Walsh	Shrewsbury FA Cup 1982
689	Carl Broomhead, Leicester	Gary Lineker	Crystal Palace Play Off Final
690	Andrew Pearson, Loughborough	Steve Walsh	Crystal Palace Play Off Final 1996
691	Paul Granger	N/A	N/A
692	Andy Moss, Leicester	Frank Worthington	Derby Play Off Final
693	Christopher Stevens, Burbage	Steve Walsh	Shrewsbury 1982
694	Peter Stevens, Wellingbrough - Northants	Keith Weller	FA Cup v Leatherhead 1975
695	David Trubshaw, Leicester	Keith Weller	Shrewsbury FA Cup 6th Round
696	Malcolm Tedd, Oadby	Frank Worthington	Derby County 1994
697	Barry Shade, Hinckley	Gary Lineker	Leeds United 1989 / 1990
698	Antony McDonagh, Hinckley	Lenny Glover	Shrewsbury FA Cup 1982
699	Gary Foley, Leicester	Keith Weller	Shrewsbury FA Cup 1982
700	Ian Middleton, Daventry - Northants	Frank Worthington	Liverpool 1972 / 1973
701	Cel Perone, Loughborough	Gary Lineker	Arsenal 1998
702	Nigel Denton, Darlington - Co. Durham	Gary Lineker	Play Off Final 1994
703	Joanne Hoare, Torquay	Gary Lineker	Derby Play Off Final
704	Henry Stewart, Manningtree	Frank Worthington	Derby Play Off Final
705	Max Henry, Manningtree	Muzzy Izzet	Tranmere Final 2000
706	Dennis Henry, Torquay	Arthur Rowley	N/A
707	Noah Nenry, Manningtree	Robbie Savage	Spurs 2001
708	Joe Brewin, Hugglescote - Coalville	Steve Claridge	Coca Cola Cup Final - Hillsborough
709	Terry Statham, Barwell	Frank Worthington	Manchester City
710	Ian Parker, Wigston Magna	Frank Worthington	Liverpool 1984
711	Sharon Delves, Hinckley	Steve Walsh	Play Off Final 1996
712	Mark Weaver, Leicester	Tony Cottee	Derby Play Off Final
713	Janice Benfield, Leicester	Graham Cross	Derby Play Off Final
714	Chris Gregory, London	Peter Shilton	Coca Cola Cup Final
715	Glenda Holliland, Littlethorpe	Robbie Savage	Fulham 2000
716	Sarah Brackenridge, Lincoln	Steve Walsh	Swindon Play Off Final
717	The Melton Bookshop	N/A	N/A
718	Karl Prime, Atherstone - Warwickshire	Steve Walsh	Crystal Palace Play Off Final 1996
719	Gordon Ridgway, Milton Keynes	Keith Weller	Coca Cola Cup Final Replay 1997
720	Wojtek Swistak, Ealing - London	Steve Walsh	Derby Play Off Final
721	John Wells, Rothwell	Arthur Rowley	Aston Villa 1958
722	Allan Wright, Leicester	Peter Shilton	Liverpool 1973
723	Andrew Johnson, Leicester	Kevin McDonald	Liverpool 1983 / 84
724	Dave Stoneleigh, Leicester	Gordon Banks	Leeds 1989
725	John Smith, Ventnor, I.O.W.	Gary Lineker	Swindon Play Off Final
726	Jean White, Leicester	Frank Worthington	FA Cup Semi Final 1949
727	Tony Moore, Coalville	N/A	N/A
728	Paul Welch, Barlestone	Gary McAllister	Shrewsbury FA Cup 1981 / 1982
729	Tim Goss, Leicester	N/A	N/A
730	David Smith, Leicester	N/A	N/A
731	Joe Ayre, Wigston	Muzzy Izzet	Crystal Palace & Wembley 1996
732	Dave Ayre, Wigston	Gordon Banks	Manchester United 1963
733	Joel Bevans, Leicester	Tommy Wright	Cambridge 1992
734	Andrew Hardy-Smith, Leicester	Keith Weller	Sunderland 1999
735	Luke Bevans, Leicester	Gary McAllister	Spurs Away 1999
736	Chris Johnson, Leicester	Lenny Glover	Shrewsbury FA Cup
737	Kevin John Smith, Wigston Fields	Jim Melrose	Liverpool Away 1981
738	Ian Gentry, Dubai UAE	Mike Stringfellow	Liverpool
739	Alistair Wood, Whetstone - Leicester	Robbie Savage	Swindon
740	Karen Colmer, Swindon	Steve Claridge	Crystal Palace Play Off Final 1996
741	Patricia Thompson, Leicester	Steve Claridge	Crystal Palace Play Off Final 1996
742	Tim Driver, York	Neil Lennon	Crystal Palace Play Off Final 1996
743	Jason Bowers, Stamford - Lincs	Tommy Wright	Wimbledon League Cup Semi Final
744	John Pasiecznik, Hadfield - Derbys	Frank Worthington	Coca Cola Cup Final Replay 1997
745	Tim Moore, Leicester	Keith Weller	Man City FA Cup 1967 / 1968
746	Chris Eyre, Wendover - Bucks	Frank Worthington	Cambridge 1992
747	Peter Simpson, Hinckley	Frank Worthington	Manchester City

TRAINERS & COACHES

Biographical notes for those men who served Fosse and City in the above roles after having played for the club are to be found elsewhere; while the entry for Gordon Lee is in the Managers' section.

> **Charlie Brown** (d. Leicester, 27.1.1927, aged 71) was Fosse's trainer throughout the final Midland League season of 1893/4, merely noted by the local press at the time as being 'well known amongst the athletes of Leicester'.

> **Jack Butler** (John Dennis; b. Colombo, Ceylon, 14.8.1894; d. London, 5.1.1961) coached City throughout most of the WW2 era, from November 1940 to May 1946. His sixteen-year stint as an Arsenal centre-half had earned him one England cap in 1924, and he had finished his playing career with Torquay United before joining Daring FC of Belgium as manager/coach in 1932, and concurrently running the Belgian national side from 1935-39. On leaving Filbert Street, where he and manager Tom Bromilow instituted a useful Colts policy that linked football and civilian employment, he initially coached for the Danish FA, then successively managed Torquay, Crystal Palace, Daring again, and Colchester United.

> **Steve Butler** (b. Birmingham, 27.1.1962) was Peter Taylor's choice of first-team coach upon his arrival at Filbert Street in the summer of 2000, having served under the manager at Gillingham as both a veteran striker and training-ground back-up, and only weeks beforehand having been re-confirmed as the No 2 with the Gills. A former soldier who played non-league for Windsor & Eton and Wokingham Town before attracting Brentford's attention in December 1984, he built up a substantial goalscoring portfolio over the next fifteen years with Maidstone, Watford, Bournemouth, Cambridge, Gillingham (twice), Peterborough and Stevenage; and his final strike had been in the Play-Off Final which elevated the Gills to Division One.

> **David Plews Coates** (b. Newcastle, 11.4.1935) joined the City coaching staff under Frank O'Farrell and stayed throughout the Bloomfield and McLintock managements, usually looking after the reserves. A former wing-half with Hull, Mansfield and Notts County, he later worked with David Pleat at Luton, as youth coach at Oxford, and as chief scout for Sunderland and Plymouth Argyle.

> **Bill Dodgin Jr** (b. Gateshead, 4.11.1931; d. June 2000) was appointed as a City coach by Jimmy Bloomfield in 1972. A former Under-23 cap, he had played for Fulham and Arsenal, coached Millwall and QPR, and returned to Craven Cottage as both coach and manager. Less than a year after arriving at Filbert Street, though, he was off for the first of two spells managing Northampton Town, and also fitted in an interim spell as Brentford boss.

> **Alex Dowdells** (b. Slamannan, Lanarkshire) came in to head the City training staff under David Halliday in 1956, after 16 years in a similar role with Celtic, and nine years as trainer to the Scottish national side. Having studied medicine at Glasgow University from 1933, and played at centre-forward for Wishaw and Shettleston, he'd initially held training posts with both Shettleston and the Scottish Junior international team before moving to Parkhead. After becoming a familiar sight as sponge-man through the bulk of the Matt Gillies era, Alex became the first and only non-player to be honoured with a City testimonial game – a Filbert Street friendly in May 1966 against a strong Scotland XI (the first chosen by new boss John Prentice), drawn 1-1. He retired to live in Norfolk.

> **Bob Dunmore** (b. 1857) was in charge of Fosse's fitness from 1898-1900, performed similar functions at Woolwich Arsenal for seven years after 1903, and later trained each of Bury and Chesterfield Town before WW1. His son Horace was a Loughborough Corinthians goalkeeper, and a Bristol Rovers trialist in 1929; while by 1934 Bob himself was being awarded mementos for long service in training Leicester Walking Club.

> **Laurie Edwards** (b. Shropshire; d. Leicester, 8.6.1962) joined City as trainer in May 33, and stayed until signing up for Chelmsford City on the eve of war. A former half-mile 'world' champion athlete (Powderhall, January 1920), and coach at Shrewsbury School and Liverpool University, he'd toured Canada with the FA XI in 1926, acted as trainer to the full England side for their games in France and Belgium in 1931, and had been an official athletics trainer to the South African team competing in the 1932 Los Angeles Olympic Games. He'd also served under George Jobey at Derby County; and for a while had a private electrical therapy practice in Leicester. Postwar, Laurie was a successful, Waterloo Cup-winning greyhound owner and breeder.

> **Mike Everitt** (Michael Dennis; b. Clacton, 16.1.1941) was another coach to serve Jimmy Bloomfield, staying with City from 1975-77. He had been a player with Arsenal, Northampton, Plymouth and Brighton; player/manager at non-league Wimbledon; and boss at Brentford. In the early 90s he was coaching Al Shabab SC in Kuwait.

> **Bill Fox** (William Henry; b. Islington, ca 1874; d. Leicester, 21.3.1935) was part of the Filbert Street scene for over 20 years. He'd become a masseur after Army service in the Boer War and in India, when his duties as a Seaforth Highlanders signaller using heliographs contributed to him going blind. He occasionally assisted Fosse, as well as county cricketers and other local sportsmen, and then was employed full-time by City throughout the 20s and early 30s. He cut his own throat after returning home from a lengthy hospital stay, and Filbert Street hosted a Boxers v Police benefit game which raised £85 for his widow.

> **Paul Leslie Franklin** (b. Hainault, 5.10.1963) was brought in as reserve-team boss by Martin O'Neill, and left shortly after his mentor. A Youth Cup-winner with Watford in 1982, who was also loaned out to Shrewsbury and Swindon after making his Vicarage Road breakthrough, he subsequently played in central defence for Reading and Wycombe, there graduating to the coaching ranks under O'Neill.

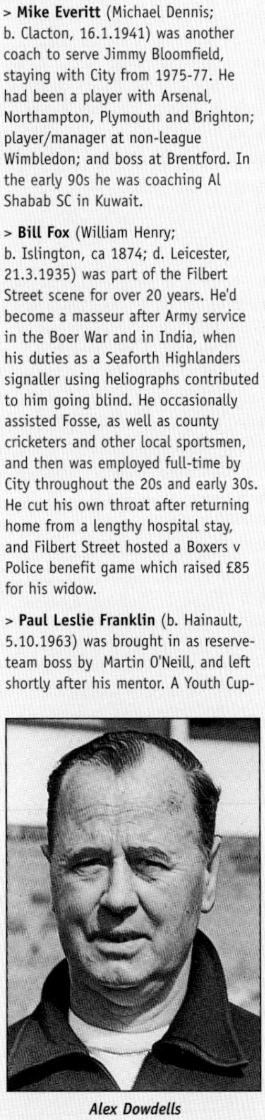

Alex Dowdells

> **Dave Gardner** (David Richmond; b. Glasgow, 31.3.1873; d. Loughborough, 5.11.1931) was City's head trainer from 1919 until his sudden death on Longcliffe golf course, serving under Peter Hodge and Willie Orr throughout the club's First Division heyday. Capped by Scotland as a Third Lanark defender in 1897, Dave had in the interim been a solid left-back for Newcastle, Grimsby, West Ham and Croydon Common, where he had been signed by Jack Bartlett and where he first took up training duties. He was welcomed to Leicester, by 'Scrutator' in the *Mail*, thus: 'As befits an old player, he will do his utmost to prove the maxim that it is good condition that counts as ability's most faithful ally'.

> **John Charles Gregory** (b. Scunthorpe, 11.5.1954) followed Brian Little into Filbert Street after a matter of weeks, and followed him again to Villa Park after a matter of days, having coached both the reserves and first team during his Leicester stay (and having turned out on occasion in the Central League). A former England midfielder whose League career took him to Northampton, Aston Villa, Brighton, QPR, Derby, Plymouth and Bolton, he had been Portsmouth coach and manager before coming to Leicester. He finally left Little's company to manage Wycombe in October 1996, then replaced him at Villa in February 1998. His father, also John, had played for West Ham, Scunthorpe and Aldershot.

> **Mike Hickman** (Michael Frederick Thomas; b. Elstead, 2.10.1946) came from Reading with Mark McGhee and Colin Lee in December 1994, and accompanied them to Wolves a year later, having taken charge of coaching the midweek Central League side. He'd been an inside-forward with Brighton, Grimsby, Blackburn and Torquay in the 60s and 70s, and had established his coaching credentials in Australia, working with the national side there. In December 1998 he moved back Down Under.

> **Alan Hill** (b. Barnsley, 3.11.1943) assumed control of all City's Football Academy operations in the summer of 2000, overseeing all youth scouting and coaching issues. A former goalkeeper with Barnsley, Rotherham and Nottingham Forest, he had remained at the City Ground for many years as a coach under Brian Clough, and also served Derby, Wolves and Notts County in backroom capacities before becoming Director of the Youth Academy at Leeds in 1998.

> **Steve Hunt** (Stephen Kenneth; b. Witton, 4.8.1956) was Brian Little's youth coach from 1991-93. The former Aston Villa, New York Cosmos, Coventry, West Brom and England striker had previously managed Willenhall Town and run Port Vale's youth set-up; and would later be noted from 1996 as assistant manager at VS Rugby.

> **John Jackson** (b. Deritend, Birmingham, 14.2.1861; d. Brighton, June 1931) was Fosse's trainer from 1896-98. A former goalkeeper with minor club Coventry Rovers, he'd been assistant trainer to Wolves when they'd won the FA Cup in 1893, had guided Loughborough to a Midland League title, and trained Liverpool to the Second Division championship in 1896. He moved on from Leicester to become inaugural trainer/manager of Brighton United in 1898, and commenced a long tenure as a licensee in the locality when that club collapsed in 1900. Only a year later, though, John was back as a prime mover in the formation of Brighton & Hove Albion, and remained with them as secretary/manager until 1905, thereafter concentrating on his pubs.

> **Bert Johnson** (William Herbert; b. Stockton-on-Tees; 4.6.1916) was Matt Gillies' coaching No 2 for much of his stay with Leicester, though he initially joined the club in 1959 as head scout. Often given a share in the credit for the tactical innovations that helped City to four Cup Finals in the early 60s, he took over as acting manager during Gillies' absence through illness in 1968, and it was his sacking later that year which prompted Gillies' immediate resignation. A devout churchman, Bert had begun his playing career in the Northern League with South Bank, Stockton and Spennymoor United before signing for Charlton as a wing-half in March 1939. He guested for Bolton alongside Gillies during the war, played in two Victory internationals for England, and took successive runners-up and winners' medals from the FA Cup Finals of 1946 and 1947. From 1953 he had been player/manager at each of Bexleyheath & Welling and Cambridge United. Upon leaving Leicester, he was chief scout for each of Nottingham Forest, Derby and Southampton, and in August 1979 became general manager at Walsall, working in tandem with player/manager Alan Buckley.

> **David Jones** (b. Whitwell, 9.4.1914; d. Scarborough, July 1998), formerly a long-serving Bury wing-half under Norman Bullock, followed his boss to Leicester as head trainer in June 1950, and stayed in this role until May 1956, when resigning to look after his Anstey Lane newsagent shop. Upon Frank King's departure in summer 1958, however, he returned to Filbert Street as Alex Dowdells' assistant, and remained on the staff until 1978. He was also a former Nottinghamshire CCC batsman.

> **Frank King** (Francis Oliver; b. Alnwick, 13.3.1917), a pre-war Blyth Spartans, Everton and Derby goalkeeper, was assistant trainer to David Jones from 1954, and left City in 1958 to take the senior trainer's role at Luton. His younger brothers Ray and George were both League footballers: the former a Port Vale and England 'B' goalie, and the latter a wandering centre-forward who started at Newcastle and whose best spell was at Barrow.

> **Cyril Lea** (b. Wrexham, 5.8.1934) assumed the youth development role with Bryan Hamilton's City set-up in 1987, and later performed similar duties for West Brom from 1989. His playing career had started with Leyton Orient in 1957, and peaked with two Welsh caps in 1965, while he was with Ipswich Town. He had coached at Ipswich, Stoke and Hull before becoming Colchester manager from 1983-86. By the mid-90s, Cyril was a Midlands-based scout for Ipswich.

> **Colin Lee** (b. Torquay, 12.6.1956) became City's assistant manager when moving from Reading with Mark McGhee and Mike Hickman in December 1994; left with the same pair a year later for Molineux; took over the Wolves hot seat himself in November 1998 after McGhee was sacked; held it until December 2000; and most recently kept Torquay in the Football League by the skin of their teeth. Primarily remembered as a player for scoring four times on his Spurs debut against Bristol Rovers, and twice for Chelsea in the Full Members Cup Final of 1986, he had commenced his senior career at Bristol City, and also featured for Hereford and Torquay before his 1977 move to White Hart Lane. At Stamford Bridge from 1980, the striker also occasionally figured at right-back and in central defence. Colin was player/youth coach at Brentford from 1987; youth coach and then briefly full manager at Watford; and coach at Elm Park from July 1991.

> **Tony McAndrew** (b. Glasow, 11.4.1956) joined City as youth coach in July 1993, having previously performed the same role with Darlington. He was part of the 'Two Macs' caretaker management partnership with Kevin MacDonald in November 1994, in the wake of Brian Little's departure, but resigned in January 1995 and rejoined Little at Villa Park. He was also No 2 to Little at Stoke from June 1998. His playing career as a defender was largely spent with Middlesbrough, though his two Ayresome spells sandwiched stints with Vancouver Whitecaps and Chelsea, and he came out of retirement to play briefly for each of Darlington and Hartlepool.

> **Seamus McDonagh** (James Martin; b. Rotherham, 6.10.1952) has been the full-time goalkeeping coach with City since the summer of 1997. An England youth international, but then capped 25 times by the Republic of Ireland, he'd started his own goalkeeping career at Rotherham in 1970, and then played for Bolton (in two spells), Everton, Notts County, Birmingham, Gillingham, Sunderland, Wichita Wings, Scarborough, Huddersfield and Spalding United.

> **Willie McLean** (b. Paisley) arrived at Leicester in the summer of 1932, assisted Laurie Edwards with City's training duties throughout most of the 30s, served during WW2 in the RAF, and returned to Filbert Street as joint trainer with George Ritchie for almost four years after the war, accompanying John Duncan's side to Wembley in 1949. A former Powderhall sprinter who played professional football in the American Soccer League for J&P Coats, he had held training roles with St Mirren and Doncaster Rovers before joining City. By the late 50s, he was masseur to Leicestershire CCC. His brother Walter was a hugely influential Scottish scout for City from the 40s to the 60s; while his son Malcolm was a City apprentice in 1962.

> **Eddie May** (b. Epping, 19.5.1943) was brought in by Jock Wallace as reserve-team coach in 1978, and stayed four years. A former rock-solid centre-half with Southend, Wrexham, Swansea and Chicago Sting, he moved on to coach Charlton Athletic after leaving Leicester. He was manager of crisis-racked Newport County for less than a month in July 1988; coached Lincoln City; managed Cardiff City (twice), Barry and Torquay; briefly co-managed Brentford; coached FinnPa in Helsinki; was director of football at Haverfordwest County; and managed Dundalk and Drogheda United during 1999/2000.

> **Jim Metcalfe** (b. Sunderland, 10.12.1899; d. Preston, 20.2.1975) had two spells as City trainer. He initially arrived from Preston North End on the eve of war in 1939, and was released in October 1940 to look after his sick wife and undertake munitions work in Lancashire; but he returned in 1949/50 to briefly succeed Willie McLean, leaving again in May 1950 to concentrate on his Preston nurseryman's business. As a player, he'd figured for South Shields (from

Malcolm Musgrove

Dave Richardson

1921-27), Preston and Nelson; and had become trainer at Deepdale in 1930. Jim was also a church organist.

> **John Moore** (b. Harthill, 21.12.1943) was brought in by David Pleat in 1989 to succeed Cyril Lea in the youth development role, renewing an old Luton Town partnership. In fact, John had been a long-serving defender (1965-72), a coach and, from 1986-87, the manager at Kenilworth Road; and would return there as reserve-team coach following his year-long City stint. His playing career had also encompassed spells with Motherwell, Brighton and Northampton.

> **Peter John Morris** (b. Shirebrook, 8.11.1943) was brought in on the 1987 break-up of the Milne/Hamilton tandem to work as assistant to the latter manager, and found himself in a caretaker role at senior level in December of that year, before the arrival of David Pleat. He took the Kettering manager's job in July 1988, switched to Boston United in June 1992, became assistant at Northampton in June 1994, and boss of King's Lynn in summer 1995. He commenced a second spell as Kettering boss in May 1998, and took his team to Wembley for the FA Trophy Final in May 2000. Peter's playing career encompassed lengthy stints with Mansfield and Ipswich, a couple of seasons at Norwich, and a graduation to player/manager status in a second Field Mill stint. He'd also been assistant at Newcastle United, and had managed Peterborough and Crewe before arriving at Filbert Street.

> **Colin Victor Murphy** (b. Croydon, 21.1.1944) was youth coach with City from August 1990 to May 1991, and a decade later returned to Filbert Street at Peter Taylor's behest as Football Co-Ordinator. Otherwise notorious for his often surreal programme notes, he has been much in demand for his coaching prowess since a relatively undistinguished and injury-hit playing career with Crystal Palace reserves and Cork Hibernians in the 60s. He became player/manager at Hastings United, joined the backroom staffs of Charlton and Nottingham Forest, became assistant boss to Dave Mackay at both Forest and Derby, and then managed Derby himself from November 1976 to September 1977. He had subsequently completed two stints at the helm of each of Lincoln and Stockport, and coaching posts at Notts County and Ittihad (Saudi Arbia) when taken on by David Pleat, and he rejoined Pleat in 1991 as No 2 at Luton. Colin managed Southend in 1992/3 (signing Stan Collymore), briefly bossed Shelbourne from December 1994, and became Notts County's general manager in June 1995, alongside former City reserve Steve Thompson. He had nine months as national coach in Vietnam from July 1997, then rejoined Pleat again, to head up Spurs' youth academy. Summer 2000 saw him first preparing to manage Cork City, then diverted by Taylor's call.

> **Malcolm Musgrove** (b. Durham, 8.7.1933) arrived from a coaching role at Aston Villa to become assistant to Frank O'Farrell in 1969, and departed with the boss for Old Trafford. The former West Ham and Leyton Orient winger, who had substantially helped to dump City out of the FA Cup in 1964 with the latter club, and who had been chairman of the PFA from 1963-66, followed his Manchester United spell with jobs as manager at Torquay and as coach with Connecticut Bi-Centennials, Chicago Sting, Exeter, Plymouth and Shrewsbury, where he remains as physiotherapist.

> **Joe Newton** was Fosse's trainer for 1895/6. Originally with Dundonian side Strathmore, he'd trained Hearts to their 1891 Scottish Cup win, and two years later was being used to endorse the beneficial effects of Bovril in press advertisements. On departure from Filbert Street, he joined Dundee.

> **Ernest Nixon** (b. Leicester; d. Leicester, 27.12.1935) was an assistant trainer to Dave Gardner, and assumed the senior role on Gardner's death in late 1931, until being replaced by Laurie Edwards in 1933. Formerly an instructor on the Army Gymnastic Staff, he showed his adaptability after leaving Filbert Street with a brief stint training local star heavyweight Reggie Meen; then ran pubs in Uppingham and Leicester (The Joiner's Arms, Sanvey Gate) until his early death.

> **Dave Richardson** was a Jock Wallace appointee at Filbert Street, though his second home became Belvoir Drive as he completely reorganised City's junior coaching, scouting and recruitment network over a successful six-year period. Bryan Hamilton passed the Youth Development Officer over for promotion in 1987, and he moved on immediately to assist Graham Taylor at Aston Villa. In fact Villa Park had been the previous base, too, for this former Middlesbrough schoolteacher, who'd played part-time for Northern League clubs Whitby Town and South Bank, and managed Whitby for two years from 1974.

> **Bob Roberts** (b. Penycae, July 1864; d. Wrexham, 15.3.1932) was a former Welsh international who trained Fosse for and through their inaugural Football League campaign of 1894/5. He'd played in two Welsh Cup Finals (1883, 1884) with his first club, Druids (also FA Cup quarter-finalists in 1883), before signing for an eight-year stay at Bolton Wanderers in April 1884. Capped nine times as a wing-half, he also briefly served Preston North End and Lincoln City, though he was twice suspended for drinking offences during his 1892/3 stint with the latter club. Before his professional football days, he'd been a boxer and a terracotta works employee.

> **John Neilson Robertson** (b Uddingston, 20.1.1953) was a member of Martin O'Neill's back-up entourage for several months before being formally named assistant manager in August 1996. Capped for

No.	Name / Home Town	Fav. LCFC player	Fav. LCFC game
748	Nick Froggatt, Loughborough	Steve Walsh	Coca Cola Cup Final Replay 1997
749	Holmes Family, Church Gresley	Steve Walsh	Derby Play Off Final
750	Gary Reader, Leicester	Steve Walsh	Derby Play Off Final
751	Nigel Carver, Leicester	Keith Weller	Arsenal 1997 / 1998
752	Steve Hyde, Birstall - Leicester	Steve Walsh	Derby Play Off Final
753	David Hickin, Barton Turf - Norwich	Frank Worthington	Liverpool
754	Andrew Eaton, Norwich	Muzzy Izzet	Shrewsbury
755	Paul Ramsell, Stoke on Trent	Graham Cross	Aston Villa 1966
756	Matthew Ramsell, Stoke on Trent	Steve Walsh	Coca Cola Cup Final 1997
757	Viv & Mike Morton, Loughborough	Steve Walsh	Wembley Play Off Final 1994
758	Elizabeth Foley, Cricklade,Wilts	Keith Weller	N/A
759	Paul Doyle, Leicester	Frank Worthington	Shrewsbury Cup 1982
760	Stanley Drewery, Leicester	Keith Weller	Derby Play Off Final
761	David Adcock, Tamworth	Frank Worthington	Shrewsbury FA Cup
762	Leslie Stones, Leicester	Keith Weller	Fulham FA Cup
763	Ryan Stones, Leicester	Neil Lennon	Shrewsbury FA Cup
764	Hayley Cooper, Melton Mowbray	Neil Lennon	Shrewsbury FA Cup
765	Rosemary Harvey, Nuneaton	Steve Claridge	Shrewsbury FA Cup
766	David Parker, Leicester	Gary Lineker	Oxford 1991
767	Lee Greet, Leicester	Gary Lineker	Worthington Cup Final 1997
768	Jonathan Mills, Market Harborough	Frank Worthington	Shrewsbury FA Cup 1982
769	Terry Gray, Ibstock	Lenny Glover	Sunderland 1999 / 2000
770	Michael Hodges, Leicester	Keith Weller	Crystal Palace Play Off Final 1996
771	John Kenny, Ashby De La Zouch	David Gibson	Manchester City 1968
772	John Konderak, Knighton, Leicester	Steve Walsh	Coca Cola Cup Final 1997
773	Tom, Emily & Ben Miles, Houghton on the Hill	Keith Weller	Crystal Palace Play Off Final 1996
774	Paul Jackson, Clanfield - Hampshire	Keith Weller	Liverpool 1972
775	Drew Murray, Helensburgh - Scotland	Larry May	Shrewsbury FA Cup Final
776	Ted Weston, Rugby	Keith Weller	Derby Play Off Final
777	Lee Beardsmore, Leicester	Tommy Wright	Newcastle Early 1990's
778	Richard Toone, Loughborough	Steve Walsh	Derby Play Off Final
779	John Clare, Stamford, Lincs	Keith Weller	Liverpool 1980
780	Kevin Partridge, Bilston	Frank Worthington	Leeds 1973
781	Glenn Murrell, Norwich	Keith Weller	Shrewsbury FA Cup 1982
782	Balbi Murrell, Cheltenham	Steve Walsh	Middlesbrough 1997
783	Ryan Nunwa, Welling - Kent	Emile Heskey	West Ham 2000
784	Peter Salmon, St. Austell, Cornwall	Peter Shilton	Tottenham 1961
785	Colin Garland, Leicester	Frank Worthington	Liverpool 1972
786	Ray Beck, Gislingham, Suffolk	Arthur Rowley	Derby Play Off Final
787	Nigel Clarke, Leicester	Keith Weller	Swindon Play Off Final
788	Derek Allen, Rushden - Northants	Lenny Glover	Shrewsbury Cup 1982
789	Philip James Ramsell, Stockport	Lenny Glover	Shrewsbury Town 1982
790	Steve Freer, Melton Mowbray	Steve Walsh	Luton 1974
791	John Hutchinson, Leicester	Frank Worthington	Crystal Palace Play Off Final 1996
792	Tom Logue, Belgrave - Leicester	Steve Walsh	Derby Play Off Final
793	Colin Boulter, Barwell, Leics	Gordon Banks	Manchester City 1968
794	Andrew Thorpe, Melton Mowbray	Gary McAllister	Worthington Cup Final 2000
795	Edward Taylor, Leicester	Frank Worthington	Fulham Worthington Cup 1999
796	SP Walker, Hinckley	Steve Walsh	Cambridge Semi
797	David James, Leicester	Lenny Glover	Crystal Palace
798	George Robinson, Leicester	Keith Weller	Manchester City FA Cup 1968
799	Peter Blandamer, Bromsgrove	Gary McAllister	Crystal Palace
800	Stefan Horeckyj, Whitehaven	Peter Shilton	Anfield 5th Round Replay 1969
801	Graham Bartlett, St Neots	Robbie Savage	Atletico Madrid 1997
802	Simon Sleath, Leicester	Steve Walsh	Crystal Palace Play Off Final 1996
803	Ian Clay, Leicester	Frank Worthington	Crystal Palace Play Off Final 1996
804	Gerard Glenton, Newfoundpool, Leicester	Steve Whitworth	Derby Play Off Final
805	Rob Glenton, Sale - Cheshire	Arthur Rowley	Manchester City 1958
806	Glynn Marshall, Leicester	Steve Walsh	Shrewsbury 1982
807	Paul Taylor, London	David Gibson	Man City FAC rep 1968
808	Barbara Taylor, Littlethorpe, Leics	Don Revie	Portsmouth FAC 1949
809	Kate Taylor, London	-	-
810	Helen Taylor, London	-	-
811	Reg Beaumont, Massachusetts, USA	-	-
812	Steve Walton, Melton Mowbray	David Gibson	City 4 Man Utd 3 1963
813	Matt Poynton, Syston, Leicester	Steve Claridge	Derby, Wembley 1994
814	Ernest Tench, Winchelsea, Australia	David Gibson	FAC Final 1969
815	Robert Pratt, Leicester	David Gibson	-
816	Robert Adam Gask, Leicester	Robbie Savage	-
817	David Gask, Charnwood, Leicester	-	-
818	Richard Worman, Keighley	Tony Cottee	Tranmere, Wembley 2000
819	Dave Smith, Oadby, Leicester	Steve Walsh	Man City FAC rep 1968
820	Helen Smith, Oadby, Leicester	Bobby Roberts	-
821	Thomas Smith, Oadby, Leicester	Steve Walsh	Derby, Wembley 1994
822	Jennifer Smith, Oadby, Leicester	Paul Ramsey	Derby, Wembley 1994
823	Paul Smith, Oadby, Leicester	-	Arsenal 3-3, 1997
824	Sally Smith, Oadby, Leicester	Emile Heskey	Tranmere, Wembley 2000
825	Mary Earp, Oadby, Leicester	-	-
826	Stephen Wann, Lancaster	-	-
827	Jack Birch, Evington, Leicester	Arthur Rowley	Luton, 1950
828	Mark Buckley, Leicester	Keith Weller	Liverpool (a) 1980-81
829	Gerald Toon, Thurnby, Leicester	Keith Weller	Liverpool (h) 1972
830	Julian Baskcomb, Barsby, Leicester	Steve Walsh	Crystal Palace, Wembley 1996
831	Ian Nettelfield, Leicester	Gary Lineker	Derby Play Off Final
832	Chris Taylor, Woodville - Derbyshire	Steve Walsh	Derby Play Off Final
833	Robert Calow, Leicester	Frank Worthington	Luton City 1974
834	Steve Wells, Shepherds Bush	-	-
835	Harvey Wells, Shepherds Bush	-	-
836	Alastair Fox, Shepherds Bush	-	-

Scotland on 28 occasions as a jinky Forest winger (and a teammate of O'Neill's for many of the Trentside glory days), he had also served Derby for two of his fifteen years in action.

> **Fred Rose** was appointed assistant trainer to City in July 1939, for the Second Division season that never was, after five years at Oldham Athletic. He'd previously been a professional sprinter.

> **Gerry Summers** (Gerald Thomas; b. Birmingham, 4.10.1933) was Gordon Milne's assistant for four years from 1982. A former West Brom, Sheffield United, Hull and Walsall player, he had coached at Wolves and West Brom, and had six-year spells as manager at each of Oxford and Gillingham. On leaving City, he took up a youth coaching role at Derby.

> **Harley Thompson**, the trainer accused of 'enticing' six Fossils from the Grimsby pitch during the last 15 minutes of the notoriously weatherbeaten match of January 1912, and suspended for two months by the League, had been with Fosse since 1905. He remained with the club as assistant when Billy Leech became the first Fossil to be elevated from the playing ranks to the senior trainer's role.

> **Chris Turner** (Christopher Robert; b. Sheffield, 15.9.1958) joined the City backroom staff in the summer of 1995 to assist David Nish with the youth team, and was soon called upon to turn out in goal for the reserves as the Zeljko Kalac work-permit saga dragged on. He was part of the acting management team in December 1995, between the McGhee and O'Neill regimes, then from July 1996 rejoined McGhee at Wolves as youth coach, replacing Rob Kelly. In February 1999 he became manager of Hartlepool United. His previous career between the sticks consisted of two spells with Sheffield Wednesday, and stints with Sunderland, Manchester United, Lincoln, Leeds and Leyton Orient, where he became joint player/manager.

> **Steve Walford** (Stephen Joseph; b. Highgate, 5.1.1958) was introduced as City's first-team coach by Martin O'Neill, who'd worked with him at both Wycombe and Norwich, and had previously played alongside him at Carrow Road. Highly esteemed for his day-to-day work with the Premiership squad, he was offered the chance to work alongside incoming manager Peter Taylor, but chose in July 2000 to follow O'Neill to Celtic. A Spurs pro from 1975, but released to rivals Arsenal after only two games, he was the Gunners' substitute in their 1979 FA Cup Final win. Then came spells with Norwich and West Ham, loans at Huddersfield, Gillingham and West Brom, globetrotting experience with Lai Sun in Hong Kong and in Turkish football, and a non-league sunset with Wycombe and Wealdstone.

SECRETARIES

The post of secretary was not nominally separated from that of manager until September 1936, when Leicester-born **George Smith** was promoted from the role of assistant secretary he had held since August 1925. Smith discharged his administrative duties until September 1940, when retiring to take the Earl of Stamford Arms, Groby. He emigrated to New Zealand in May 1957.

Tom Bromilow and Tom Mather effectively acted as secretary/managers again until the end of the war, when **Charles Alexander Maley** was appointed. A seemingly dour Scot from a footballing family (uncle Willie managed Celtic to glory, uncle Alex was the boss of the original Clydebank club, while father Tom was secretary/ manager at Manchester City and Bradford Park Avenue), Charles himself learned the backroom ropes in Bradford: as assistant at Park Avenue from 1919, similarly employed at Bradford City from 1924, and as the senior secretary at Valley Parade from 1930. He joined City in August 1945, ran a fairly formal and faintly forbidding Filbert Street administration, and stayed until retirement in May 1962. He died in Glasgow on 18th August 1965.

Eddie Plumley was his successor, immediately noted for a greater dynamism and a rather more sophisticated grasp of public relations principles. Originally a young goalkeeper on the books of Birmingham City, Eddie had shifted to the St Andrews office as an assistant in 1955. He found himself with a Cup Final on his hands in his first season at Leicester, and coped well with the changing demands on a football administrator throughout the 60s; moving on to Coventry in 1969, and later to the roles of Chief Executive and director at Watford.

City looked far afield for their next appointment, bringing **John Smith** back to England after a stint as business manager of the New York Generals (the club which later became the Cosmos). John had run the offices at Leyton Orient, the Football Combination and Queens Park Rangers before his Stateside sojourn, and was noted as something of a progressive thinker at Leicester throughout the 70s, when the club's commercial base had to be efficiently diversified. He moved on in 1979 to become Chief Executive at Luton Town, and was centrally involved during the 80s in a host of Kenilworth Road controversies over relocation, artificial pitches, and bans on away supporters.

Alan Bennett, appointed in February 1979, experienced a three month 'handover' period with Smith, while still functioning as secretary of Aston Villa. He had begun his administrative career with the Football Association, and had been assistant secretary at Chelsea before taking over the Villa Park office. He was noted, especially via his programme column, for striking a fine diplomatic balance between the demands of communication and confidentiality.

In 1994, on Alan Bennett's retirement, a restructuring took place which saw assistant (and City supporter) **Ian Silvester** promoted to Football Secretary, while director-to-be Steve Kind assumed the new role of Company Secretary, and former marketing boss Barrie Pierpoint became Chief Executive. Ian, who skilfully negotiated the problems of running a progressive sporting entity within a new corporate culture (and of the formal split between the FC and the plc), and forged a fine relationship with Martin O'Neill, left in November 1998 to take up a similar position at Leeds United (a year later additionally joining the board there); and was replaced by former Norwich City secretary **Andrew Neville**.

PHYSIOTHERAPISTS

> 1968 George Preston; 1977 Jim Peacock; 1977 John McVey; 1989 Mark Geeson; 1992-2000 Alan Smith; 1996-date Mick Yeoman, 1998-date Ian Andrews, 1999-date David Rennie.

THE BOARDROOM

Leicester Fosse Presidents (1884-1919):
Joseph Johnson, Sir Thomas Wright, Frank Ashwell, Sir John Fawke Lancelot Rolleston, A H Vass, Sir Keith Alexander Fraser, Montague John Rice.

Leicester Fosse Committee Members (1891-1897 only) included:
J P Angrave, Thomas S Ashmole, Frank Ashwell, Jimmy Atter, J A Barfoot, W J Brierley, J E Carpenter, F Harold Chitham, C Coleman, M A Cook, William John Cooper, John J Curtis (chairman 1895/6), Frank Gardner, G H Geeson, F W Green, J H Grinen, Dr Halkyard, J D Harris, W H Harris, James A Hartopp, Samuel Hudson (chairman 1893/4), Teddy Johnson, Jimmy Johnson, Joseph Johnson (treasurer to 1892), William George Jones (chairman 1896/7), C W Kilby, Ernest A Marson, G Palmer, Arthur T Porter, Sheldon Reid, T Salisbury, Thomas Seddon (treasurer 1892-95), J Simmons, H Simpson, Arthur W Staines, A J Stubbs, Charles J Walker, A West, W A Wilbourne (financial secretary 1897), T H Woollerton.

Leicester Fosse Directors (1897-1919)
E J Benn, Cliff Bentley, J S Blackwell, George W Boyling, Louis Henry Burridge , Harry Collins, Tom Collins, William John Cooper, Carter Crossland, John J Curtis, James A Hartopp, James M Hawkes, Samuel Hudson (chairman 1897-99), W Hutchinson, J Lewis, Harry Linney, Jack H Linthwaite, Ernest A Marson, W Mason, Shirley W Matthews, F C Norman, G T Oldershaw, A Pickering, Sheldon Reid, Arthur Rice, Montague John Rice, J Richards, S Scattergood, Thomas Seddon, W H Shaw, J H Smedley, S C Smith, William Smith (chairman 1911-15), William Herbert Squires (chairman 1905-11, 1915-19), Arthur W Staines, W E Stevens, A Tomkins, A H Vass (chairman 1899-1905), R Wilson, G Woodford, F W Wright, Orson J Wright (acting chairman 1905).

Leicester City Directors (from 1919) (* previously on Fosse board)
Louis Henry Burridge (* 1919-40; chairman 1926-29 & 1933-35)
Harry Collins (* 1919-21)
Carter Crossland (* 1919-28)
William Archibald Jennings (1919-21; chairman 1919-21)
Harry Linney (* 1919-24)
Arthur Needham (1919-31 & 1936-39)
Albert Ernest Pudan (1919-40; chairman 1929-31)
William Herbert Squires (* 1919-33 & 1936-40; chairman 1925-26 & 1931-33; president 1933-36)
William Tompkins (1919-32)
Montague John Rice (* president 1919-25; chairman 1921-25; dir 1929-31)
J Carter (1921-24)
Arthur Rice (* 1921-40)
Emmanuel Gregson (1921-40; chairman 1935-38)
William Archibald Tompkins (1933-40; chairman 1938-40)
Walter Sidney George Needham, OBE (1936-40 & 1941-79; chairman 1961-64 & 1975-78)
Frank Sidney Smith (1936-40)
Leslie Lovell Green (1939-40 & 1940-46)
Leonard Thomas Shipman, CBE (1939-79; chairman 1948-56 & 1970-73)
Alfred Edward Pallett (1939-79; chairman 1940-48 & 1967-70)
G McDonald (1940)
William Albert Wileman (1940-68; chairman 1956-58)
Thomas S Bloor (1941-78; chairman 1958-61 & 1973-75)
Dennis E Sharp (1946-83; chairman 1964-67 & 1978-81)
John Henry Burridge (1959-74)
Terence W Shipman (1966-98; chairman 1981-91; president 1998-date)
Thomas E Bloor (1974-86)
Colin McLeod (1976-78)
William G Page (1976-79)
William Kenneth Shooter (1979-96 & 1999-date)
Tom Smeaton (1979-98; chairman 1996-98)
Trevor L Bennett (vice-president 1983; president 1984-89)
Martin Francis George (vice-president 1983; director 1983-97 & 1999-date; chairman 1991-96)
John Michael Elsom (vice-president 1983; director 1984-date; chairman 1998-date)
Ken R Brigstock (vice-president 1985-89; president 1989-98; life president 1998-date)
Roy William Parker (vice-president 1989; director 1990-99)
John Sharp (1990-97)
Stephen Andrew Kind (1997-date)
Barrie James Pierpoint (1997-99)
Philip Henry Smith (1998-99)
Gilbert Kenneth Kinch (1998-99)
Gregory Allison Clarke (1999-date)

Sir Rodney Myerscough Walker (plc chairman 1997-date)

John Elsom